THE FA CHALLENGE CUP COMPLETE RESULTS

1871/72 to 2019/20

Tony Brown

A *SoccerData* Publication

Published in Great Britain by Tony Brown,
4 Adrian Close, Toton, Nottingham NG9 6FL.
Telephone 0115 973 6086. E-mail soccer@innotts.co.uk
On the web at www.soccerdata.com

First published 1994, as The Ultimate FA Cup Statistics Book
Second edition, with revisions, 1999, as The FA Challenge Cup Complete Results
Third edition, updated and revised, 2006
Fourth edition, updated and revised, 2012
This edition, updated and revised, 2020

© Tony Brown 1994, 1999, 2006, 2012, 2020

The right of Tony Brown to be identified as the Author of the
Work has been asserted by him in accordance with the Copyright,
Designs and Patents Act 1988.

All rights reserved. No part of this publication may be
reproduced, stored in a retrieval system, or transmitted in any
form, or by any means, electronic, mechanical, photocopying,
recording, or otherwise without the prior permission in writing of
the publisher, nor be otherwise circulated in any form or binding
or cover other than in which it is published and without a similar
condition being imposed on the subsequent publisher.

Cover design by Bob Budd

Printed by 4Edge, Hockley, Essex.

ISBN 978-1-911376-20-0

INTRODUCTION

This is the record book of the world's oldest national association football club competition. The database contains the results of over 73,000 matches and the records of 3,600 clubs. Was game number 57,462 any more important than game 56,160? One was a Cup Final with 73,000 spectators and millions of television viewers all over the world. The other was at Farnham in a preliminary round, before 74 spectators and the tea ladies. To the statistician and club historian the two games are equally important. They are both part of the rich fabric that makes up the glamour of the FA Challenge Cup.

HOW TO USE THE BOOK

The book contains every FA Cup result to the end of season 2019/20. You can treat it as a reference book and go straight to the season you are interested in. Use the bold headings at the top of each page to find the season, noting that some pages contain more than one. Alternatively, you can use the index of clubs first, so that you know which seasons to look at in the results pages for a particular club.

Please note that there was no competition for seasons 1915/16 to 1918/19 and 1940/41 to 1944/45 because of the two World Wars. The competition for 1939/40 started but was cancelled after the extra preliminary round had been played on September 2nd 1939.

The result listings include the group number (if it was a qualifying round game after 1888 or early rounds before then) and markers such as "e" to indicate extra time. A full list of the markers will be found on page 12. The group number will help you find a particular club in the qualifying rounds.

As an example of the use of the club index, say you want to follow the exploits of Gnome Athletic. You will find from the index that they appeared sixteen times between seasons 1919/20 and 1922/23. Now, imagine the letter "S" superimposed on the map of England and Wales. The start of the "S", in the North East, has the low numbered groups in the qualifying rounds. The tail of the "S", in Wales and the South West, has the high numbers.

If you know Gnome Athletic were a London club, then try groups 16 to 18. Start with the preliminary round; if they are not there, try the extra preliminary round or the first qualifying round.

Although the number of groups has changed over the years, and clubs can appear in different groups from season to season, you will find they are a handy method of following particular clubs. The group numbers were replaced for 1998/99 season onwards with a match number, but you will find the "S" shape still applies; low numbers in the North East, high numbers in the South West.

The task of finding a particular club in the qualifying rounds is complicated by the fact that they may have had an exemption to a later round. The list of dates of rounds in an appendix will show you the number of rounds played each season. This will help you see the rounds when exempt clubs may have entered.

The 'old' Wembley Stadium from the air, the home of the FA Cup Final from 1923 to 2000. The distinctive aluminium roof was added in time for the 1963 Final. It used 218,000 sq. feet of material supplied by the British Aluminium Company. Unilux transparent sheeting from U.A.M. Plastics let light through to the playing surface.

Canvey Island, Kent in November 1995. A glorious sunny day by the Thames estuary, but a nip in the air means the spectators in the free seats need to wrap up to keep warm. Brighton and Hove Albion are the visitors for a First Round match; it is Canvey Island's sixth match in that year's competition. A 2-2 draw was the result.

A SHORT HISTORY OF THE FA CUP

The meeting that started it all took place on 20th July 1871 in the Sportsmans Office in London, "when it was resolved to institute a cup competition open to all clubs belonging to the Football Association". A five-man committee was appointed on the 16th October 1871 to frame the rules; three days later Mr. J. Powell and Mr. E.C. Morley presented the first draft. There was a stipulation that the teams should have eleven players. Games with mixed numbers on each side were common at the time; the first time Nottingham Forest met the established Notts (County) club, 13 Notts men were due to play 15 of the Forest. In the event, 11 played 17! There was no concept of a "home" tie in the rules; in any case, few clubs had grounds they could call their own. An exemption from the early rounds could be given to provincial clubs to minimise travel costs.

In the first few seasons, if a game was drawn, both clubs would be allowed through to the next round, although the Committee had the discretion to ask them to play again. Ties had to be played before a set date, so a drawn game close to this deadline was almost certain to see both clubs in the next round draw.

It was a "Challenge" Cup; the significance of this was that the holder would be exempt from the next competition until the Final, where it would meet the winner of the so-called "trial" matches. The holders also had choice of ground for the final tie. Consequently, the 1871/72 winners did not play in the 1872/73 competition until the final.

It should be remembered that the rules of the game were still evolving at this time. Clubs played under the rules of their local association, and it was not until 1877 that the Sheffield and London (i.e. Football Association) rules came into alignment. The FA Cup was an important factor in this process, as clubs were obliged to play the London rules.

The game in 1871 would be a strange sight to modern eyes. No crossbars or goal nets, a single handed throw in when the ball went out of play, two umpires on the pitch to give judgements when appealed to by the players, and a playing formation that would be described today as 1-1-8. The eight man forward line would often have the appearance of a rugby scrum! However, by the late 1870s the influence of Queen's Park (Glasgow) and the Royal Engineers led to a more organised approach to the game that we might recognise today. Apart from the tackles and shoulder charges perhaps!

The first FA Cup games took place on 11th November 1871. Civil Service could only field eight men for their game against Barnes. Crystal Palace and Hitchin drew 0-0 and both were allowed through to the next round. Queen's Park of Glasgow and Donnington School in Lincolnshire were drawn together in the first round but were unable to arrange a date for deciding the tie, "owing to the short notice received". Both clubs were therefore included in the second drawing. The scorer of the first goal is generally credited to Jarvis Kenrick of Clapham Rovers, who scored in the 15th minute of a game that kicked off at 3.30pm.

The round two game between Hitchin and Royal Engineers only lasted 60 minutes, but the result was allowed to stand. The Committee met on 7th February 1872 to decide if Wanderers and Crystal Palace should "play out" their third round game that finished 0-0. Again it was agreed that both clubs would be allowed through to the next round.

The Committee met again on 13th February 1872 to decide on the design of the trophy. Two designs were considered, from Benson & Co. and Martin, Hall & Co. The latter company was chosen.

The visit of Queen's Park of Glasgow to the Oval for the semi-final with Wanderers caused a good deal of interest. A public subscription had been necessary to pay for their trip south. Their close passing style was much admired, but the game ended as a stalemate with no goals scored. Queen's Park were unable to remain for a replay and so Wanderers went through to the Final.

The Wanderers won the first competition. A crowd of 2000 at the Oval saw them beat the Royal Engineers of Chatham by one goal to nil. More spectators had been expected, but the entrance charge of one shilling was too expensive for many people. Royal Engineers were probably the favourites and had been unbeaten for the previous two seasons. In the event, the Wanderers club proved too strong, with play described as "superior to anything that has been seen at the Oval". They had to wait for the presentation of the Cup until their annual dinner in four weeks after the final.

The scorer of the Wanderers goal in the 1872 final was MP Betts, sometimes reported as "AH Chequer", or "A Harrow Chequer". There was nothing to stop a man being a member of more than one club. A glance at the names of the players in the early finals will show the same players appearing for the Old Etonians, the Wanderers and Oxford University. However, the Cup rules said a player could only appear for one club in any one season. Betts was due to play for Harrow Chequers in the first round (against the Wanderers) but the Harrow team scratched.

The size of the ball was standardised on 3rd October 1872, and an amendment made to the rules. Lillywhite's "No. 5" had emerged as the favourite; the ball had to have a circumference of "not less than 27 inches and not more than 28 inches"; balls of much larger circumference were used in the other forms of football played at the time. Late entries for the 1872/73 competition were received from Old Etonians and Harrow Chequers but were not accepted. Other rule changes saw the dropping of the clause that allowed both clubs through in the event of a draw.

As winners of the first tournament, Wanderers were exempt until the final of 1872/73. The rule giving winners exemption to the final was then dropped, although the name of the competition remains "The Challenge Cup". Queen's Park of Glasgow were given a bye through to the semi-finals because of travel problems. They then had to withdraw from their tie against Oxford University because of the business commitments of some of their team. Wanderers had choice of ground for the final, electing to play at the Lillie Bridge ground, close to where Stamford Bridge is today. They beat Oxford University by two goals to nil.

The Sheffield Association entered "en bloc" for the 1873/74 competition. They were told that entries could only be accepted from clubs supporting the Association, and not from the Sheffield Association itself. The original Sheffield club duly entered and met Shropshire Wanderers. After two drawn games the two clubs tossed a coin to see who would go through; Sheffield won.

Barnes' entry was overlooked and they were omitted from the first round draw. However, Harrow Chequers withdrew from their game against First Surrey Rifles, so Barnes were allowed to take their place.

For the first two seasons, the draw for each round was made when needed, and apart from the later rounds (due to be played at the Oval) the choice of ground was left to the two clubs involved. The ties were drawn "all at once" for 1873/74, rather than after each round was completed, rather in the way Wimbledon tennis runs today.

The question of the "home" club was becoming more important as more clubs entered the competition. The meeting of 14th July 1874 agreed a new rule: "The captains of the competing clubs shall toss for choice of ground in the first and second series of ties. In the case of drawn matches, captains of the club who lost the toss have choice for the second match, and so on alternately, but except by mutual consent, it shall not be allowable for a captain to select any ground other than that on which his club is accustomed to play. After the second series, all ties to be played at the Oval, or other ground determined by the Committee".

The term "first series" referred to the segregation of the clubs into regional areas. For the seasons prior to 1879/80, this split into "divisions" was done only when needed, since only a handful of provincial clubs were involved.

The 1874/75 result Wanderers 16 Farningham 0 was reported as the highest score ever made under FA rules. Both semi-finals were played at the Oval on 27th February 1875, with 1.30 pm and 3.15 pm kick offs.

Sheffield met Shropshire Wanderers for the third successive season in 1875/76. This was inevitable under the original rule seven as there were no other entries from their areas.

The first clubs who would later play in the Football League entered in 1877/78; Darwen, Notts County and Reading. Wanderers won the cup for the third successive season and were entitled to retain it; however, it was presented back to the Association on condition that it could not be won outright again.

In 1879/80, the increased number of provincial clubs led the Committee to introduce a formal set of "divisions" into which the competing clubs were organised. Moreover, the ties in these divisions would continue until only one club remained unbeaten. The qualifying rounds introduced in 1888/89 work in a similar way. Five divisions were needed in 1879, Northern, Western and Metropolitan. Because of the greater number of clubs in the latter category, it was subdivided into three. That meant five teams were left in the competition for the next round, resulting in one club being given a bye in the next two rounds.

Aston Villa scratched from their tie with Oxford University in 1879/80, preferring to play in the Birmingham Senior Cup. The FA Cup was popularly known as "the London Cup" at this time and many provincial clubs were not convinced they needed to enter.

1880/81 required six divisions, labelled Northern, Central and Metropolitan, the latter group now split into four. There was no zoning for the Metropolitan clubs; the Committee worked out the size of each sub-division.

The success of Northern clubs in 1881/82 led to the FA writing to Surrey CCC to say that they were departing from their normal practice of playing semi-final matches at the Oval. Blackburn Rovers met Sheffield Wednesday at St. John's Rugby Ground, Huddersfield and replayed at Whalley Range, Manchester.

The meeting of 17th April 1882 rejected the request of Blackburn Rovers that the FA should pay their fares to and from London for the Final! The Rovers were the first provincial club (if we exclude Queen's Park) to reach the Final. They lost to the Old Etonians, the last time a Southern amateur club was to take the trophy.

The 1882/83 rules were amended so that the first club out of the hat had choice of ground. This season marked the coming of age of the "protest" as a strategic weapon. Protests came in all shapes and sizes; pitches were too long or too short, umpires were biased, goals were too big or too small, players were not registered. It was alleged that Nottingham Forest had posted bills in Sheffield offering a £20 reward if anyone could prove that one of the Sheffield Wednesday players was not properly qualified.

The Committee meeting of 8th February 1883 thankfully rejected a proposal from E.H. Bambridge of the Swifts that the Challenge Cup be competed for only by representative County elevens.

Blackburn Olympic beat Old Etonians in the Final of 1883 and so began a long period of Northern domination. However, the strongest amateur club of the time were the Corinthians, formed in 1882. Their club rules prevented them from entering the Cup until the 1920s, but they beat Blackburn Rovers 8-1 just after Rovers had won the Cup for the first time in 1884, and later beat the "invincible" Preston North End team by 5-0!

The increasing number of entries was beginning to cause some organisational difficulties. A proposal at the Committee meeting of 16th March 1885 from Mr. Betts was that the Challenge Cup should be competed for by the winners of the cups of the various County Associations.

After a drawn game, the 1884/85 semi-final between Queen's Park and Nottingham Forest was played at the Merchiston Castle ground in Edinburgh.

Darwen, Blackburn Rovers and other leading clubs were believed to have made illegal payments to some of their players in the early 1880s; this led to many protests by losing clubs in the early years of the competition. Accrington was the first club to be penalised, being disqualified after beating Blackburn Park Road in 1883/84. Bolton Wanderers were drawn to play Preston Zingari in 1884/85 but both clubs withdrew because of the likelihood of disqualification.

1885 saw the FA legalise professionalism, admittedly with fairly tight constraints. A questionnaire had been sent to the clubs in April, including the question "Shall professionals be allowed to play in the FA Cup?". The Sub Committee met to agree the final proposals and these were agreed at a Special General Meeting held on 20th July 1885.

The new rules placed strict conditions on professional players. Bolton Wanderers and Preston North End were disqualified in 1885/86 for breaking the rules. Burnley fielded their reserve team to avoid the problem, but lost 11-0 to a Darwen club, the Old Wanderers.

By 1886/87 eight divisions were needed. The entries were now largely from non-Metropolitan clubs, so there were six divisions for the North and Midlands, and two for Southern clubs. Scottish clubs were included in groups one and two; Cliftonville of Belfast were in group two. Sheffield Wednesday were among the late entries that year and were not accepted. The fifth round was the first "unsegregated" round and was also known at the time as "the first round of the second series".

This was the last year of entry by the Scottish clubs; the Scottish FA barred them from competing in any tournament but their own. Irish clubs continued to enter until 1890/91, and Welsh clubs to this day.

Matters became complicated in 1887/88! After Everton had beaten Bolton Wanderers in round one, they lost to Preston in round two. Then Bolton's appeal against Everton (for playing seven ineligible players) was successful, and they were reinstated. Preston then had to play another round two game, against Bolton. The number of groups increased to nine this season.

1888/89 was the first season of the Football League. The twelve founder members were Accrington, Blackburn Rovers, Bolton Wanderers, Burnley, Everton and Preston North End from the North of England, and Aston Villa, Derby County, Notts County, Stoke, West Bromwich Albion and Wolverhampton Wanderers from the Midlands. A limit of twelve clubs was partly imposed by the twenty-two Saturdays required for each club to play their home and away matches. Darwen's playing record had declined somewhat, which is perhaps why they were not included. A rule also limited participation to one club per town, and Darwen is close to Blackburn.

The Cup competition of 1888/89 was the first season in which qualifying rounds were played. The disparity between the leading clubs and the rest had been highlighted by Preston's 26-0 victory over Hyde the previous season. As the number of entries increased, so did the number of rounds to be played. Even before the Football League, the leading clubs were starting to have problems fitting the Cup games into their schedule. Making the leading clubs exempt until later rounds made good sense.

Arrangements for the early rounds of the Cup are made during the close season, so the Football Association could not have taken the formation of the League in the summer of 1888 into account. It was decided to make 18 clubs exempt from the qualifying rounds plus the four semi-finalists from 1887/88. Of the League clubs, Stoke, Notts County and Everton were drawn to play in the qualifying rounds. Old Carthusians, Notts Rangers and Halliwell (Bolton) were among the clubs exempted.

The principles of the qualifying rounds remained unchanged to 1997/98. The clubs were organised into geographical groups to minimise travel costs. There were 10 such groups in 1888/89 and 36 in 1997/98. The clubs knocked each other out until there was just one "winner" left from each group. These group winners were then joined by the exempt clubs in the later rounds. This book does not have space to list the exempted clubs eacg season but they can be deduced by observing which ones did not play in the previous round.

The League and Cup competitions lived uneasily together for some time, with several instances on record where clubs had to play their reserve teams in the Cup in order to fulfil a scheduled League fixture. Everton withdrew in

1888/89 when drawn to play Ulster in the first qualifying round.

The first League club to lose to a non-league club was Stoke, beaten by Warwick County in the first qualifying round of the 1888/89 tournament. This was Warwick's only claim to fame in the Cup; they last entered in 1890/91, losing to Port Vale.

Of the great amateur clubs competing that year, Old Carthusians lost 4-3 at Wolves and Old Westminsters lost by the same score at Burnley.

The four semi-finalists were all League clubs, and the winners were Preston North End. Preston's unbeaten record in the League that year (never equalled) was matched by their record in winning the Cup; no goals conceded! Bury are the only club to match this feat, in 1902/03.

A new rule was carried in 1889: "That a club not having a private ground, shall provide a private or enclosed ground, to which gate money can be charged for Cup ties free of all charge to the visiting Club, or play on its opponent's ground".

The Shanghai (China) Marine Engineers Institute FC was affiliated to the Association in 1890. It is perhaps fortunate that they never entered the Cup!

The first non-League club to reach the Final was Sheffield Wednesday of the Football Alliance in 1889/90. This was the first season of the Alliance; it was absorbed into the Football League in 1892/93, most of its clubs forming the new Second Division.

The first Second Division club to win the Cup was Notts County in 1893/94. This was also the first season of the Amateur Cup. The Sheffield club had proposed a Cup for amateur clubs in 1892, but the offer was declined. However, the FA Council decided they should institute the competition. Some clubs played in both tournaments in 1893/94, notably Tottenham Hotspur, but the famous "Old Boy" clubs were not seen in the FA Cup again.

Aston Villa had to report the loss of the Cup at the FA Committee meeting in November 1895! It had been stolen from the shop window of William Shillcock, football and boot manufacturer. A £10 reward was offered, but the trophy was never seen again. The meeting in February fined the club £25, which was also the cost of a new trophy, to be made "as nearly as possible like the old cup".

There were changes to the exemption system in 1896/97. Twenty two clubs were exempt until the first round proper. Four clubs from each of the ten qualifying groups were exempt until the third qualifying round. This season is rather an oddity in Cup history; groups were involved in different rounds on the same day. Also, the same round was called "preliminary", "first qualifying" or "first preliminary", depending on the group.

Another non-League club reached the final in 1899/1900; Southampton of the Southern League. The Southern League was formed in 1894/95 and the leading clubs in its early years would certainly have done well in the Second Division of the Football League and probably the First Division as well. The First Division of the Southern League was eventually to form the Third Division of the Football League in 1920/21.

The first (and only) non-League winners were Tottenham Hotspur in 1900/01. The Spurs finished fifth in the Southern League that season.

The exemption system had three categories for this season. Twenty-two clubs were still exempt to round one. Ten were exempt to a new intermediate round after the qualifying rounds. Four from each group were exempt to the third qualifying round as before.

Coventry City withdrew from the competition in 1900/01 in order to play a fixture in the Birmingham League.

A record entry in 1904/05 saw four levels of exemptions; the three described for 1900/01, and ten clubs to a new qualifying round six. The scheme was simplified for 1905/06 by returning to two levels of exemption; twenty-four to the last qualifying round (Q4) and forty to round one. The number of qualifying groups was increased to 24.

1906/07 required further tuning; fifty-two clubs exempt until round one, twelve until qualifying round five. This lasted (with a few minor variations) until 1913/14.

A dispute led to the withdrawal of some clubs from the 1907/08 competition. The FA ruled that County Associations should permit the affiliation of professional clubs. The Surrey and Middlesex Associations remained firmly amateur, and led a breakaway group called the Amateur Football Defence Federation, later renamed the Amateur Football Association. The clubs affected did not return until the 1913/14 competition.

In 1910, the Committee passed the resolution "The present Football Association Challenge Cup, having been duplicated without the consent of the Association, be withdrawn from Competition, and a new Cup offered, the design of which should be registered". Messrs Fattorini and Sons of Bradford were awarded the contract to design the new trophy; the first winners were Bradford City in 1911! The old cup was presented to Lord Kinnaird to celebrate his 21 years as president of the Association.

The meeting of 19th July 1912 decided that extra time would be played in the final tie if necessary.

The FA Cup was popularly known as "The English Cup" through to the late 1920s. The medal engravers made the mistake of engraving this on the finalist's medals for 1914.

The outbreak of the First World War in 1914 presented the Football Association with a problem. Although supporting the enrolment of footballers into the armed forces it decided to continue with the 1914/15 competition. Many smaller clubs withdrew from the qualifying rounds, but the rounds proper were unaffected. Manchester City's proposal that extra time should be played in the first game was agreed to, and it was also ruled that replays should take place the following Saturday, despite the possible interference with League matches. One replay between Bradford City and Norwich City was played behind closed doors in Lincoln, though it is reported that many fans managed to break in to watch the game.

The exemption system returned to three levels for 1914/15; twenty-four clubs to Q5, twelve to Q6, and fifty-two to the first round.

The 1915 Cup Final is known as the "khaki final" because of the number of soldiers in the crowd. The competition was not held again until season 1919/20.

Leeds United were elected to the League in 1920/21 and withdrew from the qualifying rounds after playing two games. Similarly, Charlton Athletic withdrew in 1921/22, and Doncaster Rovers in 1923/24, after their election to the League.

1921/22 saw the largest ever number of entries accepted for the competition; 656. (A higher figure quoted in FA sources for 1920/21 is incorrect). New rules on grounds and club status helped reduce the number of entries for 1922/23.

Birmingham were missing from the 1921/22 competition because their secretary forgot to return the entry form! Queen's Park Rangers made the same mistake in 1926.

The Corinthians finally entered the tournament in 1922/23, and were given exemption until the rounds proper. This was the first season that Wembley Stadium was used for the final.

The 1925/26 competition took the shape we are familiar with today, though the number of ties per round and the number of exemptions have changed. The bulk of the clubs were divided into 26 regional groups. By qualifying round three, just two clubs were left from each group, making this round a sort of "group final". The 26 successful clubs joined 24 leading non-league clubs in qualifying round four. This left 25 victorious clubs to be joined by a further 51 clubs in round one; these included the Amateur Cup finalists from 1925, Clapton and Southall, and clubs from the Third Division of the Football League. Finally, the remaining 45 League clubs joined in round three.

Freak weather hit the South Yorkshire area on September 19th 1925, causing most of the preliminary round games to be abandoned.

The "North Eastern Daily Gazette" was amused to report that two draws had been made for the first qualifying round in 1928/29. The FA had pre-drawn the round (the usual practice) but the local committee were unaware of this and made their own draw after the preliminary round had been played.

Newport County were excluded from the 1931/32 competition because of the issue of tickets for an illegal lottery the season before. In 1932/33, Third Division Brighton and Hove Albion repeated the mistake of Birmingham and forgot to enter.

However, they decided to play through the qualifying rounds. This obviously did them no harm as they went on to defeat First Division Chelsea in round three! They scored 43 goals in eleven games that season.

The 1933 Final between Everton and Manchester City saw numbers on the player's shirts for the first time. Everton wore numbers 1 to 11, City 12 to 22. Numbers on shirts in League matches were introduced in 1939. The 1938 Final was the first broadcast live on television; radio had been at the Final since 1927.

The extra preliminary round of the 1939/40 competition had been played before the outbreak of the Second World War. The rest of the competition was cancelled.

The competition restarted in 1945/46. Entry was restricted to those who had entered in 1939/40, except by special permission of the Cup Committee. The 10/- (50p) entry fees paid in 1939 were accepted as the entry fee for 1945/46! Many clubs had closed down during the war. Of the Football League clubs, Hull City and New Brighton were unable to enter.

With no League competition that year, the Football Association decided that rounds one to six would be played over two legs, with the aggregate score deciding the tie. The first legs were generally played on a Saturday, with the second leg in the middle of the following week. Extra time was played in the second leg, ten minutes each way, and then the game continued to the finish if the scores were still level. Bad light caused some games to go to a third meeting.

Newport (Isle of Wight) had the unusual distinction of losing four games in 1945/46. They survived a third qualifying round defeat when their opponents were disqualified, lost the first leg of their round one tie, and both legs of round two!

Transport difficulties after the war caused the FA to agree that extra time should be played in the first meetings in seasons 1947/48 and 1948/49.

A steady growth in entries to 1950/51 was halted when new qualification rules were implemented. This was the last season that an extra preliminary round was needed. Further refinements led to a led to a ten percent drop in entries for 1955/56; new "yardsticks" required consideration of attendances, gate receipts and ground facilities as well as the playing ability of the club.

Changes to the competition were always under consideration. A proposal in 1954 was that all Football League clubs should enter at the same time, in a 128 club first round. In 1959, it was proposed that all amateur clubs should be excluded, together with professional clubs not in full membership, and a new tournament organised for them. The proposal was rejected, but the Committee agreed to write to Third and Fourth Division clubs to see if they were interested in an "Intermediate Cup" for those knocked out in the early stages of the Cup; they weren't!

Wembley finals seemed to bear a charmed life; a replay was not necessary until 1969/70 when Chelsea beat Leeds at Old Trafford. Subsequent replays have been held at Wembley; they were needed three years in succession from 1981 to 1983.

The question of substitutes for injured players was first discussed in 1960. They were not allowed in cup ties until the 1966/67 season. Derek Clarke of West Bromwich Albion was the first substitute to appear in the Final.

The distinction between amateur and professional players was abolished in 1974. The FA Vase competition was introduced to replace the Amateur Cup. A competition for the senior non-League clubs, the FA Trophy, was introduced in 1969/70.

Kevin Moran of Manchester United was the first player to be sent off in a final tie, against Everton in 1985. Jose Antonio Reyes of Arsenal in 2005, Pablo Zabaleta in 2013, Chris Smalling in 2016, Victor Moses in 2017 and Mateo Kovacic in 2020 also left the field early.

Penalty shoot-outs were introduced into the rounds proper in 1991/92 in order to settle replayed games that were still level after extra time. Goals scored in these shoot-outs are not included in the statistical analyses that follow. The first game to be settled on penalties was a First Round replay at Rotherham, when United beat Scunthorpe United 7-6. Penalties were also used in the qualifying rounds from 1997/98 onwards, though one tie (Oxford City v. Wycombe Wanderers in 1999/2000) needed a second replay after the first replay was abandoned in extra-time and other second replays have been necessary after matches have been declared void.

The fourth trophy came into use for the 1991/92 Final, won by Liverpool. It is an exact copy of the third trophy, which is now in honourable retirement at the FA office unless lent for exhibition.

A thorough overall of the qualifying group structure took place for the 1998/99 competition. The exemptions were changed so that the senior clubs in the non-League pyramid entered in the later qualifying rounds. The 36 groups were replaced by a wider and less formal structure, though generally still seeking to minimise travelling costs for the clubs concerned. For the first time, the 1999 Final would have gone to a penalty shoot out (rather than a replay) if the scores were level after extra time. The 2005 Final between Arsenal and Manchester United was the first to be decided on kicks from the penalty mark.

In 1999/2000 Manchester United played in FIFA's Club World Championship in Brazil. A "lucky loser" from round two, Darlington, took their place in round three.

The closure of Wembley Stadium for re-building saw the Final played at the Millennium Stadium, Cardiff, from 2001 to 2006 inclusive.

Millwall's final appearance in 2004 was the first by a second tier club since Sunderland in 1992. Cardiff City repeated the feat in 2008. The last club to win the cup whilst in the second tier was West Ham United in 1980.

Saha's goal for Everton in the 2009 final was timed at 25 seconds, a new record. The honour was previously held by Di Matteo, with a 42nd second goal for Chelsea in the 1997 final.

2009/10 saw new records set for the number of entries and the number of ties in a season.

Increasing fixture congestion led to changes to the rules governing extra time and penalties. The last semi-final to need a replay was between Manchester United and Arsenal in 1999. The following year, Aston Villa became the first winner of a semi-final on penalties when they beat Bolton Wanderers after the score was still 0-0 after extra time. Replays in quarter finals were abolished in 2016-17, and in the fifth round from 2018-19, so drawn games were settled on penalties after extra time. Up to 2008-09, the first meetings in the qualifying rounds could go to extra time if the two competing clubs agreed. Now, drawn games at 90 minutes are replayed. The full list of the current rules of the competition are on the FA's web site, www.thefa.com.

The Covid-19 outbreak during the 2019/20 season resulted in all games from Round 6 onwards having to be played behind closed doors.

The following pages list the winners of the competition and give a summary of appearances in the final rounds.

The figures in italics after the Cup Final results are the Football League (and Premier League) divisions that the two clubs were in at the time. The most common results in the Final (not including the replays) are 1-0 (40 times), 2-1 (22 times) and 2-0 (20 times).

The Roll of Honour uses present day names for the clubs throughout. Clubs are ranked in the order of wins, then appearances in the final and semi-finals.

F.A. CUP FINALS 1871/72 to 2019/20

Figures in italics are the Football League/Premiership divisions of the finalists.

Year	Match	Score	Div
1872	Wanderers v. Royal Engineers	1-0	
1873	Wanderers v. Oxford University	2-0	
1874	Oxford University v. Royal Engineers	2-0	
1875	Royal Engineers v. Old Etonians	1-1e	
rep.	Royal Engineers v. Old Etonians	2-0	
1876	Wanderers v. Old Etonians	1-1	
rep.	Wanderers v. Old Etonians	3-0	
1877	Wanderers v. Oxford University	2-1e	
1878	Wanderers v. Royal Engineers	3-1	
1879	Old Etonians v. Clapham Rovers	1-0	
1880	Clapham Rovers v. Oxford University	1-0	
1881	Old Carthusians v. Old Etonians	3-0	
1882	Old Etonians v. Blackburn Rovers	1-0	
1883	Blackburn Olympic v. Old Etonians	2-1e	
1884	Blackburn Rovers v. Queens Park	2-1	
1885	Blackburn Rovers v. Queens Park	2-0	
1886	Blackburn Rovers v. West Bromwich Albion	0-0	
rep.	Blackburn Rovers v. West Bromwich Albion	2-0	
1887	Aston Villa v. West Bromwich Albion	2-0	
1888	West Bromwich Albion v. Preston North End	2-1	
1889	Preston NE v. Wolverhampton Wanderers	3-0	*1/1*
1890	Blackburn Rovers v. Sheffield Wednesday	6-1	*1/-*
1891	Blackburn Rovers v. Notts County	3-1	*1/1*
1892	West Bromwich Albion v. Aston Villa	3-0	*1/1*
1893	Wolverhampton Wanderers v. Everton	1-0	*1/1*
1894	Notts County v. Bolton Wanderers	4-1	*2/1*
1895	Aston Villa v. West Bromwich Albion	1-0	*1/1*
1896	Sheffield Wednesday v. Wolverhampton Wan	2-1	*1/1*
1897	Aston Villa v. Everton	3-2	*1/1*
1898	Nottingham Forest v. Derby County	3-1	*1/1*
1899	Sheffield United v. Derby County	4-1	*1/1*
1900	Bury v. Southampton	4-0	*1/-*
1901	Tottenham Hotspur v. Sheffield United	2-2	*-/1*
rep.	Tottenham Hotspur v. Sheffield United	3-1	*-/1*
1902	Sheffield United v. Southampton	1-1	*1/-*
rep.	Sheffield United v. Southampton	2-1	*1/-*
1903	Bury v. Derby County	6-0	*1/1*
1904	Manchester City v. Bolton Wanderers	1-0	*1/2*
1905	Aston Villa v. Newcastle United	2-0	*1/1*
1906	Everton v. Newcastle United	1-0	*1/1*
1907	Sheffield Wednesday v. Everton	2-1	*1/1*
1908	Wolverhampton Wan. v. Newcastle United	3-1	*2/1*
1909	Manchester United v. Bristol City	1-0	*1/1*
1910	Newcastle United v. Barnsley	1-1	*1/2*
rep.	Newcastle United v. Barnsley	2-0	*1/2*
1911	Bradford City v. Newcastle United	0-0	*1/1*
rep.	Bradford City v. Newcastle United	1-0	*1/1*
1912	Barnsley v. West Bromwich Albion	0-0	*2/1*
rep.	Barnsley v. West Bromwich Albion	1-0e	*2/1*
1913	Aston Villa v. Sunderland	1-0	*1/1*
1914	Burnley v. Liverpool	1-0	*1/1*
1915	Sheffield United v. Chelsea	3-0	*1/1*
1920	Aston Villa v. Huddersfield Town	1-0e	*1/2*
1921	Tottenham Hotspur v. Wolverhampton Wan	1-0	*1/2*
1922	Huddersfield Town v. Preston North End	1-0	*1/1*
1923	Bolton Wanderers v. West Ham United	2-0	*1/2*
1924	Newcastle United v. Aston Villa	2-0	*1/1*
1925	Sheffield United v. Cardiff City	1-0	*1/1*
1926	Bolton Wanderers v. Manchester City	1-0	*1/1*
1927	Cardiff City v. Arsenal	1-0	*1/1*
1928	Blackburn Rovers v. Huddersfield Town	3-1	*1/1*
1929	Bolton Wanderers v. Portsmouth	2-0	*1/1*
1930	Arsenal v. Huddersfield Town	2-0	*1/1*
1931	West Bromwich A v. Birmingham	2-1	*2/1*
1932	Newcastle United v. Arsenal	2-1	*1/1*
1933	Everton v. Manchester City	3-0	*1/1*
1934	Manchester City v. Portsmouth	2-1	*1/1*
1935	Sheffield Wednesday v. West Bromwich Albion	4-2	*1/1*
1936	Arsenal v. Sheffield United	1-0	*1/2*
1937	Sunderland v. Preston NE	3-1	*1/1*
1938	Preston North End v. Huddersfield Town	1-0e	*1/1*
1939	Portsmouth v. Wolverhampton Wanderers	4-1	*1/1*
1946	Derby County v. Charlton Athletic	4-1e	*1/1*
1947	Charlton Athletic v. Burnley	1-0e	*1/2*
1948	Manchester United v. Blackpool	4-2	*1/1*
1949	Wolverhampton Wanderers v. Leicester City	3-1	*1/2*
1950	Arsenal v. Liverpool	2-0	*1/1*
1951	Newcastle United v. Blackpool	2-0	*1/1*
1952	Newcastle United v. Arsenal	1-0	*1/1*
1953	Blackpool v. Bolton Wanderers	4-3	*1/1*
1954	West Bromwich Albion v. Preston North End	3-2	*1/1*
1955	Newcastle United v. Manchester City	3-1	*1/1*
1956	Manchester City v. Birmingham City	3-1	*1/1*
1957	Aston Villa v. Manchester United	2-1	*1/1*
1958	Bolton Wanderers v. Manchester United	2-0	*1/1*
1959	Nottm Forest v. Luton Town	2-1	*1/1*
1960	Wolverhampton W v. Blackburn Rovers	3-0	*1/1*
1961	Tottenham Hotspur v. Leicester City	2-0	*1/1*
1962	Tottenham Hotspur v. Burnley	3-1	*1/1*
1963	Manchester United v. Leicester City	3-1	*1/1*
1964	West Ham United v. Preston North End	3-2	*1/2*
1965	Liverpool v. Leeds United	2-1e	*1/1*
1966	Everton v. Sheffield Wednesday	3-2	*1/1*
1967	Tottenham Hotspur v. Chelsea	2-1	*1/1*
1968	West Bromwich Albion v. Everton	1-0e	*1/1*
1969	Manchester City v. Leicester City	1-0	*1/1*
1970	Chelsea v. Leeds United	2-2e	*1/1*
rep.	Chelsea v. Leeds United	2-1e	*1/1*
1971	Arsenal v. Liverpool	2-1e	*1/1*
1972	Leeds United v. Arsenal	1-0	*1/1*
1973	Sunderland v. Leeds United	1-0	*2/1*
1974	Liverpool v. Newcastle United	3-0	*1/1*
1975	West Ham United v. Fulham	2-0	*1/2*
1976	Southampton v. Manchester United	1-0	*2/1*
1977	Manchester United v. Liverpool	2-1	*1/1*
1978	Ipswich Town v. Arsenal	1-0	*1/1*
1979	Arsenal v. Manchester United	3-2	*1/1*
1980	West Ham United v. Arsenal	1-0	*2/1*
1981	Tottenham Hotspur v. Manchester City	1-1e	*1/1*
rep.	Tottenham Hotspur v. Manchester City	3-2	*1/1*
1982	Tottenham Hotspur v. Queen's Park Rgs.	1-1e	*1/2*
rep.	Tottenham Hotspur v. Queen's Park Rgs.	1-0	*1/2*
1983	Manchester United v. Brighton & Hove Albion	2-2e	*1/1*
rep.	Manchester United v. Brighton & Hove Albion	4-0	*1/1*
1984	Everton v. Watford	2-0	*1/1*
1985	Manchester United v. Everton	1-0e	*1/1*
1986	Liverpool v. Everton	3-1	*1/1*
1987	Coventry City v. Tottenham Hotspur	3-2e	*1/1*
1988	Wimbledon v. Liverpool	1-0	*1/1*
1989	Liverpool v. Everton	3-2e	*1/1*
1990	Manchester United v. Crystal Palace	3-3e	*1/1*
rep.	Manchester United v. Crystal Palace	1-0	*1/1*
1991	Tottenham Hotspur v. Nottingham Forest	2-1e	*1/1*
1992	Liverpool v. Sunderland	2-0	*1/2*
1993	Arsenal v. Sheffield Wednesday	1-1e	*P/P*
rep.	Arsenal v. Sheffield Wednesday	2-1e	*P/P*
1994	Manchester United v. Chelsea	4-0	*P/P*
1995	Everton v. Manchester United	1-0	*P/P*
1996	Manchester United v. Liverpool	1-0	*P/P*
1997	Chelsea v. Middlesbrough	2-0	*P/P*
1998	Arsenal v. Newcastle United	2-0	*P/P*
1999	Manchester United v. Newcastle United	2-0	*P/P*
2000	Chelsea v. Aston Villa	1-0	*P/P*
2001	Liverpool v. Arsenal	2-1	*P/P*
2002	Arsenal v. Chelsea	2-0	*P/P*
2003	Arsenal v. Southampton	1-0	*P/P*
2004	Manchester United v. Millwall	3-0	*P/1*
2005	Arsenal v. Manchester United	0-0e	*P/P*
	Arsenal won 5-4 on penalties		
2006	Liverpool v. West Ham United	3-3e	*P/P*
	Liverpool won 3-1 on penalties		
2007	Chelsea v. Manchester United	1-0e	*P/P*
2008	Portsmouth v. Cardiff City	1-0	*P/FC*
2009	Chelsea v. Everton	2-1	*P/P*
2010	Chelsea v. Portsmouth	1-0	*P/P*
2011	Manchester City v. Stoke City	1-0	*P/P*
2012	Chelsea v. Liverpool	2-1	*P/P*
2013	Wigan Athletic v Manchester City	1-0	*P/P*
2014	Arsenal v Hull City	3-2e	*P/P*
2015	Arsenal v Aston Villa	4-0	*P/P*
2016	Manchester United v Crystal Palace	2-1e	*P/P*
2017	Arsenal v Chelsea	2-1	*P/P*
2018	Chelsea v Manchester United	1-0	*P/P*
2019	Manchester City v Watford	6-0	*P/P*
2020	Arsenal v Chelsea	2-1	*P/P*

ROLL OF HONOUR 1871/72 to 2019/20

Clubs with more than one semi-final appearance, excluding byes

	Wins	Finals	SFs
Arsenal (& Woolwich Arsenal)	14	21	30
Manchester United (& Newton Heath)	12	20	30
Tottenham Hotspur	8	9	21
Chelsea	8	14	24
Aston Villa	7	11	21
Liverpool	7	14	24
Blackburn Rovers	6	8	18
Manchester City	6	11	15
Newcastle United	6	13	17
Wanderers	5	5	3
West Bromwich Albion	5	10	20
Everton	5	13	26
Sheffield United	4	6	14
Bolton Wanderers	4	7	14
Wolverhampton Wanderers	4	8	15
West Ham United	3	5	7
Sheffield Wednesday	3	6	16
Bury	2	2	2
Nottingham Forest	2	3	12
Sunderland	2	4	12
Portsmouth	2	5	7
Old Etonians	2	6	5
Preston North End	2	7	10
Bradford City	1	1	1
Coventry City	1	1	1
Blackburn Olympic	1	1	2
Wigan Athletic	1	1	2
Wimbledon	1	1	2
Ipswich Town	1	1	3
Old Carthusians	1	1	3
Clapham Rovers	1	2	1
Charlton Athletic	1	2	2
Barnsley	1	2	3
Notts County	1	2	5
Blackpool	1	3	3
Cardiff City	1	3	4
Burnley	1	3	8
Oxford University	1	4	4
Royal Engineers	1	4	4
Leeds United	1	4	8
Southampton	1	4	12
Derby County	1	4	13
Huddersfield Town	1	5	7
Leicester City (& Fosse)		4	7
Queen's Park (Glasgow)		2	3
Crystal Palace		2	4
Watford		2	7
Birmingham City (& Small Heath)		2	9
Fulham		1	6
Millwall		1	5
Luton Town		1	4
Stoke City		1	4
Middlesbrough		1	3
Bristol City		1	2
Brighton & Hove Albion		1	2
Hull City		1	2
Queen's Park Rangers		1	1
Norwich City			3
Oldham Athletic			3
Swifts			3
Swindon Town			2
Swansea City (as Town)			2
Grimsby Town			2
Reading			2

One semi-final appearance:

Cambridge University
Chesterfield
Crewe Alexandra
Crystal Palace (original club)
Darwen
Derby Junction
Leyton Orient (& Clapton Orient)
Marlow
Old Harrovians
Plymouth Argyle
Port Vale
Rangers (Glasgow)
Shropshire Wanderers
Wrexham
Wycombe Wanderers

One or more quarter-finals:

Birmingham St George's
Bootle
Bournemouth
Bradford Park Avenue
Brentford
Brentwood
Bristol Rovers
Cambridge United
Carlisle United
Chatham
Church
Colchester United
Druids
Exeter City
Gateshead
Gillingham
Glossop
Hampstead Heathens
Hendon
Lincoln City
Maidenhead
Mansfield Town
Middlesbrough Ironopolis
Northwich Victoria
Old Foresters
Oxford United
Southport
Redcar
Old Westminsters
Peterborough United
Sheffield
Romford
Shrewsbury Town
South Shore
Stafford Road
Upton Park
Wednesbury Old Ath.
Tranmere Rovers
Wigan Athletic
Woodford Wells
York City

THE SEASON BY SEASON RESULTS

Key to the listings

The home club is listed first, unless the game was played on a neutral ground. It is possible that a few games are listed incorrectly. The convention in newspapers used to be to list the winning club first, so without a copy of the draw it is often difficult to establish which one was at home. Also, clubs originally drawn at home have the right (with the FA's permission) to play the game on the opponent's ground.

Club names are generally those in use at the time. A list in appendix five shows the clubs that changed their names. However, if different clubs have the same name, a number in brackets has been used to distinguish between them. The index of club appearances should also help to clarify which club is which. Please also see the note on page 265 on the subject of club names.

The first column shows the group number if it is a qualifying round game, and a replay indicator "r". You will also find "r2, r3" and so on for second and subsequent replays.

The following markers appear after the score:

"e" indicates that the game went to extra time. This information is often not recorded in match reports of the time and the indicator is only set when it is known for certain that extra time was played.. All drawn replays could have gone to extra time; however, in the days before floodlights, darkness would often intervene.

"P" indicates that the first named club went through as the result of a penalty shoot out after extra time; "q" that the second named club did (small "p" could not be used because of its similarity on the printed page to "P"). "q" usually means the "away club" won, but when games are played on a neutral ground it means the second named club.

"B" indicates that both clubs were allowed through to the next round. This happened a few times in 1871/72 when clubs were unable to arrange their game before the closing date for the round set by the FA Committee.

"N" indicates that the game was played on a neutral ground. However, this marker is generally not used when a club has lost the use of its ground temporarily and is playing elsewhere.

"v" indicates a void game, usually as a result of a protest by the losing club. The game will have been replayed.

"D" indicates that the home club was disqualified, usually as a result of a protest by the other club. "d" indicates the away club was disqualified.

"wo/s" shows the first club named had a walkover into the next round because the other club scratched. Void games might have caused one of the clubs to scratch rather than face the cost of a replay. Also, because entries were accepted towards the close of the previous season, some clubs may have folded before the new season started.

"wo/d" is used occasionally, to show that a game did not take place because the second named club had been disqualified.

"E" is used for the unusual occasions when both clubs were disqualified.

"T" indicates the game was settled on the toss of a coin. This only happened once, in 1873/74.

"x" indicates that the game was abandoned in extra time. The score shown is that at the end of the 90 minutes. I take the view that the game was complete at the 90 minute mark, so the second games are always described as a replay, and goals scored in the abandoned extra time are excluded. Matches abandoned before ninety minutes are not included, but note that the subsequent game are sometimes described as a replay in match reports of the time.

"w" is used just once, to indicate Darlington's 'lucky loser' status in 1999/2000, when they went through to the third round despite losing in the second round.

"np" is used in 1939/40 to indicated matches that were not played because of the threat of war.

Third place play-off games are not included. These games were originally intended to be played on the evening before the Cup Final. The results were as follows:

1970	Manchester Utd. v. Watford	2-0
1971	Stoke City v. Everton	3-2
1972	Birmingham City v. Stoke City	0-0
1973	Wolves v. Arsenal	3-1
1974	Burnley v. Leicester City	1-0

Birmingham City won the 1972 game on penalties. The first three games were played on neutral grounds, Highbury, Selhurst Park and the Hawthorns respectively. The last two were at Arsenal and Leicester respectively.

Debenhams Cup games are also not included. This short-lived competition was for the two clubs that made the most progress in the FA Cup and were not exempt until the Third Round Proper. In 1976/77, Chester beat Port Vale 4-3 on aggregate (2-0 to Port Vale at Burslem, 4-1 to Chester in Chester). In 1977/78, Blyth Spartans beat Wrexham 3-2 on aggregate (2-1 to Blyth at Wrexham, 1-1 at Blyth). Blyth later returned the trophy to the Debenhams company and for many years its whereabouts was unknown. It came to light in 2019 and was returned to Blyth.

1871/72 to 1876/77

1871/72

Round One

Barnes v Civil Service	2-0
Hampstead Heathens - Bye	
Hitchin v Crystal Palace (1)	0-0 B
Maidenhead v Marlow	2-0
Queen's Park (Glasgow) v Donnington School	B
Royal Engineers v Reigate Priory	wo/s
Upton Park v Clapham Rovers	0-3
Wanderers v Harrow Chequers	wo/s

Round Two

Barnes v Hampstead Heathens	1-1
Clapham Rovers v Wanderers	0-1
Crystal Palace (1) v Maidenhead	3-0
Hitchin v Royal Engineers	0-5
Queen's Park (Glasgow) v Donnington School	wo/s
r Barnes v Hampstead Heathens	0-1

Round Three

Queen's Park (Glasgow) - Bye	
Royal Engineers v Hampstead Heathens	3-0
Wanderers v Crystal Palace (1)	0-0 B

Semi Finals

Royal Engineers v Crystal Palace (1)	0-0 N
Wanderers v Queen's Park (Glasgow)	0-0 N
r Royal Engineers v Crystal Palace (1)	3-0 N
r Wanderers v Queen's Park (Glasgow)	wo/s

Final

Wanderers v Royal Engineers	1-0 N

1872/73

Round One

1st Surrey Rifles v Upton Park	2-0
Barnes v South Norwood	0-1
Clapham Rovers v Hitchin	wo/s
Crystal Palace (1) v Oxford University	2-3
Maidenhead v Marlow	1-0
Queen's Park (Glasgow) - Bye	
Reigate Priory v Windsor Home Park	2-4
Royal Engineers v Civil Service	3-0

Round Two

Maidenhead v 1st Surrey Rifles	3-0
Oxford University v Clapham Rovers	3-0
Queen's Park (Glasgow) - Bye	
Royal Engineers - Bye	
South Norwood v Windsor Home Park	1-0 v
r Windsor Home Park v South Norwood	3-0

Round Three

Maidenhead v Windsor Home Park	1-0
Oxford University v Royal Engineers	1-0
Queen's Park (Glasgow) - Bye	

Round Four

Oxford University v Maidenhead	4-0
Queen's Park (Glasgow) - Bye	

Semi Final

Oxford University v Queen's Park (Glasgow)	wo/s

Wanderers exempt until the final

Final

Wanderers v Oxford University	2-0 N

1873/74

Round One

1st Surrey Rifles v Barnes	0-0
Cambridge University v South Norwood	1-0
Clapham Rovers v Amateur Athletic Club	wo/s
High Wycombe v Old Etonians	wo/s
Maidenhead v Civil Service	wo/s
Pilgrims v Marlow	1-0
Royal Engineers v Brondesbury	5-0
Swifts v Crystal Palace (1)	1-0
Sheffield v Shropshire Wanderers	0-0
Trojans v Farningham	wo/s
Upton Park v Oxford University	0-4
Uxbridge v Gitanos	3-0
Wanderers v Southall	wo/s
Woodford Wells v Reigate Priory	3-2
r Barnes v 1st Surrey Rifles	1-0
r Shropshire Wanderers v Sheffield	0-0 T

Round Two

Clapham Rovers v Cambridge University	1-1
Maidenhead v High Wycombe	1-0
Oxford University v Barnes	2-0
Sheffield v Pilgrims	1-0 N
Swifts v Woodford Wells	2-1
Uxbridge v Royal Engineers	1-2
Wanderers v Trojans	wo/s
r Cambridge University v Clapham Rovers	1-1
r2 Clapham Rovers v Cambridge University	4-1 N

Round Three

Clapham Rovers v Sheffield	2-1 N
Maidenhead v Royal Engineers	0-7
Swifts - Bye	
Wanderers v Oxford University	1-1
r Oxford University v Wanderers	1-0

Semi Finals

Clapham Rovers v Oxford University	0-1
Royal Engineers v Swifts	2-0 N

Final

Oxford University v Royal Engineers	2-0 N

1874/75

Round One

Cambridge University v Crystal Palace (1)	0-0
Civil Service v Harrow Chequers	wo/s
Hitchin v Maidenhead	0-1
Marlow v Royal Engineers	0-3
Oxford University v Brondesbury	6-0
Panthers v Clapham Rovers	0-3
Reigate Priory - Bye	
Shropshire Wanderers v Sheffield	wo/s
South Norwood v Pilgrims	1-3
Southall v Leyton	0-0
Swifts v Old Etonians	0-0
Upton Park v Barnes	0-3
Wanderers v Farningham	16-0
Windsor Home Park v Uxbridge	wo/s
Woodford Wells v High Wycombe	1-0 N
r Crystal Palace (1) v Cambridge University	1-2
r Leyton v Southall	0-5
r Old Etonians v Swifts	1-1
r2 Swifts v Old Etonians	0-3

Round Two

Civil Service v Shropshire Wanderers	1-1
Clapham Rovers v Pilgrims	2-0
Maidenhead v Reigate Priory	2-1 N
Old Etonians - Bye	
Oxford University v Windsor Home Park	wo/s
Royal Engineers v Cambridge University	5-0 N
Wanderers v Barnes	5-0
Woodford Wells v Southall	3-0
r Shropshire Wanderers v Civil Service	wo/s

Round Three

Old Etonians v Maidenhead	1-0 N
Royal Engineers v Clapham Rovers	3-2 N
Shropshire Wanderers v Woodford Wells	1-1eN
Wanderers v Oxford University	1-2 N
r Woodford Wells v Shropshire Wanderers	0-2 N

Semi Finals

Old Etonians v Shropshire Wanderers	1-0 N
Royal Engineers v Oxford University	1-1 N
r Royal Engineers v Oxford University	1-0eN

Final

Royal Engineers v Old Etonians	1-1eN
r Royal Engineers v Old Etonians	2-0 N

1875/76

Round One

105th Regiment v Crystal Palace (1)	0-0
Barnes v Reigate Priory	0-1
Cambridge University v Civil Service	wo/s
Clapham Rovers v Hitchin	wo/s
Herts Rangers v Rochester	4-0
Leyton v Harrow Chequers	wo/s
Maidenhead v Ramblers	2-0
Old Etonians v Pilgrims	4-1
Oxford University v Forest School	6-0 N
Panthers v Woodford Wells	1-0 N
Royal Engineers v High Wycombe	15-0
Sheffield v Shropshire Wanderers	wo/s
South Norwood v Clydesdale	wo/s
Swifts v Marlow	2-0
Upton Park v Southall	1-0
Wanderers v 1st Surrey Rifles	5-0
r Crystal Palace (1) v 105th Regiment	3-0 N

Round Two

Clapham Rovers v Leyton	12-0
Herts Rangers v Oxford University	2-8
Old Etonians v Maidenhead	8-0
Reigate Priory v Cambridge University	0-8
Royal Engineers v Panthers	wo/s
Sheffield v Upton Park	wo/s
Swifts v South Norwood	5-0
Wanderers v Crystal Palace (1)	3-0

Round Three

Cambridge University v Oxford University	0-4 N
Old Etonians v Clapham Rovers	1-0 N
Royal Engineers v Swifts	1-3 N
Wanderers v Sheffield	2-0 N

Semi Finals

Oxford University v Old Etonians	0-1 N
Wanderers v Swifts	2-1 N

Final

Wanderers v Old Etonians	1-1 N
r Wanderers v Old Etonians	3-0 N

1876/77

Round One

105th Regiment v 1st Surrey Rifles	3-0
Barnes v Old Etonians	wo/s
Cambridge University v High Wycombe	wo/s
Clapham Rovers v Reigate Priory	5-0
Forest School v Gresham	4-1
Marlow v Herts Rangers	2-1
Oxford University v Old Salopians	wo/s
Pilgrims v Ramblers	4-1
Queen's Park (Glasgow) - Bye	
Rochester v Highbury Union	5-0
Royal Engineers v Old Harrovians	2-1
Sheffield v Trojans	wo/s
Shropshire Wanderers v Druids	wo/s
South Norwood v Saxons	4-1
Southall v Old Wykehamists	wo/s
Swifts v Reading Hornets	2-0
Upton Park v Leyton	7-0
Wanderers v Saffron Walden Town	wo/s
Wood Grange v Panthers	0-3

Round Two

Barnes v Upton Park	0-1
Cambridge University v Clapham Rovers	2-1
Forest School v Marlow	0-1
Oxford University v 105th Regiment	6-1
Panthers v Pilgrims	0-1
Queen's Park (Glasgow) - Bye	
Rochester v Swifts	1-0
Shropshire Wanderers v Royal Engineers	0-3
South Norwood v Sheffield	0-7
Southall v Wanderers	0-6

Round Three

Cambridge University v Rochester	4-0 N
Oxford University v Queen's Park (Glasgow)	wo/s
Royal Engineers v Sheffield	1-0 N
Upton Park v Marlow	2-2 N
Wanderers v Pilgrims	3-0 N
r Upton Park v Marlow	1-0 N

13

1876/77 to 1880/81

Round Four

Cambridge University v Royal Engineers	1-0 N
Oxford University v Upton Park	0-0 N
Wanderers - Bye	
r Oxford University v Upton Park	1-0 N

Semi Finals

Oxford University - Bye	
Wanderers v Cambridge University	1-0 N

Final

Wanderers v Oxford University	2-1eN

1877/78

Round One

105th Regiment v Old Harrovians	0-2
1st Surrey Rifles v Forest School	1-0
Barnes v St Mark's	wo/s
Cambridge University v Southill Park	3-1
Darwen v Manchester	3-0
Grantham v Clapham Rovers	0-2
Hawks v Minerva	5-2
Hendon (1) v Marlow	0-2
Maidenhead v Reading Hornets	10-0
Notts County v Sheffield	1-1
Old Foresters v Old Wykehamists	wo/s
Oxford University v Herts Rangers	5-2
Panthers v Wanderers	1-9
Pilgrims v Ramblers	0-0
Queen's Park (Glasgow) - Bye	
Reading v South Norwood	2-0 N
Remnants v St Stephens	4-0
Royal Engineers v Highbury Union	wo/s
Shropshire Wanderers v Druids	0-1
Swifts v Leyton	3-2
Upton Park v Rochester	3-0
Wood Grange v High Wycombe	0-4
r Pilgrims v Ramblers	1-0
r Sheffield v Notts County	3-0

Round Two

Barnes v Marlow	3-1
Cambridge University v Maidenhead	4-2e
Clapham Rovers v Swifts	4-0
Darwen v Sheffield	0-1
Druids v Queen's Park (Glasgow)	wo/s
Hawks v Remnants	0-2
High Wycombe v Wanderers	0-9
Old Harrovians v 1st Surrey Rifles	6-0
Oxford University v Old Foresters	1-0
Reading v Upton Park	0-1
Royal Engineers v Pilgrims	6-0

Round Three

Old Harrovians v Cambridge University	2-2 N
Oxford University v Clapham Rovers	3-2 N
Royal Engineers v Druids	8-0 N
Sheffield - Bye	
Upton Park v Remnants	3-0 N
Wanderers v Barnes	1-1 N
r Old Harrovians v Cambridge University	2-2e N
r Wanderers v Barnes	4-1 N
r2 Old Harrovians v Cambridge University	2-0 N

Round Four

Old Harrovians v Upton Park	3-1 N
Royal Engineers v Oxford University	3-3 N
Wanderers v Sheffield	3-0 N
r Royal Engineers v Oxford University	2-2eN
r2 Royal Engineers v Oxford University	4-2 N

Semi Finals

Royal Engineers v Old Harrovians	2-1 N
Wanderers - Bye	

Final

Wanderers v Royal Engineers	3-1 N

1878/79

Round One

Barnes v Maidenhead	1-1
Brentwood (1) v Pilgrims	1-3
Cambridge University v Herts Rangers	2-0
Clapham Rovers v Finchley	wo/s
Darwen v Birch	wo/s
Eagley - Bye	
Forest School v Rochester	7-2
Grey Friars v Marlow	2-1
Minerva v 105th Regiment	wo/s
Notts County v Nottingham Forest	1-3e
Old Harrovians v Southill Park	8-0
Oxford University v Wednesbury Strollers	7-0
Panthers v Runnymede	wo/s
Reading v Hendon (1)	1-0
Remnants v Unity	wo/s
Romford (1) v Ramblers	3-1
Royal Engineers v Old Foresters	3-0
Sheffield v Grantham	1-1
South Norwood v Leyton	wo/s
Swifts v Hawks	2-1
Upton Park v Saffron Walden Town	5-0
Wanderers v Old Etonians	2-7
r Grantham v Sheffield	1-3
r Maidenhead v Barnes	0-4

Round Two

Barnes v Upton Park	3-2e
Cambridge University v South Norwood	3-0
Clapham Rovers v Forest School	10-1
Eagley v Darwen	0-0
Grey Friars v Minerva	0-3
Nottingham Forest v Sheffield	2-0
Old Harrovians v Panthers	3-0
Oxford University v Royal Engineers	4-0
Reading v Old Etonians	0-1
Remnants v Pilgrims	6-2
Swifts v Romford (1)	3-1
r Darwen v Eagley	4-1

Round Three

Clapham Rovers v Cambridge University	1-0eN
Old Etonians v Minerva	5-2 N
Old Harrovians v Nottingham Forest	0-2 N
Oxford University v Barnes	2-1 N
Remnants v Darwen	2-3eN
Swifts - Bye	

Round Four

Clapham Rovers v Swifts	8-1 N
Nottingham Forest v Oxford University	2-1 N
Old Etonians v Darwen	5-5 N
r Old Etonians v Darwen	2-2eN
r2 Old Etonians v Darwen	6-2 N

Semi Finals

Clapham Rovers - Bye	
Old Etonians v Nottingham Forest	2-1 N

Final

Old Etonians v Clapham Rovers	1-0 N

1879/80

Round One

1 Blackburn Rovers v Tyne Association	5-1
Eagley v Darwen	0-1
Nottingham Forest v Notts County	4-0
Sheffield Providence - Bye	
Sheffield v Queen's Park (Glasgow)	wo/s
Turton v Brigg	7-0
2 Aston Villa - Bye	
Birmingham (1) v Panthers	wo/s
Henley v Reading	wo/s
Maidenhead v Calthorpe	3-1
Marlow v Oxford University	1-1
Stafford Road v Wednesbury Strollers	2-0
3 Acton v Old Carthusians	0-4
Argonauts v Hotspur	1-1
Old Etonians v Barnes	wo/s
Rochester v Wanderers	0-6
West End v Swifts	wo/s
4 Finchley v Old Harrovians	1-2
Gresham v Kildare	3-0
Grey Friars v Hanover United	2-1
Remnants v Upton Park	1-1
Royal Engineers v Cambridge University	2-0
5 Herts Rangers v Minerva	2-1
Mosquitos v St Peter's Institute	3-1
Old Foresters v Hendon (1)	1-1
Pilgrims v Clarence	5-2
Romford (1) v Clapham Rovers	0-7
South Norwood v Brentwood (1)	4-2
2r Oxford University v Marlow	1-0
3r Argonauts v Hotspur	0-1
4r Upton Park v Remnants	5-2
5r Hendon (1) v Old Foresters	2-2
5r2 Old Foresters v Hendon (1)	1-3

Round Two

1 Blackburn Rovers v Darwen	3-1
Sheffield v Sheffield Providence	3-3
Turton v Nottingham Forest	0-6
2 Birmingham (1) v Oxford University	0-6
Henley v Maidenhead	1-3
Stafford Road v Aston Villa	1-1
3 Old Etonians - Bye	
Wanderers v Old Carthusians	1-0
West End v Hotspur	1-0
4 Grey Friars v Gresham	9-0
Old Harrovians - Bye	
Royal Engineers v Upton Park	4-1
5 Clapham Rovers v South Norwood	4-1
Hendon (1) v Mosquitos	7-1
Pilgrims v Herts Rangers	wo/s
1r Sheffield v Sheffield Providence	3-0
2r Aston Villa v Stafford Road	3-1

Round Three

1 Nottingham Forest v Blackburn Rovers	6-0
Sheffield - Bye	
2 Maidenhead - Bye	
Oxford University v Aston Villa	wo/s
3 Old Etonians v Wanderers	3-1
West End - Bye	
4 Grey Friars - Bye	
Royal Engineers v Old Harrovians	2-0
5 Clapham Rovers v Pilgrims	7-0
Hendon (1) - Bye	

Round Four

1 Nottingham Forest v Sheffield	2-2 d
2 Maidenhead v Oxford University	0-1
3 Old Etonians v West End	5-1
4 Royal Engineers v Grey Friars	1-0
5 Clapham Rovers v Hendon (1)	2-0

Round Five

Clapham Rovers v Old Etonians	1-0 N
Nottingham Forest - Bye	
Oxford University v Royal Engineers	1-1eN
r Oxford University v Royal Engineers	1-0 N

Semi Finals

Clapham Rovers - Bye	
Oxford University v Nottingham Forest	1-0 N

Final

Clapham Rovers v Oxford University	1-0 N

1880/81

Round One

1 Astley Bridge v Eagley	4-0
Blackburn Rovers v Sheffield Providence	6-2
Darwen v Brigg	8-0
Sheffield v Blackburn Olympic	5-4
Sheffield Wednesday v Queen's Park (Glasgow)	wo/s
Turton v Brigg Brittania	5-0
2 Aston Villa v Wednesbury Strollers	5-3
Calthorpe v Grantham	1-2
Nottingham Forest v Caius College	wo/s
Notts County v Derbyshire	4-4
Stafford Road v Spilsby	7-0 N
3 Clapham Rovers v Finchley	15-0
Mosquitos v Upton Park	1-8
Reading v Hotspur	5-1
Swifts v Old Foresters	1-1
Weybridge Swallows v Henley	3-1
4 Brentwood (1) v Old Etonians	0-10
Grey Friars v Windsor Home Park	0-0
Herts Rangers v Barnes	6-0
Maidenhead v Old Harrovians	1-1
St Peter's Institute v Hendon (1)	1-8
5 Old Carthusians v Saffron Walden Town	7-0
Pilgrims v Old Philberdians	wo/s
Rangers (London) v Wanderers	wo/s
Rochester v Dreadnought	1-2
Royal Engineers v Remnants	0-0
6 Acton v Kildare	1-1
Marlow v Clarence	6-0
Reading Abbey v St Albans (Upton)	1-0
Romford (1) v Reading Minster	1-1 N
West End v Hanover United	1-0
2r Derbyshire v Notts County	2-4e
3r Old Foresters v Swifts	1-2
4r Old Harrovians v Maidenhead	0-1 N
r Windsor Home Park v Grey Friars	1-3
5r Remnants v Royal Engineers	0-1
6r Kildare v Acton	0-5
r Romford (1) v Reading Minster	wo/s

14

1880/81 to 1882/83

Round Two

1 Astley Bridge v Turton	0-3
Blackburn Rovers v Sheffield Wednesday	0-4
Sheffield v Darwen	1-5
2 Grantham v Stafford Road	1-1
Nottingham Forest v Aston Villa	1-2
Notts County - Bye	
3 Clapham Rovers - Bye	
Reading v Swifts	0-1
Weybridge Swallows v Upton Park	0-3
4 Grey Friars v Maidenhead	1-0
Herts Rangers - Bye	
Old Etonians v Hendon (1)	2-0
5 Old Carthusians v Dreadnought	5-1
Rangers (London) - Bye	
Royal Engineers v Pilgrims	1-0
6 Marlow v West End	4-0
Reading Abbey v Acton	2-1
Romford (1) - Bye	
2r Stafford Road v Grantham	7-1

Round Three

1 Darwen - Bye	
Turton v Sheffield Wednesday	0-2
2 Notts County v Aston Villa	1-3
Stafford Road - Bye	
3 Clapham Rovers v Swifts	2-1
Upton Park - Bye	
4 Grey Friars - Bye	
Old Etonians v Herts Rangers	3-0
5 Old Carthusians - Bye	
Royal Engineers v Rangers (London)	6-0
6 Marlow - Bye	
Romford (1) v Reading Abbey	2-0

Round Four

1 Darwen v Sheffield Wednesday	5-2
2 Aston Villa v Stafford Road	2-3
3 Clapham Rovers v Upton Park	5-4
4 Grey Friars v Old Etonians	0-4
5 Royal Engineers v Old Carthusians	1-2
6 Romford (1) v Marlow	2-1

Round Five

Darwen v Romford (1)	15-0
Old Carthusians v Clapham Rovers	3-1e
Stafford Road v Old Etonians	1-2

Semi Finals

Old Carthusians v Darwen	4-1 N
Old Etonians - Bye	

Final

Old Carthusians v Old Etonians	3-0 N

1881/82

Round One

1 Accrington v Queen's Park (Glasgow)	wo/s
Astley Bridge v Turton	2-2
Blackburn Rovers v Blackburn Park Road	9-1
Bolton Wanderers v Eagley	5-5
Bootle (1) v Blackburn Law	2-1
Darwen v Blackburn Olympic	3-1
2 Aston Villa v Nottingham Forest	4-1
Notts County v Calthorpe	wo/s
Small Heath Alliance v Derby Town	4-1
Wednesbury Old Athletic v Mitchell's St George's	9-0
Wednesbury Strollers v Stafford Road	3-1
3 Grantham v Brigg	6-0
Sheffield Heeley v Lockwood Brothers	5-1
Sheffield v Brigg Brittania	8-0
Sheffield Wednesday v Sheffield Providence	2-0
Staveley v Spilsby	5-1
4 Dreadnought v Caius College	wo/s
Marlow v Brentwood (1)	3-1 N
Reading v Hendon (1)	5-0
St Bart's Hospital v Wanderers	wo/s
West End v Remnants	3-2
5 Barnes v Rochester	3-1
Esher Leopold v Old Carthusians	0-5
Kildare v Royal Engineers	0-6
Mosquitos v Pilgrims	1-1
Old Foresters v Morton Rangers	3-0
6 Acton v Finchley	0-0
Henley v Maidenhead	0-2
Herts Rangers v Swifts	0-4
Old Etonians v Clapham Rovers	2-2
Olympic v Old Harrovians	2-4
7 Hanover United - Bye	
Hotspur v Highbury Union	1-0
Reading Minster v Windsor Home Park	1-0
Romford (1) v Rangers (London)	wo/s
Upton Park v St Albans (Upton)	3-0
Woodford Bridge v Reading Abbey	1-1
1r Eagley v Bolton Wanderers	0-1
r Turton v Astley Bridge	1-1
4r Pilgrims v Mosquitos	5-0
6r Acton v Finchley	4-0
r Clapham Rovers v Old Etonians	0-1
7r Reading Abbey v Woodford Bridge	2-1
1r2 Astley Bridge v Turton	3-3 N
1r3 Turton v Astley Bridge	2-0

Round Two

1 Blackburn Rovers v Bolton Wanderers	6-2
Darwen v Accrington	3-1
Turton v Bootle (1)	4-0
2 Aston Villa v Notts County	5-3 v
Notts County v Wednesbury Strollers	5-3 v
Wednesbury Old Athletic v Small Heath Alliance	6-0
3 Sheffield v Sheffield Heeley	0-4
Sheffield Wednesday - Bye	
Staveley v Grantham	3-1
4 Dreadnought - Bye	
Marlow v St Bart's Hospital	2-0
West End v Reading	1-1 D
5 Old Carthusians v Barnes	7-1
Old Foresters v Pilgrims	3-1
Royal Engineers - Bye	
6 Maidenhead v Acton	2-1e
Old Etonians - Bye	
Swifts v Old Harrovians	7-1
7 Hanover United v Upton Park	1-3
Reading Abbey v Hotspur	1-4
Reading Minster v Romford (1)	3-1
2r Notts County v Wednesbury Strollers	11-1 N
4r Reading v West End	wo/s

Round Three

1 Blackburn Rovers - Bye	
Darwen v Turton	4-1
2 Aston Villa v Notts County	2-2e
Wednesbury Old Athletic - Bye	
3 Sheffield Heeley - Bye	
Sheffield Wednesday v Staveley	2-2
4 Marlow v Dreadnought	2-1
Reading - Bye	
5 Old Carthusians v Royal Engineers	0-2
Old Foresters - Bye	
6 Maidenhead - Bye	
Old Etonians v Swifts	3-0
7 Hotspur v Reading Minster	0-0
Upton Park - Bye	
2r Notts County v Aston Villa	2-2e
3r Staveley v Sheffield Wednesday	0-0e
7r Reading Minster v Hotspur	0-2
2r2 Aston Villa v Notts County	4-1
3r2 Sheffield Wednesday v Staveley	5-1 N

Round Four

1 Blackburn Rovers v Darwen	5-1
2 Wednesbury Old Athletic v Aston Villa	4-2
3 Sheffield Wednesday v Sheffield Heeley	3-1 N
4 Marlow v Reading	wo/s
5 Old Foresters v Royal Engineers	2-1
6 Old Etonians v Maidenhead	6-3
7 Upton Park v Hotspur	5-0

Round Five

Old Etonians - Bye	
Old Foresters v Marlow	0-0eN
Sheffield Wednesday v Upton Park	6-0
Wednesbury Old Athletic v Blackburn Rovers	1-3
r Marlow v Old Foresters	1-0

Semi Finals

Blackburn Rovers v Sheffield Wednesday	0-0 N
Old Etonians v Marlow	5-0 N
r Sheffield Wednesday v Blackburn Rovers	1-5 N

Final

Old Etonians v Blackburn Rovers	1-0 N

1882/83

Round One

1 Grimsby Town v Queen's Park (Glasgow)	wo/s
Macclesfield (1) v Lockwood Brothers	3-4
Nottingham Forest v Brigg Brittania	wo/s
Notts County v Sheffield	6-1
Phoenix Bessemer v Grantham	wo/s
Sheffield Heeley - Bye	
Sheffield Wednesday v Spilsby	12-2
2 Aston Unity - Bye	
Aston Villa v Walsall Swifts	4-1
Chesterfield Spital v Wednesbury Old Athletic	1-7
Mitchell's St George's v Calthorpe	4-1
Small Heath Alliance v Stafford Road	3-3
Walsall Town v Staveley	4-1
3 Blackburn Olympic v Accrington	6-3
Blackburn Park Road v Darwen	1-4
Blackburn Rovers v Blackpool St John's	11-1
Church v Clitheroe	5-0
Darwen Ramblers v South Shore	5-2
Haslingden - Bye	
Irwell Springs v Lower Darwen	2-5
4 Bolton Olympic v Eagley	4-7
Bolton Wanderers v Bootle (1)	6-1
Druids v Oswestry	1-1
Halliwell v Great Lever	3-2
Northwich Victoria v Astley Bridge	3-2
Southport (1) v Liverpool Ramblers	1-1
5 Kildare v Clapham Rovers	0-3
Mosquitos v Hanover United	1-0
United Hospital v London Olympic	3-0
Windsor Home Park v Acton	3-0
6 Barnes v Brentwood	2-4
Old Etonians v Old Foresters	1-1
Rochester v Hotspur	2-0
Swifts v Highbury Union	4-1
Upton Park - Bye	
7 Etonian Ramblers v Romford (1)	6-2
Maidenhead v Old Westminsters	0-2
Pilgrims v Old Carthusians	0-6
Reading - Bye	
Royal Engineers v Woodford Bridge	3-1
8 Chatham - Bye	
Dreadnought v South Reading	1-2 v
Hornchurch (1) v Marlow	0-2
Reading Minster v Remnants	wo/s
West End v Hendon (1)	1-3
2r Stafford Road v Small Heath Alliance	6-2
4r Druids v Oswestry	2-0
r Liverpool Ramblers v Southport (1)	4-0
6r Old Foresters v Old Etonians	1-3
8r Dreadnought v South Reading	1-2

Round Two

1 Grimsby Town v Phoenix Bessemer	1-9
Lockwood Brothers v Sheffield Wednesday	0-6
Nottingham Forest v Sheffield Heeley	7-2
Notts County - Bye	
2 Aston Unity v Mitchell's St George's	3-1
Aston Villa v Wednesbury Old Athletic	4-1
Stafford Road v Walsall Town	1-4
3 Blackburn Olympic v Lower Darwen	8-1
Blackburn Rovers v Darwen	0-1
Church - Bye	
Darwen Ramblers v Haslingden	3-2
4 Bolton Wanderers v Liverpool Ramblers	3-0
Druids v Northwich Victoria	5-0
Eagley v Halliwell	3-1
5 Clapham Rovers v Hanover United	7-1
Windsor Home Park v United Hospital	3-1
6 Brentwood (1) v Old Etonians	1-2
Rochester - Bye	
Upton Park v Swifts	2-2
7 Etonian Ramblers v Old Carthusians	0-7
Old Westminsters - Bye	
Royal Engineers v Reading	8-0
8 Hendon (1) v Chatham	2-1
Marlow v Reading Minster	wo/s
South Reading - Bye	
6r Upton Park v Swifts	2-3 N

Round Three

1 Nottingham Forest v Sheffield Wednesday	2-2
Notts County v Phoenix Bessemer	4-1
2 Aston Villa v Aston Unity	3-1
Walsall Town - Bye	
3 Blackburn Olympic v Darwen Ramblers	8-0
Church v Darwen	2-2
4 Druids v Bolton Wanderers	0-0
Eagley - Bye	
5 Windsor Home Park v Clapham Rovers	0-3
6 Rochester v Old Etonians	0-7
Swifts - Bye	
7 Old Carthusians v Old Westminsters	3-2
Royal Engineers - Bye	
8 Hendon (1) v South Reading	11-1
Marlow - Bye	
1r Sheffield Wednesday v Nottingham Forest	3-2
3r Darwen v Church	0-2
4r Bolton Wanderers v Druids	1-1e
4r2 Druids v Bolton Wanderers	1-0 N

Round Four

1 Sheffield Wednesday v Notts County	1-4
2 Aston Villa v Walsall Town	2-1
3 Church v Blackburn Olympic	0-2
4 Eagley v Druids	1-2e
5 Clapham Rovers - Bye	
6 Old Etonians v Swifts	2-0
7 Old Carthusians v Royal Engineers	6-2
8 Marlow v Hendon (1)	0-3

15

1882/83 to 1884/85

Round Five

Blackburn Olympic v Druids	4-1
Hendon (1) v Old Etonians	2-4
Notts County v Aston Villa	4-3
Old Carthusians v Clapham Rovers	5-3

Semi Finals

Blackburn Olympic v Old Carthusians	4-0 N
Old Etonians v Notts County	2-1 N

Final

Blackburn Olympic v Old Etonians	2-1eN

1883/84

Round One

1	Chesterfield Spital v Rotherham Town	1-1
	Grantham v Spilsby	3-2
	Hull Town v Grimsby Town	1-3
	Middlesbrough v Staveley	1-5
	Nottingham Forest v Redcar	wo/s
	Notts County v Sheffield Heeley	3-1
	Sheffield v Lockwood Brothers	1-4
	Sheffield Wednesday - Bye	
2	Calthorpe v Walsall Town	0-9
	Derby Midland - Bye	
	Small Heath Alliance v Birmingham Excelsior	1-1
	Stafford Road v Aston Unity	5-1
	Walsall Swifts v Aston Villa	1-5
	Wednesbury Old Athletic v Mitchell's St George's	5-0
	West Bromwich Albion v Wednesbury Town	0-2
	Wolverhampton Wan. v Long Eaton Rangers	4-1
3	Accrington v Blackpool St John's	4-0
	Blackburn Olympic v Darwen Ramblers	5-1
	Blackburn Park Road v Clitheroe Low Moor	6-0
	Blackburn Rovers v Southport (1)	7-1
	Clitheroe v South Shore	3-3
	Darwen v Church	2-2
	Padiham v Lower Darwen	3-1
4	Bolton Association v Bradshaw	5-1
	Bolton Wanderers v Bolton Olympic	9-0
	Great Lever v Astley Bridge	4-1
	Halliwell v Eagley	2-5
	Hurst v Turton	3-1
	Preston North End - Bye	
	Rossendale v Irwell Springs	2-6
5	Crewe Alexandra v Queen's Park (Glasgow)	0-10
	Davenham v Macclesfield (1)	2-0
	Druids v Northwich Victoria	0-1
	Oswestry v Hartford St John's	2-0
	Stoke v Manchester	1-2
	Wrexham Olympic v Liverpool Ramblers	wo/s
6	Hanover United v Brentwood (1)	1-6
	Hendon (1) v Old Etonians	3-2
	Mosquitos v Pilgrims	3-2
	Old Westminsters v Chatham	3-0
	Romford (1) v Woodford Bridge	3-0
7	Acton v Upton Park	0-2
	Old Foresters v Dreadnought	2-1
	Reading Minster v Old Carthusians	1-10
	Reading v South Reading	2-2
	West End v Maidenhead	1-0
8	Clapham Rovers v Kildare	wo/s
	Hornchurch (1) v Marlow	0-9
	Uxbridge v Rochester	1-2
	Swifts - Bye	
	Upton Rangers v Old Wykehamists	0-7
	Windsor Home Park v Royal Engineers	5-3
1r	Chesterfield Spital v Rotherham Town	2-7
2r	Birmingham Excelsior v Small Heath Alliance	3-2
3r	Church v Darwen	0-1
r	South Shore v Clitheroe	3-2
7r	Reading v South Reading	0-4

Round Two

1	Grantham v Grimsby Town	4-0
	Lockwood Brothers v Rotherham Town	3-1 N
	Notts County v Nottingham Forest	3-0
	Staveley v Sheffield Wednesday	3-1
2	Birmingham Excelsior v Derby Midland	1-1
	Stafford Road v Aston Villa	0-5
	Walsall Town v Wednesbury Town	2-2
	Wednesbury Old Athletic v Wolverhampton Wan.	4-2
3	Accrington v Blackburn Park Road	3-2D
	Darwen v Blackburn Olympic	1-2e
	Padiham - Bye	
	South Shore v Blackburn Rovers	0-7
4	Bolton Wanderers v Bolton Association	3-0
	Eagley - Bye	
	Hurst v Irwell Springs	3-2 v
	Preston North End v Great Lever	4-1
5	Davenham v Northwich Victoria	1-5
	Queen's Park (Glasgow) v Manchester	15-0
	Wrexham Olympic v Oswestry	3-4
6	Brentwood (1) - Bye	
	Old Westminsters v Hendon (1)	2-1

	Romford (1) v Mosquitos	3-1
7	Old Carthusians v Old Foresters	2-7
	Reading v West End	1-0
	Upton Park - Bye	
8	Clapham Rovers v Rochester	7-0
	Swifts v Marlow	2-0
	Windsor Home Park v Old Wykehamists	0-1
2r	Derby Midland v Birmingham Excelsior	2-1
r	Wednesbury Town v Walsall Town	6-0
4r	Irwell Springs v Hurst	wo/s

Round Three

1	Grantham v Notts County	1-4
	Staveley v Lockwood Brothers	1-0
2	Wednesbury Old Athletic v Aston Villa	4-7
	Wednesbury Town v Derby Midland	1-0
3	Blackburn Olympic - Bye	
	Blackburn Rovers v Padiham	3-0
4	Bolton Wanderers v Irwell Springs	8-1
	Preston North End v Eagley	9-1
5	Northwich Victoria - Bye	
	Oswestry v Queen's Park (Glasgow)	1-7
6	Old Westminsters - Bye	
	Romford (1) v Brentwood (1)	1-4
7	Old Foresters - Bye	
	Reading v Upton Park	1-6
8	Clapham Rovers v Swifts	1-2
	Old Wykehamists - Bye	

Round Four

Blackburn Olympic v Old Wykehamists	6-0
Blackburn Rovers v Staveley	5-1
Northwich Victoria v Brentwood (1)	3-0
Notts County v Bolton Wanderers	2-2e
Old Westminsters v Wednesbury Town	5-0
Preston North End v Upton Park	1-1 D
Queen's Park (Glasgow) v Aston Villa	6-1
Swifts v Old Foresters	2-1
r Bolton Wanderers v Notts County	1-2

Round Five

Blackburn Olympic v Northwich Victoria	9-1
Notts County v Swifts	1-1e
Old Westminsters v Queen's Park (Glasgow)	0-1
Upton Park v Blackburn Rovers	0-3
r Swifts v Notts County	0-1 N

Semi Finals

Blackburn Rovers v Notts County	1-0 N
Queen's Park (Glasgow) v Blackburn Olympic	4-0 N

Final

Blackburn Rovers v Queen's Park (Glasgow)	2-1 N

1884/85

Round One

1	Aston Unity v Mitchell's St George's	0-5
	Aston Villa v Wednesbury Town	4-1
	Birmingham Excelsior v Small Heath Alliance	2-0
	Derby City v Walsall Town	0-7
	Derby Junction v West Bromwich Albion	1-7
	Derby Midland v Wednesbury Old Athletic	1-2
	Walsall Swifts v Stafford Road	0-0
	Wolverhampton Wan. v Derby St Luke's	0-0
2	Chesterfield Spital - Bye	
	Lockwood Brothers v Sheffield	0-3
	Long Eaton Rangers v Sheffield Wednesday	0-1
	Nottingham Forest v Rotherham Town	5-0
	Notts County v Notts Olympic	2-0
	Sheffield Heeley v Notts Wanderers	1-0
	Staveley v Notts Rangers	4-1
3	Bolton Association v Astley Bridge	wo/s
	Darwen v Bradshaw	11-0
	Fishwick Ramblers v Darwen Ramblers	2-1
	Higher Walton v Darwen Old Wanderers	1-1
	Lower Darwen v Halliwell	4-1
4	Chirk v Davenham	4-2
	Crewe Alexandra v Oswestry	2-1
	Druids v Liverpool Ramblers	6-1
	Leek v Northwich Victoria	4-3
	Macclesfield (1) v Hartford St John's	9-0
	Newtown v Stafford Rangers	wo/s
	Queen's Park (Glasgow) v Stoke	wo/s
	Wrexham Olympic v Goldenhill	1-0
5	Grantham v Grimsby Town	1-1
	Hull Town v Lincoln City	1-5
	Middlesbrough v Grimsby District	wo/s
	Newark v Spilsby	7-3
	Redcar v Sunderland	3-1
6	Accrington v Southport (1)	3-0 D
	Blackburn Park Road v Clitheroe Low Moor	3-3 D
	Blackburn Rovers v Rossendale	11-0
	Hurst v Church	2-3
	Oswaldtwistle Rovers v Blackburn Olympic	0-12

	South Shore v Rawtenstall	wo/s
	Witton v Clitheroe	wo/s
7	Acton v Old Carthusians	1-7
	Maidenhead v Old Wykehamists	0-3
	Marlow v Royal Engineers	10-1
	Reading v Rochester	2-0
	Uxbridge v Hotspur	1-3
	West End v Upton Park	3-3
8	Chatham v Windsor Home Park	wo/s
	Clapham Rovers v Hendon (1)	3-3
	Dulwich v Pilgrims	3-2
	Hanover United v Reading Minster	1-0
	Hoddesdon Town v Old Foresters	0-8
	Romford (1) v Clapton	3-2
9	Brentwood (1) v Barnes	2-0
	Casuals v South Reading	1-4
	Henley - Bye	
	Luton Wanderers v Old Etonians	1-3
	Old Westminsters v Bournemouth Rovers	6-0
	Swifts v Old Brightonians	3-0
1r	Derby St Luke's v Wolverhampton Wan.	4-2e
	r Stafford Road v Walsall Swifts	1-2
3r	Darwen Old Wanderers v Higher Walton	4-1
5r	Grimsby Town v Grantham	1-0
7r	Upton Park v West End	wo/s
8r	Hendon (1) v Clapham Rovers	6-0

Round Two

1	Birmingham Excelsior v Mitchell's St George's	2-2
	Derby St Luke's v Walsall Swifts	0-1
	Walsall Town v Aston Villa	0-2
	West Bromwich Albion v Wednesbury Old Athletic	4-2
2	Nottingham Forest v Sheffield Heeley	4-1
	Sheffield v Chesterfield Spital	4-1
	Sheffield Wednesday - Bye	
	Staveley v Notts County	0-2
3	Darwen Old Wanderers v Bolton Association	7-2
	Fishwick Ramblers v Darwen	0-2
	Lower Darwen - Bye	
4	Chirk v Wrexham Olympic	4-1
	Macclesfield (1) v Leek	1-5
	Newtown v Druids	1-1
	Queen's Park (Glasgow) v Crewe Alexandra	2-1
5	Grimsby Town v Redcar	3-1
	Lincoln City - Bye	
	Middlesbrough v Newark	4-1
6	Blackburn Rovers v Blackburn Olympic	3-2
	South Shore v Church	2-3
	Southport (1) v Clitheroe Low Moor	3-1
	Witton - Bye	
7	Hotspur v Old Wykehamists	1-2
	Old Carthusians v Marlow	5-3
	Upton Park v Reading	3-1
8	Chatham v Hendon (1)	1-0
	Hanover United v Old Foresters	2-1
	Romford (1) v Dulwich	3-0
9	Brentwood (1) v Old Etonians	2-2
	Old Westminsters v Henley	7-0
	Swifts v South Reading	3-2
1r	Mitchell's St George's v Birmingham Excelsior	2-0
4r	Druids v Newtown	6-0
9r	Old Etonians v Brentwood (1)	6-1

Round Three

1	Aston Villa v West Bromwich Albion	0-0
	Mitchell's St George's v Walsall Swifts	2-3
2	Notts County v Sheffield	5-0
	Sheffield Wednesday v Nottingham Forest	1-2
3	Darwen - Bye	
	Lower Darwen v Darwen Old Wanderers	4-2
4	Druids v Chirk	4-1
	Leek v Queen's Park (Glasgow)	2-3
5	Grimsby Town v Lincoln City	1-0
	Middlesbrough - Bye	
6	Blackburn Rovers v Witton	5-0
	Church v Southport (1)	10-0
7	Old Carthusians - Bye	
	Old Wykehamists v Upton Park	2-1
8	Hanover United v Chatham	0-2
	Romford (1) - Bye	
9	Old Etonians - Bye	
	Swifts v Old Westminsters	1-1
1r	West Bromwich Albion v Aston Villa	3-0
9r	Old Westminsters v Swifts	2-2
9r2	Swifts v Old Westminsters	2-1

Round Four

Blackburn Rovers v Romford (1)	8-0
Chatham v Lower Darwen	1-0
Church v Darwen	3-0
Old Carthusians v Grimsby Town	3-0
Old Etonians v Middlesbrough	5-2e
Queen's Park (Glasgow) v Old Wykehamists	7-0
Swifts v Nottingham Forest	0-1
Walsall Swifts v Notts County	1-4
West Bromwich Albion v Druids	1-0

16

1884/85 to 1886/87

Round Five

Blackburn Rovers - Bye	
Chatham v Old Carthusians	0-3
Church - Bye	
Nottingham Forest - Bye	
Notts County - Bye	
Old Etonians - Bye	
Queen's Park (Glasgow) - Bye	
West Bromwich Albion - Bye	

Round Six

Church v Old Carthusians	0-1
Notts County v Queen's Park (Glasgow)	2-2
Old Etonians v Nottingham Forest	0-2
West Bromwich Albion v Blackburn Rovers	0-2
r Queen's Park (Glasgow) v Notts County	2-1 N

Semi Finals

Blackburn Rovers v Old Carthusians	5-1 N
Nottingham Forest v Queen's Park (Glasgow)	1-1 N
r Queen's Park (Glasgow) v Nottingham Forest	3-0 N

Final

Blackburn Rovers v Queen's Park (Glasgow)	2-0 N

1885/86

Round One

1 Bolton Wanderers v Eagley	6-0
Halliwell v Fishwick Ramblers	2-1
Higher Walton v South Shore	3-4
Hurst v Bradshaw	2-1 v
Preston North End v Great Lever	wo/s
Queen's Park (Glasgow) v Partick Thistle	5-1
Rawtenstall v Rangers (Glasgow)	wo/s
Southport (1) v Astley Bridge	2-3
2 Accrington v Witton	5-4
Blackburn Olympic v Church	4-2 v
Clitheroe v Blackburn Rovers	0-2
Darwen Old Wanderers v Burnley	11-0
Oswaldtwistle Rovers v Lower Darwen	3-1
Padiham v Heart of Midlothian	wo/s
Rossendale v Clitheroe Low Moor	6-2
Third Lanark v Blackburn Park Road	4-2
3 Birmingham Excelsior v Derby Midland	1-2
Darwen v Derby Junction	2-2
Derby County v Mitchell's St George's	3-0
Small Heath Alliance v Burton Wanderers	9-2
Stafford Road v Matlock	7-0
Walsall Swifts - Bye	
Walsall Town v Aston Villa	0-5
Wednesbury Old Athletic v Burton Swifts	5-1
West Bromwich Albion v Aston Unity	4-1
Wolverhampton Wan. v Derby St Luke's	7-0
4 Lockwood Brothers v Notts Rangers	2-2
Long Eaton Rangers v Sheffield Wednesday	2-0
Mexborough v Staveley	1-1
Newark v Sheffield	0-3
Nottingham Forest v Mellors (Nottm)	6-2
Notts County v Rotherham Town	15-0
Notts Wanderers v Notts Olympic	2-2
Sheffield Heeley v Eckington Works	2-1
5 Bollington v Oswestry	0-5
Burslem Port Vale v Chirk	3-0
Davenham v Goldenhill	2-1
Hartford St John's v Newtown	0-0
Leek v Wrexham Olympic	6-3
Macclesfield (1) v Northwich Victoria	4-1
Stafford Rangers v Druids	1-4
Stoke v Crewe Alexandra	2-2
6 Darlington - Bye	
Gainsborough Trinity v Grantham	4-1
Lincoln City v Grimsby Town	0-2
Lincoln Lindum v Grimsby District	4-0
Middlesbrough v Horncastle	wo/s
Redcar v Sunderland	3-0
7 Chatham v Old Carthusians	0-2
Hanover United v Romford (1)	1-1
Luton Wanderers v Chesham	3-2
Marlow v Luton Town	3-0
Old Brightonians v Acton	2-1
Old Etonians v Bournemouth Rovers	wo/s
Old Westminsters v Hotspur	3-1
Old Wykehamists v Uxbridge	5-0
Upton Park v United London Swifts	4-2
8 1st Surrey Rifles v Clapham Rovers	0-12
Barnes v Lancing Old Boys	1-7
Brentwood (1) v Maidenhead	3-0
Dulwich v South Reading	1-2
Hendon (1) v Clapton	0-4
Old Harrovians v St James	wo/s
Rochester v Reading	6-1
Royal Engineers v Old Foresters	1-5
Swifts v Casuals	7-1
1r Bradshaw v Hurst	1-1
2r Church v Blackburn Olympic	2-2
3r Darwen v Derby Junction	4-0
4r Notts Olympic v Notts Wanderers	4-1
r Notts Rangers v Lockwood Brothers	4-0
r Staveley v Mexborough	wo/s
5r Crewe Alexandra v Stoke	1-0e
r Newtown v Hartford St John's	3-1
7r Romford (1) v Hanover United	3-0
1r2 Hurst v Bradshaw	3-2 N
2r2 Church v Blackburn Olympic	3-1

Round Two

1 Hurst v Halliwell	3-1 v
Preston North End v Astley Bridge	11-3
Rawtenstall v Bolton Wanderers	3-3 D
South Shore v Queen's Park (Glasgow)	wo/s
2 Blackburn Rovers v Oswaldtwistle Rovers	1-0
Church v Third Lanark	wo/s
Darwen Old Wanderers v Accrington	2-1
Rossendale v Padiham	9-1
3 Derby County v Aston Villa	2-0
Derby Midland v Walsall Swifts	1-3
Small Heath Alliance v Darwen	3-1
West Bromwich Albion v Wednesbury Old Athletic	3-2
Wolverhampton Wan. v Stafford Road	4-2
4 Long Eaton Rangers v Staveley	1-4
Nottingham Forest v Notts Olympic	4-1
Notts County v Sheffield	8-0
Sheffield Heeley v Notts Rangers	1-6
5 Davenham v Macclesfield (1)	8-1
Druids v Burslem Port Vale	2-2e
Leek v Newtown	wo/s
Oswestry v Crewe Alexandra	1-1
6 Gainsborough Trinity v Middlesbrough	1-2e
Grimsby Town v Darlington	8-0
Redcar v Lincoln Lindum	2-0
7 Marlow v Old Etonians	6-1
Old Brightonians v Old Westminsters	0-3
Old Wykehamists v Luton Wanderers	10-0
Romford (1) - Bye	
Upton Park v Old Carthusians	0-6
8 Brentwood (1) v Lancing Old Boys	6-1
Clapham Rovers - Bye	
Clapton v South Reading	1-1
Old Harrovians v Old Foresters	2-1
Swifts v Rochester	5-1
1r Halliwell v Hurst	wo/s
5r Burslem Port Vale v Druids	5-1
r Crewe Alexandra v Oswestry	wo/d
8r South Reading v Clapton	wo/d

Round Three

1 Bolton Wanderers v Preston North End	2-3 d
Halliwell v South Shore	1-6
2 Blackburn Rovers v Darwen Old Wanderers	6-1
Church v Rossendale	5-1
3 Small Heath Alliance v Derby County	4-2
West Bromwich Albion - Bye	
Wolverhampton Wan. v Walsall Swifts	2-1
4 Notts County v Notts Rangers	3-0
Staveley v Nottingham Forest	2-1
5 Davenham v Crewe Alexandra	2-1
Leek v Burslem Port Vale	2-3ev
6 Middlesbrough v Grimsby Town	2-1
Redcar - Bye	
7 Marlow v Old Wykehamists	d/d
Old Carthusians - Bye	
Old Westminsters v Romford (1)	5-1
8 Brentwood (1) - Bye	
South Reading v Clapham Rovers	wo/d
Swifts v Old Harrovians	wo/d
5r Burslem Port Vale v Leek	wo/s

Round Four

Blackburn Rovers - Bye	
Bolton Wanderers - Bye	
Burslem Port Vale - Bye	
Church - Bye	
Davenham - Bye	
Middlesbrough - Bye	
Notts County - Bye	
Old Carthusians - Bye	
Old Westminsters - Bye	
Redcar - Bye	
Small Heath Alliance - Bye	
8 South Reading v Brentwood (1)	0-3
South Shore - Bye	
Staveley - Bye	
Swifts - Bye	
3 West Bromwich Albion v Wolverhampton Wan.	3-1

Round Five

Blackburn Rovers v Staveley	7-1
Burslem Port Vale v Brentwood (1)	2-1 v
Church v Swifts	2-6
Old Westminsters v Bolton Wanderers	wo/d
Redcar v Middlesbrough	2-1
Small Heath Alliance v Davenham	2-1
South Shore v Notts County	2-1
West Bromwich Albion v Old Carthusians	1-0
r Brentwood (1) v Burslem Port Vale	3-3eN
r2 Brentwood (1) v Burslem Port Vale	wo/s

Round Six

Brentwood (1) v Blackburn Rovers	1-3
Small Heath Alliance v Redcar	2-0
South Shore v Swifts	1-2
West Bromwich Albion v Old Westminsters	6-0

Semi Finals

Blackburn Rovers v Swifts	2-1 N
West Bromwich Albion v Small Heath Alliance	4-0 N

Final

Blackburn Rovers v West Bromwich Albion	0-0 N
r Blackburn Rovers v West Bromwich Albion	2-0 N

1886/87

Round One

1 Astley Bridge v Burnley	3-3
Blackburn Rovers v Halliwell	wo/s
Bolton Wanderers v South Shore	5-3
Darwen v Heart of Midlothian	7-1
Oswaldtwistle Rovers v Witton	2-3
Queen's Park (Glasgow) v Preston North End	0-3
Renton v Accrington	1-0
Third Lanark v Higher Walton	5-0
2 Blackburn Olympic v Partick Thistle	1-3
Blackburn Park Road v Cliftonville	2-2
Bootle (1) v Great Lever	2-4
Burton Swifts v Crosswell's Brewery	0-1
Church v Rawtenstall	1-1e
Darwen Old Wanderers v Cowlairs	1-4
Fleetwood Rangers v Newton Heath	2-2 d
Rangers (Glasgow) v Everton	wo/s
3 Aston Villa v Wednesbury Old Athletic	13-0
Birmingham Excelsior v Derby Midland	3-3e
Derby County v Aston Unity	4-1
Derby St Luke's v Walsall Town	3-3e
Small Heath Alliance v Mitchell's St George's	1-3
Wellington St George's v Derby Junction	0-1
West Bromwich Albion v Burton Wanderers	6-0
Wolverhampton Wan. v Matlock	6-0
4 Cleethorpes Town v Mellors (Nottm)	2-1
Grimsby Town v Sheffield Heeley	4-1
Lockwood Brothers v Long Eaton Rangers	1-0
Nottingham Forest v Notts Olympic	3-0
Notts County v Basford Rovers	13-0
Sheffield v Notts Rangers	0-3
Staveley v Attercliffe	7-0
5 Bollington v Oswestry	2-8
Burslem Port Vale v Davenham	1-1e
Chirk v Hartford St John's	8-1
Goldenhill v Macclesfield (1)	4-2 v
Leek v Druids	2-1
Northwich Victoria v Furness Vale Rovers	10-0
Stoke v Caernarvon Wanderers	10-1
Wrexham Olympic v Crewe Alexandra	1-4
6 Bishop Auckland Church Inst. v Middlesbrough	0-1
Horncastle v Darlington	3-1
Lincoln Lindum v Grantham	0-1
Redcar v Tyne Association	4-0
South Bank v Gainsborough Trinity	0-4
Sunderland v Newcastle West End	2-1ev
7 Chatham v Bournemouth Rovers	wo/s
Crusaders v Clapton	5-0
Hendon (1) v London Caledonians	1-2
Luton Town v Hotspur	1-3
Old Carthusians v Reading	2-1
Old Foresters v Cannon	wo/s
Old Wykehamists v Hanover United	3-0
Swifts v Luton Wanderers	13-0
Watford Rovers v Swindon Town	0-1
8 1st Surrey Rifles v Upton Park	0-9
Casuals v Dulwich	2-4
Chesham v Lyndhurst	4-2
Clapham Rovers v Old Brightonians	0-6
Old Etonians v Royal Engineers	1-0
Old Harrovians v Old Westminsters	0-4
Rochester v Marlow	0-2
South Reading v Maidenhead	0-2
1r Burnley v Astley Bridge	2-2 D
2r Cliftonville v Blackburn Park Road	7-2
r Rawtenstall v Church	1-7
3r Derby Midland v Birmingham Excelsior	2-1
r Walsall Town v Derby St Luke's	6-1
5r Burslem Port Vale v Davenham	3-0e
r Macclesfield (1) v Goldenhill	2-3e
6r Newcastle West End v Sunderland	1-0

Round Two

1 Darwen v Astley Bridge	wo/s
Preston North End v Witton	6-0
Renton v Blackburn Rovers	2-2e
Third Lanark v Bolton Wanderers	2-3
2 Great Lever v Cliftonville	1-3
Partick Thistle v Fleetwood Rangers	7-0
Rangers (Glasgow) v Church	2-1
Rossendale v Cowlairs	2-10

17

1886/87 to 1887/88

3 Aston Villa v Derby Midland	6-1	
Derby County v Mitchell's St George's	1-2	
Walsall Town - Bye		
West Bromwich Albion v Derby Junction	2-1	
Wolverhampton Wan. v Crosswell's Brewery	14-0	
4 Cleethorpes Town v Lockwood Brothers	1-4	
Nottingham Forest v Grimsby Town	2-2	
Notts County v Notts Rangers	3-3	
Staveley v Rotherham Town	4-0	
5 Burslem Port Vale - Bye		
Chester v Goldenhill	1-0 D	
Crewe Alexandra v Stoke	6-4e	
Leek v Oswestry	4-2	
Northwich Victoria v Chirk	0-0	
6 Grantham v Redcar	3-2	
Horncastle - Bye		
Middlesbrough v Lincoln City	1-1	
Newcastle West End v Gainsborough Trinity	2-6	
7 Chatham v Hotspur	1-0	
Old Carthusians v Crusaders	4-2	
Old Foresters - Bye		
Old Wykehamists v London Caledonians	0-1	
Swifts v Swindon Town	7-1	
8 Chesham v Old Etonians	1-7	
Maidenhead v Dulwich	2-3e	
Marlow v Upton Park	4-0	
Old Westminsters v Old Brightonians	1-1	
1r Blackburn Rovers v Renton	0-2	
4r Grimsby Town v Nottingham Forest	0-1	
r Notts County v Notts Rangers	5-0	
5r Chirk v Northwich Victoria	3-0	
6r Lincoln City v Middlesbrough	2-0	
8r Old Westminsters v Old Brightonians	3-0	

Round Three

1 Darwen v Bolton Wanderers	4-3	
Renton v Preston North End	0-2 N	
2 Cliftonville v Partick Thistle	1-11	
Rangers (Glasgow) v Cowlairs	3-2	
3 Aston Villa v Wolverhampton Wan.	2-2e	
Walsall Town v Mitchell's St George's	2-7	
West Bromwich Albion - Bye		
4 Lockwood Brothers v Nottingham Forest	2-1	
Staveley v Notts County	0-3	
5 Chirk v Goldenhill	wo/s	
Crewe Alexandra - Bye		
Leek v Burslem Port Vale	2-2x	
6 Gainsborough Trinity v Lincoln City	2-2e	
Horncastle v Grantham	2-0	
7 Chatham v Old Foresters	1-4	
Old Carthusians v London Caledonians	wo/s	
Swifts - Bye		
8 Marlow v Dulwich	3-0	
Old Etonians v Old Westminsters	0-3	
3r Wolverhampton Wan. v Aston Villa	1-1e	
5r Burslem Port Vale v Leek	1-3 N	
6r Lincoln City v Gainsborough Trinity	1-0 N	
3r2 Wolverhampton Wan. v Aston Villa	3-3e	
3r3 Aston Villa v Wolverhampton Wan.	2-0	

Round Four

Aston Villa - Bye		
Chirk - Bye		
Crewe Alexandra v Leek	0-1	
Darwen - Bye		
Horncastle - Bye		
Lincoln City - Bye		
Lockwood Brothers - Bye		
Marlow - Bye		
3 Mitchell's St George's v West Bromwich Albion	0-1 N	
Notts County - Bye		
Old Carthusians - Bye		
Old Westminsters - Bye		
Partick Thistle - Bye		
Preston North End - Bye		
Rangers (Glasgow) - Bye		
7 Swifts v Old Foresters	0-2	

Round Five

Aston Villa v Horncastle	5-0	
Chirk v Darwen	1-2	
Leek v Old Carthusians	0-2	
Lockwood Brothers v West Bromwich Albion	0-1ev	
Notts County v Marlow	5-2	
Old Foresters v Preston North End	0-3	
Old Westminsters v Partick Thistle	1-0	
Rangers (Glasgow) v Lincoln City	3-0	
r West Bromwich Albion v Lockwood Brothers	2-1 N	

Round Six

Aston Villa v Darwen	3-2	
Notts County v West Bromwich Albion	1-4	
Old Carthusians v Preston North End	1-2e	
Rangers (Glasgow) v Old Westminsters	5-1	

Semi Finals		
Aston Villa v Rangers (Glasgow)	3-1 N	
West Bromwich Albion v Preston North End	3-1 N	
Final		
Aston Villa v West Bromwich Albion	2-0 N	

1887/88

Round One

1 Elswick Rangers v Bishop Auckland Church Inst.	3-3e	
Darlington v Gateshead Association	3-0	
Middlesbrough v Whitburn	4-0	
Newcastle West End v Redcar	5-1	
Scarborough v Shankhouse	3-5	
South Bank v Newcastle East End	3-2e	
Sunderland v Morpeth Harriers	4-2 v	
2 Accrington v Rossendale	11-0	
Blackburn Olympic - Bye		
Blackburn Park Road v Distillery	2-1 D	
Blackburn Rovers v Bury	wo/s	
Burnley v Darwen Old Wanderers	4-0 v	
Church v Cliftonville	wo/s	
Rawtenstall v Darwen	1-3	
Witton v Oswaldtwistle Rovers	4-1 v	
3 Bolton Wanderers v Everton	1-0 v	
Bootle (1) v Workington (1)	6-0	
Fleetwood Rangers v West Manchester	4-1	
Higher Walton v Heywood Central	8-1	
Hurst v Astley Bridge	5-3 v	
Liverpool Stanley v Halliwell	1-5	
Preston North End v Hyde	26-0	
South Shore v Denton	wo/s	
4 Chester v Davenham	2-3e	
Chirk v Chester St Oswald's	4-1	
Crewe Alexandra v Druids	5-0	
Leek v Northwich Victoria	2-2	
Llangollen v Oswestry	7-3 v	
Macclesfield (1) v Shrewsbury Town	1-3	
Over Wanderers v Wellington St George's	3-1	
Stoke v Burslem Port Vale	1-0	
Wrexham Olympic - Bye		
5 Aston Shakespeare v Burton Wanderers	2-3 v	
Burton Swifts v Southfield	7-0	
Oldbury Town v Aston Villa	0-4	
Small Heath Alliance v Aston Unity	6-1 v	
Stafford Road v Great Bridge Unity	2-1 v	
Walsall Swifts v Wolverhampton Wan.	1-2	
Walsall Town v Mitchell's St George's	1-2	
Warwick County v Birmingham Excelsior	1-4 v	
West Bromwich Albion v Wednesbury Old Athletic	7-1	
6 Belper Town (1) v Sheffield Wednesday	2-3	
Derby Junction v Derby St Luke's	3-2	
Ecclesfield v Derby Midland	4-1	
Long Eaton Rangers v Park Grange	6-3	
Matlock v Rotherham Town	2-3	
Owlerton v Eckington Works	2-1	
Sheffield Heeley v Attercliffe	9-0	
Sheffield v Lockwood Brothers	1-3	
Staveley v Derby County	1-2	
7 Basford Rovers v Lincoln Albion	3-2	
Cleethorpes Town v Grimsby Town	0-4	
Gainsborough Trinity v Boston (1)	7-0	
Grantham v Lincoln Lindum	4-0	
Lincoln City v Horncastle	4-1	
Mellors (Nottm) v Notts Olympic	6-3ev	
Nottingham Forest v Notts Swifts	2-1e	
Notts County v Lincoln Ramblers	9-0	
Notts Rangers v Jardines (Nottm)	10-1	
8 Chatham v Luton Town	5-1	
Hitchin v Old Wykehamists	2-5	
Lyndhurst v Crusaders	0-9	
Millwall Rovers v Casuals	wo/s	
Old Etonians v Lancing Old Boys	4-2	
Old St Mark's v East Sheen	7-2	
Old Westminsters v Clapton	4-1	
Royal Engineers v Rochester	3-0 v	
9 Chesham v Watford Rovers	4-2 v	
Hendon (1) v Old Harrovians	2-4	
Hotspur - Bye		
London Caledonians v Old Foresters	1-6	
Marlow v South Reading	4-1	
Old Brightonians v Swindon Town	1-0	
Old Carthusians v Hanover United	5-0	
Reading v Dulwich	0-2 v	
Swifts v Maidenhead	3-1	
1r Bishop Auckland Church Inst. v Elswick Rangers	0-2	
r Morpeth Harriers v Sunderland	2-3	
2r Burnley v Darwen Old Wanderers	wo/s	
r Oswaldtwistle Rovers v Witton	3-4 N	
3r Astley Bridge v Hurst	wo/s	
r Everton v Bolton Wanderers	2-2	
4r Llangollen v Oswestry	0-2	
r Northwich Victoria v Leek	4-2	
5r Aston Shakespeare v Burton Wanderers	wo/s	
r Great Bridge Unity v Stafford Road	wo/s	
r Warwick County v Birmingham Excelsior	0-5	
7r Notts Olympic v Mellors (Nottm)	1-2	
8r Royal Engineers v Rochester	wo/s	

9r Dulwich v Reading	wo/s	
r Watford Rovers v Chesham	3-1	
3r2 Bolton Wanderers v Everton	1-1	
3r3 Everton v Bolton Wanderers	2-1 D	

Round Two

1 Darlington v Elswick Rangers	4-3e	
Middlesbrough v South Bank	4-1	
Shankhouse - Bye		
Sunderland v Newcastle West End	3-1e	
2 Accrington v Burnley	3-2	
Blackburn Rovers v Blackburn Olympic	5-1	
Darwen v Church	2-0	
Distillery v Witton	2-4	
3 Astley Bridge v Halliwell	0-4	
Bootle (1) v South Shore	1-1	
Fleetwood Rangers v Higher Walton	1-3	
Preston North End v Everton	6-1 v	
4 Chirk v Shrewsbury Town	10-2	
Northwich Victoria v Crewe Alexandra	0-1	
Oswestry - Bye		
Over Wanderers v Stoke	0-2	
Wrexham Olympic v Davenham	1-2	
5 Birmingham Excelsior - Bye		
Burton Swifts v Great Bridge Unity	2-5	
Mitchell's St George's v West Bromwich Albion	0-1	
Small Heath Alliance v Aston Villa	0-4	
Wolverhampton Wan. v Aston Shakespeare	3-0	
6 Derby County v Ecclesfield	6-0	
Derby Junction v Rotherham Town	3-2	
Lockwood Brothers - Bye		
Long Eaton Rangers v Sheffield Wednesday	1-2e	
Owlerton v Sheffield Heeley	1-0	
7 Grantham v Notts Rangers	0-4	
Grimsby Town - Bye		
Lincoln City v Gainsborough Trinity	2-1	
Nottingham Forest v Mellors (Nottm)	2-0	
Notts County v Basford Rovers	wo/s	
8 Chatham v Royal Engineers	3-1	
Crusaders v Old Wykehamists	3-2	
Old Etonians v Old St Mark's	3-2	
Old Westminsters v Millwall Rovers	8-1	
9 Dulwich v Hotspur	2-1	
Marlow v Old Foresters	2-3e	
Old Harrovians v Old Brightonians	0-4	
Swifts - Bye		
Watford Rovers v Old Carthusians	1-3	
3r South Shore v Bootle (1)	0-3	

Round Three

1 Darlington v Shankhouse	0-2	
Middlesbrough v Sunderland	2-2	
2 Accrington v Blackburn Rovers	1-3	
Darwen v Witton	1-1	
3 Higher Walton v Bootle (1)	1-6	
Preston North End v Halliwell	4-0	
Bolton Wan. - Bye after Everton disqualified		
4 Crewe Alexandra - Bye		
Davenham v Chirk	2-2	
Stoke v Oswestry	3-0	
5 Aston Villa - Bye		
Birmingham Excelsior v Great Bridge Unity	1-2	
West Bromwich Albion v Wolverhampton Wan.	2-0	
6 Derby County v Owlerton	6-2	
Derby Junction v Lockwood Brothers	2-1	
Sheffield Wednesday - Bye		
7 Grimsby Town v Lincoln City	2-0	
Nottingham Forest v Notts County	2-1	
Notts Rangers - Bye		
8 Crusaders v Chatham	4-0	
Old Etonians v Old Westminsters	7-2	
9 Dulwich v Swifts	1-3	
Old Carthusians v Old Brightonians	5-0	
Old Foresters - Bye		
1r Sunderland v Middlesbrough	4-2 D	
2r Witton v Darwen	0-2	
4r Chirk v Davenham	6-1	

Round Four

Blackburn Rovers - Bye		
Chirk - Bye		
Crewe Alexandra v Swifts	2-2	
Crusaders v Sheffield Wednesday	0-1	
Darwen v Notts Rangers	3-1	
Derby County - Bye		
Derby Junction - Bye		
Great Bridge Unity v Bootle (1)	1-2	
Middlesbrough - Bye		
Nottingham Forest v Old Etonians	6-0	
Old Carthusians - Bye		
Old Foresters v Grimsby Town	4-2	
Preston North End v Bolton Wanderers	9-1	
Shankhouse v Aston Villa	0-9 N	
Stoke - Bye		
West Bromwich Albion - Bye		
r Swifts v Crewe Alexandra	3-2 v	
r2 Crewe Alexandra v Swifts	2-1 N	

18

1887/88 to 1888/90

Round Five

Aston Villa v Preston North End	1-3
Chirk v Derby Junction	1-1
Crewe Alexandra v Derby County	1-0
Darwen v Blackburn Rovers	0-3
Middlesbrough v Old Foresters	4-0
Nottingham Forest v Sheffield Wednesday	2-4
Old Carthusians v Bootle (1)	2-0
West Bromwich Albion v Stoke	4-1
r Derby Junction v Chirk	1-0

Round Six

Derby Junction v Blackburn Rovers	2-1
Middlesbrough v Crewe Alexandra	0-2
Sheffield Wednesday v Preston North End	1-3
West Bromwich Albion v Old Carthusians	4-2

Semi Finals

Preston North End v Crewe Alexandra	4-0 N
West Bromwich Albion v Derby Junction	3-0 N

Final

West Bromwich Albion v Preston North End	2-1 N

1888/89

Qualifying Round One

1 Ashington v Elswick Rangers	0-4
Birtley v Darlington	2-0e
Morpeth Harriers v Whitburn	5-0
Newcastle East End v Port Clarence	3-1
Newcastle West End v Bishop Auckland Church Inst.	7-2
Sunderland Albion v Shankhouse	8-2
2 Blackburn Olympic v Fleetwood Rangers	wo/s
Clitheroe v Blackburn Park Road	3-2
Irwell Springs v Southport Central	4-5
Rawtenstall v Rossendale	3-4
3 Gorton Villa v West Manchester	2-6
Heywood Central v Astley Bridge	2-3
Hurst v Bolton Wanderers	0-0
Liverpool Stanley v Workington (1)	3-0
Ulster v Everton	wo/s
4 Chester v Macclesfield (1)	2-2 d
Hartford St John's v Nantwich	1-7
Over Wanderers v Chester St Oswald's	1-5 d
Wrexham v Davenham	3-0
5 Burton Swifts v Leek	1-3e
Burton Wanderers v Wednesbury Old Athletic	3-0
Great Bridge Unity v Aston Shakespeare	0-1
Stoke v Warwick County	1-2
Wellington St George's v Shrewsbury Town	1-1e
6 Basford Rovers v Belper Town (1)	3-1
Beeston St John's v Notts Olympic	2-0
Notts County v Eckington Works	4-1
7 Doncaster Rovers v Rotherham Town	1-9
Middlesbrough v Ecclesfield	0-1
Park Grange v Rotherham Swifts	1-0
Scarborough v Whitby (1)	2-0
Sheffield v South Bank	3-2 v
Sheffield Heeley v Redcar	6-1
8 Grimsby Town v Lincoln City	1-1e
Horncastle v Grantham	2-1
Kettering v Newark	3-4e
9 Chesham v Lyndhurst	4-2
Luton Town v Reading	4-0
Maidenhead v Old Etonians	4-0
Old Brightonians v Hendon (1)	wo/s
Old Foresters v Schorne College	2-0e
10 Casuals v Hitchin	wo/s
Crusaders v Royal Engineers	5-1
Dulwich v London Caledonians	0-13
Lancing Old Boys v Millwall Rovers	4-0
Old Wykehamists v Chatham	1-2
Rochester v Old Harrovians	2-4
3r Bolton Wanderers v Hurst	wo/s
5r Shrewsbury Town v Wellington St George's	2-1
7r South Bank v Sheffield	4-0 N
8r Lincoln City v Grimsby Town	1-1e
8r2 Grimsby Town v Lincoln City	3-1 N

Qualifying Round Two

1 Morpeth Harriers v Birtley	3-1 v
Newcastle East End v Stockton	2-1
Newcastle West End v Sunderland Albion	3-5 v
Sunderland v Elswick Rangers	5-3
2 Blackburn Olympic v Oswaldtwistle Rovers	1-3
Clitheroe v Higher Walton	0-7
Rossendale v Darwen	4-3
South Shore v Southport Central	7-1
3 Belfast YMCA v Cliftonville	0-5
Liverpool Stanley v Astley Bridge	3-0
Ulster v Linfield Athletic	1-7
West Manchester v Bolton Wanderers	1-0 v
4 Chester v Over Wanderers	5-1
Chirk v Nantwich	12-0
Llangollen v Oswestry	6-3
Wrexham v Northwich Victoria	3-2
5 Burton Wanderers v Shrewsbury Town	4-0
Leek v Oldbury Town	4-0
Small Heath v Burslem Port Vale	3-2
Warwick County v Aston Shakespeare	4-2
6 Basford Rovers v Mellors (Nottm)	0-1
Derby Midland v Derby St Luke's	2-1
Notts County v Beeston St John's	4-2
Staveley v Matlock	4-0
7 Owlerton v Rotherham Town	3-2
Park Grange v Attercliffe	2-1 v
Scarborough v Ecclesfield	2-4
Sheffield Heeley v South Bank	2-1
8 Cleethorpes Town v Netherfield (1)	wo/s
Horncastle v Boston (1)	0-1
Jardines (Nottm) v Gainsborough Trinity	0-4
Newark v Grimsby Town	4-4e
9 Chesham v Luton Town	3-3e
Maidenhead v Old Brightonians	1-2
Swindon Town v Marlow	2-5
Watford Rovers v Old Foresters	6-0
10 Casuals v Clapton	1-3
Chatham v London Caledonians	4-0
Old Harrovians v Crusaders	0-1
Old St Mark's v Lancing Old Boys	3-1
1r Birtley v Morpeth Harriers	1-0
r Newcastle West End v Sunderland Albion	1-2e
3r Bolton Wanderers v West Manchester	wo/s
7r Park Grange v Attercliffe	4-1
8r Grimsby Town v Newark	9-0
9r Luton Town v Chesham	10-2

Qualifying Round Three

1 Birtley v Sunderland Albion	2-5
Sunderland v Newcastle East End	2-0e
2 Rossendale v Higher Walton	2-3
South Shore v Oswaldtwistle Rovers	4-0
3 Cliftonville v Liverpool Stanley	wo/s
Linfield Athletic v Bolton Wanderers	4-0
4 Chester v Llangollen	5-1
Wrexham v Chirk	2-1e
5 Burton Wanderers v Warwick County	5-1
Small Heath v Leek	4-0
6 Notts County v Derby Midland	2-1
Staveley v Mellors (Nottm)	5-0
7 Owlerton v Ecclesfield	3-2
Sheffield Heeley v Park Grange	3-1
8 Gainsborough Trinity v Boston (1)	5-3
Grimsby Town v Cleethorpes Town	5-0
9 Old Brightonians v Luton Town	3-1
Watford Rovers v Marlow	0-2
10 Clapton v Chatham	0-1
Crusaders v Old St Mark's	1-0

Qualifying Round Four

1 Sunderland Albion v Sunderland	wo/s
2 South Shore v Higher Walton	5-0
3 Cliftonville v Linfield Athletic	3-3
4 Chester v Wrexham	2-3
5 Small Heath v Burton Wanderers	9-0
6 Staveley v Notts County	1-3
7 Sheffield Heeley v Owlerton	5-1
8 Grimsby Town v Gainsborough Trinity	wo/s
9 Old Brightonians v Marlow	5-2
10 Chatham v Crusaders	0-0
3r Linfield Athletic v Cliftonville	3-3
10r Crusaders v Chatham	2-3
3r2 Linfield Athletic v Cliftonville	7-0

Round One

Accrington v Blackburn Rovers	1-1
Aston Villa v Witton	3-2
Birmingham St George's v Long Eaton Rangers	3-2
Bootle (1) v Preston North End	0-3
Burnley v Old Westminsters	4-3
Chatham v South Shore	2-1e
Crewe Alexandra v Halliwell	2-2ev
Derby County v Derby Junction	1-0
Grimsby Town v Sunderland Albion	3-1
Nottingham Forest v Linfield Athletic	2-2e
Notts County v Old Brightonians	2-0
Notts Rangers v Sheffield Wednesday	1-1
Small Heath v West Bromwich Albion	2-3
Swifts v Wrexham	3-1
Walsall Town Swifts v Sheffield Heeley	5-1
Wolverhampton Wan. v Old Carthusians	4-3
r Blackburn Rovers v Accrington	5-0
r Crewe Alexandra v Halliwell	1-5
r Nottingham Forest v Linfield Athletic	wo/s
r Sheffield Wednesday v Notts Rangers	3-0

Round Two

Aston Villa v Derby County	5-3
Blackburn Rovers v Swifts	wo/s
Chatham v Nottingham Forest	1-1e
Grimsby Town v Preston North End	0-2
Halliwell v Birmingham St George's	2-3
Sheffield Wednesday v Notts County	3-2
West Bromwich Albion v Burnley	5-1
Wolverhampton Wan. v Walsall Town Swifts	6-1
r Nottingham Forest v Chatham	2-2e
r2 Chatham v Nottingham Forest	3-2 N

Round Three

Blackburn Rovers v Aston Villa	8-1
Chatham v West Bromwich Albion	1-10
Preston North End v Birmingham St George's	2-0
Wolverhampton Wan. v Sheffield Wednesday	3-0

Semi Finals

Preston North End v West Bromwich Albion	1-0 N
Wolverhampton Wan. v Blackburn Rovers	1-1 N
r Blackburn Rovers v Wolverhampton Wan.	1-3 N

Final

Preston North End v Wolverhampton Wan.	3-0 N

1889/90

Qualifying Round One

2 Denton v Gorton Villa	1-5
Halliwell v Clitheroe	5-0
South Shore v Workington (1)	wo/s
3 Boston (1) v Gainsborough Trinity	0-2
Jardines (Nottm) v Notts Swifts	4-1
4 Derby Junction v Matlock	4-2
Heanor Town v Long Eaton Midland	7-1
5 Walsall Town Swifts v Wellington St George's	3-0
Wednesbury Old Athletic v Leek	1-0
6 Birtley v Bishop Auckland	3-1
Bishop Auckland Church Inst. v Stockton	0-9
Darlington St Augustines v Darlington	5-0
Gateshead NER v Elswick Rangers	1-0
Middlesbrough v South Bank	3-4
Newcastle East End v Shankhouse	4-0
Newcastle West End v Port Clarence	9-1
Whitburn v Morpeth Harriers	7-1
7 Attercliffe v Whitby (1)	5-0 v
Redcar v Clinton	1-0
Rotherham Swifts v Owlerton	9-1
Rotherham Town v Doncaster Rovers	2-1
Scarborough v Sheffield United	1-6
8 Chester v Over Wanderers	2-0
Chester St Oswald's v Druids	4-0
Macclesfield (1) v Hartford & Davenham United	2-4
Shrewsbury Town v Nantwich	3-2
9 Chatham v Crusaders	4-5
Millwall Athletic v Schorne College	0-4
Old Harrovians v Norwich Thorpe	2-4
Old St Mark's v Norwich CEYMS	5-5
Royal Arsenal v Lyndhurst	11-0
Watford Rovers v Swindon Town	5-3
10 Chesham v Maidenhead	0-1
Clapton v London Caledonians	wo/s
Dulwich v Old St Paul's	0-9
Old Brightonians v Marlow	4-0
Old Wykehamists v Rochester	3-4
7r Whitby (1) v Attercliffe	6-0
9r Old St Mark's v Norwich CEYMS	2-1e

Qualifying Round Two

1 Belfast North End - Bye	
Belfast YMCA - Bye	
Distillery - Bye	
Linfield Athletic v Cliftonville	4-0
2 Gorton Villa v Darwen	2-7
Higher Walton v Blackburn Park Road	wo/s
Liverpool Stanley v Halliwell	0-2
South Shore v Witton	3-1
3 Beeston St John's v Jardines (Nottm)	1-3
Gainsborough Trinity v Kettering	wo/s
Lincoln City v Notts Olympic	2-1
Notts Rangers v Beeston	3-2
4 Derby Junction v Belper Town (1)	6-1
Heanor Town v Derby Midland	2-7
Long Eaton Rangers v Staveley	1-3
Loughborough v Derby St Luke's	2-1ev
5 Burton Swifts v Great Bridge Unity	5-3e
Burton Wanderers v Wednesbury Old Athletic	2-3
Oldbury Town v Small Heath	1-3
Warwick County v Walsall Town Swifts	1-1e
6 Birtley v Newcastle West End	1-2
Darlington St Augustines v Newcastle East End	2-1
South Bank v Whitburn	3-0
Stockton v Gateshead NER	5-0
7 Redcar v Rotherham Town	1-8
Sheffield v Sheffield Walkley	2-0
Sheffield United v Sheffield Heeley	1-0
Whitby (1) v Rotherham Swifts	1-5
8 Chester v Burslem Port Vale	1-0
Chester St Oswald's v Shrewsbury Town	6-1
Hartford & Davenham United v Crewe Alexandra	0-4
Northwich Victoria v Wrexham	3-1
9 Casuals v Swifts	3-8
Crusaders v Old St Mark's	2-0
Norwich Thorpe v Royal Arsenal	2-2e
Schorne College v Watford Rovers	1-2
10 Clapton v Rochester	3-0
Maidenhead v Luton Town	1-2
Old Etonians v Old Brightonians	3-3e
Reading v Old St Paul's	3-4e

19

1888/90 to 1890/91

4r	Derby St Luke's v Loughborough	2-0
5r	Walsall Town Swifts v Warwick County	2-0
9r	Royal Arsenal v Norwich Thorpe	wo/s
10r	Old Brightonians v Old Etonians	4-1

Qualifying Round Three

1	Distillery v Belfast YMCA	wo/s
	Linfield Athletic v Belfast North End	wo/s
2	Darwen v Halliwell	4-1
	South Shore v Higher Walton	6-2
3	Jardines (Nottm) v Gainsborough Trinity	2-2
	Notts Rangers v Lincoln City	2-7
4	Derby St Luke's v Derby Midland	0-1
	Staveley v Derby Junction	2-0
5	Burton Swifts v Walsall Town Swifts	1-6
	Wednesday Old Athletic v Small Heath	1-5
6	Newcastle West End v South Bank	5-2
	Stockton v Darlington St Augustines	3-1
7	Rotherham Swifts v Rotherham Town	0-0e
	Sheffield United v Sheffield	3-0
8	Chester St Oswald's v Chester	0-3
	Crewe Alexandra v Northwich Victoria	9-0
9	Royal Arsenal v Crusaders	5-2e
	Watford Rovers v Swifts	2-5
10	Clapton v Old Brightonians	wo/s
	Old St Paul's v Luton Town	4-0
3r	Gainsborough Trinity v Jardines (Nottm)	4-1
7r	Rotherham Town v Rotherham Swifts	2-1e

Qualifying Round Four

1	Distillery v Linfield Athletic	3-3
2	South Shore v Darwen	2-0
3	Lincoln City v Gainsborough Trinity	5-3
4	Derby Midland v Staveley	6-0
5	Small Heath v Walsall Town Swifts	4-0
6	Stockton v Newcastle West End	0-1
7	Rotherham Town v Sheffield United	2-2
8	Chester v Crewe Alexandra	2-1
9	Royal Arsenal v Swifts	1-5
10	Old St Paul's v Clapton	0-6
1r	Linfield Athletic v Distillery	3-5
7r	Sheffield United v Rotherham Town	2-1

Round One

Accrington v West Bromwich Albion	3-1 v
Birmingham St George's v Notts County	4-4e
Blackburn Rovers v Sunderland	4-2e
Bolton Wanderers v Distillery	10-2
Bootle (1) v Sunderland Albion	1-3 d
Derby Midland v Nottingham Forest	3-0
Everton v Derby County	11-2
Lincoln City v Chester	2-0
Newcastle West End v Grimsby Town	1-2
Preston North End v Newton Heath	6-1
Sheffield United v Burnley	2-1
Sheffield Wednesday v Swifts	6-1
Small Heath v Clapton	3-1
South Shore v Aston Villa	2-4
Stoke v Old Westminsters	3-0
Wolverhampton Wan. v Old Carthusians	2-0
r Accrington v West Bromwich Albion	3-0
r Notts County v Birmingham St George's	6-2

Round Two

Blackburn Rovers v Grimsby Town	3-0
Bolton Wanderers v Sheffield United	13-0
Bootle (1) v Derby Midland	2-1
Notts County v Aston Villa	4-1
Preston North End v Lincoln City	4-0
Sheffield Wednesday v Accrington	2-1
Stoke v Everton	4-2
Wolverhampton Wan. v Small Heath	2-1

Round Three

Bootle (1) v Blackburn Rovers	0-7
Preston North End v Bolton Wanderers	2-3
Sheffield Wednesday v Notts County	5-0 v
Wolverhampton Wan. v Stoke	4-0 v
r Sheffield Wednesday v Notts County	2-3 v
r Wolverhampton Wan. v Stoke	8-0
r2 Sheffield Wednesday v Notts County	2-1 N

Semi Finals

Blackburn Rovers v Wolverhampton Wan.	1-0 N
Sheffield Wednesday v Bolton Wanderers	2-1 N

Final

Blackburn Rovers v Sheffield Wednesday	6-1 N

1890/91

Preliminary Round

10	Crusaders v Rochester	5-0

Qualifying Round One

1	Chester St Oswald's v Chester	0-6
	Cliftonville v Macclesfield (1)	4-3
	Nantwich v Linfield Athletic	5-4
	Northwich Victoria v Chirk	3-2
	Over Wanderers v Druids	2-3
	Rhosllanerchrugog v Shrewsbury Town	wo/s
2	Ardwick v Liverpool Stanley	12-0
	Carlisle v Bootle (1)	1-6
	Gorton Villa v Denton	4-1
	Newton Heath v Higher Walton	2-0
	Witton v Heywood Central	1-4
	Workington (1) v Clitheroe	wo/s
3	Boston (1) v Eckington Works	2-2 d
	Ecclesfield v Grimsby Town	8-2
	Gainsborough Trinity v Lincoln City	1-3
	Staveley v Sheffield Walkley	19-0
4	Derby Junction v Sheffield United	0-1
	Leicester Fosse v Burton Wanderers	0-4
	Loughborough v Derby Midland	3-2
	Matlock v Leys Recreation (Derby)	wo/s
5	Clifton v Wednesbury Old Athletic	1-7
	Kidderminster (1) v Bath City	4-1
	Langley Green Victoria v Kettering	5-0
	Oldbury Town v Wellington St George's	3-1
	Small Heath v Hednesford Town	8-0
	Warmley v Walsall Town Swifts	0-12
	Warwick County v Burslem Port Vale	1-3
6	Darlington St Augustines v Barnard Castle Athletic	3-2
	Darlington West End v Darlington St Hilda's	3-2
	Hurworth v Stockton	0-14
	Middlesbrough v Scarborough	11-0
	Port Clarence v Whitby (1)	4-1
7	Bishop Auckland v Rendel	3-0
	Elswick Rangers v Newcastle West End	2-5
	Gateshead Association v Sunderland Albion	2-8
	Morpeth Harriers v Whitburn	0-2
	Shankhouse v Birtley	5-4 v
	Southwick (1) v Bishop Auckland Church Inst.	6-0
8	Clinton v Jardines (Nottm)	3-7
	Long Eaton Rangers v Sheffield Heeley	wo/s
	Newark v Notts Olympic	4-0
	Rotherham Swifts v Attercliffe	5-2
	Rotherham Town v Sheffield	13-0
9	93rd Highland Regiment v Luton Town	7-0
	Chesham v Watford Rovers	1-2
	Hunts County v Norwich CEYMS	3-1
	Ipswich Town v Reading	2-0
	Swindon Town v Maidenhead	9-0
	Windsor Phoenix Athletic v Schorne College	6-1
	Wolverton (1) v Marlow	0-4
10	Chatham v Crusaders	1-2
	City Ramblers v Crystal Palace Engineers	wo/s
	Folkestone v Old Wykehamists	2-1
	Gravesend v Old Harrovians	4-1
	Millwall Athletic v Ilford	2-3
	Old Brightonians v Old Carthusians	3-4
	Old Etonians v Swifts	4-1
	Old St Mark's v London Caledonians	2-3e
7r	Shankhouse v Birtley	5-1

Qualifying Round Two

1	Chester v Northwich Victoria	2-0
	Cliftonville v Rhosllanerchrugog	wo/s
	Leek v Druids	2-0
	Wrexham v Nantwich	2-3
2	Bootle (1) v Newton Heath	1-0
	Halliwell v Ardwick	wo/s
	Heywood Central v Gorton Villa	9-0
	South Shore v Workington (1)	10-0
3	Doncaster Rovers v Kilnhurst	4-5
	Ecclesfield v Grantham Rovers	wo/s
	Lincoln City v Boston (1)	9-0
	Mansfield Town (1) v Staveley	0-4
4	Belper Town (1) v Leeds Albion	4-2
	Burton Swifts v Sheffield United	2-1 D
	Loughborough v Burton Wanderers	8-1
	Matlock v Derby St Luke's	1-0
5	Burslem Port Vale v Walsall Town Swifts	2-3
	Kidderminster (1) v Oldbury Town	4-0
	Langley Green Victoria v Great Bridge Unity	2-1 v
	Wednesbury Old Athletic v Small Heath	0-2 d
6	Darlington v Darlington West End	wo/s
	Darlington St Augustines v Middlesbrough	1-4
	South Bank v Port Clarence	7-2
	Stockton v Middlesbrough Ironopolis	1-2
7	Bishop Auckland v Newcastle East End	1-2
	Newcastle West End v Southwick (1)	8-1
	Shankhouse v Ashington	2-0
	Sunderland Albion v Whitburn	wo/s
8	Long Eaton Rangers v Heanor Town	7-3
	Newark v Beeston	3-1 D
	Owlerton v Rotherham Town	1-4
	Rotherham Swifts v Jardines (Nottm)	3-4
9	93rd Highland Regiment v Watford Rovers	3-2
	Norwich Thorpe v Ipswich Town	0-4
	Swindon Town v Marlow	2-0
	Windsor Phoenix Athletic v Hunts County	1-2
10	City Ramblers v Old Carthusians	0-8
	Crusaders v Folkestone	6-1
	Ilford v Gravesend	2-0
	London Caledonians v Old Etonians	6-3
5r	Great Bridge Unity v Langley Green Victoria	4-2

Qualifying Round Three

1	Leek v Cliftonville	1-2
	Nantwich v Chester	4-5
2	Halliwell v Bootle (1)	4-3
	Heywood Central v South Shore	5-0
3	Lincoln City v Ecclesfield	3-0
	Staveley v Kilnhurst	6-2
4	Loughborough v Belper Town (1)	5-2
	Sheffield United v Matlock	3-0
5	Great Bridge Unity v Kidderminster (1)	1-0 D
	Walsall Town Swifts v Wednesbury Old Athletic	5-3
6	Middlesbrough v Darlington	2-0 D
	Middlesbrough Ironopolis v South Bank	6-1
7	Newcastle East End v Shankhouse	5-0
	Newcastle West End v Sunderland Albion	0-3
8	Long Eaton Rangers v Jardines (Nottm)	4-1
	Rotherham Town v Beeston	6-1
9	93rd Highland Regiment v Swindon Town	6-0
	Ipswich Town v Hunts County	5-2
10	Ilford v Crusaders	0-7
	London Caledonians v Old Carthusians	2-0

Qualifying Round Four

1	Chester v Cliftonville	wo/s
2	Halliwell v Heywood Central	2-1
3	Lincoln City v Staveley	4-1
4	Sheffield United v Loughborough	6-1
5	Kidderminster (1) v Walsall Town Swifts	3-0
6	Middlesbrough Ironopolis v Darlington	6-0 v
7	Newcastle East End v Sunderland Albion	2-2
8	Long Eaton Rangers v Rotherham Town	2-1
9	Ipswich Town v 93rd Highland Regiment	1-4
10	Crusaders v London Caledonians	4-2
6r	Middlesbrough Ironopolis v Darlington	3-0
7r	Newcastle East End v Sunderland Albion	0-2

Round One

Accrington v Bolton Wanderers	2-2 v
Accrington v Bolton Wanderers	5-1
Aston Villa v Casuals	13-1
Burnley v Crewe Alexandra	4-2e
Chester v Lincoln City	1-0
Clapton v Nottingham Forest	0-14
Crusaders v Birmingham St George's	0-2
Darwen v Kidderminster (1)	3-1 v
Long Eaton Rangers v Wolverhampton Wan.	1-2e
Middlesbrough Ironopolis v Blackburn Rovers	1-2 v
Royal Arsenal v Derby County	1-2
Sheffield United v Notts County	1-9
Sheffield Wednesday v Halliwell	12-0
Stoke v Preston North End	3-0
Sunderland v Everton	1-0
Sunderland Albion v 93rd Highland Regiment	2-0
West Bromwich Albion v Old Westminsters	wo/s
r Darwen v Kidderminster (1)	13-0
r Middlesbrough Ironopolis v Blackburn Rovers	0-3

Round Two

Accrington v Wolverhampton Wan.	2-3e
Birmingham St George's v West Bromwich Albion	0-3
Blackburn Rovers v Chester	7-0
Darwen v Sunderland	0-2
Derby County v Sheffield Wednesday	2-3
Notts County v Burnley	2-1
Stoke v Aston Villa	3-0
Sunderland Albion v Nottingham Forest	1-1e
r Nottingham Forest v Sunderland Albion	3-3e
r2 Nottingham Forest v Sunderland Albion	5-0 N

Round Three

Blackburn Rovers v Wolverhampton Wan.	2-0
Notts County v Stoke	1-0
Sheffield Wednesday v West Bromwich Albion	0-2
Sunderland v Nottingham Forest	4-0

Semi Finals

Blackburn Rovers v West Bromwich Albion	3-2 N
Notts County v Sunderland	3-3 N
r Sunderland v Notts County	0-2 N

Final

Blackburn Rovers v Notts County	3-1 N

1891/92 to 1892/93

1891/92

Qualifying Round One

1 Bishop Auckland v Southwick (1)	4-3
Gateshead NER v Ashington	7-2
Shankhouse v Birtley	wo/s
Tow Law v Newcastle East End	1-5
Whitburn v Sunderland Olympic	3-2
2 Darlington v Port Clarence	3-0
Darlington St Augustines v South Bank	3-4
Middlesbrough Ironopolis v Hurworth	wo/s
Scarborough v West Hartlepool Rovers	4-1
Spennymoor v Whitby (1)	4-3 D
3 Barrow (1) v Fleetwood Rangers	1-3
Bury v Witton	3-1
Fairfield v South Shore	3-1 D
Heywood v North Meols	6-0
Heywood Central v Moss Bay (1)	wo/s
Higher Walton v Blackpool	4-5
Newton Heath v Ardwick	5-1
Royton v Halliwell	6-3 D
4 Attercliffe v Rotherham Town	1-2
Boston (1) v Sheffield	5-3
Gainsborough Trinity v Grantham	3-0
Grantham Rovers v Sheffield Heeley	wo/s
Grimsby Town v Long Eaton Rangers	2-1
Lincoln City v Doncaster Rovers	3-1
5 Greenhalgh's v Heanor Town	0-2
Mansfield Town (1) v Riddings	3-0
Matlock v Beeston	4-2e
Newark v Eckington Works	3-1
Staveley v Notts Olympic	3-0
6 Burslem Port Vale v Burton Wanderers	2-4
Hednesford Town v Brierley Hill Alliance	1-2
Hereford (1) v Kettering	wo/s
Leicester Fosse v Small Heath	2-6
Walsall Town Swifts v Wednesbury Old Athletic	7-2
7 Gorton Villa v Leek	6-1
Macclesfield (1) v Newtown	4-2
Nantwich v Chester St Oswald's	3-0
Prescot v Crewe Alexandra	1-7
Rhosllanerchrugog v Chester	0-1
Tranmere Rovers v Northwich Victoria	1-5
8 Clifton v Poole	5-0
Luton Town v Swindon Town	4-3
Reading v Newbury	2-1
Somerset Rovers v Bristol St George	6-3
Warmley v Southampton St Mary's	1-4
9 London Caledonians v Chesham	4-2
Maidenhead v Watford Rovers	0-5
Norwich CEYMS v Marlow	1-9
Norwich Thorpe v Old Wykehamists	1-3
Old Etonians v Hunts County	6-1
Old Westminsters v Ipswich Town	5-1
Wolverton (1) v Swifts	wo/s
10 1st Highland Light Infantry v Maidstone (1)	7-0
Casuals v Clapton	3-2
Crouch End v Ashford United	6-2
Folkestone v Old St Mark's	3-3
Ilford v Chatham	0-1
Old Cranleighans v Gravesend	2-3
Rochester v Millwall Athletic	1-2e
10r Old St Mark's v Folkestone	4-2

Qualifying Round Two

1 Bishop Auckland v Rendel	4-2
Newcastle West End v Newcastle East End	1-3
Whitburn v Gateshead NER	4-10
Willington Athletic v Shankhouse	2-2
2 Darlington v Scarborough	13-1
Middlesbrough Ironopolis v Whitby (1)	7-0
Rothwell v Leeds Albion	1-1
South Bank v Stockton	2-4
3 Blackpool v Fleetwood Rangers	4-2
Heywood Central v Bury	1-2
Newton Heath v Heywood	wo/s
South Shore v Halliwell	8-1
4 Gainsborough Trinity v Grantham Rovers	4-0
Grimsby Town v Boston (1)	10-0
Rotherham Town v Kilnhurst	5-1
Sheffield United v Lincoln City	4-1
5 Buxton v Gedling Grove	6-0
Derby Junction v Newark	1-2
Heanor Town v Staveley	2-1
Mansfield Town (1) v Matlock	4-0
6 Burton Wanderers v Small Heath	1-1
Loughborough v Hereford (1)	7-0
Stourbridge v Brierley Hill Alliance	0-2
Walsall Town Swifts v Burton Swifts	2-4
7 Chester v Wrexham	2-4
Gorton Villa v Crewe Alexandra	2-3
Nantwich v Macclesfield (1)	3-4
Northwich Victoria v Liverpool Stanley	9-0
8 Bedminster v 93rd Highland Regiment	wo/s
Clifton v Somerset Rovers	8-5
Luton Town v Windsor Phoenix Athletic	3-0
Southampton St Mary's v Reading	7-0 D
9 London Caledonians v Watford Rovers	2-1
Old Carthusians v Old Etonians	4-6
Old Wykehamists v Marlow	0-5
Wolverton (1) v Old Westminsters	0-4
10 Crouch End v Chatham	0-4
Gravesend v Old Brightonians	0-8
Millwall Athletic v 1st Highland Light Infantry	3-4
Old St Mark's v Casuals	1-5
1r Shankhouse v Willington Athletic	4-1
2r Leeds Albion v Rothwell	2-0
6r Small Heath v Burton Wanderers	2-1

Qualifying Round Three

1 Bishop Auckland v Gateshead NER	3-1
Newcastle East End v Shankhouse	3-2
2 Darlington v Leeds Albion	wo/s
Middlesbrough Ironopolis v Stockton	1-1
3 Bury v Blackpool	5-5
South Shore v Newton Heath	0-2
4 Gainsborough Trinity v Rotherham Town	3-2
Grimsby Town v Sheffield United	1-2
5 Mansfield Town (1) v Buxton	0-0
Newark v Heanor Town	0-0
6 Brierley Hill Alliance v Loughborough	7-0
Small Heath v Burton Swifts	4-2
7 Crewe Alexandra v Wrexham	3-1
Northwich Victoria v Macclesfield (1)	5-0
8 Bedminster v Luton Town	1-4
Clifton v Reading	8-2
9 Old Etonians v London Caledonians	2-3
Old Westminsters v Marlow	6-1
10 1st Highland Light Infantry v Casuals	1-4
Chatham v Old Brightonians	3-2
2r Stockton v Middlesbrough Ironopolis	1-1
3r Blackpool v Bury	4-3
5r Buxton v Mansfield Town (1)	2-2
r Heanor Town v Newark	6-1
2r2 Stockton v Middlesbrough Ironopolis	2-5
5r2 Mansfield Town (1) v Buxton	wo/d

Qualifying Round Four

1 Newcastle East End v Bishop Auckland	7-0
2 Darlington v Middlesbrough Ironopolis	0-3
3 Newton Heath v Blackpool	3-4
4 Sheffield United v Gainsborough Trinity	1-0
5 Mansfield Town (1) v Heanor Town	2-4
6 Small Heath v Brierley Hill Alliance	6-2
7 Crewe Alexandra v Northwich Victoria	1-2 v
8 Clifton v Luton Town	0-3
9 London Caledonians v Old Westminsters	2-2
10 Casuals v Chatham	1-2 d
7r Crewe Alexandra v Northwich Victoria	6-2
9r London Caledonians v Old Westminsters	0-2

Round One

Aston Villa v Heanor Town	4-1
Blackburn Rovers v Derby County	4-1
Blackpool v Sheffield United	0-3
Bootle (1) v Darwen	0-2
Crusaders v Accrington	1-4
Everton v Burnley	2-4 v
Luton Town v Middlesbrough	0-3
Nottingham Forest v Newcastle East End	2-1
Old Westminsters v West Bromwich Albion	2-3
Preston North End v Middlesbrough Ironopolis	2-2 v
Sheffield Wednesday v Bolton Wanderers	2-1 v
Small Heath v Woolwich Arsenal	5-1
Stoke v Casuals	3-0 v
Sunderland v Notts County	3-0 v
Sunderland Albion v Birmingham St George's	4-0
Wolverhampton Wan. v Crewe Alexandra	2-2e
r Crewe Alexandra v Wolverhampton Wan.	1-4
r Everton v Burnley	1-3
r Preston North End v Middlesbrough Ironopolis	6-0
r Sheffield Wednesday v Bolton Wanderers	4-1
r Stoke v Casuals	3-0
r Sunderland v Notts County	4-0

Round Two

Accrington v Sunderland	1-0 v
Aston Villa v Darwen	2-0
Burnley v Stoke	1-3
Middlesbrough v Preston North End	1-2
Sheffield Wednesday v Small Heath	2-0
Sunderland Albion v Nottingham Forest	0-1
West Bromwich Albion v Blackburn Rovers	3-1
Wolverhampton Wan. v Sheffield United	3-1
r Accrington v Sunderland	1-3

Round Three

Nottingham Forest v Preston North End	2-0
Stoke v Sunderland	2-2e
West Bromwich Albion v Sheffield Wednesday	2-1
Wolverhampton Wan. v Aston Villa	1-3
r Sunderland v Stoke	4-0

Semi Finals

Aston Villa v Sunderland	4-1 N
West Bromwich Albion v Nottingham Forest	1-1 N
r Nottingham Forest v West Bromwich Albion	1-1 N
r2 West Bromwich Albion v Nottingham Forest	6-2 N

Final

West Bromwich Albion v Aston Villa	3-0 N

1892/93

Preliminary Round

3 Ardwick v Fleetwood Rangers	1-1
West Manchester v Halliwell	3-4
6 Burton Swifts v Singers (Coventry)	3-0
9 Old Etonians v Norwich CEYMS	6-1
Old Westminsters v Norwich Thorpe	11-3
Old Wykehamists v Old Harrovians	3-0
3r Ardwick v Fleetwood Rangers	0-2

Qualifying Round One

1 Bishop Auckland v Seaham Harbour	6-1
Blyth v Shankhouse	2-3
Leadgate Park - Bye	
Mickley - Bye	
Rendel - Bye	
Southwick (1) v Gateshead NER	3-2 v
Tow Law v Ashington	3-3 d
Willington Athletic - Bye	
2 Darlington v Scarborough	wo/s
Darlington St Augustines - Bye	
Hurworth v West Hartlepool Rovers	4-1
Loftus - Bye	
Port Clarence v Wakefield	wo/s
Rothwell v Scarborough Rangers	wo/s
South Bank - Bye	
Stockton v Whitby (1)	wo/s
3 Ashton-under-Lyne v Higher Walton	3-3
Barrow (1) v Fairfield	4-1
Bury v Southport Central	9-0
Fleetwood Rangers v Workington (1)	9-1
Heywood Central v Blackpool	3-4
North Meols v Oswaldtwistle Rovers	0-6
South Shore v Rossendale	3-2 v
Stockport County v Halliwell	4-0 v
4 Attercliffe v Grimsby Town	0-2
Doncaster Rovers v Mansfield Town (1)	2-0
Gainsborough Trinity v Chesterfield	4-2ev
Grantham v Belper Town (1)	2-4
Greenhalgh's v Eckington Works	5-2
Kilnhurst v Sheffield	4-2e
Newark v Lincoln City	3-4
Rotherham Town v Grantham Rovers	4-0
5 Beeston v Gedling Grove	4-1
Kettering v Langley Mill Rangers	3-1
Kimberley v Sutton Town	2-1e
Leicester Fosse v Rushden	7-0
Loughborough v Riddings	8-1
Matlock v Heanor Town	1-1
Notts Olympic v Finedon Revellers	4-2
Wellingborough Town v Buxton	2-4
6 Brierley Hill Alliance v Wellington St George's	3-0
Burslem Port Vale v Burton Swifts	0-2
Hereford (1) v Hednesford Town	1-4
Ironbridge v Burton Wanderers	1-3
Leek v Long Eaton Rangers	1-1 d
Old Hill Wanderers v Wednesbury Old Athletic	2-3
Stourbridge v Crewe Alexandra	2-1
Walsall Town Swifts v Derby Junction	1-0e
7 Barnton Rovers v Flint	1-2
Bootle (1) v Gorton Villa	10-0
Liverpool Caledonians v Wrexham	7-1
Liverpool Stanley v Chester	1-4
Nantwich v Liverpool	0-4
Newtown v Tranmere Rovers	wo/s
Northwich Victoria v Macclesfield (1)	4-0
Rhosllanerchrugog v Prescot	3-1 D
8 Bristol St George v Chesham	2-1
Chesham Generals v Maidenhead	2-6
Cowes (1) v Swindon Town	1-2e
Marlow v Somerset Rovers	wo/s
Reading v Clifton	6-1
Southampton St Mary's v Newbury	4-1
Uxbridge v Bedminster	7-1
Warmley v Windsor & Eton	6-1
9 Hunts County v Swifts	2-3
Ipswich Town v Old Wykehamists	4-0
Luton Town v Old St Mark's	4-0
Old Etonians v 1st Sherwood Foresters	4-0
Old Westminsters v Old Brightonians	3-1
Surbiton Hill v Polytechnic	0-2
West Herts v Crusaders	2-6
Wolverton (1) v Casuals	1-3
10 Chatham v 2nd West Kent Regiment	2-2
City Ramblers v Old Cranleighans	5-1
Clapton v Rochester	4-1
Crouch End v Sheppey United	1-3
Ilford v Erith	3-2
Maidstone (1) v Ashford United	2-4

21

1892/93 to 1893/94

Millwall Athletic v Folkestone	6-1	
Woolwich Arsenal v 1st Highland Light Infantry	3-0	
1r Gateshead NER v Southwick (1)	0-5	
3r Higher Walton v Ashton-under-Lyne	wo/s	
r Rossendale v South Shore	3-0	
r Stockport County v Halliwell	4-2e	
4r Gainsborough Trinity v Chesterfield	4-2	
5r Heanor Town v Matlock	3-0	
10r Chatham v 2nd West Kent Regiment	3-3	
10r2 Chatham v 2nd West Kent Regiment	0-2 N	

Qualifying Round Two

1 Bishop Auckland v Mickley	7-0	
Rendel v Southwick (1)	2-1	
Shankhouse v Willington Athletic	4-0	
Tow Law v Leadgate Park	5-2	
2 Darlington v Darlington St Augustines	5-1	
Hurworth v Rothwell	3-2	
Port Clarence v Loftus	2-3	
South Bank v Stockton	0-9	
3 Blackpool v Oswaldtwistle Rovers	8-1	
Bury v Stockport County	8-1	
Higher Walton v Fleetwood Rangers	1-5	
Rossendale v Barrow (1)	4-0	
4 Doncaster Rovers v Grimsby Town	1-2	
Doncaster Rovers v Grimsby Town	1-1 v	
Gainsborough Trinity v Belper Town (1)	13-0	
Greenhalgh's v Lincoln City	0-3	
Kilnhurst v Rotherham Town	0-3	
5 Kettering v Beeston	6-1	
Kimberley v Buxton	0-3	
Leicester Fosse v Notts Olympic	3-3x	
Loughborough v Heanor Town	3-1	
6 Burton Wanderers v Brierley Hill Alliance	3-2	
Hednesford Town v Wednesbury Old Athletic	2-1	
Leek v Burton Swifts	0-3	
Walsall Town Swifts v Stourbridge	7-0	
7 Bootle (1) v Liverpool Caledonians	2-3	
Chester v Prescot	2-1	
Liverpool v Newtown	9-0	
Northwich Victoria v Flint	7-0	
8 Bristol St George v Marlow	2-3	
Southampton St Mary's v Maidenhead	0-4	
Swindon Town v Warmley	8-1	
Uxbridge v Reading	2-3	
9 Casuals v Crusaders	3-0	
Luton Town v Old Etonians	4-2	
Old Westminsters v Ipswich Town	4-1	
Swifts v Polytechnic	1-1	
10 Ashford United v Sheppey United	1-2	
Ilford v Clapton	0-6	
Millwall Athletic v 2nd West Kent Regiment	2-0	
Woolwich Arsenal v City Ramblers	10-1	
5r Leicester Fosse v Notts Olympic	7-0	
9r Polytechnic v Swifts	4-2	

Qualifying Round Three

1 Rendel v Bishop Auckland	1-3
Tow Law v Shankhouse	4-3eD
2 Darlington v Hurworth	wo/s
Stockton v Loftus	wo/s
3 Fleetwood Rangers v Blackpool	1-3
Rossendale v Bury	7-1
4 Grimsby Town v Gainsborough Trinity	1-0
Lincoln City v Rotherham Town	2-0
5 Kettering v Loughborough	1-2
Leicester Fosse v Buxton	1-2
6 Burton Wanderers v Hednesford Town	3-1
Walsall Town Swifts v Burton Swifts	1-3
7 Liverpool Caledonians v Chester	3-2
Northwich Victoria v Liverpool	2-1
8 Marlow v Maidenhead	3-0
Swindon Town v Reading	2-1
9 Old Westminsters v Casuals	2-5
Polytechnic v Luton Town	4-2
10 Sheppey United v Clapton	3-4
Woolwich Arsenal v Millwall Athletic	3-2

Qualifying Round Four

1 Shankhouse v Bishop Auckland	2-1
2 Darlington v Stockton	1-5
3 Blackpool v Rossendale	2-1
4 Grimsby Town v Lincoln City	5-0
5 Buxton v Loughborough	0-6 v
6 Burton Swifts v Burton Wanderers	3-2
7 Liverpool Caledonians v Northwich Victoria	2-3e
8 Marlow v Swindon Town	1-0
9 Casuals v Polytechnic	5-0
10 Woolwich Arsenal v Clapton	3-0
5r Buxton v Loughborough	0-3

Round One

Accrington v Stoke	2-1
Blackburn Rovers v Newton Heath	4-0
Blackpool v Sheffield United	1-3
Bolton Wanderers v Wolverhampton Wan.	1-1e
Burnley v Small Heath	2-0
Darwen v Aston Villa	5-4
Everton v West Bromwich Albion	4-1
Grimsby Town v Stockton	5-0
Loughborough v Northwich Victoria	1-2

Marlow v Middlesbrough Ironopolis	1-3	
Newcastle United v Middlesbrough	2-3	
Nottingham Forest v Casuals	4-0	
Notts County v Shankhouse	4-0	
Preston North End v Burton Swifts	9-2	
Sheffield Wednesday v Derby County	3-2ev	
Sunderland v Woolwich Arsenal	6-0	
r Derby County v Sheffield Wednesday	1-0ev	
r Wolverhampton Wan. v Bolton Wanderers	2-1	
r2 Sheffield Wednesday v Derby County	4-2	

Round Two

Accrington v Preston North End	1-4
Blackburn Rovers v Northwich Victoria	4-1
Darwen v Grimsby Town	2-0
Everton v Nottingham Forest	4-2
Middlesbrough Ironopolis v Notts County	3-2
Sheffield United v Sunderland	1-3
Sheffield Wednesday v Burnley	1-0
Wolverhampton Wan. v Middlesbrough	2-1e

Round Three

Blackburn Rovers v Sunderland	3-0
Everton v Sheffield Wednesday	3-0
Middlesbrough Ironopolis v Preston North End	2-2e
Wolverhampton Wan. v Darwen	5-0
r Preston North End v Middlesbrough Ironopolis	7-0

Semi Finals

Everton v Preston North End	2-2 N
Wolverhampton Wan. v Blackburn Rovers	2-1 N
r Preston North End v Everton	0-0 N
r2 Everton v Preston North End	2-1 N

Final

Wolverhampton Wan. v Everton	1-0 N

1893/94

Qualifying Round One

1 Blyth v Hebburn Argyle	4-1	
Gateshead NER v Bishop Auckland	5-0	
Howden Rangers v Tow Law	1-2	
Hurworth v Leadgate Park	1-4	
Leadgate Exiles v Middlesbrough	2-4	
Rendel v Shankhouse	5-1	
Willington Athletic v Darlington	1-0	
2 Fleetwood Rangers v Fairfield	3-1	
Heywood Central v Hurst Nook Rovers	9-0	
Nelson v Bury	2-3e	
South Shore v Blackpool	2-1	
Southport Central v Oswaldtwistle Rovers	9-0	
West Manchester v Ardwick	3-0	
Workington (1) v Higher Walton	wo/s	
3 Ardsley v Wath-upon-Dearne	2-3	
Barnsley St Peter's v Gainsborough Trinity	4-5	
Grantham Rovers v Attercliffe	3-1	
Grimsby Town v Kilnhurst	5-1	
Lincoln City v Sheffield	2-0	
Worksop Town v Rotherham Town	3-2	
4 Belper Town (1) v Ilkeston Town (1)	2-5	
Buxton v Langley Mill Rangers	3-0	
Long Eaton Rangers v Eckington Works	5-1	
Matlock v Chesterfield	0-5	
Riddings v Derby Junction	1-1e	
5 Gedling Grove v Notts Olympic	2-1	
Hucknall St Johns v Greenhalgh's	1-3e	
Loughborough v Kettering	4-1	
Rushden v Bulwell United	1-0e	
Sutton Town v Kimberley	5-2	
6 Burslem Port Vale v Burton Swifts	3-4e	
Burton Wanderers v Leek	9-0	
Coalville Town (1) v Stourbridge	0-4	
Ironbridge v Hednesford Town	3-3e	
Old Hill Wanderers v Hereford (1)	wo/s	
Redditch Town v Singers (Coventry)	4-1	
Wellington St George's v Walsall	0-3	
7 Barnton Rovers v Wrexham	3-4e	
Nantwich v Flint	3-2e	
Newtown v Macclesfield (1)	4-4	
Stockport County v Bootle (1)	wo/s	
8 Bedminster v Uxbridge	2-6	
Bristol St George v Marlow	0-4	
Cowes (1) v Weymouth	0-2	
Newbury v Clifton	2-2e	
Reading v Warmley	3-0	
Swindon Town v Maidenhead	4-0	
10 Folkestone v Clapton	2-3	
Ilford v New Brompton	6-3	
Maidstone (1) v 2nd Scots Guards	1-3	
Sheppey United v Chatham	1-0	
Sittingbourne v 1st Highland Light Infantry	0-6	
Woolwich Arsenal v Ashford United	12-0	
4r Derby Junction v Riddings	1-0	
6r Hednesford Town v Ironbridge	wo/s	
7r Macclesfield (1) v Newtown	5-1	
8r Clifton v Newbury	1-5	

Qualifying Round Two

1 Blyth v Willington Athletic	1-1	
Leadgate Park v Rendel	0-2	
Middlesbrough v Gateshead NER	2-1	
West Hartlepool Rovers v Tow Law	1-3	
2 Rossendale v Bury	1-2	
South Shore v Heywood Central	5-1	
Southport Central v Workington (1)	5-1	
West Manchester v Fleetwood Rangers	2-4	
3 Doncaster Rovers v Grantham Rovers	1-2	
Lincoln City v Grimsby Town	2-5	
Mexborough v Gainsborough Trinity	0-3	
Wath-upon-Dearne v Worksop Town	1-3	
4 Chesterfield v Derby Junction	4-0	
Ilkeston Town (1) v Buxton	4-2	
Long Eaton Rangers v Heanor Town	0-3	
Sheepbridge Works v Clay Cross Town	6-1	
5 Gedling Grove v Greenhalgh's	1-4	
Leicester Fosse v Mansfield Town (1)	1-0	
Loughborough v Newark	4-0	
Rushden v Sutton Town	6-1	
6 Brierley Hill Alliance v Burton Swifts	3-1	
Burton Wanderers v Old Hill Wanderers	5-0	
Hednesford Town v Redditch Town	wo/s	
Stourbridge v Walsall	1-3	
7 Macclesfield (1) v Chester	6-1	
Nantwich v Wrexham	2-3	
Northwich Victoria v Crewe Alexandra	0-1	
Stockport County v Tranmere Rovers	2-1	
8 Chesham v Weymouth	1-1	
Newbury v Reading	1-2	
Southampton St Mary's v Uxbridge	3-1	
Swindon Town v Marlow	1-0	
9 Norwich CEYMS v Swifts	wo/s	
Old Westminsters v Luton Town	0-1	
Polytechnic v 1st Sherwood Foresters	0-5	
Wolverton (1) v Casuals	2-0	
10 Croydon Park v 2nd Scots Guards	0-10	
Ilford v Millwall Athletic	1-3	
Sheppey United v 1st Highland Light Infantry	1-3	
Woolwich Arsenal v Clapton	6-2	
1r Blyth v Willington Athletic	0-2	
8r Weymouth v Chesham	4-3	

Qualifying Round Three

1 Middlesbrough v Tow Law	3-0
Rendel v Willington Athletic	1-3
2 Bury v Fleetwood Rangers	2-0
Southport Central v South Shore	3-4
3 Gainsborough Trinity v Worksop Town	3-2
Grantham Rovers v Grimsby Town	2-6
4 Heanor Town v Chesterfield	3-1
Ilkeston Town (1) v Sheepbridge Works	wo/s
5 Greenhalgh's v Leicester Fosse	0-5
Loughborough v Rushden	1-0
6 Burton Wanderers v Hednesford Town	7-2
Walsall v Brierley Hill Alliance	1-2
7 Crewe Alexandra v Macclesfield (1)	3-2
Stockport County v Wrexham	3-2 v
8 Reading v Southampton St Mary's	2-1
Weymouth v Swindon Town	0-4
9 Luton Town v Norwich CEYMS	5-1
Wolverton (1) v 1st Sherwood Foresters	0-2
10 2nd Scots Guards v 1st Highland Light Infantry	1-0
Woolwich Arsenal v Millwall Athletic	2-0
7r Stockport County v Wrexham	7-0

Qualifying Round Four

1 Willington Athletic v Middlesbrough	1-4
2 South Shore v Bury	3-1e
3 Grimsby Town v Gainsborough Trinity	6-1
4 Heanor Town v Ilkeston Town (1)	5-4
5 Loughborough v Leicester Fosse	0-1
6 Burton Wanderers v Brierley Hill Alliance	2-1
7 Stockport County v Crewe Alexandra	0-0e
8 Swindon Town v Reading	0-2
9 1st Sherwood Foresters v Luton Town	2-2x
10 2nd Scots Guards v Woolwich Arsenal	1-2e
7r Crewe Alexandra v Stockport County	1-2
9r Luton Town v 1st Sherwood Foresters	2-1

Round One

Aston Villa v Wolverhampton Wan.	4-2
Derby County v Darwen	2-0
Leicester Fosse v South Shore	2-1
Liverpool v Grimsby Town	3-0
Middlesbrough Ironopolis v Luton Town	2-1
Newcastle United v Sheffield United	2-0
Newton Heath v Middlesbrough	4-0
Nottingham Forest v Heanor Town	1-0e
Notts County v Burnley	1-0
Preston North End v Reading	18-0
Small Heath v Bolton Wanderers	3-4
Stockport County v Burton Wanderers	0-1
Stoke v Everton	1-0
Sunderland v Accrington	3-0
West Bromwich Albion v Blackburn Rovers	2-3
Woolwich Arsenal v Sheffield Wednesday	1-2

22

1893/94 to 1895/96

Round Two

Burton Wanderers v Notts County	1-2
Leicester Fosse v Derby County	0-0e
Liverpool v Preston North End	3-2
Newcastle United v Bolton Wanderers	1-2
Newton Heath v Blackburn Rovers	0-0e
Nottingham Forest v Middlesbrough Ironopolis	2-0
Sheffield Wednesday v Stoke	1-0
Sunderland v Aston Villa	2-2e
r Aston Villa v Sunderland	3-1
r Blackburn Rovers v Newton Heath	5-1
r Derby County v Leicester Fosse	3-0

Round Three

Bolton Wanderers v Liverpool	3-0
Derby County v Blackburn Rovers	1-4
Nottingham Forest v Notts County	1-1e
Sheffield Wednesday v Aston Villa	3-2e
r Notts County v Nottingham Forest	4-1

Semi Finals

Bolton Wanderers v Sheffield Wednesday	2-1 N
Notts County v Blackburn Rovers	1-0 N

Final

Notts County v Bolton Wanderers	4-1 N

1894/95

Preliminary Round

1 Hebburn Argyle v South Bank	1-0
Mickley v Middlesbrough Ironopolis	wo/s
Middlesbrough v Rendel	4-0
Tow Law v Leadgate Park	3-0
Trafalgar v Gateshead NER	1-3
Willington Athletic v Seaham Harbour	7-2
7 Northwich Victoria v Tranmere Rovers	3-1

Qualifying Round One

1 Bishop Auckland v Hebburn Argyle	6-1
Blyth v Shankhouse	2-0
Darlington v Darlington St Augustines	7-0
Gateshead NER v Hexham Excelsior	2-1
Howden Rangers v Saltburn Swifts	wo/s
Middlesbrough v Willington Athletic	2-1
Stockton v Mickley	3-2
Tow Law v West Hartlepool NER	3-0
2 Accrington v Bacup	0-4
Blackpool v Chorley	3-2
Fleetwood Rangers v Clitheroe	4-0
Heywood Central v Liverpool Stanley	3-2
Horwich v Rossendale	1-2
Southport Central v South Shore	1-0
West Manchester v Nelson	3-6
Workington (1) v Oswaldtwistle Rovers	2-1
3 Barnsley St Peter's v Grantham Rovers	3-1
Doncaster Rovers v Mexborough	1-2
Gainsborough Trinity v Rotherham Town	5-1
Kilnhurst v Worksop Town	1-3
Lincoln City v Grimsby Town	0-3
Sheffield v Wath-upon-Dearne	0-1
4 Chesterfield v Clay Cross Town	3-0
Derby Junction v Belper Town (1)	2-2
Heanor Town v Langley Mill Rangers	3-0
Ilkeston Town (1) v Eckington Works	4-2
Long Eaton Rangers v Sheepbridge Works	9-3
North Wingfield v Matlock	1-1
5 Gedling Grove v Rushden	0-5
Hucknall St Johns v Bulwell United	5-3
Kimberley v Peterborough (1)	6-2
Leicester Fosse v Notts Olympic	13-0
Loughborough v Kettering	4-0
Newstead Byron v Hucknall Portland	2-1
Sutton Town v Newark	1-4
6 Burton Wanderers v Walsall	3-0
Coalville Town (1) v Smethwick Carriage Works	wo/s
Old Hill Wanderers v Hereford (1)	wo/s
Redditch Town v Stafford Rangers	3-2
Stourbridge v Burslem Port Vale	5-3
7 Barnton Rovers v Hurst Nook Rovers	4-2
Chester v Macclesfield (1)	1-2
Flint v Warrington St Elphin's	13-0
Glossop North End v Tonge	4-0
Newtown v Crewe Alexandra	1-3
Northwich Victoria v Middleton	0-1
Stalybridge Rovers v Wrexham	2-3
Stockport County v Fairfield	2-3
8 Clifton v Reading	3-7
Cowes (1) v Windsor & Eton	1-2
Maidenhead v King's Own Rifles	0-1
Slough v Marlow	1-4
Southampton St Mary's v Newbury	14-0
Swindon Town v Bristol St George	4-2
Uxbridge v Weymouth	2-1
Warmley v Freemantle	3-1
9 Chesham v Casuals	1-4
Clapton v Old St Stephens	5-2
Ilford v Chesham Generals	4-0
Luton Town v City Ramblers	8-2
Norwich CEYMS v London United	wo/s
Old Castle Swifts v Wolverton LNWR	1-1
Tottenham Hotspur v West Herts	3-2
Vampires v St Albans	0-1
10 1st Highland Light Infantry v Ashford United	wo/s
Chatham v Sittingbourne	1-1
Dover v Maidstone (1)	5-1
Millwall Athletic v Folkestone	5-0
Royal Engs. Training Battalion v Sheppey United	3-3
Royal Ordnance v Eastbourne	wo/s
4r Belper Town (1) v Derby Junction	wo/s
r Matlock v North Wingfield	6-0
9r Wolverton LNWR v Old Castle Swifts	3-1
10r Sheppey United v Royal Engs. Training Battalion	0-1
r Sittingbourne v Chatham	1-2

Qualifying Round Two

1 Bishop Auckland v Tow Law	3-1
Blyth v Gateshead NER	4-2
Darlington v Stockton	2-0
Middlesbrough v Howden Rangers	4-1
2 Fleetwood Rangers v Bacup	3-0
Heywood Central v Workington (1)	2-3
Rossendale v Blackpool	2-1
Southport Central v Nelson	4-0
3 Barnsley St Peter's v Leeds	8-0
Grimsby Town v Attercliffe	2-2
Mexborough v Wath-upon-Dearne	4-0
Worksop Town v Gainsborough Trinity	3-1
4 Buxton v Riddings	3-0
Heanor Town v Long Eaton Rangers	1-3
Ilkeston Town (1) v Belper Town (1)	1-0
Matlock v Chesterfield	1-3
5 Leicester Fosse v Kimberley	7-2
Loughborough v Hucknall St Johns	4-1
Newark v Mansfield	2-1
Rushden v Newstead Byron	3-0
6 Burton Swifts v Stourbridge	3-2
Burton Wanderers v Brierley Hill Alliance	5-1
Coalville Town (1) v Redditch Town	wo/s
Old Hill Wanderers v Wellington St George's	4-2
7 Crewe Alexandra v Fairfield	3-6
Flint v Middleton	2-1
Glossop North End v Barnton Rovers	5-0
Wrexham v Macclesfield (1)	7-1
8 King's Own Rifles v Windsor & Eton	3-1
Marlow v Swindon Town	4-2
Southampton St Mary's v Reading	5-2
Warmley v Uxbridge	3-1
9 Ilford v Casuals	0-0
Norwich CEYMS v Clapton	2-3
St Albans v Luton Town	1-6
Tottenham Hotspur v Wolverton LNWR	5-3
10 1st Highland Light Infantry v Royal Scots Fusiliers	3-1
New Brompton v Chatham	3-0
Royal Engs. Training Battalion v Millwall Athletic	1-4
Royal Ordnance v Dover	6-0
3r Grimsby Town v Attercliffe	8-0
9r Casuals v Ilford	1-3

Qualifying Round Three

1 Bishop Auckland v Blyth	3-0
Darlington v Middlesbrough	0-1
2 Southport Central v Fleetwood Rangers	1-1
Workington (1) v Rossendale	wo/s
3 Grimsby Town v Worksop Town	0-1
Mexborough v Barnsley St Peter's	1-1
4 Chesterfield v Buxton	4-0
Ilkeston Town (1) v Long Eaton Rangers	0-0
5 Newark v Loughborough	0-1
Rushden v Leicester Fosse	2-3
6 Burton Wanderers v Burton Swifts	5-2
Coalville Town (1) v Old Hill Wanderers	1-1
7 Flint v Fairfield	1-2
Wrexham v Glossop North End	1-2
8 Southampton St Mary's v Marlow	7-2
Warmley v King's Own Rifles	2-0
9 Clapton v Tottenham Hotspur	0-4
Ilford v Luton Town	0-2
10 New Brompton v Millwall Athletic	0-2
Royal Ordnance v 1st Highland Light Infantry	3-0
2r Fleetwood Rangers v Southport Central	1-1e
3r Barnsley St Peter's v Mexborough	1-0
4r Long Eaton Rangers v Ilkeston Town (1)	5-2
6r Old Hill Wanderers v Coalville Town (1)	wo/s
2r2 Fleetwood Rangers v Southport Central	2-3 N

Qualifying Round Four

1 Bishop Auckland v Middlesbrough	1-3
2 Workington (1) v Southport Central	1-1
3 Barnsley St Peter's v Worksop Town	3-1
4 Long Eaton Rangers v Chesterfield	1-1
5 Leicester Fosse v Loughborough	1-1
6 Burton Wanderers v Old Hill Wanderers	5-0
7 Fairfield v Glossop North End	4-1
8 Southampton St Mary's v Warmley	5-1
9 Tottenham Hotspur v Luton Town	2-2
10 Royal Ordnance v Millwall Athletic	0-3
2r Southport Central v Workington (1)	5-0
4r Chesterfield v Long Eaton Rangers	3-0
5r Loughborough v Leicester Fosse	2-2
9r Luton Town v Tottenham Hotspur	4-0
5r2 Leicester Fosse v Loughborough	3-0

Round One

Aston Villa v Derby County	2-1
Barnsley St Peter's v Liverpool	1-1
Blackburn Rovers v Burton Wanderers	2-1
Bolton Wanderers v Woolwich Arsenal	1-0
Bury v Leicester Fosse	4-1
Darwen v Wolverhampton Wan.	0-0
Luton Town v Preston North End	0-2
Middlesbrough v Chesterfield	4-0
Newcastle United v Burnley	2-1
Newton Heath v Stoke	2-3
Sheffield United v Millwall Athletic	3-1
Sheffield Wednesday v Notts County	5-1
Small Heath v West Bromwich Albion	1-2
Southampton St Mary's v Nottingham Forest	1-4
Southport Central v Everton	0-3
Sunderland v Fairfield	11-1
r Liverpool v Barnsley St Peter's	4-0
r Wolverhampton Wan. v Darwen	2-0

Round Two

Aston Villa v Newcastle United	7-1
Bolton Wanderers v Bury	1-0
Everton v Blackburn Rovers	1-1
Liverpool v Nottingham Forest	0-2
Sheffield United v West Bromwich Albion	1-1
Sheffield Wednesday v Middlesbrough	6-1
Sunderland v Preston North End	2-0
Wolverhampton Wan. v Stoke	2-0
r Blackburn Rovers v Everton	2-3
r West Bromwich Albion v Sheffield United	2-1

Round Three

Aston Villa v Nottingham Forest	6-2
Sheffield Wednesday v Everton	2-0
Sunderland v Bolton Wanderers	2-1
West Bromwich Albion v Wolverhampton Wan.	1-0

Semi Finals

Aston Villa v Sunderland	2-1 N
West Bromwich Albion v Sheffield Wednesday	2-0 N

Final

Aston Villa v West Bromwich Albion	1-0 N

1895/96

Preliminary Round

1 Gateshead NER v Blyth	4-1
Howden-le-Wear v Bishop Auckland	0-2
Jarrow v Shankhouse	1-0
Newcastle United v Leadgate Exiles	wo/s
South Bank v Hebburn Argyle	3-1
Stockton v Saltburn Swifts	3-1
Swallwell Axwell Rovers v Newcastle East End (2)	1-2
Tow Law v Darlington	3-1
Willington Athletic v Brandon Rovers	7-2
2 Chorley v Nelson	3-1
Clitheroe v Rossendale	1-2
Oswaldtwistle Rovers v Carlisle City (1)	9-0
West Manchester v Accrington	5-1
5 Kimberley v Newark	2-1
Notts Wanderers v Coalville Town (1)	1-4
Rushden v Hucknall St Johns	2-4
Sutton Town v Notts Olympic	6-1
7 Crewe Alexandra v Tranmere Rovers	2-1
Newtown v Barnton Rovers	wo/s
Port Sunlight v Warrington St Elphin's	2-0
8 Bristol South End v Slough	5-1
Eastville Rovers v Warmley	0-2
Marlow v Cowes (1)	3-3
Oxford City v Uxbridge	2-5
Staple Hill v Bristol St George	0-4
9 Chesham Generals v Vampires	1-1
City Ramblers v Chesham	7-2
10 Swanscombe v Royal Engs. Training Battalion	1-2
8r Cowes (1) v Marlow	0-2
9r Vampires v Chesham Generals	wo/s

Qualifying Round One

1 Bishop Auckland v Stockton	4-3
Darlington St Augustines v Willington Athletic	0-5
Jarrow v Middlesbrough	0-3
Newcastle East End (2) v Leadgate Park	2-1
Newcastle United v West Hartlepool NER	8-0
Rendel v Gateshead NER	3-2
South Bank v Hexham Excelsior	5-1
Tow Law v Mickley	1-0

1895/96 to 1896/97

2 Bacup v West Manchester	6-1
Black Diamonds v Moss Bay Exchange	0-1
Blackpool v Ashton North End	7-1
Chorley v Southport Central	2-2
Fleetwood Rangers v Rossendale	2-3
Oswaldtwistle Rovers v Manchester City	wo/s
South Shore v Horwich	3-0
Workington (1) v Haliwell Rovers	wo/s
3 Attercliffe v Gainsborough Trinity	0-3
Kilnhurst v Sheffield	3-0
Leeds v Grantham Rovers	1-1
Mexborough v Doncaster Rovers	1-1
Peterborough (1) v Lincoln City	0-13
Rotherham Town v Barnsley St Peter's	1-1
Staveley v Grimsby Town	0-5
Worksop Town v Wath-upon-Dearne	1-1
4 Belper Town (1) v Langley Mill Rangers	1-0
Buxton v Long Eaton Rangers	1-2
Chesterfield v Eckington Works	1-0
Clay Cross Town v Gresley Rovers	1-5
Riddings v Derby Junction	1-2
Sheepbridge Works v Heanor Town	0-6
Swadlincote v Ilkeston Town (1)	0-2
5 Ashby Albion v Hucknall St Johns	1-2
Hucknall Portland v Sutton Town	4-5
Kettering v Gedling Grove	4-0
Kimberley v Mansfield	4-0
Leicester Fosse v Hinckley Town (1)	4-0
Leicester YMCA v Coalville Town (1)	1-3
Loughborough v Bulwell United	5-2
Newstead Byron v Stapleford Town	3-1
6 Burslem Port Vale v Hereford Thistle	wo/s
Kidderminster Harriers v Stourbridge	0-0
Redditch Town v Stafford Rangers	3-3
Singers (Coventry) v Hereford (1)	6-1
Walsall v Dresden United	1-0
Wellington St George's v Burton Swifts	1-6
Wrockwardine Wood v Brierley Hill Alliance	3-1
7 Crewe Alexandra v Stalybridge Rovers	3-1
Druids v Middleton	1-2
Fairfield v Birkenhead LNWR	0-0
Glossop North End v Macclesfield (1)	5-1
Northwich Victoria v Liverpool Stanley	2-1
Port Sunlight v Chester	1-5
Stockport County v Liverpool South End	2-0
Wrexham v Newtown	3-1
8 Bedminster v Weymouth	2-2
Bristol South End v Marlow	0-1
Eastleigh LSWR v Clifton	9-0
Freemantle v Southampton St Mary's	1-5
Reading v Bristol St George	7-2
Trowbridge Town v Swindon Town	1-3
Uxbridge v Newbury	8-1
Warmley v Windsor & Eton	4-2
9 Barking Woodville v St Albans	2-0
City Ramblers v Maidenhead	0-1
Clapton v Ilford	0-2
Luton Town v Tottenham Hotspur	1-2
Nomads v Vampires	1-4
Queen's Park Rangers v Old St Stephens	1-1
West Herts v Norwich CEYMS	2-1
Wycombe Wanderers v Wolverton LNWR	2-3
10 Ashford United v Sittingbourne	0-4
Faversham v Sheppey United	0-4
Folkestone v Royal Scots Fusiliers	wo/s
New Brompton v Millwall Athletic	0-1
Northfleet v Dartford	3-3
Romford (1) v Royal Engs. Training Battalion	0-2
Royal Scots (Chatham) v Royal Ordnance	1-3
Thames Ironworks v Chatham	0-5
2r Southport Central v Chorley	4-0
3r Barnsley St Peter's v Rotherham Town	3-7
r Doncaster Rovers v Mexborough	4-1
r Grantham Rovers v Leeds	3-0
r Wath-upon-Dearne v Worksop Town	0-5
6r Stafford Rangers v Redditch Town	1-3
r Stourbridge v Kidderminster Harriers	1-2
7r Birkenhead LNWR v Fairfield	1-3
8r Weymouth v Bedminster	3-1
9r Old St Stephens v Queen's Park Rangers	1-0
10r Dartford v Northfleet	2-3

Qualifying Round Two

1 Newcastle United v Middlesbrough	4-1
Rendel v Bishop Auckland	2-1
South Bank v Willington Athletic	2-0
Tow Law v Newcastle East End (2)	5-1
2 Bacup v Blackpool	1-2
Oswaldtwistle Rovers v Moss Bay Exchange	4-2
Rossendale v Workington (1)	4-1
Southport Central v South Shore	2-4
3 Doncaster Rovers v Rotherham Town	0-7
Grantham Rovers v Gainsborough Trinity	1-3
Kilnhurst v Grimsby Town	1-4
Worksop Town v Lincoln City	0-3
4 Belper Town (1) v Derby Junction	1-0
Chesterfield v Long Eaton Rangers	2-0
Gresley Rovers v Heanor Town	0-4
Ilkeston Town (1) v Matlock	6-0
5 Coalville Town (1) v Kettering	0-4
Kimberley v Sutton Town	2-1
Leicester Fosse v Hucknall St Johns	3-1
Loughborough v Newstead Byron	0-0

6 Burslem Port Vale v Burton Swifts	1-1
Kidderminster Harriers v Singers (Coventry)	0-0
Walsall v Redditch Town	4-0
Wellington Town v Wrockwardine Wood	1-1
7 Chester v Middleton	0-3
Fairfield v Stockport County	5-1
Northwich Victoria v Glossop North End	1-4
Wrexham v Crewe Alexandra	3-3e
8 Reading v Eastleigh LSWR	2-1
Southampton St Mary's v Marlow	5-0
Swindon Town v Warmley	2-1
Uxbridge v Weymouth	2-1
9 Barking Woodville v Ilford	1-2
Vampires v Tottenham Hotspur	4-2 v
West Herts v Old St Stephens	0-1
Wolverton LNWR v Maidenhead	1-1
10 Chatham v Sittingbourne	8-0
Millwall Athletic v Folkestone	5-0
Royal Engs. Training Battalion v Royal Ordnance	0-4
Sheppey United v Northfleet	4-1
5r Loughborough v Newstead Byron	1-0
6r Burton Swifts v Burslem Port Vale	1-0
r Singers (Coventry) v Kidderminster Harriers	2-1
r Wrockwardine Wood v Wellington Town	4-0
7r Crewe Alexandra v Wrexham	5-2
9r Maidenhead v Wolverton LNWR	0-0
r Tottenham Hotspur v Vampires	2-1
9r2 Maidenhead v Wolverton LNWR	1-0

Qualifying Round Three

1 Newcastle United v Rendel	5-0
Tow Law v South Bank	4-2
2 Rossendale v Oswaldtwistle Rovers	3-2
South Shore v Blackpool	1-2
3 Gainsborough Trinity v Rotherham Town	0-2
Lincoln City v Grimsby Town	2-4
4 Belper Town (1) v Ilkeston Town (1)	0-0
Chesterfield v Heanor Town	3-0
5 Kettering v Loughborough	2-1
Kimberley v Leicester Fosse	1-3
6 Singers (Coventry) v Burton Swifts	0-2
Wrockwardine Wood v Walsall	3-1
7 Glossop North End v Fairfield	0-2
Middleton v Crewe Alexandra	0-4
8 Southampton St Mary's v Reading	3-0
Uxbridge v Swindon Town	5-0
9 Ilford v Tottenham Hotspur	1-5
Old St Stephens v Maidenhead	4-3
10 Millwall Athletic v Sheppey United	4-0
Royal Ordnance v Chatham	1-0
4r Ilkeston Town (1) v Belper Town (1)	5-1

Qualifying Round Four

1 Newcastle United v Tow Law	4-0
2 Rossendale v Blackpool	2-4
3 Grimsby Town v Rotherham Town	4-0
4 Chesterfield v Ilkeston Town (1)	2-0
5 Leicester Fosse v Kettering	1-2
6 Burton Swifts v Wrockwardine Wood	3-1
7 Fairfield v Crewe Alexandra	2-2
8 Southampton St Mary's v Uxbridge	3-0
9 Tottenham Hotspur v Old St Stephens	2-1
10 Royal Ordnance v Millwall Athletic	1-2
7r Crewe Alexandra v Fairfield	4-3

Round One

Blackburn Rovers v West Bromwich Albion	1-2
Blackpool v Burton Swifts	4-1
Burnley v Woolwich Arsenal	6-1
Burton Wanderers v Sheffield United	1-1
Chesterfield v Newcastle United	0-4
Crewe Alexandra v Bolton Wanderers	0-4
Darwen v Grimsby Town	0-2
Derby County v Aston Villa	4-2
Liverpool v Millwall Athletic	4-1
Newton Heath v Kettering	2-1
Nottingham Forest v Everton	0-2
Small Heath v Bury	1-4
Southampton St Mary's v Sheffield Wednesday	2-3
Stoke v Tottenham Hotspur	5-0
Sunderland v Preston North End	4-1
Wolverhampton Wan. v Notts County	2-2
r Notts County v Wolverhampton Wan.	3-4
r Sheffield United v Burton Wanderers	1-0

Round Two

Blackpool v Bolton Wanderers	0-2
Burnley v Stoke	1-1
Everton v Sheffield United	3-0
Grimsby Town v West Bromwich Albion	1-1
Newcastle United v Bury	1-3
Newton Heath v Derby County	1-1
Sheffield Wednesday v Sunderland	2-1
Wolverhampton Wan. v Liverpool	2-0
r Derby County v Newton Heath	5-1
r Stoke v Burnley	7-1
r West Bromwich Albion v Grimsby Town	3-0

Round Three

Bolton Wanderers v Bury	2-0
Derby County v West Bromwich Albion	1-0
Sheffield Wednesday v Everton	4-0
Wolverhampton Wan. v Stoke	3-0

Semi Finals

Sheffield Wednesday v Bolton Wanderers	1-1 N
Wolverhampton Wan. v Derby County	2-1 N
r Sheffield Wednesday v Bolton Wanderers	3-1 N

Final

Sheffield Wednesday v Wolverhampton Wan.	2-1 N

1896/97

Preliminary Round

1 Darlington St Augustines v Stockton	0-6
Leadgate Exiles v Wallsend Park Villa	3-0
Rendel v Jarrow	3-0
Saltburn Swifts v Shankhouse	4-2
Wolsingham v West Hartlepool NER	1-2
2 Accrington Stanley v Carlisle City (1)	wo/s
Chorley v Horwich	5-1
South Shore v Ashton North End	3-1
Southport Central v Blackburn Park Road	4-2
7 Aberystwyth v Druids	0-3
Birkenhead LNWR v Newtown	1-5
9 Chesham v Barking Woodville	3-1
Chesham Generals v 3rd Grenadier Guards	6-3e
Maidenhead v 1st Coldstream Guards	5-2
Slough v 1st Scots Guards	1-6
Vampires v Watford St Marys	1-2
Windsor & Eton v South West Ham	4-1
10 Dartford v Folkestone	3-0
Gravesend United v Leytonstone	7-0
Romford (1) v Sittingbourne	3-3
Sheppey United v Thames Ironworks	8-0
Swanscombe v Ashford United	4-1
West Norwood v Enfield (1)	3-1
10r Romford (1) v Sittingbourne	wo/d

Qualifying Round One

1 Hexham Excelsior v Gateshead NER	2-1 D
Leadgate Park v Mickley	5-0
Rendel v Saltburn Swifts	1-2
Seaham Harbour v Blyth	0-5
South Bank v Howden-le-Wear	4-0
Stockton v Leadgate Exiles	3-2
West Hartlepool NER v Hebburn Argyle	1-6
Willington Athletic v Birtley	1-1
2 Chorley v Accrington Stanley	5-0
Clitheroe v Rossendale	4-1
Fleetwood Rangers v Black Diamonds	3-0
Moss Bay Exchange v West Manchester	1-4
Oldham County v Oswaldtwistle Rovers	7-0
South Shore v Bacup	3-2
Southport Central v Workington (1)	2-0
Stalybridge Rovers v Haliwell Rovers	2-1
3 Grantham Rovers v Worksop Town	2-2
Kilnhurst v Mexborough	1-0
Sheffield v Wombwell Town	7-0
4 Buxton v Gresley Rovers	2-3
Swadlincote v Belper Town (1)	5-2
5 Bulwell United v Hinckley Town (1)	2-1
Hucknall St Johns v Beeston Humber	1-1
Mansfield v Hucknall Portland	4-0
Newstead Byron v Peterborough (1)	4-1
Notts Olympic v Rushden	0-8
6 Hereford (1) v Brierley Hill Alliance	2-2
Kidderminster Harriers v Berwick Rangers	wo/s
Redditch Town v Hereford Thistle	1-6
7 Buckley v Middlewich Rangers	4-1
Liverpool South End v Llandudno Swifts	2-0
Middleton v Chester	3-2
Newtown v Bangor City	2-2
Northwich Victoria v Druids	2-4
Stockport County v Barnton Rovers	6-0
Tranmere Rovers v Warrington St Elphin's	5-1
Wrexham v Rock Ferry	0-4
8 Bristol South End v Bedminster	2-4
Bristol St George v Weymouth	3-3
Clifton v Cowes (1)	0-5
Eastleigh LSWR v Royal Artillery Portsmouth	1-7
Freemantle v Warmley	wo/s
Newbury v Eastville Rovers	1-1
Oxford Cygnets v Staple Hill	wo/s
Trowbridge Town v Reading Amateurs	1-1
9 1st Scots Guards v Windsor & Eton	2-1
Chesham v Wolverton LNWR	4-2
Chesham Generals v Watford St Marys	0-2
Crescent (Hampstead) v Nomads	wo/s
Maidenhead v West Herts	2-1
Norwich CEYMS v Wycombe Wanderers	2-1
Queen's Park Rangers v Marlow	1-3
St Luke's v Ilford	1-3

24

1896/97 to 1897/98

10	Civil Service v Northfleet	0-8
	Gravesend United v Royal Engs. Training Battalion	7-1
	Leyton v Upton Park	9-2
	New Brompton v Faversham	6-1
	Romford (1) v Dartford	1-4
	Sheppey United v Lewisham St Mary's	7-0
	Swanscombe v Fulham	5-0
	West Norwood v Mid Kent	4-1
1r	Birtley v Willington Athletic	0-2
3r	Worksop Town v Grantham Rovers	4-3
5r	Beeston Humber v Hucknall St Johns	1-2
6r	Brierley Hill Alliance v Hereford (1)	0-1
7r	Bangor City v Newtown	1-0 D
8r	Eastville Rovers v Newbury	2-1
r	Reading Amateurs v Trowbridge Town	4-3e
r	Weymouth v Bristol St George	0-1

Qualifying Round Two

1	Blyth v Saltburn Swifts	5-0
	Gateshead NER v Leadgate Park	2-2
	Hebburn Argyle v South Bank	4-0
	Stockton v Willington Athletic	6-0
2	Clitheroe v Chorley	0-2
	Fleetwood Rangers v West Manchester	1-3
	South Shore v Oldham County	0-2
	Stalybridge Rovers v Southport Central	3-1
3	Hunslet v Attercliffe	3-1
	Parkgate United v Worksop Town	0-3
	Sheffield v Leeds	2-1
	Wath-upon-Dearne v Kilnhurst	2-0
4	Coalville Town (1) v Swadlincote	1-6
	Eastwood Town (1) v Langley Mill Rangers	3-1
	Sheepbridge Works v Riddings	1-0
	Stapleford Town v Gresley Rovers	1-5
5	Gedling Grove v Rushden	1-4
	Kimberley v Bulwell United	0-4
	Mansfield v Sutton Town	2-0
	Newstead Byron v Hucknall St Johns	0-1
6	Dresden United v Kidderminster Harriers	wo/s
	Hereford (1) v Hereford Thistle	4-2
	Stourbridge v Singers (Coventry)	4-2
	Wellington Town v Wellington St George's	2-2
7	Buckley v Tranmere Rovers	2-0
	Druids v Stockport County	3-2
	Liverpool South End v Rock Ferry	2-4
	Middleton v Newtown	3-0
8	Bedminster v Freemantle	2-0
	Eastville Rovers v Bristol St George	1-0
	Oxford Cygnets v Royal Artillery Portsmouth	1-3
	Reading Amateurs v Cowes (1)	0-1
9	Chesham v Maidenhead	1-2
	Crescent (Hampstead) v Norwich CEYMS	1-4
	Marlow v Ilford	3-0
	Watford St Marys v 1st Scots Guards	1-1
10	Dartford v Northfleet	1-4
	Gravesend United v New Brompton	1-4
	Leyton v Swanscombe	2-2
	West Norwood v Sheppey United	0-4
1r	Leadgate Park v Gateshead NER	3-2
6r	Wellington St George's v Wellington Town	2-2
9r	1st Scots Guards v Watford St Marys	1-1
10r	Swanscombe v Leyton	0-1
6r2	Wellington Town v Wellington St George's	1-2 N
9r2	Watford St Marys v 1st Scots Guards	2-3

Qualifying Round Three

1	Bishop Auckland v Tow Law	1-1
	Darlington v Blyth	7-1
	Hebburn Argyle v Middlesbrough	8-1
	Leadgate Park v Stockton	1-5
2	Chorley v Stalybridge Rovers	3-2
	Darwen v Blackpool	1-2
	Nelson v Oldham County	3-1
	Newton Heath v West Manchester	7-0
3	Barnsley St Peter's v Hunslet	3-2
	Lincoln City v Gainsborough Trinity	1-0
	Sheffield v Doncaster Rovers	3-1
	Wath-upon-Dearne v Worksop Town	2-2
4	Chesterfield v Swadlincote	1-1
	Eastwood Town (1) v Ilkeston Town (1)	1-4
	Gresley Rovers v Heanor Town	3-4
	Sheepbridge Works v Long Eaton Rangers	1-1
5	Hucknall St Johns v Wellingborough Town	1-5
	Leicester Fosse v Bulwell United	3-1
	Mansfield v Loughborough	2-1
	Rushden v Kettering	0-2
6	Burslem Port Vale v Hereford (1)	wo/s
	Burton Swifts v Wrockwardine Wood	6-0
	Walsall v Dresden United	11-0
	Wellington St George's v Stourbridge	0-3
7	Crewe Alexandra v Buckley	1-0
	Druids v Rock Ferry	4-1
	Glossop North End v Macclesfield (1)	5-0
	Middleton v Fairfield	2-2
8	Bedminster v Reading	0-5
	Cowes (1) v Southampton St Mary's	0-6
	Royal Artillery Portsmouth v Eastville Rovers	wo/s
	Swindon Town v Uxbridge	3-2
9	Luton Town v 1st Scots Guards	7-0
	Maidenhead v Norwich CEYMS	5-1
	Marlow v Clapton	3-1
	Tottenham Hotspur v Old St Stephens	4-0
10	Chatham v Royal Ordnance	wo/s
	Northfleet v New Brompton	3-1
	Sheppey United v Millwall Athletic	3-3
	Woolwich Arsenal v Leyton	5-0
1r	Tow Law v Bishop Auckland	0-2
3r	Worksop Town v Wath-upon-Dearne	2-1
4r	Long Eaton Rangers v Sheepbridge Works	3-1
r	Swadlincote v Chesterfield	1-5
7r	Fairfield v Middleton	5-1
10r	Millwall Athletic v Sheppey United	3-1

Qualifying Round Four

1	Bishop Auckland v Hebburn Argyle	1-0
	Darlington v Stockton	1-3
2	Chorley v Blackpool	0-1
	Newton Heath v Nelson	3-0
3	Barnsley St Peter's v Sheffield	2-1
	Worksop Town v Lincoln City	3-3
4	Chesterfield v Heanor Town	0-2
	Ilkeston Town (1) v Long Eaton Rangers	4-2
5	Mansfield v Kettering	0-1
	Wellingborough Town v Leicester Fosse	2-3
6	Stourbridge v Burslem Port Vale	1-3
	Walsall v Burton Swifts	1-1
7	Fairfield v Crewe Alexandra	4-0
	Glossop North End v Druids	5-2
8	Reading v Southampton St Mary's	1-4
	Swindon Town v Royal Artillery Portsmouth	4-1
9	Marlow v Luton Town	0-5
	Tottenham Hotspur v Maidenhead	6-0
10	Chatham v Woolwich Arsenal	0-4
	Millwall Athletic v Northfleet	6-1
3r	Lincoln City v Worksop Town	8-0
6r	Burton Swifts v Walsall	1-0e

Qualifying Round Five

1	Stockton v Bishop Auckland	2-0
2	Newton Heath v Blackpool	2-2
3	Lincoln City v Barnsley St Peter's	1-2
4	Ilkeston Town (1) v Heanor Town	0-0
5	Kettering v Leicester Fosse	2-1
6	Burslem Port Vale v Burton Swifts	2-3
7	Glossop North End v Fairfield	2-1
8	Southampton St Mary's v Swindon Town	8-2
9	Luton Town v Tottenham Hotspur	3-0
10	Millwall Athletic v Woolwich Arsenal	4-2
2r	Blackpool v Newton Heath	1-2
4r	Heanor Town v Ilkeston Town (1)	4-2

Round One

	Aston Villa v Newcastle United	5-0
	Blackburn Rovers v Sheffield United	2-1
	Derby County v Barnsley St Peter's	8-1
	Everton v Burton Wanderers	5-2
	Grimsby Town v Bolton Wanderers	0-0
	Liverpool v Burton Swifts	4-3
	Luton Town v West Bromwich Albion	0-1
	Millwall Athletic v Wolverhampton Wan.	1-2
	Newton Heath v Kettering	5-1
	Preston North End v Manchester City	6-0
	Sheffield Wednesday v Nottingham Forest	0-1
	Small Heath v Notts County	1-2
	Southampton St Mary's v Heanor Town	1-1
	Stockton v Bury	0-0
	Stoke v Glossop North End	5-2
	Sunderland v Burnley	1-0
r	Bolton Wanderers v Grimsby Town	3-3e
r	Bury v Stockton	12-1
r	Heanor Town v Southampton St Mary's	0-1
r2	Bolton Wanderers v Grimsby Town	3-2 N

Round Two

	Aston Villa v Notts County	2-1
	Blackburn Rovers v Wolverhampton Wan.	2-1
	Derby County v Bolton Wanderers	4-1
	Everton v Bury	3-0
	Preston North End v Stoke	2-1
	Southampton St Mary's v Newton Heath	1-1
	Sunderland v Nottingham Forest	1-3
	West Bromwich Albion v Liverpool	1-2
r	Newton Heath v Southampton St Mary's	3-1

Round Three

	Derby County v Newton Heath	2-0
	Everton v Blackburn Rovers	2-0
	Liverpool v Nottingham Forest	1-1
	Preston North End v Aston Villa	1-1
r	Aston Villa v Preston North End	0-0e
r	Nottingham Forest v Liverpool	0-1
r2	Aston Villa v Preston North End	3-2 N

Semi Finals

	Aston Villa v Liverpool	3-0 N
	Everton v Derby County	3-2 N

Final

	Aston Villa v Everton	3-2 N

1897/98

Preliminary Round

1	Crook Town v Seaham Albion	6-2
	Hebburn Argyle v West Hartlepool NER	2-0
	Hexham Excelsior v Shankhouse	3-5
2	Carlisle City (1) v Accrington Stanley	0-4
	Hurst Ramblers v Oswaldtwistle Rovers	wo/s
	Trawden Forest v South Shore	4-3
8	Warmley v Staple Hill	7-1
9	3rd Grenadier Guards v West Herts	7-4
	Chesham v Uxbridge	2-1
	Norwich CEYMS v Maidenhead	1-3
	Queen's Park Rangers v Windsor & Eton	3-0
	Slough v Crouch End Vampires	1-6
10	Dartford v Mid Kent	5-2
	Metropolitan Railway v Dover	2-1
	Thames Ironworks v Redhill	3-0

Qualifying Round One

1	Birtley v Rendel	0-1
	Crook Town v Seaham Harbour	5-0
	Gateshead NER v Hebburn Argyle	1-3
	Leadgate Exiles v Shankhouse	5-0
	South Bank v Middlesbrough	2-3
	St Peter's Albion v Jarrow	0-2
	Tow Law v Darlington St Augustines	1-0
	Willington Athletic v Blyth	0-0
2	Blackburn Park Road v Halliwell Rovers	2-1
	Fleetwood Rangers v Wigan County	0-1
	Horwich v Accrington Stanley	3-1
	Hurst Ramblers v Middleton	8-1
	Moss Bay Exchange v Rochdale (1)	3-5
	Southport Central v Black Diamonds	0-2
	Stalybridge Rovers v Trawden Forest	3-0
	Workington (1) v Clitheroe	wo/s
3	Kilnhurst v Bradford (1)	3-1
	Leeds v Mexborough	1-2
	Parkgate United v Hunslet	1-1
	Wath-upon-Dearne v Worksop Town	3-0
4	Buxton v Sheepbridge Works	0-1
	Langley Mill Rangers v Heanor Town	wo/s
5	Beeston Humber v Bulwell United	1-4
	Finedon Revellers v Newstead Byron	0-0
	Kimberley v Newark	0-4
6	Hereford (1) v Kidderminster Harriers	1-2
	Stourbridge v Newport (Salop)	9-0
	Wellington Town v Berwick Rangers	6-2
	Wrockwardine Wood v Singers (Coventry)	1-0
7	Chirk v Buckley	2-0
	Druids v Bangor City	4-0
	Garston Copper Works v Birkenhead LNWR	6-0
	Middlewich Rangers v New Brighton Tower	0-6
	Oswestry United v Northwich Victoria	3-1
	Rock Ferry v Llandudno Swifts	3-0
	Stockport County v Chester	2-1
	Warrington St Elphin's v Wrexham	0-3
8	Bristol City v Clifton	9-1
	Cowes (1) v Bristol St George	2-1
	Newbury v Bedminster	1-3
	Oxford City v Freemantle	1-3
	Oxford Cygnets v Eastleigh LSWR	2-6
	Reading Amateurs v Weymouth	wo/s
	Trowbridge Town v Bedminster St Pauls	7-0
	Warmley v Eastville Rovers	0-0
9	Aylesbury United v Watford St Marys	1-4
	Brentford v 1st Coldstream Guards	6-1
	Chesham Generals v Wycombe Wanderers	3-0
	Crouch End Vampires v Chesham	3-1
	Hampstead v 2nd Coldstream Guards	0-4
	Old St Stephens v 3rd Grenadier Guards	2-4
	Queen's Park Rangers v Wolverton LNWR	2-1
	Stanley v Maidenhead	0-0
10	Folkestone v Eastbourne Swifts	1-3
	Gravesend United v Dartford	3-1
	Leyton v Grays United	1-2
	Metropolitan Railway v St Albans	2-3
	Northfleet v New Brompton	1-3
	Romford (1) v Swanscombe	2-2
	Thames Ironworks v Royal Engs. Training Battalion	2-1
	Upton Park v Ashford United	0-1
1r	Blyth v Willington Athletic	0-3
3r	Hunslet v Parkgate United	1-2
5r	Newstead Byron v Finedon Revellers	wo/s
8r	Eastville Rovers v Warmley	6-2
9r	Maidenhead v Stanley	2-0
10r	Swanscombe v Romford (1)	4-0

Qualifying Round Two

1	Crook Town v Tow Law	2-3
	Jarrow v Hebburn Argyle	0-2
	Leadgate Exiles v Willington Athletic	0-0
	Rendel v Middlesbrough	0-1
2	Black Diamonds v Blackburn Park Road	1-1
	Rochdale (1) v Horwich	1-1
	Wigan County v Hurst Ramblers	4-3
	Workington (1) v Stalybridge Rovers	wo/s
3	Attercliffe v Wombwell Town	1-0
	Halifax (1) v Sheffield	1-2

1897/98 to 1898/99

	Kilnhurst v Mexborough	1-2
	Parkgate United v Wath-upon-Dearne	4-1 v
4	Coalville Albion v Long Eaton Rangers	0-1
	Coalville Town (1) v Riddings	1-0
	Eastwood Town (1) v Sheepbridge Works	4-0
	Langley Mill Rangers v Stapleford Town	5-1
5	Bulwell United v Newark	3-1
	Hinckley Town (1) v Newstead Byron	2-1
	Hucknall St Johns v Shepshed	4-0
	Mansfield v Rothwell Town Swifts	0-2
6	Kidderminster Harriers - Bye	
	Stourbridge - Bye	
	Wellington Town - Bye	
	Wrockwardine Wood - Bye	
7	Chirk v Wrexham	2-2
	Druids v Rock Ferry	2-3
	New Brighton Tower v Garston Copper Works	6-0
	Stockport County v Oswestry United	2-1
8	Cowes (1) v Freemantle	6-0
	Eastville Rovers v Bedminster	3-2
	Reading Amateurs v Eastleigh LSWR	1-4
	Trowbridge Town v Bristol City	2-5
9	Brentford v 3rd Grenadier Guards	1-1
	Crouch End Vampires v Maidenhead	6-2
	Queen's Park Rangers v Chesham Generals	4-0
	Watford St Marys v 2nd Coldstream Guards	1-2
10	Ashford United v Grays United	2-3
	New Brompton v Eastbourne Swifts	2-0
	St Albans v Thames Ironworks	2-0
	Swanscombe v Gravesend United	1-0
1r	Willington Athletic v Leadgate Exiles	2-1
2r	Blackburn Park Road v Black Diamonds	3-2
r	Horwich v Rochdale (1)	6-2
3r	Parkgate United v Wath-upon-Dearne	1-0
7r	Wrexham v Chirk	2-0
9r	3rd Grenadier Guards v Brentford	4-1

Qualifying Round Three

1	Middlesbrough v Bishop Auckland	3-1
	Newcastle United v Willington Athletic	6-0
	Stockton v Darlington	4-0
	Tow Law v Hebburn Argyle	0-4
2	Darwen v Blackpool	3-2
	Horwich v Chorley	2-3
	Wigan County v Nelson	3-1
	Workington (1) v Blackburn Park Road	1-1
3	Gainsborough Trinity v Parkgate United	5-0
	Lincoln City v Attercliffe	5-0
	Mexborough v Barnsley	2-1
	Sheffield v Doncaster Rovers	0-4
4	Eastwood Town (1) v Belper Town (1)	2-3
	Gresley Rovers v Coalville Town (1)	2-2
	Ilkeston Town (1) v Langley Mill Rangers	6-1
	Long Eaton Rangers v Chesterfield	3-2
5	Bulwell United v Loughborough	3-0
	Hinckley Town (1) v Rushden	0-2
	Hucknall St Johns v Rothwell Town Swifts	5-0
	Kettering v Wellingborough Town	0-1
6	Burslem Port Vale v Small Heath	2-1
	Burton Swifts v Stourbridge	0-2
	Kidderminster Harriers v Wellington Town	1-0
	Wrockwardine Wood v Burton Wanderers	3-5
7	Aberystwyth v Glossop North End	1-0
	Crewe Alexandra v Wrexham	4-1
	New Brighton Tower v Fairfield	wo/s
	Stockport County v Rock Ferry	2-1
8	Cowes (1) v Royal Artillery Portsmouth	1-1
	Eastville Rovers v Eastleigh LSWR	2-0
	Reading v Swindon Town	0-0
	Southampton v Bristol City	2-0
9	3rd Grenadier Guards v Crouch End Vampires	1-4
	Clapton v Queen's Park Rangers	1-0
	Luton Town v Marlow	wo/s
	Tottenham Hotspur v 2nd Coldstream Guards	7-0
10	Millwall Athletic v Sheppey United	5-1 v
	New Brompton v Grays United	6-2
	Swanscombe v Chatham	0-5
	Woolwich Arsenal v St Albans	9-0
2r	Blackburn Park Road v Workington (1)	2-2
4r	Coalville Town (1) v Gresley Rovers	2-1
8r	Royal Artillery Portsmouth v Cowes (1)	2-2e
r	Swindon Town v Reading	3-2
10r	Sheppey United v Millwall Athletic	5-0
8r2	Blackburn Park Road v Workington (1)	3-0 N
r2	Cowes (1) v Royal Artillery Portsmouth	1-0

Qualifying Round Four

1	Middlesbrough v Hebburn Argyle	2-0
	Stockton v Newcastle United	1-4
2	Darwen v Chorley	2-2
	Wigan County v Blackburn Park Road	2-1
3	Gainsborough Trinity v Lincoln City	5-1
	Mexborough v Doncaster Rovers	0-0
4	Belper Town (1) v Ilkeston Town (1)	1-2
	Long Eaton Rangers v Coalville Town (1)	2-0
5	Hucknall St Johns v Bulwell United	2-1
	Wellingborough Town v Rushden	1-2
6	Burslem Port Vale v Kidderminster Harriers	wo/s
	Stourbridge v Burton Wanderers	0-2
7	Crewe Alexandra v New Brighton Tower	1-1
	Stockport County v Aberystwyth	5-0
8	Eastville Rovers v Cowes (1)	6-2
	Swindon Town v Southampton	1-3
9	Crouch End Vampires v Clapton	0-1
	Tottenham Hotspur v Luton Town	3-4
10	New Brompton v Chatham	1-0
	Woolwich Arsenal v Sheppey United	3-0
2r	Chorley v Darwen	0-0
3r	Doncaster Rovers v Mexborough	1-1
7r	New Brighton Tower v Crewe Alexandra	4-1
2r2	Darwen v Chorley	2-1 N
3r2	Doncaster Rovers v Mexborough	1-1xN
3r3	Doncaster Rovers v Mexborough	1-2 N

Qualifying Round Five

1	Middlesbrough v Newcastle United	0-2
2	Darwen v Wigan County	1-1
3	Mexborough v Gainsborough Trinity	0-1
4	Long Eaton Rangers v Ilkeston Town (1)	2-0
5	Hucknall St Johns v Rushden	2-1
6	Burslem Port Vale v Burton Wanderers	2-1
7	Stockport County v New Brighton Tower	0-1
8	Southampton v Eastville Rovers	8-1
9	Clapton v Luton Town	0-2
10	Woolwich Arsenal v New Brompton	4-2
2r	Wigan County v Darwen	4-0

Round One

	Burnley v Woolwich Arsenal	3-1
	Bury v Stoke	1-2
	Derby County v Aston Villa	1-0
	Everton v Blackburn Rovers	1-0
	Liverpool v Hucknall St Johns	2-0
	Long Eaton Rangers v Gainsborough Trinity	0-1
	Luton Town v Bolton Wanderers	0-1
	Manchester City v Wigan County	1-0
	Newton Heath v Walsall	1-0
	Nottingham Forest v Grimsby Town	4-0
	Notts County v Wolverhampton Wan.	0-1
	Preston North End v Newcastle United	1-2
	Sheffield United v Burslem Port Vale	1-1
	Southampton v Leicester Fosse	2-1
	Sunderland v Sheffield Wednesday	0-1
	West Bromwich Albion v New Brighton Tower	2-0
r	Burslem Port Vale v Sheffield United	2-1e

Round Two

	Bolton Wanderers v Manchester City	1-0
	Burnley v Burslem Port Vale	3-0
	Newton Heath v Liverpool	0-0
	Nottingham Forest v Gainsborough Trinity	4-0
	Southampton v Newcastle United	1-0
	Stoke v Everton	0-0
	West Bromwich Albion v Sheffield Wednesday	1-0
	Wolverhampton Wan. v Derby County	0-1
r	Everton v Stoke	5-1
r	Liverpool v Newton Heath	2-1

Round Three

	Bolton Wanderers v Southampton	0-0
	Burnley v Everton	1-3
	Derby County v Liverpool	1-1
	West Bromwich Albion v Nottingham Forest	2-3
r	Liverpool v Derby County	1-5
r	Southampton v Bolton Wanderers	4-0

Semi Finals

	Derby County v Everton	3-1 N
	Nottingham Forest v Southampton	1-1 N
r	Nottingham Forest v Southampton	2-0 N

Final

	Nottingham Forest v Derby County	3-1 N

1898/99

Preliminary Round

1	Crook Town v Shankhouse	4-1
	Hebburn Argyle v Seaham Harbour	1-0
	Rutherford College v Bishop Auckland	0-1
	South Shields (1) v Shildon United	3-1
	St Peter's Albion v Thornaby	1-0
	Tow Law v Darlington St Augustines	2-0
2	Carlisle City (1) v Trawden Forest	2-3
	Hapton v South Shore	0-5
7	Aberystwyth v Middlewich Rangers	4-1
8	Newbury v Bedminster	0-3
	Staple Hill v Eastleigh Athletic	2-1
9	1st Coldstream Guards v Barnet (1)	4-3
	3rd Grenadier Guards v Hampstead	wo/s
	Aylesbury United v Harwich & Parkeston	3-2
	Hounslow v Shepherds Bush	1-3
	Ilford v Civil Service	2-0
	Maidenhead v 2nd Coldstream Guards	2-0
	Norwich CEYMS v Slough	wo/s
	Richmond Association v Queen's Park Rangers	3-0
	St Albans v Crouch End Vampires	2-2e
	Uxbridge v Hitchin	0-2
	Watford v Chesham Town	1-0
	Wolverton LNWR v Windsor & Eton	8-0
	Wycombe Wanderers v Marlow	1-2
10	Brighton United v Romford (1)	8-2
	Chatham v London Welsh	5-0
	Folkestone v Faversham	2-1
	Leyton v Swanscombe	1-1
	Royal Engs. Training Battalion v Eastbourne Swifts	6-2
	Sittingbourne v Wandsworth	2-1
	West Norwood v Bromley	3-3
9r	Crouch End Vampires v St Albans	2-4
10r	Bromley v West Norwood	3-0
r	Swanscombe v Leyton	1-1
10r2	Leyton v Swanscombe	2-1e

Qualifying Round One

1	Birtley v Thornaby Utopians	6-0
	Bishop Auckland v Crook Town	6-0
	Howden-le-Wear v Mickley	2-2
	Leadgate Exiles v Gateshead NER	2-3
	Leadgate Park v Hebburn Argyle	0-1
	Seaham Albion v South Shields (1)	0-6
	South Bank v Willington Athletic	1-2
	St Peter's Albion v Tow Law	1-0
2	Black Diamonds v Trawden Forest	1-3
	Freetown v Halliwell Rovers	0-2
	Frizington White Star v Fleetwood Rangers	3-0
	Hindley v Blackburn Park Road	6-1
	Horwich v South Shore	0-1 v
	Oswaldtwistle Rovers v Accrington Stanley	2-4
	Southport Central v Blackpool	2-2
	Workington (1) v Rossendale United	3-1
3	Altofts v Attercliffe	0-0
	Parkgate United v Sheffield	2-0
	Swinton Town v Worksop Town	0-3
	Wath-upon-Dearne v Hunslet	1-1
4	Burton Swifts v Hugglescote Robin Hood	4-1
	Swadlincote v Langley Mill Rangers	3-0
5	Bulwell United v Finedon Revellers	9-1
	Hinckley Town (1) v Northampton Town	1-2
	Loughborough v Mansfield	4-0
	Rothwell Town Swifts v Newark	1-0
6	Coventry City v Hereford (1)	0-0
	Newtown v Druids	0-2
	Stourbridge v Shrewsbury Town	2-1
	Wellington Town v Halesowen	8-2
	Welshpool v Kidderminster Harriers	wo/s
7	Aberystwyth v 1st South Lancs Regiment	0-2
	Ashton North End v Rhyl United	13-1
	Birkenhead LNWR v Bangor City	0-1
	Congleton Hornets v Hurst Ramblers	2-0
	Middleton v Rochdale (1)	3-2
	Stalybridge Rovers v Garston Copper Works	4-0
	Warrington St Elphin's v South Liverpool	0-6
	Wrexham v Chester	3-2
8	Bedminster v Ryde	3-1
	Cowes (1) v Trowbridge Town	7-1
	Eastville Wanderers v Oxford City	1-3
	Freemantle v Andover	2-0
	Oxford Cygnets v Warmley	2-9
	Reading Ramblers v Bristol St George	1-10
	Royal Artillery Portsmouth v Weymouth	5-0
	Staple Hill v Chippenham Town	7-0
9	3rd Grenadier Guards v 1st Coldstream Guards	2-2
	Aylesbury United v Hitchin	5-1
	Lowestoft Town v Norwich CEYMS	3-0
	Marlow v 3rd Coldstream Guards	3-1
	Richmond Association v Ilford	2-0
	St Albans v Shepherds Bush	1-2
	Watford v Chesham Generals	4-0
	Wolverton LNWR v Maidenhead	wo/s
10	Brighton United v Ashford United	5-0
	Eastbourne v Sittingbourne	0-0
	Leyton v Grays United	0-1
	Leytonstone v Chatham	3-1
	Maidstone United v Folkestone	1-0
	Thames Ironworks v Royal Engs. Training Battalion	2-0
	Upton Park v Metropolitan Railway	0-3
	West Croydon v Bromley	0-1
1r	Mickley v Howden-le-Wear	wo/s
2r	Blackpool v Southport Central	1-2
r	South Shore v Horwich	2-0
3r	Attercliffe v Altofts	2-1
r	Hunslet v Wath-upon-Dearne	0-0
6r	Hereford (1) v Coventry City	1-0
9r	3rd Grenadier Guards v 1st Coldstream Guards	4-0
10r	Sittingbourne v Eastbourne	4-2
3r2	Wath-upon-Dearne v Hunslet	3-3 N
3r3	Hunslet v Wath-upon-Dearne	1-2 N

Qualifying Round Two

1	Hebburn Argyle v Birtley	1-1
	South Shields (1) v Bishop Auckland	2-0 D
	St Peter's Albion v Mickley	2-1
	Willington Athletic v Gateshead NER	2-1
2	Accrington Stanley v Frizington White Star	8-0
	Halliwell Rovers v South Shore	1-1
	Hindley v Workington (1)	2-4 v
	Southport Central v Trawden Forest	3-2
3	Bradford (1) v Parkgate United	2-2
	Doncaster Rovers v Wath-upon-Dearne	6-0
	Wombwell Town v Barnsley	0-1
	Worksop Town v Attercliffe	0-1

1898/99 to 1899/1900

4	Burton Swifts v Coalville Town (1)	4-1
	Heanor Town v Gresley Rovers	4-0
	Stapleford Town v Coalville Albion	4-1
	Swadlincote v Belper Town (1)	2-1
5	Barwell Swifts v Kimberley	4-4
	Hucknall Portland v Bulwell United	2-2
	Loughborough v Rothwell Town Swifts	7-0
	Wellingborough Town v Northampton Town	0-2 v
6	Ironbridge v Druids	1-1
	Oswestry United v Stourbridge	wo/s
	Wellington Town v Hereford (1)	wo/s
	Welshpool v Chirk	1-3
7	1st South Lancs Regiment v Congleton Hornets	2-2
	Bangor City v Ashton North End	2-1 v
	South Liverpool v Wrexham	4-2
	Stalybridge Rovers v Middleton	3-6
8	Bristol St George v Staple Hill	4-1
	Freemantle v Oxford City	2-1
	Royal Artillery Portsmouth v Cowes (1)	1-1
	Warmley v Bedminster	1-1
9	Richmond Association v Marlow	4-3
	Shepherds Bush v Aylesbury United	2-0
	Watford v Lowestoft Town	2-0
	Wolverton LNWR v 3rd Grenadier Guards	3-0
10	Brighton United v Thames Ironworks	0-0
	Grays United v Sittingbourne	4-0
	Leytonstone v Maidstone United	2-3
	Metropolitan Railway v Bromley	3-2
1r	Birtley v Hebburn Argyle	0-2
2r	South Shore v Halliwell Rovers	wo/s
r	Workington (1) v Hindley	4-0
3r	Parkgate United v Bradford (1)	8-4
5r	Bulwell United v Hucknall Portland	5-2
r	Kimberley v Barwell Swifts	7-0
r	Wellingborough Town v Northampton Town	6-1
6r	Druids v Ironbridge	5-1
7r	Ashton North End v Bangor City	wo/s
r	Congleton Hornets v 1st South Lancs Regiment	3-4
8r	Bedminster v Warmley	2-2
r	Cowes (1) v Royal Artillery Portsmouth	3-0
10r	Thames Ironworks v Brighton United	1-4
8r2	Warmley v Bedminster	2-1

Qualifying Round Three

1	Bishop Auckland v Darlington	4-1
	Jarrow v St Peter's Albion	1-0
	Middlesbrough v Hebburn Argyle	0-1
	Willington Athletic v Stockton	5-1
2	Chorley v Workington (1)	5-1
	Darwen v Wigan County	1-5
	South Shore v Accrington Stanley	5-1
	Southport Central v Nelson	3-0
3	Doncaster Rovers v Parkgate United	8-1
	Gainsborough Trinity v Barnsley	2-2
	Grimsby Town v Mexborough	5-0
	Lincoln City v Attercliffe	5-0
4	Burton Swifts v Ilkeston Town (1)	4-2
	Chesterfield v Swadlincote	8-0
	Heanor Town v Long Eaton Rangers	3-2
	Stapleford Town v Buxton	5-1
5	Kettering v Hucknall St Johns	1-0
	Leicester Fosse v Kimberley	9-0
	Loughborough v Wellingborough Town	0-0
	Rushden v Bulwell United	4-2
6	Burslem Port Vale v Wellington Town	5-0
	Burton Wanderers v Oswestry United	7-2
	Druids v Walsall	2-1
	Small Heath v Chirk	8-0
7	Ashton North End v Stockport County	2-2
	Crewe Alexandra v South Liverpool	4-1
	Glossop v New Brighton Tower	4-2
	Middleton v 1st South Lancs Regiment	3-0
8	Bristol Rovers v Reading	0-1
	Bristol St George v Freemantle	7-0
	Cowes (1) v Bristol City	0-5
	Warmley v Swindon Town	1-0
9	Clapton v Brentford	6-1
	Luton Town v Watford	2-2
	Shepherds Bush v Richmond Association	0-0
	Tottenham Hotspur v Wolverton LNWR	4-0
10	Gravesend United v Metropolitan Railway	8-2
	Maidstone United v Sheppey United	2-5
	Millwall Athletic v Brighton United	3-0
	New Brompton v Grays United	3-0
3r	Barnsley v Gainsborough Trinity	4-0
5r	Wellingborough Town v Loughborough	1-3
7r	Stockport County v Ashton North End	1-0
9r	Richmond Association v Shepherds Bush	0-2
r	Watford v Luton Town	0-1

Qualifying Round Four

1	Bishop Auckland v Jarrow	1-2
	Willington Athletic v Hebburn Argyle	1-2
2	South Shore v Chorley	1-0
	Southport Central v Wigan County	3-1
3	Doncaster Rovers v Barnsley	1-2
	Grimsby Town v Lincoln City	2-1
4	Burton Swifts v Chesterfield	1-0
	Stapleford Town v Heanor Town	1-3
5	Kettering v Loughborough	2-1
	Leicester Fosse v Rushden	2-1
6	Burslem Port Vale v Burton Wanderers	3-0
	Small Heath v Druids	10-0
7	Glossop v Crewe Alexandra	1-0
	Stockport County v Middleton	3-0
8	Bristol St George v Bristol City	0-1
	Reading v Warmley	1-1
9	Clapton v Tottenham Hotspur	1-1
	Luton Town v Shepherds Bush	4-3
10	Gravesend United v Millwall Athletic	3-1
	New Brompton v Sheppey United	2-1
8r	Reading v Warmley	3-0
9r	Tottenham Hotspur v Clapton	2-1

Qualifying Round Five

1	Hebburn Argyle v Jarrow	0-0
2	South Shore v Southport Central	3-0
3	Barnsley v Grimsby Town	0-0
4	Burton Swifts v Heanor Town	0-0
5	Kettering v Leicester Fosse	1-1
6	Small Heath v Burslem Port Vale	7-0
7	Stockport County v Glossop	0-2
8	Bristol City v Reading	3-2
9	Tottenham Hotspur v Luton Town	1-1
10	Gravesend United v New Brompton	1-1
1r	Jarrow v Hebburn Argyle	2-1
3r	Grimsby Town v Barnsley	2-1
4r	Heanor Town v Burton Swifts	1-0
5r	Leicester Fosse v Kettering	1-2
9r	Luton Town v Tottenham Hotspur	1-1
10r	New Brompton v Gravesend United	2-0
9r2	Tottenham Hotspur v Luton Town	2-0 N

Round One

	Bristol City v Sunderland	2-4
	Burnley v Sheffield United	2-2
	Everton v Jarrow	3-1
	Glossop v Newcastle United	0-1
	Heanor Town v Bury	0-3
	Liverpool v Blackburn Rovers	2-0
	New Brompton v Southampton	0-1
	Nottingham Forest v Aston Villa	2-1
	Notts County v Kettering	2-0
	Preston North End v Grimsby Town	7-0
	Sheffield Wednesday v Stoke	2-2
	Small Heath v Manchester City	3-2
	Tottenham Hotspur v Newton Heath	1-1
	West Bromwich Albion v South Shore	8-0
	Wolverhampton Wan. v Bolton Wanderers	0-0
	Woolwich Arsenal v Derby County	0-6
r	Bolton Wanderers v Wolverhampton Wan.	0-1
r	Newton Heath v Tottenham Hotspur	3-5
r	Sheffield United v Burnley	2-1
r	Stoke v Sheffield Wednesday	2-0

Round Two

	Derby County v Wolverhampton Wan.	2-1
	Everton v Nottingham Forest	0-1
	Liverpool v Newcastle United	3-1
	Notts County v Southampton	0-1
	Preston North End v Sheffield United	2-2
	Stoke v Small Heath	2-2
	Tottenham Hotspur v Sunderland	2-1
	West Bromwich Albion v Bury	2-1
r	Sheffield United v Preston North End	2-1
r	Small Heath v Stoke	1-2

Round Three

	Nottingham Forest v Sheffield United	0-1
	Southampton v Derby County	1-2
	Stoke v Tottenham Hotspur	4-1
	West Bromwich Albion v Liverpool	0-2

Semi Finals

	Derby County v Stoke	3-1 N
	Sheffield United v Liverpool	2-2 N
r	Sheffield United v Liverpool	4-4 N
r2	Sheffield United v Liverpool	1-0 N

Final

	Sheffield United v Derby County	4-1 N

1899/1900

Preliminary Round

1	Ashington v St Peter's Albion	0-1
	Birtley v Seaham Albion	wo/s
	Darlington v Tow Law	2-0
	Darlington St Augustines v Bishop Auckland	2-9
	Grangetown Athletic v Thornaby	0-3
	Leadgate Park v Howden-le-Wear	2-1
	Prudhoe v Mickley	1-1
	Thornaby Utopians v South Bank	3-3
	Whitby (1) v Stockton	4-0
2	Blackburn Park Road v Accrington Stanley	3-0
	Darwen v Great Harwood	1-1
	Middleton v Rochdale (1)	2-0
	Nelson v Trawden Forest	2-1
	Oswaldtwistle Rovers v Hapton	3-1
3	New Brighton Tower v Birkenhead	5-0
	South Liverpool v White Star Wanderers	3-0
	Winsford United v 1st South Lancs Regiment	1-1
4	Nuneaton Town v Brierley Hill Alliance	2-3
5	Attercliffe v Montrose Works	3-0
	Denaby United v Parkgate United	1-0
	Mexborough v Pyebank	6-0
6	Desborough Town v Wellingborough Town	0-5
	Rushden v Rothwell Town Swifts	4-0
7	Bromley v Deptford Town	0-2
	London Welsh v Queen's Park Rangers	2-4
	Redhill v West Croydon	4-2
8	Ashford United v Folkestone	1-0
	Barking Woodville v West Ham Garfield	0-1
	Clapton v Leyton	4-1
	Dover v Sittingbourne	2-1
	Grays United v Royal Scots Fusiliers	0-0
	Ilford v Romford (1)	6-0
	Leytonstone v Olympic	2-4
	Maidstone United v Dartford	1-2
	Sheppey United v Gravesend United	3-1
	Thames Ironworks v Royal Engineers United	6-0
	Upton Park v Olympian	4-1
	Worthing v Eastbourne	0-1
1r	Mickley v Prudhoe	3-1
r	South Bank v Thornaby Utopians	3-1
2r	Great Harwood v Darwen	0-6
3r	1st South Lancs Regiment v Winsford United	0-1
8r	Royal Scots Fusiliers v Grays United	1-3

Qualifying Round One

1	Crook Town v Darlington	1-1
	Gateshead NER v Birtley	4-0
	Leadgate Park v Bishop Auckland	2-2
	Seaham Harbour v South Shields (1)	0-5
	St Peter's Albion v Shankhouse	0-1
	Stockton St John's v South Bank	0-2
	Thornaby v Whitby (1)	2-0
	Wallsend Park Villa v Mickley	2-1
2	Darwen v Blackburn Park Road	3-2
	Freetown v Middleton	wo/s
	Heywood v Walshaw	1-2
	Oswaldtwistle Rovers v Nelson	3-0
	Workington (1) v Black Diamonds	6-0
3	Congleton Hornets v Buxton	3-1
	Nantwich v Winsford United	2-1
	Tranmere Rovers v South Liverpool	0-1
	Warrington St Elphin's v Middlewich Rangers	5-1
	Wigan County v Swinton Town	8-0
	Wirral Railway v New Brighton Tower	1-7
4	Aberystwyth v Newtown	5-7
	Dudley v Brierley Hill Alliance	8-2
	Ironbridge v Wellington Town	2-2
	Stourbridge v Coventry City	5-0
5	Attercliffe v Mexborough	1-1
	Denaby United v Sheffield	1-1
	Gainsborough Trinity v Doncaster Rovers	1-4
	Hunslet v Altofts	3-0
	Ilkeston Town (1) v Chesterfield	1-2
	Stapleford Town v Belper Town (1)	14-0
	Wath Athletic v Wombwell Town	1-2
	Worksop Town v Newark	1-1
6	Burton Wanderers v Swadlincote	2-0
	Coalville Town (1) v Gresley Rovers	3-0
	Finedon Revellers v Rushden	2-4
	Newstead Byron v Bulwell United	2-0
	Northampton Town v Wellingborough Town	1-2
7	Colchester Town v Norwich CEYMS	2-4
	Deptford Town v Wandsworth	1-4
	Dunstable Thursdays v Wolverton LNWR	0-5
	Kirkley v Harwich & Parkeston	2-1
	Queen's Park Rangers v Fulham	3-0
	Redhill v West Norwood	2-4
	Watford v Hitchin	7-1
	West Hampstead v Hampstead	10-0
8	Brighton United v Eastbourne	6-1
	Clapton v Olympic	4-0
	Dartford v Ashford United	1-0
	Eastbourne Swifts v Brighton Athletic	1-3
	Ilford v Upton Park	3-1
	Swanscombe v Dover	5-2
	Thames Ironworks v Grays United	4-0
	West Ham Garfield v Sheppey United	1-8
9	Aylesbury United v Chesham Generals	3-0
	Maidenhead v Maidenhead Norfolkians	2-4
	Reading Ramblers v Oxford City	1-1
	Richmond Association v 1st Scots Guards	2-0
10	Bristol East v Staple Hill	2-0
	Portsmouth v Ryde	10-0
1r	Bishop Auckland v Leadgate Park	5-1
r	Darlington v Crook Town	2-3
4r	Wellington Town v Ironbridge	1-0
5r	Mexborough v Attercliffe	2-0
r	Newark v Worksop Town	1-0
r	Sheffield v Denaby United	0-1
9r	Oxford City v Reading Ramblers	1-3

Qualifying Round Two

1	Bishop Auckland v Crook Town	3-2
	Gateshead NER v South Shields (1)	1-0
	South Bank v Thornaby	0-2
	Wallsend Park Villa v Shankhouse	6-0

1899/1900 to 1900/01

2	Blackpool - Bye	
	Freetown v Walshaw	2-1
	Moss Bay Exchange v Workington (1)	1-1
	Oswaldtwistle Rovers v Darwen	2-2
3	Haydock v Wigan County	1-4
	Nantwich v Warrington St Elphin's	2-1
	South Liverpool v New Brighton Tower	3-2
	Stalybridge Rovers v Congleton Hornets	2-0
4	Llandudno Swifts v Wrexham	1-2
	Oswestry United v Newtown	3-3
	Shrewsbury Town v Wellington Town	1-2
	Stourbridge v Dudley	1-4
5	Chesterfield v Stapleford Town	5-2
	Denaby United v Mexborough	2-1
	Doncaster Rovers v Newark	3-1
	Wombwell Town v Hunslet	1-2
6	Burton Wanderers v Coalville Town (1)	0-2
	Hinckley Town (1) v Barwell Swifts	7-1
	Hucknall Portland v Newstead Byron	3-2
	Wellingborough Town v Rushden	1-1
7	Norwich CEYMS v Kirkley	1-0
	Queen's Park Rangers v West Hampstead	5-0
	Watford v Wolverton LNWR	1-0
	West Norwood v Wandsworth	0-1
8	Brighton United v Brighton Athletic	9-0
	Clapton v Ilford	2-1
	Swanscombe v Dartford	1-2
	Thames Ironworks v Sheppey United	4-2
9	Chesham Town v Aylesbury United	2-0
	Reading Ramblers v Oxford Cygnets	4-2
	Shepherds Bush v Richmond Association	2-3
	Slough v Maidenhead Norfolkians	2-2
10	Bristol East v Bristol Amateurs	1-0
	Eastleigh Athletic v Freemantle	5-0
	Portsmouth v Cowes (1)	3-2
	Yeovil Casuals v Street	3-3
2r	Darwen v Oswaldtwistle Rovers	4-0
r	Workington (1) v Moss Bay Exchange	6-1
4r	Newtown v Oswestry United	1-3
6r	Rushden v Wellingborough Town	1-3
9r	Maidenhead Norfolkians v Slough	4-0
10r	Street v Yeovil Casuals	wo/s

Qualifying Round Three

1	Gateshead NER v Bishop Auckland	1-1
	Middlesbrough v Jarrow	1-2
	Wallsend Park Villa v Hebburn Argyle	1-1
	Willington Athletic v Thornaby	5-0
2	Blackpool v Southport Central	0-2
	Chorley v Workington (1)	6-1
	Darwen v Freetown	3-1
	South Shore v Newton Heath	3-1
3	Burslem Port Vale v Nantwich	2-0
	Crewe Alexandra v Wigan County	3-1
	Glossop v Stockport County	2-2
	Stalybridge Rovers v South Liverpool	1-0
4	Small Heath v Oswestry United	10-2
	Walsall v Kidderminster Harriers	6-1
	Wellington Town v Druids	4-0
	Wrexham v Dudley	3-2
5	Chesterfield v Heanor Town	6-1
	Denaby United v Hunslet	2-2
	Grimsby Town v Doncaster Rovers	3-1
	Lincoln City v Barnsley	0-1
6	Burton Swifts v Kettering	8-2
	Coalville Town (1) v Hucknall Portland	3-3
	Leicester Fosse v Wellingborough Town	3-1
	Loughborough v Hinckley Town (1)	1-2
7	Crouch End Vampires v Watford	0-3
	Lowestoft Town v Luton Town	0-2
	Norwich CEYMS v Civil Service	1-3
	Queen's Park Rangers v Wandsworth	7-1
8	Chatham v Brighton United	2-0
	Dartford v Thames Ironworks	0-7
	Millwall Athletic v Clapton	7-0
	Woolwich Arsenal v New Brompton	1-1
9	Brentford v Richmond Association	1-2
	Chesham Town v Maidenhead Norfolkians	11-3
	Marlow v Reading Ramblers	4-2
	Wycombe Wanderers v Reading	0-8
10	Bristol East v Street	4-1
	Bristol Rovers v Eastleigh Athletic	5-0
	Portsmouth v Swindon Town	2-1
	Weymouth v Bedminster	0-6
1r	Bishop Auckland v Gateshead NER	4-0
r	Hebburn Argyle v Wallsend Park Villa	2-3
3r	Stockport County v Glossop	3-0
5r	Hunslet v Denaby United	1-1e
6r	Hucknall Portland v Coalville Town (1)	4-3
8r	New Brompton v Woolwich Arsenal	0-0
5r2	Hunslet v Denaby United	4-3 N
8r2	New Brompton v Woolwich Arsenal	2-2eN
8r3	New Brompton v Woolwich Arsenal	1-1 N
8r4	New Brompton v Woolwich Arsenal	1-0 N

Qualifying Round Four

1	Jarrow v Wallsend Park Villa	3-2
	Willington Athletic v Bishop Auckland	2-0
2	Chorley v Darwen	1-1
	South Shore v Southport Central	1-1
3	Crewe Alexandra v Burslem Port Vale	2-2
	Stalybridge Rovers v Stockport County	2-0
4	Small Heath v Wrexham	6-1
	Walsall v Wellington Town	2-1
5	Chesterfield v Hunslet	6-0
	Grimsby Town v Barnsley	3-2
6	Hinckley Town (1) v Hucknall Portland	0-1
	Leicester Fosse v Burton Swifts	3-1
7	Luton Town v Watford	3-2
	Queen's Park Rangers v Civil Service	3-0
8	Millwall Athletic v Chatham	3-0
	New Brompton v Thames Ironworks	0-0
9	Chesham Town v Richmond Association	3-1
	Reading v Marlow	2-1
10	Bedminster v Bristol East	4-1
	Bristol Rovers v Portsmouth	1-1
2r	Darwen v Chorley	0-1
r	Southport Central v South Shore	4-1
3r	Burslem Port Vale v Crewe Alexandra	3-1
8r	Thames Ironworks v New Brompton	2-0
10r	Portsmouth v Bristol Rovers	4-0

Qualifying Round Five

1	Willington Athletic v Jarrow	0-0
2	Southport Central v Chorley	1-3
3	Burslem Port Vale v Stalybridge Rovers	0-1
4	Small Heath v Walsall	0-0
5	Grimsby Town v Chesterfield	3-2
6	Leicester Fosse v Hucknall Portland	6-1
7	Luton Town v Queen's Park Rangers	1-1
8	Thames Ironworks v Millwall Athletic	1-2
9	Reading v Chesham Town	7-1
10	Bedminster v Portsmouth	1-2
1r	Jarrow v Willington Athletic	4-2
4r	Walsall v Small Heath	2-0
7r	Queen's Park Rangers v Luton Town	4-1

Round One

	Bristol City v Stalybridge Rovers	2-1
	Burnley v Bury	0-1
	Derby County v Sunderland	2-2
	Jarrow v Millwall Athletic	0-2
	Manchester City v Aston Villa	1-1
	Newcastle United v Reading	2-1
	Nottingham Forest v Grimsby Town	3-0
	Notts County v Chorley	6-0
	Portsmouth v Blackburn Rovers	0-0
	Preston North End v Tottenham Hotspur	1-0
	Queen's Park Rangers v Wolverhampton Wan.	1-1
	Sheffield United v Leicester Fosse	1-0
	Sheffield Wednesday v Bolton Wanderers	1-0
	Southampton v Everton	3-0
	Stoke v Liverpool	0-0
	Walsall v West Bromwich Albion	1-1
r	Aston Villa v Manchester City	3-0
r	Blackburn Rovers v Portsmouth	1-1e
r	Liverpool v Stoke	1-0
r	Sunderland v Derby County	3-0
r	West Bromwich Albion v Walsall	6-1
r	Wolverhampton Wan. v Queen's Park Rangers	0-1e
r2	Blackburn Rovers v Portsmouth	5-0

Round Two

	Aston Villa v Bristol City	5-1
	Liverpool v West Bromwich Albion	1-1
	Nottingham Forest v Sunderland	3-0
	Notts County v Bury	0-0
	Preston North End v Blackburn Rovers	1-0
	Queen's Park Rangers v Millwall Athletic	0-2
	Sheffield United v Sheffield Wednesday	1-1
	Southampton v Newcastle United	4-1
r	Bury v Notts County	2-0
r	Sheffield Wednesday v Sheffield United	0-2
r	West Bromwich Albion v Liverpool	2-1

Round Three

	Millwall Athletic v Aston Villa	1-1
	Preston North End v Nottingham Forest	0-0
	Sheffield United v Bury	2-2
	Southampton v West Bromwich Albion	2-1
r	Aston Villa v Millwall Athletic	0-0e
r	Bury v Sheffield United	2-0
r	Nottingham Forest v Preston North End	1-0
r2	Millwall Athletic v Aston Villa	2-1 N

Semi Finals

	Bury v Nottingham Forest	1-1 N
	Southampton v Millwall Athletic	0-0 N
r	Bury v Nottingham Forest	3-2eN
r	Southampton v Millwall Athletic	3-0 N

Final

	Bury v Southampton	4-0 N

1900/01

Preliminary Round

1	Bishop Auckland v Stanley United	5-2
	Darlington v Tow Law	3-0
	Howden-le-Wear v Darlington St Augustines	0-2
	Leadgate Park v Crook Town	3-0
	Stockton v South Bank	0-2
2	Turton v Heywood	0-2
5	Altofts v Wath Athletic	2-3
	Doncaster Rovers v Rotherham Town	6-1
	Sheffield v Attercliffe	1-3
	Worksop Town v Denaby United	3-2
7	Colchester Town v Bury St Edmunds	7-0
	Great Yarmouth Town v Harwich & Parkeston	1-1
	Hampstead v West Hampstead	0-4
	King's Lynn v Kirkley	2-0
	Norwich CEYMS v Lowestoft Town	1-2
	Willesden Town v Civil Service	1-3
8	Eastbourne v Worthing	6-0
	Leyton v West Ham Garfield	1-1
	Olympic v Upton Park	5-0
	Woodford v Leytonstone	1-1
7r	Harwich & Parkeston v Great Yarmouth Town	wo/s
8r	Leytonstone v Woodford	1-10
r	West Ham Garfield v Leyton	4-1

Qualifying Round One

1	Darlington St Augustines v Darlington	1-1
	Leadgate Park v Bishop Auckland	2-2
	Mickley v St Peter's Albion	1-2
	Shankhouse v Gateshead NER	0-1
	South Bank v Thornaby Utopians	0-3
	South Shields (1) v Morpeth Harriers	1-2
	Stockton St John's v Thornaby	0-2
	Wallsend Park Villa v Prudhoe	1-1
2	Blackburn Park Road v Trawden Forest	5-1
	Freetown v Heywood	3-1
	Keswick v Frizington White Star	3-2
	Oswaldtwistle Rovers v Great Harwood	4-0
	Rochdale (1) v Rossendale United	1-0
	Workington (1) v Moss Bay Exchange	4-3
3	Birkenhead v Buckley Victoria	3-0
	Earlestown v Haydock	3-0
	Middlewich Rangers v Nantwich	0-3
	Tranmere Rovers v White Star Wanderers	0-1
4	Druids v Chirk	1-2
	Halesowen v Brierley Hill Alliance	1-2
	Rhyl United v Llandudno Swifts	3-0
	Stourbridge v Kidderminster Harriers	5-2
5	Attercliffe v Doncaster Rovers	0-2
	Belper Town (1) v Heanor Town	2-0
	Grantham Avenue v Grimsby All Saints	3-1
	Ilkeston Town (1) v Stapleford Town	2-0
	Newark v Boston (1)	6-1
	Royston United v Hunslet	1-2
	Wath Athletic v Wombwell Town	3-0
	Worksop Town v Montrose Works	7-2
6	Burton Wanderers v Gresley Rovers	2-2
	Coalville Town (1) v Swadlincote	3-1
	Hinckley Town (1) v Nuneaton Town	wo/s
	Mansfield Foresters v Bulwell United	2-1
	Newstead Byron v Hucknall Portland	wo/s
	Rothwell Town Swifts v Finedon Revellers	1-3
	Rushden v Desborough Town	4-1
7	Civil Service v West Hampstead	4-1
	Colchester Town v Lowestoft Town	2-5
	Crouch End Vampires v London Welsh	3-0
	Godalming v Redhill	4-3
	King's Lynn v Harwich & Parkeston	2-1
	West Croydon v West Norwood	5-0
8	Brighton & Hove Rangers v Eastbourne	3-0
	Eastbourne Swifts v Brighton Athletic	1-2
	Folkestone v Sittingbourne	3-3
	Maidstone United v Ashford United	4-0
	Sheppey United v Gravesend United	1-0
	Swanscombe v Grays United	0-3
	West Ham Garfield v Olympic	0-3
	Woodford v Ilford	2-3
9	Chesham Generals v Chesham Town	0-0
	Maidenhead v Maidenhead Norfolkians	wo/s
	Richmond Association v Shepherds Bush	3-2
1r	Bishop Auckland v Leadgate Park	3-1
r	Darlington v Darlington St Augustines	4-1
r	Prudhoe v Wallsend Park Villa	2-3
6r	Gresley Rovers v Burton Wanderers	1-1
8r	Sittingbourne v Folkestone	wo/s
9r	Chesham Town v Chesham Generals	0-3
6r2	Burton Wanderers v Gresley Rovers	2-4 N

Qualifying Round Two

1	Bishop Auckland v Darlington	3-0
	Morpeth Harriers v Gateshead NER	0-1
	St Peter's Albion v Wallsend Park Villa	1-5
	Thornaby Utopians v Thornaby	2-1
2	Blackburn Park Road v Oswaldtwistle Rovers	3-0
	Freetown v Rochdale (1)	0-3
	Hudsons v Southport Central	1-2
	Keswick v Workington (1)	1-2

1900/01 to 1901/02

3 Birkenhead v White Star Wanderers	0-1
Buxton - Bye	
Earlestown v Swinton Town	5-0
Nantwich v Winsford United	5-2
4 Oswestry United v Ironbridge	wo/s
Rhyl United v Chirk	0-0
Stourbridge v Brierley Hill Alliance	2-2
Welshpool v Aberystwyth	wo/s
5 Grantham Avenue v Newark	0-0
Hunslet v Wath Athletic	4-1
Ilkeston Town (1) v Belper Town (1)	6-1
Worksop Town v Doncaster Rovers	0-0
6 Finedon Revellers v Rushden	2-2
Gresley Rovers v Coalville Town (1)	2-0
Hinckley Town (1) v Loughborough	wo/s
Mansfield Foresters v Newstead Byron	1-2
7 Crouch End Vampires v Civil Service	0-1
Godalming v West Croydon	4-0
King's Lynn v Lowestoft Town	3-0
Leighton Cee Springs v Hitchin	wo/s
8 Brighton Athletic v Brighton & Hove Rangers	0-4
Grays United v Sheppey United	1-0
Maidstone United v Sittingbourne	2-2
Olympic v Ilford	1-1
9 Chesham Generals v Aylesbury United	1-0
Oxford City v Reading	
Richmond Association v 1st Coldstream Guards	wo/s
Slough v Maidenhead	2-2
10 Bristol East - Bye	
Yeovil Casuals v Street	6-1
4r Brierley Hill Alliance v Stourbridge	1-3
r Chirk v Rhyl United	wo/s
5r Doncaster Rovers v Worksop Town	2-1
r Newark v Grantham Avenue	4-2
6r Rushden v Finedon Revellers	0-1
8r Ilford v Olympic	0-2
r Sittingbourne v Maidstone United	0-0
9r Maidenhead v Slough	3-0
8r2 Maidstone United v Sittingbourne	2-0 N

Qualifying Round Three

1 Gateshead NER v Jarrow	0-1
Middlesbrough v Willington Athletic	3-3
Thornaby Utopians v Bishop Auckland	1-5
Wallsend Park Villa v Hebburn Argyle	3-0
2 Blackburn Park Road v Blackpool	0-1
Darwen v Nelson	3-1
Southport Central v Chorley	3-1
Workington (1) v Rochdale (1)	wo/s
3 Crewe Alexandra v Stalybridge Rovers	3-0
Earlestown v White Star Wanderers	2-1
Nantwich v Buxton	2-1
Stockport County v Wrexham	6-2
4 Chirk v Welshpool	8-1
Oswestry United v Coventry City	wo/s
Shrewsbury Town v Walsall	1-1
Wellington Town v Stourbridge	wo/s
5 Barnsley v Doncaster Rovers	2-1
Chesterfield v Hunslet	8-3
Ilkeston Town (1) v Newark	2-1 v
Lincoln City v Gainsborough Trinity	0-0
6 Burton Swifts v Newstead Byron	2-2
Gresley Rovers v Wellingborough Town	2-0
Hinckley Town (1) v Northampton Town	2-0
Kettering v Finedon Revellers	7-0
7 Godalming v Civil Service	1-2
King's Lynn v Luton Town	1-4
Queen's Park Rangers v Fulham	7-0
Watford v Leighton Cee Springs	10-0
8 Brighton & Hove Rangers v Chatham	1-5
Clapton v Maidstone United	8-1
Grays United v New Brompton	0-2
West Ham United v Olympic	1-0
9 Brentford v Maidenhead	3-1
Marlow v Chesham Generals	3-5
Oxford City v Reading	0-4
Richmond Association v Wycombe Wanderers	wo/s
10 Bristol Rovers - Bye	
Staple Hill - Bye	
Swindon Town v Bristol East	1-1
Weymouth v Yeovil Casuals	4-3
1r Willington Athletic v Middlesbrough	0-0
4r Walsall v Shrewsbury Town	1-0
5r Gainsborough Trinity v Lincoln City	1-1x
r Newark v Ilkeston Town (1)	2-1e
6r Burton Swifts v Newstead Byron	4-0
10r Swindon Town v Bristol East	5-0
1r2 Middlesbrough v Willington Athletic	8-0
5r2 Lincoln City v Gainsborough Trinity	3-1 N

Qualifying Round Four

1 Bishop Auckland v Wallsend Park Villa	5-0
Middlesbrough v Jarrow	3-0
2 Darwen v Blackpool	2-1
Southport Central v Workington (1)	2-0
3 Earlestown v Nantwich	2-3
Stockport County v Crewe Alexandra	1-3
4 Chirk v Walsall	0-1
Wellington Town v Oswestry United	4-0
5 Barnsley v Lincoln City	1-0
Newark v Chesterfield	0-5
6 Gresley Rovers v Kettering	1-3
Hinckley Town (1) v Burton Swifts	1-4

7 Luton Town v Civil Service	9-1
Watford v Queen's Park Rangers	1-1
8 Chatham v Clapton	2-2
New Brompton v West Ham United	1-1
9 Brentford v Richmond Association	0-1
Reading v Chesham Generals	11-0
10 Bristol Rovers v Weymouth	15-1
Swindon Town v Staple Hill	2-2
7r Queen's Park Rangers v Watford	4-1
8r Clapton v Chatham	5-1
r West Ham United v New Brompton	4-1
10r Swindon Town v Staple Hill	6-0

Qualifying Round Five

1 Middlesbrough v Bishop Auckland	4-0
2 Southport Central v Darwen	1-1
3 Crewe Alexandra v Nantwich	5-1
4 Walsall v Wellington Town	6-0
5 Barnsley v Chesterfield	1-5
6 Burton Swifts v Kettering	1-2
7 Luton Town v Queen's Park Rangers	3-0
8 West Ham United v Clapton	1-1
9 Reading v Richmond Association	2-0
10 Bristol Rovers v Swindon Town	5-1
2r Darwen v Southport Central	2-0
8r Clapton v West Ham United	2-3

Intermediate Round

Burslem Port Vale v New Brighton Tower	1-3
Chesterfield v Walsall	3-0
Darwen v Woolwich Arsenal	0-2
Grimsby Town v Middlesbrough	0-1
Kettering v Crewe Alexandra	1-0
Luton Town v Bristol Rovers	1-2
Newton Heath v Portsmouth	3-0
Reading v Bristol City	1-1
Stoke v Glossop	1-0
West Ham United v Liverpool	0-1
r Bristol City v Reading	0-0x
r2 Reading v Bristol City	2-1 N

Round One

Aston Villa v Millwall Athletic	5-0
Bolton Wanderers v Derby County	1-0
Kettering v Chesterfield	1-1
Middlesbrough v Newcastle United	3-1
Newton Heath v Burnley	0-0
Nottingham Forest v Leicester Fosse	5-1
Notts County v Liverpool	2-0
Reading v Bristol Rovers	2-0
Sheffield Wednesday v Bury	0-1
Southampton v Everton	1-3
Stoke v Small Heath	1-1
Sunderland v Sheffield United	1-2
Tottenham Hotspur v Preston North End	1-1
West Bromwich Albion v Manchester City	1-0
Wolverhampton Wan. v New Brighton Tower	5-1
Woolwich Arsenal v Blackburn Rovers	2-0
r Burnley v Newton Heath	7-1
r Chesterfield v Kettering	1-2e
r Preston North End v Tottenham Hotspur	2-4
r Small Heath v Stoke	2-1e

Round Two

Aston Villa v Nottingham Forest	0-0
Bolton Wanderers v Reading	0-1
Middlesbrough v Kettering	5-0
Notts County v Wolverhampton Wan.	2-3
Sheffield United v Everton	2-0
Small Heath v Burnley	1-0
Tottenham Hotspur v Bury	2-1
Woolwich Arsenal v West Bromwich Albion	0-1
r Nottingham Forest v Aston Villa	1-3e

Round Three

Middlesbrough v West Bromwich Albion	0-1
Reading v Tottenham Hotspur	1-1
Small Heath v Aston Villa	0-0
Wolverhampton Wan. v Sheffield United	0-4
r Aston Villa v Small Heath	1-0e
r Tottenham Hotspur v Reading	3-0

Semi Finals

Sheffield United v Aston Villa	2-2 N
Tottenham Hotspur v West Bromwich Albion	4-0 N
r Sheffield United v Aston Villa	3-0 N

Final

Tottenham Hotspur v Sheffield United	2-2 N
r Tottenham Hotspur v Sheffield United	3-1 N

1901/02

Preliminary Round

1 Grangetown Athletic v South Bank	0-1
Leadgate Park v Darlington	3-0
Scarborough v Thornaby	1-2
Stockton v Whitby (1)	4-1
West Hartlepool v Stockton St John's	4-2
2 Moss Bay Exchange v Frizington U (1)	2-0
Oswaldtwistle Rovers v Trawden Forest	7-0
5 Denaby United v Thornhill United	2-2
Mexborough St John's v Wycliffe	2-1
Rotherham Town v Roundell	2-2
Sheffield v Attercliffe	5-2
6 Wellingborough Town v Rushden	4-0
7 Bromley v West Norwood	0-3
Chiswick v Fulham	2-3
Hampstead v Willesden Town	1-3
King's Lynn v Lowestoft Town	0-3
Kirkley v Harwich & Parkeston	1-1
London Welsh v Crouch End Vampires	0-1
Lynn Swifts v Great Yarmouth Town	3-4
Norwich CEYMS v Bury St Edmunds	18-0
West Croydon v Redhill	2-6
8 Brighton & Hove Albion v Brighton Athletic	6-2
Chatham v Grays United	0-2
Eastbourne v St Leonards (1)	5-2
Eastbourne Old Town v Eastbourne Swifts	0-3
Leytonstone v West Ham Garfield	2-0
Worthing v Hastings & St Leonards (1)	0-4
5r Roundell v Rotherham Town	3-1
r Thornhill United v Denaby United	2-3
7r Harwich & Parkeston v Kirkley	1-0

Qualifying Round One

1 Darlington St Augustines v Tow Law	1-0
Hebburn Argyle v Sunderland Royal Rovers	1-2
Mickley v Gateshead NER	0-0
Morpeth Harriers v Shankhouse	5-1
South Bank v Stockton	2-2
Stanley United v Leadgate Park	0-2
West Hartlepool v Thornaby	1-3
2 Accrington Stanley v Nelson	2-1
Barrow v Black Diamonds	3-2
Frizington White Star v Moss Bay Exchange	1-2
Oswaldtwistle Rovers v Blackburn Park Road	5-2
3 Birkenhead v Chester	1-1
Haydock v Wigan United	0-5
St Helens v Earlestown	2-1
White Star Wanderers v Hudsons	1-3
Winsford United v Middlewich Rangers	1-1
4 Halesowen v Brierley Hill Alliance	2-3
Ironbridge v Stafford Rangers	2-2
Shrewsbury Town v Oswestry United	1-1
5 Belper Town (1) v Derby Hills Ivanhoe	6-1
Denaby United v Sheffield	3-0
Hunslet v Royston United	1-1
Newark v Boston (1)	5-1
Roundell v Mexborough St John's	4-0
Stapleford Town v Ilkeston Town (1)	0-4
Wath Athletic v Altofts	3-2
Worksop Town v Grantham Avenue	5-1
6 Desborough Town v Wellingborough Town	1-5
Newstead Byron v Bulwell United	wo/s
Rothwell Town Swifts v Finedon Revellers	2-1
7 Bedford Queens Works v Leighton Cee Springs	3-1
Crouch End Vampires v Fulham	4-2
Harwich & Parkeston v Great Yarmouth Town	0-1
Luton Town v Apsley	13-1
Norwich CEYMS v Lowestoft Town	1-1
Wandsworth v Godalming	0-1
West Norwood v Redhill	7-1
Willesden Town v Vulcans	5-1
8 Ashford United v Sittingbourne	0-0
Brighton & Hove Albion v Eastbourne	3-1
Chatham Amateurs v Grays United	1-2
Eastbourne Swifts v Hastings & St Leonards (1)	0-1
Leytonstone v Upton Park	1-2
Maidstone United v Folkestone	3-1
Olympic v Leyton	0-7
Swanscombe v Sheppey United	0-0
9 Chesham Generals v Chesham Town	3-1
Shepherds Bush v Southall	5-4
Slough v Windsor & Eton	3-0
10 Bridgwater v Avalon Rovers	3-2
Eastleigh Athletic v Freemantle	0-3
1r Gateshead NER v Mickley	3-0
r Stockton v South Bank	wo/s
3r Chester v Birkenhead	5-4 D
r Middlewich Rangers v Winsford United	1-4
4r Oswestry United v Shrewsbury Town	2-0
r Stafford Rangers v Ironbridge	wo/s
5r Royston United v Hunslet	wo/s
7r Lowestoft Town v Norwich CEYMS	5-0
8r Sheppey United v Swanscombe	1-0
r Sittingbourne v Ashford United	1-0

29

1901/02 to 1902/03

Qualifying Round Two

1	Darlington St Augustines v Leadgate Park	4-0
	Morpeth Harriers v Gateshead NER	2-3
	South Shields Athletic v Sunderland Royal Rovers	0-0
	Thornaby v Stockton	1-0
2	Accrington Stanley v Oswaldtwistle Rovers	1-1
	Barrow v Moss Bay Exchange	1-1
	Rochdale (1) v Black Lane Temperance	7-2
	Shaddongate United v Keswick	5-1
3	Buxton - Bye	
	Hudsons v Birkenhead	2-2
	Nantwich v Winsford United	3-0
	Wigan United v St Helens	0-1
4	Berwick Rangers v Kidderminster Harriers	3-2
	Brierley Hill Alliance v Stourbridge	4-1
	Chirk v Wrexham	0-2
	Oswestry United v Stafford Rangers	1-1
5	Belper Town (1) v Ilkeston Town (1)	2-4
	Denaby United v Roundell	3-0
	Royston United v Wath Athletic	6-2
	Worksop Town v Newark	5-1
6	Coalville Town (1) v Gresley Rovers	3-4
	Newstead Byron v Hucknall Town (1)	2-0
	Wellingborough Town v Rothwell Town Swifts	4-0
7	Crouch End Vampires v Willesden Town	3-1
	Godalming v West Norwood	0-2
	Great Yarmouth Town v Lowestoft Town	0-2
	Luton Town v Bedford Queens Works	4-2
8	Brighton & Hove Albion v Hastings & St Leonards (1)	5-0
	Grays United v Sheppey United	0-0
	Leyton v Upton Park	4-4
	Sittingbourne v Maidstone United	2-4
9	Aylesbury United v Chesham Generals	2-1
	Maidenhead Norfolkians v Slough	2-0
	Richmond Association v Shepherds Bush	1-1
10	Bridgwater v Street	1-4
	Staple Hill v Bristol East	1-1
	Trowbridge Town v Yeovil Casuals	0-5
	Whiteheads v Freemantle	1-0
1r	Sunderland Royal Rovers v South Shields Athletic	3-1
2r	Moss Bay Exchange v Barrow	1-3
r	Oswaldtwistle Rovers v Accrington Stanley	0-2
3r	Birkenhead v Hudsons	2-1
4r	Stafford Rangers v Oswestry United	0-2
8r	Sheppey United v Grays United	0-0
r	Upton Park v Leyton	0-6
9r	Shepherds Bush v Richmond Association	1-0
10r	Bristol East v Staple Hill	1-0
8r2	Grays United v Sheppey United	3-0

Qualifying Round Three

1	Bishop Auckland v Jarrow	2-0
	Darlington St Augustines v Willington Athletic	1-1
	Gateshead NER v Wallsend Park Villa	0-2
	Thornaby v Sunderland Royal Rovers	1-2
2	Barrow v Rochdale (1)	4-0
	Darwen v Accrington Stanley	2-1
	Shaddongate United v Workington (1)	0-2
	Southport Central v Blackpool	0-0
3	Buxton v Stockport County	0-2
	Glossop v St Helens	5-2
	Nantwich v Birkenhead	2-1
	Stalybridge Rovers v Crewe Alexandra	0-2
4	Berwick Rangers v Coventry City	11-2
	Brierley Hill Alliance v Walsall	1-1
	Burslem Port Vale v Wellington Town	6-0
	Oswestry United v Wrexham	1-2
5	Barnsley v Gainsborough Trinity	1-0
	Ilkeston Town (1) v Denaby United	2-1
	Royston United v Doncaster Rovers	1-3
	Worksop Town v Lincoln City	0-4
6	Gresley Rovers v Northampton Town	0-2
	Kettering v Wellingborough Town	1-0
	Newstead Byron v Hinckley Town (1)	0-2
	Whitwick White Cross v Burton United	0-3
7	Civil Service v West Norwood	1-3
	Lowestoft Town v Luton Town	1-2
	Queen's Park Rangers v Crouch End Vampires	2-0
	West Hampstead v Watford	1-2
8	Brighton & Hove Albion v Clapton	2-3
	Grays United v Maidstone United	2-0
	Leyton v West Ham United	0-1
	New Brompton v Ilford	6-1
9	Aylesbury United v Oxford City	0-4
	Maidenhead Norfolkians v Shepherds Bush	0-4
	Marlow v Brentford	0-3
	Wycombe Wanderers v Maidenhead	1-1
10	Bristol City v Bristol East	5-1
	Bristol Rovers v Whiteheads	5-0
	Street v Weymouth	0-2
	Swindon Town v Yeovil Casuals	4-0
1r	Willington Athletic v Darlington St Augustines	1-1
2r	Blackpool v Southport Central	0-0x
4r	Walsall v Brierley Hill Alliance	2-1
9r	Maidenhead v Wycombe Wanderers	0-2
1r2	Darlington St Augustines v Willington Athletic	2-0 N
2r2	Southport Central v Blackpool	2-1 N

Qualifying Round Four

1	Sunderland Royal Rovers v Darlington St Augustines	0-1
	Wallsend Park Villa v Bishop Auckland	2-2
2	Barrow v Darwen	2-3
	Southport Central v Workington (1)	4-0
3	Nantwich v Glossop	1-3
	Stockport County v Crewe Alexandra	3-2
4	Walsall v Berwick Rangers	2-1
	Wrexham v Burslem Port Vale	2-1 v
5	Ilkeston Town (1) v Barnsley	2-4
	Lincoln City v Doncaster Rovers	1-0
6	Burton United v Northampton Town	0-0
	Kettering v Hinckley Town (1)	1-1
7	Queen's Park Rangers v West Norwood	4-0
	Watford v Luton Town	1-2
8	Clapton v New Brompton	2-2
	West Ham United v Grays United	1-2
9	Brentford v Shepherds Bush	2-3
	Wycombe Wanderers v Oxford City	2-5
10	Bristol Rovers v Bristol City	1-1x
	Swindon Town v Weymouth	2-1
1r	Bishop Auckland v Wallsend Park Villa	3-2
4r	Wrexham v Burslem Port Vale	0-0
6r	Hinckley Town (1) v Kettering	2-2
r	Northampton Town v Burton United	2-0
8r	New Brompton v Clapton	2-0
10r	Bristol City v Bristol Rovers	2-3
4r2	Burslem Port Vale v Wrexham	3-1
6r2	Kettering v Hinckley Town (1)	6-0 N

Qualifying Round Five

1	Bishop Auckland v Darlington St Augustines	4-2
2	Southport Central v Darwen	2-2
3	Glossop v Stockport County	2-0
4	Burslem Port Vale v Walsall	1-2
5	Barnsley v Lincoln City	0-0
6	Kettering v Northampton Town	2-2
7	Luton Town v Queen's Park Rangers	2-0
8	New Brompton v Grays United	1-0
9	Shepherds Bush v Oxford City	1-3
10	Swindon Town v Bristol Rovers	0-1
2r	Darwen v Southport Central	2-2
5r	Lincoln City v Barnsley	3-1e
6r	Northampton Town v Kettering	2-0
2r2	Darwen v Southport Central	1-0 N

Intermediate Round

	Bishop Auckland v Burnley	2-3
	Leicester Fosse v Glossop	0-1
	Millwall Athletic v Bristol Rovers	1-1
	Newton Heath v Lincoln City	1-2
	Northampton Town v Darwen	4-1
	Oxford City v New Brighton Tower	wo/s
	Portsmouth v Small Heath	2-1
	Reading v Chesterfield	2-0
	Walsall v New Brompton	2-0
	Woolwich Arsenal v Luton Town	1-1
r	Bristol Rovers v Millwall Athletic	1-0
r	Luton Town v Woolwich Arsenal	0-2

Round One

	Blackburn Rovers v Derby County	0-2
	Bury v West Bromwich Albion	5-1
	Glossop v Nottingham Forest	1-3
	Grimsby Town v Portsmouth	1-1
	Liverpool v Everton	2-2
	Manchester City v Preston North End	1-1
	Middlesbrough v Bristol Rovers	1-1
	Northampton Town v Sheffield United	0-2
	Notts County v Reading	1-2
	Oxford City v Lincoln City	0-0
	Sheffield Wednesday v Sunderland	0-1
	Stoke v Aston Villa	2-2
	Tottenham Hotspur v Southampton	1-1
	Walsall v Burnley	1-0
	Wolverhampton Wan. v Bolton Wanderers	0-2
	Woolwich Arsenal v Newcastle United	0-2
r	Aston Villa v Stoke	1-2e
r	Bristol Rovers v Middlesbrough	1-0e
r	Everton v Liverpool	0-2
r	Lincoln City v Oxford City	4-0
r	Portsmouth v Grimsby Town	2-0
r	Preston North End v Manchester City	0-0e
r	Southampton v Tottenham Hotspur	2-2e
r2	Preston North End v Manchester City	2-4e
r2	Southampton v Tottenham Hotspur	2-1 N

Round Two

	Bristol Rovers v Stoke	0-1
	Lincoln City v Derby County	1-3
	Manchester City v Nottingham Forest	0-2
	Newcastle United v Sunderland	1-0
	Reading v Portsmouth	0-1
	Sheffield United v Bolton Wanderers	2-1
	Southampton v Liverpool	4-1
	Walsall v Bury	0-5

Round Three

	Bury v Southampton	2-3
	Newcastle United v Sheffield United	1-1
	Nottingham Forest v Stoke	2-0
	Portsmouth v Derby County	0-0
r	Derby County v Portsmouth	6-3
r	Sheffield United v Newcastle United	2-1

Semi Finals

	Sheffield United v Derby County	1-1 N
	Southampton v Nottingham Forest	3-1 N
r	Sheffield United v Derby County	1-1eN
r2	Sheffield United v Derby County	1-0 N

Final

	Sheffield United v Southampton	1-1 N
r	Sheffield United v Southampton	2-1 N

1902/03

Preliminary Round

1	Darlington St Augustines v Tow Law	1-2
	Leadgate Park v Darlington	0-5
2	Darwen v Padiham	2-2
	Frizington U (1) v Moss Bay Exchange	0-1
	Trawden Forest v Bacup	3-3
	Workington (1) v Frizington White Star	0-1
5	Rotherham Town v Attercliffe	2-0
7	Apsley v Berkhamsted Town	7-1
	Bedford Queens Works v Leighton Cee Springs	4-2
	Bromley v West Croydon	1-2
	Crouch End Vampires v West Hampstead	6-1
	Fulham v Civil Service	2-0
	Kirkley v Great Yarmouth Town	3-1
	Lowestoft Town v Norwich City	5-0
	Willesden Town v War Office	3-3
8	Chatham v Maidstone United	1-1
	Chelmsford v Olympic	1-0
	Deptford Town v Cray Wanderers	1-2
	Hove v Brighton Athletic	1-2
	Leyton v West Ham Garfield	3-1
	Leytonstone v Woodford	2-2
	Newhaven Cement Works v Hastings & St Leonards (1)	2-3
	Swanscombe v Folkestone	wo/s
	Upton Park v Boleyn Castle	4-0
2r	Bacup v Trawden Forest	4-3
r	Padiham v Darwen	2-2
7r	War Office v Willesden Town	1-2
8r	Maidstone United v Chatham	2-2
r	Woodford v Leytonstone	3-1
2r2	Padiham v Darwen	1-0 N
8r2	Maidstone United v Chatham	2-0

Qualifying Round One

1	Crook Town v Darlington St Hilda's	1-1
	Stockton v Stockton St John's	1-1
	Tow Law v Darlington	1-1
	Whitby (1) v Scarborough	3-2
	Willington Athletic v Sunderland Royal Rovers	0-3
2	Accrington Stanley v Bacup	5-0
	Barrow v Moss Bay Exchange	4-0
	Black Diamonds v Frizington White Star	wo/s
	Blackpool v Black Lane Temperance	4-1
	Padiham v Rossendale United	1-2
	Rochdale (1) v White Star Wanderers	5-1
3	St Helens Recreation v Earlestown	2-0
	St Helens Town v Wigan United	0-0
	Stockport County v Stalybridge Rovers	0-1
4	Brierley Hill Alliance v Halesowen	wo/s
	Oswestry United v Royal Welsh Warehouse	1-0
	Shrewsbury Town v Wellington Town	1-2
	Welshpool v Chirk	1-3
5	Derby Hills Ivanhoe v Stapleford Town	2-2
	Grantham Avenue v Worksop Town	2-1
	Ilkeston Town (1) v Belper Town (1)	1-3
	Newark v Boston (1)	4-1
	Sheffield v Rotherham Town	1-4
	Thornhill United v Channing Rovers	wo/s
6	Allsops v Newhall Red Rose	0-2
	Burton United v Sutton Town	wo/s
	Desborough Town v Raunds Town	6-0
	Hinckley Town (1) v Whitwick White Cross	1-1
	Irthlingborough Town v Rushden	3-1
7	Bedford Queens Works v Apsley	2-1
	Fulham v Crouch End Vampires	4-0
	Kirkley v King's Lynn	4-3
	Luton Amateur v Wolverton Town	3-0
	Norwich CEYMS v Lowestoft Town	0-5
	Richmond Town v Croydon Wanderers	1-1
	West Croydon v Godalming	1-0
	Willesden Town v Hampstead	2-1
8	Brighton & Hove Albion v Brighton Athletic	14-2
	Hastings & St Leonards (1) v St Leonards (1)	4-1
	Maidstone United v Cray Wanderers	2-1
	Shoreham v Worthing	4-2
	Sittingbourne v Swanscombe	wo/s
	Tunbridge Wells (1) v Eastbourne Old Town	5-1
	Upton Park v Chelmsford	2-1
	Woodford v Leyton	2-0
10	Basingstoke v Eastleigh Athletic	0-2
	Bristol East v Bristol St George	1-1
	North Hants Ironworks v Freemantle	3-0

1902/03 to 1903/04

1r Darlington v Tow Law	1-2
r Darlington St Hilda's v Crook Town	0-2
r Stockton v Stockton St John's	wo/s
3r Wigan United v St Helens Town	1-5
5r Stapleford Town v Derby Hills Ivanhoe	wo/s
6r Whitwick White Cross v Hinckley Town (1)	3-1e
7r Croydon Wanderers v Richmond Town	1-3
10r Bristol St George v Bristol East	1-2

Qualifying Round Two

1 Morpeth Harriers v Shankhouse	4-0
Sunderland West End v Sunderland Royal Rovers	3-4
Tow Law v Crook Town	1-1
Whitby (1) v Stockton	1-7
2 Accrington Stanley v Rossendale United	1-0
Barrow v Black Diamonds	7-1
Blackpool v Rochdale (1)	0-1
Keswick v Shaddongate United	2-0
3 Nantwich - Bye	
Rhyl - Bye	
St Helens Recreation v St Helens Town	3-0
Stalybridge Rovers v Buxton	3-0
4 Caerphilly v Aberaman	1-7
Oswestry United v Chirk	1-0
Walsall v Brierley Hill Alliance	0-2
Wellington Town v Stafford Rangers	0-3
5 Belper Town (1) v Stapleford Town	3-0
Grantham Avenue v Newark	1-1
Rotherham Town v Thornhill United	3-1
Royston United v Hemsworth	0-0
6 Burton United v Newhall Red Rose	wo/s
Gresley Rovers v Coalville Town (1)	5-2
Irthlingborough Town v Desborough Town	2-1
Market Harborough Town v Whitwick White Cross	1-4
7 Bedford Queens Works v Luton Amateur	1-2
Fulham v Willesden Town	0-0
Kirkley v Lowestoft Town	0-0
West Croydon v Richmond Town	2-1
8 Shoreham v Brighton & Hove Albion	0-12
Sittingbourne v Maidstone United	1-2
Tunbridge Wells (1) v Hastings & St Leonards (1)	1-2
Woodford v Upton Park	4-3
9 Chesham Generals v Chesham Town	2-0
Maidenhead Norfolkians v Maidenhead	4-0
Richmond Association v Southall	1-2
Wycombe Wanderers v Aylesbury United	0-2
10 Glastonbury v Bristol East	0-2
North Hants Ironworks v Eastleigh Athletic	2-2
Poole v Weymouth	3-2
Swindon Town v Chippenham Town	5-0
1r Crook Town v Tow Law	1-1e
5r Newark v Grantham Avenue	1-0
r Royston United v Hemsworth	wo/s
7r Fulham v Willesden Town	5-0
r Lowestoft Town v Kirkley	2-1
10r Eastleigh Athletic v North Hants Ironworks	3-0
1r2 Tow Law v Crook Town	0-0 d

Qualifying Round Three

1 Bishop Auckland v Morpeth Harriers	2-1
South Bank v Sunderland Royal Rovers	0-0
Tow Law v Stockton	1-5
Wallsend Park Villa v Gateshead NER	1-0
2 Keswick v Southport Central	0-3
Manchester United v Accrington Stanley	7-0
Nelson v Barrow	3-3
Oswaldtwistle Rovers v Rochdale (1)	2-0
3 Burslem Port Vale v Stalybridge Rovers	3-1
Crewe Alexandra v Glossop	0-3
St Helens Recreation v Rhyl	18-0
Wrexham v Nantwich	3-0
4 Brierley Hill Alliance v Stafford Rangers	0-1
Coventry City v Aberaman	3-1
Kidderminster Harriers v Hereford (1)	wo/s
Stourbridge v Oswestry United	7-0
5 Belper Town (1) v Barnsley	1-4
Chesterfield v Newark	6-0
Gainsborough Trinity v Doncaster Rovers	1-0
Rotherham Town v Royston United	2-1
6 Burton United v Northampton Town	2-0
Gresley Rovers v Kettering	0-1
Irthlingborough Town v Leicester Fosse	0-1
Wellingborough Town v Whitwick White Cross	3-0
7 Luton Amateur v West Norwood	5-0
Queen's Park Rangers v Luton Town	0-3
Watford v Fulham	1-1
West Croydon v Lowestoft Town	1-3
8 Brighton & Hove Albion v Grays United	5-5
Ilford v Hastings & St Leonards (1)	5-0
Maidstone United v Woodford	3-2
New Brompton v Clapton	2-0
9 Chesham Generals v Marlow	2-2
Maidenhead Norfolkians v Shepherds Bush	2-2
Oxford City v Brentford	2-2
Southall v Aylesbury United	3-2
10 Bristol East v Poole	1-1
Eastleigh Athletic v Staple Hill	7-0
Whiteheads v Street	6-0
Yeovil Casuals v Swindon Town	0-4

1r Grays United v Brighton & Hove Albion	0-3
r Sunderland Royal Rovers v South Bank	4-1
2r Barrow v Nelson	2-0
7r Fulham v Watford	3-0
9r Brentford v Oxford City	5-4
r Marlow v Chesham Generals	2-4
r Shepherds Bush v Maidenhead Norfolkians	5-1
10r Poole v Bristol East	4-3

Qualifying Round Four

1 Stockton v Bishop Auckland	1-4
Wallsend Park Villa v Sunderland Royal Rovers	0-1
2 Manchester United v Oswaldtwistle Rovers	3-2
Southport Central v Barrow	2-1
3 Glossop v Wrexham	4-0
St Helens Recreation v Burslem Port Vale	2-1
4 Coventry City v Stafford Rangers	5-2
Stourbridge v Kidderminster Harriers	2-2
5 Barnsley v Chesterfield	3-2
Gainsborough Trinity v Rotherham Town	3-0
6 Burton United v Kettering	3-1
Wellingborough Town v Leicester Fosse	4-1
7 Fulham v Luton Amateur	4-1
Luton Town v Lowestoft Town	5-1
8 Ilford v Brighton & Hove Albion	1-0
Maidstone United v New Brompton	0-3
9 Brentford v Southall	5-0
Shepherds Bush v Chesham Generals	2-0
10 Swindon Town v Poole	7-1
Whiteheads v Eastleigh Athletic	3-1
4r Kidderminster Harriers v Stourbridge	0-0e
4r2 Stourbridge v Kidderminster Harriers	0-2

Qualifying Round Five

1 Bishop Auckland v Sunderland Royal Rovers	8-0
2 Manchester United v Southport Central	4-1
3 Glossop v St Helens Recreation	5-0
4 Coventry City v Kidderminster Harriers	2-2
5 Barnsley v Gainsborough Trinity	3-2
6 Burton United v Wellingborough Town	5-1
7 Luton Town v Fulham	6-1
8 New Brompton v Ilford	4-1
9 Brentford v Shepherds Bush	2-2
10 Whiteheads v Swindon Town	0-9
4r Kidderminster Harriers v Coventry City	4-2
9r Shepherds Bush v Brentford	1-1x
9r2 Shepherds Bush v Brentford	0-1 N

Intermediate Round

Barnsley v Swindon Town	4-0
Bishop Auckland v Preston North End	1-3
Brentford v Woolwich Arsenal	1-1
Bristol City v Middlesbrough	3-1
Bristol Rovers v Millwall Athletic	2-2
Glossop v New Brompton	2-1
Lincoln City v West Ham United	2-0
Luton Town v Kidderminster Harriers	3-0
Manchester United v Burton United	1-1
Reading v Burnley	1-0
r Manchester United v Burton United	3-1
r Millwall Athletic v Bristol Rovers	0-0x
r Woolwich Arsenal v Brentford	5-0
r2 Millwall Athletic v Bristol Rovers	2-0 N

Round One

Aston Villa v Sunderland	4-1
Barnsley v Lincoln City	2-0
Blackburn Rovers v Sheffield Wednesday	0-0
Bolton Wanderers v Bristol City	0-5
Bury v Wolverhampton Wan.	1-0
Derby County v Small Heath	2-1
Everton v Portsmouth	5-0
Glossop v Stoke	2-3
Grimsby Town v Newcastle United	2-1
Manchester United v Liverpool	2-1
Millwall Athletic v Luton Town	3-0
Nottingham Forest v Reading	0-0
Notts County v Northampton	0-0
Preston North End v Manchester City	3-1
Tottenham Hotspur v West Bromwich Albion	0-0
Woolwich Arsenal v Sheffield United	1-3
r Reading v Nottingham Forest	3-6e
r Sheffield Wednesday v Blackburn Rovers	0-1
r Southampton v Notts County	2-2e
r West Bromwich Albion v Tottenham Hotspur	0-2
r2 Notts County v Southampton	2-1eN

Round Two

Aston Villa v Barnsley	4-1
Derby County v Blackburn Rovers	2-0
Everton v Manchester United	3-1
Grimsby Town v Notts County	0-2
Millwall Athletic v Preston North End	4-1
Nottingham Forest v Stoke	0-0
Sheffield United v Bury	0-1
Tottenham Hotspur v Bristol City	1-0
r Stoke v Nottingham Forest	2-0

Round Three

Bury v Notts County	1-0
Derby County v Stoke	3-0
Millwall Athletic v Everton	1-0
Tottenham Hotspur v Aston Villa	2-3

Semi Finals

Bury v Aston Villa	3-0 N
Derby County v Millwall Athletic	3-0 N

Final

Bury v Derby County	6-0 N

1903/04

Extra Preliminary Round

1 Darlington St Augustines v West Stanley	3-1
Southwick (1) v Seaham White Star	1-0
Tow Law v Darlington St Hilda's	wo/s
5 Denaby United v Roundell	2-0
Sheffield v Bolton United	4-2
8 Dartford v Cray Wanderers	2-7
Deptford Town v New Brompton Athletic	1-3
Grays United v Upton Park	2-1
Leytonstone v Wanstead	4-0
Maidstone United v Folkestone	1-1
Royal Engs. Service Batt'n v Maidstone Church Ins.	0-5
Woodford v South Weald	3-1
8r Folkestone v Maidstone United	1-3

Preliminary Round

1 Crook Town v Darlington St Augustines	2-2
Darlington v Shildon	1-1
Jarrow v Mickley	1-0
Leadgate Park v Bishop Auckland	1-1
Rutherford College v Prudhoe	5-0
Scarborough v Grangetown Athletic	1-0
Southwick (1) v Sunderland West End	1-2
Tow Law v Stanley United	0-4
West Hartlepool v Sunderland Black Watch	2-3
2 Bacup v Padiham	2-5
Colne v Accrington Stanley	0-3
Nelson v Chorley	2-2
Rossendale United v Oswaldtwistle Rovers	4-0
Workington (1) v Barrow	9-1
5 Denaby United v Mexborough Town	0-2
Grantham Avenue v Arnold (1)	4-1
Hoyland Town v Wath Athletic	2-2
Long Eaton St Helen's v Blackwell Colliery	4-2
Mexborough West End v Attercliffe	3-3
Ripley Athletic v Stapleford Town	1-1
Rockingham Colliery v Morley	3-0
Thornhill United v Sheffield	2-0
7 Bromley v Woking	5-0
Crouch End Vampires v Kensington	6-0
Croydon (1) v Croydon Wanderers	2-0
Fulham v Hampstead	3-0
Great Yarmouth Town v King's Lynn	3-0
London Welsh v Civil Service	1-4
Norwich CEYMS v Kirkley	4-1
Norwich City v Lowestoft Town	4-1
West Hampstead v War Office	1-0
8 Eastbourne v Newhaven Cement Works	5-1
Grays United v Southend Athletic	5-0
Ilford v Olympic	5-0
Maidstone Church Institute v Ashford United	0-1
Maidstone United v Sheppey United	1-0
Northfleet United v New Brompton Athletic	0-2
Romford (1) v Leytonstone	0-5
Sittingbourne v Cray Wanderers	3-2
Tunbridge Wells (1) v Hastings & St Leonards (1)	1-1
West Ham Garfield v Woodford	2-3
9 Marlow v Slough	1-2
10 Staple Hill v Wells City	4-0
1r Bishop Auckland v Leadgate Park	1-0
r Darlington St Augustines v Crook Town	4-1
r Shildon v Darlington	0-1
2r Chorley v Nelson	0-1
5r Attercliffe v Mexborough West End	1-2
r Stapleford Town v Ripley Athletic	3-2
r Wath Athletic v Hoyland Town	1-2
8r Hastings & St Leonards (1) v Tunbridge Wells (1)	0-11

Qualifying Round One

1 Bishop Auckland v Stanley United	3-0
Darlington v Darlington St Augustines	7-3
Morpeth Harriers v Ashington	1-1
Rutherford College v Sunderland Black Watch	1-2
Scarborough v Stockton St John's	4-2
Sunderland West End v Jarrow	1-1
Whitby (1) v Stockton	0-5
2 Black Diamonds v Workington (1)	0-2
Frizington White Star v Moss Bay Exchange	2-5
Nelson v Rossendale United	3-1
Padiham v Accrington Stanley	0-0

31

1903/04 to 1904/05

3	St Helens Recreation v Earlestown	4-3
	St Helens Town v Ashton Town (1)	1-1
5	Belper Town (1) v Derby Hills Ivanhoe	3-2
	Bradford City v Rockingham Colliery	6-1
	Mexborough Town v Hoyland Town	3-1
	Mexborough West End v Thornhill United	3-0
	Mirfield United v Royston United	1-1
	Newark v Boston (1)	4-1
	Stapleford Town v Long Eaton St Helen's	0-1
	Worksop Town v Grantham Avenue	2-0
6	Burton United v Gresley Rovers	2-0
	Hinckley Town (1) v Coalville Town (1)	11-0
	Irthlingborough Town v Rushden	2-2
	Wellingborough Town v Desborough Town	6-0
7	Bromley v Godalming	3-1
	Civil Service v West Hampstead	2-1
	Crouch End Vampires v Fulham	0-5
	Great Yarmouth Town v Norwich City	1-2
	Harwich & Parkeston v Norwich CEYMS	5-2
	Hitchin v Leighton Cee Springs	5-0
	Luton Amateur v Apsley	5-1
	Redhill v Croydon (1)	3-0
8	Ashford United v New Brompton Athletic	wo/s
	Eastbourne v Eastbourne Old Town	2-2
	Ilford v Grays United	0-2
	Maidstone United v Sittingbourne	2-1
	Shoreham v Brighton Amateurs	4-3
	St Leonards (1) v Tunbridge Wells (1)	3-3
	Woodford v Leytonstone	3-6
	Worthing v Horsham	2-0
9	Maidenhead Norfolkians v Maidenhead	2-1
	Slough v Reading Amateurs	2-1
	Southall v Hanwell	1-1
10	Basingstoke v North Hants Ironworks	1-4
	Freemantle v Eastleigh Athletic	2-0
	Glastonbury v Staple Hill	0-1
	Street v Bristol East	0-6
1r	Ashington v Morpeth Harriers	1-2
r	Jarrow v Sunderland West End	0-1
2r	Accrington Stanley v Padiham	4-0
3r	Ashton Town (1) v St Helens Town	3-2
5r	Royston United v Mirfield United	1-2
6r	Rushden v Irthlingborough Town	3-2
8r	Eastbourne Old Town v Eastbourne	1-0
r	Tunbridge Wells (1) v St Leonards (1)	5-1
9r	Hanwell v Southall	4-3

Qualifying Round Two

1	Darlington v Bishop Auckland	5-2
	Morpeth Harriers - Bye	
	Stockton v Scarborough	4-0
	Sunderland West End v Sunderland Black Watch	3-0
2	Accrington Stanley v Nelson	2-1
	Keswick v Shaddongate United	2-1
	Workington (1) v Moss Bay Exchange	4-0
3	Ashton Town (1) v St Helens Recreation	0-1
	Buxton - Bye	
	Heywood v Glossop	wo/s
	Nantwich v Middlewich Rangers	1-0
4	Brierley Hill Alliance v Kidderminster Harriers	wo/s
	Oswestry United v Wrexham	2-0
	Shrewsbury Town v Wellington Town	4-3
	Tranmere Rovers v Port Sunlight	3-1
5	Belper Town (1) v Long Eaton St Helen's	4-0
	Bradford City v Mirfield United	3-1
	Mexborough West End v Mexborough Town	0-2
	Newark v Worksop Town	2-2
6	Burton United v Hinckley Town (1)	2-2
	Kimberley St John's v Sutton Town	0-2
	Rothwell Town Swifts v Market Harborough Town	1-1
	Wellingborough Town v Rushden	5-0
7	Bromley v Redhill	1-1
	Fulham v Civil Service	3-3
	Harwich & Parkeston v Norwich City	2-4
	Luton Amateur v Hitchin	1-3
8	Eastbourne Old Town v Tunbridge Wells (1)	2-0
	Leytonstone v Grays United	1-0
	Maidstone United v Ashford United	0-2
	Shoreham v Worthing	0-1
9	Chesham Town - Bye	
	Maidenhead Norfolkians v Slough	1-3
	Richmond Association - Bye	
	Uxbridge v Hanwell	3-1
10	Bristol East v Staple Hill	0-2
	Freemantle v North Hants Ironworks	4-2
	Longfleet St Mary's v Yeovil Casuals	4-1
	Plymouth Argyle - Bye	
5r	Worksop Town v Newark	1-0
6r	Hinckley Town (1) v Burton United	3-3e
r	Market Harborough Town v Rothwell Town Swifts	2-1
7r	Civil Service v Fulham	0-3
r	Redhill v Bromley	5-0
6r2	Hinckley Town (1) v Burton United	1-6 N

Qualifying Round Three

1	Morpeth Harriers v Stockton	0-2
	South Bank v Willington Athletic	3-1
	Sunderland Royal Rovers v Darlington	4-2
	Sunderland West End v Wallsend Park Villa	1-1
2	Accrington Stanley v Southport Central	0-1
	Burnley v Keswick	8-0
	Darwen v Black Lane Temperance	7-1
	Workington (1) v Blackpool	2-4
3	Crewe Alexandra v Burslem Port Vale	0-0
	Nantwich v St Helens Recreation	1-1
	Stalybridge Rovers v Buxton	2-0
	Stockport County v Heywood	4-0
4	Coventry City v Walsall	2-4
	Stafford Rangers v Brierley Hill Alliance	1-0
	Stourbridge v Shrewsbury Town	1-2
	Tranmere Rovers v Oswestry United	2-2
5	Bradford City v Worksop Town	5-0
	Doncaster Rovers v Belper Town (1)	2-0
	Lincoln City v Chesterfield	0-2
	Mexborough Town v Gainsborough Trinity	0-2
6	Burton United v Kettering	3-0
	Leicester Fosse v Market Harborough Town	10-0
	Sutton Town v Whitwick White Cross	1-0 D
	Wellingborough Town v Northampton Town	2-0
7	Luton Town v Hitchin	2-1
	Norwich City v West Norwood	1-1
	Queen's Park Rangers v Fulham	1-1
	Redhill v Watford	1-6
8	Ashford United v Worthing	5-0
	Clapton v Leytonstone	4-1
	Eastbourne Old Town v Chatham	1-4
	West Ham United v Brighton & Hove Albion	4-0
9	Brentford v Uxbridge	8-0
	Shepherds Bush v Oxford City	0-3
	Slough v Chesham Town	8-3
	Wycombe Wanderers v Richmond Association	2-1
10	Freemantle v Longfleet St Mary's	2-1
	Plymouth Argyle v Whiteheads	7-0
	Swindon Town v Poole	9-0
	Weymouth v Staple Hill	0-0
1r	Wallsend Park Villa v Sunderland West End	2-0
3r	Burslem Port Vale v Crewe Alexandra	2-1
r	St Helens Recreation v Nantwich	2-3
4r	Oswestry United v Tranmere Rovers	2-1
7r	Fulham v Queen's Park Rangers	3-1
r	West Norwood v Norwich City	wo/s
10r	Staple Hill v Weymouth	3-1

Qualifying Round Four

1	South Bank v Wallsend Park Villa	2-2
	Sunderland Royal Rovers v Stockton	0-0
2	Darwen v Burnley	3-0
	Southport Central v Blackpool	3-0
3	Stalybridge Rovers v Nantwich	1-2
	Stockport County v Burslem Port Vale	0-0
4	Shrewsbury Town v Oswestry United	1-0
	Stafford Rangers v Walsall	1-2
5	Chesterfield v Bradford City	2-1
	Doncaster Rovers v Gainsborough Trinity	0-1
6	Wellingborough Town v Leicester Fosse	1-2
	Whitwick White Cross v Burton United	2-5
7	Fulham v West Norwood	4-0
	Luton Town v Watford	4-1
8	Ashford United v Chatham	0-2
	Clapton v West Ham United	0-3
9	Brentford v Oxford City	3-1
	Wycombe Wanderers v Slough	5-2
10	Plymouth Argyle v Freemantle	5-1
	Swindon Town v Staple Hill	5-0
1r	Stockton v Sunderland Royal Rovers	5-0
r	Wallsend Park Villa v South Bank	1-0
3r	Burslem Port Vale v Stockport County	6-0

Qualifying Round Five

1	Stockton v Wallsend Park Villa	2-2
2	Southport Central v Darwen	1-4
3	Nantwich v Burslem Port Vale	0-1
4	Shrewsbury Town v Walsall	1-0
5	Chesterfield v Gainsborough Trinity	0-2
6	Burton United v Leicester Fosse	1-1
7	Fulham v Luton Town	3-1
8	Chatham v West Ham United	0-5
9	Brentford v Wycombe Wanderers	4-1
10	Plymouth Argyle v Swindon Town	2-0
1r	Wallsend Park Villa v Stockton	0-1
6r	Leicester Fosse v Burton United	2-2
6r2	Leicester Fosse v Burton United	0-2 N

Intermediate Round

	Brentford v Plymouth Argyle	1-1
	Bristol Rovers v Woolwich Arsenal	1-1
	Burslem Port Vale v Burton United	3-0
	Grimsby Town v Barnsley	2-0
	Manchester United v Small Heath	1-1
	New Brompton v Bristol City	1-1
	Preston North End v Darwen	2-1
	Reading v Gainsborough Trinity	1-0
	Stockton v Shrewsbury Town	2-1
	West Ham United v Fulham	0-1
r	Bristol City v New Brompton	5-2
r	Plymouth Argyle v Brentford	4-1
r	Small Heath v Manchester United	1-1e
r	Woolwich Arsenal v Bristol Rovers	1-1
r2	Bristol Rovers v Woolwich Arsenal	0-1 N
r2	Small Heath v Manchester United	1-1eN
r3	Manchester United v Small Heath	3-1 N

Round One

	Blackburn Rovers v Liverpool	3-1
	Bristol City v Sheffield United	1-3
	Bury v Newcastle United	2-1
	Everton v Tottenham Hotspur	1-2
	Manchester City v Sunderland	3-2
	Millwall v Middlesbrough	0-2
	Notts County v Manchester United	3-3
	Plymouth Argyle v Sheffield Wednesday	2-2
	Portsmouth v Derby County	2-5
	Preston North End v Grimsby Town	1-0
	Reading v Bolton Wanderers	1-1
	Southampton v Burslem Port Vale	3-0
	Stockton v Wolverhampton Wan.	1-4
	Stoke v Aston Villa	2-3
	West Bromwich Albion v Nottingham Forest	1-1
	Woolwich Arsenal v Fulham	1-0
r	Bolton Wanderers v Reading	3-2
r	Manchester United v Notts County	2-1
r	Nottingham Forest v West Bromwich Albion	3-1
r	Sheffield Wednesday v Plymouth Argyle	2-0

Round Two

	Aston Villa v Tottenham Hotspur	0-1
	Blackburn Rovers v Nottingham Forest	3-1
	Bolton Wanderers v Southampton	4-1
	Bury v Sheffield United	1-2
	Derby County v Wolverhampton Wan.	2-2
	Preston North End v Middlesbrough	0-3
	Sheffield Wednesday v Manchester United	6-0
	Woolwich Arsenal v Manchester City	0-2
r	Wolverhampton Wan. v Derby County	2-2e
r2	Derby County v Wolverhampton Wan.	1-0 N

Round Three

	Derby County v Blackburn Rovers	2-1
	Manchester City v Middlesbrough	0-0
	Sheffield United v Bolton Wanderers	0-2
	Tottenham Hotspur v Sheffield Wednesday	1-1
r	Middlesbrough v Manchester City	1-3
r	Sheffield Wednesday v Tottenham Hotspur	2-0

Semi Finals

	Bolton Wanderers v Derby County	1-0 N
	Manchester City v Sheffield Wednesday	3-0 N

Final

	Manchester City v Bolton Wanderers	1-0 N

1904/05

Extra Preliminary Round

5	Catcliffe v Morley	wo/s
	Highthorn v Rawmarsh Albion	0-1
	Rotherham Town v Thornhill United	1-1
8	Chatham v Ashford United	4-2
	Eltham v Bromley	4-1
	Folkestone v Swanscombe	3-2
	Gravesend United v Maidstone Church Institute	4-1
	Guildford v Redhill	2-1
	Northfleet United v Sheppey United	0-1
	Sittingbourne v Cray Wanderers	1-2
5r	Thornhill United v Rotherham Town	1-0

Preliminary Round

1	Crook Town v Consett Town Swifts	4-0
	Hebburn Argyle v Mickley	2-0
	Leadgate Park v Stanley United	2-2
	Saltburn v South Bank	1-1
	Southwick (1) v Tow Law	wo/s
	Stockton v Hull City	3-3
	West Hartlepool v Willington Athletic	1-2
	West Stanley v Darlington St Augustines	1-0
	Whitby (1) v Grangetown Athletic	2-7
2	Carlisle Red Rose v Keswick	1-0
5	Catcliffe v Thorpe Hesley	0-1
	Denaby United v Rawmarsh Albion	0-0
	Grimethorpe United v Huddersfield (1)	4-1
	Heckmondwike v Mirfield United	0-1
	Hoyland Town v Sandygate Excelsior	1-2
	Mexborough Town v Thornhill United	1-0
	Rockingham Colliery v Leeds City	3-1
	Sheffield v Wombwell Rising Star	3-1
6	Gresley Rovers v Coalville Town (1)	4-0
7	Clapton Orient v Enfield	4-1
	Grays United v Harwich & Parkeston	4-0
	King's Lynn v Norwich CEYMS	5-1
	Leytonstone v Felstead	2-0
	Upton Park v Cheshunt	2-2
	Woodford v Leyton	1-4
8	Clapham v Guards Depot	0-1
	Cray Wanderers v Eltham	0-1
	Dartford v Folkestone	5-1
	Eastbourne Old Town v Rock-a-Nore	3-2
	Godalming v Croydon Wanderers	2-3
	Gravesend United v Sheppey United	0-2

1904/05

Maidstone United v Chatham		2-0
Newhaven Cement Works v Hastings & St Leonards (1)		4-5
Southern United v Croydon (1)		3-0
Steyning v Brighton Amateurs		2-0
Tunbridge Wells Rangers v Tunbridge Wells (1)		2-1
Woking v Guildford		4-1
Worthing v Horsham		3-0
9 Civil Service v Willesden Town		2-1
Kensal Rise v Middlesex Wanderers		5-0
Slough v Reading Amateurs		2-4
Staines Town v Maidenhead Norfolkians		1-2
Uxbridge v Maidenhead		8-1
Windsor & Eton v Marlow		3-1
10 Basingstoke v Freemantle		5-2
1r South Bank v Saltburn		4-2
r Stanley United v Leadgate Park		1-1e
r Stockton v Hull City		4-1
5r Rawmarsh Albion v Denaby United		0-5
7r Cheshunt v Upton Park		2-0
1r2 Stanley United v Leadgate Park		1-0

Qualifying Round One

1 Ashington v Shankhouse		1-3
Morpeth Harriers v Burradon Athletic		3-0
Scarborough v South Bank		0-3
Southwick (1) v Crook Town		5-0
Stockton v Grangetown Athletic		2-1
Sunderland West End v Hebburn Argyle		1-0
West Stanley v Stanley United		1-1
Willington Athletic v Sunderland Royal Rovers		4-2
2 Carlisle Red Rose v Frizington White Star		3-1
Carlisle United v Workington (1)		2-2
Chorley v Black Lane Temperance		3-0
Colne v Burnley Belvedere		4-0
Padiham v Nelson		0-1
Rossendale United v Oswaldtwistle Rovers		1-1
3 Brynn Central v St Helens Town		1-1
Earlestown v St Helens Recreation		2-2
4 Chirk v Welshpool		1-2
Coventry City v Halesowen		2-2
Oswestry United v Druids		1-1
Walsall v Brierley Hill Alliance		3-0
5 Blackwell v Long Eaton St Helen's		2-0
Denaby United v Sandygate Excelsior		2-0
Derby Hills Ivanhoe v Belper Town (1)		0-2
Mexborough Town v Sheffield		1-1
Mirfield United v Grimethorpe United		1-1
Newark v Grantham Avenue		7-0
Rockingham Colliery v Thorpe Hesley		1-5
Worksop Town v Boston (1)		10-1
6 Coalville United v Hinckley Town (1)		0-0
Gresley Rovers v Trent Rovers		2-1
Peterborough Town v Kettering		1-5
7 Cheshunt v Clapton Orient		0-0
Grays United v South Weald		3-0
Great Yarmouth Town v King's Lynn		5-3
Kirkley v Lowestoft Town		1-3
Leighton Cee Springs v Apsley		1-1
Leyton v Leytonstone		1-2
Luton Amateur v Biggleswade & District		3-4
Romford (1) v Southend Athletic		8-0
8 Guards Depot v Southern United		0-0
Hastings & St Leonards (1) v St Leonards (1)		6-0
Maidstone United v Eltham		4-0
Sheppey United v Dartford		3-2
Shoreham v Hove		9-0
Tunbridge Wells Rangers v Eastbourne Old Town		3-2
Woking v Croydon Wanderers		4-1
Worthing v Steyning		6-3
9 Civil Service v Kensington		5-2
Finchley v Hampstead		0-0
Kensal Rise v Richmond Association		3-0
Uxbridge v Maidenhead Norfolkians		1-0
West Hampstead v Crouch End Vampires		4-1
Windsor & Eton v Reading Amateurs		4-2
10 Brislington v Yeovil Casuals		1-3
Bristol East v Staple Hill		1-0
Cowes (2) v Ryde		4-2
Longfleet St Mary's v Poole		3-2
North Hants Ironworks v Basingstoke		4-0
Warmley Amateurs v Paulton Rovers		4-3
1r Stanley United v West Stanley		2-0
2r Oswaldtwistle Rovers v Rossendale United		4-5
r Workington (1) v Carlisle United		3-1
3r St Helens Recreation v Earlestown		1-2
r St Helens Town v Brynn Central		wo/s
4r Coventry City v Halesowen		3-2
r Oswestry United v Druids		0-0e
5r Grimethorpe United v Mirfield United		3-1
r Sheffield v Mexborough Town		2-4
6r Hinckley Town (1) v Coalville United		4-0
7r Apsley v Leighton Cee Springs		4-1
r Clapton Orient v Cheshunt		4-1
8r Southern United v Guards Depot		6-1
9r Hampstead v Finchley		2-3
4r2 Druids v Oswestry United		3-2 N

Qualifying Round Two

1 Morpeth Harriers v Shankhouse		3-0
South Bank v Stockton		2-0
Stanley United v Southwick (1)		1-1
Sunderland West End v Willington Athletic		3-0
2 Barrow v Barrow St George's		7-1
Chorley v Rossendale United		2-1
Nelson v Colne		3-1
Workington (1) v Carlisle Red Rose		0-4
3 Buxton v Fairfield		4-0
Earlestown v St Helens Town		6-0
Sandbach Ramblers v Nantwich		1-2
Stalybridge Rovers - Bye		
4 Coventry City v Walsall		2-0
Druids v Welshpool		2-1
Rhyl - Bye		
Tranmere Rovers v Port Sunlight		1-3
5 Belper Town (1) v Blackwell		1-1
Denaby United v Mexborough Town		0-2
Newark v Worksop Town		2-0
Thorpe Hesley v Grimethorpe United		1-4
6 Gresley Rovers v Hinckley Town (1)		3-1
Kettering v Irthlingborough Town		6-0
Linby Church v Kimberley St John's		5-0
Mansfield Mechanics v Sutton Town		3-3
7 Apsley v Biggleswade & District		0-2
Clapton Orient v Leytonstone		1-1
Grays United v Romford (1)		3-0
Great Yarmouth Town v Lowestoft Town		1-2
8 Hastings & St Leonards (1) v Tunbridge Wells Rangers		4-0
Maidstone United v Sheppey United		0-1
Shoreham v Worthing		5-1
Southern United v Woking		8-1
9 Chesham Town v Chesham Generals		3-0
Civil Service v Kensal Rise		1-1
West Hampstead v Finchley		2-0
Windsor & Eton v Uxbridge		3-2
10 Cowes (2) v North Hants Ironworks		4-1
Green Waves (Plymouth) - Bye		
Longfleet St Mary's v Yeovil Casuals		2-1
Warmley Amateurs v Bristol East		0-2
1r Southwick (1) v Stanley United		2-0
5r Blackwell v Belper Town (1)		1-0
6r Sutton Town v Mansfield Mechanics		2-0
7r Leytonstone v Clapton Orient		2-5
9r Kensal Rise v Civil Service		4-4
9r2 Civil Service v Kensal Rise		wo/s

Qualifying Round Three

1 Bishop Auckland v South Bank		2-1
Jarrow v Sunderland West End		0-2
Morpeth Harriers v Darlington		0-6
Southwick (1) v Wallsend Park Villa		0-4
2 Accrington Stanley v Blackpool		1-4
Barrow v Southport Central		1-3
Darwen v Chorley		4-2
Nelson v Carlisle Red Rose		9-0
3 Crewe Alexandra v Wrexham		0-3
Earlestown v Buxton		4-1
Nantwich v Glossop		1-2
Stockport County v Stalybridge Rovers		2-0
4 Druids v Rhyl		2-0
Port Sunlight v Kidderminster Harriers		0-0
Stafford Rangers v Coventry City		3-2
Stourbridge v Wellington Town		1-1
5 Blackwell v Upper Armley		1-0
Doncaster Rovers v Mexborough Town		0-0
Gainsborough Trinity v Ilkeston United		4-1
Grimethorpe United v Newark		3-2
6 Burton United v Northampton Town		2-3
Kettering v Wellingborough Town		1-1
Leicester Fosse v Linby Church		10-1
Sutton Town v Gresley Rovers		1-2
7 Hitchin v Clapton Orient		2-1
Lowestoft Town v West Norwood		3-0
Norwich City v Grays United		0-0
Watford v Biggleswade & District		7-1
8 Brighton & Hove Albion v Shoreham		7-1
Clapton v New Brompton		2-6
Sheppey United v Hastings & St Leonards (1)		0-1
Southern United v Ilford		1-2
9 Civil Service v Chesham Town		3-1
Oxford City v Wycombe Wanderers		3-0
Shepherds Bush v West Hampstead		3-3
Windsor & Eton v Southall		2-3
10 Eastleigh Athletic v Cowes (2)		3-3
Green Waves (Plymouth) v Bristol East		1-1
Longfleet St Mary's v Weymouth		0-0
Swindon Town v Whiteheads		7-0
4r Kidderminster Harriers v Port Sunlight		6-0
r Stourbridge v Wellington Town		wo/s
5r Mexborough Town v Doncaster Rovers		3-1
6r Wellingborough Town v Kettering		1-2 N
7r Norwich City v Grays United		2-3
9r West Hampstead v Shepherds Bush		1-2
10r Bristol East v Green Waves (Plymouth)		0-1
r Cowes (2) v Eastleigh Athletic		3-1
r Longfleet St Mary's v Weymouth		wo/s

Qualifying Round Four

1 Bishop Auckland v Darlington		3-1
Wallsend Park Villa v Sunderland West End		1-1
2 Blackpool v Southport Central		3-0
Nelson v Darwen		1-1
3 Earlestown v Wrexham		0-2
Glossop v Stockport County		1-1
4 Druids v Stafford Rangers		2-2
Stourbridge v Kidderminster Harriers		0-1
5 Gainsborough Trinity v Grimethorpe United		5-1
Mexborough Town v Blackwell		6-2
6 Kettering v Northampton Town		0-2
Leicester Fosse v Gresley Rovers		5-0
7 Grays United v Watford		1-3
Lowestoft Town v Hitchin		0-3
8 Hastings & St Leonards (1) v Ilford		2-3
New Brompton v Brighton & Hove Albion		0-1
9 Oxford City v Southall		3-3
Shepherds Bush v Civil Service		1-4
10 Green Waves (Plymouth) v Cowes (2)		7-0
Swindon Town v Longfleet St Mary's		8-0
1r Sunderland West End v Wallsend Park Villa		3-2
2r Darwen v Nelson		2-3
3r Stockport County v Glossop		0-0
4r Stafford Rangers v Druids		4-1
9r Southall v Oxford City		0-0
3r2 Stockport County v Glossop		1-0
9r2 Oxford City v Southall		1-6 N

Qualifying Round Five

1 Bishop Auckland v Sunderland West End		1-1
2 Blackpool v Nelson		1-0
3 Stockport County v Wrexham		4-0
4 Stafford Rangers v Kidderminster Harriers		1-0
5 Mexborough Town v Gainsborough Trinity		1-1
6 Northampton Town v Leicester Fosse		2-2
7 Watford v Hitchin		2-0
8 Brighton & Hove Albion v Ilford		5-1
9 Civil Service v Southall		1-4
10 Green Waves (Plymouth) v Swindon Town		2-1
1r Sunderland West End v Bishop Auckland		1-1
5r Gainsborough Trinity v Mexborough Town		7-0
6r Leicester Fosse v Northampton Town		2-0
1r2 Bishop Auckland v Sunderland West End		1-2 N

Qualifying Round Six

Barnsley v Burslem Port Vale		0-0
Bradford City v Sunderland West End		9-0
Chesterfield v Stockport County		2-0
Fulham v Luton Town		4-0
Green Waves (Plymouth) v Gainsborough Trinity		1-3
Queen's Park Rangers v Brentford		1-2
Southall v Leicester Fosse		0-4
Stafford Rangers v Blackpool		2-2
Watford v Lincoln City		1-1
West Ham United v Brighton & Hove Albion		1-2
r Blackpool v Stafford Rangers		3-0
r Burslem Port Vale v Barnsley		1-2
r Lincoln City v Watford		2-1

Intermediate Round

Bradford City v Millwall		1-4
Brentford v Reading		1-1
Brighton & Hove Albion v Bristol Rovers		1-2
Bristol City v Blackpool		2-1
Burnley v Lincoln City		1-1
Grimsby Town v Gainsborough Trinity		2-0
Manchester United v Fulham		2-2
Plymouth Argyle v Barnsley		2-0
Portsmouth v Chesterfield		0-0
West Bromwich Albion v Leicester Fosse		2-5
r Fulham v Manchester United		0-0e
r Lincoln City v Burnley		3-2
r Portsmouth v Chesterfield		2-0
r Reading v Brentford		2-0
r2 Manchester United v Fulham		0-1 N

Round One

Aston Villa v Leicester Fosse		5-1
Blackburn Rovers v Sheffield Wednesday		1-2
Bolton Wanderers v Bristol Rovers		1-1
Bury v Notts County		1-0
Derby County v Preston North End		0-2
Fulham v Reading		0-0
Lincoln City v Manchester City		1-2
Liverpool v Everton		1-1
Middlesbrough v Tottenham Hotspur		1-1
Newcastle United v Plymouth Argyle		1-1
Nottingham Forest v Sheffield United		2-0
Small Heath v Portsmouth		0-2
Southampton v Millwall		3-1
Stoke v Grimsby Town		2-0
Sunderland v Wolverhampton Wan.		1-1
Woolwich Arsenal v Bristol City		0-0
r Bristol City v Woolwich Arsenal		1-0
r Bristol Rovers v Bolton Wanderers		0-3
r Everton v Liverpool		2-1
r Plymouth Argyle v Newcastle United		1-1
r Reading v Fulham		0-0e
r Tottenham Hotspur v Middlesbrough		1-0
r Wolverhampton Wan. v Sunderland		1-0
r2 Fulham v Reading		1-0eN
r2 Newcastle United v Plymouth Argyle		2-0 N

Round Two

Aston Villa v Bury		3-2
Bristol City v Preston North End		0-0
Fulham v Nottingham Forest		1-0
* Manchester City v Bolton Wanderers		1-2

33

1904/05 to 1905/06

	Sheffield Wednesday v Portsmouth	2-1
	Stoke v Everton	0-4
	Tottenham Hotspur v Newcastle United	1-1
	Wolverhampton Wan. v Southampton	2-3
r	Newcastle United v Tottenham Hotspur	4-0
r	Preston North End v Bristol City	1-0

Round Three

	Aston Villa v Fulham	5-0
	Bolton Wanderers v Newcastle United	0-2
	Everton v Southampton	4-0
	Preston North End v Sheffield Wednesday	1-1
r	Sheffield Wednesday v Preston North End	3-0

Semi Finals

	Aston Villa v Everton	1-1 N
	Newcastle United v Sheffield Wednesday	1-0 N
r	Aston Villa v Everton	2-1 N

Final

	Aston Villa v Newcastle United	2-0 N

1905/06

Preliminary Round

1	Mickley v Shankhouse	wo/s
	Morpeth Harriers v Sunderland Royal Rovers	0-1
	Wallsend Park Villa v Gateshead Town	2-1
2	Crook Town v Scarborough	wo/s
	Eldon Albion v Spennymoor United	1-2
	Leadgate Park v Stanley United	3-0
	Stockton v Saltburn	2-2
	West Auckland Town v Grangetown Athletic	0-0
4	Accrington Stanley v Nelson	7-0
7	Welshpool v Chirk	3-5
	Wrexham v Rhyl	1-4
9	Rockingham Colliery v Mexborough Town	2-4
10	Thorpe Hesley v Rawmarsh Albion	4-1
12	Boston (1) v Grantham Avenue	1-2
	Sutton Town v Hucknall Constitutional	0-1
16	Chelmsford v Cheshunt	1-6
17	Staines Town v Richmond Association	0-4
	Uxbridge v Southall	wo/s
	West Hampstead v Crouch End Vampires	1-0
18	Marlow v Wycombe Wanderers	0-1
	Reading Amateurs v Slough	2-3
20	Croydon Wanderers v Redhill	0-1
21	Dartford v Chatham	0-1
	Eltham v New Brompton Athletic	2-0
22	Hastings & St Leonards (1) v Rock-a-Nore	1-0
	St Leonards (1) v Eastbourne	5-0
	Worthing v Eastbourne Old Town	2-1
23	Basingstoke v Ryde	1-3
	Poole v Salisbury (1)	2-1
	Weymouth v Whiteheads	3-2
2r	Grangetown Athletic v West Auckland Town	1-0
r	Saltburn v Stockton	1-2

Qualifying Round One

1	Southwick (1) v North Shields Athletic	4-1
	Sunderland Black Watch v Mickley	1-1
	Sunderland Royal Rovers v Willington Athletic	1-1
	Wallsend Park Villa v Sunderland West End	1-0
2	Darlington St Augustines v West Stanley	0-2
	Leadgate Park v Grangetown Athletic	1-1
	South Bank v Crook Town	3-1
	Stockton v Spennymoor United	2-2
3	Carlisle United v Carlisle Red Rose	3-0
	Keswick v Barrow St George's	3-2
	Wigton Harriers v Frizington White Star	1-1
	Workington (1) v Barrow	0-1
4	Accrington Stanley v Burnley Belvedere	5-0
	Black Lane Temperance v Padiham	2-7
	Chorley v Oswaldtwistle Rovers	1-4
	Rossendale United v Colne	7-1
5	Oldham Athletic v Ashton Town (1)	2-1
	Sandbach Ramblers v Congleton Hornets	wo/s
	Stalybridge Rovers v Buxton	2-0
6	Newton-le-Willows v Earlestown	3-3
	St Helens Recreation v Brynn Central	1-0
7	Birkenhead v Oswestry United	3-0
	Chester v Northern Nomads	2-0
	Chirk v Tranmere Rovers	1-1
	Rhyl v Whitchurch	wo/s
8	Coventry City v Worcester City	0-3
	Kidderminster Harriers v Brierley Hill Alliance	5-1
	Stafford Rangers v Dudley	1-0
	Stourbridge v Halesowen	0-1
9	Denaby United v Doncaster Rovers	4-2
	Hull City v Grimethorpe United	8-1
	Leeds City v Morley	11-0
	Mexborough Town v Upper Armley	9-0
10	Rotherham County v Thorpe Hesley	3-1
	Rotherham Main v South Kirkby Colliery	2-2
	Rotherham Town v Sheffield	4-0
	Worksop Town v Hoyland Town	4-0
11	Blackwell v Sandiacre Olympic	0-0
	Coalville Town (1) v Ilkeston United	0-0
	Gresley Rovers v Belper Town (1)	0-2
	Stapleford Town v Trent Rovers	0-0
12	Grantham Avenue v Newark	2-4
	Kimberley St John's v Hucknall Constitutional	1-2
	Mansfield Mechanics v Arnold (1)	1-0
	Mansfield Woodhouse Rangers v Linby Church	wo/s
13	Hitchin Town v Irthlingborough Town	6-1
	Luton Amateur v Kettering	2-6
14	Cromer v Kirkley	2-1
	King's Lynn v Norwich CEYMS	4-2
	Lowestoft Town v Beccles	5-1
15	Felstead v Clapton Orient	1-1
	Grays United v Leyton	2-6
	Leytonstone v Barking	1-1
	Upton Park v East Ham	1-1
16	Romford (1) v Enfield	4-1
	South Weald v Barnet Alston	3-0
	Southend Athletic v Cheshunt	0-1
	Woodford v Wanstead	0-3
17	London Caledonians v Hampstead	3-0
	Shepherds Bush v Richmond Association	3-1
	Uxbridge v Civil Service	1-2
	Willesden Town v West Hampstead	1-1
18	Aylesbury United v Wycombe Wanderers	2-2
	Chesham Generals v Maidenhead	2-4
	Chesham Town v Maidenhead Norfolkians	4-2
	Slough v Windsor & Eton	4-2
19	2nd Grenadier Guards v City of Westminster	2-0
	Chelsea v 1st Grenadier Guards	6-1
	Crystal Palace v Clapham	7-0
	Southern United v Nunhead	5-2
20	Croydon (1) v Godalming	1-1
	Guildford v West Norwood	2-3
	New Crusaders v Woking	16-0
	Redhill v Guards Depot	1-1
21	Eltham v Woolwich Polytechnic	0-2
	Maidstone Church Institute v Chatham	1-1
	Maidstone United v Bromley	3-0
	Sittingbourne v Sheppey United	1-1
22	Hastings & St Leonards (1) v Tunbridge Wells (1)	3-1
	Horsham v Tunbridge Wells Rangers	0-3
	Shoreham v Newhaven	3-1
	Worthing v St Leonards (1)	0-2
23	Cowes (2) v Poole	3-1
	Longfleet St Mary's v North Hants Ironworks	0-2
	Ryde v Eastleigh Athletic	1-2
	Weymouth v Bournemouth Gasworks Athletic	5-3
24	Brislington v Bristol East	1-0
	Radstock Town v Staple Hill	1-1
	Taunton Castle v Green Waves (Plymouth)	2-7
	Yeovil Casuals v Paulton Rovers	2-1
1r	Mickley v Sunderland Black Watch	1-0
r	Willington Athletic v Sunderland Royal Rovers	4-1
2r	Grangetown Athletic v Leadgate Park	3-0
r	Spennymoor United v Stockton	2-0
3r	Frizington White Star v Wigton Harriers	3-1
6r	Earlestown v Newton-le-Willows	7-0
7r	Tranmere Rovers v Chirk	0-1
10r	South Kirkby Colliery v Rotherham Main	4-0
11r	Ilkeston United v Coalville Town (1)	4-0
r	Sandiacre Olympic v Blackwell	0-2
r	Trent Rovers v Stapleford Town	1-0
15r	Barking v Leytonstone	1-1
r	Clapton Orient v Felstead	5-1
r	East Ham v Upton Park	1-4
17r	West Hampstead v Willesden Town	4-1
18r	Wycombe Wanderers v Aylesbury United	2-1
20r	Godalming v Croydon (1)	wo/s
r	Guards Depot v Redhill	5-2
21r	Maidstone Church Institute v Chatham	1-2
r	Sittingbourne v Sheppey United	1-3
24r	Staple Hill v Radstock Town	1-0
15r2	Leytonstone v Barking	1-5 N

Qualifying Round Two

1	Southwick (1) v Willington Athletic	9-1
	Wallsend Park Villa v Mickley	2-3
2	South Bank v Grangetown Athletic	3-1
	West Stanley v Spennymoor United	2-0
3	Barrow v Carlisle United	4-2
	Keswick v Frizington White Star	3-4
4	Oswaldtwistle Rovers v Rossendale United	2-1
	Padiham v Accrington Stanley	1-4
5	Oldham Athletic v Fairfield	8-0
	Stalybridge Rovers v Sandbach Ramblers	8-5
6	Skelmersdale United v Earlestown	1-1
	St Helens Town v St Helens Recreation	0-1
7	Birkenhead v Rhyl	2-2
	Chirk v Chester	2-0
8	Kidderminster Harriers v Halesowen	3-0
	Worcester City v Stafford Rangers	4-1
9	Denaby United v Hull City	0-2
	Leeds City v Mexborough Town	1-1
10	South Kirkby Colliery v Rotherham County	2-1
	Worksop Town v Rotherham Town	1-1
11	Belper Town (1) v Blackwell	3-1
	Ilkeston United v Trent Rovers	5-1
12	Mansfield Mechanics v Hucknall Constitutional	1-2
	Newark v Mansfield Woodhouse Rangers	5-0
13	Biggleswade & District v Wellingborough Town	wo/s
	Kettering v Hitchin Town	2-2
14	Cromer v Great Yarmouth Town	4-1
	King's Lynn v Lowestoft Town	2-0
15	Clapton Orient v Barking	3-1
	Leyton v Upton Park	5-0
16	Romford (1) v Wanstead	2-1
	South Weald v Cheshunt	3-1
17	Shepherds Bush v London Caledonians	2-0
	West Hampstead v Civil Service	6-1
18	Chesham Town v Slough	2-5
	Maidenhead v Wycombe Wanderers	1-3
19	2nd Grenadier Guards v Crystal Palace	0-3
	Southern United v Chelsea	0-1
20	New Crusaders v Guards Depot	6-0
	West Norwood v Godalming	3-0
21	Chatham v Maidstone United	2-1
	Sheppey United v Woolwich Polytechnic	2-1
22	Hastings & St Leonards (1) v Shoreham	2-0
	Tunbridge Wells Rangers v St Leonards (1)	2-0
23	Cowes (2) v Eastleigh Athletic	2-0
	Weymouth v North Hants Ironworks	3-2
24	Brislington v Staple Hill	2-3
	Green Waves (Plymouth) v Yeovil Casuals	5-1
6r	Earlestown v Skelmersdale United	3-0
7r	Rhyl v Birkenhead	2-1e
9r	Mexborough Town v Leeds City	1-1e
10r	Rotherham Town v Worksop Town	3-2 v
13r	Hitchin Town v Kettering	0-4
9r2	Leeds City v Mexborough Town	3-2
10r2	Rotherham Town v Worksop Town	4-0

Qualifying Round Three

1	Mickley v Southwick (1)	0-1
2	West Stanley v South Bank	4-0
3	Barrow v Frizington White Star	6-1
4	Accrington Stanley v Oswaldtwistle Rovers	3-1
5	Oldham Athletic v Stalybridge Rovers	1-1
6	St Helens Recreation v Earlestown	1-5
7	Rhyl v Chirk	0-0
8	Worcester City v Kidderminster Harriers	2-1
9	Hull City v Leeds City	1-1
10	Rotherham Town v South Kirkby Colliery	2-2
11	Ilkeston United v Belper Town (1)	2-0
12	Hucknall Constitutional v Newark	0-0
13	Kettering v Biggleswade & District	2-1
14	King's Lynn v Cromer	5-4
15	Leyton v Clapton Orient	1-3
16	South Weald v Romford (1)	1-0
17	West Hampstead v Shepherds Bush	1-1
18	Wycombe Wanderers v Slough	4-1
19	Crystal Palace v Chelsea	7-1
20	New Crusaders v West Norwood	7-2
21	Sheppey United v Chatham	1-1
22	Tunbridge Wells Rangers v Hastings & St Leonards (1)	4-0
23	Weymouth v Cowes (2)	3-1
24	Staple Hill v Green Waves (Plymouth)	4-0
5r	Stalybridge Rovers v Oldham Athletic	1-3
7r	Chirk v Rhyl	3-1
9r	Leeds City v Hull City	1-2
10r	South Kirkby Colliery v Rotherham Town	1-0
12r	Newark v Hucknall Constitutional	4-0
17r	Shepherds Bush v West Hampstead	1-2
21r	Chatham v Sheppey United	1-2

Qualifying Round Four

	Barrow v West Hartlepool	4-1
	Bishop Auckland v South Kirkby Colliery	1-0
	Brentford v Wycombe Wanderers	4-0
	Burton United v Accrington Stanley	3-0
	Clapton v Clapton Orient	0-2
	Crewe Alexandra v Darwen	2-0
	Crystal Palace v Luton Town	1-0
	Darlington v Bradford City	0-4
	Earlestown v Barnsley	0-2
	Gainsborough Trinity v Weymouth	12-1
	Glossop v Brighton & Hove Albion	0-1
	Hull City v Oldham Athletic	2-1
	Kettering v Ilkeston United	3-0
	King's Lynn v Chirk	8-1
	Oxford City v Burslem Port Vale	0-1
	Sheppey United v Norwich City	0-2
	Southwick (1) v New Crusaders	1-1
	Staple Hill v South Weald	0-0
	Swindon Town v West Hampstead	4-0
	Tunbridge Wells Rangers v Newark	3-0
	Walsall v Stockport County	3-3
	Watford v Southport Central	3-1
	West Stanley v Northampton Town	1-1
	Worcester City v Ilford	5-1
r	New Crusaders v Southwick (1)	wo/s
r	Northampton Town v West Stanley	3-0
r	South Weald v Staple Hill	1-4
r	Stockport County v Walsall	5-0

Round One

	Aston Villa v King's Lynn	11-0
	Birmingham v Preston North End	1-0
	Bishop Auckland v Wolverhampton Wan.	0-3
	Blackpool v Crystal Palace	1-1
	Bradford City v Barrow	3-2
	Brentford v Bristol City	2-1
	Brighton & Hove Albion v Swindon Town	3-0

1905/06 to 1906/07

Burslem Port Vale v Gainsborough Trinity 0-3
Bury v Nottingham Forest 1-1
Clapton Orient v Chesterfield 0-0
Crewe Alexandra v Barnsley 1-1
Derby County v Kettering 4-0
Everton v West Bromwich Albion 3-1
Fulham v Queen's Park Rangers 1-0
Hull City v Reading 0-1
Lincoln City v Stockport County 4-2
Liverpool v Leicester Fosse 2-1
Manchester United v Staple Hill 7-2
Middlesbrough v Bolton Wanderers 3-0
Millwall v Burton United 1-0
New Brompton v Northampton Town 2-1
New Crusaders v Plymouth Argyle 3-6
Newcastle United v Grimsby Town 6-0
Norwich City v Tunbridge Wells Rangers 1-1
Sheffield United v Manchester City 4-1
Sheffield Wednesday v Bristol Rovers 1-0
Southampton v Portsmouth 5-1
Stoke v Blackburn Rovers 1-0
Sunderland v Notts County 1-0
Tottenham Hotspur v Burnley 2-0
Woolwich Arsenal v West Ham United 1-1
Worcester City v Watford 0-6
r Barnsley v Crewe Alexandra 4-0
r Chesterfield v Clapton Orient 3-0
r Crystal Palace v Blackpool 1-1e
r Nottingham Forest v Bury 6-2
r Tunbridge Wells Rangers v Norwich City 0-5
r West Ham United v Woolwich Arsenal 2-3
r2 Blackpool v Crystal Palace 1-0 N

Round Two

Aston Villa v Plymouth Argyle 0-0
Bradford City v Wolverhampton Wan. 5-0
Brentford v Lincoln City 3-0
Brighton & Hove Albion v Middlesbrough 1-1
Derby County v Newcastle United 0-0
Everton v Chesterfield 3-0
Fulham v Nottingham Forest 1-3
Liverpool v Barnsley 1-0
Manchester United v Norwich City 3-0
New Brompton v Southampton 0-0
Sheffield United v Blackpool 1-2
Sheffield Wednesday v Millwall 1-1
Stoke v Birmingham 0-1
Sunderland v Gainsborough Trinity 1-1
Tottenham Hotspur v Reading 3-2
Woolwich Arsenal v Watford 3-0
r Middlesbrough v Brighton & Hove Albion 1-1e
r Millwall v Sheffield Wednesday 0-3
r Newcastle United v Derby County 2-1
r Plymouth Argyle v Aston Villa 1-5
r Southampton v New Brompton 1-0
r Sunderland v Gainsborough Trinity 3-0
r2 Brighton & Hove Albion v Middlesbrough 1-3 N

Round Three

Everton v Bradford City 1-0
Liverpool v Brentford 2-0
Manchester United v Aston Villa 5-1
Newcastle United v Blackpool 5-0
Sheffield Wednesday v Nottingham Forest 4-1
Southampton v Middlesbrough 6-1
Tottenham Hotspur v Birmingham 1-1
Woolwich Arsenal v Sunderland 5-0
r Birmingham v Tottenham Hotspur 2-0e

Round Four

Birmingham v Newcastle United 2-2
Everton v Sheffield Wednesday 4-3
Liverpool v Southampton 3-0
Manchester United v Woolwich Arsenal 2-3
r Newcastle United v Birmingham 3-0e

Semi Finals

Everton v Liverpool 2-0 N
Newcastle United v Woolwich Arsenal 2-0 N

Final

Everton v Newcastle United 1-0 N

1906/07

Preliminary Round

1 Ashington v Gateshead Town 3-0
Hebburn Argyle v Whitburn 2-0
Mickley v Southwick (1) 4-2
North Shields Athletic v Annfield Plain 1-1
Seaham White Star v Sunderland West End 2-1
Walker Parish Church v Sunderland Royal Rovers 2-2
Wallsend Park Villa v Newcastle East End (2) 2-1
Willington Athletic v Morpeth Harriers 1-3
2 Croft v Spennymoor United 0-2
Darlington St Augustines v Shildon 1-1
Eldon Albion v Darlington 1-2
Riley Brothers v Saltburn 1-6
Stanley United v West Stanley 1-1
West Auckland Town v Leadgate Park 1-0
West Hartlepool v South Bank 0-6
4 Darwen v Burnley Belvedere 6-1
Nelson v Rossendale United 2-3
Southport Central v Chorley 6-0
6 Altrincham v Newton-le-Willows 3-0
Skelmersdale United v Sale Holmefield 1-1
St Helens Town v St Helens Recreation 2-1
7 Nantwich v Sandbach Ramblers 4-1
Wrexham v Rhyl 7-0
9 Heckmondwike v Mirfield United 3-1
Morley v Doncaster Rovers 1-4
10 Elsecar Athletic v Rotherham Main 2-1
Rawmarsh Albion v Hoyland Silkstone 1-1
Rotherham Town v Kilnhurst Town 5-1
Sheffield v Birdwell 2-2
South Kirkby Colliery v Rotherham County 2-4
12 Grantham Avenue v Sutton Town 1-3
13 Kettering v Bedford Excelsior 4-0
Rushden Fosse v Desborough Town 2-3
15 Clapton v Leyton wo/s
East Ham v Upton Park 0-2
Grays United v Clapton Orient wo/s
Ilford v Chelmsford 1-1
Leytonstone v Southend Athletic 0-0
Limehouse Town v Woodford 2-5
Romford (1) v Barking 3-2
South Weald v Wanstead 5-0
16 Enfield v Finchley 1-1
Page Green Old Boys v Crouch End Vampires 6-6
17 Hanwell v Kingston-on-Thames 2-4
19 Clapham v Plumstead St John's 3-0
Southern United v Dorking 3-0
West Norwood v Wimbledon 2-1
20 Dartford v Sittingbourne 0-4
Maidstone United v Chatham wo/s
Sheppey United v Eltham 5-0
22 Salisbury (1) v North Hants Ironworks 5-0
24 Radstock Town v Wells City 3-2
Staple Hill v Bristol East 2-1
1r Annfield Plain v North Shields Athletic 0-3
r Sunderland Royal Rovers v Walker Parish Church 3-1
2r Shildon v Darlington St Augustines 2-1
r West Stanley v Stanley United 0-1
6r Sale Holmefield v Skelmersdale United 0-2
10r Birdwell v Sheffield 1-1
r Hoyland Silkstone v Rawmarsh Albion 1-1
15r Chelmsford v Ilford 2-1
r Southend Athletic v Leytonstone 2-5e
16r Crouch End Vampires v Page Green Old Boys 2-6
r Finchley v Enfield 2-1
10r2 Birdwell v Sheffield 3-0 N
r2 Hoyland Silkstone v Rawmarsh Albion 3-1 N

Qualifying Round One

1 Ashington v North Shields Athletic 2-2
Hebburn Argyle v Mickley 2-0
Morpeth Harriers v Seaham White Star 0-1
Sunderland Royal Rovers v Wallsend Park Villa 0-2
2 Darlington v South Bank 0-6
Saltburn v Spennymoor United 1-0
Skinningrove United v Shildon 0-5
West Auckland Town v Stanley United 1-0
3 Carlisle United v Penrith 3-0
Lancaster Town v Barrow St George's 5-1
Moresby Park v Barrow 1-8
Wigton Harriers v Keswick 2-2
4 Colne v Darwen 2-1
Halliwell Unitarians v Oswaldtwistle Rovers 0-4
Haslingden v Southport Central 0-3
Kirkham v Rossendale United 0-5
5 Burbage v Newton Heath Athletic 0-0
Buxton v Failsworth 1-0
Denton v Stalybridge Rovers 0-4
Oldham Athletic v Hyde 5-0
6 Atherton v Skelmersdale United 2-0
Northern Nomads v Earlestown 2-5
Pendlebury v Altrincham 1-2
St Helens Town v Brynn Central 1-1
7 Nantwich v Druids 4-1
Welshpool v Oswestry United 0-1
Whitchurch v Chirk 3-0
Wrexham v Tranmere Rovers 2-1
8 Stafford Rangers v Stourbridge 4-2
Walsall v Brierley Hill Alliance 0-3
Worcester City v Kidderminster Harriers 0-1
9 Castleford Town v Rockingham Colliery 4-1
Denaby United v Doncaster Rovers 0-0
Goole Town v Grimethorpe United 1-1
Heckmondwike v Darfield United 1-0
10 Birdwell v Rotherham Town 0-11
Hoyland Silkstone v Hoyland Town 1-1
Rotherham County v Elsecar Athletic 2-0
Thorpe Hesley v Wombwell Main 2-1
11 Belper Town (1) v Coalville Town (1) 4-1
Blackwell v Newhall Swifts 0-1
Long Eaton St Helen's v Ilkeston United 2-1
Sandiacre Olympic v Pinxton 1-3
12 Kimberley St John's v Arnold (1) 2-0
Newark v Mansfield Mechanics 3-0
Stanton Hill Victoria v Sutton Town 0-2
Sutton Junction v Boston Town (1) wo/s
13 Biggleswade & District v Hitchin Town 0-0
Irthlingborough Town v Desborough Town 2-0
Peterborough Town v Kettering 2-1 v
Wellingbro Redwell Stars v Luton Clarence 1-2
14 Cromer v Kirkley 6-2
King's Lynn v Harwich & Parkeston 1-0
Lowestoft Town v Norwich CEYMS 2-5
15 Chelmsford v Clapton 1-5
Leytonstone v South Weald 2-2
Romford (1) v Woodford 1-2
Upton Park v Grays United wo/s
16 Apsley v Cheshunt 7-0
Civil Service v London Caledonians 1-3
Page Green Old Boys v Barnet Alston 3-0
St Albans Abbey v Finchley 1-2
17 Kingston-on-Thames v Staines Town 2-0
Richmond Association v Uxbridge 0-1
Shepherds Bush v Windsor & Eton 2-0
Slough v Hounslow 2-2
18 Aylesbury United v Marlow 3-0
Chesham Town v Reading Amateurs 3-1
Maidenhead v Maidenhead Norfolkians 2-4
19 Clapham v Godalming 7-1
Farncombe v Croydon Wanderers wo/s
Redhill v Southern United 0-0
West Norwood v Guards Depot 2-0
20 Ashford United v Northfleet United 2-3
Maidstone Church Institute v Gravesend United 0-1
Sheppey United v Maidstone United 1-1
Sittingbourne v Margate Holy Trinity 7-1
21 Newhaven v Hove Park 1-3
Shoreham v Rock-a-Nore 0-1
Tunbridge Wells Rangers v Worthing 2-0
22 2nd Lincolnshire Regiment v Ryde 2-0
Basingstoke v Alton 5-4
Salisbury (1) v Cowes (2) 0-1
Winchester City v Eastleigh Athletic 2-4
23 Bridport v Whiteheads 0-3
Longfleet St Mary's v Poole 0-1
Yeovil Casuals v Bournemouth Gasworks Athletic 0-1
24 Chippenham Town v Paulton Rovers 0-6
Newport (Monmouth) v Frome Town 5-0
Radstock Town v Welton Rovers 3-1
Torpoint v Staple Hill 1-1
1r North Shields Athletic v Ashington 2-1
3r Keswick v Wigton Harriers 3-6
5r Burbage v Newton Heath Athletic 2-3
6r Brynn Central v St Helens Town 1-1
9r Doncaster Rovers v Denaby United 2-2
r Grimethorpe United v Goole Town 3-2e
10r Hoyland Town v Hoyland Silkstone 2-1
13r Hitchin Town v Biggleswade & District 5-1
r Kettering v Peterborough Town 4-0
15r South Weald v Leytonstone 0-1
17r Hounslow v Slough 3-1
19r Southern United v Redhill 2-2
20r Maidstone United v Sheppey United 2-0
24r Staple Hill v Torpoint 0-3
6r2 St Helens Town v Brynn Central 1-2
9r2 Denaby United v Doncaster Rovers 3-1 N
19r2 Redhill v Southern United 2-1

Qualifying Round Two

1 North Shields Athletic v Hebburn Argyle 4-1
Seaham White Star v Wallsend Park Villa 0-1
2 Shildon v South Bank 0-1
West Auckland Town v Saltburn 2-3
3 Barrow v Lancaster Town 2-1
Carlisle United v Wigton Harriers 3-1
4 Colne v Rossendale United 2-2
Oswaldtwistle Rovers v Southport Central 1-2
5 Buxton v Stalybridge Rovers 1-0
Oldham Athletic v Newton Heath Athletic 4-1
6 Atherton v Earlestown 4-2
Brynn Central v Altrincham 5-2
7 Nantwich v Whitchurch 0-2
Wrexham v Oswestry United 3-1
8 Dudley v Brierley Hill Alliance 1-2
Stafford Rangers v Kidderminster Harriers 1-1
9 Castleford Town v Heckmondwike 1-3
Grimethorpe United v Denaby United 1-1
10 Rotherham Town v Rotherham County 1-2
Thorpe Hesley v Hoyland Town 2-2
11 Long Eaton St Helen's v Newhall Swifts 0-0
Pinxton v Belper Town (1) 1-0
12 Kimberley St John's v Sutton Town 2-1 v
Newark v Sutton Junction 4-2
13 Hitchin Town v Kettering 5-0
Irthlingborough Town v Luton Clarence 1-0
14 King's Lynn v Bury St Edmunds 5-4
Norwich CEYMS v Cromer 1-0
15 Clapton v Upton Park 4-1
Woodford v Leytonstone 0-5
16 Apsley v Finchley 3-0
London Caledonians v Page Green Old Boys 3-2
17 Shepherds Bush v Hounslow 1-0
Uxbridge v Kingston-on-Thames 3-2
18 Chesham Town v Maidenhead Norfolkians 5-3
Wycombe Wanderers v Aylesbury United 3-1
19 Redhill v Clapham 1-3
West Norwood v Farncombe 6-0
20 Gravesend United v Maidstone United 1-0
Sittingbourne v Northfleet United 1-2

1906/07 to 1907/08

21	Rock-a-Nore v Hastings & St Leonards U	0-4
	Tunbridge Wells Rangers v Hove Park	10-0
22	Basingstoke v 2nd Lincolnshire Regiment	0-2
	Eastleigh Athletic v Cowes (2)	0-1
23	2nd Royal Warwicks v Bournemouth Gasworks Athletic	1-2
	Poole v Whiteheads	3-1
24	Paulton Rovers v Newport (Monmouth)	4-1
	Radstock Town v Torpoint	2-0
4r	Rossendale United v Colne	8-0
8r	Kidderminster Harriers v Stafford Rangers	4-0
9r	Denaby United v Grimethorpe United	7-1
10r	Hoyland Town v Thorpe Hesley	3-3 d
11r	Newhall Swifts v Long Eaton St Helen's	2-0
12r	Kimberley St John's v Sutton Town	0-2

Qualifying Round Three

1	North Shields Athletic v Wallsend Park Villa	3-2
2	South Bank v Saltburn	4-0
3	Barrow v Carlisle United	1-2
4	Southport Central v Rossendale United	1-0
5	Buxton v Oldham Athletic	1-3
6	Atherton v Brynn Central	3-2
7	Wrexham v Whitchurch	3-2
8	Brierley Hill Alliance v Kidderminster Harriers	1-1
9	Heckmondwike v Denaby United	3-5
10	Hoyland Town v Rotherham County	0-1
11	Newhall Swifts v Pinxton	2-0
12	Sutton Town v Newark	8-2
13	Hitchin Town v Irthlingborough Town	2-2
14	King's Lynn v Norwich CEYMS	1-4
15	Clapton v Leytonstone	1-2
16	London Caledonians v Apsley	5-0
17	Uxbridge v Shepherds Bush	4-7
18	Wycombe Wanderers v Chesham Town	1-1
19	Clapham v West Norwood	1-1
20	Gravesend United v Northfleet United	2-2
21	Tunbridge Wells Rangers v Hastings & St Leonards U	1-3
22	2nd Lincolnshire Regiment v Cowes (2)	4-1
23	Bournemouth Gasworks Athletic v Poole	2-3
24	Paulton Rovers v Radstock Town	3-0
8r	Kidderminster Harriers v Brierley Hill Alliance	10-0
13r	Irthlingborough Town v Hitchin Town	5-2
18r	Chesham Town v Wycombe Wanderers	2-1
19r	West Norwood v Clapham	7-2
20r	Northfleet United v Gravesend United	2-0

Qualifying Round Four

	2nd Lincolnshire Regiment v Hastings & St Leonards U	1-3
	Atherton v Oldham Athletic	1-1
	Carlisle United v Southport Central	0-4
	Denaby United v Rotherham County	0-0
	Irthlingborough Town v London Caledonians	4-2
	Kidderminster Harriers v Wrexham	2-1
	Leytonstone v Norwich CEYMS	6-2
	Newhall Swifts v Sutton Town	4-3
	Paulton Rovers v Poole	2-1
	Shepherds Bush v Chesham Town	5-1
	South Bank v North Shields Athletic	1-1
	West Norwood v Northfleet United	6-1
r	North Shields Athletic v South Bank	1-1
r	Oldham Athletic v Atherton	4-1
r	Rotherham County v Denaby United	2-1
r2	South Bank v North Shields Athletic	5-0

Qualifying Round Five

	Burton United v Bishop Auckland	6-0
	Crystal Palace v Rotherham County	4-0 N
	Irthlingborough Town v Shepherds Bush	2-0
	Kidderminster Harriers v Leytonstone	7-0
	New Crusaders v Hastings & St Leonards U	0-2
	Newhall Swifts v Glossop	1-2
	Northampton Town v Southport Central	2-1
	Oldham Athletic v South Bank	9-1
	Paulton Rovers v Crewe Alexandra	0-1
	Stockton v Watford	0-2
	Swindon Town v Burslem Port Vale	1-2
	West Norwood v Accrington Stanley	1-9

Round One

	Blackburn Rovers v Manchester City	2-2
	Bolton Wanderers v Brighton & Hove Albion	3-1
	Bradford City v Reading	2-0
	Brentford v Glossop	2-1
	Bristol City v Leeds City	4-1
	Bristol Rovers v Queen's Park Rangers	0-0
	Burnley v Aston Villa	1-3
	Burslem Port Vale v Irthlingborough Town	7-1
	Burton United v New Brompton	0-0
	Crewe Alexandra v Accrington Stanley	1-1
	Derby County v Chesterfield	1-1
	Everton v Sheffield United	1-0
	Fulham v Stockport County	0-0
	Gainsborough Trinity v Luton Town	0-0
	Grimsby Town v Woolwich Arsenal	1-1
	Lincoln City v Chelsea	2-2
	Liverpool v Birmingham	2-1
	Middlesbrough v Northampton Town	4-2
	Millwall v Plymouth Argyle	2-0
	Newcastle United v Crystal Palace	0-1
	Norwich City v Hastings & St Leonards U	3-1
	Nottingham Forest v Barnsley	1-1
	Notts County v Preston North End	1-0
	Oldham Athletic v Kidderminster Harriers	5-0
	Oxford City v Bury	0-3
	Portsmouth v Manchester United	2-2
	Sheffield Wednesday v Wolverhampton Wan.	3-2
	Southampton v Watford	2-1
	Sunderland v Leicester Fosse	4-1
	Tottenham Hotspur v Hull City	0-0
	West Bromwich Albion v Stoke	1-1
	West Ham United v Blackpool	2-1
r	Accrington Stanley v Crewe Alexandra	1-0
r	Barnsley v Nottingham Forest	2-1
r	Chelsea v Lincoln City	0-1e
r	Chesterfield v Derby County	1-1x
r	Fulham v Stockport County	2-1
r	Hull City v Tottenham Hotspur	0-0x
r	Luton Town v Gainsborough Trinity	2-1
r	Manchester City v Blackburn Rovers	0-1
r	Manchester United v Portsmouth	1-2
r	New Brompton v Burton United	0-0x
r	Queen's Park Rangers v Bristol Rovers	0-1
r	Stoke v West Bromwich Albion	2-2e
r	Woolwich Arsenal v Grimsby Town	3-0
r2	Chesterfield v Derby County	0-4 N
r2	New Brompton v Burton United	2-0 N
r2	Tottenham Hotspur v Hull City	1-0
r2	West Bromwich Albion v Stoke	2-0 N

Round Two

	Barnsley v Portsmouth	1-0
	Blackburn Rovers v Tottenham Hotspur	1-1
	Bolton Wanderers v Aston Villa	2-0
	Bradford City v Accrington Stanley	1-0
	Brentford v Middlesbrough	1-0
	Bristol Rovers v Millwall	3-0
	Burslem Port Vale v Notts County	2-2
	Bury v New Brompton	1-0
	Derby County v Lincoln City	1-0
	Fulham v Crystal Palace	0-0
	Luton Town v Sunderland	0-0
	Oldham Athletic v Liverpool	0-1
	Southampton v Sheffield Wednesday	1-1
	West Bromwich Albion v Norwich City	1-0
	West Ham United v Everton	1-2
	Woolwich Arsenal v Bristol City	2-1
r	Crystal Palace v Fulham	1-0
r	Notts County v Burslem Port Vale	5-0
r	Sheffield Wednesday v Southampton	3-1
r	Sunderland v Luton Town	1-0
r	Tottenham Hotspur v Blackburn Rovers	1-1e
r2	Tottenham Hotspur v Blackburn Rovers	2-1 N

Round Three

	Barnsley v Bury	1-0
	Crystal Palace v Brentford	1-1
	Everton v Bolton Wanderers	0-0
	Liverpool v Bradford City	1-0
	Notts County v Tottenham Hotspur	4-0
	Sheffield Wednesday v Sunderland	0-0
	West Bromwich Albion v Derby County	2-0
	Woolwich Arsenal v Bristol Rovers	1-0
r	Bolton Wanderers v Everton	0-3
r	Brentford v Crystal Palace	0-1
r	Sunderland v Sheffield Wednesday	0-1

Round Four

	Barnsley v Woolwich Arsenal	1-2
	Crystal Palace v Everton	1-1
	Sheffield Wednesday v Liverpool	1-0
	West Bromwich Albion v Notts County	3-1
r	Everton v Crystal Palace	4-0

Semi Finals

	Everton v West Bromwich Albion	2-1 N
	Sheffield Wednesday v Woolwich Arsenal	3-1 N

Final

	Sheffield Wednesday v Everton	2-1 N

1907/08

Preliminary Round

1	Hebburn Argyle v Ashington	3-1
	Kingston Villa v Southwick (1)	0-0
	Morpeth Harriers v Mickley	1-0
	Murton Red Star v Sunderland West End	0-0
	Seaham White Star v Whitburn	5-0
	South Shields Adelaide v North Shields Athletic	1-3
	Wallsend Park Villa v Walker Parish Church	2-0
	Willington Athletic v Sunderland Royal Rovers	1-1
2	Annfield Plain v Stanley United	2-4
	Leadgate Park v Craghead United	2-1
	Spennymoor United v Eldon Albion	1-0
	West Auckland Town v West Hartlepool	1-1
3	North Skelton v Brotton	wo/s
	Saltburn v Grangetown Athletic	5-1
4	Carlisle United v Carlisle City (1)	1-0
	Penrith v Barrow	0-2
5	Chorley v Accrington Stanley	2-1
	Eccles Borough v Salford United	1-1e
	Failsworth v Haslingden	1-3
	Nelson v Denton	2-1
	Padiham v Kirkham	1-4
	Rossendale United v Brierfield Swifts	7-1
	Southport Central v Colne	2-1
6	Altrincham v Hyde	8-0
	Chapel-en-le-Frith v Buxton	0-0
	Fairfield v Ashbourne Town	3-2
	Macclesfield Town v Wigan Town	4-1
	Newton-le-Willows v Earlestown	2-5
	Pendlebury v Atherton	0-3
	St Helens Recreation v St Helens Town	2-1
	Stalybridge Rovers v Burbage	10-0
7	Oswestry United v Nantwich	5-1
	Rhyl v Tranmere Rovers	0-2
	Welshpool v Witton Albion	1-3
8	Brierley Hill Alliance v Coventry City	2-6
	Walsall v Stafford Rangers	2-5
10	Heckmondwike v Clayton West	4-1
	Morley v Bingley	wo/s
11	Birdwell v Kilnhurst Town	1-2
	Grimethorpe United v Thorpe Hesley	4-2
	Hoyland Town v Wombwell Main	3-1
	Mexborough Town v Hoyland Silkstone	2-1
	Rotherham County v Wath Athletic	0-2
	Rotherham Main v Rawmarsh Albion	3-0
	Rotherham Town v Monckton Athletic	3-1
	South Kirkby Colliery v Darfield United	6-1
12	Coalville Town (1) v Eastwood Rangers	4-0
	Gresley Rovers v Long Eaton St Helen's	1-1
13	Grantham Avenue v Sneinton	4-0
	Newark v Market Harborough Town	5-0
	Notts Olympic v Sutton Town	2-2
14	Hitchin Town v Peterborough City (1)	1-3
	Irthlingborough Town v Raunds St Peter's	3-0
	Kettering v Raunds Town	6-1
	Luton Clarence v Desborough Town	6-0
	Rothwell Town v Wellingbro Redwell Stars	2-1
	Rushden Fosse v St Ives Town	4-1
16	Barking v Ilford	3-4
	Clapton v Chelmsford	5-2
	Clapton Orient v Custom House	3-0
	Leytonstone v South Weald	8-2
	Newportonians v Limehouse Town	4-2
	Romford (1) v Woodford	10-1
	Southend United v East Ham	3-0
	Wanstead v Leyton	wo/s
17	Apsley v Crouch End Vampires	wo/s
	Chesham Town v London Caledonians	0-3
	Finchley v Enfield	1-1
	Hampstead v St Albans Abbey	sc/sc
	Upton Park v Cheshunt	wo/s
	Watford Victoria Works v Chesham Generals	1-1
	West Hampstead v Barnet Alston	0-7
18	Aylesbury United v Marlow	5-1
	Hounslow v Slough	3-3
	Maidenhead v Windsor & Eton	0-3
	Wycombe Wanderers v Reading Amateurs	5-3
19	Clapham v Guards Depot	0-0
	Dorking v Wimbledon	6-5
	Farncombe v West Norwood	wo/s
	Godalming v Norwood Association	2-0
	Guildford v Walton-on-Thames	4-0
	Nunhead v Croydon Common	3-1
	Redhill v Summerstown	1-1
	Woking v Croydon (1)	wo/s
20	Ashford United v Sheppey United	0-5
	Bromley v Northfleet United	6-0
	Maidstone Church Institute v Eltham	wo/s
	Maidstone United v Deptford Invicta	5-2
	Margate Holy Trinity v Faversham	0-6
	Plumstead St John's v New Crusaders	wo/s
	Sittingbourne v Depot Batt. Royal Engrs	1-1
22	Cowes (2) v Winchester City	8-0
24	Radstock Town v Frome Town	5-3
r	Sunderland West End v Murton Red Star	2-0
1r	Southwick (1) v Kingston Villa	1-0
r	Sunderland Royal Rovers v Willington Athletic	2-4
2r	West Hartlepool v West Auckland Town	1-1
5r	Salford United v Eccles Borough	0-0x
6r	Buxton v Chapel-en-le-Frith	3-1
12r	Long Eaton St Helen's v Gresley Rovers	2-1
13r	Sutton Town v Notts Olympic	2-1
17r	Chesham Generals v Watford Victoria Works	2-0
r	Enfield v Finchley	0-4
18r	Slough v Hounslow	2-1
19r	Guards Depot v Clapham	0-4
r	Summerstown v Redhill	4-1
20r	Depot Batt. Royal Engrs v Sittingbourne	1-0
2r2	West Auckland Town v West Hartlepool	1-0
5r2	Salford United v Eccles Borough	1-2 N

Qualifying Round One

1	Hebburn Argyle v Willington Athletic	3-0
	Morpeth Harriers v Seaham White Star	2-3
	Southwick (1) v Sunderland West End	2-0
	Wallsend Park Villa v North Shields Athletic	2-2
2	Crook Town v Shildon	2-2
	Leadgate Park v Spennymoor United	2-2

1907/08

	West Auckland Town v Gateshead Town	2-0
	West Stanley v Stanley United	3-2
3	Darlington v South Bank	2-0
	Darlington St Augustines v North Skelton	0-0
	Guisborough Red Rose v Skinningrove United	1-3
	Scarborough v Saltburn	0-2
4	Carlisle United v Lancaster Town	4-1
	Moresby Park v Barrow St George's	3-0
	Windermere v Wigton Harriers	3-0
	Workington (1) v Barrow	6-2
5	Eccles Borough v Kirkham	1-4
	Haslingden v Burnley Belvedere	6-1
	Nelson v Chorley	1-3
	Southport Central v Rossendale United	2-0
6	Atherton v Earlestown	1-0
	Buxton v Macclesfield Town	0-0
	St Helens Recreation v Fairfield	7-0
	Stalybridge Rovers v Altrincham	4-0
7	Chester v Tranmere Rovers	0-4
	Chirk v Druids	1-1
	Witton Albion v Whitchurch	2-0
	Wrexham v Oswestry United	0-1
8	Bilston United v Stourbridge	2-0
	Coventry City v Darlaston	7-1
	Halesowen v Kidderminster Harriers	1-2
	Worcester City v Stafford Rangers	2-0
9	Castleford Town v Doncaster St James	6-1
	Denaby United v Wakefield City	13-0
	Doncaster Rovers v Goole Town	1-1
	Kippax Parish Church v Altofts	1-1
10	Heckmondwike v Worksop Town	0-2
	Mirfield United v Morley	2-0
	Sheffield v Horsforth	0-1
	Swaine Hill United v Guiseley Colliery	3-3
11	Kilnhurst Town v Grimethorpe United	3-1 v
	Rotherham Town v Hoyland Town	4-0
	South Kirkby Colliery v Mexborough Town	1-0
	Wath Athletic v Rotherham Main	2-0
12	Belper Town (1) v Coalville Town (1)	5-2
	Long Eaton St Helen's v Langley Mill Rangers	1-0
	Pinxton v Newhall Swifts	1-2
	Sandiacre Olympic v Ilkeston United	1-4
13	Arnold (1) v Mansfield Mechanics	1-6
	Grantham Avenue v Stanton Hill Victoria	3-0
	Kimberley St John's v Leicester Imperial	2-3
	Sutton Town v Newark	2-1
14	Luton Clarence v Peterborough City (1)	2-3
	Peterborough G.N. Loco v Kettering	0-2
	Rothwell Town v Biggleswade & District	1-2
	Rushden Fosse v Irthlingborough Town	1-3
15	Great Yarmouth Town v Cromer	2-0
	King's Lynn v Lowestoft Town	3-2
	Kirkley v 4th Kings Royal Rifles	1-2
	Norwich CEYMS v Bury St Edmunds	wo/s
16	Clapton v Southend United	0-1
	Clapton Orient v Romford (1)	6-3
	Leytonstone v Ilford	0-4
	Wanstead v Newportonians	0-4
17	Barnet Alston v Civil Service	wo/s
	Chesham Generals v London Caledonians	0-5
	Finchley v Apsley	3-0
	Upton Park - Bye	
18	Slough v Maidenhead Norfolkians	1-1
	Staines Town v Aylesbury United	1-1
	Uxbridge v Windsor & Eton	1-1
	Wycombe Wanderers v Shepherds Bush	1-1
19	Dorking v Farncombe	2-2
	Godalming v Clapham	1-7
	Nunhead v Summerstown	2-0
	Woking v Guildford	5-0
20	Depot Batt. Royal Engrs v Sheppey United	4-1
	Faversham v Bromley	0-3
	Maidstone Church Institute v Maidstone United	0-1
	Plumstead St John's v Gravesend United	0-0
21	Horsham v Newhaven	6-2
	Rock-a-Nore v Hastings & St Leonards U	1-6
	Tunbridge Wells Rangers v Shoreham	2-0
	Worthing v Tunbridge Wells (1)	3-0
22	Bitterne Guild v North Hants Ironworks	3-3
	Cowes (2) v Eastleigh Athletic	0-1
	Salisbury (1) v Basingstoke	5-1
	South Farnborough Ath. v Ryde	3-4
23	Bournemouth Gasworks Athletic v Yeovil	1-0
	Poole v Whiteheads	2-2
	Weymouth v Longfleet St Mary's	0-4
24	Paulton Rovers v Green Waves (Plymouth)	2-0
	Radstock Town v Bradford on Avon	5-0
	Staple Hill v Chippenham Town	5-0
	Wells City v Welton Rovers	0-5
1r	North Shields Athletic v Wallsend Park Villa	1-2
2r	Shildon v Crook Town	0-2
r	Spennymoor United v Leadgate Park	1-1
3r	Darlington St Augustines v North Skelton	2-1
6r	Macclesfield Town v Buxton	1-1x
7r	Druids v Chirk	2-1
9r	Goole Town v Doncaster Rovers	2-1
r	Kippax Parish Church v Altofts	wo/s
10r	Guiseley Colliery v Swaine Hill United	2-0
11r	Kilnhurst Town v Grimethorpe United	2-2x
18r	Aylesbury United v Staines Town	1-0
r	Maidenhead Norfolkians v Slough	8-0
r	Shepherds Bush v Wycombe Wanderers	1-0
r	Windsor & Eton v Uxbridge	3-2e
19r	Farncombe v Dorking	2-5
20r	Plumstead St John's v Gravesend United	0-2
22r	North Hants Ironworks v Bitterne Guild	1-3
23r	Whiteheads v Poole	5-1
2r2	Spennymoor United v Leadgate Park	1-3
6r2	Macclesfield Town v Buxton	3-2 N
11r2	Grimethorpe United v Kilnhurst Town	4-0
	Qualifying Round Two	
1	Hebburn Argyle v Wallsend Park Villa	2-1
	Seaham White Star v Southwick (1)	2-1
2	Crook Town v West Stanley	1-2
	West Auckland Town v Leadgate Park	1-0
3	Darlington St Augustines v Darlington	0-2
	Skinningrove United v Saltburn	2-0
4	Carlisle United v Windermere	9-1
	Workington (1) v Moresby Park	3-1
5	Chorley v Southport Central	2-1
	Haslingden v Kirkham	5-0
6	Atherton v Macclesfield Town	5-0
	St Helens Recreation v Stalybridge Rovers	7-1
7	Druids v Oswestry United	0-0
	Witton Albion v Tranmere Rovers	4-1
8	Coventry City v Bilston United	2-1
	Worcester City v Kidderminster Harriers	8-2
9	Castleford Town v Goole Town	3-2
	Kippax Parish Church v Denaby United	0-4
10	Guiseley Colliery v Mirfield United	1-1
	Worksop Town v Horsforth	1-1
11	Grimethorpe United v Wath Athletic	2-1
	Rotherham Town v South Kirkby Colliery	3-0
12	Ilkeston United v Belper Town (1)	2-1
	Long Eaton St Helen's v Newhall Swifts	2-1
13	Grantham Avenue v Mansfield Mechanics	2-2
	Sutton Town v Leicester Imperial	1-0
14	Irthlingborough Town v Biggleswade & District	1-2
	Peterborough City (1) v Kettering	1-5
15	Great Yarmouth Town v 4th Kings Royal Rifles	1-4
	Norwich CEYMS v King's Lynn	1-2
16	Clapton Orient v Newportonians	5-2
	Southend United v Ilford	3-1
17	Barnet Alston v London Caledonians	1-1
	Finchley v Upton Park	6-4
18	Maidenhead Norfolkians v Aylesbury United	5-2
	Shepherds Bush v Windsor & Eton	1-1
19	Clapham v Dorking	5-2
	Woking v Nunhead	5-1
20	Depot Batt. Royal Engrs v Bromley	0-1
	Maidstone United v Gravesend United	4-1
21	Hastings & St Leonards U v Worthing	8-2
	Horsham v Tunbridge Wells Rangers	0-3
22	Ryde v Eastleigh Athletic	1-5
	Salisbury (1) v Bitterne Guild	1-1
23	Bournemouth Gasworks Athletic v Whiteheads	1-2
	Longfleet St Mary's v Portland Prison Officers	2-2
24	Paulton Rovers v Welton Rovers	6-1
	Staple Hill v Radstock Town	1-1
7r	Oswestry United v Druids	5-1
10r	Horsforth v Worksop Town	0-2
r	Mirfield United v Guiseley Colliery	1-2
13r	Mansfield Mechanics v Grantham Avenue	4-1
17r	London Caledonians v Barnet Alston	2-1
18r	Windsor & Eton v Shepherds Bush	1-2
22r	Bitterne Guild v Salisbury (1)	1-4
23r	Portland Prison Officers v Longfleet St Mary's	3-1
24r	Radstock Town v Staple Hill	5-3
	Qualifying Round Three	
1	Hebburn Argyle v Seaham White Star	2-1
2	West Stanley v West Auckland Town	3-2
3	Darlington v Skinningrove United	6-0
4	Workington (1) v Carlisle United	2-3
5	Haslingden v Chorley	0-1 d
6	St Helens Recreation v Atherton	4-0
7	Oswestry United v Witton Albion	8-1
8	Coventry City v Worcester City	2-0
9	Castleford Town v Denaby United	2-1
10	Guiseley Colliery v Worksop Town	3-4
11	Grimethorpe United v Rotherham Town	0-4
12	Long Eaton St Helen's v Ilkeston United	0-0
13	Mansfield Mechanics v Sutton Town	2-2
14	Biggleswade & District v Kettering	2-1
15	4th Kings Royal Rifles v King's Lynn	4-1
16	Clapton Orient v Southend United	1-1
17	London Caledonians v Finchley	2-5
18	Maidenhead Norfolkians v Shepherds Bush	2-3
19	Woking v Clapham	2-0
20	Maidstone United v Bromley	6-2
21	Tunbridge Wells Rangers v Hastings & St Leonards U	0-2
22	Eastleigh Athletic v Salisbury (1)	1-3
23	Portland Prison Officers v Whiteheads	0-2
24	Radstock Town v Paulton Rovers	1-1
12r	Ilkeston United v Long Eaton St Helen's	1-0
13r	Sutton Town v Mansfield Mechanics	3-1
16r	Southend United v Clapton Orient	3-1
24r	Paulton Rovers v Radstock Town	3-1
	Qualifying Round Four	
	Biggleswade & District v Sutton Town	0-2
	Carlisle United v Darlington	7-0
	Finchley v Shepherds Bush	2-4
	Hastings & St Leonards U v Salisbury (1)	4-0
	Hebburn Argyle v West Stanley	1-4
	Ilkeston United v Rotherham Town	0-2
	Maidstone United v Woking	1-2
	Oswestry United v Coventry City	2-2
	Southend United v 4th Kings Royal Rifles	6-0
	St Helens Recreation v Haslingden	2-1
	Whiteheads v Paulton Rovers	4-5
	Worksop Town v Castleford Town	4-3
r	Coventry City v Oswestry United	2-0
	Qualifying Round Five	
	Carlisle United v Southend United	4-0
	Coventry City v Bishop Auckland	7-1
	Crewe Alexandra v Rotherham Town	1-1
	Hastings & St Leonards U v Paulton Rovers	11-2
	New Brompton v Shepherds Bush	6-0
	Northampton Town v Sutton Town	10-0
	Oldham Athletic v Darwen	8-1
	St Helens Recreation v Chesterfield	1-4
	Stockton v Burton United	2-1
	West Stanley v Glossop	0-3
	Woking v Oxford City	2-2
	Worksop Town - Bye	
r	Oxford City v Woking	1-2
r	Rotherham Town v Crewe Alexandra	2-1
	Round One	
	Aston Villa v Stockport County	3-0
	Bolton Wanderers v Woking	5-0
	Bradford City v Wolverhampton Wan.	1-1
	Brighton & Hove Albion v Preston North End	1-1
	Bristol City v Grimsby Town	0-0
	Burnley v Southampton	1-2
	Bury v Millwall	2-1
	Carlisle United v Brentford	2-2
	Chelsea v Worksop Town	9-1
	Chesterfield v Stockton	4-0
	Coventry City v Crystal Palace	2-4
	Everton v Tottenham Hotspur	1-0
	Gainsborough Trinity v Watford	1-0
	Glossop v Manchester City	0-0
	Hastings & St Leonards U v Portsmouth	0-1
	Leicester Fosse v Blackburn Rovers	2-0
	Liverpool v Derby County	4-2
	Luton Town v Fulham	3-8
	Manchester United v Blackpool	3-1
	New Brompton v Sunderland	3-1
	Newcastle United v Nottingham Forest	2-0
	Northampton Town v Bristol Rovers	0-1
	Norwich City v Sheffield Wednesday	2-0
	Notts County v Middlesbrough	2-0
	Oldham Athletic v Leeds City	2-1
	Plymouth Argyle v Barnsley	1-0
	Queen's Park Rangers v Reading	1-0
	Stoke v Lincoln City	5-0
	Swindon Town v Sheffield United	0-0
	West Bromwich Albion v Birmingham	1-1
	West Ham United v Rotherham Town	1-0
	Woolwich Arsenal v Hull City	0-0
r	Birmingham v West Bromwich Albion	1-2
r	Brentford v Carlisle United	1-3e
r	Grimsby Town v Bristol City	2-1
r	Hull City v Woolwich Arsenal	4-1
r	Manchester City v Glossop	6-0
r	Preston North End v Brighton & Hove Albion	1-1
r	Sheffield United v Swindon Town	2-3e
r	Wolverhampton Wan. v Bradford City	1-0
r2	Preston North End v Brighton & Hove Albion	0-1 N
	Round Two	
	Aston Villa v Hull City	3-0
	Bristol Rovers v Chesterfield	2-0
	Fulham v Norwich City	2-1
	Grimsby Town v Carlisle United	6-2
	Liverpool v Brighton & Hove Albion	1-1
	Manchester City v New Brompton	1-1
	Manchester United v Chelsea	1-0
	Newcastle United v West Ham United	2-0
	Notts County v Bolton Wanderers	1-1
	Oldham Athletic v Everton	0-0
	Plymouth Argyle v Crystal Palace	2-3
	Portsmouth v Leicester Fosse	1-0
	Southampton v West Bromwich Albion	1-0
	Stoke v Gainsborough Trinity	1-1
	Swindon Town v Queen's Park Rangers	2-1
	Wolverhampton Wan. v Bury	2-0
r	Bolton Wanderers v Notts County	2-1e
r	Brighton & Hove Albion v Liverpool	0-3
r	Everton v Oldham Athletic	6-1
r	Gainsborough Trinity v Stoke	2-2e
r	New Brompton v Manchester City	1-2
r2	Stoke v Gainsborough Trinity	3-1 N
	Round Three	
	Aston Villa v Manchester United	0-2
	Bolton Wanderers v Everton	3-3
	Grimsby Town v Crystal Palace	1-0
	Manchester City v Fulham	1-1
	Newcastle United v Liverpool	3-1
	Portsmouth v Stoke	0-1
	Southampton v Bristol Rovers	2-0
	Wolverhampton Wan. v Swindon Town	2-0

1907/08 to 1908/09

r	Everton v Bolton Wanderers	3-1e
r	Fulham v Manchester City	3-1

Round Four

	Everton v Southampton	0-0
	Fulham v Manchester United	2-1
	Newcastle United v Grimsby Town	5-1
	Stoke v Wolverhampton Wan.	0-1
r	Southampton v Everton	3-2

Semi Finals

	Newcastle United v Fulham	6-0 N
	Wolverhampton Wan. v Southampton	2-0 N

Final

	Wolverhampton Wan. v Newcastle United	3-1 N

1908/09

Extra Preliminary Round

5	Colne v Ramsbottom	2-0
	Darwen v Southport Central	1-0
	Halliwell Unitarians v Nelson	0-4
	Tonge v Atherton	5-2
6	Clitheroe Central v Great Harwood	1-0
	Macclesfield Town v St Helens Town	1-3
	Newton-le-Willows v Brynn Central	0-2

Preliminary Round

1	Bedlington United v Jarrow	0-0
	Mickley v Newcastle East End (2)	2-1
	Morpeth Harriers v Gateshead Town	5-1
	North Shields Athletic v Ashington	4-0
	South Shields Adelaide v Willington Athletic	0-0
	Walker Parish Church v Scotswood	2-2
	Wallsend Park Villa v Kingston Villa	2-0
2	Crook Town v Annfield Plain	0-1
	Murton Red Star v Leadgate Park	1-1
	Seaham White Star v Whitley Bay	3-0
	Sunderland Royal Rovers v Stanley United	1-3
	Sunderland West End v Bishop Auckland	1-3
	West Auckland Town v Shildon	2-4
	West Stanley v Spennymoor United	2-1
3	Skinningrove United v Darlington St Augustines	2-4
4	Lancaster Town v Barrow St George's	4-0
	Wigton Harriers v Hindpool Athletic	1-2
5	Colne v Padiham	7-2
	Darwen v Brierfield Swifts	4-1
	Eccles Borough v Earlestown	0-0
	Fleetwood v Rossendale United	1-2
	Kirkham v Haslingden	0-4
	Nelson v Bacup	7-1
	Rochdale v Accrington Stanley	3-5
	Tonge v Hyde	3-3
6	Altrincham v Pendlebury	4-1
	Buxton v St Helens Recreation	2-3
	Clitheroe Central v Burnley Belvedere	6-0
	Denton v Salford United	3-0
	Northern Nomads v Fairfield	6-0
	Oswaldtwistle Rovers v Chorley	0-0
	Sale Holmefield v Ashton Town (1)	3-0
	St Helens Town v Brynn Central	2-1
7	Druids v Rhyl	8-0
	Shrewsbury Town v Witton Albion	4-1
	Wellington Town v Oswestry United	4-1
	Wrexham v Welshpool	6-1
8	Atherstone Town v Kidderminster Harriers	2-4
	Bilston United v Stafford Rangers	1-1
	Halesowen v Willenhall Pickwick	6-2
	Nuneaton Town v Hednesford Town	2-2
	Willenhall Swifts v Darlaston	1-0
	Worcester City v Walsall	0-2
10	Mirfield United v Morley	0-0
11	Kilnhurst Town v Hickleton Main	2-2
	Monckton Athletic v Parkgate United	12-0
	Rawmarsh Albion v Hoyland Town	0-1
	Rotherham Main v Worksop Town	1-2
	Wath Athletic v Hoyland Silkstone	1-1
12	Ashbourne Town v Gresley Villa	3-2
	Coalville Town (1) v Pinxton	1-2
	Ilkeston United v Gresley Rovers	2-0
	Long Eaton St Helen's v Belper Town (1)	1-3
	Moore's Athletic v Burton United	0-6
	Newhall Swifts v Ripley	1-1
	Ripley Athletic v Newhall St Edward's	8-0
	South Normanton St Michael's v Clay Cross Works	1-1
13	Grantham Avenue v Horncastle United	5-2
	Loughborough Corinthians v Notts Olympic	0-3
	Mansfield Mechanics v Basford United	7-0
	Market Harborough Town v Leicester Nomads	3-2
	Sneinton v Sutton Town	2-2
	Sutton Junction v Notts Jardines	5-2
14	Biggleswade & District v Luton Clarence	1-2
	Desborough Town v Irthlingborough Town	4-0
	Fletton United v Luton Celtic	4-2
	Kettering v Higham Ferrers YMCI	3-1
	Kettering St Mary's v Peterborough G.N. Loco	3-1
	Peterborough City (1) v Kettering Working Men's	6-0
	Raunds Town v Wellingbro Redwell Stars	2-2
	Rushden Fosse v Rushden Windmill	2-1
16	Barking v Chelmsford	2-0
	Clapton v East Ham	6-0
	Ilford v Wanstead	3-1
	Leyton v Romford (1)	1-0
	Leytonstone v Newportonians	3-2
	London Caledonians v Southend United	0-4
	Shoeburyness Garrison v Custom House	1-0
	Tufnell Park v South Weald	4-1
17	2nd Coldstream Guards v West Hampstead	3-2
	Barnet Alston v Enfield	7-1
	Clove v Limehouse Town	wo/s
	Walthamstow Grange v Woodford	5-0
18	Maidenhead v Chesham Town	5-3
	Marlow v Uxbridge	0-6
	Slough v Wycombe Wanderers	1-3
	Yiewsley v Reading Amateurs	wo/s
19	1st Grenadier Guards v Clapham	5-2
	Croydon Common v Farncombe	10-1
	Dorking v Guards Depot	2-0
	Godalming v West Norwood	1-2
	Guildford v Nunhead	2-5
	Summerstown v Wimbledon	5-3
20	Bromley v Gravesend United	4-2
	Dartford v Sheppey United	4-1
	Deptford Invicta v Depot Batt. Royal Engrs	0-1
	Maidstone Athletic v Ashford Railway Works	0-0
	Sittingbourne v Gravesend Amateurs	2-1
22	Basingstoke v Winchester City	1-4
	Cowes (2) v Gosport United	4-0
24	Bradford on Avon v Kingswood Rovers	3-3
	Staple Hill v Welton Rovers	2-3
1r	Jarrow v Bedlington United	4-1
r	Scotswood v Walker Parish Church	3-1
r	Willington Athletic v South Shields Adelaide	0-4
2r	Leadgate Park v Murton Red Star	3-2
5r	Earlestown v Eccles Borough	4-0
r	Hyde v Tonge	5-0
6r	Chorley v Oswaldtwistle Rovers	1-0
8r	Hednesford Town v Nuneaton Town	5-1
r	Stafford Rangers v Bilston United	0-1
10r	Morley v Mirfield United	4-0
11r	Hickleton Main v Kilnhurst Town	3-1
r	Hoyland Silkstone v Wath Athletic	1-1e
12r	Clay Cross Works v South Normanton St Michael's	3-1
r	Ripley v Newhall Swifts	1-1e
13r	Sutton Town v Sneinton	4-1
14r	Wellingbro Redwell Stars v Raunds Town	6-4
20r	Ashford Railway Works v Maidstone Athletic	2-0
24r	Kingswood Rovers v Bradford on Avon	3-2
11r2	Wath Athletic v Hoyland Silkstone	2-0
12r2	Newhall Swifts v Ripley	1-2 N

Qualifying Round One

1	Mickley v Hebburn Argyle	3-1
	Morpeth Harriers v North Shields Athletic	0-0
	Scotswood v Jarrow	1-4
	South Shields Adelaide v Wallsend Park Villa	2-1
2	Annfield Plain v Craghead United	1-4
	Leadgate Park v Stanley United	2-1
	Seaham White Star v Shildon	0-1
	West Stanley v Bishop Auckland	4-0
3	Darlington v Scarborough	3-2
	Darlington St Augustines v West Hartlepool Expansion	1-4
	Hartlepools United v West Hartlepool	2-1
	Saltburn v South Bank	0-6
4	Hindpool Athletic v Moresby Park	wo/s
	Lancaster Town v Windermere	4-2
	Penrith v Barrow	1-6
	Workington (1) v Barrow Novocastrians	9-0
5	Accrington Stanley v Rossendale United	2-0
	Darwen v Haslingden	1-1
	Earlestown v Hyde	0-3
	Nelson v Colne	2-3
6	Chorley v Clitheroe Central	4-0
	Northern Nomads v St Helens Town	3-0
	Sale Holmefield v Denton	3-3
	St Helens Recreation v Altrincham	3-1
7	Chester v Druids	4-1
	Nantwich v Shrewsbury Town	2-1
	Wellington Town v Wellington St George's	2-1 v
	Whitchurch v Wrexham	0-3
8	Cannock Town v Willenhall Swifts	2-1
	Halesowen v Bilston United	1-3
	Kidderminster Harriers v Walsall	2-1
	Oldfields v Hednesford Town	1-3
9	Doncaster Rovers v Castleford Town	1-1
	Doncaster St James v Mexborough Town	0-4
	Goole Town v Denaby United	0-1
	Grimsby Rangers v Selby Mizpah	8-1
10	Bradford Park Avenue v South Kirkby Colliery	8-1
	Denby Dale v Lindley Temperance	3-1
	Morley v Clayton West	0-0
	Rothwell White Rose v Heckmondwike	2-2
11	Hickleton Main v Rotherham County	0-3
	Thorpe Hesley v Hoyland Town	2-2
	Wath Athletic v Monckton Athletic	1-1
	Worksop Town v Wombwell Main	1-3
12	Ashbourne Town v Burton United	1-4
	Belper Town (1) v Ripley	4-3
	Ilkeston United v Clay Cross Works	3-2
	Pinxton v Ripley Athletic	2-1
13	Mansfield Mechanics v Market Harborough Town	1-2
	Stanton Hill Victoria v Leicester Imperial	1-2
	Sutton Junction v Notts Olympic	2-5
	Sutton Town v Grantham Avenue	6-0
14	Desborough Town v Peterborough City (1)	4-0
	Fletton United v Kettering St Mary's	1-2
	Kettering v Rushden Fosse	3-1
	Luton Clarence v Wellingbro Redwell Stars	1-0
16	Leyton v Southend United	0-1
	Leytonstone v Barking	2-2
	Shoeburyness Garrison v Clapton	1-0
	Tufnell Park v Ilford	0-5
17	Barnet Alston v Walthamstow Grange	3-2
	Clove v Page Green Old Boys	wo/s
	Hounslow v 2nd Coldstream Guards	2-1
	St Albans City v Upton Park	1-1
18	Maidenhead Norfolkians v Uxbridge	4-4
	Shepherds Bush v Chesham Generals	2-2
	Wycombe Wanderers v Maidenhead	3-2
	Yiewsley v Aylesbury United	1-2
19	1st Grenadier Guards v Croydon (1)	2-0
	Nunhead v Dorking	8-2
	Summerstown v Woking	3-2
	West Norwood v Croydon Common	1-1
20	Bromley v Sittingbourne	3-0
	Dartford v South Ashford Invicta	wo/s
	Depot Batt. Royal Engrs v Ashford Railway Works	4-2
	Northfleet United v Plumstead St John's	5-2
21	Hastings & St Leonards U v Horsham	7-0
	Newhaven v Shoreham	2-3
	Rock-a-Nore v Worthing	1-2
	Tunbridge Wells Rangers v Bognor Regis Town	11-0
22	Cowes (2) v Salisbury (1)	2-1
	Eastleigh Athletic v Bitterne Guild	2-5
	North Hants Ironworks v Winchester City	3-2
	Ryde v South Farnborough Ath.	4-0
23	Exeter City v Weymouth	14-0
	Longfleet St Mary's v Yeovil	4-2
	Poole v Portland Prison Officers	2-2
	Whiteheads v Bournemouth Gasworks Athletic	6-4
24	Bath City v Camerton	1-0
	Radstock Town v Frome Town	1-1
	Trowbridge Town v Chippenham Town	4-0
	Welton Rovers v Kingswood Rovers	1-2
1r	North Shields Athletic v Morpeth Harriers	0-1
5r	Haslingden v Darwen	1-2
6r	Denton v Sale Holmefield	3-1
7r	Wellington St George's v Wellington Town	1-2
9r	Castleford Town v Doncaster Rovers	4-1
10r	Clayton West v Morley	3-1 v
r	Rothwell White Rose v Heckmondwike	0-2
11r	Hoyland Town v Thorpe Hesley	1-0
r	Monckton Athletic v Wath Athletic	2-3e
16r	Barking v Leytonstone	6-1
17r	Upton Park v St Albans City	3-2
18r	Chesham Generals v Shepherds Bush	0-2
r	Uxbridge v Maidenhead Norfolkians	4-1
19r	Croydon Common v West Norwood	4-2
23r	Portland Prison Officers v Poole	2-1
24r	Frome Town v Radstock Town	1-2
10r2	Morley v Clayton West	1-0

Qualifying Round Two

1	Mickley v South Shields Adelaide	0-3
	Morpeth Harriers v Jarrow	1-0
2	Craghead United v Leadgate Park	2-3
	Shildon v West Stanley	0-4
3	Darlington v West Hartlepool Expansion	4-0
	South Bank v Hartlepools United	2-2
4	Barrow v Lancaster Town	0-0
	Hindpool Athletic v Workington (1)	0-11
5	Accrington Stanley v Darwen	3-1
	Colne v Hyde	4-0
6	Northern Nomads v Denton	2-1
	St Helens Recreation v Chorley	wo/s
7	Chester v Wellington Town	3-1
	Nantwich v Wrexham	2-4
8	Bilston United v Kidderminster Harriers	1-1
	Cannock Town v Hednesford Town	1-3
9	Castleford Town v Grimsby Rangers	3-3
	Denaby United v Mexborough Town	0-1
10	Denby Dale v Bradford Park Avenue	0-11
	Heckmondwike v Morley	3-1
11	Rotherham County v Wombwell Main	6-1
	Wath Athletic v Hoyland Town	1-1
12	Burton United v Belper Town (1)	2-1
	Ilkeston United v Pinxton	6-2
13	Notts Olympic v Leicester Imperial	1-4
	Sutton Town v Market Harborough Town	2-1
14	Desborough Town v Kettering	1-1
	Luton Clarence v Kettering St Mary's	1-1
15	Great Yarmouth Town v Cromer	0-1
	Harwich & Parkeston v Kirkley	5-1
16	Barking v Ilford	1-2
	Southend United v Shoeburyness Garrison	4-0
17	Clove v Upton Park	1-1e
	Hounslow v Barnet Alston	1-3
18	Shepherds Bush v Aylesbury United	5-0
	Uxbridge v Wycombe Wanderers	1-1
19	Croydon Common v 1st Grenadier Guards	9-0
	Summerstown v Nunhead	0-3
20	Bromley v Depot Batt. Royal Engrs	0-1
	Northfleet United v Dartford	5-2

1908/09 to 1909/10

21	Hastings & St Leonards U v Tunbridge Wells Rangers	4-1
	Shoreham v Worthing	2-2
22	Bitterne Guild v North Hants Ironworks	6-1
	Ryde v Cowes (2)	0-2
23	Longfleet St Mary's v Exeter City	1-1
	Portland Prison Officers v Whiteheads	0-3
24	Radstock Town v Kingswood Rovers	0-3
	Trowbridge Town v Bath City	1-1
3r	Hartlepools United v South Bank	0-2
4r	Lancaster Town v Barrow	1-0
8r	Kidderminster Harriers v Bilston United	3-4
9r	Grimsby Rangers v Castleford Town	0-2
11r	Hoyland Town v Wath Athletic	1-3
14r	Kettering v Desborough Town	3-2
r	Luton Clarence v Kettering St Mary's	2-1
17r	Upton Park v Clove	5-1
18r	Wycombe Wanderers v Uxbridge	3-4e
21r	Worthing v Shoreham	2-5
23r	Exeter City v Longfleet St Mary's	10-1
24r	Bath City v Trowbridge Town	4-1

Qualifying Round Three

1	Morpeth Harriers v South Shields Adelaide	0-6
2	Leadgate Park v West Stanley	0-1
3	South Bank v Darlington	1-0
4	Workington (1) v Lancaster Town	8-0
5	Accrington Stanley v Colne	1-1
6	Northern Nomads v St Helens Recreation	2-1
7	Chester v Wrexham	1-3
8	Hednesford Town v Bilston United	1-0
9	Castleford Town v Mexborough Town	3-3
10	Bradford Park Avenue v Heckmondwike	wo/s
11	Rotherham County v Wath Athletic	5-0
12	Burton United v Ilkeston United	1-0
13	Leicester Imperial v Sutton Town	1-5
14	Kettering v Luton Clarence	3-0
15	Harwich & Parkeston v Cromer	1-2
16	Ilford v Southend United	1-3
17	Barnet Alston v Upton Park	4-2
18	Shepherds Bush v Uxbridge	3-2
19	Croydon Common v Nunhead	1-0
20	Northfleet United v Depot Batt. Royal Engrs	1-1
21	Hastings & St Leonards U v Shoreham	4-0
22	Cowes (2) v Bitterne Guild	4-2
23	Exeter City v Whiteheads	4-0
24	Kingswood Rovers v Bath City	2-0
5r	Colne v Accrington Stanley	2-2x
9r	Mexborough Town v Castleford Town	4-0
20r	Depot Batt. Royal Engrs v Northfleet United	0-3
5r2	Accrington Stanley v Colne	1-0 N

Qualifying Round Four

	Accrington Stanley v Northern Nomads	0-2
	Barnet Alston v Shepherds Bush	4-1
	Bradford Park Avenue v Mexborough Town	6-0
	Hastings & St Leonards U v Cowes (2)	2-0
	Hednesford Town v Wrexham	1-2
	Kettering v Sutton Town	2-1
	Kingswood Rovers v Exeter City	0-2
	Northfleet United v Croydon Common	1-1
	Rotherham County v Burton United	1-2
	Southend United v Cromer	2-0
	West Stanley v South Bank	5-2
	Workington (1) v South Shields Adelaide	4-1
r	Croydon Common v Northfleet United	4-3

Qualifying Round Five

	Barnet Alston v Exeter City	0-3
	Bradford Park Avenue v Croydon Common	1-2
	Chesterfield v Rotherham Town	3-0
	Coventry City v Carlisle United	1-1
	Gainsborough Trinity v Northern Nomads	4-0
	Hastings & St Leonards U v New Brompton	2-2
	Kettering v Burton United	2-0
	Lincoln City v Stockton	1-0
	Luton Town v Southend United	1-1
	Watford v West Stanley	4-1
	Workington (1) v Crewe Alexandra	4-1
	Wrexham v Oxford City	7-0
r	Carlisle United v Coventry City	1-1
r	New Brompton v Hastings & St Leonards U	1-2
r	Southend United v Luton Town	2-4
r2	Carlisle United v Coventry City	3-1 N

Round One

	Birmingham v Portsmouth	2-5
	Blackpool v Hastings & St Leonards U	2-0
	Bradford City v Workington (1)	2-0
	Brentford v Gainsborough Trinity	2-0
	Bristol City v Southampton	1-1
	Bristol Rovers v Burnley	1-4
	Bury v Kettering	8-0
	Chesterfield v Glossop	0-2
	Croydon Common v Woolwich Arsenal	1-1 N
	Everton v Barnsley	3-1
	Fulham v Carlisle United	4-1
	Grimsby Town v Stockport County	0-2
	Hull City v Chelsea	1-1
	Liverpool v Lincoln City	5-1
	Luton Town v Millwall	1-2
	Manchester City v Tottenham Hotspur	3-4
	Manchester United v Brighton & Hove Albion	1-0
	Newcastle United v Clapton Orient	5-0
	Northampton Town v Derby County	1-1
	Norwich City v Reading	0-0 N
	Nottingham Forest v Aston Villa	2-0
	Notts County v Blackburn Rovers	0-1
	Oldham Athletic v Leeds City	1-1
	Plymouth Argyle v Swindon Town	1-0
	Preston North End v Middlesbrough	1-0
	Queen's Park Rangers v West Ham United	0-0
	Sheffield United v Sunderland	2-3
	Sheffield Wednesday v Stoke	5-0
	Watford v Leicester Fosse	1-1
	West Bromwich Albion v Bolton Wanderers	3-1
	Wolverhampton Wan. v Crystal Palace	2-2
	Wrexham v Exeter City	1-1
r	Chelsea v Hull City	1-0
r	Crystal Palace v Wolverhampton Wan.	4-2
r	Derby County v Northampton Town	4-2
r	Exeter City v Wrexham	2-1e
r	Leeds City v Oldham Athletic	2-0
r	Leicester Fosse v Watford	3-1
r	Reading v Norwich City	1-1e
r	Southampton v Bristol City	0-2
r	West Ham United v Queen's Park Rangers	1-0
r	Woolwich Arsenal v Croydon Common	2-0
r2	Norwich City v Reading	3-2eN

Round Two

	Blackburn Rovers v Chelsea	2-1
	Bristol City v Bury	2-2
	Crystal Palace v Burnley	0-0
	Leeds City v West Ham United	1-1
	Leicester Fosse v Derby County	0-2
	Liverpool v Norwich City	2-3
	Manchester United v Everton	1-0
	Newcastle United v Blackpool	2-1
	Nottingham Forest v Brentford	1-0
	Plymouth Argyle v Exeter City	2-0
	Portsmouth v Sheffield Wednesday	2-2
	Preston North End v Sunderland	1-2
	Stockport County v Glossop	1-1
	Tottenham Hotspur v Fulham	1-0
	West Bromwich Albion v Bradford City	1-2
	Woolwich Arsenal v Millwall	1-1
r	Burnley v Crystal Palace	9-0
r	Bury v Bristol City	0-1
r	Glossop v Stockport County	1-0e
r	Millwall v Woolwich Arsenal	1-0
r	Sheffield Wednesday v Portsmouth	3-0
r	West Ham United v Leeds City	2-1e

Round Three

	Bradford City v Sunderland	0-1
	Bristol City v Norwich City	2-0
	Derby County v Plymouth Argyle	1-0
	Manchester United v Blackburn Rovers	6-1
	Nottingham Forest v Millwall	3-1
	Sheffield Wednesday v Glossop	0-1
	Tottenham Hotspur v Burnley	0-0
	West Ham United v Newcastle United	0-0
r	Burnley v Tottenham Hotspur	3-1
r	Newcastle United v West Ham United	2-1

Round Four

	Burnley v Manchester United	2-3
	Derby County v Nottingham Forest	3-0
	Glossop v Bristol City	0-0
	Newcastle United v Sunderland	2-2
r	Bristol City v Glossop	1-0
r	Sunderland v Newcastle United	0-3

Semi Finals

	Bristol City v Derby County	1-1 N
	Manchester United v Newcastle United	1-0 N
r	Bristol City v Derby County	2-1 N

Final

	Manchester United v Bristol City	1-0 N

1909/10

Extra Preliminary Round

1	Blyth Spartans v Washington United	1-1
5	Holme v Breightmet United	0-2
	Oswaldtwistle Rovers v Dobson & Barlow's	1-1
	Portsmouth Rovers (Lancs) v Bacup	0-3
	Rossendale United v Padiham	7-0
	Walkden Central v Tydesley Albion	0-0
6	Atherton v Chapel-en-le-Frith	4-0
	Hooley Hill v Denton	1-0
	Macclesfield Town v Heywood United	0-1
7	Lostock Gralam v Chirk	wo/s
11	Birdwell v Rawmarsh Albion	1-1
	Birdwell Primitive Methodists v Atlas & Norfolk Work	1-4
	Elsecar Main v Darfield United	2-0
	Grimethorpe United v Silverwood Colliery	2-0
12	Heanor United v Newhall White Rose	4-1
13	Eastwood Rangers v Netherfield Rangers	5-2
	Mansfield Wesleyans v Shepshed Albion	3-2
14	Daventry United (1) v Kettering St Mary's	wo/s
	Finedon United v Kettering Working Men's	2-3
	Leagrave United v Wellingbro Redwell Stars	0-2
	Leighton Town (1) v Hitchin Blue Cross Temp.	4-2
19	Kingston-on-Thames v Catford Southend	2-1
1r	Washington United v Blyth Spartans	3-1
5r	Dobson & Barlow's v Oswaldtwistle Rovers	2-0
r	Tydesley Albion v Walkden Central	2-2
11r	Rawmarsh Albion v Birdwell	3-1
5r2	Walkden Central v Tydesley Albion	6-3

Preliminary Round

1	Hebburn Argyle v Mickley	1-0
	Kingston Villa v Bedlington United	1-1
	North Shields Athletic v Morpeth Harriers	7-0
	South Shields Adelaide v Willington Athletic	0-0
	South Shields Parkside v Newburn	2-1
	Walker Parish Church v Ashington	2-2
	Wallsend Park Villa v Scotswood	2-0
	Washington United v Newcastle East End (2)	0-1
2	Craghead United v Sunderland West End	4-2
	Murton Red Star v West Stanley	1-2
	Seaham Harbour v Whitburn	6-0
	Shildon v Annfield Plain	1-1
	Spennymoor United v Crook Town	1-1
	Stanley United v Tow Law Town	1-1
	Sunderland Royal Rovers v West Auckland Town	1-0
3	Darlington St Augustines v Wingate Albion Comrades	1-1
	Filey United v Saltburn	1-1
	Horden Athletic v Darlington	1-1
	South Bank v Skinningrove United	4-1
	West Hartlepool Expansion v Scarborough	5-1
4	Barrow Novocastrians v Barrow	1-4
	Barrow St Mary's v Bowness Rovers	1-0
	Windermere v Barrow St George's	5-0
	Workington (1) v Wigton Harriers	4-0
5	Brierfield Swifts v Nelson	2-3
	Chorley v Colne	0-3
	Clitheroe Central v Bacup	2-1
	Darwen v Breightmet United	2-1
	Haslingden v Dobson & Barlow's	7-0
	Rochdale v Ramsbottom	1-1
	Rossendale United v Walkden Central	1-3
	Southport Central v Great Harwood	1-1
6	Ashton Town (1) v Altrincham	2-3
	Buxton v Atherton	1-1
	Eccles Borough v Hooley Hill	2-1
	Hyde v St Helens Recreation	1-0
	Newton-le-Willows v Heywood United	1-1
	Sale Holmefield v Earlestown	0-2
	Salford United v Northern Nomads	4-1
	Tonge v St Helens Town	4-2
7	Connah's Quay&Shotton v New Brighton Tower Ams	2-1
	Druids v Aberystwyth	wo/s
	Oswestry United v Rhyl	7-1
	Saltney v Nantwich	3-1
	Shrewsbury Town v Wellington Town	3-0
	Tranmere Rovers v Chester	6-0
	Wellington St George's v Lostock Gralam	1-0
	Whitchurch v Witton Albion	5-3
8	Brierley Hill Alliance v Worcester City	1-1
	Darlaston v Halesowen	1-1
	Hereford City v Cradley Heath St Luke's	0-1
	Nuneaton Town v Kidderminster Harriers	2-2
	Walsall v Cannock Town	1-2
	Wednesbury Old Athletic v Hednesford Town	1-4
	Willenhall Pickwick v Stafford Rangers	7-3
	Willenhall Swifts v Bilston United	0-3
9	Allerton Bywater Colliery v Mexborough Town	3-3
	Grimsby Rangers v Denaby United	2-3
	Grimsby Rovers v Goole Town	3-3
	Scunthorpe United v Withernsea	8-0
	Selby Mizpah v Hull Day Street Old Boys	2-1
10	Heckmondwike v Huddersfield Town	0-11
11	Hoyland Silkstone v Rawmarsh Albion	3-1
	Hoyland Town v Grimethorpe United	1-2
	Monckton Athletic v Elsecar Main	1-2
	Parkgate & Rawmarsh Utd. v Hickleton Main	4-1
	Rotherham County v Atlas & Norfolk Works	3-1
	Rotherham Town v Thorpe Hesley	7-0
	Wath Athletic v Sheffield	7-1
	Worksop Town v Wombwell Main	3-0
12	Belper Town (1) v Old Whittington Mutuals	3-0
	Coalville Town (1) v Heanor United	0-0
	Gresley Rovers v Ashbourne Town	2-1
	Gresley Villa v Newhall Swifts	0-0
	Ilkeston United v Burton United	4-0
	Long Eaton St Helen's v South Normanton St Michael's	1-0
	Pinxton v Shirebrook Athletic	3-1
	Ripley v Clay Cross Town	0-0
13	Eastwood Rangers v Notts Jardines	3-1
	Horncastle United v Basford United	2-2
	Loughborough Corinthians v Mansfield Mechanics	4-5
	Mansfield Wesleyans v Notts Olympic	1-1
	Market Harborough Town v Sutton Town	5-7
	Sneinton v Hinckley United (1)	2-1
	Stanton Hill Victoria v Leicester Nomads	2-1
	Sutton Junction v Leicester Imperial	5-0
14	Daventry United (1) v Peterborough City (1)	1-7
	Desborough Town v Leighton Town (1)	5-0
	Kettering v Higham Ferrers YMCI	16-0

1909/10

Kettering Working Men's v Raunds Town 3-1
Luton Clarence v Irthlingborough Town 7-2
Peterborough G.N. Loco v Luton Celtic 3-1
Rushden Fosse v Biggleswade & District 3-2
Wellingbro Redwell Stars v Rushden Windmill 1-10
16 Chelmsford v Newportonians 4-1
Leytonstone v Colchester Town 4-2
Romford (1) v Shoeburyness Garrison 1-4
South Weald v Ilford 0-0
Walthamstow Grange v Barking 3-5
Wanstead v Upton Park 3-2
17 Barnet Alston v Enfield 2-1
Chesham Town v Apsley 3-1
London Caledonians v Finchley 1-2
St Albans City v Tufnell Park 1-0
18 City of Westminster v Southall 1-7
Gramophone v Marlow 0-0
Hanwell v Shepherds Bush 1-3
Maidenhead v Hounslow wo/s
Maidenhead Norfolkians v Yiewsley 7-0
Slough v Staines Town 6-0
Uxbridge v Windsor & Eton 2-1
Wycombe Wanderers v Aylesbury United 4-3
19 Clapham v Old Kingstonians 1-4
Dorking v West Norwood 1-2
Farncombe v Guildford 2-7
Leatherhead (1) v Summerstown 1-2
Redhill v Kingston-on-Thames 2-1
Walton-on-Thames v Croydon (1) 1-4
Wimbledon v Guards Depot 5-0
Woking v Godalming 5-0
20 Dartford v Northfleet United 2-2
Deptford Invicta v Depot Batt. Royal Engrs 1-1
Folkestone v Sittingbourne 1-6
Plumstead St John's v Chatham 0-2
22 Basingstoke v Cowes (2) 0-11
Eastleigh Athletic v 1st Grenadier Guards 4-2
Gosport United v Farnham 1-1
Salisbury (1) v South Farnborough Ath. 3-3
23 Bournemouth Gasworks Athletic v Boscombe 0-0
Whiteheads v Portland Prison Officers 2-1
24 Kingswood Rovers v Trowbridge Town 6-4
Melksham Town v Bradford on Avon 4-5
Paulton Rovers v Chippenham Town wo/s
Radstock Town v Bath City 3-2
Swindon Amateurs v Ton Pentre wo/s
Welton Rovers v Staple Hill wo/s
1r Ashington v Walker Parish Church 3-1
r Bedlington United v Kingston Villa 4-3
r Willington Athletic v South Shields Adelaide 0-0
2r Annfield Plain v Shildon 2-4
r Crook Town v Spennymoor United 3-1
r Tow Law Town v Stanley United 0-2
3r Darlington v Horden Athletic 2-0
r Saltburn v Filey United wo/s
r Wingate Albion Comrades v Darlington St Augustines 3-1
5r Great Harwood v Southport Central 0-1
r Rochdale v Ramsbottom 4-0
6r Atherton v Buxton 3-2
r Heywood United v Newton-le-Willows 5-0
8r Halesowen v Darlaston 3-4
r Kidderminster Harriers v Nuneaton Town 1-1e
r Worcester City v Brierley Hill Alliance wo/s
9r Goole Town v Grimsby Rovers 2-3
r Mexborough Town v Allerton Bywater Colliery 3-1
12r Clay Cross Town v Ripley 0-3
r Heanor United v Coalville Town (1) 2-2
r Newhall Swifts v Gresley Villa 2-3
13r Basford United v Horncastle United 4-1
r Mansfield Wesleyans v Notts Olympic wo/s
16r Ilford v South Weald 2-0
18r Marlow v Gramophone 0-1
20r Depot Batt. Royal Engrs v Deptford Invicta 2-1
r Northfleet United v Dartford 2-1
22r Farnham v Gosport United 4-2
r South Farnborough Ath. v Salisbury (1) 0-2
23r Bournemouth Gasworks Athletic v Boscombe 1-2
1r2 South Shields Adelaide v Willington Athletic 1-2
8r2 Kidderminster Harriers v Nuneaton Town 1-1e
12r2 Heanor United v Coalville Town (1) 2-0
8r3 Nuneaton Town v Kidderminster Harriers wo/s

Qualifying Round One

1 Bedlington United v Hebburn Argyle 3-0
North Shields Athletic v Ashington 4-5
South Shields Parkside v Willington Athletic 1-1
Wallsend Park Villa v Newcastle East End (2) 3-1
2 Craghead United v Crook Town 3-2
Seaham Harbour v Leadgate Park 3-1
Stanley United v Shildon 3-2
Sunderland Royal Rovers v West Stanley 1-4
3 Darlington v West Hartlepool Expansion 2-1
Grangetown Athletic v West Hartlepool 1-0
Hartlepools United v Wingate Albion Comrades 6-3
South Bank v Saltburn 5-0
4 Barrow v Hindpool Athletic wo/s
Barrow St Luke's v Workington (1) 0-8
Barrow St Mary's v Windermere 1-4
Penrith v Kendal Swifts 3-0
5 Colne v Nelson 1-0 v
Darwen v Clitheroe Central 2-1
Haslingden v Rochdale 3-1
Walkden Central v Southport Central 2-0
6 Altrincham v Salford United 0-0
Eccles Borough v Earlestown 4-1
Heywood United v Atherton 1-1
Tonge v Hyde 0-0
7 Connah's Quay & Shotton v Saltney 1-0
Oswestry United v Wellington St George's 2-1
Shrewsbury Town v Druids 2-1
Tranmere Rovers v Whitchurch 4-2
8 Cannock Town v Willenhall Pickwick 3-0
Darlaston v Bilston United 3-2
Hednesford Town v Worcester City 1-0
Nuneaton Town v Cradley Heath St Luke's 0-0
9 Denaby United v Doncaster St James 8-1
Mexborough Town v Castleford Town 5-0
Selby Mizpah v Grimsby Rovers 2-7
York City (1) v Scunthorpe United 4-0
10 Clayton West v Skipton Town wo/s
Huddersfield Town v Mirfield United 6-0
Rothwell White Rose v Morley wo/s
Stourton United v South Kirkby Colliery 1-1
11 Elsecar Main v Hoyland Silkstone 3-0
Rotherham Town v Grimethorpe United 6-2
Wath Athletic v Rotherham County 0-2
Worksop Town v Parkgate & Rawmarsh Utd. 4-0
12 Gresley Villa v Gresley Rovers 2-2
Ilkeston United v Pinxton 1-1
Long Eaton St Helen's v Heanor United 1-5
Ripley v Belper Town (1) 1-2
13 Eastwood Rangers v Sneinton 4-2
Mansfield Mechanics v Basford United 4-0
Stanton Hill Victoria v Mansfield Wesleyans 1-1
Sutton Junction v Sutton Town 3-1
14 Kettering v Rushden Fosse 5-1
Luton Clarence v Kettering Working Men's 8-0
Peterborough G.N. Loco v Peterborough City (1) 1-2
Rushden Windmill v Desborough Town 1-2
15 Chatteris Engineers v King's Lynn 3-4
Cromer v Lowestoft Town 1-2
Norwich CEYMS v Gorleston 2-0
16 Barking v East Ham 5-1
Ilford v Wanstead 3-0
Leytonstone v Custom House 2-3
Shoeburyness Garrison v Chelmsford 3-1
17 2nd Coldstream Guards v West Hampstead 1-5
Chesham Generals v Finchley 0-3
St Albans City v Barnet Alston 1-1
Wood Green Town v Chesham Town 5-0
18 Gramophone v Slough 2-2
Maidenhead Norfolkians v Maidenhead 4-2
Shepherds Bush v Uxbridge 1-1
Wycombe Wanderers v Southall 1-0
19 Guildford v West Norwood 1-1
Redhill v Croydon (1) 8-0
Wimbledon v Summerstown 3-5
Woking v Old Kingstonians 0-1 d
20 Ashford Railway Works v Chatham 2-2
Maidstone United v Sittingbourne 3-1
Northfleet United v Sheppey United 6-5
Woolwich Polytechnic v Depot Batt. Royal Engrs 1-1
21 Horsham v Worthing 2-3
Newhaven v Southwick 0-2
Tunbridge Wells Rangers v Seaford 4-0
22 Bitterne Guild v Farnham 5-0
Eastleigh Athletic v Royal Engs. Aldershot 0-1
Salisbury (1) v Cowes (2) 4-1
Winchester City v North Hants Ironworks 6-0
23 Bournemouth (Ams) v Weymouth wo/s
Poole v Boscombe 3-2
Shaftesbury v Longfleet St Mary's 4-2
Yeovil v Whiteheads wo/s
24 Camerton v Swindon Amateurs 2-1
Kingswood Rovers v Welton Rovers 2-0
Paulton Rovers v Bradford on Avon 3-1
Radstock Town v Clevedon 2-0
1r Willington Athletic v South Shields Parkside 2-2
5r Colne v Nelson 1-1
6r Altrincham v Salford United 4-0
r Atherton v Heywood United 3-0
r Hyde v Tonge 2-2
8r Cradley Heath St Luke's v Nuneaton Town 2-1
10r South Kirkby Colliery v Stourton United 5-0
12r Gresley Villa v Gresley Rovers 3-0
r Pinxton v Ilkeston United 1-4
13r Mansfield Wesleyans v Stanton Hill Victoria 4-1
17r Barnet Alston v St Albans City 2-0
18r Slough v Gramophone 3-2
r Uxbridge v Shepherds Bush 1-0
19r West Norwood v Guildford 4-2
20r Chatham v Ashford Railway Works 3-3e
r Depot Batt. Royal Engrs v Woolwich Polytechnic 1-0
1r2 Willington Athletic v South Shields Parkside 0-2
5r2 Nelson v Colne 1-2
6r2 Tonge v Hyde 3-0 N
20r2 Chatham v Ashford Railway Works 2-1 N

Qualifying Round Two

1 Bedlington United v Ashington 3-0
South Shields Parkside v Wallsend Park Villa 1-3
2 Seaham Harbour v West Stanley 1-1
Stanley United v Craghead United 0-1
3 Grangetown Athletic v South Bank 1-3
Hartlepools United v Darlington 0-1
4 Barrow v Workington (1) 1-2
Penrith v Windermere 3-2
5 Darwen v Colne 4-0
Walkden Central v Haslingden 1-2
6 Atherton v Altrincham 1-0
Eccles Borough v Tonge 3-4
7 Connah's Quay & Shotton v Shrewsbury Town 1-2
Tranmere Rovers v Oswestry United 5-1
8 Darlaston v Cannock Town 3-1
Hednesford Town v Cradley Heath St Luke's 1-2
9 Denaby United v York City (1) 5-1
Mexborough Town v Grimsby Rovers 6-1
10 Clayton West v South Kirkby Colliery 1-5
Huddersfield Town v Rothwell White Rose 7-0
11 Rotherham County v Elsecar Main 1-2
Rotherham Town v Worksop Town 2-2
12 Gresley Villa v Heanor United 1-3
Ilkeston United v Belper Town (1) 0-0
13 Eastwood Rangers v Sutton Junction 1-3
Mansfield Mechanics v Mansfield Wesleyans 1-1
14 Desborough Town v Peterborough City (1) 3-0
Luton Clarence v Kettering 2-3
15 Lowestoft Town v Great Yarmouth Town 1-1
Norwich CEYMS v King's Lynn 0-1
16 Barking v Custom House 4-1
Shoeburyness Garrison v Ilford 2-3
17 Finchley v West Hampstead 0-0
Wood Green Town v Barnet Alston 0-3
18 Maidenhead Norfolkians v Wycombe Wanderers 1-3
Uxbridge v Slough 4-0
19 Redhill v West Norwood 2-1
Summerstown v Woking 5-4
20 Maidstone United v Chatham 1-2
Northfleet United v Depot Batt. Royal Engrs 5-1
21 Southwick v Shoreham 2-3
Tunbridge Wells Rangers v Worthing 3-2
22 Bitterne Guild v Winchester City 7-1
Salisbury (1) v Royal Engs. Aldershot 1-2
23 Poole v Shaftesbury 3-2
Yeovil v Bournemouth (Ams) 5-0
24 Kingswood Rovers v Camerton 2-1
Radstock Town v Paulton Rovers 0-2
2r West Stanley v Seaham Harbour 1-3
11r Worksop Town v Rotherham Town 2-3
12r Belper Town (1) v Ilkeston United 0-3
13r Mansfield Mechanics v Mansfield Wesleyans 1-0
15r Great Yarmouth Town v Lowestoft Town 0-1
17r West Hampstead v Finchley 4-3

Qualifying Round Three

1 Bedlington United v Wallsend Park Villa 2-2
2 Seaham Harbour v Craghead United 5-1
3 Darlington v South Bank 2-3
4 Workington (1) v Penrith 6-0
5 Darwen v Haslingden 1-7
6 Tonge v Atherton 3-1
7 Tranmere Rovers v Shrewsbury Town 0-2
8 Cradley Heath St Luke's v Darlaston 3-1
9 Mexborough Town v Denaby United 1-1
10 Huddersfield Town v South Kirkby Colliery 5-2
11 Elsecar Main v Rotherham Town 1-3
12 Ilkeston United v Heanor United 1-0
13 Sutton Junction v Mansfield Mechanics 2-3
14 Kettering v Desborough Town 3-1
15 King's Lynn v Lowestoft Town 11-2
16 Ilford v Barking 3-3
17 Barnet Alston v West Hampstead 5-1
18 Wycombe Wanderers v Uxbridge 1-0
19 Redhill v Summerstown 1-2
20 Chatham v Northfleet United 1-4
21 Tunbridge Wells Rangers v Shoreham 2-0
22 Royal Engs. Aldershot v Bitterne Guild 0-2
23 Poole v Yeovil 1-4
24 Paulton Rovers v Kingswood Rovers 0-1 v
1r Wallsend Park Villa v Bedlington United 5-1
9r Denaby United v Mexborough Town 1-1x
16r Barking v Ilford 1-2
24r Paulton Rovers v Kingswood Rovers 2-1
9r2 Denaby United v Mexborough Town 0-1 N

Qualifying Round Four

Brentford v Luton Town 2-1
Carlisle United v Tonge 1-0
Clapton v Yeovil 6-1
Coventry City v Wrexham 3-0
Cradley Heath St Luke's v Chesterfield 1-2
Crewe Alexandra v Lincoln City 2-1
Croydon Common v Northfleet United 2-2
Doncaster Rovers v Mexborough Town 0-0
Exeter City v Nunhead 7-1
Haslingden v Accrington Stanley 3-4
Hastings & St Leonards U v Ilford 3-0
Huddersfield Town v Rotherham Town 2-2
Kettering v Mansfield Mechanics 1-1
King's Lynn v Shrewsbury Town 0-1
Leyton v Bitterne Guild 9-1
New Brompton v Oxford City 9-1
South Bank v Wallsend Park Villa 3-0
Southend United v Barnet Alston 5-2
Stockton v Bishop Auckland 1-5
Stoke v Ilkeston United 2-0
Summerstown v Wycombe Wanderers 1-3
Tunbridge Wells Rangers v Paulton Rovers 2-0
Watford v Bromley 8-1
Workington (1) v Seaham Harbour 3-1

1909/10 to 1910/11

r	Mansfield Mechanics v Kettering	1-1e
r	Mexborough Town v Doncaster Rovers	2-1
r	Northfleet United v Croydon Common	1-3
r	Rotherham Town v Huddersfield Town	2-1
r2	Mansfield Mechanics v Kettering	1-2 N

Qualifying Round Five

	Accrington Stanley v Brentford	1-0
	Bishop Auckland v South Bank	1-1
	Chesterfield v Crewe Alexandra	5-2
	Clapton v Shrewsbury Town	1-1
	Croydon Common v Leyton	0-1
	Kettering v Coventry City	0-5
	Mexborough Town v Carlisle United	0-0
	Rotherham Town v New Brompton	0-1
	Southend United v Hastings & St Leonards U	4-2
	Stoke v Exeter City	0-0
	Workington (1) v Tunbridge Wells Rangers	6-0
	Wycombe Wanderers v Watford	0-4
r	Carlisle United v Mexborough Town	4-0
r	Exeter City v Stoke	1-1e
r	Shrewsbury Town v Clapton	4-1
r	South Bank v Bishop Auckland	1-4
r2	Stoke v Exeter City	2-1 N

Round One

	Birmingham v Leicester Fosse	1-4
	Blackburn Rovers v Accrington Stanley	7-1
	Blackpool v Barnsley	1-1
	Bradford City v Notts County	4-2
	Bradford Park Avenue v Bishop Auckland	8-0
	Brighton & Hove Albion v Southampton	0-1
	Bristol City v Liverpool	2-0
	Burnley v Manchester United	2-0
	Bury v Glossop	2-1
	Chelsea v Hull City	2-1
	Chesterfield v Fulham	0-0
	Crystal Palace v Swindon Town	1-3
	Derby County v Millwall	5-0
	Gainsborough Trinity v Southend United	1-1
	Grimsby Town v Bristol Rovers	0-2
	Leyton v New Brompton	0-0
	Middlesbrough v Everton	1-1
	Northampton Town v Sheffield Wednesday	0-0
	Norwich City v Queen's Park Rangers	0-0
	Nottingham Forest v Sheffield United	3-2
	Oldham Athletic v Aston Villa	1-2
	Plymouth Argyle v Tottenham Hotspur	1-1
	Portsmouth v Shrewsbury Town	3-0
	Preston North End v Coventry City	1-2
	Stockport County v Bolton Wanderers	4-1
	Stoke v Newcastle United	1-1
	Sunderland v Leeds City	1-0
	West Bromwich Albion v Clapton Orient	2-0
	West Ham United v Carlisle United	1-1
	Wolverhampton Wan. v Reading	5-0
	Woolwich Arsenal v Watford	3-0
	Workington (1) v Manchester City	1-2
r	Barnsley v Blackpool	6-0
r	Everton v Middlesbrough	5-3
r	Fulham v Chesterfield	2-1
r	New Brompton v Leyton	2-2e
r	Newcastle United v Stoke	2-1
r	Queen's Park Rangers v Norwich City	3-0
r	Sheffield Wednesday v Northampton Town	0-1
r	Southend United v Gainsborough Trinity	1-0
r	Tottenham Hotspur v Plymouth Argyle	7-1
r	West Ham United v Carlisle United	5-0
r2	Leyton v New Brompton	1-0 N

Round Two

	Aston Villa v Derby County	6-1
	Barnsley v Bristol Rovers	4-0
	Bradford City v Blackburn Rovers	1-2
	Bristol City v West Bromwich Albion	1-1
	Chelsea v Tottenham Hotspur	0-1
	Everton v Woolwich Arsenal	5-0
	Leicester Fosse v Bury	3-2
	Newcastle United v Fulham	4-0
	Northampton Town v Nottingham Forest	0-0
	Portsmouth v Coventry City	0-1
	Southampton v Manchester City	0-5
	Southend United v Queen's Park Rangers	0-0
	Stockport County v Leyton	0-2
	Sunderland v Bradford Park Avenue	3-1
	Swindon Town v Burnley	2-0
	Wolverhampton Wan. v West Ham United	1-5
r	Nottingham Forest v Northampton Town	1-0
r	Queen's Park Rangers v Southend United	3-2
r	West Bromwich Albion v Bristol City	4-2

Round Three

	Aston Villa v Manchester City	1-2
	Barnsley v West Bromwich Albion	1-0
	Coventry City v Nottingham Forest	3-1
	Everton v Sunderland	2-0
	Leyton v Leicester Fosse	0-1
	Newcastle United v Blackburn Rovers	3-1
	Queen's Park Rangers v West Ham United	1-1
	Swindon Town v Tottenham Hotspur	3-2
r	West Ham United v Queen's Park Rangers	0-1e

Round Four

	Barnsley v Queen's Park Rangers	1-0
	Coventry City v Everton	0-2
	Newcastle United v Leicester Fosse	3-0
	Swindon Town v Manchester City	2-0

Semi Finals

	Barnsley v Everton	0-0 N
	Newcastle United v Swindon Town	2-0 N
r	Barnsley v Everton	3-0 N

Final

	Newcastle United v Barnsley	1-1 N
r	Newcastle United v Barnsley	2-0 N

1910/11

Extra Preliminary Round

1	Blaydon United v Walker Church Institute	2-1
5	Leyland v Fleetwood	wo/s
8	Birmingham Corp. Tramways v Bromsgrove Rovers	4-0
	Cannock Town v Coombs Wood	3-1
	Stourbridge v Cradley Heath St Luke's	5-4
	Wednesbury Old Athletic v Stafford Rangers	wo/s
	Willenhall Pickwick v Redditch	6-0
11	Atlas Hotel v Frickley Colliery	3-0
13	Castle Donnington Town v Mapperley	4-1
	Holwell Works v Sutton Town	2-3
	Leicester Nomads v Loughborough Corinthians	1-3
	Shepshed Albion v Notts Rangers	3-2
	Sneinton v New Hucknall Colliery	5-2
14	Bedford Town (1) v Fletton United	1-0

Preliminary Round

1	Blaydon United v Newcastle City	2-0
	Blyth Spartans v Willington Athletic	5-0
	Mickley v Ashington	0-2
	Newburn v Newcastle East End (2)	2-0
	Scotswood v Hebburn Argyle	6-0
	South Shields Adelaide v Bedlington United	3-0
	South Shields Parkside v Jarrow Caledonians	1-0
	Washington United v North Shields Athletic	0-6
2	Annfield Plain v Sunderland West End	3-1
	Houghton Rovers v Leadgate Park	3-0
	Seaham Villa v Shildon	0-4
	Spennymoor United v Craghead United	0-0
	Tow Law Town v Sunderland Royal Rovers	0-0
	West Auckland Town v Seaham Harbour	1-1
	West Stanley v Crook Town	1-4
3	Darlington St Augustines v Scarborough	1-1
	Grangetown Athletic v Stockton	0-1
	Hartlepools United v Horden Athletic	5-0
	Skinningrove United v Esh Winning Rangers	1-1
5	Barnoldswick United v Southport Park Villa	3-2
	Brierfield Swifts v Padiham	2-1
	Burnley Casuals v Portsmouth Rovers (Lancs)	1-1
	Colne v Kirkham	4-0
	Darwen v Clitheroe Central	wo/s
	Great Harwood v Rossendale United	2-3
	Haslingden v Leyland	2-1
	Southport Central v Chorley	wo/s
6	Chapel-en-le-Frith v Macclesfield Town	2-7
	Denton v Buxton	0-2
	Heywood United v Walkden Central	3-0
	Rochdale v Earlestown	2-1
	St Helens Recreation v Newton-le-Willows	4-1
	Tonge v Northern Nomads	5-0
7	Denbigh Town v Middlewich	2-3
	Druids v Chester	1-3
	Ironbridge United v New Brighton Tower Amateurs	2-3
	Lostock Gralam v Connah's Quay & Shotton	0-2
	Wellington Town v Nantwich	3-2
	Whitchurch v Harrowby	2-1
	Witton Albion v Tranmere Rovers	wo/s
	Wrexham v Wellington St George's	9-1
8	Bilston United v Hednesford Town	1-2
	Cannock Town v Wednesbury Old Athletic (2)	0-0
	Darlaston v Stourbridge	3-1
	Halesowen v Hereford City	3-1
	Kidderminster Harriers v Brierley Hill Alliance	1-1
	Nuneaton Town v Birmingham Corp. Tramways	2-1
	Walsall v Willenhall Swifts	1-0
	Willenhall Pickwick v Worcester City	2-3
9	Allerton Bywater Colliery v Doncaster St James	3-3
	Denaby United v Scunthorpe United	6-0
	Doncaster Rovers v Hull Day Street Old Boys	7-0
	Goole Town v Grimsby St John's	4-1
	Grimsby Rovers v Grimsby Rangers	3-2
	Hull Oriental v Mexborough Town	1-5
11	Atlas & Norfolk Works v Wath Athletic	0-2
	Atlas Hotel v Thorpe Hesley	3-1
	Hoyland Town v Birdwell	wo/s
	Parkgate & Rawmarsh Utd. v Hoyland Silkstone	0-1
	Rotherham County v Sheffield	9-2
	Rotherham Town v Monckton Athletic	3-0
	Silverwood Colliery v Elsecar Main	2-0
	Worksop Town v Hickleton Main	6-0
12	Alfreton Town v Belper Town (1)	0-2
	Blackwell Colliery v Ashbourne Town	2-0
	Coalville Town (1) v Newhall White Rose	4-1
	Gresley Rovers v Clay Cross Town	1-1
	Heanor United v Gresley Villa	2-3
	Newhall Swifts v Long Eaton St Helen's	2-4
	Pinxton v Ripley Town & Athletic	4-0
13	Basford United v Netherfield Rangers	6-2
	Castle Donnington Town v Mansfield Mechanics	2-0
	Horncastle United v Hinckley United (1)	1-2
	Loughborough Corinthians v Notts Olympic	3-0
	Market Harborough Town v Mansfield Town	0-5
	Shepshed Albion v Leicester Imperial	1-4
	Sneinton v Notts Jardines	1-1
	Sutton Town v Sutton Junction	2-2
14	Bedford Town (1) v Higham Ferrers YMCI	wo/s
	Daventry United (1) v Raunds Town	0-1
	Desborough Town v Wellingbro Redwell Stars	4-1
	Irthlingborough Town v Leagrave United	2-1
	Kempston v Biggleswade & District	0-6
	Peterborough City (1) v Kettering Working Men's	wo/s
	Peterborough G.N. Loco v Rushden Fosse	5-1
	Rushden Windmill v Kettering	2-4
16	Barking v Chelmsford	1-2
	Custom House v Upton Park	4-0
	Leytonstone v East Ham	5-2
	Romford (1) v South Weald	0-2
	Shoeburyness Garrison v Wanstead	4-0
	Walthamstow Grange v Newportonians	3-1
17	Chesham Generals v Leighton Town (1)	2-1
	Enfield v Luton Clarence	8-1
	Finchley v Tufnell Park	1-2
	St Albans City v Luton Celtic	5-1
	West Hampstead v Apsley	3-0
18	1st Grenadier Guards v Windsor & Eton	0-0
	City of Westminster v Fulham Amateurs	1-0
	Kilburn v Wycombe Wanderers	2-2
	Ravenscourt Amateurs v Maidenhead Norfolkians	3-1
	Shepherds Bush v Uxbridge	2-2
	Slough v Gramophone	1-1
19	Croydon (1) v Walton-on-Thames	3-2
	Dorking v Wimbledon	wo/s
	Godalming v Redhill	0-2
	Guildford v Nunhead	wo/s
	Summerstown v Old Kingstonians	3-3
	West Norwood v Tooting Graveney	2-3
	Woking v Hersham United	1-1
20	Ashford Railway Works v Maidstone United	1-2
	Catford Southend v Chatham	3-0
	Folkestone v Whitstable	2-3
	Gravesend United v Depot Batt. Royal Engrs	1-0
	Northfleet United v Dartford	0-1
	Orpington v Plumstead St John's	2-3
	Sheppey United v Woolwich Polytechnic	4-1
22	Basingstoke v Salisbury (1)	0-1
	Cowes (2) v Bitterne Guild	1-1
23	Bournemouth (Ams) v Yeovil	0-2
	Longfleet St Mary's v Shaftesbury	6-1
24	Camerton v Trowbridge Town	1-1
	Cardiff City v Bath City	3-1
	Clevedon v Mardy	2-2
	Melksham Town v Paulton Rovers	1-0
	Welton Rovers v Frome Town	2-2
2r	Craghead United v Spennymoor United	1-2
r	Seaham Harbour v West Auckland Town	2-3
r	Sunderland Royal Rovers v Tow Law Town	2-1
3r	Esh Winning Rangers v Skinningrove United	wo/s
r	Scarborough v Darlington St Augustines	5-1
5r	Portsmouth Rovers (Lancs) v Burnley Casuals	4-0
8r	Brierley Hill Alliance v Kidderminster Harriers	1-3
r	Wednesbury Old Athletic v Cannock Town	2-4
9r	Allerton Bywater Colliery v Doncaster St James	wo/s
12r	Clay Cross Town v Gresley Rovers	3-3e
13r	Notts Jardines v Sneinton	1-1
r	Sutton Junction v Sutton Town	3-2
18r	Gramophone v Slough	1-0
r	Uxbridge v Shepherds Bush	3-2e
r	Windsor & Eton v 1st Grenadier Guards	2-3
r	Wycombe Wanderers v Kilburn	2-1e
19r	Old Kingstonians v Summerstown	5-0
r	Woking v Hersham United	wo/s
22r	Bitterne Guild v Cowes (2)	0-3
24r	Frome Town v Welton Rovers	3-1
r	Mardy v Clevedon	2-1
r	Trowbridge Town v Camerton	1-2
12r2	Gresley Rovers v Clay Cross Town	0-2
13r2	Notts Jardines v Sneinton	6-1

Qualifying Round One

1	Blaydon United v Ashington	0-4
	Newburn v Blyth Spartans	1-0
	Scotswood v North Shields Athletic	1-1
	South Shields Adelaide v South Shields Parkside	2-2
2	Annfield Plain v West Auckland Town	1-5
	Spennymoor United v Shildon	0-0
	Stanley United v Houghton Rovers	1-0
	Sunderland Royal Rovers v Crook Town	6-0
3	Bishop Auckland v Scarborough	2-0
	Darlington v Hartlepools United	1-1
	Willington Temperance v Esh Winning Rangers	2-1
	Wingate Albion Comrades v Stockton	3-1
4	Barrow St Luke's v Kendal Swifts	1-0
	Bowness Rovers v Wigton Harriers	1-3
	Penrith v Barrow Novocastrians	2-0

1910/11

	Windermere v Barrow	0-7
5	Barnoldswick United v Portsmouth Rovers (Lancs)	3-0
	Brierfield Swifts v Haslingden	1-5
	Colne v Rossendale United	1-0
	Southport Central v Darwen	1-0
6	Heywood United v Tonge	3-0
	Hooley Hill v Buxton	1-1
	St Helens Recreation v Macclesfield Town	3-1
	St Helens Town v Rochdale	1-2
7	Chester v Wrexham	3-0
	Middlewich v Wellington Town	wo/s
	New Brighton Tower Ams v Connah's Quay&Shotton	3-1
	Witton Albion v Whitchurch	2-1
8	Cannock Town v Darlaston	1-3
	Hednesford Town v Walsall	4-3
	Nuneaton Town v Halesowen	1-1
	Worcester City v Kidderminster Harriers	3-1
9	Allerton Bywater Colliery v Denaby United	1-1
	Doncaster Rovers v Grimsby Rovers	5-4
	Goole Town v Castleford Town	3-1
	Mexborough Town v York City (1)	4-2
10	Huddersfield Town v Horsforth	6-0
	South Kirkby Colliery v Heckmondwike	2-0
11	Atlas Hotel v Wath Athletic	0-2
	Rotherham Town v Rotherham County	2-1
	Silverwood Colliery v Hoyland Town	0-2
	Worksop Town v Hoyland Silkstone	8-0
12	Coalville Town (1) v Clay Cross Town	2-2
	Long Eaton St Helen's v Blackwell Colliery	2-5
	Pinxton v Gresley Villa	1-0
	South Normanton St Michael's v Belper Town (1)	2-1
13	Basford United v Sutton Junction	5-1
	Castle Donnington Town v Hinckley United (1)	1-4
	Mansfield Town v Loughborough Corinthians	3-0
	Notts Jardines v Leicester Imperial	0-1
14	Biggleswade & District v Irthlingborough Town	8-0
	Desborough Town v Bedford Town (1)	3-1
	Peterborough City (1) v Kettering	0-2
	Raunds Town v Peterborough G.N. Loco	4-3
15	Cambridge Utd. (1) v King's Lynn	3-1
	Harwich & Parkeston v Colchester Town	1-2
	Kirkley v Cromer	6-3
16	3rd Grenadier Guards v Chelmsford	3-2
	Shoeburyness Garrison v Custom House	0-0
	South Weald v Leytonstone	7-3
	Walthamstow Grange v Ilford	0-4
17	Chesham Town v Tufnell Park	2-2
	St Albans City v Barnet Alston	2-1
	West Hampstead v Enfield	1-1
	Wood Green Town v Chesham Generals	9-3
18	Gramophone v Aylesbury United	2-2
	Maidenhead v 1st Grenadier Guards	1-1
	Uxbridge v Ravenscourt Amateurs	0-1
	Wycombe Wanderers v City of Westminster	1-1
19	Dorking v Redhill	2-2
	Farncombe v Tooting Graveney	2-3
	Guildford v Croydon (1)	4-0
	Old Kingstonians v Woking	7-2
20	Catford Southend v Sheppey United	5-0
	Gravesend United v Plumstead St John's	1-0
	Maidstone United v Dartford	2-3
	Whitstable v Deptford Invicta	4-3
21	Horsham v Shoreham	2-2
	Southwick v Seaford	7-2
	Tunbridge Wells Rangers v Worthing	12-1
22	Cowes (2) v Winchester City	1-1
	Eastleigh Athletic v Salisbury (1)	2-0
	Royal Engs. Aldershot v Farnham	2-0
	Ryde v Southampton Cambridge	1-3
23	Bournemouth Gasworks Athletic v Longfleet St Mary's	4-3
	Green Waves (Plymouth) v Torquay Town	0-2
	Poole v Yeovil	4-0
	Weymouth v Boscombe	3-4
24	Camerton v Street	3-1
	Cardiff City v Merthyr Town	0-1
	Chippenham Town v Melksham Town	2-0
	Mardy v Frome Town	3-0 v
1r	North Shields Athletic v Scotswood	2-1
r	South Shields Parkside v South Shields Adelaide	2-3
2r	Shildon v Spennymoor United	3-0
3r	Hartlepools United v Darlington	0-1
6r	Buxton v Hooley Hill	2-4
8r	Halesowen v Nuneaton Town	2-1
9r	Denaby United v Allerton Bywater Colliery	6-1
12r	Clay Cross Town v Coalville Town (1)	0-0 d
16r	Custom House v Shoeburyness Garrison	1-1
17r	Enfield v West Hampstead	5-0
r	Tufnell Park v Chesham Town	5-0
18r	1st Grenadier Guards v Maidenhead	8-1
r	Aylesbury United v Gramophone	0-3
r	Wycombe Wanderers v City of Westminster	4-2
19r	Redhill v Dorking	5-0
21r	Shoreham v Horsham	3-1
22r	Winchester City v Cowes (2)	1-3
24r	Frome Town v Mardy	1-2
16r2	Custom House v Shoeburyness Garrison	2-0 N

Qualifying Round Two

1	Newburn v Ashington	3-1
	North Shields Athletic v South Shields Adelaide	0-0
2	Stanley United v Shildon	1-2
	West Auckland Town v Sunderland Royal Rovers	4-0
3	Bishop Auckland v Willington Temperance	3-0
	Darlington v Wingate Albion Comrades	1-1
4	Barrow St Luke's v Barrow	2-3
	Wigton Harriers v Penrith	0-1
5	Colne v Southport Central	2-0
	Haslingden v Barnoldswick United	6-0
6	Heywood United v Rochdale	3-4
	Hooley Hill v St Helens Recreation	0-0
7	New Brighton Tower Amateurs v Chester	1-3
	Witton Albion v Middlewich	4-0
8	Hednesford Town v Darlaston	3-1
	Worcester City v Halesowen	2-0
9	Denaby United v Goole Town	4-0
	Doncaster Rovers v Mexborough Town	1-0
10	Huddersfield Town v Mirfield United	2-0
	Knaresborough v South Kirkby Colliery	1-4
11	Hoyland Town v Worksop Town	2-0
	Rotherham Town v Wath Athletic	2-1
12	Blackwell Colliery v South Normanton St Michael's	1-1
	Pinxton v Clay Cross Town	0-1
13	Basford United v Mansfield Town	2-2
	Leicester Imperial v Hinckley United (1)	2-3
14	Biggleswade & District v Kettering	1-2
	Raunds Town v Desborough Town	1-1
15	Cambridge Utd. (1) v Lowestoft Town	2-1
	Kirkley v Colchester Town	3-1
16	3rd Grenadier Guards v Ilford	1-5
	South Weald v Custom House	4-3
17	Enfield v Wood Green Town	3-2
	St Albans City v Tufnell Park	0-0
18	Ravenscourt Amateurs v Gramophone	2-0
	Wycombe Wanderers v 1st Grenadier Guards	0-1
19	Guildford v Redhill	1-7
	Tooting Graveney v Old Kingstonians	0-9
20	Dartford v Whitstable	2-1
	Gravesend United v Catford Southend	0-2
21	Newhaven v Tunbridge Wells Rangers	0-6
	Shoreham v Southwick	0-1
22	Cowes (2) v Southampton Cambridge	0-1
	Eastleigh Athletic v Royal Engs. Aldershot	1-2
23	Poole v Boscombe	0-0
	Torquay Town v Bournemouth Gasworks Athletic	1-1
24	Camerton v Mardy	3-2
	Merthyr Town v Chippenham Town	5-2
1r	North Shields Athletic v South Shields Adelaide	3-3
3r	Darlington v Wingate Albion Comrades	3-3
6r	St Helens Recreation v Hooley Hill	4-0
12r	South Normanton St Michael's v Blackwell Colliery	0-2
13r	Basford United v Mansfield Town	1-3
14r	Desborough Town v Raunds Town	3-0
17r	Tufnell Park v St Albans City	3-1
23r	Bournemouth Gasworks Athletic v Torquay Town	0-1e
r	Poole v Boscombe	1-4
1r2	North Shields Athletic v South Shields Adelaide	1-0
3r2	Darlington v Wingate Albion Comrades	2-1

Qualifying Round Three

1	Newburn v North Shields Athletic	1-0
2	West Auckland Town v Shildon	3-1 v
3	Darlington v Bishop Auckland	2-0
4	Barrow v Penrith	3-1
5	Haslingden v Colne	3-3
6	Rochdale v St Helens Recreation	1-0
7	Chester v Witton Albion	7-1
8	Worcester City v Hednesford Town	2-1
9	Denaby United v Doncaster Rovers	2-1
10	South Kirkby Colliery v Huddersfield Town	1-5
11	Rotherham Town v Hoyland Town	1-0
12	Blackwell Colliery v Clay Cross Town	4-1
13	Hinckley United (1) v Mansfield Town	1-2
14	Kettering v Desborough Town	0-1
15	Kirkley v Cambridge Utd. (1)	2-2
16	Ilford v South Weald	4-1
17	Enfield v Tufnell Park	4-0
18	1st Grenadier Guards v Ravenscourt Amateurs	4-0
19	Redhill v Old Kingstonians	2-2
20	Dartford v Catford Southend	1-1
21	Tunbridge Wells Rangers v Southwick	5-2
22	Royal Engs. Aldershot v Southampton Cambridge	3-2
23	Torquay Town v Boscombe	1-0
24	Camerton v Merthyr Town	0-3
2r	West Auckland Town v Shildon	1-1x
5r	Colne v Haslingden	4-1 D
15r	Cambridge Utd. (1) v Kirkley	4-0
19r	Old Kingstonians v Redhill	0-2
20r	Dartford v Catford Southend	0-2
2r2	Shildon v West Auckland Town	2-1

Qualifying Round Four

	Carlisle United v Newburn	3-0
	Catford Southend v 1st Grenadier Guards	1-0
	Chesterfield v Desborough Town	1-0
	Clapton v Redhill	0-3 v
	Crewe Alexandra v Chester	4-3
	Croydon Common v London Caledonians	7-0
	Darlington v Shildon	5-3
	Enfield v Southend United	3-3
	Haslingden v Accrington Stanley	0-1
	Huddersfield Town v Lincoln City	1-1
	Ilkeston United v Gainsborough Trinity	0-0
	Luton Town v Cambridge Utd. (1)	9-1
	Mansfield Town v Blackwell Colliery	0-1
	Nelson v Barrow	5-0
	Oxford City v Torquay Town	2-2
	Reading v Exeter City	1-1
	Rochdale v Stockport County	0-0
	Rotherham Town v Denaby United	1-1
	Royal Engs. Aldershot v New Brompton	2-2
	Shrewsbury Town v Merthyr Town	1-0
	Stoke v Worcester City	7-0
	Tunbridge Wells Rangers v Bromley	3-0
	Watford v Ilford	3-2
	Workington (1) v Wallsend Park Villa	1-0
r	Exeter City v Reading	1-0
r	Gainsborough Trinity v Ilkeston United	0-0
r	Lincoln City v Huddersfield Town	1-0
r	New Brompton v Royal Engs. Aldershot	7-0
r	Redhill v Clapton	2-2
r	Rotherham Town v Denaby United	2-1
r	Southend United v Enfield	3-1
r	Stockport County v Rochdale	0-0
r	Torquay Town v Oxford City	3-1
r2	Clapton v Redhill	4-0
r2	Gainsborough Trinity v Ilkeston United	5-0 N
r2	Rochdale v Stockport County	1-0 N

Qualifying Round Five

	Accrington Stanley v Torquay Town	4-0
	Blackwell Colliery v Darlington	1-6
	Crewe Alexandra v Carlisle United	1-1
	Croydon Common v Workington (1)	3-1
	Gainsborough Trinity v Shrewsbury Town	4-0
	Nelson v Exeter City	3-4
	New Brompton v Catford Southend	4-1
	Rochdale v Luton Town	1-1
	Rotherham Town v Chesterfield	1-2
	Southend United v Tunbridge Wells Rangers	1-0
	Stoke v Lincoln City	4-0
	Watford v Clapton	6-0
r	Carlisle United v Crewe Alexandra	3-4
r	Luton Town v Rochdale	3-2

Round One

	Birmingham v Oldham Athletic	1-1
	Blackburn Rovers v Southend United	5-1
	Bolton Wanderers v Chesterfield	0-2
	Bradford Park Avenue v Queen's Park Rangers	5-3
	Brentford v Preston North End	0-1
	Bristol City v Crewe Alexandra	0-3
	Bristol Rovers v Hull City	0-0
	Burnley v Exeter City	2-0
	Chelsea v Leyton	0-0
	Clapton Orient v Woolwich Arsenal	1-2
	Crystal Palace v Everton	0-4
	Derby County v Plymouth Argyle	2-1
	Grimsby Town v Croydon Common	3-0 v
	Leeds City v Brighton & Hove Albion	1-3
	Leicester Fosse v Southampton	3-1
	Liverpool v Gainsborough Trinity	3-2
	Manchester United v Blackpool	2-1
	Middlesbrough v Glossop	1-0
	New Brompton v Bradford City	0-1
	Newcastle United v Bury	6-1
	Northampton Town v Luton Town	5-1
	Norwich City v Sunderland	3-1
	Portsmouth v Aston Villa	1-4
	Sheffield United v Darlington	0-1
	Sheffield Wednesday v Coventry City	1-2
	Stoke v Manchester City	1-2
	Swindon Town v Notts County	3-1
	Tottenham Hotspur v Millwall	2-1
	Watford v Barnsley	0-2
	West Bromwich Albion v Fulham	4-1
	West Ham United v Nottingham Forest	2-1
	Wolverhampton Wan. v Accrington Stanley	2-0
r	Grimsby Town v Croydon Common	8-1
r	Hull City v Bristol Rovers	1-0e
r	Leyton v Chelsea	0-2
r	Oldham Athletic v Birmingham	2-0

Round Two

	Blackburn Rovers v Tottenham Hotspur	0-0
	Bradford City v Norwich City	2-1
	Brighton & Hove Albion v Coventry City	0-0
	Burnley v Barnsley	2-0
	Chelsea v Chesterfield	4-1
	Crewe Alexandra v Grimsby Town	1-5
	Darlington v Bradford Park Avenue	2-1
	Derby County v West Bromwich Albion	2-0
	Everton v Liverpool	2-1
	Hull City v Oldham Athletic	1-0
	Manchester United v Aston Villa	2-1
	Middlesbrough v Leicester Fosse	0-0
	Newcastle United v Northampton Town	1-1
	Swindon Town v Woolwich Arsenal	1-0
	West Ham United v Preston North End	3-0
	Wolverhampton Wan. v Manchester City	1-0
r	Coventry City v Brighton & Hove Albion	2-0
r	Leicester Fosse v Middlesbrough	1-2e
r	Newcastle United v Northampton Town	1-0
r	Tottenham Hotspur v Blackburn Rovers	0-2

Round Three

	Bradford City v Grimsby Town	1-0
	Burnley v Coventry City	5-0
	Darlington v Swindon Town	0-3

1910/11 to 1911/12

	Derby County v Everton	5-0
	Middlesbrough v Blackburn Rovers	0-3
	Newcastle United v Hull City	3-2
	West Ham United v Manchester United	2-1
	Wolverhampton Wan. v Chelsea	0-2

Round Four

	Bradford City v Burnley	1-0
	Chelsea v Swindon Town	3-1
	Newcastle United v Derby County	4-0
	West Ham United v Blackburn Rovers	2-3

Semi Finals

	Bradford City v Blackburn Rovers	3-0 N
	Newcastle United v Chelsea	3-0 N

Final

	Bradford City v Newcastle United	0-0 N
r	Bradford City v Newcastle United	1-0 N

1911/12

Extra Preliminary Round

1	Blyth Spartans v Washington United	1-0
	Jarrow Croft v Wallsend Elm Villa	2-1
	New Hartley Rovers v South Shields Parkside	2-2
	Newcastle City v Blaydon United	2-1
	South Shields Albion v Jarrow Caledonians	0-2
	Walker Church Institute v Hebburn Argyle	0-1
	Willington Athletic v Mickley	1-1
2	Annfield Plain v Dipton United	2-0
	Grangetown (Sunderland) v Craghead United	1-7
	Haswell v Tow Law Town	2-0
	Seaham Villa v Crook Town	0-3
5	Brierfield Swifts v Breightmet United	1-1
	Great Harwood v Darwen	0-2
	Leyland v Chorley	1-3
	Padiham v Tottington	3-0
6	Widnes County v Alderley Edge United	3-1
7	Whitchurch v South Liverpool	0-2
	Wrexham v Rhyl	11-0
8	Bilston United v Cannock Town	2-1
	Coombs Wood v Birmingham Corp. Tramways	2-5
	Dudley v Cradley Heath St Luke's	2-1
	Kidderminster Harriers v Atherstone Town	2-0
	Redditch v Willenhall Swifts	0-1
	Stafford Rangers v Wednesbury Old Athletic (2)	3-1
	Stourbridge v Bromsgrove Rovers	2-0
9	Allerton Bywater Colliery v Cleethorpes Town	0-5
	North Lindsey Midgets v Hull Day Street Old Boys	1-2
	Reckitt's (Hull) v Driffield Town	2-1
11	Atlas & Norfolk Works v Parkgate & Rawmarsh Utd.	3-2
	Redfearns v Grimethorpe United	2-1
	Tankersley v Royston Midland Institute	0-0
12	Coalville Town (1) v Brimington Hotspur	3-0
	Gresley Colliery v Overseal Swifts	2-1
	Gresley Rovers v Burton Town	3-0
	New Whittington Exchange v Shobnall Villa	1-2
13	Castle Donnington Town v Boston Town (1)	3-2
	Eastwood Rangers v Notts Jardines	6-1
	Loughborough Corinthians v Stanton Hill Victoria	1-1
	Mansfield Mechanics v New Hucknall Colliery	3-0
	Market Harborough Town v Sneinton	3-1
	Netherfield Rangers v Horncastle United	8-0
	Notts Olympic v Sutton Junction	0-7
	Notts Rangers v Sutton Town	0-6
14	Fletton United v Stamford	2-0
16	2nd Coldstream Guards v Grays Athletic	0-0
	Leytonstone v Newportonians	1-0
	Romford (1) v Barking	1-2
	Shoeburyness Garrison v East Ham	0-1
	Walthamstow Grange v Chelmsford	5-1
19	Farncombe v Kingston-on-Thames	0-2
	Surrey Wanderers v Walton-on-Thames	2-0
20	Bronze Athletic v Woolwich Royal Artillery	wo/s
	Deptford Invicta v Ashford Railway Works	1-2
	Sittingbourne v Ramsgate Town	6-0
24	Cardiff Corinthians v Barry	2-1
	Llanelli v Milford Town	1-1
1r	Mickley v Willington Athletic	3-1
r	South Shields Parkside v New Hartley Rovers	2-1
5r	Breightmet United v Brierfield Swifts	2-1
11r	Royston Midland Institute v Tankersley	1-0
13r	Stanton Hill Victoria v Loughborough Corinthians	1-0
16r	Grays Athletic v 2nd Coldstream Guards	0-1
24r	Milford Town v Llanelli	2-3

Preliminary Round

1	Ashington v Mickley	5-2
	Bedlington United v Jarrow Croft	1-2
	Blyth Spartans v South Shields Parkside	2-1
	Hebburn Argyle v Jarrow Caledonians	0-0
	Scotswood v Newcastle City	1-1
2	Annfield Plain v Horden Athletic	0-0
	Haswell v Craghead United	1-0
	Seaham Harbour v Crook Town	1-1
	West Stanley v Esh Winning Rangers	3-0
3	Darlington St Augustines v South Bank	1-2
	Grangetown Athletic v Skinningrove United	5-0
	Spennymoor United v Saltburn	3-0
	Stockton v Eston United	0-0
5	Darwen v Chorley	1-1
	Padiham v Breightmet United	5-2
	Rossendale United v Portsmouth Rovers (Lancs)	8-0
6	Buxton v Altrincham	1-2
	Chapel-en-le-Frith v Earlestown	1-3
	Denton v Newton Heath Athletic	4-2
	Hurst v Macclesfield Town	6-1
	Hyde v Walkden Central	2-2
	St Helens Town v Widnes County	2-1
7	Connah's Quay & Shotton v Northern Nomads	0-2
	Harrowby v Wrexham	1-1
	Nantwich v Wellington St George's	3-2
	South Liverpool v Lostock Gralam	1-0
8	Bilston United v Dudley	0-4
	Brierley Hill Alliance v Stafford Rangers	6-2
	Kidderminster Harriers v Stourbridge	3-2
	Nuneaton Town v Willenhall Swifts	3-1
	Willenhall Pickwick v Birmingham Corp. Tramways	2-1
9	Grimsby St John's v Castleford Town	1-8
	Hull Day Street Old Boys v Grimsby Rovers	0-1
	Reckitt's (Hull) v Cleethorpes Town	3-3
	York City (1) v Scunthorpe United	1-2
10	Leeds United (1) v Morley	1-3
	Rothwell White Rose v Calverley	2-2
	West Vale Ramblers v Thornhill Lees Albion	1-1
11	Hickleton Main v Silverwood Colliery	3-1
	Hoyland Silkstone v Royston Midland Institute	0-2
	Redfearns v Rotherham County	2-2
	Sheffield v Atlas & Norfolk Works	1-2
12	Ashbourne Town v Shobnall Villa	1-1
	Coalville Town (1) v Ripley Town & Athletic	2-2
	Gresley Colliery v Heanor United	wo/s
	Gresley Rovers v Newhall Swifts	1-0
13	Eastwood Rangers v Castle Donnington Town	6-0
	Market Harborough Town v Sutton Town	1-1
	Netherfield Rangers v Mansfield Mechanics	0-4
	Stanton Hill Victoria v Sutton Junction	1-2
14	Daventry United (1) v Rushden Windmill	1-1
	Irthlingborough Town v Fletton United	2-0
	Peterborough City (1) v Peterborough G.N. Loco	1-0
	Wellingbro Redwell Stars v Bedford Town (1)	4-1
16	2nd Coldstream Guards v Leytonstone	1-1
	3rd Grenadier Guards v East Ham	1-0
	Walthamstow Grange v Barking	1-3
17	Barnet (2) v Luton Clarence	2-4
	Barnet Alston v Tufnell Spartan	1-1
	Chesham Generals v Luton Crusaders	0-2
	Finchley v Chesham Town	0-0
18	Fulham Amateurs v Maidenhead	1-4
	Hanwell v Southall	1-2
	Kilburn v City of Westminster	6-2
	Marlow v Shepherds Bush	0-1
	Staines Town v Maidenhead Norfolkians	1-1
	Windsor & Eton v Uxbridge	3-3
19	Croydon (1) v Summerstown	2-2
	Dorking v Woking	3-2
	Nunhead v Kingston-on-Thames	9-0
	Redhill v Sutton United	6-0
	Surrey Wanderers v Godalming	1-1
	West Norwood v Hersham United	3-1
20	Ashford Railway Works v Northfleet United	2-1
	Bronze Athletic v Woolwich Polytechnic	wo/s
	Chatham v Sheppey United	2-0
	Sittingbourne v Maidstone United	3-1
21	East Grinstead v St Leonards Amateurs	1-3
	Seaford v Vernon Athletic	0-3
	Worthing v Tunbridge Wells (1)	1-1
22	Bitterne Guild v Farnham	9-0
	South Farnborough Ath. v 1st Kings Royal Rifles	0-5
23	Portland v Frome Town	1-2
24	Bath City v Weston-Super-Mare	3-0
	Cardiff City v Cardiff Corinthians	3-0
	Llanelli v Swindon Victoria	2-3
	Welton Rovers v Paulton Rovers	3-3
1r	Jarrow Caledonians v Hebburn Argyle	0-4
r	Newcastle City v Scotswood	3-1
2r	Crook Town v Seaham Harbour	1-0
r	Horden Athletic v Annfield Plain	1-1
3r	Eston United v Stockton	2-1
5r	Chorley v Darwen	2-3
6r	Walkden Central v Hyde	1-0
7r	Wrexham v Harrowby	wo/s
9r	Cleethorpes Town v Reckitt's (Hull)	4-0
10r	Calverley v Rothwell White Rose	2-0
r	Thornhill Lees Albion v West Vale Ramblers	2-0
11r	Rotherham County v Redfearns	5-0
12r	Ripley Town & Athletic v Coalville Town (1)	1-0
r	Shobnall Villa v Ashbourne Town	2-1
13r	Sutton Town v Market Harborough Town	5-0
14r	Rushden Windmill v Daventry United (1)	wo/s
16r	Leytonstone v 2nd Coldstream Guards	2-1
17r	Barnet Alston v Tufnell Spartan	9-0
r	Chesham Town v Finchley	2-1
18r	Maidenhead Norfolkians v Staines Town	0-1
r	Uxbridge v Windsor & Eton	5-3
19r	Godalming v Surrey Wanderers	1-3
r	Summerstown v Croydon (1)	4-0
21r	Tunbridge Wells (1) v Worthing	1-1
24r	Paulton Rovers v Welton Rovers	2-4e
2r2	Annfield Plain v Horden Athletic	1-0 N
21r2	Tunbridge Wells (1) v Worthing	1-0

Qualifying Round One

1	Jarrow Croft v Ashington	0-0
	Newcastle City v Blyth Spartans	3-2
	South Shields v Newburn	1-0
	Wallsend Park Villa v Hebburn Argyle	2-2
2	Annfield Plain v Wingate Albion Comrades	1-1
	Stanley United v Crook Town	0-1
	West Auckland Town v Sunderland Royal Rovers	3-1
	West Stanley v Haswell	4-2
3	Bishop Auckland v Eston United	3-2
	Scarborough v Spennymoor United	1-3
	Shildon v Grangetown Athletic	2-1
	Willington v South Bank	7-0
4	Barrow v Penrith	7-0
	Kendal Swifts v Barrow St Luke's	3-1
	Wigton Athletic v Workington (1)	wo/s
	Wigton Harriers v Windermere	2-2
5	Colne v Barnoldswick United	5-0
	Nelson v Haslingden	3-2
	Rossendale United v Darwen	2-1
	Southport Central v Padiham	3-0
6	Heywood United v Denton	2-0
	St Helens Recreation v Hurst	2-0
	St Helens Town v Altrincham	0-2
	Walkden Central v Earlestown	3-1
7	Chester v Shrewsbury Town	6-1
	Nantwich v South Liverpool	0-3
	Northern Nomads v New Brighton Tower Amateurs	2-0
	Wrexham v Witton Albion	4-2
8	Brierley Hill Alliance v Nuneaton Town	2-1
	Hednesford Town v Dudley	3-2
	Kidderminster Harriers v Worcester City	1-0
	Willenhall Pickwick v Darlaston	0-1
9	Castleford Town v Doncaster Rovers	1-0
	Denaby United v Grimsby Rovers	3-1
	Goole Town v Cleethorpes Town	3-3
	Mexborough Town v Scunthorpe United	3-2
10	Calverley v Morley	0-1
	Knaresborough v Heckmondwike	1-0
	Mirfield United v Horsforth	3-0
	South Kirkby Colliery v Thornhill Lees Albion	3-0
11	Hickleton Main v Rotherham Town	0-5
	Royston Midland Institute v Hoyland Town	1-1
	Wath Athletic v Rotherham County	0-1
	Worksop Town v Atlas & Norfolk Works	5-1
12	Blackwell Colliery v South Normanton Colliery	3-0
	Gresley Colliery v Shobnall Villa	wo/s
	Pinxton v Ilkeston United	5-3
	Ripley Town & Athletic v Gresley Rovers	4-2
13	Eastwood Rangers v Basford United	4-0
	Hinckley United (1) v Mansfield Town	1-0
	Leicester Imperial v Sutton Junction	1-2
	Sutton Town v Mansfield Mechanics	2-3
14	Desborough Town v Biggleswade & District	3-0
	Irthlingborough Town v Wellingbro Redwell Stars	1-0
	Raunds Town v Kettering	2-3
	Rushden Windmill v Peterborough City (1)	1-5
15	Cromer v Cambridge Utd. (1)	4-0
	Harwich & Parkeston v Colchester Town	3-1
	Kirkley v Gorleston	3-1
	Lowestoft Town v King's Lynn	0-1
16	1st Grenadier Guards v Clapton	2-1
	3rd Grenadier Guards v Ilford	0-1
	Custom House v Leytonstone	2-1
	South Weald v Barking	2-0
17	Barnet Alston v Luton Clarence	1-0
	Chesham Town v St Albans City	2-2
	Enfield v Wood Green Town	3-0
	Tufnell Park v Luton Crusaders	2-0
18	Kilburn v Shepherds Bush	2-1
	Maidenhead v Staines Town	1-1
	Ravenscourt Amateurs v Southall	1-4
	Uxbridge v Wycombe Wanderers	1-4
19	Dorking v West Norwood	2-3
	Redhill v Summerstown	1-0
	Surrey Wanderers v Nunhead	2-4
	Tooting v Guildford	2-2
20	Bronze Athletic v Whitstable	1-5
	Catford Southend v Dartford	2-0
	Chatham v Ashford Railway Works	7-2
	Sittingbourne v Gravesend United	2-1
21	Shoreham v Vernon Athletic	1-2
	Southwick v Newhaven	3-4
	St Leonards Amateurs v Horsham	0-0
	Tunbridge Wells (1) v Tunbridge Wells Rangers	1-2
22	Basingstoke v 1st Kings Royal Rifles	0-2
	Bitterne Guild v Cowes (2)	3-0
	Eastleigh Athletic v Southampton Cambridge	10-1
	Royal Engs. Aldershot v Ryde	6-0
23	Bournemouth Gasworks Athletic v Street	0-0
	Frome Town v Yeovil	2-0
	Trowbridge Town v Torquay Town	1-0
	Weymouth v Longfleet St Mary's	2-0
24	Bath City v Camerton	0-2
	Cardiff City v Mardy	2-0
	Chippenham Town v Swindon Victoria	4-1
	Merthyr Town v Welton Rovers	3-1
1r	Ashington v Jarrow Croft	0-3
r	Hebburn Argyle v Wallsend Park Villa	2-3
2r	Wingate Albion Comrades v Annfield Plain	2-0
4r	Windermere v Wigton Harriers	wo/s
9r	Cleethorpes Town v Goole Town	2-2
11r	Hoyland Town v Royston Midland Institute	2-3
17r	St Albans City v Chesham Town	3-0

1911/12 to 1912/13

18r Staines Town v Maidenhead 0-3
19r Guildford v Tooting 1-0
21r Horsham v St Leonards Amateurs 2-4
23r Street v Bournemouth Gasworks Athletic 1-0
9r2 Cleethorpes Town v Goole Town 2-1 N

Qualifying Round Two

1 Jarrow Croft v Wallsend Park Villa 1-1
South Shields v Newcastle City 0-2
2 West Stanley v Crook Town 2-2
Wingate Albion Comrades v West Auckland Town 1-1
3 Bishop Auckland v Spennymoor United 3-1
Shildon v Willington 1-0
4 Barrow v Windermere 4-1
Kendal Swifts v Wigton Athletic 8-2
5 Nelson v Colne 0-2
Southport Central v Rossendale United 4-1
6 Altrincham v St Helens Recreation 2-2
Walkden Central v Heywood United 2-0 D
7 Chester v Northern Nomads 4-0
Wrexham v South Liverpool 4-3
8 Darlaston v Brierley Hill Alliance 3-0
Hednesford Town v Kidderminster Harriers 1-0
9 Castleford Town v Cleethorpes Town 1-0
Denaby United v Mexborough Town 0-1
10 Mirfield United v Morley 0-0
South Kirkby Colliery v Knaresborough 2-0
11 Rotherham County v Royston Midland Institute 3-0
Rotherham Town v Worksop Town 5-1
12 Blackwell Colliery v Pinxton 4-1
Ripley Town & Athletic v Gresley Colliery 1-0
13 Eastwood Rangers v Mansfield Mechanics 0-2
Sutton Junction v Hinckley United (1) 3-1
14 Desborough Town v Kettering 1-1
Irthlingborough Town v Peterborough City (1) 0-4
15 Cromer v Kirkley 3-0
King's Lynn v Harwich & Parkeston 1-1
16 Custom House v South Weald 6-1
Ilford v 1st Grenadier Guards 5-2
17 St Albans City v Barnet Alston 1-2
Tufnell Park v Enfield 2-2
18 Maidenhead v Kilburn 2-0
Wycombe Wanderers v Southall 1-1
19 Nunhead v Redhill 5-1
West Norwood v Guildford 5-1
20 Catford Southend v Chatham 2-1
Whitstable v Sittingbourne 3-2
21 St Leonards Amateurs v Vernon Athletic 1-0
Tunbridge Wells Rangers v Newhaven 8-0
22 Eastleigh Athletic v Bitterne Guild 1-3
Royal Engs. Aldershot v 1st Kings Royal Rifles 0-2
23 Frome Town v Street 3-0
Weymouth v Trowbridge Town 3-3
24 Camerton v Chippenham Town 3-0
Merthyr Town v Cardiff City 1-1
1r Wallsend Park Villa v Jarrow Croft 0-3
2r Crook Town v West Stanley 2-1
r West Auckland Town v Wingate Albion Comrades 1-2
6r St Helens Recreation v Altrincham wo/s
10r Morley v Mirfield United 2-0
14r Kettering v Desborough Town 2-1
15r Harwich & Parkeston v King's Lynn 4-3
17r Enfield v Tufnell Park 1-2
18r Southall v Wycombe Wanderers 2-1
23r Trowbridge Town v Weymouth 1-3
24r Cardiff City v Merthyr Town 1-2

Qualifying Round Three

1 Jarrow Croft v Newcastle City 0-0
2 Wingate Albion Comrades v Crook Town 1-2
3 Shildon v Bishop Auckland 3-1
4 Barrow v Kendal Swifts 9-0
5 Southport Central v Colne 1-0
6 Heywood United v St Helens Recreation 3-2
7 Wrexham v Chester 1-4
8 Hednesford Town v Darlaston 0-1
9 Castleford Town v Mexborough Town 1-0
10 Morley v South Kirkby Colliery 1-0
11 Rotherham Town v Rotherham County 0-1
12 Blackwell Colliery v Ripley Town & Athletic 1-2
13 Mansfield Mechanics v Sutton Junction 1-3
14 Kettering v Peterborough City (1) 0-0
15 Cromer v Harwich & Parkeston 3-0
16 Ilford v Custom House 1-1
17 Tufnell Park v Barnet Alston 0-1
18 Southall v Maidenhead 2-0
19 West Norwood v Nunhead 1-4
20 Whitstable v Catford Southend 0-0
21 Tunbridge Wells Rangers v St Leonards Amateurs 3-1
22 Bitterne Guild v 1st Kings Royal Rifles 0-2
23 Frome Town v Weymouth 3-1
24 Camerton v Merthyr Town 0-12
1r Newcastle City v Jarrow Croft 2-1
14r Peterborough City (1) v Kettering 2-1
16r Custom House v Ilford 4-0
20r Catford Southend v Whitstable 6-0

Qualifying Round Four

Accrington Stanley v Carlisle United 3-0
Barnet Alston v Cromer 1-1
Barrow v Rochdale 1-0
Brentford v 1st Kings Royal Rifles 1-1
Bromley v Catford Southend 1-1
Castleford Town v Morley 1-1
Chester v Stockport County 1-4
Crook Town v Newcastle City 2-0
Custom House v Watford 0-5
Darlaston v Crewe Alexandra 0-5
Darlington v Shildon 6-0
Exeter City v Merthyr Town 1-1
Frome Town v Oxford City 4-1
Gainsborough Trinity v Rotherham County 1-0
Heywood United v Southport Central 1-1
Lincoln City v Grimsby Town 3-2
London Caledonians v Southend United 1-3
New Brompton v Croydon Common 1-2
North Shields Athletic v Hartlepools United 2-1
Peterborough City (1) v Sutton Junction 2-3
Reading v Southall 7-1
Ripley Town & Athletic v Chesterfield 2-0
Tunbridge Wells Rangers v Nunhead 7-1
Walsall v Stoke 2-1
r 1st Kings Royal Rifles v Brentford 1-4
r Catford Southend v Bromley 0-0e
r Cromer v Barnet Alston 4-5
r Merthyr Town v Exeter City 0-0
r Morley v Castleford Town 1-2
r Southport Central v Heywood United 1-0
r2 Bromley v Catford Southend 1-2
r2 Merthyr Town v Exeter City 2-0 N

Qualifying Round Five

Castleford Town v Reading 1-2
Crewe Alexandra v Merthyr Town 4-0
Crook Town v Lincoln City 2-3
Croydon Common v Ripley Town & Athletic 4-1
Gainsborough Trinity v Tunbridge Wells Rangers 1-1
North Shields Athletic v Darlington 1-2
Southend United v Brentford 0-1
Southport Central v Frome Town 4-1
Stockport County v Catford Southend 4-0
Sutton Junction v Barnet Alston 5-0
Walsall v Accrington Stanley 2-1
Watford v Barrow 2-2
r Barrow v Watford 1-2
r Tunbridge Wells Rangers v Gainsborough Trinity 0-1

Round One

Aston Villa v Walsall 6-0
Birmingham v Barnsley 0-0
Blackburn Rovers v Norwich City 4-1
Bolton Wanderers v Woolwich Arsenal 1-0
Brentford v Crystal Palace 0-0
Bristol Rovers v Portsmouth 1-2
Bury v Millwall 2-1
Chelsea v Sheffield United 1-0
Clapton Orient v Everton 1-2
Crewe Alexandra v Blackpool 1-1
Croydon Common v Leicester Fosse 2-2
Darlington v Brighton & Hove Albion 2-1
Derby County v Newcastle United 3-0
Fulham v Burnley 2-1
Leeds City v Glossop 1-0
Lincoln City v Stockport County 2-0
Liverpool v Leyton 1-0
Luton Town v Notts County 2-4
Manchester United v Huddersfield Town 3-1
Middlesbrough v Sheffield Wednesday 0-0
Northampton Town v Bristol City 1-0
Nottingham Forest v Bradford Park Avenue 0-1
Oldham Athletic v Hull City 1-1
Preston North End v Manchester City 0-1
Queen's Park Rangers v Bradford City 0-0
Southampton v Coventry City 0-2
Southport Central v Reading 0-2
Sunderland v Plymouth Argyle 3-1
Swindon Town v Sutton Junction 5-0
Watford v Wolverhampton Wan. 0-0
West Bromwich Albion v Tottenham Hotspur 3-0
West Ham United v Gainsborough Trinity 2-1
r Barnsley v Birmingham 3-0
r Blackpool v Crewe Alexandra 2-2
r Bradford City v Queen's Park Rangers 4-0
r Crystal Palace v Brentford 4-0
r Hull City v Oldham Athletic 0-1
r Leicester Fosse v Croydon Common 6-1
r Sheffield Wednesday v Middlesbrough 1-2
r Wolverhampton Wan. v Watford 10-0
r2 Crewe Alexandra v Blackpool 1-2 N

Round Two

Aston Villa v Reading 1-1
Barnsley v Leicester Fosse 1-0
Bolton Wanderers v Blackpool 1-0
Bradford City v Chelsea 2-0
Bradford Park Avenue v Portsmouth 2-0
Coventry City v Manchester United 1-5
Crystal Palace v Sunderland 0-0
Darlington v Northampton Town 1-1
Derby County v Blackburn Rovers 1-2
Everton v Bury 1-1
Fulham v Liverpool 3-0
Leeds City v West Bromwich Albion 0-1
Manchester City v Oldham Athletic 0-1
Middlesbrough v West Ham United 1-1
Swindon Town v Notts County 2-0
Wolverhampton Wan. v Lincoln City 2-1
r Everton v Bury 6-0
r Northampton Town v Darlington 2-0
r Reading v Aston Villa 1-0
r Sunderland v Crystal Palace 1-0e
r West Ham United v Middlesbrough 2-1

Round Three

Blackburn Rovers v Wolverhampton Wan. 3-2
Bolton Wanderers v Barnsley 1-2
Bradford Park Avenue v Bradford City 0-1
Fulham v Northampton Town 2-1
Oldham Athletic v Everton 0-2
Reading v Manchester United 1-1
Sunderland v West Bromwich Albion 1-2
West Ham United v Swindon Town 1-1
r Manchester United v Reading 3-0
r Swindon Town v West Ham United 4-0

Round Four

Barnsley v Bradford City 0-0
Manchester United v Blackburn Rovers 1-1
Swindon Town v Everton 2-1
West Bromwich Albion v Fulham 3-0
r Blackburn Rovers v Manchester United 4-2e
r Bradford City v Barnsley 0-0e
r2 Barnsley v Bradford City 0-0e
r3 Barnsley v Bradford City 3-2eN

Semi Finals

Barnsley v Swindon Town 0-0 N
West Bromwich Albion v Blackburn Rovers 0-0 N
r Barnsley v Swindon Town 1-0 N
r West Bromwich Albion v Blackburn Rovers 1-0eN

Final

Barnsley v West Bromwich Albion 0-0 N
r Barnsley v West Bromwich Albion 1-0eN

1912/13

Extra Preliminary Round

1 Ashington v Birtley 5-2
Blyth Spartans v Spen Black & White 3-1
Choppington v Jarrow Caledonians 1-1
Gateshead (1) v Pelaw 5-0
Hebburn Argyle v Washington United 3-2
Langley Park (1) v Scotswood 0-2
Mickley v Blaydon United 1-1
New Hartley Rovers v Bedlington United 2-1
Rutherford College v South Shields Parkside 12-0
Wallsend Elm Villa v RGA Tynemouth 2-1
Willington Athletic v Shields Albion 1-3
8 Atherstone Town v Coombs Wood 7-1
Bromsgrove Rovers v Bilston United 1-2
Cradley Heath St Luke's v Birmingham Corp. Tramways 1-4
Rugby Town (1) v Nuneaton Town 0-2
Stourbridge v Hereford City 7-1
Wednesbury Old Athletic v Dudley Phoenix 5-0
Willenhall Pickwick v Redditch 4-1
9 Alford United v Hull Day Street Old Boys 1-4
Bridlington Albion v Bentley Colliery 0-11
Brodsworth Main Colliery v Lock Lane Woodville 3-0
Doncaster St George v Castleford United wo/s
Grimsby Haycroft Rovers v Frodingham & Brumby Utd 2-1
Grimsby St John's v Immingham 3-2
Sutton (Hull) v Grimsby Rovers 6-2
11 Cammells Sports v Frickley Colliery 0-0
Kilnhurst Town v Industry Inn 0-0
Rawmarsh Town v Darfield United 0-6
13 Grantham Avenue v Notts Jardines 3-4
Holwell Works v Whitwick Imperial 3-1
Loughborough Corinthians v Mapperley 5-0
Mansfield Town v Market Harborough Town 2-1
Netherfield Rangers v Boston Town (1) 6-0
New Hucknall Colliery v Leicester Nomads 4-1
Sneinton v Grantham 2-2
19 Cranleigh v Surrey Wanderers 2-0
Old Kingstonians v Kingston-on-Thames 1-2
South Tooting v Hersham United wo/s
Sutton United v Guards Depot 1-3
Wimbledon v Tooting 0-2
22 Poole v Salisbury (1) 1-0
Winchester City v RGA Weymouth 2-0
23 Peasedown St John's v Devizes Town 3-0
1r Blaydon United v Mickley 0-1
r Jarrow Caledonians v Choppington 1-0
11r Frickley Colliery v Cammells Sports 1-0
r Industry Inn v Kilnhurst Town 0-0e
13r Grantham v Sneinton 7-2 v
11r2 Industry Inn v Kilnhurst Town 1-1e
13r2 Sneinton v Grantham 1-2
11r3 Kilnhurst Town v Industry Inn 2-1

1912/13

Preliminary Round

1	Blyth Spartans v Ashington	3-0
	Gateshead (1) v Wallsend Elm Villa	6-1
	Jarrow Caledonians v Hebburn Argyle	1-0
	Mickley v Newcastle East End (2)	5-1
	Newcastle City v New Hartley Rovers	3-0
	Rutherford College v Scotswood	1-1
	South Shields v Shields Albion	4-0
	Wallsend Park Villa v Jarrow Croft	2-1
2	Annfield Plain v Seaham Harbour	1-0
	Grangetown (Sunderland) v Horden Athletic	0-3
	Houghton Rovers v Horden Colliery	2-1
	Murton Red Star v Leadgate Park	0-0
	Sunderland Rovers v Craghead United	1-1
	West Stanley v Dipton United	3-1
3	Eston United v South Bank	1-1
	Saltburn v Darlington St Augustines	1-3
	Skinningrove Steel Works v Grangetown Athletic	0-5
	Stanley United v Shildon	1-3
	Tow Law Town v Scarborough	0-1
5	Barnoldswick United v Brierfield Swifts	3-1
	Breightmet United v Darwen	0-1
	Great Harwood v Colne	1-2
	Haslingden v Portsmouth Rovers (Lancs)	3-1
	Leyland v Nelson	1-6
	Padiham v Coppull Central	5-0
	Southport Central v Tottington	6-1
6	Alderley Edge United v Buxton	3-2
	Altrincham v Hurst	2-0
	Hyde v Garston Gasworks	2-0
	Macclesfield Town v St Helens Town	1-1
	Newton Heath Athletic v Widnes County	3-2
	St Helens Recreation v Heywood United	1-1
	Stalybridge Celtic v Denton	1-1
7	Harrowby v Connah's Quay & Shotton	5-1
	Nantwich v Northern Nomads	1-2
	Northwich Victoria v Lostock Gralam	7-0
	Port Vale v New Brighton Tower Amateurs	7-0
	South Liverpool v Witton Albion	1-2
	Tranmere Rovers v Oswestry United	4-2
	Wellington Town v Wellington St George's	3-1
	Wrexham v Chester	2-0
8	Atherstone Town v Dudley	2-0
	Bilston United v Wednesbury Old Athletic (2)	2-0
	Brierley Hill Alliance v Birmingham Corp. Tramways	1-0
	Cannock Town v Willenhall Pickwick	1-1
	Darlaston v Hednesford Town	3-2
	Kidderminster Harriers v Stafford Rangers	0-1
	Nuneaton Town v Worcester City	1-3
	Stourbridge v Willenhall Swifts	1-1
9	Brodsworth Main Colliery v Scunthorpe United	0-3
	Castleford Town v Allerton Bywater Colliery	1-0
	Cleethorpes Town v Hull Day Street Old Boys	3-0
	Denaby United v Doncaster Rovers	1-2
	Doncaster St George v Grimsby Haycroft Rovers	4-1
	Goole Town v Bentley Colliery	3-0
	Grimsby St John's v Sutton (Hull)	5-1
	Mexborough Town v York City (1)	1-1
10	Boothtown v West Vale Ramblers	1-0
	Heckmondwike v Clarence Iron & Steel Works	3-6
	Horsforth v Halifax Town	2-4
	Mirfield United v Morley	1-0
	Rothwell White Rose v Hebden Bridge	2-2
	Thornhill Lees Albion v Calverley	0-3
11	Darfield United v Redfearns	3-1
	Hickleton Main v Rotherham County	1-4
	Hoyland Town v Atlas & Norfolk Works	4-0
	Rotherham Town v Sheffield	7-0
	Royston Midland Institute v Wath Athletic	1-2
	Silverwood Colliery v Frickley Colliery	5-0
	Tankersley v Conisborough St Peters	4-0
	Worksop Town v Kilnhurst Town	5-0
12	Ashbourne Town v Castle Donnington Town	4-0
	Blackwell Colliery v South Normanton Colliery	1-1
	Coalville Town (1) v Overseal Swifts	2-3
	Gresley Colliery v Shirebrook	3-1
	Hardwick Colliery v Gresley Rovers	1-0
	Ilkeston United v Long Eaton St Helen's	2-0
	Shepshed Albion v Ripley Town & Athletic	0-2
	South Normanton Rangers v Tibshelf Colliery	0-0
13	Grantham v New Hucknall Colliery	2-1
	Hinckley United (1) v Holwell Works	7-3
	Loughborough Corinthians v Basford United	4-0
	Mansfield Town v Notts Rangers	5-0
	Notts Jardines v Netherfield Rangers	1-3
	Notts Olympic v Stanton Hill Victoria	1-3
	Sutton Junction v Leicester Imperial	6-1
	Sutton Town v Mansfield Mechanics	2-1
14	Bedford Town (1) v Stamford	5-1
	Fletton United v Wellingbro Redwell Stars	2-0
	Peterborough G.N. Loco v Biggleswade & District	3-1
	Rushden Fosse v Raunds Town	2-3
	Rushden Windmill v Desborough Town	2-2
15	Colchester Town v Norwich CEYMS	2-1
16	Barking v Ilford	3-1
	Chelmsford v Newportonians	3-1
	Hoffmann Athletic (Chelmsford) v Grays Athletic	2-0
	Leytonstone v 3rd Grenadier Guards	4-2
	Romford (1) v Walthamstow Grange	2-3
	Shoeburyness Garrison v East Ham	2-1e
	Southend United v Southend Amateurs	5-0
17	Apsley v Wood Green Town	2-2
	Barnet Alston v Luton Crusaders	2-0
	Chesham Generals v Waltham	4-1
	Chesham Town v Luton Amateur	1-0
	Finchley v Enfield	1-3
	Luton Clarence v Tufnell Park	1-2
	Luton Reliance v Tufnell Spartan	4-2
18	Kilburn v Hanwell	2-0
	Liberty v Fulham Amateurs	4-2
	Maidenhead v Hampstead Town	2-1
	Maidenhead Norfolkians v Wycombe Wanderers	3-4
	Marlow v Uxbridge	3-5
	West London Old Boys v Shepherds Bush	4-1
	Windsor & Eton v City of Westminster	2-0
19	Dorking v Summerstown	3-1
	Guards Depot v Guildford	1-2
	Kingston-on-Thames v Farnham	4-0
	Nunhead v Tooting	6-2
	Redhill v Croydon (1)	0-6
	South Tooting v Godalming	5-3
	West Norwood v Walton-on-Thames	6-0
	Woking v Cranleigh	5-0
20	Bromley v Ashford Town (1)	3-0
	Bronze Athletic v Sheppey United	1-1
	Chatham v Ashford Railway Works	2-1
	Dartford v Maidstone United	2-0
	Gravesend United v Deptford Invicta	3-1
	Northfleet United v Sittingbourne	4-1
	Ramsgate Town v Whitstable	1-1
22	1st Kings Royal Rifles v Winchester City	2-1
	Basingstoke v Bournemouth (Ams)	2-1
	Boscombe v Portland	6-0
	Bournemouth Gasworks Athletic v Woolston	0-4
	Eastleigh Athletic v Poole	4-0
	Gosport United v Royal Engs. Aldershot	2-2
	South Farnborough Ath. v Longfleet St Mary's	5-5
	Weymouth v Cowes (2)	0-1
23	Bath City v Chippenham Town	4-2
	Camerton v Trowbridge Town	2-3
	Frome Town v Swindon Victoria	1-0
	Hanham Athletic v Peasedown St John's	1-1
	Minehead v Welton Rovers	4-0
	Paulton Rovers v Radstock Town	wo/s
	Street v Weston-Super-Mare	1-1
	Yeovil v Clevedon	2-0
24	Aberdare v Port Talbot	2-1
	Pontypridd v Lysaghts Excelsior	8-1
1r	Scotswood v Rutherford College	2-0
2r	Craghead United v Sunderland Rovers	2-3
r	Leadgate Park v Murton Red Star	2-1
3r	South Bank v Eston United	2-2
6r	St Helens Recreation v Heywood United	1-3
r	St Helens Town v Macclesfield Town	0-1
r	Stalybridge Celtic v Denton	3-0
8r	Willenhall Pickwick v Cannock Town	2-1
r	Willenhall Swifts v Stourbridge	wo/s
9r	York City (1) v Mexborough Town	1-1
10r	Hebden Bridge v Rothwell White Rose	2-1
12r	South Normanton Colliery v Blackwell Colliery	4-3
r	Tibshelf Colliery v South Normanton Rangers	5-0
14r	Desborough Town v Rushden Windmill	5-0
17r	Apsley v Wood Green Town	2-1
20r	Sheppey United v Bronze Athletic	3-1
r	Whitstable v Ramsgate Town	3-0
22r	Longfleet St Mary's v South Farnborough Ath.	1-2
r	Royal Engs. Aldershot v Gosport United	1-2
23r	Peasedown St John's v Hanham Athletic	2-1
r	Weston-Super-Mare v Street	1-2
3r2	South Bank v Eston United	3-2 N
9r2	Mexborough Town v York City (1)	2-3eN

Qualifying Round One

1	Newcastle City v Mickley	0-0
	Scotswood v Jarrow Caledonians	4-0
	South Shields v Blyth Spartans	2-1
	Wallsend Park Villa v Gateshead (1)	2-1
2	Annfield Plain v Horden Athletic	1-1
	Hartlepools United v Houghton Rovers	3-1
	Sunderland Rovers v Leadgate Park	1-0
	West Stanley v Wingate Albion Comrades	0-3
3	Darlington St Augustines v South Bank	1-1
	Shildon v Crook Town	1-1
	Spennymoor United v Grangetown Athletic	5-0
	Willington v Scarborough	0-0
4	Barrow - Bye	
	Barrow Novocastrians v Lowca	1-1
	North Lonsdale Amateurs v Penrith	wo/s
	Windermere v Barrow St Luke's	3-4
5	Colne v Haslingden	0-1
	Nelson v Darwen	3-1
	Rossendale United v Padiham	1-0
	Southport Central v Barnoldswick United	2-1
6	Alderley Edge United v Newton Heath Athletic	1-1
	Heywood United v Hyde	6-0
	Macclesfield Town v Rochdale	3-5
	Stalybridge Celtic v Altrincham	3-0
7	Harrowby v Tranmere Rovers	2-1
	Northwich Victoria v Witton Albion	2-2
	Port Vale v Northern Nomads	4-1
	Wellington Town v Wrexham	1-1
8	Atherstone Town v Willenhall Swifts	6-2
	Darlaston v Bilston United	1-1
	Willenhall Pickwick v Brierley Hill Alliance	2-0
	Worcester City v Stafford Rangers	1-0
9	Castleford Town v Doncaster Rovers	2-0
	Doncaster St George v Cleethorpes Town	1-1
	Scunthorpe United v Goole Town	2-1
	York City (1) v Grimsby St John's	7-1
10	Clarence Iron & Steel Works v Calverley	1-5
	Halifax Town v Hebden Bridge	3-2
	Knaresborough v Mirfield United	2-1
	South Kirkby Colliery v Boothtown	2-1
11	Darfield United v Wath Athletic	1-0
	Rotherham County v Silverwood Colliery	6-0
	Rotherham Town v Worksop Town	0-0
	Tankersley v Hoyland Town	0-2
12	Ashbourne Town v Hardwick Colliery	2-1
	Gresley Colliery v South Normanton Colliery	1-2
	Ilkeston United v Tibshelf Colliery	1-2
	Ripley Town & Athletic v Overseal Swifts	6-1
13	Grantham v Stanton Hill Victoria	1-1
	Hinckley United (1) v Sutton Town	2-3
	Loughborough Corinthians v Sutton Junction	2-2
	Netherfield Rangers v Mansfield Town	2-3
14	Bedford Town (1) v Irthlingborough Town	5-1
	Fletton United v Peterborough City (1)	1-7
	Peterborough G.N. Loco v Kettering	3-0
	Raunds Town v Desborough Town	2-0
15	Cambridge Utd. (1) v Kirkley	9-1
	Colchester Town v Cromer	4-0
	Gorleston v Lowestoft Town	3-2
	King's Lynn v Harwich & Parkeston	5-1
16	Barking v Custom House	0-3
	Leytonstone v Chelmsford	2-1
	Shoeburyness Garrison v Hoffmann Ath. (Chelm'rd)	1-1
	Southend United v Walthamstow Grange	6-2
17	Apsley v St Albans City	0-2
	Barnet Alston v Luton Reliance	5-2
	Chesham Town v Enfield	0-0
	Tufnell Park v Chesham Generals	3-0
18	Kilburn v West London Old Boys	3-3
	Southall v Maidenhead	3-2
	Uxbridge v Liberty	8-3
	Wycombe Wanderers v Windsor & Eton	3-1
19	Dorking v Croydon (1)	3-3
	Guildford v Nunhead	0-3
	South Tooting v Kingston-on-Thames	1-4
	West Norwood v Woking	1-4
20	Chatham v Catford Southend	3-1
	Dartford v Bromley	3-3
	Northfleet United v Sheppey United	0-1
	Whitstable v Gravesend United	4-3
21	East Grinstead v Tunbridge Wells Rangers	1-7
	Lewes v Worthing	5-2
	St Leonards Amateurs v Vernon Athletic	0-1
	Tunbridge Wells (1) v Littlehampton	3-1
22	Cowes (2) v South Farnborough Ath.	7-2
	Eastleigh Athletic v Basingstoke	2-4
	Gosport United v Boscombe	1-1
	Woolston v 1st Kings Royal Rifles	0-0
23	Paulton Rovers v Frome Town	1-3
	Peasedown St John's v Bath City	1-0
	Street v Yeovil	2-0
	Trowbridge Town v Minehead	3-0
24	Cardiff Corinthians v Llanelli	3-5
	Mardy v Aberdare	1-0
	Merthyr Town v Cardiff City	1-5
	Pontypridd v Barry	2-0
1r	Mickley v Newcastle City	1-2
2r	Horden Athletic v Annfield Plain	2-0
3r	Crook Town v Shildon	3-0
r	Scarborough v Willington	3-2
r	South Bank v Darlington St Augustines	1-0
4r	Lowca v Barrow Novocastrians	2-0
6r	Newton Heath Athletic v Alderley Edge United	2-0
7r	Witton Albion v Northwich Victoria	1-2
r	Wrexham v Wellington Town	2-2
8r	Bilston United v Darlaston	2-0
9r	Cleethorpes Town v Doncaster St George	2-0
11r	Worksop Town v Rotherham Town	1-1e
13r	Stanton Hill Victoria v Grantham	2-1e
r	Sutton Junction v Loughborough Corinthians	3-5e
16r	Hoffmann Ath. (Chelm'rd) v Shoeburyness Garrison	0-3
17r	Enfield v Chesham Town	3-0
18r	West London Old Boys v Kilburn	4-1
19r	Dorking v Croydon (1)	1-0
20r	Bromley v Dartford	1-3
22r	1st Kings Royal Rifles v Woolston	2-1
r	Boscombe v Gosport United	7-1
7r2	Wrexham v Wellington Town	3-0
11r2	Rotherham Town v Worksop Town	4-1

Qualifying Round Two

1	South Shields v Scotswood	4-1
	Wallsend Park Villa v Newcastle City	2-3
2	Hartlepools United v Wingate Albion Comrades	4-1
	Horden Athletic v Sunderland Rovers	0-0
3	Crook Town v Scarborough	1-0
	South Bank v Spennymoor United	1-1
4	Barrow v Lowca	8-0
	Barrow St Luke's v North Lonsdale Amateurs	0-1
5	Nelson v Haslingden	2-0
	Southport Central v Rossendale United	4-0
6	Newton Heath Athletic v Rochdale	0-5
	Stalybridge Celtic v Heywood United	2-0
7	Harrowby v Port Vale	0-2
	Northwich Victoria v Wrexham	5-1
8	Atherstone Town v Bilston United	2-0
	Willenhall Pickwick v Worcester City	3-2
9	Cleethorpes Town v Castleford Town	0-4
	Scunthorpe United v York City (1)	2-2

1912/13 to 1913/14

10	Calverley v South Kirkby Colliery	1-1
	Halifax Town v Knaresborough	6-0
11	Hoyland Town v Rotherham Town	0-2
	Rotherham County v Darfield United	5-1
12	Ashbourne Town v Ripley Town & Athletic	3-3
	Tibshelf Colliery v South Normanton Colliery	2-0
13	Mansfield Town v Loughborough Corinthians	5-2
	Stanton Hill Victoria v Sutton Town	1-2
14	Peterborough City (1) v Peterborough G.N. Loco	3-0
	Raunds Town v Bedford Town (1)	2-1
15	Colchester Town v Cambridge Utd. (1)	1-2
	Gorleston v King's Lynn	1-2
16	Custom House v Shoeburyness Garrison	2-0
	Leytonstone v Southend United	0-5
17	Enfield v St Albans City	2-0
	Tufnell Park v Barnet Alston	2-0
18	Uxbridge v Wycombe Wanderers	4-3
	West London Old Boys v Southall	0-1
19	Dorking v Kingston-on-Thames	0-0
	Woking v Nunhead	1-2
20	Chatham v Dartford	1-1
	Sheppey United v Whitstable	4-0
21	Tunbridge Wells (1) v Lewes	3-2
	Tunbridge Wells Rangers v Vernon Athletic	4-1
22	1st Kings Royal Rifles v Cowes (2)	7-1
	Boscombe v Basingstoke	3-1
23	Frome Town v Trowbridge Town	2-2
	Peasedown St John's v Street	1-2
24	Cardiff City v Pontypridd	2-1
	Llanelli v Mardy	2-1
2r	Sunderland Rovers v Horden Athletic	1-1
3r	Spennymoor United v South Bank	1-0
9r	York City (1) v Scunthorpe United	5-4
10r	South Kirkby Colliery v Calverley	2-0
12r	Ripley Town & Athletic v Ashbourne Town	1-1e
19r	Kingston-on-Thames v Dorking	3-0
20r	Dartford v Chatham	1-2
23r	Trowbridge Town v Frome Town	3-0
2r2	Sunderland Rovers v Horden Athletic	2-2
12r2	Ripley Town & Athletic v Ashbourne Town	4-0 N
2r3	Horden Athletic v Sunderland Rovers	1-2

Qualifying Round Three

1	Newcastle City v South Shields	1-5
2	Hartlepools United v Sunderland Rovers	2-1
3	Crook Town v Spennymoor United	1-4
4	Barrow v North Lonsdale Amateurs	0-0
5	Nelson v Southport Central	3-1
6	Rochdale v Stalybridge Celtic	2-1
7	Northwich Victoria v Port Vale	3-1
8	Atherstone Town v Willenhall Pickwick	1-2
9	York City (1) v Castleford Town	1-1
10	Halifax Town v South Kirkby Colliery	6-0
11	Rotherham County v Rotherham Town	1-0
12	Ripley Town & Athletic v Tibshelf Colliery	4-1
13	Sutton Town v Mansfield Town	3-1
14	Peterborough City (1) v Raunds Town	4-0
15	King's Lynn v Cambridge Utd. (1)	4-1
16	Custom House v Southend United	0-1
17	Tufnell Park v Enfield	2-0
18	Uxbridge v Southall	0-6
19	Nunhead v Kingston-on-Thames	0-1
20	Sheppey United v Chatham	1-1
21	Tunbridge Wells (1) v Tunbridge Wells Rangers	0-1
22	Boscombe v 1st Kings Royal Rifles	0-0
23	Street v Trowbridge Town	0-2
24	Llanelli v Cardiff City	1-4
4r	Barrow v North Lonsdale Amateurs	4-1
9r	Castleford Town v York City (1)	1-0
20r	Chatham v Sheppey United	1-1e
22r	1st Kings Royal Rifles v Boscombe	1-0
20r2	Chatham v Sheppey United	2-0

Qualifying Round Four

	Barrow v Carlisle United	4-1
	Bishop Auckland v South Shields	0-3
	Brentford v Watford	0-0
	Cardiff City v Exeter City	5-1
	Chatham v London Caledonians	0-4
	Chesterfield v Sutton Town	2-1
	Clapton v Southend United	1-2
	Croydon Common v Oxford City	3-0
	Darlington v North Shields Athletic	0-0
	Gainsborough Trinity v Peterborough City (1)	3-1
	Gillingham v Leyton	wo/s
	Glossop v Ripley Town & Athletic	2-0
	Halifax Town v Nelson	3-3
	Hartlepools United v Castleford Town	1-0
	King's Lynn v Tufnell Park	2-0
	Luton Town v Tunbridge Wells Rangers	3-0
	Northwich Victoria v Shrewsbury Town	1-2
	Rochdale v Accrington Stanley	6-1
	Rotherham County v Lincoln City	1-3
	Southall v Kingston-on-Thames	3-0
	Stockton v Spennymoor United	0-1
	Trowbridge Town v 1st Kings Royal Rifles	1-1
	Walsall v Crewe Alexandra	2-1
	Willenhall Pickwick v Stockport County	0-2
r	1st Kings Royal Rifles v Trowbridge Town	2-4
r	Nelson v Halifax Town	2-3
r	North Shields Athletic v Darlington	0-4
r	Watford v Brentford	5-1

Qualifying Round Five

	Cardiff City v Southend United	0-3
	Chesterfield v Watford	3-1
	Croydon Common v Luton Town	2-0
	Gainsborough Trinity v Hartlepools United	4-0
	Glossop v Southall	11-1
	King's Lynn v Stockport County	2-7
	Rochdale v Darlington	1-1
	Shrewsbury Town v London Caledonians	2-2
	South Shields v Lincoln City	1-0
	Spennymoor United v Gillingham	1-1
	Trowbridge Town v Barrow	1-4
	Walsall v Halifax Town	0-0
r	Darlington v Rochdale	0-1
r	Gillingham v Spennymoor United	3-0
r	Halifax Town v Walsall	1-0
r	London Caledonians v Shrewsbury Town	1-0

Round One

	Blackburn Rovers v Northampton Town	7-2
	Bradford Park Avenue v Barrow	1-1
	Bristol Rovers v Notts County	2-0
	Chelsea v Southend United	5-2
	Chesterfield v Nottingham Forest	1-4
	Croydon Common v Woolwich Arsenal	0-0
	Crystal Palace v Glossop	2-0
	Derby County v Aston Villa	1-3
	Everton v Stockport County	5-1
	Fulham v Hull City	0-2
	Gillingham v Barnsley	0-0
	Huddersfield Town v Sheffield United	3-1
	Leeds City v Burnley	2-3
	Leicester Fosse v Norwich City	1-4
	Liverpool v Bristol City	3-0
	Manchester City v Birmingham	4-0
	Manchester United v Coventry City	1-1
	Millwall v Middlesbrough	0-0
	Newcastle United v Bradford City	1-0
	Oldham Athletic v Bolton Wanderers	2-0
	Plymouth Argyle v Preston North End	2-0
	Portsmouth v Brighton & Hove Albion	1-2
	Queen's Park Rangers v Halifax Town	4-2
	Rochdale v Swindon Town	0-2
	Sheffield Wednesday v Grimsby Town	5-1
	South Shields v Gainsborough Trinity	0-1
	Southampton v Bury	1-1
	Stoke v Reading	2-2
	Sunderland v Clapton Orient	6-0
	Tottenham Hotspur v Blackpool	1-1
	West Bromwich Albion v West Ham United	1-1
	Wolverhampton Wan. v London Caledonians	3-1
r	Barnsley v Gillingham	3-1
r	Bradford Park Avenue v Barrow	1-0
r	Bury v Southampton	2-1
r	Coventry City v Manchester United	1-2
r	Middlesbrough v Millwall	4-1
r	Reading v Stoke	3-0
r	Tottenham Hotspur v Blackpool	6-1
r	West Ham United v West Bromwich Albion	2-2e
r	Woolwich Arsenal v Croydon Common	2-1
r2	West Ham United v West Bromwich Albion	3-0 N

Round Two

	Aston Villa v West Ham United	5-0
	Barnsley v Blackburn Rovers	2-3
	Bradford Park Avenue v Wolverhampton Wan.	3-0
	Brighton & Hove Albion v Everton	0-0
	Bristol Rovers v Norwich City	1-1
	Burnley v Gainsborough Trinity	4-1
	Chelsea v Sheffield Wednesday	1-1
	Crystal Palace v Bury	2-0
	Huddersfield Town v Swindon Town	1-2
	Hull City v Newcastle United	0-0
	Middlesbrough v Queen's Park Rangers	3-2
	Oldham Athletic v Nottingham Forest	5-1
	Plymouth Argyle v Manchester United	0-2
	Reading v Tottenham Hotspur	1-0
	Sunderland v Manchester City	2-0
	Woolwich Arsenal v Liverpool	1-4
r	Everton v Brighton & Hove Albion	1-0e
r	Newcastle United v Hull City	3-0
r	Norwich City v Bristol Rovers	2-2e
r	Sheffield Wednesday v Chelsea	6-0
r2	Bristol Rovers v Norwich City	1-0 N

Round Three

	Aston Villa v Crystal Palace	5-0
	Bradford Park Avenue v Sheffield Wednesday	2-1
	Bristol Rovers v Everton	0-4
	Burnley v Middlesbrough	3-1
	Liverpool v Newcastle United	1-1
	Oldham Athletic v Manchester United	0-0
	Reading v Blackburn Rovers	1-2
	Sunderland v Swindon Town	4-2
r	Manchester United v Oldham Athletic	1-2
r	Newcastle United v Liverpool	1-0

Round Four

	Blackburn Rovers v Burnley	0-1
	Bradford Park Avenue v Aston Villa	0-5
	Everton v Oldham Athletic	0-1
	Sunderland v Newcastle United	0-0
r	Newcastle United v Sunderland	2-2e
r2	Newcastle United v Sunderland	0-3

Semi Finals

	Aston Villa v Oldham Athletic	1-0 N
	Sunderland v Burnley	0-0 N
r	Sunderland v Burnley	3-2 N

Final

	Aston Villa v Sunderland	1-0 N

1913/14

Extra Preliminary Round

1	Bedlington United v Hexham Athletic	4-0
	Blyth Spartans v New Hartley Rovers	3-2
	Brighton West End v Choppington	1-0
	Gateshead Rodsley v Hebburn Argyle	1-0
	Jarrow v Rutherford College	2-1
	Jarrow Blackett v Shields Albion	1-0
	Mickley v Ashington	0-2
	Seaton Delaval v Benwell Adelaide	0-2
	Wallsend Elm Villa v Newburn	0-3
	Willington Athletic v Walker Church Institute	2-1
2	Dipton United v West Hartlepool St Josephs	4-0
	Grangetown (Sunderland) v Leadgate Park	1-5
	Houghton Rovers v Brooms	1-1
	Ryhope Villa v Hobson Wanderers	1-2
	Spen Black & White v West Hartlepool Expansion	3-3
7	Egremont (1) v Wallasey Rovers	1-2
	Hoylake v New Brighton Tower Amateurs	2-1
	Marlborough Old Boys v Dominion	3-0
8	Birmingham Corp. Tramways v Dudley Phoenix	wo/s
	Cannock Town v Stafford Rangers	1-3
	Dudley v Bromsgrove Rovers	6-0
	Hednesford Town v Cradley Heath St Luke's	1-0
	Hereford City v Darlaston	1-3
	Rugby Town (1) v Nuneaton Town	2-6
9	Brigg v Fryston Colliery	1-8
	Grimsby Rovers v Denaby United	8-1
11	Rawmarsh Town v Bolsover Colliery	3-0
	Staveley Town v Atlas & Norfolk Works	3-1
13	Arnold St Mary's v Basford United	2-2
	Grantham Avenue v Holwell Works	3-1
	Leicester Imperial v Eastwood Rangers	6-2
	New Hucknall Colliery v Mapperley	1-2
	Notts Rangers v Grantham	0-9
	Sutton Junction v Mansfield Mechanics	1-3
17	Apsley v Watford Orient	3-2 D
	Luton Trinity v Harpenden Town	2-0
	Wealdstone v Page Green Old Boys	1-3
19	Camberley & Yorktown v Sutton United	5-3
	Walton-on-Thames v Wimbledon	4-0
20	Folkestone v Margate	0-1
22	Christchurch v Wareham Town	6-2
	East Cowes Victoria v Southampton Cambridge	2-2
23	Petters United v Weston-Super-Mare	wo/s
	Swindon Victoria v Timsbury Athletic	2-0
	Torquay Town v Welton Rovers	1-1
	Yeovil v St Austell	0-2
2r	Brooms v Houghton Rovers	1-2
r	West Hartlepool Expansion v Spen Black & White	1-0
13r	Basford United v Arnold St Mary's	0-1
22r	Southampton Cambridge v East Cowes Victoria	6-1
23r	Welton Rovers v Torquay Town	2-1

Preliminary Round

1	Bedlington United v Jarrow Blackett	4-0
	Blyth Spartans v Newcastle East End (2)	3-2
	Brighton West End v Wallsend	3-0
	Gateshead (1) v Scotswood	1-0
	Jarrow v South Shields Parkside	5-0
	Newburn v Benwell Adelaide	2-2
	Newcastle City v Gateshead Rodsley	4-0
	Willington Athletic v Ashington	1-3
2	Annfield Plain v Wingate Albion Comrades	0-0
	Birtley v Washington United	3-1
	Dipton United v Horden Athletic	1-3
	Hartlepools United v Sunderland Rovers	0-0
	Houghton Rovers v Seaham Harbour	0-0
	Langley Park (1) v West Hartlepool Expansion	5-2
	Leadgate Park v Craghead United	1-2
	West Stanley v Hobson Wanderers	1-1
3	Bishop Auckland v Shildon	1-0
	Grangetown St Mary's v Darlington St Augustines	0-0
	Lingdale Mines v Grangetown Athletic	2-3
	Loftus Albion v Crook Town	0-0
	Skinningrove Steel Works v Saltburn	11-0
	South Bank v Scarborough	3-0
	Spennymoor United v Redcar	8-2
	Stanley United v Willington	1-2

1913/14

4	Barrow Novocastrians v Moresby Park	1-0
	Frizington Athletic v Barrow St Mary's	4-1
	Lancaster Town v Appleby	6-2
	Maryport v Penrith	3-3
5	Barnoldswick United v Darwen	4-1
	Breightmet United v Rossendale United	2-4
	Leyland v Great Harwood	5-1
	Padiham v Coppull Central	4-2
	Portsmouth Rovers (Lancs) v Tottington	4-2
	Southport Central v Southport Park Villa	2-0
6	Alderley Edge United v Newton Heath Athletic	0-3
	Altrincham v Widnes County	4-0
	Atherton v St Helens Town	1-2
	Heywood United v Eccles Borough	2-3
	Hyde v Denton	6-2
	Macclesfield Town v Hurst	2-0
	Sandbach Ramblers v Walkden Central	3-0
	Stalybridge Celtic v Buxton	7-0
7	Hoylake v Northern Nomads	2-3
	Marlborough Old Boys v Oswestry United	0-6
	Nantwich v Chester	3-5
	Port Vale v Harrowby	3-1
	South Liverpool v Northwich Victoria	3-1
	Tranmere Rovers v Lostock Gralam	6-1
	Wallasey Rovers v Connah's Quay & Shotton	1-0 v
	Witton Albion v Wrexham	0-5
8	Dudley v Darlaston	4-1
	Hednesford Town v Atherstone Town	4-0
	Kidderminster Harriers v Brierley Hill Alliance	0-2
	Walsall v Stafford Rangers	1-0
	Wednesbury Old Athletic v Nuneaton Town	3-2
	Willenhall Pickwick v Bilston United	0-1
	Willenhall Swifts v Redditch	2-1
	Worcester City v Birmingham Corp. Tramways	4-3
9	Brodsworth Main Colliery v Bentley Colliery	1-1
	Castleford Town v Hull Old Boys	2-0
	Cleethorpes Town v Fryston Colliery	1-1
	Goole Town v Doncaster Rovers	2-1
	Grimsby Rovers v Allerton Bywater Colliery	2-0
	Grimsby St John's v Grimsby Haycroft Rovers	0-1
	Lock Lane Woodville v York City (1)	0-10
	Mexborough Town v Scunthorpe United	2-2
10	Clarence Iron & Steel Works v Boothtown	2-1
	Hebden Bridge v Thornhill Lees Albion	4-0
	Horsforth v Rothwell White Rose	1-4
	Mirfield United v Heckmondwike	1-0
	West Vale Ramblers v Morley	2-1
11	Conisborough St Peters v Hickleton Main	4-0
	Darfield United v Kilnhurst Town	1-4
	Hoyland Town v Sheffield	6-2
	Redfearns v Frickley Colliery	0-3
	Rotherham County v Rawmarsh Town	2-0
	Silverwood Colliery v Rotherham Town	1-1
	Tankersley v Wath Athletic	1-2
	Worksop Town v Staveley Town	3-0
12	Blackwell Colliery v Overseal Swifts	8-3
	Coalville Town (1) v Ilkeston United	0-2
	Crich Town v Gresley Colliery	4-2
	Gresley Rovers v Long Eaton St Helen's	5-1
	Ripley Town & Athletic v Matlock	4-0
	Shirebrook v Shepshed Albion	4-1
	Tibshelf Colliery v Ashbourne Town	2-1
13	Boston Town (1) v Sneinton	1-1
	Grantham v Grantham Avenue	0-1
	Hinckley United (1) v Arnold St Mary's	3-1
	Leicester Imperial v Whitwick Imperial	0-1
	Mansfield Mechanics v Sutton Town	1-0
	Mansfield Town v Mapperley	3-1
	Market Harborough Town v Loughborough Corinthians	1-0
	Netherfield Rangers v Notts Olympic	3-0
14	Daventry United (1) v Fletton United	0-1
	Desborough Town v Wellingbro Redwell Stars	4-1
	Irthlingborough Town v Kettering	2-2
	Peterborough City (1) v Stamford	0-1
	Rushden Fosse v Biggleswade & District	1-0
	Rushden Windmill v Bedford Town (1)	2-2
15	Great Yarmouth Town v King's Lynn	4-0
16	Chelmsford v Southend Amateurs	2-2
	East Ham v Clapton	1-2
	Hoffmann Athletic (Chelmsford) v Barking	1-2
	Ilford v Walthamstow Grange	1-1
	Newportonians v Woodford Crusaders	0-1
	Romford (1) v Shoeburyness Garrison	4-2
17	Chesham Generals v Finchley	0-1
	Chesham Town v Wood Green Town	2-2
	Enfield v Tufnell Park	0-2
	Luton Amateur v Watford Orient	6-0
	Luton Clarence v Tufnell Spartan	4-0
	Luton Reliance v Luton Crusaders	3-1
	Luton Trinity v Barnet Alston	0-3
	St Albans City v Page Green Old Boys	1-2
18	Henley Town v West London Old Boys	1-3
	Maidenhead v Wycombe Wanderers	0-1
	Maidenhead Norfolkians v Polytechnic	3-1
	Marlow v Hampstead Town	1-3
	Shepherds Bush v Oxford City	1-1
	Slough v City of Westminster	3-2
	Uxbridge v Southall	1-4
	Windsor & Eton v Liberty	2-3
19	Camberley & Yorktown v Guildford	1-3
	Croydon (1) v Nunhead	1-2
	Hersham United v Farnham	3-0
	Kingston-on-Thames v Woking	2-2
	Summerstown v Redhill	0-2
	Tooting v Dorking	2-1
	Walton-on-Thames v South Tooting	2-4
	West Norwood v Old Kingstonians	2-0
20	Ashford Railway Works v Bronze Athletic	3-2
	Bromley v Maidstone United	0-1
	Catford Southend v Sheppey United	0-0
	Chatham v Deptford Invicta	9-0
	Dartford v Margate	3-1
	New Crusaders v Sittingbourne	0-0
	Ramsgate Town v Northfleet United	0-4
	Whitstable v Gravesend United	0-5
22	Basingstoke v Southampton Cambridge	4-2
	Bournemouth (Ams) v RGA Weymouth	5-0
	Christchurch v South Farnborough Ath.	2-0
	Gosport United v Bournemouth Gasworks Athletic	3-1
	Poole v Longfleet St Mary's	2-2
	Royal Engs. Aldershot v Boscombe	1-2
	Weymouth v Eastleigh Athletic	2-2
	Woolston v Cowes (2)	1-2
23	Chippenham Town v Camerton	2-1
	Clevedon v Welton Rovers	2-5
	Hanham Athletic v Paulton Rovers	6-0
	Melksham Town v Devizes Town	3-2
	Peasedown St John's v Trowbridge Town	1-1
	Petters United v Bath City	2-7
	St Austell v Minehead	7-1
	Street v Swindon Victoria	5-1
24	Aberdare v Mardy	3-1
	Barry v Milford Town	wo/s
	Caerleon Athletic v Pembroke Dock	2-1
	Cardiff Corinthians v Caerphilly	3-1
	Llanelli v Lysaghts Excelsior	6-1
	Newport County v Mond Nickel Works	6-0
	Pontypridd v Mid Rhondda	0-1
	Swansea Town v Port Talbot	4-0
1r	Benwell Adelaide v Newburn	7-1
2r	Hobson Wanderers v West Stanley	3-2
r	Seaham Harbour v Houghton Rovers	2-2
r	Sunderland Rovers v Hartlepools United	1-2
r	Wingate Albion Comrades v Annfield Plain	0-1
3r	Crook Town v Loftus Albion	4-1
r	Darlington St Augustines v Grangetown St Mary's	0-1
4r	Penrith v Maryport	2-1
7r	Connah's Quay & Shotton v Wallasey Rovers	2-0
9r	Bentley Colliery v Brodsworth Main Colliery	2-2e
r	Fryston Colliery v Cleethorpes Town	wo/s
r	Scunthorpe United v Mexborough Town	3-0
11r	Rotherham Town v Silverwood Colliery	2-3
13r	Boston Town (1) v Sneinton	6-0
14r	Bedford Town (1) v Rushden Windmill	1-2
r	Kettering v Irthlingborough Town	6-1
16r	Southend Amateurs v Chelmsford	3-1
r	Walthamstow Grange v Ilford	2-1
17r	Wood Green Town v Chesham Town	1-3
18r	Oxford City v Shepherds Bush	4-0
19r	Woking v Kingston-on-Thames	1-1x
20r	Sheppey United v Catford Southend	4-0
r	Sittingbourne v New Crusaders	1-3
22r	Eastleigh Athletic v Weymouth	2-0
r	Longfleet St Mary's v Poole	1-0
23r	Trowbridge Town v Peasedown St John's	3-1
2r2	Seaham Harbour v Houghton Rovers	0-1
9r2	Brodsworth Main Colliery v Bentley Colliery	4-1
19r2	Woking v Kingston-on-Thames	1-2e

Qualifying Round One

1	Ashington v Blyth Spartans	1-1
	Bedlington United v Jarrow	0-0
	Brighton West End v Benwell Adelaide	4-2
	Gateshead (1) v Newcastle City	2-3
2	Birtley v Hobson Wanderers	5-1
	Craghead United v Langley Park (1)	2-1
	Hartlepools United v Annfield Plain	6-1
	Horden Athletic v Houghton Rovers	2-0
3	Bishop Auckland v Grangetown Athletic	2-2
	Grangetown St Mary's v Crook Town	0-1
	Spennymoor United v South Bank	1-0
	Willington v Skinningrove Steel Works	8-0
4	Barrow Novocastrians v Frizington Athletic	3-3
	Lancaster Town v Carlisle United	0-0
	Lowca v Windermere	6-1
	Penrith v Barrow St Luke's	wo/s
5	Barnoldswick United v Rossendale United	5-2
	Haslingden v Nelson	0-0
	Padiham v Leyland	2-2
	Portsmouth Rovers (Lancs) v Southport Central	1-9
6	Altrincham v Sandbach Ramblers	1-1
	Newton Heath Athletic v Hyde	0-0
	St Helens Town v Eccles Borough	3-2
	Stalybridge Celtic v Macclesfield Town	1-0
7	Chester v Tranmere Rovers	2-1
	Connah's Quay & Shotton v Wrexham	1-2
	Port Vale v Northern Nomads	5-0
	South Liverpool v Oswestry United	4-2
8	Brierley Hill Alliance v Wednesbury Old Athletic (2)	3-0
	Dudley v Willenhall Swifts	3-1
	Hednesford Town v Bilston United	5-1
	Worcester City v Walsall	7-0
9	Goole Town v Castleford Town	1-0
	Grimsby Haycroft Rovers v Fryston Colliery	2-0
	Grimsby Rovers v Brodsworth Main Colliery	2-5
	York City (1) v Scunthorpe United	2-1
10	Halifax Town v West Vale Ramblers	12-0
	Hebden Bridge v Calverley	2-2
	Rothwell White Rose v Clarence Iron & Steel Works	5-1
	South Kirkby Colliery v Mirfield United	0-2
11	Conisborough St Peters v Silverwood Colliery	1-1
	Hoyland Town v Wath Athletic	0-5
	Rotherham County v Kilnhurst Town	8-1
	Worksop Town v Frickley Colliery	9-0
12	Blackwell Colliery v Shirebrook	2-3
	Gresley Rovers v South Normanton Colliery	3-2
	Ilkeston United v Ripley Town & Athletic	2-1
	Tibshelf Colliery v Crich Town	6-2
13	Grantham Avenue v Mansfield Mechanics	1-0
	Mansfield Town v Netherfield Rangers	2-2
	Market Harborough Town v Hinckley United (1)	1-5
	Whitwick Imperial v Boston Town (1)	5-1
14	Kettering v Peterborough G.N. Loco	9-0
	Raunds Town v Rushden Windmill	3-0
	Rushden Fosse v Desborough Town	1-1
	Stamford v Fletton United	7-1
15	Colchester Town v Cambridge Utd. (1)	4-0
	Cromer v Kirkley	2-1
	Harwich & Parkeston v Lowestoft Town	2-1
	Norwich CEYMS v Great Yarmouth Town	2-2
16	Clapton v Barking	3-1
	Romford (1) v Custom House	0-2
	Southend Amateurs v Leytonstone	1-8
	Woodford Crusaders v Walthamstow Grange	1-5
17	Barnet Alston v Chesham Town	4-0
	Finchley v Page Green Old Boys	1-2
	Luton Amateur v Luton Reliance	1-4
	Luton Clarence v Tufnell Park	3-2
18	Liberty v Southall	2-5
	Maidenhead Norfolkians v Hampstead Town	0-3
	Oxford City v Wycombe Wanderers	5-0
	West London Old Boys v Slough	2-0
19	Guildford v Kingston-on-Thames	1-1
	Hersham United v West Norwood	1-8
	Redhill v Nunhead	0-7
	Tooting v South Tooting	0-2
20	Chatham v Dartford	3-2
	Gravesend United v Ashford Railway Works	7-1
	Maidstone United v Sheppey United	2-1
	Northfleet United v New Crusaders	2-7
21	East Grinstead v Tunbridge Wells Rangers	2-7
	Eastbourne St Mary's v St Leonards Amateurs	2-1
	Horsham v Worthing	0-0
	Tunbridge Wells (1) v Littlehampton	5-1
22	Basingstoke v Bournemouth (Ams)	1-3
	Cowes (2) v Boscombe	2-3
	Eastleigh Athletic v Christchurch	5-1
	Gosport United v Longfleet St Mary's	6-0
23	Bath City v Chippenham Town	6-1
	Hanham Athletic v Trowbridge Town	4-1
	Street v Melksham Town	8-0
	Welton Rovers v St Austell	8-1
24	Aberdare v Llanelli	3-0
	Cardiff Corinthians v Newport County	1-6
	Mid Rhondda v Barry	3-0
	Swansea Town v Caerleon Athletic	8-1
1r	Blyth Spartans v Ashington	1-2
r	Jarrow v Bedlington United	2-0
3r	Grangetown Athletic v Bishop Auckland	3-2e
4r	Carlisle United v Lancaster Town	4-2
r	Frizington Athletic v Barrow Novocastrians	5-2
5r	Leyland v Padiham	5-3
r	Nelson v Haslingden	2-1
6r	Hyde v Newton Heath Athletic	2-1
r	Sandbach Ramblers v Altrincham	0-1
10r	Calverley v Hebden Bridge	1-5
11r	Silverwood Colliery v Conisborough St Peters	3-0
13r	Netherfield Rangers v Mansfield Town	0-4
14r	Desborough Town v Rushden Fosse	5-0
15r	Great Yarmouth Town v Norwich CEYMS	5-0
19r	Kingston-on-Thames v Guildford	2-0
21r	Worthing v Horsham	7-2

Qualifying Round Two

1	Ashington v Newcastle City	4-3
	Jarrow v Brighton West End	3-1
2	Craghead United v Horden Athletic	0-0
	Hartlepools United v Birtley	4-0
3	Crook Town v Grangetown Athletic	1-2
	Willington v Spennymoor United	3-2
4	Carlisle United v Frizington Athletic	2-1
	Lowca v Penrith	1-0
5	Nelson v Leyland	3-1
	Southport Central v Barnoldswick United	5-0
6	Hyde v St Helens Town	3-1
	Stalybridge Celtic v Altrincham	1-0
7	Chester v Port Vale	2-5
	Wrexham v South Liverpool	1-1
8	Dudley v Brierley Hill Alliance	2-1
	Worcester City v Hednesford Town	1-0
9	Goole Town v Brodsworth Main Colliery	6-1
	York City (1) v Grimsby Haycroft Rovers	7-0
10	Hebden Bridge v Mirfield United	2-4
	Rothwell White Rose v Halifax Town	1-1
11	Silverwood Colliery v Worksop Town	1-0
	Wath Athletic v Rotherham County	2-2
12	Gresley Rovers v Tibshelf Colliery	1-0
	Shirebrook v Ilkeston United	3-1
13	Grantham Avenue v Whitwick Imperial	4-0
	Mansfield Town v Hinckley United (1)	1-3
14	Raunds Town v Kettering	1-4
	Stamford v Desborough Town	3-2

1913/14 to 1914/15

15 Colchester Town v Cromer 1-1
Harwich & Parkeston v Great Yarmouth Town 2-2
16 Clapton v Custom House 2-2
Walthamstow Grange v Leytonstone 1-1
17 Luton Clarence v Luton Reliance 4-1
Page Green Old Boys v Barnet Alston 1-1
18 Hampstead Town v Southall 1-3
West London Old Boys v Oxford City 0-4
19 Nunhead v Kingston-on-Thames 4-0
South Tooting v West Norwood 1-1
20 Chatham v Maidstone United 2-1
Gravesend United v New Crusaders 3-0
21 Tunbridge Wells (1) v Eastbourne St Mary's 1-1
Tunbridge Wells Rangers v Worthing 5-1
22 Boscombe v Bournemouth (Ams) 0-1
Gosport United v Eastleigh Athletic 2-1
23 Bath City v Hanham Athletic 4-0
Street v Welton Rovers 0-1
24 Newport County v Aberdare 1-1
Swansea Town v Mid Rhondda 1-0
2r Horden Athletic v Craghead United 4-0
7r South Liverpool v Wrexham 1-0
10r Halifax Town v Rothwell White Rose 6-0
11r Rotherham County v Wath Athletic 9-1
15r Cromer v Colchester Town 3-1
r Great Yarmouth Town v Harwich & Parkeston 4-0
16r Custom House v Clapton 1-0
r Leytonstone v Walthamstow Grange 2-2
17r Barnet Alston v Page Green Old Boys 1-1
19r West Norwood v South Tooting 2-2
21r Eastbourne St Mary's v Tunbridge Wells (1) 2-1e
24r Aberdare v Newport County 1-0
16r2 Walthamstow Grange v Leytonstone 5-1
17r2 Page Green Old Boys v Barnet Alston 0-1
19r2 South Tooting v West Norwood 2-3

Qualifying Round Three

1 Jarrow v Ashington 0-0
2 Hartlepools United v Horden Athletic 4-0
3 Willington v Grangetown Athletic 5-1
4 Carlisle United v Lowca 7-1
5 Southport Central v Nelson 3-0
6 Stalybridge Celtic v Hyde 2-0
7 Port Vale v South Liverpool 5-0
8 Worcester City v Dudley 1-1
9 Goole Town v York City (1) 1-1
10 Halifax Town v Mirfield United 2-0
11 Silverwood Colliery v Rotherham County 2-2
12 Gresley Rovers v Shirebrook 1-1
13 Hinckley United (1) v Grantham Avenue 3-1
14 Stamford v Kettering 3-1
15 Cromer v Great Yarmouth Town 5-2
16 Custom House v Walthamstow Grange 0-1
17 Luton Clarence v Barnet Alston 3-2
18 Oxford City v Southall 3-0
19 Nunhead v West Norwood 3-1
20 Chatham v Gravesend United 2-1
21 Tunbridge Wells Rangers v Eastbourne St Mary's 6-2
22 Gosport United v Bournemouth (Ams) 2-2
23 Bath City v Welton Rovers 2-1
24 Swansea Town v Aberdare 4-0
1r Ashington v Jarrow 2-0
8r Dudley v Worcester City 3-2
9r York City (1) v Goole Town 2-1
11r Rotherham County v Silverwood Colliery 2-0
12r Shirebrook v Gresley Rovers 3-2e
22r Bournemouth (Ams) v Gosport United 4-0

Qualifying Round Four

Ashington v Willington 1-1
Barrow v Rochdale 3-0
Bath City v Merthyr Town 1-1
Brentford v Luton Clarence 1-0
Carlisle United v Southport Central 2-1
Chatham v Oxford City 4-0
Crewe Alexandra v Dudley 2-1
Darlington v Stockton 4-1
Gainsborough Trinity v Stockport County 3-2
Gillingham v Nunhead 2-0
Glossop v Hinckley United (1) 5-1
Hartlepools United v South Shields 0-1
Luton Town v Croydon Common 3-0
Norwich City v Walthamstow Grange 6-0
Port Vale v Coventry City 3-1
Rotherham County v Halifax Town 1-1
Shirebrook v Chesterfield 1-1
Southend United v Tunbridge Wells Rangers 3-0
Stalybridge Celtic v Accrington Stanley 2-0
Stamford v Cromer 4-1
Stoke v Shrewsbury Town 2-0
Swansea Town v Cardiff City 2-0
Watford v Bournemouth (Ams) 10-0
York City (1) v North Shields Athletic 0-2
r Chesterfield v Shirebrook 2-0
r Halifax Town v Rotherham County 5-2
r Merthyr Town v Bath City 3-0
r Willington v Ashington 4-0

Qualifying Round Five

Brentford v Southend United 1-1
Chatham v Stamford 2-0
Gainsborough Trinity v Crewe Alexandra 2-0

Gillingham v Watford 1-0
Glossop v Carlisle United 4-1
Luton Town v South Shields 0-0
Merthyr Town v Stalybridge Celtic 1-1
North Shields Athletic v Chesterfield 1-1
Norwich City v Halifax Town 2-0
Port Vale v Darlington 2-2
Stoke v Barrow 3-1
Swansea Town v Willington 3-0
r Chesterfield v North Shields Athletic 8-2
r Darlington v Port Vale 1-1x
r South Shields v Luton Town 2-0
r Southend United v Brentford 2-0
r Stalybridge Celtic v Merthyr Town 1-2
r2 Darlington v Port Vale 0-1 N

Round One

Aston Villa v Stoke 4-0
Birmingham v Southend United 2-1
Blackburn Rovers v Middlesbrough 3-0
Bolton Wanderers v Port Vale 3-0
Bradford City v Woolwich Arsenal 2-0
Bradford Park Avenue v Reading 5-1
Burnley v South Shields 3-1
Clapton Orient v Nottingham Forest 2-2
Crystal Palace v Norwich City 2-1
Derby County v Northampton Town 1-0
Gillingham v Blackpool 1-0
Glossop v Everton 2-1
Huddersfield Town v London Caledonians 3-0
Hull City v Bury 0-0
Leeds City v Gainsborough Trinity 4-2
Leicester Fosse v Tottenham Hotspur 5-5
Liverpool v Barnsley 1-1
Manchester City v Fulham 2-0
Millwall v Chelsea 0-0
Newcastle United v Sheffield United 0-5
Oldham Athletic v Brighton & Hove Albion 1-1
Plymouth Argyle v Lincoln City 4-1
Portsmouth v Exeter City 0-4
Preston North End v Bristol Rovers 5-2
Queen's Park Rangers v Bristol City 2-2
Sheffield Wednesday v Notts County 3-2
Sunderland v Chatham 9-0
Swansea Town v Merthyr Town 2-0
Swindon Town v Manchester United 1-0
West Bromwich Albion v Grimsby Town 2-0
West Ham United v Chesterfield 8-1
Wolverhampton Wan. v Southampton 3-0
r Barnsley v Liverpool 0-1
r Brighton & Hove Albion v Oldham Athletic 1-0e
r Bristol City v Queen's Park Rangers 0-2e
r Bury v Hull City 2-1
r Chelsea v Millwall 0-1
r Nottingham Forest v Clapton Orient 0-1
r Tottenham Hotspur v Leicester Fosse 2-0

Round Two

Birmingham v Huddersfield Town 1-0
Blackburn Rovers v Bury 2-0
Bolton Wanderers v Swindon Town 4-2
Brighton & Hove Albion v Clapton Orient 3-1
Burnley v Derby County 3-2
Exeter City v Aston Villa 1-2
Glossop v Preston North End 0-1
Leeds City v West Bromwich Albion 0-2
Liverpool v Gillingham 2-0
Manchester City v Tottenham Hotspur 2-1
Millwall v Bradford City 1-0
Sheffield United v Bradford Park Avenue 3-1
Sunderland v Plymouth Argyle 2-1
Swansea Town v Queen's Park Rangers 1-2
West Ham United v Crystal Palace 2-0
Wolverhampton Wan. v Sheffield Wednesday 1-1
r Sheffield Wednesday v Wolverhampton Wan. 1-0

Round Three

Aston Villa v West Bromwich Albion 2-1
Birmingham v Queen's Park Rangers 1-2
Blackburn Rovers v Manchester City 1-2
Burnley v Bolton Wanderers 3-0
Millwall v Sheffield United 0-4
Sheffield Wednesday v Brighton & Hove Albion 3-0
Sunderland v Preston North End 2-0
West Ham United v Liverpool 1-1
r Liverpool v West Ham United 5-1

Round Four

Liverpool v Queen's Park Rangers 2-1
Manchester City v Sheffield United 0-0
Sheffield Wednesday v Aston Villa 0-1
Sunderland v Burnley 0-0
r Burnley v Sunderland 2-1
r Sheffield United v Manchester City 0-0e
r2 Sheffield United v Manchester City 1-0 N

Semi Finals

Burnley v Sheffield United 0-0 N
Liverpool v Aston Villa 2-0 N
r Burnley v Sheffield United 1-0 N

Final

Burnley v Liverpool 1-0 N

1914/15

Extra Preliminary Round

1 Gateshead (1) v Lintz Institute 0-2
Gateshead Rodsley v Pandon Temperance 0-1
Jarrow Blackett v Spen Black & White 0-1
Mickley v Bedlington United 5-1
Newburn v New Hartley Rovers 5-2
Rutherford College v Blyth Spartans 0-7
Slipway (Wallsend) v Wallsend 2-0
Wallsend Elm Villa v Seaton Delaval 1-4
Washington United v Allendale Park 3-2
Willington Athletic v Newcastle East End (2) 2-0
2 Boldon Colliery v Twizell United 2-2
Esh Winning (1) v Brooms 1-1
5 Chorley v Tonge Temperance 3-0
6 Longfield v Chapel-en-le-Frith 3-2
7 Garston Gasworks v Ormskirk (1) 2-2
Nantwich v Hoylake wo/s
Northern Nomads v North Engineers (Bootle) 1-2
Skelmersdale United v Llandudno wo/s
Wallasey Borough v Connah's Quay & Shotton wo/s
8 Bilston United v Atherstone Town 2-2
Birmingham Corp. Tramways v Bloxwich Strollers 3-1
Cannock Town v Rugby Town (1) 6-0
Kidderminster Harriers v Darlaston 1-1
Nuneaton Town v Tamworth Castle 1-1
Stourbridge v Stafford Rangers 3-1
Walsall v Willenhall Pickwick 4-0
Willenhall Swifts v Hereford City wo/s
11 Bolton Athletic (Rotherham) v Hardwick Colliery 1-1
Eckington Red Rose v Holly Bush (Parkgate) 2-2
Sheffield v Grimethorpe Colliery Institute sc/sc
Tankersley v Stocksbridge Church 1-2
13 Boots Athletic v Arnold St Mary's 0-4
Grantham v Holwell Works 4-1
Leicester Imperial v Basford United 0-0
Pleasley United v New Hucknall Colliery 1-2
Sneinton v Netherfield Rangers 0-2
16 Woolwich Polytechnic v 1st Grenadier Guards wo/s
22 Bournemouth Tramways v Wareham Town wo/s
Portsmouth Amateurs v Bournemouth Wanderers wo/s
RGA Weymouth v Bournemouth Gasworks Athletic wo/s
South Farnborough Ath. v Southampton Cambridge wo/s
Thornycrofts (Basingstoke) v Salisbury (1) wo/s
23 Clevedon v Frome Town wo/s
Minehead v Babbacombe sc/sc
St Austell v Torquay Town wo/s
Trowbridge Town v Cheltenham Town sc/sc
24 Troedryhiw Stars v Caerau Rovers 4-2
2r Brooms v Esh Winning (1) 3-0
r Twizell United v Boldon Colliery 0-1
7r Ormskirk (1) v Garston Gasworks wo/s
8r Atherstone Town v Bilston United 1-2
r Darlaston v Kidderminster Harriers wo/s
r Tamworth Castle v Nuneaton Town 1-5
11r Hardwick Colliery v Bolton Athletic (Rotherham) 7-1
r Holly Bush (Parkgate) v Eckington Red Rose 1-3
13r Basford United v Leicester Imperial 1-0

Preliminary Round

1 Jarrow v Slipway (Wallsend) 0-0
Newcastle City v Newburn 2-1
Scotswood v Lintz Institute 0-1
Seaton Delaval v Benwell Adelaide 5-0
South Shields Parkside v Blyth Spartans 0-3
Spen Black & White v Ashington 1-0
Washington United v Pandon Temperance 2-1
Willington Athletic v Mickley 2-0
2 Annfield Plain v Birtley 0-2
Boldon Colliery v Houghton Rovers wo/s
Craghead United v Dipton United 2-1
Grangetown (Sunderland) v Brooms 0-3
Hobson Wanderers v Horden Athletic 1-1
Ryhope Villa v Sunderland Rovers 2-2
West Stanley v West Hartlepool St Josephs wo/s
Wingate Albion Comrades v Seaham Harbour 2-0
3 Brotton v Grangetown Athletic 2-1
Lingdale Mines v Redcar wo/s
Loftus Albion v Eston United 4-2
Scarborough v Stanley United 2-2
Shildon v Crook Town 3-1
West Auckland Town v Darlington St Augustines 0-2
4 Barrow St Mary's v Windermere wo/s
Bigrigg United v Barrow Novocastrians 6-2
Bowness Rovers v Vickerstown 1-0
Lancaster Town v Appleby 17-2
Maryport v Penrith wo/s
5 Accrington Stanley v Adlington 1-1
Barnoldswick United v Portsmouth Rovers (Lancs) 4-2
Chorley v Breightmet United 6-0

1914/15

	Great Harwood v Leyland	4-2
	Haslingden v Horwich RMI	3-1
	Nelson v Tottington	9-1
	Padiham v Rossendale United	1-3
	Southport Central v Southport Park Villa	1-0
6	Atherton v Sandbach Ramblers	4-0
	Denton v Alderley Edge United	wo/s
	Hurst v Heywood United	2-0
	Hyde v Macclesfield Town	1-1
	Newton Heath Athletic v Altrincham	1-1
	St Helens Town v Buxton	6-0
	Walkden Central v Eccles Borough	0-3
	Widnes County v Longfield	2-0
7	Chester v Lostock Gralam	wo/s
	Egremont (1) v Skelmersdale United	3-4
	Harrowby v North Engineers (Bootle)	1-2
	Nantwich v Wallasey Borough	3-0
	Oswestry United v Marlborough Old Boys	wo/s
	Tranmere Rovers v Northwich Victoria	2-2
	Witton Albion v Ormskirk (1)	1-2
	Wrexham v South Liverpool	2-1
8	Bilston United v Hednesford Town	0-0
	Brierley Hill Alliance v Dudley	3-0
	Bromsgrove Rovers v Birmingham Corp. Tramways	0-3
	Cradley Heath St Luke's v Wednesbury Old Ath.(2)	1-0
	Darlaston v Nuneaton Town	7-2
	Stoke v Stourbridge	11-0
	Walsall v Cannock Town	2-1
	Willenhall Swifts v Redditch	0-1
9	Acomb WMC (York) v Mexborough Town	0-8
	Beverley Town v Frodingham & Brumby Utd	4-1
	Brodsworth Main Colliery v York City (1)	0-1
	Bullcroft Main Colliery v Goole Town	1-3
	Cleethorpes Town v Grimsby St John's	6-0
	Grimsby Haycroft Rovers v Doncaster Rovers	0-3
	Grimsby Rovers v Bentley Colliery	wo/s
	Hull Old Boys v Scunthorpe United	1-5
10	Calverley v Boothtown	4-2
	Castleford Town v Halifax Town	2-1
	Frickley Colliery v Horsforth	wo/s
	Glasshoughton Colliery v Rothwell White Rose	1-4
	Hebden Bridge v South Kirkby Colliery	1-1
	Heckmondwike v Clarence Iron & Steel Works	2-1
	Rothwell Parish Church v Fryston Colliery	0-1
	Woodhouse Brittania v Lock Lane Woodville	2-1
11	Atlas & Norfolk Works v Darfield United	0-4
	Bolsover Colliery v Hardwick Colliery	2-1
	Eckington Red Rose v Hoyland Town	4-1
	Hickleton Main v Stocksbridge Church	1-1
	Silverwood Colliery v Rotherham Town	1-1
	Staveley Town - Bye	
	Wath Athletic v Rawmarsh Town	2-1
	Worksop Town v Kilnhurst Town	8-0
12	Ashbourne Town v Shirebrook	0-8
	Blackwell Colliery v Tutbury Town	0-2
	Ilkeston United v Matlock	2-0
	Long Eaton v Coalville Town (1)	2-2
	Ripley Town & Athletic v Newhall Swifts	2-1
	Shepshed Albion v Castle Donnington Town	6-2
	South Normanton Colliery v Gresley Rovers	3-1
	Tibshelf Colliery v Coalville Swifts	2-1
13	Basford United v Grantham	0-0
	Boston Town (1) v Arnold St Mary's	3-1
	Grantham Avenue v New Hucknall Colliery	1-2
	Mansfield Mechanics v Hinckley United (1)	2-0
	Market Harborough T v Loughborough Corinthians	4-0
	Netherfield Rangers v Notts Olympic	9-1
	Sutton Town v Mansfield Town	5-0
	Whitwick Imperial v Sutton Junction	0-2
14	Desborough Town v Bedford Town (1)	wo/s
	Peterborough City (1) v Wolverton Town	wo/s
	Peterbro' Westwood Works v Fletton United	wo/s
	Raunds Town v Irthlingborough Town	2-3
	Rushden Fosse v Biggleswade & District	3-0
	Rushden Windmill v Wellingbro Redwell Stars	0-2
15	Cambridge Town v Gorleston	wo/s
	Norwich CEYMS v King's Lynn	3-0
	Norwich St James' v Mortons Athletic	wo/s
16	Barking v East Ham	wo/s
	Clapton v Ilford	0-2
	Custom House v Shoeburyness Garrison	wo/s
	Leytonstone v Woodford Albion	wo/s
	Newportonians v Chelmsford	0-5
	Romford (1) v Woolwich	wo/s
	Walthamstow Grange v Hoffmann Ath. (Chelmsford)	wo/s
	Woolwich Polytechnic v Woodford Crusaders	0-5
17	Barnet Alston v Wealdstone	wo/s
	Hitchin Union Jack v Chesham Generals	wo/s
	Leavesden Mental Hospital v Chesham Town	wo/s
	Letchworth Athletic v St Albans City	wo/s
	Luton Amateur v Enfield	1-5
	Luton Clarence v Tufnell Spartan	wo/s
18	Hampstead Town v Sutton Court	wo/s
	Maidenhead Norfolkians v Wycombe Wanderers	wo/s
	Newbury Town v West London Old Boys	sc/sc
	Slough v Marlow	wo/s
	Southall v City of Westminster	4-1
	Uxbridge v Polytechnic	wo/s
	Windsor & Eton v Liberty	sc/sc
	Yiewsley v Maidenhead	wo/s
19	Croydon (1) v Camberley & Yorktown	wo/s
	Guildford v Woking	wo/s
	Old Kingstonians v Summerstown	3-2
	Redhill v Hersham United	wo/s
	Sutton United v Dorking	wo/s

	Tooting v Walton-on-Thames	4-0
	West Norwood v Weybridge	sc/sc
20	Charlton Athletic v Ashford Railway Works	wo/s
	Cray Wanderers v Folkestone	wo/s
	Dartford v Maidstone United	wo/s
	Margate v Gravesend United	wo/s
	Northfleet United v New Crusaders	2-1
	Ramsgate Town v Dartford Amateurs	wo/s
	Sittingbourne v Sheppey United	wo/s
	Whitstable v Catford Southend	2-1
22	Boscombe v RGA Weymouth	wo/s
	Bournemouth Tramways v Bournemouth (Ams)	wo/s
	Cowes (2) v Gosport United	wo/s
	Eastleigh Athletic v Basingstoke	wo/s
	Longfleet St Mary's v South Farnborough Ath.	wo/s
	Poole v Christchurch	sc/sc
	Portsmouth Amateurs v Woolston	wo/s
	Thornycrofts (Basingstoke) v Weymouth	wo/s
23	Bath City v St Austell	wo/s
	Camerton v Weston-Super-Mare	sc/sc
	Clevedon v Petters United	wo/s
	Hanham Athletic v Chippenham Town	wo/s
	Paulton Rovers v Yeovil	wo/s
	Swindon Victoria v Peasedown St John's	2-1
	Welton Rovers v Street	wo/s
24	Abertillery v Pembroke Dock	4-2
	Barry v Mond Nickel Works	wo/s
	Caerleon Athletic v Port Talbot	sc/sc
	Mid Rhondda v Cardiff Corinthians	wo/s
	Milford Town v Newport Barbarians	wo/s
	Newport County v Rhiwderin	8-0
	Rhymney Town v Mardy	1-0
	Troedryhiw Stars v Bargoed	2-2
1r	Slipway (Wallsend) v Jarrow	0-1
2r	Horden Athletic v Hobson Wanderers	2-1
r	Sunderland Rovers v Ryhope Villa	3-0
3r	Stanley United v Scarborough	3-0
5r	Accrington Stanley v Adlington	2-3
6r	Altrincham v Newton Heath Athletic	5-1
r	Macclesfield Town v Hyde	4-3e
7r	Tranmere Rovers v Northwich Victoria	3-2
8r	Hednesford Town v Bilston United	2-0
10r	South Kirkby Colliery v Hebden Bridge	wo/s
11r	Rotherham Town v Silverwood Colliery	3-2
r	Stocksbridge Church v Hickleton Main	3-0
12r	Coalville Town (1) v Long Eaton	1-3
13r	Grantham v Basford United	4-1e
24r	Bargoed v Troedryhiw Stars	4-2

Qualifying Round One

1	Blyth Spartans v Newcastle City	4-0
	Lintz Institute v Spen Black & White	3-1
	Seaton Delaval v Willington Athletic	0-3
	Washington United v Jarrow	0-2
2	Birtley v Craghead United	3-2
	Sunderland Rovers v Horden Athletic	4-0
	West Stanley v Brooms	0-0
	Wingate Albion Comrades v Boldon Colliery	0-1
3	Brotton v Loftus Albion	3-2
	Shildon v Lingdale Mines	3-0
	Spennymoor United v Stockton	2-0
	Stanley United v Darlington St Augustines	4-0
4	Bigrigg United v Maryport	3-2
	Carlisle United v Barrow St Mary's	4-1
	Lancaster Town v Bowness Rovers	4-1
	Lowca v Frizington Athletic	0-4
5	Adlington v Barnoldswick United	4-3
	Chorley v Nelson	1-0
	Great Harwood v Southport Central	3-3
	Rossendale United v Haslingden	1-1
6	Altrincham v St Helens Town	4-2
	Atherton v Macclesfield Town	1-2
	Denton v Hurst	1-1
	Eccles Borough v Widnes County	5-0
7	Chester v Ormskirk (1)	2-0
	North Engineers (Bootle) v Nantwich	2-3
	Tranmere Rovers v Oswestry United	13-0
	Wrexham v Skelmersdale United	2-1
8	Birmingham Corp. Tramways v Stoke	2-3
	Brierley Hill Alliance v Darlaston	5-3
	Cradley Heath St Luke's v Redditch	8-0
	Walsall v Hednesford Town	3-1
9	Beverley Town v York City (1)	0-2
	Doncaster Rovers v Cleethorpes Town	3-1
	Goole Town v Mexborough Town	1-0 v
	Grimsby Rovers v Scunthorpe United	0-4
10	Fryston Colliery v Calverley	3-0
	Heckmondwike v Castleford Town	2-2
	Rothwell White Rose v Frickley Colliery	3-0
	Woodhouse Brittania v South Kirkby Colliery	1-2
11	Bolsover Colliery v Darfield United	3-1
	Staveley Town v Stocksbridge Church	6-0
	Wath Athletic v Eckington Red Rose	2-1
	Worksop Town v Rotherham Town	2-2
12	Shepshed Albion v Ilkeston United	0-4
	Shirebrook v Long Eaton	1-1
	Tibshelf Colliery v Ripley Town & Athletic	3-1
	Tutbury Town v South Normanton Colliery	0-7
13	Boston Town (1) v Netherfield Rangers	0-1
	Grantham v Sutton Junction	1-5
	Mansfield Mechanics v Market Harborough Town	4-1
	New Hucknall Colliery v Sutton Town	1-1
14	Irthlingborough Town v Peterborough City (1)	0-2
	Kettering v Desborough Town	0-0

	Peterbro' Westwood Works v Wellingbro Redwell Stars	3-0
	Rushden Fosse v Stamford	wo/s
15	Great Yarmouth Town v Colchester Town	wo/s
	Lowestoft Town v Cromer	wo/s
	Norwich CEYMS v Cambridge Town	5-4
	Norwich St James' v Harwich & Parkeston	wo/s
16	Chelmsford v Barking	2-3
	Custom House v Woodford Crusaders	2-1
	Leytonstone v Ilford	0-0
	Walthamstow Grange v Romford (1)	3-0
17	Letchworth Athletic v Leavesden Mental Hospital	wo/s
	Luton Clarence v Hitchin Union Jack	wo/s
	Luton Reliance v Barnet Alston	0-4
	Page Green Old Boys v Enfield	2-1
18	Slough v Maidenhead Norfolkians	1-0
	Uxbridge v Southall	1-3
	Yiewsley v Hampstead Town	2-2
19	Guildford v Croydon (1)	1-0
	Kingston-on-Thames v Sutton United	sc/sc
	Redhill - Bye	
	Tooting v Old Kingstonians	0-2
20	Dartford v Charlton Athletic	0-0
	Northfleet United v Cray Wanderers	3-1
	Ramsgate Town v Whitstable	1-0
	Sittingbourne v Margate	1-0
21	Eastbourne v Southwick	wo/s
	Eastbourne St Mary's v Vernon Athletic	wo/s
	Horsham v Tunbridge Wells Rangers	3-4
	Worthing v Tunbridge Wells (1)	wo/s
22	Boscombe v Bournemouth Tramways	wo/s
	Cowes (2) v Portsmouth Amateurs	4-1
	Eastleigh Athletic v Thornycrofts (Basingstoke)	4-8
	Longfleet St Mary's - Bye	
23	Bath City v Clevedon	2-1
	Hanham Athletic v Welton Rovers	1-1
	Paulton Rovers - Bye	
	Swindon Victoria - Bye	
24	Barry v Abertillery	4-1
	Mid Rhondda v Bargoed	1-0
	Newport County v Milford Town	6-0
	Rhymney Town - Bye	
2r	Brooms v West Stanley	0-1
5r	Haslingden v Rossendale United	2-1
r	Southport Central v Great Harwood	2-1
6r	Hurst v Denton	4-2
9r	Goole Town v Mexborough Town	1-0
10r	Castleford Town v Heckmondwike	0-1
11r	Rotherham Town v Worksop Town	2-1
12r	Long Eaton v Shirebrook	0-0e
13r	Sutton Town v New Hucknall Colliery	2-1
14r	Desborough Town v Kettering	1-4
16r	Ilford v Leytonstone	2-1
18r	Hampstead Town v Yiewsley	3-0
20r	Dartford v Charlton Athletic	2-1
23r	Welton Rovers v Hanham Athletic	5-0
12r2	Shirebrook v Long Eaton	3-2e

Qualifying Round Two

1	Lintz Institute v Jarrow	2-0
	Willington Athletic v Blyth Spartans	1-0
2	Birtley v West Stanley	0-4
	Sunderland Rovers v Boldon Colliery	2-2
3	Brotton v Stanley United	1-3
	Shildon v Spennymoor United	0-0
4	Carlisle United v Lancaster Town	3-1
	Frizington Athletic v Bigrigg United	1-0
5	Adlington v Haslingden	1-4
	Southport Central v Chorley	4-1
6	Eccles Borough v Hurst	0-0
	Macclesfield Town v Altrincham	1-3
7	Tranmere Rovers v Chester	5-1
	Wrexham v Nantwich	4-2
8	Stoke v Brierley Hill Alliance	1-0
	Walsall v Cradley Heath St Luke's	5-2
9	Goole Town v York City (1)	0-0
	Scunthorpe United v Doncaster Rovers	1-0
10	Rothwell White Rose v Heckmondwike	0-2
	South Kirkby Colliery v Fryston Colliery	3-1
11	Bolsover Colliery v Rotherham Town	2-6
	Staveley Town v Wath Athletic	1-1
12	Shirebrook v Ilkeston United	2-0
	Tibshelf Colliery v South Normanton Colliery	3-2
13	Mansfield Mechanics v Sutton Junction	1-1
	Sutton Town v Netherfield Rangers	4-2
14	Peterborough City (1) v Kettering	4-3
	Peterbro' Westwood Works v Rushden Fosse	wo/s
15	Great Yarmouth Town v Norwich St James'	7-0
	Norwich CEYMS v Lowestoft Town	2-2
16	Custom House v Walthamstow Grange	1-0 v
	Ilford v Barking	4-0
17	Barnet Alston v Luton Clarence	4-2
	Letchworth Athletic v Page Green Old Boys	4-2
18	Hampstead Town - Bye	
	Southall v Slough	10-0
19	Guildford - Bye	
	Redhill v Old Kingstonians	2-2
20	Dartford v Ramsgate Town	6-2
	Sittingbourne v Northfleet United	2-2
21	Eastbourne St Mary's v Worthing	wo/s
	Tunbridge Wells Rangers v Eastbourne	wo/s
22	Longfleet St Mary's v Cowes (2)	2-5
	Thornycrofts (Basingstoke) v Boscombe	1-6
23	Paulton Rovers v Swindon Victoria	1-1
	Welton Rovers v Bath City	4-1

1914/15 & 1919/20 (No competition 1915/16 to 1918/19)

24 Barry v Mid Rhondda	0-0	
Rhymney Town v Newport County	1-3	
2r Boldon Colliery v Sunderland Rovers	0-1	
3r Spennymoor United v Shildon	1-3	
6r Hurst v Eccles Borough	1-2	
9r York City (1) v Goole Town	0-0	
11r Wath Athletic v Staveley Town	2-2e	
13r Sutton Junction v Mansfield Mechanics	1-2	
15r Norwich CEYMS v Lowestoft Town	2-0	
16r Walthamstow Grange v Custom House	3-1	
19r Redhill v Old Kingstonians	1-0	
20r Northfleet United v Sittingbourne	2-2	
23r Paulton Rovers v Swindon Victoria	0-1	
24r Mid Rhondda v Barry	0-2	
9r2 York City (1) v Goole Town	3-2 v	
11r2 Staveley Town v Wath Athletic	2-1 N	
20r2 Sittingbourne v Northfleet United	1-2	
9r3 Goole Town v York City (1)	2-0 N	

Qualifying Round Three

1 Lintz Institute v Willington Athletic	3-1
2 Sunderland Rovers v West Stanley	4-0
3 Shildon v Stanley United	3-1
4 Frizington Athletic v Carlisle United	3-1
5 Southport Central v Haslingden	1-1
6 Eccles Borough v Altrincham	0-0
7 Wrexham v Tranmere Rovers	1-1
8 Walsall v Stoke	1-0
9 Scunthorpe United v Goole Town	1-1
10 South Kirkby Colliery v Heckmondwike	0-0
11 Staveley Town v Rotherham Town	2-2
12 Shirebrook v Tibshelf Colliery	4-0
13 Sutton Town v Mansfield Mechanics	4-1
14 Peterbro' Westwood Works v Peterborough City (1)	1-9
15 Norwich CEYMS v Great Yarmouth Town	1-2
16 Ilford v Walthamstow Grange	2-1
17 Barnet Alston v Letchworth Athletic	4-2
18 Hampstead Town v Southall	3-1
19 Guildford v Redhill	1-0
20 Dartford v Northfleet United	4-3
21 Eastbourne St Mary's v Tunbridge Wells Rangers	1-2
22 Cowes (2) v Boscombe	0-1
23 Welton Rovers v Swindon Victoria	7-1
24 Newport County v Barry	4-2
5r Haslingden v Southport Central	3-3
6r Altrincham v Eccles Borough	0-1
7r Tranmere Rovers v Wrexham	0-1
9r Goole Town v Scunthorpe United	5-1
10r Heckmondwike v South Kirkby Colliery	3-1
11r Rotherham Town v Staveley Town	4-1
5r2 Southport Central v Haslingden	1-0

Qualifying Round Four

Barrow v Frizington Athletic	9-1
Boscombe v Welton Rovers	2-1
Bromley v Tunbridge Wells Rangers	2-1
Chatham v Dartford	0-0
Crewe Alexandra v Port Vale	1-1
Eccles Borough v Southport Central	2-2
Gainsborough Trinity v Peterborough City (1)	2-0
Goole Town v Sutton Town	2-0
Guildford v Hampstead Town	1-1
Hartlepools United v Bishop Auckland	6-2
Heckmondwike v Shirebrook	0-2
Ilford v Barnet Alston	0-0
Lintz Institute v Shildon	1-1
Luton Town v Great Yarmouth Town	15-0
North Shields Athletic v Hebburn Argyle	5-0
Nunhead v Brentford	0-1
Rochdale v Stalybridge Celtic	3-2
Rotherham Town v Chesterfield	2-4
Shrewsbury Town v Worcester City	1-0
South Bank v Darlington	0-4
Sunderland Rovers v Willington	4-4
Swansea Town v Newport County	1-0
Tufnell Park v Oxford City	0-2
Walsall v Wrexham	2-1
r Barnet Alston v Ilford	1-1
r Dartford v Chatham	3-6
r Hampstead Town v Guildford	2-1
r Port Vale v Crewe Alexandra	5-2
r Shildon v Lintz Institute	2-0
r Southport Central v Eccles Borough	0-2
r Willington v Sunderland Rovers	1-1
r2 Barnet Alston v Ilford	2-1 N
r2 Sunderland Rovers v Willington	4-3 N

Qualifying Round Five

Barnet Alston v Chatham	1-0
Barrow v Eccles Borough	1-2
Boscombe v Brentford	0-0
Bromley v Hampstead Town	1-1
Gainsborough Trinity v Chesterfield	0-0
North Shields Athletic v Shildon	3-2
Oxford City v Luton Town	0-1
Rochdale v Hartlepools United	2-0
Shirebrook v Goole Town	0-2
Shrewsbury Town v Walsall	2-1
Sunderland Rovers v Darlington	1-1
Swansea Town v Port Vale	1-0

r Brentford v Boscombe	0-1	
r Chesterfield v Gainsborough Trinity	3-1	
r Darlington v Sunderland Rovers	3-0	
r Hampstead Town v Bromley	2-5	

Qualifying Round Six

Bristol Rovers v Boscombe	3-0
Croydon Common v Barnet Alston	4-0
Eccles Borough v Merthyr Town	2-4
Glossop v Coventry City	3-1
Goole Town v Chesterfield	2-0
Lincoln City v Rotherham County	6-0
London Caledonians v Darlington	0-1
Luton Town v Bromley	5-1
North Shields Athletic v South Shields	1-3
Nottingham Forest v Shrewsbury Town	6-1
Rochdale v Watford	2-0
Swansea Town v Leicester Fosse	1-0

Round One

Arsenal v Merthyr Town	3-0
Aston Villa v Exeter City	2-0
Birmingham v Crystal Palace	2-2
Blackpool v Sheffield United	1-2
Bolton Wanderers v Notts County	2-1
Bradford Park Avenue v Portsmouth	1-0
Brighton & Hove Albion v Lincoln City	2-1
Bristol City v Cardiff City	2-0
Bristol Rovers v Southend United	0-0
Burnley v Huddersfield Town	3-1
Bury v Plymouth Argyle	1-1
Chelsea v Swindon Town	1-1
Croydon Common v Oldham Athletic	0-3
Darlington v Bradford City	0-1
Derby County v Leeds City	1-2
Everton v Barnsley	3-0
Grimsby Town v Northampton Town	0-3
Hull City v West Bromwich Albion	1-0
Liverpool v Stockport County	3-0
Middlesbrough v Goole Town	9-3
Millwall v Clapton Orient	2-1
Nottingham Forest v Norwich City	1-4
Preston North End v Manchester City	0-0
Queen's Park Rangers v Glossop	2-1
Reading v Wolverhampton Wan.	0-1
Rochdale v Gillingham	2-0
Sheffield Wednesday v Manchester United	1-0
South Shields v Fulham	1-2
Southampton v Luton Town	3-0
Swansea Town v Blackburn Rovers	1-0
Tottenham Hotspur v Sunderland	2-1
West Ham United v Newcastle United	2-2
r Birmingham v Crystal Palace	3-0e
r Chelsea v Swindon Town	5-2e
r Manchester City v Preston North End	3-0
r Newcastle United v West Ham United	3-2
r Plymouth Argyle v Bury	1-2
r Southend United v Bristol Rovers	3-0

Round Two

Bolton Wanderers v Millwall	0-0e
Bradford City v Middlesbrough	1-0
Brighton & Hove Albion v Birmingham	0-0e
Burnley v Southend United	6-0
Bury v Bradford Park Avenue	0-1
Chelsea v Arsenal	1-0
Everton v Bristol City	4-0
Fulham v Southampton	2-3e
Hull City v Northampton Town	2-1
Manchester City v Aston Villa	1-0
Newcastle United v Swansea Town	1-1e
Norwich City v Tottenham Hotspur	3-2
Oldham Athletic v Rochdale	3-0
Queen's Park Rangers v Leeds City	1-0
Sheffield United v Liverpool	1-0
Sheffield Wednesday v Wolverhampton Wan.	2-0
r Birmingham v Brighton & Hove Albion	3-0
r Millwall v Bolton Wanderers	2-2e
r Swansea Town v Newcastle United	0-2
r2 Bolton Wanderers v Millwall	4-1

Round Three

Birmingham v Oldham Athletic	2-3
Bolton Wanderers v Burnley	2-1e
Bradford City v Norwich City	1-1e
Manchester City v Chelsea	0-1
Queen's Park Rangers v Everton	1-2 N
Sheffield United v Bradford Park Avenue	1-0e
Sheffield Wednesday v Newcastle United	1-2
Southampton v Hull City	2-2e
r Hull City v Southampton	4-0
r Norwich City v Bradford City	0-0e
r2 Bradford City v Norwich City	2-0 N

Round Four

Bolton Wanderers v Hull City	4-2
Bradford City v Everton	0-2
Chelsea v Newcastle United	1-1e
Oldham Athletic v Sheffield United	0-0e

r Newcastle United v Chelsea	0-1e	
r Sheffield United v Oldham Athletic	3-0	

Semi Finals

Chelsea v Everton	2-0 N
Sheffield United v Bolton Wanderers	2-1 N

Final

Sheffield United v Chelsea	3-0 N

1919/20

Extra Preliminary Round

1 Newbiggin Athletic v Brighton West End	1-0
Palmers, Jarrow v Felling Colliery	3-0
Usworth Colliery v Close Works	0-4
Walker Celtic v Washington Colliery	3-2
8 Bloxwich Strollers v Wellington Town	0-0
Darlaston v Talbot Stead	5-1
Hednesford Town v Halesowen Town	5-3
Kidderminster Harriers v Redditch	4-0
Tamworth Castle v Nuneaton Town	3-3
Wednesbury Old Athletic v Cradley Heath St Luke's	1-3
11 Darfield St George v Kilnhurst United	4-0
Dearne v Prospect United	3-1
Denaby United v Mexborough	1-4
Doncaster Plant Works v Conisborough Athletic	5-2
Rotherham Amateurs v Kimberworth Old Boys	1-2
Sheffield Simplex Works v Thurnscoe Park Avenue	1-3
21 Woolwich Ordnance v Brompton	3-3
22 Thornycrofts (Woolston) v RAE Farnborough	4-0
23 Devizes Town v Clandown	1-2
Melksham Town v Timsbury Athletic	1-1
Welton Rovers v Douglas (Kingswood)	2-1
8r Nuneaton Town v Tamworth Castle	2-3
r Wellington Town v Bloxwich Strollers	4-0
21r Woolwich Ordnance v Brompton	3-1
23r Timsbury Athletic v Melksham Town	2-1

Preliminary Round

1 Ashington v Close Works	1-0
Bedlington United v Walker Celtic	1-2
Lintz Institute v Wallsend	1-0
Mickley v Blyth Spartans	0-1
Newbiggin Athletic v Seaton Delaval	1-1
Newburn v Palmers, Jarrow	0-3
Pandon Temperance v Spen Black & White	1-0
Rutherford College v Prudhoe Castle	1-2
2 Birtley v Horden Athletic	3-3
Boldon Colliery v Craghead Heros	1-0
Dipton United v Houghton	1-2
Hobson Wanderers v Durham City	1-5
Leadgate Park v South Pontop Villa	2-1
Ryhope Comrades v Annfield Plain	0-1
Seaham Harbour v Esh Winning (1)	3-1
Sunderland West End v Chopwell Institute	4-0
3 Brotton v Redcar	3-2
Crook Town v Darlington Railway Ath.	2-0
Grangetown St Mary's v Spennymoor United	1-2
Rise Carr v Scarborough	wo/s
Shildon v Stanley United	1-0 v
South Bank v Loftus Albion	4-1
Willington v St Helens United	1-0
4 Barrow Shipbuilders v Kells White Star	1-2
5 Dick, Kerrs v Kirkham & Wesham	wo/s
Fleetwood v Hamilton Central	4-5
Nelson v Accrington Stanley	2-1
Portsmouth Rovers (Lancs) v Breightmet United	0-3
6 Runcorn v Congleton Town	4-1
Widnes DS&S v Monks Hall	1-4
7 Harrowby v Lostock Gralam	0-1
Nantwich v Chester	5-0
South Liverpool v Northern Nomads	7-2
Wallasey Borough v Marlborough Old Boys	0-2
Winsford United v Northwich Victoria	2-0
Witton Albion v Wrexham	2-2
8 Bilston United v Tamworth Castle	1-0
Birmingham Corp. Tramways v Brierley Hill Alliance	1-2
Darlaston v Rugby Town (1)	4-1
Hednesford Town v Atherstone Town	5-0
Stafford Rangers v Kidderminster Harriers	4-2
Stourbridge v Cradley Heath St Luke's	3-3
Wellington Town v Bromsgrove Rovers	4-1
Willenhall v Cannock Town	5-1
9 Bentley Colliery v Bullcroft Main Colliery	wo/s
Beverley Town v Goole Chevrons	2-1
Brigg Town v Cleethorpes Town	0-14
Frodingham Athletic v Brodsworth Main Colliery	0-2
Gainsborough Trinity v Hull Old Boys	4-0
Grimsby Rovers v Grimsby Haycroft Rovers	3-1
Humber Graving Dock v National Radiator Co.	wo/s
Scunthorpe United v Goole Town	7-0
10 Acomb WMC (York) v Frickley Colliery	1-1
Boothtown v Harrogate	3-3
Castleford Town v Calverley	3-1
Halifax Town v Apperley Bridge	7-0
Leeds Steelworks v Hebden Bridge	4-2
Rothwell Athletic v Horsforth	2-1

50

1919/20

	Rothwell Parish Church v Glasshoughton Colliery	1-0
	South Kirkby Colliery v Rowntrees	5-0
11	Darfield St George v Worksop Town	3-2
	Dearne v Atlas & Norfolk Works	2-0
	Grimethorpe Colliery Inst. v Parkgate Works Sports	6-0
	Kimberworth Old Boys v Wath Athletic	1-0
	Rotherham Town v Sheffield	2-1
	Silverwood Colliery v Doncaster Plant Works	6-0
	Tankersley v Tinsley Park	6-1
	Thurnscoe Park Avenue v Mexborough	0-2
12	Chesterfield v Clay Cross Town	4-0
13	Arnold St Mary's v Grantham	0-4
	Boots Athletic v Netherfield Rangers	2-1
	Ericssons Athletic v Basford United	2-3
	Hucknall Byron v Sutton Town	1-1
	New Hucknall Colliery v Rufford Colliery	5-4
	Shirebrook v Mansfield Town	3-1
	Sneinton v Newark Athletic	2-3
	Sutton Junction v Welbeck Colliery	3-3
15	Brotherhoods Works v Bourne Town	1-0
16	Gorleston v Mortons Athletic	1-0
	Great Yarmouth Town v Norwich CEYMS	1-2
	King's Lynn DS&S v Norwich DS&S	1-2
	Leiston Works Athletic v Lowestoft Town	0-1
17	GER Romford v Custom House	0-3
	Gnome Athletic v Woodford Crusaders	2-1
	Leyton v Hoffmann Athletic (Chelmsford)	1-4
	Newportonians v Walthamstow Grange	1-5
	Shoeburyness Garrison v Jurgens (Purfleet)	wo/s
18	Barnet v Cheshunt	1-0
	Chesham United v Tufnell Spartan	6-0
	Islington Town v Page Green Old Boys	2-0
	Leavesden Mental Hospital v Waterlows (Dunstable)	1-0
19	Hampstead Town v Southall	3-1
	Handley Page v Hammersmith Comrades	wo/s
	Maidenhead United v Henley Town	12-1
	Newbury Town v Uxbridge	6-0
	Windsor & Eton v Botwell Mission	2-1
	Wycombe Wanderers v Reading United	5-2
	Yiewsley v Slough	0-11
20	Aquarius v Walton-on-Thames	2-0 v
	Camberley & Yorktown v Redhill	3-1
	Croydon (1) v Burberry Athletic	3-4
	Guards Depot v Sutton United	1-5
	Guildford v Woking	1-1
	Tooting Town v Summerstown	2-2
	West Norwood v Kingstonian	1-3
	Wimbledon v Pearl Assurance	7-0
21	Lewes v Worthing	3-6
	Maidstone United v Ashford Railway Works	2-0
	Margate v Deal Ports	12-1
	Northfleet United v Catford Southend	4-2
	Sittingbourne v Charlton Athletic	7-2
	Tunbridge Wells Rangers v Sheppey United	2-2
	Whitstable v Folkestone	2-0
	Woolwich Ordnance v Woolwich Polytechnic	2-1
22	Boscombe v Poole	9-0
	Bournemouth (Ams) v Longfleet St Mary's	wo/s
	East Cowes Victoria v Cowes (2)	2-2
	Eastleigh Athletic v Basingstoke	0-2
	Portsmouth Amateurs v White & Co's Sports	15-0
	Thornycrofts (Basingstoke) v Salisbury (1)	1-1
	Thornycrofts (Woolston) v Bournemouth Gasworks Ath.	5-0
	Weymouth v Bournemouth Tramways	1-3
23	Bath City v Yeovil & Petter's United	4-4
	Chippenham Town v Cheltenham Town	4-0
	Clandown v Swindon Victoria	4-0
	Minehead v Hanham Athletic	1-3
	Street v Frome Town	4-0
	Timsbury Athletic v Paulton Rovers	2-0
	Trowbridge Town v Peasedown St John's	2-0
	Welton Rovers v Clevedon	2-1
24	Bargoed v Abertillery	2-0
	Ebbw Vale v Barry	1-1
	Mid Rhondda v Aberdare Amateurs	wo/s
	Pontypridd v Rhiwderin	3-0
	Rogerstone v Llanelli	1-6
	Ton Pentre v Caerau Rovers	3-0
1r	Seaton Delaval v Newbiggin Athletic	0-1
2r	Horden Athletic v Birtley	1-0
3r	Shildon v Stanley United	4-3
7r	Wrexham v Witton Albion	3-2e
8r	Cradley Heath St Luke's v Stourbridge	3-2
10r	Frickley Colliery v Acomb WMC (York)	wo/s
r	Harrogate v Boothtown	3-0
13r	Sutton Town v Hucknall Byron	5-1
r	Welbeck Colliery v Sutton Junction	wo/s
20r	Summerstown v Tooting Town	3-0
r	Walton-on-Thames v Aquarius	4-1
r	Woking v Guildford	2-11
21r	Sheppey United v Tunbridge Wells Rangers	7-1
22r	Cowes (2) v East Cowes Victoria	5-2
r	Salisbury (1) v Thornycrofts (Basingstoke)	0-4
23r	Yeovil & Petter's United v Bath City	0-2
24r	Barry v Ebbw Vale	0-1

Qualifying Round One

1	Ashington v Pandon Temperance	4-0
	Lintz Institute v Prudhoe Castle	3-1
	Newbiggin Athletic v Palmers, Jarrow	1-4
	Walker Celtic v Blyth Spartans	1-2
2	Horden Athletic v Houghton	1-3
	Leadgate Park v Durham City	2-1
	Seaham Harbour v Annfield Plain	2-0
	Sunderland West End v Boldon Colliery	5-0
3	Brotton v Crook Town	0-2
	Eston United v Rise Carr	2-5
	South Bank v Willington	3-2
	Spennymoor United v Shildon	1-1
4	Carlisle United v Wigton Harriers	8-1
	Penrith v Cleator Moor Celtic	1-3
	Vickerstown v Kells White Star	0-5
	Wath Brow United v Frizington Athletic	1-3
5	Chorley v Great Harwood	1-0
	Hamilton Central v Breightmet United	1-0
	Leyland v Dick, Kerrs	3-1
	Nelson v Horwich RMI	0-1
6	Garston Gasworks v Macclesfield Town	2-1
	Glossop v Altrincham	1-1
	Monks Hall v Hurst	2-2
	Runcorn v Sandbach Ramblers	7-0
7	Crewe Alexandra v Tranmere Rovers	1-0
	Lostock Gralam v Nantwich	3-1
	South Liverpool v Winsford United	3-0
	Wrexham v Marlborough Old Boys	8-0
8	Bilston United v Wellington Town	1-1
	Brierley Hill Alliance v Darlaston	0-1
	Cradley Heath St Luke's v Stafford Rangers	2-1
	Hednesford Town v Willenhall	3-2
9	Gainsborough Trinity v Bentley Colliery	2-0
	Grimsby Rovers v Cleethorpes Town	2-4
	Humber Graving Dock v Beverley Town	5-0
	Scunthorpe United v Brodsworth Main Colliery	2-1
10	Castleford Town v Halifax Town	3-0
	Frickley Colliery v Rothwell Athletic	3-1
	Harrogate v South Kirkby Colliery	1-1
	Leeds Steelworks v Rothwell Parish Church	4-2
11	Darfield St George v Mexborough	0-1
	Grimethorpe Colliery Institute v Silverwood Colliery	2-1
	Rotherham Town v Dearne	4-2
	Tankersley v Kimberworth Old Boys	1-4
12	Chesterfield v Ilkeston United	2-1
	Eckington Red Rose v Bolsover Colliery	0-1
	South Normanton Colliery v Long Eaton	2-1
	Staveley Town v Dronfield Woodhouse	7-0
13	Basford United v Sutton Town	1-5
	Grantham v Boots Athletic	2-2
	New Hucknall Colliery v Newark Athletic	4-0
	Welbeck Colliery v Shirebrook	3-1
14	Coalville Swifts v Ashbourne Town	8-0
	Coalville Town (1) v Gresley Rovers	0-6
	Hinckley United (1) v Whitwick Imperial	4-2
	Loughborough Corinthians v Brush Works	9-1
15	Bedford Town (1) v Kettering	1-6
	Brotherhoods Works v Stamford	1-0 D
	Desborough Town v Wellingborough Town	6-0
	Fletton United v Boston (1)	2-0
16	Cambridge Town v Norwich DS&S	3-0
	Colchester Town v Gorleston	2-0
	Cromer v Lowestoft Town	1-1
	Norwich CEYMS v King's Lynn	2-6
17	Custom House v Chelmsford	0-1
	Gnome Athletic v 1st Grenadier Guards	8-1
	Leytonstone v Walthamstow Grange	3-0
	Shoeburyness Garrison v Hoffmann Ath.(Chelm'rd)	1-2
18	Enfield v Chesham United	0-1
	Leavesden Mental Hospital v Tufnell Park	2-0
	Luton Clarence v Islington Town	5-0
	St Albans City v Barnet	1-0
19	Hampstead Town v Marlow	4-1
	Slough v Newbury Town	8-2
	Windsor & Eton v Handley Page	5-0
	Wycombe Wanderers v Maidenhead United	2-1
20	Camberley & Yorktown v Summerstown	1-3
	Guildford v Kingstonian	7-1
	Sutton United v Burberry Athletic	3-0
	Wimbledon v Walton-on-Thames	3-0
21	Maidstone United v Sheppey United	0-0
	Northfleet United v Margate	7-2
	Woolwich Ordnance v Whitstable	6-0
	Worthing v Sittingbourne	2-2
22	Basingstoke v Boscombe	1-0
	Bournemouth (Ams) v Bournemouth Tramways	0-6
	Thornycrofts (Basingstoke) v Portsmouth Amateurs	0-5
	Thornycrofts (Woolston) v Cowes (2)	7-3
23	Clandown v Street	0-0
	Timsbury Athletic v Hanham Athletic	3-3
	Trowbridge Town v Chippenham Town	5-0
	Welton Rovers v Bath City	1-4
24	Cardiff Corinthians v Newport Barbarians	2-0
	Llanelli v Bargoed	1-0
	Mid Rhondda v Ebbw Vale	3-0
	Ton Pentre v Pontypridd	3-1
3r	Shildon v Spennymoor United	2-1
6r	Altrincham v Glossop	5-4
r	Hurst v Monks Hall	3-5
8r	Wellington Town v Bilston United	3-1
10r	South Kirkby Colliery v Harrogate	4-0
13r	Boots Athletic v Grantham	2-2e
16r	Lowestoft Town v Cromer	1-3
21r	Sheppey United v Maidstone United	2-1
r	Sittingbourne v Worthing	4-2
23r	Hanham Athletic v Timsbury Athletic	3-1
r	Street v Clandown	0-1
13r2	Grantham v Boots Athletic	2-0 N

Qualifying Round Two

1	Ashington v Blyth Spartans	0-3
	Lintz Institute v Palmers, Jarrow	1-0
2	Leadgate Park v Sunderland West End	4-1
	Seaham Harbour v Houghton	1-1
3	Crook Town v Shildon	1-2
	Rise Carr v South Bank	0-2
4	Carlisle United v Cleator Moor Celtic	6-1
	Kells White Star v Frizington Athletic	1-3
5	Hamilton Central v Horwich RMI	0-1
	Leyland v Chorley	0-0
6	Garston Gasworks v Runcorn	0-1
	Monks Hall v Altrincham	2-1
7	Crewe Alexandra v Wrexham	3-3
	South Liverpool v Lostock Gralam	4-1
8	Darlaston v Wellington Town	2-1
	Hednesford Town v Cradley Heath St Luke's	5-2
9	Gainsborough Trinity v Humber Graving Dock	4-0
	Scunthorpe United v Cleethorpes Town	0-1
10	Castleford Town v Leeds Steelworks	6-0
	South Kirkby Colliery v Frickley Colliery	4-2
11	Kimberworth Old Boys v Grimethorpe Colliery Inst.	3-0
	Rotherham Town v Mexborough	2-0
12	Bolsover Colliery v Staveley Town	0-1
	Chesterfield v South Normanton Colliery	5-0 D
13	Grantham v Sutton Town	3-4
	Welbeck Colliery v New Hucknall Colliery	2-2
14	Hinckley United (1) v Coalville Swifts	0-1
	Loughborough Corinthians v Gresley Rovers	3-2
15	Fletton United v Desborough Town	0-1
	Stamford v Kettering	0-2
16	Colchester Town v Cambridge Town	1-1
	King's Lynn v Cromer	3-1
17	Chelmsford v Leytonstone	0-3
	Gnome Athletic v Hoffmann Athletic (Chelmsford)	7-0
18	Leavesden Mental Hospital v Chesham United	0-2
	St Albans City v Luton Clarence	0-0
19	Hampstead Town v Windsor & Eton	3-0
	Wycombe Wanderers v Slough	3-3
20	Guildford v Summerstown	2-1
	Wimbledon v Sutton United	2-0
21	Sittingbourne v Sheppey United	0-3
	Woolwich Ordnance v Northfleet United	1-3
22	Portsmouth Amateurs v Bournemouth Tramways	0-2
	Thornycrofts (Woolston) v Basingstoke	5-1
23	Hanham Athletic v Clandown	2-4
	Trowbridge Town v Bath City	1-2
24	Cardiff Corinthians v Mid Rhondda	0-4
	Ton Pentre v Llanelli	5-2
2r	Houghton v Seaham Harbour	1-2
5r	Chorley v Leyland	1-0
7r	Wrexham v Crewe Alexandra	0-1
13r	New Hucknall Colliery v Welbeck Colliery	wo/s
16r	Cambridge Town v Colchester Town	5-2
18r	Luton Clarence v St Albans City	3-2
19r	Slough v Wycombe Wanderers	4-5

Qualifying Round Three

1	Lintz Institute v Blyth Spartans	1-0
2	Leadgate Park v Seaham Harbour	2-1
3	South Bank v Shildon	3-1
4	Carlisle United v Frizington Athletic	1-0
5	Chorley v Horwich RMI	1-1
6	Runcorn v Monks Hall	2-2
7	Crewe Alexandra v South Liverpool	1-3
8	Darlaston v Hednesford Town	3-3
9	Gainsborough Trinity v Cleethorpes Town	1-1
10	Castleford Town v South Kirkby Colliery	2-0
11	Kimberworth Old Boys v Rotherham Town	0-0
12	South Normanton Colliery v Staveley Town	1-1
13	Sutton Town v New Hucknall Colliery	4-1
14	Loughborough Corinthians v Coalville Swifts	2-0
15	Desborough Town v Kettering	1-0
16	King's Lynn v Cambridge Town	6-2
17	Leytonstone v Gnome Athletic	0-4
18	Luton Clarence v Chesham United	0-3
19	Hampstead Town v Wycombe Wanderers	4-1
20	Guildford v Wimbledon	2-1
21	Northfleet United v Sheppey United	3-4
22	Bournemouth Tramways v Thornycrofts (Woolston)	0-0
23	Clandown v Bath City	2-2
24	Ton Pentre v Mid Rhondda	2-1
5r	Horwich RMI v Chorley	4-0
6r	Monks Hall v Runcorn	1-0
8r	Hednesford Town v Darlaston	2-1
9r	Cleethorpes Town v Gainsborough Trinity	2-1 N
11r	Rotherham Town v Kimberworth Old Boys	5-4
12r	Staveley Town v South Normanton Colliery	0-0e
22r	Thornycrofts (Woolston) v Bournemouth Tramways	3-1
23r	Bath City v Clandown	3-1
12r2	Staveley Town v South Normanton Colliery	2-0eN

Qualifying Round Four

	Barrow v Carlisle United	0-0
	Bishop Auckland v Hartlepools United	1-0
	Bromley v Guildford	4-2
	Clapton v Chatham	3-2
	Darlington v South Bank	4-2
	Desborough Town v Cleethorpes Town	1-2
	Dulwich Hamlet v Nunhead	1-0
	Hampstead Town v Gnome Athletic	1-1
	Ilford v Sheppey United	1-3

1919/20 to 1920/21

	King's Lynn - Bye	
	Lintz Institute v Castleford Town	0-0
	London Caledonians v Chesham United	3-1
	Loughborough Corinthians v Sutton Town	3-0
	Newport County v Bath City	5-2
	Oxford City v Thornycrofts (Woolston)	1-2
	Rochdale v Monks Hall	1-0
	Rotherham Town v Staveley Town	2-2
	Shrewsbury Town v Hednesford Town	0-8
	Southport v South Liverpool	1-0 v
	Stalybridge Celtic v Horwich RMI	4-2
	Stockton v Leadgate Park	1-2
	Ton Pentre v Merthyr Town	0-3
	Walsall v Worcester City	3-1
	West Stanley v Scotswood	2-0
r	Carlisle United v Barrow	2-0
r	Castleford Town v Lintz Institute	1-0
r	Gnome Athletic v Hampstead Town	2-0
r	Rotherham Town v Staveley Town	7-1
r	Southport v South Liverpool	1-1
r2	South Liverpool v Southport	1-0

Qualifying Round Five

	Bishop Auckland v Darlington	2-9
	Bromley v Sheppey United	2-2
	Clapton v Gnome Athletic	1-1
	Cleethorpes Town v Castleford Town	1-3
	Dulwich Hamlet v Thornycrofts (Woolston)	1-3
	Hednesford Town v Walsall	4-2
	London Caledonians v King's Lynn	6-0
	Loughborough Corinthians v Rotherham Town	2-1
	Newport County v Merthyr Town	1-0
	Rochdale v Stalybridge Celtic	1-0
	South Liverpool v Carlisle United	3-1
	West Stanley v Leadgate Park	2-0
r	Gnome Athletic v Clapton	1-0
r	Sheppey United v Bromley	1-0e

Qualifying Round Six

	Brighton & Hove Albion v Luton Town	0-1
	Castleford Town v London Caledonians	3-2
	Darlington v Norwich City	5-0
	Gillingham v Swansea Town	1-1
	Hednesford Town v Gnome Athletic	2-2
	Newport County v Exeter City	1-0
	Northampton Town v Bristol Rovers	2-2
	Port Vale v Loughborough Corinthians	4-0
	South Liverpool v Rochdale	1-2
	Southend United v Watford	1-0
	Thornycrofts (Woolston) v Sheppey United	4-0
	West Stanley v Rotherham County	1-0
r	Bristol Rovers v Northampton Town	3-2
r	Gnome Athletic v Hednesford Town	0-3
r	Swansea Town v Gillingham	1-1
r2	Gillingham v Swansea Town	0-0 N
r3	Gillingham v Swansea Town	3-1 N

Round One

	Arsenal v Rochdale	4-2
	Aston Villa v Queen's Park Rangers	2-1
	Birmingham v Everton	2-0
	Blackburn Rovers v Wolverhampton Wan.	2-2
	Blackpool v Derby County	0-0
	Bolton Wanderers v Chelsea	0-1
	Bradford City v Portsmouth	2-0
	Bradford Park Avenue v Nottingham Forest	3-0
	Bristol Rovers v Tottenham Hotspur	1-4
	Bury v Stoke	2-0
	Cardiff City v Oldham Athletic	2-0
	Castleford Town v Hednesford Town	2-0
	Darlington v Sheffield Wednesday	0-0
	Fulham v Swindon Town	1-2
	Grimsby Town v Bristol City	1-2
	Huddersfield Town v Brentford	5-1
	Luton Town v Coventry City	2-2
	Manchester City v Clapton Orient	4-1
	Middlesbrough v Lincoln City	4-1
	Newcastle United v Crystal Palace	2-0
	Newport County v Leicester City	0-0
	Notts County v Millwall	2-0
	Plymouth Argyle v Reading	2-0
	Port Vale v Manchester United	0-1
	Preston North End v Stockport County	3-1
	Sheffield United v Southend United	3-0
	South Shields v Liverpool	1-1
	Southampton v West Ham United	0-0
	Sunderland v Hull City	6-2
	Thornycrofts (Woolston) v Burnley	0-0 N
	West Bromwich Albion v Barnsley	0-1
	West Stanley v Gillingham	3-1
r	Burnley v Thornycrofts (Woolston)	5-0
r	Coventry City v Luton Town	0-1
r	Derby County v Blackpool	1-4
r	Leicester City v Newport County	2-0
r	Liverpool v South Shields	2-0
r	Sheffield Wednesday v Darlington	0-2
r	West Ham United v Southampton	3-1
r	Wolverhampton Wan. v Blackburn Rovers	1-0

Round Two

	Birmingham v Darlington	4-0
	Bradford City v Sheffield United	2-1
	Bradford Park Avenue v Castleford Town	3-2
	Bristol City v Arsenal	1-0
	Burnley v Sunderland	1-1
	Chelsea v Swindon Town	4-0
	Leicester City v Manchester City	3-0
	Luton Town v Liverpool	0-2
	Manchester United v Aston Villa	1-2
	Newcastle United v Huddersfield Town	0-1
	Notts County v Middlesbrough	1-0
	Plymouth Argyle v Barnsley	4-1
	Preston North End v Blackpool	2-1
	Tottenham Hotspur v West Stanley	4-0
	West Ham United v Bury	6-0
	Wolverhampton Wan. v Cardiff City	1-2
r	Sunderland v Burnley	2-0

Round Three

	Aston Villa v Sunderland	1-0
	Bristol City v Cardiff City	2-1
	Chelsea v Leicester City	3-0
	Huddersfield Town v Plymouth Argyle	3-1
	Liverpool v Birmingham	2-0
	Notts County v Bradford Park Avenue	3-4
	Preston North End v Bradford City	0-3
	Tottenham Hotspur v West Ham United	3-0

Round Four

	Bristol City v Bradford City	2-0
	Chelsea v Bradford Park Avenue	4-1
	Huddersfield Town v Liverpool	2-1
	Tottenham Hotspur v Aston Villa	0-1

Semi Finals

	Aston Villa v Chelsea	3-1 N
	Huddersfield Town v Bristol City	2-1 N

Final

	Aston Villa v Huddersfield Town	1-0eN

1920/21

Extra Preliminary Round

1	Hebburn Colliery v Prudhoe Castle	3-0
	Newburn v Walker Celtic	3-2
	Preston Colliery v Heaton Stannington	6-0
	Seaton Delaval v St Peter's Albion	3-0
2	Consett Celtic v Twizell United	3-0
	Craghead United v Wingate Albion Comrades	1-1
3	Bridlington Town (1) v Redcar	6-2
	Filey Town v South Bank East End	0-2
	Haverton Hill v West Auckland Town	3-0
	Spennymoor United v Willington	1-2
7	Marine v Bromborough	4-0
	Prescot Wire Works v Old Xaverians	2-1
	St Cleopatra's Old Boys v North Engineers (Bootle)	wo/s
8	Bilston United v Kidderminster Harriers	1-3
	Bloxwich Strollers v Stafford Rangers	0-0e
	Brierley Hill Alliance v Halesowen Town	1-4
	Cannock Town v Atherstone Town	4-1
	Darlaston v Oakengates Town	3-0
	Talbot Stead v Walsall Wood	1-0
	Wednesbury Old Athletic v Wolverhampton Amateur	3-1
	Wellington St George's v Redditch	2-1
	West Birmingham v Birmingham Corp. Tramways	1-2
	Willenhall v Stourbridge	1-1
9	Barton Town (1) v Hull Dairycoates	2-2
	Bentley Colliery v Grimsby STC	4-0
	Frodingham Athletic v Gilberdyke	0-1
	Goole Shipyards v Charltons (Grimsby)	1-1
	Grimsby Haycroft Rovers v Gainsborough Albion	3-0
	Holderness Athletic v Brunswick Institute	0-2
	Hook Shipyards v West Hull Albion	4-1
	Hull Old Boys v Marfleet	wo/s
	Hull St Peter's OB v Newland Choir	1-1
	Hull Wanderers v Brodsworth Main Colliery	2-5
	Shiphams v Grimsby Rovers	3-6
	Withernsea v Sutton (Hull)	3-0
10	Allerton Bywater Colliery v Glasshoughton Colliery	3-0
	Apperley Bridge v Selby Olympia	10-1
	Halifax Town v Rowntrees	5-3
	Horsforth v Ryhill Liberal	2-1
	Leeds United v Boothtown	5-2
	Mytholmroyd v Harrogate	1-4
	Rothwell Parish Church v Hebden Bridge	2-2
11	Ardsley Athletic v Goldthorpe Colliery	7-1
	Conisborough Athletic v Wath Athletic	0-14
	Doncaster Rovers v Atlas & Norfolk Works	6-0
	Kilnhurst United v Jump WMC	0-0
	Kiveton Park Colliery v Anston United	2-0
	Maltby Main Colliery v Hemmingfield	2-0
	Rawmarsh Athletic v Denaby United	0-1
	Tankersley v Hoyland St Peter's	3-0
	Wombwell v Sheffield	4-0
	Worksop Town v Treeton Reading Room	0-0
13	Basford United v Lenton	0-5
	Players Athletic v Kirkby Collieries	2-1
15	Horncastle Town v Spilsby	3-2
	Peterbro' Westwood Works v Rushden Town	0-0
	Raunds Town v Northampton War Team	2-5
21	Bexleyheath Labour v Dartford	wo/s
	Cray Wanderers v Bostall Heath	3-3
	Newhaven v Vernon Athletic	3-1
	Whitstable v RN Depot	1-0
23	Babbacombe v Frenchay	2-1
	Cheltenham Town v Melksham & Avon United	2-2 d
	Chippenham Rovers v Welton Rovers	1-3
	Clevedon v Glastonbury	0-1
	Frome Town v Yeovil & Petter's United	3-1
	Paulton Rovers v Minehead	2-1
	Radstock Town v Warminster Town	1-0
	Spencer Moulton v Devizes Town	4-1
	Street v Torquay Town	4-3
	Swindon Victoria v Timsbury Athletic	3-0
24	Cardiff Albion v Aberdare Amateurs	wo/s
	Chepstow v Oakdale	6-0
2r	Wingate Albion Comrades v Craghead United	0-4
8r	Stafford Rangers v Bloxwich Strollers	2-2e
r	Stourbridge v Willenhall	1-2
9r	Goole Shipyards v Charltons (Grimsby)	1-2
r	Hull Dairycoates v Barton Town (1)	0-1e
r	Newland Choir v Hull St Peter's OB	1-2
10r	Hebden Bridge v Rothwell Parish Church	2-0
11r	Kilnhurst United v Jump WMC	1-0
r	Worksop Town v Treeton Reading Room	2-0
15r	Rushden Town v Peterbro' Westwood Works	4-0
21r	Bostall Heath v Cray Wanderers	6-1
8r2	Stafford Rangers v Bloxwich Strollers	1-2e

Preliminary Round

1	Ashington v Close Works	1-0
	Bedlington United v Hebburn Colliery	1-1
	Lintz Institute v Newburn	4-1
	Pandon Temperance v Mickley	1-2
	Preston Colliery v Jarrow	1-0
	Scotswood v Chopwell Institute	1-0
	Spen Black & White v Seaton Delaval	4-3
	Wallsend v Usworth Colliery	3-1
2	Annfield Plain v Esh Winning (1)	2-1
	Birtley v Craghead United	1-0
	Horden Athletic v Hobson Wanderers	3-0
	Houghton v Dipton United	2-0
	Leadgate Park v Crook Town	3-0
	Seaham Harbour v Langley Park	3-1
	Sunderland West End v Wolsingham Town	3-0
	Tow Law Town v Consett Celtic	1-0
3	Eston United v Willington	1-0
	Grangetown St Mary's v Brotton	1-0
	Hartlepools United v South Bank East End	7-0
	Haverton Hill v Rise Carr	3-2
	Loftus Albion v Bridlington Town (1)	5-1
	Scarborough v Stanley United	4-1
	South Bank v Darlington Railway Ath.	3-1
	Stockton v Shildon	4-0
4	Barrow v Vickerstown	4-0
	Barrow YMCA v Arlecdon Red Rose	0-2
	Frizington Athletic v Dalton Casuals	2-0
	Parton Athletic v Lowca	0-0
	Penrith v Distington	6-0
	Wath Brow United v Appleby	6-1
5	Dick, Kerrs v Great Harwood	1-0
	Fleetwood v Accrington Stanley	8-0
	Morecambe v Breightmet United	1-1
	Nelson v Skelmersdale United	4-1
	Portsmouth Rovers (Lancs) v Lancaster Town	2-3
6	Congleton Town v Sandbach Ramblers	6-3
	Eccles United v Glossop	10-0
	Garston Gasworks v Buxton	4-0
	Graysons v Chapel-en-le-Frith	4-3
	Hurst v Matlock Town	7-0
7	Buckley United v Marlborough Old Boys	wo/s
	Harrowby v South Liverpool	3-3
	Lostock Gralam v St Cleopatra's Old Boys	8-1
	Marine v Oswestry Town	9-2
	Nantwich v Witton Albion	4-0
	Prescot v Northern Nomads	4-2
	Prescot Wire Works v Winsford United	3-1
	Wrexham v Northwich Victoria	3-0
8	Bloxwich Strollers v Wellington Town	0-6
	Cannock Town v Wednesbury Old Athletic (2)	1-3
	Darlaston v Cradley Heath St Luke's	1-3
	Halesowen Town v Kidderminster Harriers	3-2
	Hednesford Town v Willenhall	4-1
	Walsall v Birmingham Corp. Tramways	3-0
	Wellington St George's v Shrewsbury Town	1-2
	Worcester City v Talbot Stead	1-1
9	Barton Town (1) v Hook Shipyards	1-2
	Bentley Colliery v Hull St Peter's OB	4-0
	Brodsworth Main Colliery v Humber Graving Dock	5-2
	Charltons (Grimsby) v Withernsea	5-0
	Cleethorpes Town v Gilberdyke	1-3
	Grimsby Haycroft Rovers v Grimsby Rovers	4-4
	Hull Old Boys v Gainsborough Trinity	0-5
	Scunthorpe United v Brunswick Institute	6-0
10	Allerton Bywater Colliery v Rothwell Athletic	4-0
	Apperley Bridge v Yeadon Celtic	3-1
	Bolton United v Horsforth	3-1
	Calverley v South Kirkby United	wo/s
	Halifax Town v Liversedge	3-1

1920/21

	Harrogate v Hebden Bridge	3-2
	Leeds United v Leeds Steelworks	7-0
	South Kirkby Colliery v Frickley Colliery	4-0 E
11	Denaby United v Ardsley Athletic	1-0
	Doncaster Rovers v Wombwell	0-1
	Grimethorpe Col. Inst. v Hoyland Common Weslyans	3-2
	Houghton Main Colliery v Tankersley	0-0
	Mexborough v Kilnhurst United	5-0
	Wath Athletic v Rotherham Town	0-1
	Wombwell Main v Maltby Main Colliery	4-7
	Worksop Town v Kiveton Park Colliery	1-0
12	Beighton Recreation v Tibshelf Colliery	2-4
	Blackwell Colliery v Clowne Colliery	4-3
	Dronfield Woodhouse v Chesterfield	1-11
	Hardwick Colliery v Bolsover Colliery	wo/s
	Ilkeston United v Eckington Works	3-0
	Long Eaton v South Normanton Colliery	2-1
	Ripley Colliery v Clay Cross Town	1-1
13	Arnold St Mary's v Netherfield Rangers	2-1
	Grantham v Sneinton	4-1
	Hucknall Byron v Lenton	3-0
	Mansfield Town v Sutton Junction	8-1
	New Hucknall Colliery v Boots Athletic	0-3
	Shirebrook v Ericssons Athletic	1-0
	Sutton Town v Newark Athletic	4-3
	Welbeck Colliery v Players Athletic	4-0
14	Ashbourne Town v Gresley Colliery	1-0 D
	Barwell United v Gresley Rovers	3-3
	Brush Works v Coalville Town (2)	2-4
	Burton All Saints v Bretby Colliery	1-3
	Coalville Swifts v Ashby Town	2-1
	Loughborough Corinthians v Rugby Town (1)	2-1
	Nuneaton Town v Whitwick Imperial	4-0
15	Bedford Town (1) v Kettering	1-3
	Boston (1) v Louth Town	7-1
	Boston St James v Stamford	0-7
	Fletton United v Rushden Town	2-3
	Horncastle Town v RAF Cranwell	2-2
	Irthlingborough Town v Brotherhoods Works	1-0
	Northampton War Team v Market Harborough Town	2-1
	Wellingborough Town v Desborough Town	2-4
16	Bury St Edmunds v Lowestoft Town	1-1
	Clacton Town v Leiston Works Athletic	0-1
	Gorleston v Norwich CEYMS	2-2
	Great Yarmouth Town v Cromer	3-0
	Terrington v Mortons Athletic	1-5
17	Barking v Grays Athletic	2-2
	Chelmsford v Newportonians	3-1
	Custom House v Southend Corinthians	1-0
	Shoeburyness Garrison v GER Romford	1-2
	Walthamstow Grange v Green & Silley Weir Ath.	3-1
18	Barnet v London Generals	2-1
	Enfield v Luton Amateur	2-2
	Fricker Athletic v Wood Green Town	2-0
	Hampstead Town v Polytechnic	8-0
	Leavesden Mental Hospital v Islington Town	wo/s
	St Albans City v West London Old Boys	1-0
	Vauxhall Motors (Luton) v Chiswick Town	0-0
	Wealdstone v Cheshunt	1-1
19	Henley Town v Reading United	2-4
	Maidenhead United v Newbury Town	7-1
	Marlow v Southall	1-3
	Yiewsley v Botwell Mission	1-1
20	Aquarius v Kingstonian	1-6
	Earlsfield Town v West Norwood	1-5
	Redhill v Summerstown	3-3
	Sutton United v Camberley & Yorktown	2-0
	Tooting Town v Hersham	8-2
	Woking v Walton-on-Thames	4-2
21	Ashford Railway Works v Woolwich Ordnance	0-0
	Bexleyheath Labour v Margate	1-4
	Charlton Athletic v Catford Southend	6-0
	Folkestone v Tunbridge Wells Rangers	3-1
	Maidstone United v Bostall Heath	9-0
	Sheppey United v Sittingbourne	2-1
	Whitstable v Northfleet United	2-6
	Worthing v Newhaven	3-2
22	Bournemouth (Ams) v Osborne Athletic	3-1
	Cowes (2) v Salisbury (1)	6-2
	East Cowes Victoria v Blandford	2-3
	Thornycrofts (Basingstoke) v Sholing Athletic	1-2
	Weymouth v Gosport Athletic	2-1
23	Bath City v Welton Rovers	4-2
	Cheltenham Town v Trowbridge Town	1-3
	Douglas (Kingswood) v Babbacombe	9-1
	Glastonbury v Street	2-1
	Hanham Athletic v Paulton Rovers	5-1
	Radstock Town v Clandown	0-1
	Spencer Moulton v Chippenham Town	2-2
	Swindon Victoria v Frome Town	1-1
24	Aberdare Athletic v Cardiff Albion	4-0
	Bargoed v Aberaman Athletic	0-3
	Barry v Newport Barbarians	wo/s
	Caerau Rovers v Cardiff Corinthians	2-2
	Chepstow v Abertillery	1-3
	Ebbw Vale v Llanelli	7-0
	Mid Rhondda v Pontypridd	2-1
	Rogerstone v Ton Pentre	0-10
1r	Hebburn Colliery v Bedlington United	2-1
4r	Lowca v Parton Athletic	1-1
5r	Morecambe v Breightmet United	0-2
7r	South Liverpool v Harrowby	0-1 N
8r	Talbot Stead v Worcester City	1-0
9r	Grimsby Rovers v Grimsby Haycroft Rovers	7-2
11r	Tankersley v Houghton Main Colliery	0-1
12r	Clay Cross Town v Ripley Colliery	2-0
14r	Gresley Rovers v Barwell United	2-1
15r	RAF Cranwell v Horncastle Town	6-1
16r	Lowestoft Town v Bury St Edmunds	2-0
r	Norwich CEYMS v Gorleston	0-1
17r	Grays Athletic v Barking	3-5
18r	Cheshunt v Wealdstone	4-1
r	Chiswick Town v Vauxhall Motors (Luton)	2-3
r	Luton Amateur v Enfield	2-1
19r	Botwell Mission v Yiewsley	6-1
20r	Summerstown v Redhill	3-0
21r	Woolwich Ordnance v Ashford Railway Works	0-1
23r	Chippenham Town v Spencer Moulton	2-4
r	Frome Town v Swindon Victoria	1-3
24r	Cardiff Corinthians v Caerau Rovers	5-3
4r2	Parton Athletic v Lowca	3-0

Qualifying Round One

1	Ashington v Spen Black & White	2-0
	Hebburn Colliery v Mickley	3-2
	Scotswood v Preston Colliery	1-0
	Wallsend v Lintz Institute	3-2
2	Annfield Plain v Sunderland West End	3-2
	Horden Athletic v Birtley	1-0
	Leadgate Park v Houghton	2-0 D
	Seaham Harbour v Tow Law Town	5-3
3	Eston United v South Bank	3-1
	Haverton Hill v Hartlepools United	2-2
	Loftus Albion v Stockton	2-1
	Scarborough v Grangetown St Mary's	1-0
4	Arlecdon Red Rose v Parton Athletic	3-1
	Barrow v Cleator Moor Celtic	12-0
	Carlisle United v Frizington Athletic	3-1
	Penrith v Wath Brow United	1-2
5	Breightmet United v Lancaster Town	0-5
	Chorley v Leyland	0-1
	Dick, Kerrs v Fleetwood	0-6
	Nelson v Horwich RMI	3-0
6	Congleton Town v Graysons	5-1
	Eccles United v Altrincham	1-0
	Garston Gasworks v Monks Hall	2-1
	Runcorn v Hurst	2-2
7	Buckley United v Nantwich	4-1
	Marine v Lostock Gralam	3-0
	Prescot v Harrowby	1-0
	Wrexham v Prescot Wire Works	7-0
8	Cradley Heath St Luke's v Halesowen Town	5-0
	Shrewsbury Town v Walsall	1-0
	Talbot Stead v Hednesford Town	1-4
	Wednesbury Old Athletic v Wellington Town	0-3
9	Charltons (Grimsby) v Hook Shipyards	3-0
	Gainsborough Trinity v Grimsby Rovers	7-0
	Gilberdyke v Brodsworth Main Colliery	2-2
	Scunthorpe United v Bentley Colliery	3-0
10	Apperley Bridge - Bye	
	Calverley v Bolton United	wo/s
	Halifax Town v Allerton Bywater Colliery	4-1
	Harrogate v Leeds United	wo/s
11	Denaby United v Houghton Main Colliery	1-2
	Mexborough v Rotherham Town	0-0
	Wombwell v Maltby Main Colliery	2-0
	Worksop Town v Grimethorpe Colliery Institute	5-0
12	Chesterfield v Clay Cross Town	2-1
	Hardwick Colliery v Staveley Town	1-1
	Long Eaton v Ilkeston United	1-1
	Tibshelf Colliery v Blackwell Colliery	3-3
13	Boots Athletic v Arnold St Mary's	3-0
	Grantham v Shirebrook	3-1
	Mansfield Town v Hucknall Byron	5-0
	Sutton Town v Welbeck Colliery	1-3
14	Bretby Colliery v Coalville Swifts	1-1
	Gresley Rovers v Loughborough Corinthians	3-0
	Hinckley United (1) v Coalville Town (2)	5-1
	Nuneaton Town v Gresley Colliery	9-2
15	Boston (1) v Stamford	3-2
	Irthlingborough Town v Kettering	2-5
	RAF Cranwell v Northampton War Team	2-3
	Rushden Town v Desborough Town	0-2
16	Cambridge Town v Mortons Athletic	4-0
	Colchester Town v Lowestoft Town	6-2
	Great Yarmouth Town v King's Lynn	1-0
	Leiston Works Athletic v Gorleston	1-0
17	Barking v Hoffmann Athletic (Chelmsford)	4-1
	Chelmsford v Custom House	1-2
	GER Romford v Clapton	1-0
	Walthamstow Grange v Gnome Athletic	0-2
18	Barnet v Vauxhall Motors (Luton)	8-0
	Cheshunt v Fricker Athletic	3-3
	Hampstead Town v Luton Amateur	6-0
	Leavesden Mental Hospital v St Albans City	1-1
19	Botwell Mission v Slough	1-5
	Chesham United v Reading United	2-3
	Windsor & Eton v Maidenhead United	3-1
	Wycombe Wanderers v Southall	4-1
20	Kingstonian v Woking	3-2
	Summerstown v Sutton United	1-0
	Tooting Town v Guildford	1-1
	Wimbledon v West Norwood	5-1
21	Maidstone United v Ashford Railway Works	7-1
	Margate v Charlton Athletic	0-0
	Northfleet United v Sheppey United	4-1
	Worthing v Folkestone	1-1
22	Boscombe v Blandford	1-1
	Bournemouth Tramways v Cowes (2)	2-3
	Portsmouth Amateurs v Bournemouth (Ams)	1-3
	Weymouth v Sholing Athletic	1-1
23	Clandown v Glastonbury	3-1
	Douglas (Kingswood) v Bath City	0-4
	Spencer Moulton v Swindon Victoria	2-2
	Trowbridge Town v Hanham Athletic	1-1
24	Aberaman Athletic v Barry	0-2
	Aberdare Athletic v Cardiff Corinthians	2-1
	Abertillery v Ebbw Vale	1-0
	Mid Rhondda v Ton Pentre	1-0
3r	Hartlepools United v Haverton Hill	0-0
6r	Hurst v Runcorn	5-1
9r	Brodsworth Main Colliery v Gilberdyke	wo/s
11r	Rotherham Town v Mexborough	2-2
12r	Blackwell Colliery v Tibshelf Colliery	2-0
r	Ilkeston United v Long Eaton	1-0e
r	Staveley Town v Hardwick Colliery	5-2
14r	Coalville Swifts v Bretby Colliery	4-0
18r	Fricker Athletic v Cheshunt	2-0
r	St Albans City v Leavesden Mental Hospital	3-1
20r	Guildford v Tooting Town	3-0
21r	Charlton Athletic v Margate	3-1
r	Folkestone v Worthing	1-1e
22r	Blandford v Boscombe	2-1
r	Sholing Athletic v Weymouth	3-0
23r	Hanham Athletic v Trowbridge Town	5-0
r	Swindon Victoria v Spencer Moulton	4-2
3r2	Haverton Hill v Hartlepools United	0-1 N
11r2	Mexborough v Rotherham Town	3-1eN
21r2	Worthing v Folkestone	2-1 N

Qualifying Round Two

1	Ashington v Wallsend	0-1
	Hebburn Colliery v Scotswood	1-2
2	Annfield Plain v Houghton	0-1
	Horden Athletic v Seaham Harbour	0-0
3	Eston United v Loftus Albion	4-4
	Scarborough v Hartlepools United	1-4
4	Barrow v Carlisle United	1-1
	Wath Brow United v Arlecdon Red Rose	3-1
5	Fleetwood v Nelson	5-0
	Lancaster Town v Leyland	2-2
6	Congleton Town v Garston Gasworks	1-0
	Eccles United v Hurst	2-0
7	Buckley United v Marine	1-1
	Wrexham v Prescot	2-0
8	Hednesford Town v Shrewsbury Town	3-2
	Wellington Town v Cradley Heath St Luke's	1-0
9	Charltons (Grimsby) v Scunthorpe United	1-4
	Gainsborough Trinity v Brodsworth Main Colliery	0-1
10	Calverley v Apperley Bridge	4-2
	Halifax Town v Harrogate	1-0
11	Mexborough v Houghton Main Colliery	2-2
	Wombwell v Worksop Town	1-2
12	Ilkeston United v Chesterfield	0-0
	Staveley Town v Blackwell Colliery	4-1
13	Boots Athletic v Welbeck Colliery	4-3
	Grantham v Mansfield Town	1-3
14	Coalville Swifts v Gresley Rovers	0-2
	Nuneaton Town v Hinckley United (1)	3-1
15	Boston (1) v Northampton War Team	1-2
	Desborough Town v Kettering	1-2
16	Colchester Town v Great Yarmouth Town	3-1
	Leiston Works Athletic v Cambridge Town	0-0
17	GER Romford v Custom House	2-0
	Gnome Athletic v Barking	1-1
18	Hampstead Town v Fricker Athletic	5-1
	St Albans City v Barnet	4-2
19	Slough v Reading United	1-0
	Wycombe Wanderers v Windsor & Eton	2-0
20	Guildford v Summerstown	7-2
	Kingstonian v Wimbledon	2-1
21	Charlton Athletic v Maidstone United	1-1
	Worthing v Northfleet United	0-5
22	Blandford v Bournemouth (Ams)	2-0
	Cowes (2) v Sholing Athletic	2-0
23	Bath City v Hanham Athletic	3-0
	Swindon Victoria v Clandown	2-0
24	Abertillery v Aberdare Athletic	0-2
	Mid Rhondda v Barry	0-0
2r	Seaham Harbour v Horden Athletic	5-4
3r	Loftus Albion v Eston United	3-0
4r	Carlisle United v Barrow	1-0 D
5r	Leyland v Lancaster Town	0-1
7r	Marine v Buckley United	0-2
11r	Houghton Main Colliery v Mexborough	2-1e
12r	Chesterfield v Ilkeston United	1-0
16r	Cambridge Town v Leiston Works Athletic	5-0
17r	Barking v Gnome Athletic	5-1
21r	Maidstone United v Charlton Athletic	2-0
24r	Barry v Mid Rhondda	1-0

Qualifying Round Three

1	Scotswood v Wallsend	2-0
2	Seaham Harbour v Houghton	1-1
3	Hartlepools United v Loftus Albion	2-1
4	Barrow v Wath Brow United	3-0
5	Lancaster Town v Fleetwood	1-1
6	Congleton Town v Eccles United	2-3
7	Buckley United v Wrexham	1-0
8	Hednesford Town v Wellington Town	2-1
9	Scunthorpe United v Brodsworth Main Colliery	1-1
10	Calverley v Halifax Town	2-4

1920/21 to 1921/22

11	Worksop Town v Houghton Main Colliery	3-0
12	Staveley Town v Chesterfield	2-0
13	Mansfield Town v Boots Athletic	3-0
14	Nuneaton Town v Gresley Rovers	3-1
15	Northampton War Team v Kettering	0-4
16	Colchester Town v Cambridge Town	2-1
17	Barking v GER Romford	2-2
18	St Albans City v Hampstead Town	1-2
19	Wycombe Wanderers v Slough	2-2
20	Kingstonian v Guildford	0-3
21	Maidstone United v Northfleet United	5-0
22	Cowes (2) v Blandford	1-0
23	Bath City v Swindon Victoria	1-1
24	Aberdare Athletic v Barry	2-0
2r	Houghton v Seaham Harbour	4-1
5r	Fleetwood v Lancaster Town	5-1
9r	Brodsworth Main Colliery v Scunthorpe United	1-1
17r	GER Romford v Barking	5-2
19r	Slough v Wycombe Wanderers	2-7
23r	Swindon Victoria v Bath City	2-3
9r2	Scunthorpe United v Brodsworth Main Colliery	1-0 N

Qualifying Round Four

	Aberdare Athletic v Bath City	0-0
	Bishop Auckland v West Stanley	3-2
	Blyth Spartans v Scotswood	2-0
	Bromley v Chatham	2-0
	Buckley United v Stalybridge Celtic	1-4
	Castleford Town v Halifax Town	3-1
	Colchester Town v Ilford	2-2
	Dulwich Hamlet v Nunhead	5-0
	Durham City v Barrow	4-1
	Eccles United v Crewe Alexandra	2-0
	Gillingham v Maidstone United	1-0
	Hartlepools United v Houghton	3-0
	Kettering v Luton Clarence	5-2
	Leytonstone v Tufnell Park	4-0
	London Caledonians v Guildford	4-2
	Newport County v Merthyr Town	0-0
	Nuneaton Town v Hednesford Town	0-0
	Oxford City v Hampstead Town	3-0
	Rochdale v Fleetwood	1-0
	Scunthorpe United v Mansfield Town	0-1
	Staveley Town v Worksop Town	1-3
	Thornycrofts (Woolston) v Cowes (2)	3-1
	Tranmere Rovers v Southport	1-0
	Wycombe Wanderers v GER Romford	3-2
r	Bath City v Aberdare Athletic	2-1
r	Hednesford Town v Nuneaton Town	3-2
r	Ilford v Colchester Town	2-0
r	Merthyr Town v Newport County	4-0

Qualifying Round Five

	Blyth Spartans v Durham City	1-0
	Castleford Town v Hednesford Town	1-1
	Eccles United v Stalybridge Celtic	2-0
	Gillingham v Dulwich Hamlet	2-1
	Hartlepools United v Bishop Auckland	1-1
	Kettering v Wycombe Wanderers	2-1
	London Caledonians v Leytonstone	0-3
	Merthyr Town v Bath City	0-0
	Oxford City v Bromley	1-3
	Rochdale v Tranmere Rovers	1-0
	Thornycrofts (Woolston) v Ilford	1-0
	Worksop Town v Mansfield Town	2-2
r	Bath City v Merthyr Town	1-0
r	Bishop Auckland v Hartlepools United	0-5
r	Hednesford Town v Castleford Town	2-1
r	Mansfield Town v Worksop Town	0-8

Qualifying Round Six

	Bristol Rovers v Worksop Town	9-0
	Clapton Orient v Port Vale	1-0
	Coventry City v Rochdale	1-1
	Darlington v Blyth Spartans	4-0
	Kettering v Grimsby Town	2-4
	Leytonstone v Bath City	1-1
	Lincoln City v Bromley	5-0
	Northampton Town v Gillingham	3-1
	Rotherham County v Luton Town	1-3
	Southend United v Hednesford Town	3-1
	Swansea Town v Hartlepools United	3-0
	Thornycrofts (Woolston) v Eccles United	2-3
r	Bath City v Leytonstone	2-0
r	Rochdale v Coventry City	2-1

Round One

	Aston Villa v Bristol City	2-0
	Blackburn Rovers v Fulham	1-1
	Bradford City v Barnsley	3-1
	Bradford Park Avenue v Clapton Orient	1-0
	Brentford v Huddersfield Town	1-2
	Brighton & Hove Albion v Oldham Athletic	4-1
	Crystal Palace v Manchester City	2-0
	Darlington v Blackpool	2-2
	Derby County v Middlesbrough	2-0
	Everton v Stockport County	1-0
	Grimsby Town v Norwich City	1-0
	Hull City v Bath City	3-0
	Leicester City v Burnley	3-7
	Liverpool v Manchester United	1-1
	Luton Town v Birmingham	2-1
	Millwall v Lincoln City	0-3
	Newcastle United v Nottingham Forest	1-1
	Northampton Town v Southampton	0-0
	Notts County v West Bromwich Albion	3-0
	Plymouth Argyle v Rochdale	2-0
	Preston North End v Bolton Wanderers	2-0
	Queen's Park Rangers v Arsenal	2-0
	Reading v Chelsea	0-0
	Sheffield Wednesday v West Ham United	1-0
	South Shields v Portsmouth	3-0
	Southend United v Eccles United	5-1
	Sunderland v Cardiff City	0-1
	Swansea Town v Bury	3-0
	Swindon Town v Sheffield United	1-0
	Tottenham Hotspur v Bristol Rovers	6-2
	Watford v Exeter City	3-0
	Wolverhampton Wan. v Stoke	3-2
r	Blackpool v Darlington	2-1
r	Chelsea v Reading	2-2e
r	Fulham v Blackburn Rovers	1-0
r	Manchester United v Liverpool	1-2
r	Newcastle United v Nottingham Forest	2-0
r	Southampton v Northampton Town	4-1
r2	Chelsea v Reading	3-1

Round Two

	Bradford Park Avenue v Huddersfield Town	0-1
	Brighton & Hove Albion v Cardiff City	0-0
	Burnley v Queen's Park Rangers	4-2
	Crystal Palace v Hull City	0-2
	Derby County v Wolverhampton Wan.	1-1
	Everton v Sheffield Wednesday	1-1
	Grimsby Town v Southampton	1-3
	Lincoln City v Fulham	0-0
	Newcastle United v Liverpool	1-0
	Notts County v Aston Villa	0-0
	Preston North End v Watford	4-1
	South Shields v Luton Town	0-4
	Southend United v Blackpool	1-0
	Swansea Town v Plymouth Argyle	1-2
	Swindon Town v Chelsea	0-2
	Tottenham Hotspur v Bradford City	4-0
r	Aston Villa v Notts County	1-0
r	Cardiff City v Brighton & Hove Albion	1-0
r	Fulham v Lincoln City	1-0
r	Sheffield Wednesday v Everton	0-1
r	Wolverhampton Wan. v Derby County	1-0

Round Three

	Aston Villa v Huddersfield Town	2-0
	Everton v Newcastle United	3-0
	Fulham v Wolverhampton Wan.	0-1
	Hull City v Burnley	3-0
	Luton Town v Preston North End	2-3
	Plymouth Argyle v Chelsea	0-0
	Southampton v Cardiff City	0-1
	Southend United v Tottenham Hotspur	1-4
r	Chelsea v Plymouth Argyle	0-0e
r2	Chelsea v Plymouth Argyle	2-1 N

Round Four

	Cardiff City v Chelsea	1-0
	Everton v Wolverhampton Wan.	0-1
	Hull City v Preston North End	0-0
	Tottenham Hotspur v Aston Villa	1-0
r	Preston North End v Hull City	1-0

Semi Finals

	Tottenham Hotspur v Preston North End	2-1 N
	Wolverhampton Wan. v Cardiff City	0-0 N
r	Wolverhampton Wan. v Cardiff City	3-1 N

Final

	Tottenham Hotspur v Wolverhampton Wan.	1-0 N

1921/22

Extra Preliminary Round

1	Close Works v Walker Celtic	2-1
	Felling Colliery v Pandon Temperance	1-0
	Newbiggin Athletic v Spen Black & White	0-1
	Preston Colliery v Kibblesworth	1-0
	Prudhoe Castle v St Anthony's Institute	1-0
2	Chester-le-Street v White-le-Head Rangers	3-0
	Seaham Colliery Welfare v Langley Park	3-0
3	Bridlington Town (1) v Staithes United	6-0
	Haverton Hill v Rise Carr	0-1
	Redcar v Guisborough Belmont Ath.	2-0
	Shildon v Cockfield	2-0
	South Bank v Grangetown St Mary's	5-1
	Willington v Coundon United	2-1
4	Bowthorn Recreation v Workington DS&S	0-3
	Whitehaven Athletic v Kells White Star	0-2
	Whitehaven Colliery Recreation v Workington	1-0
	Wigton Harriers v Egremont	1-0
	Windermere v Moor Row Villa Rovers	2-4
6	Glossop v Atherton	1-4
	New Brighton v Whiston	3-5
	North Liverpool v Marlborough Old Boys	3-1
	Runcorn v Old Xaverians	3-2
	Youlgrave v Chapel-en-le-Frith	1-1
7	Chester v Machynlleth	7-0
	Kinderton Victoria v Ellesmere Port Cement	wo/s
	Whitchurch v Chirk	2-0
8	Atherstone Town v Bloxwich Strollers	1-0
	Bilston United v Walsall Phoenix	6-1
	Brierley Hill Alliance v Hereford St Martins	5-0
	Darlaston v Bilston Amateurs	2-2
	Donnington Wood Institute v Oakengates Town	1-3
	Hereford Thistle v Bromsgrove Rovers	0-0
	Kidderminster Harriers v Redditch	0-0
	Nuneaton Town v Wellington Town	2-0
	Rugeley v Cannock Town	1-2
	Rushall Olympic (1) v West Birmingham	2-1
	Stourbridge v Halesowen Town	0-1
	Sunbeam v Willenhall	1-3
	Talbot Stead v Birmingham Corp. Tramways	1-1
	Wednesbury Old Athletic v Stafford Rangers	1-2
	Wellington St George's v Wolverhampton Amateur	5-1
	Worcester City v Cradley Heath St Luke's	2-2
9	Brigg Town v Goole Shipyards	2-0
	Brunswick Institute v Hornsea Town	2-0
	Earles Welfare v West Hull Albion	1-3
	Grimsby Haycroft Rovers v Cleethorpes Town	3-2
	Louth Town v Barton Town (1)	3-2
	Retford Town v British Oil & Cake Mills	8-0
10	Blakebrough & Sons v Rawden	2-0
	Boothtown v Acomb WMC (York)	5-2
	Bowling Albion v Harrogate	2-1
	Castleford & Allerton United v Glasshoughton Col.	4-0
	Frickley Colliery v Altofts West Riding Col.	1-0
	Hebden Bridge v Liversedge	0-0
	Methley Perseverance v Horsforth	5-1
	Mytholmroyd v Halifax Town	wo/s
	Rothwell Athletic v Crofton	6-1
	Rowntrees v Guiseley	wo/s
	Selby Town v Leeds Steelworks	3-1
	South Kirkby Colliery v Calverley	2-1
	Thornton United v Fryston Colliery	1-0
	Wakefield City v Allerton Bywater Colliery	wo/s
11	Ardsley Athletic v Denaby United	1-3
	Birdwell v Prospect United	3-2
	Bullcroft Main Colliery v Tankersley	3-0
	Cudworth Village v Hoyland Common Wesleyans	3-1
	Dodworth v Hoyland St Peter's	2-0
	Doncaster Rovers v Rotherham Town	2-0
	Grimethorpe Colliery Institute v Rossington Main	0-0
	Hemmingfield v Wombwell Main	4-1
	Houghton Main Colliery v Mexborough	2-2
	Maltby Main Colliery v Wath Athletic	0-0
	Mexborough Loco. Works v Laughton Common	1-0
	Monckton Athletic v Thurnscoe Park Avenue	wo/s
	Rawmarsh Athletic v Rotherham Amateurs	3-2
	Silverwood Colliery v Dinnington Main Colliery	4-3
	Treeton Reading Room v Rycroft Athletic	1-1
	Wombwell v Anston Athletic	5-1
12	Atlas & Norfolk Works v Clay Cross Town	2-0
	Chesterfield Corinthians v Woodhouse	0-1
	Clay Cross Zingari v Long Eaton	1-3
	Eckington Works v Beighton Recreation	5-1
	Handsworth v Heanor Town	2-1
	Hardwick Colliery v Matlock Town	3-2
	Kilnhurst United v Sheepbridge Works	2-1
	Marsden Moor v Darnall Wellington	1-0
	New Tupton United v Kiveton Park Colliery	3-2
	Sheffield v Grassmoor Ivanhoe	1-2
	Tinsley Park v Dronfield Woodhouse	2-0
13	Creswell Colliery v Lenton	0-0
	Ericssons Athletic v Sutton Town	1-4
	Hucknall Byron v Basford United	2-3
	Mansfield Woodhouse Excelsior v Newark Athletic	2-2
	New Hucknall Colliery v Clifton Colliery	1-3
	Sneinton v Mansfield Colliery	0-4
	Stanton Hill DS&S v Arnold St Mary's	2-0
	Sutton Junction v Rufford Colliery	1-0
	Whitwell Colliery v Pinxton	1-2
14	Burton Werneth Rangers v Loughborough Corinthians	1-5
	Netherseal Colliery v Newhall Swifts	1-1
	Shepshed Albion v Tamworth Castle	2-2
	Stableford Works v Moira United	1-0
15	Peterborough G.N. Loco v Boston St Nicholas	2-0
	Spalding United v Bourne Town	7-0
	Spilsby v Higham Ferrers Town	2-6
	Stamford v Raunds Town	5-2
	Wellingborough Town v Daventry Victoria	3-0
18	Biggleswade & District v Hitchin Blue Cross	0-0
	Chiswick Town v Edmonton	0-2
	Enfield v Cheshunt	0-0
	Harrow Weald v Wood Green Town	2-1
	Hertford Town v Luton Amateur	2-1
	Leavesden Mental Hospital v Arlington	4-1
	Letchworth Town v Waterlows (Dunstable)	0-0
	RAF Henlow v Berkhamsted Comrades	3-1
	Watford Old Boys v Finchley	1-3
20	Aldershot Excelsior v Aldershot Institute Alb.	1-1
	East Grinstead v Guildford United	1-6
	Farnham United Breweries v Sutton United	3-4
	Leyland Motors (Kingston) v Croydon (1)	1-1
	RAE Farnborough v Camberley & Yorktown	1-4
	Tooting Town v Dorking	4-1
	Wellington Works v Burberry Athletic	2-1

1921/22

	Woking v Earlsfield Town	1-0
21	Ashford Railway Works v RN Depot	3-1
	Belvedere v Bostall Heath	3-1
	Catford Southend v Folkestone	0-0
	Cray Wanderers v Sheppey United	1-3
	Dartford v Ramsgate (1)	2-1
	Hastings & St Leonards v Shoreham	1-1
	Margate v Charlton Athletic	wo/s
	Newhaven v Royal Engs. Comrades (Eastbourne)	0-2
	Southwick v Vernon Athletic	0-3
	Tunbridge Wells Rangers v Sittingbourne	0-3
	Woolwich v Bexleyheath Labour	2-1
	Woolwich Polytechnic v Whitstable	2-4
22	Basingstoke v RGA Gosport	1-2
	Gosport Athletic v Portsea Gas Company	1-0
	Harland & Wolffs v Portland United	3-1
	Osborne Athletic v Bournemouth Gasworks Athletic	1-3
	Ryde Sports v Poole	2-3
	Thornycrofts (Basingstoke) v Eastleigh Athletic	3-1
	Westham (Weymouth) v East Cowes Victoria	3-0
23	Bristol St George v Torquay Town	wo/s
	Chippenham Rovers v Timsbury Athletic	3-1
	Clevedon v Westbury United	1-3
	Clutton Wanderers v Douglas (Kingswood)	wo/s
	Devizes Town v Cheltenham Town	3-1
	Glastonbury v Calne & Harris United	2-2
	Horfield United v Salisbury Corinthians	3-1
	Melksham & Avon United v Frome Town	1-1
	Minehead v Torquay United	0-3
	Peasedown St John's v Street	4-1
	Radstock Town v Trowbridge Town	2-0
	Spencer Moulton v Chippenham Town	3-0
	Warminster Town v Paulton Rovers	1-1
	Yeovil & Petter's United v Welton Rovers	5-0
24	Aberaman Athletic v Pontypridd	1-2
	Abercarn v Llanhilleth	0-2
	Bargoed v Abertillery	1-2
	Barry v Cardiff Corinthians	1-0
	Blackwood Town v Bridgend Town (1)	1-3
	Caerau Rovers v Treherbert	1-3
	Caerphilly v Ebbw Vale	0-0
	Gilfach v Cross Keys	10-0
	Lovells Athletic v Rhymney Town	1-2
	Mardy v Oakdale	3-2
	Mid Rhondda v Aberaman United	wo/s
	Pembroke Dock v Llanelli	1-0
	Porth Athletic v Aberdare Athletic	wo/s
	Rhiwderin v Chepstow	0-6
	Rogerstone v Risca Stars	1-1
	Ton Pentre v New Tredegar	1-0
6r	Chapel-en-le-Frith v Youlgrave	1-1
8r	Birmingham Corp. Tramways v Talbot Stead	0-1
r	Bromsgrove Rovers v Hereford Thistle	wo/s
r	Cradley Heath St Luke's v Worcester City	2-1
r	Darlaston v Bilston Amateurs	7-1
r	Redditch v Kidderminster Harriers	2-0
10r	Liversedge v Hebden Bridge	4-1
11r	Mexborough v Houghton Main Colliery	1-0
r	Rossington Main v Grimethorpe Colliery Institute	2-0
r	Rycroft Athletic v Treeton Reading Room	0-1
r	Wath Athletic v Maltby Main Colliery	1-1e
13r	Lenton v Creswell Colliery	2-1
r	Newark Athletic v Mansfield Woodhouse Excelsior	4-2e
14r	Newhall Swifts v Netherseal Colliery	2-0
r	Tamworth Castle v Shepshed Albion	3-0
18r	Cheshunt v Enfield	2-3e
r	Hitchin Blue Cross v Biggleswade & District	0-2
r	Waterlows (Dunstable) v Letchworth Town	3-2
20r	Aldershot Institute Alb. v Aldershot Excelsior	2-1e
r	Croydon (1) v Leyland Motors (Kingston)	1-1
21r	Folkestone v Catford Southend	3-0
r	Shoreham v Hastings & St Leonards	3-1
23r	Calne & Harris United v Glastonbury	3-2
r	Frome Town v Melksham & Avon United	5-1
r	Paulton Rovers v Warminster Town	2-1
24r	Ebbw Vale v Caerphilly	2-1
r	Risca Stars v Rogerstone	1-4
6r2	Youlgrave v Chapel-en-le-Frith	1-5
11r2	Wath Athletic v Maltby Main Colliery	2-1 N
20r2	Croydon (1) v Leyland Motors (Kingston)	2-0 N

Preliminary Round

1	Bedlington United v Spen Black & White	2-1
	Chopwell Institute v Mickley	1-0
	Close Works v St Peter's Albion	1-0
	Felling Colliery v Newburn	1-1
	Jarrow v Scotswood	3-0
	Prudhoe Castle v Preston Colliery	0-0
	Seaton Delaval v Lintz Institute	4-0
	Wallsend v Usworth Colliery	3-1
2	Birtley v Spennymoor United	1-1
	Chester-le-Street v Consett Celtic	2-0
	Craghead United v Wingate Albion Comrades	1-0
	Esh Winning (1) v Horden Athletic	1-0
	Houghton v Hobson Wanderers	2-3
	Seaham Colliery Welfare v Dipton United	1-1
	Seaham Harbour v Annfield Plain	2-0
	Sunderland West End v Twizell United	1-0
3	Bridlington Town (1) v Brotton	3-0
	Darlington Railway Ath. v Crook Town	0-0
	Filey Town v Scarborough	0-1
	Redcar v Loftus Albion	0-4
	Shildon v Tow Law Town	5-0
	South Bank East End v South Bank	1-0
	Stockton v Stanley United	2-1
	Willington v Rise Carr	4-1
4	Appleby v Cleator Moor Celtic	2-2
	Arlecdon Red Rose v Kells White Star	3-0
	Carlisle United v Vickerstown	5-0
	Parton Athletic v Wath Brow United	1-3
	Penrith v Frizington Athletic	2-0
	Ulverston Town v Moor Row Villa Rovers	0-1
	Whitehaven Colliery Recreation v Dalton Casuals	2-2
	Workington DS&S v Wigton Harriers	3-3
5	Burscough Rangers v Chorley	1-1
	Fleetwood v Dick, Kerrs	3-0
	Great Harwood v Darwen	2-3
	Leyland v Breightmet United	4-3
	Morecambe v Horwich RMI	0-0
	Rossendale United v Cornholme	6-1
	Skelmersdale United v Portsmouth Rovers (Lancs)	1-0
6	Altrincham v North Liverpool	8-0
	Atherton v Buxton	7-0
	Chapel-en-le-Frith v Marine	3-2
	Eccles United v Prescot Wire Works	9-0
	Hurst v Prescot	1-0
	Monks Hall v Congleton Town	wo/s
	Runcorn v Garston Gasworks	2-0
	Whiston v Sandbach Ramblers	2-2
7	Buckley United v Kinderton Victoria	2-1
	Chester v Ellesmere Port Town	3-1
	Connah's Quay v Gresford	3-0
	Harrowby v Macclesfield Town	2-0
	Lostock Gralam v Whitchurch	2-1
	Nantwich v Witton Albion	4-2
	Oswestry Town v Northwich Victoria	0-0
	Winsford United v Hoylake	2-0
8	Atherstone Town v Bilston United	2-1
	Brierley Hill Alliance v Bromsgrove Rovers	1-2
	Cannock Town v Halesowen Town	4-1
	Cradley Heath St Luke's v Willenhall	3-1
	Darlaston v Rushall Olympic (1)	4-1
	Nuneaton Town v Redditch	4-0
	Oakengates Town v Talbot Stead	2-3
	Wellington St George's v Stafford Rangers	3-1
9	Brigg Town v Holderness Athletic	0-1
	Charltons (Grimsby) v Brodsworth Main Colliery	0-3
	Gainsborough Trinity v West Hull Albion	3-0
	Grimsby Haycroft Rovers v Hull Old Boys	2-1
	Grimsby Rovers v Bentley Colliery	3-2
	Hook Shipyards v Brunswick Institute	5-1
	Marfleet v Louth Town	4-1
	Scunthorpe United v Retford Town	2-1
10	Boothtown v Rowntrees	2-1
	Castleford Town v Blakebrough & Sons	6-1
	Frickley Colliery v Bowling Albion	3-0
	Liversedge v South Kirkby Colliery	1-1
	Methley Perseverance v Castleford & Allerton United	1-1
	Mytholmroyd v Rothwell Athletic	1-1
	Thornton United v Selby Town	0-2
	Wakefield City v Apperley Bridge	3-1
11	Birdwell v Rossington Main	1-1
	Bullcroft Main Colliery v Rawmarsh Athletic	1-0
	Cudworth Village v Wath Athletic	1-0
	Hemmingfield v Dodworth	5-1
	Mexborough v Denaby United	1-2
	Monckton Athletic v Silverwood Colliery	1-2
	Treeton Reading Room v Mexborough Loco. Works	1-4
	Wombwell v Doncaster Rovers	1-0
12	Blackwell Colliery v Handsworth	3-2
	Bolsover Colliery v Atlas & Norfolk Works	2-2
	Eckington Works v Hardwick Colliery	1-1
	Grassmoor Ivanhoe v Staveley Town	0-1
	Ilkeston United v New Tupton United	4-0
	South Normanton Colliery v Marsden Moor	3-1
	Tinsley Park v Kilnhurst United	4-1
	Woodhouse v Long Eaton	1-1
13	Basford United v Sutton Junction	1-1
	Clifton Colliery v Newark Athletic	2-1
	Mansfield Town v Mansfield Colliery	8-0
	Netherfield Rangers v Boots Athletic	0-8
	Shirebrook v Grantham	3-4
	Stanton Hill DS&S v Lenton	3-1
	Sutton Town v Pinxton	1-2
	Welbeck Colliery v Kirkby Collieries	6-1
14	Ashby Town v Stableford Works	2-5
	Burton All Saints v Brush Works	wo/s
	Coalville Swifts v Newhall Swifts	1-2
	Gresley Colliery v Coalville Town (2)	1-1
	Hinckley United (1) v Barwell United	7-1
	Loughborough Corinthians v Gresley Rovers	2-0
	Rugby Town (1) v Whitwick Imperial	1-2
	Tamworth Castle v Ashbourne Town	wo/s
15	Bedford Town (1) v Fletton United	1-1
	Brotherhoods Works v Wellingborough Town	3-3
	Higham Ferrers Town v Desborough Town	0-1
	Market Harborough Town v Horncastle Town	3-1
	Northampton Wanderers v Boston (1)	1-3
	Peterborough G.N. Loco v Rushden Town	4-1
	Peterbro' Westwood Works v Irthlingborough Town	1-5
	Stamford v Spalding United	2-1
16	Bury St Edmunds v Norwich CEYMS	2-3
	Clacton Town v Cromer	2-0
	Great Yarmouth Town v Lowestoft Town	5-1
	Harwich & Parkeston v Thetford REC	7-2
	King's Lynn v Norwich British Legion	1-3
17	Chelmsford v Green & Silley Weir Ath.	wo/s
	Clapton v GER Romford	4-1
	Custom House v Southend Corinthians	wo/s
	Gnome Athletic v Walthamstow Avenue	0-1
	Grays Athletic v Sterling Athletic	2-2
	Leyton v Chelmsford Rollers	wo/s
	Shoeburyness Garrison v Barking	1-5
	Walthamstow Grange v Newportonians	7-0
18	Edmonton v St Albans City	1-4
	Enfield v Biggleswade & District	1-1
	Fricker Athletic v Finchley	2-1
	Hampstead Town v Barnet	3-0
	Hertford Town v Polytechnic	2-6
	RAF Henlow v Leavesden Mental Hospital	2-0
	Waterlows (Dunstable) v Harrow Weald	1-1
	Wealdstone v Luton Clarence	0-0
19	Aylesbury United v Henley Town	4-1
	Botwell Mission v Marlow	4-1
	Henley Comrades v Reading Amateurs	1-2
	Maidenhead United v Windsor & Eton	3-2
	Newbury Town v Southall	1-1
	Uxbridge v Slough	1-1
	Yiewsley v Chesham United	0-5
20	Aldershot Institute Alb. v Tooting Town	1-0
	Croydon (1) v Camberley & Yorktown	2-3
	Guildford United v Woking	2-2
	Kingstonian v Walton-on-Thames	1-0
	Redhill v Guildford	4-0
	Sutton United v Hersham	wo/s
	Wellington Works v Summerstown	1-4
	Wimbledon v West Norwood	2-1
21	Bromley v Royal Engs. Comrades (Eastb'rne)	2-0
	Chatham v Woolwich	1-1
	Dartford v Vernon Athletic	3-1
	Sheppey United v Ashford Railway Works	4-2
	Shoreham v Northfleet United	0-6
	Sittingbourne v Margate	0-2
	Whitstable v Folkestone	2-6
	Worthing v Belvedere	2-0
22	Blandford v Bournemouth (Ams)	0-2
	Boscombe v RGA Gosport	2-0
	Cowes (2) v Poole	2-2
	Harland & Wolffs v Bournemouth Gasworks Athletic	2-0
	Portsmouth Amateurs v Gosport Athletic	2-2
	Sholing Athletic v Thornycrofts (Basingstoke)	2-0
	Thornycrofts (Woolston) v Bournemouth Tramways	1-1
	Westham (Weymouth) v Weymouth	0-3
23	Calne & Harris United v Bristol St George	1-2
	Chippenham Rovers v Paulton Rovers	1-3
	Devizes Town v Clandown	0-1
	Hanham Athletic v Westbury United	3-2
	Radstock Town v Horfield United	1-1
	Spencer Moulton v Peasedown St John's	2-1
	Torquay United v Frome Town	1-1
	Yeovil & Petter's United v Clutton Wanderers	2-0
24	Abertillery v Rogerstone	9-1
	Bridgend Town (1) v Pembroke Dock	6-2
	Chepstow v Barry	3-1
	Ebbw Vale v Ton Pentre	6-0
	Gilfach v Porth Athletic	0-4
	Mardy v Llanhilleth	7-1
	Pontypridd v Rhymney Town	8-0
	Treherbert v Mid Rhondda	0-1
1r	Newburn v Felling Colliery	1-5
r	Preston Colliery v Prudhoe Castle	3-1
2r	Dipton United v Seaham Colliery Welfare	0-3
r	Spennymoor United v Birtley	0-2
3r	Crook Town v Darlington Railway Ath.	3-1
4r	Cleator Moor Celtic v Appleby	wo/s
r	Dalton Casuals v Whitehaven Colliery Recreation	0-3
r	Wigton Harriers v Workington DS&S	2-3
5r	Chorley v Burscough Rangers	4-2
r	Horwich RMI v Morecambe	2-1
6r	Sandbach Ramblers v Whiston	1-1
7r	Northwich Victoria v Oswestry Town	3-1
10r	Castleford & Allerton United v Methley Perseverance	2-0
r	Rothwell Athletic v Mytholmroyd	6-2
r	South Kirkby Colliery v Liversedge	2-1
11r	Rossington Main v Birdwell	1-1e
12r	Atlas & Norfolk Works v Bolsover Colliery	1-0e
r	Hardwick Colliery v Eckington Works	3-2e
r	Long Eaton v Woodhouse	1-1e
13r	Sutton Junction v Basford United	5-1
14r	Gresley Colliery v Coalville Town (2)	3-0
15r	Fletton United v Bedford Town (1)	2-0e
r	Wellingborough Town v Brotherhoods Works	3-0
17r	Grays Athletic v Sterling Athletic	2-1
18r	Biggleswade & District v Enfield	1-2
r	Luton Clarence v Wealdstone	0-3
r	Waterlows (Dunstable) v Harrow Weald	wo/s
19r	Slough v Uxbridge	4-1
r	Southall v Newbury Town	3-1
20r	Woking v Guildford United	1-2e
21r	Woolwich v Chatham	0-1
22r	Bournemouth Tramways v Thornycrofts (Woolston)	2-2
r	Gosport Athletic v Portsmouth Amateurs	0-1
r	Poole v Cowes (2)	1-1
23r	Frome Town v Torquay United	1-3
r	Horfield United v Radstock Town	2-1
6r2	Sandbach Ramblers v Whiston	1-1 N
11r2	Birdwell v Rossington Main	3-0
12r2	Woodhouse v Long Eaton	3-2 N
22r2	Bournemouth Tramways v Thornycrofts (Woolston)	1-2 N
r2	Poole v Cowes (2)	0-1 N
6r3	Whiston v Sandbach Ramblers	wo/s

1921/22

Qualifying Round One

1	Close Works v Chopwell Institute	2-0
	Felling Colliery v Preston Colliery	3-1
	Jarrow v Bedlington United	1-0
	Seaton Delaval v Wallsend	0-1
2	Chester-le-Street v Sunderland West End	2-0
	Craghead United v Esh Winning (1)	1-2
	Seaham Colliery Welfare v Hobson Wanderers	0-0
	Seaham Harbour v Birtley	2-1
3	Bridlington Town (1) v Scarborough	1-1
	Crook Town v South Bank East End	9-0
	Stockton v Loftus Albion	1-0
	Willington v Shildon	0-1
4	Arlecdon Red Rose v Workington DS&S	4-1
	Carlisle United v Penrith	6-1
	Moor Row Villa Rovers v Wath Brow United	3-0
	Whitehaven Colliery Recreation v Cleator Moor Celtic	0-3
5	Chorley v Fleetwood	0-1
	Darwen v Rossendale United	5-2
	Horwich RMI v Lancaster Town	1-5
	Leyland v Skelmersdale United	2-0
6	Atherton v Whiston	2-4
	Hurst v Eccles United	0-1
	Monks Hall v Altrincham	0-1
	Runcorn v Chapel-en-le-Frith	4-1
7	Buckley United v Connah's Quay	0-0
	Chester v Lostock Gralam	2-0
	Nantwich v Harrowby	0-1
	Winsford United v Northwich Victoria	0-2
8	Atherstone Town v Cannock Town	1-2
	Bromsgrove Rovers v Darlaston	2-2
	Nuneaton Town v Talbot Stead	2-1
	Wellington St George's v Cradley Heath St Luke's	3-1
9	Brodsworth Main Colliery v Grimsby Rovers	3-1
	Grimsby Haycroft Rovers v Hook Shipyards	2-0
	Marfleet v Gainsborough Trinity	0-7
	Scunthorpe United v Holderness Athletic	10-0
10	Boothtown v Frickley Colliery	1-3
	Castleford & Allerton United v South Kirkby Colliery	2-0
	Selby Town v Castleford Town	2-2
	Wakefield City v Rothwell Athletic	3-0
11	Birdwell v Silverwood Colliery	2-0
	Cudworth Village v Bullcroft Main Colliery	0-1
	Denaby United v Mexborough Loco. Works	3-1
	Wombwell v Hemmingfield	5-1
12	Atlas & Norfolk Works v Hardwick Colliery	1-1
	Ilkeston United v South Normanton Colliery	1-0
	Tinsley Park v Staveley Town	2-2
	Woodhouse v Blackwell Colliery	2-2
13	Clifton Colliery v Pinxton	0-1
	Grantham v Boots Athletic	6-2
	Mansfield Town v Stanton Hill DS&S	6-0
	Sutton Junction v Welbeck Colliery	0-1
14	Burton All Saints v Gresley Colliery	5-0
	Loughborough Corinthians v Whitwick Imperial	2-1
	Newhall Swifts v Tamworth Castle	2-0
	Stableford Works v Hinckley United (1)	1-4
15	Boston (1) v Peterborough G.N. Loco	7-0
	Desborough Town v Market Harborough Town	4-0
	Fletton United v Wellingborough Town	1-0
	Irthlingborough Town v Stamford	4-1
16	Harwich & Parkeston v Great Yarmouth Town	6-0
	Leiston Works Athletic v Cambridge Town	2-3
	Norwich British Legion v Clacton Town	0-2
	Norwich CEYMS v Colchester Town	1-0
17	Clapton v Chelmsford	3-0
	Custom House v Grays Athletic	0-2
	Leyton v Barking	2-4
	Walthamstow Avenue v Walthamstow Grange	1-7
18	Enfield v RAF Henlow	0-2
	Hampstead Town v Wealdstone	1-0
	Polytechnic v St Albans City	2-4
	Waterlows (Dunstable) v Fricker Athletic	0-2
19	Aylesbury United v Maidenhead United	6-1
	Chesham United v Botwell Mission	3-2
	Reading Amateurs v Southall	1-0
	Wycombe Wanderers v Slough	2-2
20	Aldershot Institute Alb. v Guildford United	2-4
	Kingstonian v Camberley & Yorktown	2-2
	Sutton United v Redhill	1-1
	Wimbledon v Summerstown	0-0
21	Chatham v Bromley	2-0
	Folkestone v Sheppey United	3-1
	Margate v Northfleet United	0-1
	Worthing v Dartford	0-0
22	Bournemouth (Ams) v Boscombe	0-0
	Portsmouth Amateurs v Harland & Wolffs	0-4
	Sholing Athletic v Cowes (2)	2-1
	Weymouth v Thornycrofts (Woolston)	0-2
23	Clandown v Bristol St George	0-1
	Hanham Athletic v Yeovil & Petter's United	3-2
	Horfield United v Paulton Rovers	2-1
	Torquay United v Spencer Moulton	5-2
24	Bridgend Town (1) v Chepstow	3-1
	Mardy v Abertillery	1-0
	Pontypridd v Mid Rhondda	0-2
	Porth Athletic v Ebbw Vale	2-0
2r	Hobson Wanderers v Seaham Colliery Welfare	0-0x
3r	Scarborough v Bridlington Town (1)	2-0
7r	Connah's Quay v Buckley United	2-0
8r	Darlaston v Bromsgrove Rovers	1-0
10r	Castleford Town v Selby Town	4-2
12r	Blackwell Colliery v Woodhouse	3-1
r	Hardwick Colliery v Atlas & Norfolk Works	2-3
r	Staveley Town v Tinsley Park	1-0
19r	Slough v Wycombe Wanderers	3-1
20r	Camberley & Yorktown v Kingstonian	2-1
r	Redhill v Sutton United	2-0
r	Summerstown v Wimbledon	1-2
21r	Dartford v Worthing	1-0
22r	Boscombe v Bournemouth (Ams)	6-0
2r2	Hobson Wanderers v Seaham Colliery Welfare	3-1 N

Qualifying Round Two

1	Close Works v Wallsend	1-1
	Felling Colliery v Jarrow	0-2
2	Chester-le-Street v Esh Winning (1)	2-2
	Hobson Wanderers v Seaham Harbour	0-2
3	Crook Town v Shildon	1-1
	Stockton v Scarborough	5-3
4	Carlisle United v Arlecdon Red Rose	8-0
	Cleator Moor Celtic v Moor Row Villa Rovers	3-0
5	Fleetwood v Darwen	2-1
	Lancaster Town v Leyland	2-0
6	Altrincham v Eccles United	4-1
	Whiston v Runcorn	0-1
7	Harrowby v Chester	1-3
	Northwich Victoria v Connah's Quay	2-0
8	Darlaston v Cannock Town	8-2
	Wellington St George's v Nuneaton Town	4-2
9	Grimsby Haycroft Rovers v Gainsborough Trinity	0-7
	Scunthorpe United v Brodsworth Main Colliery	4-1
10	Castleford & Allerton United v Wakefield City	1-1
	Frickley Colliery v Castleford Town	2-1
11	Denaby United v Bullcroft Main Colliery	3-0
	Wombwell v Birdwell	1-1
12	Ilkeston United v Atlas & Norfolk Works	7-0
	Staveley Town v Blackwell Colliery	4-2
13	Mansfield Town v Grantham	2-0
	Pinxton v Welbeck Colliery	0-0
14	Burton All Saints v Newhall Swifts	3-0
	Hinckley United (1) v Loughborough Corinthians	2-6
15	Desborough Town v Boston (1)	1-2
	Fletton United v Irthlingborough Town	2-2
16	Cambridge Town v Harwich & Parkeston	1-1
	Clacton Town v Norwich CEYMS	1-2
17	Barking v Clapton	0-1
	Grays Athletic v Walthamstow Grange	2-1
18	Hampstead Town v St Albans City	2-4
	RAF Henlow v Fricker Athletic	2-1
19	Aylesbury United v Reading Amateurs	7-0
	Slough v Chesham United	2-0
20	Guildford United v Camberley & Yorktown	3-2
	Redhill v Wimbledon	0-0
21	Chatham v Dartford	3-1
	Northfleet United v Folkestone	4-2
22	Boscombe v Thornycrofts (Woolston)	1-0
	Sholing Athletic v Harland & Wolffs	1-1
23	Hanham Athletic v Horfield United	2-1
	Torquay United v Bristol St George	6-0
24	Mardy v Porth Athletic	1-0
	Mid Rhondda v Bridgend Town (1)	7-1
1r	Wallsend v Close Works	1-1e
2r	Esh Winning (1) v Chester-le-Street	1-0
3r	Shildon v Crook Town	4-0
10r	Wakefield City v Castleford & Allerton United	0-2
11r	Birdwell v Wombwell	0-1
13r	Welbeck Colliery v Pinxton	1-0
15r	Irthlingborough Town v Fletton United	2-0
16r	Harwich & Parkeston v Cambridge Town	1-5
20r	Wimbledon v Redhill	6-3
22r	Harland & Wolffs v Sholing Athletic	3-0
1r2	Close Works v Wallsend	2-1e

Qualifying Round Three

1	Jarrow v Close Works	2-2
2	Seaham Harbour v Esh Winning (1)	1-1
3	Shildon v Stockton	3-1
4	Carlisle United v Cleator Moor Celtic	2-0
5	Lancaster Town v Fleetwood	2-1
6	Runcorn v Altrincham	1-3
7	Chester v Northwich Victoria	3-3
8	Wellington St George's v Darlaston	1-2
9	Gainsborough Trinity v Scunthorpe United	2-0
10	Frickley Colliery v Castleford & Allerton United	2-0
11	Wombwell v Denaby United	3-1
12	Ilkeston United v Staveley Town	0-0
13	Welbeck Colliery v Mansfield Town	1-2
14	Loughborough Corinthians v Burton All Saints	1-3
15	Boston (1) v Irthlingborough Town	0-1
16	Norwich CEYMS v Cambridge Town	1-1
17	Grays Athletic v Clapton	1-6
18	RAF Henlow v St Albans City	0-3
19	Slough v Aylesbury United	1-1
20	Guildford United v Wimbledon	3-3
21	Chatham v Northfleet United	0-3
22	Harland & Wolffs v Boscombe	2-3
23	Torquay United v Hanham Athletic	2-2
24	Mid Rhondda v Mardy	0-0
1r	Close Works v Jarrow	3-2e
2r	Esh Winning (1) v Seaham Harbour	6-1
7r	Northwich Victoria v Chester	0-1
12r	Staveley Town v Ilkeston United	1-0
16r	Cambridge Town v Norwich CEYMS	2-1
19r	Aylesbury United v Slough	2-1
20r	Wimbledon v Guildford United	0-1
23r	Hanham Athletic v Torquay United	1-3
24r	Mardy v Mid Rhondda	0-4 N

Qualifying Round Four

	Accrington Stanley v Nelson	0-1
	Altrincham v Tranmere Rovers	4-4
	Ashington v Close Works	6-0
	Aylesbury United v Metrogas	0-0
	Barrow v Lancaster Town	2-2
	Bishop Auckland v West Stanley	2-0
	Blyth Spartans v Shildon	1-2
	Cambridge Town v Kettering	2-7
	Carlisle United v Stalybridge Celtic	0-0
	Chesterfield v Irthlingborough Town	3-0
	Clapton v St Albans City	2-3
	Crewe Alexandra v Chester	1-1
	Darlaston v Hednesford Town	3-1
	Frickley Colliery v Wombwell	1-3
	Gainsborough Trinity v Mansfield Town	1-2
	Leadgate Park v Esh Winning (1)	3-1
	Leytonstone v Ilford	1-2
	Maidstone United v Tufnell Park	1-1
	Mid Rhondda v Swindon Victoria	6-1
	Northfleet United v Guildford United	1-0
	Shrewsbury Town v Walsall	0-1
	Torquay United v Boscombe	0-1
	Worksop Town v Staveley Town	3-1
	Wrexham v Burton All Saints	4-0
r	Chester v Crewe Alexandra	1-2e
r	Lancaster Town v Barrow	1-0
r	Metrogas v Aylesbury United	5-0
r	Stalybridge Celtic v Carlisle United	3-2
r	Tranmere Rovers v Altrincham	2-4
r	Tufnell Park v Maidstone United	1-0e

Qualifying Round Five

	Ashington v Leadgate Park	2-1
	Bishop Auckland v Shildon	1-1
	Brentford v Dulwich Hamlet	3-1
	Bristol Rovers v Exeter City	0-0
	Durham City v Darlington	0-2
	Grimsby Town v Kettering	1-1
	Lancaster Town v Stockport County	2-0
	Lincoln City v Northampton Town	1-2
	Mansfield Town v Darlaston	2-0
	Metrogas v Norwich City	1-2
	Mid Rhondda v Merthyr Town	0-1
	Nelson v Rochdale	3-2
	Newport County v Bath City	2-0
	Northfleet United v Gillingham	0-0
	Nunhead v St Albans City	0-0
	Oxford City v London Caledonians	2-0
	Rotherham County v Coventry City	1-1
	Southport v Altrincham	3-0
	Stalybridge Celtic v Hartlepools United	2-0
	Swansea Town v Boscombe	4-0
	Tufnell Park v Ilford	1-0
	Walsall v Chesterfield	2-0
	Worksop Town v Wombwell	2-0
	Wrexham v Crewe Alexandra	5-2
r	Coventry City v Rotherham County	1-0
r	Exeter City v Bristol Rovers	0-2
r	Gillingham v Northfleet United	3-1
r	Kettering v Grimsby Town	0-2
r	Shildon v Bishop Auckland	2-1e
r	St Albans City v Nunhead	2-0

Qualifying Round Six

	Ashington v Stalybridge Celtic	1-0
	Brentford v Shildon	1-0
	Gillingham v St Albans City	3-1
	Grimsby Town v Tufnell Park	1-1
	Mansfield Town v Walsall	1-1
	Merthyr Town v Darlington	0-0
	Northampton Town v Lancaster Town	1-0
	Oxford City v Norwich City	1-1
	Southport v Coventry City	1-0
	Swansea Town v Bristol Rovers	2-0
	Worksop Town v Nelson	2-1
	Wrexham v Newport County	0-0
r	Darlington v Merthyr Town	1-0e
r	Newport County v Wrexham	3-0
r	Norwich City v Oxford City	3-0
r	Tufnell Park v Grimsby Town	1-2
r	Walsall v Mansfield Town	4-0

Round One

	Arsenal v Queen's Park Rangers	0-0
	Aston Villa v Derby County	6-1
	Barnsley v Norwich City	1-1
	Blackburn Rovers v Southport	1-1
	Blackpool v Watford	1-2
	Bolton Wanderers v Bury	1-0
	Bradford Park Avenue v Sheffield Wednesday	1-0
	Brentford v Tottenham Hotspur	0-2
	Brighton & Hove Albion v Sheffield United	1-0
	Bristol City v Nottingham Forest	0-0
	Burnley v Huddersfield Town	2-2
	Chelsea v West Bromwich Albion	2-4
	Everton v Crystal Palace	0-6
	Gillingham v Oldham Athletic	1-3

1921/22 to 1922/23

Grimsby Town v Notts County 1-1
Hull City v Middlesbrough 5-0
Leicester City v Clapton Orient 2-0
Manchester City v Darlington 3-1
Manchester United v Cardiff City 1-4
Millwall v Ashington 4-2
Newcastle United v Newport County 6-0
Northampton Town v Reading 3-0
Plymouth Argyle v Fulham 1-1
Port Vale v Stoke 2-4
Portsmouth v Luton Town 1-1
Preston North End v Wolverhampton Wan. 3-0
Southampton v South Shields 3-1
Sunderland v Liverpool 1-1
Swansea Town v West Ham United 0-0
Swindon Town v Leeds United 2-1
Walsall v Bradford City 3-3
Worksop Town v Southend United 1-2
r Bradford City v Walsall 4-0
r Fulham v Plymouth Argyle 1-0
r Huddersfield Town v Burnley 3-2
r Liverpool v Sunderland 5-0
r Luton Town v Portsmouth 2-1
r Norwich City v Barnsley 1-2
r Nottingham Forest v Bristol City 3-1
r Notts County v Grimsby Town 3-0
r Queen's Park Rangers v Arsenal 1-2
r Southport v Blackburn Rovers 0-2
r West Ham United v Swansea Town 1-1e
r2 Swansea Town v West Ham United 1-0 N

Round Two

Aston Villa v Luton Town 1-0
Barnsley v Oldham Athletic 3-1
Bolton Wanderers v Manchester City 1-3
Bradford City v Notts County 1-1
Bradford Park Avenue v Arsenal 2-3
Brighton & Hove Albion v Huddersfield Town 0-0
Crystal Palace v Millwall 0-0
Leicester City v Fulham 2-0
Liverpool v West Bromwich Albion 0-1
Northampton Town v Stoke 2-2
Nottingham Forest v Hull City 3-0
Preston North End v Newcastle United 3-1
Southampton v Cardiff City 1-1
Southend United v Swansea Town 0-1
Swindon Town v Blackburn Rovers 0-1
Tottenham Hotspur v Watford 1-0
r Cardiff City v Southampton 2-0
r Huddersfield Town v Brighton & Hove Albion 2-0
r Millwall v Crystal Palace 2-0
r Notts County v Bradford City 0-0e
r Stoke v Northampton Town 3-0
r2 Notts County v Bradford City 1-0 N

Round Three

Arsenal v Leicester City 3-0
Barnsley v Preston North End 1-1
Blackburn Rovers v Huddersfield Town 1-1
Cardiff City v Nottingham Forest 4-1
Millwall v Swansea Town 4-0
Stoke v Aston Villa 0-0
Tottenham Hotspur v Manchester City 2-1
West Bromwich Albion v Notts County 1-1
r Aston Villa v Stoke 4-0
r Huddersfield Town v Blackburn Rovers 5-0
r Notts County v West Bromwich Albion 2-0
r Preston North End v Barnsley 3-0

Round Four

Arsenal v Preston North End 1-1
Cardiff City v Tottenham Hotspur 1-1
Huddersfield Town v Millwall 3-0
Notts County v Aston Villa 2-2
r Aston Villa v Notts County 3-4e
r Preston North End v Arsenal 2-1e
r Tottenham Hotspur v Cardiff City 2-1

Semi Finals

Huddersfield Town v Notts County 3-1 N
Preston North End v Tottenham Hotspur 2-1 N

Final

Huddersfield Town v Preston North End 1-0 N

1922/23

Extra Preliminary Round

1 Bedlington United v Seaton Delaval 2-1
Chopwell Institute v Washington Colliery 3-1
Gateshead Town (2) v Leslies 3-2
Newburn v Lintz Institute 0-0
Scotswood v Walker Celtic 2-1
2 Annfield Plain v White-le-Head Rangers 0-0
Craghead United v Consett Swifts 2-1
Ferryhill Athletic v Trimdon Grange Colliery 4-1
Ouston Rovers v Wingate Albion Comrades 1-0
Spennymoor United v Birtley 8-1
Sunderland West End v Hetton United 2-0
Thornley Albion v Dipton United 0-0
3 Bridlington Town (1) v Eston United 3-2
South Bank East End v Filey Town 6-0
Stanley United v Willington 2-3
8 Bilston United v Talbot Stead 3-0
Bloxwich Strollers v Cannock Town 3-0
Boldmere St Michaels v Wednesbury Old Athletic (2) 1-1
Bromsgrove Rovers v Hereford Thistle 6-1
Chirk v Shrewsbury Town 1-2
Darlaston v Hednesford Town 3-2
Halesowen Town v Cradley Heath St Luke's 0-3
Kidderminster Harriers v Redditch 3-2
Leamington Town v Willenhall 1-1
Oswestry Town v Wellington Town 2-1
Stafford Rangers v Wolseley Athletic 9-1
Stourbridge v Birmingham Corp. Tramways 3-1
Wellington St George's v Oakengates Town 3-2
West Birmingham v Brierley Hill Alliance 1-6
Wolverhampton Amateur v Rugeley wo/s
Worcester City v Hereford St Martins 7-0
11 Woodhouse v Anston Athletic 0-0
13 Langwith Athletic v New Hucknall Colliery 2-0
Lenton v Basford United 1-1
14 Gresley Colliery v Moira United 0-3
Measham Town v Atherstone Town 3-1
15 Wolverton Town v Rothwell Town 2-4
18 Apsley v Welwyn 2-3
Arlesey Town v Deerfield Athletic 0-4
Biggleswade & District v Barnet 2-1
Cheshunt v Wood Green Town 0-0
Edmonton v Polytechnic 6-0
Hitchin Athletic v LNWR (Wembley) 2-4
Hitchin Blue Cross v Hertford Town 1-2
Letchworth Town v Luton Clarence 4-1
Luton Amateur v Waterlows (Dunstable) 5-0
Old Lyonian v St Neots & District 0-1
Wealdstone v Berkhamsted Town 2-0
20 Basingstoke v Aldershot Excelsior wo/s
Burberry Athletic v Nunhead 0-2
Carshalton Athletic v Croydon (1) wo/s
Egham v Aldershot Institute Alb. 2-0
Farnham United Breweries v Wellington Works 3-1
Guildford v RAE Farnborough 1-3
Gwynnes Athletic v Summerstown 2-4
Hersham v Dorking 8-2
RAMC Aldershot v Woking 0-1
Tooting Town v Kingstonian 0-1
Walton-on-Thames v Sutton United 0-5
21 Ashford Railway Works v Margate 6-2
Bexleyheath Town v Woolwich Polytechnic 7-1
Bostall Heath v Bromley 6-1
Horsham v Southwick 3-3
Sheppey United v Erith & Belvedere 1-0
Tunbridge Wells Rangers v Sittingbourne 1-1
Whitstable v Ramsgate (1) 0-0
Worthing v Shoreham 1-1
22 Bournemouth (Ams) v Bournemouth Gasworks Athletic 0-3
Eastleigh Athletic v Portsmouth Amateurs 1-4
Gosport Athletic v Salisbury (1) 2-1
Weymouth v Poole 1-0
23 Clevedon v Timsbury Athletic 4-2
Coleford Athletic v Minehead 2-0
Spencer Moulton v Yeovil & Petter's United 1-3
Warminster Town v Clutton Wanderers 1-2
1r Lintz Institute v Newburn 1-0
2r Dipton United v Thornley Albion 2-1
r White-le-Head Rangers v Annfield Plain 2-1
8r Wednesbury Old Athletic v Boldmere St Michaels 1-2
r Willenhall v Leamington Town 12-1
11r Woodhouse v Anston Athletic wo/s
13r Basford United v Lenton 2-3
18r Wood Green Town v Cheshunt 0-5
21r Ramsgate (1) v Whitstable 6-4 v
r Shoreham v Worthing 1-1e
r Sittingbourne v Tunbridge Wells Rangers 2-0
r Southwick v Horsham 4-2
21r2 Whitstable v Ramsgate (1) 3-2
r2 Worthing v Shoreham 3-2 N

Preliminary Round

1 Bedlington United v Chopwell Institute 4-1
Felling Colliery v Scotswood 2-0
Mickley v Lintz Institute 1-1
Prudhoe Castle v St Peter's Albion 0-0
Spen Black & White v Kibblesworth 5-0
St Anthony's Institute v Gateshead Town (2) 2-0
Usworth Colliery v Preston Colliery 2-1
Wallsend v Jarrow 2-1
2 Esh Winning (1) v Dipton United 1-0
Ferryhill Athletic v Sunderland West End 5-0
Horden Athletic v Craghead United 2-1
Leadgate Park v Houghton 3-1
Ouston Rovers v Langley Park 3-1
Spennymoor United v Hobson Wanderers 6-2
West Stanley v Seaham Harbour 3-0
White-le-Head Rangers v Chester-le-Street 1-1
3 Bridlington Town (1) v Grangetown St Mary's 5-3
Brotton v Loftus Albion 1-1
Cockfield v Shildon 2-1
Coundon United v Darlington Railway Ath. 3-2
Scarborough v South Bank East End 3-3
Stockton v Rise Carr 3-0
Tow Law Town v Crook Town 3-2
Willington v Haverton Hill 8-0
4 Bowthorn Recreation v Arlecdon Red Rose 4-1
Egremont v Wigton Harriers 4-4
Frizington Athletic v Whitehaven Athletic 4-2
Kendal Town v Windermere 1-1
Keswick v Cleator Moor Celtic 1-1
Moor Row Villa Rovers v Whitehaven Colliery Rec. 3-4
Penrith v Appleby 2-2
Workington v Wath Brow United 3-3
5 Burscough Rangers v Dick, Kerrs 2-7
Chorley v Darwen 2-1
Great Harwood v Lytham 2-2
Leyland Motors v Horwich RMI 2-1 D
Morecambe v Breightmet United 2-2
Rossendale United v Leyland 7-4
6 Buxton v Marlborough Old Boys 5-1
Chapel-en-le-Frith v Prescot 5-1
Eccles United v Glossop 2-0
Garston Gasworks v Youlgrave 7-0
Hurst v Whiston 5-3
Marine v Atherton 2-0
Old Xaverians v Skelmersdale United 1-3
Prescot Wire Works v Runcorn 0-0
7 Ellesmere Port Cement v Lostock Gralam 4-3
Macclesfield Town v Nantwich 3-0
Middlewich v Sandbach Ramblers 1-3
New Brighton v Chester 4-2
Northwich Victoria v Ellesmere Port Town 2-0
Winsford United v Port Sunlight 0-1
Witton Albion v West Kirby 3-0
8 Bloxwich Strollers v Wolverhampton Amateur 3-0
Boldmere St Michaels v Bilston United 0-4
Cradley Heath St Luke's v Brierley Hill Alliance 3-2
Darlaston v Willenhall 1-0
Kidderminster Harriers v Bromsgrove Rovers 3-2
Shrewsbury Town v Worcester City 3-2
Stafford Rangers v Stourbridge 3-0
Wellington St George's v Oswestry Town 4-0
9 Barton Town (1) v Hull Old Boys 0-0
Boston (1) v Cleethorpes Town 5-2
Brigg Town v Gainsborough Trinity 2-2
Grimsby Rovers v Charltons (Grimsby) 0-3
Holderness Athletic v Hull Dairycoates 0-1
Horncastle Town v Grimsby Haycroft Rovers 1-1
Retford Town v Selby Town 3-0
10 Bentley Colliery v Wombwell 1-0
Cudworth Village v Doncaster Rovers 0-4
Denaby United v Guiseley 8-0
Frickley Colliery v Brodsworth Main Colliery 0-0
Mexborough v Horsforth 4-0
South Kirkby Colliery v Liversedge 1-1
Wath Athletic v Fryston Colliery 1-1
11 Ardsley Athletic v Kiveton Park Colliery 0-1
Dinnington Main Colliery v Houghton Main Colliery 3-2
Laughton Common v Rawmarsh Athletic 3-2
Prospect United v Birdwell 1-1
Rossington Main v Woodhouse 1-2
Rotherham Amateurs v Maltby Main Colliery 0-0
Rotherham Town v Atlas & Norfolk Works 4-1
Treeton Reading Room v Sheffield 4-1
12 Alfreton Town v Staveley Town 2-1
Bolsover Colliery v Clay Cross Town 4-0
Creswell Colliery v Grassmoor Ivanhoe 2-2
Eckington Works v Heanor Town 3-2
Ilkeston United v New Tupton United 6-0
Long Eaton v Matlock Town 0-1
Pinxton v Clay Cross Zingari 6-1
South Normanton Colliery v Blackwell Colliery 5-1
13 Arnold St Mary's v Sutton Junction 0-3
Hucknall Byron v Whitwell Colliery 3-0
Lenton v Grantham 2-1
Mansfield Town v Langwith Athletic 2-1
Newark Athletic v Clifton Colliery 4-1
Shirebrook v Sneinton 4-1
Sutton Town v Boots Athletic 6-1
Welbeck Colliery v Mansfield Colliery 6-0
14 Ashby Town v Hinckley United (1) 0-1
Coalville Swifts v Barwell United 3-0
Coalville Town (2) v Nuneaton Town 0-5
Measham Town v Newhall Swifts 1-2
Moira United v Rugby Town (1) 4-2
Shepshed Albion v Loughborough Corinthians 0-4
Stableford Works v Gresley Rovers 0-6
Whitwick Imperial v Burton All Saints 4-1
15 Bedford Town (1) v Market Harborough Town 2-0
Brotherhoods Works v Desborough Town 2-2
Fletton United v Northampton Wanderers 0-0
Higham Ferrers Town v Peterborough G.N. Loco 8-0
Irthlingborough Town v Wellingborough Town 1-2
Kettering v Stamford 3-0
Peterbro' Westwood Works v Spalding United 1-4
Rothwell Town v Rushden Town 2-1
16 Bury St Edmunds v Cromer 3-1
Leiston Works Athletic v Colchester Town 1-0
Lowestoft Town v Great Yarmouth Town 2-3
Newmarket Town v Orwell Works 0-1
Norwich British Legion v King's Lynn 1-3
17 Custom House v Walthamstow Town wo/s
GER Romford v Shoeburyness Garrison 2-1
Gnome Athletic v Sterling Athletic 4-0
Leyton v Chelmsford 1-4
Walthamstow Avenue v Leytonstone 0-2
18 Biggleswade & District v Wealdstone 2-1
Enfield v Hampstead Town 2-1

1922/23

	Hertford Town v Fricker Athletic	2-3
	Leavesden Mental Hospital v Welwyn	3-1
	Letchworth Town v Cheshunt	2-1
	Luton Amateur v LNWR (Wembley)	1-1
	RAF Henlow v Deerfield Athletic	1-0
	St Neots & District v Edmonton	2-2
19	Henley Town v Slough Trading Estate	wo/s
	Maidenhead United v Reading Amateurs	3-1
	Marlow v Wycombe Wanderers	1-7
	Southall v Hanwell Athletic	5-0
	Uxbridge v Henley Comrades	4-1
	Windsor & Eton v Chesham United	1-2
	Yiewsley v Botwell Mission	2-2
20	Egham v Camberley & Yorktown	4-1
	Farnham United Breweries v Basingstoke	2-2
	Kingstonian v Sutton United	2-1
	Metrogas v Hersham	0-2
	Nunhead v Carshalton Athletic	2-1
	RAE Farnborough v Woking	1-3
	Redhill v Guildford United	0-4
	Summerstown v Wimbledon	1-2
21	Ashford Railway Works v Chatham	1-2
	Bexleyheath Town v Whitstable	1-2
	Bostall Heath v Worthing	5-0
	Catford Southend v Sittingbourne	1-2
	Folkestone v Northfleet United	3-3
	Royal Engs. Comrades (Eastb'rne) v Newhaven	4-0
	Sheppey United v Dartford	1-1
	Southwick v Vernon Athletic	1-2
22	Boscombe v Blandford	3-0
	Bournemouth Gasworks Ath. v Salisbury Corinthians	3-0
	Gosport Athletic v Weymouth	1-0
	Portsea Gas Company v East Cowes Victoria	6-0
	Ryde Sports v Osborne Athletic	1-0
	Sholing Athletic v Portsmouth Amateurs	1-1
	Thornycrofts (Woolston) v Portland United	2-1
	Westham (Weymouth) v Bournemouth Tramways	2-5
23	Frome Town v Welton Rovers	1-2
	Melksham & Avon United v Clutton Wanderers	3-2
	Radstock Town v Devizes Town	0-2
	Street v Coleford Athletic	2-5
	Torquay United v Clevedon	3-0
	Trowbridge Town v Glastonbury	8-0
	Westbury United v Calne & Harris United	3-3
	Yeovil & Petter's United v Peasedown St John's	5-2
24	Barry v Llanelli	1-0
	Bath City v Horfield United	7-1
	Bristol St George v Chippenham Town	3-0
	Cardiff Corinthians v Ton Pentre	2-0
	Clandown v Swindon Victoria	0-2
	Ebbw Vale v Paulton Rovers	4-1
	Hanham Athletic v Chippenham Rovers	2-1
	Porth Athletic v Pontypridd	2-0
1r	Lintz Institute v Mickley	1-0
r	St Peter's Albion v Prudhoe Castle	3-0
2r	Chester-le-Street v White-le-Head Rangers	1-2 d
3r	Loftus Albion v Brotton	4-1
r	South Bank East End v Scarborough	2-3e
4r	Appleby v Penrith	1-6
r	Cleator Moor Celtic v Keswick	5-1
r	Wigton Harriers v Egremont	3-1
r	Windermere v Kendal Town	0-1 d
r	Workington v Wath Brow United	2-1
5r	Lytham v Great Harwood	2-1
r	Morecambe v Breightmet United	4-0
6r	Runcorn v Prescot Wire Works	3-0
9r	Gainsborough Trinity v Brigg Town	4-1
r	Grimsby Haycroft Rovers v Horncastle Town	8-1
r	Hull Old Boys v Barton Town (1)	1-0
10r	Frickley Colliery v Brodsworth Main Colliery	1-0
r	Liversedge v South Kirkby Colliery	4-1
r	Wath Athletic v Fryston Colliery	4-1
11r	Birdwell v Prospect United	1-4
r	Maltby Main Colliery v Rotherham Amateurs	3-1
12r	Grassmoor Ivanhoe v Creswell Colliery	3-2
15r	Desborough Town v Brotherhoods Works	2-1
r	Northampton Wanderers v Fletton United	1-2
18r	Edmonton v St Neots & District	wo/s
r	LNWR (Wembley) v Luton Amateur	0-1
19r	Botwell Mission v Yiewsley	6-1
20r	Basingstoke v Farnham United Breweries	0-1
21r	Dartford v Sheppey United	2-1
r	Northfleet United v Folkestone	4-1
22r	Portsmouth Amateurs v Sholing Athletic	0-3
23r	Calne & Harris United v Westbury United	6-0
	Qualifying Round One	
1	Felling Colliery v St Peter's Albion	2-0
	Spen Black & White v Lintz Institute	0-1 d
	Usworth Colliery v Bedlington United	2-0
	Wallsend v St Anthony's Institute	5-0
2	Ferryhill Athletic v Horden Athletic	2-1
	Ouston Rovers v Leadgate Park	3-1 D
	Spennymoor United v Esh Winning (1)	3-0
	West Stanley v Chester-le-Street	1-0
3	Cockfield v Loftus Albion	3-1
	Scarborough v Willington	0-7
	Stockton v Coundon United	4-3
	Tow Law Town v Bridlington Town (1)	5-1
4	Bowthorn Recreation v Penrith	3-3
	Whitehaven Colliery Recreation v Frizington Athletic	1-1
	Wigton Harriers v Cleator Moor Celtic	1-4
	Workington v Windermere	7-0
5	Dick, Kerrs v Lancaster Town	2-0
	Horwich RMI v Chorley	1-1
	Morecambe v Lytham	1-0
	Rossendale United v Fleetwood	1-1
6	Buxton v Chapel-en-le-Frith	2-0
	Eccles United v Marine	1-0
	Garston Gasworks v Skelmersdale United	4-6
	Runcorn v Hurst	1-3
7	Ellesmere Port Cement v Macclesfield Town	2-1
	Harrowby v Witton Albion	0-2
	Northwich Victoria v New Brighton	0-1
	Port Sunlight v Sandbach Ramblers	0-0
8	Bilston United v Shrewsbury Town	1-4
	Bloxwich Strollers v Cradley Heath St Luke's	4-1
	Stafford Rangers v Kidderminster Harriers	3-1
	Wellington St George's v Darlaston	1-0
9	Gainsborough Trinity v Hull Old Boys	5-0
	Grimsby Haycroft Rovers v Retford Town	2-2
	Hull Dairycoates v Boston (1)	1-4
	Scunthorpe United v Charltons (Grimsby)	3-0
10	Castleford Town v Frickley Colliery	0-0
	Denaby United v Doncaster Rovers	0-0
	Mexborough v Bentley Colliery	4-0
	Wath Athletic v Liversedge	7-2
11	Dinnington Main Colliery v Rotherham Town	1-1
	Kiveton Park Colliery v Maltby Main Colliery	1-0
	Laughton Common v Treeton Reading Room	0-1
	Woodhouse v Prospect United	0-0
12	Alfreton Town v Bolsover Colliery	3-3
	Grassmoor Ivanhoe v Eckington Works	1-1
	Pinxton v Matlock Town	3-1
	South Normanton Colliery v Ilkeston United	1-2
13	Lenton v Sutton Town	2-3
	Mansfield Town v Shirebrook	3-1
	Sutton Junction v Newark Athletic	2-0
	Welbeck Colliery v Hucknall Byron	3-0
14	Gresley Rovers v Newhall Swifts	3-1
	Hinckley United (1) v Nuneaton Town	0-3
	Loughborough Corinthians v Coalville Swifts	1-2
	Whitwick Imperial v Moira United	1-1
15	Fletton United v Kettering	5-1
	Higham Ferrers Town v Bedford Town (1)	0-0
	Rothwell Town v Wellingborough Town	4-0
	Spalding United v Desborough Town	2-0
16	Bury St Edmunds v Harwich & Parkeston	0-1
	Cambridge Town v King's Lynn	0-1
	Great Yarmouth Town v Orwell Works	3-1
	Norwich CEYMS v Leiston Works Athletic	1-2
17	Clapton v Gnome Athletic	2-0
	Custom House v Chelmsford	1-1
	Leytonstone v Grays Athletic	1-1
	Walthamstow Grange v GER Romford	0-1
18	Edmonton v RAF Henlow	2-1
	Enfield v Letchworth Town	1-0
	Fricker Athletic v Biggleswade & District	0-1
	Luton Amateur v Leavesden Mental Hospital	0-2
19	Botwell Mission v Maidenhead United	5-3
	Chesham United v Southall	5-3
	Slough v Henley Town	8-0
	Uxbridge v Wycombe Wanderers	1-6
20	Egham v Wimbledon	0-4
	Guildford United v Nunhead	4-0
	Hersham v Farnham United Breweries	2-6
	Woking v Kingstonian	2-2
21	Bostall Heath v Dartford	1-2
	Northfleet United v Chatham	0-0
	Royal Engs. Comrades (Eastb'rne) v Vernon Athletic	1-1
	Whitstable v Sittingbourne	2-4
22	Bournemouth Tramways v Boscombe	1-2
	Gosport Athletic v Ryde Sports	2-1
	Portsea Gas Co. v Bournemouth Gasworks Ath.	3-1
	Thornycrofts (Woolston) v Sholing Athletic	1-3
23	Melksham & Avon United v Devizes Town	2-2
	Trowbridge Town v Coleford Athletic	1-1
	Welton Rovers v Torquay United	3-2
	Yeovil & Petter's United v Calne & Harris United	8-1
24	Bath City v Hanham Athletic	2-0
	Ebbw Vale v Barry	3-1
	Porth Athletic v Cardiff Corinthians	3-3
	Swindon Victoria v Bristol St George	4-0
4r	Frizington Athletic v Whitehaven Colliery Recreation	1-2
r	Penrith v Bowthorn Recreation	1-0e
5r	Chorley v Horwich RMI	1-0
r	Fleetwood v Rossendale United	2-2
7r	Sandbach Ramblers v Port Sunlight	1-0
9r	Retford Town v Grimsby Haycroft Rovers	4-1
10r	Doncaster Rovers v Denaby United	4-1
r	Frickley Colliery v Castleford Town	1-0
11r	Prospect United v Woodhouse	0-2
r	Rotherham Town v Dinnington Main Colliery	2-0
12r	Bolsover Colliery v Alfreton Town	1-2
r	Eckington Works v Grassmoor Ivanhoe	0-1
14r	Moira United v Whitwick Imperial	0-2
15r	Bedford Town (1) v Higham Ferrers Town	1-1e
17r	Chelmsford v Custom House	0-0
r	Grays Athletic v Leytonstone	1-2
20r	Kingstonian v Woking	0-3
21r	Chatham v Northfleet United	1-3
r	Vernon Athletic v Royal Engs. Comrades (Eastb'rne)	2-1e
23r	Coleford Athletic v Trowbridge Town	2-1
r	Devizes Town v Melksham & Avon United	1-2
24r	Cardiff Corinthians v Porth Athletic	2-0
5r2	Rossendale United v Fleetwood	1-3
15r2	Higham Ferrers Town v Bedford Town (1)	4-1 N
17r2	Custom House v Chelmsford	3-1
	Qualifying Round Two	
1	Felling Colliery v Usworth Colliery	2-0
	Spen Black & White v Wallsend	1-0
2	Ferryhill Athletic v West Stanley	0-0
	Spennymoor United v Leadgate Park	3-1
3	Cockfield v Willington	3-2
	Stockton v Tow Law Town	3-1
4	Cleator Moor Celtic v Workington	1-2
	Whitehaven Colliery Recreation v Penrith	2-0
5	Fleetwood v Dick, Kerrs	1-0
	Morecambe v Chorley	2-1
6	Buxton v Eccles United	0-2
	Skelmersdale United v Hurst	2-3
7	New Brighton v Witton Albion	2-1
	Sandbach Ramblers v Ellesmere Port Cement	2-0
8	Stafford Rangers v Shrewsbury Town	2-3
	Wellington St George's v Bloxwich Strollers	1-0
9	Boston (1) v Retford Town	2-1
	Gainsborough Trinity v Scunthorpe United	1-2
10	Frickley Colliery v Wath Athletic	0-0
	Mexborough v Doncaster Rovers	0-0
11	Kiveton Park Colliery v Treeton Reading Room	2-0
	Rotherham Town v Woodhouse	3-0
12	Alfreton Town v Grassmoor Ivanhoe	9-0
	Ilkeston United v Pinxton	2-0
13	Mansfield Town v Sutton Junction	3-0
	Welbeck Colliery v Sutton Town	0-2
14	Coalville Swifts v Gresley Rovers	1-0
	Nuneaton Town v Whitwick Imperial	3-2
15	Fletton United v Rothwell Town	1-0
	Higham Ferrers Town v Spalding United	3-0
16	Great Yarmouth Town v King's Lynn	0-2
	Harwich & Parkeston v Leiston Works Athletic	1-2
17	Clapton v Custom House	4-2
	GER Romford v Leytonstone	1-3
18	Biggleswade & District v Edmonton	1-1
	Enfield v Leavesden Mental Hospital	5-1
19	Chesham United v Botwell Mission	6-0
	Wycombe Wanderers v Slough	0-2
20	Farnham United Breweries v Wimbledon	2-4
	Woking v Guildford United	0-1
21	Dartford v Vernon Athletic	3-1
	Sittingbourne v Northfleet United	2-0
22	Boscombe v Sholing Athletic	2-1
	Portsea Gas Company v Gosport Athletic	1-1
23	Melksham & Avon United v Coleford Athletic	2-3
	Welton Rovers v Yeovil & Petter's United	2-1
24	Bath City v Ebbw Vale	2-0
	Cardiff Corinthians v Swindon Victoria	1-0
2r	West Stanley v Ferryhill Athletic	3-1
10r	Doncaster Rovers v Mexborough	2-1
r	Wath Athletic v Frickley Colliery	1-0
18r	Edmonton v Biggleswade & District	1-0
22r	Gosport Athletic v Portsea Gas Company	5-2
	Qualifying Round Three	
1	Felling Colliery v Spen Black & White	0-0
2	West Stanley v Spennymoor United	5-0
3	Cockfield v Stockton	1-0
4	Whitehaven Colliery Recreation v Workington	0-4
5	Morecambe v Fleetwood	0-1
6	Hurst v Eccles United	2-2
7	New Brighton v Sandbach Ramblers	5-0
8	Wellington St George's v Shrewsbury Town	2-1
9	Boston (1) v Scunthorpe United	0-1
10	Doncaster Rovers v Wath Athletic	0-0
11	Rotherham Town v Kiveton Park Colliery	1-0
12	Ilkeston United v Alfreton Town	0-0
13	Mansfield Town v Sutton Town	4-1
14	Coalville Swifts v Nuneaton Town	3-2
15	Fletton United v Higham Ferrers Town	0-0
16	King's Lynn v Leiston Works Athletic	3-1
17	Clapton v Leytonstone	3-0
18	Enfield v Edmonton	2-2
19	Chesham United v Slough	5-1
20	Guildford United v Wimbledon	4-0
21	Sittingbourne v Dartford	1-0
22	Boscombe v Gosport Athletic	4-0
23	Coleford Athletic v Welton Rovers	1-2
24	Bath City v Cardiff Corinthians	2-0
1r	Spen Black & White v Felling Colliery	0-1
6r	Eccles United v Hurst	1-0
10r	Wath Athletic v Doncaster Rovers	2-1
12r	Alfreton Town v Ilkeston United	2-1
15r	Higham Ferrers Town v Fletton United	2-2
18r	Edmonton v Enfield	5-1
15r2	Higham Ferrers Town v Fletton United	2-1e
	Qualifying Round Four	
	Barking v Clapton	3-5
	Barrow v Workington	1-0
	Carlisle United v Fleetwood	7-1
	Chesham United v Oxford City	5-2
	Chesterfield v Lincoln City	2-0
	Coalville Swifts v Mansfield Town	0-2
	Cockfield v Felling Colliery	0-1
	Durham City v West Stanley	2-1
	Edmonton v Ilford	1-1
	Exeter City v Boscombe	0-0
	Halifax Town v Rotherham Town	6-1
	Higham Ferrers Town v King's Lynn	3-1 v
	Maidstone United v Guildford United	2-1

1922/23 to 1923/24

	New Brighton v Crewe Alexandra	1-1
	Rochdale v Nelson	0-1
	Sittingbourne v Southend United	0-0
	South Bank v Blyth Spartans	1-1
	St Albans City v Dulwich Hamlet	1-1
	Tufnell Park v London Caledonians	0-3
	Wath Athletic v Alfreton Town	2-1
	Wellington St George's v Tranmere Rovers	2-1
	Welton Rovers v Bath City	1-4
	Wigan Borough v Eccles United	4-0
	Worksop Town v Scunthorpe United	4-2
r	Blyth Spartans v South Bank	3-2
r	Boscombe v Exeter City	1-3
r	Crewe Alexandra v New Brighton	0-1
r	Dulwich Hamlet v St Albans City	8-7e
r	Ilford v Edmonton	3-0
r	King's Lynn v Higham Ferrers Town	1-3
r	Southend United v Sittingbourne	4-2

Qualifying Round Five

	Aberdare Athletic v Newport County	1-1
	Accrington Stanley v Halifax Town	1-1
	Barrow v Stockport County	3-2
	Bishop Auckland v Darlington	1-2
	Blyth Spartans v Ashington	2-1
	Carlisle United v Felling Colliery	6-0
	Charlton Athletic v Northampton Town	2-0
	Chesterfield v Higham Ferrers Town	4-4
	Dulwich Hamlet v Clapton	2-2x
	Durham City v Hartlepools United	0-1
	Exeter City v Bath City	1-2
	Grimsby Town v Worksop Town	0-2
	Ilford v Chesham United	6-1
	London Caledonians v Gillingham	1-2
	Maidstone United v Brentford	0-0
	Mansfield Town v Wath Athletic	1-0
	Merthyr Town v Swansea Town	0-0
	New Brighton v Coventry City	3-0
	Port Vale v Wrexham	0-2
	Reading v Bristol Rovers	0-1
	Southend United v Norwich City	2-2
	Southport v Wigan Borough	1-1
	Stalybridge Celtic v Nelson	1-0
	Walsall v Wellington St George's	5-0
r	Brentford v Maidstone United	4-0
r	Clapton v Dulwich Hamlet	2-0
r	Halifax Town v Accrington Stanley	1-0
r	Higham Ferrers Town v Chesterfield	0-1
r	Newport County v Aberdare Athletic	1-1e
r	Norwich City v Southend United	2-1
r	Swansea Town v Merthyr Town	0-1
r	Wigan Borough v Southport	3-1
r2	Aberdare Athletic v Newport County	2-1 N

Qualifying Round Six

	Aberdare Athletic v Carlisle United	0-0
	Barrow v Bath City	2-2
	Brentford v Merthyr Town	0-1
	Charlton Athletic v Darlington	2-1
	Gillingham v Blyth Spartans	1-4
	Mansfield Town v Halifax Town	0-2
	New Brighton v Clapton	1-0
	Norwich City v Ilford	5-1
	Stalybridge Celtic v Bristol Rovers	0-0
	Walsall v Wigan Borough	1-3
	Worksop Town v Chesterfield	1-0
	Wrexham v Hartlepools United	1-0
r	Bath City v Barrow	2-0
r	Bristol Rovers v Stalybridge Celtic	1-2
r	Carlisle United v Aberdare Athletic	1-2e

Round One

	Aberdare Athletic v Preston North End	1-3
	Aston Villa v Blackburn Rovers	0-1
	Blyth Spartans v Stoke	0-3
	Bradford City v Manchester United	1-1
	Brighton & Hove Albion v Corinthians	1-1
	Bristol City v Wrexham	5-1
	Bury v Luton Town	2-1
	Cardiff City v Watford	1-1
	Chelsea v Rotherham County	1-0
	Clapton Orient v Millwall	0-2
	Derby County v Blackpool	2-0
	Everton v Bradford Park Avenue	1-1
	Huddersfield Town v Birmingham	2-1
	Hull City v West Ham United	2-3
	Leicester City v Fulham	4-0
	Liverpool v Arsenal	0-0
	Manchester City v Charlton Athletic	1-2
	Merthyr Town v Wolverhampton Wan.	0-1
	Newcastle United v Southampton	0-0
	Norwich City v Bolton Wanderers	0-2
	Nottingham Forest v Sheffield United	0-0
	Oldham Athletic v Middlesbrough	0-1
	Plymouth Argyle v Notts County	0-0
	Portsmouth v Leeds United	0-0
	Queen's Park Rangers v Crystal Palace	1-0
	Sheffield Wednesday v New Brighton	3-0
	South Shields v Halifax Town	3-1
	Sunderland v Burnley	3-1
	Swindon Town v Barnsley	0-0
	Tottenham Hotspur v Worksop Town	0-0
	West Bromwich Albion v Stalybridge Celtic	0-0
	Wigan Borough v Bath City	4-1
r	Arsenal v Liverpool	1-4
r	Barnsley v Swindon Town	2-0
r	Bradford Park Avenue v Everton	1-0
r	Corinthians v Brighton & Hove Albion	1-1eN
r	Leeds United v Portsmouth	3-1
r	Manchester United v Bradford City	2-0
r	Notts County v Plymouth Argyle	0-1
r	Sheffield United v Nottingham Forest	0-0e
r	Southampton v Newcastle United	3-1
r	Stalybridge Celtic v West Bromwich Albion	0-2
r	Tottenham Hotspur v Worksop Town	9-0
r	Watford v Cardiff City	2-2e
r2	Brighton & Hove Albion v Corinthians	1-0 N
r2	Cardiff City v Watford	2-1 N
r2	Nottingham Forest v Sheffield United	1-1eN
r3	Sheffield United v Nottingham Forest	1-0 N

Round Two

	Bolton Wanderers v Leeds United	3-1
	Brighton & Hove Albion v West Ham United	1-1
	Bristol City v Derby County	0-3
	Bury v Stoke	3-1
	Charlton Athletic v Preston North End	2-0
	Chelsea v Southampton	0-0
	Leicester City v Cardiff City	0-1
	Middlesbrough v Sheffield United	1-1
	Millwall v Huddersfield Town	0-0
	Plymouth Argyle v Bradford Park Avenue	4-1
	Sheffield Wednesday v Barnsley	2-1
	South Shields v Blackburn Rovers	0-0
	Tottenham Hotspur v Manchester United	4-0
	West Bromwich Albion v Sunderland	2-1
	Wigan Borough v Queen's Park Rangers	2-4
	Wolverhampton Wan. v Liverpool	0-2
r	Blackburn Rovers v South Shields	0-1
r	Huddersfield Town v Millwall	3-0
r	Sheffield United v Middlesbrough	3-0
r	Southampton v Chelsea	1-0
r	West Ham United v Brighton & Hove Albion	1-0

Round Three

	Bury v Southampton	0-0
	Cardiff City v Tottenham Hotspur	2-3
	Charlton Athletic v West Bromwich Albion	1-0
	Derby County v Sheffield Wednesday	1-0
	Huddersfield Town v Bolton Wanderers	1-1
	Liverpool v Sheffield United	1-2
	Queen's Park Rangers v South Shields	3-0
	West Ham United v Plymouth Argyle	2-0
r	Bolton Wanderers v Huddersfield Town	1-0
r	Southampton v Bury	1-0

Round Four

	Charlton Athletic v Bolton Wanderers	0-1
	Queen's Park Rangers v Sheffield United	0-1
	Southampton v West Ham United	1-1
	Tottenham Hotspur v Derby County	0-1
r	West Ham United v Southampton	1-1e
r2	West Ham United v Southampton	1-0 N

Semi Finals

	Bolton Wanderers v Sheffield United	1-0 N
	West Ham United v Derby County	5-2 N

Final

	Bolton Wanderers v West Ham United	2-0 N

1923/24

Extra Preliminary Round

1	Scotswood v Washington Colliery	1-2
2	Birtley v Crook Town	2-1
	Chester-le-Street v Dipton United	0-1
	Hobson Wanderers v Seaham Harbour	1-2
	Horden Athletic v Esh Winning (1)	1-0
	Langley Park v Wingate Albion Comrades	0-0
	Thornley Albion v Wingate Constitutional Ath.	4-2
	Trimdon Grange Colliery v Sunderland West End	0-0
3	Bridlington Town (1) v Haverton Hill	5-1
	Carlin How v Stockton Malleable Institute	2-2
	Eston United v Guisborough Belmont Ath.	5-2
	Grangetown St Mary's v Brotton	5-1
	Stanley United v Chilton Colliery Recreation	0-1
	West Auckland Town v Coundon United	3-0
4	Moss Bay United v Maryport	0-1
6	Hadfield v Harlandic	0-3
	North Liverpool v New Mills	0-6
	Old Xaverians v Manchester North End	0-2
	Orrell v Glossop	0-1
	Prescot v Altrincham	1-3
7	Hoylake v Whitchurch	2-1
	Wallasey United v Llandudno	1-1
8	Bilston United v Birmingham Corp. Tramways	4-2
	Evesham Town v Kidderminster Harriers	1-1
	Halesowen Town v Brierley Hill Alliance	1-1
	Hednesford Town v Stourbridge	3-1
	Hereford St Martins v Worcester City	0-5
	Hereford Thistle v Bromsgrove Rovers	2-1
	Oakengates Town v Wellington Town	5-2
	Oswestry Town v Chirk	2-1
	Redditch v Leamington Town	2-0
	Wednesbury Old Athletic v Darlaston	1-1
	Willenhall v Cradley Heath St Luke's	2-0
	Wolseley Athletic v Wolverhampton Amateur	7-0
9	Blundells v Frodingham Athletic	1-2
	Brigg Town v Hull Old Boys	1-0
	British Oil & Cake Mills v Hornsea Town	3-1
	Central Hull Rangers v Hull Dairycoates	2-0
	Cleethorpes Town - Bye	
	Driffield Town v Bourne Town	3-2
	Grimsby Haycroft Rovers v Brunswick Institute	7-1
	Reckitt's (Hull) v Marfleet	1-0
10	Castleford Town v Monckton Athletic	0-0
	Darfield v Denaby United	1-1
	York City v Castleford & Allerton United	2-1
14	Ibstock Colliery v Hinckley United (1)	0-4
	Newhall Swifts v Rugby Town (1)	0-7
	Shepshed Albion v Mountsorrel Town	2-1
15	Leighton United v Bedford Town (1)	1-1
18	Baldock Town v Hertford Town	1-3
	Barnet v Apsley	8-0
	Finchley v Waterlows (Dunstable)	0-2
	Hitchin Blue Cross v Berkhamsted Town	3-0
	Wealdstone v Arlesey Town	4-1
19	Harrow Weald v Staines Lagonda	1-4
	Henley Town v Newbury Town	0-0
	Hounslow v Witney Town	5-0
20	Aldershot Institute Alb. v Hersham	6-0
	Brighton Railway Athletic v Basingstoke	1-1
	Carshalton Athletic v Sutton United	1-0
	Dorking v RAE Farnborough	3-1
	Egham v Wellington Works	1-4
	Gwynnes Athletic v Mitcham Wanderers	0-6
	Kingstonian v Thornycrofts (Basingstoke)	3-1
	Leyland Motors (Kingston) v RAMC Aldershot	2-1
	Tooting Town v RASC	2-3
	West Norwood v Guildford	4-3
21	Erith & Belvedere v Bexleyheath Town	1-0
	Folkestone v Ashford Railway Works	0-0
	Hastings & St Leonards v East Grinstead	3-1
	Newhaven v Southwick	0-3
	RMLI Chatham v Cray Wanderers	1-2
	Sheppey United v Bostall Heath	2-0
	Shoreham v Tunbridge Wells Rangers	0-3
	Whitstable v Ramsgate (1)	0-2
22	Bournemouth Gasworks Athletic v East Cowes Victoria	6-0
	Bournemouth Tramways v Osborne Athletic	2-1
	Portland United v Poole	1-1
	Salisbury Corinthians v Cowes	1-2
	Westham (Weymouth) v Salisbury (1)	0-1
23	Green Waves (Plymouth) v Minehead	2-0
	Spencer Melksham v Clutton Wanderers	1-2
	Spencer Moulton v Radstock Town	2-1
	Taunton & Newtons United v Torquay United	0-3
	Wells City v Frome Town	2-2
	Westbury United v Calne & Harris United	1-1
2r	Sunderland West End v Trimdon Grange Colliery	2-1
r	Wingate Albion Comrades v Langley Park	4-2
3r	Stockton Malleable Institute v Carlin How	2-0
7r	Llandudno v Wallasey United	0-1
8r	Brierley Hill Alliance v Halesowen Town	1-1
r	Darlaston v Wednesbury Old Athletic (2)	4-1
r	Kidderminster Harriers v Evesham Town	2-0
10r	Denaby United v Darfield	3-1
r	Monckton Athletic v Castleford Town	0-1
15r	Bedford Town (1) v Leighton United	1-1
19r	Newbury Town v Henley Town	4-2
20r	Brighton Railway Athletic v Basingstoke	wo/s
21r	Ashford Railway Works v Folkestone	2-2
22r	Poole v Portland United	3-0
23r	Calne & Harris United v Westbury United	1-3
r	Frome Town v Wells City	2-1
8r2	Brierley Hill Alliance v Halesowen Town	0-0 N
15r2	Bedford Town (1) v Leighton United	1-2
21r2	Folkestone v Ashford Railway Works	3-1 N
8r3	Halesowen Town v Brierley Hill Alliance	wo/s

Preliminary Round

1	Chopwell Institute v Prudhoe Castle	2-2
	Jarrow v Washington Colliery	1-1
	Leslies v Walker Celtic	1-2
	Newburn v Bedlington United	1-2
	Preston Colliery v Lintz Institute	3-0
	Spen Black & White v Wallsend	1-1
	St Anthony's Institute v Felling Colliery	2-1
	St Peter's Albion v Usworth Colliery	3-0
2	Birtley v Houghton	5-2
	Craghead United v Annfield Plain	3-0
	Dipton United v Seaham Harbour	4-0
	Durham City v West Stanley	2-2
	Horden Athletic v Leadgate Park	1-2
	Spennymoor United v Wingate Albion Comrades	4-1
	Sunderland West End v Thornley Albion	0-1
	White-le-Head Rangers v Ouston Rovers	3-2
3	Eston United v Bridlington Town (1)	7-1
	Ferryhill Athletic v West Auckland Town	3-1
	Loftus Albion v South Bank East End	3-2
	Scarborough v Darlington Railway Ath.	3-0
	South Bank v Stockton	3-1

1923/24

Stockton Malleable Institute v Grangetown St Mary's 1-0
Tow Law Town v Cockfield 0-2
Willington v Chilton Colliery Recreation 0-1
4 Egremont v Bowthorn Recreation 4-2
Kendal Town v Moor Row Villa Rovers 4-0
Keswick v Penrith 1-4
Maryport v Appleby 7-1
Wath Brow United v Cleator Moor Celtic 0-6
Whitehaven Colliery Recreation v Whitehaven Athletic 4-4
Windermere v Frizington Athletic 3-2
Workington v Wigton Harriers 8-1
5 Bacup Borough v Lancaster Town 1-1
Breightmet United v Atherton 0-3
Dick, Kerrs v Rossendale United 1-3
Fleetwood v Chorley 3-1
Great Harwood v Horwich RMI 1-2
Leyland Motors v Leyland 1-2
Lytham v Darwen 3-3
Morecambe v Portsmouth Rovers (Lancs) 3-0
6 Altrincham v Marlborough Old Boys 7-1
Buxton v Harlandic 2-1
Garston Gasworks v Whiston 3-2
Hurst v Chapel-en-le-Frith 4-0
Manchester North End v Eccles United 1-1
Marine v Burscough Rangers 0-1
New Mills v Glossop 3-1
Skelmersdale United v Youlgrave 2-1
7 Chester v Ellesmere Port Cement 1-0
Ellesmere Port Town v Port Sunlight 3-1
Macclesfield Town v Witton Albion 5-1
Nantwich v Hoylake 4-1
Northwich Victoria v Sandbach Ramblers 1-1
Rhyl Athletic v Middlewich 2-1
Wallasey United v Winsford United 0-1
West Kirby v Lostock Gralam 1-4
8 Bilston United v Hereford Thistle 7-1
Bloxwich Strollers v Kidderminster Harriers 1-0
Halesowen Town v Stafford Rangers 2-1
Oakengates Town v Redditch 2-1
Shrewsbury Town v Darlaston 3-1
Wellington St George's v Wolseley Athletic 3-1
Willenhall v Oswestry Town 3-1
Worcester City v Hednesford Town 5-0
9 Boston (1) v Retford Town 4-3
Brigg Town v Central Hull Rangers 1-0
British Oil & Cake Mills v Barton Town (1) 2-1
Cleethorpes Town v Frodingham Athletic 5-0
Driffield Town v Charltons (Grimsby) 1-3
Holderness Athletic v Grimsby Haycroft Rovers 0-1
Reckitt's (Hull) v Gainsborough Trinity 1-5
Scunthorpe United v Grimsby Rovers 5-1
10 Bentley Colliery v Wombwell 0-1
Castleford Town v Horsforth 3-2
Cudworth Village v York City 0-1
Denaby United v Selby Town 9-1
Fryston Colliery v Doncaster Rovers wo/s
Mexborough v Liversedge 2-1
South Kirkby Colliery v Frickley Colliery 0-7
Wath Athletic v Brodsworth Main Colliery 4-0
11 Anston Athletic v Rotherham Amateurs 1-0
Atlas & Norfolk Works v Sheffield 6-0
Birdwell v Ardsley Athletic 2-2
Chesterfield Corinthians v Maltby Main Colliery 0-9
Dinnington Main Colliery v Bullcroft Main Colliery 1-1
Rossington Main v Prospect United 1-1
12 Blackwell Colliery v Matlock Town 0-3
Bolsover Colliery v Creswell Colliery 1-0
Hardwick Colliery v Long Eaton 0-4
South Normanton Colliery v Crich Town wo/s
Staveley Town v Heanor Town 1-2
13 Boots Athletic v New Hucknall Colliery 7-1
Grantham v Shirebrook 4-4
Mansfield Colliery v Basford United 4-1
Sneinton v Lenton 1-4
Whitwell Colliery v Clifton Colliery 5-2
14 Barwell United v Loughborough Corinthians 3-1
Burton All Saints v Atherstone Town 10-1
Coalville Swifts v Ashby Town 4-2
Coalville Town (2) v Whitwick Imperial 1-4
Gresley Rovers v Stableford Works 8-0
Measham Town v Hinckley United (1) 3-4
Moira United v Rugby Town (1) 3-2
Nuneaton Town v Shepshed Albion 3-3
15 Desborough Town v Kettering 2-1
Fletton United v Leighton United 9-1
Higham Ferrers Town v Rothwell Town 2-0
Market Harborough Town v Peterbro' Westwood Works 4-2
Peterborough City (1) v Northampton Wanderers 1-2
Rushden Town v Stamford 2-1
Wellingborough Town v Irthlingborough Town 3-4
Wolverton Town v Peterborough G.N. Loco 4-1
16 Clacton Town v Harwich & Parkeston 5-2
Cromer v Lowestoft Town 4-1
Great Yarmouth Town v Cambridge Town 4-1
King's Lynn v Newmarket Town 7-1
Kirkley v Norwich CEYMS 1-4
Leiston Works Athletic v Paxmans Athletic 1-2
Orwell Works v Colchester Town 0-4
Wisbech Town v City Wanderers (Norwich) 0-0
17 Grays Athletic v Chelmsford 2-1
Shoeburyness Garrison v Walthamstow Grange 0-1
Walthamstow Town v Walthamstow Avenue 4-0
18 Enfield v Waterlows (Dunstable) 3-1
Hertford Town v Wood Green Town 1-0
Hitchin Blue Cross v Edmonton 1-1
Leavesden Mental Hospital v Barnet 0-3
Letchworth Town v Tufnell Park 2-3
Luton Amateur v Fricker Athletic 3-6
Luton Clarence v Hampstead Town 2-5
Wealdstone v Biggleswade & District 2-1
19 Chesham United v Wycombe Wanderers 2-4
Maidenhead United v Hounslow 3-3
Marlow v Hanwell Athletic 3-3
Oxford City v Botwell Mission 1-2
Slough v Henley Comrades 13-0
Southall v Windsor & Eton 3-0
Staines Lagonda v Newbury Town 2-1
Uxbridge v Yiewsley 2-0
20 Guildford United v RASC 4-0
Kingstonian v Dorking 9-1
Leyland Motors (Kingston) v Brighton Railway Ath. 3-0ev
Redhill v Mitcham Wanderers 4-1
Summerstown v Aldershot Institute Alb. 7-0
Walton-on-Thames v Farnham United Breweries 1-7
Wellington Works v Woking 6-2
West Norwood v Carshalton Athletic 2-3
21 Cray Wanderers v Folkestone 0-6
Dartford v Woolwich Polytechnic 4-0
Erith & Belvedere v Ramsgate (1) 1-2
Hastings & St Leonards v Tunbridge Wells Rangers 2-1
Maidstone United v Chatham 0-2
Northfleet United v Sheppey United 2-2
Southwick v Vernon Athletic 3-3
Worthing v Royal Engs. Comrades (Eastb'rne) 2-0
22 Bournemouth (Ams) v Eastleigh Athletic 2-2
Bournemouth Gasworks Athletic v Sholing Athletic 3-1
Cowes v Salisbury (1) 6-2
Portsea Gas Company v Bournemouth wo/s
Portsmouth Amateurs v Bournemouth Tramways 0-3
Ryde Sports v Poole 6-2
Thornycrofts (Woolston) v Gosport Athletic 0-0
Weymouth v Blandford 9-0
23 Coleford Athletic v Clevedon 2-0
Devizes Town v Melksham & Avon United 2-0
Glastonbury v Trowbridge Town 1-2
Green Waves (Plymouth) v Torquay United 0-3
Spencer Moulton v Street 3-0
Warminster Town v Welton Rovers 1-1
Westbury United v Clutton Wanderers 3-1
Yeovil & Petter's United v Frome Town 2-0
24 Bath City v Hanham Athletic 0-1
Bristol St George v Horfield United 3-1
Cardiff Corinthians v Ebbw Vale 1-6
Chippenham Rovers v Timsbury Athletic 2-1
Llanelli v Barry 2-1
Paulton Rovers v Chippenham Town 0-0
Peasedown St John's v Clandown 5-2
Pontypridd v Swindon Victoria 8-1
1r Prudhoe Castle v Chopwell Institute 1-0
r Wallsend v Spen Black & White 1-0
r Washington Colliery v Jarrow 0-2
2r West Stanley v Durham City 1-1
4r Whitehaven Athletic v Whitehaven Colliery Recreation 0-3
5r Darwen v Lytham 4-1
r Lancaster Town v Bacup Borough 4-1
6r Eccles United v Manchester North End 1-2
7r Sandbach Ramblers v Northwich Victoria 1-2
11r Ardsley Athletic v Birdwell 4-2e
r Bullcroft Main Colliery v Dinnington Main Colliery 2-0
r Prospect United v Rossington Main 3-2
13r Shirebrook v Grantham 1-0
14r Shepshed Albion v Nuneaton Town 0-3
16r City Wanderers (Norwich) v Wisbech Town 1-0
18r Edmonton v Hitchin Blue Cross 3-2
19r Hanwell Athletic v Marlow 1-0
r Hounslow v Maidenhead United 4-1
20r Brighton Railway Athletic v Leyland Motors (Kingston 0-1
21r Sheppey United v Northfleet United 3-4
r Southwick v Vernon Athletic 2-0
22r Eastleigh Athletic v Bournemouth (Ams) 3-2
r Gosport Athletic v Thornycrofts (Woolston) 5-2
23r Welton Rovers v Warminster Town 5-2
24r Chippenham Town v Paulton Rovers 3-1
2r2 West Stanley v Durham City 0-1

Qualifying Round One

1 Jarrow v Preston Colliery 0-0
St Anthony's Institute v Wallsend 1-1
St Peter's Albion v Prudhoe Castle 2-0
Walker Celtic v Bedlington United 0-0
2 Birtley v Craghead United 1-1
Dipton United v Durham City 1-0
Leadgate Park v Spennymoor United 1-0
Thornley Albion v White-le-Head Rangers 0-0
3 Cockfield v South Bank 2-1
Eston United v Stockton Malleable Institute 3-1
Ferryhill Athletic v Scarborough 0-0
Loftus Albion v Chilton Colliery Recreation 1-1
4 Cleator Moor Celtic v Whitehaven Colliery Recreation 6-1
Kendal Town v Penrith 0-2
Windermere v Maryport 1-0
Workington v Egremont 5-1
5 Atherton v Horwich RMI 2-0
Lancaster Town v Fleetwood 1-5
Leyland v Darwen 2-2
Rossendale United v Morecambe 0-1
6 Altrincham v Hurst 2-1
Garston Gasworks v Burscough Rangers 4-2
Manchester North End v Buxton 2-4
Skelmersdale United v New Mills 1-1
7 Chester v Lostock Gralam 5-1
Ellesmere Port Town v Rhyl Athletic 2-1
Nantwich v Winsford United 1-1
Northwich Victoria v Macclesfield Town 3-1
8 Halesowen Town v Bilston United 3-2
Oakengates Town v Bloxwich Strollers 1-2
Shrewsbury Town v Worcester City 2-1
Willenhall v Wellington St George's 1-0
9 Boston (1) v British Oil & Cake Mills 8-1
Charltons (Grimsby) v Brigg Town 2-4
Cleethorpes Town v Scunthorpe United 0-6
Gainsborough Trinity v Grimsby Haycroft Rovers 4-1
10 Frickley Colliery v Wombwell 2-2
Fryston Colliery v Castleford Town 0-1
Wath Athletic v Denaby United 0-3
York City v Mexborough 1-1
11 Anston Athletic v Rotherham Town 0-0
Ardsley Athletic v Treeton Reading Room 1-1
Bullcroft Main Colliery v Atlas & Norfolk Works 2-1
Maltby Main Colliery v Prospect United 4-1
12 Alfreton Town v Pinxton 5-0
Bolsover Colliery v Grassmoor Ivanhoe wo/s
Heanor Town v Matlock Town 1-2
South Normanton Colliery v Long Eaton 4-1
13 Boots Athletic v Lenton 2-1e
Mansfield Colliery v Sutton Town 2-8
Mansfield Town v Shirebrook 1-1
Whitwell Colliery v Newark Athletic 3-1
14 Coalville Swifts v Barwell United 1-0
Gresley Rovers v Whitwick Imperial 2-0
Hinckley United (1) v Burton All Saints 4-0
Nuneaton Town v Moira United 10-2
15 Desborough Town v Wolverton Town 3-2
Irthlingborough Town v Northampton Wanderers 4-2
Market Harborough Town v Higham Ferrers Town 0-5
Rushden Town v Fletton United 1-1
16 City Wanderers (Norwich) v Great Yarmouth Town 1-0
Clacton Town v Cromer 1-3
Colchester Town v Paxmans Athletic 8-3
King's Lynn v Norwich CEYMS 5-0
17 Custom House v Walthamstow Grange 3-2
GER Romford v Barking 2-4
Grays Athletic v Walthamstow Town 4-2
Leytonstone v Sterling Athletic 6-1
18 Barnet v Fricker Athletic 2-0
Enfield v Edmonton 5-1
Hampstead Town v Tufnell Park 1-1
Hertford Town v Wealdstone 0-0
19 Slough v Staines Lagonda 1-0
Southall v Hanwell Athletic 6-0
Uxbridge v Botwell Mission 2-2
Wycombe Wanderers v Hounslow 8-2
20 Carshalton Athletic v Summerstown 0-2
Guildford United v Redhill 2-1
Kingstonian v Wellington Works 8-0
Leyland Motors (Kingston) v Farnham United Breweries 0-2
21 Dartford v Chatham 1-0
Folkestone v Hastings & St Leonards 8-1
Ramsgate (1) v Northfleet United 4-2
Southwick v Worthing 4-3
22 Bournemouth Tramways v Eastleigh Athletic 4-2
Cowes v Ryde Sports 4-0
Gosport Athletic v Bournemouth Gasworks Athletic 2-0
Portsea Gas Company v Weymouth 1-2
23 Torquay United v Coleford Athletic 6-0
Trowbridge Town v Spencer Moulton 1-0
Welton Rovers v Devizes Town 6-1
Yeovil & Petter's United v Westbury United 12-1
24 Chippenham Town v Bristol St George 4-1
Ebbw Vale v Llanelli 0-2
Hanham Athletic v Chippenham Rovers 0-0
Peasedown St John's v Pontypridd 0-8
1r Bedlington United v Walker Celtic 1-2
r Preston Colliery v Jarrow 1-0
r Wallsend v St Anthony's Institute 3-3
2r Craghead United v Birtley 4-0
r White-le-Head Rangers v Thornley Albion 0-0e
3r Chilton Colliery Recreation v Loftus Albion 3-0
r Scarborough v Ferryhill Athletic 1-3
5r Darwen v Leyland 3-2
6r New Mills v Skelmersdale United 1-2
7r Winsford United v Nantwich 2-4
10r Mexborough v York City 1-1e
r Wombwell v Frickley Colliery 1-3
11r Rotherham Town v Anston Athletic 9-0
r Treeton Reading Room v Ardsley Athletic 2-4
13r Shirebrook v Mansfield Town 4-2
15r Fletton United v Rushden Town 1-0
18r Tufnell Park v Hampstead Town 6-0
r Wealdstone v Hertford Town 5-3
19r Botwell Mission v Uxbridge 1-0
24r Chippenham Rovers v Hanham Athletic 1-3
1r2 Wallsend v St Anthony's Institute 2-3
2r2 White-le-Head Rangers v Thornley Albion 0-1 N
10r2 Mexborough v York City 3-1 N

Qualifying Round Two

1 St Peter's Albion v Preston Colliery 2-0
Walker Celtic v St Anthony's Institute 2-1
2 Leadgate Park v Craghead United 3-1
Thornley Albion v Dipton United 0-0
3 Cockfield v Chilton Colliery Recreation 2-2
Ferryhill Athletic v Eston United 6-2

1923/24 to 1924/25

4 Windermere v Penrith	2-2
Workington v Cleator Moor Celtic	6-1
5 Atherton v Morecambe	2-2
Fleetwood v Darwen	3-0
6 Altrincham v Buxton	3-1
Garston Gasworks v Skelmersdale United	2-3
7 Ellesmere Port Town v Chester	2-1
Nantwich v Northwich Victoria	2-1
8 Halesowen Town v Bloxwich Strollers	1-1
Shrewsbury Town v Willenhall	2-0
9 Boston (1) v Brigg Town	2-1
Scunthorpe United v Gainsborough Trinity	2-0
10 Castleford Town v Frickley Colliery	2-2
Denaby United v Mexborough	1-0
11 Ardsley Athletic v Rotherham Town	0-0
Maltby Main Colliery v Bullcroft Main Colliery	1-2
12 Bolsover Colliery v Alfreton Town	1-1
Matlock Town v South Normanton Colliery	0-1
13 Shirebrook v Boots Athletic	1-1
Sutton Town v Whitwell Colliery	8-0
14 Coalville Swifts v Gresley Rovers	1-1
Hinckley United (1) v Nuneaton Town	7-3
15 Desborough Town v Higham Ferrers Town	3-0
Fletton United v Irthlingborough Town	1-1
16 City Wanderers (Norwich) v Cromer	4-1
King's Lynn v Colchester Town	2-0
17 Barking v Custom House	3-2
Grays Athletic v Leytonstone	4-0
18 Barnet v Enfield	1-1
Wealdstone v Tufnell Park	0-1
19 Botwell Mission v Wycombe Wanderers	4-4
Slough v Southall	1-0
20 Guildford United v Summerstown	2-2
Kingstonian v Farnham United Breweries	0-1
21 Folkestone v Southwick	1-1
Ramsgate (1) v Dartford	1-0
22 Cowes v Gosport Athletic	0-2
Weymouth v Bournemouth Tramways	6-0
23 Torquay United v Trowbridge Town	3-0
Welton Rovers v Yeovil & Petter's United	1-2
24 Chippenham Town v Hanham Athletic	3-0
Llanelli v Pontypridd	1-0
2r Dipton United v Thornley Albion	1-1
3r Chilton Colliery Recreation v Cockfield	3-0
4r Penrith v Windermere	2-2
5r Morecambe v Atherton	3-1
8r Bloxwich Strollers v Halesowen Town	1-0
10r Frickley Colliery v Castleford Town	2-1
11r Rotherham Town v Ardsley Athletic	3-0
12r Alfreton Town v Bolsover Colliery	6-1
13r Boots Athletic v Shirebrook	0-1
14r Gresley Rovers v Coalville Swifts	2-1
15r Irthlingborough Town v Fletton United	1-4
18r Enfield v Barnet	4-2
19r Wycombe Wanderers v Botwell Mission	1-2
20r Summerstown v Guildford United	1-2
21r Southwick v Folkestone	1-4
2r2 Dipton United v Thornley Albion	1-2 N
4r2 Windermere v Penrith	1-3

Qualifying Round Three

1 St Peter's Albion v Walker Celtic	2-0
2 Thornley Albion v Leadgate Park	2-2
3 Ferryhill Athletic v Chilton Colliery Recreation	1-0
4 Penrith v Workington	1-4
5 Morecambe v Fleetwood	0-3
6 Skelmersdale United v Altrincham	2-1
7 Ellesmere Port Town v Nantwich	3-2
8 Shrewsbury Town v Bloxwich Strollers	3-1
9 Scunthorpe United v Boston (1)	2-0
10 Denaby United v Frickley Colliery	4-2
11 Rotherham Town v Bullcroft Main Colliery	2-0
12 South Normanton Colliery v Alfreton Town	3-3
13 Sutton Town v Shirebrook	1-0
14 Gresley Rovers v Hinckley United (1)	1-1
15 Fletton United v Desborough Town	1-0
16 King's Lynn v City Wanderers (Norwich)	4-0
17 Grays Athletic v Barking	0-0
18 Tufnell Park v Enfield	2-2
19 Botwell Mission v Slough	3-0
20 Guildford United v Farnham United Breweries	3-0
21 Folkestone v Ramsgate (1)	4-0
22 Weymouth v Gosport Athletic	2-2
23 Yeovil & Petter's United v Torquay United	1-1
24 Chippenham Town v Llanelli	1-1
2r Leadgate Park v Thornley Albion	1-0
12r Alfreton Town v South Normanton Colliery	1-1e
14r Hinckley United (1) v Gresley Rovers	4-1
17r Barking v Grays Athletic	2-1
18r Enfield v Tufnell Park	1-2
22r Gosport Athletic v Weymouth	1-1
23r Torquay United v Yeovil & Petter's United	2-1
24r Llanelli v Chippenham Town	6-0
12r2 Alfreton Town v South Normanton Colliery	2-0
22r2 Gosport Athletic v Weymouth	0-3 N

Qualifying Round Four

Alfreton Town v Worksop Town	2-2
Barrow v Carlisle United	1-2
Bishop Auckland v Ashington	1-2
Botwell Mission v Barking	5-3
Denaby United v Lincoln City	1-2
Ferryhill Athletic v Leadgate Park	0-0
Folkestone v Bromley	2-1
Hartlepools United v St Peter's Albion	10-1
Hinckley United (1) v Shrewsbury Town	3-1
Ilford v St Albans City	1-1
Newport County v Exeter City	0-2
Nunhead v Guildford United	2-1
Rochdale v Skelmersdale United	4-0
Scunthorpe United v Rotherham Town	0-0
Shildon v Blyth Spartans	3-1
Sittingbourne v Dulwich Hamlet	2-1
Southend United v King's Lynn	1-0
Southport v New Brighton	1-1
Sutton Town v Fletton United	1-1
Torquay United v Aberdare Athletic	0-0
Tranmere Rovers v Ellesmere Port Town	1-0
Tufnell Park v Clapton	0-1
Weymouth v Llanelli	0-1
Workington v Fleetwood	3-0
r Aberdare Athletic v Torquay United	4-0
r Fletton United v Sutton Town	1-0
r Leadgate Park v Ferryhill Athletic	3-2
r New Brighton v Southport	0-1
r Rotherham Town v Scunthorpe United	0-1
r St Albans City v Ilford	3-0
r Worksop Town v Alfreton Town	4-1

Qualifying Round Five

Aberdare Athletic v Reading	1-0
Accrington Stanley v Rochdale	1-0
Ashington v Carlisle United	2-0
Botwell Mission v Brentford	1-1 N
Clapton v Southend United	1-3 N
Coventry City v Tranmere Rovers	2-2
Exeter City v Bristol Rovers	2-2
Fletton United v Halifax Town	0-1
Folkestone v Norwich City	2-3
Hartlepools United v Shildon	3-1
Hinckley United (1) v Grimsby Town	0-3
Leadgate Park v Darlington	1-1
Llanelli v Merthyr Town	3-1
London Caledonians v Portsmouth	1-5
Northampton Town v Lincoln City	5-1
Nunhead v Gillingham	0-6
Scunthorpe United v Rotherham County	1-1
Sittingbourne v St Albans City	2-1
Stockport County v Crewe Alexandra	1-0
Walsall v Stalybridge Celtic	3-1
Wigan Borough v Nelson	1-1
Workington v Southport	1-2
Worksop Town v Chesterfield	0-2
Wrexham v Port Vale	5-1
r Brentford v Botwell Mission	2-0
r Bristol Rovers v Exeter City	0-1
r Darlington v Leadgate Park	1-0
r Nelson v Wigan Borough	0-1
r Rotherham County v Scunthorpe United	2-0
r Tranmere Rovers v Coventry City	3-2e

Qualifying Round Six

Aberdare Athletic v Walsall	1-0
Accrington Stanley v Wrexham	1-0
Ashington v Hartlepools United	2-1
Brentford v Portsmouth	1-1
Chesterfield v Grimsby Town	0-0
Darlington v Southport	3-0
Gillingham v Tranmere Rovers	1-0
Halifax Town v Rotherham County	1-0
Llanelli v Southend United	2-1
Norwich City v Stockport County	2-0
Sittingbourne v Exeter City	0-2
Wigan Borough v Northampton Town	0-6
r Grimsby Town v Chesterfield	2-0
r Portsmouth v Brentford	1-0e

Round One

Accrington Stanley v Charlton Athletic	0-0
Arsenal v Luton Town	4-1
Ashington v Aston Villa	1-5
Barnsley v Brighton & Hove Albion	0-0
Blackpool v Sheffield United	1-0
Burnley v South Shields	3-2
Cardiff City v Gillingham	0-0
Chelsea v Southampton	1-1
Corinthians v Blackburn Rovers	1-0
Crystal Palace v Tottenham Hotspur	2-0
Derby County v Bury	2-1
Everton v Preston North End	3-1
Exeter City v Grimsby Town	1-0
Fulham v Llanelli	2-0
Huddersfield Town v Birmingham	1-0
Hull City v Bolton Wanderers	2-2
Leeds United v Stoke	1-0
Liverpool v Bradford City	2-1
Manchester City v Nottingham Forest	2-0
Manchester United v Plymouth Argyle	1-0
Middlesbrough v Watford	0-1
Millwall v West Bromwich Albion	0-1
Northampton Town v Halifax Town	1-1
Norwich City v Bristol City	0-1
Oldham Athletic v Sunderland	2-1
Portsmouth v Newcastle United	2-4
Queen's Park Rangers v Notts County	1-2
Sheffield Wednesday v Leicester City	4-1
Swansea Town v Clapton Orient	1-1
Swindon Town v Bradford Park Avenue	4-0
West Ham United v Aberdare Athletic	5-0
Wolverhampton Wan. v Darlington	3-1
r Bolton Wanderers v Hull City	4-0
r Brighton & Hove Albion v Barnsley	1-0
r Charlton Athletic v Accrington Stanley	1-0
r Clapton Orient v Swansea Town	1-1e
r Gillingham v Cardiff City	0-2
r Halifax Town v Northampton Town	1-1e
r Southampton v Chelsea	2-0
r2 Halifax Town v Northampton Town	4-2 N
r2 Swansea Town v Clapton Orient	2-1 N

Round Two

Bolton Wanderers v Liverpool	1-4
Brighton & Hove Albion v Everton	5-2
Burnley v Fulham	0-0
Cardiff City v Arsenal	1-0
Charlton Athletic v Wolverhampton Wan.	0-0
Crystal Palace v Notts County	0-0
Derby County v Newcastle United	2-2
Exeter City v Watford	0-0
Manchester City v Halifax Town	2-2
Manchester United v Huddersfield Town	0-3
Sheffield Wednesday v Bristol City	1-1
Southampton v Blackpool	3-1
Swansea Town v Aston Villa	0-2
Swindon Town v Oldham Athletic	2-0
West Bromwich Albion v Corinthians	5-0
West Ham United v Leeds United	1-1
r Bristol City v Sheffield Wednesday	2-0
r Fulham v Burnley	0-1e
r Halifax Town v Manchester City	0-0e
r Leeds United v West Ham United	1-0
r Newcastle United v Derby County	2-2e
r Notts County v Crystal Palace	0-0e
r Watford v Exeter City	1-0
r Wolverhampton Wan. v Charlton Athletic	1-0
r2 Crystal Palace v Notts County	0-0eN
r2 Derby County v Newcastle United	2-2eN
r2 Manchester City v Halifax Town	3-0 N
r3 Crystal Palace v Notts County	2-1 N
r3 Newcastle United v Derby County	5-3

Round Three

Aston Villa v Leeds United	3-0
Brighton & Hove Albion v Manchester City	1-5
Burnley v Huddersfield Town	1-0
Cardiff City v Bristol City	3-0
Crystal Palace v Swindon Town	1-2
Southampton v Liverpool	0-0
Watford v Newcastle United	0-1
West Bromwich Albion v Wolverhampton Wan.	1-1
r Liverpool v Southampton	2-0
r Wolverhampton Wan. v West Bromwich Albion	0-2

Round Four

Manchester City v Cardiff City	0-0
Newcastle United v Liverpool	1-0
Swindon Town v Burnley	1-1
West Bromwich Albion v Aston Villa	0-2
r Burnley v Swindon Town	3-1
r Cardiff City v Manchester City	0-1e

Semi Finals

Aston Villa v Burnley	3-0 N
Newcastle United v Manchester City	2-0 N

Final

Newcastle United v Aston Villa	2-0 N

1924/25

Extra Preliminary Round

2 8th Durham Light Infantry v Seaham Harbour	1-1
Birtley New Town v Spennymoor United	1-0
Burnhope Institute v White-le-Head Rangers	1-2
Crook Town v Chester-le-Street	3-2
Horden Athletic v Esh Winning (1)	1-0
Seaham Colliery Welfare v Twizell United	1-0
West Stanley v Sunderland West End	1-2
Wheatley Hill Colliery v Hobson Wanderers	3-1
Wingate Albion Comrades v Annfield Plain	4-1
3 Coundon United v Tow Law Town	2-2
Haverton Hill v South Bank East End	1-2
Scarborough v Scarborough Penguins	5-2
5 Black Lane Rovers v Croston	8-2
Colne Carlton v Barnoldswick Park Villa	0-0
Horwich Central v Coppull Central	0-2
7 Barnton Victoria v Harrowby	2-0
Middlewich v Ellesmere Port Cement	0-1
Rhyl Athletic v Bangor City	0-1
West Kirby v Lostock Gralam	2-0

1924/25

8	Birmingham Corp. Tramways v Bilston United	1-1
	Bloxwich Strollers v Wolverhampton Amateur	9-0
	Brierley Hill Alliance v Leamington Town	2-2
	Bromsgrove Rovers v Redditch	1-3
	Cannock Town v Wolseley Athletic	2-1
	Darlaston v Hednesford Town	3-4
	Evesham Town v Hereford RAOC	wo/s
	Halesowen Town v Stourbridge	1-1
	Hereford Thistle v Worcester City	2-4
	Kidderminster Harriers v Hereford United	7-2
	Oswestry Town v Wellington Town	2-3
	Shrewsbury Town v Chirk	8-0
	Stafford Rangers v Cradley Heath St Luke's	2-0
	Wednesbury Old Athletic v Walsall Phoenix	3-2
	Wellington St George's v Oakengates Town	3-0
9	Cleethorpes Town v Louth Town	9-3
	Frodingham Athletic v Hull Technical College OB	wo/s
	Grimsby Rovers v Grimsby Haycroft Rovers	2-1
	Reckitt's (Hull) v Drypool Parish Church	0-4
10	Darfield v Cudworth Village	3-1
	Fryston Colliery v Wombwell	2-2
	York City v Guiseley	1-0
15	Biggleswade & District v Northampton Wanderers	wo/s
18	Baldock Town v Bishop's Stortford	1-1
	Bush Hill Park v Cheshunt	1-1
	Hampstead Town v Fricker Athletic	4-2
	Hitchin Blue Cross v Luton Clarence	1-3
	Waterlows (Dunstable) v Berkhamsted Town	1-0
19	Aylesbury United v Savoy Hotel	4-0
	Henley Town v BWI Reading	1-8
	Newbury Town v Oxford City	1-2
	Yiewsley v Polytechnic	3-0
20	Aldershot Traction Co. v Metropolitan Police	3-3
	Camberley & Yorktown v Woking	1-5
	Egham v Aldershot Albion	1-2
	Godalming v Southern Rail, Croydon	3-6
	Guildford v Leyland Motors (Kingston)	1-2
	Mitcham Wanderers v RAMC Aldershot	2-2
	Staines Lagonda v RASC	4-1
	Walton-on-Thames v Basingstoke	1-4
21	Ashford Railway Works v Northfleet United	1-3
	Bexleyheath Town v Tunbridge Wells Rangers	1-1
	Bostall Heath v Woolwich Polytechnic	7-0
	Chatham v Maidstone United	5-0
	East Grinstead v Rock-a-Nore	2-1
	Eastbourne Old Comrades v Vernon Athletic	2-1
	Hastings & St Leonards v Hove	2-2
	RM Chatham v Whitstable	0-1
	Shoreham v Newhaven	5-1
	Worthing v Horsham	3-0
22	Bournemouth (Ams) v Bournemouth Gasworks Athletic	3-2
	Fareham v Harland & Wolffs	0-1
	Poole v Burrfield Park	5-0
	Portsea Gas Company v Portsmouth Amateurs	7-0
	Ryde Sports v Osborne Athletic	6-3
	Salisbury Corinthians v Wimborne	2-0
23	Calne & Harris United v Wells City	3-1
	Green Waves (Plymouth) v Truro City	6-0
	Melksham & Avon United v Devizes Town	1-2
	Radstock Town v Frome Town	0-1
	Spencer Moulton v Warminster Town	2-2
	Taunton & Newtons United v Clutton Wanderers	2-0
2r	Seaham Harbour v 8th Durham Light Infantry	5-0
3r	Tow Law Town v Coundon United	2-1
5r	Barnoldswick Park Villa v Colne Carlton	3-2
8r	Bilston United v Birmingham Corp. Tramways	3-1
r	Leamington Town v Brierley Hill Alliance	5-2
9r	Frodingham Athletic v Hull Technical College OB	1-0
10r	Wombwell v Fryston Colliery	4-3
18r	Bishop's Stortford v Baldock Town	0-1
r	Cheshunt v Bush Hill Park	4-0
20r	Aldershot Traction Co. v Metropolitan Police	8-1
r	RAMC Aldershot v Mitcham Wanderers	2-1
21r	Bexleyheath Town v Tunbridge Wells Rangers	0-1
r	Hastings & St Leonards v Hove	1-1e
23r	Warminster Town v Spencer Moulton	2-1
21r2	Hastings & St Leonards v Hove	7-1

Preliminary Round

1	Jarrow v Bedlington United	4-0
	Seaton Delaval v Tanfield Lea Rovers	4-2
	St Anthony's Institute v Hexham	wo/s
	Usworth Colliery v Chopwell Institute	1-0
	Wallsend v Lintz Institute	4-1
	Washington Colliery v Spen Black & White	4-2
	Wood Skinners v Pandon Temperance	2-2
2	Crook Town v Craghead United	1-1
	Horden Athletic v Leadgate Park	1-3
	Seaham Harbour v Seaham Colliery Welfare	3-1
	Sunderland West End v Birtley	3-1
	Thornley Albion v Wingate Albion Comrades	1-0
	Trimdon Grange Colliery v Birtley New Town	4-2
	Wheatley Hill Colliery v Langley Park	2-1
	White-le-Head Rangers v Dipton United	2-2
3	Darlington Railway Ath. v Chilton Colliery Recreatio	2-2
	Ferryhill Athletic v Cockfield	3-1
	Grangetown St Mary's v Guisborough Belmont Ath.	2-1
	Scarborough v Eston United	2-2
	Shildon v Stanley United	3-1
	South Bank v Loftus Albion	3-2
	South Bank East End v Stockton Malleable Institute	4-3
	Tow Law Town v Willington	3-1
4	Egremont v Whitehaven Colliery Recreation	1-0
	Maryport v Keswick	3-1
	Parton Athletic v Moss Bay United	0-0
	Penrith v Frizington Athletic	7-0
	Wath Brow United v Cleator Moor Celtic	1-2
	Windermere v Bowthorn Recreation	2-2
	Workington v Wigton Harriers	3-0
5	Bacup Borough v Darwen	0-2
	Barnoldswick Park Villa v Dick, Kerrs	1-2
	Chorley v Coppull Central	1-0
	Fleetwood v Black Lane Rovers	4-0
	Horwich RMI v Portsmouth Rovers (Lancs)	4-2
	Leyland v Atherton	2-1
	Lytham v Lancaster Town	5-2
	Morecambe v Breightmet United	4-1
6	Chapel-en-le-Frith v Prescot	2-3
	Eccles United v Earle	5-1
	Glossop v Hurst	2-2
	Manchester North End v Marine	6-0
	Old Xaverians v New Mills	0-7
	Youlgrave v Burscough Rangers	0-5
7	Bangor City v Llandudno	2-1
	Ellesmere Port Town v Port Sunlight	3-1
	Hoylake v Ellesmere Port Cement	3-3
	Nantwich v Barnton Victoria	2-1
	Northwich Victoria v Sandbach Ramblers	2-1
	West Kirby v Wallasey United	wo/s
	Winsford United v Altrincham	4-0
	Witton Albion v Chester	2-0
8	Bilston United v Wednesbury Old Athletic (2)	2-1
	Cannock Town v Bloxwich Strollers	3-1
	Evesham Town v Redditch	2-1
	Shrewsbury Town v Stafford Rangers	1-1
	Stourbridge v Leamington Town	6-2
	Wellington Town v Wellington St George's	1-0
	Willenhall v Hednesford Town	4-0
	Worcester City v Kidderminster Harriers	1-0
9	Brigg Town v British Oil & Cake Mills	2-1
	Charltons (Grimsby) v Boston (1)	1-7
	Cleethorpes Town v Holderness Athletic	5-0
	Frodingham Athletic v Hull Old Boys	3-0
	Gainsborough Trinity v Grimsby Rovers	4-1
	Hull Dairycoates v Selby Olympia	7-0
	Scunthorpe United v Barton Town (1)	2-1
	Sutton (Hull) v Drypool Parish Church	3-0
10	Castleford & Allerton United v Bentley Colliery	3-0
	Castleford Town v Wath Athletic	0-0
	Frickley Colliery v Mexborough	0-0
	Liversedge v Wombwell	1-1
	Maltby Main Colliery v Darfield	4-0
	Monckton Athletic v Denaby United	1-1
	South Kirkby Colliery v Brodsworth Main Colliery	2-0
	York City v Horsforth	7-1
11	Anston Athletic v Beighton WM	4-0
	Birdwell v Sheffield	3-1
	Bullcroft Main Colliery v Ardsley Athletic	0-1
	Eckington Works v Prospect United	2-2
	Manton Colliery v Rotherham Amateurs	2-2
	Rossington Main v Treeton Reading Room	3-2
12	Bolsover Colliery v Staveley Town	1-0
	Creswell Colliery v Ilkeston United	wo/s
	Hardwick Colliery v Grassmoor Comrades	1-1
	Heanor Town v Long Eaton	2-3
	Pinxton v Chesterfield Corinthians	7-0
	South Normanton Colliery v New Tupton United	6-0
13	Basford United v Shirebrook	wo/s
	Mansfield Town v Sneinton	6-1
	New Hucknall Colliery v Langwith Colliery	0-4
	Newark Town v Grantham	0-2
	Sutton Junction v Clifton Colliery	1-0
	Sutton Town v Lenton	4-1
14	Ashby Town v Ibstock Colliery	4-2
	Atherstone Town v Gresley Rovers	1-1
	Burton Town v Stableford Works	1-1
	Coalville Swifts v Loughborough Corinthians	2-4
	Hinckley United (1) v Measham Town	5-0
	Moira United v Shepshed Albion	7-2
	Mountsorrel Town v Barwell United	1-3
	Whitwick Imperial v Nuneaton Town	1-5
15	Kettering v Market Harborough Town	8-1
	Leighton United v Higham Ferrers Town	3-7
	Peterborough G.N. Loco v Peterborough & Fletton Utd.	0-11
	Peterboro' Westwood Works v Stamford	2-3
	Rothwell Town v Biggleswade & District	1-0
	Rushden Town v Bedford Town (1)	3-1
	Wellingborough Town v Desborough Town	2-2
	Wolverton Town v Irthlingborough Town	2-0
16	Great Yarmouth Town v Cambridge Town	1-2
	Leiston Works Athletic v Clacton Town	2-1
	Lowestoft Town v Newmarket Town	8-1
	Norwich Priory Athletic v Wisbech Town	1-3
	Orwell Works v Kirkley	2-4
17	Chelmsford v Leyton	0-1
	Shoeburyness Garrison v Walthamstow Town	1-2
18	Cheshunt v Apsley	4-0
	Edmonton v Barnet	0-5
	Letchworth Town v Finchley	4-2
	Luton Amateur v Hampstead Town	0-5
	Luton Clarence v Enfield	1-5
	Tufnell Park v Wealdstone	1-2
	Waterlows (Dunstable) v Hertford Town	2-0
	Wood Green Town v Baldock Town	3-2
19	Aylesbury United v Chesham United	3-3
	BWI Reading v Henley Comrades	1-0
	Harrow Weald v Botwell Mission	1-4
	Hounslow v Uxbridge	4-2
	Maidenhead United v Marlow	3-1
	Oxford City v Slough	1-2
	Southall v Hanwell Town (1)	1-0
	Wycombe Wanderers v Yiewsley	9-1
20	Aldershot Traction Co. v Southern Rail, Croydon	2-3
	Basingstoke v Aldershot Albion	4-0
	Farnham United Breweries v RAMC Aldershot	3-2
	Guildford United v Staines Lagonda	4-1
	Leyland Motors (Kingston) v Carshalton Athletic	3-1
	Tooting Town v Thornycrofts (Basingstoke)	3-2
	West Norwood v Summerstown	0-1
	Woking v Wellington Works	4-1
21	Bostall Heath v Dartford	1-4
	Chatham v Northfleet United	3-2
	East Grinstead v Tunbridge Wells Rangers	2-5
	Eastbourne Old Comrades v Shoreham	1-1
	Hastings & St Leonards v Worthing	4-1
	Nunhead v Ramsgate (1)	wo/s
	Sheppey United v Bromley	2-6
	Whitstable v Folkestone	0-4
22	Bournemouth (Ams) v Thornycrofts (Woolston)	4-2
	Cowes v Weymouth	1-6
	Eastleigh Athletic v Portland United	0-3
	Gosport Athletic v Westham (Weymouth)	wo/s
	Harland & Wolffs v Portsea Gas Company	0-0
	Ryde Sports v Poole	1-2
	Salisbury Corinthians v Salisbury (1)	0-2
	Sholing Athletic v Bournemouth Tramways	1-2
23	Clevedon v Frome Town	6-3
	Devizes Town v Street	4-2
	Glastonbury v Warminster Town	1-4
	Minehead v Taunton & Newtons United	1-4
	Spencer Melksham v Coleford Athletic	3-3
	Torquay United v Green Waves (Plymouth)	2-0
	Trowbridge Town v Calne & Harris United	1-0
	Yeovil & Petter's United v Westbury United	9-1
24	Barry v Cardiff Corinthians	4-0
	Bristol St George v Swindon Victoria	1-0
	Chippenham Rovers v Kingswood	1-2
	Chippenham Town v Welton Rovers	2-0
	Clandown v Bath City	1-1
	Llanelli v Pontypridd	1-1
	Peasedown St John's v Hanham Athletic	1-1
	Swindon Corinthians v Paulton Rovers	3-4
1r	Pandon Temperance v Wood Skinners	0-1e
2r	Craghead United v Crook Town	0-2
r	Dipton United v White-le-Head Rangers	0-1
3r	Chilton Colliery Recreation v Darlington Railway Ath	5-0
r	Scarborough v Eston United	1-2
4r	Bowthorn Recreation v Windermere	0-3
r	Moss Bay United v Parton Athletic	3-2 v
6r	Hurst v Glossop	0-2
7r	Ellesmere Port Cement v Hoylake	wo/s
8r	Stafford Rangers v Shrewsbury Town	1-2
10r	Denaby United v Monckton Athletic	3-0
r	Mexborough v Frickley Colliery	1-3
r	Wath Athletic v Castleford Town	2-0
r	Wombwell v Liversedge	3-2
11r	Prospect United v Eckington Works	1-0
r	Rotherham Amateurs v Manton Colliery	2-4
12r	Grassmoor Comrades v Hardwick Colliery	0-0
14r	Gresley Rovers v Atherstone Town	5-0
r	Stableford Works v Burton Town	0-2
15r	Desborough Town v Wellingborough Town	5-1
19r	Chesham United v Aylesbury United	2-1
21r	Shoreham v Eastbourne Old Comrades	1-0
22r	Portsea Gas Company v Harland & Wolffs	6-0
23r	Coleford Athletic v Spencer Melksham	5-1
24r	Bath City v Clandown	2-1
r	Hanham Athletic v Peasedown St John's	4-2
r	Pontypridd v Llanelli	2-0
4r2	Parton Athletic v Moss Bay United	1-5
12r2	Grassmoor Comrades v Hardwick Colliery	4-2

Qualifying Round One

1	Jarrow v Preston Colliery	4-0
	Seaton Delaval v Wallsend	0-1
	St Anthony's Institute v Usworth Colliery	0-0
	Wood Skinners v Washington Colliery	3-0
2	Seaham Harbour v Trimdon Grange Colliery	1-1
	Thornley Albion v Crook Town	0-3
	Wheatley Hill Colliery v Sunderland West End	0-0
	White-le-Head Rangers v Leadgate Park	2-0
3	Chilton Colliery Recreation v South Bank East End	6-0
	Ferryhill Athletic v Shildon	3-0
	South Bank v Grangetown St Mary's	5-0
	Tow Law Town v Eston United	4-0
4	Egremont v Maryport	3-2
	Moss Bay United v Windermere	4-1
	Penrith v Cleator Moor Celtic	2-2
	Workington v Carlisle United	1-2
5	Dick, Kerrs v Leyland	1-0
	Fleetwood v Morecambe	4-0
	Horwich RMI v Darwen	2-4
	Lytham v Chorley	4-2
6	Glossop v Manchester North End	3-0
	New Mills v Buxton	3-4
	Prescot v Eccles United	0-0
	Skelmersdale United v Burscough Rangers	0-0
7	Bangor City v Nantwich	3-1
	Ellesmere Port Cement v West Kirby	4-0
	Northwich Victoria v Witton Albion	5-2
	Winsford United v Ellesmere Port Town	2-1

1924/25

8	Bilston United v Worcester City	0-3
	Cannock Town v Stourbridge	1-1
	Evesham Town v Wellington Town	1-3
	Willenhall v Shrewsbury Town	2-1
9	Brigg Town v Hull Dairycoates	1-1
	Frodingham Athletic v Sutton (Hull)	1-0
	Gainsborough Trinity v Cleethorpes Town	2-1
	Scunthorpe United v Boston (1)	0-0
10	Castleford & Allerton United v Frickley Colliery	0-0
	Denaby United v Wath Athletic	1-0
	Maltby Main Colliery v South Kirkby Colliery	2-0
	York City v Wombwell	1-2
11	Anston Athletic v Birdwell	2-1
	Ardsley Athletic v Manton Colliery	6-1
	Prospect United v Rossington Main	1-1
	Rotherham Town v Worksop Town	2-1
12	Alfreton Town v Creswell Colliery	3-1
	Bolsover Colliery v Long Eaton	1-0
	Matlock Town v Grassmoor Comrades	3-0
	Pinxton v South Normanton Colliery	2-1
13	Boots Athletic v Basford United	4-1
	Mansfield Town v Whitwell Colliery	7-0
	Sutton Junction v Langwith Colliery	2-1
	Sutton Town v Grantham	0-1
14	Ashby Town v Gresley Rovers	0-0
	Hinckley United (1) v Loughborough Corinthians	3-1
	Moira United v Barwell United	2-1
	Nuneaton Town v Burton Town	4-2
15	Desborough Town v Stamford	1-0
	Kettering v Higham Ferrers Town	1-0
	Rushden Town v Peterborough & Fletton Utd.	1-1
	Wolverton Town v Rothwell Town	1-1
16	Cambridge Town v Wisbech Town	1-2e
	City Wanderers (Norwich) v Lowestoft Town	1-5
	Colchester Town v Leiston Works Athletic	7-1
	King's Lynn v Kirkley	4-0
17	Barking v Leyton	0-2
	Grays Athletic v Walthamstow Town	3-1
	Leytonstone v GER Romford	4-1
	Walthamstow Avenue v Ilford	1-5
18	Cheshunt v Letchworth Town	3-4
	Hampstead Town v Enfield	7-0
	Waterlows (Dunstable) v Wealdstone	2-1
	Wood Green Town v Barnet	2-4
19	Hounslow v BWI Reading	2-1
	Maidenhead United v Chesham United	1-3
	Southall v Slough	2-1
	Wycombe Wanderers v Botwell Mission	4-0
20	Basingstoke v Southern Rail, Croydon	0-2
	Farnham United Breweries v Summerstown	0-0
	Guildford United v Leyland Motors (Kingston)	1-0
	Woking v Tooting Town	3-1
21	Bromley v Folkestone	1-2
	Chatham v Dartford	2-2
	Nunhead v Hastings & St Leonards	5-0
	Shoreham v Tunbridge Wells Rangers	1-1
22	Bournemouth (Ams) v Portland United	1-2
	Gosport Athletic v Portsea Gas Company	0-0
	Salisbury (1) v Bournemouth Tramways	1-2
	Weymouth v Poole	5-0
23	Torquay United v Taunton & Newtons United	1-1
	Trowbridge Town v Coleford Athletic	2-0
	Warminster Town v Devizes Town	4-1
	Yeovil & Petter's United v Clevedon	5-1
24	Chippenham Town v Hanham Athletic	2-0
	Kingswood v Bath City	1-0
	Paulton Rovers v Bristol St George	1-3
	Pontypridd v Barry	2-1
1r	Usworth Colliery v St Anthony's Institute	2-0
2r	Sunderland West End v Wheatley Hill Colliery	1-0
r	Trimdon Grange Colliery v Seaham Harbour	3-1
4r	Cleator Moor Celtic v Penrith	3-1
6r	Burscough Rangers v Skelmersdale United	5-0
r	Eccles United v Prescot	0-0
8r	Stourbridge v Cannock Town	4-0
9r	Boston (1) v Scunthorpe United	3-0
r	Hull Dairycoates v Brigg Town	1-1e
10r	Frickley Colliery v Castleford & Allerton United	1-1
11r	Rossington Main v Prospect United	1-0
14r	Gresley Rovers v Ashby Town	1-1e
15r	Peterborough & Fletton Utd. v Rushden Town	1-0
r	Rothwell Town v Wolverton Town	4-1
20r	Summerstown v Farnham United Breweries	4-0
21r	Dartford v Chatham	0-1
r	Tunbridge Wells Rangers v Shoreham	3-1
22r	Portsea Gas Company v Gosport Athletic	3-0
23r	Taunton & Newtons United v Torquay United	2-1
6r2	Prescot v Eccles United	0-5
9r2	Brigg Town v Hull Dairycoates	2-0
10r2	Castleford & Allerton United v Frickley Colliery	3-2
14r2	Ashby Town v Gresley Rovers	2-2e
14r3	Gresley Rovers v Ashby Town	5-2 N

Qualifying Round Two

1	Usworth Colliery v Wallsend	1-0
	Wood Skinners v Jarrow	0-0
2	Crook Town v White-le-Head Rangers	3-0
	Sunderland West End v Trimdon Grange Colliery	4-0
3	Ferryhill Athletic v Chilton Colliery Recreation	3-4
	Tow Law Town v South Bank	0-0
4	Carlisle United v Cleator Moor Celtic	5-1
	Moss Bay United v Egremont	0-2
5	Dick, Kerrs v Fleetwood	4-1
	Lytham v Darwen	0-1
6	Buxton v Eccles United	3-2
	Glossop v Burscough Rangers	3-2
7	Ellesmere Port Cement v Winsford United	0-1
	Northwich Victoria v Bangor City	1-0
8	Stourbridge v Willenhall	3-0
	Wellington Town v Worcester City	0-2
9	Boston (1) v Frodingham Athletic	8-0
	Gainsborough Trinity v Brigg Town	4-1
10	Castleford & Allerton United v Maltby Main Colliery	0-1
	Denaby United v Wombwell	1-1
11	Ardsley Athletic v Anston Athletic	9-1
	Rossington Main v Rotherham Town	3-2
12	Bolsover Colliery v Pinxton	1-1
	Matlock Town v Alfreton Town	0-3
13	Grantham v Boots Athletic	2-0
	Mansfield Town v Sutton Junction	3-0
14	Gresley Rovers v Moira United	7-2
	Nuneaton Town v Hinckley United (1)	2-0
15	Peterborough & Fletton Utd. v Kettering	1-1
	Rothwell Town v Desborough Town	0-4
16	King's Lynn v Wisbech Town	2-2
	Lowestoft Town v Colchester Town	2-0
17	Ilford v Grays Athletic	3-1
	Leytonstone v Leyton	0-3
18	Barnet v Letchworth Town	2-1
	Hampstead Town v Waterlows (Dunstable)	3-3
19	Chesham United v Hounslow	3-1
	Wycombe Wanderers v Southall	0-0
20	Southern Rail, Croydon v Guildford United	0-4
	Woking v Summerstown	0-2
21	Folkestone v Tunbridge Wells Rangers	9-0
	Nunhead v Chatham	1-2
22	Portsea Gas Company v Bournemouth Tramways	6-0
	Weymouth v Portland United	3-1
23	Trowbridge Town v Taunton & Newtons United	1-1
	Warminster Town v Yeovil & Petter's United	1-3
24	Bristol St George v Kingswood	0-0
	Pontypridd v Chippenham Town	6-1
1r	Jarrow v Wood Skinners	1-0
3r	South Bank v Tow Law Town	2-1
10r	Wombwell v Denaby United	0-0e
12r	Pinxton v Bolsover Colliery	3-1
15r	Kettering v Peterborough & Fletton Utd.	3-0
16r	Wisbech Town v King's Lynn	0-2
18r	Waterlows (Dunstable) v Hampstead Town	1-4
19r	Southall v Wycombe Wanderers	4-1
23r	Taunton & Newtons United v Trowbridge Town	3-1
24r	Kingswood v Bristol St George	0-0e
10r2	Denaby United v Wombwell	0-0eN
24r2	Bristol St George v Kingswood	3-3e
10r3	Denaby United v Wombwell	1-0 N
24r3	Kingswood v Bristol St George	0-0e
24r4	Bristol St George v Kingswood	1-2

Qualifying Round Three

1	Jarrow v Usworth Colliery	1-3
2	Crook Town v Sunderland West End	6-0
3	South Bank v Chilton Colliery Recreation	1-3
4	Egremont v Carlisle United	2-6
5	Darwen v Dick, Kerrs	4-0
6	Buxton v Glossop	4-1
7	Winsford United v Northwich Victoria	2-0
8	Worcester City v Stourbridge	3-0
9	Boston (1) v Gainsborough Trinity	3-0
10	Maltby Main Colliery v Denaby United	0-1
11	Ardsley Athletic v Rossington Main	1-1
12	Alfreton Town v Pinxton	3-1
13	Mansfield Town v Grantham	1-0
14	Nuneaton Town v Gresley Rovers	2-2
15	Kettering v Desborough Town	4-1
16	Lowestoft Town v King's Lynn	0-2
17	Ilford v Leyton	1-1
18	Hampstead Town v Barnet	2-2
19	Chesham United v Southall	0-0
20	Guildford United v Summerstown	2-2
21	Folkestone v Chatham	0-0
22	Weymouth v Portsea Gas Company	6-1
23	Taunton & Newtons United v Yeovil & Petter's United	1-2
24	Pontypridd v Kingswood	6-0
11r	Rossington Main v Ardsley Athletic	2-1
14r	Gresley Rovers v Nuneaton Town	1-2
17r	Leyton v Ilford	1-1e
18r	Barnet v Hampstead Town	3-2
19r	Southall v Chesham United	5-0
20r	Summerstown v Guildford United	0-1
21r	Chatham v Folkestone	0-1
17r2	Ilford v Leyton	2-2eN
17r3	Leyton v Ilford	3-3eN
17r4	Ilford v Leyton	0-2

Qualifying Round Four

	Aberdare Athletic v Newport County	0-0
	Alfreton Town v Nuneaton Town	3-1
	Barnet v Guildford United	3-0
	Barrow v Darwen	1-0
	Boston (1) v Worcester City	3-1
	Carlisle United v Bishop Auckland	0-1
	Chilton Colliery Recreation v Usworth Colliery	3-0
	Doncaster Rovers v Mansfield Town	3-2
	Durham City v Blyth Spartans	3-1
	Erith & Belvedere v Reading	0-2
	Hartlepools United v Ashington	0-0
	Kettering v Denaby United	3-0
	King's Lynn v St Albans City	1-1
	Kingstonian v Folkestone	0-2
	Leyton v Sittingbourne	3-0
	Lincoln City v Rossington Main	3-0
	New Brighton v Stalybridge Celtic	3-0
	Southall v Dulwich Hamlet	0-1
	Southend United v London Caledonians	3-3
	Stockton v Crook Town	0-1
	Tranmere Rovers v Crewe Alexandra	1-1
	Weymouth v Pontypridd	2-1
	Winsford United v Buxton	1-0
	Yeovil & Petter's United v Bournemouth	3-2
r	Ashington v Hartlepools United	2-0 D
r	Crewe Alexandra v Tranmere Rovers	0-2
r	London Caledonians v Southend United	1-4
r	Newport County v Aberdare Athletic	3-0
r	St Albans City v King's Lynn	8-1

Qualifying Round Five

	Alfreton Town v Lincoln City	1-0
	Barnet v Leyton	2-0
	Barrow v Wrexham	4-0
	Charlton Athletic v Dulwich Hamlet	4-0
	Crook Town v Chilton Colliery Recreation	4-3
	Darlington v Durham City	3-1
	Exeter City v Newport County	1-1
	Grimsby Town v Chesterfield	1-2
	Halifax Town v Rochdale	0-1
	Hartlepools United v Bishop Auckland	2-0
	Kettering v Gillingham	1-1
	Nelson v Winsford United	4-1
	New Brighton v Accrington Stanley	0-0
	Norwich City v Folkestone	2-0
	Port Vale v Boston (1)	6-1
	Queen's Park Rangers v Clapton	4-4
	Reading v Southend United	2-1
	Rotherham County v Doncaster Rovers	2-3
	St Albans City v Brentford	5-3
	Tranmere Rovers v Southport	1-1
	Walsall v Coventry City	1-2
	Weymouth v Merthyr Town	3-2
	Wigan Borough v Bradford Park Avenue	0-1
	Yeovil & Petter's United v Bristol Rovers	2-4
r	Accrington Stanley v New Brighton	3-2
r	Clapton v Queen's Park Rangers	0-2
r	Gillingham v Kettering	6-2
r	Newport County v Exeter City	3-3e
r	Southport v Tranmere Rovers	1-0
r2	Exeter City v Newport County	1-0 N

Qualifying Round Six

	Accrington Stanley v Chesterfield	1-0
	Alfreton Town v Port Vale	2-8
	Bristol Rovers v Weymouth	0-0
	Crook Town v Bradford Park Avenue	0-4
	Doncaster Rovers v Southport	1-0
	Exeter City v Barnet	3-0
	Gillingham v Barrow	0-0
	Hartlepools United v St Albans City	4-0
	Nelson v Coventry City	0-1
	Norwich City v Rochdale	1-0
	Queen's Park Rangers v Charlton Athletic	1-1
	Reading v Darlington	0-1
r	Barrow v Gillingham	1-1e
r	Charlton Athletic v Queen's Park Rangers	1-2
r	Weymouth v Bristol Rovers	0-2
r2	Barrow v Gillingham	1-1eN
r3	Barrow v Gillingham	1-1eN
r4	Barrow v Gillingham	2-1 N

Round One

	Accrington Stanley v Portsmouth	2-5
	Aston Villa v Port Vale	7-2
	Birmingham v Chelsea	2-0
	Blackburn Rovers v Oldham Athletic	1-0
	Blackpool v Barrow	0-0
	Bolton Wanderers v Huddersfield Town	3-0
	Bradford Park Avenue v Middlesbrough	1-0
	Bristol Rovers v Bristol City	0-1
	Bury v Sunderland	0-3
	Cardiff City v Darlington	0-0
	Coventry City v Notts County	0-2
	Crystal Palace v South Shields	2-1
	Derby County v Bradford City	0-1
	Doncaster Rovers v Norwich City	1-2
	Everton v Burnley	2-1
	Hull City v Wolverhampton Wan.	1-1
	Leicester City v Stoke	3-0
	Liverpool v Leeds United	3-0
	Millwall v Barnsley	0-0
	Newcastle United v Hartlepools United	4-1
	Nottingham Forest v Clapton Orient	1-0
	Preston North End v Manchester City	4-1
	Queen's Park Rangers v Stockport County	1-3
	Sheffield United v Corinthians	5-0
	Sheffield Wednesday v Manchester United	2-0
	Southampton v Exeter City	3-1
	Swansea Town v Plymouth Argyle	3-0
	Swindon Town v Fulham	1-2
	Tottenham Hotspur v Northampton Town	3-0
	Watford v Brighton & Hove Albion	1-1
	West Bromwich Albion v Luton Town	4-0

1924/25 to 1925/26

	West Ham United v Arsenal	0-0
r	Arsenal v West Ham United	2-2e
r	Barnsley v Millwall	2-1
r	Barrow v Blackpool	0-2
r	Brighton & Hove Albion v Watford	4-3
r	Darlington v Cardiff City	0-0e
r	Wolverhampton Wan. v Hull City	0-1e
r2	Cardiff City v Darlington	2-0 N
r2	West Ham United v Arsenal	1-0 N

Round Two

	Barnsley v Bradford City	0-3
	Birmingham v Stockport County	1-0
	Blackburn Rovers v Portsmouth	0-0
	Bradford Park Avenue v Blackpool	1-1
	Bristol City v Liverpool	0-1
	Cardiff City v Fulham	1-0
	Hull City v Crystal Palace	3-2
	Newcastle United v Leicester City	2-2
	Nottingham Forest v West Ham United	0-2
	Notts County v Norwich City	4-0
	Sheffield United v Sheffield Wednesday	3-2
	Southampton v Brighton & Hove Albion	1-0
	Sunderland v Everton	0-0
	Swansea Town v Aston Villa	1-3
	Tottenham Hotspur v Bolton Wanderers	1-1
	West Bromwich Albion v Preston North End	2-0
r	Blackpool v Bradford Park Avenue	2-1
r	Bolton Wanderers v Tottenham Hotspur	0-1
r	Everton v Sunderland	2-1
r	Leicester City v Newcastle United	1-0
r	Portsmouth v Blackburn Rovers	0-0e
r2	Blackburn Rovers v Portsmouth	1-0 N

Round Three

	Hull City v Leicester City	1-1
	Liverpool v Birmingham	2-1
	Notts County v Cardiff City	0-2
	Sheffield United v Everton	1-0
	Southampton v Bradford City	2-0
	Tottenham Hotspur v Blackburn Rovers	2-2
	West Bromwich Albion v Aston Villa	1-1
	West Ham United v Blackpool	1-1
r	Aston Villa v West Bromwich Albion	1-2
r	Blackburn Rovers v Tottenham Hotspur	3-1
r	Blackpool v West Ham United	3-0
r	Leicester City v Hull City	3-1

Round Four

	Blackburn Rovers v Blackpool	1-0
	Cardiff City v Leicester City	2-1
	Sheffield United v West Bromwich Albion	2-0
	Southampton v Liverpool	1-0

Semi Finals

	Cardiff City v Blackburn Rovers	3-1 N
	Sheffield United v Southampton	2-0 N

Final

	Sheffield United v Cardiff City	1-0 N

1925/26

Extra Preliminary Round

2	Chester-le-Street v Birtley	3-1
	Cockfield v Shildon	0-2
	Esh Winning (1) v Annfield Plain	2-1
	Horden Athletic v Thornley Albion	4-0
	Langley Park v Willington	2-5
	Seaham Colliery Welfare v Dipton United	0-2
	Seaham Harbour v Spennymoor United	4-1
	South Pontop Villa v Wingate Albion Comrades	2-3
	Stanley United v Coundon United	0-0
	Twizell United v West Auckland Town	1-1
	Wheatley Hill Colliery v Hobson Wanderers	6-0
5	Atherton v Colne Carlton	3-1
	Bacup Borough v Great Harwood	4-1
	Barnoldswick Park Villa v Hindley Green Athletic	4-3
	Breightmet United v Horwich Central	3-2
	Clitheroe v Morecambe	2-2
	Skelmersdale United v Chorley	1-4
8	Bilston United v Cradley Heath St Luke's	2-2
	Birmingham Corp. Tramways v Darlaston	3-2
	Bloxwich Strollers v Halesowen Town	3-2
	Brierley Hill Alliance v Wolverhampton Amateur	5-1
	Cannock Town v Bromsgrove Rovers	5-2
	Hednesford Town v Leamington Town	5-0
9	Central Hull Rangers v Hull Old Boys	2-1
	Goole Town v Holderness Athletic	9-0
	Grimsby Albion v Horncastle Town	3-2
	Hull Dairycoates v Drypool Parish Church	3-0
	Melton v British Oil & Cake Mills	1-1
	Reckitt's (Hull) v Brunswick Institute	2-0
	Selby Olympia v Marfleet	5-0
10	Bentley Colliery v Guiseley	3-0
	Brodsworth Main Colliery v Wath Athletic	1-6
	Methley Perseverance v South Kirkby Colliery	4-2
	Mexborough v Fryston Colliery	7-0
	Yorkshire Amateur v Castleford Town	0-7
15	Northampton Nomads v Kempston Rovers	4-1
17	Custom House v Brentwood Mental Hospital	3-3
	Grays Thurrock United v Grays Sports	wo/s
	Hoffmann Athletic (Chelmsford) v Crittall Athletic	3-1
18	Arlesey Town v Watford Old Boys	1-6
	Boxmoor v Leavesden Mental Hospital	2-4
	Harrow Weald v Luton Clarence	wo/s
	Hertford Town v Cheshunt	2-6
24	Bournemouth Gasworks Athletic v Harland & Wolffs	6-1
	Emsworth v Southampton CS	2-4
	Gosport Albion v Burrfield Park	5-5
	Gosport Athletic v RAOC Cosham	5-2
	Poole v Salisbury (1)	3-3
	RM Portsmouth v East Cowes	3-1
25	Bath City v Coleford Athletic	1-2
	Devizes Town v Calne & Harris United	4-1
	Welton Rovers v Peasedown St John's	6-2
26	Bedminster Down Sports v Clevedon	0-4
	Bideford v Glastonbury	5-0
	Cheltenham Town v Union Jack (Bristol)	3-6
	St Austell v Newquay United	3-1
	St Philips Athletic v Mid Rhondda	1-2
	Street v Weston-Super-Mare	8-0
2r	Coundon United v Stanley United	3-3e
r	West Auckland Town v Twizell United	5-2
5r	Morecambe v Clitheroe	5-0
8r	Cradley Heath St Luke's v Bilston United	3-2
9r	British Oil & Cake Mills v Melton	2-1e
17r	Brentwood Mental Hospital v Custom House	3-1
24r	Burrfield Park v Gosport Albion	0-2
r	Salisbury (1) v Poole	4-3
2r2	Stanley United v Coundon United	3-1

Preliminary Round

1	Crawcrook Albion v St Peter's Albion	2-3
	High Fell v Pelton Fell	1-1
	Jarrow v Tanfield Lea Rovers	4-0
	Preston Colliery v Wood Skinners	2-1
	Seaton Delaval v Bedlington United	4-0
	Shankhouse v Pandon Temperance	3-3
	Walker Celtic v Washington Colliery	0-1
2	Craghead United v Horden Athletic	2-2
	Dipton United v Chester-le-Street	2-1
	Shildon v West Auckland Town	3-0
	Stanley United v Seaham Harbour	0-3
	Trimdon Grange Colliery v Sunderland West End	0-2
	Wheatley Hill Colliery v Wingate Albion Comrades	0-1
	White-le-Head Rangers v Esh Winning (1)	3-0
	Willington v Ferryhill Athletic	5-2
3	Normanby Mangnesite v Scarborough	1-3
	Scarborough Penguins v Filey Town	3-3
	Stockton Malleable Institute v South Bank East End	3-1
4	Bowthorn Recreation v Keswick	1-5
	Cleator Moor Celtic v Wath Brow United	3-0
	Frizington Athletic v Whitehaven Athletic	3-5
	Kendal Town v Netherfield (Kendal)	2-1
	Moss Bay United v Wigton Harriers	0-1
	Penrith v Bowness Rovers	5-1
	Windermere v Barrow YMCA	0-2
5	Bacup Borough v Fleetwood	0-3
	Chorley v Dick, Kerrs	4-0
	Coppull Central v Burscough Rangers	2-3
	Darwen v Breightmet United	5-3
	Horwich RMI v Barnoldswick Park Villa	2-1
	Lancaster Town v Portsmouth Rovers (Lancs)	4-0
	Leyland v Lytham	1-2
	Morecambe v Atherton	3-1
6	Earle v Marine	1-0
	Eccles United v Black Lane Rovers	5-2
	Glossop v Whiston	4-1
	Manchester North End v Buxton	1-1
	New Mills v Alderley Edge United	5-1
	Prescot v Old Xaverians	4-1
	Stalybridge Celtic v Hurst	3-3
	Youlgrave v Newton Common Recreation	3-5
7	Altrincham v Witton Albion	0-0
	Harrowby v Lostock Gralam	1-0
	Llandudno v Chester	0-0
	Mold v Rhyl Athletic	1-0
	Northern Nomads v Port Sunlight	4-3
	Sandbach Ramblers v Ellesmere Port Cement	3-0
	Winsford United v Barnton Victoria	3-1
8	Bloxwich Strollers v Cannock Town	2-1
	Brierley Hill Alliance v Hednesford Town	5-2
	Cradley Heath St Luke's v Wellington St George's	5-0
	Hereford United v Wellington Town	4-5
	Redditch v Stourbridge	0-5
	Shrewsbury Town v Oswestry Town	3-2
	Stafford Rangers v Birmingham Corp. Tramways	3-0
	Willenhall v Oakengates Town	2-0
9	Barton Town (1) v Grimsby Albion	8-1
	British Oil & Cake Mills v Hull Dairycoates	0-2
	Charltons (Grimsby) v Grimsby Rovers	2-4
	Cleethorpes Town v Scunthorpe United	0-4
	Gainsborough Trinity v Brigg Town	9-0
	Goole Town v Reckitt's (Hull)	4-0
	Grimsby Haycroft Rovers v Frodingham Athletic	6-2
	Selby Olympia v Central Hull Rangers	5-3
10	Castleford & Allerton United v Liversedge	1-0
	Cudworth Village v Wath Athletic	1-3
	Darfield v Denaby United	1-3
	Frickley Colliery v Horsforth	8-1
	Mexborough v Bentley Colliery	6-1
	Monckton Athletic v Castleford Town	1-4
	Wombwell v Methley Perseverance	8-0
	York City v Maltby Main Colliery	5-3
11	Anston Athletic v Prospect United	2-2
	Ardsley Athletic v Rotherham Amateurs	3-1
	Birdwell v Beighton WM	wo/s
	Bullcroft Main Colliery v Dinnington Main Colliery	3-2
	Kilnhurst United v Hemsworth West End	1-2
	Manton Colliery v Treeton Reading Room	0-1
	Rossington Main - Bye	
	Sheffield v Mapplewell & Staincross Ath.	3-0
12	Bolsover Colliery v Grassmoor	2-2
	Creswell Colliery v Chesterfield Corinthians	8-0
	Ilkeston United v Heanor Town	2-3
	Shirebrook v Long Eaton	1-0
	Staveley Town v Blackwell Colliery	7-2
	Whitwell Colliery v South Normanton Colliery	0-0
13	Arnold Town (1) v Gedling Colliery	2-5e
	Boots Athletic v New Hucknall Colliery	2-1
	Cammell Laird (Nottm) v Langwith Colliery	0-0
	Clifton Colliery v Hucknall Byron	wo/s
	Newark Town v Lenton	6-1
	Sneinton v Basford United	4-1
	Sutton Town v Sutton Junction	3-1
14	Ashby Town v Stableford Works	0-0
	Barwell United v Measham Town	3-1
	Burton Town v Mountsorrel Town	9-0
	Gresley Colliery v Gresley Rovers	1-1
	Hinckley United (1) v Ibstock Colliery	4-0
	Loughborough Corinthians v Whitwick Imperial	5-0
	Shepshed Albion v Atherstone Town	5-1
15	Bedford Town (1) v Wellingborough Town	2-2
	Biggleswade & District v Leighton United	0-4
	Desborough Town v Peterbro' Westwood Works	9-0
	Higham Ferrers Town v Peterborough & Fletton Utd.	0-2
	Market Harborough Town v Peterborough G.N. Loco	0-2
	Northampton Nomads v Stamford	3-4
	Rushden Town v Rothwell Town	3-2
	Wolverton Town v Irthlingborough Town	1-2
16	Cambridge Town v Great Yarmouth Town	2-1
	Clacton Town v Leiston Works Athletic	0-0
	Harwich & Parkeston v Parkeston Railway	2-4
	Lowestoft Town v City Wanderers (Norwich)	3-2
	Newmarket Town v King's Lynn	0-6
	Norwich Priory Athletic v March Great Eastern United	1-0
	Wisbech Town v Beccles	9-1
17	Barking v Grays Athletic	1-2
	Bush Hill Park v Wood Green Town	1-2
	Enfield v Edmonton	5-0
	GER Romford v Chelmsford	2-1
	Hoffmann Ath. (Chelmsford) v Grays Thurrock Utd	1-10 d
	Leyton v Walthamstow Grange	3-0
	Leytonstone v Brentwood Mental Hospital	10-2
	Tufnell Park v Walthamstow Avenue	5-1
18	Apsley v Watford Old Boys	3-1
	Berkhamsted Town v Harrow Weald	1-0
	Cheshunt v Bishop's Stortford	9-0
	Hampstead Town v Finchley	2-0
	Letchworth Town v Baldock Town	0-1
	Luton Amateur v Leagrave & District	0-3
	Waterlows (Dunstable) v Leavesden Mental Hospital	1-0
	Wealdstone v Hitchin Blue Cross	4-1
19	BWI Reading v Marlow	2-1
	Botwell Mission v Hounslow	3-1
	Hanwell Town (1) v Uxbridge	1-3
	Oxford City v Maidenhead United	1-1
	Polytechnic v Old Lyonian	2-5
	Windsor & Eton v Henley Town	18-0
	Wycombe Wanderers v Newbury Town	1-6
	Yiewsley v Slough	1-2
20	Kingstonian v Redhill	0-1
	Mitcham Wanderers v Dorking	3-1
	Sutton United v Carshalton Athletic	4-2
	West Norwood v Epsom Town	1-0
	Wimbledon v Tooting Town	2-1
21	Addlestone v Aldershot Traction Co.	1-5
	Aldershot Albion v Staines Town	3-2
	Farnham United Breweries v Camberley & Yorktown	5-1
	Guildford v Egham	4-2
	RAMC Aldershot v Basingstoke	5-3
	Wellington Works v Walton-on-Thames	6-3
22	Beckenham v Catford Southend	2-1
	Bexleyheath Town v Cray Wanderers	1-1
	Bostall Heath v Whitstable	2-3
	Bromley v Woolwich Polytechnic	3-0
	Maidstone United v Erith & Belvedere	2-0
23	East Grinstead v Portslade	3-1
	Horsham Trinity v Eastbourne Old Comrades	4-6
	Newhaven v Southwick	1-4
	Shoreham v Worthing	0-5
	Vernon Athletic v Hove	0-3
24	Bournemouth (Ams) v Portland United	2-2
	Bournemouth Gasworks Ath. v Bour'mouth Tramways	1-2
	Gosport Albion v Portsmouth Amateurs	4-0
	Portsea Gas Company v Osborne Athletic	8-0
	RM Portsmouth v Gosport Athletic	2-0
	Ryde Sports v Cowes	4-2
	Salisbury (1) v Salisbury Corinthians	1-0
	Southampton CS v Thornycrofts (Basingstoke)	6-3
25	Chippenham Town v Trowbridge Town	4-1
	Clandown v Clutton Wanderers	2-0
	Coleford Athletic v Welton Rovers	1-1
	Paulton Rovers v Frome Town	4-1
	Radstock Town v Swindon Victoria	4-0

1925/26

	Spencer Moulton v Swindon Corinthians	3-2
	Warminster Town v Melksham & Avon United	3-2
	Westbury United v Devizes Town	0-0
26	Barry v Mid Rhondda	2-2
	Bideford v Wells City	0-2
	Bristol St George v Union Jack (Bristol)	1-0
	Kingswood v Hanham Athletic	2-0
	Pontypridd v Cardiff Corinthians	6-1
	Street v Clevedon	2-2
	Taunton United v St Austell	3-0
	Torquay United v Green Waves (Plymouth)	5-1
1r	Pandon Temperance v Shankhouse	1-3
r	Pelton Fell v High Fell	2-3
2r	Horden Athletic v Craghead United	4-0
3r	Filey Town v Scarborough Penguins	1-2
6r	Buxton v Manchester North End	4-2e
r	Hurst v Stalybridge Celtic	1-2
7r	Chester v Llandudno	2-1
r	Witton Albion v Altrincham	4-0
11r	Prospect United v Anston Athletic	1-1e
12r	Grassmoor v Bolsover Colliery	4-0
r	South Normanton Colliery v Whitwell Colliery	1-0
13r	Langwith Colliery v Cammell Laird (Nottm)	2-1
14r	Gresley Rovers v Gresley Colliery	4-1
r	Stableford Works v Ashby Town	2-7
15r	Wellingborough Town v Bedford Town (1)	2-1
16r	Leiston Works Athletic v Clacton Town	2-4
19r	Maidenhead United v Oxford City	3-1
22r	Cray Wanderers v Bexleyheath Town	4-2
24r	Portland United v Bournemouth (Ams)	6-1
25r	Devizes Town v Westbury United	2-0
r	Welton Rovers v Coleford Athletic	1-2
26r	Clevedon v Street	4-3
r	Mid Rhondda v Barry	2-1
11r2	Anston Athletic v Prospect United	4-3 N

Qualifying Round One

1	High Fell v Washington Colliery	2-0
	Jarrow v Shankhouse	3-1
	Preston Colliery v St Peter's Albion	3-1
	Seaton Delaval v Usworth Colliery	1-1
2	Horden Athletic v White-le-Head Rangers	1-0
	Shildon v Dipton United	2-0
	Willington v Sunderland West End	3-0
	Wingate Albion Comrades v Seaham Harbour	5-3
3	Darlington Railway Ath. v Grangetown St Mary's	0-2
	Eston United v Loftus Albion	5-1
	Guisborough Belmont Ath. v Scarborough Penguins	2-0
	Stockton Malleable Institute v Scarborough	2-5
4	Barrow YMCA v Kendal Town	1-0
	Cleator Moor Celtic v Wigton Harriers	2-1
	Penrith v Keswick	3-2
	Whitehaven Athletic v Egremont	1-2
5	Darwen v Burscough Rangers	2-1
	Fleetwood v Chorley	1-4
	Lancaster Town v Horwich RMI	8-2
	Lytham v Morecambe	2-1
6	Earle v Prescot	1-4
	New Mills v Eccles United	2-3
	Newton Common Recreation v Buxton	1-6
	Stalybridge Celtic v Glossop	5-2
7	Chester v Sandbach Ramblers	2-0
	Mold v Harrowby	4-0
	Winsford United v Northern Nomads	3-0
	Witton Albion v Bangor City	2-1
8	Bloxwich Strollers v Willenhall	1-2
	Shrewsbury Town v Stourbridge	3-1
	Stafford Rangers v Brierley Hill Alliance	3-0
	Wellington Town v Cradley Heath St Luke's	4-3
9	Goole Town v Gainsborough Trinity	0-3
	Grimsby Rovers v Barton Town (1)	3-0
	Hull Dairycoates v Selby Olympia	1-0 v
	Scunthorpe United v Grimsby Haycroft Rovers	5-1
10	Castleford & Allerton United v Mexborough	0-1
	Frickley Colliery v Castleford Town	0-1
	Wath Athletic v Denaby United	2-0
	York City v Wombwell	5-0
11	Anston Athletic v Sheffield	2-2
	Ardsley Athletic v Rossington Main	1-1
	Bullcroft Main Colliery v Hemsworth West End	0-0
	Treeton Reading Room v Birdwell	3-1
12	Alfreton Town v South Normanton Colliery	2-4
	Creswell Colliery v Heanor Town	1-1
	Matlock Town v Grassmoor	2-3
	Shirebrook v Staveley Town	2-0
13	Boots Athletic v Gedling Colliery	6-1
	Grantham v Sutton Town	0-1
	Langwith Colliery v Clifton Colliery	4-3
	Newark Town v Sneinton	5-1
14	Barwell United v Gresley Rovers	3-1
	Hinckley United (1) v Ashby Town	1-1
	Loughborough Corinthians v Burton Town	3-4
	Moira United v Shepshed Albion	6-1
15	Desborough Town v Leighton United	2-0
	Irthlingborough Town v Stamford	4-1
	Peterborough & Fletton Utd. v Wellingborough Town	6-1
	Rushden Town v Peterborough G.N. Loco	6-1
16	Cambridge Town v Wisbech Town	3-0
	Clacton Town v Parkeston Railway	0-8
	Colchester Town v King's Lynn	1-0
	Lowestoft Town v Norwich Priory Athletic	3-4
17	GER Romford v Grays Athletic	2-2
	Hoffmann Athletic (Chelmsford) v Enfield	1-2
	Tufnell Park v Leyton	0-6
	Wood Green Town v Leytonstone	1-10
18	Hampstead Town v Berkhamsted Town	8-1
	Leagrave & District v Cheshunt	1-2
	Waterlows (Dunstable) v Apsley	4-0
	Wealdstone v Baldock Town	1-1
19	BWI Reading v Windsor & Eton	0-3
	Maidenhead United v Newbury Town	0-3
	Old Lyonian v Uxbridge	2-6
	Slough v Botwell Mission	2-6
20	Nunhead v West Norwood	2-2
	Redhill v Mitcham Wanderers	5-1
	Sutton United v Summerstown	2-2
	Wimbledon v Leyland Motors (Kingston)	4-1
21	Aldershot Albion v RAMC Aldershot	2-2
	Farnham United Breweries v Guildford	6-0
	Guildford United v Aldershot Traction Co.	1-1
	Wellington Works v Woking	3-3
22	Bromley v RM Chatham	1-4
	Cray Wanderers v Whitstable	5-4
	Maidstone United v Ashford Railway Works	2-3
	Sheppey United v Beckenham	8-3
23	East Grinstead v Tunbridge Wells Rangers	1-2
	Hastings & St Leonards v Southwick	7-3
	Rock-a-Nore v Hove	3-1
	Worthing v Eastbourne Old Comrades	4-2
24	Gosport Albion v RM Portsmouth	3-5
	Portsea Gas Company v Ryde Sports	5-2
	Salisbury (1) v Bournemouth Tramways	5-1
	Southampton CS v Portland United	2-1
25	Chippenham Town v Radstock Town	2-2
	Clandown v Devizes Town	3-2
	Coleford Athletic v Spencer Moulton	0-0
	Paulton Rovers v Warminster Town	4-3
26	Bristol St George v Clevedon	4-1
	Kingswood v Wells City	4-1
	Mid Rhondda v Pontypridd	3-1
	Taunton United v Torquay United	1-2
1r	Usworth Colliery v Seaton Delaval	2-0
9r	Selby Olympia v Hull Dairycoates	0-3
11r	Hemsworth West End v Bullcroft Main Colliery	2-0
r	Rossington Main v Ardsley Athletic	1-0
r	Sheffield v Anston Athletic	4-6
12r	Heanor Town v Creswell Colliery	2-1
14r	Ashby Town v Hinckley United (1)	2-3
17r	Grays Athletic v GER Romford	2-1
18r	Baldock Town v Wealdstone	2-0
20r	Summerstown v Sutton United	0-1
r	West Norwood v Nunhead	0-3
21r	Aldershot Traction Co. v Guildford United	2-1
r	RAMC Aldershot v Aldershot Albion	9-0
r	Woking v Wellington Works	0-0x
25r	Radstock Town v Chippenham Town	0-0
r	Spencer Moulton v Coleford Athletic	0-1
21r2	Woking v Wellington Works	1-3
25r2	Chippenham Town v Radstock Town	1-2 N

Qualifying Round Two

1	Jarrow v High Fell	2-0
	Usworth Colliery v Preston Colliery	3-1
2	Horden Athletic v Wingate Albion Comrades	5-0
	Shildon v Willington	3-2
3	Eston United v Scarborough	1-1
	Grangetown St Mary's v Guisborough Belmont Ath.	2-2
4	Cleator Moor Celtic v Egremont	1-2
	Penrith v Barrow YMCA	3-1
5	Chorley v Lancaster Town	4-2
	Lytham v Darwen	3-0
6	Buxton v Stalybridge Celtic	3-0
	Eccles United v Prescot	3-1
7	Chester v Witton Albion	2-2
	Mold v Winsford United	2-0
8	Stafford Rangers v Shrewsbury Town	1-1
	Wellington Town v Willenhall	1-1
9	Grimsby Rovers v Hull Dairycoates	4-3
	Scunthorpe United v Gainsborough Trinity	2-2
10	Wath Athletic v Mexborough	2-2
	York City v Castleford Town	3-0
11	Anston Athletic v Treeton Reading Room	2-1
	Hemsworth West End v Rossington Main	4-2
12	Heanor Town v Shirebrook	3-1
	South Normanton Colliery v Grassmoor	0-1
13	Newark Town v Langwith Colliery	6-1
	Sutton Town v Boots Athletic	4-2
14	Barwell United v Hinckley United (1)	0-2
	Burton Town v Moira United	4-1
15	Desborough Town v Peterborough & Fletton Utd.	0-3
	Irthlingborough Town v Rushden Town	2-3
16	Colchester Town v Norwich Priory Athletic	9-0
	Parkeston Railway v Cambridge Town	2-3
17	Enfield v Grays Athletic	3-1
	Leytonstone v Leyton	3-5
18	Cheshunt v Waterlows (Dunstable)	3-1
	Hampstead Town v Baldock Town	10-2
19	Newbury Town v Botwell Mission	2-3
	Uxbridge v Windsor & Eton	0-4
20	Nunhead v Wimbledon	1-1
	Sutton United v Redhill	0-2
21	Farnham United Breweries v Aldershot Traction Co.	4-1
	RAMC Aldershot v Wellington Works	2-2
22	Ashford Railway Works v Cray Wanderers	5-2
	Sheppey United v RM Chatham	2-1
23	Hastings & St Leonards v Rock-a-Nore	5-0
	Worthing v Tunbridge Wells Rangers	2-1
24	Salisbury (1) v Portsea Gas Company	2-0
	Southampton CS v RM Portsmouth	1-2
25	Clandown v Coleford Athletic	3-2
	Paulton Rovers v Radstock Town	1-2
26	Bristol St George v Mid Rhondda	2-4
	Kingswood v Torquay United	2-3
3r	Guisborough Belmont Ath. v Grangetown St Mary's	1-0
r	Scarborough v Eston United	4-1
7r	Witton Albion v Chester	2-4
8r	Shrewsbury Town v Stafford Rangers	6-0
r	Willenhall v Wellington Town	1-2
9r	Gainsborough Trinity v Scunthorpe United	1-0
10r	Mexborough v Wath Athletic	2-3
20r	Wimbledon v Nunhead	5-2
21r	Wellington Works v RAMC Aldershot	1-6

Qualifying Round Three

1	Usworth Colliery v Jarrow	3-0
2	Horden Athletic v Shildon	3-1
3	Guisborough Belmont Ath. v Scarborough	1-2
4	Penrith v Egremont	2-2
5	Lytham v Chorley	2-1
6	Eccles United v Buxton	4-0
7	Chester v Mold	2-2
8	Wellington Town v Shrewsbury Town	5-1
9	Gainsborough Trinity v Grimsby Rovers	7-3
10	Wath Athletic v York City	4-1
11	Anston Athletic v Hemsworth West End	1-3
12	Grassmoor v Heanor Town	3-0
13	Newark Town v Sutton Town	2-0
14	Hinckley United (1) v Burton Town	0-1
15	Rushden Town v Peterborough & Fletton Utd.	2-0
16	Cambridge Town v Colchester Town	9-1
17	Enfield v Leyton	1-3
18	Hampstead Town v Cheshunt	0-2
19	Windsor & Eton v Botwell Mission	5-3
20	Redhill v Wimbledon	2-0
21	RAMC Aldershot v Farnham United Breweries	1-3
22	Sheppey United v Ashford Railway Works	4-1
23	Hastings & St Leonards v Worthing	3-2
24	Salisbury (1) v RM Portsmouth	4-1
25	Clandown v Radstock Town	2-2
26	Mid Rhondda v Torquay United	1-2
4r	Egremont v Penrith	2-3
7r	Mold v Chester	5-0
25r	Radstock Town v Clandown	3-3
25r2	Radstock Town v Clandown	0-2

Qualifying Round Four

	Bishop Auckland v Stockton	1-2
	Blyth Spartans v Crook Town	4-1
	Burton Town v Wellington Town	1-3
	Chesham United v Windsor & Eton	1-2
	Chilton Colliery Recreation v Usworth Colliery	3-0
	Farnham United Breweries v Salisbury (1)	2-1
	Folkestone v Dartford	1-0
	Grassmoor v Boston (1)	1-2
	Hastings & St Leonards v Chatham	0-3
	Horden Athletic v Scarborough	5-2
	Ilford v Cambridge Town	1-0
	Kettering Town v Hemsworth West End	5-0
	Leyton v Cheshunt	4-1
	Lytham v Penrith	3-0
	Mansfield Town v Gainsborough Trinity	2-0
	Mold v Eccles United	2-0
	Newark Town v Worksop Town	1-3
	Nuneaton Town v Worcester City	2-7
	Redhill v Barnet	2-2
	Sittingbourne v Sheppey United	2-2
	Torquay United v Yeovil & Petter's United	3-1
	Tow Law Town v South Bank	1-2
	Wath Athletic v Rushden Town	7-3
	Weymouth v Clandown	4-1
	Workington v Carlisle United	1-3
r	Barnet v Redhill	3-2
r	Sheppey United v Sittingbourne	0-1

Round One

	Aberdare Athletic v Bristol Rovers	4-1
	Accrington Stanley v Wrexham	4-0
	Blyth Spartans v Hartlepools United	2-2
	Boston (1) v Mansfield Town	5-2
	Bournemouth v Merthyr Town	3-0
	Bradford Park Avenue v Lincoln City	2-2
	Brentford v Barnet	3-1
	Brighton & Hove Albion v Watford	1-1
	Carlisle United v Chilton Colliery Recreation	0-2
	Charlton Athletic v Windsor & Eton	4-2
	Chatham v Sittingbourne	0-3
	Clapton v Norwich City	3-1
	Doncaster Rovers v Wellington Town	2-0
	Durham City v Ashington	4-1
	Exeter City v Swansea Town	1-3
	Farnham United Breweries v Swindon Town	1-10
	Gillingham v Southall	6-0
	Halifax Town v Rotherham United	0-3
	Horden Athletic v Darlington	2-3
	Leyton v St Albans City	1-0
	London Caledonians v Ilford	1-2
	Luton Town v Folkestone	3-0
	New Brighton v Barrow	2-0
	Northampton Town v Barnsley	3-1
	Northfleet United v Queen's Park Rangers	2-2

1925/26 to 1926/27

	Oldham Athletic v Lytham	10-1
	Rochdale v West Stanley	4-0
	South Bank v Stockton	1-4
	Southend United v Dulwich Hamlet	5-1
	Southport v Mold	1-0
	Torquay United v Reading	1-1
	Tranmere Rovers v Crewe Alexandra	0-0
	Walsall v Grimsby Town	0-1
	Wath Athletic v Chesterfield	0-5
	Weymouth v Newport County	0-1
	Wigan Borough v Nelson	3-0
	Worcester City v Kettering Town	0-0
	Worksop Town v Coventry City	1-0
r	Crewe Alexandra v Tranmere Rovers	2-1e
r	Hartlepools United v Blyth Spartans	1-1e
r	Kettering Town v Worcester City	0-0e
r	Lincoln City v Bradford Park Avenue	1-1e
r	Queen's Park Rangers v Northfleet United	2-0
r	Reading v Torquay United	1-1e
r	Watford v Brighton & Hove Albion	2-0
r2	Bradford Park Avenue v Lincoln City	2-1 N
r2	Hartlepools United v Blyth Spartans	1-1eN
r2	Kettering Town v Worcester City	2-0 N
r2	Reading v Torquay United	2-0 N
r3	Hartlepools United v Blyth Spartans	1-2 N

Round Two

	Aberdare Athletic v Luton Town	1-0
	Accrington Stanley v Blyth Spartans	5-0
	Boston (1) v Bradford Park Avenue	1-0
	Brentford v Bournemouth	1-2
	Chilton Colliery Recreation v Rochdale	1-1
	Clapton v Ilford	1-0
	Crewe Alexandra v Wigan Borough	2-2
	Doncaster Rovers v Rotherham United	0-2
	Durham City v Southport	0-3
	Kettering Town v Grimsby Town	1-1
	New Brighton v Darlington	2-0
	Northampton Town v Newport County	3-1
	Queen's Park Rangers v Charlton Athletic	1-1
	Reading v Leyton	6-0
	Southend United v Gillingham	1-0
	Stockton v Oldham Athletic	4-6
	Swansea Town v Watford	3-2
	Swindon Town v Sittingbourne	7-0
	Worksop Town v Chesterfield	1-2
r	Charlton Athletic v Queen's Park Rangers	1-0
r	Grimsby Town v Kettering Town	3-1
r	Rochdale v Chilton Colliery Recreation	1-2
r	Wigan Borough v Crewe Alexandra	2-1

Round Three

	Birmingham v Grimsby Town	2-0
	Blackburn Rovers v Preston North End	1-1
	Blackpool v Swansea Town	0-2
	Bolton Wanderers v Accrington Stanley	1-0
	Bournemouth v Reading	2-0
	Cardiff City v Burnley	2-2
	Charlton Athletic v Huddersfield Town	0-1
	Chesterfield v Clapton Orient	0-1
	Clapton v Swindon Town	2-3 N
	Corinthians v Manchester City	3-3
	Derby County v Portsmouth	0-0
	Everton v Fulham	1-1
	Hull City v Aston Villa	0-3
	Middlesbrough v Leeds United	5-1
	Millwall v Oldham Athletic	1-1
	New Brighton v Sheffield Wednesday	2-1
	Newcastle United v Aberdare Athletic	4-1
	Northampton Town v Crystal Palace	3-3
	Nottingham Forest v Bradford City	1-0
	Notts County v Leicester City	2-0
	Plymouth Argyle v Chelsea	1-2
	Port Vale v Manchester United	2-3
	Rotherham United v Bury	2-3
	Sheffield United v Stockport County	2-0
	South Shields v Chilton Colliery Recreation	3-0
	Southampton v Liverpool	0-0
	Southend United v Southport	5-2
	Sunderland v Boston (1)	8-1
	Tottenham Hotspur v West Ham United	5-0
	West Bromwich Albion v Bristol City	4-1
	Wigan Borough v Stoke City	2-5
	Wolverhampton Wan. v Arsenal	1-1
r	Arsenal v Wolverhampton Wan.	1-0
r	Burnley v Cardiff City	0-2
r	Crystal Palace v Northampton Town	2-1
r	Fulham v Everton	1-0
r	Liverpool v Southampton	1-0
r	Manchester City v Corinthians	4-0
r	Oldham Athletic v Millwall	0-1
r	Portsmouth v Derby County	1-1e
r	Preston North End v Blackburn Rovers	1-4
r2	Derby County v Portsmouth	2-0 N

Round Four

	Arsenal v Blackburn Rovers	3-1
	Bournemouth v Bolton Wanderers	2-2
	Bury v Millwall	3-3
	Cardiff City v Newcastle United	0-2
	Clapton Orient v Middlesbrough	4-2
	Crystal Palace v Chelsea	2-1
	Fulham v Liverpool	3-1
	Manchester City v Huddersfield Town	4-0
	Nottingham Forest v Swindon Town	2-0
	Notts County v New Brighton	2-0
	Sheffield United v Sunderland	1-2
	South Shields v Birmingham	2-1
	Southend United v Derby County	4-1
	Swansea Town v Stoke City	6-3
	Tottenham Hotspur v Manchester United	2-2
	West Bromwich Albion v Aston Villa	1-2
r	Bolton Wanderers v Bournemouth	6-2
r	Manchester United v Tottenham Hotspur	2-0
r	Millwall v Bury	2-0

Round Five

	Aston Villa v Arsenal	1-1
	Bolton Wanderers v South Shields	3-0
	Clapton Orient v Newcastle United	2-0
	Manchester City v Crystal Palace	11-4
	Millwall v Swansea Town	0-1
	Notts County v Fulham	0-1
	Southend United v Nottingham Forest	0-1
	Sunderland v Manchester United	3-3
r	Arsenal v Aston Villa	2-0
r	Manchester United v Sunderland	2-1

Round Six

	Clapton Orient v Manchester City	1-6
	Fulham v Manchester United	1-2
	Nottingham Forest v Bolton Wanderers	2-2
	Swansea Town v Arsenal	2-1
r	Bolton Wanderers v Nottingham Forest	0-0e
r2	Bolton Wanderers v Nottingham Forest	1-0 N

Semi Finals

	Bolton Wanderers v Swansea Town	3-0 N
	Manchester City v Manchester United	3-0 N

Final

	Bolton Wanderers v Manchester City	1-0 N

1926/27

Extra Preliminary Round

2	Cockfield v Langley Park	0-3
	Craghead United v Thornley Albion	0-0
	Crawcrook Albion v Hylton Colliery	1-2
	Seaham Colliery Welfare v Sunderland West End	2-1
	Seaham Harbour v Chopwell Institute	1-0
	South Pontop Villa v Spen Black & White	1-0
	Spennymoor United v West Auckland Town	2-1 D
	Twizell United v Stanley United	3-0
	White-le-Head Rangers v Dipton United	2-0
5	Burscough Rangers v Hindley Green Athletic	5-2
	Colne Town v Clitheroe	1-4
	Dick, Kerrs v Bacup Borough	2-1
	Horwich RMI v St Helens Town	2-4
	Skelmersdale United v Horwich Central	4-1
	Walsden United v Portsmouth Rovers (Lancs)	1-0
8	Bean (Dudley) v Kidderminster Harriers	2-5
	Cannock Town v Leamington Town	1-0
	Cradley Heath St Luke's v Bilston United	2-1
	Darlaston v Bromsgrove Rovers	5-3
	Hereford United v Halesowen Town	6-1
	Oakengates Town v Walsall Phoenix	8-2
	Redditch v Hednesford Town	1-1
	Stourbridge v Birmingham Corp. Tramways	0-4
	Wellington St George's v Bloxwich Strollers	5-3
	Whitchurch v Wolverhampton Amateur	4-1
9	Cleethorpes Town v East Hull United	5-0
	Frodingham Athletic v Grimsby YMCA	9-2
	Grimsby Albion v Brunswick Institute	4-1
	Hull Old Boys v Normanby Park Steel Works	1-2
	Reckitt's (Hull) v Barton Town (1)	0-2
	Selby OCO v Marfleet	8-0
	Spalding United v Goole Town	1-5
10	Luddendenfoot v Guiseley	0-2
15	Higham Ferrers Town v Walgrave Amber	5-2
	Stamford v Northampton Nomads	2-0
18	Aylesbury United v Ware	9-2
19	Hanwell Town (1) v Yiewsley	6-0
	Hendon Town v Civil Service	3-2
	Old Lyonian v Savoy (Southall)	4-1
	Oxford City v Cowley	2-1
25	Paulton Rovers v Spencer Moulton	6-2
	Warminster Town v Chippenham Rovers	2-1
26	Keynsham v Hanham Athletic	2-1
	Minehead v Lovells Athletic	2-3
2r	Thornley Albion v Craghead United	2-1
8r	Hednesford Town v Redditch	2-3

Preliminary Round

1	Bedlington United v Wallsend	3-0
	Blyth Spartans v Chester-le-Street	3-2
	High Fell v St Peter's Albion	1-2
	Preston Colliery v Felling Colliery	8-0
	Scotswood v Walker Celtic	1-2
	Shankhouse v Pelaw	1-2
	Usworth Colliery v Birtley	4-1
	Washington Colliery v Sunniside Rangers	3-1
2	Annfield Plain v West Auckland Town	3-1
	Hylton Colliery v Hobson Wanderers	4-0
	Seaham Harbour v Seaham Colliery Welfare	3-1
	Shildon v Horden Athletic	0-0
	South Pontop Villa v Wheatley Hill Colliery	1-0
	Tow Law Town v Langley Park	3-1
	White-le-Head Rangers v Twizell United	2-1
	Wingate Albion Comrades v Thornley Albion	2-2
3	South Bank East End v Whitby United	2-3
	Stockton Malleable Institute v Scarborough Penguins	3-1
4	Cleator Moor Celtic v Bowthorn Recreation	2-3
	Kendal Town v Windermere	1-2
	Keswick v Wath Brow United	1-0
	Moss Bay United v Frizington Athletic	1-1
	Netherfield (Kendal) v Bowness Rovers	1-1
	Ulverston Town v Penrith	2-2
	Whitehaven Athletic v Egremont	4-2
5	Burscough Rangers v St Helens Town	5-3
	Chorley v Coppull Central	5-2
	Clitheroe v Skelmersdale United	2-1 v
	Darwen v Lytham	4-2
	Dick, Kerrs v Lancaster Town	0-2
	Great Harwood v Barnoldswick Park Villa	2-1
	Morecambe v Fleetwood	6-1
	Walsden United v Breightmet United	5-3
6	Black Lane Rovers v New Mills	4-3
	Earle v Old Xaverians	1-2
	Glossop v Manchester North End	4-1
	Whiston v Harlandic	3-1
7	Altrincham v Harrowby	6-2
	Connah's Quay v Bangor City	5-0
	Llandudno v Chester	2-0
	Lostock Gralam v Barnton Victoria	0-0
	Mold v Ellesmere Port Cement	5-3
	Rhyl Athletic v Ellesmere Port Town	11-1
	Sandbach Ramblers v Winsford United	2-1
	Witton Albion v Nantwich	4-2
8	Cannock Town v Whitchurch	2-0
	Cradley Heath St Luke's v Redditch	5-2
	Darlaston v Wellington St George's	0-1
	Kidderminster Harriers v Hereford United	4-2
	Oswestry Town v Brierley Hill Alliance	4-3
	Stafford Rangers v Oakengates Town	8-2
	Willenhall v Birmingham Corp. Tramways	6-2
	Worcester City v Shrewsbury Town	0-2
9	British Oil & Cake Mills v Brigg Town	1-2
	Cleethorpes Town v Normanby Park Steel Works	2-2
	Gainsborough Trinity v Frodingham Athletic	11-1
	Goole Town v Barton Town (1)	3-2
	Grimsby Haycroft Rovers v Broughton Rangers	3-2
	Holderness Athletic v Scunthorpe United	0-10
	Hull Dairycoates v Grimsby Rovers	6-2
	Selby OCO v Grimsby Albion	4-0
10	Darfield v Wath Athletic	1-1
	Denaby United v Fryston Colliery	10-0
	Guiseley v Cudworth Village	7-2
	Liversedge v Horsforth	5-2
	Mexborough v Methley Perseverance	7-2
	Monckton Athletic v Castleford & Allerton United	4-3
	South Kirkby Colliery v Frickley Colliery	1-1
	Wombwell v Castleford Town	2-0
11	Ardsley Athletic v Norton Woodseats	4-1
	Birdwell v Anston Athletic	2-1
	Brodsworth Main Colliery v Hallam	1-1
	Eckington Works v Dinnington Main Colliery	2-0
	Maltby Main Colliery v Hemsworth West End	3-3
	Rossington Main v Markham Main Colliery	2-0
	Rotherham Amateurs v Bullcroft Main Colliery	2-1
	Sheffield v Mapplewell & Staincross Ath.	1-1
12	Alfreton Town v Bolsover Colliery	3-1
	Chesterfield Corinthians v Ilkeston United	0-9
	Grassmoor v Youlgrave	3-2
	Lewison (Ilkeston) v Matlock Town	4-6
	Long Eaton v Staveley Town	2-4
13	Clifton Colliery v Arnold Town (1)	3-1
	New Hucknall Colliery v Grantham	0-7
	Newark Town v Basford United	3-0
	Sneinton v Gedling Colliery	1-5
	Sutton Junction v Lenton	4-2
14	Ashby Town v Atherstone Town	4-1
	Barwell United v Measham Town	8-0
	Gresley Rovers v Moira United	7-1
	Loughborough Corinthians v Shepshed Albion	9-0
	Mountsorrel Town v Ibstock Colliery	2-3
	Stableford Works v Gresley Colliery	3-4
	Whitwick Imperial v Hinckley United (1)	3-7
15	Bedford Town (1) v Kempston Rovers	5-2
	Desborough Town v Peterbro' Westwood Works	2-0
	Irthlingborough Town v Peterborough & Fletton Utd.	1-6
	Leighton United v Rushden Town	2-2
	Market Harborough Town v Wolverton Town	1-3
	Rothwell Town v Higham Ferrers Town	5-1
	Stamford v Peterborough G.N. Loco	1-0
	Wellingborough Town v Biggleswade & District	4-1
16	Cambridge Town v March Great Eastern United	10-2
	Clacton Town v King's Lynn	1-3
	Lowestoft Town v Cromer	3-1
	Newmarket Town v Colchester Town	3-6
	Norwich CEYMS v City Wanderers (Norwich)	1-1
	Norwich Priory Athletic v Beccles	2-2 v
	Wisbech Town v Harwich & Parkeston	4-6
17	Barking v Wood Green Town	6-1

1926/27

	Brentwood & Warley v Crittall Athletic	1-3
	Custom House v Grays Thurrock United	1-2
	Edmonton v Tufnell Park	3-0
	GER Romford v Brentwood Mental Hospital	5-2
	Hoffmann Athletic (Chelmsford) v Grays Athletic	3-7
	Millwall United v Chelmsford	1-2
	Walthamstow Avenue v Walthamstow Grange	6-2
18	Apsley v Aylesbury United	6-0
	Chesham United v Finchley	3-4
	Hampstead Town v Berkhamsted Town	4-3
	Hitchin Blue Cross v Enfield	0-6
	Leagrave & District v Waterlows (Dunstable)	1-3
	Leavesden Mental Hospital v Wealdstone	0-2
	Letchworth Town v Baldock Town	3-2
	Watford Old Boys v Cheshunt	2-1
19	Hanwell Town (1) v Hounslow	3-4
	Maidenhead United v Henley Town	7-2
	Newbury Town v Marlow	8-0
	Old Lyonian v Hendon Town	1-4
	Oxford City v Windsor & Eton	3-3
	Slough v Polytechnic	9-0
	Uxbridge v Southall	1-1
	Wycombe Wanderers v Botwell Mission	4-1
20	Carshalton Athletic v Summerstown	4-7
	Epsom Town v Tooting Town	3-4
21	Camberley & Yorktown v Basingstoke	6-3
	Egham v Thornycrofts (Basingstoke)	4-6
	Farnham United Breweries v Walton-on-Thames	5-0
	Guildford v Staines Town	1-4
	Guildford United v Aldershot Albion	7-0
	Wellington Works v RAMC Aldershot	0-1
	Weybridge v Addlestone	3-3
	Woking v Aldershot Traction Co.	4-1
22	Ashford Railway Works v Margate	1-0
	Beckenham v Catford Southend	2-0
	Bexleyheath Town v Bostall Heath	2-1
	Bromley v Dartford	1-2
	Erith & Belvedere v Woolwich Polytechnic	5-0
	RM Chatham v Whitstable	2-0
	Sheppey United v Maidstone United	6-1
23	Eastbourne Old Comrades v Tunbridge Wells Rangers	0-5
	Horsham Trinity v East Grinstead	1-1
	Hove v Vernon Athletic	6-1
	Newhaven v Shoreham	8-2
	Southwick v Lewes	5-4
	Worthing v Bognor Regis Town	5-1
24	Poole v Dorchester Town	7-0
	Portland United v Salisbury Corinthians	5-0
	RAOC Cosham v East Cowes	7-0
	Ryde Sports v Emsworth	6-1
	Salisbury (1) v Bournemouth Tramways	4-2
	Sandown v Gosport Albion	7-4
25	Devizes Town v Clutton Wanderers	1-1
	Frome Town v Calne & Harris United	4-4
	Melksham & Avon United v Trowbridge Town	1-3
	Radstock Town v Coleford Athletic	0-0
	Swindon Victoria v Chippenham Town	1-3
	Warminster Town v Swindon Corinthians	2-4
	Welton Rovers v Paulton Rovers	1-2
	Westbury United v Clandown	2-2
26	Barry v Cardiff Corinthians	5-0
	Bristol St George v Glastonbury	6-2
	Clevedon v Bedminster Down Sports	5-0
	Green Waves (Plymouth) v Newquay	4-1
	Keynsham v Lovells Athletic	0-4
	St Austell v Taunton United	3-1
	Wells City v Kingswood	3-2
	Yeovil & Petter's United v Street	10-1
2r	Horden Athletic v Shildon	0-2
r	Thornley Albion v Wingate Albion Comrades	3-1
4r	Bowness Rovers v Netherfield (Kendal)	2-0
r	Frizington Athletic v Moss Bay United	1-0
r	Penrith v Ulverston Town	2-1
5r	Skelmersdale United v Clitheroe	2-1
7r	Barnton Victoria v Lostock Gralam	1-0
9r	Normanby Park Steel Works v Cleethorpes Town	4-2
10r	Frickley Colliery v South Kirkby Colliery	5-2
r	Wath Athletic v Darfield	1-0e
11r	Hallam v Brodsworth Main Colliery	3-3e
r	Hemsworth West End v Maltby Main Colliery	2-1e
r	Mapplewell & Staincross v Sheffield	6-0
15r	Rushden Town v Leighton United	3-1
16r	Beccles v Norwich Priory Athletic	0-3
r	City Wanderers (Norwich) v Norwich CEYMS	2-3
19r	Southall v Uxbridge	1-0
r	Windsor & Eton v Oxford City	4-1
21r	Addlestone v Weybridge	4-0
23r	East Grinstead v Horsham Trinity	4-1
25r	Clandown v Westbury United	4-1
r	Clutton Wanderers v Devizes Town	6-0
r	Coleford Athletic v Radstock Town	1-2
r	Frome Town v Calne & Harris United	5-4
11r2	Hallam v Brodsworth Main Colliery	0-2 N

Qualifying Round One

1	Bedlington United v Blyth Spartans	5-1
	Pelaw v Preston Colliery	0-4
	St Peter's Albion v Washington Colliery	4-3
	Usworth Colliery v Walker Celtic	2-4
2	Annfield Plain v Hylton Colliery	2-1
	Thornley Albion v Seaham Harbour	2-1 D
	Tow Law Town v South Pontop Villa	2-1
	White-le-Head Rangers v Shildon	1-3
3	Filey Town v Normanby Mangnesite	3-1
	Guisborough Belmont Ath. v York City	0-5
	South Bank v Stockton Malleable Institute	2-1
	Whitby United v Loftus Albion	4-2
4	Frizington Athletic v Keswick	3-2
	Penrith v Barrow YMCA	3-1
	Whitehaven Athletic v Bowthorn Recreation	7-1
	Windermere v Bowness Rovers	1-2
5	Burscough Rangers v Great Harwood	2-0
	Chorley v Skelmersdale United	4-0
	Lancaster Town v Walsden United	5-1
	Morecambe v Darwen	1-2
6	Black Lane Rovers v Whiston	4-1
	Marine v Eccles United	4-2
	Prescot v Old Xaverians	4-0
	Stalybridge Celtic v Glossop	4-0
7	Altrincham v Sandbach Ramblers	3-3
	Connah's Quay v Llandudno	3-2
	Rhyl Athletic v Mold	1-0
	Witton Albion v Barnton Victoria	2-1
8	Cannock Town v Oswestry Town	1-1
	Kidderminster Harriers v Stafford Rangers	2-0
	Shrewsbury Town v Cradley Heath St Luke's	1-1
	Willenhall v Wellington St George's	4-0
9	Brigg Town v Gainsborough Trinity	1-6
	Hull Dairycoates v Normanby Park Steel Works	1-2
	Scunthorpe United v Grimsby Haycroft Rovers	7-2
	Selby OCO v Goole Town	2-1
10	Frickley Colliery v Monckton Athletic	4-3
	Guiseley v Denaby United	1-1
	Mexborough v Liversedge	4-0
	Wombwell v Wath Athletic	0-2
11	Ardsley Athletic v Rossington Main	5-0
	Brodsworth Main Colliery v Eckington Works	6-0
	Hemsworth West End v Birdwell	5-2
	Rotherham Amateurs v Mapplewell & Staincross Ath.	0-1
12	Alfreton Town v South Normanton Colliery	4-1
	Heanor Town v Matlock Town	2-1
	Shirebrook v Ilkeston United	1-1
	Staveley Town v Grassmoor	2-0
13	Clifton Colliery v Sutton Junction	1-0
	Langwith Colliery v Boots Athletic	2-3
	Newark Town v Grantham	4-0
	Sutton Town v Gedling Colliery	3-1
14	Burton Town v Ashby Town	7-1
	Gresley Colliery v Hinckley United (1)	1-6
	Gresley Rovers v Loughborough Corinthians	1-0
	Ibstock Colliery v Barwell United	2-2
15	Peterborough & Fletton Utd. v Rushden Town	3-1
	Rothwell Town v Bedford Town (1)	7-0
	Stamford v Wolverton Town	4-2
	Wellingborough Town v Desborough Town	1-1
16	Cambridge Town v Norwich CEYMS	3-1
	Colchester Town v Harwich & Parkeston	0-0
	King's Lynn v Norwich Priory Athletic	6-0
	Parkeston Railway v Lowestoft Town	1-6
17	Chelmsford v Barking	1-1
	Crittall Athletic v Grays Thurrock United	1-2
	Edmonton v Grays Athletic	0-4
	GER Romford v Walthamstow Avenue	3-0
18	Enfield v Watford Old Boys	6-1
	Finchley v Waterlows (Dunstable)	3-3
	Hampstead Town v Letchworth Town	2-1
	Wealdstone v Apsley	3-1
19	Hendon Town v Windsor & Eton	2-5
	Maidenhead United v Hounslow	7-1
	Newbury Town v Southall	2-0
	Slough v Wycombe Wanderers	9-0
20	Leyland Motors (Kingston) v Dorking	5-1
	Mitcham Wanderers v Summerstown	3-1
	Tooting Town v West Norwood	2-1
	Wimbledon v Sutton United	3-1
21	Addlestone v Thornycrofts (Basingstoke)	4-4
	Farnham United Breweries v Camberley & Yorktown	4-2
	Guildford United v Staines Town	8-0
	Woking v RAMC Aldershot	3-2
22	Dartford v Beckenham	3-1
	Erith & Belvedere v Bexleyheath Town	2-1
	Folkestone v Ashford Railway Works	5-1
	RM Chatham v Sheppey United	4-0
23	East Grinstead v Hove	2-4
	Hastings & St Leonards v Tunbridge Wells Rangers	0-2
	Newhaven v Rock-a-Nore	8-2
	Southwick v Worthing	2-1
24	Poole v Salisbury (1)	3-2
	RAOC Cosham v Portsmouth Gas Company	4-4
	RM Portsmouth v Ryde Sports	3-1
	Sandown v Portland United	1-4
25	Chippenham Town v Clandown	0-1
	Frome Town v Radstock Town	2-4
	Swindon Corinthians v Paulton Rovers	1-0
	Trowbridge Town v Clutton Wanderers	7-4
26	Barry v Lovells Athletic	2-0
	Clevedon v Wells City	5-0
	St Austell v Green Waves (Plymouth)	1-1
	Yeovil & Petter's United v Bristol St George	3-0
7r	Sandbach Ramblers v Altrincham	2-1
8r	Cannock Town v Oswestry Town	wo/s
r	Cradley Heath St Luke's v Shrewsbury Town	6-0
10r	Denaby United v Guiseley	13-1
12r	Ilkeston United v Shirebrook	4-3
14r	Barwell United v Ibstock Colliery	3-1e
15r	Desborough Town v Wellingborough Town	2-1
16r	Harwich & Parkeston v Colchester Town	5-5
17r	Barking v Chelmsford	6-0
18r	Waterlows (Dunstable) v Finchley	2-2
21r	Addlestone v Thornycrofts (Basingstoke)	1-6
24r	Portsmouth Gas Company v RAOC Cosham	3-1
26r	Green Waves (Plymouth) v St Austell	3-4e
16r2	Colchester Town v Harwich & Parkeston	4-2 N
18r2	Waterlows (Dunstable) v Finchley	4-4x
18r3	Waterlows (Dunstable) v Finchley	3-1 N

Qualifying Round Two

1	Bedlington United v Preston Colliery	2-0
	Walker Celtic v St Peter's Albion	4-3
2	Seaham Harbour v Annfield Plain	2-3
	Tow Law Town v Shildon	5-0
3	Filey Town v Whitby United	1-3
	York City v South Bank	4-0
4	Penrith v Frizington Athletic	5-2
	Whitehaven Athletic v Bowness Rovers	3-0
5	Chorley v Burscough Rangers	2-3
	Lancaster Town v Darwen	2-0
6	Prescot v Marine	2-2
	Stalybridge Celtic v Black Lane Rovers	5-0
7	Rhyl Athletic v Witton Albion	2-2
	Sandbach Ramblers v Connah's Quay	1-1
8	Kidderminster Harriers v Cannock Town	4-3
	Willenhall v Cradley Heath St Luke's	3-0
9	Gainsborough Trinity v Normanby Park Steel Works	5-0
	Selby OCO v Scunthorpe United	0-0
10	Denaby United v Mexborough	1-1
	Frickley Colliery v Wath Athletic	2-2
11	Ardsley Athletic v Hemsworth West End	1-1
	Brodsworth Main Col. v Mapplewell&Staincross Ath.	3-1
12	Alfreton Town v Heanor Town	2-2
	Staveley Town v Ilkeston United	0-0
13	Newark Town v Boots Athletic	5-3
	Sutton Town v Clifton Colliery	4-0
14	Burton Town v Hinckley United (1)	6-0
	Gresley Rovers v Barwell United	1-3
15	Desborough Town v Stamford	2-1
	Rothwell Town v Peterborough & Fletton Utd.	0-5
16	Colchester Town v Cambridge Town	3-1
	King's Lynn v Lowestoft Town	2-3
17	GER Romford v Barking	4-7
	Grays Thurrock United v Grays Athletic	3-3
18	Hampstead Town v Enfield	2-0
	Wealdstone v Waterlows (Dunstable)	1-5
19	Maidenhead United v Slough	1-4
	Newbury Town v Windsor & Eton	7-1
20	Tooting Town v Mitcham Wanderers	2-3
	Wimbledon v Leyland Motors (Kingston)	1-3
21	Farnham Utd Breweries v Thornycrofts (Basingstoke)	2-3
	Woking v Guildford United	2-0
22	Dartford v Folkestone	2-0
	RM Chatham v Erith & Belvedere	1-3
23	Newhaven v Hove	9-0
	Southwick v Tunbridge Wells Rangers	5-2
24	Poole v Portsmouth Gas Company	7-0
	Portland United v RM Portsmouth	3-4
25	Clandown v Swindon Corinthians	4-4
	Trowbridge Town v Radstock Town	1-1
26	Clevedon v Barry	1-4
	Yeovil & Petter's United v St Austell	5-0
6r	Marine v Prescot	3-2
7r	Connah's Quay v Sandbach Ramblers	1-0
r	Witton Albion v Rhyl Athletic	0-2
9r	Scunthorpe United v Selby OCO	1-0
10r	Mexborough v Denaby United	2-0
r	Wath Athletic v Frickley Colliery	2-0
11r	Hemsworth West End v Ardsley Athletic	3-2
12r	Heanor Town v Alfreton Town	1-4
r	Ilkeston United v Staveley Town	1-1e
17r	Grays Athletic v Grays Thurrock United	3-2
25r	Radstock Town v Trowbridge Town	4-1
r	Swindon Corinthians v Clandown	1-2
12r2	Staveley Town v Ilkeston United	3-4 N

Qualifying Round Three

1	Bedlington United v Walker Celtic	3-3
2	Annfield Plain v Tow Law Town	4-3
3	York City v Whitby United	0-0
4	Whitehaven Athletic v Penrith	9-2
5	Lancaster Town v Burscough Rangers	6-1
6	Marine v Stalybridge Celtic	4-0
7	Rhyl Athletic v Connah's Quay	3-0
8	Kidderminster Harriers v Willenhall	2-2
9	Gainsborough Trinity v Scunthorpe United	3-3
10	Mexborough v Wath Athletic	2-0
11	Brodsworth Main Colliery v Hemsworth West End	3-1
12	Ilkeston United v Alfreton Town	1-0
13	Sutton Town v Newark Town	1-2
14	Barwell United v Burton Town	1-3
15	Peterborough & Fletton Utd. v Desborough Town	2-2
16	Lowestoft Town v Colchester Town	3-1
17	Barking v Grays Athletic	2-1
18	Waterlows (Dunstable) v Hampstead Town	4-2
19	Slough v Newbury Town	4-1
20	Mitcham Wanderers v Leyland Motors (Kingston)	1-4
21	Woking v Thornycrofts (Basingstoke)	5-1
22	Dartford v Erith & Belvedere	2-0
23	Newhaven v Southwick	3-0
24	RM Portsmouth v Poole	2-2
25	Radstock Town v Clandown	2-3
26	Yeovil & Petter's United v Barry	3-1
1r	Walker Celtic v Bedlington United	3-5 N
3r	York City v Whitby United	2-1

1926/27 to 1927/28

8r Willenhall v Kidderminster Harriers	3-2
9r Scunthorpe United v Gainsborough Trinity	1-0
15r Desborough Town v Peterborough & Fletton Utd.	3-1
24r Poole v RM Portsmouth	2-0

Qualifying Round Four

Annfield Plain v Jarrow	3-0
Barnet v Slough	3-1
Bishop Auckland v Esh Winning (1)	3-3
Boston (1) v Newark Town	4-2
Brodsworth Main Colliery v Mexborough	4-4
Carlisle United v Whitehaven Athletic	7-1
Chilton Colliery Recreation v West Stanley	1-0
Clandown v Poole	2-2
Crook Town v Ferryhill Athletic	1-0
Dartford v Chatham	1-1
Ilford v Kingstonian	1-3
Ilkeston United v York City	1-5
Leyland Motors (Kingston) v Barking	1-2
Lowestoft Town v Leyton	7-3
Mansfield Town v Burton Town	2-1
Redhill v Nunhead	2-4
Rhyl Athletic v Marine	6-1
Scunthorpe United v Kettering Town	1-2
Sittingbourne v Newhaven	6-0
Waterlows (Dunstable) v Desborough Town	1-2
Wellington Town v Willenhall	2-0
Weymouth v Yeovil & Petter's United	4-1
Willington v Bedlington United	3-4
Woking v Leytonstone	3-0
Workington v Lancaster Town	1-0
r Chatham v Dartford	3-1
r Esh Winning (1) v Bishop Auckland	1-2
r Mexborough v Brodsworth Main Colliery	2-1
r Poole v Clandown	1-0

Round One

Accrington Stanley v Rochdale	4-3
Annfield Plain v Chilton Colliery Recreation	2-4
Barking v Gillingham	0-0
Bishop Auckland v Bedlington United	0-1
Boston (1) v Northampton Town	1-1
Bournemouth v Swindon Town	1-1
Brighton & Hove Albion v Barnet	3-0
Carlisle United v Hartlepools United	6-2
Chatham v St Albans City	3-1
Chesterfield v Mexborough	2-1
Clapton v Brentford	1-1
Crewe Alexandra v Northern Nomads	4-1
Crystal Palace v Norwich City	0-0
Doncaster Rovers v Desborough Town	3-0
Dulwich Hamlet v Southend United	1-4
Exeter City v Aberdare Athletic	3-0
Grimsby Town v Halifax Town	3-2
Kettering Town v Coventry City	2-3
Lincoln City v Rotherham United	2-0
Luton Town v London Caledonians	4-2
Merthyr Town v Bristol City	0-2
Nelson v Stockport County	4-1
Nunhead v Kingstonian	9-0
Poole v Newport County	1-0
Reading v Weymouth	4-4
Rhyl Athletic v Stoke City	1-1
Sittingbourne v Northfleet United	1-3
Southport v Tranmere Rovers	1-1
Stockton v Ashington	1-2
Torquay United v Bristol Rovers	1-1
Walsall v Bradford Park Avenue	1-0
Watford v Lowestoft Town	10-1
Wellington Town v Mansfield Town	1-2
Wigan Borough v Barrow	2-2e
Woking v Charlton Athletic	1-3
Workington v Crook Town	1-2
Wrexham v New Brighton	1-1
York City v Worksop Town	4-1
r Barrow v Wigan Borough	0-1
r Brentford v Clapton	7-3
r Bristol Rovers v Torquay United	1-0
r Gillingham v Barking	2-0
r New Brighton v Wrexham	2-2e
r Northampton Town v Boston (1)	2-1
r Norwich City v Crystal Palace	1-0
r Reading v Weymouth	5-0
r Stoke City v Rhyl Athletic	1-1e
r Swindon Town v Bournemouth	3-4
r Tranmere Rovers v Southport	1-2
r2 Rhyl Athletic v Stoke City	2-1 N
r2 Wrexham v New Brighton	3-1 N

Round Two

Ashington v Nelson	2-1
Bristol Rovers v Bournemouth	1-1
Bristol Rovers v Charlton Athletic	4-1
Carlisle United v Bedlington United	4-0
Chilton Colliery Recreation v Accrington Stanley	0-3
Coventry City v Lincoln City	1-1
Crewe Alexandra v Wigan Borough	4-1
Doncaster Rovers v Chesterfield	0-1
Exeter City v Northampton Town	1-0
Gillingham v Brentford	1-1
Grimsby Town v York City	2-1
Luton Town v Northfleet United	6-2
Norwich City v Chatham	5-0
Nunhead v Poole	1-2
Reading v Southend United	3-2
Rhyl Athletic v Wrexham	3-1
Southport v Crook Town	2-0
Walsall v Mansfield Town	2-0
Watford v Brighton & Hove Albion	0-1
r Bournemouth v Bristol City	2-0
r Brentford v Gillingham	1-0
r Lincoln City v Coventry City	2-1

Round Three

Ashington v Nottingham Forest	0-2
Barnsley v Crewe Alexandra	6-1
Birmingham v Manchester City	4-1
Blackpool v Bolton Wanderers	1-3
Bournemouth v Liverpool	1-1
Bradford City v Derby County	2-6
Bristol Rovers v Portsmouth	3-3
Burnley v Grimsby Town	3-1
Cardiff City v Aston Villa	2-1
Carlisle United v Wolverhampton Wan.	0-2
Chelsea v Luton Town	4-0
Clapton Orient v Port Vale	1-1
Darlington v Rhyl Athletic	2-1
Everton v Poole	3-1
Exeter City v Accrington Stanley	0-2
Fulham v Chesterfield	4-3
Hull City v West Bromwich Albion	2-1
Leeds United v Sunderland	3-2
Lincoln City v Preston North End	2-4
Middlesbrough v Leicester City	5-3
Millwall v Huddersfield Town	3-1
Newcastle United v Notts County	8-1
Oldham Athletic v Brentford	2-4
Reading v Manchester United	1-1
Sheffield United v Arsenal	2-3
Sheffield Wednesday v Brighton & Hove Albion	2-0
South Shields v Plymouth Argyle	3-1
Southampton v Norwich City	3-0
Southport v Blackburn Rovers	2-0
Swansea Town v Bury	4-1
Walsall v Corinthians	0-4
West Ham United v Tottenham Hotspur	3-2
r Liverpool v Bournemouth	4-1
r Manchester United v Reading	2-2e
r Port Vale v Clapton Orient	5-1
r Portsmouth v Bristol Rovers	4-0
r2 Reading v Manchester United	2-1 N

Round Four

Barnsley v Swansea Town	1-3
Chelsea v Accrington Stanley	7-2
Corinthians v Newcastle United	1-3
Darlington v Cardiff City	0-2
Derby County v Millwall	0-2
Fulham v Burnley	0-4
Hull City v Everton	1-1
Leeds United v Bolton Wanderers	0-0
Liverpool v Southport	3-1
Port Vale v Arsenal	2-2
Preston North End v Middlesbrough	0-3
Reading v Portsmouth	3-1
Sheffield Wednesday v South Shields	1-1
Southampton v Birmingham	4-1
West Ham United v Brentford	1-1
Wolverhampton Wan. v Nottingham Forest	2-0
r Arsenal v Port Vale	1-0
r Bolton Wanderers v Leeds United	3-0
r Brentford v West Ham United	2-0
r Everton v Hull City	2-2e
r South Shields v Sheffield Wednesday	1-0
r2 Hull City v Everton	3-2eN

Round Five

Arsenal v Liverpool	2-0
Bolton Wanderers v Cardiff City	0-2
Chelsea v Burnley	2-1
Millwall v Middlesbrough	3-2
Reading v Brentford	1-0
South Shields v Swansea Town	2-2
Southampton v Newcastle United	2-1
Wolverhampton Wan. v Hull City	1-0
r Swansea Town v South Shields	2-1

Round Six

Arsenal v Wolverhampton Wan.	2-1
Chelsea v Cardiff City	0-0
Millwall v Southampton	0-0
Swansea Town v Reading	1-3
r Cardiff City v Chelsea	3-2
r Southampton v Millwall	2-0

Semi Finals

Arsenal v Southampton	2-1 N
Cardiff City v Reading	3-0 N

Final

Cardiff City v Arsenal	1-0 N

1927/28

Extra Preliminary Round

2 Bishop Auckland v Leasingthorne Colliery	6-1
Burnhope Institute v Twizell United	2-0
Chilton Colliery Recreation v Esh Winning (1)	3-2
Chopwell Institute v Craghead United	4-3
Consett v Crawcrook Albion	3-1
Dipton United v Willington	1-3
Horden Athletic v Langley Park	2-2
Spennymoor United v Stanley United	5-0
Sunderland West End v Seaham Colliery Welfare	4-2
Tow Law Town v White-le-Head Rangers	2-1
West Auckland Town v South Pontop Villa	1-3 d
West Stanley v Spen Black & White	4-1
Wheatley Hill Colliery v Hylton Colliery	2-1
4 Arlecdon Red Rose v Aspatria Athletic	1-3
Portsmouth Rovers (Lancs) v Dick, Kerrs	2-5
5 Hindley Green Athletic v Horwich Central	5-3
8 Bilston United v Stafford Rangers	1-3
Birmingham Corp. Tramways v Leamington Town	wo/s
Brierley Hill Alliance v Worcester City	5-0
Bromsgrove Rovers v Walsall Phoenix	9-1
Nuneaton Town v Stourbridge	2-3
Redditch v Hednesford Town	4-3
Shrewsbury Town v Oakengates Town	2-0
9 Grimsby Albion v Cleethorpes Town	2-3
Holderness Athletic v Barton Town (1)	1-5
Louth Town v Spalding United	3-2
Reckitt's (Hull) v Broughton Rangers	0-7
10 Pontefract Borough v Altofts West Riding Col.	1-7
11 Anston Athletic v Thorne Colliery	4-6
Ecclesfield v Grimethorpe Colliery Institute	5-3
Goldthorpe United v Maltby Main Colliery	6-2
Pilkington Recreation v Treeton Reading Room	1-1
Tankersley United v Hemsworth Colliery	2-1
15 Leighton United v Lynton Works (Bedford)	7-0
Peterbro' Westwood Works v Irthlingborough Town	wo/s
16 Great Yarmouth Town v Abbey United (Cambs)	3-1
Harwich & Parkeston v Leiston Works Athletic	2-2
Kirkley v Ipswich Works	4-2
Norwich CEYMS v Norwich Priory Athletic	2-0
Sheringham v March Great Eastern United	9-3
18 Bishop's Stortford v Stevenage Town	2-1
Chesham United v Leagrave & District	3-1
Cheshunt v Letchworth Town	2-3
Haywards Sports v Waltham Comrades	0-3e
Hitchin Blue Cross v Welwyn Garden City	2-3
Luton Amateur v Apsley	2-8
24 Gosport Athletic v Southampton CS	3-2
25 5th Royal Tank Regiment v Coleford Athletic	5-0
Bath City v Melksham	3-0
Cheltenham Town v Warminster Town	3-5
Frome Town v Clutton Wanderers	wo/s
Salisbury Corinthians v Paulton Rovers	9-0
Swindon Victoria v Salisbury (1)	2-6
Westbury United v Welton Rovers	1-1
2r Langley Park v Horden Athletic	2-2
11r Treetool Reading Room v Pilkington Recreation	1-2
16r Leiston Works Athletic v Harwich & Parkeston	0-1
25r Welton Rovers v Westbury United	3-0
2r2 Langley Park v Horden Athletic	4-1

Preliminary Round

1 Bedlington United v Howdon British Legion	3-1
Birtley v Preston Colliery	0-2
Jarrow v Chester-le-Street	2-1
Scotswood v Usworth Colliery	1-1
Shankhouse v Wallsend	4-1
St Peter's Albion v High Fell	1-0
Walker Celtic v Percy Main Amateurs	2-1
Washington Colliery v Pelaw	4-0
2 Annfield Plain v Chopwell Institute	5-3
Bishop Auckland v Wheatley Hill Colliery	6-1
Langley Park v West Stanley	0-1
Seaham Harbour v Consett	2-2
Spennymoor United v Ferryhill Athletic	4-2
Sunderland West End v Burnhope Institute	2-2
Tow Law Town v Chilton Colliery Recreation	3-3
Willington v West Auckland Town	1-1
3 Scarborough v Normanby Mangnesite	4-3
4 Barrow YMCA v Penrith	2-1
Bowness Rovers v Kendal Town	8-1
Cleator Moor Celtic v Workington	2-2
Frizington Athletic v Aspatria Athletic	2-1
Keswick v Netherfield (Kendal)	1-1
Moss Bay United v Wath Brow United	8-4
Ulverston Town v Windermere	1-0
Whitehaven Athletic v Bowthorn Recreation	3-1
5 Barnoldswick Park Villa v Walsden United	4-1
Burscough Rangers v Skelmersdale United	4-1 D
Chorley v Hindley Green Athletic	1-0
Fleetwood v Breightmet United	7-1
Great Harwood v Morecambe	2-1 v
Horwich RMI v Bacup Borough	4-0
Lancaster Town v Dick, Kerrs	2-0
Lytham v Darwen	2-0
6 Altrincham v Hurst	2-5
Bootle (2) v Earle	3-0
Bootle Celtic v Prescot	wo/s
Manchester North End v Glossop	4-3

68

1927/28

	Whiston v Old Xaverians	5-2
7	Bangor City v Nantwich	4-0
	Chester v Lostock Gralam	10-1
	Winsford United v Colwyn Bay	3-2
8	Bloxwich Strollers v Willenhall	4-2
	Cradley Heath St Luke's v Cannock Town	2-0
	Oswestry Town v Brierley Hill Alliance	5-1
	Shrewsbury Town v Wolverhampton Amateur	6-1
	Stafford Rangers v Hereford United	4-0
	Stourbridge v Redditch	1-1
	Wellington St George's v Birmingham Corp. Tramways	7-2
	Whitchurch v Bromsgrove Rovers	3-2
9	British Oil & Cake Mills v Barton Town (1)	0-1
	Broughton Rangers v Hull Dairycoates	7-0
	Frodingham Athletic v Normanby Park Steel Works	3-5
	Gainsborough Trinity v Louth Town	4-0
	Goole Town v Marfleet	7-1
	Grimsby Haycroft Rovers v Brigg Town	2-1
	Scunthorpe United v Cleethorpes Town	5-2
	Selby OCO v Hull Old Boys	5-2
10	Altofts West Riding Col. v Horsforth	0-0
	Castleford Town v Wombwell	1-0
	Cudworth Village v South Kirkby Colliery	2-1
	Frickley Colliery v Mexborough	3-3
	Guiseley v Denaby United	2-3
	Luddendenfoot v Darfield	2-6
	Monckton Athletic v Methley Perseverance	2-3
	Wath Athletic v Castleford & Allerton United	5-1
11	Ardsley Athletic v Tankersley United	5-1
	Brodsworth Main Colliery v Sheffield	9-0
	Dinnington Main Colliery v Rotherham Amateurs	0-0
	Goldthorpe United v Birdwell	5-1
	Hemsworth West End v Hallam	1-1
	Rossington Main v Ecclesfield	1-8
	Thorne Colliery v Mapplewell & Staincross Ath.	3-1
	Worksop Town v Pilkington Recreation	7-2
12	Ripley Town v Long Eaton	wo/s
	Shirebrook v Matlock Town	3-1
13	Hucknall Byron v Grantham	0-5
	New Hucknall Colliery v Sneinton	2-0
	Ransome & Marles v Sutton Junction	2-2
	Sutton Town - Bye	
14	Ibstock Colliery v Loughborough Corinthians	1-8
	Newhall United v Mountsorrel Town	wo/s
	Whitwick Imperial v Moira United	1-4
15	Desborough Town v Peterborough G.N. Loco	5-2
	Higham Ferrers Town v Peterbro' Westwood Works	8-3
	Kempston Rovers v Bedford Town (1)	3-3
	Market Harborough Town v Peterborough & Fletton Utd.	0-8
	Rushden Town v Wellingborough Town	1-0
	Stamford v Rothwell Town	2-2
	Walgrave Amber v Biggleswade & District	2-3
	Wolverton Town v Leighton United	3-1
16	Colchester Town v Clacton Town	7-0
	Cromer v Cambridge Town	0-5
	Great Yarmouth Town v City Wanderers (Norwich)	8-1
	Kirkley v Harwich & Parkeston	1-2
	Lowestoft Town v Crittall Athletic	3-1
	Newmarket Town v Parkeston Railway	3-2
	Norwich CEYMS v King's Lynn	0-6
	Sheringham v Wisbech Town	4-3
17	Chelmsford v Custom House	3-2
	Grays Athletic v Grays Thurrock United	4-0
	Millwall United v Edmonton	5-0
	Tilbury v Tufnell Park	2-2
	Walthamstow Grange v Brentwood Mental Hospital	3-1
	Wood Green Town v Walthamstow Avenue	1-5
18	Apsley v Old Lyonian	3-2
	Aylesbury United v Chesham United	2-4
	Enfield v Barnet	0-8
	Hampstead Town v Waltham Comrades	7-1
	Hendon Town v Watford Old Boys	1-3
	Letchworth Town v Bishop's Stortford	5-1
	Wealdstone v Waterlows (Dunstable)	2-7
	Welwyn Garden City v Ware	5-2
19	BWI Reading v Marlow	4-4
	Botwell Mission v Windsor & Eton	5-4
	Henley Town v Cowley	0-9
	Hounslow v Abingdon Town	3-1
	Maidenhead United v Oxford City	9-1
	Wycombe Wanderers v Uxbridge	4-4
20	Carshalton Athletic v Polytechnic	7-3
	Civil Service v Sutton United	1-7
	Epsom Town v Mitcham Wanderers	3-2
	Redhill v Dorking	7-1
	Summerstown v Leyland Motors (Kingston)	4-2
	West Norwood v Reigate Priory	7-4
21	Addlestone v Aldershot Albion	wo/s
	Aldershot v Guildford	5-1
	Farnham United Breweries v Staines Town	4-0
	Guildford City v Egham	5-1
	Thornycrofts (Basingstoke) - Bye	
	Walton-on-Thames v Aldershot Traction Co.	3-4
	Wellington Works v Camberley & Yorktown	0-7
	Woking v Weybridge	6-2
22	Ashford Railway Works v Folkestone	0-5
	Bexleyheath Town v Sheppey United	3-2
	Bostall Heath v Woolwich Polytechnic	4-1
	Maidstone United v Whitstable	4-1
	Margate v Bromley	1-4
	RM Chatham v Cray Wanderers	2-1
23	Bognor Regis Town v Vernon Athletic	5-1
	Chichester v Hove	3-1
	Hastings & St Leonards v Eastbourne Old Comrades	1-2
	Hollington United v East Grinstead	4-1
	Worthing v Rock-a-Nore	9-0
24	Blandford v Dorchester Town	6-2
	Bournemouth (Ams) v Bournemouth Tramways	1-3
	Gosport Athletic v Gosport Albion	6-4
	Portland United v Weymouth	2-5
	Portsmouth Gas Company v Emsworth	4-0
	RAOC Cosham v Osborne Athletic	7-0
	Ryde Sports v East Cowes	8-0
	Sandown v RM Portsmouth	0-14
25	5th Royal Tank Regiment v Chippenham Rovers	7-0
	Devizes Town v Swindon Corinthians	1-3
	Radstock Town v Frome Town	7-1
	Salisbury (1) v Calne & Harris United	6-2
	Spencer Moulton v Bath City	0-3
	Trowbridge Town v Clandown	4-0
	Warminster Town v Salisbury Corinthians	8-3
	Welton Rovers v Chippenham Town	10-3
26	Barry v Kingswood	3-3
	Bristol St George v St Anne's Oldland	1-1
	Clevedon v Lovells Athletic	1-7
	Keynsham v Bedminster Down Sports	3-6
	Plymouth Civil Service v St Austell	1-0
	Street v Hanham Athletic	3-4
	Wells City v Cardiff Corinthians	3-3
	Yeovil & Petter's United v Green Waves (Plymouth)	3-1
1r	Usworth Colliery v Scotswood	2-1
2r	Burnhope Institute v Sunderland West End	5-0
r	Chilton Colliery Recreation v Tow Law Town	1-2
r	Consett v Seaham Harbour	10-0
r	West Auckland Town v Willington	4-4e
4r	Netherfield (Kendal) v Keswick	3-4e
r	Workington v Cleator Moor Celtic	8-0
5r	Morecambe v Great Harwood	1-0
8r	Stourbridge v Redditch	5-2
10r	Horsforth v Altofts West Riding Col.	1-3
r	Mexborough v Frickley Colliery	0-3
11r	Hallam v Hemsworth West End	4-2
r	Rotherham Amateurs v Dinnington Main Colliery	5-2
13r	Sutton Junction v Ransome & Marles	2-3
15r	Bedford Town (1) v Kempston Rovers	1-0
r	Rothwell Town v Stamford	17-0
17r	Tufnell Park v Tilbury	4-1
19r	Marlow v BWI Reading	4-3
r	Uxbridge v Wycombe Wanderers	0-4
26r	Cardiff Corinthians v Wells City	4-3
r	Kingswood v Barry	0-2
r	St Anne's Oldland v Bristol St George	3-2 D
2r2	West Auckland Town v Willington	1-5 N

Qualifying Round One

1	Bedlington United v Washington Colliery	4-2
	Jarrow v St Peter's Albion	3-0
	Usworth Colliery v Preston Colliery	1-0
	Walker Celtic v Shankhouse	2-0
2	Bishop Auckland v Spennymoor United	1-5
	Burnhope Institute v Consett	2-1
	Tow Law Town v Annfield Plain	1-0
	West Stanley v Willington	1-0
3	Loftus Albion v Filey Town	7-4
	Scarborough v Scarborough Penguins	3-0
	South Bank East End v Stockton Malleable Institute	3-3
	York City v Whitby United	4-0
4	Barrow YMCA v Bowness Rovers	3-1
	Frizington Athletic v Moss Bay United	4-3
	Ulverston Town v Keswick	3-2
	Workington v Whitehaven Athletic	2-0
5	Barnoldswick Park Villa v Lytham	3-3
	Chorley v Fleetwood	7-0
	Horwich RMI v Skelmersdale United	3-0
	Morecambe v Lancaster Town	1-2
6	Bootle Celtic v Black Lane Rovers	0-0
	Manchester North End v Bootle (2)	3-0
	Marine v Stalybridge Celtic	0-5
	Whiston v Hurst	1-5
7	Bangor City v Connah's Quay	6-3
	Barnton Victoria v Harrowby	4-1
	Chester v Winsford United	4-0
	Rhyl Athletic v Llandudno	4-1
8	Oswestry Town v Whitchurch	5-2
	Shrewsbury Town v Cradley Heath St Luke's	1-0
	Stafford Rangers v Wellington St George's	2-1
	Stourbridge v Bloxwich Strollers	3-2
9	Broughton Rangers v Goole Town	4-3
	Gainsborough Trinity v Scunthorpe United	3-0
	Normanby Park Steel Works v Barton Town (1)	3-3
	Selby OCO v Grimsby Haycroft Rovers	3-2
10	Altofts West Riding Col. v Frickley Colliery	2-2
	Cudworth Village v Methley Perseverance	2-3
	Darfield v Castleford Town	2-2
	Wath Athletic v Denaby United	1-1
11	Brodsworth Main Colliery v Ardsley Athletic	2-2
	Ecclesfield v Goldthorpe United	2-4
	Rotherham Amateurs v Thorne Colliery	1-6
	Worksop Town v Hallam	1-0
12	Heanor Town v South Normanton Colliery	2-5
	Ilkeston United v Grassmoor	4-3
	Ripley Town v Alfreton Town	2-2
	Staveley Town v Shirebrook	3-3
13	Clifton Colliery v Ransome & Marles	0-5
	Grantham v Sutton Town	1-1
	New Hucknall Colliery v Boots Athletic	2-5
	Newark Town v Basford United	15-3
14	Gresley Colliery v Newhall United	4-1
	Gresley Rovers - Bye	
	Hinckley United (1) v Burton Town	1-1
	Loughborough Corinthians v Moira United	11-1
15	Desborough Town v Biggleswade & District	5-3
	Peterborough & Fletton Utd. v Bedford Town (1)	3-1
	Rothwell Town v Higham Ferrers Town	5-1
	Rushden Town v Wolverton Town	3-0
16	Cambridge Town v Great Yarmouth Town	2-2
	Harwich & Parkeston v Lowestoft Town	4-4
	Newmarket Town v Colchester Town	1-2
	Sheringham v King's Lynn	4-1
17	GER Romford v Chelmsford	2-3
	Grays Athletic v Walthamstow Grange	10-2
	Millwall United v Leytonstone	1-1
	Tufnell Park v Walthamstow Avenue	4-0
18	Barnet v Waterlows (Dunstable)	5-0
	Chesham United v Apsley	5-2
	Hampstead Town v Welwyn Garden City	7-4
	Letchworth Town v Watford Old Boys	2-1
19	Botwell Mission v Newbury Town	12-1
	Cowley v Marlow	12-0
	Hounslow v Wycombe Wanderers	4-1
	Maidenhead United v Slough	5-2
20	Carshalton Athletic v Summerstown	3-2
	Sutton United v Redhill	2-2
	West Norwood v Epsom Town	1-4
	Wimbledon v Tooting Town	2-0
21	Aldershot v Addlestone	8-0
	Camberley & Yorktown v Aldershot Traction Co.	0-4
	Guildford City v Woking	3-0
	Thornycrofts (Basingstoke) v Farnham Utd Breweries	3-0
22	Bromley v Bexleyheath Town	2-0
	Dartford v RM Chatham	1-0
	Erith & Belvedere v Bostall Heath	2-2
	Maidstone United v Folkestone	1-2
23	Bognor Regis Town v Hollington United	2-2
	Chichester v Newhaven	3-2
	Eastbourne Old Comrades v Worthing	2-3
	Southwick v Tunbridge Wells Rangers	1-0
24	Gosport Athletic v Blandford	4-2
	RM Portsmouth v Portsmouth Gas Company	3-1
	Ryde Sports v RAOC Cosham	3-0
	Weymouth v Bournemouth Tramways	8-1
25	Bath City v 5th Royal Tank Regiment	8-3
	Salisbury (1) v Radstock Town	2-1
	Trowbridge Town v Welton Rovers	2-3
	Warminster Town v Swindon Corinthians	3-4
26	Barry v Bedminster Down Sports	12-1
	Hanham Athletic v Bristol St George	1-1
	Lovells Athletic v Cardiff Corinthians	1-0
	Plymouth Civil Service v Yeovil & Petter's United	3-1
3r	Stockton Malleable Institute v South Bank East End	2-0
5r	Lytham v Barnoldswick Park Villa	3-1
6r	Black Lane Rovers v Bootle Celtic	1-4
9r	Barton Town (1) v Normanby Park Steel Works	3-0
10r	Castleford Town v Darfield	2-3
r	Denaby United v Wath Athletic	7-1
r	Frickley Colliery v Altofts West Riding Col.	5-1
11r	Ardsley Athletic v Brodsworth Main Colliery	2-3
12r	Alfreton Town v Ripley Town	0-3
r	Shirebrook v Staveley Town	5-1
13r	Sutton Town v Grantham	2-3
14r	Burton Town v Hinckley United (1)	5-3e
16r	Great Yarmouth Town v Cambridge Town	0-5
r	Lowestoft Town v Harwich & Parkeston	2-0
17r	Leytonstone v Millwall United	4-1
20r	Redhill v Sutton United	2-3
22r	Bostall Heath v Erith & Belvedere	1-4
23r	Hollington United v Bognor Regis Town	wo/s
26r	Bristol St George v Hanham Athletic	1-4

Qualifying Round Two

1	Bedlington United v Usworth Colliery	3-0
	Walker Celtic v Jarrow	2-1
2	Spennymoor United v Tow Law Town	3-1
	West Stanley v Burnhope Institute	3-0
3	Stockton Malleable Institute v Loftus Albion	6-2
	York City v Scarborough	1-1
4	Barrow YMCA v Frizington Athletic	2-0
	Workington v Ulverston Town	3-1
5	Lancaster Town v Horwich RMI	2-1
	Lytham v Chorley	1-1
6	Manchester North End v Hurst	2-2
	Stalybridge Celtic v Bootle Celtic	9-2
7	Bangor City v Chester	1-0
	Rhyl Athletic v Barnton Victoria	3-0
8	Shrewsbury Town v Oswestry Town	3-4
	Stourbridge v Stafford Rangers	3-2
9	Gainsborough Trinity v Barton Town (1)	3-1
	Selby OCO v Broughton Rangers	2-5
10	Darfield v Frickley Colliery	2-2
	Denaby United v Methley Perseverance	1-0
11	Brodsworth Main Colliery v Worksop Town	0-0
	Thorne Colliery v Goldthorpe United	1-0
12	Ilkeston United v Shirebrook	2-3
	Ripley Town v South Normanton Colliery	2-4
13	Grantham v Boots Athletic	8-3
	Ransome & Marles v Newark Town	2-3
14	Gresley Rovers v Burton Town	1-0
	Loughborough Corinthians v Gresley Colliery	3-1
15	Peterborough & Fletton Utd. v Rushden Town	5-0
	Rothwell Town v Desborough Town	2-4

1927/28 to 1928/29

16	Colchester Town v Cambridge Town	1-1
	Sheringham v Lowestoft Town	1-2
17	Chelmsford v Leytonstone	4-2
	Tufnell Park v Grays Athletic	1-4
18	Hampstead Town v Chesham United	2-2
	Letchworth Town v Barnet	1-4
19	Cowley v Maidenhead United	0-1
	Hounslow v Botwell Mission	4-5
20	Epsom Town v Sutton United	2-0
	Wimbledon v Carshalton Athletic	4-0
21	Aldershot v Guildford City	2-1
	Thornycrofts (Basingstoke) v Aldershot Traction Co.	2-0
22	Bromley v Erith & Belvedere	5-2
	Folkestone v Dartford	0-0
23	Southwick v Chichester	5-1
	Worthing v Hollington United	5-0
24	Gosport Athletic v Weymouth	4-4
	RM Portsmouth v Ryde Sports	1-1
25	Bath City v Swindon Corinthians	1-1
	Welton Rovers v Salisbury (1)	4-2
26	Barry v Lovells Athletic	1-1
	Plymouth Civil Service v Hanham Athletic	4-0
3r	Scarborough v York City	0-4
5r	Chorley v Lytham	1-2
6r	Hurst v Manchester North End	2-1
10r	Frickley Colliery v Darfield	5-0
11r	Worksop Town v Brodsworth Main Colliery	5-1
16r	Cambridge Town v Colchester Town	2-0
18r	Chesham United v Hampstead Town	2-3
22r	Dartford v Folkestone	3-1
24r	Ryde Sports v RM Portsmouth	3-2
r	Weymouth v Gosport Athletic	4-2
25r	Swindon Corinthians v Bath City	1-2
26r	Lovells Athletic v Barry	7-3

Qualifying Round Three

1	Walker Celtic v Bedlington United	2-4
2	Spennymoor United v West Stanley	2-1
3	York City v Stockton Malleable Institute	7-1
4	Workington v Barrow YMCA	7-1
5	Lancaster Town v Lytham	2-0
6	Stalybridge Celtic v Hurst	5-1
7	Rhyl Athletic v Bangor City	7-2
8	Stourbridge v Oswestry Town	0-0
9	Gainsborough Trinity v Broughton Rangers	5-2
10	Denaby United v Frickley Colliery	2-1
11	Thorne Colliery v Worksop Town	2-3
12	South Normanton Colliery v Shirebrook	1-3
13	Grantham v Newark Town	6-0
14	Gresley Rovers v Loughborough Corinthians	1-1
15	Desborough Town v Peterborough & Fletton Utd.	0-0
16	Lowestoft Town v Cambridge Town	3-1
17	Chelmsford v Grays Athletic	1-2
18	Hampstead Town v Barnet	2-1
19	Maidenhead United v Botwell Mission	1-6
20	Wimbledon v Epsom Town	3-2
21	Aldershot v Thornycrofts (Basingstoke)	3-1
22	Bromley v Dartford	1-1
23	Southwick v Worthing	1-3
24	Ryde Sports v Weymouth	3-3
25	Bath City v Welton Rovers	1-0
26	Lovells Athletic v Plymouth Civil Service	6-1
8r	Oswestry Town v Stourbridge	6-3
14r	Loughborough Corinthians v Gresley Rovers	0-2
15r	Peterborough & Fletton Utd. v Desborough Town	4-2
22r	Dartford v Bromley	4-0
24r	Weymouth v Ryde Sports	2-2
24r2	Ryde Sports v Weymouth	4-1 N

Qualifying Round Four

	Aldershot v Kingstonian	5-0
	Barking v Ilford	1-1
	Bath City v Lovells Athletic	1-0
	Bedlington United v Crook Town	1-3
	Botwell Mission v Grays Athletic	3-1
	Chatham v Sittingbourne	2-1
	Dartford v Worthing	3-0
	Denaby United v Boston (1)	1-1
	Dulwich Hamlet v Nunhead	3-2
	Gainsborough Trinity v Mansfield Town	5-0
	Gresley Rovers v Wellington Town	2-2
	Kettering Town v St Albans City	9-1
	Lancaster Town v Carlisle United	0-2
	Lowestoft Town v Clapton	1-6
	Oswestry Town v Stalybridge Celtic	4-3
	Peterborough & Fletton Utd. v Worksop Town	2-1
	Poole v Ryde Sports	3-3
	Rhyl Athletic v Northern Nomads	4-1
	Shildon v York City	1-1
	Shirebrook v Grantham	5-0
	Southall v Hampstead Town	3-2
	Spennymoor United v South Bank	4-1
	Stockton v Blyth Spartans	3-1
	Wimbledon v London Caledonians	1-1
	Workington v Barrow	3-1
r	Boston (1) v Denaby United	1-2
r	Ilford v Barking	4-2e
r	London Caledonians v Wimbledon	3-1
r	Ryde Sports v Poole	1-1e
r	Wellington Town v Gresley Rovers	5-1
r	York City v Shildon	1-2
r2	Ryde Sports v Poole	0-1 N

Round One

	Accrington Stanley v Lincoln City	2-5
	Aldershot v Queen's Park Rangers	2-1
	Bath City v Southall	2-0
	Botwell Mission v Peterborough & Fletton Utd.	3-4
	Bradford City v Workington	6-0
	Bristol Rovers v Walsall	4-2
	Carlisle United v Doncaster Rovers	2-1
	Coventry City v Bournemouth	2-2
	Crewe Alexandra v Ashington	2-2
	Darlington v Chesterfield	4-1
	Dartford v Crystal Palace	1-3
	Denaby United v Southport	2-3
	Durham City v Wrexham	1-1
	Exeter City v Aberdare Athletic	9-1
	Gainsborough Trinity v Stockton	6-0
	Gillingham v Plymouth Argyle	2-1
	Halifax Town v Hartlepools United	3-0
	Ilford v Dulwich Hamlet	4-0
	Kettering Town v Chatham	2-0
	Luton Town v Clapton	9-0
	Merthyr Town v Charlton Athletic	0-0
	Nelson v Bradford Park Avenue	0-3
	Newport County v Swindon Town	0-1
	Northampton Town v Leyton	8-0
	Northfleet United v London Caledonians	0-1
	Poole v Norwich City	1-1
	Rhyl Athletic v Wigan Borough	4-3
	Rochdale v Crook Town	8-2
	Shildon v New Brighton	1-3
	Shirebrook v Tranmere Rovers	1-3
	Southend United v Wellington Town	1-0
	Spennymoor United v Rotherham United	1-1
	Stockport County v Oswestry Town	5-2
	Watford v Brighton & Hove Albion	1-2
r	Ashington v Crewe Alexandra	0-2
r	Bournemouth v Coventry City	2-0
r	Charlton Athletic v Merthyr Town	2-1
r	Norwich City v Poole	5-0
r	Rotherham United v Spennymoor United	4-2
r	Wrexham v Durham City	4-0

Round Two

	Bournemouth v Bristol Rovers	6-1
	Bradford City v Rotherham United	2-3
	Bradford Park Avenue v Southport	0-2
	Charlton Athletic v Kettering Town	1-1
	Crewe Alexandra v Stockport County	2-0
	Darlington v Rochdale	2-1
	Exeter City v Ilford	5-3
	Gainsborough Trinity v Lincoln City	0-2
	Gillingham v Southend United	2-0
	London Caledonians v Bath City	1-0
	Luton Town v Norwich City	6-0
	New Brighton v Rhyl Athletic	7-2
	Northampton Town v Brighton & Hove Albion	1-0
	Peterborough & Fletton Utd. v Aldershot	2-1
	Swindon Town v Crystal Palace	0-0
	Tranmere Rovers v Halifax Town	3-1
	Wrexham v Carlisle United	1-0
r	Crystal Palace v Swindon Town	1-2
r	Kettering Town v Charlton Athletic	1-2

Round Three

	Arsenal v West Bromwich Albion	2-0
	Birmingham v Peterborough & Fletton Utd.	4-3
	Blackburn Rovers v Newcastle United	4-1
	Blackpool v Oldham Athletic	1-4
	Bolton Wanderers v Luton Town	2-1
	Bristol City v Tottenham Hotspur	1-2
	Burnley v Aston Villa	0-2
	Cardiff City v Southampton	2-1
	Charlton Athletic v Bury	1-1
	Huddersfield Town v Lincoln City	4-2
	Hull City v Leicester City	0-1
	Liverpool v Darlington	1-0
	London Caledonians v Crewe Alexandra	2-3 N
	Manchester City v Leeds United	1-0
	Manchester United v Brentford	7-1
	Middlesbrough v South Shields	3-0
	Millwall v Derby County	1-2
	New Brighton v Corinthians	2-1
	Nottingham Forest v Tranmere Rovers	1-0
	Notts County v Sheffield United	2-3
	Port Vale v Barnsley	3-0
	Portsmouth v West Ham United	0-2
	Preston North End v Everton	0-3
	Reading v Grimsby Town	4-0
	Rotherham United v Exeter City	3-3
	Sheffield Wednesday v Bournemouth	3-0
	Southport v Fulham	3-0
	Stoke City v Gillingham	6-1
	Sunderland v Northampton Town	3-3
	Swindon Town v Clapton Orient	2-1
	Wolverhampton Wan. v Chelsea	2-1
	Wrexham v Swansea Town	2-1
r	Bury v Charlton Athletic	4-3
r	Exeter City v Rotherham United	3-1
r	Northampton Town v Sunderland	0-3

Round Four

	Arsenal v Everton	4-3
	Aston Villa v Crewe Alexandra	3-0
	Bury v Manchester United	1-1
	Cardiff City v Liverpool	2-1
	Derby County v Nottingham Forest	0-0
	Exeter City v Blackburn Rovers	2-2
	Huddersfield Town v West Ham United	2-1
	Port Vale v New Brighton	3-0
	Reading v Leicester City	0-1
	Sheffield United v Wolverhampton Wan.	3-1
	Southport v Middlesbrough	0-3
	Stoke City v Bolton Wanderers	4-2
	Sunderland v Manchester City	1-2
	Swindon Town v Sheffield Wednesday	1-2
	Tottenham Hotspur v Oldham Athletic	3-0
	Wrexham v Birmingham	1-3
r	Blackburn Rovers v Exeter City	3-1
r	Manchester United v Bury	1-0
r	Nottingham Forest v Derby County	2-0

Round Five

	Arsenal v Aston Villa	4-1
	Blackburn Rovers v Port Vale	2-1
	Huddersfield Town v Middlesbrough	4-0
	Leicester City v Tottenham Hotspur	0-3
	Manchester City v Stoke City	0-1
	Manchester United v Birmingham	1-0
	Nottingham Forest v Cardiff City	2-1
	Sheffield Wednesday v Sheffield United	1-1
r	Sheffield United v Sheffield Wednesday	4-1

Round Six

	Arsenal v Stoke City	4-1
	Blackburn Rovers v Manchester United	2-0
	Huddersfield Town v Tottenham Hotspur	6-1
	Sheffield United v Nottingham Forest	3-0

Semi Finals

	Blackburn Rovers v Arsenal	1-0 N
	Huddersfield Town v Sheffield United	2-2 N
r	Huddersfield Town v Sheffield United	0-0eN
r2	Huddersfield Town v Sheffield United	1-0 N

Final

	Blackburn Rovers v Huddersfield Town	3-1 N

1928/29

Extra Preliminary Round

2	Bishop Auckland v Spen Black & White	5-2
	Consett v Cockfield	4-0
	Craghead United v Ferryhill Athletic	4-4
	Esh Winning (1) v Leasingthorne Colliery	1-2
	Seaham Harbour v Willington	1-1
	White-le-Head Rangers v Murton CW	3-0
8	Birmingham Corp. Tramways v Leamington Town	0-2
	Bloxwich Strollers v Headingley	3-1
	Bromsgrove Rovers v Bilston United	2-1
	Cradley Heath St Luke's v Hednesford Town	8-2
	Evesham Town v Walsall Phoenix	4-3
	Hereford United v Cannock Town	2-0
	Nuneaton Town v Walsall LMS	1-1
	Oakengates Town v Ledbury	4-1
	Wellington St George's v Wolverhampton Amateur	5-1
	Whitchurch v Worcester City	1-5
	Willenhall v Redditch	4-0
9	British Oil & Cake Mills v Hessle	1-0
	Reckitt's (Hull) v Hull Old Boys	2-2
10	Farsley Celtic v Harrogate	0-3
	Horsforth v Luddendenfoot	7-1
15	Biggleswade & District v Baldock Town	8-0
	Luton Amateur v Langford	4-1
	Waterlows (Dunstable) v Peterbro' Westwood Works	3-1
16	Clacton Town v Ipswich Works	wo/s
	Felixstowe Town v Harwich & Parkeston	0-4
	Newmarket Town v Severalls Athletic	0-2
	Parkeston Railway v Thetford Town	3-4
18	Berkhamsted Town v Leavesden Mental Hospital	2-3
	Hertford Town v Finchley	2-2
19	Oxford City v RAF Uxbridge	1-1
25	Calne & Harris United v Frome Town	3-1
	Chippenham Town v Radstock Town	2-2
	Coleford Athletic v Melksham	3-0
	Gloucester City v Cheltenham Town	2-1
	Spencer Moulton v Swindon Victoria	2-1
26	St Austell v Taunton Town (1)	0-4
	Weston-Super-Mare v Glastonbury	3-2
2r	Ferryhill Athletic v Craghead United	4-3
r	Willington v Seaham Harbour	1-3
8r	Walsall LMS v Nuneaton Town	3-0
9r	Hull Old Boys v Reckitt's (Hull)	3-1
18r	Finchley v Hertford Town	5-1
19r	RAF Uxbridge v Oxford City	2-0
25r	Radstock Town v Chippenham Town	2-1

1928/29

Preliminary Round

1	Jarrow v Gosforth & Coxlodge	4-0
	Pelaw v Birtley	2-1
	Scotswood v Bedlington United	1-0
	St Peter's Albion v Shankhouse	4-0
	Walker Celtic v Felling Colliery	1-1
	Wallsend v Usworth Colliery	4-2
	Washington Colliery v Walker Park	1-1
2	Annfield Plain v Sunderland West End	5-0
	Chopwell Institute v Burnhope Institute	7-2
	Consett v Tow Law Town	2-2
	Dipton United v Seaham Harbour	6-0
	Ferryhill Athletic v Leasingthorne Colliery	5-2
	Langley Park v Crawcrook Albion	1-1
	Shildon v White-le-Head Rangers	4-1
	Stanley United v Bishop Auckland	0-1
3	Bridlington Town (1) v Stockton Shamrocks	3-1
	Eston United v Filey Town	5-3
	Normanby Magnesite v South Bank East End	4-3
4	Aspatria Athletic v Cleator Moor Celtic	3-1
	Burnside (Kendal) v Ulverston Town	3-4
	Egremont v Frizington Athletic	3-2
	Kendal Town v Netherfield (Kendal)	2-2
	Keswick v Bowness Rovers	3-3
	Moss Bay United v Penrith	1-6
	Whitehaven Athletic v Bowthorn Recreation	4-1
	Windermere v Barrow YMCA	2-5
5	Breightmet United v Walsden United	5-1
	Darwen v Portsmouth Rovers (Lancs)	wo/s
	Dick, Kerrs v Burscough Rangers	4-2
	Morecambe v Great Harwood	1-0
	Skelmersdale United v Horwich Central	0-4
6	Earle v Ellesmere Port Cement	1-1
	Ellesmere Port Town v Timperley	6-1
	Harrowby v Eccles United	wo/s
	Marine v Prescot Cables	1-3
	St Helens Town v Manchester North End	0-0
	Stalybridge Celtic v Hurst	3-5
	Whiston v Glossop	4-1
7	Bangor City v Barnton Victoria	6-2
	Colwyn Bay v Macclesfield Town	2-2
	Connah's Quay v Winsford United	4-3
	Flint v Altrincham	1-0
	Lostock Gralam v Llandudno	2-1
	Northwich Victoria v Chester	3-1
	Rhyl Athletic v Sandbach Ramblers	4-1
	Witton Albion v Nantwich	5-1
8	Cradley Heath St Luke's v Hereford United	3-2
	Evesham Town v Walsall LMS	2-0
	Leamington Town v Shrewsbury Town	1-1
	Oakengates Town v Bromsgrove Rovers	6-2
	Stafford Rangers v Oswestry Town	6-4
	Wellington St George's - Bye	
	Willenhall v Bloxwich Strollers	2-0
	Worcester City v Stourbridge	8-0
9	Barton Town (1) v Scunthorpe United	2-3
	British Oil & Cake Mills v Marfleet	0-4
	Frodingham Athletic v Broughton Rangers	7-3
	Goole Town v Normanby Park Steel Works	8-2
	Grimsby Haycroft Rovers v Cleethorpes Town	2-4
	Louth Town v Boston (1)	0-2
	Selby OCO v Hull Old Boys	2-0
	Spalding United v Brigg Town	2-2
10	Castleford Town v Altofts West Riding Col.	2-5
	Frickley Colliery v South Kirkby Colliery	6-1
	Guiseley v Cudworth Village	0-4
	Methley Perseverance v Horsforth	3-0
	Mexborough v Harrogate	5-0
	Monckton Athletic v Darfield	1-5
	Wath Athletic v Denaby United	0-1
	Wombwell v Pontefract Borough	1-2
11	Ardsley Athletic v Grimethorpe Colliery Institute	3-0
	Norton Woodseats v Mapplewell & Staincross Ath.	2-1
	Rossington Main v Rotherham Amateurs	0-1
	Sheffield v Pilkington Recreation	0-5
	Treeton Reading Room v Hallam	5-1
12	Alfreton Town v Staveley Town	1-6
	Matlock Town v Markham Main Colliery	2-0
13	Lenton v Basford United	3-1
	Sutton Junction v New Hucknall Colliery	wo/s
	Sutton Town v Hucknall Byron	11-1
15	Bedford Town (1) v Luton Amateur	3-0
	Letchworth Town v Biggleswade & District	1-5
	Market Harborough Town v Peterborough G.N. Loco	3-2
	Rothwell Town v Higham Ferrers Town	2-1
	Rushden Town v Wellingborough Town	3-3
	Stamford v Desborough Town	0-0
	Waterlows (Dunstable) v Leighton United	3-2
	Wolverton Town v Kempston Rovers	2-1
16	Clacton Town v Abbey United (Cambs)	3-1
	Crittall Athletic v Harwich & Parkeston	4-1
	Great Yarmouth Town v Norwich Priory Athletic	6-0
	King's Lynn v Kirkley	2-0
	Leiston Works Athletic v Severalls Athletic	1-4
	Norwich CEYMS v Wisbech Town	4-1
	Sheringham v Lowestoft Town	1-5
	Thetford Town v Colchester Town	3-1
17	Brentwood & Warley v Walthamstow Grange	3-4
	Brentwood Mental Hospital v Grays Thurrock United	1-6
	Custom House v GER Romford	3-4
	Walthamstow Avenue v Tilbury	3-1
18	Apsley v Waltham Comrades	8-1
	Aylesbury United v Stevenage Town	6-1
	Barnet v Enfield	1-1
	Bishop's Stortford v Finchley	3-3
	Hendon Town v Chesham United	3-4
	Leavesden Mental Hospital v Wealdstone	1-2
	Watford Old Boys v Haywards Sports	4-3
	Wood Green Town v Old Johnians	2-1
19	Abingdon Town v Hounslow	1-4
	Botwell Mission v Hampstead Town	6-2
	Cowley v Old Lyonian	0-0
	Newbury Town v Uxbridge	1-2
	RAF Uxbridge v Windsor & Eton	1-2
	Slough v Marlow	4-1
	Southall v Maidenhead United	4-2
	Wycombe Wanderers v Henley Town	11-1
20	Dorking v Redhill	3-10
	Polytechnic v Mitcham Wanderers	1-10
	Reigate Priory v Leyland Motors (Kingston)	1-1
	Tooting Town v Civil Service	5-0
	West Norwood v Sutton United	0-2
21	Addlestone v Thornycrofts (Basingstoke)	3-5
	Aldershot Traction Co. v Basingstoke	6-1
	Godalming v Aldershot	1-5
	Guildford v Walton-on-Thames	2-6
	RAMC Aldershot v Camberley & Yorktown	6-4
	Staines Town v Winchester City	0-3
	Wellington Works v Egham	1-0
	Weybridge v Guildford City	1-7
22	Bostall Heath v Callender Athletic	4-6
	Folkestone v Margate	wo/s
	Maidstone United v Beckenham	0-1
	RM Chatham v Woolwich Polytechnic	4-1
	Sheppey United v Bexleyheath Town	4-0
	Whitstable v Cray Wanderers	1-5
23	Bexhill v Vernon Athletic	4-3
	Bognor Regis Town v Hove	3-3
	Tunbridge Wells Rangers v East Grinstead	7-0
24	Bournemouth (Ams) v Blandford	0-1
	Cowes v Osborne Athletic	10-2
	Dorchester Town v Bournemouth Tramways	3-3
	East Cowes v RAOC Hilsea	1-9
	Emsworth v Ryde Sports	1-1
	Portland United v Weymouth	3-1
	Portsmouth Gas Company v Gosport Athletic	0-1
25	Bath City v Swindon Corinthians	7-2
	Calne & Harris United v Clandown	3-2
	Chippenham Rovers v Devizes Town	4-2
	Coleford Athletic v Welton Rovers	1-5
	Radstock Town v Trowbridge Town	5-2
	Salisbury City (1) v Paulton Rovers	9-1
	Salisbury Corinthians v Warminster Town	2-1
	Spencer Moulton v Gloucester City	1-0
26	Bristol St George v Hanham Athletic	2-2
	Clevedon v Keynsham	1-2
	Kingswood v Street	8-2
	Lovells Athletic v Barry	3-3
	Plymouth Civil Service v Green Waves (Plymouth)	5-0
	Taunton Town (1) v Yeovil & Petter's United	1-1
	Wells City v Aberdare Athletic	wo/s
	Weston-Super-Mare v Minehead	5-2
1r	Felling Colliery v Walker Celtic	1-2
r	Walker Park v Washington Colliery	2-6
2r	Crawcrook Albion v Langley Park	3-1
r	Tow Law Town v Consett	1-3
4r	Bowness Rovers v Keswick	3-1
r	Netherfield (Kendal) v Kendal Town	wo/s
6r	Ellesmere Port Cement v Earle	2-1
r	Manchester North End v St Helens Town	1-0
7r	Macclesfield Town v Colwyn Bay	3-1
8r	Shrewsbury Town v Leamington Town	2-4
9r	Brigg Town v Spalding United	3-3e
15r	Desborough Town v Stamford	2-0
r	Wellingborough Town v Rushden Town	2-1
18r	Enfield v Barnet	2-1
r	Finchley v Bishop's Stortford	4-0
19r	Cowley v Old Lyonian	2-0
20r	Reigate Priory v Leyland Motors (Kingston)	1-2e
23r	Hove v Bognor Regis Town	1-3
24r	Bournemouth Tramways v Dorchester Town	2-1e
r	Ryde Sports v Emsworth	2-2e
26r	Barry v Lovells Athletic	2-1
r	Hanham Athletic v Bristol St George	1-3
r	Yeovil & Petter's United v Taunton Town (1)	0-3 d
9r2	Spalding United v Brigg Town	4-2
24r2	Ryde Sports v Emsworth	1-2 N

Qualifying Round One

1	Blyth Spartans v Walker Celtic	2-0
	Jarrow v St Peter's Albion	1-0
	Scotswood v Washington Colliery	4-0
	Wallsend v Pelaw	3-1
2	Bishop Auckland v Chopwell Institute	1-0
	Dipton United v Annfield Plain	2-2
	Ferryhill Athletic v Crawcrook Albion	3-1
	Shildon v Consett	1-0
3	Bridlington Town (1) v Eston United	5-1
	Loftus Albion v Scarborough Penguins	3-0
	South Bank v Normanby Magnesite	2-3
	York City v Stockton	7-1
4	Barrow YMCA v Bowness Rovers	4-1
	Netherfield (Kendal) v Egremont	0-4
	Penrith v Aspatria Athletic	6-0
	Ulverston Town v Whitehaven Athletic	1-0
5	Darwen v Breightmet United	1-0
	Dick, Kerrs v Horwich Central	4-2
	Horwich RMI v Chorley	1-0
	Morecambe v Lytham	3-2
6	Manchester North End v Ellesmere Port Town	6-3
	Northern Nomads v Hurst	3-3
	Prescot Cables v Ellesmere Port Cement	2-2
	Whiston v Harrowby	4-1
7	Bangor City v Northwich Victoria	2-2
	Connah's Quay v Witton Albion	4-2
	Macclesfield Town v Flint	2-1
	Rhyl Athletic v Lostock Gralam	3-1
8	Cradley Heath St Luke's v Willenhall	1-0
	Oakengates Town v Wellington St George's	2-1
	Stafford Rangers v Evesham Town	3-0
	Worcester City v Leamington Town	2-1
9	Boston (1) v Selby OCO	10-2
	Cleethorpes Town v Marfleet	2-0
	Frodingham Athletic v Goole Town	5-0
	Spalding United v Scunthorpe United	0-3
10	Cudworth Village v Pontefract Borough	2-2
	Denaby United v Darfield	6-1
	Frickley Colliery v Methley Perseverance	1-1
	Mexborough v Altofts West Riding Col.	3-2
11	Ardsley Athletic v Pilkington Recreation	4-2
	Norton Woodseats v Thorne Colliery	0-3
	Treeton Reading Room v Hemsworth West End	3-1
	Worksop Town v Rotherham Amateurs	6-2
12	Matlock Town v Heanor Town	2-5
	Shirebrook v Ripley Town	2-1
	South Normanton Colliery v Grassmoor	1-1
	Staveley Town v Ilkeston United	4-2
13	Boots Athletic v Grantham	0-6
	Newark Town v Lenton	5-1
	Sutton Junction v Ransome & Marles	3-2
	Sutton Town v Sneinton	7-0
14	Gresley Rovers v Burton Town	3-0
	Hinckley United (1) v Gresley Colliery	2-0
	Moira United v Loughborough Corinthians	0-6
	Whitwick Imperial v Ibstock Colliery	wo/s
15	Bedford Town (1) v Desborough Town	2-1
	Market Harborough Town v Wolverton Town	3-2
	Waterlows (Dunstable) v Rothwell Town	1-0
	Wellingborough Town v Biggleswade & District	6-0
16	Clacton Town v Norwich CEYMS	4-2
	Crittall Athletic v Thetford Town	5-3e
	Great Yarmouth Town v Lowestoft Town	0-2
	Severalls Athletic v King's Lynn	0-1
17	Chelmsford v GER Romford	1-1
	Leytonstone v Grays Athletic	2-3
	Tufnell Park v Walthamstow Avenue	2-2
	Walthamstow Grange v Grays Thurrock United	0-4
18	Aylesbury United v Enfield	0-1
	Finchley v Apsley	3-1
	Watford Old Boys v Wood Green Town	2-3
	Wealdstone v Chesham United	1-4
19	Cowley v Botwell Mission	2-1
	Southall v Wycombe Wanderers	3-3
	Uxbridge v Hounslow	0-1
	Windsor & Eton v Slough	2-1
20	Mitcham Wanderers v Wimbledon	0-3
	Nunhead v Leyland Motors (Kingston)	7-0
	Redhill v Sutton United	2-1
	Tooting Town v Epsom Town	2-1
21	Aldershot v Wellington Works	6-1
	Aldershot Traction Co. v Walton-on-Thames	2-1
	Guildford City v Winchester City	2-2
	RAMC Aldershot v Thornycrofts (Basingstoke)	4-5
22	Beckenham v Folkestone	1-6
	Bromley v Cray Wanderers	3-2
	RM Chatham v Callender Athletic	3-3
	Sheppey United v Dartford	5-0
23	Bognor Regis Town v Chichester	1-3
	Newhaven v Eastbourne Old Comrades	2-3
	Southwick v Bexhill	3-2
	Tunbridge Wells Rangers v Worthing	3-3
24	Bournemouth Tramways v Portland United	1-5
	Cowes v Emsworth	6-0
	RAOC Hilsea v Gosport Athletic	3-0
	RM Portsmouth v Blandford	2-0
25	Calne & Harris United v Salisbury Corinthians	1-2
	Radstock Town v Bath City	2-0
	Spencer Moulton v Salisbury City (1)	2-1 v
	Welton Rovers v Chippenham Rovers	5-1
26	Barry v Weston-Super-Mare	5-1
	Bristol St George v Kingswood	2-1
	Plymouth Civil Service v Yeovil & Petter's United	2-2
	Wells City v Keynsham	10-1
2r	Annfield Plain v Dipton United	4-1
6r	Hurst v Northern Nomads	4-1
r	Prescot Cables v Ellesmere Port Cement	2-0
7r	Northwich Victoria v Bangor City	0-1e
10r	Methley Perseverance v Frickley Colliery	2-1
r	Pontefract Borough v Cudworth Village	1-3
12r	Grassmoor v South Normanton Colliery	1-0
17r	GER Romford v Chelmsford	2-0
r	Walthamstow Avenue v Tufnell Park	1-0
19r	Wycombe Wanderers v Southall	1-5
21r	Winchester City v Guildford City	1-3
22r	Callender Athletic v RM Chatham	4-4
23r	Worthing v Tunbridge Wells Rangers	1-2
25r	Salisbury City (1) v Spencer Moulton	2-1
26r	Yeovil & Petter's United v Plymouth Civil Service	6-3
22r2	Callender Athletic v RM Chatham	1-0 N

1928/29

Qualifying Round Two

1	Jarrow v Blyth Spartans	4-2
	Scotswood v Wallsend	2-1
2	Annfield Plain v Ferryhill Athletic	3-0
	Shildon v Bishop Auckland	3-1
3	Bridlington Town (1) v Loftus Albion	4-2
	York City v Normanby Mangnesite	2-1
4	Egremont v Ulverston Town	2-0
	Penrith v Barrow YMCA	3-2
5	Dick, Kerrs v Horwich RMI	1-1
	Morecambe v Darwen	4-1
6	Hurst v Prescot Cables	3-2
	Manchester North End v Whiston	3-1
7	Macclesfield Town v Connah's Quay	2-1
	Rhyl Athletic v Bangor City	2-0
8	Stafford Rangers v Cradley Heath St Luke's	3-0
	Worcester City v Oakengates Town	3-0
9	Boston (1) v Frodingham Athletic	5-0
	Scunthorpe United v Cleethorpes Town	4-3
10	Cudworth Village v Mexborough	1-1
	Denaby United v Methley Perseverance	2-2
11	Ardsley Athletic v Worksop Town	1-0
	Treeton Reading Room v Thorne Colliery	3-0
12	Grassmoor v Heanor Town	5-1
	Staveley Town v Shirebrook	0-3
13	Grantham v Newark Town	0-0
	Sutton Junction v Sutton Town	3-2
14	Gresley Rovers v Whitwick Imperial	6-0
	Loughborough Corinthians v Hinckley United (1)	3-0
15	Market Harborough Town v Bedford Town (1)	1-2
	Wellingborough Town v Waterlows (Dunstable)	2-1
16	Clacton Town v Lowestoft Town	2-4
	King's Lynn v Crittall Athletic	4-0
17	Grays Athletic v GER Romford	1-1
	Walthamstow Avenue v Grays Thurrock United	3-0
18	Enfield v Finchley	2-6
	Wood Green Town v Chesham United	2-2
19	Hounslow v Southall	1-3
	Windsor & Eton v Cowley	3-1
20	Redhill v Nunhead	3-2
	Tooting Town v Wimbledon	2-1
21	Aldershot v Guildford City	0-1
	Thornycrofts (Basingstoke) v Aldershot Traction Co.	0-6
22	Folkestone v Callender Athletic	9-0
	Sheppey United v Bromley	1-2
23	Eastbourne Old Comrades v Chichester	1-1
	Tunbridge Wells Rangers v Southwick	4-4
24	Portland United v Cowes	1-0
	RAOC Hilsea v RM Portsmouth	1-0
25	Radstock Town v Welton Rovers	8-3
	Salisbury Corinthians v Salisbury City (1)	0-3
26	Bristol St George v Barry	1-3
	Yeovil & Petter's United v Wells City	5-2
5r	Horwich RMI v Dick, Kerrs	3-0
10r	Methley Perseverance v Denaby United	2-2e
r	Mexborough v Cudworth Village	4-1
13r	Newark Town v Grantham	2-3
17r	GER Romford v Grays Athletic	2-3
18r	Chesham United v Wood Green Town	9-0
23r	Chichester v Eastbourne Old Comrades	8-1
r	Southwick v Tunbridge Wells Rangers	0-1
10r2	Methley Perseverance v Denaby United	2-3 N

Qualifying Round Three

1	Jarrow v Scotswood	2-0
2	Annfield Plain v Shildon	1-1
3	York City v Bridlington Town (1)	3-0
4	Penrith v Egremont	4-1
5	Horwich RMI v Morecambe	3-1
6	Manchester North End v Hurst	4-1
7	Rhyl Athletic v Macclesfield Town	2-2
8	Worcester City v Stafford Rangers	4-2
9	Boston (1) v Scunthorpe United	0-1
10	Denaby United v Mexborough	2-1
11	Ardsley Athletic v Treeton Reading Room	4-1
12	Shirebrook v Grassmoor	1-0
13	Sutton Junction v Grantham	1-6
14	Loughborough Corinthians v Gresley Rovers	1-0
15	Bedford Town (1) v Wellingborough Town	2-2
16	Lowestoft Town v King's Lynn	6-0
17	Walthamstow Avenue v Grays Athletic	2-2
18	Chesham United v Finchley	2-2
19	Windsor & Eton v Southall	2-4
20	Tooting Town v Redhill	5-1
21	Aldershot Traction Co. v Guildford City	3-6
22	Folkestone v Bromley	8-3
23	Tunbridge Wells Rangers v Chichester	10-0
24	Portland United v RAOC Hilsea	5-1
25	Salisbury City (1) v Radstock Town	2-0
26	Barry v Yeovil & Petter's United	2-2
2r	Shildon v Annfield Plain	0-2
7r	Macclesfield Town v Rhyl Athletic	0-0
15r	Wellingborough Town v Bedford Town (1)	3-1
17r	Grays Athletic v Walthamstow Avenue	3-4e
18r	Finchley v Chesham United	2-2
26r	Yeovil & Petter's United v Barry	0-0
7r2	Macclesfield Town v Rhyl Athletic	0-2
18r2	Chesham United v Finchley	5-1 N
26r2	Yeovil & Petter's United v Barry	3-1 N

Qualifying Round Four

Ardsley Athletic v Mansfield Town	2-2
Chilton Colliery Recreation v Spennymoor United	1-2
Clapton v Barking	1-1
Durham City v Scarborough	0-3
Folkestone v Chatham	0-3
Gainsborough Trinity v Denaby United	1-0
Grantham v Scunthorpe United	2-1
Guildford City v London Caledonians	3-1
Jarrow v York City	0-0
Kettering Town v St Albans City	6-1
Kingstonian v Dulwich Hamlet	2-2
Lowestoft Town v Peterborough & Fletton Utd.	1-5
Penrith v Lancaster Town	4-9
Poole v Portland United	2-0
Rhyl Athletic v Manchester North End	3-2
Salisbury City (1) v Yeovil & Petter's United	3-3
Shirebrook v Loughborough Corinthians	2-1
Sittingbourne v Tunbridge Wells Rangers	2-1
Southall v Chesham United	2-1
Tooting Town v Woking	1-3
Walthamstow Avenue v Ilford	1-1
Wellingborough Town v Cambridge Town	3-1
West Stanley v Annfield Plain	3-3
Worcester City v Wellington Town	2-0
Workington v Horwich RMI	2-2
r Annfield Plain v West Stanley	1-1e
r Barking v Clapton	4-0
r Dulwich Hamlet v Kingstonian	4-4e
r Horwich RMI v Workington	3-0
r Ilford v Walthamstow Avenue	5-0
r Mansfield Town v Ardsley Athletic	2-0
r Yeovil & Petter's United v Salisbury City (1)	5-2
r York City v Jarrow	2-2e
r2 Annfield Plain v West Stanley	1-0 N
r Jarrow v York City	2-3 N
r Kingstonian v Dulwich Hamlet	2-3 N

Round One

Accrington Stanley v South Shields	2-1
Annfield Plain v Southport	1-4
Bradford City v Doncaster Rovers	4-1
Brentford v Brighton & Hove Albion	4-1
Bristol Rovers v Wellingborough Town	2-1
Chesterfield v Rochdale	3-2
Coventry City v Fulham	1-4
Crystal Palace v Kettering Town	2-0
Darlington v New Brighton	3-0
Exeter City v Barking	6-0
Gainsborough Trinity v Crewe Alexandra	3-1
Gillingham v Torquay United	0-0
Grantham v Rhyl Athletic	1-0
Guildford City v Queen's Park Rangers	4-2
Horwich RMI v Scarborough	1-2
Lancaster Town v Lincoln City	1-3
Leyton v Watford	0-2
Luton Town v Southend United	2-1
Merthyr Town v Dulwich Hamlet	4-2
Newport County v Woking	7-0
Northfleet United v Ilford	5-2
Norwich City v Chatham	6-1
Peterborough & Fletton Utd. v Charlton Athletic	0-2
Poole v Bournemouth	1-4
Shirebrook v Mansfield Town	2-4
Sittingbourne v Southall	2-1
Spennymoor United v Hartlepools United	5-2
Stockport County v Halifax Town	1-0
Tranmere Rovers v Rotherham United	2-1
Walsall v Worcester City	3-1
Wigan Borough v Ashington	2-0
Wrexham v Carlisle United	0-1
Yeovil & Petter's United v Plymouth Argyle	1-4
York City v Barrow	0-1
r Torquay United v Gillingham	5-1

Round Two

Accrington Stanley v Spennymoor United	7-0
Barrow v Mansfield Town	1-2
Brentford v Plymouth Argyle	0-1
Carlisle United v Lincoln City	0-1
Crystal Palace v Bristol Rovers	3-1
Fulham v Luton Town	0-0
Gainsborough Trinity v Chesterfield	2-3
Guildford City v Bournemouth	1-5
Northfleet United v Charlton Athletic	1-5
Norwich City v Newport County	6-0
Scarborough v Darlington	2-2
Stockport County v Southport	3-0
Torquay United v Exeter City	0-1
Tranmere Rovers v Bradford City	0-1
Walsall v Sittingbourne	2-1
Watford v Merthyr Town	2-0
Wigan Borough v Grantham	2-1
r Darlington v Scarborough	2-1
r Luton Town v Fulham	4-1

Round Three

Accrington Stanley v Bournemouth	1-1
Arsenal v Stoke City	2-1
Aston Villa v Cardiff City	6-1
Birmingham v Manchester City	3-1
Blackburn Rovers v Barnsley	1-0
Bolton Wanderers v Oldham Athletic	2-0
Bradford City v Stockport County	2-0
Bristol City v Liverpool	0-2
Burnley v Sheffield United	2-1
Chelsea v Everton	2-0
Chesterfield v Huddersfield Town	1-7
Darlington v Bury	2-6
Derby County v Notts County	4-3
Exeter City v Leeds United	2-2
Grimsby Town v West Bromwich Albion	1-1
Hull City v Bradford Park Avenue	1-1
Lincoln City v Leicester City	0-1
Luton Town v Crystal Palace	0-0
Millwall v Northampton Town	1-1
Norwich City v Corinthians	0-5
Nottingham Forest v Swansea Town	1-2
Plymouth Argyle v Blackpool	3-0
Port Vale v Manchester United	0-3
Portsmouth v Charlton Athletic	2-1
Reading v Tottenham Hotspur	2-0
Southampton v Clapton Orient	0-0
Swindon Town v Newcastle United	2-0
Walsall v Middlesbrough	1-1
Watford v Preston North End	1-0
West Ham United v Sunderland	1-0
Wigan Borough v Sheffield Wednesday	1-3
Wolverhampton Wan. v Mansfield Town	0-1
r Bournemouth v Accrington Stanley	2-0
r Bradford Park Avenue v Hull City	3-1
r Clapton Orient v Southampton	2-1
r Crystal Palace v Luton Town	7-0
r Leeds United v Exeter City	5-1
r Middlesbrough v Walsall	5-1
r Northampton Town v Millwall	2-2e
r West Bromwich Albion v Grimsby Town	2-0
r2 Millwall v Northampton Town	2-0 N

Round Four

Arsenal v Mansfield Town	2-0
Aston Villa v Clapton Orient	0-0
Blackburn Rovers v Derby County	1-1
Bournemouth v Watford	6-4
Burnley v Swindon Town	3-3
Chelsea v Birmingham	1-0
Huddersfield Town v Leeds United	3-0
Leicester City v Swansea Town	1-0
Liverpool v Bolton Wanderers	0-0
Manchester United v Bury	0-1
Millwall v Crystal Palace	0-0
Plymouth Argyle v Bradford Park Avenue	0-1
Portsmouth v Bradford City	2-0
Reading v Sheffield Wednesday	1-0
West Bromwich Albion v Middlesbrough	1-0
West Ham United v Corinthians	3-0
r Bolton Wanderers v Liverpool	5-2e
r Clapton Orient v Aston Villa	0-8
r Crystal Palace v Millwall	5-3
r Derby County v Blackburn Rovers	0-3
r Swindon Town v Burnley	3-2

Round Five

Blackburn Rovers v Bury	1-0
Bournemouth v West Ham United	1-1
Chelsea v Portsmouth	1-1
Huddersfield Town v Crystal Palace	5-2
Leicester City v Bolton Wanderers	1-2
Reading v Aston Villa	1-3
Swindon Town v Arsenal	0-0
West Bromwich Albion v Bradford Park Avenue	6-0
r Arsenal v Swindon Town	1-0
r Portsmouth v Chelsea	1-0
r West Ham United v Bournemouth	3-1

Round Six

Aston Villa v Arsenal	1-0
Blackburn Rovers v Bolton Wanderers	1-1
Portsmouth v West Ham United	3-2
West Bromwich Albion v Huddersfield Town	1-1
r Bolton Wanderers v Blackburn Rovers	2-1
r Huddersfield Town v West Bromwich Albion	2-1

Semi Finals

Bolton Wanderers v Huddersfield Town	3-1 N
Portsmouth v Aston Villa	1-0 N

Final

Bolton Wanderers v Portsmouth	2-0 N

1929/30

Extra Preliminary Round

2	Chopwell Institute v Willington	1-2
	Cockfield v West Hartlepool	2-1
	Evenwood Town v West Auckland Town	3-1
	Murton CW v Horden CW	6-2
	Tow Law Town v Spen Black & White	2-4

1929/30

7 Congleton Town v Linotype & Machinery 3-2
8 Bloxwich Strollers v Bilston United 5-2
Brierley Hill Alliance v Hereford United 3-2
Darlaston v Wolverhampton Amateur 7-1
Leamington Town v Birmingham Corp. Tramways 4-0
Nuneaton Town v Walsall Phoenix 13-2
Oswestry Town v Bournville Athletic 6-2
Redditch v Headingley 5-2
Shrewsbury Town v Cannock Town 12-0
Walsall LMS v Bromsgrove Rovers 2-2
Wellington Town v Evesham Town 1-1
Whitchurch v Stourbridge 4-4
Willenhall v Hednesford Town 2-3
9 Humber United v Pickering St George's 8-0
16 Abbey United (Cambs) v Newmarket Town 2-1
Harwich & Parkeston v Thetford Town 7-0
Leiston Works Athletic v Severalls Athletic 3-0
Norwich CEYMS v Gorleston 4-3
Sheringham v Cromer 2-1
18 Apsley v Standard Telephones 4-3
Cheshunt v Welwyn Garden City 5-0
Leavesden Mental Hospital v Barnet 0-0
Old Lyonian v Haywards Sports 1-8
Waltham Comrades v Wealdstone 1-6
Ware v Hertford Town 2-3
24 New Milton v Castle Hill 0-3
Newport (IOW) v Fareham 4-2
25 Chippenham Town v Garrards Athletic 1-8
Swindon Victoria v Frome Town 4-3
Warminster Town v Purton West End 4-1
26 Ebbw Vale v St Cuthbert's 2-1
Keynsham v Green Waves (Plymouth) wo/s
Minehead v J.S. Fry & Sons 2-4
Mount Hill Enterprise v Glastonbury 5-2
Street v St Philips Athletic 3-2
Taunton Town (1) v Hanham Athletic 3-0
8r Bromsgrove Rovers v Walsall LMS 3-5
r Evesham Town v Wellington Town 2-2e
r Whitchurch v Stourbridge wo/s
18r Barnet v Leavesden Mental Hospital 3-2e
8r2 Wellington Town v Evesham Town 3-2

Preliminary Round

1 Birtley v Bedlington United 2-2
Felling Colliery v Hobson Wanderers 1-0
Gosforth & Coxlodge v Pelaw 1-2
Jarrow v St Peter's Albion 1-1
Scotswood v Walker Park 3-1
Usworth Colliery v Howdon British Legion 1-1
Wallsend v Walker Celtic 3-0
Washington Colliery v Shankhouse 4-2
2 Annfield Plain v Dipton United 2-1
Burnhope Institute v Murton CW 0-0
Cockfield v Spen Black & White 2-1
Esh Winning (1) v Ferryhill Athletic 3-3
Evenwood Town v Langley Park 3-0
Shildon v Bishop Auckland 3-1
White-le-Head Rangers v Chilton Colliery Recreation 0-0
Willington v Consett 4-2
4 Cleator Moor Celtic v Frizington Athletic 1-2
Kendal Town v Netherfield (Kendal) 1-6
Keswick v Aspatria Athletic 0-3
Windermere v Bowthorn Recreation 1-0
Workington v Moss Bay United 7-0
5 Adlington v Westhoughton 4-3
Breightmet United v Skelmersdale United 4-2
Burscough Rangers v Great Harwood 6-3
Chorley v Darwen 2-1
Lancaster Town v Walsden United 5-1
Lytham v Morecambe 5-3
6 Bootle Celtic v Glossop 4-1
Earle v Timperley 3-3
Ellesmere Port Town v Whiston 3-2
Hurst v Manchester Central 1-3
Manchester North End v Northern Nomads 4-4
Marine v Ellesmere Port Cement 2-0
Prescot Cables v High Park 3-1
Runcorn v Stalybridge Celtic 3-2
7 Colwyn Bay v Nantwich 6-1
Connah's Quay v Caernarvon Athletic 1-1
Llandudno v Lostock Gralam 5-1
Macclesfield Town v Bangor City 6-0
Rhyl Athletic v Northwich Victoria 4-1
Sandbach Ramblers v Congleton Town 1-1
Winsford United v Altrincham 3-0
Witton Albion v Barnton Victoria 2-0
8 Brierley Hill Alliance v Darlaston 1-1
Cradley Heath St Luke's v Walsall LMS 4-0
Leamington Town v Oakengates Town 3-6
Nuneaton Town v Hednesford Town 3-2
Redditch v Stafford Rangers 1-4
Shrewsbury Town v Bloxwich Strollers 5-2
Wellington Town v Worcester City 5-0
Whitchurch v Oswestry Town 2-2
9 Barton Town (1) v British Oil & Cake Mills 4-0
Broughton Rangers v Humber United 4-0
Cleethorpes Town v Brigg Town 0-1
Goole Town v Louth Town 5-1
Grimsby Haycroft Rovers v Marfleet 3-0
Normanby Park Steel Works v Spalding United 2-1
Selby OCO v Frodingham & Appleby Ath. 7-1
Selby Town v Scunthorpe United 1-3
10 Altofts West Riding Col. v Mexborough 1-4 v
Cudworth Village v Frickley Colliery 1-0
Darfield v Harrogate 2-3
Denaby United v Wombwell 1-5
Horsforth v Methley Perseverance 2-4
Luddendenfoot v Farsley Celtic 0-4
Monckton Athletic v South Kirkby Colliery 1-4
Wath Athletic v Guiseley 8-0
11 Goldthorpe United v Hatfield Main 1-0
Grimethorpe Colliery Institute v Pilkington Recreati 1-1
Mapplewell & Staincross v Brodsworth Main Colliery 0-2
Owston Park Rangers v Ardsley Athletic 2-1
Sheffield v Maltby Main Colliery wo/s
Silverwood Colliery v Norton Woodseats 3-0
Worksop Town v Hallam 2-1
13 Teversal & Silverhill CW v Ransome & Marles 0-2
15 Baldock Town v Market Harborough Town 1-4
Bedford Town (1) v Leighton United 4-2
Biggleswade & District v Stamford 4-0
Higham Ferrers Town v Rothwell Town 2-0
Kempston Rovers v Desborough Town 0-2
Peterbro' Westwood Works v Wolverton Town 2-3
Rushden Town v Waterlows (Dunstable) 1-3
Wellingborough Town v Letchworth Town 5-2
16 Cambridge Town v King's Lynn 2-0
Clacton Town v Leiston Works Athletic 1-6
Colchester Town v Harwich & Parkeston 2-1
Crittall Athletic v Felixstowe Town 3-1
Kirkley & Waveney v Great Yarmouth Town 2-0
Norwich CEYMS v Norwich Priory Athletic 2-3
Sheringham v Lowestoft Town 1-1
Wisbech Town v Abbey United (Cambs) 0-4
17 Barking v Grays Thurrock United 2-4
Chelmsford v Dagenham Town 0-1
Clapton v Brentwood & Warley 3-0
GER Romford v Brentwood Mental Hospital 0-1
Grays Athletic v Romford (2) 4-1
Tilbury v Leytonstone 1-0
Tufnell Park v Custom House 3-0
Walthamstow Avenue v Walthamstow Grange 3-3
18 Apsley v Berkhamsted Town 8-2
Bishop's Stortford v Chesham United 1-4
Cheshunt v Wood Green Town 4-2
Haywards Sports v Barnet 1-5
Hendon Town v Aylesbury United 1-1
Hertford Town v Finchley 2-2
Watford Old Boys v Enfield 0-1
Wealdstone v St Albans City 4-0
19 Abingdon Town v Marlow 5-2
Hampstead Town v Hayes 2-0
Henley Town v Uxbridge 1-3
Hounslow v Cowley 3-3
Maidenhead United v Wycombe Wanderers 1-0
Oxford City v Newbury Town 5-1
Thatcham v RAF Uxbridge 1-2
Witney Town v Slough 3-1
20 Carshalton Athletic v Redhill 0-5
Epsom Town v Beddington Corner 8-3
Reigate Priory v West Norwood 3-3
Sutton United v Leyland Motors (Kingston) 6-1
Wallington v Dorking 1-5
Wimbledon v Polytechnic 15-2
Woking v Mitcham Wanderers 1-2
21 Camberley & Yorktown v Winchester City 1-2
Godalming v Basingstoke 6-1
Hersham v Wellington Works wo/s
Metropolitan Police v RAMC Aldershot 0-1
Staines Town v Guildford 1-1
Weybridge v Egham 3-3
22 Bexleyheath Town v Beckenham 3-1
Foots Cray v Margate 0-2
Whitstable v Erith & Belvedere 0-1
23 East Grinstead v Newhaven 1-1
Littlehampton v Bexhill 4-4
Worthing v Vernon Athletic 4-0
24 Dorchester Town v Bournemouth Tramways 1-2
Emsworth v Salisbury City (1) 2-2
Newport (IOW) v Cowes 2-6
Osborne Athletic v Portsmouth Gas Company 2-6
RM Portsmouth v Gosport 4-3
Ryde Sports v RAOC Hilsea 1-1
Salisbury Corinthians v Castle Hill 3-1
Weymouth v Portland United 2-3
25 Chippenham Rovers v Radstock Town 2-3
Coleford Athletic v Garrards Athletic 2-4
Devizes Town v Bath City 2-10
Melksham v Calne & Harris United 2-2
Paulton Rovers v Swindon Corinthians 1-1
Swindon Victoria v Welton Rovers 2-2
Trowbridge Town v Clandown 3-0
Warminster Town v Spencer Moulton 3-1
26 Barry v Taunton Town (1) 2-1
Bristol St George v Ebbw Vale 0-3
Clevedon v J.S. Fry & Sons 3-1
Keynsham v Lovells Athletic 2-4
St Austell v Plymouth Civil Service 1-1
Street v Mount Hill Enterprise 1-1
Wells City v Weston-Super-Mare 1-2
Yeovil & Petter's United v Kingswood 3-2
1r Bedlington United v Birtley 3-1
r Howdon British Legion v Usworth Colliery 1-2
r St Peter's Albion v Jarrow 0-1
2r Chilton Colliery Recreation v White-le-Head Rangers 3-5
r Ferryhill Athletic v Esh Winning (1) 4-2
r Murton CW v Burnhope Institute 2-0
6r Northern Nomads v Manchester North End 3-4
r Timperley v Earle 1-0 v
7r Caernarvon Athletic v Connah's Quay 3-2
r Congleton Town v Sandbach Ramblers 3-0
8r Darlaston v Brierley Hill Alliance 1-0
r Oswestry Town v Whitchurch 7-1
10r Mexborough v Altofts West Riding Col. 7-2
11r Pilkington Recreation v Grimethorpe Colliery Inst. 3-0
16r Lowestoft Town v Sheringham 3-0
17r Walthamstow Grange v Walthamstow Avenue 2-7
18r Aylesbury United v Hendon Town 2-0
r Finchley v Hertford Town 2-1
19r Cowley v Hounslow 0-2
20r West Norwood v Reigate Priory 7-0
21r Egham v Weybridge 7-1
r Guildford v Staines Town 3-1
23r Littlehampton v Bexhill 2-1
r Newhaven v East Grinstead 2-0
24r RAOC Hilsea v Ryde Sports 3-2
r Salisbury City (1) v Emsworth 4-0
25r Calne & Harris United v Melksham 0-2
r Swindon Corinthians v Paulton Rovers 5-0
r Welton Rovers v Swindon Victoria 3-0
26r Mount Hill Enterprise v Street 1-2e
r Plymouth Civil Service v St Austell 2-1
6r2 Earle v Timperley 3-1 N

Qualifying Round One

1 Felling Colliery v Usworth Colliery 5-3
Jarrow v Pelaw 1-1
Scotswood v Bedlington United 3-1
Wallsend v Washington Colliery 1-1
2 Annfield Plain v White-le-Head Rangers 4-1
Evenwood Town v Ferryhill Athletic 4-0
Shildon v Murton CW 3-0
Willington v Cockfield 3-1
3 Filey Town v Loftus Albion 2-1
South Bank v South Bank East End 2-1
Stockton v Carlin How 3-0
Whitby United v Normanby Mangnesite 4-3
4 Frizington Athletic v Aspatria Athletic 0-2
Netherfield (Kendal) v Egremont 3-1
Ulverston Town v Windermere 7-0
Workington v Penrith 9-1
5 Burscough Rangers v Adlington 4-4
Horwich RMI v Breightmet United 1-0
Lancaster Town v Dick, Kerrs 7-2
Lytham v Chorley 2-0
6 Manchester Central v Marine 7-1
Manchester North End v Ellesmere Port Town 3-1
Prescot Cables v Bootle Celtic 7-0
Runcorn v Earle 4-3
7 Caernarvon Athletic v Congleton Town 9-0
Colwyn Bay v Witton Albion 7-0
Llandudno v Winsford United 1-1
Macclesfield Town v Rhyl Athletic 4-3
8 Darlaston v Cradley Heath St Luke's 1-3
Oakengates Town v Nuneaton Town 2-1
Stafford Rangers v Oswestry Town 0-0
Wellington Town v Shrewsbury Town 1-0
9 Broughton Rangers v Barton Town (1) 2-1
Goole Town v Normanby Park Steel Works 4-0
Grimsby Haycroft Rovers v Brigg Town 2-5
Scunthorpe United v Selby OCO 1-0
10 Harrogate v Cudworth Village 9-1
Methley Perseverance v Mexborough 2-7
Wath Athletic v South Kirkby Colliery 0-3
Wombwell v Farsley Celtic 7-1
11 Goldthorpe United v Treeton wo/s
Pilkington Recreation v Silverwood Colliery 2-1
Sheffield v Brodsworth Main Colliery 1-2
Worksop Town v Owston Park Rangers 7-0
12 Grassmoor v South Normanton Colliery 1-0
Ilkeston United v Staveley Town 4-1
Ripley Town v Heanor Town 3-2
Shirebrook v Matlock Town 4-1
13 Boots Athletic v Ransome & Marles 3-3
Sneinton v Newark Town 2-4
Sutton Junction v Lenton 7-1
Sutton Town v Basford United 7-1
14 Burton Town v Moira United 8-0
Gresley Rovers - Bye
Hinckley United (1) v Gresley Colliery 2-2
Loughborough Corinthians - Bye
15 Desborough Town v Wellingborough Town 2-4
Higham Ferrers Town v Biggleswade & District 0-1
Market Harborough Town v Bedford Town (1) 6-0
Waterlows (Dunstable) v Wolverton Town 3-1
16 Abbey United (Cambs) v Crittall Athletic 0-5
Colchester Town v Norwich Priory Athletic 4-2
Kirkley & Waveney v Cambridge Town 1-4
Leiston Works Athletic v Lowestoft Town 2-0
17 Dagenham Town v Grays Athletic 5-0
Grays Thurrock United v Clapton 1-2
Tilbury v Walthamstow Avenue 2-0
Tufnell Park v Brentwood Mental Hospital 2-2

1929/30

18	Chesham United v Aylesbury United	3-0
	Cheshunt v Enfield	1-0
	Finchley v Barnet	2-2
	Wealdstone v Apsley	3-1
19	Abingdon Town v Hampstead Town	0-7
	Maidenhead United v RAF Uxbridge	3-3
	Oxford City v Uxbridge	5-3
	Witney Town v Hounslow	4-2
20	Epsom Town v Dorking	4-2
	Mitcham Wanderers v Sutton United	3-0
	Tooting Town v Redhill	2-1
	Wimbledon v West Norwood	3-0
21	Aldershot Traction Co. v Egham	0-0
	Godalming v Guildford	5-1
	Hersham v Winchester City	0-3
	Thornycrofts (Basingstoke) v RAMC Aldershot	2-3
22	Bexleyheath Town v Woolwich Polytechnic	2-0
	Erith & Belvedere v Callender Athletic	4-2
	Margate v Bostall Heath	5-0
	RM Chatham v Cray Wanderers	3-2
23	Bognor Regis Town v Tunbridge Wells Rangers	0-4
	Littlehampton v Eastbourne Old Comrades	2-4
	Southwick v Newhaven	4-1
	Worthing v Chichester	1-2
24	Cowes v Bournemouth Tramways	0-1
	RAOC Hilsea v Portland United	0-0
	RM Portsmouth v Portsmouth Gas Company	3-0
	Salisbury Corinthians v Salisbury City (1)	2-0
25	Bath City v Swindon Corinthians	6-0
	Garrards Athletic v Melksham	4-0
	Trowbridge Town v Radstock Town	4-0
	Welton Rovers v Warminster Town	3-2
26	Lovells Athletic v Clevedon	5-2
	Street v Barry	0-3
	Weston-Super-Mare v Plymouth Civil Service	3-2e
	Yeovil & Petter's United v Ebbw Vale	2-1
1r	Pelaw v Jarrow	1-3
r	Washington Colliery v Wallsend	3-2
5r	Adlington v Burscough Rangers	2-2e
7r	Llandudno v Winsford United	1-2 d
8r	Oswestry Town v Stafford Rangers	4-4
13r	Ransome & Marles v Boots Athletic	0-3
14r	Hinckley United (1) v Gresley Colliery	3-1
17r	Brentwood Mental Hospital v Tufnell Park	1-4
18r	Barnet v Finchley	3-1e
19r	RAF Uxbridge v Maidenhead United	1-6
21r	Egham v Aldershot Traction Co.	1-3
24r	Portland United v RAOC Hilsea	3-0
5r2	Adlington v Burscough Rangers	2-4 N
8r2	Oswestry Town v Stafford Rangers	2-3 N

Qualifying Round Two

1	Scotswood v Jarrow	1-0
	Washington Colliery v Felling Colliery	3-1
2	Shildon v Annfield Plain	3-1
	Willington v Evenwood Town	1-1
3	South Bank v Stockton	2-2
	Whitby United v Filey Town	8-2
4	Netherfield (Kendal) v Ulverston Town	1-2
	Workington v Aspatria Athletic	6-0
5	Horwich RMI v Lancaster Town	1-1
	Lytham v Burscough Rangers	4-1
6	Manchester Central v Runcorn	1-0
	Prescot Cables v Manchester North End	5-2
7	Llandudno v Colwyn Bay	3-2
	Macclesfield Town v Caernarvon Athletic	2-2
8	Cradley Heath St Luke's v Stafford Rangers	4-3
	Oakengates Town v Wellington Town	2-2
9	Broughton Rangers v Brigg Town	2-2
	Scunthorpe United v Goole Town	2-1
10	South Kirkby Colliery v Harrogate	2-0
	Wombwell v Mexborough	1-2
11	Brodsworth Main Colliery v Pilkington Recreation	4-2
	Worksop Town v Goldthorpe United	1-1
12	Grassmoor v Ilkeston United	1-0
	Ripley Town v Shirebrook	2-4
13	Boots Athletic v Sutton Town	7-3
	Newark Town v Sutton Junction	3-2
14	Burton Town v Loughborough Corinthians	7-1
	Gresley Rovers v Hinckley United (1)	3-3
15	Biggleswade & District v Waterlows (Dunstable)	5-2
	Market Harborough Town v Wellingborough Town	4-0
16	Cambridge Town v Leiston Works Athletic	3-0
	Crittall Athletic v Colchester Town	3-2
17	Clapton v Dagenham Town	0-7
	Tufnell Park v Tilbury	2-0
18	Barnet v Cheshunt	0-4
	Wealdstone v Chesham United	2-0
19	Hampstead Town v Oxford City	2-1
	Maidenhead United v Witney Town	6-1
20	Epsom Town v Mitcham Wanderers	1-0
	Tooting Town v Wimbledon	2-6
21	Godalming v Aldershot Traction Co.	1-1
	Winchester City v RAMC Aldershot	1-0
22	Bexleyheath Town v Margate	0-0
	RM Chatham v Erith & Belvedere	5-2
23	Southwick v Eastbourne Old Comrades	2-1
	Tunbridge Wells Rangers v Chichester	4-0
24	Portland United v Bournemouth Tramways	2-0
	Salisbury Corinthians v RM Portsmouth	2-1e
25	Bath City v Garrards Athletic	7-1
	Trowbridge Town v Welton Rovers	2-2
26	Lovells Athletic v Barry	0-1
	Yeovil & Petter's United v Weston-Super-Mare	5-0
2r	Evenwood Town v Willington	0-1
3r	Stockton v South Bank	3-0
5r	Lancaster Town v Horwich RMI	5-3
7r	Caernarvon Athletic v Macclesfield Town	4-2
8r	Wellington Town v Oakengates Town	4-2
9r	Brigg Town v Broughton Rangers	0-6
11r	Worksop Town v Goldthorpe United	4-2
14r	Hinckley United (1) v Gresley Rovers	1-0
21r	Aldershot Traction Co. v Godalming	6-0
22r	Margate v Bexleyheath Town	2-0
25r	Welton Rovers v Trowbridge Town	1-4

Qualifying Round Three

1	Scotswood v Washington Colliery	1-0
2	Shildon v Willington	3-2
3	Stockton v Whitby United	5-0
4	Workington v Ulverston Town	2-2
5	Lancaster Town v Lytham	4-2
6	Manchester Central v Prescot Cables	1-1
7	Caernarvon Athletic v Llandudno	2-0
8	Wellington Town v Cradley Heath St Luke's	7-2
9	Scunthorpe United v Broughton Rangers	7-0
10	South Kirkby Colliery v Mexborough	2-0
11	Worksop Town v Brodsworth Main Colliery	3-1
12	Grassmoor v Shirebrook	1-2
13	Newark Town v Boots Athletic	4-1
14	Burton Town v Hinckley United (1)	5-2
15	Market Harborough Town v Biggleswade & District	2-2
16	Crittall Athletic v Cambridge Town	3-3
17	Tufnell Park v Dagenham Town	3-4
18	Cheshunt v Wealdstone	1-1
19	Maidenhead United v Hampstead Town	6-0
20	Wimbledon v Epsom Town	7-1
21	Aldershot Traction Co. v Winchester City	1-1
22	Margate v RM Chatham	1-1
23	Tunbridge Wells Rangers v Southwick	4-3
24	Portland United v Salisbury Corinthians	2-0
25	Bath City v Trowbridge Town	5-2
26	Barry v Yeovil & Petter's United	4-3
4r	Ulverston Town v Workington	0-2
6r	Prescot Cables v Manchester Central	1-3
15r	Biggleswade & District v Market Harborough Town	1-1e
16r	Cambridge Town v Crittall Athletic	2-1
18r	Wealdstone v Cheshunt	2-0
21r	Winchester City v Aldershot Traction Co.	1-0
22r	RM Chatham v Margate	4-4e
15r2	Biggleswade & District v Market Harborough Town	6-1 N
22r2	RM Chatham v Margate	1-4 N

Qualifying Round Four

	Aldershot v Kingstonian	11-1
	Ashington v Stockton	4-0
	Burton Town v Caernarvon Athletic	0-2
	Cambridge Town v Kettering Town	0-3
	Dagenham Town v London Caledonians	1-0
	Dartford v Folkestone	0-0
	Dulwich Hamlet v Wealdstone	7-7
	Grantham v Newark Town	4-4
	Lancaster Town v Workington	2-2
	Nunhead v Maidenhead United	3-0
	Peterborough & Fletton Utd. v Biggleswade & District	6-1
	Poole v Bath City	1-4
	Portland United v Barry	1-1
	Scarborough v York City	1-3
	Scotswood v Shildon	2-1 D
	Scunthorpe United v South Kirkby Colliery	6-1
	Sheppey United v Margate	2-4
	Shirebrook v Manchester Central	0-2
	Sittingbourne v Northfleet United	2-4
	Southall v Leyton	0-3
	Thames v Winchester City	3-0
	Tunbridge Wells Rangers v Chatham	4-1
	Wellington Town v Boston (1)	2-2
	Wimbledon v Guildford City	5-1
	Worksop Town v Gainsborough Trinity	1-5
r	Barry v Portland United	2-0
r	Boston (1) v Wellington Town	2-3
r	Folkestone v Dartford	3-3
r	Newark Town v Grantham	1-0
r	Wealdstone v Dulwich Hamlet	1-2
r	Workington v Lancaster Town	2-2
r2	Dartford v Folkestone	3-4 N
r2	Lancaster Town v Workington	3-1 N

Round One

	Accrington Stanley v Rochdale	3-1
	Aldershot v Northampton Town	0-1
	Barrow v Newark Town	1-0
	Barry v Dagenham Town	0-0
	Bournemouth v Torquay United	2-0
	Brighton & Hove Albion v Peterborough & Fletton Utd.	4-0
	Caernarvon Athletic v Darlington	4-2
	Carlisle United v Halifax Town	2-0
	Clapton Orient v Folkestone	0-0
	Doncaster Rovers v Shildon	0-0
	Dulwich Hamlet v Plymouth Argyle	0-3
	Fulham v Thames	4-0
	Gainsborough Trinity v Port Vale	0-0
	Gillingham v Margate	0-2
	Ilford v Watford	0-3
	Leyton v Merthyr Town	4-1
	Lincoln City v Wigan Borough	3-1
	Luton Town v Queen's Park Rangers	2-3
	Mansfield Town v Manchester Central	0-2
	Nelson v Crewe Alexandra	0-3
	New Brighton v Lancaster Town	4-1
	Newport County v Kettering Town	3-2
	Norwich City v Coventry City	3-3
	Nunhead v Bristol Rovers	0-2
	Rotherham United v Ashington	3-0
	Scunthorpe United v Hartlepools United	1-0
	South Shields v Wrexham	2-4
	Southend United v Brentford	1-0
	Southport v Chesterfield	0-0
	Tunbridge Wells Rangers v Bath City	1-3
	Walsall v Exeter City	1-0
	Wellington Town v Stockport County	1-4
	Wimbledon v Northfleet United	1-4
	York City v Tranmere Rovers	2-2
r	Chesterfield v Southport	3-2
r	Coventry City v Norwich City	2-0
r	Dagenham Town v Barry	0-1 N
r	Folkestone v Clapton Orient	2-2e
r	Port Vale v Gainsborough Trinity	5-0
r	Shildon v Doncaster Rovers	1-1e
r	Tranmere Rovers v York City	0-1
r2	Clapton Orient v Folkestone	4-1 N
r2	Doncaster Rovers v Shildon	3-0 N

Round Two

	Brighton & Hove Albion v Barry	4-1
	Bristol Rovers v Accrington Stanley	4-1
	Caernarvon Athletic v Bournemouth	1-1
	Carlisle United v Crewe Alexandra	4-2
	Chesterfield v Port Vale	2-0
	Clapton Orient v Northfleet United	2-0
	Coventry City v Bath City	7-1
	Doncaster Rovers v New Brighton	1-0
	Leyton v Fulham	1-4
	Manchester Central v Wrexham	0-1
	Newport County v Walsall	2-3
	Northampton Town v Margate	6-0
	Queen's Park Rangers v Lincoln City	2-1
	Scunthorpe United v Rotherham United	3-3
	Southend United v York City	1-4
	Stockport County v Barrow	4-0
	Watford v Plymouth Argyle	1-1
r	Bournemouth v Caernarvon Athletic	5-2
r	Plymouth Argyle v Watford	3-0
r	Rotherham United v Scunthorpe United	5-4

Round Three

	Arsenal v Chelsea	2-0
	Aston Villa v Reading	5-1
	Barnsley v Bradford Park Avenue	0-1
	Birmingham v Bolton Wanderers	1-0
	Blackburn Rovers v Northampton Town	4-1
	Blackpool v Stockport County	2-1
	Bradford City v Southampton	4-1
	Brighton & Hove Albion v Grimsby Town	1-1
	Bury v Huddersfield Town	0-0
	Carlisle United v Everton	2-4
	Charlton Athletic v Queen's Park Rangers	1-1
	Chesterfield v Middlesbrough	1-1
	Clapton Orient v Bristol Rovers	1-0
	Corinthians v Millwall	2-2
	Coventry City v Sunderland	1-2
	Derby County v Bristol City	5-1
	Doncaster Rovers v Stoke City	1-0
	Fulham v Bournemouth	1-1
	Leeds United v Crystal Palace	8-1
	Liverpool v Cardiff City	1-2
	Manchester United v Swindon Town	0-2
	Newcastle United v York City	1-1
	Oldham Athletic v Wolverhampton Wan.	1-0
	Plymouth Argyle v Hull City	3-4
	Portsmouth v Preston North End	2-0
	Rotherham United v Nottingham Forest	0-5
	Sheffield United v Leicester City	2-1
	Sheffield Wednesday v Burnley	1-0
	Tottenham Hotspur v Manchester City	2-2
	Walsall v Swansea Town	2-0
	West Ham United v Notts County	4-0
	Wrexham v West Bromwich Albion	1-0
r	Bournemouth v Fulham	0-2
r	Grimsby Town v Brighton & Hove Albion	0-1
r	Huddersfield Town v Bury	3-1
r	Manchester City v Tottenham Hotspur	4-1
r	Middlesbrough v Chesterfield	4-3
r	Millwall v Corinthians	1-1e
r	Queen's Park Rangers v Charlton Athletic	0-3
r	York City v Newcastle United	1-2
r2	Millwall v Corinthians	5-1 N

Round Four

	Arsenal v Birmingham	2-2
	Aston Villa v Walsall	3-1
	Blackburn Rovers v Everton	4-1
	Derby County v Bradford Park Avenue	1-1
	Huddersfield Town v Sheffield United	2-1
	Hull City v Blackpool	3-1
	Middlesbrough v Charlton Athletic	1-1
	Millwall v Doncaster Rovers	4-0
	Newcastle United v Clapton Orient	3-1

1929/30 to 1930/31

	Nottingham Forest v Fulham	2-1
	Oldham Athletic v Sheffield Wednesday	3-4
	Portsmouth v Brighton & Hove Albion	0-1
	Sunderland v Cardiff City	2-1
	Swindon Town v Manchester City	1-1
	West Ham United v Leeds United	4-1
	Wrexham v Bradford City	0-0
r	Birmingham v Arsenal	0-1
r	Bradford City v Wrexham	2-1
r	Bradford Park Avenue v Derby County	2-1
r	Charlton Athletic v Middlesbrough	1-1e
r	Manchester City v Swindon Town	10-1
r2	Middlesbrough v Charlton Athletic	1-0eN

Round Five

	Aston Villa v Blackburn Rovers	4-1
	Huddersfield Town v Bradford City	2-1
	Manchester City v Hull City	1-2
	Middlesbrough v Arsenal	0-2
	Newcastle United v Brighton & Hove Albion	3-0
	Sheffield Wednesday v Bradford Park Avenue	5-1
	Sunderland v Nottingham Forest	2-2
	West Ham United v Millwall	4-1
r	Nottingham Forest v Sunderland	3-1

Round Six

	Aston Villa v Huddersfield Town	1-2
	Newcastle United v Hull City	1-1
	Nottingham Forest v Sheffield Wednesday	2-2
	West Ham United v Arsenal	0-3
r	Hull City v Newcastle United	1-0
r	Sheffield Wednesday v Nottingham Forest	3-1

Semi Finals

	Arsenal v Hull City	2-2 N
	Huddersfield Town v Sheffield Wednesday	2-1 N
r	Arsenal v Hull City	1-0 N

Final

	Arsenal v Huddersfield Town	2-0 N

1930/31

Extra Preliminary Round

1	Blyth Spartans v North Shields	0-2
	Chester-le-Street v Crawcrook Albion	3-3
2	Bishop Auckland v Crook Town	2-5
	Burnhope Institute v Eden CW	3-1
	Chilton Colliery Recreation v West Auckland Town	4-0
	Durham City v Cockfield	3-2
	Ferryhill Athletic v Consett	2-3
	Leasingthorne Colliery v Seaham Colliery Welfare	3-1
	Murton CW v Esh Winning (1)	2-1
	Spen Black & White v Stanley United	5-2
	Spennymoor United v Dipton United	5-2
	White-le-Head Rangers v Horden CW	2-3
7	Barnton Victoria v Lostock Gralam	2-1
	Connah's Quay & Shotton v Congleton Town	2-0
	Rhyl Athletic v Chester	4-2
8	Atherstone Town v Headingley	8-1
	Bilston United v Halesowen Town	4-0
	Birmingham Corp. Tramways v Darlaston	3-1
	Bromsgrove Rovers v Willenhall	wo/s
	Cradley Heath St Luke's v Cannock Town	7-0
	Evesham Town v Wolverhampton Amateur	8-1
	Hednesford Town v Bournville Athletic	6-2
	Hereford United v Bloxwich Strollers	6-1
	Kidderminster Harriers v Walsall Phoenix	8-0
	Leamington Town v Brierley Hill Alliance	0-3
	Oakengates Town v Nuneaton Town	2-2
	Oswestry Town v Walsall LMS	5-1
	Redditch v Stafford Rangers	4-4
	Stourbridge v Whitchurch	3-0
	Walsall Jolly Club v Boldmere St Michaels	1-2
	Wellington St George's v Shrewsbury Town	4-0
15	Luton Amateur v Hitchin Town	0-0
	St Neots & District v Leagrave & District	4-1
16	Great Yarmouth Town v Norwich CEYMS	2-3
	Ipswich Town v Harwich & Parkeston	5-0
	Sheringham v Chatteris Town	6-1
	Thetford Town v Abbey United (Cambs)	4-3
18	Apsley v Standard Telephones	8-3
	Aylesbury United v Waltham Comrades	8-3
	Finchley v Old Johnians	3-1
	Hertford Town v Hendon Town	7-1
	St Albans City v Welwyn Garden City	9-0
19	Bicester Town v Stokenchurch	4-3
	Henley Town v Suttons	3-1
	Morris Motors (Cowley) v Newbury Town	1-2
	Park Royal v Abingdon Town	7-0
	Uxbridge v Hayes	4-4
25	Frome Town v Chippenham Rovers	4-3
	Melksham v Calne & Harris United	1-1
	Swindon Victoria v Westbury United	10-1
26	Glastonbury v Clevedon	2-2
	Kingswood v Hanham Athletic	3-1
	St Cuthbert's v Street	3-0
	Wadebridge United v Westland Works	1-0
1r	Crawcrook Albion v Chester-le-Street	3-0
8r	Nuneaton Town v Oakengates Town	2-2
r	Stafford Rangers v Redditch	3-2
15r	Hitchin Town v Luton Amateur	1-3
19r	Hayes v Uxbridge	2-3e
25r	Calne & Harris United v Melksham	2-1 D
26r	Clevedon v Glastonbury	1-2
8r2	Nuneaton Town v Oakengates Town	2-3

Preliminary Round

1	Crawcrook Albion v Pelaw	3-2
	Felling Colliery v Usworth Colliery	0-2
	Gosforth & Coxlodge v Howdon British Legion	4-2
	Jarrow v Washington Colliery	1-0
	North Shields v St Peter's Albion	1-0
	Scotswood v Shankhouse	3-1
	Walker Celtic v Ashington	3-0
	Wallsend v Birtley	1-0
2	Annfield Plain v Shildon	4-3
	Crook Town v Willington	2-1
	Durham City v Tow Law Town	1-0
	Evenwood Town v Chilton Colliery Recreation	1-0
	Horden CW v Burnhope Institute	7-0
	Leasingthorne Colliery v Spennymoor United	3-3
	Murton CW v Chopwell Institute	2-1
	Spen Black & White v Consett	2-2
4	Egremont v Moss Bay United	8-3
	Kells United v Maryport	1-1
	Keswick v Cleator Moor Celtic	1-2
	Whitehaven Athletic v Penrith	5-2
5	Chorley v Great Harwood	2-0
6	Harrowby v Seaforth Albion	8-0
	Marine v Ellesmere Port Cement	3-2
	Northern Nomads v Ellesmere Port Town	4-3
	Shell Mex v Stalybridge Celtic	3-0
7	Bangor City v Altrincham	2-5
	Connah's Quay & Shotton v Colwyn Bay	6-0 D
	Nantwich v Llandudno	6-0
	Northwich Victoria v Runcorn	1-2
	Rhyl Athletic v Macclesfield Town	0-0
	Sandbach Ramblers v Linotype & Machinery	3-2
	Winsford United v Caernarvon Athletic	7-2
	Witton Albion v Barnton Victoria	2-1
8	Birmingham Corp. Tramways v Boldmere St Michaels	3-0
	Cradley Heath St Luke's v Atherstone Town	2-1
	Hednesford Town v Bromsgrove Rovers	8-1
	Hereford United v Bilston United	1-1
	Kidderminster Harriers v Brierley Hill Alliance	2-2
	Oswestry Town v Evesham Town	2-1
	Stourbridge v Stafford Rangers	4-3
	Wellington St George's v Oakengates Town	1-5
9	Barton Town (1) v British Oil & Cake Mills	8-1
	Frodingham & Appleby Ath. v Selby Town	3-1
	Goole Town v Spalding United	3-0
	Grimsby Haycroft Rovers v Normanby Park Steel Works	3-2
	Marfleet v Humber United	0-3
	Selby OCO v Cleethorpes Town	2-1
10	Denaby United v Guiseley	3-2
	Horsforth v Yorkshire Amateur	1-2
	Monckton Athletic v Cudworth Village	3-2
	Wath Athletic v Frickley Colliery	0-2
11	Ardsley Athletic v Rawmarsh Welfare	1-3
	Hallam v Brodsworth Main Colliery	2-3
	Hatfield Main v Grimethorpe Colliery Institute	5-2
	Norton Woodseats v Goldthorpe United	2-2
	Rossington Main v Highgate (Rotherham)	1-2
	Silverwood Colliery v Worksop Town	wo/s
	Thurnscoe Victoria v Sheffield	12-4
12	Buxton v South Normanton Colliery	6-1
	Eckington Town v Bolsover Colliery	2-5
13	Lenton v Basford United	3-1
	Newark Castle Rovers v Sneinton	6-1
	Ransome & Marles v Raleigh Athletic	11-1
14	Desborough Town v Moira United	wo/s
	Gresley Rovers v Rothwell Town	3-2
	Higham Ferrers Town v Rushden Town	1-4
15	Leighton United v Baldock Town	4-5
	Northampton Nomads v Biggleswade & District	1-2
	Peterborough & Fletton Utd. v Bedford Town (1)	5-2
	Peterbro' Westwood Works v Kempston Rovers	3-2
	RAF Henlow v Wolverton Town	1-2
	St Neots & District v Luton Amateur	2-0
	Stamford v Arlesey Town	5-0
	Waterlows (Dunstable) v Letchworth Town	6-1
16	Crittall Athletic v Colchester Town	2-2
	Ipswich Town v Leiston Works Athletic	5-2
	King's Lynn v Gorleston	4-1
	Kirkley & Waveney v Cambridge Town	1-2
	Lowestoft Town v Wisbech Town	1-2
	Norwich CEYMS v Cromer	3-1
	Severalls Athletic v Felixstowe Town	1-0
	Sheringham v Thetford Town	4-2
17	Barking v Brentwood Mental Hospital	2-0
	Brentwood & Warley v Grays Thurrock United	0-1
	GER Loughton v Leytonstone	1-3
	Grays Athletic v Walthamstow Avenue	3-3
	Walthamstow Grange v Custom House	5-1
18	Barnet v St Albans City	6-2
	Chesham United v Apsley	1-1
	Finchley v Aylesbury United	6-4
	Haywards Sports v Berkhamsted Town	6-3
	Hertford Town v Bishop's Stortford	3-2
	Leavesden Mental Hospital v Enfield	1-1
	Old Lyonian v Tufnell Park	1-5
	Wood Green Town v Watford Spartans	2-1
19	Bicester Town v RAF Uxbridge	1-0
	Cowley v Park Royal	0-13
	Hampstead Town v Maidenhead United	3-2
	Hounslow v Henley Town	2-3
	Marlow v Southall	2-2
	Newbury Town v Thatcham	wo/s
	Oxford City v Slough	2-0
	Uxbridge v Wycombe Wanderers	1-0
20	Carshalton Athletic v Kingstonian	0-4
	Casuals v Redhill	3-1
	Dorking v Metropolitan Police	4-4
	Epsom Town v Tooting Town	4-1
	Mitcham Wanderers v Leyland Motors (Kingston)	2-1
	Sutton United v West Norwood	1-0
	Wallington v Beddington Corner	0-2
	Woking v Whyteleafe Athletic	5-1
21	Addlestone v RAMC Aldershot	1-7
	Aldershot Traction Co. v Staines Town	4-1
	Courage & Co.'s Sports v Thornycrofts (Basingstoke)	4-3
	Egham v Basingstoke	3-3
	Godalming v Wellington Works	4-1
	Guildford v Weybridge	wo/s
	Hersham v Camberley & Yorktown	0-5
22	Beckenham v Chatham	1-2
	Bexleyheath Town v Bromley	1-4
	Bostall Heath v Canterbury Waverley	1-4
	Erith & Belvedere v RM Chatham	1-3
	Sittingbourne Paper Mills v Callender Athletic	0-2
	Tunbridge Wells Rangers v Maidstone United	3-1
	Whitstable v Ashford	1-4
	Woolwich Polytechnic v Cray Wanderers	2-6
23	East Grinstead v Newhaven	3-0
	Hove v Hastings & St Leonards	3-3
24	Bournemouth (Ams) v Blandford	3-1
	Newport (IOW) v Ryde Sports	2-1
	RAOC Hilsea v Osborne Athletic	1-1
	Salisbury City (1) v Weymouth	4-4
25	Bath City v Paulton Rovers	10-0
	Chippenham Town v Clandown	5-2
	Coleford Athletic v Garrards Athletic	1-1
	Spencer Moulton v Welton Rovers	1-5
	Swindon Corinthians v Melksham	2-1
	Swindon Victoria v Radstock Town	3-2
	Trowbridge Town v Devizes Town	5-2
	Warminster Town v Frome Town	10-5
26	Barry v Lovells Athletic	1-0
	Glastonbury v Minehead	3-2
	Keynsham v Ebbw Vale	2-0
	Kingswood v Bristol St George	1-1
	Mount Hill Enterprise v St Philips Athletic	2-2
	St Austell v Yeovil & Petter's United	1-5
	Taunton Town (1) v Wadebridge United	2-0
	Wells City v St Cuthbert's	4-1
2r	Consett v Spen Black & White	1-0
r	Spennymoor United v Leasingthorne Colliery	2-0
4r	Maryport v Kells United	2-0
7r	Macclesfield Town v Rhyl Athletic	1-3
8r	Bilston United v Hereford United	3-3e
r	Brierley Hill Alliance v Kidderminster Harriers	2-1
11r	Goldthorpe United v Norton Woodseats	4-0
16r	Colchester Town v Crittall Athletic	1-3
17r	Walthamstow Avenue v Grays Athletic	4-4
18r	Apsley v Chesham United	3-3e
r	Enfield v Leavesden Mental Hospital	1-2
19r	Southall v Marlow	3-0
20r	Metropolitan Police v Dorking	2-3
21r	Basingstoke v Egham	1-2
23r	Hastings & St Leonards v Hove	3-1
24r	Osborne Athletic v RAOC Hilsea	1-2
r	Weymouth v Salisbury City (1)	3-4e
25r	Garrards Athletic v Coleford Athletic	5-1
26r	Bristol St George v Kingswood	2-3
r	Mount Hill Enterprise v St Philips Athletic	4-3
8r2	Hereford United v Bilston United	3-3eN
17r2	Grays Athletic v Walthamstow Avenue	2-5 N
18r2	Apsley v Chesham United	0-7 N
8r3	Hereford United v Bilston United	6-4

Qualifying Round One

1	Jarrow v Usworth Colliery	8-1
	North Shields v Walker Celtic	4-1
	Scotswood v Crawcrook Albion	2-0
	Wallsend v Gosforth & Coxlodge	6-1
2	Consett v Durham City	2-1
	Crook Town v Murton CW	3-1
	Evenwood Town v Annfield Plain	4-4
	Spennymoor United v Horden CW	3-2
3	Carlin How v Normanby Magnesite	0-7
	South Bank v Filey Town	11-0
	Stockton v Whitby Albion Rangers	7-4
	Whitby United v Bridlington Town (1)	3-1
4	Cleator Moor Celtic v Maryport	3-0
	Ulverston Town v Netherfield (Kendal)	10-1
	Whitehaven Athletic v Egremont	3-0
	Workington v Aspatria Athletic	3-0
5	Chorley v Breightmet United	2-0
	Horwich RMI v Burscough Rangers	5-1
	Lytham v Dick, Kerrs	2-1
	Skelmersdale United v Darwen	4-2
6	Glossop v Whiston	1-1
	Marine v Shell Mex	1-1

1930/31

	Northern Nomads v Earle	5-1
	Prescot Cables v Harrowby	8-1
7	Colwyn Bay v Altrincham	6-1
	Rhyl Athletic v Witton Albion	4-0
	Runcorn v Sandbach Ramblers	9-3
	Winsford United v Nantwich	2-0
8	Cradley Heath St Luke's v Brierley Hill Alliance	1-2
	Hednesford Town v Oswestry Town	4-2
	Hereford United v Birmingham Corp. Tramways	2-1
	Stourbridge v Oakengates Town	2-3
9	Boston (1) v Grimsby Haycroft Rovers	6-0
	Frodingham & Appleby Ath. v Selby OCO	3-3
	Goole Town v Brigg Town	4-1
	Humber United v Barton Town (1)	4-2
10	Denaby United v Mexborough Athletic	2-2
	Monckton Athletic v Luddendenfoot	9-1
	Wombwell v Frickley Colliery	3-0
	Yorkshire Amateur v South Kirkby Colliery	3-2
11	Goldthorpe United v Silverwood Colliery	1-0
	Hatfield Main v Pilkington Recreation	2-1
	Rawmarsh Welfare v Highgate (Rotherham)	2-2
	Thurnscoe Victoria v Brodsworth Main Colliery	2-2
12	Bolsover Colliery v Matlock Town	2-0
	Buxton v Ripley Town	3-1
	Ilkeston United v Heanor Town	1-0
	Shirebrook v Grassmoor	5-0
13	Grantham v Ransome & Marles	5-0
	Lenton v Sutton Town	4-3
	Newark Town v Newark Castle Rovers	4-0
	Sutton Junction v Boots Athletic	1-5
14	Gresley Rovers v Desborough Town	4-2
	Hinckley United (1) v Market Harborough Town	1-6
	Loughborough Corinthians v Wellingborough Town	6-0
	Rushden Town v Burton Town	2-2
15	Baldock Town v Biggleswade & District	3-3
	Peterbro' Westwood Works v Wolverton Town	2-3
	St Neots & District v Peterborough & Fletton Utd.	1-5
	Stamford v Waterlows (Dunstable)	4-0
16	Ipswich Town v Severalls Athletic	6-1
	King's Lynn v Cambridge Town	3-1
	Sheringham v Crittall Athletic	2-3
	Wisbech Town v Norwich CEYMS	2-4
17	Grays Thurrock United v Barking	3-5
	Leytonstone v Clapton	1-0
	Walthamstow Avenue v Chelmsford	3-2
	Walthamstow Grange v Dagenham Town	1-2
18	Haywards Sports v Tufnell Park	1-1
	Hertford Town v Barnet	3-3
	Leavesden Mental Hospital v Finchley	0-2
	Wood Green Town v Chesham United	2-2
19	Bicester Town v Hampstead Town	2-8
	Newbury Town v Oxford City	1-4
	Southall v Park Royal	0-4
	Uxbridge v Henley Town	5-2
20	Dorking v Kingstonian	2-3
	Epsom Town v Sutton United	2-0
	Mitcham Wanderers v Beddington Corner	5-2
	Woking v Casuals	4-0
21	Aldershot Traction Co. v Guildford	3-0
	Egham v Courage & Co.'s Sports	6-3
	Godalming v Camberley & Yorktown	2-0
	Winchester City v RAMC Aldershot	3-3
22	Ashford v Cray Wanderers	8-0
	Canterbury Waverley v Callender Athletic	2-1
	Chatham v Tunbridge Wells Rangers	0-2
	RM Chatham v Bromley	0-3
23	Bexhill v Hastings & St Leonards	2-2
	Bognor Regis Town v Vernon Athletic	1-0
	Littlehampton v Southwick	1-2
	Worthing v East Grinstead	2-0
24	Bournemouth Tramways v Salisbury Corinthians	3-0
	Newport (IOW) v Poole	wo/s
	RAOC Hilsea v Dorchester Town	6-2
	Salisbury City (1) v Bournemouth (Ams)	5-1
25	Chippenham Town v Trowbridge Town	3-0
	Garrards Athletic v Swindon Victoria	1-1
	Swindon Corinthians v Warminster Town	0-0
	Welton Rovers v Bath City	0-2
26	Glastonbury v Wells City	0-5
	Keynsham v Barry	0-4
	Mount Hill Enterprise v Kingswood	0-3
	Yeovil & Petter's United v Taunton Town (1)	1-1
2r	Annfield Plain v Evenwood Town	1-1
6r	Shell Mex v Marine	4-1
r	Whiston v Glossop	1-1e
9r	Selby OCO v Frodingham & Appleby Ath.	1-3e
10r	Mexborough Athletic v Denaby United	2-1
11r	Brodsworth Main Colliery v Thurnscoe Victoria	3-0 D
r	Highgate (Rotherham) v Rawmarsh Welfare	4-2
14r	Burton Town v Rushden Town	6-3
15r	Biggleswade & District v Baldock Town	9-0
18r	Barnet v Hertford Town	7-1
r	Chesham United v Wood Green Town	5-2
r	Tufnell Park v Haywards Sports	3-2
21r	RAMC Aldershot v Winchester City	3-2
23r	Hastings & St Leonards v Bexhill	4-1
25r	Swindon Victoria v Garrards Athletic	5-1
r	Warminster Town v Swindon Corinthians	2-5
26r	Taunton Town (1) v Yeovil & Petter's United	4-1
2r2	Annfield Plain v Evenwood Town	1-2
6r2	Whiston v Glossop	4-2 N

Qualifying Round Two

1	Scotswood v Jarrow	0-1
	Wallsend v North Shields	3-1
2	Consett v Spennymoor United	4-2
	Crook Town v Evenwood Town	0-1
3	South Bank v Normanby Magnesite	5-1
	Whitby United v Stockton	5-1
4	Ulverston Town v Workington	0-3
	Whitehaven Athletic v Cleator Moor Celtic	3-3
5	Lytham v Horwich RMI	2-2
	Skelmersdale United v Chorley	1-1
6	Prescot Cables v Whiston	4-1
	Shell Mex v Northern Nomads	2-2
7	Colwyn Bay v Runcorn	5-3
	Rhyl Athletic v Winsford United	4-2
8	Hednesford Town v Brierley Hill Alliance	6-1
	Hereford United v Oakengates Town	1-0
9	Boston (1) v Humber United	2-0
	Frodingham & Appleby Ath. v Goole Town	3-2
10	Wombwell v Mexborough Athletic	1-0
	Yorkshire Amateur v Monckton Athletic	4-3
11	Goldthorpe United v Hatfield Main	4-2
	Thurnscoe Victoria v Highgate (Rotherham)	0-1
12	Ilkeston United v Bolsover Colliery	8-2
	Shirebrook v Buxton	1-1
13	Boots Athletic v Grantham	1-5
	Newark Town v Lenton	8-1
14	Burton Town v Loughborough Corinthians	1-1
	Market Harborough Town v Gresley Rovers	2-3
15	Peterborough & Fletton Utd. v Biggleswade & District	5-0
	Wolverton Town v Stamford	3-1
16	Ipswich Town v Crittall Athletic	2-3
	King's Lynn v Norwich CEYMS	3-0
17	Dagenham Town v Walthamstow Avenue	0-2
	Leytonstone v Barking	4-0
18	Barnet v Chesham United	3-2
	Finchley v Tufnell Park	2-1
19	Hampstead Town v Uxbridge	2-2
	Oxford City v Park Royal	3-1
20	Kingstonian v Woking	3-1
	Mitcham Wanderers v Epsom Town	3-1
21	Aldershot Traction Co. v Egham	1-0
	Godalming v RAMC Aldershot	1-4
22	Bromley v Ashford	5-2
	Canterbury Waverley v Tunbridge Wells Rangers	0-4
23	Hastings & St Leonards v Worthing	2-1
	Southwick v Bognor Regis Town	9-1
24	Bournemouth Tramways v Newport (IOW)	0-4
	Salisbury City (1) v RAOC Hilsea	1-0
25	Swindon Corinthians v Bath City	1-7
	Swindon Victoria v Chippenham Town	4-1
26	Taunton Town (1) v Barry	3-1
	Wells City v Kingswood	2-2
4r	Cleator Moor Celtic v Whitehaven Athletic	1-4
5r	Chorley v Skelmersdale United	2-2e
r	Horwich RMI v Lytham	4-1
6r	Northern Nomads v Shell Mex	5-2
12r	Buxton v Shirebrook	3-0
14r	Loughborough Corinthians v Burton Town	2-1
19r	Uxbridge v Hampstead Town	1-2e
26r	Kingswood v Wells City	1-3
5r2	Chorley v Skelmersdale United	5-2eN

Qualifying Round Three

1	Jarrow v Wallsend	4-1
2	Evenwood Town v Consett	2-2
3	South Bank v Whitby United	2-2
4	Workington v Whitehaven Athletic	3-0
5	Horwich RMI v Chorley	3-0
6	Northern Nomads v Prescot Cables	2-3
7	Rhyl Athletic v Colwyn Bay	1-0
8	Hednesford Town v Hereford United	1-2
9	Boston (1) v Frodingham & Appleby Ath.	3-1
10	Wombwell v Yorkshire Amateur	3-2
11	Highgate (Rotherham) v Goldthorpe United	3-2
12	Buxton v Ilkeston United	4-3
13	Newark Town v Grantham	2-0
14	Gresley Rovers v Loughborough Corinthians	2-0
15	Peterborough & Fletton Utd. v Wolverton Town	5-0
16	King's Lynn v Crittall Athletic	2-0
17	Walthamstow Avenue v Leytonstone	3-2
18	Barnet v Finchley	4-0
19	Hampstead Town v Oxford City	3-1
20	Mitcham Wanderers v Kingstonian	2-4
21	Aldershot Traction Co. v RAMC Aldershot	6-5
22	Bromley v Tunbridge Wells Rangers	2-10
23	Southwick v Hastings & St Leonards	7-2
24	Salisbury City (1) v Newport (IOW)	2-3
25	Bath City v Swindon Victoria	1-3
26	Taunton Town (1) v Wells City	2-0
2r	Consett v Evenwood Town	6-0
3r	Whitby United v South Bank	2-1

Qualifying Round Four

Boston (1) v Newark Town	0-0
Gainsborough Trinity v Hereford United	3-0
Gresley Rovers v King's Lynn	4-1
Hampstead Town v Guildford City	2-3
Jarrow v Consett	3-0
Kingstonian v Barnet	2-1
Lancaster Town v Horwich RMI	3-1
Leyton v Aldershot	1-2
London Caledonians v Dulwich Hamlet	2-4
Mansfield Town v Highgate (Rotherham)	10-1
Northfleet United v Dartford	1-0
Nunhead v Wimbledon	0-2
Peterborough & Fletton Utd. v Kettering Town	2-0
Rhyl Athletic v Prescot Cables	3-2
Scarborough v West Stanley	1-1
Scunthorpe United v Worcester City	3-0
Sheppey United v Folkestone	0-3
Sittingbourne v Southwick	8-0
Swindon Victoria v Merthyr Town	1-6
Taunton Town (1) v Newport (IOW)	5-1
Tunbridge Wells Rangers v Margate	3-2
Walthamstow Avenue v Aldershot Traction Co.	15-0
Wellington Town v Buxton	2-1
Whitby United v Wombwell	2-3
Workington v Manchester Central	2-2
r Manchester Central v Workington	0-0x
r Newark Town v Boston (1)	2-0
r West Stanley v Scarborough	0-1
r2 Workington v Manchester Central	4-0 N

Round One

Accrington Stanley v Lancaster Town	3-1
Aldershot v Peterborough & Fletton Utd.	4-1
Bristol Rovers v Merthyr Town	4-1
Carlisle United v New Brighton	3-1
Chesterfield v Notts County	1-2
Crewe Alexandra v Jarrow	1-0
Crystal Palace v Taunton Town (1)	6-0
Dulwich Hamlet v Newport County	2-2
Folkestone v Sittingbourne	5-3
Fulham v Wimbledon	1-1
Gainsborough Trinity v Scunthorpe United	1-0
Gillingham v Guildford City	7-2
Halifax Town v Mansfield Town	2-2
Hartlepools United v Stockport County	2-3
Ilford v Brentford	1-6
Lincoln City v Barrow	8-3
Luton Town v Clapton Orient	2-2
Nelson v Workington	4-0
Newark Town v Rotherham United	2-1
Northampton Town v Coventry City	1-2
Northfleet United v Exeter City	0-3
Norwich City v Swindon Town	2-0
Queen's Park Rangers v Thames	5-0
Rochdale v Doncaster Rovers	1-2
Scarborough v Rhyl Athletic	6-0
Southend United v Torquay United	0-1
Southport v Darlington	4-2
Tranmere Rovers v Gateshead	4-4
Tunbridge Wells Rangers v Kingstonian	3-0
Walsall v Bournemouth	1-0
Walthamstow Avenue v Watford	1-5
Wellington Town v Wombwell	0-0
Wrexham v Wigan Borough	2-0
York City v Gresley Rovers	3-1
r Clapton Orient v Luton Town	2-4 N
r Gateshead v Tranmere Rovers	3-2
r Mansfield Town v Halifax Town	1-2
r Newport County v Dulwich Hamlet	4-1
r Wimbledon v Fulham	0-6
r Wombwell v Wellington Town	0-3

Round Two

Accrington Stanley v Torquay United	0-1
Brentford v Norwich City	1-0
Bristol Rovers v Stockport County	4-2
Carlisle United v Tunbridge Wells Rangers	4-2
Crewe Alexandra v Queen's Park Rangers	2-4
Crystal Palace v Newark Town	6-0
Doncaster Rovers v Notts County	0-1
Exeter City v Coventry City	1-1
Fulham v Halifax Town	4-0
Gainsborough Trinity v Southport	0-4
Gateshead v Folkestone	3-2
Gillingham v Aldershot	1-3
Nelson v York City	1-1
Scarborough v Lincoln City	6-4
Walsall v Newport County	4-0
Watford v Luton Town	3-1
Wellington Town v Wrexham	2-4
r Coventry City v Exeter City	1-2
r York City v Nelson	3-2

Round Three

Aldershot v Bradford Park Avenue	0-1
Arsenal v Aston Villa	2-2
Barnsley v Bristol City	4-1
Blackburn Rovers v Walsall	1-1
Bolton Wanderers v Carlisle United	1-0
Brentford v Cardiff City	2-2
Bristol Rovers v Queen's Park Rangers	3-1
Burnley v Manchester City	3-0
Bury v Torquay United	1-1
Corinthians v Port Vale	1-3
Crystal Palace v Reading	1-1
Exeter City v Derby County	3-2
Fulham v Portsmouth	0-2
Gateshead v Sheffield Wednesday	2-6
Hull City v Blackpool	1-2
Leeds United v Huddersfield Town	2-0

1930/31 to 1931/32

	Leicester City v Brighton & Hove Albion	1-2
	Liverpool v Birmingham	0-2
	Middlesbrough v Bradford City	1-1
	Newcastle United v Nottingham Forest	4-0
	Notts County v Swansea Town	3-1
	Oldham Athletic v Watford	1-3
	Plymouth Argyle v Everton	0-2
	Scarborough v Grimsby Town	1-2
	Sheffield United v York City	1-1
	Southport v Millwall	3-1
	Stoke City v Manchester United	3-3
	Sunderland v Southampton	2-0
	Tottenham Hotspur v Preston North End	3-1
	West Bromwich Albion v Charlton Athletic	2-2
	West Ham United v Chelsea	1-3
	Wolverhampton Wan. v Wrexham	9-1
r	Aston Villa v Arsenal	1-3
r	Bradford City v Middlesbrough	2-1
r	Cardiff City v Brentford	1-2
r	Charlton Athletic v West Bromwich Albion	1-1e
r	Manchester United v Stoke City	0-0e
r	Reading v Crystal Palace	1-1e
r	Torquay United v Bury	1-2e
r	Walsall v Blackburn Rovers	0-3
r	York City v Sheffield United	0-2
r2	Crystal Palace v Reading	2-0 N
r2	Manchester United v Stoke City	4-2 N
r2	West Bromwich Albion v Charlton Athletic	3-1 N

Round Four

	Barnsley v Sheffield Wednesday	2-1
	Birmingham v Port Vale	2-0
	Blackburn Rovers v Bristol Rovers	5-1
	Bolton Wanderers v Sunderland	1-1
	Bradford City v Wolverhampton Wan.	0-0
	Bradford Park Avenue v Burnley	2-0
	Brentford v Portsmouth	0-1
	Bury v Exeter City	1-2
	Chelsea v Arsenal	2-1
	Crystal Palace v Everton	0-6
	Grimsby Town v Manchester United	1-0
	Leeds United v Newcastle United	4-1
	Sheffield United v Notts County	4-1
	Southport v Blackpool	2-1
	Watford v Brighton & Hove Albion	2-0
	West Bromwich Albion v Tottenham Hotspur	1-0
r	Sunderland v Bolton Wanderers	3-1
r	Wolverhampton Wan. v Bradford City	4-2

Round Five

	Barnsley v Wolverhampton Wan.	1-3
	Birmingham v Watford	3-0
	Chelsea v Blackburn Rovers	3-0
	Everton v Grimsby Town	5-3
	Exeter City v Leeds United	3-1
	Portsmouth v West Bromwich Albion	0-1
	Southport v Bradford Park Avenue	1-0
	Sunderland v Sheffield United	2-1

Round Six

	Birmingham v Chelsea	2-2
	Everton v Southport	9-1
	Sunderland v Exeter City	1-1
	West Bromwich Albion v Wolverhampton Wan.	1-1
r	Chelsea v Birmingham	0-3
r	Exeter City v Sunderland	2-4
r	Wolverhampton Wan. v West Bromwich Albion	1-2

Semi Finals

	Birmingham v Sunderland	2-0 N
	West Bromwich Albion v Everton	1-0 N

Final

	West Bromwich Albion v Birmingham	2-1 N

1931/32

Extra Preliminary Round

1	Birtley v Leslies	1-0
	Blyth Spartans v Shankhouse	7-1
	Chester-le-Street v Usworth Colliery	0-3
	Chopwell Institute v Bedlington United	2-3
	South Shields Corinthians v Spen Black & White	4-0
2	Blackhall Colliery Welfare v Stanley United	2-1
	Burnhope Institute v Trimdon Grange Colliery	2-3
	Chilton Colliery Recreation v Easington CW	2-2
	Durham City v Barnard Castle Athletic	2-2
	Eden CW v West Auckland Town	0-0
	Ferryhill Athletic v Cockfield	1-1
	Seaham Colliery Welfare v Willington	4-3
	Tow Law Town v Annfield Plain	4-1
7	Bedouins v Willaston White Star	1-5
8	Atherstone Town v Oswestry Town	3-1
	Birmingham Corp. Tramways v Headingley	6-2
	Bloxwich Strollers v Wolverhampton Amateur	4-2
	Bromsgrove Rovers v Cannock Town	4-4
	Evesham Town v Cradley Heath St Luke's	0-0
	Nuneaton Town v Walsall Phoenix	15-0
	Oakengates Town v Darlaston	2-1
	Redditch v Stafford Rangers	1-1
	Shrewsbury Town v Bournville Athletic	6-1
	Stourbridge v Bilston United	4-2
	Walsall LMS v Walsall Jolly Club	4-0
	Wellington Town v Leamington Town	10-1
16	4th Divisional Signals Regiment v Colchester Town	1-3
	Cambridge Town v Great Yarmouth Town	1-1
	Chatteris Town v Sheringham	5-1
	Leiston Works Athletic v Clacton Town	4-2
	Newmarket Town v Gorleston	1-3
	Stowmarket v Parkeston Railway	3-1
	Thetford Town v Cromer	3-1
18	Aylesbury United v Leavesden Mental Hospital	1-8
	Bishop's Stortford v Bletchley Town (1)	2-1
	Shredded Wheat v Hoddesdon Town	1-4
	St Albans City v Hertford Town	9-1
	Stevenage Town v Ware	4-3
	Wood Green Town v Apsley	0-5
19	Bicester Town v Windsor & Eton	1-4
	Headington United v Hounslow Town	2-8
	Newbury Town v Maidenhead United	2-3
	Stokenchurch v Marlow	2-7
	Wealdstone v Thame United	12-4
	Witney Town v Gradwell Sports	1-3
	Wycombe Wanderers v Morris Motors (Cowley)	9-1
22	Woolwich Borough Co. Ath. v RM Deal	2-2e
24	Fareham v New Milton	3-0
	Gosport v Portsmouth Albion	2-1
25	Purton v Spencer Moulton	1-4
26	Clevedon v Street	3-3
	Ebbw Vale v Llanelli	1-1
	Glastonbury v Minehead	2-0
	Gloucester City v Keynsham	4-4
	Green Waves (Plymouth) v Dartmouth United	0-2
	Hanham Athletic v Cadbury Heath YMCA	3-0
	J.S. Fry & Sons v Cheltenham Town	0-5
	Yeovil & Petter's United v Wadebridge United	11-1
2r	Barnard Castle Athletic v Durham City	0-3
r	Cockfield v Ferryhill Athletic	3-1
r	Easington CW v Chilton Colliery Recreation	6-1
r	West Auckland Town v Eden CW	3-2
8r	Cannock Town v Bromsgrove Rovers	wo/s
r	Cradley Heath St Luke's v Evesham Town	9-1
r	Stafford Rangers v Redditch	4-1
16r	Great Yarmouth Town v Cambridge Town	1-5
22r	RM Deal v Woolwich Borough Co. Ath.	2-0
26r	Keynsham v Gloucester City	5-1
r	Llanelli v Ebbw Vale	4-0
r	Street v Clevedon	5-0

Preliminary Round

1	Bedlington United v Howdon British Legion	1-2
	Blyth Spartans v Scotswood	9-0
	Crawcrook Albion v South Shields Corinthians	4-0
	Gosforth & Coxlodge v Usworth Colliery	5-0
	Jarrow v Pelaw	6-2
	North Shields v Ashington	2-1
	Walker Celtic v Dipton United	7-2
	Wallsend v Birtley	1-1
2	Blackhall Colliery Welfare v Shildon	4-1
	Consett v Horden CW	2-4
	Crook Town v Durham City	3-0
	Easington CW v Murton CW	0-0
	Leasingthorne Colliery v Cockfield	1-1
	Spennymoor United v Tow Law Town	4-0
	Trimdon Grange Colliery v Seaham Colliery Welfare	3-2
	West Auckland Town v Evenwood Town	0-2
3	Pease & Partners v Whitby Albion Rangers	7-3
4	Holme Head Works v Aspatria Athletic	wo/s
	Keswick v Windermere	3-1
	Netherfield (Kendal) v Kells United	1-6
5	Dick, Kerrs v Morecambe	4-1
	Great Harwood v Breightmet United	1-1
6	Droylsden v Ellesmere Port Cement	4-3
	Earle v Stalybridge Celtic	2-3
	Manchester North End v Peasley Cross Athletic	3-2
	Marine v Whiston	3-2
	Northern Nomads v Harrowby	10-0
	Prescot Cables v Ellesmere Port Town	9-0
	Timperley v Glossop	3-2
7	Altrincham v Colwyn Bay	5-3
	Congleton Town v Witton Albion	2-0
	Connah's Quay & Shotton v Northwich Victoria	0-0
	Macclesfield Town v Nantwich	2-0
	Rhyl v Willaston White Star	6-2
	Runcorn v Bangor City	6-4
	Sandbach Ramblers v Llandudno	3-3
	Winsford United v Lostock Gralam	4-3
8	Atherstone Town v Wellington Town	3-1
	Birmingham Corp. Tramways v Bloxwich Strollers	4-0
	Cradley Heath St Luke's v Hereford United	3-1
	Hednesford Town v Brierley Hill Alliance	2-3
	Nuneaton Town v Worcester City	4-1
	Oakengates Town v Cannock Town	4-0
	Shrewsbury Town v Walsall LMS	4-1
	Stourbridge v Stafford Rangers	4-5
9	Boston (1) v East Riding Amateurs	11-1
	Brigg Town v Normanby Park Steel Works	1-0
	British Oil & Cake Mills v Frodingham & Appleby Ath.	1-3
	Broughton Rangers v Spalding United	wo/s
	Grimsby Haycroft Rovers v Selby OCO	wo/s
	Humber United v Barton Town (1)	0-0
	Reckitt's (Hull) v Marfleet	0-2
	Selby Town v Louth Town	4-1
10	Cudworth Village v Grimethorpe Colliery Institute	0-0
	Denaby United v Ardsley Athletic	3-1
	Frickley Colliery v Luddendenfoot	7-0
	South Kirkby Colliery v Farsley Celtic	4-2
11	Highgate (Rotherham) v Hatfield Main	3-3
	Norton Woodseats v Sheffield	8-0
	Owston Park Rangers v Silverwood Colliery	4-2
	Pilkington Recreation v Brodsworth Main Colliery	3-4
	Rossington Main v Rawmarsh Welfare	2-2
	Wath Athletic v Thurnscoe Victoria	2-1
	Worksop Town v Hallam	2-2
12	Ripley Town v Heanor Town	2-2
14	Desborough Town v Peterbro' Westwood Works	6-4
	Higham Ferrers Town v Northampton Nomads	7-1
	Market Harborough Town v Rushden Town	3-5
	Peterborough & Fletton Utd. v Hinckley United (1)	3-1
	Rothwell Town v Wellingborough Town	4-3
	Wolverton Town v New Peterborough Swifts	2-2
15	Baldock Town v Letchworth Town	1-3
	Hitchin Town v Davis Athletic	6-1
	Langford v Bedford Town (1)	1-7
	RAF Henlow v St Neots & District	5-2
16	Cambridge Town v Chatteris Town	9-2
	Colchester Town v Harwich & Parkeston	2-2
	Crittall Athletic v Felixstowe Town	7-0
	Gorleston v Wisbech Town	2-1
	King's Lynn v Norwich CEYMS	4-0
	Leiston Works Athletic v Ipswich Town	3-2
	Stowmarket v Lowestoft Town	0-1
	Thetford Town v Kirkley & Waveney	0-2
17	Brentwood & Warley v Chelmsford	2-7
	Clapton v Grays Thurrock United	1-0
	Grays Athletic v Brentwood Mental Hospital	wo/s
	Leytonstone v Custom House	5-1
	Romford (2) v Jurgens (Purfleet)	2-1
18	Enfield v Stevenage Town	9-2
	Finchley v Welwyn Garden City	10-2
	Hendon Town - Bye	
	Leavesden Mental Hospital v Apsley	3-2
	Old Johnians v Bishop's Stortford	0-1
	St Albans City v Old Lyonian	3-1
	Tufnell Park v London Caledonians	2-1e
	Waltham Comrades v Hoddesdon Town	2-6
19	Abingdon Town v Park Royal	2-9
	Henley Town v Marlow	0-1
	Hounslow Town v Gradwell Sports	1-6
	Maidenhead United v Oxford City	2-1
	Slough v Windsor & Eton	6-1
	Southall v Cowley	4-2
	Wealdstone v Hampstead Town	1-1
	Wycombe Wanderers v Uxbridge	7-0
20	Carshalton Athletic v RNVR Mitcham	7-0
	Epsom Town v West Norwood	0-1
	Mitcham Wanderers v Casuals	6-2
	Redhill v Dorking	1-2
	Sutton United v Columbia	1-0
	Tooting Town v Metropolitan Police	0-0
	Walton-on-Thames v Beddington Corner	1-5
	Woking v Leyland Motors (Kingston)	5-0
21	Camberley & Yorktown v Thornycrofts (Basingstoke)	2-0
	Courage & Co.'s Sports v Basingstoke	4-1
	Guildford v Wellington Works	1-4
	Winchester City v Staines Town	7-2
22	Ashford v Sittingbourne	2-2
	Bexleyheath & Welling v RM Deal	1-2
	Bromley v Woolwich Polytechnic	2-1
	Canterbury Waverley v Maidstone United	4-2
	Cray Wanderers v Bostall Heath	2-4
	Erith & Belvedere v Sheppey United	2-1
	RM Chatham v Beckenham	4-2
	Whitstable v Chatham	0-2
23	Bexhill v Vernon Athletic	0-1
	Littlehampton v Chichester	2-3
	Newhaven v Eastbourne Old Comrades	1-2
24	Bournemouth (Ams) v Dorchester Town	4-2
	Bournemouth Tramways v Salisbury City (1)	1-2
	Cowes v Ryde Sports	3-2
	Fareham v RAOC Hilsea	3-1
	Gosport v Blandford	0-2
	Newport (IOW) v Sandown	wo/s
	Osborne Athletic v Weymouth	0-6
	Poole Town v Salisbury Corinthians	5-3
25	Chippenham Rovers v Trowbridge Town	2-5
	Chippenham Town v Melksham	4-0
	Coleford Athletic v Spencer Moulton	2-4
	Devizes Town v Bath City	0-8
	Frome Town v Calne & Harris United	2-2
	Swindon Corinthians v Radstock Town	0-2
	Swindon Victoria v Paulton Rovers	1-2
	Warminster Town v Welton Rovers	2-4
26	Barry v Lovells Athletic	1-1
	Keynsham v Hanham Athletic	1-1
	Kingswood v Cheltenham Town	2-0
	Merthyr Town v Llanelli	1-4
	Mount Hill Enterprise v Bristol St George	0-1
	Street v Glastonbury	1-1
	Taunton Town (1) v Wells City	3-1
	Yeovil & Petter's United v Dartmouth United	4-0
1r	Birtley v Wallsend	0-1
2r	Cockfield v Leasingthorne Colliery	3-1
r	Murton CW v Easington CW	1-0
5r	Breightmet United v Great Harwood	2-3
7r	Llandudno v Sandbach Ramblers	1-5

1931/32

r	Northwich Victoria v Connah's Quay & Shotton	3-1
9r	Barton Town (1) v Humber United	1-0
10r	Grimethorpe Colliery Institute v Cudworth Village	4-1
11r	Hallam v Worksop Town	1-4
r	Hatfield Main v Highgate (Rotherham)	4-0
r	Rawmarsh Welfare v Rossington Main	3-1
12r	Heanor Town v Ripley Town	0-4
14r	New Peterborough Swifts v Wolverton Town	5-0
16r	Harwich & Parkeston v Colchester Town	3-4
19r	Hampstead Town v Wealdstone	5-2
20r	Metropolitan Police v Tooting Town	3-0
22r	Sittingbourne v Ashford	2-3
25r	Calne & Harris United v Frome Town	2-3
26r	Glastonbury v Street	1-2
r	Hanham Athletic v Keynsham	3-1
r	Lovells Athletic v Barry	3-2

Qualifying Round One

1	Blyth Spartans v Wallsend	3-2
	Crawcrook Albion v Howdon British Legion	1-0
	Jarrow v Gosforth & Coxlodge	2-1
	Walker Celtic v North Shields	2-2
2	Crook Town v Blackhall Colliery Welfare	2-0
	Evenwood Town v Spennymoor United	1-1
	Horden CW v Trimdon Grange Colliery	2-0
	Murton CW v Cockfield	1-0
3	Filey Town v Carlin How	2-1
	Normanby Mangnesite v Pease & Partners	4-0
	Stockton v Bridlington Town (1)	1-1
	Whitby United v South Bank	5-2
4	Cleator Moor Celtic v Penrith	5-1
	Holme Head Works v Keswick	7-0
	Whitehaven Athletic v Maryport	8-1
	Workington v Kells United	5-1
5	Burscough Rangers v Darwen	2-2
	Chorley v Horwich RMI	1-0
	Dick, Kerrs v Great Harwood	2-0
	Skelmersdale United v Lytham	1-2
6	Droylsden v Shell Mex	3-1
	Marine v Timperley	5-0
	Northern Nomads v Stalybridge Celtic	2-3
	Prescot Cables v Manchester North End	5-2
7	Altrincham v Sandbach Ramblers	3-1
	Macclesfield Town v Congleton Town	3-1
	Rhyl v Northwich Victoria	2-1
	Runcorn v Winsford United	1-1
8	Brierley Hill Alliance v Birmingham Corp. Tramways	6-0
	Nuneaton Town v Atherstone Town	6-1
	Shrewsbury Town v Oakengates Town	1-2
	Stafford Rangers v Cradley Heath St Luke's	2-2
9	Barton Town (1) v Boston (1)	4-3
	Frodingham & Appleby Ath. v Marfleet	4-3
	Grimsby Haycroft Rovers v Broughton Rangers	1-2
	Selby Town v Brigg Town	10-0
10	Denaby United v Monckton Athletic	5-1
	Frickley Colliery v Mexborough Athletic	4-3
	Grimethorpe Colliery Institute v Yorkshire Amateur	0-3
	Wombwell v South Kirkby Colliery	0-0
11	Owston Park Rangers v Hatfield Main	4-0
	Rawmarsh Welfare v Norton Woodseats	4-0
	Wath Athletic v Brodsworth Main Colliery	1-0
	Worksop Town v Goldthorpe United	5-2
12	Bolsover Colliery v Matlock Town	0-1
	Burton Town v Buxton	4-1
	Ripley Town v Ilkeston United	1-4
	Shirebrook v Gresley Rovers	2-0
13	Basford United v Sutton Junction	5-5
	Boots Athletic - Bye	
	Lenton v Sutton Town	3-2
	Newark Castle Rovers v Ransome & Marles	2-1
14	Desborough Town v Kettering Town	0-0
	New Peterborough Swifts v Higham Ferrers Town	2-6
	Rushden Town v Peterborough & Fletton Utd.	0-1
	Stamford v Rothwell Town	7-0
15	Biggleswade & District v Waterlows (Dunstable)	2-2
	Hitchin Town v Bedford Town (1)	3-1
	Letchworth Town v Arlesey Town	4-1
	Luton Amateur v RAF Henlow	3-0
16	Colchester Town v Kirkley & Waveney	2-1
	Crittall Athletic v Lowestoft Town	0-4
	King's Lynn v Cambridge Town	3-1
	Leiston Works Athletic v Gorleston	0-0
17	Chelmsford v Walthamstow Avenue	5-1
	Clapton v Leytonstone	2-2
	Grays Athletic v Dagenham Town	0-3
	Romford (2) v Barking	1-3
18	Finchley v Bishop's Stortford	1-0
	Hendon Town v Enfield	2-5
	Hoddesdon Town v St Albans City	2-1
	Tufnell Park v Leavesden Mental Hospital	2-0
19	Hampstead Town v Southall	0-3
	Maidenhead United v Marlow	6-3
	Slough v Gradwell Sports	3-2
	Wycombe Wanderers v Park Royal	5-3
20	Beddington Corner v West Norwood	1-2
	Carshalton Athletic v Dorking	8-1
	Mitcham Wanderers v Metropolitan Police	0-3
	Woking v Sutton United	1-4
21	Aldershot Traction Co. v Camberley & Yorktown	1-3
	Courage & Co.'s Sports v Egham	6-0
	Wellington Works v Godalming	6-1
	Winchester City v RAMC Aldershot	6-0
22	Bostall Heath v RM Chatham	3-2
	Bromley v Ashford	2-1
	Canterbury Waverley v RM Deal	4-0
	Chatham v Erith & Belvedere	4-0
23	Chichester v Eastbourne Old Comrades	4-2
	East Grinstead v Hove	3-2
	Vernon Athletic v Southwick	0-4
	Worthing v Hastings & St Leonards	0-2
24	Blandford v Salisbury City (1)	0-3
	Fareham v Weymouth	2-0
	Newport (IOW) v Bournemouth (Ams)	7-1
	Poole Town v Cowes	1-2
25	Bath City v Radstock Town	2-0
	Frome Town v Spencer Moulton	2-2
	Trowbridge Town v Chippenham Town	2-1
	Welton Rovers v Paulton Rovers	1-4
26	Kingswood v Bristol St George	2-2
	Llanelli v Taunton Town (1)	3-2
	Lovells Athletic v Hanham Athletic	4-0
	Street v Yeovil & Petter's United	1-4
1r	North Shields v Walker Celtic	0-1
2r	Spennymoor United v Evenwood Town	0-1
3r	Bridlington Town (1) v Stockton	0-1
5r	Darwen v Burscough Rangers	5-3e
7r	Winsford United v Runcorn	2-1
8r	Cradley Heath St Luke's v Stafford Rangers	3-1
10r	South Kirkby Colliery v Wombwell	2-0
13r	Sutton Junction v Basford United	9-0
14r	Kettering Town v Desborough Town	5-2e
15r	Waterlows (Dunstable) v Biggleswade & District	1-0
16r	Gorleston v Leiston Works Athletic	1-0
17r	Leytonstone v Clapton	2-1
25r	Spencer Moulton v Frome Town	4-1
26r	Bristol St George v Kingswood	2-2
26r2	Kingswood v Bristol St George	1-1
26r3	Bristol St George v Kingswood	2-3

Qualifying Round Two

1	Blyth Spartans v Walker Celtic	3-2
	Jarrow v Crawcrook Albion	2-0
2	Crook Town v Horden CW	4-1
	Murton CW v Evenwood Town	3-2
3	Normanby Mangnesite v Filey Town	4-0
	Stockton v Whitby United	3-2
4	Holme Head Works v Whitehaven Athletic	1-0
	Workington v Cleator Moor Celtic	3-0
5	Chorley v Lytham	2-2
	Darwen v Dick, Kerrs	3-1
6	Prescot Cables v Marine	3-1
	Stalybridge Celtic v Droylsden	5-1
7	Macclesfield Town v Winsford United	1-1
	Rhyl v Altrincham	1-1
8	Cradley Heath St Luke's v Brierley Hill Alliance	2-0
	Nuneaton Town v Oakengates Town	2-1
9	Broughton Rangers v Selby Town	3-4
	Frodingham & Appleby Ath. v Barton Town (1)	1-4
10	Denaby United v South Kirkby Colliery	2-1
	Frickley Colliery v Yorkshire Amateur	0-2
11	Owston Park Rangers v Worksop Town	2-3
	Rawmarsh Welfare v Wath Athletic	1-0
12	Burton Town v Ilkeston United	2-0
	Matlock Town v Shirebrook	0-0
13	Lenton v Boots Athletic	2-1
	Sutton Junction v Newark Castle Rovers	7-1
14	Higham Ferrers Town v Peterborough & Fletton Utd.	1-3
	Stamford v Kettering Town	2-3
15	Hitchin Town v Waterlows (Dunstable)	1-1
	Luton Amateur v Letchworth Town	2-0
16	King's Lynn v Gorleston	1-0
	Lowestoft Town v Colchester Town	5-3
17	Chelmsford v Leytonstone	7-1
	Dagenham Town v Barking	3-1
18	Enfield v Tufnell Park	4-1
	Hoddesdon Town v Finchley	5-4
19	Slough v Southall	0-2
	Wycombe Wanderers v Maidenhead United	4-0
20	Sutton United v Carshalton Athletic	1-2
	West Norwood v Metropolitan Police	1-6
21	Courage & Co.'s Sports v Camberley & Yorktown	4-3
	Wellington Works v Winchester City	2-4
22	Bostall Heath v Canterbury Waverley	4-1
	Chatham v Bromley	2-0
23	East Grinstead v Hastings & St Leonards	1-6
	Southwick v Chichester	3-0
24	Cowes v Newport (IOW)	2-5
	Fareham v Salisbury City (1)	1-1
25	Paulton Rovers v Spencer Moulton	5-0
	Trowbridge Town v Bath City	0-4
26	Llanelli v Kingswood	3-0
	Yeovil & Petter's United v Lovells Athletic	1-0
5r	Lytham v Chorley	3-2e
7r	Altrincham v Rhyl	4-1
r	Winsford United v Macclesfield Town	0-1
12r	Shirebrook v Matlock Town	4-1
15r	Waterlows (Dunstable) v Hitchin Town	0-2
24r	Salisbury City (1) v Fareham	2-1

Qualifying Round Three

1	Blyth Spartans v Jarrow	4-1
2	Murton CW v Crook Town	1-1
3	Stockton v Normanby Mangnesite	2-2
4	Workington v Holme Head Works	6-0
5	Darwen v Lytham	3-1
6	Prescot Cables v Stalybridge Celtic	3-2
7	Altrincham v Macclesfield Town	6-4
8	Cradley Heath St Luke's v Nuneaton Town	0-0
9	Selby Town v Barton Town (1)	6-0
10	Yorkshire Amateur v Denaby United	2-1
11	Worksop Town v Rawmarsh Welfare	2-1
12	Burton Town v Shirebrook	6-4
13	Sutton Junction v Lenton	3-1
14	Peterborough & Fletton Utd. v Kettering Town	0-0
15	Hitchin Town v Luton Amateur	7-0
16	King's Lynn v Lowestoft Town	1-0
17	Chelmsford v Dagenham Town	1-1
18	Hoddesdon Town v Enfield	0-5
19	Wycombe Wanderers v Southall	2-1
20	Metropolitan Police v Carshalton Athletic	3-2
21	Winchester City v Courage & Co.'s Sports	0-0
22	Bostall Heath v Chatham	1-2
23	Hastings & St Leonards v Southwick	3-0
24	Salisbury City (1) v Newport (IOW)	3-0
25	Bath City v Paulton Rovers	2-0
26	Llanelli v Yeovil & Petter's United	0-1
2r	Crook Town v Murton CW	8-2
3r	Normanby Mangnesite v Stockton	1-1
8r	Nuneaton Town v Cradley Heath St Luke's	3-1
14r	Kettering Town v Peterborough & Fletton Utd.	0-3
17r	Dagenham Town v Chelmsford	0-2
21r	Courage & Co.'s Sports v Winchester City	3-4
3r2	Normanby Mangnesite v Stockton	1-8

Qualifying Round Four

	Altrincham v Yorkshire Amateur	1-3
	Barnet v Dulwich Hamlet	2-1
	Bath City - Bye	
	Chatham v Northfleet United	1-4
	Crook Town v Bishop Auckland	3-1
	Darwen v Prescot Cables	2-1
	Enfield v Wycombe Wanderers	6-1
	Folkestone v Dartford	1-0
	Guildford City v Ilford	4-1
	Hastings & St Leonards v Wimbledon	1-4
	Hayes v Hitchin Town	7-1
	King's Lynn v Newark Town	1-1
	Kingstonian v Metropolitan Police	1-1
	Lancaster Town v Workington	2-0
	Leyton v Chelmsford	1-2
	Margate v Tunbridge Wells Rangers	1-2
	Nelson v Manchester Central	1-3
	Nuneaton Town v Burton Town	0-2
	Nunhead v Winchester City	3-1
	Scunthorpe United v Sutton Junction	7-1
	Selby Town v Peterborough & Fletton Utd.	1-1
	Stockton v Blyth Spartans	0-3
	West Stanley v Scarborough	2-0
	Worksop Town v Gainsborough Trinity	0-2
	Yeovil & Petter's United v Salisbury City (1)	4-2
r	Kingstonian v Metropolitan Police	0-2
r	Newark Town v King's Lynn	2-1
r	Peterborough & Fletton Utd. v Selby Town	3-0

Round One

	Aldershot v Chelmsford	7-0
	Barnet v Queen's Park Rangers	3-7
	Barrow v Doncaster Rovers	3-3
	Bath City v Nunhead	9-0
	Bournemouth v Northfleet United	1-1
	Bristol Rovers v Gillingham	5-1
	Burton Town v Wigan Borough	wo/s
	Cardiff City v Enfield	8-0
	Chester v Hartlepools United	4-1
	Coventry City v Clapton Orient	2-2
	Crewe Alexandra v Gainsborough Trinity	2-2
	Crook Town v Stockport County	3-1
	Darlington v Walsall	1-0
	Darwen v Peterborough & Fletton Utd.	4-1
	Folkestone v Brighton & Hove Albion	2-5
	Fulham v Guildford City	2-0
	Gateshead v Wrexham	3-2
	Hull City v Mansfield Town	4-1
	Lancaster Town v Blyth Spartans	0-3
	Manchester Central v Lincoln City	0-3
	New Brighton v York City	3-1
	Newark Town v Halifax Town	1-1
	Northampton Town v Metropolitan Police	9-0
	Reading v Crystal Palace	0-1
	Rotherham United v Accrington Stanley	0-0
	Scunthorpe United v Rochdale	2-1
	Swindon Town v Luton Town	0-5
	Thames v Watford	2-2
	Torquay United v Southend United	1-3
	Tranmere Rovers v West Stanley	3-0
	Tunbridge Wells Rangers v Brentford	1-1
	Wimbledon v Norwich City	1-3
	Yeovil & Petter's United v Hayes	3-1
	Yorkshire Amateur v Carlisle United	1-3
r	Accrington Stanley v Rotherham United	5-0
r	Brentford v Tunbridge Wells Rangers	2-1
r	Clapton Orient v Coventry City	2-0
r	Doncaster Rovers v Barrow	1-1e
r	Gainsborough Trinity v Crewe Alexandra	1-0
r	Halifax Town v Newark Town	2-1
r	Northfleet United v Bournemouth	0-1
r	Watford v Thames	2-1e
r2	Barrow v Doncaster Rovers	1-1eN
r3	Doncaster Rovers v Barrow	1-0eN

1931/32 to 1932/33

Round Two

	Aldershot v Crook Town	1-1
	Bath City v Crystal Palace	2-1
	Bournemouth v Blyth Spartans	1-0
	Brentford v Norwich City	4-1
	Brighton & Hove Albion v Doncaster Rovers	5-0
	Burton Town v Gateshead	4-1
	Cardiff City v Clapton Orient	4-0
	Carlisle United v Darlington	0-2
	Darwen v Chester	2-1
	Fulham v Yeovil & Petter's United	0-0
	Gainsborough Trinity v Watford	2-5
	Halifax Town v Accrington Stanley	3-0
	Lincoln City v Luton Town	2-2
	New Brighton v Hull City	0-4
	Northampton Town v Southend United	3-0
	Scunthorpe United v Queen's Park Rangers	1-4
	Tranmere Rovers v Bristol Rovers	2-0
r	Crook Town v Aldershot	1-0
r	Luton Town v Lincoln City	4-1
r	Yeovil & Petter's United v Fulham	2-5

Round Three

	Arsenal v Darwen	11-1
	Barnsley v Southport	0-0
	Birmingham v Bradford City	1-0
	Blackpool v Newcastle United	1-1
	Bradford Park Avenue v Cardiff City	2-0
	Brentford v Bath City	2-0
	Brighton & Hove Albion v Port Vale	1-2
	Burnley v Derby County	0-4
	Burton Town v Blackburn Rovers	0-4
	Bury v Swansea Town	2-1
	Charlton Athletic v West Ham United	1-2
	Chesterfield v Nottingham Forest	5-2
	Darlington v Northampton Town	1-1
	Everton v Liverpool	1-2
	Grimsby Town v Exeter City	4-1
	Halifax Town v Bournemouth	1-3
	Leicester City v Crook Town	7-0
	Luton Town v Wolverhampton Wan.	1-2
	Middlesbrough v Portsmouth	1-1
	Millwall v Manchester City	2-3
	Notts County v Bristol City	2-2
	Oldham Athletic v Huddersfield Town	1-1
	Plymouth Argyle v Manchester United	4-1
	Preston North End v Bolton Wanderers	0-0
	Queen's Park Rangers v Leeds United	3-1
	Sheffield United v Corinthians	2-1
	Stoke City v Hull City	3-0
	Sunderland v Southampton	0-0
	Tottenham Hotspur v Sheffield Wednesday	2-2
	Tranmere Rovers v Chelsea	2-2
	Watford v Fulham	1-1
	West Bromwich Albion v Aston Villa	1-2
r	Bolton Wanderers v Preston North End	2-5
r	Bristol City v Notts County	3-2
r	Chelsea v Tranmere Rovers	5-3
r	Fulham v Watford	0-3
r	Huddersfield Town v Oldham Athletic	6-0
r	Newcastle United v Blackpool	1-0
r	Northampton Town v Darlington	2-0
r	Portsmouth v Middlesbrough	3-0
r	Sheffield Wednesday v Tottenham Hotspur	3-1
r	Southampton v Sunderland	2-4
r	Southport v Barnsley	4-1

Round Four

	Arsenal v Plymouth Argyle	4-2
	Bradford Park Avenue v Northampton Town	4-2
	Bury v Sheffield United	3-1
	Chelsea v West Ham United	3-1
	Chesterfield v Liverpool	2-4
	Derby County v Blackburn Rovers	3-2
	Grimsby Town v Birmingham	2-1
	Huddersfield Town v Queen's Park Rangers	5-0
	Manchester City v Brentford	6-1
	Newcastle United v Southport	1-1
	Port Vale v Leicester City	1-2
	Portsmouth v Aston Villa	1-1
	Preston North End v Wolverhampton Wan.	2-0
	Sheffield Wednesday v Bournemouth	7-0
	Sunderland v Stoke City	1-1
	Watford v Bristol City	2-1
r	Aston Villa v Portsmouth	0-1
r	Southport v Newcastle United	1-1e
r	Stoke City v Sunderland	1-1e
r2	Newcastle United v Southport	9-0 N
r2	Stoke City v Sunderland	2-1eN

Round Five

	Bury v Stoke City	3-0
	Huddersfield Town v Preston North End	4-0
	Liverpool v Grimsby Town	1-0
	Manchester City v Derby County	3-0
	Newcastle United v Leicester City	3-1
	Portsmouth v Arsenal	0-2
	Sheffield Wednesday v Chelsea	1-1
	Watford v Bradford Park Avenue	1-0
r	Chelsea v Sheffield Wednesday	2-0

Round Six

Bury v Manchester City	3-4
Huddersfield Town v Arsenal	0-1
Liverpool v Chelsea	0-2
Newcastle United v Watford	5-0

Semi Finals

Arsenal v Manchester City	1-0 N
Newcastle United v Chelsea	2-1 N

Final

Newcastle United v Arsenal	2-1 N

1932/33

Extra Preliminary Round

1	Chopwell Institute v Shankhouse	10-5
	Gosforth & Coxlodge v Dipton United	1-0
	Hebburn St Cuthbert's v Newcastle East End (2)	0-3
	Leslies v Walker Park	3-4
	North Shields v Usworth Colliery	0-0
	Rosehill v Birtley	1-1
	Scotswood v South Shields Corinthians	3-1
	Wallsend v Spen Black & White	5-1
2	Annfield Plain v Durham City	5-3
	Blackhall Colliery Welfare v Consett	4-0
	Cockfield v Eden CW	2-4
	Easington CW v Washington Colliery	4-2
	Leasingthorne Colliery v Trimdon Grange Colliery	1-2
	Spennymoor United v Dawdon Colliery Recreation	10-1
	Stanley United v Shildon	1-0
	Thornley CW v Shotton CW	2-1
	Tow Law Town v Willington	1-2
	Wardley Welfare v Chilton Colliery Recreation	2-1
	West Auckland Town v Seaham Colliery Welfare	1-2
8	Birmingham Corp. Tramways v Bromsgrove Rovers	5-0
	Bournville Athletic v Cannock Town	1-2
	Evesham Town v Leamington Town	3-1
	Hereford United v Bilston United	wo/s
	Kidderminster Harriers v Hednesford Town	5-2
	Oswestry Town v Wellington Town	3-2
	Redditch v Headingley	11-0
	Stourbridge v Worcester City	2-4
	Walsall Phoenix v Wolverhampton Amateur	2-1
	Whitchurch v Stafford Rangers	4-1
11	Bentley Colliery v Dinnington Athletic	1-3
16	4th Divisional Signals Regiment v Felixstowe Town	2-0
	Abbey United (Cambs) v Histon Institute	4-5
	Cambridge Town v Chatteris Town	6-2
	Crittall Athletic v Stowmarket	4-0
	Ipswich Town v Kirkley	0-0
	King's Lynn v Cromer	2-0
	Norwich CEYMS v Leiston Works Athletic	8-0
	Parkeston Railway v RAF Martlesham	1-4
	Severalls Athletic v Harwich & Parkeston	0-4
	Sheringham v Great Yarmouth Town	1-0
	Wisbech Town v Newmarket Town	3-2
18	Apsley v Welwyn Garden City	4-1
	Bishop's Stortford v Stevenage Town	1-0
	Bletchley Town (1) v Aylesbury United	2-3
	Hendon Town v Hertford Town	5-1
	Old Lyonian v Berkhamsted Town	3-2
	St Albans City v Chesham United	1-1
	Waltham Comrades v Watford British Legion	wo/s
19	Bicester Town v AEC Athletic	wo/s
	Marlow v Stokenchurch	6-2
	Morris Motors (Cowley) v Witney Town	4-6
	Thame United v Henley Town	5-1
	Wealdstone v Abingdon Town	9-0
22	Bexley v Woolwich Borough Co. Ath.	9-1
	Lloyds (Sittingbourne) v RM Chatham	5-1
	Maidstone United v Ashford	0-1
	UGB Sports (Charlton) v Callender Athletic	0-3
24	Shanklin & Lake v Shaftesbury	3-4
25	Calne & Harris United v Coleford Athletic	7-3
	Devizes Town v Radstock Town	4-1
	Frome Town v Street	2-5
	Garrards Athletic v Clandown	0-3
	Wells City v Swindon Corinthians	5-3
	Westbury United v Warminster Town	5-1
26	Dartmouth United v Wadebridge United	3-1
	Ebbw Vale v Merthyr Town	0-1
	Green Waves (Plymouth) v Oreston Rovers	2-2
	Hanham Athletic v Wesley Rangers	2-1
	St Philips Marsh Adult School v Clevedon	5-4
	Taunton Town (1) v St Philips Athletic	2-2
1r	Birtley v Rosehill	5-0
r	Usworth Colliery v North Shields	0-4
16r	Kirkley v Ipswich Town	2-3
18r	Chesham United v St Albans City	2-1
26r	Oreston Rovers v Green Waves (Plymouth)	4-3
r	Taunton Town (1) v St Philips Athletic	3-1

Preliminary Round

1	Blyth Spartans v Birtley	7-0
	Chester-le-Street v Howdon British Legion	2-1
	Crawcrook Albion v North Shields	1-0
	Gosforth & Coxlodge v Chopwell Institute	2-6
	Scotswood v Newcastle East End (2)	4-1
	Walker Celtic v Jarrow	2-1
	Walker Park v Pelaw	2-1
	Wallsend v Ashington	2-0
2	Bishop Auckland v Annfield Plain	1-2
	Ferryhill Athletic v Willington	2-1
	Seaham Colliery Welfare v Eden CW	2-0
	Spennymoor United v Murton CW	5-1
	Stanley United v Horden CW	3-3
	Thornley CW v Blackhall Colliery Welfare	4-1
	Trimdon Grange Colliery v Evenwood Town	3-1
	Wardley Welfare v Easington CW	1-0
4	Parton Athletic v Keswick	wo/s
	Windermere v Moss Bay United	wo/s
5	Breightmet United v Westhoughton	wo/s
	Crossens v Skelmersdale United	1-2
6	Earle v New Mills	3-1
	Northern Nomads v Shell Mex	9-1
	Prescot Cables v Ashton National	3-1
	Stalybridge Celtic v Manchester North End	4-2
	Timperley v Peasley Cross Athletic	2-11
	Whiston v Glossop	3-1
7	Altrincham v Barnton Victoria	5-0
	Colwyn Bay v Sandbach Ramblers	3-4
	Linotype & Machinery v Rhyl	0-5
	Llandudno v Witton Albion	0-3
	Lostock Gralam v Northwich Victoria	0-4
	Macclesfield Town v Congleton Town	2-1
	Nantwich v Willaston White Star	2-1
	Winsford United v Bangor City	1-2
8	Atherstone Town v Hereford United	2-4
	Brierley Hill Alliance v Oakengates Town	5-0
	Cradley Heath St Luke's v Walsall Phoenix	5-0
	Evesham Town v Worcester City	3-4
	Kidderminster Harriers v Cannock Town	2-1
	Oswestry Town v Redditch	7-2
	Shrewsbury Town v Nuneaton Town	3-1
	Whitchurch v Birmingham Corp. Tramways	8-1
9	Brigg Town v Humber United	4-3
	Goole Town v Marfleet	4-2
	Grimsby Haycroft Rovers v Brigg 2nd Lincs Sugar Co.	0-1
	Selby OCO v Louth Town	0-4
10	Cudworth Village v Farsley Celtic	5-2
	Guiseley v Luddendenfoot	6-2
	Hebden Bridge v Wombwell	2-4
	Monckton Athletic v Grimethorpe Colliery Institute	1-2
11	Denaby United v Brodsworth Main Colliery	1-1
	Hallam v Goldthorpe United	1-2
	Norton Woodseats v Owston Park Rangers	1-1
	Pilkington Recreation v Thurnscoe Victoria	2-1
	Rawmarsh Welfare v Mexborough Athletic	2-0
	Rossington Main v Wath Athletic	1-7
	Silverwood Colliery v Dinnington Athletic	1-1
	Worksop Town v Hatfield Main	5-1
12	Sandiacre Excelsior Foundry v Loughborough Cor's	3-5
13	Grantham v Ransome & Marles	2-1
	Sutton Town v Spalding United	6-1
14	Desborough Town v Peterbro' Westwood Works	3-2
	Market Harborough Town v Rushden Town	4-5
	Rothwell Town v New Peterborough Swifts	0-1
	Wellingborough Town v Wolverton Town	5-4
15	Davis Athletic v Langford	0-1
	Kempston Rovers v Biggleswade & District	2-2
	Leighton United v Baldock Town	6-3
	RAF Henlow v Sandy Albion	1-1
	St Neots & District v Arlesey Town	3-2
	Vauxhall Motors (Luton) v Bedford Town (1)	0-3
	Waterlows (Dunstable) v Hitchin Town	2-0
16	4th Divisional Signals Regiment v RAF Martlesham	0-1
	Cambridge Town v Ipswich Town	2-2
	Crittall Athletic v Colchester Town	0-2
	Gorleston v Norwich CEYMS	0-2
	Harwich & Parkeston v Clacton Town	4-2
	Histon Institute v Sheringham	2-3
	King's Lynn v Lowestoft Town	2-1
	Wisbech Town v Thetford Town	7-1
17	Barking v Chelmsford	4-2
	Clapton v South West Ham	5-2
	Dagenham Town v Romford (2)	1-4
	Grays Athletic v Tate Institute	10-1
	Heybridge v Custom House	5-3
	Jurgens (Purfleet) v Leyton	2-1
	Tilbury v Brentwood & Warley	0-2
	Walthamstow Avenue v Leytonstone	4-3
18	Apsley v Hoddesdon Town	3-1
	Bishop's Stortford v London Caledonians	2-0
	Chesham United v Ware	6-0
	Finchley v Hendon Town	0-3
	Leavesden Mental Hospital v Enfield	4-2
	Tufnell Park v Old Johnians	1-0
	Waltham Comrades v Old Lyonian	1-1
	Wood Green Town v Aylesbury United	2-1
19	Bicester Town v Headington United	2-2
	Hampstead Town v Uxbridge	6-1
	Maidenhead United v Wealdstone	4-0
	Marlow v Witney Town	3-1
	Newbury Town v Slough	0-7
	Park Royal v Thame United	9-0
	Windsor & Eton v Southall	2-1
	Wycombe Wanderers v Gradwell Sports	2-0
20	Epsom Town v West Norwood	5-1
	Metropolitan Police v Dorking	1-0
	Nunhead v Wills Sports	1-0
	Redhill v Beddington Corner	8-0
	Sutton United v Leyland Motors (Kingston)	5-0

1932/33

	Tooting & Mitcham United v PO Engineers (Beddington)	3-3
	Woking v Walton-on-Thames	5-3
21	Egham v Basingstoke	5-2
	Guildford v Aldershot Traction Co.	wo/s
	RAMC Aldershot v Thornycrofts (Basingstoke)	4-2
22	Ashford - Bye	
	Bexleyheath & Welling v Beckenham	1-2
	Bromley v Callender Athletic	2-5
	Erith & Belvedere v Bostall Heath	1-1
	Lloyds (Sittingbourne) v Canterbury Waverley	5-3
	Sheppey United v RM Deal	4-2
	Sittingbourne v Whitstable	7-2
	Woolwich Polytechnic v Bexley	0-2
23	East Grinstead v Worthing	0-1
	Eastbourne Old Comrades v Hove	2-0
	Littlehampton v Chichester	5-2
	Shoreham v Newhaven	4-2
	Southwick v Bexhill	2-0
	Vernon Athletic v Horsham	1-6
24	Bournemouth Tramways v Fareham	3-1
	Cowes v Dorchester Town	7-4
	Gosport v Osborne Athletic	4-2
	New Milton v Bournemouth (Ams)	2-7
	Newport (IOW) v Weymouth	4-1
	RAOC Hilsea v Blandford	6-0
	Ryde Sports v Shaftesbury	6-2
	Salisbury Corinthians v Salisbury City (1)	2-3
25	Calne & Harris United v Street	0-4
	Devizes Town v Wells City	1-2
	Glastonbury v Melksham	4-3
	Paulton Rovers v Swindon Victoria	1-1
	Spencer Moulton v Chippenham Rovers	8-1
	Trowbridge Town v Chippenham Town	1-2
	Welton Rovers v Clandown	1-1
	Westbury United v Purton	1-0
26	Hanham Athletic v Cadbury Heath YMCA	3-1
	Keynsham v Kingswood	1-1
	Llanelli v Lovells Athletic	4-0
	Merthyr Town v Barry	3-2
	Minehead v St Philips Marsh Adult School	1-2
	Mount Hill Enterprise v Bristol St George	2-3
	Oreston Rovers v Dartmouth United	2-3
	Taunton Town (1) v J.S. Fry & Sons	6-1
2r	Horden CW v Stanley United	5-2
11r	Brodsworth Main Colliery v Denaby United	0-1
r	Dinnington Athletic v Silverwood Colliery	3-1e
r	Owston Park Rangers v Norton Woodseats	7-2
15r	Biggleswade & District v Kempston Rovers	3-2e
r	Sandy Albion v RAF Henlow	5-3
16r	Ipswich Town v Cambridge Town	1-2
18r	Old Lyonian v Waltham Comrades	1-3
19r	Headington United v Bicester Town	2-4
20r	Tooting & Mitcham Utd v PO Engineers (Beddington)	1-5
22r	Bostall Heath v Erith & Belvedere	3-1
25r	Clandown v Welton Rovers	1-0
r	Swindon Victoria v Paulton Rovers	5-3
26r	Kingswood v Keynsham	3-2

Qualifying Round One

1	Chester-le-Street v Blyth Spartans	2-3
	Chopwell Institute v Walker Park	5-2
	Scotswood v Crawcrook Albion	0-1
	Wallsend v Walker Celtic	3-3
2	Horden CW v Trimdon Grange Colliery	4-0
	Spennymoor United v Seaham Colliery Welfare	4-1
	Thornley CW v Ferryhill Athletic	1-1
	Wardley Welfare v Annfield Plain	4-0
3	Bridlington Town (1) v Filey Town	5-2
	Normanby Mangnesite v South Bank East End	4-2
	Stockton v Whitby Albion Rangers	5-3
	Whitby United v South Bank	4-3
4	Kells United v Parton Athletic	3-1
	Whitehaven Athletic v Penrith	6-3
	Windermere v Cleator Moor Celtic	4-3
	Workington v Netherfield (Kendal)	6-1
5	Chorley v Breightmet United	1-1
	Dick, Kerrs v Lytham	1-0
	Horwich RMI v Burscough Rangers	4-1
	Morecambe v Skelmersdale United	2-2
6	Droylsden - Bye	
	Northern Nomads v Stalybridge Celtic	5-6
	Peasley Cross Athletic v Whiston	4-2
	Prescot Cables v Earle	1-0
7	Bangor City v Sandbach Ramblers	3-1
	Macclesfield Town v Altrincham	2-3
	Nantwich v Witton Albion	6-1
	Northwich Victoria v Rhyl	0-2
8	Brierley Hill Alliance v Cradley Heath St Luke's	2-1
	Hereford United v Worcester City	5-2
	Oswestry Town v Whitchurch	0-1
	Shrewsbury Town v Kidderminster Harriers	5-1
9	Brigg 2nd Lincs Sugar Co. v Brigg Town	9-0
	Broughton Rangers v Barton Town (1)	2-3
	Frodingham & Appleby Ath. v Goole Town	2-3
	Louth Town v Selby Town	2-0
10	Cudworth Village v Ardsley Athletic	4-1
	Grimethorpe Colliery Institute v South Kirkby Col.	1-4
	Guiseley v Frickley Colliery	0-7
	Wombwell v Yorkshire Amateur	2-3
11	Denaby United v Pilkington Recreation	4-1
	Rawmarsh Welfare v Dinnington Athletic	1-0
	Wath Athletic v Owston Park Rangers	2-1
	Worksop Town v Goldthorpe United	3-1
12	Ilkeston United v Shirebrook	2-0
	Loughborough Corinthians v Heanor Town	4-1
	Matlock Town v Gresley Rovers	2-3
	Ripley Town v Bolsover Colliery	6-0
13	Boston (1) v Lenton	4-1
	Grantham v Sutton Junction	8-1
	Newark Castle Rovers v Basford United	2-2
	Sutton Town v Boots Athletic	4-2
14	Higham Ferrers Town v Wellingborough Town	2-1
	Kettering Town v Rushden Town	4-0
	Peterborough & Fletton U v New Peterboro' Swifts	2-0
	Stamford v Desborough Town	1-5
15	Bedford Town (1) v Biggleswade & District	1-1
	Sandy Albion v Leighton United	7-0
	St Neots & District v Letchworth Town	2-3
	Waterlows (Dunstable) v Langford	9-1
16	Colchester Town v Sheringham	4-2
	King's Lynn v Harwich & Parkeston	0-0
	Norwich CEYMS v Cambridge Town	2-2
	Wisbech Town v RAF Martlesham	5-3
17	Barking v Brentwood & Warley	1-0
	Clapton v Walthamstow Avenue	1-3
	Heybridge v Jurgens (Purfleet)	1-1
	Romford (2) v Grays Athletic	3-1
18	Apsley v Wood Green Town	0-2
	Chesham United v Tufnell Park	1-1
	Hendon Town v Waltham Comrades	3-0
	Leavesden Mental Hospital v Bishop's Stortford	4-1
19	Hampstead Town v Bicester Town	5-2
	Marlow v Park Royal	0-2
	Windsor & Eton v Slough	1-6
	Wycombe Wanderers v Maidenhead United	3-2
20	Carshalton Athletic v Nunhead	1-5
	Epsom Town v Redhill	4-1
	Sutton United v PO Engineers (Beddington)	2-4
	Woking v Metropolitan Police	0-2
21	Camberley & Yorktown v Guildford	3-1
	Courage & Co.'s Sports v Staines Town	4-2
	Egham v Godalming	2-7
	Wellington Works v RAMC Aldershot	5-2
22	Ashford v Bexley	6-0
	Beckenham v Sittingbourne	4-3
	Callender Athletic v Lloyds (Sittingbourne)	0-1
	Sheppey United v Bostall Heath	1-0
23	Brighton & Hove Albion v Shoreham	12-0
	Eastbourne Old Comrades v Worthing	2-6
	Littlehampton v Hastings & St Leonards	1-3
	Southwick v Horsham	2-0
24	Bournemouth (Ams) v RAOC Hilsea	2-2
	Cowes v Newport (IOW)	0-1
	Gosport v Salisbury City (1)	2-2
	Ryde Sports v Bournemouth Tramways	3-1
25	Chippenham Town v Westbury United	1-5
	Spencer Moulton v Glastonbury	3-4
	Street v Wells City	3-2
	Swindon Victoria v Clandown	0-0
26	Kingswood v St Philips Marsh Adult School	0-1
	Llanelli v Bristol St George	5-0
	Merthyr Town v Hanham Athletic	10-2
	Taunton Town (1) v Dartmouth United	2-2
1r	Walker Celtic v Wallsend	0-2
2r	Ferryhill Athletic v Thornley CW	2-0
5r	Breightmet United v Chorley	1-5
r	Skelmersdale United v Morecambe	3-4e
13r	Basford United v Newark Castle Rovers	6-2
15r	Biggleswade & District v Bedford Town (1)	0-2
16r	Cambridge Town v Norwich CEYMS	3-5
r	Harwich & Parkeston v King's Lynn	5-0
17r	Jurgens (Purfleet) v Heybridge	6-0
18r	Tufnell Park v Chesham United	0-1
24r	RAOC Hilsea v Bournemouth (Ams)	4-1
r	Salisbury City (1) v Gosport	2-4
25r	Clandown v Swindon Victoria	4-2
26r	Dartmouth United v Taunton Town (1)	1-4

Qualifying Round Two

1	Blyth Spartans v Crawcrook Albion	4-1
	Chopwell Institute v Wallsend	3-2
2	Ferryhill Athletic v Horden CW	1-4
	Wardley Welfare v Spennymoor United	0-2
3	Bridlington Town (1) v Stockton	4-2
	Normanby Mangnesite v Whitby United	2-0
4	Kells United v Workington	0-7
	Windermere v Whitehaven Athletic	4-6
5	Dick, Kerrs v Morecambe	1-3
	Horwich RMI v Chorley	0-3
6	Droylsden v Prescot Cables	1-2
	Peasley Cross Athletic v Stalybridge Celtic	1-1
7	Altrincham v Nantwich	7-1
	Bangor City v Rhyl	0-0
8	Brierley Hill Alliance v Hereford United	1-1
	Shrewsbury Town v Whitchurch	3-3
9	Brigg 2nd Lincs Sugar Co. v Barton Town (1)	3-3
	Louth Town v Goole Town	2-1
10	Frickley Colliery v Yorkshire Amateur	1-3
	South Kirkby Colliery v Cudworth Village	3-0
11	Wath Athletic v Denaby United	1-1
	Worksop Town v Rawmarsh Welfare	3-1
12	Ilkeston United v Gresley Rovers	0-4
	Ripley Town v Loughborough Corinthians	1-1
13	Boston (1) v Basford United	8-0
	Sutton Town v Grantham	1-2
14	Higham Ferrers Town v Desborough Town	10-1
	Kettering Town v Peterborough & Fletton Utd.	10-0
15	Bedford Town (1) v Sandy Albion	7-1
	Waterlows (Dunstable) v Letchworth Town	1-1
16	Harwich & Parkeston v Colchester Town	4-1
	Wisbech Town v Norwich CEYMS	1-3
17	Barking v Walthamstow Avenue	1-2
	Jurgens (Purfleet) v Romford (2)	0-1
18	Leavesden Mental Hospital v Hendon Town	8-0
	Wood Green Town v Chesham United	5-2
19	Hampstead Town v Slough	1-2
	Wycombe Wanderers v Park Royal	6-1
20	Metropolitan Police v PO Engineers (Beddington)	3-2
	Nunhead v Epsom Town	0-0
21	Camberley & Yorktown v Wellington Works	1-0
	Courage & Co.'s Sports v Godalming	2-2
22	Lloyds (Sittingbourne) v Beckenham	6-1
	Sheppey United v Ashford	3-2
23	Brighton & Hove Albion v Worthing	7-1
	Hastings & St Leonards v Southwick	2-0
24	Gosport v Ryde Sports	1-3
	Newport (IOW) v RAOC Hilsea	1-5
25	Clandown v Street	1-4
	Glastonbury v Westbury United	2-3
26	Merthyr Town v Llanelli	1-0
	St Philips Marsh Adult School v Taunton Town (1)	2-1
6r	Stalybridge Celtic v Peasley Cross Athletic	5-4
7r	Rhyl v Bangor City	2-2e
8r	Hereford United v Brierley Hill Alliance	4-0
r	Whitchurch v Shrewsbury Town	0-1
9r	Barton Town (1) v Brigg 2nd Lincs Sugar Co.	2-3e
11r	Denaby United v Wath Athletic	2-1
12r	Loughborough Corinthians v Ripley Town	2-1
15r	Letchworth Town v Waterlows (Dunstable)	2-1
20r	Epsom Town v Nunhead	5-0
21r	Godalming v Courage & Co.'s Sports	1-0
7r2	Rhyl v Bangor City	2-0 N

Qualifying Round Three

1	Blyth Spartans v Chopwell Institute	3-0
2	Spennymoor United v Horden CW	2-0
3	Bridlington Town (1) v Normanby Mangnesite	3-2
4	Whitehaven Athletic v Workington	0-0
5	Morecambe v Chorley	0-3
6	Stalybridge Celtic v Prescot Cables	5-0
7	Rhyl v Altrincham	2-3
8	Hereford United v Shrewsbury Town	3-1
9	Brigg 2nd Lincs Sugar Co. v Louth Town	2-3
10	Yorkshire Amateur v South Kirkby Colliery	0-1
11	Denaby United v Worksop Town	4-0
12	Gresley Rovers v Loughborough Corinthians	6-2
13	Grantham v Boston (1)	1-1
14	Kettering Town v Higham Ferrers Town	3-0
15	Bedford Town (1) v Letchworth Town	4-2
16	Norwich CEYMS v Harwich & Parkeston	1-1
17	Walthamstow Avenue v Romford (2)	2-2
18	Leavesden Mental Hospital v Wood Green Town	6-0
19	Slough v Wycombe Wanderers	2-3
20	Metropolitan Police v Epsom Town	3-1
21	Godalming v Camberley & Yorktown	2-4
22	Lloyds (Sittingbourne) v Sheppey United	3-2
23	Hastings & St Leonards v Brighton & Hove Albion	0-9
24	RAOC Hilsea v Ryde Sports	1-2
25	Westbury United v Street	2-4
26	St Philips Marsh Adult School v Merthyr Town	0-7
4r	Workington v Whitehaven Athletic	5-2e
13r	Boston (1) v Grantham	3-2
16r	Harwich & Parkeston v Norwich CEYMS	5-3
17r	Romford (2) v Walthamstow Avenue	4-2

Qualifying Round Four

	Barnet v Brighton & Hove Albion	0-4
	Bath City v Yeovil & Petter's United	2-4
	Bridlington Town (1) v Spennymoor United	2-4
	Camberley & Yorktown v Wycombe Wanderers	0-4
	Chorley v Darwen	2-2
	Crook Town v Blyth Spartans	5-1
	Dartford v Northfleet United	2-0
	Denaby United v Louth Town	6-2
	Gresley Rovers v Gainsborough Trinity	1-1
	Guildford City v Harwich & Parkeston	2-0
	Hayes v Kingstonian	3-4
	Hereford United v Kettering Town	3-0
	Ilford v Oxford City	7-0
	Lloyds (Sittingbourne) v Wimbledon	5-1
	Margate v Leavesden Mental Hospital	1-0
	Nelson v Lancaster Town	6-0
	Newark Town v Boston (1)	0-2
	Romford (2) v Bedford Town (1)	3-1
	Ryde Sports v Metropolitan Police	1-0
	Scunthorpe United v Burton Town	4-1
	Stalybridge Celtic v Altrincham	0-0
	Street v Merthyr Town	1-1
	Tunbridge Wells Rangers v Folkestone	0-2
	West Stanley v Scarborough	2-3
	Workington v South Kirkby Colliery	3-0
r	Altrincham v Stalybridge Celtic	3-3e
r	Darwen v Chorley	5-0
r	Gainsborough Trinity v Gresley Rovers	4-2
r	Merthyr Town v Street	5-2
r2	Altrincham v Stalybridge Celtic	0-1 N

Round One

	Accrington Stanley v Hereford United	2-1
	Barrow v Gateshead	0-1

1932/33 to 1933/34

	Bristol City v Romford (2)	4-0
	Cardiff City v Bristol Rovers	1-1
	Carlisle United v Denaby United	1-0
	Chester v Rotherham United	4-0
	Clapton Orient v Aldershot	0-1
	Crewe Alexandra v Crook Town	4-0
	Crystal Palace v Brighton & Hove Albion	1-2
	Darlington v Boston (1)	1-0
	Dartford v Yeovil & Petter's United	0-0
	Doncaster Rovers v Gainsborough Trinity	4-1
	Folkestone v Norwich City	1-0
	Gillingham v Wycombe Wanderers	1-1
	Guildford City v Coventry City	1-2
	Halifax Town v Darwen	2-0
	Luton Town v Kingstonian	2-2
	Margate v Ryde Sports	5-0
	Marine v Hartlepools United	2-5
	Merthyr Town v Queen's Park Rangers	1-1
	Newport County v Ilford	4-2
	Northampton Town v Lloyds (Sittingbourne)	8-1
	Reading v Brentford	3-2
	Rochdale v Stockport County	0-2
	Southend United v Exeter City	1-1
	Southport v Nelson	3-3
	Stalybridge Celtic v Hull City	2-8
	Swindon Town v Dulwich Hamlet	4-1
	Torquay United v Bournemouth	0-0
	Tranmere Rovers v New Brighton	3-0
	Walsall v Mansfield Town	4-1
	Workington v Scunthorpe United	5-1
	Wrexham v Spennymoor United	3-0
	York City v Scarborough	1-3
r	Bournemouth v Torquay United	2-2e
r	Bristol Rovers v Cardiff City	4-1
r	Exeter City v Southend United	0-1
r	Kingstonian v Luton Town	2-3
r	Nelson v Southport	0-4
r	Queen's Park Rangers v Merthyr Town	5-1
r	Wycombe Wanderers v Gillingham	2-4
r	Yeovil & Petter's United v Dartford	4-2
r2	Torquay United v Bournemouth	3-2 N

Round Two

	Accrington Stanley v Aldershot	1-2
	Brighton & Hove Albion v Wrexham	0-0
	Bristol City v Tranmere Rovers	2-2
	Bristol Rovers v Gillingham	1-1
	Carlisle United v Hull City	1-1
	Chester v Yeovil & Petter's United	2-1
	Crewe Alexandra v Darlington	0-2
	Folkestone v Newport County	2-1
	Gateshead v Margate	5-2
	Halifax Town v Workington	2-1
	Northampton Town v Doncaster Rovers	0-1
	Reading v Coventry City	2-2
	Southend United v Scarborough	4-1
	Southport v Swindon Town	1-2
	Stockport County v Luton Town	2-3
	Torquay United v Queen's Park Rangers	1-1
	Walsall v Hartlepools United	2-1
r	Coventry City v Reading	3-3e
r	Gillingham v Bristol Rovers	1-3
r	Hull City v Carlisle United	2-1e
r	Queen's Park Rangers v Torquay United	3-1
r	Tranmere Rovers v Bristol City	3-2
r	Wrexham v Brighton & Hove Albion	2-3e
r2	Reading v Coventry City	1-0 N

Round Three

	Aldershot v Bristol Rovers	1-0
	Barnsley v Luton Town	0-0
	Birmingham v Preston North End	2-1
	Blackpool v Port Vale	2-1
	Bradford City v Aston Villa	2-2
	Bradford Park Avenue v Plymouth Argyle	5-1
	Brighton & Hove Albion v Chelsea	2-1
	Bury v Nottingham Forest	2-2
	Charlton Athletic v Bolton Wanderers	1-5
	Chester v Fulham	5-0
	Corinthians v West Ham United	0-2
	Darlington v Queen's Park Rangers	2-0
	Doncaster Rovers v Halifax Town	0-3
	Gateshead v Manchester City	1-1
	Grimsby Town v Portsmouth	3-2
	Huddersfield Town v Folkestone	2-0
	Hull City v Sunderland	0-2
	Leicester City v Everton	2-3
	Lincoln City v Blackburn Rovers	1-5
	Manchester United v Middlesbrough	1-4
	Millwall v Reading	1-1
	Newcastle United v Leeds United	0-3
	Oldham Athletic v Tottenham Hotspur	0-6
	Sheffield Wednesday v Chesterfield	2-2
	Stoke City v Southampton	1-0
	Swansea Town v Sheffield United	2-3
	Swindon Town v Burnley	1-2
	Tranmere Rovers v Notts County	2-1
	Walsall v Arsenal	2-0
	Watford v Southend United	1-1
	West Bromwich Albion v Liverpool	2-0
	Wolverhampton Wan. v Derby County	3-6
r	Aston Villa v Bradford City	2-1
r	Chesterfield v Sheffield Wednesday	4-2
r	Luton Town v Barnsley	2-0
r	Manchester City v Gateshead	9-0
r	Nottingham Forest v Bury	1-2
r	Reading v Millwall	0-2
r	Southend United v Watford	2-0

Round Four

	Aldershot v Millwall	1-0
	Aston Villa v Sunderland	0-3
	Birmingham v Blackburn Rovers	3-0
	Blackpool v Huddersfield Town	2-0
	Bolton Wanderers v Grimsby Town	2-1
	Brighton & Hove Albion v Bradford Park Avenue	2-1
	Burnley v Sheffield United	3-1
	Chester v Halifax Town	0-0
	Darlington v Chesterfield	0-2
	Everton v Bury	3-1
	Luton Town v Tottenham Hotspur	2-0
	Manchester City v Walsall	2-0
	Middlesbrough v Stoke City	4-1
	Southend United v Derby County	2-3
	Tranmere Rovers v Leeds United	0-0
	West Ham United v West Bromwich Albion	2-0
r	Halifax Town v Chester	3-2e
r	Leeds United v Tranmere Rovers	4-0

Round Five

	Bolton Wanderers v Manchester City	2-4
	Brighton & Hove Albion v West Ham United	2-2
	Burnley v Chesterfield	1-0
	Derby County v Aldershot	2-0
	Everton v Leeds United	2-0
	Halifax Town v Luton Town	0-2
	Middlesbrough v Birmingham	0-0
	Sunderland v Blackpool	1-0
r	Birmingham v Middlesbrough	3-0
r	West Ham United v Brighton & Hove Albion	1-0e

Round Six

	Burnley v Manchester City	0-1
	Derby County v Sunderland	4-4
	Everton v Luton Town	6-0
	West Ham United v Birmingham	4-0
r	Sunderland v Derby County	0-1e

Semi Finals

	Everton v West Ham United	2-1 N
	Manchester City v Derby County	3-2 N

Final

	Everton v Manchester City	3-0 N

1933/34

Extra Preliminary Round

1	Howdon British Legion v Spen Black & White	2-1
	Newcastle East End (2) v Jarrow	1-5
	Pelaw v Scotswood	4-0
	Usworth Colliery v Throckley Welfare	2-2
	West Wylam CW v Ashington	1-1
2	Bishop Auckland v Stanley United	4-3
	Cockfield v Shildon	1-1
	Durham City v Blackhall Colliery Welfare	5-0
	Easington CW v Annfield Plain	3-0
	Evenwood Town v Consett	1-2
	Murton CW v Barnard Castle Athletic	2-1
	Seaham Colliery Welfare v Crookhall CW	2-1
	Shotton CW v Trimdon Grange Colliery	1-2
	South Hetton CW v Burnhope Institute	2-0
	Tow Law Town v Tanfield Lea Rovers	2-1
	Willington v West Auckland Town	2-1
7	Bangor City v Witton Albion	4-2
	Bedouins v Middlewich Athletic	1-2
	Moulton Verdin v ICI Alkali	1-3
	Shell Mex v Willaston White Star	0-1
	Whitchurch v Barnton Victoria	0-2
8	Atherstone Town v Wolverhampton Amateur	5-3
	Bournville Athletic v Leamington Town	2-6
	Cannock Town v Headingley	6-1
	Evesham Town v Boldmere St Michaels	2-0
	Hednesford Town v Dudley Town	4-0
	Nuneaton Town v Halesowen Town	7-2
	Oakengates Town v Cradley Heath St Luke's	4-0
	Oswestry Town v Badsey Rangers	19-3
	Rugby Town (1) v Kidderminster Harriers	2-2
	Stourbridge v Bromsgrove Rovers	3-2
	Wellington Town v Redditch	6-1
	Worcester City v Birmingham Corp. Tramways	7-1
15	4th Divisional Signals Regiment v Crittall Athletic	1-5
	Brightlingsea United v Severalls Athletic	4-1
	Bury Town v Great Yarmouth Town	4-2
	Chatteris Town v Abbey United (Cambs)	2-2
	Clacton Town v Norwich YMCA	1-1
	Cromer v Sheringham	1-4
	Frosts Athletic v Norwich St Barnabas	2-2
	Gorleston v Ipswich Town	3-2
	Histon Institute v King's Lynn	1-5
	Kirkley v Lowestoft Town	0-3
	Leiston Works Athletic v Felixstowe Town	1-3
	March Great Eastern United v Chatteris Engineers	2-1
	Newmarket Town v Wisbech Town	1-1
18	Bushey United v Apsley	4-1
	Enfield v Hertford Town	1-0
	Hoddesdon Town v Welwyn Garden City	12-0
	Shredded Wheat v Old Johnians	1-2
	St Albans City v Watford British Legion	6-1
	Ware v Boxmoor St Johns	1-3
19	Aylesbury United v Maidenhead United	3-3
	Bicester Town v Stokenchurch	7-2
	Cowley v Abingdon Town	2-0
	Henley Town v Marlow	2-6
	Hounslow Town v Wealdstone	4-3
	Morris Motors (Cowley) v Newbury Town	3-2
	Southall v Civil Service	6-0
	Windsor & Eton v Uxbridge	1-3
	Witney Town v Thame United	3-1
22	Bostall Heath v London Paper Mills	1-2
	Bromley v Swanley Athletic	3-2
	Callender Athletic v Woolwich Borough Co. Ath.	3-1
	Canterbury Waverley v RM Chatham	6-0
	Cray Wanderers v Bexley	4-0
	Deal Town v Chatham	4-2
	RM Deal v Maidstone United	3-1
	Ramsgate Press Wanderers v Aylesford Paper Mills	2-2
	UGB Sports (Charlton) v Woolwich Polytechnic	1-0
24	Blandford v Hamworthy	0-3
	Dorchester Town v Poole Town	2-3
	RM Portsmouth v Totton	0-0
25	Frome Town v Trowbridge Town	2-1
26	Barry v Cardiff Corinthians	3-1
	Bristol St George v Kingswood	4-1
	Cheltenham Town v Mount Hill Enterprise	2-0
	Clevedon v Wesley Rangers	6-0
	Green Waves (Plymouth) v Dartmouth United	6-1
	Hanham Athletic v St Philips Marsh Adult School	0-0
	Keynsham v Cadbury Heath YMCA	1-0
	Lovells Athletic v Ebbw Vale	0-0
	Minehead v Street	1-3
	Plymouth United v Tiverton Town	3-3
	St Philips Athletic v J.S. Fry & Sons	5-0
	Wells City v Weston-Super-Mare	0-1
1r	Ashington v West Wylam CW	8-2
r	Throckley Welfare v Usworth Colliery	2-0
2r	Shildon v Cockfield	2-0
8r	Kidderminster Harriers v Rugby Town (1)	wo/s
15r	Abbey United (Cambs) v Chatteris Town	3-2
r	Norwich St Barnabas v Frosts Athletic	2-1
r	Norwich YMCA v Clacton Town	1-2e
r	Wisbech Town v Newmarket Town	0-1
19r	Aylesbury United v Maidenhead United	1-4
22r	Aylesford Paper Mills v Ramsgate Press Wanderers	3-3e
24r	Totton v RM Portsmouth	5-1
25r	Tiverton Town v Plymouth United	3-2
26r	Ebbw Vale v Lovells Athletic	2-1
r	St Philips Marsh Adult School v Hanham Athletic	2-1
22r2	Ramsgate Press Wanderers v Aylesford Paper Mills	2-4 N

Preliminary Round

1	Ashington v Birtley	2-0
	Blyth Spartans v Pelaw	2-1
	Chopwell Institute v Jarrow	1-3
	Howdon British Legion v Walker Park	1-2
	Rosehill v Dipton United	3-0
	Throckley Welfare v Gosforth & Coxlodge	1-3
	Walker Celtic v Shankhouse	4-0
	Wardley Welfare v Crawcrook Albion	7-3
2	Bishop Auckland v Consett	2-2
	Easington CW v South Hetton CW	6-2
	Ferryhill Athletic v Willington	2-1
	Horden CW v Durham City	1-0
	Murton CW v Trimdon Grange Colliery	3-2
	Seaham Colliery Welfare v West Stanley	0-1
	Shildon v Dawdon Colliery Recreation	4-1
	Tow Law Town v Crook Town	2-1
3	South Bank St Peters v Pease & Partners	3-0
4	Holme Head Works v Burnside (Kendal)	1-0
5	Breightmet United v Lytham	0-2
	Leyland Motors v Skelmersdale United	3-0
	Westhoughton v Rossendale United	1-0
	Wigan Athletic v Great Harwood	1-1
6	Ashton National v Whiston	3-1
	Earle v Orrell	4-2
	Glossop v Droylsden	1-0
	Harrowby v Shell Mex	2-2
	Marine v Northern Nomads	2-0
	Prescot Cables v Manchester North End	1-1
	Stalybridge Celtic v Urmston Old Boys	7-0
	Timperley v Seaforth Albion	0-6
7	Barnton Victoria v Macclesfield Town	3-3
	Colwyn Bay v Winsford United	3-1
	ICI Alkali v Middlewich Athletic	4-2
	Llandudno v Bangor City	0-2
	Lostock Gralam v Congleton Town	2-1
	Northwich Victoria v Linotype & Machinery	7-1
	Rhyl v Willaston White Star	9-3
	Sandbach Ramblers v Altrincham	2-2
8	Atherstone Town - Bye	
	Brierley Hill Alliance v Evesham Town	0-0
	Hednesford Town v Wellington Town	3-3
	Hereford United v Oakengates Town	5-1
	Kidderminster Harriers v Nuneaton Town	2-2

1933/34

	Shrewsbury Town v Oswestry Town	3-1
	Stourbridge v Cannock Town	2-0
	Worcester City v Leamington Town	4-0
9	Barton Town (1) v Humber United	1-1
	Lysaght's Sports (Scunthorpe) v Selby OCO	5-0
	Marfleet v Frodingham & Appleby Ath.	4-3
	Selby Town v Brigg Town	4-0
10	Cortonwood v Monckton Athletic	1-5
	Cudworth Village v Yorkshire Amateur	1-2
	Denaby United v Mexborough Athletic	3-0
	Goldthorpe United v Thurnscoe Victoria	1-1
	Guiseley v Wath Athletic	7-1
	Rawmarsh Welfare v Wombwell Main Welfare	4-1
	South Kirkby Colliery v Grimethorpe Colliery Inst.	1-1
11	Pilkington Recreation v Brodsworth Main Colliery	2-0
	Thorne Colliery v Sheffield	4-2
13	Johnson & Barnes v Boots Athletic	5-1
	Ransome & Marles v Lenton	wo/s
	Sutton Junction v Rufford Colliery	8-1
14	Market Harborough Town v Wellingborough Town	0-4
	Phorpres Sports v Wolverton Town	1-0
	Rothwell Town v Rushden Town	0-6
15	Bury Town v Lowestoft Town	2-1
	Clacton Town v Norwich CEYMS	2-1
	Crittall Athletic v Colchester Town	5-1
	Gorleston v Felixstowe Town	4-0
	Harwich & Parkeston v Brightlingsea United	7-2
	King's Lynn v March Great Eastern United	10-0
	Newmarket Town v Abbey United (Cambs)	3-1
	Sheringham v Norwich St Barnabas	2-3
16	Baldock Town v Luton Amateur	3-0
	Bedford Town (1) v Arlesey Town	7-0
	Biggleswade & District v St Neots & District	6-2
	Hitchin Town v Vauxhall Motors (Luton)	0-1
	Kempston Rovers v Leighton United	9-0
	Langford v Letchworth Town	0-3
	Waterlows (Dunstable) v Bedford Queens Park Rangers	3-1
17	Brentwood & Warley v Dagenham Town	0-2
	Chelmsford v South West Ham	6-2
	Clapton v Custom House	4-1
	Grays Athletic v Tilbury	1-1
	Leyton v Barking	1-1
	Leytonstone v Heybridge	5-0
	Romford (2) v Becontree Town	wo/s
18	Bishop's Stortford v Bushey United	1-3
	Boxmoor St Johns v Hendon Town	wo/s
	Finchley v Tufnell Park	1-2
	Hoddesdon Town v Enfield	5-1
	Leavesden Mental Hospital v Old Johnians	1-0
	London Caledonians v Old Lyonian	1-2
	St Albans City v Berkhamsted Town	3-3
	Wood Green Town v Stevenage Town	9-1
19	Bicester Town v Slough	2-4
	Cowley v Marlow	3-3
	Gradwell Sports v AEC Athletic	2-1
	Maidenhead United v Hounslow Town	5-2
	Oxford City v Golders Green	4-3
	Park Royal v Chesham United	4-3
	Uxbridge v Morris Motors (Cowley)	6-2
	Witney Town v Southall	2-3
20	Beddington Corner v Hersham	3-1
	Carshalton Athletic v West Norwood	3-1
	Leyland Motors (Kingston) v Dorking	4-2
	PO Engineers (Beddington) v Streatham Town	0-2
	Walton-on-Thames v Sutton United	3-2
	Wills Sports v Tooting & Mitcham United	0-5
	Woking v Epsom Town	1-1
21	Egham v Guildford	8-1
	Staines Town v Cranleigh	2-0
	Winchester City v RAMC Aldershot	5-1
22	Ashford v Deal Town	7-1
	Aylesford Paper Mills v Lloyds (Sittingbourne)	2-0
	Beckenham v Erith & Belvedere	1-1
	Bexleyheath & Welling v London Paper Mills	1-3
	Bromley v Cray Wanderers	3-1
	Callender Athletic v UGB Sports (Charlton)	2-3
	Canterbury Waverley v RM Deal	1-1
	Sheppey United v Tunbridge Wells Rangers	5-2
23	Bexhill v Hove	4-4
	East Grinstead v Newhaven	2-5
	Eastbourne Old Comrades v Chichester	5-2
	Haywards Heath v Worthing	5-3
	Horsham v Shoreham	1-4
	Littlehampton v Vernon Athletic	1-4
24	Bournemouth Tramways v Salisbury Corinthians	0-0
	Cowes v RAOC Hilsea	1-0
	Newport (IOW) v Totton	1-1
	Poole Town v Hamworthy	3-1
	Ryde Sports v Osborne Athletic	9-1
	Salisbury City (1) v Bournemouth (Ams)	2-3
	Shaftesbury v Weymouth	1-6
	Shanklin & Lake v Gosport	1-2
25	Calne & Harris United v Devizes Town	3-0
	Clandown v Chippenham Town	3-1
	Garrards Athletic - Bye	
	Melksham v Warminster Town	2-2
	Radstock Town v Welton Rovers	2-1
	Swindon Corinthians v Chippenham Rovers	9-0
	Swindon Victoria v Paulton Rovers	1-3
	Westbury United v Frome Town	1-5
26	Barry v Llanelli	0-4
	Bristol St George v St Philips Marsh Adult School	0-5
	Glastonbury v Taunton Town (1)	1-0
	Keynsham v Clevedon	5-1
	Merthyr Town v Ebbw Vale	1-0
	St Philips Athletic v Cheltenham Town	1-1
	Tiverton Town v Green Waves (Plymouth)	1-3
	Weston-Super-Mare v Street	1-1
2r	Consett v Bishop Auckland	1-3
5r	Great Harwood v Wigan Athletic	1-4
6r	Harrowby v Shell Mex	wo/s
r	Manchester North End v Prescot Cables	3-0
7r	Altrincham v Sandbach Ramblers	3-0
r	Macclesfield Town v Barnton Victoria	4-3
8r	Evesham Town v Brierley Hill Alliance	1-2
r	Nuneaton Town v Kidderminster Harriers	3-5e
r	Wellington Town v Hednesford Town	5-0
9r	Humber United v Barton Town (1)	2-1
10r	Grimethorpe Colliery Institute v South Kirkby Collie	2-2e
r	Thurnscoe Victoria v Goldthorpe United	0-0e
17r	Barking v Leyton	1-3
r	Tilbury v Grays Athletic	1-0
18r	Berkhamsted Town v St Albans City	3-1
19r	Marlow v Cowley	3-0
20r	Epsom Town v Woking	5-2e
22r	Erith & Belvedere v Beckenham	3-0
r	RM Deal v Canterbury Waverley	0-2
23r	Hove v Bexhill	4-2
24r	Salisbury Corinthians v Bournemouth Tramways	7-1
r	Totton v Newport (IOW)	0-2
25r	Warminster Town v Melksham	5-2e
26r	Cheltenham Town v St Philips Athletic	5-0
r	Street v Weston-Super-Mare	3-2
10r2	Grimethorpe Colliery Institute v South Kirkby Collie	0-2 N
r2	Thurnscoe Victoria v Goldthorpe United	2-1 N

Qualifying Round One

1	Blyth Spartans v Gosforth & Coxlodge	6-2
	Jarrow v Wardley Welfare	0-0
	Rosehill v Ashington	1-1
	Walker Celtic v Walker Park	1-4
2	Bishop Auckland v Shildon	1-6
	Ferryhill Athletic v Tow Law Town	3-0
	Horden CW v Easington CW	3-3
	Murton CW v West Stanley	2-0
3	Bridlington Town (1) v South Bank East End	2-2
	Filey Town v South Bank St Peters	0-4
	South Bank v Normanby Mangnesite	1-0
	Whitby United v Whitby Albion Rangers	6-2
4	Cleator Moor Celtic v Kells United	1-6
	Maryport v Whitehaven Athletic	1-2
	Netherfield (Kendal) v Holme Head Works	5-3
	Penrith v Windermere	3-3
5	Dick, Kerrs v Leyland Motors	3-2
	Horwich RMI v Wigan Athletic	0-3
	Lytham v Morecambe	5-1
	Westhoughton v Crossens	3-1
6	Ashton National v Marine	2-2
	Glossop v Seaforth Albion	6-2
	Manchester North End v Earle	9-1
	Stalybridge Celtic v Harrowby	6-1
7	Altrincham v Lostock Gralam	2-0
	ICI Alkali v Bangor City	1-0
	Macclesfield Town v Colwyn Bay	3-0
	Northwich Victoria v Rhyl	0-4
8	Brierley Hill Alliance v Kidderminster Harriers	3-2
	Shrewsbury Town v Hereford United	3-1
	Wellington Town v Atherstone Town	4-0
	Worcester City v Stourbridge	6-0
9	Goole Town v Lysaght's Sports (Scunthorpe)	2-1
	Humber United v Marfleet	1-1
	Louth Town v Brigg 2nd Lincs Sugar Co.	6-3
	Scunthorpe United v Selby Town	4-1
10	Denaby United v Guiseley	5-1
	Rawmarsh Welfare v Frickley Colliery	wo/s
	Thurnscoe Victoria v Monckton Athletic	4-1
	Yorkshire Amateur v South Kirkby Colliery	1-0
11	Bentley Colliery v Pilkington Recreation	3-1
	Dinnington Athletic v Thorne Colliery	2-2
	Rossington Main v Worksop Town	0-4
	Silverwood Colliery v Owston Park Rangers	2-1
12	Gresley Rovers v Matlock Town	2-3
	Heanor Town v Hinckley United (1)	9-0
	Ripley Town - Bye	
	Sandiacre Excelsior Foundry v Loughboro' Cor's	1-2
13	Basford United v Boston (1)	wo/s
	Grantham v Sutton Town	1-1
	Ransome & Marles v Johnson & Barnes	5-1
	Sutton Junction v Spalding United	3-4
14	Desborough Town v Wellingborough Town	2-5
	Higham Ferrers Town v Peterbro' Westwood Works	4-3
	Phorpres Sports v Kettering Town	2-4
	Stamford v Rushden Town	4-2
15	Clacton Town v Crittall Athletic	2-0
	Gorleston v Norwich St Barnabas	2-2
	Harwich & Parkeston v Newmarket Town	6-2
	King's Lynn v Bury Town	4-0
16	Bedford Town (1) v Waterlows (Dunstable)	5-0
	Letchworth Town v Biggleswade & District	1-1
	Sandy Albion v Baldock Town	0-3
	Vauxhall Motors (Luton) v Kempston Rovers	4-1
17	Clapton v Jurgens (Purfleet)	2-2
	Leyton v Leytonstone	3-3
	Romford (2) v Chelmsford	1-2
	Tilbury v Dagenham Town	5-2
18	Leavesden Mental Hospital v Berkhamsted Town	3-0
	Old Lyonian v Bushey United	5-0
	Tufnell Park v Boxmoor St Johns	3-3
	Wood Green Town v Hoddesdon Town	2-3
19	Marlow v Gradwell Sports	2-0
	Oxford City v Park Royal	2-0
	Southall v Maidenhead United	4-0
	Uxbridge v Slough	5-2
20	Epsom Town v Nunhead	3-0
	Leyland Motors (Kingston) v Streatham Town	2-4
	Tooting & Mitcham United v Carshalton Athletic	3-0
	Walton-on-Thames v Beddington Corner	0-1
21	Camberley & Yorktown v Wellington Works	4-1
	Egham v Courage & Co.'s Sports	4-2
	Staines Town v Thornycrofts (Basingstoke)	4-2
	Winchester City v Godalming	2-0
22	Canterbury Waverley v Ashford	4-4
	Erith & Belvedere v London Paper Mills	2-4
	Sheppey United v Bromley	3-0
	UGB Sports (Charlton) v Aylesford Paper Mills	0-0
23	Hastings & St Leonards v Southwick	5-2
	Newhaven v Hove	2-3
	Shoreham v Eastbourne Old Comrades	8-2
	Vernon Athletic v Haywards Heath	2-0
24	Bournemouth (Ams) v Salisbury Corinthians	2-0
	Cowes v Newport (IOW)	3-2
	Gosport v Weymouth	2-1
	Ryde Sports v Poole Town	4-1
25	Calne & Harris United v Frome Town	5-2
	Garrards Athletic v Clandown	1-2
	Paulton Rovers v Swindon Corinthians	1-2
	Radstock Town v Warminster Town	3-2
26	Cheltenham Town v Street	4-0
	Green Waves (Plymouth) v St Philips Marsh Ad.Sch.	3-2
	Llanelli v Keynsham	5-1
	Merthyr Town v Glastonbury	3-3
1r	Ashington v Rosehill	3-1
r	Wardley Welfare v Jarrow	2-1
2r	Horden CW v Easington CW	0-1
3r	South Bank East End v Bridlington Town (1)	1-2
4r	Windermere v Penrith	3-5e
6r	Marine v Ashton National	3-1
9r	Marfleet v Humber United	1-2
11r	Thorne Colliery v Dinnington Athletic	1-2
13r	Sutton Town v Grantham	2-0
15r	Norwich St Barnabas v Gorleston	3-1
16r	Biggleswade & District v Letchworth Town	2-0
17r	Jurgens (Purfleet) v Clapton	1-0
r	Leytonstone v Leyton	3-1
18r	Boxmoor St Johns v Tufnell Park	1-10
22r	Ashford v Canterbury Waverley	1-3
r	Aylesford Paper Mills v UGB Sports (Charlton)	1-1
26r	Glastonbury v Merthyr Town	1-2
22r2	UGB Sports (Charlton) v Aylesford Paper Mills	0-1 N

Qualifying Round Two

1	Ashington v Blyth Spartans	0-0
	Wardley Welfare v Walker Park	1-1
2	Ferryhill Athletic v Murton CW	1-1
	Shildon v Easington CW	3-1
3	South Bank v Whitby United	1-1
	South Bank St Peters v Bridlington Town (1)	1-0
4	Netherfield (Kendal) v Penrith	5-2
	Whitehaven Athletic v Kells United	1-0
5	Dick, Kerrs v Westhoughton	2-2
	Wigan Athletic v Lytham	2-1
6	Marine v Glossop	2-1
	Stalybridge Celtic v Manchester North End	3-4
7	Altrincham v ICI Alkali	1-1
	Rhyl v Macclesfield Town	0-1
8	Brierley Hill Alliance v Worcester City	4-0
	Wellington Town v Shrewsbury Town	2-2
9	Louth Town v Goole Town	4-2
	Scunthorpe United v Humber United	5-0
10	Denaby United v Thurnscoe Victoria	4-3
	Yorkshire Amateur v Rawmarsh Welfare	0-3
11	Dinnington Athletic v Bentley Colliery	3-1
	Silverwood Colliery v Worksop Town	1-0
12	Loughborough Corinthians v Heanor Town	1-3
	Ripley Town v Matlock Town	1-3
13	Basford United v Spalding United	3-7
	Sutton Town v Ransome & Marles	5-0
14	Higham Ferrers Town v Kettering Town	1-2
	Stamford v Wellingborough Town	1-0
15	Harwich & Parkeston v King's Lynn	3-2
	Norwich St Barnabas v Clacton Town	3-2
16	Baldock Town v Vauxhall Motors (Luton)	2-1
	Bedford Town (1) v Biggleswade & District	4-3
17	Chelmsford v Leytonstone	2-3
	Tilbury v Jurgens (Purfleet)	0-3
18	Hoddesdon Town v Leavesden Mental Hospital	3-1
	Old Lyonian v Tufnell Park	4-2
19	Oxford City v Marlow	10-1
	Uxbridge v Southall	0-2
20	Beddington Corner v Streatham Town	3-1
	Tooting & Mitcham United v Epsom Town	0-1
21	Camberley & Yorktown v Winchester City	5-0
	Staines Town v Egham	1-2
22	Aylesford Paper Mills v Canterbury Waverley	3-2
	London Paper Mills v Sheppey United	4-2
23	Hove v Vernon Athletic	3-2
	Shoreham v Hastings & St Leonards	2-1
24	Gosport v Cowes	1-0
	Ryde Sports v Bournemouth (Ams)	5-0
25	Calne & Harris United v Radstock Town	2-1
	Swindon Corinthians v Clandown	2-2
26	Llanelli v Green Waves (Plymouth)	9-0
	Merthyr Town v Cheltenham Town	2-4

1933/34 to 1934/35

1r	Blyth Spartans v Ashington	1-1
r	Walker Park v Wardley Welfare	1-3
2r	Murton CW v Ferryhill Athletic	3-1
3r	Whitby United v South Bank	2-1
5r	Westhoughton v Dick, Kerrs	1-5
7r	ICI Alkali v Altrincham	0-1
8r	Shrewsbury Town v Wellington Town	4-1
25r	Clandown v Swindon Corinthians	3-1
1r2	Blyth Spartans v Ashington	2-1

Qualifying Round Three

1	Wardley Welfare v Blyth Spartans	1-1
2	Murton CW v Shildon	3-1
3	South Bank St Peters v Whitby United	4-2
4	Whitehaven Athletic v Netherfield (Kendal)	3-0
5	Wigan Athletic v Dick, Kerrs	2-1
6	Manchester North End v Marine	5-3
7	Altrincham v Macclesfield Town	2-1
8	Shrewsbury Town v Brierley Hill Alliance	2-1
9	Scunthorpe United v Louth Town	4-1
10	Denaby United v Rawmarsh Welfare	1-1
11	Silverwood Colliery v Dinnington Athletic	1-2
12	Matlock Town v Heanor Town	1-2
13	Sutton Town v Spalding United	2-0
14	Kettering Town v Stamford	5-3
15	Harwich & Parkeston v Norwich St Barnabas	9-0
16	Baldock Town v Bedford Town (1)	1-6
17	Jurgens (Purfleet) v Leytonstone	0-1
18	Old Lyonian v Hoddesdon Town	3-1
19	Oxford City v Southall	4-0
20	Epsom Town v Beddington Corner	4-2
21	Egham v Camberley & Yorktown	1-1
22	Aylesford Paper Mills v London Paper Mills	0-3
23	Hove v Shoreham	2-7
24	Gosport v Ryde Sports	2-2
25	Calne & Harris United v Clandown	3-1
26	Llanelli v Cheltenham Town	2-2
1r	Blyth Spartans v Wardley Welfare	2-2
10r	Rawmarsh Welfare v Denaby United	4-1
21r	Camberley & Yorktown v Egham	1-0
24r	Ryde Sports v Gosport	5-1
26r	Cheltenham Town v Llanelli	1-2 d
1r2	Blyth Spartans v Wardley Welfare	1-0

Qualifying Round Four

	Altrincham v Wigan Athletic	3-1
	Blyth Spartans v North Shields	0-0
	Burton Town v Sutton Town	1-2
	Cheltenham Town v Calne & Harris United	10-1
	Chorley v Lancaster Town	1-1
	Dartford v Guildford City	4-0
	Darwen v Whitehaven Athletic	5-0
	Dinnington Athletic v Newark Town	3-4
	Dulwich Hamlet v Wycombe Wanderers	1-0
	Epsom Town v Leytonstone	3-1
	Gainsborough Trinity v Shrewsbury Town	0-0
	Hayes v Walthamstow Avenue	3-2
	Ilford v Harwich & Parkeston	3-1
	Kettering Town v Bedford Town (1)	4-3
	London Paper Mills v Ryde Sports	4-2
	Manchester North End v Workington	3-3
	Murton CW v Scarborough	1-1
	Northfleet United v Camberley & Yorktown	11-1
	Old Lyonian v Margate	0-2
	Oxford City v Shoreham	6-1
	Scunthorpe United v Heanor Town	4-2
	South Bank St Peters v Rawmarsh Welfare	3-2
	Stockton v Spennymoor United	2-2
	Wimbledon v Barnet	1-3
	Yeovil & Petter's United v Bath City	0-2
r	Lancaster Town v Chorley	3-2
r	North Shields v Blyth Spartans	3-1
r	Scarborough v Murton CW	2-0
r	Shrewsbury Town v Gainsborough Trinity	1-3
r	Spennymoor United v Stockton	2-1
r	Workington v Manchester North End	6-3

Round One

	Barrow v Doncaster Rovers	4-2
	Bath City v Charlton Athletic	0-0
	Bournemouth v Hayes	3-0
	Cardiff City v Aldershot	0-0
	Carlisle United v Wrexham	2-1
	Cheltenham Town v Barnet	5-1
	Chester v Darlington	6-1
	Clapton Orient v Epsom Town	4-2
	Coventry City v Crewe Alexandra	3-0
	Crystal Palace v Norwich City	3-0
	Dulwich Hamlet v Newport County	2-2
	Folkestone v Bristol Rovers	0-0
	Gainsborough Trinity v Altrincham	1-0
	Gateshead v Darwen	5-2
	Halifax Town v Barnsley	3-2
	Ilford v Swindon Town	2-4
	Kingstonian v Bristol City	1-7
	Lancaster Town v Stockport County	0-1
	London Paper Mills v Southend United	0-1
	New Brighton v Mansfield Town	0-0
	North Shields v Scarborough	3-0
	Northampton Town v Exeter City	2-0
	Northfleet United v Dartford	0-2
	Oxford City v Gillingham	1-5
	Queen's Park Rangers v Kettering Town	6-0
	Rotherham United v South Bank St Peters	3-2
	Scunthorpe United v Accrington Stanley	1-1
	Sutton Town v Rochdale	2-1
	Torquay United v Margate	1-1
	Tranmere Rovers v Newark Town	7-0
	Walsall v Spennymoor United	4-0
	Watford v Reading	0-3
	Workington v Southport	1-0
	York City v Hartlepools United	2-3
r	Accrington Stanley v Scunthorpe United	3-0
r	Aldershot v Cardiff City	3-1
r	Bristol Rovers v Folkestone	3-1
r	Charlton Athletic v Bath City	3-1
r	Mansfield Town v New Brighton	3-4
r	Margate v Torquay United	0-2
r	Newport County v Dulwich Hamlet	6-2

Round Two

	Accrington Stanley v Bristol Rovers	1-0
	Bournemouth v Tranmere Rovers	2-4
	Bristol City v Barrow	2-1
	Carlisle United v Cheltenham Town	1-2
	Charlton Athletic v Gillingham	1-0
	Gainsborough Trinity v Aldershot	0-2
	Gateshead v North Shields	1-0
	Halifax Town v Hartlepools United	1-1
	Northampton Town v Torquay United	3-0
	Queen's Park Rangers v New Brighton	1-1
	Rotherham United v Coventry City	2-1
	Southend United v Chester	2-1
	Stockport County v Crystal Palace	1-2
	Sutton Town v Reading	1-2
	Swindon Town v Dartford	1-0
	Walsall v Clapton Orient	0-0
	Workington v Newport County	3-1
r	Clapton Orient v Walsall	2-0
r	Hartlepools United v Halifax Town	1-2
r	New Brighton v Queen's Park Rangers	0-4

Round Three

	Birmingham v Sheffield United	2-1
	Bolton Wanderers v Halifax Town	3-1
	Brighton & Hove Albion v Swindon Town	3-1
	Bristol City v Derby County	1-1
	Burnley v Bury	0-0
	Charlton Athletic v Port Vale	2-0
	Chelsea v West Bromwich Albion	1-1
	Cheltenham Town v Blackpool	1-3
	Chesterfield v Aston Villa	2-2
	Crystal Palace v Aldershot	1-0
	Grimsby Town v Clapton Orient	1-0
	Hull City v Brentford	1-0
	Leeds United v Preston North End	0-1
	Leicester City v Lincoln City	3-0
	Liverpool v Fulham	1-1
	Luton Town v Arsenal	0-1
	Manchester City v Blackburn Rovers	3-1
	Manchester United v Portsmouth	1-1
	Millwall v Accrington Stanley	3-0
	Nottingham Forest v Queen's Park Rangers	4-0
	Plymouth Argyle v Huddersfield Town	1-1
	Reading v Oldham Athletic	1-2
	Rotherham United v Sheffield Wednesday	0-3
	Southampton v Northampton Town	1-1
	Stoke City v Bradford Park Avenue	3-0
	Sunderland v Middlesbrough	1-1
	Swansea Town v Notts County	1-0
	Tottenham Hotspur v Everton	3-0
	Tranmere Rovers v Southend United	3-0
	West Ham United v Bradford City	3-2
	Wolverhampton Wan. v Newcastle United	1-0
	Workington v Gateshead	4-1
r	Aston Villa v Chesterfield	2-0
r	Bury v Burnley	3-2
r	Derby County v Bristol City	1-0e
r	Fulham v Liverpool	2-3e
r	Huddersfield Town v Plymouth Argyle	6-2
r	Middlesbrough v Sunderland	1-2
r	Northampton Town v Southampton	1-0
r	Portsmouth v Manchester United	4-1
r	West Bromwich Albion v Chelsea	0-1e

Round Four

	Arsenal v Crystal Palace	7-0
	Aston Villa v Sunderland	7-2
	Birmingham v Charlton Athletic	1-0
	Brighton & Hove Albion v Bolton Wanderers	1-1
	Bury v Swansea Town	1-1
	Chelsea v Nottingham Forest	1-1
	Derby County v Wolverhampton Wan.	3-0
	Huddersfield Town v Northampton Town	0-2
	Hull City v Manchester City	2-2
	Liverpool v Tranmere Rovers	3-1
	Millwall v Leicester City	3-6
	Oldham Athletic v Sheffield Wednesday	1-1
	Portsmouth v Grimsby Town	2-0
	Stoke City v Blackpool	3-0
	Tottenham Hotspur v West Ham United	4-1
	Workington v Preston North End	1-2
r	Bolton Wanderers v Brighton & Hove Albion	6-1
r	Manchester City v Hull City	4-1
r	Nottingham Forest v Chelsea	0-3
r	Sheffield Wednesday v Oldham Athletic	6-1
r	Swansea Town v Bury	3-0

Round Five

	Arsenal v Derby County	1-0
	Birmingham v Leicester City	1-2
	Liverpool v Bolton Wanderers	0-3
	Preston North End v Northampton Town	4-0
	Sheffield Wednesday v Manchester City	2-2
	Stoke City v Chelsea	3-1
	Swansea Town v Portsmouth	0-1
	Tottenham Hotspur v Aston Villa	0-1
r	Manchester City v Sheffield Wednesday	2-0

Round Six

	Arsenal v Aston Villa	1-2
	Bolton Wanderers v Portsmouth	0-3
	Manchester City v Stoke City	1-0
	Preston North End v Leicester City	0-1

Semi Finals

	Manchester City v Aston Villa	6-1 N
	Portsmouth v Leicester City	4-1 N

Final

	Manchester City v Portsmouth	2-1 N

1934/35

Extra Preliminary Round

1	Crawcrook Albion v Gosforth & Coxlodge	4-1
	Newbiggin West End v Throckley Welfare	2-4
	Pegswood United v St Peter's Albion	1-1
	Pelaw v Usworth Colliery	1-2
	Shankhouse v Bedlington United	3-1
	Wallsend v Newburn	1-1
	Whitburn CW v Chester-le-Street	1-3
2	Annfield Plain v Dawdon Colliery Recreation	11-0
	Billingham Synthonia v Tow Law Town	5-2
	Bishop Auckland v Durham City	1-2
	Chilton Colliery Recreation v West Stanley	4-3
	Cockfield v Evenwood Town	2-3
	Crook Town v Burnhope Institute	5-1
	Seaham Colliery Welfare v Barnard Castle Athletic	8-2
	Shotton CW v Eden CW	2-6
	South Hetton CW v Blackhall Colliery Welfare	0-3
	Thornley CW v Leasingthorne Colliery	3-0
	West Auckland Town v Horden CW	2-5
	Willington v Crookhall CW	2-0
6	Denton United v Ellesmere Port Town	4-2
	Hoylake v Peasley Cross Athletic	8-0
7	Bedouins v Whitchurch	1-2
	Linotype & Machinery v Nantwich	2-6
	Witton Albion v Bangor City	2-2
8	Badsey Rangers v Bromsgrove Rovers	1-3
	Bilston Borough v Tamworth	2-2
	Birmingham Corp. Tramways v Boldmere St Michaels	4-3
	Bournville Athletic v Halesowen Town	4-1
	Cradley Heath St Luke's v Evesham Town	6-0
	Dudley Town v Hereford United	1-0
	Leamington Town v Headingley	9-0
	Nuneaton Town v Hednesford Town	6-1
	Oswestry Town v Stafford Rangers	1-2
	Redditch v Wolverhampton Amateur	5-0
	Rugby Town (1) v Atherstone Town	0-8
	Shrewsbury Town v Cannock Town	2-2
	Stourbridge v Worcester City	3-1
	Walsall Phoenix v Moor Green	2-2
	Wellington Town v Oakengates Town	3-2 N
10	Bentley Colliery v Farsley Celtic	9-1
	Cudworth Village v Wombwell Main Welfare	3-2
	Denaby United v Mexborough Athletic	1-1
	Guiseley v Brodsworth Main Colliery	6-1
	Luddendenfoot v Goldthorpe United	1-5
	Meltham Mills v Frickley Colliery	2-5
	Monckton Athletic v Thorne Colliery	0-0
	Owston Park Rangers v Wath Athletic	7-0
	Sheffield v Grimethorpe Colliery Institute	wo/s
	South Kirkby Colliery v Pilkington Recreation	3-2
	Yorkshire Amateur v Rossington Main	8-1
17	Barking v Clapton	1-0
	Romford (2) v Ford Sports (Dagenham)	3-1
18	Berkhamsted Town v Bushey United	8-2
	Bishop's Stortford v Old Johnians	1-0
	St Albans City v Apsley	1-3
	Wood Green Town v Pinner	1-3
19	Abingdon Town v Stokenchurch	5-1
	Acton v Cowley	3-1
	Banbury Spencer v Hayes	4-1
	Chesham United v AEC Athletic	10-1
	Civil Service v Headington United	3-0
	Maidenhead United v Bicester Town	6-0
	Newbury Town v Osberton Radiator (Oxford)	6-1
	Park Royal v Windsor & Eton	7-1
	Slough v RAF Halton	3-1
	Thame United v Aylesbury United	0-5
	Yiewsley v Henley Town	2-5

1934/35

20	Banstead Mental Hospital v Leyland Motors (Kingston)	2-1
	Basingstoke v RAMC Aldershot	5-0
	Carshalton Athletic v Epsom Town	0-3
	Dorking v Egham	5-4
	Hersham v PO Engineers (Beddington)	1-2
	Hounslow Town v Guildford	3-2
	Redhill v Courage & Co.'s Sports	4-0
	Staines Town v Metropolitan Police	0-2
	Sutton United v Godalming	5-0
	Thornycrofts (Basingstoke) v Beddington Corner	4-3
	Tooting & Mitcham United v Wellington Works	10-3
	Walton-on-Thames v Nunhead	3-1
	Wills Sports v Cranleigh	6-0
	Woking v Guildford City	0-2
21	Bexleyheath & Welling v Woolwich Polytechnic	9-0
	Chatham v Callender Athletic	2-0
	Cray Wanderers v Beckenham	4-0
	Gravesend United v Swanley Athletic	3-1
	RM Deal v Ashford	2-3
	Ramsgate (1) v Betteshanger CW	3-0
	Sittingbourne v Lloyds (Sittingbourne)	3-2
	Tunbridge Wells Rangers v Maidstone United	7-0
	UGB Sports (Charlton) v Bexley	3-2
	Whitstable v Deal Town	1-1
	Woolwich Borough Co. Ath. v Bostall Heath	2-3
23	Bournemouth Tramways v Lymington	4-3
	HMS Victory v Shaftesbury	wo/s
	Newport (IOW) v Ringwood Town	9-0
	Osborne Athletic v RM Portsmouth	1-6
24	Purton v Devizes Town	3-3
	Timsbury Athletic v Coleford Athletic	9-0
1r	Newburn v Wallsend	4-4
r	St Peter's Albion v Pegswood United	5-4
7r	Bangor City v Witton Albion	wo/s
8r	Moor Green v Walsall Phoenix	wo/s
r	Shrewsbury Town v Cannock Town	5-2
r	Tamworth v Bilston Borough	5-1
10r	Mexborough Athletic v Denaby United	3-1
r	Thorne Colliery v Monckton Athletic	4-1
21r	Deal Town v Whitstable	1-0
24r	Devizes Town v Purton	4-0
1r2	Newburn v Wallsend	2-4

Preliminary Round

1	Ashington v Dipton United	2-2
	Chester-le-Street v St Peter's Albion	4-3
	Howdon British Legion v Usworth Colliery	4-0
	Scotswood v Crawcrook Albion	1-5
	Throckley Welfare v North Shields	0-4
	Walker Celtic v Wardley Welfare	5-3
	Wallsend v Shankhouse	2-1
	West Wylam CW v Walker Park	3-1
2	Blackhall Colliery Welfare v Consett	2-1
	Durham City v Murton CW	1-5
	Easington CW v Annfield Plain	2-1
	Eden CW v Chilton Colliery Recreation	4-2
	Evenwood Town v Horden CW	1-2
	Seaham Colliery Welfare v Ferryhill Athletic	2-1
	Thornley CW v Billingham Synthonia	2-1
	Willington v Crook Town	3-3
3	Bridlington Town (1) v Normanby Mangnesite	1-1
	Filey Town v Scarborough Junior Imperial	2-1
	Pease & Partners v South Bank East End	2-1
	Stockton v Grangetown St Mary's	3-5
	Whitby Albion Rangers v South Bank St Peters	0-5
5	Great Harwood v Leyland Motors	2-3
	Morecambe v Crossens	4-0
	Nelson v Breightmet United	3-1
	Skelmersdale United v Rossendale United	3-2
6	Droylsden v Stalybridge Celtic	2-2
	Glossop v Manchester North End	3-1
	Marine v Hoylake	0-5
	Northern Nomads v Ashton National	3-2
	Orrell v Harrowby	6-2
	Prescot Cables v Denton United	2-3
	Seaforth Albion v Earle	1-3
	Shell Mex v Whiston	2-1
7	Altrincham v Timperley	8-2
	Colwyn Bay v Willaston White Star	6-3
	ICI Alkali v Middlewich Athletic	2-5
	Llandudno v Barnton Victoria	2-2
	Macclesfield Town v Bangor City	5-1
	Northwich Victoria v Congleton Town	2-0
	Whitchurch v Moulton Verdin	3-3
	Winsford United v Nantwich	2-1
8	Atherstone Town v Moor Green	2-0
	Birmingham Corp. Tramways v Bromsgrove Rovers	2-1
	Brierley Hill Alliance v Shrewsbury Town	2-2
	Dudley Town v Nuneaton Town	2-0
	Leamington Town v Redditch	5-0
	Stafford Rangers v Cradley Heath St Luke's	3-0
	Stourbridge v Wellington Town	6-4
	Tamworth v Bournville Athletic	5-2
9	Selby OCO v Marfleet	0-0
	Selby Town v Brigg Town	7-1
10	Bentley Colliery v Thurnscoe Victoria	3-1
	Dinnington Athletic v South Kirkby Colliery	2-0
	Frickley Colliery v Cudworth Village	5-0
	Goldthorpe United v Yorkshire Amateur	2-0
	Guiseley v Rawmarsh Welfare	0-0
	Owston Park Rangers v Silverwood Colliery	1-1
	Thorne Colliery v Mexborough Athletic	1-1
	Worksop Town v Sheffield	7-1
11	Buxton v Hinckley United (1)	1-0
	Ilkeston v Sandiacre Excelsior Foundry	4-0
	Newhall Swifts v Bolsover Colliery	6-1
	South Normanton MW v Gresley Rovers	1-5
12	Boots Athletic v Stapleford Brookhill	3-1
	Grantham v Rufford Colliery	13-0
	Ollerton Colliery v Boston United	0-3
13	Northampton Nomads v Phorpres Sports	1-6
	Rushden Town v Irchester United	3-0
14	Arlesey Town v St Neots & District	1-2
	Bedford Queens Park Rangers v Bedford North End	2-2
	Biggleswade & District v Kempston Rovers	4-0
	Hitchin Town v Baldock Town	4-0
	Luton Amateur v Leighton United	4-1
	Sandy Albion v Langford	2-2
	Vauxhall Motors (Luton) v Waterlows (Dunstable)	2-1
15	Pye Radio v Thetford Town	3-3
16	Bury Town v RAF Martlesham	4-1
	Cromer v Newmarket Town	1-1
	Felixstowe Town v Norwich YMCA	2-3
	Gorleston v Bolton & Pauls	3-0
	Ipswich Town v Norwich St Barnabas	3-2
	Kirkley v Leiston Works Athletic	5-0
	Norwich CEYMS v Lowestoft Town	0-1
	Sheringham v Frosts Athletic	0-1
17	Brightlingsea United v Crittall Athletic	1-3
	Clacton Town v Grays Athletic	1-1
	Harwich & Parkeston v Colchester Town	3-2
	Jurgens (Purfleet) v Custom House	13-2
	Leytonstone v Dagenham Town	2-2
	Romford (2) v Heybridge	5-0
	Severalls Athletic v Brentwood & Warley	2-1
	Tilbury v Barking	1-0
18	Apsley v Leavesden	3-1
	Berkhamsted Town v Old Lyonian	8-0
	Bishop's Stortford v Tufnell Park	1-2
	Enfield v Wealdstone	4-0
	Finchley v Ware	5-0
	Hertford Town v Watford British Legion	3-1
	London Caledonians v Pinner	3-2e
	Stevenage Town v Hoddesdon Town	2-3
19	Acton v Newbury Town	4-1
	Aylesbury United v Wycombe Wanderers	3-0
	Chesham United v Southall	2-5
	Civil Service v Abingdon Town	7-0
	Henley Town v Park Royal	1-4
	Maidenhead United v Banbury Spencer	6-0
	Marlow v Oxford City	3-2
	Slough v Uxbridge	0-2
20	Guildford City v Banstead Mental Hospital	5-4
	PO Engineers (Beddington) v Dorking	9-0
	Redhill v Epsom Town	3-6
	Streatham Town v Hounslow Town	1-1
	Tooting & Mitcham United v Sutton United	0-2
	Walton-on-Thames v Basingstoke	2-1
	Wills Sports v Metropolitan Police	3-1
	Winchester City v Thornycrofts (Basingstoke)	5-1
21	Bexleyheath & Welling v Cray Wanderers	3-0
	Canterbury Waverley v London Paper Mills	0-0
	Chatham v Aylesford Paper Mills	1-1
	Deal Town v Sittingbourne	0-4
	Gravesend United v Bromley	3-5
	Ramsgate (1) v Ashford	2-2
	Tunbridge Wells Rangers v Sheppey United	4-0
	UGB Sports (Charlton) v Bostall Heath	2-0
22	Brighton Mental Hospital v Haywards Heath	2-0
	Chichester v Vernon Athletic	2-2e
	Eastbourne Comrades v Bexhill	1-2
	Hastings & St Leonards v Hove	5-0
	Littlehampton v Horsham	0-5
	Southwick v Newhaven	1-0
	Worthing v East Grinstead	4-2
23	Blandford United v RM Portsmouth	3-0
	Bournemouth Tramways v Weymouth	0-2
	Dorchester Town v Totton	1-1
	Gosport v Cowes	0-1
	Newport (IOW) v Salisbury Corinthians	4-2
	Poole Town v HMS Victory	3-0
	Ryde Sports v Bournemouth (Ams)	6-2
	Salisbury City (1) v Hamworthy	4-0
24	Chippenham Town v Devizes Town	2-2
	Melksham v Westbury United	1-5
	Radstock Town v Timsbury Athletic	3-3
	Swindon Corinthians v Calne & Harris United	4-1
	Swindon Victoria v Chippenham Rovers	2-2
	Trowbridge Town v Clandown	2-1
	Warminster Town v Frome Town	2-2
	Welton Rovers v Paulton Rovers	4-1
25	Exmouth Town v Dartmouth United	2-4
26	Cardiff Corinthians v Barry	0-4
	Ebbw Vale v Merthyr Town	wo/s
	Hanham Athletic v Rose Green	2-3
	Kingswood v Keynsham	1-1
	Lovells Athletic v Cadbury Heath YMCA	6-0
	St Philips Athletic v Mount Hill Enterprise	5-5
	St Philips Marsh Adult School v Clevedon	2-0
1r	Dipton United v Ashington	2-1
2r	Crook Town v Willington	1-1
3r	Normanby Mangnesite v Bridlington Town (1)	1-0
6r	Stalybridge Celtic v Droylsden	4-1
7r	Barnton Victoria v Llandudno	4-0
r	Moulton Verdin v Whitchurch	wo/s
8r	Shrewsbury Town v Brierley Hill Alliance	3-1
9r	Marfleet v Selby OCO	1-0
10r	Mexborough Athletic v Thorne Colliery	1-2
r	Rawmarsh Welfare v Guiseley	4-0
r	Silverwood Colliery v Owston Park Rangers	3-1
14r	Bedford North End v Bedford Queens Park Rangers	0-0
r	Langford v Sandy Albion	2-2e
15r	Thetford Town v Pye Radio	3-7
16r	Newmarket Town v Cromer	6-0
17r	Dagenham Town v Leytonstone	2-0
r	Grays Athletic v Clacton Town	2-1
20r	Hounslow Town v Streatham Town	1-2
21r	Ashford v Ramsgate (1)	5-0
r	Aylesford Paper Mills v Chatham	0-0
r	London Paper Mills v Canterbury Waverley	3-0
22r	Vernon Athletic v Chichester	8-3
23r	Totton v Dorchester Town	3-2
24r	Chippenham Rovers v Swindon Victoria	1-5
r	Devizes Town v Chippenham Town	4-0
r	Frome Town v Warminster Town	5-4
r	Timsbury Athletic v Radstock Town	1-4
26r	Keynsham v Kingswood	3-2
r	Mount Hill Enterprise v St Philips Athletic	5-3
2r2	Willington v Crook Town	0-4
14r2	Bedford Queens Park Rangers v Bedford North End	1-1
r2	Langford v Sandy Albion	1-0 N
21r2	Aylesford Paper Mills v Chatham	1-0 N
14r3	Bedford North End v Bedford Queens Park Rangers	0-1 N

Qualifying Round One

1	Chester-le-Street v Howdon British Legion	3-1
	Crawcrook Albion v Wallsend	5-2
	North Shields v Dipton United	8-0
	Walker Celtic v West Wylam CW	8-1
2	Easington CW v Crook Town	1-1
	Horden CW v Blackhall Colliery Welfare	1-2
	Seaham Colliery Welfare v Eden CW	1-2
	Thornley CW v Murton CW	0-7
3	Filey Town v Normanby Mangnesite	4-0
	Pease & Partners v Scarborough	1-0
	South Bank St Peters v South Bank	1-1
	Whitby United v Grangetown St Mary's	2-0
4	Kells United - Bye	
	Netherfield (Kendal) v Cleator Moor Celtic	5-0
	Penrith - Bye	
	Whitehaven Athletic v Holme Head Works	4-4
5	Dick, Kerrs v Lytham	3-1
	Horwich RMI v Morecambe	1-3
	Skelmersdale United v Leyland Motors	2-1
	Wigan Athletic v Nelson	3-1
6	Earle v Glossop	0-1
	Hoylake v Stalybridge Celtic	0-2
	Northern Nomads v Denton United	1-2
	Shell Mex v Orrell	2-2
7	Altrincham v Barnton Victoria	8-2
	Macclesfield Town v Colwyn Bay	3-1
	Moulton Verdin v Middlewich Athletic	2-2
	Northwich Victoria v Winsford United	3-2
8	Birmingham Corp. Tramways v Leamington Town	3-0
	Shrewsbury Town v Stafford Rangers	1-0
	Stourbridge v Atherstone Town	3-0
	Tamworth v Dudley Town	1-2
9	Brigg 2nd Lincs Sugar Co. v Louth Town	1-2
	Goole Town v Frodingham & Appleby Ath.	4-1
	Lysaght's Sports (Scunthorpe) v Marfleet	2-0
	Selby Town v Barton Town (1)	4-2
10	Dinnington Athletic v Frickley Colliery	1-0
	Silverwood Colliery v Bentley Colliery	3-2
	Thorne Colliery v Rawmarsh Welfare	3-1
	Worksop Town v Goldthorpe United	4-2
11	Heanor Town v Gresley Rovers	11-0
	Ilkeston v Buxton	2-0
	Matlock Town v Ripley Town	2-2
	Newhall Swifts v Loughborough Corinthians	wo/s
12	Boston United v Newark Town	6-2
	Grantham v Basford United	8-1
	Ransome & Marles v Boots Athletic	4-2
	Sutton Town v Spalding United	4-1
13	Higham Ferrers Town v Rushden Town	1-1
	Peterbro' Westwood Works v Desborough Town	0-2
	Phorpres Sports v Wolverton Town	2-2
	Stamford v Kettering Town	0-3
14	Biggleswade & District v St Neots & District	0-2
	Hitchin Town v Langford	10-0
	Luton Amateur v Bedford Town (1)	0-9
	Vauxhall Mtrs (Luton) v Bedford Queens Park Rgrs	13-0
15	Chatteris Engineers v King's Lynn	1-6
	Chatteris Town v Pye Radio	3-2
	Histon Institute v Abbey United (Cambs)	1-1
	Wisbech Town v Cambridge Town	2-2
16	Gorleston v Bury Town	9-2
	Ipswich Town v Norwich YMCA	1-1
	Kirkley v Lowestoft Town	0-2
	Newmarket Town v Frosts Athletic	1-1
17	Crittall Athletic v Harwich & Parkeston	2-3
	Grays Athletic v Jurgens (Purfleet)	1-2
	Romford (2) v Dagenham Town	4-1
	Tilbury v Severalls Athletic	2-1
18	Apsley v Berkhamsted Town	2-0
	Finchley v London Caledonians	2-1
	Hertford Town v Enfield	0-1
	Tufnell Park v Hoddesdon Town	3-1
19	Marlow v Maidenhead United	1-2
	Park Royal v Aylesbury United	3-1
	Southall v Civil Service	2-3
	Uxbridge v Acton	4-0

1934/35

20	PO Engineers (Beddington) v Winchester City	3-1
	Streatham Town v Epsom Town	2-2
	Walton-on-Thames v Sutton United	0-4
	Wills Sports v Guildford City	2-6
21	Ashford v Aylesford Paper Mills	3-0
	Bromley v Tunbridge Wells Rangers	0-0
	Sittingbourne v Bexleyheath & Welling	2-0
	UGB Sports (Charlton) v London Paper Mills	0-4
22	Bexhill v Horsham	4-3
	Brighton Mental Hospital v Vernon Athletic	3-1
	Hastings & St Leonards v Southwick	6-1
	Worthing v Shoreham	7-1
23	Blandford United v Totton	1-2
	Newport (IOW) v Ryde Sports	1-1
	Poole Town v Cowes	4-2
	Salisbury City (1) v Weymouth	0-1
24	Devizes Town v Frome Town	2-2
	Radstock Town v Welton Rovers	3-5
	Swindon Corinthians v Swindon Victoria	3-2
	Westbury United v Trowbridge Town	1-1
25	Minehead v Dartmouth United	0-2
	Tiverton Town v Yeovil & Petter's United	1-5
	Wells City v Street	2-0
	Weston-Super-Mare v Glastonbury	0-7
26	Llanelli v Barry	1-1
	Lovells Athletic v Ebbw Vale	5-0
	Rose Green v Keynsham	2-1
	St Philips Marsh Adult School v Mount Hill Enterpris	7-0
2r	Crook Town v Easington CW	4-0
3r	South Bank v South Bank St Peters	1-0
4r	Holme Head Works v Whitehaven Athletic	1-4
6r	Orrell v Shell Mex	2-4
7r	Middlewich Athletic v Moulton Verdin	1-2
11r	Ripley Town v Matlock Town	5-2
13r	Rushden Town v Higham Ferrers Town	5-3
r	Wolverton Town v Phorpres Sports	1-2e
15r	Abbey United (Cambs) v Histon Institute	4-5e
r	Cambridge Town v Wisbech Town	7-1
16r	Frosts Athletic v Newmarket Town	1-0
r	Norwich YMCA v Ipswich Town	2-4
20r	Epsom Town v Streatham Town	7-4
21r	Tunbridge Wells Rangers v Bromley	0-1
23r	Ryde Sports v Newport (IOW)	2-1 D
24r	Frome Town v Devizes Town	2-4
r	Trowbridge Town v Westbury United	7-1
26r	Barry v Llanelli	4-1

Qualifying Round Two

1	Crawcrook Albion v Chester-le-Street	3-1
	North Shields v Walker Celtic	3-1
2	Blackhall Colliery Welfare v Crook Town	2-2
	Eden CW v Murton CW	2-1
3	Pease & Partners v Whitby United	1-1
	South Bank v Filey Town	3-1
4	Kells United v Whitehaven Athletic	2-5
	Penrith v Netherfield (Kendal)	5-3
5	Dick, Kerrs v Skelmersdale United	0-0
	Morecambe v Wigan Athletic	0-5
6	Denton United v Glossop	2-1
	Stalybridge Celtic v Shell Mex	4-2
7	Moulton Verdin v Altrincham	0-9
	Northwich Victoria v Macclesfield Town	2-1
8	Shrewsbury Town v Dudley Town	1-1
	Stourbridge v Birmingham Corp. Tramways	2-2
9	Louth Town v Selby Town	3-2
	Lysaght's Sports (Scunthorpe) v Goole Town	3-1
10	Dinnington Athletic v Thorne Colliery	2-1
	Worksop Town v Silverwood Colliery	3-1
11	Ilkeston v Heanor Town	3-3
	Ripley Town v Newhall Swifts	8-2
12	Grantham v Sutton Town	3-1
	Ransome & Marles v Boston United	2-2
13	Kettering Town v Phorpres Sports	5-1
	Rushden Town v Desborough Town	11-0
14	Hitchin Town v Bedford Town (1)	0-0
	Vauxhall Motors (Luton) v St Neots & District	4-2
15	Cambridge Town v King's Lynn	2-3
	Chatteris Town v Histon Institute	3-1
16	Gorleston v Lowestoft Town	3-2
	Ipswich Town v Frosts Athletic	2-0
17	Jurgens (Purfleet) v Harwich & Parkeston	0-3
	Tilbury v Romford (2)	2-2
18	Apsley v Enfield	0-1
	Tufnell Park v Finchley	0-1
19	Civil Service v Maidenhead United	3-1
	Uxbridge v Park Royal	1-0
20	Epsom Town v Guildford City	2-4
	PO Engineers (Beddington) v Sutton United	3-1
21	London Paper Mills v Bromley	2-1
	Sittingbourne v Ashford	2-4
22	Bexhill v Brighton Mental Hospital	0-2
	Hastings & St Leonards v Worthing	2-2
23	Newport (IOW) v Weymouth	1-1
	Poole Town v Totton	1-2
24	Devizes Town v Swindon Corinthians	5-0
	Welton Rovers v Trowbridge Town	1-0
25	Glastonbury v Dartmouth United	5-1
	Yeovil & Petter's United v Wells City	8-2
26	Barry v Lovells Athletic	2-0
	Rose Green v St Philips Marsh Adult School	1-1
2r	Crook Town v Blackhall Colliery Welfare	1-1
3r	Whitby United v Pease & Partners	2-5
5r	Skelmersdale United v Dick, Kerrs	0-2
8r	Dudley Town v Shrewsbury Town	1-1
r	Stourbridge v Birmingham Corp. Tramways	1-3
11r	Heanor Town v Ilkeston	4-3e
12r	Boston United v Ransome & Marles	5-1
14r	Bedford Town (1) v Hitchin Town	1-0
17r	Romford (2) v Tilbury	1-0
22r	Worthing v Hastings & St Leonards	4-1
23r	Weymouth v Newport (IOW)	2-1
26r	St Philips Marsh Adult School v Rose Green	4-1
2r2	Crook Town v Blackhall Colliery Welfare	3-0
8r2	Shrewsbury Town v Dudley Town	1-1 N
8r3	Shrewsbury Town v Dudley Town	3-1 N

Qualifying Round Three

1	North Shields v Crawcrook Albion	6-1
2	Crook Town v Eden CW	0-1
3	South Bank v Pease & Partners	2-1
4	Whitehaven Athletic v Penrith	2-4
5	Wigan Athletic v Dick, Kerrs	5-1
6	Denton United v Stalybridge Celtic	1-5
7	Altrincham v Northwich Victoria	0-1
8	Shrewsbury Town v Birmingham Corp. Tramways	1-4
9	Lysaght's Sports (Scunthorpe) v Louth Town	0-4
10	Worksop Town v Dinnington Athletic	0-4
11	Ripley Town v Heanor Town	1-2
12	Grantham v Boston United	1-1
13	Kettering Town v Rushden Town	3-1
14	Bedford Town (1) v Vauxhall Motors (Luton)	5-1
15	King's Lynn v Chatteris Town	6-0
16	Gorleston v Ipswich Town	2-0
17	Romford (2) v Harwich & Parkeston	1-1
18	Finchley v Enfield	1-2
19	Uxbridge v Civil Service	4-1
20	Guildford City v PO Engineers (Beddington)	2-1
21	Ashford v London Paper Mills	2-0
22	Worthing v Brighton Mental Hospital	3-1
23	Weymouth v Totton	5-0
24	Welton Rovers v Devizes Town	2-1
25	Glastonbury v Yeovil & Petter's United	1-2
26	St Philips Marsh Adult School v Barry	0-2
12r	Boston United v Grantham	3-1
17r	Harwich & Parkeston v Romford (2)	3-2

Qualifying Round Four

	Bath City v Welton Rovers	9-0
	Bedford Town (1) v Heanor Town	3-0
	Birmingham Corp. Tramways v Louth Town	2-0
	Boston United v King's Lynn	5-0
	Burton Town v Gainsborough Trinity	4-0
	Cheltenham Town v Barry	2-4
	Dartford v Enfield	3-0
	Darwen v Penrith	8-1
	Folkestone v Margate	0-0
	Gorleston v Walthamstow Avenue	2-8
	Guildford City v Worthing	3-1
	Harwich & Parkeston v Barnet	5-2
	Ilford v Golders Green	1-1
	Jarrow v Spennymoor United	0-4
	Leyton v Kingstonian	1-1
	North Shields v Blyth Spartans	0-1
	Northfleet United v Ashford	2-3
	Scunthorpe United v Kettering Town	2-2
	Shildon v Eden CW	2-1
	South Bank v Dinnington Athletic	1-1
	Stalybridge Celtic v Chorley	4-0
	Uxbridge v Wimbledon	1-1
	Wigan Athletic v Northwich Victoria	4-0
	Workington v Lancaster Town	3-0
	Yeovil & Petter's United v Weymouth	6-2
r	Dinnington Athletic v South Bank	1-0
r	Golders Green v Ilford	2-0
r	Kettering Town v Scunthorpe United	1-3
r	Kingstonian v Leyton	0-2
r	Margate v Folkestone	1-1
r	Wimbledon v Uxbridge	4-2
r2	Folkestone v Margate	4-3 N

Round One

	Aldershot v Bournemouth	4-0
	Ashford v Clapton Orient	1-4
	Barry v Northampton Town	0-1
	Bedford Town (1) v Dartford	2-3
	Blyth Spartans v Stockport County	1-1
	Brighton & Hove Albion v Folkestone	3-1
	Bristol City v Gillingham	2-0
	Bristol Rovers v Harwich & Parkeston	3-0
	Burton Town v York City	2-3
	Cardiff City v Reading	1-2
	Carlisle United v Wigan Athletic	1-6
	Charlton Athletic v Exeter City	2-2
	Chester v Dinnington Athletic	3-1
	Coventry City v Scunthorpe United	7-0
	Crewe Alexandra v Walsall	1-2
	Darwen v Boston United	1-2
	Doncaster Rovers v Barrow	0-2
	Dulwich Hamlet v Torquay United	1-2
	Gateshead v Darlington	1-4
	Guildford City v Bath City	1-2
	Halifax Town v Hartlepools United	1-1
	Mansfield Town v Accrington Stanley	6-1
	Queen's Park Rangers v Walthamstow Avenue	2-0
	Rotherham United v Spennymoor United	2-0
	Shildon v Lincoln City	2-2
	Southend United v Golders Green	10-1
	Southport v New Brighton	1-1
	Swindon Town v Newport County	4-0
	Tranmere Rovers v Stalybridge Celtic	3-1
	Watford v Corinthians	2-0
	Wimbledon v Leyton	1-1
	Workington v Birmingham Corp. Tramways	2-0
	Wrexham v Rochdale	4-1
	Yeovil & Petter's United v Crystal Palace	3-0
r	Exeter City v Charlton Athletic	5-2
r	Hartlepools United v Halifax Town	2-0
r	Leyton v Wimbledon	0-1
r	Lincoln City v Shildon	4-0
r	New Brighton v Southport	1-1e
r	Stockport County v Blyth Spartans	4-1
r2	Southport v New Brighton	1-2 N

Round Two

	Barrow v Aldershot	0-2
	Bath City v Boston United	2-1
	Clapton Orient v Chester	1-3
	Dartford v Bristol Rovers	0-1
	Hartlepools United v Coventry City	0-4
	Mansfield Town v Tranmere Rovers	4-2
	Northampton Town v Workington	0-0
	Queen's Park Rangers v Brighton & Hove Albion	1-2
	Reading v Wrexham	3-0
	Rotherham United v Bristol City	1-2
	Stockport County v Darlington	3-2
	Swindon Town v Lincoln City	4-3
	Watford v Walsall	1-1
	Wigan Athletic v Torquay United	3-2
	Wimbledon v Southend United	1-5
	Yeovil & Petter's United v Exeter City	4-1
	York City v New Brighton	1-0
r	Walsall v Watford	1-0e
r	Workington v Northampton Town	0-1

Round Three

	Aldershot v Reading	0-0
	Aston Villa v Bradford City	1-3
	Birmingham v Coventry City	5-1
	Brentford v Plymouth Argyle	0-1
	Brighton & Hove Albion v Arsenal	0-2
	Bristol City v Bury	1-1
	Bristol Rovers v Manchester United	1-3
	Burnley v Mansfield Town	4-2
	Chelsea v Luton Town	1-1
	Chester v Nottingham Forest	0-4
	Everton v Grimsby Town	6-3
	Hull City v Newcastle United	1-5
	Leeds United v Bradford Park Avenue	4-1
	Leicester City v Blackpool	2-1
	Middlesbrough v Blackburn Rovers	1-1
	Northampton Town v Bolton Wanderers	0-2
	Norwich City v Bath City	2-0
	Portsmouth v Huddersfield Town	1-1
	Preston North End v Barnsley	0-0
	Sheffield Wednesday v Oldham Athletic	3-1
	Southend United v Sheffield United	0-4
	Sunderland v Fulham	3-2
	Swansea Town v Stoke City	4-1
	Swindon Town v Chesterfield	2-1
	Tottenham Hotspur v Manchester City	1-0
	Walsall v Southampton	1-2
	West Bromwich Albion v Port Vale	2-1
	West Ham United v Stockport County	1-1
	Wigan Athletic v Millwall	1-4
	Wolverhampton Wan. v Notts County	4-0
	Yeovil & Petter's United v Liverpool	2-6
	York City v Derby County	0-1
r	Barnsley v Preston North End	0-1
r	Blackburn Rovers v Middlesbrough	1-0
r	Bury v Bristol City	2-2e
r	Huddersfield Town v Portsmouth	2-3
r	Luton Town v Chelsea	2-0
r	Reading v Aldershot	3-1
r	Stockport County v West Ham United	1-0
r2	Bristol City v Bury	2-1 N

Round Four

	Blackburn Rovers v Liverpool	1-0
	Bradford City v Stockport County	0-0
	Burnley v Luton Town	3-1
	Derby County v Swansea Town	3-0
	Leicester City v Arsenal	0-1
	Norwich City v Leeds United	3-3
	Nottingham Forest v Manchester United	0-0
	Plymouth Argyle v Bolton Wanderers	1-4
	Portsmouth v Bristol City	0-0
	Reading v Millwall	1-0
	Southampton v Birmingham	0-3
	Sunderland v Everton	1-1
	Swindon Town v Preston North End	0-2
	Tottenham Hotspur v Newcastle United	2-0
	West Bromwich Albion v Sheffield United	7-1
	Wolverhampton Wan. v Sheffield Wednesday	1-2
r	Bristol City v Portsmouth	2-0
r	Everton v Sunderland	6-4
r	Leeds United v Norwich City	1-2
r	Manchester United v Nottingham Forest	0-3
r	Stockport County v Bradford City	3-2e

1934/35 to 1935/36

Round Five

	Blackburn Rovers v Birmingham	1-2
	Bristol City v Preston North End	0-0
	Everton v Derby County	3-1
	Norwich City v Sheffield Wednesday	0-1
	Nottingham Forest v Burnley	0-0
	Reading v Arsenal	0-1
	Stockport County v West Bromwich Albion	0-5
	Tottenham Hotspur v Bolton Wanderers	1-1
r	Bolton Wanderers v Tottenham Hotspur	1-1e
r	Burnley v Nottingham Forest	3-0
r	Preston North End v Bristol City	5-0
r2	Bolton Wanderers v Tottenham Hotspur	2-0 N

Round Six

	Burnley v Birmingham	3-2
	Everton v Bolton Wanderers	1-2
	Sheffield Wednesday v Arsenal	2-1
	West Bromwich Albion v Preston North End	1-0

Semi Finals

	Sheffield Wednesday v Burnley	3-0 N
	West Bromwich Albion v Bolton Wanderers	1-1 N
r	West Bromwich Albion v Bolton Wanderers	2-0 N

Final

	Sheffield Wednesday v West Bromwich Albion	4-2 N

1935/36

1	Annfield Plain v Pelaw	6-0
	Ashington v Newburn	5-3
	Consett v Newbiggin West End	1-3
	Crookhall CW v Throckley Welfare	2-1
	Eden CW v Wardley Welfare	1-0
	Gosforth & Coxlodge v Dipton United	1-1
	Howdon British Legion v Birtley	1-2
	New Gateshead United v St Peter's Albion	5-0
	Scotswood v West Stanley	1-3
	Shankhouse v Usworth Colliery	2-2
	Stakeford Albion v Hexham	2-1
	West Wylam CW v Bedlington United	3-0
	Windy Nook v Crawcrook Albion	2-0
2	Easington CW v Witton Park Institute	5-0
	Horden CW v Shotton CW	2-2
	Stanley United v Chilton Colliery Recreation	1-1
	Trimdon Grange Colliery v Tow Law Town	3-2
7	Colwyn Bay v Barnton Victoria	4-1
	Haslington Villa v Wilmslow Albion	5-1
	Hyde United v Timperley	8-3
	Middlewich Athletic v Lostock Gralam	3-1
	Rhyl v Llandudno	2-1
	Winsford United v ICI Alkali	2-1
8	Atherstone Town v Cannock Town	3-2
	Bilston Borough v Moor Green	2-2
	Birmingham Corp. Tramways v Wolverhampton Ams	8-0
	Bromsgrove Rovers v Thynnes Athletic	3-1
	Cradley Heath St Luke's v Leamington Town	3-5
	Evesham Town v Hereford United	1-4
	Hednesford Town v Brierley Hill Alliance	3-1
	Kidderminster Harriers v Sutton Town (Birmingham)	5-1
	Oakengates Town v Stourbridge	3-1
	Oswestry Town v Dudley Town	2-4
	Redditch v Nuneaton Town	0-1
	Shirley Town v Badsey Rangers	3-2
	Shrewsbury Town v Boldmere St Michaels	3-0
	Walsall Phoenix v Bournville Athletic	2-2
	Wellington Town v Headingley	14-0
	Worcester City v Stafford Rangers	4-1
10	Cudworth Village v Yorkshire Amateur	0-1
	Farsley Celtic v Altofts West Riding Col.	2-2
	Luddendenfoot v Denaby United	0-6
	Monckton Athletic v Sheffield	1-1
	Norton Woodseats v Wombwell Main Welfare	2-0
	Owston Park Rangers v South Kirkby Colliery	2-4
	Pilkington Recreation v Firbeck Main Colliery	2-0
	Rawmarsh Welfare v Rossington Main	6-3
	Rockingham Colliery v Mexborough Athletic	1-1
	Thurnscoe Victoria v Cudworth St Mary's	1-2
17	Anglo (Purfleet) v Briggs Motor Bodies	3-3
	Barking v Hoffmann Athletic (Chelmsford)	2-1
	Crittall Athletic v Chelmsford	2-0
	Dagenham Town v Ford Sports (Dagenham)	0-0
	Eton Manor v Clapton	3-1
	Grays Athletic v Custom House	11-0
	Maldon & Heybridge v Brightlingsea United	5-1
	Severalls Athletic v Colchester Town	1-2
18	Bishop's Stortford v Pinner	3-2
	Hertford Town v Bushey United	13-2
	Letchworth Town v Watford British Legion	3-0
	London Labour v Wealdstone	1-1
	Old Lyonian v Old Johnians	1-1
	Shredded Wheat v Bedouins	3-1
	St Albans City v Hoddesdon Town	4-2
	Ware v Stevenage Town	2-6
19	AEC Athletic v Slough	2-4
	Abingdon Town v RAF Halton	1-4
	Aylesbury United v Bicester Town	4-1
	Banbury Spencer v Pressed Steel	4-0
	Hayesco Sports v Marlow	0-2
	Henley Town v Cowley	3-1
	Morris Motors (Cowley) v Thame United	5-5
	Newbury Town v Headington United	6-2
	Southall v Hayes	2-1
20	Banstead Mental Hospital v Egham	2-2
	Brookwood Hospital v Courage & Co.'s Sports	0-5
	Carshalton Athletic v Nunhead	0-4
	Godalming v RAMC Aldershot	1-1
	Hounslow Town v Hersham	1-1
	Leyland Motors (Kingston) v Camberley & Yorktown	3-2
	Metropolitan Police v Streatham Town	5-2
	Tooting & Mitcham United v Woking	1-2
	Walton-on-Thames v Cranleigh	2-2
	West Norwood v Guildford	3-2
	Wills Sports v Redhill	4-2
21	Aylesford Paper Mills v Ramsgate (1)	1-6
	Bexleyheath & Welling v Beckenham	8-2
	Bostall Heath v Darenth Training Colony	1-5
	Chatham v Callender Athletic	1-1
	Cray Wanderers v Bexley	4-2e
	Deal Town v RM Deal	1-2
	Gravesend United v Woolwich Borough Co. Ath.	3-0
	Lloyds (Sittingbourne) v Maidstone United	1-1
	Sheppey United v Betteshanger CW	5-1
	Swanley Athletic v UGB Sports (Charlton)	1-4
	Tunbridge Wells Rangers v Whitstable	7-2
23	Cowes v East Cowes	2-3
	Hamworthy v Blandford United	2-2
	Lymington v Salisbury City (1)	1-3
24	Chippenham Rovers v Swindon Victoria	2-1
	Chippenham Town v Spencer Moulton	7-3
	Paulton Rovers v Radstock Town	2-0
1r	Dipton United v Gosforth & Coxlodge	2-3
r	Usworth Colliery v Shankhouse	2-3
2r	Chilton Colliery Recreation v Stanley United	4-1
r	Shotton CW v Horden CW	2-2
8r	Bournville Athletic v Walsall Phoenix	6-2
r	Moor Green v Bilston Borough	4-0
10r	Altofts West Riding Col. v Farsley Celtic	1-0
r	Mexborough Athletic v Rockingham Colliery	6-0
r	Sheffield v Monckton Athletic	4-0
17r	Briggs Motor Bodies v Anglo (Purfleet)	3-1
r	Ford Sports (Dagenham) v Dagenham Town	0-3
18r	Old Johnians v Old Lyonian	1-0
r	Wealdstone v London Labour	2-0
19r	Thame United v Morris Motors (Cowley)	5-2
20r	Cranleigh v Walton-on-Thames	1-7
r	Egham v Banstead Mental Hospital	4-2
r	Hersham v Hounslow Town	3-2
r	RAMC Aldershot v Godalming	3-4
21r	Callender Athletic v Chatham	2-4
r	Maidstone United v Lloyds (Sittingbourne)	3-0
23r	Blandford United v Hamworthy	4-1
2r2	Shotton CW v Horden CW	1-2

Preliminary Round

1	Annfield Plain v Gosforth & Coxlodge	5-0
	Ashington v Walker Celtic	0-2
	Birtley v Stakeford Albion	1-5
	Eden CW v Crookhall CW	1-0
	Jarrow v North Shields	2-1
	New Gateshead United v West Wylam CW	3-1
	Newbiggin West End v Shankhouse	3-1
	West Stanley v Windy Nook	2-1
2	Billingham Synthonia v Crook Town	3-3
	Blackhall Colliery Welfare v Cockfield	3-2
	Easington CW v Trimdon Grange Colliery	0-0
	Evenwood Town v Ferryhill Athletic	1-3
	Horden CW v Seaham Colliery Welfare	3-2
	Murton CW v Barnard Castle Athletic	5-1
	West Auckland Town v Chilton Colliery Recreation	5-0
	Willington v Dawdon Colliery Recreation	2-0
3	Bridlington Town (1) v Cargo Fleet Works	3-1
	Normanby Mangnesite v South Bank	0-2
	Scarborough v Stockton	6-1
	Smith's Dock v Whitby United	4-1
	South Bank East End v Filey Town	3-1
	South Bank St Peters v Thornaby St Patrick	5-1
	Whitby Albion Rangers v Scarborough Junior Imperial	4-1
5	Breightmet United v Rossendale United	1-0
	Crossens v Horwich RMI	0-2
	Lytham v Leyland Motors	2-3
6	Droylsden v Glossop	1-1
	Northern Nomads v Manchester North End	7-0
	Orrell v Hoylake	4-2e
	Peasley Cross Athletic v Shell Mex	1-3
	Prescot Cables v Harrowby	10-0
	South Liverpool v Marine	1-0
	Thorndale v Earle	3-5
7	Altrincham v Macclesfield Town	4-3
	Bangor City v Colwyn Bay	1-1
	Congleton Town v Moulton Verdin	6-1
	Hyde United v Middlewich Athletic	4-1
	Linotype & Machinery v Haslington Villa	3-3
	Northwich Victoria v Willaston White Star	6-1
	Rhyl v Nantwich	9-2
	Winsford United v Whitchurch	5-0
8	Atherstone Town v Wellington Town	1-4
	Hednesford Town v Birmingham Corp. Tramways	1-2
	Hereford United v Dudley Town	1-0
	Kidderminster Harriers v Bournville Athletic	6-3
	Leamington Town v Nuneaton Town	2-1
	Oakengates Town v Shrewsbury Town	1-3
	Shirley Town v Moor Green	4-0
	Worcester City v Bromsgrove Rovers	8-1
9	Barton Town (1) v Redbourne Sports	2-4
	Brigg 2nd Lincs Sugar Co. v Marfleet	1-0
	Humber United v Hull Papermills	1-0
	Lysaght's Sports (Scunthorpe) v Appleby Frodingham	3-0
10	Altofts West Riding Col. v Worksop Town	4-2
	Denaby United v Sheffield	6-0
	Frickley Colliery v Cudworth St Mary's	3-0
	Goole Town v Pilkington Recreation	1-0
	Silverwood Colliery v Mexborough Athletic	0-2
	South Kirkby Colliery v Rawmarsh Welfare	3-5
	Thorne Colliery v Norton Woodseats	3-1
	Yorkshire Amateur v Dinnington Athletic	2-1
11	North Derby Ramblers v Hinckley United (1)	0-2
12	Bilsthorpe Colliery v Rufford Colliery	3-0
14	Arlesey Town v Bedford Town (1)	1-3
	Baldock Town v Leighton United	4-0
	Biggleswade & District v Waterlows (Dunstable)	3-3
	Eynesbury Rovers v Luton Amateur	7-0
	Kempston Rovers v Biggleswade United (1)	4-0
	Sandy Albion v Langford	3-1
	Vauxhall Motors (Luton) v St Neots & District	2-0
15	Ely City v Chatteris Engineers	0-2
	Thetford Town v Pye Radio	4-3
16	Bungay Town v RAF Martlesham	1-4
	Bury Town v Walton United	6-1
	Felixstowe Town v Stowmarket	5-2
	Frosts Athletic v Cromer	2-2
	Ipswich Town v Kirkley	wo/s
	Lowestoft Town v Norwich CEYMS	4-0
	Norwich St Barnabas v Great Yarmouth Town	0-3
	Norwich YMCA v Sheringham	1-2
17	Crittall Athletic v Colchester Town	2-2
	Eton Manor v Briggs Motor Bodies	3-1
	Ilford v Barking	1-1
	Leyton v Jurgens (Purfleet)	3-0
	Leytonstone v Grays Athletic	1-2
	Maldon & Heybridge v Clacton Town	3-1
	Romford (2) v Harwich & Parkeston	4-1
	Tilbury v Dagenham Town	1-2
18	Berkhamsted Town v London Caledonians	0-0
	Bishop's Stortford v Apsley	3-3
	Finchley v Golders Green	3-2
	Leavesden v Barnet	6-2
	Letchworth Town v Old Johnians	5-3e
	St Albans City v Shredded Wheat	3-1
	Stevenage Town v Hertford Town	1-5
	Wealdstone v Tufnell Park	4-4
19	Aylesbury United v Henley Town	7-3
	Banbury Spencer v Thame United	9-1
	Marlow v Maidenhead United	1-0
	Newbury Town v Chesham United	2-2
	Osberton Radiator (Oxford) v RAF Halton	0-3
	Park Royal v Uxbridge	1-3
	Southall v Civil Service	2-1
	Wycombe Wanderers v Slough	4-3
20	Beddington Corner v Woking	0-4
	Courage & Co.'s Sports v Godalming	3-0
	Epsom v Metropolitan Police	1-1
	Hersham v Walton-on-Thames	4-3
	PO Engineers (Beddington) v Egham	8-1
	West Norwood v Nunhead	3-3
	Wills Sports v Leyland Motors (Kingston)	4-0
	Winchester City v Sutton United	4-4
21	Ashford v Tunbridge Wells Rangers	1-1
	Bromley v Chatham	6-0
	Cray Wanderers v Bexleyheath & Welling	3-3
	Gravesend United v UGB Sports (Charlton)	4-2
	London Paper Mills v Darenth Training Colony	0-0
	Maidstone United v Sittingbourne	2-2
	RM Deal v Sheppey United	0-1
	Ramsgate (1) v Margate	1-5
22	Brighton Mental Hospital v Chichester	7-3
	Eastbourne Comrades v Southwick	2-4
	Haywards Heath v Worthing	1-6
	Horsham v Shoreham	7-3
	Littlehampton v Brighton Corp. Tramways	2-2
	Newhaven v Hove	0-5
23	Blandford United v Weymouth	0-2
	Gosport v East Cowes	3-1
	Newport (IOW) v HMS Victory	5-3
	Poole Town v Bournemouth Tramways	wo/s
	Ringwood Town v Dorchester Town	2-1
	Ryde Sports v Osborne Athletic	9-0
	Salisbury City (1) v Totton	3-0
	Salisbury Corinthians v Bournemouth (Ams)	3-1
24	Calne & Harris United v Chippenham Rovers	3-3
	Cheltenham Town v Paulton Rovers	4-0
	Chippenham Town v Warminster Town	4-5
	Clandown v Welton Rovers	1-2
	Devizes Town v Purton	4-2 D
	Frome Town v Swindon Corinthians	2-1
	Timsbury Athletic v Coleford Athletic	6-3
	Westbury United v Trowbridge Town	2-4
25	Bristol St George v St Philips Marsh Adult School	2-5
	Cardiff Corinthians v Ebbw Vale	2-0
	Llanelli v Aberdare Town	2-2
	Mount Hill Enterprise v Hanham Athletic	4-1
	St Philips Athletic v Clevedon	1-2
26	Plymouth & Stonehouse Gas Co. v Taunton Town	wo/s

1935/36

2r Crook Town v Billingham Synthonia 4-2
r Trimdon Grange Colliery v Easington CW 4-1
6r Glossop v Droylsden 5-2
7r Colwyn Bay v Bangor City 2-0
r Haslington Villa v Linotype & Machinery 4-1
14r Waterlows (Dunstable) v Biggleswade & District 2-3
16r Cromer v Frosts Athletic 1-0
17r Barking v Ilford 4-2e
r Colchester Town v Crittall Athletic 2-3
18r Apsley v Bishop's Stortford 5-3
r London Caledonians v Berkhamsted Town 3-2
r Tufnell Park v Wealdstone 1-2
19r Chesham United v Newbury Town 8-2
20r Metropolitan Police v Epsom 3-0
r Nunhead v West Norwood 2-0
r Sutton United v Winchester City 9-0
21r Bexleyheath & Welling v Cray Wanderers 3-0
r Darenth Training Colony v London Paper Mills 0-3
r Sittingbourne v Maidstone United 3-1
r Tunbridge Wells Rangers v Ashford 3-0
22r Littlehampton v Brighton Corp. Tramways 4-5
24r Chippenham Rovers v Calne & Harris United 5-1
25r Aberdare Town v Llanelli 6-1

Qualifying Round One

1 Annfield Plain v Newbiggin West End 2-1
New Gateshead United v Walker Celtic 0-1
Stakeford Albion v Eden CW 0-0
West Stanley v Jarrow 3-1
2 Blackhall Colliery Welfare v Murton CW 4-0
Ferryhill Athletic v Crook Town 7-2
West Auckland Town v Horden CW 1-2
Willington v Trimdon Grange Colliery 4-1
3 Scarborough v Bridlington Town (1) 2-0
Smith's Dock v Pease & Partners 4-1
South Bank East End v South Bank 2-3
Whitby Albion Rangers v South Bank St Peters 2-2
4 Cockermouth v Kells United 3-2 v
Holme Head Works v Whitehaven Athletic wo/s
Netherfield (Kendal) v Cleator Moor Celtic 2-1
Penrith - Bye
5 Horwich RMI v Breightmet United 7-1
Leyland Motors v Great Harwood 4-0
Morecambe v Nelson 0-1
Skelmersdale United v Dick, Kerrs 1-2
6 Denton United v Earle 5-0
Northern Nomads v Glossop 1-1
Shell Mex v Orrell 1-3
South Liverpool v Prescot Cables 1-1
7 Colwyn Bay v Congleton Town 1-1
Hyde United v Altrincham 1-1
Rhyl v Haslington Villa 7-1
Winsford United v Northwich Victoria 0-2
8 Birmingham Corp. Tramways v Leamington Town 1-2
Shirley Town v Kidderminster Harriers 1-4
Wellington Town v Hereford United 2-2
Worcester City v Shrewsbury Town 2-2
9 Brigg 2nd Lincs Sugar Co. v Brigg Town 3-2
Gainsborough Trinity v Redbourne Sports 3-0
Humber United v Selby Town 3-1
Lysaght's Sports (Scunthorpe) v Louth Town 2-4
10 Goole Town v Frickley Colliery 5-2
Mexborough Athletic v Denaby United 0-4
Rawmarsh Welfare v Altofts West Riding Col. 6-0
Yorkshire Amateur v Thorne Colliery 2-3
11 Gresley Rovers v Bolsover Colliery 1-4
Ilkeston v Heanor Town 2-5
Ripley Town v Sandiacre Excelsior Foundry 10-0
South Normanton MW v Hinckley United (1) 2-8
12 Boots Athletic v Sutton Town 1-3
Grantham v Newark Town 5-0
Ollerton Colliery v Basford United 3-1
Ransome & Marles v Bilsthorpe Colliery 4-4
13 Higham Ferrers Town v Wolverton Town 0-3
Kettering Town v Desborough Town 3-0
Peterborough United v Rushden Town 0-3
Stamford v Peterbro' Westwood Works 6-4
14 Baldock Town v Bedford Town (1) 2-5
Eynesbury Rovers v Hitchin Town 3-4
Kempston Rovers v Vauxhall Motors (Luton) 0-1
Sandy Albion v Biggleswade & District 4-3
15 Abbey United (Cambs) v Chatteris Engineers 1-1
Chatteris Town v Cambridge Town 0-8
Histon Institute v Thetford Town 1-1
King's Lynn v Wisbech Town 6-1
16 Bury Town v RAF Martlesham 5-2
Ipswich Town v Great Yarmouth Town 0-0
Lowestoft Town v Cromer 2-0
Sheringham v Felixstowe Town 3-0
17 Barking v Romford (2) 0-2
Crittall Athletic v Eton Manor 1-0
Grays Athletic v Leyton 2-6
Maldon & Heybridge v Dagenham Town 0-1
18 Apsley v Hertford Town 4-1
Leavesden v Letchworth Town 3-3
London Caledonians v Finchley 2-0
St Albans City v Wealdstone 3-1
19 Aylesbury United v Uxbridge 1-2
Chesham United v Banbury Spencer 3-1
Marlow v Southall 0-5
RAF Halton v Wycombe Wanderers 1-4
20 Metropolitan Police v Courage & Co.'s Sports 1-4
Nunhead v Wills Sports 4-0
PO Engineers (Beddington) v Hersham 4-2
Woking v Sutton United 0-0
21 Bromley v Sheppey United 4-1
London Paper Mills v Gravesend United 1-1
Margate v Sittingbourne 5-1
Tunbridge Wells Rangers v Bexleyheath & Welling 3-1
22 Bexhill v Worthing 2-0
Brighton Mental Hospital v Brighton Corp. Tramways 4-2
Horsham v Hastings & St Leonards 2-2
Southwick v Hove 3-1
23 Gosport v Weymouth 1-2
Ringwood Town v Newport (IOW) 1-7
Salisbury City (1) v Ryde Sports 4-6
Salisbury Corinthians v Poole Town 4-0
24 Cheltenham Town v Purton 8-1
Chippenham Rovers v Frome Town 3-1
Timsbury Athletic v Welton Rovers 2-4
Warminster Town v Trowbridge Town 4-4
25 Barry v Aberdare Town 6-1
Lovells Athletic v Cardiff Corinthians 7-1
Mount Hill Enterprise v Clevedon 2-5
Rose Green v St Philips Marsh Adult School 4-3
26 Dartmouth United v Tiverton Town 3-0
Glastonbury v Wells City 5-3
Plymouth & Stonehouse Gas Co. v Exmouth Town 2-1
Street v Weston-Super-Mare 7-0
1r Eden CW v Stakeford Albion 4-3
3r South Bank St Peters v Whitby Albion Rangers 8-2
4r Kells United v Cockermouth 2-1
6r Glossop v Northern Nomads 1-0
r Prescot Cables v South Liverpool 2-1
7r Altrincham v Hyde United 4-1
r Congleton Town v Colwyn Bay 4-0
8r Hereford United v Wellington Town 0-2
r Shrewsbury Town v Worcester City 1-0
12r Bilsthorpe Colliery v Ransome & Marles 1-3
15r Chatteris Engineers v Abbey United (Cambs) 3-3e
r Thetford Town v Histon Institute 5-0
16r Great Yarmouth Town v Ipswich Town 4-1
18r Letchworth Town v Leavesden 0-5
20r Sutton United v Woking 4-2
21r Gravesend United v London Paper Mills 0-5
22r Hastings & St Leonards v Horsham 2-0
24r Trowbridge Town v Warminster Town 4-0
15r2 Abbey United (Cambs) v Chatteris Engineers 1-3 N

Qualifying Round Two

1 Eden CW v West Stanley 2-2
Walker Celtic v Annfield Plain 2-2
2 Blackhall Colliery Welfare v Horden CW 2-1
Willington v Ferryhill Athletic 1-2
3 Scarborough v Smith's Dock 3-0
South Bank St Peters v South Bank 1-0
4 Kells United v Holme Head Works 1-1
Netherfield (Kendal) v Penrith 2-3
5 Dick, Kerrs v Nelson 1-1
Horwich RMI v Leyland Motors 3-2
6 Glossop v Denton United 3-0
Prescot Cables v Orrell 3-2
7 Altrincham v Northwich Victoria 1-1
Congleton Town v Rhyl 1-2
8 Kidderminster Harriers v Shrewsbury Town 2-2
Leamington Town v Wellington Town 2-1
9 Brigg 2nd Lincs Sugar Co. v Humber United 4-1
Gainsborough Trinity v Louth Town 5-0
10 Denaby United v Rawmarsh Welfare 5-2
Thorne Colliery v Goole Town 1-1
11 Bolsover Colliery v Heanor Town 2-2
Ripley Town v Hinckley United (1) 5-0
12 Grantham v Ransome & Marles 5-1
Sutton Town v Ollerton Colliery 1-4
13 Kettering Town v Wolverton Town 4-1
Stamford v Rushden Town 2-4
14 Bedford Town (1) v Sandy Albion 3-0
Hitchin Town v Vauxhall Motors (Luton) 3-2
15 Chatteris Engineers v Cambridge Town 1-3
King's Lynn v Thetford Town 2-1
16 Bury Town v Great Yarmouth Town 3-2
Lowestoft Town v Sheringham 4-1
17 Crittall Athletic v Dagenham Town 1-1
Romford (2) v Leyton 2-0
18 Leavesden v Apsley 5-2
St Albans City v London Caledonians 1-1
19 Chesham United v Uxbridge 2-5
Wycombe Wanderers v Southall 2-7
20 Courage & Co.'s Sports v PO Engineers (Beddington) 2-5
Nunhead v Sutton United 1-0
21 London Paper Mills v Bromley 2-0
Margate v Tunbridge Wells Rangers 1-0
22 Bexhill v Brighton Mental Hospital 6-2
Hastings & St Leonards v Southwick 1-2
23 Newport (IOW) v Weymouth 2-1
Salisbury Corinthians v Ryde Sports 2-1
24 Chippenham Rovers v Welton Rovers 1-0
Trowbridge Town v Cheltenham Town 1-4
25 Barry v Rose Green 7-0
Clevedon v Lovells Athletic 3-3
26 Glastonbury v Dartmouth United 7-1
Street v Plymouth & Stonehouse Gas Co. 1-2
1r Annfield Plain v Walker Celtic 2-1
r West Stanley v Eden CW 1-2
4r Holme Head Works v Kells United 0-1e
5r Nelson v Dick, Kerrs 3-4
7r Northwich Victoria v Altrincham 2-1e
8r Shrewsbury Town v Kidderminster Harriers 1-2
10r Goole Town v Thorne Colliery 6-3
11r Heanor Town v Bolsover Colliery 4-1
17r Dagenham Town v Crittall Athletic 2-1
18r London Caledonians v St Albans City 1-3
25r Lovells Athletic v Clevedon 5-1

Qualifying Round Three

1 Annfield Plain v Eden CW 2-2
2 Ferryhill Athletic v Blackhall Colliery Welfare 3-2
3 Scarborough v South Bank St Peters 2-1
4 Kells United v Penrith 7-1
5 Horwich RMI v Dick, Kerrs 4-2
6 Glossop v Prescot Cables 5-2
7 Northwich Victoria v Rhyl 3-2
8 Kidderminster Harriers v Leamington Town 6-3
9 Gainsborough Trinity v Brigg 2nd Lincs Sugar Co. 3-0
10 Denaby United v Goole Town 3-1
11 Ripley Town v Heanor Town 1-4
12 Ollerton Colliery v Grantham 1-2
13 Rushden Town v Kettering Town 3-2
14 Bedford Town (1) v Hitchin Town 1-1
15 King's Lynn v Cambridge Town 5-1
16 Bury Town v Lowestoft Town 2-2
17 Dagenham Town v Romford (2) 1-6
18 Leavesden v St Albans City 5-2
19 Uxbridge v Southall 0-1
20 Nunhead v PO Engineers (Beddington) 2-0
21 London Paper Mills v Margate 0-1
22 Southwick v Bexhill 6-1
23 Newport (IOW) v Salisbury Corinthians 3-1
24 Cheltenham Town v Chippenham Rovers 12-0
25 Barry v Lovells Athletic 2-1
26 Glastonbury v Plymouth & Stonehouse Gas Co. 1-3
1r Eden CW v Annfield Plain 1-0
14r Hitchin Town v Bedford Town (1) 4-2
16r Lowestoft Town v Bury Town 5-2

Qualifying Round Four

Blyth Spartans v Spennymoor United 1-0
Burton Town v King's Lynn 7-0
Chorley v Wigan Athletic 1-4
Dartford v Oxford City 5-1
Darwen v Lancaster Town 3-2
Eden CW v Ferryhill Athletic 0-2
Gainsborough Trinity v Heanor Town 3-2
Glossop v Kells United 2-4
Hitchin Town v Boston United 2-3
Horwich RMI v Stalybridge Celtic 1-2
Kidderminster Harriers v Lowestoft Town 4-0
Kingstonian v Nunhead 2-3
Newport (IOW) v Bath City 2-1
Northfleet United v Folkestone 1-2
Plymouth & Stonehouse Gas Co. v Cheltenham Town 1-3
Romford (2) v Guildford City 4-2
Rushden Town v Grantham 1-2
Scarborough v Shildon 2-1
Scunthorpe United v Denaby United 4-1
Southall v Enfield 4-2
Southwick v Dulwich Hamlet 0-5
Walthamstow Avenue v Leavesden 6-1
Wimbledon v Margate 1-4
Workington v Northwich Victoria 4-0
Yeovil & Petter's United v Barry 2-1

Round One

Barrow v Wrexham 4-1
Brighton & Hove Albion v Cheltenham Town 0-0
Bristol City v Crystal Palace 0-1
Cardiff City v Dartford 0-3
Chester v Gateshead 1-0
Chesterfield v Southport 3-0
Clapton Orient v Aldershot 0-0
Coventry City v Scunthorpe United 1-1
Crewe Alexandra v Boston United 4-2
Darlington v Accrington Stanley 4-2
Dulwich Hamlet v Torquay United 2-3
Exeter City v Gillingham 0-4
Gainsborough Trinity v Blyth Spartans 3-1
Grantham v Notts County 0-2
Halifax Town v Rochdale 4-0
Kidderminster Harriers v Bishop Auckland 4-1
Mansfield Town v Hartlepools United 2-3
Margate v Queen's Park Rangers 3-1
New Brighton v Workington 1-3
Newport County v Southend United 0-1
Northampton Town v Bristol Rovers 0-0
Nunhead v Watford 2-4
Oldham Athletic v Ferryhill Athletic 6-1
Reading v Corinthians 8-3
Romford (2) v Folkestone 3-3
Scarborough v Darwen 2-0
Southall v Swindon Town 3-1
Stalybridge Celtic v Kells United 4-0
Tranmere Rovers v Carlisle United 3-0
Walsall v Lincoln City 2-0
Walthamstow Avenue v Bournemouth 1-1
Wigan Athletic v Rotherham United 1-2
Yeovil & Petter's United v Newport (IOW) 0-1
York City v Burton Town 1-5
r Aldershot v Clapton Orient 0-1e
r Bournemouth v Walthamstow Avenue 8-1
r Bristol Rovers v Northampton Town 3-1

1935/36 to 1936/37

r Cheltenham Town v Brighton & Hove Albion	0-6
r Folkestone v Romford (2)	2-1e
r Scunthorpe United v Coventry City	4-2

Round Two

Bournemouth v Barrow	5-2
Chester v Reading	3-3
Chesterfield v Walsall	0-0
Crewe Alexandra v Gillingham	2-1
Dartford v Gainsborough Trinity	4-0
Folkestone v Clapton Orient	1-2
Halifax Town v Hartlepools United	1-1
Margate v Crystal Palace	3-1
Notts County v Torquay United	3-0
Oldham Athletic v Bristol Rovers	1-1
Rotherham United v Watford	1-1
Scarborough v Brighton & Hove Albion	1-1
Southall v Newport (IOW)	8-0
Southend United v Burton Town	5-0
Stalybridge Celtic v Darlington	0-1
Tranmere Rovers v Scunthorpe United	6-2
Workington v Kidderminster Harriers	5-1
r Brighton & Hove Albion v Scarborough	3-0
r Bristol Rovers v Oldham Athletic	4-1
r Hartlepools United v Halifax Town	0-0e
r Reading v Chester	3-0
r Walsall v Chesterfield	2-1
r Watford v Rotherham United	1-0
r2 Halifax Town v Hartlepools United	1-4eN

Round Three

Aston Villa v Huddersfield Town	0-1
Barnsley v Birmingham	3-3
Blackburn Rovers v Bolton Wanderers	1-1
Blackpool v Margate	3-1
Bradford City v Bournemouth	1-0
Bradford Park Avenue v Workington	3-2
Bristol Rovers v Arsenal	1-5
Burnley v Sheffield United	0-0
Clapton Orient v Charlton Athletic	3-0
Crewe Alexandra v Sheffield Wednesday	1-1
Darlington v Bury	2-3
Derby County v Dartford	3-2
Doncaster Rovers v Nottingham Forest	1-2
Everton v Preston North End	1-3
Fulham v Brighton & Hove Albion	2-1
Hartlepools United v Grimsby Town	0-0
Leicester City v Brentford	1-0
Liverpool v Swansea Town	1-0
Manchester City v Portsmouth	3-1
Middlesbrough v Southampton	1-0
Millwall v Stoke City	0-0
Norwich City v Chelsea	1-1
Notts County v Tranmere Rovers	0-0
Reading v Manchester United	1-3
Southall v Watford	1-4
Stockport County v Plymouth Argyle	2-3
Sunderland v Port Vale	2-2
Tottenham Hotspur v Southend United	4-4
Walsall v Newcastle United	0-2
West Bromwich Albion v Hull City	2-0
West Ham United v Luton Town	2-2
Wolverhampton Wan. v Leeds United	1-1
r Birmingham v Barnsley	0-2
r Bolton Wanderers v Blackburn Rovers	0-1e
r Chelsea v Norwich City	3-1
r Grimsby Town v Hartlepools United	4-1
r Leeds United v Wolverhampton Wan.	3-1
r Luton Town v West Ham United	4-0
r Port Vale v Sunderland	2-0
r Sheffield United v Burnley	2-1
r Sheffield Wednesday v Crewe Alexandra	3-1e
r Southend United v Tottenham Hotspur	1-2
r Stoke City v Millwall	4-0
r Tranmere Rovers v Notts County	4-3

Round Four

Bradford City v Blackburn Rovers	3-1
Bradford Park Avenue v West Bromwich Albion	1-1
Chelsea v Plymouth Argyle	4-1
Derby County v Nottingham Forest	2-0
Fulham v Blackpool	5-2
Leeds United v Bury	3-2
Leicester City v Watford	6-3
Liverpool v Arsenal	0-2
Manchester City v Luton Town	2-1
Middlesbrough v Clapton Orient	3-0
Port Vale v Grimsby Town	0-4
Preston North End v Sheffield United	0-0
Sheffield Wednesday v Newcastle United	1-1
Stoke City v Manchester United	0-0
Tottenham Hotspur v Huddersfield Town	1-0
Tranmere Rovers v Barnsley	2-4
r Manchester United v Stoke City	0-2
r Newcastle United v Sheffield Wednesday	3-1
r Sheffield United v Preston North End	2-0
r West Bromwich Albion v Bradford Park Avenue	1-1e
r2 Bradford Park Avenue v West Bromwich Albion	2-0 N

Round Five

Barnsley v Stoke City	2-1
Bradford City v Derby County	0-1
Bradford Park Avenue v Tottenham Hotspur	0-0
Chelsea v Fulham	0-0
Grimsby Town v Manchester City	3-2
Middlesbrough v Leicester City	2-1
Newcastle United v Arsenal	3-3
Sheffield United v Leeds United	3-1
r Arsenal v Newcastle United	3-0
r Fulham v Chelsea	3-2
r Tottenham Hotspur v Bradford Park Avenue	2-1

Round Six

Arsenal v Barnsley	4-1
Fulham v Derby County	3-0
Grimsby Town v Middlesbrough	3-1
Sheffield United v Tottenham Hotspur	3-1

Semi Finals

Arsenal v Grimsby Town	1-0 N
Sheffield United v Fulham	2-1 N

Final

Arsenal v Sheffield United	1-0 N

1936/37

Extra Preliminary Round

1 Ashington v Usworth Colliery	3-0
Consett v Whitley & Monkseaton	2-3
Crawcrook Albion v Scotswood	7-0
Dipton United v Crookhall CW	2-2
Gosforth & Coxlodge v Newcastle West End (2)	2-5
New Gateshead United v Jarrow	1-1
Newbiggin West End v West Wylam CW	6-5
Newburn v Felling Red Star	7-1
Throckley Welfare v Birtley	4-4
2 Cockfield v Tow Law Town	2-2
Crook Town v Chilton Colliery Recreation	1-3
Durham City v Shotton CW	4-3
Leasingthorne Colliery v Evenwood Town	2-2
Murton CW v Lanchester Rangers	5-1
West Auckland Town v Easington CW	0-2
7 Colwyn Bay v Whitchurch	7-1
Llandudno v Runcorn	1-2
Macclesfield Town v Haslington Villa	4-1
Witton Albion v Moulton Verdin	3-4
8 Brierley Hill Alliance v Bournville Athletic	9-1
Bromsgrove Rovers v Wolverhampton Amateur	4-2
Cannock Town v Headingley	6-1
Evesham Town v Cradley Heath St Luke's	2-4
Halesowen Town v Thynnes Athletic	4-1
Hednesford Town v Wrockwardine Wood	3-2
Hereford United v Badsey Rangers	3-3
Oakengates Town v Boldmere St Michaels	8-2
Oswestry Town v Birmingham Corp. Tramways	2-1
Shirley Town v Moor Green	2-4
Stafford Rangers v Bilston Borough	3-1
Stourbridge v Nuneaton Town	4-1
Tamworth v Dudley Town	2-3
10 Altofts West Riding Col. v Rawmarsh Welfare	4-1
Armthorpe Welfare v Goole Town	0-3
Bentley Colliery v Luddendenfoot	3-0
Cudworth St Mary's v Dinnington Athletic	1-3
Cudworth Village v Yorkshire Amateur	1-7
Farsley Celtic v Monckton Athletic	2-2
Frickley Colliery v Ryhill & Havercroft United	7-2
Meltham Mills v Upton Colliery	2-2
Norton Woodseats v Rossington Main	5-0
Ravensthorpe v Castleford Town	5-1
Rockingham Colliery v Guiseley	0-0
Sheffield v Selby Town	2-4
Thurnscoe Victoria v South Kirkby Colliery	5-2
Worksop Town v Pilkington Recreation	1-1
16 Eastern Counties United v Orwell Works	9-0
Gorleston v Holt United	1-1
17 Chelmsford v Clacton Town	2-2
Ford Sports (Dagenham) v CWS Silvertown	2-1
Harwich & Parkeston v Maldon & Heybridge	7-0
Jurgens (Purfleet) v Barking	0-2
Leytonstone v Hoffmann Athletic (Chelmsford)	1-1
18 Barnet v Old Johnians	4-1
Golders Green v Bushey United	9-0
Shredded Wheat v Berkhamsted Town	2-5
Tufnell Park v Ware	6-1
19 Aylesbury United v Henley Town	6-2
Banbury Spencer v Thatcham	7-0
Bicester Town v Cowley	3-3
Hayes v Hayesco Sports	2-1
Headington United v Pressed Steel	3-3
Morris Motors (Cowley) v Abingdon Town	5-2
RAF Halton v Maidenhead United	2-10
Windsor & Eton v Slough	4-1
Yiewsley v Marlow	4-7
20 Camberley & Yorktown v Woking	1-2
Carshalton Athletic v Cranleigh	4-1
Guildford v Metropolitan Police	2-3
Hersham v Leyland Motors (Kingston)	9-2
Redhill v Beddington Corner	4-1
West Norwood v Streatham Town	1-3
21 Aylesford Paper Mills v Betteshanger CW	8-1
Bexley v Woolwich Polytechnic	1-2
Bexleyheath & Welling v Cray Wanderers	3-1
Bostall Heath v Beckenham	1-2
Callender Athletic v Darenth Training Colony	8-1
Canterbury Waverley v Sittingbourne	7-1
Deal Town v Chatham	2-4
Lloyds (Sittingbourne) v Ashford	0-1
Whitstable v Sheppey United	3-0
Woolwich Borough Co. Ath. v Imperial Paper Mills	7-2e
23 Basingstoke v Thornycrofts (Basingstoke)	8-0
Blandford United v Bournemouth (Ams)	1-5
Gosport v HMS Excellent	4-1
HMS Victory v Lymington	1-2
Sherborne v Dorchester Town	2-0
Winchester City v Osborne Athletic	8-0
24 Purton v Melksham	3-1
Radstock Town v Twerton St Michael's	6-0
1r Birtley v Throckley Welfare	3-1
r Crookhall CW v Dipton United	2-1
r Jarrow v New Gateshead United	1-0
2r Evenwood Town v Leasingthorne Colliery	2-1
r Tow Law Town v Cockfield	4-1
8r Hereford United v Badsey Rangers	3-0
10r Guiseley v Rockingham Colliery	9-2
r Monckton Athletic v Farsley Celtic	2-1
r Pilkington Recreation v Worksop Town	1-7
r Upton Colliery v Meltham Mills	8-1
16r Holt United v Gorleston	0-2
17r Clacton Town v Chelmsford	0-1
r Hoffmann Athletic (Chelmsford) v Leytonstone	0-0
19r Cowley v Bicester Town	3-2
r Pressed Steel v Headington United	6-1
17r2 Hoffmann Athletic (Chelmsford) v Leytonstone	1-0

Preliminary Round

1 Ashington v Crawcrook Albion	7-1
Birtley v Annfield Plain	2-2
Crookhall CW v Newbiggin West End	1-1
Jarrow v Windy Nook	5-2
Newburn v Pelaw	2-1
Newcastle West End (2) v Shankhouse	4-3
West Stanley v Walker Celtic	0-2
Whitley & Monkseaton v Eden CW	2-1
2 Billingham Synthonia v Bishop Auckland	2-4
Blackhall Colliery Welfare v Tow Law Town	8-1
Chilton Colliery Recreation v Dawdon Colliery Recrea	0-3
Durham City v Murton CW	0-0
Easington CW v Evenwood Town	2-2
Ferryhill Athletic v Seaham Colliery Welfare	3-0
Spennymoor United v Willington	4-1
Trimdon Grange Colliery v Horden CW	0-1
3 Filey Town v Bridlington Town (1)	2-4
Grangetown St Mary's v Whitby United	1-1
Pease & Partners v Scarborough	0-3
Smith's Dock v Carlin How	1-3
South Bank East End v Scarborough Junior Imperial	4-2
Thornaby v South Bank	2-5
Thornaby St Patrick v Stockton	2-3
Whitby Albion Rangers v Normanby Mangnesite	2-5
5 Rossendale United v Lytham	4-3
Skelmersdale United v Morecambe	2-2
6 Glossop v Droylsden	2-2
Harrowby v Earlestown Bohemians	0-3
Manchester North End v Northern Nomads	4-0
Orrell v Earle	1-2
Prescot Cables v Marine	1-4
South Liverpool v Oakmere (Liverpool)	5-0
Thorndale v Hoylake	0-6
Urmston v Buxton	1-2
7 Altrincham v Willaston White Star	7-1
Barnton Victoria v Middlewich Athletic	5-1
Congleton Town v Timperley	6-1
ICI Alkali v Bangor City	1-2
Macclesfield Town v Linotype & Machinery	4-3
Nantwich v Colwyn Bay	4-1
Northwich Victoria v Moulton Verdin	4-1
Runcorn v Rhyl	6-2
8 Dudley Town v Halesowen Town	6-1
Hereford United v Cradley Heath St Luke's	4-1
Leamington Town v Oswestry Town	2-1
Moor Green v Hednesford Town	1-1
Shrewsbury Town v Brierley Hill Alliance	5-1
Stafford Rangers v Oakengates Town	1-2
Stourbridge v Bromsgrove Rovers	5-1
Wellington Town v Cannock Town	6-1
9 Brigg Town v Lysaght's Sports (Scunthorpe)	2-1
Ranks (Hull) v Barton Town (1)	5-5
10 Bentley Colliery v Denaby United	2-6
Dinnington Athletic v Thorne Colliery	0-0
Guiseley v Altofts West Riding Col.	3-5
Ravensthorpe v Norton Woodseats	2-2
Selby Town v Monckton Athletic	1-0
Thurnscoe Victoria v Goole Town	2-2
Upton Colliery v Worksop Town	1-2
Yorkshire Amateur v Frickley Colliery	0-4

88

1936/37

11	Danesmoor Welfare v Ilkeston	3-2
	Staveley Welfare v Leicester Nomads	3-2
12	Bilsthorpe Colliery v Boots Athletic	2-3
13	Desborough Town v Irchester United	wo/s
	Stewarts & Lloyds v Wellingborough Town	7-3
14	Baldock Town v St Neots & District	0-5
	Bedford Town (1) v Leighton United	0-1
	Eynesbury Rovers v Biggleswade United (1)	7-0
	Letchworth Town v Kempston Rovers	1-1
	Luton Amateur v Biggleswade & District	0-10
	Waterlows (Dunstable) v Arlesey Town	8-2
15	March Great Eastern United v Abbey United (Cambs)	2-0
16	Cromer v Great Yarmouth Town	2-2
	Felixstowe Town v Bury Town	0-4
	Gorleston v Lowestoft Town	0-1
	Ipswich Town v Eastern Counties United	7-0
	Norwich CEYMS v Norwich YMCA	3-0
	Norwich St Barnabas v Frosts Athletic	0-7
	Sheringham v Bungay Town	0-1
	Stowmarket v RAF Martlesham	6-1
17	Anglo (Purfleet) v Ford Sports (Dagenham)	2-3
	Briggs Motor Bodies v Barking	1-7
	Brightlingsea United v Severalls Athletic	0-2
	Colchester Town v Chelmsford	3-2
	Crittall Athletic v Harwich & Parkeston	1-1
	Dagenham Town v Tilbury	3-1
	Hoffmann Athletic (Chelmsford) v Romford (2)	0-5
	Leyton v Clapton	4-1
18	Berkhamsted Town v London Caledonians	4-2
	Enfield v Stevenage Town	11-1
	Golders Green v Pinner	5-1
	Hertford Town v Barnet	1-4
	Hoddesdon Town v Bishop's Stortford	1-4
	Leavesden v Apsley	5-3
	St Albans City v Old Lyonian	4-2
	Wealdstone v Tufnell Park	0-3
19	Aylesbury United v Wycombe Wanderers	1-2
	Banbury Spencer v Pressed Steel	7-2
	Civil Service v Chesham United	1-3
	Hayes v Maidenhead United	4-3
	Newbury Town v Cowley	2-6
	Osberton Radiator (Oxford) v Morris Motors (Cowley)	5-1
	Uxbridge v Marlow	6-1
	Windsor & Eton v AEC Athletic	8-1
20	Hersham v Tooting & Mitcham United	5-0
	Nunhead v Banstead Mental Hospital	3-2
	PO Engineers (Beddington) v Redhill	4-2
	RAMC Aldershot v Carshalton Athletic	2-2
	Streatham Town v Egham	2-1
	Sutton United v Kingstonian	1-1
	Walton-on-Thames v Metropolitan Police	2-3
	Woking v Epsom	3-1
21	Ashford v Aylesford Paper Mills	4-0
	Bexleyheath & Welling v Bromley	2-0
	Callender Athletic v Beckenham	11-0
	Maidstone United v Chatham	0-3
	RM Deal v Canterbury Waverley	0-8
	Swanley Athletic v Woolwich Borough Co. Ath.	2-1
	Whitstable v Northfleet United	1-3
	Woolwich Polytechnic v London Paper Mills	1-3
22	Bexhill v East Grinstead	4-0
	Chichester v Hove	1-4
	Hastings & St Leonards v Bognor Regis Town	11-1
	Haywards Heath v Shoreham	7-0
	Horsham v Brighton Corp. Tramways	8-2
	Littlehampton v Southwick	1-1
	Newhaven v Eastbourne Comrades	3-1
	Worthing v Vernon Athletic	2-0
23	Courage & Co.'s Sports v Cowes	0-0
	Lymington v Basingstoke	1-1
	Ryde Sports v East Cowes	3-2
	Salisbury City (1) v Poole Town	2-0
	Salisbury Corinthians v Weymouth	3-0
	Sherborne v Bournemouth (Ams)	2-4
	Totton v Newport (IOW)	0-1
	Winchester City v Gosport	1-2
24	Chippenham Rovers v Spencer Moulton	1-5
	Chippenham Town v Warminster Town	2-3
	Devizes Town v Swindon Victoria	2-4
	Paulton Rovers v Frome Town	2-2
	Radstock Town v Welton Rovers	4-1
	Swindon Corinthians v Trowbridge Town	6-3
	Timsbury Athletic v Clandown	2-3
	Westbury United v Purton	4-2
26	Barry v Ebbw Vale	2-1
	Cardiff Corinthians v Llanelli	1-2
	Clevedon v Keynsham	7-3
	Hanham Athletic v St Philips Marsh Adult School	1-3
	Lovells Athletic v Aberdare Town	wo/s
	Mount Hill Enterprise v St Philips Athletic	2-1
	Rose Green v Bristol St George	2-3
	Weston-Super-Mare v Cheltenham Town	3-13
1r	Annfield Plain v Birtley	1-5
r	Newbiggin West End v Crookhall CW	4-2
2r	Evenwood Town v Easington CW	1-1x
r	Murton CW v Durham City	6-1
3r	Whitby United v Grangetown St Mary's	0-2
5r	Morecambe v Skelmersdale United	2-0
6r	Droylsden v Glossop	1-2e
8r	Hednesford Town v Moor Green	3-2
9r	Barton Town (1) v Ranks (Hull)	0-1
10r	Goole Town v Thurnscoe Victoria	5-0e
r	Norton Woodseats v Ravensthorpe	5-1
r	Thorne Colliery v Dinnington Athletic	0-1
14r	Kempston Rovers v Letchworth Town	3-2e
16r	Great Yarmouth Town v Cromer	2-4
17r	Harwich & Parkeston v Crittall Athletic	8-2
20r	Carshalton Athletic v RAMC Aldershot	4-1
r	Kingstonian v Sutton United	3-2
22r	Southwick v Littlehampton	4-0
23r	Basingstoke v Lymington	4-2
r	Cowes v Courage & Co.'s Sports	2-3
24r	Frome Town v Paulton Rovers	4-0
2r2	Evenwood Town v Easington CW	1-3 N

Qualifying Round One

1	Ashington v Jarrow	2-0
	Newcastle West End (2) v Birtley	1-2
	Walker Celtic v Newbiggin West End	3-2
	Whitley & Monkseaton v Newburn	2-1
2	Bishop Auckland v Horden CW	3-0
	Dawdon Colliery Recreation v Spennymoor United	0-4
	Easington CW v Ferryhill Athletic	3-1
	Murton CW v Blackhall Colliery Welfare	1-0
3	Bridlington Town (1) v Stockton	2-1
	Normanby Mangnesite v Carlin How	4-1
	Scarborough v Grangetown St Mary's	1-1
	South Bank East End v South Bank	1-1
4	Kells United v Cleator Moor Celtic	4-0
	Netherfield (Kendal) v Cockermouth	4-1
	Whitehaven Wellington Villa v Whitehaven White Rose	4-3
5	Chorley v Nelson	wo/s
	Crossens v Breightmet United	1-0
	Horwich RMI v Rossendale United	3-1
	Leyland Motors v Morecambe	1-1
6	Buxton v Hoylake	3-3
	Manchester North End v Glossop	3-2
	Marine v Earle	4-1
	South Liverpool v Earlestown Bohemians	3-0
7	Congleton Town v Nantwich	1-3
	Macclesfield Town v Barnton Victoria	5-1
	Northwich Victoria v Bangor City	2-0
	Runcorn v Altrincham	7-0
8	Dudley Town v Hednesford Town	2-0
	Oakengates Town v Hereford United	2-2
	Shrewsbury Town v Wellington Town	2-2
	Stourbridge v Leamington Town	8-0
9	Appleby Frodingham v Louth Town	1-3
	Brigg Town v Boston United	2-3
	Humber United v Ranks (Hull)	0-1
	Redbourne Sports v Marfleet	1-1
10	Denaby United v Selby Town	4-1
	Goole Town v Dinnington Athletic	1-1
	Norton Woodseats v Altofts West Riding Col.	5-1
	Worksop Town v Frickley Colliery	1-3
11	Danesmoor Welfare v Ripley Town	1-5
	Heanor Town v North Derby Ramblers	1-3
	Hinckley United (1) v Bolsover Colliery	0-3
	Staveley Welfare v Sandiacre Excelsior Foundry	7-1
12	Boots Athletic v Basford United	3-0
	Newark Town v Sutton Town	1-0
	Ollerton Colliery v Grantham	1-1
	Rufford Colliery v Ransome & Marles	1-3
13	Desborough Town v Stamford	4-0
	Kettering Town v Peterborough United	0-2
	Peterbro' Westwood Works v Wolverton Town	2-2
	Rushden Town v Stewarts & Lloyds	2-0
14	Eynesbury Rovers v Waterlows (Dunstable)	1-3
	Kempston Rovers v Leighton United	1-2
	Sandy Albion v St Neots & District	1-6
	Vauxhall Motors (Luton) v Biggleswade & District	1-4
15	Chatteris Town v March Great Eastern United	3-1
	King's Lynn v Thetford Town	2-0
	Pye Radio v Cambridge Town	0-2
	Wisbech Town v Chatteris Engineers	9-0
16	Cromer v Bungay Town	4-1
	Ipswich Town v Stowmarket	8-0
	Lowestoft Town v Bury Town	2-0
	Norwich CEYMS v Frosts Athletic	0-1
17	Barking v Severalls Athletic	5-0
	Colchester Town v Romford (2)	0-3
	Dagenham Town v Harwich & Parkeston	0-2
	Ford Sports (Dagenham) v Leyton	3-2
18	Berkhamsted Town v Tufnell Park	2-1
	Enfield v Bishop's Stortford	1-0
	Golders Green v Barnet	6-2
	Leavesden v St Albans City	0-2
19	Banbury Spencer v Wycombe Wanderers	1-3
	Hayes v Chesham United	4-1
	Uxbridge v Osberton Radiator (Oxford)	2-1
	Windsor & Eton v Cowley	7-0
20	Hersham v Woking	4-0
	Nunhead v Carshalton Athletic	0-0
	PO Engineers (Beddington) v Kingstonian	1-1
	Streatham Town v Metropolitan Police	3-3e
21	Ashford v Callender Athletic	2-2
	Bexleyheath & Welling v Swanley Athletic	2-0
	Chatham v Canterbury Waverley	5-2
	Northfleet United v London Paper Mills	1-0
22	Bexhill v Horsham	1-4
	Hastings & St Leonards v Southwick	2-3
	Haywards Heath v Newhaven	1-2
	Hove v Worthing	0-7
23	Bournemouth (Ams) v Newport (IOW)	1-4
	Courage & Co.'s Sports v Salisbury City (1)	3-3
	Gosport v Salisbury Corinthians	5-3
	Ryde Sports v Basingstoke	4-0
24	Radstock Town v Frome Town	4-0
	Swindon Corinthians v Spencer Moulton	1-2
	Swindon Victoria v Westbury United	1-0
	Warminster Town v Clandown	2-0
25	Dartmouth United v Exmouth Town	2-3
	Minehead v Glastonbury	0-3
	Tiverton Town v Ilfracombe Town	3-1
	Wells City v Street	2-1
26	Barry v Llanelli	5-0
	Bristol St George v Clevedon	0-4
	Mount Hill Enterprise v Cheltenham Town	0-6
	St Philips Marsh Adult School v Lovells Athletic	0-1
3r	Scarborough v Grangetown St Mary's	4-1
r	South Bank v South Bank East End	2-1
5r	Morecambe v Leyland Motors	3-2
6r	Hoylake v Buxton	0-0
8r	Hereford United v Oakengates Town	0-1
r	Wellington Town v Shrewsbury Town	3-2
9r	Marfleet v Redbourne Sports	2-1
10r	Dinnington Athletic v Goole Town	1-1
12r	Grantham v Ollerton Colliery	5-1
13r	Wolverton Town v Peterbro' Westwood Works	3-1
20r	Carshalton Athletic v Nunhead	2-1
r	Kingstonian v PO Engineers (Beddington)	4-1
r	Metropolitan Police v Streatham Town	2-1
21r	Callender Athletic v Ashford	3-1
23r	Salisbury City (1) v Courage & Co.'s Sports	3-0
6r2	Hoylake v Buxton	0-2 N
10r2	Dinnington Athletic v Goole Town	5-1 N

Qualifying Round Two

1	Ashington v Birtley	1-2
	Whitley & Monkseaton v Walker Celtic	1-3
2	Murton CW v Easington CW	2-2
	Spennymoor United v Bishop Auckland	1-1
3	Bridlington Town (1) v Normanby Mangnesite	4-2
	South Bank v Scarborough	0-1
4	Kells United v Holme Head Works	4-2
	Netherfield (Kendal) v Whitehaven Wellington Villa	4-2
5	Horwich RMI v Crossens	5-0
	Morecambe v Chorley	5-1
6	Buxton v Marine	5-2
	South Liverpool v Manchester North End	3-1
7	Macclesfield Town v Runcorn	1-2
	Nantwich v Northwich Victoria	2-5
8	Dudley Town v Oakengates Town	1-1
	Stourbridge v Wellington Town	2-3
9	Boston United v Louth Town	4-2
	Marfleet v Ranks (Hull)	3-1
10	Denaby United v Dinnington Athletic	4-1
	Frickley Colliery v Norton Woodseats	6-1
11	Bolsover Colliery v Staveley Welfare	2-0
	Ripley Town v North Derby Ramblers	3-2
12	Grantham v Ransome & Marles	4-2
	Newark Town v Boots Athletic	4-0
13	Peterborough United v Wolverton Town	3-0
	Rushden Town v Desborough Town	1-0
14	Leighton United v Biggleswade & District	1-2
	Waterlows (Dunstable) v St Neots & District	3-3
15	Cambridge Town v King's Lynn	2-1
	Wisbech Town v Chatteris Town	7-0
16	Cromer v Frosts Athletic	4-0
	Lowestoft Town v Ipswich Town	1-1
17	Barking v Ford Sports (Dagenham)	2-2
	Romford (2) v Harwich & Parkeston	1-1
18	Enfield v Berkhamsted Town	0-0
	Golders Green v St Albans City	4-0
19	Hayes v Uxbridge	5-1
	Wycombe Wanderers v Windsor & Eton	3-1
20	Hersham v Kingstonian	1-3
	Metropolitan Police v Carshalton Athletic	4-0
21	Bexleyheath & Welling v Callender Athletic	0-1
	Northfleet United v Chatham	4-0
22	Newhaven v Southwick	0-3
	Worthing v Horsham	2-1
23	Gosport v Ryde Sports	1-2
	Salisbury City (1) v Newport (IOW)	2-1
24	Spencer Moulton v Radstock Town	1-0
	Warminster Town v Swindon Victoria	1-0
25	Tiverton Town v Exmouth Town	7-1
	Wells City v Glastonbury	5-0
26	Barry v Lovells Athletic	1-2
	Cheltenham Town v Clevedon	6-1
2r	Bishop Auckland v Spennymoor United	1-3
r	Easington CW v Murton CW	2-0
8r	Oakengates Town v Dudley Town	1-0
14r	St Neots & District v Waterlows (Dunstable)	0-2
16r	Ipswich Town v Lowestoft Town	4-0
17r	Ford Sports (Dagenham) v Barking	0-3
r	Harwich & Parkeston v Romford (2)	6-2
18r	Berkhamsted Town v Enfield	4-4
18r2	Enfield v Berkhamsted Town	4-0 N

Qualifying Round Three

1	Walker Celtic v Birtley	1-1
2	Spennymoor United v Easington CW	6-1
3	Bridlington Town (1) v Scarborough	4-6
4	Netherfield (Kendal) v Kells United	1-2
5	Horwich RMI v Morecambe	0-2
6	Buxton v South Liverpool	0-1
7	Northwich Victoria v Runcorn	1-0
8	Wellington Town v Oakengates Town	4-0

1936/37 to 1937/38

9	Boston United v Marfleet	6-0
10	Frickley Colliery v Denaby United	4-1
11	Bolsover Colliery v Ripley Town	0-3
12	Grantham v Newark Town	0-1
13	Peterborough United v Rushden Town	4-2
14	Biggleswade & District v Waterlows (Dunstable)	4-2
15	Wisbech Town v Cambridge Town	3-3
16	Ipswich Town v Cromer	11-0
17	Barking v Harwich & Parkeston	1-3
18	Enfield v Golders Green	2-1
19	Hayes v Wycombe Wanderers	5-1
20	Metropolitan Police v Kingstonian	1-4
21	Northfleet United v Callender Athletic	3-2
22	Southwick v Worthing	0-1
23	Salisbury City (1) v Ryde Sports	0-0
24	Warminster Town v Spencer Moulton	3-1
25	Wells City v Tiverton Town	6-0
26	Cheltenham Town v Lovells Athletic	3-0
1r	Birtley v Walker Celtic	0-1
15r	Cambridge Town v Wisbech Town	2-0
23r	Ryde Sports v Salisbury City (1)	1-0

Qualifying Round Four

	Biggleswade & District v Peterborough United	1-2
	Blyth Spartans v Walker Celtic	7-1
	Boston United v Newark Town	6-2
	Folkestone v Guildford City	2-1
	Frickley Colliery v Ripley Town	2-1
	Gainsborough Trinity v Scunthorpe United	0-1
	Harwich & Parkeston v Hayes	5-4
	Ipswich Town v Cambridge Town	2-1
	Kells United v Morecambe	1-4
	Kidderminster Harriers v Burton Town	3-2 D
	Lancaster Town v Stalybridge Celtic	2-4
	Margate v Dulwich Hamlet	1-2
	North Shields v Spennymoor United	2-3
	Northfleet United v Dartford	0-5
	Northwich Victoria v Wellington Town	1-1
	Oxford City v Southall	3-6
	Scarborough v Shildon	2-3
	Tunbridge Wells Rangers v Enfield	8-0
	Walthamstow Avenue v Kingstonian	5-1
	Warminster Town v Bath City	0-1
	Wells City v Ryde Sports	1-1
	Wigan Athletic v Darwen	3-0
	Workington v South Liverpool	0-2
	Worthing v Wimbledon	2-0
	Yeovil & Petter's United v Cheltenham Town	3-2
r	Ryde Sports v Wells City	8-1
r	Wellington Town v Northwich Victoria	2-0

Round One

	Accrington Stanley v Wellington Town	3-1
	Aldershot v Millwall	1-6
	Barrow v Mansfield Town	0-4
	Bath City v Tunbridge Wells Rangers	1-2
	Blyth Spartans v Wrexham	0-2
	Boston United v Spennymoor United	1-1
	Bournemouth v Harwich & Parkeston	5-1
	Burton Town v Wigan Athletic	5-1
	Cardiff City v Southall	3-1
	Carlisle United v Stockport County	2-1
	Clapton Orient v Torquay United	2-1
	Corinthians v Bristol Rovers	0-2
	Crewe Alexandra v Rochdale	5-1
	Crystal Palace v Southend United	1-1
	Dartford v Peterborough United	3-0
	Exeter City v Folkestone	3-0
	Frickley Colliery v Southport	0-2
	Gateshead v Notts County	2-0
	Halifax Town v Darlington	1-2
	Ilford v Reading	2-4
	Ipswich Town v Watford	2-1
	Lincoln City v New Brighton	1-1
	Newport County v Bristol City	3-0
	Oldham Athletic v Tranmere Rovers	1-0
	Queen's Park Rangers v Brighton & Hove Albion	5-1
	Rotherham United v Hartlepools United	4-4
	Ryde Sports v Gillingham	1-5
	Shildon v Stalybridge Celtic	4-2
	South Liverpool v Morecambe	1-0
	Swindon Town v Dulwich Hamlet	6-0
	Walsall v Scunthorpe United	3-0
	Walthamstow Avenue v Northampton Town	6-1
	Yeovil & Petter's United v Worthing	4-3
	York City v Hull City	5-2
r	Hartlepools United v Rotherham United	2-0
r	New Brighton v Lincoln City	2-3e
r	Southend United v Crystal Palace	2-0
r	Spennymoor United v Boston United	2-0

Round Two

	Accrington Stanley v Tunbridge Wells Rangers	1-0
	Bristol Rovers v Southport	2-1
	Burton Town v Darlington	1-2
	Cardiff City v Swindon Town	2-1
	Carlisle United v Clapton Orient	4-1
	Crewe Alexandra v Hartlepools United	1-1
	Ipswich Town v Spennymoor United	1-2
	Lincoln City v Oldham Athletic	2-3
	Mansfield Town v Bournemouth	0-3
	Millwall v Gateshead	7-0
	Reading v Newport County	7-2
	Shildon v Dartford	0-3
	South Liverpool v Queen's Park Rangers	0-1
	Southend United v York City	3-3
	Walsall v Yeovil & Petter's United	1-1
	Walthamstow Avenue v Exeter City	2-3
	Wrexham v Gillingham	2-0
r	Hartlepools United v Crewe Alexandra	1-2
r	Yeovil & Petter's United v Walsall	0-1
r	York City v Southend United	2-1

Round Three

	Aston Villa v Burnley	2-3
	Blackburn Rovers v Accrington Stanley	2-2
	Bradford City v York City	2-2
	Bradford Park Avenue v Derby County	0-4
	Brentford v Huddersfield Town	5-0
	Bristol Rovers v Leicester City	2-5
	Bury v Queen's Park Rangers	1-0
	Cardiff City v Grimsby Town	1-3
	Chelsea v Leeds United	4-0
	Chester v Doncaster Rovers	4-0
	Chesterfield v Arsenal	1-5
	Coventry City v Charlton Athletic	2-0
	Crewe Alexandra v Plymouth Argyle	0-2
	Dartford v Darlington	0-1
	Everton v Bournemouth	5-0
	Exeter City v Oldham Athletic	3-0
	Luton Town v Blackpool	3-3
	Manchester United v Reading	1-0
	Millwall v Fulham	2-0
	Norwich City v Liverpool	3-0
	Nottingham Forest v Sheffield United	2-4
	Portsmouth v Tottenham Hotspur	0-5
	Preston North End v Newcastle United	2-0
	Sheffield Wednesday v Port Vale	2-0
	Southampton v Sunderland	2-3
	Stoke City v Birmingham	4-1
	Swansea Town v Carlisle United	1-0
	Walsall v Barnsley	3-1
	West Bromwich Albion v Spennymoor United	7-1
	West Ham United v Bolton Wanderers	0-0
	Wolverhampton Wan. v Middlesbrough	6-1
	Wrexham v Manchester City	1-3
r	Accrington Stanley v Blackburn Rovers	3-1e
r	Blackpool v Luton Town	1-2
r	Bolton Wanderers v West Ham United	1-0
r	York City v Bradford City	1-0

Round Four

	Arsenal v Manchester United	5-0
	Bolton Wanderers v Norwich City	1-1
	Burnley v Bury	4-1
	Coventry City v Chester	2-0
	Derby County v Brentford	3-0
	Everton v Sheffield Wednesday	3-0
	Exeter City v Leicester City	3-1
	Grimsby Town v Walsall	5-1
	Luton Town v Sunderland	2-2
	Manchester City v Accrington Stanley	2-0
	Millwall v Chelsea	3-0
	Preston North End v Stoke City	5-1
	Swansea Town v York City	0-0
	Tottenham Hotspur v Plymouth Argyle	1-0
	West Bromwich Albion v Darlington	3-2
	Wolverhampton Wan. v Sheffield United	2-2
r	Norwich City v Bolton Wanderers	1-2e
r	Sheffield United v Wolverhampton Wan.	1-2
r	Sunderland v Luton Town	3-1
r	York City v Swansea Town	1-3

Round Five

	Bolton Wanderers v Manchester City	0-5
	Burnley v Arsenal	1-7
	Coventry City v West Bromwich Albion	2-3
	Everton v Tottenham Hotspur	1-1
	Grimsby Town v Wolverhampton Wan.	1-1
	Millwall v Derby County	2-1
	Preston North End v Exeter City	5-3
	Sunderland v Swansea Town	3-0
r	Tottenham Hotspur v Everton	4-3
r	Wolverhampton Wan. v Grimsby Town	6-2

Round Six

	Millwall v Manchester City	2-0
	Tottenham Hotspur v Preston North End	1-3
	West Bromwich Albion v Arsenal	3-1
	Wolverhampton Wan. v Sunderland	1-1
r	Sunderland v Wolverhampton Wan.	2-2e
r2	Sunderland v Wolverhampton Wan.	4-0 N

Semi Finals

	Preston North End v West Bromwich Albion	4-1 N
	Sunderland v Millwall	2-1 N

Final

	Sunderland v Preston North End	3-1 N

1937/38

Extra Preliminary Round

1	Amble v Gosforth & Coxlodge	2-1
	Felling Red Star v New Gateshead United	0-1
	Hexham v Crookhall CW	4-2
	Jarrow v South Shields (2)	2-1
	Newbiggin West End v West Stanley	2-4
	Scotswood v Consett	3-3
	Throckley Welfare v Close Works	4-0
	West Wylam CW v Ouston United	1-1
	Windy Nook v Crawcrook Albion	3-1
2	Barnard Castle Athletic v Evenwood Town	1-1
	Blackhall Colliery Welfare v Crook Town	6-0
	Chilton Colliery Recreation v Shotton CW	8-1
	Dawdon Colliery Recreation v Lanchester Rangers	6-0
	Ferryhill Athletic v Willington	2-1
	Furness Athletic v Durham City	1-3
	Leasingthorne v Trimdon Grange Colliery	2-2
	Seaham Colliery Welfare v Billingham Synthonia	2-1
	Tow Law Town v Cockfield	0-0
	West Auckland Town v Brandon Social	1-1
	Witton Park Institute v Leasingthorne Colliery	wo/s
6	Formby v Stanlow Social	1-4
	Tushingham Brick Works v Orrell	0-0
7	Sandbach Ramblers v Lostock Gralam	2-0
	Winsford United v Rhyl	2-0
8	Badsey Rangers v Hednesford Town	1-5
	Bilston Borough v Cradley Heath St Luke's	1-3
	Bournville Athletic v Boldmere St Michaels	0-3
	Brierley Hill Alliance v Wrockwardine Wood	5-0
	Bromsgrove Rovers v Birmingham Corp. Tramways	6-2
	Moor Green v Wolverhampton Amateur	3-1
	Oswestry Town v Halesowen Town	4-0
	Shirley Town v Headingley	3-1
	Shrewsbury Town v Evesham Town	10-2
	Worcester City v Sutton Town (Birmingham)	9-0
10	Armthorpe Welfare v Thorne Colliery	2-0
	Frickley Colliery v Bradford Rovers	2-1
	Goole Town v Meltham Mills	4-0
	Guiseley v Pilkington Recreation	0-4
	Luddendenfoot v Farsley Celtic	0-0
	Monckton Athletic v Thurnscoe Victoria	2-0
	Ravensthorpe v Upton Colliery	2-7
	Rawmarsh Welfare v Cudworth Village	0-0
	Rossington Main v Lopham Methodists	5-1
	Selby Town v Altofts West Riding Col.	5-1
	South Kirkby Colliery v Sheffield	4-1
	Worksop Town v Bentley Colliery	3-0
	Yorkshire Amateur v Ryhill & Havercroft United	4-0
14	Hitchin Town v Stewartby Works	6-1
17	Brightlingsea United v CWS Silvertown	3-4
	Eton Manor v Tilbury	1-0
	Grays Athletic v Colchester Town	4-0
18	Apsley v Bushey United	2-1
	Barnet v Hoddesdon Town	2-5
	Finchley v Northmet	1-3
	Harlow Town v Watford British Legion	5-3
	Stevenage Town v Bishop's Stortford	1-2
	Tufnell Park v Epping Town	3-0
	Wood Green Town v Old Lyonian	7-0
19	Aylesbury United v Henley Town	0-1
	Banbury Spencer v Chesham United	1-3
	Bicester Town v Abingdon Town	7-1
	Cowley v Thatcham	5-8
	Headington United v Marlow	4-2
	Maidenhead United v Lyons Club (Greenford)	3-0
	Metropolitan Railway v Slough	1-5
	Newbury Town v Osberton Radiator (Oxford)	2-9
	Pressed Steel v Morris Motors (Cowley)	3-4
	Windsor & Eton v Hounslow Town	3-0
	Yiewsley v Civil Service	2-6
20	Brookwood Hospital v 4th Royal Tank Regiment	4-3
	Cranleigh v Tooting & Mitcham United	0-5
	Epsom v RAMC Aldershot	3-0
	Godalming v Ewell & Stoneleigh	5-8
	Guildford v Camberley & Yorktown	2-4
	Leyland Motors (Kingston) v Woking	1-3
	Nunhead v West Norwood	4-0
	Sutton United v PO Engineers (Beddington)	6-0
	Venner Sports v Banstead Mental Hospital	0-1
	Wandsworth United v Redhill	0-3
21	Ashford v Ramsgate Grenville	5-0
	Aylesford Paper Mills v Cray Wanderers	6-0
	Betteshanger CW v Dover	1-7
	Bexley v Darenth Park	1-8
	Bromley v Beckenham	4-1
	Canterbury Waverley v Deal Town	9-1
	London Paper Mills v Swanley Athletic	wo/s
	RM Deal v Sittingbourne	1-8
23	East Cowes v Totton	2-4
	HMS Excellent v Portsmouth Electricity	8-4
	Salisbury Corinthians v Poole Town	4-1
	Sherborne v Weymouth	1-2
24	Calne & Harris United v Wilts County Mental Hospital	1-2
1r	Consett v Scotswood	1-1
r	Ouston United v West Wylam CW	3-2
2r	Brandon Social v West Auckland Town	2-1
r	Cockfield v Tow Law Town	4-2
r	Evenwood Town v Barnard Castle Athletic	4-1
r	Trimdon Grange Colliery v Leasingthorne	1-1x

1937/38

6r	Orrell v Tushingham Brick Works	2-2e
10r	Cudworth Village v Rawmarsh Welfare	1-2
r	Farsley Celtic v Luddendenfoot	2-0
1r2	Scotswood v Consett	1-1
2r2	Trimdon Grange Colliery v Leasingthorne	3-2
6r2	Tushingham Brick Works v Orrell	4-4xN
1r3	Consett v Scotswood	0-2
6r3	Orrell v Tushingham Brick Works	3-3eN
6r4	Orrell v Tushingham Brick Works	3-1 N

Preliminary Round

1	Annfield Plain v West Stanley	3-1
	Ashington v Newburn	4-1
	Birtley v Ouston United	2-2
	Jarrow v Amble	7-1
	Scotswood v New Gateshead United	1-2
	Usworth Colliery v Hexham	1-4
	Walker Celtic v Throckley Welfare	1-1
	Windy Nook v Whitley & Monkseaton	3-1 D
2	Brandon Social v Blackhall Colliery Welfare	2-1
	Chilton Colliery Recreation v Evenwood Town	1-0
	Dawdon Colliery Recreation v Bishop Auckland	0-0
	Durham City v Murton CW	3-1
	Easington CW v Seaham Colliery Welfare	2-5
	Ferryhill Athletic v Trimdon Grange Colliery	5-1
	Horden CW v Cockfield	1-0
	Spennymoor United v Witton Park Institute	6-1
3	Bridlington Town (1) v Normanby Mangnesite	5-0
	Grangetown St Mary's v South Bank East End	1-4
	Portrack Shamrocks v Filey Town	1-0
	Scarborough Juniors v Whitby United	2-2
	Smith's Dock v Thornaby St Patrick	2-1
	South Bank v Scarborough	1-3
	South Bank St Peters v Scarborough Junior Imperial	3-0
	Stockton v Whitby Albion Rangers	7-2
5	Great Harwood v Lytham	3-3
	Rossendale United v Breightmet United	5-0
	Skelmersdale United v Leyland Motors	1-1
6	Earle v Hoylake	2-3
	Glossop v Droylsden	wo/s
	Manchester North End v Buxton	3-1
	Orrell v Marine	0-8
	Prescot Cables v Stanlow Social	7-0
	South Liverpool v Harrowby	6-1
	Thorndale v Oakmere (Liverpool)	1-0
	Urmston v Northern Nomads	3-0
7	Haslington Villa v Sandbach Ramblers	2-3
	Llandudno v Winsford United	4-2
	Middlewich Athletic v Altrincham	wo/d
	Runcorn v Bangor City	2-0
	Timperley v Colwyn Bay	5-0
	Whitchurch v Nantwich	0-2
	Willaston White Star v Linotype & Machinery	1-0
	Witton Albion v Moulton Verdin	6-1
8	Brierley Hill Alliance v Moor Green	1-3
	Cradley Heath St Luke's v Boldmere St Michaels	5-3
	Dudley Town v Hednesford Town	3-1
	Hereford United v Shrewsbury Town	1-2
	Kidderminster Harriers v Worcester City	1-0
	Oakengates Town v Tamworth	2-2
	Oswestry Town v Stourbridge	0-5
	Shirley Town v Bromsgrove Rovers	4-1
9	Redbourne Sports v Appleby Frodingham	3-0
10	Armthorpe Welfare v Frickley Colliery	0-4
	Goole Town v Selby Town	1-3
	Monckton Athletic v Dinnington Athletic	0-1
	Norton Woodseats v Denaby United	0-3
	Rawmarsh Welfare v Worksop Town	1-2
	South Kirkby Colliery v Rossington Main	2-1
	Upton Colliery v Farsley Celtic	4-4
	Yorkshire Amateur v Pilkington Recreation	0-0
11	Coalville Town (2) v Ibstock Penistone Rovers	1-4
	Danesmoor Welfare v Leicester Nomads	1-1
	Sandiacre Excelsior Foundry v Ilkeston	wo/s
	South Normanton MW v Heanor Town	1-1
12	Boston United v Bilsthorpe Colliery	10-0
	Ollerton Colliery v Basford United	9-1
	Sutton Town v Raleigh Athletic	1-4
	Teversal & Silverhill CW v Thoresby Colliery	1-0
13	Mount Pleasant v Spalding United	1-3
14	Baldock Town v Arlesey Town	0-3
	Bedford Town (1) v Sandy Albion	6-0
	Biggleswade United (1) v Vauxhall Motors (Luton)	0-4
	Hitchin Town v Luton Amateur	6-1
	Langford v Kempston Rovers	1-3
	Leighton United v Biggleswade & District	0-5
	Letchworth Town v Eynesbury Rovers	6-2
	St Neots & District v Waterlows (Dunstable)	3-3
15	Chatteris Engineers v Newmarket Town	2-2
	March Great Eastern United v Abbey United (Cambs)	3-1
	Pye Radio v Thetford Town	1-8
	Soham Rangers v Histon Institute	1-3
16	Felixstowe Town v Frosts Athletic	1-2
	Great Yarmouth Town v Bungay Town	3-2
	Lowestoft Town v Gorleston	4-2
	Norwich CEYMS v Holt United	1-0
	Norwich YMCA v Bury Town	wo/s
	Sheringham v Norwich St Barnabas	0-3
	Stowmarket v Walton United	7-3
17	Barking v Maldon & Heybridge	6-0
	CWS Silvertown v Grays Athletic	0-4
	Clapton v Dagenham Town	4-2
	Crittall Athletic v Severalls Athletic	3-1
	Hoffmann Ath. (Chelmsford) v Ford Sports (Dag'ham)	3-2
	Leytonstone v Harwich & Parkeston	4-4
	Romford (2) v Eton Manor	4-0e
	Stork (Purfleet) v Chelmsford	0-5
18	Apsley v St Albans City	1-4
	Bishop's Stortford v Old Johnians	4-1
	Golders Green v Northmet	3-1
	Harlow Town v Berkhamsted Town	3-1
	Leavesden v Hoddesdon Town	5-2
	Tufnell Park v London Caledonians	3-1
	Wealdstone v Pinner	4-0
	Wood Green Town v Enfield	1-4
19	Chesham United v Bicester Town	4-0
	Hayes v Civil Service	2-3
	Headington United v Osberton Radiator (Oxford)	1-2
	Morris Motors (Cowley) v Oxford City	4-2
	Slough v Wycombe Wanderers	4-0
	Southall v Maidenhead United	4-1
	Thatcham v Henley Town	1-1
	Windsor & Eton v Uxbridge	5-2
20	Brookwood Hospital v Epsom	0-3
	Carshalton Athletic v Metropolitan Police	0-6
	Egham v Ewell & Stoneleigh	3-2
	Hersham v Banstead Mental Hospital	5-1
	Nunhead v Woking	6-1
	Redhill v Camberley & Yorktown	3-1
	Sutton United v Kingstonian	3-2
	Walton-on-Thames v Tooting & Mitcham United	3-1
21	Ashford v Dover	3-0
	Aylesford Paper Mills v Woolwich Polytechnic	8-0
	Bostall Heath v Callender Athletic	0-2
	Bromley v Darenth Park	4-1
	Canterbury Waverley v Sheppey United	3-0
	London Paper Mills v Chatham	2-1
	Maidstone United v Lloyds (Sittingbourne)	4-2
	Whitstable v Sittingbourne	1-3
22	Brighton Corp. Tramways v Bexhill	0-3
	East Grinstead v Hastings & St Leonards	1-5
	Haywards Heath v Vernon Athletic	4-0
	Horsham v Bognor Regis Town	2-2
	Littlehampton v Eastbourne Comrades	6-1
	Newhaven v Chichester	4-0
	Shoreham v Worthing	1-5
	Southwick v Hove	8-0
23	Courage & Co.'s Sports v Dorchester Town	3-0
	Cowes v HMS Victory	6-0
	Gosport v Newport (IOW)	1-1
	Osborne Athletic v Totton	0-5
	Ryde Sports v HMS Excellent	1-3
	Salisbury Corinthians v Weymouth	0-2
	Thornycrofts (Basingstoke) v Salisbury City (1)	1-8
	Winchester City v Basingstoke	1-3
24	Chippenham Town v Clandown	3-1
	Devizes Town v Swindon Victoria	3-1
	Purton v Warminster Town	0-4
	Radstock Town v Spencer Moulton	3-0
	Swindon Corinthians v Melksham	1-6
	Timsbury Athletic v Welton Rovers	5-1
	Trowbridge Town v Twerton St Michael's	6-0
	Wilts County Mental Hospital v Chippenham Rovers	wo/s
26	Barry v Monmouth Town	8-0
	Cardiff Corinthians v Llanelli	0-5
	Ebbw Vale v Lovells Athletic	0-3
	Gloucester City v Bristol St George	4-1
	Hanham Athletic v Mount Hill Enterprise	1-2
	St Philips Athletic v Clevedon	1-2
	St Philips Marsh Adult School v Keynsham	wo/s
1r	Ouston United v Birtley	2-2
r	Throckley Welfare v Walker Celtic	2-3
2r	Bishop Auckland v Dawdon Colliery Recreation	3-2
3r	Whitby United v Scarborough Juniors	4-3
5r	Leyland Motors v Skelmersdale United	7-3
r	Lytham v Great Harwood	2-0
8r	Tamworth v Oakengates Town	1-3
10r	Farsley Celtic v Upton Colliery	1-2
r	Pilkington Recreation v Yorkshire Amateur	1-2
11r	Heanor Town v South Normanton MW	2-3
r	Leicester Nomads v Danesmoor Welfare	3-1
14r	Waterlows (Dunstable) v St Neots & District	2-4
15r	Newmarket Town v Chatteris Engineers	5-0
17r	Harwich & Parkeston v Leytonstone	0-1
19r	Henley Town v Thatcham	8-1
22r	Bognor Regis Town v Horsham	2-3
23r	Newport (IOW) v Gosport	2-2
1r2	Birtley v Ouston United	1-0
23r2	Newport (IOW) v Gosport	2-0 N

Qualifying Round One

1	Ashington v Annfield Plain	0-1
	Birtley v Whitley & Monkseaton	1-0
	Hexham v Jarrow	1-1
	Walker Celtic v New Gateshead United	3-2
2	Bishop Auckland v Chilton Colliery Recreation	3-2
	Brandon Social v Seaham Colliery Welfare	5-2
	Durham City v Horden CW	1-1
	Ferryhill Athletic v Spennymoor United	2-2
3	Portrack Shamrocks v Bridlington Town (1)	3-1
	Scarborough v Stockton	1-0
	South Bank St Peters v Smith's Dock	2-1
	Whitby United v South Bank East End	3-1
4	Kells United v Milnthorpe Corinthians	1-1
	Netherfield (Kendal) v Holme Head Works	4-0
	Penrith v Cockermouth	0-0
	Whitehaven Wellington Villa v Cleator Moor Celtic	1-3
5	Chorley v Rossendale United	4-2
	Leyland Motors v Crossens	3-2
	Morecambe v Horwich RMI	2-2
	Wigan Athletic v Lytham	7-1
6	Manchester North End v Marine	2-2
	Prescot Cables v South Liverpool	2-2
	Thorndale v Hoylake	2-3 N
	Urmston v Glossop	4-3
7	Nantwich v Llandudno	8-0
	Sandbach Ramblers v Timperley	2-0
	Willaston White Star v Runcorn	2-7
	Witton Albion v Middlewich Athletic	6-1
8	Dudley Town v Stourbridge	0-3
	Moor Green v Kidderminster Harriers	1-1
	Oakengates Town v Cradley Heath St Luke's	1-0
	Shrewsbury Town v Shirley Town	5-2
9	Barton Town (1) v Louth Town	wo/s
	Brigg Town v Marfleet	5-0
	Old Hullensians v Ranks (Hull)	1-5
	Redbourne Sports v Lysaght's Sports (Scunthorpe)	3-0
10	Denaby United v South Kirkby Colliery	1-1
	Upton Colliery v Frickley Colliery	0-3
	Worksop Town v Selby Town	3-0
	Yorkshire Amateur v Dinnington Athletic	2-0
11	Ibstock Penistone Rovers v Ripley Town	wo/s
	Leicester Nomads v Bolsover Colliery	2-3
	Sandiacre Excelsior Foundry v North Derby Ramblers	2-5
	Staveley Welfare v South Normanton MW	4-0
12	Boots Athletic v Ransome & Marles	1-0
	Grantham v Teversal & Silverhill CW	5-1
	Newark Town v Raleigh Athletic	4-1
	Ollerton Colliery v Boston United	0-2
13	Kettering Town v Stamford	3-1
	Peterbro' Westwood Works v Rushden Town	0-5
	Spalding United v Desborough Town	2-0
	Wellingborough Town v Peterborough United	0-5
14	Bedford Town (1) v St Neots & District	3-2
	Biggleswade & District v Hitchin Town	2-2
	Kempston Rovers v Arlesey Town	3-1
	Vauxhall Motors (Luton) v Letchworth Town	4-2
15	Chatteris Town v March Great Eastern United	4-3
	King's Lynn v Cambridge Town	3-1
	Newmarket Town v Histon Institute	3-1
	Thetford Town v Wisbech Town	2-7
16	Frosts Athletic v Norwich YMCA	1-1
	Lowestoft Town v Cromer	4-1
	Norwich St Barnabas v Great Yarmouth Town	2-5
	Stowmarket v Norwich CEYMS	2-4
17	Barking v Leytonstone	1-6
	Chelmsford v Clapton	1-3
	Grays Athletic v Crittall Athletic	4-2
	Romford (2) v Hoffmann Athletic (Chelmsford)	2-3
18	Bishop's Stortford v Wealdstone	2-3
	Golders Green v Enfield	1-2
	Leavesden v Tufnell Park	1-4
	St Albans City v Harlow Town	6-1
19	Civil Service v Morris Motors (Cowley)	2-1
	Slough v Henley Town	10-1
	Southall v Chesham United	2-2
	Windsor & Eton v Osberton Radiator (Oxford)	10-2
20	Egham v Hersham	0-9
	Epsom v Walton-on-Thames	3-1
	Nunhead v Sutton United	0-2
	Redhill v Metropolitan Police	0-0
21	Aylesford Paper Mills v Bromley	0-3
	Callender Athletic v London Paper Mills	1-3
	Canterbury Waverley v Ashford	0-3
	Sittingbourne v Maidstone United	2-2
22	Bexhill v Littlehampton	1-0
	Hastings & St Leonards v Haywards Heath	3-2
	Horsham v Newhaven	5-1
	Worthing v Southwick	1-0
23	Basingstoke v Courage & Co.'s Sports	2-6
	Cowes v HMS Excellent	4-0
	Salisbury City (1) v Weymouth	1-3
	Totton v Newport (IOW)	0-0
24	Melksham v Chippenham Town	2-1
	Timsbury Athletic v Radstock Town	1-7
	Trowbridge Town v Devizes Town	3-0
	Warminster Town v Wilts County Mental Hospital	0-1
25	Exmouth Town v Street	3-4
	Frome Town v Glastonbury	2-0
	Wells City v Minehead	6-1
	Westbury United v Tiverton Town	8-0
26	Gloucester City v St Philips Marsh Adult School	5-2
	Llanelli v Mount Hill Enterprise	6-2
	Lovells Athletic v Barry	2-0
	Weston-Super-Mare v Clevedon	0-3
1r	Jarrow v Hexham	5-4
2r	Horden CW v Durham City	7-2
r	Spennymoor United v Ferryhill Athletic	3-0
4r	Cockermouth v Penrith	3-0
r	Milnthorpe Corinthians v Kells United	1-0
5r	Horwich RMI v Morecambe	5-1
6r	Marine v Manchester North End	0-3
r	South Liverpool v Prescot Cables	3-1
8r	Kidderminster Harriers v Moor Green	7-2
10r	South Kirkby Colliery v Denaby United	1-2
14r	Hitchin Town v Biggleswade & District	1-1
16r	Norwich YMCA v Frosts Athletic	0-3
19r	Chesham United v Southall	2-1
20r	Metropolitan Police v Redhill	3-0
21r	Maidstone United v Sittingbourne	0-1
23r	Newport (IOW) v Totton	9-2
14r2	Hitchin Town v Biggleswade & District	2-1 N

1937/38

Qualifying Round Two

1	Annfield Plain v Jarrow	4-1
	Walker Celtic v Birtley	2-1
2	Brandon Social v Bishop Auckland	3-3
	Horden CW v Spennymoor United	3-2
3	Portrack Shamrocks v Whitby United	2-2
	Scarborough v South Bank St Peters	2-1
4	Cleator Moor Celtic v Cockermouth	5-1
	Netherfield (Kendal) v Milnthorpe Corinthians	1-0
5	Chorley v Wigan Athletic	0-1
	Leyland Motors v Horwich RMI	1-0
6	Hoylake v Urmston	5-2
	South Liverpool v Manchester North End	2-2
7	Nantwich v Sandbach Ramblers	5-2
	Witton Albion v Runcorn	2-1
8	Kidderminster Harriers v Oakengates Town	2-0
	Shrewsbury Town v Stourbridge	0-0
9	Ranks (Hull) v Barton Town (1)	3-3
	Redbourne Sports v Brigg Town	2-1
10	Worksop Town v Frickley Colliery	2-0
	Yorkshire Amateur v Denaby United	1-1
11	North Derby Ramblers v Ibstock Penistone Rovers	2-3
	Staveley Welfare v Bolsover Colliery	1-5
12	Grantham v Boots Athletic	8-3
	Newark Town v Boston United	1-2
13	Kettering Town v Peterborough United	2-2
	Rushden Town v Spalding United	1-1
14	Hitchin Town v Bedford Town (1)	3-1
	Vauxhall Motors (Luton) v Kempston Rovers	2-2
15	Chatteris Town v Wisbech Town	1-6
	King's Lynn v Newmarket Town	6-2
16	Frosts Athletic v Norwich CEYMS	4-2
	Great Yarmouth Town v Lowestoft Town	2-3
17	Hoffmann Athletic (Chelmsford) v Clapton	2-1
	Leytonstone v Grays Athletic	3-0
18	St Albans City v Tufnell Park	2-1
	Wealdstone v Enfield	2-3
19	Civil Service v Chesham United	0-2
	Windsor & Eton v Slough	1-1
20	Epsom v Sutton United	2-4
	Hersham v Metropolitan Police	2-1
21	Ashford v Sittingbourne	1-2
	Bromley v London Paper Mills	4-2
22	Horsham v Bexhill	1-0
	Worthing v Hastings & St Leonards	1-2
23	Courage & Co.'s Sports v Weymouth	2-1
	Newport (IOW) v Cowes	1-1
24	Trowbridge Town v Radstock Town	1-2
	Wilts County Mental Hospital v Melksham	3-1
25	Street v Wells City	4-5
	Westbury United v Frome Town	2-0
26	Clevedon v Llanelli	1-2
	Gloucester City v Lovells Athletic	0-1
2r	Bishop Auckland v Brandon Social	0-3
3r	Whitby United v Portrack Shamrocks	3-2
6r	Manchester North End v South Liverpool	0-1
8r	Stourbridge v Shrewsbury Town	3-2
9r	Barton Town (1) v Ranks (Hull)	2-1
10r	Denaby United v Yorkshire Amateur	0-1
13r	Peterborough United v Kettering Town	0-1
r	Spalding United v Rushden Town	2-2
14r	Kempston Rovers v Vauxhall Motors (Luton)	1-3
19r	Slough v Windsor & Eton	2-6
23r	Cowes v Newport (IOW)	1-0
13r2	Rushden Town v Spalding United	4-0

Qualifying Round Three

1	Walker Celtic v Annfield Plain	2-1
2	Horden CW v Brandon Social	0-0
3	Scarborough v Whitby United	2-0
4	Netherfield (Kendal) v Cleator Moor Celtic	5-1
5	Wigan Athletic v Leyland Motors	3-0
6	South Liverpool v Hoylake	5-0
7	Nantwich v Witton Albion	1-3
8	Kidderminster Harriers v Stourbridge	3-2
9	Redbourne Sports v Barton Town (1)	8-0
10	Yorkshire Amateur v Worksop Town	0-1
11	Bolsover Colliery v Ibstock Penistone Rovers	5-1
12	Grantham v Boston United	0-0
13	Kettering Town v Rushden Town	3-1
14	Vauxhall Motors (Luton) v Hitchin Town	3-1
15	Wisbech Town v King's Lynn	0-1
16	Frosts Athletic v Lowestoft Town	1-1
17	Hoffmann Athletic (Chelmsford) v Leytonstone	2-1
18	Enfield v St Albans City	3-1
19	Windsor & Eton v Chesham United	1-3
20	Sutton United v Hersham	1-2
21	Bromley v Sittingbourne	2-0
22	Horsham v Hastings & St Leonards	3-3
23	Cowes v Courage & Co.'s Sports	8-1
24	Radstock Town v Wilts County Mental Hospital	5-1
25	Westbury United v Wells City	3-2
26	Lovells Athletic v Llanelli	0-1
2r	Brandon Social v Horden CW	0-1
12r	Boston United v Grantham	2-3e
16r	Lowestoft Town v Frosts Athletic	8-1
22r	Hastings & St Leonards v Horsham	1-6

Qualifying Round Four

Bromley v Wimbledon	3-0
Burton Town v Bolsover Colliery	10-1
Cheltenham Town v Bath City	4-1
Chesham United v Tunbridge Wells Rangers	3-3
Dartford v Leyton	3-0
Enfield v Horsham	3-3
Gainsborough Trinity v Redbourne Sports	3-0
Guildford City v Cowes	3-0
Hersham v Folkestone	2-2
Hoffmann Athletic (Chelmsford) v Ipswich Town	0-3
Horden CW v Blyth Spartans	0-0
Ilford v Corinthians	1-2
Kettering Town v Vauxhall Motors (Luton)	7-3
Kidderminster Harriers v Witton Albion	4-1
King's Lynn v Lowestoft Town	2-1
Netherfield (Kendal) v Workington	2-2
North Shields v Scarborough	0-1
Northwich Victoria v Wigan Athletic	0-1
Radstock Town v Yeovil & Petter's United	0-3
Scunthorpe United v Grantham	4-2
Shildon v Walker Celtic	0-0
South Liverpool v Darwen	0-0
Stalybridge Celtic v Lancaster Town	1-2
Westbury United v Llanelli	3-2
Worksop Town v Wellington Town	0-2
r Blyth Spartans v Horden CW	1-0e
r Darwen v South Liverpool	2-6
r Folkestone v Hersham	5-1
r Horsham v Enfield	0-1
r Tunbridge Wells Rangers v Chesham United	4-0
r Walker Celtic v Shildon	3-2
r Workington v Netherfield (Kendal)	7-3

Round One

Accrington Stanley v Lancaster Town	1-1
Barrow v Crewe Alexandra	0-1
Bournemouth v Dartford	0-0
Brighton & Hove Albion v Tunbridge Wells Rangers	5-1
Bristol City v Enfield	3-0
Bristol Rovers v Queen's Park Rangers	1-8
Burton Town v Rotherham United	1-1
Corinthians v Southend United	0-2
Crystal Palace v Kettering Town	2-2
Darlington v Scarborough	0-2
Doncaster Rovers v Blyth Spartans	7-0
Dulwich Hamlet v Aldershot	1-2
Exeter City v Folkestone	1-0
Gillingham v Swindon Town	3-4
Guildford City v Reading	1-0
Hartlepools United v Southport	3-1
Hull City v Scunthorpe United	4-0
Kidderminster Harriers v Newport County	2-2
King's Lynn v Bromley	0-4
New Brighton v Workington	5-0
Northampton Town v Cardiff City	1-2
Port Vale v Gainsborough Trinity	1-1
Rochdale v Lincoln City	1-1
Torquay United v Clapton Orient	1-2
Tranmere Rovers v Carlisle United	2-1
Walker Celtic v Bradford City	1-1
Walsall v Gateshead	4-0
Watford v Cheltenham Town	3-0
Wellington Town v Mansfield Town	1-2
Westbury United v Walthamstow Avenue	1-3
Wigan Athletic v South Liverpool	1-4
Wrexham v Oldham Athletic	2-1
Yeovil & Petter's United v Ipswich Town	2-1
York City v Halifax Town	1-1
r Bradford City v Walker Celtic	11-3
r Dartford v Bournemouth	0-6
r Gainsborough Trinity v Port Vale	2-1e
r Halifax Town v York City	0-1
r Kettering Town v Crystal Palace	0-4
r Lancaster Town v Accrington Stanley	1-1e
r Lincoln City v Rochdale	2-0
r Newport County v Kidderminster Harriers	4-1
r Rotherham United v Burton Town	3-0
r2 Accrington Stanley v Lancaster Town	4-0 N

Round Two

Accrington Stanley v Crystal Palace	0-1
Cardiff City v Bristol City	1-1
Clapton Orient v York City	2-2
Crewe Alexandra v New Brighton	2-2
Doncaster Rovers v Guildford City	4-0
Exeter City v Hull City	1-2
Mansfield Town v Lincoln City	2-1
Newport County v Bournemouth	2-1
Rotherham United v Aldershot	1-3
Scarborough v Bromley	4-1
South Liverpool v Brighton & Hove Albion	1-1
Swindon Town v Queen's Park Rangers	2-1
Tranmere Rovers v Hartlepools United	3-1
Walthamstow Avenue v Southend United	0-1
Watford v Walsall	3-0
Wrexham v Bradford City	1-2
Yeovil & Petter's United v Gainsborough Trinity	2-1
r Brighton & Hove Albion v South Liverpool	6-0
r Bristol City v Cardiff City	0-2
r New Brighton v Crewe Alexandra	4-1
r York City v Clapton Orient	1-0

Round Three

Aldershot v Notts County	1-3
Arsenal v Bolton Wanderers	3-1
Birmingham v Blackpool	0-1
Bradford City v Chesterfield	1-1
Bradford Park Avenue v Newport County	7-4
Brentford v Fulham	3-1
Bury v Brighton & Hove Albion	2-0
Charlton Athletic v Cardiff City	5-0
Chelsea v Everton	0-1
Crystal Palace v Liverpool	0-0
Derby County v Stoke City	1-2
Doncaster Rovers v Sheffield United	0-2
Grimsby Town v Swindon Town	1-1
Huddersfield Town v Hull City	3-1
Leeds United v Chester	3-1
Manchester United v Yeovil & Petter's United	3-0
Mansfield Town v Leicester City	1-2
Middlesbrough v Stockport County	2-0
Millwall v Manchester City	2-2
New Brighton v Plymouth Argyle	1-0
Norwich City v Aston Villa	2-3
Nottingham Forest v Southampton	3-1
Preston North End v West Ham United	3-0
Scarborough v Luton Town	1-1
Sheffield Wednesday v Burnley	1-1
Southend United v Barnsley	2-2
Sunderland v Watford	1-0
Swansea Town v Wolverhampton Wan.	0-4
Tottenham Hotspur v Blackburn Rovers	3-2
Tranmere Rovers v Portsmouth	1-2
West Bromwich Albion v Newcastle United	1-0
York City v Coventry City	3-2
r Barnsley v Southend United	2-1
r Burnley v Sheffield Wednesday	3-1
r Chesterfield v Bradford City	1-1e
r Liverpool v Crystal Palace	3-1e
r Luton Town v Scarborough	5-1
r Manchester City v Millwall	3-1
r Swindon Town v Grimsby Town	2-1e
r2 Bradford City v Chesterfield	0-2 N

Round Four

Aston Villa v Blackpool	4-0
Barnsley v Manchester United	2-2
Bradford Park Avenue v Stoke City	1-1
Brentford v Portsmouth	2-1
Charlton Athletic v Leeds United	2-1
Chesterfield v Burnley	3-2
Everton v Sunderland	0-1
Huddersfield Town v Notts County	1-0
Luton Town v Swindon Town	2-1
Manchester City v Bury	3-1
New Brighton v Tottenham Hotspur	0-0
Nottingham Forest v Middlesbrough	1-3
Preston North End v Leicester City	2-0
Sheffield United v Liverpool	1-1
Wolverhampton Wan. v Arsenal	1-2
York City v West Bromwich Albion	3-2
r Liverpool v Sheffield United	1-0
r Manchester United v Barnsley	1-0
r Stoke City v Bradford Park Avenue	1-2
r Tottenham Hotspur v New Brighton	5-2

Round Five

Arsenal v Preston North End	0-1
Brentford v Manchester United	2-0
Charlton Athletic v Aston Villa	1-1
Chesterfield v Tottenham Hotspur	2-2
Liverpool v Huddersfield Town	0-1
Luton Town v Manchester City	1-3
Sunderland v Bradford Park Avenue	1-0
York City v Middlesbrough	1-0
r Aston Villa v Charlton Athletic	2-2e
r Tottenham Hotspur v Chesterfield	2-1
r2 Aston Villa v Charlton Athletic	4-1 N

Round Six

Aston Villa v Manchester City	3-2
Brentford v Preston North End	0-3
Tottenham Hotspur v Sunderland	0-1
York City v Huddersfield Town	0-0
r Huddersfield Town v York City	2-1

Semi Finals

Huddersfield Town v Sunderland	3-1 N
Preston North End v Aston Villa	2-1 N

Final

Preston North End v Huddersfield Town	1-0eN

1938/39

1938/39

Extra Preliminary Round

1	Chopwell Colliery v Ouston United	2-4
	Close Works v Newburn	0-1
	Consett v Shankhouse	5-2
	Crawcrook Albion v Amble	2-1
	Crookhall CW v Ashington	2-1
	Gosforth & Coxlodge v Crookhall Rovers	1-3
	Hexham v South Shields (2)	0-1
	Newbiggin CW v Scotswood	2-1
2	Barnard Castle Athletic v West Auckland Town	0-4
	Blackhall Colliery Welfare v Middleton Wanderers	16-1
	Crook Town v Washington Chemical Works	2-0
	Evenwood Town v Seaham Colliery Welfare	3-2
	Lanchester Rangers v Chilton Colliery Recreation	2-1
	Langley Park Villa v Shotton CW	4-1
	Stanley United v Usworth Colliery	4-1
	Willington v Dawdon Colliery Recreation	1-1
7	Barnton Victoria v Moulton Verdin	0-2
	Macclesfield Town v Timperley	7-1
	Sandbach Ramblers v Nantwich	1-2
	Whitchurch v Wardle & Barbridge Utd.	1-0
	Winsford United v Rhyl	2-2
8	Brierley Hill Alliance v Sutton Town (Birmingham)	5-1
	Headingley v Thynnes Athletic	1-4
	Moor Green v Bournville Athletic	2-3
	Oakengates Town v Badsey Rangers	1-2
	Oswestry Town v Hereford United	3-1
	Solihull v Evesham Town	3-2
	Stafford Rangers v Bilston Borough	4-0
	Walsall Jolly Club v Wrockwardine Wood	wo/s
	Wolverhampton Amateur v Birmingham Transport	2-2
10	Bentley Colliery v South Kirkby Colliery	2-1
	Brodsworth Main Colliery v Dinnington Athletic	4-3
	Denaby United v Upton Colliery	4-0
	East Bierley v Ravensthorpe	2-3
	Goole Town v Bradford Rovers	4-1
	Guiseley v Meltham Mills	6-1
	Lopham Methodists v Armthorpe Welfare	3-1
	Monckton Athletic v Thurnscoe Victoria	0-1
	Ossett Town v Farsley Celtic	3-3
	Pilkington Recreation v Thorne Colliery	2-3
	Rawmarsh Welfare v Rossington Main	3-0
	Selby Town v Golcar (Huddersfield)	wo/s
	Sheffield v Norton Woodseats	3-4
	Yorkshire Amateur v Luddendenfoot	3-1
17	Briggs Motor Bodies v Barking	0-1
	Crittall Athletic v Brantham Athletic	4-0
	Ford Sports (Dagenham) v Severalls Athletic	3-3
	Maldon & Heybridge v Port of London Authority	3-1
	Tilbury v Clacton Town	4-0
18	Barnet v Welwyn Garden City	7-0
	Berkhamsted Town v Old Johnians	7-1
	Bishop's Stortford v Watford British Legion	9-0
	Finchley v Northmet	4-2
	Golders Green v Pinner	4-1
	Hertford Town v Hoxton Manor	1-3
	Saffron Walden Town v Hoddesdon Town	0-3
	Tufnell Park v Old Lyonian	7-0
	Ware v Stevenage Town	1-3
	Wood Green Town v London Caledonians	0-0
19	Henley Town v Pressed Steel	3-2
	Maidenhead United v Hounslow Town	5-4
	Newbury Town v Abingdon Town	5-1
	Osberton Radiator (Oxford) v Headington United	2-5
	Oxford City v Banbury Spencer	1-1
	Southall v Redford Sports (Wycombe)	2-2
	Thame United v Aylesbury United	1-6
	Thatcham v Morris Motors (Cowley)	0-3
	Wycombe Wanderers v Hayes	2-5
	Yiewsley v Marlow	3-2
20	Camberley & Yorktown v PO Engineers (Beddington)	0-2
	Cobham v Carshalton Athletic	2-3
	Egham v Godalming	0-3
	Guildford v Leyland Motors (Kingston)	0-6
	Nunhead v Woking	2-1
	RAMC Aldershot v Banstead Mental Hospital	4-0
	Tooting & Mitcham United v Cranleigh	5-0
	Walton-on-Thames v Wandsworth United	10-2
21	Bexley v Woolwich Polytechnic	2-5
	Darenth Park v Aylesford Paper Mills	5-1
	Maidstone United v Margate	wo/s
	RM Deal v Lloyds (Sittingbourne)	2-5
	Ramsgate Grenville v Whitstable	2-2
	Sheppey United v Dover	4-0
	UGB Sports (Charlton) v Beckenham	wo/s
23	Basingstoke v Winchester City	4-1
	Bournemouth (Ams) v Bridport	5-0
	Fareham v East Cowes	8-1
	HMS Victory v Totton	0-2
	Osborne Athletic v Gosport	0-2
	Portsmouth Electricity v Sandown	0-0
2r	Dawdon Colliery Recreation v Willington	2-4
7r	Rhyl v Winsford United	2-1
8r	Birmingham Transport v Wolverhampton Amateur	3-0
10r	Farsley Celtic v Ossett Town	1-5
17r	Severalls Athletic v Ford Sports (Dagenham)	1-3
18r	London Caledonians v Wood Green Town	3-2
19r	Banbury Spencer v Oxford City	2-1
r	Redford Sports (Wycombe) v Southall	0-1
21r	Whitstable v Ramsgate Grenville	4-2
23r	Sandown v Portsmouth Electricity	0-2

Preliminary Round

1	Annfield Plain v Crawcrook Albion	3-3
	Consett v Crookhall Rovers	4-0
	Crookhall CW v Newcastle West End (2)	3-0
	Jarrow v Newburn	3-2
	Newbiggin CW v Ouston United	3-3
	North Shields v Whitley & Monkseaton	9-0
	Throckley Welfare v South Shields (2)	1-2
	Walker Celtic v Blyth Spartans	2-1
2	Birtley v Spennymoor United	2-7
	Bishop Auckland v Horden CW	0-1
	Cockfield v Lanchester Rangers	7-1
	Evenwood Town v Stanley United	1-1
	Shildon v Blackhall Colliery Welfare	6-1
	Tow Law Town v Brandon Social	0-6
	West Auckland Town v Crook Town	3-1
	Willington v Langley Park Villa	1-2
3	Billingham Synthonia v Stockton	2-1
	Furness Athletic v Bridlington Town (1)	2-3
	Grangetown St Mary's v South Bank	2-1
	South Bank East End v Scarborough Juniors	0-3
	South Bank St Peters v Billingham South	0-4
	Whitby Albion Rangers v Normanby Mangnesite	1-2
	Whitby United v Filey Town	7-0
5	Lytham v Great Harwood	1-2
	Morecambe v Crossens	4-2
	Skelmersdale United v Rossendale United	3-0
6	Earle v Harrowby	6-3
	Earlestown Bohemians v Stanlow Social	2-0
	Earlestown White Star v Formby	3-3
	Garston Woodcutters v Oakmere (Liverpool)	8-2
	Orrell v Marine	1-6
	Sandhurst (Liverpool) v Prescot Cables	4-3
	Stoneycroft v Thorndale	6-2
	Tushingham Brick Works v Prescot B.I.C.C	3-2
7	Buxton v Haslington Villa	3-1
	Fodens Motor Works v Nantwich	5-3
	Llandudno v Runcorn	2-4
	Macclesfield Town v Moulton Verdin	2-0
	Rhyl v Glossop	3-2
	Whitchurch v Bangor City	1-1
	Willaston White Star v Linotype & Machinery	5-5
	Witton Albion v Middlewich Athletic	6-0
8	Badsey Rangers - Bye	
	Bournville Athletic v Walsall Jolly Club	1-1
	Brierley Hill Alliance v Kidderminster Harriers	0-0
	Cradley Heath St Luke's v Tamworth	2-2e
	Oswestry Town v Boldmere St Michaels	4-3
	Solihull v Worcester City	0-3
	Stafford Rangers v Stourbridge	2-1
	Thynnes Athletic v Birmingham Transport	1-5
10	Bentley Colliery v Rawmarsh Welfare	1-4
	Frickley Colliery v Brodsworth Main Colliery	3-3
	Goole Town v Ossett Town	3-0
	Norton Woodseats v Lopham Methodists	2-1
	Selby Town v Guiseley	3-0
	Thorne Colliery v Worksop Town	3-1
	Thurnscoe Victoria v Denaby United	0-1
	Yorkshire Amateur v Ravensthorpe	3-2
11	Bilsthorpe Colliery v Raleigh Athletic	1-1
	Ollerton Colliery v Basford United	4-0
	Ransome & Marles v Teversal & Silverhill CW	4-1
13	Stamford v Holbeach United	1-1
	Wellingborough Town v Stewarts & Lloyds	1-0
14	Arlesey Town v St Neots & District	2-3
	Baldock Town v Wolverton Town	0-5
	Bedford Town (1) v Eynesbury Rovers	4-2
	Hitchin Town v Luton Amateur	0-0
	Kempston Rovers v Stewartby Works	3-2
	Leighton United v Letchworth Town	2-5
	Sandy Albion v Waterlows (Dunstable)	0-6
	Vauxhall Motors (Luton) v Biggleswade & District	1-3
15	Abbey United (Cambs) v Histon Institute	2-1
16	Bungay Town v Walton United	4-0
	Eastern Coachworks v Holt United	0-1
	Felixstowe Town v Cromer	1-1
	Norwich St Barnabas v RAF Martlesham	0-1
	Sheringham v Orwell Works	2-4
17	Barking v Chelmsford City	1-2
	Brightlingsea United v Leyton	0-4
	Crittall Athletic v Grays Athletic	6-2
	Eton Manor v Clapton	5-0
	Ford Sports (Dagenham) v Maldon & Heybridge	0-0
	Harwich & Parkeston v Tilbury	1-3
	Hoffmann Athletic (Chelmsford) v Dagenham Town	5-1
	Romford (2) v Stork (Purfleet)	12-1
18	Apsley v St Albans City	2-1
	Finchley v Enfield	1-4
	Hoddesdon Town v Berkhamsted Town	3-1
	Hoxton Manor v Bishop's Stortford	3-1
	Leavesden v Barnet	1-2
	Stevenage Town v Harlow Town	6-1
	Tufnell Park v Golders Green	0-1
	Wealdstone v London Caledonians	6-0
19	Aylesbury United v Bicester Town	5-0
	Henley Town v Headington United	2-5
	Maidenhead United v Windsor & Eton	1-1
	Morris Motors (Cowley) v Banbury Spencer	0-2
	Newbury Town v Chesham United	1-1
	Slough v Uxbridge	3-0
	Southall v Civil Service	2-0e
	Yiewsley v Hayes	1-1
20	Carshalton Athletic v Redhill	1-4
	Epsom v West Norwood	2-0
	Godalming v PO Engineers (Beddington)	2-1
	Hersham v Nunhead	1-2
	Kingstonian v RAMC Aldershot	6-0
	Metropolitan Police v Wimbledon	5-1
	Tooting & Mitcham Utd v Leyland Motors (Kingston)	2-2
	Walton-on-Thames v Sutton United	0-3
21	Ashford v Betteshanger CW	wo/s
	Canterbury Waverley v Lloyds (Sittingbourne)	3-1
	Cray Wanderers v Chatham	2-1
	Darenth Park v Callender Athletic	2-3
	London Paper Mills v Bostall Heath	5-0
	Sittingbourne v Sheppey United	1-3
	Whitstable v Maidstone United	1-3
	Woolwich Polytechnic v UGB Sports (Charlton)	0-4
22	Bexhill v Littlehampton	0-1
	Bognor Regis Town v East Grinstead	4-1
	Chichester v Southwick	2-5
	Hastings & St Leonards v Hove	4-1
	Haywards Heath v Newhaven	4-0
	Horsham v Eastbourne Comrades	3-2
	Shoreham v Worthing	1-8
	Vernon Athletic v Brighton Corp. Tramways	0-4
23	Basingstoke v Salisbury City (1)	0-1
	Cowes v Ryde Sports	1-1
	Fareham v Totton	1-1
	HMS Excellent v Newport (IOW)	2-3
	Poole Town v Bournemouth (Ams)	1-0
	Portsmouth Electricity v Gosport	4-3
	Salisbury Corinthians v Thornycrofts (Basingstoke)	2-0
	Weymouth v Dorchester Town	3-1
24	Clandown v Swindon Corinthians	5-2
	Devizes Town v Spencer Moulton	3-0
	Frome Town v Westbury United	2-1
	Paulton Rovers v Swindon Victoria	3-1
	Trowbridge Town v Purton	3-1
	Twerton St Michael's v Melksham	2-5
	Warminster Town v Chippenham Town	9-2
	Wilts County Mental Hospital v Wootton Bassett Town	6-0
25	Aberdare (2) v Cardiff Corinthians	4-3
	Barry v Monmouth Town	4-1
	Hanham Athletic v Weston-Super-Mare	3-0
	Llanelli v Ebbw Vale	3-0
	St Philips Marsh Adult Sch. v Mount Hill Enterprise	3-2
26	Newton Corinthians v Peasedown MW	3-2
1r	Crawcrook Albion v Annfield Plain	3-2e
r	Ouston United v Newbiggin CW	5-1
2r	Stanley United v Evenwood Town	3-1
6r	Formby v Earlestown White Star	4-2
7r	Bangor City v Whitchurch	6-1
r	Linotype & Machinery v Willaston White Star	4-0
8r	Kidderminster Harriers v Brierley Hill Alliance	6-0
r	Tamworth v Cradley Heath St Luke's	3-0
r	Walsall Jolly Club v Bournville Athletic	3-0
10r	Brodsworth Main Colliery v Frickley Colliery	0-5
11r	Raleigh Athletic v Bilsthorpe Colliery	3-1e
13r	Stamford v Holbeach United	wo/s
14r	Luton Amateur v Hitchin Town	1-6
16r	Cromer v Felixstowe Town	3-0
17r	Maldon & Heybridge v Ford Sports (Dagenham)	0-7
19r	Chesham United v Newbury Town	7-1
r	Hayes v Yiewsley	8-0
r	Windsor & Eton v Maidenhead United	7-1
20r	Tooting & Mitcham Utd v Leyland Motors (Kingston)	6-1
23r	Ryde Sports v Cowes	5-1
r	Totton v Fareham	2-3

Qualifying Round One

1	Crawcrook Albion v Consett	1-3
	Jarrow v Walker Celtic	1-2
	North Shields v Crookhall CW	5-1
	South Shields (2) v Ouston United	9-2
2	Horden CW v West Auckland Town	3-0
	Langley Park Villa v Brandon Social	5-0
	Shildon v Cockfield	6-2
	Stanley United v Spennymoor United	2-3
3	Billingham Synthonia v Normanby Mangnesite	3-2
	Portrack Shamrocks v Billingham South	0-1
	Scarborough Juniors v Bridlington Town (1)	1-2
	Whitby United v Grangetown St Mary's	2-1
4	Cleator Moor Celtic - Bye	
	Cockermouth v Milnthorpe Corinthians	4-2
	Kells United v Whitehaven Wellington Villa	3-2
	Netherfield (Kendal) v Penrith	2-0
5	Chorley v Great Harwood	6-2
	Horwich RMI v Skelmersdale United	4-5
	Leyland Motors v Morecambe	2-0
	Wigan Athletic v Breightmet United	3-0
6	Earlestown Bohemians v Formby	4-0
	Garston Woodcutters v Tushingham Brick Works	1-1
	Marine v Sandhurst (Liverpool)	14-0
	Stoneycroft v Earle	3-3
7	Bangor City v Macclesfield Town	3-1
	Buxton v Witton Albion	2-4
	Rhyl v Fodens Motor Works	3-0
	Runcorn v Linotype & Machinery	9-3
8	Badsey Rangers v Kidderminster Harriers	1-8
	Stafford Rangers v Oswestry Town	1-1
	Walsall Jolly Club v Tamworth	1-5
	Worcester City v Birmingham Transport	1-1
9	Lysaght's Sports (Scunthorpe) v Brigg Town	4-2
	Marfleet v Old Hullensians	6-2

1938/39

	Ranks (Hull) v Appleby Frodingham	1-4
	Scunthorpe United v Barton Town (1)	9-1
10	Frickley Colliery v Goole Town	7-0
	Norton Woodseats v Selby Town	4-3
	Thorne Colliery v Denaby United	4-1
	Yorkshire Amateur v Rawmarsh Welfare	2-1
11	Boston United v Sutton Town	6-1
	Grantham v Ollerton Colliery	1-2
	Raleigh Athletic v Newark Town	1-5
	Ransome & Marles v Boots Athletic	6-0
12	Bolsover Colliery v Gresley Rovers	9-3
	Burton Town v Sandiacre Excelsior Foundry	16-2
	Heanor Town v Hinckley United (1)	0-8
	Ibstock Penistone Rovers v Coalville Town (2)	3-1
13	Desborough Town v Stamford	2-2
	Peterborough United v Kettering Town	2-1
	Spalding United v Peterbro' Westwood Works	4-2
	Wellingborough Town v Rushden Town	2-3
14	Hitchin Town v Letchworth Town	3-4
	Kempston Rovers v Biggleswade & District	5-7
	St Neots & District v Wolverton Town	4-2
	Waterlows (Dunstable) v Bedford Town (1)	0-0
15	Cambridge Town v Abbey United (Cambs)	3-0
	King's Lynn v Thetford Town	7-0
	March Great Eastern United v Chatteris Engineers	2-3
	Wisbech Town v Chatteris Town	12-1
16	Bungay Town v Holt United	0-6
	Cromer v Orwell Works	7-1
	Gorleston v Lowestoft Town	0-1
	RAF Martlesham v Great Yarmouth Town	3-5
17	Crittall Athletic v Eton Manor	2-1
	Ford Sports (Dagenham) v Chelmsford City	2-6
	Leyton v Hoffmann Athletic (Chelmsford)	5-1
	Tilbury v Romford (2)	1-5
18	Enfield v Barnet	0-2
	Golders Green v Wealdstone	0-0
	Hoxton Manor v Apsley	0-4
	Stevenage Town v Hoddesdon Town	3-4
19	Aylesbury United v Southall	1-1
	Chesham United v Hayes	1-3
	Headington United v Windsor & Eton	2-3
	Slough v Banbury Spencer	0-2
20	Epsom v Redhill	1-4
	Godalming v Sutton United	2-5
	Metropolitan Police v Kingstonian	2-2
	Nunhead v Tooting & Mitcham United	2-3
21	Ashford v London Paper Mills	3-0
	Callender Athletic v Cray Wanderers	5-2
	Canterbury Waverley v Sheppey United	4-3
	Maidstone United v UGB Sports (Charlton)	1-5e
22	Haywards Heath v Bognor Regis Town	3-0
	Horsham v Worthing	4-4
	Littlehampton v Hastings & St Leonards	1-4
	Southwick v Brighton Corp. Tramways	6-0
23	Newport (IOW) v Poole Town	2-1
	Portsmouth Electricity v Salisbury Corinthians	2-5
	Salisbury City (1) v Ryde Sports	2-2
	Weymouth v Fareham	1-1
24	Frome Town v Trowbridge Town	1-4
	Melksham v Warminster Town	2-2
	Paulton Rovers v Clandown	1-0
	Wilts County Mental Hospital v Devizes Town	0-1
25	Barry v Llanelli	2-1
	Gloucester City v Clevedon	1-1
	Hanham Athletic v Aberdare (2)	1-9
	Lovells Athletic v St Philips Marsh Adult School	3-2
26	Glastonbury v Street	1-1
	Newton Corinthians v Exmouth Town	5-1
	Radstock Town v Welton Rovers	6-3
	Timsbury Athletic v Wells City	1-5
6r	Earle v Stoneycroft	2-4
r	Tushingham Brick Works v Garston Woodcutters	3-4
8r	Birmingham Transport v Worcester City	3-1
r	Oswestry Town v Stafford Rangers	4-3
13r	Stamford v Desborough Town	5-1
14r	Bedford Town (1) v Waterlows (Dunstable)	1-1
18r	Wealdstone v Golders Green	1-2
19r	Southall v Aylesbury United	4-1
20r	Kingstonian v Metropolitan Police	1-2
22r	Worthing v Horsham	5-2
23r	Fareham v Weymouth	1-4
r	Ryde Sports v Salisbury City (1)	5-0
24r	Warminster Town v Melksham	2-3
25r	Clevedon v Gloucester City	1-3
26r	Street v Glastonbury	3-1
14r2	Bedford Town (1) v Waterlows (Dunstable)	2-3

Qualifying Round Two

1	Consett v North Shields	0-0
	Walker Celtic v South Shields (2)	1-4
2	Langley Park Villa v Horden CW	0-3
	Shildon v Spennymoor United	5-2
3	Billingham South v Billingham Synthonia	5-0
	Bridlington Town (1) v Whitby United	4-0
4	Kells United v Cleator Moor Celtic	4-3
	Netherfield (Kendal) v Cockermouth	6-3
5	Leyland Motors v Chorley	1-1
	Wigan Athletic v Skelmersdale United	1-1
6	Marine v Earlestown Bohemians	2-2
	Stoneycroft v Garston Woodcutters	2-1
7	Rhyl v Runcorn	1-4
	Witton Albion v Bangor City	0-1
8	Kidderminster Harriers v Birmingham Transport	1-1
	Oswestry Town v Tamworth	3-1
9	Lysaght's Sports (Scunthorpe) v Marfleet	2-1
	Scunthorpe United v Appleby Frodingham	4-1
10	Norton Woodseats v Frickley Colliery	2-5
	Thorne Colliery v Yorkshire Amateur	1-3
11	Boston United v Newark Town	5-1
	Ollerton Colliery v Ransome & Marles	4-1
12	Bolsover Colliery v Ibstock Penistone Rovers	4-2
	Burton Town v Hinckley United (1)	3-1
13	Rushden Town v Peterborough United	4-4
	Spalding United v Stamford	1-1
14	Letchworth Town v Biggleswade & District	0-1
	St Neots & District v Waterlows (Dunstable)	3-2
15	Chatteris Engineers v Cambridge Town	1-2
	King's Lynn v Wisbech Town	0-0
16	Cromer v Holt United	2-1
	Great Yarmouth Town v Lowestoft Town	4-4
17	Chelmsford City v Crittall Athletic	4-3
	Romford (2) v Leyton	6-2
18	Golders Green v Barnet	3-2
	Hoddesdon Town v Apsley	1-2
19	Hayes v Banbury Spencer	5-2
	Southall v Windsor & Eton	1-1
20	Metropolitan Police v Redhill	1-1
	Tooting & Mitcham United v Sutton United	2-2
21	Callender Athletic v Ashford	1-2
	Canterbury Waverley v UGB Sports (Charlton)	4-0
22	Hastings & St Leonards v Southwick	7-6
	Worthing v Haywards Heath	1-5
23	Ryde Sports v Newport (IOW)	0-1
	Salisbury Corinthians v Weymouth	4-2
24	Devizes Town v Paulton Rovers	3-0
	Trowbridge Town v Melksham	4-1
25	Barry v Lovells Athletic	1-0
	Gloucester City v Aberdare (2)	4-0
26	Street v Newton Corinthians	7-2
	Wells City v Radstock Town	1-2
1r	North Shields v Consett	2-1
5r	Chorley v Leyland Motors	5-1
r	Skelmersdale United v Wigan Athletic	1-2
6r	Earlestown Bohemians v Marine	1-5
8r	Birmingham Transport v Kidderminster Harriers	1-3
13r	Peterborough United v Rushden Town	3-1
r	Stamford v Spalding United	2-3
15r	Wisbech Town v King's Lynn	1-0
16r	Lowestoft Town v Great Yarmouth Town	2-0
19r	Windsor & Eton v Southall	1-4
20r	Redhill v Metropolitan Police	1-0
r	Sutton United v Tooting & Mitcham United	3-2

Qualifying Round Three

1	South Shields (2) v North Shields	1-2
2	Shildon v Horden CW	0-1
3	Billingham South v Bridlington Town (1)	2-1
4	Kells United v Netherfield (Kendal)	1-5
5	Wigan Athletic v Chorley	3-3
6	Marine v Stoneycroft	4-0
7	Bangor City v Runcorn	1-4
8	Kidderminster Harriers v Oswestry Town	7-1
9	Scunthorpe United v Lysaght's Sports (Scunthorpe)	11-3
10	Frickley Colliery v Yorkshire Amateur	4-2
11	Boston United v Ollerton Colliery	1-1
12	Burton Town v Bolsover Colliery	11-0
13	Spalding United v Peterborough United	2-3
14	St Neots & District v Biggleswade & District	3-2
15	Wisbech Town v Cambridge Town	1-0
16	Lowestoft Town v Cromer	5-3
17	Romford (2) v Chelmsford City	1-3
18	Apsley v Golders Green	2-1
19	Hayes v Southall	2-1
20	Sutton United v Redhill	2-3
21	Ashford v Canterbury Waverley	0-1
22	Haywards Heath v Hastings & St Leonards	0-4
23	Newport (IOW) v Salisbury Corinthians	2-1
24	Trowbridge Town v Devizes Town	4-1
25	Gloucester City v Barry	1-2
26	Radstock Town v Street	1-5
5r	Chorley v Wigan Athletic	5-1
11r	Ollerton Colliery v Boston United	1-2

Qualifying Round Four

	Apsley v Leytonstone	4-1
	Canterbury Waverley v Guildford City	0-1
	Chelmsford City v Dulwich Hamlet	5-1
	Chorley v Netherfield (Kendal)	3-1
	Colchester United v Ilford	4-1
	Dartford v Corinthians	3-3
	Ferryhill Athletic v North Shields	3-7
	Folkestone v Redhill	7-3
	Gainsborough Trinity v Frickley Colliery	7-0
	Gillingham v Tunbridge Wells Rangers	2-4
	Hayes v Newport (IOW)	1-0
	Horden CW v Billingham South	4-1
	Kidderminster Harriers v Burton Town	1-1
	Lancaster City v Northwich Victoria	3-2
	Lowestoft Town v Wisbech Town	2-1
	Peterborough United v St Neots & District	1-0
	Runcorn v Darwen	7-1
	Scunthorpe United v Boston United	2-1
	Shrewsbury Town v Wellington Town	0-1
	South Liverpool v Workington	2-2
	Stalybridge Celtic v Marine	3-2
	Street v Bath City	1-0
	Trowbridge Town v Cheltenham Town	1-3
	Walthamstow Avenue v Hastings & St Leonards	11-2
	Yeovil & Petter's United v Barry	5-2
r	Burton Town v Kidderminster Harriers	1-3
r	Corinthians v Dartford	2-1
r	Workington v South Liverpool	3-1

Round One

	Aldershot v Guildford City	1-1
	Bournemouth v Bristol City	2-1
	Bristol Rovers v Peterborough United	4-1
	Bromley v Apsley	2-1
	Chelmsford City v Kidderminster Harriers	4-0
	Cheltenham Town v Cardiff City	1-1
	Chester v Bradford City	3-1
	Clapton Orient v Hayes	3-1
	Crystal Palace v Queen's Park Rangers	1-1
	Darlington v Stalybridge Celtic	4-0
	Doncaster Rovers v New Brighton	4-2
	Folkestone v Colchester United	2-1
	Gainsborough Trinity v Gateshead	2-1
	Halifax Town v Rochdale	7-3
	Hartlepools United v Accrington Stanley	2-1
	Horden CW v Chorley	1-1
	Hull City v Rotherham United	4-1
	Ipswich Town v Street	7-0
	Lincoln City v Barrow	4-1
	North Shields v Stockport County	1-4
	Oldham Athletic v Crewe Alexandra	2-2
	Reading v Newport County	3-3
	Runcorn v Wellington Town	3-0
	Scarborough v Southport	0-0
	Scunthorpe United v Lancaster City	4-2
	Southend United v Corinthians	3-0
	Swindon Town v Lowestoft Town	6-0
	Torquay United v Exeter City	3-1
	Walsall v Carlisle United	4-1
	Walthamstow Avenue v Tunbridge Wells Rangers	4-1
	Watford v Northampton Town	4-1
	Workington v Mansfield Town	1-1
	Wrexham v Port Vale	1-2
	Yeovil & Petter's United v Brighton & Hove Albion	2-1
r	Cardiff City v Cheltenham Town	1-0
r	Chorley v Horden CW	1-2
r	Crewe Alexandra v Oldham Athletic	1-0
r	Guildford City v Aldershot	3-4
r	Mansfield Town v Workington	2-1
r	Newport County v Reading	3-1
r	Queen's Park Rangers v Crystal Palace	3-0
r	Southport v Scarborough	5-3

Round Two

	Bristol Rovers v Bournemouth	0-3
	Cardiff City v Crewe Alexandra	1-0
	Chelmsford City v Darlington	3-1
	Chester v Hull City	2-2
	Folkestone v Yeovil & Petter's United	1-1
	Gainsborough Trinity v Doncaster Rovers	0-1
	Halifax Town v Mansfield Town	1-1
	Hartlepools United v Queen's Park Rangers	0-2
	Horden CW v Newport County	2-3
	Ipswich Town v Torquay United	4-1
	Lincoln City v Bromley	8-1
	Port Vale v Southend United	0-1
	Runcorn v Aldershot	3-1
	Scunthorpe United v Watford	1-2
	Southport v Swindon Town	2-0
	Stockport County v Walthamstow Avenue	0-0
	Walsall v Clapton Orient	4-2
r	Hull City v Chester	0-1
r	Mansfield Town v Halifax Town	3-3e
r	Walthamstow Avenue v Stockport County	1-3
r	Yeovil & Petter's United v Folkestone	1-0
r2	Mansfield Town v Halifax Town	0-0eN
r3	Mansfield Town v Halifax Town	1-2 N

Round Three

	Aston Villa v Ipswich Town	1-1
	Barnsley v Stockport County	1-2
	Birmingham v Halifax Town	2-0
	Blackburn Rovers v Swansea Town	2-0
	Blackpool v Sheffield United	1-2
	Brentford v Newcastle United	0-2
	Cardiff City v Charlton Athletic	1-0
	Chelmsford City v Southampton	4-1
	Chelsea v Arsenal	2-1
	Chester v Coventry City	1-0
	Chesterfield v Southend United	1-1
	Derby County v Everton	0-1
	Fulham v Bury	6-0
	Grimsby Town v Tranmere Rovers	6-0
	Huddersfield Town v Nottingham Forest	0-0
	Leeds United v Bournemouth	3-1
	Leicester City v Stoke City	1-1
	Liverpool v Luton Town	3-0
	Middlesbrough v Bolton Wanderers	0-0
	Newport County v Walsall	0-2
	Norwich City v Manchester City	0-5
	Notts County v Burnley	3-1
	Portsmouth v Lincoln City	4-0
	Queen's Park Rangers v West Ham United	1-2
	Runcorn v Preston North End	2-4
	Sheffield Wednesday v Yeovil & Petter's United	1-1

1938/39, 1939/40 & 1945/46 (1939/40 cancelled, no competition 1940/41 to 1944/45)

	Southport v Doncaster Rovers	1-1
	Sunderland v Plymouth Argyle	3-0
	Tottenham Hotspur v Watford	7-1
	West Bromwich Albion v Manchester United	0-0
	Wolverhampton Wan. v Bradford Park Avenue	3-1
	York City v Millwall	0-5
r	Bolton Wanderers v Middlesbrough	0-0e
r	Doncaster Rovers v Southport	2-1
r	Ipswich Town v Aston Villa	1-2
r	Manchester United v West Bromwich Albion	1-5
r	Nottingham Forest v Huddersfield Town	0-3
r	Southend United v Chesterfield	4-3e
r	Stoke City v Leicester City	1-2
r	Yeovil & Petter's United v Sheffield Wednesday	1-2
r2	Bolton Wanderers v Middlesbrough	0-1 N

Round Four

	Birmingham v Chelmsford City	6-0
	Blackburn Rovers v Southend United	4-2
	Cardiff City v Newcastle United	0-0
	Chelsea v Fulham	3-0
	Everton v Doncaster Rovers	8-0
	Leeds United v Huddersfield Town	2-4
	Liverpool v Stockport County	5-1
	Middlesbrough v Sunderland	0-2
	Millwall v Grimsby Town	2-2
	Notts County v Walsall	0-0
	Portsmouth v West Bromwich Albion	2-0
	Preston North End v Aston Villa	2-0
	Sheffield United v Manchester City	2-0
	Sheffield Wednesday v Chester	1-1
	West Ham United v Tottenham Hotspur	3-3
	Wolverhampton Wan. v Leicester City	5-1
r	Chester v Sheffield Wednesday	1-1e
r	Grimsby Town v Millwall	3-2
r	Newcastle United v Cardiff City	4-1
r	Tottenham Hotspur v West Ham United	1-1e
r	Walsall v Notts County	4-0
r2	Sheffield Wednesday v Chester	2-0 N
r2	West Ham United v Tottenham Hotspur	2-1 N

Round Five

	Birmingham v Everton	2-2
	Chelsea v Sheffield Wednesday	1-1
	Huddersfield Town v Walsall	3-0
	Newcastle United v Preston North End	1-2
	Portsmouth v West Ham United	2-0
	Sheffield United v Grimsby Town	0-0
	Sunderland v Blackburn Rovers	1-1
	Wolverhampton Wan. v Liverpool	4-1
r	Blackburn Rovers v Sunderland	0-0e
r	Everton v Birmingham	2-1
r	Grimsby Town v Sheffield United	1-0
r	Sheffield Wednesday v Chelsea	0-0e
r2	Blackburn Rovers v Sunderland	1-0 N
r2	Chelsea v Sheffield Wednesday	3-1 N

Round Six

	Chelsea v Grimsby Town	0-1
	Huddersfield Town v Blackburn Rovers	1-1
	Portsmouth v Preston North End	1-0
	Wolverhampton Wan. v Everton	2-0
r	Blackburn Rovers v Huddersfield Town	1-2

Semi Finals

	Portsmouth v Huddersfield Town	2-1 N
	Wolverhampton Wan. v Grimsby Town	5-0 N

Final

	Portsmouth v Wolverhampton Wan.	4-1 N

1939/40

Extra Preliminary Round

1	Amble v Chopwell Colliery	8-4
	Annfield Plain v Gosforth & Coxlodge	5-0
	Ashington v Whitley & Monkseaton	2-1
	Crookhall CW v Newcastle West End (2)	1-1
	Reyrolles v Shankhouse	5-2
	Throckley Welfare v Scotswood	1-2
2	Birtley v Trimdon Grange Colliery	2-1
	Holiday's Sports v Brandon Social	2-0
	Usworth Colliery v Dawdon Colliery Recreation	5-1
	Washington Chemical Works v Chilton Colliery Rec.	2-1
7	Buxton v Wilmslow Albion	4-0
	Moulton Verdin v Middlewich Athletic	np
	Nantwich v Haslington Villa	5-1
	Willaston White Star v Cheadle	np
10	Armthorpe Welfare v Rossington Main	5-0
	Bentley Colliery v Meltham Mills	1-1
	Brodsworth Main Colliery v Bradford Rovers	4-3
	Goole Town v Luddendenfoot	8-1
	Grimethorpe Rovers v Ossett Town	4-2
	Guiseley v Rawmarsh Welfare	1-3
	Ravensthorpe v Farsley Celtic	np
	Upton Colliery v South Kirkby Colliery	3-5
	Worksop Town v Pilkington Recreation	1-0
16	Norwich YMCA v Norwich Electricity Works	np
17	Clapton v Dagenham Town	4-2
	Harwich & Parkeston v Esso (Purfleet)	np
18	Berkhamsted Town v Barnet	1-2
	Enfield v London Caledonians	np
	Epping Town v Ware	1-3
	Harlow Town v Welwyn Garden City	2-3
	Harrow Town v Finchley	0-3
	Kings Langley v Hertford Town	np
	Saffron Walden Town v Leavesden	np
	St Albans City v Bishop's Stortford	6-1
	Stevenage Town v Bushey United	4-0
	Tufnell Park v Pinner	np
	Wealdstone v Old Johnians	7-3
	Wood Green Town v Old Lyonian	np
19	Civil Service v Lyons Club (Greenford)	np
	Hounslow Town v Wycombe Wanderers	0-3
	Maidenhead United v Yiewsley	4-0
	Newbury Town v Bicester Town	1-2
	Osberton Radiator (Oxford) v Pressed Steel	3-5
	Oxford City v Headington United	np
	Redford Sports (Wycombe) v Uxbridge	4-0
	Slough v Marlow	np
20	Camberley & Yorktown v PO Engineers (Wallington)	np
	Egham v Woking	0-12
	Kingstonian v Banstead Mental Hospital	np
	Vickers Armstrong v Guildford	np
	Walton-on-Thames v Leyland Motors (Kingston)	2-1
	Wimbledon v Venner Sports	np
21	Gravesend United v Bexley	1-3
	Maidstone United v Margate	2-2
	RM Deal v Whitstable	np
23	Bournemouth Gasworks Athletic v Bournemouth (Ams)	4-0
	Fareham v Gosport	1-3
	HMS Victory v East Cowes	np
	Hamworthy v Sherborne	np
	Thornycrofts (Basingstoke) v Winchester City	np
	Trafalgar Sports (Portsmouth) v Osborne Athletic	np
24	Calne & Harris United v Pewsey YM	np

1945/46

Extra Preliminary Round

19	Aylesbury United v Chesham United	5-0
	Banbury Spencer v Headington United	8-1
	Pressed Steel v Morris Motors (Cowley)	1-0
	Uxbridge v Lyons Club (Greenford)	11-1

Preliminary Round

2	Shildon v Usworth Colliery	7-1
9	Ossett Town v Thorne Colliery	1-3
18	Apsley v Kings Langley	4-7
	Edgware Town v Barnet	1-4
	Harrow Town v Berkhamsted Town	8-0
	Hertford Town v Enfield	3-6
	Hoddesdon Town v Bishop's Stortford	0-0
	Pinner v Wealdstone	1-2
	St Albans City v Finchley	4-3
	Tufnell Park v Welwyn Garden City	11-1
19	Aylesbury United v Osberton Radiator (Oxford)	5-0
	Hayes v Maidenhead United	4-1
	Hounslow Town v Slough United	4-4e
	Marlow v Yiewsley	3-4
	Newbury Town v Banbury Spencer	0-8
	Oxford City v Uxbridge	4-0
	Windsor & Eton v Pressed Steel	11-1
	Wycombe Wanderers v Southall	0-2
20	Banstead Mental Hospital v Metropolitan Police	0-2
	Epsom v Woking	1-8
	Sutton United v Guildford	6-0
	Tooting & Mitcham United v Kingstonian	5-2
22	East Grinstead v Horsham	2-2
23	Thornycrofts (Basingstoke) v Totton	1-3
24	Chippenham Town v Devizes Town	9-0
	Purton v Swindon GWR Corinthians	0-6
18r	Bishop's Stortford v Hoddesdon Town	4-1
19r	Slough United v Hounslow Town	3-1
22r	Horsham v East Grinstead	1-0

Qualifying Round One

1	Annfield Plain v Ashington	1-2
	Consett v Shankhouse	6-0
	Gosforth & Coxlodge v Throckley	0-2
	Newburn v Amble	3-1
2	Blackhall Colliery Welfare v Seaham Colliery Welfare	4-2
	Ferryhill Athletic v Shildon	1-3
	Spennymoor United v Tow Law Town	4-1
	Stanley United v West Auckland Town	5-0
5	Leyland Motors v Skelmersdale United	1-2
6	Bangor City v Rhyl	4-1 D
	Hurst v Earle	9-2
	Northwich Victoria v Fodens Motor Works	0-4
	Witton Albion v Glossop	8-2
7	Hednesford Town v Nuneaton Borough	2-2
	Hereford United v Moor Green	0-8
	Tamworth v Bournville Athletic	2-5
	Worcester City v Birmingham City Transport	8-0
9	East Bierley v Thorne Colliery	3-3
	Goole Town v Yorkshire Amateur	0-1
	Guiseley v Frickley Colliery	3-3
	Meltham Mills v South Kirkby Colliery	1-7
10	Brodsworth Main Colliery v Firbeck Main Colliery	1-1
	Grimethorpe Rovers v Denaby United	1-5
	Monckton Athletic v Upton Colliery	6-2
	Rawmarsh Welfare v Norton Woodseats	3-1
13	Kettering Town v Peterbro' Westwood Works	5-0
14	Bedford Avenue v Bedford Town (1)	0-0
	Hitchin Town v Vauxhall Motors (Luton)	3-2e
15	Abbey United (Cambs) v Cambridge Town	0-8
	Chatteris Engineers v Newmarket Town	0-1
17	Eton Manor v Romford (2)	1-1
	Ford Sports (Dagenham) v Hoffmann Ath. (Chelm'rd)	4-2
	Leyton v Grays Athletic	1-1
18	Enfield v Bishop's Stortford	8-1
	Harrow Town v Kings Langley	7-1
	St Albans City v Wealdstone	2-2
	Tufnell Park v Barnet	1-1
19	Aylesbury United v Oxford City	1-2
	Hayes v Southall	1-1
	Windsor & Eton v Banbury Spencer	0-3
	Yiewsley v Slough United	2-2
20	Metropolitan Police v Woking	1-4
	Redhill v Tooting & Mitcham United	1-5
	Sutton United v Wimbledon	7-0
	Walton & Hersham v Epsom Town (2)	11-0
21	Erith & Belvedere v Gravesend United	3-3
	Sheppey United v Bromley	1-5
	Woolwich Polytechnic v Lloyds (Sittingbourne)	1-1
22	Hastings & St Leonards v Bexhill Town	wo/s
	Horsham v Worthing	4-2
	Newhaven v Haywards Heath	2-2
	Southwick v Bognor Regis Town	4-1
23	East Cowes Victoria v Sandown	9-1
	Ryde Sports v Cowes	1-3
	Salisbury Corinthians v Gosport Borough Ath.	2-6
	Totton v Newport (IOW)	0-4
24	Clandown v Chippenham Town	0-1
	Paulton Rovers v Swindon GWR Corinthians	4-3
	Pewsey YM v Trowbridge Town	1-3
	Westbury United v Swindon Victoria	4-3
25	Aberaman & Aberdare v Llanelli	6-1 D
	Barry Town v Clevedon	10-0
	Ebbw Vale v Cardiff Corinthians	3-1 D
7r	Nuneaton Borough v Hednesford Town	5-2
9r	Frickley Colliery v Guiseley	7-0
r	Thorne Colliery v East Bierley	1-6
10r	Firbeck Main Colliery v Brodsworth Main Colliery	3-4
14r	Bedford Town (1) v Bedford Avenue	0-4
17r	Grays Athletic v Leyton	0-3
r	Romford (2) v Eton Manor	4-3
18r	Barnet v Tufnell Park	3-1
r	Wealdstone v St Albans City	3-0
19r	Slough United v Yiewsley	2-2
r	Southall v Hayes	2-1
21r	Gravesend United v Erith & Belvedere	2-1
r	Lloyds (Sittingbourne) v Woolwich Polytechnic	4-0
22r	Haywards Heath v Newhaven	5-0
19r2	Slough United v Yiewsley	2-0

Qualifying Round Two

1	Ashington v Consett	1-1
	Throckley v Newburn	0-0
2	Shildon v Blackhall Colliery Welfare	6-1
	Spennymoor United v Stanley United	6-1
3	Billingham Synthonia - Bye	
	Stockton v Whitby United	4-0
4	Milnthorpe Corinthians v Kells Welfare Centre	4-5
	Netherfield (Kendal) - Bye	
5	Chorley v Wigan Athletic	5-2
	Darwen v Skelmersdale United	2-2
6	Rhyl v Fodens Motor Works	5-1
	Witton Albion v Hurst	6-1
7	Bournville Athletic v Moor Green	6-5e
	Nuneaton Borough v Worcester City	1-0
8	Lysaght's Sports (Scunthorpe) - Bye	
	Scunthorpe United - Bye	
9	South Kirkby Colliery v Frickley Colliery	0-2
	Yorkshire Amateur v East Bierley	3-0
10	Brodsworth Main Colliery v Denaby United	2-3
	Rawmarsh Welfare v Monckton Athletic	2-1
11	Coalville Town (3) - Bye	
	Gresley Rovers - Bye	
12	Grantham v Basford United	6-1
	Ollerton Colliery v Boston United	4-2
13	Rushden Town v Peterborough United	1-9
	Wellingborough Town v Kettering Town	2-5
14	Hitchin Town v Bedford Avenue	0-2
	Letchworth Town v Leighton United	3-0
15	Cambridge Town v King's Lynn	4-1
	Wisbech Town v Newmarket Town	5-0
16	Leiston - Bye	
	Lowestoft Town - Bye	
17	Leyton v Ford Sports (Dagenham)	6-2
	Romford (2) v Crittall Athletic	7-1
18	Barnet v Enfield	5-0
	Harrow Town v Wealdstone	1-1
19	Banbury Spencer v Slough United	2-5
	Oxford City v Southall	2-1
20	Sutton United v Walton & Hersham	4-0
	Woking v Tooting & Mitcham United	1-2
21	Bromley v Gravesend United	2-0
	Ramsgate Athletic v Lloyds (Sittingbourne)	3-3
22	Hastings & St Leonards v Horsham	6-1
	Haywards Heath v Southwick	5-1

1945/46 ("s" indicates a second-leg match) to 1946/47

23 Cowes v East Cowes Victoria 4-2
Newport (IOW) v Gosport Borough Ath. 2-0
24 Paulton Rovers v Westbury United 4-0
Trowbridge Town v Chippenham Town 3-1
25 Barry Town v Cardiff Corinthians 6-1
Llanelli v Monmouth Town 7-0
26 Radstock Town - Bye
Welton Rovers v Peasedown MW 3-7
1r Consett v Ashington 3-0
r Newburn v Throckley 1-2
5r Skelmersdale United v Darwen 2-3
18r Wealdstone v Harrow Town 6-1
21r Lloyds (Sittingbourne) v Ramsgate Athletic 3-1

Qualifying Round Three

1 Throckley v Consett 2-4
2 Shildon v Spennymoor United 3-2
3 Stockton v Billingham Synthonia 4-1
4 Kells Welfare Centre v Netherfield (Kendal) 1-2
5 Chorley v Darwen 1-0
6 Rhyl v Witton Albion 2-2
7 Nuneaton Borough v Bournville Athletic 8-1 D
8 Scunthorpe United v Lysaght's Sports (Scunthorpe) 4-1
9 Frickley Colliery v Yorkshire Amateur 0-4
10 Rawmarsh Welfare v Denaby United 5-1
11 Gresley Rovers v Coalville Town (3) 0-7
12 Grantham v Ollerton Colliery 2-1
13 Kettering Town v Peterborough United 2-1
14 Bedford Avenue v Letchworth Town 1-0
15 Wisbech Town v Cambridge Town 3-1
16 Leiston v Lowestoft Town 2-2 d
17 Romford (2) v Leyton 4-1
18 Barnet v Wealdstone 3-0
19 Slough United v Oxford City 3-1
20 Tooting & Mitcham United v Sutton United 3-3
21 Lloyds (Sittingbourne) v Bromley 3-4
22 Haywards Heath v Hastings & St Leonards 1-0
23 Newport (IOW) v Cowes 0-1 d
24 Trowbridge Town v Paulton Rovers 7-0
25 Llanelli v Barry Town 1-7
26 Peasedown MW v Radstock Town 7-0
6r Witton Albion v Rhyl 3-1
20r Sutton United v Tooting & Mitcham United 5-1

Qualifying Round Four

Barnet v Ilford 5-2
Barry Town v Lovells Athletic 1-5
Bromley v Shorts Sports 2-0
Chelmsford City v Leiston 9-0
Cheltenham Town v Peasedown MW 1-1
Consett v Stockton 2-3
Dulwich Hamlet v Romford (2) 1-2
Gillingham v Sutton United 3-9
Grantham v Bedford Avenue 6-1
Guildford City v Newport (IOW) 1-2
Kettering Town v Coalville Town (3) 2-1
Leytonstone v Slough United 3-3
Netherfield (Kendal) v Lancaster City 2-0
Rawmarsh Welfare v Gainsborough Trinity 1-3
Scarborough v North Shields 2-4
Scunthorpe United v Yorkshire Amateur 1-2
Shrewsbury Town v Bournville Athletic 6-2
Stalybridge Celtic v Runcorn 3-0
Trowbridge Town v Haywards Heath 6-0
Walthamstow Avenue v Clapton 4-0
Wellington Town v Kidderminster Harriers 5-2
Willington v Shildon 3-2
Wisbech Town v Colchester United 5-0
Witton Albion v Marine 2-3
Workington v Chorley 1-2
r Peasedown MW v Cheltenham Town 0-1
r Slough United v Leytonstone 3-1

Round One

Barnet v Queen's Park Rangers 2-6
Barrow v Netherfield (Kendal) 1-0
Bath City v Cheltenham Town 3-2
Brighton & Hove Albion v Romford (2) 3-1
Bromley v Slough United 6-1
Carlisle United v North Shields 5-1
Chorley v Accrington Stanley 2-1
Clapton Orient v Newport (IOW) 2-1
Crewe Alexandra v Wrexham 4-2
Darlington v Stockton 2-0
Doncaster Rovers v Rotherham United 0-1
Halifax Town v York City 1-0
Hartlepools United v Gateshead 1-2
Kettering Town v Grantham 1-5
Lovells Athletic v Bournemouth 4-1
Mansfield Town v Gainsborough Trinity 3-0
Marine v Stalybridge Celtic 4-0
Northampton Town v Chelmsford City 5-1
Notts County v Bradford City 2-2
Port Vale v Wellington Town 4-0
Reading v Aldershot 3-1
Shrewsbury Town v Walsall 5-0
South Liverpool v Tranmere Rovers 1-1
Southport v Oldham Athletic 1-2
Stockport County v Rochdale 1-2
Sutton United v Walthamstow Avenue 1-4
Swindon Town v Bristol Rovers 1-0
Torquay United v Newport County 0-1

Trowbridge Town v Exeter City 1-3
Watford v Southend United 1-1
Willington v Bishop Auckland 0-5
Wisbech Town v Ipswich Town 0-3
Yeovil & Petter's United v Bristol City 2-2
Yorkshire Amateur v Lincoln City 1-0
s Accrington Stanley v Chorley 2-0
s Aldershot v Reading 7-3
s Bishop Auckland v Willington 0-2
s Bournemouth v Lovells Athletic 3-2
s Bradford City v Notts County 1-2
s Bristol City v Yeovil & Petter's United 3-0
s Bristol Rovers v Swindon Town 4-1
s Chelmsford City v Northampton Town 0-5
s Cheltenham Town v Bath City 0-2
s Exeter City v Trowbridge Town 7-2
s Gainsborough Trinity v Mansfield Town 4-2e
s Gateshead v Hartlepools United 6-2
s Grantham v Kettering Town 2-2
s Ipswich Town v Wisbech Town 5-0
s Lincoln City v Yorkshire Amateur 5-1
s Netherfield (Kendal) v Barrow 2-2
s Newport (IOW) v Clapton Orient 2-0
s Newport County v Torquay United 1-1
s North Shields v Carlisle United 2-3
s Oldham Athletic v Southport 3-1
s Queen's Park Rangers v Barnet 2-1
s Rochdale v Stockport County 1-1
s Romford (2) v Brighton & Hove Albion 1-1
s Rotherham United v Doncaster Rovers 2-1
s Slough United v Bromley 1-0
s Southend United v Watford 0-3
s Stalybridge Celtic v Marine 3-3
s Stockton v Darlington 1-4
s Tranmere Rovers v South Liverpool 6-1
s Walsall v Shrewsbury Town 4-1
s Walthamstow Avenue v Sutton United 7-2
s Wellington Town v Port Vale 0-2
s Wrexham v Crewe Alexandra 3-0
s York City v Halifax Town 4-2

Round Two

Aldershot v Newport (IOW) 7-0
Barrow v Carlisle United 4-2
Bishop Auckland v York City 1-2
Bristol City v Bristol Rovers 4-2
Bromley v Watford 1-3
Darlington v Gateshead 2-4
Grantham v Mansfield Town 1-2
Lovells Athletic v Bath City 2-1
Newport County v Exeter City 5-1
Northampton Town v Notts County 3-1
Oldham Athletic v Accrington Stanley 2-1
Port Vale v Marine 3-1
Queen's Park Rangers v Ipswich Town 4-0
Rotherham United v Lincoln City 2-1
Shrewsbury Town v Wrexham 0-1
Tranmere Rovers v Rochdale 3-1
Walthamstow Avenue v Brighton & Hove Albion 1-1
s Accrington Stanley v Oldham Athletic 3-1
s Bath City v Lovells Athletic 2-5
s Brighton & Hove Albion v Walthamstow Avenue 4-2
s Bristol Rovers v Bristol City 0-2
s Carlisle United v Barrow 3-4
s Exeter City v Newport County 1-3
s Gateshead v Darlington 1-2
s Ipswich Town v Queen's Park Rangers 0-2
s Lincoln City v Rotherham United 1-1
s Mansfield Town v Grantham 2-1
s Marine v Port Vale 1-1
s Newport (IOW) v Aldershot 0-5
s Notts County v Northampton Town 1-0
s Rochdale v Tranmere Rovers 3-0
s Watford v Bromley 1-1
s Wrexham v Shrewsbury Town 1-1
s York City v Bishop Auckland 3-0

Round Three

Accrington Stanley v Manchester United 2-2
Aldershot v Plymouth Argyle 2-0
Birmingham City v Portsmouth 1-0
Bolton Wanderers v Blackburn Rovers 1-0
Bradford Park Avenue v Port Vale 2-1
Bristol City v Swansea Town 5-1
Bury v Rochdale 3-3
Cardiff City v West Bromwich Albion 1-1
Charlton Athletic v Fulham 3-1
Chelsea v Leicester City 1-1
Chester v Liverpool 0-2
Chesterfield v York City 1-1
Coventry City v Aston Villa 2-1
Grimsby Town v Sunderland 1-3
Huddersfield Town v Sheffield United 1-1
Leeds United v Middlesbrough 4-4
Lovells Athletic v Wolverhampton Wan. 2-4
Luton Town v Derby County 0-6
Manchester City v Barrow 6-2
Mansfield Town v Sheffield Wednesday 0-0
Newcastle United v Barnsley 4-2
Northampton Town v Millwall 2-2
Norwich City v Brighton & Hove Albion 1-2
Nottingham Forest v Watford 1-1
Preston North End v Everton 2-1

Queen's Park Rangers v Crystal Palace 0-0
Rotherham United v Gateshead 2-2
Southampton v Newport County 4-3
Stoke City v Burnley 3-1
Tottenham Hotspur v Brentford 2-2
West Ham United v Arsenal 6-0
Wrexham v Blackpool 1-4
s Arsenal v West Ham United 1-0
s Aston Villa v Coventry City 2-0
s Barnsley v Newcastle United 3-0
s Barrow v Manchester City 2-2
s Blackburn Rovers v Bolton Wanderers 1-3
s Blackpool v Wrexham 4-1
s Brentford v Tottenham Hotspur 2-0
s Brighton & Hove Albion v Norwich City 4-1
s Burnley v Stoke City 2-1
s Crystal Palace v Queen's Park Rangers 0-0x
s Derby County v Luton Town 3-0
s Everton v Preston North End 2-2e
s Fulham v Charlton Athletic 2-1
s Gateshead v Rotherham United 0-2
s Leicester City v Chelsea 0-2
s Liverpool v Chester 2-1
s Manchester United v Accrington Stanley 5-1
s Middlesbrough v Leeds United 7-2
s Millwall v Northampton Town 3-0
s Newport County v Southampton 1-2
s Plymouth Argyle v Aldershot 0-1
s Port Vale v Bradford Park Avenue 1-1
s Portsmouth v Birmingham City 0-0
s Rochdale v Bury 2-4
s Sheffield United v Huddersfield Town 2-0
s Sheffield Wednesday v Mansfield Town 5-0
s Sunderland v Grimsby Town 2-1
s Swansea Town v Bristol City 2-2
s Watford v Nottingham Forest 1-1e
s West Bromwich Albion v Cardiff City 4-0
s Wolverhampton Wan. v Lovells Athletic 8-1
s York City v Chesterfield 3-2e
r Nottingham Forest v Watford 0-1eN
r Queen's Park Rangers v Crystal Palace 1-0 N

Round Four

Barnsley v Rotherham United 3-0
Birmingham City v Watford 5-0
Blackpool v Middlesbrough 3-2
Bolton Wanderers v Liverpool 5-0
Bradford Park Avenue v Manchester City 1-3
Brighton & Hove Albion v Aldershot 3-0
Bristol City v Brentford 2-1
Charlton Athletic v Wolverhampton Wan. 5-2
Chelsea v West Ham United 2-0
Derby County v West Bromwich Albion 1-0
Manchester United v Preston North End 1-0
Millwall v Aston Villa 2-4
Sheffield Wednesday v York City 5-1
Southampton v Queen's Park Rangers 0-1
Stoke City v Sheffield United 2-0
Sunderland v Bury 3-1
s Aldershot v Brighton & Hove Albion 1-4
s Aston Villa v Millwall 9-1
s Brentford v Bristol City 5-0
s Bury v Sunderland 5-4e
s Liverpool v Bolton Wanderers 2-0
s Manchester City v Bradford Park Avenue 2-8
s Middlesbrough v Blackpool 3-2e
s Preston North End v Manchester United 3-1
s Queen's Park Rangers v Southampton 4-3
s Rotherham United v Barnsley 2-1
s Sheffield United v Stoke City 3-2
s Watford v Birmingham City 1-1
s West Bromwich Albion v Derby County 1-3
s West Ham United v Chelsea 1-0
s Wolverhampton Wan. v Charlton Athletic 1-1
s York City v Sheffield Wednesday 1-6
r Blackpool v Middlesbrough 0-1eN

Round Five

Barnsley v Bradford Park Avenue 0-1
Bolton Wanderers v Middlesbrough 1-0
Brighton & Hove Albion v Derby County 1-4
Chelsea v Aston Villa 0-1
Preston North End v Charlton Athletic 1-1
Queen's Park Rangers v Brentford 1-3
Stoke City v Sheffield Wednesday 2-0
Sunderland v Birmingham City 1-0
s Aston Villa v Chelsea 1-0
s Birmingham City v Sunderland 3-1
s Bradford Park Avenue v Barnsley 1-1
s Brentford v Queen's Park Rangers 0-0
s Charlton Athletic v Preston North End 6-0
s Derby County v Brighton & Hove Albion 6-0
s Middlesbrough v Bolton Wanderers 1-1
s Sheffield Wednesday v Stoke City 0-0

Round Six

Aston Villa v Derby County 3-4
Bradford Park Avenue v Birmingham City 2-2
Charlton Athletic v Brentford 6-3
Stoke City v Bolton Wanderers 0-2
s Birmingham City v Bradford Park Avenue 6-0
s Bolton Wanderers v Stoke City 0-0

1945/46 and 1946/47

s Brentford v Charlton Athletic		1-3
s Derby County v Aston Villa		1-1

Semi Finals

Charlton Athletic v Bolton Wanderers		2-0 N
Derby County v Birmingham City		1-1 N
r Derby County v Birmingham City		4-0eN

Final

Derby County v Charlton Athletic		4-1eN

1946/47

Extra Preliminary Round

2 Horden CW v Easington CW		3-3
Langley Park CW v Evenwood Town		0-2
17 Barking v London Transport		9-0
Brentwood & Warley v Tilbury		3-4
Harwich & Parkeston v Dagenham British Legion		8-1
18 Enfield v Wood Green Town		1-1e
Finchley v Polytechnic		2-0
Hatfield United v Chipperfield		2-3
Hertford Town v Leavesden		6-2
Pinner v Hendon		2-3
Saffron Walden Town v Ware		4-2
Twickenham v Acton Town		1-2
Welwyn Garden City v Berkhamsted Town		2-2
19 Aylesbury United v Morris Motors (Cowley)		2-1
Bicester Town v Headington United		2-3
Henley Town v Uxbridge		6-6e
Hounslow Town v Maidenhead United		1-4
Metal & Produce Recovery Depot v Chesham United		1-1
Redford Sports (Wycombe) v Yiewsley		3-7
Wycombe Wanderers v Marlow		2-0
23 Trafalgar Sports (Portsmouth) v RAOC Hilsea		2-6
24 Calne & Harris United v Warminster Town		3-4
Hanham Athletic v Soundwell		1-2
Hoffmann Ath. (Stonehouse) v Frome Town		7-0
Spencer Moulton v Melksham		2-4
Wootton Bassett Town v Dilton Rovers		5-0
2r Easington CW v Horden CW		2-0
18r Berkhamsted Town v Welwyn Garden City		4-2
r Wood Green Town v Enfield		4-3e
19r Chesham United v Metal & Produce Recovery Depot		5-0
r Uxbridge v Henley Town		3-1

Preliminary Round

1 Annfield Plain v Shankhouse		wo/s
Eden Colliery v Crook CW		2-8
Gosforth & Coxlodge v Amble		6-2
Murton CW v South Shields (2)		3-2
2 Brandon CW v Stanley United		3-3
Ferryhill Athletic v Blackhall Colliery Welfare		2-1
Seaham Colliery Welfare v Dawdon Colliery Welfare		7-0
Shildon v Easington CW		2-2
Spennymoor United v Willington		7-2
Tow Law Town v Chilton & Windlestone		1-3
Trimdon Grange Colliery v Evenwood Town		3-3
West Auckland Town v Usworth Colliery		wo/s
4 Distington v Lowca		1-7
Frizington United v Haig United		3-2
Kells Welfare Centre v William Colliery (Whitehaven)		4-0
Parton United v Salterbeck		wo/s
Penrith v Cleator Moor Celtic		1-5
Scalegill v Moss Bay		2-4
5 Great Harwood v Horwich RMI		2-6
Lytham v Leyland Motors		1-1
Nelson v Morecambe		1-2
Wigan Athletic v Crossens		3-2
7 Buxton v Hyde United		2-2
Ellesmere Port Town v Nantwich		9-0
Llandudno v Northwich Victoria		3-4
8 Atherstone Town v Boldmere St Michaels		4-2
Birmingham City Transport v Stourbridge		0-5
Bromsgrove Rovers v Dudley Town		0-3
Hednesford Town v Hereford United		0-3
Nuneaton Borough v Darlaston		3-1
9 Brodsworth Main Col. v Lysaght's Sports (Scun'rpe)		9-1
Denaby United v Maltby Main Colliery		4-1
Harworth Colliery Athletic v Upton Colliery		8-1
Matlock Town v Sheffield		2-5
Rawmarsh Welfare v Firbeck Main Colliery		5-1
Scunthorpe United v Norton Woodseats		5-2
Thurnscoe Victoria v Wombwell Athletic		0-5
Wombwell Main Welfare v Grimethorpe Rovers		2-2
10 Kiveton Park Colliery v Ossett Town		1-2
Selby Town v Meltham Mills		6-0
Thorne Colliery v Bradford United		0-0
14 Arlesey Town v Biggleswade Town		1-2
Bedford Town (1) v Wolverton Town		1-1
Eynesbury Rovers v Waterlows (Dunstable)		1-0
Vauxhall Motors (Luton) v Luton Amateur		2-4
17 Barking v Severalls Athletic		wo/s
Crittall Athletic v Woodford Town (1)		4-2
Ekco (Southend) v Eton Manor		2-0
Ford Sports (Dagenham) v Clapton		2-4e
Harwich & Parkeston v Ilford		3-2
Leyton v Hoffmann Athletic (Chelmsford)		3-0
Romford (2) v Grays Athletic		2-1
Tilbury v Clacton Town		3-0
18 Bishop's Stortford v Chipperfield		2-1
Edgware Town v Harrow Town		1-2e
Finchley v Hendon		3-1
Hertford Town v Saffron Walden Town		7-2
Hoddesdon Town v Berkhamsted Town		4-3
St Albans City v Apsley		5-1
Wealdstone v Tufnell Park		6-1
Wood Green Town v Acton Town		4-0
19 Aylesbury United v Osberton Radiator (Oxford)		6-2
Hayes v Pressed Steel		7-1
Headington United v Banbury Spencer		3-2
Slough United v Lyons Club (Greenford)		4-2
Southall v Wycombe Wanderers		2-5
Uxbridge v Chesham United		7-2
Windsor & Eton v Oxford City		4-2
Yiewsley v Maidenhead United		3-3
20 Epsom v Metropolitan Police		0-5
Kingstonian v Epsom Town (2)		wo/s
Redhill v Tooting & Mitcham United		3-9
Vickers Armstrong v PO Engineers (Wallington)		5-0
Walton & Hersham v Guildford		11-0
Wimbledon v Carshalton Athletic		3-0
21 Callender Athletic v Woolwich Polytechnic		2-3
Chatham v Folkestone		0-8
Dartford v Sheppey United		2-5
Erith & Belvedere v Gravesend & Northfleet		3-3
Lloyds (Sittingbourne) v Shorts Sports		4-2
Maidstone United v Margate		3-1
Ramsgate Athletic v Dover		9-0
Whitstable v Ashford		3-10
22 Bexhill Town v Hove		5-2
East Grinstead v Shoreham		11-0
Eastbourne v Newhaven		4-1
Hastings & St Leonards v Worthing		3-3
Littlehampton v Bognor Regis Town		1-2
23 Basingstoke Town v Salisbury Corinthians		1-1
Bournemouth (Ams) v Poole Town		2-4
Bournemouth Gasworks Athletic v Weymouth S.A.A.		wo/s
East Cowes Victoria v Portsmouth Electricity		4-1
RAOC Hilsea v Cowes		4-3
Ryde Sports v Gosport Borough Ath.		1-8
Sandown v Newport (IOW)		3-3
Thornycroft Athletic v Andover		2-0
24 Clandown v Purton		8-3
Devizes Town v Westbury United		1-2
Melksham v Swindon Victoria		4-1
Odd Down v Soundwell		0-3
Paulton Rovers v Hoffmann Ath. (Stonehouse)		2-4
Swindon GWR Corinthians v Wootton Bassett Town		5-1
Trowbridge Town v Chippenham Town		6-0
Warminster Town v Pewsey YM		4-6
25 Ebbw Vale v Llanelli		2-2
Merthyr Tydfil v Cardiff Corinthians		4-1
Weston-Super-Mare St Johns v Gloucester City		0-5
26 Street v Wells City		2-2
2r Easington CW v Shildon		2-4
r Evenwood Town v Trimdon Grange Colliery		2-1
r Stanley United v Brandon CW		1-3
5r Lytham v Leyland Motors		0-3
7r Hyde United v Buxton		2-3 d
9r Grimethorpe Rovers v Wombwell Main Welfare		6-1
10r Bradford United v Thorne Colliery		1-2
14r Wolverton Town v Bedford Town (1)		1-2e
19r Maidenhead United v Yiewsley		3-0
21r Gravesend & Northfleet v Erith & Belvedere		4-1
22r Worthing v Hastings & St Leonards		2-2e
23r Newport (IOW) v Sandown		3-2
r Salisbury Corinthians v Basingstoke Town		2-2e
25r Llanelli v Ebbw Vale		5-2
26r Wells City v Street		1-2
22r2 Worthing v Hastings & St Leonards		3-2 N
23r2 Salisbury Corinthians v Basingstoke Town		2-1 N

Qualifying Round One

1 Annfield Plain v Newburn		1-2
Consett v Gosforth & Coxlodge		7-0
Murton CW v Ashington		1-3
Throckley v Crook CW		2-5
2 Brandon CW v Evenwood Town		2-1
Ferryhill Athletic v Chilton & Windlestone		3-1
Shildon v Spennymoor United		3-3
West Auckland Town v Seaham Colliery Welfare		0-3
3 Brigham & Cowan (Hull) v Billingham Synthonia		2-2
Portrack Shamrocks v Hull Amateur		5-1
Stockton - Bye		
Whitby Albion Rangers v Whitby		2-6
4 Kells Welfare Centre v Lowca		1-2
Moss Bay v Milnthorpe Corinthians		2-3
Netherfield (Kendal) v Frizington United		7-2
Parton United v Cleator Moor Celtic		2-4
5 Chorley v Hurst		4-1
Darwen v Horwich RMI		1-1
Morecambe v Wigan Athletic		0-3
Skelmersdale United v Leyland Motors		4-3
6 Earle - Bye		
Haydock C&B Recreation - Bye		
Orrell v Newton YMCA		1-2
Prescot Cables v St Helens Town		wo/s
7 Fodens Motor Works v Bangor City		3-6
Glossop v Rhyl		2-6
Hyde United v Ellesmere Port Town		1-2
Stalybridge Celtic v Northwich Victoria		4-3
8 Atherstone Town v Nuneaton Borough		1-4
Dudley Town v Stourbridge		1-1
Hereford United v Bournville Athletic		1-0
Worcester City v Moor Green		1-1
9 Brodsworth Main Colliery v Denaby United		1-1
Rawmarsh Welfare v Grimethorpe Rovers		4-0
Scunthorpe United v Harworth Colliery Athletic		5-2
Sheffield v Wombwell Athletic		2-4
10 Dinnington Athletic v Frickley Colliery		3-4
Goole Town v Yorkshire Amateur		2-4
Ossett Town v South Kirkby Colliery		0-2
Selby Town v Thorne Colliery		0-0
11 Brush Sports - Bye		
Coalville Town (3) - Bye		
Gresley Rovers - Bye		
Ibstock Penistone Rovers - Bye		
12 Basford United v Ollerton Colliery		2-1
Boston United - Bye		
Grantham - Bye		
Ransome & Marles v Boots Athletic		3-1
13 Kettering Town v Rushden Town		2-0
Peterborough United v Wellingborough Town		6-0
Peterbro' Westwood Works - Bye		
Stewarts & Lloyds - Bye		
14 Biggleswade Town v Bedford Avenue		1-7
Leighton United v Eynesbury Rovers		2-1
Letchworth Town v Hitchin Town		0-2
Luton Amateur v Bedford Town (1)		1-5
15 Cambridge Town - Bye		
Chatteris Town - Bye		
King's Lynn - Bye		
Newmarket Town - Bye		
16 Gothic (Norwich) v Gorleston		1-1
Great Yarmouth Town v Old Grammarians (Ipswich)		5-1
Leiston - Bye		
Lowestoft Town - Bye		
17 Crittall Athletic v Clapton		3-1
Harwich & Parkeston v Barking		0-3
Romford (2) v Ekco (Southend)		3-0
Tilbury v Leyton		4-1
18 Harrow Town v Wealdstone		4-3
Hoddesdon Town v Bishop's Stortford		3-2
St Albans City v Hertford Town		5-1
Wood Green Town v Finchley		2-4
19 Aylesbury United v Headington United		2-3
Slough United v Windsor & Eton		3-3
Uxbridge v Maidenhead United		2-1
Wycombe Wanderers v Hayes		3-4
20 Sutton United v Metropolitan Police		7-0
Vickers Armstrong v Kingstonian		1-1
Walton & Hersham v Tooting & Mitcham United		1-1
Woking v Wimbledon		2-6
21 Folkestone v Ramsgate Athletic		2-1
Lloyds (Sittingbourne) v Gravesend & Northfleet		1-4
Maidstone United v Ashford		3-5
Woolwich Polytechnic v Sheppey United		0-0
22 Bexhill Town v East Grinstead		3-1
Haywards Heath v Bognor Regis Town		0-1
Southwick v Horsham		5-3
Worthing v Eastbourne		3-5
23 Newport (IOW) v Bournemouth Gasworks Athletic		0-1
Poole Town v East Cowes Victoria		1-0
Salisbury Corinthians v Gosport Borough Ath.		2-2
Thornycroft Athletic v RAOC Hilsea		1-2
24 Hoffmann Ath. (Stonehouse) v Clandown		2-1
Melksham v Swindon GWR Corinthians		3-2
Trowbridge Town v Soundwell		6-2
Westbury United v Pewsey YM		2-1
25 Barry Town v Clevedon		4-1
Lovells Athletic v Aberaman & Aberdare		1-0
Merthyr Tydfil v Llanelli		5-2
St Philips Marsh Adult School v Gloucester City		2-0
26 Dartmouth United v Plymouth United		5-2
Peasedown MW v Glastonbury		1-0
Street v Somerton Amateurs		2-0
Welton Rovers v Radstock Town		2-4
2r Spennymoor United v Shildon		4-2
3r Billingham Synthonia v Brigham & Cowan (Hull)		wo/s
5r Horwich RMI v Darwen		0-2
8r Moor Green v Worcester City		1-6
r Stourbridge v Dudley Town		0-1
9r Denaby United v Brodsworth Main Colliery		2-1
10r Thorne Colliery v Selby Town		2-1
16r Gothic (Norwich) v Gorleston		6-0
19r Windsor & Eton v Slough United		2-4
20r Kingstonian v Vickers Armstrong		3-2
r Tooting & Mitcham United v Walton & Hersham		2-1
21r Sheppey United v Woolwich Polytechnic		1-3
23r Gosport Borough Ath. v Salisbury Corinthians		2-1

Qualifying Round Two

1 Crook CW v Consett		2-1
Newburn v Ashington		3-3
2 Brandon CW v Seaham Colliery Welfare		1-1
Spennymoor United v Ferryhill Athletic		2-0
3 Portrack Shamrocks v Billingham Synthonia		2-1
Whitby v Stockton		0-2
4 Lowca v Cleator Moor Celtic		3-3
Netherfield (Kendal) v Milnthorpe Corinthians		6-2
5 Skelmersdale United v Chorley		1-1
Wigan Athletic v Darwen		1-2
6 Earle v Prescot Cables		0-3
Haydock C&B Recreation v Newton YMCA		1-1
7 Bangor City v Stalybridge Celtic		4-1
Rhyl v Ellesmere Port Town		4-4

97

1946/47 & 1947/48

8	Hereford United v Worcester City	3-0
	Nuneaton Borough v Dudley Town	2-1
9	Rawmarsh Welfare v Scunthorpe United	0-3
	Wombwell Athletic v Denaby United	4-2
10	South Kirkby Colliery v Frickley Colliery	2-1
	Yorkshire Amateur v Thorne Colliery	1-0
11	Brush Sports v Gresley Rovers	7-0
	Coalville Town (3) v Ibstock Penistone Rovers	14-0
12	Basford United v Ransome & Marles	0-7
	Grantham v Boston United	1-2
13	Peterborough United v Peterbro' Westwood Works	3-0
	Stewarts & Lloyds v Kettering Town	1-1
14	Bedford Avenue v Hitchin Town	0-8
	Leighton United v Bedford Town (1)	2-5
15	King's Lynn v Cambridge Town	0-2
	Newmarket Town v Chatteris Town	0-2
16	Leiston v Great Yarmouth Town	3-1
	Lowestoft Town v Gothic (Norwich)	2-5
17	Barking v Crittall Athletic	3-0
	Tilbury v Romford (2)	2-1
18	Finchley v Hoddesdon Town	4-2
	St Albans City v Harrow Town	2-5
19	Hayes v Slough United	6-3
	Uxbridge v Headington United	5-2
20	Sutton United v Kingstonian	3-1
	Tooting & Mitcham United v Wimbledon	1-0
21	Ashford v Gravesend & Northfleet	1-1
	Woolwich Polytechnic v Folkestone	0-3
22	Bognor Regis Town v Bexhill Town	2-1
	Southwick v Eastbourne	5-5e
23	Poole Town v Gosport Borough Ath.	3-0
	RAOC Hilsea v Bournemouth Gasworks Athletic	2-2
24	Hoffmann Ath. (Stonehouse) v Melksham	5-1
	Trowbridge Town v Westbury United	4-0
25	Merthyr Tydfil v Lovells Athletic	4-2
	St Philips Marsh Adult School v Barry Town	1-6
26	Peasedown MW v Dartmouth United	1-1
	Radstock Town v Street	2-1
1r	Ashington v Newburn	6-1
2r	Seaham Colliery Welfare v Brandon CW	2-0
4r	Cleator Moor Celtic v Lowca	0-5
5r	Chorley v Skelmersdale United	1-1
6r	Newton YMCA v Haydock C&B Recreation	1-3
7r	Ellesmere Port Town v Rhyl	1-3
13r	Kettering Town v Stewarts & Lloyds	4-2
21r	Gravesend & Northfleet v Ashford	3-2
22r	Eastbourne v Southwick	4-1
23r	Bournemouth Gasworks Athletic v RAOC Hilsea	6-2
26r	Dartmouth United v Peasedown MW	3-1
5r2	Skelmersdale United v Chorley	1-0

Qualifying Round Three

1	Ashington v Crook CW	7-1
2	Seaham Colliery Welfare v Spennymoor United	0-4
3	Stockton v Portrack Shamrocks	9-1
4	Lowca v Netherfield (Kendal)	0-1
5	Skelmersdale United v Darwen	1-1
6	Prescot Cables v Haydock C&B Recreation	2-2
7	Bangor City v Rhyl	5-3
8	Hereford United v Nuneaton Borough	5-0
9	Wombwell Athletic v Scunthorpe United	2-5
10	South Kirkby Colliery v Yorkshire Amateur	1-2
11	Brush Sports v Coalville Town (3)	4-3
12	Boston United v Ransome & Marles	3-1
13	Peterborough United v Kettering Town	4-1
14	Bedford Town (1) v Hitchin Town	2-2
15	Chatteris Town v Cambridge Town	1-6
16	Gothic (Norwich) v Leiston	4-4
17	Barking v Tilbury	3-0
18	Finchley v Harrow Town	4-3
19	Hayes v Uxbridge	3-2
20	Tooting & Mitcham United v Sutton United	3-5
21	Folkestone v Gravesend & Northfleet	1-2
22	Eastbourne v Bognor Regis Town	4-1
23	Poole Town v Bournemouth Gasworks Athletic	4-2 v
24	Hoffmann Ath. (Stonehouse) v Trowbridge Town	3-4
25	Merthyr Tydfil v Barry Town	3-0
26	Radstock Town v Dartmouth United	1-3
5r	Darwen v Skelmersdale United	6-4
6r	Haydock C&B Recreation v Prescot Cables	1-0
14r	Hitchin Town v Bedford Town (1)	3-2e
16r	Leiston v Gothic (Norwich)	0-2
23r	Bournemouth Gasworks Athletic v Poole Town	2-3

Qualifying Round Four

	Barking v Leytonstone	1-4
	Brush Sports v Shrewsbury Town	5-1
	Chelmsford City v Cambridge Town	0-4
	Cheltenham Town v Hereford United	1-1
	Colchester United v Gothic (Norwich)	5-1
	Darwen v Lancaster City	2-5
	Eastbourne v Finchley	3-7
	Gravesend & Northfleet v Walthamstow Avenue	1-0
	Guildford City v Gillingham	1-2
	Hayes v Dulwich Hamlet	4-2
	Marine v Haydock C&B Recreation	7-0
	Merthyr Tydfil v Bath City	7-1
	Netherfield (Kendal) v Workington	1-3
	North Shields v Ashington	1-1
	Peterborough United v Hitchin Town	4-1
	Poole Town v Trowbridge Town	2-0
	Scunthorpe United v Boston United	4-1
	South Bank v Spennymoor United	0-3
	South Liverpool v Bangor City	2-2
	Stockton v Scarborough	5-1
	Sutton United v Bromley	2-0
	Wellington Town v Kidderminster Harriers	3-1
	Witton Albion v Runcorn	1-2
	Yeovil Town v Dartmouth United	10-2
	Yorkshire Amateur v Gainsborough Trinity	3-3
r	Ashington v North Shields	1-1x
r	Bangor City v South Liverpool	0-4
r	Gainsborough Trinity v Yorkshire Amateur	6-2
r	Hereford United v Cheltenham Town	3-4
r2	North Shields v Ashington	3-1

Round One

	Aldershot v Cheltenham Town	4-2
	Barnet v Sutton United	3-0
	Barrow v Halifax Town	0-0
	Bournemouth v Exeter City	4-2
	Bristol City v Hayes	9-3
	Brush Sports v Southend United	1-6
	Carlisle United v Runcorn	4-0
	Doncaster Rovers v Accrington Stanley	2-2
	Gainsborough Trinity v Darlington	1-2
	Gateshead v Bradford City	3-1
	Gillingham v Gravesend & Northfleet	4-1
	Hartlepools United v North Shields	6-0
	Hull City v New Brighton	0-0
	Ipswich Town v Torquay United	2-0
	Lancaster City v Spennymoor United	1-0
	Leyton Orient v Notts County	1-2
	Leytonstone v Walsall	1-6
	Merthyr Tydfil v Bristol Rovers	3-1
	Northampton Town v Mansfield Town	2-0
	Norwich City v Brighton & Hove Albion	7-2
	Oldham Athletic v Tranmere Rovers	1-0
	Port Vale v Finchley	5-0
	Queen's Park Rangers v Poole Town	2-2
	Reading v Colchester United	5-0
	Rochdale v Bishop Auckland	6-1
	Rotherham United v Crewe Alexandra	2-0
	South Liverpool v Workington	2-1
	Stockport County v Southport	2-0
	Stockton v Lincoln City	2-4
	Swindon Town v Cambridge Town	4-1
	Wellington Town v Watford	1-1
	Wrexham v Marine	5-0
	Yeovil Town v Peterborough United	2-2
	York City v Scunthorpe United	0-1
r	Accrington Stanley v Doncaster Rovers	0-5
r	Halifax Town v Barrow	1-0e
r	New Brighton v Hull City	1-2e
r	Peterborough United v Yeovil Town	1-0
r	Poole Town v Queen's Park Rangers	0-6
r	Watford v Wellington Town	1-0

Round Two

	Barnet v Southend United	2-9
	Bournemouth v Aldershot	4-2
	Bristol City v Gillingham	1-2
	Darlington v Hull City	1-2
	Gateshead v Lancaster City	4-0
	Halifax Town v Stockport County	1-1
	Lincoln City v Wrexham	1-1
	Merthyr Tydfil v Reading	1-3
	Norwich City v Queen's Park Rangers	4-4
	Notts County v Swindon Town	2-1
	Oldham Athletic v Doncaster Rovers	1-2
	Peterborough United v Northampton Town	1-1
	Rochdale v Hartlepools United	6-1
	Rotherham United v Scunthorpe United	4-1
	South Liverpool v Carlisle United	2-3
	Walsall v Ipswich Town	0-0
	Watford v Port Vale	1-1
r	Ipswich Town v Walsall	0-1
r	Northampton Town v Peterborough United	1-1e
r	Port Vale v Watford	2-1
r	Queen's Park Rangers v Norwich City	2-0
r	Stockport County v Halifax Town	2-1
r	Wrexham v Lincoln City	3-3e
r2	Lincoln City v Wrexham	2-1 N
r2	Northampton Town v Peterborough United	8-1 N

Round Three

	Blackburn Rovers v Hull City	1-1
	Bolton Wanderers v Stockport County	5-1
	Bournemouth v Derby County	0-2
	Bradford Park Avenue v Manchester United	0-3
	Brentford v Cardiff City	1-0
	Burnley v Aston Villa	5-1
	Charlton Athletic v Rochdale	3-1
	Chelsea v Arsenal	1-1
	Chester v Plymouth Argyle	2-0
	Chesterfield v Sunderland	2-1
	Coventry City v Newport County	5-2
	Doncaster Rovers v Portsmouth	2-3
	Everton v Southend United	4-2
	Fulham v Birmingham City	1-2
	Huddersfield Town v Barnsley	3-4
	Lincoln City v Nottingham Forest	0-1
	Luton Town v Notts County	6-0
	Manchester City v Gateshead	3-0
	Millwall v Port Vale	0-3
	Newcastle United v Crystal Palace	6-2
	Northampton Town v Preston North End	1-2
	Queen's Park Rangers v Middlesbrough	1-1
	Reading v Grimsby Town	2-2
	Sheffield United v Carlisle United	3-0
	Sheffield Wednesday v Blackpool	4-1
	Southampton v Bury	5-1
	Swansea Town v Gillingham	4-1
	Tottenham Hotspur v Stoke City	2-2
	Walsall v Liverpool	2-5
	West Bromwich Albion v Leeds United	2-1
	West Ham United v Leicester City	1-2
	Wolverhampton Wan. v Rotherham United	3-0
r	Arsenal v Chelsea	1-1e
r	Grimsby Town v Reading	3-1
r	Hull City v Blackburn Rovers	0-3
r	Middlesbrough v Queen's Park Rangers	3-1
r	Stoke City v Tottenham Hotspur	1-0
r2	Arsenal v Chelsea	0-2 N

Round Four

	Birmingham City v Portsmouth	1-0
	Blackburn Rovers v Port Vale	2-0
	Bolton Wanderers v Manchester City	3-3
	Brentford v Leicester City	0-0
	Burnley v Coventry City	2-0
	Chelsea v Derby County	2-2
	Chester v Stoke City	0-0
	Liverpool v Grimsby Town	2-0
	Luton Town v Swansea Town	2-0
	Manchester United v Nottingham Forest	0-2
	Middlesbrough v Chesterfield	2-1
	Newcastle United v Southampton	3-1
	Preston North End v Barnsley	6-0
	Sheffield Wednesday v Everton	2-1
	West Bromwich Albion v Charlton Athletic	1-2
	Wolverhampton Wan. v Sheffield United	0-0
r	Derby County v Chelsea	1-0e
r	Leicester City v Brentford	0-0e
r	Manchester City v Bolton Wanderers	1-0
r	Sheffield United v Wolverhampton Wan.	2-0
r	Stoke City v Chester	3-2
r2	Leicester City v Brentford	4-1 N

Round Five

	Birmingham City v Manchester City	5-0
	Charlton Athletic v Blackburn Rovers	1-0
	Liverpool v Derby County	1-0
	Luton Town v Burnley	0-0
	Newcastle United v Leicester City	1-1
	Nottingham Forest v Middlesbrough	2-2
	Sheffield Wednesday v Preston North End	0-2
	Stoke City v Sheffield United	0-1
r	Burnley v Luton Town	3-0
r	Leicester City v Newcastle United	1-2
r	Middlesbrough v Nottingham Forest	6-2

Round Six

	Charlton Athletic v Preston North End	2-1
	Liverpool v Birmingham City	4-1
	Middlesbrough v Burnley	1-1
	Sheffield United v Newcastle United	0-2
r	Burnley v Middlesbrough	1-0e

Semi Finals

	Burnley v Liverpool	0-0eN
	Charlton Athletic v Newcastle United	4-0 N
r	Burnley v Liverpool	1-0 N

Final

	Charlton Athletic v Burnley	1-0eN

1947/48

Extra Preliminary Round

2	Blackhall Colliery Welfare v Willington	2-1
	Dawdon Colliery Welfare v Horden CW	0-0
	Easington CW v Shotton CW	4-1
	Murton CW v Stanley United	2-2e
4	Cockermouth v Pica	6-1
7	Droylsden v Wilmslow Albion	2-0
9	Appleby Frodingham v Dinnington Athletic	4-1
	Armthorpe Welfare v Matlock Town	3-1
	Barton Town (1) v Grimethorpe Athletic	3-4
	Bentley Colliery v Winterton Rangers	2-4
	Harworth Colliery Athletic v Pilkington Recreation	7-3
	Monckton Athletic v Brodsworth Main Colliery	1-2
	Wombwell Athletic v Firbeck Main Colliery	4-3
17	Clapton v Rainham Town	2-1
	Upminster v Grays Athletic	0-1
	West Thurrock Athletic v Ford Sports (Dagenham)	3-0
18	Civil Service v Harlow Town	2-0
	Edgware Town v Acton Town	9-0
	Hemel Hempstead Town v Berkhamsted Town	3-4
	Leavesden v Willesden	7-1
	Pinner v Saffron Walden Town	2-0
	Sawbridgeworth v Crown & Manor	4-1

1947/48

	Tufnell Park v Royston Town	4-3e
	Ware v Edmonton Borough	2-3
	Welwyn Garden City v Enfield	1-5
	Wood Green Town v Chipperfield	1-4
19	Abingdon Town v Aylesbury United	2-4
	Banbury Spencer v Oxford City	5-0
	Henley Town v Lyons Club (Greenford)	1-7
	Marlow v Maidenhead United	0-2
	Pressed Steel v Huntley & Palmers	0-3
	Redford Sports (Wycombe) v Southall	0-5
	Wallingford Town v Chesham United	4-2e
	Wycombe Wanderers v Hounslow Town	4-2
	Yiewsley v Windsor & Eton	3-3e
21	Betteshanger CW v Aylesford Paper Mills	3-2
	Lloyds (Sittingbourne) v Chatham Town	2-4
	Sittingbourne v Bexley	3-4
	Whitstable v Chatham	wo/s
23	Andover v Pirelli General Cables	7-0
	Cowes v Newport (IOW)	1-3
	Lymington v Portland United	1-2
	Weymouth v Longfleet St Mary's	4-1
	Winchester City v Salisbury (2)	0-1
24	Chippenham Town v Odd Down	4-2
	Frome Town v Welton Rovers	1-2
	Warminster Town v Clandown	3-4
	Wootton Bassett Town v Pewsey Vale	0-2
2r	Horden CW v Dawdon Colliery Welfare	9-0
r	Stanley United v Murton CW	2-2
19r	Windsor & Eton v Yiewsley	3-2
2r2	Stanley United v Murton CW	1-2

Preliminary Round

1	Annfield Plain v Amble	5-2
	Birtley v Blyth Spartans	0-2
	Newbiggin CW v West Stanley	1-5
	South Shields (2) v Radcliffe Welfare United	13-0
2	Chilton Athletic v Shildon	2-3
	Crook CW v Murton CW	1-2e
	Easington CW v Brandon CW	2-0
	Ferryhill Athletic v Consett	3-2e
	Horden CW v Spennymoor United	2-0
	Seaham Colliery Welfare v Langley Park CW	5-1
	Tow Law Town v Evenwood Town	4-6
	West Auckland Town v Blackhall Colliery Welfare	5-3
3	Filey Town v South Bank East End	3-2
	Guisborough v Cargo Fleet Works	4-1
	Whitby Albion Rangers v South Bank St Peters	2-0
4	Appleby v Milnthorpe Corinthians	3-9
	Bowthorn United v Kells Welfare Centre	2-2
	Florence & Ullcoats Utd. v Frizington United	1-3
	Lowca v Penrith	3-2e
	Netherfield (Kendal) v Cockermouth	10-2
	Parton United v Cleator Moor Celtic	3-1
	Scalegill v Moss Bay	1-0
	William Colliery (Whitehaven) v Distington	8-2
5	De Havilland (Bolton) v Morecambe	1-3
	Fleetwood v Great Harwood	7-1
	Lytham v Bacup Borough	0-1
6	Burscough v Bangor City	3-1
	Earlestown v Haydock C&B Recreation	3-0
	Formby v Wigan Athletic	0-4
	Llandudno v Earle	2-7
	Newton YMCA v Orrell	1-2
	Rhyl v Crossens	10-0
	Skelmersdale United v Stoneycroft	8-0
	St Helens Town v Prescot Cables	0-1
7	Ashton United v Winsford United	2-0
	Buxton v Macclesfield Town	6-1
	Congleton Town v Witton Albion	3-3
	Droylsden v Youlgrave	6-6e
	Ellesmere Port Town v Lostock Gralam	3-0
	Fodens Motor Works v Hyde United	1-2
	Nantwich v Altrincham	1-8
	Northwich Victoria v Wheelock Albion	8-1
8	Boldmere St Michaels v Hednesford Town	0-1
	Bournville Athletic v Birmingham City Transport	0-3
	Darlaston v Worcester City	1-2
	Halesowen Town v Cradley Heath	4-1
	Hereford United v Thynnes Athletic	11-0
	Moor Green v Stafford Rangers	2-7
	Oswestry Town v Bromsgrove Rovers	1-4
	Stourbridge v Dudley Town	1-0
9	Armthorpe Welfare v Norton Woodseats	1-4
	Brodsworth Main Colliery v Rawmarsh Welfare	3-4
	Grimethorpe Athletic v Thurnscoe Victoria	wo/s
	Harworth Colliery Athletic v Wombwell Athletic	4-1
	Lysaght's Sports (Scunthorpe) v Kiveton Park Col.	4-1
	Maltby Main Colliery v Appleby Frodingham	1-4
	Scunthorpe United v Sheffield	5-1
	Winterton Rangers v Denaby United	1-2
10	Bradford United v Luddendenfoot	1-0
	Ossett Town v Meltham Mills	5-1
	Upton Colliery v Goole Town	1-3
12	Boots Athletic v Ilkeston Town (2)	0-4
	Gedling Colliery v Holbeach United	6-1
	Spalding United v Ollerton Colliery	3-2
	Stamford v Bourne Town	4-0
14	Arlesey Town v Leighton United	2-0
	Bedford Queens Works v Letchworth Town	1-8
	Bedford Town (1) v Eynesbury Rovers	7-4
	Biggleswade Town v St Neots & District	9-1
	Hitchin Town v Waterlows (Dunstable)	8-0
	Kempston Rovers v Bedford Avenue	4-1
	Vauxhall Motors (Luton) v Stewartby Works	7-1
	Wolverton Town v Luton Amateur	4-2
15	Histon Institute v Abbey United (Cambs)	6-4
	March Town v Wisbech Town	4-2
16	Gorleston v Whitton United	2-4
	Norwich CEYMS v Cromer	0-0e
17	Crittall Athletic v Tilbury	3-2
	Dagenham British Legion v London Transport	4-1
	Eton Manor v Ekco (Southend)	2-3
	Grays Athletic v Ilford	3-2
	Leyton v Harwich & Parkeston	1-2
	Romford (2) v Barking	1-3
	West Thurrock Athletic v Clapton	4-1
	Woodford Town (1) v Brentwood & Warley	1-8
18	Edgware Town v Pinner	7-0
	Finchley v Civil Service	3-2e
	Harrow Town v Tufnell Park	4-0
	Hoddesdon Town v Edmonton Borough	5-3
	Sawbridgeworth v Berkhamsted Town	1-6
	St Albans City v Chipperfield	1-0
	Twickenham v Leavesden	1-3
	Wealdstone v Enfield	2-0
19	Banbury Spencer v Osberton Radiator (Oxford)	8-2
	Bicester Town v Metal & Produce Recovery Depot	1-3
	Hayes v Windsor & Eton	3-1
	Headington United v Wallingford Town	4-0
	Huntley & Palmers v Aylesbury United	4-1
	Maidenhead United v Lyons Club (Greenford)	7-2
	Slough United v Southall	0-1
	Wycombe Wanderers v Uxbridge	3-1
20	Epsom v Brookwood Hospital	4-3
	Metropolitan Police v Walton & Hersham	4-6e
	Redhill v Guildford	9-0
	Woking v Leatherhead	2-0
21	Ashford v Whitstable	4-1
	Betteshanger CW v Woolwich Polytechnic	2-1
	Dartford v Erith & Belvedere	3-2e
	Dover v Gravesend & Northfleet	1-5
	Folkestone v Callender Athletic	6-0
	Maidstone United v Ramsgate Athletic	3-4
	Margate v Chatham Town	3-0
	Sheppey United v Bexley	3-2
22	Chichester City (1) v Eastbourne Comrades	5-2
	East Grinstead v Newhaven	5-2
	Hastings & St Leonards v Horsham	1-2
23	Bitterne Nomads v Thornycroft Athletic	2-3
	Bournemouth Gasworks Athletic v Portland United	4-0
	Gosport Borough Ath. v East Cowes Victoria	2-0
	Newport (IOW) v Weymouth	5-2
	Poole Town v Bournemouth (Ams)	3-2
	Salisbury (2) v Basingstoke Town	5-1
	Salisbury Corinthians v Andover	1-2
	Sandown v Ryde Sports	2-2
24	Devizes Town v Purton	4-0
	Paulton Rovers v Radstock Town	5-1
	Peasedown MW v Clandown	2-3
	Swindon GWR Corinthians v Pewsey Vale	2-1
	Swindon Victoria v Melksham	4-2
	Welton Rovers v Trowbridge Town	0-2
	Westbury United v Chippenham Town	3-0
	Wilts County Mental Hospital v Dilton Rovers	4-0
25	Barry Town v Aberaman & Aberdare	2-0
	Ebbw Vale v Hoffmann Ath. (Stonehouse)	2-0
	Gloucester City v Hanham Athletic	2-4
	Llanelli v Cardiff Corinthians	3-0
	Merthyr Tydfil v Clevedon	2-1
	Soundwell v Bristol Aeroplane Co.	2-0
	St Philips Marsh Adult School v Lovells Athletic	1-5
	Stonehouse v Weston-Super-Mare St Johns	4-7
26	Oak Villa v Newton Abbot Spurs	1-2
4r	Kells Welfare Centre v Bowthorn United	1-3
7r	Droylsden v Youlgrave	2-1
r	Witton Albion v Congleton Town	7-0
16r	Cromer v Norwich CEYMS	1-3
23r	Ryde Sports v Sandown	4-1

Qualifying Round One

1	Annfield Plain v South Shields (2)	2-4
	Ashington v West Stanley	4-3
	Blyth Spartans v Throckley	4-0
	Newburn v Gosforth & Coxlodge	2-0
2	Evenwood Town v Seaham Colliery Welfare	3-1
	Ferryhill Athletic v Shildon	1-0
	Murton CW v Easington CW	2-3
	West Auckland Town v Horden CW	1-0
3	Billingham Synthonia v Portrack Shamrocks	1-3
	Guisborough v Whitby Albion Rangers	1-2
	South Bank v Stockton	2-3e
	Whitby v Filey Town	4-2
4	Bowthorn United v Lowca	4-2
	Netherfield (Kendal) v Scalegill	5-1
	Parton United v Frizington United	3-2
	William Col. (Whitehaven) v Milnthorpe Corinthians	3-4
5	Bacup Borough v Morecambe	2-3
	Darwen v Fleetwood	1-3
	Leyland Motors v Horwich RMI	1-2
	Nelson v Chorley	2-1
6	Burscough v Rhyl	0-3
	Earlestown v Wigan Athletic	0-1
	Orrell v Prescot Cables	0-6
	Skelmersdale United v Earle	3-2
7	Altrincham v Hyde United	4-1
	Ashton United v Witton Albion	2-6
	Buxton v Northwich Victoria	2-0
	Ellesmere Port Town v Droylsden	2-2e
8	Bromsgrove Rovers v Worcester City	3-2
	Halesowen Town v Birmingham City Transport	2-1
	Hednesford Town v Stourbridge	2-3
	Hereford United v Stafford Rangers	2-1
9	Denaby United v Appleby Frodingham	4-1
	Grimethorpe Athletic v Lysaght's Sports (Scunthorpe)	4-2
	Harworth Colliery Athletic v Norton Woodseats	0-1
	Scunthorpe United v Rawmarsh Welfare	8-0
10	Bradford United v South Kirkby Colliery	4-2
	Frickley Colliery v Selby Town	1-3
	Goole Town v Ossett Town	3-1
	Yorkshire Amateur v Thorne Colliery	0-0e
11	Coalville Town (3) v Atherstone Town	1-0
	Gresley Rovers v Nuneaton Borough	3-2
	Moira United v Brush Sports	1-3
	Tamworth v Ibstock Penistone Rovers	6-0
12	Basford United v Stamford	3-1
	Boston United v Gedling Colliery	5-3
	Ilkeston Town (2) v Ransome & Marles	2-1e
	Spalding United v Grantham	0-4
13	Desborough Town v Stewarts & Lloyds	1-0
	Kettering Town - Bye	
	Peterbro' Westwood Works v Peterborough United	0-5
	Wellingborough Town v Rushden Town	0-3
14	Bedford Town (1) v Arlesey Town	2-0
	Biggleswade Town v Kempston Rovers	4-5
	Vauxhall Motors (Luton) v Letchworth Town	2-2e
	Wolverton Town v Hitchin Town	1-2
15	Cambridge Town v King's Lynn	3-1e
	Chatteris Town v Bury Town	2-5
	Histon Institute v Parson Drove United	3-2e
	Newmarket Town v March Town	2-3
16	Gothic (Norwich) v Sheringham	3-1
	Leiston v Old Grammarians (Ipswich)	8-2
	Norwich CEYMS v Great Yarmouth Town	1-6
	Whitton United v Lowestoft Town	3-5
17	Barking v Crittall Athletic	3-1e
	Ekco (Southend) v Dagenham British Legion	3-0
	Grays Athletic v West Thurrock Athletic	3-0
	Harwich & Parkeston v Brentwood & Warley	1-4
18	Berkhamsted Town v Harrow Town	3-4
	Hoddesdon Town v Edgware Town	1-2
	Leavesden v St Albans City	2-1
	Wealdstone v Finchley	5-4e
19	Maidenhead United v Huntley & Palmers	5-2
	Metal & Produce Recovery Depot v Banbury Spencer	0-3
	Southall v Headington United	2-1
	Wycombe Wanderers v Hayes	1-0
20	Kingstonian v Epsom	10-1
	Sutton United v Carshalton Athletic	1-3
	Walton & Hersham v Redhill	2-2e
	Woking v Tooting & Mitcham United	2-3
21	Folkestone v Betteshanger CW	5-1
	Gravesend & Northfleet v Ashford	4-0
	Margate v Dartford	0-3
	Ramsgate Athletic v Sheppey United	4-2
22	Bognor Regis Town v Shoreham	1-1e
	East Grinstead v Bexhill Town	7-1
	Horsham v Haywards Heath	1-1e
	Worthing v Chichester City (1)	3-2
23	Bournemouth Gasworks Athletic v Gosport Borough Ath.	0-3
	Poole Town v Andover	2-1
	Ryde Sports v Thornycroft Athletic	3-0
	Salisbury (2) v Newport (IOW)	0-0
24	Paulton Rovers v Clandown	4-3 v
	Swindon GWR Corinthians v Westbury United	1-4
	Trowbridge Town v Devizes Town	4-1
	Wilts County Mental Hospital v Swindon Victoria	5-3
25	Ebbw Vale v Llanelli	3-2
	Merthyr Tydfil v Hanham Athletic	9-0
	Soundwell v Barry Town	0-10
	Weston-Super-Mare St Johns v Lovells Athletic	1-4
26	Plymouth United v Dartmouth United	1-2
	St Austell v Glastonbury	2-1
	Street v Somerton Amateurs	9-1
	Wells City v Newton Abbot Spurs	0-1
7r	Droylsden v Ellesmere Port Town	4-1
10r	Thorne Colliery v Yorkshire Amateur	4-3
14r	Letchworth Town v Vauxhall Motors (Luton)	1-5
20r	Redhill v Walton & Hersham	2-1
22r	Haywards Heath v Horsham	3-8
r	Shoreham v Bognor Regis Town	2-5
23r	Newport (IOW) v Salisbury (2)	2-0
24r	Clandown v Paulton Rovers	6-0

Qualifying Round Two

1	Newburn v Blyth Spartans	1-5
	South Shields (2) v Ashington	3-1
2	Ferryhill Athletic v Evenwood Town	4-0
	West Auckland Town v Easington CW	0-1
3	Portrack Shamrocks v Whitby	0-1
	Stockton v Whitby Albion Rangers	8-1
4	Bowthorn United v Parton United	3-4
	Netherfield (Kendal) v Milnthorpe Corinthians	4-1
5	Fleetwood v Morecambe	2-0
	Nelson v Horwich RMI	4-1
6	Prescot Cables v Skelmersdale United	1-1e
	Wigan Athletic v Rhyl	2-1
7	Altrincham v Droylsden	4-1
	Witton Albion v Buxton	6-3
8	Bromsgrove Rovers v Halesowen Town	1-1e
	Stourbridge v Hereford United	4-0
9	Norton Woodseats v Grimethorpe Athletic	7-1
	Scunthorpe United v Denaby United	1-0

1947/48 to 1948/49

10 Goole Town v Thorne Colliery	2-0	
Selby Town v Bradford United	3-1	
11 Brush Sports v Tamworth	3-1e	
Gresley Rovers v Coalville Town (3)	3-0	
12 Grantham v Basford United	7-0	
Ilkeston Town (2) v Boston United	1-0	
13 Desborough Town v Peterborough United	1-2	
Rushden Town v Kettering Town	1-2	
14 Hitchin Town v Bedford Town (1)	2-3	
Kempston Rovers v Vauxhall Motors (Luton)	1-2	
15 Bury Town v Cambridge Town	2-1	
March Town v Histon Institute	1-0	
16 Gothic (Norwich) v Leiston	3-1	
Lowestoft Town v Great Yarmouth Town	2-3	
17 Barking v Brentwood & Warley	0-0e	
Grays Athletic v Ekco (Southend)	1-0	
18 Edgware Town v Wealdstone	1-2	
Leavesden v Harrow Town	3-2	
19 Banbury Spencer v Maidenhead United	4-0	
Southall v Wycombe Wanderers	3-3e	
20 Kingstonian v Tooting & Mitcham United	0-2	
Redhill v Carshalton Athletic	5-2	
21 Folkestone v Ramsgate Athletic	4-1	
Gravesend & Northfleet v Dartford	0-1	
22 Bognor Regis Town v Worthing	1-3	
Horsham v East Grinstead	5-2	
23 Gosport Borough Ath. v Newport (IOW)	5-2	
Ryde Sports v Poole Town	2-1e	
24 Trowbridge Town v Clandown	4-3	
Wilts County Mental Hospital v Westbury United	1-3	
25 Barry Town v Ebbw Vale	2-0	
Merthyr Tydfil v Lovells Athletic	2-1	
26 Newton Abbot Spurs v Street	2-4	
St Austell v Dartmouth United	5-2	
6r Skelmersdale United v Prescot Cables	0-3	
8r Halesowen Town v Bromsgrove Rovers	1-2	
17r Brentwood & Warley v Barking	2-3e	
19r Wycombe Wanderers v Southall	1-2	

Qualifying Round Three

1 Blyth Spartans v South Shields (2)	0-3
2 Easington CW v Ferryhill Athletic	3-3
3 Whitby v Stockton	1-3
4 Parton United v Netherfield (Kendal)	1-4
5 Fleetwood v Nelson	1-1
6 Wigan Athletic v Prescot Cables	3-0
7 Witton Albion v Altrincham	4-2
8 Bromsgrove Rovers v Stourbridge	2-0
9 Scunthorpe United v Norton Woodseats	2-1
10 Selby Town v Goole Town	0-5
11 Brush Sports v Gresley Rovers	5-1
12 Grantham v Ilkeston Town (2)	11-1
13 Kettering Town v Peterborough United	3-4
14 Vauxhall Motors (Luton) v Bedford Town (1)	1-1e
15 Bury Town v March Town	3-0
16 Gothic (Norwich) v Great Yarmouth Town	2-3
17 Barking v Grays Athletic	0-2
18 Leavesden v Wealdstone	1-3
19 Southall v Banbury Spencer	3-4e
20 Redhill v Tooting & Mitcham United	1-0
21 Dartford v Folkestone	1-0
22 Horsham v Worthing	1-0e
23 Gosport Borough Ath. v Ryde Sports	1-2
24 Westbury United v Trowbridge Town	0-3
25 Barry Town v Merthyr Tydfil	3-4
26 St Austell v Street	1-2
2r Ferryhill Athletic v Easington CW	3-1
5r Nelson v Fleetwood	2-1
14r Bedford Town (1) v Vauxhall Motors (Luton)	0-2

Qualifying Round Four

Bishop Auckland v North Shields	3-2
Bromsgrove Rovers v Brush Sports	5-2
Colchester United v Chelmsford City	3-1
Ferryhill Athletic v Stockton	1-1
Gillingham v Barnet	3-1e
Grantham v Goole Town	3-3e
Grays Athletic v Banbury Spencer	0-1
Great Yarmouth Town v Bury Town	3-0
Guildford City v Dulwich Hamlet	5-2
Horsham v Redhill	2-1
Kidderminster Harriers v Cheltenham Town	2-4
Lancaster City v Nelson	5-1
Marine v Wigan Athletic	3-1
Merthyr Tydfil v Bath City	2-1
Ryde Sports v Trowbridge Town	0-1
Scarborough v South Shields (2)	2-3
Scunthorpe United v Gainsborough Trinity	4-2
South Liverpool v Runcorn	2-3
Street v Yeovil Town	2-1
Vauxhall Motors (Luton) v Peterborough United	2-1
Walthamstow Avenue v Dartford	0-1
Wealdstone v Bromley	0-2
Wellington Town v Shrewsbury Town	1-2
Witton Albion v Stalybridge Celtic	2-3
Workington v Netherfield (Kendal)	2-1
r Goole Town v Grantham	2-3
r Stockton v Ferryhill Athletic	3-2

Round One

Aldershot v Bromsgrove Rovers	2-1
Barrow v Carlisle United	3-2
Bournemouth v Guildford City	2-0
Bristol City v Leytonstone	3-2
Bromley v Reading	3-3e
Cheltenham Town v Street	5-0
Chester v Bishop Auckland	3-1
Colchester United v Banbury Spencer	2-1
Crewe Alexandra v South Shields (2)	4-1
Crystal Palace v Port Vale	2-1
Dartford v Bristol City	0-0e
Exeter City v Northampton Town	1-1e
Gateshead v Bradford City	1-3
Gillingham v Leyton Orient	1-0
Great Yarmouth Town v Shrewsbury Town	1-4
Hartlepools United v Darlington	1-0
Hull City v Southport	1-1e
Lincoln City v Workington	0-2
New Brighton v Marine	4-0
Newport County v Southend United	3-2
Norwich City v Merthyr Tydfil	3-0
Notts County v Horsham	9-1
Oldham Athletic v Lancaster City	6-0
Runcorn v Scunthorpe United	4-2
Stockport County v Accrington Stanley	3-1
Stockton v Grantham	2-1
Swindon Town v Ipswich Town	4-2
Tranmere Rovers v Stalybridge Celtic	2-0
Trowbridge Town v Brighton & Hove Albion	1-1e
Vauxhall Motors (Luton) v Walsall	1-2 N
Watford v Torquay United	1-1e
Wimbledon v Mansfield Town	0-1
Wrexham v Halifax Town	5-0
York City v Rochdale	0-1
r Brighton & Hove Albion v Trowbridge Town	5-0
r Bristol City v Dartford	9-2
r Northampton Town v Exeter City	2-0
r Reading v Bromley	3-0
r Southport v Hull City	2-3
r Torquay United v Watford	3-0

Round Two

Aldershot v Swindon Town	0-0e
Bournemouth v Bradford City	1-0
Bristol City v Crystal Palace	0-1e
Bristol Rovers v New Brighton	4-0
Colchester United v Wrexham	1-0
Hartlepools United v Brighton & Hove Albion	1-1e
Hull City v Cheltenham Town	4-2
Northampton Town v Torquay United	1-1e
Norwich City v Walsall	2-2e
Notts County v Stockton	1-1e
Oldham Athletic v Mansfield Town	0-1
Reading v Newport County	3-0
Rochdale v Gillingham	1-1e
Runcorn v Barrow	0-1
Stockport County v Shrewsbury Town	1-1x
Tranmere Rovers v Chester	0-1
Workington v Crewe Alexandra	1-2
r Brighton & Hove Albion v Hartlepools United	2-1
r Gillingham v Rochdale	3-0
r Shrewsbury Town v Stockport County	2-2e
r Stockton v Notts County	1-4 N
r Swindon Town v Aldershot	2-0
r Torquay United v Northampton Town	2-0
r Walsall v Norwich City	3-2
r2 Stockport County v Shrewsbury Town	3-2eN

Round Three

Arsenal v Bradford Park Avenue	0-1
Aston Villa v Manchester United	4-6
Birmingham City v Notts County	0-2
Blackburn Rovers v West Ham United	0-0e
Blackpool v Leeds United	4-0
Bolton Wanderers v Tottenham Hotspur	0-2e
Bournemouth v Wolverhampton Wan.	1-2
Bristol Rovers v Swansea Town	3-0
Burnley v Swindon Town	0-2
Cardiff City v Sheffield Wednesday	1-2e
Charlton Athletic v Newcastle United	2-1
Chelsea v Barrow	5-0
Colchester United v Huddersfield Town	1-0
Coventry City v Walsall	2-1
Crewe Alexandra v Sheffield United	3-1
Crystal Palace v Chester	0-1
Derby County v Chesterfield	2-0
Fulham v Doncaster Rovers	2-0
Gillingham v Queen's Park Rangers	1-1e
Grimsby Town v Everton	1-4
Hull City v Middlesbrough	1-3
Leicester City v Bury	1-0
Liverpool v Nottingham Forest	4-1
Manchester City v Barnsley	2-1
Mansfield Town v Stoke City	2-4
Millwall v Preston North End	1-2
Plymouth Argyle v Luton Town	2-4
Portsmouth v Brighton & Hove Albion	4-1
Rotherham United v Brentford	0-3
Southampton v Sunderland	1-0
Stockport County v Torquay United	3-0
West Bromwich Albion v Reading	2-0

r Queen's Park Rangers v Gillingham	3-1
r West Ham United v Blackburn Rovers	2-4e

Round Four

Blackpool v Chester	4-0
Brentford v Middlesbrough	1-2
Charlton Athletic v Stockport County	3-0
Colchester United v Bradford Park Avenue	3-2
Crewe Alexandra v Derby County	0-3
Fulham v Bristol Rovers	5-2
Leicester City v Sheffield Wednesday	2-1
Luton Town v Coventry City	3-2
Manchester City v Chelsea	2-0e
Manchester United v Liverpool	3-0 N
Portsmouth v Preston North End	1-3
Queen's Park Rangers v Stoke City	3-0
Southampton v Blackburn Rovers	3-2
Swindon Town v Notts County	1-0
Tottenham Hotspur v West Bromwich Albion	3-1
Wolverhampton Wan. v Everton	1-1e
r Everton v Wolverhampton Wan.	3-2e

Round Five

Blackpool v Colchester United	5-0
Fulham v Everton	1-1e
Manchester City v Preston North End	0-1
Manchester United v Charlton Athletic	2-0 N
Middlesbrough v Derby County	1-2
Queen's Park Rangers v Luton Town	3-1
Southampton v Swindon Town	3-0
Tottenham Hotspur v Leicester City	5-2
r Everton v Fulham	0-1

Round Six

Fulham v Blackpool	0-2
Manchester United v Preston North End	4-1
Queen's Park Rangers v Derby County	1-1e
Southampton v Tottenham Hotspur	0-1
r Derby County v Queen's Park Rangers	5-0

Semi Finals

Blackpool v Tottenham Hotspur	3-1eN
Manchester United v Derby County	3-1 N

Final

Manchester United v Blackpool	4-2 N

1948/49

Extra Preliminary Round

1 Cramlington Welfare v Hexham Hearts	3-4
Eldon Albion v South Hetton CW	0-5
Murton CW v Shildon	6-2
Shankhouse v Alnwick Town	4-1
2 Crook CW v Horden CW	0-3
Dawdon Colliery Welfare v Cockfield	4-1
Jarrow v Morpeth Town	2-1
Langley Park CW v Eppleton CW	3-4
Lynemouth Welfare v Shilbottle CW	1-2
Shotton CW v Seaham Colliery Welfare	1-4
Silksworth CW v Willington	4-3
Spennymoor United v Blackhall Colliery Welfare	3-0
Stanley United v Consett	3-3
Tow Law Town v Seaham United	7-2
6 Bangor City v Orrell	8-1
Earlestown v UGB St Helens	5-1
St Helens Town v Prescot B.I.C.C.	4-2
7 Ashton United v Mossley	3-0
Barnton v Nantwich	5-1
Ellesmere Port Town v Northwich Victoria	0-2
Harrowby v Glossop	2-11
Lostock Gralam v Wheelock Albion	4-0
Macclesfield Town v Shell (Ellesmere Port)	6-3
8 Bournville Athletic v Hednesford Town	2-3
Cradley Heath v Brierley Hill Alliance	4-1
Lye Town v Boldmere St Michaels	2-5
Sutton Town (Birmingham) v Lockheed Leamington	1-0
Thynnes Athletic v Staffordshire Casuals	wo/s
9 Creswell Colliery v Hardwick Colliery	wo/s
Hoyland Common Athletic v Staveley Welfare	5-1
Maltby Main Colliery v Beighton Miners Welfare	1-3
Steel, Peech & Tozer Social Ser. v Bolsover Colliery	4-2
10 Appleby Frodingham v Laceby	2-4
Armthorpe Welfare v South Kirkby Colliery	2-5
Bentley Colliery v Upton Colliery	3-1
Bradford United v Harrogate Hotspurs	4-2
Brigg Town v Winterton Rangers	3-2
David Brown Athletic v Ossett Town	0-11
Farsley Celtic v Liversedge	6-0
Frickley Colliery v Brodsworth Main Colliery	4-3
Hessle Old Boys (Hull) v Meltham Mills	2-3
New Waltham v Luddington (Scunthorpe)	3-1
Thorne Colliery v Barton Town (1)	2-0
12 Heanor Athletic v Linby Colliery	0-1
Rufford Colliery v Raleigh Athletic	0-2

1948/49

14	Arlesey Town v Bedford Avenue	5-2
	St Neots St Mary v Baldock Town	0-4
	Wolverton Town v Luton Amateur	1-5
17	Brentwood & Warley v Hoffmann Athletic (Chelmsford)	8-0
	Brightlingsea United v Harwich & Parkeston	1-3
	Clacton Town v Briggs Sports	1-0
	Clapton v Chingford Town	0-1
	Dagenham British Legion v Colchester Casuals	3-2
	Eton Manor v London Transport	5-0
	Harlow Town v Bishop's Stortford	1-4
	Romford (2) v Ford Sports (Dagenham)	5-0
	Tilbury v Rainham Town	2-0
	Upminster v Sawbridgeworth	2-2e
	Woodford Town (1) v Saffron Walden Town	6-1
18	Acton Town v Wingate	1-8
	Edmonton Borough v Finchley	0-2
	Enfield v Civil Service	8-0
	Lyons Club (Greenford) v Wood Green Town	3-1
	Pinner v Hoddesdon Town	0-7
	Polytechnic v Ware	1-0
	Ruislip Manor v Tufnell Park	6-2e
	Ruislip Town v Stevenage Town	2-4e
	St Albans City v De Havilland Vampires	5-0
	Welwyn Garden City v Hendon	0-3
	Willesden v Chipperfield	8-1
19	Abingdon Town v St Frideswides (Oxford)	4-3
	Aylesbury United v Pressed Steel	4-1
	Berkhamsted Town v Rickmansworth Town	3-1
	Chesham United v Hemel Hempstead Town	6-2
	Headington United v Osberton Radiator (Oxford)	4-2
	Marlow v Slough Centre	2-3
	Metal & Produce Recovery Depot v Wallingford Town	1-3
	N.A.C Athletic (Banbury) v Huntley & Palmers	2-3 N
	Oxford City v Henley Town	9-1
	Slough Town v Hayes	2-1
	Southall v Windsor & Eton	3-1e
	Uxbridge v Yiewsley	1-1e
20	Cobham v Post Office Telecoms	2-2e
	Epsom v Dorking	4-0
	McLaren Sports v Farnham Town	2-4
	Vickers Armstrong v Leatherhead	1-4
21	Ashford v Woolwich Polytechnic	2-0
	Callender Athletic v Aylesford Paper Mills	6-0
	Chatham Town v Dover	2-3
	Margate v Canterbury City	3-1
	Tonbridge v Bexley	5-0
23	Basingstoke Town v Bitterne Nomads	1-2
	Botley v Winchester City	1-3
	Dorchester Town v Hamworthy	3-2
	East Cowes Victoria v Sandown	6-1
	Pirelli General Cables v Romsey Town	2-5
	Portland United v Longfleet St Mary's	2-4
	RAOC Hilsea v Lymington	3-0
	Weymouth v Bournemouth (Ams)	8-3
24	Calne & Harris United v Peasedown MW	1-3
	Chippenham United v Radstock Town	6-1
	Devizes Town v Melksham	2-1
	Frome Town v Paulton Rovers	2-0
	Salisbury (2) v Purton	1-0
	Somerton Amateurs v Coleford Athletic	0-4
	Spencer Moulton v West End Rovers	10-3
	Swindon GWR Corinthians v Wootton Bassett Town	6-3
	Welton Rovers v Odd Down	5-1
25	Bristol Aeroplane Co. v Hoffmann Ath. (Stonehouse)	0-4
	Clevedon v Wells Amateurs	wo/s
	Gloucester City v Cinderford Town	4-0
	Hanham Athletic v Bristol St George	2-0
	Ilminster Town v Bideford	1-5
	Soundwell v Stonehouse	9-3
	Tavistock v Taunton	7-2
	Tiverton Town v Barnstaple Town	2-3
2r	Consett v Stanley United	2-1 v
17r	Sawbridgeworth v Upminster	1-2
19r	Yiewsley v Uxbridge	3-3e
20r	Post Office Telecoms v Cobham	1-6
2r2	Stanley United v Consett	3-2
19r2	Yiewsley v Uxbridge	0-3

Preliminary Round

1	Amble v Blyth Spartans	0-4
	Annfield Plain v Gosforth & Coxlodge	2-1
	Ashington v West Stanley	1-0
	Hexham Hearts v Birtley	5-0
	Newbiggin CW v North Shields	2-5
	Radcliffe Welfare United v Shankhouse	1-5
	South Hetton CW v Ferryhill Athletic	1-1
	West Auckland Town v Murton CW	0-1
2	Dawdon Colliery Welfare v Spennymoor United	1-3
	Easington CW v Eppleton CW	6-1
	Evenwood Town v Chilton Athletic	3-2
	Horden CW v East Tanfield CW	wo/s
	Jarrow v Newburn	0-3
	Shilbottle CW v South Shields (2)	1-4
	Stanley United v Silksworth CW	3-1
	Tow Law Town v Seaham Colliery Welfare	0-1
3	Billingham St John v Cargo Fleet Works	4-5
	Billingham Synthonia v Guisborough	5-1
	Bridlington Central Utd. v Whitby	4-1
	Filey Town v Whitby Albion Rangers	3-1
	South Bank St Peters v Smith's Dock	0-2
4	Appleby v Florence & Ullcoats Utd.	3-6
	Cockermouth v Moresby Welfare Centre	6-3
	Lowca v Parton United	0-1
	Milnthorpe Corinthians v Frizington United	8-2
	Moss Bay v Cleator Moor Celtic	6-2
	Netherfield (Kendal) v Kells Welfare Centre	5-1
	Penrith v Bowthorn United	9-2
	Scalegill v High Duty Alloys (Distington)	3-8
5	Atherton Collieries v Lytham	4-1
	Clitheroe v Great Harwood	5-2
	Darwen v Barnoldswick & District	2-0
	De Havilland (Bolton) v Nelson	0-1
	Leyland Motors v Chorley	1-0
	Morecambe v Fleetwood	0-1
	Rossendale United v Bacup Borough	2-0
6	Bangor City v Crossens	6-0
	Burscough v Marine	4-1
	Earle v St Helens Town	1-2
	Formby v Haydock C&B Recreation	4-2
	Llandudno v Newton YMCA	0-1
	Rhyl v Earlestown	2-1
	Stoneycroft v Prescot Cables	0-7
	Wigan Athletic v Skelmersdale United	2-1
7	Altrincham v Witton Albion	0-4
	Barnton v Fodens Motor Works	wo/s
	Hyde United v Ashton United	2-1
	Lostock Gralam v Buxton	1-4
	Macclesfield Town v Northwich Victoria	0-3
	Matlock Town v Congleton Town	3-8
	Wilmslow Albion v Port Sunlight	0-6
	Winsford United v Glossop	3-1
8	Bromsgrove Rovers v Oswestry Town	5-0
	Darlaston v Moor Green	2-1
	Halesowen Town v Cradley Heath	2-0
	Hednesford Town v Thynnes Athletic	10-0
	Hereford United v Boldmere St Michaels	6-1
	Stafford Rangers v Sutton Town (Birmingham)	2-1
	Stourbridge v Dudley Town	3-1
	Worcester City v Birmingham City Transport	4-0
9	Creswell Colliery v Sheffield	2-0
	Denaby United v Kilnhurst Colliery	1-0
	Dinnington Athletic v Beighton Miners Welfare	5-1
	Kiveton Park Colliery v Wombwell Athletic	1-1e
	Monckton Athletic v Firbeck Main Colliery	1-2
	Norton Woodseats v Grimethorpe Athletic	2-1
	Rawmarsh Welfare v Harworth Colliery Athletic	1-4
	Steel,Peech&Tozer Soc. Ser. v Hoyland Common A.	2-1
10	Bentley Colliery v South Kirkby Colliery	1-3
	Bradford United v New Waltham	8-4
	Farsley Celtic v Thorne Colliery	2-1
	Frickley Colliery v Lysaght's Sports (Scunthorpe)	4-0
	Goole Town v Brigg Town	6-3
	Pilkington Recreation v Ossett Town	2-5
	Selby Town v Laceby	4-2
	Yorkshire Amateur v Meltham Mills	2-1
11	Ibstock Penistone Rovers v Bedworth Town	1-4
	Moira United v Rugby Town (2)	8-3
	Morris Sports (Loughborough) v Hinckley Athletic	1-5
	Whitwick Colliery v Nuneaton Borough	2-0
12	Basford United v Ollerton Colliery	0-3
	Boots Athletic v Ransome & Marles	0-6
	Bourne Town v Raleigh Athletic	0-5
	Grantham v Gedling Colliery	3-1e
	Ilkeston Town (2) v Sherwood Colliery	3-0
	Linby Colliery v Stamford	3-2
	South Normanton MW v Holbeach United	5-1
	Spalding United v Boston United	2-1e
13	Northampton Amateurs v Symingtons Recreation	1-4
14	Bedford Queens Works v Stewartby Works	1-2
	Bedford Town (1) v Kempston Rovers	7-0
	Biggleswade Town v Eynesbury Rovers	3-1
	Hitchin Town v Arlesey Town	0-0e
	Leighton United v St Neots & District	2-0
	Letchworth Town v Luton Amateur	3-0
	Potton United v Waterlows (Dunstable)	2-1
	Vauxhall Motors (Luton) v Baldock Town	1-1e
15	Abbey United (Cambs) v Wisbech Town	1-1e
	Newmarket Town v Chatteris Town	9-2
	Royston Town v King's Lynn	1-6
	Sawston United v Parson Drove United	2-8
16	Gorleston v Whitton United	5-3
	Leiston v Stoke United	1-1e
	Lowestoft Town v Sheringham	6-0
	Norwich CEYMS v Cromer	2-0
	Old Grammarians (Ipswich) v Achilles (Ipswich)	1-9
	Stowmarket Corinthians v Norwich School OB Union	8-0
17	Barking v Dagenham British Legion	4-0
	Brentwood & Warley v Eton Manor	2-1
	Crittall Athletic v Upminster	2-2e
	Harwich & Parkeston v Clacton Town	2-2e
	Ilford v Chingford Town	2-3
	Leyton v Tilbury	2-0
	Romford (2) v Grays Athletic	3-0
	Woodford Town (1) v Bishop's Stortford	3-2
18	Edgware Town v Finchley	0-0e
	Harrow Town v Crown & Manor	7-1
	Hendon v Hoddesdon Town	2-1
	Lyons Club (Greenford) v Enfield	0-5
	Ruislip Manor v Wingate	4-3
	St Albans City v Polytechnic	3-0
	Stevenage Town v Leavesden	2-3
	Wealdstone v Willesden	4-0
19	Abingdon Town v Wallingford Town	2-2e
	Berkhamsted Town v Slough Town	3-1
	Chesham United v Maidenhead United	1-4
	Headington United v Banbury Spencer	1-3
	Huntley & Palmers v Aylesbury United	3-2
	Oxford City v Bicester Town	6-1
	Southall v Slough Centre	2-2e
	Uxbridge v Wycombe Wanderers	4-3e
20	Epsom v Sutton United	2-2e
	Farnham Town v Hounslow Town	2-4
	Leatherhead v Cobham	2-0
	Metropolitan Police v Camberley	7-2
	Redhill v Brookwood Hospital	11-1
	Tooting & Mitcham United v Guildford	6-1
	Walton & Hersham v Twickenham	11-1
	Woking v Carshalton Athletic	1-1e
21	Bromley v Folkestone	2-1
	Callender Athletic v Dartford	1-2
	Dover v Tonbridge	4-2
	Gravesend & Northfleet v Sittingbourne	3-1
	Lloyds (Sittingbourne) v Erith & Belvedere	5-1
	Ramsgate Athletic v Betteshanger CW	6-1
	Sheppey United v Margate	5-4e
	Whitstable v Ashford	0-1e
22	Chichester City (1) v Bexhill Town	3-5e
	Haywards Heath v Hastings & St Leonards	wo/s
	Horsham v Lancing Athletic	wo/s
	Littlehampton Town v Southwick	7-2
	Shoreham v Hove	2-1
	Worthing v Eastbourne Comrades	4-3
23	Cowes v East Cowes Victoria	1-2
	Dorchester Town v Ryde Sports	0-2
	Gosport Borough Ath. v Bournemouth Gasworks Athletic	0-1
	Longfleet St Mary's v Winchester City	4-2
	Newport (IOW) v Bitterne Nomads	4-0
	Poole Town v Romsey Town	5-3
	RAOC Hilsea v Thornycroft Athletic	2-3
	Weymouth v Andover	3-0
24	Chippenham United v Trowbridge Town	1-2
	Coleford Athletic v Clandown	1-4
	Devizes Town v Salisbury Corinthians	3-0
	Frome Town v Peasedown MW	3-7
	Swindon GWR Corinthians v Welton Rovers	2-3
	Warminster Town v Swindon Victoria	3-1
	Westbury United v Spencer Moulton	2-1
	Wilts County Mental Hospital v Salisbury (2)	0-3
25	Bideford v Oak Villa	6-0
	Dartmouth United v Clevedon	1-3
	Gloucester City v Barnstaple Town	5-2
	Hanham Athletic v Hoffmann Ath. (Stonehouse)	3-1
	Soundwell v St Austell	4-3
	Street v Tavistock	6-1
	Wells City v Newton Abbot Spurs	4-2
	Weston-Super-Mare St Johns v Glastonbury	1-1
1r	Ferryhill Athletic v South Hetton CW	1-2
9r	Wombwell Athletic v Kiveton Park Colliery	4-1
14r	Arlesey Town v Hitchin Town	2-3
r	Baldock Town v Vauxhall Motors (Luton)	2-5
15r	Wisbech Town v Abbey United (Cambs)	8-0
16r	Leiston v Stoke United	6-1
17r	Clacton Town v Harwich & Parkeston	2-3
r	Upminster v Crittall Athletic	2-0
18r	Finchley v Edgware Town	2-1
19r	Slough Centre v Southall	0-2
r	Wallingford Town v Abingdon Town	2-0
20r	Carshalton Athletic v Woking	4-7
r	Sutton United v Epsom	2-0
25r	Glastonbury v Weston-Super-Mare St Johns	9-0

Qualifying Round One

1	Annfield Plain v Shankhouse	7-1
	Blyth Spartans v Ashington	2-1
	North Shields v Hexham Hearts	0-0
	South Hetton CW v Murton CW	0-1
2	Evenwood Town v Seaham Colliery Welfare	3-1
	Horden CW v Spennymoor United	3-1
	South Shields (2) v Newburn	5-2
	Stanley United v Easington CW	3-2
3	Billingham Synthonia v Cargo Fleet Works	11-1
	Filey Town v Portrack Shamrocks	1-2
	Smith's Dock v South Bank East End	2-1
	South Bank v Bridlington Central Utd.	10-0
4	Milnthorpe Corinthians v Cockermouth	11-0
	Moss Bay v High Duty Alloys (Distington)	2-3
	Netherfield (Kendal) v Florence & Ullcoats Utd.	10-0
	Parton United v Penrith	1-3
5	Clitheroe v Horwich RMI	3-1
	Darwen v Atherton Collieries	3-2
	Fleetwood v Nelson	1-0
	Leyland Motors v Rossendale United	2-2
6	Bangor City v Burscough	4-2
	Formby v St Helens Town	0-1
	Newton YMCA v Rhyl	1-4
	Wigan Athletic v Prescot Cables	1-2
7	Barnton v Hyde United	0-2
	Congleton Town v Winsford United	2-2
	Northwich Victoria v Port Sunlight	5-0
	Witton Albion v Buxton	3-0
8	Bromsgrove Rovers v Stourbridge	3-2
	Hednesford Town v Worcester City	4-2
	Hereford United v Halesowen Town	2-0
	Stafford Rangers v Darlaston	4-3
9	Denaby United v Wombwell Athletic	3-1
	Dinnington Athletic v Creswell Colliery	3-2
	Harworth Col. Ath. v Steel,Peech&Tozer Soc. Serv.	2-0
	Norton Woodseats v Firbeck Main Colliery	2-1
10	Frickley Colliery v South Kirkby Colliery	3-0
	Goole Town v Bradford United	4-2
	Ossett Town v Farsley Celtic	3-2
	Yorkshire Amateur v Selby Town	0-4
11	Bedworth Town v Whitwick Colliery	1-3

1948/49

	Coalville Town (3) v Brush Sports	0-4
	Gresley Rovers v Hinckley Athletic	4-3e
	Tamworth v Moira United	6-2
12	Grantham v Raleigh Athletic	6-0
	Ilkeston Town (2) v Linby Colliery	0-3
	Ransome & Marles v Ollerton Colliery	2-0
	South Normanton MW v Spalding United	1-3
13	Desborough Town v Peterbro' Westwood Works	wo/s
	Kettering Town v Rushden Town	2-2
	Peterborough United v Symingtons Recreation	4-0
	Wellingborough Town v Stewarts & Lloyds	1-0
14	Bedford Town (1) v Vauxhall Motors (Luton)	1-2
	Biggleswade Town v Letchworth Town	4-4e
	Hitchin Town v Leighton United	4-2
	Stewartby Works v Potton United	1-6
15	Histon Institute v March Town	2-1
	King's Lynn v Bury Town	7-0
	Parson Drove United v Newmarket Town	3-2
	Wisbech Town v Cambridge Town	4-4e
16	Gothic (Norwich) v Leiston	5-2
	Great Yarmouth Town v Stowmarket Corinthians	3-2
	Lowestoft Town v Gorleston	3-1
	Norwich CEYMS v Achilles (Ipswich)	3-4
17	Barking v Harwich & Parkeston	2-1
	Brentwood & Warley v Woodford Town (1)	5-0
	Leyton v Chingford Town	3-2
	Romford (2) v Upminster	2-1
18	Finchley v Hendon	1-2
	Leavesden v St Albans City	1-4
	Ruislip Manor v Enfield	3-5
	Wealdstone v Harrow Town	2-1
19	Berkhamsted Town v Banbury Spencer	1-2
	Oxford City v Huntley & Palmers	2-1e
	Uxbridge v Southall	1-0
	Wallingford Town v Maidenhead United	1-3
20	Hounslow Town v Tooting & Mitcham United	1-3
	Leatherhead v Sutton United	0-2
	Metropolitan Police v Woking	0-2
	Walton & Hersham v Redhill	1-2
21	Gravesend & Northfleet v Bromley	4-1
	Lloyds (Sittingbourne) v Dartford	1-2
	Ramsgate Athletic v Ashford	4-0
	Sheppey United v Dover	2-4
22	Bexhill Town v Shoreham	5-1
	Bognor Regis Town v Littlehampton Town	3-0
	Haywards Heath v Horsham	0-1
	Worthing v East Grinstead	2-0
23	East Cowes Victoria v Bournemouth Gasworks Athletic	3-1
	Longfleet St Mary's v Thornycroft Athletic	4-0
	Newport (IOW) v Weymouth	2-4
	Ryde Sports v Poole Town	0-1
24	Clandown v Welton Rovers	2-1
	Salisbury (2) v Peasedown MW	3-2
	Trowbridge Town v Warminster Town	4-1
	Westbury United v Devizes Town	3-2
25	Glastonbury v Soundwell	4-3
	Gloucester City v Clevedon	8-2
	Hanham Athletic v Wells City	4-3
	Street v Bideford	4-1
26	Barry Town v Ebbw Vale	4-1
	Llanelli v Cardiff Corinthians	1-1
	Merthyr Tydfil - Bye	
	Troedryhiw v Lovells Athletic	1-2
1r	Hexham Hearts v North Shields	1-2
5r	Rossendale United v Leyland Motors	4-2
7r	Winsford United v Congleton Town	2-0
13r	Rushden Town v Kettering Town	0-1
14r	Letchworth Town v Biggleswade Town	3-3e
15r	Cambridge Town v Wisbech Town	5-2
26r	Cardiff Corinthians v Llanelli	0-2
14r2	Letchworth Town v Biggleswade Town	0-4

Qualifying Round Two

1	Blyth Spartans v North Shields	2-1
	Murton CW v Annfield Plain	1-2
2	Evenwood Town v Horden CW	1-2
	Stanley United v South Shields (2)	2-3ed
3	Smith's Dock v Billingham Synthonia	2-5
	South Bank v Portrack Shamrocks	1-3
4	High Duty Alloys (Distington) v Penrith	4-4
	Netherfield (Kendal) v Milnthorpe Corinthians	9-2
5	Clitheroe v Fleetwood	0-3
	Rossendale United v Darwen	4-0
6	Rhyl v Prescot Cables	2-1
	St Helens Town v Bangor City	0-4
7	Northwich Victoria v Witton Albion	1-3
	Winsford United v Hyde United	4-0
8	Bromsgrove Rovers v Hednesford Town	8-3
	Stafford Rangers v Hereford United	3-5
9	Harworth Colliery Athletic v Denaby United	2-0e
	Norton Woodseats v Dinnington Athletic	2-1
10	Frickley Colliery v Goole Town	3-1
	Ossett Town v Selby Town	1-4
11	Brush Sports v Tamworth	4-3
	Gresley Rovers v Whitwick Colliery	0-3
12	Linby Colliery v Grantham	1-2
	Spalding United v Ransome & Marles	0-1
13	Kettering Town v Desborough Town	2-2
	Wellingborough Town v Peterborough United	2-3
14	Biggleswade Town v Vauxhall Motors (Luton)	1-4
	Potton United v Hitchin Town	1-1e
15	Histon Institute v King's Lynn	3-4
	Parson Drove United v Cambridge Town	1-3
16	Gothic (Norwich) v Achilles (Ipswich)	4-0
	Great Yarmouth Town v Lowestoft Town	2-0
17	Barking v Leyton	3-0
	Romford (2) v Brentwood & Warley	3-1
18	Hendon v Enfield	3-0
	St Albans City v Wealdstone	0-5
19	Banbury Spencer v Uxbridge	3-1
	Oxford City v Maidenhead United	8-0
20	Redhill v Woking	4-3
	Sutton United v Tooting & Mitcham United	0-1
21	Dartford v Ramsgate Athletic	2-0
	Gravesend & Northfleet v Dover	4-1
22	Horsham v Bexhill Town	4-0
	Worthing v Bognor Regis Town	1-4
23	East Cowes Victoria v Poole Town	1-2
	Longfleet St Mary's v Weymouth	0-4
24	Trowbridge Town v Salisbury (2)	4-1
	Westbury United v Clandown	0-0
25	Glastonbury v Gloucester City	1-1
	Hanham Athletic v Street	2-5
26	Barry Town v Llanelli	3-1
	Lovells Athletic v Merthyr Tydfil	3-1
4r	Penrith v High Duty Alloys (Distington)	3-2
13r	Desborough Town v Kettering Town	0-3
14r	Hitchin Town v Potton United	3-1
24r	Clandown v Westbury United	1-2
25r	Gloucester City v Glastonbury	3-1

Qualifying Round Three

1	Blyth Spartans v Annfield Plain	0-2
2	Stanley United v Horden CW	1-3
3	Billingham Synthonia v Portrack Shamrocks	5-0
4	Netherfield (Kendal) v Penrith	2-1
5	Fleetwood v Rossendale United	0-1
6	Bangor City v Rhyl	0-2
7	Winsford United v Witton Albion	0-1
8	Bromsgrove Rovers v Hereford United	2-4
9	Harworth Colliery Athletic v Norton Woodseats	1-6
10	Selby Town v Frickley Colliery	2-0
11	Whitwick Colliery v Brush Sports	1-2
12	Ransome & Marles v Grantham	2-0
13	Peterborough United v Kettering Town	2-1
14	Vauxhall Motors (Luton) v Hitchin Town	2-1
15	King's Lynn v Cambridge Town	4-5e
16	Gothic (Norwich) v Great Yarmouth Town	3-2
17	Romford (2) v Barking	3-2
18	Hendon v Wealdstone	4-2e
19	Banbury Spencer v Oxford City	2-3
20	Tooting & Mitcham United v Redhill	5-1
21	Gravesend & Northfleet v Dartford	0-1
22	Horsham v Bognor Regis Town	1-2
23	Weymouth v Poole Town	4-2
24	Trowbridge Town v Westbury United	8-0
25	Gloucester City v Street	4-1
26	Barry Town v Lovells Athletic	1-3

Qualifying Round Four

	Barnet v Hendon	5-4e
	Bath City v Gloucester City	2-3
	Billingham Synthonia v Annfield Plain	2-1
	Bognor Regis Town v Dulwich Hamlet	1-8
	Cambridge Town v Gothic (Norwich)	6-1
	Guildford City v Chelmsford City	0-2e
	Hereford United v Oxford City	4-3e
	Kidderminster Harriers v Brush Sports	5-2
	Lovells Athletic v Yeovil Town	2-3
	Netherfield (Kendal) v Rossendale United	3-1
	Norton Woodseats v Gainsborough Trinity	2-4e
	Peterborough United v Ransome & Marles	3-1
	Rhyl v South Liverpool	3-0
	Romford (2) v Gillingham	2-1e
	Runcorn v Stalybridge Celtic	3-1
	Scarborough v Bishop Auckland	3-0 v
	Scunthorpe United v Selby Town	2-1
	Stockton v Horden CW	1-2
	Tooting & Mitcham United v Kingstonian	1-1e
	Vauxhall Motors (Luton) v Walthamstow Avenue	0-2
	Wellington Town v Cheltenham Town	2-1
	Weymouth v Trowbridge Town	2-0e
	Wimbledon v Dartford	1-2
	Witton Albion v Shrewsbury Town	4-0
	Workington v Lancaster City	1-1e
r	Bishop Auckland v Scarborough	0-3
r	Kingstonian v Tooting & Mitcham United	2-4
r	Lancaster City v Workington	2-2e
r2	Workington v Lancaster City	2-1 N

Round One

	Barnet v Exeter City	2-6
	Bradford City v Doncaster Rovers	4-3
	Colchester United v Reading	2-4
	Crewe Alexandra v Billingham Synthonia	5-0
	Crystal Palace v Bristol City	0-1e
	Dartford v Leyton Orient	2-3
	Gainsborough Trinity v Witton Albion	1-0
	Gateshead v Netherfield (Kendal)	3-0
	Halifax Town v Scunthorpe United	0-0e
	Hartlepools United v Chester	1-3
	Hull City v Accrington Stanley	3-1
	Ipswich Town v Aldershot	0-3
	Kidderminster Harriers v Hereford United	0-3
	Leytonstone v Watford	2-1
	Mansfield Town v Gloucester City	4-0
	Millwall v Tooting & Mitcham United	1-0
	New Brighton v Carlisle United	1-0
	Newport County v Brighton & Hove Albion	3-1
	Northampton Town v Dulwich Hamlet	2-1
	Norwich City v Wellington Town	1-0
	Notts County v Port Vale	2-1
	Peterborough United v Torquay United	0-1
	Rhyl v Scarborough	0-2
	Rochdale v Barrow	1-1eN
	Southend United v Swansea Town	1-2e
	Southport v Horden CW	2-1
	Tranmere Rovers v Darlington	1-3
	Walsall v Bristol Rovers	2-1
	Walthamstow Avenue v Cambridge Town	3-2
	Weymouth v Chelmsford City	2-1
	Workington v Stockport County	0-3
	Wrexham v Oldham Athletic	0-3
	Yeovil Town v Romford (2)	4-0
	York City v Runcorn	2-1
r	Barrow v Rochdale	2-0
r	Scunthorpe United v Halifax Town	1-0

Round Two

	Aldershot v Chester	1-0
	Bradford City v New Brighton	0-0
	Bristol City v Swansea Town	3-1
	Crewe Alexandra v Millwall	3-2
	Darlington v Leyton Orient	1-0
	Exeter City v Hereford United	2-1
	Gateshead v Scarborough	3-0
	Hull City v Reading	0-0e
	Leytonstone v Newport County	3-4e
	Mansfield Town v Northampton Town	2-1e
	Notts County v Barrow	3-2
	Scunthorpe United v Stockport County	0-1
	Southport v York City	2-2e
	Torquay United v Norwich City	3-1
	Walsall v Gainsborough Trinity	4-3
	Walthamstow Avenue v Oldham Athletic	2-2e
	Weymouth v Yeovil Town	0-4
r	New Brighton v Bradford City	1-0
r	Oldham Athletic v Walthamstow Avenue	3-1
r	Reading v Hull City	1-2
r	York City v Southport	0-2

Round Three

	Arsenal v Tottenham Hotspur	3-0
	Aston Villa v Bolton Wanderers	1-1e
	Barnsley v Blackpool	0-1
	Birmingham City v Leicester City	1-1e
	Blackburn Rovers v Hull City	1-2e
	Brentford v Middlesbrough	3-2e
	Bristol City v Chelsea	1-3
	Burnley v Charlton Athletic	2-1e
	Crewe Alexandra v Sunderland	0-2
	Derby County v Southport	4-1
	Everton v Manchester City	1-0
	Fulham v Walsall	0-1e
	Gateshead v Aldershot	3-1
	Grimsby Town v Exeter City	2-1
	Leeds United v Newport County	1-3
	Lincoln City v West Bromwich Albion	0-1
	Luton Town v West Ham United	3-1
	Manchester United v Bournemouth	6-0
	Newcastle United v Bradford Park Avenue	0-2
	Nottingham Forest v Liverpool	2-2e
	Oldham Athletic v Cardiff City	2-3
	Plymouth Argyle v Notts County	0-1e
	Portsmouth v Stockport County	7-0
	Preston North End v Mansfield Town	2-1
	Queen's Park Rangers v Huddersfield Town	0-0e
	Rotherham United v Darlington	4-2
	Sheffield United v New Brighton	5-2
	Sheffield Wednesday v Southampton	2-1
	Swindon Town v Stoke City	1-3
	Torquay United v Coventry City	1-0
	Wolverhampton Wan. v Chesterfield	6-0
	Yeovil Town v Bury	3-1
r	Bolton Wanderers v Aston Villa	0-0e
r	Huddersfield Town v Queen's Park Rangers	5-0
r	Leicester City v Birmingham City	1-1e
r	Liverpool v Nottingham Forest	4-0
r2	Aston Villa v Bolton Wanderers	2-1e
r2	Birmingham City v Leicester City	1-2

Round Four

	Aston Villa v Cardiff City	1-2
	Brentford v Torquay United	1-0
	Chelsea v Everton	2-0
	Derby County v Arsenal	1-0
	Gateshead v West Bromwich Albion	1-3e
	Grimsby Town v Hull City	2-3
	Leicester City v Preston North End	2-0
	Liverpool v Notts County	1-0
	Luton Town v Walsall	4-0
	Manchester United v Bradford Park Avenue	1-1e
	Newport County v Huddersfield Town	3-3e
	Portsmouth v Sheffield Wednesday	2-1
	Rotherham United v Burnley	0-1
	Sheffield United v Wolverhampton Wan.	0-3
	Stoke City v Blackpool	1-1e

1948/49 to 1949/50

	Yeovil Town v Sunderland	2-1e
r	Blackpool v Stoke City	0-1
r	Bradford Park Avenue v Manchester United	1-1e
r	Huddersfield Town v Newport County	1-3
r2	Manchester United v Bradford Park Avenue	5-0

Round Five

	Brentford v Burnley	4-2
	Derby County v Cardiff City	2-1
	Luton Town v Leicester City	5-5e
	Manchester United v Yeovil Town	8-0
	Portsmouth v Newport County	3-2e
	Stoke City v Hull City	0-2
	West Bromwich Albion v Chelsea	3-0
	Wolverhampton Wan. v Liverpool	3-1
r	Leicester City v Luton Town	5-3

Round Six

	Brentford v Leicester City	0-2
	Hull City v Manchester United	0-1
	Portsmouth v Derby County	2-1
	Wolverhampton Wan. v West Bromwich Albion	1-0

Semi Finals

	Leicester City v Portsmouth	3-1 N
	Manchester United v Wolverhampton Wan.	1-1eN
r	Manchester United v Wolverhampton Wan.	0-1 N

Final

	Wolverhampton Wan. v Leicester City	3-1 N

1949/50

Extra Preliminary Round

1	Amble v Newbiggin CW	0-2
	Ashington v Wardley Welfare	5-2
	Birtley v Heaton Stannington	2-2
	Cramlington Welfare v West Sleekburn Welfare	3-1
	Lynemouth Welfare v Jarrow	6-2
	Shankhouse v Newburn	1-4
	Shilbottle CW v Gosforth & Coxlodge	2-3
	Usworth Colliery v Boldon CW	0-2
2	Blackhall Colliery Welfare v Tow Law Town	1-0
	Chilton Athletic v Langley Park CW	4-1
	Dawdon Colliery Welfare v Crook CW	0-1
	Eppleton CW v Consett	2-3
	Shotton CW v Spennymoor United	2-2
	Silksworth CW v Cockfield	1-0
	Willington v Seaham United	8-0
6	Bootle Athletic v Stoneycroft	5-1
	Earlestown v Crossens	2-1
	Haydock C&B Recreation v Prescot B.I.C.C	5-2
	Hoylake Athletic v Southport Leyland Road	9-5
	Marine v Formby	1-0
	Newton YMCA v Earle	3-4
	Wigan Athletic v UGB St Helens	2-0
7	Barnton v Knutsford	1-1
	Congleton Town v Wilmslow Albion	8-2
	Ellesmere Port Town v Buxton	2-3
	Matlock Town v Port Sunlight	0-2
	Mossley v Ashton United	2-1
	Shell (Ellesmere Port) v Atherton Collieries	5-1
	Stork v Droylsden United	2-5
8	Bilston v Oswestry Town	1-0
	Bournville Athletic v Cradley Heath	1-6
	Moor Green v Boldmere St Michaels	3-2
	Sutton Town (Birmingham) v Halesowen Town	3-0
	Thynnes Athletic v Darlaston	0-6
9	Bolsover Colliery v Kiveton Park Colliery	2-1
	Creswell Colliery v Maltby Main Colliery	3-0
	Parkhouse Colliery v Jump Home Guard	6-0
	Steel, Peech & Tozer Social Ser. v Rawmarsh Welfare	1-4
	Stocksbridge Works v Wombwell Athletic	4-1
10	Appleby Frodingham v Brigg Town	1-1
	Armthorpe Welfare v Farsley Celtic	4-5
	Bentley Colliery v Upton Colliery	9-1
	Brodsworth Main Colliery v Meltham	3-2
	Brunswick Institute v Ferrybridge Amateur	7-3
	Lysaght's Sports (Scunthorpe) v Thorne Colliery	3-1
	Pilkington Recreation v Laceby	2-1
	Winterton Rangers v Ashby Institute	1-4
12	Alford United v Skegness Town	6-4
	Basford United v Stanton Ironworks	0-1
	Boots Athletic v Measham Imperial	1-2
	Boston United v Holbeach United	7-0
	Bourne Town v Rufford Colliery	5-3
	Cinderhill Colliery v Heanor Athletic	0-7
	Ilkeston Town (2) v Sutton Town	2-3
	Langold WMC v Raleigh Athletic	3-3
	Ollerton Colliery v Gedling Colliery	0-4
	Parliament Street Methodists v Teversal & Silverhill	2-5
	South Normanton MW v Sherwood Colliery	3-0
	Spalding United v Stamford	1-0
	Worksop Town v Bestwood Colliery	2-1
14	Arlesey Town v Huntingdon United	4-5
	Bedford Avenue v Bedford St Cuthberts	1-1
	Bedford Corinthians v Houghton Rangers	1-4
	Potton United v Luton Amateur	1-2e
17	Briggs Sports v Crittall Athletic	7-0
	Clapton v Brightlingsea United	4-0
	Eton Manor v Clacton Town	2-1
	Harwich & Parkeston v Chingford Town	4-2
	Rainham Town v Woodford Town (1)	2-1
	Saffron Walden Town v Colchester Casuals	2-3
	Sawbridgeworth v Tilbury	0-6
	Stansted v Grays Athletic	0-5
18	Crown & Manor v Tufnell Park	2-1
	Edgware Town v Hoddesdon Town	1-1
	Harrow Town v Wingate	0-2
	Hatfield Town v Ruislip Town	6-2
	Hertford Town v Finchley	3-5
	Lyons Club (Greenford) v Pinner	3-2
	Ruislip Manor v Acton Town	4-2
	Stevenage Town v Willesden	2-2
	Wembley v Ware	2-2e
	Wood Green Town v Polytechnic	1-0
19	Aylesbury United v Bicester Town	5-2
	Chesham United v Dickinsons (Apsley)	3-0
	Headington United v Huntley & Palmers	9-4
	Hemel Hempstead Town v Marlow	6-0
	Henley Town v Pressed Steel	4-2
	Osberton Radiator (Oxford) v Abingdon Town	5-0
	Rickmansworth Town v Yiewsley	2-2
	Slough Town v Slough Centre	1-0
	Southall v Berkhamsted Town	1-0
	Windsor & Eton v Hayes	2-3
20	Epsom v Guildford	6-0
	Leatherhead v Hounslow Town	2-6
	McLaren Sports v Camberley	3-1
21	Callender Athletic v Folkestone	0-7
	Margate v Faversham Town	1-3
	Sheppey United v Ashford	1-0
	Sittingbourne v Erith & Belvedere	0-2
	Snowdown CW v Whitstable	2-1
23	Bournemouth (Ams) v Bournemouth Gasworks Athletic	1-0
	Cowes v Lymington	4-0
	Dorchester Town v Blandford United	2-1
	Hamworthy v Portland United	0-1
	Ryde Sports v Andover	1-0
	Thornycroft Athletic v Sandown	5-0
	Totton v Basingstoke Town	3-0
	Winchester City v Newport (IOW)	1-2
24	Chippenham Town v Timsbury Athletic	7-0
	Coleford Athletic v Swindon Victoria	2-5
	Frome Town v Chippenham United	1-3
	Spencer Moulton v Devizes Town	1-3
	Swindon GWR Corinthians v Calne & Harris United	3-2
	Wootton Bassett Town v Warminster Town	4-5
26	Llanelli v Hoffmann Ath. (Stonehouse)	6-1
	St Philips Marsh Adult School v Mount Hill Enterpris	1-2
1r	Heaton Stannington v Birtley	2-2
2r	Spennymoor United v Shotton CW	4-2
7r	Knutsford v Barnton	2-1
10r	Brigg Town v Appleby Frodingham	4-1
12r	Raleigh Athletic v Langold WMC	0-2
14r	Bedford St Cuthberts v Bedford Avenue	0-0e
18r	Edgware Town v Hoddesdon Town	3-0
r	Ware v Wembley	2-2
r	Willesden v Stevenage Town	7-2
19r	Yiewsley v Rickmansworth Town	2-0
1r2	Heaton Stannington v Birtley	4-3
14r2	Bedford Avenue v Bedford St Cuthberts	3-2e
18r2	Wembley v Ware	1-5 N

Preliminary Round

1	Alnwick Town v Ashington	2-4
	Blyth Spartans v Annfield Plain	3-0
	Boldon CW v Heaton Stannington	1-2
	Morpeth Town v Gosforth & Coxlodge	2-2
	Newbiggin CW v Cramlington Welfare	3-0
	North Shields v Newburn	7-0
	South Shields (2) v Lynemouth Welfare	9-2
	West Stanley v Hexham Hearts	0-0
2	Blackhall Colliery Welfare v Consett	1-4
	Crook CW v Easington CW	3-6
	Evenwood Town v Stanley United	5-1
	Horden CW v Ferryhill Athletic	8-4
	Seaham Colliery Welfare v Shildon	1-1
	Silksworth CW v West Auckland Town	3-3
	South Hetton CW v Chilton Athletic	5-1
	Willington v Spennymoor United	2-2
3	Bridlington Central Utd. v Cargo Fleet Works	8-0
	South Bank East End v Whitby	2-5
4	Aspatria Spartans v Cleator Moor Celtic	3-1
	Cockermouth v Bowthorn United	8-2
	Scalegill v Florence & Ullcoats Utd.	6-4
5	Barnoldswick & District v Nelson	1-3
	Chorley v De Havilland (Bolton)	5-0
	Clitheroe v Lytham	4-2
	Fleetwood v Galgate	5-3
	Great Harwood v Bacup Borough	1-1
	Morecambe v Leyland Motors	4-5
	Rossendale United v Horwich RMI	5-2
6	Bootle Athletic v Earlestown	5-1
	Burscough v Marine	2-1
	Earle v Orrell	wo/s
	Haydock C&B Recreation v Bangor City	1-2
	Hoylake Athletic v St Helens Town	0-3
	Prescot Cables v Skelmersdale United	3-0
	Rhyl v Llandudno	2-0
	South Liverpool v Wigan Athletic	0-1
7	Altrincham v Mossley	2-3
	Congleton Town v Shell (Ellesmere Port)	6-3
	Droylsden United v Nantwich	10-1
	Glossop v Hyde United	1-2
	Knutsford v Northwich Victoria	0-9
	Lostock Gralam v Buxton	1-2
	Macclesfield Town v Port Sunlight	3-2
	Winsford United v Wheelock Albion	9-1
8	Bilston v Darlaston	2-1
	Birmingham City Transport v Cradley Heath	1-5
	Hednesford Town v Dudley Town	0-1
	Lye Town v Brierley Hill Alliance	2-0
	Moor Green v Bromsgrove Rovers	2-2
	Stafford Rangers v Worcester City	3-0
	Stourbridge v Kidderminster Harriers	0-0
	Sutton Town (Birmingham) v Staffordshire Casuals	4-0
9	Beighton Miners Welfare v Grimethorpe Athletic	5-1
	Bolsover Colliery v Creswell Colliery	4-5
	Denaby United v Sheffield	3-1
	Firbeck Main Colliery v Staveley Welfare	2-3
	Harworth Colliery Athletic v Stocksbridge Works	2-2
	Hoyland Common Athletic v Kilnhurst Colliery	2-1
	Norton Woodseats v Dinnington Athletic	3-1
	Rawmarsh Welfare v Parkhouse Colliery	6-3
10	Bentley Colliery v Ashby Institute	3-1
	Brodsworth Main Colliery v South Kirkby Colliery	2-0
	Brunswick Institute v Farsley Celtic	0-3
	Frickley Colliery v Yorkshire Amateur	1-0
	Goole Town v Barton Town (1)	5-1
	Luddington (Scunthorpe) v Brigg Town	1-7
	Ossett Town v Pilkington Recreation	7-0
	Selby Town v Lysaght's Sports (Scunthorpe)	5-0
11	Barwell Athletic v Coalville Town (3)	3-0
	Bedworth Town v Nuneaton Borough	1-3
	Hinckley Athletic v Morris Sports (Loughborough)	11-0
	Ibstock Penistone Rovers v Tamworth	0-2
	Rugby Town (2) v Moira United	2-3
	Shepshed Albion v Atherstone Town	0-0
12	Alford United v Bourne Town	3-3
	Boston United v Teversal & Silverhill CW	2-1
	Gedling Colliery v Langold WMC	2-0
	Linby Colliery v Grantham	1-2
	South Normanton MW v Worksop Town	1-1
	Spalding United v Heanor Athletic	3-2
	Stanton Ironworks v Ransome & Marles	3-5
	Sutton Town v Measham Imperial	3-2
13	Corby Town v Rothwell Town	7-1
14	Baldock Town v Leighton United	2-0
	Bedford Town (1) v Kempston Rovers	2-0
	Eynesbury Rovers v Wolverton Town & BR	2-1
	Hitchin Town v Houghton Rangers	5-0
	Huntingdon United v Bedford Avenue	4-2
	Letchworth Town v St Neots St Mary	8-1
	St Neots & District v Vauxhall Motors (Luton)	3-2
	Stewartby Works v Luton Amateur	3-6
15	Abbey United (Cambs) v Wisbech Town	2-1
	March Town v Parson Drove United	4-0
	Newmarket Town v Chatteris Town	4-4
	Royston Town v Bury Town	0-6
	South Lynn v Wimblington Old Boys	4-0
16	Felixstowe United v Norwich School Old Boys Union	0-5
	Gorleston v Holt United	4-1
	Great Yarmouth Town v Cromer	1-1
	Leiston v Achilles (Ipswich)	0-5
	Sheringham v Stowmarket Corinthians	0-1
	Whitton United v Churchmans Sports (Ipswich)	3-0
17	Barking v Eton Manor	1-1
	Briggs Sports v Dagenham British Legion	10-1
	Clapton v Harlow Town	7-1
	Grays Athletic v Colchester Casuals	5-1
	Harwich & Parkeston v Brentwood & Warley	4-2
	Ilford v Ford Sports (Dagenham)	4-1
	Rainham Town v Upminster	1-2
	Tilbury v Leyton	2-2
18	Civil Service v Hatfield Town	0-3
	Finchley v Enfield	0-2
	Hendon v Wealdstone	0-4
	Lyons Club (Greenford) v Crown & Manor	0-4
	Ruislip Manor v St Albans City	1-2
	Welwyn Garden City v Edgware Town	0-2
	Wingate v Ware	1-5
	Wood Green Town v Willesden	0-1
19	Hayes v Banbury Spencer	1-0
	Hemel Hempstead Town v Headington United	3-1
	Henley Town v Yiewsley	0-3
	Maidenhead United v Osberton Radiator (Oxford)	1-1
	Oxford City v N.A.C Athletic (Banbury)	5-2
	Slough Town v Aylesbury United	3-2
	Southall v Wycombe Wanderers	6-2
	Uxbridge v Chesham United	2-0
20	Epsom v Cobham	4-2
	Hounslow Town v Wimbledon	2-2
	Redhill v Dorking	7-3
	Sutton United v Kingstonian	0-1
	Tooting & Mitcham United v Farnham Town	4-0
	Vickers Armstrong v McLaren Sports	7-2
	Walton & Hersham v Carshalton Athletic	2-2
	Woking v Metropolitan Police	1-0
21	Aylesford Paper Mills v Bowater Lloyds	1-10
	Canterbury City v Chatham Town	2-1
	Dover v Bexley	7-2
	Faversham Town v Erith & Belvedere	0-1
	Folkestone v Snowdown CW	1-1
	Gravesend & Northfleet v Sheppey United	4-0
	Ramsgate Athletic v Betteshanger CW	6-0

1949/50

	Tonbridge v Woolwich Polytechnic	3-1
22	Bexhill Town v Littlehampton Town	3-4
	Chichester City (1) v Eastbourne Comrades	2-2
	Hastings United v Shoreham	3-0
	Haywards Heath v East Grinstead	5-1
	Hove v Newhaven	3-2
23	Bournemouth (Ams) v Thornycroft Athletic	5-2
	East Cowes Victoria v Gosport Borough Ath.	4-1
	Longfleet St Mary's v Portland United	0-1
	Pirelli General Cables v Cowes	3-4
	Poole Town v RAOC Hilsea	9-1
	Romsey Town v Dorchester Town	1-4
	Ryde Sports v Newport (IOW)	1-1
	Weymouth v Totton	6-3
24	Bath City v Roundway Hospital (Devizes)	7-1
	Clandown v Peasedown MW	3-1
	Devizes Town v Chippenham Town	4-4
	Melksham v Swindon GWR Corinthians	2-1
	Paulton Rovers v Purton	4-0
	Salisbury (2) v Warminster Town	8-0
	Swindon Victoria v Trowbridge Town	0-7
	Westbury United v Chippenham United	1-2
25	Bideford v Newton Abbot Spurs	1-1
	Bridgwater Town (1) v Taunton	1-1
	Glastonbury v Wells City	1-4
	Ilminster Town v Street	4-1
	St Austell v Oak Villa	4-1
	Tavistock v Barnstaple Town	0-4
	Tiverton Town v Dartmouth United	2-2
	Truro City v Ilfracombe Town	2-6
26	Barry Town v Soundwell	3-1
	Cardiff Corinthians v Mount Hill Enterprise	0-1
	Clevedon v Hanham Athletic	2-1
	Llanelli v Stonehouse	4-1
	Merthyr Tydfil v Ebbw Vale	5-1
	Troedryhiw v Bristol Aeroplane Co.	3-0
	Weston-Super-Mare v Gloucester City	2-3
	Weston-Super-Mare St Johns v Lovells Athletic	2-7
1r	Gosforth & Coxlodge v Morpeth Town	3-1
r	Hexham Hearts v West Stanley	2-1
2r	Shildon v Seaham Colliery Welfare	2-3
r	Spennymoor United v Willington	2-4
r	West Auckland Town v Silksworth CW	2-5
5r	Bacup Borough v Great Harwood	5-1
8r	Bromsgrove Rovers v Moor Green	4-1
r	Kidderminster Harriers v Stourbridge	2-3
9r	Stocksbridge Works v Harworth Colliery Athletic	8-4
11r	Atherstone Town v Shepshed Albion	8-2
12r	Bourne Town v Alford United	5-3
r	Worksop Town v South Normanton MW	1-2
15r	Chatteris Town v Newmarket Town	1-4
16r	Cromer v Great Yarmouth Town	3-4
17r	Barking v Eton Manor	5-3
r	Leyton v Tilbury	2-3
19r	Osberton Radiator (Oxford) v Maidenhead United	1-0e
20r	Carshalton Athletic v Walton & Hersham	0-8
r	Wimbledon v Hounslow Town	5-0
21r	Snowdown CW v Folkestone	1-1
22r	Eastbourne Comrades v Chichester City (1)	6-0
23r	Newport (IOW) v Ryde Sports	3-5
24r	Chippenham Town v Devizes Town	4-3
25r	Dartmouth United v Tiverton Town	2-0
r	Newton Abbot Spurs v Bideford	2-4
r	Taunton v Bridgwater Town (1)	1-3
21r2	Folkestone v Snowdown CW	1-2eN

Qualifying Round One

1	Ashington v Heaton Stannington	2-3
	Gosforth & Coxlodge v Blyth Spartans	0-4
	North Shields v Newbiggin CW	3-0
	South Shields (2) v Hexham Hearts	3-1
2	Evenwood Town v Consett	1-4
	Seaham Colliery Welfare v Easington CW	1-1
	Silksworth CW v South Hetton CW	0-0
	Willington v Horden CW	2-2
3	Portrack Shamrocks v Bridlington Central Utd.	1-0
	South Bank St Peters v Filey Town	4-2
	Whitby v Billingham Synthonia	2-2
	Whitby Albion Rangers v South Bank	1-2
4	Aspatria Spartans v Milnthorpe Corinthians	6-1
	Cockermouth v Kells Welfare Centre	1-3
	Penrith v Netherfield (Kendal)	2-3
	Scalegill v High Duty Alloys (Distington)	wo/s
5	Chorley v Bacup Borough	3-1
	Darwen v Nelson	0-5
	Fleetwood v Clitheroe	3-0
	Rossendale United v Leyland Motors	5-1
6	Bootle Athletic v Prescot Cables	2-1
	Earle v Rhyl	1-3
	St Helens Town v Bangor City	0-3
	Wigan Athletic v Burscough	1-1
7	Buxton v Hyde United	3-0
	Macclesfield Town v Congleton Town	1-2
	Mossley v Northwich Victoria	3-2
	Winsford United v Droylsden United	2-3
8	Bromsgrove Rovers v Bilston	2-1
	Cradley Heath v Lye Town	1-0
	Dudley Town v Sutton Town (Birmingham)	0-0
	Stourbridge v Stafford Rangers	0-3
9	Denaby United v Beighton Miners Welfare	0-2
	Hoyland Common Athletic v Creswell Colliery	1-1
	Rawmarsh Welfare v Staveley Welfare	3-2
	Stocksbridge Works v Norton Woodseats	3-2
10	Bentley Colliery v Farsley Celtic	4-2
	Frickley Colliery v Goole Town	1-1
	Ossett Town v Brodsworth Main Colliery	1-3
	Selby Town v Brigg Town	2-1
11	Barwell Athletic v Atherstone Town	2-2
	Brush Sports v Tamworth	2-0
	Hinckley Athletic v Gresley Rovers	1-3
	Nuneaton Borough v Moira United	7-1
12	Boston United v Grantham	2-3
	Ransome & Marles v Gedling Colliery	4-6
	South Normanton MW v Bourne Town	3-2
	Sutton Town v Spalding United	0-4
13	Kettering Town v Northampton Amateurs	5-1
	Peterborough United v Desborough Town	5-1
	Rushden Town v Symingtons Recreation	0-3
	Wellingborough Town v Corby Town	0-5
14	Bedford Town (1) v Luton Amateur	2-0
	Eynesbury Rovers v Hitchin Town	0-1
	Huntingdon United v Baldock Town	2-3
	St Neots & District v Letchworth Town	3-1
15	Bury Town v Cambridge Town	0-1
	Histon Institute v South Lynn	3-2
	King's Lynn v March Town	3-2
	Newmarket Town v Abbey United (Cambs)	1-0
16	Gorleston v Achilles (Ipswich)	5-0
	Gothic (Norwich) v Lowestoft Town	1-3
	Great Yarmouth Town v Whitton United	4-1
	Stowmarket Corinthians v Norwich School OB Union	3-3
17	Barking v Clapton	4-1
	Briggs Sports v Harwich & Parkeston	0-0
	Ilford v Grays Athletic	1-2
	Tilbury v Upminster	2-2
18	Enfield v Wealdstone	0-0
	Hatfield Town v Willesden	4-1
	St Albans City v Crown & Manor	4-1
	Ware v Edgware Town	0-2e
19	Hemel Hempstead Town v Uxbridge	1-4
	Oxford City v Slough Town	1-1
	Southall v Osberton Radiator (Oxford)	3-1
	Yiewsley v Hayes	2-2
20	Vickers Armstrong v Tooting & Mitcham United	2-4
	Walton & Hersham v Redhill	1-0
	Wimbledon v Kingstonian	0-0
	Woking v Epsom	1-2
21	Bowater Lloyds v Canterbury City	2-3
	Dover v Snowdown CW	2-0
	Erith & Belvedere v Tonbridge	3-0
	Ramsgate Athletic v Gravesend & Northfleet	0-0
22	Eastbourne Comrades v Horsham	0-1
	Hastings United v Hove	14-2
	Haywards Heath v Bognor Regis Town	7-0
	Worthing v Littlehampton Town	5-0
23	Bournemouth (Ams) v Portland United	3-1
	Cowes v Dorchester Town	5-1
	Poole Town v East Cowes Victoria	5-1
	Ryde Sports v Weymouth	2-6
24	Bath City v Salisbury (2)	0-2
	Clandown v Chippenham United	3-0
	Melksham v Paulton Rovers	3-8
	Trowbridge Town v Chippenham Town	3-1
25	Bideford v Ilminster Town	6-0
	Dartmouth United v Bridgwater Town (1)	2-0
	Ilfracombe Town v St Austell	2-3
	Wells City v Barnstaple Town	1-0
26	Barry Town v Gloucester City	1-1
	Clevedon v Troedryhiw	2-1
	Llanelli v Merthyr Tydfil	0-3
	Lovells Athletic v Mount Hill Enterprise	4-1
2r	Easington CW v Seaham Colliery Welfare	2-1
r	Horden CW v Willington	4-0
r	South Hetton CW v Silksworth CW	0-2
3r	Billingham Synthonia v Whitby	3-0
6r	Burscough v Wigan Athletic	1-5
8r	Sutton Town (Birmingham) v Dudley Town	0-1
9r	Creswell Colliery v Hoyland Common Athletic	0-2
10r	Goole Town v Frickley Colliery	1-0
11r	Atherstone Town v Barwell Athletic	4-3
16r	Stowmarket Corinthians v Norwich School OB Union	3-3
17r	Harwich & Parkeston v Briggs Sports	0-0e
r	Upminster v Tilbury	2-4
18r	Wealdstone v Enfield	2-0
19r	Hayes v Yiewsley	3-2
r	Slough Town v Oxford City	4-2e
20r	Kingstonian v Wimbledon	1-1
21r	Gravesend & Northfleet v Ramsgate Athletic	2-1
26r	Gloucester City v Barry Town	1-0
16r2	Stowmarket Corinthians v Norwich School OB Union	3-0
17r2	Harwich & Parkeston v Briggs Sports	3-0
20r2	Kingstonian v Wimbledon	6-3

Qualifying Round Two

1	Blyth Spartans v Heaton Stannington	5-1
	North Shields v South Shields (2)	2-0
2	Horden CW v Easington CW	2-1
	Silksworth CW v Consett	2-1
3	South Bank v Billingham Synthonia	0-1
	South Bank St Peters v Portrack Shamrocks	2-2
4	Aspatria Spartans v Scalegill	1-0
	Netherfield (Kendal) v Kells Welfare Centre	2-0
5	Chorley v Rossendale United	2-3
	Fleetwood v Nelson	3-2
6	Rhyl v Bangor City	4-1
	Wigan Athletic v Bootle Athletic	6-1
7	Congleton Town v Droylsden United	1-2
	Mossley v Buxton	2-1
8	Cradley Heath v Bromsgrove Rovers	1-2
	Stafford Rangers v Dudley Town	2-2
9	Hoyland Common Athletic v Beighton Miners Welfare	3-2
	Stocksbridge Works v Rawmarsh Welfare	1-2
10	Goole Town v Bentley Colliery	1-1
	Selby Town v Brodsworth Main Colliery	1-0 D
11	Atherstone Town v Nuneaton Borough	2-2
	Gresley Rovers v Brush Sports	3-2
12	South Normanton MW v Grantham	0-3
	Spalding United v Gedling Colliery	5-2
13	Corby Town v Symingtons Recreation	6-1
	Kettering Town v Peterborough United	0-5
14	Bedford Town (1) v St Neots & District	3-0
	Hitchin Town v Baldock Town	4-1
15	Cambridge Town v Newmarket Town	1-0
	Histon Institute v King's Lynn	2-2
16	Gorleston v Stowmarket Corinthians	4-2
	Lowestoft Town v Great Yarmouth Town	3-2
17	Barking v Grays Athletic	4-0
	Harwich & Parkeston v Tilbury	0-2
18	Edgware Town v Hatfield Town	5-1
	St Albans City v Wealdstone	0-1
19	Slough Town v Hayes	1-2
	Southall v Uxbridge	4-1
20	Epsom v Kingstonian	1-3
	Tooting & Mitcham United v Walton & Hersham	1-1
21	Dover v Erith & Belvedere	3-0
	Gravesend & Northfleet v Canterbury City	5-1
22	Hastings United v Horsham	4-1
	Worthing v Haywards Heath	2-4
23	Bournemouth (Ams) v Cowes	3-3
	Weymouth v Poole Town	4-0
24	Clandown v Salisbury (2)	1-6
	Paulton Rovers v Trowbridge Town	1-4
25	Bideford v Wells City	1-1
	Dartmouth United v St Austell	2-1
26	Gloucester City v Clevedon	3-0
	Lovells Athletic v Merthyr Tydfil	1-0
3r	Portrack Shamrocks v South Bank St Peters	2-1
8r	Dudley Town v Stafford Rangers	1-0
10r	Bentley Colliery v Goole Town	2-4
11r	Nuneaton Borough v Atherstone Town	1-1
15r	King's Lynn v Histon Institute	5-2
20r	Walton & Hersham v Tooting & Mitcham United	1-2e
23r	Cowes v Bournemouth (Ams)	4-0
25r	Wells City v Bideford	2-3e
11r2	Nuneaton Borough v Atherstone Town	2-1

Qualifying Round Three

1	Blyth Spartans v North Shields	1-5
2	Horden CW v Silksworth CW	3-1
3	Billingham Synthonia v Portrack Shamrocks	3-1
4	Aspatria Spartans v Netherfield (Kendal)	2-4
5	Fleetwood v Rossendale United	5-0
6	Rhyl v Wigan Athletic	2-0
7	Droylsden United v Mossley	1-3
8	Bromsgrove Rovers v Dudley Town	3-1
9	Rawmarsh Welfare v Hoyland Common Athletic	4-2
10	Brodsworth Main Colliery v Goole Town	1-1
11	Nuneaton Borough v Gresley Rovers	2-2
12	Spalding United v Grantham	0-2
13	Corby Town v Peterborough United	1-0
14	Bedford Town (1) v Hitchin Town	2-0
15	King's Lynn v Cambridge Town	3-1
16	Lowestoft Town v Gorleston	0-3
17	Barking v Tilbury	1-2
18	Edgware Town v Wealdstone	0-1
19	Hayes v Southall	4-1
20	Kingstonian v Tooting & Mitcham United	5-3
21	Gravesend & Northfleet v Dover	5-0
22	Haywards Heath v Hastings United	0-1
23	Cowes v Weymouth	1-5
24	Trowbridge Town v Salisbury (2)	1-0
25	Bideford v Dartmouth United	4-2
26	Gloucester City v Lovells Athletic	3-0
10r	Goole Town v Brodsworth Main Colliery	8-2
11r	Gresley Rovers v Nuneaton Borough	2-3

Qualifying Round Four

Barnet v Chelmsford City	2-6
Bideford v Gloucester City	1-1
Billingham Synthonia v Horden CW	1-1
Bromsgrove Rovers v Shrewsbury Town	5-2
Corby Town v Gravesend & Northfleet	1-6
Fleetwood v Lancaster City	4-1
Gorleston v Tilbury	1-1
Grantham v Gainsborough Trinity	2-0
Guildford City v Gillingham	2-3
Hastings United v Bedford Town (1)	2-0
Hereford United v Cheltenham Town	1-1
King's Lynn v Dartford	1-1
Leytonstone v Hayes	3-2
Mossley v Runcorn	1-0
Netherfield (Kendal) v Workington	2-0
North Shields v Scarborough	1-1
Rhyl v Stalybridge Celtic	6-0
Romford (2) v Kingstonian	3-0
Scunthorpe United v Goole Town	0-0
Stockton v Bishop Auckland	7-0
Walthamstow Avenue v Dulwich Hamlet	3-3

1949/50 to 1950/51

	Wealdstone v Colchester United	1-0
	Wellington Town v Nuneaton Borough	3-4
	Weymouth v Trowbridge Town	3-3
	Witton Albion v Rawmarsh Welfare	3-0
r	Cheltenham Town v Hereford United	2-2e
r	Dartford v King's Lynn	1-2
r	Dulwich Hamlet v Walthamstow Avenue	1-3
r	Gloucester City v Bideford	3-1
r	Goole Town v Scunthorpe United	2-0
r	Horden CW v Billingham Synthonia	0-1
r	Scarborough v North Shields	1-3e
r	Tilbury v Gorleston	2-1
r	Trowbridge Town v Weymouth	1-2
r2	Hereford United v Cheltenham Town	4-2

Round One

	Accrington Stanley v Hartlepools United	0-1
	Bradford City v Fleetwood	9-0
	Bromley v Watford	1-2
	Carlisle United v Lincoln City	1-0
	Chester v Goole Town	4-1
	Crystal Palace v Newport County	0-3
	Darlington v Crewe Alexandra	2-2
	Doncaster Rovers v New Brighton	5-1
	Gateshead v York City	3-1
	Gloucester City v Norwich City	2-3
	Gravesend & Northfleet v Torquay United	1-3
	Hastings United v Gillingham	1-3
	Hereford United v Bromsgrove Rovers	3-0
	Ipswich Town v Brighton & Hove Albion	2-1
	Leyton Orient v Southend United	0-2
	Leytonstone v Chelmsford City	1-2
	Mansfield Town v Walsall	4-1
	Millwall v Exeter City	3-5
	Netherfield (Kendal) v North Shields	4-3
	Northampton Town v Walthamstow Avenue	4-1
	Nottingham Forest v Bristol City	1-0
	Notts County v Tilbury	4-0
	Nuneaton Borough v King's Lynn	2-1
	Oldham Athletic v Stockton	4-0
	Port Vale v Wealdstone	1-0
	Rhyl v Rochdale	0-3
	Southport v Barrow	1-1
	Stockport County v Billingham Synthonia	3-0
	Swindon Town v Bristol Rovers	1-0
	Tranmere Rovers v Halifax Town	2-1
	Weymouth v Aldershot	2-2
	Witton Albion v Mossley	0-1
	Wrexham v Grantham	4-1
	Yeovil Town v Romford (2)	4-1
r	Aldershot v Weymouth	2-3
r	Barrow v Southport	0-1
r	Crewe Alexandra v Darlington	1-0

Round Two

	Carlisle United v Swindon Town	2-0
	Chelmsford City v Ipswich Town	1-1
	Crewe Alexandra v Oldham Athletic	1-1
	Doncaster Rovers v Mansfield Town	1-0
	Exeter City v Chester	2-0
	Hartlepools United v Norwich City	1-1
	Newport County v Gateshead	1-1
	Northampton Town v Torquay United	4-2
	Nottingham Forest v Stockport County	0-2
	Nuneaton Borough v Mossley	0-0
	Port Vale v Tranmere Rovers	1-0
	Rochdale v Notts County	1-2
	Southport v Bradford City	2-1
	Watford v Netherfield (Kendal)	6-0
	Weymouth v Hereford United	2-1
	Wrexham v Southend United	2-2
	Yeovil Town v Gillingham	3-1
r	Gateshead v Newport County	1-2e
r	Ipswich Town v Chelmsford City	1-0e
r	Mossley v Nuneaton Borough	0-3
r	Norwich City v Hartlepools United	5-1
r	Oldham Athletic v Crewe Alexandra	0-0e
r	Southend United v Wrexham	2-0
r2	Crewe Alexandra v Oldham Athletic	0-3 N

Round Three

	Arsenal v Sheffield Wednesday	1-0
	Aston Villa v Middlesbrough	2-2
	Blackburn Rovers v Liverpool	0-0
	Blackpool v Southend United	4-0
	Bradford Park Avenue v Bournemouth	0-1
	Brentford v Chelsea	0-1
	Bury v Rotherham United	5-4
	Cardiff City v West Bromwich Albion	2-2
	Carlisle United v Leeds United	2-5
	Charlton Athletic v Fulham	2-2
	Chesterfield v Yeovil Town	3-1
	Coventry City v Bolton Wanderers	1-2
	Exeter City v Nuneaton Borough	3-0
	Luton Town v Grimsby Town	3-4
	Manchester City v Derby County	3-5
	Manchester United v Weymouth	4-0
	Newport County v Port Vale	1-2
	Northampton Town v Southampton	1-1
	Notts County v Burnley	1-4
	Oldham Athletic v Newcastle United	2-7
	Plymouth Argyle v Wolverhampton Wan.	1-1
	Portsmouth v Norwich City	1-1
	Queen's Park Rangers v Everton	0-2
	Reading v Doncaster Rovers	2-3
	Sheffield United v Leicester City	3-1
	Southport v Hull City	0-0
	Stockport County v Barnsley	4-2
	Stoke City v Tottenham Hotspur	0-1
	Sunderland v Huddersfield Town	6-0
	Swansea Town v Birmingham City	3-0
	Watford v Preston North End	2-2
	West Ham United v Ipswich Town	5-1
r	Fulham v Charlton Athletic	1-2
r	Hull City v Southport	5-0
r	Liverpool v Blackburn Rovers	2-1
r	Middlesbrough v Aston Villa	0-0e
r	Norwich City v Portsmouth	0-2
r	Preston North End v Watford	0-1
r	Southampton v Northampton Town	2-3
r	West Bromwich Albion v Cardiff City	0-1
r	Wolverhampton Wan. v Plymouth Argyle	3-0
r2	Aston Villa v Middlesbrough	0-3 N

Round Four

	Arsenal v Swansea Town	2-1
	Blackpool v Doncaster Rovers	2-1
	Bournemouth v Northampton Town	1-1
	Burnley v Port Vale	2-1
	Bury v Derby County	2-2
	Charlton Athletic v Cardiff City	1-1
	Chelsea v Newcastle United	3-0
	Chesterfield v Middlesbrough	3-2
	Leeds United v Bolton Wanderers	1-1
	Liverpool v Exeter City	3-1
	Portsmouth v Grimsby Town	5-0
	Stockport County v Hull City	0-0
	Tottenham Hotspur v Sunderland	5-1
	Watford v Manchester United	0-1
	West Ham United v Everton	1-2
	Wolverhampton Wan. v Sheffield United	0-0
r	Bolton Wanderers v Leeds United	2-3e
r	Cardiff City v Charlton Athletic	2-0
r	Derby County v Bury	5-2
r	Hull City v Stockport County	0-2
r	Northampton Town v Bournemouth	2-1
r	Sheffield United v Wolverhampton Wan.	3-4

Round Five

	Arsenal v Burnley	2-0
	Chesterfield v Chelsea	1-1
	Derby County v Northampton Town	4-2
	Everton v Tottenham Hotspur	1-0
	Leeds United v Cardiff City	3-1
	Manchester United v Portsmouth	3-3
	Stockport County v Liverpool	1-2
	Wolverhampton Wan. v Blackpool	0-0
r	Blackpool v Wolverhampton Wan.	1-0
r	Chelsea v Chesterfield	3-0
r	Portsmouth v Manchester United	1-3

Round Six

	Arsenal v Leeds United	1-0
	Chelsea v Manchester United	2-0
	Derby County v Everton	1-2
	Liverpool v Blackpool	2-1

Semi Finals

	Arsenal v Chelsea	2-2 N
	Liverpool v Everton	2-0 N
r	Chelsea v Arsenal	0-1eN

Final

	Arsenal v Liverpool	2-0 N

1950/51

Extra Preliminary Round

1	Alnwick Town v Newbiggin CW	4-0
	Boldon CW v Morpeth Town	3-1
	Lynemouth Welfare v West Stanley	2-9
	Newburn v Wardley Welfare	3-1
	Shankhouse v Cramlington Welfare	2-6
	South Shields Ex-schoolboys v Annfield Plain	1-1
2	Brandon CW v Ushaw Moor	0-1
	Cockfield v Shildon	0-3
	Evenwood Town v Langley Park CW	5-2
	Ferryhill Athletic v Crook Town	1-2
	Seaham Colliery Welfare v Eppleton CW	1-2
	South Hetton CW v Stanley United	2-1
	Spennymoor United v Blackhall Colliery Welfare	1-2
	West Auckland Town v Chilton Athletic	2-1
	Wingate Welfare v Murton CW	4-2
6	Burscough v St Helens Town	3-1
	Cromptons Recreation v UGB St Helens	3-0
	Crossens v Skelmersdale United	0-12
	Flint Town United v Liverpool Police	4-2
7	Ellesmere Port Town v Wallasey Transport	wo/s
8	Moor Green v Lye Town	2-2
	Oswestry Town v Hednesford Town	2-1
	Sutton Town (Birmingham) v Stourbridge	0-3
9	Hallam v Worksop Town	2-4
10	Ashby Institute v Armthorpe Welfare	8-1
	Barton Town (1) v Upton Colliery	5-3
	Brigg Town v Lysaght's Sports (Scunthorpe)	3-1
	Meltham v Marsden	2-3
	Ossett Town v Brunswick Institute	5-2
	Thorne Colliery v Pilkington Recreation	2-2
	Yorkshire Amateur v Harrogate Town	4-1
12	Basford United v Langold WMC	1-5
	Heanor Athletic v Bourne Town	3-1
	Holbeach United v Bentinck Colliery Welfare	2-0
	Parliament Street Methodists v Linby Colliery	3-4
	Ransome & Marles v Mablethorpe United	6-0
	Retford Town v Boots Athletic	2-0
	Rufford Colliery v Neville's Athletic	7-3
	Sherwood Colliery v Ilkeston Town (2)	0-8
	Skegness Town v Boston United	3-10
	Stamford v Raleigh Athletic	1-1
	Sutton Town v Shirebrook	0-1
	Teversal & Silverhill CW v Long Eaton Town	2-2
14	Bedford Avenue v Bedford St Cuthberts	6-1
	Bedford Queens Works v Lynton Works (Bedford)	6-5
	Biggleswade Town v Dunstable Town	6-0
	Letchworth Town v Arlesey Town	3-2
	Marston Shelton Rovers v Bedford Corinthians	3-0
	Shefford Town v Huntingdon United	3-3
	St Ives Town v Kempston Rovers	2-1
	Vauxhall Motors (Luton) v Stewartby Works	5-0
	Wolverton Town & BR v Eynesbury Rovers	3-2
	Wootton Blue Cross v Waterlows (Dunstable)	2-0
16	Beccles v Diss Town	4-2
	Eastern Coachworks v Fakenham Town	8-2
	Haverhill Rovers v Bungay Town	2-2
	Sheringham v Felixstowe United	3-1
	Sudbury Town v Churchmans Sports (Ipswich)	4-0
	Wymondham Town v Norwich School Old Boys Union	1-5
17	Bishop's Stortford v Leyton	2-1
18	Cheshunt v Hoddesdon Town	4-2
	Enfield v Pinner	5-0
	Finchley v Stevenage Town	5-0
	Polytechnic v Hertford Town	2-6
	Tufnell Park v Harrow Town	6-3
	Ware v Wood Green Town	4-0
19	Amersham Town v Wycombe Wanderers	0-13
	Buckingham Town v Yiewsley	1-5
	Chesham United v Witney Town	4-2
	Headington United v Kidlington	6-0
	Hemel Hempstead Town v Banbury Spencer	1-1
	Leavesden v Morris Motors (Cowley)	8-1
	Marlow v Aylesbury United	2-4
	N.A.C Athletic (Banbury) v Huntley & Palmers	1-5
	Osberton Radiator (Oxford) v Pressed Steel	1-2
	Slough Centre v Abingdon Town	2-2e
	Windsor & Eton v Maidenhead United	1-1
20	Chertsey Town v Wimbledon	1-3
	Metropolitan Police v Surbiton Town	2-1
	Redhill v Vickers Armstrong	2-2
	Sutton United v Banstead Athletic	3-1
	Woking v Carshalton Athletic	2-2
21	Betteshanger CW v Folkestone	1-0
	Margate v Ashford	1-2
	Whitstable v Chatham Town	1-0
23	Basingstoke Town v Alton Town	1-2
	Dorchester Town v Portland United	6-3
	Longfleet St Mary's v Hamworthy	1-1
	Newport (IOW) v Totton	4-0
	Ryde Sports v Andover	2-1
	Shaftesbury v Bournemouth Gasworks Athletic	2-1
	Thornycroft Athletic v Pirelli General Cables	5-5
24	Chippenham United v Coleford Athletic	6-0
	Frome Town v Bath City	0-5
	Odd Down v Corsham Town	0-6
	Peasedown MW v Chippenham Town	0-3
	Purton v Pewsey Vale	5-3
	Radstock Town v Westbury United	2-3
	Shepton Mallet Town v Devizes Town	1-5
	Swindon British Rail v Melksham	4-1
	Warminster Town v Timsbury Athletic	6-2
	Welton Rovers v Swindon Victoria	5-4
	Wootton Bassett Town v Spencer Moulton	2-1
25	Ilfracombe Town v Ilminster Town	8-2
	Newquay v Weston-Super-Mare St Johns	7-0
	Plymouth United v Green Waves (Plymouth)	0-4
	St Blazey v Exmouth Town	3-3
	Taunton v Wadebridge Town	4-2
	Truro City v Callington	4-3
1r	Annfield Plain v South Shields Ex-schoolboys	3-1
8r	Lye Town v Moor Green	3-1
10r	Pilkington Recreation v Thorne Colliery	3-5
12r	Long Eaton Town v Teversal & Silverhill CW	3-2
r	Raleigh Athletic v Stamford	5-2
14r	Huntingdon United v Shefford Town	5-4
15r	Crook Town v Ferryhill Athletic	4-4
16r	Bungay Town v Haverhill Rovers	2-1e
19r	Abingdon Town v Slough Centre	4-3
r	Banbury Spencer v Hemel Hempstead Town	5-1
r	Maidenhead United v Windsor & Eton	2-1
20r	Carshalton Athletic v Woking	7-4e
r	Vickers Armstrong v Redhill	4-2
23r	Hamworthy v Longfleet St Mary's	1-0
r	Pirelli General Cables v Thornycroft Athletic	3-2
25r	Exmouth Town v St Blazey	1-4
15r2	Ferryhill Athletic v Crook Town	0-4

1950/51

Preliminary Round

1	Alnwick Town v Newburn	10-2
	Amble v Hexham Hearts	1-1
	Ashington v Annfield Plain	3-1
	Birtley v Gosforth & Coxlodge	1-4
	Boldon CW v West Stanley	1-4
	Cramlington Welfare v West Sleekburn Welfare	5-1
	Heaton Stannington v South Shields (2)	0-3
	Shilbottle CW v Blyth Spartans	1-6
2	Crook Town v Ushaw Moor	2-2
	Dawdon Colliery Welfare v Blackhall Colliery Welfare	1-1
	Easington CW v Wingate Welfare	3-1
	Horden CW v Eppleton CW	1-0
	Shildon v Evenwood Town	3-5
	Shotton CW v Consett	1-8
	Silksworth CW v Tow Law Town	3-3
	West Auckland Town v South Hetton CW	4-0
3	Bridlington Central Utd. v Smith's Dock	6-3
	Filey Town v Head Wrightsons	3-7
	Skinningrove Works v Whitby Town	0-5
	South Bank East End v Bridlington Trinity	1-1
4	Cleator Moor Celtic v Holme Head Works	1-0
	Frizington United v Threlkeld	5-1
	Millom Town v Florence & Ullcoats Utd.	2-3
	Milnthorpe Corinthians v Bowthorn United	5-2
	Penrith v Moss Bay	12-0
5	Chorley v Darwen	1-2
	Clitheroe v Leyland Motors	1-1
	Fleetwood v Lytham	3-1
	Great Harwood v Horwich RMI	1-4
	Lancaster City v Barnoldswick & District	5-1
	Morecambe v Bacup Borough	0-4
6	Bootle Athletic v Earle	2-1
	Cromptons Recreation v Formby	2-1
	Flint Town United v Llandudno	2-0
	Haydock C&B Recreation v Burscough	1-3
	Hoylake Athletic v Prescot Cables	2-7
	Skelmersdale United v Bangor City	1-0
	South Liverpool v Wigan Athletic	0-0
	Stoneycroft v Marine	3-5
7	Congleton Town v Buxton	3-1
	Droylsden United v Macclesfield Town	5-5
	Glossop v Altrincham	1-4
	Hyde United v Atherton Collieries	5-0
	Matlock Town v Stalybridge Celtic	2-4
	Nantwich v Ellesmere Port Town	4-3
	Runcorn v Mossley	3-1
	Winsford United v Ashton United	2-0
8	Bilston v Wellington Town	1-3
	Bournville Athletic v Hereford United	1-5
	Brierley Hill Alliance v Darlaston	7-1
	Cradley Heath v Stourbridge	0-1
	Kidderminster Harriers v Halesowen Town	3-0
	Lye Town v Boldmere St Michaels	2-1
	Oswestry Town v Shrewsbury Town	wo/s
	Stafford Rangers v Dudley Town	1-2
9	Creswell Colliery v Staveley Welfare	9-0
	Grimethorpe Athletic v Stocksbridge Works	1-2
	Jump Home Guard v Parkhouse Colliery	3-3
	Kilnhurst Colliery v Beighton Miners Welfare	0-3
	Parkgate Welfare v Denaby United	2-0
	Rawmarsh Welfare v Norton Woodseats	0-0
	Steel,Peech&Tozer Soc. Ser. v Maltby Main Col.	2-0
	Worksop Town v Sheffield	2-1
10	Ashby Institute v Thorne Colliery	2-1
	Barton Town (1) v Frickley Colliery	1-3
	Brigg Town v Bentley Colliery	4-0
	Farsley Celtic v Appleby Frodingham	1-0
	Goole Town v Brodsworth Main Colliery	5-0
	Selby Town v South Kirkby Colliery	4-1
	Winterton Rangers v Ossett Town	1-3
	Yorkshire Amateur v Marsden	2-0
11	Barwell Athletic v Whitwick Colliery	1-2
	Bedworth Town v Morris Sports (Loughborough)	3-1
	Coalville Town (3) v Brush Sports	2-2
	Coventry Amateurs v Atherstone Town	2-3
	Ibstock Penistone Rovers v Tamworth	2-0
	Moira United v Lockheed Leamington	0-1
	Newhall United v Hinckley Athletic	2-2
12	Boston United v South Normanton MW	3-2
	Grantham v Heanor Athletic	5-1
	Ilkeston Town (2) v Long Eaton Town	0-4
	Langold WMC v Holbeach United	2-1
	Linby Colliery v Retford Town	3-0
	Raleigh Athletic v Gedling Colliery	1-1
	Ransome & Marles v Spalding United	0-1
	Rufford Colliery v Shirebrook	0-2
14	Baldock Town v Huntingdon United	1-3
	Bedford Avenue v Wootton Blue Cross	0-4
	Hitchin Town v Marston Shelton Rovers	2-1
	Leighton United v Bedford Queens Works	5-1
	Letchworth Town v Biggleswade Town	2-2
	Potton United v Bedford Town (1)	2-6
	St Neots & District v St Ives Town	5-2
	Wolverton Town & BR v Vauxhall Motors (Luton)	6-3
15	Parson Drove United v Wimblington Old Boys	4-1
	South Lynn v Chatteris Town	0-1
	Wisbech Town v Bury Town	1-0
16	Bungay Town v Leiston	1-4
	Cromer v Sudbury Town	0-4
	Gorleston v Eastern Coachworks	0-1
	Great Yarmouth Town v Norwich School Old Boys Union	3-2
	Holt United v Thetford Town	1-4
	Sheringham v Gothic (Norwich)	0-3
	Stowmarket Corinthians v Beccles	7-3
	Whitton United v Lowestoft Town	1-3
17	Brentwood & Warley v Tilbury	0-1
	Briggs Sports v Clacton Town	2-0
	Chingford Town v Ilford	1-0
	Eton Manor v Barking	2-4
	Harwich & Parkeston v Bishop's Stortford	5-3
	Rainham Town v Crittall Athletic	0-0
	Romford (2) v Grays Athletic	7-1
	Woodford Town (1) v Clapton	4-0
18	Barnet v Hendon	2-3
	Cheshunt v Ware	2-1
	Enfield v Willesden	5-1
	Hatfield Town v Civil Service	1-2
	Hayes v Southall	3-0
	Hertford Town v Wealdstone	1-3
	St Albans City v Finchley	1-0
	Tufnell Park v Edgware Town	0-2
19	Aylesbury United v Uxbridge	2-2
	Berkhamsted Town v Bicester Town	1-1
	Chesham United v Abingdon Town	5-0
	Headington United v Slough Town	3-4
	Huntley & Palmers v Banbury Spencer	1-2
	Leavesden v Yiewsley	1-2
	Maidenhead United v Wycombe Wanderers	0-2
	Oxford City v Pressed Steel	5-4
20	Camberley v Cobham	3-0
	Carshalton Athletic v Vickers Armstrong	4-2
	Dorking v Dulwich Hamlet	wo/s
	Kingstonian v Farnham Town	6-1
	Leatherhead v Walton & Hersham	1-3
	Metropolitan Police v Hounslow Town	4-4
	Sutton United v Tooting & Mitcham United	0-0
	Wimbledon v Guildford	9-3
21	Aylesford Paper Mills v Tonbridge	0-3
	Betteshanger CW v Erith & Belvedere	2-1
	Bowater Lloyds v Faversham Town	4-1
	Canterbury City v Sittingbourne	0-1
	Dover v Snowdown CW	1-2
	Gravesend & Northfleet v Sheppey United	5-2
	Maidstone United v Ramsgate Athletic	5-2
	Whitstable v Ashford	0-2
22	Arundel v Bognor Regis Town	1-0
	Bexhill Town v Haywards Heath	0-1
	East Grinstead v Littlehampton Town	6-1
	Eastbourne v Shoreham	2-1
	Eastbourne Comrades v Newhaven	0-0
	Horsham v Hove	4-2
	Lancing Athletic v Hastings United	2-3
	Southwick v Worthing	1-2
23	Blandford United v Gosport Borough Ath.	4-1
	Cowes v Bournemouth (Ams)	1-1
	Newport (IOW) v Winchester City	5-1
	Pirelli General Cables v Hamworthy	1-2
	RAOC Hilsea v Poole Town	0-5
	Romsey Town v East Cowes Victoria	3-2
	Ryde Sports v Dorchester Town	3-3
	Shaftesbury v Alton Town	1-5
24	Bath City v Chippenham Town	2-0
	Chippenham United v Purton	4-1
	Clandown v Calne & Harris United	3-0
	Corsham Town v Warminster Town	3-2
	Devizes Town v Wootton Bassett Town	4-0
	Paulton Rovers v Trowbridge Town	1-1
	Swindon British Rail v Welton Rovers	1-5
	Westbury United v Salisbury (2)	1-6
25	Bideford v Dartmouth United	7-1
	Bridgwater Town (1) v Glastonbury	1-1
	Green Waves (Plymouth) v Truro City	2-3
	Newquay v St Austell	3-0
	Oak Villa v Barnstaple Town	2-6
	St Blazey v Ilfracombe Town	0-6
	Street v Tiverton Town	7-0
	Taunton v Wells City	3-2
26	Barry Town v Soundwell	4-0
	Cinderford Town v St Philips Marsh Adult School	2-1
	Clevedon v Douglas (Kingswood)	5-0
	Hanham Athletic v Troedyrhiw	0-2
	Llanelli v Ebbw Vale	2-0
	Lovells Athletic v Stonehouse	2-2
	Merthyr Tydfil v Bristol St George	11-3
	Mount Hill Enterprise v Hoffmann Ath. (Stonehouse)	1-1
1r	Hexham Hearts v Amble	wo/s
2r	Blackhall Colliery Welfare v Dawdon Colliery Welfare	3-1
r	Tow Law Town v Silksworth CW	2-0
r	Ushaw Moor v Crook Town	3-2
3r	Bridlington Trinity v South Bank East End	4-2
5r	Leyland Motors v Clitheroe	2-0
6r	Wigan Athletic v South Liverpool	3-2
7r	Macclesfield Town v Droylsden United	7-2
9r	Norton Woodseats v Rawmarsh Welfare	4-2
r	Parkhouse Colliery v Jump Home Guard	7-1
11r	Brush Sports v Coalville Town (3)	2-1
r	Hinckley Athletic v Newhall United	2-1
12r	Gedling Colliery v Raleigh Athletic	8-1
14r	Biggleswade Town v Letchworth Town	3-2
17r	Crittall Athletic v Rainham Town	2-1
19r	Bicester Town v Berkhamsted Town	2-1
r	Uxbridge v Aylesbury United	1-1
20r	Metropolitan Police v Hounslow Town	1-2
r	Tooting & Mitcham United v Sutton United	1-0
22r	Newhaven v Eastbourne Comrades	3-0
23r	Bournemouth (Ams) v Cowes	4-2
r	Dorchester Town v Ryde Sports	4-2
24r	Trowbridge Town v Paulton Rovers	4-1
25r	Glastonbury v Bridgwater Town (1)	7-0
26r	Hoffmann Ath. (Stonehouse) v Mount Hill Enterprise	2-1
r	Stonehouse v Lovells Athletic	1-0
19r2	Aylesbury United v Uxbridge	4-1

Qualifying Round One

1	Ashington v West Stanley	2-1
	Cramlington Welfare v Gosforth & Coxlodge	5-2
	Hexham Hearts v Alnwick Town	2-1
	South Shields (2) v Blyth Spartans	0-2
2	Evenwood Town v Easington CW	3-2
	Horden CW v Consett	4-0
	Tow Law Town v West Auckland Town	3-2
	Ushaw Moor v Blackhall Colliery Welfare	1-3
3	Bridlington Central Utd. v Head Wrightsons	4-5
	Scarborough v Bridlington Trinity	7-2
	South Bank St Peters v South Bank	1-4
	Whitby Town v Cargo Fleet Works	10-2
4	Florence & Ullcoats Utd. v Aspatria Spartans	2-5
	Frizington United v Kells Welfare Centre	wo/s
	Milnthorpe Corinthians v Netherfield (Kendal)	0-5
	Penrith v Cleator Moor Celtic	1-2
5	Bacup Borough v Darwen	2-0
	Leyland Motors v Fleetwood	1-1
	Nelson v Lancaster City	5-2
	Rossendale United v Horwich RMI	6-5
6	Burscough v Bootle Athletic	2-0
	Marine v Cromptons Recreation	0-1
	Skelmersdale United v Prescot Cables	6-2
	Wigan Athletic v Flint Town United	1-1
7	Altrincham v Macclesfield Town	3-1
	Runcorn v Nantwich	4-1
	Stalybridge Celtic v Hyde United	2-6
	Winsford United v Congleton Town	4-0
8	Dudley Town v Stourbridge	0-0
	Kidderminster Harriers v Hereford United	0-1
	Oswestry Town v Lye Town	2-1
	Wellington Town v Brierley Hill Alliance	3-1
9	Beighton Miners Welfare v Worksop Town	1-1
	Norton Woodseats v Steel, Peech & Tozer Social Ser.	9-0
	Parkgate Welfare v Stocksbridge Works	0-2
	Parkhouse Colliery v Creswell Colliery	1-2
10	Ashby Institute v Brigg Town	0-3
	Farsley Celtic v Frickley Colliery	3-1
	Ossett Town v Selby Town	1-3
	Yorkshire Amateur v Goole Town	0-4
11	Atherstone Town v Lockheed Leamington	2-4
	Brush Sports v Whitwick Colliery	5-2
	Gresley Rovers v Bedworth Town	0-2
	Hinckley Athletic v Ibstock Penistone Rovers	4-0
12	Grantham v Boston United	0-0
	Langold WMC v Long Eaton Town	5-1
	Linby Colliery v Shirebrook	2-0
	Spalding United v Gedling Colliery	8-0
13	Corby Town - Bye	
	Peterborough United v Symingtons Recreation	3-0
	Rushden Town v Kettering Town	2-2
	Wellingborough Town v Desborough Town	2-0
14	Biggleswade Town v Wootton Blue Cross	1-2
	Huntingdon United v Hitchin Town	1-5
	Leighton United v Bedford Town (1)	2-8
	Wolverton Town & BR v St Neots & District	3-2
15	Chatteris Town v Newmarket Town	0-2
	Histon Institute v Parson Drove United	1-0
	King's Lynn v Abbey United (Cambs)	2-2
	Wisbech Town v March Town United	0-2
16	Eastern Coachworks v Sudbury Town	2-2
	Great Yarmouth Town v Gothic (Norwich)	3-0
	Leiston v Lowestoft Town	0-1
	Stowmarket Corinthians v Thetford Town	5-0
17	Barking v Briggs Sports	2-2
	Chingford Town v Crittall Athletic	3-2
	Romford (2) v Tilbury	5-1
	Woodford Town (1) v Harwich & Parkeston	3-2
18	Civil Service v Enfield	2-5
	Hayes v Cheshunt	7-1
	Hendon v Edgware Town	7-1
	Wealdstone v St Albans City	1-5
19	Banbury Spencer v Bicester Town	4-0
	Chesham United v Wycombe Wanderers	1-1
	Slough Town v Oxford City	2-2
	Yiewsley v Aylesbury United	2-2
20	Carshalton Athletic v Hounslow Town	1-0
	Kingstonian v Dorking	4-0
	Tooting & Mitcham United v Camberley	3-2
	Wimbledon v Walton & Hersham	0-2
21	Betteshanger CW v Ashford	2-1
	Bowater Lloyds v Snowdown CW	1-1
	Sittingbourne v Maidstone United	2-0
	Tonbridge v Gravesend & Northfleet	1-0
22	Arundel v Hastings United	0-2
	Eastbourne v Horsham	3-2
	Newhaven v East Grinstead	1-2
	Worthing v Haywards Heath	1-2
23	Alton Town v Hamworthy	9-0
	Blandford United v Bournemouth (Ams)	6-2
	Newport (IOW) v Poole Town	6-6
	Romsey Town v Dorchester Town	1-1
24	Clandown v Devizes Town	2-0
	Salisbury (2) v Chippenham United	2-1
	Trowbridge Town v Corsham Town	6-1
	Welton Rovers v Bath City	2-1

1950/51

25	Bideford v Barnstaple Town	2-2
	Newquay v Ilfracombe Town	5-2
	Street v Taunton	3-0
	Truro City v Glastonbury	2-4
26	Cinderford Town v Barry Town	0-2
	Clevedon v Llanelli	2-2
	Merthyr Tydfil v Hoffmann Ath. (Stonehouse)	7-0
	Stonehouse v Troedryhiw	3-1
5r	Fleetwood v Leyland Motors	2-4
6r	Flint Town United v Wigan Athletic	1-3
8r	Stourbridge v Dudley Town	1-3
9r	Worksop Town v Beighton Miners Welfare	5-3
12r	Boston United v Grantham	4-1
13r	Kettering Town v Rushden Town	4-0
15r	Abbey United (Cambs) v King's Lynn	0-1
16r	Sudbury Town v Eastern Coachworks	0-1
17r	Briggs Sports v Barking	2-1
19r	Aylesbury United v Yiewsley	2-0e
r	Oxford City v Slough Town	1-2
r	Wycombe Wanderers v Chesham United	4-2
21r	Snowdown CW v Bowater Lloyds	2-0
23r	Dorchester Town v Romsey Town	2-0e
r	Poole Town v Newport (IOW)	1-0
25r	Barnstaple Town v Bideford	3-1
26r	Llanelli v Clevedon	7-1

Qualifying Round Two

1	Ashington v Hexham Hearts	0-0
	Cramlington Welfare v Blyth Spartans	2-0
2	Horden CW v Evenwood Town	4-0
	Tow Law Town v Blackhall Colliery Welfare	0-0
3	Scarborough v South Bank	3-2
	Whitby Town v Head Wrightsons	4-2
4	Cleator Moor Celtic v Aspatria Spartans	8-3
	Frizington United v Netherfield (Kendal)	1-2
5	Bacup Borough v Rossendale United	3-2
	Nelson v Leyland Motors	4-1
6	Burscough v Skelmersdale United	3-2
	Wigan Athletic v Cromptons Recreation	1-0
7	Altrincham v Winsford United	3-2
	Runcorn v Hyde United	1-1
8	Dudley Town v Oswestry Town	0-1
	Wellington Town v Hereford United	1-4
9	Norton Woodseats v Worksop Town	1-3
	Stocksbridge Works v Creswell Colliery	6-3
10	Goole Town v Brigg Town	3-1
	Selby Town v Farsley Celtic	2-3
11	Brush Sports v Bedworth Town	3-2
	Hinckley Athletic v Lockheed Leamington	7-0
12	Boston United v Linby Colliery	0-4
	Spalding United v Langold WMC	2-2
13	Corby Town v Wellingborough Town	5-0
	Kettering Town v Peterborough United	2-2
14	Bedford Town (1) v Wolverton Town & BR	3-1
	Wootton Blue Cross v Hitchin Town	3-4
15	King's Lynn v March Town United	6-0
	Newmarket Town v Histon Institute	1-3
16	Eastern Coachworks v Lowestoft Town	1-1
	Great Yarmouth Town v Stowmarket Corinthians	2-1
17	Romford (2) v Briggs Sports	2-2
	Woodford Town (1) v Chingford Town	1-1
18	Enfield v St Albans City	2-0
	Hendon v Hayes	2-0
19	Aylesbury United v Wycombe Wanderers	0-2
	Banbury Spencer v Slough Town	1-1
20	Carshalton Athletic v Kingstonian	1-1
	Tooting & Mitcham United v Walton & Hersham	2-1
21	Betteshanger CW v Snowdown CW	0-0
	Tonbridge v Sittingbourne	3-1
22	East Grinstead v Haywards Heath	1-5
	Eastbourne v Hastings United	5-4
23	Alton Town v Blandford United	9-0
	Poole Town v Dorchester Town	1-3
24	Salisbury (2) v Clandown	4-2
	Welton Rovers v Trowbridge Town	0-2
25	Glastonbury v Barnstaple Town	3-0
	Newquay v Street	1-2
26	Llanelli v Merthyr Tydfil	5-5
	Stonehouse v Barry Town	1-1
1r	Hexham Hearts v Ashington	2-6
2r	Blackhall Colliery Welfare v Tow Law Town	3-0
7r	Hyde United v Runcorn	3-0
12r	Langold WMC v Spalding United	1-2
13r	Peterborough United v Kettering Town	1-2
16r	Lowestoft Town v Eastern Coachworks	2-1
17r	Briggs Sports v Romford (2)	1-2
r	Chingford Town v Woodford Town (1)	0-4
19r	Slough Town v Banbury Spencer	5-1
20r	Kingstonian v Carshalton Athletic	2-4
21r	Snowdown CW v Betteshanger CW	1-0
26r	Barry Town v Stonehouse	3-2
r	Merthyr Tydfil v Llanelli	1-2

Qualifying Round Three

1	Ashington v Cramlington Welfare	3-1
2	Horden CW v Blackhall Colliery Welfare	4-1
3	Scarborough v Whitby Town	3-0
4	Cleator Moor Celtic v Netherfield (Kendal)	2-1
5	Bacup Borough v Nelson	0-2
6	Burscough v Wigan Athletic	0-2
7	Hyde United v Altrincham	1-1
8	Oswestry Town v Hereford United	1-2
9	Worksop Town v Stocksbridge Works	1-2
10	Farsley Celtic v Goole Town	3-2
11	Hinckley Athletic v Brush Sports	0-1
12	Spalding United v Linby Colliery	2-2
13	Corby Town v Kettering Town	1-5
14	Hitchin Town v Bedford Town (1)	2-3
15	King's Lynn v Histon Institute	3-1
16	Lowestoft Town v Great Yarmouth Town	1-2
17	Woodford Town (1) v Romford (2)	2-2
18	Enfield v Hendon	2-4
19	Slough Town v Wycombe Wanderers	1-1
20	Carshalton Athletic v Tooting & Mitcham United	1-3
21	Tonbridge v Snowdown CW	1-1
22	Eastbourne v Haywards Heath	4-2
23	Alton Town v Dorchester Town	2-2
24	Salisbury (2) v Trowbridge Town	1-0
25	Street v Glastonbury	0-1
26	Llanelli v Barry Town	1-1
7r	Altrincham v Hyde United	1-2
12r	Linby Colliery v Spalding United	3-1
17r	Romford (2) v Woodford Town (1)	1-1
19r	Wycombe Wanderers v Slough Town	2-0
21r	Snowdown CW v Tonbridge	3-6
23r	Dorchester Town v Alton Town	1-0
26r	Barry Town v Llanelli	1-2
17r2	Woodford Town (1) v Romford (2)	2-1

Qualifying Round Four

	Ashington v Farsley Celtic	2-1
	Billingham Synthonia v Scarborough	1-3
	Bishop Auckland v Horden CW	2-0
	Bromley v Leytonstone	3-1
	Bromsgrove Rovers v Kettering Town	3-2
	Dorchester Town v Glastonbury	1-4
	Gainsborough Trinity v Brush Sports	3-1
	Gloucester City v Salisbury (2)	2-1
	Guildford City v Bedford Town (1)	0-0
	Hereford United v Scunthorpe United	1-0
	Hyde United v Nelson	2-2
	King's Lynn v Dartford	1-1
	Linby Colliery v Nuneaton Borough	3-1
	Llanelli v Weymouth	5-0
	Rhyl v Wigan Athletic	0-0
	Stocksbridge Works v Worcester City	2-2
	Stockton v North Shields	0-1
	Tonbridge v Hendon	3-3
	Tooting & Mitcham United v Great Yarmouth Town	5-3
	Walthamstow Avenue v Eastbourne	2-0
	Witton Albion v Northwich Victoria	4-2
	Woodford Town (1) v Colchester United	1-7
	Workington v Cleator Moor Celtic	0-1
	Wycombe Wanderers v Chelmsford City	0-4
	Yeovil Town v Cheltenham Town	2-4
r	Bedford Town (1) v Guildford City	1-2
r	Dartford v King's Lynn	3-0
r	Hendon v Tonbridge	1-2
r	Nelson v Hyde United	3-0
r	Wigan Athletic v Rhyl	2-3
r	Worcester City v Stocksbridge Works	3-0

Round One

	Aldershot v Bromley	2-2
	Bishop Auckland v York City	2-2
	Bournemouth v Colchester United	1-0
	Bradford City v Oldham Athletic	2-2
	Bristol City v Gloucester City	4-0
	Bristol Rovers v Llanelli	1-1
	Bromsgrove Rovers v Hereford United	1-3
	Carlisle United v Barrow	2-1
	Chelmsford City v Tonbridge	2-2
	Chester v Bradford Park Avenue	1-2
	Cleator Moor Celtic v Tranmere Rovers	0-5 N
	Crewe Alexandra v North Shields	4-0
	Crystal Palace v Millwall	1-4
	Darlington v Rotherham United	2-7
	Gainsborough Trinity v Plymouth Argyle	0-3
	Glastonbury v Exeter City	1-2
	Guildford City v Dartford	1-5
	Halifax Town v Ashington	2-3
	Leyton Orient v Ipswich Town	1-2
	Linby Colliery v Gillingham	1-4
	Lincoln City v Southport	1-1
	Mansfield Town v Walthamstow Avenue	1-0
	Newport County v Walsall	4-2
	Norwich City v Watford	2-0
	Nottingham Forest v Torquay United	6-1
	Port Vale v New Brighton	3-2
	Reading v Cheltenham Town	3-1
	Rochdale v Willington	3-1
	Scarborough v Rhyl	1-2
	Southend United v Swindon Town	0-3
	Tooting & Mitcham United v Brighton & Hove Albion	2-3
	Witton Albion v Nelson	1-2
	Worcester City v Hartlepools United	1-4
	Wrexham v Accrington Stanley	1-0
r	Bromley v Aldershot	0-1
r	Llanelli v Bristol Rovers	1-1e
r	Oldham Athletic v Bradford City	2-1
r	Southport v Lincoln City	3-2
r	Tonbridge v Chelmsford City	0-1e
r	York City v Bishop Auckland	2-1
r2	Bristol Rovers v Llanelli	3-1eN

Round Two

	Aldershot v Bournemouth	3-0
	Ashington v Rochdale	1-2
	Brighton & Hove Albion v Ipswich Town	2-0
	Bristol City v Wrexham	2-1
	Bristol Rovers v Gillingham	2-2
	Chelmsford City v Mansfield Town	1-4
	Crewe Alexandra v Plymouth Argyle	2-2
	Exeter City v Swindon Town	3-0
	Hartlepools United v Oldham Athletic	1-2
	Hereford United v Newport County	0-3
	Millwall v Bradford Park Avenue	1-1
	Port Vale v Nelson	3-2
	Reading v Dartford	4-0
	Rhyl v Norwich City	0-1
	Rotherham United v Nottingham Forest	3-1
	Southport v Carlisle United	1-3
	York City v Tranmere Rovers	2-1
r	Bradford Park Avenue v Millwall	0-1
r	Gillingham v Bristol Rovers	1-1e
r	Plymouth Argyle v Crewe Alexandra	3-0
r2	Bristol Rovers v Gillingham	2-1 N

Round Three

	Arsenal v Carlisle United	0-0
	Aston Villa v Burnley	2-0
	Birmingham City v Manchester City	2-0
	Bolton Wanderers v York City	2-0
	Brighton & Hove Albion v Chesterfield	2-1
	Bristol City v Blackburn Rovers	2-1
	Bristol Rovers v Aldershot	5-1
	Charlton Athletic v Blackpool	2-2
	Derby County v West Bromwich Albion	2-2
	Fulham v Sheffield Wednesday	1-0
	Grimsby Town v Exeter City	3-3
	Huddersfield Town v Tottenham Hotspur	2-0
	Hull City v Everton	2-0
	Leeds United v Middlesbrough	1-0
	Leicester City v Preston North End	0-3
	Luton Town v Portsmouth	2-0
	Manchester United v Oldham Athletic	4-1
	Mansfield Town v Swansea Town	2-0
	Newcastle United v Bury	4-1
	Newport County v Reading	3-2
	Northampton Town v Barnsley	3-1
	Norwich City v Liverpool	3-1
	Notts County v Southampton	3-4
	Plymouth Argyle v Wolverhampton Wan.	1-2
	Queen's Park Rangers v Millwall	3-4
	Rochdale v Chelsea	2-3
	Rotherham United v Doncaster Rovers	2-1
	Sheffield United v Gateshead	1-0
	Stockport County v Brentford	2-1
	Stoke City v Port Vale	2-2
	Sunderland v Coventry City	2-0
	West Ham United v Cardiff City	2-1
r	Blackpool v Charlton Athletic	3-0
r	Carlisle United v Arsenal	1-4
r	Exeter City v Grimsby Town	4-2
r	Port Vale v Stoke City	0-1
r	West Bromwich Albion v Derby County	0-1

Round Four

	Arsenal v Northampton Town	3-2
	Blackpool v Stockport County	2-1
	Bristol City v Brighton & Hove Albion	1-0
	Derby County v Birmingham City	1-3
	Exeter City v Chelsea	1-1
	Hull City v Rotherham United	2-0
	Luton Town v Bristol Rovers	1-2
	Manchester United v Leeds United	4-0
	Millwall v Fulham	0-1
	Newcastle United v Bolton Wanderers	3-2
	Newport County v Norwich City	0-2
	Preston North End v Huddersfield Town	0-2
	Sheffield United v Mansfield Town	0-0
	Stoke City v West Ham United	1-0
	Sunderland v Southampton	2-0
	Wolverhampton Wan. v Aston Villa	3-1
r	Chelsea v Exeter City	2-0
r	Mansfield Town v Sheffield United	2-1

Round Five

	Birmingham City v Bristol City	2-0
	Blackpool v Mansfield Town	2-0
	Bristol Rovers v Hull City	3-0
	Chelsea v Fulham	1-1
	Manchester United v Arsenal	1-0
	Stoke City v Newcastle United	2-4
	Sunderland v Norwich City	3-1
	Wolverhampton Wan. v Huddersfield Town	2-0
r	Fulham v Chelsea	3-0

Round Six

	Birmingham City v Manchester United	1-0
	Blackpool v Fulham	1-0
	Newcastle United v Bristol Rovers	0-0
	Sunderland v Wolverhampton Wan.	1-1
r	Bristol Rovers v Newcastle United	1-3
r	Wolverhampton Wan. v Sunderland	3-1

1950/51 to 1951/52

Semi Finals

	Blackpool v Birmingham City	0-0 N
	Newcastle United v Wolverhampton Wan.	0-0 N
r	Birmingham City v Blackpool	1-2 N
r	Wolverhampton Wan. v Newcastle United	1-2 N

Final

	Newcastle United v Blackpool	2-0 N

1951/52

Preliminary Round

7	Chorley v Horwich RMI	2-5
	Stalybridge Celtic v Darwen	2-2
8	Marine v Liverpool Police	4-0
	Prescot Cables v Llandudno	3-1
	South Liverpool v Bangor City	1-1
9	Bedworth Town v Rugby Town (2)	2-2
	Bournville Athletic v Tamworth	1-3
	Darlaston v Atherstone Town	1-1
	Moor Green v Burton Albion	2-4
10	Brierley Hill Alliance v Lye Town	4-2
	Oswestry Town v Dudley Town	5-2
	Stourbridge v Bilston	5-0
	Wellington Town v Halesowen Town	4-0
11	Buxton v Hyde United	2-1
	Congleton Town v Glossop	wo/s
15	Ashby Institute v Skegness Town	3-6
17	Bentinck Colliery Welfare v Creswell Colliery	1-2
	Bestwood Colliery v Cinderhill Colliery	1-1
	Sutton Town v Linby Colliery	2-2
24	Bowater Lloyds v Ramsgate Athletic	2-2
	Faversham Town v Snowdown CW	0-3
	Folkestone v Chatham Town	4-0
	Gravesend & Northfleet v Maidstone United	2-2
	Margate v Canterbury City	6-1
	Sheppey United v Betteshanger CW	1-3
	Sittingbourne v Deal Town	2-2
	Whitstable v Dover	0-4
25	Bognor Regis Town v Bexhill Town	1-1
	East Grinstead v Haywards Heath	3-5
	Hastings United v Ashford Town	1-3
	Horsham v Eastbourne	2-3
	Littlehampton Town v Tonbridge	1-7
	Redhill v Chichester City (1)	3-0
	Southwick v Lancing Athletic	1-1
	Worthing v Shoreham	3-2
26	Ilford v Brentwood & Warley	1-1
	Tilbury v Briggs Sports	0-4
27	Letchworth Town v Clapton	0-2
	Stevenage Town v Woodford Town (1)	1-4
28	Dorking v Croydon Rovers	wo/s
	Epsom v Woking	3-4
	Farnham Town v Hounslow Town	3-5
	Metropolitan Police v Tooting & Mitcham United	2-3
	Sutton United v Carshalton Athletic	3-3
	Wimbledon v Erith & Belvedere	0-1
29	Headington United v Oxford City	2-2
	Huntley & Palmers v Abingdon Town	6-2
	Marlow v Hemel Hempstead Town	4-3
	Windsor & Eton v Bicester Town	3-2
	Witney Town v Chesham United	1-3
30	Berkhamsted Town v Edgware Town	3-1
	Maidenhead United v Yiewsley	4-1
	Uxbridge v Harrow Town	3-2
	Wealdstone v Southall	2-1
33	Calne & Harris United v Melksham Town	4-0
	Chippenham Town v Spencer Moulton	4-0
	Frome Town v Devizes Town	1-0
	Warminster Town v Corsham Town	3-5
	Westbury United v Andover	5-1
34	Chippenham United v Weston-Super-Mare	4-0
	Clevedon v Bath City	1-3
	Hanham Athletic v Paulton Rovers	0-7
	Peasedown MW v Bristol St George	3-1
	Radstock Town v Wells City	1-3
36	Bridgwater Town (1) v Minehead	2-1
	Dartmouth United v Oak Villa	4-1
	Ilminster Town v Ilfracombe Town	4-3
	Newquay v Wadebridge Town	3-1
	St Austell v Tavistock	3-0
	Taunton v Bideford	1-1
	Tiverton Town v Barnstaple Town	1-2
	Truro City v Newton Abbot	5-3
7r	Darwen v Stalybridge Celtic	2-0
8r	Bangor City v South Liverpool	2-1
9r	Atherstone Town v Darlaston	1-4
r	Rugby Town (2) v Bedworth Town	1-6
17r	Cinderhill Colliery v Bestwood Colliery	4-0
r	Linby Colliery v Sutton Town	1-0
24r	Deal Town v Sittingbourne	1-3
r	Maidstone United v Gravesend & Northfleet	0-3
r	Ramsgate Athletic v Bowater Lloyds	7-0
25r	Bexhill Town v Bognor Regis Town	3-0
r	Lancing Athletic v Southwick	0-1
26r	Brentwood & Warley v Ilford	3-3
28r	Carshalton Athletic v Sutton United	2-3
29r	Oxford City v Headington United	0-3
36r	Bideford v Taunton	8-2
26r2	Ilford v Brentwood & Warley	2-3

Qualifying Round One

1	Alnwick Town v Cramlington Welfare	5-0
	Amble v Shankhouse	3-4
	Newburn v Blyth Spartans	1-1
	West Sleekburn Welfare v Hexham Hearts	2-2
2	Boldon CW v Consett	3-5
	Dawdon Colliery Welfare v Annfield Plain	3-0
	Gosforth & Coxlodge v Easington CW	2-3
	South Shields (2) v Heaton Stannington	4-0
3	Evenwood Town v Crook Town	1-3
	Shildon v Stanley United	3-0
	West Auckland Town v Spennymoor United	2-4
	Willington v Tow Law Town	4-4
4	Blackhall Colliery Welfare v Ushaw Moor	2-1
	Chilton Athletic v Eppleton CW	4-2
	Horden CW v Seaham Colliery Welfare	9-1
	Murton CW v Silksworth CW	3-2
5	Billingham Synthonia v Skinningrove Works	6-0
	Ferryhill Athletic v South Bank	3-4
	Head Wrightsons v Bridlington Trinity	2-3
	Whitby Town v Bridlington Central Utd.	6-2
6	Burscough v Morecambe	2-2
	Fleetwood v Great Harwood	5-0
	Lancaster City v Bacup Borough	2-0
	Netherfield (Kendal) v Clitheroe	2-0
7	Lytham v Darwen	1-3
	Mossley v Leyland Motors	3-0
	Rossendale United v Horwich RMI	4-2
	Skelmersdale United v Ashton United	5-1
8	Bootle Athletic v Bangor City	1-1
	Ellesmere Port Town v Flint Town United	2-2
	Runcorn v Marine	2-1
	St Helens Town v Prescot Cables	2-2
9	Darlaston v Bedworth Town	1-2
	Hednesford Town v Tamworth	0-0
	Nuneaton Borough v Burton Albion	2-2
	Sutton Town (Birmingham) v Boldmere St Michaels	2-0
10	Cradley Heath v Brierley Hill Alliance	1-5
	Kidderminster Harriers v Stafford Rangers	3-2
	Stourbridge v Oswestry Town	4-0
	Worcester City v Wellington Town	3-4
11	Macclesfield Town v Buxton	0-0
	Nantwich v Congleton Town	2-2
	Northwich Victoria v Linotype & Machinery	6-2
	Winsford United v Altrincham	2-0
12	Frickley Colliery v Hallam	3-1
	South Kirkby Colliery v Grimethorpe Athletic	4-0
	Stocksbridge Works v Denaby United	1-1
	Upton Colliery v Sheffield	3-3
13	Brunswick Institute v Norton Woodseats	0-2
	Langold WMC v Brodsworth Main Colliery	3-2
	Rawmarsh Welfare v Beighton Miners Welfare	2-0
	Worksop Town v Bentley Colliery	5-1
14	Goole Town v Harrogate Town	7-3
	Ossett Town v Bradford United	wo/s
	Selby Town v Farsley Celtic	1-1
	Yorkshire Amateur v Pilkington Recreation	5-2
15	Alford United v Skegness Town	1-3
	Boston United v Barton Town (1)	5-3
	Bourne Town v Retford Town	2-4
	Holbeach United v Lysaght's Sports (Scunthorpe)	5-0
16	Boots Athletic v Basford United	2-2
	Ilkeston Town (2) v Gedling Colliery	7-3
	Long Eaton Town v Gresley Rovers	1-1
	Newhall United v Matlock Town	4-0
17	Parliament Street Methodists v Linby Colliery	2-3
	Raleigh Athletic v Creswell Colliery	2-4
	Ransome & Marles v Players Athletic	4-1
	Shirebrook v Cinderhill Colliery	5-1
18	Rushden Town v Corby Town	0-6
	Spalding United v Kettering Town	1-7
	Stamford v Wellingborough Town	5-3
	Symingtons Recreation v Desborough Town	1-3
19	Hinckley Athletic v Barwell Athletic	1-1
	Moira United v Ibstock Penistone Rovers	5-1
	South Normanton MW v Coalville Town (3)	6-0
	Whitwick Colliery v Brush Sports	0-3
20	Bedford Town (1) v Biggleswade Town	3-2
	Hitchin Town v Eynesbury Rovers	1-7
	Vauxhall Motors (Luton) v Potton United	0-0
	Wolverton Town & BR v Luton Amateur	6-1
21	Huntingdon United v Wisbech Town	0-2
	King's Lynn v Chatteris Town	14-1
	March Town United v Abbey United (Cambs)	1-1
	St Neots & District v Histon Institute	6-3
22	Gorleston v Beccles	5-1
	Great Yarmouth Town v Bungay Town	4-2
	Sheringham v Gothic (Norwich)	0-2
	Wymondham Town v Cromer	1-4
23	Diss Town v Sudbury Town	0-4
	Stowmarket v Bury Town	0-3
	Thetford Town v Lowestoft Town	4-4
	Whitton United v Leiston	4-1
24	Betteshanger CW v Gravesend & Northfleet	3-1
	Dover v Ramsgate Athletic	4-0
	Folkestone v Margate	3-1
	Snowdown CW v Sittingbourne	4-2
25	Bexhill Town v Tonbridge	0-4
	Haywards Heath v Eastbourne	1-2
	Redhill v Ashford Town	2-3
	Southwick v Worthing	6-7
26	Clacton Town v Briggs Sports	0-1
	Grays Athletic v Brentwood & Warley	1-2
	Harwich & Parkeston v Dagenham	2-2
	Romford (2) v Barking	1-0
27	Cheshunt v Leyton	1-2
	Enfield v Woodford Town (1)	0-2
	Eton Manor v Clapton	1-0
	Finchley v Tufnell Park Edmonton	2-1
28	Kingstonian v Tooting & Mitcham United	3-1
	Sutton United v Erith & Belvedere	2-2
	Walton & Hersham v Hounslow Town	0-6
	Woking v Dorking	5-1
29	Aylesbury United v Marlow	4-1
	Banbury Spencer v Huntley & Palmers	2-1
	Headington United v Chesham United	5-2
	Wycombe Wanderers v Windsor & Eton	6-1
30	Hayes v Berkhamsted Town	5-0
	Slough Town v Barnet	2-2
	St Albans City v Maidenhead United	3-1
	Wealdstone v Uxbridge	2-1
31	Basingstoke Town v Cowes	4-3
	Gosport Borough Ath. v Newport (IOW)	2-3
	Totton v Ryde Sports	3-0
	Winchester City v Alton Town	2-2
32	Blandford United v Lymington	1-3
	Bridport v Bournemouth Gasworks Athletic	2-2
	Portland United v Dorchester Town	1-1
	Shaftesbury v Poole Town	1-4
33	Corsham Town v Frome Town	2-7
	Salisbury (2) v Calne & Harris United	2-0
	Trowbridge Town v Chippenham Town	2-2
	Welton Rovers v Westbury United	2-2
34	Clandown v Paulton Rovers	3-1
	Glastonbury v Bath City	2-2
	Street v Chippenham United	0-3
	Wells City v Peasedown MW	2-2
35	Cinderford Town v Ebbw Vale	1-5
	Llanelli v Lovells Athletic	2-0
	Stonehouse v Gloucester City	1-2
	Troedryhiw v Barry Town	1-3
36	Dartmouth United v Newquay	1-0
	Ilminster Town v Bridgwater Town (1)	1-1
	St Austell v Bideford	1-1
	Truro City v Barnstaple Town	2-3
1r	Blyth Spartans v Newburn	1-0
r	Hexham Hearts v West Sleekburn Welfare	6-0
3r	Tow Law Town v Willington	1-2
6r	Morecambe v Burscough	0-1
8r	Bangor City v Bootle Athletic	2-0
r	Flint Town United v Ellesmere Port Town	3-1
r	Prescot Cables v St Helens Town	2-1
9r	Burton Albion v Nuneaton Borough	2-4
r	Tamworth v Hednesford Town	2-4
11r	Buxton v Macclesfield Town	2-0
r	Congleton Town v Nantwich	3-1
12r	Denaby United v Stocksbridge Works	2-1
r	Sheffield v Upton Colliery	0-2
14r	Farsley Celtic v Selby Town	4-2
16r	Basford United v Boots Athletic	2-0
r	Gresley Rovers v Long Eaton Town	0-2
19r	Barwell Athletic v Hinckley Athletic	2-7
20r	Potton United v Vauxhall Motors (Luton)	4-3
21r	Abbey United (Cambs) v March Town United	3-4
23r	Lowestoft Town v Thetford Town	5-0
26r	Dagenham v Harwich & Parkeston	2-1
28r	Erith & Belvedere v Sutton United	1-1
30r	Barnet v Slough Town	1-6
31r	Alton Town v Winchester City	3-1
32r	Bournemouth Gasworks Athletic v Bridport	3-1
r	Dorchester Town v Portland United	2-3
33r	Chippenham Town v Trowbridge Town	2-1
r	Westbury United v Welton Rovers	0-3
34r	Bath City v Glastonbury	3-1
r	Peasedown MW v Wells City	0-2
36r	Bideford v St Austell	5-0
r	Bridgwater Town (1) v Ilminster Town	4-2
28r2	Sutton United v Erith & Belvedere	3-0

Qualifying Round Two

1	Alnwick Town v Shankhouse	2-0
	Blyth Spartans v Hexham Hearts	4-0
2	Dawdon Colliery Welfare v Consett	0-3
	South Shields (2) v Easington CW	2-2
3	Crook Town v Willington	2-1
	Shildon v Spennymoor United	0-2
4	Chilton Athletic v Blackhall Colliery Welfare	0-0
	Murton CW v Horden CW	0-3
5	Bridlington Trinity v Billingham Synthonia	0-6
	Whitby Town v South Bank	3-2
6	Lancaster City v Fleetwood	2-3
	Netherfield (Kendal) v Burscough	4-2
7	Darwen v Mossley	1-0
	Rossendale United v Skelmersdale United	1-1
8	Bangor City v Runcorn	1-0
	Prescot Cables v Flint Town United	3-1
9	Bedworth Town v Hednesford Town	3-0
	Nuneaton Borough v Sutton Town (Birmingham)	5-1
10	Brierley Hill Alliance v Kidderminster Harriers	1-2
	Stourbridge v Wellington Town	1-3
11	Buxton v Winsford United	4-0
	Congleton Town v Northwich Victoria	1-0
12	Frickley Colliery v Denaby United	4-1
	Upton Colliery v South Kirkby Colliery	2-2
13	Rawmarsh Welfare v Langold WMC	2-0
	Worksop Town v Norton Woodseats	1-0
14	Farsley Celtic v Yorkshire Amateur	2-3
	Ossett Town v Goole Town	2-3

1951/52

15	Boston United v Retford Town	6-1
	Skegness Town v Holbeach United	4-0
16	Basford United v Newhall United	1-1
	Long Eaton Town v Ilkeston Town (2)	0-3
17	Linby Colliery v Ransome & Marles	5-1
	Shirebrook v Creswell Colliery	2-2
18	Corby Town v Kettering Town	1-2
	Desborough Town v Stamford	2-1
19	Brush Sports v Moira United	2-0
	Hinckley Athletic v South Normanton MW	2-2
20	Bedford Town (1) v Eynesbury Rovers	3-0
	Potton United v Wolverton Town & BR	2-5
21	King's Lynn v Wisbech Town	2-0
	March Town United v St Neots & District	1-0
22	Gorleston v Cromer	3-0
	Great Yarmouth Town v Gothic (Norwich)	0-3
23	Bury Town v Lowestoft Town	2-0
	Whitton United v Sudbury Town	1-2
24	Dover v Folkestone	0-2
	Snowdown CW v Betteshanger CW	0-2
25	Eastbourne v Ashford Town	2-2
	Tonbridge v Worthing	11-1
26	Brentwood & Warley v Dagenham	3-3
	Briggs Sports v Romford (2)	1-1
27	Eton Manor v Leyton	0-1
	Woodford Town (1) v Finchley	3-1
28	Sutton United v Kingstonian	2-2
	Woking v Hounslow Town	0-6
29	Banbury Spencer v Aylesbury United	0-4
	Headington United v Wycombe Wanderers	3-2 D
30	St Albans City v Slough Town	1-1
	Wealdstone v Hayes	2-0
31	Basingstoke Town v Alton Town	2-5
	Newport (IOW) v Totton	6-1
32	Bournemouth Gasworks Athletic v Portland United	1-3
	Lymington v Poole Town	3-2
33	Chippenham Town v Welton Rovers	5-1
	Frome Town v Salisbury (2)	2-3
34	Clandown v Bath City	1-3
	Wells City v Chippenham United	1-5
35	Barry Town v Llanelli	0-0
	Gloucester City v Ebbw Vale	1-2
36	Bideford v Dartmouth United	7-0
	Bridgwater Town (1) v Barnstaple Town	1-3
2r	Easington CW v South Shields (2)	1-1
4r	Blackhall Colliery Welfare v Chilton Athletic	1-0
7r	Skelmersdale United v Rossendale United	3-0
12r	South Kirkby Colliery v Upton Colliery	2-3
16r	Newhall United v Basford United	3-0
17r	Creswell Colliery v Shirebrook	1-0
19r	South Normanton MW v Hinckley Athletic	1-2
25r	Ashford Town v Eastbourne	4-0
26r	Dagenham v Brentwood & Warley	1-2
r	Romford (2) v Briggs Sports	6-2
28r	Kingstonian v Sutton United	2-3
30r	Slough Town v St Albans City	4-0
35r	Llanelli v Barry Town	2-2
2r2	South Shields (2) v Easington CW	2-1
35r2	Barry Town v Llanelli	4-0 N

Qualifying Round Three

1	Blyth Spartans v Alnwick Town	4-3
2	Consett v South Shields (2)	4-0
3	Crook Town v Spennymoor United	0-2
4	Blackhall Colliery Welfare v Horden CW	3-1
5	Whitby Town v Billingham Synthonia	2-3
6	Fleetwood v Netherfield (Kendal)	3-0
7	Skelmersdale United v Darwen	1-1
8	Bangor City v Prescot Cables	1-0
9	Bedworth Town v Nuneaton Borough	1-1
10	Wellington Town v Kidderminster Harriers	3-2
11	Buxton v Congleton Town	2-0
12	Frickley Colliery v Upton Colliery	5-0
13	Rawmarsh Welfare v Worksop Town	2-1
14	Goole Town v Yorkshire Amateur	3-0
15	Skegness Town v Boston United	2-1
16	Ilkeston Town (2) v Newhall United	6-1
17	Creswell Colliery v Linby Colliery	2-0
18	Kettering Town v Desborough Town	2-0
19	Hinckley Athletic v Brush Sports	2-3
20	Bedford Town (1) v Wolverton Town & BR	5-1
21	March Town United v King's Lynn	1-4
22	Gorleston v Gothic (Norwich)	5-0
23	Bury Town v Sudbury Town	1-1
24	Folkestone v Betteshanger CW	2-0
25	Ashford Town v Tonbridge	1-1
26	Romford (2) v Brentwood & Warley	3-1
27	Leyton v Woodford Town (1)	3-2
28	Hounslow Town v Sutton United	1-4
29	Wycombe Wanderers v Aylesbury United	1-2
30	Wealdstone v Slough Town	5-0
31	Newport (IOW) v Alton Town	5-1
32	Lymington v Portland United	1-1
33	Salisbury (2) v Chippenham Town	1-1
34	Chippenham United v Bath City	0-3
35	Barry Town v Ebbw Vale	4-2
36	Barnstaple Town v Bideford	2-1
7r	Darwen v Skelmersdale United	0-1
9r	Nuneaton Borough v Bedworth Town	1-2
23r	Sudbury Town v Bury Town	2-2
25r	Tonbridge v Ashford Town	4-0
32r	Portland United v Lymington	1-2
33r	Chippenham Town v Salisbury (2)	2-1
23r2	Bury Town v Sudbury Town	2-4

Qualifying Round Four

	Ashington v Blyth Spartans	0-2
	Aylesbury United v Hendon	4-3
	Bangor City v New Brighton	2-1
	Bath City v Barry Town	0-2
	Billingham Synthonia v North Shields	2-1
	Bromsgrove Rovers v Bedford Town (1)	2-5
	Brush Sports v Wellington Town	3-1
	Cheltenham Town v Merthyr Tydfil	2-3
	Chippenham Town v Newport (IOW)	3-1
	Folkestone v Sutton United	1-1
	Frickley Colliery v Buxton	1-1
	Gainsborough Trinity v Creswell Colliery	5-2
	Goole Town v Spennymoor United	4-3
	Gorleston v Romford (2)	1-0
	Guildford City v Dartford	2-1
	Ilkeston Town (2) v Grantham	2-1
	Kettering Town v Bedworth Town	4-2
	King's Lynn v Sudbury Town	1-0
	Leyton v Walthamstow Avenue	0-0
	Leytonstone v Chelmsford City	2-1
	Lymington v Barnstaple Town	1-1
	Peterborough United v Hereford United	1-1
	Rawmarsh Welfare v Skegness Town	4-2
	Rhyl v Fleetwood	7-2
	Scarborough v Blackhall Colliery Welfare	0-0
	Skelmersdale United v Nelson	0-3
	Stockton v Consett	2-0
	Tonbridge v Wealdstone	2-0
	Wigan Athletic v Witton Albion	2-2
	Yeovil Town v Weymouth	1-1
r	Barnstaple Town v Lymington	3-1
r	Blackhall Colliery Welfare v Scarborough	5-3
r	Buxton v Frickley Colliery	3-1
r	Hereford United v Peterborough United	1-0
r	Sutton United v Folkestone	1-3
r	Walthamstow Avenue v Leyton	1-2e
r	Weymouth v Yeovil Town	2-1
r	Witton Albion v Wigan Athletic	3-3e
r2	Wigan Athletic v Witton Albion	1-3

Round One

	Accrington Stanley v Chester	1-2
	Aylesbury United v Watford	0-5
	Bangor City v Southport	2-2
	Barnstaple Town v Folkestone	2-2
	Barrow v Chesterfield	0-2
	Blackhall Colliery Welfare v Workington	2-5
	Blyth Spartans v Bishop Auckland	2-1
	Bradford City v Carlisle United	6-1
	Brighton & Hove Albion v Bristol City	1-2
	Bristol Rovers v Kettering Town	3-0
	Brush Sports v Weymouth	2-3
	Colchester United v Port Vale	3-1
	Crewe Alexandra v Lincoln City	2-4
	Crystal Palace v Gillingham	0-1
	Grimsby Town v Darlington	4-0
	Guildford City v Hereford United	4-1
	Hartlepools United v Rhyl	2-0
	Ilkeston Town (2) v Rochdale	0-2
	King's Lynn v Exeter City	1-3
	Leyton v Chippenham Town	3-0
	Leyton Orient v Gorleston	2-2
	Leytonstone v Shrewsbury Town	2-0
	Merthyr Tydfil v Ipswich Town	2-2e
	Millwall v Plymouth Argyle	1-0
	Nelson v Oldham Athletic	0-4
	Newport County v Barry Town	4-0
	Norwich City v Northampton Town	3-2
	Rawmarsh Welfare v Buxton	1-4
	Reading v Walsall	1-0
	Scunthorpe United v Billingham Synthonia	5-0
	Southend United v Bournemouth	6-1
	Stockport County v Gateshead	2-2
	Stockton v Mansfield Town	1-1
	Swindon Town v Bedford Town (1)	2-0
	Tonbridge v Aldershot	0-0
	Torquay United v Bromley	3-2
	Tranmere Rovers v Goole Town	4-2
	Witton Albion v Gainsborough Trinity	2-1
	Wrexham v Halifax Town	3-0
	York City v Bradford Park Avenue	1-1
r	Aldershot v Tonbridge	3-2e
r	Bradford Park Avenue v York City	1-1e
r	Folkestone v Barnstaple Town	5-2
r	Gateshead v Stockport County	1-1e
r	Gorleston v Leyton Orient	0-0e
r	Ipswich Town v Merthyr Tydfil	1-0
r	Mansfield Town v Stockton	0-2
r	Southport v Bangor City	3-0
r2	Leyton Orient v Gorleston	5-4 N
r2	Stockport County v Gateshead	1-2 N
r2	York City v Bradford Park Avenue	0-4 N

Round Two

	Bradford Park Avenue v Bradford City	3-2
	Bristol Rovers v Weymouth	2-0
	Buxton v Aldershot	4-3
	Chester v Leyton	5-2
	Colchester United v Bristol City	2-1
	Gateshead v Guildford City	2-0
	Gillingham v Rochdale	0-3
	Ipswich Town v Exeter City	4-0
	Leytonstone v Newport County	2-2
	Lincoln City v Grimsby Town	3-1
	Millwall v Scunthorpe United	0-0
	Norwich City v Chesterfield	3-1
	Reading v Southport	1-1
	Southend United v Oldham Athletic	5-0
	Stockton v Folkestone	2-1
	Swindon Town v Torquay United	3-3
	Tranmere Rovers v Blyth Spartans	1-1
	Watford v Hartlepools United	1-2
	Witton Albion v Workington	3-3
	Wrexham v Leyton Orient	1-1
r	Blyth Spartans v Tranmere Rovers	1-1x
r	Leyton Orient v Wrexham	3-2e
r	Newport County v Leytonstone	3-0
r	Scunthorpe United v Millwall	3-0
r	Southport v Reading	1-1e
r	Torquay United v Swindon Town	1-1e
r	Workington v Witton Albion	1-0
r2	Reading v Southport	2-0 N
r2	Swindon Town v Torquay United	3-1 N
r2	Tranmere Rovers v Blyth Spartans	2-2eN
r3	Tranmere Rovers v Blyth Spartans	5-1 N

Round Three

	Barnsley v Colchester United	3-0
	Bradford Park Avenue v Sheffield Wednesday	2-1
	Brentford v Queen's Park Rangers	3-1
	Bristol Rovers v Preston North End	2-0
	Burnley v Hartlepools United	1-0
	Cardiff City v Swindon Town	1-1
	Chelsea v Chester	2-2
	Doncaster Rovers v Buxton	2-0
	Fulham v Birmingham City	0-1
	Huddersfield Town v Tranmere Rovers	1-2
	Ipswich Town v Gateshead	2-2
	Leicester City v Coventry City	1-1
	Leyton Orient v Everton	0-0
	Liverpool v Workington	1-0
	Luton Town v Charlton Athletic	1-0
	Manchester City v Wolverhampton Wan.	2-2
	Manchester United v Hull City	0-2
	Middlesbrough v Derby County	2-2
	Newcastle United v Aston Villa	4-2
	Norwich City v Arsenal	0-5
	Nottingham Forest v Blackburn Rovers	2-2
	Notts County v Stockton	4-0
	Portsmouth v Lincoln City	4-0
	Reading v Swansea Town	0-3
	Rochdale v Leeds United	0-2
	Rotherham United v Bury	2-1
	Scunthorpe United v Tottenham Hotspur	0-3
	Sheffield United v Newport County	2-0
	Southend United v Southampton	3-0
	Sunderland v Stoke City	0-0
	West Bromwich Albion v Bolton Wanderers	4-0
	West Ham United v Blackpool	2-1
r	Blackburn Rovers v Nottingham Forest	2-0
r	Chester v Chelsea	2-3e
r	Coventry City v Leicester City	4-1
r	Derby County v Middlesbrough	0-2
r	Everton v Leyton Orient	1-3
r	Gateshead v Ipswich Town	3-3e
r	Stoke City v Sunderland	3-1
r	Swindon Town v Cardiff City	1-0e
r	Wolverhampton Wan. v Manchester City	4-1
r2	Ipswich Town v Gateshead	1-2eN

Round Four

	Arsenal v Barnsley	4-0
	Birmingham City v Leyton Orient	0-1
	Blackburn Rovers v Hull City	2-0
	Burnley v Coventry City	2-0
	Chelsea v Tranmere Rovers	4-0
	Gateshead v West Bromwich Albion	0-2 N
	Leeds United v Bradford Park Avenue	2-0
	Liverpool v Wolverhampton Wan.	2-1
	Luton Town v Brentford	2-2
	Middlesbrough v Doncaster Rovers	1-4
	Notts County v Portsmouth	1-3
	Southend United v Bristol Rovers	2-1
	Swansea Town v Rotherham United	3-0
	Swindon Town v Stoke City	1-1
	Tottenham Hotspur v Newcastle United	0-3
	West Ham United v Sheffield United	0-0
r	Brentford v Luton Town	0-0e
r	Sheffield United v West Ham United	4-2
r	Stoke City v Swindon Town	0-1
r2	Luton Town v Brentford	3-2eN

Round Five

	Blackburn Rovers v West Bromwich Albion	1-0
	Burnley v Liverpool	2-0
	Leeds United v Chelsea	1-1
	Leyton Orient v Arsenal	0-3
	Luton Town v Swindon Town	3-1
	Portsmouth v Doncaster Rovers	4-0
	Southend United v Sheffield United	1-2
	Swansea Town v Newcastle United	0-1
r	Chelsea v Leeds United	1-1e
r2	Leeds United v Chelsea	1-5 N

1951/52 to 1952/53

	Round Six	
	Blackburn Rovers v Burnley	3-1
	Luton Town v Arsenal	2-3
	Portsmouth v Newcastle United	2-4
	Sheffield United v Chelsea	0-1
	Semi Finals	
	Chelsea v Arsenal	1-1 N
	Newcastle United v Blackburn Rovers	0-0 N
r	Arsenal v Chelsea	3-0 N
r	Blackburn Rovers v Newcastle United	1-2 N
	Final	
	Newcastle United v Arsenal	1-0 N

1952/53

	Preliminary Round	
6	Penrith v Burscough	4-4
7	Leyland Motors v Horwich RMI	0-3
	Lytham v Droylsden	2-0
8	Earlestown v Prescot Cables	0-2
	Llandudno v Bootle Athletic	1-1
	Marine v Ellesmere Port Town	3-3
	Runcorn v Bangor City	2-2
9	Boldmere St Michaels v Rugby Town (2)	2-2
	Lockheed Leamington v Nuneaton Borough	1-2
	Moor Green v Burton Albion	1-1
	Tamworth v Hednesford Town	0-2
10	Darlaston v Stourbridge	2-1
	Halesowen Town v Brierley Hill Alliance	1-4
	Kidderminster Harriers v Dudley Town	4-0
	Stafford Rangers v Bilston	0-1
15	Ashby Institute v Brigg Town	2-3
	Boston United v Barton Town (1)	7-1
	Retford Town v Holbeach United	2-1
17	Parliament Street Methodists v Linby Colliery	0-6
	Raleigh Athletic v Ransome & Marles	1-4
18	Rushden Town v Wellingborough Town	3-1
20	Dunstable Town v Hitchin Town	2-4
21	Chatteris Town v Cambridge United	0-4
24	Betteshanger CW v Deal Town	2-0
	Chatham Town v Dover	0-6
	Maidstone United v Bromley	0-6
	Margate v Gravesend & Northfleet	1-4
	Ramsgate Athletic v Snowdown CW	4-2
	Sheppey United v Bowater Lloyds	5-1
	Sittingbourne v Faversham Town	3-1
	Tunbridge Wells United v Canterbury City	2-1
25	Bexhill Town v Shoreham	2-0
	East Grinstead v Redhill	4-2
	Hastings United v Chichester City (1)	4-0
	Haywards Heath v Southwick	2-2
	Horsham v Worthing	1-4
	Lancing Athletic v Eastbourne	6-6
	Littlehampton Town v Bognor Regis Town	4-3
	Newhaven v Ashford Town	2-4
26	Barking v Ilford	1-1
	Brentwood & Warley v Dagenham	1-3
27	Enfield v Woodford Town (1)	3-3
28	Bexleyheath & Welling v Carshalton Athletic	1-5
	Epsom v Dulwich Hamlet	2-2
	Kingstonian v Erith & Belvedere	5-0
	Metropolitan Police v Wimbledon	1-5
	Walton & Hersham v Tooting & Mitcham United	0-1
	Woking v Dorking	4-1
29	Aylesbury United v Chesham United	4-1
	Banbury Spencer v Maidenhead United	1-1
	Huntley & Palmers v Witney Town	4-2
	Marlow v Headington United	0-8
	Oxford City v Wycombe Wanderers	1-4
30	Berkhamsted Town v Barnet	1-5
	Harrow Town v Uxbridge	1-8
	Hayes v Yiewsley	6-1
	Slough Centre v Slough Town	2-1
	Southall v Edgware Town	1-3
	Windsor & Eton v Wealdstone	0-4
32	Blandford United v Dorchester Town	2-5
33	Andover v Frome Town	2-3
	Calne & Harris United v Trowbridge Town	0-4
	Corsham Town v Chippenham Town	1-4
	Melksham Town v Warminster Town	0-2
	Salisbury (2) v Welton Rovers	7-1
34	Clandown v Glastonbury	0-4
	Hanham Athletic v Paulton Rovers	0-1
	Peasedown MW v Clevedon	6-2
	Street v Bristol St George	2-0
35	Gloucester City v Llanelli	1-1
36	Barnstaple Town v Dartmouth United	5-1
	Minehead v Bideford	1-4
	Newquay v Truro City	7-1
	Newton Abbot v Ilfracombe Town	1-1
	St Blazey v Penzance	3-1
	Tavistock v Bridgwater Town (1)	1-2
	Tiverton Town v Taunton	1-2
	Wadebridge Town v St Austell	4-5
6r	Burscough v Penrith	3-1
8r	Bangor City v Runcorn	3-2e
r	Bootle Athletic v Llandudno	1-0
r	Ellesmere Port Town v Marine	2-1
9r	Burton Albion v Moor Green	3-0
r	Rugby Town (2) v Boldmere St Michaels	2-1
25r	Eastbourne v Lancing Athletic	1-2e
r	Southwick v Haywards Heath	0-1e
26r	Ilford v Barking	4-2
27r	Woodford Town (1) v Enfield	4-2
28r	Dulwich Hamlet v Epsom	4-2
29r	Maidenhead United v Banbury Spencer	3-0
35r	Llanelli v Gloucester City	5-0
36r	Ilfracombe Town v Newton Abbot	2-1

	Qualifying Round One	
1	Alnwick Town v West Sleekburn Welfare	4-1
	Amble v Ashington	0-4
	Cramlington Welfare v Hexham Hearts	0-1
	Newburn v Shankhouse	4-1
2	Annfield Plain v Boldon CW	6-2
	Dawdon Colliery Welfare v South Shields (2)	1-2
	Easington CW v Heaton Stannington	3-0
	Gosforth & Coxlodge v Consett	0-5
3	Evenwood Town v Tow Law Town	1-0
	Shildon v Crook Town	0-4
	Stanley United v Spennymoor United	2-4
	Willington v West Auckland Town	2-4
4	Seaham Colliery Welfare v Horden CW	1-3
	Silksworth CW v Murton CW	7-0
	Ushaw Moor v Chilton Athletic	2-0
5	Billingham Synthonia v South Bank	3-2
	Ferryhill Athletic v Skinningrove Works	7-0
	Head Wrightsons v Bridlington Central Utd.	2-0
6	Burscough v Lancaster City	1-0
	Clitheroe v Fleetwood	1-1
	Morecambe v Great Harwood	1-0
	Netherfield (Kendal) v Bacup Borough	5-0
7	Ashton United v Skelmersdale United	7-2
	Horwich RMI v Chorley	5-3
	Mossley v Lytham	3-1
	Rossendale United v Darwen	2-0
8	Bangor City v St Helens Town	2-0
	Bootle Athletic v New Brighton	1-1
	Ellesmere Port Town v South Liverpool	4-0
	Prescot Cables v Flint Town United	1-1
9	Bournville Athletic v Rugby Town (2)	0-2
	Burton Albion v Bedworth Town	1-2
	Hednesford Town v Nuneaton Borough	1-1
	Sutton Town (Birmingham) v Atherstone Town	1-2
10	Bromsgrove Rovers v Darlaston	3-2
	Cradley Heath v Bilston	2-2
	Kidderminster Harriers v Oswestry Town	2-0
	Lye Town v Brierley Hill Alliance	1-3
11	Macclesfield Town v Congleton Town	3-0
	Northwich Victoria v Winsford United	1-1
	Stalybridge Celtic v Hyde United	3-2
12	Denaby United v Stocksbridge Works	2-1
	Frickley Colliery v Upton Colliery	2-2
	Grimethorpe Athletic v Sheffield	3-1
	South Kirkby Colliery v Hallam	2-1
13	Brodsworth Main Colliery v Norton Woodseats	0-5
	Brunswick Institute v Beighton Miners Welfare	0-2
	Langold WMC v Bentley Colliery	2-0
	Worksop Town v Rawmarsh Welfare	3-3
14	Farsley Celtic v Ossett Town	1-0
15	Boston United v Alford United	5-4
	Bourne Town v Grantham	0-5
	Lysaght's Sports (Scunthorpe) v Skegness Town	1-9
	Retford Town v Brigg Town	8-2
16	Basford United v Boots Athletic	0-1
	Gresley Rovers v Gedling Colliery	3-1
	Ilkeston Town (2) v Long Eaton Town	7-2
	Newhall United v Matlock Town	3-2
17	Creswell Colliery v Sutton Town	2-0
	Linby Colliery v Bestwood Colliery	3-0
	Players Athletic v Shirebrook	8-5
	Ransome & Marles v Cinderhill Colliery	1-0
18	Desborough Town v Corby Town	1-4
	Kettering Town v Rushden Town	1-0
	Spalding United v Stamford	1-0
	Symingtons Recreation v Peterborough United	2-5
19	Brush Sports v Ibstock Penistone Rovers	5-0
	Coalville Town (3) v Moira United	7-1
	Hinckley Athletic v Whitwick Colliery	2-3
	South Normanton MW v Barwell Athletic	4-0
20	Bedford Town (1) v Potton United	6-0
	Biggleswade Town v Wolverton Town & BR	0-3
	Hitchin Town v Luton Amateur	5-0
	Vauxhall Motors (Luton) v Eynesbury Rovers	2-4
21	Cambridge United v March Town United	3-1
	Huntingdon United v Cambridge City	0-3
	King's Lynn v St Neots & District	4-1
	Wisbech Town v Histon Institute	3-0
22	Beccles v Bungay Town	3-1
	Gothic (Norwich) v Wymondham Town	6-0
	Great Yarmouth Town v Cromer	13-0
23	Bury Town v Leiston	9-1
	Diss Town v Lowestoft Town	1-4
	Stowmarket v Thetford Town	4-0
	Whitton United v Sudbury Town	0-4
24	Betteshanger CW v Ramsgate Athletic	1-2
	Bromley v Gravesend & Northfleet	0-1
	Dover v Sheppey United	2-0
	Tunbridge Wells United v Sittingbourne	2-4
25	Ashford Town v Hastings United	1-3
	Bexhill Town v Lancing Athletic	1-2
	East Grinstead v Haywards Heath	1-0
	Littlehampton Town v Worthing	0-3
26	Clacton Town v Romford (2)	1-1
	Dagenham v Briggs Sports	2-2
	Grays Athletic v Harwich & Parkeston	6-2
	Tilbury v Ilford	1-0
27	Cheshunt v Tufnell Park Edmonton	2-1
	Clapton v Finchley	1-2
	Letchworth Town v Eton Manor	1-1
	Woodford Town (1) v Stevenage Town	2-1
28	Carshalton Athletic v Kingstonian	3-0
	Dulwich Hamlet v Tooting & Mitcham United	2-1
	Sutton United v Hounslow Town	3-2
	Woking v Wimbledon	1-2
29	Headington United v Aylesbury United	4-2
	Hemel Hempstead Town v Abingdon Town	6-0
	Maidenhead United v Bicester Town	2-0
	Wycombe Wanderers v Huntley & Palmers	4-2
30	Barnet v St Albans City	1-2
	Edgware Town v Slough Centre	2-1
	Hayes v Uxbridge	0-3
	Wealdstone v Hendon	0-1
31	Basingstoke Town v Totton	3-1
	Cowes v Newport (IOW)	0-1
	Ryde Sports v Alton Town	3-4e
	Winchester City v Gosport Borough Ath.	1-0
32	Bournemouth Gasworks Athletic v Poole Town	3-0
	Bridport v Dorchester Town	0-2
	Ilminster Town v Lymington	2-1
	Portland United v Shaftesbury	3-1
33	Frome Town v Devizes Town	3-6
	Salisbury (2) v Westbury United	4-1
	Spencer Moulton v Chippenham Town	0-3
	Warminster Town v Trowbridge Town	1-1
34	Chippenham United v Wells City	2-2
	Paulton Rovers v Bath City	2-7
	Peasedown MW v Radstock Town	3-0
	Street v Glastonbury	1-2
35	Cinderford Town v Cheltenham Town	1-1
	Lovells Athletic v Llanelli	0-1
	Stonehouse v Ebbw Vale	0-1
	Troedryhiw v Barry Town	3-8
36	Barnstaple Town v Taunton	1-1
	Ilfracombe Town v Bideford	3-0
	Newquay v St Blazey	1-3
	St Austell v Bridgwater Town (1)	2-3
6r	Fleetwood v Clitheroe	1-2
8r	Flint Town United v Prescot Cables	3-0
r	New Brighton v Bootle Athletic	1-0
9r	Nuneaton Borough v Hednesford Town	2-5
10r	Bilston v Cradley Heath	3-1
11r	Winsford United v Northwich Victoria	4-2
12r	Upton Colliery v Frickley Colliery	0-2
13r	Rawmarsh Welfare v Worksop Town	3-2
26r	Briggs Sports v Dagenham	0-0x
r	Romford (2) v Clacton Town	1-3
27r	Eton Manor v Letchworth Town	1-1e
33r	Trowbridge Town v Warminster Town	4-1
34r	Wells City v Chippenham United	3-1
35r	Cheltenham Town v Cinderford Town	5-0
36r	Taunton v Barnstaple Town	3-5
26r2	Briggs Sports v Dagenham	1-3
27r2	Letchworth Town v Eton Manor	0-3 N

	Qualifying Round Two	
1	Alnwick Town v Newburn	0-1
	Hexham Hearts v Ashington	3-5
2	Easington CW v Consett	2-2
	South Shields (2) v Annfield Plain	3-1
3	Crook Town v Spennymoor United	1-2
	West Auckland Town v Evenwood Town	1-2
4	Horden CW v Blackhall Colliery Welfare	3-0
	Ushaw Moor v Silksworth CW	4-1
5	Billingham Synthonia v Head Wrightsons	6-1
	Ferryhill Athletic v Whitby Town	4-0
6	Burscough v Netherfield (Kendal)	2-4
	Clitheroe v Morecambe	0-1
7	Ashton United v Horwich RMI	2-1
	Mossley v Rossendale United	1-0
8	Bangor City v New Brighton	2-0
	Ellesmere Port Town v Flint Town United	1-2
9	Atherstone Town v Rugby Town (2)	2-0
	Hednesford Town v Bedworth Town	0-3
10	Bromsgrove Rovers v Bilston	1-0
	Kidderminster Harriers v Brierley Hill Alliance	1-1
11	Stalybridge Celtic v Altrincham	2-2
	Winsford United v Macclesfield Town	1-0
12	Denaby United v Grimethorpe Athletic	1-0
	Frickley Colliery v South Kirkby Colliery	4-0
13	Beighton Miners Welfare v Rawmarsh Welfare	6-0
	Langold WMC v Norton Woodseats	0-4
14	Goole Town v Farsley Celtic	3-3
	Selby Town v Yorkshire Amateur	2-1
15	Retford Town v Boston United	1-4
	Skegness Town v Grantham	2-0
16	Boots Athletic v Newhall United	2-2
	Gresley Rovers v Ilkeston Town (2)	0-5
17	Creswell Colliery v Ransome & Marles	3-0
	Linby Colliery v Players Athletic	6-0
18	Corby Town v Kettering Town	1-1
	Spalding United v Peterborough United	2-2
19	Brush Sports v Coalville Town (3)	3-1
	South Normanton MW v Whitwick Colliery	3-0
20	Eynesbury Rovers v Bedford Town (1)	0-4

1952/53

	Hitchin Town v Wolverton Town & BR	6-2
21	Cambridge City v King's Lynn	3-3
	Cambridge United v Wisbech Town	0-0
22	Gothic (Norwich) v Great Yarmouth Town	0-5
	Sheringham v Beccles	2-2
23	Bury Town v Stowmarket	1-1
	Sudbury Town v Lowestoft Town	4-0
24	Dover v Ramsgate Athletic	5-3
	Gravesend & Northfleet v Sittingbourne	3-0
25	East Grinstead v Lancing Athletic	0-1
	Worthing v Hastings United	2-2
26	Clacton Town v Tilbury	6-2
	Dagenham v Grays Athletic	0-1
27	Cheshunt v Eton Manor	0-1
	Finchley v Woodford Town (1)	2-0
28	Dulwich Hamlet v Wimbledon	3-3
	Sutton United v Carshalton Athletic	0-2
29	Headington United v Maidenhead United	2-0
	Hemel Hempstead Town v Wycombe Wanderers	1-2
30	St Albans City v Hendon	1-1
	Uxbridge v Edgware Town	2-1
31	Basingstoke Town v Alton Town	2-0
	Winchester City v Newport (IOW)	1-3
32	Bournemouth Gasworks Athletic v Portland United	5-1
	Dorchester Town v Ilminster Town	6-1
33	Devizes Town v Trowbridge Town	0-3
	Salisbury (2) v Chippenham Town	3-1
34	Bath City v Wells City	2-0
	Peasedown MW v Glastonbury	0-1
35	Cheltenham Town v Barry Town	0-3
	Ebbw Vale v Llanelli	0-3
36	Barnstaple Town v Bridgwater Town (1)	4-2
	Ilfracombe Town v St Blazey	2-0
2r	Consett v Easington CW	3-0
10r	Brierley Hill Alliance v Kidderminster Harriers	1-2
11r	Altrincham v Stalybridge Celtic	2-1
14r	Farsley Celtic v Goole Town	3-4
16r	Newhall United v Boots Athletic	0-2
18r	Kettering Town v Corby Town	0-2
r	Peterborough United v Spalding United	3-0
21r	King's Lynn v Cambridge City	5-1
r	Wisbech Town v Cambridge United	2-3e
22r	Beccles v Sheringham	2-1
23r	Stowmarket v Bury Town	2-4
25r	Hastings United v Worthing	1-3
28r	Wimbledon v Dulwich Hamlet	5-2
30r	Hendon v St Albans City	3-1

Qualifying Round Three

1	Newburn v Ashington	1-4
2	Consett v South Shields (2)	4-0
3	Evenwood Town v Spennymoor United	1-1
4	Horden CW v Ushaw Moor	3-1
5	Billingham Synthonia v Ferryhill Athletic	5-0
6	Netherfield (Kendal) v Morecambe	3-1
7	Ashton United v Mossley	2-1
8	Bangor City v Flint Town United	4-2
9	Atherstone Town v Bedworth Town	1-1
10	Bromsgrove Rovers v Kidderminster Harriers	0-2
11	Winsford United v Altrincham	0-1
12	Frickley Colliery v Denaby United	1-1
13	Beighton Miners Welfare v Norton Woodseats	1-1
14	Selby Town v Goole Town	4-1
15	Boston United v Skegness Town	3-2
16	Ilkeston Town (2) v Boots Athletic	4-0
17	Linby Colliery v Creswell Colliery	0-0
18	Corby Town v Peterborough United	0-0
19	Brush Sports v South Normanton MW	3-1
20	Hitchin Town v Bedford Town (1)	2-3
21	Cambridge United v King's Lynn	0-0
22	Great Yarmouth Town v Beccles	2-1
23	Bury Town v Sudbury Town	3-0
24	Gravesend & Northfleet v Dover	2-1
25	Lancing Athletic v Worthing	2-0
26	Grays Athletic v Clacton Town	2-1
27	Eton Manor v Finchley	0-1
28	Carshalton Athletic v Wimbledon	3-4
29	Headington United v Wycombe Wanderers	6-2
30	Hendon v Uxbridge	3-1
31	Basingstoke Town v Newport (IOW)	2-4
32	Dorchester Town v Bournemouth Gasworks Athletic	2-1
33	Salisbury (2) v Trowbridge Town	0-2
34	Glastonbury v Bath City	0-3
35	Barry Town v Llanelli	1-1
36	Barnstaple Town v Ilfracombe Town	0-0
3r	Spennymoor United v Evenwood Town	4-1
9r	Bedworth Town v Atherstone Town	2-0
12r	Denaby United v Frickley Colliery	3-4
13r	Norton Woodseats v Beighton Miners Welfare	1-3
17r	Creswell Colliery v Linby Colliery	0-0e
18r	Peterborough United v Corby Town	5-3
21r	King's Lynn v Cambridge United	4-0
35r	Llanelli v Barry Town	3-0
36r	Ilfracombe Town v Barnstaple Town	1-0
17r2	Creswell Colliery v Linby Colliery	0-5

Qualifying Round Four

	Ashington v Billingham Synthonia	4-0
	Ashton United v Altrincham	3-1
	Bath City v Trowbridge Town	3-0
	Boston United v Frickley Colliery	3-2
	Brush Sports v Hereford United	0-1
	Buxton v Beighton Miners Welfare	2-3
	Chelmsford City v Finchley	0-0
	Consett v North Shields	1-3
	Dartford v Hendon	0-3
	Dorchester Town v Weymouth	1-5
	Folkestone v Tonbridge	0-0
	Gainsborough Trinity v Ilkeston Town (2)	5-1
	Gorleston v Leytonstone	1-4
	Grays Athletic v King's Lynn	0-0
	Great Yarmouth Town v Bury Town	2-0
	Guildford City v Headington United	2-1
	Horden CW v Blyth Spartans	2-1
	Kidderminster Harriers v Bedworth Town	1-1
	Lancing Athletic v Newport (IOW)	1-5
	Llanelli v Ilfracombe Town	1-0
	Nelson v Rhyl	1-3
	Peterborough United v Bedford Town (1)	2-1
	Scarborough v Stockton	5-1
	Selby Town v Linby Colliery	4-2
	Spennymoor United v Bishop Auckland	1-1
	Wellington Town v Worcester City	1-0
	Wigan Athletic v Netherfield (Kendal)	2-3
	Wimbledon v Gravesend & Northfleet	4-2
	Witton Albion v Bangor City	0-2
	Yeovil Town v Merthyr Tydfil	1-0
r	Bedworth Town v Kidderminster Harriers	0-2
r	Bishop Auckland v Spennymoor United	2-1
r	Finchley v Chelmsford City	3-0
r	King's Lynn v Grays Athletic	0-2
r	Tonbridge v Folkestone	4-4e
r2	Folkestone v Tonbridge	0-2 N

Round One

	Aldershot v Millwall	0-0
	Bath City v Southend United	3-1
	Beighton Miners Welfare v Wrexham	0-3 N
	Boston United v Oldham Athletic	1-2
	Bradford City v Rhyl	4-0
	Bradford Park Avenue v Rochdale	2-1
	Chester v Hartlepools United	0-1
	Chesterfield v Workington	1-0
	Coventry City v Bristol City	2-0
	Crystal Palace v Reading	1-1
	Darlington v Grimsby Town	2-3
	Gainsborough Trinity v Netherfield (Kendal)	1-1
	Gateshead v Crewe Alexandra	2-0
	Grays Athletic v Llanelli	0-5
	Guildford City v Great Yarmouth Town	2-2
	Halifax Town v Ashton United	1-1
	Hendon v Northampton Town	0-0
	Horden CW v Accrington Stanley	1-2
	Ipswich Town v Bournemouth	2-2
	Kidderminster Harriers v Finchley	0-1
	Leyton v Hereford United	0-0
	Leyton Orient v Bristol Rovers	1-1
	Leytonstone v Watford	0-2
	Newport County v Walsall	2-1
	North Shields v Stockport County	3-6
	Peterborough United v Torquay United	2-1
	Port Vale v Exeter City	2-1
	Queen's Park Rangers v Shrewsbury Town	2-2
	Scarborough v Mansfield Town	0-8
	Scunthorpe United v Carlisle United	1-0
	Selby Town v Bishop Auckland	1-5
	Southport v Bangor City	3-1
	Swindon Town v Newport (IOW)	5-0
	Tonbridge v Norwich City	2-2
	Tranmere Rovers v Ashington	8-1
	Walthamstow Avenue v Wimbledon	2-2
	Wellington Town v Gillingham	1-1
	Weymouth v Colchester United	1-1
	Yeovil Town v Brighton & Hove Albion	1-4
	York City v Barrow	1-2
r	Ashton United v Halifax Town	1-2
r	Bournemouth v Ipswich Town	2-2e
r	Bristol Rovers v Leyton Orient	1-0
r	Colchester United v Weymouth	4-0
r	Gillingham v Wellington Town	3-0
r	Great Yarmouth Town v Guildford City	1-0
r	Hereford United v Leyton	3-2
r	Millwall v Aldershot	7-1
r	Netherfield (Kendal) v Gainsborough Trinity	0-3
r	Northampton Town v Hendon	2-0
r	Norwich City v Tonbridge	1-0
r	Reading v Crystal Palace	1-3
r	Shrewsbury Town v Queen's Park Rangers	2-2e
r	Wimbledon v Walthamstow Avenue	0-3
r2	Ipswich Town v Bournemouth	3-2 N
r2	Queen's Park Rangers v Shrewsbury Town	1-4 N

Round Two

	Accrington Stanley v Mansfield Town	0-2
	Barrow v Millwall	2-2
	Bishop Auckland v Coventry City	1-4
	Bradford City v Ipswich Town	1-1
	Bradford Park Avenue v Gateshead	1-2
	Brighton & Hove Albion v Norwich City	2-0
	Colchester United v Llanelli	3-2
	Finchley v Crystal Palace	3-1
	Great Yarmouth Town v Wrexham	1-2
	Grimsby Town v Bath City	1-0
	Halifax Town v Southport	4-2
	Hereford United v Scunthorpe United	0-0
	Newport County v Gainsborough Trinity	2-1
	Peterborough United v Bristol Rovers	0-1
	Port Vale v Oldham Athletic	0-3
	Shrewsbury Town v Chesterfield	0-0
	Stockport County v Gillingham	3-1
	Swindon Town v Northampton Town	2-0
	Tranmere Rovers v Hartlepools United	2-1
	Walthamstow Avenue v Watford	1-1
r	Chesterfield v Shrewsbury Town	2-4
r	Ipswich Town v Bradford City	5-1
r	Millwall v Barrow	4-1
r	Scunthorpe United v Hereford United	2-1
r	Watford v Walthamstow Avenue	1-2e

Round Three

	Arsenal v Doncaster Rovers	4-0
	Aston Villa v Middlesbrough	3-1
	Barnsley v Brighton & Hove Albion	4-3
	Bolton Wanderers v Fulham	3-1
	Brentford v Leeds United	2-1
	Derby County v Chelsea	4-4
	Everton v Ipswich Town	3-2
	Gateshead v Liverpool	1-0
	Grimsby Town v Bury	1-3
	Halifax Town v Cardiff City	3-1
	Huddersfield Town v Bristol Rovers	2-0
	Hull City v Charlton Athletic	3-1
	Leicester City v Notts County	2-4
	Lincoln City v Southampton	1-1
	Luton Town v Blackburn Rovers	6-1
	Manchester City v Swindon Town	7-0
	Mansfield Town v Nottingham Forest	0-1
	Millwall v Manchester United	0-1
	Newcastle United v Swansea Town	3-0
	Newport County v Sheffield United	1-4
	Oldham Athletic v Birmingham City	1-3
	Plymouth Argyle v Coventry City	4-1
	Portsmouth v Burnley	1-1
	Preston North End v Wolverhampton Wan.	5-2
	Rotherham United v Colchester United	2-2
	Sheffield Wednesday v Blackpool	1-2
	Shrewsbury Town v Finchley	2-0
	Stoke City v Wrexham	2-1
	Sunderland v Scunthorpe United	1-1
	Tranmere Rovers v Tottenham Hotspur	1-1
	Walthamstow Avenue v Stockport County	2-1
	West Ham United v West Bromwich Albion	1-4
r	Burnley v Portsmouth	3-1
r	Chelsea v Derby County	1-0e
r	Colchester United v Rotherham United	0-2
r	Scunthorpe United v Sunderland	1-2
r	Southampton v Lincoln City	2-1
r	Tottenham Hotspur v Tranmere Rovers	9-1

Round Four

	Arsenal v Bury	6-2
	Aston Villa v Brentford	0-0
	Blackpool v Huddersfield Town	1-0
	Bolton Wanderers v Notts County	1-1
	Burnley v Sunderland	2-0
	Chelsea v West Bromwich Albion	1-1
	Everton v Nottingham Forest	4-1
	Halifax Town v Stoke City	1-0
	Hull City v Gateshead	1-2
	Manchester City v Luton Town	1-1
	Manchester United v Walthamstow Avenue	1-1
	Newcastle United v Rotherham United	1-3
	Plymouth Argyle v Barnsley	1-0
	Preston North End v Tottenham Hotspur	2-2
	Sheffield United v Birmingham City	1-1
	Shrewsbury Town v Southampton	1-4
r	Birmingham City v Sheffield United	3-1
r	Brentford v Aston Villa	1-2
r	Luton Town v Manchester City	5-1
r	Notts County v Bolton Wanderers	2-2e
r	Tottenham Hotspur v Preston North End	1-0
r	Walthamstow Avenue v Manchester United	2-5 N
r	West Bromwich Albion v Chelsea	0-0e
r2	Bolton Wanderers v Notts County	1-0 N
r2	Chelsea v West Bromwich Albion	1-1eN
r3	West Bromwich Albion v Chelsea	0-4 N

Round Five

	Blackpool v Southampton	1-1
	Burnley v Arsenal	0-2
	Chelsea v Birmingham City	0-4
	Everton v Manchester United	2-1
	Halifax Town v Tottenham Hotspur	0-3
	Luton Town v Bolton Wanderers	0-1
	Plymouth Argyle v Gateshead	0-1
	Rotherham United v Aston Villa	1-3
r	Southampton v Blackpool	1-2

Round Six

	Arsenal v Blackpool	1-2
	Aston Villa v Everton	0-1
	Birmingham City v Tottenham Hotspur	1-1
	Gateshead v Bolton Wanderers	0-1
r	Tottenham Hotspur v Birmingham City	2-2e
r2	Birmingham City v Tottenham Hotspur	0-1 N

1952/53 to 1953/54

Semi Finals

	Blackpool v Tottenham Hotspur	2-1 N
	Bolton Wanderers v Everton	4-3 N

Final

	Blackpool v Bolton Wanderers	4-3 N

1953/54

Preliminary Round

7	Ashton United v Leyland Motors	5-1
	Darwen v Rossendale United	2-0
8	Bootle Athletic v Pwllheli & District	0-2
	Runcorn v New Brighton	3-1
	St Helens Town v Bangor City	2-2
9	Lockheed Leamington v Boldmere St Michaels	7-0
	Rugby Town (2) v Moor Green	5-1
	Sutton Town (Birmingham) v Bournville Athletic	3-2
10	Cradley Heath v Brierley Hill Alliance	0-6
	Dudley Town v Bilston	1-2
	Halesowen Town v Stafford Rangers	1-2
	Lye Town v Worcester City	3-5
	Stourbridge v Oswestry Town	2-0
21	Holbeach United v Histon	0-1
	St Neots & District v Huntingdon United	4-1
24	Betteshanger CW v Walton & Hersham	3-2
	Bexleyheath & Welling v Dulwich Hamlet	1-3
	Canterbury City v Tunbridge Wells United	0-2
	Chatham Town v Tooting & Mitcham United	1-3
	Ramsgate Athletic v Bowater Lloyds	wo/s
	Sittingbourne v Carshalton Athletic	2-1
	Snowdown CW v Guildford City	1-3
	Sutton United v Deal Town	3-5
25	East Grinstead v Southwick	4-2
	Haywards Heath v Bexhill Town	3-0
	Horsham v Littlehampton Town	3-1
	Lancing Athletic v Newhaven	2-1
	Redhill v Bognor Regis Town	2-0
	Shoreham v Hastings United	0-3
	Worthing v Eastbourne	2-4
26	Briggs Sports v Clacton Town	4-3
	Dagenham v Brentwood & Warley	4-0
	Leyton v Tilbury	2-1
	Woodford Town (1) v Chelmsford City	0-3
28	Bromley v Wimbledon	1-2
	Dover v Hounslow Town	1-2
	Epsom v Dorking	1-1
	Kingstonian v Woking	3-1
	Margate v Gravesend & Northfleet	5-1
	Sheppey United v Maidstone United	2-2
29	Abingdon Town v Oxford City	0-5
	Banbury Spencer v Wycombe Wanderers	2-1
	Bicester Town v Maidenhead United	0-5
	Chesham United v Huntley & Palmers	3-1
30	Barnet v Wealdstone	1-2
	Berkhamsted Town v Hemel Hempstead Town	3-3
	Edgware Town v Southall	0-1
	Harrow Town v Hendon	2-3
	Slough Centre v Slough Town	4-1
	Uxbridge v Hayes	2-2
	Windsor & Eton v Yiewsley	3-3
33	Calne & Harris United v Chippenham Town	0-2
	Devizes Town v Trowbridge Town	2-11
	Melksham Town v Andover	1-5
	Spencer Moulton v Westbury United	6-2
34	Bristol St George v Radstock Town	4-3
	Clandown v Wells City	1-0
	Clevedon v Glastonbury	0-1
	Hanham Athletic v Paulton Rovers	4-1
35	Lovells Athletic v Cinderford Town	1-3
36	Dartmouth United v St Austell	2-1
	Newquay v Minehead	2-1
	Newton Abbot v Wadebridge Town	1-3
	Taunton v St Blazey	0-2
	Tavistock v Barnstaple Town	1-3
	Tiverton Town v Ilfracombe Town	2-3
8r	Bangor City v St Helens Town	5-1
28r	Dorking v Epsom	0-1
r	Maidstone United v Sheppey United	3-1
30r	Hayes v Uxbridge	2-3e
r	Hemel Hempstead Town v Berkhamsted Town	4-2e
r	Yiewsley v Windsor & Eton	2-1

Qualifying Round One

1	Alnwick Town v Shankhouse	9-0
	Amble v Newburn	3-3
	Ashington v West Sleekburn Welfare	1-2
	Hexham Hearts v Cramlington Welfare	3-3
2	Boldon CW v Heaton Stannington	2-1
	Consett v Easington CW	2-2
	Dawdon Colliery Welfare v Annfield Plain	1-4
	Gosforth & Coxlodge v South Shields (2)	0-5
3	Crook Town v Stanley United	0-1
	Shildon v Tow Law Town	4-0
	Spennymoor United v West Auckland Town	6-0
	Willington v Evenwood Town	2-0
4	Horden CW v Silksworth CW	1-0
	Murton CW v Blackhall Colliery Welfare	2-1
	Seaham Colliery Welfare v Chilton Athletic	2-2
5	Billingham Synthonia v Whitby Town	2-1
	Bridlington Central Utd. v South Bank	4-0
	Ferryhill Athletic v Skinningrove Works	18-0
6	Burscough v Bacup Borough	4-1
	Fleetwood v Netherfield (Kendal)	3-1
	Great Harwood v Lancaster City	1-4
	Penrith v Morecambe	1-6
7	Droylsden v Lytham	2-4
	Horwich RMI v Darwen	1-1
	Mossley v Ashton United	3-2
	Skelmersdale United v Chorley	1-1
8	Bangor City v Prescot Cables	1-2
	Earlestown v Runcorn	1-4
	Flint Town United v Ellesmere Port Town	3-2
	Marine v Pwllheli & District	1-1
9	Burton Albion v Bedworth Town	2-1
	Nuneaton Borough v Lockheed Leamington	1-0
	Sutton Town (Birmingham) v Rugby Town (2)	1-1
	Tamworth v Atherstone Town	0-1
10	Bilston v Kidderminster Harriers	0-2
	Darlaston v Worcester City	0-0
	Stafford Rangers v Bromsgrove Rovers	2-3
	Stourbridge v Brierley Hill Alliance	0-5
11	Congleton Town v Hyde United	5-5
	Northwich Victoria v Winsford United	0-0
	Stalybridge Celtic v Macclesfield Town	1-0
12	Denaby United v Frickley Colliery	1-2
	Retford Town v Upton Colliery	3-4
	Sheffield v Stocksbridge Works	2-2
	South Kirkby Colliery v Hallam	1-2
13	Beighton Miners Welfare v Langold WMC	5-2
	Brodsworth Main Colliery v Worksop Town	1-4
	Brunswick Institute v Bentley Colliery	0-4
	Rawmarsh Welfare v Norton Woodseats	1-1
14	Goole Town v Ossett Town	4-2
15	Bourne Town v Boston United	1-4
	Brigg Town v Skegness Town	4-1
	Grantham v Ashby Institute	2-2
	Lysaght's Sports (Scunthorpe) v Barton Town (1)	2-2
16	Basford United v Newhall United	0-0
	Gresley Rovers v Ilkeston Town (2)	2-1
	Matlock Town v Boots Athletic	5-0
	South Normanton MW v Gedling Colliery	1-0
17	Bestwood Colliery v Cinderhill Colliery	3-1
	Creswell Colliery v Ransome & Marles	1-0
	Shirebrook MW v Parliament Street Methodists	5-1
	Sutton Town v Linby Colliery	3-2
18	Corby Town v Spalding United	6-2
	Rushden Town v Kettering Town	1-1
	Stamford v Wellingborough Town	5-0
	Symingtons Recreation v Desborough Town	0-3
19	Brush Sports v Coalville Town (3)	2-0
	Hinckley Athletic v Players Athletic	5-0
20	Luton Amateur v Dunstable Town	1-3
	Potton United v Bedford Town (1)	1-5
	Vauxhall Motors (Luton) v Eynesbury Rovers	6-2
	Wolverton Town & BR v Biggleswade Town	0-2
21	Histon v Cambridge City	2-5
	March Town United v King's Lynn	3-1
	St Neots & District v Cambridge United	0-3
	Wisbech Town v Chatteris Town	6-0
22	Beccles v Sheringham	7-1
	Bungay Town v Wymondham Town	3-3
	Gothic (Norwich) v Gorleston	1-10
23	Lowestoft Town v Bury Town	2-1
	Stowmarket v Leiston	2-0
	Sudbury Town v Diss Town	2-1
24	Betteshanger CW v Tooting & Mitcham United	1-0
	Deal Town v Ramsgate Athletic	0-0
	Guildford City v Sittingbourne	2-0
	Tunbridge Wells United v Dulwich Hamlet	3-1
25	Ashford Town v East Grinstead	4-0
	Hastings United v Horsham	4-1
	Haywards Heath v Lancing Athletic	1-3
	Redhill v Eastbourne	0-1
26	Barking v Erith & Belvedere	1-2
	Chelmsford City v Romford (2)	3-2
	Dagenham v Briggs Sports	1-3
	Leyton v Ilford	0-2
27	Eton Manor v Clapton	4-3
	Hitchin Town v Letchworth Town	3-3
	Stevenage Town v Cheshunt	6-1
	Tufnell Park Edmonton v Enfield	2-0
28	Hounslow Town v Dartford	0-0
	Maidstone United v Margate	1-3
	Metropolitan Police v Epsom	1-2
	Wimbledon v Kingstonian	1-1
29	Aylesbury United v Headington United	1-2
	Banbury Spencer v Oxford City	2-0
	Chesham United v Marlow	2-0
	Witney Town v Maidenhead United	0-1
30	Hendon v Hemel Hempstead Town	2-1
	Slough Centre v St Albans City	0-1
	Uxbridge v Yiewsley	0-1
	Wealdstone v Southall	2-1
31	Alton Town v Gosport Borough Ath.	3-2
	Basingstoke Town v Newport (IOW)	0-5
32	Bournemouth Gasworks Athletic v Bridport	8-0
	Dorchester Town v Lymington	9-0
	Ilminster Town v Poole Town	3-2
	Portland United v Shaftesbury	11-1
33	Frome Town v Chippenham Town	2-6
	Salisbury (2) v Andover	2-1
	Spencer Moulton v Welton Rovers	3-5
	Warminster Town v Trowbridge Town	2-2
34	Chippenham United v Bridgwater Town (1)	3-1
	Clandown v Glastonbury	2-4
	Hanham Athletic v Bristol St George	0-2
	Peasedown MW v Street	1-4
35	Gloucester City v Cinderford Town	6-1
	Merthyr Tydfil v Cheltenham Town	3-2
	Stonehouse v Barry Town	0-6
	Troedryhiw v Ebbw Vale	2-3
36	Dartmouth United v Wadebridge Town	2-3
	Ilfracombe Town v Bideford	0-4
	Penzance v Barnstaple Town	0-6
	St Blazey v Newquay	4-2
1r	Cramlington Welfare v Hexham Hearts	2-5
r	Newburn v Amble	wo/s
2r	Easington CW v Consett	1-3
4r	Chilton Athletic v Seaham Colliery Welfare	0-2
7r	Chorley v Skelmersdale United	0-2
r	Darwen v Horwich RMI	3-2e
8r	Pwllheli & District v Marine	4-0
9r	Rugby Town (2) v Sutton Town (Birmingham)	4-1
10r	Worcester City v Darlaston	3-1
11r	Hyde United v Congleton Town	0-1
r	Winsford United v Northwich Victoria	1-1
12r	Stocksbridge Works v Sheffield	0-0e
13r	Norton Woodseats v Rawmarsh Welfare	6-0
15r	Ashby Institute v Grantham	2-1
r	Barton Town (1) v Lysaght's Sports (Scunthorpe)	1-2
16r	Newhall United v Basford United	2-3
18r	Kettering Town v Rushden Town	3-1
22r	Bungay Town v Wymondham Town	4-1
24r	Ramsgate Athletic v Deal Town	1-0
27r	Letchworth Town v Hitchin Town	0-1
28r	Dartford v Hounslow Town	0-3
r	Kingstonian v Wimbledon	4-2
33r	Trowbridge Town v Warminster Town	8-2
11r2	Winsford United v Northwich Victoria	2-0 N
12r2	Sheffield v Stocksbridge Works	1-1
12r3	Sheffield v Stocksbridge Works	3-1

Qualifying Round Two

1	Hexham Hearts v Alnwick Town	3-2
	West Sleekburn Welfare v Newburn	0-1
2	Boldon CW v South Shields (2)	3-3
	Consett v Annfield Plain	2-3
3	Spennymoor United v Stanley United	2-1
	Willington v Shildon	3-0
4	Murton CW v Ushaw Moor	1-1
	Seaham Colliery Welfare v Horden CW	0-2
5	Billingham Synthonia v Bridlington Central Utd.	4-1
	Ferryhill Athletic v Head Wrightsons	7-1
6	Burscough v Lancaster City	2-1
	Fleetwood v Morecambe	1-2
7	Lytham v Skelmersdale United	1-2
	Mossley v Darwen	2-0
8	Flint Town United v Runcorn	1-3
	Prescot Cables v Pwllheli & District	0-1
9	Burton Albion v Atherstone Town	3-0
	Rugby Town (2) v Nuneaton Borough	1-2
10	Brierley Hill Alliance v Worcester City	2-0
	Kidderminster Harriers v Bromsgrove Rovers	2-1
11	Altrincham v Stalybridge Celtic	2-1
	Winsford United v Congleton Town	1-0
12	Frickley Colliery v Sheffield	2-1
	Hallam v Upton Colliery	0-5
13	Beighton Miners Welfare v Norton Woodseats	2-1
	Bentley Colliery v Worksop Town	1-2
14	Farsley Celtic v Goole Town	0-1
	Yorkshire Amateur v Selby Town	3-3
15	Ashby Institute v Brigg Town	4-3
	Lysaght's Sports (Scunthorpe) v Boston United	0-4 N
16	Basford United v South Normanton MW	0-5
	Gresley Rovers v Matlock Town	2-0
17	Bestwood Colliery v Creswell Colliery	0-7
	Sutton Town v Shirebrook MW	1-1
18	Desborough Town v Kettering Town	0-4
	Stamford v Corby Town	3-2
19	Raleigh Athletic v Hinckley Athletic	0-3
	Whitwick Colliery v Brush Sports	3-5
20	Biggleswade Town v Bedford Town (1)	0-0
	Dunstable Town v Vauxhall Motors (Luton)	3-2
21	Cambridge City v Cambridge United	1-3
	Wisbech Town v March Town United	4-1
22	Beccles v Gorleston	1-5
	Cromer v Bungay Town	2-0
23	Lowestoft Town v Sudbury Town	3-0
	Stowmarket v Whitton United	4-1
24	Betteshanger CW v Tunbridge Wells United	1-2
	Ramsgate Athletic v Guildford City	2-4
25	Eastbourne v Hastings United	2-7
	Lancing Athletic v Ashford Town	1-3
26	Chelmsford City v Erith & Belvedere	2-1
	Ilford v Briggs Sports	1-1
27	Eton Manor v Hitchin Town	1-1
	Tufnell Park Edmonton v Stevenage Town	2-1
28	Hounslow Town v Epsom	4-1
	Kingstonian v Margate	2-1
29	Chesham United v Banbury Spencer	1-0
	Headington United v Maidenhead United	4-0
30	Hendon v Yiewsley	2-2
	Wealdstone v St Albans City	2-0
31	Cowes v Alton Town	5-0
	Newport (IOW) v Winchester City	7-0
32	Dorchester Town v Portland United	1-3
	Ilminster Town v Bournemouth Gasworks Athletic	0-4

1953/54 to 1954/55

33	Chippenham Town v Salisbury (2)	4-2
	Welton Rovers v Trowbridge Town	0-3
34	Chippenham United v Bristol St George	4-1
	Street v Glastonbury	2-1
35	Barry Town v Gloucester City	2-1
	Merthyr Tydfil v Ebbw Vale	3-0
36	Barnstaple Town v Wadebridge Town	2-2
	Bideford v St Blazey	1-3
2r	South Shields (2) v Boldon CW	9-2
4r	Ushaw Moor v Murton CW	4-1
14r	Selby Town v Yorkshire Amateur	4-1
17r	Shirebrook MW v Sutton Town	4-3
20r	Bedford Town (1) v Biggleswade Town	5-0
26r	Briggs Sports v Ilford	5-0
27r	Hitchin Town v Eton Manor	7-1
30r	Yiewsley v Hendon	2-0
36r	Wadebridge Town v Barnstaple Town	3-4

Qualifying Round Three

1	Hexham Hearts v Newburn	5-4
2	Annfield Plain v South Shields (2)	0-1
3	Spennymoor United v Willington	2-1
4	Horden CW v Ushaw Moor	4-2
5	Billingham Synthonia v Ferryhill Athletic	1-2
6	Morecambe v Burscough	0-1
7	Skelmersdale United v Mossley	1-3
8	Pwllheli & District v Runcorn	2-2
9	Burton Albion v Nuneaton Borough	1-1
10	Kidderminster Harriers v Brierley Hill Alliance	2-0
11	Winsford United v Altrincham	3-1
12	Upton Colliery v Frickley Colliery	2-3
13	Worksop Town v Beighton Miners Welfare	3-2
14	Goole Town v Selby Town	1-3
15	Ashby Institute v Boston United	2-3
16	Gresley Rovers v South Normanton MW	5-1
17	Creswell Colliery v Shirebrook MW	3-4
18	Stamford v Kettering Town	3-3
19	Brush Sports v Hinckley Athletic	2-1
20	Dunstable Town v Bedford Town (1)	2-4
21	Cambridge United v Wisbech Town	1-0
22	Cromer v Gorleston	2-6
23	Stowmarket v Lowestoft Town	4-2
24	Tunbridge Wells United v Guildford City	0-2
25	Hastings United v Ashford Town	2-1
26	Chelmsford City v Briggs Sports	1-0
27	Hitchin Town v Tufnell Park Edmonton	5-1
28	Hounslow Town v Kingstonian	6-1
29	Headington United v Chesham United	2-0
30	Yiewsley v Wealdstone	0-3
31	Newport (IOW) v Cowes	4-2
32	Portland United v Bournemouth Gasworks Athletic	4-1
33	Chippenham Town v Trowbridge Town	3-2
34	Chippenham United v Street	4-1
35	Merthyr Tydfil v Barry Town	3-3
36	St Blazey v Barnstaple Town	3-5
8r	Runcorn v Pwllheli & District	3-0
9r	Nuneaton Borough v Burton Albion	3-1
18r	Kettering Town v Stamford	12-0
35r	Barry Town v Merthyr Tydfil	2-3

Qualifying Round Four

	Bath City v Barnstaple Town	2-1
	Blyth Spartans v North Shields	4-2
	Brush Sports v Hereford United	2-2
	Buxton v Kettering Town	0-3
	Chelmsford City v Great Yarmouth Town	0-0
	Chippenham Town v Weymouth	2-4
	Ferryhill Athletic v South Shields (2)	2-0
	Folkestone v Finchley	0-1
	Gorleston v Bedford Town (1)	0-2
	Guildford City v Tonbridge	4-0
	Hexham Hearts v Horden CW	2-2
	Hounslow Town v Hastings United	1-2
	Kidderminster Harriers v Wellington Town	1-2
	Leytonstone v Hitchin Town	0-1
	Llanelli v Portland United	6-5
	Mossley v Rhyl	1-1
	Nelson v Winsford United	1-0
	Newport (IOW) v Chippenham United	3-1
	Nuneaton Borough v Gresley Rovers	4-1
	Peterborough United v Grays Athletic	4-1
	Scarborough v Stockton	6-1
	Selby Town v Frickley Colliery	2-0
	Shirebrook MW v Boston United	2-5
	Spennymoor United v Bishop Auckland	3-1
	Stowmarket v Cambridge United	0-5
	Wealdstone v Headington United	0-3
	Wigan Athletic v Burscough	2-1
	Witton Albion v Runcorn	2-0 d
	Worksop Town v Gainsborough Trinity	2-2
	Yeovil Town v Merthyr Tydfil	2-1
r	Gainsborough Trinity v Worksop Town	2-1
r	Great Yarmouth Town v Chelmsford City	1-0
r	Hereford United v Brush Sports	3-0
r	Horden CW v Hexham Hearts	2-0
r	Rhyl v Mossley	2-0

Round One

	Aldershot v Wellington Town	5-3
	Barnsley v York City	5-2
	Bath City v Walsall	0-3
	Blyth Spartans v Accrington Stanley	0-1
	Brighton & Hove Albion v Coventry City	5-1
	Cambridge United v Newport County	2-2
	Colchester United v Millwall	1-1
	Crewe Alexandra v Bradford City	0-0
	Darlington v Port Vale	1-3
	Exeter City v Hereford United	1-1
	Finchley v Southend United	1-3
	Gainsborough Trinity v Chesterfield	1-4
	Gateshead v Tranmere Rovers	1-2
	Great Yarmouth Town v Crystal Palace	1-0
	Grimsby Town v Rochdale	2-0
	Halifax Town v Rhyl	0-0
	Hartlepools United v Mansfield Town	1-1
	Harwich & Parkeston v Headington United	2-3
	Hastings United v Guildford City	1-0
	Hitchin Town v Peterborough United	1-3
	Horden CW v Wrexham	0-1
	Ipswich Town v Reading	4-1
	Leyton Orient v Kettering Town	3-0
	Northampton Town v Llanelli	3-0
	Nuneaton Borough v Watford	3-0
	Queen's Park Rangers v Shrewsbury Town	2-0
	Scunthorpe United v Boston United	9-0
	Selby Town v Bradford Park Avenue	0-2
	Southampton v Bournemouth	1-1
	Southport v Carlisle United	1-0
	Spennymoor United v Barrow	0-3
	Stockport County v Chester	4-2
	Swindon Town v Newport (IOW)	2-1
	Torquay United v Bristol City	1-3
	Walthamstow Avenue v Gillingham	1-0
	Weymouth v Bedford Town (1)	2-0
	Wigan Athletic v Scarborough	4-0
	Witton Albion v Nelson	4-1
	Workington v Ferryhill Athletic	3-0
	Yeovil Town v Norwich City	0-2
r	Bournemouth v Southampton	3-1
r	Bradford City v Crewe Alexandra	0-1
r	Hereford United v Exeter City	2-0
r	Mansfield Town v Hartlepools United	0-3
r	Millwall v Colchester United	4-0
r	Newport County v Cambridge United	1-2
r	Rhyl v Halifax Town	4-3e

Round Two

	Accrington Stanley v Tranmere Rovers	2-2
	Barrow v Great Yarmouth Town	5-2
	Cambridge United v Bradford Park Avenue	1-2
	Hastings United v Swindon Town	4-1
	Ipswich Town v Walthamstow Avenue	2-2
	Leyton Orient v Weymouth	4-0
	Millwall v Headington United	3-3
	Northampton Town v Hartlepools United	1-1
	Norwich City v Barnsley	2-1
	Peterborough United v Aldershot	2-1
	Queen's Park Rangers v Nuneaton Borough	1-1
	Rhyl v Bristol City	0-3
	Scunthorpe United v Bournemouth	1-0
	Southend United v Chesterfield	1-2
	Southport v Port Vale	1-1
	Stockport County v Workington	2-1
	Walsall v Crewe Alexandra	3-0
	Wigan Athletic v Hereford United	4-1
	Witton Albion v Grimsby Town	1-1
	Wrexham v Brighton & Hove Albion	1-1
r	Brighton & Hove Albion v Wrexham	1-1e
r	Grimsby Town v Witton Albion	6-1
r	Hartlepools United v Northampton Town	1-0e
r	Headington United v Millwall	1-0
r	Nuneaton Borough v Queen's Park Rangers	1-2
r	Port Vale v Southport	2-0
r	Tranmere Rovers v Accrington Stanley	5-1
r	Walthamstow Avenue v Ipswich Town	0-1
r2	Wrexham v Brighton & Hove Albion	3-1 N

Round Three

	Arsenal v Aston Villa	5-1
	Barrow v Swansea Town	2-2
	Blackpool v Luton Town	1-1
	Bolton Wanderers v Liverpool	1-0
	Bradford Park Avenue v Manchester City	2-5
	Brentford v Hull City	0-0
	Bristol City v Rotherham United	1-3
	Bristol Rovers v Blackburn Rovers	0-1
	Burnley v Manchester United	5-3
	Cardiff City v Peterborough United	3-1
	Chesterfield v Bury	2-0
	Derby County v Preston North End	0-2
	Everton v Notts County	2-1
	Grimsby Town v Fulham	5-5
	Hastings United v Norwich City	3-3
	Ipswich Town v Oldham Athletic	3-3
	Leeds United v Tottenham Hotspur	3-3
	Lincoln City v Walsall	1-1
	Middlesbrough v Leicester City	0-0
	Newcastle United v Wigan Athletic	2-2
	Plymouth Argyle v Nottingham Forest	2-0
	Portsmouth v Charlton Athletic	3-3
	Queen's Park Rangers v Port Vale	0-1
	Sheffield Wednesday v Sheffield United	1-1
	Stockport County v Headington United	0-0
	Stoke City v Hartlepools United	6-2
	Sunderland v Doncaster Rovers	0-2
	Tranmere Rovers v Leyton Orient	2-2
	West Bromwich Albion v Chelsea	1-0
	West Ham United v Huddersfield Town	4-0
	Wolverhampton Wan. v Birmingham City	1-2
	Wrexham v Scunthorpe United	3-3
r	Charlton Athletic v Portsmouth	2-3e
r	Fulham v Grimsby Town	3-1
r	Headington United v Stockport County	1-0
r	Hull City v Brentford	2-2e
r	Leicester City v Middlesbrough	3-2
r	Leyton Orient v Tranmere Rovers	4-1
r	Luton Town v Blackpool	0-0e
r	Norwich City v Hastings United	3-0
r	Oldham Athletic v Ipswich Town	0-1
r	Scunthorpe United v Wrexham	3-1
r	Sheffield United v Sheffield Wednesday	1-3
r	Swansea Town v Barrow	4-2
r	Tottenham Hotspur v Leeds United	1-0
r	Walsall v Lincoln City	1-1e
r	Wigan Athletic v Newcastle United	2-3
r2	Blackpool v Luton Town	1-1eN
r2	Brentford v Hull City	2-5 N
r2	Lincoln City v Walsall	2-1 N
r3	Luton Town v Blackpool	0-2 N

Round Four

	Arsenal v Norwich City	1-2
	Blackburn Rovers v Hull City	2-2
	Burnley v Newcastle United	1-1
	Cardiff City v Port Vale	0-2
	Everton v Swansea Town	3-0
	Headington United v Bolton Wanderers	2-4
	Ipswich Town v Birmingham City	1-0
	Leyton Orient v Fulham	2-1
	Lincoln City v Preston North End	0-2
	Manchester City v Tottenham Hotspur	0-1
	Plymouth Argyle v Doncaster Rovers	0-2
	Scunthorpe United v Portsmouth	1-1
	Sheffield Wednesday v Chesterfield	0-0
	Stoke City v Leicester City	0-0
	West Bromwich Albion v Rotherham United	4-0
	West Ham United v Blackpool	1-1
r	Blackpool v West Ham United	3-1
r	Chesterfield v Sheffield Wednesday	2-4
r	Hull City v Blackburn Rovers	2-1
r	Leicester City v Stoke City	3-1
r	Newcastle United v Burnley	1-0
r	Portsmouth v Scunthorpe United	2-2e
r2	Scunthorpe United v Portsmouth	0-4 N

Round Five

	Bolton Wanderers v Portsmouth	0-0
	Hull City v Tottenham Hotspur	1-1
	Leyton Orient v Doncaster Rovers	3-1
	Norwich City v Leicester City	1-2
	Port Vale v Blackpool	2-0
	Preston North End v Ipswich Town	6-1
	Sheffield Wednesday v Everton	3-1
	West Bromwich Albion v Newcastle United	3-2
r	Portsmouth v Bolton Wanderers	1-2
r	Tottenham Hotspur v Hull City	2-0

Round Six

	Leicester City v Preston North End	1-1
	Leyton Orient v Port Vale	0-1
	Sheffield Wednesday v Bolton Wanderers	1-1
	West Bromwich Albion v Tottenham Hotspur	3-0
r	Bolton Wanderers v Sheffield Wednesday	0-2
r	Preston North End v Leicester City	2-2e
r2	Leicester City v Preston North End	1-3 N

Semi Finals

	Preston North End v Sheffield Wednesday	2-0 N
	West Bromwich Albion v Port Vale	2-1 N

Final

	West Bromwich Albion v Preston North End	3-2 N

1954/55

Preliminary Round

1	Heaton Stannington v Lynemouth Welfare	3-3
	Newburn v Ashington	1-6
	Shankhouse v Alnwick Town	5-1
	South Shields (2) v North Shields	1-4
7	Bacup Borough v Rossendale United	1-0
	Chorley v Ashton United	2-1
	Horwich RMI v Skelmersdale United	1-0
	Nelson v Lytham	3-0
8	Llandudno v New Brighton	6-2
	Marine v Earlestown	4-0
	Pwllheli & District v Prescot Cables	7-0
	South Liverpool v Bangor City	1-3
9	Bedworth Town v Rugby Town (2)	2-3
	Burton Albion v Tamworth	1-0
	Lockheed Leamington v Bournville Athletic	7-1
	Sutton Town (Birmingham) v Bloxwich Strollers	0-3

1954/55

10	Brierley Hill Alliance v Stourbridge	0-3
	Bromsgrove Rovers v Darlaston	4-3
	Halesowen Town v Kidderminster Harriers	1-4
	Lye Town v Cradley Heath	3-2
	Redditch v Oswestry Town	0-1
	Stafford Rangers v Dudley Town	3-1
	Worcester City v Hednesford Town	2-3
11	Congleton Town v Northwich Victoria	2-5
	Hyde United v Winsford United	3-1
	Lostock Gralam v Linotype & Machinery	5-0
19	Heanor Town v Whitwick Colliery	2-5
21	Cambridge City v Exning United	2-1
	Chatteris Town v March Town United	1-3
	Histon v Warboys Town	4-2
	Holbeach United v St Neots & District	4-1
	Somersham Town v Newmarket Town	3-0
	Thetford Town v Ely City	2-0
	Wisbech Town v King's Lynn	1-1
24	Bexleyheath & Welling v Tooting & Mitcham United	3-3
	Canterbury City v Sutton United	3-0
	Deal Town v Ashford Town	0-2
	Ramsgate Athletic v Sittingbourne	1-1
	Walton & Hersham v Chatham Town	1-1
25	Arundel v Wigmore Athletic	4-0
	Bexhill Town v Haywards Heath	2-5
	Bognor Regis Town v Redhill	3-2
	Littlehampton Town v Southwick	3-1
	Newhaven v Eastbourne	2-2
	Shoreham v Horsham	1-6
	Tunbridge Wells United v East Grinstead	5-0
26	Aveley v Ilford	0-0
	Barking v Woodford Town (1)	3-2
	Brentwood & Warley v Rainham Town	0-1
	Briggs Sports v Leytonstone	1-4
	Chelmsford City v Clacton Town	2-0
	Dagenham v Tilbury	3-1
	Leyton v Grays Athletic	2-0
	Romford (2) v Harwich & Parkeston	3-1
27	Barnet v Royston Town	11-0
	Enfield v Bishop's Stortford	3-1
	Eton Manor v St Albans City	0-1
	Shefford Town v Letchworth Town	1-0
	Stevenage Town v Welwyn Garden City	5-2
	Tufnell Park Edmonton v Clapton	0-4
	Ware v Hitchin Town	2-3
28	Dorking v Epsom	1-3
	Dover v Woking	2-1
	Erith & Belvedere v Margate	0-4
	Gravesend & Northfleet v Folkestone	5-1
	Maidstone United v Bromley	1-3
	Tonbridge v Sheppey United	6-0
	Vickers (Weybridge) v Dartford	0-6
29	Aylesbury United v Wycombe Wanderers	0-1
	Bicester Town v Abingdon Town	5-2
	Huntley & Palmers v Banbury Spencer	0-3
	Maidenhead United v Marlow	2-2
	Oxford City v Witney Town	4-3
	Slough Town v Windsor & Eton	6-2
30	Berkhamsted Town v Hendon	0-3
	Edgware Town v Hayes	0-2
	Finchley v Kingstonian	3-3
	Hemel Hempstead Town v Wingate	2-2
	Hounslow Town v Uxbridge	2-2
	Metropolitan Police v Harrow Town	1-1
	Wealdstone v Wimbledon	2-4
	Yiewsley v Southall	1-0
33	Calne & Harris United v Bulford United	1-1
	Frome Town v Chippenham Town	4-2
	Welton Rovers v Swindon Victoria	3-7
	Westbury United v Warminster Town	2-0
34	Clevedon v Bridgwater Town (1)	0-4
	Street v Weston-Super-Mare	3-2
35	Lovells Athletic v Ebbw Vale	3-2
36	Bodmin Town v Wadebridge Town	2-0
	Minehead v Dartmouth United	3-3
	Newquay v Bideford	5-1
	St Austell v Penzance	3-1
	St Blazey v Ilfracombe Town	1-1
	Taunton v Barnstaple Town	3-3
	Tavistock v Tiverton Town	5-2
1r	Lynemouth Welfare v Heaton Stannington	2-3
21r	King's Lynn v Wisbech Town	8-1
24r	Chatham Town v Walton & Hersham	0-4
r	Sittingbourne v Ramsgate Athletic	2-1
r	Tooting & Mitcham United v Bexleyheath & Welling	4-1
25r	Eastbourne v Newhaven	3-0
26r	Ilford v Aveley	3-0
29r	Marlow v Maidenhead United	0-2
30r	Harrow Town v Metropolitan Police	1-5
r	Kingstonian v Finchley	3-1
r	Uxbridge v Hounslow Town	1-7
r	Wingate v Hemel Hempstead Town	1-3
33r	Bulford United v Calne & Harris United	6-3
36r	Barnstaple Town v Taunton	6-0
r	Dartmouth United v Minehead	3-5
r	Ilfracombe Town v St Blazey	5-2

Qualifying Round One

1	Ashington v Heaton Stannington	6-1
	Gosforth & Coxlodge v Cramlington Welfare	1-5
	North Shields v Shankhouse	5-1
	West Sleekburn Welfare v Hexham Hearts	3-2
2	Boldon CW v Silksworth CW	2-0
	Dawdon Colliery Welfare v Consett	2-1
	Easington CW v Birtley	7-2
	Seaham Colliery Welfare v Annfield Plain	1-2
3	Cockfield v Ferryhill Athletic	1-1
	Evenwood Town v Stockton	4-0
	Shildon v Willington	1-2
	Tow Law Town v Stanley United	0-1
4	Blackhall Colliery Welfare v Murton CW	2-0
	Durham City v Ushaw Moor	4-3
	Shotton CW v Trimdon Grange Colliery	5-1
	Wolsingham Welfare v Chilton Athletic	7-3
5	Billingham Synthonia v Bridlington Central Utd.	2-2
	North Skelton Athletic v Bridlington Trinity	9-1
	Scarborough v Head Wrightsons	3-0
	South Bank v Whitby Town	2-0
6	Burscough v Penrith	4-0
	Great Harwood v Netherfield (Kendal)	2-3
	Lancaster City v Milnthorpe Corinthians	8-1
	Morecambe v Fleetwood	2-2
7	Bacup Borough v Chorley	1-2
	Darwen v Horwich RMI	1-0
	Droylsden v Mossley	1-2
	Nelson v Leyland Motors	8-2
8	Flint Town United v St Helens Town	5-2
	Marine v Ellesmere Port Town	1-0
	Pwllheli & District v Bangor City	2-1
	Runcorn v Llandudno	6-0
9	Birch Coppice Colliery v Atherstone Town	0-3
	Burton Albion v Bloxwich Strollers	6-1
	Lockheed Leamington v Moor Green	4-5
	Rugby Town (2) v Boldmere St Michaels	5-1
10	Bilston v Lye Town	4-2
	Kidderminster Harriers v Hednesford Town	2-3
	Oswestry Town v Bromsgrove Rovers	1-2
	Stafford Rangers v Stourbridge	0-1
11	Altrincham v Northwich Victoria	3-2
	Hyde United v Buxton	3-0
	Lostock Gralam v Macclesfield Town	2-5
	Nantwich v Stalybridge Celtic	1-2
12	Hallam v Sheffield	1-3
	Retford Town v Denaby United	1-4
	South Kirkby Colliery v Langwith MW	3-6
	Upton Colliery v Frickley Colliery	4-3
13	Beighton Miners Welfare v Brunswick Institute	6-0
	Brodsworth Main Colliery v Norton Woodseats	0-4
	Rawmarsh Welfare v Bentley Colliery	2-1
	Worksop Town v Langold WMC	4-0
15	Alford United v Ashby Institute	4-2
	Brigg Town v Boston United	0-2
	Grantham v Barton Town (1)	5-2
	Skegness Town v Lysaght's Sports (Scunthorpe)	4-0
16	Basford United v Gresley Rovers	1-7
	Boots Athletic v Ilkeston Town (2)	1-6
	Matlock Town v Gedling Colliery	1-1
	South Normanton MW v Newhall United	2-1
17	Linby Colliery v Bestwood Colliery	5-0
	Parliament Street Methodists v Creswell Colliery	2-5
	Ransome & Marles v Sutton Town	0-3
	Shirebrook MW v Cinderhill Colliery	5-0
18	Bourne Town v Symingtons Recreation	3-2
	Rushden Town v Desborough Town	3-1
	Spalding United v Corby Town	2-3
	Stamford v Wellingborough Town	2-2
19	Brush Sports v Players Athletic	2-0
	Hinckley Athletic v Long Eaton Town	7-1
	Raleigh Athletic v Moira United	3-2
	Whitwick Colliery v Coalville Town (3)	14-0
20	Dunstable Town v Biggleswade Town	2-3
	Potton United v Vauxhall Motors (Luton)	1-0
	Wolverton Town & BR v Bletchley & Wipac Sports	1-0
21	Histon v Thetford Town	1-2
	King's Lynn v Huntingdon United	9-0
	March Town United v Cambridge City	1-0
	Somersham Town v Holbeach United	1-7
22	Beccles v Wymondham Town	2-0
	Gorleston v Sheringham	4-0
	Gothic (Norwich) v Cromer	7-2
	North Walsham Athletic v Bungay Town	3-2
23	Diss Town v Stowmarket	1-3
	Haverhill Rovers v Bury Town	4-6
	Leiston v Sudbury Town	2-3
	Lowestoft Town v Whitton United	3-0
24	Ashford Town v Snowdown CW	1-1
	Canterbury City v Dulwich Hamlet	2-2
	Sittingbourne v Tooting & Mitcham United	2-1
	Walton & Hersham v Carshalton Athletic	0-0
25	Eastbourne v Littlehampton Town	5-3
	Horsham v Arundel	2-0
	Tunbridge Wells United v Haywards Heath	4-0
	Worthing v Bognor Regis Town	3-3
26	Barking v Rainham Town	1-1
	Ilford v Dagenham	3-3
	Leyton v Romford (2)	4-2
	Leytonstone v Chelmsford City	0-0
27	Barnet v Hitchin Town	2-0
	Clapton v St Albans City	1-1
	Shefford Town v Hoddesdon Town	2-5
	Stevenage Town v Enfield	1-2
28	Dartford v Dover	1-2
	Gravesend & Northfleet v Tonbridge	1-2
	Margate v Bromley	4-2
	Whitstable v Epsom	0-0
29	Chesham United v Banbury Spencer	1-0
	Maidenhead United v Bicester Town	3-2
	Slough Centre v Wycombe Wanderers	1-3
	Slough Town v Oxford City	2-3
30	Hayes v Wimbledon	1-1
	Hemel Hempstead Town v Metropolitan Police	0-0
	Hendon v Yiewsley	2-1
	Kingstonian v Hounslow Town	3-4
31	Basingstoke Town v Andover	3-1
	Cowes v Chichester City (1)	6-0
32	Dorchester Town v Poole Town	2-1
33	Devizes Town v Trowbridge Town	2-5
	Salisbury (2) v Frome Town	2-3
	Swindon Victoria v Bulford United	2-2
	Westbury United v Melksham Town	1-2
34	Clandown v Street	2-0
	Peasedown MW v Chippenham United	3-1
	Radstock Town v Hanham Athletic	4-1
	Wells City v Bridgwater Town (1)	2-1
35	Barry Town v Cheltenham Town	1-1
	Cinderford Town v Gloucester City	0-3
	Llanelli v Merthyr Tydfil	1-2
	Lovells Athletic v Stonehouse	7-1
36	Bodmin Town v Minehead	3-3
	Ilfracombe Town v Newquay	2-0
	St Austell v Tavistock	3-4
	Truro City v Barnstaple Town	1-3
3r	Ferryhill Athletic v Cockfield	2-1
5r	Bridlington Central Utd. v Billingham Synthonia	3-2
6r	Fleetwood v Morecambe	3-1e
16r	Gedling Colliery v Matlock Town	6-1
18r	Wellingborough Town v Stamford	2-0
24r	Carshalton Athletic v Walton & Hersham	2-0
r	Dulwich Hamlet v Canterbury City	0-2
r	Snowdown CW v Ashford Town	5-0
25r	Bognor Regis Town v Worthing	4-1
26r	Chelmsford City v Leytonstone	2-1e
r	Dagenham v Ilford	3-4
r	Rainham Town v Barking	1-2
27r	St Albans City v Clapton	0-1
28r	Epsom v Whitstable	1-4
30r	Metropolitan Police v Hemel Hempstead Town	3-2
r	Wimbledon v Hayes	0-2
33r	Bulford United v Swindon Victoria	1-3
35r	Cheltenham Town v Barry Town	1-2
36r	Minehead v Bodmin Town	2-2
36r2	Bodmin Town v Minehead	2-3

Qualifying Round Two

1	Ashington v North Shields	2-0
	Cramlington Welfare v West Sleekburn Welfare	1-7
2	Annfield Plain v Boldon CW	3-1
	Easington CW v Dawdon Colliery Welfare	3-2
3	Ferryhill Athletic v Evenwood Town	3-0
	Willington v Stanley United	0-1
4	Blackhall Colliery Welfare v Durham City	2-2
	Wolsingham Welfare v Shotton CW	2-2
5	Bridlington Central Utd. v North Skelton Athletic	1-6
	Scarborough v South Bank	4-1
6	Lancaster City v Burscough	2-3
	Netherfield (Kendal) v Fleetwood	7-0
7	Chorley v Nelson	4-2
	Darwen v Mossley	3-1
8	Flint Town United v Marine	5-1
	Runcorn v Pwllheli & District	0-1
9	Atherstone Town v Rugby Town (2)	2-1
	Burton Albion v Moor Green	3-2
10	Bilston v Hednesford Town	1-4e
	Bromsgrove Rovers v Stourbridge	3-1
11	Hyde United v Macclesfield Town	3-1
	Stalybridge Celtic v Altrincham	2-1
12	Denaby United v Langwith MW	6-0
	Upton Colliery v Sheffield	3-2
13	Rawmarsh Welfare v Beighton Miners Welfare	1-0
	Worksop Town v Norton Woodseats	3-3
14	Farsley Celtic v Ossett Town	2-1
	Goole Town v Harrogate Railway Athletic	4-2
15	Alford United v Skegness Town	2-2
	Grantham v Boston United	2-2
16	Gresley Rovers v Gedling Colliery	3-2
	South Normanton MW v Ilkeston Town (2)	1-5
17	Creswell Colliery v Sutton Town	6-0
	Shirebrook MW v Linby Colliery	0-4
18	Bourne Town v Corby Town	1-4
	Wellingborough Town v Rushden Town	2-1
19	Brush Sports v Hinckley Athletic	3-4
	Raleigh Athletic v Whitwick Colliery	0-1
20	Eynesbury Rovers v Wolverton Town & BR	3-2
	Potton United v Biggleswade Town	2-5
21	Holbeach United v King's Lynn	2-2
	Thetford Town v March Town United	0-3
22	Beccles v Gothic (Norwich)	3-1
	North Walsham Athletic v Gorleston	1-4
23	Stowmarket v Bury Town	2-3
	Sudbury Town v Lowestoft Town	3-1
24	Canterbury City v Carshalton Athletic	2-1
	Sittingbourne v Snowdown CW	2-1
25	Bognor Regis Town v Eastbourne	4-2
	Horsham v Tunbridge Wells United	2-3
26	Chelmsford City v Barking	2-2
	Leyton v Ilford	2-1
27	Barnet v Hoddesdon Town	3-0
	Clapton v Enfield	1-0

1954/55 to 1955/56

28	Dover v Whitstable	2-1
	Tonbridge v Margate	2-2
29	Chesham United v Maidenhead United	5-5
	Oxford City v Wycombe Wanderers	4-1
30	Hayes v Hendon	3-3
	Metropolitan Police v Hounslow Town	2-4
31	Basingstoke Town v Winchester City	0-2
	Gosport Borough Ath. v Cowes	2-1
32	Dorchester Town v Bournemouth Gasworks Athletic	4-0
	Portland United v Bridport	4-2
33	Melksham Town v Swindon Victoria	4-2
	Trowbridge Town v Frome Town	1-1
34	Clandown v Wells City	0-2
	Radstock Town v Peasedown MW	4-3
35	Barry Town v Gloucester City	1-4
	Merthyr Tydfil v Lovells Athletic	3-1
36	Barnstaple Town v Ilfracombe Town	2-0
	Tavistock v Minehead	4-2
4r	Durham City v Blackhall Colliery Welfare	4-1
r	Shotton CW v Wolsingham Welfare	2-3
13r	Norton Woodseats v Worksop Town	1-2
15r	Boston United v Grantham	1-0e
r	Skegness Town v Alford United	5-1
21r	King's Lynn v Holbeach United	3-1
26r	Barking v Chelmsford City	1-1e
28r	Margate v Tonbridge	0-1e
29r	Maidenhead United v Chesham United	5-3e
30r	Hendon v Hayes	2-3
33r	Frome Town v Trowbridge Town	4-0
26r2	Chelmsford City v Barking	3-2 N

Qualifying Round Three

1	Ashington v West Sleekburn Welfare	2-1
2	Annfield Plain v Easington CW	5-1
3	Stanley United v Ferryhill Athletic	3-1
4	Durham City v Wolsingham Welfare	1-3
5	North Skelton Athletic v Scarborough	0-4
6	Burscough v Netherfield (Kendal)	0-1
7	Darwen v Chorley	1-1
8	Flint Town United v Pwllheli & District	2-3
9	Atherstone Town v Burton Albion	1-2
10	Hednesford Town v Bromsgrove Rovers	1-2
11	Hyde United v Stalybridge Celtic	8-1
12	Denaby United v Upton Colliery	2-0
13	Rawmarsh Welfare v Worksop Town	0-3
14	Farsley Celtic v Goole Town	2-0
15	Skegness Town v Boston United	2-6
16	Gresley Rovers v Ilkeston Town (2)	2-2
17	Creswell Colliery v Linby Colliery	3-1
18	Corby Town v Wellingborough Town	8-0
19	Whitwick Colliery v Hinckley Athletic	2-2
20	Eynesbury Rovers v Biggleswade Town	3-2
21	King's Lynn v March Town United	1-3
22	Gorleston v Beccles	4-0
23	Sudbury Town v Bury Town	3-1
24	Canterbury City v Sittingbourne	2-1
25	Tunbridge Wells United v Bognor Regis Town	4-0
26	Leyton v Chelmsford City	0-1
27	Clapton v Barnet	0-1
28	Tonbridge v Dover	3-2
29	Oxford City v Maidenhead United	4-1
30	Hounslow Town v Hayes	2-1
31	Winchester City v Gosport Borough Ath.	3-0
32	Portland United v Dorchester Town	1-5
33	Melksham Town v Frome Town	0-2
34	Wells City v Radstock Town	4-0
35	Gloucester City v Merthyr Tydfil	0-1
36	Barnstaple Town v Tavistock	12-1
7r	Chorley v Darwen	5-4
16r	Ilkeston Town (2) v Gresley Rovers	5-4
19r	Hinckley Athletic v Whitwick Colliery	4-1

Qualifying Round Four

	Annfield Plain v Blyth Spartans	1-2
	Ashington v Scarborough	2-3
	Barnet v Great Yarmouth Town	2-0
	Barnstaple Town v Yeovil Town	3-1
	Bedford Town (1) v March Town United	5-2
	Burton Albion v Wellington Town	0-1
	Cambridge United v Eynesbury Rovers	3-1
	Chorley v Netherfield (Kendal)	1-4
	Corby Town v Worksop Town	3-1
	Denaby United v Creswell Colliery	2-5
	Frome Town v Weymouth	3-1
	Gorleston v Chelmsford City	1-2
	Hastings United v Guildford City	1-0
	Headington United v Tonbridge	1-0
	Hinckley Athletic v Bromsgrove Rovers	2-1
	Horden CW v Spennymoor United	1-0
	Hounslow Town v Canterbury City	3-0
	Hyde United v Witton Albion	6-3
	Ilkeston Town (2) v Kettering Town	1-1
	Merthyr Tydfil v Bath City	3-1
	Nuneaton Borough v Hereford United	3-2
	Peterborough United v Boston United	1-2
	Pwllheli & District v Rhyl	0-3
	Selby Town v Gainsborough Trinity	4-2
	Stanley United v Wolsingham Welfare	5-1
	Sudbury Town v Walthamstow Avenue	0-2
	Tunbridge Wells United v Oxford City	3-1
	Wells City v Newport (IOW)	1-4
	Wigan Athletic v Farsley Celtic	3-1
	Winchester City v Dorchester Town	0-1
r	Kettering Town v Ilkeston Town (2)	4-2

Round One

	Accrington Stanley v Creswell Colliery	7-1
	Aldershot v Chelmsford City	3-1
	Barnet v Southampton	1-4
	Barnsley v Wigan Athletic	3-2
	Barnstaple Town v Bournemouth	1-4
	Barrow v Darlington	1-1
	Bishop Auckland v Kettering Town	5-1
	Boston United v Blyth Spartans	1-1
	Bradford City v Mansfield Town	3-1
	Bradford Park Avenue v Southport	2-0
	Brentford v Nuneaton Borough	2-1
	Brighton & Hove Albion v Tunbridge Wells United	5-0
	Bristol City v Southend United	1-2
	Corby Town v Watford	0-2
	Crook Town v Stanley United	5-3
	Dorchester Town v Bedford Town (1)	2-0
	Frome Town v Leyton Orient	0-3
	Gateshead v Chester	6-0
	Gillingham v Newport County	2-0
	Grimsby Town v Halifax Town	2-1
	Hartlepools United v Chesterfield	1-0
	Hinckley Athletic v Newport (IOW)	4-3
	Horden CW v Scunthorpe United	0-1
	Hounslow Town v Hastings United	2-4
	Merthyr Tydfil v Wellington Town	1-1
	Millwall v Exeter City	3-2
	Netherfield (Kendal) v Wrexham	3-3
	Northampton Town v Coventry City	0-1
	Norwich City v Headington United	4-2
	Oldham Athletic v Crewe Alexandra	1-0
	Queen's Park Rangers v Walthamstow Avenue	2-2
	Reading v Colchester United	3-3
	Selby Town v Rhyl	2-1
	Stockport County v Carlisle United	0-1
	Swindon Town v Crystal Palace	0-2
	Torquay United v Cambridge United	4-0
	Tranmere Rovers v Rochdale	3-3
	Walsall v Shrewsbury Town	5-2
	Workington v Hyde United	5-1
	York City v Scarborough	3-2
r	Blyth Spartans v Boston United	5-4
r	Colchester United v Reading	1-2
r	Darlington v Barrow	2-1
r	Rochdale v Tranmere Rovers	1-0
r	Walthamstow Avenue v Queen's Park Rangers	2-2e
r	Wellington Town v Merthyr Tydfil	1-6
r	Wrexham v Netherfield (Kendal)	4-0
r2	Queen's Park Rangers v Walthamstow Avenue	0-4 N

Round Two

	Blyth Spartans v Torquay United	1-3
	Bournemouth v Oldham Athletic	1-0
	Bradford City v Merthyr Tydfil	7-1
	Bradford Park Avenue v Southend United	2-3
	Brentford v Crook Town	4-1
	Carlisle United v Watford	2-2
	Coventry City v Scunthorpe United	4-0
	Crystal Palace v Bishop Auckland	2-4
	Dorchester Town v York City	2-5
	Gateshead v Barnsley	3-3
	Gillingham v Reading	1-1
	Grimsby Town v Southampton	4-1
	Hartlepools United v Aldershot	4-0
	Leyton Orient v Workington	0-1
	Millwall v Accrington Stanley	3-2
	Norwich City v Brighton & Hove Albion	0-0
	Rochdale v Hinckley Athletic	2-1
	Selby Town v Hastings United	0-2
	Walthamstow Avenue v Darlington	0-3
	Wrexham v Walsall	1-2
r	Barnsley v Gateshead	0-1
r	Brighton & Hove Albion v Norwich City	5-1
r	Reading v Gillingham	5-3
r	Watford v Carlisle United	4-1

Round Three

	Arsenal v Cardiff City	1-0
	Blackburn Rovers v Swansea Town	0-2
	Blackpool v York City	0-2
	Bolton Wanderers v Millwall	3-1
	Bournemouth v West Bromwich Albion	0-1
	Brentford v Bradford City	1-1
	Brighton & Hove Albion v Aston Villa	2-2
	Bristol Rovers v Portsmouth	2-1
	Bury v Stoke City	1-1
	Chelsea v Walsall	2-0
	Derby County v Manchester City	1-3
	Everton v Southend United	3-1
	Fulham v Preston North End	2-3
	Gateshead v Tottenham Hotspur	0-2
	Grimsby Town v Wolverhampton Wan.	2-5
	Hartlepools United v Darlington	1-1
	Huddersfield Town v Coventry City	3-3
	Hull City v Birmingham City	0-2
	Ipswich Town v Bishop Auckland	2-2
	Leeds United v Torquay United	2-2
	Lincoln City v Liverpool	1-1
	Luton Town v Workington	5-0
	Middlesbrough v Notts County	1-4
	Plymouth Argyle v Newcastle United	0-1
	Reading v Manchester United	1-1
	Rochdale v Charlton Athletic	1-3
	Rotherham United v Leicester City	1-0
	Sheffield United v Nottingham Forest	1-3
	Sheffield Wednesday v Hastings United	2-1
	Sunderland v Burnley	1-0
	Watford v Doncaster Rovers	1-2
	West Ham United v Port Vale	2-2
r	Aston Villa v Brighton & Hove Albion	4-2
r	Bishop Auckland v Ipswich Town	3-0
r	Bradford City v Brentford	2-2e
r	Coventry City v Huddersfield Town	1-2e
r	Darlington v Hartlepools United	2-2e
r	Liverpool v Lincoln City	1-0e
r	Manchester United v Reading	4-1
r	Port Vale v West Ham United	3-1
r	Stoke City v Bury	1-1x
r	Torquay United v Leeds United	4-0
r2	Brentford v Bradford City	1-0 N
r2	Bury v Stoke City	3-3eN
r2	Hartlepools United v Darlington	2-0 N
r3	Stoke City v Bury	2-2eN
r4	Bury v Stoke City	2-3eN

Round Four

	Birmingham City v Bolton Wanderers	2-1
	Bishop Auckland v York City	1-3
	Bristol Rovers v Chelsea	1-3
	Doncaster Rovers v Aston Villa	0-0
	Everton v Liverpool	0-4
	Hartlepools United v Nottingham Forest	1-1
	Manchester City v Manchester United	2-0
	Newcastle United v Brentford	3-2
	Preston North End v Sunderland	3-3
	Rotherham United v Luton Town	1-5
	Sheffield Wednesday v Notts County	1-1
	Swansea Town v Stoke City	3-1
	Torquay United v Huddersfield Town	0-1
	Tottenham Hotspur v Port Vale	4-2
	West Bromwich Albion v Charlton Athletic	2-4
	Wolverhampton Wan. v Arsenal	1-0
r	Aston Villa v Doncaster Rovers	2-2e
r	Nottingham Forest v Hartlepools United	2-1e
r	Notts County v Sheffield Wednesday	1-0e
r	Sunderland v Preston North End	2-0
r2	Doncaster Rovers v Aston Villa	1-1eN
r3	Aston Villa v Doncaster Rovers	0-0xN
r4	Doncaster Rovers v Aston Villa	3-1 N

Round Five

	Birmingham City v Doncaster Rovers	2-1
	Liverpool v Huddersfield Town	0-2
	Luton Town v Manchester City	0-2
	Nottingham Forest v Newcastle United	1-1
	Notts County v Chelsea	1-0
	Swansea Town v Sunderland	2-2
	Wolverhampton Wan. v Charlton Athletic	4-1
	York City v Tottenham Hotspur	3-1
r	Newcastle United v Nottingham Forest	2-2e
r	Sunderland v Swansea Town	1-0
r2	Newcastle United v Nottingham Forest	2-1e

Round Six

	Birmingham City v Manchester City	0-1
	Huddersfield Town v Newcastle United	1-1
	Notts County v York City	0-1
	Sunderland v Wolverhampton Wan.	2-0
r	Newcastle United v Huddersfield Town	2-0e

Semi Finals

	Manchester City v Sunderland	1-0 N
	Newcastle United v York City	1-1 N
r	York City v Newcastle United	0-2 N

Final

	Newcastle United v Manchester City	3-1 N

1955/56

Preliminary Round

7	Chorley v Darwen	4-0
	Horwich RMI v Skelmersdale United	3-2
	Leyland Motors v Bacup Borough	2-1
	Mossley v Lytham	1-1
8	Bangor City v Llandudno	3-3
	Prescot Cables v Marine	4-3
	South Liverpool v Ellesmere Port Town	4-2
	St Helens Town v Pwllheli & District	1-1
9	Atherstone Town v Burton Albion	1-2
	Boldmere St Michaels v Sutton Town (Birmingham)	2-2
	Moor Green v Bloxwich Strollers	2-2
10	Bilston v Stafford Rangers	1-5
	Brierley Hill Alliance v Kidderminster Harriers	1-1
	Dudley Town v Hednesford Town	1-4
	Halesowen Town v Bromsgrove Rovers	2-1
	Redditch v Worcester City	0-1

1955/56

	Stourbridge v Oswestry Town	6-0
11	Linotype & Machinery v Hyde United	2-4
	Nantwich v Congleton Town	0-1
	Northwich Victoria v Altrincham	2-2
	Winsford United v Witton Albion	4-1
21	Cambridge City v March Town United	2-2
	Chatteris Town v Cambridge United	2-1
	Exning United v Ely City	2-4
	Holbeach United v Newmarket Town	6-0
	King's Lynn v Histon	6-1
	Wisbech Town v Warboys Town	5-0
24	Ashford Town v Tooting & Mitcham United	1-0
	Canterbury City v Sutton United	2-1
	Carshalton Athletic v Dulwich Hamlet	4-1
	Chatham Town v Ramsgate Athletic	1-6
	Sittingbourne v Bexleyheath & Welling	4-2
	Snowdown CW v Walton & Hersham	4-0
25	Bexhill Town v Littlehampton Town	2-3
	East Grinstead v Newhaven	2-1
	Eastbourne v Wigmore Athletic	4-2
	Horsham v Redhill	1-3
	Shoreham v Bognor Regis Town	1-6
	Worthing v Lancing Athletic	5-0
26	Aveley v Brentwood & Warley	5-1
	Barking v Leyton	2-2
	Dagenham v Romford (2)	2-1
	Grays Athletic v Chelmsford City	1-0
	Ilford v Briggs Sports	0-3
	Leytonstone v Harwich & Parkeston	2-1
	Rainham Town v Clacton Town	1-3
	Woodford Town (1) v Tilbury	4-2
27	Bishop's Stortford v Eton Manor	1-2
	Enfield v Letchworth Town	3-1
	Hertford Town v St Albans City	1-2
	Stevenage Town v Barnet	1-3
	Ware v Shefford Town	7-2
	Welwyn Garden City v Clapton	0-3
28	Bromley v Margate	0-1
	Dartford v Gravesend & Northfleet	0-3
	Dover v Whitstable	5-1
	Erith & Belvedere v Dorking	3-3
	Maidstone United v Sheppey United	1-1
	Tonbridge v Betteshanger CW	8-2
	Woking v Folkestone	1-1
29	Aylesbury United v Slough Centre	3-1
	Marlow v Maidenhead United	1-2
	Slough Town v Bicester Town	4-0
	Windsor & Eton v Chesham United	2-2
	Witney Town v Wycombe Wanderers	0-0
30	Berkhamsted Town v Kingstonian	2-2
	Harrow Town v Uxbridge	3-3
	Hayes v Finchley	1-4
	Hounslow Town v Metropolitan Police	3-3
	Wembley v Wealdstone	2-3
	Wimbledon v Edgware Town	4-1
	Yiewsley v Southall	0-0
33	Bulford United v Welton Rovers	1-1
	Frome Town v Trowbridge Town	4-3
	Warminster Town v Melksham Town	3-1
34	Clandown v Bath City	0-0
	Clevedon v Chippenham United	0-2
	Wells City v Bridgwater Town (1)	2-1
36	Bodmin Town v Ilfracombe Town	4-3
	Penzance v Newquay	4-2
	St Austell v Truro City	1-8
	St Blazey v Tavistock	3-1
	Taunton v Barnstaple Town	2-1
7r	Lytham v Mossley	1-0
8r	Llandudno v Bangor City	1-0
r	Pwllheli & District v St Helens Town	3-1
9r	Bloxwich Strollers v Moor Green	0-2
r	Sutton Town (Birmingham) v Boldmere St Michaels	4-2
10r	Kidderminster Harriers v Brierley Hill Alliance	4-2
11r	Altrincham v Northwich Victoria	0-2
21r	March Town United v Cambridge City	3-1
26r	Leyton v Barking	1-0
28r	Dorking v Erith & Belvedere	5-1
r	Folkestone v Woking	2-1
r	Sheppey United v Maidstone United	0-4
29r	Chesham United v Windsor & Eton	2-0
r	Wycombe Wanderers v Witney Town	15-1
30r	Kingstonian v Berkhamsted Town	6-0
r	Metropolitan Police v Hounslow Town	0-4
r	Southall v Yiewsley	2-1
r	Uxbridge v Harrow Town	1-2
33r	Welton Rovers v Bulford United	1-3
34r	Bath City v Clandown	4-0

Qualifying Round One

1	Ashington v Gosforth & Coxlodge	7-0
	Hexham Hearts v North Shields	2-4
	Newburn v Cramlington Welfare	1-2
	South Shields (2) v Alnwick Town	5-0
2	Consett v Dawdon Colliery Welfare	4-0
	Seaham Colliery Welfare v Easington CW	1-3
	Silksworth CW v Annfield Plain	9-5
3	Shildon v Stockton	3-0
	Stanley United v West Auckland Town	0-1
	Tow Law Town v Evenwood Town	3-1
	Willington v Cockfield	3-1
4	Durham City v Chilton Athletic	4-2
	Murton CW v Blackhall Colliery Welfare	4-2
5	Bridlington Central Utd. v North Skelton Athletic	3-0
6	Lancaster City v Burscough	2-0
	Milnthorpe Corinthians v Morecambe	5-2
7	Ashton United v Nelson	1-1
	Leyland Motors v Horwich RMI	1-0
	Lytham v Chorley	1-4
	Rossendale United v Droylsden	4-3
8	Earlestown v South Liverpool	1-1
	Flint Town United v Runcorn	0-0
	New Brighton v Llandudno	4-0
	Pwllheli & District v Prescot Cables	4-1
9	Burton Albion v Tamworth	2-0
	Lockheed Leamington v Moor Green	2-1
	Rugby Town (2) v Bedworth Town	2-2
	Sutton Town (Birmingham) v Bournville Athletic	2-2
10	Darlaston v Stourbridge	2-7
	Hednesford Town v Halesowen Town	0-1
	Kidderminster Harriers v Wellington Town	2-1
	Stafford Rangers v Worcester City	1-2
11	Buxton v Lostock Gralam	2-1
	Congleton Town v Hyde United	1-3
	Macclesfield Town v Northwich Victoria	0-4
	Stalybridge Celtic v Winsford United	1-1
12	Denaby United v Retford Town	5-0
	Langwith MW v Hallam	1-2
	Stocksbridge Works v Sheffield	8-2
	Upton Colliery v Frickley Colliery	0-3
13	Brodsworth Main Colliery v Langold WMC	1-2
	Norton Woodseats v Beighton Miners Welfare	1-2
	Worksop Town v Brunswick Institute	8-0
14	Yorkshire Amateur v Ossett Town	1-2
15	Brigg Town v Bourne Town	2-2
	Grantham v Ashby Institute	4-2
	Skegness Town v Barton Town (1)	7-2
17	Ransome & Marles v Creswell Colliery	6-1
18	Corby Town v Kettering Town	2-1
	Desborough Town v Rothwell Town	0-0
	Stamford v Rushden Town	1-5
	Wellingborough Town v Spalding United	1-9
19	Long Eaton Town v Whitwick Colliery	2-3
20	Bedford Town (1) v Biggleswade Town	4-0
	Potton United v Eynesbury Rovers	0-2
	Wolverton Town & BR v Dunstable Town	0-2
21	Ely City v Thetford Town	4-3
	King's Lynn v Chatteris Town	4-2
	March Town United v St Neots & District	3-1
	Wisbech Town v Holbeach United	2-2
22	Bungay Town v Beccles	0-2
	Cromer v Wymondham Town	1-2
	Sheringham v Great Yarmouth Town	0-0
23	Bury Town v Whitton United	3-2
	Lowestoft Town v Haverhill Rovers	9-0
	Stowmarket v Diss Town	7-0
	Sudbury Town v Leiston	14-1
24	Ashford Town v Ramsgate Athletic	2-5
	Deal Town v Canterbury City	2-2
	Sittingbourne v Tunbridge Wells United	2-0
	Snowdown CW v Carshalton Athletic	0-1
25	Bognor Regis Town v East Grinstead	3-1
	Eastbourne v Redhill	0-2
	Southwick v Littlehampton Town	2-1
	Worthing v Haywards Heath	4-1
26	Briggs Sports v Grays Athletic	0-0
	Clacton Town v Woodford Town (1)	3-0
	Leyton v Aveley	3-0
	Leytonstone v Dagenham	0-3
27	Clapton v St Albans City	0-0
	Eton Manor v Barnet	3-2
	Hitchin Town v Ware	5-0
	Hoddesdon Town v Enfield	2-5
28	Dorking v Folkestone	3-1
	Epsom v Dover	3-2
	Gravesend & Northfleet v Margate	1-2
	Tonbridge v Maidstone United	0-1
29	Abingdon Town v Slough Town	0-3
	Banbury Spencer v Aylesbury United	7-0
	Oxford City v Chesham United	2-1
	Wycombe Wanderers v Maidenhead United	4-2
30	Harrow Town v Wealdstone	0-7
	Hemel Hempstead Town v Hounslow Town	1-0
	Southall v Kingstonian	1-1
	Wimbledon v Finchley	0-1
31	Andover v Gosport Borough Ath.	5-0
	Basingstoke Town v Fareham Town	3-3
	Cowes v Bournemouth Gasworks Athletic	4-1
	Winchester City v Chichester City (1)	2-2
33	Bulford United v Calne & Harris United	4-1
	Devizes Town v Salisbury (2)	0-2
	Frome Town v Warminster Town	2-1
	Westbury United v Chippenham Town	1-1
34	Bath City v Chippenham United	3-3
	Glastonbury v Street	1-3
	Radstock Town v Weston-Super-Mare	2-3
	Wells City v Peasedown MW	2-1
35	Cheltenham Town v Lovells Athletic	1-2
	Ebbw Vale v Gloucester City	2-2
	Llanelli v Cinderford Town	5-0
	Stonehouse v Barry Town	3-4
36	Bideford v Minehead	4-0
	Penzance v Truro City	3-1
	Taunton v St Blazey	0-2
	Wadebridge Town v Bodmin Town	2-5
7r	Nelson v Ashton United	1-4
8r	Runcorn v Flint Town United	4-3
r	South Liverpool v Earlestown	3-1
9r	Bedworth Town v Rugby Town (2)	2-2
r	Bournville Athletic v Sutton Town (Birmingham)	1-4
11r	Winsford United v Stalybridge Celtic	6-0
15r	Bourne Town v Brigg Town	2-3
18r	Rothwell Town v Desborough Town	5-0
21r	Holbeach United v Wisbech Town	0-2
22r	Great Yarmouth Town v Sheringham	3-2
24r	Canterbury City v Deal Town	2-1
26r	Grays Athletic v Briggs Sports	0-0e
27r	St Albans City v Clapton	4-1
30r	Kingstonian v Southall	0-1
31r	Chichester City (1) v Winchester City	1-3
r	Fareham Town v Basingstoke Town	3-2
33r	Chippenham Town v Westbury United	0-1
34r	Chippenham United v Bath City	1-0
35r	Gloucester City v Ebbw Vale	4-1
9r2	Bedworth Town v Rugby Town (2)	3-1
26r2	Briggs Sports v Grays Athletic	1-0

Qualifying Round Two

1	North Shields v Ashington	3-1
	South Shields (2) v Cramlington Welfare	5-3
2	Boldon CW v Consett	1-2
	Easington CW v Silksworth CW	4-2
3	Tow Law Town v West Auckland Town	1-4
	Willington v Shildon	3-3
4	Murton CW v Ferryhill Athletic	0-2
	Wolsingham Welfare v Durham City	2-2
5	Bridlington Central Utd. v Whitby Town	4-4
	South Bank v Billingham Synthonia	0-1
6	Fleetwood v Milnthorpe Corinthians	0-0
	Lancaster City v Penrith	2-0
7	Ashton United v Leyland Motors	2-1
	Rossendale United v Chorley	2-1
8	New Brighton v Pwllheli & District	4-2
	Runcorn v South Liverpool	1-1
9	Bedworth Town v Burton Albion	1-1
	Lockheed Leamington v Sutton Town (Birmingham)	3-4
10	Halesowen Town v Stourbridge	3-0
	Kidderminster Harriers v Worcester City	2-0
11	Hyde United v Northwich Victoria	1-3
	Winsford United v Buxton	5-1
12	Denaby United v Stocksbridge Works	3-2
	Hallam v Frickley Colliery	0-2
13	Langold WMC v Bentley Colliery	1-2
	Worksop Town v Beighton Miners Welfare	3-0
14	Goole Town v Harrogate Railway Athletic	6-0
	Ossett Town v Farsley Celtic	3-2
15	Alford United v Grantham	0-3
	Skegness Town v Brigg Town	3-1
16	Gresley Rovers v Boots Athletic	0-1
	Ilkeston Town (2) v South Normanton MW	3-1
17	Linby Colliery v Sutton Town	3-3
	Shirebrook MW v Ransome & Marles	3-1
18	Rushden Town v Rothwell Town	3-3
	Spalding United v Corby Town	1-3
19	Heanor Town v Brush Sports	1-2
	Players Athletic v Whitwick Colliery	1-4
20	Dunstable Town v Bedford Town (1)	0-4
	Eynesbury Rovers v Bletchley & Wipac Sports	5-0
21	King's Lynn v March Town United	1-1
	Wisbech Town v Ely City	3-2
22	Beccles v Wymondham Town	2-2
	Great Yarmouth Town v Gorleston	2-0
23	Bury Town v Lowestoft Town	2-3
	Sudbury Town v Stowmarket	4-0
24	Ramsgate Athletic v Canterbury City	1-1
	Sittingbourne v Carshalton Athletic	0-0
25	Bognor Regis Town v Redhill	2-2
	Southwick v Worthing	1-2
26	Dagenham v Briggs Sports	0-1
	Leyton v Clacton Town	4-0
27	Enfield v St Albans City	4-2
	Eton Manor v Hitchin Town	3-3
28	Epsom v Dorking	3-2
	Maidstone United v Margate	1-4
29	Banbury Spencer v Oxford City	3-1
	Slough Town v Wycombe Wanderers	3-3
30	Hemel Hempstead Town v Finchley	2-5
	Wealdstone v Southall	1-2
31	Andover v Winchester City	2-1
	Cowes v Fareham Town	2-3
32	Poole Town v Bridport	3-1
	Portland United v Ilminster Town	5-0
33	Frome Town v Westbury United	2-2
	Salisbury (2) v Bulford United	3-0
34	Street v Chippenham United	3-6
	Weston-Super-Mare v Wells City	5-1
35	Barry Town v Gloucester City	5-2
	Llanelli v Lovells Athletic	0-3
36	Bideford v St Blazey	4-1
	Penzance v Bodmin Town	4-3
3r	Shildon v Willington	7-3
4r	Durham City v Wolsingham Welfare	2-0
5r	Whitby Town v Bridlington Central Utd.	0-1
6r	Milnthorpe Corinthians v Fleetwood	2-5
8r	South Liverpool v Runcorn	1-3
9r	Burton Albion v Bedworth Town	3-2
17r	Sutton Town v Linby Colliery	3-2
18r	Rothwell Town v Rushden Town	3-2
21r	March Town United v King's Lynn	1-0
22r	Wymondham Town v Beccles	1-2
24r	Canterbury City v Ramsgate Athletic	2-5
r	Carshalton Athletic v Sittingbourne	1-2

1955/56 to 1956/57

25r Redhill v Bognor Regis Town	4-0
27r Hitchin Town v Eton Manor	2-1
29r Wycombe Wanderers v Slough Town	1-0
33r Westbury United v Frome Town	1-2

Qualifying Round Three

1 South Shields (2) v North Shields	0-1
2 Consett v Easington CW	1-4
3 West Auckland Town v Shildon	1-1
4 Durham City v Ferryhill Athletic	0-0
5 Bridlington Central Utd. v Billingham Synthonia	1-0
6 Fleetwood v Lancaster City	1-1
7 Ashton United v Rossendale United	1-0
8 Runcorn v New Brighton	0-1
9 Burton Albion v Sutton Town (Birmingham)	6-3
10 Kidderminster Harriers v Halesowen Town	0-0
11 Northwich Victoria v Winsford United	2-2
12 Frickley Colliery v Denaby United	3-5
13 Worksop Town v Bentley Colliery	9-2
14 Goole Town v Ossett Town	2-1
15 Grantham v Skegness Town	3-3
16 Ilkeston Town (2) v Boots Athletic	9-0
17 Sutton Town v Shirebrook MW	4-1
18 Corby Town v Rothwell Town	3-1
19 Brush Sports v Whitwick Colliery	1-0
20 Eynesbury Rovers v Bedford Town (1)	1-4
21 Wisbech Town v March Town United	1-1
22 Beccles v Great Yarmouth Town	1-4
23 Lowestoft Town v Sudbury Town	0-0
24 Sittingbourne v Ramsgate Athletic	1-1
25 Worthing v Redhill	1-4
26 Briggs Sports v Leyton	1-2
27 Hitchin Town v Enfield	3-1
28 Epsom v Margate	1-3
29 Banbury Spencer v Wycombe Wanderers	1-2
30 Southall v Finchley	3-0
31 Fareham Town v Andover	2-2
32 Portland United v Poole Town	1-4
33 Salisbury (2) v Frome Town	3-0
34 Chippenham United v Weston-Super-Mare	3-2
35 Barry Town v Lovells Athletic	1-3
36 Penzance v Bideford	2-2
3r Shildon v West Auckland Town	5-3
4r Ferryhill Athletic v Durham City	0-2
6r Lancaster City v Fleetwood	3-1
10r Halesowen Town v Kidderminster Harriers	1-0
11r Winsford United v Northwich Victoria	1-2
15r Skegness Town v Grantham	3-0
21r March Town United v Wisbech Town	3-0
23r Sudbury Town v Lowestoft Town	4-1
24r Ramsgate Athletic v Sittingbourne	3-2
31r Andover v Fareham Town	0-2
36r Bideford v Penzance	2-0

Qualifying Round Four

Ashton United v Wigan Athletic	5-0
Bedford Town (1) v Walthamstow Avenue	6-0
Bideford v Yeovil Town	0-3
Blyth Spartans v Shildon	2-4
Brush Sports v Burton Albion	0-2
Chippenham United v Salisbury (2)	2-6
Dorchester Town v Newport (IOW)	3-0
Durham City v Bridlington Central Utd.	5-2
Guildford City v Ramsgate Athletic	2-2
Headington United v Margate	2-4
Hereford United v Nuneaton Borough	8-1
Hinckley Athletic v Halesowen Town	1-4
Horden CW v Easington CW	0-1
Ilkeston Town (2) v Peterborough United	1-3
Leyton v Hitchin Town	3-1
Lovells Athletic v Merthyr Tydfil	2-0
March Town United v Great Yarmouth Town	1-0
Netherfield (Kendal) v Lancaster City	2-0
Northwich Victoria v Denaby United	3-1
Poole Town v Weymouth	2-3
Redhill v Hastings United	2-2
Rhyl v New Brighton	3-1
Scarborough v North Shields	4-3
Selby Town v Goole Town	2-4
Skegness Town v Gainsborough Trinity	1-1
Spennymoor United v Crook Town	2-2
Sudbury Town v Southall	4-4
Sutton Town v Boston United	2-8
Worksop Town v Corby Town	1-0
Wycombe Wanderers v Fareham Town	3-1
r Crook Town v Spennymoor United	5-0
r Gainsborough Trinity v Skegness Town	0-2
r Hastings United v Redhill	4-0
r Ramsgate Athletic v Guildford City	3-2
r Southall v Sudbury Town	2-2e
r2 Southall v Sudbury Town	7-2

Round One

Accrington Stanley v Wrexham	3-1
Barrow v Crewe Alexandra	0-0
Bedford Town (1) v Leyton	3-0
Bishop Auckland v Durham City	3-1
Boston United v Northwich Victoria	3-2
Bradford City v Oldham Athletic	3-1
Brentford v March Town United	4-0
Brighton & Hove Albion v Newport County	8-1
Chesterfield v Chester	1-0
Coventry City v Exeter City	0-1
Crook Town v Derby County	2-2
Crystal Palace v Southampton	0-0
Darlington v Carlisle United	0-0
Easington CW v Tranmere Rovers	0-2
Gillingham v Shrewsbury Town	1-1
Goole Town v Halifax Town	1-2
Halesowen Town v Hendon	2-4
Hartlepools United v Gateshead	3-0
Hastings United v Southall	6-1
Leyton Orient v Lovells Athletic	7-1
Mansfield Town v Stockport County	2-0
Margate v Walsall	2-2
Netherfield (Kendal) v Grimsby Town	1-5
Northampton Town v Millwall	4-1
Norwich City v Dorchester Town	4-0
Peterborough United v Ipswich Town	3-1
Reading v Bournemouth	1-0
Rhyl v Bradford Park Avenue	0-3
Rochdale v York City	0-1
Scunthorpe United v Shildon	3-0
Skegness Town v Worksop Town	0-4
Southend United v Queen's Park Rangers	2-0
Southport v Ashton United	6-1
Swindon Town v Hereford United	4-0
Torquay United v Colchester United	2-0
Watford v Ramsgate Athletic	5-3
Weymouth v Salisbury (2)	3-2
Workington v Scarborough	4-2
Wycombe Wanderers v Burton Albion	1-3
Yeovil Town v Aldershot	1-1
r Aldershot v Yeovil Town	1-1e
r Carlisle United v Darlington	0-0e
r Crewe Alexandra v Barrow	2-3e
r Derby County v Crook Town	5-1
r Shrewsbury Town v Gillingham	4-1e
r Southampton v Crystal Palace	2-0
r Walsall v Margate	6-1
r2 Darlington v Carlisle United	3-1 N
r2 Yeovil Town v Aldershot	0-3 N

Round Two

Bedford Town (1) v Watford	3-2
Bishop Auckland v Scunthorpe United	0-0
Bradford City v Worksop Town	2-2
Bradford Park Avenue v Workington	4-3
Brighton & Hove Albion v Norwich City	1-2
Chesterfield v Hartlepools United	1-2
Darlington v Accrington Stanley	0-1
Derby County v Boston United	1-6
Exeter City v Hendon	6-2
Halifax Town v Burton Albion	0-0
Leyton Orient v Brentford	4-1
Northampton Town v Hastings United	4-1
Reading v Aldershot	2-2
Shrewsbury Town v Torquay United	0-0
Southport v Grimsby Town	0-0
Swindon Town v Peterborough United	1-1
Tranmere Rovers v Barrow	0-3
Walsall v Southampton	2-1
Weymouth v Southend United	0-1
York City v Mansfield Town	2-1
r Aldershot v Reading	3-0e
r Burton Albion v Halifax Town	1-0
r Grimsby Town v Southport	3-2
r Peterborough United v Swindon Town	1-2e
r Scunthorpe United v Bishop Auckland	2-0
r Torquay United v Shrewsbury Town	5-1
r Worksop Town v Bradford City	1-0

Round Three

Aldershot v Barnsley	1-2
Arsenal v Bedford Town (1)	2-2
Aston Villa v Hull City	1-1
Bolton Wanderers v Huddersfield Town	3-0
Bradford Park Avenue v Middlesbrough	0-4
Bristol Rovers v Manchester United	4-0
Bury v Burnley	0-1
Charlton Athletic v Burton Albion	7-0
Doncaster Rovers v Nottingham Forest	3-0
Everton v Bristol City	3-1
Exeter City v Stoke City	0-0
Hartlepools United v Chelsea	0-1
Leeds United v Cardiff City	1-2
Leyton Orient v Plymouth Argyle	1-0
Lincoln City v Southend United	2-3
Liverpool v Accrington Stanley	2-0
Luton Town v Leicester City	0-4
Manchester City v Blackpool	2-1
Northampton Town v Blackburn Rovers	1-2
Notts County v Fulham	0-1
Portsmouth v Grimsby Town	3-1
Rotherham United v Scunthorpe United	1-1
Sheffield United v Barrow	5-0
Sheffield Wednesday v Newcastle United	1-3
Sunderland v Norwich City	4-2
Swansea Town v York City	1-2
Swindon Town v Worksop Town	1-0
Torquay United v Birmingham City	1-7
Tottenham Hotspur v Boston United	4-0
Walsall v Port Vale	0-1
West Ham United v Preston North End	5-2
Wolverhampton Wan. v West Bromwich Albion	1-2
r Bedford Town (1) v Arsenal	1-2e
r Hull City v Aston Villa	1-2
r Scunthorpe United v Rotherham United	4-2
r Stoke City v Exeter City	3-0

Round Four

Arsenal v Aston Villa	4-1
Barnsley v Blackburn Rovers	0-1
Bolton Wanderers v Sheffield United	1-2
Bristol Rovers v Doncaster Rovers	1-1
Burnley v Chelsea	1-1
Charlton Athletic v Swindon Town	2-1
Fulham v Newcastle United	4-5
Leicester City v Stoke City	3-3
Leyton Orient v Birmingham City	0-4
Liverpool v Scunthorpe United	3-3
Port Vale v Everton	2-3
Southend United v Manchester City	0-1
Tottenham Hotspur v Middlesbrough	3-1
West Bromwich Albion v Portsmouth	2-0
West Ham United v Cardiff City	2-1
York City v Sunderland	0-0
r Chelsea v Burnley	1-1e
r Doncaster Rovers v Bristol Rovers	1-0
r Scunthorpe United v Liverpool	1-2e
r Stoke City v Leicester City	2-1
r Sunderland v York City	2-1
r2 Burnley v Chelsea	2-2eN
r3 Chelsea v Burnley	0-0eN
r4 Burnley v Chelsea	0-2 N

Round Five

Charlton Athletic v Arsenal	0-2
Doncaster Rovers v Tottenham Hotspur	0-2
Everton v Chelsea	1-0
Manchester City v Liverpool	0-0
Newcastle United v Stoke City	2-1
Sheffield United v Sunderland	0-0
West Bromwich Albion v Birmingham City	0-1
West Ham United v Blackburn Rovers	0-0
r Blackburn Rovers v West Ham United	2-3
r Liverpool v Manchester City	1-2
r Sunderland v Sheffield United	1-0

Round Six

Arsenal v Birmingham City	1-3
Manchester City v Everton	2-1
Newcastle United v Sunderland	0-2
Tottenham Hotspur v West Ham United	3-3
r West Ham United v Tottenham Hotspur	1-2

Semi Finals

Birmingham City v Sunderland	3-0 N
Manchester City v Tottenham Hotspur	1-0 N

Final

Manchester City v Birmingham City	3-1 N

1956/57

Preliminary Round

7 Lytham v Horwich RMI	1-7
Rossendale United v Mossley	0-1
Skelmersdale United v Ashton United	3-0
8 Bangor City v Pwllheli & District	2-2
New Brighton v Prescot Cables	1-0
Runcorn v Flint Town United	1-1
South Liverpool v Earle	7-0
St Helens Town v Marine	2-2
9 Sutton Coldfield Town v Moor Green	3-2
10 Bilston v Wellington Town	1-1
Brierley Hill Alliance v Stourbridge	0-2
Bromsgrove Rovers v Cradley Heath	3-3
Halesowen Town v Stafford Rangers	2-3
Kidderminster Harriers v Dudley Town	3-0
Redditch v Hednesford Town	4-1
Worcester City v Darlaston	7-0
11 Altrincham v Northwich Victoria	4-3
Hyde United v Stalybridge Celtic	4-4
Lostock Gralam v Leek Town	2-1
Macclesfield Town v Ellesmere Port Town	2-1
Stockton Heath v Winsford United	4-5
Witton Albion v Buxton	2-1
21 Cambridge City v Warboys Town	2-1
Chatteris Town v St Neots & District	0-2
Histon v Ely City	2-5
Holbeach United v Cambridge United	2-2
Newmarket Town v March Town United	1-6
24 Ashford Town v Whitstable	3-1
Betteshanger CW v Maidstone United	1-0
Chatham Town v Ramsgate Athletic	2-4
Dartford v Gravesend & Northfleet	2-2
Deal Town v Sittingbourne	3-5
Folkestone v Canterbury City	0-1
Margate v Sheppey United	8-1
Snowdown CW v Dover	0-0

117

1956/57

25	Haywards Heath v Eastbourne	2-3
	Littlehampton Town v Lancing Athletic	1-2
	Newhaven v Bognor Regis Town	1-5
	Worthing v Southwick	3-2
26	Barking v Tilbury	4-1
	Briggs Sports v Leyton	4-0
	Chelmsford City v Ilford	1-0
	Dagenham v Brentwood & Warley	0-1
	Harwich & Parkeston v Clacton Town	0-0
	Leytonstone v Aveley	6-2
	Romford (2) v Grays Athletic	4-2
	Woodford Town (1) v Rainham Town	0-5
27	Barnet v Stevenage Town	2-1
	Bishop's Stortford v Enfield	3-0
	Letchworth Town v St Albans City	1-0
	Ware v Hitchin Town	1-1
28	Bromley v Metropolitan Police	5-3
	Dorking v Tunbridge Wells United	0-1
	Dulwich Hamlet v Woking	1-2
	Epsom v Bexleyheath & Welling	1-3
	Erith & Belvedere v Sutton United	4-3
	Kingstonian v Tonbridge	2-2
	Wimbledon v Tooting & Mitcham United	1-5
29	Abingdon Town v Banbury Spencer	0-3
	Maidenhead United v Huntley & Palmers	5-1
30	Finchley v Hemel Hempstead Town	5-0
	Uxbridge v Berkhamsted Town	3-2
	Wealdstone v Hayes	2-4
	Wembley v Edgware Town	4-1
	Yiewsley v Hendon	1-0
33	Chippenham Town v Calne & Harris United	9-2
34	Wells City v Street	1-1
35	Cheltenham Town v Lovells Athletic	3-0
36	Minehead v Wadebridge Town	2-3
	St Blazey v Bideford	2-5
8r	Flint Town United v Runcorn	1-2
r	Marine v St Helens Town	2-1
r	Pwllheli & District v Bangor City	4-1
10r	Cradley Heath v Bromsgrove Rovers	0-1
r	Wellington Town v Bilston	3-2e
11r	Stalybridge Celtic v Hyde United	4-4e
21r	Cambridge United v Holbeach United	5-0
24r	Dover v Snowdown CW	1-2
r	Gravesend & Northfleet v Dartford	3-2e
26r	Clacton Town v Harwich & Parkeston	2-1
27r	Hitchin Town v Ware	5-2
28r	Tonbridge v Kingstonian	6-1
34r	Street v Wells City	0-0
11r2	Hyde United v Stalybridge Celtic	6-1
34r2	Street v Wells City	2-0

Qualifying Round One

1	Cramlington Welfare v Gosforth & Coxlodge	3-1
	Morpeth Town v North Shields	0-5
	South Shields (2) v Alnwick Town	3-0
	Whitley Bay v Ashington	1-3
2	Dawdon Colliery Welfare v Consett	0-2
	Shotton CW v Wingate Welfare	4-2
3	Cockfield v Stanley United	2-3
	Evenwood Town v Tow Law Town	4-0
	Shildon v West Auckland Town	2-2
	Wolsingham Welfare v Willington	1-8
4	Ferryhill Athletic v Horden CW	0-3
	Spennymoor United v Blackhall Colliery Welfare	1-1
5	Billingham Synthonia v Bridlington Central Utd.	2-1
6	Fleetwood v Lancaster City	3-0
	Milnthorpe Corinthians v Burscough	2-1
7	Bacup Borough v Mossley	2-8
	Chorley v Nelson	4-1
	Darwen v Leyland Motors	1-0
	Horwich RMI v Skelmersdale United	2-1
8	Llandudno v Earlestown	0-2
	Marine v New Brighton	1-3
	Pwllheli & District v South Liverpool	1-4
	Stork v Runcorn	2-2
9	Atherstone Town v Boldmere St Michaels	4-0
	Bournville Athletic v Bedworth Town	0-4
	Lockheed Leamington v Rugby Town (2)	3-1
	Sutton Coldfield Town v Tamworth	1-7
10	Kidderminster Harriers v Redditch	1-0
	Stafford Rangers v Oswestry Town	1-1
	Wellington Town v Stourbridge	8-2
	Worcester City v Bromsgrove Rovers	0-1
11	Altrincham v Macclesfield Town	1-3
	Congleton Town v Hyde United	3-3
	Linotype & Machinery v Winsford United	1-1
	Lostock Gralam v Witton Albion	1-0
12	Retford Town v Denaby United	3-3
13	Hallam v Norton Woodseats	2-2
14	Harrogate Railway Athletic v Ossett Town	3-2
15	Ashby Institute v Louth United	0-0
	Barton Town (1) v Alford United	0-1
	Bourne Town v Brigg Town	2-0
	Grantham v Skegness Town	2-1
16	Gresley Rovers v Belper Town	7-3
	South Normanton MW v Clay Cross & Danesmoor Welf.	3-5
17	Langwith MW v Creswell Colliery	1-2
	Sutton Town v Shirebrook MW	3-2
18	Rothwell Town v Corby Town	0-1
	Rushden Town v Stamford	3-1
	Spalding United v Kettering Town	3-2
19	Brush Sports v Hinckley Athletic	2-2
	Long Eaton Town v Players Athletic	9-0
20	Biggleswade Town v Vauxhall Motors (Luton)	2-3
21	Cambridge United v Ely City	2-5
	King's Lynn v St Neots & District	4-0
	Thetford Town v Cambridge City	0-2
	Wisbech Town v March Town United	0-0
22	Great Yarmouth Town v Gorleston	5-1
23	Bury Town v Haverhill Rovers	1-1
	Diss Town v Whitton United	6-3
	Lowestoft Town v Leiston	8-1
24	Ashford Town v Canterbury City	1-2
	Gravesend & Northfleet v Betteshanger CW	7-1
	Ramsgate Athletic v Sittingbourne	1-2
	Snowdown CW v Margate	2-2
25	Eastbourne v Bexhill Town	4-1
	Lancing Athletic v Bognor Regis Town	0-2
	Wigmore Athletic v Horsham	1-4
	Worthing v Redhill	2-2
26	Barking v Brentwood & Warley	2-2
	Briggs Sports v Romford (2)	0-1
	Chelmsford City v Rainham Town	6-0
	Clacton Town v Leytonstone	1-1
27	Barnet v Eton Manor	0-3
	Bishop's Stortford v Hoddesdon Town	1-0
	Letchworth Town v Hertford Town	0-0
	Shefford Town v Hitchin Town	2-6
28	Bromley v Erith & Belvedere	6-0
	Carshalton Athletic v Bexleyheath & Welling	4-9
	Tonbridge v Tooting & Mitcham United	3-3
	Tunbridge Wells United v Woking	3-0
29	Aylesbury United v Slough Town	3-0
	Maidenhead United v Oxford City	2-3
	Marlow v Windsor & Eton	6-1
	Witney Town v Banbury Spencer	1-0
30	Finchley v Wembley	1-0
	Harrow Town v Southall	0-3
	Hayes v Hounslow Town	0-2
	Uxbridge v Yiewsley	1-4
31	Chichester City (1) v Andover	2-3
	Cowes v Gosport Borough Ath.	1-4
33	Devizes Town v Chippenham Town	0-2
	Melksham Town v Westbury United	2-2
	Trowbridge Town v Frome Town	5-0
	Warminster Town v Salisbury (2)	1-6
34	Bath City v Clandown	2-0
	Bridgwater Town (1) v Clevedon	4-0
	Peasedown MW v Glastonbury	0-2
	Street v Chippenham United	1-2
35	Ebbw Vale v Cheltenham Town	2-5
	Gloucester City v Barry Town	3-1
	Llanelli v Merthyr Tydfil	5-1
	Stonehouse v Cinderford Town	1-4
36	Ilfracombe Town v Bideford	1-2
	Tavistock v Newquay	3-4
	Truro City v Penzance	3-4
	Wadebridge Town v Taunton	0-6
3r	West Auckland Town v Shildon	2-1
4r	Blackhall Colliery Welfare v Spennymoor United	0-4
8r	Runcorn v Stork	3-2
10r	Oswestry Town v Stafford Rangers	0-4
11r	Hyde United v Congleton Town	6-2
r	Winsford United v Linotype & Machinery	2-1
12r	Denaby United v Retford Town	3-0
13r	Norton Woodseats v Hallam	0-0
15r	Louth United v Ashby Institute	5-0
19r	Hinckley Athletic v Brush Sports	5-1e
21r	March Town United v Wisbech Town	2-1
23r	Haverhill Rovers v Bury Town	1-6
24r	Margate v Snowdown CW	1-0
25r	Redhill v Worthing	7-2
26r	Brentwood & Warley v Barking	2-1
r	Leytonstone v Clacton Town	0-1
27r	Hertford Town v Letchworth Town	3-0
28r	Tooting & Mitcham United v Tonbridge	2-1
33r	Westbury United v Melksham Town	4-2
13r2	Hallam v Norton Woodseats	1-3

Qualifying Round Two

1	Cramlington Welfare v South Shields (2)	0-6
	North Shields v Ashington	1-0
2	Annfield Plain v Consett	4-2
	Shotton CW v Boldon CW	3-0
3	Evenwood Town v Willington	2-1
	West Auckland Town v Stanley United	0-0
4	Horden CW v Chilton Athletic	10-0
	Spennymoor United v Durham City	3-1
5	North Skelton Athletic v Billingham Synthonia	1-3
	Whitby Town v South Bank	5-1
6	Fleetwood v Penrith	2-1
	Milnthorpe Corinthians v Morecambe	1-4
7	Darwen v Mossley	1-1
	Horwich RMI v Chorley	3-0
8	Earlestown v New Brighton	1-6
	Runcorn v South Liverpool	0-1
9	Atherstone Town v Lockheed Leamington	4-0 v
	Tamworth v Bedworth Town	1-4
10	Bromsgrove Rovers v Kidderminster Harriers	4-0
	Wellington Town v Stafford Rangers	4-1
11	Hyde United v Lostock Gralam	5-2
	Winsford United v Macclesfield Town	2-2
12	Bentley Colliery v Upton Colliery	2-1
	Frickley Colliery v Denaby United	3-2
13	Norton Woodseats v Sheffield	2-1
	Stocksbridge Works v Beighton Miners Welfare	8-2
14	Farsley Celtic v Yorkshire Amateur	1-0
	Goole Town v Harrogate Railway Athletic	4-0
15	Bourne Town v Grantham	2-8
	Louth United v Alford United	1-1
16	Clay Cross & Danesmoor Welf. v Gresley Rovers	3-1
	Ilkeston Town (2) v Boots Athletic	2-0
17	Creswell Colliery v Ransome & Marles	0-6
	Linby Colliery v Sutton Town	0-3
18	Corby Town v Wellingborough Town	6-0
	Rushden Town v Spalding United	0-3
19	Heanor Town v Whitwick Colliery	2-0
	Long Eaton Town v Hinckley Athletic	3-4
20	Dunstable Town v Vauxhall Motors (Luton)	3-0
	Wolverton Town & BR v Eynesbury Rovers	4-3
21	Cambridge City v Ely City	0-1
	March Town United v King's Lynn	4-1
22	Bungay Town v Beccles	2-2
	Sheringham v Great Yarmouth Town	0-2
23	Diss Town v Bury Town	2-4
	Lowestoft Town v Sudbury Town	0-1
24	Margate v Canterbury City	2-0
	Sittingbourne v Gravesend & Northfleet	1-0
25	Horsham v Eastbourne	2-0
	Redhill v Bognor Regis Town	3-0
26	Brentwood & Warley v Clacton Town	0-1
	Chelmsford City v Romford (2)	4-0
27	Bishop's Stortford v Eton Manor	0-2
	Hertford Town v Hitchin Town	0-1
28	Bexleyheath & Welling v Bromley	2-5
	Tunbridge Wells United v Tooting & Mitcham United	2-3
29	Aylesbury United v Oxford City	2-0
	Witney Town v Marlow	1-1
30	Finchley v Yiewsley	1-2
	Southall v Hounslow Town	2-1
31	Andover v Bournemouth Gasworks Athletic	3-2
	Winchester City v Gosport Borough Ath.	3-0
32	Poole Town v Bridport	3-0
	Portland United v Ilminster Town	9-0
33	Salisbury (2) v Chippenham Town	1-2
	Trowbridge Town v Westbury United	5-2
34	Bath City v Bridgwater Town (1)	1-2
	Glastonbury v Chippenham United	3-2
35	Gloucester City v Cheltenham Town	1-2
	Llanelli v Cinderford Town	3-0
36	Bideford v Newquay	4-0
	Penzance v Taunton	1-1
3r	Stanley United v West Auckland Town	2-0
7r	Mossley v Darwen	3-0
9r	Lockheed Leamington v Atherstone Town	2-1
11r	Macclesfield Town v Winsford United	4-1
15r	Alford United v Louth United	2-1
22r	Beccles v Bungay Town	4-4e
29r	Marlow v Witney Town	0-4
36r	Taunton v Penzance	3-3e
22r2	Bungay Town v Beccles	3-0 N
36r2	Taunton v Penzance	3-2 N

Qualifying Round Three

1	North Shields v South Shields (2)	1-1
2	Shotton CW v Annfield Plain	2-3
3	Evenwood Town v Stanley United	5-1
4	Horden CW v Spennymoor United	3-0
5	Whitby Town v Billingham Synthonia	2-3
6	Fleetwood v Morecambe	3-3
7	Horwich RMI v Mossley	1-0
8	New Brighton v South Liverpool	6-1
9	Bedworth Town v Lockheed Leamington	2-4
10	Bromsgrove Rovers v Wellington Town	1-0
11	Macclesfield Town v Hyde United	4-4
12	Bentley Colliery v Frickley Colliery	1-2
13	Stocksbridge Works v Norton Woodseats	3-2
14	Goole Town v Farsley Celtic	9-0
15	Alford United v Grantham	1-2
16	Clay Cross & Danesmoor Welf. v Ilkeston Town (2)	1-8
17	Sutton Town v Ransome & Marles	4-1
18	Corby Town v Spalding United	3-1
19	Hinckley Athletic v Heanor Town	4-1
20	Dunstable Town v Wolverton Town & BR	3-1
21	Ely City v March Town United	2-0
22	Great Yarmouth Town v Bungay Town	4-0
23	Bury Town v Sudbury Town	0-0
24	Sittingbourne v Margate	2-3
25	Horsham v Redhill	2-1
26	Chelmsford City v Clacton Town	2-2
27	Eton Manor v Hitchin Town	3-1
28	Tooting & Mitcham United v Bromley	4-0
29	Aylesbury United v Witney Town	7-0
30	Southall v Yiewsley	0-1
31	Winchester City v Andover	0-2
32	Poole Town v Portland United	2-0
33	Chippenham Town v Trowbridge Town	4-1
34	Glastonbury v Bridgwater Town (1)	4-3
35	Cheltenham Town v Llanelli	4-0
36	Taunton v Bideford	1-7
1r	South Shields (2) v North Shields	2-1
6r	Morecambe v Fleetwood	3-2
11r	Hyde United v Macclesfield Town	3-3e
23r	Sudbury Town v Bury Town	3-1
26r	Clacton Town v Chelmsford City	0-0e
11r2	Macclesfield Town v Hyde United	3-5 N
26r2	Chelmsford City v Clacton Town	1-2

Qualifying Round Four

Bideford v Dorchester Town	1-1
Billingham Synthonia v Crook Town	8-3

1956/57 to 1957/58

Blyth Spartans v Annfield Plain	3-0
Boston United v Grantham	6-3
Burton Albion v Hinckley Athletic	6-1
Cheltenham Town v Andover	2-1
Chippenham Town v Weymouth	0-0
Clacton Town v Yiewsley	2-3
Corby Town v Peterborough United	1-5
Dunstable Town v Eton Manor	5-1
Easington CW v Evenwood Town	0-3
Ely City v Sudbury Town	1-0
Goole Town v Gainsborough Trinity	2-1
Headington United v Guildford City	0-2
Horsham v Hastings United	0-2
Ilkeston Town (2) v Sutton Town	2-2
Lockheed Leamington v Hereford United	1-4
Morecambe v Horwich RMI	3-2
New Brighton v Hyde United	4-1
Nuneaton Borough v Bromsgrove Rovers	1-2
Poole Town v Newport (IOW)	0-3
Rhyl v Frickley Colliery	2-0
Selby Town v Stocksbridge Works	3-1
South Shields (2) v Horden CW	1-0
Tooting & Mitcham United v Aylesbury United	3-1
Walthamstow Avenue v Great Yarmouth Town	6-0
Wigan Athletic v Netherfield (Kendal)	2-2
Worksop Town v Scarborough	1-4
Wycombe Wanderers v Margate	2-4
Yeovil Town v Glastonbury	3-1
r Dorchester Town v Bideford	3-0
r Netherfield (Kendal) v Wigan Athletic	3-3e
r Sutton Town v Ilkeston Town (2)	1-2e
r Weymouth v Chippenham Town	4-1
r2 Wigan Athletic v Netherfield (Kendal)	2-0

Round One

Accrington Stanley v Morecambe	4-1
Bishop Auckland v Tranmere Rovers	2-1
Boston United v Bradford Park Avenue	0-2
Bournemouth v Burton Albion	8-0
Brentford v Guildford City	3-0
Brighton & Hove Albion v Millwall	1-1
Carlisle United v Billingham Synthonia	6-1
Cheltenham Town v Reading	1-2
Chester v Barrow	0-0
Colchester United v Southend United	1-4
Crewe Alexandra v Wrexham	2-2
Crystal Palace v Walthamstow Avenue	2-0
Darlington v Evenwood Town	7-2
Derby County v Bradford City	2-1
Ely City v Torquay United	2-6
Exeter City v Plymouth Argyle	0-2
Halifax Town v Oldham Athletic	2-3
Hartlepools United v Selby Town	3-1
Hereford United v Aldershot	3-2
Hull City v Gateshead	4-0
Ilkeston Town (2) v Blyth Spartans	1-5
Ipswich Town v Hastings United	4-0
Mansfield Town v Workington	1-1
Margate v Dunstable Town	3-1
New Brighton v Stockport County	3-3
Newport (IOW) v Watford	0-6
Norwich City v Bedford Town (1)	2-4
Queen's Park Rangers v Dorchester Town	4-0
Rhyl v Scarborough	3-2
Scunthorpe United v Rochdale	1-0
South Shields (2) v Chesterfield	2-2
Southampton v Northampton Town	2-0
Southport v York City	0-0
Swindon Town v Coventry City	2-1
Tooting & Mitcham United v Bromsgrove Rovers	2-1
Walsall v Newport County	0-1
Weymouth v Shrewsbury Town	1-0
Wigan Athletic v Goole Town	1-2
Yeovil Town v Peterborough United	1-3
Yiewsley v Gillingham	2-2
r Barrow v Chester	3-1
r Chesterfield v South Shields (2)	4-0
r Gillingham v Yiewsley	2-0
r Millwall v Brighton & Hove Albion	3-1
r Stockport County v New Brighton	2-3
r Workington v Mansfield Town	2-1
r Wrexham v Crewe Alexandra	2-1
r York City v Southport	2-1

Round Two

Accrington Stanley v Oldham Athletic	2-1
Blyth Spartans v Hartlepools United	0-1
Brentford v Crystal Palace	1-1
Carlisle United v Darlington	2-1
Chesterfield v Barrow	4-1
Derby County v New Brighton	1-3
Gillingham v Newport County	1-2
Goole Town v Workington	2-2
Hereford United v Southend United	2-3
Hull City v York City	2-1
Millwall v Margate	4-0
Peterborough United v Bradford Park Avenue	3-0
Reading v Bedford Town (1)	1-0
Rhyl v Bishop Auckland	3-1
Scunthorpe United v Wrexham	0-0
Southampton v Weymouth	3-2
Swindon Town v Bournemouth	0-1
Tooting & Mitcham United v Queen's Park Rangers	0-2

Torquay United v Plymouth Argyle	1-0
Watford v Ipswich Town	1-3
r Crystal Palace v Brentford	3-2e
r Workington v Goole Town	0-1
r Wrexham v Scunthorpe United	6-2e

Round Three

Arsenal v Stoke City	4-2
Barnsley v Port Vale	3-3
Bolton Wanderers v Blackpool	2-3
Bournemouth v Accrington Stanley	2-0
Bristol City v Rotherham United	4-1
Burnley v Chesterfield	7-0
Bury v Portsmouth	1-3
Carlisle United v Birmingham City	3-3
Doncaster Rovers v West Bromwich Albion	1-1
Everton v Blackburn Rovers	1-0
Hartlepools United v Manchester United	3-4
Huddersfield Town v Sheffield United	0-0
Hull City v Bristol Rovers	3-4
Ipswich Town v Fulham	2-3
Leeds United v Cardiff City	1-2
Leyton Orient v Chelsea	0-2
Luton Town v Aston Villa	2-2
Middlesbrough v Charlton Athletic	1-1
Millwall v Crystal Palace	2-0
New Brighton v Torquay United	2-1
Newcastle United v Manchester City	1-1
Newport County v Southampton	3-3
Nottingham Forest v Goole Town	6-0
Notts County v Rhyl	1-3
Peterborough United v Lincoln City	2-2
Preston North End v Sheffield Wednesday	0-0
Southend United v Liverpool	2-1
Sunderland v Queen's Park Rangers	4-0
Tottenham Hotspur v Leicester City	2-0
West Ham United v Grimsby Town	5-3
Wolverhampton Wan. v Swansea Town	5-3
Wrexham v Reading	1-1
r Aston Villa v Luton Town	2-0
r Birmingham City v Carlisle United	4-0
r Charlton Athletic v Middlesbrough	2-3
r Lincoln City v Peterborough United	4-5e
r Manchester City v Newcastle United	4-5e
r Port Vale v Barnsley	0-1
r Reading v Wrexham	1-2
r Sheffield United v Huddersfield Town	1-1e
r Sheffield Wednesday v Preston North End	2-2e
r Southampton v Newport County	0-1
r West Bromwich Albion v Doncaster Rovers	2-0
r2 Huddersfield Town v Sheffield United	2-1 N
r2 Preston North End v Sheffield Wednesday	5-1 N

Round Four

Blackpool v Fulham	6-2
Bristol City v Rhyl	3-0
Bristol Rovers v Preston North End	1-4
Burnley v New Brighton	9-0
Cardiff City v Barnsley	0-1
Everton v West Ham United	2-1
Huddersfield Town v Peterborough United	3-1
Middlesbrough v Aston Villa	2-3
Millwall v Newcastle United	2-1
Newport County v Arsenal	0-2
Portsmouth v Nottingham Forest	1-3
Southend United v Birmingham City	1-6
Tottenham Hotspur v Chelsea	4-0
West Bromwich Albion v Sunderland	4-2
Wolverhampton Wan. v Bournemouth	0-1
Wrexham v Manchester United	0-5

Round Five

Aston Villa v Bristol City	2-1
Barnsley v Nottingham Forest	1-2
Blackpool v West Bromwich Albion	0-0
Bournemouth v Tottenham Hotspur	3-1
Huddersfield Town v Burnley	1-2
Manchester United v Everton	1-0
Millwall v Birmingham City	1-4
Preston North End v Arsenal	3-3
r Arsenal v Preston North End	2-1
r West Bromwich Albion v Blackpool	2-1

Round Six

Birmingham City v Nottingham Forest	0-0
Bournemouth v Manchester United	1-2
Burnley v Aston Villa	1-1
West Bromwich Albion v Arsenal	2-2
r Arsenal v West Bromwich Albion	1-2
r Aston Villa v Burnley	2-0
r Nottingham Forest v Birmingham City	0-1

Semi Finals

Aston Villa v West Bromwich Albion	2-2 N
Manchester United v Birmingham City	2-0 N
r West Bromwich Albion v Aston Villa	0-1 N

Final

Aston Villa v Manchester United	2-1 N

1957/58

Preliminary Round

7	Ashton United v Skelmersdale United	3-1
	Bacup Borough v Lytham	3-0
	Horwich RMI v Mossley	1-1
	Leyland Motors v Cromptons Recreation	2-2
8	Earlestown v Prescot Cables	1-6
	Runcorn v Pwllheli & District	3-0
	Stork v South Liverpool	3-2
9	Bilston v Darlaston	2-0
	Lockheed Leamington v Brierley Hill Alliance	1-4
	Sutton Coldfield Town v Nuneaton Borough	2-2
	Worcester City v Hednesford Town	4-1
10	Kidderminster Harriers v Wellington Town	0-2
	Lye Town v Dudley Town	6-0
	Moor Green v Boldmere St Michaels	0-1
	Tamworth v Oswestry Town	1-2
11	Congleton Town v Stalybridge Celtic	2-0
	Ellesmere Port Town v Stockton Heath	3-0
	Lostock Gralam v Altrincham	3-4
	Macclesfield Town v Winsford United	5-4
	Northwich Victoria v Buxton	4-2
21	Chatteris Town v Ely City	1-1
	Histon v Cambridge City	1-2
	King's Lynn v Holbeach United	2-1
	March Town United v Thetford Town	3-1
	Soham Town Rangers v Warboys Town	4-2
	St Neots Town v Somersham Town	6-0
	Wisbech Town v Newmarket Town	6-0
23	Haverhill Rovers v Diss Town	6-1
24	Bettershanger CW v Snowdown CW	2-0
	Deal Town v Dartford	1-1
	Dover v Folkestone	2-1
	Gravesend & Northfleet v Ashford Town	3-1
	Maidstone United v Whitstable	1-3
	Ramsgate Athletic v Chatham Town	5-1
	Sheppey United v Sittingbourne	2-5
25	Eastbourne United v Horsham	1-1
	Littlehampton Town v Bexhill Town	3-1
	Newhaven v Eastbourne	2-1
	Worthing v Haywards Heath	1-1
26	Brentwood & Warley v Harwich & Parkeston	0-0
	Chelmsford City v Briggs Sports	3-0
	Grays Athletic v Dagenham	2-1
	Hornchurch & Upminster v Leytonstone	1-1
	Leyton v Woodford Town (1)	5-0
	Rainham Town v Aveley	2-1
	Romford (2) v Clacton Town	1-1
	Tilbury v Ilford	0-0
27	Enfield v Cheshunt	3-0
	Eton Manor v Hertford Town	3-1
	Hoddesdon Town v St Albans City	2-2
	Letchworth Town v Barnet	2-1
	Shefford Town v Clapton	2-8
	Tufnell Park Edmonton v Bishop's Stortford	2-1
	Ware v Hitchin Town	3-1
28	Bexleyheath & Welling v Tonbridge	1-0
	Bromley v Epsom	4-2
	Dorking v Sutton United	1-1
	Dulwich Hamlet v Metropolitan Police	8-0
	Erith & Belvedere v Tunbridge Wells United	1-3
	Kingstonian v Woking	3-5
	Wimbledon v Walton & Hersham	1-3
29	Abingdon Town v Maidenhead United	1-0
	Headington United v Aylesbury United	3-0
	Huntley & Palmers v Windsor & Eton	4-2
	Slough Town v Witney Town	5-2
30	Finchley v Hayes	3-3
	Hounslow Town v Harrow Town	2-0
	Southall v Edgware Town	4-0
	Wealdstone v Hendon	0-5
	Wembley v Berkhamsted Town	3-0
33	Salisbury (2) v Westbury United	4-2
35	Lovells Athletic v Merthyr Tydfil	3-2
36	Ilfracombe Town v Barnstaple Town	1-7
	Newquay v St Austell	2-0
	Tavistock v St Blazey	4-3
7r	Cromptons Recreation v Leyland Motors	5-1
r	Mossley v Horwich RMI	2-1
9r	Nuneaton Borough v Sutton Coldfield Town	3-1
21r	Ely City v Chatteris Town	0-1
24r	Dartford v Deal Town	2-1
25r	Haywards Heath v Worthing	3-3x
r	Horsham v Eastbourne United	2-0
26r	Clacton Town v Romford (2)	2-2e
r	Harwich & Parkeston v Brentwood & Warley	1-1e
r	Ilford v Tilbury	2-1
r	Leytonstone v Hornchurch & Upminster	3-3e
27r	St Albans City v Hoddesdon Town	4-1
28r	Sutton United v Dorking	5-0
30r	Hayes v Finchley	0-1e
25r2	Worthing v Haywards Heath	7-1
26r2	Brentwood & Warley v Harwich & Parkeston	2-0e
r	Leytonstone v Hornchurch & Upminster	0-2
r2	Romford (2) v Clacton Town	2-4 N

Qualifying Round One

1	Alnwick Town v South Bank	8-3
	Boldon CW v Blackhall Colliery Welfare	4-2
	Easington CW v Wolsingham Welfare	11-2

1957/58

2	Crook Town v Consett	4-3
	Stanley United v Chilton Athletic	3-1
	West Auckland Town v Whitley Bay	1-2
3	Shotton CW v Shildon	0-3
	Tow Law Town v Whitby Town	2-2
	Willington v Stockton	1-0
4	North Shields v Annfield Plain	4-1
	Spennymoor United v Ferryhill Athletic	2-2
5	Cockfield v Cramlington Welfare	5-0
	Durham City v Gosforth & Coxlodge	8-3
6	Burscough v Fleetwood	4-3
	Clitheroe v Milnthorpe Corinthians	4-0
	Lancaster City v Morecambe	1-2
	Netherfield (Kendal) v Penrith	5-2
7	Bacup Borough v Mossley	1-1
	Chorley v Nelson	5-1
	Cromptons Recreation v Darwen	2-1
	Rossendale United v Ashton United	2-2
8	Flint Town United v Bangor City	1-1
	Marine v Stork	0-1
	Runcorn v Prescot Cables	0-1
	St Helens Town v Llandudno	3-5
9	Bedworth Town v Atherstone Town	2-1
	Brierley Hill Alliance v Halesowen Town	3-2
	Nuneaton Borough v Bilston	2-0
	Worcester City v Rugby Town (2)	1-1
10	Lye Town v Boldmere St Michaels	4-2
	Oswestry Town v Stafford Rangers	3-0
	Stourbridge v Bournville Athletic	3-1
	Wellington Town v Cradley Heath	7-1
11	Altrincham v Macclesfield Town	4-3
	Ellesmere Port Town v Hyde United	5-0
	Linotype & Machinery v Northwich Victoria	3-6
	Witton Albion v Congleton Town	4-0
15	Alford United v Bourne Town	1-0
	Ashby Institute v Brigg Town	2-5
	Gainsborough Trinity v Louth United	4-2
	Skegness Town v Grantham	1-1
16	Belper Town v Clay Cross & Danesmoor Welf.	3-1
	Matlock Town v Gresley Rovers	2-3
	South Normanton MW v Ilkeston Town (2)	2-2
17	Ransome & Marles v Worksop Town	2-1
18	Corby Town v Rothwell Town	2-1
	Kettering Town v Stamford	4-1
	Rushden Town v Spalding United	2-2
19	Brush Sports v Hinckley Athletic	0-1
20	Eynesbury Rovers v Dunstable Town	1-3
21	Cambridge City v King's Lynn	1-6
	Cambridge United v St Neots Town	6-2
	Chatteris Town v Wisbech Town	0-5
	March Town United v Soham Town Rangers	4-2
22	Bungay Town v Great Yarmouth Town	0-2
23	Bury Town v Leiston	8-1
	Haverhill Rovers v Lowestoft Town	2-4
	Sudbury Town v Stowmarket	1-3
	Whitton United v Long Melford	2-0
24	Betteshanger CW v Ramsgate Athletic	1-0
	Dover v Dartford	1-3
	Gravesend & Northfleet v Sittingbourne	3-1
	Whitstable v Canterbury City	2-2
25	Horsham v Redhill	1-2
	Littlehampton Town v Bognor Regis Town	3-3
	Newhaven v Lancing Athletic	1-0
	Southwick v Worthing	3-2
26	Chelmsford City v Clacton Town	4-0
	Hornchurch & Upminster v Leyton	1-1
	Ilford v Grays Athletic	4-3
	Rainham Town v Brentwood & Warley	2-0
27	Clapton v St Albans City	3-1
	Enfield v Eton Manor	2-0
	Letchworth Town v Tufnell Park Edmonton	1-1
	Ware v Stevenage Town	3-0
28	Dulwich Hamlet v Carshalton Athletic	4-0
	Tunbridge Wells United v Bexleyheath & Welling	1-4
	Walton & Hersham v Sutton United	3-3
	Woking v Bromley	1-5
29	Chesham United v Abingdon Town	5-1
	Headington United v Banbury Spencer	1-0
	Marlow v Huntley & Palmers	4-1
	Slough Town v Oxford City	1-2
30	Finchley v Hendon	4-0
	Hemel Hempstead Town v Hounslow Town	1-2
	Uxbridge v Southall	1-2
	Wembley v Yiewsley	0-1
31	Andover v Chichester City (1)	2-3
	Basingstoke Town v Alton Town	4-2
	Cowes v Winchester City	0-0
33	Calne & Harris United v Warminster Town	1-2
	Devizes Town v Chippenham Town	1-5
	Melksham Town v Frome Town	0-0
	Salisbury (2) v Trowbridge Town	0-3
34	Bath City v Weston-Super-Mare	5-0
	Clandown v Clevedon	2-4
	Glastonbury v Street	5-0
	Wells City v Chippenham United	2-1
35	Cheltenham Town v Lovells Athletic	0-0
	Cinderford Town v Gloucester City	2-1
	Ebbw Vale v Llanelli	5-5
	Stonehouse v Barry Town	0-2
36	Barnstaple Town v Minehead	5-1
	Tavistock v Penzance	1-3
	Truro City v Newquay	3-1
	Wadebridge Town v Bideford	0-2
3r	Whitby Town v Tow Law Town	5-1
4r	Ferryhill Athletic v Spennymoor United	4-2
7r	Ashton United v Rossendale United	1-0
r	Mossley v Bacup Borough	3-1
8r	Bangor City v Flint Town United	5-1
9r	Rugby Town (2) v Worcester City	0-2
15r	Grantham v Skegness Town	2-0
16r	Ilkeston Town (2) v South Normanton MW	2-0
18r	Spalding United v Rushden Town	8-0
24r	Canterbury City v Whitstable	1-5
25r	Bognor Regis Town v Littlehampton Town	5-4e
26r	Leyton v Hornchurch & Upminster	4-1
27r	Tufnell Park Edmonton v Letchworth Town	0-1
28r	Sutton United v Walton & Hersham	0-4
31r	Winchester City v Cowes	0-1
33r	Frome Town v Melksham Town	2-3
35r	Llanelli v Ebbw Vale	3-2
r	Lovells Athletic v Cheltenham Town	0-0
35r2	Cheltenham Town v Lovells Athletic	2-4

Qualifying Round Two

1	Easington CW v Boldon CW	2-1
	Newburn v Alnwick Town	0-2
2	Whitley Bay v Crook Town	0-5
	Wingate Welfare v Stanley United	2-11
3	Bridlington Central Utd. v Shildon	0-3
	Willington v Whitby Town	5-2
4	Horden CW v Ferryhill Athletic	3-1
	North Shields v Ashington	0-0
5	Cockfield v Evenwood Town	2-5
	Morpeth Town v Durham City	1-2
6	Morecambe v Clitheroe	1-0
	Netherfield (Kendal) v Burscough	0-2
7	Ashton United v Cromptons Recreation	4-1
	Mossley v Chorley	1-4
8	Prescot Cables v Bangor City	4-2
	Stork v Llandudno	1-1
9	Bedworth Town v Worcester City	1-1
	Brierley Hill Alliance v Nuneaton Borough	4-2
10	Lye Town v Oswestry Town	1-4
	Stourbridge v Wellington Town	2-3
11	Altrincham v Ellesmere Port Town	2-0
	Witton Albion v Northwich Victoria	3-2
12	Denaby United v Upton Colliery	5-1
	Frickley Colliery v Retford Town	1-0
13	Beighton Miners Welfare v Norton Woodseats	1-2
	Hallam v Sheffield	5-2
14	Stocksbridge Works v Ossett Town	1-1
	Yorkshire Amateur v Farsley Celtic	1-1
15	Alford United v Gainsborough Trinity	2-1
	Brigg Town v Grantham	1-1
16	Boots Athletic v Gresley Rovers	1-3
	Ilkeston Town (2) v Belper Town	2-4
17	Ransome & Marles v Creswell Colliery	3-4
	Shirebrook MW v Sutton Town	2-3
18	Corby Town v Kettering Town	3-1
	Wellingborough Town v Spalding United	1-1
19	Hinckley Athletic v Long Eaton United	4-4
	Players Athletic v Heanor Town	0-5
20	Dunstable Town v Vauxhall Motors (Luton)	1-6
	Wolverton Town & BR v Biggleswade Town	7-0
21	King's Lynn v Wisbech Town	2-2
	March Town United v Cambridge United	4-1
22	Gorleston v Sheringham	3-0
	Great Yarmouth Town v Beccles	4-0
23	Bury Town v Lowestoft Town	2-1
	Whitton United v Stowmarket	2-4
24	Dartford v Gravesend & Northfleet	0-1
	Whitstable v Betteshanger CW	2-0
25	Bognor Regis Town v Newhaven	5-1
	Redhill v Southwick	3-0
26	Chelmsford City v Leyton	5-0
	Rainham Town v Ilford	4-3
27	Enfield v Clapton	2-3
	Ware v Letchworth Town	3-0
28	Bexleyheath & Welling v Dulwich Hamlet	3-1
	Walton & Hersham v Bromley	1-0
29	Chesham United v Marlow	2-2
	Oxford City v Headington United	0-2
30	Hounslow Town v Southall	0-0
	Yiewsley v Finchley	4-1
31	Basingstoke Town v Cowes	2-5
	Chichester City (1) v Gosport Borough Ath.	5-3
32	Ilminster Town v Bridport	1-2
	Portland United v Poole Town	3-1
33	Chippenham Town v Trowbridge Town	1-1
	Melksham Town v Warminster Town	7-2
34	Clevedon v Bath City	1-1
	Glastonbury v Wells City	3-0
35	Barry Town v Cinderford Town	3-0
	Llanelli v Lovells Athletic	4-2
36	Bideford v Penzance	5-1
	Truro City v Barnstaple Town	2-5
4r	Ashington v North Shields	3-1
8r	Llandudno v Stork	0-2
9r	Worcester City v Bedworth Town	3-0
14r	Farsley Celtic v Yorkshire Amateur	1-2
r	Ossett Town v Stocksbridge Works	3-4
15r	Grantham v Brigg Town	2-0
18r	Spalding United v Wellingborough Town	4-1
19r	Long Eaton United v Hinckley Athletic	1-9
21r	Wisbech Town v King's Lynn	4-1
29r	Marlow v Chesham United	5-1
30r	Southall v Hounslow Town	0-2
33r	Trowbridge Town v Chippenham Town	3-0
34r	Bath City v Clevedon	4-1

Qualifying Round Three

1	Easington CW v Alnwick Town	6-4
2	Crook Town v Stanley United	1-1
3	Shildon v Willington	1-2
4	Horden CW v Ashington	3-1
5	Evenwood Town v Durham City	1-2
6	Morecambe v Burscough	6-2
7	Ashton United v Chorley	2-3
8	Stork v Prescot Cables	1-3
9	Worcester City v Brierley Hill Alliance	4-0
10	Oswestry Town v Wellington Town	2-2
11	Witton Albion v Altrincham	3-2
12	Frickley Colliery v Denaby United	2-1
13	Norton Woodseats v Hallam	4-0
14	Stocksbridge Works v Yorkshire Amateur	2-3
15	Alford United v Grantham	1-0
16	Belper Town v Gresley Rovers	2-1
17	Sutton Town v Creswell Colliery	2-1
18	Spalding United v Corby Town	4-0
19	Heanor Town v Hinckley Athletic	3-1
20	Wolverton Town & BR v Vauxhall Motors (Luton)	2-1
21	March Town United v Wisbech Town	1-1e
22	Gorleston v Great Yarmouth Town	3-2
23	Stowmarket v Bury Town	2-3
24	Whitstable v Gravesend & Northfleet	0-3
25	Bognor Regis Town v Redhill	0-3
26	Chelmsford City v Rainham Town	6-0
27	Clapton v Ware	2-0
28	Walton & Hersham v Bexleyheath & Welling	3-1
29	Headington United v Marlow	1-0
30	Hounslow Town v Yiewsley	3-1
31	Cowes v Chichester City (1)	3-1
32	Portland United v Bridport	2-1
33	Melksham Town v Trowbridge Town	0-6
34	Bath City v Glastonbury	2-1
35	Llanelli v Barry Town	1-1
36	Barnstaple Town v Bideford	2-3
2r	Stanley United v Crook Town	0-4
10r	Wellington Town v Oswestry Town	0-1
21r	Wisbech Town v March Town United	2-1e
35r	Barry Town v Llanelli	1-0

Qualifying Round Four

	Barry Town v Bath City	1-2
	Bedford Town (1) v Walthamstow Avenue	1-1
	Boston United v Alford United	4-0
	Bromsgrove Rovers v Worcester City	3-3
	Chorley v Wigan Athletic	1-2
	Clapton v Bury Town	3-2
	Cowes v Trowbridge Town	2-2
	Crook Town v Blyth Spartans	3-0
	Durham City v Willington	2-0
	Easington CW v Billingham Synthonia	2-3
	Gorleston v Chelmsford City	1-0
	Guildford City v Gravesend & Northfleet	1-1
	Headington United v Margate	0-2
	Heanor Town v Hereford United	1-5
	Hounslow Town v Wisbech Town	2-3
	New Brighton v Rhyl	2-3
	Newport (IOW) v Portland United	5-0
	Norton Woodseats v Witton Albion	0-0
	Oswestry Town v Burton Albion	5-1
	Peterborough United v Wolverton Town & BR	7-0
	Prescot Cables v Morecambe	3-0
	Scarborough v Selby Town	2-2
	South Shields (2) v Horden CW	4-2
	Spalding United v Belper Town	2-1
	Sutton Town v Frickley Colliery	0-1
	Tooting & Mitcham United v Redhill	1-3
	Walton & Hersham v Hastings United	3-1
	Weymouth v Dorchester Town	2-2
	Yeovil Town v Bideford	3-1
	Yorkshire Amateur v Goole Town	1-2
r	Dorchester Town v Weymouth	2-1
r	Gravesend & Northfleet v Guildford City	0-1
r	Selby Town v Scarborough	2-2e
r	Trowbridge Town v Cowes	4-1
r	Walthamstow Avenue v Bedford Town (1)	1-0
r	Witton Albion v Norton Woodseats	6-1e
r	Worcester City v Bromsgrove Rovers	2-1
r2	Scarborough v Selby Town	1-0e

Round One

Aldershot v Worcester City	0-0
Bath City v Exeter City	2-1
Bishop Auckland v Bury	0-0
Boston United v Billingham Synthonia	5-2
Bradford City v Scarborough	6-0
Brighton & Hove Albion v Walsall	2-1
Carlisle United v Rhyl	5-1
Chester v Gateshead	4-3
Clapton v Queen's Park Rangers	1-1
Coventry City v Walthamstow Avenue	1-0
Dorchester Town v Wycombe Wanderers	3-2
Durham City v Spalding United	3-1
Gillingham v Gorleston	10-1
Guildford City v Yeovil Town	2-2
Hartlepools United v Prescot Cables	5-0
Hull City v Crewe Alexandra	2-1
Mansfield Town v Halifax Town	2-0
Margate v Crystal Palace	2-3
Millwall v Brentford	1-0

1957/58 to 1958/59

Newport (IOW) v Hereford United	0-3
Northampton Town v Newport County	3-0
Norwich City v Redhill	6-1
Oldham Athletic v Bradford Park Avenue	2-0
Oswestry Town v Bournemouth	1-5
Peterborough United v Torquay United	3-3
Plymouth Argyle v Watford	6-2
Port Vale v Shrewsbury Town	2-1
Reading v Swindon Town	1-0
Rochdale v Darlington	0-2
Scunthorpe United v Goole Town	2-1
South Shields (2) v Frickley Colliery	3-2
Southport v Wigan Athletic	1-2
Stockport County v Barrow	2-1
Tranmere Rovers v Witton Albion	2-1
Trowbridge Town v Southend United	0-2
Walton & Hersham v Southampton	1-6
Wisbech Town v Colchester United	1-0
Workington v Crook Town	8-1
Wrexham v Accrington Stanley	0-1
York City v Chesterfield	1-0
r Bury v Bishop Auckland	4-1
r Queen's Park Rangers v Clapton	3-1
r Torquay United v Peterborough United	1-0
r Worcester City v Aldershot	2-2e
r Yeovil Town v Guildford City	1-0
r2 Aldershot v Worcester City	3-2eN

Round Two

Aldershot v Coventry City	4-1
Carlisle United v Accrington Stanley	1-1
Chester v Bradford City	3-3
Crystal Palace v Southampton	1-0
Darlington v Boston United	5-3
Durham City v Tranmere Rovers	0-3
Hereford United v Queen's Park Rangers	6-1
Millwall v Gillingham	1-1
Northampton Town v Bournemouth	4-1
Norwich City v Brighton & Hove Albion	1-1
Oldham Athletic v Workington	1-5
Plymouth Argyle v Dorchester Town	5-2
Port Vale v Hull City	2-2
Reading v Wisbech Town	2-1
Scunthorpe United v Bury	2-0
South Shields (2) v York City	1-3
Stockport County v Hartlepools United	2-1
Torquay United v Southend United	1-1
Wigan Athletic v Mansfield Town	1-1
Yeovil Town v Bath City	2-0
r Accrington Stanley v Carlisle United	3-2
r Bradford City v Chester	3-1
r Brighton & Hove Albion v Norwich City	1-2
r Gillingham v Millwall	6-1
r Hull City v Port Vale	4-3e
r Mansfield Town v Wigan Athletic	3-1
r Southend United v Torquay United	2-1

Round Three

Accrington Stanley v Bristol City	2-2
Bristol Rovers v Mansfield Town	5-0
Burnley v Swansea Town	4-2
Crystal Palace v Ipswich Town	0-1
Doncaster Rovers v Chelsea	0-2
Fulham v Yeovil Town	4-0
Hereford United v Sheffield Wednesday	0-3
Huddersfield Town v Charlton Athletic	2-2
Hull City v Barnsley	1-1
Leeds United v Cardiff City	1-2
Leyton Orient v Reading	1-0
Lincoln City v Wolverhampton Wan.	0-1
Liverpool v Southend United	1-1
Middlesbrough v Derby County	5-0
Northampton Town v Arsenal	3-1
Norwich City v Darlington	1-2
Nottingham Forest v Gillingham	2-0
Notts County v Tranmere Rovers	2-0
Plymouth Argyle v Newcastle United	1-6
Portsmouth v Aldershot	5-1
Preston North End v Bolton Wanderers	0-3
Rotherham United v Blackburn Rovers	1-4
Scunthorpe United v Bradford City	1-0
Sheffield United v Grimsby Town	5-1
Stockport County v Luton Town	3-0
Stoke City v Aston Villa	1-1
Sunderland v Everton	2-2
Tottenham Hotspur v Leicester City	4-0
West Bromwich Albion v Manchester City	5-1
West Ham United v Blackpool	5-1
Workington v Manchester United	1-3
York City v Birmingham City	3-0
r Aston Villa v Stoke City	3-3e
r Barnsley v Hull City	0-2
r Bristol City v Accrington Stanley	3-1
r Charlton Athletic v Huddersfield Town	1-0
r Everton v Sunderland	3-1
r Southend United v Liverpool	2-3
r2 Stoke City v Aston Villa	2-0 N

Round Four

Bristol Rovers v Burnley	2-2
Cardiff City v Leyton Orient	4-1
Chelsea v Darlington	3-3
Everton v Blackburn Rovers	1-2
Fulham v Charlton Athletic	1-1
Liverpool v Northampton Town	3-1
Manchester United v Ipswich Town	2-0
Newcastle United v Scunthorpe United	1-3
Notts County v Bristol City	1-2
Sheffield Wednesday v Hull City	4-3
Stoke City v Middlesbrough	3-1
Tottenham Hotspur v Sheffield United	0-3
West Bromwich Albion v Nottingham Forest	3-3
West Ham United v Stockport County	3-2
Wolverhampton Wan. v Portsmouth	5-1
York City v Bolton Wanderers	0-0
r Bolton Wanderers v York City	3-0
r Burnley v Bristol Rovers	2-3
r Charlton Athletic v Fulham	0-2
r Darlington v Chelsea	4-1e
r Nottingham Forest v West Bromwich Albion	1-5

Round Five

Bolton Wanderers v Stoke City	3-1
Bristol City v Bristol Rovers	3-4
Cardiff City v Blackburn Rovers	0-0
Manchester United v Sheffield Wednesday	3-0
Scunthorpe United v Liverpool	0-1
Sheffield United v West Bromwich Albion	1-1
West Ham United v Fulham	2-3
Wolverhampton Wan. v Darlington	6-1
r Blackburn Rovers v Cardiff City	2-1
r West Bromwich Albion v Sheffield United	4-1

Round Six

Blackburn Rovers v Liverpool	2-1
Bolton Wanderers v Wolverhampton Wan.	2-1
Fulham v Bristol Rovers	3-1
West Bromwich Albion v Manchester United	2-2
r Manchester United v West Bromwich Albion	1-0

Semi Finals

Bolton Wanderers v Blackburn Rovers	2-1 N
Manchester United v Fulham	2-2 N
r Fulham v Manchester United	3-5 N

Final

Bolton Wanderers v Manchester United	2-0 N

1958/59

Preliminary Round

7 Ashton United v Leyland Motors	4-1
Bacup Borough v Droylsden	4-1
Chorley v Mossley	1-0
Cromptons Recreation v Horwich RMI	1-4
Rossendale United v Lytham	1-0
8 Flint Town United v Marine	4-3
Llandudno v Stork	7-0
Prescot Cables v Earlestown	4-3
Runcorn v South Liverpool	7-1
9 Bilston v Lockheed Leamington	6-1
Darlaston v Evesham United	1-3
Halesowen Town v Bedworth Town	2-2
10 Lye Town v Bournville Athletic	1-0
Moor Green v Cradley Heath	5-3
Stafford Rangers v Dudley Town	11-0
11 Hyde United v Lostock Gralam	2-0
Linotype & Machinery v Witton Albion	1-2
Macclesfield Town v Ellesmere Port Town	1-3
Stalybridge Celtic v Winsford United	1-1
13 Beighton Miners Welfare v Belper Town	2-5
15 Boston United v Alford United	3-0
16 Burton Albion v Atherstone Town	3-2
19 Ely City v Holbeach United	3-5
Histon v Wisbech Town	0-5
March Town United v Chatteris Town	5-2
Soham Town Rangers v Warboys Town	4-1
21 Clacton Town v Harwich & Parkeston	0-1
22 Ashford United v Betteshanger CW	10-1
23 Bexhill Town v Arundel	2-3
Bognor Regis Town v Littlehampton Town	5-1
Crawley Town v Horsham	0-1
Eastbourne v Haywards Heath	1-1
Southwick v Lancing Athletic	3-1
24 Aveley v Barking	0-1
25 Cheshunt v Bishop's Stortford	3-2
Ware v Hemel Hempstead Town	2-2
26 Dorking v Wimbledon	2-1
Dulwich Hamlet v Epsom	5-2
Kingstonian v Carshalton Athletic	1-5
Redhill v Walton & Hersham	3-2
27 Abingdon Town v Maidenhead United	0-2
Aylesbury United v Wokingham Town	2-2
Banbury Spencer v Oxford City	0-3
Chesham United v Huntley & Palmers	3-0
Windsor & Eton v Marlow	4-3
28 Staines Town v Harrow Town	2-2
29 Erith & Belvedere v Chatham Town	8-0
Tunbridge Wells United v Maidstone United	3-1
30 Briggs Sports v Clapton	2-2
31 Fareham Town v Ryde Sports	4-2
35 Barry Town v Cheltenham Town	2-0
36 Minehead v Bideford	3-4
Wadebridge Town v Penzance	4-1
9r Bedworth Town v Halesowen Town	4-2
11r Winsford United v Stalybridge Celtic	5-1
23r Haywards Heath v Eastbourne	3-1
25r Hemel Hempstead Town v Ware	1-0
27r Wokingham United v Aylesbury United	4-2
28r Harrow Town v Staines Town	2-3
30r Clapton v Briggs Sports	1-3

Qualifying Round One

1 Bridlington Central Utd. v Chilton Athletic	2-3
South Bank v West Auckland Town	0-1
2 Consett v Whitby Town	2-1
Willington v Shotton CW	6-0
3 Alnwick Town v Cockfield	3-3
Annfield Plain v Whitley Bay	1-1
4 Evenwood Town v Easington CW	8-1
Shildon v Horden CW	2-6
5 Billingham Synthonia v Tow Law Town	2-4
Ferryhill Athletic v Morpeth Town	1-1
Stockton v Spennymoor United	4-5
6 Burscough v Netherfield (Kendal)	2-2
Fleetwood v Clitheroe	6-2
Milnthorpe Corinthians v Penrith	2-0
Morecambe v Lancaster City	5-2
7 Ashton United v Skelmersdale United	1-3
Bacup Borough v Nelson	2-3
Chorley v Horwich RMI	2-1
Darwen v Rossendale United	3-1
8 Bangor City v New Brighton	0-0
Llandudno v St Helens Town	3-0
Prescot Cables v Pwllheli & District	8-0
Runcorn v Flint Town United	0-1
9 Bedworth Town v Sutton Coldfield Town	1-1
Bilston v Rugby Town (2)	2-1
Boldmere St Michaels v Evesham United	2-4
Hednesford Town v Brierley Hill Alliance	0-6
10 Bromsgrove Rovers v Lye Town	4-2
Moor Green v Wellington Town	0-8
Oswestry Town v Kidderminster Harriers	5-3
Stafford Rangers v Stourbridge	4-1
11 Congleton Town v Buxton	1-5
Ellesmere Port Town v Northwich Victoria	3-1
Winsford United v Hyde United	1-2
Witton Albion v Stockton Heath	2-4
12 Denaby United v Yorkshire Amateur	4-2
East End Park WMC v Upton Colliery	1-0
Farsley Celtic v Selby Town	1-3
Stocksbridge Works v Frickley Colliery	3-3
13 Belper Town v Sheffield	2-3
Clay Cross & Danesmoor Welf. v South Normanton MW	2-3
Hallam v Boots Athletic	3-1
Norton Woodseats v Matlock Town	4-1
14 Creswell Colliery v Sutton Town	0-3
Players Athletic v Worksop Town	0-4
Ransome & Marles v Heanor Town	1-5
Shirebrook MW v Retford Town	0-1
15 Boston United v Louth United	5-2
Bourne Town v Skegness Town	1-2
Brigg Town v Ashby Institute	3-1
Grantham v Gainsborough Trinity	1-4
16 Burton Albion v Nuneaton Borough	0-3
Gresley Rovers v Tamworth	1-3
Hinckley Athletic v Brush Sports	1-2
Long Eaton United v Ilkeston Town (2)	2-0
17 Corby Town v Stamford	7-2
Rushden Town v Rothwell Town	5-2
Spalding United v Kettering Town	4-6
18 Biggleswade Town v Vauxhall Motors (Luton)	1-2
Eynesbury Rovers v Wolverton Town & BR	3-0
Hitchin Town v Dunstable Town	6-2
Stevenage Town v Letchworth Town	3-2
19 Cambridge United v Cambridge City	2-1
March Town United v St Neots Town	0-1
Soham Town Rangers v Holbeach United	1-3
Wisbech Town v Somersham Town	7-0
20 Bungay Town v Sheringham	4-3
Gorleston v Diss Town	3-2
Great Yarmouth Town v Thetford Town	4-4
Lowestoft Town v King's Lynn	0-1
21 Harwich & Parkeston v Sudbury Town	1-1
Leiston v Whitton United	2-6
Long Melford v Haverhill Rovers	2-2
Stowmarket v Newmarket Town	3-1
22 Ashford Town v Snowdown CW	6-0
Deal Town v Whitstable	3-4
Dover v Canterbury City	0-2
Ramsgate Athletic v Folkestone	3-2
23 Arundel v Newhaven	5-3
Bognor Regis Town v Haywards Heath	0-2
Eastbourne United v Southwick	3-1
Horsham v Worthing	5-2
24 Barking v Tilbury	3-1
Grays Athletic v Woodford Town (1)	0-1
Leyton v Brentwood & Warley	2-2
Rainham Town v Leytonstone	2-1
25 Barnet v St Albans City	1-2
Berkhamsted Town v Hemel Hempstead Town	2-2
Cheshunt v Hoddesdon Town	4-0
Hertford Town v Enfield	0-2

121

1958/59

26	Bromley v Tooting & Mitcham United	2-2
	Carshalton Athletic v Metropolitan Police	5-0
	Dorking v Sutton United	1-4
	Redhill v Dulwich Hamlet	1-0
27	Headington United v Windsor & Eton	7-0
	Maidenhead United v Witney Town	7-2
	Oxford City v Chesham United	5-2
	Wokingham Town v Slough Town	3-2
28	Hounslow Town v Yiewsley	0-2
	Southall v Hayes	0-2
	Staines Town v Wembley	3-6
	Wealdstone v Uxbridge	2-1
29	Bexleyheath & Welling v Tonbridge	1-1
	Dartford v Tunbridge Wells United	3-3
	Erith & Belvedere v Sittingbourne	0-4
	Sheppey United v Gravesend & Northfleet	2-6
30	Briggs Sports v Hornchurch & Upminster	4-4
	Edgware Town v Dagenham	0-4
	Eton Manor v Romford (2)	2-9
	Hendon v Finchley	3-2
31	Andover v Winchester City	4-1
	Basingstoke Town v Alton Town	2-2
	Cowes v Chichester City (1)	5-4
	Fareham Town v Gosport Borough Ath.	6-2
32	Bridport v Salisbury (2)	2-5
	Poole Town v Frome Town	7-1
	Portland United v Ilminster Town	7-0
33	Calne & Harris United v Trowbridge Town	2-7
	Devizes Town v Chippenham Town	2-6
	Melksham Town v Chippenham United	1-6
34	Bridgwater Town (1) v Street	2-0
	Clandown v Taunton	1-3
	Glastonbury v Clevedon	0-0
	Weston-Super-Mare v Wells City	2-1
35	Barry Town v Merthyr Tydfil	1-4
	Gloucester City v Cinderford Town	3-2
	Lovells Athletic v Llanelli	1-1
	Stonehouse v Ebbw Vale	1-0
36	Barnstaple Town v Truro City	3-0
	Bideford v Tavistock	3-0
	Ilfracombe Town v Wadebridge Town	4-4
	St Blazey v Newquay	2-1
3r	Cockfield v Alnwick Town	3-2
r	Whitley Bay v Annfield Plain	2-1
5r	Morpeth Town v Ferryhill Athletic	0-2
6r	Netherfield (Kendal) v Burscough	2-1
8r	New Brighton v Bangor City	3-2
9r	Sutton Coldfield Town v Bedworth Town	2-3
12r	Frickley Colliery v Stocksbridge Works	0-3
20r	Thetford Town v Great Yarmouth Town	3-3
21r	Haverhill Rovers v Long Melford	4-2
r	Sudbury Town v Harwich & Parkeston	0-2
24r	Brentwood & Warley v Leyton	2-1
25r	Hemel Hempstead Town v Berkhamsted Town	1-2
26r	Tooting & Mitcham United v Bromley	5-1
29r	Tonbridge v Bexleyheath & Welling	6-5e
r	Tunbridge Wells United v Dartford	1-2e
30r	Hornchurch & Upminster v Briggs Sports	3-2
31r	Alton Town v Basingstoke Town	3-2
34r	Clevedon v Glastonbury	0-2
35r	Llanelli v Lovells Athletic	1-1
36r	Wadebridge Town v Ilfracombe Town	2-1
20r2	Thetford Town v Great Yarmouth Town	4-5
35r2	Lovells Athletic v Llanelli	3-2

Qualifying Round Two

1	Stanley United v Chilton Athletic	4-2
	West Auckland Town v Redcar Albion	3-0
2	Consett v Ashington	3-2
	Wolsingham Welfare v Willington	1-4
3	Cockfield v Blackhall Colliery Welfare	1-2
	Cramlington Welfare v Whitley Bay	3-4
4	Evenwood Town v Newburn	7-2
	North Shields v Horden CW	4-1
5	Spennymoor United v Ferryhill Athletic	3-3
	Tow Law Town v Boldon CW	4-1
6	Milnthorpe Corinthians v Netherfield (Kendal)	1-2
	Morecambe v Fleetwood	4-2
7	Darwen v Chorley	1-1
	Skelmersdale United v Nelson	2-0
8	Llandudno v Prescot Cables	5-4
	New Brighton v Flint Town United	3-0
9	Bedworth Town v Bilston	0-1
	Brierley Hill Alliance v Evesham United	4-0
10	Oswestry Town v Bromsgrove Rovers	3-0
	Wellington Town v Stafford Rangers	3-1
11	Buxton v Hyde United	3-0
	Stockton Heath v Ellesmere Port Town	0-2
12	Denaby United v East End Park WMC	2-0
	Stocksbridge Works v Selby Town	1-1
13	Norton Woodseats v Hallam	4-1
	South Normanton MW v Sheffield	1-4
14	Retford Town v Heanor Town	1-1
	Worksop Town v Sutton Town	3-3
15	Gainsborough Trinity v Brigg Town	6-2
	Skegness Town v Boston United	0-3
16	Long Eaton United v Brush Sports	1-2
	Tamworth v Nuneaton Borough	1-1
17	Kettering Town v Corby Town	5-1
	Rushden Town v Wellingborough Town	1-0
18	Eynesbury Rovers v Vauxhall Motors (Luton)	0-3
	Stevenage Town v Hitchin Town	3-4
19	Cambridge United v Holbeach United	1-2
	Wisbech Town v St Neots Town	4-0
20	Great Yarmouth Town v Bungay Town	2-1
	King's Lynn v Gorleston	6-1
21	Stowmarket v Haverhill Rovers	5-1
	Whitton United v Harwich & Parkeston	0-2
22	Ramsgate Athletic v Canterbury City	0-2
	Whitstable v Ashford Town	1-2
23	Eastbourne United v Haywards Heath	3-1
	Horsham v Arundel	5-1
24	Rainham Town v Brentwood & Warley	3-1
	Woodford Town (1) v Barking	2-1
25	Enfield v Berkhamsted Town	6-0
	St Albans City v Cheshunt	2-3
26	Sutton United v Carshalton Athletic	1-1
	Tooting & Mitcham United v Redhill	7-1
27	Headington United v Oxford City	3-2
	Maidenhead United v Wokingham Town	4-0
28	Wealdstone v Hayes	2-1
	Yiewsley v Wembley	3-1
29	Gravesend & Northfleet v Dartford	1-1
	Tonbridge v Sittingbourne	0-2
30	Hendon v Dagenham	3-1
	Romford (2) v Hornchurch & Upminster	2-3
31	Andover v Fareham Town	1-0
	Cowes v Alton Town	1-2
32	Poole Town v Salisbury (2)	2-1
	Portland United v Warminster Town	3-0
33	Chippenham Town v Westbury United	3-0
	Chippenham United v Trowbridge Town	1-2
34	Glastonbury v Taunton	1-1
	Weston-Super-Mare v Bridgwater Town (1)	1-3
35	Lovells Athletic v Gloucester City	2-3
	Stonehouse v Merthyr Tydfil	2-3
36	Barnstaple Town v Bideford	0-2
	St Blazey v Wadebridge Town	2-2
5r	Ferryhill Athletic v Spennymoor United	2-1
7r	Chorley v Darwen	5-1
12r	Selby Town v Stocksbridge Works	1-2e
14r	Heanor Town v Retford Town	7-1
r	Sutton Town v Worksop Town	4-3
16r	Nuneaton Borough v Tamworth	1-0
26r	Carshalton Athletic v Sutton United	3-4
29r	Dartford v Gravesend & Northfleet	2-4
34r	Taunton v Glastonbury	4-0
36r	Wadebridge Town v St Blazey	3-1

Qualifying Round Three

1	West Auckland Town v Stanley United	3-3
2	Consett v Willington	0-0
3	Blackhall Colliery Welfare v Whitley Bay	2-2
4	Evenwood Town v North Shields	1-0
5	Tow Law Town v Ferryhill Athletic	2-0
6	Netherfield (Kendal) v Morecambe	0-0
7	Skelmersdale United v Chorley	2-2
8	Llandudno v New Brighton	0-1
9	Bilston v Brierley Hill Alliance	2-2
10	Wellington Town v Oswestry Town	2-3
11	Ellesmere Port Town v Buxton	2-2
12	Denaby United v Stocksbridge Works	2-1
13	Sheffield v Norton Woodseats	2-0
14	Sutton Town v Heanor Town	1-3
15	Boston United v Gainsborough Trinity	1-1
16	Nuneaton Borough v Brush Sports	2-1
17	Rushden Town v Kettering Town	0-1
18	Vauxhall Motors (Luton) v Hitchin Town	0-2
19	Wisbech Town v Holbeach United	4-0
20	Great Yarmouth Town v King's Lynn	0-1
21	Harwich & Parkeston v Stowmarket	1-0
22	Ashford Town v Canterbury City	1-1
23	Horsham v Eastbourne United	3-1
24	Woodford Town (1) v Rainham Town	2-0
25	Cheshunt v Enfield	3-1
26	Sutton United v Tooting & Mitcham United	1-8
27	Maidenhead United v Headington United	1-6
28	Yiewsley v Wealdstone	1-2
29	Sittingbourne v Gravesend & Northfleet	4-4
30	Hornchurch & Upminster v Hendon	0-1
31	Andover v Alton Town	3-2
32	Portland United v Poole Town	1-0
33	Chippenham Town v Trowbridge Town	2-2
34	Bridgwater Town (1) v Taunton	1-2
35	Merthyr Tydfil v Gloucester City	2-1
36	Bideford v Wadebridge Town	7-1
1r	Stanley United v West Auckland Town	2-0
2r	Willington v Consett	1-2
3r	Whitley Bay v Blackhall Colliery Welfare	5-0
6r	Morecambe v Netherfield (Kendal)	7-1
7r	Chorley v Skelmersdale United	3-0
9r	Brierley Hill Alliance v Bilston	4-2
11r	Buxton v Ellesmere Port Town	4-1
15r	Gainsborough Trinity v Boston United	2-2e
22r	Canterbury City v Ashford Town	2-4e
29r	Gravesend & Northfleet v Sittingbourne	2-0
33r	Trowbridge Town v Chippenham Town	3-0
15r2	Gainsborough Trinity v Boston United	1-3 N

Qualifying Round Four

	Bath City v Trowbridge Town	3-1
	Bedford Town (1) v Wisbech Town	3-4
	Bideford v Yeovil Town	1-4
	Bishop Auckland v Stanley United	4-1
	Blyth Spartans v Durham City	1-0
	Buxton v New Brighton	4-0
	Chelmsford City v Harwich & Parkeston	2-0
	Cheshunt v King's Lynn	0-6
	Consett v Whitley Bay	3-0
	Crook Town v Evenwood Town	3-0
	Goole Town v Denaby United	1-2
	Gravesend & Northfleet v Margate	0-0
	Guildford City v Andover	1-0
	Hastings United v Ashford Town	1-1
	Heanor Town v Scarborough	2-2
	Hendon v Wycombe Wanderers	1-3
	Hitchin Town v Woodford Town (1)	1-1
	Merthyr Tydfil v Taunton	2-1
	Morecambe v Chorley	2-0
	Nuneaton Borough v Hereford United	2-2
	Oswestry Town v Kettering Town	1-3
	Peterborough United v Walthamstow Avenue	3-0
	Portland United v Newport (IOW)	2-2
	Rhyl v Wigan Athletic	1-0
	Sheffield v Boston United	0-3
	Tooting & Mitcham United v Horsham	4-0
	Tow Law Town v South Shields (2)	2-3
	Wealdstone v Headington United	2-4
	Weymouth v Dorchester Town	3-0
	Worcester City v Brierley Hill Alliance	3-0
r	Ashford Town v Hastings United	2-1
r	Hereford United v Nuneaton Borough	3-1
r	Margate v Gravesend & Northfleet	4-3
r	Newport (IOW) v Portland United	3-1
r	Scarborough v Heanor Town	2-3
r	Woodford Town (1) v Hitchin Town	2-3

Round One

	Accrington Stanley v Workington	5-1
	Ashford Town v Crystal Palace	0-1
	Brentford v Exeter City	3-2
	Bury v York City	1-0
	Buxton v Crook Town	4-1
	Chelmsford City v Worcester City	0-0
	Chester v Boston United	3-2
	Chesterfield v Rhyl	3-0
	Colchester United v Bath City	2-0
	Crewe Alexandra v South Shields (2)	2-2
	Denaby United v Oldham Athletic	0-2
	Doncaster Rovers v Consett	5-0
	Gateshead v Bradford Park Avenue	1-4
	Guildford City v Hereford United	1-2
	Hartlepools United v Rochdale	1-1
	Headington United v Margate	3-2
	Heanor Town v Carlisle United	1-5
	Hitchin Town v Millwall	1-1
	Hull City v Stockport County	0-1
	King's Lynn v Merthyr Tydfil	2-1
	Mansfield Town v Bradford City	3-4
	Morecambe v Blyth Spartans	1-2
	Newport (IOW) v Shrewsbury Town	0-0
	Northampton Town v Wycombe Wanderers	2-0
	Norwich City v Ilford	3-1
	Notts County v Barrow	1-2
	Peterborough United v Kettering Town	2-2
	Plymouth Argyle v Gillingham	2-2
	Southampton v Woking	4-1
	Southend United v Yeovil Town	0-0
	Southport v Halifax Town	0-2
	Swindon Town v Aldershot	5-0
	Tooting & Mitcham United v Bournemouth	3-1
	Torquay United v Port Vale	1-0
	Tranmere Rovers v Bishop Auckland	8-1
	Walsall v Queen's Park Rangers	0-1
	Watford v Reading	1-1
	Weymouth v Coventry City	2-5
	Wisbech Town v Newport County	2-2
	Wrexham v Darlington	1-2
r	Gillingham v Plymouth Argyle	1-4
r	Kettering Town v Peterborough United	2-3e
r	Millwall v Hitchin Town	2-1
r	Newport County v Wisbech Town	4-1e
r	Reading v Watford	0-2
r	Rochdale v Hartlepools United	3-3e
r	Shrewsbury Town v Newport (IOW)	5-0
r	South Shields (2) v Crewe Alexandra	5-0
r	Worcester City v Chelmsford City	3-1
r	Yeovil Town v Southend United	1-0
r2	Hartlepools United v Rochdale	2-1eN

Round Two

	Accrington Stanley v Buxton	6-1
	Barrow v Hartlepools United	2-0
	Blyth Spartans v Stockport County	3-4
	Bradford Park Avenue v Bradford City	0-2
	Brentford v King's Lynn	3-1
	Carlisle United v Chesterfield	0-0
	Chester v Bury	1-1
	Colchester United v Yeovil Town	1-1
	Coventry City v Plymouth Argyle	1-3
	Crystal Palace v Shrewsbury Town	2-2
	Halifax Town v Darlington	1-1
	Hereford United v Newport County	0-2
	Oldham Athletic v South Shields (2)	2-0
	Peterborough United v Headington United	4-2
	Queen's Park Rangers v Southampton	0-1
	Swindon Town v Norwich City	1-1
	Tooting & Mitcham United v Northampton Town	2-1
	Torquay United v Watford	2-0
	Tranmere Rovers v Doncaster Rovers	1-2

1958/59 to 1959/60

Worcester City v Millwall	5-2	
r Bury v Chester	2-1	
r Chesterfield v Carlisle United	1-0	
r Darlington v Halifax Town	3-0	
r Norwich City v Swindon Town	1-0	
r Shrewsbury Town v Crystal Palace	2-2e	
r Yeovil Town v Colchester United	1-7	
r2 Crystal Palace v Shrewsbury Town	4-1 N	

Round Three

Accrington Stanley v Darlington	3-0
Aston Villa v Rotherham United	2-1
Barrow v Wolverhampton Wan.	2-4
Blackburn Rovers v Leyton Orient	4-2
Brentford v Barnsley	2-0
Brighton & Hove Albion v Bradford City	0-2
Bristol Rovers v Charlton Athletic	0-4
Bury v Arsenal	0-1
Colchester United v Chesterfield	2-0
Derby County v Preston North End	2-2
Doncaster Rovers v Bristol City	0-2
Everton v Sunderland	4-0
Fulham v Peterborough United	0-0
Grimsby Town v Manchester City	2-2
Ipswich Town v Huddersfield Town	1-0
Leicester City v Lincoln City	1-1
Luton Town v Leeds United	5-1
Middlesbrough v Birmingham City	0-1
Newcastle United v Chelsea	1-4
Newport County v Torquay United	0-0
Norwich City v Manchester United	3-0
Plymouth Argyle v Cardiff City	0-3
Portsmouth v Swansea Town	3-1
Scunthorpe United v Bolton Wanderers	0-2
Sheffield United v Crystal Palace	2-0
Sheffield Wednesday v West Bromwich Albion	0-2
Southampton v Blackpool	1-2
Stockport County v Burnley	1-3
Stoke City v Oldham Athletic	5-1
Tooting & Mitcham United v Nottingham Forest	2-2
Tottenham Hotspur v West Ham United	2-0
Worcester City v Liverpool	2-1
r Lincoln City v Leicester City	0-2
r Manchester City v Grimsby Town	1-2
r Nottingham Forest v Tooting & Mitcham United	3-0
r Peterborough United v Fulham	0-1
r Preston North End v Derby County	4-2e
r Torquay United v Newport County	0-1

Round Four

Accrington Stanley v Portsmouth	0-0
Birmingham City v Fulham	1-1
Blackburn Rovers v Burnley	1-2
Bristol City v Blackpool	1-1
Charlton Athletic v Everton	2-2
Chelsea v Aston Villa	1-2
Colchester United v Arsenal	2-2
Leicester City v Luton Town	1-1
Norwich City v Cardiff City	3-2
Nottingham Forest v Grimsby Town	4-1
Preston North End v Bradford City	3-2
Stoke City v Ipswich Town	0-1
Tottenham Hotspur v Newport County	4-1
West Bromwich Albion v Brentford	2-0
Wolverhampton Wan. v Bolton Wanderers	1-2
Worcester City v Sheffield United	0-2
r Arsenal v Colchester United	4-0
r Blackpool v Bristol City	1-0
r Everton v Charlton Athletic	4-1e
r Fulham v Birmingham City	2-3
r Luton Town v Leicester City	4-1
r Portsmouth v Accrington Stanley	4-1

Round Five

Arsenal v Sheffield United	2-2
Birmingham City v Nottingham Forest	1-1
Blackpool v West Bromwich Albion	3-1
Bolton Wanderers v Preston North End	2-2
Burnley v Portsmouth	1-0
Everton v Aston Villa	1-4
Ipswich Town v Luton Town	2-5
Tottenham Hotspur v Norwich City	1-1
r Norwich City v Tottenham Hotspur	1-0
r Nottingham Forest v Birmingham City	1-1e
r Preston North End v Bolton Wanderers	1-1e
r Sheffield United v Arsenal	3-0
r2 Birmingham City v Nottingham Forest	0-5 N
r2 Bolton Wanderers v Preston North End	1-0 N

Round Six

Aston Villa v Burnley	0-0
Blackpool v Luton Town	1-1
Nottingham Forest v Bolton Wanderers	2-1
Sheffield United v Norwich City	1-1
r Burnley v Aston Villa	0-2
r Luton Town v Blackpool	1-0
r Norwich City v Sheffield United	3-2

Semi Finals

Luton Town v Norwich City	1-1 N
Nottingham Forest v Aston Villa	1-0 N
r Norwich City v Luton Town	0-1 N

Final

Nottingham Forest v Luton Town	2-1 N

1959/60

Preliminary Round

7 Droylsden v Darwen	2-1
Nelson v Ashton United	0-0
Rossendale United v Lytham	4-4
Skelmersdale United v Mossley	0-0
8 New Brighton v Marine	1-0
South Liverpool v Pwllheli & District	3-4
St Helens Town v Earlestown	0-2
Stork v Runcorn	1-2
9 Bilston v Lockheed Leamington	3-2
10 Bromsgrove Rovers v Stafford Rangers	2-1
11 Lostock Gralam v Linotype & Machinery	0-1
Stockton Heath v Congleton Town	0-3
Winsford United v Northwich Victoria	0-3
Witton Albion v Stalybridge Celtic	3-3
16 Brush Sports v Long Eaton United	2-1
22 Betteshanger CW v Ramsgate Athletic	2-2
23 Bognor Regis Town v Eastbourne	1-2
Crawley Town v Southwick	6-1
Horsham v Hastings United	1-3
Lancing Athletic v Newhaven	2-1
Littlehampton Town v Arundel	1-2
Worthing v Eastbourne United	3-1
24 Aveley v Leytonstone	1-2
Brentwood & Warley v Tilbury	1-2
26 Bromley v Redhill	5-0
Metropolitan Police v Carshalton Athletic	1-3
Walton & Hersham v Kingstonian	0-2
Wimbledon v Dorking	6-0
Woking v Epsom	3-0
27 Maidenhead United v Huntley & Palmers	4-1
Windsor & Eton v Aylesbury United	2-3
Witney Town v Oxford City	0-1
Wokingham Town v Slough Town	5-2
28 Hayes v Wealdstone	2-1
29 Chatham Town v Sheppey United	0-3
Erith & Belvedere v Tonbridge	0-2
30 Ford United v Hendon	1-2
35 Cheltenham Town v Lovells Athletic	1-0
36 Bideford v Tavistock	4-3
7r Ashton United v Nelson	1-2
r Lytham v Rossendale United	2-1
r Mossley v Skelmersdale United	3-0
11r Stalybridge Celtic v Witton Albion	1-2
22r Ramsgate Athletic v Betteshanger CW	0-1

Qualifying Round One

1 Billingham Synthonia v Murton CW	3-5
Scarborough v Ashington	2-2
2 Consett v Evenwood Town	2-1
Ferryhill Athletic v Bridlington Town	0-0
3 Horden CW v North Shields	2-2
4 Shotton CW v Spennymoor United	0-2
5 Tow Law Town v Whitby Town	2-1
6 Fleetwood v Clitheroe	2-2
Lancaster City v Burscough	2-4
Milnthorpe Corinthians v Netherfield (Kendal)	0-3
Penrith v Morecambe	1-0
7 Altrincham v Droylsden	7-1
Horwich RMI v Bacup Borough	1-2
Mossley v Chorley	2-1
Nelson v Lytham	2-2
8 Bangor City v New Brighton	3-2
Earlestown v Pwllheli & District	5-2
Prescot Cables v Flint Town United	4-0
Runcorn v Llandudno	3-2
9 Brierley Hill Alliance v Rugby Town (2)	2-2
Evesham United v Bedworth Town	2-0
Halesowen Town v Bilston	2-4
Sutton Coldfield Town v Hednesford Town	2-3
10 Cradley Heath v Stourbridge	0-5
Kidderminster Harriers v Bournville Athletic	7-1
Moor Green v Bromsgrove Rovers	2-4
Wellington Town v Oswestry Town	1-1
11 Buxton v Linotype & Machinery	4-1
Congleton Town v Northwich Victoria	0-3
Macclesfield Town v Ellesmere Port Town	2-3
Witton Albion v Hyde United	2-1
12 Farsley Celtic v Upton Colliery	5-2
Frickley Colliery v East End Park WMC	1-0
Selby Town v Denaby United	1-3
Yorkshire Amateur v Goole Town	1-3
13 Norton Woodseats v Boots Athletic	2-1
Sheffield v Worksop Town	2-3
Stocksbridge Works v Matlock Town	1-3
14 Retford Town v Heanor Town	2-2
Shirebrook MW v Sutton Town	1-1
South Normanton MW v Ransome & Marles	3-0
15 Bourne Town v Louth United	4-1
Brigg Town v Ashby Institute	1-1
Gainsborough Trinity v Alford United	4-1
Skegness Town v Grantham	5-0
16 Burton Albion v Nuneaton Borough	1-4
Gresley Rovers v Atherstone Town	2-2
Hinckley Athletic v Brush Sports	0-1
Tamworth v Ilkeston Town (2)	2-2
17 Rushden Town v Stamford	3-2
Wellingborough Town v Rothwell Town	3-2
18 Letchworth Town v Dunstable Town	5-0
Stevenage Town v Vauxhall Motors (Luton)	0-1
Wolverton Town & BR v Hitchin Town	2-1
19 Chatteris Town v March Town United	1-2
Ely City v Cambridge United	0-3
Histon v Cambridge City	1-4
St Neots Town v Holbeach United	1-1
20 Gorleston v Diss Town	2-2
Lowestoft Town v Sheringham	6-2
Thetford Town v Great Yarmouth Town	2-4
21 Newmarket Town v Clacton Town	1-4
Stowmarket v Sudbury Town	0-3
Whitton United v Harwich & Parkeston	1-2
22 Canterbury City v Snowdown CW	1-0
Deal Town v Ashford Town	0-1
Dover v Betteshanger CW	0-0
Whitstable v Folkestone	1-6
23 Hastings United v Bexhill Town	4-1
Haywards Heath v Eastbourne	3-3
Lancing Athletic v Arundel	2-3
Worthing v Crawley Town	1-6
24 Barking v Leytonstone	0-1
Grays Athletic v Tilbury	2-1
Ilford v Rainham Town	4-1
Woodford Town (1) v Leyton	1-1
25 Hertford Town v Cheshunt	7-0
Hoddesdon Town v St Albans City	2-0
Ware v Enfield	1-7
26 Carshalton Athletic v Kingstonian	2-4
Sutton United v Leatherhead	6-0
Wimbledon v Bromley	3-0
Woking v Dulwich Hamlet	3-0
27 Abingdon Town v Maidenhead United	1-1
Aylesbury United v Oxford City	1-4
Marlow v Banbury Spencer	0-3
Wokingham Town v Chesham United	4-1
28 Hounslow Town v Wembley	6-0
Southall v Harrow Town	1-0
Staines Town v Hayes	1-2
Yiewsley v Uxbridge	2-1
29 Bexleyheath & Welling v Sittingbourne	5-1
Dartford v Sheppey United	4-1
Gravesend & Northfleet v Tonbridge	2-0
Tunbridge Wells United v Maidstone United	1-1
30 Clapton v Hornchurch & Upminster	2-4
Dagenham v Walthamstow Avenue	1-1
Edgware Town v Hendon	0-1
Romford (2) v Finchley	1-3
31 Andover v Gosport Borough Ath.	0-0
Basingstoke Town v Alton Town	5-2
Cowes v Newport (IOW)	2-0
Winchester City v Fareham Town	1-4
32 Portland United v Salisbury (2)	2-3
Warminster Town v Frome Town	1-1
33 Devizes Town v Chippenham United	3-2
Melksham Town v Trowbridge Town	2-4
Westbury United v Chippenham Town	3-1
34 Bridgwater Town (1) v Minehead	2-1
Glastonbury v Street	2-1
Taunton v Weston-Super-Mare	7-0
35 Cinderford Town v Merthyr Tydfil	1-1
Ebbw Vale v Barry Town	2-2
Gloucester City v Cheltenham Town	1-3
Stonehouse v Llanelli	0-5
36 Barnstaple Town v Newquay	wo/s
Penzance v Bideford	3-5
Truro City v Ilfracombe Town	wo/s
Wadebridge Town v St Blazey	3-2
1r Ashington v Scarborough	0-0
2r Bridlington Town v Ferryhill Athletic	1-2
3r North Shields v Horden CW	3-1
6r Clitheroe v Fleetwood	1-0
7r Lytham v Nelson	2-0
9r Rugby Town (2) v Brierley Hill Alliance	1-0
10r Oswestry Town v Wellington Town	3-1
14r Heanor Town v Retford Town	4-0
r Sutton Town v Shirebrook MW	3-4
15r Ashby Institute v Brigg Town	1-5
16r Atherstone Town v Gresley Rovers	2-0
r Ilkeston Town (2) v Tamworth	2-1
19r Holbeach United v St Neots Town	3-2e
20r Diss Town v Gorleston	2-2
22r Betteshanger CW v Dover	3-1
23r Eastbourne v Haywards Heath	4-2
24r Leyton v Woodford Town (1)	1-0
27r Maidenhead United v Abingdon Town	3-1
29r Maidstone United v Tunbridge Wells United	2-3e
30r Walthamstow Avenue v Dagenham	4-0
31r Gosport Borough Ath. v Andover	0-1
32r Frome Town v Warminster Town	1-2
35r Barry Town v Ebbw Vale	6-1
r Merthyr Tydfil v Cinderford Town	2-0
1r2 Scarborough v Ashington	1-0 N
20r2 Gorleston v Diss Town	2-1

123

1959/60

Qualifying Round Two

1	Annfield Plain v Bedlington Mechanics	4-1
	Murton CW v Scarborough	2-5
2	Easington CW v Boldon CW	0-2
	Ferryhill Athletic v Consett	2-4
3	North Shields v Newburn	5-0
	Shildon v Redcar Albion	4-0
4	Spennymoor United v South Bank	3-1
	Stockton v Stanley United	4-2
5	Tow Law Town v West Auckland Town	4-4
	Willington v Whitley Bay	4-1
6	Burscough v Netherfield (Kendal)	4-1
	Clitheroe v Penrith	6-3
7	Altrincham v Mossley	3-2
	Lytham v Bacup Borough	2-1
8	Bangor City v Runcorn	4-1
	Earlestown v Prescot Cables	0-1
9	Bilston v Rugby Town (2)	5-1
	Evesham United v Hednesford Town	3-1
10	Bromsgrove Rovers v Stourbridge	4-0
	Kidderminster Harriers v Oswestry Town	0-2
11	Buxton v Witton Albion	1-2
	Northwich Victoria v Ellesmere Port Town	0-3
12	Denaby United v Farsley Celtic	2-0
	Frickley Colliery v Goole Town	1-3
13	Belper Town v Norton Woodseats	3-2
	Matlock Town v Worksop Town	3-1
14	Creswell Colliery v Heanor Town	2-5
	South Normanton MW v Shirebrook MW	6-1
15	Brigg Town v Skegness Town	0-3
	Gainsborough Trinity v Bourne Town	4-1
16	Atherstone Town v Ilkeston Town (2)	0-2
	Brush Sports v Nuneaton Borough	4-3
17	Spalding United v Corby Town	1-2
	Wellingborough Town v Rushden Town	0-2
18	Biggleswade Town v Letchworth Town	1-2
	Wolverton Town & BR v Vauxhall Motors (Luton)	5-1
19	Cambridge City v March Town United	5-1
	Cambridge United v Holbeach United	3-0
20	Bungay Town v Gorleston	1-0
	Great Yarmouth Town v Lowestoft Town	6-2
21	Bury Town v Clacton Town	6-5
	Harwich & Parkeston v Sudbury Town	4-2
22	Ashford Town v Folkestone	1-0
	Betteshanger CW v Canterbury City	6-0
23	Arundel v Hastings United	2-5
	Crawley Town v Eastbourne	2-2
24	Grays Athletic v Ilford	2-2
	Leytonstone v Leyton	1-3
25	Bishop's Stortford v Hertford Town	0-1
	Enfield v Hoddesdon Town	15-0
26	Kingstonian v Woking	0-3
	Wimbledon v Sutton United	0-1
27	Maidenhead United v Wokingham Town	5-0
	Oxford City v Banbury Spencer	5-1
28	Hayes v Hounslow Town	1-0
	Southall v Yiewsley	1-1
29	Dartford v Tunbridge Wells United	0-2
	Gravesend & Northfleet v Bexleyheath & Welling	4-3
30	Hendon v Hornchurch & Upminster	0-2
	Walthamstow Avenue v Finchley	4-0
31	Basingstoke Town v Fareham Town	4-1
	Cowes v Andover	3-0
32	Poole Town v Bridport	4-0
	Warminster Town v Salisbury (2)	0-5
33	Calne & Harris United v Devizes Town	7-2
	Westbury United v Trowbridge Town	1-3
34	Ilminster Town v Bridgwater Town (1)	1-3
	Taunton v Glastonbury	0-0
35	Barry Town v Llanelli	2-0
	Cheltenham Town v Merthyr Tydfil	2-2
36	Barnstaple Town v Wadebridge Town	9-1
	Bideford v Truro City	6-2
5r	West Auckland Town v Tow Law Town	5-2
23r	Eastbourne v Crawley Town	1-2
24r	Ilford v Grays Athletic	2-4e
28r	Yiewsley v Southall	1-2
34r	Glastonbury v Taunton	2-1
35r	Merthyr Tydfil v Cheltenham Town	0-1

Qualifying Round Three

1	Annfield Plain v Scarborough	2-3
2	Boldon CW v Consett	0-4
3	Shildon v North Shields	2-0
4	Stockton v Spennymoor United	1-1
5	Willington v West Auckland Town	0-2
6	Clitheroe v Burscough	1-2
7	Lytham v Altrincham	1-1
8	Prescot Cables v Bangor City	4-1
9	Evesham United v Bilston	2-1
10	Oswestry Town v Bromsgrove Rovers	3-1
11	Ellesmere Port Town v Witton Albion	4-1
12	Goole Town v Denaby United	0-1
13	Belper Town v Matlock Town	2-3
14	Heanor Town v South Normanton MW	2-1
15	Skegness Town v Gainsborough Trinity	0-0
16	Ilkeston Town (2) v Brush Sports	1-1
17	Corby Town v Rushden Town	2-2
18	Letchworth Town v Wolverton Town & BR	3-2
19	Cambridge United v Cambridge City	0-1
20	Bungay Town v Great Yarmouth Town	1-4
21	Bury Town v Harwich & Parkeston	2-0
22	Ashford Town v Betteshanger CW	3-0
23	Crawley Town v Hastings United	2-2
24	Leyton v Grays Athletic	1-1
25	Hertford Town v Enfield	2-3
26	Sutton United v Woking	3-3
27	Oxford City v Maidenhead United	3-0
28	Southall v Hayes	1-1
29	Tunbridge Wells United v Gravesend & Northfleet	0-3
30	Walthamstow Avenue v Hornchurch & Upminster	7-1
31	Basingstoke Town v Cowes	2-1
32	Poole Town v Salisbury (2)	0-1
33	Calne & Harris United v Trowbridge Town	1-6
34	Bridgwater Town (1) v Glastonbury	3-1
35	Barry Town v Cheltenham Town	1-4
36	Barnstaple Town v Bideford	1-1
4r	Spennymoor United v Stockton	1-0
7r	Altrincham v Lytham	3-0
15r	Gainsborough Trinity v Skegness Town	3-0
16r	Brush Sports v Ilkeston Town (2)	1-2e
17r	Rushden Town v Corby Town	2-1
23r	Hastings United v Crawley Town	5-2
24r	Grays Athletic v Leyton	6-2
26r	Woking v Sutton United	1-3
28r	Hayes v Southall	4-1
36r	Bideford v Barnstaple Town	1-5

Qualifying Round Four

Barnstaple Town v Trowbridge Town	1-0
Bedford Town (1) v Hayes	5-3
Bishop Auckland v Scarborough	1-2
Blyth Spartans v Spennymoor United	4-0
Cambridge City v Headington United	2-3
Cheltenham Town v Bridgwater Town (1)	0-0
Consett v South Shields (2)	0-0
Ellesmere Port Town v Burscough	1-2
Enfield v Rushden Town	3-0
Gainsborough Trinity v Heanor Town	4-2
Gravesend & Northfleet v Ashford Town	1-2
Grays Athletic v Chelmsford City	1-3
Ilkeston Town (2) v Matlock Town	2-6
Kettering Town v Boston United	1-0
Letchworth Town v King's Lynn	3-4
Margate v Guildford City	1-0
Oswestry Town v Evesham United	4-1
Peterborough United v Bury Town	7-1
Prescot Cables v Altrincham	1-0
Salisbury (2) v Basingstoke Town	2-2
Shildon v Denaby United	6-1
Sutton United v Hastings United	2-3
Tooting & Mitcham United v Wisbech Town	1-2
Walthamstow Avenue v Great Yarmouth Town	2-1
West Auckland Town v Durham City	2-2
Weymouth v Dorchester Town	0-1
Wigan Athletic v Rhyl	1-1
Worcester City v Hereford United	0-3
Wycombe Wanderers v Oxford City	1-0
Yeovil Town v Bath City	0-2
r Basingstoke Town v Salisbury (2)	1-2
r Bridgwater Town (1) v Cheltenham Town	0-1
r Durham City v West Auckland Town	0-0e
r Rhyl v Wigan Athletic	3-1e
r South Shields (2) v Consett	2-2e
r2 Consett v South Shields (2)	5-5e
r2 West Auckland Town v Durham City	4-1
r3 South Shields (2) v Consett	1-0

Round One

Accrington Stanley v Mansfield Town	1-2
Barnsley v Bradford City	3-3
Bath City v Millwall	3-1
Bedford Town (1) v Gillingham	0-4
Bradford Park Avenue v Scarborough	6-1
Brentford v Ashford Town	5-0
Burscough v Crewe Alexandra	1-3
Bury v Hartlepools United	5-0
Cheltenham Town v Watford	0-0
Colchester United v Queen's Park Rangers	2-3
Coventry City v Southampton	1-1
Crook Town v Matlock Town	2-2
Crystal Palace v Chelmsford City	5-1
Darlington v Prescot Cables	4-0
Doncaster Rovers v Gainsborough Trinity	3-3
Dorchester Town v Port Vale	1-2
Enfield v Headington United	4-3
Exeter City v Barnstaple Town	4-0
Gateshead v Halifax Town	3-4
Hastings United v Notts County	1-2
Kettering Town v Margate	1-1
King's Lynn v Aldershot	3-1
Newport County v Hereford United	4-2
Norwich City v Reading	1-1
Peterborough United v Shrewsbury Town	4-3
Rhyl v Grimsby Town	1-2
Rochdale v Carlisle United	2-2
Salisbury (2) v Barnet	1-0
Shildon v Oldham Athletic	1-1
South Shields (2) v Chesterfield	2-1
Southend United v Oswestry Town	6-0
Southport v Workington	2-2
Swindon Town v Walsall	2-3
Torquay United v Northampton Town	7-1
Tranmere Rovers v Chester	0-1
Walthamstow Avenue v Bournemouth	2-3
West Auckland Town v Stockport County	2-6
Wrexham v Blyth Spartans	2-1
Wycombe Wanderers v Wisbech Town	4-2
York City v Barrow	3-1
r Bradford City v Barnsley	2-1
r Carlisle United v Rochdale	1-3e
r Gainsborough Trinity v Doncaster Rovers	0-1
r Margate v Kettering Town	3-2
r Matlock Town v Crook Town	0-1
r Oldham Athletic v Shildon	3-0
r Reading v Norwich City	2-1
r Southampton v Coventry City	5-1
r Watford v Cheltenham Town	3-0
r Workington v Southport	3-0

Round Two

Bury v Oldham Athletic	2-1
Crook Town v York City	0-1
Doncaster Rovers v Darlington	3-2
Enfield v Bournemouth	1-5
Exeter City v Brentford	3-1
Gillingham v Torquay United	2-2
Grimsby Town v Wrexham	2-3
Mansfield Town v Chester	2-0
Margate v Crystal Palace	0-0
Notts County v Bath City	0-1
Queen's Park Rangers v Port Vale	3-3
Reading v King's Lynn	4-2
Rochdale v Bradford City	1-1
Salisbury (2) v Newport County	0-1
South Shields (2) v Bradford Park Avenue	1-5
Southampton v Southend United	3-0
Stockport County v Crewe Alexandra	0-0
Walsall v Peterborough United	2-3
Watford v Wycombe Wanderers	5-1
Workington v Halifax Town	1-0
r Bradford City v Rochdale	2-1
r Crewe Alexandra v Stockport County	2-0
r Crystal Palace v Margate	3-0
r Port Vale v Queen's Park Rangers	2-1
r Torquay United v Gillingham	1-2

Round Three

Aston Villa v Leeds United	2-1
Bath City v Brighton & Hove Albion	0-1
Blackpool v Mansfield Town	3-0
Bournemouth v York City	1-0
Bradford City v Everton	3-0
Bristol City v Charlton Athletic	2-3
Bristol Rovers v Doncaster Rovers	0-0
Bury v Bolton Wanderers	1-1
Cardiff City v Port Vale	0-2
Chelsea v Bradford Park Avenue	5-1
Crewe Alexandra v Workington	2-0
Derby County v Manchester United	2-4
Exeter City v Luton Town	1-2
Fulham v Hull City	5-0
Gillingham v Swansea Town	1-4
Huddersfield Town v West Ham United	1-1
Ipswich Town v Peterborough United	2-3
Lincoln City v Burnley	1-1
Liverpool v Leyton Orient	2-1
Manchester City v Southampton	1-5
Newcastle United v Wolverhampton Wan.	2-2
Newport County v Tottenham Hotspur	0-4
Nottingham Forest v Reading	1-0
Rotherham United v Arsenal	2-2
Scunthorpe United v Crystal Palace	1-0
Sheffield United v Portsmouth	3-0
Sheffield Wednesday v Middlesbrough	2-1
Stoke City v Preston North End	1-1
Sunderland v Blackburn Rovers	1-1
Watford v Birmingham City	2-1
West Bromwich Albion v Plymouth Argyle	3-2
Wrexham v Leicester City	1-2
r Arsenal v Rotherham United	1-1e
r Blackburn Rovers v Sunderland	4-1
r Bolton Wanderers v Bury	4-2
r Burnley v Lincoln City	2-0
r Doncaster Rovers v Bristol Rovers	1-2
r Preston North End v Stoke City	3-1
r West Ham United v Huddersfield Town	1-5
r Wolverhampton Wan. v Newcastle United	4-2
r2 Rotherham United v Arsenal	2-0 N

Round Four

Blackburn Rovers v Blackpool	1-1
Bradford City v Bournemouth	3-1
Bristol Rovers v Preston North End	3-3
Chelsea v Aston Villa	1-2
Crewe Alexandra v Tottenham Hotspur	2-2
Huddersfield Town v Luton Town	0-1
Leicester City v Fulham	2-1
Liverpool v Manchester United	1-3
Rotherham United v Brighton & Hove Albion	1-1
Scunthorpe United v Port Vale	0-1
Sheffield United v Nottingham Forest	3-0
Sheffield Wednesday v Peterborough United	2-0
Southampton v Watford	2-2
Swansea Town v Burnley	0-0
West Bromwich Albion v Bolton Wanderers	2-0
Wolverhampton Wan. v Charlton Athletic	2-1

1959/60 to 1960/61

r	Blackpool v Blackburn Rovers	0-3
r	Brighton & Hove Albion v Rotherham United	1-1e
r	Burnley v Swansea Town	2-1
r	Preston North End v Bristol Rovers	5-1
r	Tottenham Hotspur v Crewe Alexandra	13-2
r	Watford v Southampton	1-0
r2	Rotherham United v Brighton & Hove Albion	0-6 N

Round Five

	Bradford City v Burnley	2-2
	Leicester City v West Bromwich Albion	2-1
	Luton Town v Wolverhampton Wan.	1-4
	Manchester United v Sheffield Wednesday	0-1
	Port Vale v Aston Villa	1-2
	Preston North End v Brighton & Hove Albion	2-1
	Sheffield United v Watford	3-2
	Tottenham Hotspur v Blackburn Rovers	1-3
r	Burnley v Bradford City	5-0

Round Six

	Aston Villa v Preston North End	2-0
	Burnley v Blackburn Rovers	3-3
	Leicester City v Wolverhampton Wan.	1-2
	Sheffield United v Sheffield Wednesday	0-2
r	Blackburn Rovers v Burnley	2-0e

Semi Finals

	Blackburn Rovers v Sheffield Wednesday	2-1 N
	Wolverhampton Wan. v Aston Villa	1-0 N

Final

	Wolverhampton Wan. v Blackburn Rovers	3-0 N

1960/61

Preliminary Round

6	Wigan Athletic v Prescot Cables	2-0
7	South Liverpool v Pwllheli & District	1-5
8	Rossendale United v Mossley	1-1
11	Stourbridge v Oswestry Town	1-4
13	Matlock Town v Creswell Colliery	6-0
19	Lowestoft Town v Sheringham	5-1
8r	Mossley v Rossendale United	5-2

Qualifying Round One

1	Bridlington Town v Durham City	6-0
	Shotton CW v Murton CW	2-2
	Whitby Town v Stockton	1-2
2	Bedlington Mechanics v Billingham Synthonia	5-2
	West Auckland Town v Annfield Plain	2-4
3	Ashington v Newburn	2-1
	Ferryhill Athletic v Evenwood Town	3-2
4	North Shields v Spennymoor United	6-2
	Scarborough v Whitley Bay	4-1
5	Burscough v Milnthorpe Corinthians	2-1
	Fleetwood v Clitheroe	3-2
	Morecambe v Lancaster City	7-4
	Netherfield (Kendal) v Penrith	5-0
6	Earlestown v Altrincham	4-3
	Marine v Horwich RMI	2-0
	Skelmersdale United v St Helens Town	3-2
	Wigan Athletic v Ashton United	3-2
7	Flint Town United v Bangor City	1-2
	New Brighton v Llandudno	3-1
	Pwllheli & District v Ellesmere Port Town	1-4
	Runcorn v Stork	6-0
8	Darwen v Bacup Borough	0-1
	Lytham v Hyde United	2-4
	Mossley v Chorley	0-1
	Nelson v Stalybridge Celtic	6-2
9	Buxton v Linotype & Machinery	1-3
	Lostock Gralam v Congleton Town	0-0
	Northwich Victoria v Macclesfield Town	0-3
	Winsford United v Witton Albion	1-0
10	Bedworth Town v Brierley Hill Alliance	4-1
	Evesham United v Bilston	1-3
	Hednesford Town v Halesowen Town	2-3
	Lockheed Leamington v Rugby Town (2)	4-0
11	Cradley Heath v Redditch	1-3
	Moor Green v Kidderminster Harriers	2-3
	Oswestry Town v Bromsgrove Rovers	3-2
	Stafford Rangers v Wellington Town	0-1
12	East End Park WMC v Retford Town	0-2
	Gainsborough Trinity v Denaby United	0-3
	Goole Town v Frickley Colliery	2-4
	Selby Town v Yorkshire Amateur	3-2
13	Belper Town v South Normanton MW	3-2
	Matlock Town v Heanor Town	0-1
	Shirebrook MW v Alfreton Town	1-6
	Worksop Town v Sutton Town	2-2
14	Grantham v Skegness Town	3-4
	Holbeach United v Alford United	7-1
	Louth United v Spalding United	1-0
15	Atherstone Town v Hinckley Athletic	0-3
	Ilkeston Town (2) v Burton Albion	3-1
	Loughborough United v Long Eaton United	5-1
	Nuneaton Borough v Tamworth	1-4
16	Corby Town v Kettering Town	1-2
	Eynesbury Rovers v St Neots Town	1-9
	Rushden Town v Rothwell Town	1-0
	Stamford v Wellingborough Town	2-1
17	Hitchin Town v Biggleswade Town	4-0
	St Albans City v Dunstable Town	2-1
	Stevenage Town v Letchworth Town	2-2
	Vauxhall Motors (Luton) v Wolverton Town & BR	2-0
18	Bury Town v Cambridge City	0-3
	Cambridge United v Newmarket Town	5-1
	Ely City v Chatteris Town	6-2
	Histon v March Town United	1-2
19	Gorleston v Bungay Town	0-1
	Harwich & Parkeston v Clacton Town	0-4
	Lowestoft Town v Great Yarmouth Town	4-1
	Stowmarket v Sudbury Town	2-3
20	Betteshanger CW v Deal Town	1-7
	Dover v Canterbury City	4-1
	Ramsgate Athletic v Folkestone	1-1
	Snowdown CW v Whitstable	6-1
21	Arundel v Crawley Town	3-0
	Horsham v Bognor Regis Town	3-1
	Littlehampton Town v Lancing Athletic	6-3e
	Southwick v Worthing	2-2
22	Eastbourne v Newhaven	2-1
	Eastbourne United v Tunbridge Wells United	1-2
	Tonbridge v Bexhill Town	2-2
23	Aveley v Brentwood & Warley	2-5
	Grays Athletic v Barking	2-3
	Rainham Town v Ilford	2-3
	Tilbury v Woodford Town (1)	2-2
24	Barnet v Hounslow Town	5-1
	Cheshunt v Bishop's Stortford	0-2
	Hertford Town v Ware	5-1
	Wealdstone v Harrow Town	1-2
25	Epsom v Carshalton Athletic	0-1
	Marlow v Slough Town	0-1
	Staines Town v Dulwich Hamlet	0-2
	Sutton United v Redhill	4-0
26	Bromley v Kingstonian	2-3
	Leatherhead v Dorking	1-2
	Walton & Hersham v Metropolitan Police	5-1
	Wimbledon v Woking	5-1
27	Abingdon Town v Banbury Spencer	4-2
	Chesham United v Aylesbury United	5-1
	Oxford City v Huntley & Palmers	6-1
	Witney Town v Wokingham Town	2-5
28	Edgware Town v Finchley	3-1
	Southall v Hayes	2-1
	Uxbridge v Yiewsley	2-1
	Windsor & Eton v Maidenhead United	2-4
29	Cray Wanderers v Dartford	4-5
	Erith & Belvedere v Bexleyheath & Welling	3-6
	Maidstone United v Gravesend & Northfleet	2-1
	Sheppey United v Sittingbourne	1-4
30	Clapton v Leyton	1-0
	Hornchurch & Upminster v Ford United	1-0
	Leytonstone v Dagenham	3-0
	Romford (2) v Wembley	7-0
31	Fareham Town v Alton Town	4-3
	Newport (IOW) v Cowes	1-2
32	Poole Town v Bridport	6-3
	Warminster Town v Portland United	3-1
33	Calne & Harris United v Devizes Town	2-5
	Melksham Town v Westbury United	3-2
	Trowbridge Town v Chippenham Town	1-1
34	Street v Weston-Super-Mare	0-8
35	Barry Town v Ebbw Vale	9-0
	Gloucester City v Cheltenham Town	1-4
	Lovells Athletic v Llanelli	2-3
	Merthyr Tydfil v Stonehouse	5-2
36	Truro City v Bideford	2-2
	Wadebridge Town v St Blazey	2-7
1r	Murton CW v Shotton CW	3-1
9r	Congleton Town v Lostock Gralam	2-0
13r	Sutton Town v Worksop Town	3-0
17r	Letchworth Town v Stevenage Town	2-6
20r	Folkestone v Ramsgate Athletic	4-1
21r	Worthing v Southwick	2-3e
22r	Bexhill Town v Tonbridge	1-2
23r	Woodford Town (1) v Tilbury	1-2
33r	Chippenham Town v Trowbridge Town	0-1
36r	Bideford v Truro City	4-2

Qualifying Round Two

1	Bridlington Town v Murton CW	5-0
	Stockton v Boldon CW	2-2
2	Annfield Plain v Shildon	1-4
	Horden CW v Bedlington Mechanics	3-1
3	Ashington v Silksworth CW	6-1
	South Bank v Ferryhill Athletic	3-4
4	Consett v North Shields	3-2
	Scarborough v Willington	5-2
5	Fleetwood v Netherfield (Kendal)	0-4
	Morecambe v Burscough	2-2
6	Earlestown v Skelmersdale United	2-4
	Marine v Wigan Athletic	1-5
7	Bangor City v Runcorn	2-1
	New Brighton v Ellesmere Port Town	0-0
8	Bacup Borough v Nelson	0-2
	Hyde United v Chorley	1-1
9	Congleton Town v Winsford United	3-1
	Macclesfield Town v Linotype & Machinery	1-1
10	Bilston v Lockheed Leamington	1-3
	Halesowen Town v Bedworth Town	5-2
11	Kidderminster Harriers v Oswestry Town	2-1
	Redditch v Wellington Town	0-3
12	Frickley Colliery v Denaby United	3-0
	Retford Town v Selby Town	1-2
13	Alfreton Town v Belper Town	1-7
	Sutton Town v Heanor Town	4-2
14	Louth United v Holbeach United	0-3
	Skegness Town v Ransome & Marles	5-1
15	Ilkeston Town (2) v Tamworth	3-1
	Loughborough United v Hinckley Athletic	2-1
16	Kettering Town v Stamford	3-0
	Rushden Town v St Neots Town	0-5
17	Hitchin Town v Vauxhall Motors (Luton)	3-0
	Stevenage Town v St Albans City	1-1
18	Cambridge United v March Town United	7-3
	Ely City v Cambridge City	1-8
19	Bungay Town v Sudbury Town	4-2
	Clacton Town v Lowestoft Town	6-2
20	Dover v Snowdown CW	5-3
	Folkestone v Deal Town	5-1
21	Horsham v Southwick	10-1
	Littlehampton Town v Arundel	3-2
22	Eastbourne v Hastings United	0-7
	Tunbridge Wells United v Tonbridge	1-2
23	Barking v Tilbury	3-3
	Ilford v Brentwood & Warley	0-2
24	Bishop's Stortford v Barnet	4-2
	Harrow Town v Hertford Town	3-2
25	Carshalton Athletic v Slough Town	5-2
	Sutton United v Dulwich Hamlet	4-2
26	Dorking v Wimbledon	4-3
	Walton & Hersham v Kingstonian	3-1
27	Chesham United v Wokingham Town	2-2
	Oxford City v Abingdon Town	1-1
28	Maidenhead United v Uxbridge	4-0
	Southall v Edgware Town	2-2
29	Bexleyheath & Welling v Sittingbourne	1-0
	Maidstone United v Dartford	1-3
30	Hornchurch & Upminster v Clapton	2-1
	Leytonstone v Romford (2)	1-3
31	Chichester City (1) v Cowes	6-3
	Fareham Town v Andover	3-3
32	Poole Town v Frome Town	4-1
	Weymouth v Warminster Town	5-1
33	Melksham Town v Chippenham United	2-5
	Trowbridge Town v Devizes Town	2-2
34	Bridgwater Town (1) v Minehead	4-1
	Glastonbury v Weston-Super-Mare	2-2
35	Cheltenham Town v Merthyr Tydfil	4-0
	Llanelli v Barry Town	0-0
36	Barnstaple Town v St Blazey	1-1
	Bideford v Penzance	5-2
1r	Boldon CW v Stockton	3-1
5r	Burscough v Morecambe	1-2
7r	Ellesmere Port Town v New Brighton	0-1
8r	Chorley v Hyde United	3-1
9r	Linotype & Machinery v Macclesfield Town	0-3
17r	St Albans City v Stevenage Town	2-2e
23r	Tilbury v Barking	3-1
27r	Abingdon Town v Oxford City	2-1
r	Wokingham Town v Chesham United	1-2
28r	Edgware Town v Southall	3-2
31r	Andover v Fareham Town	3-2
33r	Devizes Town v Trowbridge Town	2-3
34r	Weston-Super-Mare v Glastonbury	2-0
35r	Barry Town v Llanelli	1-2
36r	St Blazey v Barnstaple Town	1-2
17r2	St Albans City v Stevenage Town	3-2

Qualifying Round Three

1	Bridlington Town v Boldon CW	11-2
2	Horden CW v Shildon	5-1
3	Ferryhill Athletic v Ashington	2-1
4	Consett v Scarborough	1-2
5	Netherfield (Kendal) v Morecambe	2-0
6	Skelmersdale United v Wigan Athletic	0-0
7	Bangor City v New Brighton	3-0
8	Nelson v Chorley	7-4
9	Congleton Town v Macclesfield Town	0-3
10	Lockheed Leamington v Halesowen Town	6-1
11	Wellington Town v Kidderminster Harriers	1-0
12	Selby Town v Frickley Colliery	1-3
13	Belper Town v Sutton Town	1-2
14	Holbeach United v Skegness Town	1-0
15	Ilkeston Town (2) v Loughborough United	0-3
16	Kettering Town v St Neots Town	2-0
17	Hitchin Town v St Albans City	4-0
18	Cambridge United v Cambridge City	1-1
19	Bungay Town v Clacton Town	0-1
20	Dover v Folkestone	1-0
21	Horsham v Littlehampton Town	2-3
22	Tonbridge v Hastings United	1-2
23	Tilbury v Brentwood & Warley	1-3
24	Harrow Town v Bishop's Stortford	8-4
25	Carshalton Athletic v Sutton United	2-2
26	Dorking v Walton & Hersham	1-1
27	Chesham United v Abingdon Town	1-2
28	Maidenhead United v Edgware Town	3-3
29	Bexleyheath & Welling v Dartford	5-0
30	Romford (2) v Hornchurch & Upminster	3-0
31	Chichester City (1) v Andover	2-1
32	Weymouth v Poole Town	1-1
33	Trowbridge Town v Chippenham United	2-1

1960/61 to 1961/62

34 Weston-Super-Mare v Bridgwater Town (1)	0-1
35 Cheltenham Town v Llanelli	2-0
36 Barnstaple Town v Bideford	1-0
6r Wigan Athletic v Skelmersdale United	2-1
18r Cambridge City v Cambridge United	1-1e
25r Sutton United v Carshalton Athletic	3-0
26r Walton & Hersham v Dorking	2-1
28r Edgware Town v Maidenhead United	0-2
32r Poole Town v Weymouth	3-4
18r2 Cambridge City v Cambridge United	1-2

Qualifying Round Four

Ashford Town v Margate	1-1
Bangor City v Netherfield (Kendal)	1-0
Barnstaple Town v Bath City	1-2
Bedford Town (1) v King's Lynn	1-4
Bexleyheath & Welling v Sutton United	1-3
Brentwood & Warley v Oxford United	0-4
Bridgwater Town (1) v Cheltenham Town	0-0
Bridlington Town v South Shields (2)	5-3
Chelmsford City v Wisbech Town	3-3
Chichester City (1) v Dorchester Town	4-1
Clacton Town v Cambridge United	2-1
Crook Town v Bishop Auckland	1-2
Dover v Littlehampton Town	2-1
Harrow Town v Maidenhead United	2-3
Hastings United v Guildford City	2-1
Hitchin Town v Abingdon Town	2-0
Holbeach United v Loughborough United	1-2
Horden CW v Blyth Spartans	1-3
Kettering Town v Boston United	1-1
Lockheed Leamington v Hereford United	1-2
Nelson v Macclesfield Town	2-3
Romford (2) v Enfield	2-1
Scarborough v Ferryhill Athletic	1-0
Sutton Town v Frickley Colliery	2-1
Trowbridge Town v Yeovil Town	0-4
Walthamstow Avenue v Walton & Hersham	4-1
Wellington Town v Worcester City	1-1
Weymouth v Salisbury (2)	1-1
Wigan Athletic v Rhyl	1-1
Wycombe Wanderers v Tooting & Mitcham United	2-1
r Boston United v Kettering Town	1-3
r Cheltenham Town v Bridgwater Town (1)	1-2
r Margate v Ashford Town	1-2
r Rhyl v Wigan Athletic	2-1
r Salisbury (2) v Weymouth	0-2
r Wisbech Town v Chelmsford City	1-4
r Worcester City v Wellington Town	3-2

Round One

Accrington Stanley v Barrow	2-1
Aldershot v Notts County	2-0
Ashford Town v Gillingham	1-2
Bangor City v Wrexham	1-0
Bishop Auckland v Bridlington Town	3-2
Bradford City v Scarborough	0-0
Bridgwater Town (1) v Hereford United	3-0
Bristol City v Chichester City (1)	11-0
Chelmsford City v Port Vale	2-3
Chester v Carlisle United	0-1
Chesterfield v Doncaster Rovers	3-3
Clacton Town v Southend United	1-3
Colchester United v Maidenhead United	5-0
Crewe Alexandra v Rochdale	1-1
Crystal Palace v Hitchin Town	6-2
Darlington v Grimsby Town	2-0
Dover v Peterborough United	1-4
Exeter City v Bournemouth	1-1
Gateshead v Barnsley	0-0
Halifax Town v Hartlepools United	5-1
Hendon v Oxford United	2-2
Hull City v Sutton Town	3-0
Loughborough United v King's Lynn	0-0
Mansfield Town v Blyth Spartans	3-1
Northampton Town v Hastings United	2-1
Queen's Park Rangers v Walthamstow Avenue	3-2
Reading v Millwall	6-2
Rhyl v Oldham Athletic	0-1
Shrewsbury Town v Newport County	4-1
Southport v Macclesfield Town	7-2
Stockport County v Workington	1-0
Sutton United v Romford (2)	2-2
Swindon Town v Bath City	2-2
Tranmere Rovers v Bury	1-0
Walsall v Yeovil Town	0-1
Watford v Brentford	2-2
Weymouth v Torquay United	1-3
Worcester City v Coventry City	1-4
Wycombe Wanderers v Kettering Town	1-2
York City v Bradford Park Avenue	0-0
r Barnsley v Gateshead	2-0
r Bath City v Swindon Town	4-6
r Bournemouth v Exeter City	3-1
r Bradford Park Avenue v York City	0-2
r Brentford v Watford	0-2
r Doncaster Rovers v Chesterfield	0-1
r King's Lynn v Loughborough United	3-0
r Oxford United v Hendon	3-2
r Rochdale v Crewe Alexandra	1-2
r Romford (2) v Sutton United	5-0
r Scarborough v Bradford City	1-3e

Round Two

Accrington Stanley v Mansfield Town	3-0
Aldershot v Colchester United	3-1
Bangor City v Southport	1-1
Bournemouth v Yeovil Town	3-1
Bradford City v Barnsley	1-2
Chesterfield v Oldham Athletic	4-4
Crystal Palace v Watford	0-0
Darlington v Hull City	1-1
Gillingham v Southend United	3-2
Halifax Town v Crewe Alexandra	2-2
King's Lynn v Bristol City	2-2
Oxford United v Bridgwater Town (1)	2-1
Port Vale v Carlisle United	2-1
Queen's Park Rangers v Coventry City	1-2
Reading v Kettering Town	4-2
Romford (2) v Northampton Town	1-5
Stockport County v Bishop Auckland	2-0
Swindon Town v Shrewsbury Town	0-1
Torquay United v Peterborough United	1-3
Tranmere Rovers v York City	1-1
r Bristol City v King's Lynn	3-0
r Crewe Alexandra v Halifax Town	3-0
r Hull City v Darlington	1-1e
r Oldham Athletic v Chesterfield	0-3
r Southport v Bangor City	3-1
r Watford v Crystal Palace	1-0
r York City v Tranmere Rovers	2-1
r2 Darlington v Hull City	1-1xN
r3 Hull City v Darlington	0-0eN
r4 Darlington v Hull City	0-3 N

Round Three

Aldershot v Shrewsbury Town	1-1
Brighton & Hove Albion v Derby County	3-1
Bristol Rovers v Aston Villa	1-1
Burnley v Bournemouth	1-0
Cardiff City v Manchester City	1-1
Chelsea v Crewe Alexandra	1-2
Chesterfield v Blackburn Rovers	0-0
Everton v Sheffield United	0-1
Gillingham v Leyton Orient	2-6
Hull City v Bolton Wanderers	0-1
Leicester City v Oxford United	3-1
Lincoln City v West Bromwich Albion	3-1
Liverpool v Coventry City	3-2
Luton Town v Northampton Town	4-0
Manchester United v Middlesbrough	3-0
Newcastle United v Fulham	5-0
Nottingham Forest v Birmingham City	0-2
Plymouth Argyle v Bristol City	0-1
Portsmouth v Peterborough United	1-2
Preston North End v Accrington Stanley	1-1
Reading v Barnsley	1-1
Rotherham United v Watford	1-0
Scunthorpe United v Blackpool	6-2
Sheffield Wednesday v Leeds United	2-0
Southampton v Ipswich Town	7-1
Stockport County v Southport	3-1
Sunderland v Arsenal	2-1
Swansea Town v Port Vale	3-0
Tottenham Hotspur v Charlton Athletic	3-2
West Ham United v Stoke City	2-2
Wolverhampton Wan. v Huddersfield Town	1-1
York City v Norwich City	1-1
r Accrington Stanley v Preston North End	0-4
r Aston Villa v Bristol Rovers	4-0
r Barnsley v Reading	3-1e
r Blackburn Rovers v Chesterfield	3-0
r Huddersfield Town v Wolverhampton Wan.	2-1
r Manchester City v Cardiff City	0-0e
r Norwich City v York City	1-0
r Shrewsbury Town v Aldershot	2-2e
r Stoke City v West Ham United	1-0
r2 Aldershot v Shrewsbury Town	2-0 N
r2 Cardiff City v Manchester City	0-2eN

Round Four

Birmingham City v Rotherham United	4-0
Bolton Wanderers v Blackburn Rovers	3-3
Brighton & Hove Albion v Burnley	3-3
Huddersfield Town v Barnsley	1-1
Leicester City v Bristol City	5-1
Liverpool v Sunderland	0-2
Luton Town v Manchester City	3-1
Newcastle United v Stockport County	4-0
Peterborough United v Aston Villa	1-1
Scunthorpe United v Norwich City	1-4
Sheffield United v Lincoln City	3-1
Sheffield Wednesday v Manchester United	1-1
Southampton v Leyton Orient	0-1
Stoke City v Aldershot	0-0
Swansea Town v Preston North End	2-1
Tottenham Hotspur v Crewe Alexandra	5-1
r Aldershot v Stoke City	0-0e
r Aston Villa v Peterborough United	2-1
r Barnsley v Huddersfield Town	1-0
r Blackburn Rovers v Bolton Wanderers	4-0
r Burnley v Brighton & Hove Albion	2-0
r Manchester United v Sheffield Wednesday	2-7
r2 Stoke City v Aldershot	3-0 N

Round Five

Aston Villa v Tottenham Hotspur	0-2
Barnsley v Luton Town	1-0
Birmingham City v Leicester City	1-1
Burnley v Swansea Town	4-0
Leyton Orient v Sheffield Wednesday	0-2
Newcastle United v Stoke City	3-1
Norwich City v Sunderland	0-1
Sheffield United v Blackburn Rovers	2-1
r Leicester City v Birmingham City	2-1

Round Six

Leicester City v Barnsley	0-0
Newcastle United v Sheffield United	1-3
Sheffield Wednesday v Burnley	0-0
Sunderland v Tottenham Hotspur	1-1
r Barnsley v Leicester City	1-2
r Burnley v Sheffield Wednesday	2-0
r Tottenham Hotspur v Sunderland	5-0

Semi Finals

Leicester City v Sheffield United	0-0 N
Tottenham Hotspur v Burnley	3-0 N
r Sheffield United v Leicester City	0-0eN
r2 Leicester City v Sheffield United	2-0eN

Final

Tottenham Hotspur v Leicester City	2-0 N

1961/62

Preliminary Round

1 South Bank v Annfield Plain	4-2
2 Ashington v Spennymoor United	3-2
5 Altrincham v Earlestown	6-1
6 Ellesmere Port Town v Llandudno	5-3
7 Bacup Borough v Darwen	1-5
8 Mossley v Congleton Town	1-2
10 Bromsgrove Rovers v Moor Green	2-0

Qualifying Round One

1 North Shields v Easington CW	3-0
South Bank v Newburn	0-3
Stockton v Bridlington Town	2-3
Willington v Shotton CW	2-2
2 Ashington v Silksworth CW	4-1
Bedlington Mechanics v Whitby Town	4-2
Ryhope CW v Billingham Synthonia	1-2
Stanley United v Durham City	5-1
3 Evenwood Town v Murton CW	3-3
Ferryhill Athletic v Horden CW	0-1
Shildon v Tow Law Town	3-3
Whitley Bay v Boldon CW	5-2
4 Burscough v Lancaster City	2-0
Fleetwood v Milnthorpe Corinthians	9-1
Morecambe v Clitheroe	4-2
Netherfield (Kendal) v Penrith	2-3
5 Altrincham v Marine	3-3
Horwich RMI v Ashton United	0-2
Prescot Cables v St Helens Town	3-1
Skelmersdale United v Wigan Athletic	0-4
6 Ellesmere Port Town v Pwllheli & District	2-0
New Brighton v Flint Town United	7-0
Runcorn v Bangor City	2-0
South Liverpool v Stork	4-0
7 Darwen v Lytham	3-1
Hyde United v Chorley	3-0
Nelson v Leyland Motors	4-0
Rossendale United v Stalybridge Celtic	1-2
8 Congleton Town v Lostock Gralam	4-2
Linotype & Machinery v Buxton	1-1
Macclesfield Town v Droylsden	4-0
Northwich Victoria v Witton Albion	2-1
9 Bedworth Town v Halesowen Town	3-0
Evesham United v Brierley Hill Alliance	1-5
Hednesford Town v Bilston	3-6
Lockheed Leamington v Rugby Town (2)	1-2
10 Bromsgrove Rovers v Redditch	4-0
Oswestry Town v Kidderminster Harriers	1-1
Stafford Rangers v Sankey of Wellington	2-2
Stourbridge v Wellington Town	1-0
11 East End Park WMC v Yorkshire Amateur	1-1
Goole Town v Farsley Celtic	5-1
Selby Town v Frickley Colliery	4-1
12 Creswell Colliery v Worksop Town	1-2
Gainsborough Trinity v Norton Woodseats	6-0
Retford Town v Denaby United	5-0
13 Arnold St Mary's v Matlock Town	1-5
Heanor Town v Belper Town	4-2
Shirebrook MW v Alfreton Town	1-8
South Normanton MW v Sutton Town	2-6
14 Boston United v Louth United	3-4
Holbeach United v Grantham	0-2
Ransome & Marles v Alford United	1-4
Skegness Town v Spalding United	1-1
15 Atherstone Town v Long Eaton United	3-2
Ilkeston Town (2) v Hinckley Athletic	1-1

126

1961/62

	Loughborough United v Burton Albion	2-6
	Nuneaton Borough v Tamworth	3-0
16	Bourne Town v Rushden Town	2-1
	Rothwell Town v Eynesbury Rovers	6-2
	St Neots Town v Corby Town	0-2
	Stamford v Wellingborough Town	5-0
17	Bedford Town (1) v Letchworth Town	8-0
	Hitchin Town v Biggleswade Town	2-1
	St Albans City v Cambridge City	1-2
	Vauxhall Motors (Luton) v Wolverton Town & BR	2-2
18	Chatteris Town v Cambridge United	1-5
	Histon v Bury Town	2-3
	March Town United v Newmarket Town	0-2
	Sudbury Town v Ely City	5-3
19	Bungay Town v Clacton Town	0-6
	Great Yarmouth Town v Gorleston	1-0
	Sheringham v Lowestoft Town	3-5
	Stowmarket v Harwich & Parkeston	2-2
20	Dover v Deal Town	4-0
	Whitstable v Canterbury City	0-4
21	Crawley Town v Worthing	5-0
	Lancing Athletic v Haywards Heath	1-4
	Littlehampton Town v Horsham	5-3
22	Eastbourne United v Bexhill Town	5-2
	Tunbridge Wells United v Maidstone United	1-0
23	Aveley v Ilford	2-2
	Grays Athletic v Brentwood & Warley	3-2
	Rainham Town v Barking	0-1
	Tilbury v Woodford Town (1)	6-0
24	Enfield v Hertford Town	8-1
	Harrow Town v Bishop's Stortford	7-1
	Hounslow Town v Barnet	2-4
	Wealdstone v Ware	5-0
25	Epsom & Ewell v Dulwich Hamlet	1-2
	Redhill v Carshalton Athletic	1-0
	Slough Town v Sutton United	4-1
	Tooting & Mitcham United v Marlow	7-1
26	Bromley v Metropolitan Police	4-0
	Leatherhead v Kingstonian	2-2
	Walton & Hersham v Dorking	2-2
	Wimbledon v Woking	5-1
27	Abingdon Town v Huntley & Palmers	2-0
	Chesham United v Banbury Spencer	1-4
	Oxford City v Aylesbury United	5-2
	Witney Town v Wokingham Town	0-4
28	Edgware Town v Southall	2-1
	Maidenhead United v Hayes	8-2
	Uxbridge v Finchley	1-2
	Windsor & Eton v Yiewsley	0-2
29	Dartford v Sittingbourne	5-0
	Gravesend & Northfleet v Bexleyheath & Welling	2-2
	Sheppey United v Erith & Belvedere	2-2
30	Hendon v Leyton	9-1
	Hornchurch v Dagenham	2-6
	Leytonstone v Clapton	1-1
	Romford (2) v Wembley	6-2
31	Andover v Alton Town	5-1
	Basingstoke Town v Chichester City (1)	3-0
	Cowes v Newbury Town	3-1
	Fareham Town v Newport (IOW)	2-3
32	Bridport v Swanage Town	3-1
	Warminster Town v Dorchester Town	1-6
33	Chippenham United v Cheltenham Town	2-6
	Melksham Town v Calne & Harris United	6-0
	Trowbridge Town v Devizes Town	2-2
34	Street v Frome Town	0-2
	Weston-Super-Mare v Westbury United	5-3
35	Gloucester City v Stonehouse	5-1
	Lovells Athletic v Barry Town	2-3
	Merthyr Tydfil v Llanelli	5-0
36	Bideford v Truro City	5-3
1r	Shotton CW v Willington	2-3
3r	Murton CW v Evenwood Town	2-3
r	Tow Law Town v Shildon	1-5
5r	Marine v Altrincham	2-2
8r	Buxton v Linotype & Machinery	6-1
10r	Kidderminster Harriers v Oswestry Town	1-1
r	Sankey of Wellington v Stafford Rangers	5-1
11r	Yorkshire Amateur v East End Park WMC	0-2
14r	Spalding United v Skegness Town	0-3
15r	Hinckley Athletic v Ilkeston Town (2)	2-1e
17r	Wolverton Town & BR v Vauxhall Motors (Luton)	0-3
19r	Harwich & Parkeston v Stowmarket	7-2
23r	Ilford v Aveley	3-0
26r	Dorking v Walton & Hersham	1-3
r	Kingstonian v Leatherhead	4-2
29r	Bexleyheath & Welling v Gravesend & Northfleet	4-1
r	Erith & Belvedere v Sheppey United	2-1
30r	Clapton v Leytonstone	1-2
33r	Devizes Town v Trowbridge Town	0-2
5r2	Marine v Altrincham	0-1
10r2	Kidderminster Harriers v Oswestry Town	4-0
	Qualifying Round Two	
1	Bridlington Town v North Shields	1-2
	Willington v Newburn	3-2
2	Bedlington Mechanics v Billingham Synthonia	1-0
	Stanley United v Ashington	1-4
3	Shildon v Evenwood Town	4-2
	Whitley Bay v Horden CW	0-4
4	Fleetwood v Burscough	1-1
	Penrith v Morecambe	1-2
5	Ashton United v Altrincham	3-3
	Wigan Athletic v Prescot Cables	1-1
6	New Brighton v Ellesmere Port Town	1-2
	South Liverpool v Runcorn	0-0
7	Hyde United v Darwen	5-1
	Stalybridge Celtic v Nelson	1-0
8	Buxton v Congleton Town	2-3
	Northwich Victoria v Macclesfield Town	1-0
9	Brierley Hill Alliance v Bedworth Town	2-0
	Rugby Town (2) v Bilston	1-0
10	Kidderminster Harriers v Bromsgrove Rovers	0-2
	Sankey of Wellington v Stourbridge	2-0
11	East End Park WMC v Goole Town	1-1
	Harrogate Town v Selby Town	1-2
12	Stocksbridge Works v Retford Town	0-0
	Worksop Town v Gainsborough Trinity	4-3
13	Heanor Town v Matlock Town	4-2
	Sutton Town v Alfreton Town	5-0
14	Grantham v Louth United	2-1
	Skegness Town v Alford United	6-1
15	Hinckley Athletic v Atherstone Town	3-1
	Nuneaton Borough v Burton Albion	1-0
16	Rothwell Town v Bourne Town	1-2
	Stamford v Corby Town	1-1
17	Cambridge City v Vauxhall Motors (Luton)	7-0
	Hitchin Town v Bedford Town (1)	3-2
18	Cambridge United v Sudbury Town	5-1
	Newmarket Town v Bury Town	2-6
19	Clacton Town v Harwich & Parkeston	3-4
	Great Yarmouth Town v Lowestoft Town	2-0
20	Folkestone v Dover	2-3
	Ramsgate Athletic v Canterbury City	2-1
21	Bognor Regis Town v Littlehampton Town	1-1
	Crawley Town v Haywards Heath	3-2
22	Newhaven v Eastbourne United	1-6
	Tonbridge v Tunbridge Wells United	1-3
23	Grays Athletic v Ilford	3-1
	Tilbury v Barking	2-1
24	Harrow Town v Enfield	0-4
	Wealdstone v Barnet	1-1
25	Dulwich Hamlet v Tooting & Mitcham United	3-1
	Slough Town v Redhill	2-0
26	Kingstonian v Bromley	2-1
	Wimbledon v Walton & Hersham	1-2
27	Banbury Spencer v Abingdon Town	4-1
	Wokingham Town v Oxford City	0-3
28	Maidenhead United v Edgware Town	1-0
	Yiewsley v Finchley	2-0
29	Cray Wanderers v Erith & Belvedere	3-4
	Dartford v Bexleyheath & Welling	4-0
30	Dagenham v Hendon	3-1
	Romford (2) v Leytonstone	3-1
31	Andover v Basingstoke Town	7-1
	Newport (IOW) v Cowes	0-0
32	Poole Town v Dorchester Town	0-1
	Portland United v Bridport	4-3
33	Cheltenham Town v Melksham Town	5-2
	Chippenham Town v Trowbridge Town	1-1
34	Glastonbury v Weston-Super-Mare	1-1
	Minehead v Frome Town	3-0
35	Ebbw Vale v Merthyr Tydfil	1-2
	Gloucester City v Barry Town	0-0
36	Penzance v Barnstaple Town	2-3
	Wadebridge Town v Bideford	1-4
4r	Burscough v Fleetwood	5-2
5r	Altrincham v Ashton United	3-1
r	Prescot Cables v Wigan Athletic	1-3
6r	Runcorn v South Liverpool	2-0
11r	Goole Town v East End Park WMC	2-1
12r	Retford Town v Stocksbridge Works	2-5
16r	Corby Town v Stamford	3-1
21r	Littlehampton Town v Bognor Regis Town	0-2
24r	Barnet v Wealdstone	9-0
31r	Cowes v Newport (IOW)	5-1
33r	Trowbridge Town v Chippenham Town	0-2
34r	Weston-Super-Mare v Glastonbury	2-2e
35r	Barry Town v Gloucester City	2-1
34r2	Glastonbury v Weston-Super-Mare	0-3
	Qualifying Round Three	
1	Willington v North Shields	2-4
2	Ashington v Bedlington Mechanics	2-2
3	Shildon v Horden CW	1-0
4	Burscough v Morecambe	1-8
5	Altrincham v Wigan Athletic	1-1
6	Ellesmere Port Town v Runcorn	4-3
7	Hyde United v Stalybridge Celtic	2-2
8	Congleton Town v Northwich Victoria	1-2
9	Brierley Hill Alliance v Rugby Town (2)	2-1
10	Bromsgrove Rovers v Sankey of Wellington	1-2
11	Goole Town v Selby Town	2-2
12	Worksop Town v Stocksbridge Works	3-1
13	Heanor Town v Sutton Town	5-1
14	Grantham v Skegness Town	3-1
15	Hinckley Athletic v Nuneaton Borough	2-2
16	Bourne Town v Corby Town	1-5
17	Hitchin Town v Cambridge City	2-1
18	Cambridge United v Bury Town	3-2
19	Harwich & Parkeston v Great Yarmouth Town	5-1
20	Dover v Ramsgate Athletic	3-2
21	Crawley Town v Bognor Regis Town	2-1
22	Eastbourne United v Tunbridge Wells United	1-5
23	Grays Athletic v Tilbury	1-1
24	Enfield v Barnet	2-4
25	Dulwich Hamlet v Slough Town	5-1
26	Kingstonian v Walton & Hersham	4-1
27	Banbury Spencer v Oxford City	3-1
28	Maidenhead United v Yiewsley	2-3
29	Dartford v Erith & Belvedere	3-1
30	Dagenham v Romford (2)	1-1
31	Andover v Cowes	2-1
32	Portland United v Dorchester Town	0-3
33	Cheltenham Town v Chippenham Town	2-0
34	Weston-Super-Mare v Minehead	1-0
35	Barry Town v Merthyr Tydfil	2-0
36	Barnstaple Town v Bideford	1-2
2r	Bedlington Mechanics v Ashington	1-4
5r	Wigan Athletic v Altrincham	3-1
7r	Stalybridge Celtic v Hyde United	0-0x
11r	Selby Town v Goole Town	1-0
15r	Nuneaton Borough v Hinckley Athletic	1-1e
23r	Tilbury v Grays Athletic	2-1
30r	Romford (2) v Dagenham	4-1
7r2	Hyde United v Stalybridge Celtic	1-2 N
15r2	Hinckley Athletic v Nuneaton Borough	3-1 N
	Qualifying Round Four	
	Ashford Town v Dover	3-1
	Banbury Spencer v Yiewsley	4-0
	Barnet v Hitchin Town	3-2
	Barry Town v Bideford	2-1
	Bath City v Bridgwater Town (1)	0-2
	Cheltenham Town v Weston-Super-Mare	0-1
	Corby Town v Worksop Town	2-2
	Crawley Town v Tunbridge Wells United	1-2
	Crook Town v Shildon	1-2
	Dartford v Hastings United	4-1
	Dorchester Town v Weymouth	3-3
	Dulwich Hamlet v King's Lynn	1-2
	Gateshead v Selby Town	1-1
	Grantham v Hinckley Athletic	2-1
	Harwich & Parkeston v Kingstonian	6-0
	Kettering Town v Heanor Town	2-0
	Margate v Guildford City	6-2
	Morecambe v Wigan Athletic	2-0
	North Shields v Blyth Spartans	1-2
	Northwich Victoria v Ellesmere Port Town	1-0
	Oxford United v Salisbury (2)	3-2
	Rhyl v Stalybridge Celtic	4-0
	Romford (2) v Cambridge United	2-1
	Sankey of Wellington v Hereford United	0-1
	Scarborough v Ashington	2-2
	South Shields (2) v Bishop Auckland	2-1
	Wisbech Town v Chelmsford City	3-3
	Worcester City v Brierley Hill Alliance	0-1
	Wycombe Wanderers v Tilbury	3-1
	Yeovil Town v Andover	4-0
r	Ashington v Scarborough	2-0
r	Chelmsford City v Wisbech Town	1-0
r	Selby Town v Gateshead	0-3
r	Weymouth v Dorchester Town	2-0
r	Worksop Town v Corby Town	2-1e
	Round One	
	Aldershot v Tunbridge Wells United	3-1
	Barry Town v Queen's Park Rangers	1-1
	Bournemouth v Margate	0-3
	Bradford City v York City	1-0
	Bradford Park Avenue v Port Vale	0-1
	Brentford v Oxford United	3-0
	Bridgwater Town (1) v Weston-Super-Mare	0-0
	Brierley Hill Alliance v Grantham	3-0
	Bristol City v Hereford United	1-1
	Chelmsford City v King's Lynn	1-2
	Chester v Ashington	4-1
	Coventry City v Gillingham	2-0
	Crewe Alexandra v Lincoln City	2-0
	Crystal Palace v Portsmouth	3-0
	Darlington v Carlisle United	0-4
	Doncaster Rovers v Chesterfield	0-4
	Exeter City v Dartford	3-3
	Hartlepools United v Blyth Spartans	5-1
	Hull City v Rhyl	5-0
	Mansfield Town v Grimsby Town	3-2
	Morecambe v South Shields (2)	2-1
	Northampton Town v Millwall	2-0
	Notts County v Yeovil Town	4-2
	Oldham Athletic v Shildon	5-2
	Peterborough United v Colchester United	3-3
	Reading v Newport County	1-1
	Rochdale v Halifax Town	2-0
	Shrewsbury Town v Banbury Spencer	7-1
	Southend United v Watford	0-2
	Southport v Northwich Victoria	1-0
	Stockport County v Accrington Stanley	0-1
	Swindon Town v Kettering Town	2-2
	Torquay United v Harwich & Parkeston	5-1
	Tranmere Rovers v Gateshead	2-3
	Walthamstow Avenue v Romford (2)	2-3
	West Auckland Town v Barnsley	3-3
	Weymouth v Barnet	1-0
	Workington v Worksop Town	2-0
	Wrexham v Barrow	3-2
	Wycombe Wanderers v Ashford Town	0-0
r	Ashford Town v Wycombe Wanderers	3-0
r	Barnsley v West Auckland Town	2-0
r	Colchester United v Peterborough United	2-2e
r	Dartford v Exeter City	2-1
r	Hereford United v Bristol City	2-5

1961/62 to 1962/63

r	Kettering Town v Swindon Town	3-0
r	Newport County v Reading	1-0
r	Queen's Park Rangers v Barry Town	7-0
r	Weston-Super-Mare v Bridgwater Town (1)	0-1
r2	Peterborough United v Colchester United	3-0 N

Round Two

	Aldershot v Brentford	2-2
	Ashford Town v Queen's Park Rangers	0-3
	Barnsley v Carlisle United	1-2
	Bridgwater Town (1) v Crystal Palace	0-3
	Bristol City v Dartford	8-2
	Chester v Morecambe	0-1
	Chesterfield v Oldham Athletic	2-2
	Coventry City v King's Lynn	1-2
	Crewe Alexandra v Port Vale	1-1
	Gateshead v Workington	0-2
	Hartlepools United v Accrington Stanley	2-1
	Hull City v Bradford City	0-2
	Margate v Notts County	1-1
	Northampton Town v Kettering Town	3-0
	Rochdale v Wrexham	1-2
	Romford (2) v Watford	1-3
	Shrewsbury Town v Brierley Hill Alliance	3-0
	Southport v Mansfield Town	4-2
	Torquay United v Peterborough United	1-4
	Weymouth v Newport County	1-0
r	Brentford v Aldershot	2-0
r	Notts County v Margate	3-1
r	Oldham Athletic v Chesterfield	4-2e
r	Port Vale v Crewe Alexandra	3-0

Round Three

	Arsenal v Bradford City	3-0
	Aston Villa v Crystal Palace	4-3
	Birmingham City v Tottenham Hotspur	3-3
	Blackpool v West Bromwich Albion	0-0
	Brentford v Leyton Orient	1-1
	Brighton & Hove Albion v Blackburn Rovers	0-3
	Bristol City v Walsall	0-0
	Bristol Rovers v Oldham Athletic	1-1
	Burnley v Queen's Park Rangers	6-1
	Bury v Sheffield United	0-0
	Charlton Athletic v Scunthorpe United	1-0
	Everton v King's Lynn	4-0
	Fulham v Hartlepools United	3-1
	Huddersfield Town v Rotherham United	4-3
	Ipswich Town v Luton Town	1-1
	Leeds United v Derby County	2-2
	Leicester City v Stoke City	1-1
	Liverpool v Chelsea	4-3
	Manchester United v Bolton Wanderers	2-1
	Middlesbrough v Cardiff City	1-0
	Morecambe v Weymouth	0-1
	Newcastle United v Peterborough United	0-1
	Norwich City v Wrexham	3-1
	Notts County v Manchester City	0-1
	Plymouth Argyle v West Ham United	3-0
	Port Vale v Northampton Town	3-1
	Preston North End v Watford	3-2
	Sheffield Wednesday v Swansea Town	1-0
	Southampton v Sunderland	2-2
	Southport v Shrewsbury Town	1-3
	Wolverhampton Wan. v Carlisle United	3-1
	Workington v Nottingham Forest	1-2
r	Derby County v Leeds United	3-1
r	Leyton Orient v Brentford	2-1
r	Luton Town v Ipswich Town	1-1e
r	Oldham Athletic v Bristol Rovers	2-0
r	Sheffield United v Bury	2-2e
r	Stoke City v Leicester City	5-2
r	Sunderland v Southampton	3-0
r	Tottenham Hotspur v Birmingham City	4-2
r	Walsall v Bristol City	4-1
r	West Bromwich Albion v Blackpool	2-1
r2	Bury v Sheffield United	0-2 N
r2	Ipswich Town v Luton Town	5-1 N

Round Four

	Aston Villa v Huddersfield Town	2-1
	Burnley v Leyton Orient	1-1
	Charlton Athletic v Derby County	2-1
	Everton v Manchester City	2-0
	Fulham v Walsall	2-2
	Manchester United v Arsenal	1-0
	Norwich City v Ipswich Town	1-1
	Nottingham Forest v Sheffield Wednesday	0-2
	Oldham Athletic v Liverpool	1-2
	Peterborough United v Sheffield United	1-3
	Plymouth Argyle v Tottenham Hotspur	1-5
	Preston North End v Weymouth	2-0
	Shrewsbury Town v Middlesbrough	2-2
	Stoke City v Blackburn Rovers	0-1
	Sunderland v Port Vale	0-0
	Wolverhampton Wan. v West Bromwich Albion	1-2
r	Ipswich Town v Norwich City	1-2
r	Leyton Orient v Burnley	0-1
r	Middlesbrough v Shrewsbury Town	5-1
r	Port Vale v Sunderland	3-1
r	Walsall v Fulham	0-2

Round Five

	Aston Villa v Charlton Athletic	2-1
	Blackburn Rovers v Middlesbrough	2-1
	Burnley v Everton	3-1
	Fulham v Port Vale	1-0
	Liverpool v Preston North End	0-0
	Manchester United v Sheffield Wednesday	0-0
	Sheffield United v Norwich City	3-1
	West Bromwich Albion v Tottenham Hotspur	2-4
r	Preston North End v Liverpool	0-0e
r	Sheffield Wednesday v Manchester United	0-2
r2	Liverpool v Preston North End	0-1 N

Round Six

	Fulham v Blackburn Rovers	2-2
	Preston North End v Manchester United	0-0
	Sheffield United v Burnley	0-1
	Tottenham Hotspur v Aston Villa	2-0
r	Blackburn Rovers v Fulham	0-1
r	Manchester United v Preston North End	2-1

Semi Finals

	Burnley v Fulham	1-1 N
	Tottenham Hotspur v Manchester United	3-1 N
r	Fulham v Burnley	1-2 N

Final

	Tottenham Hotspur v Burnley	3-1 N

1962/63

Qualifying Round One

1	Ashington v Willington	4-3
	Boldon CW v Ferryhill Athletic	1-2
	South Bank v Ryhope CW	0-0
	Stockton v Penrith	2-1
2	Billingham Synthonia v Horden CW	2-2
	Easington CW v Stanley United	1-6
	Evenwood Town v Annfield Plain	0-0
3	Bedlington Mechanics v Whitby Town	3-1
	Consett v Spennymoor United	2-0
	Shildon v Durham City	3-1
4	Burscough v Fleetwood	1-4
	Clitheroe v Lancaster City	4-1
	Horwich RMI v Netherfield (Kendal)	2-2
	Wigan Athletic v Milnthorpe Corinthians	5-0
5	Altrincham v Marine	1-0
	Ashton United v Prescot Cables	2-0
	Earlestown v St Helens Town	1-3
	South Liverpool v Skelmersdale United	3-1
6	Bangor City v New Brighton	4-0
	Borough United v Stork	4-0
	Ellesmere Port Town v Pwllheli & District	3-0
	Llandudno v Runcorn	2-3
7	Bacup Borough v Stalybridge Celtic	0-3
	Chorley v Lytham	10-2
	Hyde United v Nelson	3-0
	Leyland Motors v Rossendale United	1-5
8	Droylsden v Macclesfield Town	3-3
	Linotype & Machinery v Mossley	1-2
	Lostock Gralam v Northwich Victoria	3-1
	Winsford United v Witton Albion	3-0
9	Bilston v Hednesford Town	2-3
	Nuneaton Borough v Halesowen Town	6-0
	Rugby Town (2) v Stourbridge	2-1
10	Bromsgrove Rovers v Oswestry Town	7-1
	Congleton Town v Wellington Town	1-1
	Kidderminster Harriers v Sankey of Wellington	1-0
	Moor Green v Stafford Rangers	0-6
11	Bridlington Town v Scarborough	1-1
	Farsley Celtic v Goole Town	1-0
	Selby Town v Ossett Albion	1-5
12	Creswell Colliery v Frickley Colliery	1-4
	Denaby United v Retford Town	4-0
	Gainsborough Trinity v Stocksbridge Works	3-1
	Norton Woodseats v Worksop Town	1-3
13	Alfreton Town v Heanor Town	1-0
	Arnold St Mary's v Matlock Town	3-2
	Belper Town v South Normanton MW	wo/s
	Buxton v Sutton Town	2-1
14	Alford United v Holbeach United	1-1
	Grantham v Louth United	5-2
	Spalding United v Boston United	1-3
15	Atherstone Town v Ilkeston Town (2)	1-1
	Burton Albion v Long Eaton United	1-1
	Gresley Rovers v Tamworth	2-2
	Hinckley Athletic v Loughborough United	4-2
16	Bourne Town v Rushden Town	4-1
	Eynesbury Rovers v St Neots Town	0-5
	Wellingborough Town v Corby Town	0-0
17	Bedford Town (1) v Wolverton Town & BR	8-0
	Biggleswade Town v Letchworth Town	3-3
	Cambridge City v St Albans City	3-0
	Hitchin Town v Vauxhall Motors (Luton)	0-0
18	Bury Town v Chatteris Town	4-1
	March Town United v Ely City	4-1
19	Great Yarmouth Town v Bungay Town	3-2e
	Lowestoft Town v Clacton Town	4-2
	Stowmarket v Gorleston	2-1
20	Canterbury City v Folkestone	0-3
	Sheppey United v Dover	0-1
	Sittingbourne v Whitstable	10-0
21	Haywards Heath v Lancing	4-0
	Lewes v Horsham	5-1
	Worthing v Bognor Regis Town	1-2
22	Eastbourne v Tunbridge Wells United	3-4
	Eastbourne United v Tonbridge	4-3
	Hastings United v Maidstone United	0-0
	Newhaven v Bexhill Town	0-0
23	Aveley v Woodford Town (1)	1-0
	Barking v Ilford	0-4
	Brentwood & Warley v Rainham Town	3-2
	Grays Athletic v Tilbury	1-2
24	Barnet v Hertford Town	2-0
	Bishop's Stortford v Ware	1-0
	Harlow Town v Wealdstone	0-2
	Stevenage Town v Enfield	0-2
25	Carshalton Athletic v Marlow	4-0
	Dulwich Hamlet v Redhill	6-1
	Epsom & Ewell v Slough Town	1-3
	Ruislip Manor v Tooting & Mitcham United	0-2
26	Dorking v Metropolitan Police	2-3
	Kingstonian v Walton & Hersham	5-0
	Leatherhead v Wimbledon	1-4
	Petter Sports v Woking	0-2
27	Aylesbury United v Huntley & Palmers	8-0
	Banbury Spencer v Oxford City	0-2
	Harrow Town v Wokingham Town	5-2
	Hemel Hempstead Town v Chesham United	3-0
28	Edgware Town v Yiewsley	0-3
	Finchley v Southall	4-0
	Hayes v Uxbridge	3-0
	Maidenhead United v Windsor & Eton	2-1
29	Bromley v Bexleyheath & Welling	2-1
	Gravesend & Northfleet v Chatham Town	2-1
	Sutton United v Cray Wanderers	4-1
30	Clapton v Hornchurch	2-3
	Dagenham v Leyton	0-3
	Ford United v Wembley	8-1
	Hendon v Leytonstone	1-0
31	Alton Town v Newport (IOW)	2-0
	Andover v Cowes	4-1
	Basingstoke Town v Fareham Town	4-2
	Chichester City (1) v Newbury Town	2-3
32	Bridport v Portland United	1-5
	Swanage Town v Poole Town	0-8
33	Melksham Town v Devizes Town	0-5
	Salisbury (2) v Chippenham Town	2-2
34	Bridgwater Town (1) v Weston-Super-Mare	1-1
	Glastonbury v Frome Town	0-6
35	Barry Town v Stonehouse	2-0
	Cheltenham Town v Llanelli	1-0
	Ebbw Vale v Lovells Athletic	1-1
	Gloucester City v Merthyr Tydfil	3-2
36	Falmouth Town v Barnstaple Town	1-1
	Truro City v Bideford	0-3
1r	Ryhope CW v South Bank	2-1
2r	Annfield Plain v Evenwood Town	2-1
r	Horden CW v Billingham Synthonia	4-2
4r	Netherfield (Kendal) v Horwich RMI	3-2e
8r	Macclesfield Town v Droylsden	2-2x
10r	Wellington Town v Congleton Town	2-0
11r	Scarborough v Bridlington Town	5-2
14r	Holbeach United v Alford United	6-4
15r	Ilkeston Town (2) v Atherstone Town	1-2
r	Long Eaton United v Burton Albion	0-3
r	Tamworth v Gresley Rovers	4-1
16r	Corby Town v Wellingborough Town	1-0
17r	Letchworth Town v Biggleswade Town	1-1x
r	Vauxhall Motors (Luton) v Hitchin Town	0-3
22r	Maidstone United v Hastings United	4-2
r	Newhaven v Bexhill Town	0-2
33r	Chippenham Town v Salisbury (2)	3-1
34r	Weston-Super-Mare v Bridgwater Town (1)	0-0
35r	Lovells Athletic v Ebbw Vale	4-1
36r	Barnstaple Town v Falmouth Town	1-3
8r2	Droylsden v Macclesfield Town	3-2 N
17r2	Letchworth Town v Biggleswade Town	0-3 N
34r2	Bridgwater Town (1) v Weston-Super-Mare	3-1

Qualifying Round Two

1	Ferryhill Athletic v Ryhope CW	2-2
	Stockton v Ashington	wo/s
2	Annfield Plain v Whitley Bay	2-2
	Stanley United v Horden CW	0-1
3	Consett v North Shields	1-1
	Shildon v Bedlington Mechanics	4-0
4	Clitheroe v Netherfield (Kendal)	0-4
	Wigan Athletic v Fleetwood	8-1
5	Altrincham v Ashton United	4-2
	St Helens Town v South Liverpool	2-1
6	Bangor City v Ellesmere Port Town	1-2
	Runcorn v Borough United	0-1
7	Chorley v Hyde United	2-2
	Rossendale United v Stalybridge Celtic	2-4
8	Droylsden v Mossley	0-0
	Lostock Gralam v Winsford United	0-3
9	Nuneaton Borough v Lockheed Leamington	2-1
	Rugby Town (2) v Hednesford Town	2-0

1962/63

10	Bromsgrove Rovers v Kidderminster Harriers	0-0
	Stafford Rangers v Wellington Town	0-2
11	Ossett Albion v Farsley Celtic	2-1
	Scarborough v Harrogate Town	5-1
12	Denaby United v Gainsborough Trinity	1-2
	Worksop Town v Frickley Colliery	1-0
13	Alfreton Town v Arnold St Mary's	0-4
	Belper Town v Buxton	3-4
14	Boston United v Grantham	3-2
	Holbeach United v Skegness Town	2-3
15	Atherstone Town v Burton Albion	2-1
	Hinckley Athletic v Tamworth	0-0
16	Bourne Town v Stamford	5-1
	Corby Town v St Neots Town	1-0
17	Cambridge City v Biggleswade Town	5-0
	Hitchin Town v Bedford Town (1)	2-5
18	Bury Town v Cambridge United	0-2
	March Town United v Sudbury Town	1-3
19	Great Yarmouth Town v Harwich & Parkeston	1-3
	Stowmarket v Lowestoft Town	1-2
20	Dover v Ramsgate Athletic	4-1
	Sittingbourne v Folkestone	2-2
21	Bognor Regis Town v Haywards Heath	2-5
	Lewes v Littlehampton Town	6-2
22	Eastbourne United v Tunbridge Wells United	0-1
	Maidstone United v Bexhill Town	5-0
23	Ilford v Brentwood & Warley	4-1
	Tilbury v Aveley	2-1
24	Bishop's Stortford v Wealdstone	0-2
	Enfield v Barnet	4-1
25	Carshalton Athletic v Dulwich Hamlet	2-3
	Slough Town v Tooting & Mitcham United	0-4
26	Metropolitan Police v Kingstonian	1-2
	Wimbledon v Woking	4-2
27	Hemel Hempstead Town v Aylesbury United	2-0
	Oxford City v Harrow Town	4-2
28	Finchley v Hayes	1-1
	Maidenhead United v Yiewsley	3-2
29	Bromley v Erith & Belvedere	2-3
	Gravesend & Northfleet v Sutton United	2-1
30	Hendon v Ford United	2-1
	Hornchurch v Leyton	1-2
31	Andover v Basingstoke Town	2-1
	Newbury Town v Alton Town	1-9
32	Poole Town v Warminster Town	10-1
	Portland United v Dorchester Town	1-3
33	Chippenham Town v Westbury United	4-1
	Devizes Town v Trowbridge Town	2-3
34	Bridgwater Town (1) v Taunton	5-1
	Frome Town v Minehead	2-2
35	Cheltenham Town v Lovells Athletic	5-1
	Gloucester City v Barry Town	3-0
36	Bideford v Wadebridge Town	0-0
	Falmouth Town v St Blazey	1-0
1r	Ryhope CW v Ferryhill Athletic	1-0
2r	Whitley Bay v Annfield Plain	0-1
3r	North Shields v Consett	5-2
7r	Hyde United v Chorley	3-0
8r	Mossley v Droylsden	1-2e
10r	Kidderminster Harriers v Bromsgrove Rovers	1-3
15r	Tamworth v Hinckley Athletic	0-1
20r	Folkestone v Sittingbourne	1-2
28r	Hayes v Finchley	1-2
34r	Minehead v Frome Town	4-0
36r	Wadebridge Town v Bideford	2-5

Qualifying Round Three

1	Ryhope CW v Stockton	1-2
2	Horden CW v Annfield Plain	2-0
3	Shildon v North Shields	3-3
4	Netherfield (Kendal) v Wigan Athletic	0-3
5	St Helens Town v Altrincham	1-3
6	Borough United v Ellesmere Port Town	0-1
7	Stalybridge Celtic v Hyde United	1-1
8	Winsford United v Droylsden	0-1
9	Rugby Town (2) v Nuneaton Borough	1-0
10	Wellington Town v Bromsgrove Rovers	2-0
11	Ossett Albion v Scarborough	1-2
12	Worksop Town v Gainsborough Trinity	0-0
13	Buxton v Arnold St Mary's	6-3
14	Boston United v Skegness Town	1-0
15	Hinckley Athletic v Atherstone Town	3-1
16	Corby Town v Bourne Town	4-1
17	Bedford Town (1) v Cambridge City	2-1
18	Cambridge United v Sudbury Town	6-0
19	Lowestoft Town v Harwich & Parkeston	4-0
20	Sittingbourne v Dover	2-1
21	Haywards Heath v Lewes	0-3
22	Tunbridge Wells United v Maidstone United	0-1
23	Tilbury v Ilford	1-0
24	Wealdstone v Enfield	1-5
25	Tooting & Mitcham United v Dulwich Hamlet	5-1
26	Wimbledon v Kingstonian	3-2
27	Oxford City v Hemel Hempstead Town	4-3
28	Maidenhead United v Finchley	3-1
29	Gravesend & Northfleet v Erith & Belvedere	5-0
30	Hendon v Leyton	4-1
31	Alton Town v Andover	1-1
32	Dorchester Town v Poole Town	0-3
33	Chippenham Town v Trowbridge Town	0-1
34	Bridgwater Town (1) v Minehead	1-3
35	Gloucester City v Cheltenham Town	1-2
36	Falmouth Town v Bideford	1-1
3r	North Shields v Shildon	5-2
7r	Hyde United v Stalybridge Celtic	3-0
12r	Gainsborough Trinity v Worksop Town	2-1
31r	Andover v Alton Town	4-1
36r	Bideford v Falmouth Town	0-3

Qualifying Round Four

	Altrincham v Rhyl	2-3
	Bedford Town (1) v Wisbech Town	1-0
	Blyth Spartans v Horden CW	2-1
	Boston United v Kettering Town	2-0
	Brierley Hill Alliance v Hinckley Athletic	1-3
	Cambridge United v Lowestoft Town	4-0
	Chelmsford City v Romford (2)	2-0
	Dartford v Maidstone United	2-0
	Falmouth Town v Bath City	2-1
	Gainsborough Trinity v Buxton	0-0
	Gateshead v West Auckland Town	2-2
	Gravesend & Northfleet v Lewes	1-0
	Guildford City v Sittingbourne	0-0
	Hendon v Andover	1-1
	King's Lynn v Corby Town	2-1
	Maidenhead United v Tilbury	2-1
	Margate v Ashford Town	2-0
	Minehead v Cheltenham Town	0-1
	Morecambe v Droylsden	1-0
	North Shields v Stockton	2-2
	Poole Town v Weymouth	0-0
	Rugby Town (2) v Wellington Town	1-1
	Scarborough v Hyde United	1-0
	South Shields (2) v Bishop Auckland	2-1
	Tooting & Mitcham United v Enfield	2-3
	Walthamstow Avenue v Wycombe Wanderers	1-1
	Wigan Athletic v Ellesmere Port Town	2-0
	Wimbledon v Oxford City	6-1
	Worcester City v Hereford United	0-2
	Yeovil Town v Trowbridge Town	4-0
r	Andover v Hendon	5-4
r	Buxton v Gainsborough Trinity	4-1
r	Sittingbourne v Guildford City	1-0
r	Stockton v North Shields	3-3e
r	Wellington Town v Rugby Town (2)	4-0
r	West Auckland Town v Gateshead	0-2
r	Weymouth v Poole Town	0-2
r	Wycombe Wanderers v Walthamstow Avenue	3-1
r2	North Shields v Stockton	4-2

Round One

	Aldershot v Brentford	1-0
	Andover v Gillingham	0-1
	Barnsley v Rhyl	4-0
	Bedford Town (1) v Cambridge United	2-1
	Blyth Spartans v Morecambe	2-1
	Boston United v King's Lynn	1-2
	Bristol City v Wellington Town	4-2
	Bristol Rovers v Port Vale	0-2
	Buxton v Barrow	2-2
	Carlisle United v Hartlepools United	2-1
	Chelmsford City v Shrewsbury Town	2-6
	Cheltenham Town v Enfield	3-6
	Chester v Tranmere Rovers	0-2
	Chesterfield v Stockport County	4-1
	Coventry City v Bournemouth	1-0
	Crewe Alexandra v Scarborough	1-1
	Crystal Palace v Hereford United	2-0
	Falmouth Town v Oxford United	1-2
	Gateshead v Wigan Athletic	2-1
	Gravesend & Northfleet v Exeter City	3-2
	Halifax Town v Bradford Park Avenue	1-0
	Hinckley Athletic v Sittingbourne	3-0
	Hounslow Town v Mansfield Town	3-3
	Hull City v Crook Town	5-4
	Lincoln City v Darlington	1-1
	Maidenhead United v Wycombe Wanderers	0-3
	Millwall v Margate	3-1
	North Shields v Workington	2-2
	Northampton Town v Torquay United	1-2
	Notts County v Peterborough United	0-3
	Oldham Athletic v Bradford City	2-5
	Queen's Park Rangers v Newport County	3-2
	South Shields (2) v Doncaster Rovers	0-0
	Southend United v Brighton & Hove Albion	2-1
	Southport v Wrexham	1-1
	Swindon Town v Reading	4-2
	Watford v Poole Town	2-2
	Wimbledon v Colchester United	2-1
	Yeovil Town v Dartford	3-2
	York City v Rochdale	0-0
r	Barrow v Buxton	3-1
r	Darlington v Lincoln City	1-2
r	Doncaster Rovers v South Shields (2)	2-1
r	Mansfield Town v Hounslow Town	9-2
r	Poole Town v Watford	1-2
r	Rochdale v York City	1-2
r	Scarborough v Crewe Alexandra	2-3e
r	Workington v North Shields	7-2
r	Wrexham v Southport	3-2

Round Two

	Barnsley v Chesterfield	2-1
	Blyth Spartans v Carlisle United	0-2
	Bradford City v Gateshead	3-2
	Bristol City v Wimbledon	2-1
	Crystal Palace v Mansfield Town	2-2
	Doncaster Rovers v Tranmere Rovers	1-4
	Gillingham v Bedford Town (1)	3-0
	Gravesend & Northfleet v Wycombe Wanderers	3-1
	Hull City v Workington	2-0
	King's Lynn v Oxford United	1-2
	Lincoln City v Halifax Town	1-0
	Millwall v Coventry City	0-0
	Peterborough United v Enfield	1-0
	Port Vale v Aldershot	2-0
	Queen's Park Rangers v Hinckley Athletic	7-2
	Shrewsbury Town v Torquay United	2-1
	Southend United v Watford	0-2
	Wrexham v Barrow	5-2
	Yeovil Town v Swindon Town	0-2
	York City v Crewe Alexandra	2-1
r	Coventry City v Millwall	2-1
r	Mansfield Town v Crystal Palace	7-2

Round Three

	Arsenal v Oxford United	5-1
	Barnsley v Everton	0-3
	Birmingham City v Bury	3-3
	Blackburn Rovers v Middlesbrough	1-1
	Bradford City v Newcastle United	1-6
	Bristol City v Aston Villa	1-1
	Carlisle United v Gravesend & Northfleet	0-1
	Charlton Athletic v Cardiff City	1-0
	Derby County v Peterborough United	2-0
	Gillingham v Port Vale	2-4
	Grimsby Town v Leicester City	1-3
	Leeds United v Stoke City	3-1
	Leyton Orient v Hull City	1-1
	Lincoln City v Coventry City	1-5
	Luton Town v Swindon Town	0-2
	Manchester United v Huddersfield Town	5-0
	Mansfield Town v Ipswich Town	2-3
	Norwich City v Blackpool	1-1
	Nottingham Forest v Wolverhampton Wan.	4-3
	Plymouth Argyle v West Bromwich Albion	1-5
	Portsmouth v Scunthorpe United	1-1
	Preston North End v Sunderland	1-4
	Sheffield United v Bolton Wanderers	3-1
	Shrewsbury Town v Sheffield Wednesday	1-1
	Southampton v York City	5-0
	Swansea Town v Queen's Park Rangers	2-0
	Tottenham Hotspur v Burnley	0-3
	Tranmere Rovers v Chelsea	2-2
	Walsall v Manchester City	0-1
	Watford v Rotherham United	2-0
	West Ham United v Fulham	0-0
	Wrexham v Liverpool	0-3
r	Aston Villa v Bristol City	3-2
r	Blackpool v Norwich City	1-3e
r	Bury v Birmingham City	2-0
r	Chelsea v Tranmere Rovers	3-1
r	Fulham v West Ham United	1-2
r	Hull City v Leyton Orient	0-2e
r	Middlesbrough v Blackburn Rovers	3-1
r	Scunthorpe United v Portsmouth	1-2
r	Sheffield Wednesday v Shrewsbury Town	2-1

Round Four

	Arsenal v Sheffield Wednesday	2-0
	Burnley v Liverpool	1-1
	Charlton Athletic v Chelsea	0-3
	Gravesend & Northfleet v Sunderland	1-1
	Leicester City v Ipswich Town	3-1
	Leyton Orient v Derby County	3-0
	Manchester City v Bury	1-0
	Manchester United v Aston Villa	1-0
	Middlesbrough v Leeds United	0-2
	Norwich City v Newcastle United	5-0
	Port Vale v Sheffield United	1-2
	Portsmouth v Coventry City	1-1
	Southampton v Watford	3-1
	Swindon Town v Everton	1-5
	West Bromwich Albion v Nottingham Forest	0-0
	West Ham United v Swansea Town	1-0
r	Coventry City v Portsmouth	2-2e
r	Liverpool v Burnley	2-1e
r	Nottingham Forest v West Bromwich Albion	2-1e
r	Sunderland v Gravesend & Northfleet	5-2
r2	Portsmouth v Coventry City	1-2 N

Round Five

	Arsenal v Liverpool	1-2
	Coventry City v Sunderland	2-1
	Leyton Orient v Leicester City	0-1
	Manchester City v Norwich City	1-2
	Manchester United v Chelsea	2-1
	Nottingham Forest v Leeds United	3-0
	Southampton v Sheffield United	1-0
	West Ham United v Everton	1-0

Round Six

	Coventry City v Manchester United	1-3
	Liverpool v West Ham United	1-0
	Norwich City v Leicester City	0-2
	Nottingham Forest v Southampton	1-1
r	Southampton v Nottingham Forest	3-3e

1962/63 to 1963/64

r2	Nottingham Forest v Southampton	0-5 N

Semi Finals

Leicester City v Liverpool	1-0 N
Manchester United v Southampton	1-0 N

Final

Manchester United v Leicester City	3-1 N

1963/64

Qualifying Round One

1	Annfield Plain v Stanley United	1-2
	Ashington v Billingham Synthonia	1-1
	South Bank v Spennymoor United	2-5
	Whitby Town v Willington	4-2
2	North Shields v Consett	3-2
	Penrith v Scarborough	1-3
	Tow Law Town v Stockton	4-0
	Whitley Bay v Durham City	4-0
3	Bishop Auckland v Horden CW	0-0
	Shildon v Ryhope CW	0-1
	West Auckland Town v Boldon CW	4-1
4	Clitheroe v Netherfield (Kendal)	0-1
	Horwich RMI v Burscough	0-3
	Milnthorpe Corinthians v Lancaster City	0-5
5	Ashton United v St Helens Town	5-2
	Earlestown v Altrincham	0-10
	Marine v Skelmersdale United	2-2
	South Liverpool v Prescot Cables	3-0
6	Borough United v Pwllheli & District	7-2
	Ellesmere Port Town v Bangor City	0-1
	Llandudno v Runcorn	0-4
	Stork v New Brighton	2-2
7	Chorley v Stalybridge Celtic	2-1
	Hyde United v Rossendale United	6-2
	Nelson v Bacup Borough	5-1
8	Lostock Gralam v Witton Albion	4-1
	Macclesfield Town v Winsford United	1-0
	Northwich Victoria v Droylsden	2-1
9	Bilston v Rugby Town (2)	1-4
	Halesowen Town v Brierley Hill Alliance	1-0
	Hednesford Town v Nuneaton Borough	3-4
	Stourbridge v Lockheed Leamington	0-1
10	Bromsgrove Rovers v Wellington Town	1-3
	Kidderminster Harriers v Stafford Rangers	4-1
	Sankey of Wellington v Worcester City	2-3
11	Bridlington Town v Harrogate Town	3-3
	Farsley Celtic v Yorkshire Amateur	0-0
	Frickley Colliery v Ossett Albion	3-0
	Selby Town v Goole Town	0-0
12	Denaby United v Worksop Town	0-5
	Gainsborough Trinity v Stocksbridge Works	4-0
	Retford Town v Creswell Colliery	4-0
13	Belper Town v Alfreton Town	5-3
	Buxton v Sutton Town	1-1
	Matlock Town v Arnold St Mary's	4-1
14	Grantham v Louth United	3-0
	Holbeach United v Boston United	2-2
15	Burton Albion v Tamworth	0-1
	Gresley Rovers v Loughborough United	1-3
	Long Eaton United v Atherstone Town	2-2
16	Bourne Town v Desborough Town	6-1
	Corby Town v St Neots Town	3-0
	Rothwell Town v Rushden Town	0-3
	Wellingborough Town v Eynesbury Rovers	3-0
17	Biggleswade Town v Wolverton Town & BR	4-1
	Hitchin Town v Vauxhall Motors (Luton)	4-2
	St Albans City v Bletchley Town	3-0
18	Chatteris Town v March Town United	4-0
	Ely City v Bury Town	0-4
19	Harwich & Parkeston v Clacton Town	5-2
	Lowestoft Town v Gorleston	5-0
20	Canterbury City v Whitstable	7-1
	Dover v Sheppey United	1-2
	Ramsgate Athletic v Deal Town	4-2
21	Bognor Regis Town v Lewes	0-4
	Haywards Heath v Crawley Town	3-3
	Horsham v Littlehampton Town	1-2
	Worthing v Lancing	0-0
22	Eastbourne v Tunbridge Wells United	1-1
	Eastbourne United v Tonbridge	0-1
	Maidstone United v Bexhill Town	1-0
23	Barking v Rainham Town	3-1
	Brentwood & Warley v Aveley	2-4
	Grays Athletic v Tilbury	1-3
	Woodford Town (1) v Ilford	1-3
24	Barnet v Stevenage Town	4-2
	Bishop's Stortford v Harrow Town	1-2
	Harlow Town v Ware	2-2
	Wealdstone v Hertford Town	0-1
25	Carshalton Athletic v Redhill	2-0
	Dulwich Hamlet v Walthamstow Avenue	0-3
	Epsom & Ewell v Slough Town	2-1
	Tooting & Mitcham United v Marlow	5-0
26	Dorking v Woking	2-3
	Guildford City v Petter Sports	8-2
	Kingstonian v Walton & Hersham	3-1
27	Aylesbury United v Maidenhead United	2-3
	Banbury Spencer v Huntley & Palmers	4-0
	Newbury Town v Hemel Hempstead Town	0-0
	Oxford City v Chesham United	5-0
28	Edgware Town v Uxbridge	1-2
	Finchley v Hounslow	4-0
	Hayes v Windsor & Eton	2-1
	Yiewsley v Southall	2-2
29	Bromley v Chatham Town	4-1
	Cray Wanderers v Dartford	1-0
	Sittingbourne v Erith & Belvedere	3-3
30	Dagenham v Leyton	2-1
	Ford United v Clapton	2-3
	Hendon v Leytonstone	4-2
	Wembley v Hornchurch	0-2
31	Andover v Newport (IOW)	2-0
	Basingstoke Town v Fareham Town	4-3
	Cowes v Alton Town	5-1
32	Dorchester Town v Poole Town	1-0
	Portland United v Bridport	2-4
33	Devizes Town v Trowbridge Town	0-5
	Melksham Town v Chippenham Town	0-2
34	Frome Town v Minehead	1-3
	Glastonbury v Weston-Super-Mare	2-5
35	Cheltenham Town v Abergavenny Thursdays	7-2
	Gloucester City v Merthyr Tydfil	2-2
	Lovells Athletic v Barry Town	1-1
	Stonehouse v Llanelli	1-1
36	Barnstaple Town v St Austell	4-2
1r	Billingham Synthonia v Ashington	0-2
3r	Horden CW v Bishop Auckland	2-1
5r	Skelmersdale United v Marine	3-0
6r	New Brighton v Stork	2-2e
11r	Goole Town v Selby Town	3-2
r	Harrogate Town v Bridlington Town	0-2
r	Yorkshire Amateur v Farsley Celtic	0-4
13r	Sutton Town v Buxton	2-0e
14r	Boston United v Holbeach United	0-1
15r	Atherstone Town v Long Eaton United	1-3
21r	Crawley Town v Haywards Heath	7-2
r	Lancing v Worthing	3-2
22r	Tunbridge Wells United v Eastbourne	2-0
24r	Ware v Harlow Town	0-0e
27r	Hemel Hempstead Town v Newbury Town	6-0
28r	Southall v Yiewsley	0-3
29r	Erith & Belvedere v Sittingbourne	1-2
35r	Barry Town v Lovells Athletic	3-1
r	Llanelli v Stonehouse	1-0
r	Merthyr Tydfil v Gloucester City	2-3
6r2	New Brighton v Stork	3-0
24r2	Ware v Harlow Town	2-1e

Qualifying Round Two

1	Stanley United v Ashington	3-0
	Whitby Town v Spennymoor United	2-2
2	Scarborough v North Shields	2-1
	Tow Law Town v Whitley Bay	3-1
3	Ferryhill Athletic v Ryhope CW	4-1
	Horden CW v West Auckland Town	1-0
4	Fleetwood v Lancaster City	1-2
	Netherfield (Kendal) v Burscough	2-0
5	Ashton United v South Liverpool	2-2
	Skelmersdale United v Altrincham	0-3
6	Borough United v New Brighton	1-1
	Runcorn v Bangor City	1-2
7	Chorley v Nelson	6-1
	Lytham v Hyde United	1-1
8	Lostock Gralam v Northwich Victoria	4-4
	Mossley v Macclesfield Town	0-5
9	Nuneaton Borough v Halesowen Town	2-1
	Rugby Town (2) v Lockheed Leamington	1-1
10	Moor Green v Kidderminster Harriers	1-2
	Wellington Town v Worcester City	0-1
11	Bridlington Town v Goole Town	4-1
	Frickley Colliery v Farsley Celtic	3-0
12	Norton Woodseats v Gainsborough Trinity	1-6
	Worksop Town v Retford Town	2-0
13	Belper Town v Matlock Town	2-3
	Heanor Town v Sutton Town	5-1
14	Grantham v Holbeach United	2-0
	Skegness Town v Stamford	2-4
15	Ilkeston Town (2) v Loughborough United	1-1
	Tamworth v Long Eaton United	3-1
16	Corby Town v Bourne Town	4-2
	Rushden Town v Wellingborough Town	0-2
17	Biggleswade Town v St Albans City	5-4
	Letchworth Town v Hitchin Town	1-2
18	Chatteris Town v Bury Town	0-5
	Sudbury Town v Cambridge City	2-4
19	Bungay Town v Great Yarmouth Town	2-2
	Harwich & Parkeston v Lowestoft Town	3-2
20	Canterbury City v Ramsgate Athletic	0-1
	Folkestone v Sheppey United	2-0
21	Lewes v Lancing	3-0
	Littlehampton Town v Crawley Town	0-4
22	Hastings United v Tonbridge	2-5
	Tunbridge Wells United v Maidstone United	1-3
23	Barking v Ilford	1-2
	Tilbury v Aveley	3-3
24	Barnet v Hertford Town	3-1
	Ware v Harrow Town	2-1
25	Carshalton Athletic v Tooting & Mitcham United	0-3
	Epsom & Ewell v Walthamstow Avenue	0-8
26	Leatherhead v Kingstonian	3-2
	Woking v Guildford City	0-2
27	Banbury Spencer v Maidenhead United	2-3
	Hemel Hempstead Town v Oxford City	5-0
28	Hayes v Finchley	3-1
	Uxbridge v Yiewsley	0-0
29	Bexley United v Bromley	0-0
	Sittingbourne v Cray Wanderers	1-1
30	Dagenham v Hornchurch	2-0
	Hendon v Clapton	8-0
31	Andover v Cowes	1-1
	Chichester City (1) v Basingstoke Town	1-2
32	Dorchester Town v Bridport	1-0
	Warminster Town v Salisbury (2)	2-2
33	Trowbridge Town v Chippenham Town	1-1
	Westbury United v Welton Rovers	0-3
34	Minehead v Weston-Super-Mare	3-1
	Taunton v Bridgwater Town (1)	1-3
35	Barry Town v Llanelli	0-1
	Gloucester City v Cheltenham Town	1-2
36	Bideford v Barnstaple Town	2-0
	Wadebridge Town v St Blazey	1-1
1r	Spennymoor United v Whitby Town	0-2
5r	South Liverpool v Ashton United	3-1
6r	New Brighton v Borough United	3-1
7r	Hyde United v Lytham	5-0
8r	Northwich Victoria v Lostock Gralam	4-0
9r	Lockheed Leamington v Rugby Town (2)	2-2e
15r	Loughborough United v Ilkeston Town (2)	4-0
19r	Great Yarmouth Town v Bungay Town	2-1
23r	Aveley v Tilbury	2-1
28r	Yiewsley v Uxbridge	2-1e
29r	Bromley v Bexley United	2-2e
r	Cray Wanderers v Sittingbourne	0-1
31r	Cowes v Andover	4-2
32r	Salisbury (2) v Warminster Town	4-0
33r	Chippenham Town v Trowbridge Town	2-4
36r	St Blazey v Wadebridge Town	8-1
9r2	Rugby Town (2) v Lockheed Leamington	1-2
29r2	Bexley United v Bromley	1-0

Qualifying Round Three

1	Stanley United v Whitby Town	2-0
2	Scarborough v Tow Law Town	0-2
3	Horden CW v Ferryhill Athletic	3-2
4	Netherfield (Kendal) v Lancaster City	2-0
5	Altrincham v South Liverpool	3-0
6	Bangor City v New Brighton	2-0
7	Chorley v Hyde United	2-0
8	Northwich Victoria v Macclesfield Town	1-1
9	Nuneaton Borough v Lockheed Leamington	0-2
10	Worcester City v Kidderminster Harriers	4-1
11	Frickley Colliery v Bridlington Town	1-0
12	Worksop Town v Gainsborough Trinity	1-3
13	Matlock Town v Heanor Town	0-1
14	Grantham v Stamford	4-2
15	Tamworth v Loughborough United	0-0
16	Corby Town v Wellingborough Town	3-1
17	Biggleswade Town v Hitchin Town	2-2e
18	Bury Town v Cambridge City	0-3
19	Harwich & Parkeston v Great Yarmouth Town	2-1
20	Ramsgate Athletic v Folkestone	1-3
21	Crawley Town v Lewes	0-2
22	Maidstone United v Tonbridge	1-5
23	Aveley v Ilford	0-1
24	Ware v Barnet	1-6
25	Walthamstow Avenue v Tooting & Mitcham United	3-6
26	Guildford City v Leatherhead	5-1
27	Maidenhead United v Hemel Hempstead Town	2-1
28	Hayes v Yiewsley	2-0
29	Sittingbourne v Bexley United	0-2
30	Hendon v Dagenham	3-0
31	Cowes v Basingstoke Town	3-1
32	Dorchester Town v Salisbury (2)	1-1
33	Trowbridge Town v Welton Rovers	3-0
34	Minehead v Bridgwater Town (1)	0-1
35	Cheltenham Town v Llanelli	0-1
36	Bideford v St Blazey	3-1
8r	Macclesfield Town v Northwich Victoria	1-0
15r	Loughborough United v Tamworth	2-0
17r	Hitchin Town v Biggleswade Town	5-1
32r	Salisbury (2) v Dorchester Town	1-3

Qualifying Round Four

Altrincham v Rhyl	3-1
Barnet v Wycombe Wanderers	6-3
Bath City v Falmouth Town	2-0
Bedford Town (1) v Cambridge City	2-2
Blyth Spartans v Tow Law Town	1-0
Bridgwater Town (1) v Llanelli	0-0
Cambridge United v Hitchin Town	4-1
Chelmsford City v Romford (2)	2-0
Cowes v Yeovil Town	0-1
Enfield v Hendon	3-1
Folkestone v Ashford Town	3-0
Gateshead v South Shields (2)	5-3
Gravesend & Northfleet v Lewes	2-1
Guildford City v Bexley United	0-0
Harwich & Parkeston v King's Lynn	4-0
Hayes v Tooting & Mitcham United	1-2
Heanor Town v Gainsborough Trinity	2-0
Hereford United v Hinckley Athletic	1-1
Horden CW v Netherfield (Kendal)	0-3

1963/64 to 1964/65

Ilford v Maidenhead United	1-3
Kettering Town v Grantham	3-1
Lockheed Leamington v Corby Town	2-2
Loughborough United v Worcester City	4-1
Macclesfield Town v Frickley Colliery	1-3
Margate v Tonbridge	2-1
Morecambe v Chorley	3-4
Stanley United v Crook Town	0-2
Trowbridge Town v Bideford	2-2
Weymouth v Dorchester Town	3-0
Wigan Athletic v Bangor City	1-1
r Bangor City v Wigan Athletic	1-0
r Bexley United v Guildford City	3-0
r Bideford v Trowbridge Town	2-4
r Cambridge City v Bedford Town (1)	2-3
r Corby Town v Lockheed Leamington	2-0
r Hinckley Athletic v Hereford United	1-1e
r Llanelli v Bridgwater Town (1)	0-1
r2 Hereford United v Hinckley Athletic	3-2eN

Round One

Altrincham v Wrexham	0-0
Barnsley v Stockport County	1-0
Barrow v Bangor City	3-2
Bexley United v Wimbledon	1-5
Bournemouth v Bristol Rovers	1-3
Bradford City v Port Vale	1-2
Bradford Park Avenue v Heanor Town	3-1
Brentford v Margate	2-2
Bridgwater Town (1) v Luton Town	0-3
Brighton & Hove Albion v Colchester United	0-1
Cambridge United v Chelmsford City	0-1
Chester v Blyth Spartans	3-2
Corby Town v Bristol City	1-3
Crook Town v Chesterfield	1-2
Crystal Palace v Harwich & Parkeston	8-2
Darlington v Gateshead	1-4
Doncaster Rovers v Tranmere Rovers	3-0
Exeter City v Shrewsbury Town	2-1
Hartlepools United v Lincoln City	0-1
Hereford United v Newport County	1-1
Hull City v Crewe Alexandra	2-2
Kettering Town v Millwall	1-1
Maidenhead United v Bath City	0-2
Netherfield (Kendal) v Loughborough United	6-1
Notts County v Frickley Colliery	2-1
Oldham Athletic v Mansfield Town	3-2
Oxford United v Folkestone	2-0
Peterborough United v Watford	1-1
Queen's Park Rangers v Gillingham	4-1
Reading v Enfield	2-2
Rochdale v Chorley	2-1
Southport v Walsall	2-1
Sutton United v Aldershot	0-4
Tooting & Mitcham United v Gravesend & Northfleet	1-2
Torquay United v Barnet	6-2
Trowbridge Town v Coventry City	1-6
Weymouth v Bedford Town (1)	1-1
Workington v Halifax Town	4-1
Yeovil Town v Southend United	1-0
York City v Carlisle United	2-5
r Bedford Town (1) v Weymouth	1-0
r Crewe Alexandra v Hull City	0-3
r Enfield v Reading	2-4e
r Margate v Brentford	0-2
r Millwall v Kettering Town	2-3
r Newport County v Hereford United	4-0
r Watford v Peterborough United	2-1e
r Wrexham v Altrincham	3-0

Round Two

Barnsley v Rochdale	3-1
Brentford v Gravesend & Northfleet	1-0
Carlisle United v Gateshead	4-3
Chelmsford City v Bedford Town (1)	0-1
Chester v Barrow	0-2
Colchester United v Queen's Park Rangers	0-1
Coventry City v Bristol Rovers	1-2
Doncaster Rovers v Notts County	1-1
Exeter City v Bristol City	0-2
Lincoln City v Southport	2-0
Luton Town v Reading	2-1
Netherfield (Kendal) v Chesterfield	1-1
Newport County v Watford	2-0
Oldham Athletic v Bradford Park Avenue	2-0
Oxford United v Kettering Town	2-1
Port Vale v Workington	2-1
Torquay United v Aldershot	2-3
Wimbledon v Bath City	2-2
Wrexham v Hull City	0-2
Yeovil Town v Crystal Palace	3-1
r Bath City v Wimbledon	4-0
r Chesterfield v Netherfield (Kendal)	4-1
r Notts County v Doncaster Rovers	1-2

Round Three

Arsenal v Wolverhampton Wan.	2-1
Aston Villa v Aldershot	0-0
Bath City v Bolton Wanderers	1-1
Birmingham City v Port Vale	1-2
Blackburn Rovers v Grimsby Town	4-0
Brentford v Middlesbrough	2-1
Bristol Rovers v Norwich City	2-1
Burnley v Rotherham United	1-1
Cardiff City v Leeds United	0-1
Carlisle United v Queen's Park Rangers	2-0
Doncaster Rovers v Bristol City	2-2
Fulham v Luton Town	4-1
Hull City v Everton	1-1
Ipswich Town v Oldham Athletic	6-3
Leicester City v Leyton Orient	2-3
Lincoln City v Sheffield United	0-4
Liverpool v Derby County	5-0
Newcastle United v Bedford Town (1)	1-2
Newport County v Sheffield Wednesday	3-2
Nottingham Forest v Preston North End	0-0
Oxford United v Chesterfield	1-0
Plymouth Argyle v Huddersfield Town	0-1
Scunthorpe United v Barnsley	2-2
Southampton v Manchester United	2-3
Stoke City v Portsmouth	4-1
Sunderland v Northampton Town	2-0
Swansea Town v Barrow	4-1
Swindon Town v Manchester City	2-1
Tottenham Hotspur v Chelsea	1-1
West Bromwich Albion v Blackpool	2-2
West Ham United v Charlton Athletic	3-0
Yeovil Town v Crystal Palace	0-2
r Aldershot v Aston Villa	2-1
r Barnsley v Scunthorpe United	3-2e
r Blackpool v West Bromwich Albion	0-1
r Bolton Wanderers v Bath City	3-0
r Bristol City v Doncaster Rovers	2-0
r Chelsea v Tottenham Hotspur	2-0
r Everton v Hull City	2-1
r Preston North End v Nottingham Forest	1-0
r Rotherham United v Burnley	2-3

Round Four

Aldershot v Swindon Town	1-2
Barnsley v Bury	2-1
Bedford Town (1) v Carlisle United	0-3
Blackburn Rovers v Fulham	2-0
Bolton Wanderers v Preston North End	2-2
Burnley v Newport County	2-1
Chelsea v Huddersfield Town	1-2
Ipswich Town v Stoke City	1-1
Leeds United v Everton	1-1
Leyton Orient v West Ham United	1-1
Liverpool v Port Vale	0-0
Manchester United v Bristol Rovers	4-1
Oxford United v Brentford	2-2
Sheffield United v Swansea Town	1-1
Sunderland v Bristol City	6-1
West Bromwich Albion v Arsenal	3-3
r Arsenal v West Bromwich Albion	2-0
r Brentford v Oxford United	1-2
r Everton v Leeds United	2-0
r Port Vale v Liverpool	1-2e
r Preston North End v Bolton Wanderers	2-1
r Stoke City v Ipswich Town	1-0
r Swansea Town v Sheffield United	4-0
r West Ham United v Leyton Orient	3-0

Round Five

Arsenal v Liverpool	0-1
Barnsley v Manchester United	0-4
Burnley v Huddersfield Town	3-0
Oxford United v Blackburn Rovers	3-1
Preston North End v Carlisle United	1-0
Stoke City v Swansea Town	2-2
Sunderland v Everton	3-1
Swindon Town v West Ham United	1-3
r Swansea Town v Stoke City	2-0

Round Six

Liverpool v Swansea Town	1-2
Manchester United v Sunderland	3-3
Oxford United v Preston North End	1-2
West Ham United v Burnley	3-2
r Sunderland v Manchester United	2-2e
r2 Sunderland v Manchester United	1-5 N

Semi Finals

Preston North End v Swansea Town	2-1 N
West Ham United v Manchester United	3-1 N

Final

West Ham United v Preston North End	3-2 N

1964/65

1 Consett v Boldon CW	5-1
Penrith v Willington	4-2
South Bank v Evenwood Town	1-4
2 Bishop Auckland v Shildon	4-1
Ferryhill Athletic v Billingham Synthonia	5-0
Murton CW v North Shields	2-5
3 Annfield Plain v Durham City	2-0
Ryhope CW v Stanley United	3-2
4 Clitheroe v Morecambe	1-2
Fleetwood v Milnthorpe Corinthians	3-0
Horwich RMI v Accrington (2)	5-2
Lancaster City v Burscough	1-1
Marine v Altrincham	1-3
Skelmersdale United v Droylsden	0-0
South Liverpool v Ashton United	2-1
St Helens Town v Prescot Cables	4-1
6 Ellesmere Port Town v Rhyl	6-1
New Brighton v Llandudno	8-3
Runcorn v Holyhead Town	5-2
Stork v Borough United	0-4
7 Hyde United v Bacup Borough	9-0
Nelson v Lytham	2-1
Rossendale United v Great Harwood	1-0
Stalybridge Celtic v Chorley	5-1
8 Macclesfield Town v Oswestry Town	2-0
Northwich Victoria v Mossley	5-2
Winsford United v Congleton Town	2-1
Witton Albion v Lostock Gralam	4-0
9 Halesowen Town v Bilston	1-1
Lockheed Leamington v Hednesford Town	4-3
Rugby Town (2) v Moor Green	4-0
Stourbridge v Brierley Hill Alliance	3-2
10 Kidderminster Harriers v Redditch	1-1
Stafford Rangers v Sankey of Wellington	3-3
Wellington Town v Dudley Town	1-3
Worcester City v Bromsgrove Rovers	4-0
11 Farsley Celtic v Scarborough	0-0
Ossett Albion v Harrogate Town	3-0
Selby Town v Bridlington Trinity	1-5
Yorkshire Amateur v Bridlington Town	0-1
12 Gainsborough Trinity v Goole Town	1-3
Retford Town v Norton Woodseats	5-1
Stocksbridge Works v Frickley Colliery	1-4
Worksop Town v Mexborough Town	2-1
13 Belper Town v Alfreton Town	2-2
Heanor Town v Buxton	2-1
Matlock Town v Creswell Colliery	4-1
Sutton Town v Arnold	2-2
14 Boston United v Spalding United	0-14
Louth United v Holbeach United	2-5
Stamford v Skegness Town	1-1
15 Gresley Rovers v Atherstone Town	3-5
Long Eaton United v Ilkeston Town (2)	1-3
Loughborough United v Nuneaton Borough	1-2
Tamworth v Burton Albion	2-0
16 Desborough Town v Bourne Town	2-1
Rushden Town v Rothwell Town	2-3
Wellingborough Town v St Neots Town	0-2
17 Hitchin Town v Biggleswade Town	2-2
St Albans City v Letchworth Town	3-2
Vauxhall Motors (Luton) v Cheshunt	0-2
Wolverton Town & BR v Bletchley Town	0-1
18 Bury Town v Soham Town Rangers	2-1
Chatteris Town v Cambridge City	1-2
Ely City v Haverhill Rovers	5-1
March Town United v Wisbech Town	1-3
19 Clacton Town v Gorleston	9-1
Sudbury Town v Great Yarmouth Town	1-0
20 Dover v Canterbury City	0-2
Ramsgate Athletic v Folkestone	1-2
Sheppey United v Ashford Town	0-1
Whitstable v Deal Town	2-7
21 Bognor Regis Town v Redhill	1-3
Horsham v Haywards Heath	3-3
Littlehampton Town v Lewes	1-3
22 Eastbourne v Bexhill Town	4-0
Maidstone United v Hastings United	1-3
Tunbridge Wells Rangers v Tonbridge	1-3
23 Barking v Walthamstow Avenue	1-2
Grays Athletic v Brentwood & Warley	0-2
Ilford v Hornchurch	3-4
Tilbury v Aveley	1-1
24 Harlow Town v Barnet	0-2
Hertford Town v Harrow Town	2-0
Stevenage Town v Hatfield Town	5-0
Ware v Bishop's Stortford	1-3
25 Dulwich Hamlet v Wokingham Town	0-0
Marlow v Epsom & Ewell	1-7
Slough Town v Metropolitan Police	4-1
Tooting & Mitcham United v Carshalton Athletic	1-4
26 Kingstonian v Dorking	2-0
Petter Sports v Leatherhead	0-5
Walton & Hersham v Chertsey Town	4-1
Woking v Guildford City	1-3
27 Chesham United v Aylesbury United	5-0
Huntley & Palmers v Hemel Hempstead Town	0-6
Newbury Town v Abingdon Town	2-0
Oxford City v Banbury Spencer	2-1
28 Hillingdon Borough v Hayes	1-2
Hounslow v Finchley	1-4
Uxbridge v Southall	0-3
Windsor & Eton v Corinthian Casuals	2-2
29 Chatham Town v Bromley	3-1
Dartford v Cray Wanderers	5-0
Erith & Belvedere v Sutton United	0-4
Sittingbourne v Bexley United	0-3
30 Ford United v Clapton	3-1
Leyton v Hendon	2-3
Leytonstone v Ruislip Manor	7-1
Wembley v Dagenham	2-2

1964/65

31	Andover v Alton Town	4-1
	Cowes v Chichester City (1)	5-4
	Newport (IOW) v Fareham Town	1-5
32	Poole Town v Bridport	2-0
	Salisbury (2) v Dorchester Town	3-3
33	Melksham Town v Cheltenham Town	0-4
	Trowbridge Town v Chippenham Town	3-1
34	Minehead v Weston-Super-Mare	2-1
	Taunton v Frome Town	0-1
35	Barry Town v Stonehouse	2-1
	Gloucester City v Abergavenny Thursdays	3-1
	Lovells Athletic v Llanelli	1-1
	Merthyr Tydfil v Cinderford Town	4-1
36	Newton Abbot Spurs v Falmouth Town	1-1
	St Austell v Bideford	3-5
	Wadebridge Town v St Blazey	2-6
4r	Burscough v Lancaster City	1-2
5r	Droylsden v Skelmersdale United	1-2
9r	Bilston v Halesowen Town	0-3
10r	Sankey of Wellington v Stafford Rangers	3-0
11r	Scarborough v Farsley Celtic	0-0e
13r	Alfreton Town v Belper Town	0-3
r	Arnold v Sutton Town	2-0
14r	Skegness Town v Stamford	4-0
17r	Biggleswade Town v Hitchin Town	2-4
21r	Haywards Heath v Horsham	1-2
23r	Aveley v Tilbury	2-0
25r	Wokingham Town v Dulwich Hamlet	2-0
28r	Corinthian Casuals v Windsor & Eton	1-2
30r	Dagenham v Wembley	3-0
32r	Dorchester Town v Salisbury (2)	1-3
35r	Llanelli v Lovells Athletic	2-1
36r	Falmouth Town v Newton Abbot Spurs	3-2
11r2	Scarborough v Farsley Celtic	5-0

Qualifying Round Two

1	Penrith v Evenwood Town	3-1
	Stockton v Consett	2-3
2	Bishop Auckland v North Shields	2-3
	Horden CW v Ferryhill Athletic	4-1
3	Ashington v Tow Law Town	0-0
	Ryhope CW v Annfield Plain	1-1
4	Horwich RMI v Lancaster City	1-1
	Morecambe v Fleetwood	6-1
5	Altrincham v St Helens Town	4-1
	Skelmersdale United v South Liverpool	2-2
6	Ellesmere Port Town v New Brighton	4-0
	Runcorn v Borough United	0-2
7	Hyde United v Nelson	1-3
	Rossendale United v Stalybridge Celtic	0-3
8	Macclesfield Town v Northwich Victoria	4-1
	Winsford United v Witton Albion	1-1
9	Halesowen Town v Lockheed Leamington	2-4
	Rugby Town (2) v Stourbridge	5-0
10	Dudley Town v Worcester City	0-3
	Kidderminster Harriers v Sankey of Wellington	3-0
11	Bridlington Trinity v Bridlington Town	4-4
	Scarborough v Ossett Albion	2-1
12	Frickley Colliery v Worksop Town	2-0
	Goole Town v Retford Town	0-1
13	Belper Town v Heanor Town	2-1
	Matlock Town v Arnold	1-3
14	Grantham v Holbeach United	1-1
	Skegness Town v Spalding United	0-3
15	Atherstone Town v Ilkeston Town (2)	4-2
	Nuneaton Borough v Tamworth	2-1
16	Eynesbury Rovers v Rothwell Town	3-1
	St Neots Town v Desborough Town	3-0
17	Cheshunt v Bletchley Town	1-1
	Hitchin Town v St Albans City	4-0
18	Bury Town v Cambridge City	0-2
	Ely City v Wisbech Town	0-2
19	Clacton Town v Sudbury Town	0-0
	Harwich & Parkeston v Lowestoft Town	2-3
20	Ashford Town v Deal Town	2-2
	Canterbury City v Folkestone	3-1
21	Crawley Town v Horsham	5-0
	Lewes v Redhill	2-2
22	Eastbourne United v Hastings United	1-7
	Tonbridge v Eastbourne	2-0
23	Hornchurch v Aveley	4-0
	Walthamstow Avenue v Brentwood & Warley	1-0
24	Barnet v Hertford Town	0-0
	Stevenage Town v Bishop's Stortford	4-1
25	Slough Town v Carshalton Athletic	2-0
	Wokingham Town v Epsom & Ewell	2-4
26	Kingstonian v Leatherhead	1-1
	Walton & Hersham v Guildford City	1-5
27	Chesham United v Hemel Hempstead Town	1-1
	Newbury Town v Oxford City	0-2
28	Finchley v Southall	4-0
	Windsor & Eton v Hayes	0-1
29	Chatham Town v Dartford	2-4
	Sutton United v Bexley United	1-1
30	Ford United v Hendon	2-5
	Leytonstone v Dagenham	4-0
31	Basingstoke Town v Cowes	4-2
	Fareham Town v Andover	2-1
32	Salisbury (2) v Poole Town	1-1
	Warminster Town v Portland United	1-3
33	Trowbridge Town v Cheltenham Town	1-3
	Westbury United v Devizes Town	0-3
34	Frome Town v Minehead	1-3
	Welton Rovers v Glastonbury	4-0
35	Gloucester City v Llanelli	0-1
	Merthyr Tydfil v Barry Town	4-0
36	Barnstaple Town v Bideford	0-0
	St Blazey v Falmouth Town	2-1
3r	Annfield Plain v Ryhope CW	2-0
r	Tow Law Town v Ashington	0-0
4r	Lancaster City v Horwich RMI	2-1
5r	South Liverpool v Skelmersdale United	5-3
8r	Witton Albion v Winsford United	2-1
11r	Bridlington Town v Bridlington Trinity	3-1
14r	Holbeach United v Grantham	0-1
17r	Bletchley Town v Cheshunt	1-0
19r	Sudbury Town v Clacton Town	4-2
20r	Deal Town v Ashford Town	4-2
21r	Redhill v Lewes	4-3
24r	Hertford Town v Barnet	0-2
26r	Leatherhead v Kingstonian	1-0
27r	Hemel Hempstead Town v Chesham United	3-2
29r	Bexley United v Sutton United	3-1
32r	Poole Town v Salisbury (2)	0-1
36r	Bideford v Barnstaple Town	3-0
3r2	Ashington v Tow Law Town	1-2

Qualifying Round Three

1	Penrith v Consett	3-3
2	North Shields v Horden CW	0-2
3	Annfield Plain v Tow Law Town	3-2
4	Morecambe v Lancaster City	1-2
5	Altrincham v South Liverpool	0-3
6	Ellesmere Port Town v Borough United	4-0
7	Nelson v Stalybridge Celtic	2-3
8	Macclesfield Town v Witton Albion	2-1
9	Lockheed Leamington v Rugby Town (2)	2-3
10	Kidderminster Harriers v Worcester City	2-2
11	Scarborough v Bridlington Town	3-1
12	Retford Town v Frickley Colliery	3-0
13	Belper Town v Arnold	3-3
14	Spalding United v Grantham	4-0
15	Atherstone Town v Nuneaton Borough	1-1
16	St Neots Town v Eynesbury Rovers	7-0
17	Hitchin Town v Bletchley Town	0-4
18	Cambridge City v Wisbech Town	1-2
19	Sudbury Town v Lowestoft Town	0-5
20	Canterbury City v Deal Town	4-1
21	Redhill v Crawley Town	1-6
22	Tonbridge v Hastings United	3-0
23	Walthamstow Avenue v Hornchurch	3-1
24	Barnet v Stevenage Town	2-0
25	Epsom & Ewell v Slough Town	0-1
26	Leatherhead v Guildford City	1-2
27	Hemel Hempstead Town v Oxford City	1-1
28	Finchley v Hayes	1-2
29	Dartford v Bexley United	3-1
30	Hendon v Leytonstone	2-1
31	Fareham Town v Basingstoke Town	3-3
32	Salisbury (2) v Portland United	5-1
33	Cheltenham Town v Devizes Town	6-1
34	Minehead v Welton Rovers	0-3
35	Llanelli v Merthyr Tydfil	2-7
36	St Blazey v Bideford	0-3
1r	Consett v Penrith	1-0
10r	Worcester City v Kidderminster Harriers	1-2
13r	Arnold v Belper Town	1-0
15r	Nuneaton Borough v Atherstone Town	2-5
27r	Oxford City v Hemel Hempstead Town	4-2
31r	Basingstoke Town v Fareham Town	1-2

Qualifying Round Four

	Annfield Plain v Horden CW	3-2
	Arnold v Corby Town	0-2
	Atherstone Town v Hereford United	1-3
	Barnet v Walthamstow Avenue	3-3
	Bath City v Merthyr Tydfil	4-1
	Bedford Town (1) v Cambridge United	1-4
	Bideford v Cheltenham Town	1-0
	Canterbury City v Crawley Town	3-0
	Chelmsford City v Oxford City	6-2
	Consett v South Shields (2)	0-4
	Dartford v Tonbridge	3-1
	Gateshead v Netherfield (Kendal)	1-4
	Gravesend & Northfleet v Margate	1-0
	Guildford City v Maidenhead United	9-0
	Hayes v Wycombe Wanderers	7-0
	Hendon v Slough Town	3-1
	Kidderminster Harriers v Rugby Town (2)	5-1
	King's Lynn v St Neots Town	6-0
	Lancaster City v Bangor City	2-3
	Lowestoft Town v Kettering Town	1-3
	Macclesfield Town v Ellesmere Port Town	2-1
	Retford Town v South Liverpool	2-3
	Salisbury (2) v Yeovil Town	2-1
	Scarborough v Blyth Spartans	4-3
	Spalding United v Hinckley Athletic	3-1
	Stalybridge Celtic v Wigan Athletic	2-4
	Welton Rovers v Bridgwater Town (1)	1-0
	Weymouth v Fareham Town	3-2
	Wimbledon v Romford (2)	1-1
	Wisbech Town v Bletchley Town	3-2
r	Romford (2) v Wimbledon	2-1
r	Walthamstow Avenue v Barnet	1-4

Round One

	Barnet v Cambridge United	2-1
	Barrow v Grimsby Town	1-1
	Bournemouth v Gravesend & Northfleet	7-0
	Bradford Park Avenue v Doncaster Rovers	2-3
	Bristol City v Brighton & Hove Albion	1-0
	Canterbury City v Torquay United	0-6
	Chester v Crewe Alexandra	5-0
	Chesterfield v South Shields (2)	2-0
	Colchester United v Bideford	3-3
	Corby Town v Hartlepools United	1-3
	Crook Town v Carlisle United	1-0
	Dartford v Aldershot	1-1
	Exeter City v Hayes	1-0
	Guildford City v Gillingham	2-2
	Halifax Town v South Liverpool	2-2
	Kidderminster Harriers v Hull City	1-4
	King's Lynn v Shrewsbury Town	0-1
	Luton Town v Southend United	1-0
	Macclesfield Town v Wrexham	1-2
	Millwall v Kettering Town	2-0
	Netherfield (Kendal) v Barnsley	1-3
	Newport County v Spalding United	5-3
	Notts County v Chelmsford City	2-0
	Oldham Athletic v Hereford United	4-0
	Oxford United v Mansfield Town	0-1
	Peterborough United v Salisbury (2)	5-1
	Port Vale v Hendon	2-1
	Queen's Park Rangers v Bath City	2-0
	Reading v Watford	3-1
	Romford (2) v Enfield	0-0
	Scarborough v Bradford City	1-0
	Scunthorpe United v Darlington	1-2
	Southport v Annfield Plain	6-1
	Stockport County v Wigan Athletic	2-1
	Tranmere Rovers v Lincoln City	0-0
	Walsall v Bristol Rovers	0-2
	Welton Rovers v Weymouth	1-1
	Wisbech Town v Brentford	0-2
	Workington v Rochdale	2-0
	York City v Bangor City	5-1
r	Aldershot v Dartford	1-0
r	Bideford v Colchester United	1-2
r	Enfield v Romford (2)	0-0e
r	Gillingham v Guildford City	1-0
r	Grimsby Town v Barrow	2-2e
r	Lincoln City v Tranmere Rovers	1-0
r	South Liverpool v Halifax Town	4-2
r	Weymouth v Welton Rovers	4-3
r2	Barrow v Grimsby Town	0-2 N
r2	Romford (2) v Enfield	2-4 N

Round Two

	Aldershot v Reading	1-3
	Barnsley v Chester	2-5
	Bournemouth v Bristol City	0-3
	Brentford v Notts County	4-0
	Bristol Rovers v Weymouth	4-1
	Chesterfield v York City	2-1
	Crook Town v Oldham Athletic	0-1
	Doncaster Rovers v Scarborough	0-0
	Enfield v Barnet	4-4
	Exeter City v Shrewsbury Town	1-2
	Hartlepools United v Darlington	0-0
	Hull City v Lincoln City	1-1
	Luton Town v Gillingham	1-0
	Millwall v Port Vale	4-0
	Newport County v Mansfield Town	3-0
	Queen's Park Rangers v Peterborough United	3-3
	South Liverpool v Workington	0-2
	Stockport County v Grimsby Town	1-0
	Torquay United v Colchester United	2-0
	Wrexham v Southport	2-3
r	Barnet v Enfield	3-0
r	Darlington v Hartlepools United	4-1
r	Lincoln City v Hull City	3-1
r	Peterborough United v Queen's Park Rangers	2-1
r	Scarborough v Doncaster Rovers	1-2

Round Three

	Aston Villa v Coventry City	3-0
	Barnet v Preston North End	2-3
	Bolton Wanderers v Workington	4-1
	Bristol City v Sheffield United	1-1
	Bristol Rovers v Stockport County	0-0
	Burnley v Brentford	1-1
	Cardiff City v Charlton Athletic	1-2
	Chelsea v Northampton Town	4-1
	Chesterfield v Peterborough United	0-3
	Crystal Palace v Bury	5-1
	Darlington v Arsenal	0-2
	Doncaster Rovers v Huddersfield Town	0-1
	Everton v Sheffield Wednesday	2-2
	Fulham v Millwall	3-3
	Leeds United v Southport	3-0
	Leicester City v Blackburn Rovers	2-2
	Luton Town v Sunderland	0-3
	Manchester City v Shrewsbury Town	1-1
	Manchester United v Chester	2-1
	Middlesbrough v Oldham Athletic	6-2
	Nottingham Forest v Norwich City	1-0
	Plymouth Argyle v Derby County	4-2

1964/65 to 1965/66

Portsmouth v Wolverhampton Wan.	0-0
Reading v Newport County	2-2
Rotherham United v Lincoln City	5-1
Southampton v Leyton Orient	3-1
Stoke City v Blackpool	4-1
Swansea Town v Newcastle United	1-0
Swindon Town v Ipswich Town	1-2
Torquay United v Tottenham Hotspur	3-3
West Bromwich Albion v Liverpool	1-2
West Ham United v Birmingham City	4-2
r Blackburn Rovers v Leicester City	1-2
r Brentford v Burnley	0-2
r Millwall v Fulham	2-0
r Newport County v Reading	0-1
r Sheffield United v Bristol City	3-0
r Sheffield Wednesday v Everton	0-3
r Shrewsbury Town v Manchester City	3-1
r Stockport County v Bristol Rovers	3-2
r Tottenham Hotspur v Torquay United	5-1
r Wolverhampton Wan. v Portsmouth	3-2

Round Four

Charlton Athletic v Middlesbrough	1-1
Leeds United v Everton	1-1
Leicester City v Plymouth Argyle	5-0
Liverpool v Stockport County	1-1
Millwall v Shrewsbury Town	1-2
Peterborough United v Arsenal	2-1
Preston North End v Bolton Wanderers	1-2
Reading v Burnley	1-1
Sheffield United v Aston Villa	0-2
Southampton v Crystal Palace	1-2
Stoke City v Manchester United	0-0
Sunderland v Nottingham Forest	1-3
Swansea Town v Huddersfield Town	1-0
Tottenham Hotspur v Ipswich Town	5-0
West Ham United v Chelsea	0-1
Wolverhampton Wan. v Rotherham United	2-2
r Burnley v Reading	1-0
r Everton v Leeds United	1-2
r Manchester United v Stoke City	1-0
r Middlesbrough v Charlton Athletic	2-1
r Rotherham United v Wolverhampton Wan.	0-3
r Stockport County v Liverpool	0-2

Round Five

Aston Villa v Wolverhampton Wan.	1-1
Bolton Wanderers v Liverpool	0-1
Chelsea v Tottenham Hotspur	1-0
Crystal Palace v Nottingham Forest	3-1
Leeds United v Shrewsbury Town	2-0
Manchester United v Burnley	2-1
Middlesbrough v Leicester City	0-3
Peterborough United v Swansea Town	0-0
r Swansea Town v Peterborough United	0-2
r Wolverhampton Wan. v Aston Villa	0-0e
r2 Aston Villa v Wolverhampton Wan.	1-3 N

Round Six

Chelsea v Peterborough United	5-1
Crystal Palace v Leeds United	0-3
Leicester City v Liverpool	0-0
Wolverhampton Wan. v Manchester United	3-5
r Liverpool v Leicester City	1-0

Semi Finals

Leeds United v Manchester United	0-0 N
Liverpool v Chelsea	2-0 N
r Manchester United v Leeds United	0-1 N

Final

Liverpool v Leeds United	2-1eN

1965/66

Qualifying Round One

1 Blyth Spartans v Ryhope CW	4-3
Ferryhill Athletic v Stanley United	1-3
Shildon v Horden CW	0-4
Whitley Bay v Annfield Plain	11-0
2 Billingham Synthonia v Whitby Town	1-2
Bishop Auckland v South Bank	5-1
Durham City v Willington	0-8
Spennymoor United v North Shields	2-0
3 Ashington v West Auckland Town	3-1
Boldon CW v Tow Law Town	2-1
Consett v Murton CW	7-0
Stockton v Evenwood Town	3-0
4 Clitheroe v Lancaster City	2-0
Horwich RMI v Burscough	2-1
Milnthorpe Corinthians v Fleetwood	1-7
Morecambe v Penrith	2-0
5 Ashton Utd v St Helens Town	2-4
Droylsden v Marine	3-3
Prescot Town v Altrincham	1-2
Skelmersdale United v Leyland Motors	2-2
6 Ellesmere Port Town v Runcorn	3-1
Holyhead Town v New Brighton	0-2
Rhyl v Borough United	1-1
Stork v Colwyn Bay	0-2
7 Chorley v Nelson	6-0
Great Harwood v Hyde United	1-4
Lytham v Bacup Borough	2-0
Rossendale United v Darwen	3-2
8 Macclesfield Town v Winsford United	7-0
Mossley v Northwich Victoria	1-4
Oswestry Town v Congleton Town	6-0
Witton Albion v Stalybridge Celtic	4-0
9 Bilston v Rugby Town (2)	2-1
Brierley Hill Alliance v Hednesford Town	1-1
Lockheed Leamington v Nuneaton Borough	3-1
Stourbridge v Bedworth Town	8-0
10 Dudley Town v Wellington Town	0-0
Kidderminster Harriers v Redditch	3-0
Stafford Rangers v Bromsgrove Rovers	1-1
Worcester City v Lower Gornal Athletic	4-2
11 Bridlington Trinity v Selby Town	3-2
Farsley Celtic v Harrogate Town	0-1
Ossett Albion v Bridlington Town	0-0
Yorkshire Amateur v Hull Brunswick	2-4
12 Gainsborough Trinity v Retford Town	1-0
Goole Town v Mexborough Town	4-2
Norton Woodseats v Frickley Colliery	0-3
Stocksbridge Works v Denaby United	1-4
13 Arnold v Matlock Town	1-1
Belper Town v Buxton	1-1
Heanor Town v Alfreton Town	5-3
Sutton Town v Worksop Town	2-2
14 Grantham v Spalding United	3-0
Holbeach United v Louth United	2-0
Skegness Town v Boston United	3-2
Stamford v Boston	0-1
15 Burton Albion v Loughborough United	1-0
Gresley Rovers v Ilkeston Town (2)	0-2
Long Eaton United v Atherstone Town	7-2
Tamworth v Hinckley Athletic	1-1
16 Desborough Town v St Neots Town	3-0
Eynesbury Rovers v Rothwell Town	0-2
Rushden Town v Bourne Town	4-4
Wellingborough Town v Biggleswade Town	3-0
17 Bletchley Town v Vauxhall Motors (Luton)	3-2
Hitchin Town v Letchworth Town	4-1
St Albans City v Dunstable Town	3-0
Wolverton Town v BR v Amersham Town	2-2
18 Cambridge City v Soham Town Rangers	8-1
Chatteris Town v Ely City	2-3
March Town United v Bury Town	1-2
Wisbech Town v Newmarket Town	5-1
19 Great Yarmouth Town v Gorleston	6-4
Harwich & Parkeston v Clacton Town	2-2
Lowestoft Town v Thetford Town	10-2
Sudbury Town v Haverhill Rovers	3-0
20 Canterbury City v Ramsgate Athletic	2-1
Deal Town v Dover	2-2
Folkestone v Margate	2-1
Whitstable v Herne Bay	1-3
21 Crawley Town v Haywards Heath	3-0
Horsham v Sutton United	2-2
Lancing v Lewes	3-1
Redhill v Carshalton Athletic	2-2
22 Eastbourne v Tonbridge	1-4
Eastbourne United v Hastings United	0-4
Maidstone United v Bexhill Town	4-0
Tunbridge Wells Rangers v Ashford Town	4-1
23 Brentwood Town (1) v Tilbury	0-2
Grays Athletic v Hornchurch	1-0
Ilford v Barking	2-4
Walthamstow Avenue v Aveley	4-0
24 Bishop's Stortford v Stevenage Town	1-1
Harlow Town v Harrow Town	3-1
Hertford Town v Wealdstone	1-2
Ware v Cheshunt	3-1
25 Dulwich Hamlet v Tooting & Mitcham United	3-2
Marlow v Metropolitan Police	0-4
Slough Town v Wembley	5-3
Wokingham Town v Bracknell Town	6-0
26 Dorking v Walton & Hersham	1-1
Guildford City v Kingstonian	3-2
Leatherhead v Chertsey Town	3-3
Woking v Addlestone	9-0
27 Aylesbury United v Huntley & Palmers	3-3
Banbury United v Chesham United	2-0
Hemel Hempstead Town v Abingdon Town	6-0
Oxford City v Maidenhead United	5-2
28 Hayes v Windsor & Eton	1-2
Hillingdon Borough v Corinthian Casuals	1-2
Hounslow v Southall	2-3
Uxbridge v Finchley	1-7
29 Bexley United v Chatham Town	6-2
Bromley v Erith & Belvedere	3-2
Cray Wanderers v Sheppey United	0-1
Sittingbourne v Faversham Town	9-0
30 Clapton v Leytonstone	0-9
Dagenham v Ford United	2-2
Leyton v Woodford Town (1)	3-2
Ruislip Manor v Rainham Town	1-5
31 Basingstoke Town v Littlehampton Town	6-0
Chichester City (1) v Cowes	3-6
Fareham Town v Alton Town	7-3
Newport (IOW) v Bognor Regis Town	2-1
32 Poole Town v Bridport	3-2
Portland United v Dorchester Town	4-1
Salisbury (2) v Newbury Town	4-0
Warminster Town v Andover	0-4
33 Chippenham Town v Melksham Town	5-1
Westbury United v Trowbridge Town	1-3
34 Bridgwater Town (1) v Taunton	1-0
Glastonbury v Frome Town	0-1
Weston-Super-Mare v Minehead	2-1
35 Cinderford Town v Merthyr Tydfil	1-1
Gloucester City v Llanelli	1-0
Lovells Athletic v Barry Town	6-1
Stonehouse v Abergavenny Thursdays	2-1
5r Leyland Motors v Skelmersdale United	1-2
r Marine v Droylsden	1-0
6r Borough United v Rhyl	1-0
9r Hednesford Town v Brierley Hill Alliance	1-3
10r Bromsgrove Rovers v Stafford Rangers	1-2
r Wellington Town v Dudley Town	1-2
11r Bridlington Town v Ossett Albion	1-2
13r Buxton v Belper Town	6-3
r Matlock Town v Arnold	2-2x
r Worksop Town v Sutton Town	6-2
15r Hinckley Athletic v Tamworth	4-2
16r Bourne Town v Rushden Town	4-1
17r Amersham Town v Wolverton Town & BR	0-2
19r Clacton Town v Harwich & Parkeston	0-5
20r Dover v Deal Town	3-0
21r Carshalton Athletic v Redhill	3-0
r Sutton United v Horsham	3-2
24r Stevenage Town v Bishop's Stortford	2-0
26r Chertsey Town v Leatherhead	2-5e
r Walton & Hersham v Dorking	4-1
27r Huntley & Palmers v Aylesbury United	1-0
30r Ford United v Dagenham	1-2
35r Merthyr Tydfil v Cinderford Town	4-0
13r2 Arnold v Matlock Town	1-2

Qualifying Round Two

1 Blyth Spartans v Horden CW	0-2
Stanley United v Whitley Bay	2-2
2 Spennymoor United v Bishop Auckland	0-0
Willington v Whitby Town	1-2
3 Boldon CW v Consett	1-1
Stockton v Ashington	3-1
4 Clitheroe v Morecambe	2-1
Horwich RMI v Fleetwood	3-3
5 Altrincham v Marine	4-0
St Helens Town v Skelmersdale United	0-3
6 Borough United v New Brighton	3-0
Ellesmere Port Town v Colwyn Bay	1-2
7 Chorley v Rossendale United	1-1
Lytham v Hyde United	1-3
8 Macclesfield Town v Witton Albion	9-0
Oswestry Town v Northwich Victoria	3-1
9 Bilston v Stourbridge	0-1
Lockheed Leamington v Brierley Hill Alliance	2-3
10 Dudley Town v Worcester City	0-3
Stafford Rangers v Kidderminster Harriers	0-2
11 Bridlington Trinity v Hull Brunswick	6-0
Ossett Albion v Harrogate Town	1-1
12 Frickley Colliery v Goole Town	1-3
Gainsborough Trinity v Denaby United	4-1
13 Heanor Town v Buxton	5-1
Matlock Town v Worksop Town	1-3
14 Grantham v Boston	7-0
Skegness Town v Holbeach United	2-2
15 Burton Albion v Hinckley Athletic	8-1
Long Eaton United v Ilkeston Town (2)	3-2
16 Bourne Town v Rothwell Town	3-1
Desborough Town v Wellingborough Town	1-2
17 Bletchley Town v Wolverton Town & BR	2-1
St Albans City v Hitchin Town	2-0
18 Bury Town v Ely City	5-0
Cambridge City v Wisbech Town	1-1
19 Lowestoft Town v Great Yarmouth Town	4-2
Sudbury Town v Harwich & Parkeston	1-2
20 Canterbury City v Herne Bay	1-0
Folkestone v Dover	1-1
21 Lancing v Carshalton Athletic	0-2
Sutton United v Crawley Town	0-1
22 Maidstone United v Hastings United	1-5
Tonbridge v Tunbridge Wells Rangers (2)	4-1
23 Barking v Grays Athletic	0-1
Tilbury v Walthamstow Avenue	0-0
24 Stevenage Town v Ware	1-1
Wealdstone v Harlow Town	5-1
25 Dulwich Hamlet v Wokingham Town	1-2
Slough Town v Metropolitan Police	0-1
26 Leatherhead v Guildford City	2-2
Walton & Hersham v Woking	0-4
27 Hemel Hempstead Town v Banbury United	5-1
Huntley & Palmers v Oxford City	1-4
28 Finchley v Southall	2-2
Windsor & Eton v Corinthian Casuals	0-6
29 Bromley v Sittingbourne	0-2
Sheppey United v Bexley United	1-3
30 Leyton v Dagenham	3-2
Leytonstone v Rainham Town	5-0
31 Basingstoke Town v Fareham Town	0-2
Cowes v Newport (IOW)	3-3
32 Andover v Salisbury (2)	0-3
Poole Town v Portland United	0-2

133

1965/66 to 1966/67

33	Cheltenham Town v Chippenham Town	4-1
	Devizes Town v Trowbridge Town	3-2
34	Frome Town v Bridgwater Town (1)	1-1
	Welton Rovers v Weston-Super-Mare	1-1
35	Lovells Athletic v Gloucester City	1-2
	Merthyr Tydfil v Stonehouse	6-2
36	Bideford v Barnstaple Town	2-2
	St Blazey v Falmouth Town	4-1
1r	Whitley Bay v Stanley United	1-0
2r	Bishop Auckland v Spennymoor United	1-4
3r	Consett v Boldon CW	5-0
4r	Fleetwood v Horwich RMI	2-1
7r	Hyde United v Lytham	4-0
r	Rossendale United v Chorley	0-3
11r	Harrogate Town v Ossett Albion	2-3
14r	Holbeach United v Skegness Town	0-1
18r	Wisbech Town v Cambridge City	1-0
20r	Dover v Folkestone	2-3
23r	Walthamstow Avenue v Tilbury	5-4e
24r	Stevenage Town v Ware	4-1
26r	Guildford City v Leatherhead	3-0
28r	Southall v Finchley	2-1e
31r	Newport (IOW) v Cowes	0-3
34r	Bridgwater Town (1) v Frome Town	0-1
r	Weston-Super-Mare v Welton Rovers	0-3
36r	Barnstaple Town v Bideford	2-2e
36r2	Bideford v Barnstaple Town	4-1 N

Qualifying Round Three

1	Horden CW v Whitley Bay	1-0
2	Whitby Town v Spennymoor United	4-3
3	Consett v Stockton	2-0
4	Fleetwood v Clitheroe	3-1
5	Altrincham v Skelmersdale United	4-1
6	Borough United v Colwyn Bay	1-1
7	Hyde United v Chorley	1-1
8	Oswestry Town v Macclesfield Town	3-2
9	Brierley Hill Alliance v Stourbridge	1-2
10	Kidderminster Harriers v Worcester City	2-2
11	Ossett Albion v Bridlington Trinity	2-0
12	Goole Town v Gainsborough Trinity	3-4
13	Heanor Town v Worksop Town	3-2
14	Skegness Town v Grantham	0-7
15	Long Eaton United v Burton Albion	1-2
16	Bourne Town v Wellingborough Town	2-2
17	St Albans City v Bletchley Town	0-1
18	Bury Town v Wisbech Town	0-3
19	Harwich & Parkeston v Lowestoft Town	4-2
20	Folkestone v Canterbury City	1-0
21	Crawley Town v Carshalton Athletic	3-0
22	Hastings United v Tonbridge	1-1
23	Grays Athletic v Walthamstow Avenue	1-3
24	Wealdstone v Stevenage Town	6-5
25	Metropolitan Police v Wokingham Town	3-2
26	Guildford City v Woking	6-0
27	Hemel Hempstead Town v Oxford City	0-1
28	Southall v Corinthian Casuals	2-2
29	Bexley United v Sittingbourne	4-2
30	Leyton v Leytonstone	0-3
31	Fareham Town v Cowes	4-2
32	Salisbury (2) v Portland United	0-3
33	Devizes Town v Cheltenham Town	2-8
34	Welton Rovers v Frome Town	4-1
35	Gloucester City v Merthyr Tydfil	1-1
36	St Blazey v Bideford	2-2
6r	Colwyn Bay v Borough United	2-1
7r	Chorley v Hyde United	4-1
10r	Worcester City v Kidderminster Harriers	1-2
16r	Wellingborough Town v Bourne Town	3-2
22r	Tonbridge v Hastings United	3-1
28r	Corinthian Casuals v Southall	3-2
35r	Merthyr Tydfil v Gloucester City	1-1
36r	Bideford v St Blazey	3-2e
35r2	Gloucester City v Merthyr Tydfil	0-1

Qualifying Round Four

	Bangor City v Altrincham	3-3
	Bath City v Welton Rovers	3-1
	Burton Albion v Gainsborough Trinity	3-2
	Cambridge United v Bedford Town (1)	1-2
	Cheltenham Town v Hereford United	0-1
	Corby Town v King's Lynn	2-1
	Enfield v Corinthian Casuals	0-3
	Fareham Town v Wimbledon	0-3
	Fleetwood v Colwyn Bay	2-1
	Folkestone v Bexley United	4-1
	Gateshead v Horden CW	3-1
	Grantham v Heanor Town	4-4
	Gravesend & Northfleet v Crawley Town	1-0
	Guildford City v Bletchley Town	4-0
	Metropolitan Police v Wycombe Wanderers	2-3
	Oswestry Town v Kidderminster Harriers	3-4
	Portland United v Yeovil Town	1-1
	Romford (2) v Chelmsford City	2-1
	Scarborough v Netherfield (Kendal)	3-1
	South Liverpool v Ossett Albion	3-0
	South Shields (2) v Consett	3-0
	Stourbridge v Merthyr Tydfil	1-3
	Tonbridge v Dartford	0-0
	Walthamstow Avenue v Leytonstone	2-5
	Wealdstone v Oxford City	2-0
	Wellingborough Town v Harwich & Parkeston	1-0
	Weymouth v Bideford	1-1
	Whitby Town v Crook Town	1-1
	Wigan Athletic v Chorley	4-0
	Wisbech Town v Kettering Town	6-1
r	Altrincham v Bangor City	3-2
r	Bideford v Weymouth	1-3
r	Crook Town v Whitby Town	4-1
r	Dartford v Tonbridge	6-2
r	Heanor Town v Grantham	1-2
r	Yeovil Town v Portland United	1-0

Round One

	Aldershot v Wellingborough Town	2-1
	Altrincham v Scarborough	6-0
	Barnet v Dartford	0-2
	Barrow v Grimsby Town	1-2
	Bath City v Newport County	2-0
	Bournemouth v Weymouth	0-0
	Bradford Park Avenue v Hull City	2-3
	Brentford v Yeovil Town	2-1
	Brighton & Hove Albion v Wisbech Town	10-1
	Chesterfield v Chester	0-2
	Colchester United v Queen's Park Rangers	3-3
	Corby Town v Burton Albion	6-3
	Corinthian Casuals v Watford	1-5
	Crewe Alexandra v Scunthorpe United	3-0
	Darlington v Bradford City	3-2
	Doncaster Rovers v Wigan Athletic	2-2
	Exeter City v Bedford Town (1)	1-2
	Fleetwood v Rochdale	2-2
	Gateshead v Crook Town	4-2
	Gillingham v Folkestone	1-2
	Grantham v Hendon	4-1
	Guildford City v Wycombe Wanderers	2-2
	Hartlepools United v Workington	3-1
	Leytonstone v Hereford United	0-1
	Lincoln City v Barnsley	1-3
	Mansfield Town v Oldham Athletic	1-3
	Millwall v Wealdstone	3-1
	Oxford United v Port Vale	2-2
	Peterborough United v Kidderminster Harriers	2-1
	Reading v Bristol Rovers	3-2
	Romford (2) v Luton Town	1-1
	Shrewsbury Town v Torquay United	2-1
	South Shields (2) v York City	3-1
	Southend United v Notts County	3-1
	Southport v Halifax Town	2-0
	Swindon Town v Merthyr Tydfil	5-1
	Tranmere Rovers v Stockport County	0-1
	Walsall v Swansea Town	6-3
	Wimbledon v Gravesend & Northfleet	4-1
	Wrexham v South Liverpool	4-1
r	Luton Town v Romford (2)	1-0
r	Port Vale v Oxford United	3-2
r	Queen's Park Rangers v Colchester United	4-0
r	Rochdale v Fleetwood	5-0
r	Weymouth v Bournemouth	1-4
r	Wigan Athletic v Doncaster Rovers	3-1
r	Wycombe Wanderers v Guildford City	0-1

Round Two

	Aldershot v Walsall	0-2
	Barnsley v Grimsby Town	1-1
	Bournemouth v Bath City	5-3
	Brighton & Hove Albion v Bedford Town (1)	1-1
	Chester v Wigan Athletic	2-1
	Corby Town v Luton Town	2-2
	Crewe Alexandra v South Shields (2)	3-1
	Darlington v Oldham Athletic	0-1
	Gateshead v Hull City	0-4
	Grantham v Swindon Town	1-6
	Hartlepools United v Wrexham	2-0
	Hereford United v Millwall	1-0
	Port Vale v Dartford	1-0
	Queen's Park Rangers v Guildford City	3-0
	Reading v Brentford	5-0
	Rochdale v Altrincham	1-3
	Shrewsbury Town v Peterborough United	3-2
	Southend United v Watford	2-1
	Southport v Stockport County	3-3
	Wimbledon v Folkestone	0-1
r	Bedford Town (1) v Brighton & Hove Albion	2-1
r	Grimsby Town v Barnsley	2-0e
r	Luton Town v Corby Town	0-1
r	Stockport County v Southport	0-2

Round Three

	Aston Villa v Leicester City	1-2
	Bedford Town (1) v Hereford United	2-1
	Birmingham City v Bristol City	3-2
	Blackburn Rovers v Arsenal	3-0
	Blackpool v Manchester City	1-1
	Bolton Wanderers v West Bromwich Albion	3-0
	Bournemouth v Burnley	1-1
	Cardiff City v Port Vale	2-1
	Carlisle United v Crystal Palace	3-0
	Charlton Athletic v Preston North End	2-3
	Chester v Newcastle United	1-3
	Derby County v Manchester United	2-5
	Everton v Sunderland	3-0
	Folkestone v Crewe Alexandra	1-5
	Grimsby Town v Portsmouth	0-0
	Huddersfield Town v Hartlepools United	3-1
	Hull City v Southampton	1-0
	Leeds United v Bury	6-0
	Leyton Orient v Norwich City	1-3
	Liverpool v Chelsea	1-2
	Northampton Town v Nottingham Forest	1-2
	Oldham Athletic v West Ham United	2-2
	Plymouth Argyle v Corby Town	6-0
	Queen's Park Rangers v Shrewsbury Town	0-0
	Reading v Sheffield Wednesday	2-3
	Rotherham United v Southend United	3-2
	Sheffield United v Fulham	3-1
	Southport v Ipswich Town	0-0
	Stoke City v Walsall	0-2
	Swindon Town v Coventry City	1-2
	Tottenham Hotspur v Middlesbrough	4-0
	Wolverhampton Wan. v Altrincham	5-0
r	Burnley v Bournemouth	7-0
r	Ipswich Town v Southport	2-3
r	Manchester City v Blackpool	3-1
r	Portsmouth v Grimsby Town	1-3
r	Shrewsbury Town v Queen's Park Rangers	1-0
r	West Ham United v Oldham Athletic	2-1

Round Four

	Bedford Town (1) v Everton	0-3
	Birmingham City v Leicester City	1-2
	Bolton Wanderers v Preston North End	1-1
	Chelsea v Leeds United	1-0
	Crewe Alexandra v Coventry City	1-1
	Hull City v Nottingham Forest	2-0
	Manchester City v Grimsby Town	2-0
	Manchester United v Rotherham United	0-0
	Newcastle United v Sheffield Wednesday	1-2
	Norwich City v Walsall	3-2
	Plymouth Argyle v Huddersfield Town	0-2
	Shrewsbury Town v Carlisle United	0-0
	Southport v Cardiff City	2-0
	Tottenham Hotspur v Burnley	4-3
	West Ham United v Blackburn Rovers	3-3
	Wolverhampton Wan. v Sheffield United	3-0
r	Blackburn Rovers v West Ham United	4-1
r	Carlisle United v Shrewsbury Town	1-1e
r	Coventry City v Crewe Alexandra	4-1
r	Preston North End v Bolton Wanderers	3-2
r	Rotherham United v Manchester United	0-1e
r2	Shrewsbury Town v Carlisle United	4-3eN

Round Five

	Chelsea v Shrewsbury Town	3-2
	Everton v Coventry City	3-0
	Huddersfield Town v Sheffield Wednesday	1-2
	Hull City v Southport	2-0
	Manchester City v Leicester City	2-2
	Norwich City v Blackburn Rovers	2-2
	Preston North End v Tottenham Hotspur	2-1
	Wolverhampton Wan. v Manchester United	2-4
r	Blackburn Rovers v Norwich City	3-2
r	Leicester City v Manchester City	0-1

Round Six

	Blackburn Rovers v Sheffield Wednesday	1-2
	Chelsea v Hull City	2-2
	Manchester City v Everton	0-0
	Preston North End v Manchester United	1-1
r	Everton v Manchester City	0-0e
r	Hull City v Chelsea	1-3
r	Manchester United v Preston North End	3-1
r2	Everton v Manchester City	2-0 N

Semi Finals

	Everton v Manchester United	1-0 N
	Sheffield Wednesday v Chelsea	2-0 N

Final

	Everton v Sheffield Wednesday	3-2 N

1966/67

Qualifying Round One

1	Annfield Plain v Ferryhill Athletic	2-2
	Billingham Synthonia v Evenwood Town	1-0
	Consett v Whitby Town	2-3
	Murton CW v Durham City	4-2
2	Blyth Spartans v Whitley Bay	4-1
	Stanley United v Ryhope CW	1-0
	Stockton v Boldon CW	2-2
	Tow Law Town v West Auckland Town	5-0
3	Ashington v North Shields	2-2
	South Bank v Shildon	4-3
	Spennymoor United v Horden CW	0-2
	Willington v Bishop Auckland	0-3
4	Fleetwood v Penrith	3-1
	Lytham v Nelson	0-1
	Morecambe v Milnthorpe Corinthians	7-0
	Netherfield (Kendal) v Leyland Motors	4-1
5	Lostock Gralam v Winsford United	3-2
	Rhyl v St Helens Town	5-1

1966/67

	Runcorn v Linotype & Machinery	5-2
	Skelmersdale United v Nantwich	4-3
6	Borough United v Oswestry Town	2-3
	Kirkby Town v Marine	2-0
	Llandudno v Bangor City	0-1
	New Brighton v Colwyn Bay	3-1
7	Burscough v Rossendale United	2-3
	Chorley v Horwich RMI	1-0
	Darwen v Bacup Borough	2-3
	Lancaster City v Clitheroe	1-1
8	Ellesmere Port Town v Witton Albion	0-0
	Mossley v Prescot Town	6-2
	Northwich Victoria v Congleton Town	5-0
	Stalybridge Celtic v Hyde United	2-2
9	Hinckley Athletic v Worcester City	0-4
	Redditch v Stratford Town	0-2
	Rugby Town (2) v Bromsgrove Rovers	4-2
	Tamworth v Lockheed Leamington	4-2
10	Brierley Hill Alliance v Wellington Town	2-1
	Halesowen Town v Lower Gornal Athletic	2-3
	Hednesford Town v Bilston	4-4
	Stourbridge v Dudley Town	5-3
11	Buxton v Worksop Town	1-2
	Long Eaton United v Matlock Town	2-4
	Macclesfield Town v Alfreton Town	2-1
	Sutton Town v Ilkeston Town (2)	1-0
12	Bridlington Town v Selby Town	4-0
	Goole Town v Hull Brunswick	3-1
	Harrogate Town v Barton Town (2)	0-4
	Scarborough v Bridlington Trinity	1-2
13	Farsley Celtic v Yorkshire Amateur	1-0
	Gainsborough Trinity v Ossett Albion	3-0
	Mexborough Town v Denaby United	0-2
	Retford Town v Frickley Colliery	4-0
14	Boston United v Stamford	4-0
	King's Lynn v Skegness Town	4-3
	Louth United v Boston	0-3
	Spalding United v Holbeach United	5-2
15	Atherstone Town v Nuneaton Borough	1-6
	Belper Town v Gresley Rovers	4-2
	Burton Albion v Arnold	2-0
	Loughborough United v Bedworth Town	2-2
16	Desborough Town v Wellingborough Town	2-1
	Eynesbury Rovers v Rushden Town	0-0
	March Town United v Chatteris Town	4-3
	St Neots Town v Ely City	4-2
17	Bishop's Stortford v Soham Town Rangers	2-0
	Cambridge City v Letchworth Town	5-3
	Cambridge United v Biggleswade Town	6-0
	Newmarket Town v Bury Town	1-1
18	Gorleston v Sudbury Town	1-3
	Great Yarmouth Town v Haverhill Rovers	0-3
	Harwich & Parkeston v Clacton Town	4-2
	Lowestoft Town v Gothic (Norwich)	6-0
19	Chesham United v Wembley	1-0
	Hemel Hempstead Town v Huntley & Palmers	1-0
	Hitchin Town v Banbury United	1-4
	Southall v Dunstable Town	3-0
20	Deal Town v Sittingbourne	1-1
	Hastings United v Tonbridge	1-0
	Herne Bay v Canterbury City	0-4
	Ramsgate Athletic v Dover	2-1
21	Crawley Town v Worthing	4-0
	Eastbourne United v Lancing	2-0
	Haywards Heath v Bexhill Town	0-1
	Maidstone United v Eastbourne	2-2
22	Bromley v Tunbridge Wells Rangers (2)	0-1
	Dulwich Hamlet v Redhill	2-1
	Leytonstone v Ashford Town	2-2
	Margate v Chatham Town	2-1
23	Egham Town v Wolverton Town & BR	2-2
	Hounslow v St Albans City	2-0
	Oxford City v Addlestone	8-0
	Wokingham Town v Harrow Borough	1-3
24	Chertsey Town v Walthamstow Avenue	1-3
	Enfield v Leyton	7-0
	Hillingdon Borough v Aylesbury United	6-0
	Stevenage Town v Erith & Belvedere	0-0
25	Clapton v Walton & Hersham	3-2
	Finchley v Marlow	4-1
	Hoddesdon Town v Bletchley Town	0-7
	Slough Town v Dagenham	2-0
26	Grays Athletic v Maidenhead United	0-0
	Leatherhead v Barking	1-0
	Malden Town v Feltham	1-0
	Vauxhall Motors (Luton) v Corinthian Casuals	1-2
27	Bexley United v Woodford Town (1)	5-1
	Croydon Amateurs v Hornchurch	1-2
	Hayes v Amersham Town	4-1
	Tooting & Mitcham United v Brentwood Town (1)	2-3
28	Carshalton Athletic v Ware	2-4
	Harlow Town v Cray Wanderers	0-0
	Ilford v Barnet	0-2
	Uxbridge v Edgware Town	1-2
29	Crittall Athletic v Tilbury	1-0
	Hampton v Metropolitan Police	0-2
	Kingstonian v Aveley	5-2
	Sutton United v Hatfield Town	4-0
30	Basingstoke Town v Woking	1-2
	Dorking v Horsham	0-3
	Fleet Town v Alton Town	6-1
	Littlehampton Town v Bognor Regis Town	3-3
31	Ford United v Cheshunt	0-1
	Hertford Town v Epsom & Ewell	2-1e
	Ruislip Manor v Rainham Town	1-2
32	Chichester City (1) v Waterlooville	2-2
	Fareham Town v Newport (IOW)	5-1
	Newbury Town v Andover	0-3
	Salisbury (2) v Cowes	4-1
33	Dorchester Town v Warminster Town	5-0
	Glastonbury v Portland United	2-2
	Poole Town v Bridport	7-0
	Street v Frome Town	1-1
34	Chippenham Town v Westbury United	4-2
	Melksham Town v Trowbridge Town	0-4
	Stonehouse v Weston-Super-Mare	3-2
	Welton Rovers v Devizes Town	2-0
35	Barry Town v Merthyr Tydfil	0-1
	Cinderford Town v Llanelli	2-0
	Gloucester City v Abergavenny Thursdays	4-1
	Lovells Athletic v Cheltenham Town	0-3
36	Bridgwater Town (1) v Barnstaple Town	0-1
	Falmouth Town v Bideford	0-3
	St Blazey v St Austell	0-2
	Taunton v Minehead	1-4
1r	Ferryhill Athletic v Annfield Plain	2-2
2r	Boldon CW v Stockton	0-0
3r	North Shields v Ashington	2-4
7r	Clitheroe v Lancaster City	0-1
8r	Hyde United v Stalybridge Celtic	3-1
r	Witton Albion v Ellesmere Port Town	3-1
10r	Bilston v Hednesford Town	2-3
15r	Bedworth Town v Loughborough United	1-2
16r	Rushden Town v Eynesbury Rovers	6-3
17r	Bury Town v Newmarket Town	2-1
20r	Sittingbourne v Deal Town	6-2
21r	Eastbourne v Maidstone United	1-3
22r	Ashford Town v Leytonstone	4-0
23r	Wolverton Town & BR v Egham Town	6-1
24r	Erith & Belvedere v Stevenage Town	0-3
26r	Maidenhead United v Grays Athletic	3-1
28r	Cray Wanderers v Harlow Town	3-1
30r	Bognor Regis Town v Littlehampton Town	1-4
32r	Waterlooville v Chichester City (1)	4-1
33r	Frome Town v Street	1-3
r	Portland United v Glastonbury	4-2
1r2	Annfield Plain v Ferryhill Athletic	3-2
2r2	Stockton v Boldon CW	4-1

Qualifying Round Two

1	Annfield Plain v Murton CW	4-0
	Whitby Town v Billingham Synthonia	1-1
2	Blyth Spartans v Tow Law Town	3-3
	Stanley United v Stockton	4-4
3	Bishop Auckland v South Bank	3-1
	Horden CW v Ashington	2-1
4	Fleetwood v Netherfield (Kendal)	2-2
	Nelson v Morecambe	0-4
5	Lostock Gralam v Skelmersdale United	1-1
	Rhyl v Runcorn	3-3
6	Kirkby Town v Bangor City	0-1
	Oswestry Town v New Brighton	2-4
7	Chorley v Bacup Borough	2-0
	Rossendale United v Lancaster City	3-3
8	Mossley v Northwich Victoria	1-1
	Witton Albion v Hyde United	4-1
9	Stratford Town v Rugby Town (2)	0-2
	Worcester City v Tamworth	0-1
10	Brierley Hill Alliance v Stourbridge	5-0
	Lower Gornal Athletic v Hednesford Town	0-3
11	Matlock Town v Macclesfield Town	2-2
	Worksop Town v Sutton Town	3-0
12	Bridlington Town v Bridlington Trinity	0-2
	Goole Town v Barton Town (2)	3-3
13	Farsley Celtic v Retford Town	2-0
	Gainsborough Trinity v Denaby United	2-1
14	Boston United v Spalding United	2-0
	King's Lynn v Boston	2-1
15	Belper Town v Burton Albion	1-3
	Nuneaton Borough v Loughborough United	8-2
16	Desborough Town v St Neots Town	1-2
	Rushden Town v March Town United	4-0
17	Bishop's Stortford v Bury Town	2-5
	Cambridge City v Cambridge United	1-0
18	Haverhill Rovers v Harwich & Parkeston	2-0
	Sudbury Town v Lowestoft Town	1-2
19	Chesham United v Southall	4-3
	Hemel Hempstead Town v Banbury United	6-3
20	Hastings United v Canterbury City	2-0
	Sittingbourne v Ramsgate Athletic	1-3
21	Crawley Town v Maidstone United	1-0
	Eastbourne United v Bexhill Town	3-2
22	Dulwich Hamlet v Ashford Town	1-4
	Tunbridge Wells Rangers v Margate	0-4
23	Hounslow v Oxford City	0-3
	Wolverton Town & BR v Harrow Borough	4-1
24	Enfield v Hillingdon Borough	3-0
	Walthamstow Avenue v Stevenage Town	0-2
25	Clapton v Slough Town	0-2
	Finchley v Bletchley Town	0-0
26	Maidenhead United v Leatherhead	0-2
	Malden Town v Corinthian Casuals	1-1
27	Bexley United v Brentwood Town (1)	3-2
	Hornchurch v Hayes	1-0
28	Cray Wanderers v Barnet	1-4
	Ware v Edgware Town	2-2
29	Crittall Athletic v Sutton United	1-2
	Metropolitan Police v Kingstonian	2-2
30	Horsham v Fleet Town	3-0
	Woking v Littlehampton Town	2-1
31	Cheshunt v Rainham Town	5-2
	Windsor & Eton v Hertford Town	2-2
32	Fareham Town v Andover	1-0
	Waterlooville v Salisbury (2)	0-2
33	Dorchester Town v Street	2-0
	Portland United v Poole Town	0-2
34	Chippenham Town v Welton Rovers	0-4
	Trowbridge Town v Stonehouse	5-0
35	Cinderford Town v Gloucester City	2-2
	Merthyr Tydfil v Cheltenham Town	1-3
36	Barnstaple Town v Minehead	1-2
	Bideford v St Austell	5-0
1r	Billingham Synthonia v Whitby Town	1-0
2r	Stockton v Stanley United	3-1eN
r	Tow Law Town v Blyth Spartans	2-3e
4r	Netherfield (Kendal) v Fleetwood	2-1e
5r	Runcorn v Rhyl	2-2
r	Skelmersdale United v Lostock Gralam	5-1
7r	Lancaster City v Rossendale United	2-1
8r	Northwich Victoria v Mossley	3-1
11r	Macclesfield Town v Matlock Town	6-1
12r	Barton Town (2) v Goole Town	0-2
25r	Bletchley Town v Finchley	0-1
26r	Corinthian Casuals v Malden Town	3-2e
28r	Edgware Town v Ware	1-0
29r	Kingstonian v Metropolitan Police	2-1
31r	Hertford Town v Windsor & Eton	4-1
35r	Gloucester City v Cinderford Town	0-3
5r2	Rhyl v Runcorn	3-1

Qualifying Round Three

1	Billingham Synthonia v Annfield Plain	4-0
2	Blyth Spartans v Stockton	4-2
3	Horden CW v Bishop Auckland	0-1
4	Morecambe v Netherfield (Kendal)	2-1
5	Rhyl v Skelmersdale United	2-0
6	Bangor City v New Brighton	6-6
7	Chorley v Lancaster City	3-0
8	Northwich Victoria v Witton Albion	1-6
9	Rugby Town (2) v Tamworth	2-2
10	Hednesford Town v Brierley Hill Alliance	6-0
11	Macclesfield Town v Worksop Town	3-1
12	Goole Town v Bridlington Trinity	4-0
13	Gainsborough Trinity v Farsley Celtic	1-1
14	King's Lynn v Boston United	2-5
15	Burton Albion v Nuneaton Borough	0-1
16	Rushden Town v St Neots Town	0-3
17	Bury Town v Cambridge City	3-3
18	Lowestoft Town v Haverhill Rovers	4-4
19	Hemel Hempstead Town v Chesham United	2-3
20	Hastings United v Ramsgate Athletic	2-1
21	Eastbourne United v Crawley Town	1-1
22	Ashford Town v Margate	1-0
23	Oxford City v Wolverton Town & BR	3-2
24	Enfield v Stevenage Town	2-2
25	Finchley v Slough Town	3-2
26	Leatherhead v Corinthian Casuals	2-1
27	Hornchurch v Bexley United	2-2
28	Barnet v Edgware Town	4-1
29	Kingstonian v Sutton United	0-2
30	Horsham v Woking	2-1
31	Cheshunt v Hertford Town	0-0
32	Fareham Town v Salisbury (2)	2-2
33	Poole Town v Dorchester Town	1-0
34	Trowbridge Town v Welton Rovers	0-3
35	Cinderford Town v Cheltenham Town	2-3
36	Minehead v Bideford	5-0
6r	New Brighton v Bangor City	0-1
9r	Tamworth v Rugby Town (2)	2-1e
13r	Farsley Celtic v Gainsborough Trinity	0-1
17r	Cambridge City v Bury Town	1-0
18r	Haverhill Rovers v Lowestoft Town	4-6
21r	Crawley Town v Eastbourne United	2-2e
24r	Stevenage Town v Enfield	1-1e
27r	Bexley United v Hornchurch	0-3
31r	Hertford Town v Cheshunt	0-1
32r	Salisbury (2) v Fareham Town	1-2
21r2	Eastbourne United v Crawley Town	3-2
24r2	Enfield v Stevenage Town	2-0

Qualifying Round Four

Altrincham v Wigan Athletic	2-4
Barnet v Enfield	1-2
Bath City v Weymouth	2-2
Bedford Town (1) v Romford (2)	1-1
Boston United v Grantham	1-4
Cheltenham Town v Yeovil Town	3-3
Chorley v Bangor City	3-3
Corby Town v Cambridge City	0-2
Crook Town v Bishop Auckland	4-4
Dartford v Wimbledon	2-2
Folkestone v Gravesend & Northfleet	3-2
Gainsborough Trinity v Goole Town	1-0
Gateshead v Blyth Spartans	1-3
Guildford City v Ashford Town	1-1
Hereford United v Kidderminster Harriers	1-1
Hornchurch v Chelmsford City	0-4
Horsham v Hastings United	2-1
Leatherhead v Chesham United	1-2
Lowestoft Town v Kettering Town	3-1
Macclesfield Town v Nuneaton Borough	1-1
Oxford City v Finchley	5-1

1966/67 to 1967/68

Poole Town v Minehead	1-0
South Liverpool v Morecambe	1-1
South Shields (2) v Billingham Synthonia	2-0
St Neots Town v Wisbech Town	2-0
Sutton United v Eastbourne United	7-2
Tamworth v Hednesford Town	1-1
Welton Rovers v Fareham Town	4-1
Witton Albion v Rhyl	4-2
Wycombe Wanderers v Cheshunt	8-0
r Ashford Town v Guildford City	2-0
r Bangor City v Chorley	4-3
r Bishop Auckland v Crook Town	2-0
r Hednesford Town v Tamworth	1-3
r Kidderminster Harriers v Hereford United	2-4
r Morecambe v South Liverpool	1-0
r Nuneaton Borough v Macclesfield Town	2-0
r Romford (2) v Bedford Town (1)	1-2
r Weymouth v Bath City	0-1
r Wimbledon v Dartford	3-0
r Yeovil Town v Cheltenham Town	3-1

Round One

Aldershot v Torquay United	2-1
Ashford Town v Cambridge City	4-1
Barnsley v Southport	3-1
Bath City v Sutton United	1-0
Bishop Auckland v Blyth Spartans	1-1
Bournemouth v Welton Rovers	3-0
Bradford City v Port Vale	1-2
Bradford Park Avenue v Witton Albion	3-2
Brentford v Chelmsford City	1-0
Chester v Middlesbrough	2-5
Crewe Alexandra v Grimsby Town	1-1
Darlington v Stockport County	0-0
Enfield v Chesham United	6-0
Exeter City v Luton Town	1-1
Folkestone v Swansea Town	2-2
Gainsborough Trinity v Colchester United	0-1
Gillingham v Tamworth	4-1
Grantham v Wimbledon	2-1
Halifax Town v Doncaster Rovers	2-2
Hendon v Reading	1-3
Horsham v Swindon Town	0-3
Lincoln City v Scunthorpe United	3-4
Mansfield Town v Bangor City	4-1
Newport County v Brighton & Hove Albion	1-2
Oldham Athletic v Notts County	3-1
Orient v Lowestoft Town	2-1
Oxford City v Bristol Rovers	2-2
Peterborough United v Hereford United	4-1
Queen's Park Rangers v Poole Town	3-2
Rochdale v Barrow	1-3
Shrewsbury Town v Hartlepools United	5-2
South Shields (2) v Workington	1-4
Tranmere Rovers v Wigan Athletic	1-1
Walsall v St Neots Town	2-0
Watford v Southend United	1-0
Wealdstone v Nuneaton Borough	0-2
Wrexham v Chesterfield	3-2
Wycombe Wanderers v Bedford Town (1)	1-1
Yeovil Town v Oxford United	1-3
York City v Morecambe	0-0
r Bedford Town (1) v Wycombe Wanderers	3-3e
r Blyth Spartans v Bishop Auckland	0-0e
r Bristol Rovers v Oxford City	4-0
r Doncaster Rovers v Halifax Town	1-3e
r Grimsby Town v Crewe Alexandra	0-1
r Luton Town v Exeter City	2-0
r Morecambe v York City	1-1e
r Stockport County v Darlington	1-1e
r Swansea Town v Folkestone	7-2
r Wigan Athletic v Tranmere Rovers	0-1
r2 Bishop Auckland v Blyth Spartans	3-3eN
r2 Darlington v Stockport County	4-2 N
r2 Wycombe Wanderers v Bedford Town (1)	1-1x
r2 York City v Morecambe	1-0 N
r3 Bedford Town (1) v Wycombe Wanderers	3-2
r3 Blyth Spartans v Bishop Auckland	1-4 N

Round Two

Aldershot v Reading	1-0
Barnsley v Port Vale	1-1
Barrow v Tranmere Rovers	2-1
Bath City v Brighton & Hove Albion	0-5
Bishop Auckland v Halifax Town	0-0
Bradford Park Avenue v Workington	3-1
Bristol Rovers v Luton Town	3-2
Colchester United v Peterborough United	0-3
Crewe Alexandra v Darlington	2-1
Enfield v Watford	2-4
Grantham v Oldham Athletic	0-4
Mansfield Town v Scunthorpe United	2-1
Middlesbrough v York City	1-1
Nuneaton Borough v Swansea Town	2-0
Orient v Brentford	0-0
Oxford United v Bedford Town (1)	1-1
Queen's Park Rangers v Bournemouth	2-0
Shrewsbury Town v Wrexham	5-1
Swindon Town v Ashford Town	5-0
Walsall v Gillingham	3-1

r Bedford Town (1) v Oxford United	1-0
r Brentford v Orient	3-1
r Halifax Town v Bishop Auckland	7-0
r Port Vale v Barnsley	1-3
r York City v Middlesbrough	0-0e
r2 Middlesbrough v York City	4-1 N

Round Three

Aldershot v Brighton & Hove Albion	0-0
Barnsley v Cardiff City	1-1
Barrow v Southampton	2-2
Bedford Town (1) v Peterborough United	2-6
Birmingham City v Blackpool	2-1
Blackburn Rovers v Carlisle United	1-2
Bolton Wanderers v Crewe Alexandra	1-0
Bradford Park Avenue v Fulham	1-3
Bristol Rovers v Arsenal	0-3
Burnley v Everton	0-0
Bury v Walsall	2-0
Charlton Athletic v Sheffield United	0-1
Coventry City v Newcastle United	3-4
Halifax Town v Bristol City	1-1
Huddersfield Town v Chelsea	1-2
Hull City v Portsmouth	1-1
Ipswich Town v Shrewsbury Town	4-1
Leeds United v Crystal Palace	3-0
Manchester City v Leicester City	2-1
Manchester United v Stoke City	2-0
Mansfield Town v Middlesbrough	2-0
Millwall v Tottenham Hotspur	0-0
Northampton Town v West Bromwich Albion	1-3
Norwich City v Derby County	3-0
Nottingham Forest v Plymouth Argyle	2-1
Nuneaton Borough v Rotherham United	1-1
Oldham Athletic v Wolverhampton Wan.	2-2
Preston North End v Aston Villa	0-1
Sheffield Wednesday v Queen's Park Rangers	3-0
Sunderland v Brentford	5-2
Watford v Liverpool	0-0
West Ham United v Swindon Town	3-3
r Brighton & Hove Albion v Aldershot	3-1
r Bristol City v Halifax Town	4-1
r Cardiff City v Barnsley	2-1
r Everton v Burnley	2-1
r Liverpool v Watford	3-1
r Portsmouth v Hull City	2-2e
r Rotherham United v Nuneaton Borough	1-0
r Southampton v Barrow	3-0
r Swindon Town v West Ham United	3-1
r Tottenham Hotspur v Millwall	1-0
r Wolverhampton Wan. v Oldham Athletic	4-1
r2 Hull City v Portsmouth	1-3 N

Round Four

Bolton Wanderers v Arsenal	0-0
Brighton & Hove Albion v Chelsea	1-1
Bristol City v Southampton	1-0
Cardiff City v Manchester City	1-1
Fulham v Sheffield United	1-1
Ipswich Town v Carlisle United	2-0
Leeds United v West Bromwich Albion	5-0
Liverpool v Aston Villa	1-0
Manchester United v Norwich City	1-2
Nottingham Forest v Newcastle United	3-0
Rotherham United v Birmingham City	0-1
Sheffield Wednesday v Mansfield Town	4-0
Sunderland v Peterborough United	7-1
Swindon Town v Bury	2-1
Tottenham Hotspur v Portsmouth	3-1
Wolverhampton Wan. v Everton	1-1
r Arsenal v Bolton Wanderers	3-0
r Birmingham City v Rotherham United	2-1
r Chelsea v Brighton & Hove Albion	4-0
r Everton v Wolverhampton Wan.	3-1
r Manchester City v Cardiff City	3-1
r Sheffield United v Fulham	3-1

Round Five

Birmingham City v Arsenal	1-0
Chelsea v Sheffield United	2-0
Everton v Liverpool	1-0
Manchester City v Ipswich Town	1-1
Norwich City v Sheffield Wednesday	1-3
Nottingham Forest v Swindon Town	0-0
Sunderland v Leeds United	1-1
Tottenham Hotspur v Bristol City	2-0
r Ipswich Town v Manchester City	0-3
r Leeds United v Sunderland	1-1e
r Swindon Town v Nottingham Forest	1-1e
r2 Nottingham Forest v Swindon Town	3-0 N
r2 Sunderland v Leeds United	1-2 N

Round Six

Birmingham City v Tottenham Hotspur	0-0
Chelsea v Sheffield Wednesday	1-0
Leeds United v Manchester City	1-0
Nottingham Forest v Everton	3-2
r Tottenham Hotspur v Birmingham City	6-0

Semi Finals

Chelsea v Leeds United	1-0 N
Tottenham Hotspur v Nottingham Forest	2-1 N

Final

Tottenham Hotspur v Chelsea	2-1 N

1967/68

Preliminary Round

1 Spennymoor United v Boldon CW	5-0
2 Horden CW v North Shields	1-0
9 Stafford Rangers v Lower Gornal Athletic	0-1
11 Thorne Colliery v Selby Town	3-4
12 Yorkshire Amateur v Worksop Town	1-0
13 Tamworth v Sutton Town	5-1
14 Wisbech Town v Spalding United	1-1
15 Rugby Town (2) v Loughborough United	3-0
16 Stamford v St Neots Town	0-4
17 Wellingborough Town v Soham Town Rangers	3-1
18 Thetford Town v Sudbury Town	2-2
19 Wembley v Wealdstone	2-0
35 Stonehouse v Merthyr Tydfil	0-6
14r Spalding United v Wisbech Town	2-3
18r Sudbury Town v Thetford Town	2-0

Qualifying Round One

1 Billingham Synthonia v Whitby Town	2-6
Ferryhill Athletic v Bedlington CW	2-1
Gateshead v Blyth Spartans	1-1
Stockton v Spennymoor United	0-3
2 Annfield Plain v West Auckland Town	2-2
Ashington v Horden CW	3-2
Consett v Crook Town	1-2
Tow Law Town v South Bank	5-1
3 Evenwood Town v Ryhope CW	0-6
Shildon v Murton CW	3-3
Stanley United v Whitley Bay	3-2
Willington v Durham City	1-3
4 Fleetwood v Netherfield (Kendal)	2-3
Great Harwood v Leyland Motors	3-1
Lancaster City v Milnthorpe Corinthians	3-0
Penrith v Nelson	4-0
5 Linotype & Machinery v Runcorn	1-3
Lostock Gralam v New Brighton	1-1
Nantwich v Kirkby Town	1-2
Winsford United v Northwich Victoria	1-0
6 Bangor City v Pwllheli & District	6-0
Holyhead Town v Porthmadog	4-0
Marine v Oswestry Town	2-3
Rhyl v South Liverpool	2-1
7 Chorley v St Helens Town	1-1
Darwen v Ellesmere Port Town	0-2
Droylsden v Burscough	1-1
Stalybridge Celtic v Prescot Town	1-1
8 Horwich RMI v Wigan Rovers	3-1
Hyde United v Mossley	3-0
Macclesfield Town v Bacup Borough	7-0
Witton Albion v Rossendale United	6-1
9 Bilston v Dudley Town	0-1
Brierley Hill Alliance v Burton Albion	1-1
Bromsgrove Rovers v Lower Gornal Athletic	2-0
Hinckley Athletic v Darlaston	0-1
10 Hednesford Town v Wellington Town	0-5
Lockheed Leamington v Stourbridge	0-1
Redditch v Halesowen Town	2-3
Worcester City v Stratford Town	2-0
11 Barton Town (2) v Hull Brunswick	5-2
Bridlington Town v Brigg Town	0-0
Bridlington Trinity v Selby Town	1-2
Scarborough v Goole Town	1-1
12 Denaby United v Ossett Albion	4-0
Farsley Celtic v Gainsborough Trinity	2-1
Frickley Colliery v Yorkshire Amateur	5-0
Retford Town v Mexborough Town	2-1
13 Alfreton Town v Matlock Town	1-2
Buxton v Eastwood Hanley	4-6
Congleton Town v Tamworth	0-5
Norton Woodseats v Ilkeston Town (2)	2-1
14 Boston v Louth United	0-0
Boston United v Holbeach United	1-1
Bourne Town v Wisbech Town	4-0
Skegness Town v King's Lynn	0-2
15 Arnold v Heanor Town	3-0
Atherstone Town v Belper Town	2-0
Bedworth Town v Rugby Town (2)	2-0
Long Eaton United v Gresley Rovers	2-0
16 Biggleswade Town v Rothwell Town	1-1
Cambridge City v Desborough Town	4-0
Chatteris Town v St Neots Town	1-2
Rushden Town v Histon	8-0
17 Cambridge United v March Town United	6-0
Ely City v Haverhill Rovers	5-1
Newmarket Town v Kettering Town	0-1
Wellingborough Town v Eynesbury Rovers	4-0

136

1967/68

18	Bury Town v Harwich & Parkeston	2-1
	Clacton Town v Gothic (Norwich)	3-2
	Gorleston v Sudbury Town	0-2
	Lowestoft Town v Great Yarmouth Town	3-0
19	Aylesbury United v Maidenhead United	2-2
	Banbury United v Dunstable Town	2-0
	Bletchley Town v Wembley	3-4
	Marlow v Letchworth Town	3-1
20	Chesham United v Leytonstone	0-3
	Cheshunt v Erith & Belvedere	4-4
	Dulwich Hamlet v Amersham Town	2-1
	St Albans City v Hitchin Town	0-0
21	Barnet v Walton & Hersham	3-2
	Clapton v Leatherhead	2-1
	Huntley & Palmers v Barking	1-2
	Windsor & Eton v Malden Town	3-1
22	Carshalton Athletic v Staines Town	2-2
	Croydon Amateurs v Hayes	0-1
	Harlow Town v Brentwood Town (1)	0-2
	Uxbridge v Metropolitan Police	3-1
23	Hampton v Southall	2-0
	Hemel Hempstead Town v Kingstonian	1-0
	Ilford v Grays Athletic	1-0
	Walthamstow Avenue v Leyton	2-0
24	Bexley United v Tilbury	2-0
	Epsom & Ewell v Stevenage Town	1-3
	Hillingdon Borough v Aveley	4-0
	Tooting & Mitcham United v Sutton United	1-3
25	Crittall Athletic v Vauxhall Motors (Luton)	3-0
	Finchley v Hoddesdon Town	0-1
	Harrow Borough v Baldock Town	1-0
	Ware v Hounslow	3-2
26	Dagenham v Redhill	1-0
	Dartford v Gravesend & Northfleet	4-0
	Ford United v Cray Wanderers	1-2
	Ruislip Manor v Hornchurch	0-1
27	Feltham v Hertford Town	1-1e
	Hatfield Town v Bishop's Stortford	1-2
	Slough Town v Corinthian Casuals	3-0
	Wolverton Town & BR v Rainham Town	4-1
28	Canterbury City v Tonbridge	1-2
	Chatham Town v Maidstone United	4-2
	Dover v Bromley	4-0
	Whitstable Town v Sittingbourne	1-1
29	Deal Town v Sheppey United	2-0
	Hastings United v Margate	0-1
	Herne Bay v Bexhill Town	0-2
	Snowdown CW v Ramsgate Athletic	0-4
30	Basingstoke Town v Woking	5-1
	Chichester City (1) v Dorking	2-0
	Crawley Town v Alton Town	1-0
	Wokingham Town v Fleet Town	2-1
31	Eastbourne v Littlehampton Town	1-1
	Eastbourne United v Horsham	2-0
	Haywards Heath v Bognor Regis Town	2-1
	Worthing v Lancing	0-1
32	Cowes v Thornycroft Athletic	2-1
	Fareham Town v Salisbury (2)	2-2
	Newport (IOW) v Andover	4-3
	Waterlooville v Selsey	2-2
33	Frome Town v Trowbridge Town	1-0
	Minehead v Street	4-1
	Portland United v Bridport	3-1
	Warminster Town v Taunton	0-9
34	Devizes Town v Poole Town	0-4
	Dorchester Town v Glastonbury	1-0
	Westbury United v Chippenham Town	0-0
35	Abergavenny Thursdays v Llanelli	0-2
	Barry Town v Cinderford Town	1-0
	Cheltenham Town v Merthyr Tydfil	2-1
	Lovells Athletic v Gloucester City	0-4
36	Bideford v St Blazey	3-2
	Falmouth Town v Penzance	4-1
	Wadebridge Town v Barnstaple Town	7-1
1r	Blyth Spartans v Gateshead	2-1
2r	West Auckland Town v Annfield Plain	2-0
3r	Murton CW v Shildon	1-1
5r	New Brighton v Lostock Gralam	1-2
7r	Burscough v Droylsden	5-2
r	Prescot Town v Stalybridge Celtic	0-1
r	St Helens Town v Chorley	0-3
9r	Burton Albion v Brierley Hill Alliance	2-1
11r	Brigg Town v Bridlington Town	1-0
r	Goole Town v Scarborough	2-1
14r	Holbeach United v Boston United	0-2
r	Louth United v Boston	4-0
16r	Rothwell Town v Biggleswade Town	5-2
19r	Maidenhead United v Aylesbury United	4-2
20r	Erith & Belvedere v Cheshunt	4-3
r	Hitchin Town v St Albans City	3-1
22r	Staines Town v Carshalton Athletic	1-1
27r	Hertford Town v Feltham	8-0
28r	Sittingbourne v Whitstable Town	3-3
31r	Littlehampton Town v Eastbourne	1-2
32r	Salisbury (2) v Fareham Town	5-1
r	Selsey v Waterlooville	3-2
34r	Chippenham Town v Westbury United	3-2
3r2	Shildon v Murton CW	1-2
22r2	Staines Town v Carshalton Athletic	2-3
28r2	Whitstable Town v Sittingbourne	3-2 N

Qualifying Round Two

1	Ferryhill Athletic v Spennymoor United	0-0
	Whitby Town v Blyth Spartans	2-0
2	Tow Law Town v Crook Town	2-0
	West Auckland Town v Ashington	0-1
3	Durham City v Murton CW	3-0
	Ryhope CW v Stanley United	1-0
4	Netherfield (Kendal) v Great Harwood	1-2
	Penrith v Lancaster City	0-3
5	Runcorn v Lostock Gralam	5-2
	Winsford United v Kirkby Town	3-0
6	Bangor City v Holyhead Town	3-1
	Rhyl v Oswestry Town	4-0
7	Chorley v Ellesmere Port Town	2-2
	Stalybridge Celtic v Burscough	1-1
8	Horwich RMI v Hyde United	0-3
	Witton Albion v Macclesfield Town	0-2
9	Darlaston v Bromsgrove Rovers	0-0
	Dudley Town v Burton Albion	0-4
10	Wellington Town v Stourbridge	2-2
	Worcester City v Halesowen Town	1-1
11	Barton Town (2) v Brigg Town	3-3
	Goole Town v Selby Town	2-0
12	Denaby United v Farsley Celtic	2-2
	Retford Town v Frickley Colliery	2-0
13	Matlock Town v Eastwood Hanley	4-1
	Norton Woodseats v Tamworth	1-2
14	Boston United v Louth United	1-0
	King's Lynn v Bourne Town	3-1
15	Arnold v Atherstone Town	2-1
	Long Eaton United v Bedworth Town	2-0
16	Rothwell Town v Cambridge City	1-7
	Rushden Town v St Neots Town	4-0
17	Cambridge United v Ely City	3-1
	Kettering Town v Wellingborough Town	1-1
18	Bury Town v Clacton Town	3-2
	Lowestoft Town v Sudbury Town	3-1
19	Maidenhead United v Banbury United	1-3
	Marlow v Wembley	0-3
20	Hitchin Town v Dulwich Hamlet	3-1
	Leytonstone v Erith & Belvedere	4-0
21	Barnet v Clapton	9-0
	Windsor & Eton v Barking	2-1
22	Carshalton Athletic v Hayes	3-2
	Uxbridge v Brentwood Town (1)	1-4
23	Hampton v Hemel Hempstead Town	3-2
	Walthamstow Avenue v Ilford	1-0
24	Bexley United v Stevenage Town	1-2
	Sutton United v Hillingdon Borough	5-1
25	Crittall Athletic v Hoddesdon Town	2-0
	Ware v Harrow Borough	4-1
26	Dagenham v Dartford	2-1
	Hornchurch v Cray Wanderers	2-4
27	Slough Town v Hertford Town	3-0
	Wolverton Town & BR v Bishop's Stortford	1-3
28	Tonbridge v Chatham Town	2-1
	Whitstable Town v Dover	1-7
29	Deal Town v Margate	1-4
	Ramsgate Athletic v Bexhill Town	4-1
30	Basingstoke Town v Chichester City (1)	3-4
	Wokingham Town v Crawley Town	1-5
31	Eastbourne v Eastbourne United	2-0
	Lancing v Haywards Heath	1-1
32	Cowes v Salisbury (2)	1-1
	Selsey v Newport (IOW)	1-3
33	Frome Town v Minehead	1-1
	Taunton v Portland United	2-0
34	Dorchester Town v Chippenham Town	4-1
	Poole Town v Melksham Town	5-0
35	Gloucester City v Cheltenham Town	0-1
	Llanelli v Barry Town	0-0
36	Bideford v St Austell	2-0
	Falmouth Town v Wadebridge Town	6-0
1r	Spennymoor United v Ferryhill Athletic	4-2
7r	Burscough v Stalybridge Celtic	3-1e
r	Ellesmere Port Town v Chorley	3-2
9r	Bromsgrove Rovers v Darlaston	5-0
10r	Halesowen Town v Worcester City	0-0
r	Stourbridge v Wellington Town	1-0
11r	Brigg Town v Barton Town (2)	2-2
12r	Farsley Celtic v Denaby United	3-1
17r	Wellingborough Town v Kettering Town	1-3
31r	Haywards Heath v Lancing	1-1
32r	Salisbury (2) v Cowes	5-1
33r	Minehead v Frome Town	2-1
35r	Barry Town v Llanelli	4-0
10r2	Worcester City v Halesowen Town	2-0
11r2	Barton Town (2) v Brigg Town	1-0
31r2	Lancing v Haywards Heath	3-0 N

Qualifying Round Three

1	Whitby Town v Spennymoor United	0-1
2	Tow Law Town v Ashington	3-2
3	Ryhope CW v Durham City	4-3
4	Great Harwood v Lancaster City	3-1
5	Runcorn v Winsford United	7-1
6	Bangor City v Rhyl	4-0
7	Ellesmere Port Town v Burscough	3-2
8	Hyde United v Macclesfield Town	0-2
9	Burton Albion v Bromsgrove Rovers	5-1
10	Stourbridge v Worcester City	4-0
11	Barton Town (2) v Goole Town	1-1
12	Farsley Celtic v Retford Town	0-1
13	Matlock Town v Tamworth	2-0
14	Boston United v King's Lynn	2-0
15	Arnold v Long Eaton United	1-0
16	Cambridge City v Rushden Town	1-0
17	Cambridge United v Kettering Town	3-0
18	Bury Town v Lowestoft Town	0-1
19	Banbury United v Wembley	3-2
20	Leytonstone v Hitchin Town	2-1
21	Barnet v Windsor & Eton	7-1
22	Carshalton Athletic v Brentwood Town (1)	0-2
23	Hampton v Walthamstow Avenue	4-5
24	Stevenage Town v Sutton United	2-3
25	Crittall Athletic v Ware	1-2
26	Dagenham v Cray Wanderers	1-0
27	Slough Town v Bishop's Stortford	5-1
28	Tonbridge v Dover	4-2
29	Margate v Ramsgate Athletic	6-4
30	Chichester City (1) v Crawley Town	1-0
31	Eastbourne v Lancing	4-0
32	Salisbury (2) v Newport (IOW)	3-0
33	Minehead v Taunton	2-2
34	Dorchester Town v Poole Town	3-2
35	Barry Town v Cheltenham Town	2-2
36	Falmouth Town v Bideford	3-1
11r	Goole Town v Barton Town (2)	4-1
33r	Taunton v Minehead	1-2
35r	Cheltenham Town v Barry Town	3-1e

Qualifying Round Four

	Arnold v Stourbridge	4-2
	Bishop Auckland v Ryhope CW	2-2
	Boston United v Bedford Town (1)	1-1
	Brentwood Town (1) v Walthamstow Avenue	1-3
	Burton Albion v Kidderminster Harriers	1-4
	Chelmsford City v Banbury United	2-0
	Corby Town v Cambridge City	2-2
	Dorchester Town v Salisbury (2)	1-2
	Eastbourne v Margate	0-9
	Ellesmere Port Town v Runcorn	1-2
	Goole Town v Bangor City	2-0
	Great Harwood v Altrincham	0-1
	Guildford City v Chichester City (1)	0-0
	Hendon v Romford (2)	1-2
	Hereford United v Cheltenham Town	3-2
	Lowestoft Town v Cambridge United	2-2
	Minehead v Falmouth Town	1-2
	Nuneaton Borough v Matlock Town	1-0
	Retford Town v Grantham	4-4
	Slough Town v Leytonstone	2-2
	South Shields (2) v Tow Law Town	2-2
	Spennymoor United v Morecambe	1-0
	Sutton United v Barnet	2-2
	Tonbridge v Folkestone	5-1
	Ware v Oxford City	0-2
	Weymouth v Bath City	1-1
	Wigan Athletic v Macclesfield Town	1-1
	Wimbledon v Ashford Town	3-0
	Wycombe Wanderers v Dagenham	0-2
	Yeovil Town v Welton Rovers	2-0
r	Barnet v Sutton United	3-1
r	Bath City v Weymouth	0-1
r	Bedford Town (1) v Boston United	2-3e
r	Cambridge City v Corby Town	0-1
r	Cambridge United v Lowestoft Town	1-2
r	Chichester City (1) v Guildford City	0-3
r	Grantham v Retford Town	3-1
r	Leytonstone v Slough Town	2-1
r	Macclesfield Town v Wigan Athletic	3-0
r	Ryhope CW v Bishop Auckland	4-1
r	Tow Law Town v South Shields (2)	1-0

Round One

	Arnold v Bristol Rovers	0-3
	Barrow v Oldham Athletic	2-0
	Bournemouth v Northampton Town	2-0
	Bradford City v Wrexham	7-1
	Brentford v Guildford City	2-2
	Brighton & Hove Albion v Southend United	1-0
	Chelmsford City v Oxford United	3-3
	Chesterfield v Barnsley	2-0
	Corby Town v Boston United	0-3
	Dagenham v Tonbridge	1-0
	Goole Town v Spennymoor United	0-0
	Grantham v Altrincham	0-3
	Grimsby Town v Bradford Park Avenue	1-1
	Halifax Town v Crewe Alexandra	3-2
	Hartlepools United v Bury	2-3
	Hereford United v Barnet	3-2
	Leytonstone v Walsall	0-1
	Lowestoft Town v Watford	0-1
	Luton Town v Oxford City	2-1
	Newport County v Gillingham	3-0
	Nuneaton Borough v Exeter City	0-0
	Peterborough United v Falmouth Town	5-2
	Port Vale v Chester	1-2
	Reading v Aldershot	6-2
	Runcorn v Notts County	1-0
	Ryhope CW v Workington	0-1
	Scunthorpe United v Skelmersdale United	2-0
	Shrewsbury Town v Darlington	3-0
	Southport v Lincoln City	3-1
	Stockport County v Macclesfield Town	1-1
	Swansea Town v Enfield	2-0
	Swindon Town v Salisbury (2)	4-0
	Torquay United v Colchester United	1-1
	Tow Law Town v Mansfield Town	5-1
	Tranmere Rovers v Rochdale	5-1

1967/68 to 1968/69

Walthamstow Avenue v Kidderminster Harriers	2-1
Weymouth v Orient	0-2
Wimbledon v Romford (2)	3-0
Yeovil Town v Margate	1-3
York City v Doncaster Rovers	0-1
r Bradford Park Avenue v Grimsby Town	4-1
r Colchester United v Torquay United	2-1
r Exeter City v Nuneaton Borough	0-0e
r Guildford City v Brentford	2-1
r Macclesfield Town v Stockport County	2-1
r Oxford United v Chelmsford City	3-3e
r Spennymoor United v Goole Town	3-1
r2 Chelmsford City v Oxford United	1-0 N
r2 Nuneaton Borough v Exeter City	0-1 N

Round Two

Altrincham v Barrow	1-2
Boston United v Orient	1-1
Bradford City v Bury	2-3
Bradford Park Avenue v Tranmere Rovers	2-3
Chelmsford City v Colchester United	0-2
Chester v Chesterfield	0-1
Doncaster Rovers v Workington	1-1
Exeter City v Walsall	1-3
Guildford City v Newport County	0-1
Halifax Town v Scunthorpe United	1-0
Macclesfield Town v Spennymoor United	2-0
Margate v Peterborough United	0-4
Reading v Dagenham	1-1
Southport v Runcorn	4-2
Swansea Town v Brighton & Hove Albion	2-1
Swindon Town v Luton Town	3-2
Tow Law Town v Shrewsbury Town	1-1
Walthamstow Avenue v Bournemouth	1-3
Watford v Hereford United	3-0
Wimbledon v Bristol Rovers	0-4
r Dagenham v Reading	0-1
r Orient v Boston United	2-1
r Shrewsbury Town v Tow Law Town	6-2
r Workington v Doncaster Rovers	1-2e

Round Three

Aston Villa v Millwall	3-0
Barrow v Leicester City	1-2
Blackpool v Chesterfield	2-1
Bournemouth v Liverpool	0-0
Bristol City v Bristol Rovers	0-0
Burnley v West Ham United	1-3
Chelsea v Ipswich Town	3-0
Colchester United v West Bromwich Albion	1-1
Coventry City v Charlton Athletic	3-0
Doncaster Rovers v Swansea Town	0-2
Fulham v Macclesfield Town	4-2
Halifax Town v Birmingham City	2-4
Leeds United v Derby County	2-0
Manchester City v Reading	0-0
Manchester United v Tottenham Hotspur	2-2
Middlesbrough v Hull City	1-1
Newcastle United v Carlisle United	0-1
Norwich City v Sunderland	1-1
Nottingham Forest v Bolton Wanderers	4-2
Orient v Bury	1-0
Peterborough United v Portsmouth	0-1
Queen's Park Rangers v Preston North End	1-3
Rotherham United v Wolverhampton Wan.	1-0
Sheffield Wednesday v Plymouth Argyle	3-0
Shrewsbury Town v Arsenal	1-1
Southampton v Newport County	1-1
Southport v Everton	0-1
Stoke City v Cardiff City	4-1
Swindon Town v Blackburn Rovers	1-0
Tranmere Rovers v Huddersfield Town	2-1
Walsall v Crystal Palace	1-1
Watford v Sheffield United	0-1
r Arsenal v Shrewsbury Town	2-0
r Bristol Rovers v Bristol City	1-2
r Crystal Palace v Walsall	1-2
r Hull City v Middlesbrough	2-2e
r Liverpool v Bournemouth	4-1
r Newport County v Southampton	2-3
r Reading v Manchester City	0-7
r Sunderland v Norwich City	0-1
r Tottenham Hotspur v Manchester United	1-0e
r West Bromwich Albion v Colchester United	4-0
r2 Middlesbrough v Hull City	1-0 N

Round Four

Aston Villa v Rotherham United	0-1
Birmingham City v Orient	3-0
Carlisle United v Everton	0-2
Chelsea v Norwich City	1-0
Coventry City v Tranmere Rovers	1-1
Fulham v Portsmouth	0-0
Leeds United v Nottingham Forest	2-1
Manchester City v Leicester City	0-0
Middlesbrough v Bristol City	1-1
Sheffield United v Blackpool	2-1
Sheffield Wednesday v Swindon Town	2-1
Stoke City v West Ham United	0-3
Swansea Town v Arsenal	0-1
Tottenham Hotspur v Preston North End	3-1
Walsall v Liverpool	0-0

West Bromwich Albion v Southampton	1-1
r Bristol City v Middlesbrough	2-1
r Leicester City v Manchester City	4-3
r Liverpool v Walsall	5-2
r Portsmouth v Fulham	1-0
r Southampton v West Bromwich Albion	2-3
r Tranmere Rovers v Coventry City	2-0

Round Five

Arsenal v Birmingham City	1-1
Everton v Tranmere Rovers	2-0
Leeds United v Bristol City	2-0
Portsmouth v West Bromwich Albion	1-2
Rotherham United v Leicester City	1-1
Sheffield Wednesday v Chelsea	2-2
Tottenham Hotspur v Liverpool	1-1
West Ham United v Sheffield United	1-2
r Birmingham City v Arsenal	2-1
r Chelsea v Sheffield Wednesday	2-0
r Leicester City v Rotherham United	2-0e
r Liverpool v Tottenham Hotspur	2-1

Round Six

Birmingham City v Chelsea	1-0
Leeds United v Sheffield United	1-0
Leicester City v Everton	1-3
West Bromwich Albion v Liverpool	0-0
r Liverpool v West Bromwich Albion	1-1e
r2 West Bromwich Albion v Liverpool	2-1 N

Semi Finals

Everton v Leeds United	1-0 N
West Bromwich Albion v Birmingham City	2-0 N

Final

West Bromwich Albion v Everton	1-0eN

1968/69

Preliminary Round

4 Fleetwood v Milnthorpe Corinthians	5-0
Nelson v Netherfield (Kendal)	0-4 N
5 Nantwich v Sandbach Ramblers	5-4
6 Rhyl v Prescot Town	5-1
7 Droylsden v Skelmersdale United	0-3
8 Mossley v Guinness Exports	3-1
9 Burton Albion v Bromsgrove Rovers	1-3
Hinckley Athletic v Lower Gornal Athletic	1-1
10 Lockheed Leamington v Hednesford Town	2-2
Stratford Town v Wellington Town	1-3
11 Goole Town v Barton Town (2)	4-1
12 Mexborough Town v Denaby United	1-1
13 Ilkeston Town (2) v Wombwell Sporting	1-1
15 Belper Town v Bedworth Town	2-2
Long Eaton United v Loughborough United	2-1
16 Desborough Town v Chatteris Town	3-0
Rushden Town v St Neots Town	0-1
17 March Town United v Cambridge United	1-1
19 Marlow v Banbury United	1-4
22 Hayes v Brentwood Town (1)	1-3
31 Horsham v Bognor Regis Town	2-3
32 Selsey v Andover	1-0
34 Poole Town v Melksham Town	4-0
9r Lower Gornal Athletic v Hinckley Athletic	3-2
10r Hednesford Town v Lockheed Leamington	4-1
12r Denaby United v Mexborough Town	3-2
13r Wombwell Sporting v Ilkeston Town (2)	1-5
15r Bedworth Town v Belper Town	3-2
17r Cambridge United v March Town United	5-0

Qualifying Round One

1 Durham City v Willington	1-0
Murton CW v Ferryhill Athletic	1-0
North Shields v Boldon CW	3-0
Whitley Bay v Shildon	0-1
2 Consett v Ryhope CW	2-0
Crook Town v Stockton	2-3
Evenwood Town v Annfield Plain	7-1
West Auckland Town v Stanley United	3-2
3 Billingham Synthonia v Ashington	2-0
Bishop Auckland v Gateshead	2-1
Blyth Spartans v Spennymoor United	4-3
Horden CW v Whitby Town	2-1
4 Clitheroe v Great Harwood	0-0
Fleetwood v Penrith	0-0
Lancaster City v Lytham	7-3
Morecambe v Netherfield (Kendal)	4-0
5 Congleton Town v Winsford United	0-1
Kirkby Town v New Brighton	3-1
Lostock Gralam v Nantwich	4-2
Northwich Victoria v Linotype & Machinery	3-0
6 Holyhead Town v Bangor City	2-3
Marine v Rhyl	0-0
Pwllheli & District v Porthmadog	0-5
South Liverpool v Oswestry Town	4-2
7 Burscough v Ellesmere Port Town	3-1
Darwen v Skelmersdale United	1-4

St Helens Town v Chorley	0-0
Stalybridge Celtic v Leyland Motors	3-2
8 Ashton United v Witton Albion	1-6
Bacup Borough v Rossendale United	0-1
Hyde United v Mossley	2-2
Wigan Rovers v Horwich RMI	1-1
9 Brierley Hill Alliance v Lower Gornal Athletic	1-5
Bromsgrove Rovers v Stafford Rangers	1-1
Dudley Town v Bilston	0-2
Tamworth v Darlaston	1-2
10 Alvechurch v Redditch	3-2
Halesowen Town v Wellington Town	0-1
Hednesford Town v Worcester City	1-2
Stourbridge v Lye Town	7-4
11 Ashby Institute v Selby Town	0-3
Bridlington Town v Hull Brunswick	1-1
Brigg Town v Goole Town	1-5
Scarborough v Bridlington Trinity	0-0
12 Farsley Celtic v Retford Town	1-2
Gainsborough Trinity v Denaby United	4-0
Hatfield Main v Yorkshire Amateur	5-0
Worksop Town v Frickley Colliery	2-4
13 Alfreton Town v Matlock Town	1-2
Eastwood Hanley v Ilkeston Town (2)	2-3
Norton Woodseats v Buxton	0-3
Rawmarsh Welfare v Sutton Town	0-0
14 Bourne Town v Wisbech Town	2-3
Holbeach United v Spalding United	1-1
Louth United v Boston	3-1
Skegness Town v King's Lynn	0-3
15 Atherstone Town v Long Eaton United	4-2
Bedworth Town v Rugby Town (2)	3-3
Eastwood Town v Heanor Town	2-2
Gresley Rovers v Arnold	1-0
16 Bedford Town (1) v Histon	5-0
Cambridge City v St Neots Town	0-0
Desborough Town v Stamford	0-4
Rothwell Town v Biggleswade Town	2-3
17 Ely City v Newmarket Town	4-1
Kettering Town v Cambridge United	1-0
Potton United v Wellingborough Town	1-2
Soham Town Rangers v Eynesbury Rovers	6-0
18 Clacton Town v Thetford Town	4-2
Gorleston v Harwich & Parkeston	2-1
Great Yarmouth Town v Bury Town	0-0
Sudbury Town v Gothic (Norwich)	4-0
19 Aylesbury United v Wembley	1-0
Bletchley Town v Maidenhead United	0-0
Letchworth Town v Banbury United	2-3
Wealdstone v Dunstable Town	3-2
20 Amersham Town v Erith & Belvedere	1-5
Dulwich Hamlet v Woodford Town (1)	0-1
Hitchin Town v Cheshunt	3-1
Wycombe Wanderers v St Albans City	0-0
21 Barking v Windsor & Eton	0-1
Clapton v Malden Town	1-1
Leatherhead v Molesey	5-0
Walton & Hersham v Huntley & Palmers	7-1
22 Banstead Athletic v Uxbridge	1-1
Carshalton Athletic v Metropolitan Police	4-5
Harlow Town v Brentwood Town (1)	0-3
Staines Town v Croydon Amateurs	0-4
23 Grays Athletic v Southall	1-4
Hampton v Kingstonian	1-6
Ilford v Edmonton (2)	0-1
Leyton v Hemel Hempstead Town	3-2
24 Aveley v Tooting & Mitcham United	0-1
Bexley United v Sutton United	1-0
Hillingdon Borough v Bromley	7-0
Tilbury v Epsom & Ewell	1-0
25 Crittall Athletic v Ware	1-1
Finchley v Hounslow	2-2
Hoddesdon Town v Baldock Town	1-1
Vauxhall Motors (Luton) v Harrow Borough	6-1
26 Dagenham v Ruislip Manor	2-2
Dartford v Hornchurch	4-0
Gravesend & Northfleet v Cray Wanderers	1-3
Redhill v Ford United	3-0
27 Bishop's Stortford v Wolverton Town & BR	6-0
Corinthian Casuals v Rainham Town	6-4
Hertford Town v Hendon	0-0
Slough Town v Feltham	2-1
28 Canterbury City v Whitstable Town	1-0
Chatham Town v Sittingbourne	1-6
Dover v Tonbridge	5-2
Maidstone United v Ashford Town	1-2
29 Deal Town v Snowdown CW	2-2
Folkestone v Margate	1-3
Hastings United v Ramsgate Athletic	1-1
Sheppey United v Herne Bay	1-1
30 Chichester City (1) v Fleet Town	1-0
Dorking v Addlestone	1-2
Fareham Town v Wokingham Town	2-3
Woking v Crawley Town	2-1
31 Eastbourne v Lancing	2-0
Haywards Heath v Bognor Regis Town	1-1
Littlehampton Town v Eastbourne United	1-2
Southwick v Worthing	1-1
32 Cowes v Thornycroft Athletic	0-1
Newport (IOW) v Selsey	3-2
Ryde Sports v Salisbury (2)	1-7
Waterlooville v Basingstoke Town	2-1
33 Bridport v Warminster Town	9-1
Minehead v Frome Town	1-2
Street v Bridgwater Town (1)	2-2

138

1968/69

	Trowbridge Town v Portland United	3-0
34	Chippenham Town v Welton Rovers	2-4
	Dorchester Town v Poole Town	2-5
	Gloucester City v Devizes Town	3-1
	Westbury United v Glastonbury	3-1
35	Abergavenny Thursdays v Stonehouse	4-1
	Cheltenham Town v Lovells Athletic	2-1
	Llanelli v Ton Pentre	2-1
	Merthyr Tydfil v Cinderford Town	1-4
36	Bideford v Barnstaple Town	2-2
	Penzance v Falmouth Town	3-4
	St Blazey v Nanpean Rovers	2-2
4r	Great Harwood v Clitheroe	0-1
r	Penrith v Fleetwood	0-5
6r	Rhyl v Marine	0-1
7r	Chorley v St Helens Town	0-1
8r	Horwich RMI v Wigan Rovers	2-0
r	Mossley v Hyde United	2-1
9r	Stafford Rangers v Bromsgrove Rovers	2-1
11r	Bridlington Trinity v Scarborough	1-1x
r	Hull Brunswick v Bridlington Town	3-2
13r	Sutton Town v Rawmarsh Welfare	4-1
14r	Spalding United v Holbeach United	2-5
15r	Heanor Town v Eastwood Town	5-1
r	Rugby Town (2) v Bedworth Town	0-2
16r	St Neots Town v Cambridge City	3-3e
18r	Bury Town v Great Yarmouth Town	1-0
19r	Maidenhead United v Bletchley Town	1-0
20r	St Albans City v Wycombe Wanderers	1-0
21r	Malden Town v Clapton	2-1e
22r	Uxbridge v Banstead Athletic	3-1
25r	Baldock Town v Hoddesdon Town	0-2
r	Hounslow v Finchley	4-2e
r	Ware v Crittall Athletic	2-1
26r	Ruislip Manor v Dagenham	1-6
27r	Hendon v Hertford Town	1-0
29r	Herne Bay v Sheppey United	3-5
r	Ramsgate Athletic v Hastings United	0-1
r	Snowdown CW v Deal Town	2-1
31r	Bognor Regis Town v Haywards Heath	2-3
r	Worthing v Southwick	4-4x
33r	Bridgwater Town (1) v Street	2-1
36r	Barnstaple Town v Bideford	0-1e
r	Nanpean Rovers v St Blazey	1-1
11r2	Scarborough v Bridlington Trinity	3-1e
16r2	Cambridge City v St Neots Town	3-0
31r2	Southwick v Worthing	5-3 N
36r2	Nanpean Rovers v St Blazey	2-0

Qualifying Round Two

1	Murton CW v North Shields	0-4
	Shildon v Durham City	3-1
2	Consett v Evenwood Town	4-3
	Stockton v West Auckland Town	2-1
3	Bishop Auckland v Horden CW	2-1
	Blyth Spartans v Billingham Synthonia	1-2
4	Fleetwood v Clitheroe	2-0
	Lancaster City v Morecambe	2-4
5	Northwich Victoria v Lostock Gralam	2-1
	Winsford United v Kirkby Town	2-4
6	Porthmadog v Bangor City	1-8
	South Liverpool v Marine	2-0
7	St Helens Town v Skelmersdale United	0-1
	Stalybridge Celtic v Burscough	2-2
8	Horwich RMI v Mossley	1-5
	Witton Albion v Rossendale United	4-3
9	Bilston v Lower Gornal Athletic	3-0
	Stafford Rangers v Darlaston	2-0
10	Stourbridge v Wellington Town	0-2
	Worcester City v Alvechurch	0-0
11	Scarborough v Goole Town	0-2
	Selby Town v Hull Brunswick	2-1
12	Frickley Colliery v Gainsborough Trinity	2-1
	Hatfield Main v Retford Town	2-2
13	Buxton v Ilkeston Town (2)	1-0
	Sutton Town v Matlock Town	0-1
14	King's Lynn v Louth United	3-1
	Wisbech Town v Holbeach United	3-1
15	Bedworth Town v Heanor Town	2-2
	Gresley Rovers v Atherstone Town	0-4
16	Biggleswade Town v Cambridge City	2-1
	Stamford v Bedford Town (1)	1-0
17	Soham Town Rangers v Kettering Town	0-1
	Wellingborough Town v Ely City	3-1
18	Clacton Town v Gorleston	2-3
	Sudbury Town v Bury Town	1-1
19	Aylesbury United v Maidenhead United	2-1
	Wealdstone v Banbury United	3-1
20	Hitchin Town v Woodford Town (1)	3-1
	St Albans City v Erith & Belvedere	3-2
21	Walton & Hersham v Leatherhead	4-1
	Windsor & Eton v Malden Town	2-2
22	Croydon Amateurs v Brentwood Town (1)	0-2
	Uxbridge v Metropolitan Police	2-2
23	Leyton v Edmonton (2)	1-1
	Southall v Kingstonian	0-0
24	Tilbury v Hillingdon Borough	0-3
	Tooting & Mitcham United v Bexley United	0-1
25	Vauxhall Motors (Luton) v Hoddesdon Town	1-0
	Ware v Hounslow	3-2
26	Dagenham v Dartford	1-2
	Redhill v Cray Wanderers	1-0
27	Bishop's Stortford v Corinthian Casuals	9-0
	Slough Town v Hendon	2-1
28	Canterbury City v Sittingbourne	2-0
	Dover v Ashford Town	2-3
29	Hastings United v Snowdown CW	7-3
	Sheppey United v Margate	0-6
30	Woking v Addlestone	5-2
	Wokingham Town v Chichester City (1)	5-0
31	Eastbourne United v Haywards Heath	3-0
	Southwick v Eastbourne	1-2
32	Salisbury (2) v Thornycroft Athletic	4-0
	Waterlooville v Newport (IOW)	3-0
33	Bridport v Frome Town	1-4
	Trowbridge Town v Bridgwater Town (1)	2-3
34	Poole Town v Westbury United	4-0
	Welton Rovers v Gloucester City	1-2
35	Abergavenny Thursdays v Cheltenham Town	2-2
	Cinderford Town v Llanelli	3-0
36	Falmouth Town v Bideford	2-1
	Wadebridge Town v Nanpean Rovers	1-1
7r	Burscough v Stalybridge Celtic	2-4
10r	Alvechurch v Worcester City	0-1
12r	Retford Town v Hatfield Main	1-0
15r	Heanor Town v Bedworth Town	1-0
18r	Bury Town v Sudbury Town	3-2
21r	Malden Town v Windsor & Eton	3-2
22r	Metropolitan Police v Uxbridge	3-3
23r	Edmonton (2) v Leyton	2-1
r	Kingstonian v Southall	3-1
35r	Cheltenham Town v Abergavenny Thursdays	3-2
36r	Nanpean Rovers v Wadebridge Town	0-7
22r2	Metropolitan Police v Uxbridge	3-1

Qualifying Round Three

1	North Shields v Shildon	2-1
2	Stockton v Consett	0-3
3	Billingham Synthonia v Bishop Auckland	0-2
4	Morecambe v Fleetwood	1-0
5	Northwich Victoria v Kirkby Town	4-2
6	Bangor City v South Liverpool	3-1
7	Skelmersdale United v Stalybridge Celtic	3-1
8	Mossley v Witton Albion	2-0
9	Bilston v Stafford Rangers	3-2
10	Wellington Town v Worcester City	2-3
11	Goole Town v Selby Town	3-0
12	Frickley Colliery v Retford Town	0-0
13	Buxton v Matlock Town	0-3
14	King's Lynn v Wisbech Town	5-3
15	Atherstone Town v Heanor Town	3-2
16	Biggleswade Town v Stamford	1-2
17	Kettering Town v Wellingborough Town	4-1
18	Bury Town v Gorleston	4-1
19	Wealdstone v Aylesbury United	2-1
20	Hitchin Town v St Albans City	0-2
21	Walton & Hersham v Malden Town	4-0
22	Brentwood Town (1) v Metropolitan Police	2-1
23	Edmonton (2) v Kingstonian	1-1
24	Hillingdon Borough v Bexley United	3-0
25	Vauxhall Motors (Luton) v Ware	3-3
26	Redhill v Dartford	2-4
27	Slough Town v Bishop's Stortford	2-0
28	Ashford Town v Canterbury City	3-4
29	Margate v Hastings United	4-0
30	Woking v Wokingham Town	3-2
31	Eastbourne United v Eastbourne	2-3
32	Waterlooville v Salisbury (2)	4-2
33	Bridgwater Town (1) v Frome Town	0-1
34	Poole Town v Gloucester City	1-1
35	Cinderford Town v Cheltenham Town	1-3
36	Wadebridge Town v Falmouth Town	2-2
12r	Retford Town v Frickley Colliery	0-0
23r	Kingstonian v Edmonton (2)	2-0
25r	Ware v Vauxhall Motors (Luton)	2-1eN
34r	Gloucester City v Poole Town	1-2
36r	Falmouth Town v Wadebridge Town	3-1
12r2	Retford Town v Frickley Colliery	3-0

Qualifying Round Four

	Altrincham v Wigan Athletic	2-0
	Barnet v Enfield	4-2
	Bath City v Yeovil Town	0-2
	Bilston v Matlock Town	2-0
	Bishop Auckland v Goole Town	2-3
	Boston United v Grantham	2-2
	Corby Town v St Albans City	0-1
	Eastbourne v Canterbury City	2-2
	Falmouth Town v Waterlooville	2-2
	Frome Town v Cheltenham Town	1-2
	Guildford City v Dartford	0-1
	Hereford United v Worcester City	4-1
	Hillingdon Borough v Brentwood Town (1)	0-0
	Kettering Town v Atherstone Town	2-0
	King's Lynn v Lowestoft Town	3-0
	Kingstonian v Chelmsford City	3-3
	Margate v Walton & Hersham	1-0
	Mossley v Morecambe	1-2
	North Shields v Tow Law Town	1-3
	Northwich Victoria v Skelmersdale United	1-3
	Nuneaton Borough v Kidderminster Harriers	1-1
	Oxford City v Romford (2)	7-1
	Retford Town v Macclesfield Town	0-2
	Runcorn v Bangor City	1-4
	Slough Town v Wealdstone	1-1
	South Shields (2) v Consett	1-1
	Stamford v Bury Town	0-2
	Ware v Walthamstow Avenue	1-0
	Weymouth v Poole Town	1-1
	Wimbledon v Woking	0-2
r	Brentwood Town (1) v Hillingdon Borough	2-0e
r	Canterbury City v Eastbourne	4-2
r	Chelmsford City v Kingstonian	5-3
r	Consett v South Shields (2)	0-6
r	Grantham v Boston United	2-1
r	Kidderminster Harriers v Nuneaton Borough	3-0
r	Poole Town v Weymouth	0-1
r	Waterlooville v Falmouth Town	1-1e
r	Wealdstone v Slough Town	2-0
r2	Falmouth Town v Waterlooville	0-2

Round One

	Altrincham v Crewe Alexandra	0-1
	Bangor City v Morecambe	2-3
	Barnet v Brentwood Town (1)	1-1
	Barnsley v Rochdale	0-0
	Bilston v Halifax Town	1-3
	Bradford City v Chester	1-2
	Brentford v Woking	2-0
	Brighton & Hove Albion v Kidderminster Harriers	2-2
	Bristol Rovers v Peterborough United	3-1
	Bury Town v Bournemouth	0-0 N
	Cheltenham Town v Watford	0-4
	Chesterfield v Skelmersdale United	2-0
	Colchester United v Chesham United	5-0
	Darlington v Grimsby Town	2-0
	Dartford v Aldershot	3-1
	Doncaster Rovers v Notts County	1-0
	Exeter City v Newport County	0-0
	Goole Town v Barrow	1-3
	Grantham v Chelmsford City	2-1
	Hartlepool v Rotherham United	1-1
	Hereford United v Torquay United	0-0
	Leytonstone v Walsall	0-1
	Luton Town v Ware	6-1
	Macclesfield Town v Lincoln City	1-3
	Mansfield Town v Tow Law Town	4-1
	Northampton Town v Margate	3-1
	Orient v Gillingham	1-1
	Oxford City v Swansea Town	2-3
	Reading v Plymouth Argyle	1-0
	Shrewsbury Town v Port Vale	1-1
	South Shields (2) v York City	0-6
	Southend United v King's Lynn	9-0
	Stockport County v Bradford Park Avenue	3-0
	Swindon Town v Canterbury City	1-0
	Tranmere Rovers v Southport	0-1
	Waterlooville v Kettering Town	1-2
	Wealdstone v St Albans City	1-1
	Weymouth v Yeovil Town	2-1
	Workington v Scunthorpe United	2-0
	Wrexham v Oldham Athletic	4-2
r	Bournemouth v Bury Town	3-0
r	Brentwood Town (1) v Barnet	1-0
r	Gillingham v Orient	2-1
r	Kidderminster Harriers v Brighton & Hove Albion	0-1
r	Newport County v Exeter City	1-3
r	Port Vale v Shrewsbury Town	3-1
r	Rochdale v Barnsley	0-1
r	Rotherham United v Hartlepool	3-0
r	St Albans City v Wealdstone	1-0
r	Torquay United v Hereford United	4-2

Round Two

	Bournemouth v Bristol Rovers	0-0
	Brighton & Hove Albion v Northampton Town	1-2
	Chester v Lincoln City	1-1
	Chesterfield v Wrexham	2-1
	Colchester United v Exeter City	0-1
	Darlington v Barnsley	0-0
	Doncaster Rovers v Southport	2-1
	Grantham v Swindon Town	0-2
	Halifax Town v Crewe Alexandra	1-1
	Kettering Town v Dartford	5-0
	Luton Town v Gillingham	3-1
	Port Vale v Workington	0-0
	Reading v Torquay United	0-0
	Rotherham United v Mansfield Town	2-2
	Southend United v Brentwood Town (1)	10-1
	St Albans City v Walsall	1-1
	Stockport County v Barrow	2-0
	Watford v Brentford	1-0
	Weymouth v Swansea Town	1-1
	York City v Morecambe	2-0
r	Barnsley v Darlington	1-0e
r	Bristol Rovers v Bournemouth	1-0
r	Crewe Alexandra v Halifax Town	1-3e
r	Lincoln City v Chester	2-1
r	Mansfield Town v Rotherham United	1-0
r	Swansea Town v Weymouth	2-0
r	Torquay United v Reading	1-2
r	Walsall v St Albans City	3-1
r	Workington v Port Vale	1-2

Round Three

	Aston Villa v Queen's Park Rangers	2-1
	Barnsley v Leicester City	1-1
	Birmingham City v Lincoln City	2-1
	Blackburn Rovers v Stockport County	2-0

1968/69 to 1969/70

	Bolton Wanderers v Northampton Town	2-1
	Bristol Rovers v Kettering Town	1-1
	Burnley v Derby County	3-1
	Bury v Huddersfield Town	1-2
	Cardiff City v Arsenal	0-0
	Charlton Athletic v Crystal Palace	0-0
	Chelsea v Carlisle United	2-0
	Coventry City v Blackpool	3-1
	Everton v Ipswich Town	2-1
	Exeter City v Manchester United	1-3
	Hull City v Wolverhampton Wan.	1-3
	Liverpool v Doncaster Rovers	2-0
	Manchester City v Luton Town	1-0
	Mansfield Town v Sheffield United	2-1
	Middlesbrough v Millwall	1-1
	Newcastle United v Reading	4-0
	Oxford United v Southampton	1-1
	Portsmouth v Chesterfield	3-0
	Preston North End v Nottingham Forest	3-0
	Sheffield Wednesday v Leeds United	1-1
	Sunderland v Fulham	1-4
	Swansea Town v Halifax Town	0-1
	Swindon Town v Southend United	0-2
	Walsall v Tottenham Hotspur	0-1
	Watford v Port Vale	2-0
	West Bromwich Albion v Norwich City	3-0
	West Ham United v Bristol City	3-2
	York City v Stoke City	0-2
r	Arsenal v Cardiff City	2-0
r	Crystal Palace v Charlton Athletic	0-2
r	Kettering Town v Bristol Rovers	1-2
r	Leeds United v Sheffield Wednesday	1-3
r	Leicester City v Barnsley	2-1
r	Millwall v Middlesbrough	1-0
r	Southampton v Oxford United	2-0

Round Four

	Arsenal v Charlton Athletic	2-0
	Blackburn Rovers v Portsmouth	4-0
	Bolton Wanderers v Bristol Rovers	1-2
	Everton v Coventry City	2-0
	Fulham v West Bromwich Albion	1-2
	Huddersfield Town v West Ham United	0-2
	Liverpool v Burnley	2-1
	Manchester United v Watford	1-1
	Mansfield Town v Southend United	2-1
	Millwall v Leicester City	0-1
	Newcastle United v Manchester City	0-0
	Preston North End v Chelsea	0-0
	Sheffield Wednesday v Birmingham City	2-2
	Southampton v Aston Villa	2-2
	Stoke City v Halifax Town	1-1
	Tottenham Hotspur v Wolverhampton Wan.	2-1
r	Aston Villa v Southampton	2-1
r	Birmingham City v Sheffield Wednesday	2-1
r	Chelsea v Preston North End	2-1
r	Halifax Town v Stoke City	0-3
r	Manchester City v Newcastle United	2-0
r	Watford v Manchester United	0-2

Round Five

	Birmingham City v Manchester United	2-2
	Blackburn Rovers v Manchester City	1-4
	Chelsea v Stoke City	3-2
	Everton v Bristol Rovers	1-0
	Leicester City v Liverpool	0-0
	Mansfield Town v West Ham United	3-0
	Tottenham Hotspur v Aston Villa	3-2
	West Bromwich Albion v Arsenal	1-0
r	Liverpool v Leicester City	0-1
r	Manchester United v Birmingham City	6-2

Round Six

Chelsea v West Bromwich Albion	1-2
Manchester City v Tottenham Hotspur	1-0
Manchester United v Everton	0-1
Mansfield Town v Leicester City	0-1

Semi Finals

Leicester City v West Bromwich Albion	1-0 N
Manchester City v Everton	1-0 N

Final

Manchester City v Leicester City	1-0 N

1969/70

Preliminary Round

1	Whitby Town v West Auckland Town	3-1
2	Ferryhill Athletic v Boldon CW	2-0
4	Darwen v Penrith	3-0
5	Congleton Town v Winsford United	0-6
6	Prescot Town v Runcorn	1-6
7	Hyde United v Stalybridge Celtic	1-1
9	Darlaston v Dudley Town	1-2
	Lower Gornal Athletic v Brierley Hill Alliance	4-2
10	Stourbridge v Stratford Town	5-1
	Telford United v Lockheed Leamington	3-1
11	Winterton Rangers v Selby Town	5-2
12	Kiveton Park United v Yorkshire Amateur	1-3
13	Ilkeston Town (2) v Matlock Town	1-2
	Norton Woodseats v Buxton	1-0
14	Boston United v Wisbech Town	2-1
15	Gresley Rovers v Long Eaton United	3-0
	Loughborough United v Bedworth United	1-1
16	Rothwell Town v Rushden Town	0-2
	St Neots Town v Chatteris Town	3-0
17	March Town United v Newmarket Town	1-1
	Soham Town Rangers v Ely City	1-1
18	Great Yarmouth Town v Harwich & Parkeston	0-1
	Sudbury Town v Gorleston	1-3
19	Marlow v Maidenhead United	4-1
	Wealdstone v Bletchley Town	2-1
21	Hatfield Town v Windsor & Eton	0-2
22	Guildford City v Uxbridge	4-1
23	Enfield v Southall	1-1
24	Canvey Island v Tooting & Mitcham United	0-0
25	Hazells (Aylesbury) v Ware	3-2
26	Egham Town v Ruislip Manor	1-1
27	Chertsey Town v Wolverton Town & BR	0-2
28	Tunbridge Wells v Whitstable Town	2-1
30	Dorking v Fleet Town	1-0
	Woking v Chichester City (1)	4-1
31	Horsham v Lancing	3-0
	Littlehampton Town v Eastbourne United	3-0
32	Ryde Sports v Salisbury (2)	1-1
33	Street v Frome Town	1-3
	Trowbridge Town v Minehead	2-3
34	Glastonbury v Melksham Town	5-1
	Poole Town v Devizes Town	6-1
7r	Stalybridge Celtic v Hyde United	0-2
15r	Bedworth United v Loughborough United	2-1
17r	Ely City v Soham Town Rangers	2-3
r	Newmarket Town v March Town United	3-0
23r	Southall v Enfield	1-1
24r	Tooting & Mitcham United v Canvey Island	4-1
26r	Ruislip Manor v Egham Town	1-2
32r	Salisbury (2) v Ryde Sports	3-2
23r2	Enfield v Southall	6-2

Qualifying Round One

1	Bedlington CW v Whitby Town	0-1
	Stockton v Blyth Spartans	3-3
	Willington v Evenwood Town	2-4
	Wingate (Durham) v Murton CW	3-0
2	Bishop Auckland v Washington	4-1
	Crook Town v Ferryhill Athletic	3-3
	Horden CW v Shildon	0-1
	Ryhope CW v Ashington	0-1
3	Consett v Annfield Plain	2-3
	Gateshead v Durham City	5-0
	Spennymoor United v South Bank	1-0
	Whitley Bay v Stanley United	2-1
4	Clitheroe v Fleetwood	1-5
	Great Harwood v Netherfield (Kendal)	1-3
	Lancaster City v Darwen	1-0
	Milnthorpe Corinthians v Lytham	1-1
5	Linotype & Machinery v Kirkby Town	0-1
	Nantwich v Northwich Victoria	2-3
	New Brighton v Winsford United	2-1
	Sandbach Ramblers v Lostock Gralam	0-1
6	Marine v South Liverpool	2-3
	Oswestry Town v Runcorn	0-1
	Porthmadog v Rhyl	1-3
	Pwllheli & District v Bethesda Athletic	0-6
7	Burscough v Leyland Motors	5-2
	Droylsden v St Helens Town	1-0
	Ellesmere Port Town v Hyde United	1-1
	Wigan Athletic v Chorley	1-1
8	Horwich RMI v Guinness Exports	3-1
	New Mills v Mossley	0-1
	Rossendale United v Witton Albion	3-1
	Wigan Rovers v Formby	0-6
9	Bilston v Stafford Rangers	0-1
	Bromsgrove Rovers v Dudley Town	0-1
	Lower Gornal Athletic v Tamworth	1-1
	Moor Green v Highgate United	1-1
10	Hednesford Town v Worcester City	2-1
	Lye Town v Alvechurch	2-3
	Redditch United v Stourbridge	0-0
	Telford United v Halesowen Town	7-3
11	Ashby Institute v Bridlington Trinity	1-0
	Bridlington Town v Barton Town (2)	3-5
	Hull Brunswick v Winterton Rangers	2-0
	Scarborough v Brigg Town	4-1
12	Frickley Colliery v Farsley Celtic	2-1
	Mexborough Town v Worksop Town	3-3
	Retford Town v Yorkshire Amateur	4-0
	Thackley v Gainsborough Trinity	1-4
13	Alfreton Town v Sutton Town	2-1
	Eastwood Hanley v Matlock Town	2-3
	Norton Woodseats v Wombwell Sporting	1-3
	Rawmarsh Welfare v Heanor Town	1-1
14	Boston v King's Lynn	2-3
	Holbeach United v Bourne Town	1-2
	Louth United v Skegness Town	0-1
	Spalding United v Boston United	0-4
15	Atherstone Town v Rugby Town (2)	1-2
	Bedworth United v Arnold	0-0
	Belper Town v Gresley Rovers	0-3
	Eastwood Town v Burton Albion	0-1
16	Bedford Town (1) v Corby Town	2-3
	Cambridge City v Stamford	7-0
	Desborough Town v Rushden Town	1-2
	St Neots Town v Biggleswade Town	2-3
17	Cambridge United v Wellingborough Town	5-0
	Eynesbury Rovers v Newmarket Town	2-3
	Letchworth Town v Irthlingborough Diamonds	2-3
	Soham Town Rangers v Potton United	2-2
18	Clacton Town v Thetford Town	2-1
	Gorleston v Bury Town	1-2
	Gothic (Norwich) v Harwich & Parkeston	0-1
	Lowestoft Town v Haverhill Rovers	6-1
19	Banbury United v Wembley	2-1
	Dunstable Town v Marlow	4-2
	Stevenage Athletic v Leighton Town	1-3
	Wealdstone v Aylesbury United	0-0
20	Cheshunt v Amersham Town	3-0
	Erith & Belvedere v St Albans City	2-1
	Hitchin Town v Chesham United	5-0
	Wycombe Wanderers v Dulwich Hamlet	2-1
21	Clapton v Barking	0-5
	Leatherhead v Walton & Hersham	0-1
	Malden Town v Windsor & Eton	4-0
	Molesey v Huntley & Palmers	1-1
22	Carshalton Athletic v Banstead Athletic	2-1
	Hayes v Staines Town	2-2
	Metropolitan Police v Guildford City	1-0
	Whyteleafe v Croydon Amateurs	1-1
23	Edmonton (2) v Hemel Hempstead Town	2-0
	Hampton v Grays Athletic	1-2
	Ilford v Leyton	2-0
	Kingstonian v Enfield	1-3 v
24	Aveley v Bromley	1-2
	Epsom & Ewell v Tilbury	0-1
	Hillingdon Borough v Tooting & Mitcham United	0-0
	Walthamstow Avenue v Bexley United	1-1
25	Baldock Town v Harrow Borough	3-0
	Finchley v Braintree & Crittall Ath.	1-1
	Hoddesdon Town v Vauxhall Motors (Luton)	4-2
	Hounslow v Hazells (Aylesbury)	6-1
26	Dagenham v Cray Wanderers	3-0
	Gravesend & Northfleet v Redhill	0-1
	Hornchurch v Egham Town	1-1
	Romford (2) v Ford United	2-2
27	Bishop's Stortford v Hendon	1-2
	Harlow Town v Corinthian Casuals	2-2
	Hertford Town v Slough Town	1-0
	Rainham Town v Wolverton Town & BR	1-0
28	Ashford Town v Dover	0-0
	Chatham Town v Canterbury City	1-6
	Maidstone United v Tonbridge	5-4
	Sittingbourne v Tunbridge Wells	0-1
29	Folkestone v Herne Bay	0-0
	Hastings United v Deal Town	4-0
	Ramsgate Athletic v Snowdown CW	8-1
	Sheppey United v Brett Sports	3-1
30	Basingstoke Town v Wokingham Town	1-2
	Crawley Town v Dorking	4-0
	East Grinstead v Alton Town	1-3
	Woking v Addlestone	3-3
31	Eastbourne v Worthing	5-1
	Haywards Heath v Horsham	1-2
	Littlehampton Town v Bognor Regis Town	1-0
	Southwick v Arundel	2-1
32	Andover v Newport (IOW)	4-1
	Fareham Town v Cowes	3-0
	Selsey v Waterlooville	3-4
	Thornycroft Athletic v Salisbury (2)	3-4
33	Bridport v Warminster Town	9-3
	Minehead v Bridgwater Town (1)	2-0
	Portland United v Frome Town	1-1
	Taunton v Bath City	2-4
34	Chippenham Town v Westbury United	3-2
	Dorchester Town v Glastonbury	1-2
	Poole Town v Welton Rovers	1-1
	Weston-Super-Mare v Spencer Moulton	11-2
35	Cinderford Town v Abergavenny Thursdays	2-3
	Llanelli v Stonehouse	1-2
	Merthyr Tydfil v Barry Town	2-1
	Ton Pentre v Gloucester City	2-2
36	Barnstaple Town v St Blazey	3-1
	Bideford v Falmouth Town	1-2
	Wadebridge Town v Nanpean Rovers	8-0
1r	Blyth Spartans v Stockton	8-2
2r	Ferryhill Athletic v Crook Town	0-1
4r	Lytham v Milnthorpe Corinthians	1-5
7r	Chorley v Wigan Athletic	2-5
r	Hyde United v Ellesmere Port Town	1-0
9r	Highgate United v Moor Green	3-2
r	Tamworth v Lower Gornal Athletic	4-2
10r	Stourbridge v Redditch United	3-0
12r	Worksop Town v Mexborough Town	6-1
13r	Heanor Town v Rawmarsh Welfare	0-1
15r	Arnold v Bedworth United	6-1
17r	Potton United v Soham Town Rangers	2-1
19r	Aylesbury United v Wealdstone	1-3
21r	Huntley & Palmers v Molesey	3-1e
22r	Croydon Amateurs v Whyteleafe	1-1e
r	Staines Town v Hayes	1-0 N
23r	Kingstonian v Enfield	0-3
24r	Bexley United v Walthamstow Avenue	2-2e
r	Tooting & Mitcham United v Hillingdon Borough	1-2
25r	Braintree & Crittall Ath. v Finchley	2-0
26r	Egham Town v Hornchurch	0-0x
r	Ford United v Romford (2)	2-4

1969/70

27r	Corinthian Casuals v Harlow Town	4-1
28r	Dover v Ashford Town	2-4
29r	Herne Bay v Folkestone	1-1e
30r	Addlestone v Woking	2-0
33r	Frome Town v Portland United	2-0
34r	Welton Rovers v Poole Town	2-1
35r	Gloucester City v Ton Pentre	0-1
22r2	Croydon Amateurs v Whyteleafe	0-1
24r2	Bexley United v Walthamstow Avenue	0-2
26r2	Hornchurch v Egham Town	5-2e
29r2	Folkestone v Herne Bay	1-0

Qualifying Round Two

1	Blyth Spartans v Evenwood Town	1-1
	Whitby Town v Wingate (Durham)	3-1
2	Bishop Auckland v Ashington	3-0
	Crook Town v Shildon	0-4
3	Spennymoor United v Gateshead	2-2
	Whitley Bay v Annfield Plain	7-1
4	Fleetwood v Netherfield (Kendal)	3-0
	Lancaster City v Milnthorpe Corinthians	3-0
5	Lostock Gralam v Northwich Victoria	0-5
	New Brighton v Kirkby Town	1-2
6	Bethesda Athletic v Rhyl	1-3
	Runcorn v South Liverpool	1-1
7	Hyde United v Burscough	0-1
	Wigan Athletic v Droylsden	4-1
8	Formby v Horwich RMI	1-2
	Mossley v Rossendale United	0-0
9	Dudley Town v Highgate United	3-0
	Tamworth v Stafford Rangers	3-3
10	Stourbridge v Alvechurch	1-1
	Telford United v Hednesford Town	4-3
11	Ashby Institute v Scarborough	0-2
	Hull Brunswick v Barton Town (2)	1-1
12	Gainsborough Trinity v Worksop Town	2-1
	Retford Town v Frickley Colliery	1-1
13	Alfreton Town v Wombwell Sporting	1-1
	Matlock Town v Rawmarsh Welfare	2-2
14	Boston United v Bourne Town	0-0
	King's Lynn v Skegness Town	2-1
15	Arnold v Rugby Town (2)	0-3
	Gresley Rovers v Burton Albion	0-3
16	Biggleswade Town v Cambridge City	0-2
	Rushden Town v Corby Town	2-1
17	Cambridge United v Potton United	10-0
	Newmarket Town v Irthlingborough Diamonds	3-1
18	Bury Town v Clacton Town	3-1
	Harwich & Parkeston v Lowestoft Town	0-1
19	Dunstable Town v Leighton Town	3-1
	Wealdstone v Banbury United	1-0
20	Hitchin Town v Cheshunt	3-1
	Wycombe Wanderers v Erith & Belvedere	2-0
21	Huntley & Palmers v Walton & Hersham	0-9
	Malden Town v Barking	2-2
22	Metropolitan Police v Carshalton Athletic	1-4
	Whyteleafe v Staines Town	1-2
23	Edmonton (2) v Ilford	2-1
	Enfield v Grays Athletic	7-1
24	Hillingdon Borough v Bromley	4-1
	Walthamstow Avenue v Tilbury	2-2
25	Baldock Town v Hoddesdon Town	0-1
	Hounslow v Braintree & Crittall Ath.	2-2
26	Hornchurch v Dagenham	0-2
	Romford (2) v Redhill	2-0
27	Corinthian Casuals v Hertford Town	1-2
	Rainham Town v Hendon	1-1
28	Ashford Town v Maidstone United	1-0
	Tunbridge Wells v Canterbury City	3-4
29	Folkestone v Ramsgate Athletic	1-1
	Sheppey United v Hastings United	0-6
30	Addlestone v Wokingham Town	0-1
	Crawley Town v Alton Town	1-0
31	Horsham v Southwick	2-0
	Littlehampton Town v Eastbourne	2-0
32	Andover v Waterlooville	2-1
	Salisbury (2) v Fareham Town	1-0
33	Frome Town v Bath City	1-4
	Minehead v Bridport	2-0
34	Glastonbury v Weston-Super-Mare	3-1
	Welton Rovers v Chippenham Town	2-2
35	Merthyr Tydfil v Abergavenny Thursdays	3-2
	Ton Pentre v Stonehouse	2-0
36	Falmouth Town v Penzance	1-0
	Wadebridge Town v Barnstaple Town	4-2
1r	Evenwood Town v Blyth Spartans	2-1
3r	Gateshead v Spennymoor United	0-1
6r	South Liverpool v Runcorn	5-0
8r	Rossendale United v Mossley	0-1
9r	Stafford Rangers v Tamworth	0-3
10r	Alvechurch v Stourbridge	1-3
11r	Barton Town (2) v Hull Brunswick	1-2
12r	Frickley Colliery v Retford Town	3-0
13r	Rawmarsh Welfare v Matlock Town	3-2
r	Wombwell Sporting v Alfreton Town	1-2
14r	Boston United v Bourne Town	2-0
21r	Barking v Malden Town	4-0
24r	Tilbury v Walthamstow Avenue	2-2e
25r	Braintree & Crittall Ath. v Hounslow	2-0
27r	Hendon v Rainham Town	7-2
29r	Ramsgate Athletic v Folkestone	1-0
34r	Chippenham Town v Welton Rovers	2-1
24r2	Tilbury v Walthamstow Avenue	3-1

Qualifying Round Three

1	Evenwood Town v Whitby Town	0-2
2	Bishop Auckland v Shildon	2-1
3	Whitley Bay v Spennymoor United	2-3
4	Fleetwood v Lancaster City	3-1
5	Northwich Victoria v Kirkby Town	0-2
6	South Liverpool v Rhyl	2-0
7	Wigan Athletic v Burscough	1-1
8	Mossley v Horwich RMI	2-1
9	Tamworth v Dudley Town	2-0
10	Telford United v Stourbridge	3-0
11	Scarborough v Hull Brunswick	5-1
12	Gainsborough Trinity v Frickley Colliery	3-2
13	Alfreton Town v Rawmarsh Welfare	3-1
14	King's Lynn v Boston United	2-1
15	Rugby Town (2) v Burton Albion	1-0
16	Cambridge City v Rushden Town	4-1
17	Cambridge United v Newmarket Town	6-0
18	Bury Town v Lowestoft Town	1-3
19	Wealdstone v Dunstable Town	4-0
20	Wycombe Wanderers v Hitchin Town	1-0
21	Walton & Hersham v Barking	4-1
22	Staines Town v Carshalton Athletic	1-2
23	Edmonton (2) v Enfield	1-4
24	Tilbury v Hillingdon Borough	1-2
25	Hoddesdon Town v Braintree & Crittall Ath.	1-1
26	Romford (2) v Dagenham	1-2
27	Hertford Town v Hendon	2-4
28	Ashford Town v Canterbury City	1-1
29	Ramsgate Athletic v Hastings United	2-1
30	Wokingham Town v Crawley Town	2-5
31	Littlehampton Town v Horsham	3-2
32	Andover v Salisbury (2)	0-0
33	Minehead v Bath City	3-0
34	Chippenham Town v Glastonbury	2-2
35	Ton Pentre v Merthyr Tydfil	4-2
36	Wadebridge Town v Falmouth Town	0-5
7r	Burscough v Wigan Athletic	2-3
25r	Braintree & Crittall Ath. v Hoddesdon Town	3-1e
28r	Canterbury City v Ashford Town	1-4e
32r	Salisbury (2) v Andover	3-0
34r	Glastonbury v Chippenham Town	7-0

Qualifying Round Four

	Alfreton Town v Goole Town	3-0
	Ashford Town v Walton & Hersham	0-1
	Bangor City v Fleetwood	2-1
	Brentwood Town (1) v Lowestoft Town	1-0
	Carshalton Athletic v Ramsgate Athletic	1-0
	Chelmsford City v Cambridge United	3-2
	Falmouth Town v Ton Pentre	1-1
	Glastonbury v Cheltenham Town	0-0
	Grantham v Gainsborough Trinity	5-0
	Hendon v Cambridge City	1-0
	Hereford United v Rugby Town (2)	3-1
	Hillingdon Borough v Dartford	1-1
	Kettering Town v Braintree & Crittall Ath.	4-0
	Leytonstone v Dagenham	0-4
	Littlehampton Town v Margate	0-1
	Macclesfield Town v Altrincham	3-0
	Minehead v Yeovil Town	0-0
	Mossley v Morecambe	4-1
	Nuneaton Borough v Tamworth	2-4
	Oxford City v King's Lynn	2-0
	Salisbury (2) v Weymouth	0-1
	South Liverpool v Kirkby Town	0-0
	South Shields (2) v Bishop Auckland	2-2
	Spennymoor United v Tow Law Town	1-0
	Telford United v Kidderminster Harriers	2-1
	Wealdstone v Enfield	0-1
	Whitby Town v Scarborough	3-1
	Wigan Athletic v Skelmersdale United	2-0
	Wimbledon v Crawley Town	0-0
	Wycombe Wanderers v Barnet	0-0
r	Barnet v Wycombe Wanderers	3-0
r	Bishop Auckland v South Shields (2)	1-3
r	Cheltenham Town v Glastonbury	4-1
r	Crawley Town v Wimbledon	0-0e
r	Dartford v Hillingdon Borough	0-0e
r	Kirkby Town v South Liverpool	4-3e
r	Ton Pentre v Falmouth Town	1-1e
r	Yeovil Town v Minehead	0-0e
r2	Crawley Town v Wimbledon	0-2
r2	Falmouth Town v Ton Pentre	1-0
r2	Hillingdon Borough v Dartford	4-1
r2	Minehead v Yeovil Town	0-5

Round One

	Alfreton Town v Barrow	1-1
	Bangor City v Kirkby Town	6-0
	Bournemouth v Luton Town	1-1
	Bradford City v Grimsby Town	2-1
	Brentford v Plymouth Argyle	0-0
	Brentwood Town (1) v Reading	1-0
	Brighton & Hove Albion v Enfield	2-1
	Bury v Mansfield Town	2-2
	Chelmsford City v Hereford United	1-2
	Cheltenham Town v Oxford City	0-2
	Dagenham v Sutton United	0-1
	Darlington v Barnsley	0-0
	Doncaster Rovers v Crewe Alexandra	1-1
	Exeter City v Fulham	2-0
	Falmouth Town v Peterborough United	1-4
	Halifax Town v Chester	3-3
	Hartlepool v North Shields	3-0
	Hendon v Carshalton Athletic	5-3
	Hillingdon Borough v Wimbledon	2-0
	Kettering Town v Swansea Town	0-2
	Lincoln City v Southport	2-0
	Macclesfield Town v Scunthorpe United	1-1
	Margate v Aldershot	2-7
	Newport County v Colchester United	2-1
	Northampton Town v Weymouth	0-0
	Notts County v Rotherham United	0-3
	Oldham Athletic v Grantham	3-1
	South Shields (2) v Bradford Park Avenue	2-1
	Southend United v Gillingham	0-0
	Spennymoor United v Wrexham	1-4
	Stockport County v Mossley	1-1
	Tamworth v Torquay United	2-1
	Telford United v Bristol Rovers	0-3
	Tranmere Rovers v Chesterfield	3-0
	Walsall v Orient	0-0
	Walton & Hersham v Barnet	0-1
	Wigan Athletic v Port Vale	1-1
	Workington v Rochdale	2-1
	Yeovil Town v Shrewsbury Town	2-3
	York City v Whitby Town	2-0
r	Barnsley v Darlington	2-0
r	Barrow v Alfreton Town	0-0e
r	Chester v Halifax Town	1-0
r	Crewe Alexandra v Doncaster Rovers	0-1
r	Gillingham v Southend United	2-1
r	Luton Town v Bournemouth	3-1
r	Mansfield Town v Bury	2-0
r	Mossley v Stockport County	0-1
r	Orient v Walsall	0-2
r	Plymouth Argyle v Brentford	2-0
r	Port Vale v Wigan Athletic	2-2e
r	Scunthorpe United v Macclesfield Town	4-2
r	Weymouth v Northampton Town	1-3
r2	Alfreton Town v Barrow	2-2eN
r2	Port Vale v Wigan Athletic	1-0eN
r3	Barrow v Alfreton Town	2-0 N

Round Two

	Aldershot v Bristol Rovers	3-1
	Bangor City v York City	0-0
	Barnet v Sutton United	0-2
	Barnsley v Barrow	3-0
	Bradford City v Lincoln City	3-0
	Brighton & Hove Albion v Walsall	1-1
	Chester v Doncaster Rovers	1-1
	Gillingham v Tamworth	6-0
	Hartlepool v Wrexham	0-1
	Hendon v Brentwood Town (1)	0-2
	Hillingdon Borough v Luton Town	2-1
	Newport County v Hereford United	2-1
	Northampton Town v Exeter City	1-1
	Oxford City v Swansea Town	1-5
	Peterborough United v Plymouth Argyle	2-0
	Port Vale v Tranmere Rovers	2-2
	Rotherham United v Workington	3-0
	Shrewsbury Town v Mansfield Town	1-2
	South Shields (2) v Oldham Athletic	0-0
	Stockport County v Scunthorpe United	0-0
r	Doncaster Rovers v Chester	0-2
r	Exeter City v Northampton Town	0-0e
r	Oldham Athletic v South Shields (2)	1-2
r	Scunthorpe United v Stockport County	4-0
r	Tranmere Rovers v Port Vale	3-1
r	Walsall v Brighton & Hove Albion	1-1e
r	York City v Bangor City	2-0
r2	Brighton & Hove Albion v Walsall	0-0eN
r2	Northampton Town v Exeter City	2-1 N
r3	Brighton & Hove Albion v Walsall	1-2 N

Round Three

	Arsenal v Blackpool	1-1
	Aston Villa v Charlton Athletic	1-1
	Blackburn Rovers v Swindon Town	0-4
	Bolton Wanderers v Watford	1-2
	Bradford City v Tottenham Hotspur	2-2
	Brentwood Town (1) v Northampton Town	0-1
	Burnley v Wolverhampton Wan.	3-0
	Chelsea v Birmingham City	3-0
	Chester v Bristol City	2-1
	Coventry City v Liverpool	1-1
	Crystal Palace v Walsall	2-0
	Gillingham v Newport County	1-0
	Hillingdon Borough v Sutton United	0-0
	Huddersfield Town v Aldershot	1-1
	Hull City v Manchester City	0-1
	Ipswich Town v Manchester United	0-1
	Leeds United v Swansea Town	2-1
	Leicester City v Sunderland	1-0
	Mansfield Town v Barnsley	3-2
	Middlesbrough v West Ham United	2-1
	Norwich City v Wrexham	1-2
	Nottingham Forest v Carlisle United	0-0
	Oxford United v Stoke City	0-0
	Portsmouth v Tranmere Rovers	1-2
	Preston North End v Derby County	1-1

1969/70 to 1970/71

Queen's Park Rangers v South Shields (2) 4-1
Rotherham United v Peterborough United 0-1
Scunthorpe United v Millwall 2-1
Sheffield United v Everton 2-1
Sheffield Wednesday v West Bromwich Albion 2-1
Southampton v Newcastle United 3-0
York City v Cardiff City 1-1
r Aldershot v Huddersfield Town 3-1
r Blackpool v Arsenal 3-2
r Cardiff City v York City 1-1e
r Carlisle United v Nottingham Forest 2-1
r Charlton Athletic v Aston Villa 1-0
r Derby County v Preston North End 4-1
r Liverpool v Coventry City 3-0
r Stoke City v Oxford United 3-2
r Sutton United v Hillingdon Borough 4-1
r Tottenham Hotspur v Bradford City 5-0
r2 Cardiff City v York City 1-3eN

Round Four

Blackpool v Mansfield Town 0-2
Carlisle United v Aldershot 2-2
Charlton Athletic v Queen's Park Rangers 2-3
Chelsea v Burnley 2-2
Derby County v Sheffield United 3-0
Gillingham v Peterborough United 5-1
Liverpool v Wrexham 3-1
Manchester United v Manchester City 3-0
Middlesbrough v York City 4-1
Sheffield Wednesday v Scunthorpe United 1-2
Southampton v Leicester City 1-1
Sutton United v Leeds United 0-6
Swindon Town v Chester 4-2
Tottenham Hotspur v Crystal Palace 0-0
Tranmere Rovers v Northampton Town 0-0
Watford v Stoke City 1-0
r Aldershot v Carlisle United 1-4
r Burnley v Chelsea 1-3e
r Crystal Palace v Tottenham Hotspur 1-0
r Leicester City v Southampton 4-2e
r Northampton Town v Tranmere Rovers 2-1

Round Five

Carlisle United v Middlesbrough 1-2
Crystal Palace v Chelsea 1-4
Leeds United v Mansfield Town 2-0
Liverpool v Leicester City 0-0
Northampton Town v Manchester United 2-8
Queen's Park Rangers v Derby County 1-0
Swindon Town v Scunthorpe United 3-1
Watford v Gillingham 2-1
r Leicester City v Liverpool 0-2

Round Six

Middlesbrough v Manchester United 1-1
Queen's Park Rangers v Chelsea 2-4
Swindon Town v Leeds United 0-2
Watford v Liverpool 1-0
r Manchester United v Middlesbrough 2-1

Semi Finals

Chelsea v Watford 5-1 N
Manchester United v Leeds United 0-0 N
r Manchester United v Leeds United 0-0eN
r2 Manchester United v Leeds United 0-1 N

Final

Chelsea v Leeds United 2-2eN
r Chelsea v Leeds United 2-1eN

1970/71

Preliminary Round

3 Bishop Auckland v Boldon CW 3-0
5 Marine v Prescot Town 2-1
Mossley v Eastwood Hanley 0-1
7 Lostock Gralam v Stalybridge Celtic 0-7
Northwich Victoria v Buxton 2-0
8 New Mills v Chorley 0-2
9 Stafford Rangers v Brierley Hill Alliance 1-2
10 Highgate United v Worcester City 0-5
Lockheed Leamington v Bromsgrove Rovers 1-3
13 Gainsborough Trinity v Sutton Town 2-1
Heanor Town v Belper Town 3-1
15 Burton Albion v Loughborough United 1-0
Gresley Rovers v Atherstone Town 0-1
16 St Neots Town v Corby Town 1-4
18 Harwich & Parkeston v Sudbury Town 1-2
Haverhill Rovers v Gorleston 0-7
19 Wealdstone v Hatfield Town 2-0
21 Ware v Grays Athletic 0-1
24 Uxbridge v Bromley 0-0
25 Wolverton Town & BR v Baldock Town 1-0
28 Tunbridge Wells v Deal Town 2-1
29 Folkestone v Snowdon CW 4-3
Hastings United v Canterbury City 2-0
30 Chichester City (1) v Horsham 5-2
Dorking v Banstead Athletic 2-0
31 Woking v East Grinstead 2-0
32 Fareham Town v Thornycroft Athletic 1-2
Fleet Town v Basingstoke Town 0-3
33 Welton Rovers v Frome Town 5-1
34 Dorchester Town v Trowbridge Town 1-2
Poole Town v Chippenham Town 4-0
24r Bromley v Uxbridge 3-1

Qualifying Round One

1 Annfield Plain v Gateshead 1-5
Durham City v Consett 0-0
Ferryhill Athletic v Crook Town 3-1
Spennymoor United v Bedlington CW 2-0
2 Billingham Synthonia v Whitley Bay 2-4
Blyth Spartans v Willington 2-1
Evenwood Town v Tow Law Town 3-0
West Auckland Town v Stockton 1-0
3 Horden CW v Stanley United 0-0
North Shields v Bishop Auckland 2-0
Shildon v Ryhope CW 3-1
South Bank v Washington 2-2
4 Clitheroe v Fleetwood 3-1
Great Harwood v Leyland Motors 5-2
Netherfield (Kendal) v Lancaster City 1-3
Penrith v Morecambe 3-1
5 Ellesmere Port Town v Eastwood Hanley 3-0
New Brighton v Nantwich 1-1
Sandbach Ramblers v Marine 0-2
Skelmersdale United v Congleton Town 3-0
6 Oswestry Town v Kirkby Town 2-0
Porthmadog v Holyhead Town 6-0
Pwllheli & District v Rhyl 0-6
Runcorn v Winsford United 0-2
7 Horwich RMI v Northwich Victoria 2-0
Prestwich Heys v Burscough 2-3
South Liverpool v Stalybridge Celtic 1-1
St Helens Town v Rossendale United 0-2
8 Bacup Borough v Droylsden 1-3
Formby v Ashton United 2-0
Hyde United v Guinness Exports 3-1
Witton Albion v Chorley 4-1
9 Coventry Amateurs v Dudley Town 1-2
Hednesford Town v Nuneaton Borough 1-2
Moor Green v Lye Town 2-2
Stourbridge v Brierley Hill Alliance 3-0
10 Alvechurch v Bilston 2-0
Halesowen Town v Bromsgrove Rovers 1-2
Kidderminster Harriers v Worcester City 1-0
Stratford Town v Redditch United 1-2
11 Bridlington Trinity v Farsley Celtic 1-0
Goole Town v Yorkshire Amateur 2-1
Scarborough v Bridlington Town 1-0
Winterton Rangers v Selby Town 3-1
12 Barton Town (2) v Brigg Town 1-1
Frickley Colliery v Ashby Institute 1-0
Norton Woodseats v Mexborough Town 7-3
Rawmarsh Welfare v Dinnington Athletic 0-1
13 Alfreton Town v Arnold 3-1
Eastwood Town v Heanor Town 0-1
Retford Town v Matlock Town 2-1
Worksop Town v Gainsborough Trinity 0-1
14 Boston United v Holbeach United 4-0
Louth United v Boston 0-1
Spalding United v Skegness Town 1-1
Stamford v Lincoln United 2-5
15 Bedworth United v Atherstone Town 1-2
Hinckley Athletic v Newhall United 1-1
Long Eaton United v Ilkeston Town (2) 1-1
Rugby Town (2) v Burton Albion 0-2
16 Cambridge City v Desborough Town 5-1
Irthlingborough Diamonds v Histon 2-1
Rothwell Town v Potton United 1-0
Wellingborough Town v Corby Town 4-1
17 Ely City v King's Lynn 1-2
March Town United v Chatteris Town 2-1
Soham Town Rangers v Rushden Town 1-0
Wisbech Town v Bourne Town 2-1
18 Bury Town v Clacton Town 0-2
Great Yarmouth Town v Gorleston 2-2
Newmarket Town v Lowestoft Town 3-3
Thetford Town v Sudbury Town 1-1
19 Bedford Town (1) v Letchworth Town 3-0
Biggleswade Town v Leighton Town 1-4
St Albans City v Marlow 2-0
Wembley v Wealdstone 0-2
20 Finchley v Hitchin Town 2-2
Metropolitan Police v Erith & Belvedere 0-1
Romford (2) v Rainham Town 11-0
Walton & Hersham v Chertsey Town 5-0
21 Bexley United v Hertford Town 2-2
Leatherhead v Barking 3-1
Vauxhall Motors (Luton) v Tooting & Mitcham United 1-2
Windsor & Eton v Grays Athletic 0-1
22 Chesham United v Cheshunt 0-1
Dulwich Hamlet v Addlestone 2-2
Guildford City v Epsom & Ewell 5-0
Stevenage Athletic v Woodford Town (1) 3-1
23 Hoddesdon Town v Ilford 1-1
Kingstonian v Hemel Hempstead Town 2-0
Tilbury v Slough Town 1-1
Wokingham Town v Cray Wanderers 1-3
24 Bishop's Stortford v Canvey Island 5-3
Hampton v Dartford 0-1
Hounslow v Harrow Borough 0-1 v
Walthamstow Avenue v Bromley 1-4
25 Aylesbury United v Banbury United 0-3
Bletchley Town v Witney Town 1-0
Maidenhead United v Dunstable Town 0-1
Wycombe Wanderers v Wolverton Town & BR 8-1
26 Edmonton (2) v Ford United 1-2
Hornchurch v Corinthian Casuals 3-2
Southall v Redhill 2-4
Staines Town v Leytonstone 0-1
27 Aveley v Braintree & Crittall Ath. 2-1
Clapton v Feltham 3-0
Hayes v Harlow Town 3-0
Leyton v Boreham Wood 2-4
28 Chatham Town v Gravesend & Northfleet 1-4
Herne Bay v Ashford Town 2-1
Sheppey United v Ramsgate Athletic 1-2
Tonbridge v Tunbridge Wells 5-0
29 Bexhill Town v Brett Sports 1-1
Dover v Hastings United 0-1
Sittingbourne v Maidstone United 0-5
Whitstable Town v Folkestone 2-7
30 Bognor Regis Town v Dorking 2-1
Eastbourne United v Eastbourne Town 1-3
Ringmer v Arundel 5-2
Selsey v Chichester City (1) 2-4
31 Crawley Town v Haywards Heath 3-0
Lancing v Carshalton Athletic 1-2
Southwick v Littlehampton Town 2-3
Worthing v Woking 0-2
32 Cowes v Basingstoke Town 1-3
Gosport Borough v Alton Town 5-1
Ryde Sports v Newport (IOW) 0-3
Waterlooville v Thornycroft Athletic 1-1
33 Bridport v Glastonbury 0-0
Minehead v Bridgwater Town (1) 1-1
Taunton Town v Street 6-2
Weston-Super-Mare v Welton Rovers 1-2
34 Andover v Bath City 0-1
Devizes Town v Poole Town 1-5
Salisbury (2) v Portland United 3-0
Westbury United v Trowbridge Town 1-3
35 Cinderford Town v Gloucester City 3-2
Llanelli v Barry Town 1-0
Stonehouse v Merthyr Tydfil 1-2
Ton Pentre v Abergavenny Thursdays 4-1
36 Barnstaple Town v Bideford 1-7
Falmouth Town v Truro City 5-1
St Blazey v Penzance 3-3
Wadebridge Town v Saltash United 1-3
1r Consett v Durham City 1-3
3r Stanley United v Horden CW 1-1
r Washington v South Bank 1-0
5r Nantwich v New Brighton 0-2
7r Stalybridge Celtic v South Liverpool 0-2
9r Lye Town v Moor Green 2-0
12r Brigg Town v Barton Town (2) 3-0
14r Skegness Town v Spalding United 1-2
15r Ilkeston Town (2) v Long Eaton United 0-0
r Newhall United v Hinckley Athletic 4-1
18r Gorleston v Great Yarmouth Town 2-1
r Lowestoft Town v Newmarket Town 3-0
r Sudbury Town v Thetford Town 0-1
20r Hitchin Town v Finchley 4-1
21r Hertford Town v Bexley United 1-2
22r Addlestone v Dulwich Hamlet 1-2
23r Ilford v Hoddesdon Town 2-0
r Slough Town v Tilbury 2-0
24r Hounslow v Harrow Borough 2-2
29r Brett Sports v Bexhill Town 0-2
32r Thornycroft Athletic v Waterlooville 0-0
33r Bridgwater Town (1) v Minehead 2-3
r Glastonbury v Bridport 2-0
36r Penzance v St Blazey 1-2
3r2 Horden CW v Stanley United 1-2
15r2 Long Eaton United v Ilkeston Town (2) 2-0
24r2 Harrow Borough v Hounslow 1-1
32r2 Waterlooville v Thornycroft Athletic 1-0
24r3 Hounslow v Harrow Borough 2-3

Qualifying Round Two

1 Ferryhill Athletic v Durham City 1-0
Spennymoor United v Gateshead 0-1
2 Blyth Spartans v West Auckland Town 6-1
Evenwood Town v Whitley Bay 1-0
3 Stanley United v Shildon 1-0
Washington v North Shields 1-0
4 Clitheroe v Penrith 0-2
Lancaster City v Great Harwood 1-1
5 New Brighton v Ellesmere Port Town 1-3
Skelmersdale United v Marine 2-1
6 Rhyl v Porthmadog 2-1
Winsford United v Oswestry Town 0-0
7 Burscough v South Liverpool 0-3
Rossendale United v Horwich RMI 3-1
8 Droylsden v Witton Albion 2-3
Hyde United v Formby 0-1
9 Dudley Town v Stourbridge 1-2
Nuneaton Borough v Lye Town 3-0
10 Alvechurch v Kidderminster Harriers 2-2
Redditch United v Bromsgrove Rovers 2-2

142

1970/71

11 Bridlington Trinity v Goole Town 0-0
Winterton Rangers v Scarborough 1-2
12 Brigg Town v Dinnington Athletic 1-1
Norton Woodseats v Frickley Colliery 0-0
13 Alfreton Town v Gainsborough Trinity 1-2
Retford Town v Heanor Town 1-2
14 Boston United v Lincoln United 1-0
Spalding United v Boston 2-2
15 Long Eaton United v Atherstone Town 2-1
Newhall United v Burton Albion 1-3
16 Cambridge City v Wellingborough Town 2-2
Rothwell Town v Irthlingborough Diamonds 1-1
17 King's Lynn v Wisbech Town 4-0
Soham Town Rangers v March Town United 2-0
18 Clacton Town v Thetford Town 2-0
Lowestoft Town v Gorleston 4-2
19 Leighton Town v Wealdstone 1-1
St Albans City v Bedford Town (1) 1-1
20 Hitchin Town v Walton & Hersham 1-1
Romford (2) v Erith & Belvedere 0-0
21 Bexley United v Grays Athletic 1-3
Tooting & Mitcham United v Leatherhead 1-2
22 Cheshunt v Stevenage Athletic 3-1
Guildford City v Dulwich Hamlet 2-1
23 Ilford v Cray Wanderers 3-0
Slough Town v Kingstonian 3-0
24 Bishop's Stortford v Bromley 2-1
Harrow Borough v Dartford 0-7
25 Banbury United v Wycombe Wanderers 0-3
Dunstable Town v Bletchley Town 1-0
26 Ford United v Leytonstone 0-2
Redhill v Hornchurch 0-0
27 Aveley v Boreham Wood 3-3
Hayes v Clapton 1-0
28 Gravesend & Northfleet v Tonbridge 0-1
Ramsgate Athletic v Herne Bay 0-0
29 Bexhill Town v Folkestone 1-1
Maidstone United v Hastings United 0-2
30 Eastbourne Town v Bognor Regis Town 2-4
Ringmer v Chichester City (1) 4-0
31 Crawley Town v Woking 3-1
Littlehampton Town v Carshalton Athletic 2-3
32 Gosport Borough v Waterlooville 2-3
Newport (IOW) v Basingstoke Town 2-2
33 Glastonbury v Welton Rovers 1-0
Taunton Town v Minehead 1-2
34 Bath City v Trowbridge Town 3-0
Salisbury (2) v Poole Town 0-1
35 Cinderford Town v Ton Pentre 0-1
Merthyr Tydfil v Llanelli 1-1
36 Bideford v Saltash United 3-1
St Blazey v Falmouth Town 3-2
4r Great Harwood v Lancaster City 3-0
6r Oswestry Town v Winsford United 1-0
10r Bromsgrove Rovers v Redditch United 3-0
r Kidderminster Harriers v Alvechurch 7-1
11r Goole Town v Bridlington Trinity 0-0
12r Dinnington Athletic v Brigg Town 0-1
r Frickley Colliery v Norton Woodseats 2-1
14r Boston v Spalding United 3-0
16r Irthlingborough Diamonds v Rothwell Town 5-0
r Wellingborough Town v Cambridge City 2-2
19r Bedford Town (1) v St Albans City 2-3
r Wealdstone v Leighton Town 0-1
20r Erith & Belvedere v Romford (2) 1-1
r Walton & Hersham v Hitchin Town 3-0
26r Hornchurch v Redhill 2-1
27r Boreham Wood v Aveley 0-3
28r Herne Bay v Ramsgate Athletic 3-1
29r Folkestone v Bexhill Town 4-2
32r Basingstoke Town v Newport (IOW) 1-0
35r Llanelli v Merthyr Tydfil 0-2
11r2 Bridlington Trinity v Goole Town 4-1
16r2 Wellingborough Town v Cambridge City 1-2 N
20r2 Romford (2) v Erith & Belvedere 1-0

Qualifying Round Three

1 Gateshead v Ferryhill Athletic 0-0
2 Blyth Spartans v Evenwood Town 2-1
3 Stanley United v Washington 0-2
4 Great Harwood v Penrith 3-2
5 Ellesmere Port Town v Skelmersdale United 0-1
6 Oswestry Town v Rhyl 1-1
7 Rossendale United v South Liverpool 1-3
8 Formby v Witton Albion 1-1
9 Nuneaton Borough v Stourbridge 2-1
10 Bromsgrove Rovers v Kidderminster Harriers 2-2
11 Scarborough v Bridlington Trinity 2-2
12 Frickley Colliery v Brigg Town 4-2
13 Heanor Town v Gainsborough Trinity 0-2
14 Boston v Boston United 0-4
15 Long Eaton United v Burton Albion 1-3
16 Irthlingborough Diamonds v Cambridge City 2-2
17 King's Lynn v Soham Town Rangers 6-0
18 Lowestoft Town v Clacton Town 2-1
19 St Albans City v Leighton Town 2-1
20 Romford (2) v Walton & Hersham 1-1
21 Leatherhead v Grays Athletic 3-0
22 Guildford City v Cheshunt 1-1
23 Slough Town v Ilford 4-2
24 Dartford v Bishop's Stortford 1-1
25 Dunstable Town v Wycombe Wanderers 0-4
26 Hornchurch v Leytonstone 1-2
27 Hayes v Aveley 2-3
28 Herne Bay v Tonbridge 4-1
29 Hastings United v Folkestone 0-0
30 Bognor Regis Town v Ringmer 1-2
31 Carshalton Athletic v Crawley Town 0-4
32 Basingstoke Town v Waterlooville 0-0
33 Minehead v Glastonbury 1-0
34 Poole Town v Bath City 1-0
35 Merthyr Tydfil v Ton Pentre 2-0
36 St Blazey v Bideford 2-6
1r Ferryhill Athletic v Gateshead 2-0
6r Rhyl v Oswestry Town 2-1
8r Witton Albion v Formby 3-1
10r Kidderminster Harriers v Bromsgrove Rovers 2-1
11r Bridlington Trinity v Scarborough 0-5
16r Cambridge City v Irthlingborough Diamonds 3-0
20r Walton & Hersham v Romford (2) 3-3
22r Cheshunt v Guildford City 2-0
24r Bishop's Stortford v Dartford 3-1
29r Folkestone v Hastings United 4-2
32r Waterlooville v Basingstoke Town 1-0
20r2 Romford (2) v Walton & Hersham 2-3

Qualifying Round Four

Altrincham v Great Harwood 1-1
Aveley v Leytonstone 0-0
Bangor City v Witton Albion 1-1
Bishop's Stortford v Cheshunt 5-2
Blyth Spartans v South Shields (2) 1-1
Chelmsford City v King's Lynn 2-0
Cheltenham Town v Burton Albion 2-2
Folkestone v Crawley Town 0-0
Frickley Colliery v Boston United 1-3
Grantham v Gainsborough Trinity 1-1
Hendon v St Albans City 0-0
Hereford United v Kidderminster Harriers 5-0
Herne Bay v Margate 0-1
Leatherhead v Wimbledon 1-2
Lowestoft Town v Barnet 0-0
Merthyr Tydfil v Minehead 0-2
Oxford City v Cambridge City 4-1
Poole Town v Yeovil Town 1-2
Rhyl v South Liverpool 3-3
Scarborough v Ferryhill Athletic 3-0
Skelmersdale United v Wigan Athletic 1-1
Slough Town v Hillingdon Borough 3-3
Tamworth v Nuneaton Borough 1-1
Walton & Hersham v Sutton United 1-0
Washington v Bradford Park Avenue 0-3
Waterlooville v Ringmer 2-3
Weymouth v Bideford 3-0
Wycombe Wanderers v Kettering Town 5-0
r Barnet v Lowestoft Town 2-0
r Burton Albion v Cheltenham Town 0-3
r Crawley Town v Folkestone 3-2
r Gainsborough Trinity v Grantham 3-3e
r Great Harwood v Altrincham 2-1
r Hillingdon Borough v Slough Town 0-2
r Leytonstone v Aveley 2-3
r Nuneaton Borough v Tamworth 2-2e
r South Liverpool v Rhyl 2-2e
r South Shields (2) v Blyth Spartans 3-0
r St Albans City v Hendon 1-2
r Wigan Athletic v Skelmersdale United 5-0
r Witton Albion v Bangor City 2-3
r2 Grantham v Gainsborough Trinity 2-1 N
r2 Nuneaton Borough v Tamworth 1-3
r2 Rhyl v South Liverpool 1-0

Round One

Barnet v Newport County 6-1
Barnsley v Bradford Park Avenue 1-0
Bradford City v Macclesfield Town 3-2
Brentford v Gillingham 2-1
Brighton & Hove Albion v Cheltenham Town 4-0
Chesterfield v Halifax Town 2-0
Colchester United v Ringmer 3-0
Crawley Town v Chelmsford City 1-1
Crewe Alexandra v Doncaster Rovers 0-0
Dagenham v Margate 2-0
Darlington v Bangor City 5-1
Enfield v Cambridge United 0-1
Fulham v Bristol Rovers 1-2
Grantham v Stockport County 2-1
Great Harwood v Rotherham United 2-6
Grimsby Town v Bury 0-1
Hendon v Aldershot 0-2
Hereford United v Northampton Town 2-2
Lincoln City v Barrow 2-1
Mansfield Town v Wrexham 2-0
Minehead v Shrewsbury Town 1-2
Notts County v Port Vale 1-0
Oxford City v Bournemouth 1-1
Peterborough United v Wimbledon 3-1
Preston North End v Chester 1-1
Reading v Bishop's Stortford 6-1
Rhyl v Hartlepool 1-0
Rochdale v Oldham Athletic 2-0
Scarborough v Workington 2-3
South Shields (2) v Wigan Athletic 1-1
Southend United v Weymouth 7-0
Southport v Boston United 0-2
Swansea City v Exeter City 4-1
Tamworth v York City 0-0
Torquay United v Aston Villa 3-1
Tranmere Rovers v Scunthorpe United 1-1
Walsall v Plymouth Argyle 3-0
Walton & Hersham v Telford United 2-5
Wycombe Wanderers v Slough Town 1-1
Yeovil Town v Aveley 1-0
r Bournemouth v Oxford City 8-1
r Chelmsford City v Crawley Town 6-1
r Chester v Preston North End 1-0
r Doncaster Rovers v Crewe Alexandra 1-3
r Northampton Town v Hereford United 1-2
r Scunthorpe United v Tranmere Rovers 0-0e
r Slough Town v Wycombe Wanderers 1-0
r Wigan Athletic v South Shields (2) 2-0
r York City v Tamworth 5-0
r2 Tranmere Rovers v Scunthorpe United 0-1eN

Round Two

Aldershot v Bristol Rovers 1-1
Boston United v York City 1-2
Bournemouth v Yeovil Town 0-1
Brentford v Walsall 1-0
Bury v Notts County 1-1
Chelmsford City v Torquay United 0-1
Chester v Crewe Alexandra 1-0
Chesterfield v Workington 0-0
Colchester United v Cambridge United 3-0
Darlington v Rochdale 0-2
Grantham v Rotherham United 1-4
Hereford United v Brighton & Hove Albion 1-2
Lincoln City v Bradford City 2-2
Rhyl v Barnsley 0-0
Scunthorpe United v Mansfield Town 3-0
Shrewsbury Town v Reading 2-2
Slough Town v Barnet 0-1
Southend United v Dagenham 1-0
Swansea City v Telford United 6-2
Wigan Athletic v Peterborough United 2-1
r Barnsley v Rhyl 1-1e
r Bradford City v Lincoln City 2-2e
r Bristol Rovers v Aldershot 1-3
r Notts County v Bury 3-0
r Reading v Shrewsbury Town 1-0
r Workington v Chesterfield 3-2
r2 Lincoln City v Bradford City 4-1 N
r2 Rhyl v Barnsley 2-0 N

Round Three

Barnet v Colchester United 0-1
Blackpool v West Ham United 4-0
Cardiff City v Brighton & Hove Albion 1-0
Chester v Derby County 1-2
Crystal Palace v Chelsea 2-2
Everton v Blackburn Rovers 2-0
Huddersfield Town v Birmingham City 1-1
Hull City v Charlton Athletic 3-0
Leicester City v Notts County 2-0
Liverpool v Aldershot 1-0
Manchester City v Wigan Athletic 1-0
Manchester United v Middlesbrough 0-0
Newcastle United v Ipswich Town 1-1
Nottingham Forest v Luton Town 1-1
Oxford United v Burnley 3-0
Portsmouth v Sheffield United 2-0
Queen's Park Rangers v Swindon Town 1-2
Rochdale v Coventry City 2-1
Rotherham United v Leeds United 0-0
Southampton v Bristol City 3-0
Southend United v Carlisle United 0-3
Stoke City v Millwall 2-1
Sunderland v Orient 0-3
Swansea City v Rhyl 6-1
Torquay United v Lincoln City 4-3
Tottenham Hotspur v Sheffield Wednesday 4-1
Watford v Reading 5-0
West Bromwich Albion v Scunthorpe United 0-0
Wolverhampton Wan. v Norwich City 5-1
Workington v Brentford 0-1
Yeovil Town v Arsenal 0-3
York City v Bolton Wanderers 2-0
r Birmingham City v Huddersfield Town 0-2
r Chelsea v Crystal Palace 2-0
r Ipswich Town v Newcastle United 2-1
r Leeds United v Rotherham United 3-2
r Luton Town v Nottingham Forest 3-4
r Middlesbrough v Manchester United 2-1
r Scunthorpe United v West Bromwich Albion 1-3

Round Four

Cardiff City v Brentford 0-2
Carlisle United v Tottenham Hotspur 2-3
Chelsea v Manchester City 0-3
Derby County v Wolverhampton Wan. 2-1
Everton v Middlesbrough 3-0
Hull City v Blackpool 2-0
Leeds United v Swindon Town 4-0
Leicester City v Torquay United 3-0
Liverpool v Swansea City 3-0
Nottingham Forest v Orient 1-1
Oxford United v Watford 1-1
Portsmouth v Arsenal 1-1
Rochdale v Colchester United 3-3

1970/71 to 1971/72

	Stoke City v Huddersfield Town	3-3
	West Bromwich Albion v Ipswich Town	1-1
	York City v Southampton	3-3
r	Arsenal v Portsmouth	3-2
r	Colchester United v Rochdale	5-0
r	Huddersfield Town v Stoke City	0-0e
r	Ipswich Town v West Bromwich Albion	3-0
r	Orient v Nottingham Forest	0-1
r	Southampton v York City	3-2
r	Watford v Oxford United	1-2
r2	Stoke City v Huddersfield Town	1-0 N

Round Five

	Colchester United v Leeds United	3-2
	Everton v Derby County	1-0
	Hull City v Brentford	2-1
	Leicester City v Oxford United	1-1
	Liverpool v Southampton	1-0
	Manchester City v Arsenal	1-2
	Stoke City v Ipswich Town	0-0
	Tottenham Hotspur v Nottingham Forest	2-1
r	Ipswich Town v Stoke City	0-1
r	Oxford United v Leicester City	1-3e

Round Six

	Everton v Colchester United	5-0
	Hull City v Stoke City	2-3
	Leicester City v Arsenal	0-0
	Liverpool v Tottenham Hotspur	0-0
r	Arsenal v Leicester City	1-0
r	Tottenham Hotspur v Liverpool	0-1

Semi Finals

	Arsenal v Stoke City	2-2 N
	Liverpool v Everton	2-1 N
r	Stoke City v Arsenal	0-2 N

Final

	Arsenal v Liverpool	2-1eN

1971/72

Preliminary Round

5	Ellesmere Port Town v Formby	2-1
7	New Mills v Sandbach Ramblers	3-1
8	Hyde United v Kirkby Town	2-2
9	Brierley Hill Alliance v Bromsgrove Rovers	0-2
10	Kidderminster Harriers v Lye Town	3-1
11	Bridlington Town v Bridlington Trinity	2-1
12	Frickley Colliery v Mexborough Town	3-2
13	Louth United v Lincoln United	0-1
16	Histon v Rothwell Town	4-2
17	March Town United v Skegness Town	1-2
18	Harwich & Parkeston v Lowestoft Town	2-2
19	Desborough Town v Irthlingborough Diamonds	1-2
20	Kingstonian v Leighton Town	4-1
21	Hornchurch v Metropolitan Police	1-4
22	Romford (2) v St Albans City	3-0
25	Ilford v Staines Town	2-3
27	Hertford Town v Leytonstone	1-1
28	Ramsgate Athletic v Sittingbourne	1-1
32	Gosport Borough v Newport (IOW)	0-0
33	Minehead v Poole Town	1-2
34	Chippenham Town v Frome Town	1-0
35	Llanelli v Merthyr Tydfil	0-3
8r	Kirkby Town v Hyde United	1-2
18r	Lowestoft Town v Harwich & Parkeston	1-2
27r	Leytonstone v Hertford Town	2-1
28r	Sittingbourne v Ramsgate Athletic	0-1
32r	Newport (IOW) v Gosport Borough	4-0

Qualifying Round One

1	Billingham Synthonia v Ferryhill Athletic	0-2
	Bishop Auckland v Stanley United	4-1
	Gateshead v Tow Law Town	3-0
	Wingate (Durham) v North Shields	0-1
2	Bedlington CW v Ryhope CW	5-1
	Blyth Spartans v Boldon CW	3-2
	Crook Town v Consett	1-4
	Washington v Willington	1-1
3	Annfield Plain v Durham City	0-5
	Shildon v Evenwood Town	1-1
	Spennymoor United v Horden CW	4-2
	Stockton v Whitley Bay	2-2
4	Bacup Borough v Fleetwood	0-0
	Lancaster City v Penrith	6-1
	Morecambe v Accrington Stanley (2)	2-0
	Netherfield (Kendal) v Rossendale United	2-4
5	Chorley v Marine	3-0
	Droylsden v Ellesmere Port Town	0-3
	Leyland Motors v Ormskirk	1-4
	Radcliffe Borough v Burscough	2-3
6	Oswestry Town v Porthmadog	2-1
	Pwllheli & District v Connah's Quay Nomads	0-3
	Runcorn v New Brighton	2-0
	South Liverpool v Northwich Victoria	1-0
7	Altrincham v Buxton	1-0
	Eastwood Hanley v Winsford United	1-0
	Nantwich v New Mills	3-1
	Stalybridge Celtic v Witton Albion	0-1
8	Ashton United v Clitheroe	2-1
	Great Harwood v Prescot Town	7-1
	Horwich RMI v Hyde United	1-1
	Mossley v Prestwich Heys	2-2
9	Alvechurch v Moor Green	4-0
	Atherstone Town v Bromsgrove Rovers	3-1
	Darlaston v Warley	2-1
	Dudley Town v Worcester City	0-1
10	Hednesford Town v Redditch United	0-2
	Highgate United v Kidderminster Harriers	3-1
	Lockheed Leamington v Stourbridge	2-1
	Lower Gornal Athletic v Halesowen Town	2-2
11	Barton Town (2) v Bridlington Town	1-0
	Goole Town v Selby Town	3-0
	Hull Brunswick v Whitby Town	1-3
	Scarborough v Ashby Institute	6-0
12	Denaby United v Emley	3-0
	Farsley Celtic v Frickley Colliery	0-1
	Glossop v Worksop Town	0-1
	Rawmarsh Welfare v Yorkshire Amateur	1-1
13	Arnold v Brigg Town	2-0
	Eastwood Town v Retford Town	2-2
	Gainsborough Trinity v Lincoln United	2-3
	Norton Woodseats v Winterton Rangers	0-3
14	Alfreton Town v Bilston	4-0
	Heanor Town v Newhall United	1-0
	Long Eaton United v Sutton Coldfield Town	3-1
	Loughborough United v Nuneaton Borough	0-5
15	Belper Town v Burton Albion	0-0
	Gresley Rovers v Stafford Rangers	0-4
	Ilkeston Town (2) v Bedworth United	1-2
	Matlock Town v Sutton Town	1-3
16	Chatteris Town v Soham Town Rangers	3-0
	Ely City v Histon	4-0
	Kettering Town v Cambridge City	6-1
	St Neots Town v Wellingborough Town	1-3
17	Boston v Bourne Town	1-5
	Holbeach United v Stamford	1-4
	King's Lynn v Skegness Town	4-1
	Spalding United v Wisbech Town	0-1
18	Bury Town v Clacton Town	2-0
	Gorleston v Sudbury Town	0-3
	Great Yarmouth Town v Harwich & Parkeston	1-3
	Newmarket Town v Thetford Town	1-4
19	Banbury United v Bedford Town (1)	2-2
	Biggleswade Town v Rushden Town	2-1
	Corby Town v Irthlingborough Diamonds	0-1
	Potton United v Witney Town	0-1
20	Bromley v Civil Service	10-0
	Finchley v Stevenage Athletic	0-1
	Hayes v Kingstonian	2-0
	Marlow v Wembley	0-3
21	Boreham Wood v Cheshunt	2-1
	Harrow Borough v Wealdstone	0-1
	Hoddesdon Town v Metropolitan Police	2-1
	Walthamstow Avenue v Woodford Town (1)	1-0
22	Braintree & Crittall Ath. v Chertsey Town	2-1
	Cray Wanderers v Ware	3-0
	Letchworth Town v Romford (2)	1-2
	Slough Town v Woking	1-1
23	Bexley United v Clapton	2-1
	Erith & Belvedere v Leatherhead	2-2
	Hemel Hempstead Town v Addlestone	2-2
	Hitchin Town v Tilbury	2-2
24	Barking v Bishop's Stortford	0-1
	Corinthian Casuals v Harlow Town	0-2 N
	Guildford City v Aylesbury United	2-0
	Hampton v Bletchley Town	2-1
25	Carshalton Athletic v Chesham United	2-1
	Dartford v Walton & Hersham	1-1
	Ford United v Staines Town	1-4
	Tooting & Mitcham United v Windsor & Eton	1-1
26	Dulwich Hamlet v Dunstable Town	1-0
	Feltham v Redhill	1-3
	Grays Athletic v Sutton United	2-4
	Hounslow v Uxbridge	0-2
27	Aveley v Banstead Athletic	1-0
	Gravesend & Northfleet v Southall	2-2
	Hatfield Town v Leytonstone	0-4
	Maidenhead United v Wycombe Wanderers	2-0
28	Ashford Town v Bexhill Town	2-0
	Deal Town v Tonbridge	1-1
	Dover v Ramsgate Athletic	2-1
	Snowdown CW v Whitstable Town	1-4
29	Canterbury City v Chatham Town	5-1
	Folkestone v Sheppey United	6-2
	Herne Bay v Faversham Town	3-1
	Maidstone United v Tunbridge Wells	6-1
30	Arundel v Bognor Regis Town	1-0
	Chichester City (1) v Haywards Heath	3-1
	Eastbourne United v Burgess Hill Town	0-2
	Hastings United v Southwick	1-1
31	Crawley Town v Eastbourne Town	4-0
	East Grinstead v Ringmer	2-0
	Horsham v Lewes	2-0
	Littlehampton Town v Worthing	0-1
32	Alton Town v Cowes	3-2
	Fareham Town v Selsey	8-2
	Fleet Town v Newport (IOW)	1-1
	Ryde Sports v Thornycroft Athletic	1-4
33	Bridgwater Town (1) v Bridport	1-0
	Dorchester Town v Taunton Town	3-2
	Glastonbury v Poole Town	2-1
	Trowbridge Town v Street	4-2
34	Basingstoke Town v Welton Rovers	2-1
	Bath City v Chippenham Town	2-1
	Melksham Town v Andover	1-3
	Salisbury (2) v Westbury United	4-0
35	Abergavenny Thursdays v Barry Town	1-0
	Cinderford Town v Ton Pentre	1-1
	Gloucester City v Merthyr Tydfil	2-3
	Stonehouse v Weston-Super-Mare	4-2
36	Barnstaple Town v Bideford	1-3
	Falmouth Town v Truro City	3-2
	Saltash United v Wadebridge Town	2-3
	St Blazey v Newquay	4-0
2r	Willington v Washington	1-0
3r	Evenwood Town v Shildon	4-3
r	Whitley Bay v Stockton	5-2
4r	Fleetwood v Bacup Borough	3-0
8r	Hyde United v Horwich RMI	2-0
r	Prestwich Heys v Mossley	1-2
10r	Halesowen Town v Lower Gornal Athletic	1-3
12r	Yorkshire Amateur v Rawmarsh Welfare	4-2
13r	Retford Town v Eastwood Town	0-3
15r	Burton Albion v Belper Town	2-0
19r	Bedford Town (1) v Banbury United	1-0
22r	Woking v Slough Town	0-2
23r	Addlestone v Hemel Hempstead Town	1-1
r	Leatherhead v Erith & Belvedere	3-0
r	Tilbury v Hitchin Town	3-2
25r	Walton & Hersham v Dartford	1-0
r	Windsor & Eton v Tooting & Mitcham United	2-0
27r	Southall v Gravesend & Northfleet	3-1
28r	Tonbridge v Deal Town	2-0
30r	Southwick v Hastings United	1-1
32r	Newport (IOW) v Fleet Town	5-2
35r	Ton Pentre v Cinderford Town	3-1
23r2	Hemel Hempstead Town v Addlestone	1-4
30r2	Hastings United v Southwick	2-1

Qualifying Round Two

1	Gateshead v Bishop Auckland	3-2
	North Shields v Ferryhill Athletic	3-1
2	Bedlington CW v Consett	0-0
	Blyth Spartans v Willington	3-1
3	Durham City v Spennymoor United	2-0
	Whitley Bay v Evenwood Town	3-1
4	Fleetwood v Lancaster City	0-2
	Rossendale United v Morecambe	2-2
5	Burscough v Chorley	2-1
	Ormskirk v Ellesmere Port Town	0-1
6	Oswestry Town v Connah's Quay Nomads	3-1
	South Liverpool v Runcorn	1-0
7	Altrincham v Eastwood Hanley	4-1
	Witton Albion v Nantwich	0-1
8	Ashton United v Great Harwood	3-2
	Mossley v Hyde United	0-0
9	Darlaston v Alvechurch	0-4
	Worcester City v Atherstone Town	0-0
10	Lockheed Leamington v Highgate United	0-2
	Lower Gornal Athletic v Redditch United	0-0
11	Goole Town v Barton Town (2)	3-2
	Whitby Town v Scarborough	0-2
12	Denaby United v Worksop Town	1-2
	Yorkshire Amateur v Frickley Colliery	0-0
13	Arnold v Eastwood Town	2-4
	Winterton Rangers v Lincoln United	3-1
14	Alfreton Town v Heanor Town	3-1
	Nuneaton Borough v Long Eaton United	2-0
15	Burton Albion v Stafford Rangers	1-2
	Sutton Town v Bedworth United	2-2
16	Kettering Town v Chatteris Town	2-0
	Wellingborough Town v Ely City	4-2
17	Bourne Town v Stamford	3-1
	Wisbech Town v King's Lynn	0-4
18	Bury Town v Sudbury Town	2-0
	Thetford Town v Harwich & Parkeston	0-0
19	Bedford Town (1) v Biggleswade Town	3-0
	Witney Town v Irthlingborough Diamonds	3-0
20	Bromley v Stevenage Athletic	1-1
	Wembley v Hayes	1-6
21	Boreham Wood v Wealdstone	1-1
	Walthamstow Avenue v Hoddesdon Town	2-0
22	Braintree & Crittall Ath. v Cray Wanderers	1-0
	Slough Town v Romford (2)	0-1
23	Bexley United v Leatherhead	3-2
	Tilbury v Addlestone	3-0
24	Bishop's Stortford v Harlow Town	4-2
	Hampton v Guildford City	1-1
25	Carshalton Athletic v Walton & Hersham	0-0
	Windsor & Eton v Staines Town	2-1
26	Dulwich Hamlet v Redhill	0-1
	Uxbridge v Sutton United	1-3
27	Aveley v Southall	1-1
	Maidenhead United v Leytonstone	1-0
28	Ashford Town v Tonbridge	3-1
	Whitstable Town v Dover	0-5
29	Canterbury City v Folkestone	1-3
	Maidstone United v Herne Bay	3-0
30	Arundel v Chichester City (1)	0-0
	Hastings United v Burgess Hill Town	4-1
31	Crawley Town v East Grinstead	3-0
	Worthing v Horsham	1-3

1971/72

32	Alton Town v Fareham Town	0-1
	Thornycroft Athletic v Newport (IOW)	4-1
33	Bridgwater Town (1) v Dorchester Town	1-0
	Trowbridge Town v Glastonbury	0-0
34	Andover v Basingstoke Town	1-3
	Salisbury (2) v Bath City	2-1
35	Abergavenny Thursdays v Ton Pentre	0-2
	Stonehouse v Merthyr Tydfil	0-2
36	Bideford v Falmouth Town	3-1
	Wadebridge Town v St Blazey	6-1
2r	Consett v Bedlington CW	4-1
4r	Morecambe v Rossendale United	0-1
8r	Hyde United v Mossley	2-0
9r	Atherstone Town v Worcester City	1-0
10r	Redditch United v Lower Gornal Athletic	3-1
12r	Frickley Colliery v Yorkshire Amateur	3-1
15r	Bedworth United v Sutton Town	0-1
18r	Harwich & Parkeston v Thetford Town	1-0
20r	Stevenage Athletic v Bromley	2-4
21r	Wealdstone v Boreham Wood	0-2
24r	Guildford City v Hampton	2-1
25r	Walton & Hersham v Carshalton Athletic	5-1
27r	Southall v Aveley	3-3
30r	Chichester City (1) v Arundel	1-1
33r	Glastonbury v Trowbridge Town	0-5
27r2	Aveley v Southall	2-1
30r2	Arundel v Chichester City (1)	2-7

Qualifying Round Three

1	Gateshead v North Shields	0-1
2	Blyth Spartans v Consett	8-1
3	Whitley Bay v Durham City	3-1
4	Lancaster City v Rossendale United	1-4
5	Burscough v Ellesmere Port Town	0-1
6	Oswestry Town v South Liverpool	2-0
7	Altrincham v Nantwich	1-1
8	Ashton United v Hyde United	2-2
9	Alvechurch v Atherstone Town	3-0
10	Redditch United v Highgate United	3-0
11	Scarborough v Goole Town	2-0
12	Worksop Town v Frickley Colliery	1-1
13	Eastwood Town v Winterton Rangers	1-2
14	Alfreton Town v Nuneaton Borough	0-4
15	Stafford Rangers v Sutton Town	2-0
16	Kettering Town v Wellingborough Town	2-1
17	Bourne Town v King's Lynn	0-3
18	Bury Town v Harwich & Parkeston	1-0
19	Bedford Town (1) v Witney Town	2-2
20	Bromley v Hayes	3-0
21	Boreham Wood v Walthamstow Avenue	2-2
22	Romford (2) v Braintree & Crittall Ath.	2-0
23	Bexley United v Tilbury	1-1
24	Bishop's Stortford v Guildford City	2-2
25	Walton & Hersham v Windsor & Eton	2-2
26	Redhill v Sutton United	0-2
27	Aveley v Maidenhead United	1-1
28	Ashford Town v Dover	0-2
29	Folkestone v Maidstone United	2-0
30	Chichester City (1) v Hastings United	1-1
31	Crawley Town v Horsham	3-1
32	Fareham Town v Thornycroft Athletic	5-1
33	Bridgwater Town (1) v Trowbridge Town	2-1
34	Basingstoke Town v Salisbury (2)	5-2
35	Ton Pentre v Merthyr Tydfil	2-1
36	Bideford v Wadebridge Town	4-1
7r	Nantwich v Altrincham	1-4 N
8r	Hyde United v Ashton United	3-1
12r	Frickley Colliery v Worksop Town	3-1
19r	Witney Town v Bedford Town (1)	2-0 N
21r	Walthamstow Avenue v Boreham Wood	2-1
23r	Tilbury v Bexley United	2-1
24r	Guildford City v Bishop's Stortford	1-1
25r	Windsor & Eton v Walton & Hersham	0-1 N
27r	Maidenhead United v Aveley	3-2
30r	Hastings United v Chichester City (1)	9-1
24r2	Bishop's Stortford v Guildford City	1-2

Qualifying Round Four

	Alvechurch v Oxford City	2-2
	Basingstoke Town v Fareham Town	2-2
	Bradford Park Avenue v South Shields (2)	0-1
	Bridgwater Town (1) v Yeovil Town	2-0
	Bromley v Guildford City	0-1
	Bury Town v King's Lynn	1-3
	Folkestone v Romford (2)	0-2
	Frickley Colliery v Grantham	3-0
	Hastings United v Crawley Town	0-0
	Hendon v Barnet	2-2
	Hereford United v Cheltenham Town	3-0
	Hyde United v Bangor City	1-3
	Kettering Town v Chelmsford City	4-1
	Macclesfield Town v Ellesmere Port Town	1-2
	Maidenhead United v Walton & Hersham	2-1
	Margate v Wimbledon	1-0
	Nuneaton Borough v Tamworth	3-1
	Oswestry Town v Altrincham	0-3
	Redditch United v Ton Pentre	3-0
	Rossendale United v Stafford Rangers	6-3
	Scarborough v North Shields	1-0
	Sutton United v Witney Town	0-1
	Tilbury v Enfield	0-1
	Walthamstow Avenue v Dover	0-0
	Weymouth v Bideford	3-1
	Whitley Bay v Blyth Spartans	1-1
	Wigan Athletic v Rhyl	2-1
	Winterton Rangers v Boston United	0-3
r	Barnet v Hendon	2-0
r	Blyth Spartans v Whitley Bay	2-1
r	Crawley Town v Hastings United	3-2
r	Dover v Walthamstow Avenue	1-0
r	Fareham Town v Basingstoke Town	1-1e
r	Oxford City v Alvechurch	1-1e
r2	Alvechurch v Oxford City	1-1eN
r2	Basingstoke Town v Fareham Town	2-1
r3	Oxford City v Alvechurch	0-0eN
r4	Oxford City v Alvechurch	0-0eN
r5	Oxford City v Alvechurch	0-1 N

Round One

	Aldershot v Alvechurch	4-2
	Barrow v Darlington	0-2
	Basingstoke Town v Northampton Town	1-5
	Blackburn Rovers v Port Vale	1-1
	Bolton Wanderers v Bangor City	3-0
	Bournemouth v Margate	11-0
	Bridgwater Town (1) v Reading	0-3
	Brighton & Hove Albion v Hillingdon Borough	7-1
	Bristol Rovers v Telford United	3-0
	Cambridge United v Weymouth	2-1
	Chester v Mansfield Town	1-1
	Chesterfield v Oldham Athletic	3-0
	Colchester United v Shrewsbury Town	1-4
	Crawley Town v Exeter City	0-0
	Crewe Alexandra v Blyth Spartans	0-1
	Doncaster Rovers v Stockport County	1-2
	Ellesmere Port Town v Boston United	0-3
	Enfield v Maidenhead United	2-0
	Frickley Colliery v Rotherham United	2-2
	Gillingham v Plymouth Argyle	3-2
	Guildford City v Dover	0-0
	Hartlepool v Scarborough	6-1
	Kettering Town v Barnet	2-4
	King's Lynn v Hereford United	0-0
	Lincoln City v Bury	1-2
	Notts County v Newport County	6-0
	Redditch United v Peterborough United	1-1
	Rochdale v Barnsley	1-3
	Rossendale United v Altrincham	1-0
	Skelmersdale United v Tranmere Rovers	0-4
	South Shields (2) v Scunthorpe United	3-3
	Southend United v Aston Villa	1-0
	Southport v Workington	1-3
	Swansea City v Brentford	1-1
	Torquay United v Nuneaton Borough	1-0
	Walsall v Dagenham	4-1
	Wigan Athletic v Halifax Town	2-1
	Witney Town v Romford (2)	0-3
	Wrexham v Bradford City	5-1
	York City v Grimsby Town	4-2
r	Brentford v Swansea City	2-3
r	Dover v Guildford City	0-2
r	Exeter City v Crawley Town	2-0
r	Hereford United v King's Lynn	1-0
r	Mansfield Town v Chester	4-3
r	Peterborough United v Redditch United	6-0
r	Port Vale v Blackburn Rovers	3-1
r	Rotherham United v Frickley Colliery	4-0
r	Scunthorpe United v South Shields (2)	2-3

Round Two

	Barnet v Torquay United	1-4
	Barnsley v Chesterfield	0-0
	Blyth Spartans v Stockport County	1-0
	Boston United v Hartlepool	2-1
	Bournemouth v Southend United	2-0
	Brighton & Hove Albion v Walsall	1-1
	Bristol Rovers v Cambridge United	3-0
	Hereford United v Northampton Town	0-0
	Mansfield Town v Tranmere Rovers	2-2
	Peterborough United v Enfield	4-0
	Port Vale v Darlington	1-0
	Reading v Aldershot	1-0
	Romford (2) v Gillingham	0-1
	Rossendale United v Bolton Wanderers	1-4 N
	Rotherham United v York City	1-1
	Shrewsbury Town v Guildford City	2-1
	South Shields (2) v Notts County	1-3
	Swansea City v Exeter City	0-0
	Workington v Bury	1-3
	Wrexham v Wigan Athletic	4-0
r	Chesterfield v Barnsley	1-0
r	Exeter City v Swansea City	0-1
r	Northampton Town v Hereford United	2-2e
r	Tranmere Rovers v Mansfield Town	4-2
r	Walsall v Brighton & Hove Albion	2-1
r	York City v Rotherham United	2-3e
r2	Hereford United v Northampton Town	2-1eN

Round Three

	Birmingham City v Port Vale	3-0
	Blackpool v Chelsea	0-1
	Blyth Spartans v Reading	2-2
	Bolton Wanderers v Torquay United	2-1
	Boston United v Portsmouth	0-1
	Burnley v Huddersfield Town	0-1
	Bury v Rotherham United	1-1
	Charlton Athletic v Tranmere Rovers	0-0
	Crystal Palace v Everton	2-2
	Derby County v Shrewsbury Town	2-0
	Leeds United v Bristol Rovers	4-1
	Manchester City v Middlesbrough	1-1
	Millwall v Nottingham Forest	3-1
	Newcastle United v Hereford United	2-2
	Norwich City v Hull City	0-3
	Orient v Wrexham	3-0
	Oxford United v Liverpool	0-3
	Peterborough United v Ipswich Town	0-2
	Preston North End v Bristol City	4-2
	Queen's Park Rangers v Fulham	1-1
	Sheffield United v Cardiff City	1-3
	Southampton v Manchester United	1-1
	Stoke City v Chesterfield	2-1
	Sunderland v Sheffield Wednesday	3-0
	Swansea City v Gillingham	1-0
	Swindon Town v Arsenal	0-2
	Tottenham Hotspur v Carlisle United	1-1
	Walsall v Bournemouth	1-0
	Watford v Notts County	1-4
	West Bromwich Albion v Coventry City	1-2
	West Ham United v Luton Town	2-1
	Wolverhampton Wan. v Leicester City	1-1
r	Carlisle United v Tottenham Hotspur	1-3
r	Everton v Crystal Palace	3-2
r	Fulham v Queen's Park Rangers	2-1
r	Hereford United v Newcastle United	2-1e
r	Leicester City v Wolverhampton Wan.	2-0
r	Manchester United v Southampton	4-1e
r	Middlesbrough v Manchester City	1-0
r	Reading v Blyth Spartans	6-1
r	Rotherham United v Bury	2-1
r	Tranmere Rovers v Charlton Athletic	4-2

Round Four

	Birmingham City v Ipswich Town	1-0
	Cardiff City v Sunderland	1-1
	Chelsea v Bolton Wanderers	3-0
	Coventry City v Hull City	0-1
	Derby County v Notts County	6-0
	Everton v Walsall	2-1
	Hereford United v West Ham United	0-0
	Huddersfield Town v Fulham	3-0
	Leicester City v Orient	0-2
	Liverpool v Leeds United	0-0
	Millwall v Middlesbrough	2-2
	Portsmouth v Swansea City	2-0
	Preston North End v Manchester United	0-2
	Reading v Arsenal	1-2
	Tottenham Hotspur v Rotherham United	2-0
	Tranmere Rovers v Stoke City	2-2
r	Leeds United v Liverpool	2-0
r	Middlesbrough v Millwall	2-1
r	Stoke City v Tranmere Rovers	2-0
r	Sunderland v Cardiff City	1-1e
r	West Ham United v Hereford United	3-1
r2	Cardiff City v Sunderland	3-1 N

Round Five

	Birmingham City v Portsmouth	3-1
	Cardiff City v Leeds United	0-2
	Derby County v Arsenal	2-2
	Everton v Tottenham Hotspur	0-2
	Huddersfield Town v West Ham United	4-2
	Manchester United v Middlesbrough	0-0
	Orient v Chelsea	3-2
	Stoke City v Hull City	4-1
r	Arsenal v Derby County	0-0e
r	Middlesbrough v Manchester United	0-3
r2	Derby County v Arsenal	0-1 N

Round Six

	Birmingham City v Huddersfield Town	3-1
	Leeds United v Tottenham Hotspur	2-1
	Manchester United v Stoke City	1-1
	Orient v Arsenal	0-1
r	Stoke City v Manchester United	2-1e

Semi Finals

	Arsenal v Stoke City	1-1 N
	Leeds United v Birmingham City	3-0 N
r	Stoke City v Arsenal	1-2 N

Final

	Leeds United v Arsenal	1-0 N

1972/73

1972/73

Preliminary Round

5	Ormskirk v Chorley	3-3
7	Prestwich Heys v Horwich RMI	3-3
8	Winsford United v Northwich Victoria	3-1
9	Moor Green v Darlaston	2-1
10	Sutton Coldfield Town v Highgate United	0-0
11	Whitby Town v Goole Town	0-1
12	Rawmarsh Welfare v Glossop	0-1
13	Winterton Rangers v Frickley Colliery	2-0
14	Norton Woodseats v Heanor Town	0-0
15	Nuneaton Borough v Kidderminster Harriers	1-1
16	Rushden Town v Long Eaton United	0-1
17	Spalding United v Kettering Town	0-2
18	Thetford Town v King's Lynn	2-1
19	Soham Town Rangers v Histon	0-2
20	Slough Town v Bedford Town (1)	1-0
21	Hitchin Town v Dunstable Town	3-0
22	Tilbury v Ilford	2-1
23	Hertford Town v Bromley	2-1
24	Sutton United v Corinthian Casuals	3-1
25	Southall v Dulwich Hamlet	0-1
26	Walton & Hersham v Metropolitan Police	1-1
27	Wembley v Hayes	1-3
28	Sheppey United v Dover	2-2
29	Tonbridge v Maidstone United	1-1
30	Lewes v Eastbourne United	3-0
31	Ringmer v Haywards Heath	0-1
32	Newport (IOW) v Cowes	2-0
33	Stonehouse v Cinderford Town	4-0
34	Welton Rovers v Melksham Town	2-0
35	Ton Pentre v Merthyr Tydfil	3-3
36	Truro City v Falmouth Town	1-0
5r	Chorley v Ormskirk	1-0
7r	Horwich RMI v Prestwich Heys	4-1
10r	Highgate United v Sutton Coldfield Town	2-0
14r	Heanor Town v Norton Woodseats	2-1
15r	Kidderminster Harriers v Nuneaton Borough	0-1
26r	Metropolitan Police v Walton & Hersham	1-6
28r	Dover v Sheppey United	1-0
29r	Maidstone United v Tonbridge	1-2
35r	Merthyr Tydfil v Ton Pentre	1-0

Qualifying Round One

1	Billingham Synthonia v Stanley United	3-2
	Crook Town v Ashington	2-0
	Evenwood Town v Annfield Plain	2-0
	Tow Law Town v Boldon CW	1-1
2	Gateshead v West Auckland Town	1-0
	Horden CW v North Shields	0-2
	Shildon v Murton CW	3-4
	Spennymoor United v Stockton	5-1
3	Consett v Ryhope CW	3-1
	Durham City v Ferryhill Athletic	1-2
	Whitley Bay v Bishop Auckland	0-1
	Wingate (Durham) v Willington	1-4
4	Bacup Borough v Morecambe	1-0
	Great Harwood v Clitheroe	4-1
	Lancaster City v Fleetwood	3-1
	Netherfield (Kendal) v Penrith	3-0
5	Accrington Stanley (2) v Darwen	1-1
	Burscough v Wigan Rovers	2-0
	Chorley v Formby	2-1
	Runcorn v Leyland Motors	8-0
6	Blaenau Ffestiniog v Oswestry Town	1-2
	Nantwich v Connah's Quay Nomads	3-2
	New Brighton v Marine	1-4
	Porthmadog v South Liverpool	0-0
7	Buxton v Altrincham	0-0
	Droylsden v Ashton United	1-2
	Horwich RMI v Hyde United	3-3
	New Mills v Radcliffe Borough	1-3
8	Eastwood Hanley v Congleton Town	2-1
	Ellesmere Port Town v Leek Town	2-1
	Sandbach Ramblers v Witton Albion	0-7
	Winsford United v Prescot Town	1-0
9	Brierley Hill Alliance v Tamworth	2-1
	Burton Albion v Atherstone Town	1-0
	Gresley Rovers v Warley	0-1
	Moor Green v Dudley Town	2-1
10	Halesowen Town v Bilston	1-4
	Hednesford Town v Bromsgrove Rovers	1-5
	Highgate United v Lower Gornal Athletic	6-0
	Stourbridge v Worcester City	2-1
11	Denaby United v Hatfield Main	1-1
	Farsley Celtic v Bridlington Town	3-2
	Goole Town v Scarborough	0-0
	Selby Town v Yorkshire Amateur	0-2
12	Emley v Macclesfield Town	1-2
	Glossop v Mexborough Town	3-2
	Mossley v Stalybridge Celtic	1-1
	Stocksbridge Works v Bradford Park Avenue	1-3
13	Bridlington Trinity v Ashby Institute	2-1
	Brigg Town v Barton Town (2)	1-3
	Retford Town v Worksop Town	1-2
	Winterton Rangers v Gainsborough Trinity	1-3
14	Belper Town v Alfreton Town	1-1
	Eastwood Town v Arnold	3-3
	Heanor Town v Ilkeston Town (2)	0-0
	Matlock Town v Sutton Town	1-1
15	Alvechurch v Oldbury United	3-1
	Bedworth United v Rugby Town (2)	0-3
	Lye Town v Redditch United	1-0
	Nuneaton Borough v Lockheed Leamington	4-1
16	Desborough Town v Enderby Town	1-2
	Irthlingborough Diamonds v Hinckley Athletic	1-1
	Long Eaton United v Loughborough United	3-0
	Rothwell Town v Wellingborough Town	1-5
17	Corby Town v Boston	3-1
	Holbeach United v Bourne Town	0-1
	Kettering Town v Louth United	4-0
	Skegness Town v Stamford	3-1
18	Gorleston v Chatteris Town	0-2
	Great Yarmouth Town v Ely City	2-2
	March Town United v Wisbech Town	1-1
	Thetford Town v Lowestoft Town	4-2
19	Clacton Town v Bury Town	1-4
	Harwich & Parkeston v Cambridge City	1-3
	Histon v Potton United	1-3
	St Neots Town v Sudbury Town	1-1
20	Aylesbury United v Oxford City	1-1
	Banbury United v Wokingham Town	4-1
	Chesham United v Witney Town	0-1
	Slough Town v Bletchley Town	0-0
21	Bishop's Stortford v Epping Town	1-0
	Harlow Town v Uxbridge	1-0
	Hitchin Town v Fleet Town	2-1
	Vauxhall Motors (Luton) v Edmonton (2)	0-0
22	Hatfield Town v Biggleswade Town	1-4
	Hemel Hempstead Town v Dartford	2-9
	Maidenhead United v Woking	0-1
	Tilbury v Kingstonian	0-0
23	Addlestone v Croydon	1-0
	Barking v Rainham Town	1-0
	Gravesend & Northfleet v St Albans City	1-1
	Hertford Town v Ford United	2-0
24	Cheshunt v Wimbledon	0-4
	Clapton v Aveley	1-2
	Stevenage Athletic v Ware	1-0
	Sutton United v Marlow	5-1
25	Bexley United v Bracknell Town	1-0
	Carshalton Athletic v Molesey	0-0
	Dulwich Hamlet v Hampton	1-2
	Hornchurch v Walthamstow Avenue	0-8
26	Letchworth Town v Egham Town	1-2
	Leytonstone v Hounslow	1-0
	Tooting & Mitcham United v Wycombe Wanderers	1-3
	Walton & Hersham v Staines Town	3-0
27	Finchley v Leyton	2-0
	Harrow Borough v Erith & Belvedere	0-0
	Hayes v Hoddesdon Town	4-1
	Wealdstone v Windsor & Eton	0-0
28	Chatham Town v Ashford Town	0-2
	Cray Wanderers v Canterbury City	2-1
	Dover v Hastings United	2-1
	Herne Bay v Tunbridge Wells	5-0
29	Faversham Town v Bexhill Town	0-2
	Folkestone v Deal Town	4-1
	Sittingbourne v Whitstable Town	2-0
	Tonbridge v Ramsgate Athletic	1-1
30	Bognor Regis Town v Dorking	3-0
	Burgess Hill Town v Peacehaven & Telscombe	1-3
	Leatherhead v Worthing	3-0
	Lewes v Horsham	1-0
31	Chichester City (1) v Pagham	0-0
	Eastbourne Town v Arundel	0-5
	Haywards Heath v Littlehampton Town	2-2
	Redhill v Southwick	1-0
32	Alton Town v Farnborough Town	2-0
	Basingstoke Town v Winchester City	1-1
	Gosport Borough v Ryde Sports	2-0
	Newport (IOW) v Fareham Town	2-6
33	Bath City v Cheltenham Town	0-0
	Chippenham Town v Devizes Town	0-4
	Gloucester City v Trowbridge Town	2-2
	Stonehouse v Glastonbury	0-1
34	Dorchester Town v Andover	1-1
	Frome Town v Bridport	4-2
	Salisbury (2) v Westbury United	9-1
	Welton Rovers v Poole Town	2-0
35	Bridgwater Town (1) v Ferndale Athletic	3 0
	Llanelli v Barry Town	0-1
	Merthyr Tydfil v Minehead	1-0
	Taunton Town v Weston-Super-Mare	3-1
36	Barnstaple Town v Bodmin Town	3-1
	Bideford v Penzance	3-2
	St Blazey v Wadebridge Town	1-2
	Truro City v Newquay	2-1
1r	Boldon CW v Tow Law Town	0-3
5r	Darwen v Accrington Stanley (2)	2-4
6r	South Liverpool v Porthmadog	2-1
7r	Altrincham v Buxton	4-1
r	Hyde United v Horwich RMI	1-0
11r	Hatfield Main v Denaby United	0-0
r	Scarborough v Goole Town	1-0
12r	Stalybridge Celtic v Mossley	4-3e
14r	Alfreton Town v Belper Town	4-1
r	Arnold v Eastwood Town	0-5
r	Ilkeston Town (2) v Heanor Town	0-2
r	Sutton Town v Matlock Town	3-2
16r	Hinckley Athletic v Irthlingborough Diamonds	1-2
18r	Ely City v Great Yarmouth Town	3-1
r	Wisbech Town v March Town United	3-0
19r	Sudbury Town v St Neots Town	6-1
20r	Bletchley Town v Slough Town	0-3
r	Oxford City v Aylesbury United	3-0
21r	Edmonton (2) v Vauxhall Motors (Luton)	0-2
22r	Kingstonian v Tilbury	1-2
23r	St Albans City v Gravesend & Northfleet	1-0
25r	Molesey v Carshalton Athletic	4-1
27r	Erith & Belvedere v Harrow Borough	2-1
r	Windsor & Eton v Wealdstone	0-3
29r	Ramsgate Athletic v Tonbridge	0-3
31r	Littlehampton Town v Haywards Heath	1-2
r	Pagham v Chichester City (1)	1-2
32r	Winchester City v Basingstoke Town	1-1
33r	Cheltenham Town v Bath City	3-2
r	Trowbridge Town v Gloucester City	2-0
34r	Andover v Dorchester Town	2-1
11r2	Denaby United v Hatfield Main	1-2
32r2	Basingstoke Town v Winchester City	0-0
32r3	Winchester City v Basingstoke Town	0-3

Qualifying Round Two

1	Crook Town v Tow Law Town	4-2
	Evenwood Town v Billingham Synthonia	0-0
2	Murton CW v Gateshead	2-4
	Spennymoor United v North Shields	1-1
3	Consett v Willington	1-2
	Ferryhill Athletic v Bishop Auckland	3-2
4	Great Harwood v Netherfield (Kendal)	5-0
	Lancaster City v Bacup Borough	2-1
5	Accrington Stanley (2) v Runcorn	1-1
	Burscough v Chorley	1-1
6	Marine v Oswestry Town	3-1
	Nantwich v South Liverpool	1-1
7	Altrincham v Radcliffe Borough	3-2
	Ashton United v Hyde United	1-1
8	Eastwood Hanley v Witton Albion	3-0
	Ellesmere Port Town v Winsford United	1-0
9	Brierley Hill Alliance v Warley	5-2
	Burton Albion v Moor Green	2-1
10	Bilston v Stourbridge	3-2
	Bromsgrove Rovers v Highgate United	2-1
11	Farsley Celtic v Scarborough	0-1
	Hatfield Main v Yorkshire Amateur	1-2
12	Bradford Park Avenue v Stalybridge Celtic	2-1
	Macclesfield Town v Glossop	3-0
13	Barton Town (2) v Gainsborough Trinity	2-2
	Bridlington Trinity v Worksop Town	0-1
14	Alfreton Town v Sutton Town	3-0
	Eastwood Town v Heanor Town	2-0
15	Alvechurch v Lye Town	4-0
	Rugby Town (2) v Nuneaton Borough	0-1
16	Enderby Town v Wellingborough Town	2-1
	Irthlingborough Diamonds v Long Eaton United	2-1
17	Bourne Town v Kettering Town	1-5
	Corby Town v Skegness Town	0-2
18	Chatteris Town v Wisbech Town	3-1
	Ely City v Thetford Town	2-0
19	Bury Town v Sudbury Town	1-1
	Cambridge City v Potton United	3-1
20	Banbury United v Slough Town	2-1
	Oxford City v Witney Town	0-4
21	Bishop's Stortford v Hitchin Town	4-1
	Vauxhall Motors (Luton) v Harlow Town	2-1
22	Biggleswade Town v Woking	0-2
	Dartford v Tilbury	4-3
23	Addlestone v St Albans City	0-1
	Barking v Hertford Town	1-0
24	Aveley v Sutton United	1-2
	Wimbledon v Stevenage Athletic	3-1
25	Bexley United v Walthamstow Avenue	1-0
	Molesey v Hampton	0-0
26	Egham Town v Wycombe Wanderers	2-6
	Leytonstone v Walton & Hersham	2-2
27	Erith & Belvedere v Hayes	1-2
	Finchley v Wealdstone	0-2
28	Ashford Town v Herne Bay	6-0
	Cray Wanderers v Dover	0-2
29	Bexhill Town v Sittingbourne	0-0
	Folkestone v Tonbridge	0-1
30	Bognor Regis Town v Leatherhead	2-0
	Peacehaven & Telscombe v Lewes	0-1
31	Arundel v Haywards Heath	1-2
	Chichester City (1) v Redhill	1-2
32	Alton Town v Gosport Borough	8-1
	Basingstoke Town v Fareham Town	3-1
33	Cheltenham Town v Trowbridge Town	4-0
	Devizes Town v Glastonbury	7-2
34	Andover v Salisbury (2)	0-1
	Frome Town v Welton Rovers	1-1
35	Barry Town v Merthyr Tydfil	1-0
	Bridgwater Town (1) v Taunton Town	0-4
36	Barnstaple Town v Wadebridge Town	3-0
	Bideford v Truro City	8-0
1r	Billingham Synthonia v Evenwood Town	2-1
2r	North Shields v Spennymoor United	2-2
5r	Chorley v Burscough	1-2
r	Runcorn v Accrington Stanley (2)	2-1
6r	South Liverpool v Nantwich	1-0
7r	Hyde United v Ashton United	2-2
13r	Gainsborough Trinity v Barton Town (2)	3-1
19r	Sudbury Town v Bury Town	1-3
25r	Hampton v Molesey	1-0
26r	Walton & Hersham v Leytonstone	3-0
29r	Sittingbourne v Bexhill Town	1-0
34r	Welton Rovers v Frome Town	0-1

1972/73 to 1973/74

2r2	Spennymoor United v North Shields	1-0
7r2	Ashton United v Hyde United	2-1

Qualifying Round Three

1	Crook Town v Billingham Synthonia	0-3
2	Gateshead v Spennymoor United	0-4
3	Ferryhill Athletic v Willington	1-5
4	Lancaster City v Great Harwood	1-0
5	Burscough v Runcorn	2-2
6	Marine v South Liverpool	0-2
7	Ashton United v Altrincham	1-3
8	Ellesmere Port Town v Eastwood Hanley	2-2
9	Burton Albion v Brierley Hill Alliance	0-1
10	Bromsgrove Rovers v Bilston	1-1
11	Scarborough v Yorkshire Amateur	2-2
12	Macclesfield Town v Bradford Park Avenue	1-0
13	Gainsborough Trinity v Worksop Town	1-0
14	Eastwood Town v Alfreton Town	0-4
15	Nuneaton Borough v Alvechurch	2-0
16	Irthlingborough Diamonds v Enderby Town	0-4
17	Kettering Town v Skegness Town	7-0
18	Ely City v Chatteris Town	3-3
19	Cambridge City v Bury Town	0-1
20	Banbury United v Witney Town	0-0
21	Bishop's Stortford v Vauxhall Motors (Luton)	2-0
22	Dartford v Woking	3-2
23	Barking v St Albans City	3-2
24	Sutton United v Wimbledon	3-1
25	Hampton v Bexley United	0-0
26	Walton & Hersham v Wycombe Wanderers	1-0
27	Hayes v Wealdstone	3-1
28	Dover v Ashford Town	1-2
29	Tonbridge v Sittingbourne	4-1
30	Lewes v Bognor Regis Town	1-1
31	Haywards Heath v Redhill	1-2
32	Basingstoke Town v Alton Town	0-2
33	Devizes Town v Cheltenham Town	1-0
34	Frome Town v Salisbury (2)	0-0
35	Barry Town v Taunton Town	0-0
36	Bideford v Barnstaple Town	1-2
5r	Runcorn v Burscough	2-3
8r	Ellesmere Port Town v Eastwood Hanley	2-0
10r	Bilston v Bromsgrove Rovers	1-0
11r	Yorkshire Amateur v Scarborough	0-2
18r	Chatteris Town v Ely City	2-4
20r	Witney Town v Banbury United	1-2
25r	Bexley United v Hampton	4-1
30r	Bognor Regis Town v Lewes	3-1
34r	Salisbury (2) v Frome Town	0-1
35r	Taunton Town v Barry Town	2-0

Qualifying Round Four

	Alfreton Town v Nuneaton Borough	0-2
	Alton Town v Devizes Town	2-0
	Altrincham v Ellesmere Port Town	1-1
	Ashford Town v Guildford City	3-4
	Barking v Hayes	1-2
	Barnstaple Town v Weymouth	1-0
	Billingham Synthonia v South Shields (2)	1-1
	Bilston v Brierley Hill Alliance	3-0
	Bishop's Stortford v Dagenham	1-1
	Bognor Regis Town v Bexley United	1-0
	Burscough v Wigan Athletic	1-3
	Bury Town v Boston United	1-3
	Crawley Town v Chelmsford City	0-2
	Ely City v Kettering Town	1-2
	Enderby Town v Telford United	0-2
	Frome Town v Banbury United	1-1
	Gainsborough Trinity v Grantham	1-2
	Hillingdon Borough v Redhill	0-0
	Lancaster City v Barrow	3-1
	Macclesfield Town v South Liverpool	0-1
	Margate v Sutton United	2-0
	Rossendale United v Bangor City	1-2
	Scarborough v Blyth Spartans	2-1
	Skelmersdale United v Rhyl	0-4
	Tonbridge v Romford (2)	0-0
	Walton & Hersham v Dartford	2-2
	Willington v Spennymoor United	0-2
	Yeovil Town v Taunton Town	4-1
r	Banbury United v Frome Town	3-0
r	Dagenham v Bishop's Stortford	0-4
r	Dartford v Walton & Hersham	0-1
r	Ellesmere Port Town v Altrincham	1-2
r	Redhill v Hillingdon Borough	0-1
r	Romford (2) v Tonbridge	1-2
r	South Shields (2) v Billingham Synthonia	2-1

Round One

	Altrincham v Notts County	0-1
	Banbury United v Barnet	0-2
	Barnsley v Halifax Town	1-1
	Barnstaple Town v Bilston	0-2
	Bolton Wanderers v Chester	1-1
	Boston United v Lancaster City	1-2
	Bournemouth v Cambridge United	5-1
	Bradford City v Grantham	3-0
	Chelmsford City v Hillingdon Borough	2-0
	Chesterfield v Rhyl	4-2
	Colchester United v Bognor Regis Town	6-0
	Crewe Alexandra v Stafford Rangers	1-0
	Darlington v Wrexham	1-1
	Doncaster Rovers v Bury	3-1
	Enfield v Bishop's Stortford	1-1
	Gillingham v Reading	1-2
	Grimsby Town v Wigan Athletic	2-1
	Hartlepool v Scunthorpe United	0-0
	Hayes v Bristol Rovers	1-0
	Lincoln City v Blackburn Rovers	2-2
	Margate v Swansea City	1-0
	Newport County v Alton Town	5-1
	Oldham Athletic v Scarborough	1-1
	Peterborough United v Northampton Town	1-0
	Plymouth Argyle v Hendon	1-0
	Port Vale v Southport	2-1
	Rochdale v Bangor City	1-2
	Rotherham United v South Shields (2)	4-0
	South Liverpool v Tranmere Rovers	0-2
	Southend United v Aldershot	0-2
	Spennymoor United v Shrewsbury Town	1-1
	Stockport County v Workington	1-0
	Telford United v Nuneaton Borough	3-2
	Tonbridge v Charlton Athletic	0-5
	Torquay United v Hereford United	3-0
	Walsall v Kettering Town	3-3
	Walton & Hersham v Exeter City	2-1
	Watford v Guildford City	4-2
	Yeovil Town v Brentford	2-1
	York City v Mansfield Town	2-1
r	Bishop's Stortford v Enfield	1-0
r	Blackburn Rovers v Lincoln City	4-1
r	Chester v Bolton Wanderers	0-1
r	Halifax Town v Barnsley	2-1
r	Kettering Town v Walsall	1-2
r	Scarborough v Oldham Athletic	2-1
r	Scunthorpe United v Hartlepool	0-0e
r	Shrewsbury Town v Spennymoor United	3-1
r	Wrexham v Darlington	5-0
r2	Hartlepool v Scunthorpe United	1-2eN

Round Two

	Bangor City v York City	2-3
	Barnet v Bilston	1-1
	Bishop's Stortford v Peterborough United	2-2
	Blackburn Rovers v Crewe Alexandra	0-1
	Bolton Wanderers v Shrewsbury Town	3-0
	Bournemouth v Colchester United	0-0
	Bradford City v Tranmere Rovers	2-1
	Chelmsford City v Telford United	5-0
	Grimsby Town v Chesterfield	2-2
	Notts County v Lancaster City	2-1
	Port Vale v Wrexham	1-0
	Reading v Hayes	0-0
	Rotherham United v Stockport County	0-1
	Scarborough v Doncaster Rovers	1-2
	Scunthorpe United v Halifax Town	3-2
	Torquay United v Newport County	0-1
	Walsall v Charlton Athletic	1-2
	Walton & Hersham v Margate	0-1
	Watford v Aldershot	2-0
	Yeovil Town v Plymouth Argyle	0-2
r	Bilston v Barnet	0-1
r	Chesterfield v Grimsby Town	0-1
r	Colchester United v Bournemouth	0-2
r	Hayes v Reading	0-1
r	Peterborough United v Bishop's Stortford	3-1

Round Three

	Arsenal v Leicester City	2-2
	Bradford City v Blackpool	2-1
	Brighton & Hove Albion v Chelsea	0-2
	Burnley v Liverpool	0-0
	Carlisle United v Huddersfield Town	2-2
	Charlton Athletic v Bolton Wanderers	1-1
	Chelmsford City v Ipswich Town	1-3
	Crystal Palace v Southampton	2-0
	Everton v Aston Villa	3-2
	Grimsby Town v Preston North End	0-0
	Luton Town v Crewe Alexandra	2-0
	Manchester City v Stoke City	3-2
	Margate v Tottenham Hotspur	0-6
	Millwall v Newport County	3-0
	Newcastle United v Bournemouth	2-0
	Norwich City v Leeds United	1-1
	Notts County v Sunderland	1-1
	Orient v Coventry City	1-4
	Peterborough United v Derby County	0-1
	Plymouth Argyle v Middlesbrough	1-0
	Port Vale v West Ham United	0-1
	Portsmouth v Bristol City	1-1
	Queen's Park Rangers v Barnet	0-0
	Reading v Doncaster Rovers	2-0
	Scunthorpe United v Cardiff City	2-3
	Sheffield Wednesday v Fulham	2-0
	Stockport County v Hull City	0-0
	Swindon Town v Birmingham City	2-0
	Watford v Sheffield United	0-1
	West Bromwich Albion v Nottingham Forest	1-1
	Wolverhampton Wan. v Manchester United	1-0
	York City v Oxford United	0-1
r	Barnet v Queen's Park Rangers	0-3
r	Bolton Wanderers v Charlton Athletic	4-0
r	Bristol City v Portsmouth	4-1
r	Huddersfield Town v Carlisle United	0-1
r	Hull City v Stockport County	2-0e
r	Leeds United v Norwich City	1-1e
r	Leicester City v Arsenal	1-2
r	Liverpool v Burnley	3-0
r	Nottingham Forest v West Bromwich Albion	0-0e
r	Preston North End v Grimsby Town	0-1
r	Sunderland v Notts County	2-0
r2	Norwich City v Leeds United	0-5 N
r2	West Bromwich Albion v Nottingham Forest	3-1 N

Round Four

	Arsenal v Bradford City	2-0
	Bolton Wanderers v Cardiff City	2-2
	Carlisle United v Sheffield United	2-1
	Chelsea v Ipswich Town	2-0
	Coventry City v Grimsby Town	1-0
	Derby County v Tottenham Hotspur	1-1
	Everton v Millwall	0-2
	Hull City v West Ham United	1-0
	Leeds United v Plymouth Argyle	2-1
	Liverpool v Manchester City	0-0
	Newcastle United v Luton Town	0-2
	Oxford United v Queen's Park Rangers	0-2
	Sheffield Wednesday v Crystal Palace	1-1
	Sunderland v Reading	1-1
	West Bromwich Albion v Swindon Town	2-0
	Wolverhampton Wan. v Bristol City	1-0
r	Cardiff City v Bolton Wanderers	1-1e
r	Crystal Palace v Sheffield Wednesday	1-1e
r	Manchester City v Liverpool	2-0
r	Reading v Sunderland	1-3
r	Tottenham Hotspur v Derby County	3-5e
r2	Bolton Wanderers v Cardiff City	1-0 N
r2	Sheffield Wednesday v Crystal Palace	3-2 N

Round Five

	Bolton Wanderers v Luton Town	0-1
	Carlisle United v Arsenal	1-2
	Coventry City v Hull City	3-0
	Derby County v Queen's Park Rangers	4-2
	Leeds United v West Bromwich Albion	2-0
	Manchester City v Sunderland	2-2
	Sheffield Wednesday v Chelsea	1-2
	Wolverhampton Wan. v Millwall	1-0
r	Sunderland v Manchester City	3-1

Round Six

	Chelsea v Arsenal	2-2
	Derby County v Leeds United	0-1
	Sunderland v Luton Town	2-0
	Wolverhampton Wan. v Coventry City	2-0
r	Arsenal v Chelsea	2-1

Semi Finals

	Leeds United v Wolverhampton Wan.	1-0 N
	Sunderland v Arsenal	2-1 N

Final

	Sunderland v Leeds United	1-0 N

1973/74

Preliminary Round

5	Ormskirk v Leyland Motors	2-0
7	New Brighton v Hyde United	1-1
8	Oswestry Town v Northwich Victoria	1-3
9	Sutton Coldfield Town v Eastwood Town	0-2
10	Oldbury United v Lye Town	0-1
11	Stocksbridge Works v Prestwich Heys	4-4
12	Rawmarsh Welfare v Hatfield Main	2-1
13	Retford Town v Louth United	2-1
14	Matlock Town v Heanor Town	3-0
15	Redditch United v AP Leamington	1-3
17	Thetford Town v Spalding United	3-0
18	Soham Town Rangers v Lowestoft Town	1-2
19	Letchworth Town v Ely City	2-1
20	Stevenage Athletic v Rushden Town	6-1
21	Wealdstone v Marlow	2-0
22	Feltham v Edmonton & Haringey	1-3
23	Kingstonian v Grays Athletic	4-0
24	Wembley v Southall	0-1
25	Rainham Town v Horsham	1-2
26	Maidenhead United v Hemel Hempstead Town	2-0
27	Sutton United v Metropolitan Police	3-0
28	Woking v Tonbridge	2-1
29	Ramsgate v Herne Bay	2-1
30	Tunbridge Wells v Ringmer	5-1
31	Waterlooville v Sidley United	4-0
32	Newport (IOW) v Fareham Town	1-1
34	Westbury United v Salisbury (2)	0-2
35	Welton Rovers v Mangotsfield United	1-4
36	Truro City v Penzance	0-2
7r	Hyde United v New Brighton	2-1
11r	Prestwich Heys v Stocksbridge Works	6-0
32r	Fareham Town v Newport (IOW)	0-1

1973/74

Qualifying Round One

1	Consett v Durham City	2-2
	North Shields v Spennymoor United	2-0
	Stanley United v Willington	1-6
	West Auckland Town v Whitley Bay	1-1
2	Annfield Plain v Murton CW	0-1
	Billingham Synthonia v Ashington	1-4
	Crook Town v Horden CW	1-3
	Wingate (Durham) v Whitby Town	2-1
3	Bishop Auckland v Gateshead	wo/s
	Boldon CW v Evenwood Town	0-1
	Shildon v Ferryhill Athletic	2-1
	Stockton v Tow Law Town	2-4
4	Bacup Borough v Fleetwood	2-3
	Barrow v Accrington Stanley (2)	0-4
	Netherfield (Kendal) v Rossendale United	3-2
	Penrith v Chorley	0-1
5	Burscough v Formby	1-1
	Clitheroe v Ormskirk	1-4
	Great Harwood v South Liverpool	0-1
	Morecambe v Darwen	0-0
6	Connah's Quay Nomads v Prescot Town	5-1
	Marine v Blaenau Ffestiniog	0-0
	Runcorn v Witton Albion	2-0
	Winsford United v Porthmadog	1-2
7	Altrincham v Glossop	3-1
	Congleton Town v Hyde United	2-0
	Horwich RMI v Skelmersdale United	3-1
	Nantwich Town v Ellesmere Port Town	5-0
8	Ashton United v Macclesfield Town	0-3
	Eastwood Hanley v Northwich Victoria	1-1
	New Mills v Stalybridge Celtic	0-2
	Sandbach Ramblers v Leek Town	0-4
9	Atherstone Town v Darlaston	1-0
	Belper Town v Eastwood Town	0-0
	Dudley Town v Tamworth	1-2
	Ilkeston Town (2) v Brereton Social	2-2
10	Brierley Hill Alliance v Hednesford Town	1-1
	Gornal Athletic v Lye Town	0-0
	Highgate United v Worcester City	1-1
	Nuneaton Borough v Gresley Rovers	3-0
11	Buxton v Farsley Celtic	1-0
	Droylsden v Prestwich Heys	1-4
	Mossley v Yorkshire Amateur	2-0
	Radcliffe Borough v Emley	1-2
12	Barton Town (2) v Bradford Park Avenue	0-2
	Bridlington Town v Rawmarsh Welfare	5-0
	Goole Town v Winterton Rangers	2-0
	Mexborough Town v Bridlington Trinity	3-2
13	Ashby Institute v Frickley Colliery	0-0
	Brigg Town v Retford Town	1-0
	Gainsborough Trinity v Sutton Town	1-2
	Norton Woodseats v Denaby United	0-4
14	Alfreton Town v Burton Albion	3-1
	Arnold v Matlock Town	1-1
	Enderby Town v Worksop Town	2-4
	Long Eaton United v Bilston	1-3
15	Alvechurch v Halesowen Town	2-0
	Bedworth United v AP Leamington	1-0
	Hinckley Athletic v Stourbridge	2-4
	Moor Green v Bromsgrove Rovers	1-1
16	Cinderford Town v Kidderminster Harriers	1-1
	Evesham United v Banbury United	2-2
	Oxford City v Witney Town	0-1
	Stonehouse v Gloucester City	1-1
17	Boston v Holbeach United	0-2
	Bury Town v Thetford Town	0-4
	Skegness Town v Wisbech Town	2-3
	Stamford v Desborough Town	1-0
18	Chatteris Town v Harwich & Parkeston	0-4
	Clacton Town v Lowestoft Town	2-1
	King's Lynn v Sudbury Town	1-0
	March Town United v Great Yarmouth Town	2-2
19	Bedford Town (1) v Cambridge City	2-0
	Biggleswade Town v Letchworth Town	2-0
	Corby Town v Wellingborough Town	1-0
	Histon v Bourne Town	1-0
20	Bletchley Town v Potton United	3-0
	Hitchin Town v Stevenage Athletic	1-1
	Rothwell Town v Vauxhall Motors (Luton)	1-0
	St Neots Town v Irthlingborough Diamonds	3-1
21	Aylesbury United v Hatfield Town	3-2
	Chesham United v Wealdstone	1-1
	Hertford Town v Wokingham Town	5-1
	Ware v Dunstable Town	2-0
22	Addlestone v Boreham Wood	1-3
	Bexley United v Edmonton & Haringey	3-0
	Dulwich Hamlet v Romford (2)	0-1
	Finchley v Bracknell Town	1-0
23	Cheshunt v Dagenham	2-2
	Clapton v Kingstonian	0-1
	Dartford v St Albans City	4-1
	Hampton v Cray Wanderers	3-3
24	Barking v Egham Town	0-2
	Bromley v Southall	0-1
	Epsom & Ewell v Wimbledon	1-5
	Staines Town v Croydon	2-0
25	Aveley v Harlow Town	2-1
	Carshalton Athletic v Horsham	0-3
	Harrow Borough v Tooting & Mitcham United	2-1
	Leyton v Crawley Town	2-2
26	Corinthian Casuals v Epping Town	0-2
	Dorking v Maidenhead United	0-2
	Gravesend & Northfleet v Walthamstow Avenue	6-1
	Hounslow v Edgware Town	2-0
27	Erith & Belvedere v Leatherhead	1-6
	Hornchurch v Sutton United	0-0
	Leytonstone v Windsor & Eton	2-0
	Redhill v Ilford	0-1
28	Chatham Town v Molesey	3-0
	Farnborough Town v Woking	2-2
	Tilbury v Wycombe Wanderers	0-3
	Uxbridge v Fleet Town	1-1
29	Ashford Town v Eastbourne United	4-0
	Bexhill Town v Ramsgate	0-2
	Hastings United v Sittingbourne	3-5
	Maidstone United v Canterbury City	4-2
30	Deal Town v Folkestone	1-1
	Dover v Tunbridge Wells	5-0
	Lewes v Whitstable Town	4-1
	Sheppey United v Faversham Town	2-3
31	Eastbourne Town v Peacehaven & Telscombe	3-2
	Haywards Heath v Waterlooville	1-1
	Pagham v Worthing	0-0
	Southwick v Littlehampton Town	0-3
32	Alton Town v Cowes	2-0
	Arundel v Newport (IOW)	0-2
	Bognor Regis Town v Ryde Sports	3-0
	Gosport Borough v Chichester City (1)	8-0
33	Basingstoke Town v Frome Town	2-0
	Bath City v Andover	3-0
	Hungerford Town v Trowbridge Town	1-1
	Melksham Town v Chippenham Town	4-2
34	Bridgwater Town (1) v Dorchester Town	3-3
	Bridport v Salisbury (2)	0-1
	Poole Town v Weymouth	0-3
	Taunton Town v Devizes Town	3-1
35	Barry Town v Merthyr Tydfil	0-3
	Everwarm v Mangotsfield United	0-4
	Llanelli v Weston-Super-Mare	1-0
	Ton Pentre v Glastonbury	1-2
36	Barnstaple Town v Minehead	2-1
	Bideford v Penzance	4-1
	Newquay v Wadebridge Town	1-0
	St Blazey v Falmouth Town	1-3
1r	Durham City v Consett	3-1
r	Whitley Bay v West Auckland Town	4-1
5r	Darwen v Morecambe	3-2
r	Formby v Burscough	4-1
6r	Blaenau Ffestiniog v Marine	0-0
8r	Northwich Victoria v Eastwood Hanley	4-1
9r	Brereton Social v Ilkeston Town (2)	1-1
r	Eastwood Town v Belper Town	0-3
10r	Hednesford Town v Brierley Hill Alliance	2-1
r	Lye Town v Gornal Athletic	5-0
r	Worcester City v Highgate United	1-2
13r	Frickley Colliery v Ashby Institute	2-1
14r	Matlock Town v Arnold	3-4
15r	Bromsgrove Rovers v Moor Green	1-0
16r	Banbury United v Evesham United	2-0
r	Gloucester City v Stonehouse	0-1
r	Kidderminster Harriers v Cinderford Town	1-3
18r	Great Yarmouth Town v March Town United	2-2
20r	Stevenage Athletic v Hitchin Town	1-1
21r	Wealdstone v Chesham United	2-4
23r	Cray Wanderers v Hampton	1-3
r	Dagenham v Cheshunt	2-2
25r	Crawley Town v Leyton	3-2e
27r	Sutton United v Hornchurch	2-0
28r	Fleet Town v Uxbridge	3-1
r	Woking v Farnborough Town	2-2e
30r	Folkestone v Deal Town	6-2
31r	Waterlooville v Haywards Heath	3-1
r	Worthing v Pagham	3-1
33r	Trowbridge Town v Hungerford Town	4-2
34r	Dorchester Town v Bridgwater Town (1)	0-1
6r2	Marine v Blaenau Ffestiniog	1-0
9r2	Ilkeston Town (2) v Brereton Social	1-0
18r2	March Town United v Great Yarmouth Town	0-1
20r2	Hitchin Town v Stevenage Athletic	3-2
23r2	Cheshunt v Dagenham	0-0
28r2	Farnborough Town v Woking	1-2
23r3	Dagenham v Cheshunt	2-1

Qualifying Round Two

1	North Shields v Whitley Bay	0-0
	Willington v Durham City	3-1
2	Ashington v Murton CW	2-1
	Horden CW v Wingate (Durham)	3-2
3	Evenwood Town v Tow Law Town	2-2
	Shildon v Bishop Auckland	1-3
4	Chorley v Fleetwood	0-0
	Netherfield (Kendal) v Accrington Stanley (2)	2-1
5	Darwen v Formby	0-1
	South Liverpool v Ormskirk	0-1
6	Porthmadog v Connah's Quay Nomads	2-0
	Runcorn v Marine	0-0
7	Horwich RMI v Congleton Town	2-0
	Nantwich Town v Altrincham	0-3
8	Leek Town v Macclesfield Town	2-2
	Stalybridge Celtic v Northwich Victoria	3-1
9	Ilkeston Town (2) v Atherstone Town	2-0
	Tamworth v Belper Town	3-0
10	Highgate United v Lye Town	1-0
	Nuneaton Borough v Hednesford Town	1-0
11	Emley v Buxton	1-2
	Mossley v Prestwich Heys	1-1
12	Goole Town v Bridlington Town	3-1
	Mexborough Town v Bradford Park Avenue	1-1
13	Denaby United v Frickley Colliery	0-3
	Sutton Town v Brigg Town	1-1
14	Bilston v Alfreton Town	0-2
	Worksop Town v Arnold	1-0
15	Bromsgrove Rovers v Alvechurch	1-2
	Stourbridge v Bedworth United	5-2
16	Stonehouse v Cinderford Town	1-2
	Witney Town v Banbury United	1-2
17	Stamford v Holbeach United	3-1
	Wisbech Town v Thetford Town	3-1
18	Great Yarmouth Town v Harwich & Parkeston	1-2
	King's Lynn v Clacton Town	3-1
19	Corby Town v Biggleswade Town	1-0
	Histon v Bedford Town (1)	2-1
20	Rothwell Town v Hitchin Town	1-7
	St Neots Town v Bletchley Town	0-3
21	Hertford Town v Chesham United	2-0
	Ware v Aylesbury United	1-0
22	Finchley v Boreham Wood	0-1
	Romford (2) v Bexley United	2-2
23	Dartford v Kingstonian	1-3
	Hampton v Dagenham	0-5
24	Staines Town v Egham Town	2-0
	Wimbledon v Southall	2-1
25	Crawley Town v Aveley	2-3
	Harrow Borough v Horsham	1-0
26	Gravesend & Northfleet v Maidenhead United	2-3
	Hounslow v Epping Town	1-2
27	Ilford v Leatherhead	1-1
	Leytonstone v Sutton United	3-2
28	Fleet Town v Chatham Town	2-4
	Wycombe Wanderers v Woking	1-0
29	Maidstone United v Ashford Town	1-1
	Sittingbourne v Ramsgate	1-1
30	Faversham Town v Folkestone	1-1
	Lewes v Dover	1-1
31	Littlehampton Town v Eastbourne Town	2-2
	Worthing v Waterlooville	2-1
32	Bognor Regis Town v Newport (IOW)	1-0
	Gosport Borough v Alton Town	1-1
33	Melksham Town v Basingstoke Town	0-6
	Trowbridge Town v Bath City	0-0
34	Taunton Town v Bridgwater Town (1)	1-0
	Weymouth v Salisbury (2)	2-0
35	Glastonbury v Merthyr Tydfil	0-0
	Llanelli v Mangotsfield United	1-2
36	Falmouth Town v Barnstaple Town	4-1
	Newquay v Bideford	1-1
1r	Whitley Bay v North Shields	1-1
3r	Tow Law Town v Evenwood Town	1-0
4r	Fleetwood v Chorley	1-1
6r	Marine v Runcorn	0-1
8r	Macclesfield Town v Leek Town	4-2
11r	Prestwich Heys v Mossley	2-3
12r	Bradford Park Avenue v Mexborough Town	4-2
13r	Brigg Town v Sutton Town	0-1
22r	Bexley United v Romford (2)	3-1
27r	Leatherhead v Ilford	2-0
29r	Ashford Town v Maidstone United	0-2
r	Ramsgate v Sittingbourne	2-0
30r	Dover v Lewes	1-2
r	Folkestone v Faversham Town	4-1
31r	Eastbourne Town v Littlehampton Town	0-1
32r	Alton Town v Gosport Borough	2-1
33r	Bath City v Trowbridge Town	2-4
35r	Merthyr Tydfil v Glastonbury	3-1
36r	Bideford v Newquay	6-1
1r2	Whitley Bay v North Shields	2-2
4r2	Chorley v Fleetwood	3-2
1r3	North Shields v Whitley Bay	3-0

Qualifying Round Three

1	Willington v North Shields	3-0
2	Horden CW v Ashington	1-1
3	Bishop Auckland v Tow Law Town	3-1
4	Chorley v Netherfield (Kendal)	0-1
5	Formby v Ormskirk	1-0
6	Porthmadog v Runcorn	0-2
7	Altrincham v Horwich RMI	4-0
8	Macclesfield Town v Stalybridge Celtic	2-1
9	Ilkeston Town (2) v Tamworth	2-3
10	Nuneaton Borough v Highgate United	1-4
11	Buxton v Mossley	2-1
12	Bradford Park Avenue v Goole Town	3-3
13	Frickley Colliery v Sutton Town	2-1
14	Alfreton Town v Worksop Town	2-1
15	Alvechurch v Stourbridge	3-2
16	Cinderford Town v Banbury United	2-2
17	Stamford v Wisbech Town	4-2
18	Harwich & Parkeston v King's Lynn	1-2
19	Histon v Corby Town	0-2
20	Bletchley Town v Hitchin Town	1-1
21	Ware v Hertford Town	0-0
22	Boreham Wood v Bexley United	1-0
23	Dagenham v Kingstonian	3-2
24	Staines Town v Wimbledon	1-1
25	Aveley v Harrow Borough	1-0
26	Epping Town v Maidenhead United	3-0
27	Leatherhead v Leytonstone	0-0
28	Chatham Town v Wycombe Wanderers	0-7
29	Maidstone United v Ramsgate	3-1
30	Folkestone v Lewes	5-1
31	Littlehampton Town v Worthing	0-2

1973/74 to 1974/75

32 Alton Town v Bognor Regis Town	1-2
33 Basingstoke Town v Trowbridge Town	0-1
34 Taunton Town v Weymouth	1-2
35 Merthyr Tydfil v Mangotsfield United	2-0
36 Falmouth Town v Bideford	3-3
2r Ashington v Horden CW	2-1
12r Goole Town v Bradford Park Avenue	4-1
16r Banbury United v Cinderford Town	4-1
20r Hitchin Town v Bletchley Town	2-0
21r Hertford Town v Ware	3-1
24r Wimbledon v Staines Town	4-3
27r Leytonstone v Leatherhead	1-0
36r Bideford v Falmouth Town	1-1
36r2 Falmouth Town v Bideford	2-2
36r3 Bideford v Falmouth Town	2-2
36r4 Falmouth Town v Bideford	1-2

Qualifying Round Four

Banbury United v Tamworth	2-0
Barnet v Hendon	2-2
Bideford v Trowbridge Town	2-2
Bishop Auckland v South Shields (2)	0-1
Bishop's Stortford v Dagenham	1-1
Blyth Spartans v Netherfield (Kendal)	2-0
Boreham Wood v Aveley	2-2
Buxton v Alfreton Town	2-2
Corby Town v Boston United	1-2
Epping Town v Chelmsford City	1-2
Folkestone v Guildford City	2-3
Formby v Goole Town	3-0
Grantham v Kettering Town	3-1
Hayes v Enfield	1-1
Hillingdon Borough v Hertford Town	2-1
Hitchin Town v Bognor Regis Town	2-1
King's Lynn v Stamford	3-1
Lancaster City v Altrincham	1-1
Leytonstone v Margate	0-0
Macclesfield Town v Merthyr Tydfil	0-0
Rhyl v Frickley Colliery	0-4
Runcorn v Bangor City	2-2
Stafford Rangers v Alvechurch	1-1
Telford United v Highgate United	2-0
Willington v Ashington	1-0
Wimbledon v Maidstone United	1-0
Worthing v Wycombe Wanderers	0-3
Yeovil Town v Weymouth	1-1
r Alfreton Town v Buxton	2-1
r Altrincham v Lancaster City	1-0
r Alvechurch v Stafford Rangers	2-0
r Aveley v Boreham Wood	1-2
r Bangor City v Runcorn	1-2
r Dagenham v Bishop's Stortford	2-1
r Enfield v Hayes	0-1
r Hendon v Barnet	3-0
r Margate v Leytonstone	1-3
r Merthyr Tydfil v Macclesfield Town	2-1
r Trowbridge Town v Bideford	1-1
r Weymouth v Yeovil Town	2-2
r2 Bideford v Trowbridge Town	1-1
r2 Yeovil Town v Weymouth	0-1
r3 Trowbridge Town v Bideford	2-3

Round One

Alfreton Town v Blyth Spartans	0-0
Altrincham v Hartlepool	2-0
Banbury United v Northampton Town	0-0
Bideford v Bristol Rovers	0-2
Boston United v Hayes	0-0
Bournemouth v Charlton Athletic	1-0
Bradford City v Workington	2-0
Cambridge United v Gillingham	3-2
Chester v Telford United	1-0
Chesterfield v Barnsley	0-0
Colchester United v Peterborough United	2-3
Crewe Alexandra v Scarborough	0-0
Dagenham v Aldershot	0-4
Doncaster Rovers v Lincoln City	1-0
Exeter City v Alvechurch	0-1
Formby v Oldham Athletic	0-2
Halifax Town v Frickley Colliery	6-1
Hendon v Leytonstone	3-0
Hereford United v Torquay United	3-1
Hillingdon Borough v Grantham	0-4
Hitchin Town v Guildford City	1-1
Huddersfield Town v Wigan Athletic	2-0
King's Lynn v Wimbledon	1-0
Plymouth Argyle v Brentford	2-1
Reading v Slough Town	3-0
Rochdale v South Shields (2)	2-0
Rotherham United v Southport	2-1
Runcorn v Grimsby Town	0-1
Scunthorpe United v Darlington	1-0
Southend United v Boreham Wood	3-0
Stockport County v Port Vale	0-1
Tranmere Rovers v Bury	2-1
Walsall v Swansea City	1-0
Walton & Hersham v Brighton & Hove Albion	0-0
Watford v Chelmsford City	1-0
Weymouth v Merthyr Tydfil	0-1
Willington v Blackburn Rovers	0-0
Wrexham v Shrewsbury Town	1-1
Wycombe Wanderers v Newport County	3-1
York City v Mansfield Town	0-0

r Barnsley v Chesterfield	2-1
r Blackburn Rovers v Willington	6-1
r Blyth Spartans v Alfreton Town	2-1
r Brighton & Hove Albion v Walton & Hersham	0-4
r Guildford City v Hitchin Town	1-4
r Hayes v Boston United	1-2e
r Mansfield Town v York City	5-3
r Northampton Town v Banbury United	3-2
r Scarborough v Crewe Alexandra	2-1
r Shrewsbury Town v Wrexham	0-1

Round Two

Aldershot v Cambridge United	1-2
Alvechurch v King's Lynn	6-1
Barnsley v Bradford City	1-1
Blackburn Rovers v Altrincham	0-0
Boston United v Hitchin Town	1-0
Chester v Huddersfield Town	3-2
Doncaster Rovers v Tranmere Rovers	3-0
Grantham v Rochdale	1-1
Grimsby Town v Blyth Spartans	1-1
Halifax Town v Oldham Athletic	0-1
Hereford United v Walton & Hersham	3-0
Mansfield Town v Scunthorpe United	1-1
Merthyr Tydfil v Hendon	0-3
Northampton Town v Bristol Rovers	1-2
Plymouth Argyle v Walsall	1-0
Port Vale v Scarborough	2-1
Southend United v Reading	2-0
Watford v Bournemouth	0-1
Wrexham v Rotherham United	3-0
Wycombe Wanderers v Peterborough United	1-3
r Altrincham v Blackburn Rovers	0-2
r Blyth Spartans v Grimsby Town	0-2
r Bradford City v Barnsley	2-1
r Rochdale v Grantham	3-5e
r Scunthorpe United v Mansfield Town	1-0

Round Three

Aston Villa v Chester	3-1
Birmingham City v Cardiff City	5-2
Bolton Wanderers v Stoke City	3-2
Bradford City v Alvechurch	4-2
Bristol City v Hull City	1-1
Cambridge United v Oldham Athletic	2-2
Carlisle United v Sunderland	0-0
Chelsea v Queen's Park Rangers	0-0
Crystal Palace v Wrexham	0-2
Derby County v Boston United	0-0
Everton v Blackburn Rovers	3-0
Fulham v Preston North End	1-0
Grantham v Middlesbrough	0-2
Grimsby Town v Burnley	0-2
Ipswich Town v Sheffield United	3-2
Leicester City v Tottenham Hotspur	1-0
Liverpool v Doncaster Rovers	2-2
Manchester United v Plymouth Argyle	1-0
Millwall v Scunthorpe United	1-1
Newcastle United v Hendon	1-1
Norwich City v Arsenal	0-1
Nottingham Forest v Bristol Rovers	4-3
Orient v Bournemouth	2-1
Oxford United v Manchester City	2-5
Peterborough United v Southend United	3-1
Port Vale v Luton Town	1-1
Portsmouth v Swindon Town	3-3
Sheffield Wednesday v Coventry City	0-0
Southampton v Blackpool	2-1
West Bromwich Albion v Notts County	4-0
West Ham United v Hereford United	1-1
Wolverhampton Wan. v Leeds United	1-1
r Boston United v Derby County	1-6
r Coventry City v Sheffield Wednesday	3-1
r Doncaster Rovers v Liverpool	0-2
r Hendon v Newcastle United	0-4 N
r Hereford United v West Ham United	2-1
r Hull City v Bristol City	0-1
r Leeds United v Wolverhampton Wan.	1-0
r Luton Town v Port Vale	4-2
r Oldham Athletic v Cambridge United	3-3e
r Queen's Park Rangers v Chelsea	1-0
r Scunthorpe United v Millwall	1-0
r Sunderland v Carlisle United	0-1
r Swindon Town v Portsmouth	0-1
r2 Cambridge United v Oldham Athletic	1-2 N

Round Four

Arsenal v Aston Villa	1-1
Coventry City v Derby County	0-0
Everton v West Bromwich Albion	0-0
Fulham v Leicester City	1-1
Hereford United v Bristol City	1-1
Liverpool v Carlisle United	0-0
Luton Town v Bradford City	3-0
Manchester United v Ipswich Town	0-1
Newcastle United v Scunthorpe United	1-1
Nottingham Forest v Manchester City	4-1
Oldham Athletic v Burnley	1-4
Peterborough United v Leeds United	1-4
Portsmouth v Orient	0-0
Queen's Park Rangers v Birmingham City	2-0
Southampton v Bolton Wanderers	3-3

Wrexham v Middlesbrough	1-0
r Aston Villa v Arsenal	2-0
r Bolton Wanderers v Southampton	0-2e
r Carlisle United v Liverpool	0-2
r Derby County v Coventry City	0-1e
r Leicester City v Fulham	2-1e
r Orient v Portsmouth	1-1e
r Scunthorpe United v Newcastle United	0-3
r West Bromwich Albion v Everton	1-0
r2 Portsmouth v Orient	2-0 N

Round Five

Bristol City v Leeds United	1-1
Burnley v Aston Villa	1-0
Coventry City v Queen's Park Rangers	0-0
Liverpool v Ipswich Town	2-0
Luton Town v Leicester City	0-4
Nottingham Forest v Portsmouth	1-0
Southampton v Wrexham	0-1
West Bromwich Albion v Newcastle United	0-3
r Leeds United v Bristol City	0-1
r Queen's Park Rangers v Coventry City	3-2

Round Six

Bristol City v Liverpool	0-1
Burnley v Wrexham	1-0
Newcastle United v Nottingham Forest	4-3 v
Queen's Park Rangers v Leicester City	0-2
r Newcastle United v Nottingham Forest	0-0 N
r2 Newcastle United v Nottingham Forest	1-0 N

Semi Finals

Liverpool v Leicester City	0-0 N
Newcastle United v Burnley	2-0 N
r Leicester City v Liverpool	1-3 N

Final

Liverpool v Newcastle United	3-0 N

1974/75

Preliminary Round

1 Evenwood Town v Spennymoor United	2-2
2 Boldon CW v West Auckland Town	4-0
4 Clitheroe v Barrow	4-8
5 Bacup Borough v Accrington Stanley (2)	3-3
7 Marine v Ormskirk	wo/s
11 Bedworth United v Alfreton Town	0-1
14 Darlaston v Bilston	1-2
17 Corby Town v Cambridge City	2-1
20 Epping Town v Boreham Wood	3-0
21 Marlow v Aylesbury United	3-3
22 Edmonton & Haringey v Cheshunt	2-1
23 Cray Wanderers v Aveley	4-2
24 Dagenham v Bromley	2-2
25 Corinthian Casuals v Barking	4-2
26 Hampton v Burnham (1)	2-0
27 Egham Town v Addlestone	1-3
28 Deal Town v Ashford Town	0-4
30 Eastbourne United v Bexhill Town	2-3
31 Burgess Hill Town v Arundel	2-2
32 Basingstoke Town v Andover	1-0
33 Devizes Town v Bath City	2-3
34 Dorchester Town v Bridgwater Town (1)	3-2
35 Cinderford Town v Barry Town	2-2
1r Spennymoor United v Evenwood Town	4-0
5r Accrington Stanley (2) v Bacup Borough	4-1
21r Aylesbury United v Marlow	1-1
24r Bromley v Dagenham	2-4
31r Arundel v Burgess Hill Town	1-1
35r Barry Town v Cinderford Town	0-0x
21r2 Marlow v Aylesbury United	1-0
31r2 Burgess Hill Town v Arundel	1-0
35r2 Cinderford Town v Barry Town	2-0

Qualifying Round One

1 Bishop Auckland v Stanley United	wo/s
Crook Town v Wingate (Durham)	1-4
Spennymoor United v Durham City	6-2
Whitley Bay v North Shields	1-1
2 Ashington v Horden CW	2-1
Boldon CW v Shildon	2-3
Ferryhill Athletic v Tow Law Town	0-3
Willington v Consett	4-1
3 Barton Town (2) v Winterton Rangers	2-2
Bridlington Town v South Bank	1-0
Goole Town v Stockton	3-0
Whitby Town v Bridlington Trinity	1-1
4 Barrow v Rossendale United	1-0
Burscough v Lancaster City	0-1
Fleetwood v Netherfield (Kendal)	0-2
Penrith v Darwen	0-3
5 Accrington Stanley (2) v Radcliffe Borough	1-1
Ashton United v Great Harwood	1-0
Formby v Horwich RMI	0-2
Prestwich Heys v Chorley	0-0

149

1974/75

6	Bethesda Athletic v South Liverpool	1-0
	Blaenau Ffestiniog v Oswestry Town	0-0
	New Brighton v Porthmadog	2-1
	Rhyl v Ellesmere Port Town	wo/s
7	Marine v Witton Albion	4-1
	Northwich Victoria v Sandbach Ramblers	2-3
	St Helens Town v Skelmersdale United	0-1
	Winsford United v Prescot Town	5-1
8	Buxton v Runcorn	0-1
	Eastwood Hanley v Mossley	1-3
	Leek Town v Nantwich Town	1-2
	New Mills v Hyde United	0-1
9	Droylsden v Yorkshire Amateur	1-1
	Emley v Glossop	4-1
	Frickley Colliery v Stalybridge Celtic	2-2
	Stocksbridge Works v Farsley Celtic	1-3
10	Ashby Institute v Worksop Town	0-1
	Brigg Town v Matlock Town	0-1
	Gainsborough Trinity v Mexborough Town	5-1
	Retford Town v Denaby United	3-0
11	Alfreton Town v Tamworth	1-1
	Arnold v Ilkeston Town (2)	0-0
	Enderby Town v Long Eaton United	3-1
	Sutton Town v Eastwood Town	0-2
12	Belper Town v Stafford Rangers	0-0
	Burton Albion v Heanor Town	0-0
	Gresley Rovers v Hednesford Town	1-0
	Macclesfield Town v Congleton Town	2-0
13	Bromsgrove Rovers v Worcester City	0-3
	Dudley Town v AP Leamington	1-3
	Halesowen Town v Lye Town	1-2
	Warley County Borough v Evesham United	2-0
14	Bilston v Stourbridge	3-0
	Brierley Hill Alliance v Kidderminster Harriers	1-2
	Highgate United v Oldbury United	2-1
	Redditch United v Gornal Athletic	2-1
15	Alvechurch v Sutton Coldfield Town	3-0
	Atherstone Town v Hinckley Athletic	5-1
	Coventry Sporting v Moor Green	1-0
	Nuneaton Borough v Banbury United	3-0
16	Boston v Spalding United	4-0
	Bourne Town v Louth United	1-0
	King's Lynn v Parson Drove United	9-0
	Skegness Town v Holbeach United	3-0
17	Chatteris Town v St Neots Town	0-2
	Corby Town v Wisbech Town	2-0
	March Town United v Soham Town Rangers	2-1
	Stamford v Histon	1-3
18	Bedford Town (1) v Wellingborough Town	2-1
	Biggleswade Town v Potton United	0-0
	Irthlingborough Diamonds v Rothwell Town	3-1
	Rushden Town v Desborough Town	2-1
19	Bury Town v Thetford Town	4-1
	Clacton Town v Harwich & Parkeston	1-0
	Great Yarmouth Town v Lowestoft Town	3-3
	Sudbury Town v Ely City	5-0
20	Dunstable Town v Hertford Town	3-2
	Epping Town v St Albans City	0-0
	Hemel Hempstead Town v Hitchin Town	2-3
	Letchworth Town v Hatfield Town	1-0
21	Chesham United v Vauxhall Motors (Luton)	1-0
	Marlow v Wycombe Wanderers	0-1
	Oxford City v Witney Town	1-1
	Wolverton Town & BR v Milton Keynes City	1-2
22	Edgware Town v Harlow Town	1-2
	Edmonton & Haringey v Ware	0-1
	Finchley v Hoddesdon Town	0-1
	Stevenage Athletic v Enfield	1-0
23	Bexley United v Grays Athletic	0-1
	Cray Wanderers v Walthamstow Avenue	2-0
	Erith & Belvedere v Leyton	5-0
	Sutton United v Dulwich Hamlet	4-2
24	Croydon v Leatherhead	0-2
	Dagenham v Tilbury	3-1
	Hornchurch v Metropolitan Police	2-1
	Redhill v Epsom & Ewell	3-0
25	Carshalton Athletic v Leytonstone	0-1
	Corinthian Casuals v Wembley	1-2
	Harrow Borough v Molesey	0-0
	Romford (2) v Gravesend & Northfleet	2-0
26	Farnborough Town v Staines Town	1-1
	Hampton v Wealdstone	2-2
	Southall v Tooting & Mitcham United	0-0
	Uxbridge v Hounslow	2-1
27	Addlestone v Wokingham Town	0-0
	Bracknell Town v Wimbledon	1-3
	Maidenhead United v Windsor & Eton	4-1
	Woking v Kingstonian	2-2
28	Ashford Town v Sittingbourne	0-0
	Canterbury City v Herne Bay	4-0
	Folkestone & Shepway v Ramsgate	0-0
	Sheppey United v Dover	1-3
29	Eastbourne Town v Maidstone United	0-0
	Hastings United v Tonbridge	0-0
	Medway v Whitstable Town	4-2
	Tunbridge Wells v Faversham Town	0-0
30	Bexhill Town v Southwick	0-6
	Crawley Town v Peacehaven & Telscombe	3-0
	Lewes v Ringmer	2-4
	Sidley United v Haywards Heath	1-3
31	Bognor Regis Town v Horsham	1-2
	Burgess Hill Town v Worthing	2-0
	Fareham Town v Littlehampton Town	1-1
	Pagham v Chichester City (1)	3-3
32	Alton Town v Newport (IOW)	3-2
	Basingstoke Town v Waterlooville	3-1
	Gosport Borough v Ryde Sports	7-1
	Salisbury (2) v Cowes	3-0
33	Bath City v Weston-Super-Mare	3-0
	Chippenham Town v Melksham Town	3-0
	Mangotsfield United v Trowbridge Town	2-1
	Westbury United v Hungerford Town	1-3
34	Bridport v Poole Town	1-6
	Dorchester Town v Weymouth	1-3
	Glastonbury v Taunton Town	2-2
	Welton Rovers v Frome Town	1-1
35	Cheltenham Town v Llanelli	3-2
	Cinderford Town v Ton Pentre	3-2
	Gloucester City v Merthyr Tydfil	3-2
	Stonehouse v Everwarm	1-1
36	Barnstaple Town v Wadebridge Town	0-4
	Falmouth Town v Newquay	2-0
	Penzance v Bideford	1-2
	St Blazey v Minehead	1-1
1r	North Shields v Whitley Bay	1-3
3r	Bridlington Trinity v Whitby Town	0-1
r	Winterton Rangers v Barton Town (2)	1-0
5r	Chorley v Prestwich Heys	6-1
r	Radcliffe Borough v Accrington Stanley (2)	0-1
6r	Oswestry Town v Blaenau Ffestiniog	1-0
9r	Stalybridge Celtic v Frickley Colliery	2-0
r	Yorkshire Amateur v Droylsden	4-4
11r	Ilkeston Town (2) v Arnold	0-1
r	Tamworth v Alfreton Town	1-0
12r	Heanor Town v Burton Albion	1-3
r	Stafford Rangers v Belper Town	4-0
18r	Potton United v Biggleswade Town	2-1
19r	Lowestoft Town v Great Yarmouth Town	3-2
20r	St Albans City v Epping Town	2-2
21r	Witney Town v Oxford City	0-0
25r	Molesey v Harrow Borough	0-1
26r	Staines Town v Farnborough Town	0-1
r	Tooting & Mitcham United v Southall	3-1
r	Wealdstone v Hampton	2-0
27r	Kingstonian v Woking	1-2
r	Wokingham Town v Addlestone	1-1
28r	Ramsgate v Folkestone & Shepway	2-0
r	Sittingbourne v Ashford Town	1-2
29r	Faversham Town v Tunbridge Wells	3-2
r	Maidstone United v Eastbourne Town	5-3
r	Tonbridge v Hastings United	1-2
31r	Chichester City (1) v Pagham	5-4
r	Littlehampton Town v Fareham Town	1-1
34r	Frome Town v Welton Rovers	1-2
r	Taunton Town v Glastonbury	4-0
35r	Everwarm v Stonehouse	4-1
36r	Minehead v St Blazey	4-1
9r2	Droylsden v Yorkshire Amateur	0-1
20r2	Epping Town v St Albans City	1-2
21r2	Oxford City v Witney Town	1-0
27r2	Addlestone v Wokingham Town	1-3
31r2	Fareham Town v Littlehampton Town	0-1

Qualifying Round Two

1	Spennymoor United v Wingate (Durham)	3-0
	Whitley Bay v Bishop Auckland	2-2
2	Shildon v Willington	2-4
	Tow Law Town v Ashington	0-4
3	Bridlington Town v Goole Town	1-0
	Winterton Rangers v Whitby Town	3-2
4	Barrow v Darwen	0-2
	Lancaster City v Netherfield (Kendal)	2-1
5	Accrington Stanley (2) v Chorley	2-0
	Ashton United v Horwich RMI	0-2
6	Bethesda Athletic v Rhyl	2-2
	Oswestry Town v New Brighton	2-1
7	Marine v Winsford United	1-1
	Sandbach Ramblers v Skelmersdale United	2-1
8	Mossley v Nantwich Town	5-1
	Runcorn v Hyde United	3-0
9	Emley v Stalybridge Celtic	3-1
	Yorkshire Amateur v Farsley Celtic	0-2
10	Matlock Town v Gainsborough Trinity	2-1
	Worksop Town v Retford Town	1-0
11	Arnold v Enderby Town	0-0
	Tamworth v Eastwood Town	1-1
12	Burton Albion v Gresley Rovers	0-0
	Stafford Rangers v Macclesfield Town	3-0
13	AP Leamington v Lye Town	3-1
	Worcester City v Warley County Borough	5-0
14	Bilston v Redditch United	0-2
	Kidderminster Harriers v Highgate United	5-2
15	Alvechurch v Nuneaton Borough	1-3
	Atherstone Town v Coventry Sporting	5-0
16	Boston v Skegness Town	1-1
	Bourne Town v King's Lynn	2-2
17	Corby Town v Histon	3-2
	St Neots Town v March Town United	2-3
18	Bedford Town (1) v Rushden Town	2-0
	Potton United v Irthlingborough Diamonds	5-3
19	Bury Town v Sudbury Town	0-2
	Clacton Town v Lowestoft Town	3-0
20	Dunstable Town v Hitchin Town	0-0
	St Albans City v Letchworth Town	1-0
21	Chesham United v Oxford City	4-1
	Wycombe Wanderers v Milton Keynes City	2-0
22	Harlow Town v Hoddesdon Town	1-0
	Ware v Stevenage Athletic	0-3
23	Cray Wanderers v Sutton United	1-5
	Grays Athletic v Erith & Belvedere	0-1
24	Dagenham v Redhill	3-0
	Leatherhead v Hornchurch	5-0
25	Leytonstone v Harrow Borough	1-0
	Wembley v Romford (2)	2-3
26	Farnborough Town v Tooting & Mitcham United	2-2
	Wealdstone v Uxbridge	2-0
27	Wimbledon v Maidenhead United	4-0
	Wokingham Town v Woking	2-1
28	Ashford Town v Dover	1-0
	Canterbury City v Ramsgate	2-1
29	Maidstone United v Hastings United	6-0
	Medway v Faversham Town	2-1
30	Crawley Town v Ringmer	2-2
	Southwick v Haywards Heath	3-2
31	Burgess Hill Town v Chichester City (1)	4-1
	Horsham v Littlehampton Town	1-0
32	Alton Town v Gosport Borough	2-2
	Basingstoke Town v Salisbury (2)	1-1
33	Bath City v Hungerford Town	6-1
	Chippenham Town v Mangotsfield United	0-2
34	Poole Town v Taunton Town	2-0
	Weymouth v Welton Rovers	7-1
35	Cheltenham Town v Gloucester City	4-1
	Cinderford Town v Everwarm	2-1
36	Minehead v Falmouth Town	3-2
	Wadebridge Town v Bideford	3-3
1r	Bishop Auckland v Whitley Bay	4-3
6r	Rhyl v Bethesda Athletic	2-2
7r	Winsford United v Marine	1-4
11r	Eastwood Town v Tamworth	5-3
r	Enderby Town v Arnold	1-0
12r	Gresley Rovers v Burton Albion	0-1
16r	King's Lynn v Bourne Town	1-0
r	Skegness Town v Boston	1-2
20r	Hitchin Town v Dunstable Town	2-1
26r	Tooting & Mitcham United v Farnborough Town	6-1
30r	Ringmer v Crawley Town	2-1
32r	Gosport Borough v Alton Town	0-1
r	Salisbury (2) v Basingstoke Town	3-1
36r	Bideford v Wadebridge Town	4-2
6r2	Bethesda Athletic v Rhyl	0-3

Qualifying Round Three

1	Bishop Auckland v Spennymoor United	4-2
2	Ashington v Willington	2-2
3	Bridlington Town v Winterton Rangers	1-1
4	Lancaster City v Darwen	3-0
5	Horwich RMI v Accrington Stanley (2)	0-2
6	Oswestry Town v Rhyl	2-1
7	Sandbach Ramblers v Marine	0-1
8	Mossley v Runcorn	1-0
9	Emley v Farsley Celtic	1-2
10	Matlock Town v Worksop Town	6-2
11	Enderby Town v Eastwood Town	1-0
12	Burton Albion v Stafford Rangers	0-0
13	AP Leamington v Worcester City	2-1
14	Kidderminster Harriers v Redditch United	1-1
15	Atherstone Town v Nuneaton Borough	1-1
16	King's Lynn v Boston	1-0
17	March Town United v Corby Town	0-4
18	Potton United v Bedford Town (1)	1-2
19	Clacton Town v Sudbury Town	2-1
20	Hitchin Town v St Albans City	2-1
21	Chesham United v Wycombe Wanderers	1-3
22	Harlow Town v Stevenage Athletic	0-0
23	Erith & Belvedere v Sutton United	1-5
24	Leatherhead v Dagenham	0-0
25	Leytonstone v Romford (2)	0-1
26	Tooting & Mitcham United v Wealdstone	1-0
27	Wimbledon v Wokingham Town	2-0
28	Canterbury City v Ashford Town	2-2
29	Maidstone United v Medway	7-0
30	Ringmer v Southwick	1-3
31	Horsham v Burgess Hill Town	5-0
32	Alton Town v Salisbury (2)	1-3
33	Mangotsfield United v Bath City	1-3
34	Poole Town v Weymouth	0-3
35	Cheltenham Town v Cinderford Town	3-2
36	Minehead v Bideford	2-1
2r	Willington v Ashington	1-5
3r	Winterton Rangers v Bridlington Town	0-2
12r	Stafford Rangers v Burton Albion	2-0
14r	Redditch United v Kidderminster Harriers	2-2
15r	Nuneaton Borough v Atherstone Town	2-0
22r	Stevenage Athletic v Harlow Town	0-2
24r	Dagenham v Leatherhead	1-3
28r	Ashford Town v Canterbury City	4-0
14r2	Kidderminster Harriers v Redditch United	3-0 N

Qualifying Round Four

AP Leamington v Corby Town	1-0
Altrincham v Accrington Stanley (2)	3-0
Ashington v Gateshead United	1-3
Barnet v Hitchin Town	1-1
Bath City v Yeovil Town	2-1
Blyth Spartans v Scarborough	3-1
Bridlington Town v Farsley Celtic	0-4
Cheltenham Town v Salisbury (2)	4-1
Clacton Town v Romford (2)	1-2
Enderby Town v Boston United	1-2
Guildford & Dorking Utd. v Wimbledon	0-3
Hendon v Maidstone United	0-2

1974/75 to 1975/76

Hillingdon Borough v Ashford Town	1-2
Horsham v Chelmsford City	1-3
Kettering Town v Bedford Town (1)	3-3
King's Lynn v Stafford Rangers	1-3
Lancaster City v Bishop Auckland	1-1
Marine v Telford United	2-1
Matlock Town v Bangor City	3-0
Minehead v Weymouth	0-3
Mossley v Oswestry Town	1-3
Nuneaton Borough v Grantham	1-1
Slough Town v Sutton United	1-0
Southwick v Hayes	2-1
Tooting & Mitcham United v Harlow Town	3-0
Walton & Hersham v Leatherhead	1-7
Wigan Athletic v Kidderminster Harriers	4-0
Wycombe Wanderers v Margate	2-1
r Bedford Town (1) v Kettering Town	0-0
r Bishop Auckland v Lancaster City	2-1
r Grantham v Nuneaton Borough	2-3
r Hitchin Town v Barnet	2-0
r2 Kettering Town v Bedford Town (1)	2-0

Round One

AP Leamington v Southend United	1-2
Ashford Town v Walsall	1-3
Barnsley v Halifax Town	1-2
Bishop Auckland v Morecambe	5-0
Bishop's Stortford v Leatherhead	0-0
Blyth Spartans v Preston North End	1-1
Bournemouth v Southwick	5-0
Brighton & Hove Albion v Aldershot	3-1
Bury v Southport	4-2
Chelmsford City v Charlton Athletic	0-1
Chesterfield v Boston United	3-1
Crewe Alexandra v Gateshead United	2-2
Darlington v Workington	1-0
Dartford v Plymouth Argyle	2-3
Exeter City v Newport County	1-2
Farsley Celtic v Tranmere Rovers	0-2 N
Grimsby Town v Huddersfield Town	1-0
Hartlepool v Bradford City	1-0
Hereford United v Gillingham	1-0
Hitchin Town v Cambridge United	0-0
Mansfield Town v Wrexham	3-1
Matlock Town v Blackburn Rovers	1-4
Nuneaton Borough v Maidstone United	2-2
Oswestry Town v Doncaster Rovers	1-3
Peterborough United v Weymouth	0-0
Port Vale v Lincoln City	2-2
Rochdale v Marine	0-0
Romford (2) v Ilford	0-2
Rotherham United v Chester	1-0
Scunthorpe United v Altrincham	1-1
Shrewsbury Town v Wigan Athletic	1-1
Slough Town v Brentford	1-4
Stockport County v Stafford Rangers	0-0
Swansea City v Kettering Town	1-1
Swindon Town v Reading	4-0
Tooting & Mitcham United v Crystal Palace	1-2
Torquay United v Northampton Town	0-1
Watford v Colchester United	0-1
Wimbledon v Bath City	1-0
Wycombe Wanderers v Cheltenham Town	3-1
r Altrincham v Scunthorpe United	3-1
r Cambridge United v Hitchin Town	3-0
r Gateshead United v Crewe Alexandra	1-0e
r Kettering Town v Swansea City	3-1
r Leatherhead v Bishop's Stortford	2-0
r Lincoln City v Port Vale	2-0
r Maidstone United v Nuneaton Borough	2-0
r Marine v Rochdale	1-2e
r Preston North End v Blyth Spartans	5-1
r Stafford Rangers v Stockport County	1-0
r Weymouth v Peterborough United	3-3e
r Wigan Athletic v Shrewsbury Town	2-1
r2 Peterborough United v Weymouth	3-0

Round Two

Altrincham v Gateshead United	3-0
Bishop Auckland v Preston North End	0-2
Blackburn Rovers v Darlington	1-0
Brighton & Hove Albion v Brentford	1-0
Cambridge United v Hereford United	2-0
Chesterfield v Doncaster Rovers	1-0
Grimsby Town v Bury	1-1
Hartlepool v Lincoln City	0-0
Ilford v Southend United	0-2
Leatherhead v Colchester United	1-0
Newport County v Walsall	1-3
Peterborough United v Charlton Athletic	3-0
Plymouth Argyle v Crystal Palace	2-1
Rochdale v Tranmere Rovers	1-1
Rotherham United v Northampton Town	2-1
Stafford Rangers v Halifax Town	2-1
Swindon Town v Maidstone United	3-1
Wigan Athletic v Mansfield Town	1-1
Wimbledon v Kettering Town	2-0
Wycombe Wanderers v Bournemouth	0-0
r Bournemouth v Wycombe Wanderers	1-2
r Bury v Grimsby Town	2-1
r Lincoln City v Hartlepool	1-0
r Mansfield Town v Wigan Athletic	3-1
r Tranmere Rovers v Rochdale	1-0

Round Three

Arsenal v York City	1-1
Blackburn Rovers v Bristol Rovers	1-2
Bolton Wanderers v West Bromwich Albion	0-0
Brighton & Hove Albion v Leatherhead	0-1
Burnley v Wimbledon	0-1
Bury v Millwall	2-2
Chelsea v Sheffield Wednesday	3-2
Coventry City v Norwich City	2-0
Everton v Altrincham	1-1
Fulham v Hull City	1-1
Leeds United v Cardiff City	4-1
Leicester City v Oxford United	3-1
Liverpool v Stoke City	2-0
Luton Town v Birmingham City	0-1
Manchester City v Newcastle United	0-2
Manchester United v Walsall	0-0
Mansfield Town v Cambridge United	1-0
Nottingham Forest v Tottenham Hotspur	1-1
Notts County v Portsmouth	3-1
Oldham Athletic v Aston Villa	0-3
Orient v Derby County	2-2
Peterborough United v Tranmere Rovers	1-0
Plymouth Argyle v Blackpool	2-0
Preston North End v Carlisle United	0-1
Sheffield United v Bristol City	2-0
Southampton v West Ham United	1-2
Southend United v Queen's Park Rangers	2-2
Stafford Rangers v Rotherham United	0-0
Sunderland v Chesterfield	2-0
Swindon Town v Lincoln City	2-0
Wolverhampton Wan. v Ipswich Town	1-2
Wycombe Wanderers v Middlesbrough	0-0
r Altrincham v Everton	0-2 N
r Derby County v Orient	2-1
r Hull City v Fulham	2-2e
r Middlesbrough v Wycombe Wanderers	1-0
r Millwall v Bury	1-1e
r Queen's Park Rangers v Southend United	2-0
r Rotherham United v Stafford Rangers	0-2
r Tottenham Hotspur v Nottingham Forest	0-1
r Walsall v Manchester United	3-2e
r West Bromwich Albion v Bolton Wanderers	4-0
r York City v Arsenal	1-3e
r2 Bury v Millwall	2-0 N
r2 Fulham v Hull City	1-0 N

Round Four

Aston Villa v Sheffield United	4-1
Bury v Mansfield Town	1-2
Carlisle United v West Bromwich Albion	3-2
Chelsea v Birmingham City	0-1
Coventry City v Arsenal	1-1
Derby County v Bristol Rovers	2-0
Fulham v Nottingham Forest	0-0
Ipswich Town v Liverpool	1-0
Leeds United v Wimbledon	0-0
Leicester City v Leatherhead	3-2
Middlesbrough v Sunderland	3-1
Plymouth Argyle v Everton	1-3
Queen's Park Rangers v Notts County	3-0
Stafford Rangers v Peterborough United	1-2 N
Walsall v Newcastle United	1-0
West Ham United v Swindon Town	1-1
r Arsenal v Coventry City	3-0
r Nottingham Forest v Fulham	1-1e
r Swindon Town v West Ham United	1-2
r Wimbledon v Leeds United	0-1 N
r2 Fulham v Nottingham Forest	1-1e
r3 Nottingham Forest v Fulham	1-2

Round Five

Arsenal v Leicester City	0-0
Birmingham City v Walsall	2-1
Derby County v Leeds United	0-1
Everton v Fulham	1-2
Ipswich Town v Aston Villa	3-2
Mansfield Town v Carlisle United	0-1
Peterborough United v Middlesbrough	1-1
West Ham United v Queen's Park Rangers	2-1
r Leicester City v Arsenal	1-1e
r Middlesbrough v Peterborough United	2-0
r2 Leicester City v Arsenal	0-1e

Round Six

Arsenal v West Ham United	0-2
Birmingham City v Middlesbrough	1-0
Carlisle United v Fulham	0-1
Ipswich Town v Leeds United	0-0
r Leeds United v Ipswich Town	1-1e
r2 Ipswich Town v Leeds United	0-0eN
r3 Leeds United v Ipswich Town	2-3 N

Semi Finals

Fulham v Birmingham City	1-1 N
West Ham United v Ipswich Town	0-0 N
r Birmingham City v Fulham	0-1eN
r Ipswich Town v West Ham United	1-2 N

Final

West Ham United v Fulham	2-0 N

1975/76

Preliminary Round

1 Horden CW v Bridlington Town	1-1
2 Evenwood Town v Bridlington Trinity	2-3
3 Crook Town v Barrow	3-0
4 Louth United v Barton Town (2)	0-0
5 Mossley v Emley	2-0
6 Horwich RMI v Farsley Celtic	1-1
7 Great Harwood v Burscough	2-1
8 Porthmadog v Bethesda Athletic	3-2
9 New Brighton v Bacup Borough	3-1
10 Eastwood Hanley v Buxton	2-3
11 Hednesford Town v Brereton Social	1-1
12 Enderby Town v Atherstone Town	2-1
13 Hinckley Athletic v Dudley Town	0-4
14 Alvechurch v Evesham United	1-1
Llanelli v Mangotsfield United	0-2
15 Coventry Sporting v Bromsgrove Rovers	3-0
16 Kidderminster Harriers v Bedworth United	0-1
17 Milton Keynes City v Didcot Town	3-1
18 Corby Town v Boston	0-0
19 King's Lynn v Gorleston	2-0
20 Lowestoft Town v Harwich & Parkeston	4-3
21 Grays Athletic v Barnet	1-2
22 Epsom & Ewell v Corinthian Casuals	4-2
23 Harrow Borough v Barking	2-2
24 Harlow Town v Clacton Town	2-3
25 Hertford Town v Burnham (1)	0-2
26 Hatfield Town v Edmonton & Haringey	1-0
27 Hoddesdon Town v Dunstable Town	1-2
28 Gravesend & Northfleet v Chertsey Town	1-1
29 Folkestone & Shepway v Canterbury City	1-2
30 Maidstone United v Eastbourne United	5-0
31 Haywards Heath v Burgess Hill Town	0-4
32 Littlehampton Town v Chichester City (1)	1-1
33 Guildford & Dorking Utd. v Arundel	7-0
34 Fareham Town v Bath City	1-0
35 Melksham Town v Devizes Town	2-0
36 Penzance v Bideford	5-1
1r Bridlington Town v Horden CW	4-1
4r Barton Town (2) v Louth United	1-3
6r Farsley Celtic v Horwich RMI	1-1
11r Brereton Social v Hednesford Town	1-1
14r Evesham United v Alvechurch	0-1
18r Boston v Corby Town	1-2
23r Barking v Harrow Borough	2-0
28r Chertsey Town v Gravesend & Northfleet	0-2
32r Chichester City (1) v Littlehampton Town	0-2
6r2 Horwich RMI v Farsley Celtic	2-1
11r2 Hednesford Town v Brereton Social	3-3
11r3 Brereton Social v Hednesford Town	0-2

Qualifying Round One

1 Bishop Auckland v North Shields	0-1
Eppleton CW v Ferryhill Athletic	1-0
Whitby Town v Wingate (Durham)	4-0
Willington v Bridlington Town	4-2
2 Billingham Synthonia v Shildon	1-1
Durham City v Easington CW	1-3
South Bank v West Auckland Town	2-0
Tow Law Town v Bridlington Trinity	1-0
3 Ashington v Netherfield (Kendal)	0-2
Boldon CW v Consett	2-0
Penrith v Whitley Bay	1-0
Spennymoor United v Crook Town	1-1
4 Ashby Institute v Mexborough Town	0-1
Brigg Town v Goole Town	2-1
Retford Town v Skegness Town	0-0
Selby Town v Louth United	1-0
5 Denaby United v Stocksbridge Works	4-1
Frickley Colliery v Gainsborough Trinity	3-0
Winterton Rangers v Yorkshire Amateur	4-2
Worksop Town v Mossley	1-0
6 Clitheroe v Lancaster City	1-2
Fleetwood v Glossop	2-0
Leyland Motors v Rossendale United	1-8
Radcliffe Borough v Horwich RMI	4-0
7 Accrington Stanley (2) v Hyde United	2-3
Darwen v Droylsden	2-3
Prescot Town v Stalybridge Celtic	1-1
Prestwich Heys v Great Harwood	0-1
8 Bangor City v Pwllheli & District	2-0
Formby v Marine	0-1
Rhyl v St Helens Town	4-2
Runcorn v Porthmadog	5-3
9 Ashton United v Skelmersdale United	1-2
Chorley v Nantwich Town	1-0
South Liverpool v Witton Albion	0-3
Winsford United v New Brighton	4-1
10 Armitage v Leek Town	0-3
Congleton Town v Curzon Ashton	4-3
New Mills v Oswestry Town	1-1
Northwich Victoria v Buxton	2-0
11 Arnold v Long Eaton United	2-1
Burton Albion v Darlaston	1-3
Macclesfield Town v Sutton Town	0-0

151

1975/76

	Sutton Coldfield Town v Hednesford Town	1-0
12	Alfreton Town v Gresley Rovers	2-0
	Bilston v Eastwood Town	3-1
	Heanor Town v Tividale	2-6
	Moor Green v Enderby Town	0-1
13	Belper Town v Ilkeston Town (2)	1-0
	Gornal Athletic v Highgate United	1-0
	Nuneaton Borough v Tamworth	2-1
	Stourbridge v Dudley Town	0-1
14	Barry Town v Everwarm	1-1
	Mangotsfield United v Merthyr Tydfil	0-1
	Ton Pentre v Worcester City	4-3
	Welton Rovers v Alvechurch	1-3
15	Brierley Hill Alliance v Gloucester City	2-1
	Chippenham Town v Cinderford Town	2-4
	Halesowen Town v Warley County Borough	2-1
	Oldbury United v Coventry Sporting	0-0
16	Banbury United v Lye Town	1-0
	Cheltenham Town v Desborough Town	1-1
	Oxford City v Wolverton Town & BR	2-0
	Rothwell Town v Bedworth United	1-0
17	Aylesbury United v Redditch United	2-1
	Irthlingborough Diamonds v AP Leamington	1-2
	Rushden Town v Witney Town	0-3
	Wellingborough Town v Milton Keynes City	0-1
18	Bedford Town (1) v Ely City	2-0
	Bourne Town v Chatteris Town	4-0
	Parson Drove United v Thetford Town	5-5
	Stamford v Corby Town	3-2
19	Bury Town v St Neots Town	1-1
	Great Yarmouth Town v Holbeach United	1-0
	Soham Town Rangers v Wisbech Town	1-0
	Spalding United v King's Lynn	3-3
20	Cambridge City v March Town United	5-1
	Histon v Letchworth Town	0-2
	Potton United v Sudbury Town	2-1
	Stowmarket v Lowestoft Town	0-1
21	Aveley v Hornchurch	1-1
	Chesham United v Epping Town	3-0
	Staines Town v Tring Town	2-0
	Sutton United v Barnet	1-1
22	Bexley United v Hillingdon Borough	0-2
	Cray Wanderers v Dulwich Hamlet	1-3
	Leyton-Wingate v Tilbury	1-1
	Southall & Ealing Boro. v Epsom & Ewell	1-1
23	Addlestone v Metropolitan Police	2-0
	Bracknell Town v Feltham	1-1
	St Albans City v Tooting & Mitcham United	3-3
	Stevenage Athletic v Barking	2-1
24	Cheshunt v Hemel Hempstead Town	2-2
	Clapton v Finchley	2-0
	Romford (2) v Ware	3-1
	Ruislip Manor v Clacton Town	0-2
25	Boreham Wood v Hounslow	2-0
	Dagenham v Edgware Town	5-1
	Wealdstone v Woking	1-1
	Windsor & Eton v Burnham (1)	1-1
26	Carshalton Athletic v Kingstonian	0-2
	Egham Town v Hampton	2-0
	Marlow v Wokingham Town	2-0
	Tonbridge v Hatfield Town	5-0
27	Biggleswade Town v Maidenhead United	0-1
	Enfield v Hayes	3-0
	Uxbridge v Wembley	1-3
	Vauxhall Motors (Luton) v Dunstable Town	0-1
28	Bromley v Leytonstone	3-1
	Croydon v Erith & Belvedere	1-1
	Molesey v Willesden	4-1
	Walthamstow Avenue v Gravesend & Northfleet	2-1
29	Bexhill Town v Margate	0-8
	Deal Town v Eastbourne Town	1-1
	Sheppey United v Whitstable Town	5-1
	Sidley United v Canterbury City	0-2
30	Dover v Peacehaven & Telscombe	4-1
	Faversham Town v Herne Bay	2-1
	Ramsgate v Sittingbourne	4-1
	Ringmer v Maidstone United	1-1
31	Ashford Town v Lewes	2-1
	Crawley Town v Hastings United	2-1
	Medway v Tunbridge Wells	1-3
	Redhill v Burgess Hill Town	1-0
32	Bognor Regis Town v Newport (IOW)	1-3
	Cowes v Gosport Borough	0-2
	Poole Town v Worthing	1-0
	Waterlooville v Littlehampton Town	2-2
33	Alton Town v Horsham	2-1
	Basingstoke Town v Farnborough Town	2-1
	Pagham v Southwick	1-1
	Ryde Sports v Guildford & Dorking Utd.	0-4
34	Andover v Frome Town	1-1
	Bridport v Dorchester Town	4-3
	Salisbury (2) v Trowbridge Town	3-1
	Swaythling v Fareham Town	2-0
35	Bridgwater Town (1) v Minehead	1-2
	Glastonbury v Hungerford Town	2-1
	Stonehouse v Yeovil Town	0-6
	Weston-Super-Mare v Melksham Town	3-0
36	Barnstaple Town v St Blazey	9-1
	Falmouth Town v Newquay	5-1
	Taunton Town v Wadebridge Town	2-3
	Tiverton Town v Penzance	1-3
2r	Shildon v Billingham Synthonia	3-2
3r	Crook Town v Spennymoor United	1-2
4r	Skegness Town v Retford Town	0-2
7r	Stalybridge Celtic v Prescot Town	1-2e
10r	Oswestry Town v New Mills	5-3
11r	Sutton Town v Macclesfield Town	0-4
14r	Everwarm v Barry Town	0-1
15r	Coventry Sporting v Oldbury United	3-1
16r	Desborough Town v Cheltenham Town	2-3
18r	Thetford Town v Parson Drove United	5-0
19r	King's Lynn v Spalding United	1-1
r	St Neots Town v Bury Town	2-0
21r	Barnet v Sutton United	1-2
r	Hornchurch v Aveley	3-1
22r	Epsom & Ewell v Southall & Ealing Boro.	3-3
r	Tilbury v Leyton-Wingate	11-0
23r	Feltham v Bracknell Town	3-2
r	Tooting & Mitcham United v St Albans City	4-0
24r	Hemel Hempstead Town v Cheshunt	0-2
25r	Burnham (1) v Windsor & Eton	1-0
r	Woking v Wealdstone	3-5e
28r	Erith & Belvedere v Croydon	1-3
29r	Eastbourne Town v Deal Town	1-0
30r	Maidstone United v Ringmer	3-1
32r	Littlehampton Town v Waterlooville	1-3
33r	Southwick v Pagham	3-1
34r	Frome Town v Andover	5-3
19r2	Spalding United v King's Lynn	5-2
22r2	Southall & Ealing Boro. v Epsom & Ewell	5-1

Qualifying Round Two

1	Eppleton CW v North Shields	1-1
	Willington v Whitby Town	2-0
2	Easington CW v Shildon	1-3
	Tow Law Town v South Bank	2-1
3	Boldon CW v Netherfield (Kendal)	1-1
	Spennymoor United v Penrith	2-0
4	Brigg Town v Mexborough Town	2-3
	Selby Town v Retford Town	0-2
5	Frickley Colliery v Denaby United	2-2
	Worksop Town v Winterton Rangers	4-3
6	Fleetwood v Lancaster City	1-1
	Radcliffe Borough v Rossendale United	2-2
7	Droylsden v Hyde United	3-2
	Great Harwood v Prescot Town	5-1
8	Marine v Bangor City	1-0
	Runcorn v Rhyl	4-1
9	Chorley v Skelmersdale United	3-1
	Winsford United v Witton Albion	3-2
10	Congleton Town v Leek Town	1-3
	Northwich Victoria v Oswestry Town	3-1
11	Darlaston v Arnold	0-1
	Sutton Coldfield Town v Macclesfield Town	0-2
12	Bilston v Alfreton Town	2-2
	Enderby Town v Tividale	0-1
13	Dudley Town v Nuneaton Borough	0-1
	Gornal Athletic v Belper Town	2-0
14	Alvechurch v Ton Pentre	1-0
	Barry Town v Merthyr Tydfil	5-2
15	Cinderford Town v Brierley Hill Alliance	0-1
	Coventry Sporting v Halesowen Town	2-0
16	Cheltenham Town v Banbury United	2-0
	Rothwell Town v Oxford City	0-1
17	AP Leamington v Aylesbury United	3-1
	Milton Keynes City v Witney Town	2-1
18	Bourne Town v Bedford Town (1)	1-5
	Stamford v Thetford Town	2-0
19	Great Yarmouth Town v St Neots Town	3-2
	Spalding United v Soham Town Rangers	8-2
20	Letchworth Town v Cambridge City	0-1
	Lowestoft Town v Potton United	3-3
21	Chesham United v Hornchurch	2-0
	Sutton United v Staines Town	5-1
22	Dulwich Hamlet v Hillingdon Borough	5-1
	Southall & Ealing Boro. v Tilbury	2-1
23	Feltham v Addlestone	2-6
	Stevenage Athletic v Tooting & Mitcham United	2-2
24	Clacton Town v Romford (2)	1-1
	Clapton v Cheshunt	1-2
25	Burnham (1) v Wealdstone	0-2
	Dagenham v Boreham Wood	4-0
26	Egham Town v Kingstonian	0-1
	Tonbridge v Marlow	2-2
27	Dunstable Town v Wembley	0-2
	Enfield v Maidenhead United	6-0
28	Croydon v Bromley	2-1
	Walthamstow Avenue v Molesey	1-2
29	Canterbury City v Sheppey United	6-2
	Eastbourne Town v Margate	0-2
30	Faversham Town v Dover	0-4
	Maidstone United v Ramsgate	1-2
31	Crawley Town v Ashford Town	4-1
	Redhill v Tunbridge Wells	4-1
32	Gosport Borough v Newport (IOW)	2-2
	Waterlooville v Poole Town	3-0
33	Basingstoke Town v Alton Town	5-0
	Guildford & Dorking Utd. v Southwick	2-2
34	Bridport v Frome Town	0-3
	Swaythling v Salisbury (2)	0-1
35	Glastonbury v Minehead	0-4
	Weston-Super-Mare v Yeovil Town	0-0
36	Falmouth Town v Barnstaple Town	4-0
	Penzance v Wadebridge Town	2-1
1r	North Shields v Eppleton CW	0-1
3r	Netherfield (Kendal) v Boldon CW	3-2
5r	Denaby United v Frickley Colliery	0-2
6r	Lancaster City v Fleetwood	2-1
r	Rossendale United v Radcliffe Borough	4-1
12r	Alfreton Town v Bilston	2-1
20r	Potton United v Lowestoft Town	1-3
23r	Tooting & Mitcham United v Stevenage Athletic	2-0
24r	Romford (2) v Clacton Town	3-2
26r	Marlow v Tonbridge	1-3
32r	Newport (IOW) v Gosport Borough	1-1
33r	Southwick v Guildford & Dorking Utd.	3-2
35r	Yeovil Town v Weston-Super-Mare	4-0
32r2	Gosport Borough v Newport (IOW)	2-0

Qualifying Round Three

1	Willington v Eppleton CW	2-1
2	Tow Law Town v Shildon	4-1
3	Spennymoor United v Netherfield (Kendal)	3-0
4	Retford Town v Mexborough Town	1-2
5	Worksop Town v Frickley Colliery	1-1
6	Rossendale United v Lancaster City	2-1
7	Great Harwood v Droylsden	1-1
8	Runcorn v Marine	0-0
9	Winsford United v Chorley	2-0
10	Northwich Victoria v Leek Town	1-1
11	Macclesfield Town v Arnold	3-1
12	Tividale v Alfreton Town	0-0
13	Nuneaton Borough v Gornal Athletic	1-1
14	Alvechurch v Barry Town	3-1
15	Coventry Sporting v Brierley Hill Alliance	2-1
16	Oxford City v Cheltenham Town	0-0
17	Milton Keynes City v AP Leamington	0-1
18	Stamford v Bedford Town (1)	0-2
19	Spalding United v Great Yarmouth Town	2-0
20	Lowestoft Town v Cambridge City	1-0
21	Sutton United v Chesham United	3-1
22	Southall & Ealing Boro. v Dulwich Hamlet	2-2
23	Tooting & Mitcham United v Addlestone	4-2
24	Romford (2) v Cheshunt	1-0
25	Wealdstone v Dagenham	2-0
26	Tonbridge v Kingstonian	0-0
27	Wembley v Enfield	1-0
28	Molesey v Croydon	0-4
29	Canterbury City v Margate	2-0
30	Ramsgate v Dover	0-2
31	Redhill v Crawley Town	1-1
32	Waterlooville v Gosport Borough	4-0
33	Southwick v Basingstoke Town	2-1
34	Salisbury (2) v Frome Town	1-0
35	Yeovil Town v Minehead	1-0
36	Penzance v Falmouth Town	0-3
5r	Frickley Colliery v Worksop Town	1-1
7r	Droylsden v Great Harwood	1-1
8r	Marine v Runcorn	1-0
10r	Leek Town v Northwich Victoria	1-0
12r	Alfreton Town v Tividale	0-1
13r	Gornal Athletic v Nuneaton Borough	0-3
16r	Cheltenham Town v Oxford City	2-0
22r	Dulwich Hamlet v Southall & Ealing Boro.	1-2
26r	Kingstonian v Tonbridge	3-1
31r	Crawley Town v Redhill	1-0
5r2	Worksop Town v Frickley Colliery	2-0
7r2	Great Harwood v Droylsden	0-1

Qualifying Round Four

	AP Leamington v Tividale	3-2
	Bedford Town (1) v Lowestoft Town	6-1
	Blyth Spartans v Rossendale United	0-0
	Chelmsford City v Bishop's Stortford	0-2
	Coventry Sporting v Spalding United	2-0
	Crawley Town v Dover	0-0
	Croydon v Wycombe Wanderers	2-2
	Droylsden v Gateshead United	0-4
	Falmouth Town v Yeovil Town	1-5
	Grantham v Leek Town	4-0
	Hendon v Canterbury City	1-0
	Hitchin Town v Romford (2)	0-1
	Kettering Town v Boston United	3-4
	Leatherhead v Ilford	1-0
	Mexborough Town v Macclesfield Town	1-2
	Nuneaton Borough v Cheltenham Town	2-1
	Salisbury (2) v Weymouth	4-5
	Slough Town v Walton & Hersham	1-2
	Southall & Ealing Boro. v Tooting & Mitcham United	1-4
	Stafford Rangers v Alvechurch	1-1
	Sutton United v Waterlooville	1-1
	Telford United v Winsford United	1-1
	Tow Law Town v Spennymoor United	0-2
	Wealdstone v Southwick	3-1
	Wembley v Dartford	0-1
	Willington v Morecambe	2-2
	Wimbledon v Kingstonian	6-1
	Worksop Town v Marine	0-0
r	Alvechurch v Stafford Rangers	1-2
r	Dover v Crawley Town	6-0
r	Marine v Worksop Town	4-0
r	Morecambe v Willington	4-1
r	Rossendale United v Blyth Spartans	1-0
r	Waterlooville v Sutton United	1-3
r	Winsford United v Telford United	5-4
r	Wycombe Wanderers v Croydon	5-2

Round One

	AP Leamington v Stafford Rangers	2-3
	Aldershot v Wealdstone	4-3
	Boston United v Lincoln City	0-1

1975/76 to 1976/77

Bradford City v Chesterfield	1-0
Brentford v Northampton Town	2-0
Bury v Doncaster Rovers	4-2
Cardiff City v Exeter City	6-2
Colchester United v Dover	3-3
Coventry Sporting v Tranmere Rovers	2-0 N
Crystal Palace v Walton & Hersham	1-0
Darlington v Chester	0-0
Dartford v Bishop's Stortford	1-4
Grantham v Port Vale	2-2
Grimsby Town v Gateshead United	1-3
Halifax Town v Altrincham	3-1
Hartlepool v Stockport County	3-0
Hendon v Reading	1-0
Hereford United v Torquay United	2-0
Leatherhead v Cambridge United	2-0
Mansfield Town v Wrexham	1-1
Marine v Barnsley	3-1
Newport County v Swindon Town	2-2
Nuneaton Borough v Wimbledon	0-1
Peterborough United v Winsford United	4-1
Preston North End v Scunthorpe United	2-1
Romford (2) v Tooting & Mitcham United	0-1
Rossendale United v Shrewsbury Town	0-1
Rotherham United v Crewe Alexandra	2-1
Scarborough v Morecambe	2-0
Sheffield Wednesday v Macclesfield Town	3-1
Southend United v Swansea City	2-0
Spennymoor United v Southport	4-1
Sutton United v Bournemouth	1-1
Walsall v Huddersfield Town	0-1
Watford v Brighton & Hove Albion	0-3
Weymouth v Gillingham	0-2
Wigan Athletic v Matlock Town	4-1
Workington v Rochdale	1-1
Wycombe Wanderers v Bedford Town (1)	0-0
Yeovil Town v Millwall	1-1
r Bedford Town (1) v Wycombe Wanderers	2-2e
r Bournemouth v Sutton United	1-0
r Chester v Darlington	2-0
r Dover v Colchester United	4-1e
r Millwall v Yeovil Town	2-2e
r Port Vale v Grantham	4-1
r Rochdale v Workington	2-1e
r Swindon Town v Newport County	3-0
r Wrexham v Mansfield Town	1-1e
r2 Mansfield Town v Wrexham	2-1 N
r2 Wycombe Wanderers v Bedford Town (1)	2-1
r2 Yeovil Town v Millwall	0-1 N

Round Two

Aldershot v Bishop's Stortford	2-0
Bournemouth v Hereford United	2-2
Bury v Spennymoor United	3-0
Cardiff City v Wycombe Wanderers	1-0
Coventry Sporting v Peterborough United	0-4 N
Gateshead United v Rochdale	1-1
Gillingham v Brighton & Hove Albion	0-1
Hendon v Swindon Town	0-1
Huddersfield Town v Port Vale	2-1
Leatherhead v Tooting & Mitcham United	0-0
Mansfield Town v Lincoln City	1-2
Marine v Hartlepool	1-1
Millwall v Crystal Palace	1-1
Rotherham United v Bradford City	0-3
Scarborough v Preston North End	3-2
Sheffield Wednesday v Wigan Athletic	2-0
Shrewsbury Town v Chester	3-1
Southend United v Dover	4-1
Stafford Rangers v Halifax Town	1-3
Wimbledon v Brentford	0-2
r Crystal Palace v Millwall	2-1
r Hartlepool v Marine	6-3
r Hereford United v Bournemouth	2-0
r Rochdale v Gateshead United	3-1
r Tooting & Mitcham United v Leatherhead	2-1e

Round Three

Aldershot v Lincoln City	1-2
Blackpool v Burnley	1-0
Brentford v Bolton Wanderers	0-0
Charlton Athletic v Sheffield Wednesday	2-1
Chelsea v Bristol Rovers	1-1
Coventry City v Bristol City	2-1
Derby County v Everton	2-1
Fulham v Huddersfield Town	2-3
Hull City v Plymouth Argyle	1-1
Ipswich Town v Halifax Town	3-1
Leicester City v Sheffield United	3-0
Luton Town v Blackburn Rovers	2-0
Manchester City v Hartlepool	6-0
Manchester United v Oxford United	2-1
Middlesbrough v Bury	0-0
Norwich City v Rochdale	1-1
Nottingham Forest v Peterborough United	0-0
Notts County v Leeds United	0-1
Orient v Cardiff City	0-1
Portsmouth v Birmingham City	1-1
Queen's Park Rangers v Newcastle United	0-0
Scarborough v Crystal Palace	1-2
Shrewsbury Town v Bradford City	1-2
Southampton v Aston Villa	1-1
Southend United v Brighton & Hove Albion	2-1
Sunderland v Oldham Athletic	2-0
Swindon Town v Tooting & Mitcham United	2-2
Tottenham Hotspur v Stoke City	1-1
West Bromwich Albion v Carlisle United	3-1
West Ham United v Liverpool	0-2
Wolverhampton Wan. v Arsenal	3-0
York City v Hereford United	2-1
r Aston Villa v Southampton	1-2e
r Birmingham City v Portsmouth	0-1
r Bolton Wanderers v Brentford	2-0
r Bristol Rovers v Chelsea	0-1
r Bury v Middlesbrough	3-2
r Newcastle United v Queen's Park Rangers	2-1
r Peterborough United v Nottingham Forest	1-0
r Plymouth Argyle v Hull City	1-4
r Rochdale v Norwich City	0-0e
r Stoke City v Tottenham Hotspur	2-1
r Tooting & Mitcham United v Swindon Town	2-1
r2 Norwich City v Rochdale	2-1

Round Four

Bradford City v Tooting & Mitcham United	3-1
Charlton Athletic v Portsmouth	1-1
Coventry City v Newcastle United	1-1
Derby County v Liverpool	1-0
Huddersfield Town v Bolton Wanderers	0-1
Ipswich Town v Wolverhampton Wan.	0-0
Leeds United v Crystal Palace	0-1
Leicester City v Bury	1-0
Manchester United v Peterborough United	3-1
Norwich City v Luton Town	2-0
Southampton v Blackpool	3-1
Southend United v Cardiff City	2-1
Stoke City v Manchester City	1-0
Sunderland v Hull City	1-0
West Bromwich Albion v Lincoln City	3-2
York City v Chelsea	0-2
r Newcastle United v Coventry City	5-0
r Portsmouth v Charlton Athletic	0-3
r Wolverhampton Wan. v Ipswich Town	1-0

Round Five

Bolton Wanderers v Newcastle United	3-3
Chelsea v Crystal Palace	2-3
Derby County v Southend United	1-0
Leicester City v Manchester United	1-2
Norwich City v Bradford City	1-2
Stoke City v Sunderland	0-0
West Bromwich Albion v Southampton	1-1
Wolverhampton Wan. v Charlton Athletic	3-0
r Newcastle United v Bolton Wanderers	0-0e
r Southampton v West Bromwich Albion	4-0
r Sunderland v Stoke City	2-1
r2 Bolton Wanderers v Newcastle United	1-2 N

Round Six

Bradford City v Southampton	0-1
Derby County v Newcastle United	4-2
Manchester United v Wolverhampton Wan.	1-1
Sunderland v Crystal Palace	0-1
r Wolverhampton Wan. v Manchester United	2-3e

Semi Finals

Manchester United v Derby County	2-0 N
Southampton v Crystal Palace	2-0 N

Final

Southampton v Manchester United	1-0 N

1976/77

Preliminary Round

1 North Shields v Spennymoor United	0-0
Washington v West Auckland Town	3-1
2 Crook Town v Eppleton CW	4-1
Evenwood Town v Lancaster City	1-1
3 Horden CW v Wingate (Durham)	2-3
4 Frickley Athletic v Yorkshire Amateur	3-0
5 Frecheville Community v Winterton Rangers	0-1
6 Darwen v Radcliffe Borough	3-1
7 New Brighton v Skelmersdale United	1-1
Stalybridge Celtic v Witton Albion	1-3
8 Prescot Town v St Helens Town	4-1
South Liverpool v Winsford United	0-4
9 Congleton Town v Worksop Town	1-2
10 Eastwood Hanley v Heanor Town	2-2
Hyde United v Leek Town	2-1
11 Hinckley Athletic v Tividale	0-1
12 Friar Lane Old Boys v Warley County Borough	2-0
13 Dudley Town v Halesowen Town	3-1
Kidderminster Harriers v Redditch United	1-2
14 AP Leamington v Moor Green	1-0
Nuneaton Borough v Racing Club Warwick	2-1
15 Dunstable v Witney Town	0-4
16 Louth United v Wisbech Town	2-2
17 Harwich & Parkeston v Thetford Town	4-2
18 March Town United v Stowmarket	0-3
19 Rushden Town v Wolverton Town & BR	1-0
20 Croydon v Guildford & Dorking Utd.	1-0
Medway v Rainham Town	3-3
22 Enfield v Hampton	1-0
Hertford Town v Romford (2)	1-1
23 Feltham v Hornchurch	0-1
Marlow v Milton Keynes City	0-0
24 Hayes v Leyton-Wingate	2-0
Molesey v St Albans City	2-1
25 Edmonton & Haringey v Kingstonian	0-1
Letchworth Garden City v Maidenhead United	5-1
26 Harrow Borough v Willesden	3-1
27 Ruislip Manor v Wokingham Town	2-2
28 Newport (IOW) v Wigmore Athletic	2-0
29 Horsham YMCA v Worthing	2-0
30 Margate v Sittingbourne	2-2
31 Herne Bay v Whitstable Town	4-1
32 Farnborough Town v Salisbury (2)	4-0
33 Glastonbury v Barry Town	1-0
34 Everwarm v Llanelli	0-1
Gloucester City v Trowbridge Town	1-1
35 Clevedon Town v Weston-Super-Mare	1-1
36 Penzance v Yeovil Town	2-7
1r Spennymoor United v North Shields	4-1
2r Lancaster City v Evenwood Town	4-0
7r Skelmersdale United v New Brighton	0-2
10r Heanor Town v Eastwood Hanley	2-0
16r Wisbech Town v Louth United	2-0
20r Rainham Town v Medway	2-1
22r Romford (2) v Hertford Town	1-2
23r Milton Keynes City v Marlow	0-1
27r Wokingham Town v Ruislip Manor	3-1
30r Sittingbourne v Margate	0-1
34r Trowbridge Town v Gloucester City	1-2
35r Weston-Super-Mare v Clevedon Town	3-0

Qualifying Round One

1 Heaton Stannington v Shildon	0-3
Washington v Barrow	0-2
Whitby Town v Spennymoor United	3-3
Whitley Bay v Boldon CA	5-0
2 Consett v Easington CW	1-1
Lancaster City v Bishop Auckland	1-1
Penrith v Crook Town	0-2
South Bank v Carlisle City	3-0
3 Annfield Plain v Billingham Synthonia	3-2
Ferryhill Athletic v Netherfield (Kendal)	0-1
Tow Law Town v Wingate (Durham)	3-1
Willington v Durham City	3-3
4 Appleby Frodingham Ath. v Bridlington Town	5-3
Farsley Celtic v Goole Town	1-4
Mexborough Town v Frickley Athletic	2-0
Selby Town v Bridlington Trinity	0-2
5 Barton Town (2) v Brigg Town	2-2
Emley v Gainsborough Trinity	4-1
Retford Town v Winterton Rangers	0-3
Sutton Town v Denaby United	0-1
6 Accrington Stanley (2) v Bacup Borough	5-0
Clitheroe v Formby	0-0
Great Harwood v Darwen	1-1
Mossley v Chorley	5-2
7 Nantwich Town v Northwich Victoria	0-1
Porthmadog v New Brighton	3-4
Rhyl v Macclesfield Town	1-1
Witton Albion v Curzon Ashton	3-1
8 Bangor City v Prescot Town	6-0
Bethesda Athletic v Oswestry Town	2-1
Prestwich Heys v Runcorn	0-1
Winsford United v Burscough	0-0
9 Alfreton Town v Belper Town	2-0
Droylsden v Glossop	3-2
Horwich RMI v Worksop Town	1-1
Rossendale United v Buxton	0-5
10 Burton Albion v Eastwood Town	1-1
Hyde United v Ashton United	4-1
Long Eaton United v Heanor Town	3-0
New Mills v Brereton Social	5-2
11 Arnold v Atherstone Town	1-0
Hednesford Town v Ilkeston Town (2)	1-0
Oldbury United v Tividale	0-4
Telford United v Gresley Rovers	3-1
12 Armitage v Bedworth United	2-1
Darlaston v Highgate United	2-1
Sutton Coldfield Town v Friar Lane Old Boys	3-0
Tamworth v Coventry Sporting	1-1
13 Desborough Town v Enderby Town	0-1
Redditch United v Alvechurch	2-0
Stratford Town v Dudley Town	0-2
V.S. Rugby v Bilston	1-4
14 Gornal Athletic v Lye Town	1-3
Nuneaton Borough v Brierley Hill Alliance	2-0
Rothwell Town v AP Leamington	0-0
Stourbridge v Bromsgrove Rovers	1-3
15 Aylesbury United v Banbury United	1-3
Didcot Town v Oxford City	1-0
Thame United v Witney Town	1-0
Tring Town v Chesham United	0-3
16 Boston v Bourne Town	2-0
King's Lynn v Parson Drove United	3-2
Skegness Town v Wisbech Town	0-2
Stamford v Holbeach United	3-2
17 Clacton Town v Bury Town	1-2
Gorleston v Lowestoft Town	1-1
Newmarket Town v Harwich & Parkeston	1-1

153

1976/77

Sudbury Town v Great Yarmouth Town 1-1
18 Bedford Town (1) v Chatteris Town 7-1
Histon v Potton United 1-4
Spalding United v Corby Town 0-3
St Neots Town v Stowmarket 1-0
19 Barton Rovers v Cambridge City 3-0
Irthlingborough Diamonds v Soham Town Rangers 2-2
Vauxhall Motors (Luton) v Rushden Town 0-0
Wellingborough Town v Ely City 3-1
20 Corinthian Casuals v Grays Athletic 0-1
Rainham Town v Aveley 1-2
Tonbridge v Croydon 0-1
Woking v Burgess Hill Town 3-1
21 Cray Wanderers v Erith & Belvedere 2-2
Gravesend & Northfleet v Maidstone United 0-0
Redhill v Bromley 0-1
Three Bridges v Faversham Town 3-3
22 Camberley Town v Epsom & Ewell 1-1
Hertford Town v Boreham Wood 1-2
Tilbury v Enfield 2-2
Uxbridge v Bracknell Town 0-1
23 Dagenham v Stevenage Athletic wo/s
Epping Town v Hoddesdon Town 3-2
Marlow v Carshalton Athletic 1-2
Southall & Ealing Boro. v Hornchurch 2-1
24 Harlow Town v Hillingdon Borough 2-2
Molesey v Burnham (1) 2-1
Staines Town v Hayes 3-1
Ware v Edgware Town 2-0
25 Dulwich Hamlet v Hemel Hempstead Town 0-0
Letchworth Garden City v Addlestone 1-0
Walthamstow Avenue v Kingstonian 1-4
Wealdstone v Clapton 5-1
26 Barnet v Egham Town 6-1
Hatfield Town v Hounslow 2-0
Leytonstone v Harrow Borough 2-0
Slough Town v Finchley 2-2
27 Barking v Chertsey Town 6-1
Metropolitan Police v Sutton United 0-3
Wembley v Wokingham Town 1-1
Windsor & Eton v Cheshunt 3-2
28 Basingstoke Town v Chichester City (1) 10-0
Horsham v Selsey 4-0
Swaythling v Newport (IOW) 4-0
Waterlooville v Cowes 9-0
29 Bognor Regis Town v Bexhill Town 1-2
Eastbourne Town v Lewes 0-3
Littlehampton Town v Horsham YMCA 0-1
Tunbridge Wells v Crawley Town 2-0
30 Dover v Eastbourne United 3-1
Folkestone & Shepway v Sidley United 3-0
Haywards Heath v Ringmer 3-1
Sheppey United v Margate 2-2
31 Ashford Town v Canterbury City 1-0
Hastings United v Peacehaven & Telscombe 5-0
Ramsgate v Herne Bay 2-1
Southwick v Deal Town 2-0
32 Alton Town v Andover 1-0
Fareham Town v Gosport Borough 1-1
Hungerford Town v Farnborough Town 0-3
Poole Town v Dorchester Town 2-0
33 Ammanford Town v Evesham United 1-0 v
Chippenham Town v Devizes Town 1-3
Frome Town v Mangotsfield United 1-5
Worcester City v Glastonbury 3-2
34 Cinderford Town v Melksham Town 1-1
Llanelli v Calne Town 2-1
Merthyr Tydfil v Gloucester City 4-1
Ton Pentre v Cheltenham Town 1-1
35 Barnstaple Town v Bath City 2-1
Bridport v Minehead 2-4
Taunton Town v Weston-Super-Mare 1-0
Welton Rovers v Bideford 1-2
36 Bridgwater Town (1) v Falmouth Town 2-4
Newquay v St Blazey 0-0
Tiverton Town v Yeovil Town 0-2
Wadebridge Town v Ilminster Town 1-1
2r Bishop Auckland v Lancaster City 2-0
3r Durham City v Willington 3-3
5r Brigg Town v Barton Town (2) 3-2
6r Darwen v Great Harwood 0-3
r Formby v Clitheroe 3-1
7r Macclesfield Town v Rhyl 1-2
8r Burscough v Winsford United 1-3
9r Worksop Town v Horwich RMI 1-0
10r Eastwood Town v Burton Albion 1-2
12r Coventry Sporting v Tamworth 2-0
14r AP Leamington v Rothwell Town 2-0
17r Great Yarmouth Town v Sudbury Town 0-1
r Harwich & Parkeston v Newmarket Town 8-1
r Lowestoft Town v Gorleston 2-0
19r Rushden Town v Vauxhall Motors (Luton) 1-2
r Soham Town Rangers v Irthlingborough Diamonds 4-3
21r Erith & Belvedere v Cray Wanderers 2-3
r Faversham Town v Three Bridges 2-1
r Maidstone United v Gravesend & Northfleet 3-1
22r Enfield v Tilbury 3-1
r Epsom & Ewell v Camberley Town 1-0
24r Hillingdon Borough v Harlow Town 2-0
25r Hemel Hempstead Town v Dulwich Hamlet 1-2
26r Finchley v Slough Town 0-4
27r Wokingham Town v Wembley 1-1
30r Margate v Sheppey United 2-0
32r Gosport Borough v Fareham Town 0-5
33r Ammanford Town v Evesham United 1-5 N

34r Cheltenham Town v Ton Pentre 4-0
r Melksham Town v Cinderford Town 0-1
36r Ilminster Town v Wadebridge Town 1-0
r St Blazey v Newquay 1-3
3r2 Willington v Durham City 2-3
27r2 Wembley v Wokingham Town 0-1

Qualifying Round Two

1 Barrow v Shildon 2-1
Whitby Town v Whitley Bay 2-0
2 Bishop Auckland v Consett 3-0
Crook Town v South Bank 1-0
3 Annfield Plain v Netherfield (Kendal) 1-1
Tow Law Town v Durham City 1-2
4 Appleby Frodingham Ath. v Goole Town 0-0
Mexborough Town v Bridlington Trinity 3-2
5 Brigg Town v Emley 1-2
Winterton Rangers v Denaby United 2-1
6 Accrington Stanley (2) v Formby 0-3
Great Harwood v Mossley 6-0
7 New Brighton v Rhyl 1-3
Witton Albion v Northwich Victoria 1-3
8 Bangor City v Bethesda Athletic 4-2
Winsford United v Runcorn 1-0
9 Alfreton Town v Droylsden 0-1
Worksop Town v Buxton 3-0
10 Hyde United v Burton Albion 0-1
Long Eaton United v New Mills 3-0
11 Arnold v Hednesford Town 0-0
Tividale v Telford United 0-3
12 Armitage v Darlaston 1-1
Sutton Coldfield Town v Coventry Sporting 2-1
13 Dudley Town v Bilston 4-1
Redditch United v Enderby Town 0-0
14 AP Leamington v Bromsgrove Rovers 1-1
Nuneaton Borough v Lye Town 2-0
15 Banbury United v Didcot Town 3-2
Thame United v Chesham United 0-1
16 Boston v King's Lynn 2-1
Wisbech Town v Stamford 1-1
17 Bury Town v Lowestoft Town 2-3
Harwich & Parkeston v Sudbury Town 3-1 N
18 Bedford Town (1) v Potton United 4-1
St Neots Town v Corby Town 3-0
19 Barton Rovers v Soham Town Rangers 5-0
Vauxhall Motors (Luton) v Wellingborough Town 1-3
20 Aveley v Grays Athletic 1-0
Croydon v Woking 0-0
21 Bromley v Faversham Town 2-0
Cray Wanderers v Maidstone United 2-1
22 Boreham Wood v Epsom & Ewell 1-1
Enfield v Bracknell Town 5-2
23 Carshalton Athletic v Epping Town 1-1
Southall & Ealing Boro. v Dagenham 0-1
24 Molesey v Hillingdon Borough 1-1
Staines Town v Ware 3-1
25 Kingstonian v Wealdstone 0-2
Letchworth Garden City v Dulwich Hamlet 0-1
26 Barnet v Hatfield Town 3-0
Leytonstone v Slough Town 1-1
27 Barking v Sutton United 1-1
Wokingham Town v Windsor & Eton 2-1
28 Basingstoke Town v Horsham 2-0
Swaythling v Waterlooville 0-3
29 Bexhill Town v Lewes 0-3
Horsham YMCA v Tunbridge Wells 1-1
30 Dover v Haywards Heath 2-0
Margate v Folkestone & Shepway 2-2
31 Ashford Town v Hastings United 0-1
Ramsgate v Southwick 1-1
32 Alton Town v Fareham Town 0-0
Farnborough Town v Poole Town 1-1
33 Devizes Town v Mangotsfield United 0-1
Worcester City v Evesham United 3-1
34 Llanelli v Cinderford Town 3-2
Merthyr Tydfil v Cheltenham Town 3-3
35 Barnstaple Town v Minehead 1-2
Taunton Town v Bideford 4-2
36 Falmouth Town v Newquay 8-0
Yeovil Town v Ilminster Town 10-1
3r Netherfield (Kendal) v Annfield Plain 6-0
4r Goole Town v Appleby Frodingham Ath. 1-0
11r Hednesford Town v Arnold 3-0
12r Darlaston v Armitage 1-0
13r Enderby Town v Redditch United 1-0
14r Bromsgrove Rovers v AP Leamington 2-1
16r Stamford v Wisbech Town 3-0
20r Woking v Croydon 2-0
22r Epsom & Ewell v Boreham Wood 2-1
23r Epping Town v Carshalton Athletic 1-1
24r Hillingdon Borough v Molesey 2-1
26r Slough Town v Leytonstone 1-0
27r Sutton United v Barking 1-4
29r Tunbridge Wells v Horsham YMCA 0-2
30r Folkestone & Shepway v Margate 2-4 v
31r Southwick v Ramsgate 1-2
32r Fareham Town v Alton Town 1-0
r Poole Town v Farnborough Town 3-1
34r Cheltenham Town v Merthyr Tydfil 1-1
23r2 Carshalton Athletic v Epping Town 4-2
30r2 Folkestone & Shepway v Margate 3-4
34r2 Merthyr Tydfil v Cheltenham Town 4-0

Qualifying Round Three

1 Barrow v Whitby Town 2-2
2 Bishop Auckland v Crook Town 1-1
3 Netherfield (Kendal) v Durham City 1-1
4 Goole Town v Mexborough Town 7-1
5 Emley v Winterton Rangers 4-7
6 Formby v Great Harwood 0-0
7 Northwich Victoria v Rhyl 0-0
8 Winsford United v Bangor City 1-1
9 Droylsden v Worksop Town 1-0
10 Burton Albion v Long Eaton United 5-0
11 Hednesford Town v Telford United 0-0
12 Darlaston v Sutton Coldfield Town 1-0
13 Enderby Town v Dudley Town 0-1
14 Nuneaton Borough v Bromsgrove Rovers 2-0
15 Banbury United v Chesham United 1-4
16 Boston v Stamford 1-0
17 Lowestoft Town v Harwich & Parkeston 0-3
18 Bedford Town (1) v St Neots Town 3-0
19 Barton Rovers v Wellingborough Town 1-1
20 Aveley v Woking 1-1
21 Cray Wanderers v Bromley 0-2
22 Epsom & Ewell v Enfield 1-1
23 Carshalton Athletic v Dagenham 3-3
24 Hillingdon Borough v Staines Town 2-0
25 Dulwich Hamlet v Wealdstone 0-2
26 Barnet v Slough Town 0-1
27 Barking v Wokingham Town 3-1
28 Basingstoke Town v Waterlooville 1-2
29 Lewes v Horsham YMCA 4-4
30 Dover v Margate 3-2
31 Hastings United v Ramsgate 2-0
32 Fareham Town v Poole Town 0-1
33 Mangotsfield United v Worcester City 0-2
34 Llanelli v Merthyr Tydfil 3-6
35 Minehead v Taunton Town 2-1
36 Falmouth Town v Yeovil Town 2-0
1r Whitby Town v Barrow 3-4
2r Crook Town v Bishop Auckland 1-0
3r Durham City v Netherfield (Kendal) 1-2
6r Great Harwood v Formby 3-0
7r Rhyl v Northwich Victoria 1-3
8r Bangor City v Winsford United 4-1
11r Telford United v Hednesford Town 3-0
19r Wellingborough Town v Barton Rovers 1-2
20r Woking v Aveley 4-0
22r Enfield v Epsom & Ewell 1-0
23r Dagenham v Carshalton Athletic 2-1
29r Horsham YMCA v Lewes 2-4

Qualifying Round Four

Altrincham v Grantham 1-0
Barton Rovers v Nuneaton Borough 2-3
Blyth Spartans v Gateshead United 0-3
Boston v Bangor City 1-0
Bromley v Walton & Hersham 9-3
Burton Albion v Northwich Victoria 0-1
Chelmsford City v Leatherhead 0-4
Chesham United v Worcester City 4-2
Crook Town v Netherfield (Kendal) 2-1
Dagenham v Dartford 1-1
Darlaston v Kettering Town 1-1
Dover v Hitchin Town 2-2
Dudley Town v Bedford Town (1) 1-0
Enfield v Ilford 2-2
Falmouth Town v Minehead 1-1
Goole Town v Boston United 1-1
Hillingdon Borough v Hastings United 2-1
Lewes v Harwich & Parkeston 1-1
Marine v Barrow 1-1
Morecambe v Great Harwood 2-0
Poole Town v Weymouth 2-3
Telford United v Matlock Town 2-5
Tooting & Mitcham United v Barking 1-1
Waterlooville v Hendon 4-1
Wealdstone v Bishop's Stortford 3-2
Winterton Rangers v Droylsden 3-3
Woking v Slough Town 0-0
Wycombe Wanderers v Merthyr Tydfil 3-1
r Barking v Tooting & Mitcham United 1-2
r Barrow v Marine 3-1
r Boston United v Goole Town 1-3
r Dartford v Dagenham 3-2
r Droylsden v Winterton Rangers 3-2
r Harwich & Parkeston v Lewes 3-1
r Hitchin Town v Dover 3-1
r Ilford v Enfield 0-4
r Kettering Town v Darlaston 2-0
r Minehead v Falmouth Town 3-0
r Slough Town v Woking 0-1

Round One

Aldershot v Portsmouth 1-1
Barnsley v Boston 3-1
Barrow v Goole Town 0-2
Bournemouth v Newport County 0-0
Brentford v Chesham United 2-0
Brighton & Hove Albion v Crystal Palace 2-2
Bury v Workington 6-0
Cambridge United v Colchester United 1-1
Chester v Hartlepool 1-0
Crewe Alexandra v Preston North End 1-1

1976/77 to 1977/78

Crook Town v Nuneaton Borough	1-4
Doncaster Rovers v Shrewsbury Town	2-2
Droylsden v Grimsby Town	0-0
Dudley Town v York City	1-1
Enfield v Harwich & Parkeston	0-0
Exeter City v Southend United	1-1
Gillingham v Watford	0-1
Huddersfield Town v Mansfield Town	0-0
Kettering Town v Oxford United	1-1
Leatherhead v Northampton Town	2-0
Lincoln City v Morecambe	1-0
Matlock Town v Wigan Athletic	2-0
Reading v Wealdstone	1-0
Rochdale v Northwich Victoria	1-1
Rotherham United v Altrincham	5-0
Scarborough v Darlington	0-0
Scunthorpe United v Chesterfield	1-2
Sheffield Wednesday v Stockport County	2-0
Southport v Port Vale	1-2
Stafford Rangers v Halifax Town	0-0
Swansea City v Minehead	0-1
Swindon Town v Bromley	7-0
Tooting & Mitcham United v Dartford	4-2
Torquay United v Hillingdon Borough	1-2
Tranmere Rovers v Peterborough United	0-4
Walsall v Bradford City	0-0
Waterlooville v Wycombe Wanderers	1-2
Weymouth v Hitchin Town	1-1
Wimbledon v Woking	1-0
Wrexham v Gateshead United	6-0
r Bradford City v Walsall	0-2
r Colchester United v Cambridge United	2-0
r Crystal Palace v Brighton & Hove Albion	1-1e
r Darlington v Scarborough	4-1
r Grimsby Town v Droylsden	5-3
r Halifax Town v Stafford Rangers	1-0
r Harwich & Parkeston v Enfield	0-3
r Hitchin Town v Weymouth	2-2e
r Mansfield Town v Huddersfield Town	2-1
r Newport County v Bournemouth	3-0
r Northwich Victoria v Rochdale	0-0e
r Oxford United v Kettering Town	0-1
r Portsmouth v Aldershot	2-1
r Preston North End v Crewe Alexandra	2-2e
r Shrewsbury Town v Doncaster Rovers	4-3
r Southend United v Exeter City	2-1e
r York City v Dudley Town	4-1
r2 Brighton & Hove Albion v Crystal Palace	0-1 N
r2 Crewe Alexandra v Preston North End	0-3 N
r2 Rochdale v Northwich Victoria	1-2 N
r2 Weymouth v Hitchin Town	3-3eN
r3 Hitchin Town v Weymouth	3-1 N

Round Two

Bury v Shrewsbury Town	0-0
Chesterfield v Walsall	1-1
Colchester United v Brentford	3-2
Crystal Palace v Enfield	4-0
Darlington v Sheffield Wednesday	1-0
Grimsby Town v Chester	0-1
Halifax Town v Preston North End	1-0
Hillingdon Borough v Watford	2-3
Hitchin Town v Swindon Town	1-1
Kettering Town v Tooting & Mitcham United	1-0
Leatherhead v Wimbledon	1-3
Lincoln City v Nuneaton Borough	6-0
Mansfield Town v Matlock Town	2-5
Northwich Victoria v Peterborough United	4-0
Port Vale v Barnsley	3-0
Portsmouth v Minehead	2-1
Rotherham United v York City	0-0
Southend United v Newport County	3-0
Wrexham v Goole Town	1-1
Wycombe Wanderers v Reading	1-2
r Goole Town v Wrexham	0-1
r Shrewsbury Town v Bury	2-1
r Swindon Town v Hitchin Town	3-1e
r Walsall v Chesterfield	0-0e
r York City v Rotherham United	1-1e
r2 Chesterfield v Walsall	0-1 N
r2 Rotherham United v York City	2-1e

Round Three

Birmingham City v Portsmouth	1-0
Blackpool v Derby County	0-0
Burnley v Lincoln City	2-2
Cardiff City v Tottenham Hotspur	1-0
Carlisle United v Matlock Town	5-1
Charlton Athletic v Blackburn Rovers	1-1
Coventry City v Millwall	1-0
Darlington v Orient	2-2
Everton v Stoke City	2-0
Fulham v Swindon Town	3-3
Halifax Town v Luton Town	0-1
Hereford United v Reading	1-0
Hull City v Port Vale	1-1
Ipswich Town v Bristol City	4-1
Kettering Town v Colchester United	2-3
Leeds United v Norwich City	5-2
Leicester City v Aston Villa	0-1
Liverpool v Crystal Palace	0-0
Manchester City v West Bromwich Albion	1-1
Manchester United v Walsall	1-0

Northwich Victoria v Watford	3-2
Nottingham Forest v Bristol Rovers	1-1
Notts County v Arsenal	0-1
Oldham Athletic v Plymouth Argyle	3-0
Queen's Park Rangers v Shrewsbury Town	2-1
Sheffield United v Newcastle United	0-0
Southampton v Chelsea	1-1
Southend United v Chester	0-4
Sunderland v Wrexham	2-2
West Ham United v Bolton Wanderers	2-1
Wimbledon v Middlesbrough	0-0
Wolverhampton Wan. v Rotherham United	3-2
r Blackburn Rovers v Charlton Athletic	2-0
r Bristol Rovers v Nottingham Forest	1-1e
r Chelsea v Southampton	0-3e
r Crystal Palace v Liverpool	2-3
r Derby County v Blackpool	3-2
r Lincoln City v Burnley	0-1
r Middlesbrough v Wimbledon	1-0
r Newcastle United v Sheffield United	3-1
r Orient v Darlington	0-0e
r Port Vale v Hull City	3-1e
r Swindon Town v Fulham	5-0
r West Bromwich Albion v Manchester City	0-1
r Wrexham v Sunderland	1-0
r2 Darlington v Orient	0-3 N
r2 Nottingham Forest v Bristol Rovers	6-0 N

Round Four

Arsenal v Coventry City	3-1
Aston Villa v West Ham United	3-0
Birmingham City v Leeds United	1-2
Blackburn Rovers v Orient	3-0
Cardiff City v Wrexham	3-2
Chester v Luton Town	1-0
Colchester United v Derby County	1-1
Ipswich Town v Wolverhampton Wan.	2-2
Liverpool v Carlisle United	3-0
Manchester United v Queen's Park Rangers	1-0
Middlesbrough v Hereford United	4-0
Newcastle United v Manchester City	1-3
Northwich Victoria v Oldham Athletic	1-3 N
Nottingham Forest v Southampton	3-3
Port Vale v Burnley	2-1
Swindon Town v Everton	2-2
r Derby County v Colchester United	1-0
r Everton v Swindon Town	2-1
r Southampton v Nottingham Forest	2-1
r Wolverhampton Wan. v Ipswich Town	1-0

Round Five

Aston Villa v Port Vale	3-0
Cardiff City v Everton	1-2
Derby County v Blackburn Rovers	3-1
Leeds United v Manchester City	1-0
Liverpool v Oldham Athletic	3-1
Middlesbrough v Arsenal	4-1
Southampton v Manchester United	2-2
Wolverhampton Wan. v Chester	1-0
r Manchester United v Southampton	2-1

Round Six

Everton v Derby County	2-0
Liverpool v Middlesbrough	2-0
Manchester United v Aston Villa	2-1
Wolverhampton Wan. v Leeds United	0-1

Semi Finals

Liverpool v Everton	2-2 N
Manchester United v Leeds United	2-1 N
r Everton v Liverpool	0-3 N

Final

Manchester United v Liverpool	2-1 N

1977/78

Preliminary Round

1 North Shields v West Auckland Town	1-1
Wallsend Town v Whitby Town	2-3
2 Eppleton CW v South Bank	1-0
Horden CW v Spennymoor United	2-2
3 Wingate (Durham) v Annfield Plain	2-1
4 Winterton Rangers v Appleby Frodingham Ath.	0-1
5 Yorkshire Amateur v Barton Town (2)	0-2
6 Skelmersdale United v Accrington Stanley (2)	0-3
7 Runcorn v Bacup Borough	4-0
8 Witton Albion v Bangor City	1-1
9 Winsford United v Ashton United	1-1
10 Sutton Town v Belper Town	2-1
11 Heanor Town v Leek Town	2-2
Ilkeston Town (2) v Tamworth	0-0
12 Cheltenham Town v Moor Green	4-1
Halesowen Town v Oldbury United	2-1
13 Kidderminster Harriers v Sutton Coldfield Town	5-2
Stourbridge v Tividale	1-1
14 Wolverton Town & BR v Banbury United	1-1

15 V.S. Rugby v Bedworth United	0-0
16 Spalding United v Arnold	2-3
17 Wisbech Town v Clacton Town	5-0
18 Sudbury Town v Bury Town	1-1
19 Kempston Rovers v Potton United	2-1
Milton Keynes City v Rushden Town	0-2
20 Didcot Town v Leytonstone	2-2
Hounslow v Molesey	2-1
21 Clapton v Metropolitan Police	4-1
Hillingdon Borough v Slough Town	3-3
22 Harwich & Parkeston v Southall & Ealing Boro.	4-0
Romford (2) v Walthamstow Avenue	1-1
23 Gravesend & Northfleet v Staines Town	4-0
Leyton-Wingate v Uxbridge	2-0
24 Hatfield Town v Marlow	1-2
Ilford v Woking	1-0
25 Kingstonian v Tilbury	0-1
Ruislip Manor v Windsor & Eton	1-3
26 Willesden v Bedford Town (1)	4-3
27 Tunbridge Wells v Canterbury City	5-0
28 Sheppey United v Bexhill Town	1-2
29 Whitstable Town v Ashford Town	0-1
30 Littlehampton Town v Three Bridges	0-1
Southwick v Waterlooville	0-1
31 Wigmore Athletic v East Grinstead	1-3
32 Yeovil Town v Alton Town	2-2
33 Taunton Town v Bath City	1-2
34 Clevedon Town v Mangotsfield United	4-0
Glastonbury v Merthyr Tydfil	0-1
35 Melksham Town v Welton Rovers	1-0
Trowbridge Town v Weston-Super-Mare	1-1
36 Wadebridge Town v Barnstaple Town	0-7
1r West Auckland Town v North Shields	2-1
2r Spennymoor United v Horden CW	3-1
8r Bangor City v Witton Albion	2-0
9r Ashton United v Winsford United	0-2
11r Leek Town v Heanor Town	2-0
r Tamworth v Ilkeston Town (2)	1-0
13r Tividale v Stourbridge	1-0
14r Banbury United v Wolverton Town & BR	4-1
15r Bedworth United v V.S. Rugby	0-1
18r Bury Town v Sudbury Town	2-0
20r Leytonstone v Didcot Town	1-0
21r Slough Town v Hillingdon Borough	0-1
22r Walthamstow Avenue v Romford (2)	3-2
32r Alton Town v Yeovil Town	0-4
35r Weston-Super-Mare v Trowbridge Town	2-1

Qualifying Round One

1 Bishop Auckland v West Auckland Town	3-0
Boldon CA v Carlisle City	3-1
Netherfield (Kendal) v Willington	4-0
Tow Law Town v Whitby Town	0-4
2 Billingham Synthonia v Eppleton CW	2-0
Bridlington Town v Durham City	1-1
Easington CW v Whitley Bay	4-4
Ferryhill Athletic v Spennymoor United	2-4
3 Consett v Wingate (Durham)	1-1
Crook Town v Evenwood Town	3-0
Penrith v Washington	3-3
Shildon v Blyth Spartans	0-3
4 Bridlington Trinity v Appleby Frodingham Ath.	1-2
Brigg Town v Farsley Celtic	2-0
Frickley Athletic v North Ferriby United	3-1
Gainsborough Trinity v Ashby Institute	1-0
5 Emley v Barton Town (2)	3-2
Goole Town v Louth United	6-1
Retford Town v Worksop Town	1-2
Selby Town v Denaby United	3-1
6 Burscough v Accrington Stanley (2)	2-2
Chorley v Clitheroe	5-1
Great Harwood v Prestwich Heys	1-1
Horwich RMI v Barrow	1-0
7 Droylsden v Runcorn	0-2
Formby v Lancaster City	1-0
Lytham v Rossendale United	0-1
Prescot Town v Darwen	0-1
8 Nantwich Town v Bangor City	1-1
Oswestry Town v Porthmadog	2-0
Radcliffe Borough v South Liverpool	2-6
Rhyl v Congleton Town	0-0
9 Glossop v Winsford United	0-2
Macclesfield Town v Mossley	0-2
New Brighton v St Helens Town	1-2
New Mills v Curzon Ashton	1-2
10 Gresley Rovers v Sutton Town	2-2
Hednesford Town v Hyde United	1-0
Long Eaton United v Stalybridge Celtic	0-2
Mexborough Town v Buxton	1-3
11 Alfreton Town v Leek Town	0-1
Darlaston v Eastwood Town	3-0
Friar Lane Old Boys v Telford United	1-2
Hinckley Athletic v Tamworth	0-0
12 Atherstone Town v Cheltenham Town	0-0
Bilston v Brierley Hill Alliance	1-2
Burton Albion v Stratford Town	1-0
Gornal Athletic v Halesowen Town	1-3
13 AP Leamington v Tividale	3-1
Alvechurch v Kidderminster Harriers	2-2
Dudley Town v Gloucester City	1-1
Highgate United v Willenhall Town	2-1
14 Lye Town v Banbury United	3-3
Oxford City v Racing Club Warwick	2-0
Redditch United v Wellingborough Town	1-3

155

1977/78

	Thame United v Bromsgrove Rovers	1-3
15	Corby Town v V.S. Rugby	1-1
	Coventry Sporting v Enderby Town	1-1
	Irthlingborough Diamonds v Stamford	3-1
	Rothwell Town v Bourne Town	4-1
16	Chatteris Town v Arnold	1-6
	Ely City v Holbeach United	1-2
	March Town United v Skegness Town	2-1
	Parson Drove United v Boston	0-2
17	King's Lynn v Wisbech Town	1-2
	Lowestoft Town v Newmarket Town	4-1
	Soham Town Rangers v Great Yarmouth Town	0-2
	St Neots Town v Thetford Town	2-1
18	Cambridge City v Bury Town	1-1
	Felixstowe Town v Gorleston	2-4
	Harlow Town v Stowmarket	5-0
	Histon v Chelmsford City	0-1
19	Aylesbury United v Kempston Rovers	0-3
	Barton Rovers v Hemel Hempstead Town	1-1
	Hertford Town v Tring Town	1-1
	Letchworth Garden City v Rushden Town	3-0
20	Aveley v Leytonstone	0-2
	Barnet v Camberley Town	4-1
	Carshalton Athletic v St Albans City	2-3
	Erith & Belvedere v Hounslow	4-2
21	Addlestone v Clapton	0-1
	Barking v Chalfont St Peter	5-2
	Cheshunt v Walton & Hersham	3-2
	Grays Athletic v Hillingdon Borough	1-1
22	Billericay Town v Harwich & Parkeston	1-1
	Corinthian Casuals v Epping Town	5-1
	Haringey Borough v Ware	2-2
	Rainham Town v Walthamstow Avenue	0-5
23	Berkhamsted Town v Gravesend & Northfleet	0-5
	Dulwich Hamlet v Egham Town	1-0
	Enfield v Wembley	6-0
	Hornchurch v Leyton-Wingate	0-1
24	Basingstoke Town v Marlow	2-0
	Burnham (1) v Chertsey Town	0-1
	Hampton v Wokingham Town	3-0
	Hayes v Ilford	0-2
25	Bracknell Town v Tilbury	1-2
	Epsom & Ewell v Feltham	1-1
	Harrow Borough v Witney Town	1-1
	Maidenhead United v Windsor & Eton	3-0
26	Chesham United v Willesden	5-0
	Edgware Town v Dunstable	4-1
	Finchley v Vauxhall Motors (Luton)	1-0
	Hoddesdon Town v Boreham Wood	0-1
27	Croydon v Tunbridge Wells	3-3
	Hastings United v Margate	2-2
	Medway v Sutton United	0-1
	Snowdown CW v Cray Wanderers	2-1
28	Burgess Hill Town v Bexhill Town	2-1
	Crawley Town v Deal Town	3-1
	Dover v Maidstone United	0-1
	Herne Bay v Bromley	2-2
29	Lewes v Ashford Town	1-0
	Peacehaven & Telscombe v Ramsgate	1-1
	Sidley United v Tonbridge	0-0
	Sittingbourne v Haywards Heath	0-2
30	Andover v Three Bridges	2-0
	Bognor Regis Town v Farnborough Town	0-2
	Horsham v Worthing	4-1
	Newport (IOW) v Waterlooville	0-0
31	Eastbourne United v East Grinstead	4-0
	Faversham Town v Folkestone & Shepway	0-3
	Horsham YMCA v Ringmer	1-0
	Redhill v Eastbourne Town	0-1
32	Frome Town v Yeovil Town	2-1
	Gosport Borough v Hungerford Town	0-0
	Poole Town v Selsey	4-1
	Salisbury (2) v Cowes	5-1
33	Bridport v Bath City	0-3
	Dorchester Town v Fareham Town	0-0
	Ilminster Town v Swaythling	0-2
	Newbury Town v Bridgwater Town (1)	0-1
34	Bridgend Town v Clevedon Town	4-3
	Calne Town v Chippenham Town	3-1
	Cinderford Town - Bye	
	Evesham United v Merthyr Tydfil	0-0
35	Barry Town v Melksham Town	4-1
	Forest Green Rovers v Larkhall Athletic	3-2
	Llanelli v Worcester City	1-1
	Ton Pentre v Weston-Super-Mare	2-2
36	Chard Town v Barnstaple Town	1-0
	Falmouth Town v Newquay	0-1
	Penzance v Tiverton Town	2-2
	St Blazey v Bideford	0-1
2r	Durham City v Bridlington Town	1-0
r	Whitley Bay v Easington CW	3-2
3r	Washington v Penrith	1-0
r	Wingate (Durham) v Consett	1-4
6r	Accrington Stanley (2) v Burscough	0-1
r	Prestwich Heys v Great Harwood	1-5
8r	Bangor City v Nantwich Town	4-1
r	Congleton Town v Rhyl	0-2
10r	Sutton Town v Gresley Rovers	2-1
11r	Tamworth v Hinckley Athletic	1-1
12r	Cheltenham Town v Atherstone Town	1-0
13r	Gloucester City v Dudley Town	1-2
r	Kidderminster Harriers v Alvechurch	1-1
14r	Banbury United v Lye Town	2-1
15r	Enderby Town v Coventry Sporting	1-0
r	V.S. Rugby v Corby Town	0-2
18r	Bury Town v Cambridge City	1-2
19r	Hemel Hempstead Town v Barton Rovers	3-1
r	Tring Town v Hertford Town	2-3e
21r	Hillingdon Borough v Grays Athletic	4-1
22r	Harwich & Parkeston v Billericay Town	1-4
r	Ware v Haringey Borough	3-3
25r	Feltham v Epsom & Ewell	2-1e
r	Witney Town v Harrow Borough	2-1
27r	Margate v Hastings United	1-2
r	Tunbridge Wells v Croydon	0-2
28r	Bromley v Herne Bay	5-0
29r	Ramsgate v Peacehaven & Telscombe	1-0
r	Tonbridge v Sidley United	8-1
30r	Waterlooville v Newport (IOW)	0-1
32r	Hungerford Town v Gosport Borough	3-0
33r	Fareham Town v Dorchester Town	1-2
34r	Merthyr Tydfil v Evesham United	2-1
35r	Weston-Super-Mare v Ton Pentre	3-2
r	Worcester City v Llanelli	2-0
36r	Tiverton Town v Penzance	3-1
11r2	Hinckley Athletic v Tamworth	2-1 N
13r2	Alvechurch v Kidderminster Harriers	0-1
22r2	Ware v Haringey Borough	0-1

Qualifying Round Two

1	Boldon CA v Whitby Town	2-1
	Netherfield (Kendal) v Bishop Auckland	1-1
2	Durham City v Spennymoor United	1-2
	Whitley Bay v Billingham Synthonia	3-1
3	Crook Town v Blyth Spartans	1-1
	Washington v Consett	0-3
4	Brigg Town v Gainsborough Trinity	1-0
	Frickley Athletic v Appleby Frodingham Ath.	1-2
5	Goole Town v Selby Town	7-0
	Worksop Town v Emley	4-2
6	Chorley v Horwich RMI	1-0
	Great Harwood v Burscough	0-1
7	Formby v Darwen	2-2
	Rossendale United v Runcorn	1-2
8	Oswestry Town v Rhyl	1-2
	South Liverpool v Bangor City	2-2
9	Mossley v Curzon Ashton	1-0
	New Brighton v Winsford United	1-3
10	Hednesford Town v Buxton	1-0
	Stalybridge Celtic v Sutton Town	6-0
11	Darlaston v Hinckley Athletic	0-1
	Telford United v Leek Town	3-0
12	Brierley Hill Alliance v Halesowen Town	0-1
	Burton Albion v Cheltenham Town	2-1
13	Dudley Town v AP Leamington	0-2
	Highgate United v Kidderminster Harriers	0-2
14	Oxford City v Bromsgrove Rovers	2-1
	Wellingborough Town v Banbury United	1-2
15	Enderby Town v Rothwell Town	5-0
	Irthlingborough Diamonds v Corby Town	1-2
16	Holbeach United v Boston	0-1
	March Town United v Arnold	3-8
17	Lowestoft Town v Great Yarmouth Town	4-1
	St Neots Town v Wisbech Town	4-4
18	Gorleston v Chelmsford City	1-1
	Harlow Town v Cambridge City	1-0
19	Hemel Hempstead Town v Letchworth Garden City	2-2
	Hertford Town v Kempston Rovers	1-0
20	Barnet v Erith & Belvedere	2-1
	St Albans City v Leytonstone	2-0
21	Barking v Hillingdon Borough	1-3
	Cheshunt v Clapton	2-1
22	Corinthian Casuals v Walthamstow Avenue	0-2
	Haringey Borough v Billericay Town	1-3
23	Dulwich Hamlet v Leyton-Wingate	1-1
	Enfield v Gravesend & Northfleet	2-1
24	Chertsey Town v Ilford	1-1
	Hampton v Basingstoke Town	1-1
25	Feltham v Maidenhead United	3-2
	Witney Town v Tilbury	0-3
26	Edgware Town v Boreham Wood	2-2
	Finchley v Chesham United	2-2
27	Hastings United v Snowdown CW	5-1
	Sutton United v Croydon	2-0
28	Crawley Town v Bromley	3-2
	Maidstone United v Burgess Hill Town	5-0
29	Ramsgate v Haywards Heath	2-0
	Tonbridge v Lewes	1-0
30	Farnborough Town v Newport (IOW)	3-0
	Horsham v Andover	3-2
31	Folkestone & Shepway v Eastbourne Town	5-2
	Horsham YMCA v Eastbourne United	4-1
32	Hungerford Town v Salisbury (2)	0-1
	Poole Town v Frome Town	0-2
33	Dorchester Town v Bridgwater Town (1)	4-3
	Swaythling v Bath City	1-1
34	Calne Town v Merthyr Tydfil	0-4
	Cinderford Town v Bridgend Town	0-4
35	Forest Green Rovers v Weston-Super-Mare	0-2
	Worcester City v Barry Town	1-0
36	Newquay v Bideford	2-3
	Tiverton Town v Chard Town	2-0
1r	Bishop Auckland v Netherfield (Kendal)	1-1e
3r	Blyth Spartans v Crook Town	3-0
7r	Darwen v Formby	2-0
8r	Bangor City v South Liverpool	1-0
17r	Wisbech Town v St Neots Town	2-1
18r	Chelmsford City v Gorleston	5-0
19r	Letchworth Garden City v Hemel Hempstead Town	4-3e
23r	Leyton-Wingate v Dulwich Hamlet	2-1e
24r	Basingstoke Town v Hampton	0-2
r	Ilford v Chertsey Town	6-1
26r	Boreham Wood v Edgware Town	4-2
r	Chesham United v Finchley	0-0e
33r	Bath City v Swaythling	3-0
1r2	Netherfield (Kendal) v Bishop Auckland	3-4
26r2	Finchley v Chesham United	3-2 N

Qualifying Round Three

1	Bishop Auckland v Boldon CA	3-2
2	Whitley Bay v Spennymoor United	2-2
3	Consett v Blyth Spartans	1-4
4	Appleby Frodingham Ath. v Brigg Town	2-2
5	Worksop Town v Goole Town	2-2
6	Burscough v Chorley	3-0
7	Runcorn v Darwen	2-0
8	Bangor City v Rhyl	1-0
9	Winsford United v Mossley	1-1
10	Stalybridge Celtic v Hednesford Town	1-1
11	Telford United v Hinckley Athletic	1-0e
12	Burton Albion v Halesowen Town	1-0
13	Kidderminster Harriers v AP Leamington	1-2
14	Banbury United v Oxford City	1-0
15	Corby Town v Enderby Town	1-2
16	Arnold v Boston	2-0
17	Wisbech Town v Lowestoft Town	0-3
18	Harlow Town v Chelmsford City	1-1
19	Hertford Town v Letchworth Garden City	0-3
20	St Albans City v Barnet	2-4
21	Cheshunt v Hillingdon Borough	1-0
22	Billericay Town v Walthamstow Avenue	3-1
23	Enfield v Leyton-Wingate	4-0
24	Hampton v Ilford	1-1
25	Tilbury v Feltham	4-1
26	Finchley v Boreham Wood	1-5
27	Sutton United v Hastings United	1-0
28	Maidstone United v Crawley Town	1-1
29	Tonbridge v Ramsgate	2-0
30	Horsham v Farnborough Town	2-0
31	Horsham YMCA v Folkestone & Shepway	2-2
32	Frome Town v Salisbury (2)	2-2
33	Bath City v Dorchester Town	2-0
34	Bridgend Town v Merthyr Tydfil	1-3
35	Worcester City v Weston-Super-Mare	1-1
36	Tiverton Town v Bideford	0-0
2r	Spennymoor United v Whitley Bay	4-1
4r	Brigg Town v Appleby Frodingham Ath.	1-2
5r	Goole Town v Worksop Town	2-2
9r	Mossley v Winsford United	3-3
10r	Hednesford Town v Stalybridge Celtic	2-1
18r	Chelmsford City v Harlow Town	2-1e
24r	Ilford v Hampton	1-1e
28r	Crawley Town v Maidstone United	1-1
31r	Folkestone & Shepway v Horsham YMCA	3-0
32r	Salisbury (2) v Frome Town	1-0
35r	Weston-Super-Mare v Worcester City	1-2
36r	Bideford v Tiverton Town	3-0
5r2	Goole Town v Worksop Town	3-1 N
9r2	Mossley v Winsford United	2-0 N
24r2	Hampton v Ilford	2-0
28r2	Crawley Town v Maidstone United	1-4 N

Qualifying Round Four

	Appleby Frodingham Ath. v Mossley	0-2
	Arnold v Telford United	3-0
	Bideford v Banbury United	1-0
	Bishop Auckland v Blyth Spartans	0-1
	Boreham Wood v Dartford	3-2
	Boston United v AP Leamington	1-2
	Burscough v Morecambe	0-0
	Chelmsford City v Folkestone & Shepway	0-3
	Goole Town v Matlock Town	2-1
	Grantham v Burton Albion	0-2
	Hampton v Barnet	1-2
	Hendon v Billericay Town	3-2
	Hitchin Town v Kettering Town	2-2
	Horsham v Enfield	0-4
	Leatherhead v Cheshunt	4-1
	Letchworth Garden City v Enderby Town	0-0
	Lowestoft Town v Bishop's Stortford	2-0
	Marine v Wigan Athletic	0-3
	Merthyr Tydfil v Bath City	1-2
	Northwich Victoria v Stafford Rangers	2-2
	Nuneaton Borough v Hednesford Town	2-1
	Runcorn v Altrincham	2-1
	Salisbury (2) v Minehead	1-1
	Spennymoor United v Bangor City	2-1
	Tilbury v Tonbridge	4-3
	Tooting & Mitcham United v Sutton United	3-0
	Wealdstone v Maidstone United	2-1
	Worcester City v Weymouth	2-2
r	Enderby Town v Letchworth Garden City	1-0
r	Kettering Town v Hitchin Town	2-1
r	Minehead v Salisbury (2)	2-1
r	Morecambe v Burscough	0-1
r	Stafford Rangers v Northwich Victoria	2-1
r	Weymouth v Worcester City	2-1

1977/78 to 1978/79

Round One

AP Leamington v Enderby Town	6-1
Arnold v Port Vale	0-0
Barnet v Peterborough United	1-2
Barnsley v Huddersfield Town	1-0
Bath City v Plymouth Argyle	0-0
Blyth Spartans v Burscough	1-0
Boreham Wood v Swindon Town	0-0
Bradford City v Crewe Alexandra	0-1
Brentford v Folkestone & Shepway	2-0
Carlisle United v Stafford Rangers	2-0
Chester v Darlington	4-1
Chesterfield v Halifax Town	1-0
Colchester United v Bournemouth	1-1
Doncaster Rovers v Shrewsbury Town	0-1
Enfield v Wimbledon	3-0
Gillingham v Weymouth	1-1
Leatherhead v Swansea City	0-0
Lowestoft Town v Cambridge United	0-2
Minehead v Wycombe Wanderers	2-0
Newport County v Exeter City	1-1
Nuneaton Borough v Oxford United	2-0
Portsmouth v Bideford	3-1
Preston North End v Lincoln City	3-2
Reading v Aldershot	3-1
Rotherham United v Mossley	3-0
Scarborough v Rochdale	4-2
Sheffield Wednesday v Bury	1-0
Southport v Runcorn	2-2
Spennymoor United v Goole Town	3-1
Stockport County v Scunthorpe United	3-0
Tilbury v Kettering Town	0-1 v
Tooting & Mitcham United v Northampton Town	1-2
Torquay United v Southend United	1-2
Tranmere Rovers v Hartlepool United	1-1
Walsall v Dagenham	1-0
Watford v Hendon	2-0
Wealdstone v Hereford United	0-0
Wigan Athletic v York City	1-0
Workington v Grimsby Town	0-2
Wrexham v Burton Albion	2-0
r Bournemouth v Colchester United	0-0e
r Exeter City v Newport County	4-2
r Hartlepool United v Tranmere Rovers	3-1
r Hereford United v Wealdstone	2-3
r Plymouth Argyle v Bath City	2-0
r Port Vale v Arnold	5-2
r Runcorn v Southport	1-0
r Swansea City v Leatherhead	2-1
r Swindon Town v Boreham Wood	2-0
r Tilbury v Kettering Town	2-2
r Weymouth v Gillingham	0-1
r2 Bournemouth v Colchester United	1-4 N
r2 Kettering Town v Tilbury	2-3

Round Two

AP Leamington v Southend United	0-0
Blyth Spartans v Chesterfield	1-0
Carlisle United v Chester	3-1
Crewe Alexandra v Scarborough	0-0
Gillingham v Peterborough United	1-1
Grimsby Town v Barnsley	2-0
Hartlepool United v Runcorn	4-2
Minehead v Exeter City	0-3
Northampton Town v Enfield	0-2
Nuneaton Borough v Tilbury	1-2
Plymouth Argyle v Cambridge United	1-0
Portsmouth v Swansea City	2-2
Preston North End v Wrexham	0-2
Rotherham United v Spennymoor United	6-0
Shrewsbury Town v Stockport County	1-1
Swindon Town v Brentford	2-1
Walsall v Port Vale	1-1
Watford v Colchester United	2-0
Wealdstone v Reading	2-1
Wigan Athletic v Sheffield Wednesday	1-0
r Peterborough United v Gillingham	2-0
r Port Vale v Walsall	1-3
r Scarborough v Crewe Alexandra	2-0
r Southend United v AP Leamington	4-0
r Stockport County v Shrewsbury Town	1-2
r Swansea City v Portsmouth	2-1

Round Three

Birmingham City v Wigan Athletic	4-0
Blackburn Rovers v Shrewsbury Town	2-1
Blyth Spartans v Enfield	1-0
Brighton & Hove Albion v Scarborough	3-0
Bristol City v Wrexham	4-4
Burnley v Fulham	1-0
Cardiff City v Ipswich Town	0-2
Carlisle United v Manchester United	1-1
Charlton Athletic v Notts County	0-2
Chelsea v Liverpool	4-2
Derby County v Southend United	3-2
Everton v Aston Villa	4-1
Exeter City v Wolverhampton Wan.	2-2
Grimsby Town v Southampton	0-0
Hartlepool United v Crystal Palace	2-1
Hull City v Leicester City	0-1
Leeds United v Manchester City	1-2
Luton Town v Oldham Athletic	1-1
Mansfield Town v Plymouth Argyle	1-0
Middlesbrough v Coventry City	3-0
Nottingham Forest v Swindon Town	4-1
Orient v Norwich City	1-1
Peterborough United v Newcastle United	1-1
Queen's Park Rangers v Wealdstone	4-0
Rotherham United v Millwall	1-1
Sheffield United v Arsenal	0-5
Stoke City v Tilbury	4-0
Sunderland v Bristol Rovers	0-1
Tottenham Hotspur v Bolton Wanderers	2-2
Walsall v Swansea City	4-1
West Bromwich Albion v Blackpool	4-1
West Ham United v Watford	1-0
r Bolton Wanderers v Tottenham Hotspur	2-1e
r Manchester United v Carlisle United	4-2
r Millwall v Rotherham United	2-0
r Newcastle United v Peterborough United	2-0
r Norwich City v Orient	0-1
r Oldham Athletic v Luton Town	1-2
r Southampton v Grimsby Town	0-0e
r Wolverhampton Wan. v Exeter City	3-1
r Wrexham v Bristol City	3-0
r2 Grimsby Town v Southampton	1-4 N

Round Four

Arsenal v Wolverhampton Wan.	2-1
Bolton Wanderers v Mansfield Town	1-0
Brighton & Hove Albion v Notts County	1-2
Bristol Rovers v Southampton	2-0
Chelsea v Burnley	6-2
Derby County v Birmingham City	2-1
Ipswich Town v Hartlepool United	4-1
Manchester United v West Bromwich Albion	1-1
Middlesbrough v Everton	3-2
Millwall v Luton Town	4-0
Newcastle United v Wrexham	2-2
Nottingham Forest v Manchester City	2-1
Orient v Blackburn Rovers	3-1
Stoke City v Blyth Spartans	2-3
Walsall v Leicester City	1-0
West Ham United v Queen's Park Rangers	1-1
r Queen's Park Rangers v West Ham United	6-1
r West Bromwich Albion v Manchester United	3-2e
r Wrexham v Newcastle United	4-1

Round Five

Arsenal v Walsall	4-1
Bristol Rovers v Ipswich Town	2-2
Derby County v West Bromwich Albion	2-3
Middlesbrough v Bolton Wanderers	2-0
Millwall v Notts County	2-1
Orient v Chelsea	0-0
Queen's Park Rangers v Nottingham Forest	1-1
Wrexham v Blyth Spartans	1-1
r Blyth Spartans v Wrexham	1-2 N
r Chelsea v Orient	1-2
r Ipswich Town v Bristol Rovers	3-0
r Nottingham Forest v Queen's Park Rangers	1-1e
r2 Nottingham Forest v Queen's Park Rangers	3-1

Round Six

Middlesbrough v Orient	0-0
Millwall v Ipswich Town	1-6
West Bromwich Albion v Nottingham Forest	2-0
Wrexham v Arsenal	2-3
r Orient v Middlesbrough	2-1

Semi Finals

Arsenal v Orient	3-0 N
Ipswich Town v West Bromwich Albion	3-1 N

Final

Ipswich Town v Arsenal	1-0 N

1978/79

Preliminary Round

1 Carlisle City v Annfield Plain	4-2
Consett v Eppleton CW	1-1
2 Crook Town v South Bank	1-2
3 Billingham Synthonia v Tow Law Town	2-1
4 Farsley Celtic v Bridlington Town	0-1
North Ferriby United v Selby Town	2-0
5 Accrington Stanley (2) v Lancaster City	1-2
6 Formby v Ashton United	3-1
7 Mossley v Burscough	2-1
Nantwich Town v Prescot Town	1-2
8 Leek Town v Bangor City	2-2
Macclesfield Town v Marine	2-4
9 Alfreton Town v Mexborough Town	2-5
10 Appleby Frodingham Ath. v Eastwood Town	1-2
11 Heanor Town v Boston United	0-3
Holbeach United v Louth United	1-4
12 Bourne Town v Arnold	0-3
Desborough Town v Friar Lane Old Boys	0-3
13 Halesowen Town v Bilston	2-0
Kidderminster Harriers v Moor Green	5-0
14 Brierley Hill Alliance v Alvechurch	0-2
Burton Albion v Oxford City	0-1
15 Bromsgrove Rovers v Lye Town	3-1
16 Banbury United v Thame United	4-2
17 Bury Town v King's Lynn	1-2
18 Gorleston v Cambridge City	1-0
Haverhill Rovers v Lowestoft Town	0-0
19 Corby Town v Barton Rovers	0-1
Newmarket Town v Olney Town	1-2
20 Egham Town v Camberley Town	2-3
Farnborough Town v Maidenhead United	1-0
21 Grays Athletic v Cheshunt	5-1
Harlow Town v Hemel Hempstead Town	1-1
22 Hampton v Banstead Athletic	2-0
Harrow Borough v Hertford Town	0-2
23 Chesham United v Berkhamsted Town	3-3
Finchley v Hillingdon Borough	0-0
24 Didcot Town v Aylesbury United	1-1
Feltham v Hayes	2-0
25 Clapton v Barking	1-6
Felixstowe Town v Hoddesdon Town	1-0
26 Gravesend & Northfleet v Aveley	6-2
Haringey Borough v Ilford	1-3
27 Folkestone & Shepway v Bromley	2-1
Margate v Redhill	2-0
28 East Grinstead v Canterbury City	1-2
Herne Bay v Horsham YMCA	1-1
29 Eastbourne United v Ashford Town	1-0
Faversham Town v Hastings United	1-3
30 Epsom & Ewell v Addlestone	2-0
Horsham v Littlehampton Town	4-0
31 Burgess Hill Town v Alton Town	1-3
Cowes v Fareham Town	0-0
32 Forest Green Rovers v Calne Town	8-1
Frome Town v Gloucester City	0-3
33 Barry Town v Mangotsfield United	2-0
34 Andover v Newbury Town	1-1
35 Glastonbury v Bath City	0-3
Ilminster Town v Poole Town	1-0
36 Liskeard Athletic v Barnstaple Town	1-0
Newquay v Penzance	2-2
1r Eppleton CW v Consett	0-7
8r Bangor City v Leek Town	1-2
18r Lowestoft Town v Haverhill Rovers	2-0
21r Hemel Hempstead Town v Harlow Town	0-4
23r Berkhamsted Town v Chesham United	1-0
24r Aylesbury United v Didcot Town	2-1
28r Horsham YMCA v Herne Bay	1-0
31r Fareham Town v Cowes	2-0
34r Newbury Town v Andover	1-2
36r Penzance v Newquay	2-1

Qualifying Round One

1 Ashington v Bishop Auckland	0-1
Evenwood Town v North Shields	2-2
Guisborough Town v Consett	2-2
Spennymoor United v Carlisle City	2-1
2 Gateshead (2) v Horden CW	1-0
Shildon v Whitley Bay	3-1
Wallsend Town v Ferryhill Athletic	1-0
Wingate (Durham) v South Bank	0-0
3 Boldon CA v Durham City	2-0
Easington CW v West Auckland Town	2-1
Washington v Newcastle Blue Star	3-2
Willington v Billingham Synthonia	0-1
4 Bridlington Trinity v Emley	1-0
Whitby Town v Worsbrough Bridge MW	3-3
Winterton Rangers v North Ferriby United	0-0
Yorkshire Amateur v Bridlington Town	0-0
5 Chorley v Darwen	3-0
Fleetwood Town v Netherfield (Kendal)	0-0
Lytham v Barrow	0-2
Penrith v Lancaster City	0-4
6 Clitheroe v Curzon Ashton	0-1
Hyde United v Skelmersdale United	1-1
Leyland Motors v Horwich RMI	1-2
South Liverpool v Formby	0-3
7 Buxton v Glossop	3-1
Radcliffe Borough v Runcorn	0-6
Rhyl v Prescot Town	2-0
Witton Albion v Mossley	4-2
8 Congleton Town v Droylsden	1-2
New Brighton v Prestwich Heys	1-3
Porthmadog v Marine	3-1
Stalybridge Celtic v Leek Town	3-1
9 Frickley Athletic v Hednesford Town	0-2
New Mills v Denaby United	2-0
Oswestry Town v St Helens Town	1-1
Winsford United v Mexborough Town	3-0
10 Barton Town (2) v Boston	1-3
Brigg Town v Spalding United	1-1
Grantham v Ashby Institute	5-3
Worksop Town v Eastwood Town	2-1
11 Enderby Town v Gainsborough Trinity	3-4
Retford Town v Stamford	2-1
Skegness Town v Louth United	0-1
Sutton Town v Boston United	0-0
12 Atherstone Town v Belper Town	2-0
Hinckley Athletic v Long Eaton United	5-0
Irthlingborough Diamonds v Friar Lane Old Boys	3-0
Wellingborough Town v Arnold	1-1
13 Dudley Town v Gresley Rovers	3-0
Racing Club Warwick v Tamworth	1-1

157

1978/79

	Stratford Town v Kidderminster Harriers	2-2
	Telford United v Halesowen Town	0-1
14	Bedworth United v Brereton Social	0-0
	Redditch United v Tividale	3-2
	Sutton Coldfield Town v Oxford City	3-0
	Wolverton Town & BR v Alvechurch	1-2
15	Darlaston v Evesham United	1-1
	Highgate United v Stourbridge	2-1
	Milton Keynes City v Coventry Sporting	2-0
	Worcester City v Bromsgrove Rovers	1-0
16	Gornal Athletic v Kempston Rovers	0-2
	Oldbury United v Willenhall Town	1-1
	V.S. Rugby v Dunstable	2-0
	Witney Town v Banbury United	0-2
17	Great Yarmouth Town v Harwich & Parkeston	1-1
	Histon v Parson Drove United	3-1
	March Town United v Chatteris Town	4-1
	St Neots Town v King's Lynn	1-0
18	Clacton Town v Ely City	0-4
	Soham Town Rangers v Sudbury Town	2-0
	Stowmarket v Lowestoft Town	0-1
	Thetford Town v Gorleston	1-5
19	Bedford Town (1) v Bishop's Stortford	2-1
	Potton United v Rushden Town	0-1
	Rothwell Town v Olney Town	1-1
	Wisbech Town v Barton Rovers	0-2
20	Carshalton Athletic v Chertsey Town	3-0
	Ruislip Manor v Southall & Ealing Boro.	0-3
	Slough Town v Farnborough Town	2-0
	Walton & Hersham v Camberley Town	2-3
21	Corinthian Casuals v Edgware Town	0-0
	Leyton-Wingate v Tilbury	1-0
	Metropolitan Police v Harlow Town	1-0
	Wembley v Grays Athletic	0-0
22	Chalfont St Peter v Epping Town	0-0
	Staines Town v Willesden	2-1
	Sutton United v Hertford Town	2-1
	Windsor & Eton v Hampton	1-0
23	Boreham Wood v Burnham (1)	3-2
	Kingstonian v Tring Town	1-0
	Molesey v Hillingdon Borough	2-2
	Uxbridge v Berkhamsted Town	2-1
24	Barnet v Bracknell Town	2-1
	Hounslow v St Albans City	1-1
	Marlow v Feltham	1-1e
	Wokingham Town v Aylesbury United	2-0
25	Billericay Town v Chelmsford City	2-1
	Hornchurch v Leytonstone	1-1
	Letchworth Garden City v Felixstowe Town	5-1
	Ware v Barking	0-2
26	Cray Wanderers v Dulwich Hamlet	1-2
	Ilford - Bye	
	Rainham Town v Walthamstow Avenue	0-4
	Welling United v Gravesend & Northfleet	1-2
27	Croydon v Erith & Belvedere	1-0
	Snowdown CW v Tonbridge	0-3
	Three Bridges v Margate	0-2
	Whitstable Town v Folkestone & Shepway	1-1
28	Dover v Eastbourne Town	3-0
	Lewes v Ramsgate	1-1
	Maidstone United v Horsham YMCA	2-0
	Sheppey United v Canterbury City	1-4
29	Crawley Town v Bexhill Town	1-1
	Medway v Sidley United	4-1
	Ringmer v Hastings United	0-2
	Sittingbourne v Eastbourne United	1-4
30	Chichester City (1) v Dorking Town	1-1
	Selsey v Tunbridge Wells	2-3
	Southwick v Horsham	1-2
	Woking v Epsom & Ewell	3-1
31	Arundel v Bognor Regis Town	2-3
	Haywards Heath v Wigmore Athletic	4-0
	Waterlooville v Fareham Town	2-0
	Worthing v Alton Town	4-1
32	Cheltenham Town v Clevedon Town	6-1
	Llanelli v Shepton Mallet Town	1-3
	Melksham Town v Gloucester City	1-0
	Trowbridge Town v Forest Green Rovers	1-0
33	Chippenham Town v Cinderford Town	2-2
	Larkhall Athletic v Paulton Rovers	3-3
	Merthyr Tydfil v Bridgend Town	4-0
	Ton Pentre v Barry Town	0-1
34	Bridport v Dorchester Town	0-1
	Hungerford Town v Swaythling	5-1
	Newport (IOW) v Basingstoke Town	0-1
	Yeovil Town v Andover	4-0
35	Bridgwater Town (1) v Chard Town	1-0
	Salisbury (2) v Welton Rovers	4-0
	Tiverton Town v Ilminster Town	1-0
	Weston-Super-Mare v Bath City	1-2
36	Bideford v Falmouth Town	2-1
	Saltash United v Penzance	8-1
	St Blazey v Taunton Town	0-3
	Wadebridge Town v Liskeard Athletic	0-2
1r	Consett v Guisborough Town	3-2
r	North Shields v Evenwood Town	1-0
2r	South Bank v Wingate (Durham)	1-1
4r	Bridlington Town v Yorkshire Amateur	2-3
r	North Ferriby United v Winterton Rangers	0-1
r	Worsbrough Bridge MW v Whitby Town	0-1
5r	Netherfield (Kendal) v Fleetwood Town	1-1
6r	Skelmersdale United v Hyde United	0-1
9r	St Helens Town v Oswestry Town	0-0
10r	Spalding United v Brigg Town	3-4
11r	Boston United v Sutton Town	4-0
12r	Arnold v Wellingborough Town	2-1
13r	Kidderminster Harriers v Stratford Town	7-0
r	Tamworth v Racing Club Warwick	1-0
14r	Brereton Social v Bedworth United	3-2
15r	Evesham United v Darlaston	2-4
16r	Willenhall Town v Oldbury United	2-0
17r	Harwich & Parkeston v Great Yarmouth Town	4-1
19r	Olney Town v Rothwell Town	0-1
21r	Edgware Town v Corinthian Casuals	4-0
r	Grays Athletic v Wembley	4-1
22r	Epping Town v Chalfont St Peter	1-1
23r	Hillingdon Borough v Molesey	2-1
24r	Feltham v Marlow	3-0e
r	St Albans City v Hounslow	4-2
25r	Leytonstone v Hornchurch	4-1
27r	Folkestone & Shepway v Whitstable Town	5-0
28r	Ramsgate v Lewes	3-0
29r	Crawley Town v Bexhill Town	1-1
30r	Dorking Town v Chichester City (1)	3-2
33r	Cinderford Town v Chippenham Town	2-1
r	Paulton Rovers v Larkhall Athletic	2-1
2r2	Wingate (Durham) v South Bank	0-0 N
5r2	Fleetwood Town v Netherfield (Kendal)	2-0
9r2	Oswestry Town v St Helens Town	3-2 N
22r2	Chalfont St Peter v Epping Town	0-0 N
29r2	Bexhill Town v Crawley Town	0-1 N
2r3	South Bank v Wingate (Durham)	2-1 N
22r3	Epping Town v Chalfont St Peter	1-2 N

Qualifying Round Two

1	Bishop Auckland v Consett	0-0
	North Shields v Spennymoor United	0-3
2	Gateshead (2) v Wallsend Town	6-0
	Shildon v South Bank	2-1
3	Boldon CA v Washington	3-2
	Easington CW v Billingham Synthonia	1-3
4	Bridlington Trinity v Winterton Rangers	2-2
	Whitby Town v Yorkshire Amateur	1-2
5	Chorley v Barrow	2-1
	Fleetwood Town v Lancaster City	1-1
6	Curzon Ashton v Horwich RMI	1-2
	Hyde United v Formby	2-2
7	Buxton v Rhyl	2-0
	Runcorn v Witton Albion	3-1
8	Droylsden v Porthmadog	3-1
	Prestwich Heys v Stalybridge Celtic	1-1
9	Hednesford Town v New Mills	4-0
	Oswestry Town v Winsford United	0-1
10	Boston v Grantham	0-1
	Brigg Town v Worksop Town	1-1
11	Gainsborough Trinity v Louth United	1-1
	Retford Town v Boston United	1-4
12	Atherstone Town v Irthlingborough Diamonds	1-3
	Hinckley Athletic v Arnold	1-0
13	Dudley Town v Kidderminster Harriers	2-0
	Tamworth v Halesowen Town	0-2
14	Brereton Social v Sutton Coldfield Town	3-2
	Redditch United v Alvechurch	1-0
15	Darlaston v Milton Keynes City	5-0
	Highgate United v Worcester City	0-0
16	Kempston Rovers v V.S. Rugby	3-1
	Willenhall Town v Banbury United	2-0
17	Harwich & Parkeston v March Town United	1-1
	Histon v St Neots Town	0-1
18	Ely City v Lowestoft Town	1-2
	Soham Town Rangers v Gorleston	0-3
19	Bedford Town (1) v Rothwell Town	5-2
	Rushden Town v Barton Rovers	1-1
20	Carshalton Athletic v Slough Town	1-2
	Southall & Ealing Boro. v Camberley Town	2-2
21	Edgware Town v Metropolitan Police	1-0
	Leyton-Wingate v Grays Athletic	2-0
22	Chalfont St Peter v Sutton United	0-2
	Staines Town v Windsor & Eton	0-0
23	Boreham Wood v Hillingdon Borough	0-2
	Kingstonian v Uxbridge	3-0
24	Barnet v Feltham	3-2
	St Albans City v Wokingham Town	0-0
25	Billericay Town v Letchworth Garden City	5-1
	Leytonstone v Barking	1-2
26	Dulwich Hamlet v Ilford	4-0
	Walthamstow Avenue v Gravesend & Northfleet	2-3
27	Croydon v Margate	0-2
	Tonbridge v Folkestone & Shepway	2-3
28	Dover v Maidstone United	0-0
	Ramsgate v Canterbury City	1-0
29	Crawley Town v Hastings United	1-2
	Medway v Eastbourne United	0-0
30	Dorking Town v Horsham	0-2
	Tunbridge Wells v Woking	0-2
31	Bognor Regis Town v Waterlooville	0-2
	Haywards Heath v Worthing	1-2
32	Cheltenham Town v Melksham Town	6-0
	Shepton Mallet Town v Trowbridge Town	1-2
33	Cinderford Town v Merthyr Tydfil	0-1
	Paulton Rovers v Barry Town	1-2
34	Dorchester Town v Basingstoke Town	1-0
	Hungerford Town v Yeovil Town	4-4
35	Bridgwater Town (1) v Tiverton Town	5-1e
	Salisbury (2) v Bath City	0-2
36	Bideford v Saltash United	2-0
	Taunton Town v Liskeard Athletic	6-0
1r	Consett v Bishop Auckland	2-1
4r	Winterton Rangers v Bridlington Trinity	2-1
5r	Lancaster City v Fleetwood Town	0-1
6r	Formby v Hyde United	2-1
8r	Stalybridge Celtic v Prestwich Heys	4-1
10r	Worksop Town v Brigg Town	1-1
11r	Louth United v Gainsborough Trinity	1-2
15r	Worcester City v Highgate United	3-2
17r	March Town United v Harwich & Parkeston	2-1
19r	Barton Rovers v Rushden Town	3-1
20r	Camberley Town v Southall & Ealing Boro.	1-3
22r	Windsor & Eton v Staines Town	1-0
24r	Wokingham Town v St Albans City	4-1
28r	Maidstone United v Dover	1-0
29r	Eastbourne United v Medway	0-0
34r	Yeovil Town v Hungerford Town	3-0
10r2	Brigg Town v Worksop Town	0-2 N
29r2	Medway v Eastbourne United	0-6 N

Qualifying Round Three

1	Spennymoor United v Consett	0-0
2	Shildon v Gateshead (2)	1-8
3	Billingham Synthonia v Boldon CA	0-0
4	Yorkshire Amateur v Winterton Rangers	1-0
5	Fleetwood Town v Chorley	0-1
6	Formby v Horwich RMI	0-0
7	Runcorn v Buxton	1-1
8	Stalybridge Celtic v Droylsden	1-1
9	Winsford United v Hednesford Town	1-2
10	Worksop Town v Grantham	0-0
11	Boston United v Gainsborough Trinity	3-0
12	Hinckley Athletic v Irthlingborough Diamonds	1-2
13	Halesowen Town v Dudley Town	0-1
14	Redditch United v Brereton Social	0-0
15	Worcester City v Darlaston	7-1
16	Willenhall Town v Kempston Rovers	0-2
17	St Neots Town v March Town United	2-3
18	Gorleston v Lowestoft Town	3-1
19	Barton Rovers v Bedford Town (1)	0-2
20	Southall & Ealing Boro. v Slough Town	1-0
21	Leyton-Wingate v Edgware Town	1-1
22	Windsor & Eton v Sutton United	0-1
23	Kingstonian v Hillingdon Borough	0-0
24	Wokingham Town v Barnet	0-4
25	Barking v Billericay Town	2-0
26	Gravesend & Northfleet v Dulwich Hamlet	1-1
27	Folkestone & Shepway v Margate	0-2
28	Ramsgate v Maidstone United	1-3
29	Eastbourne United v Hastings United	2-1
30	Woking v Horsham	5-2
31	Worthing v Waterlooville	1-1
32	Trowbridge Town v Cheltenham Town	0-4
33	Barry Town v Merthyr Tydfil	0-2
34	Yeovil Town v Dorchester Town	2-1
35	Bath City v Bridgwater Town (1)	7-1
36	Taunton Town v Bideford	3-0
1r	Consett v Spennymoor United	1-2
3r	Boldon CA v Billingham Synthonia	2-4e
6r	Horwich RMI v Formby	5-1
7r	Buxton v Runcorn	0-4
8r	Droylsden v Stalybridge Celtic	3-1
10r	Grantham v Worksop Town	0-3
14r	Brereton Social v Redditch United	0-1
21r	Edgware Town v Leyton-Wingate	3-1
23r	Hillingdon Borough v Kingstonian	3-2
26r	Dulwich Hamlet v Gravesend & Northfleet	0-1
31r	Waterlooville v Worthing	3-0

Qualifying Round Four

	AP Leamington v Hednesford Town	0-0
	Barking v Bedford Town (1)	3-1
	Bath City v Worcester City	1-1
	Billingham Synthonia v Blyth Spartans	0-1
	Cheltenham Town v Yeovil Town	1-2
	Chorley v Yorkshire Amateur	4-2
	Dagenham v Irthlingborough Diamonds	0-0
	Droylsden v Goole Town	2-0
	Dudley Town v Worksop Town	0-1
	Edgware Town v Barnet	0-1
	Gateshead (2) v Workington	1-1
	Gorleston v Enfield	2-6
	Gravesend & Northfleet v Eastbourne United	3-1
	Hendon v Hitchin Town	1-3
	Hillingdon Borough v Tooting & Mitcham United	2-1
	Kettering Town v Boston United	1-3
	March Town United v Southall & Ealing Boro.	2-1
	Margate v Woking	1-7
	Merthyr Tydfil v Minehead	2-0
	Morecambe v Horwich RMI	3-1
	Northwich Victoria v Southport	0-0
	Nuneaton Borough v Matlock Town	2-2
	Spennymoor United v Runcorn	0-0
	Stafford Rangers v Redditch United	2-1
	Sutton United v Dartford	0-2
	Taunton Town v Weymouth	0-2
	Waterlooville v Maidstone United	1-2
	Wealdstone v Kempston Rovers	1-0
r	Hednesford Town v AP Leamington	2-3
r	Irthlingborough Diamonds v Dagenham	1-2
r	Matlock Town v Nuneaton Borough	2-2
r	Runcorn v Spennymoor United	2-1
r	Southport v Northwich Victoria	2-0
r	Worcester City v Bath City	2-1
r	Workington v Gateshead (2)	3-2
r2	Nuneaton Borough v Matlock Town	2-1 N

1978/79 to 1979/80

Round One

Aldershot v Weymouth	1-1
Altrincham v Southport	4-3
Barnet v Woking	3-3
Barnsley v Worksop Town	5-1
Blackpool v Lincoln City	2-1
Bournemouth v Hitchin Town	2-1
Bradford City v Port Vale	1-0
Carlisle United v Halifax Town	1-0
Chester v Runcorn	1-1
Chorley v Scarborough	0-1
Colchester United v Oxford United	4-2
Darlington v Chesterfield	1-1
Dartford v AP Leamington	1-2
Doncaster Rovers v Huddersfield Town	2-1
Exeter City v Brentford	1-0
Gravesend & Northfleet v Wimbledon	0-0
Hartlepool United v Grimsby Town	1-0
Hereford United v Newport County	0-1
Hull City v Stafford Rangers	2-1
Leatherhead v Merthyr Tydfil	2-1
Maidstone United v Wycombe Wanderers	1-0
Mansfield Town v Shrewsbury Town	0-2
Nuneaton Borough v Crewe Alexandra	0-2
Portsmouth v Northampton Town	2-0
Reading v Gillingham	0-0
Rochdale v Droylsden	0-1
Rotherham United v Workington	3-0
Scunthorpe United v Sheffield Wednesday	1-1
Southend United v Peterborough United	3-2
Stockport County v Morecambe	5-1
Swansea City v Hillingdon Borough	4-1
Swindon Town v March Town United	2-0
Tranmere Rovers v Boston United	2-1
Walsall v Torquay United	0-2
Watford v Dagenham	3-0
Wealdstone v Enfield	0-5
Wigan Athletic v Bury	2-2
Worcester City v Plymouth Argyle	2-0
Yeovil Town v Barking	0-1
York City v Blyth Spartans	1-1
r Blyth Spartans v York City	3-5e
r Bury v Wigan Athletic	4-1
r Chesterfield v Darlington	0-1
r Gillingham v Reading	1-2e
r Runcorn v Chester	0-5
r Sheffield Wednesday v Scunthorpe United	1-0
r Weymouth v Aldershot	0-2
r Wimbledon v Gravesend & Northfleet	1-0
r Woking v Barnet	3-3e
r2 Woking v Barnet	3-0 N

Round Two

AP Leamington v Torquay United	0-1
Barking v Aldershot	1-2
Barnsley v Rotherham United	1-1
Bury v Blackpool	3-1
Carlisle United v Hull City	3-0
Crewe Alexandra v Hartlepool United	0-1
Darlington v Chester	2-1
Doncaster Rovers v Shrewsbury Town	0-3
Droylsden v Altrincham	0-2
Leatherhead v Colchester United	1-1
Maidstone United v Exeter City	1-0
Newport County v Worcester City	0-0
Portsmouth v Reading	0-1
Stockport County v Bradford City	4-2
Swansea City v Woking	2-2
Swindon Town v Enfield	3-0
Tranmere Rovers v Sheffield Wednesday	1-1
Watford v Southend United	1-1
Wimbledon v Bournemouth	1-1
York City v Scarborough	3-0
r Bournemouth v Wimbledon	1-2e
r Colchester United v Leatherhead	4-0
r Rotherham United v Barnsley	2-1
r Sheffield Wednesday v Tranmere Rovers	4-0
r Southend United v Watford	1-0
r Woking v Swansea City	3-5e
r Worcester City v Newport County	1-2

Round Three

Birmingham City v Burnley	0-2
Blackburn Rovers v Millwall	2-1
Brighton & Hove Albion v Wolverhampton Wan.	2-3
Bristol City v Bolton Wanderers	3-1
Charlton Athletic v Maidstone United	1-1
Coventry City v West Bromwich Albion	2-2
Darlington v Colchester United	0-1
Fulham v Queen's Park Rangers	2-0
Hartlepool United v Leeds United	2-6
Ipswich Town v Carlisle United	3-2
Leicester City v Norwich City	3-0
Manchester City v Rotherham United	0-0
Manchester United v Chelsea	3-0
Middlesbrough v Crystal Palace	1-1
Newcastle United v Torquay United	3-1
Newport County v West Ham United	2-1
Nottingham Forest v Aston Villa	2-0
Notts County v Reading	4-2
Orient v Bury	3-2
Preston North End v Derby County	3-0
Sheffield United v Aldershot	0-0
Sheffield Wednesday v Arsenal	1-1
Shrewsbury Town v Cambridge United	3-1
Southend United v Liverpool	0-0
Stoke City v Oldham Athletic	0-1
Sunderland v Everton	2-1
Swansea City v Bristol Rovers	0-1
Swindon Town v Cardiff City	3-0
Tottenham Hotspur v Altrincham	1-1
Wimbledon v Southampton	0-2
Wrexham v Stockport County	6-2
York City v Luton Town	2-0
r Aldershot v Sheffield United	1-0
r Altrincham v Tottenham Hotspur	0-3 N
r Arsenal v Sheffield Wednesday	1-1e
r Crystal Palace v Middlesbrough	1-0
r Liverpool v Southend United	3-0
r Maidstone United v Charlton Athletic	1-2
r Rotherham United v Manchester City	2-4
r West Bromwich Albion v Coventry City	4-0
r2 Sheffield Wednesday v Arsenal	2-2eN
r3 Arsenal v Sheffield Wednesday	3-3eN
r4 Sheffield Wednesday v Arsenal	0-2 N

Round Four

Aldershot v Swindon Town	2-1
Arsenal v Notts County	2-0
Bristol Rovers v Charlton Athletic	1-0
Burnley v Sunderland	1-1
Crystal Palace v Bristol City	3-0
Fulham v Manchester United	1-1
Ipswich Town v Orient	0-0
Liverpool v Blackburn Rovers	1-0
Newcastle United v Wolverhampton Wan.	1-1
Newport County v Colchester United	0-0
Nottingham Forest v York City	3-1
Oldham Athletic v Leicester City	3-1
Preston North End v Southampton	0-1
Shrewsbury Town v Manchester City	2-0
Tottenham Hotspur v Wrexham	3-3
West Bromwich Albion v Leeds United	3-3
r Colchester United v Newport County	1-0
r Manchester United v Fulham	1-0
r Orient v Ipswich Town	0-2
r Sunderland v Burnley	0-3
r West Bromwich Albion v Leeds United	2-0e
r Wolverhampton Wan. v Newcastle United	1-0
r Wrexham v Tottenham Hotspur	2-3e

Round Five

Aldershot v Shrewsbury Town	2-2
Colchester United v Manchester United	0-1
Crystal Palace v Wolverhampton Wan.	0-1
Ipswich Town v Bristol Rovers	6-1
Liverpool v Burnley	3-0
Nottingham Forest v Arsenal	0-1
Oldham Athletic v Tottenham Hotspur	0-1
West Bromwich Albion v Southampton	1-1
r Shrewsbury Town v Aldershot	3-1e
r Southampton v West Bromwich Albion	2-1e

Round Six

Ipswich Town v Liverpool	0-1
Southampton v Arsenal	1-1
Tottenham Hotspur v Manchester United	1-1
Wolverhampton Wan. v Shrewsbury Town	1-1
r Arsenal v Southampton	2-0
r Manchester United v Tottenham Hotspur	2-0
r Shrewsbury Town v Wolverhampton Wan.	1-3

Semi Finals

Arsenal v Wolverhampton Wan.	2-0 N
Manchester United v Liverpool	2-2 N
r Liverpool v Manchester United	0-1 N

Final

Arsenal v Manchester United	3-2 N

1979/80

Preliminary Round

1 Crook Town v Annfield Plain	5-2
Ferryhill Athletic v Willington	2-1
2 Evenwood Town v Billingham Synthonia	1-2
Shildon v Wingate (Durham)	2-2
3 Guisborough Town v Newcastle Blue Star	3-2
South Bank v Whitby Town	4-1
4 Farsley Celtic v Accrington Stanley (2)	0-2
Lytham v Rossendale United	1-1
5 Emley v Barrow	1-0
Lancaster City v Witton Albion	3-1
6 New Brighton v Macclesfield Town	1-7
Rhyl v Winsford United	1-5
7 Formby v Bangor City	2-2
Oswestry Town v Radcliffe Borough	1-0
8 Hyde United v Ashton United	1-3
Mexborough Town Athletic v Yorkshire Amateur	6-1
9 Bridlington Trinity v Appleby Frodingham Ath.	6-0
Normanby Park Steel Works v Whitby Town	1-3
10 Denaby United v Alfreton Town	0-2
Heanor Town v Winterton Rangers	0-5
11 Eastwood Town v Ashby Institute	3-1
Holbeach United v Skegness Town	2-2
12 Brierley Hill Alliance v Belper Town	0-2
Leek Town v Tamworth	0-2
13 Halesowen Town v Alvechurch	1-1
Long Eaton United v Tividale	3-1
14 Hinckley Athletic v Atherstone Town	wo/s
Rothwell Town v Willenhall Town	0-2
15 Desborough Town v Bedworth United	1-1
Histon v V.S. Rugby	0-2
16 Potton United v Chatteris Town	1-1
Spalding United v Wisbech Town	1-3
17 Great Yarmouth Town v Chelmsford City	1-3
Newmarket Town v Sudbury Town	1-3
18 Cambridge City v Basildon United	1-2
Lowestoft Town v Harlow Town	1-2
19 Chalfont St Peter v Banbury United	0-1
Haverhill Rovers v Wolverton Town & BR	4-0
20 Marlow v Bracknell Town	2-3
Staines Town v Wellingborough Town	0-1
21 Epping Town v Aveley	2-2
Milton Keynes City v Wokingham Town	4-1
22 Clapton v Basingstoke Town	3-0
Haringey Borough v Willesden	0-1
23 Leyton-Wingate v Barton Rovers	3-1
Walthamstow Avenue v Windsor & Eton	4-2
24 Grays Athletic v Aylesbury United	0-2
Harefield United v Walton & Hersham	1-4
25 Dunstable v Carshalton Athletic	1-2
Hoddesdon Town v Ruislip Manor	1-2 N
26 Egham Town v Addlestone	0-2
Hastings United v Welling United	0-4
27 Faversham Town v Bromley	0-2
Horsham v Whitstable Town	2-1
28 Herne Bay v Eastbourne Town	0-2
Ramsgate v Snowdown CW	3-1
29 Peacehaven & Telscombe v Ashford Town	0-0
Southwick v Worthing	2-3
30 Gosport Borough v Andover	2-1
Pagham v Wigmore Athletic	0-0
31 Epsom & Ewell v Arundel	1-1
Newport (IOW) v Selsey	4-0
32 Gloucester City v Bridgend Town	0-2
Moreton Town v Ton Pentre	0-2
33 Devizes Town v Cheltenham Town	0-1
Weston-Super-Mare v Llanelli	2-0
34 Didcot Town v Alton Town	0-0
Melksham Town v Trowbridge Town	1-3
35 Frome Town v Bideford	0-1
Ilminster Town v Shepton Mallet Town	0-0
36 Falmouth Town v Barnstaple Town	1-2
2r Wingate (Durham) v Shildon	4-3
4r Rossendale United v Lytham	4-0
7r Bangor City v Formby	0-1
11r Skegness Town v Holbeach United	2-1
13r Alvechurch v Halesowen Town	6-0
15r Bedworth United v Desborough Town	6-0
16r Chatteris Town v Potton United	1-2e
21r Aveley v Epping Town	0-1
29r Ashford Town v Peacehaven & Telscombe	2-1
30r Wigmore Athletic v Pagham	0-2
31r Arundel v Epsom & Ewell	0-1
34r Alton Town v Didcot Town	0-2
35r Shepton Mallet Town v Ilminster Town	0-1

Qualifying Round One

1 Boldon CA v Ashington	0-1
Easington CW v Consett	0-4
Gateshead (2) v Crook Town	2-2
North Shields v Ferryhill Athletic	4-2
2 Carlisle City v Bishop Auckland	2-2
Horden CW v Durham City	6-0
Wallsend Town v Billingham Synthonia	1-4
Washington v Wingate (Durham)	3-2
3 Brandon United v Spennymoor United	3-2
Peterlee Newtown v Eppleton CW	2-1
Tow Law Town v Guisborough Town	1-0
West Auckland Town v South Bank	1-3
4 Burscough v Chorley	6-1
Leyland Motors v Curzon Ashton	1-4
Netherfield (Kendal) v Accrington Stanley (2)	4-0
Penrith v Rossendale United	0-1
5 Clitheroe v Droylsden	0-2
Horwich RMI v Darwen	4-1
Prescot Town v Emley	1-0
Skelmersdale United v Lancaster City	1-4
6 Fleetwood Town v Mossley	1-4
New Mills v Glossop	1-2
South Liverpool v Winsford United	2-2
St Helens Town v Macclesfield Town	1-2
7 Caernarfon Town v Northwich Victoria	0-0
Nantwich Town v Colwyn Bay	2-0
Porthmadog v Formby	0-2
Prestwich Heys v Oswestry Town	0-1
8 Buxton v Matlock Town	3-1
Marine v Congleton Town	3-0
Stalybridge Celtic v Ashton United	1-2
Worsbrough Bridge MW v Mexborough Town Athletic	0-2
9 Barton Town (2) v Goole Town	0-1
Frickley Athletic v Bridlington Town	5-0

159

1979/80

	Selby Town v Bridlington Trinity	0-1
	Thackley v Whitby Town	2-2
10	Arnold v Worksop Town	2-3
	Gresley Rovers v Burton Albion	1-3
	Louth United v Alfreton Town	2-2
	Sutton Town v Winterton Rangers	2-0
11	Bourne Town v Boston	0-2
	Gainsborough Trinity v Brigg Town	1-1
	North Ferriby United v Eastwood Town	2-1
	Retford Town v Skegness Town	0-3
12	Bilston v Telford United	1-2
	Coventry Sporting v Belper Town	1-0
	Highgate United v Brereton Social	0-2
	Moor Green v Tamworth	2-1
13	Darlaston v Hednesford Town	1-2
	Kidderminster Harriers v Friar Lane Old Boys	2-0
	Lye Town v Alvechurch	1-1
	Oldbury United v Long Eaton United	0-1
14	Bromsgrove Rovers v Dudley Town	0-1
	Racing Club Warwick v Gornal Athletic	1-1
	Rushden Town v Hinckley Athletic	2-3
	Sutton Coldfield Town v Willenhall Town	3-2
15	Corby Town v Irthlingborough Diamonds	1-0
	Enderby Town v Saffron Walden Town	5-0
	Olney Town v Bedworth United	0-4
	Soham Town Rangers v V.S. Rugby	0-0
16	Ely City v Boston United	1-2
	St Neots Town v Grantham	4-2
	Stamford v Potton United	2-0
	Thetford Town v Wisbech Town	1-2
17	Felixstowe Town v March Town United	3-2
	King's Lynn v Gorleston	2-0
	Parson Drove United v Chelmsford City	2-0
	Stowmarket v Sudbury Town	0-1
18	Bishop's Stortford v Billericay Town	1-2
	Clacton Town v Bury Town	0-2
	Harwich & Parkeston v Basildon United	2-0
	Hornchurch v Harlow Town	0-3
19	Berkhamsted Town v Bedford Town (1)	1-4
	Chesham United v Boreham Wood	2-0
	Hertford Town v Banbury United	3-1
	Letchworth Garden City v Haverhill Rovers	1-1
20	Harrow Borough v Witney Town	1-3
	St Albans City v Kempston Rovers	0-2
	Thame United v Bracknell Town	6-5
	Tring Town v Wellingborough Town	2-1
21	Cheshunt v Barking	1-5
	Hemel Hempstead Town v Edgware Town	1-2
	Tilbury v Epping Town	3-0
	Uxbridge v Milton Keynes City	1-0
22	Buckingham Town v Hendon	0-7
	Feltham v Burnham (1)	1-2
	Maidenhead United v Clapton	1-0
	Metropolitan Police v Willesden	1-1
23	Chertsey Town v Hillingdon Borough	0-1
	Southall & Ealing Boro. v Leytonstone/Ilford	0-3
	Ware v Leyton-Wingate	2-1
	Wembley v Walthamstow Avenue	0-1
24	Crawley Town v Slough Town	0-0
	Hampton v Finchley	2-1
	Hayes v Aylesbury United	2-0
	Rainham Town v Walton & Hersham	2-2
25	Corinthian Casuals v Woking	1-6
	Farnborough Town v Cray Wanderers	0-1
	Hounslow v Carshalton Athletic	2-0
	Kingstonian v Ruislip Manor	2-0
26	Banstead Athletic v Sutton United	0-2
	Erith & Belvedere v Burgess Hill Town	0-0
	Molesey v Addlestone	2-3
	Sittingbourne v Welling United	2-2
27	Canterbury City v Dulwich Hamlet	1-1
	Chatham Town v Horsham	2-2
	Haywards Heath v Dover	0-3
	Margate v Bromley	4-1
28	East Grinstead v Gravesend & Northfleet	1-4
	Lewes v Folkestone & Shepway	2-1
	Ringmer v Eastbourne Town	3-3
	Sheppey United v Ramsgate	1-1
29	Bexhill Town v Croydon	0-2 N
	Bognor Regis Town v Redhill	5-0
	Three Bridges v Ashford Town	0-2
	Tonbridge v Worthing	2-3
30	Dorking Town v Eastbourne United	1-1
	Littlehampton Town v Fareham Town	0-8
	Swaythling v Gosport Borough	1-4
	Tunbridge Wells v Pagham	2-2
31	Camberley Town v Waterlooville	1-2
	Horsham YMCA v Chichester City (1)	4-2
	Poole Town v Epsom & Ewell	3-1
	Salisbury (2) v Newport (IOW)	4-3
32	Cinderford Town v Redditch United	1-2
	Mangotsfield United v Clevedon Town	2-6
	Oxford City v Bridgend Town	0-0
	Stourbridge v Ton Pentre	2-1
33	Chippenham Town v Merthyr Tydfil	0-3
	Forest Green Rovers v Clandown	3-2
	Paulton Rovers v Cheltenham Town	0-2
	Welton Rovers v Weston-Super-Mare	0-4
34	Barry Town v Bath City	2-1
	Hungerford Town v Calne Town	3-1
	Newbury Town v Didcot Town	2-1
	Taunton Town v Trowbridge Town	0-1
35	Bridgwater Town (1) v Yeovil Town	0-0
	Glastonbury v Bridport	2-1
	Liskeard Athletic v Bideford	3-1
	Saltash United v Ilminster Town	3-0
36	Dorchester Town v Wadebridge Town	2-0
	Penzance v Newquay	1-4
	St Blazey v Barnstaple Town	0-2
	Tiverton Town v Chard Town	2-1
1r	Crook Town v Gateshead (2)	2-0
2r	Bishop Auckland v Carlisle City	2-2e
6r	Winsford United v South Liverpool	3-1
7r	Northwich Victoria v Caernarfon Town	4-0
9r	Whitby Town v Thackley	2-0
10r	Alfreton Town v Louth United	4-2
11r	Brigg Town v Gainsborough Trinity	1-5
13r	Alvechurch v Lye Town	1-2
14r	Gornal Athletic v Racing Club Warwick	2-3
15r	V.S. Rugby v Soham Town Rangers	3-0
19r	Haverhill Rovers v Letchworth Garden City	1-0
22r	Willesden v Metropolitan Police	1-1
24r	Slough Town v Crawley Town	3-0
r	Walton & Hersham v Rainham Town	5-2
26r	Burgess Hill Town v Erith & Belvedere	0-0x
r	Welling United v Sittingbourne	5-0
27r	Dulwich Hamlet v Canterbury City	4-0
r	Horsham v Chatham Town	1-2
28r	Eastbourne Town v Ringmer	2-0
r	Ramsgate v Sheppey United	5-2
30r	Eastbourne United v Dorking Town	4-1
r	Pagham v Tunbridge Wells	1-2
32r	Bridgend Town v Oxford City	5-2
35r	Yeovil Town v Bridgwater Town (1)	2-0
2r2	Carlisle City v Bishop Auckland	0-5 N
22r2	Willesden v Metropolitan Police	0-3
26r2	Erith & Belvedere v Burgess Hill Town	2-0 N

Qualifying Round Two

1	Crook Town v Ashington	2-3
	North Shields v Consett	3-0
2	Billingham Synthonia v Bishop Auckland	0-1
	Washington v Horden CW	0-5
3	South Bank v Peterlee Newtown	3-2
	Tow Law Town v Brandon United	0-4
4	Netherfield (Kendal) v Burscough	0-2
	Rossendale United v Curzon Ashton	2-0
5	Lancaster City v Horwich RMI	4-0
	Prescot Town v Droylsden	2-2
6	Macclesfield Town v Mossley	0-0
	Winsford United v Glossop	2-0
7	Formby v Northwich Victoria	1-1
	Oswestry Town v Nantwich Town	2-0
8	Ashton United v Buxton	1-1
	Mexborough Town Athletic v Marine	0-1
9	Bridlington Trinity v Goole Town	0-2
	Whitby Town v Frickley Athletic	3-2
10	Alfreton Town v Worksop Town	3-1
	Sutton Town v Burton Albion	1-1
11	North Ferriby United v Boston	1-3
	Skegness Town v Gainsborough Trinity	2-0
12	Coventry Sporting v Telford United	2-4
	Moor Green v Brereton Social	2-1
13	Long Eaton United v Kidderminster Harriers	0-1
	Lye Town v Hednesford Town	1-0
14	Hinckley Athletic v Dudley Town	2-1 v
	Sutton Coldfield Town v Racing Club Warwick	3-0
15	Bedworth United v Corby Town	1-0
	V.S. Rugby v Enderby Town	0-1
16	Stamford v Boston United	0-5
	Wisbech Town v St Neots Town	5-2
17	Parson Drove United v Felixstowe Town	2-0
	Sudbury Town v King's Lynn	1-2
18	Harlow Town v Bury Town	2-1
	Harwich & Parkeston v Billericay Town	3-1
19	Haverhill Rovers v Chesham United	0-0
	Hertford Town v Bedford Town (1)	0-2
20	Thame United v Witney Town	0-1
	Tring Town v Kempston Rovers	5-0
21	Tilbury v Barking	0-1
	Uxbridge v Edgware Town	0-2
22	Maidenhead United v Hendon	2-2
	Metropolitan Police v Burnham (1)	1-1
23	Walthamstow Avenue v Leytonstone/Ilford	2-2
	Ware v Hillingdon Borough	1-1
24	Hayes v Slough Town	2-4
	Walton & Hersham v Hampton	1-1
25	Hounslow v Woking	2-3
	Kingstonian v Cray Wanderers	1-0
26	Addlestone v Sutton United	0-0
	Welling United v Erith & Belvedere	1-0
27	Chatham Town v Dover	1-1
	Margate v Dulwich Hamlet	1-0
28	Eastbourne Town v Gravesend & Northfleet	0-2
	Ramsgate v Lewes	1-0
29	Ashford Town v Croydon	0-2
	Worthing v Bognor Regis Town	1-2
30	Gosport Borough v Eastbourne United	1-0
	Tunbridge Wells v Fareham Town	1-2
31	Poole Town v Waterlooville	0-0
	Salisbury (2) v Horsham YMCA	3-1
32	Bridgend Town v Redditch United	0-0
	Stourbridge v Clevedon Town	2-3
33	Cheltenham Town v Merthyr Tydfil	0-2
	Weston-Super-Mare v Forest Green Rovers	3-1
34	Newbury Town v Barry Town	1-2
	Trowbridge Town v Hungerford Town	0-2
35	Liskeard Athletic v Yeovil Town	0-1
	Saltash United v Glastonbury	4-0
36	Barnstaple Town v Dorchester Town	0-0
	Tiverton Town v Newquay	3-3
5r	Droylsden v Prescot Town	1-0
6r	Mossley v Macclesfield Town	3-2e
7r	Northwich Victoria v Formby	2-0
8r	Buxton v Ashton United	1-1
10r	Burton Albion v Sutton Town	3-2e
14r	Dudley Town v Hinckley Athletic	1-0
19r	Chesham United v Haverhill Rovers	3-0
22r	Burnham (1) v Metropolitan Police	3-3e
r	Hendon v Maidenhead United	0-3
23r	Hillingdon Borough v Ware	3-0
r	Leytonstone/Ilford v Walthamstow Avenue	3-1
24r	Hampton v Walton & Hersham	1-5
26r	Sutton United v Addlestone	0-3
27r	Dover v Chatham Town	0-1
31r	Waterlooville v Poole Town	0-2e
32r	Redditch United v Bridgend Town	2-3
36r	Dorchester Town v Barnstaple Town	1-3
r	Newquay v Tiverton Town	0-1
8r2	Ashton United v Buxton	2-2 N
22r2	Metropolitan Police v Burnham (1)	1-0
8r3	Buxton v Ashton United	1-3 N

Qualifying Round Three

1	North Shields v Ashington	2-1
2	Horden CW v Bishop Auckland	4-1
3	South Bank v Brandon United	1-2
4	Rossendale United v Burscough	0-4
5	Lancaster City v Droylsden	0-0
6	Winsford United v Mossley	0-1
7	Oswestry Town v Northwich Victoria	1-1
8	Marine v Ashton United	4-0
9	Whitby Town v Goole Town	2-2
10	Burton Albion v Alfreton Town	2-0
11	Skegness Town v Boston	1-1
12	Moor Green v Telford United	2-1
13	Kidderminster Harriers v Lye Town	2-1
14	Sutton Coldfield Town v Dudley Town	4-1
15	Enderby Town v Bedworth United	0-0
16	Wisbech Town v Boston United	1-5
17	King's Lynn v Parson Drove United	0-1
18	Harlow Town v Harwich & Parkeston	1-0
19	Chesham United v Bedford Town (1)	0-0
20	Tring Town v Witney Town	0-2
21	Edgware Town v Barking	0-3
22	Metropolitan Police v Maidenhead United	0-1
23	Leytonstone/Ilford v Hillingdon Borough	2-1
24	Walton & Hersham v Slough Town	0-2
25	Kingstonian v Woking	0-2
26	Welling United v Addlestone	3-1
27	Chatham Town v Margate	0-1
28	Ramsgate v Gravesend & Northfleet	2-2
29	Bognor Regis Town v Croydon	0-1
30	Fareham Town v Gosport Borough	1-0
31	Salisbury (2) v Poole Town	3-0
32	Clevedon Town v Bridgend Town	0-2
33	Weston-Super-Mare v Merthyr Tydfil	2-2
34	Hungerford Town v Barry Town	3-1
35	Saltash United v Yeovil Town	3-3
36	Tiverton Town v Barnstaple Town	2-1
5r	Droylsden v Lancaster City	2-0
7r	Northwich Victoria v Oswestry Town	4-1
9r	Goole Town v Whitby Town	2-1
11r	Boston v Skegness Town	2-2
15r	Bedworth United v Enderby Town	0-1e
19r	Bedford Town (1) v Chesham United	0-1
28r	Gravesend & Northfleet v Ramsgate	2-1
33r	Merthyr Tydfil v Weston-Super-Mare	3-1
35r	Yeovil Town v Saltash United	2-1
11r2	Boston v Skegness Town	1-0

Qualifying Round Four

	Barnet v Wycombe Wanderers	0-2
	Blyth Spartans v Marine	2-2
	Boston v AP Leamington	2-2
	Boston United v Nuneaton Borough	1-1
	Bridgend Town v Hungerford Town	1-1
	Burton Albion v Parson Drove United	1-0
	Chesham United v Maidstone United	3-1
	Dagenham v Barking	2-4
	Dartford v Leytonstone/Ilford	0-2
	Enderby Town v Northwich Victoria	0-1
	Gravesend & Northfleet v Welling United	2-1
	Harlow Town v Margate	1-0
	Hitchin Town v Enfield	1-2
	Horden CW v Burscough	0-2
	Leatherhead v Croydon	1-1
	Merthyr Tydfil v Maidenhead United	2-1
	Minehead v Witney Town	1-0
	Moor Green v Runcorn	2-0
	Morecambe v Droylsden	3-2
	Mossley v Goole Town	2-1
	North Shields v Brandon United	1-2
	Salisbury (2) v Worcester City	2-1
	Slough Town v Tooting & Mitcham United	4-0
	Southport v Workington	1-3
	Sutton Coldfield Town v Kidderminster Harriers	3-3
	Tiverton Town v Fareham Town	1-2
	Wealdstone v Woking	1-0
	Yeovil Town v Weymouth	2-1
r	AP Leamington v Boston	1-0
r	Croydon v Leatherhead	3-0

1979/80 to 1980/81

r Hungerford Town v Bridgend Town	5-0
r Kidderminster Harriers v Sutton Coldfield Town	3-2e
r Marine v Blyth Spartans	0-5
r Nuneaton Borough v Boston United	2-1

Round One

Aldershot v Exeter City	4-1
Altrincham v Crewe Alexandra	3-0
Barking v Oxford United	1-0
Barnsley v Hartlepool United	5-2
Blackpool v Wigan Athletic	1-1
Blyth Spartans v Mansfield Town	0-2
Brandon United v Bradford City	0-3 N
Burton Albion v Bury	0-2
Carlisle United v Hull City	3-3
Chester v Workington	5-1
Colchester United v Plymouth Argyle	1-1
Darlington v Huddersfield Town	1-1
Enfield v Yeovil Town	0-1
Fareham Town v Merthyr Tydfil	2-3
Gillingham v Wimbledon	0-0
Gravesend & Northfleet v Torquay United	0-1
Grimsby Town v Chesterfield	1-1
Halifax Town v Scarborough	2-0
Harlow Town v Leytonstone/Ilford	2-1
Hereford United v Northampton Town	1-0
Kidderminster Harriers v Blackburn Rovers	0-2
Minehead v Chesham United	1-2
Morecambe v Rotherham United	1-1
Nuneaton Borough v Northwich Victoria	3-3
Peterborough United v Bournemouth	1-2
Port Vale v Doncaster Rovers	1-3
Portsmouth v Newport County	1-0
Reading v Kettering Town	4-2
Rochdale v Scunthorpe United	2-1
Salisbury (2) v Millwall	1-2 N
Sheffield United v Burscough	3-0
Sheffield Wednesday v Lincoln City	3-0
Slough Town v Hungerford Town	3-1
Stafford Rangers v Moor Green	3-2
Swindon Town v Brentford	4-1
Tranmere Rovers v AP Leamington	9-0
Walsall v Stockport County	2-0
Wealdstone v Southend United	0-1
Wycombe Wanderers v Croydon	0-3
York City v Mossley	5-2
r Chesterfield v Grimsby Town	2-3
r Huddersfield Town v Darlington	0-1
r Hull City v Carlisle United	0-2
r Northwich Victoria v Nuneaton Borough	3-0
r Plymouth Argyle v Colchester United	0-1e
r Rotherham United v Morecambe	2-0
r Wigan Athletic v Blackpool	2-0
r Wimbledon v Gillingham	4-2

Round Two

Blackburn Rovers v Stafford Rangers	2-0
Bury v York City	0-0
Carlisle United v Sheffield Wednesday	3-0
Chesham United v Merthyr Tydfil	1-1
Chester v Barnsley	1-0
Colchester United v Bournemouth	1-0
Croydon v Millwall	1-1 N
Darlington v Bradford City	0-1
Doncaster Rovers v Mansfield Town	1-2
Grimsby Town v Sheffield United	2-0
Hereford United v Aldershot	1-2
Northwich Victoria v Wigan Athletic	2-2
Reading v Barking	3-1
Rotherham United v Altrincham	0-2
Southend United v Harlow Town	1-1
Torquay United v Swindon Town	3-3
Tranmere Rovers v Rochdale	2-2
Walsall v Halifax Town	1-1
Wimbledon v Portsmouth	0-0
Yeovil Town v Slough Town	1-0
r Halifax Town v Walsall	1-1e
r Harlow Town v Southend United	1-0
r Merthyr Tydfil v Chesham United	1-3
r Millwall v Croydon	3-2e
r Portsmouth v Wimbledon	3-3e
r Rochdale v Tranmere Rovers	2-1
r Swindon Town v Torquay United	3-2
r Wigan Athletic v Northwich Victoria	1-0
r York City v Bury	0-2
r2 Halifax Town v Walsall	2-0e
r2 Wimbledon v Portsmouth	0-1

Round Three

Altrincham v Orient	1-1
Birmingham City v Southampton	2-1
Blackburn Rovers v Fulham	1-1
Bristol City v Derby County	6-2
Bristol Rovers v Aston Villa	1-2
Burnley v Stoke City	1-0
Cardiff City v Arsenal	0-0
Carlisle United v Bradford City	3-2
Chelsea v Wigan Athletic	0-1
Chesham United v Cambridge United	0-2
Everton v Aldershot	4-1
Halifax Town v Manchester City	1-0
Leeds United v Nottingham Forest	1-4
Leicester City v Harlow Town	1-1
Liverpool v Grimsby Town	5-0
Luton Town v Swindon Town	0-2
Mansfield Town v Brighton & Hove Albion	0-2
Millwall v Shrewsbury Town	5-1
Newcastle United v Chester	0-2
Notts County v Wolverhampton Wan.	1-3
Oldham Athletic v Coventry City	0-1
Portsmouth v Middlesbrough	1-1
Preston North End v Ipswich Town	0-3
Queen's Park Rangers v Watford	1-2
Reading v Colchester United	2-0
Rochdale v Bury	1-1
Sunderland v Bolton Wanderers	0-1
Swansea City v Crystal Palace	2-2
Tottenham Hotspur v Manchester United	1-1
West Bromwich Albion v West Ham United	1-1
Wrexham v Charlton Athletic	6-0
Yeovil Town v Norwich City	0-3
r Arsenal v Cardiff City	2-1
r Bury v Rochdale	3-2
r Crystal Palace v Swansea City	3-3e
r Fulham v Blackburn Rovers	0-1
r Harlow Town v Leicester City	1-0
r Manchester United v Tottenham Hotspur	0-1e
r Middlesbrough v Portsmouth	3-0
r Orient v Altrincham	2-1
r West Ham United v West Bromwich Albion	2-1
r2 Swansea City v Crystal Palace	2-1 N

Round Four

Arsenal v Brighton & Hove Albion	2-0
Birmingham City v Middlesbrough	2-1
Blackburn Rovers v Coventry City	1-0
Bolton Wanderers v Halifax Town	2-0
Bristol City v Ipswich Town	1-2
Bury v Burnley	1-0
Cambridge United v Aston Villa	1-1
Carlisle United v Wrexham	0-0
Chester v Millwall	2-0
Everton v Wigan Athletic	3-0
Nottingham Forest v Liverpool	0-2
Orient v West Ham United	2-3
Swansea City v Reading	4-1
Swindon Town v Tottenham Hotspur	0-0
Watford v Harlow Town	4-3
Wolverhampton Wan. v Norwich City	1-1
r Aston Villa v Cambridge United	4-1
r Norwich City v Wolverhampton Wan.	2-3
r Tottenham Hotspur v Swindon Town	2-1
r Wrexham v Carlisle United	3-1

Round Five

Blackburn Rovers v Aston Villa	1-1
Bolton Wanderers v Arsenal	1-1
Everton v Wrexham	5-2
Ipswich Town v Chester	2-1
Liverpool v Bury	2-0
Tottenham Hotspur v Birmingham City	3-1
West Ham United v Swansea City	2-0
Wolverhampton Wan. v Watford	0-3
r Arsenal v Bolton Wanderers	3-0
r Aston Villa v Blackburn Rovers	1-0

Round Six

Everton v Ipswich Town	2-1
Tottenham Hotspur v Liverpool	0-1
Watford v Arsenal	1-2
West Ham United v Aston Villa	1-0

Semi Finals

Arsenal v Liverpool	0-0 N
West Ham United v Everton	1-1 N
r Everton v West Ham United	1-2 N
r Liverpool v Arsenal	1-1eN
r2 Arsenal v Liverpool	1-1eN
r3 Liverpool v Arsenal	0-1 N

Final

West Ham United v Arsenal	1-0 N

1980/81

Preliminary Round

1 Carlisle City v Farsley Celtic	1-4
Peterlee Newtown v West Auckland Town	1-1
2 Bridlington Trinity v Eppleton CW	3-0
Netherfield (Kendal) v Washington	3-2
3 Easington CW v South Bank	0-2
Whitby Town v Yorkshire Amateur	3-1
4 Consett v Crook Town	0-2
Thackley v Wingate (Durham)	1-1
5 Emley v Fleetwood Town	0-3
New Brighton v Worsbrough Bridge MW	1-3
6 Formby v Glossop	0-2
Prescot Cables v South Liverpool	2-1
7 Caernarfon Town v Chorley	0-2
Porthmadog v Skelmersdale United	1-1
8 Denaby United v Frickley Athletic	1-3
Rossendale United v Worksop Town	1-1
9 Buxton v Eastwood Town	1-2
Nantwich Town v Winterton Rangers	0-0
10 Desborough Town v Friar Lane Old Boys	2-1
Normanby Park Steel Works v Sutton Town	0-0
11 Gainsborough Trinity v Heanor Town	3-1
March Town United v Stamford	2-1
12 Bilston v Congleton Town	3-2
Walsall Wood v Winsford United	0-3
13 Gresley Rovers v Highgate United	1-1
Redditch United v Witton Albion	0-0
14 Histon v Irthlingborough Diamonds	3-0
Tamworth v Wolverton Town	3-0
15 Brierley Hill Alliance v Darlaston	0-2
Racing Club Warwick v V.S. Rugby	1-2
16 Brereton Social v Evesham United	1-1
Cinderford Town v Forest Green Rovers	0-0
Oxford City v Cheltenham Town	0-2
17 Chatteris Town v Great Yarmouth Town	1-1
St Neots Town v Thetford Town	3-1
18 Bury Town v Felixstowe Town	2-1
Potton United v Wisbech Town	0-1
19 Edgware Town v Hoddesdon Town	4-3
Tiptree United v Wootton Blue Cross	3-0
20 Hayes v Hemel Hempstead Town	2-0
Newmarket Town v Wellingborough Town	1-0
21 Dulwich Hamlet v Hampton	3-1
Milton Keynes City v Southall	0-2
22 Carshalton Athletic v Feltham	2-0
Staines Town v Willesden	0-1
23 Chertsey Town v Dunstable	2-1
Walton & Hersham v Woodford Town (1)	3-0
24 Epping Town v Haringey Borough	2-1
Rainham Town v Uxbridge	3-4
25 Arundel v Kingstonian	0-2
Egham Town v Molesey	3-1
Worthing v Basingstoke Town	0-1
26 Cheshunt v Clapton	0-1
Hornchurch v Walthamstow Avenue	2-3
27 Cray Wanderers v Dorking Town	1-1
Tilbury v Peacehaven & Telscombe	1-0
28 Crawley Town v Deal Town	2-1
Haywards Heath v Whitstable Town	1-0
29 Chatham Town v Eastbourne United	2-1
Herne Bay v Tonbridge	0-3
30 Horsham v Lewes	1-6
Ringmer v Tunbridge Wells	3-1
31 Bracknell Town v Poole Town	1-5
Three Bridges v Wokingham Town	0-1
32 Chichester City (1) v Devizes Town	1-1
Newbury Town v Pagham	1-0
33 Calne Town v Chippenham Town	0-1
Mangotsfield United v Lye Town	0-2
34 Bath City v Glastonbury	7-1
Paulton Rovers v Weston-Super-Mare	0-3
35 Chard Town v Clevedon Town	1-1
Shepton Mallet Town v Welton Rovers	2-1
36 Newquay v Ottery St Mary	8-0
Saltash United v Wadebridge Town	5-0
1r West Auckland Town v Peterlee Newtown	3-4e
4r Wingate (Durham) v Thackley	0-1
7r Skelmersdale United v Porthmadog	3-1
8r Worksop Town v Rossendale United	3-1
9r Winterton Rangers v Nantwich Town	0-1
10r Sutton Town v Normanby Park Steel Works	2-3
13r Highgate United v Gresley Rovers	3-1
r Witton Albion v Redditch United	5-1
16r Evesham United v Brereton Social	3-2e
r Forest Green Rovers v Cinderford Town	0-0
17r Great Yarmouth Town v Chatteris Town	3-2
27r Dorking Town v Cray Wanderers	0-2
32r Devizes Town v Chichester City (1)	1-3
35r Clevedon Town v Chard Town	4-1
16r2 Cinderford Town v Forest Green Rovers	1-2 N

Qualifying Round One

1 Annfield Plain v Billingham Synthonia	2-3
Guisborough Town v Gateshead (2)	2-3
North Shields v Tow Law Town	0-0
Peterlee Newtown v Farsley Celtic	0-2
2 Ashington v Bishop Auckland	0-3
Brandon United v Shildon	0-0
Ferryhill Athletic v Evenwood Town	2-2
Netherfield (Kendal) v Bridlington Trinity	1-2
3 Barrow v Boldon CA	8-1
Horden CW v Willington	1-0
Spennymoor United v Wallsend Town	2-0
Whitby Town v South Bank	3-0
4 Goole Town v Whitley Bay	1-0
Newcastle Blue Star v Bridlington Town	3-1
Penrith v Durham City	6-0
Thackley v Crook Town	1-0
5 Accrington Stanley (2) v Darwen	2-0
Lytham v Leyland Motors	0-2
Southport v St Helens Town	1-3
Worsbrough Bridge MW v Fleetwood Town	0-4
6 Burscough v Prestwich Heys	2-1
Clitheroe v Curzon Ashton	0-2
Lancaster City v Hyde United	1-1
Prescot Cables v Glossop	2-0
7 Bangor City v Bootle	0-2
Marine v Rhyl	3-0

161

1980/81

	Oswestry Town v Colwyn Bay	0-1
	Skelmersdale United v Chorley	0-1
8	Appleby Frodingham Ath. v Ashby Institute	5-0
	Droylsden v Stalybridge Celtic	1-1
	North Ferriby United v Horwich RMI	1-0
	Worksop Town v Frickley Athletic	3-2
9	Alfreton Town v Brigg Town	2-1
	Leek Town v Mexborough Town Athletic	2-1
	Nantwich Town v Eastwood Town	0-0
	Northwich Victoria v New Mills	1-0
10	Arnold v Barton Town (2)	0-1
	Boston United v Skegness Town	3-0
	Long Eaton United v Grantham	0-0
	Normanby Park Steel Works v Desborough Town	0-4
11	Boston v Spalding United	6-1
	Corby Town v Ely City	1-0
	Ilkeston Town (2) v Holbeach United	0-0
	March Town United v Gainsborough Trinity	1-2
12	Armitage v Belper Town	1-2
	Burton Albion v Willenhall Town	2-2
	Stourbridge v Macclesfield Town	6-2
	Winsford United v Bilston	4-2 N
13	Bedworth United v Gornal Athletic	2-0
	Oldbury United v Matlock Town	4-0
	Sutton Coldfield Town v Telford United	1-0
	Witton Albion v Highgate United	3-1
14	Coventry Sporting v Hinckley Athletic	2-3
	Enderby Town v Tividale	3-1
	Soham Town Rangers v King's Lynn	1-1
	Tamworth v Histon	3-0
15	Alvechurch v Banbury United	0-2
	Moor Green v Rothwell Town	4-0
	Moreton Town v Dudley Town	0-1
	V.S. Rugby v Darlaston	3-1
16	Cheltenham Town v Forest Green Rovers	3-2
	Evesham United v Buckingham Town	0-1
	Halesowen Town v Didcot Town	1-1
	Kidderminster Harriers v Hednesford Town	3-0
17	Bourne Town v Cambridge City	0-0
	Lowestoft Town v Harwich & Parkeston	0-2
	Parson Drove United v Stowmarket	0-1
	St Neots Town v Great Yarmouth Town	0-1
18	Bedford Town (1) v Bishop's Stortford	3-2
	Haverhill Rovers v Gorleston	2-3
	Hitchin Town v Rushden Town	3-0
	Wisbech Town v Bury Town	1-2
19	Chelmsford City v Clacton Town	0-0
	Leytonstone/Ilford v Wembley	0-1
	Sudbury Town v Letchworth Garden City	0-3
	Tiptree United v Edgware Town	0-1
20	Berkhamsted Town v Finchley	1-2
	Kempston Rovers v Hertford Town	3-0
	Newmarket Town v Hayes	1-1
	Witney Town v Ruislip Manor	2-1
21	Billericay Town v Chalfont St Peter	1-1
	Chesham United v St Albans City	0-1
	Marlow v Harrow Borough	1-2
	Southall v Dulwich Hamlet	0-8
22	Addlestone & Weybridge T v Boreham Wood	2-2
	Leyton-Wingate v Harefield United	0-3
	Maidenhead United v Thame United	1-0
	Willesden v Carshalton Athletic	0-2
23	Barton Rovers v Camberley Town	3-0
	Metropolitan Police v Hounslow	2-3
	Slough Town v Ware	5-1
	Walton & Hersham v Chertsey Town	1-0
24	Aylesbury United v Burnham (1)	2-0
	Hillingdon Borough v Hendon	0-0
	Uxbridge v Epping Town	1-0
	Woking v Tring Town	2-1
25	Basingstoke Town v Egham Town	2-3
	Kingstonian v Banstead Athletic	1-0
	Tooting & Mitcham United v Windsor & Eton	0-3
	Waterlooville v Horsham YMCA	2-0
26	Aveley v Basildon United	2-0
	Dartford v Saffron Walden Town	4-1
	Grays Athletic v Erith & Belvedere	0-0
	Walthamstow Avenue v Clapton	5-0
27	Burgess Hill Town v Canterbury City	1-2
	Faversham Town v Dover	0-2
	Tilbury v Cray Wanderers	4-1
	Welling United v Sheppey United	4-2
28	Ashford Town v Corinthian Casuals	4-1
	Epsom & Ewell v Eastbourne Town	1-0
	Haywards Heath v Crawley Town	0-1
	Margate v Sittingbourne	1-1
29	Bexhill Town v Bromley	0-7 N
	Folkestone v East Grinstead	6-2
	Maidstone United v Ramsgate	6-0
	Tonbridge v Chatham Town	1-1
30	Croydon v Southwick	1-0
	Gosport Borough v Hastings United	0-0
	Redhill v Littlehampton Town	0-2
	Ringmer v Lewes	3-3
31	Alton Town v Andover	0-3
	Hungerford Town v Wick	5-1
	Sutton United v Steyning Town	3-1
	Wokingham Town v Poole Town	0-1
32	Bognor Regis Town v Bridport	3-1
	Fareham Town v Newport (IOW)	2-0
	Frome Town v Farnborough Town	1-1
	Newbury Town v Chichester City (1)	2-0
33	Barry Town v Bromsgrove Rovers	1-0
	Llanelli v Clandown	2-0
	Lye Town v Chippenham Town	1-1

	Worcester City v Malvern Town	1-1
34	Almondsbury Greenway v Barnstaple Town	0-1
	Bath City v Weston-Super-Mare	2-1
	Bridgend Town v Ton Pentre	0-1
	Melksham Town v Ilminster Town	7-0
35	Bideford v Bridgwater Town (1)	2-1
	Gloucester City v Dorchester Town	1-0
	Salisbury (2) v Trowbridge Town	1-1
	Shepton Mallet Town v Clevedon Town	1-4
36	Falmouth Town v Liskeard Athletic	1-1
	Saltash United v Newquay	4-0
	St Blazey v Penzance	1-2
	Tiverton Town v Taunton Town	0-5
1r	Tow Law Town v North Shields	4-2e
2r	Evenwood Town v Ferryhill Athletic	2-1
r	Shildon v Brandon United	1-0e
6r	Curzon Ashton v Clitheroe	2-2
r	Hyde United v Lancaster City	3-1
8r	Stalybridge Celtic v Droylsden	2-1
9r	Eastwood Town v Nantwich Town	1-0
10r	Grantham v Long Eaton United	2-2
11r	Holbeach United v Ilkeston Town (2)	1-0
12r	Willenhall Town v Burton Albion	1-2
14r	King's Lynn v Soham Town Rangers	2-1
16r	Didcot Town v Halesowen Town	0-1
17r	Cambridge City v Bourne Town	0-1
19r	Clacton Town v Chelmsford City	1-2
20r	Hayes v Newmarket Town	5-0
21r	Chalfont St Peter v Billericay Town	0-3
22r	Boreham Wood v Addlestone & Weybridge Town	0-2
24r	Hendon v Hillingdon Borough	3-2
26r	Erith & Belvedere v Grays Athletic	1-3
28r	Sittingbourne v Margate	3-4
29r	Chatham Town v Tonbridge	1-0
30r	Hastings United v Gosport Borough	3-4e
r	Lewes v Ringmer	6-2
32r	Farnborough Town v Frome Town	1-0
33r	Chippenham Town v Lye Town	0-2
r	Malvern Town v Worcester City	0-2
35r	Trowbridge Town v Salisbury (2)	2-1
36r	Liskeard Athletic v Falmouth Town	2-3
6r2	Clitheroe v Curzon Ashton	0-1 N
10r2	Grantham v Long Eaton United	3-0

Qualifying Round Two

1	Billingham Synthonia v Farsley Celtic	2-0
	Gateshead (2) v Tow Law Town	2-0
2	Bishop Auckland v Bridlington Trinity	1-0
	Evenwood Town v Shildon	2-0
3	Barrow v Whitby Town	1-1
	Spennymoor United v Horden CW	1-2
4	Newcastle Blue Star v Thackley	2-0
	Penrith v Goole Town	2-0
5	Accrington Stanley (2) v Fleetwood Town	1-1
	Leyland Motors v St Helens Town	0-4
6	Curzon Ashton v Prescot Cables	1-4
	Hyde United v Burscough	1-2
7	Bootle v Chorley	0-1
	Colwyn Bay v Marine	2-2
8	Appleby Frodingham Ath. v Worksop Town	0-2
	North Ferriby United v Stalybridge Celtic	0-0
9	Alfreton Town v Eastwood Town	1-0
	Leek Town v Northwich Victoria	1-1
10	Barton Town (2) v Desborough Town	4-1
	Grantham v Boston United	1-3
11	Corby Town v Gainsborough Trinity	2-0
	Holbeach United v Boston	0-3
12	Belper Town v Winsford United	2-2
	Stourbridge v Burton Albion	1-1
13	Bedworth United v Witton Albion	1-2
	Oldbury United v Sutton Coldfield Town	0-3
14	Hinckley Athletic v Tamworth	2-1
	King's Lynn v Enderby Town	2-0
15	Banbury United v V.S. Rugby	3-3
	Dudley Town v Moor Green	0-0
16	Buckingham Town v Cheltenham Town	2-1
	Halesowen Town v Kidderminster Harriers	1-4
17	Bourne Town v Great Yarmouth Town	0-2
	Harwich & Parkeston v Stowmarket	2-1
18	Bedford Town (1) v Bury Town	4-0
	Gorleston v Hitchin Town	0-1
19	Chelmsford City v Edgware Town	3-1
	Letchworth Garden City v Wembley	0-0
20	Finchley v Hayes	0-1
	Kempston Rovers v Witney Town	2-1
21	Billericay Town v Dulwich Hamlet	1-2
	Harrow Borough v St Albans City	3-4
22	Addlestone & Weybridge T v Carshalton Athletic	1-0
	Harefield United v Maidenhead United	0-0
23	Barton Rovers v Walton & Hersham	1-0
	Hounslow v Slough Town	1-3
24	Aylesbury United v Uxbridge	6-0
	Hendon v Woking	1-1
25	Kingstonian v Egham Town	2-1
	Waterlooville v Windsor & Eton	0-0
26	Aveley v Walthamstow Avenue	2-0
	Grays Athletic v Dartford	2-0
27	Canterbury City v Tilbury	2-1
	Dover v Welling United	2-0
28	Ashford Town v Crawley Town	3-0
	Epsom & Ewell v Margate	3-1
29	Bromley v Chatham Town	4-0
	Folkestone v Maidstone United	0-2
30	Gosport Borough v Lewes	2-1
	Littlehampton Town v Croydon	0-3
31	Andover v Poole Town	0-2
	Sutton United v Hungerford Town	2-0
32	Bognor Regis Town v Newbury Town	1-2
	Farnborough Town v Fareham Town	1-0
33	Barry Town v Lye Town	1-1
	Llanelli v Worcester City	0-3
34	Barnstaple Town v Bath City	0-1
	Melksham Town v Ton Pentre	0-3
35	Bideford v Clevedon Town	2-1
	Gloucester City v Trowbridge Town	0-1
36	Falmouth Town v Saltash United	2-1
	Penzance v Taunton Town	2-3
3r	Whitby Town v Barrow	1-2
5r	Fleetwood Town v Accrington Stanley (2)	3-2
7r	Marine v Colwyn Bay	4-0
8r	Stalybridge Celtic v North Ferriby United	3-0
9r	Northwich Victoria v Leek Town	1-0
12r	Burton Albion v Stourbridge	2-1
r	Winsford United v Belper Town	5-0
15r	Moor Green v Dudley Town	2-1
r	V.S. Rugby v Banbury United	1-3
19r	Wembley v Letchworth Garden City	3-1
22r	Maidenhead United v Harefield United	5-1
24r	Woking v Hendon	1-4
25r	Windsor & Eton v Waterlooville	4-1
33r	Lye Town v Barry Town	1-2

Qualifying Round Three

1	Gateshead (2) v Billingham Synthonia	3-0
2	Evenwood Town v Bishop Auckland	0-1
3	Horden CW v Barrow	0-0
4	Penrith v Newcastle Blue Star	1-0
5	St Helens Town v Fleetwood Town	0-1
6	Burscough v Prescot Cables	4-0
7	Marine v Chorley	3-0
8	Stalybridge Celtic v Worksop Town	0-0
9	Northwich Victoria v Alfreton Town	3-2
10	Boston United v Barton Town (2)	2-0
11	Boston v Corby Town	0-1
12	Burton Albion v Winsford United	2-2
13	Sutton Coldfield Town v Witton Albion	2-1
14	King's Lynn v Hinckley Athletic	5-1
15	Moor Green v Banbury United	0-2
16	Kidderminster Harriers v Buckingham Town	2-1
17	Harwich & Parkeston v Great Yarmouth Town	1-0
18	Hitchin Town v Bedford Town (1)	3-2
19	Wembley v Chelmsford City	3-1
20	Kempston Rovers v Hayes	0-2
21	St Albans City v Dulwich Hamlet	2-1
22	Maidenhead United v Addlestone & Weybridge T	0-0
23	Slough Town v Barton Rovers	0-1
24	Hendon v Aylesbury United	1-1
25	Windsor & Eton v Kingstonian	1-1
26	Grays Athletic v Aveley	0-1
27	Dover v Canterbury City	2-2
28	Epsom & Ewell v Ashford Town	1-0
29	Maidstone United v Bromley	2-0
30	Croydon v Gosport Borough	0-1
31	Sutton United v Poole Town	4-1
32	Farnborough Town v Newbury Town	4-1
33	Worcester City v Barry Town	1-1
34	Ton Pentre v Bath City	1-3
35	Trowbridge Town v Bideford	2-3
36	Taunton Town v Falmouth Town	1-0
3r	Barrow v Horden CW	2-3e
8r	Worksop Town v Stalybridge Celtic	1-2
12r	Winsford United v Burton Albion	1-3
22r	Addlestone & Weybridge T v Maidenhead United	5-0
24r	Aylesbury United v Hendon	1-0e
25r	Kingstonian v Windsor & Eton	2-3
27r	Canterbury City v Dover	3-3
33r	Barry Town v Worcester City	2-3
27r2	Canterbury City v Dover	0-2

Qualifying Round Four

AP Leamington v Barton Rovers	0-1
Addlestone & Weybridge T v Bideford	3-0
Aylesbury United v Barnet	1-1
Blyth Spartans v Horden CW	7-0
Burscough v Morecambe	2-0
Burton Albion v Penrith	1-0
Corby Town v Boston United	0-1
Enfield v Epsom & Ewell	5-0
Fleetwood Town v Stalybridge Celtic	1-0
Gravesend & Northfleet v Aveley	4-0
Harlow Town v Wealdstone	1-1
Harwich & Parkeston v St Albans City	2-2
Hayes v Yeovil Town	1-1
Hitchin Town v Sutton Coldfield Town	0-1
Kettering Town v Banbury United	3-0
Kidderminster Harriers v Nuneaton Borough	1-0
King's Lynn v Stafford Rangers	1-3
Leatherhead v Bath City	1-0
Maidstone United v Barking	2-0
Marine v Gateshead (2)	1-0 D
Merthyr Tydfil v Farnborough Town	0-1
Minehead v Sutton United	2-0
Northwich Victoria v Runcorn	2-1
Wembley v Dover	1-1
Weymouth v Taunton Town	0-0
Windsor & Eton v Gosport Borough	2-0
Worcester City v Wycombe Wanderers	1-1

1980/81 to 1981/82

Workington v Bishop Auckland	4-1	
r Barnet v Aylesbury United	0-0e	
r Dover v Wembley	2-3	
r St Albans City v Harwich & Parkeston	3-0	
r Taunton Town v Weymouth	0-3	
r Wealdstone v Harlow Town	0-1	
r Wycombe Wanderers v Worcester City	1-0	
r Yeovil Town v Hayes	2-0	
r2 Barnet v Aylesbury United	1-0e	

Round One

Barnet v Minehead	2-2
Blackpool v Fleetwood Town	4-0
Blyth Spartans v Burton Albion	2-1
Boston United v Rotherham United	0-4
Brentford v Addlestone & Weybridge T	2-2
Burnley v Scarborough	1-0
Burscough v Altrincham	1-2
Chester v Barnsley	1-2
Colchester United v Portsmouth	3-0
Darlington v Bury	0-2
Enfield v Wembley	3-0
Exeter City v Leatherhead	5-0
Gillingham v Dagenham	2-1
Gravesend & Northfleet v St Albans City	1-2
Harlow Town v Charlton Athletic	0-2
Hull City v Halifax Town	2-1
Kettering Town v Maidstone United	1-1
Kidderminster Harriers v Millwall	1-1
Lincoln City v Gateshead (2)	1-0
Mansfield Town v Rochdale	3-1
Mossley v Crewe Alexandra	1-0
Northampton Town v Peterborough United	1-4
Northwich Victoria v Huddersfield Town	1-1
Oxford United v Aldershot	1-0
Plymouth Argyle v Newport County	2-0
Port Vale v Bradford City	4-2
Reading v Fulham	1-2
Scunthorpe United v Hartlepool United	3-1
Southend United v Hereford United	0-1
Stockport County v Sheffield United	0-0
Sutton Coldfield Town v Doncaster Rovers	0-2
Swindon Town v Weymouth	3-2
Torquay United v Barton Rovers	2-0
Tranmere Rovers v York City	0-0
Walsall v Stafford Rangers	3-0
Wigan Athletic v Chesterfield	2-2
Wimbledon v Windsor & Eton	7-2
Workington v Carlisle United	0-0
Wycombe Wanderers v Bournemouth	0-3
Yeovil Town v Farnborough Town	2-1
r Brentford v Addlestone & Weybridge T	2-0
r Carlisle United v Workington	4-1
r Chesterfield v Wigan Athletic	2-0
r Huddersfield Town v Northwich Victoria	6-0
r Maidstone United v Kettering Town	0-0e
r Millwall v Kidderminster Harriers	1-0
r Minehead v Barnet	1-2
r Sheffield United v Stockport County	3-2e
r York City v Tranmere Rovers	1-2e
r2 Maidstone United v Kettering Town	3-1

Round Two

Barnet v Peterborough United	0-1
Burnley v Port Vale	1-1
Bury v Lincoln City	2-0
Carlisle United v Walsall	3-0
Charlton Athletic v Bournemouth	2-1
Colchester United v Yeovil Town	1-1
Doncaster Rovers v Blackpool	2-1
Enfield v Hereford United	2-0
Fulham v Brentford	1-0
Gillingham v Maidstone United	0-0
Hull City v Blyth Spartans	1-1
Millwall v Exeter City	0-1
Mossley v Mansfield Town	1-3
Plymouth Argyle v Oxford United	3-0
Rotherham United v Barnsley	0-1
Scunthorpe United v Altrincham	0-0
Sheffield United v Chesterfield	1-1
St Albans City v Torquay United	1-1
Tranmere Rovers v Huddersfield Town	0-3
Wimbledon v Swindon Town	2-0
r Altrincham v Scunthorpe United	1-0
r Blyth Spartans v Hull City	2-2e
r Chesterfield v Sheffield United	1-0
r Maidstone United v Gillingham	0-0e
r Port Vale v Burnley	2-0
r Torquay United v St Albans City	4-1
r Yeovil Town v Colchester United	0-2
r2 Gillingham v Maidstone United	0-2
r2 Hull City v Blyth Spartans	2-1eN

Round Three

Barnsley v Torquay United	2-1
Birmingham City v Sunderland	1-1
Bury v Fulham	1-1
Colchester United v Watford	0-1
Derby County v Bristol City	0-0
Everton v Arsenal	2-0
Huddersfield Town v Shrewsbury Town	0-3
Hull City v Doncaster Rovers	1-0

Ipswich Town v Aston Villa	1-0
Leeds United v Coventry City	1-1
Leicester City v Cardiff City	3-0
Liverpool v Altrincham	4-1
Maidstone United v Exeter City	2-4
Manchester City v Crystal Palace	4-0
Manchester United v Brighton & Hove Albion	2-2
Mansfield Town v Carlisle United	2-2
Newcastle United v Sheffield Wednesday	2-1
Norwich City v Cambridge United	1-0
Nottingham Forest v Bolton Wanderers	3-3
Notts County v Blackburn Rovers	2-1
Orient v Luton Town	1-3
Peterborough United v Chesterfield	1-1
Plymouth Argyle v Charlton Athletic	1-2
Port Vale v Enfield	1-1
Preston North End v Bristol Rovers	3-4
Queen's Park Rangers v Tottenham Hotspur	0-0
Southampton v Chelsea	3-1
Stoke City v Wolverhampton Wan.	2-2
Swansea City v Middlesbrough	0-5
West Bromwich Albion v Grimsby Town	3-0
West Ham United v Wrexham	1-1
Wimbledon v Oldham Athletic	0-0
r Bolton Wanderers v Nottingham Forest	0-1e
r Brighton & Hove Albion v Manchester United	0-2
r Bristol City v Derby County	2-0
r Carlisle United v Mansfield Town	2-1
r Chesterfield v Peterborough United	1-2
r Coventry City v Leeds United	1-0
r Enfield v Port Vale	3-0
r Fulham v Bury	0-0e
r Oldham Athletic v Wimbledon	0-1
r Sunderland v Birmingham City	1-2e
r Tottenham Hotspur v Queen's Park Rangers	3-1
r Wolverhampton Wan. v Stoke City	2-1
r Wrexham v West Ham United	0-0e
r2 Bury v Fulham	0-1 N
r2 Wrexham v West Ham United	1-0e

Round Four

Barnsley v Enfield	1-1
Carlisle United v Bristol City	1-1
Coventry City v Birmingham City	3-2
Everton v Liverpool	2-1
Fulham v Charlton Athletic	1-2
Leicester City v Exeter City	1-1
Manchester City v Norwich City	6-0
Middlesbrough v West Bromwich Albion	1-0
Newcastle United v Luton Town	2-1
Nottingham Forest v Manchester United	1-0
Notts County v Peterborough United	0-1
Shrewsbury Town v Ipswich Town	0-0
Southampton v Bristol Rovers	3-1
Tottenham Hotspur v Hull City	2-0
Watford v Wolverhampton Wan.	1-1
Wrexham v Wimbledon	2-1
r Bristol City v Carlisle United	5-0
r Enfield v Barnsley	0-3 N
r Exeter City v Leicester City	3-1
r Ipswich Town v Shrewsbury Town	3-0
r Wolverhampton Wan. v Watford	2-1

Round Five

Ipswich Town v Charlton Athletic	2-0
Middlesbrough v Barnsley	2-1
Newcastle United v Exeter City	1-1
Nottingham Forest v Bristol City	2-1
Peterborough United v Manchester City	0-1
Southampton v Everton	0-0
Tottenham Hotspur v Coventry City	3-1
Wolverhampton Wan. v Wrexham	3-1
r Everton v Southampton	1-0e
r Exeter City v Newcastle United	4-0

Round Six

Everton v Manchester City	2-2
Middlesbrough v Wolverhampton Wan.	1-1
Nottingham Forest v Ipswich Town	3-3
Tottenham Hotspur v Exeter City	2-0
r Ipswich Town v Nottingham Forest	1-0
r Manchester City v Everton	3-1
r Wolverhampton Wan. v Middlesbrough	3-1e

Semi Finals

Manchester City v Ipswich Town	1-0eN
Tottenham Hotspur v Wolverhampton Wan.	2-2eN
r Wolverhampton Wan. v Tottenham Hotspur	0-3 N

Final

Tottenham Hotspur v Manchester City	1-1eN
r Tottenham Hotspur v Manchester City	3-2 N

1981/82

Preliminary Round

1	Newcastle Blue Star v Whitley Bay	0-0
	Peterlee Newtown v South Bank	0-2
	Willington v Eppleton CW	0-0
2	Boldon CA v Tow Law Town	1-5
	Lancaster City v Percy Main Amateurs	3-1
	Wallsend Town v Evenwood Town	1-4
3	Chester-le-Street Town v West Auckland Town	1-0
	Guisborough Town v Shildon	3-1
4	Bridlington Town v Thackley	1-3
	Farsley Celtic v Mexborough Town Athletic	1-1
5	Appleby Frodingham Ath. v Buxton	2-2
	Bridlington Trinity v Winterton Rangers	3-1
6	Accrington Stanley (2) v South Liverpool	2-1
	Clitheroe v Netherfield (Kendal)	0-1
7	Horwich RMI v Skelmersdale United	4-0
	Marine v Prestwich Heys	2-0
	Witton Albion v Macclesfield Town	3-1
8	Congleton Town v Belper Town	0-2
	Rhyl v Winsford United	0-1
	Telford United v Oswestry Town	4-0
9	Colwyn Bay v Matlock Town	3-3
	Prescot Cables v St Helens Town	4-1
	Shifnal Town v New Mills	5-0
10	Alfreton Town v Ashby Institute	5-0 N
	Boston v Holbeach United	5-0
11	Eastwood Town v Friar Lane Old Boys	3-0
	Heanor Town v Worksop Town	1-3
12	Bilston v Rushall Olympic	0-0
	Hednesford Town v Moor Green	3-0
	Long Eaton United v Halesowen Town	1-3
13	Brereton Social v Tamworth	0-3
	Gresley Rovers v Redditch United	2-1
14	Blakenall v Desborough Town	1-1
	Dudley Town v Stourbridge	3-0
15	Tividale v Milton Keynes City	3-0
	Wellingborough Town v Brierley Hill Alliance	wo/s
16	Bury Town v Spalding United	2-0
	Great Yarmouth Town v Saffron Walden Town	4-0
17	Gorleston v Chelmsford City	2-0
	March Town United v Soham Town Rangers	1-1
18	Bedford Town (1) v Hoddesdon Town	4-0
	Chatteris City v Felixstowe Town	3-1
19	Histon v Leyton-Wingate	1-4
	Sudbury Town v Epping Town	3-3
20	Abingdon Town v Hendon	1-2
	Irthlingborough Diamonds v Harefield United	2-1
21	Didcot Town v Willesden	wo/s
	Wootton Blue Cross v Slough Town	2-2
22	Edgware Town v Staines Town	3-1
	Hounslow v Kingstonian	1-3
	Thame United v Haringey Borough	1-0
23	Billericay Town v Tiptree United	1-0
	Erith & Belvedere v Rainham Town	2-1
24	Egham Town v Marlow	1-1
	Newbury Town v Burnham (1)	4-3
25	Clapton v Whyteleafe	1-0
	Dartford v Redhill	2-2
26	Arundel v Wick	1-4
	Waterlooville v Pagham	0-3
	Woking v Newport (IOW)	1-0
27	Burgess Hill Town v Molesey	4-0
	Horsham YMCA v Uxbridge	1-1
28	Bognor Regis Town v Haywards Heath	5-1
	Metropolitan Police v Worthing	1-2
	Steyning Town v Three Bridges	0-0
29	Chertsey Town v Lewes	2-5
	Dorking Town v Basingstoke Town	0-2
30	Chatham Town v Hastings United	1-4
	Croydon v Ringmer	1-0
31	Eastbourne United v Tonbridge	0-2
	Southwick v Thanet United	0-1
	Whitstable Town v Sheppey United	2-2
32	Chichester City (1) v Poole Town	1-5
	Hungerford Town v Chippenham Town	4-0
33	Bridgend Town v Paulton Rovers	6-0
	Clandown v Gloucester City	1-3
34	Barry Town v Ton Pentre	2-0
	Cinderford Town v Llanelli	1-2
35	Almondsbury Greenway v Wellington (Somerset)	1-1
	Bridport v Ottery St Mary	5-0
36	Barnstaple Town v Tiverton Town	3-1
	Falmouth Town v Penzance	2-2
1r	Eppleton CW v Willington	0-2
r	Whitley Bay v Newcastle Blue Star	3-1
4r	Mexborough Town Athletic v Farsley Celtic	2-1e
5r	Buxton v Appleby Frodingham Ath.	3-0
9r	Matlock Town v Colwyn Bay	2-2
12r	Rushall Olympic v Bilston	1-3
14r	Desborough Town v Blakenall	2-6
17r	Soham Town Rangers v March Town United	0-4
19r	Epping Town v Sudbury Town	2-4
21r	Slough Town v Wootton Blue Cross	4-2
24r	Marlow v Egham Town	1-1
25r	Redhill v Dartford	1-0e
27r	Uxbridge v Horsham YMCA	2-1
28r	Three Bridges v Steyning Town	1-3
31r	Sheppey United v Whitstable Town	1-2
35r	Wellington (Somerset) v Almondsbury Greenway	3-0
36r	Penzance v Falmouth Town	2-2

1981/82

9r2	Colwyn Bay v Matlock Town	1-4 N
24r2	Egham Town v Marlow	7-4e
36r2	Falmouth Town v Penzance	1-0

Qualifying Round One

1	Annfield Plain v Durham City	2-3
	Morecambe v Consett	2-3
	South Bank v Barrow	3-2
	Whitley Bay v Willington	3-1
2	Ashington v Crook Town	4-2
	Horden CW v Brandon United	1-1
	Lancaster City v Billingham Synthonia	1-0
	Tow Law Town v Evenwood Town	4-2
3	Ferryhill Athletic v Chester-le-Street Town	2-2
	Gateshead (2) v Spennymoor United	1-1
	Guisborough Town v Seaham Red Star	2-3
	North Shields v Wingate (Durham)	2-1
4	Bishop Auckland v Ossett Albion	4-0
	Emley v Thackley	2-1
	Frickley Athletic v Whitby Town	2-0
	Mexborough Town Athletic v Goole Town	1-6
5	Barton Town (2) v Buxton	1-3
	Bridlington Trinity v Denaby United	2-0
	Brigg Town v Curzon Ashton	0-0
	Stalybridge Celtic v Yorkshire Amateur	2-1
6	Chorley v Accrington Stanley (2)	0-0
	Droylsden v Southport	1-0
	Netherfield (Kendal) v Leyland Motors	3-2
	Penrith v Rossendale United	2-1
7	Ashton United v Lytham	1-1
	Fleetwood Town v Hyde United	1-1
	Horwich RMI v Witton Albion	2-0
	Marine v Formby	4-0
8	Bangor City v Glossop	6-0
	Belper Town v Telford United	0-6
	Burscough v Darwen	4-0
	Winsford United v Caernarfon Town	2-3
9	Armitage v Nantwich Town	0-2
	Matlock Town v Shifnal Town	1-1
	Prescot Cables v Bootle	3-1
	Runcorn v Leek Town	3-0
10	Arnold v Alfreton Town	1-2
	Boston v Gainsborough Trinity	0-0
	Boston United v Sutton Town	2-1
	Bourne Town v North Ferriby United	1-2
11	Corby Town v Enderby Town	2-1
	Grantham v Eastwood Town	1-0
	Ilkeston Town (2) v Hinckley Athletic	2-0
	Worksop Town v Skegness Town	2-1
12	Alvechurch v Evesham United	2-0
	Bilston v Halesowen Town	2-3
	Burton Albion v Coventry Sporting	3-1
	Hednesford Town v Bedworth United	1-1
13	Darlaston v Tamworth	1-2
	Gresley Rovers v Racing Club Warwick	1-1
	Kidderminster Harriers v Shepshed Charterhouse	1-2
	Oldbury United v Willenhall Town	0-2
14	Bromsgrove Rovers v Blakenall	2-0
	Dudley Town v Malvern Town	0-2
	Highgate United v Kempston Rovers	2-2
	Sutton Coldfield Town v Buckingham Town	2-1
15	Lye Town v Wellingborough Town	2-1
	Nuneaton Borough v Rushden Town	6-0
	Tividale v Walsall Wood	3-0
	V.S. Rugby v Wolverton Town	5-0
16	Cambridge City v Bury Town	1-1
	Great Yarmouth Town v Parson Drove United	3-2
	King's Lynn v Thetford Town	0-0
	Lowestoft Town v Stamford	1-0
17	Harwich & Parkeston v Wisbech Town	1-2
	Heybridge Swifts v Gorleston	2-1
	March Town United v St Neots Town	1-0
	Newmarket Town v Letchworth Garden City	1-0
18	Barton Rovers v Haverhill Rovers	1-0
	Chatteris Town v Ely City	3-3
	Clacton Town v Ware	1-0
	Potton United v Bedford Town (1)	1-1
19	Basildon United v Walthamstow Avenue	1-2
	St Albans City v Grays Athletic	2-1
	Stowmarket v Leyton-Wingate	2-3
	Sudbury Town v Dunstable	1-1
20	Ampthill Town v Hendon	0-1
	Banbury United v Hemel Hempstead Town	2-1
	Irthlingborough Diamonds v Chesham United	1-0
	Rothwell Town v Tring Town	1-3
21	Bracknell Town v Wokingham Town	1-2
	Hitchin Town v Southall	1-2
	Slough Town v Chalfont St Peter	2-1
	Witney Town v Didcot Town	3-0
22	Aylesbury United v Feltham	0-1
	Berkhamsted Town v Hampton	0-3
	Edgware Town v Thame United	1-3
	Kingstonian v Boreham Wood	2-0
23	Aveley v Welling United	1-1
	Cray Wanderers v Billericay Town	0-4
	Erith & Belvedere v Leytonstone/Ilford	2-2
	Hornchurch v Woodford Town (1)	0-0
24	Camberley Town v Newbury Town	0-2
	Egham Town v Maidenhead United	1-2
	Harrow Borough v Oxford City	4-2
	Wealdstone v Salisbury (2)	4-0
25	Corinthian Casuals v Clapton	3-3
	Finchley v Sittingbourne	4-3
	Hayes v Tilbury	1-1
	Redhill v Hertford Town	1-2
26	Andover v Pagham	1-2
	Banstead Athletic v Horsham	2-0
	Farnborough Town v Horndean	5-0
	Wick v Woking	2-1
27	Crawley Town v Burgess Hill Town	0-1
	Littlehampton Town v Carshalton Athletic	0-3
	Uxbridge v Peacehaven & Telscombe	2-2
	Windsor & Eton v Walton & Hersham	3-4
28	Addlestone & Weybridge T v Ruislip Manor	3-1
	Bromley v Fareham Town	0-5
	Steyning Town v Dulwich Hamlet	1-1
	Worthing v Bognor Regis Town	0-0
29	Basingstoke Town v Tooting & Mitcham United	2-1
	Cheshunt v Lewes	2-2
	Hillingdon Borough v Tunbridge Wells	7-2
	Wembley v East Grinstead	2-1
30	Croydon v Bexhill Town	wo/s
	Eastbourne Town v Canterbury City	0-2
	Epsom & Ewell v Herne Bay	2-1
	Hastings United v Faversham Town	5-0
31	Ashford Town v Hastings Town	1-0
	Dover v Folkestone	4-1
	Thanet United v Deal Town	2-2
	Tonbridge v Whitstable Town	3-1
32	Eastleigh v Poole Town	2-1
	Frome Town v Trowbridge Town	2-1
	Gosport Borough v Melksham Town	0-1
	Hungerford Town v Dorchester Town	1-2
33	Calne Town v Bridgend Town	1-2
	Devizes Town v Shepton Mallet Town	1-0
	Gloucester City v Forest Green Rovers	2-1
	Worcester City v Moreton Town	5-2
34	Bath City v Mangotsfield United	3-0
	Cheltenham Town v Barry Town	4-0
	Clevedon Town v Welton Rovers	3-1
	Llanelli v Haverfordwest County	1-2
35	Bridgwater Town (1) v Wellington (Somerset)	2-0
	Bridport v Liskeard Athletic	2-2
	Glastonbury v Weston-Super-Mare	3-1
	Taunton Town v Saltash United	1-0
36	Bideford v St Blazey	4-1
	Chard Town v Barnstaple Town	1-2
	Falmouth Town v Newquay	2-0
	Ilminster Town v Torrington	0-2
2r	Brandon United v Horden CW	1-3
3r	Chester-le-Street Town v Ferryhill Athletic	2-1
r	Spennymoor United v Gateshead (2)	3-0
5r	Curzon Ashton v Brigg Town	4-1
6r	Accrington Stanley (2) v Chorley	0-0
7r	Hyde United v Fleetwood Town	2-1
r	Lytham v Ashton United	3-1
9r	Shifnal Town v Matlock Town	2-0
10r	Gainsborough Trinity v Boston	1-2
12r	Bedworth United v Hednesford Town	3-0
13r	Racing Club Warwick v Gresley Rovers	1-3
14r	Kempston Rovers v Highgate United	1-2
16r	Bury Town v Cambridge City	1-1
r	Thetford Town v King's Lynn	0-1
18r	Bedford Town (1) v Potton United	4-1
r	Ely City v Chatteris Town	2-1
19r	Dunstable v Sudbury Town	3-1
23r	Leytonstone/Ilford v Erith & Belvedere	3-0
r	Welling United v Aveley	1-1
r	Woodford Town (1) v Hornchurch	2-1e
25r	Clapton v Corinthian Casuals	1-2e
r	Tilbury v Hayes	0-0
27r	Peacehaven & Telscombe v Uxbridge	1-3
28r	Bognor Regis Town v Worthing	1-0
r	Dulwich Hamlet v Steyning Town	3-0
29r	Lewes v Cheshunt	3-3
31r	Deal Town v Thanet United	2-1
35r	Liskeard Athletic v Bridport	3-1
6r2	Chorley v Accrington Stanley (2)	4-0
16r2	Cambridge City v Bury Town	1-2
23r2	Aveley v Welling United	0-0
25r2	Hayes v Tilbury	0-0
29r2	Cheshunt v Lewes	0-2
23r3	Welling United v Aveley	3-2
25r3	Tilbury v Hayes	1-1
25r4	Hayes v Tilbury	4-0

Qualifying Round Two

1	South Bank v Durham City	4-1
	Whitley Bay v Consett	1-0
2	Lancaster City v Ashington	1-3
	Tow Law Town v Horden CW	1-4
3	Chester-le-Street Town v Spennymoor United	1-1
	Seaham Red Star v North Shields	0-1
4	Emley v Bishop Auckland	1-4
	Goole Town v Frickley Athletic	2-3
5	Bridlington Trinity v Curzon Ashton	0-1
	Buxton v Stalybridge Celtic	1-0
6	Chorley v Penrith	0-1
	Netherfield (Kendal) v Droylsden	1-1
7	Horwich RMI v Hyde United	0-4
	Marine v Lytham	0-0
8	Caernarfon Town v Bangor City	3-2
	Telford United v Burscough	3-0
9	Prescot Cables v Nantwich Town	1-1
	Shifnal Town v Runcorn	0-3
10	Boston v North Ferriby United	1-2
	Boston United v Alfreton Town	2-0
11	Grantham v Corby Town	0-1
	Worksop Town v Ilkeston Town (2)	2-3
12	Bedworth United v Alvechurch	0-1
	Halesowen Town v Burton Albion	0-0
13	Gresley Rovers v Willenhall Town	3-3
	Tamworth v Shepshed Charterhouse	2-2
14	Bromsgrove Rovers v Sutton Coldfield Town	1-0
	Malvern Town v Highgate United	2-1
15	Lye Town v Nuneaton Borough	1-2
	Tividale v V.S. Rugby	2-2
16	Bury Town v King's Lynn	0-5
	Great Yarmouth Town v Lowestoft Town	3-1
17	Heybridge Swifts v Wisbech Town	2-2
	March Town United v Newmarket Town	5-5
18	Bedford Town (1) v Barton Rovers	2-0
	Ely City v Clacton Town	2-1
19	Dunstable v Walthamstow Avenue	3-2
	Leyton-Wingate v St Albans City	2-2
20	Hendon v Banbury United	2-2
	Irthlingborough Diamonds v Tring Town	1-1
21	Slough Town v Wokingham Town	1-5
	Witney Town v Southall	4-1
22	Kingstonian v Hampton	1-0
	Thame United v Feltham	1-1
23	Billericay Town v Welling United	3-1
	Leytonstone/Ilford v Woodford Town (1)	2-1
24	Maidenhead United v Harrow Borough	0-2
	Newbury Town v Wealdstone	1-6
25	Corinthian Casuals v Hayes	2-1
	Hertford Town v Finchley	4-3
26	Pagham v Banstead Athletic	2-2
	Wick v Farnborough Town	2-2
27	Burgess Hill Town v Walton & Hersham	2-1
	Uxbridge v Carshalton Athletic	0-3
28	Bognor Regis Town v Addlestone & Weybridge T	0-0
	Dulwich Hamlet v Fareham Town	1-2
29	Basingstoke Town v Hillingdon Borough	4-2
	Lewes v Wembley	1-2
30	Croydon v Epsom & Ewell	1-1
	Hastings United v Canterbury City	4-1
31	Deal Town v Ashford Town	1-2
	Tonbridge v Dover	2-2
32	Dorchester Town v Frome Town	3-0
	Eastleigh v Melksham Town	3-1
33	Bridgend Town v Worcester City	1-3
	Gloucester City v Devizes Town	2-4
34	Cheltenham Town v Bath City	2-2
	Haverfordwest County v Clevedon Town	3-2
35	Bridgwater Town (1) v Taunton Town	1-1
	Liskeard Athletic v Glastonbury	2-0
36	Barnstaple Town v Bideford	0-1
	Falmouth Town v Torrington	1-0
3r	Spennymoor United v Chester-le-Street Town	1-0
6r	Droylsden v Netherfield (Kendal)	3-1e
7r	Lytham v Marine	2-6
9r	Nantwich Town v Prescot Cables	0-1
12r	Burton Albion v Halesowen Town	2-0
13r	Shepshed Charterhouse v Tamworth	2-0
r	Willenhall Town v Gresley Rovers	3-1
15r	V.S. Rugby v Tividale	0-2
17r	Newmarket Town v March Town United	0-2
r	Wisbech Town v Heybridge Swifts	2-1e
19r	St Albans City v Leyton-Wingate	4-1
20r	Banbury United v Hendon	3-4e
r	Tring Town v Irthlingborough Diamonds	1-0
22r	Feltham v Thame United	1-2e
26r	Banstead Athletic v Pagham	7-1
r	Farnborough Town v Wick	3-0
28r	Addlestone & Weybridge T v Bognor Regis Town	2-0
30r	Epsom & Ewell v Croydon	4-0
31r	Dover v Tonbridge	5-2e
34r	Bath City v Cheltenham Town	1-2
35r	Taunton Town v Bridgwater Town (1)	1-0

Qualifying Round Three

1	Whitley Bay v South Bank	0-2
2	Horden CW v Ashington	0-0
3	Spennymoor United v North Shields	2-2
4	Bishop Auckland v Frickley Athletic	3-0
5	Buxton v Curzon Ashton	4-1
6	Penrith v Droylsden	3-2
7	Hyde United v Marine	3-1
8	Telford United v Caernarfon Town	1-2
9	Runcorn v Prescot Cables	4-1
10	Boston United v North Ferriby United	4-0
11	Corby Town v Ilkeston Town (2)	8-1
12	Burton Albion v Alvechurch	2-0
13	Shepshed Charterhouse v Willenhall Town	1-5
14	Bromsgrove Rovers v Malvern Town	4-1
15	Nuneaton Borough v Tividale	5-2
16	King's Lynn v Great Yarmouth Town	5-1
17	Wisbech Town v March Town United	2-1
18	Bedford Town (1) v Ely City	1-0
19	St Albans City v Dunstable	1-5
20	Hendon v Tring Town	4-0
21	Witney Town v Wokingham Town	2-0
22	Thame United v Kingstonian	1-2
23	Billericay Town v Leytonstone/Ilford	0-0
24	Wealdstone v Harrow Borough	1-4
25	Corinthian Casuals v Hertford Town	2-0
26	Farnborough Town v Banstead Athletic	4-0
27	Burgess Hill Town v Carshalton Athletic	1-5
28	Addlestone & Weybridge T v Fareham Town	2-0
29	Wembley v Basingstoke Town	5-1
30	Epsom & Ewell v Hastings United	2-4

1981/82 to 1982/83

31 Dover v Ashford Town	2-1
32 Eastleigh v Dorchester Town	2-4
33 Worcester City v Devizes Town	4-1
34 Cheltenham Town v Haverfordwest County	4-0
35 Taunton Town v Liskeard Athletic	2-1
36 Bideford v Falmouth Town	1-0
2r Ashington v Horden CW	1-3e
3r North Shields v Spennymoor United	1-5
23r Leytonstone/Ilford v Billericay Town	1-0

Qualifying Round Four

Addlestone & Weybridge T v Taunton Town	2-2
Barnet v Corinthian Casuals	2-0
Bedford Town (1) v Wisbech Town	3-0
Bideford v Kingstonian	1-0
Boston United v Dunstable	3-1
Caernarfon Town v Bishop Auckland	0-2
Cheltenham Town v Dorchester Town	1-3
Dover v Leatherhead	1-1
Gravesend & Northfleet v Dagenham	0-0
Harlow Town v Corby Town	1-0
Hastings United v Wembley	2-0
Hendon v Harrow Borough	2-1
Horden CW v Hyde United	2-0
Kettering Town v King's Lynn	2-1
Leytonstone/Ilford v Carshalton Athletic	2-0
Maidstone United v Barking	0-1
Minehead v Worcester City	1-0
Nuneaton Borough v Bromsgrove Rovers	2-1
Penrith v Northwich Victoria	1-0
Scarborough v Blyth Spartans	2-3
South Bank v Mossley	0-1
Spennymoor United v Runcorn	0-1
Stafford Rangers v AP Leamington	3-0
Weymouth v Farnborough Town	3-0
Willenhall Town v Burton Albion	2-1
Witney Town v Wycombe Wanderers	0-1
Workington v Buxton	4-1
Yeovil Town v Merthyr Tydfil	3-0
r Dagenham v Gravesend & Northfleet	6-3
r Leatherhead v Dover	0-1
r Taunton Town v Addlestone & Weybridge T	0-0
r2 Taunton Town v Addlestone & Weybridge T	4-2

Round One

Aldershot v Leytonstone/Ilford	2-0
Bedford Town (1) v Wimbledon	0-2
Bideford v Barking	1-2
Bishop Auckland v Nuneaton Borough	4-1
Bishop's Stortford v Sutton United	2-2
Blyth Spartans v Walsall	1-2
Boston United v Kettering Town	0-1
Bournemouth v Reading	1-0
Brentford v Exeter City	2-0
Bristol City v Torquay United	0-0
Bristol Rovers v Fulham	1-2
Burnley v Runcorn	0-0
Chesterfield v Preston North End	4-1
Colchester United v Newport County	2-0
Dagenham v Yeovil Town	2-2
Darlington v Carlisle United	2-2
Dorchester Town v Minehead	3-3
Dover v Oxford United	0-2
Enfield v Hastings United	2-0
Halifax Town v Peterborough United	0-3
Harlow Town v Barnet	0-0
Hendon v Wycombe Wanderers	1-1
Hereford United v Southend United	3-1
Horden CW v Blackpool	0-1 N
Lincoln City v Port Vale	2-2
Mansfield Town v Doncaster Rovers	0-1
Penrith v Chester	1-0
Plymouth Argyle v Gillingham	0-0
Portsmouth v Millwall	1-1
Rochdale v Hull City	2-2
Scunthorpe United v Bradford City	1-0
Sheffield United v Altrincham	2-2
Stafford Rangers v York City	1-2
Stockport County v Mossley	3-1
Swindon Town v Taunton Town	2-1
Tranmere Rovers v Bury	1-1
Weymouth v Northampton Town	0-0
Wigan Athletic v Hartlepool United	2-2
Willenhall Town v Crewe Alexandra	0-1
Workington v Huddersfield Town	1-1
r Altrincham v Sheffield United	3-0
r Barnet v Harlow Town	1-0
r Bury v Tranmere Rovers	3-1
r Carlisle United v Darlington	3-1
r Gillingham v Plymouth Argyle	1-0
r Hartlepool United v Wigan Athletic	1-0
r Huddersfield Town v Workington	5-0
r Hull City v Rochdale	2-2e
r Millwall v Portsmouth	3-2e
r Minehead v Dorchester Town	0-4
r Northampton Town v Weymouth	6-2
r Port Vale v Lincoln City	0-0e
r Runcorn v Burnley	1-2
r Sutton United v Bishop's Stortford	2-1
r Torquay United v Bristol City	1-2
r Wycombe Wanderers v Hendon	2-0
r Yeovil Town v Dagenham	0-1e

r2 Hull City v Rochdale	1-0eN
r2 Port Vale v Lincoln City	2-0

Round Two

Aldershot v Oxford United	2-2
Barnet v Wycombe Wanderers	2-0
Brentford v Colchester United	1-1
Bristol City v Northampton Town	3-0
Bury v Burnley	1-1
Carlisle United v Bishop Auckland	1-0 N
Chesterfield v Huddersfield Town	0-1
Crewe Alexandra v Scunthorpe United	1-3
Dagenham v Millwall	1-2
Doncaster Rovers v Penrith	3-0
Dorchester Town v Bournemouth	1-1
Enfield v Wimbledon	4-1
Gillingham v Barking	1-1
Hereford United v Fulham	1-0
Hull City v Hartlepool United	2-0
Kettering Town v Blackpool	0-3
Peterborough United v Walsall	2-1
Port Vale v Stockport County	4-1
Swindon Town v Sutton United	2-1
York City v Altrincham	0-0
r Altrincham v York City	4-3
r Bournemouth v Dorchester Town	2-1e
r Burnley v Bury	2-1e
r Colchester United v Brentford	1-0
r Gillingham v Barking	3-1e
r Oxford United v Aldershot	4-2

Round Three

Barnet v Brighton & Hove Albion	0-0
Barnsley v Blackpool	0-2
Birmingham City v Ipswich Town	2-3
Bolton Wanderers v Derby County	3-1
Bournemouth v Oxford United	0-2
Burnley v Altrincham	6-1
Carlisle United v Huddersfield Town	2-3
Chelsea v Hull City	0-0
Coventry City v Sheffield Wednesday	3-1
Doncaster Rovers v Cambridge United	2-1
Enfield v Crystal Palace	2-3
Gillingham v Oldham Athletic	2-1
Leicester City v Southampton	3-1
Luton Town v Swindon Town	2-1
Manchester City v Cardiff City	3-1
Millwall v Grimsby Town	1-6
Newcastle United v Colchester United	1-1
Nottingham Forest v Wrexham	1-3
Notts County v Aston Villa	0-6
Orient v Charlton Athletic	1-0
Peterborough United v Bristol City	0-1
Queen's Park Rangers v Middlesbrough	1-1
Rotherham United v Sunderland	1-1
Scunthorpe United v Hereford United	1-1
Shrewsbury Town v Port Vale	1-0
Stoke City v Norwich City	0-1
Swansea City v Liverpool	0-4
Tottenham Hotspur v Arsenal	1-0
Watford v Manchester United	1-0
West Bromwich Albion v Blackburn Rovers	3-2
West Ham United v Everton	2-1
Wolverhampton Wan. v Leeds United	1-3
r Brighton & Hove Albion v Barnet	3-1
r Colchester United v Newcastle United	3-4e
r Hereford United v Scunthorpe United	4-1
r Hull City v Chelsea	0-2
r Middlesbrough v Queen's Park Rangers	2-3e
r Sunderland v Rotherham United	1-0

Round Four

Blackpool v Queen's Park Rangers	0-0
Brighton & Hove Albion v Oxford United	0-3
Bristol City v Aston Villa	0-1
Chelsea v Wrexham	0-0
Crystal Palace v Bolton Wanderers	1-0
Gillingham v West Bromwich Albion	0-1
Hereford United v Leicester City	0-1
Huddersfield Town v Orient	1-1
Luton Town v Ipswich Town	0-3
Manchester City v Coventry City	1-3
Newcastle United v Grimsby Town	1-2
Norwich City v Doncaster Rovers	2-1
Shrewsbury Town v Burnley	1-0
Sunderland v Liverpool	0-3
Tottenham Hotspur v Leeds United	1-0
Watford v West Ham United	2-0
r Orient v Huddersfield Town	2-0
r Queen's Park Rangers v Blackpool	5-1
r Wrexham v Chelsea	1-1e
r2 Wrexham v Chelsea	1-2

Round Five

Chelsea v Liverpool	2-0
Coventry City v Oxford United	4-0
Crystal Palace v Orient	0-0
Leicester City v Watford	2-0
Queen's Park Rangers v Grimsby Town	3-1
Shrewsbury Town v Ipswich Town	2-1

Tottenham Hotspur v Aston Villa	1-0
West Bromwich Albion v Norwich City	1-0
r Orient v Crystal Palace	0-1

Round Six

Chelsea v Tottenham Hotspur	2-3
Leicester City v Shrewsbury Town	5-2
Queen's Park Rangers v Crystal Palace	1-0
West Bromwich Albion v Coventry City	2-0

Semi Finals

Queen's Park Rangers v West Bromwich Albion	1-0 N
Tottenham Hotspur v Leicester City	2-0 N

Final

Tottenham Hotspur v Queen's Park Rangers	1-1eN
r Tottenham Hotspur v Queen's Park Rangers	1-0 N

1982/83

Preliminary Round

1 Barrow v Crook Town	2-0
Consett v Lancaster City	0-3
2 Bridlington Trinity v Whitley Bay	3-1
Gateshead (2) v Durham City	1-1
3 Ashington v Chester-le-Street Town	2-2
Morecambe v Whitby Town	2-0
4 Frickley Athletic v Shildon	5-3
Harrogate Town v West Auckland Town	3-0
5 South Liverpool v Horwich RMI	1-4
Stalybridge Celtic v Burscough	1-1
6 Chorley v Formby	5-0
Lytham v Southport	1-2
7 Bootle v Droylsden	3-0
Clitheroe v Leyland Motors	0-1
8 Gresley Rovers v Worksop Town	2-4
Skelmersdale United v Prestwich Heys	0-4
9 Winsford United v Blakenall	1-2
Witton Albion v Ilkeston Town (2)	2-0
10 Denaby United v Shepshed Charterhouse	1-3
Goole Town v North Ferriby United	1-0
11 Arnold v Hinckley Athletic	0-1
Boston v Bourne Town	1-3
12 Long Eaton United v Wednesfield Social	1-0
Matlock Town v Dudley Town	0-2
Sutton Town v Heanor Town	2-1
13 Friar Lane Old Boys v Milton Keynes City	1-1
Lye Town v Bridgnorth Town	0-2
Malvern Town v Racing Club Warwick	0-0
14 Highgate United v Chipping Norton Town	3-0
Sutton Coldfield Town v Walsall Borough	4-2
15 Buckingham Town v Desborough Town	1-0
Kidderminster Harriers v Redditch United	0-0
16 Cambridge City v March Town United	0-0
Spalding United v Irthlingborough Diamonds	0-1
17 Great Yarmouth Town v Ampthill Town	2-0
Wellingborough Town v Basildon United	5-2
18 Haverhill Rovers v Epping Town	3-0
Heybridge Swifts v Thetford Town	1-0
Wootton Blue Cross v Kempston Rovers	2-0
19 Saffron Walden Town v Ruislip Manor	5-2
20 Barton Rovers v Cheshunt	2-0
Chelmsford City v Finchley	3-1
21 Chalfont St Peter v Rainham Town	2-1
Hounslow v Cray Wanderers	2-5
22 Berkhamsted Town v Dulwich Hamlet	3-3
Hemel Hempstead Town v Hillingdon Borough	0-0
23 Abingdon Town v Aylesbury United	3-2
Harefield United v Croydon	0-4
24 Dorking Town v Arundel	2-1
Wokingham Town v Andover	6-1
25 Metropolitan Police v Sittingbourne	1-2
Woking v Chatham Town	0-0
26 Ashford Town v Sheppey United	0-2
Faversham Town v Peacehaven & Telscombe	2-0
27 Tooting & Mitcham United v Molesey	3-1
Tunbridge Wells v Canterbury City	0-3
28 Chertsey Town v Bromley	1-12
Herne Bay v Bognor Regis Town	0-1
29 Dartford v Whitehawk	5-2
Epsom & Ewell v Walton & Hersham	1-2
30 Littlehampton Town v Newport (IOW)	0-3
Worthing v Fleet Town	7-1
31 AFC Totton v Marlow	1-0
Waterlooville v Bracknell Town	1-2
32 Poole Town v Basingstoke Town	0-0
Salisbury (2) v Calne Town	3-2
33 Moreton Town v Ton Pentre	2-2
Paulton Rovers v Bristol Manor Farm	0-2
34 Barry Town v Haverfordwest County	2-0
Cinderford Town v Melksham Town	3-0
Mangotsfield United v Newbury Town	3-2
35 Bridport v Wimborne Town	2-3
St Blazey v Clandown	3-1
36 Liskeard Athletic v Ottery St Mary	1-0
Penzance v Wellington (Somerset)	2-1
2r Durham City v Gateshead (2)	2-2
3r Chester-le-Street Town v Ashington	2-1

165

1982/83

5r	Burscough v Stalybridge Celtic	4-1
13r	Milton Keynes City v Friar Lane Old Boys	1-4e
r	Racing Club Warwick v Malvern Town	4-3
15r	Redditch United v Kidderminster Harriers	2-3
16r	March Town United v Cambridge City	3-2
22r	Dulwich Hamlet v Berkhamsted Town	6-0
r	Hillingdon Borough v Hemel Hempstead Town	0-1
25r	Chatham Town v Woking	2-1
32r	Basingstoke Town v Poole Town	2-0
33r	Ton Pentre v Moreton Town	4-1
2r2	Gateshead (2) v Durham City	2-1 N

Qualifying Round One

1	Ferryhill Athletic v Barrow	0-1
	Newcastle Blue Star v Lancaster City	1-2
	Wingate (Durham) v Annfield Plain	1-3
	Yorkshire Amateur v Bishop Auckland	0-1
2	Evenwood Town v Horden CW	1-3
	Farsley Celtic v Bridlington Trinity	3-0
	North Shields v Eppleton CW	6-0
	Peterlee Newtown v Gateshead (2)	1-2
3	Emley v South Bank	3-6
	Guisborough Town v Chester-le-Street Town	0-0
	Tow Law Town v Morecambe	3-5
	Willington v Brandon United	0-5
4	Accrington Stanley (2) v Harrogate Town	1-1
	Billingham Synthonia v Seaham Red Star	0-1
	Fleetwood Town v Spennymoor United	1-2
	Netherfield (Kendal) v Frickley Athletic	0-2
5	Colwyn Bay v Caernarfon Town	0-3
	New Mills v Horwich RMI	0-3
	Oswestry Town v Burscough	2-1
	Prescot Cables v Marine	2-1
6	Curzon Ashton v Rhyl	4-1
	Darwen v Southport	2-0
	Rossendale United v Chorley	0-3
	Thackley v Runcorn	0-0
7	Ashton United v Leyland Motors	6-2
	Macclesfield Town v Bangor City	3-1
	Ossett Albion v Hyde United	1-2
	St Helens Town v Bootle	0-4
8	Eastwood Town v Prestwich Heys	4-2
	Glossop v Worksop Town	2-5
	Hednesford Town v Congleton Town	1-2
	Telford United v Buxton	3-0
9	Bilston v Blakenall	2-2
	Nantwich Town v Witton Albion	0-3
	Oldbury United v Burton Albion	0-0
	Shifnal Town v Leek Town	1-0
10	Alfreton Town v Shepshed Charterhouse	0-4
	Brigg Town v Goole Town	1-1
	Gainsborough Trinity v Appleby Frodingham Ath.	2-2
	Stamford v Nuneaton Borough	1-1
11	Armitage v Willenhall Town	3-2
	Belper Town v Mexborough Town Athletic	1-1
	Grantham v Hinckley Athletic	2-0
	Winterton Rangers v Bourne Town	4-3
12	Holbeach United v Long Eaton United	3-1
	Moor Green v Sutton Town	4-0
	Rushall Olympic v Dudley Town	1-1
	Tividale v Bromsgrove Rovers	0-1
13	Coventry Sporting v AP Leamington	0-4
	Rushden Town v Bridgnorth Town	0-2
	Stourbridge v Friar Lane Old Boys	3-0
	Tamworth v Racing Club Warwick	2-1
14	Alvechurch v Worcester City	2-4
	Enderby Town v Sutton Coldfield Town	1-4
	Rothwell Town v Darlaston	3-1
	V.S. Rugby v Highgate United	3-1
15	Banbury United v Kidderminster Harriers	0-2
	Flackwell Heath v Bedworth United	0-1
	Halesowen Town v Corby Town	1-2
	Mile Oak Rovers & Youth v Buckingham Town	2-0
16	Ely City v Lowestoft Town	1-3
	Felixstowe Town v Irthlingborough Diamonds	1-1
	Gorleston v King's Lynn	2-3
	Skegness Town v March Town United	3-0
17	Billericay Town v Wisbech Town	3-1
	Chatteris Town v Great Yarmouth Town	1-6
	Hitchin Town v Wellingborough Town	0-4
	Ware v Soham Town Rangers	1-1
18	Aveley v Haverhill Rovers	5-0
	Edgware Town v Bedford Town (1)	wo/s
	Walthamstow Avenue v Wootton Blue Cross	2-0
	Woodford Town (1) v Heybridge Swifts	3-1
19	Hayes v Saffron Walden Town	2-1
	Hornchurch v Harwich & Parkeston	1-0
	Newmarket Town v Boreham Wood	0-3
	Tring Town v Dunstable	1-0
20	Grays Athletic v Barton Rovers	1-0
	Royston Town v Leytonstone/Ilford	0-5
	Sudbury Town v Chelmsford City	1-1
	Tilbury v Stowmarket	3-2
21	Chesham United v Cray Wanderers	3-2
	Clapton v Chalfont St Peter	3-1
	Feltham v Tiptree United	3-0
	Letchworth Garden City v Harrow Borough	0-6
22	Haringey Borough v Hemel Hempstead Town	0-3
	Leyton-Wingate v Dulwich Hamlet	2-2
	Merstham v Hendon	0-2
	Wealdstone v Hertford Town	5-0
23	Erith & Belvedere v Wembley	1-2
	Hampton v Croydon	2-0
	Hoddesdon Town v Windsor & Eton	0-2
	St Albans City v Abingdon Town	4-1
24	Dorking Town v Staines Town	0-5
	Horsham v Kingstonian	0-3
	Three Bridges v Uxbridge	0-0
	Whyteleafe v Wokingham Town	0-0
25	Folkestone v Burnham (1)	2-0
	Hastings Town v Chatham Town	2-7
	Ringmer v Addlestone & Weybridge T	2-1
	Southall v Sittingbourne	1-1
26	Egham Town v Faversham Town	0-0
	Horley Town v Carshalton Athletic	1-2
	Southwick v Banstead Athletic	2-2
	Welling United v Sheppey United	2-0
27	Burgess Hill Town v Canterbury City	2-2
	Deal Town v Redhill	3-1
	Lewes v Tooting & Mitcham United	2-3
	Steyning Town v Dover	3-4
28	Eastbourne Town v Bognor Regis Town	1-3
	Hailsham Town v Thanet United	0-3
	Pagham v Hastings United	1-3
	Whitstable Town v Bromley	1-0
29	Haywards Heath v Dartford	1-6
	Horsham YMCA v Ramsgate	1-1
	Tonbridge v Walton & Hersham	2-0
	Wick v Corinthian Casuals	1-2
30	Crawley Town v Worthing	1-2
	Eastleigh v Newport (IOW)	2-2
	Fareham Town v Farnborough Town	2-3
	Horndean v Eastbourne United	1-1
31	Brockenhurst v AFC Totton	1-2
	Gosport Borough v Bracknell Town	1-0
	Maidenhead United v Chichester City (1)	4-2
	Oxford City v Dorchester Town	2-2
32	Chippenham Town v Basingstoke Town	1-1
	Devizes Town v Camberley Town	1-0
	Frome Town v Witney Town	1-1
	Slough Town v Salisbury (2)	2-0
33	Gloucester City v Llanelli	1-0
	Thame United v Cheltenham Town	2-3
	Trowbridge Town v Ton Pentre	2-0
	Welton Rovers v Bristol Manor Farm	0-0
34	Bridgend Town v Cinderford Town	2-1
	Bridgwater Town (1) v Mangotsfield United	1-1
	Forest Green Rovers v Barry Town	2-3
	Hungerford Town v Merthyr Tydfil	0-3
35	Bath City v Taunton Town	2-2
	Clevedon Town v St Blazey	0-2
	Falmouth Town v Wimborne Town	1-2
	Glastonbury v Barnstaple Town	1-1
36	Chard Town v Penzance	2-1
	Shepton Mallet Town v Torrington	3-0
	Tiverton Town v Liskeard Athletic	2-2
	Weston-Super-Mare v Bideford	1-4
3r	Chester-le-Street Town v Guisborough Town	3-0
4r	Harrogate Town v Accrington Stanley (2)	3-1
6r	Runcorn v Thackley	2-1
9r	Blakenall v Bilston	1-2e
r	Burton Albion v Oldbury United	1-0
10r	Appleby Frodingham Ath. v Gainsborough Trinity	0-0
r	Goole Town v Brigg Town	7-2
r	Nuneaton Borough v Stamford	5-0
11r	Mexborough Town Athletic v Belper Town	0-3
12r	Dudley Town v Rushall Olympic	0-1
16r	Irthlingborough Diamonds v Felixstowe Town	3-1
17r	Soham Town Rangers v Ware	4-2
20r	Chelmsford City v Sudbury Town	3-1
22r	Dulwich Hamlet v Leyton-Wingate	2-0
24r	Uxbridge v Three Bridges	1-2e
r	Wokingham Town v Whyteleafe	1-0e
25r	Sittingbourne v Southall	1-3
26r	Banstead Athletic v Southwick	0-1
r	Faversham Town v Egham Town	1-3
27r	Canterbury City v Burgess Hill Town	2-1e
29r	Ramsgate v Horsham YMCA	2-1
30r	Eastbourne United v Horndean	3-2
r	Newport (IOW) v Eastleigh	1-3e
31r	Dorchester Town v Oxford City	1-0
32r	Basingstoke Town v Chippenham Town	3-2
r	Witney Town v Frome Town	2-2
33r	Bristol Manor Farm v Welton Rovers	1-0
34r	Mangotsfield United v Bridgwater Town (1)	1-2
35r	Barnstaple Town v Glastonbury	4-1
r	Taunton Town v Bath City	2-4e
36r	Liskeard Athletic v Tiverton Town	2-1
10r2	Gainsborough Trinity v Appleby Frodingham Ath.	2-1
32r2	Frome Town v Witney Town	2-1

Qualifying Round Two

1	Bishop Auckland v Annfield Plain	2-3
	Lancaster City v Barrow	0-0
2	Gateshead (2) v Farsley Celtic	5-1
	Horden CW v North Shields	0-1
3	Chester-le-Street Town v Morecambe	1-5
	South Bank v Brandon United	2-1
4	Frickley Athletic v Harrogate Town	3-1
	Spennymoor United v Seaham Red Star	2-1
5	Caernarfon Town v Prescot Cables	4-1
	Horwich RMI v Oswestry Town	5-1
6	Chorley v Darwen	0-0
	Runcorn v Curzon Ashton	3-0
7	Ashton United v Bootle	0-0
	Hyde United v Macclesfield Town	2-5
8	Telford United v Congleton Town	3-2
	Worksop Town v Eastwood Town	1-1
9	Burton Albion v Shifnal Town	2-4
	Witton Albion v Bilston	4-2
10	Goole Town v Shepshed Charterhouse	0-2
	Nuneaton Borough v Gainsborough Trinity	3-3
11	Armitage v Belper Town	1-1
	Winterton Rangers v Grantham	0-0
12	Bromsgrove Rovers v Moor Green	2-2
	Holbeach United v Rushall Olympic	1-0
13	AP Leamington v Bridgnorth Town	6-1
	Stourbridge v Tamworth	3-2
14	Sutton Coldfield Town v V.S. Rugby	2-1
	Worcester City v Rothwell Town	3-1
15	Corby Town v Bedworth United	1-0
	Mile Oak Rovers & Youth v Kidderminster Harriers	2-7
16	King's Lynn v Lowestoft Town	2-1
	Skegness Town v Irthlingborough Diamonds	0-0
17	Billericay Town v Soham Town Rangers	5-3
	Great Yarmouth Town v Wellingborough Town	1-1
18	Aveley v Walthamstow Avenue	1-3
	Edgware Town v Woodford Town (1)	0-1
19	Boreham Wood v Hayes	3-0
	Tring Town v Hornchurch	2-2
20	Chelmsford City v Grays Athletic	3-2
	Leytonstone/Ilford v Tilbury	1-1
21	Chesham United v Clapton	3-1
	Harrow Borough v Feltham	2-3
22	Hemel Hempstead Town v Dulwich Hamlet	1-2
	Hendon v Wealdstone	1-1
23	St Albans City v Hampton	1-3
	Wembley v Windsor & Eton	1-3
24	Kingstonian v Three Bridges	4-3
	Wokingham Town v Staines Town	2-0
25	Ringmer v Folkestone	0-2
	Southall v Chatham Town	2-2
26	Carshalton Athletic v Southwick	3-1
	Egham Town v Welling United	2-0
27	Dover v Deal Town	0-3
	Tooting & Mitcham United v Canterbury City	2-0
28	Hastings United v Thanet United	1-2
	Whitstable Town v Bognor Regis Town	0-3
29	Corinthian Casuals v Ramsgate	1-0 N
	Tonbridge v Dartford	2-3
30	Farnborough Town v Eastbourne United	2-1
	Worthing v Eastleigh	3-1
31	Dorchester Town v Maidenhead United	1-1
	Gosport Borough v AFC Totton	2-2
32	Basingstoke Town v Slough Town	2-2
	Frome Town v Devizes Town	4-2
33	Cheltenham Town v Gloucester City	5-1
	Trowbridge Town v Bristol Manor Farm	3-0
34	Bridgend Town v Bridgwater Town (1)	1-0
	Merthyr Tydfil v Barry Town	3-1
35	Bath City v Barnstaple Town	4-2
	Wimborne Town v St Blazey	3-2
36	Bideford v Shepton Mallet Town	3-1
	Liskeard Athletic v Chard Town	3-1
1r	Barrow v Lancaster City	1-0
6r	Darwen v Chorley	0-3
7r	Bootle v Ashton United	0-1
8r	Eastwood Town v Worksop Town	3-1
10r	Gainsborough Trinity v Nuneaton Borough	2-0
11r	Belper Town v Armitage	0-1
r	Grantham v Winterton Rangers	4-0
12r	Moor Green v Bromsgrove Rovers	1-0
16r	Irthlingborough Diamonds v Skegness Town	1-0
17r	Wellingborough Town v Great Yarmouth Town	2-0
19r	Hornchurch v Tring Town	0-0
20r	Tilbury v Leytonstone/Ilford	2-2
22r	Wealdstone v Hendon	3-2e
25r	Chatham Town v Southall	4-2e
31r	AFC Totton v Gosport Borough	2-1
r	Maidenhead United v Dorchester Town	0-2
32r	Slough Town v Basingstoke Town	2-0
19r2	Hornchurch v Tring Town	0-3
20r2	Leytonstone/Ilford v Tilbury	2-1

Qualifying Round Three

1	Barrow v Annfield Plain	8-0
2	Gateshead (2) v North Shields	2-4
3	Morecambe v South Bank	1-1
4	Frickley Athletic v Spennymoor United	1-1
5	Horwich RMI v Caernarfon Town	2-2
6	Chorley v Runcorn	2-2
7	Ashton United v Macclesfield Town	0-2
8	Eastwood Town v Telford United	2-2
9	Witton Albion v Shifnal Town	0-2
10	Shepshed Charterhouse v Gainsborough Trinity	3-0
11	Grantham v Armitage	3-1
12	Holbeach United v Moor Green	2-1
13	Stourbridge v AP Leamington	1-1
14	Sutton Coldfield Town v Worcester City	2-4
15	Kidderminster Harriers v Corby Town	1-3
16	Irthlingborough Diamonds v King's Lynn	1-2
17	Wellingborough Town v Billericay Town	1-1
18	Walthamstow Avenue v Woodford Town (1)	2-0
19	Boreham Wood v Tring Town	3-0
20	Chelmsford City v Leytonstone/Ilford	0-0
21	Chesham United v Feltham	1-0
22	Dulwich Hamlet v Wealdstone	0-0
23	Hampton v Windsor & Eton	1-2
24	Wokingham Town v Kingstonian	2-2
25	Chatham Town v Folkestone	1-1
26	Egham Town v Carshalton Athletic	0-2
27	Tooting & Mitcham United v Deal Town	8-1

1982/83 to 1983/84

28 Bognor Regis Town v Thanet United	3-0
29 Dartford v Corinthian Casuals	2-1
30 Worthing v Farnborough Town	1-0
31 AFC Totton v Dorchester Town	1-0
32 Slough Town v Frome Town	3-0
33 Trowbridge Town v Cheltenham Town	1-1
34 Bridgend Town v Merthyr Tydfil	1-3
35 Wimborne Town v Bath City	1-0
36 Liskeard Athletic v Bideford	1-2
3r South Bank v Morecambe	1-0
4r Spennymoor United v Frickley Athletic	1-1
5r Caernarfon Town v Horwich RMI	0-2
6r Runcorn v Chorley	4-0
8r Telford United v Eastwood Town	4-0
13r AP Leamington v Stourbridge	2-0
17r Billericay Town v Wellingborough Town	1-2
20r Leytonstone/Ilford v Chelmsford City	0-0
22r Wealdstone v Dulwich Hamlet	2-1
24r Kingstonian v Wokingham Town	1-1
25r Folkestone v Chatham Town	5-0
33r Cheltenham Town v Trowbridge Town	1-0
4r2 Frickley Athletic v Spennymoor United	2-3
20r2 Chelmsford City v Leytonstone/Ilford	2-1
24r2 Wokingham Town v Kingstonian	2-0

Qualifying Round Four

AFC Totton v Windsor & Eton	0-0
Barking v Folkestone	0-2
Boreham Wood v Dartford	1-1
Boston United v Shifnal Town	4-1
Chelmsford City v Chesham United	1-3
Cheltenham Town v Weymouth	0-0
Corby Town v Holbeach Utd	0-1
Dagenham v Tooting & Mitcham United	2-0
Gravesend & Northfleet v Maidstone United	1-2
Harlow Town v Bishop's Stortford	1-1
Horwich RMI v Runcorn	2-2
Kettering Town v AP Leamington	3-1
Macclesfield Town v Stafford Rangers	3-1
Mossley v South Bank	1-0
North Shields v Barrow	2-1
Northwich Victoria v Blyth Spartans	3-0
Scarborough v Spennymoor United	4-2
Shepshed Charterhouse v King's Lynn	2-1
Slough Town v Bideford	7-1
Telford United v Grantham	3-0
Walthamstow Avenue v Carshalton Athletic	1-1
Wealdstone v Sutton United	3-1
Wimborne Town v Merthyr Tydfil	1-0
Wokingham Town v Leatherhead	1-0
Worcester City v Wellingborough Town	2-1
Workington v Penrith	2-2
Worthing v Minehead	2-2
Yeovil Town v Bognor Regis Town	4-2
r Bishop's Stortford v Harlow Town	4-0
r Carshalton Athletic v Walthamstow Avenue	2-1e
r Dartford v Boreham Wood	2-1e
r Minehead v Worthing	0-3
r Penrith v Workington	0-2
r Runcorn v Horwich RMI	0-1
r Weymouth v Cheltenham Town	4-0
r Windsor & Eton v AFC Totton	1-0

Round One

Aldershot v Wimborne Town	4-0
Altrincham v Rochdale	2-1
Blackpool v Horwich RMI	3-0
Boston United v Crewe Alexandra	3-1
Bournemouth v Southend United	0-2
Brentford v Windsor & Eton	7-0
Bristol Rovers v Wycombe Wanderers	1-0
Carshalton Athletic v Barnet	4-0
Chesham United v Yeovil Town	0-1
Chester v Northwich Victoria	1-1
Chesterfield v Peterborough United	2-2
Colchester United v Torquay United	0-2
Darlington v Scunthorpe United	0-1
Enfield v Newport County	0-0
Gillingham v Dagenham	1-0
Halifax Town v North Shields	0-1
Hartlepool United v Lincoln City	3-0
Holbeach United v Wrexham	0-4 N
Huddersfield Town v Mossley	1-0
Hull City v Sheffield United	1-1
Macclesfield Town v Worcester City	1-5
Mansfield Town v Stockport County	3-2
Northampton Town v Wimbledon	2-2
Orient v Bristol City	4-1
Oxford United v Folkestone	5-2
Plymouth Argyle v Exeter City	2-0
Port Vale v Bradford City	0-1
Portsmouth v Hereford United	4-1
Preston North End v Shepshed Charterhouse	5-1
Reading v Bishop's Stortford	1-2
Slough Town v Millwall	1-0
Swindon Town v Wealdstone	2-0
Tranmere Rovers v Scarborough	4-2
Walsall v Kettering Town	3-0
Weymouth v Maidstone United	4-3
Wigan Athletic v Telford United	0-0
Wokingham Town v Cardiff City	1-1
Workington v Doncaster Rovers	1-2
Worthing v Dartford	2-1

York City v Bury	3-1
r Cardiff City v Wokingham Town	3-0
r Newport County v Enfield	4-2
r Northwich Victoria v Chester	3-1e
r Peterborough United v Chesterfield	2-1
r Sheffield United v Hull City	2-0
r Telford United v Wigan Athletic	2-1
r Wimbledon v Northampton Town	0-2

Round Two

Altrincham v Huddersfield Town	0-1
Boston United v Sheffield United	1-1
Bristol Rovers v Plymouth Argyle	2-2
Cardiff City v Weymouth	2-3
Gillingham v Northampton Town	1-1
Hartlepool United v York City	1-1
Mansfield Town v Bradford City	1-1
Newport County v Orient	1-0
North Shields v Walsall	0-3
Oxford United v Worthing	4-0
Peterborough United v Doncaster Rovers	5-2
Portsmouth v Aldershot	1-3
Preston North End v Blackpool	2-1
Scunthorpe United v Northwich Victoria	2-1
Slough Town v Bishop's Stortford	1-4
Southend United v Yeovil Town	3-0
Swindon Town v Brentford	2-2
Telford United v Tranmere Rovers	1-1
Torquay United v Carshalton Athletic	4-1
Worcester City v Wrexham	2-1
r Bradford City v Mansfield Town	3-2
r Brentford v Swindon Town	1-3e
r Northampton Town v Gillingham	3-2
r Plymouth Argyle v Bristol Rovers	1-0
r Sheffield United v Boston United	5-1
r Tranmere Rovers v Telford United	2-1
r York City v Hartlepool United	4-0

Round Three

Arsenal v Bolton Wanderers	2-1
Blackburn Rovers v Liverpool	1-2
Bradford City v Barnsley	0-1
Brighton & Hove Albion v Newcastle United	1-1
Cambridge United v Weymouth	1-0
Carlisle United v Burnley	2-2
Charlton Athletic v Ipswich Town	2-3
Coventry City v Worcester City	3-1
Crystal Palace v York City	2-1
Derby County v Nottingham Forest	2-0
Huddersfield Town v Chelsea	1-1
Leeds United v Preston North End	3-0
Leicester City v Notts County	2-3
Luton Town v Peterborough United	3-0
Manchester United v West Ham United	2-0
Middlesbrough v Bishop's Stortford	2-2
Newport County v Everton	1-1
Northampton Town v Aston Villa	0-1
Norwich City v Swansea City	2-1
Oldham Athletic v Fulham	0-2
Oxford United v Torquay United	1-1
Scunthorpe United v Grimsby Town	0-0
Sheffield United v Stoke City	0-0
Shrewsbury Town v Rotherham United	2-1
Southend United v Sheffield Wednesday	0-0
Sunderland v Manchester City	0-0
Swindon Town v Aldershot	7-0
Tottenham Hotspur v Southampton	1-0
Tranmere Rovers v Wolverhampton Wan.	0-1
Walsall v Birmingham City	0-0
Watford v Plymouth Argyle	2-0
West Bromwich Albion v Queen's Park Rangers	3-2
r Birmingham City v Walsall	1-0e
r Bishop's Stortford v Middlesbrough	1-2
r Burnley v Carlisle United	3-1
r Chelsea v Huddersfield Town	2-0
r Everton v Newport County	2-1
r Grimsby Town v Scunthorpe United	2-0
r Manchester City v Sunderland	2-1
r Newcastle United v Brighton & Hove Albion	0-1
r Sheffield Wednesday v Southend United	2-2e
r Stoke City v Sheffield United	3-2
r Torquay United v Oxford United	2-1
r2 Sheffield Wednesday v Southend United	2-1

Round Four

Arsenal v Leeds United	1-1
Aston Villa v Wolverhampton Wan.	1-0
Brighton & Hove Albion v Manchester City	4-0
Burnley v Swindon Town	3-1
Cambridge United v Barnsley	1-0
Coventry City v Norwich City	2-2
Crystal Palace v Birmingham City	1-0
Derby County v Chelsea	2-1
Everton v Shrewsbury Town	2-1
Ipswich Town v Grimsby Town	2-0
Liverpool v Stoke City	2-0
Luton Town v Manchester United	0-2
Middlesbrough v Notts County	2-0
Torquay United v Sheffield Wednesday	2-3
Tottenham Hotspur v West Bromwich Albion	2-1
Watford v Fulham	1-1
r Fulham v Watford	1-2

r Leeds United v Arsenal	1-1e
r Norwich City v Coventry City	2-1e
r2 Arsenal v Leeds United	2-1

Round Five

Aston Villa v Watford	4-1
Cambridge United v Sheffield Wednesday	1-2
Crystal Palace v Burnley	0-0
Derby County v Manchester United	0-1
Everton v Tottenham Hotspur	2-0
Liverpool v Brighton & Hove Albion	1-2
Middlesbrough v Arsenal	1-1
Norwich City v Ipswich Town	1-0
r Arsenal v Middlesbrough	3-2
r Burnley v Crystal Palace	0-1

Round Six

Arsenal v Aston Villa	2-0
Brighton & Hove Albion v Norwich City	1-0
Burnley v Sheffield Wednesday	1-1
Manchester United v Everton	1-0
r Sheffield Wednesday v Burnley	5-0

Semi Finals

Brighton & Hove Albion v Sheffield Wednesday	2-1 N
Manchester United v Arsenal	2-1 N

Final

Manchester United v Brighton & Hove Albion	2-2eN
r Manchester United v Brighton & Hove Albion	4-0 N

1983/84

Preliminary Round

1 Chester-le-Street Town v Shildon	2-0
Easington Colliery v Whitley Bay	2-0
Fleetwood Town v Newcastle Blue Star	2-1
Peterlee Newtown v Netherfield (Kendal)	1-0
2 Gretna v Consett	3-1
Guisborough Town v Ferryhill Athletic	2-1
3 Durham City v Ashington	2-0
Ryhope Community Association v Harrogate Town	1-3
4 Accrington Stanley (2) v Crook Town	3-1
Seaham Red Star v Bridlington Trinity	7-0
5 Chadderton v Denaby United	1-0
Colwyn Bay v Emley	2-3
6 Droylsden v Prestwich Heys	1-2
Radcliffe Borough v Ossett Albion	2-1
7 Alfreton Town v Ashton United	0-1
Formby v North Ferriby United	2-1
Prescot Cables v Lytham	0-0
Warrington Town v Stalybridge Celtic	0-3
8 Congleton Town v Caernarfon Town	1-0
Wren Rovers v Appleby Frodingham Ath.	3-2e
9 Belper Town v Bilston	3-3
Brigg Town v Hednesford Town	0-0
10 Boston v Gresley Rovers	1-3
Winterton Rangers v Friar Lane Old Boys	1-0
11 Eastwood Hanley v Desborough Town	1-0
Highgate United v Bridgnorth Town	1-2
12 Lye Town v Willenhall Town	1-0
Skegness Town v Tividale	2-4
13 Blakenall v Buckingham Town	0-1
Bourne Town v Chipping Norton Town	4-2
Racing Club Warwick v Banbury United	3-1
Wigston Fields v Coventry Sporting	3-1
14 Boldmere St Michaels v Dudley Town	0-2
March Town United v Bromsgrove Rovers	3-2
15 Ely City v Armitage	3-2
Rothwell Town v Newmarket Town	2-0
16 Bury Town v Tiptree United	3-3
Soham Town Rangers v Harwich & Parkeston	1-0
17 Ampthill Town v Rushden Town	2-1
Stevenage Borough v Milton Keynes City	2-0
18 Lowestoft Town v Letchworth Garden City	2-0
19 Stowmarket v Cheshunt	1-0
Wootton Blue Cross v Basildon United	1-1
20 Aylesbury United v Harefield United	2-0
Clapton v Cray Wanderers	2-3
Dorking Town v Berkhamsted Town	1-0
Kingsbury Town v Addlestone & Weybridge T	0-1
21 Bracknell Town v Burnham (1)	0-2
Molesey v Erith & Belvedere	0-2
22 Chalfont St Peter v Finchley	2-1
Royston Town v Epping Town	4-1
23 Hornchurch v Crawley Town	1-0
St Albans City v Banstead Athletic	10-0
24 Haringey Borough v Canterbury City	1-4
Metropolitan Police v Horsham YMCA	0-1
25 Hoddesdon Town v Merstham	1-0
Horsham v Burgess Hill Town	0-0
Sittingbourne v Ringmer	3-0
Three Bridges v Hemel Hempstead Town	3-2
26 Beckenham Town v Ashford Town	1-3
Woking v Hailsham Town	1-2
27 Eastbourne United v Arundel	1-0
Lancing v Faversham Town	3-1
28 Chertsey Town v Peacehaven & Telscombe	0-1

167

1983/84

	Lewes v Tunbridge Wells	2-2
29	Walton & Hersham v Fleet Town	1-1
	Whitehawk v Horndean	3-0
30	Tonbridge v Marlow	3-0
	Wick v Newport (IOW)	2-1
31	Romsey Town v Chippenham Town	1-1
	Salisbury (2) v Flackwell Heath	1-0
32	Newbury Town v Devizes Town	4-2
	Road Sea Southampton v Oxford City	4-1
33	Brockenhurst v Clandown	1-1
	Llanelli v Clevedon Town	3-0
34	Barry Town v Calne Town	4-1
	Bristol Manor Farm v Glastonbury	0-1
	Chard Town v Taunton Town	2-1
	Mangotsfield United v Ton Pentre	3-1
35	Haverfordwest County v Weston-Super-Mare	1-0
	Paulton Rovers v Wellington (Somerset)	2-1
36	Falmouth Town v Bridgwater Town (1)	0-1
	Saltash United v Barnstaple Town	3-1
7r	Lytham v Prescot Cables	0-3
9r	Bilston v Belper Town	1-0
r	Hednesford Town v Brigg Town	3-0
16r	Tiptree United v Bury Town	0-1
19r	Basildon United v Wootton Blue Cross	2-0
25r	Horsham v Burgess Hill Town	2-0
28r	Tunbridge Wells v Lewes	0-3
29r	Fleet Town v Walton & Hersham	0-4
31r	Chippenham Town v Romsey Town	0-1e
33r	Clandown v Brockenhurst	3-0

Qualifying Round One

1	Chester-le-Street Town v Barrow	1-0
	Easington Colliery v Peterlee Newtown	2-1
	Fleetwood Town v Tow Law Town	1-2
	Horden CW v West Auckland Town	5-1
2	Brandon United v Guisborough Town	0-0
	Evenwood Town v North Shields	0-3
	Gretna v Annfield Plain	1-0
	Morecambe v Guiseley	1-0
3	Billingham Synthonia v Lancaster City	0-1e
	Eppleton CW v Durham City	0-2
	Harrogate Town v Whitby Town	2-4
	Yorkshire Amateur v Spennymoor United	4-1
4	Bishop Auckland v Thackley	2-2
	Clitheroe v South Bank	0-0
	Seaham Red Star v Gateshead (2)	1-3
	Willington v Accrington Stanley (2)	1-1
5	Bootle v Bangor City	0-1
	Chadderton v South Liverpool	1-4
	Chorley v Burscough	2-0
	Nantwich Town v Emley	1-1
6	Buxton v Curzon Ashton	2-1
	Farsley Celtic v Horwich RMI	1-4
	Radcliffe Borough v Southport	1-3
	St Helens Town v Prestwich Heys	0-1
7	Ashton United v Runcorn	0-1
	Hyde United v Darwen	3-0
	Prescot Cables v Rhyl	0-5
	Stalybridge Celtic v Formby	8-1
8	Leyland Motors v Congleton Town	1-3
	Marine v Heanor Town	3-2
	Tamworth v Macclesfield Town	1-6
	Wren Rovers v Oswestry Town	0-2
9	Arnold v Bilston	1-2
	Hednesford Town v Frickley Athletic	1-2
	Leek Town v Goole Town	1-1
	Witton Albion v Glossop	1-1
10	Coleshill Town v Gresley Rovers	1-3
	Hinckley Athletic v Shepshed Charterhouse	0-1
	Matlock Town v Winsford United	2-2
	Winterton Rangers v Eastwood Town	0-3
11	Eastwood Hanley v Leicester United	0-2
	Gainsborough Trinity v Ilkeston Town (2)	6-0
	Rushall Olympic v Grantham	1-1
	Sutton Town v Bridgnorth Town	0-2
12	Long Eaton United v Lye Town	1-1
	Mile Oak Rovers & Youth v Corby Town	0-1
	Tividale v AP Leamington	0-5
	Worksop Town v Wisbech Town	1-2
13	Bourne Town v Shifnal Town	1-4
	Racing Club Warwick v Alvechurch	2-2
	Sutton Coldfield Town v Spalding United	2-1
	Wigston Fields v Buckingham Town	1-4
14	Chatteris Town v Wellingborough Town	0-2
	Dudley Town v Irthlingborough Diamonds	3-1
	Stourbridge v Stamford	2-1
	Walsall Borough v March Town United	1-2
15	Halesowen Town v King's Lynn	6-0
	Nuneaton Borough v Oldbury United	1-2
	Rothwell Town v Burton Albion	1-5
	Wednesfield Social v Ely City	4-0
16	Bury Town v V.S. Rugby	0-2
	Chelmsford City v Gorleston	5-1
	Great Yarmouth Town v Holbeach United	3-1
	Heybridge Swifts v Soham Town Rangers	1-0
17	Barton Rovers v Kidderminster Harriers	0-1
	Bedworth United v Dunstable	3-2
	Stevenage Borough v Moor Green	0-0
	Thame United v Ampthill Town	2-1
18	Billericay Town v Thetford Town	3-0
	Felixstowe Town v Rainham Town	3-1
	Haverhill Rovers v Lowestoft Town	0-1
	Sudbury Town v Walthamstow Avenue	1-1
19	Basildon United v Leytonstone/Ilford	1-0
	Cambridge City v Wealdstone	1-2
	Saffron Walden Town v Stowmarket	3-0
	Woodford Town (1) v Aveley	0-2
20	Addlestone & Weybridge T v Cray Wanderers	3-1
	Aylesbury United v Boreham Wood	2-0
	Dorking Town v Hendon	1-1
	Harrow Borough v Ware	9-0
21	Burnham (1) v Hitchin Town	1-2
	Hayes v Wembley	1-3
	Hillingdon v Erith & Belvedere	2-1
	Tilbury v Chesham United	0-1
22	Feltham v Whyteleafe	0-1
	Hounslow v Slough Town	0-3
	Royston Town v Hampton	1-7
	Uxbridge v Chalfont St Peter	4-2
23	Edgware Town v Windsor & Eton	0-5
	Hornchurch v Tring Town	3-2
	Leyton-Wingate v St Albans City	1-2
	Staines Town v Grays Athletic	1-0
24	Canterbury City v Bognor Regis Town	0-3
	Corinthian Casuals v Camberley Town	2-0
	Hertford Town v Horsham YMCA	1-1
	Southall v Carshalton Athletic	3-3
25	Chatham Town v Epsom & Ewell	1-2
	Hoddesdon Town v Dartford	0-4
	Sittingbourne v Horsham	1-1
	Three Bridges v Croydon	5-1
26	Ashford Town v Deal Town	5-0
	Bromley v Horley Town	3-1
	Eastbourne Town v Hailsham Town	0-1
	Herne Bay v Gravesend & Northfleet	1-3
27	Dulwich Hamlet v Ramsgate	5-0
	Haywards Heath v Folkestone	2-6
	Lancing v Hastings United	2-2
	Redhill v Eastbourne United	1-1
28	Dover Athletic v Lewes	1-4
	Egham Town v Sheppey United	2-1
	Littlehampton Town v Leatherhead	0-2
	Peacehaven & Telscombe v Fisher Athletic	0-3
29	Hastings Town v Tooting & Mitcham United	3-4
	Thanet United v Pagham	1-1
	Walton & Hersham v Welling United	1-0
	Whitstable Town v Whitehawk	1-2
30	Chichester City (1) v Tonbridge	1-2
	Kingstonian v Steyning Town	2-0
	Southwick v Worthing	1-2
	Wick v Farnborough Town	1-2
31	Abingdon Town v Wokingham Town	0-3
	Dorchester Town v Eastleigh	0-0
	Romsey Town v Gosport Borough	0-2
	Sholing Sports v Salisbury (2)	2-1
32	Andover v AFC Totton	1-3
	Fareham Town v Maidenhead United	1-1
	Hungerford Town v Newbury Town	2-1
	Road Sea Southampton v Waterlooville	0-0
33	Basingstoke Town v Llanelli	2-1
	Clandown v Trowbridge Town	4-2
	Forest Green Rovers v Wimborne Town	6-0
	Witney Town v Moreton Town	2-1
34	Barry Town v Chard Town	2-0
	Bridgend Town v Redditch United	1-0
	Glastonbury v Cheltenham Town	0-0
	Mangotsfield United v Melksham Town	4-0
35	Bath City v Shepton Mallet Town	4-0
	Cinderford Town v Merthyr Tydfil	1-2
	Haverfordwest County v Gloucester City	1-2
	Welton Rovers v Paulton Rovers	2-0
36	Frome Town v Torrington	1-1
	Saltash United v Poole Town	0-1
	St Blazey v Bridgwater Town (1)	3-1
	Tiverton Town v Bideford	1-6
2r	Guisborough Town v Brandon United	1-2
4r	Accrington Stanley (2) v Willington	3-0
r	South Bank v Clitheroe	0-0
r	Thackley v Bishop Auckland	1-4
5r	Emley v Nantwich Town	6-2
9r	Glossop v Witton Albion	2-0
r	Goole Town v Leek Town	4-0
10r	Winsford United v Matlock Town	2-1
11r	Grantham v Rushall Olympic	3-0
12r	Lye Town v Long Eaton United	4-3
13r	Alvechurch v Racing Club Warwick	5-1
17r	Moor Green v Stevenage Borough	1-0e
18r	Walthamstow Avenue v Sudbury Town	2-0
20r	Hendon v Dorking Town	4-1
24r	Carshalton Athletic v Southall	3-4
r	Horsham YMCA v Hertford Town	2-2
25r	Horsham v Sittingbourne	1-2
27r	Eastbourne United v Redhill	2-1
r	Hastings United v Lancing	2-0
29r	Pagham v Thanet United	0-1
31r	Eastleigh v Dorchester Town	0-2e
32r	Maidenhead United v Fareham Town	0-1
r	Waterlooville v Road Sea Southampton	2-1
34r	Cheltenham Town v Glastonbury	4-0
36r	Torrington v Frome Town	0-3
4r2	Clitheroe v South Bank	1-0
24r2	Hertford Town v Horsham YMCA	2-0

Qualifying Round Two

1	Easington Colliery v Tow Law Town	0-0
	Horden CW v Chester-le-Street Town	6-1
2	Brandon United v Gretna	1-0
	Morecambe v North Shields	2-2
3	Durham City v Whitby Town	1-3
	Lancaster City v Yorkshire Amateur	2-2
4	Accrington Stanley (2) v Gateshead (2)	1-1
	Bishop Auckland v Clitheroe	1-0
5	Chorley v Bangor City	2-4
	Emley v South Liverpool	1-3
6	Buxton v Horwich RMI	0-1
	Prestwich Heys v Southport	0-1
7	Hyde United v Runcorn	3-0
	Stalybridge Celtic v Rhyl	2-0
8	Congleton Town v Oswestry Town	3-0
	Marine v Macclesfield Town	0-3
9	Bilston v Frickley Athletic	1-1
	Glossop v Goole Town	4-0
10	Gresley Rovers v Eastwood Town	0-1
	Winsford United v Shepshed Charterhouse	3-1
11	Bridgnorth Town v Leicester United	2-1
	Gainsborough Trinity v Grantham	2-0
12	Lye Town v AP Leamington	4-4
	Wisbech Town v Corby Town	2-2
13	Buckingham Town v Alvechurch	2-1
	Sutton Coldfield Town v Shifnal Town	5-4
14	March Town United v Dudley Town	3-2
	Stourbridge v Wellingborough Town	2-3
15	Oldbury United v Halesowen Town	2-0
	Wednesfield Social v Burton Albion	1-2
16	Chelmsford City v Great Yarmouth Town	4-2
	Heybridge Swifts v V.S. Rugby	2-2
17	Bedworth United v Kidderminster Harriers	2-1
	Thame United v Moor Green	4-4
18	Billericay Town v Walthamstow Avenue	2-2
	Lowestoft Town v Felixstowe Town	3-0
19	Aveley v Wealdstone	1-1
	Saffron Walden Town v Basildon United	2-4
20	Addlestone & Weybridge T v Hendon	2-1
	Harrow Borough v Aylesbury United	0-0
21	Hillingdon v Hitchin Town	0-1
	Wembley v Chesham United	0-0
22	Uxbridge v Hampton	0-1
	Whyteleafe v Slough Town	0-5
23	St Albans City v Hornchurch	3-0
	Staines Town v Windsor & Eton	2-2
24	Corinthian Casuals v Southall	3-2 N
	Hertford Town v Bognor Regis Town	1-1
25	Epsom & Ewell v Dartford	1-2
	Sittingbourne v Three Bridges	3-0
26	Bromley v Gravesend & Northfleet	0-4
	Hailsham Town v Ashford Town	1-3
27	Dulwich Hamlet v Folkestone	1-2
	Eastbourne United v Hastings United	0-0
28	Egham Town v Leatherhead	1-5
	Lewes v Fisher Athletic	0-2
29	Thanet United v Tooting & Mitcham United	0-7
	Whitehawk v Walton & Hersham	4-1
30	Kingstonian v Worthing	3-2
	Tonbridge v Farnborough Town	1-2
31	Dorchester Town v Wokingham Town	0-3
	Sholing Sports v Gosport Borough	0-0
32	Fareham Town v AFC Totton	0-3
	Hungerford Town v Waterlooville	3-3
33	Basingstoke Town v Clandown	1-1
	Witney Town v Forest Green Rovers	2-2
34	Barry Town v Mangotsfield United	4-2
	Bridgend Town v Cheltenham Town	0-2
35	Bath City v Merthyr Tydfil	0-1
	Welton Rovers v Gloucester City	1-4
36	Frome Town v Bideford	0-0
	St Blazey v Poole Town	0-3
1r	Tow Law Town v Easington Colliery	1-1
2r	North Shields v Morecambe	4-2e
3r	Yorkshire Amateur v Lancaster City	0-2
4r	Gateshead (2) v Accrington Stanley (2)	1-2
9r	Frickley Athletic v Bilston	2-0
12r	AP Leamington v Lye Town	4-0
r	Corby Town v Wisbech Town	3-2e
16r	V.S. Rugby v Heybridge Swifts	2-0
17r	Moor Green v Thame United	4-2
18r	Walthamstow Avenue v Billericay Town	0-0
19r	Wealdstone v Aveley	2-0
20r	Aylesbury United v Harrow Borough	1-2
21r	Chesham United v Wembley	3-2e
23r	Windsor & Eton v Staines Town	2-0
24r	Bognor Regis Town v Hertford Town	2-0
27r	Hastings United v Eastbourne United	1-0
31r	Gosport Borough v Sholing Sports	4-0
32r	Waterlooville v Hungerford Town	3-0
33r	Clandown v Basingstoke Town	0-2
r	Forest Green Rovers v Witney Town	1-2
36r	Bideford v Frome Town	0-2
1r2	Easington Colliery v Tow Law Town	1-0
18r2	Walthamstow Avenue v Billericay Town	2-1

Qualifying Round Three

1	Horden CW v Easington Colliery	3-2
2	North Shields v Brandon United	2-0
3	Lancaster City v Whitby Town	2-2
4	Bishop Auckland v Accrington Stanley (2)	4-1
5	Bangor City v South Liverpool	1-0
6	Horwich RMI v Southport	2-1
7	Hyde United v Stalybridge Celtic	2-0
8	Macclesfield Town v Congleton Town	6-0

1983/84 to 1984/85

9 Glossop v Frickley Athletic	2-3
10 Winsford United v Eastwood Town	0-1
11 Gainsborough Trinity v Bridgnorth Town	1-1
12 Corby Town v AP Leamington	2-2
13 Sutton Coldfield Town v Buckingham Town	2-1
14 Wellingborough Town v March Town United	1-0
15 Oldbury United v Burton Albion	0-3
16 Chelmsford City v V.S. Rugby	2-2
17 Bedworth United v Moor Green	2-1
18 Walthamstow Avenue v Lowestoft Town	0-0
19 Wealdstone v Basildon United	3-1
20 Harrow Borough v Addlestone & Weybridge T	1-0
21 Chesham United v Hitchin Town	0-2
22 Slough Town v Hampton	3-2
23 Windsor & Eton v St Albans City	4-1
24 Corinthian Casuals v Bognor Regis Town	3-1
25 Dartford v Sittingbourne	2-2
26 Gravesend & Northfleet v Ashford Town	1-1
27 Folkestone v Hastings United	2-0
28 Leatherhead v Fisher Athletic	0-4
29 Tooting & Mitcham United v Whitehawk	3-0
30 Kingstonian v Farnborough Town	2-4
31 Wokingham Town v Gosport Borough	2-1
32 AFC Totton v Waterlooville	1-1
33 Witney Town v Basingstoke Town	2-2
34 Cheltenham Town v Barry Town	3-1
35 Merthyr Tydfil v Gloucester City	3-2
36 Frome Town v Poole Town	2-3
3r Whitby Town v Lancaster City	7-3
11r Bridgnorth Town v Gainsborough Trinity	1-4
12r AP Leamington v Corby Town	3-0
16r V.S. Rugby v Chelmsford City	1-2e
18r Lowestoft Town v Walthamstow Avenue	0-2
25r Sittingbourne v Dartford	1-4
26r Ashford Town v Gravesend & Northfleet	3-2e
32r Waterlooville v AFC Totton	3-0
33r Basingstoke Town v Witney Town	2-1e

Qualifying Round Four

AP Leamington v Wellingborough Town	3-0
Bangor City v Scarborough	2-1
Barking v Ashford Town	3-0
Basingstoke Town v Worcester City	1-1
Boston United v Stafford Rangers	3-1
Chelmsford City v Bedworth United	2-1
Corinthian Casuals v Merthyr Tydfil	1-0
Dartford v Tooting & Mitcham United	2-0
Eastwood Town v Wycombe Wanderers	2-2
Fisher Athletic v Harrow Borough	1-1
Folkestone v Dagenham	1-1
Frickley Athletic v North Shields	1-0
Harlow Town v Barnet	1-1
Hitchin Town v Gainsborough Trinity	0-1
Horwich RMI v Macclesfield Town	0-0
Hyde United v Blyth Spartans	1-1
Kettering Town v Sutton Coldfield Town	3-2
Maidstone United v Sutton United	1-1
Penrith v Horden CW	3-0
Poole Town v Slough Town	3-0
Walthamstow Avenue v Burton Albion	0-0
Waterlooville v Wokingham Town	3-2
Wealdstone v Bishop's Stortford	1-0
Weymouth v Farnborough Town	1-1
Whitby Town v Bishop Auckland	4-2
Windsor & Eton v Cheltenham Town	1-0
Workington v Mossley	0-0
Yeovil Town v Minehead	2-2
r Barnet v Harlow Town	5-1
r Blyth Spartans v Hyde United	2-4
r Burton Albion v Walthamstow Avenue	3-1
r Dagenham v Folkestone	3-0
r Farnborough Town v Weymouth	3-2
r Harrow Borough v Fisher Athletic	4-2
r Macclesfield Town v Horwich RMI	4-3
r Minehead v Yeovil Town	2-4e
r Mossley v Workington	1-0
r Sutton United v Maidstone United	1-3
r Worcester City v Basingstoke Town	3-1
r Wycombe Wanderers v Eastwood Town	2-1

Round One

AP Leamington v Gillingham	0-1
Aldershot v Worcester City	1-1
Barking v Farnborough Town	2-1
Barnet v Bristol Rovers	0-0
Boston United v Bury	0-3
Bournemouth v Walsall	4-0
Bradford City v Wigan Athletic	0-0
Burnley v Hyde United	2-0
Burton Albion v Windsor & Eton	1-2
Chelmsford City v Wycombe Wanderers	0-0
Chester City v Chesterfield	1-2
Corinthian Casuals v Bristol City	0-0
Dagenham v Brentford	2-2
Darlington v Mossley	5-0
Exeter City v Maidstone United	1-1
Frickley Athletic v Altrincham	0-1
Gainsborough Trinity v Blackpool	0-2
Halifax Town v Whitby Town	2-3
Kettering Town v Swindon Town	0-7
Macclesfield Town v York City	0-0
Mansfield Town v Doncaster Rovers	3-0
Millwall v Dartford	2-1
Northampton Town v Waterlooville	1-1
Northwich Victoria v Bangor City	1-1
Oxford United v Peterborough United	2-0
Penrith v Hull City	0-2
Poole Town v Newport County	0-0
Port Vale v Lincoln City	1-2
Reading v Hereford United	2-0
Rochdale v Crewe Alexandra	1-0
Rotherham United v Hartlepool United	0-0
Scunthorpe United v Preston North End	1-0
Southend United v Plymouth Argyle	0-0
Telford United v Stockport County	3-0
Torquay United v Colchester United	1-2
Tranmere Rovers v Bolton Wanderers	2-2
Wealdstone v Enfield	1-1
Wimbledon v Orient	2-1
Wrexham v Sheffield United	1-5
Yeovil Town v Harrow Borough	0-1
r Bangor City v Northwich Victoria	1-0
r Bolton Wanderers v Tranmere Rovers	4-1e
r Brentford v Dagenham	2-1
r Bristol City v Corinthian Casuals	4-0
r Bristol Rovers v Barnet	3-1
r Enfield v Wealdstone	2-2e
r Hartlepool United v Rotherham United	0-1e
r Maidstone United v Exeter City	2-1
r Newport County v Poole Town	3-1
r Plymouth Argyle v Southend United	2-0e
r Waterlooville v Northampton Town	1-1e
r Wigan Athletic v Bradford City	4-2
r Worcester City v Aldershot	2-1
r Wycombe Wanderers v Chelmsford City	1-2
r York City v Macclesfield Town	2-0
r2 Northampton Town v Waterlooville	2-0
r2 Wealdstone v Enfield	2-0

Round Two

Bangor City v Blackpool	1-1
Bolton Wanderers v Mansfield Town	2-0
Brentford v Wimbledon	3-2
Bristol Rovers v Bristol City	1-2
Chesterfield v Burnley	2-2
Colchester United v Wealdstone	4-0
Darlington v Altrincham	0-0
Gillingham v Chelmsford City	6-1
Harrow Borough v Newport County	1-3
Lincoln City v Telford United	0-0
Maidstone United v Worcester City	3-2
Millwall v Swindon Town	2-3
Northampton Town v Telford United	1-1
Plymouth Argyle v Barking	2-1
Reading v Oxford United	1-1
Rotherham United v Hull City	2-1
Scunthorpe United v Bury	2-0
Wigan Athletic v Whitby Town	1-0
Windsor & Eton v Bournemouth	0-0
York City v Rochdale	0-2
r Altrincham v Darlington	0-2
r Blackpool v Bangor City	2-1
r Bournemouth v Windsor & Eton	2-0
r Burnley v Chesterfield	3-2
r Oxford United v Reading	3-0
r Sheffield United v Lincoln City	1-0
r Telford United v Northampton Town	3-2

Round Three

Aston Villa v Norwich City	1-1
Blackburn Rovers v Chelsea	1-0
Blackpool v Manchester City	2-1
Bolton Wanderers v Sunderland	0-3
Bournemouth v Manchester United	2-0
Brighton & Hove Albion v Swansea City	2-0
Burnley v Oxford United	0-0
Cambridge United v Derby County	0-3
Cardiff City v Ipswich Town	0-3
Carlisle United v Swindon Town	1-1
Colchester United v Charlton Athletic	0-1
Coventry City v Wolverhampton Wan.	1-1
Crystal Palace v Leicester City	1-0
Darlington v Maidstone United	4-1
Fulham v Tottenham Hotspur	0-0
Gillingham v Brentford	5-3
Huddersfield Town v Queen's Park Rangers	2-1
Leeds United v Scunthorpe United	1-1
Liverpool v Newcastle United	4-0
Luton Town v Watford	2-2
Middlesbrough v Arsenal	3-2
Nottingham Forest v Southampton	1-2
Notts County v Bristol City	2-2
Plymouth Argyle v Newport County	2-2
Portsmouth v Grimsby Town	2-1
Rochdale v Telford United	1-4
Rotherham United v West Bromwich Albion	0-0
Sheffield United v Birmingham City	1-1
Sheffield Wednesday v Barnsley	1-0
Shrewsbury Town v Oldham Athletic	3-0
Stoke City v Everton	0-2
West Ham United v Wigan Athletic	1-0
r Birmingham City v Sheffield United	2-0
r Bristol City v Notts County	0-2
r Newport County v Plymouth Argyle	0-1
r Norwich City v Aston Villa	3-0
r Oxford United v Burnley	2-1
r Scunthorpe United v Leeds United	1-1e
r Swindon Town v Carlisle United	3-1
r Tottenham Hotspur v Fulham	2-0
r Watford v Luton Town	4-3e
r West Bromwich Albion v Rotherham United	3-0
r Wolverhampton Wan. v Coventry City	1-1e
r2 Coventry City v Wolverhampton Wan.	3-0
r2 Scunthorpe United v Leeds United	4-2

Round Four

Brighton & Hove Albion v Liverpool	2-0
Charlton Athletic v Watford	0-2
Crystal Palace v West Ham United	1-1
Derby County v Telford United	3-2
Everton v Gillingham	0-0
Huddersfield Town v Notts County	1-2
Middlesbrough v Bournemouth	2-0
Oxford United v Blackpool	2-1
Plymouth Argyle v Darlington	2-1
Portsmouth v Southampton	0-1
Sheffield Wednesday v Coventry City	3-2
Shrewsbury Town v Ipswich Town	2-0
Sunderland v Birmingham City	1-2
Swindon Town v Blackburn Rovers	1-2
Tottenham Hotspur v Norwich City	0-2
West Bromwich Albion v Scunthorpe United	1-0
r Gillingham v Everton	0-0e
r Norwich City v Tottenham Hotspur	2-1
r West Ham United v Crystal Palace	2-0
r2 Gillingham v Everton	0-3

Round Five

Birmingham City v West Ham United	3-0
Blackburn Rovers v Southampton	0-1
Derby County v Norwich City	2-1
Everton v Shrewsbury Town	3-0
Notts County v Middlesbrough	1-0
Oxford United v Sheffield Wednesday	0-3
Watford v Brighton & Hove Albion	3-1
West Bromwich Albion v Plymouth Argyle	0-1

Round Six

Birmingham City v Watford	1-3
Notts County v Everton	1-2
Plymouth Argyle v Derby County	0-0
Sheffield Wednesday v Southampton	0-0
r Derby County v Plymouth Argyle	0-1
r Southampton v Sheffield Wednesday	5-1

Semi Finals

Everton v Southampton	1-0eN
Watford v Plymouth Argyle	1-0 N

Final

Everton v Watford	2-0 N

1984/85

Preliminary Round

1 Brandon United v Harrogate Town	3-0
Shildon v Crook Town	0-1
Yorkshire Amateur v Consett	0-1
2 Esh Winning v Guisborough Town	0-1
Ferryhill Athletic v Guiseley	1-2
3 Chester-le-Street Town v Lancaster City	3-0
Peterlee Newtown v Eppleton CW	5-1
Thackley v Darwen	0-2
4 Billingham Town v Coundon Three Tuns	1-0
Bridlington Trinity v Easington Colliery	0-2
5 Colwyn Bay v Lytham	1-0
Nantwich Town v Droylsden	0-0
Rossendale United v Denaby United	1-2
6 Alfreton Town v Eastwood Hanley	4-2
Burscough v Emley	2-1
7 Caernarfon Town v Garforth Miners	4-1
Radcliffe Borough v Clitheroe	1-0
Shifnal Town v Chadderton	2-2
8 Arnold v Ilkeston Town (2)	1-4
Long Eaton United v Curzon Ashton	3-0
Prescot Cables v Ashton United	0-0
9 Blakenall v Mile Oak Rovers & Youth	2-0
Ossett Albion v Formby	1-4
St Helens Town v Coleshill Town	6-1
10 Appleby Frodingham Ath. v Glossop	2-0
Dudley Town v Heanor Town	4-0
11 Brigg Town v Tamworth	0-2
Walsall Borough v Gresley Rovers	1-4
Wednesfield Social v Friar Lane Old Boys	0-0
12 Boldmere St Michaels v Halesowen Town	2-2
Desborough Town v Racing Club Warwick	3-0
13 Chatteris Town v Oldswinford	1-4
Stamford v Irthlingborough Diamonds	0-2
Wisbech Town v Evesham Union	3-0
14 Malvern Town v Redditch United	1-5
Milton Keynes City v Rothwell Town	0-3
15 Coventry Sporting v Spalding United	3-0
Stevenage Borough v Holbeach United	8-0

169

1984/85

	Wootton Blue Cross v Histon	3-2
16	Abingdon Town v Baldock Town	1-3
	Ampthill Town v Barton Rovers	1-0
17	Boreham Wood v Haverhill Rovers	2-1
	Sudbury Town v Edgware Town	8-1
	Wembley v Bourne Town	2-1
18	Arlesey Town v Cheshunt	2-2
	Bury Town v Great Yarmouth Town	3-0
19	Cambridge City v Hoddesdon Town	3-1 N
	Stowmarket v Gorleston	1-1
	Tilbury v Epping Town	0-1
20	Felixstowe Town v Harwich & Parkeston	3-0
	Finchley v Hornchurch	1-2
21	Braintree Town v Hillingdon	0-0
	Bromley v Cray Wanderers	4-0
	Leyton-Wingate v Burnham (1)	1-0
22	Clapton v Dunstable	0-2
	Crockenhill v Grays Athletic	0-3
23	Erith & Belvedere v Rainham Town	2-2
	Southall v Maidenhead United	1-2
	Tring Town v Kingsbury Town	3-1
24	Addlestone & Weybridge T v Letchworth Garden City	7-0
	Chatham Town v Metropolitan Police	2-3
25	Horley Town v Ruislip Manor	0-3
	Steyning Town v Redhill	1-2
26	Chertsey Town v Lancing	0-0
	Haywards Heath v Merstham	2-0
27	Banstead Athletic v Lewes	2-3
	Littlehampton Town v Canterbury City	1-1
	Whitstable Town v Burgess Hill Town	1-0
28	Deal Town v Hastings Town	2-2
	Dover Athletic v Horsham	0-0
29	Chichester City (1) v Kingstonian	0-1
	Southwick v Egham Town	1-1
	Walton & Hersham v Eastbourne United	1-0
30	Basingstoke Town v Dorking (2)	2-0
	Camberley Town v Eastbourne Town	0-0e
31	Fleet Town v Petersfield United	1-1
	Salisbury (2) v Marlow	3-1
	Thame United v Hungerford Town	2-11
32	Andover v Calne Town	6-0
	Brockenhurst v Chippenham Town	1-3
33	Chard Town v Shepton Mallet Town	0-2
	Wellington (Somerset) v Devizes Town	5-1
	Welton Rovers v Clevedon Town	0-0
34	Cinderford Town v Forest Green Rovers	1-2
	Clandown v Haverfordwest County	0-1
35	Bideford v Bristol Manor Farm	2-1
	Dorchester Town v Bridgwater Town (1)	wo/s
	Trowbridge Town v Molesey	4-1
36	Barnstaple Town v St Blazey	4-1
	Paulton Rovers v Taunton Town	2-1
5r	Droylsden v Nantwich Town	2-0
7r	Chadderton v Shifnal Town	2-1
8r	Ashton United v Prescot Cables	3-1
11r	Friar Lane Old Boys v Wednesfield Social	0-0
12r	Halesowen Town v Boldmere St Michaels	1-1
15r	Spalding United v Coventry Sporting	2-3e
18r	Cheshunt v Arlesey Town	0-1
19r	Gorleston v Stowmarket	3-0
21r	Hillingdon v Braintree Town	0-0
23r	Rainham Town v Erith & Belvedere	3-1
26r	Lancing v Chertsey Town	1-0e
27r	Canterbury City v Littlehampton Town	6-0
28r	Hastings Town v Deal Town	3-1
r	Horsham v Dover Athletic	0-1
29r	Egham Town v Southwick	2-1
30r	Eastbourne Town v Camberley Town	2-1
31r	Petersfield United v Fleet Town	1-3
33r	Clevedon Town v Welton Rovers	1-0
11r2	Friar Lane Old Boys v Wednesfield Social	2-1e
12r2	Halesowen Town v Boldmere St Michaels	1-0
21r2	Hillingdon v Braintree Town	0-2

Qualifying Round One

1	Billingham Synthonia v Brandon United	2-1
	Consett v Gateshead (2)	0-2
	Crook Town v Durham City	3-1
	Newcastle Blue Star v Horden CW	3-0
2	Blyth Spartans v Guisborough Town	1-1
	Guiseley v West Auckland Town	1-1
	Netherfield (Kendal) v South Bank	0-4
	Seaham Red Star v Tow Law Town	3-3
3	Ashington v Whitley Bay	3-1
	Bishop Auckland v Chester-le-Street Town	4-3
	Darwen v Gretna	1-2
	Peterlee Newtown v Evenwood Town	4-0
4	Easington Colliery v Wren Rovers	2-2e
	North Shields v Billingham Town	7-2
	Ryhope Community Association v Spennymoor United	4-2
	Willington v Whitby Town	2-5
5	Barrow v Colwyn Bay	4-0
	Bootle v Marine	0-2
	Denaby United v Buxton	3-3
	Droylsden v Fleetwood Town	4-0
6	Burscough v Skelmersdale United	3-0
	Leek Town v Runcorn	2-1
	Leyland Motors v Southport	0-4
	Morecambe v Alfreton Town	0-1
7	Belper Town v Rhyl	1-1
	Chadderton v Oswestry Town	0-0
	Frickley Athletic v Caernarfon Town	3-0
	Radcliffe Borough v Farsley Celtic	5-2
8	Accrington Stanley (2) v Ilkeston Town (2)	2-1
	Armitage v Witton Albion	0-4
	Ashton United v Hyde United	0-0
	Long Eaton United v Hednesford Town	1-3
9	Bilston Town v South Liverpool	3-2 N
	Chorley v Blakenall	5-1
	Formby v Lye Town	5-2
	St Helens Town v Congleton Town	2-0
10	Dudley Town v Paget Rangers	1-1
	Hinckley Athletic v Stalybridge Celtic	1-3
	Horwich RMI v Appleby Frodingham Ath.	3-0
	North Ferriby United v Winsford United	2-2
11	Boston v Matlock Town	1-4
	Eastwood Town v Tamworth	1-0
	Friar Lane Old Boys v Goole Town	1-1
	Gresley Rovers v Lincoln United	6-1
12	Desborough Town v Wigston Fields	0-0
	Grantham v Halesowen Town	0-2
	Stourbridge v Sutton Town	2-0
	Tividale v Worksop Town	1-2
13	Bromsgrove Rovers v Shepshed Charterhouse	2-5
	Gainsborough Trinity v Oldswinford	3-0
	Irthlingborough Diamonds v Leicester United	3-0
	Wisbech Town v Nuneaton Borough	2-6
14	Bridgnorth Town v Redditch United	3-2
	Rothwell Town v Wolverton Town	2-1
	Rushall Olympic v Kidderminster Harriers	1-2
	Rushden Town v Stafford Rangers	3-3
15	Banbury United v Willenhall Town	1-4
	Bedworth United v Coventry Sporting	0-0
	Stevenage Borough v Soham Town Rangers	2-1
	Wootton Blue Cross v Burton Albion	0-4
16	Ampthill Town v Oxford City	1-4
	Chalfont St Peter v Oldbury United	0-0
	Hertford Town v Sutton Coldfield Town	2-2
	Moor Green v Baldock Town	2-1
17	Alvechurch v Boreham Wood	4-1
	Berkhamsted Town v V.S. Rugby	0-0
	Sudbury Town v Flackwell Heath	2-0
	Wembley v AP Leamington	3-1
18	Bury Town v Saffron Walden Town	0-2
	Corby Town v Arlesey Town	2-1
	Hemel Hempstead Town v King's Lynn	0-2
	Newmarket Town v Wellingborough Town	1-2
19	Aveley v March Town United	5-0
	Billericay Town v Cambridge City	1-1
	Epping Town v Lowestoft Town	3-4
	Gorleston v Haringey Borough	1-1
20	Basildon United v Felixstowe Town	4-0
	Hornchurch v Woodford Town (1)	2-1
	Royston Town v Chelmsford City	0-3
	Tiptree United v Harlow Town	0-4
21	Aylesbury United v Hayes	3-2
	Bromley v Heybridge Swifts	1-1
	Buckingham Town v Braintree Town	2-2
	Leyton-Wingate v Chesham United	2-2
22	Grays Athletic v St Albans City	3-0
	Harefield United v Sutton United	0-2
	Hendon v Dunstable	1-3
	Hounslow v Wealdstone	2-5
23	Beckenham Town v Hitchin Town	0-2
	Fisher Athletic v Rainham Town	6-1
	Maidenhead United v Potton United	0-2
	Tring Town v Hampton	1-0
24	Addlestone & Weybridge T v Corinthian Casuals	3-0
	Metropolitan Police v Ware	5-0
	Tunbridge Wells v Leytonstone/Ilford	0-2
	Uxbridge v Welling United	0-1
25	Crawley Town v Ruislip Manor	2-1
	Herne Bay v Walthamstow Avenue	0-3
	Ringmer v Redhill	2-3
	Tonbridge v Folkestone	0-1
26	Carshalton Athletic v Lancing	4-0
	Haywards Heath v Woking	2-0
	Thanet United v Sittingbourne	2-3
	Whyteleafe v Staines Town	0-1
27	Arundel v Worthing	2-2
	Ashford Town v Lewes	1-2
	Canterbury City v Faversham Town	3-0
	Whitstable Town v Croydon	0-0
28	Dover Athletic v Three Bridges	1-0
	Hastings United v Hastings Town	2-1
	Pagham v Leatherhead	0-5
	Sheppey United v Whitehawk	2-0
29	Bracknell Town v Tooting & Mitcham United	0-3
	Dulwich Hamlet v Kingstonian	0-2
	Egham Town v Hailsham Town	3-0
	Walton & Hersham v Gravesend & Northfleet	0-1
30	Bognor Regis Town v Basingstoke Town	2-2
	Eastbourne Town v Wick	9-2
	Horndean v Epsom & Ewell	1-3
	Horsham YMCA v Wokingham Town	1-8
31	Eastleigh v AFC Totton	0-2
	Farnborough Town v Fleet Town	5-1
	Hungerford Town v Gosport Borough	2-1
	Salisbury (2) v Newport (IOW)	4-1
32	Chippenham Town v Sholing Sports	3-0
	Fareham Town v Andover	2-1
	Melksham Town v Road Sea Southampton	0-3
	Newbury Town v Slough Town	1-5
33	Bridgend Town v Witney Town	0-2
	Clevedon Town v Waterlooville	3-2
	Poole Town v Shepton Mallet Town	2-1
	Wellington (Somerset) v Glastonbury	2-3
34	Barry Town v Forest Green Rovers	3-2
	Haverfordwest County v Moreton Town	2-2
	Llanelli v Gloucester City	2-5
	Mangotsfield United v Highgate United	0-0
35	Cheltenham Town v Bideford	0-0
	Dorchester Town v Weston-Super-Mare	4-2
	Saltash United v Merthyr Tydfil	0-0
	Ton Pentre v Trowbridge Town	1-1
36	Bath City v Barnstaple Town	4-1
	Paulton Rovers v Wimborne Town	0-4
	Torrington v Frome Town	0-1
	Wadebridge Town v Minehead	0-2
2r	Guisborough Town v Blyth Spartans	3-1
r	Tow Law Town v Seaham Red Star	3-1
r	West Auckland Town v Guiseley	2-1e
4r	Wren Rovers v Easington Colliery	4-2
5r	Buxton v Denaby United	0-1
7r	Oswestry Town v Chadderton	4-0
r	Rhyl v Belper Town	1-0
8r	Hyde United v Ashton United	2-4
10r	Paget Rangers v Dudley Town	2-3
r	Winsford United v North Ferriby United	3-1
11r	Goole Town v Friar Lane Old Boys	4-1e
12r	Wigston Fields v Desborough Town	1-1
14r	Stafford Rangers v Rushden Town	1-3
15r	Coventry Sporting v Bedworth United	2-3
16r	Oldbury United v Chalfont St Peter	1-1
r	Sutton Coldfield Town v Hertford Town	2-1
17r	V.S. Rugby v Berkhamsted Town	3-1
19r	Billericay Town v Cambridge City	1-3e
r	Haringey Borough v Gorleston	0-2
21r	Braintree Town v Buckingham Town	1-2e
r	Chesham United v Leyton-Wingate	1-0
r	Heybridge Swifts v Bromley	2-1
27r	Croydon v Whitstable Town	5-0
r	Worthing v Arundel	4-1
30r	Basingstoke Town v Bognor Regis Town	0-1
34r	Highgate United v Mangotsfield United	1-3e
r	Moreton Town v Haverfordwest County	1-1
35r	Bideford v Cheltenham Town	0-2
r	Merthyr Tydfil v Saltash United	1-0e
r	Trowbridge Town v Ton Pentre	0-3
12r2	Desborough Town v Wigston Fields	1-2
16r2	Chalfont St Peter v Oldbury United	1-3
34r2	Moreton Town v Haverfordwest County	3-5eE

Qualifying Round Two

1	Crook Town v Gateshead (2)	1-2
	Newcastle Blue Star v Billingham Synthonia	1-0
2	Tow Law Town v Guisborough Town	4-3
	West Auckland Town v South Bank	0-6
3	Ashington v Bishop Auckland	0-5
	Peterlee Newtown v Gretna	0-0
4	Whitby Town v North Shields	1-1
	Wren Rovers v Ryhope Community Association	2-3
5	Droylsden v Denaby United	0-0
	Marine v Barrow	3-0
6	Burscough v Leek Town	2-0
	Southport v Alfreton Town	1-1
7	Radcliffe Borough v Oswestry Town	0-1
	Rhyl v Frickley Athletic	0-2
8	Hednesford Town v Ashton United	3-0
	Witton Albion v Accrington Stanley (2)	4-0
9	Bilston Town v Chorley	0-1 N
	Formby v St Helens Town	1-0
10	Dudley Town v Stalybridge Celtic	1-1
	Winsford United v Horwich RMI	2-1
11	Gresley Rovers v Goole Town	0-2
	Matlock Town v Eastwood Town	2-0
12	Wigston Fields v Stourbridge	1-6
	Worksop Town v Halesowen Town	0-3
13	Irthlingborough Diamonds v Nuneaton Borough	0-5
	Shepshed Charterhouse v Gainsborough Trinity	2-5
14	Rothwell Town v Kidderminster Harriers	1-4
	Rushden Town v Bridgnorth Town	0-1
15	Stevenage Borough v Burton Albion	0-2
	Willenhall Town v Bedworth United	3-0
16	Oxford City v Oldbury United	3-0
	Sutton Coldfield Town v Moor Green	0-3
17	Sudbury Town v Wembley	0-0
	V.S. Rugby v Alvechurch	5-0
18	Saffron Walden Town v King's Lynn	0-0
	Wellingborough Town v Corby Town	1-4
19	Aveley v Cambridge City	2-1
	Gorleston v Lowestoft Town	1-0
20	Harlow Town v Basildon United	1-1
	Hornchurch v Chelmsford City	1-1
21	Aylesbury United v Buckingham Town	0-0
	Heybridge Swifts v Chesham United	0-0
22	Grays Athletic v Sutton United	3-1
	Wealdstone v Dunstable	6-0
23	Hitchin Town v Fisher Athletic	1-1
	Potton United v Tring Town	0-2
24	Metropolitan Police v Leytonstone/Ilford	3-1
	Welling United v Addlestone & Weybridge T	2-1
25	Folkestone v Redhill	3-0
	Walthamstow Avenue v Crawley Town	1-0
26	Haywards Heath v Sittingbourne	0-3
	Staines Town v Carshalton Athletic	4-2
27	Canterbury City v Croydon	2-1
	Worthing v Lewes	3-0
28	Dover Athletic v Leatherhead	1-4
	Sheppey United v Hastings United	0-1

1984/85

29 Egham Town v Gravesend & Northfleet	1-0
Tooting & Mitcham United v Kingstonian	2-2
30 Eastbourne Town v Epsom & Ewell	2-4
Wokingham Town v Bognor Regis Town	1-2
31 AFC Totton v Farnborough Town	1-1
Salisbury (2) v Hungerford Town	0-0
32 Chippenham Town v Road Sea Southampton	2-2
Slough Town v Fareham Town	2-0
33 Glastonbury v Clevedon Town	1-2
Witney Town v Poole Town	1-1
34 Gloucester City - Bye	
Mangotsfield United v Barry Town	1-1
35 Dorchester Town v Merthyr Tydfil	0-0
Ton Pentre v Cheltenham Town	2-3
36 Minehead v Bath City	0-0
Wimborne Town v Frome Town	1-3
3r Gretna v Peterlee Newtown	2-0
4r North Shields v Whitby Town	2-2
5r Denaby United v Droylsden	2-0
6r Alfreton Town v Southport	3-0
10r Stalybridge Celtic v Dudley Town	3-1
17r Wembley v Sudbury Town	2-2
18r King's Lynn v Saffron Walden Town	2-1
20r Basildon United v Harlow Town	2-3
r Chelmsford City v Hornchurch	6-1
21r Buckingham Town v Aylesbury United	4-0
r Chesham United v Heybridge Swifts	1-2
23r Fisher Athletic v Hitchin Town	3-1e
29r Kingstonian v Tooting & Mitcham United	0-4e
31r Farnborough Town v AFC Totton	5-1e
r Hungerford Town v Salisbury (2)	3-0
32r Road Sea Southampton v Chippenham Town	1-2
33r Poole Town v Witney Town	0-0
34r Barry Town v Mangotsfield United	3-1
35r Merthyr Tydfil v Dorchester Town	3-0
36r Bath City v Minehead	3-0
4r2 Whitby Town v North Shields	2-0
17r2 Sudbury Town v Wembley	0-3
33r2 Witney Town v Poole Town	3-1eN

Qualifying Round Three

1 Gateshead (2) v Newcastle Blue Star	1-1
2 South Bank v Tow Law Town	1-2
3 Gretna v Bishop Auckland	0-2
4 Ryhope Community Association v Whitby Town	1-1
5 Denaby United v Marine	0-1
6 Burscough v Alfreton Town	2-2
7 Oswestry Town v Frickley Athletic	1-1
8 Hednesford Town v Witton Albion	2-2
9 Formby v Chorley	3-2
10 Stalybridge Celtic v Winsford United	5-0
11 Goole Town v Matlock Town	4-2
12 Stourbridge v Halesowen Town	1-1
13 Nuneaton Borough v Gainsborough Trinity	2-0
14 Kidderminster Harriers v Bridgnorth Town	3-2
15 Burton Albion v Willenhall Town	2-1
16 Oxford City v Moor Green	1-2
17 Wembley v V.S. Rugby	1-5
18 King's Lynn v Corby Town	0-0
19 Gorleston v Aveley	0-4
20 Chelmsford City v Harlow Town	1-2
21 Heybridge Swifts v Buckingham Town	0-0
22 Grays Athletic v Wealdstone	2-1
23 Tring Town v Fisher Athletic	1-1
24 Metropolitan Police v Welling United	3-1
25 Folkestone v Walthamstow Avenue	1-0
26 Sittingbourne v Staines Town	1-1
27 Canterbury City v Worthing	2-1
28 Leatherhead v Hastings United	1-2
29 Egham Town v Tooting & Mitcham United	0-0
30 Epsom & Ewell v Bognor Regis Town	4-5
31 Hungerford Town v Farnborough Town	3-3
32 Chippenham Town v Slough Town	1-0
33 Clevedon Town v Witney Town	2-3
34 Gloucester City v Barry Town	1-3
35 Merthyr Tydfil v Cheltenham Town	4-1
36 Frome Town v Bath City	3-1
1r Newcastle Blue Star v Gateshead (2)	3-1e
4r Whitby Town v Ryhope Community Association	5-1
6r Alfreton Town v Burscough	2-3e
7r Frickley Athletic v Oswestry Town	2-0
8r Witton Albion v Hednesford Town	2-2
12r Halesowen Town v Stourbridge	3-4e
18r Corby Town v King's Lynn	0-3
21r Buckingham Town v Heybridge Swifts	1-0
23r Fisher Athletic v Tring Town	5-0
26r Staines Town v Sittingbourne	3-0
29r Tooting & Mitcham United v Egham Town	1-0
31r Farnborough Town v Hungerford Town	4-1
8r2 Witton Albion v Hednesford Town	2-3

Qualifying Round Four

Aveley v Dagenham	0-1
Barnet v Boston United	3-1
Bishop Auckland v Macclesfield Town	1-2
Bishop's Stortford v Maidstone United	1-0
Bognor Regis Town v Frome Town	2-0
Buckingham Town v Barking	3-1
Canterbury City v Enfield	0-1
Farnborough Town v Chippenham Town	2-1
Folkestone v Fisher Athletic	2-2
Frickley Athletic v Moor Green	5-0
Grays Athletic v Dartford	1-3

Harlow Town v Metropolitan Police	1-3
Hastings United v Staines Town	1-1
Hednesford Town v Nuneaton Borough	0-4
Kettering Town v Harrow Borough	1-1
Kidderminster Harriers v King's Lynn	1-1
Marine v Whitby Town	0-1
Merthyr Tydfil v Barry Town	1-1
Mossley v Goole Town	0-1
Newcastle Blue Star v Burscough	0-0
Penrith v Formby	3-2
Stalybridge Celtic v Workington	1-0
Stourbridge v V.S. Rugby	1-1
Tow Law Town v Scarborough	1-0
Weymouth v Worcester City	3-1
Windsor & Eton v Tooting & Mitcham United	5-0
Wycombe Wanderers v Burton Albion	1-1
Yeovil Town v Witney Town	3-1
r Barry Town v Merthyr Tydfil	1-1
r Burscough v Newcastle Blue Star	0-4
r Burton Albion v Wycombe Wanderers	2-1
r Fisher Athletic v Folkestone	2-0
r Harrow Borough v Kettering Town	0-2
r King's Lynn v Kidderminster Harriers	1-0
r Staines Town v Hastings United	2-1e
r V.S. Rugby v Stourbridge	2-0e
r2 Barry Town v Merthyr Tydfil	3-2

Round One

Bangor City v Tranmere Rovers	1-1
Barry Town v Reading	1-2
Blackpool v Altrincham	0-1
Bradford City v Tow Law Town	7-2
Brentford v Bishop's Stortford	4-0
Bristol Rovers v King's Lynn	2-1
Buckingham Town v Orient	0-2
Burton Albion v Leicester City	2-0
Cambridge United v Peterborough United	0-2
Dagenham v Swindon Town	0-0
Darlington v Chester City	3-2
Exeter City v Enfield	2-2
Fisher Athletic v Bristol City	0-1
Frickley Athletic v Stalybridge Celtic	2-1
Gillingham v Windsor & Eton	2-1
Halifax Town v Goole Town	2-0
Hartlepool United v Derby County	2-1
Hereford United v Farnborough Town	3-0
Hull City v Bolton Wanderers	2-1
Kettering Town v Bournemouth	0-0
Lincoln City v Telford United	1-1
Macclesfield Town v Port Vale	1-2
Mansfield Town v Rotherham United	2-1
Metropolitan Police v Dartford	0-3
Newport County v Aldershot	1-1
Northampton Town v V.S. Rugby	2-2
Northwich Victoria v Crewe Alexandra	3-1
Nuneaton Borough v Scunthorpe United	1-1
Penrith v Burnley	0-9
Plymouth Argyle v Barnet	3-0
Preston North End v Bury	4-3
Rochdale v Doncaster Rovers	1-2
Southend United v Colchester United	2-2
Stockport County v Walsall	1-2
Swansea City v Bognor Regis Town	1-1
Torquay United v Yeovil Town	2-0
Weymouth v Millwall	0-3
Whitby Town v Chesterfield	1-3
Wrexham v Wigan Athletic	0-2
York City v Newcastle Blue Star	2-0
r Aldershot v Newport County	4-0
r Bognor Regis Town v Swansea City	3-1
r Bournemouth v Kettering Town	3-2
r Colchester United v Southend United	3-2e
r Enfield v Exeter City	3-0
r Scunthorpe United v Nuneaton Borough	2-1e
r Swindon Town v Dagenham	1-2e
r Telford United v Lincoln City	2-1
r Tranmere Rovers v Bangor City	7-0
r V.S. Rugby v Northampton Town	0-1

Round Two

Aldershot v Burton Albion	0-2
Altrincham v Doncaster Rovers	1-3
Bradford City v Mansfield Town	2-1
Brentford v Northampton Town	2-2
Bristol City v Bristol Rovers	1-3
Burnley v Halifax Town	3-1
Colchester United v Gillingham	0-5
Dagenham v Peterborough United	1-0
Darlington v Frickley Athletic	1-0
Dartford v Bournemouth	1-1
Hartlepool United v York City	0-2
Millwall v Enfield	1-0
Orient v Torquay United	3-0
Plymouth Argyle v Hereford United	0-0
Port Vale v Scunthorpe United	4-1
Preston North End v Telford United	1-4
Reading v Bognor Regis Town	6-2
Tranmere Rovers v Hull City	0-3
Walsall v Chesterfield	1-0
Wigan Athletic v Northwich Victoria	2-1
r Bournemouth v Dartford	4-1
r Hereford United v Plymouth Argyle	2-0
r Northampton Town v Brentford	0-2

Round Three

Barnsley v Reading	4-3
Birmingham City v Norwich City	0-0
Brighton & Hove Albion v Hull City	1-0
Bristol Rovers v Ipswich Town	1-2
Burton Albion v Leicester City	1-6 v
Carlisle United v Dagenham	1-0
Chelsea v Wigan Athletic	2-2
Coventry City v Manchester City	2-1
Doncaster Rovers v Queen's Park Rangers	1-0
Fulham v Sheffield Wednesday	2-3
Gillingham v Cardiff City	2-1
Hereford United v Arsenal	1-1
Leeds United v Everton	0-2
Liverpool v Aston Villa	3-0
Luton Town v Stoke City	1-1
Manchester United v Bournemouth	3-0
Middlesbrough v Darlington	0-0
Millwall v Crystal Palace	1-1
Nottingham Forest v Newcastle United	1-1
Notts County v Grimsby Town	2-2
Oldham Athletic v Brentford	2-1
Orient v West Bromwich Albion	2-1
Portsmouth v Blackburn Rovers	0-0
Shrewsbury Town v Oxford United	0-2
Southampton v Sunderland	4-0
Telford United v Bradford City	2-1
Tottenham Hotspur v Charlton Athletic	1-1
Watford v Sheffield United	5-0
West Ham United v Port Vale	4-1
Wimbledon v Burnley	3-1
Wolverhampton Wan. v Huddersfield Town	1-1
York City v Walsall	3-0
r Arsenal v Hereford United	7-2
r Blackburn Rovers v Portsmouth	2-1
r Burton Albion v Leicester City	0-1 N
r Charlton Athletic v Tottenham Hotspur	1-2
r Crystal Palace v Millwall	1-2
r Darlington v Middlesbrough	2-1
r Grimsby Town v Notts County	4-2
r Huddersfield Town v Wolverhampton Wan.	3-1
r Newcastle United v Nottingham Forest	1-3e
r Norwich City v Birmingham City	1-1e
r Stoke City v Luton Town	2-3
r Wigan Athletic v Chelsea	0-5
r2 Birmingham City v Norwich City	1-1e
r3 Norwich City v Birmingham City	1-0

Round Four

Barnsley v Brighton & Hove Albion	2-1
Chelsea v Millwall	2-3
Darlington v Telford United	1-1
Everton v Doncaster Rovers	2-0
Grimsby Town v Watford	1-3
Ipswich Town v Gillingham	3-2
Leicester City v Carlisle United	1-0
Liverpool v Tottenham Hotspur	1-0
Luton Town v Huddersfield Town	2-0
Manchester United v Coventry City	2-1
Nottingham Forest v Wimbledon	0-0
Orient v Southampton	0-2
Oxford United v Blackburn Rovers	0-1
Sheffield Wednesday v Oldham Athletic	5-1
West Ham United v Norwich City	2-1
York City v Arsenal	1-0
r Telford United v Darlington	3-0
r Wimbledon v Nottingham Forest	1-0

Round Five

Blackburn Rovers v Manchester United	0-2e
Everton v Telford United	3-0
Ipswich Town v Sheffield Wednesday	3-2
Luton Town v Watford	0-0
Millwall v Leicester City	2-0
Southampton v Barnsley	1-2
Wimbledon v West Ham United	1-1
York City v Liverpool	1-1
r Liverpool v York City	7-0
r Watford v Luton Town	2-2e
r West Ham United v Wimbledon	5-1
r2 Luton Town v Watford	1-0

Round Six

Barnsley v Liverpool	0-4
Everton v Ipswich Town	2-2
Luton Town v Millwall	1-0
Manchester United v West Ham United	4-2
r Ipswich Town v Everton	0-1

Semi Finals

Everton v Luton Town	2-1eN
Manchester United v Liverpool	2-2eN
r Liverpool v Manchester United	1-2 N

Final

Manchester United v Everton	1-0eN

171

1985/86

1985/86

Preliminary Round

1	Bridlington Trinity v Netherfield (Kendal)	4-0
	Ferryhill Athletic v West Auckland Town	2-2
2	Crook Town v Evenwood Town	5-1
	Farsley Celtic v Seaham Red Star	2-0
	Langley Park v Horden CW	2-6
3	Ashington v Durham City	0-2
	Eppleton CW v Yorkshire Amateur	5-1
4	Easington Colliery v Billingham Town	2-3
	Lancaster City v Willington	1-0
	Shildon v Esh Winning	3-1
5	Garforth Town v Northallerton Town	1-2
	Norton & Stockton Ancients v Shotton Comrades	1-1
	Thackley v Fleetwood Town	0-1
6	Accrington Stanley (2) v Darwen	2-0
	Rossendale United v Guiseley	1-0
7	Chadderton v Ashton United	2-2
	Emley v Belper Town	1-1
	Nantwich Town v Glossop	1-0
8	Caernarfon Town v Congleton Town	1-1
	Warrington Town v Eastwood Town	3-1
9	Colwyn Bay v Leyland Motors	3-1
	Leek Town v Armitage	0-0
10	Ilkeston Town (2) v Lincoln United	5-0
	Radcliffe Borough v North Ferriby United	2-2
11	Arnold v Shifnal Town	4-0 N
	Boldmere St Michaels v Heanor Town	2-0e
12	Gresley Rovers v Friar Lane Old Boys	8-0
	Oldswinford v Highgate United	2-1
	Spalding United v Coventry Sporting	1-2ed
13	Boston v Atherstone United	0-2
	Desborough Town v Oldbury United	2-3
14	Paget Rangers v Rushall Olympic	2-2
	Sutton Coldfield Town v Lye Town	1-2
	Wellingborough Town v Wigston Fields	4-0
15	Blakenall v Tamworth	0-4
	Stevenage Borough v AP Leamington	2-1
16	Holbeach United v Rushden Town	1-1
	Rothwell Town v Hemel Hempstead Town	3-3
	Royston Town v March Town United	2-7
17	Chatteris Town v Newmarket Town	0-3
	Sudbury Town v Tiptree United	2-0
18	Histon v Soham Town Rangers	3-0
	Stowmarket v Flackwell Heath	3-0
19	Chalfont St Peter v Banbury United	2-1
	Lowestoft Town v Bury Town	2-0
20	Great Yarmouth Town v Burnham & Hillingdon	2-0
	St Albans City v Wolverton Town	1-1
	Wootton Blue Cross v Woodford Town (1)	0-1
21	Barton Rovers v Chesham United	2-1
	Harwich & Parkeston v Hoddesdon Town	2-3e
22	Chatham Town v Southall	1-1
	Hampton v Chertsey Town	2-0
	Hertford Town v Harefield United	1-1
23	Clapton v Leytonstone/Ilford	3-2 D
	Uxbridge v Corinthian Casuals	3-1
24	Crockenhill v Hounslow	0-1
	Edgware Town v Erith & Belvedere	1-1
	Kingsbury Town v Leyton-Wingate	1-1
25	Fleet Town v Sheppey United	0-2
	Tilbury v Maidenhead United	2-0 N
26	Camberley Town v Bromley	2-2
	Rainham Town v Littlehampton Town	1-2
	Thanet United v Chichester City (1)	3-1
27	Hailsham Town v Dorking (2)	4-4
	Ringmer v Whitstable Town	2-1
28	Horley Town v Walton & Hersham	0-5
	Three Bridges v Lewes	2-3
	Tonbridge v Horsham	3-0
29	Eastbourne United v Dover Athletic	4-2
	Hastings Town v Burgess Hill Town	1-0
	Horsham YMCA v Whyteleafe	0-3
30	Ashford Town v Faversham Town	5-1
	Deal Town v Southwick	1-4
	Lancing v Hythe Town	0-3
31	Devizes Town v Pagham	2-2
	Horndean v Calne Town	1-1
32	AFC Totton v Sholing Sports	2-0
	Brockenhurst v Warminster Town	1-3
	Newbury Town v Melksham Town	2-1
33	Bridgend Town v Poole Town	0-1
	Bristol Manor Farm v Chard Town	2-0
	Wimborne Town v Weston-Super-Mare	2-5
34	Dorchester Town v Clandown	0-0
	Maesteg Park Athletic v Forest Green Rovers	0-1
	Welton Rovers v Mangotsfield United	1-3
35	Llanelli v Minehead	2-3
	Saltash United v Barnstaple Town	1-0
	Shortwood United v Sharpness	1-1
36	Glastonbury v Exmouth Town	0-5
	Ottery St Mary v Torrington	1-0
	St Blazey v Shepton Mallet Town	1-0
1r	West Auckland Town v Ferryhill Athletic	1-2
5r	Shotton Comrades v Norton & Stockton Ancients	2-2
7r	Ashton United v Chadderton	2-1
r	Belper Town v Emley	0-1
8r	Congleton Town v Caernarfon Town	1-0
9r	Armitage v Leek Town	0-2
10r	North Ferriby United v Radcliffe Borough	1-2
14r	Rushall Olympic v Paget Rangers	3-0

16r	Hemel Hempstead Town v Rothwell Town	1-0
r	Rushden Town v Holbeach United	3-3
20r	Wolverton Town v St Albans City	0-2
22r	Harefield United v Hertford Town	3-0
r	Southall v Chatham Town	2-0
24r	Erith & Belvedere v Edgware Town	1-0
r	Leyton-Wingate v Kingsbury Town	3-0
26r	Bromley v Camberley Town	4-0
27r	Dorking (2) v Hailsham Town	3-0
31r	Calne Town v Horndean	0-0
r	Pagham v Devizes Town	4-1
34r	Clandown v Dorchester Town	0-0
35r	Sharpness v Shortwood United	1-1
5r2	Shotton Comrades v Norton & Stockton Ancients	5-2
16r2	Rushden Town v Holbeach United	1-0
31r2	Horndean v Calne Town	2-1
34r2	Dorchester Town v Clandown	1-2
35r2	Sharpness v Shortwood United	5-1

Qualifying Round One

1	Brandon United v Barrow	5-0
	Bridlington Trinity v Alnwick Town	1-0
	Ferryhill Athletic v Bishop Auckland	0-3
	Newcastle Blue Star v Guisborough Town	2-1
2	Bridlington Town v Scarborough	0-1
	Farsley Celtic v Blyth Spartans	1-2
	Horden CW v Crook Town	2-3
	Ryhope Community Association v Whitley Bay	1-3
3	Billingham Synthonia v Gateshead (2)	0-4
	Durham City v Chester-le-Street Town	2-3
	Eppleton CW v Spennymoor United	2-4
	South Bank v Darlington Cleveland Bridge	4-0
4	Harrogate Town v Morecambe	0-2
	Lancaster City v Gretna	0-4
	Shildon v Billingham Town	1-2
	Tow Law Town v Consett	1-0
5	Fleetwood Town v North Shields	2-2
	Northallerton Town v Shotton Comrades	1-2
	Penrith v Peterlee Newtown	1-3
	Wingate (Durham) v Workington	4-2
6	Accrington Stanley (2) v Droylsden	4-1
	Burscough v Armthorpe Welfare	1-1
	Prescot Cables v Runcorn	1-2
	Rossendale United v Mossley	1-2
7	Ashton United v Stalybridge Celtic	0-1
	Bootle v Chorley	0-1
	Emley v Nantwich Town	1-0
	Southport v Clitheroe	4-2
8	Congleton Town v Curzon Ashton	1-0
	Rhyl v Wren Rovers	3-1
	Skelmersdale United v Horwich RMI	2-2
	Warrington Town v Formby	1-3
9	Colwyn Bay v St Helens Town	0-3
	Eastwood Hanley v Hyde United	0-0
	Leek Town v Winsford United	2-0
	Oswestry Town v GKN Sankey	1-1
10	Goole Town v Skegness Town	3-2
	Ilkeston Town (2) v Buxton	2-2
	Radcliffe Borough v Ossett Albion	0-0
	Sutton Town v Marine	2-2
11	Arnold v Tividale	6-1
	Boldmere St Michaels v South Liverpool	1-1
	Denaby United v Long Eaton United	0-0
	Leicester United v Witton Albion	0-1
12	Alfreton Town v Bourne Town	6-0
	Brigg Town v Worksop Town	0-1
	Oldswinford v Gresley Rovers	2-2
	Spalding United v Matlock Town	2-2
13	Atherstone United v Bilston Town	3-3
	Bridgnorth Town v Mile Oak Rovers & Youth	0-1
	Bromsgrove Rovers v Gainsborough Trinity	1-1
	Oldbury United v Grantham	1-1
14	Halesowen Town v Racing Club Warwick	2-0
	Irthlingborough Diamonds v Shepshed Charterhouse	3-2
	Lye Town v Stafford Rangers	1-3
	Rushall Olympic v Wellingborough Town	0-2
15	Hednesford Town v Milton Keynes Borough	2-1
	Stevenage Borough v Kidderminster Harriers	0-2
	Tamworth v Walsall Borough	2-1
	Wisbech Town v Dudley Town	2-0
16	Hemel Hempstead Town v Nuneaton Borough	1-3
	Hinckley Athletic v Willenhall Town	2-1
	Moor Green v Wednesfield Social	5-0
	Rushden Town v March Town United	2-3
17	Berkhamsted Town v Bedworth United	0-0
	Newmarket Town v Stamford	1-6
	Sudbury Town v Stourbridge	0-0
	Witney Town v Saffron Walden Town	3-0
18	Histon v Finchley	3-1
	Hitchin Town v Haverhill Rovers	1-1
	Letchworth Garden City v Corby Town	2-3
	Stowmarket v V.S. Rugby	2-2
19	Barking v Cheshunt	4-1
	Basildon United v Alvechurch	1-3
	Chalfont St Peter v King's Lynn	1-1
	Lowestoft Town v Braintree Town	1-2
20	Felixstowe Town v Gorleston	4-0
	Great Yarmouth Town v Heybridge Swifts	0-1
	Harlow Town v Cambridge City	2-1
	Woodford Town (1) v St Albans City	1-0
21	Abingdon Town v Tring Town	0-1
	Barton Rovers v Walthamstow Avenue	1-2
	Hoddesdon Town v Dunstable	1-3
	Wembley v Boreham Wood	2-0

22	Arlesey Town v Aylesbury United	1-2
	Grays Athletic v Burnham (1)	wo/s
	Hampton v Southall	3-1
	Harefield United v Aveley	0-0
23	Chelmsford City v Alma Swanley	2-0
	Leytonstone/Ilford v Marlow	0-2
	Uxbridge v Buckingham Town	0-1
	Ware v Billericay Town	1-0
24	Baldock Town v Harrow Borough	0-2
	Egham Town v Hornchurch	1-1
	Erith & Belvedere v Crawley Town	1-1
	Hounslow v Leyton-Wingate	1-2
25	Bracknell Town v Hayes	1-1
	Leatherhead v Redhill	0-2
	Sheppey United v Fisher Athletic	1-1
	Tilbury v Tunbridge Wells	2-1 N
26	Gravesend & Northfleet v Littlehampton Town	2-1e
	Ruislip Manor v Hendon	1-0
	Sutton United v Beckenham Town	5-0
	Thanet United v Bromley	2-2
27	Dorking (2) v Welling United	1-7
	Merstham v Slough Town	0-4
	Ringmer v Woking	1-3
	Staines Town v Molesey	3-1
28	Herne Bay v Carshalton Athletic	1-5
	Kingstonian v Whitehawk	1-0
	Lewes v Tonbridge	0-1
	Walton & Hersham v Hastings United	wo/s
29	Cray Wanderers v Canterbury City	1-1
	Hastings Town v Epsom & Ewell	2-1
	Sittingbourne v Banstead Athletic	1-2
	Whyteleafe v Eastbourne United	2-1
30	Dulwich Hamlet v Eastbourne Town	3-1
	Haywards Heath v Croydon	3-5
	Hythe Town v Ashford Town	1-0
	Southwick v Folkestone	1-1
31	Horndean v Tooting & Mitcham United	2-3
	Newport (IOW) v Metropolitan Police	3-2
	Pagham v Petersfield United	2-0
	Worthing v Waterlooville	3-0
32	Arundel v Basingstoke Town	1-3
	Fareham Town v Salisbury (2)	2-2
	Newbury Town v AFC Totton	3-3
	Warminster Town v Wokingham Town	1-1
33	Andover v Hungerford Town	1-3
	Bristol Manor Farm v Gosport Borough	1-1
	Oxford City v Malvern Town	7-2
	Poole Town v Weston-Super-Mare	5-1
34	Forest Green Rovers v Clandown	0-1
	Gloucester City v Ton Pentre	0-0
	Mangotsfield United v Frome Town	1-3
	Redditch United v Road Sea Southampton	1-1
35	Barry Town v Paulton Rovers	2-2
	Minehead v Cheltenham Town	1-1
	Saltash United v Sharpness	1-2
	Trowbridge Town v Chippenham Town	1-3
36	Bath City v Taunton Town	4-1
	Bideford v Merthyr Tydfil	1-1
	Exmouth Town v Ottery St Mary	2-0
	St Blazey v Clevedon Town	2-4
5r	North Shields v Fleetwood Town	2-1
6r	Armthorpe Welfare v Burscough	0-1
8r	Horwich RMI v Skelmersdale United	3-0
9r	GKN Sankey v Oswestry Town	1-0
r	Hyde United v Eastwood Hanley	1-2
10r	Buxton v Ilkeston Town (2)	4-1
r	Marine v Sutton Town	6-0
r	Ossett Albion v Radcliffe Borough	0-3
11r	Long Eaton United v Denaby United	1-0
r	South Liverpool v Boldmere St Michaels	5-0
12r	Gresley Rovers v Oldswinford	5-3
r	Matlock Town v Spalding United	0-0
13r	Bilston Town v Atherstone United	0-2
r	Gainsborough Trinity v Bromsgrove Rovers	1-2
r	Grantham v Oldbury United	2-1
17r	Bedworth United v Berkhamsted Town	1-2
r	Stourbridge v Sudbury Town	1-0
18r	Haverhill Rovers v Hitchin Town	0-0
r	V.S. Rugby v Stowmarket	3-2
19r	King's Lynn v Chalfont St Peter	1-2
22r	Aveley v Harefield United	2-0
24r	Crawley Town v Erith & Belvedere	3-0
r	Hornchurch v Egham Town	0-1e
25r	Fisher Athletic v Sheppey United	2-2
r	Hayes v Bracknell Town	2-1
26r	Bromley v Thanet United	2-1
29r	Canterbury City v Cray Wanderers	5-0
30r	Folkestone v Southwick	1-1
32r	AFC Totton v Newbury Town	2-0
r	Salisbury (2) v Fareham Town	0-5
r	Wokingham Town v Warminster Town	3-2
33r	Gosport Borough v Bristol Manor Farm	2-2
34r	Road Sea Southampton v Redditch United	3-2
r	Ton Pentre v Gloucester City	3-3
35r	Cheltenham Town v Minehead	1-2
r	Paulton Rovers v Barry Town	0-2
36r	Merthyr Tydfil v Bideford	1-1
12r2	Matlock Town v Spalding United	3-2e
18r2	Hitchin Town v Haverhill Rovers	3-0
25r2	Sheppey United v Fisher Athletic	0-4
30r2	Southwick v Folkestone	3-1e
33r2	Gosport Borough v Bristol Manor Farm	4-3
34r2	Ton Pentre v Gloucester City	2-1
36r2	Bideford v Merthyr Tydfil	2-0

1985/86

Qualifying Round Two

1	Bridlington Trinity v Brandon United	6-2
	Newcastle Blue Star v Bishop Auckland	1-3
2	Crook Town v Scarborough	0-1
	Whitley Bay v Blyth Spartans	1-2
3	South Bank v Chester-le-Street Town	2-0
	Spennymoor United v Gateshead (2)	1-2
4	Billingham Town v Morecambe	0-5
	Tow Law Town v Gretna	0-1
5	Peterlee Newtown v North Shields	2-1
	Shotton Comrades v Wingate (Durham)	0-2
6	Accrington Stanley (2) v Runcorn	1-1
	Burscough v Mossley	0-3
7	Emley v Chorley	1-4
	Southport v Stalybridge Celtic	2-0
8	Congleton Town v Horwich RMI	2-2
	Rhyl v Formby	5-0
9	GKN Sankey v Leek Town	1-1
	St Helens Town v Eastwood Hanley	2-0
10	Goole Town v Buxton	3-1
	Radcliffe Borough v Marine	0-4
11	Arnold v Witton Albion	0-2
	Long Eaton United v South Liverpool	2-3
12	Alfreton Town v Matlock Town	2-0
	Gresley Rovers v Worksop Town	1-0
13	Atherstone United v Bromsgrove Rovers	4-0
	Mile Oak Rovers & Youth v Grantham	1-3
14	Halesowen Town v Stafford Rangers	3-2
	Wellingborough Town v Irthlingborough Diamonds	1-1
15	Hednesford Town v Kidderminster Harriers	1-5
	Tamworth v Wisbech Town	2-1
16	March Town United v Hinckley Athletic	1-2
	Moor Green v Nuneaton Borough	1-4
17	Stamford v Berkhamsted Town	3-0
	Witney Town v Stourbridge	0-0
18	Histon v Corby Town	0-1
	Hitchin Town v V.S. Rugby	0-0
19	Barking v Chalfont St Peter	0-2
	Braintree Town v Alvechurch	2-1
20	Harlow Town v Heybridge Swifts	1-0
	Woodford Town (1) v Felixstowe Town	3-1
21	Dunstable v Tring Town	3-2
	Wembley v Walthamstow Avenue	1-3
22	Grays Athletic v Aveley	2-1
	Hampton v Aylesbury United	0-1
23	Chelmsford City v Buckingham Town	1-0
	Marlow v Ware	2-3
24	Egham Town v Crawley Town	0-6
	Leyton-Wingate v Harrow Borough	2-2
25	Redhill v Fisher Athletic	0-2
	Tilbury v Hayes	0-0
26	Bromley v Ruislip Manor	3-2
	Sutton United v Gravesend & Northfleet	0-1
27	Staines Town v Welling United	0-3
	Woking v Slough Town	1-5
28	Kingstonian v Walton & Hersham	3-1
	Tonbridge v Carshalton Athletic	0-2
29	Banstead Athletic v Hastings Town	0-1
	Whyteleafe v Canterbury City	1-2
30	Dulwich Hamlet v Southwick	1-1
	Hythe Town v Croydon	1-5
31	Pagham v Newport (IOW)	3-5
	Worthing v Tooting & Mitcham United	5-1
32	AFC Totton v Basingstoke Town	1-1
	Fareham Town v Wokingham Town	1-0
33	Oxford City v Gosport Borough	2-1
	Poole Town v Hungerford Town	3-2
34	Clandown v Road Sea Southampton	1-2
	Ton Pentre v Frome Town	2-1
35	Barry Town v Minehead	5-1
	Sharpness v Chippenham Town	2-3
36	Bath City v Clevedon Town	1-0
	Exmouth Town v Bideford	2-1
6r	Runcorn v Accrington Stanley (2)	9-1
8r	Horwich RMI v Congleton Town	2-0
9r	Leek Town v GKN Sankey	5-4e
14r	Irthlingborough Diamonds v Wellingborough Town	4-2
17r	Stourbridge v Witney Town	1-0
18r	V.S. Rugby v Hitchin Town	3-1
24r	Harrow Borough v Leyton-Wingate	2-3
25r	Hayes v Tilbury	1-2
30r	Southwick v Dulwich Hamlet	2-1
32r	Basingstoke Town v AFC Totton	1-2

Qualifying Round Three

1	Bishop Auckland v Bridlington Trinity	3-2
2	Blyth Spartans v Scarborough	1-1
3	South Bank v Gateshead (2)	2-2
4	Gretna v Morecambe	0-2
5	Peterlee Newtown v Wingate (Durham)	2-1
6	Mossley v Runcorn	0-2
7	Southport v Chorley	1-3
8	Rhyl v Horwich RMI	2-0
9	Leek Town v St Helens Town	0-1
10	Goole Town v Marine	0-5
11	South Liverpool v Witton Albion	5-0
12	Alfreton Town v Gresley Rovers	0-1
13	Grantham v Atherstone United	0-2
14	Halesowen Town v Irthlingborough Diamonds	2-2
15	Kidderminster Harriers v Tamworth	4-3
16	Nuneaton Borough v Hinckley Athletic	0-0
17	Stourbridge v Stamford	4-0
18	V.S. Rugby v Corby Town	2-0
19	Chalfont St Peter v Braintree Town	1-1
20	Harlow Town v Woodford Town (1)	3-0
21	Walthamstow Avenue v Dunstable	0-0
22	Grays Athletic v Aylesbury United	2-2
23	Chelmsford City v Ware	1-0
24	Crawley Town v Leyton-Wingate	2-3
25	Fisher Athletic v Tilbury	2-1
26	Gravesend & Northfleet v Bromley	2-3
27	Welling United v Slough Town	0-0
28	Kingstonian v Carshalton Athletic	2-0
29	Hastings Town v Canterbury City	3-0
30	Southwick v Croydon	0-1
31	Worthing v Newport (IOW)	4-0
32	Fareham Town v AFC Totton	0-0
33	Oxford City v Poole Town	4-1
34	Ton Pentre v Road Sea Southampton	1-1
35	Barry Town v Chippenham Town	2-2
36	Bath City v Exmouth Town	2-0
2r	Scarborough v Blyth Spartans	3-1
3r	Gateshead (2) v South Bank	1-1
14r	Irthlingborough Diamonds v Halesowen Town	1-2
16r	Hinckley Athletic v Nuneaton Borough	0-1
19r	Braintree Town v Chalfont St Peter	2-0
21r	Dunstable v Walthamstow Avenue	2-0
22r	Aylesbury United v Grays Athletic	1-0 N
27r	Slough Town v Welling United	2-1
32r	AFC Totton v Fareham Town	0-3
34r	Road Sea Southampton v Ton Pentre	1-2
35r	Chippenham Town v Barry Town	0-1
3r2	Gateshead (2) v South Bank	1-2

Qualifying Round Four

	Aylesbury United v Harlow Town	0-0 N
	Bangor City v South Liverpool	1-1
	Barnet v Enfield	0-7
	Bath City v Croydon	4-1
	Bromley v Maidstone United	0-2
	Chelmsford City v Kettering Town	1-0
	Chorley v Marine	4-2
	Dagenham v Atherstone United	5-1
	Dartford v Worcester City	2-0
	Dunstable v Nuneaton Borough	0-2
	Farnborough Town v Hastings Town	3-2
	Fisher Athletic v Fareham Town	1-2
	Frickley Athletic v Northwich Victoria	2-1
	Halesowen Town v Braintree Town	2-1
	Kidderminster Harriers v Bishop's Stortford	3-4
	Leyton-Wingate v Gresley Rovers	2-0
	Macclesfield Town v South Bank	3-1
	Morecambe v St Helens Town	1-1
	Rhyl v Runcorn	0-2
	Scarborough v Bishop Auckland	4-1
	Slough Town v Kingstonian	2-2
	Stourbridge v V.S. Rugby	1-1
	Ton Pentre v Weymouth	1-3
	Whitby Town v Peterlee Newtown	2-2
	Windsor & Eton v Oxford City	2-2
	Worthing v Bognor Regis Town	1-2
	Wycombe Wanderers v Burton Albion	1-0
	Yeovil Town v Barry Town	4-1
r	Harlow Town v Aylesbury United	1-2
r	Kingstonian v Slough Town	1-1
r	Oxford City v Windsor & Eton	0-1
r	Peterlee Newtown v Whitby Town	0-1
r	South Liverpool v Bangor City	3-2e
r	St Helens Town v Morecambe	0-1
r	V.S. Rugby v Stourbridge	3-1
r2	Slough Town v Kingstonian	2-1

Round One

	Bishop's Stortford v Peterborough United	2-2
	Bournemouth v Dartford	0-0
	Brentford v Bristol Rovers	1-3
	Bury v Chester City	2-0
	Chelmsford City v Weymouth	1-0
	Chorley v Altrincham	0-2
	Dagenham v Cambridge United	2-1
	Derby County v Crewe Alexandra	5-1
	Enfield v Bognor Regis Town	0-2
	Exeter City v Cardiff City	2-1
	Fareham Town v Maidstone United	0-3
	Farnborough Town v Bath City	0-4
	Frickley Athletic v Halesowen Town	1-1
	Gillingham v Northampton Town	3-0
	Halifax Town v Scunthorpe United	1-3
	Lincoln City v Blackpool	0-1
	Macclesfield Town v Hartlepool United	1-2
	Mansfield Town v Port Vale	1-1
	Notts County v Scarborough	6-1
	Nuneaton Borough v Burnley	2-3
	Plymouth Argyle v Aldershot	1-0
	Reading v Wealdstone	1-0
	Rochdale v Darlington	2-1
	Rotherham United v Wolverhampton Wan.	6-0
	Runcorn v Boston United	2-2
	Slough Town v Aylesbury United	2-2
	Southend United v Newport County	0-1
	Stockport County v Telford United	0-1
	Swansea City v Leyton-Wingate	2-0
	Swindon Town v Bristol City	0-0
	Tranmere Rovers v Chesterfield	2-2
	V.S. Rugby v Orient	2-2
	Walsall v Preston North End	7-3
	Whitby Town v South Liverpool	1-0
	Wigan Athletic v Doncaster Rovers	4-1
	Windsor & Eton v Torquay United	1-1
	Wrexham v Bolton Wanderers	3-1
	Wycombe Wanderers v Colchester United	2-0
	Yeovil Town v Hereford United	2-4
	York City v Morecambe	0-0
r	Aylesbury United v Slough Town	2-5 N
r	Boston United v Runcorn	1-1e
r	Bristol City v Swindon Town	4-2
r	Chesterfield v Tranmere Rovers	0-1
r	Dartford v Bournemouth	0-2
r	Halesowen Town v Frickley Athletic	1-3
r	Morecambe v York City	0-2 N
r	Orient v V.S. Rugby	4-1
r	Peterborough United v Bishop's Stortford	3-1
r	Port Vale v Mansfield Town	1-0
r	Torquay United v Windsor & Eton	3-0
r2	Runcorn v Boston United	4-1

Round Two

	Blackpool v Altrincham	1-2
	Bournemouth v Dagenham	4-1
	Bristol City v Exeter City	1-2
	Derby County v Telford United	6-1
	Gillingham v Bognor Regis Town	6-1
	Hartlepool United v Frickley Athletic	0-1
	Newport County v Torquay United	1-1
	Notts County v Wrexham	2-2
	Orient v Slough Town	2-2
	Peterborough United v Bath City	1-0
	Plymouth Argyle v Maidstone United	3-0
	Port Vale v Walsall	0-0
	Reading v Hereford United	2-0
	Rotherham United v Burnley	4-1
	Runcorn v Wigan Athletic	1-1
	Scunthorpe United v Rochdale	2-2
	Swansea City v Bristol Rovers	1-2
	Tranmere Rovers v Bury	1-1
	Wycombe Wanderers v Chelmsford City	2-0
	York City v Whitby Town	3-1
r	Bury v Tranmere Rovers	2-1
r	Rochdale v Scunthorpe United	2-1
r	Slough Town v Orient	2-3
r	Torquay United v Newport County	2-3e
r	Walsall v Port Vale	2-1
r	Wigan Athletic v Runcorn	4-0
r	Wrexham v Notts County	0-3

Round Three

	Birmingham City v Altrincham	1-2
	Bristol Rovers v Leicester City	3-1
	Bury v Barnsley	2-0
	Carlisle United v Queen's Park Rangers	1-0
	Charlton Athletic v West Ham United	0-1
	Coventry City v Watford	1-3
	Crystal Palace v Luton Town	1-2
	Everton v Exeter City	1-0
	Frickley Athletic v Rotherham United	1-3
	Gillingham v Derby County	1-1
	Grimsby Town v Arsenal	3-4
	Huddersfield Town v Reading	0-0
	Hull City v Plymouth Argyle	2-2
	Ipswich Town v Bradford City	4-4
	Liverpool v Norwich City	5-0
	Manchester United v Rochdale	2-0
	Middlesbrough v Southampton	1-3
	Millwall v Wimbledon	3-1
	Newcastle United v Brighton & Hove Albion	0-2
	Nottingham Forest v Blackburn Rovers	1-1
	Oldham Athletic v Orient	1-2
	Oxford United v Tottenham Hotspur	1-1
	Peterborough United v Leeds United	1-0
	Portsmouth v Aston Villa	2-2
	Sheffield United v Fulham	2-0
	Sheffield Wednesday v West Bromwich Albion	2-2
	Shrewsbury Town v Chelsea	0-1
	Stoke City v Notts County	0-2
	Sunderland v Newport County	2-0
	Walsall v Manchester City	1-3
	Wigan Athletic v Bournemouth	3-0
	York City v Wycombe Wanderers	2-0
r	Aston Villa v Portsmouth	3-2e
r	Blackburn Rovers v Nottingham Forest	3-2
r	Bradford City v Ipswich Town	0-1e
r	Derby County v Gillingham	3-1e
r	Plymouth Argyle v Hull City	0-1
r	Reading v Huddersfield Town	2-1e
r	Tottenham Hotspur v Oxford United	2-1e
r	West Bromwich Albion v Sheffield Wednesday	2-3

Round Four

	Arsenal v Rotherham United	5-1
	Aston Villa v Millwall	1-1
	Chelsea v Liverpool	1-2
	Everton v Blackburn Rovers	3-1
	Hull City v Brighton & Hove Albion	2-3
	Luton Town v Bristol Rovers	4-0
	Manchester City v Watford	1-1
	Notts County v Tottenham Hotspur	1-1
	Peterborough United v Carlisle United	1-0
	Reading v Bury	1-1

1985/86 to 1986/87

	Sheffield United v Derby County	0-1
	Sheffield Wednesday v Orient	5-0
	Southampton v Wigan Athletic	3-0
	Sunderland v Manchester United	0-0
	West Ham United v Ipswich Town	0-0
	York City v Altrincham	2-0
r	Bury v Reading	3-0
r	Ipswich Town v West Ham United	1-1e
r	Manchester United v Sunderland	3-0
r	Millwall v Aston Villa	1-0
r	Tottenham Hotspur v Notts County	5-0
r	Watford v Manchester City	0-0e
r2	Ipswich Town v West Ham United	0-1e
r2	Manchester City v Watford	1-3

Round Five

	Derby County v Sheffield Wednesday	1-1
	Luton Town v Arsenal	2-2
	Peterborough United v Brighton & Hove Albion	2-2
	Southampton v Millwall	0-0
	Tottenham Hotspur v Everton	1-2
	Watford v Bury	1-1
	West Ham United v Manchester United	1-1
	York City v Liverpool	1-1
r	Arsenal v Luton Town	0-0e
r	Brighton & Hove Albion v Peterborough United	1-0
r	Bury v Watford	0-3
r	Liverpool v York City	3-1e
r	Manchester United v West Ham United	0-2
r	Millwall v Southampton	0-1
r	Sheffield Wednesday v Derby County	2-0
r2	Luton Town v Arsenal	3-0

Round Six

	Brighton & Hove Albion v Southampton	0-2
	Liverpool v Watford	0-0
	Luton Town v Everton	2-2
	Sheffield Wednesday v West Ham United	2-1
r	Everton v Luton Town	1-0
r	Watford v Liverpool	1-2e

Semi Finals

	Everton v Sheffield Wednesday	2-1eN
	Liverpool v Southampton	2-0eN

Final

	Liverpool v Everton	3-1 N

1986/87

Preliminary Round

1	Alnwick Town v Guisborough Town	1-0
	Consett v Annfield Plain	0-0
	Ferryhill Athletic v Darlington Cleveland Bridge	1-2
2	Ashington v Seaham Red Star	3-2
	Bridlington Town v Murton	2-0
	North Shields v Denaby United	3-1
3	Norton & Stockton Ancients v Newcastle Blue Star	1-1
	Ryhope Community Association v Farsley Celtic	1-1
4	Durham City v Shildon	2-1
	Fleetwood Town v Clitheroe	2-0
	Northallerton Town v Guiseley	0-4
5	Darwen v West Auckland Town	2-0
	Langley Park v Evenwood Town	0-0
	Thackley v Netherfield (Kendal)	1-0
6	Ashton United v Ossett Albion	3-2
	Curzon Ashton v Armthorpe Welfare	2-2
	Penrith v Glossop	6-2
7	Accrington Stanley (2) v Lancaster City	0-1
	Chadderton v Irlam Town	0-1
	Ilkeston Town (2) v Emley	1-3
8	Bootle v Belper Town	2-0
	Burscough v Kirkby Town (2)	2-0
	Formby v Droylsden	1-1
9	Colwyn Bay v Rossendale United	1-1
	Congleton Town v Bridgnorth Town	0-0
	Radcliffe Borough v Eastwood Hanley	3-3
10	Sutton Town v Stalybridge Celtic	6-2
	Walsall Wood v Skelmersdale United	0-1
11	Bilston Town v Lye Town	1-2
	Brigg Town v Arnold	5-4
	Friar Lane Old Boys v Leicester United	0-2
12	Oldswinford v Boldmere St Michaels	3-3
	Rothwell Town v Tividale	3-2
	Wellingborough Town v Sutton Coldfield Town	1-3
13	Coventry Sporting v Racing Club Warwick	3-1
	Highgate United v Banbury United	1-3
	Mile Oak Rovers & Youth v AP Leamington	1-1
14	Bourne Town v Tamworth	0-2
	Gresley Rovers v Wolverton Town	0-2
	Rushall Olympic v Moor Green	2-3
15	Spalding United v Rushden Town	0-0
	Stevenage Borough v Milton Keynes Borough	3-2
16	Barton Rovers v Saffron Walden Town	1-1
	Hemel Hempstead Town v Baldock Town	2-2
	March Town United v Histon	1-1
17	Berkhamsted Town v Tiptree United	1-1
	Felixstowe Town v Ely City	0-1
	Royston Town v Finchley	2-3
18	Aveley v Hornchurch	0-1
	Basildon United v Potton United	3-1
	Hoddesdon Town v Great Yarmouth Town	0-2 N
19	Cheshunt v Rainham Town	1-2
	Sudbury Town v Gorleston	5-0
20	Billericay Town v Stowmarket Town	0-2
	Harwich & Parkeston v Collier Row	2-0
	Soham Town Rangers v Hertford Town	0-1
21	Boreham Wood v Egham Town	2-2
	Edgware Town v Corinthian Casuals	2-2
	Rayners Lane v Burnham & Hillingdon	1-0
22	Chesham United v Metropolitan Police	1-8
	Crockenhill v Feltham	1-5
	Kingsbury Town v Erith & Belvedere	0-0
23	Alma Swanley v Southall	4-0
	Clapton v Yeading	0-1
	Desborough Town v Flackwell Heath	1-1
24	Merstham v Leytonstone/Ilford	0-6
	Tring Town v Chertsey Town	1-3
25	Burgess Hill Town v Staines Town	0-2
	Chatham Town v Vauxhall Motors (Luton)	0-0
	Sittingbourne v Dorking (2)	1-1
26	Epsom & Ewell v Three Bridges	1-2
	Horsham YMCA v Haringey Borough	0-3
	Redhill v Maidenhead United	3-2
27	Dover Athletic v Tunbridge Wells	0-0
	Leatherhead v Eastbourne Town	1-1
	Molesey v Wick	0-3
28	Arundel v Ringmer	0-0
	Camberley Town v Shoreham	4-0
	Tonbridge v Haywards Heath	2-0
29	Horndean v Woking	2-3
	Lancing v Peacehaven & Telscombe	4-0
	Thanet United v Lewes	0-2
30	Ashford Town v Steyning Town	1-0
	Eastbourne United v Portfield	1-1
	Sheppey United v Chichester City (1)	2-1
31	Andover v Sholing Sports	1-0
	Devizes Town v Farnham Town	1-1
	Petersfield United v Hailsham Town	2-1
32	Brockenhurst v Westbury United	2-0
	Clandown v Abingdon Town	3-1
	Havant Town v Radstock Town	1-1
33	Shortwood United v Melksham Town	2-3
	Trowbridge Town v Hungerford Town	4-0
34	Bristol Manor Farm v Evesham United	0-2
	Clevedon Town v Paulton Rovers	1-0
	Maesteg Park Athletic v Llanelli	2-3
35	Ottery St Mary v Merthyr Tydfil	0-1
	Saltash United v Gloucester City	0-0
36	Welton Rovers v Taunton Town	1-0
	Weston-Super-Mare v Torrington	1-0
1r	Annfield Plain v Consett	3-1
3r	Farsley Celtic v Ryhope Community Association	3-2
r	Newcastle Blue Star v Norton & Stockton Ancients	6-0 N
5r	Evenwood Town v Langley Park	2-1
6r	Armthorpe Welfare v Curzon Ashton	4-1
8r	Droylsden v Formby	3-1
9r	Bridgnorth Town v Congleton Town	4-0
r	Eastwood Hanley v Radcliffe Borough	1-0
r	Rossendale United v Colwyn Bay	3-2e
12r	Boldmere St Michaels v Oldswinford	3-1
13r	AP Leamington v Mile Oak Rovers & Youth	1-0
15r	Rushden Town v Spalding United	2-4
16r	Baldock Town v Hemel Hempstead Town	1-0e
r	Histon v March Town United	1-1
r	Saffron Walden Town v Barton Rovers	3-1
17r	Tiptree United v Berkhamsted Town	2-1
21r	Corinthian Casuals v Edgware Town	1-0 N
r	Egham Town v Boreham Wood	1-3
22r	Erith & Belvedere v Kingsbury Town	1-0
23r	Flackwell Heath v Desborough Town	1-2
25r	Dorking (2) v Sittingbourne	2-1
r	Vauxhall Motors (Luton) v Chatham Town	0-2e
27r	Eastbourne Town v Leatherhead	3-1 N
r	Tunbridge Wells v Dover Athletic	1-2
28r	Ringmer v Arundel	0-0x
30r	Portfield v Eastbourne United	1-0
31r	Farnham Town v Devizes Town	1-4
32r	Radstock Town v Havant Town	0-1e
35r	Gloucester City v Saltash United	0-2
16r2	March Town United v Histon	3-2
28r2	Ringmer v Arundel	0-3

Qualifying Round One

1	Annfield Plain v Alnwick Town	2-3
	Barrow v Easington Colliery	0-3
	Bedlington Terriers v Chester-le-Street Town	1-2
	Harrogate Town v Darlington Cleveland Bridge	4-1
2	Ashington v Bridlington Town	2-4
	Bishop Auckland v Gateshead (2)	2-0
	Morecambe v Esh Winning	8-0
	Whitley Bay v North Shields	2-3
3	Eppleton CW v Brandon United	1-1
	Farsley Celtic v Newcastle Blue Star	1-3
	South Bank v Billingham Town	1-1
	Workington v Billingham Synthonia	2-1
4	Blyth Spartans v Crook Town	1-1
	Fleetwood Town v Durham City	2-0
	Gretna v Horden CW	6-1
	Yorkshire Amateur v Guiseley	0-1
5	Bridlington Trinity v Peterlee Newtown	1-1
	Evenwood Town v Darwen	2-0
	Tow Law Town v Spennymoor United	0-2
	Wren Rovers v Thackley	3-1
6	Armthorpe Welfare v Ashton United	2-1
	Chorley v Horwich RMI	2-1
	St Helens Town v Heanor Town	6-0
	Warrington Town v Penrith	0-2
7	Hyde United v Rhyl	1-1
	Irlam Town v Lancaster City	1-1
	Leyland Motors v Emley	0-2
	Southport v Garforth Town	1-1
8	Burscough v Bootle	2-2
	Caernarfon Town v Marine	2-0
	Mossley v Eastwood Town	3-3
	Winsford United v Droylsden	2-0
9	Bridgnorth Town v Rossendale United	1-1
	Buxton v Leek Town	1-0
	Oldbury United v Eastwood Hanley	0-0
	Oswestry Town v Prescot Cables	1-0 D
10	Long Eaton United v Northwich Victoria	1-4
	Skelmersdale United v Sutton Town	1-0
	Witton Albion v Hednesford Town	0-2
	Worksop Town v Armitage	7-0
11	Brigg Town v Lye Town	0-2
	Goole Town v Scarborough	2-1
	North Ferriby United v Leicester United	3-3
	South Liverpool v GKN Sankey	2-3
12	Alfreton Town v Gainsborough Trinity	0-0
	Boldmere St Michaels v Rothwell Town	0-1
	Grantham v Wednesfield Social	5-1
	Wisbech Town v Sutton Coldfield Town	0-2
13	Banbury United v Coventry Sporting	4-2
	Hinckley Athletic v Kidderminster Harriers	0-1
	Matlock Town v Malvern Town	1-3
	Wigston Fields v AP Leamington	2-1
14	Atherstone United v Moor Green	2-1
	Shepshed Charterhouse v Stafford Rangers	0-1
	Willenhall Town v Paget Rangers	1-0
	Wolverton Town v Tamworth	0-0
15	Dudley Town v Arlesey Town	5-2 N
	Halesowen Town v Ampthill Town	4-0 N
	Letchworth Garden City v Burton Albion	1-1
	Stevenage Borough v Spalding United	1-0
16	Alvechurch v Bedworth United	1-1
	Baldock Town v Saffron Walden Town	1-0
	Bromsgrove Rovers v Holbeach United	2-0
	Wootton Blue Cross v March Town United	1-2
17	Corby Town v Irthlingborough Diamonds	3-0
	Ely City v Tiptree United	1-4
	Kettering Town v Lowestoft Town	2-1
	Ware v Finchley	5-2
18	Basildon United v Hornchurch	0-2
	Braintree Town v Cambridge City	1-1
	King's Lynn v Haverhill Rovers	wo/s
	Newmarket Town v Great Yarmouth Town	2-0
19	Chatteris Town v Harlow Town	2-2
	Stamford v Bury Town	2-3
	Sudbury Town v Rainham Town	4-1
	Tilbury v Witham Town	3-1
20	Grays Athletic v Hitchin Town	6-1
	Harwich & Parkeston v Stowmarket Town	2-2
	Walthamstow Avenue v Heybridge Swifts	3-2 N
	Woodford Town (1) v Hertford Town	2-0
21	Aylesbury United v Barking	1-0
	Harefield United v Corinthian Casuals	3-0
	Kingstonian v Cray Wanderers	2-0
	Rayners Lane v Boreham Wood	2-5
22	Feltham v Metropolitan Police	0-5
	Fisher Athletic v Harrow Borough	1-0
	Tooting & Mitcham United v Hampton	1-2
	Walton & Hersham v Erith & Belvedere	2-2
23	Chalfont St Peter v Hayes	0-3
	Sutton United v Hounslow	2-0
	Uxbridge v Desborough Town	4-0
	Yeading v Alma Swanley	4-4
24	Bracknell Town v Croydon	2-0
	Chertsey Town v Leytonstone/Ilford	1-1
	Hendon v Banstead Athletic	2-2
	Welling United v Darenth Heathside	6-0
25	Barnet v Dulwich Hamlet	0-2
	Chatham Town v Staines Town	1-2
	St Albans City v Ruislip Manor	1-2
	Wembley v Dorking (2)	1-0
26	Buckingham Town v Dunstable	2-2
	Haringey Borough v Three Bridges	1-0
	Whyteleafe v Redhill	0-2
	Wokingham Town v Marlow	4-0
27	Bromley v Carshalton Athletic	2-2
	Leyton-Wingate v Faversham Town	1-1
	Whitehawk v Eastbourne Town	2-3
	Wick v Dover Athletic	0-4
28	Camberley Town v Arundel	0-1
	Canterbury City v Folkestone	0-1
	Whitstable Town v Tonbridge	2-1
	Worthing v Herne Bay	0-1
29	Crawley Town v Gravesend & Northfleet	1-0
	Eastleigh v Lewes	1-1
	Hastings Town v Horsham	3-2
	Lancing v Woking	2-4
30	Gosport Borough v Newport (IOW)	1-1
	Portfield v Ashford Town	1-7
	Southwick v Hythe Town	1-0
	Waterlooville v Sheppey United	0-1
31	Devizes Town v Andover	5-2
	Fareham Town v Oxford City	2-1
	Newbury Town v Petersfield United	2-1

1986/87

Road Sea Southampton v Littlehampton Town 7-1
32 AFC Totton v Calne Town 1-0
Brockenhurst v Havant Town 1-2
Chippenham Town v Poole Town 3-1
Wimborne Town v Clandown 2-2
33 Frome Town v Redditch United 0-2
Salisbury (2) v Bridgend Town 2-1
Stourbridge v Abingdon United 1-1
Trowbridge Town v Melksham Town 3-2
34 Basingstoke Town v Ton Pentre 0-2
Evesham United v Clevedon Town 1-1
Sharpness v Llanelli 4-1
Witney Town v Mangotsfield United 2-3
35 Cheltenham Town v Bideford 3-4
Dorchester Town v Barry Town 1-1
Forest Green Rovers v Yate Town 2-0
Saltash United v Merthyr Tydfil 1-0
36 Exmouth Town v Glastonbury 5-0
Minehead v Tiverton Town 1-0
St Blazey v Barnstaple Town 1-1
Weston-Super-Mare v Welton Rovers 1-0
3r Billingham Town v South Bank 0-2
r Brandon United v Eppleton CW 2-1
4r Crook Town v Blyth Spartans 0-1
5r Peterlee Newtown v Bridlington Trinity 2-0
7r Garforth Town v Southport 1-1x
r Lancaster City v Irlam Town 2-1
r Rhyl v Hyde United 3-4
8r Bootle v Burscough 2-1
r Eastwood Town v Mossley 1-1
9r Eastwood Hanley v Oldbury United 0-1
r Rossendale United v Bridgnorth Town 3-2
11r Leicester United v North Ferriby United 4-2 N
12r Gainsborough Trinity v Alfreton Town 2-1
14r Tamworth v Wolverton Town 2-2
15r Burton Albion v Letchworth Garden City 5-1
16r Bedworth United v Alvechurch 1-0
18r Cambridge City v Braintree Town 3-0
19r Harlow Town v Chatteris Town 1-0
20r Stowmarket Town v Harwich & Parkeston 1-3
22r Erith & Belvedere v Walton & Hersham 0-1
23r Alma Swanley v Yeading 0-1 N
24r Banstead Athletic v Hendon 0-1
r Leytonstone/Ilford v Chertsey Town 0-1 N
26r Dunstable v Buckingham Town 1-2
27r Carshalton Athletic v Bromley 4-2e
r Faversham Town v Leyton-Wingate 0-1
29r Lewes v Eastleigh 1-2
30r Newport (IOW) v Gosport Borough 3-2
32r Clandown v Wimborne Town 1-2
33r Abingdon United v Stourbridge 0-0
34r Clevedon Town v Evesham United 2-1
35r Barry Town v Dorchester Town 3-4
36r Barnstaple Town v St Blazey 0-0
7r2 Southport v Garforth Town 2-1e
8r2 Eastwood Town v Mossley 2-0e
14r2 Tamworth v Wolverton Town 0-2
33r2 Stourbridge v Abingdon United 2-1
36r2 St Blazey v Barnstaple Town 0-2

Qualifying Round Two

1 Alnwick Town v Easington Colliery 0-3
Harrogate Town v Chester-le-Street Town 1-1
2 Bridlington Town v Morecambe 0-1
North Shields v Bishop Auckland 0-0
3 Newcastle Blue Star v South Bank 0-0
Workington v Brandon United 0-0
4 Fleetwood Town v Gretna 1-3
Guiseley v Blyth Spartans 0-2
5 Evenwood Town v Spennymoor United 0-5
Wren Rovers v Peterlee Newtown 2-2
6 Armthorpe Welfare v St Helens Town 1-1
Penrith v Chorley 1-2
7 Emley v Hyde United 2-2
Lancaster City v Southport 1-1
8 Bootle v Eastwood Town 2-2
Winsford United v Caernarfon Town 1-3
9 Oldbury United v Buxton 3-1
Rossendale United v Prescot Cables 2-1
10 Skelmersdale United v Hednesford Town 2-1
Worksop Town v Northwich Victoria 0-2
11 Leicester United v Goole Town 0-1
Lye Town v GKN Sankey 4-1
12 Rothwell Town v Grantham 0-1
Sutton Coldfield Town v Gainsborough Trinity 0-1
13 Banbury United v Malvern Town 1-2
Wigston Fields v Kidderminster Harriers 0-5
14 Atherstone United v Stafford Rangers 2-4
Wolverton Town v Willenhall Town 2-0
15 Halesowen Town v Burton Albion 2-0
Stevenage Borough v Dudley Town 2-0
16 Baldock Town v Bromsgrove Rovers 0-1
March Town United v Bedworth United 1-0
17 Tiptree United v Kettering Town 0-3
Ware v Corby Town 1-2
18 Hornchurch v King's Lynn 1-1
Newmarket Town v Cambridge City 1-2
19 Sudbury Town v Bury Town 0-2
Tilbury v Harlow Town 2-1 D
20 Harwich & Parkeston v Walthamstow Avenue 4-1
Woodford Town (1) v Grays Athletic 2-1
21 Boreham Wood v Kingstonian 2-2
Harefield United v Aylesbury United 2-2
22 Metropolitan Police v Hampton 2-2
Walton & Hersham v Fisher Athletic 0-0
23 Uxbridge v Hayes 3-1
Yeading v Sutton United 4-1
24 Chertsey Town v Hendon 0-1
Welling United v Bracknell Town 2-1
25 Staines Town v Ruislip Manor 0-0
Wembley v Dulwich Hamlet 2-1
26 Haringey Borough v Wokingham Town 4-2
Redhill v Buckingham Town 2-4
27 Dover Athletic v Leyton-Wingate 2-1
Eastbourne Town v Carshalton Athletic 0-1
28 Arundel v Herne Bay 1-3
Whitstable Town v Folkestone 2-1
29 Eastleigh v Crawley Town 0-1
Woking v Hastings Town 4-0
30 Ashford Town v Southwick 0-0
Sheppey United v Newport (IOW) 1-1
31 Devizes Town v Road Sea Southampton 0-2
Newbury Town v Fareham Town 0-5
32 Havant Town v AFC Totton 1-1
Wimborne Town v Chippenham Town 1-1
33 Stourbridge v Redditch United 2-1
Trowbridge Town v Salisbury (2) 2-0
34 Clevedon Town v Mangotsfield United 2-0
Sharpness v Ton Pentre 0-1
35 Forest Green Rovers v Dorchester Town 4-2
Saltash United v Bideford 1-2
36 Minehead v Barnstaple Town 2-1
Weston-Super-Mare v Exmouth Town 2-3
1r Chester-le-Street Town v Harrogate Town 3-1
2r Bishop Auckland v North Shields 4-2
3r Brandon United v Workington 0-1
r South Bank v Newcastle Blue Star 1-2e
5r Peterlee Newtown v Wren Rovers 2-0
6r St Helens Town v Armthorpe Welfare 0-1
7r Hyde United v Emley 1-4
r Southport v Lancaster City 3-1
8r Eastwood Town v Bootle 1-1
18r King's Lynn v Hornchurch 2-0
21r Aylesbury United v Harefield United 2-0
r Kingstonian v Boreham Wood 0-1
22r Fisher Athletic v Walton & Hersham 3-2e
r Hampton v Metropolitan Police 2-0
25r Ruislip Manor v Staines Town 0-2
30r Newport (IOW) v Sheppey United 1-0
r Southwick v Ashford Town 1-0
32r AFC Totton v Havant Town 1-0
r Chippenham Town v Wimborne Town 0-1
8r2 Bootle v Eastwood Town 1-1
8r3 Eastwood Town v Bootle 1-0

Qualifying Round Three

1 Easington Colliery v Chester-le-Street Town 1-1
2 Morecambe v Bishop Auckland 1-2
3 Newcastle Blue Star v Workington 1-1
4 Gretna v Blyth Spartans 5-2
5 Spennymoor United v Peterlee Newtown 1-0
6 Armthorpe Welfare v Chorley 0-2
7 Southport v Emley 3-3
8 Eastwood Town v Caernarfon Town 0-4
9 Rossendale United v Oldbury United 1-2
10 Skelmersdale United v Northwich Victoria 2-3
11 Lye Town v Goole Town 1-3
12 Grantham v Gainsborough Trinity 1-2
13 Malvern Town v Kidderminster Harriers 0-2
14 Wolverton Town v Stafford Rangers 1-4
15 Stevenage Borough v Halesowen Town 1-3
16 Bromsgrove Rovers v March Town United 1-0
17 Kettering Town v Corby Town 2-0
18 King's Lynn v Cambridge City 1-0
19 Bury Town v Harlow Town 2-1
20 Harwich & Parkeston v Woodford Town (1) 1-2
21 Boreham Wood v Aylesbury United 0-1
22 Hampton v Fisher Athletic 0-0
23 Yeading v Uxbridge 1-0
24 Hendon v Welling United 0-1
25 Staines Town v Wembley 1-1
26 Haringey Borough v Buckingham Town 1-2
27 Dover Athletic v Carshalton Athletic 3-3
28 Herne Bay v Whitstable Town 1-0
29 Woking v Crawley Town 3-1
30 Southwick v Newport (IOW) 2-0
31 Road Sea Southampton v Fareham Town 0-3
32 AFC Totton v Wimborne Town 0-0
33 Trowbridge Town v Stourbridge 1-1
34 Clevedon Town v Ton Pentre 0-4
35 Bideford v Forest Green Rovers 2-1
36 Exmouth Town v Minehead 3-4
1r Chester-le-Street Town v Easington Colliery 5-3
3r Workington v Newcastle Blue Star 0-1
7r Emley v Southport 4-4e
22r Fisher Athletic v Hampton 2-1
25r Wembley v Staines Town 4-1
27r Carshalton Athletic v Dover Athletic 1-3
32r Wimborne Town v AFC Totton 1-0
33r Stourbridge v Trowbridge Town 0-4
7r2 Southport v Emley 2-0

Qualifying Round Four

Bath City v Yeovil Town 2-1
Bideford v Dartford 0-2
Bishop's Stortford v Fisher Athletic 2-0
Boston United v Gainsborough Trinity 6-0
Bromsgrove Rovers v Buckingham Town 2-0
Chelmsford City v Kidderminster Harriers 2-1
Chester-le-Street Town v Caernarfon Town 2-3
Chorley v Bishop Auckland 3-2
Dagenham v Wealdstone 0-3
Enfield v Bury Town 1-1
Farnborough Town v Herne Bay 4-0
Goole Town v Nuneaton Borough 1-2
Halesowen Town v Oldbury United 2-2
Kettering Town v Windsor & Eton 1-0
King's Lynn v Woodford Town (1) 1-3
Macclesfield Town v Southport 0-1
Northwich Victoria v Stafford Rangers 0-1
Slough Town v Dover Athletic 1-1
Southwick v Maidstone United 1-1
Spennymoor United v Gretna 2-0
Ton Pentre v Minehead 5-1
Trowbridge Town v Fareham Town 0-0
Wembley v Welling United 2-3
Whitby Town v Newcastle Blue Star 2-0
Wimborne Town v Bognor Regis Town 2-5
Woking v Weymouth 1-0
Wycombe Wanderers v V.S. Rugby 1-5
Yeading v Aylesbury United 1-3
r Bury Town v Enfield 0-1
r Dover Athletic v Slough Town 2-3e
r Fareham Town v Trowbridge Town 4-1
r Maidstone United v Southwick 1-1
r Oldbury United v Halesowen Town 1-2
r2 Maidstone United v Southwick 2-2
r3 Southwick v Maidstone United 1-5

Round One

Aldershot v Torquay United 1-0
Bath City v Aylesbury United 3-2
Bishop's Stortford v Colchester United 1-1
Bournemouth v Fareham Town 7-2
Bristol City v V.S. Rugby 3-1
Bristol Rovers v Brentford 0-0
Bromsgrove Rovers v Newport County 0-1
Caernarfon Town v Stockport County 1-0
Chester City v Rotherham United 1-1
Chorley v Wolverhampton Wan. 1-1 N
Darlington v Mansfield Town 2-1
Dartford v Enfield 1-1
Exeter City v Cambridge United 1-1
Frickley Athletic v Altrincham 0-0
Halifax Town v Bolton Wanderers 1-1
Hereford United v Fulham 3-3
Kettering Town v Gillingham 0-3
Middlesbrough v Blackpool 3-0
Northampton Town v Peterborough United 3-0
Notts County v Carlisle United 1-1
Nuneaton Borough v Rochdale 0-3
Port Vale v Stafford Rangers 1-0
Preston North End v Bury 5-1
Runcorn v Boston United 1-1
Scunthorpe United v Southport 2-0
Slough Town v Bognor Regis Town 1-1
Southend United v Halesowen Town 4-1
Spennymoor United v Tranmere Rovers 2-3
Swindon Town v Farnborough Town 4-0
Telford United v Burnley 3-0
Ton Pentre v Cardiff City 1-4
Walsall v Chesterfield 2-0
Wealdstone v Swansea City 1-1
Welling United v Maidstone United 1-1
Whitby Town v Doncaster Rovers 2-2
Wigan Athletic v Lincoln City 3-1
Woking v Chelmsford City 1-1
Woodford Town (1) v Orient 0-1
Wrexham v Hartlepool United 2-1
York City v Crewe Alexandra 3-1
r Altrincham v Frickley Athletic 4-0
r Bognor Regis Town v Slough Town 0-1
r Bolton Wanderers v Halifax Town 1-1e
r Boston United v Runcorn 1-2e
r Brentford v Bristol Rovers 2-0
r Cambridge United v Exeter City 2-0
r Carlisle United v Notts County 0-3
r Chelmsford City v Woking 2-1
r Colchester United v Bishop's Stortford 2-0
r Doncaster Rovers v Whitby Town 3-2
r Enfield v Dartford 3-0
r Fulham v Hereford United 4-0
r Maidstone United v Welling United 4-1
r Rotherham United v Chester City 1-1e
r Swansea City v Wealdstone 4-1
r Wolverhampton Wan. v Chorley 1-1e
r2 Chester City v Rotherham United 1-0
r2 Chorley v Wolverhampton Wan. 3-0 N
r2 Halifax Town v Bolton Wanderers 1-3

Round Two

Aldershot v Colchester United 3-2
Bolton Wanderers v Tranmere Rovers 2-0
Bournemouth v Orient 0-1
Bristol City v Bath City 1-1
Caernarfon Town v York City 0-0
Cardiff City v Brentford 2-0

1986/87 to 1987/88

	Chester City v Doncaster Rovers	3-1
	Chorley v Preston North End	0-0 N
	Darlington v Wigan Athletic	0-5
	Fulham v Newport County	2-0
	Gillingham v Chelmsford City	2-0
	Maidstone United v Cambridge United	1-0
	Notts County v Middlesbrough	0-1
	Rochdale v Wrexham	1-4
	Scunthorpe United v Runcorn	1-0
	Southend United v Northampton Town	4-4
	Swansea City v Slough Town	3-0
	Swindon Town v Enfield	3-0
	Telford United v Altrincham	1-0
	Walsall v Port Vale	5-0
r	Bristol City v Bath City	3-0
r	Northampton Town v Southend United	3-2
r	Preston North End v Chorley	5-0
r	York City v Caernarfon Town	1-2

Round Three

	Aldershot v Oxford United	3-0
	Aston Villa v Chelsea	2-2
	Bristol City v Plymouth Argyle	1-1
	Caernarfon Town v Barnsley	0-0
	Charlton Athletic v Walsall	1-2
	Coventry City v Bolton Wanderers	3-0
	Crystal Palace v Nottingham Forest	1-0
	Everton v Southampton	2-1
	Fulham v Swindon Town	0-1
	Grimsby Town v Stoke City	1-1
	Ipswich Town v Birmingham City	0-1
	Luton Town v Liverpool	0-0
	Manchester United v Manchester City	1-0
	Middlesbrough v Preston North End	0-1
	Millwall v Cardiff City	0-0
	Newcastle United v Northampton Town	2-1
	Norwich City v Huddersfield Town	1-1
	Oldham Athletic v Bradford City	1-1
	Orient v West Ham United	1-1
	Portsmouth v Blackburn Rovers	2-0
	Queen's Park Rangers v Leicester City	5-2
	Reading v Arsenal	1-3
	Sheffield United v Brighton & Hove Albion	0-0
	Sheffield Wednesday v Derby County	1-0
	Shrewsbury Town v Hull City	1-2
	Swansea City v West Bromwich Albion	3-2
	Telford United v Leeds United	1-2 N
	Tottenham Hotspur v Scunthorpe United	3-2
	Watford v Maidstone United	3-1
	Wigan Athletic v Gillingham	2-1
	Wimbledon v Sunderland	2-1
	Wrexham v Chester City	1-2
r	Barnsley v Caernarfon Town	1-0
r	Bradford City v Oldham Athletic	5-1
r	Brighton & Hove Albion v Sheffield United	1-2
r	Cardiff City v Millwall	2-2e
r	Chelsea v Aston Villa	2-1e
r	Huddersfield Town v Norwich City	2-4
r	Liverpool v Luton Town	0-0e
r	Plymouth Argyle v Bristol City	3-1e
r	Stoke City v Grimsby Town	1-1e
r	West Ham United v Orient	4-1
r2	Cardiff City v Millwall	1-0
r2	Luton Town v Liverpool	3-0
r2	Stoke City v Grimsby Town	6-0

Round Four

	Aldershot v Barnsley	1-1
	Arsenal v Plymouth Argyle	6-1
	Bradford City v Everton	0-1
	Chester City v Sheffield Wednesday	1-1
	Luton Town v Queen's Park Rangers	1-1
	Manchester United v Coventry City	0-1
	Newcastle United v Preston North End	2-0
	Stoke City v Cardiff City	2-1
	Swansea City v Hull City	0-1
	Swindon Town v Leeds United	1-2
	Tottenham Hotspur v Crystal Palace	4-0
	Walsall v Birmingham City	1-0
	Watford v Chelsea	1-0
	West Ham United v Sheffield United	4-0
	Wigan Athletic v Norwich City	1-0
	Wimbledon v Portsmouth	4-0
r	Barnsley v Aldershot	3-0
r	Queen's Park Rangers v Luton Town	2-1
r	Sheffield Wednesday v Chester City	3-1

Round Five

	Arsenal v Barnsley	2-0
	Leeds United v Queen's Park Rangers	2-1
	Sheffield Wednesday v West Ham United	1-1
	Stoke City v Coventry City	0-1
	Tottenham Hotspur v Newcastle United	1-0
	Walsall v Watford	1-1
	Wigan Athletic v Hull City	3-0
	Wimbledon v Everton	3-1
r	Watford v Walsall	4-4e
r	West Ham United v Sheffield Wednesday	0-2
r2	Walsall v Watford	0-1

Round Six

Arsenal v Watford	1-3
Sheffield Wednesday v Coventry City	1-3
Wigan Athletic v Leeds United	0-2
Wimbledon v Tottenham Hotspur	0-2

Semi Finals

Coventry City v Leeds United	3-2eN
Tottenham Hotspur v Watford	4-1 N

Final

Coventry City v Tottenham Hotspur	3-2eN

1987/88

Preliminary Round

1	Clitheroe v Bridlington Trinity	4-0
	Harrogate Town v Esh Winning	2-1
	Seaham Red Star v Shildon	2-0
2	Alnwick Town v Durham City	1-1
	Bridlington Town v Accrington Stanley (2)	1-0
	Ossett Albion v Chester-le-Street Town	1-1
3	Annfield Plain v West Auckland Town	0-4
	Crook Town v Bedlington Terriers	2-1
	Ferryhill Athletic v Langley Park	3-0
4	Ashington v Guiseley	3-1
	Evenwood Town v Leyland Motors	0-2
	Penrith v Horden CW	7-0
5	Lancaster City v Darwen	0-4
	Norton & Stockton Ancients v Farsley Celtic	4-5
	Shotton Comrades v Garforth Town	2-1
6	Guisborough Town v Armthorpe Welfare	2-0
	Peterlee Newtown v Denaby United	1-3
	Rossendale United v Northallerton Town	3-0
7	Burscough v Warrington Town	1-2 N
	Droylsden v Belper Town	4-2
	St Helens Town v Curzon Ashton	6-2
8	Ashton United v Kirkby Town (2)	2-0
	Glossop v Heanor Town	2-3
	Stalybridge Celtic v Congleton Town	2-0
9	Alfreton Town v Formby	3-0
	Colwyn Bay v Winsford United	3-0
	Skelmersdale United v Radcliffe Borough	0-1
10	Brigg Town v Oakham United	4-0
	Leek Town v GKN Sankey	3-3
	Long Eaton United v Sutton Town	1-3
11	Hednesford Town v Arnold	0-1
	Holbeach United v Walsall Wood	1-4
	Moor Green v Tividale	3-1
12	Grantham v Chatteris Town	2-2
	Tamworth v Gresley Rovers	3-2
	Wisbech Town v Brackley Town	1-0
13	Oldswinford v Racing Club Warwick	0-1
	Wednesfield Social v Hinckley Athletic	0-1
	Wellingborough Town v Spalding United	3-2
	Wolverton Town v Ashtree Highfield	0-2
14	Baker Perkins v Rushall Olympic	2-2
	Highgate United v Bilston Town	1-1
	Hinckley Town v Bridgnorth Town	2-1
15	Chasetown v Evesham United	0-2
	Dudley Town v Rothwell Town	1-1 N
	Northampton Spencer v Atherstone United	2-5
16	Chalfont St Peter v Arlesey Town	1-1
	Coventry Sporting v Barton Rovers	2-1
	Stamford v Vauxhall Motors (Luton)	0-0
17	Banbury United v Edgware Town	3-0
	Soham Town Rangers v Hemel Hempstead Town	0-0
	Wootton Blue Cross v Berkhamsted Town	0-0
18	Bourne Town v Milton Keynes Borough	1-4
	Gorleston v Chesham United	1-0
	Tiptree United v Aveley	0-4
19	Baldock Town v Hampton	1-0
	Great Yarmouth Town v Tilbury	0-0
	Uxbridge v Haringey Borough	2-2
20	Felixstowe Town v Walthamstow Avenue	1-2
	Lowestoft Town v Kingsbury Town	0-1
	Tring Town v Harlow Town	0-2
21	Hoddesdon Town v Southall	2-0 N
	Newmarket Town v Dunstable	0-3
	Watton United v Royston Town	0-1
22	Hertford Town v Potton United	1-1
	Staines Town v Ware	0-0
	Sudbury Town v Hounslow	1-1
23	Basildon United v Cray Wanderers	1-3
	Corinthian Casuals v Camberley Town	1-1
	Finchley v Kempston Rovers	1-0
24	Chatham Town v Collier Row	4-1
	Darenth Heathside v Leatherhead	2-1
	Feltham v Alma Swanley	5-0 N
	Heybridge Swifts v Dorking (2)	1-1
25	Erith & Belvedere v Wivenhoe Town	0-0
	Flackwell Heath v Crockenhill	0-3
	Hornchurch v Horsham YMCA	7-0
26	Rainham Town v Sittingbourne	1-1
	Three Bridges v Gravesend & Northfleet	0-0
	Witham Town v Burgess Hill Town	1-0
27	Maidenhead United v Tunbridge Wells	1-1
	Petersfield United v Wick	1-1
	Thatcham Town v Worthing	0-3
28	Epsom & Ewell v Arundel	4-0
	Faversham Town v Shoreham	1-1
	Sheppey United v Metropolitan Police	1-3
29	Beckenham Town v Hailsham Town	2-2
	Horsham v Whitehawk	0-0
	Thanet United v Canterbury City	3-0
30	Hastings Town v Lancing	0-1
	Ringmer v Eastbourne United	1-5
	Tonbridge v Folkestone	5-2
31	Bracknell Town v Peacehaven & Telscombe	1-0
	Egham Town v Portfield	1-1
	Haywards Heath v Steyning Town	4-0
32	Abingdon United v Oxford City	1-1
	Melksham Town v Andover	2-0
	Shortwood United v Waterlooville	1-6
33	Eastleigh v Swanage Town & Herston	1-1
	Frome Town v Poole Town	1-0
	Newbury Town v Welton Rovers	2-2
34	Bridgend Town v Weston-Super-Mare	1-3
	Gloucester City v Westbury United	7-0
	Hungerford Town v Yate Town	1-1
35	Devizes Town v Paulton Rovers	0-0
	Llanelli v Barnstaple Town	1-2
	Salisbury (2) v Barry Town	0-1
	Torrington v Glastonbury	3-0
36	Ottery St Mary v Chippenham Town	1-0
	St Blazey v Tiverton Town	4-4
	Taunton Town v Clandown	2-0
2r	Chester-le-Street Town v Ossett Albion	2-1
r	Durham City v Alnwick Town	1-1
10r	GKN Sankey v Leek Town	2-3
12r	Chatteris Town v Grantham	1-0
14r	Bilston Town v Highgate United	0-0
r	Rushall Olympic v Baker Perkins	3-0
15r	Rothwell Town v Dudley Town	2-1
16r	Arlesey Town v Chalfont St Peter	1-0
r	Vauxhall Motors (Luton) v Stamford	3-2
17r	Berkhamsted Town v Wootton Blue Cross	2-0
r	Hemel Hempstead Town v Soham Town Rangers	1-0
19r	Haringey Borough v Uxbridge	2-3
r	Tilbury v Great Yarmouth Town	0-2
22r	Hounslow v Sudbury Town	1-3
r	Potton United v Hertford Town	1-2
r	Ware v Staines Town	1-1e
23r	Camberley Town v Corinthian Casuals	2-0
24r	Dorking (2) v Heybridge Swifts	2-1
25r	Wivenhoe Town v Erith & Belvedere	4-2
26r	Gravesend & Northfleet v Three Bridges	2-1
r	Sittingbourne v Rainham Town	2-3
27r	Tunbridge Wells v Maidenhead United	4-3
r	Wick v Petersfield United	4-3
28r	Shoreham v Faversham Town	2-0
29r	Hailsham Town v Beckenham Town	2-4
r	Whitehawk v Horsham	2-0
31r	Portfield v Egham Town	1-3
32r	Oxford City v Abingdon United	3-0
33r	Swanage Town & Herston v Eastleigh	3-1
r	Welton Rovers v Newbury Town	2-4
34r	Yate Town v Hungerford Town	1-0
35r	Paulton Rovers v Devizes Town	1-0
36r	Tiverton Town v St Blazey	5-2
2r2	Alnwick Town v Durham City	0-0
14r2	Bilston Town v Highgate United	2-0
22r2	Ware v Staines Town	4-2
2r3	Durham City v Alnwick Town	1-2

Qualifying Round One

1	Bishop Auckland v Workington	5-2
	Clitheroe v Whitley Bay	2-0
	Murton v Seaham Red Star	0-1
	Willington v Harrogate Town	0-3
2	Billingham Synthonia v Alnwick Town	2-0
	Billingham Town v Bridlington Town	0-3
	Blyth Spartans v Gateshead (2)	2-1
	Chester-le-Street Town v Consett	2-1
3	Ferryhill Athletic v Gretna	1-2
	Fleetwood Town v West Auckland Town	3-2
	Netherfield (Kendal) v Crook Town	1-1
	North Shields v Barrow	1-1
4	Easington Colliery v Leyland Motors	2-1
	Newcastle Blue Star v Morecambe	1-0
	Penrith v Brandon United	2-1
	Ryhope Community Association v Ashington	1-1
5	Darlington Cleveland Bridge v Shotton Comrades	2-0
	Darwen v Tow Law Town	2-2
	South Bank v Spennymoor United	1-0
	Wren Rovers v Farsley Celtic	1-2
6	Emley v Southport	2-0
	Rossendale United v Worksop Town	1-1
	Stockton (2) v Denaby United	1-0
	Thackley v Guisborough Town	1-1
7	Horwich RMI v South Liverpool	1-1
	Ilkeston Town (2) v St Helens Town	1-1
	North Ferriby United v Droylsden	2-3
	Warrington Town v Northwich Victoria	1-1
8	Bangor City v Marine	2-2
	Bootle v Ashton United	1-0
	Chadderton v Heanor Town	1-0
	Stalybridge Celtic v Macclesfield Town	1-1
9	Alfreton Town v Witton Albion	4-2
	Buxton v Rhyl	6-3
	Irlam Town v Radcliffe Borough	1-0
	Prescot Cables v Colwyn Bay	0-1

1987/88

10	Eastwood Hanley v Leek Town	0-0
	Hyde United v Mossley	1-0 N
	Mile Oak Rovers & Youth v Brigg Town	1-2
	Sutton Town v Goole Town	1-2
11	Eastwood Town v Arnold	1-2
	Halesowen Harriers v Moor Green	1-1
	Matlock Town v Gainsborough Trinity	3-3
	Walsall Wood v Stafford Rangers	0-3
12	Boldmere St Michaels v Chatteris Town	2-2
	Paget Rangers v Tamworth	1-4
	Shepshed Charterhouse v Stourbridge	2-0
	Wisbech Town v Kettering Town	2-0
13	Desborough Town v Racing Club Warwick	2-2
	Halesowen Town v Ashtree Highfield	1-1
	Hinckley Athletic v Bedworth United	2-3
	Wellingborough Town v Leicester United	1-1
14	Friar Lane Old Boys v Bilston Town	2-2
	Rushall Olympic v Oldbury United	0-2
	Sutton Coldfield Town v Hinckley Town	1-1
	Willenhall Town v Bromsgrove Rovers	3-2
15	Alvechurch v Redditch United	1-1
	Atherstone United v Malvern Town	1-1
	Lye Town v Evesham United	1-0
	Rushden Town v Rothwell Town	1-4
16	AP Leamington v Coventry Sporting	2-1
	Arlesey Town v Buckingham Town	0-4
	Boreham Wood v Vauxhall Motors (Luton)	2-0
	Corby Town v Worcester City	1-1
17	Berkhamsted Town v Hitchin Town	3-1
	Ely City v Hemel Hempstead Town	1-1
	Irthlingborough Diamonds v Banbury United	3-1
	Witney Town v Barnet	0-3
18	Aveley v Bury Town	2-2
	Haverhill Rovers v Milton Keynes Borough	1-1
	King's Lynn v March Town United	1-2
	Letchworth Garden City v Gorleston	1-0
19	Cambridge City v Harwich & Parkeston	2-0
	Canvey Island v Baldock Town	0-1
	Clapton v Great Yarmouth Town	1-2
	Uxbridge v Barking	4-1
20	Billericay Town v Kingsbury Town	0-3
	Harlow Town v Woodford Town (1)	1-0
	Histon v Walthamstow Avenue	2-1
	Leytonstone/Ilford v St Albans City	2-0
21	Hoddesdon Town v Wembley	1-3
	Leyton-Wingate v Stevenage Borough	1-1
	Ruislip Manor v Royston Town	3-2
	Stowmarket Town v Dunstable	1-3
22	Aylesbury United v Wycombe Wanderers	2-0
	Braintree Town v Sudbury Town	0-4
	Grays Athletic v Hertford Town	1-3
	Ware v Hendon	0-1
23	Camberley Town v Welling United	0-2
	Cray Wanderers v Burnham	1-1
	Harrow Borough v Yeading	2-0
	Walton & Hersham v Finchley	3-0
24	Crawley Town v Chatham Town	1-3
	Dorking (2) v Fisher Athletic	0-2
	Feltham v Hayes	1-3 N
	Rayners Lane v Darenth Heathside	1-2
25	Bromley v Ashford Town	5-2
	Harefield United v Crockenhill	3-1
	Redhill v Hornchurch	3-3
	Wivenhoe Town v Sutton United	0-3
26	Carshalton Athletic v Kingstonian	1-0
	Gravesend & Northfleet v Herne Bay	6-1
	Malden Vale v Witham Town	1-3
	Saffron Walden Town v Rainham Town	2-1
27	Basingstoke Town v Dulwich Hamlet	3-0
	Marlow v Tunbridge Wells	5-1
	Pagham v Worthing	2-2
	Wick v Tooting & Mitcham United	1-1
28	Metropolitan Police v Dover Athletic	3-1
	Molesey v Epsom & Ewell	1-2
	Ramsgate v Shoreham	2-0
	Southwick v Croydon	1-3
29	Banstead Athletic v Beckenham Town	5-3
	Merstham v Thanet United	1-3
	Whitehawk v Littlehampton Town	1-2
	Windsor & Eton v Woking	0-0
30	Eastbourne United v Hythe Town	6-2
	Horndean v Tonbridge	0-2
	Whyteleafe v Lancing	2-0
	Wokingham Town v Lewes	3-0
31	Bracknell Town v Abingdon Town	3-2
	Chertsey Town v Haywards Heath	3-1
	Chichester City (1) v Egham Town	1-1
	Newport (IOW) v AFC Totton	2-0
32	Calne Town v Oxford City	1-5
	Gosport Borough v Yeovil Town	0-1
	Havant Town v Waterlooville	0-2
	Melksham Town v Wimborne Town	1-3
33	Fareham Town v Trowbridge Town	1-0
	Frome Town v Weymouth	2-2
	Radstock Town v Newbury Town	5-0
	Sholing Sports v Swanage Town & Herston	1-3
34	Bristol Manor Farm v Weston-Super-Mare	0-3
	Cheltenham Town v Dorchester Town	4-1
	Gloucester City v Ton Pentre	1-2
	Mangotsfield United v Yate Town	1-0
35	Barry Town v Clevedon Town	5-1
	Merthyr Tydfil v Paulton Rovers	2-0
	Minehead v Barnstaple Town	1-1
	Torrington v Forest Green Rovers	0-3
36	Bideford v Exmouth Town	1-1
	Maesteg Park Athletic v Tiverton Town	0-1
	Sharpness v Ottery St Mary	1-4
	Taunton Town v Saltash United	0-3
3r	Barrow v North Shields	3-0
r	Crook Town v Netherfield (Kendal)	2-1
4r	Ashington v Ryhope Community Association	1-2
5r	Tow Law Town v Darwen	3-2
6r	Guisborough Town v Thackley	0-0
r	Worksop Town v Rossendale United	2-4
7r	Northwich Victoria v Warrington Town	5-1
r	South Liverpool v Horwich RMI	3-4
r	St Helens Town v Ilkeston Town (2)	1-1
8r	Macclesfield Town v Stalybridge Celtic	5-1
r	Marine v Bangor City	3-1
10r	Leek Town v Eastwood Hanley	2-0
11r	Gainsborough Trinity v Matlock Town	0-3
r	Moor Green v Halesowen Harriers	2-1
12r	Chatteris Town v Boldmere St Michaels	0-3
13r	Ashtree Highfield v Halesowen Town	0-1
r	Leicester United v Wellingborough Town	1-0
r	Racing Club Warwick v Desborough Town	4-0
14r	Bilston Town v Friar Lane Old Boys	3-2
r	Hinckley Town v Sutton Coldfield Town	2-1
15r	Malvern Town v Atherstone United	0-2
r	Redditch United v Alvechurch	1-3
16r	Worcester City v Corby Town	3-1
17r	Hemel Hempstead Town v Ely City	2-1
18r	Bury Town v Aveley	3-1
r	Milton Keynes Borough v Haverhill Rovers	0-4
21r	Stevenage Borough v Leyton-Wingate	2-3
23r	Burnham v Cray Wanderers	2-1
25r	Hornchurch v Redhill	1-3
27r	Tooting & Mitcham United v Wick	3-0
r	Worthing v Pagham	0-2
29r	Woking v Windsor & Eton	6-3e
31r	Egham Town v Chichester City (1)	0-2
33r	Weymouth v Frome Town	3-0
35r	Barnstaple Town v Minehead	1-0
36r	Exmouth Town v Bideford	0-2
6r2	Guisborough Town v Thackley	1-0
7r2	Ilkeston Town (2) v St Helens Town	1-4 N

Qualifying Round Two

1	Clitheroe v Harrogate Town	0-0
	Seaham Red Star v Bishop Auckland	0-1
2	Bridlington Town v Blyth Spartans	1-2
	Chester-le-Street Town v Billingham Synthonia	1-1
3	Crook Town v Barrow	0-1
	Gretna v Fleetwood Town	1-2
4	Penrith v Easington Colliery	1-2
	Ryhope Community Association v Newcastle Blue Star	0-2
5	Darlington Cleveland Bridge v South Bank	2-1
	Tow Law Town v Farsley Celtic	2-1
6	Rossendale United v Guisborough Town	2-3
	Stockton (2) v Emley	0-1
7	Northwich Victoria v Droylsden	2-1
	St Helens Town v Horwich RMI	0-0
8	Bootle v Marine	2-2
	Macclesfield Town v Chadderton	5-0
9	Alfreton Town v Irlam Town	2-0
	Colwyn Bay v Buxton	2-2
10	Goole Town v Brigg Town	1-3
	Leek Town v Hyde United	2-1
11	Arnold v Matlock Town	2-3
	Stafford Rangers v Moor Green	2-3
12	Boldmere St Michaels v Shepshed Charterhouse	1-2
	Wisbech Town v Tamworth	2-3
13	Bedworth United v Racing Club Warwick	1-2
	Halesowen Town v Leicester United	5-1
14	Bilston Town v Willenhall Town	0-3
	Oldbury United v Hinckley Town	5-2
15	Atherstone United v Lye Town	1-0
	Rothwell Town v Alvechurch	1-2
16	AP Leamington v Worcester City	0-6
	Buckingham Town v Boreham Wood	0-0
17	Berkhamsted Town v Hemel Hempstead Town	3-3
	Irthlingborough Diamonds v Barnet	0-4
18	Bury Town v Letchworth Garden City	1-1
	Haverhill Rovers v March Town United	0-1
19	Great Yarmouth Town v Cambridge City	3-1
	Uxbridge v Baldock Town	1-0
20	Harlow Town v Kingsbury Town	1-1
	Histon v Leytonstone/Ilford	1-2
21	Dunstable v Leyton-Wingate	0-1
	Wembley v Ruislip Manor	1-1
22	Hendon v Hertford Town	1-2
	Sudbury Town v Aylesbury United	1-1
23	Burnham v Harrow Borough	2-1
	Welling United v Walton & Hersham	2-1
24	Chatham Town v Fisher Athletic	0-3
	Hayes v Darenth Heathside	4-1
25	Harefield United v Bromley	2-3
	Sutton United v Redhill	3-1
26	Gravesend & Northfleet v Witham Town	1-0
	Saffron Walden Town v Carshalton Athletic	1-5
27	Marlow v Basingstoke Town	1-1
	Tooting & Mitcham United v Pagham	0-0
28	Metropolitan Police v Epsom & Ewell	3-0
	Ramsgate v Croydon	0-1
29	Banstead Athletic v Woking	0-0
	Littlehampton Town v Thanet United	0-3
30	Eastbourne United v Tonbridge	0-0
	Whyteleafe v Wokingham Town	3-3
31	Bracknell Town v Chichester City (1)	4-0
	Chertsey Town v Newport (IOW)	0-1
32	Waterlooville v Yeovil Town	1-1
	Wimborne Town v Oxford City	2-1
33	Swanage Town & Herston v Fareham Town	0-2
	Weymouth v Radstock Town	3-0
34	Mangotsfield United v Cheltenham Town	1-1
	Ton Pentre v Weston-Super-Mare	1-2
35	Barnstaple Town v Forest Green Rovers	1-2
	Barry Town v Merthyr Tydfil	0-1
36	Saltash United v Ottery St Mary	7-1
	Tiverton Town v Bideford	4-2
1r	Harrogate Town v Clitheroe	2-1
2r	Billingham Synthonia v Chester-le-Street Town	4-3
7r	Horwich RMI v St Helens Town	2-3
8r	Marine v Bootle	1-0
9r	Buxton v Colwyn Bay	2-5
16r	Boreham Wood v Buckingham Town	2-1
17r	Hemel Hempstead Town v Berkhamsted Town	1-4
18r	Letchworth Garden City v Bury Town	3-1
20r	Kingsbury Town v Harlow Town	2-2
21r	Ruislip Manor v Wembley	0-5
22r	Aylesbury United v Sudbury Town	2-1
27r	Basingstoke Town v Marlow	2-1
r	Pagham v Tooting & Mitcham United	3-4 N
29r	Woking v Banstead Athletic	1-0
30r	Tonbridge v Eastbourne United	3-1
r	Wokingham Town v Whyteleafe	1-0
32r	Yeovil Town v Waterlooville	3-2
34r	Cheltenham Town v Mangotsfield United	2-0
20r2	Kingsbury Town v Harlow Town	3-2

Qualifying Round Three

1	Harrogate Town v Bishop Auckland	1-1
2	Billingham Synthonia v Blyth Spartans	5-2
3	Fleetwood Town v Barrow	0-0
4	Easington Colliery v Newcastle Blue Star	3-0
5	Tow Law Town v Darlington Cleveland Bridge	4-0
6	Guisborough Town v Emley	3-2
7	Northwich Victoria v St Helens Town	3-2
8	Macclesfield Town v Marine	0-0
9	Alfreton Town v Colwyn Bay	1-1
10	Brigg Town v Leek Town	3-2
11	Moor Green v Matlock Town	3-2
12	Tamworth v Shepshed Charterhouse	3-2
13	Racing Club Warwick v Halesowen Town	1-3
14	Oldbury United v Willenhall Town	0-1
15	Atherstone United v Alvechurch	4-3
16	Boreham Wood v Worcester City	1-3
17	Berkhamsted Town v Barnet	0-3
18	Letchworth Garden City v March Town United	2-2
19	Uxbridge v Great Yarmouth Town	0-2
20	Kingsbury Town v Leytonstone/Ilford	0-1
21	Wembley v Leyton-Wingate	2-2
22	Hertford Town v Aylesbury United	0-4
23	Welling United v Burnham	3-1
24	Hayes v Fisher Athletic	2-0
25	Sutton United v Bromley	0-0
26	Gravesend & Northfleet v Carshalton Athletic	2-6
27	Tooting & Mitcham United v Basingstoke Town	0-0
28	Metropolitan Police v Croydon	0-1
29	Thanet United v Woking	1-1
30	Tonbridge v Wokingham Town	0-0
31	Bracknell Town v Newport (IOW)	4-1
32	Wimborne Town v Yeovil Town	0-4
33	Weymouth v Fareham Town	2-2
34	Weston-Super-Mare v Cheltenham Town	1-2
35	Merthyr Tydfil v Forest Green Rovers	3-1
36	Saltash United v Tiverton Town	3-0
1r	Bishop Auckland v Harrogate Town	2-0
3r	Barrow v Fleetwood Town	3-2
8r	Marine v Macclesfield Town	1-2
9r	Colwyn Bay v Alfreton Town	1-0
18r	March Town United v Letchworth Garden City	2-3
21r	Leyton-Wingate v Wembley	5-1
25r	Bromley v Sutton United	1-2
27r	Basingstoke Town v Tooting & Mitcham United	4-1
29r	Woking v Thanet United	0-2e
30r	Wokingham Town v Tonbridge	2-1
33r	Fareham Town v Weymouth	1-2

Qualifying Round Four

Bath City v Slough Town	3-1
Boston United v Welling United	1-1
Caernarfon Town v Billingham Synthonia	0-2
Carshalton Athletic v Wokingham Town	2-1
Cheltenham Town v Bracknell Town	2-1
Chorley v Frickley Athletic	2-0
Colwyn Bay v Tow Law Town	2-1
Enfield v Aylesbury United	1-2
Farnborough Town v Saltash United	4-2
Great Yarmouth Town v Dagenham	0-2
Guisborough Town v Bishop Auckland	1-2
Halesowen Town v Bishop's Stortford	1-0
Hayes v Moor Green	2-0
Letchworth Garden City v Chelmsford City	0-1
Leyton-Wingate v Atherstone United	0-0
Leytonstone/Ilford v Worcester City	0-1
Lincoln City v Brigg Town	4-1
Macclesfield Town v Whitby Town	3-1
Maidstone United v Dartford	2-0
Merthyr Tydfil v Croydon	3-0
Northwich Victoria v Easington Colliery	3-0

1987/88 to 1988/89

Runcorn v Barrow	2-1
Sutton United v Basingstoke Town	3-0
Tamworth v Wealdstone	2-0
Thanet United v Bognor Regis Town	0-4
V.S. Rugby v Nuneaton Borough	3-0
Weymouth v Yeovil Town	1-3
Willenhall Town v Barnet	0-6
r Atherstone United v Leyton-Wingate	4-2
r Welling United v Boston United	3-2

Round One

Altrincham v Wigan Athletic	0-2
Barnet v Hereford United	0-1
Billingham Synthonia v Halifax Town	2-4 N
Bishop Auckland v Blackpool	1-4
Bognor Regis Town v Torquay United	0-3
Brentford v Brighton & Hove Albion	0-2
Bristol City v Aylesbury United	1-0
Bristol Rovers v Merthyr Tydfil	6-0
Burnley v Bolton Wanderers	0-1
Cambridge United v Farnborough Town	2-1
Chelmsford City v Bath City	1-2
Chester City v Runcorn	0-1
Chorley v Hartlepool United	0-2
Colchester United v Tamworth	3-0
Dagenham v Maidstone United	0-2
Doncaster Rovers v Rotherham United	1-1
Gillingham v Fulham	2-1
Halesowen Town v Kidderminster Harriers	2-2
Hayes v Swansea City	0-1
Leyton Orient v Exeter City	2-0
Lincoln City v Crewe Alexandra	2-1
Macclesfield Town v Carlisle United	4-2
Northampton Town v Newport County	2-1
Northwich Victoria v Colwyn Bay	1-0
Notts County v Chesterfield	3-3
Peterborough United v Cardiff City	2-1
Preston North End v Mansfield Town	1-1
Rochdale v Wrexham	0-2
Scarborough v Grimsby Town	1-2
Scunthorpe United v Bury	3-1
Southend United v Walsall	0-0
Sunderland v Darlington	2-0
Sutton United v Aldershot	3-0
Telford United v Stockport County	1-1
Tranmere Rovers v Port Vale	2-2
V.S. Rugby v Atherstone United	0-0
Welling United v Carshalton Athletic	3-2
Wolverhampton Wan. v Cheltenham Town	5-1
Worcester City v Yeovil Town	1-1
York City v Burton Albion	0-0
r Atherstone United v V.S. Rugby	0-2
r Burton Albion v York City	1-2
r Chesterfield v Notts County	0-1
r Kidderminster Harriers v Halesowen Town	4-0
r Mansfield Town v Preston North End	4-2
r Port Vale v Tranmere Rovers	3-1
r Rotherham United v Doncaster Rovers	2-0
r Stockport County v Telford United	2-0
r Walsall v Southend United	2-1
r Yeovil Town v Worcester City	1-0

Round Two

Bristol City v Torquay United	0-1
Cambridge United v Yeovil Town	0-1
Colchester United v Hereford United	3-2
Gillingham v Walsall	2-1
Grimsby Town v Halifax Town	0-0
Leyton Orient v Swansea City	2-0
Macclesfield Town v Rotherham United	4-0
Maidstone United v Kidderminster Harriers	1-1
Mansfield Town v Lincoln City	4-3
Northampton Town v Brighton & Hove Albion	1-2
Northwich Victoria v Blackpool	0-2
Peterborough United v Sutton United	1-3
Port Vale v Notts County	2-0
Runcorn v Stockport County	0-1
Scunthorpe United v Sunderland	2-1
V.S. Rugby v Bristol Rovers	1-1
Welling United v Bath City	0-1
Wigan Athletic v Wolverhampton Wan.	1-3
Wrexham v Bolton Wanderers	1-2
York City v Hartlepool United	1-1
r Bristol Rovers v V.S. Rugby	4-0
r Halifax Town v Grimsby Town	0-1
r Hartlepool United v York City	3-1
r Kidderminster Harriers v Maidstone United	2-2e
r2 Kidderminster Harriers v Maidstone United	0-0e
r3 Maidstone United v Kidderminster Harriers	2-1

Round Three

Arsenal v Millwall	2-0
Barnsley v Bolton Wanderers	3-1
Blackburn Rovers v Portsmouth	1-2
Bradford City v Wolverhampton Wan.	2-1
Brighton & Hove Albion v Bournemouth	2-0
Coventry City v Torquay United	2-0
Derby County v Chelsea	1-3
Gillingham v Birmingham City	0-3
Halifax Town v Nottingham Forest	0-4
Hartlepool United v Luton Town	1-2
Huddersfield Town v Manchester City	2-2
Ipswich Town v Manchester United	1-2
Leeds United v Aston Villa	1-2
Mansfield Town v Bath City	4-0
Newcastle United v Crystal Palace	1-0
Oldham Athletic v Tottenham Hotspur	2-4
Oxford United v Leicester City	2-0
Plymouth Argyle v Colchester United	2-0
Port Vale v Macclesfield Town	1-0
Reading v Southampton	0-1
Scunthorpe United v Blackpool	0-0
Sheffield United v Maidstone United	1-0
Sheffield Wednesday v Everton	1-1
Shrewsbury Town v Bristol Rovers	2-1
Stockport County v Leyton Orient	1-2
Stoke City v Liverpool	0-0
Sutton United v Middlesbrough	1-1
Swindon Town v Norwich City	0-0
Watford v Hull City	1-1
West Ham United v Charlton Athletic	2-0
Wimbledon v West Bromwich Albion	4-1
Yeovil Town v Queen's Park Rangers	0-3
r Blackpool v Scunthorpe United	1-0
r Everton v Sheffield Wednesday	1-1e
r Hull City v Watford	2-2e
r Liverpool v Stoke City	1-0
r Manchester City v Huddersfield Town	0-0e
r Middlesbrough v Sutton United	1-0e
r Norwich City v Swindon Town	0-2
r2 Everton v Sheffield Wednesday	1-1e
r2 Huddersfield Town v Manchester City	0-3
r2 Watford v Hull City	1-0
r3 Sheffield Wednesday v Everton	0-5

Round Four

Aston Villa v Liverpool	0-2
Barnsley v Birmingham City	0-2
Blackpool v Manchester City	1-1
Bradford City v Oxford United	4-2
Brighton & Hove Albion v Arsenal	1-2
Coventry City v Watford	0-1
Everton v Middlesbrough	1-1
Leyton Orient v Nottingham Forest	1-2
Luton Town v Southampton	2-1
Manchester United v Chelsea	2-0
Mansfield Town v Wimbledon	1-2
Newcastle United v Swindon Town	5-0
Plymouth Argyle v Shrewsbury Town	1-0
Port Vale v Tottenham Hotspur	2-1
Portsmouth v Sheffield United	2-1
Queen's Park Rangers v West Ham United	3-1
r Manchester City v Blackpool	2-1
r Middlesbrough v Everton	2-2e
r2 Everton v Middlesbrough	2-1

Round Five

Arsenal v Manchester United	2-1
Birmingham City v Nottingham Forest	0-1
Everton v Liverpool	0-1
Manchester City v Plymouth Argyle	3-1
Newcastle United v Wimbledon	1-3
Port Vale v Watford	0-0
Portsmouth v Bradford City	3-0
Queen's Park Rangers v Luton Town	1-1
r Luton Town v Queen's Park Rangers	1-0
r Watford v Port Vale	2-0

Round Six

Arsenal v Nottingham Forest	1-2
Luton Town v Portsmouth	3-1
Manchester City v Liverpool	0-4
Wimbledon v Watford	2-1

Semi Finals

Liverpool v Nottingham Forest	2-1 N
Luton Town v Wimbledon	1-2 N

Final

Wimbledon v Liverpool	1-0 N

1988/89

Preliminary Round

1 Cleator Moor Celtic v Bridlington Town	0-0
Esh Winning v Ryhope Community Association	1-1
Evenwood Town v Bedlington Terriers	2-0
Farsley Celtic v Netherfield (Kendal)	2-2
2 Crook Town v Ferryhill Athletic	0-4
Leyland Motors v Bridlington Trinity	0-1
Workington v Murton	1-1
3 Durham City v Guiseley	1-2
Harrogate Town v Stockton (2)	1-1
Norton & Stockton Ancients v Darwen	1-0
4 Annfield Plain v Denaby United	1-0
Ashington v Rossendale United	2-4
Shildon v Willington	6-2
Wren Rovers v Whitley Bay	0-3
5 Clitheroe v Lancaster City	2-2
Ossett Albion v Northallerton Town	2-2
West Auckland Town v South Bank	0-0
6 Armthorpe Welfare v Darlington Cleveland Bridge	3-1
Emley v Langley Park	4-1
Peterlee Newtown v Droylsden	1-2
7 Formby v Congleton Town	0-7
Harworth Colliery Institute v Belper Town	0-0
Irlam Town v Oakham United	3-1
St Helens Town v Ashton United	0-1
8 Bootle v Arnold	0-1
Glossop v Prescot Cables	0-0
Radcliffe Borough v Ilkeston Town (2)	2-1
9 Bilston Town v Alfreton Town	4-0
Leek Town v Heanor Town	3-0
Long Eaton United v Bridgnorth Town	0-5
Warrington Town v Curzon Ashton	3-2
10 Boston v Sutton Town	2-0
Grantham v Borrowash Victoria	2-1
Hinckley Athletic v West Winsford Town	3-0
11 Harrisons v Dudley Town	0-2
Hednesford Town v Eastwood Town	1-3
Walsall Wood v Louth United	0-0
12 Gresley Rovers v Paget Rangers	2-0
Hinckley Town v Stourbridge	2-0
Rothwell Town v Mile Oak Rovers & Youth	1-5
13 Brackley Town v Spalding United	1-0
Desborough Town v Witney Town	2-2
Highgate United v Rushden Town	0-4
Tividale v Rushall Olympic	1-4
14 Chatteris Town v Racing Club Warwick	2-2
Northampton Spencer v Irthlingborough Diamonds	0-1
Wednesfield Social v Chasetown	2-3
15 Evesham United v King's Lynn	3-0
Histon v Wisbech Town	0-2
Holbeach United v Banbury United	1-4
Leighton Town v MK Wolverton Town	2-0
16 Berkhamsted Town v March Town United	2-2
Bourne Town v Baker Perkins	1-1
Saffron Walden v Ely City	2-0
17 Edgware Town v Hitchin Town	1-4
Ware v Lowestoft Town	2-0
Wivenhoe Town v Clacton Town	3-0
18 Basildon United v Braintree Town	2-4
Heybridge Swifts v Gorleston	3-1
Soham Town Rangers v Watton United	0-1
19 Aveley v Halstead Town	2-2
Barkingside v Uxbridge	1-2
Potton United v Welwyn Garden City	2-0
Thetford Town v Harlow Town	2-2
20 Canvey Island v Stowmarket Town	2-3
Kempston Rovers v Beckenham Town	0-1
Leatherhead v Hounslow	1-1
Tiptree United v Dunstable	1-1
21 Billericay Town v Haverhill Rovers	0-1
Finchley v Wootton Blue Cross	1-0
Staines Town v Newmarket Town	3-0
22 Arlesey Town v Hoddesdon Town	1-1
Chesham United v Hornchurch	1-1
Felixstowe Town v Baldock Town	1-1
Purfleet v Metropolitan Police	0-1
23 Burgess Hill Town v Harefield United	2-1
Hanwell Town v Corinthian Casuals	4-0
Merstham v Clapton	3-3
24 Darenth Heathside v Hertford Town	0-1
Flackwell Heath v Camberley Town	3-2
Gravesend & Northfleet v Tunbridge Wells	2-1
Redhill v Malden Vale	0-1
25 Collier Row v Rainham Town	0-3
Ruislip v Crockenhill	2-0
Stevenage Borough v Rayners Lane	6-1
26 Cray Wanderers v Tilbury	1-4
Hailsham Town v Ruislip Manor	0-0
Sheppey United v Maidenhead United	1-1
27 Chatham Town v Dorking (2)	1-5
Shoreham v Eastbourne United	1-2
Sittingbourne v Hastings Town	2-3
Yeading v Haywards Heath	2-3
28 Feltham v Hythe Town	1-1
Folkestone v Ringmer	2-0
Peacehaven & Telscombe v Ramsgate	0-1
29 Molesey v Herne Bay	7-0
Tonbridge v Canterbury City	2-3
Whyteleafe v Arundel	6-0
30 Corinthian v Wick	2-1
Horndean v Banstead Athletic	2-3
Whitehawk v Lancing	2-0
31 Abingdon Town v Havant Town	4-2
Chichester City (1) v Petersfield United	2-1
Pagham v Oxford City	w/o/s
Salisbury (2) v Newbury Town	4-2
32 Calne Town v Thatcham Town	0-1
Chippenham Town v Andover	4-0
Hungerford Town v Eastleigh	0-0
33 Devizes Town v Sholing Sports	3-2
Taunton Town v Poole Town	1-1
Trowbridge Town v Romsey Town	2-0
34 Minehead v Sharpness	0-4
Radstock Town v Cwmbran Town	2-2
Tiverton Town v Bridgend Town	7-2
35 Bideford v Shortwood United	1-1
Bristol Manor Farm v Barry Town	0-1
Frome Town v St Blazey	4-1

178

1988/89

36	Clandown v Yate Town	0-2
	Paulton Rovers v Barnstaple Town	2-1
	Welton Rovers v Exmouth Town	0-5
1r	Bridlington Town v Cleator Moor Celtic	4-1
r	Netherfield (Kendal) v Farsley Celtic	0-3
r	Ryhope Community Association v Esh Winning	2-3
2r	Murton v Workington	2-4
3r	Harrogate Town v Stockton (2)	2-1
5r	Lancaster City v Clitheroe	1-0
r	Northallerton Town v Ossett Albion	2-1
r	South Bank v West Auckland Town	2-0
7r	Belper Town v Harworth Colliery Institute	1-5
8r	Prescot Cables v Glossop	1-0
11r	Louth United v Walsall Wood	1-3
13r	Witney Town v Desborough Town	1-0
14r	Racing Club Warwick v Chatteris Town	6-0
16r	Baker Perkins v Bourne Town	0-1
r	March Town United v Berkhamsted Town	4-2
19r	Halstead Town v Aveley	3-3x
r	Harlow Town v Thetford Town	4-1
20r	Dunstable v Tiptree United	1-1
r	Hounslow v Leatherhead	1-2
22r	Baldock Town v Felixstowe Town	4-0
r	Hoddesdon Town v Arlesey Town	1-3
r	Hornchurch v Chesham United	5-6
23r	Clapton v Merstham	2-1
26r	Maidenhead United v Sheppey United	0-1
r	Ruislip Manor v Hailsham Town	0-2
28r	Hythe Town v Feltham	2-5
32r	Eastleigh v Hungerford Town	0-1
33r	Poole Town v Taunton Town	1-0
34r	Radstock Town v Cwmbran Town	1-0
35r	Shortwood United v Bideford	2-1e
19r2	Aveley v Halstead Town	1-4
20r2	Tiptree United v Dunstable	0-0
20r3	Dunstable v Tiptree United	0-1

Qualifying Round One

1	Bishop Auckland v Evenwood Town	4-0
	Esh Winning v Farsley Celtic	1-1
	Guisborough Town v Alnwick Town	3-0
	North Shields v Bridlington Town	1-1
2	Horden CW v Ferryhill Athletic	0-2
	Spennymoor United v Bridlington Trinity	3-0
	Tow Law Town v Consett	2-0
	Workington v Gateshead (2)	0-0
3	Billingham Town v Guiseley	1-0
	Harrogate Town v Billingham Synthonia	1-3
	Newcastle Blue Star v Norton & Stockton Ancients	4-0
	Seaham Red Star v Accrington Stanley (2)	0-0
4	Blyth Spartans v Rossendale United	1-0
	Brandon United v Annfield Plain	2-0
	Gretna v Chester-le-Street Town	5-0
	Shildon v Whitley Bay	1-5
5	Barrow v Lancaster City	3-1
	Morecambe v Skelmersdale United	3-3
	Northallerton Town v Easington Colliery	2-0
	Shotton Comrades v South Bank	1-1
6	Armthorpe Welfare v Fleetwood Town	2-2
	Burscough v Emley	0-1
	Horwich RMI v Droylsden	3-3
	Marine v Thackley	5-0
7	Bangor City v Irlam Town	2-2
	Colwyn Bay v Ashton United	0-0
	Congleton Town v Harworth Colliery Institute	1-1
	Southport v Penrith	1-0
8	Eastwood Hanley v Prescot Cables	2-0
	Northwich Victoria v Arnold	5-0
	Radcliffe Borough v Hyde United	0-2
	Stalybridge Celtic v Chadderton	1-4
9	Bilston Town v Warrington Town	0-0
	Mossley v Bridgnorth Town	2-0 N
	Rhyl v Ashtree Highfield	4-1
	South Liverpool v Leek Town	1-1
10	Frickley Athletic v Boldmere St Michaels	2-1
	Hinckley Athletic v Buxton	1-3
	North Ferriby United v Grantham	3-2
	Witton Albion v Boston	0-0
11	Eastwood Town v Brigg Town	3-1
	Matlock Town v Walsall Wood	2-3
	Oldbury United v Dudley Town	2-3
	Worksop Town v Sutton Coldfield Town	1-2
12	Boston United v Coventry Sporting	8-1
	Gainsborough Trinity v Gresley Rovers	2-2
	Lye Town v Hinckley Town	0-3
	Mile Oak Rovers & Youth v Goole Town	3-1
13	Brackley Town v Rushall Olympic	1-2
	Leicester United v Rushden Town	4-1
	Shepshed Charterhouse v Witney Town	3-2
	Stafford Rangers v Halesowen Harriers	2-0
14	Irthlingborough Diamonds v Moor Green	1-1
	Tamworth v Racing Club Warwick	3-0
	Wellingborough Town v Chasetown	1-2
	Willenhall Town v Malvern Town	3-3
15	Atherstone United v Wisbech Town	4-0
	Leighton Town v Banbury United	0-0
	Nuneaton Borough v Stamford	2-0
	Redditch United v Evesham United	2-1
16	Barton Rovers v Saffron Walden Town	1-0
	Bedworth United v Bourne Town	1-1
	Bromsgrove Rovers v Chalfont St Peter	1-1
	March Town United v Alvechurch	1-2
17	Boreham Wood v Hitchin Town	2-0
	Bury Town v Wivenhoe Town	0-0
	Great Yarmouth Town v Milton Keynes Borough	3-0
	Ware v Kettering Town	0-3
18	Bishop's Stortford v Heybridge Swifts	3-1
	Braintree Town v Corby Town	2-0
	Hendon v Harwich & Parkeston	5-1
	Witham Town v Watton United	2-1
19	Cambridge City v Potton United	5-1
	Leyton-Wingate v Hampton	1-1
	Sudbury Town v Harlow Town	3-1
	Uxbridge v Halstead Town	0-2
20	Barking v Beckenham Town	0-0
	Barnet v Epsom & Ewell	7-0
	Grays Athletic v Tiptree United	5-0
	Leatherhead v Stowmarket Town	1-0
21	Buckingham Town v Finchley	0-3
	Letchworth Garden City v Cheshunt	1-2
	Staines Town v Harrow Borough	2-0
	Wycombe Wanderers v Haverhill Rovers	4-1
22	Hayes v Chesham United	1-0
	Hemel Hempstead Town v Baldock Town	5-1
	Metropolitan Police v Arlesey Town	1-1
	Wealdstone v Vauxhall Motors (Luton)	2-1
23	Clapton v Leytonstone/Ilford	0-1
	Erith & Belvedere v Hanwell Town	0-1
	Horsham v Walton & Hersham	1-5
	Wembley v Burgess Hill Town	3-1
24	Dartford v Flackwell Heath	7-1
	Gravesend & Northfleet v Hertford Town	1-3
	St Albans City v Malden Vale	1-0
	Wokingham Town v Kingsbury Town	2-1
25	Burnham v Rainham Town	2-2
	Dulwich Hamlet v Three Bridges	1-0
	Royston Town v Stevenage Borough	0-1
	Ruislip v Marlow	1-1
26	Carshalton Athletic v Lewes	3-1
	Crawley Town v Hailsham Town	2-1
	Sheppey United v Bromley	1-4
	Tring Town v Tilbury	2-1
27	Ashford Town v Dorking (2)	2-1
	Croydon v Hastings Town	1-2
	Dover Athletic v Egham Town	2-0
	Haywards Heath v Eastbourne United	3-2
28	Chertsey Town v Feltham	0-0
	Kingstonian v Folkestone	4-1
	Ramsgate v Fisher Athletic	0-2
	Thanet United v Portfield	1-0
29	Horsham YMCA v Molesey	1-2
	Southwick v Littlehampton Town	5-0
	Whyteleafe v Tooting & Mitcham United	2-1
	Woking v Canterbury City	3-0
30	Banstead Athletic v Windsor & Eton	0-2
	Bracknell Town v Whitehawk	1-2
	Steyning Town v Corinthian	5-1
	Worthing v AFC Totton	3-2
31	Basingstoke Town v Abingdon Town	3-1
	Fareham Town v Chichester City (1)	3-0
	Newport (IOW) v Bashley	1-1
	Salisbury (2) v Pagham	2-3
32	Abingdon United v Hungerford Town	1-2
	Thame United v Westbury United	3-1
	Thatcham Town v Gosport Borough	1-3
	Waterlooville v Chippenham Town	2-0
33	Chard Town v Poole Town	0-3
	Forest Green Rovers v Devizes Town	5-0
	Trowbridge Town v Weymouth	1-2
	Wimborne Town v Weston-Super-Mare	3-5
34	Clevedon Town v Tiverton Town	1-2
	Melksham Town v Gloucester City	0-5
	Merthyr Tydfil v Sharpness	3-0
	Radstock Town v Cheltenham Town	0-2
35	Barry Town v Worcester City	0-2
	Dorchester Town v Frome Town	3-1
	Maesteg Park Athletic v Shortwood United	1-0
	Mangotsfield United v Torrington	6-0
36	Falmouth Town v Glastonbury	3-0
	Paulton Rovers v Saltash United	1-4
	Swanage Town & Herston v Yate Town	2-1
	Ton Pentre v Exmouth Town	0-1
1r	Bridlington Town v North Shields	1-1
r	Farsley Celtic v Esh Winning	2-1
2r	Gateshead (2) v Workington	1-0
3r	Accrington Stanley (2) v Seaham Red Star	2-1
5r	Skelmersdale United v Morecambe	1-2
r	South Bank v Shotton Comrades	3-1
6r	Droylsden v Horwich RMI	1-2e
r	Fleetwood Town v Armthorpe Welfare	5-0
7r	Ashton United v Colwyn Bay	2-1
r	Harworth Colliery Institute v Congleton Town	1-0
r	Irlam Town v Bangor City	1-4
9r	Leek Town v South Liverpool	2-1
r	Warrington Town v Bilston Town	3-2
10r	Boston v Witton Albion	0-2
12r	Gresley Rovers v Gainsborough Trinity	3-1
14r	Malvern Town v Willenhall Town	0-0
r	Moor Green v Irthlingborough Diamonds	4-3
15r	Banbury United v Leighton Town	2-1
16r	Bourne Town v Bedworth United	3-4
r	Chalfont St Peter v Bromsgrove Rovers	0-3
17r	Wivenhoe Town v Bury Town	0-2
19r	Hampton v Leyton-Wingate	0-1
20r	Beckenham Town v Barking	0-1
22r	Arlesey Town v Metropolitan Police	2-0
25r	Marlow v Ruislip	3-0
r	Rainham Town v Burnham	1-1
28r	Feltham v Chertsey Town	1-0
31r	Bashley v Newport (IOW)	1-0
1r2	North Shields v Bridlington Town	1-2
14r2	Willenhall Town v Malvern Town	0-2
25r2	Burnham v Rainham Town	3-1

Qualifying Round Two

1	Bridlington Town v Bishop Auckland	2-1
	Guisborough Town v Farsley Celtic	0-0
2	Ferryhill Athletic v Spennymoor United	0-2
	Tow Law Town v Gateshead (2)	3-2
3	Accrington Stanley (2) v Billingham Synthonia	1-1
	Billingham Town v Newcastle Blue Star	2-1
4	Brandon United v Blyth Spartans	4-2
	Gretna v Whitley Bay	1-1
5	Morecambe v Northallerton Town	3-2
	South Bank v Barrow	0-0
6	Emley v Horwich RMI	5-0
	Marine v Fleetwood Town	2-4
7	Ashton United v Bangor City	1-3
	Southport v Harworth Colliery Institute	2-0
8	Chadderton v Hyde United	1-5
	Eastwood Hanley v Northwich Victoria	0-1
9	Leek Town v Mossley	2-0
	Rhyl v Warrington Town	1-1
10	Frickley Athletic v Buxton	1-0
	North Ferriby United v Witton Albion	2-2
11	Dudley Town v Walsall Wood	2-1
	Sutton Coldfield Town v Eastwood Town	1-0
12	Boston United v Mile Oak Rovers & Youth	5-0
	Hinckley Town v Gresley Rovers	1-0
13	Leicester United v Shepshed Charterhouse	1-0
	Stafford Rangers v Rushall Olympic	1-0
14	Chasetown v Tamworth	0-1
	Malvern Town v Moor Green	0-2
15	Nuneaton Borough v Banbury United	1-1
	Redditch United v Atherstone United	2-1
16	Barton Rovers v Bedworth United	1-3
	Bromsgrove Rovers v Alvechurch	2-2
17	Boreham Wood v Bury Town	0-0
	Great Yarmouth Town v Kettering Town	0-3
18	Hendon v Braintree Town	3-1
	Witham Town v Bishop's Stortford	2-3
19	Leyton-Wingate v Halstead Town	7-1
	Sudbury Town v Cambridge City	2-1
20	Barnet v Leatherhead	4-3
	Grays Athletic v Barking	1-1
21	Cheshunt v Staines Town	1-2
	Finchley v Wycombe Wanderers	0-3
22	Hemel Hempstead Town v Hayes	2-3
	Wealdstone v Arlesey Town	1-0
23	Hanwell Town v Wembley	0-1
	Walton & Hersham v Leytonstone/Ilford	3-2
24	Dartford v St Albans City	1-1
	Wokingham Town v Hertford Town	3-1
25	Dulwich Hamlet v Marlow	1-0
	Stevenage Borough v Burnham	3-2 D
26	Carshalton Athletic v Bromley	1-1
	Tring Town v Crawley Town	1-2
27	Ashford Town v Hastings Town	2-1
	Dover Athletic v Haywards Heath	5-2
28	Feltham v Kingstonian	0-0
	Thanet United v Fisher Athletic	1-3
29	Molesey v Woking	1-1
	Southwick v Whyteleafe	0-1
30	Steyning Town v Whitehawk	1-3
	Worthing v Windsor & Eton	0-4
31	Bashley v Pagham	4-3
	Fareham Town v Basingstoke Town	3-0
32	Hungerford Town v Waterlooville	0-2
	Thame United v Gosport Borough	1-3
33	Poole Town v Forest Green Rovers	2-4
	Weston-Super-Mare v Weymouth	0-1
34	Gloucester City v Cheltenham Town	3-0
	Tiverton Town v Merthyr Tydfil	0-1
35	Maesteg Park Athletic v Dorchester Town	0-2
	Mangotsfield United v Worcester City	0-1
36	Falmouth Town v Saltash United	2-2
	Swanage Town & Herston v Exmouth Town	1-1
1r	Farsley Celtic v Guisborough Town	0-1
3r	Billingham Synthonia v Accrington Stanley (2)	5-1
4r	Whitley Bay v Gretna	1-0
5r	Barrow v South Bank	1-0
9r	Warrington Town v Rhyl	2-0
10r	Witton Albion v North Ferriby United	3-1
15r	Banbury United v Nuneaton Borough	1-0
16r	Alvechurch v Bromsgrove Rovers	3-3
17r	Bury Town v Boreham Wood	1-4
20r	Barking v Grays Athletic	0-3
24r	St Albans City v Dartford	2-4
26r	Bromley v Carshalton Athletic	4-2
28r	Kingstonian v Feltham	3-0
29r	Woking v Molesey	1-0
36r	Exmouth Town v Swanage Town & Herston	3-0
r	Saltash United v Falmouth Town	5-0
16r2	Bromsgrove Rovers v Alvechurch	2-0

Qualifying Round Three

1	Guisborough Town v Bridlington Town	1-1
2	Tow Law Town v Spennymoor United	2-2
3	Billingham Synthonia v Billingham Town	3-0
4	Whitley Bay v Brandon United	0-1
5	Morecambe v Barrow	0-0
6	Fleetwood Town v Emley	2-2

1988/89 to 1989/90

7	Southport v Bangor City	3-0
8	Hyde United v Northwich Victoria	1-1
9	Warrington Town v Leek Town	1-2
10	Frickley Athletic v Witton Albion	3-1
11	Sutton Coldfield Town v Dudley Town	0-1
12	Boston United v Hinckley Town	3-4
13	Stafford Rangers v Leicester United	1-1
14	Moor Green v Tamworth	1-1
15	Banbury United v Redditch United	2-3
16	Bromsgrove Rovers v Bedworth United	3-1
17	Kettering Town v Boreham Wood	4-0
18	Hendon v Bishop's Stortford	5-3
19	Leyton-Wingate v Sudbury Town	1-2
20	Barnet v Grays Athletic	0-1
21	Staines Town v Wycombe Wanderers	0-1
22	Wealdstone v Hayes	1-2
23	Walton & Hersham v Wembley	2-1
24	Wokingham Town v Dartford	1-2
25	Dulwich Hamlet v Burnham	1-1
26	Bromley v Crawley Town	2-2
27	Dover Athletic v Ashford Town	3-0
28	Fisher Athletic v Kingstonian	1-1
29	Whyteleafe v Woking	0-2
30	Windsor & Eton v Whitehawk	1-1
31	Bashley v Fareham Town	1-2
32	Gosport Borough v Waterlooville	0-1
33	Weymouth v Forest Green Rovers	3-0
34	Gloucester City v Merthyr Tydfil	0-1
35	Worcester City v Dorchester Town	1-1
36	Saltash United v Exmouth Town	2-2
1r	Bridlington Town v Guisborough Town	0-1
2r	Spennymoor United v Tow Law Town	2-2
5r	Barrow v Morecambe	5-1
6r	Emley v Fleetwood Town	2-2
8r	Northwich Victoria v Hyde United	3-0
13r	Leicester United v Stafford Rangers	2-3
14r	Tamworth v Moor Green	4-6
25r	Burnham v Dulwich Hamlet	2-3
26r	Crawley Town v Bromley	1-0e
28r	Kingstonian v Fisher Athletic	1-4
30r	Whitehawk v Windsor & Eton	1-0
35r	Dorchester Town v Worcester City	1-2
36r	Exmouth Town v Saltash United	4-3
2r2	Spennymoor United v Tow Law Town	1-2e
6r2	Fleetwood Town v Emley	3-1

Qualifying Round Four

	Aylesbury United v Sudbury Town	1-1
	Barrow v Whitby Town	1-1
	Bognor Regis Town v Whitehawk	2-2
	Bromsgrove Rovers v Moor Green	2-0
	Caernarfon Town v Brandon United	1-1
	Chelmsford City v Halesowen Town	1-3
	Crawley Town v Merthyr Tydfil	3-3
	Dagenham v Burton Albion	2-0
	Dudley Town v Grays Athletic	3-3
	Exmouth Town v Woking	1-5
	Fareham Town v Dover Athletic	1-1
	Farnborough Town v Waterlooville	2-3
	Fisher Athletic v Dulwich Hamlet	3-3
	Fleetwood Town v Runcorn	1-3
	Frickley Athletic v Chorley	1-1
	Hayes v Redditch United	1-0
	Leek Town v Guisborough Town	0-0
	Macclesfield Town v Altrincham	0-0
	Newport County v Weymouth	2-1
	Northwich Victoria v Billingham Synthonia	2-0
	Slough Town v Dartford	1-2
	Southport v Tow Law Town	2-1
	Stafford Rangers v Kidderminster Harriers	2-1
	Sutton United v Walton & Hersham	1-1
	V.S. Rugby v Hendon	1-1
	Welling United v Hinckley Town	1-1
	Worcester City v Yeovil Town	1-2
	Wycombe Wanderers v Kettering Town	1-2
r	Altrincham v Macclesfield Town	4-0
r	Brandon United v Caernarfon Town	2-0
r	Chorley v Frickley Athletic	0-1
r	Dover Athletic v Fareham Town	0-1
r	Dulwich Hamlet v Fisher Athletic	0-3
r	Grays Athletic v Dudley Town	2-0
r	Guisborough Town v Leek Town	1-0
r	Hendon v V.S. Rugby	2-0
r	Hinckley Town v Welling United	0-3
r	Merthyr Tydfil v Crawley Town	3-1
r	Sudbury Town v Aylesbury United	0-1
r	Walton & Hersham v Sutton United	0-3
r	Whitby Town v Barrow	1-3
r	Whitehawk v Bognor Regis Town	0-2

Round One

	Aldershot v Hayes	1-0
	Altrincham v Lincoln City	3-2
	Bath City v Grays Athletic	2-0
	Blackpool v Scunthorpe United	2-1
	Bognor Regis Town v Exeter City	2-1
	Bolton Wanderers v Chesterfield	0-0
	Brentford v Halesowen Town	2-0
	Bristol City v Southend United	3-1
	Bristol Rovers v Fisher Athletic	3-0
	Burnley v Chester City	0-2
	Cardiff City v Hereford United	3-0
	Dagenham v Sutton United	0-4
	Darlington v Notts County	1-2
	Doncaster Rovers v Brandon United	0-0
	Enfield v Leyton Orient	1-1
	Frickley Athletic v Northwich Victoria	0-2
	Fulham v Colchester United	0-1
	Gillingham v Peterborough United	3-3
	Grimsby Town v Wolverhampton Wan.	1-0
	Guisborough Town v Bury	0-1 N
	Halifax Town v York City	1-0
	Hartlepool United v Wigan Athletic	2-0
	Huddersfield Town v Rochdale	1-1
	Kettering Town v Dartford	2-1
	Mansfield Town v Sheffield United	1-1
	Newport County v Maidstone United	1-2
	Preston North End v Tranmere Rovers	1-1
	Reading v Hendon	4-2
	Rotherham United v Barrow	3-1
	Runcorn v Wrexham	2-2
	Scarborough v Stockport County	2-1
	Southport v Port Vale	0-2
	Stafford Rangers v Crewe Alexandra	2-2
	Swansea City v Northampton Town	3-1
	Telford United v Carlisle United	1-1
	Torquay United v Fareham Town	2-2
	Waterlooville v Aylesbury United	1-4
	Welling United v Bromsgrove Rovers	3-0
	Woking v Cambridge United	1-4
	Yeovil Town v Merthyr Tydfil	3-2
r	Carlisle United v Telford United	4-1
r	Chesterfield v Bolton Wanderers	2-3
r	Crewe Alexandra v Stafford Rangers	3-2
r	Doncaster Rovers v Brandon United	2-1
r	Fareham Town v Torquay United	2-3
r	Leyton Orient v Enfield	2-2e
r	Peterborough United v Gillingham	1-0e
r	Rochdale v Huddersfield Town	3-4
r	Sheffield United v Mansfield Town	2-1
r	Tranmere Rovers v Preston North End	3-0
r	Wrexham v Runcorn	2-3
r2	Leyton Orient v Enfield	0-1

Round Two

	Aldershot v Bristol City	1-1
	Altrincham v Halifax Town	0-3
	Aylesbury United v Sutton United	0-1
	Bath City v Welling United	0-0
	Blackpool v Bury	3-0
	Bognor Regis Town v Cambridge United	0-1
	Bolton Wanderers v Port Vale	1-2
	Colchester United v Swansea City	2-2
	Doncaster Rovers v Sheffield United	1-3
	Enfield v Cardiff City	1-4
	Grimsby Town v Rotherham United	3-2
	Hartlepool United v Notts County	1-0
	Huddersfield Town v Chester City	1-0
	Kettering Town v Bristol Rovers	2-1
	Northwich Victoria v Tranmere Rovers	1-2
	Peterborough United v Brentford	0-0
	Reading v Maidstone United	1-1
	Runcorn v Crewe Alexandra	0-3
	Scarborough v Carlisle United	0-1
	Yeovil Town v Torquay United	1-1
r	Brentford v Peterborough United	3-2
r	Bristol City v Aldershot	0-0e
r	Maidstone United v Reading	1-2
r	Swansea City v Colchester United	1-3
r	Torquay United v Yeovil Town	1-0
r	Welling United v Bath City	3-2
r2	Aldershot v Bristol City	2-2e
r3	Bristol City v Aldershot	1-0

Round Three

	Barnsley v Chelsea	4-0
	Birmingham City v Wimbledon	0-1
	Blackpool v Bournemouth	0-1
	Bradford City v Tottenham Hotspur	1-0
	Brighton & Hove Albion v Leeds United	1-2
	Cardiff City v Hull City	1-2
	Carlisle United v Liverpool	0-3
	Charlton Athletic v Oldham Athletic	2-1
	Crewe Alexandra v Aston Villa	2-3
	Derby County v Southampton	1-1
	Hartlepool United v Bristol City	1-0
	Huddersfield Town v Sheffield United	0-1
	Kettering Town v Halifax Town	1-1
	Manchester City v Leicester City	1-0
	Manchester United v Queen's Park Rangers	0-0
	Middlesbrough v Grimsby Town	1-2
	Millwall v Luton Town	3-2
	Newcastle United v Watford	0-0
	Nottingham Forest v Ipswich Town	3-0
	Plymouth Argyle v Cambridge United	2-0
	Port Vale v Norwich City	1-3
	Portsmouth v Swindon Town	1-1
	Sheffield Wednesday v Torquay United	5-1
	Shrewsbury Town v Colchester United	0-3
	Stoke City v Crystal Palace	1-0
	Sunderland v Oxford United	1-1
	Sutton United v Coventry City	2-1
	Tranmere Rovers v Reading	1-1
	Walsall v Brentford	1-1
	Welling United v Blackburn Rovers	0-1
	West Bromwich Albion v Everton	1-1
	West Ham United v Arsenal	2-2
r	Arsenal v West Ham United	0-1
r	Brentford v Walsall	1-0
r	Everton v West Bromwich Albion	1-0
r	Halifax Town v Kettering Town	2-3
r	Oxford United v Sunderland	2-0
r	Queen's Park Rangers v Manchester United	2-2e
r	Reading v Tranmere Rovers	2-1
r	Southampton v Derby County	1-2e
r	Swindon Town v Portsmouth	2-0
r	Watford v Newcastle United	2-2e
r2	Manchester United v Queen's Park Rangers	3-0
r2	Newcastle United v Watford	0-0e
r3	Watford v Newcastle United	1-0e

Round Four

	Aston Villa v Wimbledon	0-1
	Blackburn Rovers v Sheffield Wednesday	2-1
	Bradford City v Hull City	1-2
	Brentford v Manchester City	3-1
	Charlton Athletic v Kettering Town	2-1
	Grimsby Town v Reading	1-1
	Hartlepool United v Bournemouth	1-1
	Manchester United v Oxford United	4-0
	Millwall v Liverpool	0-2
	Norwich City v Sutton United	8-0
	Nottingham Forest v Leeds United	2-0
	Plymouth Argyle v Everton	1-1
	Sheffield United v Colchester United	3-3
	Stoke City v Barnsley	3-3
	Swindon Town v West Ham United	0-0
	Watford v Derby County	2-1
r	Barnsley v Stoke City	2-1
r	Bournemouth v Hartlepool United	5-2
r	Colchester United v Sheffield United	0-2
r	Everton v Plymouth Argyle	4-0
r	Reading v Grimsby Town	1-2
r	West Ham United v Swindon Town	1-0

Round Five

	Barnsley v Everton	0-1
	Blackburn Rovers v Brentford	0-2
	Bournemouth v Manchester United	1-1
	Charlton Athletic v West Ham United	0-1
	Hull City v Liverpool	2-3
	Norwich City v Sheffield United	3-2
	Watford v Nottingham Forest	0-3
	Wimbledon v Grimsby Town	3-1
r	Manchester United v Bournemouth	1-0

Round Six

	Everton v Wimbledon	1-0
	Liverpool v Brentford	4-0
	Manchester United v Nottingham Forest	0-1
	West Ham United v Norwich City	0-0
r	Norwich City v West Ham United	3-1

Semi Finals

	Everton v Norwich City	1-0 N
	Liverpool v Nottingham Forest	3-1 N

Final

	Liverpool v Everton	3-2eN

1989/90

Preliminary Round

1	Alnwick Town v Peterlee Newtown	1-1
	Cleator Moor Celtic v Thackley	1-1
	Harworth Colliery Institute v Ashington	0-3
	Horden CW v Whitley Bay	0-3
2	Clitheroe v Bedlington Terriers	4-0
	Consett v Ferryhill Athletic	1-3
	Darlington Cleveland Bridge v Bridlington Trinity	wo/s
	Northallerton Town v Netherfield (Kendal)	3-3
3	Langley Park v Guiseley	5-4
	Norton & Stockton Ancients v South Bank	1-7
	Washington v Chester-le-Street Town	0-0
4	Annfield Plain v Shotton Comrades	2-3
	Crook Town v Workington	0-0
	Prudhoe East End v Harrogate Town	1-0
	Seaham Red Star v Easington Colliery	1-0
5	Darwen v Lancaster City	0-3
	Esh Winning v North Shields	2-6
	Evenwood Town v Durham City	0-1
	Penrith v Murton	2-3
6	Atherton LR v Accrington Stanley (2)	1-1
	Droylsden v Blackpool (Wren) Rovers	3-2
	Prescot Cables v Ossett Albion	2-1
	Skelmersdale United v Curzon Ashton	1-1
7	Burscough v Bootle	2-0
	Colwyn Bay v Ilkeston Town (2)	5-1 N
	Congleton Town v Irlam Town	1-1
	Glossop v Maine Road	0-4
8	Heanor Town v Formby	2-0
	Leyland Motors v Rossendale United	0-1
	Sheffield v Armthorpe Welfare	1-0

1989/90

9	Belper Town v Ashton United	1-0
	Oakham United v Worksop Town	4-2
	Radcliffe Borough v Bridgnorth Town	2-2
	Walsall Wood v Winsford United	2-0
10	Brigg Town v St Helens Town	0-2
	Chadderton v Gresley Rovers	1-2
	Mile Oak Rovers & Youth v Warrington Town	1-2
	North Ferriby United v Long Eaton United	1-0
11	Eastwood Town v Grantham Town	1-2
	Friar Lane Old Boys v Farsley Celtic	1-2
	Hinckley Athletic v Highgate United	2-0
12	Chasetown v Spalding United	2-2
	Nuneaton Borough v Willenhall Town	1-1
	Princes End United v Alfreton Town	0-2
	Sutton Town v Rushall Olympic	1-1
13	Brackley Town v Coventry Sporting	wo/s
	Stratford Town v Wellingborough Town	0-0
	Sutton Coldfield Town v Harrisons	7-0
14	Bilston Town v Desborough Town	1-1
	Hednesford Town v Lye Town	0-2
	MK Wolverton Town v Irthlingborough Diamonds	2-1
	Tividale v Stourbridge	1-3
15	Halesowen Harriers v Rushden Town	2-5
	March Town United v Chatteris Town	5-0
	Oldbury United v King's Lynn	1-1
	Soham Town Rangers v Rothwell Town	0-1
16	Hitchin Town v Leicester United	3-1
	Northampton Spencer v Paget Rangers	3-3
	Racing Club Warwick v Haverhill Rovers	1-1
	Wisbech Town v Eynesbury Rovers	5-0
17	Braintree Town v Newmarket Town	1-1
	Great Yarmouth Town v Stevenage Borough	0-2
	Langford v Canvey Island	0-3
	Purfleet v Stamford	1-1
18	Basildon United v Stowmarket Town	0-1
	Bury Town v Clapton	0-5
	Lowestoft Town v Gorleston	2-1
	Saffron Walden Town v Burnham Ramblers	2-1
19	Barkingside v Harlow Town	2-5
	Heybridge Swifts v Ford United	1-1
	Welwyn Garden City v Halstead Town	1-1
	Witham Town v Clacton Town	2-1
20	Felixstowe Town v Tring Town	0-2
	Ware v Tiptree United	2-1
	Wivenhoe Town v Harwich & Parkeston	2-0
	Wootton Blue Cross v Cheshunt	0-2
21	Aveley v Chesham United	0-0
	Baldock Town v Cray Wanderers	3-0
	Boreham Wood v Harefield United	1-0
	Hoddesdon Town v Berkhamsted Town	2-3 N
22	Beckenham Town v Walthamstow Pennant	0-5
	Burgess Hill Town v Wandsworth & Norwood	1-2
	Yeading v Buckingham Town	4-0
23	Barton Rovers v Chipstead	0-0
	Billericay Town v Dunstable	0-1
	Darenth Heathside v Hertford Town	3-3
	Edgware Town v Burnham	1-3
24	Hounslow v Horsham YMCA	2-2
	Letchworth Garden City v Royston Town	1-3
	Northwood v Hampton	1-3
	Rayners Lane v Wembley	1-0
25	Collier Row v Corinthian	3-1
	Epsom & Ewell v Metropolitan Police	0-0
	Hailsham Town v Eton Manor	2-2
	Lewes v Hanwell Town	2-1
26	Erith & Belvedere v Chatham Town	5-1
	Hornchurch v Merstham	2-1
	Ruislip Manor v Portfield	0-0
	Southwick v Rainham Town	3-0
27	Herne Bay v Horsham	3-1
	Lancing v Canterbury City	0-1
	Tooting & Mitcham United v Worthing	2-2
28	Molesey v Ringmer	1-0
	Peacehaven & Telscombe v Corinthian Casuals	0-0
	Three Bridges v Banstead Athletic	1-0
	Tunbridge Wells v Deal Town	1-1
29	Croydon v Havant Town	3-2 N
	Eastbourne United v Steyning Town	5-2
	Egham Town v Sheppey United	4-1
	Margate v Wick	2-1
30	Abingdon United v Newport (IOW)	1-4
	Andover v Camberley Town	2-2
	Flackwell Heath v Horndean	3-0
	Haywards Heath Town v AFC Totton	1-2
31	Bournemouth (Ams) v Bracknell Town	2-0
	Chertsey Town v Arundel	3-1
	Littlehampton Town v Calne Town	1-1
	Witney Town v Chichester City (1)	4-1
32	Petersfield United v Poole Town	0-4
	Romsey Town v Westbury United	5-1
	Salisbury (2) v Sholing Sports	6-0
	Wimborne Town v Swanage Town & Herston	0-2
33	Bridgend Town v Cwmbran Town	0-1
	Newbury Town v Bristol Manor Farm	2-2
	Thame United v Frome Town	7-0
	Welton Rovers v Thatcham Town	0-5
34	Chard Town v Yate Town	2-1
	Glastonbury v Maesteg Park Athletic	0-1
	Sharpness v Chippenham Town	1-1
	Tiverton Town v Trowbridge Town	1-1
35	Evesham United v Malvern Town	0-1
	Paulton Rovers v Radstock Town	4-2
	Ton Pentre v Mangotsfield United	2-2
36	Clevedon Town v Ilfracombe Town	0-1
	Taunton Town v Minehead	9-1
	Torrington v Falmouth Town	1-1
1r	Peterlee Newtown v Alnwick Town	1-2
r	Thackley v Cleator Moor Celtic	1-3
2r	Netherfield (Kendal) v Northallerton Town	2-1
3r	Chester-le-Street Town v Washington	2-1
4r	Workington v Crook Town	0-1
6r	Accrington Stanley (2) v Atherton LR	5-2
r	Curzon Ashton v Skelmersdale United	2-0
7r	Irlam Town v Congleton Town	0-2
9r	Bridgnorth Town v Radcliffe Borough	0-2
12r	Rushall Olympic v Sutton Town	3-0
r	Spalding United v Chasetown	3-0
r	Willenhall Town v Nuneaton Borough	1-0
13r	Wellingborough Town v Stratford Town	3-4
14r	Desborough Town v Bilston Town	2-1
15r	King's Lynn v Oldbury United	3-1
16r	Haverhill Rovers v Racing Club Warwick	1-0
r	Paget Rangers v Northampton Spencer	2-0
17r	Newmarket Town v Braintree Town	1-0
r	Stamford v Purfleet	1-2
19r	Ford United v Heybridge Swifts	0-2
r	Halstead Town v Welwyn Garden City	4-2
21r	Chesham United v Aveley	1-2
23r	Chipstead v Barton Rovers	2-3
r	Hertford Town v Darenth Heathside	4-1
24r	Horsham YMCA v Hounslow	0-1
25r	Eton Manor v Hailsham Town	0-1
r	Metropolitan Police v Epsom & Ewell	0-2
26r	Portfield v Ruislip Manor	0-2
27r	Worthing v Tooting & Mitcham United	0-1
28r	Corinthian Casuals v Peacehaven & Telscombe	1-2 N
r	Deal Town v Tunbridge Wells	2-1
30r	Camberley Town v Andover	1-5
31r	Calne Town v Littlehampton Town	0-1
33r	Bristol Manor Farm v Newbury Town	3-1
34r	Chippenham Town v Sharpness	1-0
r	Trowbridge Town v Tiverton Town	3-1
35r	Mangotsfield United v Ton Pentre	1-1
36r	Falmouth Town v Torrington	4-2
35r2	Ton Pentre v Mangotsfield United	3-3
35r3	Mangotsfield United v Ton Pentre	3-1

Qualifying Round One

1	Ashington v Alnwick Town	0-5
	Billingham Town v Spennymoor United	1-1
	Cleator Moor Celtic v Barrow	1-4
	Whitley Bay v Willington	6-0
2	Billingham Synthonia v Guisborough Town	2-0
	Clitheroe v Ferryhill Athletic	2-2
	Darlington Cleveland Bridge v Gateshead (2)	0-1
	Netherfield (Kendal) v Ryhope Community Association	3-1
3	Bishop Auckland v Chester-le-Street Town	3-2
	Langley Park v Brandon United	3-1
	South Bank v Shildon	2-0
	Whitby Town v Hebburn	1-3
4	Crook Town v West Auckland Town	5-1
	Gretna v Tow Law Town	3-5
	Prudhoe East End v Seaham Red Star	0-0
	Shotton Comrades v Bridlington Town	0-5
5	Lancaster City v Durham City	0-1
	Murton v Blyth Spartans	0-3
	Newcastle Blue Star v Stockton (2)	1-1
	North Shields v Whickham	1-0
6	Accrington Stanley (2) v Borrowash Victoria	4-0
	Curzon Ashton v Prescot Cables	2-0
	Droylsden v Fleetwood Town	0-0
	Mossley v South Liverpool	0-0
7	Burscough v Maine Road	1-2
	Caernarfon Town v Horwich RMI	3-1
	Colwyn Bay v Morecambe	4-1 N
	Congleton Town v Denaby United	2-1
8	Bangor City v Heanor Town	3-1
	Marine v Eastwood Hanley	1-1
	Rossendale United v Vauxhall G.M.	2-1
	Sheffield v Hyde United	0-1
9	Belper Town v Arnold Town	2-2
	Radcliffe Borough v Rhyl	1-2
	Southport v Stalybridge Celtic	3-2
	Walsall Wood v Oakham United	0-1
10	Buxton v Emley	3-1
	Gresley Rovers v Witton Albion	2-2
	St Helens Town v Sandwell Borough	0-1
	Warrington Town v North Ferriby United	1-0
11	Dudley Town v Boston	0-1
	Goole Town v Farsley Celtic	1-0
	Grantham Town v Louth United	2-1
	Hinckley Athletic v Frickley Athletic	1-3
12	Alfreton Town v Rocester	1-0
	Boston United v Leek Town	3-3
	Rushall Olympic v Matlock Town	0-1
	Willenhall Town v Spalding United	1-1
13	Alvechurch v Bedworth United	0-1
	Brackley Town v Shepshed Charterhouse	2-1
	Gainsborough Trinity v Sutton Coldfield Town	1-2
	Stratford Town v Histon	2-0
14	Desborough Town v Atherstone United	1-0
	Lye Town v Stourbridge	2-0
	MK Wolverton Town v Baker Perkins	2-1
	Stafford Rangers v Hinckley Town	1-0
15	Boldmere St Michaels v Tamworth	2-3
	King's Lynn v Bromsgrove Rovers	0-3
	Rothwell Town v March Town United	0-1
	Rushden Town v Holbeach United	4-5
16	Haverhill Rovers v Corby Town	1-1
	Hitchin Town v Wisbech Town	3-2
	Moor Green v Redditch United	0-1
	Paget Rangers v Ely City	2-1
17	Bishop's Stortford v Barnet	0-1
	Canvey Island v Purfleet	3-0
	Newmarket Town v Leighton Town	1-0
	Stevenage Borough v Cambridge City	3-5
18	Barking v Hendon	1-1
	Clapton v Sudbury Town	1-2
	Lowestoft Town v Arlesey Town	1-1
	Stowmarket Town v Saffron Walden Town	5-3
19	Halstead Town v Harlow Town	3-2
	Heybridge Swifts v Grays Athletic	2-1
	Redbridge Forest v Dartford	2-4
	Witham Town v Finchley	3-1
20	St Albans City v Wealdstone	1-2
	Tring Town v Leyton-Wingate	0-4
	Ware v Cheshunt	2-0
	Wivenhoe Town v Potton United	3-0
21	Aveley v Boreham Wood	0-1
	Baldock Town v Wycombe Wanderers	0-2
	Berkhamsted Town v East Thurrock United	1-0
	Harrow Borough v Gravesend & Northfleet	1-2
22	Slough Town v Walthamstow Pennant	5-1
	Uxbridge v Hemel Hempstead Town	1-0
	Wandsworth & Norwood v Carshalton Athletic	1-1
	Yeading v Chalfont St Peter	0-0
23	Barton Rovers v Windsor & Eton	2-0
	Crawley Town v Staines Town	0-1
	Dunstable v Vauxhall Motors (Luton)	3-0
	Hertford Town v Burnham	0-1
24	Bromley v Kingsbury Town	1-1
	Hampton v Fisher Athletic	3-1
	Rayners Lane v Hounslow	1-2
	Royston Town v Feltham	2-1
25	Collier Row v Dulwich Hamlet	1-2
	Dorking (2) v Tilbury	1-2
	Hailsham Town v Tonbridge	2-0
	Lewes v Epsom & Ewell	2-0
26	Hornchurch v Erith & Belvedere	1-2
	Kingstonian v Woking	1-5
	Ruislip Manor v Ashford Town	1-3
	Southwick v Shoreham	5-0
27	Canterbury City v Tooting & Mitcham United	2-0
	Folkestone v Leatherhead	2-1
	Herne Bay v Dover Athletic	0-6
	Redhill v Ramsgate	1-0
28	Deal Town v Whitstable Town	1-3
	Hastings Town v Walton & Hersham	0-3
	Peacehaven & Telscombe v Molesey	0-1
	Three Bridges v Hythe Town	0-2
29	Croydon v Wokingham Town	0-3 N
	Eastbourne United v Malden Vale	1-2
	Egham Town v Margate	0-1
	Whyteleafe v Sittingbourne	1-0
30	AFC Totton v Whitehawk	4-2
	Andover v Devizes Town	2-0
	Flackwell Heath v Newport (IOW)	0-2
	Pagham v Marlow	0-1
31	Basingstoke Town v Bashley	1-1
	Chertsey Town v Eastleigh	4-0
	Littlehampton Town v Waterlooville	3-1
	Witney Town v Bournemouth (Ams)	1-0
32	Gosport Borough v Hungerford Town	2-0
	Romsey Town v Fareham Town	1-1
	Salisbury (2) v Poole Town	1-1
	Swanage Town & Herston v Melksham Town	4-0
33	Banbury United v Maidenhead United	1-3
	Bristol Manor Farm v Cwmbran Town	0-1
	Thame United v Abingdon Town	0-3
	Thatcham Town v Stroud	2-2
34	Chard Town v Dorchester Town	0-2
	Cheltenham Town v Saltash United	1-0
	Chippenham Town v Weston-Super-Mare	1-2
	Maesteg Park Athletic v Trowbridge Town	1-2
35	Gloucester City v Mangotsfield United	4-0
	Malvern Town v Barry Town	1-5
	Paulton Rovers v Shortwood United	2-3
	Worcester City v Clandown	3-0
36	Exmouth Town v Ilfracombe Town	2-0
	Falmouth Town v St Blazey	1-1
	Taunton Town v Bideford	3-0
	Weymouth v Barnstaple Town	2-0
1r	Spennymoor United v Billingham Town	2-1
2r	Ferryhill Athletic v Clitheroe	1-1
4r	Seaham Red Star v Prudhoe East End	3-2
5r	Stockton (2) v Newcastle Blue Star	1-3
6r	Fleetwood Town v Droylsden	1-1
r	South Liverpool v Mossley	0-3
8r	Eastwood Hanley v Marine	1-2e
9r	Arnold Town v Belper Town	3-1
10r	Witton Albion v Gresley Rovers	1-0
12r	Leek Town v Boston United	0-3
r	Spalding United v Willenhall Town	0-2
16r	Corby Town v Haverhill Rovers	2-3
18r	Arlesey Town v Lowestoft Town	0-4
r	Hendon v Barking	2-2
22r	Carshalton Athletic v Wandsworth & Norwood	3-1
r	Chalfont St Peter v Yeading	0-5
24r	Kingsbury Town v Bromley	2-2
31r	Bashley v Basingstoke Town	2-3e
32r	Fareham Town v Romsey Town	1-2
r	Poole Town v Salisbury (2)	3-1
33r	Stroud v Thatcham Town	2-1
36r	St Blazey v Falmouth Town	1-0

1989/90

2r2	Clitheroe v Ferryhill Athletic	2-4
6r2	Fleetwood Town v Droylsden	0-1
18r2	Barking v Hendon	1-2
24r2	Bromley v Kingsbury Town	2-0

Qualifying Round Two

1	Barrow v Alnwick Town	3-1
	Spennymoor United v Whitley Bay	2-4
2	Billingham Synthonia v Netherfield (Kendal)	0-0
	Gateshead (2) v Ferryhill Athletic	3-0
3	Hebburn v South Bank	0-0
	Langley Park v Bishop Auckland	2-5
4	Bridlington Town v Seaham Red Star	2-1
	Tow Law Town v Crook Town	4-2
5	Blyth Spartans v Durham City	4-1
	Newcastle Blue Star v North Shields	1-1
6	Droylsden v Curzon Ashton	0-1
	Mossley v Accrington Stanley (2)	3-1
7	Caernarfon Town v Congleton Town	1-2
	Colwyn Bay v Maine Road	2-1 N
8	Hyde United v Bangor City	2-1
	Marine v Rossendale United	2-0
9	Rhyl v Oakham United	2-0
	Southport v Arnold Town	2-1
10	Buxton v Sandwell Borough	1-1
	Witton Albion v Warrington Town	2-0
11	Boston v Grantham Town	1-2
	Frickley Athletic v Goole Town	1-1
12	Boston United v Alfreton Town	1-0
	Matlock Town v Willenhall Town	5-0
13	Bedworth United v Stratford Town	3-0
	Brackley Town v Sutton Coldfield Town	1-2
14	Desborough Town v Lye Town	1-1
	Stafford Rangers v MK Wolverton Town	2-0
15	Bromsgrove Rovers v March Town United	4-0
	Tamworth v Holbeach United	1-0
16	Haverhill Rovers v Hitchin Town	2-3
	Redditch United v Paget Rangers	5-0
17	Barnet v Newmarket Town	4-2
	Cambridge City v Canvey Island	3-0
18	Hendon v Lowestoft Town	7-0
	Sudbury Town v Stowmarket Town	3-2
19	Dartford v Witham Town	3-1
	Heybridge Swifts v Halstead Town	1-0
20	Leyton-Wingate v Ware	2-1
	Wealdstone v Wivenhoe Town	0-1
21	Gravesend & Northfleet v Berkhamsted Town	1-0
	Wycombe Wanderers v Boreham Wood	3-1
22	Carshalton Athletic v Slough Town	0-2
	Uxbridge v Yeading	1-0
23	Barton Rovers v Burnham	1-1
	Staines Town v Dunstable	1-0
24	Bromley v Royston Town	3-0
	Hampton v Hounslow	2-0
25	Dulwich Hamlet v Lewes	4-1
	Tilbury v Hailsham Town	2-2
26	Ashford Town v Erith & Belvedere	0-1
	Woking v Southwick	4-1
27	Dover Athletic v Canterbury City	0-0
	Folkestone v Redhill	1-1
28	Hythe Town v Molesey	2-1
	Walton & Hersham v Whitstable Town	0-1
29	Whyteleafe v Malden Vale	2-0
	Wokingham Town v Margate	1-0
30	AFC Totton v Newport (IOW)	1-3
	Marlow v Andover	3-2
31	Basingstoke Town v Chertsey Town	3-1
	Littlehampton Town v Witney Town	0-4
32	Gosport Borough v Swanage Town & Herston	1-1
	Romsey Town v Poole Town	1-2
33	Abingdon Town v Cwmbran Town	0-0
	Maidenhead United v Stroud	2-0
34	Cheltenham Town v Weston-Super-Mare	7-0
	Dorchester Town v Trowbridge Town	0-0
35	Barry Town v Gloucester City	2-2
	Worcester City v Shortwood United	3-0
36	Taunton Town v Exmouth Town	0-0
	Weymouth v St Blazey	2-0
2r	Netherfield (Kendal) v Billingham Synthonia	1-2
3r	South Bank v Hebburn	3-0
5r	North Shields v Newcastle Blue Star	4-2
10r	Sandwell Borough v Buxton	1-1
11r	Goole Town v Frickley Athletic	1-0
14r	Lye Town v Desborough Town	5-2
23r	Burnham v Barton Rovers	3-2
25r	Hailsham Town v Tilbury	1-1
27r	Canterbury City v Dover Athletic	0-2
r	Redhill v Folkestone	0-1
32r	Swanage Town & Herston v Gosport Borough	0-2
33r	Cwmbran Town v Abingdon Town	3-4
34r	Trowbridge Town v Dorchester Town	0-2
35r	Gloucester City v Barry Town	2-0
36r	Exmouth Town v Taunton Town	2-2
10r2	Buxton v Sandwell Borough	3-2
25r2	Tilbury v Hailsham Town	2-3 N
36r2	Taunton Town v Exmouth Town	0-0
36r3	Exmouth Town v Taunton Town	1-0

Qualifying Round Three

1	Barrow v Whitley Bay	2-2
2	Gateshead (2) v Billingham Synthonia	0-2
3	Bishop Auckland v South Bank	1-1
4	Bridlington Town v Tow Law Town	0-0
5	Blyth Spartans v North Shields	0-3
6	Curzon Ashton v Mossley	1-1
7	Colwyn Bay v Congleton Town	1-1 N
8	Hyde United v Marine	0-1
9	Rhyl v Southport	0-3
10	Witton Albion v Buxton	1-1
11	Goole Town v Grantham Town	2-1
12	Matlock Town v Boston United	1-1
13	Sutton Coldfield Town v Bedworth United	1-2
14	Lye Town v Stafford Rangers	1-2
15	Bromsgrove Rovers v Tamworth	2-0
16	Hitchin Town v Redditch United	0-2
17	Cambridge City v Barnet	3-4
18	Sudbury Town v Hendon	1-2
19	Heybridge Swifts v Dartford	0-1
20	Leyton-Wingate v Wivenhoe Town	0-0
21	Wycombe Wanderers v Gravesend & Northfleet	1-1
22	Slough Town v Uxbridge	0-0
23	Burnham v Staines Town	0-1
24	Hampton v Bromley	0-1
25	Dulwich Hamlet v Hailsham Town	1-1
26	Erith & Belvedere v Woking	1-1
27	Dover Athletic v Folkestone	0-1
28	Hythe Town v Whitstable Town	2-0
29	Wokingham Town v Whyteleafe	1-1
30	Newport (IOW) v Marlow	0-1
31	Witney Town v Basingstoke Town	0-2
32	Poole Town v Gosport Borough	1-0
33	Abingdon Town v Maidenhead United	3-1
34	Dorchester Town v Cheltenham Town	2-1
35	Gloucester City v Worcester City	4-2
36	Exmouth Town v Weymouth	2-0
1r	Whitley Bay v Barrow	3-1
3r	South Bank v Bishop Auckland	1-3
4r	Tow Law Town v Bridlington Town	0-0
6r	Mossley v Curzon Ashton	3-1
7r	Congleton Town v Colwyn Bay	4-0
10r	Buxton v Witton Albion	4-6e
12r	Boston United v Matlock Town	0-1
20r	Wivenhoe Town v Leyton-Wingate	2-0
21r	Gravesend & Northfleet v Wycombe Wanderers	1-1
22r	Uxbridge v Slough Town	1-2e
25r	Hailsham Town v Dulwich Hamlet	3-4 N
26r	Woking v Erith & Belvedere	5-0
29r	Whyteleafe v Wokingham Town	1-2
4r2	Tow Law Town v Bridlington Town	3-2
21r2	Gravesend & Northfleet v Wycombe Wanderers	0-3

Qualifying Round Four

	Abingdon Town v Slough Town	0-3
	Aylesbury United v Hendon	4-1
	Basingstoke Town v Marlow	1-1
	Billingham Synthonia v North Shields	2-1
	Bognor Regis Town v Dorchester Town	1-1
	Bromsgrove Rovers v V.S. Rugby	1-0
	Burton Albion v Barnet	2-2
	Chorley v Marine	1-1
	Congleton Town v Witton Albion	1-0
	Darlington v Runcorn	4-2
	Dartford v Dagenham	3-1
	Dulwich Hamlet v Merthyr Tydfil	2-2
	Exmouth Town v Farnborough Town	1-4
	Folkestone v Gloucester City	0-1
	Hythe Town v Hayes	0-0
	Kidderminster Harriers v Chelmsford City	2-2
	Matlock Town v Enfield	3-1
	Mossley v Bishop Auckland	1-1
	Northwich Victoria v Goole Town	2-0
	Poole Town v Bath City	2-2
	Redditch United v Bedworth United	1-1
	Southport v Whitley Bay	1-3
	Stafford Rangers v Wycombe Wanderers	4-1
	Staines Town v Yeovil Town	0-3
	Tow Law Town v Altrincham	2-0
	Welling United v Bromley	5-2
	Wivenhoe Town v Halesowen Town	0-0
	Wokingham Town v Woking	1-3
r	Barnet v Burton Albion	1-0
r	Bath City v Poole Town	3-0
r	Bedworth United v Redditch United	0-2
r	Bishop Auckland v Mossley	3-0
r	Chelmsford City v Kidderminster Harriers	1-3e
r	Dorchester Town v Bognor Regis Town	5-1
r	Halesowen Town v Wivenhoe Town	3-2
r	Hayes v Hythe Town	3-0
r	Marine v Chorley	0-0
r	Marlow v Basingstoke Town	1-2
r	Merthyr Tydfil v Dulwich Hamlet	4-2
r2	Marine v Chorley	3-0

Round One

	Aldershot v Cambridge United	0-1
	Aylesbury United v Southend United	1-0
	Basingstoke Town v Bromsgrove Rovers	3-0
	Bath City v Fulham	2-2
	Bishop Auckland v Tow Law Town	2-0
	Blackpool v Bolton Wanderers	2-1
	Brentford v Colchester United	0-1
	Bristol City v Barnet	2-0
	Bristol Rovers v Reading	1-1
	Burnley v Stockport County	1-1
	Cardiff City v Halesowen Town	1-0
	Carlisle United v Wrexham	3-0
	Crewe Alexandra v Congleton Town	2-0
	Darlington v Northwich Victoria	6-2
	Dartford v Exeter City	1-1
	Doncaster Rovers v Notts County	1-0
	Farnborough Town v Hereford United	0-1
	Gillingham v Welling United	0-0
	Gloucester City v Dorchester Town	1-0
	Hartlepool United v Huddersfield Town	0-2
	Kettering Town v Northampton Town	0-1
	Kidderminster Harriers v Swansea City	2-3
	Leyton Orient v Birmingham City	0-1
	Lincoln City v Billingham Synthonia	1-0
	Macclesfield Town v Chester City	1-1
	Maidstone United v Yeovil Town	2-1
	Marine v Rochdale	0-1 N
	Peterborough United v Hayes	1-1
	Preston North End v Tranmere Rovers	1-0
	Redditch United v Merthyr Tydfil	1-3
	Rotherham United v Bury	0-0
	Scarborough v Whitley Bay	0-1
	Scunthorpe United v Matlock Town	4-1
	Shrewsbury Town v Chesterfield	2-3
	Slough Town v Woking	1-2
	Stafford Rangers v Halifax Town	2-3
	Sutton United v Torquay United	1-1
	Telford United v Walsall	0-3
	Wigan Athletic v Mansfield Town	2-0
	York City v Grimsby Town	1-2
r	Bury v Rotherham United	1-2
r	Chester City v Macclesfield Town	3-2
r	Exeter City v Dartford	4-1
r	Fulham v Bath City	2-1
r	Hayes v Peterborough United	0-1
r	Reading v Bristol Rovers	1-1e
r	Stockport County v Burnley	1-2
r	Torquay United v Sutton United	4-0
r	Welling United v Gillingham	1-0
r2	Bristol Rovers v Reading	0-1

Round Two

	Basingstoke Town v Torquay United	2-3
	Blackpool v Chester City	3-0
	Bristol City v Fulham	2-1
	Cambridge United v Woking	3-1
	Cardiff City v Gloucester City	2-2
	Chesterfield v Huddersfield Town	0-2
	Colchester United v Birmingham City	0-2
	Crewe Alexandra v Bishop Auckland	1-1
	Darlington v Halifax Town	3-0
	Grimsby Town v Doncaster Rovers	1-0
	Hereford United v Merthyr Tydfil	3-2
	Maidstone United v Exeter City	1-1
	Northampton Town v Aylesbury United	0-0
	Reading v Welling United	0-0
	Rochdale v Lincoln City	3-0
	Scunthorpe United v Burnley	2-2
	Swansea City v Peterborough United	3-1
	Walsall v Rotherham United	1-0
	Whitley Bay v Preston North End	2-0
	Wigan Athletic v Carlisle United	2-0
r	Aylesbury United v Northampton Town	0-1e
r	Bishop Auckland v Crewe Alexandra	0-2
r	Burnley v Scunthorpe United	1-1e
r	Exeter City v Maidstone United	3-2
r	Gloucester City v Cardiff City	0-1
r	Welling United v Reading	1-1e
r2	Burnley v Scunthorpe United	5-0
r2	Reading v Welling United	0-0e
r3	Welling United v Reading	1-2

Round Three

	Birmingham City v Oldham Athletic	1-1
	Blackburn Rovers v Aston Villa	2-2
	Blackpool v Burnley	1-0
	Brighton & Hove Albion v Luton Town	4-1
	Bristol City v Swindon Town	2-1
	Cambridge United v Darlington	0-0
	Cardiff City v Queen's Park Rangers	0-0
	Charlton Athletic v Bradford City	1-1
	Chelsea v Crewe Alexandra	1-1
	Crystal Palace v Portsmouth	2-1
	Exeter City v Norwich City	1-1
	Hereford United v Walsall	2-1
	Huddersfield Town v Grimsby Town	3-1
	Hull City v Newcastle United	0-1
	Leeds United v Ipswich Town	0-1
	Leicester City v Barnsley	1-2
	Manchester City v Millwall	0-0
	Middlesbrough v Everton	0-0
	Northampton Town v Coventry City	1-0
	Nottingham Forest v Manchester United	0-1
	Plymouth Argyle v Oxford United	0-1
	Port Vale v Derby County	1-1
	Reading v Sunderland	2-1
	Rochdale v Whitley Bay	1-0
	Sheffield United v Bournemouth	2-0
	Stoke City v Arsenal	0-1
	Swansea City v Liverpool	0-0
	Torquay United v West Ham United	1-0
	Tottenham Hotspur v Southampton	1-3
	Watford v Wigan Athletic	2-0
	West Bromwich Albion v Wimbledon	2-0
	Wolverhampton Wan. v Sheffield Wednesday	1-2

1989/90 to 1990/91

r	Aston Villa v Blackburn Rovers	3-1
r	Bradford City v Charlton Athletic	0-3
r	Crewe Alexandra v Chelsea	0-2
r	Darlington v Cambridge United	1-3
r	Derby County v Port Vale	2-3
r	Everton v Middlesbrough	1-1e
r	Liverpool v Swansea City	8-0
r	Millwall v Manchester City	1-1e
r	Norwich City v Exeter City	2-0
r	Oldham Athletic v Birmingham City	1-0
r	Queen's Park Rangers v Cardiff City	2-0
r2	Everton v Middlesbrough	1-0
r2	Millwall v Manchester City	3-1

Round Four

	Arsenal v Queen's Park Rangers	0-0
	Aston Villa v Port Vale	6-0
	Barnsley v Ipswich Town	2-0
	Blackpool v Torquay United	1-0
	Bristol City v Chelsea	3-1
	Crystal Palace v Huddersfield Town	4-0
	Hereford United v Manchester United	0-1
	Millwall v Cambridge United	1-1
	Norwich City v Liverpool	0-0
	Oldham Athletic v Brighton & Hove Albion	2-1
	Reading v Newcastle United	3-3
	Rochdale v Northampton Town	3-0
	Sheffield United v Watford	1-1
	Sheffield Wednesday v Everton	1-2
	Southampton v Oxford United	1-0
	West Bromwich Albion v Charlton Athletic	1-0
r	Cambridge United v Millwall	1-0e
r	Liverpool v Norwich City	3-1
r	Newcastle United v Reading	4-1
r	Queen's Park Rangers v Arsenal	2-0
r	Watford v Sheffield United	1-2

Round Five

	Blackpool v Queen's Park Rangers	2-2
	Bristol City v Cambridge United	0-0
	Crystal Palace v Rochdale	1-0
	Liverpool v Southampton	3-0
	Newcastle United v Manchester United	2-3
	Oldham Athletic v Everton	2-2
	Sheffield United v Barnsley	2-2
	West Bromwich Albion v Aston Villa	0-2
r	Barnsley v Sheffield United	0-0e
r	Cambridge United v Bristol City	1-1e
r	Everton v Oldham Athletic	1-1e
r	Queen's Park Rangers v Blackpool	0-0e
r2	Barnsley v Sheffield United	0-1e
r2	Cambridge United v Bristol City	5-1
r2	Oldham Athletic v Everton	2-1e
r2	Queen's Park Rangers v Blackpool	3-0

Round Six

	Cambridge United v Crystal Palace	0-1
	Oldham Athletic v Aston Villa	3-0
	Queen's Park Rangers v Liverpool	2-2
	Sheffield United v Manchester United	0-1
r	Liverpool v Queen's Park Rangers	1-0

Semi Finals

	Crystal Palace v Liverpool	4-3eN
	Manchester United v Oldham Athletic	3-3eN
r	Manchester United v Oldham Athletic	2-1eN

Final

	Manchester United v Crystal Palace	3-3eN
r	Manchester United v Crystal Palace	1-0 N

1990/91

Preliminary Round

1	Ashington v Prudhoe East End	1-4
	North Shields v Whickham	2-0
	Shildon v Garforth Town	3-1
	Willington v Cleator Moor Celtic	0-1
2	Bedlington Terriers v Norton & Stockton Ancients	0-4
	Billingham Town v Brandon United	1-0
	Blackpool (Wren) Rovers v Accrington Stanley (2)	2-4
	West Auckland Town v Annfield Plain	4-2
3	Chester-le-Street Town v Easington Colliery	0-2
	Ferryhill Athletic v Blackpool Mechanics	3-1
	Langley Park v Washington	2-0
	Netherfield (Kendal) v Murton	0-3
	Penrith v Harrogate Railway Athletic	0-5
4	Crook Town v Horden CW	1-2
	Great Harwood Town v Harrogate Town	2-2
	Northallerton Town v Clitheroe	4-2
	Shotton Comrades v Esh Winning	1-2
5	Darlington Cleveland Bridge v Evenwood Town	0-1
	Darwen v Peterlee Newtown	2-0
	Hebburn v Ryhope Community Association	0-2 N
	Lancaster City v Thackley	2-0
	Whitby Town v Leyland DAF	2-0
6	Ashton United v Denaby United	0-2
	Bridgnorth Town v Vauxhall G.M.	1-1
	Irlam Town v Formby	2-0
	Knowsley United v Ossett Town	1-1
7	Atherton LR v Rossendale United	3-1
	Burscough v Maine Road	0-3
	Farsley Celtic v Ossett Albion	1-1
	Glossop v Skelmersdale United	1-1
8	Armthorpe Welfare v Sheffield	3-0
	Bootle v Winsford United	1-0
	Chadderton v Radcliffe Borough	1-2
	Prescot AFC v Emley	1-1
9	Belper Town v St Helens Town	2-3
	Hednesford Town v Guiseley	2-0
	Long Eaton United v Oakham United	1-1
	Newtown (2) v Eastwood Town	1-1
	Salford City v Warrington Town	0-3
10	Borrowash Victoria v Gresley Rovers	1-2
	North Ferriby United v Leicester United	1-2
	Sutton Town v Rocester	2-2
	Willenhall Town v Brigg Town	1-1
11	Alfreton Town v Rushall Olympic	2-2
	Louth United v Princes End United	1-1
	Nuneaton Borough v Hinckley Town	4-1
	Paget Rangers v Boldmere St Michaels	2-0
12	Alvechurch v Desborough Town	2-1
	Arnold Town v Wednesfield	1-1
	Stratford Town v Highgate United	3-1
	Wellingborough Town v Tividale	1-0
13	Dudley Town v Corby Town	1-1
	Eastwood Hanley v West Midlands Police	0-2
	Heanor Town v Halesowen Harriers	0-4
	Hinckley Athletic v Friar Lane Old Boys	3-1
	Solihull Borough v Banbury United	0-0
14	Brackley Town v Walsall Wood	1-0
	Chasetown v Evesham United	0-2
	Irthlingborough Diamonds v Buckingham Town	3-4
	Oldbury United v Wolverton	0-0
15	Boston v King's Lynn	2-0
	Holbeach United v Potton United	1-2
	Mile Oak Rovers & Youth v Stourbridge	0-5
	Sandwell Borough v Northampton Spencer	4-1
16	Malvern Town v Soham Town Rangers	3-0
	Rothwell Town v Stamford	7-2
	Welwyn Garden City v Chalfont St Peter	1-2
	Wisbech Town v Barton Rovers	1-1
17	Baker Perkins v Letchworth Garden City	5-2
	Boreham Wood v Gorleston	2-0
	Haverhill Rovers v Eynesbury Rovers	1-1
	Leighton Town v Spalding United	0-1
	Lowestoft Town v Mirrlees Blackstone	1-0
18	Bourne Town v Ely City	3-0
	Great Yarmouth Town v Langford	2-2
	Newmarket Town v Cheshunt	2-1
	Wembley v Bury Town	1-0
19	Braintree Town v Collier Row	1-0
	Clapton v Felixstowe Town	5-2
	Ford United v Kingsbury Town	3-1
	Rayners Lane v Hoddesdon Town	2-1
	Tiptree United v Harlow Town	0-1
20	Cray Wanderers v Waltham Abbey	3-1
	Halstead Town v Canvey Island	1-1
	Hemel Hempstead Town v Metropolitan Police	1-2
	Ruislip Manor v Northwood	2-1
	Stowmarket Town v Saffron Walden Town	1-1
21	Arlesey Town v Walthamstow Pennant	0-4
	Burnham Ramblers v Hornchurch	0-2
	Chesham United v Baldock Town	4-1
	Clacton Town v Hertford Town	0-1
22	Barkingside v Aveley	2-1
	East Thurrock United v Stevenage Borough	0-1
	Harwich & Parkeston v Berkhamsted Town	4-1
	Witham Town v Basildon United	2-3
	Wootton Blue Cross v Hounslow	1-3
23	Banstead Athletic v Malden Vale	1-0
	Flackwell Heath v Tring Town	5-0
	Molesey v Vauxhall Motors (Luton)	1-1
	Ware v Corinthian Casuals	0-0
24	Alma Swanley v Purfleet	1-2
	Billericay Town v Hanwell Town	4-0
	Croydon v Egham Town	0-4
	Eton Manor v Edgware Town	0-2
	Tilbury v Southall	0-0
25	Chertsey Town v Walton & Hersham	0-3
	Croydon Athletic v Andover	2-2
	Harefield United v Merstham	0-1
	Horsham YMCA v Darenth Heathside	3-2
	Royston Town v Rainham Town	1-1
26	Chipstead v Littlehampton Town	2-3
	Horsham v Epsom & Ewell	2-0
	Slade Green v Ringmer	2-0
	Tonbridge v Shoreham	2-1
	Tooting & Mitcham United v Hastings Town	1-1
27	Peacehaven & Telscombe v Selsey	8-1
	Ramsgate v Margate	0-1
	Southwick v Corinthian	1-0
	Steyning Town v Whitehawk	1-2
28	Ashford Town v Leatherhead	3-1
	Cove v Haywards Heath Town	4-0
	Oakwood v Camberley Town	5-0
	Sheppey United v Pagham	0-2
	Sittingbourne v Burgess Hill Town	2-0
29	Arundel v Chatham Town	2-3
	Canterbury City v Dorking (2)	0-0
	Eastbourne United v Tunbridge Wells	6-5
	Three Bridges v Wick	1-3
30	Bracknell Town v Hampton	2-3
	Havant Town v Horndean	3-0
	Lancing v Lewes	0-3
	Langney Sports v Portfield	3-0
31	Bournemouth (Ams) v Thatcham Town	1-0
	Feltham v Thame United	2-0
	Hungerford Town v Fareham Town	1-0
	Salisbury (2) v Uxbridge	1-1
	Sholing Sports v Abingdon United	1-3
32	AFC Totton v Warminster Town	2-3
	Chichester City (1) v AFC Lymington	1-5
	Newbury Town v Eastleigh	2-1
	Trowbridge Town v Clandown	7-1
33	Calne Town v Paulton Rovers	2-0
	Melksham Town v Keynsham Town	2-1
	Romsey Town v Frome Town	1-0
	Westbury United v Stroud	1-1
34	Barry Town v Minehead	2-1
	Clevedon Town v Dawlish Town	3-3
	Cwmbran Town v Mangotsfield United	0-4
	Shortwood United v St Blazey	1-2
	Swanage Town & Herston v Devizes Town	4-0
35	Bridgend Town v Ton Pentre	2-1
	Maesteg Park Athletic v Sharpness	wo/s
	Radstock Town v Weston-Super-Mare	0-3
	Yate Town v Glastonbury	4-0
36	Ilfracombe Town v Barnstaple Town	4-0
	Saltash United v Torrington	1-1
	St Austell v Falmouth Town	0-4
	Tiverton Town v Welton Rovers	4-1
	Wimborne Town v Bideford	3-2
4r	Harrogate Town v Great Harwood Town	2-1
6r	Ossett Town v Knowsley United	2-3e
r	Vauxhall G.M. v Bridgnorth Town	4-1
7r	Ossett Albion v Farsley Celtic	0-2
r	Skelmersdale United v Glossop	0-2
8r	Emley v Prescot AFC	2-1e
9r	Eastwood Town v Newtown (2)	2-1
r	Long Eaton United v Oakham United	0-1
10r	Brigg Town v Willenhall Town	1-1
r	Rocester v Sutton Town	1-0
11r	Princes End United v Louth United	1-0
r	Rushall Olympic v Alfreton Town	3-0
12r	Wednesfield v Arnold Town	1-0
13r	Banbury United v Solihull Borough	1-1
r	Corby Town v Dudley Town	1-0
14r	Wolverton v Oldbury United	2-1
16r	Barton Rovers v Wisbech Town	2-1
17r	Eynesbury Rovers v Haverhill Rovers	0-2
18r	Langford v Great Yarmouth Town	0-1e
20r	Canvey Island v Halstead Town	1-7
r	Saffron Walden Town v Stowmarket Town	2-1
23r	Vauxhall Motors (Luton) v Molesey	0-5
r	Ware v Corinthian Casuals	0-1
24r	Southall v Tilbury	1-3
25r	Andover v Croydon Athletic	7-1
r	Rainham Town v Royston Town	1-2
26r	Hastings Town v Tooting & Mitcham United	0-2
29r	Dorking (2) v Canterbury City	4-1
31r	Uxbridge v Salisbury (2)	1-2
33r	Stroud v Westbury United	3-0
34r	Dawlish Town v Clevedon Town	2-3
36r	Torrington v Saltash United	2-5
10r2	Brigg Town v Willenhall Town	1-3
13r2	Solihull Borough v Banbury United	2-2
13r3	Banbury United v Solihull Borough	3-4

Qualifying Round One

1	Alnwick Town v Fleetwood Town	0-5
	Durham City v Prudhoe East End	0-3
	North Shields v Gateshead (2)	1-1
	Shildon v Cleator Moor Celtic	2-1
2	Accrington Stanley (2) v West Auckland Town	3-0
	Billingham Town v Guisborough Town	1-2
	Blyth Spartans v Bridlington Town	2-0
	Gretna v Norton & Stockton Ancients	5-1
3	Easington Colliery v Colne Dynamos	wo/s
	Ferryhill Athletic v South Bank	1-1
	Harrogate Railway Athletic v Murton	2-0
	Langley Park v Tow Law Town	2-1
4	Harrogate Town v Esh Winning	1-3
	Northallerton Town v Billingham Synthonia	2-0
	Stockton (2) v Spennymoor United	0-2
	Workington v Horden CW	1-1
5	Lancaster City v Darwen	1-0
	Ryhope Community Association v Consett	1-2
	Seaham Red Star v Evenwood Town	1-1
	Whitby Town v Newcastle Blue Star	4-7
6	Caernarfon Town v Denaby United	wo/s
	Knowsley United v Colwyn Bay	0-0
	Morecambe v Horwich RMI	2-2
	Vauxhall G.M. v Irlam Town	0-2
7	Altrincham v Rhyl	3-2
	Farsley Celtic v Bangor City	0-0
	Harworth Colliery Institute v Atherton LR	1-2
	Maine Road v Glossop	1-0
8	Armthorpe Welfare v Southport	1-2
	Chorley v Mossley	4-0
	Ilkeston Town (2) v Bootle	2-3
	Radcliffe Borough v Emley	0-0

1990/91

9	Eastwood Town v Hednesford Town	1-1
	Oakham United v Hyde United	1-2
	South Liverpool v Warrington Town	2-0
	St Helens Town v Curzon Ashton	0-3
10	Droylsden v Stalybridge Celtic	1-1
	Leicester United v Rocester	1-0
	Willenhall Town v Marine	0-0
	Worksop Town v Gresley Rovers	2-1
11	Blakenall v Rushall Olympic	3-2
	Frickley Athletic v Gainsborough Trinity	4-3
	Nuneaton Borough v Goole Town	1-0
	Paget Rangers v Princes End United	1-2
12	Alvechurch v Wellingborough Town	4-1
	Bilston Town v Wednesfield	6-0
	Stratford Town v Buxton	1-4
	Witton Albion v Congleton Town	2-0
13	Burton Albion v Halesowen Harriers	2-0
	Corby Town v Solihull Borough	3-0
	Hinckley Athletic v Grantham Town	2-1
	West Midlands Police v Matlock Town	0-6
14	Brackley Town v Buckingham Town	1-1
	Racing Club Warwick v Evesham United	0-0
	Shepshed Charterhouse v Lye Town	3-1
	Wolverton v Atherstone United	2-2
15	Bedworth United v Sutton Coldfield Town	1-5
	Boston v Bromsgrove Rovers	0-3
	March Town United v Sandwell Borough	1-1
	Potton United v Stourbridge	1-1
16	Barton Rovers v Redditch United	0-2
	Chalfont St Peter v Malvern Town	2-6
	Histon v Rothwell Town	2-1
	Moor Green v Tamworth	1-2
17	Boreham Wood v Baker Perkins	0-0
	Boston United v Lowestoft Town	7-0
	Haverhill Rovers v V.S. Rugby	1-1
	Spalding United v Rushden Town	0-3
18	Finchley v Great Yarmouth Town	1-2
	Newmarket Town v Cambridge City	1-2
	Sudbury Town v Heybridge Swifts	1-3
	Wembley v Bourne Town	4-1
19	Clapton v Barnet	0-2 N
	Ford United v St Albans City	3-1
	Hitchin Town v Braintree Town	0-1
	Rayners Lane v Harlow Town	0-3
20	Cray Wanderers v Ruislip Manor	2-3
	Metropolitan Police v Hendon	1-3
	Saffron Walden Town v Wealdstone	0-4
	Wivenhoe Town v Halstead Town	3-1
21	Biggleswade Town v Hornchurch	2-2
	Chesham United v Hertford Town	0-0
	Enfield v Barking	4-1
	Walthamstow Pennant v Chelmsford City	0-3
22	Barkingside v Redbridge Forest	1-3
	Fisher Athletic v Harwich & Parkeston	0-0
	Hounslow v Basildon United	4-3
	Stevenage Borough v Bishop's Stortford	2-3
23	Banstead Athletic v Molesey	3-3
	Beckenham Town v Flackwell Heath	0-2
	Corinthian Casuals v Grays Athletic	1-5
	Dagenham v Burnham	1-1
24	Edgware Town v Harrow Borough	1-0
	Egham Town v Purfleet	2-1
	Leyton-Wingate v Billericay Town	0-0
	Tilbury v Witney Town	1-1
25	Andover v Horsham YMCA	3-0
	Marlow v Merstham	3-0
	Royston Town v Yeading	3-2
	Walton & Hersham v Bromley	2-3
26	Littlehampton Town v Dulwich Hamlet	2-0
	Tonbridge v Hythe Town	3-1
	Tooting & Mitcham United v Horsham	0-0
	Whyteleafe v Slade Green	2-1
27	Folkestone v Bognor Regis Town	1-2
	Margate v Gravesend & Northfleet	2-2
	Peacehaven & Telscombe v Southwick	4-1
	Redhill v Whitehawk	2-3
28	Cove v Windsor & Eton	1-3
	Dover Athletic v Ashford Town	1-0
	Pagham v Oakwood	4-0
	Sittingbourne v Whitstable Town	1-1
29	Carshalton Athletic v Erith & Belvedere	3-0
	Eastbourne United v Crawley Town	0-2
	Wick v Dorking (2)	0-3
	Worthing v Chatham Town	3-0
30	Hampton v Hailsham Town	0-1
	Havant Town v Langney Sports	4-0
	Herne Bay v Lewes	0-1
	Kingstonian v Staines Town	2-1
31	Abingdon United v Farnborough Town	0-1
	Bournemouth (Ams) v Abingdon Town	2-1
	Salisbury (2) v Hungerford Town	2-0
	Slough Town v Feltham	8-0
32	Chippenham Town v AFC Lymington	1-1
	Trowbridge Town v Newbury Town	3-0
	Warminster Town v Wokingham Town	0-1
	Wycombe Wanderers v Maidenhead United	3-0
33	Chard Town v Romsey Town	4-4
	Melksham Town v Calne Town	2-1
	Stroud v Gosport Borough	4-1
	Waterlooville v Newport (IOW)	1-1
34	Barry Town v Clevedon Town	0-0
	Mangotsfield United v Bashley	2-2
	St Blazey v Weymouth	0-2
	Taunton Town v Swanage Town & Herston	1-2
35	Bristol Manor Farm v Bridgend Town	1-1
	Cheltenham Town v Exmouth Town	2-2
	Weston-Super-Mare v Maesteg Park Athletic	2-2
	Yate Town v Worcester City	1-3
36	Falmouth Town v Dorchester Town	2-4
	Liskeard Athletic v Wimborne Town	5-2
	Saltash United v Poole Town	1-1
	Tiverton Town v Ilfracombe Town	5-1
1r	Gateshead (2) v North Shields	0-1
3r	South Bank v Ferryhill Athletic	1-0
4r	Horden CW v Workington	2-1
5r	Evenwood Town v Seaham Red Star	0-2
6r	Colwyn Bay v Knowsley United	3-0
r	Horwich RMI v Morecambe	3-0
7r	Bangor City v Farsley Celtic	3-0
8r	Emley v Radcliffe Borough	1-0e
9r	Hednesford Town v Eastwood Town	1-1
10r	Marine v Willenhall Town	2-2
r	Stalybridge Celtic v Droylsden	1-2
14r	Atherstone United v Wolverton	4-1
r	Buckingham Town v Brackley Town	1-1
r	Evesham United v Racing Club Warwick	5-1
15r	Sandwell Borough v March Town United	2-2
r	Stourbridge v Potton United	7-0
17r	Baker Perkins v Boreham Wood	1-2
r	V.S. Rugby v Haverhill Rovers	5-0
21r	Hertford Town v Chesham United	1-5
r	Hornchurch v Biggleswade Town	3-1
22r	Harwich & Parkeston v Fisher Athletic	2-1
23r	Burnham v Dagenham	1-2
r	Molesey v Banstead Athletic	2-0
24r	Billericay Town v Leyton-Wingate	1-0
r	Witney Town v Tilbury	2-1
26r	Horsham v Tooting & Mitcham United	1-2
27r	Gravesend & Northfleet v Margate	1-4
28r	Whitstable Town v Sittingbourne	1-4e
32r	AFC Lymington v Chippenham Town	1-0
33r	Newport (IOW) v Waterlooville	3-0
r	Romsey Town v Chard Town	3-0
34r	Bashley v Mangotsfield United	6-3e
r	Clevedon Town v Barry Town	0-3
35r	Bridgend Town v Bristol Manor Farm	3-0
r	Exmouth Town v Cheltenham Town	3-3
r	Maesteg Park Athletic v Weston-Super-Mare	0-4
36r	Poole Town v Saltash United	2-2e
9r2	Eastwood Town v Hednesford Town	2-3
10r2	Marine v Willenhall Town	4-1
14r2	Buckingham Town v Brackley Town	2-0
15r2	Sandwell Borough v March Town United	1-0
35r2	Cheltenham Town v Exmouth Town	3-0
36r2	Saltash United v Poole Town	3-1

Qualifying Round Two

1	Prudhoe East End v North Shields	0-1
	Shildon v Fleetwood Town	0-4
2	Accrington Stanley (2) v Blyth Spartans	2-1
	Gretna v Guisborough Town	2-2
3	Easington Colliery v Langley Park	1-1
	Harrogate Railway Athletic v South Bank	1-0
4	Esh Winning v Spennymoor United	1-3
	Horden CW v Northallerton Town	0-3
5	Lancaster City v Newcastle Blue Star	0-2
	Seaham Red Star v Consett	1-1
6	Caernarfon Town v Colwyn Bay	2-6
	Irlam Town v Horwich RMI	1-3
7	Atherton LR v Bangor City	0-0
	Maine Road v Altrincham	0-1
8	Bootle v Southport	2-0
	Emley v Chorley	0-1
9	Hednesford Town v Hyde United	2-2
	South Liverpool v Curzon Ashton	1-0
10	Leicester United v Droylsden	0-0
	Worksop Town v Marine	1-3
11	Blakenall v Nuneaton Borough	3-3
	Princes End United v Frickley Athletic	0-4
12	Alvechurch v Witton Albion	2-7
	Bilston Town v Buxton	2-1
13	Burton Albion v Hinckley Athletic	4-0
	Corby Town v Matlock Town	2-0
14	Buckingham Town v Shepshed Charterhouse	2-4
	Evesham United v Atherstone United	1-2
15	Sandwell Borough v Bromsgrove Rovers	0-2
	Stourbridge v Sutton Coldfield Town	1-2
16	Histon v Redditch United	1-1
	Malvern Town v Tamworth	3-3
17	Boreham Wood v Rushden Town	1-0
	Boston United v V.S. Rugby	3-1
18	Great Yarmouth Town v Cambridge City	0-4
	Wembley v Heybridge Swifts	2-2
19	Braintree Town v Barnet	0-2
	Harlow Town v Ford United	1-0
20	Ruislip Manor v Hendon	2-1
	Wivenhoe Town v Wealdstone	0-0
21	Chesham United v Enfield	0-3
	Hornchurch v Chelmsford City	1-2
22	Harwich & Parkeston v Redbridge Forest	1-3
	Hounslow v Bishop's Stortford	1-5
23	Flackwell Heath v Grays Athletic	2-2
	Molesey v Dagenham	1-2
24	Billericay Town v Edgware Town	1-0
	Egham Town v Witney Town	1-0
25	Andover v Bromley	2-0
	Marlow v Royston Town	2-2
26	Tooting & Mitcham United v Littlehampton Town	1-2
	Whyteleafe v Tonbridge	0-2
27	Peacehaven & Telscombe v Bognor Regis Town	3-1
	Whitehawk v Margate	0-1
28	Dover Athletic v Sittingbourne	2-0
	Pagham v Windsor & Eton	0-3
29	Dorking (2) v Carshalton Athletic	2-0
	Worthing v Crawley Town	3-2
30	Havant Town v Kingstonian	0-4
	Lewes v Hailsham Town	0-3
31	Salisbury (2) v Bournemouth (Ams)	4-0
	Slough Town v Farnborough Town	2-3
32	AFC Lymington v Wokingham Town	1-1
	Trowbridge Town v Wycombe Wanderers	0-0
33	Melksham Town v Newport (IOW)	0-2
	Romsey Town v Stroud	1-0
34	Barry Town v Bashley	0-2
	Swanage Town & Herston v Weymouth	1-1
35	Bridgend Town v Worcester City	1-7
	Weston-Super-Mare v Cheltenham Town	0-2
36	Liskeard Athletic v Dorchester Town	5-1
	Tiverton Town v Saltash United	4-2
2r	Guisborough Town v Gretna	1-3
3r	Langley Park v Easington Colliery	0-1
5r	Consett v Seaham Red Star	2-0
7r	Bangor City v Atherton LR	4-0
9r	Hyde United v Hednesford Town	5-2e
10r	Droylsden v Leicester United	2-2
11r	Nuneaton Borough v Blakenall	3-0
16r	Redditch United v Histon	1-0
r	Tamworth v Malvern Town	5-1
18r	Heybridge Swifts v Wembley	3-1e
20r	Wealdstone v Wivenhoe Town	2-1
23r	Grays Athletic v Flackwell Heath	2-0
25r	Royston Town v Marlow	0-2e
32r	Wokingham Town v AFC Lymington	2-1
r	Wycombe Wanderers v Trowbridge Town	2-1e
34r	Weymouth v Swanage Town & Herston	2-1
10r2	Leicester United v Droylsden	4-3e

Qualifying Round Three

1	Fleetwood Town v North Shields	2-0
2	Accrington Stanley (2) v Gretna	2-1
3	Harrogate Railway Athletic v Easington Colliery	2-0
4	Spennymoor United v Northallerton Town	2-0
5	Newcastle Blue Star v Consett	3-0
6	Horwich RMI v Colwyn Bay	1-3
7	Altrincham v Bangor City	3-0
8	Chorley v Bootle	6-2
9	Hyde United v South Liverpool	1-1
10	Leicester United v Marine	0-2
11	Frickley Athletic v Nuneaton Borough	1-0
12	Witton Albion v Bilston Town	4-0
13	Corby Town v Burton Albion	0-1
14	Shepshed Charterhouse v Atherstone United	2-3
15	Sutton Coldfield Town v Bromsgrove Rovers	0-0
16	Tamworth v Redditch United	2-0
17	Boreham Wood v Boston United	1-1
18	Heybridge Swifts v Cambridge City	1-0
19	Harlow Town v Barnet	1-3
20	Ruislip Manor v Wealdstone	1-0
21	Enfield v Chelmsford City	1-1
22	Bishop's Stortford v Redbridge Forest	2-1
23	Dagenham v Grays Athletic	3-1
24	Egham Town v Billericay Town	1-1
25	Andover v Marlow	0-1
26	Littlehampton Town v Tonbridge	0-0
27	Peacehaven & Telscombe v Margate	1-0
28	Windsor & Eton v Dover Athletic	1-1
29	Dorking (2) v Worthing	1-1
30	Kingstonian v Hailsham Town	4-0
31	Salisbury (2) v Farnborough Town	0-3
32	Wycombe Wanderers v Wokingham Town	4-1
33	Newport (IOW) v Romsey Town	0-1
34	Bashley v Weymouth	2-2
35	Cheltenham Town v Worcester City	4-2
36	Tiverton Town v Liskeard Athletic	1-0
9r	South Liverpool v Hyde United	3-1
15r	Bromsgrove Rovers v Sutton Coldfield Town	4-2e
17r	Boston United v Boreham Wood	4-0
21r	Chelmsford City v Enfield	1-0
24r	Billericay Town v Egham Town	1-2
26r	Tonbridge v Littlehampton Town	2-3
28r	Dover Athletic v Windsor & Eton	3-0
29r	Worthing v Dorking (2)	2-4
34r	Weymouth v Bashley	2-3

Qualifying Round Four

Accrington Stanley (2) v Fleetwood Town	0-2
Barnet v Heybridge Swifts	3-1
Bishop Auckland v South Liverpool	1-0
Bishop's Stortford v Atherstone United	0-1
Bromsgrove Rovers v Kidderminster Harriers	1-2
Burton Albion v Tamworth	0-0
Chelmsford City v Kettering Town	0-0
Chorley v Harrogate Railway Athletic	3-1
Colwyn Bay v Whitley Bay	1-4
Dagenham v Aylesbury United	0-2
Dartford v Boston United	1-1
Dorking (2) v Cheltenham Town	2-3
Dover Athletic v Merthyr Tydfil	0-0
Farnborough Town v Gloucester City	4-1

1990/91 to 1991/92

Frickley Athletic v Witton Albion	0-2
Halesowen Town v Ruislip Manor	5-2
Hayes v Kingstonian	2-0
Macclesfield Town v Altrincham	2-2
Marine v Stafford Rangers	1-1
Northwich Victoria v Spennymoor United	1-1
Romsey Town v Littlehampton Town	1-2
Runcorn v Newcastle Blue Star	1-0
Telford United v Egham Town	2-0
Tiverton Town v Peacehaven & Telscombe	3-2
Welling United v Bashley	1-0
Woking v Bath City	2-1
Wycombe Wanderers v Basingstoke Town	6-0
Yeovil Town v Marlow	3-1
r Altrincham v Macclesfield Town	3-0
r Boston United v Dartford	2-1e
r Kettering Town v Chelmsford City	1-2
r Merthyr Tydfil v Dover Athletic	2-0
r Spennymoor United v Northwich Victoria	2-1e
r Stafford Rangers v Marine	2-1
r Tamworth v Burton Albion	3-2e

Round One

Aldershot v Tiverton Town	6-2
Altrincham v Huddersfield Town	1-2
Atherstone United v Fleetwood Town	3-1
Aylesbury United v Walsall	0-1
Barnet v Chelmsford City	2-2
Birmingham City v Cheltenham Town	1-0
Bishop Auckland v Barrow	0-1
Blackpool v Grimsby Town	2-0
Boston United v Wycombe Wanderers	1-1
Bournemouth v Gillingham	2-1
Bradford City v Shrewsbury Town	0-0
Brentford v Yeovil Town	5-0
Cardiff City v Hayes	0-0
Chester City v Doncaster Rovers	2-2
Chesterfield v Spennymoor United	3-2
Chorley v Bury	2-1
Colchester United v Reading	2-1
Darlington v York City	1-1
Exeter City v Cambridge United	1-2
Fulham v Farnborough Town	2-1
Halesowen Town v Tranmere Rovers	1-2
Halifax Town v Wrexham	3-2
Hereford United v Peterborough United	1-1
Leyton Orient v Southend United	3-2
Lincoln City v Crewe Alexandra	1-4
Littlehampton Town v Northampton Town	0-4
Maidstone United v Torquay United	4-1
Merthyr Tydfil v Sutton United	1-1
Preston North End v Mansfield Town	0-1
Rochdale v Scunthorpe United	1-1
Rotherham United v Stockport County	1-0
Runcorn v Hartlepool United	0-3
Scarborough v Leek Town	0-2
Stafford Rangers v Burnley	1-3
Swansea City v Welling United	5-2
Tamworth v Whitley Bay	4-6
Telford United v Stoke City	0-0
Wigan Athletic v Carlisle United	5-0
Witton Albion v Bolton Wanderers	1-2
Woking v Kidderminster Harriers	0-0
r Chelmsford City v Barnet	0-2
r Doncaster Rovers v Chester City	1-2e
r Hayes v Cardiff City	1-0 N
r Kidderminster Harriers v Woking	1-1e
r Peterborough United v Hereford United	2-1
r Scunthorpe United v Rochdale	2-1e
r Shrewsbury Town v Bradford City	2-1
r Stoke City v Telford United	1-0
r Sutton United v Merthyr Tydfil	0-1
r Wycombe Wanderers v Boston United	4-0
r York City v Darlington	1-0
r2 Kidderminster Harriers v Woking	1-2

Round Two

Aldershot v Maidstone United	2-1
Barnet v Northampton Town	0-0
Birmingham City v Brentford	1-3
Bournemouth v Hayes	1-0
Burnley v Stoke City	2-0
Chesterfield v Bolton Wanderers	3-4
Colchester United v Leyton Orient	0-0
Crewe Alexandra v Atherstone United	1-0
Fulham v Cambridge United	0-0
Huddersfield Town v Blackpool	0-2
Leek Town v Chester City	1-1
Mansfield Town v York City	2-1
Rotherham United v Halifax Town	1-1
Scunthorpe United v Tranmere Rovers	3-2
Shrewsbury Town v Chorley	1-0
Swansea City v Walsall	2-1
Whitley Bay v Barrow	0-1
Wigan Athletic v Hartlepool United	2-0
Woking v Merthyr Tydfil	5-1
Wycombe Wanderers v Peterborough United	1-1
r Cambridge United v Fulham	2-1
r Chester City v Leek Town	4-0
r Halifax Town v Rotherham United	1-2
r Leyton Orient v Colchester United	4-1
r Northampton Town v Barnet	0-1
r Peterborough United v Wycombe Wanderers	2-0

Round Three

Arsenal v Sunderland	2-1
Aston Villa v Wimbledon	1-1
Barnet v Portsmouth	0-5
Barnsley v Leeds United	1-1
Blackburn Rovers v Liverpool	1-1
Blackpool v Tottenham Hotspur	0-1
Bolton Wanderers v Barrow	1-0
Brighton & Hove Albion v Scunthorpe United	3-2
Bristol Rovers v Crewe Alexandra	0-2
Burnley v Manchester City	0-1
Charlton Athletic v Everton	1-2
Chelsea v Oxford United	1-3
Chester City v Bournemouth	2-3
Coventry City v Wigan Athletic	1-1
Crystal Palace v Nottingham Forest	0-0
Hull City v Notts County	2-5
Leyton Orient v Swindon Town	1-1
Manchester United v Queen's Park Rangers	2-1
Mansfield Town v Sheffield Wednesday	0-2
Middlesbrough v Plymouth Argyle	0-0
Millwall v Leicester City	2-1
Newcastle United v Derby County	2-0
Norwich City v Bristol City	2-1
Oldham Athletic v Brentford	3-1
Port Vale v Peterborough United	2-1
Sheffield United v Luton Town	1-3
Shrewsbury Town v Watford	4-1
Southampton v Ipswich Town	3-2
Swansea City v Rotherham United	0-0
West Bromwich Albion v Woking	2-4
West Ham United v Aldershot	0-0
Wolverhampton Wan. v Cambridge United	0-1
r Leeds United v Barnsley	4-0
r Liverpool v Blackburn Rovers	3-0
r Nottingham Forest v Crystal Palace	2-2e
r Plymouth Argyle v Middlesbrough	1-2
r Rotherham United v Swansea City	4-0
r Swindon Town v Leyton Orient	1-0
r West Ham United v Aldershot	6-1
r Wigan Athletic v Coventry City	0-1
r Wimbledon v Aston Villa	1-0e
r2 Nottingham Forest v Crystal Palace	3-0

Round Four

Arsenal v Leeds United	0-0
Cambridge United v Middlesbrough	2-0
Coventry City v Southampton	1-1
Crewe Alexandra v Rotherham United	1-0
Everton v Woking	1-0
Liverpool v Brighton & Hove Albion	2-2
Luton Town v West Ham United	1-1
Manchester United v Bolton Wanderers	1-0
Millwall v Sheffield Wednesday	4-4
Newcastle United v Nottingham Forest	2-2
Norwich City v Swindon Town	3-1
Notts County v Oldham Athletic	2-0
Port Vale v Manchester City	1-2
Portsmouth v Bournemouth	5-1
Shrewsbury Town v Wimbledon	1-0
Tottenham Hotspur v Oxford United	4-2
r Brighton & Hove Albion v Liverpool	2-3
r Leeds United v Arsenal	1-1e
r Nottingham Forest v Newcastle United	3-0
r Sheffield Wednesday v Millwall	2-0
r Southampton v Coventry City	2-0
r West Ham United v Luton Town	5-0
r2 Arsenal v Leeds United	0-0e
r3 Leeds United v Arsenal	1-2

Round Five

Cambridge United v Sheffield Wednesday	4-0
Liverpool v Everton	0-0
Norwich City v Manchester United	2-1
Notts County v Manchester City	1-0
Portsmouth v Tottenham Hotspur	1-2
Shrewsbury Town v Arsenal	0-1
Southampton v Nottingham Forest	1-1
West Ham United v Crewe Alexandra	1-0
r Everton v Liverpool	4-4e
r Nottingham Forest v Southampton	3-1
r2 Everton v Liverpool	1-0

Round Six

Arsenal v Cambridge United	2-1
Norwich City v Nottingham Forest	0-1
Tottenham Hotspur v Notts County	2-1
West Ham United v Everton	2-1

Semi Finals

Nottingham Forest v West Ham United	4-0 N
Tottenham Hotspur v Arsenal	3-1 N

Final

Tottenham Hotspur v Nottingham Forest	2-1eN

1991/92

Preliminary Round

1 Alnwick Town v Chester-le-Street Town	4-3
Brandon United v Shotton Comrades	7-1
Darwen v Hebburn	1-1
Esh Winning v Netherfield (Kendal)	1-3
2 Ashington v Crook Town	3-1
Bridlington Town v Evenwood Town	5-1
Clitheroe v Langley Park	4-4
Consett v Willington	5-0
3 Darlington Cleveland Bridge v Horden CW	3-2
Garforth Town v Whickham	4-1
Prudhoe East End v Bedlington Terriers	0-2
Spennymoor United v Easington Colliery	1-0
4 Durham City v South Bank	4-0
Great Harwood Town v Eccleshill United	6-0
Penrith v Ferryhill Athletic	1-0
Stockton (2) v Billingham Town	2-4
5 Blackpool (Wren) Rovers v Thackley	3-2
Seaham Red Star v Peterlee Newtown	3-2
Shildon v Washington	3-1
West Auckland Town v Denaby United	3-5e
6 Burscough v Leyland DAF	wo/s
Irlam Town v Curzon Ashton	0-0
Knowsley United v Atherton LR	5-1
Prescot AFC v Chadderton	3-2
Sheffield v Congleton Town	2-0
7 Ashton United v Rhyl	0-0
Liversedge v Maine Road	3-1
Newtown (2) v Glossop	4-2
Salford City v Warrington Town	0-0
8 Harworth Colliery Institute v Maltby MW	2-1
Lancaster City v Winsford United	1-5
Newcastle Town v Ossett Albion	2-0
Radcliffe Borough v Nantwich Town	0-1
9 Armthorpe Welfare v Vauxhall G.M.	1-1
Ossett Town v North Ferriby United	2-0
Rossendale United v Heanor Town	2-4
Worksop Town v Brigg Town	3-1
10 Belper Town v Arnold Town	2-0
Eastwood Town v Farsley Celtic	2-4
Grantham Town v Ilkeston Town (2)	1-5
St Helens Town v Borrowash Victoria	1-3
11 Boston v Harrogate Town	2-3
Dudley Town v Lincoln United	1-4
Holbeach United v Hinckley Athletic	2-3
Rocester v Oakham United	1-3
Sandwell Borough v Alfreton Town	1-2
12 Hinckley (1) v Bridgnorth Town	2-4
Irthlingborough Diamonds v Wednesfield	2-2
Oldbury United v Blakenall	1-2
Solihull Borough v Spalding United	1-0
Tamworth v Lye Town	2-2
13 Hinckley Town v Boldmere St Michaels	3-1
Racing Club Warwick v Rushall Olympic	2-1
Stourbridge v Long Buckby	1-0
Willenhall Town v Wellingborough Town	6-1
14 Banbury United v Stratford Town	4-1
Hednesford Town v Northampton Spencer	1-1
Highgate United v Chasetown	0-3
Stamford v Paget Rangers	1-1
Walsall Wood v Raunds Town	1-1
15 Chalfont St Peter v Flackwell Heath	2-0
Evesham United v Rothwell Town	3-1
Malvern Town v Halesowen Harriers	3-2
Tring Town v Hemel Hempstead Town	0-3
16 Desborough Town v Vauxhall Motors (Luton)	wo/s
Edgware Town v Southall	4-0
Rushden Town v Friar Lane Old Boys	3-2
Waltham Abbey v Stevenage Borough	0-1
17 Aveley v Felixstowe Town	2-0
Barton Rovers v Bourne Town	3-4
Braintree Town v Bury Town	2-1
Mirrlees Blackstone v Great Yarmouth Town	2-1
Wisbech Town v Burnham Ramblers	4-3
18 Collier Row v Saffron Walden Town	2-2
Hitchin Town v Tiptree United	1-1
King's Lynn v Haverhill Rovers	5-2
Leyton-Wingate v Eynesbury Rovers	6-0
Purfleet v Gorleston	3-1
19 Arlesey Town v Clapton	0-1
March Town United v Histon	1-1
Sudbury Town v Barking	2-2
Walthamstow Pennant v Langford	3-2
20 Canvey Island v Harwich & Parkeston	0-2
East Thurrock United v Royston Town	1-1
Haringey Borough v Watton United	5-0
Letchworth Garden City v Potton United	1-1
Lowestoft Town v Rainham Town	1-0
21 Barkingside v Baldock Town	1-1
Ford United v Hornchurch	2-1
Halstead Town v Hoddesdon Town	3-2
Ware v Milton Keynes Borough	5-1
22 Basildon United v Brimsdown Rovers	0-1e
Newmarket Town v Biggleswade Town	1-1
Witham Town v Welwyn Garden City	3-1
Wolverton v Uxbridge	1-0
23 Cheshunt v Tilbury	0-3
Darenth Heathside v Croydon	0-3
Leighton Town v Kingsbury Town	3-2
Yeading v Rayners Lane	8-0

185

1991/92

24 Beckenham Town v Wingate & Finchley	1-0	
Burnham v Feltham & Hounslow Boro.	1-1 N	
Dulwich Hamlet v Harefield United	2-1	
Egham Town v Wembley	0-1	
Hertford Town v Northwood	3-2	
25 Corinthian v Merstham	6-0	
Horsham YMCA v Erith & Belvedere	1-2	
Molesey v Ringmer	4-0	
Shoreham v Sheppey United	0-3	
26 Chertsey Town v Worthing	2-2	
Chichester City (1) v Chipstead	1-3	
Faversham Town v Eastbourne Town	0-0	
Whyteleafe v Ashford Town	2-0	
27 Canterbury City v Arundel	1-0	
Chatham Town v Steyning Town	1-3	
Cove v Slade Green	2-1	
Leatherhead v Corinthian Casuals	3-1	
Tunbridge Wells v Burgess Hill Town	0-2	
28 Lewes v Three Bridges	4-3	
Metropolitan Police v Hastings Town	2-4	
Tooting & Mitcham United v Redhill	2-0	
Whitstable Town v Eastbourne United	0-1	
29 Epsom & Ewell v Walton & Hersham	1-5	
Hampton v Haywards Heath Town	3-0	
Hythe Town v Croydon Athletic	4-4	
Lancing v Wick	4-1	
Langney Sports v Southwick	0-1	
30 Bracknell Town v Portfield	2-2	
Newbury Town v Horndean	1-0	
Oakwood v Havant Town	0-3	
Selsey v Malden Vale	2-1	
31 AFC Totton v AFC Lymington	2-2	
Buckingham Town v Abingdon United	1-0	
Horsham v Hungerford Town	2-1	
Sholing Sports v Maidenhead United	0-6	
32 Bournemouth (Ams) v Abingdon Town	1-2	
Calne Town v Westbury United	1-2	
Fareham Town v Thatcham Town	1-5	
Thame United v Eastleigh	1-1	
33 Chard Town v Witney Town	1-2	
Cwmbran Town v Paulton Rovers	1-0	
Glastonbury v Keynsham Town	1-0	
Gosport Borough v Clevedon Town	1-3	
34 Barry Town v Ton Pentre	3-1	
Bridgend Town v Chippenham Town	2-0	
Radstock Town v Devizes Town	0-2	
Yate Town v Bristol Manor Farm	4-1	
35 Dawlish Town v Maesteg Park Athletic	1-2	
Frome Town v Exmouth Town	3-1	
Melksham Town v Welton Rovers	1-1	
Shortwood United v Weston-Super-Mare	3-0	
36 Bideford v Falmouth Town	2-3	
Clandown v Ilfracombe Town	1-3	
St Blazey v Minehead	0-3	
Torrington v Barnstaple Town	3-1	
1r Hebburn v Darwen	2-1	
2r Clitheroe v Langley Park	1-1e	
6r Curzon Ashton v Irlam Town	4-1	
7r Rhyl v Ashton United	1-0	
r Warrington Town v Salford City	1-0	
9r Vauxhall G.M. v Armthorpe Welfare	1-2e	
12r Lye Town v Tamworth	1-3	
r Wednesfield v Irthlingborough Diamonds	3-3	
14r Northampton Spencer v Hednesford Town	1-1	
r Raunds Town v Walsall Wood	3-1	
18r Saffron Walden Town v Collier Row	2-3	
r Tiptree United v Hitchin Town	1-0	
19r Barking v Sudbury Town	2-2	
r Histon v March Town United	2-1	
20r Potton United v Letchworth Garden City	2-0	
21r Baldock Town v Barkingside	5-0	
22r Biggleswade Town v Newmarket Town	2-2e	
24r Feltham & Hounslow Boro. v Burnham	0-4	
26r Eastbourne Town v Faversham Town	0-4 N	
r Worthing v Chertsey Town	4-1	
29r Croydon Athletic v Hythe Town	2-1	
30r Portfield v Bracknell Town	2-1e	
31r AFC Lymington v AFC Totton	3-2	
32r Eastleigh v Thame United	0-2	
35r Welton Rovers v Melksham Town	1-2	
2r2 Langley Park v Clitheroe	1-0 N	
12r2 Irthlingborough Diamonds v Wednesfield	1-2	
14r2 Hednesford Town v Northampton Spencer	1-0	
19r2 Sudbury Town v Barking	2-1	
22r2 Biggleswade Town v Newmarket Town	1-0	

Qualifying Round One

1 Alnwick Town v Brandon United	1-1	
Netherfield (Kendal) v Billingham Synthonia	3-2	
Newcastle Blue Star v Hebburn	5-1	
Workington v Gateshead (2)	0-1	
2 Annfield Plain v North Shields	0-4	
Ashington v Consett	0-4	
Bridlington Town v Blyth Spartans	3-2	
Northallerton Town v Langley Park	1-0	
3 Cleator Moor Celtic v Gretna	0-7	
Darlington Cleveland Bridge v Murton	1-3	
Spennymoor United v Bedlington Terriers	0-1	
Whitby Town v Garforth Town	0-1	
4 Dunston Federation Brewery v Guisborough Town	1-0	
Durham City v Tow Law Town	1-0	
Morecambe v Great Harwood Town	1-0	
Penrith v Billingham Town	4-2	

5 Denaby United v Harrogate Railway Athletic	1-0	
Fleetwood Town v Blackpool (Wren) Rovers	3-2	
Norton & Stockton Ancients v Guiseley	0-4	
Seaham Red Star v Shildon	3-0 v	
6 Buxton v Burscough	4-2	
Curzon Ashton v Bangor City	1-1	
Knowsley United v Sheffield	2-0	
Prescot AFC v Accrington Stanley (2)	0-5	
7 Caernarfon Town v Colwyn Bay	1-1	
Marine v Liversedge	4-0	
Rhyl v Newtown (2)	1-0	
Warrington Town v Hyde United	1-0	
8 Bootle v Newcastle Town	2-1	
Flixton v Mossley	1-1	
Harworth Colliery Institute v Droylsden	0-1	
Winsford United v Nantwich Town	3-0	
9 Eastwood Hanley v Northwich Victoria	2-1	
Heanor Town v Armthorpe Welfare	0-2	
Ossett Town v Southport	0-1	
Stalybridge Celtic v Worksop Town	4-0	
10 Borrowash Victoria v Belper Town	2-0	
Farsley Celtic v Emley	0-1	
Horwich RMI v Ilkeston Town (2)	1-0	
Skelmersdale United v Macclesfield Town	0-4	
11 Alfreton Town v Hinckley Athletic	1-0	
Goole Town v Oakham United	0-1	
Harrogate Town v Frickley Athletic	2-2	
Lincoln United v Gainsborough Trinity	3-1	
12 Blakenall v Boston United	1-2	
Bridgnorth Town v Matlock Town	1-2	
Moor Green v Tamworth	0-3	
Solihull Borough v Wednesfield	3-0	
13 Hinckley Town v Leicester United	2-0	
Shepshed Albion v Stourbridge	2-0	
West Midlands Police v Burton Albion	0-1	
Willenhall Town v Racing Club Warwick	2-1	
14 Banbury United v Hednesford Town	2-1	
Chasetown v Bilston Town	0-0	
Raunds Town v Gresley Rovers	1-1	
V.S. Rugby v Stamford	2-0	
15 APV Peterborough City v Alvechurch	0-0	
Chalfont St Peter v Nuneaton Borough	0-4	
Corby Town v Hemel Hempstead Town	1-0	
Evesham United v Malvern Town	2-4	
16 Bedworth United v Bromsgrove Rovers	0-2	
Desborough Town v Rushden Town	2-4	
Redditch United v Edgware Town	5-1	
Stevenage Borough v Sutton Coldfield Town	0-2	
17 Aveley v Heybridge Swifts	0-2	
Bishop's Stortford v Mirrlees Blackstone	1-1	
Bourne Town v Braintree Town	0-3	
Wisbech Town v Kettering Town	0-3	
18 Harlow Town v Leyton-Wingate	4-1 N	
King's Lynn v Cambridge City	3-3	
Purfleet v Collier Row	2-2	
Tiptree United v Dagenham	1-0	
19 Clacton Town v Billericay Town	1-2	
Clapton v Chelmsford City	1-5	
Enfield v Walthamstow Pennant	4-0	
Sudbury Town v Histon	1-0	
20 East Thurrock United v Grays Athletic	1-1	
Harwich & Parkeston v Potton United	2-1	
Lowestoft Town v Boreham Wood	2-1	
Redbridge Forest v Haringey Borough	5-0	
21 Dartford v Ware	5-1	
Ford United v Wivenhoe Town	3-1	
Halstead Town v Baldock Town	2-3	
Stowmarket Town v Hendon	1-4	
22 Biggleswade Town v Brimsdown Rovers	1-2e	
Chesham United v Wolverton	5-1	
Thetford Town v St Albans City	0-2	
Witham Town v Wealdstone	1-3	
23 Berkhamsted Town v Harrow Borough	3-2	
Slough Town v Croydon	2-2	
Tilbury v Leighton Town	1-1	
Yeading v Ruislip Manor	3-1	
24 Dulwich Hamlet v Burnham	1-0	
Fisher Athletic v Beckenham Town	4-0	
Hertford Town v Staines Town	2-0	
Wembley v Windsor & Eton	1-2	
25 Banstead Athletic v Wokingham Town	1-2	
Corinthian v Erith & Belvedere	1-3	
Hailsham Town v Sheppey United	1-1	
Molesey v Crawley Town	1-5	
26 Dover Athletic v Chipstead	6-0	
Faversham Town v Carshalton Athletic	3-2	
Whitehawk v Bromley	0-2	
Whyteleafe v Worthing	1-2	
27 Cove v Burgess Hill Town	1-1	
Gravesend & Northfleet v Canterbury City	2-1	
Leatherhead v Dorking (2)	1-2	
Steyning Town v Bognor Regis Town	0-1	
28 Eastbourne United v Lewes	1-4	
Herne Bay v Kingstonian	0-2	
Peacehaven & Telscombe v Hastings Town	2-1	
Tooting & Mitcham United v Margate	2-1	
29 Lancing v Hampton	1-3	
Southwick v Sittingbourne	1-3	
Tonbridge v Croydon Athletic	2-1	
Walton & Hersham v Littlehampton Town	1-1	
30 Camberley Town v Marlow	1-3	
Portfield v Havant Town	1-2	
Romsey Town v Newbury Town	2-1	
Selsey v Andover	2-1	

31 AFC Lymington v Bashley	2-4	
Horsham v Buckingham Town	1-0	
Newport (IOW) v Maidenhead United	0-3	
Pagham v Basingstoke Town	1-3	
32 Poole Town v Westbury United	3-1	
Swanage Town & Herston v Waterlooville	1-1	
Thame United v Abingdon Town	2-0	
Thatcham Town v Salisbury (2)	1-1	
33 Brockenhurst v Dorchester Town	1-2	
Clevedon Town v Witney Town	2-2	
Glastonbury v Trowbridge Town	0-4	
Mangotsfield United v Cwmbran Town	4-2	
34 Bridgend Town v Cheltenham Town	3-3	
Taunton Town v Devizes Town	2-0	
Wimborne Town v Weymouth	1-2	
Yate Town v Barry Town	0-3	
35 Gloucester City v Shortwood United	4-1	
Maesteg Park Athletic v Frome Town	4-0	
Melksham Town v Worcester City	1-8	
Stroud v Bath City	1-3	
36 Falmouth Town v Minehead	2-0	
Saltash United v Ilfracombe Town	6-0	
St Austell v Liskeard Athletic	2-3	
Torrington v Tiverton Town	2-2	
1r Brandon United v Alnwick Town	0-1	
5r Shildon v Seaham Red Star	2-1	
6r Bangor City v Curzon Ashton	1-2	
7r Colwyn Bay v Caernarfon Town	2-1	
8r Mossley v Flixton	2-1	
11r Harrogate Town v Frickley Athletic	3-3	
14r Bilston Town v Chasetown	0-1	
r Gresley Rovers v Raunds Town	2-0	
15r Alvechurch v APV Peterborough City	3-2	
17r Mirrlees Blackstone v Bishop's Stortford	2-0	
18r Cambridge City v King's Lynn	1-2e	
r Collier Row v Purfleet	0-1	
20r Grays Athletic v East Thurrock United	2-1	
23r Croydon v Slough Town	0-3	
r Leighton Town v Tilbury	1-0	
25r Sheppey United v Hailsham Town	4-1	
27r Burgess Hill Town v Cove	4-0	
29r Littlehampton Town v Walton & Hersham	2-1	
32r Salisbury (2) v Thatcham Town	3-0	
r Waterlooville v Swanage Town & Herston	2-0	
33r Witney Town v Clevedon Town	1-0	
34r Cheltenham Town v Bridgend Town	5-0	
36r Tiverton Town v Torrington	3-2e	
11r2 Frickley Athletic v Harrogate Town	3-2	

Qualifying Round Two

1 Gateshead (2) v Alnwick Town	6-0	
Netherfield (Kendal) v Newcastle Blue Star	2-1	
2 Bridlington Town v Northallerton Town	4-0	
North Shields v Consett	3-1	
3 Gretna v Bedlington Terriers	3-1	
Murton v Garforth Town	3-1	
4 Dunston Federation Brewery v Penrith	2-2	
Durham City v Morecambe	1-4	
5 Denaby United v Fleetwood Town	1-0	
Guiseley v Shildon	5-1	
6 Accrington Stanley (2) v Knowsley United	2-2	
Curzon Ashton v Buxton	1-0	
7 Colwyn Bay v Rhyl	2-0	
Warrington Town v Marine	0-0	
8 Droylsden v Bootle	1-1	
Mossley v Winsford United	1-1	
9 Eastwood Hanley v Armthorpe Welfare	3-2	
Southport v Stalybridge Celtic	1-2	
10 Emley v Horwich RMI	4-2	
Macclesfield Town v Borrowash Victoria	1-2	
11 Frickley Athletic v Alfreton Town	4-1	
Lincoln United v Oakham United	2-0	
12 Boston United v Tamworth	1-1	
Matlock Town v Solihull Borough	2-1	
13 Burton Albion v Willenhall Town	4-1	
Hinckley Town v Shepshed Albion	3-3	
14 Chasetown v Banbury United	1-1	
Gresley Rovers v V.S. Rugby	3-3	
15 Alvechurch v Malvern Town	3-0	
Nuneaton Borough v Corby Town	2-2	
16 Bromsgrove Rovers v Rushden Town	1-0	
Sutton Coldfield Town v Redditch United	1-3	
17 Heybridge Swifts v Mirrlees Blackstone	1-1	
Kettering Town v Braintree Town	3-1	
18 King's Lynn v Purfleet	4-2	
Tiptree United v Harlow Town	0-6	
19 Billericay Town v Sudbury Town	3-1	
Chelmsford City v Enfield	1-1	
20 Grays Athletic v Redbridge Forest	3-1	
Lowestoft Town v Harwich & Parkeston	1-0	
21 Ford United v Dartford	0-1	
Hendon v Baldock Town	1-2	
22 St Albans City v Brimsdown Rovers	1-1	
Wealdstone v Chesham United	2-4	
23 Berkhamsted Town v Leighton Town	2-0	
Yeading v Slough Town	0-0	
24 Hertford Town v Dulwich Hamlet	2-1	
Windsor & Eton v Fisher Athletic	3-2	
25 Crawley Town v Sheppey United	2-0	
Wokingham Town v Erith & Belvedere	1-2	
26 Bromley v Worthing	3-1	
Faversham Town v Dover Athletic	0-0	
27 Bognor Regis Town v Burgess Hill Town	1-2	
Dorking (2) v Gravesend & Northfleet	3-4	

1991/92

28	Kingstonian v Lewes	3-2
	Tooting & Mitcham United v Peacehaven & Telscombe	2-0
29	Littlehampton Town v Hampton	1-3
	Sittingbourne v Tonbridge	1-2
30	Marlow v Havant Town	2-1
	Selsey v Romsey Town	1-6
31	Bashley v Maidenhead United	1-1
	Basingstoke Town v Horsham	1-1
32	Salisbury (2) v Poole Town	2-0
	Waterlooville v Thame United	3-3
33	Dorchester Town v Witney Town	3-2
	Trowbridge Town v Mangotsfield United	3-0
34	Cheltenham Town v Taunton Town	8-0
	Weymouth v Barry Town	1-1
35	Bath City v Maesteg Park Athletic	5-2
	Worcester City v Gloucester City	2-1
36	Liskeard Athletic v Falmouth Town	5-1
	Tiverton Town v Saltash United	0-0
4r	Penrith v Dunston Federation Brewery	6-6e
6r	Knowsley United v Accrington Stanley (2)	2-1e
7r	Marine v Warrington Town	1-0
8r	Bootle v Droylsden	1-3
r	Winsford United v Mossley	6-0
12r	Tamworth v Boston United	1-0e
13r	Shepshed Albion v Hinckley Town	3-2
14r	Banbury United v Chasetown	1-2e
r	V.S. Rugby v Gresley Rovers	3-0
15r	Corby Town v Nuneaton Borough	1-0e
17r	Mirrlees Blackstone v Heybridge Swifts	0-1
19r	Enfield v Chelmsford City	2-1
22r	Brimsdown Rovers v St Albans City	2-0
23r	Slough Town v Yeading	1-0
26r	Dover Athletic v Faversham Town	2-1
31r	Horsham v Basingstoke Town	2-1e
r	Maidenhead United v Bashley	1-0
32r	Thame United v Waterlooville	3-2e
34r	Barry Town v Weymouth	2-3e
36r	Saltash United v Tiverton Town	1-2
4r2	Penrith v Dunston Federation Brewery	2-1e

Qualifying Round Three

1	Gateshead (2) v Netherfield (Kendal)	0-0
2	North Shields v Bridlington Town	0-2
3	Gretna v Murton	3-0
4	Penrith v Morecambe	0-3
5	Guiseley v Denaby United	1-1
6	Knowsley United v Curzon Ashton	2-0
7	Colwyn Bay v Marine	4-3
8	Winsford United v Droylsden	3-2
9	Eastwood Hanley v Stalybridge Celtic	1-2
10	Borrowash Victoria v Emley	0-3
11	Frickley Athletic v Lincoln United	0-0
12	Matlock Town v Tamworth	0-2
13	Burton Albion v Shepshed Albion	3-2
14	Chasetown v V.S. Rugby	0-0
15	Alvechurch v Corby Town	2-0
16	Bromsgrove Rovers v Redditch United	2-0
17	Kettering Town v Heybridge Swifts	3-0
18	King's Lynn v Harlow Town	2-3
19	Billericay Town v Enfield	1-3
20	Lowestoft Town v Grays Athletic	1-2
21	Baldock Town v Dartford	2-2
22	Brimsdown Rovers v Chesham United	2-2
23	Berkhamsted Town v Slough Town	1-4
24	Hertford Town v Windsor & Eton	1-2
25	Erith & Belvedere v Crawley Town	1-2
26	Bromley v Dover Athletic	0-3
27	Burgess Hill Town v Gravesend & Northfleet	0-1
28	Kingstonian v Tooting & Mitcham United	0-0
29	Hampton v Tonbridge	2-2
30	Marlow v Romsey Town	2-0
31	Horsham v Maidenhead United	1-1
32	Thame United v Salisbury (2)	0-4
33	Dorchester Town v Trowbridge Town	1-0
34	Weymouth v Cheltenham Town	4-0
35	Bath City v Worcester City	1-2
36	Liskeard Athletic v Tiverton Town	1-3
1r	Netherfield (Kendal) v Gateshead (2)	0-3
5r	Denaby United v Guiseley	1-2
11r	Lincoln United v Frickley Athletic	3-2
14r	V.S. Rugby v Chasetown	3-0
21r	Dartford v Baldock Town	1-2e
22r	Chesham United v Brimsdown Rovers	2-1
28r	Tooting & Mitcham United v Kingstonian	2-3
29r	Tonbridge v Hampton	3-0e
31r	Maidenhead United v Horsham	0-1

Qualifying Round Four

	Aylesbury United v Chesham United	1-1
	Baldock Town v Halesowen Town	1-1
	Barrow v Bridlington Town	0-1
	Chorley v Emley	2-2
	Colchester United v Burton Albion	5-0
	Colwyn Bay v Morecambe	0-2
	Enfield v V.S. Rugby	2-1
	Gravesend & Northfleet v Harlow Town	1-1
	Grays Athletic v Atherstone United	0-2
	Gretna v Stalybridge Celtic	3-2
	Guiseley v Bishop Auckland	2-1
	Hayes v Dorchester Town	1-0
	Horsham v Crawley Town	0-0
	Kettering Town v Stafford Rangers	0-0
	Leek Town v Lincoln United	0-2
	Merthyr Tydfil v Windsor & Eton	1-1
	Runcorn v Gateshead (2)	1-0
	Salisbury (2) v Farnborough Town	1-7
	Slough Town v Kingstonian	2-1
	Tamworth v Bromsgrove Rovers	0-1
	Telford United v Knowsley United	1-0
	Tiverton Town v Dover Athletic	1-0
	Tonbridge v Yeovil Town	1-2
	Welling United v Alvechurch	5-1
	Weymouth v Sutton United	1-1
	Whitley Bay v Witton Albion	1-4
	Winsford United v Altrincham	3-2
	Worcester City v Marlow	1-2
r	Chesham United v Aylesbury United	1-3
r	Crawley Town v Horsham	3-0
r	Emley v Chorley	1-1x
r	Halesowen Town v Baldock Town	1-0
r	Harlow Town v Gravesend & Northfleet	1-0
r	Stafford Rangers v Kettering Town	0-2
r	Sutton United v Weymouth	3-0
r	Windsor & Eton v Merthyr Tydfil	1-0
r2	Chorley v Emley	0-1

Round One

	Aldershot v Enfield	0-1
	Atherstone United v Hereford United	0-0
	Barnet v Tiverton Town	5-0
	Blackpool v Grimsby Town	2-1
	Bournemouth v Bromsgrove Rovers	3-1
	Brentford v Gillingham	3-3
	Bridlington Town v York City	1-2
	Burnley v Doncaster Rovers	1-1
	Bury v Bradford City	0-1
	Carlisle United v Crewe Alexandra	1-1
	Chester City v Guiseley	1-0
	Colchester United v Exeter City	0-0
	Crawley Town v Northampton Town	4-2
	Darlington v Chesterfield	2-1
	Emley v Bolton Wanderers	0-3 N
	Fulham v Hayes	0-2
	Gretna v Rochdale	0-0
	Halesowen Town v Farnborough Town	2-2
	Hartlepool United v Shrewsbury Town	3-2
	Huddersfield Town v Lincoln United	7-0
	Kettering Town v Wycombe Wanderers	1-1
	Kidderminster Harriers v Aylesbury United	0-1
	Leyton Orient v Welling United	2-1
	Maidstone United v Sutton United	1-0
	Mansfield Town v Preston North End	0-1
	Morecambe v Hull City	0-1
	Peterborough United v Harlow Town	7-0
	Scarborough v Wigan Athletic	0-2
	Scunthorpe United v Rotherham United	1-1
	Slough Town v Reading	3-3
	Stockport County v Lincoln City	3-1
	Stoke City v Telford United	0-0
	Swansea City v Cardiff City	2-1
	Torquay United v Birmingham City	3-0
	Tranmere Rovers v Runcorn	3-0
	West Bromwich Albion v Marlow	6-0
	Windsor & Eton v Woking	2-4
	Witton Albion v Halifax Town	1-1
	Wrexham v Winsford United	5-2
	Yeovil Town v Walsall	1-1
r	Crewe Alexandra v Carlisle United	5-3e
r	Doncaster Rovers v Burnley	1-3
r	Exeter City v Colchester United	0-0P
r	Farnborough Town v Halesowen Town	4-0
r	Gillingham v Brentford	1-3
r	Halifax Town v Witton Albion	1-2e
r	Hereford United v Atherstone United	3-0
r	Reading v Slough Town	2-1
r	Rochdale v Gretna	3-1
r	Rotherham United v Scunthorpe United	3-3P
r	Telford United v Stoke City	2-1
r	Walsall v Yeovil Town	0-1e
r	Wycombe Wanderers v Kettering Town	0-2

Round Two

	Aylesbury United v Hereford United	2-3
	Blackpool v Hull City	0-1
	Bolton Wanderers v Bradford City	3-1
	Bournemouth v Brentford	2-1
	Burnley v Rotherham United	2-0
	Crewe Alexandra v Chester City	2-0
	Darlington v Hartlepool United	1-2
	Enfield v Barnet	1-4
	Exeter City v Swansea City	0-0
	Hayes v Crawley Town	0-2
	Leyton Orient v West Bromwich Albion	2-1
	Maidstone United v Kettering Town	1-2
	Peterborough United v Reading	0-0
	Preston North End v Witton Albion	5-1
	Rochdale v Huddersfield Town	1-2
	Torquay United v Farnborough Town	1-1
	Wigan Athletic v Stockport County	2-0
	Woking v Yeovil Town	3-0
	Wrexham v Telford United	1-0
	York City v Tranmere Rovers	1-1
r	Farnborough Town v Torquay United	4-3
r	Reading v Peterborough United	1-0
r	Swansea City v Exeter City	1-2
r	Tranmere Rovers v York City	2-1

Round Three

	Aston Villa v Tottenham Hotspur	0-0
	Blackburn Rovers v Kettering Town	4-1
	Bolton Wanderers v Reading	2-0
	Bournemouth v Newcastle United	0-0
	Brighton & Hove Albion v Crawley Town	5-0
	Bristol City v Wimbledon	1-1
	Bristol Rovers v Plymouth Argyle	5-0
	Burnley v Derby County	2-2
	Charlton Athletic v Barnet	3-1
	Coventry City v Cambridge United	1-1
	Crewe Alexandra v Liverpool	0-4
	Everton v Southend United	1-0
	Exeter City v Portsmouth	1-2
	Huddersfield Town v Millwall	0-4
	Hull City v Chelsea	0-2
	Ipswich Town v Hartlepool United	1-1
	Leeds United v Manchester United	0-1
	Leicester City v Crystal Palace	1-0
	Middlesbrough v Manchester City	2-1
	Norwich City v Barnsley	1-0
	Nottingham Forest v Wolverhampton Wan.	1-0
	Notts County v Wigan Athletic	2-0
	Oldham Athletic v Leyton Orient	1-1
	Oxford United v Tranmere Rovers	3-1
	Preston North End v Sheffield Wednesday	0-2
	Sheffield United v Luton Town	4-0
	Southampton v Queen's Park Rangers	2-0
	Sunderland v Port Vale	3-0
	Swindon Town v Watford	3-2
	West Ham United v Farnborough Town	1-1
	Woking v Hereford United	0-0
	Wrexham v Arsenal	2-1
r	Cambridge United v Coventry City	1-0
r	Derby County v Burnley	2-0
r	Hartlepool United v Ipswich Town	0-2
r	Hereford United v Woking	2-1e
r	Leyton Orient v Oldham Athletic	4-2e
r	Newcastle United v Bournemouth	2-2q
r	Tottenham Hotspur v Aston Villa	0-1
r	West Ham United v Farnborough Town	1-0
r	Wimbledon v Bristol City	0-1

Round Four

	Bolton Wanderers v Brighton & Hove Albion	2-1
	Bristol Rovers v Liverpool	1-1
	Cambridge United v Swindon Town	0-3
	Charlton Athletic v Sheffield United	0-0
	Chelsea v Everton	1-0
	Derby County v Aston Villa	3-4
	Ipswich Town v Bournemouth	3-0
	Leicester City v Bristol City	1-2
	Norwich City v Millwall	2-1
	Nottingham Forest v Hereford United	2-0
	Notts County v Blackburn Rovers	2-1
	Oxford United v Sunderland	2-3
	Portsmouth v Leyton Orient	2-0
	Sheffield Wednesday v Middlesbrough	1-2
	Southampton v Manchester United	0-0
	West Ham United v Wrexham	2-2
r	Liverpool v Bristol Rovers	2-1
r	Manchester United v Southampton	2-2q
r	Sheffield United v Charlton Athletic	3-1
r	Wrexham v West Ham United	0-1

Round Five

	Bolton Wanderers v Southampton	2-2
	Chelsea v Sheffield United	1-0
	Ipswich Town v Liverpool	0-0
	Norwich City v Notts County	3-0
	Nottingham Forest v Bristol City	4-1
	Portsmouth v Middlesbrough	1-1
	Sunderland v West Ham United	1-1
	Swindon Town v Aston Villa	1-2
r	Liverpool v Ipswich Town	3-2e
r	Middlesbrough v Portsmouth	2-4
r	Southampton v Bolton Wanderers	3-2e
r	West Ham United v Sunderland	2-3

Round Six

	Chelsea v Sunderland	1-1
	Liverpool v Aston Villa	1-0
	Portsmouth v Nottingham Forest	1-0
	Southampton v Norwich City	0-0
r	Norwich City v Southampton	2-1e
r	Sunderland v Chelsea	2-1

Semi Finals

	Liverpool v Portsmouth	1-1eN
	Norwich City v Sunderland	0-1 N
r	Liverpool v Portsmouth	0-0PN

Final

	Liverpool v Sunderland	2-0 N

1992/93

1992/93

Preliminary Round

1	Easington Colliery v Shotton Comrades	2-1
	Hebburn v Annfield Plain	1-1
	Newcastle Blue Star v Whickham	0-0
	Workington v West Auckland Town	3-2
2	Bamber Bridge v Prudhoe East End	4-0
	Ferryhill Athletic v Spennymoor United	2-3
	Peterlee Newtown v Evenwood Town	1-0
	Shildon v Blackpool (Wren) Rovers	2-0
	Willington v Whitby Town	1-5
3	Armthorpe Welfare v Brandon United	2-0
	Chester-le-Street Town v Billingham Town	0-1
	Darlington Cleveland Bridge v Consett	0-1
	Esh Winning v Alnwick Town	0-0
4	Crook Town v Norton & Stockton Ancients	0-3
	Horden CW v Darwen	1-1
	Northallerton Town v Langley Park	6-1
	Ossett Town v Dunston Federation Brewery	1-2
	South Bank v Bedlington Terriers	5-0
5	Eccleshill United v Harworth Colliery Institute	3-2
	St Helens Town v Tow Law Town	3-2
	Stockton (2) v Washington	3-1
	Yorkshire Amateur v Seaham Red Star	1-3
6	Ashton United v Garforth Town	1-2
	Chadderton v Lancaster City	2-1
	Formby v Bootle	1-2
	Salford City v North Ferriby United	0-1
7	Great Harwood Town v Prescot AFC	2-1
	Irlam Town v Atherton LR	1-2
	Rossendale United v Sheffield	2-2
	Thackley v Radcliffe Borough	2-1
8	Burscough v Bradford Park Avenue	1-1
	Harrogate Town v Louth United	4-3
	Mickleover RBL v Belper Town	0-2
	Warrington Town v Skelmersdale United	6-1
9	Arnold Town v Liversedge	4-0 N
	Clitheroe v Immingham Town	2-1
	Flixton v Worksop Town	1-1
	Hucknall Town v Grantham Town	2-1
10	Congleton Town v Eastwood Town	2-0
	Denaby United v Heanor Town	2-5
	Ilkeston Town (2) v Harrogate Railway Athletic	7-0
	Nantwich Town v Maltby MW	1-1
11	Alfreton Town v Oakham United	2-1
	Bedworth United v Walsall Wood	1-0
	Halesowen Harriers v Wednesfield	2-2
	Lye Town v Barwell	1-1 N
	West Midlands Police v Bridgnorth Town	5-2
12	Bilston Town v Newcastle Town	1-3
	Gresley Rovers v Highgate United	4-2
	Hinckley Town v Willenhall Town	1-1
	Pelsall Villa v Oldbury United	0-0
13	Leicester United v Dudley Town	3-0
	Nuneaton Borough v Boldmere St Michaels	2-1
	Raunds Town v Rocester	2-2
	Stratford Town v Hinckley Athletic	6-2
14	Northampton Spencer v Rushall Olympic	1-1
	Sandwell Borough v Malvern Town	4-0
	Stewarts & Lloyds (2) v Evesham United	4-2
	Sutton Coldfield Town v West Bromwich Town	0-0
15	Boston v Banbury United	4-1
	Histon v Long Buckby	1-2
	Rushden & Diamonds v Desborough Town	2-0
	Stourport Swifts v Stourbridge	0-5
16	Bourne Town v Peterborough City	3-2
	Eynesbury Rovers v Milton Keynes Borough	4-5
	Hitchin Town v Chatteris Town	3-1
	Wisbech Town v Wellingborough Town	10-0
17	Chalfont St Peter v Hoddesdon Town	1-0
	Cheshunt v Spalding United	0-0
	Letchworth Garden City v Haverhill Rovers	1-1
	March Town United v Braintree Town	1-3
18	Brook House v Aveley	1-1
	Harwich & Parkeston v Leighton Town	3-3
	Purfleet v Great Yarmouth Town	4-1
	Rainham Town v Mirrlees Blackstone	2-0 N
	Watton United v Burnham Ramblers	1-0
19	Biggleswade Town v Barking	1-3 N
	Gorleston v Clapton	5-2
	Haringey Borough v Bury Town	5-2
	Leyton v Felixstowe Town	5-4
	Norwich United v Edgware Town	1-0
20	Halstead Town v Waltham Abbey	1-1
	Newmarket Town v Langford	4-0
	Royston Town v Potton United	1-2
	Sudbury Town v Saffron Walden Town	6-1
	Tilbury v Collier Row	3-2
21	Flackwell Heath v Walthamstow Pennant	2-0
	Ware v Stowmarket Town	1-2
	Wealdstone v Tiptree United	2-1
	Witham Town v Wingate & Finchley	4-3
22	Basildon United v Tring Town	1-0
	Brightlingsea United v Fisher Athletic	1-2
	Rayners Lane v Ashford Town (Middlesex)	2-2
	Ruislip Manor v Hornchurch	1-0
	Uxbridge v Southall	4-2
23	Burnham v Canvey Island	1-0 N
	Harefield United v Barkingside	0-1
	Viking Sports v Bishop's Stortford	0-1
	Wembley v Welwyn Garden City	5-0
24	Beckenham Town v Feltham & Hounslow Boro.	2-0
	East Thurrock United v Chipstead	1-0
	Kingsbury Town v Oakwood	4-3
	Molesey v Northwood	3-1
	Redhill v Boreham Wood	1-5
25	Haywards Heath Town v Bedfont	0-1
	Lewes v Leatherhead	1-0
	Metropolitan Police v Ford United	0-0
	Three Bridges v Alma Swanley	0-3
26	Deal Town v Epsom & Ewell	3-0
	Merstham v Malden Vale	0-0
	Portfield v Faversham Town	2-4
	Whyteleafe v Pagham	5-1
	Wick v Ashford Town	1-1
27	Banstead Athletic v Eastbourne United	2-1
	Croydon Athletic v Arundel	7-3
	Dorking (2) v Hythe Town	wo/s
	Herne Bay v Camberley Town	3-3
	Walton & Hersham v Peacehaven & Telscombe	2-1
28	Canterbury City v Bracknell Town	4-1
	Egham Town v Selsey	2-1
	Hailsham Town v Steyning Town	3-1
	Sheppey United v Croydon	0-1
	Worthing v Chatham Town	8-0
29	Corinthian v Cove	1-0
	Lancing v Littlehampton Town	2-3
	Tunbridge Wells v Margate	0-4
	Worthing United v Langney Sports	1-4
30	AFC Totton v Havant Town	0-1
	Horsham YMCA v Eastbourne Town	4-3
	Whitehawk v Chichester City (1)	5-2ev
	Whitstable Town v Sittingbourne	1-2
31	Andover v Ringmer	5-0
	Poole Town v Abingdon United	0-1
	Ryde Sports v Southwick	1-2
	Sholing Sports v Bemerton Heath Harlequins	1-2
	Shoreham v Witney Town	0-3
32	Eastleigh v Newport (IOW)	1-2
	Fleet Town v Abingdon Town	1-2
	Oxford City v Devizes Town	2-3
	Wimborne Town v Bournemouth (Ams)	1-1
33	Gosport Borough v Calne Town	0-4
	Petersfield United v Chippenham Town	0-1
	Shortwood United v Brockenhurst	0-4
	Welton Rovers v Hungerford Town	4-1
	Westbury United v Thatcham Town	0-5
34	Cinderford Town v Newbury Town	3-0
	Melksham Town v Swanage Town & Herston	1-5
	Minehead v AFC Lymington	2-2
	Paulton Rovers v Bristol Manor Farm	0-2
35	Clevedon Town v Yate Town	4-1
	Dawlish Town v Newport AFC	0-3
	Forest Green Rovers v Barnstaple Town	4-2
	Taunton Town v Barri	0-3
36	Exmouth Town v Elmore	1-2
	Ilfracombe Town v Truro City	3-4
	St Blazey v Falmouth Town	1-4
	Torrington v Bideford	1-0
1r	Annfield Plain v Hebburn	5-1
r	Whickham v Newcastle Blue Star	0-2
3r	Alnwick Town v Esh Winning	2-1
4r	Darwen v Horden CW	5-0
7r	Rossendale United v Sheffield	1-2e
8r	Burscough v Bradford Park Avenue	1-2e
9r	Worksop Town v Flixton	3-0
10r	Maltby MW v Nantwich Town	2-3e
11r	Barwell v Lye Town	1-3
r	Wednesfield v Halesowen Harriers	2-3
12r	Oldbury United v Pelsall Villa	4-4
r	Willenhall Town v Hinckley Town	2-1
13r	Rocester v Raunds Town	3-4
14r	Rushall Olympic v Northampton Spencer	3-2e
r	West Bromwich Town v Sutton Coldfield Town	0-2
17r	Haverhill Rovers v Letchworth Garden City	3-4e
r	Spalding United v Cheshunt	0-5
18r	Aveley v Brook House	1-0
r	Leighton Town v Harwich & Parkeston	2-0
20r	Halstead Town v Waltham Abbey	3-4
22r	Ashford Town (Middlesex) v Rayners Lane	0-1
25r	Ford United v Metropolitan Police	0-2
26r	Ashford Town v Wick	3-1
r	Malden Vale v Merstham	3-1
27r	Camberley Town v Herne Bay	2-3e
30r	Chichester City (1) v Whitehawk	1-3
32r	Bournemouth (Ams) v Wimborne Town	1-3
34r	AFC Lymington v Minehead	2-1
12r2	Pelsall Villa v Oldbury United	1-0e

Qualifying Round One

1	Annfield Plain v Newcastle Blue Star	0-1
	Durham City v Bishop Auckland	1-1
	Easington Colliery v Workington	1-1
	Penrith v Blyth Spartans	1-2
2	Bamber Bridge v Peterlee Newtown	1-1
	Gateshead (2) v Billingham Synthonia	3-1
	Shildon v Whitby Town	0-2
	Spennymoor United v Gretna	4-0
3	Alnwick Town v Consett	0-0
	Armthorpe Welfare v Billingham Town	2-2
	Murton v Guisborough Town	1-2
	Ossett Albion v Netherfield (Kendal)	1-3
4	Darwen v Northallerton Town	1-6
	Dunston Federation Brewery v Norton & Stockton Ancie	7-0
	Fleetwood Town v Guiseley	3-2
	South Bank v North Shields	wo/s
5	Chorley v Knowsley United	1-1
	Maine Road v Morecambe	2-1
	Seaham Red Star v Eccleshill United	3-2
	St Helens Town v Stockton (2)	3-4
6	Brigg Town v Bridlington Town	2-1
	Chadderton v Bootle	3-0
	North Ferriby United v Garforth Town	1-0
	Southport v Buxton	0-0
7	Altrincham v Curzon Ashton	3-0
	Atherton LR v Great Harwood Town	1-1
	Caernarfon Town v Colwyn Bay	1-4
	Thackley v Sheffield	1-3
8	Bradford Park Avenue v Belper Town	2-0
	Harrogate Town v Warrington Town	1-2
	Hyde United v Accrington Stanley (2)	1-5
	Stocksbridge Park Steels v Stalybridge Celtic	0-4
9	Clitheroe v Hucknall Town	1-3
	Glossop North End v Macclesfield Town	0-1
	Goole Town v Horwich RMI	0-1
	Worksop Town v Arnold Town	5-3
10	Blakenall v Droylsden	4-3
	Congleton Town v Nantwich Town	0-0
	Heanor Town v Ilkeston Town (2)	2-1
	Marine v Emley	5-0
11	Alfreton Town v Stafford Rangers	0-0
	Frickley Athletic v Lincoln United	0-0
	Halesowen Harriers v Lye Town	2-1
	West Midlands Police v Bedworth United	1-2
12	Mossley v Borrowash Victoria	0-0
	Newcastle Town v Gresley Rovers	0-1
	Paget Rangers v Gainsborough Trinity	1-3
	Pelsall Villa v Willenhall Town	1-0
13	Northwich Victoria v Winsford United	4-1
	Nuneaton Borough v Leicester United	3-1
	Raunds Town v Stratford Town	0-0
	Rothwell Town v Matlock Town	0-2
14	Leek Town v Burton Albion	3-2
	Racing Club Warwick v Eastwood Hanley	0-2
	Rushall Olympic v Sandwell Borough	3-0
	Stewarts & Lloyds (2) v Sutton Coldfield Town	1-3
15	Arlesey Town v Shepshed Albion	0-1
	Boston v Stourbridge	3-4
	Hednesford Town v Tamworth	1-1
	Long Buckby v Rushden & Diamonds	0-1
16	Barton Rovers v Moor Green	2-3
	Bourne Town v Milton Keynes Borough	3-2
	Hitchin Town v Wisbech Town	4-2
	V.S. Rugby v Alvechurch	wo/s
17	Chasetown v Redditch United	1-0
	Cheshunt v Chalfont St Peter	1-0
	Hemel Hempstead Town v Solihull Borough	1-2
	Letchworth Garden City v Braintree Town	0-4
18	Boston United v King's Lynn	2-1
	Leighton Town v Aveley	2-4
	Purfleet v Watton United	6-1
	Rainham Town v Corby Town	0-1
19	Haringey Borough v Gorleston	0-0
	Heybridge Swifts v Cambridge City	2-4
	Leyton v Lowestoft Town	4-2
	Norwich United v Barking	2-1
20	Baldock Town v Waltham Abbey	3-2
	Chelmsford City v Grays Athletic	0-0
	Sudbury Town v Potton United	3-2
	Tilbury v Newmarket Town	1-1
21	Dagenham & Redbridge v Billericay Town	1-1
	Flackwell Heath v Stowmarket Town	0-5
	Kempston Rovers v Wivenhoe Town	3-4
	Wealdstone v Witham Town	2-1
22	Rayners Lane v Uxbridge	1-1
	Ruislip Manor v Basildon United	3-1
	St Albans City v Brimsdown Rovers	3-1
	Stevenage Borough v Fisher Athletic	7-1
23	Barkingside v Wembley	1-3
	Burnham v Bishop's Stortford	3-2 N
	Hertford Town v Hendon	0-2
	Slade Green v Harlow Town	wo/s
24	Boreham Wood v Chesham United	2-2
	Harrow Borough v Berkhamsted Town	0-2
	Kingsbury Town v Beckenham Town	2-3
	Molesey v East Thurrock United	4-2
25	Alma Swanley v Bedfont	1-0
	Corinthian Casuals v Slough Town	1-1
	Metropolitan Police v Lewes	2-1
	Staines Town v Yeading	0-3
26	Ashford Town v Faversham Town	1-1
	Deal Town v Malden Vale	4-0
	Horsham v Dartford	wo/s
	Whyteleafe v Windsor & Eton	1-3
27	Banstead Athletic v Herne Bay	4-1
	Croydon Athletic v Dorking (2)	1-2
	Tonbridge v Dover Athletic	0-0
	Walton & Hersham v Wokingham Town	2-0
28	Burgess Hill Town v Hastings Town	0-2
	Croydon v Canterbury City	0-0
	Egham Town v Worthing	1-1
	Hailsham Town v Bromley	2-3
29	Chertsey Town v Gravesend & Northfleet	3-2
	Kingstonian v Dulwich Hamlet	4-0
	Langney Sports v Littlehampton Town	3-1
	Margate v Corinthian	0-0
30	Carshalton Athletic v Erith & Belvedere	1-2
	Fareham Town v Tooting & Mitcham United	2-0
	Havant Town v Horsham YMCA	2-1
	Whitehawk v Sittingbourne	0-1

1992/93

31	Abingdon United v Bemerton Heath Harlequins	0-5
	Andover v Hampton	0-6
	Bognor Regis Town v Romsey Town	9-2
	Southwick v Witney Town	2-5
32	Abingdon Town v Devizes Town	4-0
	Buckingham Town v Maidenhead United	1-1
	Newport (IOW) v Wimborne Town	2-3
	Thame United v Bashley	2-3
33	Brockenhurst v Basingstoke Town	1-0
	Chippenham Town v Thatcham Town	1-2
	Salisbury (2) v Trowbridge Town	6-2
	Welton Rovers v Calne Town	1-4
34	AFC Lymington v Bristol Manor Farm	3-3
	Mangotsfield United v Dorchester Town	0-1
	Swanage Town & Herston v Cinderford Town	1-2
	Waterlooville v Cheltenham Town	0-0
35	Barri v Clevedon Town	1-3
	Forest Green Rovers v Newport AFC	1-2
	Frome Town v Worcester City	1-2
	Gloucester City v Weston-Super-Mare	2-3
36	Falmouth Town v Elmore	2-0
	Glastonbury v Bath City	0-4
	Truro City v Torrington	2-0
	Weymouth v Saltash United	1-0
1r	Bishop Auckland v Durham City	5-2
r	Workington v Easington Colliery	1-0
2r	Peterlee Newtown v Bamber Bridge	0-2
3r	Billingham Town v Armthorpe Welfare	2-0
r	Consett v Alnwick Town	2-0
5r	Knowsley United v Chorley	2-1
6r	Buxton v Southport	1-2
7r	Great Harwood Town v Atherton LR	1-2
10r	Nantwich Town v Congleton Town	2-1
11r	Lincoln United v Frickley Athletic	0-1
r	Stafford Rangers v Alfreton Town	3-0
12r	Borrowash Victoria v Mossley	0-1
13r	Stratford Town v Raunds Town	1-2
15r	Tamworth v Hednesford Town	2-4
19r	Gorleston v Haringey Borough	1-0
20r	Grays Athletic v Chelmsford City	2-1
r	Newmarket Town v Tilbury	1-0
21r	Billericay Town v Dagenham & Redbridge	1-4
22r	Uxbridge v Rayners Lane	0-1
24r	Chesham United v Boreham Wood	9-1
25r	Slough Town v Corinthian Casuals	4-3
26r	Faversham Town v Ashford Town	0-2
27r	Dover Athletic v Tonbridge	2-1e
28r	Canterbury City v Croydon	2-1
r	Worthing v Egham Town	7-1
29r	Corinthian v Margate	1-1
32r	Maidenhead United v Buckingham Town	2-1e
34r	Bristol Manor Farm v AFC Lymington	0-2 N
r	Cheltenham Town v Waterlooville	2-0
29r2	Corinthian v Margate	0-4 N

Qualifying Round Two

1	Blyth Spartans v Workington	6-0
	Newcastle Blue Star v Bishop Auckland	0-1
2	Bamber Bridge v Spennymoor United	0-4
	Gateshead (2) v Whitby Town	5-2
3	Consett v Netherfield (Kendal)	3-4
	Guisborough Town v Billingham Town	3-0
4	Dunston Federation Brewery v South Bank	2-0
	Fleetwood Town v Northallerton Town	1-2
5	Knowsley United v Stockton (2)	0-2
	Seaham Red Star v Maine Road	1-1
6	North Ferriby United v Brigg Town	0-2
	Southport v Chadderton	2-0
7	Altrincham v Sheffield	3-1
	Atherton LR v Colwyn Bay	1-2
8	Accrington Stanley (2) v Bradford Park Avenue	2-0
	Warrington Town v Stalybridge Celtic	0-3
9	Horwich RMI v Worksop Town	1-1
	Hucknall Town v Macclesfield Town	1-1
10	Marine v Heanor Town	2-0
	Nantwich Town v Blakenall	1-0
11	Bedworth United v Stafford Rangers	1-1
	Frickley Athletic v Halesowen Harriers	8-2
12	Gresley Rovers v Gainsborough Trinity	1-4
	Mossley v Pelsall Villa	1-2
13	Northwich Victoria v Raunds Town	0-2
	Nuneaton Borough v Matlock Town	2-1
14	Leek Town v Rushall Olympic	0-1
	Sutton Coldfield Town v Eastwood Hanley	2-1
15	Hednesford Town v Rushden & Diamonds	4-1
	Stourbridge v Shepshed Albion	0-0
16	Bourne Town v Moor Green	4-8
	V.S. Rugby v Hitchin Town	3-0
17	Chasetown v Braintree Town	0-2
	Cheshunt v Solihull Borough	0-0
18	Boston United v Aveley	1-2
	Purfleet v Corby Town	2-2
19	Cambridge City v Norwich United	6-1
	Gorleston v Leyton	1-2
20	Grays Athletic v Sudbury Town	1-0
	Newmarket Town v Baldock Town	2-2
21	Dagenham & Redbridge v Stowmarket Town	6-1
	Wealdstone v Wivenhoe Town	1-1
22	Ruislip Manor v Stevenage Borough	1-3
	St Albans City v Rayners Lane	5-1
23	Hendon v Burnham	6-0
	Wembley v Slade Green	3-2
24	Berkhamsted Town v Beckenham Town	0-0
	Molesey v Chesham United	0-4
25	Metropolitan Police v Slough Town	0-1
	Yeading v Alma Swanley	7-1
26	Ashford Town v Windsor & Eton	2-2
	Horsham v Deal Town	1-6
27	Dorking (2) v Walton & Hersham	4-2
	Dover Athletic v Banstead Athletic	0-0
28	Hastings Town v Canterbury City	1-2
	Worthing v Bromley	2-1
29	Kingstonian v Langney Sports	2-2
	Margate v Chertsey Town	1-4
30	Erith & Belvedere v Havant Town	1-1
	Sittingbourne v Fareham Town	3-2
31	Bognor Regis Town v Bemerton Heath Harlequins	1-1
	Witney Town v Hampton	3-1
32	Abingdon Town v Maidenhead United	2-0
	Bashley v Wimborne Town	3-1
33	Calne Town v Brockenhurst	0-1
	Salisbury (2) v Thatcham Town	4-0
34	AFC Lymington v Dorchester Town	1-1
	Cheltenham Town v Cinderford Town	3-0
35	Newport AFC v Worcester City	3-0
	Weston-Super-Mare v Clevedon Town	0-4
36	Falmouth Town v Bath City	0-3
	Weymouth v Truro City	3-2
5r	Maine Road v Seaham Red Star	1-1e
9r	Macclesfield Town v Hucknall Town	3-1
r	Worksop Town v Horwich RMI	1-5
11r	Stafford Rangers v Bedworth United	1-0
15r	Shepshed Albion v Stourbridge	4-2
17r	Solihull Borough v Cheshunt	4-0
18r	Corby Town v Purfleet	1-0
20r	Baldock Town v Newmarket Town	2-6
21r	Wivenhoe Town v Wealdstone	0-2
24r	Beckenham Town v Berkhamsted Town	0-1
26r	Windsor & Eton v Ashford Town	2-3
27r	Banstead Athletic v Dover Athletic	1-2
29r	Langney Sports v Kingstonian	1-1e
30r	Havant Town v Erith & Belvedere	5-4
31r	Bemerton Heath Harlequins v Bognor Regis Town	2-2e
34r	Dorchester Town v AFC Lymington	2-4
5r2	Maine Road v Seaham Red Star	0-5
29r2	Kingstonian v Langney Sports	3-1e
31r2	Bognor Regis Town v Bemerton Heath Harlequins	1-1e
31r3	Bemerton Heath Harlequins v Bognor Regis Town	1-0

Qualifying Round Three

1	Bishop Auckland v Blyth Spartans	1-3
2	Spennymoor United v Gateshead (2)	0-7
3	Netherfield (Kendal) v Guisborough Town	4-1
4	Dunston Federation Brewery v Northallerton Town	0-3
5	Seaham Red Star v Stockton (2)	1-2
6	Brigg Town v Southport	0-1
7	Colwyn Bay v Altrincham	3-3
8	Stalybridge Celtic v Accrington Stanley (2)	1-2
9	Macclesfield Town v Horwich RMI	1-0
10	Nantwich Town v Marine	0-1
11	Stafford Rangers v Frickley Athletic	3-0
12	Gainsborough Trinity v Pelsall Villa	4-2
13	Nuneaton Borough v Raunds Town	4-0
14	Sutton Coldfield Town v Rushall Olympic	0-0
15	Shepshed Albion v Hednesford Town	1-2
16	Moor Green v V.S. Rugby	1-2
17	Solihull Borough v Braintree Town	4-1
18	Corby Town v Aveley	1-2
19	Leyton v Cambridge City	3-0
20	Newmarket Town v Grays Athletic	1-0
21	Wealdstone v Dagenham & Redbridge	1-6
22	Stevenage Borough v St Albans City	3-3
23	Wembley v Hendon	1-0
24	Chesham United v Berkhamsted Town	3-0
25	Slough Town v Yeading	2-1
26	Ashford Town v Deal Town	3-1
27	Dorking (2) v Dover Athletic	1-0
28	Worthing v Canterbury City	3-1
29	Chertsey Town v Kingstonian	1-3
30	Sittingbourne v Havant Town	3-2
31	Witney Town v Bemerton Heath Harlequins	1-0
32	Abingdon Town v Bashley	4-2
33	Brockenhurst v Salisbury (2)	1-3
34	AFC Lymington v Cheltenham Town	0-1
35	Newport AFC v Clevedon Town	1-1
36	Bath City v Weymouth	2-0
7r	Altrincham v Colwyn Bay	1-1e
14r	Rushall Olympic v Sutton Coldfield Town	1-1e
22r	St Albans City v Stevenage Borough	2-1
35r	Clevedon Town v Newport AFC	1-1e
7r2	Altrincham v Colwyn Bay	3-1
14r2	Rushall Olympic v Sutton Coldfield Town	1-2
35r2	Newport AFC v Clevedon Town	4-2

Qualifying Round Four

	Abingdon Town v Merthyr Tydfil	0-0
	Accrington Stanley (2) v Northallerton Town	3-1
	Ashford Town v Slough Town	1-2
	Barrow v Southport	0-0
	Blyth Spartans v Stockton (2)	1-1
	Cheltenham Town v Worthing	3-2
	Crawley Town v Yeovil Town	1-2
	Enfield v Aylesbury United	0-0
	Farnborough Town v Dorking (2)	1-1
	Gainsborough Trinity v Altrincham	0-2
	Gateshead (2) v Whitley Bay	3-0
	Halesowen Town v V.S. Rugby	1-2
	Hednesford Town v Dagenham & Redbridge	1-3
	Kettering Town v Corby Town	2-1
	Kidderminster Harriers v Atherstone United	2-0
	Kingstonian v Welling United	2-1
	Netherfield (Kendal) v Macclesfield Town	1-1
	Newmarket Town v Hayes	0-2
	Newport AFC v Sutton United	1-4
	Runcorn v Marine	1-4
	Sittingbourne v Marlow	1-1
	Solihull Borough v Chesham United	3-1
	Stafford Rangers v Bromsgrove Rovers	3-0
	Sutton Coldfield Town v Leyton	6-1
	Telford United v St Albans City	1-2
	Tiverton Town v Bath City	0-0
	Wembley v Nuneaton Borough	1-1
	Witney Town v Salisbury (2)	1-2
r	Aylesbury United v Enfield	2-1
r	Bath City v Tiverton Town	2-1
r	Dorking (2) v Farnborough Town	2-0
r	Macclesfield Town v Netherfield (Kendal)	5-0
r	Marlow v Sittingbourne	2-1
r	Merthyr Tydfil v Abingdon Town	2-1
r	Nuneaton Borough v Wembley	0-0e
r	Southport v Barrow	3-2e
r	Stockton (2) v Blyth Spartans	1-2
r2	Wembley v Nuneaton Borough	1-2

Round One

	Accrington Stanley (2) v Gateshead (2)	3-2
	Blackpool v Rochdale	1-1
	Blyth Spartans v Southport	1-2
	Bolton Wanderers v Sutton Coldfield Town	2-1
	Bournemouth v Barnet	0-0
	Bradford City v Preston North End	1-1
	Brighton & Hove Albion v Hayes	2-0
	Burnley v Scarborough	2-1
	Bury v Witton Albion	2-0
	Cardiff City v Bath City	2-3
	Chester City v Altrincham	1-1
	Colchester United v Slough Town	4-0
	Crewe Alexandra v Wrexham	6-1
	Dagenham & Redbridge v Leyton Orient	4-5
	Darlington v Hull City	1-2
	Doncaster Rovers v Hartlepool United	1-2
	Dorking (2) v Plymouth Argyle	2-3
	Exeter City v Kidderminster Harriers	1-0
	Gillingham v Kettering Town	3-2
	Kingstonian v Peterborough United	1-1
	Lincoln City v Stafford Rangers	0-0
	Macclesfield Town v Chesterfield	0-0
	Marine v Halifax Town	4-1
	Marlow v Salisbury (2)	3-3
	Northampton Town v Fulham	3-1
	Reading v Birmingham City	1-0
	Rotherham United v Walsall	4-0
	Scunthorpe United v Huddersfield Town	0-0
	Shrewsbury Town v Mansfield Town	3-1
	Solihull Borough v V.S. Rugby	2-2
	St Albans City v Cheltenham Town	1-2
	Stoke City v Port Vale	0-0
	Sutton United v Hereford United	1-2
	Swansea City v Maidstone United	wo/s
	Torquay United v Yeovil Town	2-5
	West Bromwich Albion v Aylesbury United	8-0
	Wigan Athletic v Carlisle United	3-1
	Woking v Nuneaton Borough	3-2
	Wycombe Wanderers v Merthyr Tydfil	3-1
	York City v Stockport County	1-3
r	Altrincham v Chester City	2-0
r	Barnet v Bournemouth	1-2
r	Chesterfield v Macclesfield Town	2-2q
r	Huddersfield Town v Scunthorpe United	2-1e
r	Peterborough United v Kingstonian	9-1 v
r	Port Vale v Stoke City	3-1
r	Preston North End v Bradford City	4-5
r	Rochdale v Blackpool	1-0e
r	Salisbury (2) v Marlow	2-2q
r	Stafford Rangers v Lincoln City	2-1
r	V.S. Rugby v Solihull Borough	2-1e
r2	Peterborough United v Kingstonian	1-0

Round Two

	Accrington Stanley (2) v Crewe Alexandra	1-6 N
	Altrincham v Port Vale	1-4
	Bath City v Northampton Town	2-2
	Bolton Wanderers v Rochdale	4-0
	Bradford City v Huddersfield Town	0-2
	Brighton & Hove Albion v Woking	1-1
	Burnley v Shrewsbury Town	1-1
	Cheltenham Town v Bournemouth	1-1
	Exeter City v Swansea City	2-5
	Gillingham v Colchester United	1-1
	Hartlepool United v Southport	4-0
	Macclesfield Town v Stockport County	0-2
	Marine v Stafford Rangers	3-2
	Plymouth Argyle v Peterborough United	3-2
	Reading v Leyton Orient	3-0
	Rotherham United v Hull City	1-0
	V.S. Rugby v Marlow	0-0
	Wigan Athletic v Bury	1-1
	Wycombe Wanderers v West Bromwich Albion	2-2
	Yeovil Town v Hereford United	0-0
r	Bournemouth v Cheltenham Town	3-0

1992/93 to 1993/94

r Bury v Wigan Athletic	1-0
r Colchester United v Gillingham	2-3
r Hereford United v Yeovil Town	1-2
r Marlow v V.S. Rugby	2-0
r Northampton Town v Bath City	3-0
r Shrewsbury Town v Burnley	1-2
r West Bromwich Albion v Wycombe Wanderers	1-0
r Woking v Brighton & Hove Albion	1-2

Round Three

Aston Villa v Bristol Rovers	1-1
Blackburn Rovers v Bournemouth	3-1
Bolton Wanderers v Liverpool	2-2
Brentford v Grimsby Town	0-2
Brighton & Hove Albion v Portsmouth	1-0
Cambridge United v Sheffield Wednesday	1-2
Crewe Alexandra v Marine	3-1
Derby County v Stockport County	2-1
Gillingham v Huddersfield Town	0-0
Hartlepool United v Crystal Palace	1-0
Ipswich Town v Plymouth Argyle	3-1
Leeds United v Charlton Athletic	1-1
Leicester City v Barnsley	2-2
Luton Town v Bristol City	2-0
Manchester City v Reading	1-1
Manchester United v Bury	2-0
Middlesbrough v Chelsea	2-1
Newcastle United v Port Vale	4-0
Northampton Town v Rotherham United	0-1
Norwich City v Coventry City	1-0
Nottingham Forest v Southampton	2-1
Notts County v Sunderland	0-2
Oldham Athletic v Tranmere Rovers	2-2
Queen's Park Rangers v Swindon Town	3-0
Sheffield United v Burnley	2-2
Southend United v Millwall	1-0
Swansea City v Oxford United	1-1
Tottenham Hotspur v Marlow	5-1
Watford v Wolverhampton Wan.	1-4
West Bromwich Albion v West Ham United	0-2
Wimbledon v Everton	0-0
Yeovil Town v Arsenal	1-3
r Barnsley v Leicester City	1-1P
r Bristol Rovers v Aston Villa	0-3
r Burnley v Sheffield United	2-4
r Charlton Athletic v Leeds United	1-3
r Everton v Wimbledon	1-2
r Huddersfield Town v Gillingham	2-1
r Liverpool v Bolton Wanderers	0-2
r Oxford United v Swansea City	2-2q
r Reading v Manchester City	0-4
r Tranmere Rovers v Oldham Athletic	3-0

Round Four

Arsenal v Leeds United	2-2
Aston Villa v Wimbledon	1-1
Barnsley v West Ham United	4-1
Crewe Alexandra v Blackburn Rovers	0-3
Huddersfield Town v Southend United	1-2
Luton Town v Derby County	1-5
Manchester United v Brighton & Hove Albion	1-0
Norwich City v Tottenham Hotspur	0-2
Nottingham Forest v Middlesbrough	1-1
Queen's Park Rangers v Manchester City	1-2
Rotherham United v Newcastle United	1-1
Sheffield United v Hartlepool United	1-0
Sheffield Wednesday v Sunderland	1-0
Swansea City v Grimsby Town	0-0
Tranmere Rovers v Ipswich Town	1-2
Wolverhampton Wan. v Bolton Wanderers	0-2
r Grimsby Town v Swansea City	2-0
r Leeds United v Arsenal	2-3e
r Middlesbrough v Nottingham Forest	0-3
r Newcastle United v Rotherham United	2-0
r Wimbledon v Aston Villa	0-0P

Round Five

Arsenal v Nottingham Forest	2-0
Blackburn Rovers v Newcastle United	1-0
Derby County v Bolton Wanderers	3-1
Ipswich Town v Grimsby Town	4-0
Manchester City v Barnsley	2-0
Sheffield United v Manchester United	2-1
Sheffield Wednesday v Southend United	2-0
Tottenham Hotspur v Wimbledon	3-2

Round Six

Blackburn Rovers v Sheffield United	0-0
Derby County v Sheffield Wednesday	3-3
Ipswich Town v Arsenal	2-4
Manchester City v Tottenham Hotspur	2-4
r Sheffield United v Blackburn Rovers	2-2P
r Sheffield Wednesday v Derby County	1-0

Semi Finals

Arsenal v Tottenham Hotspur	1-0 N
Sheffield Wednesday v Sheffield United	2-1eN

Final

Arsenal v Sheffield Wednesday	1-1eN
r Arsenal v Sheffield Wednesday	2-1eN

1993/94

Preliminary Round

1 Billingham Synthonia v Darlington Cleveland Social	3-0
Billingham Town v Alnwick Town	1-1
Consett v Willington	5-2
Yorkshire Amateur v Brandon United	2-1
2 Esh Winning v Gretna	0-1
Evenwood Town v Ferryhill Athletic	3-1
Harrogate Town v Peterlee Newtown	5-2
Horden CW v Hebburn	4-4
3 Pickering Town v Penrith	5-2
Ryhope Community Association v Prudhoe East End	0-3
Shildon v South Shields (3)	wo/s
4 Lancaster City v Whickham	3-1
Murton v Durham City	3-2
Tow Law Town v West Auckland Town	1-0
Workington v Crook Town	0-2
5 Alfreton Town v Armthorpe Welfare	3-2
Atherton LR v Blackpool (Wren) Rovers	1-1
Belper Town v Bamber Bridge	1-2
Blidworth MW v Arnold Town	1-4
6 Caernarfon Town v Burscough	0-0
Clitheroe v Congleton Town	1-0
Warrington Town v Bradford Park Avenue	5-0
7 Eccleshill United v Denaby United	2-2
Flixton v Farsley Celtic	2-0
Glasshoughton Welfare v Glossop North End	0-2
8 Great Harwood Town v Guiseley	1-5
Hucknall Town v Chadderton	4-0
Immingham Town v Ilkeston Town (2)	1-3
Ossett Town v Harworth Colliery Institute	5-3
9 Lincoln United v Mossley	4-2
Maine Road v Maltby MW	0-1
Newcastle Town v Ossett Albion	1-1
Oldham Town v North Ferriby United	1-3
10 Radcliffe Borough v Salford City	1-3
Rossendale United v Rossington Main	3-0
Skelmersdale United v Thackley	0-1
Stocksbridge Park Steels v St Helens Town	1-2
11 Wednesfield v Eastwood Town	1-0
West Bromwich Town v Willenhall Town	1-3 N
Winterton Rangers v Prescot AFC	2-0
12 Armitage '90 v Banbury United	1-0
Bilston Town v Bridgnorth Town	0-2
Boldmere St Michaels v Blakenall	2-0
Chasetown v Barwell	2-1
13 Desborough Town v Evesham United	1-0
Dudley Town v Eastwood Hanley	2-1
Halesowen Harriers v Leicester United	2-4
Hinckley Town v Hinckley Athletic	2-1
14 Daventry Town v Oldbury United	0-3
Long Buckby v Redditch United	2-2
Lye Town v Northampton Spencer	1-2
Racing Club Warwick v Pershore Town	1-2
15 Rocester v Rushden & Diamonds	0-1
Rothwell Town v Rushall Olympic	2-0
Stewarts & Lloyds (2) v Stratford Town	1-3
Stourport Swifts v Stourbridge	0-0
16 Billericay Town v Bourne Town	5-2
Bishop's Stortford v Boston	4-0
Brightlingsea United v Canvey Island	1-3
Bury Town v Burnham Ramblers	1-2
17 Fakenham Town v Great Yarmouth Town	2-2
Felixstowe Town v Gorleston	1-1
Haverhill Rovers v Eynesbury Rovers	1-2
Histon v Heybridge Swifts	0-9
18 March Town United v Saffron Walden Town	3-2
Mirrlees Blackstone v King's Lynn	0-1
Stamford v Tiptree United	4-1
Sudbury Town v Stowmarket Town	4-1
19 Lowestoft Town v Tamworth	3-2
Watton Town v Barking	3-1 N
Wisbech Town v Brimsdown Rovers	3-1
20 Biggleswade Town v Barton Rovers	0-3 N
Brook House v Boreham Wood	2-1
Chatteris Town v Cornard United	2-3
21 Clapton v Cheshunt	1-1
Dunstable v Collier Row	2-2
Edgware Town v Feltham & Hounslow Boro.	3-0
22 Ford United v Haringey Borough	1-1
Hanwell Town v Harefield United	1-2
Hertford Town v Kempston Rovers	0-1
Hornchurch v Hoddesdon Town	1-1
23 Langford v Leighton Town	2-1
Northwood v Royston Town	3-0
Rainham Town v Purfleet	1-5
Ruislip Manor v Letchworth Garden City	4-3
24 Southall v Ware	1-0
Staines Town v Uxbridge	1-0
Tilbury v Tring Town	1-1
Walthamstow Pennant v Wingate & Finchley	2-3
25 Bedfont v Beckenham Town	wo/s
Bracknell Town v Bognor Regis Town	3-3
Burgess Hill Town v Arundel	3-0
26 Croydon v Corinthian Casuals	5-0
Eastbourne United v Egham Town	5-1
Horsham YMCA v Croydon Athletic	2-2
27 Erith & Belvedere v Godalming & Guildford	2-1
Faversham Town v Fisher '93	3-0 D
Hailsham Town v Epsom & Ewell	1-4
Horsham v Herne Bay	1-2
28 Langney Sports v Malden Vale	2-1
Lewes v Littlehampton Town	3-1
Merstham v Pagham	1-4
Oakwood v Metropolitan Police	1-1
29 Portfield v Steyning Town	1-0
Ramsgate v Selsey	1-1
Redhill v Ringmer	1-2
Southwick v Slade Green	2-1
30 Tonbridge v Whitehawk	4-1
Tooting & Mitcham United v Tunbridge Wells	7-0
Whyteleafe v Three Bridges	5-1
Windsor & Eton v Wick	1-4
31 Bournemouth (Ams) v Brockenhurst	0-1
Cove v Walton & Hersham	2-1
Fareham Town v Eastleigh	1-1
Shoreham v Buckingham Town	0-2
32 Gosport Borough v Hungerford Town	0-3
Newbury Town v Lancing	6-1
Oxford City v Newport (IOW)	0-7
Peacehaven & Telscombe v Fleet Town	2-1
33 AFC Totton v Ryde Sports	1-1e
Poole Town v Swanage Town & Herston	5-0
Thame United v Petersfield United	wo/s
Wimborne Town v Westbury United	5-0
34 Barnstaple Town v Exmouth Town	4-0
Bideford v Chippenham Town	2-2
Bridport v Bristol Manor Farm	4-0
Elmore v Devizes Town	2-1
35 Frome Town v Glastonbury	3-3
Melksham Town v Falmouth Town	1-0
Moreton Town v Minehead	2-0
Odd Down v Ilfracombe Town	1-1
36 Dawlish Town v Taunton Town	0-12
Shortwood United v St Blazey	3-2
Torrington v Yate Town	1-4
Weston-Super-Mare v Welton Rovers	6-1
1r Alnwick Town v Billingham Town	1-2
2r Hebburn v Horden CW	2-1
5r Blackpool (Wren) Rovers v Atherton LR	1-6
6r Burscough v Caernarfon Town	2-0
7r Denaby United v Eccleshill United	2-1
9r Ossett Albion v Newcastle Town	1-2
14r Redditch United v Long Buckby	3-1
15r Stourbridge v Stourport Swifts	1-2
17r Gorleston v Felixstowe Town	0-2 N
r Great Yarmouth Town v Fakenham Town	3-1
21r Cheshunt v Clapton	2-1
r Collier Row v Dunstable	0-1
22r Haringey Borough v Ford United	2-0
r Hoddesdon Town v Hornchurch	0-3 N
24r Tring Town v Tilbury	0-4
25r Bognor Regis Town v Bracknell Town	5-0
26r Croydon Athletic v Horsham YMCA	5-2
28r Metropolitan Police v Oakwood	3-1
29r Selsey v Ramsgate	3-3
31r Eastleigh v Fareham Town	4-1
33r Ryde Sports v AFC Totton	1-3
34r Chippenham Town v Bideford	3-0
35r Glastonbury v Frome Town	0-1e
r Ilfracombe Town v Odd Down	2-2e
29r2 Selsey v Ramsgate	0-1 d
35r2 Odd Down v Ilfracombe Town	1-0

Qualifying Round One

1 Billingham Town v Billingham Synthonia	0-3
Chester-le-Street Town v Consett	2-3
Gateshead (2) v Blyth Spartans	4-0
Yorkshire Amateur v Dunston Federation Brewery	1-3
2 Barrow v Guisborough Town	3-1
Evenwood Town v Hebburn	0-0
Gretna v Seaham Red Star	3-1
Harrogate Railway Athletic v Harrogate Town	1-2
3 Bishop Auckland v Netherfield (Kendal)	1-4
Newcastle Blue Star v Prudhoe East End	3-2
Pickering Town v Northallerton Town	0-2
Shildon v Easington Colliery	0-1
4 Lancaster City v Stockton (2)	2-1
Tow Law Town v Murton	3-3
Whitby Town v Crook Town	5-1
Whitley Bay v Spennymoor United	1-6
5 Alfreton Town v Bamber Bridge	2-3
Arnold Town v Leek Town	1-3
Ashton United v Atherton LR	4-0
Northwich Victoria v Emley	2-2
6 Bootle v Burscough	5-1
Clitheroe v Curzon Ashton	2-2
Stalybridge Celtic v Fleetwood Town	6-0
Warrington Town v Matlock Town	3-0
7 Bridlington Town v Frickley Athletic	2-0
Darwen v Flixton	1-1
Denaby United v Morecambe	0-4
Glossop North End v Goole Town	2-2
8 Buxton v Gainsborough Trinity	2-1
Guiseley v Ilkeston Town (2)	3-1
Heanor Town v Hucknall Town	1-2
Ossett Town v Winsford United	1-1

190

1993/94

9	Chorley v Horwich RMI	3-1
	Lincoln United v Nantwich Town	2-0
	Liversedge v Newcastle Town	3-2
	Maltby MW v North Ferriby United	1-1
10	Colwyn Bay v Hyde United	4-1
	Rossendale United v St Helens Town	1-1
	Salford City v Knowsley United	1-1
	Sheffield v Thackley	1-4
11	Droylsden v Brigg Town	1-1
	Willenhall Town v West Midlands Police	1-2
	Winterton Rangers v Nuneaton Borough	1-7
	Worksop Town v Wednesfield	1-1
12	Armitage '90 v Boldmere St Michaels	3-0
	Bedworth United v Bridgnorth Town	2-1
	Bromsgrove Rovers v Gresley Rovers	1-1
	Chasetown v Solihull Borough	0-1
13	Desborough Town v Raunds Town	1-3
	Dudley Town v Hinckley Town	1-1
	Grantham Town v Leicester United	3-1
	Telford United v Halesowen Town	4-0
14	Atherstone United v Hednesford Town	2-1
	Northampton Spencer v Pershore Town	0-1
	Oldbury United v Pelsall Villa	1-1
	Paget Rangers v Redditch United	1-1
15	Burton Albion v Moor Green	2-1
	Rothwell Town v Stourbridge	7-1
	Rushden & Diamonds v Sutton Coldfield Town	2-0
	Sandwell Borough v Stratford Town	5-0
16	Basildon United v Canvey Island	1-1
	Billericay Town v Aveley	1-1
	Bishop's Stortford v Burnham Ramblers	2-0
	Boston United v Braintree Town	1-1
17	Cambridge City v Berkhamsted Town	4-1
	Felixstowe Town v Heybridge Swifts	1-1
	Great Yarmouth Town v Hendon	2-2
	Harwich & Parkeston v Eynesbury Rovers	4-1
18	Chelmsford City v Newmarket Town	0-0
	King's Lynn v Sudbury Town	2-1
	March Town United v Wivenhoe Town	3-6
	Spalding United v Stamford	1-2
19	Corby Town v Watton United	4-0
	Lowestoft Town v Witham Town	1-0
	Stevenage Borough v Wembley	2-2
	Wisbech Town v East Thurrock United	1-1
20	Baldock Town v Brook House	6-0
	Barton Rovers v Arlesey Town	1-0
	Cornard United v Halstead Town	0-1
	Dagenham & Redbridge v Hitchin Town	1-0
21	Chalfont St Peter v Dunstable	1-0
	Chesham United v St Albans City	5-0
	Cheshunt v Burnham	0-2
	Edgware Town v Flackwell Heath	2-0
22	Enfield v Welling United	4-1
	Harefield United v Hornchurch	1-2
	Haringey Borough v Hampton	0-0
	Hemel Hempstead Town v Kempston Rovers	2-1
23	Grays Athletic v Yeading	0-2
	Kingsbury Town v Northwood	2-1
	Langford v Purfleet	1-4
	Ruislip Manor v Leyton	3-1
24	Harrow Borough v Wealdstone	3-1
	Staines Town v Chertsey Town	1-2
	Tilbury v Southall	3-2
	Viking Sports v Wingate & Finchley	3-0
25	Banstead Athletic v Bognor Regis Town	0-3
	Bedfont v Canterbury City	0-1
	Burgess Hill Town v Chatham Town	0-1
	Kingstonian v Ashford Town	2-1
26	Corinthian v Croydon Athletic	3-0
	Croydon v Chipstead	4-1
	Eastbourne United v Greenwich Borough	0-2
	Hastings Town v Molesey	1-5
27	Erith & Belvedere v Deal Town	4-3
	Fisher '93 v Herne Bay	3-3
	Gravesend & Northfleet v Epsom & Ewell	3-0
	Sittingbourne v Dover Athletic	1-1
28	Bromley v Dulwich Hamlet	3-1
	Langney Sports v Leatherhead	3-8
	Lewes v Metropolitan Police	1-1
	Margate v Pagham	6-0
29	Carshalton Athletic v Havant Town	2-0
	Ringmer v Southwick	1-0
	Selsey v Basingstoke Town	2-3
	Sheppey United v Portfield	1-1
30	Dorking (2) v Worthing	4-1
	Tonbridge v Bemerton Heath Harlequins	3-0
	Tooting & Mitcham United v Wick	3-1
	Whitstable Town v Whyteleafe	2-1
31	Bashley v Abingdon Town	2-1
	Brockenhurst v Eastleigh	1-4
	Buckingham Town v Andover	0-1
	Calne Town v Cove	5-1
32	Dorchester Town v Wokingham Town	1-0
	Hungerford Town v Newport (IOW)	0-2
	Maidenhead United v Newbury Town	1-2
	Peacehaven & Telscombe v AFC Lymington	1-1
33	Poole Town v Wimborne Town	0-0
	Thame United v Witney Town	1-1
	Thatcham Town v AFC Totton	4-2
	Waterlooville v Salisbury (2)	1-0
34	Bridport v Elmore	2-3
	Chippenham Town v Weymouth	0-5
	Cinderford Town v Barnstaple Town	1-1
	Gloucester City v Clevedon Town	1-2
35	Frome Town v Moreton Town	0-0
	Mangotsfield United v Melksham Town	3-0
	Odd Down v Forest Green Rovers	2-2
	Trowbridge Town v Newport AFC	1-1
36	Paulton Rovers v Yate Town	2-1
	Shortwood United v Weston-Super-Mare	1-3
	Taunton Town v Saltash United	3-0
	Worcester City v Tiverton Town	1-1
2r	Hebburn v Evenwood Town	0-3
4r	Murton v Tow Law Town	1-2
5r	Emley v Northwich Victoria	2-0
6r	Curzon Ashton v Clitheroe	0-1
7r	Flixton v Darwen	3-0
r	Goole Town v Glossop North End	1-0
8r	Winsford United v Ossett Town	3-1
9r	North Ferriby United v Maltby MW	4-2
10r	Knowsley United v Salford City	6-0
r	St Helens Town v Rossendale United	1-0
11r	Brigg Town v Droylsden	0-1
r	Wednesfield v Worksop Town	0-2
12r	Gresley Rovers v Bromsgrove Rovers	0-1
13r	Hinckley Town v Dudley Town	2-3e
14r	Pelsall Villa v Oldbury United	3-0
r	Redditch United v Paget Rangers	2-1
16r	Aveley v Billericay Town	1-3e
r	Braintree Town v Boston United	1-2
r	Canvey Island v Basildon United	1-0
17r	Hendon v Great Yarmouth Town	4-2
r	Heybridge Swifts v Felixstowe Town	5-1
18r	Newmarket Town v Chelmsford City	1-1e
19r	East Thurrock United v Wisbech Town	1-0
r	Wembley v Stevenage Borough	1-1e
22r	Hampton v Haringey Borough	1-2
27r	Dover Athletic v Sittingbourne	1-2
r	Herne Bay v Fisher '93	3-2
28r	Metropolitan Police v Lewes	3-2
29r	Portfield v Sheppey United	0-3
32r	AFC Lymington v Peacehaven & Telscombe	2-0
33r	Wimborne Town v Poole Town	2-0
r	Witney Town v Thame United	1-2e
34r	Barnstaple Town v Cinderford Town	3-1
35r	Forest Green Rovers v Odd Down	1-3
r	Moreton Town v Frome Town	1-0
r	Newport AFC v Trowbridge Town	0-5
36r	Tiverton Town v Worcester City	4-2
18r2	Chelmsford City v Newmarket Town	3-0 N
19r2	Wembley v Stevenage Borough	0-1 N

Qualifying Round Two

1	Dunston Federation Brewery v Billingham Synthonia	1-1
	Gateshead (2) v Consett	3-1
2	Barrow v Harrogate Town	6-1
	Gretna v Evenwood Town	8-1
3	Netherfield (Kendal) v Newcastle Blue Star	3-2
	Northallerton Town v Easington Colliery	4-1
4	Lancaster City v Tow Law Town	3-2
	Spennymoor United v Whitby Town	2-3
5	Emley v Ashton United	2-0
	Leek Town v Bamber Bridge	5-3
6	Stalybridge Celtic v Bootle	2-2
	Warrington Town v Clitheroe	2-2
7	Bridlington Town v Flixton	2-1
	Morecambe v Goole Town	3-2
8	Buxton v Hucknall Town	2-0
	Winsford United v Guiseley	2-1
9	Chorley v Liversedge	2-1
	Lincoln United v North Ferriby United	1-5
10	Colwyn Bay v Thackley	4-1
	Knowsley United v St Helens Town	2-1
11	Droylsden v Worksop Town	1-1
	Nuneaton Borough v West Midlands Police	3-3e
12	Bromsgrove Rovers v Bedworth United	2-0
	Solihull Borough v Armitage '90	2-2
13	Raunds Town v Dudley Town	3-1
	Telford United v Grantham Town	2-2
14	Atherstone United v Redditch United	0-0
	Pelsall Villa v Pershore Town	1-2
15	Burton Albion v Sandwell Borough	3-2
	Rushden & Diamonds v Rothwell Town	1-1
16	Billericay Town v Bishop's Stortford	1-3
	Boston United v Canvey Island	2-3
17	Cambridge City v Harwich & Parkeston	3-0
	Hendon v Heybridge Swifts	5-2
18	Chelmsford City v Stamford	5-2
	Wivenhoe Town v King's Lynn	2-2
19	Lowestoft Town v East Thurrock United	1-2
	Stevenage Borough v Corby Town	4-3
20	Barton Rovers v Halstead Town	1-2
	Dagenham & Redbridge v Baldock Town	2-1
21	Burnham v Edgware Town	1-3
	Chesham United v Chalfont St Peter	5-0
22	Enfield v Hemel Hempstead Town	1-0
	Haringey Borough v Hornchurch	1-3
23	Ruislip Manor v Purfleet	1-1
	Yeading v Kingsbury Town	5-2
24	Chertsey Town v Tilbury	2-0
	Harrow Borough v Viking Sports	6-0
25	Canterbury City v Chatham Town	1-4
	Kingstonian v Bognor Regis Town	1-1
26	Croydon v Greenwich Borough	0-1
	Molesey v Corinthian	2-0
27	Erith & Belvedere v Herne Bay	2-1
	Sittingbourne v Gravesend & Northfleet	0-2
28	Bromley v Margate	0-3
	Leatherhead v Metropolitan Police	3-5
29	Basingstoke Town v Ringmer	3-0
	Carshalton Athletic v Sheppey United	5-1
30	Dorking (2) v Whitstable Town	4-0
	Tonbridge v Tooting & Mitcham United	0-2
31	Andover v Eastleigh	3-0
	Bashley v Calne Town	3-1
32	AFC Lymington v Newport (IOW)	0-1
	Dorchester Town v Newbury Town	0-3
33	Thame United v Wimborne Town	2-3
	Waterlooville v Thatcham Town	3-0
34	Clevedon Town v Barnstaple Town	2-2
	Weymouth v Elmore	3-0
35	Odd Down v Moreton Town	0-2
	Trowbridge Town v Mangotsfield United	0-0
36	Taunton Town v Weston-Super-Mare	2-4
	Tiverton Town v Paulton Rovers	2-1
1r	Billingham Synthonia v Dunston Federation Brewery	1-0
6r	Bootle v Stalybridge Celtic	1-3
r	Clitheroe v Warrington Town	0-2
11r	West Midlands Police v Nuneaton Borough	0-3
r	Worksop Town v Droylsden	3-0
12r	Armitage '90 v Solihull Borough	2-3e
13r	Grantham Town v Telford United	1-3
14r	Redditch United v Atherstone United	1-1
15r	Rothwell Town v Rushden & Diamonds	0-2
18r	King's Lynn v Wivenhoe Town	1-4
23r	Purfleet v Ruislip Manor	1-0
25r	Bognor Regis Town v Kingstonian	1-6
34r	Barnstaple Town v Clevedon Town	2-1
35r	Mangotsfield United v Trowbridge Town	2-2e
14r2	Redditch United v Atherstone United	1-3 N
35r2	Trowbridge Town v Mangotsfield United	2-3 N

Qualifying Round Three

1	Billingham Synthonia v Gateshead (2)	1-1
2	Gretna v Barrow	2-1
3	Northallerton Town v Netherfield (Kendal)	4-3
4	Lancaster City v Whitby Town	1-2
5	Leek Town v Emley	1-0
6	Warrington Town v Stalybridge Celtic	0-1
7	Morecambe v Bridlington Town	2-0
8	Winsford United v Buxton	6-1
9	North Ferriby United v Chorley	1-1
10	Knowsley United v Colwyn Bay	3-0
11	Nuneaton Borough v Worksop Town	4-1
12	Solihull Borough v Bromsgrove Rovers	1-2
13	Raunds Town v Telford United	0-4
14	Pershore Town v Atherstone United	1-0
15	Rushden & Diamonds v Burton Albion	4-0
16	Bishop's Stortford v Canvey Island	0-1
17	Hendon v Cambridge City	0-1
18	Wivenhoe Town v Chelmsford City	2-0
19	East Thurrock United v Stevenage Borough	1-5
20	Halstead Town v Dagenham & Redbridge	1-3
21	Edgware Town v Chesham United	1-2
22	Hornchurch v Enfield	1-4
23	Purfleet v Yeading	1-2
24	Chertsey Town v Harrow Borough	1-3
25	Chatham Town v Kingstonian	1-2
26	Greenwich Borough v Molesey	0-4
27	Erith & Belvedere v Gravesend & Northfleet	0-1
28	Metropolitan Police v Margate	5-2
29	Basingstoke Town v Carshalton Athletic	1-3
30	Tooting & Mitcham United v Dorking (2)	2-0
31	Andover v Bashley	0-2
32	Newport (IOW) v Newbury Town	4-2
33	Wimborne Town v Waterlooville	0-1
34	Weymouth v Barnstaple Town	2-1
35	Moreton Town v Mangotsfield United	1-1
36	Weston-Super-Mare v Tiverton Town	0-0
1r	Gateshead (2) v Billingham Synthonia	0-1
9r	Chorley v North Ferriby United	2-1
35r	Mangotsfield United v Moreton Town	1-2
36r	Tiverton Town v Weston-Super-Mare	0-2

Qualifying Round Four

Altrincham v Accrington Stanley (2)	0-2
Aylesbury United v Marlow	1-2
Bashley v Carshalton Athletic	1-1
Billingham Synthonia v Leek Town	1-1
Cambridge City v Dagenham & Redbridge	2-2
Cheltenham Town v Bath City	1-1
Chesham United v Kidderminster Harriers	1-4
Chorley v Marine	0-2
Crawley Town v Merthyr Tydfil	2-1
Hayes v Slough Town	0-2
Kettering Town v Canvey Island	3-1
Kingstonian v Metropolitan Police	0-1
Macclesfield Town v Southport	5-3
Molesey v Tooting & Mitcham United	0-0
Pershore Town v Yeading	1-3
Rushden & Diamonds v Bromsgrove Rovers	1-3
Stafford Rangers v Knowsley United	1-1
Stalybridge Celtic v Whitby Town	0-0
Stevenage Borough v Nuneaton Borough	1-2
Sutton United v Moreton Town	0-0
Telford United v Morecambe	2-0
V.S. Rugby v Harrow Borough	2-2
Waterlooville v Gravesend & Northfleet	1-3
Weston-Super-Mare v Newport (IOW)	2-0

1993/94 to 1994/95

Weymouth v Farnborough Town		1-4
Winsford United v Gretna		0-0
Witton Albion v Northallerton Town		2-1
Wivenhoe Town v Enfield		1-2
r Bath City v Cheltenham Town		4-2
r Carshalton Athletic v Bashley		4-2
r Dagenham & Redbridge v Cambridge City		0-2
r Gretna v Winsford United		5-0
r Harrow Borough v V.S. Rugby		1-2
r Knowsley United v Stafford Rangers		2-2e
r Leek Town v Billingham Synthonia		2-1
r Moreton Town v Sutton United		0-2
r Tooting & Mitcham United v Molesey		1-2
r Whitby Town v Stalybridge Celtic		0-1
r2 Knowsley United v Stafford Rangers		1-0

Round One

Accrington Stanley (2) v Scunthorpe United	2-3 N
Barnet v Carshalton Athletic	2-1
Bolton Wanderers v Gretna	3-2
Bournemouth v Brighton & Hove Albion	4-2
Bradford City v Chester City	0-0
Bristol Rovers v Wycombe Wanderers	1-2
Burnley v York City	0-0
Cambridge City v Hereford United	0-1
Cambridge United v Reading	0-0
Chesterfield v Rochdale	0-1
Colchester United v Sutton United	3-4
Crewe Alexandra v Darlington	4-2
Enfield v Cardiff City	0-0
Farnborough Town v Exeter City	1-3
Halifax Town v West Bromwich Albion	2-1
Kidderminster Harriers v Kettering Town	3-0
Knowsley United v Carlisle United	1-4 N
Leek Town v Wigan Athletic	2-2
Leyton Orient v Gravesend & Northfleet	2-1
Macclesfield Town v Hartlepool United	2-0
Mansfield Town v Preston North End	1-2
Marlow v Plymouth Argyle	0-2
Metropolitan Police v Crawley Town	0-2
Molesey v Bath City	0-4
Northampton Town v Bromsgrove Rovers	1-2
Port Vale v Blackpool	2-0
Rotherham United v Stockport County	1-2
Runcorn v Hull City	0-2 N
Scarborough v Bury	1-0
Shrewsbury Town v Doncaster Rovers	1-1
Slough Town v Torquay United	1-2
Stalybridge Celtic v Marine	1-1
Swansea City v Nuneaton Borough	1-1
Telford United v Huddersfield Town	1-1
V.S. Rugby v Brentford	0-3
Witton Albion v Lincoln City	0-2
Woking v Weston-Super-Mare	2-2
Wrexham v Walsall	1-1
Yeading v Gillingham	0-0 N
Yeovil Town v Fulham	1-0
r Cardiff City v Enfield	1-0
r Chester City v Bradford City	1-0
r Doncaster Rovers v Shrewsbury Town	1-2e
r Gillingham v Yeading	3-1
r Huddersfield Town v Telford United	1-0
r Marine v Stalybridge Celtic	4-4q
r Nuneaton Borough v Swansea City	2-1e
r Reading v Cambridge United	1-2
r Walsall v Wrexham	2-0
r Weston-Super-Mare v Woking	0-1
r Wigan Athletic v Leek Town	3-0
r York City v Burnley	2-3

Round Two

Bath City v Hereford United	2-1
Bournemouth v Nuneaton Borough	1-1
Brentford v Cardiff City	1-3
Burnley v Rochdale	4-1
Carlisle United v Stalybridge Celtic	3-1
Chester City v Hull City	2-0
Crawley Town v Barnet	1-2
Crewe Alexandra v Macclesfield Town	2-1
Kidderminster Harriers v Woking	1-0
Leyton Orient v Exeter City	1-1
Lincoln City v Bolton Wanderers	1-3
Plymouth Argyle v Gillingham	2-0
Port Vale v Huddersfield Town	1-0
Shrewsbury Town v Preston North End	0-1
Stockport County v Halifax Town	5-1
Torquay United v Sutton United	0-1
Walsall v Scunthorpe United	1-1
Wigan Athletic v Scarborough	1-0
Wycombe Wanderers v Cambridge United	1-0
Yeovil Town v Bromsgrove Rovers	0-2
r Exeter City v Leyton Orient	2-2P
r Nuneaton Borough v Bournemouth	0-1
r Scunthorpe United v Walsall	0-0P

Round Three

Birmingham City v Kidderminster Harriers	1-2
Blackburn Rovers v Portsmouth	3-3
Bolton Wanderers v Everton	1-1
Bristol City v Liverpool	1-1
Bromsgrove Rovers v Barnsley	1-2
Cardiff City v Middlesbrough	2-2
Charlton Athletic v Burnley	3-0
Chelsea v Barnet	0-0
Exeter City v Aston Villa	0-1
Grimsby Town v Wigan Athletic	1-0
Leeds United v Crewe Alexandra	3-1
Luton Town v Southend United	1-0
Manchester City v Leicester City	4-1
Millwall v Arsenal	0-1
Newcastle United v Coventry City	2-0
Notts County v Sutton United	3-2
Oldham Athletic v Derby County	2-1
Oxford United v Tranmere Rovers	2-0
Peterborough United v Tottenham Hotspur	1-1
Plymouth Argyle v Chester City	1-0
Preston North End v Bournemouth	2-1
Sheffield United v Manchester United	0-1
Sheffield Wednesday v Nottingham Forest	1-1
Southampton v Port Vale	1-1
Stockport County v Queen's Park Rangers	2-1
Stoke City v Bath City	0-0
Sunderland v Carlisle United	1-1
Swindon Town v Ipswich Town	1-1
West Ham United v Watford	2-1
Wimbledon v Scunthorpe United	3-0
Wolverhampton Wan. v Crystal Palace	1-0
Wycombe Wanderers v Norwich City	0-2
r Bath City v Stoke City	1-4
r Carlisle United v Sunderland	0-1e
r Chelsea v Barnet	4-0
r Everton v Bolton Wanderers	2-3e
r Ipswich Town v Swindon Town	2-1e
r Liverpool v Bristol City	0-1
r Middlesbrough v Cardiff City	1-2e
r Nottingham Forest v Sheffield Wednesday	0-2
r Port Vale v Southampton	1-0
r Portsmouth v Blackburn Rovers	1-3
r Tottenham Hotspur v Peterborough United	1-1P

Round Four

Bolton Wanderers v Arsenal	2-2
Cardiff City v Manchester City	1-0
Charlton Athletic v Blackburn Rovers	0-0
Chelsea v Sheffield Wednesday	1-1
Grimsby Town v Aston Villa	1-2
Ipswich Town v Tottenham Hotspur	3-0
Kidderminster Harriers v Preston North End	1-0
Newcastle United v Luton Town	1-1
Norwich City v Manchester United	0-2
Notts County v West Ham United	1-1
Oldham Athletic v Stoke City	0-0
Oxford United v Leeds United	2-2
Plymouth Argyle v Barnsley	2-2
Port Vale v Wolverhampton Wan.	0-2
Stockport County v Bristol City	0-4
Wimbledon v Sunderland	2-1
r Arsenal v Bolton Wanderers	1-3e
r Barnsley v Plymouth Argyle	1-0
r Blackburn Rovers v Charlton Athletic	0-1
r Leeds United v Oxford United	2-3e
r Luton Town v Newcastle United	2-0
r Sheffield Wednesday v Chelsea	1-3e
r Stoke City v Oldham Athletic	0-1
r West Ham United v Notts County	1-0e

Round Five

Bolton Wanderers v Aston Villa	1-0
Bristol City v Charlton Athletic	1-1
Cardiff City v Luton Town	1-2
Kidderminster Harriers v West Ham United	0-1
Oldham Athletic v Barnsley	1-0
Oxford United v Chelsea	1-2
Wimbledon v Manchester United	0-3
Wolverhampton Wan. v Ipswich Town	1-1
r Charlton Athletic v Bristol City	2-0
r Ipswich Town v Wolverhampton Wan.	1-2

Round Six

Bolton Wanderers v Oldham Athletic	0-1
Chelsea v Wolverhampton Wan.	1-0
Manchester United v Charlton Athletic	3-1
West Ham United v Luton Town	0-0
r Luton Town v West Ham United	3-2

Semi Finals

Chelsea v Luton Town	2-0 N
Manchester United v Oldham Athletic	1-1eN
r Manchester United v Oldham Athletic	4-1 N

Final

Manchester United v Chelsea	4-0 N

1994/95

Preliminary Round

1	Brandon United v Alnwick Town	5-2
	Crook Town v Billingham Town	1-1
	Dunston Fed. Brewery v Darlington Cleveland Soc.	1-0
	Seaham Red Star v Easington Colliery	3-1
2	Guisborough Town v Eppleton CW	2-0
	Harrogate Town v Esh Winning	7-0
	Murton v Hebburn	3-2
	Stockton (2) v RTM Newcastle	2-2
3	Evenwood Town v Consett	0-3
	Penrith v Tow Law Town	2-3
	Ryhope Community Association v Pickering Town	1-5
	South Shields (3) v Prudhoe Town	7-1
4	Clitheroe v Bamber Bridge	1-0
	Farsley Celtic v Great Harwood Town	3-1
	West Auckland Town v Workington	1-1
	Willington v Whickham	2-1
5	Alfreton Town v Ashton United	3-1
	Atherton Collieries v Blidworth MW	1-1
	Belper Town v Blackpool (Wren) Rovers	2-1
	Chadderton v Armthorpe Welfare	3-2
	Yorkshire Amateur v Atherton LR	0-1
6	Arnold Town v Castleton Gabriels	3-2
	Bradford Park Avenue v Burscough	0-3
	Caernarfon Town v Darwen	3-1
	Congleton Town v Curzon Ashton	4-2
	Hatfield Main v Brigg Town	1-2
7	Denaby United v Hallam	1-1
	Fleetwood Town v Eastwood Town	0-3
	Glasshoughton Welfare v Eccleshill United	1-0
	Goole Town v Glossop North End	0-2
8	Bootle v Maltby MW	0-0
	Immingham Town v Heanor Town	1-2 N
	Liversedge v Ilkeston Town (2)	2-2
	Maine Road v Louth United	3-1
9	Nantwich Town v Newcastle Town	2-1
	Ossett Town v Mossley	0-0
	Prescot AFC v Pontefract Collieries	2-0
	Thackley v Radcliffe Borough	0-2
10	Ossett Albion v Rossendale United	1-4
	Sheffield v Rossington Main	3-1
	St Helens Town v Salford City	7-1
	Winterton Rangers v Stocksbridge Park Steels	3-0
11	Armitage '90 v Brierley Hill Town	1-1
	Blakenall v Banbury United	3-2
	Bolehall Swifts v Barwell	3-1
	Long Buckby v Northampton Spencer	3-3
12	Cogenhoe United v Eastwood Hanley	1-1
	Grantham Town v Leicester United	2-0
	Hinckley Athletic v Hinckley Town	2-1
	Stratford Town v Halesowen Harriers	0-2
	Wednesfield v Desborough Town	1-1
13	Bridgnorth Town v Bilston Town	3-1
	Lye Town v Racing Club Warwick	2-0 N
	Oldbury United v Moor Green	1-3
	Pelsall Villa v Newport Pagnell Town	2-0
14	Dudley Town v Rothwell Town	2-1
	Sandwell Borough v Stourbridge	1-1
	Stapenhill v Rushall Olympic	2-1
	Sutton Coldfield Town v Stourport Swifts	2-3
15	Evesham United v Tamworth	1-3
	Hucknall Town v West Midlands Police	0-0e
	Redditch United v Bedworth United	7-0
	Westfields v Wellingborough Town	1-1
16	Bourne Town v Billericay Town	1-4
	Bury Town v Boston Town	0-4
	Cornard United v Chatteris Town	2-0
	Lowestoft Town v Diss Town	2-2
17	Burnham Ramblers v King's Lynn	2-3
	Eynesbury Rovers v Gorleston	2-3
	Haverhill Rovers v Great Yarmouth Town	2-1
	Holbeach United v Heybridge Swifts	1-2
18	Hertford Town v Saffron Walden Town	2-5
	Mirrlees Blackstone v Stamford	2-2
	Newmarket Town v Soham Town Rangers	4-2
	Spalding United v March Town United	1-0
	Stowmarket Town v Tiptree United	2-2
19	Brimsdown Rovers v Sudbury Wanderers	1-1
	Kingsbury Town v Kempston Rovers	1-4
	Wisbech Town v Fakenham Town	3-0
	Witham Town v Watton United	1-0
20	Arlesey Town v Brook House	1-2
	Aveley v Wootton Blue Cross	1-1
	Berkhamsted Town v Baldock Town	1-3
	Bowers United v Barking	1-4
21	Burnham v Clapton	4-0 N
	Chalfont St Peter v Dunstable	wo/s
	Collier Row v Cheshunt	2-1
	Feltham & Hounslow Boro. v Biggleswade Town	1-0
22	Ford United v Haringey Borough	2-1
	Hoddesdon Town v Harefield United	1-1 N
	Ruislip Manor v Flackwell Heath	5-0
	Thamesmead Town v Bedfont	0-3
23	Hillingdon Borough v Royston Town	2-2
	Langford v Southall	1-2
	Leatherhead v Letchworth Garden City	8-0
	Leighton Town v Leyton	2-2
	Romford v Wingate & Finchley	2-0

1994/95

24	Slade Green v Tilbury	0-3
	Stotfold v Tower Hamlets	2-1
	Tring Town v Wealdstone	0-1
	Walthamstow Pennant v Ware	2-2
	Welwyn Garden City v Viking Sports	1-1
25	Arundel v Burgess Hill Town	1-3
	Banstead Athletic v Ash United	wo/s
	Bracknell Town v Ashford Town	1-3
	Hampton v Pagham	1-0
26	Corinthian v Crowborough Athletic	9-0
	Croydon v Three Bridges	7-0
	Eastbourne Town v Egham Town	1-7 N
	Tonbridge v Chipstead	1-1
	Uxbridge v Corinthian Casuals	1-0
27	Folkestone Invicta v Hailsham Town	2-0
	Herne Bay v Langney Sports	3-0
	Horsham YMCA v Lancing	2-1
	Northwood v Godalming & Guildford	2-1
	Worthing v Horsham	1-0
28	Canterbury City v Newhaven	6-0
	Croydon Athletic v Malden Vale	5-2
	Lewes v Fisher '93	0-1
	Littlehampton Town v Merstham	2-7 N
	Oakwood v Peacehaven & Telscombe	0-3
29	Hanwell Town v Whyteleafe	1-2
	Ramsgate v Redhill	4-0
	Shoreham v Ringmer	1-0
	Steyning Town v Sheppey United	0-2
30	Epsom & Ewell v Wembley	1-3
	Selsey v Portfield	1-4
	Whitstable Town v Tunbridge Wells	2-3
	Windsor & Eton v Whitehawk	1-0
31	Abingdon Town v Cove	0-0
	Bemerton Heath Harlequins v Aldershot Town	0-4
	Bournemouth (Ams) v Basingstoke Town	0-0
	Buckingham Town v Brockenhurst	1-0
32	Fareham Town v Eastleigh	3-1
	Fleet Town v Oxford City	3-1
	Hungerford Town v Gosport Borough	3-2
	Maidenhead United v Havant Town	0-1
33	Poole Town v Witney Town	3-0
	Ryde Sports v Thatcham Town	3-2
	Salisbury (2) v AFC Totton	5-0
	Thame United v Devizes Town	2-0
34	Bridport v Backwell United	1-2
	Elmore v Chippenham Town	4-0
	Forest Green Rovers v Cinderford Town	0-0
	Yate Town v Swanage Town & Herston	2-1
35	Glastonbury v Frome Town	4-1
	Ilfracombe Town v Paulton Rovers	0-2
	Melksham Town v Keynsham Town	4-1
	Odd Down v Newport AFC	0-6
36	Bideford v Falmouth Town	2-1
	Calne Town v Torrington	1-3
	Taunton Town v Clevedon Town	3-2
	Welton Rovers v Saltash United	1-1
1r	Billingham Town v Crook Town	1-2
2r	RTM Newcastle v Stockton (2)	6-1
4r	Workington v West Auckland Town	1-2
5r	Blidworth MW v Atherton Collieries	1-3
7r	Hallam v Denaby United	1-0
8r	Ilkeston Town (2) v Liversedge	4-1
r	Maltby MW v Bootle	1-0
9r	Mossley v Ossett Town	3-0
11r	Brierley Hill Town v Armitage '90	1-3e
r	Northampton Spencer v Long Buckby	2-1
12r	Desborough Town v Wednesfield	2-1
r	Eastwood Hanley v Cogenhoe United	0-0e
14r	Sandwell Borough v Stourbridge	2-0
15r	Wellingborough Town v Westfields	1-3
r	West Midlands Police v Hucknall Town	1-1e
16r	Diss Town v Lowestoft Town	3-3e
18r	Stamford v Mirrlees Blackstone	4-1
r	Tiptree United v Stowmarket Town	3-1
19r	Sudbury Wanderers v Brimsdown Rovers	1-0
20r	Wootton Blue Cross v Aveley	1-3
22r	Harefield United v Hoddesdon Town	1-0
23r	Leyton v Leighton Town	1-0e
r	Royston Town v Hillingdon Borough	1-2
24r	Viking Sports v Welwyn Garden City	0-1
r	Ware v Walthamstow Pennant	4-0
26r	Chipstead v Tonbridge	0-3
31r	Basingstoke Town v Bournemouth (Ams)	3-1
r	Cove v Abingdon Town	1-0
34r	Cinderford Town v Forest Green Rovers	3-2eN
36r	Saltash United v Welton Rovers	4-0
12r2	Cogenhoe United v Eastwood Hanley	2-4
15r2	Hucknall Town v West Midlands Police	0-1
16r2	Diss Town v Lowestoft Town	1-0

Qualifying Round One

1	Barrow v Chester-le-Street Town	4-1
	Crook Town v Blyth Spartans	0-2
	Dunston Federation Brewery v Brandon United	2-0
	Seaham Red Star v Billingham Synthonia	2-2
2	Bishop Auckland v Harrogate Railway Athletic	2-0
	Harrogate Town v Gretna	4-1
	Murton v Guisborough Town	1-1
	RTM Newcastle v Gateshead (2)	0-3
3	Consett v Northallerton Town	1-1
	South Shields (3) v Netherfield (Kendal)	0-0
	Spennymoor United v Shildon	4-1
	Tow Law Town v Pickering Town	4-0
4	Clitheroe v Willington	1-2
	Durham City v Peterlee Newtown	5-0
	Farsley Celtic v Whitley Bay	3-0
	West Auckland Town v Whitby Town	0-2
5	Alfreton Town v Guiseley	2-2
	Atherton Collieries v Buxton	2-0
	Atherton LR v Belper Town	1-1
	Chadderton v Winsford United	1-1
6	Arnold Town v Congleton Town	1-2
	Brigg Town v Morecambe	0-4
	Burscough v Horwich RMI	1-0
	Caernarfon Town v Chorley	2-2
7	Colwyn Bay v Flixton	4-0
	Glasshoughton Welfare v Worksop Town	0-5
	Glossop North End v Eastwood Town	2-2
	Hallam v Hyde United	0-3
8	Droylsden v Lincoln United	0-3
	Ilkeston Town (2) v Lancaster City	2-2
	Maine Road v Heanor Town	1-0 N
	Maltby MW v Knowsley United	0-4
9	Emley v Oldham Town	4-1
	Mossley v Northwich Victoria	2-4
	Prescot AFC v Nantwich Town	1-3
	Radcliffe Borough v North Ferriby United	1-0
10	Frickley Athletic v Skelmersdale United	1-1
	Rossendale United v Matlock Town	1-2
	St Helens Town v Warrington Town	0-4
	Winterton Rangers v Sheffield	0-1
11	Armitage '90 v Blakenall	2-2
	Atherstone United v Boldmere St Michaels	1-1
	Bolehall Swifts v Solihull Borough	2-3
	Northampton Spencer v Hednesford Town	1-4
12	Desborough Town v Chasetown	1-0
	Eastwood Hanley v Rushden & Diamonds	1-0
	Grantham Town v Burton Albion	2-4
	Halesowen Harriers v Hinckley Athletic	3-3
13	Bridgnorth Town v Pershore Town	1-1
	Corby Town v Paget Rangers	0-5 N
	Lye Town v Moor Green	1-5
	Pelsall Villa v Raunds Town	0-1
14	Dudley Town v Leek Town	0-1
	Rocester v Stewarts & Lloyds (2)	1-0
	Sandwell Borough v Gresley Rovers	1-2
	Stourport Swifts v Stapenhill	2-1
15	Halesowen Town v Willenhall Town	2-1
	Redditch United v Westfields	1-1
	Tamworth v Telford United	1-1
	West Midlands Police v Gainsborough Trinity	0-0
16	Bishop's Stortford v Braintree Town	1-1
	Boston Town v Basildon United	1-0
	Cornard United v Billericay Town	0-4
	Diss Town v Sudbury Town	1-0
17	Boston United v Harwich & Parkeston	2-0
	Haverhill Rovers v Felixstowe Town	1-1
	Heybridge Swifts v Gorleston	0-0
	King's Lynn v Halstead Town	0-1
18	Newmarket Town v Hitchin Town	1-2
	Saffron Walden Town v Stevenage Borough	1-4
	Spalding United v Cambridge City	0-3
	Stamford v Tiptree United	2-3
19	Chelmsford City v Barton Rovers	1-0
	Kempston Rovers v Wisbech Town	2-4
	Sudbury Wanderers v Hendon	0-1
	Witham Town v Wivenhoe Town	2-0
20	Aveley v Edgware Town	1-2
	Aylesbury United v Boreham Wood	3-1
	Barking v Canvey Island	3-1
	Brook House v Baldock Town	0-7
21	Chalfont St Peter v Collier Row	2-2
	Chesham United v Concord Rangers	4-2
	Dagenham & Redbridge v Feltham & Hounslow Boro.	3-1
	East Thurrock United v Burnham	0-2
22	Bedfont v Purfleet	0-3
	Enfield v Hemel Hempstead Town	5-2
	Harefield United v Hornchurch	0-3
	Ruislip Manor v Ford United	2-1
23	Hillingdon Borough v Southall	2-1
	Leatherhead v Hayes	1-1
	Romford v Grays Athletic	4-3
24	Leyton v St Albans City	1-2
	Stotfold v Yeading	1-3
	Tilbury v Staines Town	0-1
	Wealdstone v Harrow Borough	0-1
	Welwyn Garden City v Ware	1-2
25	Ashford Town v Chatham Town	5-0
	Bromley v Bognor Regis Town	3-2
	Burgess Hill Town v Banstead Athletic	4-3
	Hampton v Gravesend & Northfleet	1-1
26	Corinthian v Hastings Town	1-2
	Croydon v Carshalton Athletic	0-0
	Tonbridge v Egham Town	3-1 N
	Uxbridge v Dorking (2)	1-1
27	Folkestone Invicta v Sittingbourne	1-0
	Herne Bay v Dulwich Hamlet	1-3
	Northwood v Erith & Belvedere	3-0
	Worthing v Horsham YMCA	5-3
28	Canterbury City v Peacehaven & Telscombe	1-2
	Croydon Athletic v Metropolitan Police	2-2
	Fisher '93 v Kingstonian	2-4
	Margate v Merstham	2-0
29	Molesey v Southwick	1-1
	Ramsgate v Shoreham	0-0
	Sheppey United v Chertsey Town	0-1
	Whyteleafe v Dover Athletic	0-0
30	Portfield v Tooting & Mitcham United	0-3
	Walton & Hersham v Wick	3-0
	Wembley v Tunbridge Wells	4-1
	Windsor & Eton v Welling United	0-1
31	Basingstoke Town v Newport (IOW)	2-4
	Buckingham Town v Aldershot Town	2-1
	Cove v Andover	0-2
	Wokingham Town v Bicester Town	5-0
32	Dorchester Town v AFC Lymington	3-1
	Fareham Town v Hungerford Town	1-2
	Fleet Town v Newbury Town	0-1e
	Havant Town v Bashley	1-1
33	Poole Town v Ryde Sports	5-1
	Salisbury (2) v Worcester City	2-0
	Thame United v Wimborne Town	0-0
	Waterlooville v Westbury United	1-0
34	Backwell United v Elmore	0-6
	Cinderford Town v Mangotsfield United	3-2 N
	Gloucester City v Exmouth Town	3-0
	Yate Town v Merthyr Tydfil	0-3
35	Glastonbury v Barnstaple Town	0-3
	Newport AFC v Melksham Town	4-1
	Paulton Rovers v Moreton Town	2-0
	Trowbridge Town v Minehead	7-0
36	Bideford v Saltash United	4-0
	Taunton Town v Weston-Super-Mare	2-2
	Tiverton Town v St Blazey	7-1
	Torrington v Weymouth	2-0
1r	Billingham Synthonia v Seaham Red Star	2-0
2r	Guisborough Town v Murton	3-4e
3r	Netherfield (Kendal) v South Shields (3)	0-1
r	Northallerton Town v Consett	1-3
5r	Belper Town v Atherton LR	0-2
r	Guiseley v Alfreton Town	4-2
r	Winsford United v Chadderton	5-6
6r	Chorley v Caernarfon Town	2-1
7r	Eastwood Town v Glossop North End	1-1e
8r	Lancaster City v Ilkeston Town (2)	3-1
10r	Skelmersdale United v Frickley Athletic	1-4
11r	Blakenall v Armitage '90	2-0
r	Boldmere St Michaels v Atherstone United	0-1
12r	Hinckley Athletic v Halesowen Harriers	2-1e
13r	Pershore Town v Bridgnorth Town	0-2
15r	Gainsborough Trinity v West Midlands Police	6-0
r	Telford United v Tamworth	4-1
r	Westfields v Redditch United	2-3
16r	Braintree Town v Bishop's Stortford	3-0
17r	Felixstowe Town v Haverhill Rovers	2-0
r	Gorleston v Heybridge Swifts	0-2
21r	Collier Row v Chalfont St Peter	2-1
23r	Hayes v Leatherhead	4-0
25r	Gravesend & Northfleet v Hampton	1-0
26r	Carshalton Athletic v Croydon	5-0
r	Dorking (2) v Uxbridge	3-1
28r	Metropolitan Police v Croydon Athletic	0-1
29r	Dover Athletic v Whyteleafe	3-0
r	Shoreham v Ramsgate	2-0
r	Southwick v Molesey	0-1
32r	Bashley v Havant Town	3-1
33r	Wimborne Town v Thame United	3-3e
36r	Weston-Super-Mare v Taunton Town	3-2
7r2	Glossop North End v Eastwood Town	3-5e
33r2	Thame United v Wimborne Town	3-1e

Qualifying Round Two

1	Barrow v Billingham Synthonia	5-2
	Blyth Spartans v Dunston Federation Brewery	3-2
2	Bishop Auckland v Gateshead (2)	3-1
	Harrogate Town v Murton	1-0
3	South Shields (3) v Tow Law Town	2-2
	Spennymoor United v Consett	3-2
4	Durham City v Farsley Celtic	1-0
	Whitby Town v Willington	6-1
5	Chadderton v Atherton Collieries	1-2
	Guiseley v Atherton LR	3-1
6	Burscough v Congleton Town	0-0
	Morecambe v Chorley	4-2
7	Colwyn Bay v Hyde United	2-2
	Worksop Town v Eastwood Town	0-2
8	Lancaster City v Maine Road	3-2
	Lincoln United v Knowsley United	3-2
9	Emley v Radcliffe Borough	2-0
	Northwich Victoria v Nantwich Town	10-0
10	Frickley Athletic v Matlock Town	3-1
	Warrington Town v Sheffield	2-1
11	Atherstone United v Hednesford Town	3-4
	Solihull Borough v Blakenall	4-0
12	Desborough Town v Burton Albion	0-2
	Eastwood Hanley v Hinckley Athletic	2-2
13	Paget Rangers v Bridgnorth Town	2-1
	Raunds Town v Moor Green	1-2
14	Gresley Rovers v Stourport Swifts	4-0
	Rocester v Leek Town	0-4
15	Gainsborough Trinity v Redditch United	3-1
	Halesowen Town v Telford United	1-1
16	Boston Town v Billericay Town	1-2
	Braintree Town v Diss Town	2-1
17	Boston United v Halstead Town	3-0
	Felixstowe Town v Heybridge Swifts	1-5
18	Hitchin Town v Tiptree United	3-3
	Stevenage Borough v Cambridge City	0-2
19	Chelmsford City v Witham Town	1-0
	Hendon v Wisbech Town	2-1

1994/95

20 Aylesbury United v Edgware Town 2-0
Barking v Baldock Town 2-2
21 Burnham v Collier Row 0-1
Chesham United v Dagenham & Redbridge 2-0
22 Enfield v Purfleet 3-1
Hornchurch v Ruislip Manor 0-1
23 Hayes v Romford 1-2
St Albans City v Hillingdon Borough 11-1
24 Staines Town v Harrow Borough 5-3
Yeading v Ware 8-0
25 Ashford Town v Burgess Hill Town 3-2
Bromley v Gravesend & Northfleet 2-2
26 Dorking (2) v Carshalton Athletic 0-8
Hastings Town v Tonbridge 1-1
27 Folkestone Invicta v Worthing 1-2
Northwood v Dulwich Hamlet 1-4
28 Croydon Athletic v Kingstonian 1-2
Margate v Peacehaven & Telscombe 1-1
29 Chertsey Town v Shoreham 1-0
Molesey v Dover Athletic 1-4
30 Walton & Hersham v Tooting & Mitcham United 3-0
Welling United v Wembley 1-4
31 Newport (IOW) v Buckingham Town 1-0
Wokingham Town v Andover 3-0
32 Bashley v Hungerford Town 3-0
Dorchester Town v Newbury Town 4-2
33 Salisbury (2) v Poole Town 3-2
Waterlooville v Thame United 4-0
34 Elmore v Cinderford Town 4-5
Gloucester City v Merthyr Tydfil 7-1
35 Barnstaple Town v Newport AFC 1-2
Trowbridge Town v Paulton Rovers 4-1
36 Tiverton Town v Weston-Super-Mare 4-2
Torrington v Bideford 1-5
3r Tow Law Town v South Shields (3) 2-1
6r Congleton Town v Burscough 3-3e
7r Hyde United v Colwyn Bay 8-0
12r Hinckley Athletic v Eastwood Hanley 0-1
15r Telford United v Halesowen Town 3-1
18r Tiptree United v Hitchin Town 2-4
20r Baldock Town v Barking 3-2
25r Gravesend & Northfleet v Bromley 1-1e
26r Tonbridge v Hastings Town 0-1
28r Peacehaven & Telscombe v Margate 3-5e
6r2 Burscough v Congleton Town 2-2e
25r2 Gravesend & Northfleet v Bromley 1-0
6r3 Congleton Town v Burscough 5-2e

Qualifying Round Three

1 Blyth Spartans v Barrow 3-1
2 Harrogate Town v Bishop Auckland 0-3
3 Tow Law Town v Spennymoor United 0-0
4 Whitby Town v Durham City 1-1
5 Guiseley v Atherton Collieries 3-1
6 Congleton Town v Morecambe 0-3
7 Eastwood Town v Hyde United 1-1
8 Lancaster City v Lincoln United 5-1
9 Northwich Victoria v Emley 2-1
10 Warrington Town v Frickley Athletic 2-0
11 Solihull Borough v Hednesford Town 3-0
12 Eastwood Hanley v Burton Albion 0-1
13 Moor Green v Paget Rangers 4-1
14 Gresley Rovers v Leek Town 3-1
15 Gainsborough Trinity v Telford United 0-3
16 Billericay Town v Braintree Town 1-1
17 Heybridge Swifts v Boston United 3-0
18 Hitchin Town v Cambridge City 3-3
19 Hendon v Chelmsford City 0-1
20 Baldock Town v Aylesbury United 0-2
21 Collier Row v Chesham United 0-1
22 Ruislip Manor v Enfield 0-3
23 St Albans City v Romford 1-0
24 Yeading v Staines Town 4-1
25 Ashford Town v Gravesend & Northfleet 2-1
26 Hastings Town v Carshalton Athletic 2-2
27 Worthing v Dulwich Hamlet 2-1
28 Margate v Kingstonian 0-1
29 Chertsey Town v Dover Athletic 0-0
30 Wembley v Walton & Hersham 0-1
31 Newport (IOW) v Wokingham Town 3-0
32 Bashley v Dorchester Town 1-1
33 Salisbury (2) v Waterlooville 3-3
34 Gloucester City v Cinderford Town 2-0
35 Newport AFC v Trowbridge Town 2-2
36 Bideford v Tiverton Town 1-8
3r Spennymoor United v Tow Law Town 2-1e
4r Durham City v Whitby Town 3-1
7r Hyde United v Eastwood Town 3-0
16r Braintree Town v Billericay Town 3-3e
18r Cambridge City v Hitchin Town 2-3
26r Carshalton Athletic v Hastings Town 1-2
29r Dover Athletic v Chertsey Town 1-0
32r Dorchester Town v Bashley 0-2
33r Waterlooville v Salisbury (2) 0-1
35r Trowbridge Town v Newport AFC 1-1e
16r2 Billericay Town v Braintree Town 2-3e
35r2 Trowbridge Town v Newport AFC 3-1

Qualifying Round Four

Accrington Stanley (2) v Spennymoor United 0-1
Altrincham v Marine 2-1
Bishop Auckland v Macclesfield Town 2-2
Braintree Town v Gresley Rovers 0-2
Burton Albion v Hitchin Town 0-1
Cheltenham Town v Bashley 1-1
Chesham United v Bromsgrove Rovers 1-1
Dover Athletic v Kingstonian 1-2
Gloucester City v Worthing 1-1
Guiseley v Durham City 6-0
Halifax Town v Lancaster City 3-1
Hastings Town v Crawley Town 1-1
Hyde United v Warrington Town 1-1
Marlow v Sutton United 1-0
Moor Green v Aylesbury United 1-1
Morecambe v Witton Albion 0-1
Newport (IOW) v Trowbridge Town 1-0
Northwich Victoria v Blyth Spartans 2-0
Nuneaton Borough v Heybridge Swifts 2-2
Salisbury (2) v Ashford Town 2-3
Solihull Borough v Kettering Town 2-4
Southport v Stalybridge Celtic 2-1
St Albans City v Enfield 0-0
Stafford Rangers v Slough Town 0-4
Tiverton Town v Farnborough Town 4-4
V.S. Rugby v Chelmsford City 0-0
Walton & Hersham v Yeovil Town 3-2
Yeading v Telford United 1-0
r Aylesbury United v Moor Green 3-1
r Bashley v Cheltenham Town 2-1
r Bromsgrove Rovers v Chesham United 0-1
r Chelmsford City v V.S. Rugby 2-1
r Crawley Town v Hastings Town 3-2e
r Enfield v St Albans City 4-2
r Farnborough Town v Tiverton Town 1-5
r Heybridge Swifts v Nuneaton Borough 3-2
r Macclesfield Town v Bishop Auckland 0-1e
r Warrington Town v Hyde United 0-2
r Worthing v Gloucester City 2-1

Round One

Altrincham v Southport 3-2
Ashford Town v Fulham 2-2
Barnet v Woking 4-4
Bath City v Bristol Rovers 0-5
Birmingham City v Slough Town 4-0
Bishop Auckland v Bury 0-0
Bournemouth v Worthing 3-1
Bradford City v Scunthorpe United 1-1
Burnley v Shrewsbury Town 2-1
Cambridge United v Brentford 2-2
Chesham United v Bashley 0-1
Chester City v Witton Albion 2-0
Chesterfield v Scarborough 0-0
Crewe Alexandra v Gresley Rovers 7-1
Doncaster Rovers v Huddersfield Town 1-4
Enfield v Cardiff City 1-0
Exeter City v Crawley Town 1-0
Guiseley v Carlisle United 1-4 N
Halifax Town v Runcorn 1-1
Hereford United v Hitchin Town 2-2
Heybridge Swifts v Gillingham 0-2 N
Hull City v Lincoln City 0-1
Hyde United v Darlington 1-3
Kettering Town v Plymouth Argyle 0-1
Kidderminster Harriers v Torquay United 1-1
Kingstonian v Brighton & Hove Albion 2-1
Mansfield Town v Northwich Victoria 3-1
Marlow v Oxford United 2-0
Newport (IOW) v Aylesbury United 2-3
Peterborough United v Northampton Town 4-0
Port Vale v Hartlepool United 6-0
Preston North End v Blackpool 1-0
Tiverton Town v Leyton Orient 1-3
Walsall v Rochdale 3-0
Walton & Hersham v Swansea City 0-2
Wigan Athletic v Spennymoor United 4-0
Wrexham v Stockport County 1-0
Wycombe Wanderers v Chelmsford City 4-0
Yeading v Colchester United 2-2
York City v Rotherham United 3-3
r Brentford v Cambridge United 1-2
r Bury v Bishop Auckland 1-1P
r Colchester United v Yeading 7-1
r Fulham v Ashford Town 5-3e
r Hitchin Town v Hereford United 4-2
r Rotherham United v York City 3-0
r Runcorn v Halifax Town 1-3e
r Scarborough v Chesterfield 2-0
r Scunthorpe United v Bradford City 3-2e
r Torquay United v Kidderminster Harriers 1-0
r Woking v Barnet 1-0

Round Two

Altrincham v Wigan Athletic 1-0
Bashley v Swansea City 0-1
Birmingham City v Scunthorpe United 0-0
Carlisle United v Darlington 2-0
Chester City v Burnley 1-2
Crewe Alexandra v Bury 1-2
Enfield v Torquay United 1-1
Exeter City v Colchester United 1-2
Gillingham v Fulham 1-1
Halifax Town v Mansfield Town 0-0
Hitchin Town v Wycombe Wanderers 0-5
Kingstonian v Aylesbury United 1-4
Leyton Orient v Bristol Rovers 0-2
Lincoln City v Huddersfield Town 1-0
Marlow v Woking 2-1
Peterborough United v Cambridge United 0-2
Plymouth Argyle v Bournemouth 2-1
Preston North End v Walsall 1-1
Scarborough v Port Vale 1-0
Wrexham v Rotherham United 5-2
r Fulham v Gillingham 1-2e
r Mansfield Town v Halifax Town 2-1
r Scunthorpe United v Birmingham City 1-2
r Torquay United v Enfield 0-1
r Walsall v Preston North End 4-0

Round Three

Barnsley v Aston Villa 0-2
Birmingham City v Liverpool 0-0
Bristol City v Stoke City 0-0
Bury v Tranmere Rovers 2-2
Cambridge United v Burnley 2-4
Chelsea v Charlton Athletic 3-0
Coventry City v West Bromwich Albion 1-1
Crystal Palace v Lincoln City 5-1
Everton v Derby County 1-0
Gillingham v Sheffield Wednesday 1-2
Grimsby Town v Norwich City 0-1
Leicester City v Enfield 2-0
Luton Town v Bristol Rovers 1-1
Mansfield Town v Wolverhampton Wan. 2-3
Millwall v Arsenal 0-0
Newcastle United v Blackburn Rovers 1-1
Nottingham Forest v Plymouth Argyle 2-0
Notts County v Manchester City 2-2
Portsmouth v Bolton Wanderers 3-1
Queen's Park Rangers v Aylesbury United 4-0
Reading v Oldham Athletic 1-3
Scarborough v Watford 0-0
Sheffield United v Manchester United 0-2
Southampton v Southend United 2-0
Sunderland v Carlisle United 1-1
Swansea City v Middlesbrough 1-1
Swindon Town v Marlow 2-0
Tottenham Hotspur v Altrincham 3-0
Walsall v Leeds United 1-1
Wimbledon v Colchester United 1-0
Wrexham v Ipswich Town 2-1
Wycombe Wanderers v West Ham United 0-2
r Arsenal v Millwall 0-2
r Blackburn Rovers v Newcastle United 1-2
r Bristol Rovers v Luton Town 0-1
r Carlisle United v Sunderland 1-3
r Leeds United v Walsall 5-2e
r Liverpool v Birmingham City 1-1P
r Manchester City v Notts County 5-2
r Middlesbrough v Swansea City 1-2
r Stoke City v Bristol City 1-3e
r Tranmere Rovers v Bury 3-0
r Watford v Scarborough 2-0
r West Bromwich Albion v Coventry City 1-2

Round Four

Bristol City v Everton 0-1
Burnley v Liverpool 0-0
Coventry City v Norwich City 0-0
Leeds United v Oldham Athletic 3-2
Luton Town v Southampton 1-1
Manchester City v Aston Villa 1-0
Manchester United v Wrexham 5-2
Millwall v Chelsea 0-0
Newcastle United v Swansea City 3-0
Nottingham Forest v Crystal Palace 1-2
Portsmouth v Leicester City 0-1
Queen's Park Rangers v West Ham United 1-0
Sheffield Wednesday v Wolverhampton Wan. 0-0
Sunderland v Tottenham Hotspur 1-4
Tranmere Rovers v Wimbledon 0-2
Watford v Swindon Town 1-0
r Chelsea v Millwall 1-1q
r Liverpool v Burnley 1-0
r Norwich City v Coventry City 3-1e
r Southampton v Luton Town 6-0
r Wolverhampton Wan. v Sheffield Wednesday 1-1P

Round Five

Everton v Norwich City 5-0
Liverpool v Wimbledon 1-1
Manchester United v Leeds United 3-1
Newcastle United v Manchester City 3-1
Queen's Park Rangers v Millwall 1-0
Tottenham Hotspur v Southampton 1-1
Watford v Crystal Palace 0-0
Wolverhampton Wan. v Leicester City 1-0
r Crystal Palace v Watford 1-0e
r Southampton v Tottenham Hotspur 2-6e
r Wimbledon v Liverpool 0-2

Round Six

Crystal Palace v Wolverhampton Wan. 1-1
Everton v Newcastle United 1-0
Liverpool v Tottenham Hotspur 1-2
Manchester United v Queen's Park Rangers 2-0
r Wolverhampton Wan. v Crystal Palace 1-4

1994/95 to 1995/96

Semi Finals

	Manchester United v Crystal Palace	2-2eN
	Tottenham Hotspur v Everton	1-4 N
r	Manchester United v Crystal Palace	2-0 N

Final

	Everton v Manchester United	1-0 N

1995/96

Preliminary Round

1	Consett v Prudhoe Town	3-1
	Guisborough Town v Gretna	1-0
	Liversedge v Blackpool (Wren) Rovers	1-4
	Willington v Dunston Federation Brewery	0-0
2	Brandon United v Chester-le-Street Town	1-4
	Netherfield (Kendal) v Evenwood Town	10-1
	RTM Newcastle v Harrogate Railway Athletic	1-2
	South Shields (3) v Pickering Town	3-4
3	Alnwick Town v Glasshoughton Welfare	1-3
	Esh Winning v Stockton (2)	3-1
	Seaham Red Star v Billingham Town	1-2
	Whitley Bay v Easington Colliery	3-0
	Workington v Hebburn	8-1
4	Darlington Cleveland Social v Billingham Synthonia	0-3
	Ryhope Community Association v Morpeth Town	2-2e
	Shotton Comrades v Shildon	1-1
	Tadcaster Albion v Bedlington Terriers	1-1
	Washington v Garforth Town	1-0 D
5	Burscough v Northallerton '94	2-2
	Chadderton v Eastwood Town	0-1
	Eccleshill United v Atherton LR	3-2
	Lincoln United v Stocksbridge Park Steels	3-2
	Prescot Cables v Atherton Collieries	3-0
6	Arnold Town v Maine Road	2-0
	Belper Town v Worksop Town	2-3
	Glossop North End v Nantwich Town	1-2
	Radcliffe Borough v Alfreton Town	3-2
	Sheffield v Caernarfon Town	wo/s
7	Brigg Town v Clitheroe	1-1
	Leigh RMI v Flixton	2-0
	Maltby MW v Mossley	3-3
	North Ferriby United v Heanor Town	2-4
8	Blidworth MW v Rossendale United	0-0
	Denaby United v Hucknall Town	4-0
	Farsley Celtic v Oldham Town	2-2
	St Helens Town v Bootle	1-2
	Winterton Rangers v Darwen	2-0
9	Armthorpe Welfare v Bradford Park Avenue	1-1
	Crook Town v Kimberley Town	3-2
	Ossett Town v Castleton Gabriels	3-2
	Trafford v Fleetwood Town	2-1
10	Goole Town v Great Harwood Town	2-2
	Louth United v Harworth Colliery Institute	4-0
	Ossett Albion v Hatfield Main	1-3
	Rossington Main v Immingham Town	1-1
	Salford City v Newcastle Town	1-2
11	Hinckley Athletic v Ashton United	1-1
	Pontefract Collieries v Oakham United	4-1
	Thackley v Cheadle Town	5-2
	Yorkshire Amateur v Borrowash Victoria	2-4
12	Bilston Town v Blakenall	0-0
	Redditch United v Bridgnorth Town	2-2
	Rocester v Desborough Town	0-0e
	Shifnal Town v Willenhall Town	0-0
	West Midlands Police v Raunds Town	1-1
13	Chasetown v Halesowen Harriers	2-1
	Stourport Swifts v Armitage '90	0-1
	Tamworth v Hinckley Town	3-1
	Wellingborough Town v Bolehall Swifts	0-4
	Westfields v Corby Town	1-1
14	Brierley Hill Town v Sandwell Borough	0-0
	Northampton Spencer v Cogenhoe United	2-2
	Pelsall Villa v Dudley Town	1-1
	Shepshed Dynamo v Grantham Town	0-1
	Stapenhill v Lye Town	1-2
15	Leicester United v Barwell	0-0
	Newport Pagnell Town v Boldmere St Michaels	0-2
	Pershore Town v Evesham United	1-1
	Wednesfield v Banbury United	2-2
16	Knypersley Victoria v Stratford Town	0-3 N
	Long Buckby v Stewarts & Lloyds (2)	2-1
	Oldbury United v Darlaston	4-0
	Rothwell Town v Rushall Olympic	2-0
17	East Thurrock United v Tiptree United	1-1
	Eynesbury Rovers v Witham Town	4-1
	Gorleston v Diss Town	1-5
	Halstead Town v Stamford	1-1
	Wisbech Town v Tring Town	4-0
18	Basildon United v Saffron Walden Town	1-2
	King's Lynn v Wivenhoe Town	3-0
	Newmarket Town v Boston Town	0-1
	Spalding United v Harwich & Parkeston	2-3
	Wroxham v Canvey Island	0-0
19	Aveley v Stowmarket Town	0-0
	Burnham Ramblers v Holbeach United	1-3
	Bury Town v Collier Row	1-2
	Great Yarmouth Town v Bourne Town	2-1
	March Town United v Fakenham Town	1-0
20	Cheshunt v Wealdstone	0-1
	East Ham United v Sudbury Wanderers	0-7
	Hertford Town v Ware	2-1
	Leyton Pennant v Clacton Town	2-2
	Tufnell Park (2) v Potton United	1-0
21	Bedford Town v Edgware Town	1-4
	Biggleswade Town v Berkhamsted Town	0-4 N
	Felixstowe Town v Burnham	1-1
	Hillingdon Borough v Cornard United	2-0
	Hornchurch v Bowers United	3-0
22	Brook House v Welwyn Garden City	0-0
	Haverhill Rovers v Hampton	0-1
	Lowestoft Town v Chalfont St Peter	2-2
	Northwood v Ford United	3-2
	Uxbridge v Kempston Rovers	4-0
23	Brimsdown Rovers v Barton Rovers	0-2
	Hadleigh United v Southall	1-0
	Harefield United v Hoddesdon Town	0-1
	Soham Town Rangers v Stotfold	1-1
	Tilbury v Woodbridge Town	1-2
24	Barking v Royston Town	1-0
	Clapton v Leighton Town	2-1
	Concord Rangers v Wootton Blue Cross	2-1
	Flackwell Heath v Potters Bar Town	1-0
	Metropolitan Police v Viking Sports	7-0
25	Bedfont v Langford	0-0
	Bracknell Town v Kingsbury Town	0-0
	Hanwell Town v Wingate & Finchley	2-4e
	Harlow Town v Thamesmead Town	2-3
	Milton Keynes v Leatherhead	0-4
26	Corinthian Casuals v Stamco	3-0
	Egham Town v Dartford	1-3
	Fisher '93 v Merstham	0-0
	Lewes v Lancing	2-1
	Three Bridges v Camberley Town	0-5
27	Croydon v Dorking (2)	5-2
	Epsom & Ewell v Tooting & Mitcham United	0-4
	Folkestone Invicta v Peacehaven & Telscombe	1-1
	Shoreham v Corinthian	4-2
	Tonbridge v Croydon Athletic	3-1
28	Banstead Athletic v Burgess Hill Town	3-1
	Bognor Regis Town v Whitehawk	4-3
	Chatham Town v Whyteleafe	3-1
	Raynes Park Vale v Canterbury City	3-0
	Southwick v Littlehampton Town	1-1
29	Chipstead v Horsham	0-4
	Herne Bay v Horsham YMCA	1-1
	Redhill v Tunbridge Wells	3-1
	Wick v Portfield	3-2
30	Crowborough Athletic v Godalming & Guildford	1-3
	Sheppey United v Arundel	2-0
	Slade Green v Langney Sports	0-2
	Whitstable Town v Hailsham Town	3-2
31	Aldershot Town v Selsey	5-0
	Buckingham Town v Newbury Town	wo/s
	Ringmer v Bicester Town	1-0
	Steyning Town v Cove	3-0
	Thatcham Town v Oakwood	2-1
32	AFC Totton v Fleet Town	3-1
	Abingdon Town v Andover	3-2
	Hungerford Town v Poole Town	5-0
	Thame United v Maidenhead United	4-0
	Witney Town v BAT Sports	5-0
33	Basingstoke Town v Westbury United	2-2
	Bemerton Heath Harlequins v Ryde Sports	2-3
	Bournemouth (Ams) v Wimborne Town	0-4
	Calne Town v Lymington	2-0
	Fareham Town v Weymouth	1-1
34	Brockenhurst v Swanage Town & Herston	0-0
	Chippenham Town v Paulton Rovers	0-0
	Gosport Borough v Eastleigh	2-0
	Melksham Town v Bridport	1-2
	Welton Rovers v Odd Down	2-0
35	Clevedon Town v Mangotsfield United	1-5
	Devizes Town v Bristol Manor Farm	1-1
	Glastonbury v Tuffley Rovers	1-5
	Worcester City v Yate Town	1-2
36	Backwell United v Elmore	0-1
	Barnstaple Town v Minehead	2-0
	Falmouth Town v Frome Town	3-0
	Saltash United v Torrington	3-2
	Weston-Super-Mare v St Blazey	7-0
1r	Dunston Federation Brewery v Willington	5-2
4r	Bedlington Terriers v Tadcaster Albion	3-0
r	Morpeth Town v Ryhope Community Association	3-1e
r	Shildon v Shotton Comrades	2-1e
5r	Northallerton '94 v Burscough	1-2
7r	Clitheroe v Brigg Town	1-0
r	Mossley v Maltby MW	4-0
8r	Oldham Town v Farsley Celtic	0-2
r	Rossendale United v Blidworth MW	3-0
9r	Bradford Park Avenue v Armthorpe Welfare	1-0
10r	Great Harwood Town v Goole Town	3-2
r	Rossington Main v Immingham Town	1-4
11r	Ashton United v Hinckley Athletic	1-3
12r	Blakenall v Bilston Town	2-1e
r	Bridgnorth Town v Redditch United	1-4
r	Raunds Town v West Midlands Police	3-2
r	Rocester v Desborough Town	2-4
r	Willenhall Town v Shifnal Town	0-1
13r	Corby Town v Westfields	7-5
14r	Cogenhoe United v Northampton Spencer	1-0
r	Dudley Town v Pelsall Villa	1-0
r	Sandwell Borough v Brierley Hill Town	5-3
15r	Banbury United v Wednesfield	0-3
r	Barwell v Leicester United	1-1e
r	Evesham United v Pershore Town	3-2
17r	Stamford v Halstead Town	3-3e
r	Tiptree United v East Thurrock United	6-2
18r	Canvey Island v Wroxham	3-1
19r	Stowmarket Town v Aveley	3-4
20r	Clacton Town v Leyton Pennant	0-4
21r	Burnham v Felixstowe Town	2-3
22r	Chalfont St Peter v Lowestoft Town	4-1
r	Welwyn Garden City v Brook House	0-2
23r	Stotfold v Soham Town Rangers	4-1
25r	Kingsbury Town v Bracknell Town	0-0e
r	Langford v Bedfont	1-1e
26r	Merstham v Fisher '93	0-2
27r	Peacehaven & Telscombe v Folkestone Invicta	4-1
28r	Southwick v Littlehampton Town	1-0
29r	Horsham YMCA v Herne Bay	1-4
33r	Basingstoke Town v Westbury United	5-1
r	Weymouth v Fareham Town	3-2
34r	Paulton Rovers v Chippenham Town	1-1e
r	Swanage Town & Herston v Brockenhurst	1-1e
35r	Bristol Manor Farm v Devizes Town	3-1
15r2	Barwell v Leicester United	3-4 N
17r2	Stamford v Halstead Town	1-2 N
25r2	Bedfont v Langford	0-4 N
r2	Kingsbury Town v Bracknell Town	1-1e
34r2	Brockenhurst v Swanage Town & Herston	1-0 N
r2	Chippenham Town v Paulton Rovers	0-2 N
25r3	Bracknell Town v Kingsbury Town	3-2

Qualifying Round One

1	Barrow v Consett	3-0
	Durham City v Blackpool (Wren) Rovers	1-1
	Gateshead (2) v Dunston Federation Brewery	3-2
	Guisborough Town v Murton	1-0
2	Bishop Auckland v Harrogate Railway Athletic	2-1
	Lancaster City v Pickering Town	2-1
	Netherfield (Kendal) v Peterlee Newtown	2-4
	Tow Law Town v Chester-le-Street Town	3-3
3	Esh Winning v West Auckland Town	1-2
	Spennymoor United v Glasshoughton Welfare	1-0
	Whitby Town v Billingham Town	0-1
	Whitley Bay v Workington	1-2
4	Billingham Synthonia v Shildon	3-1
	Blyth Spartans v Garforth Town	6-0
	Harrogate Town v Bedlington Terriers	1-2
	Morpeth Town v Whickham	1-2
5	Eastwood Town v Buxton	2-1
	Eccleshill United v Lincoln United	2-3
	Frickley Athletic v Prescot Cables	0-0
	Northwich Victoria v Burscough	5-0
6	Gainsborough Trinity v Arnold Town	2-0
	Morecambe v Sheffield	7-0
	Nantwich Town v Droylsden	3-0
	Worksop Town v Radcliffe Borough	4-0
7	Bamber Bridge v Heanor Town	4-1
	Guiseley v Leigh RMI	3-0
	Leek Town v Clitheroe	1-1
	Mossley v Hallam	1-0
8	Chorley v Farsley Celtic	2-2
	Denaby United v Bootle	3-0
	Hyde United v Winterton Rangers	6-0 N
	Rossendale United v Colwyn Bay	1-4
9	Accrington Stanley (2) v Ossett Town	2-1
	Crook Town v Curzon Ashton	1-1
	Knowsley United v Bradford Park Avenue	0-0 N
	Warrington Town v Trafford	2-2
10	Hatfield Main v Ilkeston Town (2)	0-2
	Marine v Louth United	4-0
	Matlock Town v Great Harwood Town	5-2
	Newcastle Town v Immingham Town	5-0
11	Congleton Town v Pontefract Collieries	3-1
	Emley v Thackley	6-0
	Hinckley Athletic v Kidsgrove Athletic	3-1
	Winsford United v Borrowash Victoria	1-0
12	Halesowen Town v Blakenall	3-2
	Raunds Town v Desborough Town	3-0
	Redditch United v Moor Green	1-3
	Telford United v Shifnal Town	4-0
13	Atherstone United v Armitage '90	2-2
	Bolehall Swifts v Tamworth	0-1
	Chasetown v Solihull Borough	1-3
	Hednesford Town v Corby Town	3-1
14	Gresley Rovers v Dudley Town	1-2
	Lye Town v Eastwood Hanley	1-2
	Rushden & Diamonds v Grantham Town	4-1
	Sandwell Borough v Cogenhoe United	2-1
15	Boldmere St Michaels v Bedworth United	1-2
	Paget Rangers v Wednesfield	1-0
	Stourbridge v Evesham United	2-2
	V.S. Rugby v Leicester United	1-2
16	Burton Albion v Stratford Town	4-0
	Long Buckby v Sutton Coldfield Town	2-1
	Racing Club Warwick v Oldbury United	1-0
	Stafford Rangers v Rothwell Town	6-1
17	Boston United v Wisbech Town	1-2
	Diss Town v Heybridge Swifts	0-2
	Eynesbury Rovers v Halstead Town	7-1
	Sudbury Town v Tiptree United	3-0
18	Bishop's Stortford v Boston Town	2-2
	Cambridge City v Canvey Island	2-3
	Harwich & Parkeston v Braintree Town	0-1
	Saffron Walden Town v King's Lynn	0-2

1995/96

19	Billericay Town v Aveley	2-0
	Chelmsford City v Collier Row	1-0
	Great Yarmouth Town v Mirrlees Blackstone	2-1
	March Town United v Holbeach United	0-3
20	Arlesey Town v Leyton Pennant	3-0
	Grays Athletic v Wealdstone	2-2
	Sudbury Wanderers v Watton United	3-1
	Tufnell Park (2) v Hertford Town	2-2
21	Berkhamsted Town v Hillingdon Borough	3-2
	Dagenham & Redbridge v Hornchurch	4-0
	Edgware Town v Chesham United	0-1
	Purfleet v Felixstowe Town	4-0
22	Boreham Wood v Chalfont St Peter	1-0
	Hampton v Staines Town	1-2
	Northwood v Uxbridge	0-5
	Stevenage Borough v Brook House	0-0e
23	Hoddesdon Town v Woodbridge Town	0-2
	Romford v Hadleigh United	1-0
	St Albans City v Barton Rovers	4-1
	Stotfold v Hemel Hempstead Town	2-1
24	Baldock Town v Metropolitan Police	2-1
	Barking v Clapton	1-3
	Concord Rangers v Hayes	0-3
	Hendon v Flackwell Heath	8-0
25	Bracknell Town v Thamesmead Town	1-1
	Harrow Borough v Leatherhead	2-1
	Wembley v Langford	3-0
	Wingate & Finchley v Ruislip Manor	2-3
26	Corinthian Casuals v Margate	2-5
	Farnborough Town v Dartford	1-0
	Fisher '93 v Lewes	7-0
	Walton & Hersham v Camberley Town	4-0
27	Ashford Town v Tonbridge	2-0
	Chertsey Town v Shoreham	2-2
	Croydon v Hastings Town	2-3
	Tooting & Mitcham United v Peacehaven & Telscombe	0-0
28	Chatham Town v Ramsgate	1-1
	Dover Athletic v Bognor Regis Town	1-2
	Dulwich Hamlet v Southwick	7-1
	Raynes Park Vale v Banstead Athletic	1-2
29	Bromley v Herne Bay	3-1
	Erith & Belvedere v Redhill	4-1
	Horsham v Sittingbourne	0-5
	Welling United v Wick	2-0
30	Carshalton Athletic v Sheppey United	3-1
	Gravesend & Northfleet v Godalming & Guildford	7-0
	Langney Sports v Windsor & Eton	1-3
	Molesey v Whitstable Town	4-1
31	Aldershot Town v Pagham	4-0
	Thatcham Town v Steyning Town	5-1
	Wokingham Town v Ringmer	3-1
	Worthing v Buckingham Town	1-1
32	Abingdon Town v Newport (IOW)	2-3
	Oxford City v Witney Town	1-1
	Salisbury City v Hungerford Town	5-2
	Thame United v AFC Totton	1-1
33	Basingstoke Town v Havant Town	2-1
	Dorchester Town v Wimborne Town	2-2
	Ryde Sports v Weymouth	1-1
	Waterlooville v Calne Town	5-0
34	Bridport v Merthyr Tydfil	0-3
	Newport AFC v Brockenhurst	5-0
	Paulton Rovers v Welton Rovers	1-1
	Trowbridge Town v Gosport Borough	8-1
35	Cheltenham Town v Yate Town	5-0
	Forest Green Rovers v Mangotsfield United	2-1
	Gloucester City v Bristol Manor Farm	8-0
	Tuffley Rovers v Cinderford Town	0-4
36	Bideford v Elmore	2-2
	Falmouth Town v Weston-Super-Mare	1-1
	Saltash United v Taunton Town	1-2
	Tiverton Town v Barnstaple Town	9-0
1r	Blackpool (Wren) Rovers v Durham City	1-5
2r	Chester-le-Street Town v Tow Law Town	1-3
5r	Prescot Cables v Frickley Athletic	2-2e
7r	Clitheroe v Leek Town	2-2e
8r	Farsley Celtic v Chorley	1-2
9r	Bradford Park Avenue v Knowsley United	3-2e
r	Curzon Ashton v Crook Town	2-1
r	Trafford v Warrington Town	4-3e
13r	Armitage '90 v Atherstone United	3-3e
15r	Evesham United v Stourbridge	3-0
18r	Boston Town v Bishop's Stortford	5-2
20r	Hertford Town v Tufnell Park (2)	5-1
r	Wealdstone v Grays Athletic	4-3
22r	Brook House v Stevenage Borough	1-5 N
25r	Thamesmead Town v Bracknell Town	2-3e
27r	Peacehaven & Telscombe v Tooting & Mitcham United	0-1
r	Shoreham v Chertsey Town	1-3
28r	Ramsgate v Chatham Town	0-2
31r	Buckingham Town v Worthing	0-0e
32r	AFC Totton v Thame United	0-4
r	Witney Town v Oxford City	3-1e
33r	Weymouth v Ryde Sports	2-1
r	Wimborne Town v Dorchester Town	0-2
34r	Welton Rovers v Paulton Rovers	2-1e
36r	Elmore v Bideford	2-6
r	Weston-Super-Mare v Falmouth Town	5-0
5r2	Prescot Cables v Frickley Athletic	0-1 N
7r2	Clitheroe v Leek Town	0-0e
13r2	Armitage '90 v Atherstone United	5-4
31r2	Worthing v Buckingham Town	2-2
7r3	Leek Town v Clitheroe	1-0
31r3	Buckingham Town v Worthing	6-1

Qualifying Round Two

1	Durham City v Guisborough Town	2-1
	Gateshead (2) v Barrow	2-2
2	Bishop Auckland v Tow Law Town	2-1
	Lancaster City v Peterlee Newtown	3-0
3	Billingham Town v West Auckland Town	1-0
	Workington v Spennymoor United	2-4
4	Bedlington Terriers v Whickham	1-0
	Billingham Synthonia v Blyth Spartans	0-2
5	Frickley Athletic v Eastwood Town	2-4
	Lincoln United v Northwich Victoria	1-4
6	Gainsborough Trinity v Nantwich Town	5-0
	Worksop Town v Morecambe	2-3
7	Bamber Bridge v Mossley	0-2
	Guiseley v Leek Town	4-0
8	Chorley v Colwyn Bay	1-2
	Denaby United v Hyde United	1-2
9	Accrington Stanley (2) v Bradford Park Avenue	1-2
	Trafford v Curzon Ashton	1-2
10	Matlock Town v Ilkeston Town (2)	1-2
	Newcastle Town v Marine	0-1
11	Congleton Town v Hinckley Athletic	1-1
	Emley v Winsford United	1-1
12	Halesowen Town v Moor Green	1-0
	Raunds Town v Telford United	1-2
13	Armitage '90 v Solihull Borough	2-3
	Tamworth v Hednesford Town	1-2
14	Rushden & Diamonds v Eastwood Hanley	1-0
	Sandwell Borough v Dudley Town	2-1
15	Evesham United v Bedworth United	2-0
	Leicester United v Paget Rangers	3-2
16	Burton Albion v Stafford Rangers	1-1
	Racing Club Warwick v Long Buckby	2-0
17	Eynesbury Rovers v Wisbech Town	3-3
	Sudbury Town v Heybridge Swifts	2-1
18	Canvey Island v Braintree Town	2-0
	King's Lynn v Boston Town	5-1
19	Billericay Town v Great Yarmouth Town	2-0
	Holbeach United v Chelmsford City	0-0
20	Arlesey Town v Sudbury Wanderers	1-2
	Hertford Town v Wealdstone	1-0
21	Berkhamsted Town v Dagenham & Redbridge	1-2
	Purfleet v Chesham United	3-1
22	Boreham Wood v Staines Town	0-1
	Uxbridge v Stevenage Borough	0-1
23	Romford v Stotfold	4-1
	Woodbridge Town v St Albans City	1-1
24	Baldock Town v Hayes	0-1
	Clapton v Hendon	2-3
25	Bracknell Town v Harrow Borough	2-1
	Wembley v Ruislip Manor	3-0
26	Fisher '93 v Farnborough Town	1-4
	Walton & Hersham v Margate	2-2
27	Ashford Town v Hastings Town	3-1
	Tooting & Mitcham United v Chertsey Town	2-2
28	Banstead Athletic v Bognor Regis Town	0-3
	Dulwich Hamlet v Chatham Town	2-1
29	Erith & Belvedere v Sittingbourne	2-2
	Welling United v Bromley	2-2
30	Carshalton Athletic v Windsor & Eton	4-3
	Molesey v Gravesend & Northfleet	0-6
31	Thatcham Town v Buckingham Town	0-1
	Wokingham Town v Aldershot Town	1-2
32	Salisbury City v Newport (IOW)	1-3
	Thame United v Witney Town	1-1
33	Dorchester Town v Basingstoke Town	2-0
	Weymouth v Waterlooville	1-0
34	Newport AFC v Merthyr Tydfil	3-3
	Welton Rovers v Trowbridge Town	1-2
35	Forest Green Rovers v Cheltenham Town	3-0
	Gloucester City v Cinderford Town	0-1
36	Bideford v Taunton Town	4-3
	Weston-Super-Mare v Tiverton Town	1-1
1r	Barrow v Gateshead (2)	1-0
11r	Hinckley Athletic v Congleton Town	1-0
r	Winsford United v Emley	2-1
16r	Stafford Rangers v Burton Albion	2-3
17r	Wisbech Town v Eynesbury Rovers	6-1
19r	Chelmsford City v Holbeach United	3-1e
23r	St Albans City v Woodbridge Town	2-0
26r	Margate v Walton & Hersham	0-1
27r	Chertsey Town v Tooting & Mitcham United	1-2
29r	Bromley v Welling United	3-3e
r	Sittingbourne v Erith & Belvedere	6-1
32r	Witney Town v Thame United	2-3
34r	Merthyr Tydfil v Newport AFC	1-2
36r	Tiverton Town v Weston-Super-Mare	1-0
29r2	Welling United v Bromley	1-2

Qualifying Round Three

1	Barrow v Durham City	1-1
2	Bishop Auckland v Lancaster City	0-1
3	Spennymoor United v Billingham Town	6-1
4	Blyth Spartans v Bedlington Terriers	3-1
5	Northwich Victoria v Eastwood Town	0-0
6	Morecambe v Gainsborough Trinity	6-2
7	Guiseley v Mossley	6-1
8	Hyde United v Colwyn Bay	1-2 N
9	Bradford Park Avenue v Curzon Ashton	2-1
10	Marine v Ilkeston Town (2)	0-0
11	Winsford United v Hinckley Athletic	3-2
12	Telford United v Halesowen Town	4-1
13	Hednesford Town v Solihull Borough	2-2
14	Sandwell Borough v Rushden & Diamonds	1-6
15	Leicester United v Evesham United	0-1
16	Burton Albion v Racing Club Warwick	2-0
17	Wisbech Town v Sudbury Town	1-0
18	King's Lynn v Canvey Island	1-0 D
19	Chelmsford City v Billericay Town	1-1
20	Hertford Town v Sudbury Wanderers	0-2
21	Dagenham & Redbridge v Purfleet	1-1
22	Stevenage Borough v Staines Town	2-0
23	St Albans City v Romford	3-1
24	Hendon v Hayes	0-3
25	Bracknell Town v Wembley	4-1
26	Farnborough Town v Walton & Hersham	3-2
27	Tooting & Mitcham United v Ashford Town	0-1
28	Bognor Regis Town v Dulwich Hamlet	4-2
29	Bromley v Sittingbourne	1-1
30	Gravesend & Northfleet v Carshalton Athletic	2-1
31	Buckingham Town v Aldershot Town	0-1
32	Thame United v Newport (IOW)	1-1
33	Weymouth v Dorchester Town	2-3
34	Trowbridge Town v Newport AFC	2-0
35	Forest Green Rovers v Cinderford Town	1-1
36	Tiverton Town v Bideford	4-1
1r	Durham City v Barrow	0-1
5r	Eastwood Town v Northwich Victoria	1-2e
10r	Ilkeston Town (2) v Marine	1-2e
13r	Solihull Borough v Hednesford Town	1-2
19r	Billericay Town v Chelmsford City	2-1
21r	Purfleet v Dagenham & Redbridge	2-1
29r	Sittingbourne v Bromley	3-2e
32r	Newport (IOW) v Thame United	3-1
35r	Cinderford Town v Forest Green Rovers	1-1e
35r2	Forest Green Rovers v Cinderford Town	1-3

Qualifying Round Four

	Ashford Town v Aldershot Town	2-0
	Aylesbury United v Stevenage Borough	1-3
	Billericay Town v Wisbech Town	1-1
	Blyth Spartans v Guiseley	2-0
	Burton Albion v Bracknell Town	3-1
	Canvey Island v Hednesford Town	2-0
	Cinderford Town v Bath City	3-2
	Farnborough Town v Yeovil Town	2-1
	Gravesend & Northfleet v Marlow	1-1
	Hayes v Sudbury Wanderers	4-0
	Hitchin Town v St Albans City	2-1
	Kettering Town v Bromsgrove Rovers	0-0
	Kingstonian v Trowbridge Town	3-1
	Macclesfield Town v Northwich Victoria	0-1
	Marine v Bradford Park Avenue	2-0
	Newport (IOW) v Bashley	1-1
	Nuneaton Borough v Evesham United	6-1
	Purfleet v Rushden & Diamonds	1-1
	Runcorn v Halifax Town	2-1
	Sittingbourne v Dorchester Town	1-2
	Spennymoor United v Lancaster City	1-0
	Stalybridge Celtic v Colwyn Bay	2-2
	Sutton United v Crawley Town	4-1
	Telford United v Southport	3-0
	Tiverton Town v Bognor Regis Town	1-4
	Winsford United v Barrow	0-3
	Witton Albion v Morecambe	3-2
	Yeading v Slough Town	0-2
r	Bashley v Newport (IOW)	2-3
r	Bromsgrove Rovers v Kettering Town	2-2e
r	Colwyn Bay v Stalybridge Celtic	3-0
r	Marlow v Gravesend & Northfleet	3-3e
r	Rushden & Diamonds v Purfleet	3-1
r	Wisbech Town v Billericay Town	2-0
r2	Gravesend & Northfleet v Marlow	4-0
r2	Kettering Town v Bromsgrove Rovers	1-2

Round One

Altrincham v Crewe Alexandra	0-2
Barnet v Woking	2-2
Barrow v Nuneaton Borough	2-1
Blackpool v Chester City	2-1
Bognor Regis Town v Ashford Town	1-1
Bournemouth v Bristol City	0-0
Bradford City v Burton Albion	4-3
Brentford v Farnborough Town	1-1
Burnley v Walsall	1-3
Bury v Blyth Spartans	0-2
Canvey Island v Brighton & Hove Albion	2-2
Carlisle United v Preston North End	1-2
Cinderford Town v Bromsgrove Rovers	2-1
Exeter City v Peterborough United	0-1
Fulham v Swansea City	7-0
Gravesend & Northfleet v Colchester United	2-0
Hartlepool United v Darlington	2-4
Hereford United v Stevenage Borough	2-1
Hitchin Town v Bristol Rovers	2-1
Hull City v Wrexham	0-0
Kidderminster Harriers v Sutton United	2-2
Kingstonian v Wisbech Town	5-1
Mansfield Town v Doncaster Rovers	4-2
Newport (IOW) v Enfield	1-1
Northampton Town v Hayes	1-0
Northwich Victoria v Scunthorpe United	1-3
Oxford United v Dorchester Town	9-1
Rochdale v Rotherham United	5-3
Runcorn v Wigan Athletic	1-1
Rushden & Diamonds v Cardiff City	1-3

1995/96 to 1996/97

Scarborough v Chesterfield	0-2
Shrewsbury Town v Marine	11-2
Slough Town v Plymouth Argyle	0-2
Spennymoor United v Colwyn Bay	0-1
Stockport County v Lincoln City	5-0
Swindon Town v Cambridge United	4-1
Telford United v Witton Albion	2-1
Torquay United v Leyton Orient	1-0
Wycombe Wanderers v Gillingham	1-1
York City v Notts County	0-1
r Ashford Town v Bognor Regis Town	0-1
r Brighton & Hove Albion v Canvey Island	4-1
r Bristol City v Bournemouth	0-1
r Enfield v Newport (IOW)	2-1
r Farnborough Town v Brentford	0-4
r Gillingham v Wycombe Wanderers	1-0
r Sutton United v Kidderminster Harriers	1-1P
r Wigan Athletic v Runcorn	4-2
r Woking v Barnet	2-1e
r Wrexham v Hull City	0-0P

Round Two

Barrow v Wigan Athletic	0-4
Blackpool v Colwyn Bay	2-0
Bournemouth v Brentford	0-1
Bradford City v Preston North End	2-1
Cinderford Town v Gravesend & Northfleet	1-1
Crewe Alexandra v Mansfield Town	2-0
Enfield v Woking	1-1
Fulham v Brighton & Hove Albion	0-0
Gillingham v Hitchin Town	3-0
Hereford United v Sutton United	2-0
Kingstonian v Plymouth Argyle	1-2
Oxford United v Northampton Town	2-0
Peterborough United v Bognor Regis Town	4-0
Rochdale v Darlington	2-2
Scunthorpe United v Shrewsbury Town	1-1
Stockport County v Blyth Spartans	2-0
Swindon Town v Cardiff City	2-0
Telford United v Notts County	0-2
Torquay United v Walsall	1-1
Wrexham v Chesterfield	3-2
r Brighton & Hove Albion v Fulham	0-0q
r Darlington v Rochdale	0-1
r Gravesend & Northfleet v Cinderford Town	3-0
r Shrewsbury Town v Scunthorpe United	2-1
r Walsall v Torquay United	8-4e
r Woking v Enfield	2-1

Round Three

Arsenal v Sheffield United	1-1
Aston Villa v Gravesend & Northfleet	3-0
Barnsley v Oldham Athletic	0-0
Birmingham City v Wolverhampton Wan.	1-1
Bradford City v Bolton Wanderers	0-3
Charlton Athletic v Sheffield Wednesday	2-0
Chelsea v Newcastle United	1-1
Crewe Alexandra v West Bromwich Albion	4-3
Crystal Palace v Port Vale	0-0
Derby County v Leeds United	2-4
Everton v Stockport County	2-2
Fulham v Shrewsbury Town	1-1
Grimsby Town v Luton Town	7-1
Hereford United v Tottenham Hotspur	1-1
Huddersfield Town v Blackpool	2-1
Ipswich Town v Blackburn Rovers	0-0
Leicester City v Manchester City	0-0
Liverpool v Rochdale	7-0
Manchester United v Sunderland	2-2
Millwall v Oxford United	3-3
Norwich City v Brentford	1-2
Notts County v Middlesbrough	1-2
Peterborough United v Wrexham	1-0
Plymouth Argyle v Coventry City	1-3
Reading v Gillingham	3-1
Southampton v Portsmouth	3-0
Stoke City v Nottingham Forest	1-1
Swindon Town v Woking	2-0
Tranmere Rovers v Queen's Park Rangers	0-2
Walsall v Wigan Athletic	1-0
Watford v Wimbledon	1-1
West Ham United v Southend United	2-0
r Blackburn Rovers v Ipswich Town	0-1e
r Manchester City v Leicester City	5-0
r Newcastle United v Chelsea	2-2q
r Nottingham Forest v Stoke City	2-0
r Oldham Athletic v Barnsley	2-1
r Oxford United v Millwall	1-0
r Port Vale v Crystal Palace	4-3e
r Sheffield United v Arsenal	1-0
r Shrewsbury Town v Fulham	2-1
r Stockport County v Everton	2-3
r Sunderland v Manchester United	1-2
r Tottenham Hotspur v Hereford United	5-1
r Wimbledon v Watford	1-0
r Wolverhampton Wan. v Birmingham City	2-1

Round Four

Bolton Wanderers v Leeds United	0-1
Charlton Athletic v Brentford	3-2
Coventry City v Manchester City	2-2
Everton v Port Vale	2-2
Huddersfield Town v Peterborough United	2-0
Ipswich Town v Walsall	1-0
Middlesbrough v Wimbledon	0-0
Nottingham Forest v Oxford United	1-1
Queen's Park Rangers v Chelsea	1-2
Reading v Manchester United	0-3
Sheffield United v Aston Villa	0-1
Shrewsbury Town v Liverpool	0-4
Southampton v Crewe Alexandra	1-1
Swindon Town v Oldham Athletic	1-0
Tottenham Hotspur v Wolverhampton Wan.	1-1
West Ham United v Grimsby Town	1-1
r Crewe Alexandra v Southampton	2-3
r Grimsby Town v West Ham United	3-0
r Manchester City v Coventry City	2-1
r Oxford United v Nottingham Forest	0-3
r Port Vale v Everton	2-1
r Wimbledon v Middlesbrough	1-0
r Wolverhampton Wan. v Tottenham Hotspur	0-2

Round Five

Grimsby Town v Chelsea	0-0
Huddersfield Town v Wimbledon	2-2
Ipswich Town v Aston Villa	1-3
Leeds United v Port Vale	0-0
Liverpool v Charlton Athletic	2-1
Manchester United v Manchester City	2-1
Nottingham Forest v Tottenham Hotspur	2-2
Swindon Town v Southampton	1-1
r Chelsea v Grimsby Town	4-1
r Port Vale v Leeds United	1-2
r Southampton v Swindon Town	2-0
r Tottenham Hotspur v Nottingham Forest	1-1q
r Wimbledon v Huddersfield Town	3-1

Round Six

Chelsea v Wimbledon	2-2
Leeds United v Liverpool	0-0
Manchester United v Southampton	2-0
Nottingham Forest v Aston Villa	0-1
r Liverpool v Leeds United	3-0
r Wimbledon v Chelsea	1-3

Semi Finals

Liverpool v Aston Villa	3-0 N
Manchester United v Chelsea	2-1 N

Final

Manchester United v Liverpool	1-0 N

1996/97

Preliminary Round

1 Eastwood Hanley v Crook Town	0-1
Hebburn v Dunston Federation Brewery	0-5
Ossett Town v Armthorpe Welfare	3-1
St Helens Town v Peterlee Newtown	2-2
Workington v Worksop Town	1-0
2 Alnwick Town v Consett	0-0
Esh Winning v Oldham Town	1-3
Harrogate Town v Whitley Bay	6-0
Northallerton Town v Morpeth Town	0-1
Pontefract Collieries v Pickering Town	1-2
3 Blackpool (Wren) Rovers v Hucknall Town	1-2
Bootle v Seaham Red Star	2-0
Brandon United v Tadcaster Albion	3-1
Flixton v RTM Newcastle	4-1
Ryhope Community Association v Arnold Town	1-2
4 Ferryhill Athletic v Yorkshire Amateur	1-2 N
Harrogate Railway Athletic v Stockton (2)	5-2
Nantwich Town v South Shields (3)	5-0
Netherfield (Kendal) v Shildon	3-0
Ossett Albion v Brigg Town	2-1
5 Ashington v Ashfield United	4-5
Murton v Congleton Town	1-0
Newcastle Town v Denaby United	1-0
Willington v Borrowash Victoria	2-1
6 Eccleshill United v Hallam	2-1
Glasshoughton Welfare v Matlock Town	1-2
Trafford v Clitheroe	2-1
Washington v Bridgnorth Town	0-0
7 Cheadle Town v Burscough	0-0
Hatfield Main v Farsley Celtic	0-0
Shotton Comrades v Garforth Town	0-4
Whitby Town v Whickham	6-2
8 Droylsden v Stocksbridge Park Steels	1-5
Kidsgrove Athletic v Chester-le-Street Town	0-3
Louth United v Guisborough Town	2-2
Rossendale United v Castleton Gabriels	1-1
Thackley v Selby Town	0-4
9 Belper Town v Leigh RMI	1-1
Heanor Town v Sheffield	3-4
Horden CW v Atherton Collieries	0-4
Shifnal Town v Chadderton	1-2
10 Evenwood Town v Darwen	3-1
Harworth Colliery Institute v Blidworth MW	0-0
Liversedge v Atherton LR	0-0
Stapenhill v Salford City	3-0
11 Blakenall v Glossop North End	3-0
Kimberley Town v Rossington Main	1-1
North Ferriby United v Great Harwood Town	4-0
Prudhoe Town v Maine Road	1-1
12 Banbury United v V.S. Rugby	0-1
Bedworth United v Paget Rangers	2-2
Halesowen Harriers v Long Buckby	2-2
Rocester v Bolehall Swifts	5-1
Wellingborough Town v Cogenhoe United	0-3
13 Barwell v Bilston Town	0-2
Chasetown v Boldmere St Michaels	2-0
Desborough Town v Lye Town	4-0
Stafford Rangers v Redditch United	1-1
West Midlands Police v Westfields	1-2
14 Dudley Town v Tamworth	1-3
Newport Pagnell Town v Wednesfield	0-1
Northampton Spencer v Oldbury United	1-0
Rushall Olympic v Pelsall Villa	1-3
Willenhall Town v Hinckley Town	1-0
15 Knypersley Victoria v Wednesfield	4-0 N
Stourport Swifts v Pershore Town	0-4
Stratford Town v Shepshed Dynamo	0-2
Sutton Coldfield Town v Moor Green	0-0
16 Burnham Ramblers v Great Yarmouth Town	1-1
Maldon Town v Fakenham Town	2-2
Rothwell Town v Bourne Town	5-1
Watton United v Bedford Town	1-4
Wingate & Finchley v Spalding United	0-1
17 Haverhill Rovers v Holbeach United	5-1
Lowestoft Town v Boston Town	1-2
Tilbury v Diss Town	1-1
Witham Town v Grantham Town	2-5
Wroxham v Great Wakering Rovers	2-2
18 Bury Town v Milton Keynes	4-1
East Thurrock United v Mirrlees Blackstone	4-2
March Town United v Barkingside	2-1
Saffron Walden Town v Newmarket Town	2-2
Wivenhoe Town v Raunds Town	2-2
19 Basildon United v Woodbridge Town	0-2
Corby Town v Eynesbury Rovers	5-1
Cornard United v Gorleston	0-2
Haringey Borough v Hornchurch	0-3
Soham Town Rangers v Stamford	0-2
20 Arlesey Town v Potton United	3-1
Harefield United v Halstead Town	2-4
Leyton Pennant v Collier Row and Romford	0-0
Southend Manor v Braintree Town	0-5
Tiptree United v Hadleigh Town	1-0
21 Berkhamsted Town v Chesham United	2-3
Concord Rangers v Barking	2-2
Hoddesdon Town v Stotfold	0-1 N
Potters Bar Town v Cheshunt	5-1
Ruislip Manor v Clacton Town	1-1
22 Felixstowe Port & Town v Clapton	0-1
Hillingdon Borough v Stowmarket Town	1-4
Langford v Brackley Town	0-4
Royston Town v Southall	1-0
Uxbridge v Leighton Town	2-1
23 Brimsdown Rovers v Tring Town	1-3
Edgware Town v Flackwell Heath	1-1
Erith & Belvedere v Kingsbury Town	2-2
Ford United v Harwich & Parkeston	1-0
Welwyn Garden City v Wootton Blue Cross	2-0
24 Biggleswade Town v London Colney	0-1
Bowers United v Hanwell Town	2-1
Hemel Hempstead Town v Ware	1-0
Sheppey United v Harlow Town	1-2
Stansted v Aveley	2-1
25 Bedfont v Tunbridge Wells	1-2
Margate v Banstead Athletic	0-1
Peacehaven & Telscombe v Dorking (2)	5-0
Portfield v Three Bridges	1-3
Selsey v Thamesmead Town	3-1
26 Ashford Town (Middlesex) v Slade Green	2-0
Dartford v Horsham	1-1
Shoreham v Wealdstone	0-1
Southwick v Oakwood	0-2
Wick v Herne Bay	0-2
27 Croydon Athletic v Lewes	1-3
Langney Sports v Chalfont St Peter	3-2
Merstham v Deal Town	5-1
Mile Oak v Lancing	0-1
Worthing v Fisher Athletic (London)	1-4
28 Pagham v Northwood	1-4
Raynes Park Vale v Burnham	7-0
Ringmer v Steyning Town	1-0
Tonbridge Angels v Leatherhead	1-6
Whitehawk v Whitstable Town	3-0
29 Arundel v Canterbury City	2-2
Hailsham Town v Redhill	1-3
Hassocks v Egham Town	2-0
St Leonards Stamcroft v Metropolitan Police	2-0
Viking Sports v Corinthian	4-1
30 Burgess Hill Town v Epsom & Ewell	1-1
Corinthian Casuals v Chipstead	2-3
East Grinstead v Folkestone Invicta	6-1
Horsham YMCA v Littlehampton Town	3-3
Whyteleafe v Chatham Town	1-0
31 Cove v Ash United	0-3
Eastleigh v Hungerford Town	1-1
Wimborne Town v Andover	2-0
Wokingham Town v Fareham Town	2-0
32 Bemerton Heath Harlequins v Bicester Town	6-1 N
Lymington v Windsor & Eton	0-1
Maidenhead United v Havant Town		

197

1996/97

	Thatcham Town v Brockenhurst	2-0
33	Bournemouth (Ams) v Abingdon Town	1-3
	Fleet Town v Waterlooville	2-0
	Godalming & Guildford v Carterton Town	5-2
	Gosport Borough v Ryde Sports	2-1
	Portsmouth Royal Navy v Camberley Town	1-6
34	Cirencester Town v Yate Town	1-0
	Devizes Town v Westbury United	2-0
	Falmouth Town v Barnstaple Town	3-0
	Mangotsfield United v Chippenham Town	6-1
	Melksham Town v Bridgwater Town	2-1
35	Endsleigh v Bristol Manor Farm	0-3
	Glastonbury v Calne Town	2-4
	St Blazey v Minehead	2-0
	Torrington v Paulton Rovers	3-0
	Weston-Super-Mare v Brislington	2-0
36	Bridport v Clevedon Town	0-1
	Frome Town v Elmore	3-0
	Tuffley Rovers v Taunton Town	2-5
	Welton Rovers v Saltash United	3-2
1r	Peterlee Newtown v St Helens Town	1-2
2r	Consett v Alnwick Town	2-0
6r	Bridgnorth Town v Washington	2-1
7r	Burscough v Cheadle Town	2-0
r	Farsley Celtic v Hatfield Main	2-1
8r	Castleton Gabriels v Rossendale United	2-4e
r	Guisborough Town v Louth United	4-1
9r	Leigh RMI v Belper Town	3-1
10r	Atherton LR v Liversedge	2-2e
r	Blidworth MW v Harworth Colliery Institute	2-2e
11r	Maine Road v Prudhoe Town	1-2
r	Rossington Main v Kimberley Town	3-0
12r	Long Buckby v Halesowen Harriers	1-1e
r	Paget Rangers v Bedworth United	1-2
13r	Redditch United v Stafford Rangers	0-1
15r	Moor Green v Sutton Coldfield Town	3-2
16r	Great Yarmouth Town v Burnham Ramblers	3-1
r	Maldon Town v Fakenham Town	2-0
17r	Diss Town v Tilbury	1-0
r	Great Wakering Rovers v Wroxham	0-1
18r	Newmarket Town v Saffron Walden Town	3-0
r	Raunds Town v Wivenhoe Town	3-0
20r	Collier Row and Romford v Leyton Pennant	1-0
21r	Barking v Concord Rangers	1-0
r	Clacton Town v Ruislip Manor	3-2
23r	Flackwell Heath v Edgware Town	1-1e
r	Kingsbury Town v Erith & Belvedere	0-1
26r	Horsham v Dartford	1-0
r	Oakwood v Southwick	1-2
29r	Redhill v Hailsham Town	2-1
30r	Chatham Town v Whyteleafe	2-0
r	Chipstead v Corinthian Casuals	2-4
31r	Andover v Wimborne Town	0-1
r	Fareham Town v Wokingham Town	4-1
10r2	Atherton LR v Liversedge	2-2e
r2	Blidworth MW v Harworth Colliery Institute	2-1
12r2	Halesowen Harriers v Long Buckby	2-1
23r2	Flackwell Heath v Edgware Town	0-3
10r3	Liversedge v Atherton LR	1-3e

Qualifying Round One

1	Billingham Town v Dunston Federation Brewery	2-0
	Buxton v Ossett Town	1-2
	St Helens Town v Gateshead (2)	0-0
	Workington v Crook Town	3-1
2	Bishop Auckland v Pickering Town	3-1
	Durham City v Morpeth Town	5-1
	Harrogate Town v Consett	0-1
	Oldham Town v Halifax Town	2-3
3	Brandon United v Morecambe	0-6
	Flixton v Bootle	2-0
	Gretna v Arnold Town	1-1
	Guiseley v Hucknall Town	4-0
4	Accrington Stanley (2) v Ossett Albion	1-1
	Ashton United v Harrogate Railway Athletic	3-0
	Netherfield (Kendal) v Nantwich Town	3-1
	Yorkshire Amateur v Stalybridge Celtic	0-1
5	Bradford Park Avenue v Ashfield United	1-0
	Easington Colliery v Winsford United	2-7
	Murton v Frickley Athletic	1-3
	Willington v Newcastle Town	1-3
6	Bridgnorth Town v Trafford	2-1
	Eastwood Town v Eccleshill United	1-0
	Matlock Town v Leek Town	0-1
	Tow Law Town v Gainsborough Trinity	1-1
7	Farsley Celtic v Knowsley United	1-0
	Garforth Town v Whitby Town	1-3
	Mossley v Burscough	3-1
	Warrington Town v Hyde United	0-1
8	Burton Albion v Guisborough Town	1-0
	Emley v Selby Town	3-0
	Rossendale United v Southport	0-5
	Stocksbridge Park Steels v Chester-le-Street Town	4-2
9	Billingham Synthonia v Atherton Collieries	1-0
	Leigh RMI v Alfreton Town	2-0
	Radcliffe Borough v Marine	0-2
	Sheffield v Chadderton	2-1
10	Atherton LR v Ilkeston Town (2)	1-0
	Blidworth MW v Stapenhill	0-1
	Curzon Ashton v Evenwood Town	1-0
	West Auckland Town v Bamber Bridge	1-3
11	Bedlington Terriers v Prudhoe Town	4-0
	Lincoln United v Lancaster City	2-2
	North Ferriby United v Chorley	4-1
	Rossington Main v Blakenall	1-2
12	Atherstone United v Cogenhoe United	3-1
	Bedworth United v V.S. Rugby	3-3
	Hinckley Athletic v Halesowen Harriers	5-1
	Rocester v Kettering Town	0-3
13	Desborough Town v Leicester United	wo/s
	Gresley Rovers v Chasetown	2-1
	Stafford Rangers v Bilston Town	0-1
	Westfields v Rushden & Diamonds	0-4
14	Evesham United v Pelsall Villa	4-0
	Racing Club Warwick v Northampton Spencer	1-1
	Tamworth v Willenhall Town	4-1
	Wednesfield v Hednesford Town	0-0
15	Moor Green v Solihull Borough	1-2
	Pershore Town v Knypersley Victoria	1-2
	Sandwell Borough v Shepshed Dynamo	0-0
	Stourbridge v Halesowen Town	1-0
16	Bishop's Stortford v Bedford Town	2-0
	Maldon Town v Boston United	2-7
	Rothwell Town v Spalding United	2-3
	Sudbury Wanderers v Great Yarmouth Town	1-1
17	Cambridge City v Diss Town	6-1
	Canvey Island v Haverhill Rovers	3-1
	Grantham Town v Boston Town	2-0
	Wroxham v King's Lynn	3-2
18	Bury Town v Heybridge Swifts	0-0
	Chelmsford City v March Town United	5-0
	Raunds Town v East Thurrock United	2-4
	Wisbech Town v Newmarket Town	2-1
19	Billericay Town v Woodbridge Town	4-0
	Corby Town v Stamford	4-1
	Gorleston v Sudbury Town	1-2
	Purfleet v Hornchurch	5-1
20	Arlesey Town v Stevenage Borough	0-3
	Baldock Town v Tiptree United	2-0
	Collier Row and Romford v Halstead Town	1-1
	Marlow v Braintree Town	0-2
21	Chesham United v Barking	3-1
	Grays Athletic v Clacton Town	6-0
	Hertford Town v Potters Bar Town	1-2
	Stotfold v Hayes	0-2
22	Brackley Town v Dagenham & Redbridge	1-1
	Harrow Borough v Stowmarket Town	4-1
	Uxbridge v Clapton	5-1
	Wembley v Royston Town	0-2
23	Barton Rovers v Erith & Belvedere	2-2
	Boreham Wood v Tring Town	8-1
	Edgware Town v Ford United	3-3
	Welwyn Garden City v Aylesbury United	1-4
24	Hampton v Harlow Town	2-1
	Hemel Hempstead Town v Stansted	0-1
	St Albans City v London Colney	0-0
	Yeading v Bowers United	6-0
25	Banstead Athletic v Peacehaven & Telscombe	1-3
	Bracknell Town v Selsey	4-2
	Carshalton Athletic v Tunbridge Wells	6-0
	Three Bridges v Farnborough Town	1-6
26	Dulwich Hamlet v Ashford Town (Middlesex)	2-0
	Horsham v Wealdstone	1-0
	Southwick v Welling United	1-2
	Walton & Hersham v Herne Bay	1-1
27	Aldershot Town v Merstham	8-1
	Fisher Athletic (London) v Chalfont St Peter	3-2
	Hendon v Croydon Athletic	2-0
	Mile Oak v Dover Athletic	0-3 N
28	Hastings Town v Burnham	2-0
	Molesey v Whitstable Town	3-1
	Ringmer v Chertsey Town	1-2
	Tonbridge Angels v Northwood	2-0
29	Bromley v Viking Sports	4-0
	Croydon v Egham Town	3-1
	Redhill v Crawley Town	0-1
	St Leonards Stamcroft v Arundel	4-1
30	Chatham Town v Burgess Hill Town	1-2
	Horsham YMCA v Sittingbourne	2-3
	Staines Town v Folkestone Invicta	2-0
	Tooting & Mitcham United v Corinthian Casuals	5-0
31	Buckingham Town v Hungerford Town	3-6
	Fareham Town v Worcester City	2-1
	Wimborne Town v Cove	5-0
	Witney Town v Oxford City	1-1
32	Basingstoke Town v Gloucester City	0-3
	Havant Town v Bashley	0-3
	Thame United v Lymington	1-1
	Thatcham Town v Bemerton Heath Harlequins	1-1
33	Fleet Town v Abingdon Town	0-3
	Gosport Borough v Cheltenham Town	0-1
	Salisbury City v Godalming & Guildford	0-0
	Weymouth v Camberley Town	2-0
34	Bideford v Melksham Town	2-6
	Cirencester Town v Falmouth Town	2-0
	Devizes Town v Bath City	2-2
	Newport AFC v Mangotsfield United	5-2
35	Forest Green Rovers v Torrington	4-5
	St Blazey v Merthyr Tydfil	0-7
	Trowbridge Town v Calne Town	3-0
	Weston-Super-Mare v Bristol Manor Farm	4-0
36	Backwell United v Yeovil Town	0-6
	Clevedon Town v Dorchester Town	4-1
	Tiverton Town v Frome Town	3-0
	Welton Rovers v Taunton Town	0-6
1r	Gateshead (2) v St Helens Town	5-1
3r	Arnold Town v Gretna	3-0
4r	Ossett Albion v Accrington Stanley (2)	2-1
6r	Gainsborough Trinity v Tow Law Town	2-0
11r	Lancaster City v Lincoln United	3-2
12r	V.S. Rugby v Bedworth United	0-3
13r	Hednesford Town v Wednesfield	6-0
14r	Northampton Spencer v Racing Club Warwick	2-2e
15r	Shepshed Dynamo v Sandwell Borough	5-2
16r	Great Yarmouth Town v Sudbury Wanderers	0-1
18r	Heybridge Swifts v Bury Town	3-0
20r	Halstead Town v Collier Row and Romford	4-0
22r	Dagenham & Redbridge v Brackley Town	1-0
23r	Erith & Belvedere v Barton Rovers	1-2
r	Ford United v Edgware Town	2-3
24r	St Albans City v London Colney	4-1
26r	Herne Bay v Walton & Hersham	1-0
31r	Oxford City v Witney Town	2-3e
32r	Bemerton Heath Harlequins v Thatcham Town	2-3
r	Lymington v Thame United	1-1e
33r	Godalming & Guildford v Salisbury City	0-2
34r	Bath City v Devizes Town	3-1
14r2	Racing Club Warwick v Northampton Spencer	5-1
32r2	Thame United v Lymington	3-1

Qualifying Round Two

1	Billingham Town v Workington	0-1
	Gateshead (2) v Ossett Town	5-1
2	Durham City v Consett	1-1
	Halifax Town v Bishop Auckland	1-4
3	Arnold Town v Flixton	0-0
	Morecambe v Guiseley	4-1
4	Ashton United v Netherfield (Kendal)	2-0
	Stalybridge Celtic v Ossett Albion	4-1
5	Frickley Athletic v Bradford Park Avenue	1-0
	Winsford United v Newcastle Town	0-1
6	Gainsborough Trinity v Bridgnorth Town	2-1
	Leek Town v Eastwood Town	1-0
7	Farsley Celtic v Mossley	3-1
	Hyde United v Whitby Town	0-1
8	Burton Albion v Stocksbridge Park Steels	2-1
	Southport v Emley	1-1
9	Leigh RMI v Billingham Synthonia	1-1
	Marine v Sheffield	1-0
10	Atherton LR v Curzon Ashton	3-2
	Bamber Bridge v Stapenhill	5-3
11	Lancaster City v Blakenall	6-0
	North Ferriby United v Bedlington Terriers	1-0
12	Hinckley Athletic v Bedworth United	1-1
	Kettering Town v Atherstone United	0-0
13	Desborough Town v Bilston Town	2-2
	Rushden & Diamonds v Gresley Rovers	4-0
14	Hednesford Town v Evesham United	6-1
	Racing Club Warwick v Tamworth	0-5
15	Solihull Borough v Shepshed Dynamo	1-1
	Stourbridge v Knypersley Victoria	0-0
16	Boston United v Bishop's Stortford	3-0
	Sudbury Wanderers v Spalding United	3-2
17	Canvey Island v Grantham Town	1-1
	Wroxham v Cambridge City	1-1
18	Heybridge Swifts v Chelmsford City	1-1
	Wisbech Town v East Thurrock United	2-1
19	Billericay Town v Corby Town	0-0
	Sudbury Town v Purfleet	2-1
20	Braintree Town v Halstead Town	3-1
	Stevenage Borough v Baldock Town	1-1
21	Hayes v Grays Athletic	1-1
	Potters Bar Town v Chesham United	0-4 N
22	Dagenham & Redbridge v Harrow Borough	0-0
	Royston Town v Uxbridge	0-5
23	Aylesbury United v Boreham Wood	0-3
	Barton Rovers v Edgware Town	1-2
24	Hampton v Stansted	2-2
	St Albans City v Yeading	1-1
25	Bracknell Town v Peacehaven & Telscombe	5-2
	Farnborough Town v Carshalton Athletic	3-2
26	Herne Bay v Horsham	1-0
	Welling United v Dulwich Hamlet	2-1
27	Dover Athletic v Aldershot Town	2-0
	Hendon v Fisher Athletic (London)	0-0
28	Chertsey Town v Hastings Town	2-3
	Molesey v Tonbridge Angels	0-0
29	Crawley Town v Bromley	0-4
	Croydon v St Leonards Stamcroft	0-7
30	Sittingbourne v Tooting & Mitcham United	4-5
	Staines Town v Burgess Hill Town	2-1 N
31	Fareham Town v Hungerford Town	4-2
	Witney Town v Wimborne Town	2-1
32	Bashley v Thame United	4-3
	Gloucester City v Thatcham Town	1-3
33	Cheltenham Town v Salisbury City	4-3
	Weymouth v Abingdon Town	1-0
34	Bath City v Newport AFC	5-2
	Melksham Town v Cirencester Town	0-1
35	Merthyr Tydfil v Torrington	3-1
	Trowbridge Town v Weston-Super-Mare	2-1
36	Clevedon Town v Tiverton Town	0-2
	Yeovil Town v Taunton Town	0-0
2r	Consett v Durham City	wo/s
3r	Flixton v Arnold Town	2-0
8r	Emley v Southport	2-3e
9r	Billingham Synthonia v Leigh RMI	2-3
12r	Atherstone United v Kettering Town	1-6
r	Bedworth United v Hinckley Athletic	3-1
13r	Bilston Town v Desborough Town	5-2
15r	Knypersley Victoria v Stourbridge	1-0
r	Shepshed Dynamo v Solihull Borough	1-0
17r	Cambridge City v Wroxham	2-0

1996/97 to 1997/98

r Grantham Town v Canvey Island	0-1
18r Chelmsford City v Heybridge Swifts	2-1
19r Corby Town v Billericay Town	1-1e
20r Baldock Town v Stevenage Borough	1-2
21r Grays Athletic v Hayes	0-0e
22r Harrow Borough v Dagenham & Redbridge	0-2
24r Stansted v Hampton	2-1
r Yeading v St Albans City	0-1
27r Fisher Athletic (London) v Hendon	0-1
28r Tonbridge Angels v Molesey	1-2
36r Taunton Town v Yeovil Town	3-5
19r2 Corby Town v Billericay Town	3-1
21r2 Hayes v Grays Athletic	2-0

Qualifying Round Three

1 Gateshead (2) v Workington	4-0
2 Bishop Auckland v Consett	0-1
3 Morecambe v Flixton	6-2
4 Stalybridge Celtic v Ashton United	2-1
5 Frickley Athletic v Newcastle Town	1-1
6 Leek Town v Gainsborough Trinity	2-0
7 Farsley Celtic v Whitby Town	0-1
8 Southport v Burton Albion	4-1
9 Leigh RMI v Marine	2-0
10 Atherton LR v Bamber Bridge	1-1
11 North Ferriby United v Lancaster City	0-2
12 Kettering Town v Bedworth United	0-1
13 Rushden & Diamonds v Bilston Town	1-0
14 Hednesford Town v Tamworth	4-2
15 Shepshed Dynamo v Knypersley Victoria	1-0
16 Boston United v Sudbury Wanderers	10-1
17 Cambridge City v Canvey Island	0-3
18 Chelmsford City v Wisbech Town	2-3
19 Sudbury Town v Corby Town	1-0
20 Stevenage Borough v Braintree Town	3-1
21 Hayes v Chesham United	1-0
22 Dagenham & Redbridge v Uxbridge	3-0
23 Boreham Wood v Edgware Town	3-2
24 St Albans City v Stansted	5-0
25 Farnborough Town v Bracknell Town	3-2
26 Welling United v Herne Bay	2-0
27 Dover Athletic v Hendon	0-1
28 Hastings Town v Molesey	2-1
29 Bromley v St Leonards Stamcroft	1-1
30 Tooting & Mitcham United v Staines Town	0-1
31 Fareham Town v Witney Town	0-1
32 Bashley v Thatcham Town	0-1
33 Cheltenham Town v Weymouth	1-0
34 Bath City v Cirencester Town	2-0
35 Merthyr Tydfil v Trowbridge Town	1-0
36 Tiverton Town v Yeovil Town	0-2
5r Newcastle Town v Frickley Athletic	2-1
10r Bamber Bridge v Atherton LR	2-0
29r St Leonards Stamcroft v Bromley	2-5

Qualifying Round Four

Ashford Town v Kingstonian	3-1
Barrow v Altrincham	1-1
Bath City v Cheltenham Town	0-0
Bedworth United v Boston United	0-2
Boreham Wood v Thatcham Town	5-0
Bromley v Sutton United	1-0
Canvey Island v Sudbury Town	0-1
Cinderford Town v Farnborough Town	0-4
Colwyn Bay v Nuneaton Borough	1-0
Gateshead (2) v Consett	0-1
Gravesend & Northfleet v Stevenage Borough	1-5
Hastings Town v Hendon	1-1
Hayes v Slough Town	1-0
Hednesford Town v Telford United	2-0
Hitchin Town v Wisbech Town	1-2
Lancaster City v Morecambe	1-1
Leigh RMI v Runcorn	2-4
Merthyr Tydfil v Yeovil Town	2-1
Newcastle Town v Bamber Bridge	4-0
Newport (IOW) v Dagenham & Redbridge	1-4
Rushden & Diamonds v Bognor Regis Town	2-0
Shepshed Dynamo v Bromsgrove Rovers	2-0
Spennymoor United v Southport	2-2
Staines Town v Welling United	0-1 N
Stalybridge Celtic v Leek Town	1-0
Whitby Town v Blyth Spartans	2-1
Witney Town v St Albans City	0-4
Witton Albion v Kidderminster Harriers	1-4
r Altrincham v Barrow	4-0
r Cheltenham Town v Bath City	4-1e
r Hendon v Hastings Town	2-0
r Morecambe v Lancaster City	2-2e
r Southport v Spennymoor United	2-1
r2 Morecambe v Lancaster City	4-2

Round One

Ashford Town v Dagenham & Redbridge	2-2
Blackpool v Wigan Athletic	1-0
Boreham Wood v Rushden & Diamonds	1-1
Boston United v Morecambe	3-0
Brentford v Bournemouth	2-0
Bristol Rovers v Exeter City	1-2
Bromley v Enfield	1-3
Burnley v Lincoln City	2-1
Cambridge United v Welling United	3-0
Cardiff City v Hendon	2-0

Carlisle United v Shepshed Dynamo	6-0
Chester City v Stalybridge Celtic	3-0
Chesterfield v Bury	1-0
Colchester United v Wycombe Wanderers	1-2
Crewe Alexandra v Kidderminster Harriers	4-1
Farnborough Town v Barnet	2-2
Gillingham v Hereford United	1-0
Hartlepool United v York City	0-0
Hednesford Town v Southport	2-1
Leyton Orient v Merthyr Tydfil	2-1
Macclesfield Town v Rochdale	0-2
Mansfield Town v Consett	4-0
Newcastle Town v Notts County	0-2
Northampton Town v Watford	0-1
Northwich Victoria v Walsall	2-2
Peterborough United v Cheltenham Town	0-0
Plymouth Argyle v Fulham	5-0
Preston North End v Altrincham	4-1
Runcorn v Darlington	1-4
Scunthorpe United v Rotherham United	4-1
Shrewsbury Town v Scarborough	1-1
Stevenage Borough v Hayes	2-2
Stockport County v Doncaster Rovers	2-1
Sudbury Town v Brighton & Hove Albion	0-0
Swansea City v Bristol City	1-1
Torquay United v Luton Town	0-1
Whitby Town v Hull City	0-0 N
Wisbech Town v St Albans City	1-2
Woking v Millwall	2-2
Wrexham v Colwyn Bay	1-1
r Barnet v Farnborough Town	1-0
r Brighton & Hove Albion v Sudbury Town	1-1q
r Bristol City v Swansea City	1-0
r Cheltenham Town v Peterborough United	1-3e
r Dagenham & Redbridge v Ashford Town	1-1q
r Hayes v Stevenage Borough	0-2
r Hull City v Whitby Town	8-4e
r Millwall v Woking	0-1
r Rushden & Diamonds v Boreham Wood	2-3
r Scarborough v Shrewsbury Town	1-0
r Walsall v Northwich Victoria	3-1
r Wrexham v Colwyn Bay	2-0
r York City v Hartlepool United	3-0

Round Two

Barnet v Wycombe Wanderers	3-3
Blackpool v Hednesford Town	0-1
Bristol City v St Albans City	9-2
Cambridge United v Woking	0-2
Cardiff City v Gillingham	0-2
Carlisle United v Darlington	1-0
Chester City v Boston United	1-0
Chesterfield v Scarborough	2-0
Enfield v Peterborough United	1-1
Hull City v Crewe Alexandra	1-5
Leyton Orient v Stevenage Borough	1-2
Luton Town v Boreham Wood	2-1
Mansfield Town v Stockport County	0-3
Notts County v Rochdale	3-1
Plymouth Argyle v Exeter City	4-1
Preston North End v York City	2-3
Sudbury Town v Brentford	1-3
Walsall v Burnley	1-1
Watford v Ashford Town	5-0
Wrexham v Scunthorpe United	2-2
r Burnley v Walsall	1-1P
r Peterborough United v Enfield	4-1
r Scunthorpe United v Wrexham	2-3e
r Wycombe Wanderers v Barnet	3-2

Round Three

Arsenal v Sunderland	1-1
Barnsley v Oldham Athletic	2-0
Birmingham City v Stevenage Borough	2-0
Blackburn Rovers v Port Vale	1-0
Brentford v Manchester City	0-1
Carlisle United v Tranmere Rovers	1-0
Charlton Athletic v Newcastle United	1-1
Chelsea v West Bromwich Albion	3-0
Chesterfield v Bristol City	2-0
Coventry City v Woking	1-1
Crewe Alexandra v Wimbledon	1-1
Crystal Palace v Leeds United	2-2
Everton v Swindon Town	3-0
Gillingham v Derby County	0-2
Hednesford Town v York City	1-0
Leicester City v Southend United	2-0
Liverpool v Burnley	1-0
Luton Town v Bolton Wanderers	1-1
Manchester United v Tottenham Hotspur	2-0
Middlesbrough v Chester City	6-0
Norwich City v Sheffield United	1-0
Nottingham Forest v Ipswich Town	3-0
Notts County v Aston Villa	0-0
Plymouth Argyle v Peterborough United	0-1
Queen's Park Rangers v Huddersfield Town	1-1
Reading v Southampton	3-1
Sheffield Wednesday v Grimsby Town	7-1
Stoke City v Stockport County	0-2
Watford v Oxford United	2-0
Wolverhampton Wan. v Portsmouth	1-2
Wrexham v West Ham United	1-1
Wycombe Wanderers v Bradford City	0-2

r Aston Villa v Notts County	3-0
r Bolton Wanderers v Luton Town	6-2
r Huddersfield Town v Queen's Park Rangers	1-2
r Leeds United v Crystal Palace	1-0
r Newcastle United v Charlton Athletic	2-1e
r Sunderland v Arsenal	0-2
r West Ham United v Wrexham	0-1
r Wimbledon v Crewe Alexandra	2-0
r Woking v Coventry City	1-2

Round Four

Arsenal v Leeds United	0-1
Birmingham City v Stockport County	3-1
Blackburn Rovers v Coventry City	1-2
Bolton Wanderers v Chesterfield	2-3
Carlisle United v Sheffield Wednesday	0-2
Chelsea v Liverpool	4-2
Derby County v Aston Villa	3-1
Everton v Bradford City	2-3
Leicester City v Norwich City	2-1
Manchester City v Watford	3-1
Manchester United v Wimbledon	1-1
Middlesbrough v Hednesford Town	3-2
Newcastle United v Nottingham Forest	1-2
Peterborough United v Wrexham	2-4
Portsmouth v Reading	3-0
Queen's Park Rangers v Barnsley	3-2
r Wimbledon v Manchester United	1-0

Round Five

Birmingham City v Wrexham	1-3
Bradford City v Sheffield Wednesday	0-1
Chesterfield v Nottingham Forest	1-0
Derby County v Coventry City	3-2
Leeds United v Portsmouth	2-3
Leicester City v Chelsea	2-2
Manchester City v Middlesbrough	0-1
Wimbledon v Queen's Park Rangers	2-1
r Chelsea v Leicester City	1-0e

Round Six

Chesterfield v Wrexham	1-0
Derby County v Middlesbrough	0-2
Portsmouth v Chelsea	1-4
Sheffield Wednesday v Wimbledon	0-2

Semi Finals

Chelsea v Wimbledon	3-0 N
Middlesbrough v Chesterfield	3-3eN
r Middlesbrough v Chesterfield	3-0 N

Final

Chelsea v Middlesbrough	2-0 N

1997/98

Preliminary Round

1 Atherton Collieries v Maine Road	1-2
Billingham Synthonia v Brandon United	1-1
Harrogate Railway Athletic v South Shields (3)	2-3
Matlock Town v Curzon Ashton	3-1
Skelmersdale United v Pickering Town	3-2
2 Bedlington Terriers v Glapwell	6-1
Blackpool (Wren) Rovers v Burscough	1-4
Denaby United v West Auckland Town	3-1
Droylsden v Cheadle Town	4-1
Seaham Red Star v Ossett Town	1-1
3 Blidworth MW v Rossendale United	3-5
Buxton v Ilkeston Town (2)	0-1
Peterlee Newtown v Warrington Town	1-2
Pontefract Collieries v Ossett Albion	2-2
Tow Law Town v RTM Newcastle	1-2
4 Arnold Town v Shildon	3-1
Billingham Town v Brodsworth MW	3-0
Kidsgrove Athletic v Whitley Bay	1-1
Maltby Main v Shotton Comrades	0-1
Netherfield (Kendal) v Chadderton	1-1
5 Chester-le-Street T v Ryhope Community Assoc.	0-2
Congleton Town v Darwen	1-1
Great Harwood Town v Stockton (2)	2-1
Louth United v Glasshoughton Welfare	1-0
St Helens Town v Sheffield	3-1
6 Belper Town v Glossop North End	2-2
Bootle v Bradford Park Avenue	3-1
Eccleshill United v Thackley	1-1
Evenwood Town v Durham City	0-3
Parkgate v Nantwich Town	2-0
7 Crook Town v Mossley	0-2
Gretna v Haslingden	4-2
Liversedge v Willington	3-0
Morpeth Town v Horden CW	5-0
Tadcaster Albion v Stocksbridge Park Steels	0-3
8 Atherton LR v Hucknall Town	0-1
Brigg Town v Eastwood Town	1-0
Guisborough Town v Worksop Town	2-3
Hebburn v Garforth Town	0-5
Oldham Town v Northallerton Town	4-2

199

1997/98

9	Borrowash Victoria v Jarrow Roofing Boldon CA	1-2
	Castleton Gabriels v Clitheroe	0-1
	Flixton v Staveley MW	2-3
	Hatfield Main v Dunston Federation Brewery	2-3
	Selby Town v Lincoln United	1-3
10	Harrogate Town v Armthorpe Welfare	1-1
	Heanor Town v Salford City	1-0
	Penrith v Trafford	3-0
	Yorkshire Amateur v Easington Colliery	1-4
11	Bridgnorth Town v Dudley Town	wo/s
	Eynesbury Rovers v Pershore Town	1-2
	Fakenham Town v Stourbridge	0-1
	Stratford Town v Desborough Town	1-3
12	Banbury United v Rushall Olympic	3-2
	Blakenall v Great Yarmouth Town	1-3
	Hinckley United v Wednesfield	2-0
	Soham Town Rangers v Stewarts & Lloyds (2)	1-1
13	Boston Town v Stapenhill	0-2
	Brackley Town v Cogenhoe United	1-0
	Rocester v West Midlands Police	1-1
	Stafford Rangers v Ely City	1-1
	Sutton Coldfield Town v Stowmarket Town	1-3
14	Lowestoft Town v Watton United	wo/s
	Lye Town v Evesham United	2-1
	Raunds Town v Shifnal Town	6-0
	Sandwell Borough v Spalding United	0-4
15	Pelsall Villa v Barwell	2-3
	Racing Club Warwick v St Neots Town	3-1
	Redditch United v Wellingborough Town	4-0
	Willenhall Town v Gorleston	4-1
16	Diss Town v Bloxwich Town	1-0
	Histon v Oldbury United	2-0
	Newmarket Town v Stamford	4-4
	V.S. Rugby v Chasetown	1-0
17	Long Buckby v Boldmere St Michaels	2-4
	Northampton Spencer v Warboys Town	0-0
	Stourport Swifts v Woodbridge Town	1-5
	Wroxham v Paget Rangers	3-1
18	Flackwell Heath v Barkingside	5-0
	Folkestone Invicta v Marlow	3-4
	Littlehampton Town v Southend Manor	6-2
	Welwyn Garden City v East Thurrock United	2-3
19	Chatham Town v Banstead Athletic	0-7 N
	Ford United v Great Wakering Rovers	0-4
	Grays Athletic v Langford	10-0
	Pagham v Camberley Town	1-3
20	Corinthian Casuals v Aveley	0-2
	Croydon v Mile Oak	2-1
	Horsham v Northwood	3-1
	Tunbridge Wells v Chichester City (1)	4-4
21	Egham Town v Burnham	1-1
	Langney Sports v Southall	2-1
	Leatherhead v Wealdstone	2-0
	Whitstable Town v Dorking (2)	1-1
22	Epsom & Ewell v Canterbury City	0-1
	Godalming & Guildford v Tonbridge Angels	0-6
	Redhill v Ware	1-1
	Worthing v Eastbourne Town	8-1
23	Leighton Town v Ashford Town (Middlesex)	2-1
	Lewes v Tilbury	0-1
	Ringmer v Wick	0-1
	Wingate & Finchley v Corinthian	1-1
24	Croydon Athletic v Beaconsfield SYCOB	5-2
	Erith Town v Harlow Town	0-3
	Hailsham Town v Metropolitan Police	0-4
	Wivenhoe Town v Chipstead	4-0
25	Hassocks v Barton Rovers	1-2
	Hillingdon Borough v Stotfold	4-2
	Sheppey United v Windsor & Eton	2-3 N
	Tiptree United v Clapton	1-4
26	Halstead Town v Berkhamsted Town	0-3
	Kingsbury Town v Portfield	1-2
	Milton Keynes v Viking Sports	1-1
	Witham Town v Deal Town	1-1
27	Hythe United v Chalfont St Peter	3-2
	Oakwood v Potters Bar Town	2-1
	Peacehaven & Telscombe v Potton United	0-3
	Romford v Hertford Town	2-0
28	London Colney v Fisher Athletic (London)	0-2
	Selsey v Wembley	0-3
	Three Bridges v Whitehawk	1-2
	Wootton Blue Cross v Hemel Hempstead Town	3-2
29	Hornchurch v Arundel	2-2
	Maldon Town v Ruislip Manor	0-3
	Royston Town v Shoreham	0-0
	Slade Green v Erith & Belvedere	1-1
30	Arlesey Town v March Town United	2-1
	Barking v Basildon United	3-1
	Hanwell Town v Tring Town	3-1
	Horsham YMCA v Dartford	2-4
	Thamesmead Town v Saltdean United	3-3
31	Abingdon Town v Devizes Town	1-1
	Bridgwater Town v Brislington	1-0
	Cirencester Town v Tuffley Rovers	3-4
	Cove v Brockenhurst	1-3
	Paulton Rovers v Fareham Town	5-0
32	Bashley v Torrington	9-0
	Chippenham Town v Eastleigh	0-0
	Frome Town v Wokingham Town	0-5
	Lymington v Endsleigh	6-0 N
	Westfields v Westbury United	2-1
33	Odd Down v Backwell United	3-1
	St Blazey v Trowbridge Town	1-0
	Tiverton Town v Weymouth	2-0
	Wimborne Town v Falmouth Town	3-2
34	Clevedon Town v Bemerton Heath Harlequins	4-0
	Elmore v Hungerford Town	4-5
	Fleet Town v Thame United	0-0
	Welton Rovers v Calne Town	1-5
35	Bournemouth (Ams) v Gosport Borough	2-4
	Bridport v Buckingham Town	1-2
	Didcot Town v Taunton Town	1-5
	Glastonbury v Chard Town	0-2
	Newport AFC v Maidenhead United	2-1
36	Andover v Portsmouth Royal Navy	3-4
	Barnstaple Town v Carterton Town	1-4
	Melksham Town v Yate Town	2-1
	Minehead v Mangotsfield United	0-1
	Waterlooville v Reading Town	2-0
1r	Brandon United v Billingham Synthonia	2-5
2r	Ossett Town v Seaham Red Star	1-0
3r	Ossett Albion v Pontefract Collieries	0-3
4r	Chadderton v Netherfield (Kendal)	1-2
r	Whitley Bay v Kidsgrove Athletic	3-3P
5r	Darwen v Congleton Town	4-3
6r	Glossop North End v Belper Town	1-2
r	Thackley v Eccleshill United	0-2
10r	Armthorpe Welfare v Harrogate Town	1-3
12r	Soham Town Rangers v Stewarts & Lloyds (2)	1-3
13r	Ely City v Stafford Rangers	1-3
r	West Midlands Police v Rocester	0-3
16r	Stamford v Newmarket Town	1-4
17r	Warboys Town v Northampton Spencer	2-3
20r	Chichester City (1) v Tunbridge Wells	4-1
21r	Burnham v Egham Town	1-1P
r	Dorking (2) v Whitstable Town	3-3P
22r	Ware v Redhill	4-1
23r	Corinthian v Wingate & Finchley	0-2
26r	Deal Town v Witham Town	3-0e
r	Viking Sports v Milton Keynes	1-0
29r	Arundel v Hornchurch	4-3
r	Shoreham v Royston Town	2-1
r	Slade Green v Erith & Belvedere	3-5
30r	Saltdean United v Thamesmead Town	4-0
31r	Devizes Town v Abingdon Town	0-3
32r	Eastleigh v Chippenham Town	0-1
34r	Thame United v Fleet Town	1-3e

Qualifying Round One

1	Billingham Synthonia v Maine Road	0-0
	Gateshead (2) v Matlock Town	2-0
	South Shields (3) v Skelmersdale United	3-0
	Witton Albion v Gainsborough Trinity	0-5
2	Burscough v Bedlington Terriers	3-3
	Denaby United v Ossett Town	2-3
	Halifax Town v Droylsden	4-1
	Leigh RMI v Accrington Stanley (2)	1-0
3	Chorley v Pontefract Collieries	3-1
	Ilkeston Town (2) v Rossendale United	3-0
	Radcliffe Borough v Bishop Auckland	1-3
	Warrington Town v RTM Newcastle	1-2
4	Billingham Town v Arnold Town	0-1
	Whitby Town v Netherfield (Kendal)	6-2
	Whitley Bay v Shotton Comrades	0-0
	Winsford United v Leek Town	1-0
5	Darwen v Ryhope Community Association	1-2
	Great Harwood Town v St Helens Town	1-1
	Hyde United v Louth United	3-0
	Lancaster City v Consett	2-2
6	Bootle v Belper Town	2-3
	Durham City v Knowsley United	wo/s
	Eccleshill United v Parkgate	1-2
	Workington v Emley	0-3
7	Frickley Athletic v Morpeth Town	3-3
	Gretna v Mossley	3-0
	Liversedge v Stocksbridge Park Steels	3-3
	North Ferriby United v Barrow	2-1
8	Brigg Town v Hucknall Town	3-0
	Newcastle Town v Garforth Town	3-5
	Spennymoor United v Blyth Spartans	1-1
	Worksop Town v Oldham Town	4-2
9	Bamber Bridge v Dunston Federation Brewery	1-1
	Clitheroe v Jarrow Roofing Boldon CA	4-3
	Marine v Ashton United	1-0
	Staveley MW v Lincoln United	1-5
10	Ashington v Farsley Celtic	0-2
	Guiseley v Alfreton Town	3-0
	Harrogate Town v Easington Colliery	2-2
	Heanor Town v Penrith	1-2
11	Bridgnorth Town v Desborough Town	1-1
	Bury Town v Nuneaton Borough	1-2
	Pershore Town v Stourbridge	0-7
	Telford United v Bedworth United	1-2
12	Great Yarmouth Town v Banbury United	2-1
	Hinckley United v Stewarts & Lloyds (2)	5-0
	Kettering Town v Mirrlees Blackstone	1-0
	Shepshed Dynamo v Cambridge City	0-3
13	Brackley Town v Stapenhill	4-0
	Rocester v Stowmarket Town	3-2
	Sudbury Wanderers v Stafford Rangers	3-0
	Tamworth v Bromsgrove Rovers	1-2
14	Holbeach United v Gresley Rovers	3-6
	Knypersley Victoria v Atherstone United	1-0
	Lye Town v Lowestoft Town	2-3
	Raunds Town v Spalding United	2-4
15	Barwell v Willenhall Town	1-2
	Felixstowe Port & Town v Halesowen Town	2-5
	Racing Club Warwick v Redditch United	1-2
	Rothwell Town v Corby Town	2-1
16	Bourne Town v King's Lynn	1-3
	Diss Town v V.S. Rugby	0-1
	Histon v Newmarket Town	1-3
	Moor Green v Bilston Town	0-2
17	Boldmere St Michaels v Wroxham	1-0
	Halesowen Harriers v Grantham Town	0-1
	Northampton Spencer v Woodbridge Town	1-1
	Solihull Borough v Burton Albion	2-0
18	Chertsey Town v Heybridge Swifts	1-1
	Flackwell Heath v East Thurrock United	1-0
	Marlow v Littlehampton Town	2-2
	Whyteleafe v Crawley Town	3-2
19	Banstead Athletic v Camberley Town	2-2
	Brimsdown Rovers v Canvey Island	1-2
	Great Wakering Rovers v Grays Athletic	1-2
	St Leonards Stamcroft v Bishop's Stortford	1-0
20	Aveley v Chichester City (1)	2-1
	Burnham Ramblers v Hastings Town	0-1
	Croydon v Horsham	2-1
	Hitchin Town v Bognor Regis Town	0-2
21	Burnham v Dorking (2)	1-3 N
	Concord Rangers v Purfleet	0-1
	Langney Sports v Leatherhead	2-1
	Sittingbourne v Molesey	5-0
22	Canterbury City v Worthing	1-1
	Cheshunt v Sutton United	0-4
	Tonbridge Angels v Ware	1-0
	Welling United v Leyton Pennant	3-0
23	Baldock Town v Slough Town	0-0
	Leighton Town v Wingate & Finchley	1-2
	Tilbury v Wick	3-1
	Walton & Hersham v Hampton	2-0
24	Bedford United v Kingstonian	0-5
	Croydon Athletic v Wivenhoe Town	0-4
	Harlow Town v Metropolitan Police	0-2
	Uxbridge v Dover Athletic	0-2
25	Barton Rovers v Clapton	1-0
	Bedfont v Chesham United	2-4
	Gravesend & Northfleet v Braintree Town	3-3
	Hillingdon Borough v Windsor & Eton	0-2
26	Berkhamsted Town v Deal Town	1-1
	Burgess Hill Town v Harrow Borough	1-3
	Margate v Bracknell Town	5-0
	Portfield v Viking Sports	2-1
27	Clacton Town v Stansted	2-7
	Hythe United v Romford	4-7
	Oakwood v Potton United	0-1
	Yeading v Chelmsford City	4-2
28	Edgware Town v Aylesbury United	2-5
	Fisher Athletic (London) v Wootton Blue Cross	5-0
	Harwich & Parkeston v Carshalton Athletic	1-1
	Wembley v Whitehawk	3-1
29	Arundel v Erith & Belvedere	1-4
	Bedford Town v Dulwich Hamlet	1-1
	Ruislip Manor v Shoreham	4-1
	Tooting & Mitcham United v Billericay Town	1-2
30	Barking v Arlesey Town	4-1
	Hanwell Town v Saltdean United	3-2
	Herne Bay v Dartford	1-2
	Staines Town v Bromley	3-1
31	Bridgwater Town v Abingdon Town	1-1
	Merthyr Tydfil v Brockenhurst	7-2
	Thatcham Town v Cheltenham Town	0-1
	Tuffley Rovers v Paulton Rovers	1-3
32	Chippenham Town v Bashley	3-2
	Wokingham Town v Westfields	1-1
	Worcester City v Lymington	3-2
	Yeovil Town v Witney Town	1-1
33	Downton v Forest Green Rovers	0-4
	Odd Down v Wimborne Town	1-4
	Oxford City v Dorchester Town	1-1
	St Blazey v Tiverton Town	0-2
34	Bideford v Bath City	0-2
	Clevedon Town v Calne Town	1-1
	Havant Town v Basingstoke Town	1-1
	Hungerford Town v Fleet Town	1-4
35	Buckingham Town v Gosport Borough	1-1
	Salisbury City v Chard Town	3-0
	Taunton Town v Newport AFC	3-2
	Weston-Super-Mare v Cinderford Town	0-0
36	Carterton Town v Portsmouth Royal Navy	0-1
	Gloucester City v Mangotsfield United	3-0
	Melksham Town v Waterlooville	1-2
	Newport (IOW) v Aldershot Town	2-1
1r	Maine Road v Billingham Synthonia	2-2P
2r	Bedlington Terriers v Burscough	1-2
4r	Shotton Comrades v Whitley Bay	1-0
5r	Consett v Lancaster City	1-2
r	St Helens Town v Great Harwood Town	3-1
7r	Morpeth Town v Frickley Athletic	4-1
r	Stocksbridge Park Steels v Liversedge	2-3
8r	Blyth Spartans v Spennymoor United	1-0
9r	Dunston Federation Brewery v Bamber Bridge	2-3
10r	Easington Colliery v Harrogate Town	4-1
11r	Desborough Town v Bridgnorth Town	1-3
17r	Woodbridge Town v Northampton Spencer	3-1
18r	Heybridge Swifts v Chertsey Town	2-1e
r	Littlehampton Town v Marlow	2-2q
19r	Camberley Town v Banstead Athletic	2-1
22r	Worthing v Canterbury City	4-1
23r	Slough Town v Baldock Town	5-0
25r	Braintree Town v Gravesend & Northfleet	3-1
26r	Deal Town v Berkhamsted Town	2-1
28r	Carshalton Athletic v Harwich & Parkeston	4-0
29r	Dulwich Hamlet v Bedford Town	2-0

1997/98

31r	Abingdon Town v Bridgwater Town	1-2e
32r	Westfields v Wokingham Town	1-3
r	Witney Town v Yeovil Town	1-2
33r	Dorchester Town v Oxford City	1-0
34r	Basingstoke Town v Havant Town	2-0
r	Calne Town v Clevedon Town	2-1
35r	Cinderford Town v Weston-Super-Mare	0-1
r	Gosport Borough v Buckingham Town	1-2

Qualifying Round Two

1	Gateshead (2) v Gainsborough Trinity	1-4
	South Shields (3) v Maine Road	2-0
2	Burscough v Ossett Town	1-4
	Halifax Town v Leigh RMI	4-0
3	Chorley v Bishop Auckland	2-2
	Ilkeston Town (2) v RTM Newcastle	7-1
4	Arnold Town v Shotton Comrades	2-0
	Whitby Town v Winsford United	1-4
5	Hyde United v Lancaster City	4-1
	Ryhope Community Association v St Helens Town	2-1
6	Belper Town v Parkgate	2-2
	Durham City v Emley	0-5
7	Gretna v Liversedge	3-1
	Morpeth Town v North Ferriby United	0-0
8	Brigg Town v Worksop Town	1-1
	Garforth Town v Blyth Spartans	0-1
9	Bamber Bridge v Marine	1-3
	Clitheroe v Lincoln United	1-3
10	Guiseley v Farsley Celtic	0-0
	Penrith v Easington Colliery	6-3
11	Bedworth United v Nuneaton Borough	1-1
	Stourbridge v Bridgnorth Town	2-1
12	Hinckley United v Great Yarmouth Town	2-0
	Kettering Town v Cambridge City	1-1
13	Brackley Town v Rocester	0-0
	Sudbury Wanderers v Bromsgrove Rovers	1-1
14	Knypersley Victoria v Gresley Rovers	3-1
	Spalding United v Lowestoft Town	2-1
15	Redditch United v Willenhall Town	3-1
	Rothwell Town v Halesowen Town	1-1
16	Bilston Town v King's Lynn	1-2
	Newmarket Town v V.S. Rugby	1-2
17	Solihull Borough v Grantham Town	2-1
	Woodbridge Town v Boldmere St Michaels	4-2
18	Marlow v Flackwell Heath	2-3
	Whyteleafe v Heybridge Swifts	0-2
19	Grays Athletic v Camberley Town	1-2
	St Leonards Stamcroft v Canvey Island	2-0
20	Bognor Regis Town v Hastings Town	2-1
	Croydon v Aveley	2-0
21	Langney Sports v Dorking (2)	3-0
	Sittingbourne v Purfleet	2-1
22	Tonbridge Angels v Worthing	3-0
	Welling United v Sutton United	2-2
23	Tilbury v Wingate & Finchley	3-0
	Walton & Hersham v Slough Town	0-0
24	Dover Athletic v Kingstonian	0-4
	Metropolitan Police v Wivenhoe Town	2-2
25	Braintree Town v Chesham United	3-0
	Windsor & Eton v Barton Rovers	2-5
26	Margate v Harrow Borough	4-0
	Portfield v Deal Town	1-1
27	Potton United v Romford	1-6
	Yeading v Stansted	3-0
28	Aylesbury United v Carshalton Athletic	0-3
	Wembley v Fisher Athletic (London)	1-3
29	Billericay Town v Dulwich Hamlet	2-1
	Ruislip Manor v Erith & Belvedere	0-0
30	Barking v Hanwell Town	3-0
	Dartford v Staines Town	1-2
31	Bridgwater Town v Paulton Rovers	2-4
	Merthyr Tydfil v Cheltenham Town	0-2
32	Chippenham Town v Wokingham Town	1-1
	Worcester City v Yeovil Town	1-2
33	Dorchester Town v Forest Green Rovers	1-0
	Tiverton Town v Wimborne Town	11-1
34	Basingstoke Town v Bath City	1-1
	Fleet Town v Calne Town	2-3
35	Buckingham Town v Taunton Town	0-2
	Salisbury City v Weston-Super-Mare	2-2
36	Gloucester City v Newport (IOW)	2-1
	Portsmouth Royal Navy v Waterlooville	1-1
3r	Bishop Auckland v Chorley	2-3
6r	Parkgate v Belper Town	0-2
7r	North Ferriby United v Morpeth Town	1-0
8r	Worksop Town v Brigg Town	3-1
10r	Farsley Celtic v Guiseley	1-4
11r	Nuneaton Borough v Bedworth United	6-0
12r	Cambridge City v Kettering Town	2-4e
13r	Bromsgrove Rovers v Sudbury Wanderers	2-0
r	Rocester v Brackley Town	2-1e
15r	Halesowen Town v Rothwell Town	4-1e
22r	Sutton United v Welling United	2-1
23r	Slough Town v Walton & Hersham	0-0P
24r	Wivenhoe Town v Metropolitan Police	2-1e
26r	Deal Town v Portfield	2-1
29r	Erith & Belvedere v Ruislip Manor	3-0
32r	Wokingham Town v Chippenham Town	0-1
34r	Bath City v Basingstoke Town	1-3
35r	Weston-Super-Mare v Salisbury City	2-2q
36r	Waterlooville v Portsmouth Royal Navy	7-0

Qualifying Round Three

1	Gainsborough Trinity v South Shields (3)	3-2
2	Halifax Town v Ossett Town	5-0
3	Chorley v Ilkeston Town (2)	1-3
4	Winsford United v Arnold Town	1-1
5	Hyde United v Ryhope Community Association	8-0
6	Emley v Belper Town	2-1
7	North Ferriby United v Gretna	2-0
8	Blyth Spartans v Worksop Town	4-0
9	Marine v Lincoln United	1-1
10	Guiseley v Penrith	1-2
11	Nuneaton Borough v Stourbridge	4-1
12	Kettering Town v Hinckley United	0-1
13	Bromsgrove Rovers v Rocester	2-1
14	Knypersley Victoria v Spalding United	3-1
15	Halesowen Town v Redditch United	2-2
16	King's Lynn v V.S. Rugby	4-3
17	Solihull Borough v Woodbridge Town	6-0
18	Heybridge Swifts v Flackwell Heath	4-0
19	St Leonards Stamcroft v Camberley Town	1-3
20	Bognor Regis Town v Croydon	1-1
21	Sittingbourne v Langney Sports	2-1
22	Sutton United v Tonbridge Angels	5-1
23	Slough Town v Tilbury	6-1
24	Kingstonian v Wivenhoe Town	1-0
25	Braintree Town v Barton Rovers	4-1
26	Margate v Deal Town	2-1
27	Yeading v Romford	0-2
28	Carshalton Athletic v Fisher Athletic (London)	1-0
29	Billericay Town v Erith & Belvedere	4-1
30	Staines Town v Barking	3-1
31	Cheltenham Town v Paulton Rovers	5-0
32	Yeovil Town v Chippenham Town	4-0
33	Dorchester Town v Tiverton Town	0-1
34	Basingstoke Town v Calne Town	0-0
35	Salisbury City v Taunton Town	3-0
36	Gloucester City v Waterlooville	2-0
4r	Arnold Town v Winsford United	0-0q
9r	Lincoln United v Marine	4-1e
15r	Redditch United v Halesowen Town	0-3
20r	Croydon v Bognor Regis Town	2-2q
34r	Calne Town v Basingstoke Town	1-2

Qualifying Round Four

	Altrincham v Morecambe	0-2
	Basingstoke Town v Braintree Town	5-1
	Billericay Town v Camberley Town	1-1
	Blyth Spartans v Kidderminster Harriers	2-1
	Bognor Regis Town v Farnborough Town	0-0
	Bromsgrove Rovers v Romford	2-0
	Cheltenham Town v Sutton United	1-0
	Enfield v Carshalton Athletic	1-2
	Gainsborough Trinity v Halifax Town	2-1
	Gloucester City v Wisbech Town	1-1
	Halesowen Town v Northwich Victoria	0-2
	Heybridge Swifts v Ashford Town	5-2
	Hinckley United v Colwyn Bay	1-2
	Ilkeston Town (2) v Hyde United	3-2
	King's Lynn v Salisbury City	5-0
	Knypersley Victoria v Boston United	0-1
	Nuneaton Borough v Emley	2-3
	Runcorn v Lincoln United	1-2
	Rushden & Diamonds v Boreham Wood	1-1
	Sittingbourne v Hereford United	2-2
	Slough Town v Kingstonian	2-1
	Southport v North Ferriby United	2-0
	St Albans City v Hendon	1-2
	Staines Town v Margate	0-3
	Stalybridge Celtic v Solihull Borough	3-3
	Tiverton Town v Sudbury Town	5-0
	Winsford United v Penrith	2-0
	Yeovil Town v Hayes	1-1
r	Boreham Wood v Rushden & Diamonds	1-0e
r	Camberley Town v Billericay Town	0-1
r	Farnborough Town v Bognor Regis Town	2-1
r	Hayes v Yeovil Town	1-0
r	Hereford United v Sittingbourne	3-0
r	Solihull Borough v Stalybridge Celtic	4-3e
r	Wisbech Town v Gloucester City	3-2

Round One

	Barnet v Watford	1-2
	Billericay Town v Wisbech Town	2-3
	Blackpool v Blyth Spartans	4-3
	Bournemouth v Heybridge Swifts	3-0
	Brentford v Colchester United	2-2
	Bristol City v Millwall	1-0
	Bristol Rovers v Gillingham	2-2
	Carlisle United v Wigan Athletic	0-1
	Carshalton Athletic v Stevenage Borough	0-0
	Cheltenham Town v Tiverton Town	2-1
	Chester City v Winsford United	2-1
	Chesterfield v Northwich Victoria	1-0
	Darlington v Solihull Borough	1-1
	Exeter City v Northampton Town	1-1
	Farnborough Town v Dagenham & Redbridge	0-1
	Hartlepool United v Macclesfield Town	2-4
	Hayes v Boreham Wood	0-1
	Hendon v Leyton Orient	2-2
	Hereford United v Brighton & Hove Albion	2-1
	Hull City v Hednesford Town	0-2
	Ilkeston Town (2) v Boston United	2-1
	King's Lynn v Bromsgrove Rovers	1-0
	Lincoln City v Gainsborough Trinity	1-1
	Luton Town v Torquay United	0-1
	Margate v Fulham	1-2
	Morecambe v Emley	1-1
	Notts County v Colwyn Bay	2-0
	Oldham Athletic v Mansfield Town	1-1
	Plymouth Argyle v Cambridge United	0-0
	Preston North End v Doncaster Rovers	3-2
	Rochdale v Wrexham	0-2
	Rotherham United v Burnley	3-3
	Scunthorpe United v Scarborough	2-1
	Shrewsbury Town v Grimsby Town	1-1
	Slough Town v Cardiff City	1-1
	Southport v York City	0-4
	Swansea City v Peterborough United	1-4
	Walsall v Lincoln United	2-0
	Woking v Southend United	0-2
	Wycombe Wanderers v Basingstoke Town	2-2
r	Basingstoke Town v Wycombe Wanderers	2-2P
r	Burnley v Rotherham United	0-3
r	Cambridge United v Plymouth Argyle	3-2e
r	Cardiff City v Slough Town	3-2e
r	Colchester United v Brentford	0-0P
r	Emley v Morecambe	3-3P
r	Gillingham v Bristol Rovers	0-2
r	Grimsby Town v Shrewsbury Town	4-0
r	Leyton Orient v Hendon	0-1
r	Lincoln City v Gainsborough Trinity	3-2
r	Mansfield Town v Oldham Athletic	0-1
r	Northampton Town v Exeter City	2-1
r	Solihull Borough v Darlington	3-3q
r	Stevenage Borough v Carshalton Athletic	5-0

Round Two

	Bournemouth v Bristol City	3-1
	Cambridge United v Stevenage Borough	1-1
	Cardiff City v Hendon	3-1
	Cheltenham Town v Boreham Wood	1-1
	Chester City v Wrexham	0-2
	Colchester United v Hereford United	1-1
	Fulham v Southend United	1-0
	Grimsby Town v Chesterfield	2-2
	Hednesford Town v Darlington	0-1
	Lincoln City v Emley	2-2
	Macclesfield Town v Walsall	0-7
	Northampton Town v Basingstoke Town	1-1
	Oldham Athletic v Blackpool	2-1
	Peterborough United v Dagenham & Redbridge	3-2
	Preston North End v Notts County	2-2
	Rotherham United v King's Lynn	6-0
	Scunthorpe United v Ilkeston Town (2)	1-1
	Torquay United v Watford	1-1
	Wigan Athletic v York City	2-1
	Wisbech Town v Bristol Rovers	0-2
r	Basingstoke Town v Northampton Town	0-0q
r	Boreham Wood v Cheltenham Town	0-2
r	Chesterfield v Grimsby Town	0-2
r	Emley v Lincoln City	3-3P
r	Hereford United v Colchester United	1-1P
r	Ilkeston Town (2) v Scunthorpe United	1-2
r	Notts County v Preston North End	1-2e
r	Stevenage Borough v Cambridge United	2-1
r	Watford v Torquay United	2-1e

Round Three

	Arsenal v Port Vale	0-0
	Barnsley v Bolton Wanderers	1-0
	Blackburn Rovers v Wigan Athletic	4-2
	Bournemouth v Huddersfield Town	0-1
	Bristol Rovers v Ipswich Town	1-1
	Cardiff City v Oldham Athletic	1-0
	Charlton Athletic v Nottingham Forest	4-1
	Chelsea v Manchester United	3-5
	Cheltenham Town v Reading	1-1
	Crewe Alexandra v Birmingham City	1-2
	Crystal Palace v Scunthorpe United	2-0
	Darlington v Wolverhampton Wan.	0-4
	Derby County v Southampton	2-0
	Everton v Newcastle United	0-1
	Grimsby Town v Norwich City	3-0
	Hereford United v Tranmere Rovers	0-3
	Leeds United v Oxford United	4-0
	Leicester City v Northampton Town	4-0
	Liverpool v Coventry City	1-3
	Manchester City v Bradford City	2-0
	Peterborough United v Walsall	0-2
	Portsmouth v Aston Villa	2-2
	Preston North End v Stockport County	1-2
	Queen's Park Rangers v Middlesbrough	2-2
	Rotherham United v Sunderland	1-5
	Sheffield United v Bury	1-1
	Swindon Town v Stevenage Borough	1-2
	Tottenham Hotspur v Fulham	3-1
	Watford v Sheffield Wednesday	1-1
	West Bromwich Albion v Stoke City	3-1
	West Ham United v Emley	2-1
	Wimbledon v Wrexham	0-0
r	Aston Villa v Portsmouth	1-0
r	Bury v Sheffield United	1-2
r	Ipswich Town v Bristol Rovers	1-0
r	Middlesbrough v Queen's Park Rangers	2-0
r	Port Vale v Arsenal	1-1q

1997/98 to 1998/99

r	Reading v Cheltenham Town	2-1
r	Sheffield Wednesday v Watford	0-0P
r	Wrexham v Wimbledon	2-3

Round Four

	Aston Villa v West Bromwich Albion	4-0
	Birmingham City v Stockport County	2-1
	Cardiff City v Reading	1-1
	Charlton Athletic v Wolverhampton Wan.	1-1
	Coventry City v Derby County	2-0
	Crystal Palace v Leicester City	3-0
	Huddersfield Town v Wimbledon	0-1
	Ipswich Town v Sheffield United	1-1
	Leeds United v Grimsby Town	2-0
	Manchester City v West Ham United	1-2
	Manchester United v Walsall	5-1
	Middlesbrough v Arsenal	1-2
	Sheffield Wednesday v Blackburn Rovers	0-3
	Stevenage Borough v Newcastle United	1-1
	Tottenham Hotspur v Barnsley	1-1
	Tranmere Rovers v Sunderland	1-0
r	Barnsley v Tottenham Hotspur	3-1
r	Newcastle United v Stevenage Borough	2-1
r	Reading v Cardiff City	1-1P
r	Sheffield United v Ipswich Town	1-0
r	Wolverhampton Wan. v Charlton Athletic	3-0

Round Five

	Arsenal v Crystal Palace	0-0
	Aston Villa v Coventry City	0-1
	Leeds United v Birmingham City	3-2
	Manchester United v Barnsley	1-1
	Newcastle United v Tranmere Rovers	1-0
	Sheffield United v Reading	1-0
	West Ham United v Blackburn Rovers	2-2
	Wimbledon v Wolverhampton Wan.	1-1
r	Barnsley v Manchester United	3-2
r	Blackburn Rovers v West Ham United	1-1q
r	Crystal Palace v Arsenal	1-2
r	Wolverhampton Wan. v Wimbledon	2-1

Round Six

	Arsenal v West Ham United	1-1
	Coventry City v Sheffield United	1-1
	Leeds United v Wolverhampton Wan.	0-1
	Newcastle United v Barnsley	3-1
r	Sheffield United v Coventry City	1-1P
r	West Ham United v Arsenal	1-1q

Semi Finals

Arsenal v Wolverhampton Wan.	1-0 N
Newcastle United v Sheffield United	1-0 N

Final

Arsenal v Newcastle United	2-0 N

1998/99

Preliminary Round

1	Ashton United v Willington	5-2
2	Thackley v Hebburn	2-1
3	Atherton Collieries v Armthorpe Welfare	1-2
4	Stockton (2) v Liversedge	1-4
5	Rossendale United v Brigg Town	0-3
6	Ashington v Horden CW	2-1e
7	Sheffield v Atherton LR	2-4 N
8	Trafford v Peterlee Newtown	4-1
9	Ramsbottom United v Maine Road	0-0
10	Harrogate Town v Burscough	1-2
11	Tadcaster Albion v Ossett Town	1-0
12	Guisborough Town v Rossington Main	1-3
13	Shotton Comrades v Jarrow Roofing Boldon CA	1-2
14	Flixton v Northallerton Town	3-0
15	Marske United v Billingham Synthonia	1-1
16	Oldham Town v Warrington Town	0-2
17	Bacup Borough v Blackpool (Wren) Rovers	wo/s
18	Bradford Park Avenue v Easington Colliery	4-1
19	Yorkshire Amateur v Witton Albion	1-3
20	Durham City v Dunston Federation Brewery	2-0
21	Sandwell Borough v Blakenall	0-3
22	Boston Town v Blackstones	2-0
23	Shepshed Dynamo v Barwell	1-1
24	Sutton Coldfield Town v V.S. Rugby	1-0
25	Hinckley United v Rushall Olympic	2-0
26	Lye Town v Racing Club Warwick	0-1
27	Oldbury United v Shifnal Town	2-0
28	Stafford Rangers v Boldmere St Michaels	3-0
29	Matlock Town v Redditch United	4-1
30	Halesowen Harriers v Stourport Swifts	2-1
31	Bridgnorth Town v Borrowash Victoria	3-3
32	Corby Town v Leek CSOB	0-4
33	Chelmsford City v Fakenham Town	6-0
34	Canvey Island v Stansted	6-1
35	Eynesbury Rovers v Southall	3-3
36	Tring Town v Waltham Abbey	0-2 d
37	Bowers United v Wootton Blue Cross	5-3
38	Felixstowe Port & Town v Ford Sports (Daventry)	1-2
39	Leyton Pennant v Wembley	2-1
40	Stotfold v Sudbury Town	2-2
41	Harpenden Town v Burnham	3-2
42	Potton United v Baldock Town	0-3
43	Hornchurch v London Colney	1-1
44	Marlow v Hemel Hempstead Town	2-1
45	Bury Town v Tilbury	1-1
46	Kingsbury Town v Grays Athletic	4-4
47	Stowmarket Town v Gorleston	5-1
48	Potters Bar Town v Wealdstone	2-2
49	Witney Town v Northwood	3-0
50	Arlesey Town v Barking	0-2
51	Welwyn Garden City v East Thurrock United	6-1
52	Ford United v Wellingborough Town	2-0
53	Burnham Ramblers v Soham Town Rangers	2-1
54	Halstead Town v Flackwell Heath	3-0
55	Wisbech Town v Bedford Town	2-3
56	Desborough Town v Cheshunt	1-0
57	Farnham Town v Hailsham Town	1-1
58	Molesey v Oxford City	1-4
59	Deal Town v Hillingdon Borough	4-1
60	Egham Town v Fisher Athletic (London)	2-2
61	St Leonards v Wick	2-1
62	Cowes Sports v Dorking (2)	1-2
63	Godalming & Guildford v Banstead Athletic	1-2
64	Dartford v Reading Town	0-0
65	Folkestone Invicta v Tonbridge Angels	2-3
66	Ashford Town v Margate	1-1
67	Littlehampton Town v Fleet Town	1-4
68	Fareham Town v Croydon	0-2
69	Portfield v Eastleigh	1-1
70	Abingdon Town v Maidenhead United	0-3
71	Ashford Town (Middlesex) v Erith & Belvedere	1-3
72	Bashley v Ramsgate	4-2
73	Chatham Town v Horsham	1-1
74	Eastbourne Town v Herne Bay	1-0
75	Wokingham Town v Camberley Town	0-2
76	Burgess Hill Town v Thame United	1-0
77	Torrington v Melksham Town	0-1
78	Cirencester Town v Chippenham Town	3-2
79	Falmouth Town v Devizes Town	1-0
80	Newport AFC v Weston-Super-Mare	0-0
81	Elmore v Yate Town	1-0
82	Paulton Rovers v Bemerton Heath Harlequins	2-1
83	Minehead v Frome Town	4-0
84	Backwell United v Calne Town	2-1
85	Bideford v Barnstaple Town	1-2
86	Bridgwater Town v Welton Rovers	5-0
9r	Maine Road v Ramsbottom United	1-2
15r	Billingham Synthonia v Marske United	3-0
23r	Barwell v Shepshed Dynamo	3-3q
31r	Borrowash Victoria v Bridgnorth Town	0-2
35r	Southall v Eynesbury Rovers	6-0
40r	Sudbury Town v Stotfold	2-1
43r	London Colney v Hornchurch	1-0
45r	Tilbury v Bury Town	3-2
46r	Grays Athletic v Kingsbury Town	7-0
48r	Wealdstone v Potters Bar Town	5-3
57r	Hailsham Town v Farnham Town	3-2
60r	Fisher Athletic (London) v Egham Town	6-0
64r	Reading Town v Dartford	0-3
66r	Margate v Ashford Town	1-2
69r	Eastleigh v Portfield	1-2
73r	Horsham v Chatham Town	3-1
80r	Weston-Super-Mare v Newport AFC	1-0

Qualifying Round One

1	Billingham Town v Denaby United	7-3
2	Ashington v Louth United	0-2
3	Atherton LR v Chester-le-Street Town	0-4
4	Prescot Cables v Liversedge	5-2
5	Crook Town v Farsley Celtic	1-4
6	Eccleshill United v Penrith	2-2
7	Brigg Town v Garforth Town	1-0
8	Tadcaster Albion v Armthorpe Welfare	1-1
9	Seaham Red Star v Netherfield (Kendal)	2-2
10	Warrington Town v North Ferriby United	0-4
11	Bootle v Bradford Park Avenue	2-3
12	Glasshoughton Welfare v Salford City	3-1 D
13	Consett v Newcastle Blue Star	1-2
14	West Auckland Town v Rossington Main	5-0
15	Chadderton v Ryhope Community Association	1-1
16	St Helens Town v Brandon United	3-1
17	Radcliffe Borough v Clitheroe	2-1
18	Evenwood Town v Durham City	4-1
19	Droylsden v Maltby Main	2-2
20	Flixton v Brodsworth MW	3-0
21	Ossett Albion v Workington	1-1
22	Ashton United v Tow Law Town	2-1
23	Great Harwood Town v Whitley Bay	3-3
24	South Shields (3) v Witton Albion	0-2
25	Morpeth Town v Skelmersdale United	2-0
26	Parkgate v Cheadle Town	4-2
27	Ramsbottom United v Shildon	3-0
28	Trafford v Mossley	1-2
29	Bedlington Terriers v Pickering Town	11-1
30	Billingham Synthonia v Darwen	7-0
31	Gretna v Harrogate Railway Athletic	0-0
32	Whickham v Stocksbridge Park Steels	0-2
33	Thackley v Bacup Borough	2-0
34	Selby Town v Curzon Ashton	6-0
35	Burscough v Jarrow Roofing Boldon CA	2-0
36	Staveley MW v Leek CSOB	1-3
37	Racing Club Warwick v Willenhall Town	1-0
38	Boston Town v Eastwood Town	0-5
39	Stapenhill v Spalding United	1-0
40	Belper Town v Alfreton Town	3-0
41	Rocester v Holbeach United	3-0
42	Shepshed Dynamo v Bloxwich Town	4-1
43	Glapwell v Matlock Town	1-2
44	Lincoln United v Wednesfield	3-0
45	Halesowen Harriers v Nantwich Town	1-2
46	West Midlands Police v Stratford Town	1-0
47	Blakenall v Hinckley United	1-0
48	Congleton Town v Bilston Town	5-3
49	Moor Green v Pelsall Villa	6-1
50	Bourne Town v Glossop North End	1-2
51	Sutton Coldfield Town v Kidsgrove Athletic	2-1
52	Arnold Town v Knypersley Victoria	3-1
53	Stamford v Buxton	2-3
54	Newcastle Town v Chasetown	1-3
55	Paget Rangers v Solihull Borough	1-1
56	Oldbury United v Stourbridge	1-6
57	Bridgnorth Town v Hucknall Town	0-4
58	Stafford Rangers v Bedworth United	1-1
59	Wroxham v Stewarts & Lloyds (2)	3-0
60	Chalfont St Peter v St Neots Town	3-3
61	Beaconsfield SYCOB v Concord Rangers	2-1
62	London Colney v Braintree Town	1-3
63	Banbury United v Harpenden Town	3-1
64	Hertford Town v Barkingside	0-0
65	Leighton Town v Ford Sports (Daventry)	1-2
66	Canvey Island v Histon	5-3e
67	Edgware Town v Grays Athletic	2-3
68	Northampton Spencer v Chelmsford City	1-4
69	Bowers United v Halstead Town	1-3
70	Burnham Ramblers v Basildon United	2-2
71	Marlow v Tiptree United	1-2
72	Woodbridge Town v Southall	4-2
73	Buckingham Town v Wealdstone	0-1
74	Bedford United v Royston Town	0-3
75	Ford United v Barton Rovers	1-1
76	Yaxley v Berkhamsted Town	2-5
77	Clapton v Tilbury	2-0
78	Harlow Town v Diss Town	5-0
79	Sudbury Town v Ruislip Manor	4-0
80	Barking v Warboys Town	3-2
81	Newmarket Town v Great Yarmouth Town	0-0
82	Ware v Leyton Pennant	3-2
83	Ely City v Harwich & Parkeston	0-4
84	Brook House v Aveley	1-3
85	Yeading v Welwyn Garden City	1-2
86	Staines Town v Lowestoft Town	1-1
87	Stowmarket Town v Romford	0-1
88	Desborough Town v Raunds Town	1-2
89	Tring Town v Wingate & Finchley	0-1
90	Clacton Town v Bedford Town	1-1
91	Long Buckby v Witney Town	1-2
92	Sudbury Wanderers v Uxbridge	0-0
93	Witham Town v Hitchin Town	1-0
94	Brackley Town v Wivenhoe Town	0-2
95	Baldock Town v Great Wakering Rovers	1-3
96	Sheppey United v Lymington & New Milton	0-0
97	East Preston v Peacehaven & Telscombe	6-0
98	Thatcham Town v Ashford Town	3-4
99	Oxford City v Chertsey Town	3-2
100	Bedfont v Whitstable Town	5-2
101	Fisher Athletic (London) v BAT Sports	4-0
102	Corinthian Casuals v Worthing	1-2
103	Havant & Waterlooville v Hassocks	1-0
104	Thamesmead Town v Horsham YMCA	3-0
105	Burgess Hill Town v Saltdean United	1-3
106	Arundel v Camberley Town	0-7
107	Horsham v Bracknell Town	2-2
108	Gosport Borough v Croydon	0-2
109	Slade Green v Hungerford Town	2-4
110	Fleet Town v Dartford	3-2
111	Chipstead v Redhill	2-0
112	Langney Sports v Hailsham Town	3-1
113	AFC Newbury v Tooting & Mitcham United	1-2
114	Eastbourne Town v Tunbridge Wells	2-2
115	Metropolitan Police v Canterbury City	2-2
116	Leatherhead v Whitehawk	5-0
117	Viking Sports v Bashley	1-5
118	Sandhurst Town v Tonbridge Angels	0-1
119	Bognor Regis Town v Newport (IOW)	2-4
120	Andover v Deal Town	2-5
121	Epsom & Ewell v Shoreham	2-1
122	Windsor & Eton v Chichester City (1)	1-1
123	Portsmouth Royal Navy v Raynes Park Vale	4-2
124	Whyteleafe v Banstead Athletic	2-2
125	Maidenhead United v Selsey	2-1
126	Brockenhurst v Dorking (2)	1-7
127	Ash United v Pagham	7-1
128	Hythe United v Croydon Athletic	2-1
129	Portfield v Sittingbourne	1-2
130	Lewes v Erith & Belvedere	1-2
131	St Leonards v Erith Town	2-0
132	Ringmer v Didcot Town	1-0
133	Falmouth Town v Wimborne Town	3-1
134	Tuffley Rovers v Minehead	0-3
135	Mangotsfield United v Melksham Town	2-1
136	Tiverton Town v Weston-Super-Mare	2-0
137	Paulton Rovers v Glastonbury	8-1
138	Taunton Town v Bournemouth (Ams)	4-0
139	Barnstaple Town v Evesham United	1-0
140	Bridgwater Town v Bridport	1-0
141	Cirencester Town v Odd Down	2-2
142	St Blazey v EFC Cheltenham	3-2

1998/99

143	Brislington v Pershore Town	3-3
144	Westbury United v Elmore	3-3
145	Backwell United v Downton	10-1
146	Clevedon Town v Cinderford Town	1-1
6r	Penrith v Eccleshill United	6-0
8r	Armthorpe Welfare v Tadcaster Albion	0-0q
9r	Netherfield (Kendal) v Seaham Red Star	8-1
15r	Ryhope Community Association v Chadderton	2-1
19r	Maltby Main v Droylsden	0-2
21r	Workington v Ossett Albion	2-2q
23r	Whitley Bay v Great Harwood Town	1-2
31r	Harrogate Railway Athletic v Gretna	2-1
55r	Solihull Borough v Paget Rangers	4-2
58r	Bedworth United v Stafford Rangers	1-2
60r	St Neots Town v Chalfont St Peter	0-3
64r	Barkingside v Hertford Town	3-2e
70r	Basildon United v Burnham Ramblers	2-0
75r	Barton Rovers v Ford United	0-1
81r	Great Yarmouth Town v Newmarket Town	2-2q
86r	Lowestoft Town v Staines Town	2-2P
90r	Bedford Town v Clacton Town	2-0
92r	Uxbridge v Sudbury Wanderers	3-2e
96r	Lymington & New Milton v Sheppey United	1-2
107r	Bracknell Town v Horsham	3-4e
114r	Tunbridge Wells v Eastbourne Town	2-4
115r	Canterbury City v Metropolitan Police	1-1P
122r	Chichester City (1) v Windsor & Eton	0-4
124r	Banstead Athletic v Whyteleafe	1-2
141r	Odd Down v Cirencester Town	0-2
143r	Pershore Town v Brislington	4-2
144r	Elmore v Westbury United	4-0
146r	Cinderford Town v Clevedon Town	0-0P

Qualifying Round Two

1	Selby Town v Frickley Athletic	1-2
2	Colwyn Bay v Emley	0-1
3	Whitby Town v Accrington Stanley (2)	4-2
4	Radcliffe Borough v Ryhope Community Association	2-0
5	Billingham Synthonia v Mossley	0-0
6	Louth United v Brigg Town	0-2
7	Ashton United v Altrincham	1-0
8	Flixton v Spennymoor United	4-0
9	Thackley v Guiseley	1-1
10	Netherfield (Kendal) v Lancaster City	1-3
11	Bradford Park Avenue v Stocksbridge Park Steels	1-0
12	Runcorn v Blyth Spartans	0-0
13	Hyde United v Gainsborough Trinity	4-0
14	Morpeth Town v Ossett Albion	0-0
15	Gateshead (2) v Bishop Auckland	3-0
16	Droylsden v St Helens Town	6-0
17	Bedlington Terriers v Bamber Bridge	1-1
18	Penrith v Chorley	1-1
19	Stalybridge Celtic v Worksop Town	1-2
20	Great Harwood Town v Marine	1-3
21	Witton Albion v Salford City	7-2
22	Ramsbottom United v Billingham Town	3-0
23	North Ferriby United v Newcastle Blue Star	5-3
24	Burscough v Evenwood Town	2-2
25	Leigh RMI v Winsford United	1-0
26	Tadcaster Albion v Farsley Celtic	1-2
27	Harrogate Railway Athletic v Prescot Cables	1-1
28	Chester-le-Street Town v West Auckland Town	1-1
29	Grantham Town v West Midlands Police	4-0
30	Cambridge City v Glossop North End	1-1
31	Congleton Town v Boston United	1-0
32	Parkgate v Sutton Coldfield Town	0-3
33	Racing Club Warwick v Stourbridge	0-1
34	Arnold Town v Matlock Town	1-1
35	Belper Town v Stafford Rangers	1-2
36	Blakenall v Lincoln United	1-0
37	Shepshed Dynamo v Gresley Rovers	1-2
38	Nantwich Town v Raunds Town	1-1
39	Stapenhill v Rothwell Town	0-4
40	Ilkeston Town (2) v Moor Green	2-0
41	Atherstone United v Nuneaton Borough	0-0
42	Solihull Borough v Hucknall Town	0-1
43	Halesowen Town v Eastwood Town	2-2
44	Chasetown v Buxton	0-1
45	Leek CSOB v Tamworth	2-3
46	Rocester v Burton Albion	0-1
47	Bromsgrove Rovers v King's Lynn	1-1
48	Dorking (2) v Carshalton Athletic	0-5
49	Sheppey United v Leatherhead	0-0
50	Witney Town v Wroxham	1-1
51	Grays Athletic v Ashford Town	2-0
52	Sudbury Town v Sittingbourne	0-0
53	Bedfont v Chipstead	0-2
54	Dagenham & Redbridge v Eastbourne Town	4-0
55	Welwyn Garden City v Great Wakering Rovers	2-2
56	Ash United v Walton & Hersham	1-5
57	Clapton v Purfleet	0-1
58	Bishop's Stortford v Aldershot Town	0-2
59	Banbury United v Epsom & Ewell	2-2
60	Tooting & Mitcham United v Lowestoft Town	2-3
61	Wivenhoe Town v Harlow Town	1-3
62	Fisher Athletic (London) v Halstead Town	1-2
63	Hendon v Chelmsford City	1-1
64	Slough Town v Fleet Town	1-1
65	Romford v St Albans City	1-2
66	Ware v Braintree Town	1-1
67	Boreham Wood v Saltdean United	4-0
68	Berkhamsted Town v Langney Sports	1-1
69	Tiptree United v Royston Town	0-1
70	Barking v Beaconsfield SYCOB	1-0
71	Witham Town v Hythe United	5-2
72	Whyteleafe v Bedford Town	2-1
73	Aylesbury United v Horsham	3-1
74	St Leonards v Sutton United	0-1
75	East Preston v Worthing	0-2
76	Croydon v Enfield	0-4
77	Billericay Town v Tonbridge Angels	4-0
78	Basildon United v Barkingside	2-2
79	Ford Sports (Daventry) v Aveley	2-1
80	Crawley Town v Canterbury City	5-0
81	Wingate & Finchley v Canvey Island	0-5
82	Heybridge Swifts v Bashley	3-1
83	Uxbridge v Maidenhead United	0-5
84	Dulwich Hamlet v Deal Town	1-0
85	Bromley v Chesham United	2-1
86	Wealdstone v Newport (IOW)	0-0
87	Hungerford Town v Portsmouth Royal Navy	6-0
88	Havant & Waterlooville v Hampton	5-1
89	Harwich & Parkeston v Chalfont St Peter	0-2
90	Erith & Belvedere v Windsor & Eton	0-1
91	Ford United v Woodbridge Town	1-1
92	Harrow Borough v Thamesmead Town	3-0
93	Gravesend & Northfleet v Oxford City	3-1
94	Newmarket Town v Hastings Town	1-1
95	Camberley Town v Ringmer	2-1
96	Bath City v Cirencester Town	3-1
97	Dorchester Town v Salisbury City	0-3
98	Mangotsfield United v Worcester City	0-1
99	Taunton Town v Cinderford Town	3-1
100	Pershore Town v St Blazey	1-3
101	Minehead v Bridgwater Town	0-0
102	Elmore v Barnstaple Town	0-1
103	Backwell United v Basingstoke Town	1-1
104	Falmouth Town v Tiverton Town	1-0
105	Merthyr Tydfil v Weymouth	0-2
106	Gloucester City v Paulton Rovers	2-1
5r	Mossley v Billingham Synthonia	1-0
9r	Guiseley v Thackley	2-1
12r	Blyth Spartans v Runcorn	2-4
14r	Ossett Albion v Morpeth Town	2-2q
17r	Bamber Bridge v Bedlington Terriers	4-4q
18r	Chorley v Penrith	1-0e
24r	Evenwood Town v Burscough	0-6
27r	Prescot Cables v Harrogate Railway Athletic	2-0
28r	West Auckland Town v Chester-le-Street Town	2-0
30r	Glossop North End v Cambridge City	1-1P
34r	Matlock Town v Arnold Town	0-2
38r	Raunds Town v Nantwich Town	2-0
41r	Nuneaton Borough v Atherstone United	3-0
43r	Eastwood Town v Halesowen Town	0-1
47r	King's Lynn v Bromsgrove Rovers	2-1e
49r	Leatherhead v Sheppey United	3-1e
50r	Wroxham v Witney Town	2-3
52r	Sittingbourne v Sudbury Town	1-2
55r	Great Wakering Rovers v Welwyn Garden City	3-4
59r	Epsom & Ewell v Banbury United	0-1
63r	Chelmsford City v Hendon	2-3
64r	Fleet Town v Slough Town	0-2
66r	Braintree Town v Ware	4-1
68r	Langney Sports v Berkhamsted Town	0-0P
78r	Barkingside v Basildon United	3-3q
86r	Newport (IOW) v Wealdstone	3-2e
91r	Woodbridge Town v Ford United	1-2
94r	Hastings Town v Newmarket Town	2-1e
101r	Bridgwater Town v Minehead	0-1
103r	Basingstoke Town v Backwell United	1-0

Qualifying Round Three

1	West Auckland Town v Hyde United	2-0
2	Mossley v Lancaster City	0-1
3	Whitby Town v Bedlington Terriers	1-1
4	Doncaster Rovers v Flixton	2-0
5	Runcorn v North Ferriby United	1-1
6	Gateshead (2) v Barrow	2-1
7	Bradford Park Avenue v Ashton United	0-1
8	Emley v Marine	0-0
9	Morpeth Town v Prescot Cables	1-0
10	Morecambe v Farsley Celtic	4-2
11	Frickley Athletic v Witton Albion	1-0
12	Guiseley v Chorley	1-1
13	Droylsden v Northwich Victoria	2-0
14	Worksop Town v Leigh RMI	1-2
15	Radcliffe Borough v Burscough	0-1
16	Ramsbottom United v Southport	0-5
17	Kidderminster Harriers v Blakenall	3-1
18	Halesowen Town v Gresley Rovers	1-2
19	Sutton Coldfield Town v Telford United	1-1
20	Congleton Town v Hednesford Town	1-1
21	Buxton v Leek Town	0-0
22	Stafford Rangers v Arnold Town	5-1
23	Burton Albion v Nuneaton Borough	2-1
24	Glossop North End v Grantham Town	2-3
25	Brigg Town v Tamworth	0-2
26	Raunds Town v Rothwell Town	2-2
27	Ilkeston Town (2) v King's Lynn	1-2
28	Hucknall Town v Stourbridge	0-0
29	Hastings Town v Yeovil Town	0-3
30	Hereford United v Newport (IOW)	2-3
31	Crawley Town v Billericay Town	1-0
32	Worcester City v Falmouth Town	2-1
33	Gravesend & Northfleet v Dover Athletic	0-0
34	Farnborough Town v Heybridge Swifts	2-0
35	Basingstoke Town v Chalfont St Peter	2-0
36	Taunton Town v Kettering Town	4-3
37	Dulwich Hamlet v Purfleet	2-2
38	Welling United v Weymouth	3-2
39	Barnstaple Town v Cheltenham Town	0-1
40	Dagenham & Redbridge v Chipstead	2-0
41	Rushden & Diamonds v Forest Green Rovers	2-0
42	Welwyn Garden City v Ford United	2-2
43	Hayes v Bromley	1-0
44	Maidenhead United v Kingstonian	2-4
45	Royston Town v Boreham Wood	0-2
46	Minehead v Woking	1-5
47	Witney Town v Stevenage Borough	1-2
48	Gloucester City v Sudbury Town	10-0
49	Slough Town v Halstead Town	3-1
50	Braintree Town v Camberley Town	1-3
51	Langney Sports v Harrow Borough	4-1
52	Worthing v Whyteleafe	0-2
53	Leatherhead v Windsor & Eton	2-0
54	Grays Athletic v Aldershot Town	0-1
55	Walton & Hersham v Bath City	2-2
56	Aylesbury United v Carshalton Athletic	0-1
57	St Albans City v Basildon United	3-0
58	Lowestoft Town v Canvey Island	4-2
59	Banbury United v Enfield	0-4
60	Hungerford Town v Salisbury City	1-1
61	Ford Sports (Daventry) v Sutton United	2-2
62	Havant & Waterlooville v Witham Town	0-0
63	Harlow Town v Hendon	2-4
64	St Blazey v Barking	1-0
3r	Bedlington Terriers v Whitby Town	1-1P
5r	North Ferriby United v Runcorn	2-1 D
8r	Marine v Emley	1-4
12r	Chorley v Guiseley	1-2
19r	Telford United v Sutton Coldfield Town	1-0
20r	Hednesford Town v Congleton Town	1-0
21r	Leek Town v Buxton	3-0
26r	Rothwell Town v Raunds Town	0-1e
28r	Stourbridge v Hucknall Town	3-0
33r	Dover Athletic v Gravesend & Northfleet	3-2
37r	Purfleet v Dulwich Hamlet	1-3
42r	Ford United v Welwyn Garden City	4-2
55r	Bath City v Walton & Hersham	3-0
60r	Salisbury City v Hungerford Town	3-2
61r	Sutton United v Ford Sports (Daventry)	3-0
62r	Witham Town v Havant & Waterlooville	0-4

Qualifying Round Four

1	Runcorn v Ashton United	5-3
2	King's Lynn v West Auckland Town	0-1
3	Tamworth v Grantham Town	2-1
4	Droylsden v Leigh RMI	1-2
5	Southport v Stourbridge	4-0
6	Leek Town v Lancaster City	0-3
7	Telford United v Burscough	2-1
8	Doncaster Rovers v Guiseley	3-1
9	Morpeth Town v Burton Albion	0-1
10	Frickley Athletic v Gresley Rovers	0-0
11	Morecambe v Hednesford Town	1-2
12	Emley v Gateshead (2)	1-1
13	Stafford Rangers v Bedlington Terriers	1-2
14	Aldershot Town v Woking	0-0
15	St Albans City v Kingstonian	1-1
16	Enfield v Raunds Town	2-0
17	Havant & Waterlooville v Hayes	2-2
18	Dagenham & Redbridge v Stevenage Borough	0-3
19	Lowestoft Town v Ford United	1-3
20	Hendon v Bath City	4-0
21	Basingstoke Town v Dover Athletic	2-2
22	Boreham Wood v Sutton United	1-0
23	Worcester City v Langney Sports	7-0
24	Welling United v Whyteleafe	2-1
25	Leatherhead v Rushden & Diamonds	1-1
26	Kidderminster Harriers v Gloucester City	2-1
27	Farnborough Town v Yeovil Town	1-3
28	Carshalton Athletic v Salisbury City	0-6
29	Dulwich Hamlet v Newport (IOW)	3-2
30	Cheltenham Town v Taunton Town	3-2
31	St Blazey v Camberley Town	0-2
32	Crawley Town v Slough Town	0-0
10r	Gresley Rovers v Frickley Athletic	2-1
12r	Gateshead (2) v Emley	0-3
14r	Woking v Aldershot Town	2-1e
15r	Kingstonian v St Albans City	1-1P
17r	Hayes v Havant & Waterlooville	1-1P
21r	Dover Athletic v Basingstoke Town	1-2
25r	Rushden & Diamonds v Leatherhead	4-0
32r	Slough Town v Crawley Town	3-2

Round One

Basingstoke Town v Bournemouth	1-2
Bedlington Terriers v Colchester United	4-1
Boreham Wood v Luton Town	2-3
Brentford v Camberley Town	5-0
Bristol Rovers v Welling United	3-0
Cardiff City v Chester City	6-0
Cheltenham Town v Lincoln City	0-1
Darlington v Burnley	3-2 N
Dulwich Hamlet v Southport	0-1
Emley v Rotherham United	1-1 N
Enfield v York City	2-2
Fulham v Leigh RMI	1-1
Hartlepool United v Carlisle United	2-1
Hednesford Town v Barnet	3-1
Hendon v Notts County	0-0

1998/99 to 1999/2000

Kingstonian v Burton Albion 1-0
Leyton Orient v Brighton & Hove Albion 4-2
Macclesfield Town v Slough Town 2-2
Manchester City v Halifax Town 3-0
Mansfield Town v Hayes 2-1
Northampton Town v Lancaster City 2-1
Oldham Athletic v Gillingham 2-0
Plymouth Argyle v Kidderminster Harriers 0-0
Preston North End v Ford United 3-0
Reading v Stoke City 0-1
Runcorn v Stevenage Borough 1-1
Rushden & Diamonds v Shrewsbury Town 1-0
Salisbury City v Hull City 0-2
Scarborough v Rochdale 1-1
Southend United v Doncaster Rovers 0-1
Swansea City v Millwall 3-0
Tamworth v Exeter City 2-2
Telford United v Cambridge United 0-2
Walsall v Gresley Rovers 1-0
Wigan Athletic v Blackpool 4-3
Woking v Scunthorpe United 0-1
Worcester City v Torquay United 0-1
Wrexham v Peterborough United 1-0
Wycombe Wanderers v Chesterfield 1-0
Yeovil Town v West Auckland Town 2-2
r Exeter City v Tamworth 4-1
r Kidderminster Harriers v Plymouth Argyle 0-0q
r Leigh RMI v Fulham 0-2
r Notts County v Hendon 3-0
r Rochdale v Scarborough 2-0
r Rotherham United v Emley 3-1
r Slough Town v Macclesfield Town 1-1q
r Stevenage Borough v Runcorn 2-0
r West Auckland Town v Yeovil Town 1-1q
r York City v Enfield 2-1

Round Two

Cardiff City v Hednesford Town 3-1
Darlington v Manchester City 1-1
Doncaster Rovers v Rushden & Diamonds 0-0
Exeter City v Bristol Rovers 2-2
Fulham v Hartlepool United 4-2
Kingstonian v Leyton Orient 0-0
Lincoln City v Stevenage Borough 4-1
Luton Town v Hull City 1-2
Macclesfield Town v Cambridge United 4-1
Mansfield Town v Southport 1-2
Notts County v Wigan Athletic 1-1
Oldham Athletic v Brentford 1-1
Preston North End v Walsall 2-0
Rochdale v Rotherham United 0-0
Scunthorpe United v Bedlington Terriers 2-0
Swansea City v Stoke City 1-0
Torquay United v Bournemouth 0-1
Wrexham v York City 2-1
Wycombe Wanderers v Plymouth Argyle 1-1
Yeovil Town v Northampton Town 2-0
r Brentford v Oldham Athletic 2-2q
r Bristol Rovers v Exeter City 5-0
r Leyton Orient v Kingstonian 2-1
r Manchester City v Darlington 1-0e
r Plymouth Argyle v Wycombe Wanderers 3-2
r Rotherham United v Rochdale 4-0
r Rushden & Diamonds v Doncaster Rovers 4-2
r Wigan Athletic v Notts County 0-0q

Round Three

Aston Villa v Hull City 3-0
Blackburn Rovers v Charlton Athletic 2-0
Bolton Wanderers v Wolverhampton Wan. 1-2
Bournemouth v West Bromwich Albion 1-0
Bradford City v Grimsby Town 2-1
Bristol City v Everton 0-2
Bury v Stockport County 0-3
Cardiff City v Yeovil Town 1-1
Coventry City v Macclesfield Town 7-0
Crewe Alexandra v Oxford United 1-3
Leicester City v Birmingham City 4-2
Lincoln City v Sunderland 0-1
Manchester United v Middlesbrough 3-1
Newcastle United v Crystal Palace 2-1
Nottingham Forest v Portsmouth 0-1
Oldham Athletic v Chelsea 0-2
Plymouth Argyle v Derby County 0-3
Port Vale v Liverpool 0-3
Preston North End v Arsenal 2-4
Queen's Park Rangers v Huddersfield Town 0-1
Rotherham United v Bristol Rovers 0-1
Rushden & Diamonds v Leeds United 0-0
Sheffield United v Notts County 1-1
Sheffield Wednesday v Norwich City 4-1
Southampton v Fulham 1-1
Southport v Leyton Orient 0-2
Swindon Town v Barnsley 0-0
Tottenham Hotspur v Watford 5-2
Tranmere Rovers v Ipswich Town 0-1
West Ham United v Swansea City 1-1
Wimbledon v Manchester City 1-0
Wrexham v Scunthorpe United 4-3
r Barnsley v Swindon Town 3-1
r Fulham v Southampton 1-0
r Leeds United v Rushden & Diamonds 3-1
r Notts County v Sheffield United 3-4e
r Swansea City v West Ham United 1-0
r Yeovil Town v Cardiff City 1-2e

Round Four

Aston Villa v Fulham 0-2
Barnsley v Bournemouth 3-1
Blackburn Rovers v Sunderland 1-0
Bristol Rovers v Leyton Orient 3-0
Everton v Ipswich Town 1-0
Leicester City v Coventry City 0-3
Manchester United v Liverpool 2-1
Newcastle United v Bradford City 3-0
Oxford United v Chelsea 1-1
Portsmouth v Leeds United 1-5
Sheffield United v Cardiff City 4-1
Sheffield Wednesday v Stockport County 2-0
Swansea City v Derby County 0-1
Wimbledon v Tottenham Hotspur 1-1
Wolverhampton Wan. v Arsenal 1-2
Wrexham v Huddersfield Town 1-1
r Chelsea v Oxford United 4-2
r Huddersfield Town v Wrexham 2-1
r Tottenham Hotspur v Wimbledon 3-0

Round Five

Arsenal v Sheffield United 2-1 v
Barnsley v Bristol Rovers 4-1
Everton v Coventry City 2-1
Huddersfield Town v Derby County 2-2
Leeds United v Tottenham Hotspur 1-1
Manchester United v Fulham 1-0
Newcastle United v Blackburn Rovers 0-0
Sheffield Wednesday v Chelsea 0-1
r Arsenal v Sheffield United 2-1
r Blackburn Rovers v Newcastle United 0-1
r Derby County v Huddersfield Town 3-1
r Tottenham Hotspur v Leeds United 2-0

Round Six

Arsenal v Derby County 1-0
Barnsley v Tottenham Hotspur 0-1
Manchester United v Chelsea 0-0
Newcastle United v Everton 4-1
r Chelsea v Manchester United 0-2

Semi Finals

Manchester United v Arsenal 0-0eN
Newcastle United v Tottenham Hotspur 2-0eN
r Manchester United v Arsenal 2-1eN

Final

Manchester United v Newcastle United 2-0 N

1999/2000

Preliminary Round

1 Shildon v Thornaby-on-Tees 1-3
2 Glasshoughton Welfare v Hebburn 0-1
3 Brandon United v Ossett Town 0-3
4 Bradford Park Avenue v Prescot Cables 1-0
5 Workington v Burscough 1-2
6 Garforth Town v Armthorpe Welfare 0-4
7 Dunston Federation Brewery v Maine Road 1-0 N
8 Atherton Collieries v Ramsbottom United 1-2
9 Marske United v Ashington 1-1
10 Cheadle Town v Warrington Town 0-3
11 Morpeth Town v Harrogate Town 2-1
12 Tow Law Town v Tadcaster Albion 6-0
13 Chester-le-Street Town v St Helens Town 1-3
14 Liversedge v Hallam 2-1 N
15 Billingham Town v Fleetwood Freeport 1-2
16 Farsley Celtic v Guisborough Town 1-1
17 Accrington Stanley (2) v Peterlee Newtown 3-0
18 Rossendale United v Chadderton 2-1
19 Netherfield (Kendal) v Oldham Town 3-0
20 Harrogate Railway Athletic v Willington 1-0
21 Bootle v Jarrow Roofing Boldon CA 0-0
22 Crook Town v Yorkshire Amateur 2-0
23 Louth United v Kennek Ryhope CA 2-1
24 Flixton v Northallerton Town 2-1
25 Ashton United v Clitheroe 2-1
26 Goole AFC v Trafford 1-1
27 Woodley Sports v Ossett Albion 2-1
28 Pickering Town v Horden CW 4-1
29 Denaby United v Chorley 0-2
30 Darwen v Billingham Synthonia 0-1
31 Brodsworth MW v South Shields (3) 1-0
32 Mossley v Atherton LR 2-1
33 Parkgate v Eccleshill United 1-5
34 Thackley v Consett 0-1
35 North Ferriby United v Witton Albion 1-0
36 Penrith v Shotton Comrades 4-0
37 Salford City v Evenwood Town 2-0
38 Radcliffe Borough v Durham City 2-1
39 Selby Town v Bedlington Terriers 0-3
40 Bacup Borough v Sheffield 2-2
41 Curzon Ashton v Brigg Town 0-1
42 Skelmersdale United v Whitley Bay 5-2
43 Easington Colliery v Newcastle Blue Star 2-2
44 Seaham Red Star v West Auckland Town 2-1
45 Gretna v Rossington Main 5-0
46 Brackley Town v Long Buckby 2-1
47 Bromsgrove Rovers v Stourbridge 1-3
48 Blackstones v Willenhall Town 0-0
49 Rocester v Spalding United 2-3
50 Stamford v Corby Town 3-1
51 Belper Town v Stourport Swifts 2-2
52 Boston Town v Boldmere St Michaels 1-0
53 Stratford Town v Leek CSOB 4-1
54 Borrowash Victoria v Sutton Coldfield Town 0-1
55 Matlock Town v Chasetown 1-0
56 Moor Green v Paget Rangers 3-0
57 Barwell v Staveley MW 1-1
58 Redditch United v Kings Norton Town 1-0
59 Stafford Rangers v Glossop North End 2-0
60 Lincoln United v Mickleover Sports 1-2
61 Alfreton Town v Congleton Town 1-2
62 Ford Sports (Daventry) v Nantwich Town 1-2
63 Racing Club Warwick v Blakenall 1-2
64 Shepshed Dynamo v Raunds Town 0-3
65 Bilston Town v Oadby Town 2-4
66 Wednesfield v Oldbury United 1-6
67 Desborough Town v Northampton Spencer 2-3
68 Glapwell v Stapenhill 3-1
69 Bridgnorth Town v Hinckley United 1-3
70 Wellingborough Town v Kidsgrove Athletic 3-0
71 Gresley Rovers v Eastwood Town 0-1
72 Holbeach United v Pelsall Villa 2-0
73 Newcastle Town v Sandwell Borough 1-0
74 V.S. Rugby v Solihull Borough 1-2
75 Bourne Town v Stewarts & Lloyds (2) 0-2
76 Knypersley Victoria v Bedworth United 0-2 N
77 Shifnal Town v Rushall Olympic 3-3
78 Yaxley v Arnold Town 2-2e
79 Halesowen Harriers v West Midlands Police 4-0
80 St Neots Town v Hornchurch 2-1
81 Potters Bar Town v Flackwell Heath 3-3
82 Great Wakering Rovers v Staines Town 0-0
83 Chalfont St Peter v Barking 0-6
84 Stotfold v Wembley 0-0
85 Grays Athletic v Basildon United 7-1
86 Diss Town v Sudbury Town 1-6
87 Ely City v Witham Town 2-3
88 Berkhamsted Town v Bishop's Stortford 2-2
89 Tiptree United v London Colney 2-0
90 Wealdstone v Clacton Town 1-0
91 Fakenham Town v Brook House 3-2
92 Southend Manor v Ilford 4-0
93 Southall v Witney Town 2-5
94 Felixstowe Port & Town v Wingate & Finchley 1-3
95 Watton United v Arlesey Town 0-1 N
96 Saffron Walden Town v Kempston Rovers 5-0
97 Romford v Maldon Town 1-0
98 Burnham v Wisbech Town 0-1
99 Harwich & Parkeston v Harlow Town 2-3
100 Bury Town v Warboys Town 3-3
101 Concord Rangers v East Thurrock United 2-2
102 Uxbridge v Wroxham 0-1
103 Ruislip Manor v Leighton Town 2-0
104 Gorleston v Lowestoft Town 1-1
105 Wivenhoe Town v Bedford Town 0-1
106 Banbury United v Milton Keynes City 2-0
107 Burnham Ramblers v Hoddesdon Town 1-2
108 Great Yarmouth Town v Tilbury 5-3
109 Braintree Town v Leyton Pennant 1-1
110 Hemel Hempstead Town v Harpenden Town 4-0
111 Soham Town Rangers v Buckingham Town 7-0
112 Aveley v Stansted 1-0
113 Histon v Hullbridge Sports 1-0
114 Wootton Blue Cross v Cheshunt 0-2
115 Waltham Abbey v Yeading 1-1
116 Ware v Newmarket Town 3-0
117 Stowmarket Town v Welwyn Garden City 3-0
118 Baldock Town v Potton United 6-0
119 Bowers United v Hanwell Town 4-0
120 Ford United v Edgware Town 5-1
121 Woodbridge Town v Chelmsford City 1-5
122 Halstead Town v Royston Town 1-3
123 Beaconsfield SYCOB v Eynesbury Rovers 3-0
124 Hertford Town v Barkingside wo/s
125 Northwood v Clapton 8-0
126 Marlow v Barton Rovers 2-2
127 Kingsbury Town v Tring Town 2-1
128 East Cowes Victoria v Sittingbourne 0-1
129 Folkestone Invicta v Croydon Athletic 4-2
130 Bracknell Town v Camberley Town 2-2
131 Cobham v Farnham Town 1-1
132 Ashford Town (Middlesex) v Langney Sports 1-2
133 Saltdean United v Beckenham Town 1-0
134 Eastbourne Town v Three Bridges 0-0
135 Ash United v Chatham Town 1-2
136 Newport (IOW) v North Leigh 2-0
137 Erith & Belvedere v Wick 0-2
138 Abingdon Town v Peacehaven & Telscombe 6-0
139 Thamesmead Town v Reading Town 2-2
140 Chipstead v Tonbridge Angels 0-5
141 Hillingdon Borough v St Leonards 0-0
142 Leatherhead v Cowes Sports 0-1
143 Merstham v Corinthian Casuals 1-5
144 Hailsham Town v Littlehampton Town 5-4e
145 Molesey v Ringmer 3-1
146 Bedfont v Tunbridge Wells 4-0

1999/2000

147	Raynes Park Vale v Fisher Athletic (London)	1-2
148	Viking Greenford v Whitstable Town	3-2
149	Erith Town v Dorking (2)	0-0
150	Ashford Town v East Preston	2-1
151	Shoreham v Abingdon United	1-2
152	Windsor & Eton v Bromley	0-0
153	Oxford City v Gosport Borough	5-1
154	Herne Bay v Canterbury City	1-0
155	Epsom & Ewell v Worthing	0-3
156	Redhill v Slade Green	2-0
157	Deal Town v Greenwich Borough	5-0
158	Fleet Town v Lewes	1-3
159	Hastings Town v Southwick	6-1
160	Bognor Regis Town v Didcot Town	2-1
161	Sandhurst Town v AFC Newbury	0-0
162	Thatcham Town v Lordswood	4-2
163	Chichester City (1) v Selsey	2-2
164	Wokingham Town v Sheppey United	1-4
165	Cray Wanderers v Portfield	2-2
166	Whyteleafe v Lancing	4-3
167	Whitehawk v Maidenhead United	0-1
168	Egham Town v Croydon	2-0
169	Metropolitan Police v Chertsey Town	2-1
170	Horsham v Hassocks	0-1
171	Fareham Town v Carterton Town	0-1
172	Godalming & Guildford v Horsham YMCA	1-2
173	Hythe United v Burgess Hill Town	0-0
174	Arundel v Portsmouth Royal Navy	1-2
175	Banstead Athletic v Thame United	0-2
176	Ramsgate v Dartford	2-1
177	Christchurch v Bridport	1-1 N
178	Frome Town v Cinderford Town	0-4
179	Mangotsfield United v Hungerford Town	3-0
180	Falmouth Town v Bideford	1-2
181	Bridgwater Town v Lymington & New Milton	0-5
182	Minehead v Elmore	1-3
183	AFC Totton v Weston-Super-Mare	1-2
184	Bashley v Calne Town	6-1
185	Chippenham Town v Bournemouth (Ams)	1-0
186	Street v Eastleigh	0-1
187	Welton Rovers v Warminster Town	4-0
188	Yate Town v Taunton Town	0-3
189	Tiverton Town v Pershore Town	7-1
190	Bemerton Heath Harlequins v Brislington	0-1
191	Melksham Town v Evesham United	1-3
192	Downton v Barnstaple Town	3-6
193	St Blazey v Brockenhurst	3-1
194	Backwell United v Andover	5-1
195	Westbury United v Devizes Town	0-1
196	Paulton Rovers v Odd Down	1-2
197	Cirencester Town v BAT Sports	3-0
9r	Ashington v Marske United	1-2
16r	Guisborough Town v Farsley Celtic	0-1
21r	Jarrow Roofing Boldon CA v Bootle	1-1P
26r	Trafford v Goole AFC	6-3
40r	Sheffield v Bacup Borough	4-0
43r	Newcastle Blue Star v Easington Colliery	4-0
48r	Willenhall Town v Blackstones	4-2
51r	Stourport Swifts v Belper Town	1-2
57r	Staveley MW v Barwell	5-3
77r	Rushall Olympic v Shifnal Town	0-1e
78r	Yaxley v Arnold Town	1-2
81r	Flackwell Heath v Potters Bar Town	1-0
82r	Staines Town v Great Wakering Rovers	5-0
84r	Wembley v Stotfold	2-1
88r	Bishop's Stortford v Berkhamsted Town	3-3P
100r	Bury Town v Warboys Town	2-2q
101r	East Thurrock United v Concord Rangers	4-2
104r	Lowestoft Town v Gorleston	1-2e
109r	Leyton Pennant v Braintree Town	1-2
115r	Yeading v Waltham Abbey	1-3
126r	Barton Rovers v Marlow	1-3
130r	Camberley Town v Bracknell Town	1-3
131r	Farnham Town v Cobham	3-2
134r	Three Bridges v Eastbourne Town	1-1q
139r	Reading Town v Thamesmead Town	1-0
141r	St Leonards v Hillingdon Borough	4-1
149r	Dorking (2) v Erith Town	1-2
152r	Bromley v Windsor & Eton	3-0
161r	AFC Newbury v Sandhurst Town	5-2
163r	Selsey v Chichester City (1)	4-2
165r	Portfield v Cray Wanderers	2-3
173r	Burgess Hill Town v Hythe United	3-0
177r	Bridport v Christchurch	2-4

Qualifying Round One

1	Crook Town v Armthorpe Welfare	5-0
2	Rossendale United v Ossett Town	1-1
3	Consett v Accrington Stanley (2)	0-2
4	Liversedge v Woodley Sports	3-2
5	Bradford Park Avenue v Skelmersdale United	2-1
6	Thornaby-on-Tees v Tow Law Town	1-5
7	Brigg Town v Harrogate Railway Athletic	4-0
8	St Helens Town v Pickering Town	1-1
9	Trafford v Jarrow Roofing Boldon CA	3-3
10	Hebburn v Louth United	2-2
11	Ramsbottom United v Fleetwood Freeport	1-2
12	Farsley Celtic v Burscough	1-1
13	Mossley v Gretna	0-2
14	Eccleshill United v Marske United	4-0
15	Ashton United v Flixton	2-0
16	Radcliffe Borough v Warrington Town	8-1
17	Chorley v Seaham Red Star	3-0
18	Penrith v Morpeth Town	0-2
19	Sheffield v Brodsworth MW	1-0
20	North Ferriby United v Netherfield (Kendal)	3-2
21	Newcastle Blue Star v Billingham Synthonia	1-1
22	Dunston Federation Brewery v Salford City	1-0
23	Bedlington Terriers v Stocksbridge Park Steels	2-0
24	Stourbridge v Belper Town	0-2
25	Stafford Rangers v Matlock Town	2-2
26	Northampton Spencer v Boston Town	1-1
27	Hinckley United v Glapwell	1-0
28	Solihull Borough v Sutton Coldfield Town	1-0
29	Wellingborough Town v Newcastle Town	2-2
30	Oldbury United v Stratford Town	2-0
31	Willenhall Town v Oadby Town	1-1
32	Stamford v Brackley Town	3-1
33	Shifnal Town v Congleton Town	2-3
34	Bedworth United v Redditch United	1-3
35	Moor Green v Mickleover Sports	3-2
36	Staveley MW v Blakenall	1-3
37	Eastwood Town v Holbeach United	3-0
38	Halesowen Harriers v Arnold Town	1-4
39	Nantwich Town v Stewarts & Lloyds (2)	3-0
40	Spalding United v Raunds Town	1-0
41	Bishop's Stortford v Hemel Hempstead Town	4-2
42	Banbury United v Gorleston	6-3
43	Cheshunt v Waltham Abbey	1-0
44	Wingate & Finchley v Braintree Town	3-2
45	Great Yarmouth Town v Warboys Town	2-3
46	East Thurrock United v Baldock Town	1-2
47	Romford v Southend Manor	4-1
48	Fakenham Town v Staines Town	1-3
49	Saffron Walden Town v Hoddesdon Town	3-1
50	Wisbech Town v Wroxham	3-1
51	Ruislip Manor v Beaconsfield SYCOB	0-1
52	Barking v Grays Athletic	0-1
53	Sudbury Town v Flackwell Heath	1-0
54	Hertford Town v Royston Town	0-2
55	Arlesey Town v Bowers United	4-1
56	Wealdstone v Ford United	1-1
57	Marlow v Histon	7-2
58	Kingsbury Town v Chelmsford City	0-1
59	Tiptree United v Witney Town	1-2
60	Ware v Soham Town Rangers	1-1
61	Wembley v Harlow Town	3-1
62	Bedford Town v Aveley	0-0
63	Northwood v Stowmarket Town	2-0
64	St Neots Town v Witham Town	0-4
65	Ashford Town v Fisher Athletic (London)	0-2
66	Farnham Town v Selsey	3-0
67	Hailsham Town v Sittingbourne	1-3
68	Bedfont v Reading Town	5-1
69	Worthing v Saltdean United	2-1
70	Maidenhead United v Viking Greenford	5-0
71	Horsham YMCA v Cray Wanderers	3-0
72	Folkestone Invicta v Ramsgate	1-3
73	St Leonards v Bognor Regis Town	0-1
74	Eastbourne Town v Langney Sports	0-4
75	Lewes v Erith Town	3-3
76	Tonbridge Angels v Abingdon Town	3-0
77	Molesey v Hastings Town	0-3
78	Thame United v Wick	3-1
79	Abingdon United v Oxford City	0-6
80	Deal Town v Metropolitan Police	2-0
81	Thatcham Town v Cowes Sports	4-6
82	Carterton Town v Herne Bay	1-4
83	Corinthian Casuals v Sheppey United	4-0
84	Hassocks v Bromley	1-1
85	Redhill v Burgess Hill Town	1-1
86	AFC Newbury v Portsmouth Royal Navy	3-1
87	Chatham Town v Newport (IOW)	2-3
88	Egham Town v Whyteleafe	1-3
89	Bracknell Town v Tooting & Mitcham United	2-4
90	Elmore v Welton Rovers	0-3
91	Lymington & New Milton v Bideford	3-0
92	Devizes Town v Weston-Super-Mare	0-2
93	Mangotsfield United v Odd Down	1-1
94	Backwell United v Bashley	5-0
95	Cinderford Town v Barnstaple Town	0-1
96	Tiverton Town v Evesham United	4-3
97	Christchurch v Brislington	1-0
98	Cirencester Town v Taunton Town	2-2
99	Torrington v Wimborne Town	0-2
100	Chippenham Town v St Blazey	2-1
101	Tuffley Rovers v Eastleigh	2-1
2r	Ossett Town v Rossendale United	2-0
8r	Pickering Town v St Helens Town	3-2e
9r	Jarrow Roofing Boldon CA v Trafford	1-3
10r	Louth United v Hebburn	4-2
12r	Burscough v Farsley Celtic	0-3
21r	Billingham Synthonia v Newcastle Blue Star	3-2
25r	Matlock Town v Stafford Rangers	0-4
26r	Boston Town v Northampton Spencer	4-6
29r	Newcastle Town v Wellingborough Town	1-2
31r	Oadby Town v Willenhall Town	3-1
56r	Ford United v Wealdstone	2-3
60r	Soham Town Rangers v Ware	2-1
62r	Aveley v Bedford Town	1-2e
75r	Erith Town v Lewes	3-4
84r	Bromley v Hassocks	2-1
85r	Burgess Hill Town v Redhill	3-0
93r	Odd Down v Mangotsfield United	1-2
98r	Taunton Town v Cirencester Town	4-0

Qualifying Round Two

1	Guiseley v Pickering Town	6-0
2	Gateshead (2) v Winsford United	3-0
3	Ossett Town v Spennymoor United	2-1
4	Morpeth Town v Tow Law Town	2-1
5	Worksop Town v Bishop Auckland	2-3
6	Lancaster City v Fleetwood Freeport	wo/s
7	Gainsborough Trinity v Eccleshill United	2-0
8	Leigh RMI v Blyth Spartans	5-3
9	Hyde United v Crook Town	1-1
10	Barrow v Marine	2-2
11	Ashton United v Brigg Town	0-2
12	Accrington Stanley (2) v Whitby Town	0-2
13	Trafford v Bamber Bridge	2-2
14	Billingham Synthonia v North Ferriby United	1-2
15	Liversedge v Dunston Federation Brewery	1-2
16	Stalybridge Celtic v Colwyn Bay	1-0
17	Emley v Louth United	2-0
18	Sheffield v Farsley Celtic	0-0
19	Runcorn v Gretna	2-0
20	Bradford Park Avenue v Droylsden	2-2
21	Radcliffe Borough v Chorley	0-1
22	Frickley Athletic v Bedlington Terriers	0-1
23	Nantwich Town v Hucknall Town	1-0
24	Solihull Borough v Ilkeston Town (2)	3-4
25	Moor Green v Atherstone United	2-1
26	Redditch United v Burton Albion	0-1
27	Tamworth v Spalding United	6-2
28	Boston United v Oldbury United	3-1
29	Oadby Town v Halesowen Town	2-1
30	Leek Town v Blakenall	0-2
31	Belper Town v Arnold Town	4-2
32	Grantham Town v Northampton Spencer	6-0
33	Hinckley United v Wellingborough Town	2-0
34	Stamford v Congleton Town	1-1
35	Stafford Rangers v Eastwood Town	1-3
36	Wisbech Town v Billericay Town	1-3
37	Bishop's Stortford v Wingate & Finchley	1-1
38	Warboys Town v Witney Town	0-2
39	Sudbury Town v Dagenham & Redbridge	1-2
40	Canvey Island v Boreham Wood	3-1
41	Heybridge Swifts v Romford	1-2
42	Purfleet v Banbury United	0-0
43	Northwood v Rothwell Town	3-3
44	Cambridge City v Arlesey Town	3-1
45	Beaconsfield SYCOB v King's Lynn	0-3
46	Saffron Walden Town v Hitchin Town	1-4
47	Aylesbury United v Chelmsford City	1-3
48	Bedford Town v St Albans City	0-2
49	Chesham United v Baldock Town	1-3
50	Royston Town v Wembley	1-3
51	Soham Town Rangers v Enfield	1-3
52	Staines Town v Wealdstone	0-3
53	Marlow v Harrow Borough	1-4
54	Hendon v Grays Athletic	2-0
55	Cheshunt v Witham Town	0-0
56	Aldershot Town v Lewes	6-1
57	Thame United v Whyteleafe	0-1
58	Hampton & Richmond Boro. v Bognor Regis Town	1-1
59	Ramsgate v Margate	0-3
60	Burgess Hill Town v Bedfont	2-2
61	Walton & Hersham v Maidenhead United	0-2
62	Tooting & Mitcham United v Oxford City	0-2
63	Farnham Town v Herne Bay	2-2
64	Hastings Town v AFC Newbury	3-1
65	Carshalton Athletic v Sittingbourne	2-2
66	Tonbridge Angels v Farnborough Town	0-2
67	Horsham YMCA v Corinthian Casuals	4-0
68	Newport (IOW) v Dulwich Hamlet	1-1
69	Slough Town v Cowes Sports	3-1
70	Havant & Waterlooville v Langney Sports	2-2
71	Bromley v Crawley Town	4-1
72	Gravesend & Northfleet v Fisher Athletic (London)	1-1
73	Deal Town v Worthing	2-2
74	Christchurch v Worcester City	2-3
75	Clevedon Town v Tiverton Town	2-1
76	Taunton Town v Dorchester Town	3-0
77	Newport County (2) v Wimborne Town	1-1
78	Barnstaple Town v Backwell United	2-3
79	Weymouth v Gloucester City	0-0
80	Bath City v Weston-Super-Mare	4-0
81	Lymington & New Milton v Tuffley Rovers	1-1
82	Welton Rovers v Salisbury City	1-3
83	Chippenham Town v Mangotsfield United	2-0
84	Basingstoke Town v Merthyr Tydfil	0-0
9r	Crook Town v Hyde United	2-1
10r	Marine v Barrow	3-2
13r	Bamber Bridge v Trafford	2-1
18r	Farsley Celtic v Sheffield	2-0
20r	Droylsden v Bradford Park Avenue	2-1e
34r	Congleton Town v Stamford	2-0
37r	Wingate & Finchley v Bishop's Stortford	3-2
42r	Banbury United v Purfleet	0-1
43r	Rothwell Town v Northwood	2-0
55r	Witham Town v Cheshunt	0-2
58r	Bognor Regis Town v Hampton & Richmond Boro.	0-0P
60r	Bedfont v Burgess Hill Town	0-2
63r	Herne Bay v Farnham Town	1-1Pv
65r	Sittingbourne v Carshalton Athletic	0-1
68r	Dulwich Hamlet v Newport (IOW)	4-1
70r	Langney Sports v Havant & Waterlooville	2-1
72r	Fisher Athletic (London) v Gravesend & Northfleet	2-1
73r	Worthing v Deal Town	3-0
77r	Wimborne Town v Newport County (2)	0-3

1999/2000 to 2000/01

79r Gloucester City v Weymouth	2-1
81r Tuffley Rovers v Lymington & New Milton	0-5
84r Merthyr Tydfil v Basingstoke Town	2-1
63r2 Farnham Town v Herne Bay	1-2

Qualifying Round Three

1 Dunston Federation Brewery v Runcorn	0-2
2 Bamber Bridge v Morpeth Town	3-0
3 Stalybridge Celtic v Farsley Celtic	4-2
4 Bishop Auckland v Bedlington Terriers	1-1
5 Lancaster City v Whitby Town	2-2
6 Marine v Chorley	2-0
7 North Ferriby United v Guiseley	1-3
8 Droylsden v Gainsborough Trinity	2-2
9 Leigh RMI v Crook Town	1-1
10 Gateshead (2) v Brigg Town	4-0
11 Ossett Town v Emley	0-0
12 Enfield v Billericay Town	2-0
13 Wembley v Canvey Island	0-3
14 Chelmsford City v Moor Green	1-0
15 Belper Town v Tamworth	1-2
16 Wingate & Finchley v Ilkeston Town (2)	0-5
17 Hitchin Town v Grantham Town	2-1
18 Eastwood Town v Oadby Town	3-0
19 Romford v Congleton Town	6-0
20 Cambridge City v King's Lynn	1-0
21 Baldock Town v Cheshunt	5-1
22 Wealdstone v Rothwell Town	1-1
23 Dagenham & Redbridge v Burton Albion	0-2
24 St Albans City v Nantwich Town	4-2
25 Hendon v Blakenall	2-1
26 Boston United v Purfleet	4-0
27 Witney Town v Hinckley United	2-1
28 Chippenham Town v Worthing	1-1
29 Dulwich Hamlet v Hastings Town	2-1
30 Bath City v Farnborough Town	3-1
31 Maidenhead United v Salisbury City	0-1
32 Gloucester City v Merthyr Tydfil	2-3
33 Whyteleafe v Langney Sports	1-0
34 Backwell United v Oxford City	2-4
35 Bognor Regis Town v Bromley	1-0
36 Fisher Athletic (London) v Aldershot Town	1-2
37 Herne Bay v Horsham YMCA	0-3
38 Worcester City v Harrow Borough	3-2
39 Slough Town v Carshalton Athletic	1-0
40 Newport County (2) v Burgess Hill Town	1-2
41 Lymington & New Milton v Clevedon Town	3-1
42 Taunton Town v Margate	0-3
4r Bedlington Terriers v Bishop Auckland	0-1
5r Whitby Town v Lancaster City	2-2q
8r Gainsborough Trinity v Droylsden	1-2
9r Crook Town v Leigh RMI	2-1
11r Emley v Ossett Town	4-1
22r Rothwell Town v Wealdstone	2-0
28r Worthing v Chippenham Town	3-1

Qualifying Round Four

1 Nuneaton Borough v Guiseley	2-3
2 Droylsden v Eastwood Town	0-2
3 Telford United v Gateshead (2)	0-0
4 Scarborough v Tamworth	0-1
5 Doncaster Rovers v Crook Town	7-0
6 Southport v Emley	1-1
7 Northwich Victoria v Hednesford Town	2-2
8 Morecambe v Bishop Auckland	1-0
9 Marine v Runcorn	1-1
10 Altrincham v Stalybridge Celtic	0-0
11 Lancaster City v Bamber Bridge	0-0
12 Worthing v Dover Athletic	1-1
13 Oxford City v Salisbury City	2-1
14 Hendon v Margate	1-0
15 Bognor Regis Town v Whyteleafe	0-1
16 Welling United v Kidderminster Harriers	2-0
17 Merthyr Tydfil v Hitchin Town	2-0
18 Dulwich Hamlet v Hayes	0-0
19 Kingstonian v Boston United	0-0
20 Rushden & Diamonds v Sutton United	4-1
21 Ilkeston Town (2) v Romford	3-0
22 Worcester City v Forest Green Rovers	2-5
23 Yeovil Town v Witney Town	2-1
24 Woking v Burton Albion	1-1
25 Enfield v Baldock Town	1-1 N
26 Lymington & New Milton v Aldershot Town	1-3
27 Rothwell Town v Kettering Town	1-1
28 Canvey Island v St Albans City	3-3
29 Stevenage Borough v Bath City	1-1
30 Horsham YMCA v Chelmsford City	2-3
31 Hereford United v Burgess Hill Town	4-1
32 Slough Town v Cambridge City	1-1
3r Gateshead (2) v Telford United	2-1
6r Emley v Southport	0-2
7r Hednesford Town v Northwich Victoria	1-0
9r Runcorn v Marine	3-2q
10r Stalybridge Celtic v Altrincham	2-1 v
11r Bamber Bridge v Lancaster City	4-3e
12r Dover Athletic v Worthing	0-1e
18r Hayes v Dulwich Hamlet	3-0
19r Boston United v Kingstonian	0-3
24r Burton Albion v Woking	3-1
25r Baldock Town v Enfield	2-2qN
27r Kettering Town v Rothwell Town	2-1
28r St Albans City v Canvey Island	2-1
29r Bath City v Stevenage Borough	1-0

32r Cambridge City v Slough Town	3-2
10r2 Stalybridge Celtic v Altrincham	3-2e

Round One

Aldershot Town v Hednesford Town	1-1
Barnet v Burnley	0-1
Bath City v Hendon	0-2
Blackpool v Stoke City	2-0
Brentford v Plymouth Argyle	2-2
Bristol City v Mansfield Town	3-2
Bristol Rovers v Preston North End	0-1
Burton Albion v Rochdale	0-0
Cambridge City v Wigan Athletic	0-2
Cambridge United v Gateshead (2)	1-0
Cheltenham Town v Gillingham	1-1
Chesterfield v Enfield	1-2
Darlington v Southport	2-1
Doncaster Rovers v Halifax Town	0-2
Exeter City v Eastwood Town	2-1
Forest Green Rovers v Guiseley	6-0
Hartlepool United v Millwall	1-0
Hayes v Runcorn	2-1
Hereford United v York City	1-0
Ilkeston Town (2) v Carlisle United	2-1
Leyton Orient v Cardiff City	1-1
Lincoln City v Welling United	1-0
Luton Town v Kingstonian	4-2
Macclesfield Town v Hull City	0-0
Merthyr Tydfil v Stalybridge Celtic	2-2
Notts County v Bournemouth	1-1
Oldham Athletic v Chelmsford City	4-0
Oxford United v Morecambe	3-2
Peterborough United v Brighton & Hove Albion	1-1
Reading v Yeovil Town	4-2
Rotherham United v Worthing	3-0
Rushden & Diamonds v Scunthorpe United	2-0
Shrewsbury Town v Northampton Town	2-1
St Albans City v Bamber Bridge	0-2
Swansea City v Colchester United	2-1
Tamworth v Bury	2-2
Torquay United v Southend United	1-0
Whyteleafe v Chester City	0-0
Wrexham v Kettering Town	1-1
Wycombe Wanderers v Oxford City	1-1
r Bournemouth v Notts County	4-2
r Brighton & Hove Albion v Peterborough United	3-0
r Bury v Tamworth	2-1e
r Cardiff City v Leyton Orient	3-1
r Chester City v Whyteleafe	3-1
r Gillingham v Cheltenham Town	3-2
r Hednesford Town v Aldershot Town	1-2
r Hull City v Macclesfield Town	4-0
r Kettering Town v Wrexham	0-2
r Plymouth Argyle v Brentford	2-1e
r Rochdale v Burton Albion	3-0
r Stalybridge Celtic v Merthyr Tydfil	3-1
r Wycombe Wanderers v Oxford City	1-1ev
r2 Oxford City v Wycombe Wanderers	0-1 N

Round Two

Blackpool v Hendon	2-0
Bournemouth v Bristol City	0-2
Burnley v Rotherham United	2-0
Bury v Cardiff City	0-0
Cambridge United v Bamber Bridge	1-0
Exeter City v Aldershot Town	2-0
Forest Green Rovers v Torquay United	0-3
Gillingham v Darlington	3-1w
Hayes v Hull City	2-2
Hereford United v Hartlepool United	1-0
Ilkeston Town (2) v Rushden & Diamonds	1-1
Luton Town v Lincoln City	2-2
Oldham Athletic v Swansea City	1-0
Plymouth Argyle v Brighton & Hove Albion	0-0
Preston North End v Enfield	0-0
Reading v Halifax Town	1-1
Shrewsbury Town v Oxford United	2-2
Stalybridge Celtic v Chester City	1-2
Wrexham v Rochdale	2-1
Wycombe Wanderers v Wigan Athletic	2-2
r Brighton & Hove Albion v Plymouth Argyle	1-2
r Cardiff City v Bury	1-0e
r Enfield v Preston North End	0-3
r Halifax Town v Reading	0-1
r Hull City v Hayes	3-2e
r Lincoln City v Luton Town	0-1
r Oxford United v Shrewsbury Town	2-1e
r Rushden & Diamonds v Ilkeston Town (2)	3-0
r Wigan Athletic v Wycombe Wanderers	2-1

Round Three

Arsenal v Blackpool	3-1
Aston Villa v Darlington	2-1
Bolton Wanderers v Cardiff City	1-0
Cambridge United v Crystal Palace	2-0
Charlton Athletic v Swindon Town	2-1
Chester City v Manchester City	1-4
Crewe Alexandra v Bradford City	1-2
Derby County v Burnley	0-1
Exeter City v Everton	0-0
Fulham v Luton Town	2-2
Grimsby Town v Stockport County	3-2

Hereford United v Leicester City	0-0
Huddersfield Town v Liverpool	0-2
Hull City v Chelsea	1-6
Ipswich Town v Southampton	0-1
Leeds United v Port Vale	2-0
Norwich City v Coventry City	1-3
Nottingham Forest v Oxford United	1-1
Preston North End v Oldham Athletic	2-1
Queen's Park Rangers v Torquay United	1-1
Reading v Plymouth Argyle	1-1
Sheffield United v Rushden & Diamonds	1-1
Sheffield Wednesday v Bristol City	1-0
Sunderland v Portsmouth	1-1
Tottenham Hotspur v Newcastle United	1-1
Tranmere Rovers v West Ham United	1-0
Walsall v Gillingham	1-1
Watford v Birmingham City	0-1
West Bromwich Albion v Blackburn Rovers	2-2
Wigan Athletic v Wolverhampton Wan.	0-1
Wimbledon v Barnsley	1-0
Wrexham v Middlesbrough	2-1
r Blackburn Rovers v West Bromwich Albion	2-0e
r Everton v Exeter City	1-0
r Gillingham v Walsall	2-1e
r Leicester City v Hereford United	2-1e
r Luton Town v Fulham	0-3
r Newcastle United v Tottenham Hotspur	6-1
r Oxford United v Nottingham Forest	1-3
r Plymouth Argyle v Reading	1-0
r Rushden & Diamonds v Sheffield United	1-1q
r Torquay United v Queen's Park Rangers	2-3

Round Four

Arsenal v Leicester City	0-0
Aston Villa v Southampton	1-0
Charlton Athletic v Queen's Park Rangers	1-0
Chelsea v Nottingham Forest	2-0
Coventry City v Burnley	3-0
Everton v Birmingham City	2-0
Fulham v Wimbledon	3-0
Gillingham v Bradford City	3-1
Grimsby Town v Bolton Wanderers	0-2
Liverpool v Blackburn Rovers	0-1
Manchester City v Leeds United	2-5
Newcastle United v Sheffield United	4-1
Plymouth Argyle v Preston North End	0-3
Sheffield Wednesday v Wolverhampton Wan.	1-1
Tranmere Rovers v Sunderland	1-0
Wrexham v Cambridge United	1-2
r Leicester City v Arsenal	0-0P
r Wolverhampton Wan. v Sheffield Wednesday	0-0q

Round Five

Aston Villa v Leeds United	3-2
Blackburn Rovers v Newcastle United	1-2
Cambridge United v Bolton Wanderers	1-3
Chelsea v Leicester City	2-1
Coventry City v Charlton Athletic	2-3
Everton v Preston North End	2-0
Fulham v Tranmere Rovers	1-2
Gillingham v Sheffield Wednesday	3-1

Round Six

Bolton Wanderers v Charlton Athletic	1-0
Chelsea v Gillingham	5-0
Everton v Aston Villa	1-2
Tranmere Rovers v Newcastle United	2-3

Semi Finals

Aston Villa v Bolton Wanderers	0-0PN
Chelsea v Newcastle United	2-1 N

Final

Chelsea v Aston Villa	1-0 N

2000/01

Extra Preliminary Round

1 Brigg Town v Willington	3-0
2 Eccleshill United v Sheffield	2-3
3 South Shields (3) v Garforth Town	2-1 N
4 Tow Law Town v St Helens Town	2-0
5 Squires Gate v West Auckland Town	1-2
6 Guisborough Town v Chadderton	1-1
7 Armthorpe Welfare v Penrith	0-1
8 Pelsall Villa v Kidsgrove Athletic	1-1
9 Holbeach United v Halesowen Harriers	1-0
10 Royston Town v Newmarket Town	0-5
11 Haringey Borough v Concord Rangers	4-1
12 Raunds Town v Soham Town Rangers	2-3
13 Buckingham Town v Halstead Town	4-1
14 Lowestoft Town v Fakenham Town	2-3
15 Yate Town v Brislington	0-3
16 Melksham Town v Falmouth Town	1-0
17 Wimborne Town v Bridport	2-0
6r Chadderton v Guisborough Town	4-1
8r Kidsgrove Athletic v Pelsall Villa	1-3e

206

2000/01

Preliminary Round

1	Louth United v North Ferriby United	1-5
2	Witton Albion v Oldham Town	4-3
3	Trafford v Flixton	1-0
4	Marske United v South Shields (3)	3-1
5	Consett v Hallam	2-1
6	Yorkshire Amateur v Parkgate	5-0
7	Workington v Farsley Celtic	0-1
8	Bradford Park Avenue v Brandon United	1-0
9	Kennek Ryhope CA v Salford City	0-5
10	Whitley Bay v Ashington	2-1
11	Gretna v Ramsbottom United	0-0
12	Glasshoughton Welfare v West Auckland Town	0-2
13	Billingham Synthonia v Brigg Town	1-1
14	Goole AFC v Jarrow Roofing Boldon CA	3-0
15	Castleton Gabriels v Harrogate Railway Athletic	2-3
16	Tow Law Town v Newcastle Blue Star	2-2
17	Chadderton v Hebburn	2-3
18	Prescot Cables v Bedlington Terriers	0-2
19	Maine Road v Easington Colliery	2-2
20	Bacup Borough v Harrogate Town	0-4
21	Shotton Comrades v Atherton LR	1-2
22	Clitheroe v Shildon	4-1
23	Mossley v Hatfield Main	4-1
24	Winsford United v Selby Town	1-1
25	Durham City v Thackley	4-0
26	Skelmersdale United v Guiseley	1-1
27	Brodsworth MW v Blackpool Mechanics	2-2
28	Horden CW v Crook Town	3-0
29	Darwen v Penrith	2-2
30	Dunston Federation Brewery v Curzon Ashton	2-0
31	Great Harwood Town v Northallerton Town	2-0
32	Radcliffe Borough v Rossington Main	3-1
33	Denaby United v Warrington Town	0-2
34	Ossett Town v Chorley	0-1
35	Atherton Collieries v Morpeth Town	2-0
36	Evenwood Town v Tadcaster Albion	1-2
37	Woodley Sports v Ashton United	0-3
38	Sheffield v Rossendale United	2-1 N
39	Seaham Red Star v Pontefract Collieries	3-1
40	Peterlee Newtown v Fleetwood Freeport	4-4
41	Thornaby-on-Tees v Esh Winning	4-0
42	Abbey Hey v Stocksbridge Park Steels	1-2
43	Liversedge v Chester-le-Street Town	1-1
44	Billingham Town v Ossett Albion	2-0
45	Cheadle Town v Bridlington Town (2)	0-1
46	Kendal Town v Pickering Town	3-1
47	Boston Town v Leek CSOB	2-3
48	Spalding United v Glossop North End	4-0
49	Bilston Town v Sandwell Borough	3-0
50	Staveley MW v Belper Town	1-2
51	Gedling Town v Boldmere St Michaels	5-1
52	Oadby Town v Willenhall Town	2-1
53	Redditch United v Arnold Town	3-2
54	Newcastle Town v Buxton	2-0
55	Stamford v Rushall Olympic	2-0
56	Holbeach United v Glapwell	2-1
57	Atherstone United v Pelsall Villa	2-1
58	Bourne Town v Shepshed Dynamo	1-2
59	Corby Town v Knypersley Victoria	1-0
60	Cradley Town v Paget Rangers	1-2
61	Gresley Rovers v Matlock Town	1-1
62	Racing Club Warwick v Stourport Swifts	1-2
63	West Midlands Police v Bedworth United	1-1
64	Eastwood Town v Rocester	3-1
65	Hinckley United v Nantwich Town	7-0
66	Stapenhill v Bridgnorth Town	1-0
67	Stratford Town v Stafford Town	1-1
68	Blakenall v Oldbury United	0-1
69	Borrowash Victoria v Grantham Town	0-3
70	Barwell v Lincoln United	0-0
71	Blackstones v Shifnal Town	4-1
72	Congleton Town v Wednesfield	0-0
73	Solihull Borough v Mickleover Sports	2-1
74	Stourbridge v V.S. Rugby	0-0
75	Chasetown v Alfreton Town	0-1
76	Sutton Coldfield Town v Bromsgrove Rovers	1-1
77	Saffron Walden Town v Histon	1-2 N
78	Tiptree United v Buckingham Town	6-2
79	Flackwell Heath v Bishop's Stortford	0-2
80	Wroxham v Ford United	0-3
81	Felixstowe & Walton United v Waltham Abbey	2-3
82	Edgware Town v Stowmarket Town	2-2
83	Chelmsford City v Sawbridgeworth	3-1
84	Northampton Spencer v Southall	0-0e
85	Yeading v Basildon United	wo/s
86	Boreham Wood v Great Wakering Rovers	3-0
87	Bugbrooke St Michaels v Newmarket Town	0-3
88	Potters Bar Town v Leighton Town	2-1
89	Cogenhoe United v Desborough Town	4-1
90	Bowers United v Bedford United	1-1
91	Chalfont St Peter v Harwich & Parkeston	1-1
92	Ware v Yaxley	3-2
93	Hemel Hempstead Town v Romford	6-1
94	Wingate & Finchley v Wivenhoe Town	2-1
95	Woodbridge Town v Marlow	3-0
96	Baldock Town v Ruislip Manor	2-0
97	Uxbridge v Holmer Green	6-1
98	Barking v Haringey Borough	2-1
99	Wootton Blue Cross v London Colney	2-2
100	Ilford v Mildenhall Town	1-4
101	Wellingborough Town v Tring Town	0-0
102	Great Yarmouth Town v Kempston Rovers	4-1
103	Braintree Town v Banbury United	6-0
104	Witney Town v Beaconsfield SYCOB	0-3
105	Harlow Town v Diss Town	2-3
106	Burnham Ramblers v Burnham	1-0
107	Hanwell Town v Stotfold	1-2
108	Hullbridge Sports v Welwyn Garden City	0-1
109	Witham Town v Bedford Town	0-3
110	Southend Manor v AFC Sudbury	1-4
111	St Neots Town v Milton Keynes City	5-0
112	Tilbury v Fakenham Town	1-0
113	Rothwell Town v Northwood	0-2
114	Leyton Pennant v East Thurrock United	2-2
115	Eynesbury Rovers v Stewarts & Lloyds (2)	2-4
116	Arlesey Town v Aveley	7-1
117	Brackley Town v Wealdstone	0-3
118	Long Buckby v Clapton	0-1
119	Ford Sports (Daventry) v Hertford Town	1-1
120	Maldon Town v Bury Town	3-3
121	Berkhamsted Town v Hornchurch	4-1
122	Wembley v Gorleston	1-1 d
123	Potton United v Ely City	0-2
124	Ipswich Wanderers v Wisbech Town	3-1
125	Brentwood v Staines Town	2-4
126	Brook House v Kingsbury Town	6-0
127	Cheshunt v Clacton Town	2-2e
128	AFC Wallingford v Warboys Town	2-1
129	Hoddesdon Town v St Margaretsbury	1-2 N
130	Barton Rovers v Soham Town Rangers	0-2
131	Moneyfields v Epsom & Ewell	0-2
132	Sandhurst Town v Andover	0-4
133	Chertsey Town v Abingdon Town	3-1
134	Thatcham Town v Corinthian Casuals	2-0
135	Eastbourne Town v Selsey	1-1
136	Camberley Town v Saltdean United	0-1
137	Bashley v North Leigh	3-0
138	Littlehampton Town v Peacehaven & Telscombe	2-0
139	Beckenham Town v Aylesbury United	0-1
140	Walton & Hersham v Croydon Athletic	3-1
141	Chichester City United v Abingdon United	2-2
142	Lordswood v Horsham	1-3
143	Cowes Sports v Cray Wanderers	1-0
144	Burgess Hill Town v Brockenhurst	4-1
145	Banstead Athletic v Farnham Town	4-0
146	St Leonards v Three Bridges	1-1
147	Lewes v Dorking (2)	3-0
148	Tooting & Mitcham United v Worthing	3-0
149	Southwick v Langney Sports	0-5
150	Viking Greenford v Merstham	1-4
151	Sittingbourne v Godalming & Guildford	2-0
152	Whitchurch United v AFC Newbury	0-2
153	Thamesmead Town v Herne Bay	1-2
154	Greenwich Borough v Hythe United	1-0 D
155	Shoreham v Oxford City	1-10
156	Erith Town v Hassocks	2-2
157	Ashford Town v Walton Casuals	4-1
158	Wokingham Town v Bedfont	0-3
159	Dartford v Deal Town	3-1
160	Chipstead v Ashford Town (Middlesex)	0-1
161	Fareham Town v Ringmer	1-1
162	Gosport Borough v Slade Green	1-1
163	Windsor & Eton v Whitstable Town	1-0
164	Portsmouth Royal Navy v Ash United	1-4
165	Reading Town v Lancing	2-0
166	Newport (IOW) v Arundel	5-2
167	Metropolitan Police v Leatherhead	2-1
168	Hungerford Town v Bromley	0-2
169	East Preston v Redhill	1-0
170	Tunbridge Wells v VCD Athletic	1-2
171	Carterton Town v Thame United	1-1
172	Hillingdon Borough v Bracknell Town	1-3
173	Eastbourne United v Egham Town	1-4
174	Horsham YMCA v Cobham	2-0
175	Wick v Erith & Belvedere	1-0
176	Tonbridge Angels v Eastleigh	0-0
177	Lymington & New Milton v Didcot Town	2-1
178	Hailsham Town v Whyteleafe	1-2
179	Chatham Town v Molesey	3-1
180	Chessington & Hook United v Hastings Town	1-6
181	Bognor Regis Town v Cove	2-3
182	BAT Sports v Sheppey United	0-0
183	Fleet Town v Ramsgate	1-0
184	Whitehawk v AFC Totton	0-3
185	Paulton Rovers v Street	4-0
186	Westbury United v Bristol Manor Farm	1-3
187	Downton v Bournemouth (Ams)	4-0
188	Bemerton Heath Harlequins v Tiverton Town	0-4
189	Cinderford Town v Bridgwater Town	0-3
190	Devizes Town v Melksham Town	1-1
191	Chippenham Town v St Blazey	1-1
192	Tuffley Rovers v Taunton Town	4-1
193	Brislington v Calne Town	3-2
194	Weston-Super-Mare v Wimborne Town	2-1
195	Welton Rovers v Shortwood United	1-1
196	Elmore v Barnstaple Town	3-4
197	Frome Town v Bishop Sutton	2-0
198	Evesham United v Bideford	3-1
199	Odd Down v Gloucester City	0-2
200	Cirencester Town v Minehead	1-0
201	Mangotsfield United v Christchurch	4-2
202	Backwell United v Torrington	5-2
11r	Ramsbottom United v Gretna	3-2
13r	Brigg Town v Billingham Synthonia	1-0
16r	Newcastle Blue Star v Tow Law Town	2-1
19r	Easington Colliery v Maine Road	3-2
24r	Selby Town v Winsford United	2-0
26r	Guiseley v Skelmersdale United	4-0
27r	Blackpool Mechanics v Brodsworth MW	3-2
29r	Penrith v Darwen	0-1
40r	Fleetwood Freeport v Peterlee Newtown	3-0
43r	Chester-le-Street Town v Liversedge	0-3
61r	Matlock Town v Gresley Rovers	4-1
63r	Bedworth United v West Midlands Police	2-0
67r	Stafford Town v Stratford Town	0-0P
70r	Lincoln United v Barwell	2-4e
72r	Wednesfield v Congleton Town	0-1
74r	V.S. Rugby v Stourbridge	2-2q
76r	Bromsgrove Rovers v Sutton Coldfield Town	3-2
82r	Stowmarket Town v Edgware Town	1-0
84r	Southall v Northampton Spencer	0-2
90r	Bedford United v Bowers United	3-1
91r	Harwich & Parkeston v Chalfont St Peter	1-1P
99r	London Colney v Wootton Blue Cross	2-2P
101r	Tring Town v Wellingborough Town	2-1e
114r	East Thurrock United v Leyton Pennant	3-0
119r	Hertford Town v Ford Sports (Daventry)	2-3
120r	Bury Town v Maldon Town	0-2
127r	Clacton Town v Cheshunt	2-3e
135r	Selsey v Eastbourne Town	3-1
141r	Abingdon United v Chichester City United	2-1
146r	Three Bridges v St Leonards	2-3
156r	Hassocks v Erith Town	3-1
161r	Ringmer v Fareham Town	0-2
162r	Slade Green v Gosport Borough	1-2
171r	Thame United v Carterton Town	0-0q
176r	Eastleigh v Tonbridge Angels	0-1
182r	Sheppey United v BAT Sports	2-2P
190r	Melksham Town v Devizes Town	0-1
191r	St Blazey v Chippenham Town	0-3
195r	Shortwood United v Welton Rovers	1-0

Qualifying Round One

1	Warrington Town v Clitheroe	0-2
2	Tadcaster Albion v Horden CW	0-1
3	Stocksbridge Park Steels v Darwen	1-0
4	Harrogate Railway Athletic v Bedlington Terriers	1-5
5	West Auckland Town v Selby Town	3-1
6	Guiseley v Farsley Celtic	0-1
7	Thornaby-on-Tees v Marske United	0-1
8	Seaham Red Star v Great Harwood Town	7-0
9	Easington Colliery v Yorkshire Amateur	2-1
10	Blackpool Mechanics v Radcliffe Borough	0-1
11	Goole AFC v Ramsbottom United	2-1
12	Durham City v Newcastle Blue Star	3-1
13	Chorley v Trafford	3-2
14	North Ferriby United v Ashton United	2-2
15	Witton Albion v Atherton Collieries	1-0
16	Mossley v Hebburn	2-0
17	Harrogate Town v Billingham Town	0-2
18	Dunston Federation Brewery v Fleetwood Freeport	1-2
19	Atherton LR v Sheffield	1-5
20	Whitley Bay v Consett	3-1
21	Brigg Town v Liversedge	5-1
22	Bradford Park Avenue v Salford City	0-1
23	Bridlington Town (2) v Kendal Town	3-1
24	Redditch United v Belper Town	2-3
25	Hinckley United v Gedling Town	3-0
26	Bromsgrove Rovers v Oldbury United	1-1
27	Bilston Town v Solihull Borough	1-5
28	Grantham Town v Bedworth United	3-1
29	Paget Rangers v Stafford Town	0-2
30	Atherstone United v Stourport Swifts	0-1
31	Stourbridge v Stamford	2-3
32	Leek CSOB v Holbeach United	1-1
33	Stapenhill v Barwell	1-1
34	Shepshed Dynamo v Oadby Town	4-2
35	Newcastle Town v Corby Town	2-0
36	Congleton Town v Eastwood Town	4-3
37	Blackstones v Matlock Town	2-3
38	Alfreton Town v Spalding United	3-2
39	Cogenhoe United v Maldon Town	2-3
40	Northampton Spencer v Mildenhall Town	0-2
41	Waltham Abbey v St Neots Town	4-2
42	Wealdstone v Ware	4-0
43	Stewarts & Lloyds (2) v Baldock Town	1-3
44	Ford United v Welwyn Garden City	3-0
45	Tilbury v Chelmsford City	1-3
46	Stotfold v London Colney	1-1
47	Uxbridge v Potters Bar Town	5-1
48	Braintree Town v Clapton	5-0
49	St Margaretsbury v Boreham Wood	1-0
50	Soham Town Rangers v Ford Sports (Daventry)	3-1
51	Ely City v Tring Town	2-2
52	Newmarket Town v Wingate & Finchley	3-3
53	Yeading v Beaconsfield SYCOB	2-3
54	Arlesey Town v Histon	1-2
55	Bedford Town v Staines Town	3-1
56	Woodbridge Town v Burnham Ramblers	3-1
57	AFC Sudbury v Brook House	5-1
58	Barking v Berkhamsted Town	2-3
59	Ipswich Wanderers v Bedford United	1-0
60	Hemel Hempstead Town v Cheshunt	3-0
61	Diss Town v Bishop's Stortford	0-5
62	East Thurrock United v Northwood	1-4
63	Tiptree United v Stowmarket Town	1-3
64	Harwich & Parkeston v AFC Wallingford	1-2
65	Wembley v Great Yarmouth Town	2-0
66	Cowes Sports v Horsham YMCA	1-1
67	Littlehampton Town v Hythe United	1-1
68	Selsey v Reading Town	4-0
69	Carterton Town v St Leonards	3-1

2000/01

70	East Preston v Merstham	3-3
71	Thatcham Town v Gosport Borough	1-1
72	Newport (IOW) v Bashley	1-1
73	Fareham Town v Herne Bay	0-0
74	Sittingbourne v Horsham	0-3
75	Ashford Town v Bracknell Town	1-2
76	Fleet Town v Walton & Hersham	3-1
77	AFC Totton v Egham Town	0-0
78	Lymington & New Milton v Oxford City	0-1
79	Abingdon United v Tooting & Mitcham United	4-1
80	Aylesbury United v Bedfont	4-3
81	VCD Athletic v Epsom & Ewell	4-4
82	Windsor & Eton v Chatham Town	1-0
83	Langney Sports v Ashford Town (Middlesex)	3-2
84	Ash United v Hastings Town	2-4
85	AFC Newbury v Wick	2-0
86	Whyteleafe v Burgess Hill Town	4-0
87	Lewes v Cove	2-2
88	Dartford v Chertsey Town	1-1
89	Bromley v Metropolitan Police	1-2
90	Andover v Saltdean United	2-3
91	Banstead Athletic v Sheppey United	3-1
92	Tonbridge Angels v Hassocks	3-0
93	Weston-Super-Mare v Shortwood United	0-0
94	Bridgwater Town v Downton	2-1
95	Tuffley Rovers v Chippenham Town	0-1
96	Backwell United v Devizes Town	1-2
97	Gloucester City v Evesham United	2-1
98	Barnstaple Town v Cirencester Town	1-5
99	Brislington v Paulton Rovers	2-3
100	Mangotsfield United v Frome Town	4-2
101	Tiverton Town v Bristol Manor Farm	1-0 v
14r	Ashton United v North Ferriby United	4-3e
26r	Oldbury United v Bromsgrove Rovers	2-0
32r	Holbeach United v Leek CSOB	3-1
33r	Barwell v Stapenhill	5-1
46r	London Colney v Stotfold	2-3
51r	Tring Town v Ely City	3-2e
52r	Wingate & Finchley v Newmarket Town	4-1
66r	Horsham YMCA v Cowes Sports	6-0
67r	Hythe United v Littlehampton Town	0-1e
70r	Merstham v East Preston	3-1
71r	Gosport Borough v Thatcham Town	1-1q
72r	Bashley v Newport (IOW)	0-2
73r	Herne Bay v Fareham Town	2-1
77r	Egham Town v AFC Totton	1-3
81r	Epsom & Ewell v VCD Athletic	2-0
87r	Cove v Lewes	1-2
88r	Chertsey Town v Dartford	0-2
93r	Shortwood United v Weston-Super-Mare	3-2
101r	Bristol Manor Farm v Tiverton Town	1-4

Qualifying Round Two

1	Emley v Salford City	3-1
2	Gateshead (2) v Bishop Auckland	2-1
3	Stalybridge Celtic v Blyth Spartans	2-0
4	Witton Albion v Fleetwood Freeport	1-1
5	Durham City v Accrington Stanley (2)	2-2
6	Bamber Bridge v Marske United	1-1
7	Spennymoor United v Bedlington Terriers	0-3
8	Marine v Colwyn Bay	4-3
9	Sheffield v Farsley Celtic	2-1
10	Barrow v Droylsden	3-0
11	Ashton United v Goole AFC	1-1
12	Altrincham v Mossley	0-3
13	Frickley Athletic v Stocksbridge Park Steels	1-0
14	Clitheroe v Hyde United	1-2
15	Horden CW v Gainsborough Trinity	1-3
16	Bridlington Town (2) v Billingham Town	1-1
17	Whitley Bay v Worksop Town	2-1
18	Burscough v Runcorn	2-1
19	Brigg Town v Lancaster City	2-2
20	Radcliffe Borough v West Auckland Town	4-1
21	Chorley v Whitby Town	0-2
22	Seaham Red Star v Easington Colliery	0-3
23	Alfreton Town v Hinckley United	1-1
24	Holbeach United v Belper Town	1-3
25	Oldbury United v Stourport Swifts	2-3
26	Stamford v Tamworth	1-1
27	Stafford Town v Moor Green	2-1
28	Shepshed Dynamo v Ilkeston Town (2)	0-3
29	Hucknall Town v Congleton Town	4-0
30	Barwell v Grantham Town	0-3
31	Matlock Town v King's Lynn	1-2
32	Solihull Borough v Stafford Rangers	1-1
33	Halesowen Town v Burton Albion	0-2
34	Newcastle Town v Leek Town	1-1
35	Histon v Bishop's Stortford	1-2
36	Hendon v St Margaretsbury	3-2
37	Ford United v Soham Town Rangers	3-1
38	Heybridge Swifts v AFC Sudbury	1-1
39	Chesham United v AFC Wallingford	3-2
40	Hitchin Town v Maidenhead United	1-1
41	Cambridge City v Stotfold	3-0
42	Chelmsford City v Grays Athletic	1-1
43	Purfleet v Ipswich Wanderers	3-1
44	Canvey Island v Braintree Town	1-1
45	Hemel Hempstead Town v Northwood	3-4
46	Mildenhall Town v Beaconsfield SYCOB	3-0
47	Harrow Borough v Tring Town	3-0
48	Stowmarket Town v Wealdstone	1-2
49	Woodbridge Town v Wembley	0-0
50	Baldock Town v St Albans City	0-0
51	Uxbridge v Berkhamsted Town	3-2
52	Maldon Town v Waltham Abbey	3-1
53	Billericay Town v Wingate & Finchley	5-1
54	Bedford Town v Enfield	0-0
55	Farnborough Town v Oxford City	3-3
56	Fisher Athletic (London) v Newport (IOW)	4-2
57	Dartford v Abingdon United	3-2
58	Windsor & Eton v Hampton & Richmond Boro.	0-3
59	Carshalton Athletic v Croydon	1-1
60	Margate v Banstead Athletic	0-1
61	Herne Bay v Aylesbury United	0-5
62	Carterton Town v Havant & Waterlooville	1-4
63	Saltdean United v AFC Totton	4-2
64	Tonbridge Angels v Slough Town	2-0
65	Crawley Town v Aldershot Town	1-2
66	Gravesend & Northfleet v AFC Newbury	4-0
67	Lewes v Langney Sports	2-0
68	Fleet Town v Thatcham Town	1-2
69	Whyteleafe v Horsham YMCA	2-1
70	Metropolitan Police v Welling United	1-4
71	Horsham v Epsom & Ewell	5-1
72	Folkestone Invicta v Hastings Town	1-1
73	Bracknell Town v Merstham	3-1
74	Littlehampton Town v Sutton United	0-5
75	Selsey v Dulwich Hamlet	1-2
76	Basingstoke Town v Bath City	1-1
77	Gloucester City v Chippenham Town	1-1
78	Mangotsfield United v Paulton Rovers	4-2
79	Worcester City v Cirencester Town	2-1
80	Newport County (2) v Merthyr Tydfil	0-4
81	Clevedon Town v Salisbury City	2-4
82	Tiverton Town v Shortwood United	2-0
83	Weymouth v Dorchester Town	0-1
84	Devizes Town v Bridgwater Town	2-1
4r	Fleetwood Freeport v Witton Albion	1-2
5r	Accrington Stanley (2) v Durham City	4-2
6r	Marske United v Bamber Bridge	0-2
11r	Goole AFC v Ashton United	2-3
16r	Billingham Town v Bridlington Town (2)	3-1
19r	Lancaster City v Brigg Town	3-4e
23r	Hinckley United v Alfreton Town	2-1e
26r	Tamworth v Stamford	1-1P
32r	Stafford Rangers v Solihull Borough	0-0P
34r	Leek Town v Newcastle Town	3-2e
38r	AFC Sudbury v Heybridge Swifts	3-2
40r	Maidenhead United v Hitchin Town	1-1P
42r	Grays Athletic v Chelmsford City	2-1
44r	Braintree Town v Canvey Island	2-3
49r	Wembley v Woodbridge Town	1-4
50r	St Albans City v Baldock Town	1-2e
54r	Enfield v Bedford Town	1-1P
55r	Oxford City v Farnborough Town	1-2
59r	Croydon v Carshalton Athletic	2-2P
72r	Hastings Town v Folkestone Invicta	2-0
76r	Bath City v Basingstoke Town	2-0e
77r	Chippenham Town v Gloucester City	3-5

Qualifying Round Three

1	Sheffield v Ashton United	3-0
2	Marine v Radcliffe Borough	0-2
3	Mossley v Frickley Athletic	1-1
4	Stalybridge Celtic v Billingham Town	1-1
5	Hyde United v Brigg Town	2-1
6	Witton Albion v Burscough	0-0
7	Bamber Bridge v Gateshead (2)	1-1
8	Emley v Barrow	1-2
9	Bedlington Terriers v Accrington Stanley (2)	5-2
10	Easington Colliery v Whitby Town	1-0
11	Gainsborough Trinity v Whitley Bay	0-0
12	AFC Sudbury v Leek Town	1-1
13	Harrow Borough v Stafford Town	0-0
14	Mildenhall Town v Grays Athletic	0-2
15	Purfleet v Grantham Town	2-2
16	Bishop's Stortford v Billericay Town	1-2
17	Enfield v Stourport Swifts	3-1
18	Stafford Rangers v Chesham United	0-2
19	Wealdstone v Belper Town	2-3
20	Hendon v Ford United	2-1
21	Canvey Island v King's Lynn	2-1
22	Tamworth v Burton Albion	1-1
23	Ilkeston Town (2) v Baldock Town	3-0
24	Northwood v Uxbridge	5-1
25	Cambridge City v Maldon Town	3-2
26	Hucknall Town v Maidenhead United	3-2
27	Woodbridge Town v Hinckley United	0-2
28	Bracknell Town v Banstead Athletic	1-0
29	Welling United v Tonbridge Angels	1-0
30	Hastings Town v Horsham	2-3
31	Saltdean United v Devizes Town	1-2
32	Bath City v Sutton United	3-0
33	Tiverton Town v Gloucester City	1-3
34	Dartford v Havant & Waterlooville	0-4
35	Fisher Athletic (London) v Aldershot Town	1-2
36	Merthyr Tydfil v Hampton & Richmond Boro.	0-3
37	Farnborough Town v Aylesbury United	0-2
38	Worcester City v Thatcham Town	3-1
39	Gravesend & Northfleet v Croydon	4-1
40	Dulwich Hamlet v Lewes	1-1
41	Dorchester Town v Salisbury City	4-3
42	Whyteleafe v Mangotsfield United	1-3
3r	Frickley Athletic v Mossley	3-0e
4r	Billingham Town v Stalybridge Celtic	3-0
6r	Burscough v Witton Albion	6-1
7r	Gateshead (2) v Bamber Bridge	3-1
11r	Whitley Bay v Gainsborough Trinity	2-0
12r	Leek Town v AFC Sudbury	1-2
13r	Stafford Town v Harrow Borough	1-3
15r	Grantham Town v Purfleet	1-0e
22r	Burton Albion v Tamworth	3-1
40r	Lewes v Dulwich Hamlet	0-0q

Qualifying Round Four

1	Gateshead (2) v Billingham Town	4-2
2	Easington Colliery v Chester City	0-2
3	Barrow v Whitley Bay	6-1
4	Burscough v Radcliffe Borough	1-1
5	Sheffield v Northwich Victoria	1-5 N
6	Bedlington Terriers v Morecambe	1-3
7	Scarborough v Leigh RMI	3-4
8	Doncaster Rovers v Southport	2-2
9	Frickley Athletic v Hyde United	1-0
10	Boston United v Burton Albion	1-1
11	Hinckley United v Telford United	1-1
12	Nuneaton Borough v Stevenage Borough	1-1
13	Hucknall Town v Ilkeston Town (2)	0-1
14	Harrow Borough v Enfield	2-1
15	Hendon v Dagenham & Redbridge	1-3
16	Rushden & Diamonds v Grantham Town	5-4
17	Cambridge City v Canvey Island	0-2
18	Belper Town v AFC Sudbury	2-3
19	Billericay Town v Hednesford Town	0-0
20	Northwood v Grays Athletic	1-1
21	Chesham United v Kettering Town	0-2
22	Forest Green Rovers v Bath City	3-1
23	Havant & Waterlooville v Gloucester City	1-1
24	Aylesbury United v Bracknell Town	0-1
25	Gravesend & Northfleet v Mangotsfield United	4-0
26	Dorchester Town v Welling United	1-1
27	Yeovil Town v Horsham	1-1
28	Hayes v Dulwich Hamlet	4-2
29	Aldershot Town v Dover Athletic	1-0
30	Kingstonian v Devizes Town	5-2
31	Hampton & Richmond Boro. v Worcester City	5-0
32	Woking v Hereford United	1-0
4r	Radcliffe Borough v Burscough	2-1
8r	Southport v Doncaster Rovers	1-0
10r	Burton Albion v Boston United	3-2
11r	Telford United v Hinckley United	4-1
12r	Stevenage Borough v Nuneaton Borough	1-2
19r	Hednesford Town v Billericay Town	2-1e
20r	Grays Athletic v Northwood	1-0
23r	Gloucester City v Havant & Waterlooville	2-3
26r	Welling United v Dorchester Town	2-4e
27r	Horsham v Yeovil Town	0-2

Round One

	Aldershot Town v Brighton & Hove Albion	2-6
	Barnet v Hampton & Richmond Boro.	2-1
	Barrow v Leyton Orient	0-2
	Blackpool v Telford United	3-1
	Bournemouth v Swansea City	2-0
	Brentford v Kingstonian	1-3
	Bury v Northwich Victoria	1-1
	Cambridge United v Rochdale	2-1
	Canvey Island v Port Vale	4-4
	Cardiff City v Bristol Rovers	5-1
	Carlisle United v Woking	5-1
	Cheltenham Town v Shrewsbury Town	4-1
	Chester City v Plymouth Argyle	1-1
	Chesterfield v Bristol City	0-1
	Dagenham & Redbridge v Hayes	3-1
	Darlington v AFC Sudbury	6-1
	Forest Green Rovers v Morecambe	0-3
	Gravesend & Northfleet v Notts County	1-2 N
	Halifax Town v Gateshead (2)	0-2
	Havant & Waterlooville v Southport	1-2
	Hednesford Town v Oldham Athletic	2-4
	Kettering Town v Hull City	0-0
	Kidderminster Harriers v Burton Albion	0-0
	Lincoln City v Bracknell Town	4-0
	Luton Town v Rushden & Diamonds	1-0
	Macclesfield Town v Oxford United	0-1
	Mansfield Town v Peterborough United	1-1
	Millwall v Leigh RMI	3-0
	Northampton Town v Frickley Athletic	4-0
	Radcliffe Borough v York City	1-4 N
	Reading v Grays Athletic	4-0
	Scunthorpe United v Hartlepool United	3-1
	Stoke City v Nuneaton Borough	0-0
	Swindon Town v Ilkeston Town (2)	4-1
	Torquay United v Southend United	1-1
	Walsall v Exeter City	4-0
	Wigan Athletic v Dorchester Town	3-1
	Wrexham v Rotherham United	0-1
	Wycombe Wanderers v Harrow Borough	3-0
	Yeovil Town v Colchester United	5-1
r	Burton Albion v Kidderminster Harriers	2-4
r	Hull City v Kettering Town	0-1
r	Northwich Victoria v Bury	1-0
r	Nuneaton Borough v Stoke City	1-0
r	Peterborough United v Mansfield Town	4-0
r	Plymouth Argyle v Chester City	1-2e
r	Port Vale v Canvey Island	1-2e
r	Southend United v Torquay United	2-1e

2000/01 to 2001/02

Round Two

	Blackpool v Yeovil Town	0-1
	Bournemouth v Nuneaton Borough	3-0
	Bristol City v Kettering Town	3-1
	Cardiff City v Cheltenham Town	3-1
	Chester City v Oxford United	3-2
	Darlington v Luton Town	0-0
	Kidderminster Harriers v Carlisle United	0-2
	Lincoln City v Dagenham & Redbridge	0-1
	Millwall v Wycombe Wanderers	0-0
	Morecambe v Cambridge United	2-1
	Northwich Victoria v Leyton Orient	3-3
	Peterborough United v Oldham Athletic	1-1
	Rotherham United v Northampton Town	1-0
	Scunthorpe United v Brighton & Hove Albion	2-1
	Southend United v Canvey Island	2-1
	Southport v Kingstonian	1-2
	Swindon Town v Gateshead (2)	5-0
	Walsall v Barnet	2-1
	Wigan Athletic v Notts County	1-1
	York City v Reading	2-2
r	Leyton Orient v Northwich Victoria	3-2e
r	Luton Town v Darlington	2-0
r	Notts County v Wigan Athletic	2-1e
r	Oldham Athletic v Peterborough United	0-1
r	Reading v York City	1-3
r	Wycombe Wanderers v Millwall	2-1

Round Three

	Blackburn Rovers v Chester City	2-0
	Bolton Wanderers v Yeovil Town	2-1
	Bournemouth v Gillingham	2-3
	Bradford City v Middlesbrough	0-1
	Burnley v Scunthorpe United	2-2
	Cardiff City v Crewe Alexandra	1-1
	Carlisle United v Arsenal	0-1
	Charlton Athletic v Dagenham & Redbridge	1-1
	Chelsea v Peterborough United	5-0
	Derby County v West Bromwich Albion	3-2
	Fulham v Manchester United	1-2
	Huddersfield Town v Bristol City	0-2
	Leeds United v Barnsley	1-0
	Leicester City v York City	3-0
	Leyton Orient v Tottenham Hotspur	0-1
	Liverpool v Rotherham United	3-0
	Luton Town v Queen's Park Rangers	3-3
	Manchester City v Birmingham City	3-2
	Morecambe v Ipswich Town	0-3
	Newcastle United v Aston Villa	1-1
	Nottingham Forest v Wolverhampton Wan.	0-1
	Portsmouth v Tranmere Rovers	1-2
	Preston North End v Stockport County	0-1
	Sheffield Wednesday v Norwich City	2-1
	Southampton v Sheffield United	1-0
	Southend United v Kingstonian	0-1
	Sunderland v Crystal Palace	0-0
	Swindon Town v Coventry City	0-2
	Walsall v West Ham United	2-3
	Watford v Everton	1-2
	Wimbledon v Notts County	2-2
	Wycombe Wanderers v Grimsby Town	1-1
r	Aston Villa v Newcastle United	1-0
r	Crewe Alexandra v Cardiff City	2-1
r	Crystal Palace v Sunderland	2-4e
r	Dagenham & Redbridge v Charlton Athletic	0-1e
r	Grimsby Town v Wycombe Wanderers	1-3
r	Notts County v Wimbledon	0-1e
r	Queen's Park Rangers v Luton Town	2-1e
r	Scunthorpe United v Burnley	1-1P

Round Four

	Aston Villa v Leicester City	1-2
	Blackburn Rovers v Derby County	0-0
	Bolton Wanderers v Scunthorpe United	5-1
	Bristol City v Kingstonian	1-1
	Charlton Athletic v Tottenham Hotspur	2-4
	Crewe Alexandra v Stockport County	0-1
	Everton v Tranmere Rovers	0-3
	Gillingham v Chelsea	2-4
	Leeds United v Liverpool	0-2
	Manchester City v Coventry City	1-0
	Manchester United v West Ham United	0-1
	Middlesbrough v Wimbledon	0-0
	Queen's Park Rangers v Arsenal	0-6
	Southampton v Sheffield Wednesday	3-1
	Sunderland v Ipswich Town	1-0
	Wycombe Wanderers v Wolverhampton Wan.	2-1
r	Derby County v Blackburn Rovers	2-5
r	Kingstonian v Bristol City	0-1
r	Wimbledon v Middlesbrough	3-1e

Round Five

	Arsenal v Chelsea	3-1
	Bolton Wanderers v Blackburn Rovers	1-1
	Leicester City v Bristol City	3-0
	Liverpool v Manchester City	4-2
	Southampton v Tranmere Rovers	0-0
	Sunderland v West Ham United	0-1
	Tottenham Hotspur v Stockport County	4-0
	Wycombe Wanderers v Wimbledon	2-2
r	Blackburn Rovers v Bolton Wanderers	3-0
r	Tranmere Rovers v Southampton	4-3
r	Wimbledon v Wycombe Wanderers	2-2q

Round Six

Arsenal v Blackburn Rovers	3-0
Leicester City v Wycombe Wanderers	1-2
Tranmere Rovers v Liverpool	2-4
West Ham United v Tottenham Hotspur	2-3

Semi Finals

Arsenal v Tottenham Hotspur	2-1 N
Liverpool v Wycombe Wanderers	2-1 N

Final

Liverpool v Arsenal	2-1 N

2001/02

Extra Preliminary Round

1	Newcastle Blue Star v Hebburn	5-0
2	Prescot Cables v Salford City	2-4
3	Brigg Town v Great Harwood Town	2-2
4	Brandon United v St Helens Town	3-2
5	Clitheroe v Rossington Main	1-3
6	Flixton v Maine Road	0-0
7	Marske United v Abbey Hey	8-1
8	Lymington & New Milton v Burgess Hill Town	0-6
9	Slade Green v Chipstead	5-1
10	Saltdean United v Walton Casuals	3-3
11	Ramsgate v AFC Newbury	2-1
12	Street v Frome Town	1-2
3r	Great Harwood Town v Brigg Town	0-1e
6r	Maine Road v Flixton	2-0
10r	Walton Casuals v Saltdean United	7-0

Preliminary Round

1	Warrington Town v Ashington	0-0
2	Spennymoor United v Mossley	4-2
3	Hatfield Main v Salford City	0-2
4	Eccleshill United v Chester-le-Street Town	3-1
5	Woodley Sports v Gretna	1-2
6	Yorkshire Amateur v Shildon	3-6
7	Ossett Town v Tadcaster Albion	5-1
8	Curzon Ashton v Louth United	3-4
9	Guisborough Town v Bacup Borough	1-0
10	Esh Winning v Ashton United	0-3
11	West Auckland Town v Harrogate Town	2-2
12	Horden CW v Evenwood Town	2-0
13	Northallerton Town v Chorley	0-3
14	Shotton Comrades v Pickering Town	1-5
15	Selby Town v South Shields (3)	3-2
16	Rossington Main v Stocksbridge Park Steels	1-5
17	Marske United v Maine Road	3-3
18	Chadderton v Maltby Main	0-2
19	Billingham Synthonia v Tow Law Town	4-2
20	Squires Gate v Oldham Town	2-0
21	Brigg Town v Morpeth Town	3-1
22	Kendal Town v Consett	4-0
23	Farsley Celtic v Trafford	1-0
24	Radcliffe Borough v Atherton LR	3-3
25	Skelmersdale United v Jarrow Roofing Boldon CA	2-0
26	Willington v Durham City	0-8
27	Sheffield v Dunston Federation Brewery	1-1
28	Fleetwood Freeport v Pontefract Collieries	4-0
29	Blackpool Mechanics v Ramsbottom United	0-2
30	Witton Albion v Atherton Collieries	4-0
31	Workington v Penrith	1-0
32	Liversedge v Darwen	2-2
33	Garforth Town v Rossendale United	0-4
34	Parkgate v Crook Town	3-3
35	Cheadle Town v North Ferriby United	4-1
36	Harrogate Railway Athletic v Bridlington Town (2)	2-0
37	Peterlee Newtown v Castleton Gabriels	4-0
38	Armthorpe Welfare v Hallam	0-1
39	Easington Colliery v Denaby United	4-3
40	Glasshoughton Welfare v Winsford United	0-2
41	Seaham Red Star v Brandon United	0-7
42	Thornaby v Billingham Town	0-3
43	Ossett Albion v Bedlington Terriers	0-3
44	Newcastle Blue Star v Whitley Bay	0-8
45	Brodsworth MW v Guiseley	1-4
46	Thackley v Goole AFC	1-0
47	Buxton v Atherstone United	1-3
48	Boston Town v Borrowash Victoria	2-2
49	Willenhall Town v Solihull Borough	1-6
50	Bourne Town v Eastwood Town	1-2
51	Belper Town v Paget Rangers	1-0
52	Pelsall Villa v Knypersley Victoria	1-2
53	Stafford Town v Cradley Town	5-0
54	Oadby Town v Leek Town	0-3
55	Blackstones v Bromsgrove Rovers	0-1
56	Mickleover Sports v Stapenhill	1-0
57	Matlock Town v Holbeach United	3-1
58	Bloxwich United v Gresley Rovers	0-2
59	Halesowen Harriers v Redditch United	0-4
60	Leek CSOB v Nantwich Town	2-3 d
61	Stamford v Congleton Town	3-2
62	Arnold Town v Kidsgrove Athletic	4-1
63	Corby Town v Alfreton Town	1-2
64	Bilston Town v Gedling Town	4-2
65	Halesowen Town v Chasetown	2-0
66	Grantham Town v Glapwell	3-2
67	Rocester v Boldmere St Michaels	2-1
68	Oldbury United v Bedworth United	0-4
69	Newcastle Town v Shepshed Dynamo	3-1
70	Glossop North End v Stourbridge	0-1
71	Shifnal Town v Rushall Olympic	0-4
72	Barwell v Racing Club Warwick	2-0
73	Stourport Swifts v Rugby United	5-1
74	Staveley MW v Stratford Town	1-0
75	Bridgnorth Town v Sutton Coldfield Town	2-3
76	Lincoln United v Spalding United	3-0
77	Clacton Town v Tiptree United	2-1
78	Hullbridge Sports v Concord Rangers	0-1
79	Rothwell Town v Hornchurch	2-2
80	Burnham v Flackwell Heath	4-0
81	Northwood v Bishop's Stortford	3-3
82	Witham Town v Saffron Walden Town	6-0
83	AFC Wallingford v Mildenhall Town	1-2
84	Stotfold v Harlow Town	0-2
85	AFC Sudbury v Witney Town	wo/s
86	Potters Bar Town v Staines Town	0-5
87	Romford v Southend Manor	1-2
88	Wivenhoe Town v Harwich & Parkeston	0-2
89	Leyton v Felixstowe & Walton United	2-1
90	Wroxham v Aveley	2-1
91	Ford United v Royston Town	3-2 N
92	Maldon Town v Buckingham Town	0-0
93	Leighton Town v Dunstable Town	1-4
94	Aylesbury United v Brentwood	10-1
95	Long Buckby v Berkhamsted Town	0-9
96	London Colney v Soham Town Rangers	1-2
97	Wisbech Town v Bowers United	3-2
98	Woodbridge Town v Diss Town	1-2
99	Hertford Town v Haringey Borough	3-1
100	Kingsbury Town v Wootton Blue Cross	0-3
101	St Neots Town v Northampton Spencer	5-0
102	Wingate & Finchley v Barking & East Ham United	0-0
103	Fakenham Town v Marlow	4-3
104	Yeading v Ilford	3-1
105	Somersett Ambury V&E v Clapton	5-0
106	Beaconsfield SYCOB v Brackley Town	2-3
107	Hemel Hempstead Town v Holmer Green	4-0
108	Burnham Ramblers v Leyton Pennant	0-2
109	Bedford United v Newmarket Town	0-1
110	Southall v Uxbridge	1-11
111	St Margaretsbury v Gorleston	3-1
112	Tilbury v Wealdstone	1-1
113	Barton Rovers v Cheshunt	1-3
114	Bury Town v Great Wakering Rovers	1-2
115	Bugbrooke St Michaels v Histon	0-0
116	Tring Town v Cogenhoe United	0-2
117	Arlesey Town v Chalfont St Peter	4-0
118	Stowmarket Town v Ruislip Manor	4-3
119	Desborough Town v Great Yarmouth Town	1-2
120	Yaxley v Raunds Town	2-1
121	Banbury United v Ware	4-0 D
122	Hoddesdon Town v Wellingborough Town	6-1 N
123	Brook House v Hanwell Town	2-1
124	Ipswich Wanderers v Kempston Rovers	3-1
125	Lowestoft Town v Wembley	3-4
126	East Thurrock United v Sawbridgeworth	3-0
127	Milton Keynes City v Edgware Town	2-0
128	Ford Sports (Daventry) v Stewarts & Lloyds (2)	0-1
129	Brockenhurst v Three Bridges	3-1
130	Fareham Town v Chessington United	2-0
131	Horsham v Dulwich Hamlet	2-0
132	Banstead Athletic v Carshalton Athletic	0-2
133	Fisher Athletic (London) v Ashford Town (Middlesex)	3-0
134	Tooting & Mitcham United v Burgess Hill Town	0-0
135	Walton Casuals v Horsham YMCA	0-4
136	Thamesmead Town v Corinthian Casuals	1-1
137	Walton & Hersham v Slade Green	4-0
138	Lordswood v Hungerford Town	4-2
139	Hastings Town v Ringmer	3-0
140	Whyteleafe v Eastbourne United	2-0
141	Greenwich Borough v Cowes Sports	2-2
142	Whitehawk v Leatherhead	2-2
143	Chatham Town v Moneyfields	1-1
144	Hillingdon Borough v BAT Sports	2-3e
145	Egham Town v Cobham	3-0
146	Molesey v Arundel	2-1
147	Hassocks v Ashford Town	3-2
148	Hailsham Town v Peacehaven & Telscombe	0-1
149	Tonbridge Angels v AFC Totton	4-1
150	VCD Athletic v Chichester City United	1-3
151	Dartford v Eastbourne Town	3-1
152	Eastbourne Borough v Whitchurch United	3-1
153	Selsey v Littlehampton Town	0-2
154	Thame United v Worthing	3-2
155	Cove v Erith & Belvedere	1-3
156	Windsor & Eton v Fleet Town	3-1
157	Bracknell Town v Reading Town	5-0
158	Ramsgate v Andover	1-4
159	Croydon Athletic v Erith Town	6-2
160	Bedfont v Epsom & Ewell	5-0
161	Abingdon United v Lancing	2-1
162	Redhill v Oxford City	2-2
163	Sandhurst Town v Deal Town	2-3
164	Lewes v Slough Town	3-0

2001/02

165 Abingdon Town v Bognor Regis Town 1-3
166 Blackfield & Langley v Chertsey Town 2-5
167 Beckenham Town v Dorking (2) 2-2
168 Metropolitan Police v Carterton Town 2-1
169 Wick v Bashley 2-2
170 Thatcham Town v North Leigh 3-1
171 Chessington & Hook United v Didcot Town 2-0
172 Whitstable Town v Merstham 4-0
173 Wokingham Town v Sittingbourne 0-4
174 Eastleigh v Tunbridge Wells 2-2
175 Ash United v East Preston 3-0
176 Godalming & Guildford v Gosport Borough 0-3
177 Herne Bay v St Leonards 0-2
178 Bromley v Pagham 2-0
179 Hythe Town v Camberley Town 1-0
180 Cray Wanderers v Southwick 3-0
181 Torrington v Elmore 0-1
182 St Blazey v Bishop Sutton 4-2
183 Chard Town v Evesham United 0-4
184 Bournemouth (Ams) v Dorchester Town 3-1
185 Frome Town v Melksham Town 2-0
186 Downton v Falmouth Town 0-3
187 Backwell United v Christchurch 0-1
188 Cinderford Town v Bideford 1-1
189 Swindon Supermarine v Calne Town 1-1
190 Yate Town v Shortwood United 1-3
191 Mangotsfield United v Clevedon Town 1-0
192 Weston-Super-Mare v Taunton Town 0-0
193 Cirencester Town v Gloucester City 2-1
194 Clevedon United v Barnstaple Town 3-3
195 Highworth Town v Welton Rovers 2-0
196 Devizes Town v Odd Down 0-3
197 Minehead v Bemerton Heath Harlequins 4-1
198 Bridgwater Town v Fairford Town 0-0
199 Brislington v Paulton Rovers 3-1
200 Tuffley Rovers v Wimborne Town 2-5
201 Westbury United v Bristol Manor Farm 1-4
202 Shepton Mallet v Chippenham Town 1-1
1r Ashington v Warrington Town 3-0
11r Harrogate Town v West Auckland Town 4-1
17r Maine Road v Marske United 0-0P
24r Atherton LR v Radcliffe Borough 2-5
27r Dunston Federation Brewery v Sheffield 3-1
32r Darwen v Liversedge 0-1
34r Crook Town v Parkgate 1-0
48r Boston Town v Borrowash Victoria 1-0
79r Hornchurch v Rothwell Town 2-0 N
81r Bishop's Stortford v Northwood 0-1
92r Buckingham Town v Maldon Town 2-4
102r Barking & East Ham United v Wingate & Finchley 1-2
112r Wealdstone v Tilbury 2-1
115r Histon v Bugbrooke St Michaels 3-1
134r Burgess Hill Town v Tooting & Mitcham United 1-3e
136r Corinthian Casuals v Thamesmead Town 3-1e
141r Cowes Sports v Greenwich Borough 0-3
142r Leatherhead v Whitehawk 2-0
143r Moneyfields v Chatham Town 4-0
162r Oxford City v Redhill 4-0
167r Dorking (2) v Beckenham Town 1-0
169r Bashley v Wick 3-2
174r Tunbridge Wells v Eastleigh 2-3
188r Bideford v Cinderford Town 3-1
189r Calne Town v Swindon Supermarine 0-1
192r Taunton Town v Weston-Super-Mare 1-3
194r Barnstaple Town v Clevedon United 2-1
198r Fairford Town v Bridgwater Town 1-2
202r Chippenham Town v Shepton Mallet 3-0

Qualifying Round One

1 Spennymoor United v Cheadle Town 2-0
2 Horden CW v Witton Albion 1-2
3 Stocksbridge Park Steels v Easington Colliery 3-2
4 Rossendale United v Guisborough Town 3-2
5 Dunston Federation Brewery v Hallam 3-1
6 Brandon United v Kendal Town 1-3
7 Louth United v Durham City 0-3
8 Squires Gate v Ossett Town 3-2
9 Crook Town v Pickering Town 1-1
10 Farsley Celtic v Radcliffe Borough 3-1
11 Ramsbottom United v Ashington 6-1
12 Chorley v Maine Road 1-2
13 Whitley Bay v Workington 1-0
14 Ashton United v Skelmersdale United 4-2
15 Billingham Synthonia v Liversedge 0-2
16 Selby Town v Gretna 0-2
17 Guiseley v Eccleshill United 1-2
18 Bedlington Terriers v Peterlee Newtown 2-0
19 Shildon v Brigg Town 2-8
20 Salford City v Harrogate Town 2-3
21 Billingham Town v Fleetwood Freeport 7-0
22 Thackley v Maltby Main 2-1
23 Harrogate Railway Athletic v Winsford United 1-1
24 Alfreton Town v Newcastle Town 0-2
25 Belper Town v Leek Town 1-1
26 Matlock Town v Bilston Town 2-2
27 Mickleover Sports v Bromsgrove Rovers 1-2
28 Halesowen Town v Staveley MW 2-0
29 Arnold Town v Rushall Olympic 2-2
30 Gresley Rovers v Redditch United 1-1
31 Stamford v Grantham Town 0-3
32 Lincoln United v Stourport Swifts 3-3
33 Rocester v Barwell 1-2
34 Atherstone United v Bedworth United 1-1
35 Stourbridge v Knypersley Victoria 3-2
36 Solihull Borough v Sutton Coldfield Town 4-1
37 Stafford Town v Boston Town 2-1
38 Eastwood Town v Leek CSOB 5-0
39 Great Yarmouth Town v Hoddesdon Town 0-1
40 Great Wakering Rovers v Northwood 2-3
41 Uxbridge v Wroxham 0-3
42 Hertford Town v St Margaretsbury 0-4
43 Mildenhall Town v Wingate & Finchley 1-5
44 Fakenham Town v Leyton 1-1
45 Southend Manor v Diss Town 0-0
46 Hornchurch v Wisbech Town 1-2
47 Wootton Blue Cross v Harwich & Parkeston 2-0
48 Somersett Ambury V&E v Stewarts & Lloyds (2) 3-0
49 Ware v Wealdstone 1-5
50 Clacton Town v Leyton Pennant 3-0
51 St Neots Town v Ipswich Wanderers 0-2
52 Burnham v Soham Town Rangers 4-3
53 Aylesbury United v AFC Sudbury 4-3
54 Brackley Town v Ford United 1-1
55 Witham Town v Harlow Town 1-1
56 Concord Rangers v Stowmarket Town 1-2
57 Yeading v Staines Town 1-1
58 Dunstable Town v Cogenhoe United 1-1
59 Berkhamsted Town v Brook House 3-2
60 Wembley v Maldon Town 2-1
61 Arlesey Town v Cheshunt 2-0
62 Histon v Yaxley 3-0
63 Newmarket Town v Hemel Hempstead Town 3-1
64 East Thurrock United v Milton Keynes City 2-1
65 Chessington & Hook United v Eastleigh 2-5
66 Chertsey Town v Fisher Athletic (London) 0-6
67 Oxford City v Leatherhead 2-0
68 Dartford v Deal Town 1-1
69 Horsham YMCA v Thame United 0-0
70 Erith & Belvedere v Greenwich Borough 3-2
71 Hastings Town v Chichester City United 3-0
72 Horsham v Tonbridge Angels 2-0
73 Eastbourne Borough v Whyteleafe 3-2
74 Bracknell Town v Cray Wanderers 3-1
75 Sittingbourne v Lewes 1-1
76 Brockenhurst v Bedfont 3-3
77 Littlehampton Town v Gosport Borough 3-3
78 Carshalton Athletic v Peacehaven & Telscombe 1-0
79 Molesey v Walton & Hersham 0-0
80 Andover v Moneyfields 2-1
81 Tooting & Mitcham United v Corinthian Casuals 0-2
82 Fareham Town v Thatcham Town 2-1
83 Windsor & Eton v Lordswood 4-0
84 Egham Town v Metropolitan Police 0-0
85 Hassocks v Ash United 1-1
86 St Leonards v BAT Sports 3-0
87 Bashley v Bognor Regis Town 3-0
88 Dorking (2) v Whitstable Town 1-2
89 Abingdon United v Croydon Athletic 0-5
90 Bromley v Hythe Town 1-0
91 Christchurch v Bristol Manor Farm 2-0
92 Bideford v Wimborne Town 1-0
93 Chippenham Town v Frome Town 3-0
94 Elmore v Swindon Supermarine 1-2
95 Cirencester Town v Bournemouth (Ams) 5-0
96 Evesham United v Bridgwater Town 1-3
97 Weston-Super-Mare v Mangotsfield United 3-4
98 Falmouth Town v Odd Down 2-1
99 Highworth Town v Brislington 2-1
100 St Blazey v Shortwood United 5-0
101 Minehead v Barnstaple Town 0-2
9r Pickering Town v Crook Town 1-0
23r Winsford United v Harrogate Railway Athletic 1-4
25r Leek Town v Belper Town 1-2
26r Bilston Town v Matlock Town 4-2
29r Rushall Olympic v Arnold Town 0-3
30r Redditch United v Gresley Rovers 2-1
32r Stourport Swifts v Lincoln United 1-0
34r Bedworth United v Atherstone United 0-1
44r Leyton v Fakenham Town 3-0
45r Diss Town v Southend Manor 1-2
54r Ford United v Brackley Town 4-2eN
55r Harlow Town v Witham Town 7-2
57r Staines Town v Yeading 1-4
58r Cogenhoe United v Dunstable Town 2-2q
68r Deal Town v Dartford 0-3
69r Thame United v Horsham YMCA 2-0
75r Lewes v Sittingbourne 6-3
76r Bedfont v Brockenhurst 2-3e
77r Gosport Borough v Littlehampton Town 3-0
79r Walton & Hersham v Molesey 0-1
84r Metropolitan Police v Egham Town 1-1q
85r Ash United v Hassocks 0-3

Qualifying Round Two

1 Blyth Spartans v Eccleshill United 5-0
2 Barrow v Kendal Town 3-0
3 Maine Road v Marine 0-2
4 Durham City v Lancaster City 0-0
5 Spennymoor United v Billingham Town 6-1
6 Gretna v Brigg Town 3-3
7 Witton Albion v Whitley Bay 4-2
8 Gainsborough Trinity v Dunston Federation Brewery 5-1
9 Whitby Town v Ramsbottom United 5-2
10 Emley v Bamber Bridge 1-0
11 Vauxhall Motors v Hyde United 2-1
12 Worksop Town v Bishop Auckland 3-1
13 Gateshead (2) v Runcorn 2-4
14 Ashton United v Stocksbridge Park Steels 1-1
15 Harrogate Town v Burscough 1-1
16 Liversedge v Harrogate Railway Athletic 3-3
17 Thackley v Rossendale United 0-3
18 Squires Gate v Bedlington Terriers 2-2
19 Pickering Town v Accrington Stanley (2) 1-2
20 Bradford Park Avenue v Droylsden 3-2
21 Colwyn Bay v Farsley Celtic 2-2
22 Altrincham v Frickley Athletic 4-1
23 Redditch United v Kettering Town 0-0
24 Grantham Town v Ilkeston Town (2) 2-1
25 Moor Green v Halesowen Town 0-2
26 Newcastle Town v Stafford Rangers 0-1
27 Stourport Swifts v Solihull Borough 2-0
28 Bromsgrove Rovers v Tamworth 2-2
29 Bilston Town v Hinckley United 1-3
30 Stourbridge v Atherstone United 0-2
31 Arnold Town v Burton Albion 1-1
32 Eastwood Town v Hucknall Town 0-1
33 Belper Town v Barwell 2-1
34 Hednesford Town v Stafford Town 4-3
35 Boreham Wood v Harlow Town 2-2
36 Bedford Town v Leyton 3-0
37 Clacton Town v Heybridge Swifts 3-2
38 Southend Manor v Hendon 1-2
39 Hoddesdon Town v Berkhamsted Town 0-2
40 Ford United v Yeading 1-2 N
41 Northwood v Ipswich Wanderers 5-1
42 Grays Athletic v Wingate & Finchley 4-1
43 Purfleet v Wealdstone 3-2
44 Chesham United v East Thurrock United 2-0
45 King's Lynn v Harrow Borough 1-0
46 St Albans City v Billericay Town 0-1
47 Hampton & Richmond Boro. v Hitchin Town 1-1
48 Burnham v Wroxham 1-3
49 Dunstable Town v Cambridge City 2-3
50 Aylesbury United v Arlesey Town 2-0
51 Wembley v St Margaretsbury 1-4
52 Wisbech Town v Stowmarket Town 0-2
53 Wootton Blue Cross v Histon 0-1
54 Braintree Town v Chelmsford City 0-1
55 Canvey Island v Somersett Ambury V&E 9-1
56 Newmarket Town v Enfield 1-3
57 Lewes v Gosport Borough 0-0
58 Croydon Athletic v Dartford 2-2
59 Windsor & Eton v Oxford City 0-4
60 Andover v Bashley 1-1
61 Basingstoke Town v Corinthian Casuals 6-0
62 Bracknell Town v Horsham 1-3
63 Maidenhead United v Aldershot Town 1-1
64 Brockenhurst v Kingstonian 2-1
65 Fareham Town v Crawley Town 1-1
66 Hassocks v Bromley 2-0
67 Erith & Belvedere v Whitstable Town 3-0
68 Carshalton Athletic v Croydon 1-2
69 Thame United v Havant & Waterlooville 3-4
70 Welling United v Egham Town 1-0
71 Sutton United v Eastleigh 5-1
72 Molesey v Folkestone Invicta 1-3
73 Fisher Athletic (London) v St Leonards 3-1
74 Gravesend & Northfleet v Eastbourne Borough 1-0
75 Hastings Town v Newport (IOW) 0-2
76 Christchurch v Cirencester Town 1-3
77 Salisbury City v Tiverton Town 3-3
78 Bath City v Bideford 1-3
79 Merthyr Tydfil v Bridgwater Town 4-1
80 Barnstaple Town v Worcester City 0-5
81 Mangotsfield United v Falmouth Town 10-1
82 Highworth Town v Weymouth 0-3
83 St Blazey v Chippenham Town 3-1
84 Swindon Supermarine v Newport County (2) 1-1
4r Lancaster City v Durham City 2-1
6r Brigg Town v Gretna 2-1
14r Stocksbridge Park Steels v Ashton United 2-1e
15r Burscough v Harrogate Town 2-2q
16r Harrogate Railway Athletic v Liversedge 2-1
18r Bedlington Terriers v Squires Gate 4-0
21r Farsley Celtic v Colwyn Bay 3-1e
23r Kettering Town v Redditch United 2-0
28r Tamworth v Bromsgrove Rovers 1-0e
31r Burton Albion v Arnold Town 4-0
35r Harlow Town v Boreham Wood 0-0P
47r Hitchin Town v Hampton & Richmond Boro. 2-1e
57r Gosport Borough v Lewes 0-2
58r Dartford v Croydon Athletic 4-2
60r Bashley v Andover 0-2
63r Aldershot Town v Maidenhead United 1-0
65r Crawley Town v Fareham Town 4-0
77r Tiverton Town v Salisbury City 3-1
84r Newport County (2) v Swindon Supermarine 3-1

Qualifying Round Three

1 Farsley Celtic v Brigg Town 2-2
2 Vauxhall Motors v Harrogate Town 3-1
3 Lancaster City v Stocksbridge Park Steels 2-1
4 Emley v Accrington Stanley (2) 1-0
5 Worksop Town v Gainsborough Trinity 4-0
6 Altrincham v Witton Albion 4-1
7 Barrow v Rossendale United 1-1
8 Whitby Town v Spennymoor United 3-0
9 Runcorn v Bedlington Terriers 2-2
10 Marine v Bradford Park Avenue 4-2
11 Blyth Spartans v Harrogate Railway Athletic 1-2
12 Chesham United v Cambridge City 0-1
13 King's Lynn v Clacton Town 3-2

2001/02 to 2002/03

14 Halesowen Town v Canvey Island	0-2
15 St Margaretsbury v Stafford Rangers	0-3
16 Belper Town v Stowmarket Town	2-1
17 Bedford Town v Hednesford Town	2-0
18 Burton Albion v Berkhamsted Town	2-1
19 Enfield v Yeading	3-4
20 Hucknall Town v Stourport Swifts	2-0
21 Billericay Town v Grantham Town	2-1
22 Kettering Town v Northwood	3-0
23 Hendon v Hitchin Town	0-0
24 Tamworth v Wroxham	3-1
25 Aylesbury United v Atherstone United	3-1
26 Chelmsford City v Harlow Town	1-1
27 Purfleet v Grays Athletic	1-1
28 Histon v Hinckley United	3-3
29 Aldershot Town v Sutton United	3-0
30 Basingstoke Town v Bideford	3-1
31 Merthyr Tydfil v Mangotsfield United	3-3
32 Welling United v Newport (IOW)	3-0
33 Horsham v Folkestone Invicta	1-2
34 Fisher Athletic (London) v Erith & Belvedere	4-0
35 Andover v Newport County (2)	0-4
36 Dartford v Gravesend & Northfleet	0-2
37 Cirencester Town v Brockenhurst	2-0
38 Croydon v Havant & Waterlooville	0-1
39 Weymouth v Crawley Town	3-1
40 Lewes v Hassocks	3-1
41 St Blazey v Worcester City	2-3
42 Tiverton Town v Oxford City	3-1
1r Brigg Town v Farsley Celtic	4-3e
7r Rossendale United v Barrow	3-3q
9r Bedlington Terriers v Runcorn	4-1
23r Hitchin Town v Hendon	3-1e
26r Harlow Town v Chelmsford City	3-0
27r Grays Athletic v Purfleet	3-2
28r Hinckley United v Histon	2-0
31r Mangotsfield United v Merthyr Tydfil	4-1

Qualifying Round Four

1 Stalybridge Celtic v Bedlington Terriers	2-1
2 Harrogate Railway Athletic v Morecambe	2-3
3 Telford United v Northwich Victoria	1-1
4 Doncaster Rovers v Emley	3-2
5 Boston United v Brigg Town	0-1
6 Leigh RMI v Worksop Town	2-4
7 Barrow v Chester City	1-0
8 Altrincham v Nuneaton Borough	3-0
9 Marine v Southport	1-1
10 Whitby Town v Scarborough	3-1
11 Lancaster City v Vauxhall Motors	2-2
12 King's Lynn v Farnborough Town	0-4
13 Dover Athletic v Hereford United	0-1
14 Harlow Town v Bedford Town	1-2
15 Havant & Waterlooville v Barnet	1-1
16 Grays Athletic v Margate	2-0
17 Belper Town v Worcester City	2-2
18 Yeading v Aylesbury United	0-5
19 Hayes v Yeovil Town	3-1
20 Hucknall Town v Cambridge City	1-1
21 Woking v Newport County (2)	0-0
22 Folkestone Invicta v Welling United	1-1
23 Mangotsfield United v Lewes	0-0
24 Stevenage Borough v Kettering Town	0-0
25 Burton Albion v Gravesend & Northfleet	0-2
26 Fisher Athletic (London) v Forest Green Rovers	1-3
27 Aldershot Town v Hitchin Town	2-1
28 Billericay Town v Tiverton Town	1-2
29 Basingstoke Town v Dagenham & Redbridge	2-2
30 Weymouth v Hinckley United	1-2
31 Tamworth v Cirencester Town	2-1
32 Canvey Island v Stafford Rangers	5-1
3r Northwich Victoria v Telford United	2-1
9r Southport v Marine	2-1
11r Vauxhall Motors v Lancaster City	0-1
15r Barnet v Havant & Waterlooville	3-0
17r Worcester City v Belper Town	3-1
20r Cambridge City v Hucknall Town	3-1
21r Newport County (2) v Woking	3-1
22r Welling United v Folkestone Invicta	5-1
23r Lewes v Mangotsfield United	2-0
24r Kettering Town v Stevenage Borough	2-1
29r Dagenham & Redbridge v Basingstoke Town	3-0

Round One

Aldershot Town v Bristol Rovers	0-0
Altrincham v Lancaster City	1-1
Barnet v Carlisle United	0-0
Bedford Town v Peterborough United	0-0
Blackpool v Newport County (2)	2-2
Bournemouth v Worksop Town	3-0
Brentford v Morecambe	4-0
Brighton & Hove Albion v Shrewsbury Town	1-0
Bristol City v Leyton Orient	0-1
Cambridge United v Notts County	1-1
Cardiff City v Tiverton Town	3-1
Colchester United v York City	0-0
Dagenham & Redbridge v Southport	1-0
Doncaster Rovers v Scunthorpe United	2-3
Exeter City v Cambridge City	3-0
Grays Athletic v Hinckley United	1-2
Halifax Town v Farnborough Town	2-1

Hayes v Wycombe Wanderers	3-4
Hereford United v Wrexham	1-0
Huddersfield Town v Gravesend & Northfleet	2-1
Kettering Town v Cheltenham Town	1-6
Kidderminster Harriers v Darlington	0-1
Lincoln City v Bury	1-1
Macclesfield Town v Forest Green Rovers	2-2
Mansfield Town v Oxford United	1-0
Northwich Victoria v Hull City	2-5
Oldham Athletic v Barrow	1-1
Port Vale v Aylesbury United	3-0
Reading v Welling United	1-0
Southend United v Luton Town	3-2
Stalybridge Celtic v Chesterfield	0-3
Stoke City v Lewes	2-0
Swansea City v Queen's Park Rangers	4-0
Swindon Town v Hartlepool United	3-1
Tamworth v Rochdale	1-1
Torquay United v Northampton Town	1-2
Tranmere Rovers v Brigg Town	4-1
Whitby Town v Plymouth Argyle	1-1
Wigan Athletic v Canvey Island	0-1
Worcester City v Rushden & Diamonds	0-1
r Barrow v Oldham Athletic	0-1
r Bristol Rovers v Aldershot Town	1-0
r Bury v Lincoln City	1-1q
r Carlisle United v Barnet	1-0
r Forest Green Rovers v Macclesfield Town	1-1q
r Lancaster City v Altrincham	1-4e
r Newport County (2) v Blackpool	1-4e
r Notts County v Cambridge United	2-0
r Peterborough United v Bedford Town	2-1
r Plymouth Argyle v Whitby Town	3-2
r Rochdale v Tamworth	1-0
r York City v Colchester United	2-2P

Round Two

Altrincham v Darlington	1-2
Blackpool v Rochdale	2-0
Brighton & Hove Albion v Rushden & Diamonds	2-1
Canvey Island v Northampton Town	1-0
Cardiff City v Port Vale	3-0
Chesterfield v Southend United	1-1
Exeter City v Dagenham & Redbridge	0-0
Halifax Town v Stoke City	1-1
Hinckley United v Cheltenham Town	0-2
Hull City v Oldham Athletic	2-3
Leyton Orient v Lincoln City	2-1
Macclesfield Town v Swansea City	4-1
Mansfield Town v Huddersfield Town	4-0
Peterborough United v Bournemouth	1-0
Plymouth Argyle v Bristol Rovers	1-1
Scunthorpe United v Brentford	3-2
Swindon Town v Hereford United	3-2
Tranmere Rovers v Carlisle United	6-1
Wycombe Wanderers v Notts County	3-0
York City v Reading	2-0
r Bristol Rovers v Plymouth Argyle	3-2
r Dagenham & Redbridge v Exeter City	3-0
r Southend United v Chesterfield	2-0
r Stoke City v Halifax Town	3-0

Round Three

Aston Villa v Manchester United	2-3
Barnsley v Blackburn Rovers	1-1
Brighton & Hove Albion v Preston North End	0-2
Burnley v Canvey Island	4-1
Cardiff City v Leeds United	2-1
Charlton Athletic v Blackpool	2-1
Cheltenham Town v Oldham Athletic	2-1
Coventry City v Tottenham Hotspur	0-2
Crewe Alexandra v Sheffield Wednesday	2-1
Dagenham & Redbridge v Ipswich Town	1-4
Darlington v Peterborough United	2-2
Derby County v Bristol Rovers	1-3
Grimsby Town v York City	0-0
Leicester City v Mansfield Town	2-1
Liverpool v Birmingham City	3-0
Macclesfield Town v West Ham United	0-3
Manchester City v Swindon Town	2-0
Millwall v Scunthorpe United	2-1
Newcastle United v Crystal Palace	2-0
Norwich City v Chelsea	0-0
Portsmouth v Leyton Orient	1-4
Rotherham United v Southampton	2-1
Sheffield United v Nottingham Forest	1-0
Southend United v Tranmere Rovers	1-3
Stockport County v Bolton Wanderers	1-4
Stoke City v Everton	0-1
Sunderland v West Bromwich Albion	1-2
Walsall v Bradford City	2-0
Watford v Arsenal	2-4
Wimbledon v Middlesbrough	0-0
Wolverhampton Wan. v Gillingham	0-1
Wycombe Wanderers v Fulham	2-2
r Blackburn Rovers v Barnsley	3-1
r Chelsea v Norwich City	4-0
r Fulham v Wycombe Wanderers	1-0
r Middlesbrough v Wimbledon	2-0
r Peterborough United v Darlington	2-0
r York City v Grimsby Town	1-0

Round Four

Arsenal v Liverpool	1-0
Charlton Athletic v Walsall	1-2
Chelsea v West Ham United	1-1
Cheltenham Town v Burnley	2-1
Everton v Leyton Orient	4-1
Gillingham v Bristol Rovers	1-0
Ipswich Town v Manchester City	1-4
Middlesbrough v Manchester United	2-0
Millwall v Blackburn Rovers	0-1
Peterborough United v Newcastle United	2-4
Preston North End v Sheffield United	2-1
Rotherham United v Crewe Alexandra	2-4
Tottenham Hotspur v Bolton Wanderers	4-0
Tranmere Rovers v Cardiff City	3-1
West Bromwich Albion v Leicester City	1-0
York City v Fulham	0-2
r West Ham United v Chelsea	2-3

Round Five

Arsenal v Gillingham	5-2
Chelsea v Preston North End	3-1
Everton v Crewe Alexandra	0-0
Middlesbrough v Blackburn Rovers	1-1
Newcastle United v Manchester City	1-0
Tottenham Hotspur v Tranmere Rovers	4-0
Walsall v Fulham	1-2
West Bromwich Albion v Cheltenham Town	1-0
r Crewe Alexandra v Everton	1-2

Round Six

Middlesbrough v Everton	3-0
Newcastle United v Arsenal	1-1
Tottenham Hotspur v Chelsea	0-4
West Bromwich Albion v Fulham	0-1
r Arsenal v Newcastle United	3-0

Semi Finals

Arsenal v Middlesbrough	1-0 N
Chelsea v Fulham	1-0 N

Final

Arsenal v Chelsea	2-0 N

2002/03

Extra Preliminary Round

1 Flixton v Goole AFC	1-1
2 Holker Old Boys v Bridlington Town (2)	0-2
3 West Auckland Town v Winsford United	2-1
4 Penrith v Brandon United	3-2
5 Marske United v Salford City	1-4
6 Maltby Main v Billingham Synthonia	0-6
7 Consett v Pontefract Collieries	4-1
8 Chester-le-Street Town v Northallerton Town	3-1
9 Morpeth Town v Curzon Ashton	3-2
10 Nelson v Norton & Stockton Ancients	0-0e
11 Ramsbottom United v Thackley	1-0
12 Horden CW v Armthorpe Welfare	2-1
13 Bridgnorth Town v Gedling Town	4-2
14 Stratford Town v Stourbridge	4-1
15 Mickleover Sports v Shirebrook Town	3-1
16 Leek CSOB v Nantwich Town	0-3
17 Grosvenor Park v Stafford Town	2-0
18 Newmarket Town v Ely City	2-3 d
19 Dereham Town v AFC Wallingford	1-3
20 Saffron Walden Town v Hullbridge Sports	0-1
21 Bedford United & Valerio v Brook House	0-1
22 Potters Bar Town v Milton Keynes City	1-2
23 Sawbridgeworth v Harwich & Parkeston	2-0
24 Raunds Town v Ruislip Manor	1-0
25 Stotfold v Broxbourne Borough V&E	0-0
26 Tiptree United v Ipswich Wanderers	1-1
27 Ilford v Kempston Rovers	3-0
28 Walton Casuals v Whitehawk	0-4
29 Littlehampton Town v Godalming & Guildford	0-6
30 Greenwich Borough v Three Bridges	1-4
31 Deal Town v Chichester City United	2-2
32 Lymington & New Milton v East Preston	2-2
33 Moneyfields v Burgess Hill Town	1-0
34 Alton Town v Didcot Town	1-1
35 Horsham YMCA v Eastleigh	1-3
36 AFC Totton v Southwick	3-2
37 Ramsgate v Maidstone United (2)	1-1
38 Chessington United v Ringmer	0-1
39 Farnham Town v Reading Town	1-3
40 Paulton Rovers v Downton	5-1
41 Highworth Town v Fairford Town	2-2
42 Street v Keynsham Town	3-1
43 Portland United v Welton Rovers	6-2
44 Bishop Sutton v Melksham Town	2-1
45 Christchurch v Willand Rovers	3-0 N
1r Goole AFC v Flixton	0-0P
10r Norton & Stockton Ancients v Nelson	1-2
25r Broxbourne Borough V&E v Stotfold	1-5

211

2002/03

26r	Ipswich Wanderers v Tiptree United	3-3P
31r	Chichester City United v Deal Town	2-3
32r	East Preston v Lymington & New Milton	1-2
34r	Didcot Town v Alton Town	1-0
37r	Maidstone United (2) v Ramsgate	1-0
41r	Fairford Town v Highworth Town	1-4
	Preliminary Round	
1	Shildon v Salford City	2-4
2	Morpeth Town v Woodley Sports	1-0
3	Hatfield Main v Shotton Comrades	0-1
4	Selby Town v Newcastle Blue Star	0-0
5	Fleetwood Town v Workington	1-1
6	Skelmersdale United v Penrith	1-3
7	Brigg Town v Kendal Town	2-4
8	Whitley Bay v Harrogate Railway Athletic	2-2
9	Guisborough Town v Blackpool Mechanics	2-0
10	Farsley Celtic v Seaham Red Star	4-4
11	Glasshoughton Welfare v Jarrow Roofing Boldon CA	1-3
12	Goole AFC v Mossley	0-3
13	Nelson v Bishop Auckland	2-3
14	Ossett Town v Worsbrough Bridge MW	0-2
15	Great Harwood Town v Winterton Rangers	0-0
16	Horden CW v Trafford	2-1
17	Evenwood Town v Durham City	1-4
18	Prescot Cables v Witton Albion	3-6
19	Parkgate v St Helens Town	2-2
20	Squires Gate v Lincoln United	1-2
21	Tow Law Town v Tadcaster Albion	2-1
22	Abbey Hey v Bamber Bridge	0-0
23	Louth United v Cheadle Town	4-1
24	Ramsbottom United v Chadderton	3-0
25	Matlock Town v Pickering Town	2-2
26	Maine Road v Guiseley	1-2
27	Spennymoor United v Consett	4-0
28	Chester-le-Street Town v Hall Road Rangers	2-0
29	Atherton LR v Rossington Main	0-2
30	Ashington v Colne	7-0
31	Willington v Atherton Collieries	0-0
32	Chorley v Liversedge	5-0
33	Warrington Town v Esh Winning	2-2
34	Bacup Borough v Bridlington Town (2)	1-2 N
35	Bedlington Terriers v Brodsworth MW	3-0
36	Alnwick Town v Crook Town	1-2
37	Garforth Town v Yorkshire Amateur	3-1
38	Stocksbridge Park Steels v Oldham Town	17-1
39	Rossendale United v Ossett Albion	0-1
40	Thornaby v Dunston Federation Brewery	1-1
41	Clitheroe v Radcliffe Borough	1-3
42	Sheffield v West Auckland Town	0-4
43	South Shields (3) v Hallam	1-2
44	Easington Colliery v Hebburn	1-3
45	Washington v North Ferriby United	0-2
46	Peterlee Newtown v Billingham Synthonia	2-1
47	Billingham Town v Gretna	wo/s
48	Darwen v Eccleshill United	1-3
49	Stourport Swifts v Alfreton Town	1-4
50	Rocester v Congleton Town	3-0
51	Kidsgrove Athletic v Buxton	4-1
52	Rushall Olympic v Sutton Coldfield Town	1-4
53	Staveley MW v Boston Town	0-1
54	Halesowen Harriers v Shepshed Dynamo	1-3
55	Newcastle Town v Leek Town	0-1
56	Belper Town v Gresley Rovers	0-1
57	Mickleover Sports v Cradley Town	2-1
58	Redditch United v Grosvenor Park	2-1
59	Bourne Town v Eastwood Town	1-1
60	Bedworth United v Causeway United	1-1
61	Histon v Quorn	2-3
62	Oadby Town v Rugby United	2-2
63	Atherstone United v Studley	3-0
64	Stratford Town v Ludlow Town	3-1
65	Biddulph Victoria v Bridgnorth Town	2-0
66	Nantwich Town v Holbeach United	4-0
67	Chasetown v Spalding United	0-1
68	Corby Town v Stamford	0-6
69	Arnold Town v Racing Club Warwick	1-0
70	King's Lynn v Deeping Rangers	1-0
71	Willenhall Town v Glapwell	1-0
72	Pelsall Villa v Borrowash Victoria	1-1
73	Shifnal Town v Blackstones	1-4
74	Glossop North End v Boldmere St Michaels	1-0
75	Solihull Borough v Oldbury United	2-0
76	Barwell v Bromsgrove Rovers	1-1
77	Long Buckby v Marlow	0-2
78	Newmarket Town v Ilford	1-3
79	Barking & East Ham United v Soham Town Rangers	4-3
80	Hullbridge Sports v Edgware Town	2-5
81	Great Yarmouth Town v Holmer Green	2-1
82	Desborough Town v Romford	1-2
83	Southall Town v Wroxham	1-6
84	Northampton Spencer v Yaxley	1-1
85	Banbury United v Berkhamsted Town	1-1
86	Hoddesdon Town v AFC Sudbury	0-2 N
87	Cheshunt v Wembley	3-0
88	Maldon Town v Flackwell Heath	1-1
89	Leighton Town v Royston Town	2-2
90	Chalfont St Peter v Hemel Hempstead Town	0-3
91	Clacton Town v Sawbridgeworth	3-1
92	Wealdstone v Leyton	1-3
93	Cogenhoe United v Diss Town	0-2
94	Bowers United v Arlesey Town	1-4
95	Wivenhoe Town v Yeading	0-3
96	Stotfold v Hornchurch	1-1

97	St Neots Town v Stansted	6-0
98	Bury Town v Barton Rovers	1-2
99	Lowestoft Town v Uxbridge	0-2
100	Raunds Town v Burnham Ramblers	5-1
101	Wootton Blue Cross v Brackley Town	3-1
102	Stewarts & Lloyds (2) v Ford Sports (Daventry)	1-0
103	Harlow Town v Aveley	0-1
104	Stowmarket Town v Southall	1-6
105	Wisbech Town v Woodbridge Town	3-1
106	Brook House v Burnham	2-3
107	Hanwell Town v Great Wakering Rovers	0-3
108	Mildenhall Town v London Colney	0-0
109	Tilbury v Gorleston	4-3 N
110	Concord Rangers v Hertford Town	2-3
111	Ware v Milton Keynes City	5-1
112	Haringey Borough v Northwood	0-1
113	Ipswich Wanderers v Leyton Pennant	2-3
114	Letchworth v Staines Town	1-1
115	Clapton v Beaconsfield SYCOB	0-3
116	Witham Town v Wingate & Finchley	0-5
117	Dunstable Town v St Margaretsbury	0-2
118	East Thurrock United v Harefield United	1-2
119	Buckingham Town v Tring Town	3-0
120	Rothwell Town v Kingsbury Town	3-1
121	Brentwood v AFC Wallingford	2-2
122	Fakenham Town v Southend Manor	1-3
123	Wick v Abingdon United	1-4
124	Merstham v St Leonards	3-4
125	Three Bridges v Didcot Town	3-1
126	Erith Town v Ringmer	0-3
127	North Leigh v Cowes Sports	0-5
128	Bromley v Abingdon Town	3-2
129	Lymington & New Milton v Dulwich Hamlet	1-1
130	Redhill v Peacehaven & Telscombe	1-3
131	Gosport Borough v Wantage Town	2-1
132	Oxford City v Cray Wanderers	0-1
133	Deal Town v Hythe Town	4-2
134	Eastleigh v Erith & Belvedere	5-0
135	Fisher Athletic (London) v Wokingham Town	7-0
136	Whyteleafe v Reading Town	1-0
137	Whitstable Town v Chipstead	1-2
138	Croydon Athletic v Eastbourne Borough	0-0
139	AFC Totton v Thamesmead Town	2-0
140	Molesey v Hassocks	3-0
141	Bedfont v Whitehawk	3-1
142	Saltdean United v VCD Athletic	0-3
143	Beckenham Town v Croydon	1-2
144	Brockenhurst v Fleet Town	3-2
145	Newport (IOW) v Blackfield & Langley	1-1
146	Moneyfields v BAT Sports	0-2
147	Chertsey Town v Arundel	4-1
148	Tunbridge Wells v Ashford Town (Middlesex)	2-1
149	Fareham Town v Tooting & Mitcham United	1-1
150	Eastbourne Town v Windsor & Eton	1-1
151	Godalming & Guildford v Whitchurch United	3-0
152	Thame United v Slough Town	1-2
153	Pagham v Bracknell Town	3-2
154	Sandhurst Town v Herne Bay	2-6
155	Sittingbourne v Slade Green	2-2
156	Metropolitan Police v Lancing	4-0
157	Camberley Town v Cove	0-1
158	Horsham v Lordswood	2-2
159	Lewes v Thatcham Town	1-0
160	Chatham Town v Egham Town	0-0
161	Bognor Regis Town v Worthing	1-0
162	Banstead Athletic v Leatherhead	1-4
163	Westfield v Dorking (2)	1-2
164	Tonbridge Angels v Maidstone United (2)	2-3
165	Hillingdon Borough v Chessington & Hook United	2-2
166	Corinthian Casuals v Epsom & Ewell	1-1
167	Walton & Hersham v Andover	2-1
168	Ashford Town v Carshalton Athletic	1-3
169	AFC Newbury v Hailsham Town	2-1
170	Selsey v Ash United	3-0
171	Eastbourne United v Cobham	0-3
172	Dartford v Carterton Town	2-2
173	Chard Town v Swindon Supermarine	2-0
174	Frome Town v Shortwood United	0-1
175	Bishop Sutton v Cinderford Town	1-3
176	Torrington v Westbury United	2-1
177	Odd Down v Paulton Rovers	0-2
178	Clevedon Town v Bitton	2-2
179	Highworth Town v Cirencester Town	3-0
180	Hungerford Town v Shepton Mallet	2-0
181	Bridport v Taunton Town	2-3
182	Elmore v Backwell United	1-2
183	Bashley v Mangotsfield United	2-2
184	Salisbury City v Bideford	1-2
185	Barnstaple Town v Team Bath	0-3
186	Corsham Town v Portland United	3-1
187	Devizes Town v Ilfracombe Town	5-2
188	Bournemouth (Ams) v Bridgwater Town	3-0
189	Falmouth Town v Bristol Manor Farm	2-0
190	Merthyr Tydfil v Christchurch	5-0
191	Porthleven v Dorchester Town	0-5
192	Tuffley Rovers v St Blazey	0-1
193	Minehead v Gloucester City	0-2
194	Weston-Super-Mare v Calne Town	4-0
195	Yate Town v Hallen	4-2
196	Dawlish Town v Wimborne Town	0-3
197	Brislington v Evesham United	2-2
198	Street v Bemerton Heath Harlequins	1-3
4r	Newcastle Blue Star v Selby Town	2-4
5r	Workington v Fleetwood Town	1-0e
8r	Harrogate Railway Athletic v Whitley Bay	5-4

10r	Seaham Red Star v Farsley Celtic	1-6
15r	Winterton Rangers v Great Harwood Town	0-0q
19r	St Helens Town v Parkgate	3-1
22r	Bamber Bridge v Abbey Hey	2-2q
25r	Pickering Town v Matlock Town	0-1
31r	Atherton Collieries v Willington	5-1
33r	Esh Winning v Warrington Town	3-1e
40r	Dunston Federation Brewery v Thornaby	2-1
59r	Eastwood Town v Bourne Town	3-1
60r	Causeway United v Bedworth United	1-2e
62r	Rugby United v Oadby Town	2-3
72r	Borrowash Victoria v Pelsall Villa	1-4
76r	Bromsgrove Rovers v Barwell	4-3
84r	Yaxley v Northampton Spencer	5-1e
85r	Berkhamsted Town v Banbury United	1-4
88r	Flackwell Heath v Maldon Town	1-0
89r	Royston Town v Leighton Town	3-0
96r	Hornchurch v Stotfold	4-4q
108r	London Colney v Mildenhall Town	1-0
114r	Staines Town v Letchworth	1-0 N
121r	AFC Wallingford v Brentwood	4-1
129r	Dulwich Hamlet v Lymington & New Milton	1-3
138r	Eastbourne Borough v Croydon Athletic	4-1
145r	Blackfield & Langley v Newport (IOW)	0-3
149r	Tooting & Mitcham United v Fareham Town	1-0
150r	Windsor & Eton v Eastbourne Town	4-2
155r	Slade Green v Sittingbourne	3-1
158r	Lordswood v Horsham	1-2
160r	Egham Town v Chatham Town	0-1
165r	Chessington & Hook United v Hillingdon Borough	1-3
166r	Epsom & Ewell v Corinthian Casuals	1-2
172r	Carterton Town v Dartford	1-0
178r	Bitton v Clevedon Town	1-2
183r	Mangotsfield United v Bashley	0-1
197r	Evesham United v Brislington	3-2
	Qualifying Round One	
1	Eccleshill United v St Helens Town	3-2
2	Bedlington Terriers v Ossett Albion	1-0
3	Radcliffe Borough v Abbey Hey	4-1
4	Esh Winning v Harrogate Railway Athletic	1-2
5	Horden CW v Shotton Comrades	4-1
6	Dunston Federation Brewery v Selby Town	2-0
7	Kendal Town v North Ferriby United	2-1
8	Workington v Mossley	2-1
9	Hallam v Stocksbridge Park Steels	2-3
10	Bishop Auckland v Rossington Main	3-3
11	Jarrow Roofing Boldon CA v Billingham Town	2-4
12	Morpeth Town v Guisborough Town	0-1
13	West Auckland Town v Chorley	6-3
14	Chester-le-Street Town v Penrith	2-0
15	Great Harwood Town v Crook Town	1-1
16	Bridlington Town (2) v Garforth Town	1-0
17	Tow Law Town v Matlock Town	5-4
18	Witton Albion v Ramsbottom United	1-1
19	Farsley Celtic v Lincoln United	3-1
20	Durham City v Worsbrough Bridge MW	5-1
21	Guiseley v Hebburn	3-0
22	Peterlee Newtown v Louth United	4-0
23	Spennymoor United v Ashington	1-1
24	Atherton Collieries v Salford City	1-0
25	Alfreton Town v Kidsgrove Athletic	0-1
26	Nantwich Town v Rocester	2-0
27	Eastwood Town v Redditch United	1-2
28	Stamford v Oadby Town	3-1
29	Boston Town v Sutton Coldfield Town	1-1
30	King's Lynn v Quorn	4-1
31	Blackstones v Pelsall Villa	2-2
32	Bromsgrove Rovers v Gresley Rovers	5-0
33	Solihull Borough v Glossop North End	9-0
34	Willenhall Town v Atherstone United	0-2
35	Mickleover Sports v Shepshed Dynamo	0-1
36	Arnold Town v Biddulph Victoria	1-1
37	Leek Town v Spalding United	2-1
38	Stratford Town v Bedworth United	1-2
39	Stewarts & Lloyds (2) v Burnham	0-1
40	Rothwell Town v Southend Manor	3-2
41	Cheshunt v Edgware Town	4-0
42	Hertford Town v AFC Wallingford	1-4
43	Royston Town v London Colney	3-2
44	Hemel Hempstead Town v St Neots Town	7-1
45	Ilford v Clacton Town	2-3
46	Wootton Blue Cross v Wroxham	2-1
47	Raunds Town v AFC Sudbury	1-3
48	Barking & East Ham United v Banbury United	1-0
49	Leyton Pennant v Great Yarmouth Town	3-3
50	Staines Town v Uxbridge	1-2 N
51	Harefield United v Barton Rovers	2-1
52	Tilbury v Yeading	0-2 N
53	Beaconsfield SYCOB v Great Wakering Rovers	5-0
54	Northwood v Wisbech Town	1-2
55	Aveley v Stotfold	2-2
56	Diss Town v Romford	3-0
57	St Margaretsbury v Arlesey Town	1-2
58	Southall v Yaxley	2-3
59	Flackwell Heath v Buckingham Town	2-1
60	Leyton v Marlow	0-1
61	Wingate & Finchley v Ware	2-0
62	Bromley v BAT Sports	2-1
63	Herne Bay v Cowes Sports	3-2
64	Peacehaven & Telscombe v Carterton Town	1-2
65	Walton & Hersham v Cove	3-0
66	Horsham v Slade Green	3-0
67	Lewes v Brockenhurst	2-1

2002/03

68	Eastleigh v Croydon	2-0
69	Abingdon United v Leatherhead	2-3
70	Chatham Town v Godalming & Guildford	2-3
71	Molesey v Fisher Athletic (London)	3-0
72	Bognor Regis Town v Windsor & Eton	4-1
73	VCD Athletic v Bedfont	2-1
74	Tunbridge Wells v Selsey	2-2
75	Newport (IOW) v Maidstone United (2)	0-4
76	Metropolitan Police v Corinthian Casuals	1-0
77	Hillingdon Borough v Lymington & New Milton	2-3
78	Gosport Borough v Deal Town	2-1
79	Eastbourne Borough v AFC Newbury	6-2
80	St Leonards v Slough Town	1-2
81	Tooting & Mitcham United v Cobham	0-0
82	AFC Totton v Pagham	3-1
83	Carshalton Athletic v Dorking (2)	4-0
84	Cray Wanderers v Whyteleafe	1-0
85	Ringmer v Chertsey Town	1-2
86	Chipstead v Three Bridges	1-3
87	St Blazey v Bournemouth (Ams)	1-0
88	Team Bath v Backwell United	3-1
89	Torrington v Hungerford Town	0-1
90	Yate Town v Bideford	0-4
91	Bemerton Heath Harlequins v Shortwood United	2-1
92	Merthyr Tydfil v Chard Town	2-0
93	Weston-Super-Mare v Wimborne Town	3-1
94	Clevedon Town v Dorchester Town	2-0
95	Gloucester City v Bashley	3-0
96	Devizes Town v Taunton Town	0-1
97	Falmouth Town v Evesham United	1-2
98	Highworth Town v Cinderford Town	2-3
99	Paulton Rovers v Corsham Town	2-1
10r	Rossington Main v Bishop Auckland	1-1P
15r	Crook Town v Great Harwood Town	1-1q
18r	Ramsbottom United v Witton Albion	2-3
23r	Ashington v Spennymoor United	1-2
29r	Sutton Coldfield Town v Boston Town	2-0
31r	Pelsall Villa v Blackstones	3-2
36r	Biddulph Victoria v Arnold Town	1-2
49r	Great Yarmouth Town v Leyton Pennant	5-1
55r	Stotfold v Aveley	0-2
74r	Selsey v Tunbridge Wells	2-1
81r	Cobham v Tooting & Mitcham United	0-3

Qualifying Round Two

1	Chester-le-Street Town v Harrogate Railway Athletic	5-5
2	Colwyn Bay v West Auckland Town	4-0
3	Hyde United v Tow Law Town	7-3
4	Guisborough Town v Guiseley	3-3
5	Stocksbridge Park Steels v Ashton United	0-2
6	Stalybridge Celtic v Workington	2-2
7	Bedlington Terriers v Vauxhall Motors	1-2
8	Durham City v Peterlee Newtown	3-0
9	Gainsborough Trinity v Frickley Athletic	3-2
10	Whitby Town v Bradford Park Avenue	0-4
11	Harrogate Town v Great Harwood Town	2-0
12	Marine v Eccleshill United	2-2
13	Runcorn FC Halton v Wakefield & Emley	2-0
14	Bridlington Town (2) v Witton Albion	3-1
15	Droylsden v Farsley Celtic	4-3
16	Altrincham v Kendal Town	1-0
17	Accrington Stanley (2) v Billingham Town	2-0
18	Spennymoor United v Atherton Collieries	5-0
19	Horden CW v Worksop Town	0-4
20	Rossington Main v Radcliffe Borough	0-7
21	Lancaster City v Blyth Spartans	2-4
22	Dunston Federation Brewery v Burscough	2-0
23	Gateshead (2) v Barrow	3-4
24	Shepshed Dynamo v Stafford Rangers	0-2
25	Bedford Town v Pelsall Villa	6-1
26	King's Lynn v Cambridge City	1-0
27	Bromsgrove Rovers v Tamworth	1-2
28	Bedworth United v Moor Green	1-4
29	Ilkeston Town (2) v Atherstone United	7-0
30	Sutton Coldfield Town v Halesowen Town	0-2
31	Hednesford Town v Hucknall Town	0-0
32	Redditch United v Leek Town	1-1
33	Nantwich Town v Arnold Town	0-3
34	Solihull Borough v Grantham Town	0-2
35	Worcester City v Stamford	3-3
36	Hinckley United v Kidsgrove Athletic	3-0
37	Walton & Hersham v Chesham United	1-0
38	Harefield United v AFC Sudbury	4-4
39	Grays Athletic v Marlow	1-0
40	Molesey v Hitchin Town	3-1
41	Hendon v Tooting & Mitcham United	3-0
42	Leatherhead v Bromley	1-1
43	Godalming & Guildford v Hampton & Richmond Boro.	0-1
44	AFC Wallingford v Eastbourne Borough	0-1
45	Clacton Town v Kingstonian	2-3
46	Billericay Town v Yeading	3-1
47	Hayes v Bognor Regis Town	6-0
48	AFC Totton v Slough Town	2-2
49	Rothwell Town v Barking & East Ham United	1-0
50	Maidenhead United v Welling United	1-2
51	Lewes v Eastleigh	0-0
52	Horsham v Yaxley	2-0
53	Havant & Waterlooville v Harrow Borough	2-1
54	Diss Town v Chertsey Town	2-3
55	Canvey Island v Folkestone Invicta	2-1
56	Carshalton Athletic v Chelmsford City	1-1
57	Maidstone United (2) v Boreham Wood	2-5
58	Heybridge Swifts v Sutton United	1-1
59	Uxbridge v Braintree Town	1-2
60	Hastings United (2) v Selsey	4-1
61	Flackwell Heath v Royston Town	2-2
62	Hemel Hempstead Town v Cray Wanderers	3-1
63	Enfield v Bishop's Stortford	1-5
64	Beaconsfield SYCOB v Gosport Borough	1-2
65	Burnham v Herne Bay	0-1
66	Aldershot Town v Aylesbury United	3-1
67	Dover Athletic v Basingstoke Town	2-0
68	Lymington & New Milton v Cheshunt	3-1
69	Carterton Town v Arlesey Town	0-6
70	Crawley Town v Great Yarmouth Town	3-0
71	Wisbech Town v VCD Athletic	6-1
72	Wootton Blue Cross v Purfleet	0-4
73	Three Bridges v Aveley	1-3
74	Ford United v Metropolitan Police	4-2
75	St Albans City v Wingate & Finchley	2-0
76	Tiverton Town v Taunton Town	1-1
77	Bath City v Merthyr Tydfil	5-0
78	Weston-Super-Mare v Clevedon Town	2-0
79	Gloucester City v Newport County (2)	1-1
80	Team Bath v Bemerton Heath Harlequins	6-1
81	Bideford v St Blazey	3-1
82	Hungerford Town v Paulton Rovers	2-1
83	Evesham United v Cinderford Town	1-1
84	Chippenham Town v Weymouth	1-4
1r	Harrogate Railway Athletic v Chester-le-Street Town	7-2e
4r	Guiseley v Guisborough Town	1-0
6r	Workington v Stalybridge Celtic	3-1
12r	Eccleshill United v Marine	2-3e
31r	Hucknall Town v Hednesford Town	3-3P
32r	Leek Town v Redditch United	1-2
35r	Stamford v Worcester City	1-2
38r	AFC Sudbury v Harefield United	5-0
42r	Bromley v Leatherhead	2-4
48r	Slough Town v AFC Totton	2-0
51r	Eastleigh v Lewes	2-4e
56r	Chelmsford City v Carshalton Athletic	1-0e
58r	Sutton United v Heybridge Swifts	1-2
61r	Royston Town v Flackwell Heath	0-0q
76r	Taunton Town v Tiverton Town	0-2
79r	Newport County (2) v Gloucester City	4-0
83r	Cinderford Town v Evesham United	0-5

Qualifying Round Three

1	Harrogate Railway Athletic v Workington	4-0
2	Droylsden v Spennymoor United	0-0
3	Accrington Stanley (2) v Harrogate Town	0-0
4	Bradford Park Avenue v Bridlington Town (2)	3-5
5	Vauxhall Motors v Gainsborough Trinity	6-1
6	Durham City v Blyth Spartans	1-1
7	Barrow v Hyde United	3-1
8	Ashton United v Runcorn FC Halton	0-3
9	Dunston Federation Brewery v Marine	0-1
10	Colwyn Bay v Radcliffe Borough	1-2
11	Guiseley v Altrincham	2-1
12	Ilkeston Town (2) v King's Lynn	6-1
13	Redditch United v Arnold Town	0-1
14	Hinckley United v Tamworth	1-3
15	Moor Green v Halesowen Town	3-1
16	Wisbech Town v Bedford Town	1-0
17	Hucknall Town v Worcester City	1-0
18	Grantham Town v Worksop Town	1-0
19	Stafford Rangers v Rothwell Town	3-0
20	Canvey Island v Aveley	2-0
21	Billericay Town v Braintree Town	4-0
22	Heybridge Swifts v Herne Bay	1-0
23	Hemel Hempstead Town v Arlesey Town	1-2
24	Dover Athletic v Welling United	2-2
25	Molesey v Chertsey Town	3-1
26	Bishop's Stortford v Eastbourne Borough	1-0
27	Flackwell Heath v Purfleet	1-0
28	Grays Athletic v Hayes	2-1
29	AFC Sudbury v Walton & Hersham	2-0
30	Hastings United (2) v Hendon	2-1
31	Slough Town v Hampton & Richmond Boro.	4-2
32	St Albans City v Chelmsford City	1-0
33	Boreham Wood v Kingstonian	2-0
34	Leatherhead v Ford United	1-2
35	Horsham v Hungerford Town	1-0
36	Havant & Waterlooville v Evesham United	4-0
37	Weston-Super-Mare v Bath City	0-5
38	Bideford v Gosport Borough	3-1
39	Aldershot Town v Lewes	2-0
40	Newport County (2) v Team Bath	0-3
41	Lymington & New Milton v Crawley Town	0-2
42	Tiverton Town v Weymouth	4-2
2r	Spennymoor United v Droylsden	3-2
3r	Harrogate Town v Accrington Stanley (2)	3-2
6r	Blyth Spartans v Durham City	3-1
24r	Welling United v Dover Athletic	1-3

Qualifying Round Four

1	Wisbech Town v Harrogate Town	0-2
2	Blyth Spartans v Runcorn FC Halton	1-3
3	Morecambe v Grantham Town	3-1
4	Telford United v Doncaster Rovers	0-2
5	Ilkeston Town (2) v Stafford Rangers	0-5
6	Burton Albion v Halifax Town	2-1
7	Moor Green v Leigh RMI	2-1
8	Harrogate Railway Athletic v Marine	4-2
9	Arnold Town v Scarborough	0-2
10	Northwich Victoria v Spennymoor United	3-1
11	Hucknall Town v Vauxhall Motors	1-1
12	Guiseley v Tamworth	3-3
13	Southport v Bridlington Town (2)	4-1
14	Radcliffe Borough v Chester City	2-4
15	Nuneaton Borough v Barrow	1-1
16	AFC Sudbury v St Albans City	1-2
17	Bishop's Stortford v Boreham Wood	1-1
18	Heybridge Swifts v Bideford	2-0
19	Bath City v Yeovil Town	1-1
20	Slough Town v Canvey Island	3-2
21	Aldershot Town v Dagenham & Redbridge	0-4
22	Hastings United (2) v Kettering Town	0-0
23	Havant & Waterlooville v Billericay Town	3-1
24	Hereford United v Arlesey Town	1-0
25	Horsham v Team Bath	0-0
26	Gravesend & Northfleet v Margate	1-2
27	Forest Green Rovers v Ford United	2-1
28	Flackwell Heath v Crawley Town	1-4
29	Dover Athletic v Woking	1-1
30	Barnet v Tiverton Town	0-2
31	Grays Athletic v Stevenage Borough	1-2
32	Molesey v Farnborough Town	0-6
11r	Vauxhall Motors v Hucknall Town	5-1
12r	Tamworth v Guiseley	2-3
15r	Barrow v Nuneaton Borough	4-3
17r	Boreham Wood v Bishop's Stortford	4-1
19r	Yeovil Town v Bath City	3-1
22r	Kettering Town v Hastings United (2)	0-5
25r	Team Bath v Horsham	1-1P
29r	Woking v Dover Athletic	1-2

Round One

	Barnsley v Blackpool	1-4
	Barrow v Moor Green	2-0
	Bournemouth v Doncaster Rovers	2-1
	Bristol Rovers v Runcorn FC Halton	0-0
	Bury v Plymouth Argyle	0-3
	Carlisle United v Lincoln City	2-1
	Chesterfield v Morecambe	1-2
	Colchester United v Chester City	0-1
	Dagenham & Redbridge v Havant & Waterlooville	3-2
	Dover Athletic v Oxford United	0-1
	Farnborough Town v Harrogate Town	5-1
	Forest Green Rovers v Exeter City	0-0
	Hereford United v Wigan Athletic	0-1
	Heybridge Swifts v Bristol City	0-7
	Hull City v Macclesfield Town	0-3
	Kidderminster Harriers v Rushden & Diamonds	2-2
	Leyton Orient v Margate	1-1
	Luton Town v Guiseley	4-0
	Northampton Town v Boston United	3-2
	Northwich Victoria v Scunthorpe United	0-3
	Oldham Athletic v Burton Albion	2-2
	Port Vale v Crewe Alexandra	0-1
	Rochdale v Peterborough United	3-2
	Scarborough v Cambridge United	0-0
	Shrewsbury Town v Stafford Rangers	4-0
	Slough Town v Harrogate Railway Athletic	1-2
	Southend United v Hartlepool United	1-1
	Southport v Notts County	4-2
	Stevenage Borough v Hastings United (2)	1-0
	Stockport County v St Albans City	4-1
	Swindon Town v Huddersfield Town	1-0
	Team Bath v Mansfield Town	2-4
	Tiverton Town v Crawley Town	1-1
	Torquay United v Boreham Wood	5-0
	Tranmere Rovers v Cardiff City	2-2
	Vauxhall Motors v Queen's Park Rangers	0-0 N
	Wrexham v Darlington	0-2
	Wycombe Wanderers v Brentford	2-4
	Yeovil Town v Cheltenham Town	0-2
	York City v Swansea City	2-1
r	Burton Albion v Oldham Athletic	2-2q
r	Cambridge United v Scarborough	2-1e
r	Cardiff City v Tranmere Rovers	2-1
r	Crawley Town v Tiverton Town	3-2
r	Exeter City v Forest Green Rovers	2-1
r	Hartlepool United v Southend United	1-2
r	Margate v Leyton Orient	1-0 N
r	Queen's Park Rangers v Vauxhall Motors	1-1q
r	Runcorn FC Halton v Bristol Rovers	1-3e
r	Rushden & Diamonds v Kidderminster Harriers	2-1

Round Two

Blackpool v Torquay United	3-1
Bristol Rovers v Rochdale	1-1
Cambridge United v Northampton Town	2-2
Crawley Town v Dagenham & Redbridge	1-2
Crewe Alexandra v Mansfield Town	3-0
Darlington v Stevenage Borough	4-1
Exeter City v Rushden & Diamonds	3-1
Harrogate Railway Athletic v Bristol City	1-3
Macclesfield Town v Vauxhall Motors	2-0
Margate v Cardiff City	0-3 N
Morecambe v Chester City	3-2
Oldham Athletic v Cheltenham Town	1-2
Oxford United v Swindon Town	1-0
Scunthorpe United v Carlisle United	0-0
Shrewsbury Town v Barrow	3-1
Southend United v Bournemouth	1-1
Southport v Farnborough Town	0-3
Stockport County v Plymouth Argyle	0-3
Wigan Athletic v Luton Town	3-0
York City v Brentford	1-2

2002/03 to 2003/04

r Bournemouth v Southend United 3-2
r Carlisle United v Scunthorpe United 0-1
r Northampton Town v Cambridge United 0-1
r Rochdale v Bristol Rovers 3-2

Round Three

Arsenal v Oxford United 2-0
Aston Villa v Blackburn Rovers 1-4
Blackpool v Crystal Palace 1-2
Bolton Wanderers v Sunderland 1-1
Bournemouth v Crewe Alexandra 0-0
Brentford v Derby County 1-0
Cambridge United v Millwall 1-1
Cardiff City v Coventry City 2-2
Charlton Athletic v Exeter City 3-1
Chelsea v Middlesbrough 1-0
Darlington v Farnborough Town 2-3
Fulham v Birmingham City 3-1
Gillingham v Sheffield Wednesday 4-1
Grimsby Town v Burnley 2-2
Ipswich Town v Morecambe 4-0
Leicester City v Bristol City 2-0
Macclesfield Town v Watford 0-2
Manchester City v Liverpool 0-1
Manchester United v Portsmouth 4-1
Norwich City v Brighton & Hove Albion 3-1
Plymouth Argyle v Dagenham & Redbridge 2-2
Preston North End v Rochdale 1-2
Rotherham United v Wimbledon 0-3
Scunthorpe United v Leeds United 0-2
Sheffield United v Cheltenham Town 4-0
Shrewsbury Town v Everton 2-1
Southampton v Tottenham Hotspur 4-0
Stoke City v Wigan Athletic 3-0
Walsall v Reading 0-0
West Bromwich Albion v Bradford City 3-1
West Ham United v Nottingham Forest 3-2
Wolverhampton Wan. v Newcastle United 3-2
r Burnley v Grimsby Town 4-0
r Coventry City v Cardiff City 3-0
r Crewe Alexandra v Bournemouth 2-2q
r Dagenham & Redbridge v Plymouth Argyle 2-0
r Millwall v Cambridge United 3-2
r Reading v Walsall 1-1q
r Sunderland v Bolton Wanderers 2-0e

Round Four

Arsenal v Farnborough Town 5-1
Blackburn Rovers v Sunderland 3-3
Brentford v Burnley 0-3
Crystal Palace v Liverpool 0-0
Fulham v Charlton Athletic 3-0
Gillingham v Leeds United 1-1
Manchester United v West Ham United 6-0
Norwich City v Dagenham & Redbridge 1-0
Rochdale v Coventry City 2-0
Sheffield United v Ipswich Town 4-3
Shrewsbury Town v Chelsea 0-4
Southampton v Millwall 1-1
Stoke City v Bournemouth 3-0
Walsall v Wimbledon 1-0
Watford v West Bromwich Albion 1-0
Wolverhampton Wan. v Leicester City 4-1
r Leeds United v Gillingham 2-1
r Liverpool v Crystal Palace 0-2
r Millwall v Southampton 1-2e
r Sunderland v Blackburn Rovers 2-2P

Round Five

Crystal Palace v Leeds United 1-2
Fulham v Burnley 1-1
Manchester United v Arsenal 0-2
Sheffield United v Walsall 2-0
Southampton v Norwich City 2-0
Stoke City v Chelsea 0-2
Sunderland v Watford 0-1
Wolverhampton Wan. v Rochdale 3-1
r Burnley v Fulham 3-0

Round Six

Arsenal v Chelsea 2-2
Sheffield United v Leeds United 1-0
Southampton v Wolverhampton Wan. 2-0
Watford v Burnley 2-0
r Chelsea v Arsenal 1-3

Semi Finals

Arsenal v Sheffield United 1-0 N
Southampton v Watford 2-1 N

Final

Arsenal v Southampton 1-0 N

2003/04

Extra Preliminary Round

1 Skelmersdale United v Glasshoughton Welfare 7-2
2 Brodsworth MW v Pickering Town 0-1
3 St Helens Town v Trafford 0-2
4 Garforth Town v Whickham 0-3
5 Holker Old Boys v Penrith 1-0
6 Colne v Mossley 2-3
7 Norton & Stockton Ancients v Evenwood Town 0-2
8 Ossett Albion v Alnwick Town 5-2
9 Washington Nissan v Jarrow Roofing Boldon CA 1-2
10 Shotton Comrades v Newcastle Blue Star 1-4
11 Dunston Federation Brewery v Abbey Hey 1-0
12 Eccleshill United v Warrington Town 1-2
13 Oldham Town v Northallerton Town 3-2
14 Fleetwood Town v Darwen 1-0
15 Blackstones v Gedling Town 1-4
16 Holbeach United v Staveley MW 1-1
17 Carlton Town v Shirebrook Town 0-3
18 Lincoln Moorlands v Arnold Town 1-0
19 Nantwich Town v Stratford Town 1-2
20 Cradley Town v Daventry Town 2-0
21 Maldon Town v Holmer Green 4-1
22 Stotfold v London Colney 1-2
23 Wroxham v Halstead Town 4-1
24 Brentwood v Haringey Borough 0-2
25 Kingsbury Town v Stowmarket Town 1-2
26 Harpenden Town v Woodbridge Town 6-1
27 Needham Market v Norwich United 0-3
28 Romford v Bury Town 0-2
29 Tiptree United v Cogenhoe United 0-1
30 Northampton Spencer v Desborough Town 2-2
31 Broxbourne Borough V&E v Yaxley 0-2
32 Mildenhall Town v Ilford 2-1
33 St Margaretsbury v Henley Town 0-0
34 Bedford United & Valerio v Harefield United 1-0
35 Southend Manor v Buckingham Town 1-1
36 Ruislip Manor v Ely City 2-2
37 Hadleigh United v Wootton Blue Cross 0-1
38 Brackley Town v Hullbridge Sports 2-1
39 Royston Town v Ford Sports (Daventry) 0-3
40 Great Yarmouth Town v Southall Town 4-1
41 St Leonards v Arundel 1-4
42 Thatcham Town v Selsey 6-0
43 East Preston v Andover 2-3
44 Walton Casuals v Westfield 5-0
45 Brockenhurst v VCD Athletic 2-3
46 Wokingham Town v Chertsey Town 2-0
47 Chichester City United v Tunbridge Wells 4-1
48 Sandhurst Town v Camberley Town 2-1
49 Didcot Town v Ramsgate 2-1
50 Saltdean United v Cray Wanderers 0-4
51 Bedfont v Littlehampton Town 4-0
52 Horsham YMCA v Gosport Borough 3-3
53 Eastbourne United v Lordswood 1-0
54 BAT Sports v Cobham 3-1
55 Carterton Town v Hungerford Town 1-0
56 Lancing v Whitehawk 0-3
57 AFC Totton v Erith Town 3-0
58 Reading Town v Lymington & New Milton 1-2
59 Barnstaple Town v Exmouth Town 2-3
60 Highworth Town v Shortwood United 3-1
61 Frome Town v Tuffley Rovers 1-0
62 Shepton Mallet v Falmouth Town 0-1
63 Minehead v Liskeard Athletic 2-0
64 Devizes Town v Christchurch 0-4
65 Chard Town v Paulton Rovers 0-3
16r Staveley MW v Holbeach United 3-2
30r Desborough Town v Northampton Spencer 4-2
33r Henley Town v St Margaretsbury 0-3
35r Buckingham Town v Southend Manor 4-1e
36r Ely City v Ruislip Manor 0-2
52r Gosport Borough v Horsham YMCA 1-0

Preliminary Round

1 Brigg Town v Billingham Town 2-2
2 Maine Road v Ashington 2-4
3 Bishop Auckland v Flixton 8-0
4 Harrogate Railway Athletic v Hatfield Main wo/s
5 Armthorpe Welfare v Louth United wo/s
6 Chadderton v Holker Old Boys 1-2
7 Peterlee Newtown v Bridlington Town (2) 1-2
8 Mossley v Curzon Ashton 1-1
9 Bamber Bridge v Prescot Cables 3-1
10 Stocksbridge Park Steels v Squires Gate 2-1
11 Goole AFC v Rossendale United 2-4
12 Witton Albion v Nelson 4-1
13 Thackley v Ossett Town 0-1
14 Skelmersdale United v Atherton LR 3-0
15 Pontefract Collieries v Clitheroe 0-2
16 Blackpool Mechanics v Colwyn Bay 1-1
17 Crook Town v Guiseley 2-3
18 Tow Law Town v Salford City 1-1
19 South Shields (3) v Bedlington Terriers 0-0
20 Willington v Consett 0-5
21 Fleetwood Town v Parkgate 3-0
22 Newcastle Blue Star v Dunston Federation Brewery 1-2
23 Billingham Synthonia v Chorley 1-1
24 Hyde United v Hallam 6-1
25 Liversedge v Gateshead (2) 3-1
26 Guisborough Town v Kendal Town 1-1
27 Tadcaster Albion v Winsford United 0-4
28 Great Harwood Town v North Ferriby United 0-3
29 Cheadle Town v Chester-le-Street Town 1-2
30 Woodley Sports v Ramsbottom United 1-1
31 Durham City v Rossington Main 0-0
32 Horden CW v Brandon United 0-1
33 Esh Winning v Bacup Borough 1-3
34 Whickham v Hebburn Town 2-2
35 Thornaby v Easington Colliery 5-1
36 Shildon v Workington 2-1
37 Selby Town v Washington 0-0
38 Maltby Main v West Auckland Town 1-0
39 Sheffield v Jarrow Roofing Boldon CA 1-0
40 Pickering Town v Whitley Bay 2-0
41 Evenwood Town v Oldham Town 3-5 N
42 Hall Road Rangers v Trafford 1-1
43 Marske United v Winterton Rangers 3-0
44 Warrington Town v Yorkshire Amateur 1-0
45 Prudhoe Town v Morpeth Town 2-0
46 Ossett Albion v Alsager Town 2-1
47 Seaham Red Star v Murton 3-4
48 Atherton Collieries v Farsley Celtic 0-3
49 Gresley Rovers v Buxton 1-1
50 Stamford v Bourne Town 2-0
51 Shepshed Dynamo v Congleton Town 0-1
52 Shirebrook Town v Matlock Town 2-1
53 Grosvenor Park v Glapwell 0-0
54 Quorn v Gedling Town 0-1
55 Studley v Rushall Olympic 3-0
56 Oadby Town v Stratford Town 5-1
57 Corby Town v Lincoln United 2-1
58 Bedworth United v Halesowen Town 0-2
59 Belper Town v Boston Town 1-1
60 Mickleover Sports v Ludlow Town 3-0
61 Chasetown v Sutton Coldfield Town 1-2
62 Kidsgrove Athletic v Rugby United 1-3
63 Borrowash Victoria v Biddulph Victoria 3-4
64 Racing Club Warwick v Stafford Town 0-1
65 Rocester v Ilkeston Town (2) 1-1
66 Staveley MW v Sutton Town (2) 0-1
67 Pelsall Villa v Atherstone United wo/s
68 Eastwood Town v Deeping Rangers 2-2
69 Lincoln Moorlands v Leek Town 1-2
70 Spalding United v Glossop North End 3-0
71 Stourport Swifts v Boldmere St Michaels 1-0
72 Cradley Town v Bromsgrove Rovers 0-4
73 Solihull Borough v Stone Dominoes 3-0
74 Leek CSOB v Redditch United 2-3
75 Barwell v Oldbury United 3-1
76 Newcastle Town v Willenhall Town 3-0
77 Causeway United v Stourbridge 2-0
78 Long Eaton United v Norton United 0-0
79 Haverhill Rovers v Gorleston wo/s
80 Burnham v Arlesey Town 1-7
81 Burnham Ramblers v Potters Bar Town 4-1
82 Dunstable Town v Saffron Walden Town wo/s
83 Leighton Town v Wootton Blue Cross 3-1
84 Mildenhall Town v Tring Town wo/s
85 Sawbridgeworth v AFC Wallingford 2-2
86 Newmarket Town v Wembley 5-0
87 Chalfont St Peter v Chesham United 0-6
88 Boreham Wood v Desborough Town 2-1
89 Ware v London Colney 2-2
90 Enfield Town v Clacton Town 2-1
91 Norwich United v Leyton 2-2
92 AFC Sudbury v Diss Town 4-3
93 Histon v Yeading 7-0
94 Hampton & Richmond Boro. v Great Wakering Rovers 3-0
95 Harpenden Town v St Margaretsbury 1-3
96 Haringey Borough v Dereham Town 1-3
97 Barton Rovers v Rothwell Town 2-2
98 Stewarts & Lloyds (2) v Fakenham Town 3-0
99 Tilbury v Milton Keynes City wo/s
100 Bedford United & Valerio v St Neots Town 0-2
101 Beaconsfield SYCOB v Ipswich Wanderers 1-1
102 Wisbech Town v Aveley 1-2
103 Stowmarket Town v Waltham Forest 0-2
104 Stanway Rovers v Staines Town 0-1
105 Wivenhoe Town v Bowers United 7-0
106 Cheshunt v Harlow Town 2-3
107 Cogenhoe United v Maldon Town 1-2
108 Wingate & Finchley v Bury Town 3-2
109 Edgware Town v Clapton 2-2
110 Uxbridge v Stansted 7-0
111 Great Yarmouth Town v Berkhamsted Town 0-1
112 Raunds Town v Hoddesdon Town 1-0
113 Buckingham Town v Ford Sports (Daventry) 2-0
114 Hertford Town v Lowestoft Town 2-4
115 Yaxley v Barking & East Ham United 2-1
116 Ruislip Manor v Soham Town Rangers 1-4
117 Enfield v Hemel Hempstead Town 1-1
118 Wroxham v Banbury United 6-1
119 Flackwell Heath v Concord Rangers 4-1
120 Long Buckby v King's Lynn 1-5
121 Hanwell Town v East Thurrock United 2-2
122 Witham Town v Marlow 2-0
123 Brook House v Wealdstone 1-4
124 Brackley Town v Harwich & Parkeston 4-2
125 Greenwich Borough v Maidstone United (2) 1-1
126 Hailsham Town v Cowes Sports 0-1
127 Chessington & Hook United v Merstham 2-0
128 Leatherhead v Moneyfields 3-1
129 Windsor & Eton v Metropolitan Police 0-1
130 Dartford v Bashley 1-0

214

2003/04

131	Walton & Hersham v Walton Casuals	0-2
132	Three Bridges v Redhill	1-1
133	Tonbridge Angels v BAT Sports	4-0
134	Fisher Athletic (London) v Bedfont	3-4
135	Blackfield & Langley v Thamesmead Town	1-3
136	Abingdon United v Cove	3-2
137	Banstead Athletic v Winchester City	0-2
138	Arundel v Hassocks	4-0
139	Tooting & Mitcham United v Ashford Town (Middlesex)	3-1
140	Chipstead v Ringmer	1-2
141	Croydon v Hythe Town	1-1
142	Abingdon Town v Chichester City United	3-1
143	Whitchurch United v Withdean 2000	4-1
144	Worthing v Ash United	7-0
145	Fleet Town v Epsom & Ewell	1-0
146	Slade Green v Hartley Wintney	1-2
147	Egham Town v Thame United	1-8
148	Sidlesham v Sittingbourne	0-2
149	AFC Totton v AFC Newbury	3-1
150	Didcot Town v Eastbourne Town	4-1
151	Ashford Town v Eastbourne United	3-0
152	Gosport Borough v Erith & Belvedere	2-4
153	Hastings United (2) v Bracknell Town	1-3
154	Southwick v Burgess Hill Town	1-4
155	VCD Athletic v Eastleigh	2-1
156	Beckenham Town v Sandhurst Town	2-5
157	Slough Town v East Grinstead Town	5-0 N
158	Dulwich Hamlet v Folkestone Invicta	1-3
159	Wokingham Town v Deal Town	0-1
160	Dorking (2) v Lewes	3-5
161	Hillingdon Borough v Corinthian Casuals	2-0
162	Wick v Whyteleafe	0-5
163	Oxford City v Farnham Town	6-1
164	Molesey v Godalming & Guildford	1-2
165	Croydon Athletic v Herne Bay	2-1
166	Bromley v North Leigh	2-1
167	Whitehawk v Lymington & New Milton	0-2
168	Thatcham Town v Alton Town	1-2
169	Whitstable Town v Raynes Park Vale	1-3
170	Cray Wanderers v Pagham	4-0
171	Peacehaven & Telscombe v Chessington United	2-1
172	Horsham v Newport (IOW)	1-2
173	Carterton Town v Fareham Town	1-2
174	Chatham Town v Andover	2-4
175	Bitton v Christchurch	3-4
176	Bideford v Swindon Supermarine	1-3
177	Backwell United v Fairford Town	2-0
178	Bishop Sutton v Falmouth Town	1-0
179	Bridport v Street	2-0
180	Cinderford Town v Brislington	1-3
181	Melksham Town v Mangotsfield United	0-4
182	Evesham United v Hallen	3-3
183	Taunton Town v Bournemouth (Ams)	1-1
184	St Blazey v Willand Rovers	5-0
185	Highworth Town v Portland United	4-3
186	Westbury United v Keynsham Town	2-2
187	Minehead v Welton Rovers	2-2
188	Bemerton Heath Harlequins v Torrington	3-2
189	Bristol Manor Farm v Gloucester City	0-5
190	Frome Town v Clevedon Town	1-1
191	Porthleven v Team Bath	0-4
192	Salisbury City v Odd Down	4-0
193	Elmore v Wimborne Town	1-3
194	Downton v Exmouth Town	3-4
195	Yate Town v Cirencester Town	1-2
196	Paulton Rovers v Calne Town	2-0
197	Bridgwater Town v Corsham Town	0-1
198	Dawlish Town v Clevedon United	1-2
1r	Billingham Town v Brigg Town	1-0 N
8r	Curzon Ashton v Mossley	2-3e
16r	Colwyn Bay v Blackpool Mechanics	3-1
18r	Salford City v Tow Law Town	4-3
19r	Bedlington Terriers v South Shields (3)	4-1
23r	Chorley v Billingham Synthonia	3-1e
26r	Kendal Town v Guisborough Town	2-2q
30r	Ramsbottom United v Woodley Sports	3-0
31r	Rossington Main v Durham City	0-1
34r	Hebburn Town v Whickham	1-2
37r	Washington v Selby Town	3-3q
42r	Trafford v Hall Road Rangers	3-1
49r	Buxton v Gresley Rovers	4-0
53r	Glapwell v Grosvenor Park	2-0
59r	Boston Town v Belper Town	0-1
66r	Ilkeston Town (2) v Rocester	3-1
68r	Deeping Rangers v Eastwood Town	1-2
78r	Norton United v Long Eaton United	0-2
85r	AFC Wallingford v Sawbridgeworth	2-0
89r	London Colney v Ware	0-1e
91r	Leyton v Norwich United	2-1
97r	Rothwell Town v Barton Rovers	3-0
101r	Ipswich Wanderers v Beaconsfield SYCOB	2-1
109r	Clapton v Edgware Town	0-1
117r	Hemel Hempstead Town v Enfield	2-3
121r	East Thurrock United v Hanwell Town	6-3e
125r	Maidstone United (2) v Greenwich Borough	1-0
133r	Redhill v Three Bridges	0-3 N
141r	Hythe Town v Croydon	1-1P
182r	Hallen v Evesham United	2-1e
183r	Bournemouth (Ams) v Taunton Town	0-5
186r	Keynsham Town v Westbury United	2-5
187r	Welton Rovers v Minehead	2-1
190r	Clevedon Town v Frome Town	2-3e

Qualifying Round One

1	Witton Albion v Holker Old Boys	7-0
2	Stocksbridge Park Steels v Prudhoe Town	6-1
3	Mossley v Hyde United	1-6
4	Rossendale United v Harrogate Railway Athletic	2-1
5	Clitheroe v Brandon United	0-1
6	Maltby Main v Colwyn Bay	4-2
7	Winsford United v Marske United	2-1
8	Oldham Town v Liversedge	3-2
9	Ossett Albion v Ossett Town	0-0
10	Durham City v Shildon	0-2
11	Ashington v Ramsbottom United	3-1
12	Thornaby v Guisborough Town	1-2
13	Armthorpe Welfare v Whickham	0-0
14	Bamber Bridge v Bacup Borough	2-0
15	Guiseley v Trafford	1-0
16	Bishop Auckland v Pickering Town	0-1
17	Chester-le-Street Town v Murton	2-0
18	Warrington Town v North Ferriby United	6-1
19	Chorley v Selby Town	2-1
20	Dunston Federation Brewery v Billingham Town	2-2
21	Farsley Celtic v Sheffield	1-1
22	Bridlington Town (2) v Salford City	5-0
23	Skelmersdale United v Consett	2-0
24	Fleetwood Town v Bedlington Terriers	3-2
25	Stourport Swifts v Rugby United	0-3
26	Oadby Town v Stamford	0-2
27	Barwell v Newcastle Town	2-5
28	Glapwell v Gedling Town	1-2
29	Shirebrook Town v Stafford Town	2-0
30	Studley v Bromsgrove Rovers	0-1
31	Solihull Borough v Redditch United	0-3
32	Long Eaton United v Ilkeston Town (2)	0-2
33	Mickleover Sports v Eastwood Town	0-0
34	Sutton Coldfield Town v Causeway United	1-1
35	Pelsall Villa v Belper Town	0-4
36	Corby Town v Halesowen Town	1-1
37	Spalding United v Sutton Town (2)	2-2
38	Congleton Town v Leek Town	1-0
39	Biddulph Victoria v Buxton	1-1
40	Newmarket Town v Brackley Town	6-1
41	Hampton & Richmond Boro. v Dunstable Town	1-0
42	Harlow Town v St Neots Town	1-0
43	Waltham Forest v Rothwell Town	1-3
44	Dereham Town v Tilbury	1-4
45	Aveley v Lowestoft Town	1-2
46	Wealdstone v Uxbridge	0-1
47	Leyton v Arlesey Town	4-0
48	Edgware Town v Enfield Town	0-1
49	Ware v Buckingham Town	2-2
50	Wingate & Finchley v Raunds Town	3-1
51	Mildenhall Town v Histon	1-6
52	AFC Wallingford v Ipswich Wanderers	2-0
53	Berkhamsted Town v AFC Sudbury	0-9
54	Chesham United v Yaxley	2-0
55	Wroxham v Flackwell Heath	2-2
56	East Thurrock United v Staines Town	2-1
57	Wivenhoe Town v Soham Town Rangers	2-3
58	Boreham Wood v Maldon Town	2-1
59	St Margaretsbury v Leighton Town	2-2
60	Haverhill Rovers v Burnham Ramblers	1-2
61	King's Lynn v Stewarts & Lloyds (2)	2-2
62	Enfield v Witham Town	4-0
63	Whitchurch United v Tooting & Mitcham United	0-3
64	Raynes Park Vale v Folkestone Invicta	0-2
65	Lymington & New Milton v Erith & Belvedere	1-0
66	Cray Wanderers v Sandhurst Town	4-1
67	Deal Town v Leatherhead	1-2
68	Ashford Town v Bromley	1-1
69	Tonbridge Angels v Lewes	1-1
70	Hillingdon Borough v Oxford City	1-1
71	Chessington & Hook United v Thamesmead Town	1-4
72	Slough Town v Godalming & Guildford	2-0
73	Metropolitan Police v Winchester City	2-3
74	Fareham Town v Newport (IOW)	1-2
75	Hythe Town v Alton Town	3-1
76	Burgess Hill Town v Abingdon United	2-1
77	Thame United v VCD Athletic	4-2
78	Worthing v Walton Casuals	4-1
79	Dartford v Peacehaven & Telscombe	3-0
80	Sittingbourne v Whyteleafe	1-0
81	Andover v Arundel	5-0
82	Abingdon Town v Ringmer	4-3
83	Bracknell Town v Hartley Wintney	3-2
84	Three Bridges v Fleet Town	1-2
85	Croydon Athletic v Bedfont	7-1
86	AFC Totton v Didcot Town	1-3
87	Maidstone United (2) v Cowes Sports	4-0
88	Clevedon United v Frome Town	4-1
89	Paulton Rovers v Bemerton Heath Harlequins	2-0
90	Gloucester City v Team Bath	0-0
91	Christchurch v Westbury United	2-3
92	Mangotsfield United v Bridport	4-3
93	Cirencester Town v Swindon Supermarine	2-1
94	Corsham Town v Brislington	1-2
95	Salisbury City v Taunton Town	4-1
96	Exmouth Town v St Blazey	2-2
97	Hallen v Highworth Town	1-2
98	Backwell United v Wimborne Town	1-4
99	Welton Rovers v Bishop Sutton	3-3
9r	Ossett Town v Ossett Albion	1-3
13r	Whickham v Armthorpe Welfare	2-1
20r	Billingham Town v Dunston Federation Brewery	0-1
21r	Sheffield v Farsley Celtic	1-3e
33r	Eastwood Town v Mickleover Sports	1-0
34r	Causeway United v Sutton Coldfield Town	0-3
36r	Halesowen Town v Corby Town	3-2
37r	Sutton Town (2) v Spalding United	0-5
39r	Buxton v Biddulph Victoria	3-2
49r	Buckingham Town v Ware	2-1e
55r	Flackwell Heath v Wroxham	1-0
59r	Leighton Town v St Margaretsbury	0-1
61r	Stewarts & Lloyds (2) v King's Lynn	0-3
68r	Bromley v Ashford Town	1-0
69r	Lewes v Tonbridge Angels	2-1
70r	Oxford City v Hillingdon Borough	2-1
90r	Team Bath v Gloucester City	0-2
96r	St Blazey v Exmouth Town	3-3q
99r	Bishop Sutton v Welton Rovers	1-0

Qualifying Round Two

1	Frickley Athletic v Shildon	0-0
2	Whitby Town v Winsford United	3-0
3	Runcorn FC Halton v Guiseley	3-0
4	Droylsden v Burscough	2-2
5	Pickering Town v Ossett Albion	0-1
6	Vauxhall Motors v Southport	3-1
7	Dunston Federation Brewery v Fleetwood Town	1-1
8	Bridlington Town (2) v Farsley Celtic	2-2
9	Stocksbridge Park Steels v Brandon United	3-2
10	Ashton United v Hyde United	1-1
11	Blyth Spartans v Bamber Bridge	3-0
12	Marine v Rossendale United	3-1
13	Chester-le-Street Town v Bradford Park Avenue	0-2
14	Maltby Main v Ashington	2-3
15	Barrow v Harrogate Town	2-0
16	Lancaster City v Altrincham	2-0
17	Gainsborough Trinity v Skelmersdale United	6-0
18	Witton Albion v Wakefield & Emley	0-1
19	Guisborough Town v Stalybridge Celtic	2-2
20	Chorley v Whickham	5-0
21	Radcliffe Borough v Oldham Town	2-1
22	Spennymoor United v Warrington Town	0-2
23	Gedling Town v Alfreton Town	1-0
24	Newcastle Town v Sutton Coldfield Town	2-1
25	Cambridge City v Ilkeston Town (2)	3-1
26	Hednesford Town v Bromsgrove Rovers	0-2
27	Rothwell Town v Bedford Town	0-1
28	Stafford Rangers v Grantham Town	1-2
29	Redditch United v Shirebrook Town	1-1
30	Spalding United v Halesowen Town	1-2
31	Stamford v Kettering Town	0-3
32	Hucknall Town v Congleton Town	1-1
33	Soham Town Rangers v Histon	0-2
34	Buxton v Belper Town	1-0
35	Nuneaton Borough v Worcester City	1-0
36	Worksop Town v King's Lynn	2-2
37	Rugby United v Eastwood Town	1-3
38	Moor Green v Hinckley United	1-2
39	Basingstoke Town v Cray Wanderers	1-0
40	Sutton United v Bishop's Stortford	0-0
41	Buckingham Town v Thurrock	1-2
42	Bromley v Dartford	3-0
43	Sittingbourne v East Thurrock United	1-2
44	Boreham Wood v Burgess Hill Town	4-0
45	Bracknell Town v Tilbury	4-2
46	Hendon v Enfield	4-0
47	Canvey Island v Uxbridge	6-1
48	Wingate & Finchley v Oxford City	1-2
49	Hampton & Richmond Boro. v Kingstonian	2-1
50	Heybridge Swifts v Worthing	3-3
51	Lowestoft Town v Lewes	2-1
52	Hythe Town v Maidstone United (2)	0-4
53	Leyton v Leatherhead	1-0
54	Slough Town v Welling United	1-1
55	Thame United v Thamesmead Town	4-0
56	Abingdon Town v Chesham United	1-2
57	Hornchurch v Billericay Town	2-1
58	Newmarket Town v Fleet Town	3-0
59	Braintree Town v Aylesbury United	3-2
60	St Albans City v Grays Athletic	2-4
61	Hayes v Tooting & Mitcham United	4-2
62	Enfield Town v Carshalton Athletic	0-1
63	Hitchin Town v Folkestone Invicta	0-0
64	Ford United v Didcot Town	3-1
65	Croydon Athletic v AFC Wallingford	2-0
66	Northwood v AFC Sudbury	2-4
67	Dover Athletic v Maidenhead United	4-0
68	Burnham Ramblers v St Margaretsbury	1-3
69	Eastbourne Borough v Chelmsford City	2-2
70	Harrow Borough v Flackwell Heath	0-0
71	Harlow Town v Crawley Town	0-4
72	Newport County (2) v Weymouth	3-2
73	Bognor Regis Town v Havant & Waterlooville	0-4
74	Newport (IOW) v Tiverton Town	2-1
75	Weston-Super-Mare v Dorchester Town	4-1
76	Paulton Rovers v Bishop Sutton	4-1
77	Mangotsfield United v Wimborne Town	3-0
78	Brislington v Bath City	0-2
79	Salisbury City v Westbury United	1-1
80	Chippenham Town v Winchester City	2-1
81	Gloucester City v Merthyr Tydfil	2-0
82	Lymington & New Milton v Clevedon United	8-2
83	Cirencester Town v Andover	3-2
84	Exmouth Town v Highworth Town	0-1
1r	Shildon v Frickley Athletic	5-1
4r	Burscough v Droylsden	1-2e
7r	Fleetwood Town v Dunston Federation Brewery	1-2

2003/04 to 2004/05

8r	Farsley Celtic v Bridlington Town (2)	3-0
10r	Hyde United v Ashton United	1-2
19r	Stalybridge Celtic v Guisborough Town	3-1
29r	Shirebrook Town v Redditch United	2-2P
32r	Congleton Town v Hucknall Town	3-2e
36r	King's Lynn v Worksop Town	1-4
40r	Bishop's Stortford v Sutton United	1-1P
50r	Worthing v Heybridge Swifts	2-0
54r	Welling United v Slough Town	4-1
63r	Folkestone Invicta v Hitchin Town	3-0
69r	Chelmsford City v Eastbourne Borough	0-2
70r	Flackwell Heath v Harrow Borough	0-1
79r	Westbury United v Salisbury City	1-2

Qualifying Round Three

1	Ashton United v Barrow	2-1
2	Farsley Celtic v Worksop Town	3-0
3	Shirebrook Town v Shildon	1-3
4	Nuneaton Borough v Runcorn FC Halton	1-1
5	Ashington v Grantham Town	1-3
6	Gedling Town v Stalybridge Celtic	0-1
7	Eastwood Town v Stocksbridge Park Steels	1-1
8	Newcastle Town v Ossett Albion	1-1
9	Marine v Dunston Federation Brewery	1-2
10	Blyth Spartans v Halesowen Town	2-1
11	Bradford Park Avenue v Vauxhall Motors	1-1
12	Warrington Town v Whitby Town	0-0
13	Wakefield & Emley v Hinckley United	0-2
14	Droylsden v Gainsborough Trinity	0-2
15	Buxton v Radcliffe Borough	2-1
16	Chorley v Lancaster City	1-1
17	Congleton Town v Bromsgrove Rovers	0-2
18	Kettering Town v St Margaretsbury	2-0
19	Folkestone Invicta v Welling United	1-1
20	Bromley v Thurrock	1-1
21	Histon v Newmarket Town	0-0
22	Hornchurch v Carshalton Athletic	5-0
23	Canvey Island v Dover Athletic	4-3
24	Ford United v Worthing	3-2
25	Cambridge City v Lowestoft Town	3-0
26	Maidstone United (2) v Bishop's Stortford	1-1
27	Hayes v Boreham Wood	1-1
28	East Thurrock United v AFC Sudbury	1-1
29	Leyton v Bedford Town	3-0
30	Grays Athletic v Hendon	3-0
31	Braintree Town v Eastbourne Borough	0-4
32	Crawley Town v Croydon Athletic	6-1
33	Basingstoke Town v Bracknell Town	0-0
34	Gloucester City v Chippenham Town	4-3
35	Thame United v Bath City	3-0
36	Oxford City v Cirencester Town	0-3
37	Havant & Waterlooville v Salisbury City	3-4
38	Newport (IOW) v Harrow Borough	2-2
39	Newport County (2) v Mangotsfield United	3-6
40	Weston-Super-Mare v Chesham United	1-1
41	Lymington & New Milton v Highworth Town	2-0
42	Paulton Rovers v Hampton & Richmond Boro.	2-1
4r	Runcorn FC Halton v Nuneaton Borough	2-2P
7r	Stocksbridge Park Steels v Eastwood Town	3-2
8r	Ossett Albion v Newcastle Town	4-4P
11r	Vauxhall Motors v Bradford Park Avenue	1-3
12r	Whitby Town v Warrington Town	2-1
16r	Lancaster City v Chorley	1-0
19r	Welling United v Folkestone Invicta	2-2P
20r	Thurrock v Bromley	3-0
21r	Newmarket Town v Histon	0-1
26r	Bishop's Stortford v Maidstone United (2)	3-2
27r	Boreham Wood v Hayes	3-1
28r	AFC Sudbury v East Thurrock United	1-1q
33r	Bracknell Town v Basingstoke Town	1-0
38r	Harrow Borough v Newport (IOW)	2-0
40r	Chesham United v Weston-Super-Mare	1-2

Qualifying Round Four

1	Ossett Albion v Stalybridge Celtic	0-1
2	Dunston Federation Brewery v Lancaster City	0-1
3	Ashton United v Grantham Town	1-2
4	Blyth Spartans v Chester City	0-1
5	Bromsgrove Rovers v Whitby Town	2-2
6	Burton Albion v Buxton	6-0
7	Morecambe v Shrewsbury Town	2-4
8	Telford United v Tamworth	3-3
9	Scarborough v Hinckley United	3-1
10	Farsley Celtic v Gainsborough Trinity	1-1
11	Accrington Stanley (2) v Leigh RMI	2-0
12	Northwich Victoria v Halifax Town	1-0
13	Runcorn FC Halton v Bradford Park Avenue	0-1
14	Shildon v Stocksbridge Park Steels	6-0
15	Leyton v Histon	1-2
16	Eastbourne Borough v Stevenage Borough	2-2
17	Bracknell Town v Barnet	0-3
18	Thame United v Farnborough Town	1-2
19	Grays Athletic v Margate	3-3
20	Welling United v Weston-Super-Mare	2-3
21	Boreham Wood v Kettering Town	1-0
22	Forest Green Rovers v Aldershot Town	1-3
23	Thurrock v Dagenham & Redbridge	2-1
24	Harrow Borough v Hereford United	1-6
25	Bishop's Stortford v Gloucester City	2-0
26	Salisbury City v Lymington & New Milton	5-1
27	Cambridge City v Ford United	2-3
28	Mangotsfield United v Canvey Island	1-2
29	Hornchurch v Paulton Rovers	1-0
30	East Thurrock United v Woking	1-1
31	Cirencester Town v Crawley Town	2-4
32	Exeter City v Gravesend & Northfleet	0-0
5r	Whitby Town v Bromsgrove Rovers	2-1
8r	Tamworth v Telford United	2-3
10r	Gainsborough Trinity v Farsley Celtic	3-0
16r	Stevenage Borough v Eastbourne Borough	1-0
19r	Margate v Grays Athletic	3-3q
30r	Woking v East Thurrock United	2-0
32r	Gravesend & Northfleet v Exeter City	3-3P

Round One

	Accrington Stanley (2) v Huddersfield Town	1-0
	Barnet v Stalybridge Celtic	2-2
	Blackpool v Boreham Wood	4-0
	Bournemouth v Bristol Rovers	1-0
	Bradford Park Avenue v Bristol City	2-5
	Brentford v Gainsborough Trinity	7-1
	Bury v Rochdale	1-2
	Cheltenham Town v Hull City	3-1
	Chester City v Gravesend & Northfleet	0-1
	Colchester United v Oxford United	1-0
	Farnborough Town v Weston-Super-Mare	0-1
	Grantham Town v Leyton Orient	1-2
	Grays Athletic v Aldershot Town	1-2
	Grimsby Town v Queen's Park Rangers	1-0
	Hartlepool United v Whitby Town	4-0
	Hornchurch v Darlington	2-0
	Kidderminster Harriers v Northwich Victoria	2-1
	Lancaster City v Cambridge United	1-2
	Lincoln City v Brighton & Hove Albion	3-1
	Macclesfield Town v Boston United	3-0
	Mansfield Town v Bishop's Stortford	6-0
	Northampton Town v Plymouth Argyle	3-2
	Notts County v Shildon	7-2
	Oldham Athletic v Carlisle United	3-0
	Peterborough United v Hereford United	2-0
	Port Vale v Ford United	2-2
	Scarborough v Doncaster Rovers	1-0
	Scunthorpe United v Shrewsbury Town	2-1
	Sheffield Wednesday v Salisbury City	4-0
	Southend United v Canvey Island	1-1
	Stevenage Borough v Stockport County	2-1
	Swansea City v Rushden & Diamonds	3-0
	Telford United v Crawley Town	3-2
	Thurrock v Luton Town	1-1
	Torquay United v Burton Albion	1-2
	Tranmere Rovers v Chesterfield	3-2
	Woking v Histon	3-1
	Wycombe Wanderers v Swindon Town	4-1
	Yeovil Town v Wrexham	4-1
	York City v Barnsley	1-2
r	Canvey Island v Southend United	2-3
r	Ford United v Port Vale	1-2e
r	Luton Town v Thurrock	3-1
r	Stalybridge Celtic v Barnet	0-2

Round Two

	Bournemouth v Accrington Stanley (2)	1-1
	Bristol City v Barnsley	0-0
	Burton Albion v Hartlepool United	0-1
	Cheltenham Town v Leyton Orient	3-1
	Colchester United v Aldershot Town	1-0
	Gravesend & Northfleet v Notts County	1-2
	Hornchurch v Tranmere Rovers	0-1
	Macclesfield Town v Cambridge United	1-1
	Northampton Town v Weston-Super-Mare	4-1
	Oldham Athletic v Blackpool	2-5
	Peterborough United v Grimsby Town	3-2
	Port Vale v Scarborough	0-1
	Rochdale v Luton Town	0-2
	Scunthorpe United v Sheffield Wednesday	2-2
	Southend United v Lincoln City	3-0
	Swansea City v Stevenage Borough	2-1
	Telford United v Brentford	3-0
	Woking v Kidderminster Harriers	0-3
	Wycombe Wanderers v Mansfield Town	1-1
	Yeovil Town v Barnet	5-1
r	Accrington Stanley (2) v Bournemouth	0-0P
r	Barnsley v Bristol City	2-1
r	Cambridge United v Macclesfield Town	2-2q
r	Mansfield Town v Wycombe Wanderers	3-2
r	Sheffield Wednesday v Scunthorpe United	0-0q

Round Three

	Accrington Stanley (2) v Colchester United	0-0
	Aston Villa v Manchester United	1-2
	Barnsley v Scunthorpe United	0-0
	Birmingham City v Blackburn Rovers	4-0
	Bradford City v Luton Town	1-2
	Cardiff City v Sheffield United	0-1
	Coventry City v Peterborough United	2-1
	Crewe Alexandra v Telford United	0-1
	Everton v Norwich City	3-1
	Fulham v Cheltenham Town	2-1
	Gillingham v Charlton Athletic	3-2
	Ipswich Town v Derby County	3-0
	Kidderminster Harriers v Wolverhampton Wan.	1-1
	Leeds United v Arsenal	1-4
	Manchester City v Leicester City	2-2
	Mansfield Town v Burnley	0-2
	Middlesbrough v Notts County	2-0
	Millwall v Walsall	2-1
	Northampton Town v Rotherham United	1-1
	Nottingham Forest v West Bromwich Albion	1-0
	Portsmouth v Blackpool	2-1
	Preston North End v Reading	3-3
	Southampton v Newcastle United	0-3
	Southend United v Scarborough	1-1
	Sunderland v Hartlepool United	1-0
	Swansea City v Macclesfield Town	2-1
	Tottenham Hotspur v Crystal Palace	3-0
	Tranmere Rovers v Bolton Wanderers	1-1
	Watford v Chelsea	2-2
	Wigan Athletic v West Ham United	1-2
	Wimbledon v Stoke City	1-1
	Yeovil Town v Liverpool	0-2
r	Bolton Wanderers v Tranmere Rovers	1-2e
r	Chelsea v Watford	4-0
r	Colchester United v Accrington Stanley (2)	2-1
r	Leicester City v Manchester City	1-3
r	Reading v Preston North End	1-2
r	Rotherham United v Northampton Town	1-2
r	Scarborough v Southend United	1-0
r	Scunthorpe United v Barnsley	2-0
r	Stoke City v Wimbledon	0-1
r	Wolverhampton Wan. v Kidderminster Harriers	2-0

Round Four

	Arsenal v Middlesbrough	4-1
	Birmingham City v Wimbledon	1-0
	Burnley v Gillingham	3-1
	Coventry City v Colchester United	1-1
	Everton v Fulham	1-1
	Ipswich Town v Sunderland	1-2
	Liverpool v Newcastle United	2-1
	Luton Town v Tranmere Rovers	0-1
	Manchester City v Tottenham Hotspur	1-1
	Northampton Town v Manchester United	0-3
	Nottingham Forest v Sheffield United	0-3
	Portsmouth v Scunthorpe United	2-1
	Scarborough v Chelsea	0-1
	Swansea City v Preston North End	2-1
	Telford United v Millwall	0-2
	Wolverhampton Wan. v West Ham United	1-3
r	Colchester United v Coventry City	3-1
r	Fulham v Everton	2-1e
r	Tottenham Hotspur v Manchester City	3-4

Round Five

	Arsenal v Chelsea	2-1
	Fulham v West Ham United	0-0
	Liverpool v Portsmouth	1-1
	Manchester United v Manchester City	4-2
	Millwall v Burnley	1-0
	Sheffield United v Colchester United	1-0
	Sunderland v Birmingham City	1-1
	Tranmere Rovers v Swansea City	2-1
r	Birmingham City v Sunderland	0-2e
r	Portsmouth v Liverpool	1-0
r	West Ham United v Fulham	0-3

Round Six

	Manchester United v Fulham	2-1
	Millwall v Tranmere Rovers	0-0
	Portsmouth v Arsenal	1-5
	Sunderland v Sheffield United	1-0
r	Tranmere Rovers v Millwall	1-2

Semi Finals

	Manchester United v Arsenal	1-0 N
	Millwall v Sunderland	1-0 N

Final

	Manchester United v Millwall	3-0 N

2004/05

Extra Preliminary Round

1	Hebburn Town v Silsden	1-4
2	Maine Road v Durham City	3-2
3	Skelmersdale United v Brodsworth MW	3-1 N
4	Newcastle Blue Star v Liversedge	1-4
5	Winterton Rangers v Goole AFC	1-1
6	Curzon Ashton v Morpeth Town	1-3
7	Norton & Stockton Ancients v Yorkshire Amateur	1-0
8	Tadcaster Albion v Fleetwood Town	2-5
9	Rossington Main v Washington Nissan	1-2
10	Nelson v Chester-le-Street Town	0-1
11	St Helens Town v Newcastle Benfield Saints	4-3
12	Peterlee Newtown v Colne	1-1
13	Parkgate v Kennek Ryhope CA	3-1e
14	Holbeach United v Alvechurch	0-1
15	Barwell v Oldbury United	1-0
16	Cradley Town v Chasetown	0-4
17	Biddulph Victoria v Staveley MW	3-1
18	Causeway United v Leek CSOB	4-3
19	Boldmere St Michaels v Norton United	1-3
20	Coalville Town v Daventry Town	3-0

2004/05

21 Lowestoft Town v AFC Wallingford	8-0
22 Woodbridge Town v Ware	2-0
23 Concord Rangers v Ilford	1-3
24 Norwich United v Harefield United	2-0
25 North Greenford United v Clapton	3-3e
26 Chalfont St Peter v Wroxham	2-10
27 Great Yarmouth Town v Long Melford	1-1
28 Bury Town v Hullbridge Sports	6-0
29 Tiptree United v Ruislip Manor	2-2
30 Witham Town v Dereham Town	0-1
31 Enfield Town v Leverstock Green	0-0
32 Wembley v Edgware Town	0-2
33 Hanwell Town v Hadleigh United	6-1
34 Royston Town v Harpenden Town	3-0
35 Bowers & Pitsea v London Colney	0-0
36 AFC Sudbury v Haringey Borough	5-1
37 Ely City v Brook House	1-2
38 Felixstowe & Walton United v Leiston	1-1
39 Wisbech Town v Sawbridgeworth	0-1
40 Enfield v March Town United	5-3
41 Buckingham Town v Kingsbury Town	4-2
42 Ipswich Wanderers v St Neots Town	6-1
43 Haverhill Rovers v Needham Market	5-0
44 Potters Bar Town v Clacton Town	0-0
45 Newmarket Town v Ford Sports (Daventry)	1-1
46 Cove v Fareham Town	0-2
47 VCD Athletic v Godalming & Guildford	2-0
48 Camberley Town v Thatcham Town	1-0
49 Lordswood v Winchester City	1-4
50 Chessington United v Chichester City United	3-3
51 Walton Casuals v Three Bridges	2-0
52 Hythe Town v Littlehampton Town	1-1
53 Wick v Saltdean United	2-0
54 Broadbridge Heath v Brockenhurst	0-2
55 Selsey v Merstham	1-2
56 Moneyfields v Redhill	4-1
57 Arundel v Whitstable Town	1-3
58 Greenwich Borough v Eastbourne United	6-3 D
59 Whitehawk v AFC Totton	1-1
60 Slade Green v Reading Town	0-0
61 Bishop Sutton v Frome Town	1-1
62 Hamworthy United v Liskeard Athletic	1-0
63 Willand Rovers v St Blazey	1-4
64 Highworth Town v Falmouth Town	2-1
65 Devizes Town v Exmouth Town	1-4
66 Street v Welton Rovers	4-2
67 Bristol Manor Farm v Bridport	2-3
68 Bishop's Cleeve v Minehead	7-0
69 Tuffley Rovers v Barnstaple Town	0-3
70 Portland United v Bridgwater Town	0-3
71 Keynsham Town v Saltash United	0-1
72 Downton v Porthleven	0-1
73 Backwell United v Odd Down	3-2
5r Goole AFC v Winterton Rangers	1-0
12r Colne v Peterlee Newtown	2-0
25r Clapton v North Greenford United	0-1
27r Long Melford v Great Yarmouth Town	2-1e
29r Ruislip Manor v Tiptree United	6-2
31r Leverstock Green v Enfield Town	1-3
35r London Colney v Bowers & Pitsea	7-5e
38r Leiston v Felixstowe & Walton United	4-1
44r Clacton Town v Potters Bar Town	0-1
45r Ford Sports (Daventry) v Newmarket Town	2-1
50r Chichester City United v Chessington United	5-0
52r Littlehampton Town v Hythe Town	3-2
59r AFC Totton v Whitehawk	4-4P
60r Reading Town v Slade Green	2-1
61r Frome Town v Bishop Sutton	1-0e

Preliminary Round

1 Warrington Town v Pontefract Collieries	3-0
2 South Shields (3) v Blackpool Mechanics	3-5
3 Flixton v Parkgate	5-2
4 Willington v Woodley Sports	0-9
5 Maltby Main v Penrith	7-1
6 Abbey Hey v Squires Gate	0-1
7 Holker Old Boys v Hall Road Rangers	2-0 N
8 North Shields v Ashington	0-1
9 Consett v Crook Town	1-1
10 Atherton Collieries v Alsager Town	1-2
11 Jarrow Roofing Boldon CA v Retford United	1-1
12 Prudhoe Town v Sheffield	0-1
13 Chadderton v Norton & Stockton Ancients	2-1
14 Northallerton Town v Billingham Town	1-1
15 Marske United v Colwyn Bay	0-1
16 Harrogate Railway Athletic v Esh Winning	1-1
17 Pickering Town v Bedlington Terriers	1-0
18 Padiham v Billingham Synthonia	1-5
19 Silsden v Hallam	1-1
20 Clitheroe v Tow Law Town	6-1
21 St Helens Town v West Auckland Town	0-3
22 Kendal Town v Eccleshill United	4-1
23 Bacup Borough v Chorley	0-3
24 Cheadle Town v Maine Road	0-3
25 Horden CW v AFC Telford United	1-0
26 Armthorpe Welfare v Thackley	1-1
27 Ossett Albion v Washington	0-0
28 Great Harwood Town v Glasshoughton Welfare	0-2
29 Seaham Red Star v Whickham	3-3
30 Guisborough Town v Brigg Town	1-3
31 Cammell Laird v Goole AFC	2-0
32 Mossley v Selby Town	3-0
33 Thornaby v Easington Colliery	2-1
34 Fleetwood Town v Alnwick Town	6-0
35 Chester-le-Street Town v Colne	0-2
36 Ramsbottom United v Evenwood Town	3-0
37 Darwen v Brandon United	0-0
38 Washington Nissan v Dunston Federation Brewery	1-1
39 Shildon v Garforth Town	2-0
40 Oldham Town v Atherton LR	0-0
41 Trafford v North Ferriby United	4-2
42 Whitley Bay v Salford City	3-1
43 Rossendale United v Liversedge	1-4
44 Winsford United v Morpeth Town	2-1
45 Skelmersdale United v Stocksbridge Park Steels	1-1
46 Shepshed Dynamo v Racing Club Warwick	3-2
47 Congleton Town v Carlton Town	0-1
48 Causeway United v Lincoln Moorlands	1-1
49 Eastwood Town v Willenhall Town	1-2
50 Gedling Town v Coalville Town	0-3
51 Stourbridge v Norton United	1-3
52 Glossop North End v Ludlow Town	2-3
53 Stratford Town v Mickleover Sports	2-1
54 Bedworth United v Quorn	2-0
55 Long Eaton United v Spalding United	0-3
56 Boston Town v Stone Dominoes	1-2
57 Chasetown v Belper Town	2-2
58 Borrowash Victoria v Biddulph Victoria	1-0
59 Arnold Town v Rocester	1-4
60 Kidsgrove Athletic v Newcastle Town	1-4
61 Rushall Olympic v Bourne Town	3-0
62 Blackstones v Barwell	1-2
63 Sutton Coldfield Town v Nantwich Town	1-0
64 Buxton v Stourport Swifts	1-1
65 Sutton Town (2) v Oadby Town	2-1
66 Shirebrook Town v Bromsgrove Rovers	3-1
67 Alvechurch v Ilkeston Town (2)	1-3
68 Gresley Rovers v Studley	1-0
69 Corby Town v Westfields	1-2
70 Deeping Rangers v Glapwell	2-0
71 Cogenhoe United v Woodford United	7-0
72 Soham Town Rangers v Leighton Town	1-0
73 Sawbridgeworth v Haverhill Rovers	0-3
74 Rothwell Town v Berkhamsted Town	2-3
75 Enfield Town v AFC Sudbury	2-1
76 Royston Town v Barkingside	0-5
77 Brackley Town v Stowmarket Town	5-2
78 Fakenham Town v Gorleston	2-3
79 Enfield v Long Buckby	1-0
80 Great Wakering Rovers v Maldon Town	1-1
81 London Colney v St Margaretsbury	2-2
82 East Thurrock United v Halstead Town	3-3
83 Bedford United & Valerio v Potton United	0-3
84 Ford Sports (Daventry) v Southend Manor	1-1
85 Long Melford v Woodbridge Town	1-0
86 Stanway Rovers v Boreham Wood	0-3
87 Desborough Town v North Greenford United	1-4
88 Potters Bar Town v Uxbridge	1-7
89 Flackwell Heath v Hanwell Town	2-2
90 Brook House v Romford	4-0
91 Norwich United v Thame United	0-1
92 Wroxham v Beaconsfield SYCOB	0-1
93 Holmer Green v Newport Pagnell Town	2-1
94 Diss Town v Barking & East Ham United	0-2
95 Burnham Ramblers v Waltham Forest	0-3
96 Harlow Town v Buckingham Town	3-1
97 Harwich & Parkeston v Stansted	3-2
98 Arlesey Town v Godmanchester Rovers	3-0
99 Yaxley v Stotfold	1-2
100 Raunds Town v Hertford Town	1-1
101 Hoddesdon Town v Barton Rovers	1-10 N
102 Ruislip Manor v Henley Town	1-1
103 Lowestoft Town v Northampton Spencer	7-1
104 Leiston v Tilbury	0-2
105 Wingate & Finchley v Fleet Town	4-1
106 Dereham Town v Marlow	0-2
107 Eton Manor v Cornard United	1-3
108 Ilford v Wivenhoe Town	0-1
109 Mildenhall Town v Aveley	1-1
110 Wootton Blue Cross v Broxbourne Borough V&E	1-0
111 Edgware Town v Ipswich Wanderers	1-0
112 Bury Town v Brentwood	2-1
113 Hungerford Town v Dorking (2)	1-2
114 Frimley Green v Raynes Park Vale	1-2
115 Lymington & New Milton v Sittingbourne	1-1
116 Molesey v Westfield	5-0
117 Walton & Hersham v Leatherhead	1-2
118 Hastings United (2) v Croydon	3-1
119 Pagham v Tunbridge Wells	1-2
120 Ramsgate v Lancing	7-0
121 Newport (IOW) v Walton Casuals	0-0
122 Horsham v Chipstead	3-0
123 Hillingdon Borough v Ashford Town (Middlesex)	0-1
124 Moneyfields v Tooting & Mitcham United	0-5
125 Metropolitan Police v Alton Town	4-3
126 Bedfont v Bracknell Town	0-3
127 Herne Bay v Gosport Borough	1-2
128 Oxford City v Abingdon Town	7-0
129 Rye & Iden United v East Preston	0-0
130 Cobham v Hailsham Town	0-3
131 Fisher Athletic (London) v Eastbourne Town	5-0
132 North Leigh v Deal Town	3-1
133 Sandhurst Town v Southwick	4-2
134 Cray Wanderers v Epsom & Ewell	4-0
135 Whyteleafe v Erith & Belvedere	2-4
136 AFC Wimbledon v Ashford Town	3-0
137 Hartley Wintney v Ash United	1-2
138 Croydon Athletic v Farnham Town	5-0
139 Burgess Hill Town v Brockenhurst	1-2
140 Dartford v Horsham YMCA	5-0
141 Wantage Town v Carterton Town	1-2
142 Peacehaven & Telscombe v AFC Totton	1-3
143 Abingdon United v Cowes Sports	2-1
144 Whitstable Town v Wick	6-0
145 Bashley v Camberley Town	2-1
146 Hassocks v Merstham	1-3
147 Sidlesham v Didcot Town	0-5
148 Maidstone United (2) v Chichester City United	3-1
149 Thamesmead Town v Eastbourne United	1-0
150 Chatham Town v Reading Town	1-1
151 Banstead Athletic v Littlehampton Town	3-1
152 Corinthian Casuals v Winchester City	0-3
153 BAT Sports v Egham Town	3-0
154 Ringmer v Andover	3-2
155 Erith Town v Steyning Town	5-3
156 AFC Newbury v East Grinstead Town	3-0
157 Dulwich Hamlet v Burnham	2-1
158 Chessington & Hook United v Bromley	0-1
159 Mile Oak v Fareham Town	1-0
160 VCD Athletic v Chertsey Town	5-1
161 Evesham United v Saltash United	3-1
162 Bournemouth (Ams) v Shepton Mallet	3-2
163 Backwell United v Bridgwater Town	2-1
164 Wimborne Town v Yate Town	1-2
165 Swindon Supermarine v Calne Town	1-0
166 Paulton Rovers v St Blazey	0-1
167 Bitton v Hamworthy United	2-0
168 Exmouth Town v Wootton Bassett Town	3-2
169 Torrington v Barnstaple Town	0-3
170 Dawlish Town v Corsham Town	0-2
171 Bridport v Chard Town	1-1
172 Hallen v Melksham Town	2-0
173 Bodmin Town v Clevedon United	4-0
174 Bemerton Heath Harlequins v Westbury United	3-1
175 Brislington v Bishop's Cleeve	0-1
176 Taunton Town v Frome Town	2-3
177 Christchurch v Clevedon Town	1-2
178 Highworth Town v Elmore	6-0
179 Porthleven v Bideford	1-6
180 Mangotsfield United v Shortwood United	3-2
181 Cinderford Town v Street	1-1
182 Fairford Town v Almondsbury Town	4-0
9r Crook Town v Consett	3-1
11r Retford United v Jarrow Roofing Boldon CA	1-0
14r Billingham Town v Northallerton Town	1-0e
16r Esh Winning v Harrogate Railway Athletic	7-3
19r Hallam v Silsden	1-3
26r Thackley v Armthorpe Welfare	1-4
27r Washington v Ossett Albion	0-1e
29r Whickham v Seaham Red Star	4-0
37r Brandon United v Darwen	4-1e
38r Dunston Federation Brewery v Washington Nissan	4-1
40r Atherton LR v Oldham Town	1-0e
45r Stocksbridge Park Steels v Skelmersdale United	0-2
48r Lincoln Moorlands v Causeway United	0-3
57r Belper Town v Chasetown	2-0
64r Stourport Swifts v Buxton	1-1P
80r Maldon Town v Great Wakering Rovers	3-1
81r St Margaretsbury v London Colney	2-1
82r Halstead Town v East Thurrock United	1-0
84r Southend Manor v Ford Sports (Daventry)	3-1
89r Hanwell Town v Flackwell Heath	2-3
100r Hertford Town v Raunds Town	1-0
102r Henley Town v Ruislip Manor	0-1
109r Aveley v Mildenhall Town	3-0
115r Sittingbourne v Lymington & New Milton	1-2
121r Walton Casuals v Newport (IOW)	1-1P
129r East Preston v Rye & Iden United	3-1
150r Reading Town v Chatham Town	2-3
171r Chard Town v Bridport	0-1
181r Street v Cinderford Town	2-1e

Qualifying Round One

1 Frickley Athletic v Chadderton	4-1
2 Billingham Synthonia v Whitby Town	1-3
3 Clitheroe v Wakefield & Emley	2-2
4 Billingham Town v Ossett Town	1-0
5 Marine v Farsley Celtic	1-1
6 Bridlington Town (2) v Cammell Laird	1-5
7 Flixton v Dunston Federation Brewery	1-6
8 Hyde United v Maine Road	3-0
9 West Auckland Town v Ashington	0-2
10 Thornaby v Esh Winning	1-2
11 Colne v Sheffield	2-1
12 Guiseley v Chorley	0-0
13 Witton Albion v Winsford United	0-1
14 Burscough v Retford United	1-0
15 Alsager Town v Radcliffe Borough	0-1
16 Atherton LR v Whickham	3-0
17 Gateshead (2) v Pickering Town	2-0
18 Ramsbottom United v Colwyn Bay	2-1
19 Brigg Town v Whitley Bay	3-1
20 Brandon United v Liversedge	1-4
21 Bishop Auckland v Workington	1-2
22 Kendal Town v Prescot Cables	1-1
23 Crook Town v Glasshoughton Welfare	1-3
24 Spennymoor United v Fleetwood Town	1-1
25 Horden CW v Warrington Town	1-1
26 Mossley v Ossett Albion	3-2
27 Armthorpe Welfare v Maltby Main	1-2
28 Bamber Bridge v Blackpool Mechanics	6-0
29 Shildon v Woodley Sports	1-1
30 Blyth Spartans v Skelmersdale United	0-2

2004/05

31 Holker Old Boys v Silsden 2-2
32 Trafford v Squires Gate 1-2
33 Westfields v Carlton Town 1-2
34 Ludlow Town v Newcastle Town 5-1
35 Matlock Town v Shirebrook Town 2-1
36 Grantham Town v Shepshed Dynamo 2-4
37 Rugby United v Hednesford Town 2-2
38 Ilkeston Town (2) v Gresley Rovers 0-3
39 Spalding United v Causeway United 4-0
40 Solihull Borough v Leek Town 0-1
41 Sutton Town (2) v Stone Dominoes 1-1
42 Stamford v Bedworth United 1-0
43 Borrowash Victoria v Halesowen Town 0-5
44 Norton United v Lincoln United 0-1
45 Deeping Rangers v Coalville Town 2-2
46 Sutton Coldfield Town v Stratford Town 2-1 D
47 Willenhall Town v Barwell 1-0
48 Belper Town v Rocester 2-0
49 Stourport Swifts v Rushall Olympic 1-2
50 Harrow Borough v Potton United 2-0
51 Uxbridge v Staines Town 4-3
52 Brook House v Northwood 1-1
53 Southend Manor v Billericay Town 0-3
54 Histon v Hampton & Richmond Boro. 2-0
55 Cheshunt v Barton Rovers 2-2
56 Haverhill Rovers v Wivenhoe Town 0-1
57 Heybridge Swifts v Barking & East Ham United 1-0
58 Thame United v Gorleston 3-3
59 Lowestoft Town v Boreham Wood 0-1
60 Wingate & Finchley v Halstead Town 2-3
61 Hendon v Holmer Green 1-0
62 Wealdstone v Banbury United 2-1
63 Dunstable Town v St Margaretsbury 5-0
64 Maldon Town v King's Lynn 2-3
65 Wootton Blue Cross v Stotfold 1-2
66 Hemel Hempstead Town v North Greenford United 5-1
67 Marlow v Long Melford 1-2
68 Hertford Town v Bury Town 0-0
69 Cornard United v Aylesbury United 0-6
70 Chelmsford City v Yeading 0-1
71 Beaconsfield SYCOB v Hitchin Town 5-3
72 Enfield v Arlesey Town 1-4
73 Leyton v Tilbury 1-0
74 Waltham Forest v Cogenhoe United 2-1
75 Ruislip Manor v Harwich & Parkeston 1-1
76 Harlow Town v Enfield Town 0-1
77 Braintree Town v Soham Town Rangers 2-0
78 Aveley v Berkhamsted Town 2-1
79 Chesham United v Bedford Town 1-1
80 Brackley Town v Flackwell Heath 2-2
81 Edgware Town v Barkingside 4-1
82 Gosport Borough v Eastleigh 1-2
83 Didcot Town v Tooting & Mitcham United 2-2
84 Whitstable Town v Hailsham Town 4-0
85 Leatherhead v Cray Wanderers 1-0
86 East Preston v Merstham 1-0
87 Ash United v Maidstone United (2) 2-2
88 Dartford v Dorking (2) 0-1
89 Banstead Athletic v Oxford City 2-3
90 VCD Athletic v Brockenhurst 0-0
91 Chatham Town v Windsor & Eton 1-1
92 Thamesmead Town v Worthing 2-1
93 Ringmer v Erith Town 1-1
94 Tonbridge Angels v Winchester City 2-1
95 Bracknell Town v Sandhurst Town 0-2
96 AFC Newbury v BAT Sports 4-0
97 Croydon Athletic v Slough Town 0-1
98 Metropolitan Police v Dulwich Hamlet 3-4
99 AFC Totton v Tunbridge Wells 2-1
100 Ashford Town (Middlesex) v Bashley 3-1
101 Horsham v Abingdon United 4-3
102 Fisher Athletic (London) v Bromley 2-2
103 Dover Athletic v AFC Wimbledon 0-1
104 Raynes Park Vale v Folkestone Invicta 0-6
105 Kingstonian v Ramsgate 0-2
106 Carterton Town v Erith & Belvedere 1-1
107 Molesey v Lymington & New Milton 0-2
108 Hastings United (2) v Mile Oak 2-0
109 North Leigh v Walton Casuals 1-0
110 Chippenham Town v Bitton 4-0
111 Hallen v Bemerton Heath Harlequins 2-0
112 Bridport v Bath City 1-4
113 Fairford Town v Bideford 0-0
114 Highworth Town v Bishop's Cleeve 3-5
115 Street v Gloucester City 3-2
116 Clevedon Town v Merthyr Tydfil 1-2
117 St Blazey v Evesham United 1-2
118 Swindon Supermarine v Corsham Town 0-1
119 Exmouth Town v Salisbury City 1-2
120 Bodmin Town v Cirencester Town 0-3
121 Frome Town v Backwell United 2-2
122 Tiverton Town v Mangotsfield United 3-2
123 Barnstaple Town v Bournemouth (Ams) 3-1
124 Yate Town v Team Bath 0-1
3r Wakefield & Emley v Clitheroe 0-0q
5r Farsley Celtic v Marine 4-0
12r Chorley v Guiseley 2-1
22r Prescot Cables v Kendal Town 5-2
24r Fleetwood Town v Spennymoor United 3-2e
25r Warrington Town v Horden CW 1-2
29r Woodley Sports v Shildon 0-2
31r Silsden v Holker Old Boys 1-2
37r Hednesford Town v Rugby United 2-1
41r Stone Dominoes v Sutton Town (2) 3-0
45r Coalville Town v Deeping Rangers 3-1

52r Northwood v Brook House 3-0
55r Barton Rovers v Cheshunt 3-4e
58r Gorleston v Thame United 3-5
68r Bury Town v Hertford Town 1-1q
75r Harwich & Parkeston v Ruislip Manor 2-0
79r Bedford Town v Chesham United 4-1e
80r Flackwell Heath v Brackley Town 2-0
83r Tooting & Mitcham United v Didcot Town 2-0
87r Maidstone United (2) v Ash United 2-0
90r Brockenhurst v VCD Athletic 1-0
91r Windsor & Eton v Chatham Town 3-0
93r Erith Town v Ringmer 3-0
102r Bromley v Fisher Athletic (London) 1-0
106r Erith & Belvedere v Carterton Town 4-3
113r Bideford v Fairford Town 2-0
121r Backwell United v Frome Town 1-3e

Qualifying Round Two

1 Holker Old Boys v Harrogate Town 0-3
2 Horden CW v Frickley Athletic 3-0
3 Bradford Park Avenue v Squires Gate 2-1
4 Maltby Main v Ashton United 1-3
5 Whitby Town v Mossley 0-2
6 Glasshoughton Welfare v Clitheroe 2-1
7 Barrow v Stalybridge Celtic 3-3
8 Gateshead (2) v Chorley 4-1
9 Brigg Town v Colne 1-0
10 Lancaster City v Esh Winning 3-2
11 Altrincham v Farsley Celtic 4-1
12 Ramsbottom United v Southport 0-2
13 Fleetwood Town v Runcorn FC Halton 1-1
14 Atherton LR v Hyde United 2-3
15 Dunston Federation Brewery v Cammell Laird 2-2
16 Billingham Town v Vauxhall Motors 1-3
17 Liversedge v Prescot Cables 3-0
18 Skelmersdale United v Burscough 2-3
19 Bamber Bridge v Workington 1-5
20 Ashington v Droylsden 1-3
21 Radcliffe Borough v Shildon 3-3
22 Willenhall Town v Shepshed Dynamo 0-0
23 Matlock Town v Alfreton Town 0-5
24 Spalding United v Belper Town 5-4
25 Gainsborough Trinity v Halesowen Town 2-3
26 Redditch United v Histon 2-3
27 King's Lynn v Ludlow Town 1-0
28 Leek Town v Nuneaton Borough 1-1
29 Worcester City v Cambridge City 1-3
30 Coalville Town v Rushall Olympic 2-1
31 Gresley Rovers v Hucknall Town 2-2
32 Hinckley United v Stamford 3-1
33 Moor Green v Carlton Town 5-0
34 Stafford Rangers v Kettering Town 2-2
35 Worksop Town v Stone Dominoes 3-0
36 Stratford Town v Hednesford Town 1-0
37 Lincoln United v Winsford United 5-0
38 Bishop's Stortford v Hayes 3-4
39 Lewes v Brockenhurst 1-2
40 Slough Town v Welling United 4-1
41 Bromley v Thamesmead Town 3-0
42 Oxford City v Leyton 0-1
43 Dorking (2) v Billericay Town 0-1
44 Whitstable Town v Maidenhead United 0-0
45 Dunstable Town v AFC Wimbledon 0-3
46 Ramsgate v Dulwich Hamlet 3-6
47 Halstead Town v Thurrock 0-3
48 Cheshunt v Northwood 3-0
49 Edgware Town v North Leigh 0-1
50 Wealdstone v Grays Athletic 3-1
51 Eastbourne Borough v Sutton United 3-4
52 Tooting & Mitcham United v Hemel Hempstead Town 2-2
53 Harwich & Parkeston v Hornchurch 0-3
54 Margate v Waltham Forest 2-1
55 Carshalton Athletic v Hastings United (2) 1-3
56 Erith & Belvedere v Flackwell Heath 0-1
57 Harrow Borough v Folkestone Invicta 2-2
58 Yeading v Long Melford 2-0
59 Tonbridge Angels v Braintree Town 1-1
60 Sandhurst Town v Leatherhead 0-2
61 Erith Town v Horsham 2-3
62 Heybridge Swifts v St Albans City 0-2 d
63 Maidstone United (2) v Redbridge 2-1
64 Boreham Wood v Aveley 2-1
65 Beaconsfield SYCOB v Windsor & Eton 1-2
66 Arlesey Town v Wivenhoe Town 2-3
67 Ashford Town (Middlesex) v Hertford Town 3-1
68 Enfield Town v Thame United 0-1
69 East Preston v Uxbridge 1-0
70 Bedford Town v Hendon 1-3
71 Stotfold v Aylesbury United 1-1
72 Dorchester Town v Weymouth 0-1
73 Corsham Town v Newport County (2) 0-2
74 Basingstoke Town v AFC Newbury 2-4
75 Eastleigh v Barnstaple Town 5-0
76 Street v Merthyr Tydfil 1-2
77 Bishop's Cleeve v AFC Totton 4-1
78 Salisbury City v Frome Town 1-1
79 Havant & Waterlooville v Bath City 0-2
80 Team Bath v Hallen 0-0
81 Tiverton Town v Bideford 0-0
82 Bognor Regis Town v Cirencester Town 4-3
83 Evesham United v Weston-Super-Mare 1-3
84 Lymington & New Milton v Chippenham Town 3-2
7r Stalybridge Celtic v Barrow 3-2e
13r Runcorn FC Halton v Fleetwood Town 2-1 N

15r Cammell Laird v Dunston Federation Brewery 2-0
21r Shildon v Radcliffe Borough 0-2
22r Shepshed Dynamo v Willenhall Town 3-3q
28r Nuneaton Borough v Leek Town 1-2
31r Hucknall Town v Gresley Rovers 3-1
34r Kettering Town v Stafford Rangers 0-1
44r Maidenhead United v Whitstable Town 1-1P
52r Hemel Hempstead Town v Tooting & Mitcham United 0-3
57r Folkestone Invicta v Harrow Borough 1-1q
59r Braintree Town v Tonbridge Angels 2-0
71r Aylesbury United v Stotfold 4-2
78r Frome Town v Salisbury City 0-3
80r Hallen v Team Bath 0-0P
81r Bideford v Tiverton Town 1-3

Qualifying Round Three

1 Hinckley United v Mossley 6-1
2 Ashton United v Burscough 0-3
3 Halesowen Town v Glasshoughton Welfare 4-1
4 Leek Town v Stalybridge Celtic 2-1
5 Altrincham v Hucknall Town 3-3
6 Stratford Town v Southport 0-3
7 Liversedge v Harrogate Town 3-2
8 Horden CW v Gateshead (2) 2-3
9 Vauxhall Motors v Workington 1-0
10 Runcorn FC Halton v Stafford Rangers 0-1
11 Cammell Laird v Alfreton Town 2-3
12 Worksop Town v Droylsden 3-2
13 Lancaster City v King's Lynn 1-0
14 Lincoln United v Hyde United 1-2
15 Radcliffe Borough v Moor Green 1-0
16 Willenhall Town v Coalville Town 1-2
17 Bradford Park Avenue v Brigg Town 1-2
18 Leyton v Hendon 1-1
19 Hayes v Wivenhoe Town 2-0
20 Heybridge Swifts v Yeading 2-3
21 Wealdstone v Boreham Wood 5-1
22 Sutton United v Bromley 2-2
23 Maidenhead United v Windsor & Eton 2-1
24 Hornchurch v Dulwich Hamlet 9-0
25 Tooting & Mitcham United v Cambridge City 2-4
26 Slough Town v Cheshunt 4-0
27 Histon v Horsham 5-0
28 Harrow Borough v Flackwell Heath 0-1
29 AFC Wimbledon v Thurrock 0-2
30 Leatherhead v Maidstone United (2) 2-1
31 Braintree Town v Margate 3-1
32 Aylesbury United v Ashford Town (Middlesex) 0-1
33 East Preston v Billericay Town 0-2
34 Spalding United v Hastings United (2) 1-0
35 Brockenhurst v Bath City 0-3
36 Tiverton Town v Eastleigh 3-3
37 Bognor Regis Town v AFC Newbury 2-0
38 Hallen v Bishop's Cleeve 3-2
39 Merthyr Tydfil v Lymington & New Milton 0-1
40 North Leigh v Newport County (2) 0-0
41 Weston-Super-Mare v Salisbury City 1-3
42 Weymouth v Thame United 1-1
5r Hucknall Town v Altrincham 1-0
18r Hendon v Leyton 3-1e
22r Bromley v Sutton United 2-1
36r Eastleigh v Tiverton Town 0-1e
40r Newport County (2) v North Leigh 6-2
42r Thame United v Weymouth 2-1

Qualifying Round Four

1 Southport v Hyde United 3-1
2 Northwich Victoria v Vauxhall Motors 1-2
3 Hinckley United v Burton Albion 0-0
4 Hereford United v Radcliffe Borough 2-1
5 Brigg Town v Halesowen Town 1-4
6 Carlisle United v York City 3-1
7 Halifax Town v Leek Town 2-2
8 Tamworth v Burscough 2-1
9 Stafford Rangers v Gateshead (2) 2-1
10 Morecambe v Hucknall Town 5-1
11 Worksop Town v Alfreton Town 1-1
12 Accrington Stanley (2) v Leigh RMI 0-2
13 Lancaster City v Scarborough 1-1
14 Liversedge v Coalville Town 0-0
15 Billericay Town v Flackwell Heath 3-0
16 Barnet v Farnborough Town 2-1
17 Thame United v Forest Green Rovers 0-5
18 Canvey Island v Hallen 4-1
19 Lymington & New Milton v Woking 1-1
20 Dagenham & Redbridge v Crawley Town 2-1
21 Hornchurch v Gravesend & Northfleet 3-2
22 Exeter City v Braintree Town 2-0
23 Slough Town v Salisbury City 3-2
24 Bath City v Leatherhead 1-0
25 Aldershot Town v Maidenhead United 2-1
26 Hayes v Ashford Town (Middlesex) 4-0
27 Thurrock v Spalding United 6-0
28 Stevenage Borough v Hendon 5-0
29 Tiverton Town v Newport County (2) 4-1
30 Wealdstone v Histon 0-2
31 Bromley v Cambridge City 0-3
32 Bognor Regis Town v Yeading 0-2
3r Burton Albion v Hinckley United 1-1q
7r Leek Town v Halifax Town 0-1e
11r Alfreton Town v Worksop Town 2-1e
13r Scarborough v Lancaster City 0-1
14r Coalville Town v Liversedge 2-0

2004/05 to 2005/06

19r	Woking v Lymington & New Milton	4-2

Round One

	Aldershot Town v Canvey Island	4-0
	Alfreton Town v Macclesfield Town	1-1
	Barnet v Bath City	1-2
	Billericay Town v Stevenage Borough	0-1
	Blackpool v Tamworth	3-0
	Boston United v Hornchurch	5-2
	Bradford City v Rushden & Diamonds	0-1
	Bristol City v Brentford	1-1
	Bristol Rovers v Carlisle United	1-1
	Bury v Vauxhall Motors	5-2
	Cambridge City v Leigh RMI	2-1
	Cheltenham Town v Swansea City	1-3
	Darlington v Yeovil Town	3-3
	Exeter City v Grimsby Town	1-0
	Forest Green Rovers v Bournemouth	1-1
	Halifax Town v Cambridge United	3-1
	Hartlepool United v Lincoln City	3-0
	Hayes v Wrexham	0-4
	Hinckley United v Torquay United	2-0
	Histon v Shrewsbury Town	2-0
	Hull City v Morecambe	3-2
	Leyton Orient v Dagenham & Redbridge	3-1
	Mansfield Town v Colchester United	1-1
	Milton Keynes Dons v Lancaster City	1-0
	Northampton Town v Barnsley	1-0
	Notts County v Woking	2-0
	Peterborough United v Tranmere Rovers	2-1
	Port Vale v Kidderminster Harriers	3-1
	Rochdale v Oxford United	2-1
	Scunthorpe United v Chesterfield	2-0
	Slough Town v Walsall	2-1
	Southend United v Luton Town	0-3
	Southport v Hereford United	1-3
	Stafford Rangers v Chester City	0-2
	Stockport County v Huddersfield Town	3-1
	Swindon Town v Sheffield Wednesday	4-1
	Thurrock v Oldham Athletic	0-1
	Tiverton Town v Doncaster Rovers	1-3
	Wycombe Wanderers v Coalville Town	1-0
	Yeading v Halesowen Town	2-1
r	Bournemouth v Forest Green Rovers	3-1
r	Brentford v Bristol City	1-1P
r	Carlisle United v Bristol Rovers	1-0e
r	Colchester United v Mansfield Town	4-1
r	Macclesfield Town v Alfreton Town	2-0
r	Yeovil Town v Darlington	1-0

Round Two

	Blackpool v Port Vale	1-0
	Bournemouth v Carlisle United	2-1
	Cambridge City v Milton Keynes Dons	0-1
	Exeter City v Doncaster Rovers	2-1
	Halifax Town v Chester City	1-3
	Hartlepool United v Aldershot Town	5-1
	Hereford United v Boston United	2-3
	Hinckley United v Brentford	0-0
	Histon v Yeovil Town	1-3
	Hull City v Macclesfield Town	4-0
	Northampton Town v Bury	1-0
	Oldham Athletic v Leyton Orient	4-0
	Peterborough United v Bath City	2-0
	Rushden & Diamonds v Colchester United	2-5
	Scunthorpe United v Wrexham	2-0
	Slough Town v Yeading	1-3
	Stevenage Borough v Rochdale	0-2
	Stockport County v Swansea City	0-0
	Swindon Town v Notts County	1-1
	Wycombe Wanderers v Luton Town	0-3
r	Brentford v Hinckley United	2-1
r	Notts County v Swindon Town	2-0
r	Swansea City v Stockport County	2-1

Round Three

	Arsenal v Stoke City	2-1
	Birmingham City v Leeds United	3-0
	Bournemouth v Chester City	2-1
	Burnley v Liverpool	1-0
	Cardiff City v Blackburn Rovers	1-1
	Charlton Athletic v Rochdale	4-1
	Chelsea v Scunthorpe United	3-1
	Coventry City v Crewe Alexandra	3-0
	Derby County v Wigan Athletic	2-1
	Hartlepool United v Boston United	0-0
	Hull City v Colchester United	0-2
	Ipswich Town v Bolton Wanderers	1-3
	Leicester City v Blackpool	2-2
	Luton Town v Brentford	0-2
	Manchester United v Exeter City	0-0
	Milton Keynes Dons v Peterborough United	0-2
	Northampton Town v Southampton	1-3
	Notts County v Middlesbrough	1-2
	Oldham Athletic v Manchester City	1-0
	Plymouth Argyle v Everton	1-3
	Portsmouth v Gillingham	1-0
	Preston North End v West Bromwich Albion	0-2
	Queen's Park Rangers v Nottingham Forest	0-3
	Reading v Swansea City	1-1
	Rotherham United v Yeovil Town	0-3
	Sheffield United v Aston Villa	3-1
	Sunderland v Crystal Palace	2-1
	Tottenham Hotspur v Brighton & Hove Albion	2-1
	Watford v Fulham	1-1
	West Ham United v Norwich City	1-0
	Wolverhampton Wan. v Millwall	2-0
	Yeading v Newcastle United	0-2 N
r	Blackburn Rovers v Cardiff City	3-2
r	Blackpool v Leicester City	0-1
r	Boston United v Hartlepool United	0-1
r	Exeter City v Manchester United	0-2
r	Fulham v Watford	2-0
r	Swansea City v Reading	0-1e

Round Four

	Arsenal v Wolverhampton Wan.	2-0
	Blackburn Rovers v Colchester United	3-0
	Brentford v Hartlepool United	0-0
	Burnley v Bournemouth	2-0
	Charlton Athletic v Yeovil Town	3-2
	Chelsea v Birmingham City	2-0
	Derby County v Fulham	1-1
	Everton v Sunderland	3-0
	Manchester United v Middlesbrough	3-0
	Newcastle United v Coventry City	3-1
	Nottingham Forest v Peterborough United	1-0
	Oldham Athletic v Bolton Wanderers	0-1
	Reading v Leicester City	1-2
	Southampton v Portsmouth	2-1
	West Bromwich Albion v Tottenham Hotspur	1-1
	West Ham United v Sheffield United	1-1
r	Fulham v Derby County	4-2e
r	Hartlepool United v Brentford	0-1
r	Sheffield United v West Ham United	1-1P
r	Tottenham Hotspur v West Bromwich Albion	3-1

Round Five

	Arsenal v Sheffield United	1-1
	Bolton Wanderers v Fulham	1-0
	Burnley v Blackburn Rovers	0-0
	Charlton Athletic v Leicester City	1-2
	Everton v Manchester United	0-2
	Newcastle United v Chelsea	1-0
	Southampton v Brentford	2-2
	Tottenham Hotspur v Nottingham Forest	1-1
r	Blackburn Rovers v Burnley	2-1
r	Brentford v Southampton	1-3
r	Nottingham Forest v Tottenham Hotspur	0-3
r	Sheffield United v Arsenal	0-0q

Round Six

	Blackburn Rovers v Leicester City	1-0
	Bolton Wanderers v Arsenal	0-1
	Newcastle United v Tottenham Hotspur	1-0
	Southampton v Manchester United	0-4

Semi Finals

	Arsenal v Blackburn Rovers	3-0 N
	Manchester United v Newcastle United	4-1 N

Final

	Arsenal v Manchester United	0-0PN

Arsenal won 5-4 on penalties a.e.t.

2005/06

Extra Preliminary Round

1	Newcastle Benfield Bay Plastics v Bedlington Terrie	2-4
2	Bacup Borough v Pickering Town	0-5
3	Jarrow Roofing Boldon CA v Sheffield	0-4
4	Blackpool Mechanics v Newcastle Blue Star	1-2
5	Nelson v Retford United	2-4
6	Esh Winning v Ashington	4-4
7	Prudhoe Town v Horden CW	1-3
8	Skelmersdale United v Liversedge	1-0
9	Curzon Ashton v Darwen	1-0
10	Oldham Town v Morpeth Town	1-0
11	Guisborough Town v Great Harwood Town	1-1
12	Cheadle Town v Abbey Hey	3-2
13	Brandon United v Billingham Synthonia	0-5
14	Tow Law Town v Squires Gate	2-0
15	Formby v Consett	1-1
16	Winsford United v Alsager Town	1-1
17	Flixton v Hebburn Town	1-2
18	Rossington Main v Garforth Town	1-1
19	Cammell Laird v West Allotment Celtic	4-1
20	West Auckland Town v Shildon	2-1
21	Winterton Rangers v North Shields	1-0
22	Studley v Oadby Town	1-3
23	Sutton Town (2) v Loughborough Dynamo	5-1
24	Stourbridge v Glossop North End	3-0 N
25	Borrowash Victoria v Ford Sports (Daventry)	1-1
26	Long Eaton United v Quorn	2-1
27	Congleton Town v Romulus	2-0
28	Norton United v Alvechurch	1-0
29	Shirebrook Town v Teversal	2-3
30	Oldbury United v Racing Club Warwick	2-1
31	Witham Town v Hadleigh United	1-0
32	Hullbridge Sports v Wisbech Town	2-5
33	Chalfont St Peter v Buckingham Town	1-0
34	Brook House v Leiston	1-1
35	Wembley v St Neots Town	0-2
36	Aylesbury Vale v Kirkley (2)	2-2
37	Ware v Sporting Bengal United	2-0
38	Concord Rangers v Kingsbury Town	0-1
39	Harpenden Town v Sawbridgeworth	2-1
40	Soham Town Rangers v Yaxley	2-1
41	Stanway Rovers v Norwich United	4-1
42	Fakenham Town v Long Buckby	2-0
43	Gorleston v North Greenford United	2-4
44	Haringey Borough v Felixstowe & Walton United	0-3
45	Bowers & Pitsea v Stotfold	2-2
46	London APSA v Halstead Town	0-2
47	Broxbourne Borough V&E v Holmer Green	1-4
48	Eton Manor v Leverstock Green	0-1
49	St Margaretsbury v St Ives Town	2-1
50	Wootton Blue Cross v Desborough Town	2-0
51	Romford v Waltham Abbey	1-3
52	Biggleswade United v Haverhill Rovers	6-0
53	Harefield United v Langford	2-3
54	Southend Manor v Woodford United	0-1
55	Woodbridge Town v Lowestoft Town	3-3
56	Saffron Walden Town v Flackwell Heath	1-1
57	Erith Town v Hassocks	0-3
58	Thamesmead Town v Abingdon United	2-4
59	Saltdean United v Wantage Town	0-0
60	AFC Totton v Milton United (Oxon)	5-0
61	Eastbourne United v Ash United	1-2
62	Hythe Town v Raynes Park Vale	4-1
63	Moneyfields v Abingdon Town	6-1
64	Fareham Town v Selsey	0-0
65	Gosport Borough v Sandhurst Town	6-1
66	East Grinstead Town v VCD Athletic	0-7
67	AFC Newbury v Farnham Town	2-2
68	Erith & Belvedere v Hamble ASSC	4-2
69	Lancing v Whitehawk	1-2
70	Westfield v Godalming Town	1-2
71	Chichester City United v East Preston	1-2
72	Sidley United v Pagham	3-1
73	Sevenoaks Town v Chertsey Town	4-2
74	Andover v Didcot Town	4-4
75	Hungerford Town v North Leigh	0-4
76	Horsham YMCA v Hailsham Town	1-0
77	Three Bridges v Shoreham	2-0
78	Westbury United v Newquay	2-1
79	Willand Rovers v Hamworthy United	0-1
80	Tuffley Rovers v Elmore	0-0
81	Bishop's Cleeve v Corsham Town	1-0
82	Hallen v Porthleven	3-0
83	Calne Town v Shortwood United	0-2
84	Minehead v Almondsbury Town	1-2
85	Slimbridge v Wimborne Town	0-1
86	Odd Down v Portland United	2-0
6r	Ashington v Esh Winning	1-0
11r	Great Harwood Town v Guisborough Town	3-3P
15r	Consett v Formby	5-1
16r	Alsager Town v Winsford United	0-1
18r	Garforth Town v Rossington Main	3-0
25r	Ford Sports (Daventry) v Borrowash Victoria	1-2
34r	Leiston v Brook House	1-3
36r	Kirkley (2) v Aylesbury Vale	0-3
45r	Stotfold v Bowers & Pitsea	3-3P
55r	Lowestoft Town v Woodbridge Town	5-0
56r	Flackwell Heath v Saffron Walden Town	3-1
59r	Wantage Town v Saltdean United	0-2
64r	Selsey v Fareham Town	3-2
67r	Farnham Town v AFC Newbury	2-3
74r	Didcot Town v Andover	2-0
80r	Elmore v Tuffley Rovers	1-0

Preliminary Round

1	Bridlington Town (2) v Whitley Bay	2-2
2	Tow Law Town v Padiham	1-3
3	Colne v Chadderton	1-2
4	Warrington Town v Penrith	2-2
5	Ramsbottom United v Marske United	3-1
6	Thornaby v Peterlee Newtown	3-0
7	Hebburn Town v Winterton Rangers	1-1
8	Cheadle Town v Bamber Bridge	2-1
9	Pontefract Collieries v Bishop Auckland	2-3
10	Eccleshill United v Chester-le-Street Town	1-2
11	Selby Town v Billingham Town	1-3
12	Skelmersdale United v Colwyn Bay	2-0
13	Crook Town v St Helens Town	0-3
14	Curzon Ashton v Garforth Town	1-0
15	Rossendale United v Sunderland Nissan	1-1
16	Norton & Stockton Ancients v Great Harwood Town	0-4
17	Spennymoor Town v Consett	0-2
18	Durham City v Brodsworth MW	5-0
19	Seaham Red Star v Atherton Collieries	2-0
20	Cammell Laird v Alnwick Town	6-0
21	Brigg Town v Holker Old Boys	4-0
22	Retford United v Parkgate	4-3
23	Horden CW v Kendal Town	1-2
24	Tadcaster Albion v Chorley	2-2
25	Oldham Town v Hall Road Rangers	2-0
26	Pickering Town v Ashington	2-2
27	Washington v Stocksbridge Park Steels	0-0
28	Thackley v South Shields (3)	2-0
29	Newcastle Blue Star v Hallam	2-0 N
30	Sheffield v Mossley	2-2
31	Yorkshire Amateur v Bedlington Terriers	2-1

2005/06

32	Glasshoughton Welfare v Woodley Sports	0-2
33	Maine Road v Armthorpe Welfare	0-2
34	Billingham Synthonia v Fleetwood Town	2-0
35	Ossett Albion v Dunston Federation Brewery	0-3
36	Atherton LR v Goole AFC	1-1
37	Whickham v West Auckland Town	1-5
38	Harrogate Railway Athletic v Clitheroe	1-2
39	New Mills v Salford City	0-2
40	Trafford v Silsden	3-1
41	Northallerton Town v Winsford United	4-0
42	Willenhall Town v Blackstones	1-0
43	Shepshed Dynamo v Carlton Town	4-1
44	Newcastle Town v Buxton	1-1
45	Chasetown v Causeway United	2-0
46	Congleton Town v Corby Town	1-2
47	Solihull Borough v Eccleshall	2-0
48	Westfields v Sutton Coldfield Town	3-0
49	Rushall Olympic v Gedling Town	0-2
50	Bromsgrove Rovers v Bourne Town	4-1
51	Glapwell v Barwell	3-1
52	Spalding United v Staveley MW	0-1
53	Nantwich Town v Gresley Rovers	3-1
54	Long Eaton United v Boston Town	4-2
55	Coalville Town v Borrowash Victoria	3-0
56	Deeping Rangers v Norton United	0-0
57	Stourport Swifts v Stratford Town	1-2
58	Oldbury United v Stone Dominoes	4-0
59	Bedworth United v Rocester	3-1
60	Oadby Town v Stamford	3-3
61	Malvern Town v Mickleover Sports	4-3
62	Cradley Town v Biddulph Victoria	2-1
63	Holbeach United v Boldmere St Michaels	0-2
64	Teversal v Pegasus Juniors	1-1
65	Leamington v Sutton Town (2)	0-0
66	Lincoln Moorlands v Eastwood Town	0-0
67	Belper Town v Leek CSOB	1-0
68	South Normanton Athletic v Arnold Town	1-0
69	Stourbridge v Kidsgrove Athletic	2-2
70	Ilford v Brackley Town	0-2
71	Long Melford v AFC Sudbury	0-1
72	Wootton Blue Cross v Barton Rovers	1-1
73	Ware v Northampton Spencer	2-4
74	AFC Hornchurch v Chalfont St Peter	0-0
75	Barkingside v Leverstock Green	2-2e
76	Harlow Town v Newport Pagnell Town	4-2
77	Uxbridge v Great Wakering Rovers	2-3
78	Tiptree United v Potton United	2-3
79	Bury Town v Ely City	1-1
80	Needham Market v Diss Town	2-5
81	Marlow v Arlesey Town	2-3
82	Welwyn Garden City v Aylesbury Vale	2-0
83	St Neots Town v Hemel Hempstead Town	1-4
84	Harwich & Parkeston v Holmer Green	2-2
85	Aveley v Kingsbury Town	5-1
86	Brentwood Town v Thame United	1-0
87	Fakenham Town v Waltham Forest	1-4
88	Berkhamsted Town v Newmarket Town	2-0
89	Mildenhall Town v Potters Bar Town	3-1
90	Stotfold v Clapton	1-2
91	Barking & East Ham United v St Margaretsbury	1-1
92	Leighton Town v Wroxham	1-1
93	Soham Town Rangers v Enfield Town	1-2
94	Cogenhoe United v Hanwell Town	4-1
95	March Town United v Harpenden Town	4-1
96	Stowmarket Town v Ipswich Wanderers	2-2
97	Oxhey Jets v Lowestoft Town	1-2
98	Royston Town v Clacton Town	1-2
99	Burnham Ramblers v Flackwell Heath	4-3
100	Southall v Enfield	5-0
101	Felixstowe & Walton United v Dunstable Town	1-2
102	Tilbury v Wivenhoe Town	0-3
103	London Colney v Rothwell Town	2-3
104	Raunds Town v Beaconsfield SYCOB	0-2
105	Woodford United v Wisbech Town	1-0
106	Boreham Wood v Dereham Town	3-0
107	Great Yarmouth Town v Stanway Rovers	2-3
108	Henley Town v Witham Town	2-4
109	Tring Athletic v Biggleswade United	1-2
110	North Greenford United v Brook House	1-6
111	Waltham Abbey v Wingate & Finchley	6-2
112	Langford v Stansted	1-2
113	Hertford Town v Ruislip Manor	1-2
114	Halstead Town v Cornard United	7-0
115	Lymington & New Milton v Dover Athletic	0-2
116	Mile Oak v Camberley Town	1-1 D
117	Horsham YMCA v Corinthian Casuals	2-0
118	Moneyfields v Rye & Iden United	4-0
119	Lordswood v Saltdean United	3-2
120	Carterton v Didcot Town	0-3
121	Kingstonian v Ringmer	2-1
122	Tonbridge Angels v Horsham	3-1
123	Ashford Town v Slade Green	3-1
124	Cobham v Egham Town	0-2
125	Reading Town v Eastbourne Town	1-3
126	Molesey v Burgess Hill Town	2-4
127	Bashley v Hythe Town	4-0
128	Ash United v Leatherhead	1-1
129	Herne Bay v Sevenoaks Town	3-2
130	Burnham v Selsey	2-0
131	Sittingbourne v Chessington & Hook United	2-4
132	Erith & Belvedere v Tooting & Mitcham United	1-2
133	Croydon Athletic v Redhill	4-2
134	Oxford City v Newport (IOW)	3-2
135	East Preston v Cowes Sports	0-1
136	Chatham Town v North Leigh	2-0
137	Metropolitan Police v Bracknell Town	0-0
138	VCD Athletic v Hastings United (2)	0-2
139	Croydon v Frimley Green	1-1
140	Mole Valley Predators v Gosport Borough	0-8
141	Winchester City v Maidstone United (2)	0-3
142	Sidlesham v Bedfont	1-2
143	Thatcham Town v Cove	3-0
144	Chipstead v Brockenhurst	4-2
145	Whitstable Town v Fleet Town	3-3
146	Godalming Town v Dulwich Hamlet	1-2
147	Ashford Town (Middlesex) v Whyteleafe	3-1
148	Merstham v Ramsgate	1-4
149	Steyning Town v Cray Wanderers	0-6
150	BAT Sports v Abingdon United	0-3
151	Dartford v Dorking (2)	1-2
152	Epsom & Ewell v AFC Newbury	6-1
153	Hillingdon Borough v Hassocks	0-0
154	Banstead Athletic v Alton Town	1-0
155	Whitehawk v AFC Totton	0-2
156	Three Bridges v Walton Casuals	1-0
157	Wick v Arundel	1-1
158	Littlehampton Town v Tunbridge Wells	1-1 N
159	Sidley United v Deal Town	1-1 N
160	Elmore v Torrington	2-0
161	Shortwood United v Bodmin Town	2-3
162	Liskeard Athletic v Brislington	2-0
163	Melksham Town v Westbury United	2-2
164	Hamworthy United v Backwell United	4-0
165	Frome Town v St Blazey	0-0
166	Hallen v Swindon Supermarine	1-3
167	Almondsbury Town v Cinderford Town	3-5
168	Penzance v Street	2-2
169	Bemerton Heath Harlequins v Ilfracombe Town	1-0
170	Chard Town v Wimborne Town	0-0
171	Shepton Mallet v Bournemouth (Ams)	0-2
172	Taunton Town v Bristol Manor Farm	1-0
173	Highworth Town v Welton Rovers	1-0
174	Bridgwater Town v Paulton Rovers	0-1
175	Barnstaple Town v Clevedon United	4-1
176	Odd Down v Exmouth Town	3-2
177	Bitton v Dawlish Town	2-1
178	Witney United v Clevedon Town	0-0
179	Fairford Town v Devizes Town	0-0
180	Christchurch v Bishop Sutton	5-0
181	Bishop's Cleeve v Bideford	3-1
182	Bridport v Falmouth Town	0-3
1r	Whitley Bay v Bridlington Town (2)	4-0
4r	Penrith v Warrington Town	1-2e
7r	Winterton Rangers v Hebburn Town	0-2
15r	Sunderland Nissan v Rossendale United	1-4
24r	Chorley v Tadcaster Albion	2-0
26r	Ashington v Pickering Town	1-2
27r	Stocksbridge Park Steels v Washington	1-1P
30r	Mossley v Sheffield	1-0
36r	Goole AFC v Atherton LR	2-0
44r	Buxton v Newcastle Town	1-2
56r	Norton United v Deeping Rangers	1-0
60r	Stamford v Oadby Town	0-1e
64r	Pegasus Juniors v Teversal	3-2
65r	Sutton Town (2) v Leamington	2-2q
66r	Eastwood Town v Lincoln Moorlands	3-2e
69r	Kidsgrove Athletic v Stourbridge	5-2
72r	Barton Rovers v Wootton Blue Cross	4-1e
74r	Chalfont St Peter v AFC Hornchurch	1-2
75r	Leverstock Green v Barkingside	3-4
79r	Ely City v Bury Town	0-8
84r	Holmer Green v Harwich & Parkeston	2-5
91r	St Margaretsbury v Barking & East Ham United	2-0
92r	Wroxham v Leighton Town	4-1
96r	Ipswich Wanderers v Stowmarket Town	3-1
128r	Leatherhead v Ash United	3-2
137r	Bracknell Town v Metropolitan Police	0-2
139r	Frimley Green v Croydon	0-2
145r	Fleet Town v Whitstable Town	2-1
153r	Hassocks v Hillingdon Borough	2-1e
157r	Arundel v Wick	1-2
158r	Tunbridge Wells v Littlehampton Town	2-2P
159r	Deal Town v Sidley United	2-1
163r	Westbury United v Melksham Town	2-3
165r	St Blazey v Frome Town	8-0
168r	Street v Penzance	0-0q
170r	Wimborne Town v Chard Town	2-0
178r	Clevedon Town v Witney United	3-2
179r	Devizes Town v Fairford Town	0-3

Qualifying Round One

1	Oldham Town v Great Harwood Town	1-2
2	Wakefield & Emley v Blyth Spartans	1-2
3	Armthorpe Welfare v Mossley	3-1
4	Goole AFC v Clitheroe	5-3
5	Billingham Synthonia v Retford United	4-2
6	Trafford v Yorkshire Amateur	4-1
7	Kendal Town v Witton Albion	2-3
8	Durham City v Hebburn Town	0-2
9	Runcorn FC Halton v Skelmersdale United	2-3
10	Curzon Ashton v Chester-le-Street Town	0-2
11	Burscough v Ashton United	3-2
12	Pickering Town v Farsley Celtic	1-2
13	Cammell Laird v Radcliffe Borough	2-1
14	Stocksbridge Park Steels v Ossett Town	1-3
15	Chorley v Bishop Auckland	0-0
16	Dunston Federation Brewery v Thackley	4-1
17	Woodley Sports v Prescot Cables	2-4 N
18	Seaham Red Star v Consett	0-4
19	Bradford Park Avenue v Padiham	1-1
20	Marine v Cheadle Town	4-0
21	St Helens Town v Northallerton Town	3-3
22	Frickley Athletic v Chadderton	2-0
23	Gateshead (2) v Warrington Town	4-0
24	Guiseley v Salford City	0-1
25	Rossendale United v Billingham Town	2-2
26	Thornaby v West Auckland Town	4-3
27	Whitby Town v Newcastle Blue Star	2-1
28	North Ferriby United v Brigg Town	3-1
29	Whitley Bay v Ramsbottom United	1-2
30	Willenhall Town v Malvern Town	1-1
31	Bedworth United v Solihull Borough	1-1
32	Stratford Town v Glapwell	1-3
33	Bromsgrove Rovers v Newcastle Town	2-0
34	Ilkeston Town (2) v Coalville Town	1-0
35	Kidsgrove Athletic v Leamington	0-1
36	Staveley MW v Norton United	2-1
37	Halesowen Town v South Normanton Athletic	5-3
38	Leek Town v Long Eaton United	7-0
39	Westfields v Belper Town	1-2
40	Oadby Town v Oldbury United	3-3
41	Boldmere St Michaels v Nantwich Town	0-3
42	Matlock Town v Pegasus Juniors	4-0
43	Cradley Town v Eastwood Town	0-6
44	Grantham Town v Lincoln United	4-0
45	Chasetown v Gedling Town	2-1
46	AFC Telford United v Rugby Town	1-1
47	Corby Town v Shepshed Dynamo	2-0 N
48	Chesham United v Brackley Town	0-1
49	St Margaretsbury v Billericay Town	0-0
50	Northwood v March Town United	3-0
51	Rothwell Town v Wivenhoe Town	1-3
52	Welwyn Garden City v Beaconsfield SYCOB	3-2
53	Ruislip Manor v Redbridge	1-1
54	Wroxham v Diss Town	2-0
55	Woodford United v Harwich & Parkeston	5-0
56	East Thurrock United v Harrow Borough	1-2
57	Hampton & Richmond Boro. v Witham Town	3-0
58	Halstead Town v Lowestoft Town	1-3
59	Aveley v Burnham Ramblers	1-2
60	Brentwood Town v Great Wakering Rovers	3-1
61	Barkingside v Maldon Town	1-6
62	Brook House v Clacton Town	9-1
63	Bedford Town v AFC Sudbury	2-2
64	AFC Hornchurch v Stansted	2-0
65	Cogenhoe United v Clapton	4-2
66	Heybridge Swifts v Arlesey Town	1-0
67	Stanway Rovers v Wealdstone	0-0
68	Chelmsford City v Harlow Town	1-1
69	Ipswich Wanderers v Hemel Hempstead Town	1-1
70	Potton United v Leyton	0-1
71	Hitchin Town v Waltham Forest	4-1
72	Enfield Town v Waltham Abbey	3-0
73	Bury Town v Boreham Wood	2-2
74	Northampton Spencer v Aylesbury United	1-2
75	Staines Town v Dunstable Town	1-1
76	Hendon v Biggleswade United	6-0
77	Southall v Mildenhall Town	6-3
78	Banbury United v King's Lynn	2-1
79	Berkhamsted Town v Barton Rovers	3-0
80	Cheshunt v Braintree Town	1-2
81	Slough Town v Oxford City	4-1
82	Camberley Town v Epsom & Ewell	1-0
83	Cray Wanderers v Kingstonian	4-1
84	Fleet Town v Thatcham Town	3-2
85	Lordswood v AFC Totton	1-2
86	Didcot Town v Herne Bay	0-0
87	Bashley v Dover Athletic	0-1
88	Burgess Hill Town v Walton & Hersham	0-4
89	Abingdon United v Dulwich Hamlet	1-1
90	Banstead Athletic v Moneyfields	3-0
91	Three Bridges v Chipstead	1-3
92	Croydon Athletic v Ramsgate	1-3
93	Bedfont v Bromley	1-4
94	Horsham YMCA v Croydon	1-2
95	AFC Wimbledon v Ashford Town (Middlesex)	2-2
96	Ashford Town v Windsor & Eton	0-3
97	Maidstone United (2) v Burnham	1-2
98	Folkestone Invicta v Egham Town	3-1
99	Chessington & Hook United v Hassocks	0-3
100	Wick v Worthing	0-4
101	Eastbourne Town v Gosport Borough	1-2
102	Margate v Cowes Sports	4-0
103	Dorking (2) v Deal Town	1-3
104	Fisher Athletic (London) v Tooting & Mitcham United	6-2
105	Chatham Town v Leatherhead	3-4
106	Metropolitan Police v Tunbridge Wells	2-0
107	Hastings United (2) v Tonbridge Angels	3-3
108	Swindon Supermarine v Melksham Town	1-0
109	Fairford Town v Bishop's Cleeve	0-1
110	Liskeard Athletic v Bitton	1-1
111	Cirencester Town v Wimborne Town	5-3
112	Bath City v Cinderford Town	1-0
113	Clevedon Town v Salisbury City	1-1
114	Taunton Town v Odd Down	3-0
115	Paulton Rovers v Barnstaple Town	3-2
116	Chippenham Town v Falmouth Town	4-0
117	Penzance v Bemerton Heath Harlequins	0-1
118	Gloucester City v Christchurch	0-0
119	Tiverton Town v Evesham United	1-1
120	Yate Town v Bodmin Town	2-0
121	Merthyr Tydfil v St Blazey	3-2
122	Bournemouth (Ams) v Mangotsfield United	1-1
123	Hamworthy United v Team Bath	0-2

2005/06

124	Highworth Town v Elmore	2-1
15r	Bishop Auckland v Chorley	2-1
19r	Padiham v Bradford Park Avenue	1-4
21r	Northallerton Town v St Helens Town	2-3
25r	Billingham Town v Rossendale United	2-3
30r	Malvern Town v Willenhall Town	1-0
31r	Solihull Borough v Bedworth United	3-2
40r	Oldbury United v Oadby Town	0-3
46r	Rugby Town v AFC Telford United	2-3e
49r	Billericay Town v St Margaretsbury	2-3e
53r	Redbridge v Ruislip Manor	2-1
63r	AFC Sudbury v Bedford Town	2-1e
67r	Wealdstone v Stanway Rovers	3-0
68r	Harlow Town v Chelmsford City	0-1
69r	Hemel Hempstead Town v Ipswich Wanderers	4-1
73r	Boreham Wood v Bury Town	4-2
75r	Dunstable Town v Staines Town	0-1e
86r	Herne Bay v Didcot Town	2-6
89r	Dulwich Hamlet v Abingdon United	3-2
95r	Ashford Town (Middlesex) v AFC Wimbledon	0-2
107r	Tonbridge Angels v Hastings United (2)	2-1
110r	Bitton v Liskeard Athletic	1-0
113r	Salisbury City v Clevedon Town	4-2
118r	Christchurch v Gloucester City	3-0
119r	Evesham United v Tiverton Town	0-1
122r	Mangotsfield United v Bournemouth (Ams)	7-0

Qualifying Round Two

1	Consett v Ossett Town	1-5
2	Billingham Synthonia v North Ferriby United	0-3
3	Blyth Spartans v Prescot Cables	1-0
4	Armthorpe Welfare v Rossendale United	0-2
5	Dunston Federation Brewery v Thornaby	1-1
6	Trafford v Whitby Town	1-1
7	Harrogate Town v Great Harwood Town	3-0
8	Chester-le-Street Town v Leigh RMI	1-3
9	Marine v Cammell Laird	1-1
10	Worksop Town v Witton Albion	0-1
11	Skelmersdale United v Bishop Auckland	0-0
12	Hyde United v Lancaster City	2-1
13	St Helens Town v Alfreton Town	0-2
14	Vauxhall Motors v Ramsbottom United	2-0
15	Barrow v Hebburn Town	5-1
16	Farsley Celtic v Bradford Park Avenue	2-0
17	Gainsborough Trinity v Goole AFC	2-2
18	Frickley Athletic v Northwich Victoria	1-4
19	Droylsden v Burscough	1-2
20	Salford City v Gateshead (2)	1-0
21	Stalybridge Celtic v Workington	0-0
22	Bromsgrove Rovers v Hinckley United	3-1
23	Leamington v Oadby Town	2-2
24	Chasetown v Belper Town	3-3
25	Brackley Town v Banbury United	1-1
26	Eastwood Town v Cambridge City	1-1
27	Nuneaton Borough v AFC Telford United	3-1
28	Matlock Town v Corby Town	2-0
29	Glapwell v Halesowen Town	0-1
30	Redditch United v Woodford United	1-1
31	Malvern Town v Histon	1-4
32	Hednesford Town v Moor Green	2-0
33	Leek Town v Grantham Town	1-0
34	Kettering Town v Stafford Rangers	1-0
35	Cogenhoe United v Staveley MW	3-2
36	Solihull Borough v Ilkeston Town (2)	3-0
37	Nantwich Town v Hucknall Town	0-1
38	Thurrock v Hemel Hempstead Town	3-2
39	Boreham Wood v Welling United	0-2
40	Wivenhoe Town v Heybridge Swifts	1-4
41	Bognor Regis Town v Basingstoke Town	1-1
42	Yeading v Maidenhead United	3-0
43	Hendon v Metropolitan Police	0-0
44	AFC Hornchurch v Worthing	1-4
45	Burnham v Lowestoft Town	1-1
46	Bromley v Chipstead	2-1
47	Staines Town v Croydon	1-1
48	Redbridge v Eastbourne Borough	2-2
49	Deal Town v Hitchin Town	1-3
50	Chelmsford City v Dover Athletic	1-0
51	AFC Wimbledon v Walton & Hersham	0-3
52	Cray Wanderers v Camberley Town	4-1
53	Leyton v Lewes	0-1
54	St Margaretsbury v Folkestone Invicta	0-1
55	Braintree Town v Didcot Town	2-0
56	Brentwood Town v Windsor & Eton	1-2
57	Wroxham v Slough Town	2-0
58	Fisher Athletic (London) v Tonbridge Angels	2-3
59	Northwood v Aylesbury United	0-0
60	Margate v Carshalton Athletic	1-0
61	Hayes v Brook House	1-1
62	Welwyn Garden City v AFC Sudbury	4-2
63	Hassocks v Dulwich Hamlet	0-1
64	Ramsgate v Southall	1-0
65	Farnborough Town v Berkhamsted Town	3-0
66	Enfield Town v St Albans City	1-1
67	Sutton United v Maldon Town	2-0
68	Banstead Athletic v Wealdstone	1-4
69	Harrow Borough v Burnham Ramblers	2-1
70	Hampton & Richmond Boro. v Leatherhead	1-1
71	Fleet Town v Bishop's Stortford	0-2
72	Highworth Town v Tiverton Town	1-7
73	Yate Town v Salisbury City	0-2
74	Christchurch v Cirencester Town	0-2
75	Worcester City v Bemerton Heath Harlequins	7-0
76	Taunton Town v Merthyr Tydfil	1-1
77	Gosport Borough v Bath City	3-4
78	Mangotsfield United v Swindon Supermarine	4-2
79	Bishop's Cleeve v Bitton	3-0
80	Dorchester Town v Team Bath	4-2
81	Weston-Super-Mare v Weymouth	2-2
82	Chippenham Town v Newport County (2)	4-0
83	AFC Totton v Paulton Rovers	2-1
84	Eastleigh v Havant & Waterlooville	0-0
5r	Thornaby v Dunston Federation Brewery	2-1
6r	Whitby Town v Trafford	6-0
9r	Cammell Laird v Marine	3-1
11r	Bishop Auckland v Skelmersdale United	1-2
17r	Goole AFC v Gainsborough Trinity	1-2
21r	Workington v Stalybridge Celtic	2-1e
23r	Oadby Town v Leamington	1-1q
24r	Belper Town v Chasetown	1-4
25r	Banbury United v Brackley Town	5-2
26r	Cambridge City v Eastwood Town	3-1
30r	Woodford United v Redditch United	2-2P
41r	Basingstoke Town v Bognor Regis Town	2-1
43r	Metropolitan Police v Hendon	1-0
45r	Lowestoft Town v Burnham	1-1q
47r	Croydon v Staines Town	1-2
48r	Eastbourne Borough v Redbridge	5-1
59r	Aylesbury United v Northwood	2-0
61r	Brook House v Hayes	0-4
66r	St Albans City v Enfield Town	3-0
70r	Leatherhead v Hampton & Richmond Boro.	2-1
76r	Merthyr Tydfil v Taunton Town	2-1
81r	Weymouth v Weston-Super-Mare	1-0
84r	Havant & Waterlooville v Eastleigh	4-1

Qualifying Round Three

1	Northwich Victoria v North Ferriby United	1-0
2	Vauxhall Motors v Skelmersdale United	4-3
3	Leigh RMI v Gainsborough Trinity	1-1
4	Rossendale United v Blyth Spartans	0-1
5	Leek Town v Thornaby	2-1
6	Matlock Town v Ossett Town	3-6
7	Harrogate Town v Witton Albion	2-0
8	Hucknall Town v Cammell Laird	2-2
9	Alfreton Town v Whitby Town	2-1
10	Burscough v Workington	2-0
11	Salford City v Farsley Celtic	0-1
12	Hyde United v Barrow	2-3
13	Thurrock v Solihull Borough	1-0
14	Banbury United v Hednesford Town	3-4
15	Leamington v Woodford United	2-0
16	Cogenhoe United v Chasetown	1-1
17	Hayes v Bishop's Stortford	2-0
18	Wroxham v Aylesbury United	1-1
19	Cambridge City v Hitchin Town	4-1
20	Heybridge Swifts v Braintree Town	1-1
21	Harrow Borough v Welling United	0-1
22	Wealdstone v Burnham	2-4
23	Halesowen Town v Bromsgrove Rovers	0-2
24	Histon v Welwyn Garden City	2-1
25	St Albans City v Kettering Town	0-0
26	Nuneaton Borough v Chelmsford City	1-1
27	Bishop's Cleeve v AFC Totton	1-1
28	Metropolitan Police v Eastbourne Borough	3-3
29	Bromley v Mangotsfield United	0-0
30	Worcester City v Tonbridge Angels	3-0
31	Cirencester Town v Havant & Waterlooville	2-1
32	Worthing v Basingstoke Town	2-4
33	Yeading v Dorchester Town	1-1
34	Merthyr Tydfil v Salisbury City	2-1
35	Folkestone Invicta v Staines Town	2-0
36	Tiverton Town v Windsor & Eton	2-1
37	Leatherhead v Farnborough Town	0-2
38	Chippenham Town v Sutton United	1-0
39	Ramsgate v Walton & Hersham	1-0
40	Margate v Cray Wanderers	0-3
41	Lewes v Dulwich Hamlet	1-0
42	Weymouth v Bath City	1-0
3r	Gainsborough Trinity v Leigh RMI	2-1
8r	Cammell Laird v Hucknall Town	0-1
16r	Chasetown v Cogenhoe United	4-3e
18r	Aylesbury United v Wroxham	4-2
20r	Braintree Town v Heybridge Swifts	3-1
25r	Kettering Town v St Albans City	4-0
26r	Chelmsford City v Nuneaton Borough	1-2e
27r	AFC Totton v Bishop's Cleeve	0-4
28r	Eastbourne Borough v Metropolitan Police	3-2
29r	Mangotsfield United v Bromley	0-1
33r	Dorchester Town v Yeading	3-2

Qualifying Round Four

1	Harrogate Town v Scarborough	1-0
2	Tamworth v Altrincham	3-1
3	Southport v Kidderminster Harriers	1-0
4	Hucknall Town v Burscough	0-0
5	Blyth Spartans v Chasetown	2-2
6	Northwich Victoria v Barrow	4-1
7	Gainsborough Trinity v York City	0-4
8	Ossett Town v Leamington	2-3
9	Accrington Stanley (2) v Worcester City	1-1
10	Hednesford Town v Vauxhall Motors	3-0
11	Halifax Town v Farsley Celtic	2-0
12	Burton Albion v Leek Town	2-0
13	Hereford United v Alfreton Town	0-0
14	Bromsgrove Rovers v Morecambe	0-2
15	Crawley Town v Braintree Town	0-1
16	Canvey Island v Burnham	1-1
17	Kettering Town v Gravesend & Northfleet	3-0
18	Dorchester Town v Welling United	1-2
19	Bromley v Aldershot Town	0-1
20	Histon v Hayes	3-1
21	Grays Athletic v Cray Wanderers	2-0
22	Nuneaton Borough v Tiverton Town	0-0
23	Exeter City v Stevenage Borough	0-1
24	Woking v Thurrock	3-0
25	Basingstoke Town v Chippenham Town	0-1
26	Cambridge City v Lewes	2-1
27	Merthyr Tydfil v Farnborough Town	2-0
28	Aylesbury United v Folkestone Invicta	0-2
29	Forest Green Rovers v Dagenham & Redbridge	2-3
30	Ramsgate v Cirencester Town	3-0
31	Weymouth v Cambridge United	2-1
32	Bishop's Cleeve v Eastbourne Borough	0-1
4r	Burscough v Hucknall Town	6-2
5r	Chasetown v Blyth Spartans	1-0
9r	Worcester City v Accrington Stanley (2)	3-2
13r	Alfreton Town v Hereford United	1-1q
16r	Burnham v Canvey Island	2-1
22r	Tiverton Town v Nuneaton Borough	0-1

Round One

	Barnet v Southend United	0-1
	Barnsley v Darlington	1-0
	Bournemouth v Tamworth	1-2
	Bradford City v Tranmere Rovers	2-1
	Bristol City v Notts County	0-2
	Burnham v Aldershot Town	1-3
	Burscough v Gillingham	3-2
	Bury v Scunthorpe United	2-2
	Cambridge City v Hereford United	0-1
	Chasetown v Oldham Athletic	1-1
	Cheltenham Town v Carlisle United	1-0
	Chester City v Folkestone Invicta	2-1
	Chippenham Town v Worcester City	1-1
	Colchester United v Leamington	9-1
	Doncaster Rovers v Blackpool	4-1
	Eastbourne Borough v Oxford United	1-1
	Grimsby Town v Bristol Rovers	1-2
	Halifax Town v Rushden & Diamonds	1-1
	Hartlepool United v Dagenham & Redbridge	2-1
	Histon v Hednesford Town	4-0
	Huddersfield Town v Welling United	4-1
	Kettering Town v Stevenage Borough	1-3
	Leyton Orient v Chesterfield	0-0
	Lincoln City v Milton Keynes Dons	1-1
	Macclesfield Town v Yeovil Town	1-1
	Merthyr Tydfil v Walsall	1-2
	Morecambe v Northwich Victoria	1-3
	Nottingham Forest v Weymouth	1-1
	Nuneaton Borough v Ramsgate	2-0
	Peterborough United v Burton Albion	0-0
	Port Vale v Wrexham	2-1
	Rochdale v Brentford	0-1
	Rotherham United v Mansfield Town	3-4
	Shrewsbury Town v Braintree Town	4-1
	Southport v Woking	1-1
	Stockport County v Swansea City	2-0
	Swindon Town v Boston United	2-2
	Torquay United v Harrogate Town	1-1
	Wycombe Wanderers v Northampton Town	1-3
	York City v Grays Athletic	0-3
r	Boston United v Swindon Town	4-1
r	Burton Albion v Peterborough United	1-0
r	Chesterfield v Leyton Orient	1-2
r	Harrogate Town v Torquay United	0-0q
r	Milton Keynes Dons v Lincoln City	2-1
r	Oldham Athletic v Chasetown	4-0
r	Oxford United v Eastbourne Borough	3-0
r	Rushden & Diamonds v Halifax Town	0-0P
r	Scunthorpe United v Bury	1-0e
r	Weymouth v Nottingham Forest	0-2
r	Woking v Southport	1-0e
r	Worcester City v Chippenham Town	1-0
r	Yeovil Town v Macclesfield Town	4-0

Round Two

	Aldershot Town v Scunthorpe United	0-1
	Barnsley v Bradford City	1-1
	Boston United v Doncaster Rovers	1-2
	Burton Albion v Burscough	4-1
	Cheltenham Town v Oxford United	1-1
	Chester City v Nottingham Forest	3-0
	Hartlepool United v Tamworth	1-2
	Hereford United v Stockport County	0-2
	Mansfield Town v Grays Athletic	3-0
	Nuneaton Borough v Histon	2-2
	Oldham Athletic v Brentford	1-1
	Port Vale v Bristol Rovers	1-1
	Rushden & Diamonds v Leyton Orient	0-1
	Shrewsbury Town v Colchester United	1-2
	Southend United v Milton Keynes Dons	1-2
	Stevenage Borough v Northampton Town	2-2
	Torquay United v Notts County	2-1
	Walsall v Yeovil Town	2-0
	Woking v Northwich Victoria	0-0
	Worcester City v Huddersfield Town	0-1
r	Bradford City v Barnsley	3-5e
r	Brentford v Oldham Athletic	1-0
r	Bristol Rovers v Port Vale	0-1

2005/06 to 2006/07

r	Histon v Nuneaton Borough	1-2
r	Northampton Town v Stevenage Borough	2-0
r	Northwich Victoria v Woking	2-1
r	Oxford United v Cheltenham Town	1-2

Round Three

	Arsenal v Cardiff City	2-1
	Barnsley v Walsall	1-1
	Blackburn Rovers v Queen's Park Rangers	3-0
	Brighton & Hove Albion v Coventry City	0-1
	Burton Albion v Manchester United	0-0
	Chelsea v Huddersfield Town	2-1
	Cheltenham Town v Chester City	2-2
	Crystal Palace v Northampton Town	4-1
	Derby County v Burnley	2-1
	Fulham v Leyton Orient	1-2
	Hull City v Aston Villa	0-1
	Ipswich Town v Portsmouth	0-1
	Leicester City v Tottenham Hotspur	3-2
	Luton Town v Liverpool	3-5
	Manchester City v Scunthorpe United	3-1
	Millwall v Everton	1-1
	Newcastle United v Mansfield Town	1-0
	Norwich City v West Ham United	1-2
	Nuneaton Borough v Middlesbrough	1-1
	Port Vale v Doncaster Rovers	2-1
	Preston North End v Crewe Alexandra	2-1
	Sheffield United v Colchester United	1-2
	Sheffield Wednesday v Charlton Athletic	2-4
	Southampton v Milton Keynes Dons	4-3
	Stockport County v Brentford	2-3
	Stoke City v Tamworth	0-0
	Sunderland v Northwich Victoria	3-0
	Torquay United v Birmingham City	0-0
	Watford v Bolton Wanderers	0-3
	West Bromwich Albion v Reading	1-1
	Wigan Athletic v Leeds United	1-1
	Wolverhampton Wan. v Plymouth Argyle	1-0
r	Birmingham City v Torquay United	2-0
r	Chester City v Cheltenham Town	0-1
r	Everton v Millwall	1-0
r	Leeds United v Wigan Athletic	3-3q
r	Manchester United v Burton Albion	5-0
r	Middlesbrough v Nuneaton Borough	5-2
r	Reading v West Bromwich Albion	3-2e
r	Tamworth v Stoke City	1-1q
r	Walsall v Barnsley	2-0

Round Four

	Aston Villa v Port Vale	3-1
	Bolton Wanderers v Arsenal	1-0
	Brentford v Sunderland	2-1
	Charlton Athletic v Leyton Orient	2-1
	Cheltenham Town v Newcastle United	0-2
	Colchester United v Derby County	3-1
	Coventry City v Middlesbrough	1-1
	Everton v Chelsea	1-1
	Leicester City v Southampton	0-1
	Manchester City v Wigan Athletic	1-0
	Portsmouth v Liverpool	1-2
	Preston North End v Crystal Palace	1-1
	Reading v Birmingham City	1-1
	Stoke City v Walsall	2-1
	West Ham United v Blackburn Rovers	4-2
	Wolverhampton Wan. v Manchester United	0-3
r	Birmingham City v Reading	2-1
r	Chelsea v Everton	4-1
r	Crystal Palace v Preston North End	1-2
r	Middlesbrough v Coventry City	1-0

Round Five

	Aston Villa v Manchester City	1-1
	Bolton Wanderers v West Ham United	0-0
	Charlton Athletic v Brentford	3-1
	Chelsea v Colchester United	3-1
	Liverpool v Manchester United	1-0
	Newcastle United v Southampton	1-0
	Preston North End v Middlesbrough	0-2
	Stoke City v Birmingham City	0-1
r	Manchester City v Aston Villa	2-1
r	West Ham United v Bolton Wanderers	2-1e

Round Six

	Birmingham City v Liverpool	0-7
	Charlton Athletic v Middlesbrough	0-0
	Chelsea v Newcastle United	1-0
	Manchester City v West Ham United	1-2
r	Middlesbrough v Charlton Athletic	4-2

Semi Finals

	Liverpool v Chelsea	2-1 N
	West Ham United v Middlesbrough	1-0 N

Final

	Liverpool v West Ham United	3-3PN

Liverpool won 3-1 on penalties a.e.t.

2006/07

Extra Preliminary Round

1	Atherton Collieries v New Mills	1-2
2	Sunderland Nissan v Darlington Railway Ath. (2)	5-0
3	Glasshoughton Welfare v Bacup Borough	2-0
4	Hall Road Rangers v Durham City	0-1
5	Atherton LR v Parkgate	5-1
6	Congleton Town v Winsford United	1-0
7	Dunston Federation v Holker Old Boys	4-0
8	Cheadle Town v Crook Town	3-1
9	Whickham v Marske United	1-2
10	Jarrow Roofing Boldon CA v Billingham Synthonia	5-2
11	Whitley Bay v Northallerton Town	2-1
12	Hebburn Town v Alnwick Town	3-1
13	Selby Town v Morpeth Town	3-3
14	Salford City v Shildon	0-1
15	Billingham Town v Borrowash Victoria	5-2
16	Bishop Auckland v Squires Gate	3-1
17	Thackley v Ramsbottom United	1-1
18	Prudhoe Town v Consett	0-5
19	Blackpool Mechanics v Armthorpe Welfare	2-0 D
20	Ashington v Thornaby	0-0
21	Daisy Hill v Winterton Rangers	1-1
22	West Allotment Celtic v Norton & Stockton Ancients	1-1
23	Brandon United v Seaham Red Star	3-5
24	Liversedge v Nelson	2-0
25	Oldham Town v Trafford	1-3
26	Pickering Town v Formby	4-0
27	Chadderton v Rossington Main	2-1
28	Retford United v Tadcaster Albion	6-0
29	Garforth Town v Penrith	2-0
30	Silsden v Hallam	1-1
31	Tow Law Town v St Helens Town	1-1
32	Glossop North End v North Shields	2-0
33	Norton United v Colne	1-5
34	Newcastle Blue Star v South Shields (3)	3-1
35	Teversal v Loughborough Dynamo	0-3
36	Blackstones v Oadby Town	1-1
37	Quorn v Arnold Town	6-0
38	Mickleover Sports v Glapwell	1-0
39	Staveley MW v Boston Town	1-5
40	Atherstone Town v Carlton Town	3-2
41	Eccleshall v Pegasus Juniors	1-1
42	Ford Sports (Daventry) v Racing Club Warwick	2-2
43	Deeping Rangers v Lincoln Moorlands	5-4
44	Coalville Town v Studley	4-0
45	St Margaretsbury v Eton Manor	1-1
46	Dereham Town v Brentwood Town	3-1
47	Sawbridgeworth v St Neots Town	1-2
48	Haverhill Rovers v Welwyn Garden City	2-0
49	Felixstowe & Walton United v Potton United	0-1
50	Holmer Green v Wootton Blue Cross	1-3
51	Halstead Town v Harefield United	0-0
52	Broxbourne Borough V&E v Colney Heath	1-0
53	Fakenham Town v Norwich United	4-0
54	Stanway Rovers v Leverstock Green	0-1
55	Wembley v Thame United	3-0
56	Hertford Town v Stotfold	1-2
57	Cogenhoe United v Saffron Walden Town	2-2
58	Needham Market v Desborough Town	2-1
59	Bowers & Pitsea v Haringey Borough	2-0
60	Ruislip Manor v Aylesbury Vale	3-1
61	Mildenhall Town v Kirkley (2)	8-2
62	Lowestoft Town v Stansted	3-1
63	Barkingside v Clacton Town	2-1
64	Biggleswade Town v Clapton	4-2
65	Chalfont St Peter v Hullbridge Sports	0-1
66	Langford v Ely City	2-4 N
67	Gorleston v Tiptree United	0-1
68	March Town United v St Ives Town	3-3
69	Stowmarket Town v Soham Town Rangers	1-1
70	Walsham Le Willows v Leiston	1-4
71	Long Melford v Cornard United	1-3
72	Long Buckby v London APSA	2-1
73	Tring Athletic v Diss Town	2-1e
74	Royston Town v Harwich & Parkeston	2-2
75	Newport Pagnell Town v Romford	0-1
76	Oxhey Jets v Concord Rangers	3-0
77	Ipswich Wanderers v Woodbridge Town	2-2
78	London Colney v Raunds Town	0-1
79	Newmarket Town v Southend Manor	4-1
80	Arundel v Dorking (2)	5-0
81	Farnham Town v Three Bridges	0-1
82	Moneyfields v Oakwood	2-1
83	Croydon v Sandhurst Town	1-2
84	Wick v Westfield	1-1
85	East Preston v Milton United (Oxon)	3-1
86	Ash United v Deal Town	5-0
87	Chessington & Hook United v Mile Oak	3-1
88	Saltdean United v Lancing	0-1
89	North Leigh v AFC Newbury	wo/s
90	Epsom & Ewell v Henley Town	wo/s
91	Brockenhurst v Hamble ASSC	1-2
92	Guildford City (2) v Whitstable Town	0-1
93	Reading Town v Thamesmead Town	3-4
94	Egham Town v Hungerford Town	2-3
95	Rye United v Bedfont Green	0-2 N
96	Hassocks v Wantage Town	1-0
97	Frimley Green v VT	1-5
98	Lymington Town v Sidley United	0-4 N
99	Sporting Bengal United v Slade Green	0-2
100	Selsey v AFC Totton	0-5
101	Redhill v Cowes Sports	1-2
102	Eastbourne United v Cobham	0-0
103	Abingdon Town v Camberley Town	3-0
104	Raynes Park Vale v Shoreham	1-6
105	Hythe Town v Lordswood	2-2
106	Herne Bay v Erith & Belvedere	1-6
107	Erith Town v Hailsham Town	0-2
108	Banstead Athletic v Worthing United	1-2
109	Carterton v Gosport Borough	1-0
110	Devizes Town v Calne Town	3-0
111	Almondsbury Town v Odd Down	0-1
112	Christchurch v Bitton	3-1
113	Shortwood United v Backwell United	4-2
114	Fairford Town v Harrow Hill	2-0
115	Westbury United v Slimbridge	2-3
116	Welton Rovers v Wimborne Town	2-0
117	St Blazey v Bodmin Town	1-0
118	Corsham Town v Shepton Mallet	4-0
119	Melksham Town v Torrington	2-1
120	Bemerton Heath Harlequins v Downton	1-3
121	Bristol Manor Farm v Barnstaple Town	0-0
122	Liskeard Athletic v Sherborne Town	4-1
123	Witney United v Highworth Town	2-1
124	Bournemouth (Ams) v Minehead	2-0
125	Wadebridge Town v Elmore	1-1 N
126	Brislington v Dawlish Town	0-1
127	Hamworthy United v Hallen	1-2
128	Penzance v Clevedon United	1-2
129	Porthleven v Newquay	0-1
13r	Morpeth Town v Selby Town	3-1e
17r	Ramsbottom United v Thackley	0-1
20r	Thornaby v Ashington	3-2
21r	Winterton Rangers v Daisy Hill	3-0
22r	Norton & Stockton Ancients v West Allotment Celtic	6-1
30r	Hallam v Silsden	3-2
31r	St Helens Town v Tow Law Town	2-1
36r	Oadby Town v Blackstones	3-2
41r	Pegasus Juniors v Eccleshall	0-3
42r	Racing Club Warwick v Ford Sports (Daventry)	4-1
45r	Eton Manor v St Margaretsbury	1-1P
51r	Harefield United v Halstead Town	3-1
57r	Saffron Walden Town v Cogenhoe United	6-2
68r	St Ives Town v March Town United	2-1
69r	Soham Town Rangers v Stowmarket Town	1-4
74r	Harwich & Parkeston v Royston Town	4-1
77r	Woodbridge Town v Ipswich Wanderers	1-3
84r	Westfield v Wick	0-0PN
102r	Cobham v Eastbourne United	2-1
105r	Lordswood v Hythe Town	0-6
121r	Barnstaple Town v Bristol Manor Farm	5-3
125r	Elmore v Wadebridge Town	3-2

Preliminary Round

1	Pontefract Collieries v Woodley Sports	0-3
2	Spennymoor Town v Bamber Bridge	3-1
3	Trafford v Brodsworth MW	4-1
4	Bridlington Town (2) v Bishop Auckland	1-2
5	Cammell Laird v Morpeth Town	2-0
6	Norton & Stockton Ancients v Darwen	5-1
7	Consett v Rossendale United	1-1
8	Eccleshill United v Glasshoughton Welfare	2-1
9	Garforth Town v Chorley	1-2
10	Guisborough Town v Hallam	0-3
11	Goole AFC v Bradford Park Avenue	5-3
12	Pickering Town v New Mills	0-1
13	Atherton LR v Clitheroe	0-3
14	Glossop North End v Seaham Red Star	2-1
15	Shildon v Harrogate Railway Athletic	0-3
16	Bedlington Terriers v Curzon Ashton	1-4
17	St Helens Town v Skelmersdale United	0-3
18	Alsager Town v Cheadle Town	6-0
19	Sheffield v Retford United	0-0
20	Liversedge v Newcastle Blue Star	2-2
21	Yorkshire Amateur v Warrington Town	1-5
22	Abbey Hey v Chadderton	1-2
23	Thornaby v Chester-le-Street Town	0-2
24	Jarrow Roofing Boldon CA v Thackley	5-4
25	Colwyn Bay v Ossett Albion	1-1
26	Whitley Bay v Stocksbridge Park Steels	1-0
27	Maine Road v Armthorpe Welfare	1-2
28	Sunderland Nissan v Horden CW	3-2
29	Winterton Rangers v West Auckland Town	3-0
30	Marske United v Brigg Town	3-1
31	Hebburn Town v Flixton	3-3
32	Padiham v Colne	3-2
33	Billingham Town v Congleton Town	4-0
34	Long Eaton United v Washington	1-0
35	Wakefield v Dunston Federation	3-2
36	Newcastle Benfield Bay Plastics v Ryton	3-3
37	Esh Winning v Durham City	3-5
38	Rocester v Oldbury United	1-0
39	Eccleshall v Shepshed Dynamo	0-2
40	Kidsgrove Athletic v Spalding United	2-0
41	Tipton Town v Rushall Olympic	1-0
42	Coalville Town v Chasetown	0-0
43	Nantwich Town v Deeping Rangers	1-2
44	Gresley Rovers v South Normanton Athletic	1-1
45	Stratford Town v Bourne Town	2-2
46	Buxton v Atherstone Town	4-1
47	Eastwood Town v Bromsgrove Rovers	5-5
48	Gedling Town v Holbeach United	4-0
49	Newcastle Town v Stourbridge	2-1e
50	Sutton Coldfield Town v Leek CSOB	3-0

2006/07

51	Alvechurch v Bedworth United	1-2
52	Solihull Borough v Sutton Town (2)	6-2
53	Belper Town v Boston Town	2-2
54	Shirebrook Town v Barwell	3-1
55	Westfields v Racing Club Warwick	3-0
56	Quorn v Malvern Town	3-0
57	Romulus v Stourport Swifts	0-0
58	Oadby Town v Cradley Town	7-0
59	Loughborough Dynamo v Willenhall Town	1-2
60	Biddulph Victoria v Boldmere St Michaels	2-2
61	Leamington v Stone Dominoes	6-0
62	Causeway United v Mickleover Sports	3-2
63	Great Yarmouth Town v Needham Market	0-2
64	Tilbury v Romford	0-2
65	Cornard United v St Ives Town	1-3
66	Wroxham v Aylesbury United	1-1
67	Arlesey Town v Ilford	2-2
68	Harefield United v Wivenhoe Town	1-4
69	Broxbourne Borough V&E v Stotfold	1-1
70	Long Buckby v Flackwell Heath	3-2
71	Harwich & Parkeston v Leiston	0-4
72	Marlow v Waltham Forest	0-2
73	Barkingside v Maldon Town	0-2
74	Haverhill Rovers v Wootton Blue Cross	3-0
75	Uxbridge v Potton United	0-2
76	Wisbech Town v Mildenhall Town	4-1
77	Biggleswade United v AFC Hornchurch	2-4
78	Raunds Town v Enfield	1-1
79	Bowers & Pitsea v Dunstable Town	0-1
80	Leverstock Green v Beaconsfield SYCOB	2-3
81	Stowmarket Town v Dereham Town	0-2
82	Northampton Spencer v Chesham United	2-3
83	St Neots Town v Brackley Town	2-2
84	Hadleigh United v Rothwell Town	2-3
85	Great Wakering Rovers v Newmarket Town	4-1
86	Hullbridge Sports v Yaxley	0-2
87	Tiptree United v Ipswich Wanderers	2-1
88	Lowestoft Town v Witham Town	2-0
89	Barton Rovers v Barking	0-1
90	Biggleswade Town v Leighton Town	0-0
91	Potters Bar Town v Waltham Abbey	2-2
92	Ruislip Manor v Enfield Town	2-1
93	Hanwell Town v Buckingham Town	2-2
94	Ely City v Woodford United	0-3
95	Bury Town v Brook House	6-1
96	Berkhamsted Town v AFC Sudbury	2-6
97	Eton Manor v Wingate & Finchley	0-2
98	Hillingdon Borough v Tring Athletic	1-2
99	Burnham Ramblers v Ware	0-0
100	Harlow Town v Saffron Walden Town	0-1
101	Aveley v Oxhey Jets	0-1
102	Canvey Island v Fakenham Town	4-1
103	Wembley v Redbridge	0-3
104	Hailsham Town v AFC Totton	0-1
105	Kingstonian v Pagham	3-1
106	Hungerford Town v Littlehampton Town	1-0
107	Croydon Athletic v Arundel	4-2
108	Fareham Town v Carterton	1-2
109	Cowes Sports v Sandhurst Town	1-0
110	Dover Athletic v Bracknell Town	3-0
111	Whyteleafe v Ash United	3-2
112	Fleet Town v Thatcham Town	1-0
113	Walton Casuals v Cray Wanderers	2-3
114	Sevenoaks Town v Moneyfields	1-3
115	Dulwich Hamlet v Three Bridges	3-0
116	Colliers Wood United v Chipstead	1-1
117	AFC Wallingford v Burnham	1-0
118	Peacehaven & Telscombe v Whitehawk	0-1
119	Ashford Town v Bedfont Green	7-0
120	Epsom & Ewell v Leatherhead	0-2
121	Bedfont v Whitstable Town	0-1
122	Maidstone United (2) v Burgess Hill Town	2-1
123	Godalming Town v North Greenford United	1-1
124	Slade Green v Cobham	2-2
125	Sittingbourne v Thamesmead Town	3-1
126	Eastbourne Town v VCD Athletic	2-2
127	Hassocks v Newport (IOW)	2-0
128	Ardley United v Ringmer	3-0
129	Hythe Town v VT	1-3e
130	Lymington & New Milton v Shoreham	4-2
131	Cove v Tooting & Mitcham United	0-6
132	Oxford City v Abingdon United	2-2
133	Hastings United (2) v Merstham	0-0
134	Sidley United v Worthing United	0-1
135	Winchester City v Chatham Town	4-3
136	Horsham YMCA v Molesey	1-2
137	Lancing v North Leigh	3-1
138	East Preston v Horley Town	wo/s
139	Andover v Corinthian Casuals	1-1
140	Windsor & Eton v Bashley	1-2
141	Metropolitan Police v Chessington & Hook United	7-0
142	Chertsey Town v Abingdon Town	3-2
143	Hamble ASSC v East Grinstead Town	1-1
144	Tunbridge Wells v Dartford	0-5
145	Westfield v Alton Town	2-5
146	Didcot Town v Erith & Belvedere	2-1
147	Penryn Athletic v Slimbridge	2-3
148	Liskeard Athletic v Welton Rovers	1-0
149	Saltash United v Barnstaple Town	3-3
150	Odd Down v Bridgwater Town	0-1
151	Downton v Christchurch	2-1
152	Radstock Town v Elmore	3-1
153	Melksham Town v Cinderford Town	1-2
154	Street v Bishop's Cleeve	0-1
155	Tavistock v Bridport	4-2
156	Fairford Town v Bournemouth (Ams)	3-1
157	Poole Town v Taunton Town	0-1
158	Evesham United v Clevedon United	6-0
159	Bideford v Hallen	2-1
160	Falmouth Town v Bishop Sutton	1-2
161	Paulton Rovers v Witney United	1-1
162	Devizes Town v Swindon Supermarine	1-1
163	Chard Town v Willand Rovers	0-4
164	Shortwood United v Truro City	0-5
165	Corsham Town v Dawlish Town	3-1
166	Newquay v St Blazey	1-1
7r	Rossendale United v Consett	2-1
19r	Retford United v Sheffield	1-1q
20r	Newcastle Blue Star v Liversedge	3-2
25r	Ossett Albion v Colwyn Bay	4-2
31r	Flixton v Hebburn Town	3-0
36r	Ryton v Newcastle Benfield Bay Plastics	0-2
42r	Chasetown v Coalville Town	3-1
44r	South Normanton Athletic v Gresley Rovers	1-1q
45r	Bourne Town v Stratford Town	2-3
47r	Bromsgrove Rovers v Eastwood Town	2-0
53r	Boston Town v Belper Town	1-2
57r	Stourport Swifts v Romulus	0-5
60r	Boldmere St Michaels v Biddulph Victoria	7-0
66r	Aylesbury United v Wroxham	1-2
67r	Ilford v Arlesey Town	1-2e
69r	Stotfold v Broxbourne Borough V&E	0-4
78r	Enfield v Raunds Town	1-2
83r	Brackley Town v St Neots Town	4-0
90r	Leighton Town v Biggleswade Town	2-0
91r	Waltham Abbey v Potters Bar Town	1-2
93r	Buckingham Town v Hanwell Town	3-2
99r	Ware v Burnham Ramblers	1-2
116r	Chipstead v Colliers Wood United	1-2
123r	North Greenford United v Godalming Town	4-2e
124r	Cobham v Slade Green	2-0
126r	VCD Athletic v Eastbourne Town	1-0 N
132r	Abingdon United v Oxford City	3-4e
133r	Merstham v Hastings United (2)	2-4e
139r	Corinthian Casuals v Andover	3-4e
143r	East Grinstead Town v Hamble ASSC	1-3
149r	Barnstaple Town v Saltash United	0-1
161r	Witney United v Paulton Rovers	1-2
162r	Swindon Supermarine v Devizes Town	3-0
166r	St Blazey v Newquay	3-1

Qualifying Round One

1	Chorley v North Ferriby United	1-3
2	Durham City v Alsager Town	2-0 N
3	Eccleshill United v Flixton	1-2
4	Witton Albion v Sheffield	3-2
5	Armthorpe Welfare v Burscough	1-3
6	Cammell Laird v Newcastle Benfield Bay Plastics	0-2
7	Fleetwood Town v Jarrow Roofing Boldon CA	3-0
8	Guiseley v Mossley	2-1
9	Long Eaton United v Warrington Town	1-3
10	Glossop North End v New Mills	3-1
11	Chadderton v Trafford	1-1
12	Winterton Rangers v Kendal Town	0-5
13	Hallam v Sunderland Nissan	2-1
14	Clitheroe v Marine	0-2
15	Radcliffe Borough v Skelmersdale United	1-2
16	Whitby Town v Frickley Athletic	2-4
17	Harrogate Railway Athletic v Marske United	3-4
18	Gateshead (2) v Rossendale United	3-1
19	Whitley Bay v Norton & Stockton Ancients	3-2
20	Newcastle Blue Star v Prescot Cables	0-4
21	Chester-le-Street Town v Wakefield	0-1
22	Woodley Sports v Bishop Auckland	4-0 N
23	Ossett Town v Ossett Albion	1-2
24	Curzon Ashton v Billingham Town	4-2
25	Goole AFC v Spennymoor Town	4-1
26	Ashton United v Padiham	4-2
27	Sutton Coldfield Town v Newcastle Town	3-0
28	Oadby Town v Grantham Town	4-2
29	Bedworth United v Matlock Town	1-3
30	AFC Telford United v Halesowen Town	2-4
31	Gresley Rovers v Quorn	0-1
32	Rugby Town v Deeping Rangers	4-1
33	Kidsgrove Athletic v Leek Town	0-0
34	Romulus v Shirebrook Town	6-0
35	Hednesford Town v Gedling Town	1-1
36	Shepshed Dynamo v Chasetown	0-2
37	Causeway United v Boldmere St Michaels	2-0
38	Tipton Town v Buxton	1-1
39	Belper Town v Westfields	4-0
40	Rocester v Leamington	1-0
41	Ilkeston Town (2) v Bromsgrove Rovers	1-1
42	Corby Town v Solihull Borough	1-3
43	Lincoln United v Stamford	2-2
44	Willenhall Town v Stratford Town	2-3
45	Canvey Island v Lowestoft Town	1-3
46	Boreham Wood v St Ives Town	8-2
47	Hendon v Arlesey Town	4-0
48	Potters Bar Town v Wealdstone	2-1
49	Hitchin Town v Saffron Walden Town	1-1
50	Hemel Hempstead Town v Leyton	6-3
51	AFC Sudbury v Waltham Forest	1-0
52	Woodford United v Wroxham	3-1
53	Great Wakering Rovers v Burnham Ramblers	2-1
54	Redbridge v AFC Hornchurch	1-2
55	Heybridge Swifts v Potton United	6-1
56	Buckingham Town v Raunds Town	1-4
57	Hampton & Richmond Boro. v Billericay Town	1-1
58	Dunstable Town v Leiston	3-2
59	Haverhill Rovers v Broxbourne Borough V&E	3-1
60	Banbury United v Beaconsfield SYCOB	5-1
61	Wingate & Finchley v East Thurrock United	1-2
62	Tiptree United v Brackley Town	0-4
63	Maldon Town v Staines Town	2-1
64	Tring Athletic v King's Lynn	1-5
65	Wivenhoe Town v Yaxley	1-2
66	Long Buckby v Rothwell Town	1-2
67	Bury Town v Wisbech Town	0-2
68	Oxhey Jets v Ruislip Manor	1-0
69	Harrow Borough v Northwood	2-0
70	Romford v Leighton Town	3-0
71	Chesham United v Cheshunt	2-3
72	Barking v Chelmsford City	1-4
73	Needham Market v Dereham Town	3-4
74	Worthing v Colliers Wood United	3-0
75	Ashford Town v Tonbridge Angels	1-3
76	Cobham v Slough Town	1-2
77	Sittingbourne v Hassocks	3-0
78	Margate v Fleet Town	0-0
79	Maidenhead United v Carterton	1-1
80	Dover Athletic v Alton Town	6-1
81	Dartford v Hastings United (2)	0-2
82	Whyteleafe v Folkestone Invicta	1-2
83	Ashford Town (Middlesex) v Maidstone United (2)	4-0
84	Molesey v Leatherhead	1-1
85	Hungerford Town v Ardley United	3-0
86	Tooting & Mitcham United v Lancing	6-0
87	Bromley v AFC Totton	4-0
88	Cowes Sports v Lymington & New Milton	1-2
89	Oxford City v Chertsey Town	5-0
90	North Greenford United v VT	0-1
91	Kingstonian v Ramsgate	1-2
92	Andover v Carshalton Athletic	0-2
93	Walton & Hersham v Dulwich Hamlet	3-0
94	Whitstable Town v Croydon Athletic	1-0
95	Winchester City v Cray Wanderers	2-2
96	Bashley v VCD Athletic	5-0
97	AFC Wimbledon v Horsham	1-0
98	Worthing United v Hamble ASSC	3-2
99	Didcot Town v Whitehawk	6-1
100	Moneyfields v AFC Wallingford	3-1
101	East Preston v Metropolitan Police	1-3
102	Fairford Town v Cinderford Town	0-3
103	Downton v Team Bath	0-7
104	St Blazey v Saltash United	3-1
105	Cirencester Town v Merthyr Tydfil	2-3
106	Bishop Sutton v Bishop's Cleeve	0-0
107	Radstock Town v Evesham United	1-6
108	Mangotsfield United v Paulton Rovers	1-0
109	Taunton Town v Swindon Supermarine	2-2
110	Bath City v Tiverton Town	0-0
111	Bideford v Bridgwater Town	2-2
112	Willand Rovers v Tavistock	4-0
113	Clevedon Town v Truro City	1-1
114	Gloucester City v Liskeard Athletic	0-0
115	Yate Town v Slimbridge	1-2
116	Chippenham Town v Corsham Town	2-0
11r	Trafford v Chadderton	3-1
33r	Leek Town v Kidsgrove Athletic	0-1
35r	Gedling Town v Hednesford Town	1-0
38r	Buxton v Tipton Town	2-1
41r	Bromsgrove Rovers v Ilkeston Town (2)	0-1
43r	Stamford v Lincoln United	1-2
49r	Saffron Walden Town v Hitchin Town	1-1q
57r	Billericay Town v Hampton & Richmond Boro.	0-0P
78r	Fleet Town v Margate	0-1
79r	Carterton v Maidenhead United	2-3
84r	Leatherhead v Molesey	3-0
95r	Cray Wanderers v Winchester City	2-2P
106r	Bishop's Cleeve v Bishop Sutton	5-1
109r	Swindon Supermarine v Taunton Town	2-3
110r	Tiverton Town v Bath City	1-3
111r	Bridgwater Town v Bideford	0-2
113r	Truro City v Clevedon Town	0-1
114r	Liskeard Athletic v Gloucester City	0-3

Qualifying Round Two

1	North Ferriby United v Whitley Bay	0-2
2	Leigh RMI v Woodley Sports	0-2
3	Droylsden v Worksop Town	2-0
4	Burscough v Blyth Spartans	1-2
5	Trafford v Glossop North End	5-0
6	Marske United v Skelmersdale United	0-2
7	Farsley Celtic v Wakefield	3-0
8	Witton Albion v Vauxhall Motors	3-0
9	Prescot Cables v Marine	1-2
10	Hyde United v Newcastle Benfield Bay Plastics	0-2
11	Scarborough v Lancaster City	1-1
12	Ashton United v Gainsborough Trinity	0-2
13	Durham City v Hallam	5-1 N
14	Flixton v Barrow	1-2
15	Ossett Albion v Workington	2-1
16	Curzon Ashton v Harrogate Town	0-2
17	Guiseley v Gateshead (2)	1-0
18	Fleetwood Town v Goole AFC	4-2
19	Stalybridge Celtic v Frickley Athletic	1-1
20	Kendal Town v Warrington Town	1-1
21	Raunds Town v Stratford Town	1-2
22	Halesowen Town v Chasetown	3-1
23	Sutton Coldfield Town v Cambridge City	0-2
24	Worcester City v Romulus	2-2
25	Solihull Borough v Alfreton Town	1-1

2006/07

26	Histon v Matlock Town	0-1
27	Lincoln United v Hucknall Town	0-2
28	Redditch United v Wisbech Town	2-3
29	Oadby Town v Nuneaton Borough	0-6
30	Kidsgrove Athletic v Rothwell Town	6-0
31	Gedling Town v Rocester	0-2
32	Belper Town v Quorn	1-1
33	King's Lynn v Causeway United	3-1
34	Ilkeston Town (2) v Rugby Town	1-3
35	Kettering Town v Yaxley	5-1
36	Moor Green v Hinckley United	4-2
37	Buxton v Woodford United	0-1
38	East Thurrock United v Maidenhead United	1-2
39	Cray Wanderers v Leatherhead	1-1
40	Ramsgate v Yeading	0-1
41	Heybridge Swifts v Didcot Town	2-2
42	Braintree Town v Brackley Town	0-2
43	Hemel Hempstead Town v Harrow Borough	4-2
44	AFC Wimbledon v Oxhey Jets	3-0
45	Worthing United v Romford	4-2
46	Hastings United (2) v Metropolitan Police	1-1
47	Hendon v Lewes	0-2
48	Fisher Athletic (London) v Sittingbourne	7-1
49	Maldon Town v Potters Bar Town	0-0
50	Sutton United v Bishop's Stortford	1-3
51	Haverhill Rovers v Eastbourne Borough	1-0
52	Farnborough Town v Slough Town	2-0
53	Worthing v Cheshunt	0-0
54	Great Wakering Rovers v Carshalton Athletic	0-1
55	Lowestoft Town v Bromley	0-1
56	Tooting & Mitcham United v AFC Sudbury	2-3
57	Folkestone Invicta v Welling United	1-1
58	Whitstable Town v Margate	1-2
59	Walton & Hersham v Ashford Town (Middlesex)	2-2
60	Billericay Town v Hayes	0-0
61	Thurrock v Dover Athletic	0-3
62	Tonbridge Angels v Banbury United	1-1
63	Bedford Town v Dunstable Town	3-2
64	Hitchin Town v Bognor Regis Town	0-0
65	Boreham Wood v AFC Hornchurch	0-2
66	Dereham Town v Chelmsford City	2-2
67	Dorchester Town v Cinderford Town	3-0
68	Bishop's Cleeve v Oxford City	3-1
69	Eastleigh v Gloucester City	3-2
70	Clevedon Town v Willand Rovers	3-1
71	Slimbridge v Chippenham Town	3-1
72	Lymington & New Milton v Basingstoke Town	0-0
73	Bideford v Newport County (2)	0-3
74	Bashley v Taunton Town	3-1
75	Moneyfields v Evesham United	0-4
76	Bath City v Merthyr Tydfil	0-0
77	Havant & Waterlooville v Team Bath	3-1
78	VT v Salisbury City	0-3
79	Weston-Super-Mare v Hungerford Town	1-2
80	Mangotsfield United v St Blazey	3-1
11r	Lancaster City v Scarborough	1-2
19r	Frickley Athletic v Stalybridge Celtic	0-1
20r	Warrington Town v Kendal Town	3-2
24r	Romulus v Worcester City	1-3
25r	Alfreton Town v Solihull Borough	1-3e
32r	Quorn v Belper Town	3-1
39r	Leatherhead v Cray Wanderers	4-2
41r	Didcot Town v Heybridge Swifts	1-3
46r	Metropolitan Police v Hastings United (2)	5-1
49r	Potters Bar Town v Maldon Town	3-2e
53r	Cheshunt v Worthing	1-0
57r	Welling United v Folkestone Invicta	3-1
59r	Ashford Town (Middlesex) v Walton & Hersham	3-1e
60r	Hayes v Billericay Town	2-1
62r	Banbury United v Tonbridge Angels	1-2
64r	Bognor Regis Town v Hitchin Town	0-1
66r	Chelmsford City v Dereham Town	4-0
72r	Basingstoke Town v Lymington & New Milton	1-0
76r	Merthyr Tydfil v Bath City	3-2

Qualifying Round Three

1	Ossett Albion v Scarborough	1-1
2	Durham City v Barrow	0-1 N
3	Gainsborough Trinity v Woodley Sports	2-0
4	Droylsden v Skelmersdale United	3-2
5	Whitley Bay v Blyth Spartans	2-2
6	Trafford v Harrogate Town	0-1
7	Guiseley v Newcastle Benfield Bay Plastics	0-1
8	Marine v Stalybridge Celtic	3-2
9	Witton Albion v Farsley Celtic	1-1
10	Fleetwood Town v Warrington Town	2-0
11	Halesowen Town v King's Lynn	1-2
12	Nuneaton Borough v Hucknall Town	0-1
13	Bedford Town v Moor Green	0-2
14	Solihull Borough v Wisbech Town	1-2
15	Cambridge City v Matlock Town	0-0
16	Woodford United v AFC Sudbury	1-3
17	Kettering Town v Rocester	2-1
18	Worcester City v Hemel Hempstead Town	1-1
19	Bishop's Stortford v Stratford Town	2-0
20	Rugby Town v Chelmsford City	1-3
21	Haverhill Rovers v Kidsgrove Athletic	2-1
22	Quorn v Brackley Town	0-0
23	Mangotsfield United v Leatherhead	1-1
24	Bashley v Hungerford Town	1-2
25	Maidenhead United v Worthing United	3-1
26	Dorchester Town v Lewes	0-4
27	Heybridge Swifts v Dover Athletic	2-3
28	Hayes v Bromley	1-3
29	Margate v Potters Bar Town	1-2
30	AFC Hornchurch v Welling United	1-1
31	Clevedon Town v Hitchin Town	1-1
32	Fisher Athletic (London) v Metropolitan Police	6-1
33	Cheshunt v Tonbridge Angels	1-2
34	Eastleigh v Salisbury City	0-1
35	Newport County (2) v Bishop's Cleeve	4-2
36	AFC Wimbledon v Evesham United	2-1
37	Merthyr Tydfil v Slimbridge	2-0
38	Havant & Waterlooville v Carshalton Athletic	2-0
39	Farnborough Town v Yeading	1-1
40	Basingstoke Town v Ashford Town (Middlesex)	3-0
1r	Scarborough v Ossett Albion	2-0
5r	Blyth Spartans v Whitley Bay	1-2
9r	Farsley Celtic v Witton Albion	1-0e
15r	Matlock Town v Cambridge City	2-3e
18r	Hemel Hempstead Town v Worcester City	0-2
22r	Brackley Town v Quorn	2-1
23r	Leatherhead v Mangotsfield United	4-1
30r	Welling United v AFC Hornchurch	3-1
31r	Hitchin Town v Clevedon Town	2-2q
39r	Yeading v Farnborough Town	3-0

Qualifying Round Four

1	Barrow v Marine	3-2
2	Stafford Rangers v Scarborough	3-0
3	Tamworth v Harrogate Town	3-1
4	Gainsborough Trinity v Whitley Bay	2-0
5	King's Lynn v Hucknall Town	3-0
6	Newcastle Benfield Bay Plastics v York City	0-1
7	Fleetwood Town v Wisbech Town	3-0
8	Rushden & Diamonds v Altrincham	3-0
9	Burton Albion v Halifax Town	1-0
10	Northwich Victoria v Cambridge United	2-0
11	Farsley Celtic v Cambridge City	2-1
12	Southport v Kettering Town	0-1
13	Kidderminster Harriers v Droylsden	5-1
14	Moor Green v Morecambe	1-2
15	Worcester City v Basingstoke Town	1-1
16	Crawley Town v Lewes	2-3
17	Dover Athletic v Bishop's Stortford	0-0
18	Hungerford Town v Weymouth	0-3
19	Woking v Potters Bar Town	3-2
20	Maidenhead United v Merthyr Tydfil	1-0
21	Welling United v Clevedon Town	0-3
22	Stevenage Borough v Forest Green Rovers	4-1
23	Tonbridge Angels v Newport County (2)	0-1
24	Dagenham & Redbridge v Oxford United	0-1
25	Yeading v St Albans City	2-1
26	Haverhill Rovers v Aldershot Town	0-4
27	Exeter City v AFC Wimbledon	2-1
28	AFC Sudbury v Leatherhead	1-2
29	Chelmsford City v Gravesend & Northfleet	1-0
30	Grays Athletic v Bromley	1-2
31	Fisher Athletic (London) v Salisbury City	0-1
32	Brackley Town v Havant & Waterlooville	0-2
15r	Basingstoke Town v Worcester City	1-1P
17r	Bishop's Stortford v Dover Athletic	3-2

Round One

	Barrow v Bristol Rovers	2-3
	Bishop's Stortford v King's Lynn	3-5
	Bournemouth v Boston United	4-0
	Bradford City v Crewe Alexandra	4-0
	Brentford v Doncaster Rovers	0-1
	Brighton & Hove Albion v Northwich Victoria	8-0
	Burton Albion v Tamworth	1-2
	Chelmsford City v Aldershot Town	1-1
	Cheltenham Town v Scunthorpe United	0-0
	Chesterfield v Basingstoke Town	0-1
	Clevedon Town v Chester City	1-4
	Exeter City v Stockport County	1-2
	Farsley Celtic v Milton Keynes Dons	0-0
	Gainsborough Trinity v Barnet	1-3
	Gillingham v Bromley	4-1
	Havant & Waterlooville v Millwall	1-2 N
	Huddersfield Town v Blackpool	0-1
	Kettering Town v Oldham Athletic	3-4
	Lewes v Darlington	1-4
	Leyton Orient v Notts County	2-1
	Macclesfield Town v Walsall	0-0
	Mansfield Town v Accrington Stanley (2)	1-0
	Morecambe v Kidderminster Harriers	2-1
	Newport County (2) v Swansea City	1-3
	Northampton Town v Grimsby Town	0-0
	Nottingham Forest v Yeading	5-0
	Peterborough United v Rotherham United	3-0
	Port Vale v Lincoln City	2-1
	Rochdale v Hartlepool United	1-1
	Rushden & Diamonds v Yeovil Town	3-1
	Salisbury City v Fleetwood Town	3-0
	Shrewsbury Town v Hereford United	0-0
	Stafford Rangers v Maidenhead United	1-1
	Swindon Town v Carlisle United	3-1
	Torquay United v Leatherhead	2-1
	Tranmere Rovers v Woking	4-2
	Weymouth v Bury	2-2
	Wrexham v Stevenage Borough	1-0
	Wycombe Wanderers v Oxford United	2-1
	York City v Bristol City	0-1
r	Aldershot Town v Chelmsford City	2-0
r	Bury v Weymouth	4-3
r	Grimsby Town v Northampton Town	0-2
r	Hartlepool United v Rochdale	0-0P
r	Hereford United v Shrewsbury Town	2-0
r	Maidenhead United v Stafford Rangers	0-2
r	Milton Keynes Dons v Farsley Celtic	2-0
r	Scunthorpe United v Cheltenham Town	2-0
r	Walsall v Macclesfield Town	0-1

Round Two

	Aldershot Town v Basingstoke Town	1-1
	Barnet v Northampton Town	4-1
	Bradford City v Millwall	0-0
	Brighton & Hove Albion v Stafford Rangers	3-0
	Bristol City v Gillingham	4-3
	Bristol Rovers v Bournemouth	1-1
	Bury v Chester City	2-2
	Darlington v Swansea City	1-3
	Hereford United v Port Vale	4-0
	King's Lynn v Oldham Athletic	0-2
	Macclesfield Town v Hartlepool United	2-1
	Mansfield Town v Doncaster Rovers	1-1
	Milton Keynes Dons v Blackpool	0-2
	Rushden & Diamonds v Tamworth	1-2
	Salisbury City v Nottingham Forest	1-1
	Scunthorpe United v Wrexham	0-2
	Stockport County v Wycombe Wanderers	2-1
	Swindon Town v Morecambe	1-0
	Torquay United v Leyton Orient	1-1
	Tranmere Rovers v Peterborough United	1-2
r	Basingstoke Town v Aldershot Town	1-3
r	Bournemouth v Bristol Rovers	0-1
r	Chester City v Bury	1-3 d
r	Doncaster Rovers v Mansfield Town	2-0
r	Leyton Orient v Torquay United	1-2
r	Millwall v Bradford City	1-0e
r	Nottingham Forest v Salisbury City	2-0

Round Three

	Barnet v Colchester United	2-1
	Birmingham City v Newcastle United	2-2
	Blackpool v Aldershot Town	4-2
	Bristol City v Coventry City	3-3
	Bristol Rovers v Hereford United	1-0
	Cardiff City v Tottenham Hotspur	0-0
	Chelsea v Macclesfield Town	6-1
	Chester City v Ipswich Town	0-0
	Crystal Palace v Swindon Town	2-1
	Derby County v Wrexham	3-1
	Doncaster Rovers v Bolton Wanderers	0-4
	Everton v Blackburn Rovers	1-4
	Hull City v Middlesbrough	1-1
	Leicester City v Fulham	2-2
	Liverpool v Arsenal	1-3
	Manchester United v Aston Villa	2-1
	Nottingham Forest v Charlton Athletic	2-0
	Peterborough United v Plymouth Argyle	1-1
	Portsmouth v Wigan Athletic	2-1
	Preston North End v Sunderland	1-0
	Queen's Park Rangers v Luton Town	2-2
	Reading v Burnley	3-2
	Sheffield United v Swansea City	0-3
	Sheffield Wednesday v Manchester City	1-1
	Southend United v Barnsley	1-1
	Stoke City v Millwall	2-0
	Tamworth v Norwich City	1-4
	Torquay United v Southampton	0-2
	Watford v Stockport County	4-1
	West Bromwich Albion v Leeds United	3-1
	West Ham United v Brighton & Hove Albion	3-0
	Wolverhampton Wan. v Oldham Athletic	2-2
r	Barnsley v Southend United	0-2
r	Coventry City v Bristol City	0-2
r	Fulham v Leicester City	4-3
r	Ipswich Town v Chester City	1-0
r	Luton Town v Queen's Park Rangers	1-0
r	Manchester City v Sheffield Wednesday	2-1
r	Middlesbrough v Hull City	4-3
r	Newcastle United v Birmingham City	1-5
r	Oldham Athletic v Wolverhampton Wan.	0-2
r	Plymouth Argyle v Peterborough United	2-1
r	Tottenham Hotspur v Cardiff City	4-0

Round Four

	Arsenal v Bolton Wanderers	1-1
	Barnet v Plymouth Argyle	0-2
	Birmingham City v Reading	2-3
	Blackpool v Norwich City	1-1
	Bristol City v Middlesbrough	2-2
	Chelsea v Nottingham Forest	3-0
	Crystal Palace v Preston North End	0-2
	Derby County v Bristol Rovers	1-0
	Fulham v Stoke City	3-0
	Ipswich Town v Swansea City	1-0
	Luton Town v Blackburn Rovers	0-4
	Manchester City v Southampton	3-1
	Manchester United v Portsmouth	2-1
	Tottenham Hotspur v Southend United	3-1
	West Ham United v Watford	0-1
	Wolverhampton Wan. v West Bromwich Albion	0-3
r	Bolton Wanderers v Arsenal	1-3e
r	Middlesbrough v Bristol City	2-2P
r	Norwich City v Blackpool	3-2e

2006/07 to 2007/08

Round Five

	Arsenal v Blackburn Rovers	0-0
	Chelsea v Norwich City	4-0
	Fulham v Tottenham Hotspur	0-4
	Manchester United v Reading	1-1
	Middlesbrough v West Bromwich Albion	2-2
	Plymouth Argyle v Derby County	2-0
	Preston North End v Manchester City	1-3
	Watford v Ipswich Town	1-0
r	Blackburn Rovers v Arsenal	1-0
r	Reading v Manchester United	2-3
r	West Bromwich Albion v Middlesbrough	1-1q

Round Six

	Blackburn Rovers v Manchester City	2-0
	Chelsea v Tottenham Hotspur	3-3
	Middlesbrough v Manchester United	2-2
	Plymouth Argyle v Watford	0-1
r	Manchester United v Middlesbrough	1-0
r	Tottenham Hotspur v Chelsea	1-2

Semi Finals

Chelsea v Blackburn Rovers	2-1eN
Manchester United v Watford	4-1 N

Final

Chelsea v Manchester United	1-0eN

2007/08

Extra Preliminary Round

1	Guisborough Town v Norton & Stockton Ancients	1-3
2	West Auckland Town v Bedlington Terriers	2-1
3	Billingham Town v Eccleshill United	6-1
4	Winterton Rangers v Armthorpe Welfare	3-2
5	Glasshoughton Welfare v Liversedge	1-1
6	Horden CW v Sunderland Nissan	2-1
7	Thackley v Ashington	0-1
8	Darlington Railway Ath. v Yorkshire Amateur	6-0
9	Whitley Bay v Dunston Federation	0-1
10	Hall Road Rangers v Tadcaster Albion	6-1
11	Spennymoor Town v North Shields	3-0
12	Hebburn Town v Tow Law Town	1-3
13	Crook Town v Sunderland RCA	2-2
14	Morpeth Town v Seaham Red Star	3-0
15	Pontefract Collieries v Selby Town	0-0
16	Thornaby v South Shields (3)	2-3
17	Jarrow Roofing Boldon CA v West Allotment Celtic	2-1
18	Brandon United v Durham City	0-5
19	Washington v Pickering Town	1-3
20	Esh Winning v Whickham	1-0
21	Ryton v Silsden	3-4
22	Billingham Synthonia v Northallerton Town	2-1
23	Bottesford Town v Shildon	1-2
24	Team Northumbria v Consett	0-11
25	Chester-le-Street Town v Bishop Auckland	1-1
26	Ashton Town v Ramsbottom United	4-2
27	Daisy Hill v Congleton Town	0-4
28	AFC Emley v Darwen	3-0
29	Rossington Main v Atherton Collieries	2-2
30	Chadderton v Winsford United	3-4
31	Holker Old Boys v St Helens Town	2-3e
32	Blackpool Mechanics v Maine Road	1-3
33	Formby v Oldham Town	2-3
34	Squires Gate v Penrith	1-3
35	Flixton v Bootle	2-1
36	Trafford v Atherton LR	1-0
37	Nelson v Hallam	0-2
38	Salford City v Padiham	6-3
39	Abbey Hey v Bacup Borough	1-2
40	Brodsworth MW v Parkgate	2-3
41	Dinnington Town v Maltby Main	2-1
42	Glossop North End v Eccleshall	2-0
43	Highgate United v Shirebrook Town	2-1
44	Castle Vale v Brierley Hill & Withymoor	3-3
45	Loughborough Dynamo v Stapenhill	1-1
46	Tividale v Mickleover Sports	1-4
47	Nuneaton Griff v Rainworth MW	0-3
48	Pegasus Juniors v New Mills	0-0
49	Glapwell v Dudley Town	2-2
50	Shifnal Town v Arnold Town	1-1
51	Ledbury Town v Boldmere St Michaels	2-6
52	Oadby Town v Racing Club Warwick	1-0
53	Teversal v Coventry Sphinx	2-2
54	Market Drayton Town v Studley	1-1
55	Long Eaton United v Bridgnorth Town	2-1
56	Coalville Town v Rocester	1-2
57	Gornal Athletic v Meir KA	0-3
58	Norton United v Oldbury United	1-1
59	Westfields v Friar Lane & Epworth	3-2
60	Borrowash Victoria v Biddulph Victoria	0-1
61	Cradley Town v Gedling Town	1-3
62	Cadbury Athletic v Alvechurch	1-1
63	South Normanton Athletic v Lye Town	1-0
64	Barwell v Newcastle Town	1-1
65	Tipton Town v Leek CSOB	1-1
66	Coleshill Town v Wellington (Hereford)	1-1
67	Wroxham v Hadleigh United	3-0
68	Walsham Le Willows v Stowmarket Town	3-0
69	Woodbridge Town v Great Yarmouth Town	5-0
70	St Ives Town v Cornard United	3-2
71	Bourne Town v Haverhill Rovers	2-3
72	Mildenhall Town v Leiston	3-0
73	Holbeach United v Wisbech Town	2-1
74	Dereham Town v Fakenham Town	12-0
75	Felixstowe & Walton United v Debenham LC	2-2
76	Long Melford v Blackstones	0-2
77	Needham Market v Lowestoft Town	4-1
78	Soham Town Rangers v St Neots Town	5-2
79	Deeping Rangers v Lincoln Moorlands	5-0
80	Yaxley v March Town United	1-0
81	Brimsdown Rovers v Burnham Ramblers	1-2
82	Sporting Bengal United v London APSA	0-0e
83	Saffron Walden Town v Wootton Blue Cross	2-2
84	Daventry United v Raunds Town	0-2
85	Northampton Spencer v Clapton	3-2
86	FC Clacton v Desborough Town	1-1
87	Biggleswade United v Broxbourne Borough V&E	1-1
88	Welwyn Garden City v Bowers & Pitsea	3-1
89	Bedfont v Oxhey Jets	0-2
90	Tring Athletic v Ruislip Manor	2-1
91	Stansted v Hullbridge Sports	2-0
92	Hertford Town v Cogenhoe United	1-0
93	Potton United v Romford	3-2
94	Long Buckby v Hoddesdon Town	3-1
95	Barkingside v Stewarts & Lloyds (2)	5-3
96	Halstead Town v Wellingborough Town (2)	2-2
97	Eton Manor v Colney Heath	3-1
98	London Colney v Langford	0-1
99	Bedfont Green v Stanway Rovers	2-2
100	Cockfosters v Southend Manor	3-2
101	Tiptree United v Sawbridgeworth	2-2
102	Barking v Harefield United	4-0
103	Leverstock Green v Stotfold	0-3
104	Haringey Borough v Wembley	2-2
105	Biggleswade Town v Concord Rangers	1-3
106	North Greenford United v Royston Town	5-0
107	Tunbridge Wells v Chessington & Hook United	3-4
108	Three Bridges v Wealden	1-0
109	Camberley Town v Worthing United	2-0
110	Frimley Green v Colliers Wood United	1-2
111	Dorking (2) v Selsey	0-1
112	Whitehawk v VCD Athletic	0-1
113	Redhill v Sidley United	3-1
114	Farnham Town v Ringmer	1-4
115	Raynes Park Vale v Deal Town	3-3
116	Westfield v Banstead Athletic	0-2
117	Eastbourne United v Sevenoaks Town	1-3
118	Erith Town v Cobham	3-1
119	Lancing v Faversham Town	1-1
120	Lordswood v Bookham	1-1
121	Herne Bay v East Grinstead Town	0-0
122	Epsom & Ewell v Crowborough Athletic	1-7
123	Merstham v Hythe Town	2-3
124	Croydon v Saltdean United	wo/s
125	Peacehaven & Telscombe v East Preston	1-2
126	Pagham v Hailsham Town	1-1
127	Wick v Chertsey Town	2-2
128	Thamesmead Town v Egham Town	4-1
129	Shoreham v Horley Town	0-1
130	Hassocks v Rye United	1-0
131	Mile Oak v Guildford City (2)	0-2
132	VT v Cowes Sports	5-0
133	Corsham Town v Wantage Town	5-1
134	Fareham Town v Carterton	1-1
135	Highworth Town v Wootton Bassett Town	0-0
136	Bournemouth (Ams) v Beaconsfield SYCOB	2-3
137	Henley Town v Westbury United	3-2
138	Christchurch v Aylesbury Vale	6-1
139	Sandhurst Town v Newport Pagnell Town	2-0
140	Kidlington v Shrivenham	1-1
141	Buckingham Town v Chalfont St Peter	1-3
142	Hamble ASSC v Alton Town	1-0
143	Bemerton Heath Harlequins v Reading Town	5-3
144	Brockenhurst v Witney United	2-0
145	Abingdon Town v Ardley United	2-1
146	Flackwell Heath v Moneyfields	1-2
147	Thame United v Downton	1-2
148	Holmer Green v Melksham Town	0-1
149	North Leigh v Devizes Town	4-0
150	New Milton Town v AFC Totton	1-5
151	Bicester Town v Milton United (Oxon)	1-1
152	Hungerford Town v Calne Town	0-0
153	Lymington Town v AFC Wallingford	4-1 N
154	Marlow United v Cove	1-2
155	Minehead v Harrow Hill	4-0
156	Saltash United v Almondsbury Town	2-1
157	Shortwood United v Bishop Sutton	1-0
158	Shepton Mallet v Radstock Town	2-2
159	Bitton v Bideford	2-0
160	Street v Wimborne Town	2-5
161	Barnstaple Town v Clevedon United	4-0
162	Liskeard Athletic v Shaftesbury	2-2
163	Tavistock v Bodmin Town	1-3
164	Keynsham Town v St Blazey	1-2
165	Poole Town v Dawlish Town	0-2
166	Hamworthy United v Torrington	wo/s
167	Hallen v Fairford Town	4-2
168	Bridport v Welton Rovers	0-5
169	Chard Town v Sherborne Town	1-3
170	Odd Down v Bristol Manor Farm	2-0
171	Falmouth Town v Frome Town	1-2
5r	Liversedge v Glasshoughton Welfare	4-3
13r	Sunderland RCA v Crook Town	0-3
15r	Selby Town v Pontefract Collieries	1-0e
25r	Bishop Auckland v Chester-le-Street Town	1-2
29r	Atherton Collieries v Rossington Main	5-0
44r	Brierley Hill & Withymoor v Castle Vale	4-0
45r	Stapenhill v Loughborough Dynamo	1-2e
48r	New Mills v Pegasus Juniors	5-1
49r	Dudley Town v Glapwell	0-5 N
50r	Arnold Town v Shifnal Town	1-1q
53r	Coventry Sphinx v Teversal	2-2q
54r	Studley v Market Drayton Town	0-4
58r	Oldbury United v Norton United	1-0eN
62r	Alvechurch v Cadbury Athletic	6-0
64r	Newcastle Town v Barwell	1-2e
65r	Leek CSOB v Tipton Town	0-4
66r	Wellington (Hereford) v Coleshill Town	3-2
75r	Debenham LC v Felixstowe & Walton United	2-0
82r	London APSA v Sporting Bengal United	4-3 N
83r	Wootton Blue Cross v Saffron Walden Town	1-6
86r	Desborough Town v FC Clacton	2-3
87r	Broxbourne Borough V&E v Biggleswade United	2-1
96r	Wellingborough Town (2) v Halstead Town	2-0
99r	Stanway Rovers v Bedfont Green	2-1
101r	Sawbridgeworth v Tiptree United	2-4e
104r	Wembley v Haringey Borough	3-0
115r	Deal Town v Raynes Park Vale	4-2
119r	Faversham Town v Lancing	3-0
120r	Bookham v Lordswood	1-2
121r	East Grinstead Town v Herne Bay	1-3
126r	Hailsham Town v Pagham	2-0
127r	Chertsey Town v Wick	3-0
134r	Carterton v Fareham Town	0-3
135r	Wootton Bassett Town v Highworth Town	2-1
140r	Shrivenham v Kidlington	1-2
151r	Milton United (Oxon) v Bicester Town	0-1
152r	Calne Town v Hungerford Town	0-3
158r	Radstock Town v Shepton Mallet	0-2
162r	Shaftesbury v Liskeard Athletic	0-3

Preliminary Round

1	Jarrow Roofing Boldon CA v Norton & Stockton Anc.	1-0
2	Chester-le-Street Town v Billingham Synthonia	2-1
3	Winterton Rangers v Morpeth Town	1-0
4	Selby Town v Pickering Town	4-0
5	Marske United v Horden CW	1-1
6	Wakefield v West Auckland Town	1-1
7	Ashington v Newcastle Blue Star	1-3
8	Liversedge v Dunston Federation	2-0
9	Bridlington Town (2) v Newcastle Benfield	1-2
10	Durham City v Silsden	2-2
11	Spennymoor Town v Garforth Town	3-2
12	Shildon v Goole AFC	5-4
13	Brigg Town v South Shields (3)	4-0
14	Tow Law Town v Billingham Town	0-0
15	Hall Road Rangers v Crook Town	1-0
16	Esh Winning v Harrogate Railway Athletic	1-4
17	Consett v Darlington Railway Ath. (2)	4-0
18	Ossett Albion v Bradford Park Avenue	0-1
19	Cheadle Town v Ashton Town	3-0
20	Chorley v Warrington Town	2-0
21	Atherton Collieries v Bacup Borough	3-1
22	Parkgate v Alsager Town	2-1
23	Clitheroe v St Helens Town	3-2
24	Colwyn Bay v Congleton Town	2-2
25	Maine Road v Skelmersdale United	0-3
26	Winsford United v Penrith	1-3
27	Radcliffe Borough v Lancaster City	3-0
28	Colne v Nantwich Town	1-3
29	Trafford v FC United of Manchester	2-5 N
30	Woodley Sports v Mossley	1-1 N
31	Rossendale United v Dinnington Town	0-2
32	AFC Emley v Hallam	2-2
33	Flixton v Salford City	1-0
34	Cammell Laird v Sheffield	2-0
35	Bamber Bridge v Oldham Town	2-0
36	Stocksbridge Park Steels v Curzon Ashton	3-2
37	Leamington v Shifnal Town	1-0
38	Bromyard Town v Shepshed Dynamo	1-4
39	Retford United v Tipton Town	1-2
40	Rushall Olympic v Boldmere St Michaels	3-0
41	Pelsall Villa v Quorn	1-6
42	Causeway United v Westfields	1-1
43	Glapwell v Stone Dominoes	1-0
44	Mickleover Sports v Long Eaton United	0-0
45	Bolehall Swifts v Alvechurch	1-3
46	Brierley Hill & Withymoor v Staveley MW	1-0
47	Sutton Coldfield Town v Romulus	1-1
48	Evesham United v Gresley Rovers	1-0
49	Loughborough Dynamo v Market Drayton Town	1-1
50	New Mills v Atherstone Town	1-3
51	Rocester v Wellington (Hereford)	1-0
52	Southam United v Stratford Town	0-2
53	Stourbridge v Highgate United	2-1
54	Barwell v Biddulph Victoria	0-4
55	Chasetown v Oadby Town	4-1
56	South Normanton Athletic v Bedworth United	1-1
57	Teversal v Rainworth MW	0-0
58	Barnt Green Spartak v Willenhall Town	3-2 v
59	Carlton Town v Pilkington XXX	2-1
60	Meir KA v Gedling Town	1-1
61	Oldbury United v Kidsgrove Athletic	1-3 N
62	Belper Town v Stourport Swifts	3-3
63	Malvern Town v Glossop North End	3-0
64	Deeping Rangers v Dereham Town	0-0

2007/08

65 Diss Town v Kirkley & Pakefield	0-1
66 Ipswich Wanderers v Needham Market	1-10
67 Ely City v Boston Town	0-1
68 Yaxley v Soham Town Rangers	0-3
69 Spalding United v Norwich United	5-1
70 Blackstones v Grantham Town	0-0
71 Walsham Le Willows v Haverhill Rovers	0-0
72 Mildenhall Town v St Ives Town	2-1
73 Holbeach United v Newmarket Town	2-0
74 Debenham LC v Gorleston	2-0
75 Woodbridge Town v Wroxham	0-2
76 AFC Sudbury v Bury Town	2-3
77 Stanway Rovers v Saffron Walden Town	0-3
78 Wivenhoe Town v Concord Rangers	0-4
79 Tilbury v Great Wakering Rovers	0-4
80 Hillingdon Borough v Barking	0-0
81 Tring Athletic v Hertford Town	4-4
82 Enfield Town v AFC Hayes	2-1
83 Rothwell Town v Canvey Island	2-1
84 Dunstable Town v Wingate & Finchley	3-1
85 Aveley v Berkhamsted Town	2-1
86 Harwich & Parkeston v Ilford	2-0
87 Northwood v Uxbridge	1-0
88 Bedford v Broxbourne Borough V&E	0-3
89 Arlesey Town v Brentwood Town	0-1
90 Langford v Potters Bar Town	0-0
91 Waltham Forest v Wellingborough Town (2)	1-1
92 Wembley v Ware	1-4
93 Leighton Town v FC Clacton	3-1
94 Maldon Town v Eton Manor	5-0
95 Barkingside v Hanwell Town	2-1
96 Stotfold v Potton United	7-2
97 Welwyn Garden City v Cockfosters	1-1
98 Oxhey Jets v Burnham Ramblers	1-4
99 Tiptree United v London APSA	2-0 D
100 Raunds Town v Edgware Town	1-5
101 Long Buckby v Barton Rovers	1-1
102 Witham Town v Waltham Abbey	2-3
103 Stansted v St Margaretsbury	4-1
104 Northampton Spencer v North Greenford United	2-1
105 Redbridge v Woodford United	1-2
106 Corinthian Casuals v Deal Town	1-2
107 Arundel v Molesey	1-1
108 Walton & Hersham v Hassocks	3-0
109 Burgess Hill Town v Banstead Athletic	7-0
110 Dartford v Leatherhead	3-0
111 Slade Green v Croydon	1-6
112 Ringmer v Chatham Town	1-4
113 Selsey v Lordswood	1-0
114 Sittingbourne v Chertsey Town	1-0
115 Camberley Town v Ash United	0-0
116 Metropolitan Police v Croydon Athletic	0-1
117 Eastbourne Town v Kingstonian	2-1
118 Colliers Wood United v Faversham Town	7-6
119 Redhill v Dover Athletic	0-1
120 Herne Bay v Guildford City (2)	2-0
121 Erith & Belvedere v Ashford Town	2-0
122 Dulwich Hamlet v Three Bridges	2-0
123 Horley Town v East Preston	0-0
124 Walton Casuals v Sevenoaks Town	1-3
125 Thamesmead Town v Whitstable Town	3-1
126 Erith Town v VCD Athletic	1-0
127 Littlehampton Town v Chipstead	3-2
128 Tooting & Mitcham United v Cray Wanderers	1-2
129 Crowborough Athletic v Hailsham Town	1-1
130 Hythe Town v Whyteleafe	2-1
131 Godalming Town v Worthing	2-2
132 Horsham YMCA v Chessington & Hook United	4-1
133 Wootton Bassett Town v Bracknell Town	2-1
134 Slough Town v Fleet Town	1-4 N
135 Windsor & Eton v Marlow	1-1
136 Melksham Town v Bicester Town	4-0
137 Burnham v Brockenhurst	1-1
138 Christchurch v Didcot Town	2-4
139 Chalfont St Peter v Hamble ASSC	1-0
140 Winchester City v Moneyfields	0-2
141 Fareham Town v Sandhurst Town	3-3
142 Beaconsfield SYCOB v Hungerford Town	0-0
143 Farnborough v Chesham United	0-2
144 Aylesbury United v Newport (IOW)	4-2
145 Henley Town v Bemerton Heath Harlequins	3-2
146 Abingdon Town v AFC Totton	2-3
147 Downton v Abingdon United	1-1
148 Cove v Gosport Borough	1-6
149 Andover v Oxford City	3-4
150 North Leigh v VT	1-1
151 Corsham Town v Lymington Town	2-1
152 Kidlington v Thatcham Town	2-3e
153 Bitton v Slimbridge	wo/s
154 Brislington v Wimborne Town	0-5
155 Dawlish Town v Bishop's Cleeve	1-2
156 Shepton Mallet v Hallen	0-2
157 Shortwood United v Frome Town	2-1
158 Cinderford Town v Elmore	3-2
159 Paulton Rovers v St Blazey	1-1
160 Bridgwater Town v Minehead	3-1
161 Barnstaple Town v Truro City	0-6
162 Sherborne Town v Liskeard Athletic	3-2
163 Willand Rovers v Hamworthy United	2-3
164 Bodmin Town v Ilfracombe Town	4-0
165 Saltash United v Taunton Town	2-3
166 Welton Rovers v Odd Down	1-0
5r Horden CW v Marske United	2-1
6r West Auckland Town v Wakefield	1-0
10r Silsden v Durham City	0-3
14r Billingham Town v Tow Law Town	3-2
24r Congleton Town v Colwyn Bay	1-5
30r Mossley v Woodley Sports	1-2
32r AFC Emley v Hallam	1-2
42r Westfields v Causeway United	2-3e
44r Long Eaton United v Mickleover Sports	3-4
47r Romulus v Sutton Coldfield Town	4-4q
49r Market Drayton Town v Loughborough Dynamo	4-0
56r Bedworth United v South Normanton Athletic	1-0
57r Rainworth MW v Teversal	2-1
58r Willenhall Town v Barnt Green Spartak	3-1
60r Gedling Town v Meir KA	5-0
62r Stourport Swifts v Belper Town	2-5
64r Dereham Town v Deeping Rangers	0-1
70r Grantham Town v Blackstones	2-1e
71r Haverhill Rovers v Walsham Le Willows	4-2
80r Barking v Hillingdon Borough	1-1q
81r Hertford Town v Tring Athletic	2-0
90r Potters Bar Town v Langford	5-1
91r Wellingborough Town (2) v Waltham Forest	0-2
97r Cockfosters v Welwyn Garden City	0-1
101r Barton Rovers v Long Buckby	5-0
107r Molesey v Arundel	1-2
115r Ash United v Camberley Town	0-3
123r East Preston v Horley Town	1-1q
129r Hailsham Town v Crowborough Athletic	1-1q
131r Worthing v Godalming Town	3-0
135r Marlow v Windsor & Eton	0-3
137r Brockenhurst v Burnham	3-0
141r Sandhurst Town v Fareham Town	0-0P
142r Hungerford Town v Beaconsfield SYCOB	0-3
147r Abingdon United v Downton	5-2
150r VT v North Leigh	2-1
159r St Blazey v Paulton Rovers	0-3

Qualifying Round One

1 Bradford Park Avenue v Scarborough	wo/s
2 West Auckland Town v Winterton Rangers	3-2
3 Newcastle Benfield v Newcastle Blue Star	2-1
4 Whitby Town v Shildon	3-2
5 Chester-le-Street Town v Harrogate Railway Athletic	1-1
6 Consett v Ossett Town	3-0
7 Hall Road Rangers v Billingham Town	2-3
8 Gateshead (2) v Selby Town	6-1
9 Liversedge v North Ferriby United	1-0
10 Spennymoor Town v Brigg Town	2-1
11 Horden CW v Jarrow Roofing Boldon CA	1-1
12 Durham City v Guiseley	1-3 N
13 Dinnington Town v Penrith	2-2
14 Flixton v Bamber Bridge	2-2
15 Fleetwood Town v FC United of Manchester	2-1
16 Witton Albion v Prescot Cables	1-2
17 Hallam v Woodley Sports	0-1
18 Frickley Athletic v Stocksbridge Park Steels	1-2
19 Nantwich Town v Ashton United	3-2
20 Chorley v Clitheroe	2-2
21 Colwyn Bay v Parkgate	2-1
22 Skelmersdale United v Marine	2-0
23 Radcliffe Borough v Cammell Laird	4-1
24 Atherton Collieries v Cheadle Town	2-5
25 Worksop Town v Kendal Town	0-1
26 Stourbridge v Leamington	2-0
27 Kidsgrove Athletic v Willenhall Town	2-0
28 Rushall Olympic v Atherstone Town	4-1
29 Rocester v Chasetown	0-1
30 Belper Town v Causeway United	3-0
31 Bromsgrove Rovers v Shepshed Dynamo	1-1
32 Glapwell v Rugby Town	3-2
33 Quorn v Alvechurch	5-0
34 Halesowen Town v Malvern Town	4-0
35 Biddulph Victoria v Rainworth MW	1-3
36 Sutton Coldfield Town v Ilkeston Town (2)	2-1
37 Carlton Town v Matlock Town	2-4
38 Hednesford Town v Stratford Town	0-0
39 Evesham United v Tipton Town	1-1
40 Brierley Hill & Withymoor v Market Drayton Town	1-2
41 Bedworth United v Eastwood Town	2-1
42 Gedling Town v Mickleover Sports	3-1
43 Leek Town v Buxton	1-2
44 Holbeach United v Debenham LC	0-2
45 Kirkley & Pakefield v Wroxham	2-1
46 Boston Town v Soham Town Rangers	0-4
47 Bury Town v Deeping Rangers	2-0
48 Lincoln United v King's Lynn	0-3
49 Needham Market v Grantham Town	0-1
50 Stamford v Spalding United	5-0
51 Mildenhall Town v Haverhill Rovers	1-1
52 Hemel Hempstead Town v East Thurrock United	4-0
53 Hillingdon Borough v Northampton Spencer	1-0
54 Dunstable Town v Waltham Abbey	1-0
55 Hertford Town v Barkingside	3-3
56 Edgware Town v Potters Bar Town	2-0
57 Chelmsford City v Burnham Ramblers	5-0
58 Barton Rovers v Corby Town	0-0
59 Harwich & Parkeston v Woodford United	0-0
60 Rothwell Town v Enfield Town	1-1
61 Broxbourne Borough V&E v Bedford Town	1-1
62 Saffron Walden Town v Maldon Town	1-2
63 AFC Hornchurch v Cheshunt	3-1
64 Welwyn Garden City v Billericay Town	2-8
65 Hendon v Aveley	1-1
66 Boreham Wood v Northwood	1-0
67 Ware v Great Wakering Rovers	0-0
68 Stotfold v Stansted	4-2
69 Wealdstone v Waltham Forest	1-0
70 Harrow Borough v Hitchin Town	2-3
71 Harlow Town v Concord Rangers	2-0
72 Brackley Town v Staines Town	0-0
73 Heybridge Swifts v Leyton	4-3
74 Ashford Town (Middlesex) v Leighton Town	0-1
75 Brentwood Town v London APSA	4-0
76 Dulwich Hamlet v Deal Town	2-2
77 Hythe Town v Littlehampton Town	3-1
78 Burgess Hill Town v Dover Athletic	0-2
79 Herne Bay v Sevenoaks Town	1-0
80 Worthing v Croydon	0-0
81 Horsham v Arundel	7-1
82 Chatham Town v Margate	0-3
83 Dartford v Sittingbourne	1-1
84 Folkestone Invicta v Horsham YMCA	1-1
85 Horley Town v Erith Town	0-1
86 Croydon Athletic v Tonbridge Angels	1-1
87 Cray Wanderers v AFC Wimbledon	2-6
88 Maidstone United (2) v Erith & Belvedere	3-0
89 Eastbourne Town v Walton & Hersham	1-1
90 Camberley Town v Colliers Wood United	4-2
91 Thamesmead Town v Carshalton Athletic	2-4
92 Crowborough Athletic v Selsey	2-1
93 Hastings United (2) v Ramsgate	0-1
94 VT v Bashley	1-1
95 Didcot Town v Windsor & Eton	0-1
96 Sandhurst Town v Chalfont St Peter	1-6
97 Banbury United v Aylesbury United	1-4
98 Fleet Town v Gosport Borough	0-0
99 Oxford City v Swindon Supermarine	4-2
100 Abingdon United v AFC Totton	1-1
101 Corsham Town v Melksham Town	1-0
102 Moneyfields v Thatcham Town	1-0
103 Chesham United v Henley Town	5-1
104 Brockenhurst v Wootton Bassett Town	1-1
105 Beaconsfield SYCOB v Chippenham Town	1-1
106 Mangotsfield United v Taunton Town	3-0
107 Yate Town v Gloucester City	1-5
108 Tiverton Town v Shortwood United	0-3
109 Hamworthy United v Bishop's Cleeve	3-3
110 Bridgwater Town v Paulton Rovers	0-2
111 Hallen v Sherborne Town	2-0
112 Cirencester Town v Cinderford Town	1-1
113 Team Bath v Bodmin Town	2-0
114 Welton Rovers v Truro City	0-2
115 Clevedon Town v Wimborne Town	4-0
116 Bitton v Merthyr Tydfil	2-4
5r Harrogate Railway Athletic v Chester-le-Street Town	3-0
11r Jarrow Roofing Boldon CA v Horden CW	1-2
13r Penrith v Dinnington Town	1-2e
14r Bamber Bridge v Flixton	3-1
20r Clitheroe v Chorley	1-1P
31r Shepshed Dynamo v Bromsgrove Rovers	0-2
38r Stratford Town v Hednesford Town	0-1
39r Tipton Town v Evesham United	0-2
51r Haverhill Rovers v Mildenhall Town	0-0P
55r Barkingside v Hertford Town	3-1
58r Corby Town v Barton Rovers	3-1
59r Woodford United v Harwich & Parkeston	3-1
60r Enfield Town v Rothwell Town	2-2P
61r Bedford Town v Broxbourne Borough V&E	2-0
65r Aveley v Hendon	2-3
67r Great Wakering Rovers v Ware	4-5
72r Staines Town v Brackley Town	0-0P
76r Deal Town v Dulwich Hamlet	1-3e
80r Croydon v Worthing	0-1
83r Sittingbourne v Dartford	1-5
84r Horsham YMCA v Folkestone Invicta	0-2
86r Tonbridge Angels v Croydon Athletic	4-2e
89r Walton & Hersham v Eastbourne Town	2-1
94r Bashley v VT	4-3e
98r Gosport Borough v Fleet Town	1-3
100r AFC Totton v Abingdon United	4-1
104r Wootton Bassett Town v Brockenhurst	1-5
105r Chippenham Town v Beaconsfield SYCOB	2-0
109r Bishop's Cleeve v Hamworthy United	0-1
112r Cinderford Town v Cirencester Town	1-2

Qualifying Round Two

1 Liversedge v Kendal Town	0-3
2 Consett v Workington	0-2
3 Barrow v Colwyn Bay	5-0
4 Billingham Town v Fleetwood Town	0-4
5 Skelmersdale United v Southport	0-1
6 Prescot Cables v Guiseley	1-1
7 Dinnington Town v Cheadle Town	2-1
8 Harrogate Railway Athletic v Leigh RMI	4-1
9 Bradford Park Avenue v Whitby Town	4-0
10 Stalybridge Celtic v Hyde United	1-0
11 Bamber Bridge v Burscough	2-1
12 Gainsborough Trinity v Stocksbridge Park Steels	6-1
13 Harrogate Town v Nantwich Town	2-2
14 West Auckland Town v Newcastle Benfield	1-0
15 Gateshead (2) v Vauxhall Motors	1-3
16 Clitheroe v Spennymoor Town	8-2
17 Blyth Spartans v Radcliffe Borough	2-1
18 Horden CW v Woodley Sports	0-5
19 Cambridge City v Chasetown	1-1
20 Kettering Town v Redditch United	3-1
21 Bromsgrove Rovers v Nuneaton Borough	1-1
22 Rainworth MW v Kidsgrove Athletic	2-0
23 Matlock Town v AFC Telford United	3-1
24 Stourbridge v King's Lynn	0-5

226

2007/08

25 Soham Town Rangers v Solihull Moors 0-3
26 Hinckley United v Grantham Town 4-2
27 Boston United v Buxton 4-1
28 Quorn v Evesham United 1-3
29 Tamworth v Worcester City 1-0
30 Hednesford Town v Alfreton Town 0-0
31 Rushall Olympic v Sutton Coldfield Town 2-0
32 Glapwell v Market Drayton Town 4-4
33 Belper Town v Hucknall Town 2-1
34 Halesowen Town v Bedworth United 2-1
35 Stamford v Gedling Town 3-1
36 Horsham v Bury Town 3-2
37 Hayes & Yeading United v Herne Bay 2-2
38 Dulwich Hamlet v Chalfont St Peter 2-1
39 Crowborough Athletic v Staines Town 1-5
40 Boreham Wood v Bedford Town 3-3
41 Ware v Thurrock 3-2
42 Haverhill Rovers v Hitchin Town 1-1
43 Dartford v Camberley Town 2-2
44 Fisher Athletic (London) v Margate 3-4
45 Hemel Hempstead Town v Chelmsford City 0-2
46 Welling United v Barkingside 2-1
47 Billericay Town v Maidstone United (2) 2-0
48 Tonbridge Angels v Maldon Town 2-2
49 Dunstable Town v Lewes 0-2
50 St Albans City v Bishop's Stortford 1-2
51 Kirkley & Pakefield v Leighton Town 1-2
52 Brentwood Town v Harlow Town 2-0
53 Chesham United v Stotfold 1-1
54 Worthing v Walton & Hersham 3-0
55 Hampton & Richmond Boro. v Braintree Town 3-1
56 Hendon v AFC Hornchurch 1-1
57 Sutton United v Woodford United 1-1
58 Debenham LC v AFC Wimbledon 1-5
59 Ramsgate v Corby Town 0-1
60 Folkestone Invicta v Windsor & Eton 0-0
61 Hythe Town v Dover Athletic 2-1
62 Enfield Town v Hillingdon Borough 2-2
63 Erith Town v Heybridge Swifts 0-3 N
64 Aylesbury United v Bromley 1-1
65 Carshalton Athletic v Wealdstone 0-1
66 Eastbourne Borough v Edgware Town 2-0
67 Merthyr Tydfil v AFC Totton 2-2
68 Brockenhurst v Maidenhead United 0-6
69 Oxford City v Weston-Super-Mare 3-4
70 Bognor Regis Town v Havant & Waterlooville 1-2
71 Chippenham Town v Hallen 2-0
72 Dorchester Town v Paulton Rovers 1-1
73 Gloucester City v Shortwood United 0-2 N
74 Basingstoke Town v Newport County (2) 0-1
75 Truro City v Bath City 0-1
76 Corsham Town v Bashley 1-2
77 Moneyfields v Team Bath 1-8
78 Hamworthy United v Eastleigh 1-3
79 Cirencester Town v Clevedon Town 0-1
80 Fleet Town v Mangotsfield United 2-0
6r Guiseley v Prescot Cables 1-0
13r Nantwich Town v Harrogate Town 1-2
19r Chasetown v Cambridge City 2-1e
21r Nuneaton Borough v Bromsgrove Rovers 2-0
30r Alfreton Town v Hednesford Town 1-2
32r Market Drayton Town v Glapwell 1-2
37r Herne Bay v Hayes & Yeading United 0-3
40r Bedford Town v Boreham Wood 2-3
42r Hitchin Town v Haverhill Rovers 5-0
43r Camberley Town v Dartford 0-0q
48r Maldon Town v Tonbridge Angels 0-3e
53r Stotfold v Chesham United 2-1
56r AFC Hornchurch v Hendon 2-1
57r Woodford United v Sutton United 0-2
60r Windsor & Eton v Folkestone Invicta 0-1
62r Hillingdon Borough v Enfield Town 2-1 N
64r Bromley v Aylesbury United 4-2e
67r AFC Totton v Merthyr Tydfil 0-0q
72r Paulton Rovers v Dorchester Town 2-0

Qualifying Round Three

1 Harrogate Railway Athletic v Matlock Town 3-2
2 Harrogate Town v Clitheroe 2-0
3 Barrow v Fleetwood Town 2-1
4 West Auckland Town v Bamber Bridge 2-2
5 Dinnington Town v Bradford Park Avenue 1-7
6 Belper Town v Southport 0-3
7 Gainsborough Trinity v Blyth Spartans 1-0
8 Stalybridge Celtic v Workington 0-5
9 Kendal Town v Woodley Sports 4-0
10 Guiseley v Vauxhall Motors 2-3
11 Rushall Olympic v Hednesford Town 2-0
12 Chasetown v Rainworth MW 2-0
13 Tamworth v King's Lynn 2-1
14 Boston United v Hinckley United 4-1
15 Evesham United v Halesowen Town 3-0
16 Glapwell v Corby Town 0-3
17 Kettering Town v Solihull Moors 1-2
18 Nuneaton Borough v Stamford 4-1
19 Wealdstone v Bishop's Stortford 1-0
20 Brentwood Town v Staines Town 0-3
21 Heybridge Swifts v Billericay Town 2-2
22 Leighton Town v Boreham Wood 3-1
23 AFC Hornchurch v Dulwich Hamlet 2-1
24 Hitchin Town v Margate 4-3
25 Eastbourne Borough v Welling United 2-1
26 Hayes & Yeading United v Chelmsford City 1-0
27 AFC Wimbledon v Horsham 0-0
28 Lewes v Sutton United 1-0
29 Folkestone Invicta v Hillingdon Borough 1-0
30 Worthing v Hampton & Richmond Boro. 0-2
31 Hythe Town v Ware 1-3
32 Bromley v Dartford 1-0
33 Stotfold v Tonbridge Angels 0-5
34 Team Bath v Weston-Super-Mare 1-0
35 Eastleigh v Clevedon Town 5-0
36 Havant & Waterlooville v Fleet Town 2-1
37 Merthyr Tydfil v Paulton Rovers 2-0
38 Newport County (2) v Bath City 1-2
39 Maidenhead United v Shortwood United 3-0
40 Chippenham Town v Bashley 5-1
4r Bamber Bridge v West Auckland Town 5-1
21r Billericay Town v Heybridge Swifts 2-0
27r Horsham v AFC Wimbledon 1-1P

Qualifying Round Four

1 Evesham United v Halifax Town 0-0
2 Corby Town v Droylsden 1-2
3 Kendal Town v Altrincham 0-1
4 Rushden & Diamonds v Solihull Moors 5-0
5 Burton Albion v Tamworth 2-1
6 Histon v Bamber Bridge 4-1
7 Stafford Rangers v Cambridge United 1-1
8 Southport v Northwich Victoria 1-3
9 Farsley Celtic v Barrow 1-1
10 Bradford Park Avenue v Gainsborough Trinity 0-4
11 Workington v Boston United 1-0
12 York City v Rushall Olympic 6-0
13 Kidderminster Harriers v Vauxhall Motors 3-1
14 Harrogate Railway Athletic v Harrogate Town 2-1
15 Chasetown v Nuneaton Borough 2-1
16 Weymouth v Hitchin Town 1-1
17 AFC Hornchurch v Team Bath 0-1
18 Maidenhead United v Hayes & Yeading United 1-0
19 Salisbury City v Stevenage Borough 0-0
20 Merthyr Tydfil v Oxford United 1-2
21 Hampton & Richmond Boro. v Wealdstone 1-0
22 Bath City v Torquay United 0-2
23 Crawley Town v Aldershot Town 1-1
24 Chippenham Town v Horsham 2-3
25 Eastleigh v Forest Green Rovers 3-3
26 Eastbourne Borough v Bromley 2-1
27 Ware v Tonbridge Angels 3-1
28 Folkestone Invicta v Billericay Town 0-2
29 Grays Athletic v Lewes 1-1
30 Woking v Staines Town 0-1
31 Ebbsfleet United v Exeter City 1-3
32 Havant & Waterlooville v Leighton Town 3-0
1r Halifax Town v Evesham United 2-1
7r Cambridge United v Stafford Rangers 5-1
9r Barrow v Farsley Celtic 2-1
16r Hitchin Town v Weymouth 0-1
19r Stevenage Borough v Salisbury City 1-0
23r Aldershot Town v Crawley Town 1-0
25r Forest Green Rovers v Eastleigh 4-1
29r Lewes v Grays Athletic 2-0

Round One

Accrington Stanley (2) v Huddersfield Town 2-3
Altrincham v Millwall 1-2
Barnet v Gillingham 2-1
Barrow v Bournemouth 1-1
Billericay Town v Swansea City 1-2
Bradford City v Chester City 1-0
Bury v Workington 4-1
Cambridge United v Aldershot Town 2-1
Carlisle United v Grimsby Town 1-1
Cheltenham Town v Brighton & Hove Albion 1-1
Chesterfield v Tranmere Rovers 1-2
Crewe Alexandra v Milton Keynes Dons 2-1
Darlington v Northampton Town 1-1
Eastbourne Borough v Weymouth 0-4
Exeter City v Stevenage Borough 4-0
Forest Green Rovers v Rotherham United 2-2
Gainsborough Trinity v Hartlepool United 0-6
Halifax Town v Burton Albion 0-4
Hampton & Richmond Boro. v Dagenham & Redbridge 0-3
Harrogate Railway Athletic v Droylsden 2-0
Hereford United v Leeds United 0-0
Horsham v Maidenhead United 4-1
Leyton Orient v Bristol Rovers 1-1
Lincoln City v Nottingham Forest 1-1
Luton Town v Brentford 1-1
Mansfield Town v Lewes 3-0
Morecambe v Port Vale 0-2
Notts County v Histon 3-0
Oldham Athletic v Doncaster Rovers 2-2
Oxford United v Northwich Victoria 3-1
Peterborough United v Wrexham 4-1
Rushden & Diamonds v Macclesfield Town 3-1
Southend United v Rochdale 2-1
Stockport County v Staines Town 1-1
Team Bath v Chasetown 0-2
Torquay United v Yeovil Town 4-1
Walsall v Shrewsbury Town 2-0
Ware v Kidderminster Harriers 0-2
Wycombe Wanderers v Swindon Town 1-2
York City v Havant & Waterlooville 0-1
r Bournemouth v Barrow 3-2e
r Brentford v Luton Town 0-2
r Brighton & Hove Albion v Cheltenham Town 2-1
r Bristol Rovers v Leyton Orient 3-3P
r Doncaster Rovers v Oldham Athletic 1-2
r Grimsby Town v Carlisle United 1-0
r Leeds United v Hereford United 0-1
r Northampton Town v Darlington 2-1
r Nottingham Forest v Lincoln City 3-1
r Rotherham United v Forest Green Rovers 0-3
r Staines Town v Stockport County 1-1P

Round Two

Bradford City v Tranmere Rovers 0-3
Bristol Rovers v Rushden & Diamonds 5-1
Burton Albion v Barnet 1-1
Bury v Exeter City 1-0
Cambridge United v Weymouth 1-0
Dagenham & Redbridge v Kidderminster Harriers 3-1
Harrogate Railway Athletic v Mansfield Town 2-3
Hereford United v Hartlepool United 2-0
Horsham v Swansea City 1-1
Huddersfield Town v Grimsby Town 3-0
Luton Town v Nottingham Forest 1-0
Millwall v Bournemouth 2-1
Northampton Town v Walsall 1-1
Notts County v Havant & Waterlooville 0-1
Oldham Athletic v Crewe Alexandra 1-0
Oxford United v Southend United 0-0
Port Vale v Chasetown 1-1
Staines Town v Peterborough United 0-5
Swindon Town v Forest Green Rovers 3-2
Torquay United v Brighton & Hove Albion 0-2
r Barnet v Burton Albion 1-0
r Chasetown v Port Vale 1-0
r Southend United v Oxford United 3-0
r Swansea City v Horsham 6-2
r Walsall v Northampton Town 1-0

Round Three

Aston Villa v Manchester United 0-2
Barnsley v Blackpool 2-1
Blackburn Rovers v Coventry City 1-4
Bolton Wanderers v Sheffield United 0-1
Brighton & Hove Albion v Mansfield Town 1-2
Bristol City v Middlesbrough 1-2
Burnley v Arsenal 0-2
Charlton Athletic v West Bromwich Albion 1-1
Chasetown v Cardiff City 1-3
Chelsea v Queen's Park Rangers 1-0
Colchester United v Peterborough United 1-3
Derby County v Sheffield Wednesday 2-2
Everton v Oldham Athletic 0-1
Fulham v Bristol Rovers 2-2
Huddersfield Town v Birmingham City 2-1
Ipswich Town v Portsmouth 0-1
Luton Town v Liverpool 1-1
Norwich City v Bury 1-1
Plymouth Argyle v Hull City 3-2
Preston North End v Scunthorpe United 1-0
Southampton v Leicester City 2-0
Southend United v Dagenham & Redbridge 5-2
Stoke City v Newcastle United 0-0
Sunderland v Wigan Athletic 0-3
Swansea City v Havant & Waterlooville 1-1
Swindon Town v Barnet 1-1
Tottenham Hotspur v Reading 2-2
Tranmere Rovers v Hereford United 2-2
Walsall v Millwall 0-0
Watford v Crystal Palace 2-0
West Ham United v Manchester City 0-0
Wolverhampton Wan. v Cambridge United 2-1
r Barnet v Swindon Town 1-1P
r Bristol Rovers v Fulham 0-0
r Bury v Norwich City 2-1
r Havant & Waterlooville v Swansea City 4-2
r Hereford United v Tranmere Rovers 1-0
r Liverpool v Luton Town 5-0
r Manchester City v West Ham United 1-0
r Millwall v Walsall 2-1
r Newcastle United v Stoke City 4-1
r Reading v Tottenham Hotspur 0-1
r Sheffield Wednesday v Derby County 1-1q
r West Bromwich Albion v Charlton Athletic 2-2P

Round Four

Arsenal v Newcastle United 3-0
Barnet v Bristol Rovers 0-1
Coventry City v Millwall 2-1
Derby County v Preston North End 1-4
Hereford United v Cardiff City 1-2
Liverpool v Havant & Waterlooville 5-2
Manchester United v Tottenham Hotspur 3-1
Mansfield Town v Middlesbrough 0-2
Oldham Athletic v Huddersfield Town 0-1
Peterborough United v West Bromwich Albion 0-3
Portsmouth v Plymouth Argyle 2-1
Sheffield United v Manchester City 2-1
Southampton v Bury 2-0
Southend United v Barnsley 0-1
Watford v Wolverhampton Wan. 1-4
Wigan Athletic v Chelsea 1-2

2007/08 to 2008/09

Round Five

	Bristol Rovers v Southampton	1-0
	Cardiff City v Wolverhampton Wan.	2-0
	Chelsea v Huddersfield Town	3-1
	Coventry City v West Bromwich Albion	0-5
	Liverpool v Barnsley	1-2
	Manchester United v Arsenal	4-0
	Preston North End v Portsmouth	0-1
	Sheffield United v Middlesbrough	0-0
r	Middlesbrough v Sheffield United	1-0

Round Six

Barnsley v Chelsea	1-0
Bristol Rovers v West Bromwich Albion	1-5
Manchester United v Portsmouth	0-1
Middlesbrough v Cardiff City	0-2

Semi Finals

Cardiff City v Barnsley	1-0 N
Portsmouth v West Bromwich Albion	1-0 N

Final

Portsmouth v Cardiff City	1-0 N

2008/09

Extra Preliminary Round

1	Bedlington Terriers v Chester-le-Street Town	1-0
2	Consett v Pontefract Collieries	5-1
3	South Shields (3) v Hebburn Town	5-1
4	Horden CW v Sunderland Nissan	1-3
5	Northallerton Town v Whitley Bay	1-3
6	Glasshoughton Welfare v Billingham Synthonia	2-2
7	Crook Town v North Shields	6-1
8	Pickering Town v Liversedge	4-1
9	West Auckland Town v Hall Road Rangers	2-1
10	Jarrow Roofing Boldon CA v Spennymoor Town	2-1
11	Team Northumbria v Esh Winning	4-1
12	West Allotment Celtic v Sunderland RCA	2-1
13	Shildon v Leeds Carnegie	3-0
14	Armthorpe Welfare v Yorkshire Amateur	5-0
15	Marske United v Whickham	0-1
16	Billingham Town v Brandon United	2-2
17	Morpeth Town v Ryton	0-2
18	Washington v Stokesley SC	0-0
19	Bishop Auckland v Darlington Railway Ath. (2)	3-2
20	Seaham Red Star v Selby Town	1-3
21	Bridlington Town (2) v Guisborough Town	3-2
22	Norton & Stockton Ancients v Newcastle Benfield	0-1
23	Silsden v Eccleshill United	4-1
24	Ashington v Thackley	1-0
25	Thornaby v Tow Law Town	0-3
26	Dunston Federation v Tadcaster Albion	4-0
27	Cheadle Town v Newcastle Town	1-2
28	Leek CSOB v AFC Fylde	1-4
29	Maltby Main v Bottesford Town	3-4
30	Dinnington Town v Atherton LR	1-2
31	Parkgate v Norton United	1-2
32	Darwen v Penrith	4-7
33	Holker Old Boys v St Helens Town	2-2
34	Formby v AFC Emley	3-1
35	Winsford United v Nostell MW	3-3
36	Bootle v Eccleshall	5-1
37	Abbey Hey v Flixton	1-1
38	Barton Town Old Boys v Winterton Rangers	1-3
39	Maine Road v Chadderton	2-1
40	Brodsworth MW v Ashton Town	2-1
41	Oldham Town v Ashton Athletic	2-0
42	Congleton Town v AFC Blackpool	2-2
43	Ramsbottom United v Hallam	2-0
44	Alsager Town v Padiham	0-1
45	Runcorn Linnets v Rossington Main	3-2
46	Colne v Daisy Hill	4-1
47	Atherton Collieries v Bacup Borough	1-2
48	Squires Gate v Biddulph Victoria	3-1
49	AFC Wulfrunians v Pilkington XXX	1-1
50	Arnold Town v Long Eaton United	1-2
51	Tipton Town v Teversal	2-0
52	Highgate United v Brierley Hill & Withymoor	wo/s
53	Racing Club Warwick v Cadbury Athletic	6-2
54	Westfields v Gedling MW	7-1
55	Stratford Town v Pershore Town	2-0
56	Shirebrook Town v Causeway United	3-2
57	Gedling Town v Stapenhill	wo/s
58	New Mills v Friar Lane & Epworth	1-2
59	Borrowash Victoria v Market Drayton Town	2-4
60	Coventry Sphinx v Barwell	1-2
61	Tividale v Coleshill Town	1-3
62	Wellington (Hereford) v Mickleover Sports	1-4
63	Dunkirk v Alvechurch	1-4
64	Heather St Johns v Cradley Town	0-3
65	Ledbury Town v Bromyard Town	2-3
66	Staveley MW v Bridgnorth Town	3-1
67	Goodrich v Meir KA	1-1
68	Pegasus Juniors v Glossop North End	1-4
69	Rocester v Nuneaton Griff	0-1
70	Southam United v Boldmere St Michaels	3-1
71	Hinckley Downes v Shawbury United	4-2
72	Heath Hayes v Shifnal Town	1-3
73	Oadby Town v Oldbury United	0-3
74	Ellesmere Rangers v Dudley Sports	4-0
75	Dudley Town v Rainworth MW	1-2
76	Brocton v Lye Town	1-1
77	Gornal Athletic v Pelsall Villa	3-1
78	GSA Sports v Coalville Town	1-3
79	Stone Dominoes v Walsall Wood	3-2
80	Bolehall Swifts v Studley	1-3
81	Castle Vale v Barrow Town	0-2
82	Yaxley v Lincoln Moorlands Railway	4-3
83	Sleaford Town v Ely City	3-2
84	Haverhill Rovers v March Town United	2-2
85	Stowmarket Town v Ipswich Wanderers	2-2
86	St Neots Town v Holbeach United	7-1
87	Mildenhall Town v Felixstowe & Walton United	8-0
88	Gorleston v Fakenham Town	3-5
89	Woodbridge Town v Newmarket Town	1-0
90	Diss Town v Walsham Le Willows	1-2
91	Hadleigh United v Great Yarmouth Town	0-1
92	Whitton United v Cornard United	1-1
93	Leiston v Blackstones	2-1
94	Long Melford v Boston Town	2-5
95	Thetford Town v Needham Market	0-1
96	Debenham LC v Dereham Town	0-1
97	Lowestoft Town v St Ives Town	2-1
98	Wisbech Town v Norwich United	1-1
99	Deeping Rangers v Bourne Town	3-0
100	Wroxham v Kirkley & Pakefield	1-0
101	Raunds Town v Harwich & Parkeston	2-2
102	FC Clacton v St Margaretsbury	2-0
103	Rothwell Corinthians v Langford	2-3
104	Erith Town v Potton United	7-1
105	Clapton v Stewarts & Lloyds (2)	0-3
106	Cockfosters v Ampthill Town	0-1
107	Tring Athletic v Berkhamsted Town	5-3
108	Desborough Town v Saffron Walden Town	4-4
109	Southend Manor v AFC Kempston Rovers	2-1
110	North Greenford United v Tiptree United	0-1
111	Kentish Town v Wellingborough Town (2)	1-1
112	Tokyngton Manor v Biggleswade United	2-3
113	Cogenhoe United v Northampton Spencer	0-1
114	Stotfold v Colney Heath	3-1
115	Kingsbury London Tigers v Eton Manor	1-0
116	Long Buckby v Broxbourne Borough V&E	0-2
117	Hanwell Town v Wootton Blue Cross	3-2
118	London Colney v Sporting Bengal United	1-1
119	Stanway Rovers v Welwyn Garden City	4-0
120	Halstead Town v London APSA	4-1
121	Haringey Borough v Bedfont	1-3
122	Wivenhoe Town v Barkingside	1-4
123	Hullbridge Sports v Leverstock Green	2-1
124	Oxhey Jets v Hertford Town	5-0
125	Hoddesdon Town v Stansted	2-3
126	Wembley v Royston Town	1-1
127	Bedfont Green v Barking	4-0
128	Brimsdown Rovers v Hatfield Town	0-2
129	Bowers & Pitsea v Harefield United	1-2
130	Romford v Biggleswade Town	3-0
131	Daventry United v Burnham Ramblers	0-0
132	Selsey v Egham Town	1-0
133	Three Bridges v VCD Athletic	2-3
134	Mile Oak v Bookham	3-0
135	Hailsham Town v Worthing United	1-0
136	Ash United v Sevenoaks Town	0-4
137	Westfield v East Preston	0-3
138	Banstead Athletic v Colliers Wood United	0-2
139	Hassocks v Shoreham	0-1
140	Slade Green v Tunbridge Wells	1-1
141	Ringmer v Rye United	4-3e
142	Pagham v Hythe Town	1-5
143	Dorking (2) v Chessington & Hook United	2-1
144	Littlehampton Town v Peacehaven & Telscombe	2-5
145	Whitehawk v Croydon	0-0
146	Eastbourne United v Epsom & Ewell	2-4
147	Crawley Down v Chichester City United	2-2
148	Cobham v Southwick	1-1
149	Erith & Belvedere v Lancing	4-0
150	Wick v Molesey	0-3
151	Wealden v East Grinstead Town	3-4
152	Frimley Green v Guildford City (2)	1-0
153	Faversham Town v Horsham YMCA	0-2
154	Redhill v Herne Bay	1-2
155	Camberley Town v Lordswood	1-1
156	Sidley United v Farnham Town	4-2
157	Chertsey Town v Deal Town	2-2
158	Lingfield v Arundel	0-3
159	Horley Town v Raynes Park Vale	2-2
160	Bournemouth (Ams) v Fareham Town	2-1
161	New Milton Town v Amesbury Town	5-0
162	Westbury United v Hamble ASSC	0-0
163	Brockenhurst v Reading Town	2-1
164	Aylesbury Vale v Highworth Town	4-2e
165	Kidlington v Sandhurst Town	4-1
166	Christchurch v Melksham Town	2-1
167	Witney United v Buckingham Town	2-0
168	Milton United (Oxon) v Lymington Town	1-2
169	Hartley Wintney v Cove	3-1
170	VT v Newport Pagnell Town	0-2
171	Hungerford Town v Marlow United	0-0
172	Devizes Town v Calne Town	2-2
173	Downton v Abingdon Town	2-0
174	Chalfont St Peter v Ardley United	4-3
175	Bicester Town v Bristol Manor Farm	1-0
176	Thame United v Bitton	0-0
177	Bemerton Heath Harlequins v Almondsbury Town	1-4
178	Corsham Town v Moneyfields	0-2
179	Shortwood United v Henley Town	5-0
180	Harrow Hill v Alresford Town	4-1
181	Cowes Sports v Alton Town	4-3
182	Ringwood Town v Hallen	1-0
183	Carterton v Newport (IOW)	2-1
184	Flackwell Heath v Wootton Bassett Town	1-1
185	Wantage Town v Brading Town	1-3
186	Fairford Town v Shrivenham	4-1
187	Chard Town v Street	2-2
188	Elmore v Bodmin Town	0-4
189	Willand Rovers v Wadebridge Town	6-0
190	Welton Rovers v Poole Town	0-1
191	Launceston v Sherborne Town	3-0
192	Liskeard Athletic v Larkhall Athletic	0-5
193	Ilfracombe Town v Tavistock	1-4
194	Bideford v Keynsham Town	4-2
195	Shaftesbury v Falmouth Town	2-2
196	Odd Down v Bishop Sutton	2-1
197	Gillingham Town v Saltash United	2-2
198	Radstock Town v Brislington	1-2
199	Bridport v Barnstaple Town	2-1
200	Dawlish Town v Wimborne Town	0-0
201	Minehead v Clevedon United	0-3
202	St Blazey v Hamworthy United	0-2
203	Frome Town v Shepton Mallet	3-1
6r	Billingham Synthonia v Glasshoughton Welfare	5-1
16r	Brandon United v Billingham Town	1-2
18r	Stokesley SC v Washington	2-0
33r	St Helens Town v Holker Old Boys	1-0
35r	Nostell MW v Winsford United	3-0
37r	Flixton v Abbey Hey	3-1e
42r	AFC Blackpool v Congleton Town	1-4
49r	Pilkington XXX v AFC Wulfrunians	2-1
67r	Meir KA v Goodrich	4-4P
76r	Lye Town v Brocton	5-1
84r	March Town United v Haverhill Rovers	2-0
85r	Ipswich Wanderers v Stowmarket Town	2-0
92r	Cornard United v Whitton United	3-3P
98r	Norwich United v Wisbech Town	1-3
101r	Harwich & Parkeston v Raunds Town	0-3
108r	Saffron Walden Town v Desborough Town	2-1
111r	Wellingborough Town (2) v Kentish Town	2-0
118r	Sporting Bengal United v London Colney	1-0
126r	Royston Town v Wembley	4-0
131r	Burnham Ramblers v Daventry United	5-3
140r	Tunbridge Wells v Slade Green	2-1
145r	Croydon v Whitehawk	4-3
147r	Chichester City United v Crawley Down	3-1
148r	Southwick v Cobham	1-3
155r	Lordswood v Camberley Town	2-4
157r	Deal Town v Chertsey Town	1-2
159r	Raynes Park Vale v Horley Town	3-1
162r	Hamble ASSC v Westbury United	2-2q
171r	Marlow United v Hungerford Town	2-2P
172r	Calne Town v Devizes Town	3-0
176r	Bitton v Thame United	3-0
184r	Wootton Bassett Town v Flackwell Heath	1-6
187r	Street v Chard Town	5-1e
195r	Falmouth Town v Shaftesbury	4-2
197r	Saltash United v Gillingham Town	2-4
200r	Wimborne Town v Dawlish Town	3-2e

Preliminary Round

1	Ashington v Ossett Albion	2-1
2	Team Northumbria v Bedlington Terriers	0-3
3	Armthorpe Welfare v Crook Town	1-1
4	Wakefield v Stokesley SC	2-0
5	South Shields (3) v Selby Town	0-4
6	Sunderland Nissan v Newcastle Blue Star	1-2
7	West Allotment Celtic v Shildon	1-3
8	West Auckland Town v Durham City	0-5
9	Bishop Auckland v Consett	3-3
10	Goole AFC v Newcastle Benfield	0-4
11	Billingham Town v Whitley Bay	0-4
12	FC Halifax Town v Silsden	0-0
13	Whickham v Pickering Town	0-2
14	Jarrow Roofing Boldon CA v Bridlington Town (2)	2-2
15	Garforth Town v Tow Law Town	1-0
16	Billingham Synthonia v Ryton	0-2
17	Dunston Federation v Harrogate Railway Athletic	1-0
18	Newcastle Town v Skelmersdale United	0-1
19	Oldham Town v Rossendale United	1-1
20	Bootle v Padiham	1-0
21	Trafford v Stocksbridge Park Steels	2-4
22	Congleton Town v Squires Gate	1-1
23	Penrith v Clitheroe	1-3
24	Bottesford Town v Flixton	2-2
25	Lancaster City v Salford City	1-2
26	Norton United v Leek Town	1-3
27	Mossley v Ramsbottom United	3-1
28	Formby v Colne	0-5
29	Brigg Town v Maine Road	2-2
30	Radcliffe Borough v Winterton Rangers	1-2
31	Warrington Town v Nostell MW	0-0
32	Bacup Borough v St Helens Town	3-1
33	Chorley v Atherton LR	0-1
34	AFC Fylde v Sheffield	1-1
35	Woodley Sports v Brodsworth MW	0-0
36	Curzon Ashton v Runcorn Linnets	4-0
37	Bamber Bridge v Colwyn Bay	4-3
38	Hinckley Downes v Gornal Athletic	0-4
39	Atherstone Town v Quorn	1-0

2008/09

40	Malvern Town v Coalville Town	1-3
41	Oldbury United v Friar Lane & Epworth	0-1
42	Long Eaton United v Rushall Olympic	1-0
43	Glapwell v Market Drayton Town	2-1
44	Ellesmere Rangers v Bromsgrove Rovers	2-1
45	Loughborough Dynamo v Tipton Town	0-1
46	Shirebrook Town v Studley	1-3
47	Stone Dominoes v Rainworth MW	1-2
48	Nuneaton Town v Gedling Town	1-0
49	Westfields v Stratford Town	2-4
50	Chasetown v Carlton Town	5-0
51	Kidsgrove Athletic v Pilkington XXX	3-0
52	Highgate United v Romulus	1-4
53	Sutton Coldfield Town v Cradley Town	2-3
54	Gresley Rovers v Alvechurch	4-1
55	Shepshed Dynamo v Mickleover Sports	3-2
56	Retford United v Barrow Town	3-1
57	Glossop North End v Belper Town	1-2
58	Meir KA v Nuneaton Griff	1-0
59	Lye Town v Southam United	1-2
60	Leamington v Staveley MW	4-0
61	Willenhall Town v Bedworth United	0-0
62	Racing Club Warwick v Stourport Swifts	0-2
63	Coleshill Town v Shifnal Town	2-3
64	Bromyard Town v Barwell	1-5
65	Spalding United v Yaxley	2-3
66	Soham Town Rangers v Needham Market	0-2
67	Leiston v March Town United	3-1
68	Wisbech Town v Mildenhall Town	2-2
69	Fakenham Town v Boston Town	0-4
70	Grantham Town v Woodbridge Town	4-1
71	Walsham Le Willows v Sleaford Town	1-2
72	Dereham Town v Stamford	2-2
73	AFC Sudbury v Lowestoft Town	1-1
74	Ipswich Wanderers v Cornard United	1-1
75	Great Yarmouth Town v Wroxham	2-2
76	St Neots Town v Lincoln United	2-3
77	Deeping Rangers v Bury Town	1-2
78	Brentwood Town v Erith Town	2-1
79	Dulwich Hamlet v Broxbourne Borough V&E	1-1
80	Great Wakering Rovers v Bedfont Green	4-0
81	Langford v Arlesey Town	0-1
82	Oxhey Jets v Ilford	5-2
83	Northwood v Metropolitan Police	0-2
84	Northampton Spencer v Wingate & Finchley	2-2
85	Bedfont v Tiptree United	2-4
86	Barton Rovers v Burnham Ramblers	2-1
87	Leyton v Romford	2-1
88	Ampthill Town v Dunstable Town	0-4
89	Halstead Town v Stotfold	1-2
90	East Thurrock United v Hatfield Town	4-2
91	FC Clacton v Stansted	4-0
92	Barkingside v Stanway Rovers	0-4
93	Cheshunt v Southend Manor	2-1
94	Tilbury v Leighton Town	0-2
95	Stewarts & Lloyds (2) v Corinthian Casuals	3-2
96	Hanwell Town v Aveley	0-5
97	Witham Town v Maldon Town	3-3
98	Waltham Forest v Thamesmead Town	0-1
99	Harefield United v Saffron Walden Town	1-1
100	Ware v Sporting Bengal United	4-0
101	Concord Rangers v Kingsbury London Tigers	2-0
102	Rothwell Town v Hullbridge Sports	2-0
103	Hillingdon Borough v Enfield Town	3-1
104	Redbridge v Uxbridge	1-3
105	Croydon Athletic v Wellingborough Town (2)	3-1
106	Tring Athletic v Biggleswade United	1-2
107	AFC Hayes v Royston Town	1-3
108	Woodford United v Raunds Town	1-1
109	Potters Bar Town v Waltham Abbey	1-1
110	Walton Casuals v Molesey	2-0
111	Mile Oak v Arundel	0-2
112	Horsham YMCA v Tunbridge Wells	3-1
113	Sevenoaks Town v Folkestone Invicta	4-4
114	Ashford Town v Leatherhead	3-2
115	Herne Bay v Chipstead	2-2
116	Epsom & Ewell v Frimley Green	2-1
117	Whitstable Town v Selsey	1-0
118	Camberley Town v Worthing	0-6
119	Hythe Town v Walton & Hersham	2-1
120	Crowborough Athletic v Ringmer	3-1
121	East Preston v Erith & Belvedere	1-2
122	Sittingbourne v Chertsey Town	2-1
123	Burgess Hill Town v Hailsham Town	2-0
124	Cobham v Merstham	0-2
125	Shoreham v Kingstonian	1-3
126	Chatham Town v Dorking (2)	2-2
127	East Grinstead Town v Colliers Wood United	0-3
128	Raynes Park Vale v Godalming Town	1-2
129	Whyteleafe v Peacehaven & Telscombe	0-0
130	VCD Athletic v Croydon	3-1
131	Sidley United v Eastbourne Town	1-2
132	Cray Wanderers v Chichester City United	4-1
133	AFC Totton v Moneyfields	2-1
134	Westbury United v Fairford Town	0-6
135	Cowes Sports v Lymington Town	4-0
136	Aylesbury Vale v Burnham	1-1
137	Aylesbury United v Windsor & Eton	2-0
138	Ringwood Town v Marlow	2-2
139	Chalfont St Peter v Harrow Hill	2-1
140	Didcot Town v Bournemouth (Ams)	5-0
141	Carterton v North Leigh	0-1
142	Newport Pagnell Town v Cirencester Town	1-0
143	Gosport Borough v Hartley Wintney	5-0
144	Kidlington v Almondsbury Town	2-3
145	Chesham United v Brading Town	5-1
146	Fleet Town v Brockenhurst	1-1
147	Bitton v Bishop's Cleeve	2-1
148	Witney United v Thatcham Town	2-2
149	Beaconsfield SYCOB v Marlow United	1-0
150	Shortwood United v Christchurch	2-0
151	Abingdon United v Slough Town	1-1
152	Andover v Calne Town	1-3
153	New Milton Town v Downton	1-2
154	Flackwell Heath v Winchester City	3-4
155	Bracknell Town v Bicester Town	3-0
156	Bodmin Town v Bridgwater Town	0-3
157	Launceston v Paulton Rovers	0-2
158	Clevedon United v Taunton Town	0-3
159	Odd Down v Wimborne Town	0-2
160	Street v Bideford	3-3
161	Cinderford Town v Frome Town	0-1
162	Falmouth Town v Truro City	0-4
163	Poole Town v Willand Rovers	2-1
164	Hamworthy United v Brislington	3-2
165	Larkhall Athletic v Tavistock	6-2
166	Bridport v Gillingham Town	3-0
3r	Crook Town v Armthorpe Welfare	3-0
9r	Consett v Bishop Auckland	4-1
12r	Silsden v FC Halifax Town	1-3
14r	Bridlington Town (2) v Jarrow Roofing Boldon CA	2-1
19r	Rossendale United v Oldham Town	3-0
22r	Squires Gate v Congleton Town	0-3
24r	Flixton v Bottesford Town	7-5
29r	Maine Road v Brigg Town	1-2
31r	Nostell MW v Warrington Town	1-2
34r	Sheffield v AFC Fylde	4-0
35r	Brodsworth MW v Woodley Sports	0-2
61r	Bedworth United v Willenhall Town	2-3e
68r	Mildenhall Town v Wisbech Town	4-0
72r	Stamford v Dereham Town	1-0
73r	Lowestoft Town v AFC Sudbury	2-2P
74r	Cornard United v Ipswich Wanderers	3-0
75r	Wroxham v Great Yarmouth Town	3-0
79r	Broxbourne Borough V&E v Dulwich Hamlet	1-2
84r	Wingate & Finchley v Northampton Spencer	4-0
97r	Maldon Town v Witham Town	1-4
99r	Saffron Walden Town v Harefield United	2-0
108r	Raunds Town v Woodford United	0-0P
109r	Waltham Abbey v Potters Bar Town	1-0
113r	Folkestone Invicta v Sevenoaks Town	4-1
115r	Chipstead v Herne Bay	2-0e
126r	Dorking (2) v Chatham Town	0-1
129r	Peacehaven & Telscombe v Whyteleafe	1-3
136r	Burnham v Aylesbury Vale	1-2
138r	Marlow v Ringwood Town	4-0
146r	Brockenhurst v Fleet Town	0-1
148r	Thatcham Town v Witney United	3-1e
151r	Slough Town v Abingdon United	5-2
160r	Bideford v Street	2-1

Qualifying Round One

1	Bedlington Terriers v Bradford Park Avenue	0-1
2	Selby Town v Guiseley	2-4
3	Garforth Town v Ossett Town	1-0
4	Newcastle Benfield v Bridlington Town (2)	1-1
5	Ashington v Durham City	0-6
6	Whitby Town v Dunston Federation	3-2
7	Consett v North Ferriby United	4-4
8	Wakefield v Crook Town	4-3
9	Ryton v FC Halifax Town	0-4
10	Newcastle Blue Star v Shildon	2-0
11	Pickering Town v Whitley Bay	0-1
12	Congleton Town v Prescot Cables	0-2
13	Sheffield v Colne	3-2
14	Woodley Sports v Rossendale United	1-3
15	Bacup Borough v Cammell Laird	3-0
16	Brigg Town v Stocksbridge Park Steels	0-4
17	Clitheroe v Leek Town	1-1
18	Buxton v Bootle	3-1
19	Frickley Athletic v Skelmersdale United	1-0
20	Nantwich Town v FC United of Manchester	0-0
21	Flixton v Mossley	1-4
22	Bamber Bridge v Witton Albion	1-2
23	Salford City v Atherton LR	5-0
24	Curzon Ashton v Leigh Genesis	1-0
25	Winterton Rangers v Warrington Town	4-2
26	Ashton United v Kendal Town	2-3
27	Marine v Worksop Town	1-5
28	Hednesford Town v Atherstone Town	1-2
29	Shepshed Dynamo v Stourport Swifts	7-0
30	Friar Lane & Epworth v Rugby Town	0-0
31	Cradley Town v Ellesmere Rangers	2-2
32	Stourbridge v Rainworth MW	0-0
33	Gresley Rovers v Chasetown	2-4
34	Meir KA v Halesowen Town	1-1
35	Shifnal Town v Long Eaton United	0-1
36	Gornal Athletic v Southam United	0-0
37	Retford United v Willenhall Town	1-1
38	Ilkeston Town (2) v Matlock Town	4-1
39	Coalville Town v Studley	2-1
40	Romulus v Stratford Town	2-1
41	Eastwood Town v Kidsgrove Athletic	4-0
42	Leamington v Evesham United	0-3
43	Belper Town v Barwell	3-2
44	Boston United v Glapwell	6-1
45	Nuneaton Town v Tipton Town	3-1
46	Cambridge City v Lowestoft Town	2-0
47	Cornard United v Leiston	0-5
48	Grantham Town v Wroxham	3-4
49	Lincoln United v Mildenhall Town	3-2
50	Bury Town v Boston Town	3-1
51	Sleaford Town v Stamford	2-6
52	Needham Market v Yaxley	2-2
53	Boreham Wood v Biggleswade United	3-0
54	Hillingdon Borough v East Thurrock United	0-6
55	Royston Town v Hendon	2-4
56	Ware v Barton Rovers	1-1
57	Stewarts & Lloyds (2) v Croydon Athletic	5-1
58	Tiptree United v Stanway Rovers	1-3
59	Billericay Town v FC Clacton	4-1
60	Oxhey Jets v Dulwich Hamlet	1-5
61	Hemel Hempstead Town v Harrow Borough	1-1
62	Thamesmead Town v Great Wakering Rovers	2-1
63	Metropolitan Police v Corby Town	0-3
64	Wingate & Finchley v Witham Town	2-0
65	Stotfold v Leighton Town	0-3
66	Hitchin Town v Concord Rangers	5-0
67	Leyton v Brackley Town	2-4
68	Canvey Island v Dunstable Town	1-5
69	Raunds Town v Ashford Town (Middlesex)	0-3
70	Heybridge Swifts v Uxbridge	1-1
71	Cheshunt v Staines Town	0-3
72	Saffron Walden Town v AFC Hornchurch	0-2
73	Harlow Town v Aveley	5-1
74	Brentwood Town v Arlesey Town	1-1
75	Waltham Abbey v Rothwell Town	0-1
76	Wealdstone v Bedford Town	2-2
77	Dartford v Hastings United (2)	3-2
78	Crowborough Athletic v Walton Casuals	1-0
79	Burgess Hill Town v Epsom & Ewell	5-2
80	Horsham v Colliers Wood United	1-0
81	Horsham YMCA v Whyteleafe	1-1
82	Folkestone Invicta v Ramsgate	1-0
83	Erith & Belvedere v Sittingbourne	2-0
84	Worthing v Margate	5-1
85	Godalming Town v Arundel	1-1
86	Carshalton Athletic v Eastbourne Town	4-1
87	Kingstonian v Ashford Town	3-0
88	Sutton United v Cray Wanderers	3-1
89	Merstham v Whitstable Town	2-1
90	Hythe Town v VCD Athletic	0-0
91	Tonbridge Angels v Dover Athletic	1-2
92	Chipstead v Chatham Town	1-0
93	Maidstone United (2) v Tooting & Mitcham United	2-1
94	Bracknell Town v Oxford City	2-0 D
95	Aylesbury Vale v Downton	2-0
96	Shortwood United v Didcot Town	3-2
97	Farnborough v Slough Town	1-0
98	Fleet Town v Cowes Sports	3-0
99	Newport Pagnell Town v Marlow	2-1
100	Aylesbury United v Almondsbury Town	1-0
101	Chalfont St Peter v Gloucester City	5-3
102	Chippenham Town v Banbury United	2-0
103	Calne Town v Bashley	0-5
104	Bitton v Beaconsfield SYCOB	3-2
105	Fairford Town v Gosport Borough	1-2
106	Winchester City v AFC Totton	0-3
107	North Leigh v Chesham United	2-3
108	Thatcham Town v Swindon Supermarine	1-0
109	Frome Town v Bideford	1-1
110	Paulton Rovers v Larkhall Athletic	3-0
111	Bridgwater Town v Mangotsfield United	1-3
112	Hamworthy United v Taunton Town	2-1
113	Truro City v Yate Town	3-1
114	Clevedon Town v Bridport	4-1
115	Wimborne Town v Tiverton Town	0-1
116	Poole Town v Merthyr Tydfil	3-0
4r	Bridlington Town (2) v Newcastle Benfield	1-2
7r	North Ferriby United v Consett	6-1
17r	Leek Town v Clitheroe	0-1
20r	FC United of Manchester v Nantwich Town	3-4
30r	Rugby Town v Friar Lane & Epworth	5-3
31r	Ellesmere Rangers v Cradley Town	1-3
32r	Rainworth MW v Stourbridge	1-3
34r	Halesowen Town v Meir KA	8-1
36r	Southam United v Gornal Athletic	2-1
37r	Willenhall Town v Retford United	1-3
52r	Yaxley v Needham Market	0-3
56r	Barton Rovers v Ware	1-2
61r	Harrow Borough v Hemel Hempstead Town	1-2
70r	Uxbridge v Heybridge Swifts	1-3
74r	Arlesey Town v Brentwood Town	1-0
76r	Bedford Town v Wealdstone	1-1P
81r	Whyteleafe v Horsham YMCA	2-0
85r	Arundel v Godalming Town	1-2
90r	VCD Athletic v Hythe Town	3-0
109r	Bideford v Frome Town	1-3e

Qualifying Round Two

1	Nantwich Town v FC Halifax Town	4-1
2	Kendal Town v Mossley	1-2
3	Southport v Vauxhall Motors	3-2
4	Frickley Athletic v Clitheroe	1-0
5	North Ferriby United v Newcastle Blue Star	1-4
6	Whitby Town v Blyth Spartans	2-2
7	Stocksbridge Park Steels v Curzon Ashton	1-2
8	Wakefield v Fleetwood Town	0-3
9	Droylsden v Bradford Park Avenue	2-1
10	Winterton Rangers v Newcastle Benfield	1-1
11	Durham City v Rossendale United	4-0
12	Whitley Bay v Hyde United	3-1
13	Guiseley v Garforth Town	2-2

2008/09

14	Buxton v Burscough	1-0
15	Prescot Cables v Salford City	2-1
16	Workington v Harrogate Town	0-0
17	Gateshead (2) v Witton Albion	1-1
18	Stalybridge Celtic v Farsley Celtic	4-0
19	Sheffield v Bacup Borough	4-1
20	Coalville Town v Stafford Rangers	2-1
21	Evesham United v Nuneaton Town	2-2
22	Lincoln United v Eastwood Town	0-1
23	Rugby Town v Long Eaton United	5-1
24	Shepshed Dynamo v Alfreton Town	1-2
25	Chasetown v Rothwell Town	1-1
26	Hucknall Town v Cradley Town	3-0
27	Belper Town v Redditch United	4-1
28	Boston United v Stamford	2-1
29	Retford United v Romulus	3-1
30	Stourbridge v Brackley Town	1-1
31	Halesowen Town v Gainsborough Trinity	3-0
32	Southam United v Atherstone Town	1-1
33	Stewarts & Lloyds (2) v Ilkeston Town (2)	2-3
34	King's Lynn v Worksop Town	2-1
35	AFC Telford United v Corby Town	3-2
36	Worcester City v Tamworth	0-1
37	Hinckley United v Solihull Moors	4-1
38	Bromley v AFC Hornchurch	0-1
39	Thurrock v Boreham Wood	0-5
40	Dunstable Town v Chipstead	2-3
41	Folkestone Invicta v Horsham	1-2
42	Wroxham v Heybridge Swifts	2-1
43	Burgess Hill Town v Bognor Regis Town	0-0
44	Bedford Town v AFC Wimbledon	2-2
45	Welling United v Whyteleafe	1-1
46	Bishop's Stortford v Wingate & Finchley	3-2
47	Hitchin Town v Stanway Rovers	0-0
48	St Albans City v Harlow Town	0-0
49	Erith & Belvedere v Godalming Town	0-2
50	Dulwich Hamlet v Hendon	2-2
51	Merstham v Thamesmead Town	1-1
52	Leighton Town v Crowborough Athletic	0-1
53	Dartford v Hampton & Richmond Boro.	0-1
54	Staines Town v Hayes & Yeading United	0-0
55	Maidstone United (2) v Fisher Athletic (London)	3-2
56	Bury Town v Chelmsford City	2-1
57	Hemel Hempstead Town v Ware	1-2
58	Carshalton Athletic v Leiston	1-2
59	Sutton United v Billericay Town	3-1
60	Cambridge City v Worthing	1-1
61	Kingstonian v Braintree Town	4-0
62	Dover Athletic v Needham Market	3-1
63	East Thurrock United v VCD Athletic	3-0
64	Arlesey Town v Ashford Town (Middlesex)	1-4
65	Paulton Rovers v Bitton	1-0
66	Fleet Town v Newport Pagnell Town	5-0
67	Poole Town v Frome Town	1-3
68	Bath City v Clevedon Town	2-0
69	Aylesbury United v Mangotsfield United	4-1
70	Weston-Super-Mare v Chesham United	2-4
71	Eastleigh v Farnborough	1-0
72	AFC Totton v Thatcham Town	2-1
73	Havant & Waterlooville v Shortwood United	2-2
74	Bashley v Maidenhead United	2-1
75	Basingstoke Town v Hamworthy United	3-1
76	Oxford City v Tiverton Town	2-1
77	Aylesbury Vale v Gosport Borough	1-1
78	Dorchester Town v Newport County (2)	2-2
79	Chalfont St Peter v Team Bath	0-1
80	Truro City v Chippenham Town	1-1
6r	Blyth Spartans v Whitby Town	5-2
10r	Newcastle Benfield v Winterton Rangers	2-1e
13r	Garforth Town v Guiseley	1-3
16r	Harrogate Town v Workington	0-0P
17r	Witton Albion v Gateshead (2)	1-3
21r	Nuneaton Town v Evesham United	1-2
25r	Rothwell Town v Chasetown	2-5e
30r	Brackley Town v Stourbridge	1-0
32r	Atherstone Town v Southam United	3-1e
43r	Bognor Regis Town v Burgess Hill Town	0-2
44r	AFC Wimbledon v Bedford Town	3-0
45r	Whyteleafe v Welling United	2-0
47r	Stanway Rovers v Hitchin Town	0-2
48r	Harlow Town v St Albans City	3-2
50r	Hendon v Dulwich Hamlet	2-1
51r	Thamesmead Town v Merstham	1-5
54r	Hayes & Yeading United v Staines Town	5-3e
60r	Worthing v Cambridge City	2-1
73r	Shortwood United v Havant & Waterlooville	0-1
77r	Gosport Borough v Aylesbury Vale	4-0
78r	Newport County (2) v Dorchester Town	1-2
80r	Chippenham Town v Truro City	4-2

Qualifying Round Three

1	Belper Town v Prescot Cables	4-1
2	Guiseley v Sheffield	3-3
3	Buxton v Blyth Spartans	0-1
4	Curzon Ashton v Mossley	4-3
5	Retford United v Newcastle Benfield	1-0
6	Droylsden v Gateshead (2)	3-2
7	Eastwood Town v Harrogate Town	2-2
8	Alfreton Town v Ilkeston Town (2)	0-0
9	Stalybridge Celtic v Durham City	1-6
10	Fleetwood Town v Frickley Athletic	2-0
11	Whitley Bay v Nantwich Town	1-5
12	Newcastle Blue Star v Hucknall Town	4-0
13	Southport v Boston United	0-2
14	AFC Hornchurch v Merstham	2-0
15	Boreham Wood v Brackley Town	0-1
16	Hendon v AFC Telford United	1-2
17	Hitchin Town v Hinckley United	1-2
18	Kingstonian v Hayes & Yeading United	1-3
19	Hampton & Richmond Boro. v Whyteleafe	2-0
20	Tamworth v East Thurrock United	3-1
21	Wroxham v King's Lynn	0-2
22	Leiston v Coalville Town	1-0
23	Dover Athletic v AFC Wimbledon	0-0
24	Evesham United v Chasetown	2-0
25	Halesowen Town v Maidstone United (2)	1-4
26	Bishop's Stortford v Rugby Town	2-1
27	Harlow Town v Crowborough Athletic	1-1
28	Bury Town v Worthing	1-0
29	Atherstone Town v Chipstead	1-1
30	Ware v Sutton United	1-2
31	Havant & Waterlooville v Godalming Town	2-1
32	Horsham v Paulton Rovers	2-1
33	Basingstoke Town v Bashley	2-2
34	Oxford City v Chesham United	2-1
35	AFC Totton v Fleet Town	5-2
36	Ashford Town (Middlesex) v Chippenham Town	1-0
37	Frome Town v Team Bath	2-2
38	Burgess Hill Town v Eastleigh	2-1
39	Dorchester Town v Gosport Borough	1-0
40	Bath City v Aylesbury United	0-1
2r	Sheffield v Guiseley	2-1
7r	Harrogate Town v Eastwood Town	0-2
8r	Ilkeston Town (2) v Alfreton Town	1-3
23r	AFC Wimbledon v Dover Athletic	2-0
27r	Crowborough Athletic v Harlow Town	0-2
29r	Chipstead v Atherstone Town	3-0
33r	Bashley v Basingstoke Town	0-3
37r	Team Bath v Frome Town	4-0

Qualifying Round Four

1	Hinckley United v Curzon Ashton	1-1
2	Kettering Town v Burton Albion	3-0
3	Tamworth v Barrow	0-4
4	King's Lynn v Kidderminster Harriers	1-5
5	Boston United v Cambridge United	2-3
6	Newcastle Blue Star v Altrincham	1-2
7	Droylsden v Belper Town	0-0
8	Durham City v Histon	2-2
9	Retford United v Alfreton Town	1-3
10	Northwich Victoria v AFC Telford United	0-3
11	Blyth Spartans v Sheffield	3-1
12	York City v Mansfield Town	0-0
13	Fleetwood Town v Nantwich Town	4-3
14	Wrexham v Eastwood Town	0-0
15	Stevenage Borough v Horsham	2-2
16	Woking v Ebbsfleet United	2-2
17	Hampton & Richmond Boro. v Brackley Town	0-1
18	Oxford United v Hayes & Yeading United	2-0
19	Maidstone United (2) v AFC Wimbledon	0-1
20	Team Bath v Salisbury City	1-0
21	Dorchester Town v Bishop's Stortford	1-0
22	Oxford City v Eastbourne Borough	0-1
23	Ashford Town (Middlesex) v Forest Green Rovers	0-0
24	Evesham United v Rushden & Diamonds	2-0
25	Bury Town v Basingstoke Town	4-1
26	Burgess Hill Town v Harlow Town	0-3
27	Grays Athletic v AFC Totton	2-0
28	Aylesbury United v Sutton United	0-1
29	Torquay United v Chipstead	4-1
30	Leiston v Lewes	1-1
31	Crawley Town v Havant & Waterlooville	0-3
32	Weymouth v AFC Hornchurch	1-2
1r	Curzon Ashton v Hinckley United	1-1P
7r	Belper Town v Droylsden	1-2
8r	Histon v Durham City	5-2
12r	Mansfield Town v York City	1-0
14r	Eastwood Town v Wrexham	2-0
15r	Horsham v Stevenage Borough	1-4
16r	Ebbsfleet United v Woking	1-0
23r	Forest Green Rovers v Ashford Town (Middlesex)	4-0
30r	Lewes v Leiston	1-3

Round One

	AFC Hornchurch v Peterborough United	0-1
	AFC Telford United v Southend United	2-2
	AFC Wimbledon v Wycombe Wanderers	1-4
	Accrington Stanley (2) v Tranmere Rovers	0-0
	Aldershot Town v Rotherham United	1-1
	Alfreton Town v Bury Town	4-2
	Barnet v Rochdale	1-1
	Blyth Spartans v Shrewsbury Town	3-1
	Bournemouth v Bristol Rovers	1-0
	Brighton & Hove Albion v Hartlepool United	3-3
	Bury v Gillingham	0-1
	Carlisle United v Grays Athletic	1-1
	Cheltenham Town v Oldham Athletic	2-2
	Chester City v Millwall	0-3
	Chesterfield v Mansfield Town	3-1
	Colchester United v Leyton Orient	0-1
	Crewe Alexandra v Ebbsfleet United	1-0
	Curzon Ashton v Exeter City	3-2
	Darlington v Droylsden	0-0
	Eastbourne Borough v Barrow	0-0
	Eastwood Town v Brackley Town	2-1
	Harlow Town v Macclesfield Town	0-2
	Havant & Waterlooville v Brentford	1-3
	Hereford United v Dagenham & Redbridge	0-0
	Histon v Swindon Town	1-0
	Huddersfield Town v Port Vale	3-4
	Kettering Town v Lincoln City	1-1
	Kidderminster Harriers v Cambridge United	1-0
	Leeds United v Northampton Town	1-1
	Leicester City v Stevenage Borough	3-0
	Leiston v Fleetwood Town	0-0
	Luton Town v Altrincham	0-0
	Milton Keynes Dons v Bradford City	1-2
	Morecambe v Grimsby Town	2-1
	Oxford United v Dorchester Town	0-0
	Sutton United v Notts County	0-1
	Team Bath v Forest Green Rovers	0-1
	Torquay United v Evesham United	2-0
	Walsall v Scunthorpe United	1-3
	Yeovil Town v Stockport County	1-1
r	Altrincham v Luton Town	0-0q
r	Barrow v Eastbourne Borough	4-0
r	Dagenham & Redbridge v Hereford United	2-1
r	Dorchester Town v Oxford United	1-3e
r	Droylsden v Darlington	1-0
r	Fleetwood Town v Leiston	2-0
r	Grays Athletic v Carlisle United	0-2
r	Hartlepool United v Brighton & Hove Albion	2-1
r	Lincoln City v Kettering Town	1-2
r	Northampton Town v Leeds United	2-5
r	Oldham Athletic v Cheltenham Town	0-1
r	Rochdale v Barnet	3-2e
r	Rotherham United v Aldershot Town	0-3
r	Southend United v AFC Telford United	2-0
r	Stockport County v Yeovil Town	5-0
r	Tranmere Rovers v Accrington Stanley (2)	1-0

Round Two

	Barrow v Brentford	2-1
	Bournemouth v Blyth Spartans	0-0
	Bradford City v Leyton Orient	1-2
	Carlisle United v Crewe Alexandra	0-2
	Chesterfield v Droylsden	2-2
	Eastwood Town v Wycombe Wanderers	2-0
	Fleetwood Town v Hartlepool United	2-3
	Forest Green Rovers v Rochdale	2-0
	Gillingham v Stockport County	0-0
	Histon v Leeds United	1-0
	Kidderminster Harriers v Curzon Ashton	2-0
	Leicester City v Dagenham & Redbridge	3-2
	Millwall v Aldershot Town	3-0
	Morecambe v Cheltenham Town	2-3
	Notts County v Kettering Town	1-1
	Peterborough United v Tranmere Rovers	0-0
	Port Vale v Macclesfield Town	1-3
	Scunthorpe United v Alfreton Town	4-0
	Southend United v Luton Town	3-1
	Torquay United v Oxford United	2-0
r	Blyth Spartans v Bournemouth	1-0
r	Droylsden v Chesterfield	2-1 D
r	Kettering Town v Notts County	2-1
r	Stockport County v Gillingham	1-2
r	Tranmere Rovers v Peterborough United	1-2e

Round Three

	Arsenal v Plymouth Argyle	3-1
	Birmingham City v Wolverhampton Wan.	0-2
	Blyth Spartans v Blackburn Rovers	0-1
	Cardiff City v Reading	2-0
	Charlton Athletic v Norwich City	1-1
	Chelsea v Southend United	1-1
	Cheltenham Town v Doncaster Rovers	0-0
	Coventry City v Kidderminster Harriers	2-0
	Forest Green Rovers v Derby County	3-4
	Gillingham v Aston Villa	1-2
	Hartlepool United v Stoke City	2-0
	Histon v Swansea City	1-2
	Hull City v Newcastle United	0-0
	Ipswich Town v Chesterfield	3-0
	Kettering Town v Eastwood Town	2-1
	Leicester City v Crystal Palace	0-0
	Leyton Orient v Sheffield United	1-4
	Macclesfield Town v Everton	0-1
	Manchester City v Nottingham Forest	0-3
	Middlesbrough v Barrow	2-1
	Millwall v Crewe Alexandra	2-2
	Portsmouth v Bristol City	0-0
	Preston North End v Liverpool	0-2
	Queen's Park Rangers v Burnley	0-0
	Sheffield Wednesday v Fulham	1-2
	Southampton v Manchester United	0-3
	Sunderland v Bolton Wanderers	2-1
	Torquay United v Blackpool	1-0
	Tottenham Hotspur v Wigan Athletic	3-1
	Watford v Scunthorpe United	1-0
	West Bromwich Albion v Peterborough United	1-1
	West Ham United v Barnsley	3-0
r	Bristol City v Portsmouth	0-2
r	Burnley v Queen's Park Rangers	2-1e
r	Crewe Alexandra v Millwall	2-3
r	Crystal Palace v Leicester City	2-1
r	Doncaster Rovers v Cheltenham Town	3-0
r	Newcastle United v Hull City	0-1
r	Norwich City v Charlton Athletic	0-1
r	Peterborough United v West Bromwich Albion	0-2
r	Southend United v Chelsea	1-4

2008/09 to 2009/10

Round Four

	Cardiff City v Arsenal	0-0
	Chelsea v Ipswich Town	3-1
	Derby County v Nottingham Forest	1-1
	Doncaster Rovers v Aston Villa	0-0
	Hartlepool United v West Ham United	0-2
	Hull City v Millwall	2-0
	Kettering Town v Fulham	2-4
	Liverpool v Everton	1-1
	Manchester United v Tottenham Hotspur	2-1
	Portsmouth v Swansea City	0-2
	Sheffield United v Charlton Athletic	2-1
	Sunderland v Blackburn Rovers	0-0
	Torquay United v Coventry City	0-1
	Watford v Crystal Palace	4-3
	West Bromwich Albion v Burnley	2-2
	Wolverhampton Wan. v Middlesbrough	1-2
r	Arsenal v Cardiff City	4-0
r	Aston Villa v Doncaster Rovers	3-1
r	Blackburn Rovers v Sunderland	2-1e
r	Burnley v West Bromwich Albion	3-1
r	Everton v Liverpool	1-0e
r	Nottingham Forest v Derby County	2-3

Round Five

	Arsenal v Burnley	3-0
	Blackburn Rovers v Coventry City	2-2
	Derby County v Manchester United	1-4
	Everton v Aston Villa	3-1
	Sheffield United v Hull City	1-1
	Swansea City v Fulham	1-1
	Watford v Chelsea	1-3
	West Ham United v Middlesbrough	1-1
r	Coventry City v Blackburn Rovers	1-0
r	Fulham v Swansea City	2-1
r	Hull City v Sheffield United	2-1
r	Middlesbrough v West Ham United	2-0

Round Six

Arsenal v Hull City	2-1
Coventry City v Chelsea	0-2
Everton v Middlesbrough	2-1
Fulham v Manchester United	0-4

Semi Finals

Chelsea v Arsenal	2-1 N
Everton v Manchester United	0-0PN

Final

Chelsea v Everton	2-1 N

2000/10

Extra Preliminary Round

1	Bridlington Town (2) v Esh Winning	0-0
2	Spennymoor Town v Ashington	5-1
3	Seaham Red Star v Morpeth Town	1-4
4	Sunderland RCA v Ryton	1-3
5	Bedlington Terriers v Thackley	2-0
6	Hebburn Town v Eccleshill United	7-0
7	Jarrow Roofing Boldon CA v Armthorpe Welfare	2-1
8	Whickham v Chester-le-Street Town	2-0 D
9	Scarborough Athletic v Guisborough Town	1-2
10	Selby Town v Leeds Carnegie	0-0
11	Consett v Billingham Town	5-0
12	Team Northumbria v Marske United	4-0
13	Hall Road Rangers v Bishop Auckland	2-6
14	Norton & Stockton Ancients v Pickering Town	3-0
15	Shildon v Northallerton Town	0-0
16	South Shields (3) v Newcastle Benfield	1-4
17	Pontefract Collieries v Penrith	1-4
18	Stokesley SC v Crook Town	3-1
19	West Auckland Town v Brandon United	2-2
20	Whitley Bay v Dunston UTS	2-2
21	Billingham Synthonia v Birtley Town	1-1
22	Horden CW v Tow Law Town	0-0
23	West Allotment Celtic v Liversedge	3-2
24	Silsden v Colne	3-1
25	Congleton Town v Dinnington Town	3-2
26	Abbey Hey v Hallam	1-6
27	Chadderton v Atherton Collieries	2-2
28	Maltby Main v Rossington Main	1-3
29	Parkgate v St Helens Town	1-3
30	Holker Old Boys v Padiham	0-2
31	Bacup Borough v Atherton LR	1-1
32	Maine Road v Alsager Town	3-1
33	Squires Gate v Staveley MW	2-2
34	Ashton Athletic v Bootle	1-2
35	Runcorn Linnets v AFC Emley	4-1
36	Nostell MW v Oldham Town	2-1
37	Ramsbottom United v Cheadle Town	5-1
38	Flixton v Winsford United	3-3
39	Formby v Glossop North End	1-1
40	Meir KA v Tipton Town	0-4
41	Bewdley Town v Alvechurch	0-2
42	Cradley Town v Biddulph Victoria	3-3
43	Eccleshall v Tividale	1-3
44	Westfields v Bolehall Swifts	5-0
45	Stone Dominoes v Cadbury Athletic	7-0
46	Causeway United v Wellington (Hereford)	3-1 N
47	Studley v Pershore Town	1-0
48	Dudley Sports v Southam United	2-1
49	Coleshill Town v Bridgnorth Town	2-0
50	Pegasus Juniors v Ellesmere Rangers	5-1
51	Norton United v Newcastle Town	2-5
52	Dudley Town v Walsall Wood	3-2
53	Coventry Sphinx v Bromyard Town	3-2
54	Heath Hayes v Lye Town	2-1
55	Brocton v Shifnal Town	5-1
56	Castle Vale v Goodrich	4-2
57	Stratford Town v Pilkington XXX	5-0
58	AFC Wulfrunians v Boldmere St Michaels	2-0
59	Rocester v Wednesfield	2-1
60	Nuneaton Griff v Shawbury United	3-1
61	Highgate United v Malvern Town	3-3
62	Holwell Sports v Ellistown	2-2
63	Hinckley Downes v Boston Town	1-4
64	Borrowash Victoria v Greenwood Meadows	3-0
65	Barwell v Long Eaton United	1-2
66	Holbrook MW v Heanor Town	5-0
67	Radford v Rainworth MW	0-3
68	Oadby Town v Kirby Muxloe	2-3
69	Bardon Hill v Arnold Town	3-2
70	Coalville Town v Barrow Town	3-2
71	Bottesford Town v New Mills	1-5
72	Dunkirk v Winterton Rangers	1-3
73	Lincoln Moorlands Railway v St Andrews	2-3
74	Shirebrook Town v Holbeach United	2-2
75	Sleaford Town v Loughborough University	2-0
76	Gresley v Heather St Johns	2-2
77	Teversal v Bourne Town	1-1
78	Deeping Rangers v Friar Lane & Epworth	1-1
79	Gedling MW v Blackstones	1-1
80	Gedling Town v Barton Town Old Boys	2-2
81	Long Buckby v Hadleigh United	3-2
82	Cornard United v Gorleston	0-4
83	Yaxley v Rothwell Corinthians	1-2
84	Great Yarmouth Town v Raunds Town	1-1
85	Ely City v Wisbech Town	0-1
86	Whitton United v Daventry Town	0-5
87	Walsham Le Willows v Kirkley & Pakefield	1-1
88	St Ives Town v Daventry United	6-1
89	Needham Market v Felixstowe & Walton United	1-0
90	Wellingborough Town (2) v Wroxham	0-2
91	Woodbridge Town v St Neots Town	1-4
92	Desborough Town v Newmarket Town	4-1
93	Diss Town v Cogenhoe United	2-3
94	Dereham Town v Leiston	3-1
95	Godmanchester Rovers v Haverhill Rovers	0-0
96	Stewarts & Lloyds (2) v Norwich United	1-2
97	Northampton Spencer v March Town United	1-0
98	Stowmarket Town v Mildenhall Town	0-3
99	Clapton v Kingsbury London Tigers	2-5
100	St Margaretsbury v Hullbridge Sports	0-0
101	Thame United v Bedford	1-0
102	Wembley v Basildon United	2-3
103	Erith Town v Ampthill Town	2-0
104	Leverstock Green v Burnham Ramblers	2-1
105	Oxhey Jets v Brimsdown Rovers	0-1
106	Eton Manor v Stanway Rovers	1-2
107	Wootton Blue Cross v Sporting Bengal United	1-0
108	Hertford Town v Newport Pagnell Town	1-2
109	Flackwell Heath v Welwyn Garden City	4-0
110	Bicester Town v Dunstable Town	1-4
111	FC Clacton v London APSA	2-1
112	Tiptree United v Colney Heath	3-2
113	Buckingham Town v Hanwell Town	1-3
114	Broxbourne Borough V&E v Enfield 1893	1-4
115	Biggleswade United v Stotfold	2-0
116	Hillingdon Borough v Kentish Town	2-3
117	Hatfield Town v Southend Manor	2-2
118	London Colney v Harwich & Parkeston	4-1
119	Halstead Town v Wivenhoe Town	1-1
120	Potton United v Hoddesdon Town	2-2
121	North Greenford United v Cockfosters	0-2
122	Stansted v Royston Town	2-5 N
123	Chalfont St Peter v Tokyngton Manor	3-2
124	Witham Town v Saffron Walden Town	2-1
125	Barkingside v Bowers & Pitsea	1-4
126	Crawley Green v Cranfield United	3-1
127	Langford v Aylesbury	0-6
128	Barking v Tring Athletic	2-3
129	Harefield United v Haringey Borough	1-1
130	Tunbridge Wells v Sevenoaks Town	2-2
131	Raynes Park Vale v Farnham Town	2-2
132	Hailsham Town v Lingfield	1-7
133	Worthing United v Badshot Lea	0-2
134	Hartley Wintney v Holmesdale	1-2
135	Wick v Frimley Green	4-0
136	Deal Town v Arundel	3-2
137	Littlehampton Town v Cobham	1-1
138	Southwick v Herne Bay	2-1
139	Chessington & Hook United v Chertsey Town	0-2
140	Egham Town v Ringmer	2-2
141	Whitehawk v Hythe Town	1-2
142	Banstead Athletic v Pagham	1-1
143	Camberley Town v East Preston	1-2
144	Oakwood v Lordswood	2-4
145	Croydon v Shoreham	2-5
146	East Grinstead Town v Feltham (2)	4-1
147	Eastbourne United v Redhill	3-1
148	Erith & Belvedere v Sandhurst Town	1-1
149	Wealden v Epsom & Ewell	1-3
150	Cove v Bookham	4-0
151	Crowborough Athletic v Bedfont	1-1
152	Faversham Town v Slade Green	8-0
153	Binfield v Colliers Wood United	3-5
154	Peacehaven & Telscombe v Mile Oak	1-3
155	Lancing v Selsey	0-2
156	Dorking (2) v Horley Town	0-0
157	Crawley Down v Westfield (Sussex)	4-1
158	Molesey v Sidley United	2-1
159	Guildford City (2) v St Francis Rangers	4-1
160	Three Bridges v Chichester City	1-3
161	Hassocks v Ash United	1-4
162	Wootton Bassett Town v Westbury United	2-2
163	New Milton Town v Cowes Sports	4-1
164	Petersfield Town v Brockenhurst	0-2
165	Ringwood Town v Christchurch	2-1
166	Downton v Calne Town	1-1
167	Milton United (Oxon) v Corsham Town	3-0
168	Bournemouth (Ams) v Highworth Town	1-2
169	Fareham Town v Moneyfields	1-2
170	Hamble ASSC v Wantage Town	2-2
171	Romsey Town v Hayling United	3-0
172	Lydney Town v Totton & Eling	0-5
173	Alresford Town v Shaftesbury	8-0
174	Warminster Town v Amesbury Town	5-1
175	Bitton v Newport (IOW)	1-1
176	Laverstock & Ford v Alton Town	1-3
177	Devizes Town v Shrivenham	0-5
178	Almondsbury Town v Longwell Green Sports	2-0
179	Marlow United v Hallen	1-2
180	Ardley United v Witney United	2-2
181	Kidlington v Abingdon Town	1-0
182	Winchester City v Bemerton Heath Harlequins	1-4
183	Brading Town v Fairford Town	1-0
184	Carterton v Bristol Manor Farm	2-2
185	Shortwood United v Blackfield & Langley	1-0
186	Reading Town v Melksham Town	2-0
187	Lymington Town v Harrow Hill	6-0 N
188	Wellington (Somerset) v Bideford	1-3 N
189	Launceston v Clevedon United	2-0
190	Bridport v Keynsham Town	3-1
191	Gillingham Town v Cullompton Rangers	5-1
192	Larkhall Athletic v Shepton Mallet	4-1
193	Radstock Town v Wimborne Town	0-1
194	Dawlish Town v Elmore	3-0
195	Barnstaple Town v Tavistock	3-1
196	Bishop Sutton v Bodmin Town	1-2
197	Willand Rovers v Street	2-2
198	Buckland Athletic v Hamworthy United	1-1
199	Saltash United v Chard Town	6-2
200	Portishead Town v Brislington	1-1
201	Ilfracombe Town v Falmouth Town	0-1
202	Sherborne Town v St Blazey	4-1
203	Poole Town v Welton Rovers	3-2
1r	Esh Winning v Bridlington Town (2)	2-2q
10r	Leeds Carnegie v Selby Town	1-3
15r	Northallerton Town v Shildon	1-2
19r	Brandon United v West Auckland Town	2-1
20r	Dunston UTS v Whitley Bay	0-2
21r	Birtley Town v Billingham Synthonia	1-3
22r	Tow Law Town v Horden CW	1-2
27r	Atherton Collieries v Chadderton	3-1
31r	Atherton LR v Bacup Borough	1-0e
33r	Staveley MW v Squires Gate	2-2P
38r	Winsford United v Flixton	4-6
39r	Glossop North End v Formby	3-1
42r	Biddulph Victoria v Cradley Town	0-1
61r	Malvern Town v Highgate United	2-1
62r	Ellistown v Holwell Sports	2-1
74r	Holbeach United v Shirebrook Town	1-2
76r	Heather St Johns v Gresley	1-0
77r	Bourne Town v Teversal	3-0
78r	Friar Lane & Epworth v Deeping Rangers	3-0
79r	Blackstones v Gedling MW	2-1
80r	Barton Town Old Boys v Gedling Town	2-1
84r	Raunds Town v Great Yarmouth Town	1-3
87r	Kirkley & Pakefield v Walsham Le Willows	1-0
95r	Haverhill Rovers v Godmanchester Rovers	0-1
100r	Hullbridge Sports v St Margaretsbury	0-1
117r	Southend Manor v Hatfield Town	0-3
119r	Wivenhoe Town v Halstead Town	1-4
120r	Hoddesdon Town v Potton United	2-0 N
129r	Haringey Borough v Harefield United	1-3
130r	Sevenoaks Town v Tunbridge Wells	2-1
131r	Farnham Town v Raynes Park Vale	0-3
137r	Cobham v Littlehampton Town	2-1
140r	Ringmer v Egham Town	2-0
142r	Pagham v Banstead Athletic	1-1P
148r	Sandhurst Town v Erith & Belvedere	2-4
151r	Bedfont v Crowborough Athletic	3-2
156r	Horley Town v Dorking (2)	3-0
162r	Westbury United v Wootton Bassett Town	2-3
166r	Calne Town v Downton	1-0
170r	Wantage Town v Hamble ASSC	4-1
175r	Newport (IOW) v Bitton	2-1
180r	Witney United v Ardley United	2-1
184r	Bristol Manor Farm v Carterton	1-1P
197r	Street v Willand Rovers	0-1
198r	Hamworthy United v Buckland Athletic	3-2
200r	Brislington v Portishead Town	1-2

2009/10

Preliminary Round

No	Match	Score
1	Bedlington Terriers v Garforth Town	2-3
2	Chester-le-Street Town v Norton & Stockton Ancients	0-5
3	Morpeth Town v Billingham Synthonia	4-3
4	Selby Town v Ryton	1-2
5	Bridlington Town (2) v Shildon	1-0
6	Wakefield v Guisborough Town	0-0
7	Team Northumbria v Ossett Albion	1-2
8	Stokesley SC v Spennymoor Town	1-3
9	Jarrow Roofing Boldon CA v Penrith	2-0
10	Hebburn Town v Bishop Auckland	3-4
11	Horden CW v West Allotment Celtic	2-2
12	Newcastle Benfield v Whitley Bay	1-2
13	Brandon United v FC Halifax Town	0-6
14	Consett v Harrogate Railway Athletic	0-0
15	Warrington Town v Leigh Genesis	1-0
16	Clitheroe v Staveley MW	1-1
17	Padiham v AFC Fylde	2-4
18	Bootle v Woodley Sports	1-4
19	Silsden v Hallam	1-4
20	Sheffield v Flixton	4-0
21	Trafford v Rossendale United	2-2
22	Rossington Main v Glossop North End	1-2
23	Curzon Ashton v Lancaster City	2-2
24	Chorley v Nostell MW	2-1
25	Colwyn Bay v St Helens Town	2-4
26	Cammell Laird v Mossley	2-1
27	Maine Road v Ramsbottom United	2-1
28	Atherton LR v Prescot Cables	1-0
29	Atherton Collieries v Radcliffe Borough	0-1
30	Bamber Bridge v Runcorn Linnets	6-0
31	Witton Albion v Congleton Town	0-1
32	Salford City v Skelmersdale United	3-2
33	Castle Vale v Studley	5-1
34	Kidsgrove Athletic v Alvechurch	1-0
35	Dudley Town v Bromsgrove Rovers	3-3
36	Nuneaton Griff v Stratford Town	1-4
37	Coventry Sphinx v Stourport Swifts	4-4
38	Heath Hayes v Tividale	0-1
39	Pegasus Juniors v Willenhall Town	2-2
40	Malvern Town v Cradley Town	1-1
41	Atherstone Town v Romulus	1-2
42	Stone Dominoes v Market Drayton Town	0-1
43	Coleshill Town v Causeway United	0-2
44	Dudley Sports v Rocester	2-0
45	Chasetown v AFC Wulfrunians	1-1
46	Sutton Coldfield Town v Tipton Town	2-1
47	Leek Town v Bedworth United	2-3
48	Newcastle Town v Westfields	1-2
49	Brocton v Rushall Olympic	0-2
50	Carlton Town v New Mills	4-2
51	Borrowash Victoria v Quorn	0-0
52	Blackstones v Shepshed Dynamo	3-2
53	Barton Town Old Boys v Kirby Muxloe	6-3
54	Brigg Town v Spalding United	4-0
55	Lincoln United v Friar Lane & Epworth	5-2
56	Winterton Rangers v St Andrews	6-1
57	Coalville Town v Bardon Hill	0-1
58	Glapwell v Ellistown	3-1
59	Sleaford Town v Stamford	3-1
60	Rainworth MW v Heather St Johns	3-1
61	Long Eaton United v Loughborough Dynamo	0-2
62	Grantham Town v Mickleover Sports	2-2
63	Shirebrook Town v Boston Town	0-2
64	Belper Town v Holbrook MW	1-1
65	Bourne Town v Goole AFC	3-1
66	Desborough Town v Daventry Town	1-1
67	Norwich United v Long Buckby	0-1
68	Woodford United v AFC Sudbury	1-2
69	Rothwell Town v Bury Town	0-1
70	Needham Market v Wisbech Town	4-0
71	Lowestoft Town v Great Yarmouth Town	3-0
72	Kirkley & Pakefield v Cogenhoe United	4-0
73	Gorleston v Northampton Spencer	1-1
74	Rothwell Corinthians v Godmanchester Rovers	0-0
75	Dereham Town v Wroxham	3-0
76	Soham Town Rangers v St Ives Town	0-0
77	Mildenhall Town v St Neots Town	3-0
78	Great Wakering Rovers v Waltham Forest	0-0
79	Windsor & Eton v Bowers & Pitsea	3-1
80	Northwood v St Margaretsbury	3-1
81	Potters Bar Town v Cockfosters	1-1
82	Harlow Town v Kingsbury London Tigers	1-1
83	Chesham United v Chalfont St Peter	2-0
84	Marlow v Ilford	3-0
85	Witham Town v London Colney	3-6
86	Newport Pagnell Town v Heybridge Swifts	0-2
87	Aylesbury United v Tiptree United	2-1
88	Hanwell Town v Concord Rangers	1-3
89	Enfield Town v Leverstock Green	2-0
90	Enfield 1893 v Crawley Green	7-0
91	Harefield United v Biggleswade Town	2-1
92	FC Clacton v Hitchin Town	0-1
93	Barton Rovers v Ware	2-3
94	Thame United v Wootton Blue Cross	2-0
95	Thamesmead Town v Tilbury	4-2
96	Leighton Town v Aylesbury	0-0
97	Burnham v Kentish Town	2-1
98	Biggleswade United v Halstead Town	1-2
99	Stanway Rovers v Beaconsfield SYCOB	2-0
100	Cheshunt v Maldon Town	2-3
101	Tring Athletic v Slough Town	0-4
102	Dunstable Town v Wingate & Finchley	0-2
103	Arlesey Town v Hatfield Town	2-0
104	Hoddesdon Town v Royston Town	0-1 N
105	Erith Town v Basildon United	3-0
106	Brimsdown Rovers v Flackwell Heath	2-4
107	East Thurrock United v Brentwood Town	2-0
108	Redbridge v Romford	0-1
109	Croydon Athletic v Godalming Town	2-0
110	Sittingbourne v Horley Town	0-0
111	Worthing v Raynes Park Vale	4-0
112	Merstham v Faversham Town	2-2
113	Dulwich Hamlet v Sevenoaks Town	1-1
114	Ashford Town v Mile Oak	6-1
115	Folkestone Invicta v AFC Hayes	1-0
116	Selsey v Epsom & Ewell	1-0
117	Chertsey Town v Metropolitan Police	0-1
118	Gosport Borough v East Preston	0-1
119	Lordswood v Whitstable Town	1-1
120	Horsham YMCA v Wick	5-3
121	Shoreham v Crawley Down	1-2
122	Chichester City v AFC Totton	1-3
123	Pagham v Walton Casuals	1-2
124	Fleet Town v Walton & Hersham	1-1
125	Lingfield v Southwick	0-0 N
126	Burgess Hill Town v Chipstead	2-3
127	Andover v Molesey	2-3
128	Chatham Town v Eastbourne United	1-1
129	East Grinstead Town v Cove	4-2
130	Cobham v VT	0-6
131	Leatherhead v Bedfont Green	3-0
132	Guildford City (2) v Ramsgate	3-1
133	Hythe Town v Eastbourne Town	4-0
134	Ash United v Erith & Belvedere	4-0
135	Bedfont v Colliers Wood United	4-2
136	Holmesdale v Badshot Lea	1-3
137	Deal Town v Ringmer	4-1
138	Corinthian Casuals v VCD Athletic	1-3
139	Whyteleafe v Uxbridge	0-1
140	Hallen v Lymington Town	0-0
141	Shortwood United v Romsey Town	5-1
142	Highworth Town v Bemerton Heath Harlequins	1-0
143	Totton & Eling v Kidlington	1-4 N
144	Wootton Bassett Town v Brockenhurst	0-1
145	Yate Town v Alton Town	3-1
146	Mangotsfield United v Bracknell Town	2-0
147	Calne Town v Shrivenham	0-1
148	Bishop's Cleeve v Reading Town	3-1
149	Bristol Manor Farm v Warminster Town	4-4
150	North Leigh v Milton United (Oxon)	2-1
151	Almondsbury Town v Cinderford Town	2-1
152	Wantage Town v Newport (IOW)	5-0
153	Moneyfields v Hungerford Town	3-4
154	Ringwood Town v Abingdon United	1-3
155	Brading Town v Alresford Town	3-2
156	Witney United v New Milton Town	3-1
157	Cirencester Town v Thatcham Town	2-1
158	Wimborne Town v Sherborne Town	2-1
159	Paulton Rovers v Bideford	3-1
160	Falmouth Town v Willand Rovers	1-1
161	Taunton Town v Bodmin Town	2-1
162	Poole Town v Barnstaple Town	7-2
163	Launceston v Bridgwater Town	2-3
164	Bridport v Dawlish Town	3-3
165	Gillingham Town v Portishead Town	6-0
166	Larkhall Athletic v Saltash United	0-2
167	Hamworthy United v Frome Town	3-2
6r	Guisborough Town v Wakefield	1-0
11r	West Allotment Celtic v Horden CW	2-3e
14r	Harrogate Railway Athletic v Consett	1-1P
16r	Staveley MW v Clitheroe	1-3
21r	Rossendale United v Trafford	3-1
23r	Lancaster City v Curzon Ashton	3-2
35r	Bromsgrove Rovers v Dudley Town	3-0
37r	Stourport Swifts v Coventry Sphinx	0-2
39r	Willenhall Town v Pegasus Juniors	0-2
40r	Cradley Town v Malvern Town	2-1
45r	AFC Wulfrunians v Chasetown	2-2P
51r	Quorn v Borrowash Victoria	4-1
62r	Mickleover Sports v Grantham Town	3-1
64r	Holbrook MW v Belper Town	1-0
66r	Daventry Town v Desborough Town	2-1
73r	Northampton Spencer v Gorleston	3-2
74r	Godmanchester Rovers v Rothwell Corinthians	3-0
76r	St Ives Town v Soham Town Rangers	2-1e
78r	Waltham Forest v Great Wakering Rovers	1-0
81r	Cockfosters v Potters Bar Town	1-4
82r	Kingsbury London Tigers v Harlow Town	2-1
96r	Aylesbury v Leighton Town	1-0
110r	Horley Town v Sittingbourne	0-2
112r	Faversham Town v Merstham	4-4P
113r	Sevenoaks Town v Dulwich Hamlet	0-2
119r	Whitstable Town v Lordswood	2-1e
124r	Walton & Hersham v Fleet Town	2-2P
125r	Southwick v Lingfield	0-3
128r	Eastbourne United v Chatham Town	1-2e
140r	Lymington Town v Hallen	0-4
149r	Warminster Town v Bristol Manor Farm	2-4
160r	Willand Rovers v Falmouth Town	2-1
164r	Dawlish Town v Bridport	1-2

Qualifying Round One

No	Match	Score
1	Horden CW v Durham City	2-2
2	North Ferriby United v Harrogate Railway Athletic	2-0
3	Ossett Albion v Newcastle Blue Star	8-0
4	Kendal Town v Guisborough Town	9-1
5	Spennymoor Town v Ryton	6-0
6	Morpeth Town v Ossett Town	0-1
7	Norton & Stockton Ancients v FC Halifax Town	0-4
8	Bridlington Town (2) v Whitby Town	0-1
9	Bradford Park Avenue v Bishop Auckland	4-1
10	Jarrow Roofing Boldon CA v Garforth Town	1-0
11	Guiseley v Whitley Bay	2-0
12	Hallam v Burscough	0-4
13	Cammell Laird v St Helens Town	3-1
14	Maine Road v Bamber Bridge	1-4
15	Clitheroe v Stocksbridge Park Steels	0-2
16	Atherton LR v Congleton Town	1-1
17	Warrington Town v Nantwich Town	1-0
18	Worksop Town v Frickley Athletic	1-1
19	Lancaster City v Ashton United	0-3
20	Glossop North End v Chorley	2-3
21	AFC Fylde v Rossendale United	4-1
22	Salford City v Marine	2-1
23	Woodley Sports v Radcliffe Borough	0-1 N
24	Sheffield v FC United of Manchester	1-3
25	Causeway United v Bedworth United	0-0
26	Westfields v Sutton Coldfield Town	0-6
27	Hednesford Town v Pegasus Juniors	1-4
28	Evesham United v Tividale	0-0
29	Cradley Town v Stratford Town	0-1
30	Bromsgrove Rovers v Stourbridge	1-1
31	Kidsgrove Athletic v AFC Wulfrunians	2-3
32	Coventry Sphinx v Rushall Olympic	1-0
33	Leamington v Market Drayton Town	0-2
34	Romulus v Castle Vale	2-1
35	Rugby Town v Dudley Sports	6-0
36	Rainworth MW v Holbrook MW	2-1
37	Bourne Town v Boston Town	3-1
38	Buxton v Winterton Rangers	2-1
39	Retford United v Lincoln United	1-1
40	Bardon Hill v Barton Town Old Boys	5-0
41	Blackstones v Hucknall Town	2-4
42	Quorn v Mickleover Sports	0-2
43	Brigg Town v Nuneaton Town	0-5
44	Matlock Town v Sleaford Town	1-1 N
45	Glapwell v Carlton Town	0-1
46	Boston United v Loughborough Dynamo	4-2
47	Lowestoft Town v Dereham Town	3-1
48	Godmanchester Rovers v Northampton Spencer	1-2
49	St Ives Town v Kirkley & Pakefield	1-2
50	Bury Town v King's Lynn	2-0
51	AFC Sudbury v Needham Market	0-2
52	Long Buckby v Mildenhall Town	1-1
53	Cambridge City v Daventry Town	2-0
54	Harefield United v Maldon Town	3-1
55	Canvey Island v Hitchin Town	3-3
56	Enfield 1893 v Halstead Town	3-3
57	Flackwell Heath v Royston Town	2-1
58	Chesham United v Harrow Borough	1-1
59	Erith Town v Aylesbury	3-3
60	Heybridge Swifts v Stanway Rovers	1-1
61	Waltham Abbey v Enfield Town	0-1
62	Thamesmead Town v Windsor & Eton	1-2
63	Arlesey Town v Wealdstone	1-2
64	Thame United v Burnham	0-2
65	East Thurrock United v Ware	4-1
66	Northwood v Wingate & Finchley	2-2
67	Hemel Hempstead Town v Slough Town	1-1
68	Marlow v Hendon	0-2
69	AFC Hornchurch v Billericay Town	0-3
70	Aylesbury United v Potters Bar Town	0-0
71	London Colney v Aveley	1-1
72	Boreham Wood v Waltham Forest	1-0
73	Bedford Town v Kingsbury London Tigers	5-1
74	Romford v Concord Rangers	1-1
75	Guildford City (2) v East Preston	4-4
76	Molesey v Bashley	2-3
77	Walton & Hersham v Cray Wanderers	2-1
78	Chatham Town v Walton Casuals	0-0
79	Farnborough v Hastings United (2)	2-1
80	Whitstable Town v Carshalton Athletic	2-1
81	Crawley Down v Ashford Town (Middlesex)	2-3
82	Leatherhead v Ashford Town	2-0
83	Uxbridge v Ash United	4-3
84	Bognor Regis Town v Kingstonian	1-4
85	Folkestone Invicta v Sittingbourne	0-1
86	Maidstone United (2) v Bedfont	2-1
87	Hythe Town v Faversham Town	2-1
88	AFC Totton v VCD Athletic	5-0
89	Lingfield v Badshot Lea	4-4
90	Chipstead v Dartford	1-6
91	Tooting & Mitcham United v Horsham	4-2
92	Deal Town v Selsey	1-1
93	VT v Dulwich Hamlet	1-0
94	Tonbridge Angels v Metropolitan Police	1-0
95	Croydon Athletic v Worthing	0-1
96	Horsham YMCA v East Grinstead Town	1-0
97	Margate v Sutton United	2-2
98	Almondsbury Town v Yate Town	1-1
99	Brading Town v Hallen	1-1
100	Banbury United v Chippenham Town	0-0
101	Brackley Town v Swindon Supermarine	1-0
102	Bishop's Cleeve v Brockenhurst	5-2
103	Oxford City v Kidlington	4-2
104	Mangotsfield United v Wantage Town	3-0
105	Shortwood United v Witney United	3-3
106	Highworth Town v Abingdon United	0-3
107	Hungerford Town v Bristol Manor Farm	4-0
108	Didcot Town v Shrivenham	5-0
109	Cirencester Town v North Leigh	2-1
110	Bridgwater Town v Hamworthy United	3-1

2009/10

111	Saltash United v Gillingham Town	1-1
112	Truro City v Bridport	1-1
113	Taunton Town v Merthyr Tydfil	0-3
114	Willand Rovers v Poole Town	1-0
115	Paulton Rovers v Tiverton Town	1-0
116	Clevedon Town v Wimborne Town	4-2
1r	Durham City v Horden CW	1-3
16r	Congleton Town v Atherton LR	5-0
18r	Frickley Athletic v Worksop Town	2-1
25r	Bedworth United v Causeway United	3-0
28r	Tividale v Evesham United	1-2e
30r	Stourbridge v Bromsgrove Rovers	3-1
39r	Lincoln United v Retford United	2-1
44r	Sleaford Town v Matlock Town	1-2
52r	Mildenhall Town v Long Buckby	4-3e
55r	Hitchin Town v Canvey Island	0-1
56r	Halstead Town v Enfield 1893	1-1q
58r	Harrow Borough v Chesham United	0-2
59r	Aylesbury v Erith Town	2-1
60r	Stanway Rovers v Heybridge Swifts	0-0q
66r	Wingate & Finchley v Northwood	3-1
67r	Slough Town v Hemel Hempstead Town	2-1
70r	Potters Bar Town v Aylesbury United	2-0
71r	Aveley v London Colney	4-2
74r	Concord Rangers v Romford	6-0
75r	East Preston v Guildford City (2)	2-2P
78r	Walton Casuals v Chatham Town	2-1e
89r	Badshot Lea v Lingfield	2-1
92r	Selsey v Deal Town	3-0
97r	Sutton United v Margate	3-2e
98r	Yate Town v Almondsbury Town	1-2
99r	Hallen v Brading Town	3-0
100r	Chippenham Town v Banbury United	3-2
105r	Witney United v Shortwood United	2-1
111r	Gillingham Town v Saltash United	6-5e
112r	Bridport v Truro City	0-7

Qualifying Round Two

1	Whitby Town v Vauxhall Motors	0-5
2	Warrington Town v Radcliffe Borough	1-1
3	Congleton Town v Frickley Athletic	0-1
4	Lincoln United v Jarrow Roofing Boldon CA	2-1
5	Kendal Town v Ossett Town	2-0
6	Droylsden v FC Halifax Town	0-2
7	Horden CW v Burscough	1-4
8	Blyth Spartans v Ossett Albion	7-1
9	North Ferriby United v FC United of Manchester	0-1
10	Hyde United v Salford City	2-2
11	Chorley v Ashton United	2-1
12	Southport v Spennymoor Town	3-1
13	Bradford Park Avenue v Harrogate Town	4-0
14	Northwich Victoria v Bardon Hill	8-0
15	Fleetwood Town v Farsley Celtic	3-1
16	Workington v Cammell Laird	4-1
17	Stocksbridge Park Steels v Stalybridge Celtic	2-7
18	Guiseley v Bamber Bridge	2-0
19	Buxton v AFC Fylde	5-0
20	Coventry Sphinx v Stafford Rangers	2-2
21	Matlock Town v Bury Town	2-2
22	Nuneaton Town v Carlton Town	1-1
23	Bedford Town v Romulus	2-1
24	Evesham United v Stourbridge	0-1
25	Alfreton Town v AFC Wulfrunians	6-0
26	Bedworth United v Rainworth MW	2-1
27	AFC Telford United v Pegasus Juniors	4-1
28	Sutton Coldfield Town v Needham Market	3-1
29	Hinckley United v Kirkley & Pakefield	2-1
30	Lowestoft Town v Boston United	1-0
31	Redditch United v Stratford Town	1-1
32	Market Drayton Town v Gainsborough Trinity	1-2
33	Ilkeston Town (2) v Mildenhall Town	4-1
34	Eastwood Town v Corby Town	2-1
35	Worcester City v Bourne Town	3-0
36	Mickleover Sports v Solihull Moors	3-4
37	Rugby Town v Hucknall Town	1-3
38	Cambridge City v Northampton Spencer	4-1
39	Enfield 1893 v Chelmsford City	0-5
40	Walton Casuals v Selsey	1-0
41	Canvey Island v Tooting & Mitcham United	0-2
42	Heybridge Swifts v St Albans City	1-0
43	Burnham v Aveley	1-1
44	Chesham United v Billericay Town	4-2
45	Sutton United v Uxbridge	3-0
46	Lewes v Leatherhead	1-1
47	Bishop's Stortford v Thurrock	2-3
48	Hythe Town v Woking	2-2
49	Tonbridge Angels v Horsham YMCA	4-0
50	Dover Athletic v East Preston	8-0
51	Boreham Wood v Wealdstone	2-4
52	Windsor & Eton v Farnborough	0-1
53	Hendon v Kingstonian	2-1
54	Potters Bar Town v Whitstable Town	3-0
55	Bromley v Flackwell Heath	2-0
56	Braintree Town v Hampton & Richmond Boro.	0-0
57	Harefield United v Maidstone United (2)	0-2
58	Wingate & Finchley v Aylesbury	2-2
59	Sittingbourne v Staines Town	2-3
60	Worthing v Dartford	1-2
61	Welling United v East Thurrock United	2-0
62	Walton & Hersham v Enfield Town	3-2
63	Ashford Town (Middlesex) v Badshot Lea	1-0
64	Slough Town v Concord Rangers	2-0
65	Bishop's Cleeve v Weymouth	3-0
66	Dorchester Town v Hungerford Town	4-0
67	Bashley v Gloucester City	1-2
68	Gillingham Town v Mangotsfield United	3-3
69	Abingdon United v Cirencester Town	0-0
70	Willand Rovers v Bath City	0-5
71	Almondsbury Town v AFC Totton	1-4
72	Weston-Super-Mare v Havant & Waterlooville	0-1
73	Brackley Town v Basingstoke Town	0-1
74	Clevedon Town v Newport County (2)	1-3
75	Chippenham Town v Merthyr Tydfil	4-1
76	Witney United v Eastleigh	1-6
77	VT v Oxford City	0-1
78	Bridgwater Town v Hallen	1-0
79	Maidenhead United v Truro City	2-5
80	Didcot Town v Paulton Rovers	0-2
2r	Radcliffe Borough v Warrington Town	3-1
10r	Salford City v Hyde United	1-0
20r	Stafford Rangers v Coventry Sphinx	2-3
21r	Bury Town v Matlock Town	2-0e
22r	Carlton Town v Nuneaton Town	0-3
31r	Stratford Town v Redditch United	0-2
43r	Aveley v Burnham	3-1
46r	Leatherhead v Lewes	0-1e
48r	Woking v Hythe Town	5-1
56r	Hampton & Richmond Boro. v Braintree Town	4-1
58r	Aylesbury v Wingate & Finchley	2-1
68r	Mangotsfield United v Gillingham Town	3-0
69r	Cirencester Town v Abingdon United	3-1

Qualifying Round Three

1	Salford City v Blyth Spartans	2-2
2	Fleetwood Town v Vauxhall Motors	3-2
3	Northwich Victoria v Chorley	4-1
4	Buxton v Bradford Park Avenue	2-2
5	Guiseley v Kendal Town	1-1
6	Workington v Radcliffe Borough	3-0
7	Alfreton Town v Southport	2-2
8	FC Halifax Town v Burscough	1-0
9	FC United of Manchester v Stalybridge Celtic	3-3
10	Lincoln United v Frickley Athletic	1-1
11	Cambridge City v Hinckley United	0-5
12	Solihull Moors v Redditch United	0-2
13	Stourbridge v Hucknall Town	0-0
14	Ilkeston Town (2) v Eastwood Town	1-1
15	Bury Town v Bedford Town	1-1
16	Coventry Sphinx v Bedworth United	0-1
17	Lowestoft Town v Sutton Coldfield Town	0-0
18	AFC Telford United v Worcester City	0-0
19	Nuneaton Town v Gainsborough Trinity	1-0
20	Hampton & Richmond Boro. v Aveley	1-1
21	Dartford v Chelmsford City	1-4
22	Wealdstone v Lewes	3-0
23	Thurrock v Potters Bar Town	4-2
24	Hendon v Ashford Town (Middlesex)	0-0
25	Tonbridge Angels v Bromley	0-2
26	Dover Athletic v Welling United	2-0
27	Tooting & Mitcham United v Slough Town	3-2
28	Sutton United v Walton & Hersham	1-0
29	Aylesbury v Chesham United	4-3
30	Walton Casuals v Staines Town	0-3
31	Woking v Maidstone United (2)	2-0
32	Heybridge Swifts v Farnborough	0-0
33	Paulton Rovers v Newport County (2)	1-0
34	Dorchester Town v Gloucester City	1-2
35	Oxford City v Cirencester Town	2-0
36	Eastleigh v Basingstoke Town	2-0
37	Bishop's Cleeve v Bath City	1-4
38	Truro City v Mangotsfield United	1-1
39	AFC Totton v Bridgwater Town	3-2
40	Havant & Waterlooville v Chippenham Town	1-2
1r	Blyth Spartans v Salford City	2-1
4r	Bradford Park Avenue v Buxton	0-1
5r	Kendal Town v Guiseley	1-0
7r	Southport v Alfreton Town	2-1
9r	Stalybridge Celtic v FC United of Manchester	0-1
10r	Frickley Athletic v Lincoln United	1-1q
13r	Hucknall Town v Stourbridge	1-6
14r	Eastwood Town v Ilkeston Town (2)	1-3
15r	Bedford Town v Bury Town	3-4
17r	Sutton Coldfield Town v Lowestoft Town	1-2
18r	Worcester City v AFC Telford United	0-1
20r	Aveley v Hampton & Richmond Boro.	1-2
24r	Ashford Town (Middlesex) v Hendon	2-2q
32r	Farnborough v Heybridge Swifts	3-0e
38r	Mangotsfield United v Truro City	1-1P

Qualifying Round Four

1	Hinckley United v Histon	2-1
2	Nuneaton Town v Kendal Town	1-0
3	FC Halifax Town v Wrexham	0-1
4	Gateshead (2) v Southport	3-0
5	Workington v Rushden & Diamonds	0-3
6	Mansfield Town v Altrincham	3-0
7	Buxton v Stourbridge	0-4
8	Blyth Spartans v AFC Telford United	0-0
9	Ilkeston Town (2) v Tamworth	2-0
10	Lincoln United v Cambridge United	1-3
11	Kettering Town v Redditch United	1-1
12	Northwich Victoria v FC United of Manchester	3-0
13	Barrow v Chester City	1-1
14	Kidderminster Harriers v Fleetwood Town	0-0
15	York City v Bedworth United	2-0
16	Hendon v Woking	0-5
17	Gloucester City v Lowestoft Town	1-1
18	Farnborough v Salisbury City	0-0
19	Mangotsfield United v Forest Green Rovers	1-2
20	Crawley Town v AFC Wimbledon	1-1
21	Oxford City v Bury Town	2-1
22	Bromley v Ebbsfleet United	3-0
23	Chelmsford City v Stevenage Borough	1-2
24	Aylesbury v Wealdstone	2-4
25	Dover Athletic v Eastleigh	3-5
26	Hayes & Yeading United v Staines Town	0-1
27	Luton Town v Grays Athletic	3-0
28	Oxford United v Thurrock	2-0
29	Bath City v AFC Totton	3-2
30	Paulton Rovers v Chippenham Town	3-0
31	Tooting & Mitcham United v Eastbourne Borough	3-3
32	Hampton & Richmond Boro. v Sutton United	1-3
8r	AFC Telford United v Blyth Spartans	4-0
11r	Redditch United v Kettering Town	0-1e
13r	Chester City v Barrow	0-4
14r	Fleetwood Town v Kidderminster Harriers	3-1
17r	Lowestoft Town v Gloucester City	4-2
18r	Salisbury City v Farnborough	4-2
20r	AFC Wimbledon v Crawley Town	3-1
31r	Eastbourne Borough v Tooting & Mitcham United	3-4e

Round One

	AFC Telford United v Lincoln City	1-3
	Accrington Stanley (2) v Salisbury City	2-1
	Aldershot Town v Bury	2-0
	Barnet v Darlington	3-1
	Barrow v Eastleigh	2-1
	Bristol Rovers v Southampton	2-3
	Bromley v Colchester United	0-4
	Burton Albion v Oxford City	3-2
	Cambridge United v Ilkeston Town (2)	4-0
	Carlisle United v Morecambe	2-2
	Chesterfield v Bournemouth	1-3
	Forest Green Rovers v Mansfield Town	1-1
	Gateshead (2) v Brentford	2-2
	Gillingham v Southend United	3-0
	Grimsby Town v Bath City	0-2
	Hartlepool United v Kettering Town	0-1
	Hereford United v Sutton United	2-0
	Huddersfield Town v Dagenham & Redbridge	6-1
	Luton Town v Rochdale	3-3
	Millwall v AFC Wimbledon	4-1
	Milton Keynes Dons v Macclesfield Town	1-0
	Northampton Town v Fleetwood Town	2-1
	Northwich Victoria v Charlton Athletic	1-0
	Notts County v Bradford City	2-1
	Nuneaton Town v Exeter City	0-4
	Oldham Athletic v Leeds United	0-2
	Oxford United v Yeovil Town	1-0
	Paulton Rovers v Norwich City	0-7
	Port Vale v Stevenage Borough	1-1
	Rushden & Diamonds v Hinckley United	3-1
	Shrewsbury Town v Staines Town	0-1
	Stockport County v Tooting & Mitcham United	5-0
	Stourbridge v Walsall	0-1
	Swindon Town v Woking	1-0
	Torquay United v Cheltenham Town	3-1
	Tranmere Rovers v Leyton Orient	1-1
	Wealdstone v Rotherham United	2-3
	Wrexham v Lowestoft Town	1-0
	Wycombe Wanderers v Brighton & Hove Albion	4-4
	York City v Crewe Alexandra	3-2
r	Brentford v Gateshead (2)	5-2
r	Brighton & Hove Albion v Wycombe Wanderers	2-0
r	Leyton Orient v Tranmere Rovers	0-1
r	Mansfield Town v Forest Green Rovers	1-2
r	Morecambe v Carlisle United	0-1
r	Rochdale v Luton Town	0-2
r	Stevenage Borough v Port Vale	0-1

Round Two

	Accrington Stanley (2) v Barnet	2-2
	Bath City v Forest Green Rovers	1-2
	Bournemouth v Notts County	1-2
	Brentford v Walsall	1-0
	Brighton & Hove Albion v Rushden & Diamonds	3-2
	Cambridge United v York City	1-2
	Carlisle United v Norwich City	3-1
	Gillingham v Burton Albion	1-0
	Hereford United v Colchester United	0-1
	Kettering Town v Leeds United	1-1
	Milton Keynes Dons v Exeter City	4-3
	Northampton Town v Southampton	2-3
	Northwich Victoria v Lincoln City	1-3
	Oxford United v Barrow	1-1
	Port Vale v Huddersfield Town	0-1
	Rotherham United v Luton Town	2-2
	Staines Town v Millwall	1-1
	Stockport County v Torquay United	0-4 N
	Tranmere Rovers v Aldershot Town	0-0
	Wrexham v Swindon Town	0-1
r	Aldershot Town v Tranmere Rovers	1-2
r	Barnet v Accrington Stanley (2)	0-1
r	Barrow v Oxford United	3-1
r	Leeds United v Kettering Town	5-1e
r	Luton Town v Rotherham United	3-0
r	Millwall v Staines Town	4-0

2009/10 to 2010/11

Round Three

	Accrington Stanley (2) v Gillingham	1-0
	Aston Villa v Blackburn Rovers	3-1
	Blackpool v Ipswich Town	1-2
	Bolton Wanderers v Lincoln City	4-0
	Brentford v Doncaster Rovers	0-1
	Bristol City v Cardiff City	1-1
	Chelsea v Watford	5-0
	Everton v Carlisle United	3-1
	Fulham v Swindon Town	1-0
	Huddersfield Town v West Bromwich Albion	0-2
	Leicester City v Swansea City	2-1
	Manchester United v Leeds United	0-1
	Middlesbrough v Manchester City	0-1
	Millwall v Derby County	1-1
	Milton Keynes Dons v Burnley	1-2
	Nottingham Forest v Birmingham City	0-0
	Notts County v Forest Green Rovers	2-1
	Plymouth Argyle v Newcastle United	0-0
	Portsmouth v Coventry City	1-1
	Preston North End v Colchester United	7-0
	Reading v Liverpool	1-1
	Scunthorpe United v Barnsley	1-0
	Sheffield United v Queen's Park Rangers	1-1
	Sheffield Wednesday v Crystal Palace	1-2
	Southampton v Luton Town	1-0
	Stoke City v York City	3-1
	Sunderland v Barrow	3-0
	Torquay United v Brighton & Hove Albion	0-1
	Tottenham Hotspur v Peterborough United	4-0
	Tranmere Rovers v Wolverhampton Wan.	0-1
	West Ham United v Arsenal	1-2
	Wigan Athletic v Hull City	4-1
r	Birmingham City v Nottingham Forest	1-0
r	Cardiff City v Bristol City	1-0
r	Coventry City v Portsmouth	1-2e
r	Derby County v Millwall	1-1P
r	Liverpool v Reading	1-2e
r	Newcastle United v Plymouth Argyle	3-0
r	Queen's Park Rangers v Sheffield United	2-3

Round Four

	Accrington Stanley (2) v Fulham	1-3
	Aston Villa v Brighton & Hove Albion	3-2
	Bolton Wanderers v Sheffield United	2-0
	Cardiff City v Leicester City	4-2
	Derby County v Doncaster Rovers	1-0
	Everton v Birmingham City	1-2
	Notts County v Wigan Athletic	2-2
	Portsmouth v Sunderland	2-1
	Preston North End v Chelsea	0-2
	Reading v Burnley	1-0
	Scunthorpe United v Manchester City	2-4
	Southampton v Ipswich Town	2-1
	Stoke City v Arsenal	3-1
	Tottenham Hotspur v Leeds United	2-2
	West Bromwich Albion v Newcastle United	4-2
	Wolverhampton Wan. v Crystal Palace	2-2
r	Crystal Palace v Wolverhampton Wan.	3-1
r	Leeds United v Tottenham Hotspur	1-3
r	Wigan Athletic v Notts County	0-2

Round Five

	Bolton Wanderers v Tottenham Hotspur	1-1
	Chelsea v Cardiff City	4-1
	Crystal Palace v Aston Villa	2-2
	Derby County v Birmingham City	1-2
	Fulham v Notts County	4-0
	Manchester City v Stoke City	1-1
	Reading v West Bromwich Albion	2-2
	Southampton v Portsmouth	1-4
r	Aston Villa v Crystal Palace	3-1
r	Stoke City v Manchester City	3-1e
r	Tottenham Hotspur v Bolton Wanderers	4-0
r	West Bromwich Albion v Reading	2-3e

Round Six

	Chelsea v Stoke City	2-0
	Fulham v Tottenham Hotspur	0-0
	Portsmouth v Birmingham City	2-0
	Reading v Aston Villa	2-4
r	Tottenham Hotspur v Fulham	3-1

Semi Finals

Chelsea v Aston Villa	3-0 N
Portsmouth v Tottenham Hotspur	2-0eN

Final

Chelsea v Portsmouth	1-0 N

2010/11

Extra Preliminary Round

1	Ryton v Scarborough Athletic	0-1
2	Liversedge v Whitley Bay	0-3
3	Brandon United v Chester-le-Street Town	1-2
4	Shildon v Sunderland RCA	4-3
5	Pickering Town v South Shields (3)	1-4
6	Ashington v Billingham Town	4-1
7	Tow Law Town v Jarrow Roofing Boldon CA	0-2
8	West Auckland Town v Whickham	2-1
9	West Allotment Celtic v Tadcaster Albion	1-2
10	Norton & Stockton Ancients v Penrith	2-1
11	Guisborough Town v Armthorpe Welfare	0-3
12	Bishop Auckland v Consett	3-3
13	Brighouse Town v Dunston UTS	1-2
14	Hebburn Town v Marske United	1-1
15	Whitehaven v Team Northumbria	4-1
16	Esh Winning v Northallerton Town	0-4
17	Pontefract Collieries v Selby Town	0-2
18	Silsden v Crook Town	2-2
19	Hall Road Rangers v Newcastle Benfield	2-2
20	Bridlington Town (2) v Horden CW	5-1
21	Stokesley SC v Thackley	1-1
22	Leeds Carnegie v Billingham Synthonia	0-0
23	Spennymoor Town v Bedlington Terriers	1-0
24	Morpeth Town v AFC Emley	1-2
25	Seaham Red Star v North Shields	0-1
26	Irlam v Chadderton	1-2
27	Rossendale United v Formby	3-1
28	Ashton Athletic v Parkgate	0-2
29	Hallam v Atherton Collieries	2-3
30	Ramsbottom United v Winsford United	4-1
31	Leek CSOB v Bootle	1-1
32	New Mills v Alsager Town	10-2
33	Holker Old Boys v Abbey Hey	1-1
34	Daisy Hill v Congleton Town	0-8
35	Glossop North End v Wigan Robin Park	2-2
36	Runcorn Linnets v Maine Road	1-1
37	Atherton LR v Nelson	wo/s
38	Staveley MW v Padiham	5-0
39	Flixton v Bacup Borough	0-3
40	Nostell MW v St Helens Town	1-1
41	Colne v Ashton Town	2-0
42	Cheadle Town v Squires Gate	3-0
43	Hemsworth MW v AFC Liverpool	4-1
44	Willenhall Town v Bartley Green	0-6
45	Coalville Town v Stone Dominoes	1-1
46	Loughborough University v Stratford Town	1-4
47	Boldmere St Michaels v Westfields	0-1
48	Coventry Sphinx v Castle Vale	3-0
49	Pegasus Juniors v Heather St Johns	1-1
50	Causeway United v Ellesmere Rangers	2-1 N
51	Rocester v Pilkington XXX	1-2
52	Eccleshall v Southam United	3-0
53	Cradley Town v Malvern Town	3-4
54	Shifnal Town v Dudley Town	1-1
55	Kirby Muxloe v Walsall Wood	4-2
56	Alvechurch v Tipton Town	0-5
57	Bardon Hill v Bewdley Town	2-5
58	Tividale v Oadby Town	1-2
59	Pelsall Villa v Dosthill Colts	0-2
60	Bridgnorth Town v Highgate United	4-0
61	Castle Vale JKS v Ledbury Town	wo/s
62	AFC Wulfrunians v Heath Hayes	1-3
63	Brocton v Coleshill Town	4-4
64	Nuneaton Griff v Studley	2-1
65	Norton United v Hinckley (2)	1-0
66	Biddulph Victoria v Wellington (Hereford)	1-1
67	Wednesfield v Bolehall Swifts	2-0
68	Gedling Town v Boston Town	2-4
69	Blackstones v Maltby Main	1-1
70	Heanor Town v Borrowash Victoria	0-0
71	Long Eaton United v Barton Town Old Boys	1-1
72	Holbeach United v Radcliffe Olympic	0-1
73	Wisbech Town v St Andrews	5-0
74	Rossington Main v Shirebrook Town	0-3
75	Greenwood Meadows v Winterton Rangers	3-4
76	Teversal v Bottesford Town	0-0
77	Barrow Town v Arnold Town	2-1
78	Dunkirk v Dinnington Town	4-3
79	Gedling MW v Holwell Sports	2-2
80	Holbrook Sports v Sleaford Town	4-0
81	Lincoln Moorlands Railway v Friar Lane & Epworth	3-1
82	Deeping Rangers v Gresley	0-2
83	Haverhill Rovers v Hadleigh United	2-1
84	Diss Town v Daventry United	1-2
85	Brantham Athletic v Woodbridge Town	4-2
86	St Neots Town v Dereham Town	2-0
87	Potton United v Stewarts & Lloyds (2)	1-2
88	Newmarket Town v Yaxley	3-0
89	Whitton United v Thetford Town	1-1
90	Northampton Spencer v Leiston	0-2
91	Wellingborough Town (2) v Kirkley & Pakefield	3-0
92	Walsham Le Willows v Long Buckby	1-4
93	Team Bury v Ampthill Town	2-1
94	Ely City v Raunds Town	4-0
95	Wroxham v Rothwell Corinthians	5-1
96	Felixstowe & Walton United v Mildenhall Town	4-1
97	Great Yarmouth Town v Norwich United	0-4
98	March Town United v Gorleston	1-0
99	St Ives Town v Cogenhoe United	2-3
100	Rothwell Town v Desborough Town	3-4
101	Godmanchester Rovers v AFC Kempston Rovers	1-1
102	Welwyn Garden City v St Margaretsbury	1-2
103	Biggleswade United v Newport Pagnell Town	1-4
104	Saffron Walden Town v Mauritius Sports Association	3-2
105	Hadley v Barking	0-0
106	Kentish Town v Stansted	1-0 N
107	Chalfont St Peter v Stotfold	1-0
108	Clapton v Stanway Rovers	0-4
109	Burnham Ramblers v Hoddesdon Town	2-1
110	Oxhey Jets v Hatfield Town	3-2
111	Bethnal Green United v Basildon United	4-0
112	Bowers & Pitsea v Dunstable Town	4-1
113	Takeley v Hertford Town	0-4
114	Cockfosters v Hullbridge Sports	2-1
115	Kingsbury London Tigers v FC Clacton	1-2 N
116	Witham Town v Wembley	3-0
117	Colney Heath v Broxbourne Borough V&E	3-0
118	Langford v Aylesbury United	1-3
119	Tring Athletic v Enfield 1893	2-0
120	Leverstock Green v Harefield United	1-2
121	Haringey Borough v Hillingdon Borough	3-0
122	London APSA v Halstead Town	3-3
123	Hanwell Town v London Colney	1-3
124	Royston Town v Crawley Green	1-2
125	Eton Manor v Bedford	3-0
126	Barkingside v Southend Manor	0-2
127	Cobham v Wick	2-0
128	Hassocks v Eastbourne United	7-1
129	Farnham Town v Badshot Lea	2-1
130	Molesey v Hartley Wintney	0-2
131	Croydon v Crowborough Athletic	5-2
132	Chessington & Hook United v Raynes Park Vale	1-2
133	Alresford Town v Herne Bay	5-2
134	St Francis Rangers v Banstead Athletic	1-3
135	Sidley United v Lancing	0-3 N
136	Binfield v Crawley Down	3-2
137	Horley Town v Ash United	4-1
138	East Grinstead Town v Holyport	2-0
139	Camberley Town v Petersfield Town	2-1
140	Cove v Three Bridges	1-1
141	Alton Town v Chichester City	4-1
142	Erith Town v Colliers Wood United	2-1
143	Arundel v Hailsham Town	4-1
144	Greenwich Borough v South Park	1-2
145	Epsom & Ewell v Shoreham	3-0
146	Holmesdale v Erith & Belvedere	0-2
147	Mile Oak v Tunbridge Wells	0-1
148	Egham Town v Guildford City (2)	1-3
149	Littlehampton Town v Beckenham Town	1-1 N
150	Hythe Town v Bookham	4-0
151	Selsey v Worthing United	1-4
152	Lordswood v Pagham	1-5
153	Norton Sports v Redhill	2-0
154	Flackwell Heath v Oakwood	2-1
155	Deal Town v Sandhurst Town	3-0
156	Frimley Green v Peacehaven & Telscombe	0-4
157	Lingfield v Sevenoaks Town	1-0 N
158	Dorking (2) v Bracknell Town	0-5
159	Mole Valley SCR v Chertsey Town	0-5
160	VCD Athletic v AFC Uckfield	3-1
161	East Preston v Ringmer	1-4
162	Brading Town v Romsey Town	1-1
163	Bradford Town v Wootton Bassett Town	1-1
164	Fairford Town v Lydney Town	0-0
165	Christchurch v Hamble ASSC	0-1
166	Ringwood Town v Cowes Sports	5-0
167	Thame United v Shrivenham	3-0
168	Hayling United v Blackfield & Langley	1-2
169	Lymington Town v Moneyfields	1-3 N
170	Highworth Town v Melksham Town	2-1
171	Bournemouth (Ams) v Abingdon Town	1-0
172	Totton & Eling v Bemerton Heath Harlequins	2-0
173	Wantage Town v Shortwood United	2-3
174	Downton v Bitton	0-2
175	Hallen v Winchester City	4-1
176	Milton United (Oxon) v Witney United	0-2
177	Bristol Manor Farm v Ardley United	5-3
178	Calne Town v Corsham Town	2-1 D
179	Amesbury Town v Almondsbury UWE	0-5
180	Newport (IOW) v Kidlington	1-0
181	New Milton Town v Longwell Green Sports	1-1
182	Bicester Town v Westbury United	0-2
183	Warminster Town v Reading Town	1-2
184	Fareham Town v Clanfield 85	3-1
185	Laverstock & Ford v Hook Norton	6-1
186	Brockenhurst v Old Woodstock Town	0-1
187	Larkhall Athletic v Gillingham Town	5-1
188	Bridport v Welton Rovers	3-0
189	Launceston v Bodmin Town	0-3
190	Willand Rovers v Merthyr Town (2)	2-0
191	Sherborne Town v Portishead Town	2-1
192	Elmore v Hamworthy United	1-5
193	St Blazey v Torpoint Athletic	1-1
194	Odd Down v Verwood Town	1-1
195	Street v Barnstaple Town	4-1
196	Buckland Athletic v Radstock Town	4-4
197	Brislington v Wellington (Hereford)	0-1
198	Keynsham Town v Tavistock	0-2
199	Saltash United v Bishop Sutton	1-1
200	Poole Town v Dawlish Town	3-0
201	Ilfracombe Town v Falmouth Town	4-4
12r	Consett v Bishop Auckland	2-3
14r	Marske United v Hebburn Town	2-0

2010/11

18r Crook Town v Silsden	1-0
19r Newcastle Benfield v Hall Road Rangers	3-1
21r Thackley v Stokesley SC	2-1
22r Billingham Synthonia v Leeds Carnegie	3-1
31r Bootle v Leek CSOB	6-0
33r Abbey Hey v Holker Old Boys	0-1
35r Wigan Robin Park v Glossop North End	0-1
36r Maine Road v Runcorn Linnets	3-4
40r St Helens Town v Nostell MW	2-2P
45r Stone Dominoes v Coalville Town	0-3
49r Heather St Johns v Pegasus Juniors	5-1
54r Dudley Town v Shifnal Town	2-0
63r Coleshill Town v Brocton	2-1
66r Wellington (Hereford) v Biddulph Victoria	1-1q
69r Maltby Main v Blackstones	0-0P
70r Borrowash Victoria v Heanor Town	2-1
71r Barton Town Old Boys v Long Eaton United	1-0
76r Bottesford Town v Teversal	3-1
79r Holwell Sports v Gedling MW	3-4
89r Thetford Town v Whitton United	0-2
101r AFC Kempston Rovers v Godmanchester Rovers	4-0
105r Barking v Hadley	1-0
122r Halstead Town v London APSA	2-0
140r Three Bridges v Cove	4-1
149r Beckenham Town v Littlehampton Town	3-0
162r Romsey Town v Brading Town	0-4
163r Wootton Bassett Town v Bradford Town	3-3P
164r Lydney Town v Fairford Town	3-1
181r Longwell Green Sports v New Milton Town	3-2
193r Torpoint Athletic v St Blazey	5-1
194r Verwood Town v Odd Down	1-4
196r Radstock Town v Buckland Athletic	3-2
199r Bishop Sutton v Saltash United	4-4P
201r Falmouth Town v Ilfracombe Town	1-2

Preliminary Round

1 Spennymoor Town v Crook Town	2-0
2 Selby Town v Ossett Albion	0-4
3 Chester-le-Street Town v Scarborough Athletic	2-1
4 South Shields (3) v Dunston UTS	1-1
5 Newcastle Benfield v North Shields	3-3
6 Armthorpe Welfare v Marske United	2-4
7 Wakefield v Ashington	2-3
8 AFC Emley v Northallerton Town	0-1
9 Garforth Town v Tadcaster Albion	0-1
10 Jarrow Roofing Boldon CA v Durham City	1-2
11 Thackley v Harrogate Railway Athletic	5-0
12 Billingham Synthonia v West Auckland Town	0-3
13 Shildon v Bridlington Town (2)	1-0
14 Whitehaven v Norton & Stockton Ancients	1-5
15 Bishop Auckland v Whitley Bay	2-2
16 Radcliffe Borough v Lancaster City	2-1
17 Hemsworth MW v Bamber Bridge	0-0
18 Holker Old Boys v Trafford	0-2
19 Curzon Ashton v Congleton Town	0-0
20 Cheadle Town v Ramsbottom United	1-3
21 Skelmersdale United v AFC Fylde	3-1
22 New Mills v Chadderton	3-1
23 Bacup Borough v Clitheroe	5-3
24 Staveley MW v Parkgate	1-3
25 Bootle v Warrington Town	1-2
26 Atherton Collieries v Prescot Cables	2-2
27 St Helens Town v Glossop North End	1-1
28 Sheffield v Colne	3-1
29 Leigh Genesis v Runcorn Linnets	1-0
30 Salford City v Chorley	2-1
31 Atherton LR v Woodley Sports	0-0
32 Rossendale United v Cammell Laird	5-2
33 Mossley v Witton Albion	2-0
34 Rugby Town v Atherstone Town	1-1
35 Castle Vale JKS v Wednesfield	3-3
36 Pilkington XXX v Bromsgrove Rovers	wo/s
37 Leek Town v Eccleshall	0-1
38 Bridgnorth Town v Coventry Sphinx	1-1
39 Kidsgrove Athletic v Biddulph Victoria	0-0
40 Causeway United v Bartley Green	2-2 N
41 Bewdley Town v Sutton Coldfield Town	2-3
42 Tipton Town v Stratford Town	3-1
43 Heather St Johns v Coleshill Town	2-3
44 Westfields v Market Drayton Town	0-2
45 Oadby Town v Malvern Town	2-0
46 Stourport Swifts v Dosthill Colts	3-3
47 Bedworth United v Dudley Town	6-1
48 Rushall Olympic v Romulus	0-0
49 Kirby Muxloe v Norton United	1-3
50 Coalville Town v Heath Hayes	5-1
51 Newcastle Town v Nuneaton Griff	5-0
52 Lincoln United v Boston Town	2-2
53 Bottesford Town v Barrow Town	2-1
54 Loughborough Dynamo v Shepshed Dynamo	1-1
55 Gresley v Quorn	4-0
56 Barton Town Old Boys v Shirebrook Town	1-4
57 Dunkirk v Grantham Town	2-2
58 Spalding United v Goole AFC	1-0
59 Brigg Town v Rainworth MW	6-2
60 Maltby Main v Winterton Rangers	0-1
61 Glapwell v Lincoln Moorlands Railway	0-6
62 Carlton Town v Borrowash Victoria	2-1
63 Gedling MW v Barwell	0-1
64 Radcliffe Olympic v Wisbech Town	1-0
65 Belper Town v Holbrook Sports	1-3
66 Long Buckby v Daventry United	4-1
67 Norwich United v AFC Kempston Rovers	2-2
68 Wellingborough Town (2) v Haverhill Rovers	1-1

69 Daventry Town v Needham Market	2-3
70 Whitton United v Woodford United	0-3
71 Stewarts & Lloyds (2) v Soham Town Rangers	2-1
72 AFC Sudbury v Stamford	2-2
73 March Town United v Desborough Town	1-2
74 Felixstowe & Walton United v Team Bury	2-1
75 Wroxham v Ely City	2-2
76 Cogenhoe United v Leiston	0-3
77 Newmarket Town v Biggleswade Town	1-5
78 Brantham Athletic v St Neots Town	1-2
79 North Greenford United v Bowers & Pitsea	4-2
80 Arlesey Town v Aylesbury	1-1
81 Witham Town v Ilford	0-0
82 Kentish Town v Bethnal Green United	1-3 N
83 Crawley Green v Harefield United	2-0
84 Barking v Redbridge	0-1
85 Waltham Forest v Enfield Town	0-3
86 Hitchin Town v Ware	2-1
87 Halstead Town v Stanway Rovers	1-2
88 Burnham Ramblers v Haringey Borough	5-1
89 Oxhey Jets v St Margaretsbury	4-1
90 Burnham v Chalfont St Peter	2-1
91 Marlow v London Colney	1-2
92 Uxbridge v Tilbury	0-1
93 Tring Athletic v AFC Hayes	3-2
94 Southend Manor v Brentwood Town	0-4
95 Newport Pagnell Town v Potters Bar Town	3-2
96 Colney Heath v FC Clacton	0-0
97 Harlow Town v Barton Rovers	1-0
98 Aylesbury United v Eton Manor	3-2
99 Maldon & Tiptree v Hertford Town	4-2
100 Romford v Beaconsfield SYCOB	3-1
101 Leighton Town v Heybridge Swifts	2-2
102 East Thurrock United v Waltham Abbey	3-0
103 Cheshunt v Cockfosters	2-2
104 Saffron Walden Town v Great Wakering Rovers	1-1
105 Wingate & Finchley v Northwood	0-0
106 Thamesmead Town v Beckenham Town	2-3
107 Binfield v Camberley Town	5-1
108 AFC Totton v Sholing	1-2
109 Norton Sports v Banstead Athletic	2-0
110 Hartley Wintney v Whitehawk	2-2
111 Fleet Town v Bedfont Town	4-0
112 Corinthian Casuals v Lingfield	2-0
113 Epsom & Ewell v Flackwell Heath	3-2
114 Deal Town v Hythe Town	2-4
115 Whitstable Town v Croydon	3-0
116 Cobham v Alresford Town	2-2
117 Leatherhead v Burgess Hill Town	0-2
118 Peacehaven & Telscombe v Ashford Town (Middlesex)	1-2
119 Chipstead v Whyteleafe	4-3
120 Guildford City (2) v Three Bridges	2-1
121 Ramsgate v Godalming Town	1-1
122 Walton & Hersham v Bracknell Town	3-0
123 Erith Town v Ashford Town	wo/s
124 Faversham Town v Pagham	2-0
125 Chertsey Town v Chatham Town	2-1
126 Alton Town v Merstham	2-1
127 Raynes Park Vale v East Grinstead Town	1-4
128 VCD Athletic v Eastbourne Town	1-1
129 Walton Casuals v Worthing United	3-0
130 Horley Town v Metropolitan Police	0-6
131 Sittingbourne v Andover	0-2
132 Tunbridge Wells v Dulwich Hamlet	3-3
133 Lancing v Slough Town	1-4
134 Hassocks v Farnham Town	3-2
135 Bognor Regis Town v Ringmer	1-0
136 Worthing v Arundel	6-0
137 South Park v Horsham YMCA	4-0
138 Gosport Borough v Erith & Belvedere	0-0
139 Old Woodstock Town v Laverstock & Ford	6-3
140 Bitton v Fareham Town	2-0
141 Reading Town v Newport (IOW)	1-4 N
142 Almondsbury UWE v Wootton Bassett Town	0-1
143 Blackfield & Langley v Almondsbury Town	0-2
144 Bournemouth (Ams) v Highworth Town	0-2
145 Cinderford Town v North Leigh	2-1
146 Hallen v Bristol Manor Farm	3-4
147 Hungerford Town v Moneyfields	2-1
148 Corsham Town v Brading Town	0-1
149 Bishop's Cleeve v Westbury United	4-0
150 Thatcham Town v Witney United	2-2
151 Thame United v Lydney Town	2-1
152 Ringwood Town v Yate Town	4-1
153 Mangotsfield United v Abingdon United	5-0
154 Totton & Eling v Shortwood United	0-0
155 Longwell Green Sports v Hamble ASSC	0-3
156 Bridgwater Town v Street	1-0
157 Frome Town v Ilfracombe Town	1-0
158 Bideford v Wimborne Town	1-2
159 Willand Rovers v Radstock Town	1-0
160 Paulton Rovers v Larkhall Athletic	4-1
161 Bridport v Clevedon Town	0-6
162 Wellington (Hereford) v Bodmin Town	0-3 N
163 Torpoint Athletic v Odd Down	1-1
164 Poole Town v Bishop Sutton	3-0
165 Hamworthy United v Sherborne Town	2-2
166 Tavistock v Taunton Town	1-2
4r Dunston UTS v South Shields (3)	3-0
5r North Shields v Newcastle Benfield	0-1
15r Whitley Bay v Bishop Auckland	3-1
17r Bamber Bridge v Hemsworth MW	4-1
19r Congleton Town v Curzon Ashton	1-2e
26r Prescot Cables v Atherton Collieries	2-0
27r Glossop North End v St Helens Town	3-1e

31r Woodley Sports v Atherton LR	3-0 N
34r Atherstone Town v Rugby Town	0-3
35r Wednesfield v Castle Vale JKS	6-0
38r Coventry Sphinx v Bridgnorth Town	1-0
39r Biddulph Victoria v Kidsgrove Athletic	0-4
40r Bartley Green v Causeway United	4-2e
46r Dosthill Colts v Stourport Swifts	1-0
48r Romulus v Rushall Olympic	4-2
52r Boston Town v Lincoln United	2-4
54r Shepshed Dynamo v Loughborough Dynamo	2-3
57r Grantham Town v Dunkirk	2-3e
67r AFC Kempston Rovers v Norwich United	3-2
68r Haverhill Rovers v Wellingborough Town (2)	1-3
72r Stamford v AFC Sudbury	2-1
75r Ely City v Wroxham	1-1P
80r Aylesbury v Arlesey Town	1-2
81r Ilford v Witham Town	0-0P
96r FC Clacton v Colney Heath	1-5
101r Heybridge Swifts v Leighton Town	0-1
103r Cockfosters v Cheshunt	1-2
104r Great Wakering Rovers v Saffron Walden Town	3-1
105r Northwood v Wingate & Finchley	3-1
110r Whitehawk v Hartley Wintney	4-0
116r Alresford Town v Cobham	0-4
121r Godalming Town v Ramsgate	3-0
128r Eastbourne Town v VCD Athletic	2-1e
132r Dulwich Hamlet v Tunbridge Wells	0-1
138r Erith & Belvedere v Gosport Borough	2-1
150r Witney United v Thatcham Town	2-4
154r Shortwood United v Totton & Eling	1-3e
163r Odd Down v Torpoint Athletic	0-1
165r Sherborne Town v Hamworthy United	3-0

Qualifying Round One

1 Tadcaster Albion v Shildon	1-1
2 Ossett Albion v Whitley Bay	1-2
3 Durham City v Dunston UTS	1-3 N
4 North Ferriby United v Ossett Town	2-1
5 Ashington v Northallerton Town	3-1
6 Norton & Stockton Ancients v Chester-le-Street Town	2-1
7 West Auckland Town v Bradford Park Avenue	3-1
8 Newcastle Benfield v Spennymoor Town	1-0
9 Thackley v Marske United	3-1
10 FC Halifax Town v Whitby Town	2-0
11 FC United of Manchester v Radcliffe Borough	3-0
12 Parkgate v Warrington Town	1-3
13 Nantwich Town v Burscough	4-0
14 Salford City v Northwich Victoria	0-1
15 Curzon Ashton v New Mills	1-1
16 Prescot Cables v Ashton United	2-2
17 Frickley Athletic v Kendal Town	3-2
18 Marine v Colwyn Bay	1-1
19 Bamber Bridge v Bacup Borough	2-0
20 Rossendale United v Leigh Genesis	3-4
21 Stocksbridge Park Steels v Trafford	4-2
22 Glossop North End v Mossley	0-4
23 Ramsbottom United v Skelmersdale United	0-2
24 Woodley Sports v Sheffield	2-2 N
25 Wednesfield v Rugby Town	5-1
26 Stourbridge v Romulus	2-0
27 Evesham United v Coleshill Town	1-3
28 Leamington v Brackley Town	2-2
29 Pilkington XXX v Market Drayton Town	0-2
30 Oadby Town v Dosthill Colts	2-1
31 Coventry Sphinx v Sutton Coldfield Town	1-0
32 Tipton Town v Norton United	1-0
33 Kidsgrove Athletic v Chasetown	3-0
34 Coalville Town v Eccleshall	5-0
35 Bartley Green v Bedworth United	1-1
36 Hednesford Town v Newcastle Town	1-2
37 Winterton Rangers v Radcliffe Olympic	2-2
38 Bottesford Town v Buxton	0-3
39 Lincoln Moorlands Railway v Gresley	2-2
40 Matlock Town v Worksop Town	3-1
41 Spalding United v Brigg Town	2-2
42 Holbrook Sports v Loughborough Dynamo	1-3
43 Barwell v Hucknall Town	2-0
44 Shirebrook Town v Lincoln United	1-3
45 Carlton Town v Dunkirk	1-1
46 Retford United v Mickleover Sports	0-5
47 Cambridge City v Long Buckby	3-0
48 Lowestoft Town v Desborough Town	7-1
49 Ely City v Stewarts & Lloyds (2)	0-1
50 Woodford United v Bury Town	1-3
51 Felixstowe & Walton United v Wellingborough Town (2)	2-1
52 Needham Market v AFC Kempston Rovers	6-1
53 Leiston v St Neots Town	3-2
54 Biggleswade Town v Stamford	3-3
55 Great Wakering Rovers v Harrow Borough	2-4
56 Brentwood Town v Aylesbury United	4-0
57 Wealdstone v Tring Athletic	7-0
58 Hemel Hempstead Town v Concord Rangers	1-2
59 Burnham v Colney Heath	2-1
60 Romford v Crawley Green	1-1
61 North Greenford United v Northwood	2-1
62 Ilford v Maldon & Tiptree	0-1
63 AFC Hornchurch v Oxhey Jets	8-2
64 Canvey Island v Newport Pagnell Town	4-1
65 Redbridge v London Colney	2-0
66 Grays Athletic v Windsor & Eton	1-0 N
67 Stanway Rovers v Bedford Town	1-1
68 Arlesey Town v Enfield Town	0-2
69 Billericay Town v Tilbury	1-0
70 East Thurrock United v Leighton Town	2-1

2010/11

71	Hendon v Cheshunt	4-1
72	Hitchin Town v Aveley	2-1
73	Harlow Town v Bethnal Green United	1-1
74	Burnham Ramblers v Chesham United	0-3
75	Hythe Town v Epsom & Ewell	2-0
76	Sholing v Hassocks	5-0
77	Corinthian Casuals v Erith & Belvedere	1-2
78	Cobham v Chipstead	0-1
79	Sutton United v Alton Town	1-2
80	Carshalton Athletic v Tunbridge Wells	2-1
81	Tonbridge Angels v Guildford City (2)	0-1
82	Tooting & Mitcham United v Walton Casuals	4-1
83	Godalming Town v Metropolitan Police	1-2
84	Erith Town v Slough Town	1-0
85	Beckenham Town v Norton Sports	3-2
86	Burgess Hill Town v Eastbourne Town	3-2
87	Fleet Town v Faversham Town	3-1
88	Folkestone Invicta v Horsham	4-2
89	Kingstonian v Croydon Athletic	wo/s
90	Whitstable Town v East Grinstead Town	1-0
91	Ashford Town (Middlesex) v Worthing	1-1
92	Whitehawk v Maidstone United (2)	3-1
93	Cray Wanderers v South Park	1-0
94	Binfield v Margate	0-3
95	Bognor Regis Town v Hastings United (2)	3-2
96	Walton & Hersham v Bashley	1-4
97	Andover v Chertsey Town	0-4 N
98	Bitton v Old Woodstock Town	2-3
99	Oxford City v Mangotsfield United	0-1
100	Swindon Supermarine v Brading Town	4-0
101	Banbury United v Chippenham Town	1-2
102	Newport (IOW) v Bishop's Cleeve	0-3
103	Thatcham Town v Thame United	0-1
104	Almondsbury Town v Bristol Manor Farm	1-1
105	Hungerford Town v Totton & Eling	6-2
106	Highworth Town v Salisbury City	1-1
107	Hamble ASSC v Wootton Bassett Town	1-1
108	Cinderford Town v Ringwood Town	5-0
109	Cirencester Town v Didcot Town	0-0
110	Tiverton Town v Paulton Rovers	1-1
111	Truro City v Bridgwater Town	8-2
112	Torpoint Athletic v Clevedon Town	2-4
113	Wimborne Town v Sherborne Town	1-3
114	Bodmin Town v Poole Town	1-4
115	Taunton Town v Weymouth	1-2
116	Frome Town v Willand Rovers	1-0
1r	Shildon v Tadcaster Albion	4-2e
15r	New Mills v Curzon Ashton	3-2
16r	Ashton United v Prescot Cables	4-0
18r	Colwyn Bay v Marine	2-0
24r	Sheffield v Woodley Sports	3-1
28r	Brackley Town v Leamington	2-0
35r	Bedworth United v Bartley Green	4-0
37r	Radcliffe Olympic v Winterton Rangers	2-0
39r	Gresley v Lincoln Moorlands Railway	1-2
41r	Brigg Town v Spalding United	4-0
45r	Dunkirk v Carlton Town	1-2e
54r	Stamford v Biggleswade Town	3-0
60r	Crawley Green v Romford	1-2
67r	Bedford Town v Stanway Rovers	2-0
73r	Bethnal Green United v Harlow Town	0-4
91r	Worthing v Ashford Town (Middlesex)	5-1
104r	Bristol Manor Farm v Almondsbury Town	2-2P
106r	Salisbury City v Highworth Town	5-0
107r	Wootton Bassett Town v Hamble ASSC	0-2
109r	Didcot Town v Cirencester Town	3-1
110r	Paulton Rovers v Tiverton Town	2-0

Qualifying Round Two

1	Frickley Athletic v Newcastle Benfield	2-1
2	Bamber Bridge v Warrington Town	1-1
3	Norton & Stockton Ancients v Leigh Genesis	2-1
4	New Mills v Harrogate Town	0-2
5	Vauxhall Motors v Blyth Spartans	5-1
6	North Ferriby United v Stocksbridge Park Steels	5-2
7	Dunston UTS v Mossley	1-2
8	Ashington v Thackley	1-0
9	Colwyn Bay v Guiseley	1-1
10	Nantwich Town v Whitley Bay	2-3
11	FC United of Manchester v Gainsborough Trinity	2-1
12	Hyde FC v Droylsden	0-0
13	Ashton United v FC Halifax Town	1-2
14	Stalybridge Celtic v Alfreton Town	1-1
15	Shildon v Skelmersdale United	2-0
16	Sheffield v Northwich Victoria	2-2
17	Workington v West Auckland Town	2-1
18	Boston United v Worcester City	2-3
19	Lincoln Moorlands Railway v Ilkeston Town (2)	wo/s
20	Tipton Town v Market Drayton Town	2-0
21	Eastwood Town v Stafford Rangers	1-1
22	Brigg Town v Nuneaton Town	3-3
23	Coleshill Town v Lincoln United	5-1
24	Hinckley United v Coventry Sphinx	2-0
25	Oadby Town v Radcliffe Olympic	1-3
26	Barwell v Coalville Town	3-2
27	Loughborough Dynamo v Redditch United	0-2
28	Stewarts & Lloyds (2) v Mickleover Sports	2-2
29	Brackley Town v Buxton	1-3
30	Carlton Town v Matlock Town	0-1
31	Bedworth United v Corby Town	0-1
32	Newcastle Town v Wednesfield	5-3
33	Solihull Moors v Kidsgrove Athletic	2-0
34	AFC Telford United v Stourbridge	5-2
35	Hythe Town v Erith & Belvedere	4-1
36	Erith Town v Dover Athletic	1-5
37	Bury Town v Grays Athletic	2-2
38	Chesham United v Wealdstone	2-2
39	Braintree Town v Welling United	2-0
40	Tooting & Mitcham United v Staines Town	1-4
41	Bishop's Stortford v Bromley	2-2
42	Cambridge City v Hitchin Town	2-2
43	Billericay Town v Concord Rangers	1-1
44	Folkestone Invicta v Leiston	1-1
45	Lewes v Harlow Town	2-0
46	AFC Hornchurch v Brentwood Town	0-0
47	East Thurrock United v Carshalton Athletic	1-1
48	Hendon v Maldon & Tiptree	2-1
49	Enfield Town v Worthing	1-0
50	North Greenford United v Felixstowe & Walton United	1-1
51	Needham Market v Chipstead	0-0
52	Romford v Hampton & Richmond Boro.	0-4
53	Canvey Island v Whitstable Town	1-0
54	Redbridge v Harrow Borough	1-2
55	Burnham v Whitehawk	2-6
56	Bedford Town v Boreham Wood	0-2
57	Thurrock v Stamford	3-1
58	Cray Wanderers v Ebbsfleet United	2-2
59	St Albans City v Beckenham Town	3-1
60	Metropolitan Police v Burgess Hill Town	2-1
61	Margate v Kingstonian	1-1
62	Dartford v Lowestoft Town	2-1
63	Chelmsford City v Chertsey Town	7-0
64	Hamble ASSC v Old Woodstock Town	2-1
65	Eastleigh v Bognor Regis Town	2-0
66	Sholing v Salisbury City	2-2
67	Chippenham Town v Farnborough	0-1
68	Havant & Waterlooville v Frome Town	1-0
69	Mangotsfield United v Dorchester Town	1-4
70	Paulton Rovers v Didcot Town	0-1
71	Bristol Manor Farm v Basingstoke Town	2-2
72	Sherborne Town v Hungerford Town	1-2
73	Bashley v Fleet Town	2-2
74	Poole Town v Thame United	1-1
75	Guildford City (2) v Clevedon Town	1-2
76	Bishop's Cleeve v Woking	1-2
77	Gloucester City v Weston-Super-Mare	0-2
78	Swindon Supermarine v Weymouth	3-0
79	Maidenhead United v Truro City	1-0
80	Alton Town v Cinderford Town	2-2
2r	Warrington Town v Bamber Bridge	4-2
9r	Guiseley v Colwyn Bay	3-0
12r	Droylsden v Hyde FC	3-1
14r	Alfreton Town v Stalybridge Celtic	1-2e
16r	Northwich Victoria v Sheffield	1-2
21r	Stafford Rangers v Eastwood Town	1-3
22r	Nuneaton Town v Brigg Town	2-0
28r	Mickleover Sports v Stewarts & Lloyds (2)	3-2e
37r	Grays Athletic v Bury Town	1-4
38r	Wealdstone v Chesham United	4-1
41r	Bromley v Bishop's Stortford	2-1
42r	Hitchin Town v Cambridge City	0-2
43r	Concord Rangers v Billericay Town	1-0e
44r	Leiston v Folkestone Invicta	2-1
46r	Brentwood Town v AFC Hornchurch	1-0
47r	Carshalton Athletic v East Thurrock United	3-2
50r	Felixstowe & Walton United v North Greenford United	0-3
51r	Chipstead v Needham Market	0-2
58r	Ebbsfleet United v Cray Wanderers	4-2
61r	Kingstonian v Margate	1-1P
66r	Salisbury City v Sholing	5-1
71r	Basingstoke Town v Bristol Manor Farm	1-0
73r	Fleet Town v Bashley	0-2
74r	Thame United v Poole Town	0-1e
80r	Cinderford Town v Alton Town	2-1e

Qualifying Round Three

1	FC Halifax Town v Harrogate Town	4-0
2	Sheffield v Frickley Athletic	1-1
3	Guiseley v Whitley Bay	3-0
4	Norton & Stockton Ancients v FC United of Manchester	2-5
5	Workington v Shildon	2-1
6	North Ferriby United v Vauxhall Motors	2-2
7	Warrington Town v Stalybridge Celtic	1-3
8	Lincoln Moorlands Railway v Mossley	1-1
9	Ashington v Droylsden	1-4
10	Solihull Moors v Barwell	1-1
11	Mickleover Sports v Newcastle Town	1-2
12	Buxton v AFC Telford United	1-1
13	Redditch United v Hinckley United	1-0
14	Corby Town v Worcester City	2-1
15	Matlock Town v Eastwood Town	0-3
16	Nuneaton Town v Coleshill Town	6-0
17	Radcliffe Olympic v Tipton Town	3-3
18	Chelmsford City v Bromley	2-2
19	Leiston v North Greenford United	5-0
20	Brentwood Town v Woking	1-1
21	Harrow Borough v Hampton & Richmond Boro.	2-1
22	St Albans City v Kingstonian	0-0
23	Metropolitan Police v Wealdstone	1-1
24	Lewes v Thurrock	2-1
25	Needham Market v Ebbsfleet United	0-1
26	Whitehawk v Hendon	1-2
27	Boreham Wood v Enfield Town	3-1
28	Carshalton Athletic v Braintree Town	4-1
29	Concord Rangers v Hythe Town	0-1
30	Dover Athletic v Cambridge City	3-1
31	Bury Town v Staines Town	2-2
32	Canvey Island v Dartford	2-2
33	Swindon Supermarine v Hungerford Town	4-0
34	Salisbury City v Weston-Super-Mare	1-0
35	Didcot Town v Basingstoke Town	0-4
36	Havant & Waterlooville v Dorchester Town	4-1
37	Farnborough v Hamble ASSC	2-0
38	Poole Town v Bashley	1-0
39	Clevedon Town v Eastleigh	0-5
40	Cinderford Town v Maidenhead United	0-4
2r	Frickley Athletic v Sheffield	1-2
6r	Vauxhall Motors v North Ferriby United	1-1P
8r	Mossley v Lincoln Moorlands Railway	4-1
10r	Barwell v Solihull Moors	3-1
12r	AFC Telford United v Buxton	2-2q
17r	Tipton Town v Radcliffe Olympic	2-0
18r	Bromley v Chelmsford City	0-3
20r	Woking v Brentwood Town	1-0
22r	Kingstonian v St Albans City	1-2
23r	Wealdstone v Metropolitan Police	1-2e
31r	Staines Town v Bury Town	2-0
32r	Dartford v Canvey Island	3-3P

Qualifying Round Four

1	Mossley v Darlington	2-6
2	Sheffield v Tipton Town	2-2
3	Guiseley v Redditch United	2-1
4	Fleetwood Town v Buxton	2-1
5	Altrincham v Gateshead (2)	0-2
6	Vauxhall Motors v Newcastle Town	1-0
7	FC United of Manchester v Barrow	1-0
8	Workington v Nuneaton Town	1-1
9	Tamworth v Grimsby Town	1-1
10	Kidderminster Harriers v York City	0-2
11	FC Halifax Town v Mansfield Town	0-1
12	Wrexham v Southport	1-2
13	Stalybridge Celtic v Eastwood Town	1-2
14	Droylsden v Barwell	3-0
15	Woking v Eastleigh	3-2
16	Hythe Town v Staines Town	2-0
17	Eastbourne Borough v Harrow Borough	2-4
18	Cambridge United v Lewes	3-0
19	Corby Town v Salisbury City	3-0
20	Newport County (2) v Crawley Town	0-1
21	Luton Town v St Albans City	4-0
22	Farnborough v Dover Athletic	1-1
23	Kettering Town v Rushden & Diamonds	1-2
24	Carshalton Athletic v Chelmsford City	1-1
25	Hendon v Metropolitan Police	0-0
26	Leiston v Dartford	0-0
27	Basingstoke Town v AFC Wimbledon	0-1
28	Swindon Supermarine v Bath City	0-0
29	Havant & Waterlooville v Histon	2-0
30	Forest Green Rovers v Maidenhead United	1-0
31	Poole Town v Hayes & Yeading United	1-3
32	Ebbsfleet United v Boreham Wood	3-0
2r	Tipton Town v Sheffield	2-0
8r	Nuneaton Town v Workington	1-0
9r	Grimsby Town v Tamworth	0-1
22r	Dover Athletic v Farnborough	5-0
24r	Chelmsford City v Carshalton Athletic	3-2
25r	Metropolitan Police v Hendon	0-2
26r	Dartford v Leiston	3-2
28r	Bath City v Swindon Supermarine	3-4

Round One

AFC Wimbledon v Ebbsfleet United	0-0
Accrington Stanley (2) v Oldham Athletic	3-2
Barnet v Charlton Athletic	0-0
Bournemouth v Tranmere Rovers	5-3
Brentford v Aldershot Town	1-1
Brighton & Hove Albion v Woking	0-0
Burton Albion v Oxford United	1-0
Bury v Exeter City	2-0
Cambridge United v Huddersfield Town	0-0
Carlisle United v Tipton Town	6-0
Chelmsford City v Hendon	3-2
Cheltenham Town v Morecambe	1-0
Colchester United v Bradford City	4-3
Corby Town v Luton Town	1-1
Dagenham & Redbridge v Leyton Orient	1-1
Darlington v Bristol Rovers	2-1
Dartford v Port Vale	1-1
Fleetwood Town v Walsall	1-1
Forest Green Rovers v Northampton Town	0-3
Gillingham v Dover Athletic	0-2
Guiseley v Crawley Town	0-5
Harrow Borough v Chesterfield	0-2
Hartlepool United v Vauxhall Motors	0-0
Havant & Waterlooville v Droylsden	0-2
Hayes & Yeading United v Wycombe Wanderers	1-2
Hereford United v Hythe Town	5-1
Lincoln City v Nuneaton Town	1-0
Macclesfield Town v Southend United	2-2
Mansfield Town v Torquay United	0-1
Notts County v Gateshead (2)	2-0
Plymouth Argyle v Swindon Town	0-4
Rochdale v FC United of Manchester	2-3
Rotherham United v York City	0-0
Rushden & Diamonds v Yeovil Town	0-1
Southampton v Shrewsbury Town	2-0
Southport v Sheffield Wednesday	2-5
Stevenage v Milton Keynes Dons	0-0
Stockport County v Peterborough United	1-1
Swindon Supermarine v Eastwood Town	2-1

2010/11 to 2011/12

	Tamworth v Crewe Alexandra	2-1
r	Aldershot Town v Brentford	1-0
r	Charlton Athletic v Barnet	1-0
r	Ebbsfleet United v AFC Wimbledon	2-3e
r	Huddersfield Town v Cambridge United	2-1
r	Leyton Orient v Dagenham & Redbridge	3-2
r	Luton Town v Corby Town	4-2
r	Milton Keynes Dons v Stevenage	1-1q
r	Peterborough United v Stockport County	4-1
r	Port Vale v Dartford	4-0
r	Southend United v Macclesfield Town	2-2q
r	Vauxhall Motors v Hartlepool United	0-1
r	Walsall v Fleetwood Town	2-0
r	Woking v Brighton & Hove Albion	2-2q
r	York City v Rotherham United	3-0

Round Two

	AFC Wimbledon v Stevenage	0-2
	Brighton & Hove Albion v FC United of Manchester	1-1
	Burton Albion v Chesterfield	3-1
	Bury v Peterborough United	1-2
	Carlisle United v Tamworth	3-2
	Charlton Athletic v Luton Town	2-2
	Colchester United v Swindon Supermarine	1-0
	Crawley Town v Swindon Town	1-1
	Darlington v York City	0-2
	Dover Athletic v Aldershot Town	2-0
	Droylsden v Leyton Orient	1-1
	Hartlepool United v Yeovil Town	4-2
	Hereford United v Lincoln City	2-2
	Huddersfield Town v Macclesfield Town	6-0
	Notts County v Bournemouth	3-1
	Port Vale v Accrington Stanley (2)	1-0
	Sheffield Wednesday v Northampton Town	3-2
	Southampton v Cheltenham Town	3-0
	Torquay United v Walsall	1-0
	Wycombe Wanderers v Chelmsford City	3-1
r	FC United of Manchester v Brighton & Hove Albion	0-4
r	Leyton Orient v Droylsden	8-2e
r	Lincoln City v Hereford United	3-4
r	Luton Town v Charlton Athletic	1-3
r	Swindon Town v Crawley Town	2-3e

Round Three

	Arsenal v Leeds United	1-1
	Blackburn Rovers v Queen's Park Rangers	1-0
	Bolton Wanderers v York City	2-0
	Brighton & Hove Albion v Portsmouth	3-1
	Bristol City v Sheffield Wednesday	0-3
	Burnley v Port Vale	4-2
	Burton Albion v Middlesbrough	2-1
	Chelsea v Ipswich Town	7-0
	Coventry City v Crystal Palace	2-1
	Crawley Town v Derby County	2-1
	Doncaster Rovers v Wolverhampton Wan.	2-2
	Fulham v Peterborough United	6-2
	Huddersfield Town v Dover Athletic	2-0
	Hull City v Wigan Athletic	2-3
	Leicester City v Manchester City	2-2
	Manchester United v Liverpool	1-0
	Millwall v Birmingham City	1-4
	Norwich City v Leyton Orient	0-1
	Preston North End v Nottingham Forest	1-2
	Reading v West Bromwich Albion	1-0
	Scunthorpe United v Everton	1-5
	Sheffield United v Aston Villa	1-3
	Southampton v Blackpool	2-0
	Stevenage v Newcastle United	3-1
	Stoke City v Cardiff City	1-1
	Sunderland v Notts County	1-2
	Swansea City v Colchester United	4-0
	Torquay United v Carlisle United	1-0
	Tottenham Hotspur v Charlton Athletic	3-0
	Watford v Hartlepool United	4-1
	West Ham United v Barnsley	2-0
	Wycombe Wanderers v Hereford United	0-1
r	Cardiff City v Stoke City	0-2e
r	Leeds United v Arsenal	1-3
r	Manchester City v Leicester City	4-2
r	Wolverhampton Wan. v Doncaster Rovers	5-0

Round Four

	Arsenal v Huddersfield Town	2-1
	Aston Villa v Blackburn Rovers	3-1
	Birmingham City v Coventry City	3-2
	Bolton Wanderers v Wigan Athletic	0-0
	Burnley v Burton Albion	3-1
	Everton v Chelsea	1-1
	Fulham v Tottenham Hotspur	4-0
	Notts County v Manchester City	1-1
	Sheffield Wednesday v Hereford United	4-1
	Southampton v Manchester United	1-2
	Stevenage v Reading	1-2
	Swansea City v Leyton Orient	1-2
	Torquay United v Crawley Town	0-1
	Watford v Brighton & Hove Albion	0-1
	West Ham United v Nottingham Forest	3-2
	Wolverhampton Wan. v Stoke City	0-1
r	Chelsea v Everton	1-1e
r	Manchester City v Notts County	5-0
r	Wigan Athletic v Bolton Wanderers	0-1

Round Five

	Birmingham City v Sheffield Wednesday	3-0
	Everton v Reading	0-1
	Fulham v Bolton Wanderers	0-1
	Leyton Orient v Arsenal	1-1
	Manchester City v Aston Villa	3-0
	Manchester United v Crawley Town	1-0
	Stoke City v Brighton & Hove Albion	3-0
	West Ham United v Burnley	5-1
r	Arsenal v Leyton Orient	5-0

Round Six

Birmingham City v Bolton Wanderers	2-3
Manchester City v Reading	1-0
Manchester United v Arsenal	2-0
Stoke City v West Ham United	2-1

Semi Finals

Bolton Wanderers v Stoke City	0-5 N
Manchester City v Manchester United	1-0 N

Final

Manchester City v Stoke City	1-0 N

2011/12

Extra Preliminary Round

1	Bedlington Terriers v Whickham	1-0
2	Tow Law Town v Marske United	1-2
3	Stokesley SC v Newcastle Benfield	1-6
4	Penrith v North Shields	1-1
5	West Allotment Celtic v Northallerton Town	1-1
6	Spennymoor Town v Esh Winning	1-0
7	Ryton & Crawcrook Albion v Ashington	0-1
8	Gillford Park v Hebburn Town	1-2
9	Newton Aycliffe v Billingham Synthonia	2-7
10	Crook Town v Billingham Town	2-6
11	Chester-le-Street Town v South Shields (3)	1-1
12	West Auckland Town v Dunston UTS	2-2
13	Jarrow Roofing Boldon CA v Guisborough Town	1-2
14	Sunderland RCA v Birtley Town	7-0
15	Shildon v Consett	2-1
16	Whitehaven v Norton & Stockton Ancients	3-0
17	Whitley Bay v Bishop Auckland	2-1
18	Scarborough Athletic v Hallam	4-0
19	Thackley v Askern Villa	2-1
20	Maltby Main v Glasshoughton Welfare	1-2
21	Silsden v Rossington Main	1-1
22	Pontefract Collieries v Yorkshire Amateur	2-0
23	Parkgate v Grimsby Borough	4-1
24	AFC Emley v Hall Road Rangers	1-4
25	Hemsworth MW v Tadcaster Albion	1-2
26	Nostell MW v Armthorpe Welfare	2-3
27	Selby Town v Liversedge	1-4
28	Pickering Town v Dinnington Town	2-0
29	Staveley MW v Winterton Rangers	4-0
30	Barton Town Old Boys v Bridlington Town (2)	2-2
31	Squires Gate v Colne	1-0
32	Formby v Alsager Town	3-0
33	Winsford United v Maine Road	1-1
34	Runcorn Town v Brighouse Town	4-1
35	Padiham v Ashton Athletic	1-2
36	Holker Old Boys v Leek CSOB	3-0
37	Bacup Borough v AFC Blackpool	2-3
38	St Helens Town v Atherton LR	0-2
39	Atherton Collieries v Irlam	4-0
40	Chadderton v Cheadle Town	2-8
41	Congleton Town v Eccleshill United	3-1
42	Barnoldswick Town v Ramsbottom United	0-2
43	Bootle v Wigan Robin Park	2-0
44	AFC Liverpool v Runcorn Linnets	2-2
45	Retford United v Gresley	0-2
46	Holbeach United v Lincoln Moorlands Railway	3-1
47	Deeping Rangers v Spalding United	2-1
48	Holbrook Sports v Greenwood Meadows	1-1
49	Glossop North End v Boston Town	2-4
50	Dunkirk v Arnold Town	0-2
51	Radcliffe Olympic v Heanor Town	2-3
52	Borrowash Victoria v Sleaford Town	5-1
53	Gedling MW v Louth Town	0-0
54	Shirebrook Town v Blackstones	2-1
55	Nuneaton Griff v Stratford Town	0-7
56	Rocester v Wolverhampton Casuals	3-1
57	Southam United v Tipton Town	0-2
58	Coleshill Town v Brocton	5-1
59	Highgate United v Willenhall Town	2-0
60	Westfields v Norton United	2-4
61	Castle Vale v Heath Hayes	3-1
62	Bustleholme v Eccleshall	0-1
63	Lye Town v Coventry Sphinx	0-5
64	Studley v Walsall Wood	2-1
65	Boldmere St Michaels v Bartley Green	5-2
66	Malvern Town v Causeway United	0-0
67	Bridgnorth Town v Ellesmere Rangers	6-0
68	Atherstone Town v Cadbury Athletic	1-0
69	Tividale v Alvechurch	1-2
70	Gornal Athletic v Shifnal Town	2-2
71	Stone Dominoes v Wellington (Hereford)	3-2
72	Cradley Town v Continental Star	2-2
73	Bloxwich United v AFC Wulfrunians	2-2
74	Pegasus Juniors v Bewdley Town	1-1
75	Loughborough University v Friar Lane & Epworth	wo/s
76	Thrapston Town v Irchester United	3-2
77	Oadby Town v Northampton Spencer	6-1
78	Rushden & Higham United v Cogenhoe United	2-3
79	Rothwell Corinthians v Wellingborough Town (2)	1-0
80	Bugbrooke St Michaels v Anstey Nomads	2-1
81	Long Eaton United v Huntingdon Town	0-4
82	Long Buckby v Stewarts & Lloyds (2)	1-0
83	Thurnby Nirvana v Desborough Town	3-3
84	Rothwell Town v Raunds Town	2-1
85	Barrow Town v Kirby Muxloe	3-2
86	Daventry United v Bardon Hill	2-1
87	Yaxley v Godmanchester Rovers	0-2
88	Stanway Rovers v Hadleigh United	2-3
89	King's Lynn Town v Whitton United	6-1
90	Woodbridge Town v Gorleston	2-2
91	St Ives Town v Debenham LC	3-2
92	Wroxham v Dereham Town	3-1
93	Ipswich Wanderers v Newmarket Town	3-1
94	Mildenhall Town v Brantham Athletic	0-4
95	Walsham Le Willows v Thetford Town	3-1
96	March Town United v Kirkley & Pakefield	2-1
97	Ely City v Diss Town	4-0
98	Stowmarket Town v Haverhill Rovers	1-4
99	Felixstowe & Walton United v Norwich United	1-0
100	Long Melford v Saffron Walden Town	wo/s
101	Wisbech Town v Halstead Town	4-0
102	Great Yarmouth Town v FC Clacton	0-3
103	Burnham Ramblers v Barking	1-1
104	Hadley v Cockfosters	2-2
105	Haringey Borough v AFC Kempston Rovers	2-0
106	Witham Town v Bedford	4-1
107	St Margaretsbury v Dunstable Town	0-3
108	Enfield 1893 v London Colney	3-1
109	Kings Langley v Stotfold	5-2 D
110	Colney Heath v Langford	3-1
111	Clapton v Stansted	0-1
112	Crawley Green v Berkhamsted	1-2
113	Hullbridge Sports v Royston Town	1-3
114	Broxbourne Borough V&E v Hoddesdon Town	4-0
115	Haringey & Waltham Dev'ment v Bowers & Pitsea	4-1
116	Sawbridgeworth Town v Hatfield Town	2-2
117	AFC Dunstable v Eton Manor	3-1 N
118	Biggleswade United v Leverstock Green	2-1
119	Takeley v Southend Manor	3-3
120	London APSA v Basildon United	1-0
121	Oxhey Jets v Wodson Park	6-0
122	Barkingside v Hertford Town	1-3
123	Bethnal Green United v Kentish Town	2-1
124	Holmer Green v Harefield United	2-4
125	Sandhurst Town v Thame United	2-3
126	Witney Town v Newport Pagnell Town	0-4
127	Tring Athletic v Hanwell Town	1-0
128	Wokingham & Emmbrook v Holyport	4-1
129	Staines Lammas v Clanfield 85	3-0
130	Bedfont Sports v Bicester Town	wo/s
131	Old Woodstock Town v Wantage Town	1-2
132	Ascot United v Wembley	1-2
133	Abingdon Town v Milton United (Oxon)	4-0
134	Kidlington v Hillingdon Borough	4-2
135	Hanworth Villa v Shrivenham	4-2
136	Ardley United v Flackwell Heath	3-0
137	Aylesbury United v Bracknell Town	4-0
138	Reading Town v Binfield	0-0
139	Molesey v Egham Town	0-3
140	Raynes Park Vale v Hassocks	3-1
141	Farnham Town v Guildford City (2)	1-0
142	Wick v Redhill	0-3
143	VCD Athletic v Bookham	1-1
144	Erith & Belvedere v St Francis Rangers	2-0
145	Lancing v Horsham YMCA	2-2
146	Chichester City v Fisher	2-2
147	Pagham v Herne Bay	1-2
148	Colliers Wood United v Chessington & Hook United	1-1
149	Ringmer v Deal Town	0-2
150	Arundel v Sidley United	2-2
151	Three Bridges v Camberley Town	1-6
152	Sevenoaks Town v Ash United	4-0
153	Shoreham v Holmesdale	3-1
154	Corinthian v Dorking (2)	4-3
155	Mole Valley SCR v Lordswood	2-3
156	Westfield v Peacehaven & Telscombe	3-6
157	Tunbridge Wells v Warlingham	1-0
158	South Park v AFC Uckfield	1-0
159	Greenwich Borough v Horley Town	1-2
160	Banstead Athletic v Woodstock Sports	3-0
161	Beckenham Town v Littlehampton Town	3-1
162	Erith Town v Crowborough Athletic	6-2
163	Selsey v Mile Oak	2-2
164	Epsom & Ewell v Croydon	3-1
165	Cobham v Badshot Lea	2-2
166	Hailsham Town v Lingfield	0-4
167	Bridport v Hayling United	2-2
168	Cowes Sports v Newport (IOW)	1-4
169	Verwood Town v Horndean	0-4
170	Romsey Town v Brading Town	0-1
171	Downton v Brockenhurst	3-3
172	Alresford Town v Devizes Town	4-0
173	Totton & Eling v Fareham Town	5-1
174	Cove v AFC Portchester	0-2
175	Petersfield Town v Hartley Wintney	1-2
176	Hamworthy United v Bournemouth (Ams)	1-2

2011/12

177	Shrewton United v Fleet Spurs	1-0
178	Winchester City v Ringwood Town	5-0
179	Whitchurch United v Bemerton Heath Harlequins	3-2
180	Alton Town v New Milton Town	1-1
181	Lymington Town v Sherborne Town	3-2 N
182	Blackfield & Langley v GE Hamble	3-1
183	Gillingham Town v Newbury (2)	1-2
184	Moneyfields v Christchurch	2-0
185	Welton Rovers v Larkhall Athletic	0-5
186	Melksham Town v Almondsbury UWE	3-2
187	Hallen v Calne Town	3-0
188	Fairford Town v Wellington (Hereford)	3-0
189	Street v Shortwood United	0-2
190	Radstock Town v Wootton Bassett Town	2-1
191	Brislington v Lydney Town	4-1
192	Pewsey Vale v Bishop Sutton	0-2
193	Slimbridge v Bradford Town	3-1
194	Merthyr Town (2) v Bitton	2-2
195	Bristol Manor Farm v Longwell Green Sports	1-1
196	Hengrove Athletic v Wells City	0-3
197	Highworth Town v Odd Down	1-4
198	Corsham Town v Cadbury Heath	1-6
199	Bodmin Town v Falmouth Town	6-3
200	Tavistock v Dawlish Town	wo/s
201	St Blazey v Saltash United	1-0
202	Chard Town v Torpoint Athletic	1-2
203	Willand Rovers v Barnstaple Town	0-1
204	Ilfracombe Town v Buckland Athletic	0-4
4r	North Shields v Penrith	0-1
5r	Northallerton Town v West Allotment Celtic	2-1e
11r	South Shields (3) v Chester-le-Street Town	2-1
12r	Dunston UTS v West Auckland Town	5-1
21r	Rossington Main v Silsden	2-2q
30r	Bridlington Town (2) v Barton Town Old Boys	2-3
33r	Maine Road v Winsford United	1-0 N
44r	Runcorn Linnets v AFC Liverpool	3-1
48r	Greenwood Meadows v Holbrook Sports	0-2
53r	Louth Town v Gedling MW	2-1
66r	Causeway United v Malvern Town	5-0 N
70r	Shifnal Town v Gornal Athletic	3-4e
72r	Continental Star v Cradley Town	3-2
73r	AFC Wulfrunians v Bloxwich United	3-0
74r	Bewdley Town v Pegasus Juniors	2-1e
83r	Desborough Town v Thurnby Nirvana	0-5
90r	Gorleston v Woodbridge Town	2-1
103r	Barking v Burnham Ramblers	0-1
104r	Cockfosters v Hadley	0-0P
116r	Hatfield Town v Sawbridgeworth Town	2-1
119r	Southend Manor v Takeley	3-2
138r	Binfield v Reading Town	3-0
143r	Bookham v VCD Athletic	0-2
145r	Horsham YMCA v Lancing	2-5
146r	Fisher v Chichester City	6-1
148r	Chessington & Hook United v Colliers Wood United	2-1
150r	Arundel v Sidley United	5-1e
163r	Mile Oak v Selsey	1-2
165r	Badshot Lea v Cobham	4-1
167r	Hayling United v Bridport	0-2
171r	Brockenhurst v Downton	4-2
180r	New Milton Town v Alton Town	0-6
194r	Bitton v Merthyr Town (2)	1-2
195r	Longwell Green Sports v Bristol Manor Farm	3-2

Preliminary Round

1	Newcastle Benfield v South Shields (3)	1-1
2	Dunston UTS v Durham City	4-0
3	Spennymoor Town v Sunderland RCA	1-0
4	Guisborough Town v Shildon	0-1
5	Bedlington Terriers v Billingham Town	6-0
6	Whitley Bay v Marske United	2-0
7	Hebburn Town v Whitehaven	2-2
8	Penrith v Billingham Synthonia	3-2
9	Ashington v Northallerton Town	2-1
10	Wakefield v Thackley	1-0
11	Liversedge v Pickering Town	2-2
12	Armthorpe Welfare v Brigg Town	2-0
13	Silsden v Harrogate Railway Athletic	1-1
14	Pontefract Collieries v Tadcaster Albion	2-3
15	Garforth Town v Sheffield	3-2
16	Ossett Town v Glasshoughton Welfare	0-0
17	Scarborough Athletic v Barton Town Old Boys	2-2
18	Goole AFC v Staveley MW	1-1
19	Parkgate v Hall Road Rangers	2-2
20	AFC Blackpool v AFC Fylde	1-1
21	Ramsbottom United v Salford City	2-1
22	Trafford v Cheadle Town	3-0
23	Ossett Albion v Witton Albion	0-6
24	Cammell Laird v Atherton LR	3-1
25	Clitheroe v Skelmersdale United	4-0
26	Prescot Cables v Warrington Town	0-2
27	Mossley v Runcorn Linnets	0-0
28	Formby v Lancaster City	1-4
29	Squires Gate v Atherton Collieries	1-0
30	Curzon Ashton v Bamber Bridge	1-1
31	Woodley Sports v Bootle	3-1 N
32	Radcliffe Borough v Holker Old Boys	3-0
33	Maine Road v Ashton Athletic	0-0
34	Congleton Town v Runcorn Town	0-6
35	Deeping Rangers v Belper Town	2-1
36	New Mills v Rainworth MW	3-2
37	Arnold Town v Lincoln United	5-1
38	Grantham Town v Stamford	1-0
39	Gresley v Shirebrook Town	1-1
40	Hucknall Town v Holbeach United	0-0
41	Borrowash Victoria v Carlton Town	1-3
42	Holbrook Sports v Louth Town	1-3
43	Heanor Town v Boston Town	2-1
44	Castle Vale v AFC Wulfrunians	1-1
45	Causeway United v Leek Town	3-4
46	Newcastle Town v Studley	6-2
47	Stourport Swifts v Stone Dominoes	1-1
48	Alvechurch v Eccleshall	1-1
49	Bedworth United v Sutton Coldfield Town	2-1
50	Rugby Town v Gornal Athletic	0-0
51	Kidsgrove Athletic v Atherstone Town	5-1
52	Rocester v Halesowen Town	2-1
53	Stratford Town v Coventry Sphinx	2-1
54	Market Drayton Town v Bewdley Town	0-2
55	Continental Star v Bridgnorth Town	1-2
56	Romulus v Norton United	3-1 N
57	Tipton Town v Highgate United	4-1
58	Boldmere St Michaels v Coleshill Town	2-2
59	Shepshed Dynamo v Thrapston Town	0-0
60	Rothwell Town v Barrow Town	2-7
61	Thurnby Nirvana v St Neots Town	2-0
62	Cogenhoe United v Loughborough Dynamo	1-2
63	Rothwell Corinthians v Long Buckby	2-5
64	Woodford United v Daventry Town	0-0
65	Quorn v Oadby Town	0-0
66	Loughborough University v Godmanchester Rovers	4-1
67	Coalville Town v Daventry United	3-4
68	Bugbrooke St Michaels v Huntingdon Town	1-2
69	Leiston v FC Clacton	5-0
70	Needham Market v Felixstowe & Walton United	4-1
71	Haverhill Rovers v Brantham Athletic	3-2
72	Ely City v Walsham Le Willows	1-1
73	King's Lynn Town v Soham Town Rangers	2-1
74	March Town United v Wisbech Town	1-1
75	Hadleigh United v Heybridge Swifts	1-4
76	St Ives Town v AFC Sudbury	0-0
77	Maldon & Tiptree v Ipswich Wanderers	9-0
78	Wroxham v Long Melford	1-0
79	Gorleston v Harlow Town	2-0
80	Burnham Ramblers v Hertford Town	3-3
81	AFC Dunstable v Grays Athletic	2-3
82	Dunstable Town v Bethnal Green United	1-1
83	Romford v Royston Town	3-2
84	Potters Bar Town v Broxbourne Borough V&E	1-3
85	Stotfold v Enfield Town	2-1
86	Tilbury v Biggleswade United	3-1
87	Hatfield Town v Enfield 1893	1-1
88	Great Wakering Rovers v Oxhey Jets	1-1
89	Haringey Borough v Berkhamsted	0-1
90	Cheshunt v Southend Manor	0-0
91	Waltham Forest v Ilford	1-1
92	Waltham Abbey v Ware	6-1
93	Colney Heath v Brentwood Town	0-1
94	Barton Rovers v Witham Town	3-0
95	Stansted v London APSA	4-0
96	Cockfosters v Redbridge	1-2
97	Biggleswade Town v Haringey & Waltham Development	5-5
98	Newport Pagnell Town v Thame United	1-1
99	Wokingham & Emmbrook v Kidlington	3-0
100	Bedfont Sports v Hanworth Villa	1-1
101	Beaconsfield SYCOB v Northwood	2-1
102	Abingdon Town v Didcot Town	2-2
103	Slough Town v Binfield	3-1
104	Wantage Town v Abingdon United	1-2
105	Leighton Town v Uxbridge	2-0
106	Aylesbury United v North Leigh	0-0
107	Wembley v Ardley United	1-1
108	AFC Hayes v Tring Athletic	4-2
109	Chalfont St Peter v Aylesbury	4-2
110	Burnham v Ashford Town (Middlesex)	2-1
111	North Greenford United v Bedfont Town	2-1
112	Staines Lammas v Harefield United	2-2
113	Marlow v Thatcham Town	1-0
114	Chatham Town v Croydon Athletic	1-0
115	Badshot Lea v Chertsey Town	0-1
116	Folkestone Invicta v Whyteleafe	2-2
117	Corinthian v Maidstone United (2)	0-9
118	Walton & Hersham v Tunbridge Wells	3-1
119	Thamesmead Town v Burgess Hill Town	3-0
120	Lingfield v Fisher	4-1 N
121	Crawley Down v Farnham Town	2-1
122	Erith & Belvedere v Selsey	4-1
123	Merstham v Egham Town	1-1
124	Dulwich Hamlet v Eastbourne Town	2-0
125	Sittingbourne v Peacehaven & Telscombe	2-1
126	Whitstable Town v Worthing	1-3
127	Epsom & Ewell v Chipstead	1-2
128	Banstead Athletic v Arundel	3-1
129	Whitehawk v Ramsgate	0-0
130	Beckenham Town v Walton Casuals	3-1
131	Chessington & Hook United v Hythe Town	0-1
132	Lordswood v VCD Athletic	0-1
133	Bognor Regis Town v Camberley Town	5-1
134	Shoreham v Lancing	1-0
135	Herne Bay v Deal Town	3-0
136	Horley Town v Corinthian Casuals	3-1
137	Raynes Park Vale v Faversham Town	0-1
138	Sevenoaks Town v Redhill	1-3
139	Erith Town v South Park	2-0
140	Totton & Eling v Bournemouth (Ams)	1-2
141	Sholing v Newbury (2)	9-1
142	Shrewton United v Hungerford Town	0-1
143	Fleet Town v Alton Town	4-3
144	Wimborne Town v Godalming Town	1-2
145	Whitchurch United v Brading Town	2-1
146	AFC Portchester v Newport (IOW)	2-2
147	Moneyfields v Gosport Borough	2-1
148	Winchester City v Blackfield & Langley	1-3
149	Poole Town v Andover	wo/s
150	Alresford Town v Hartley Wintney	1-4
151	Lymington Town v Brockenhurst	1-1
152	Horndean v Bridport	3-1
153	Yate Town v Melksham Town	10-1
154	Merthyr Town (2) v Longwell Green Sports	1-0
155	Slimbridge v Cadbury Heath	1-2
156	Fairford Town v Cinderford Town	1-3
157	Shortwood United v Bishop Sutton	1-1
158	Paulton Rovers v Clevedon Town	1-2
159	Mangotsfield United v Hallen	1-0 D
160	Larkhall Athletic v Odd Down	4-0
161	Bishop's Cleeve v Wells City	0-1
162	Radstock Town v Brislington	1-2
163	St Blazey v Tavistock	1-2
164	Barnstaple Town v Bodmin Town	1-2
165	Taunton Town v Buckland Athletic	1-1
166	Bideford v Tiverton Town	4-0
167	Torpoint Athletic v Bridgwater Town	2-5
1r	South Shields (3) v Newcastle Benfield	0-3
7r	Whitehaven v Hebburn Town	2-4
11r	Pickering Town v Liversedge	3-3P
13r	Harrogate Railway Athletic v Silsden	2-0
16r	Glasshoughton Welfare v Ossett Town	1-3
17r	Barton Town Old Boys v Scarborough Athletic	0-1
18r	Staveley MW v Goole AFC	3-1
19r	Hall Road Rangers v Parkgate	2-0 D
20r	AFC Fylde v AFC Blackpool	3-2
27r	Runcorn Linnets v Mossley	4-0
30r	Bamber Bridge v Curzon Ashton	3-2
33r	Ashton Athletic v Maine Road	2-3
39r	Shirebrook Town v Gresley	2-3e
40r	Holbeach United v Hucknall Town	1-3e
44r	AFC Wulfrunians v Castle Vale	3-3P
47r	Stone Dominoes v Stourport Swifts	2-1
48r	Eccleshall v Alvechurch	2-3
50r	Gornal Athletic v Rugby Town	4-3
58r	Coleshill Town v Boldmere St Michaels	0-1
59r	Thrapston Town v Shepshed Dynamo	2-1
64r	Daventry Town v Woodford United	5-0
65r	Oadby Town v Quorn	1-3e
72r	Walsham Le Willows v Ely City	1-2
74r	Wisbech Town v March Town United	3-2
76r	AFC Sudbury v St Ives Town	3-2e
80r	Hertford Town v Burnham Ramblers	2-2P
82r	Dunstable Town v Bethnal Green United	3-0
87r	Enfield 1893 v Hatfield Town	1-2
88r	Oxhey Jets v Great Wakering Rovers	1-0
90r	Southend Manor v Cheshunt	4-2
91r	Ilford v Waltham Forest	2-3
97r	Haringey & Waltham Development v Biggleswade Town	1-2
98r	Thame United v Newport Pagnell Town	1-1P
100r	Hanworth Villa v Bedfont Sports	2-0
102r	Didcot Town v Abingdon Town	3-2e
106r	North Leigh v Aylesbury United	4-2
107r	Ardley United v Wembley	1-2
112r	Harefield United v Staines Lammas	0-2
116r	Whyteleafe v Folkestone Invicta	1-2
123r	Egham Town v Merstham	2-3
129r	Ramsgate v Whitehawk	0-1
146r	Newport (IOW) v AFC Portchester	2-1
151r	Brockenhurst v Lymington Town	2-1
157r	Bishop Sutton v Shortwood United	4-1
165r	Buckland Athletic v Taunton Town	0-2

Qualifying Round One

1	Spennymoor Town v Dunston UTS	3-0
2	Bedlington Terriers v Newcastle Benfield	4-0
3	Kendal Town v Whitley Bay	1-0
4	Hebburn Town v Penrith	2-0
5	Shildon v Ashington	0-0
6	Armthorpe Welfare v Stocksbridge Park Steels	1-1
7	Garforth Town v Frickley Athletic	0-2
8	Pickering Town v Staveley MW	2-2
9	Parkgate v Whitby Town	1-3
10	Wakefield v Ossett Town	4-0
11	North Ferriby United v Worksop Town	1-0
12	Bradford Park Avenue v Harrogate Railway Athletic	8-0
13	Tadcaster Albion v Scarborough Athletic	3-0
14	Ashton United v Runcorn Town	5-1
15	FC United of Manchester v Woodley Sports	1-1
16	Bamber Bridge v Warrington Town	0-4
17	Squires Gate v Runcorn Linnets	0-0
18	Ramsbottom United v Nantwich Town	1-2
19	Lancaster City v Maine Road	5-1
20	AFC Fylde v Chorley	1-1
21	Witton Albion v Marine	2-0
22	Burscough v Clitheroe	2-2
23	Cammell Laird v Radcliffe Borough	1-2
24	Trafford v Northwich Victoria	0-2
25	Deeping Rangers v New Mills	5-1
26	Louth Town v Buxton	0-2
27	Grantham Town v Arnold Town	2-0
28	Mickleover Sports v Gresley	4-2
29	Matlock Town v Hucknall Town	2-0
30	Carlton Town v Heanor Town	1-0
31	Romulus v Bridgnorth Town	1-2 N
32	Evesham United v Rocester	4-0
33	Leamington v Boldmere St Michaels	5-0
34	Leek Town v Tipton Town	2-0
35	Kidsgrove Athletic v Gornal Athletic	3-0

2011/12

36	Chasetown v Alvechurch	6-2
37	Rushall Olympic v Bedworth United	1-0
38	Bewdley Town v Stourbridge	1-2
39	Redditch United v Hednesford Town	0-2
40	AFC Wulfrunians v Stafford Rangers	2-3
41	Newcastle Town v Stratford Town	5-5
42	Barwell v Stone Dominoes	3-2
43	Thurnby Nirvana v Barrow Town	1-1
44	Long Buckby v Thrapston Town	4-1
45	Huntingdon Town v Daventry Town	1-3
46	Quorn v Loughborough University	2-1
47	Loughborough Dynamo v Daventry United	3-1
48	Cambridge City v Maldon & Tiptree	2-2
49	Needham Market v Ely City	1-1
50	Leiston v AFC Sudbury	0-1
51	Bury Town v Gorleston	3-0
52	Heybridge Swifts v Lowestoft Town	1-2
53	Wisbech Town v Wroxham	1-4
54	King's Lynn Town v Haverhill Rovers	1-0
55	Tilbury v Arlesey Town	1-2
56	Waltham Forest v Hitchin Town	2-0
57	St Albans City v Berkhamsted	0-0
58	Wingate & Finchley v Redbridge	0-3
59	Barton Rovers v Hatfield Town	1-1
60	AFC Hornchurch v Concord Rangers	1-3
61	Canvey Island v Stansted	4-1
62	Hemel Hempstead Town v Brentwood Town	0-0
63	Grays Athletic v Aveley	1-2
64	Hertford Town v Oxhey Jets	0-1
65	East Thurrock United v Bedford Town	1-0
66	Biggleswade Town v Waltham Abbey	3-1
67	Billericay Town v Stotfold	4-0
68	Dunstable Town v Broxbourne Borough V&E	7-0
69	Southend Manor v Romford	4-2
70	Burnham v Chalfont St Peter	1-0
71	Leatherhead v North Leigh	5-1
72	Chesham United v Staines Lammas	3-2
73	Wokingham & Emmbrook v North Greenford United	1-2
74	Leighton Town v Abingdon United	4-1
75	Oxford City v Didcot Town	1-1
76	Banbury United v Slough Town	1-3
77	AFC Hayes v Hendon	0-3
78	Harrow Borough v Marlow	2-0
79	Thame United v Brackley Town	2-0
80	Hanworth Villa v Wembley	1-0
81	Wealdstone v Beaconsfield SYCOB	0-2
82	Carshalton Athletic v Faversham Town	3-0
83	Herne Bay v Erith Town	2-3
84	Margate v Tooting & Mitcham United	3-0
85	Chertsey Town v Lewes	4-1
86	Hastings United (2) v Cray Wanderers	0-3
87	Bognor Regis Town v Sittingbourne	1-0
88	Beckenham Town v Metropolitan Police	4-2
89	Chatham Town v Worthing	0-1
90	Banstead Athletic v Maidstone United (2)	1-9
91	Merstham v Walton & Hersham	2-1
92	Crawley Down v VCD Athletic	0-2
93	Horley Town v Dulwich Hamlet	0-4
94	Chipstead v Redhill	3-1
95	Shoreham v Thamesmead Town	0-2
96	Hythe Town v Erith & Belvedere	5-2
97	Folkestone Invicta v Whitehawk	0-3
98	Horsham v Lingfield	2-2
99	Hungerford Town v Horndean	3-1
100	Whitchurch United v Brockenhurst	2-0
101	Sholing v Blackfield & Langley	2-1
102	Poole Town v Kingstonian	3-0
103	Bournemouth (Ams) v Newport (IOW)	2-1
104	Hartley Wintney v Bashley	1-0
105	AFC Totton v Fleet Town	2-0
106	Godalming Town v Moneyfields	1-1
107	Chippenham Town v Wells City	3-0 D
108	Merthyr Town (2) v Cinderford Town	1-1
109	Yate Town v Larkhall Athletic	1-0
110	Swindon Supermarine v Cirencester Town	3-2
111	Hallen v Frome Town	2-2
112	Clevedon Town v Brislington	3-2
113	Bishop Sutton v Cadbury Heath	0-4
114	Bideford v Bridgwater Town	2-1
115	Weymouth v Taunton Town	0-0
116	Tavistock v Bodmin Town	1-3
5r	Ashington v Shildon	2-2P
6r	Stocksbridge Park Steels v Armthorpe Welfare	3-1
8r	Staveley MW v Pickering Town	4-0
15r	Woodley Sports v FC United of Manchester	1-4 N
17r	Runcorn Linnets v Squires Gate	1-0
20r	Chorley v AFC Fylde	0-1
22r	Clitheroe v Burscough	5-2
41r	Stratford Town v Newcastle Town	6-2
43r	Barrow Town v Thurnby Nirvana	3-1
48r	Maldon & Tiptree v Cambridge City	2-1
49r	Ely City v Needham Market	3-4e
57r	Berkhamsted v St Albans City	0-3
59r	Hatfield Town v Barton Rovers	2-1
62r	Brentwood Town v Hemel Hempstead Town	0-0q
75r	Didcot Town v Oxford City	0-3
98r	Lingfield v Horsham	2-4eN
106r	Moneyfields v Godalming Town	1-3
108r	Cinderford Town v Merthyr Town (2)	2-0e
111r	Frome Town v Hallen	1-1P
115r	Taunton Town v Weymouth	1-3

Qualifying Round Two

1	Northwich Victoria v Nantwich Town	1-2
2	Stalybridge Celtic v Guiseley	1-2
3	Workington v Droylsden	1-2
4	FC Halifax Town v Tadcaster Albion	2-1
5	Wakefield v Kendal Town	1-4 N
6	Stocksbridge Park Steels v Colwyn Bay	3-1
7	Clitheroe v Radcliffe Borough	1-3
8	Staveley MW v Hyde FC	0-3
9	Blyth Spartans v Bedlington Terriers	2-1
10	Ashton United v Spennymoor Town	0-3
11	AFC Fylde v Gainsborough Trinity	2-2
12	Hebburn Town v Runcorn Linnets	1-0
13	FC United of Manchester v Lancaster City	0-1
14	Bradford Park Avenue v Warrington Town	3-1
15	Whitby Town v North Ferriby United	2-1
16	Frickley Athletic v Harrogate Town	1-1
17	Altrincham v Witton Albion	0-2
18	Ashington v Vauxhall Motors	3-3
19	Histon v Corby Town	1-1
20	Mickleover Sports v Barrow Town	1-4
21	Stafford Rangers v Stratford Town	2-4
22	Deeping Rangers v Leek Town	0-2
23	Buxton v Rushall Olympic	1-2
24	Matlock Town v Hinckley United	1-3
25	Eastwood Town v Evesham United	0-3
26	Barwell v Stourbridge	0-2
27	Chasetown v Grantham Town	1-2
28	Bridgnorth Town v Long Buckby	0-2
29	Carlton Town v Hednesford Town	0-1
30	Daventry Town v Leamington	2-1
31	Needham Market v Nuneaton Town	0-3
32	Solihull Moors v Loughborough Dynamo	2-0
33	Boston United v Kidsgrove Athletic	0-0
34	King's Lynn Town v Quorn	4-2
35	Chipstead v Billericay Town	0-3
36	Oxhey Jets v Hendon	1-2
37	Hanworth Villa v Aveley	1-0
38	Cray Wanderers v Erith Town	5-0
39	Arlesey Town v Hampton & Richmond Boro.	6-2
40	Redbridge v Bury Town	1-0
41	Slough Town v Boreham Wood	3-2
42	East Thurrock United v St Albans City	3-3
43	Southend Manor v Chertsey Town	4-2
44	Dover Athletic v Carshalton Athletic	3-0
45	North Greenford United v Hythe Town	2-1
46	Chelmsford City v Tonbridge Angels	3-0
47	Sutton United v Dulwich Hamlet	5-1
48	Wroxham v Concord Rangers	2-2
49	Dartford v Harrow Borough	5-0
50	Margate v Thamesmead Town	0-0
51	Bromley v Welling United	2-1
52	Leighton Town v Hatfield Town	3-0
53	Whitehawk v Maldon & Tiptree	0-0
54	Staines Town v Beaconsfield SYCOB	0-0
55	Burnham v Horsham	2-2
56	Dunstable Town v Chesham United	2-1
57	Biggleswade Town v Leatherhead	1-1
58	Canvey Island v Bishop's Stortford	0-1
59	Waltham Forest v Eastbourne Borough	0-1
60	Maidstone United (2) v Bognor Regis Town	2-3
61	Merstham v AFC Sudbury	0-2
62	Lowestoft Town v Hemel Hempstead Town	3-0
63	VCD Athletic v Thurrock	2-2
64	Worthing v Beckenham Town	0-0
65	Havant & Waterlooville v Sholing	4-1
66	Frome Town v Basingstoke Town	0-0
67	Thame United v Oxford City	1-3
68	Bournemouth (Ams) v Truro City	0-0
69	Dorchester Town v Weston-Super-Mare	0-1
70	Whitchurch United v Gloucester City	0-2
71	Wells City v Woking	0-7
72	Salisbury City v Swindon Supermarine	3-0
73	Yate Town v Bodmin Town	1-1
74	Godalming Town v Worcester City	2-1
75	Poole Town v Cadbury Heath	4-0
76	Eastleigh v Cinderford Town	3-1
77	Weymouth v Hungerford Town	3-3
78	Hartley Wintney v Bideford	2-1
79	Maidenhead United v Farnborough	1-1
80	Clevedon Town v AFC Totton	1-2
11r	Gainsborough Trinity v AFC Fylde	2-1e
16r	Harrogate Town v Frickley Athletic	1-2
18r	Vauxhall Motors v Ashington	0-1
19r	Corby Town v Histon	3-1e
33r	Kidsgrove Athletic v Boston United	2-0
42r	St Albans City v East Thurrock United	1-3
48r	Concord Rangers v Wroxham	1-2
50r	Thamesmead Town v Margate	1-6
53r	Maldon & Tiptree v Whitehawk	2-1
54r	Beaconsfield SYCOB v Staines Town	0-2
55r	Horsham v Burnham	2-3
57r	Leatherhead v Biggleswade Town	2-1
63r	Thurrock v VCD Athletic	1-0
64r	Beckenham Town v Worthing	1-2
66r	Basingstoke Town v Frome Town	3-0
68r	Truro City v Bournemouth (Ams)	3-2
73r	Bodmin Town v Yate Town	4-1
77r	Hungerford Town v Weymouth	1-3
79r	Farnborough v Maidenhead United	2-3

Qualifying Round Three

1	Nantwich Town v Kendal Town	2-1
2	Radcliffe Borough v Hebburn Town	2-4
3	Lancaster City v FC Halifax Town	0-3
4	Whitby Town v Blyth Spartans	1-2
5	Gainsborough Trinity v Frickley Athletic	2-0
6	Hyde FC v Bradford Park Avenue	0-1
7	Ashington v Guiseley	1-0
8	Witton Albion v Spennymoor Town	3-1
9	Droylsden v Stocksbridge Park Steels	4-1
10	King's Lynn Town v Stratford Town	3-2
11	Daventry Town v Nuneaton Town	1-2
12	Hednesford Town v Corby Town	2-4
13	Kidsgrove Athletic v Long Buckby	2-1
14	Hinckley United v Leek Town	3-3
15	Solihull Moors v Grantham Town	3-2
16	Barrow Town v Rushall Olympic	0-3
17	Stourbridge v Evesham United	5-0
18	Billericay Town v Leatherhead	0-3
19	Worthing v Staines Town	0-2
20	Redbridge v Dunstable Town	3-0
21	Eastbourne Borough v AFC Sudbury	1-0
22	Lowestoft Town v Chelmsford City	2-5
23	Cray Wanderers v Dartford	1-2
24	Maldon & Tiptree v Hendon	1-3
25	Thurrock v Arlesey Town	0-0
26	Burnham v Bishop's Stortford	2-5
27	Slough Town v Hanworth Villa	2-2
28	East Thurrock United v North Greenford United	3-3
29	Dover Athletic v Wroxham	3-1
30	Margate v Bromley	2-3
31	Southend Manor v Leighton Town	5-0
32	Sutton United v Bognor Regis Town	4-0
33	Basingstoke Town v Hartley Wintney	4-0
34	Bodmin Town v Godalming Town	1-1
35	Gloucester City v Truro City	7-2
36	AFC Totton v Weymouth	4-2
37	Eastleigh v Oxford City	1-3
38	Salisbury City v Poole Town	6-1
39	Weston-Super-Mare v Havant & Waterlooville	3-2
40	Maidenhead United v Woking	4-1
14r	Leek Town v Hinckley United	1-2
25r	Arlesey Town v Thurrock	4-1
27r	Hanworth Villa v Slough Town	3-1
28r	North Greenford United v East Thurrock United	0-3
34r	Godalming Town v Bodmin Town	5-1

Qualifying Round Four

1	Tamworth v King's Lynn Town	2-1
2	Droylsden v Blyth Spartans	0-0
3	Stourbridge v Rushall Olympic	5-0
4	Kidsgrove Athletic v Bradford Park Avenue	0-2
5	Gateshead (2) v Hebburn Town	3-0
6	Grimsby Town v Ashington	5-0
7	Wrexham v York City	2-1
8	Mansfield Town v Fleetwood Town	1-1
9	Nantwich Town v Nuneaton Town	1-0
10	Alfreton Town v Lincoln City	1-1
11	AFC Telford United v Gainsborough Trinity	5-0
12	Southport v Stockport County	1-0
13	Solihull Moors v FC Halifax Town	0-1
14	Kidderminster Harriers v Corby Town	0-0
15	Darlington v Hinckley United	1-1
16	Witton Albion v Barrow	1-4
17	Dover Athletic v Bath City	0-1
18	Bishop's Stortford v Salisbury City	1-2
19	Eastbourne Borough v East Thurrock United	1-2
20	Chelmsford City v Gloucester City	1-1
21	Hayes & Yeading United v Cambridge United	2-6
22	Godalming Town v Maidenhead United	0-5
23	Sutton United v Leatherhead	3-3
24	Weston-Super-Mare v Oxford City	2-3
25	AFC Totton v Hanworth Villa	3-2
26	Basingstoke Town v Staines Town	2-1
27	Arlesey Town v Forest Green Rovers	2-1
28	Dartford v Bromley	1-2
29	Luton Town v Hendon	5-1
30	Kettering Town v Southend Manor	3-1
31	Redbridge v Ebbsfleet United	2-0
32	Newport County (2) v Braintree Town	4-3
2r	Blyth Spartans v Droylsden	2-1
8r	Fleetwood Town v Mansfield Town	5-0
10r	Lincoln City v Alfreton Town	1-2
14r	Corby Town v Kidderminster Harriers	4-1
15r	Hinckley United v Darlington	3-0
20r	Gloucester City v Chelmsford City	0-1
23r	Leatherhead v Sutton United	2-3e

Round One

AFC Totton v Bradford Park Avenue	8-1
AFC Wimbledon v Scunthorpe United	0-0
Alfreton Town v Carlisle United	0-4
Barrow v Rotherham United	1-2
Blyth Spartans v Gateshead (2)	0-2
Bournemouth v Gillingham	3-3
Bradford City v Rochdale	1-0
Brentford v Basingstoke Town	1-0
Bristol Rovers v Corby Town	3-1
Bury v Crawley Town	0-2
Cambridge United v Wrexham	2-2

2011/12 to 2012/13

	Chelmsford City v AFC Telford United	4-0
	Chesterfield v Torquay United	1-3
	Crewe Alexandra v Colchester United	1-4
	Dagenham & Redbridge v Bath City	1-1
	East Thurrock United v Macclesfield Town	0-3
	Exeter City v Walsall	1-1
	FC Halifax Town v Charlton Athletic	0-4
	Fleetwood Town v Wycombe Wanderers	2-0
	Hartlepool United v Stevenage	0-1
	Hereford United v Yeovil Town	0-3
	Hinckley United v Tamworth	2-2
	Leyton Orient v Bromley	3-0
	Luton Town v Northampton Town	1-0
	Maidenhead United v Aldershot Town	1-1
	Milton Keynes Dons v Nantwich Town	6-0
	Morecambe v Sheffield Wednesday	1-2
	Newport County (2) v Shrewsbury Town	0-1
	Notts County v Accrington Stanley (2)	4-1
	Oldham Athletic v Burton Albion	3-1
	Plymouth Argyle v Stourbridge	3-3
	Port Vale v Grimsby Town	0-0
	Preston North End v Southend United	0-0
	Redbridge v Oxford City	0-0
	Salisbury City v Arlesey Town	3-1
	Sheffield United v Oxford United	3-0
	Southport v Barnet	1-2
	Sutton United v Kettering Town	1-0
	Swindon Town v Huddersfield Town	4-1
	Tranmere Rovers v Cheltenham Town	0-1
r	Aldershot Town v Maidenhead United	2-0
r	Bath City v Dagenham & Redbridge	1-3e
r	Gillingham v Bournemouth	3-2
r	Grimsby Town v Port Vale	1-0
r	Oxford City v Redbridge	1-2e
r	Scunthorpe United v AFC Wimbledon	0-1
r	Southend United v Preston North End	1-0
r	Stourbridge v Plymouth Argyle	2-0
r	Tamworth v Hinckley United	1-0
r	Walsall v Exeter City	3-2e
r	Wrexham v Cambridge United	2-1

Round Two

	AFC Totton v Bristol Rovers	1-6
	Barnet v Milton Keynes Dons	1-3
	Bradford City v AFC Wimbledon	3-1
	Brentford v Wrexham	0-1
	Charlton Athletic v Carlisle United	2-0
	Chelmsford City v Macclesfield Town	1-1
	Colchester United v Swindon Town	0-1
	Crawley Town v Redbridge	5-0
	Dagenham & Redbridge v Walsall	1-1
	Fleetwood Town v Yeovil Town	2-2
	Gateshead (2) v Tamworth	1-2
	Leyton Orient v Gillingham	0-1
	Luton Town v Cheltenham Town	2-4
	Salisbury City v Grimsby Town	0-0
	Sheffield United v Torquay United	3-2
	Sheffield Wednesday v Aldershot Town	1-0
	Shrewsbury Town v Rotherham United	2-1
	Southend United v Oldham Athletic	1-1
	Stourbridge v Stevenage	0-3
	Sutton United v Notts County	0-2
r	Grimsby Town v Salisbury City	2-3e
r	Macclesfield Town v Chelmsford City	1-0
r	Oldham Athletic v Southend United	1-0
r	Walsall v Dagenham & Redbridge	0-0q
r	Yeovil Town v Fleetwood Town	0-2

Round Three

	Arsenal v Leeds United	1-0
	Barnsley v Swansea City	2-4
	Birmingham City v Wolverhampton Wan.	0-0
	Brighton & Hove Albion v Wrexham	1-1
	Bristol Rovers v Aston Villa	1-3
	Chelsea v Portsmouth	4-0
	Coventry City v Southampton	1-2
	Crawley Town v Bristol City	1-0
	Dagenham & Redbridge v Millwall	0-0
	Derby County v Crystal Palace	1-0
	Doncaster Rovers v Notts County	0-2
	Everton v Tamworth	2-0
	Fleetwood Town v Blackpool	1-5
	Fulham v Charlton Athletic	4-0
	Gillingham v Stoke City	1-3
	Hull City v Ipswich Town	3-1
	Liverpool v Oldham Athletic	5-1
	Macclesfield Town v Bolton Wanderers	2-2
	Manchester City v Manchester United	2-3
	Middlesbrough v Shrewsbury Town	1-0
	Milton Keynes Dons v Queen's Park Rangers	1-1
	Newcastle United v Blackburn Rovers	2-1
	Norwich City v Burnley	4-1
	Nottingham Forest v Leicester City	0-0
	Peterborough United v Sunderland	0-2
	Reading v Stevenage	0-1
	Sheffield United v Salisbury City	3-1
	Sheffield Wednesday v West Ham United	1-0
	Swindon Town v Wigan Athletic	2-1
	Tottenham Hotspur v Cheltenham Town	3-0
	Watford v Bradford City	4-2
	West Bromwich Albion v Cardiff City	4-2
r	Bolton Wanderers v Macclesfield Town	2-0
r	Leicester City v Nottingham Forest	4-0
r	Millwall v Dagenham & Redbridge	5-0
r	Queen's Park Rangers v Milton Keynes Dons	1-0
r	Wolverhampton Wan. v Birmingham City	0-1
r	Wrexham v Brighton & Hove Albion	1-1q

Round Four

	Arsenal v Aston Villa	3-2
	Blackpool v Sheffield Wednesday	1-1
	Bolton Wanderers v Swansea City	2-1
	Brighton & Hove Albion v Newcastle United	1-0
	Derby County v Stoke City	0-2
	Everton v Fulham	2-1
	Hull City v Crawley Town	0-1
	Leicester City v Swindon Town	2-0
	Liverpool v Manchester United	2-1
	Millwall v Southampton	1-1
	Queen's Park Rangers v Chelsea	0-1
	Sheffield United v Birmingham City	0-4
	Stevenage v Notts County	1-0
	Sunderland v Middlesbrough	1-1
	Watford v Tottenham Hotspur	0-1
	West Bromwich Albion v Norwich City	1-2
r	Middlesbrough v Sunderland	1-2e
r	Sheffield Wednesday v Blackpool	0-3
r	Southampton v Millwall	2-3

Round Five

	Chelsea v Birmingham City	1-1
	Crawley Town v Stoke City	0-2
	Everton v Blackpool	2-0
	Liverpool v Brighton & Hove Albion	6-1
	Millwall v Bolton Wanderers	0-2
	Norwich City v Leicester City	1-2
	Stevenage v Tottenham Hotspur	0-0
	Sunderland v Arsenal	2-0
r	Birmingham City v Chelsea	0-2
r	Tottenham Hotspur v Stevenage	3-1

Round Six

	Chelsea v Leicester City	5-2
	Everton v Sunderland	1-1
	Liverpool v Stoke City	2-1
	Tottenham Hotspur v Bolton Wanderers	3-1
r	Sunderland v Everton	0-2

Semi Finals

Chelsea v Tottenham Hotspur	5-1 N
Liverpool v Everton	2-1 N

Final

Chelsea v Liverpool	2-1 N

2012/13

Extra Preliminary Round

1	Dunston UTS v Armthorpe Welfare	2-1
2	Liversedge v West Auckland Town	2-4
3	Crook Town v Penrith	2-1
4	Thackley v Hebburn Town	1-3
5	Jarrow Roofing Boldon CA v Pickering Town	1-1
6	Newton Aycliffe v Holker Old Boys	1-1
7	Tadcaster Albion v Consett	1-1
8	Ashington v Sunderland RCA	1-1
9	Chester-le-Street Town v Billingham Town	0-0
10	South Shields (3) v Darlington Railway Ath. (2)	0-0
11	Northallerton Town v Guisborough Town	4-5
12	Billingham Synthonia v Celtic Nation	0-1
13	Marske United v Stokesley SC	1-0
14	North Shields v Birtley Town	1-1
15	Durham City v Newcastle Benfield	2-1
16	Washington v Esh Winning	1-3
17	Tow Law Town v Bishop Auckland	0-2
18	Eccleshill United v Glasshoughton Welfare	4-2
19	Spennymoor Town v Scarborough Athletic	1-0
20	Bedlington Terriers v Morpeth Town	2-1
21	Pontefract Collieries v Norton & Stockton Ancients	2-2
22	Silsden v Brighouse Town	2-3
23	Whitehaven v Shildon	0-6
24	West Allotment Celtic v Selby Town	2-1
25	Bridlington Town (2) v Whitley Bay	1-2
26	Daisy Hill v Formby	0-5
27	AFC Blackpool v AFC Liverpool	3-6
28	Dinnington Town v Atherton Collieries	0-2
29	Irlam v Hallam	5-3
30	Bootle v Alsager Town	4-1
31	Maine Road v Squires Gate	3-0
32	Atherton LR v Rossington Main	4-2
33	St Helens Town v Abbey Hey	1-5
34	Padiham v Wigan Robin Park	1-0
35	Hemsworth MW v Runcorn Linnets	1-1
36	Colne v Congleton Town	0-0
37	Stockport Sports v Ashton Athletic	0-0 N
38	Cheadle Town v Maltby Main	1-1
39	Parkgate v Runcorn Town	2-3
40	AFC Emley v Chadderton	0-2
41	Staveley MW v Hall Road Rangers	2-1
42	Nostell MW v Winsford United	0-1
43	Barton Town Old Boys v Barnoldswick Town	2-0
44	Winterton Rangers v Bacup Borough	0-3 N
45	Shepshed Dynamo v Heanor Town	0-3
46	Long Eaton United v Dunkirk	0-1
47	Blackstones v Barrow Town	5-1
48	Spalding United v Blaby & Whetstone Athletic	1-2
49	Arnold Town v Holbeach United	0-2
50	Shirebrook Town v Kirby Muxloe	0-1
51	Boston Town v Quorn	0-2
52	Glossop North End v Louth Town	0-0
53	Retford United v Bardon Hill	2-1
54	Oadby Town v Anstey Nomads	3-1
55	Holbrook Sports v Deeping Rangers	3-1
56	Thurnby Nirvana v Lincoln Moorlands Railway	4-2
57	St Andrews v Borrowash Victoria	1-2
58	Sleaford Town v Holwell Sports	2-0
59	Teversal v Loughborough University	1-2
60	Causeway United v Continental Star	1-1 N
61	Norton United v Alvechurch	2-2
62	Highgate United v Wellington (Hereford)	1-1
63	Coleshill Town v AFC Wulfrunians	1-1
64	Bloxwich United v Studley	2-3
65	Brocton v Bewdley Town	2-2
66	Dudley Sports v Heath Hayes	2-2
67	Boldmere St Michaels v Bridgnorth Town	1-3
68	Pilkington XXX v Atherstone Town	5-4
69	Stone Dominoes v Rocester	0-3
70	Dudley Town v Southam United	4-1
71	Eccleshall v Stourport Swifts	0-1
72	Lye Town v Bartley Green	2-2
73	Cradley Town v Shifnal Town	3-0
74	Tipton Town v Wolverhampton Casuals	0-1
75	Ellesmere Rangers v Coventry Sphinx	0-4
76	Gornal Athletic v Malvern Town	4-0
77	Earlswood Town v Nuneaton Griff	3-3
78	Shawbury United v Westfields	2-4
79	Pegasus Juniors v Long Buckby	2-1
80	Tividale v Stratford Town	5-2
81	Willenhall Town v Sporting Khalsa	1-1
82	Godmanchester Rovers v Thetford Town	2-1
83	Irchester United v Huntingdon Town	0-1
84	Ely City v Rothwell Corinthians	7-1
85	Peterboro' Northern Star v Wellingboro' Whitworths	5-1
86	Dereham Town v Stewarts & Lloyds (2)	3-1
87	Rushden & Higham United v Bugbrooke St Michaels	1-3
88	Fakenham Town v St Ives Town	0-1
89	Thrapston Town v Cogenhoe United	2-1
90	Wellingborough Town (2) v March Town United	2-1
91	Wisbech Town v Desborough Town	1-1
92	Northampton Spencer v Yaxley	1-1
93	Brantham Athletic v Mildenhall Town	1-0
94	Wivenhoe Town v Haverhill Rovers	1-1
95	FC Clacton v Halstead Town	1-3
96	Felixstowe & Walton United v Team Bury	3-1
97	Walsham Le Willows v Burnham Ramblers	1-3
98	Barkingside v Great Yarmouth Town	1-1
99	Kirkley & Pakefield v Sawbridgeworth Town	1-1
100	Norwich United v Stansted	2-1
101	Gorleston v Stanway Rovers	3-1
102	Takeley v Newmarket Town	2-1
103	London APSA v Long Melford	3-1 N
104	Basildon United v Diss Town	1-0
105	Debenham LC v Whitton United	0-2
106	Southend Manor v Hullbridge Sports	1-0
107	Woodbridge Town v Great Wakering Rovers	1-2
108	Bowers & Pitsea v Eton Manor	1-3
109	Ipswich Wanderers v Hadleigh United	0-3
110	AFC Dunstable v Ampthill Town	4-1
111	Hanworth Villa v Bethnal Green United	2-2
112	Hoddesdon Town v Berkhamsted	1-1 N
113	Wodson Park v Colney Heath	0-4
114	Bedfont Sports v Tring Athletic	0-1
115	Haringey Borough v AFC Kempston Rovers	1-3
116	Staines Lammas v Barking	4-4
117	Wembley v Langford	3-2
118	Biggleswade United v Cranfield United	2-0
119	Dunstable Town v Broxbourne Borough V&E	wo/s
120	Hadley v Hertford Town	2-0
121	Hanwell Town v Haringey & Waltham Development	1-3
122	Harefield United v Hillingdon Borough	3-1
123	Crawley Green v Stotfold	1-2
124	London Colney v Hatfield Town	3-0
125	Kings Langley v St Margaretsbury	1-1
126	Aylesbury United v Enfield 1893	4-0
127	London Lions v Clapton	4-0 N
128	Cockfosters v Sporting Bengal United	3-1
129	Oxhey Jets v Leverstock Green	5-2
130	Ardley United v Holyport	4-2
131	Kidlington v Shrivenham	2-2
132	Cove v Slimbridge	2-0
133	Reading Town v Newport Pagnell Town	1-6
134	Hartley Wintney v Holmer Green	2-1
135	Old Woodstock Town v Wantage Town	1-4
136	Bracknell Town v Binfield	2-1
137	Ascot United v Sandhurst Town	6-1
138	Thame United v Newbury (2)	1-0
139	Witney Town v Marlow	1-1
140	Wokingham & Emmbrook v Camberley Town	0-2
141	Abingdon Town v Fairford Town	1-0
142	Flackwell Heath v Windsor	0-1
143	Erith Town v Ringmer	2-4
144	Littlehampton Town v Molesey	4-0
145	Tunbridge Wells v Beckenham Town	1-4
146	Peacehaven & Telscombe v Banstead Athletic	2-1
147	Chessington & Hook United v Warlingham	2-2

2012/13

148 Cobham v South Park 1-1
149 Pagham v Sevenoaks Town 2-1
150 Arundel v Epsom & Ewell 1-2
151 Lordswood v Erith & Belvedere 3-2
152 Dorking (2) v VCD Athletic 3-4
153 Redhill v Whyteleafe 1-0
154 Deal Town v Ashford United 1-2
155 Lingfield v AFC Uckfield 4-2 N
156 Hailsham Town v Greenwich Borough 2-4
157 Fisher v East Preston 1-1
158 Mole Valley SCR v Badshot Lea 1-1
159 Horley Town v Holmesdale 5-1
160 Lancing v Selsey 6-1
161 Egham Town v Westfield 4-0
162 Chichester City v Crowborough Athletic 2-5
163 Shoreham v Colliers Wood United 2-2
164 St Francis Rangers v Rye United 0-1
165 Corinthian v Croydon 3-2
166 Hassocks v Sidley United 0-1
167 Raynes Park Vale v Horsham YMCA 8-0
168 Bitton v Bristol Manor Farm 3-1
169 Bemerton Heath Harlequins v Hamworthy United 1-2
170 Winterbourne United v Moneyfields 1-2
171 Hallen v Fawley 4-0
172 Farnham Town v Alresford Town 0-3
173 Highworth Town v Corsham Town 3-1
174 GE Hamble v Whitchurch United 2-0
175 Almondsbury UWE v Petersfield Town 1-1
176 East Cowes Victoria Athletic v Verwood Town 3-2
177 Downton v Ash United 4-1
178 Fareham Town v Hayling United 3-0
179 Wootton Bassett Town v Calne Town 4-2
180 Horndean v Brockenhurst 2-1
181 Totton & Eling v Fleet Spurs 3-2
182 Alton Town v Bradford Town 3-0
183 Ringwood Town v Cadbury Heath 1-5
184 Longwell Green Sports v Melksham Town 0-0
185 Christchurch v Cowes Sports 5-0
186 Romsey Town v Lymington Town 4-0
187 New Milton Town v Newport (IOW) 0-2
188 Blackfield & Langley v AFC Portchester 6-1
189 Bournemouth (Ams) v Pewsey Vale 0-1
190 Plymouth Parkway v Welton Rovers 3-1
191 Gillingham Town v Tavistock 5-0
192 Bodmin Town v Brislington 3-1
193 Bishop Sutton v Radstock Town 3-2
194 Street v Hengrove Athletic 1-3
195 Chard Town v Ilfracombe Town 1-0
196 Wells City v Barnstaple Town 3-2
197 Larkhall Athletic v Willand Rovers 2-1
198 Odd Down v Saltash United 3-1
199 Buckland Athletic v Bridport 2-1
200 Sherborne Town v Elmore 3-1
5r Pickering Town v Jarrow Roofing Boldon CA 2-4
6r Holker Old Boys v Newton Aycliffe 3-0
7r Consett v Tadcaster Albion 2-3e
8r Sunderland RCA v Ashington 1-2
9r Billingham Town v Chester-le-Street Town 1-0
10r Darlington Railway Ath. v South Shields (3) 5-6
14r Birtley Town v North Shields 2-0
21r Norton & Stockton Ancients v Pontefract Collieries 5-2e
35r Runcorn Linnets v Hemsworth MW 2-2q
36r Congleton Town v Colne 5-2
37r Ashton Athletic v Stockport Sports 2-1
38r Maltby Main v Cheadle Town 1-0
52r Louth Town v Glossop North End 1-2e
60r Continental Star v Causeway United 3-0
61r Alvechurch v Norton United 1-2
62r Wellington (Hereford) v Highgate United 3-3P
63r AFC Wulfrunians v Coleshill Town 3-2e
65r Bewdley Town v Brocton 1-0
66r Heath Hayes v Dudley Sports 2-1e
72r Bartley Green v Lye Town 1-2
77r Nuneaton Griff v Earlswood Town 3-1
81r Sporting Khalsa v Willenhall Town 3-2
91r Desborough Town v Wisbech Town 2-5
92r Yaxley v Northampton Spencer 3-1
94r Haverhill Rovers v Wivenhoe Town 2-0
98r Great Yarmouth Town v Barkingside 3-0 N
99r Sawbridgeworth Town v Kirkley & Pakefield 3-7
111r Hanworth Villa v Bethnal Green United 5-1
112r Berkhamsted v Hoddesdon Town 2-1
116r Barking v Staines Lammas 0-1
125r St Margaretsbury v Kings Langley 3-2
131r Shrivenham v Kidlington 6-3
139r Marlow v Witney Town 4-3
147r Warlingham v Chessington & Hook United 2-3
148r South Park v Cobham 3-0
157r East Preston v Fisher 1-0
158r Badshot Lea v Mole Valley SCR 4-1
163r Colliers Wood United v Shoreham 4-1
175r Petersfield Town v Almondsbury UWE 2-3e
184r Melksham Town v Longwell Green Sports 3-1

Preliminary Round

1 Harrogate Railway Athletic v South Shields (3) 1-1
2 Birtley Town v West Auckland Town 1-4
3 Jarrow Roofing Boldon CA v Farsley AFC 2-3
4 Shildon v Guisborough Town 1-1
5 Bishop Auckland v Esh Winning 7-1
6 Ossett Town v Goole AFC 1-0
7 Garforth Town v Wakefield 1-0
8 Tadcaster Albion v Norton & Stockton Ancients 3-0
9 Brighouse Town v Eccleshill United 1-2
10 Hebburn Town v Ossett Albion 1-3
11 Dunston UTS v Celtic Nation 1-2 d
12 Crook Town v Holker Old Boys 4-4
13 Marske United v Ashington 1-4
14 Spennymoor Town v West Allotment Celtic 3-0
15 Whitley Bay v Bedlington Terriers 0-3
16 Durham City v Billingham Town 2-1
17 Staveley MW v Bamber Bridge 3-3
18 Chadderton v Maltby Main 0-1
19 Ashton Athletic v Lancaster City 2-2
20 Padiham v Burscough 0-0
21 Mossley v Bootle 0-3
22 Maine Road v Bacup Borough 2-1
23 Barton Town Old Boys v Cammell Laird 1-2
24 Atherton Collieries v Congleton Town 2-1
25 Ramsbottom United v Brigg Town 3-0
26 Winsford United v Trafford 0-2
27 AFC Liverpool v Prescot Cables 0-1
28 Irlam v Runcorn Town 3-5
29 Atherton LR v Warrington Town 0-3
30 Formby v Skelmersdale United 1-3
31 Northwich Victoria v Curzon Ashton 0-0
32 Sheffield v Abbey Hey 1-2
33 Clitheroe v Radcliffe Borough 2-2
34 Salford City v Hemsworth MW 5-1
35 Loughborough Dynamo v Glossop North End 3-0
36 Lincoln United v Thurnby Nirvana 1-2
37 New Mills v Mickleover Sports 2-2
38 Holbrook Sports v Belper Town 1-6
39 Coalville Town v Loughborough University 5-3
40 Stamford v Borrowash Victoria 1-0
41 Kirby Muxloe v Holbeach United 0-2
42 Blaby & Whetstone Athletic v Heanor Town 2-1
43 Carlton Town v Oadby Town 3-2
44 Hucknall Town v Retford United 0-1
45 Sleaford Town v Rainworth MW 1-2
46 Blackstones v Gresley 1-3
47 Quorn v Dunkirk 2-1
48 Chasetown v Rocester 2-1
49 Cradley Town v Norton United 4-4
50 Studley v Rugby Town 1-4
51 Halesowen Town v Dudley Town 1-2
52 Gornal Athletic v Coventry Sphinx 6-0
53 Leek Town v Evesham United 2-1
54 Market Drayton Town v Newcastle Town 2-1
55 Heath Hayes v Tividale 3-4
56 Sporting Khalsa v Nuneaton Griff 1-1
57 AFC Wulfrunians v Kidsgrove Athletic 1-0
58 Stourport Swifts v Continental Star 1-1
59 Wellington (Hereford) v Bewdley Town 3-5
60 Lye Town v Bridgnorth Town 0-1
61 Westfields v Romulus 2-1
62 Sutton Coldfield Town v Pegasus Juniors 2-1
63 Wolverhampton Casuals v Pilkington XXX 2-0
64 Godmanchester Rovers v Daventry Town 3-4
65 Peterborough Northern Star v Thrapston Town 3-1
66 Bugbrooke St Michaels v Ely City 2-2
67 Huntingdon Town v St Ives Town 3-2
68 Dereham Town v Woodford United 3-0
69 Wisbech Town v Yaxley 3-0
70 Wellingborough Town (2) v King's Lynn Town 1-3
71 Soham Town Rangers v Burnham Ramblers 5-1
72 Great Yarmouth Town v Witham Town 1-8
73 Grays Athletic v Takeley 1-0
74 Tilbury v Brantham Athletic 5-1
75 AFC Sudbury v Ilford 5-0
76 Kirkley & Pakefield v Southend Manor 0-2
77 Harlow Town v Hadleigh United 1-2
78 Halstead Town v Brentwood Town 0-6
79 Needham Market v Gorleston 6-2
80 Eton Manor v Norwich United 0-2
81 Felixstowe & Walton United v Heybridge Swifts 1-1
82 Whitton United v Aveley 0-3
83 Basildon United v Haverhill Rovers 1-0
84 Maldon & Tiptree v London APSA 9-1
85 Wroxham v Great Wakering Rovers 2-0
86 St Margaretsbury v Leighton Town 0-0
87 London Colney v Harefield United 1-2
88 Haringey & Waltham Development v Waltham Abbey 1-2
89 Biggleswade United v Ware 0-1
90 Ashford Town (Middlesex) v Tring Athletic 2-2
91 AFC Kempston Rovers v Cockfosters 2-0
92 London Lions v Oxhey Jets 3-1 N
93 Berkhamsted v Hadley 3-1
94 Cheshunt v Potters Bar Town 2-2
95 Aylesbury United v Northwood 2-5
96 Hanworth Villa v Royston Town 1-2
97 Colney Heath v Stotfold 1-1
98 Staines Lammas v Barton Rovers 0-2
99 AFC Dunstable v Redbridge 5-0
100 Biggleswade Town v AFC Hayes 3-0
101 Uxbridge v Wembley 2-2
102 Romford v Waltham Forest 1-4
103 North Greenford United v Dunstable Town 2-4
104 Bishop's Cleeve v Ascot United 2-1
105 Cinderford Town v Abingdon Town 5-0
106 Didcot Town v Abingdon United 2-1
107 Camberley Town v Chalfont St Peter 0-5
108 Hungerford Town v Beaconsfield SYCOB 5-2
109 Aylesbury v Windsor 0-2
110 Wantage Town v Hartley Wintney 4-1
111 Newport Pagnell Town v Ardley United 6-2
112 Fleet Town v Marlow 0-2
113 North Leigh v Thame United 6-0
114 Cirencester Town v Merthyr Town (2) 0-1
115 Cove v Thatcham Town 2-5
116 Bracknell Town v Shrivenham 2-0
117 Lordswood v Pagham 0-0
118 Chertsey Town v Beckenham Town 1-4
119 Horley Town v Leatherhead 1-1
120 Lancing v South Park 0-1
121 Epsom & Ewell v Three Bridges 2-1
122 Badshot Lea v Egham Town 2-1
123 Chipstead v Crowborough Athletic 5-2
124 Sittingbourne v Burnham 2-1
125 Faversham Town v Ringmer 3-0
126 Chatham Town v Peacehaven & Telscombe 2-1
127 Crawley Down v Tooting & Mitcham United 1-3
128 Slough Town v Corinthian 4-2
129 Horsham v Raynes Park Vale 2-2
130 Merstham v Walton & Hersham 1-5
131 VCD Athletic v Whitstable Town 2-1
132 Burgess Hill Town v Littlehampton Town 0-3
133 Redhill v Corinthian Casuals 3-0
134 Godalming Town v Ramsgate 5-2
135 Herne Bay v Folkestone Invicta 1-3
136 Dulwich Hamlet v Hythe Town 1-0
137 Maidstone United (2) v Colliers Wood United 4-1
138 Guildford City (2) v East Preston 5-3
139 Eastbourne Town v Chessington & Hook United 2-0
140 Walton Casuals v Thamesmead Town 1-2
141 Ashford United v Lingfield 1-3
142 Worthing v Rye United 5-1
143 Greenwich Borough v Sidley United 2-2
144 Christchurch v Alresford Town 2-1
145 Highworth Town v Shortwood United 1-0
146 Blackfield & Langley v Downton 1-0
147 Mangotsfield United v Bitton 2-0
148 Yate Town v Poole Town 5-0
149 GE Hamble v Totton & Eling 0-1
150 Pewsey Vale v Melksham Town 2-3
151 Moneyfields v Newport (IOW) 0-1
152 Sholing v East Cowes Victoria Athletic 4-0
153 Cadbury Heath v Almondsbury UWE 2-3
154 Hallen v Swindon Supermarine 1-4
155 Horndean v Romsey Town 2-0
156 Wootton Bassett Town v Hamworthy United 1-0
157 Wimborne Town v Fareham Town 0-1
158 Winchester City v Alton Town 3-0
159 Gillingham Town v Bishop Sutton 3-3
160 Wells City v Bodmin Town 0-4
161 Clevedon Town v Tiverton Town 2-0
162 Buckland Athletic v Hengrove Athletic 5-0
163 Sherborne Town v Odd Down 2-0
164 Larkhall Athletic v Bridgwater Town 3-2
165 Paulton Rovers v Taunton Town 1-1
166 Chard Town v Plymouth Parkway 1-4
1r South Shields (3) v Harrogate Railway Athletic 1-0
4r Guisborough Town v Shildon 0-6
12r Holker Old Boys v Crook Town 3-1
17r Bamber Bridge v Staveley MW 5-2
19r Lancaster City v Ashton Athletic 4-1
20r Burscough v Padiham 2-1e
31r Curzon Ashton v Northwich Victoria 2-2P
33r Radcliffe Borough v Clitheroe 0-1
37r Mickleover Sports v New Mills 1-1e
49r Norton United v Cradley Town 5-0
56r Nuneaton Griff v Sporting Khalsa 5-1
58r Continental Star v Stourport Swifts 1-3
66r Ely City v Bugbrooke St Michaels 1-3
81r Heybridge Swifts v Felixstowe & Walton United 4-0
86r Leighton Town v St Margaretsbury 2-3
90r Tring Athletic v Ashford Town (Middlesex) 0-2
94r Potters Bar Town v Cheshunt 3-1
97r Stotfold v Colney Heath 3-7
101r Wembley v Uxbridge 0-5
117r Pagham v Lordswood 1-1P
119r Leatherhead v Horley Town 3-0
129r Raynes Park Vale v Horsham 1-3
143r Sidley United v Greenwich Borough 0-1 N
159r Bishop Sutton v Gillingham Town 2-3
165r Taunton Town v Paulton Rovers 3-2

Qualifying Round One

1 Spennymoor Town v South Shields (3) 2-0
2 Tadcaster Albion v Holker Old Boys 3-0
3 Durham City v Shildon 1-3
4 Farsley AFC v Ossett Albion 1-1
5 Ossett Town v Whitby Town 1-1
6 Bedlington Terriers v Bishop Auckland 0-1
7 Dunston UTS v Kendal Town 3-3
8 Ashington v West Auckland Town 2-3
9 Eccleshill United v North Ferriby United 0-2
10 Blyth Spartans v Garforth Town 1-0
11 Abbey Hey v Atherton Collieries 2-1
12 Warrington Town v Maine Road 1-0
13 Burscough v Witton Albion 2-4
14 Worksop Town v Frickley Athletic 0-2
15 Skelmersdale United v Clitheroe 1-0
16 Lancaster City v Salford City 0-4
17 Chorley v Nantwich Town 2-0
18 Bootle v Bamber Bridge 1-2
19 Prescot Cables v Ashton United 1-3
20 Stocksbridge Park Steels v Marine 0-3
21 FC United of Manchester v Cammell Laird 5-0
22 Runcorn Town v Trafford 0-4
23 Curzon Ashton v Maltby Main 8-1
24 AFC Fylde v Ramsbottom United 3-1
25 Retford United v New Mills 2-2

2012/13

26	Matlock Town v Belper Town	2-2
27	Holbeach United v Stamford	1-2
28	Eastwood Town v Blaby & Whetstone Athletic	1-1
29	Quorn v Buxton	1-2
30	Thurnby Nirvana v Gresley	2-2
31	Loughborough Dynamo v Grantham Town	2-2
32	Rainworth MW v Carlton Town	2-2
33	Coalville Town v Ilkeston FC	0-1
34	Dudley Town v Nuneaton Griff	0-1
35	Rugby Town v Bedworth United	1-1
36	Chasetown v Market Drayton Town	1-1
37	Redditch United v Hednesford Town	0-3
38	Norton United v Westfields	2-5
39	Barwell v AFC Wulfrunians	3-0
40	Bridgnorth Town v Rushall Olympic	3-1
41	Leamington v Stourbridge	2-2
42	Sutton Coldfield Town v Gornal Athletic	0-3
43	Stourport Swifts v Stafford Rangers	1-1
44	Wolverhampton Casuals v Tividale	1-1
45	Leek Town v Bewdley Town	5-1
46	Cambridge City v Huntingdon Town	7-0
47	Daventry Town v King's Lynn Town	1-1
48	St Neots Town v Peterborough Northern Star	5-0
49	Wisbech Town v Kettering Town	0-0
50	Bugbrooke St Michaels v Dereham Town	1-4
51	Tilbury v Lowestoft Town	0-2
52	Heybridge Swifts v AFC Sudbury	4-1
53	Soham Town Rangers v Maldon & Tiptree	0-2
54	Basildon United v Thurrock	0-3
55	Bury Town v Canvey Island	3-0
56	Wroxham v Brentwood Town	0-5
57	Leiston v Southend Manor	5-1
58	Concord Rangers v Needham Market	1-0
59	East Thurrock United v Witham Town	2-0
60	Grays Athletic v Norwich United	2-1
61	Aveley v Hadleigh United	6-1
62	Dunstable Town v Ashford Town (Middlesex)	2-2
63	AFC Kempston Rovers v Hampton & Richmond Boro.	0-3
64	Chesham United v Northwood	0-1
65	Enfield Town v St Margaretsbury	2-0
66	Harrow Borough v St Albans City	1-3
67	London Lions v AFC Dunstable	2-4 N
68	Hemel Hempstead Town v Waltham Forest	2-5
69	Waltham Abbey v Bedford Town	1-0
70	Hendon v Potters Bar Town	1-1
71	Uxbridge v Berkhamsted	3-4
72	Ware v Hitchin Town	0-5
73	Barton Rovers v Arlesey Town	0-1
74	Colney Heath v Harefield United	1-2
75	Wingate & Finchley v Royston Town	1-1
76	Wealdstone v Biggleswade Town	2-0
77	Bishop's Cleeve v Bracknell Town	6-0
78	Chalfont St Peter v Newport Pagnell Town	3-2
79	Windsor v Didcot Town	0-1
80	Cinderford Town v Merthyr Town (2)	1-1
81	Hungerford Town v Banbury United	1-1
82	North Leigh v Wantage Town	6-1
83	Marlow v Thatcham Town	1-3
84	Littlehampton Town v Eastbourne Town	0-1
85	VCD Athletic v Horsham	0-1
86	Slough Town v Lingfield	4-1
87	Faversham Town v Margate	2-2
88	Bognor Regis Town v Epsom & Ewell	4-0
89	Badshot Lea v Folkestone Invicta	3-2
90	Godalming Town v Dulwich Hamlet	2-2
91	Leatherhead v Tooting & Mitcham United	3-1
92	Greenwich Borough v Cray Wanderers	0-1
93	Redhill v Lewes	1-3
94	Beckenham Town v Metropolitan Police	1-7
95	South Park v Walton & Hersham	1-1
96	Chipstead v Maidstone United (2)	0-4
97	Pagham v Carshalton Athletic	0-0
98	Guildford City (2) v Kingstonian	0-3
99	Whitehawk v Sittingbourne	5-0
100	Thamesmead Town v Worthing	2-0
101	Hastings United (2) v Chatham Town	3-1
102	Fareham Town v Christchurch	2-1
103	Newport (IOW) v Horndean	2-0
104	Chippenham Town v Mangotsfield United	3-1
105	Blackfield & Langley v Almondsbury UWE	4-0
106	Totton & Eling v Weymouth	2-2
107	Winchester City v Yate Town	1-2
108	Swindon Supermarine v AFC Totton	0-6
109	Wootton Bassett Town v Highworth Town	3-1
110	Sholing v Melksham Town	4-0
111	Bashley v Gosport Borough	1-1
112	Plymouth Parkway v Buckland Athletic	1-1
113	Gillingham Town v Taunton Town	0-0
114	Bideford v Bodmin Town	2-2
115	Larkhall Athletic v Frome Town	0-0
116	Clevedon Town v Sherborne Town	5-0
4r	Ossett Albion v Farsley AFC	1-0
5r	Whitby Town v Ossett Town	1-0
7r	Kendal Town v Dunston UTS	4-2e
26r	Belper Town v Matlock Town	3-0
28r	Blaby & Whetstone Athletic v Eastwood Town	1-3
30r	Gresley v Thurnby Nirvana	4-1
31r	Grantham Town v Loughborough Dynamo	3-1
32r	Carlton Town v Rainworth MW	3-1
35r	Bedworth United v Rugby Town	1-0e
36r	Market Drayton Town v Chasetown	1-2e
41r	Stourbridge v Leamington	1-2
43r	Stafford Rangers v Stourport Swifts	2-1e
44r	Tividale v Wolverhampton Casuals	4-2
47r	King's Lynn Town v Daventry Town	2-3e
49r	Kettering Town v Wisbech Town	3-0
62r	Ashford Town (Middlesex) v Dunstable Town	3-0e
70r	Potters Bar Town v Hendon	0-3
75r	Royston Town v Wingate & Finchley	2-3e
80r	Merthyr Town (2) v Cinderford Town	3-0
81r	Banbury United v Hungerford Town	0-2
87r	Margate v Faversham Town	3-0
90r	Dulwich Hamlet v Godalming Town	2-2P
95r	Walton & Hersham v South Park	0-1
97r	Carshalton Athletic v Pagham	3-0
106r	Weymouth v Totton & Eling	3-0
111r	Gosport Borough v Bashley	3-2e
112r	Buckland Athletic v Plymouth Parkway	5-1
113r	Taunton Town v Gillingham Town	1-3
114r	Bodmin Town v Bideford	2-3e
115r	Frome Town v Larkhall Athletic	4-0

Qualifying Round Two

1	Bishop Auckland v AFC Fylde	1-2
2	FC Halifax Town v Abbey Hey	6-0
3	Curzon Ashton v Bradford Park Avenue	1-3
4	Blyth Spartans v Workington	1-1
5	Shildon v Altrincham	0-3
6	Ashton United v Marine	0-2
7	Salford City v FC United of Manchester	2-3
8	Trafford v Spennymoor Town	5-3
9	Stalybridge Celtic v Vauxhall Motors	1-0
10	Bamber Bridge v Guiseley	0-1
11	Kendal Town v Witton Albion	4-2
12	Colwyn Bay v Warrington Town	3-2
13	Gainsborough Trinity v Chester FC	1-1
14	Tadcaster Albion v Skelmersdale United	4-1
15	Whitby Town v Droylsden	4-3
16	North Ferriby United v Ossett Albion	1-2
17	West Auckland Town v Harrogate Town	2-2
18	Chorley v Frickley Athletic	1-3
19	Gornal Athletic v Worcester City	0-4
20	Boston United v Kettering Town	1-0
21	Solihull Moors v Westfields	1-1
22	Hinckley United v Tividale	5-3
23	Cambridge City v Grantham Town	3-1
24	Eastwood Town v Histon	3-5
25	Nuneaton Griff v Hednesford Town	2-3
26	Gresley v Stafford Rangers	3-2
27	Carlton Town v New Mills	4-3
28	Brackley Town v Daventry Town	4-0
29	Dereham Town v Chasetown	2-1
30	Ilkeston FC v Belper Town	2-2
31	Stamford v Buxton	1-3
32	Leek Town v Bridgnorth Town	3-0
33	Barwell v Bedworth United	3-2
34	Corby Town v Leamington	3-2
35	Northwood v AFC Dunstable	1-1
36	Wealdstone v Lowestoft Town	1-2
37	Ashford Town (Middlesex) v St Albans City	2-6
38	Hayes & Yeading United v Heybridge Swifts	3-2
39	Carshalton Athletic v Chalfont St Peter	0-1
40	Hendon v Lewes	3-0
41	St Neots Town v Boreham Wood	1-2
42	Chelmsford City v Leatherhead	2-1
43	Dover Athletic v Tonbridge Angels	2-1
44	Brentwood Town v Maldon & Tiptree	1-1
45	Badshot Lea v Leiston	4-2
46	Aveley v Margate	1-4
47	Waltham Abbey v Eastbourne Borough	2-4
48	Billericay Town v AFC Hornchurch	3-1
49	Concord Rangers v Welling United	1-1
50	Enfield Town v Bishop's Stortford	1-4
51	Cray Wanderers v Thamesmead Town	3-1
52	Waltham Forest v Hampton & Richmond Boro.	0-1
53	Whitehawk v Hitchin Town	1-1
54	South Park v Harefield United	0-0
55	Arlesey Town v Dulwich Hamlet	1-0
56	Staines Town v Hastings United (2)	2-3
57	Berkhamsted v Metropolitan Police	0-3
58	Slough Town v Eastbourne Town	5-1
59	Bury Town v Wingate & Finchley	2-1
60	Horsham v Thurrock	1-2
61	Sutton United v Bromley	0-1
62	Grays Athletic v Maidstone United (2)	0-5
63	Kingstonian v East Thurrock United	2-3
64	Bishop's Cleeve v Chippenham Town	1-2
65	Truro City v AFC Totton	2-3
66	Dorchester Town v Wootton Bassett Town	4-0
67	Buckland Athletic v Bath City	1-2
68	Gloucester City v Thatcham Town	2-1
69	Gillingham Town v Sholing	1-3
70	North Leigh v Havant & Waterlooville	1-0
71	Basingstoke Town v Weymouth	3-1
72	Merthyr Town (2) v Hungerford Town	0-0
73	Frome Town v Weston-Super-Mare	0-2
74	Didcot Town v Clevedon Town	3-1
75	Newport (IOW) v Salisbury City	0-3
76	Gosport Borough v Bideford	2-0
77	Fareham Town v Blackfield & Langley	0-2
78	Farnborough v Eastleigh	1-2
79	Maidenhead United v Bognor Regis Town	4-2
80	Yate Town v Oxford City	2-1
4r	Workington v Blyth Spartans	1-0
13r	Chester FC v Gainsborough Trinity	2-1e
17r	Harrogate Town v West Auckland Town	5-1
21r	Westfields v Solihull Moors	1-2
30r	Belper Town v Ilkeston FC	1-5
35r	AFC Dunstable v Northwood	0-3
44r	Maldon & Tiptree v Brentwood Town	1-1q
49r	Welling United v Concord Rangers	2-1
53r	Hitchin Town v Whitehawk	5-0
54r	Harefield United v South Park	1-4
72r	Hungerford Town v Merthyr Town (2)	1-1q

Qualifying Round Three

1	Ilkeston FC v Gresley	4-2
2	Chester FC v FC Halifax Town	1-1
3	Hednesford Town v Buxton	2-2
4	AFC Fylde v Solihull Moors	4-1
5	Carlton Town v Bradford Park Avenue	1-3
6	Colwyn Bay v Guiseley	1-1
7	Stalybridge Celtic v Whitby Town	3-1
8	Barwell v Workington	1-1
9	Hinckley United v Ossett Albion	2-2
10	FC United of Manchester v Kendal Town	3-1
11	Leek Town v Altrincham	0-2
12	Trafford v Marine	1-3
13	Harrogate Town v Frickley Athletic	3-2
14	Tadcaster Albion v Boston United	0-2
15	Hastings United (2) v Hitchin Town	2-2
16	Histon v Corby Town	1-1
17	Cambridge City v Billericay Town	1-1
18	Margate v Slough Town	0-1
19	Dereham Town v Metropolitan Police	1-1
20	South Park v Brentwood Town	3-1
21	Chalfont St Peter v Bishop's Stortford	1-1
22	Cray Wanderers v Chelmsford City	1-2
23	Dover Athletic v Bromley	1-2
24	Northwood v Boreham Wood	0-4
25	East Thurrock United v Maidstone United (2)	3-0
26	Bury Town v Hampton & Richmond Boro.	4-0
27	St Albans City v Lowestoft Town	0-1
28	Eastbourne Borough v Hendon	2-2
29	Arlesey Town v Brackley Town	4-3
30	Welling United v Thurrock	1-1
31	Weston-Super-Mare v Worcester City	1-1
32	Dorchester Town v Basingstoke Town	1-0
33	Yate Town v North Leigh	2-1
34	Gloucester City v Eastleigh	1-0
35	Chippenham Town v Badshot Lea	3-1
36	Didcot Town v Maidenhead United	1-0
37	AFC Totton v Merthyr Town (2)	3-2
38	Bath City v Gosport Borough	1-1
39	Sholing v Blackfield & Langley	1-3
40	Hayes & Yeading United v Salisbury City	2-1
2r	FC Halifax Town v Chester FC	3-1
3r	Buxton v Hednesford Town	2-1e
6r	Guiseley v Colwyn Bay	3-1
8r	Workington v Barwell	2-0
9r	Ossett Albion v Hinckley United	1-0
15r	Hitchin Town v Hastings United (2)	1-2
16r	Corby Town v Histon	2-1
17r	Billericay Town v Cambridge City	2-4
19r	Metropolitan Police v Dereham Town	2-0
21r	Bishop's Stortford v Chalfont St Peter	3-1
28r	Hendon v Eastbourne Borough	2-1e
30r	Thurrock v Welling United	1-3
31r	Worcester City v Weston-Super-Mare	1-0
38r	Gosport Borough v Bath City	3-1

Qualifying Round Four

1	Alfreton Town v Gateshead (2)	2-0
2	Hyde FC v Harrogate Town	1-1
3	FC United of Manchester v Hereford United	0-2
4	Barrow v Tamworth	2-0
5	Guiseley v Buxton	2-0
6	Grimsby Town v Kidderminster Harriers	2-4
7	Bradford Park Avenue v Ossett Albion	4-1
8	Wrexham v Southport	2-0
9	AFC Fylde v Ilkeston FC	1-1
10	Boston United v Altrincham	1-3
11	Lincoln City v FC Halifax Town	0-0
12	Macclesfield Town v Marine	3-1
13	Workington v Mansfield Town	1-2
14	Stockport County v Stalybridge Celtic	5-3
15	AFC Telford United v Nuneaton Town	2-2
16	South Park v Metropolitan Police	0-3
17	Didcot Town v Arlesey Town	0-1
18	Forest Green Rovers v Dartford	1-1
19	Yate Town v Newport County (2)	3-3
20	Slough Town v Gosport Borough	0-0
21	Hastings United (2) v Blackfield & Langley	3-0
22	Bromley v Worcester City	1-0
23	Chelmsford City v East Thurrock United	2-2
24	Hayes & Yeading United v Boreham Wood	2-3
25	AFC Totton v Cambridge City	2-3
26	Welling United v Bishop's Stortford	1-3
27	Braintree Town v Lowestoft Town	3-2
28	Dorchester Town v Bury Town	3-1
29	Cambridge United v Luton Town	0-2
30	Gloucester City v Chippenham Town	1-0
31	Corby Town v Hendon	1-2
32	Woking v Ebbsfleet United	0-1
2r	Harrogate Town v Hyde FC	1-0 N
9r	Ilkeston FC v AFC Fylde	0-1
11r	FC Halifax Town v Lincoln City	0-2
15r	Nuneaton Town v AFC Telford United	1-0e
18r	Dartford v Forest Green Rovers	1-4
19r	Newport County (2) v Yate Town	1-3e
20r	Gosport Borough v Slough Town	1-2
23r	East Thurrock United v Chelmsford City	4-4q

2012/13 to 2013/14

Round One

	AFC Fylde v Accrington Stanley (2)	1-4
	Aldershot Town v Hendon	2-1
	Barnet v Oxford United	0-2
	Bishop's Stortford v Hastings United (2)	1-2
	Boreham Wood v Brentford	0-2
	Bournemouth v Dagenham & Redbridge	4-0
	Braintree Town v Tranmere Rovers	0-3
	Bristol Rovers v Sheffield United	1-2
	Burton Albion v Altrincham	3-3
	Bury v Exeter City	1-0
	Cambridge City v Milton Keynes Dons	0-0
	Carlisle United v Ebbsfleet United	4-2
	Chelmsford City v Colchester United	3-1
	Cheltenham Town v Yate Town	3-0
	Chesterfield v Hartlepool United	6-1
	Coventry City v Arlesey Town	3-0
	Crewe Alexandra v Wycombe Wanderers	4-1
	Doncaster Rovers v Bradford Park Avenue	3-1
	Dorchester Town v Plymouth Argyle	1-0
	Fleetwood Town v Bromley	3-0
	Forest Green Rovers v Port Vale	2-3
	Gillingham v Scunthorpe United	4-0
	Gloucester City v Leyton Orient	0-2
	Guiseley v Barrow	2-2
	Hereford United v Shrewsbury Town	3-1
	Kidderminster Harriers v Oldham Athletic	0-2
	Lincoln City v Walsall	1-1
	Luton Town v Nuneaton Town	1-1
	Mansfield Town v Slough Town	0-0
	Metropolitan Police v Crawley Town	1-2
	Morecambe v Rochdale	1-1
	Northampton Town v Bradford City	1-1
	Portsmouth v Notts County	0-2
	Preston North End v Yeovil Town	3-0
	Rotherham United v Stevenage	3-2
	Southend United v Stockport County	3-0
	Swindon Town v Macclesfield Town	0-2
	Torquay United v Harrogate Town	0-1
	Wrexham v Alfreton Town	2-4
	York City v AFC Wimbledon	1-1
r	AFC Wimbledon v York City	4-3e
r	Altrincham v Burton Albion	0-2
r	Barrow v Guiseley	1-0
r	Bradford City v Northampton Town	3-3P
r	Milton Keynes Dons v Cambridge City	6-1
r	Nuneaton Town v Luton Town	0-2
r	Rochdale v Morecambe	0-1
r	Slough Town v Mansfield Town	1-1q
r	Walsall v Lincoln City	2-3e

Round Two

	Accrington Stanley (2) v Oxford United	3-3
	Alfreton Town v Leyton Orient	2-4
	Barrow v Macclesfield Town	1-1
	Bradford City v Brentford	1-1
	Bury v Southend United	1-1
	Carlisle United v Bournemouth	1-3
	Cheltenham Town v Hereford United	1-1
	Coventry City v Morecambe	2-1
	Crawley Town v Chelmsford City	3-0
	Crewe Alexandra v Burton Albion	0-1
	Fleetwood Town v Aldershot Town	2-3
	Harrogate Town v Hastings United (2)	1-1
	Lincoln City v Mansfield Town	3-3
	Luton Town v Dorchester Town	2-1
	Milton Keynes Dons v AFC Wimbledon	2-1
	Oldham Athletic v Doncaster Rovers	3-1
	Preston North End v Gillingham	2-0
	Rotherham United v Notts County	1-1
	Sheffield United v Port Vale	2-1
	Tranmere Rovers v Chesterfield	2-1
r	Brentford v Bradford City	4-2e
r	Hastings United (2) v Harrogate Town	1-1P
r	Hereford United v Cheltenham Town	1-2e
r	Macclesfield Town v Barrow	4-1
r	Mansfield Town v Lincoln City	2-1
r	Notts County v Rotherham United	0-3
r	Oxford United v Accrington Stanley (2)	2-0
r	Southend United v Bury	1-1P

Round Three

	Aldershot Town v Rotherham United	3-1
	Aston Villa v Ipswich Town	2-1
	Barnsley v Burnley	1-0
	Blackburn Rovers v Bristol City	2-0
	Bolton Wanderers v Sunderland	2-2
	Brighton & Hove Albion v Newcastle United	2-0
	Charlton Athletic v Huddersfield Town	0-1
	Cheltenham Town v Everton	1-5
	Crawley Town v Reading	1-3
	Crystal Palace v Stoke City	0-0
	Derby County v Tranmere Rovers	5-0
	Fulham v Blackpool	1-1
	Hull City v Leyton Orient	1-1
	Leeds United v Birmingham City	1-1
	Leicester City v Burton Albion	2-0
	Luton Town v Wolverhampton Wan.	1-0
	Macclesfield Town v Cardiff City	2-1
	Manchester City v Watford	3-0
	Mansfield Town v Liverpool	1-2
	Middlesbrough v Hastings United (2)	4-1
	Millwall v Preston North End	1-0
	Nottingham Forest v Oldham Athletic	2-3
	Oxford United v Sheffield United	0-3
	Peterborough United v Norwich City	0-3
	Queen's Park Rangers v West Bromwich Albion	1-1
	Sheffield Wednesday v Milton Keynes Dons	0-0
	Southampton v Chelsea	1-5
	Southend United v Brentford	2-2
	Swansea City v Arsenal	2-2
	Tottenham Hotspur v Coventry City	3-0
	West Ham United v Manchester United	2-2
	Wigan Athletic v Bournemouth	1-1
r	Arsenal v Swansea City	1-0
r	Birmingham City v Leeds United	1-2
r	Blackpool v Fulham	1-2e
r	Bournemouth v Wigan Athletic	0-1
r	Brentford v Southend United	2-1
r	Leyton Orient v Hull City	1-2e
r	Manchester United v West Ham United	1-0
r	Milton Keynes Dons v Sheffield Wednesday	2-0
r	Stoke City v Crystal Palace	4-1
r	Sunderland v Bolton Wanderers	0-2
r	West Bromwich Albion v Queen's Park Rangers	0-1

Round Four

	Bolton Wanderers v Everton	1-2
	Brentford v Chelsea	2-2
	Brighton & Hove Albion v Arsenal	2-3
	Derby County v Blackburn Rovers	0-3
	Huddersfield Town v Leicester City	1-1
	Hull City v Barnsley	0-1
	Leeds United v Tottenham Hotspur	2-1
	Macclesfield Town v Wigan Athletic	0-1
	Manchester United v Fulham	4-1
	Middlesbrough v Aldershot Town	2-1
	Millwall v Aston Villa	2-1
	Norwich City v Luton Town	0-1
	Oldham Athletic v Liverpool	3-2
	Queen's Park Rangers v Milton Keynes Dons	2-4
	Reading v Sheffield United	4-0
	Stoke City v Manchester City	0-1
r	Chelsea v Brentford	4-0
r	Leicester City v Huddersfield Town	1-2

Round Five

	Arsenal v Blackburn Rovers	0-1
	Huddersfield Town v Wigan Athletic	1-4
	Luton Town v Millwall	0-3
	Manchester City v Leeds United	4-0
	Manchester United v Reading	2-1
	Middlesbrough v Chelsea	0-2
	Milton Keynes Dons v Barnsley	1-3
	Oldham Athletic v Everton	2-2
r	Everton v Oldham Athletic	3-1

Round Six

	Everton v Wigan Athletic	0-3
	Manchester City v Barnsley	5-0
	Manchester United v Chelsea	2-2
	Millwall v Blackburn Rovers	0-0
r	Blackburn Rovers v Millwall	0-1
r	Chelsea v Manchester United	1-0

Semi Finals

Manchester City v Chelsea	2-1 N
Wigan Athletic v Millwall	2-0 N

Final

Wigan Athletic v Manchester City	1-0 N

2013/14

Extra Preliminary Round

1	Darlington Railway Ath. v Newton Aycliffe	1-5
2	Thackley v Guisborough Town	1-3
3	Glasshoughton Welfare v Jarrow Roofing Boldon CA	2-3
4	Colne v South Shields (3)	1-1
5	Brighouse Town v Seaham Red Star	3-1
6	Ashington v Pontefract Collieries	9-0
7	Dunston UTS v Pickering Town	4-1
8	Garforth Town v Shildon	1-4
9	Silsden v Bridlington Town (2)	1-2
10	Crook Town v Billingham Town	4-2
11	Northallerton Town v Whitehaven	2-4
12	Morpeth Town v Liversedge	6-0
13	Billingham Synthonia v West Allotment Celtic	4-0
14	Spennymoor Town v Sunderland RCA	2-1
15	Team Northumbria v Whitley Bay	2-1
16	Bishop Auckland v Tadcaster Albion	0-0
17	Albion Sports v North Shields	2-0
18	Hebburn Town v Barnoldswick Town	2-2
19	Penrith v Newcastle Benfield	3-1
20	Marske United v Consett	3-1
21	Tow Law Town v West Auckland Town	0-5
22	Durham City v Hall Road Rangers	6-1
23	Runcorn Town v Winterton Rangers	7-2
24	Stockport Sports v Winsford United	1-2
25	Worksop Parramore v AFC Blackpool	2-0
26	Maltby Main v Congleton Town	1-4
27	Bacup & Rossendale Borough v Formby	1-4
28	Bootle v Squires Gate	2-1
29	Barton Town Old Boys v Nostell MW	2-1
30	Maine Road v Runcorn Linnets	0-3
31	Parkgate v Shirebrook Town	0-3
32	AFC Emley v Wigan Robin Park	3-2
33	AFC Liverpool v Cheadle Town	1-0
34	Armthorpe Welfare v Glossop North End	1-4
35	Alsager Town v Atherton Collieries	1-3
36	Staveley MW v Ashton Town	2-1
37	West Didsbury & Chorlton v Abbey Hey	2-0
38	St Helens Town v Ashton Athletic	2-2
39	Boldmere St Michaels v Tipton Town	0-2
40	Bolehall Swifts v Causeway United	2-2
41	Bewdley Town v Coventry Sphinx	0-3
42	Rocester v Atherstone Town	3-3
43	Gornal Athletic v Ellesmere Rangers	1-2
44	Westfields v Lye Town	2-3
45	Studley v Stafford Town	5-0
46	Heath Hayes v Black Country Rangers	1-3
47	Walsall Wood v Continental Star	4-1
48	Norton United v Southam United	7-1
49	Tividale v Alvechurch	3-0
50	Stourport Swifts v Coleshill Town	3-1
51	AFC Wulfrunians v Earlswood Town	4-1
52	Wolverhampton Casuals v Pegasus Juniors	7-1
53	Nuneaton Griff v Brocton	2-3
54	Shawbury United v Dudley Town	0-0
55	Thurnby Nirvana v Kirby Muxloe	0-0
56	Quorn v Holbrook Sports	5-1
57	Retford United v Heanor Town	3-1
58	Graham Street Primitives v Shepshed Dynamo	1-3
59	Harborough Town v Teversal	2-1
60	Dunkirk v Barrow Town	4-0
61	Stewarts & Lloyds (2) v Arnold Town	1-1
62	Lincoln Moorlands Railway v Long Eaton United	2-4
63	Basford United v Holwell Sports	1-0
64	Borrowash Victoria v Louth Town	2-1
65	Desborough Town v Oadby Town	3-1
66	Blaby & Whetstone Athletic v Heather St Johns	2-0
67	Loughborough University v Hucknall Town	wo/s
68	Gorleston v Deeping Rangers	2-1
69	Boston Town v Great Yarmouth Town	3-2
70	Godmanchester Rovers v Blackstones	6-3
71	Holbeach United v Norwich United	2-1
72	Thetford Town v Diss Town	1-0
73	Ely City v Sleaford Town	0-3
74	Yaxley v Peterborough Northern Star	0-3
75	Huntingdon Town v Fakenham Town	4-1
76	Spalding United v Eynesbury Rovers	4-2
77	Swaffham Town v Wisbech Town	2-1
78	FC Clacton v Sporting Bengal United	3-1
79	Great Wakering Rovers v Halstead Town	5-0
80	Whitton United v London APSA	4-1
81	Kirkley & Pakefield v Brightlingsea Regent	2-2
82	Stansted v Brantham Athletic	0-0
83	Clapton v Stanway Rovers	0-0
84	Sawbridgeworth Town v Mildenhall Town	1-6
85	Haverhill Rovers v Eton Manor	3-1
86	Newmarket Town v Ilford	3-1
87	Ipswich Wanderers v Wivenhoe Town	0-0
88	Barking v Bowers & Pitsea	3-1
89	Woodbridge Town v Hullbridge Sports	0-2
90	Basildon United v Southend Manor	2-2
91	Walsham Le Willows v Tower Hamlets	0-1
92	Takeley v Hadleigh United	0-2
93	Felixstowe & Walton United v Saffron Walden Town	3-0
94	Berkhamsted v AFC Dunstable	2-1
95	Hadley v Oxhey Jets	1-1
96	AFC Kempston Rovers v Wembley	0-1
97	Wellingborough Town (2) v Greenhouse London	3-3
98	Hoddesdon Town v St Margaretsbury	1-1
99	Kings Langley v Long Buckby	3-1
100	Newport Pagnell Town v Hatfield Town	2-0
101	Hillingdon Borough v Leverstock Green	4-2
102	Cogenhoe United v Tring Athletic	0-0
103	London Lions v Stotfold	1-1
104	Irchester United v Biggleswade United	0-2
105	Harefield United v Woodford United	3-0
106	Codicote v Crawley Green	1-1
107	Holmer Green v Ampthill Town	2-3
108	Hertford Town v Colney Heath	2-1
109	Northampton Spencer v Bugbrooke St Michaels	2-0
110	Haringey Borough v Rushden & Higham United	6-0
111	Enfield 1893 v London Tigers	0-0
112	Cockfosters v Hanwell Town	1-1
113	London Colney v AFC Rushden & Diamonds	1-1
114	Sandhurst Town v Farnham Town	2-2
115	Tadley Calleva v Ascot United	2-4 d
116	Bracknell Town v Fairford Town	2-1
117	Holyport v Hanworth Villa	2-7
118	Staines Lammas v Badshot Lea	0-2
119	Ardley United v Thame United	4-1
120	Camberley Town v Chinnor	2-0
121	Reading Town v Wantage Town	0-5
122	Frimley Green v Ash United	3-2
123	Flackwell Heath v Binfield	0-0
124	Bedfont Sports v Abingdon United	2-2
125	Westfield v Shrivenham	2-1
126	Cheltenham Saracens v Slimbridge	0-0
127	Cove v Carterton	5-0
128	Newbury (2) v Windsor	1-4
129	Kidlington v Hartley Wintney	1-1

2013/14

130 Abingdon Town v Highmoor Ibis 1-5
131 Dorking (2) v Shoreham 1-4
132 Alton Town v Selsey 3-1
133 Dorking Wanderers v Canterbury City 5-0
134 East Preston v Crowborough Athletic 0-0
135 Ashford United v Worthing United 0-0
136 Sevenoaks Town v Horley Town 1-4
137 Erith Town v Sidley United wo/s
138 Whyteleafe v Epsom & Ewell 3-3
139 Holmesdale v East Grinstead Town 1-0
140 Horsham YMCA v Hassocks 2-3
141 Molesey v Hailsham Town 8-1
142 Littlehampton Town v St Francis Rangers 3-1
143 Chichester City v Chessington & Hook United 1-8
144 Pagham v Tunbridge Wells 2-4
145 Mole Valley SCR v South Park 0-1
146 Cray Valley Paper Mills v Lancing 1-1
147 Arundel v Rye United 0-0
148 Beckenham Town v Corinthian 1-2
149 Epsom Athletic v Croydon 1-3
150 Lordswood v Eastbourne United 1-4
151 Raynes Park Vale v Lingfield 2-1
152 Greenwich Borough v Ringmer 2-2
153 Fisher v Deal Town 1-2
154 Colliers Wood United v AFC Croydon Athletic 6-2
155 Newport (IOW) v Verwood Town 4-1
156 Bournemouth (Ams) v Highworth Town 3-1
157 Team Solent v AFC Portchester 1-3
158 Bradford Town v Longwell Green Sports 1-2
159 Horndean v Calne Town 7-2
160 Cowes Sports v Fawley 4-1
161 Wootton Bassett Town v Totton & Eling 0-2
162 Alresford Town v Winchester City 0-3
163 Downton v Sholing 1-3
164 Melksham Town v Hamworthy United 3-3
165 Christchurch v Sherborne Town 1-2
166 Bitton v Pewsey Vale 4-1
167 Folland Sports v Winterbourne United 4-1
168 Moneyfields v Cadbury Heath 2-1
169 Hallen v Whitchurch United 1-1
170 Corsham Town v Gillingham Town 3-1
171 Petersfield Town v Blackfield & Langley 4-3
172 Bemerton Heath Harlequins v Fareham Town 1-4
173 Romsey Town v Brockenhurst 1-4
174 Bristol Manor Farm v Oldland Abbotonians 9-3
175 East Cowes Victoria Athletic v Lymington Town 0-3
176 Hengrove Athletic v Bridport 0-2
177 Willand Rovers v Larkhall Athletic 0-4
178 St Blazey v Tavistock 1-0
179 Bishop Sutton v Odd Down 1-1
180 Shepton Mallet v Street 0-0
181 AFC St Austell v Ilfracombe Town 1-4
182 Buckland Athletic v Wells City 0-3
183 Barnstaple Town v Brislington 0-2
184 Plymouth Parkway v Saltash United 2-1
185 Radstock Town v Bodmin Town 1-4
4r South Shields (3) v Colne 2-1
16r Tadcaster Albion v Bishop Auckland 0-3
18r Barnoldswick Town v Hebburn Town 0-2
38r Ashton Athletic v St Helens Town 1-0
40r Causeway United v Bolehall Swifts 0-4
42r Atherstone Town v Rocester 1-0
54r Dudley Town v Shawbury United 1-2
55r Kirby Muxloe v Thurnby Nirvana 2-2P
61r Arnold Town v Stewarts & Lloyds (2) 2-1
81r Brightlingsea Regent v Kirkley & Pakefield 1-2
82r Brantham Athletic v Stansted 6-1
83r Stanway Rovers v Clapton 0-1
87r Wivenhoe Town v Ipswich Wanderers 0-1
90r Southend Manor v Basildon United 1-2
95r Oxhey Jets v Hadley 0-1
97r Greenhouse London v Wellingborough Town (2) 5-3e
98r St Margaretsbury v Hoddesdon Town 4-1
102r Tring Athletic v Cogenhoe United 3-0
103r Stotfold v London Lions 1-0
106r Crawley Green v Codicote 3-1
111r London Tigers v Enfield 1893 2-1
112r Hanwell Town v Cockfosters 0-1
113r AFC Rushden & Diamonds v London Colney 6-1
114r Farnham Town v Sandhurst Town 4-1
123r Binfield v Flackwell Heath 3-2
124r Abingdon United v Bedfont Sports 0-1
126r Slimbridge v Cheltenham Saracens 1-1q
129r Hartley Wintney v Kidlington 5-2
134r Crowborough Athletic v East Preston 2-3
135r Worthing United v Ashford United 0-1
138r Epsom & Ewell v Whyteleafe 1-6
146r Lancing v Cray Valley Paper Mills 0-4
147r Arundel v Rye United 1-2
152r Ringmer v Greenwich Borough 1-3
164r Hamworthy United v Melksham Town 3-1e
169r Whitchurch United v Hallen 0-2
179r Odd Down v Bishop Sutton 1-2
180r Street v Shepton Mallet 2-0

Preliminary Round

1 Kendal Town v Crook Town 2-4
2 Billingham Synthonia v Brighouse Town 1-1
3 Jarrow Roofing Boldon CA v Dunston UTS 2-1
4 Whitehaven v Team Northumbria 0-2
5 Hebburn Town v Marske United 1-2
6 Padiham v Clitheroe 3-1
7 Scarborough Athletic v Ashington 4-1
8 Newton Aycliffe v Spennymoor Town 3-3
9 Farsley AFC v Lancaster City 1-3
10 Albion Sports v South Shields (3) 3-3
11 Shildon v Penrith 0-2
12 Goole AFC v Bishop Auckland 0-2
13 Guisborough Town v Bridlington Town (2) 1-1
14 Durham City v Morpeth Town 1-1
15 Harrogate Railway Athletic v West Auckland Town 2-2
16 Formby v Northwich Victoria 0-3
17 Bootle v Barton Town Old Boys 4-1
18 Ossett Town v AFC Emley 3-0
19 Mossley v Worksop Parramore 1-1
20 Atherton Collieries v Radcliffe Borough 1-1
21 Bamber Bridge v Staveley MW 1-0
22 Cammell Laird v Salford City 2-0
23 Prescot Cables v Congleton Town 0-0
24 Sheffield v Shirebrook Town 1-1
25 Curzon Ashton v Ashton Athletic 4-0
26 Warrington Town v Winsford United 5-1
27 Ossett Albion v Runcorn Linnets 1-3
28 Runcorn Town v Glossop North End 0-1
29 Wakefield v New Mills 0-2
30 West Didsbury & Chorlton v Burscough 0-3
31 Ramsbottom United v AFC Liverpool 5-0
32 Newcastle Town v Shawbury United 2-1
33 Rugby Town v Norton United 1-1
34 Tividale v Wolverhampton Casuals 3-0
35 Stourport Swifts v AFC Wulfrunians 1-1
36 Black Country Rangers v Halesowen Town 1-2
37 Chasetown v Romulus 3-1
38 Sutton Coldfield Town v Bedworth United 1-0
39 Coventry Sphinx v Lye Town 2-1
40 Leek Town v Walsall Wood 2-2
41 Atherstone Town v Studley 3-1
42 Market Drayton Town v Kidsgrove Athletic 1-3
43 Evesham United v Bolehall Swifts 2-1
44 Brocton v Ellesmere Rangers 6-0
45 Tipton Town v Stratford Town 1-0
46 Loughborough Dynamo v Eastwood Town 0-1
47 Kettering Town v Gresley 0-2
48 Basford United v Quorn 2-2
49 Dunkirk v Rainworth MW 1-1
50 Coalville Town v Lincoln United 7-1
51 Desborough Town v Loughborough University 2-4
52 Kirby Muxloe v Blaby & Whetstone Athletic 0-2
53 Carlton Town v Borrowash Victoria 2-0
54 Arnold Town v Brigg Town 2-2
55 Long Eaton United v Shepshed Dynamo 4-0
56 Mickleover Sports v Harborough Town 8-0
57 Belper Town v Retford United 5-0
58 Sleaford Town v Godmanchester Rovers 2-0
59 Swaffham Town v Huntingdon Town 0-2
60 Spalding United v Holbeach United 4-0
61 Gorleston v Thetford Town 4-1
62 Peterborough Northern Star v Wroxham 2-4
63 St Ives Town v Soham Town Rangers 3-1
64 Boston Town v Dereham Town 1-3
65 Brantham Athletic v Barkingside 1-0
66 Clapton v Mildenhall Town 0-2
67 AFC Sudbury v Ipswich Wanderers 4-1
68 Waltham Abbey v Whitton United 1-1
69 Basildon United v Heybridge Swifts 0-3
70 Harlow Town v Tower Hamlets 4-1
71 Aveley v Waltham Forest 7-0
72 Tilbury v Kirkley & Pakefield 2-0
73 Witham Town v Newmarket Town 0-0
74 Thurrock v Felixstowe & Walton United 3-0
75 Brentwood Town v Great Wakering Rovers 3-2
76 Needham Market v Haverhill Rovers 3-2
77 FC Clacton v Hullbridge Sports 3-0
78 Redbridge v Burnham Ramblers 1-3
79 Hadleigh United v Romford 0-5
80 Maldon & Tiptree v Barking 1-1
81 St Margaretsbury v London Tigers 1-0
82 Kings Langley v Newport Pagnell Town 2-1
83 Uxbridge v Stotfold 5-1
84 Ware v Wembley 1-5
85 Crawley Green v Dunstable Town 0-3
86 Barton Rovers v Ampthill Town 4-0
87 Haringey Borough v AFC Hayes 2-1
88 Potters Bar Town v Greenhouse London 0-3
89 North Greenford United v Tring Athletic 3-0
90 Royston Town v Northampton Spencer 3-3
91 Cockfosters v Hadley 2-1
92 Daventry Town v Hillingdon Borough 1-0
93 Berkhamsted v Harefield United 4-1
94 Northwood v AFC Rushden & Diamonds 1-2
95 Hertford Town v Cheshunt 4-2
96 Leighton Town v Biggleswade United 1-3
97 Bedfont Sports v North Leigh 1-3
98 Beaconsfield SYCOB v Bracknell Town 5-3
99 Badshot Lea v Hartley Wintney 2-3
100 Wantage Town v Didcot Town 2-3
101 Marlow v Chertsey Town 1-2
102 Slough Town v Cirencester Town 1-1
103 Ashford Town (Middlesex) v Bishop's Cleeve 0-0
104 Binfield v Cheltenham Saracens 0-0
105 Shortwood United v Egham Town 2-1
106 Ardley United v Hanworth Villa 1-0
107 Chalfont St Peter v Tadley Calleva 5-3
108 Fleet Town v Westfield 0-1
109 Windsor v Highmoor Ibis 1-3
110 Aylesbury v Thatcham Town 2-1
111 Frimley Green v Cove 0-2
112 Cinderford Town v Aylesbury United 1-3
113 Farnham Town v Camberley Town 0-3
114 Erith & Belvedere v Chatham Town 0-5
115 Littlehampton Town v Greenwich Borough 1-0
116 Raynes Park Vale v Alton Town 4-4
117 Eastbourne United v Herne Bay 2-2
118 Guildford City (2) v South Park 0-4
119 Folkestone Invicta v Molesey 3-3
120 Colliers Wood United v East Preston 1-3
121 Merstham v Deal Town 4-2
122 Croydon v Whyteleafe 0-2
123 Hastings United (2) v Ramsgate 1-0
124 Leatherhead v Tooting & Mitcham United 1-0
125 Shoreham v Walton Casuals 2-1
126 Crawley Down Gatwick v Guernsey 1-3
127 Horley Town v Holmesdale 5-3
128 Dorking Wanderers v Hassocks 0-0
129 Walton & Hersham v Horsham 0-2
130 Chipstead v Rye United 3-2
131 Eastbourne Town v Corinthian 1-0
132 Faversham Town v Worthing 5-1
133 VCD Athletic v Burgess Hill Town 1-3
134 Chessington & Hook United v Sittingbourne 0-1
135 Corinthian Casuals v Erith Town 3-0
136 Peacehaven & Telscombe v Ashford United 4-0
137 Three Bridges v Hythe Town 2-1
138 Tunbridge Wells v Whitstable Town 0-0
139 Cray Valley Paper Mills v Redhill 0-2
140 Corsham Town v Sherborne Town 2-0
141 Moneyfields v Longwell Green Sports 2-2
142 Godalming Town v AFC Portchester 0-1
143 Bournemouth (Ams) v Hallen 2-4
144 Winchester City v Swindon Supermarine 3-0
145 Yate Town v Cowes Sports 2-1
146 Bristol Manor Farm v Lymington Town 7-1
147 Petersfield Town v Horndean 1-2
148 Wimborne Town v Hamworthy United 1-3
149 Newport (IOW) v Fareham Town 0-2
150 Brockenhurst v Folland Sports 2-0
151 Totton & Eling v Sholing 0-0
152 Mangotsfield United v Bitton 3-0
153 Taunton Town v Bridgwater Town 1-1
154 Bridport v Merthyr Town (2) 2-3
155 Clevedon Town v Bishop Sutton 4-1
156 Plymouth Parkway v Ilfracombe Town 4-1
157 Street v Paulton Rovers 1-0
158 Wells City v Bodmin Town 3-2
159 Brislington v St Blazey 4-0
160 Larkhall Athletic v Tiverton Town 1-0
2r Brighouse Town v Billingham Synthonia 4-0
8r Spennymoor Town v Newton Aycliffe 3-0
10r South Shields (3) v Albion Sports 1-2
13r Bridlington Town (2) v Guisborough Town 2-4
14r Morpeth Town v Durham City 3-2
15r West Auckland Town v Harrogate Town 4-2
19r Worksop Parramore v Mossley 3-2
20r Radcliffe Borough v Atherton Collieries 2-1
23r Congleton Town v Prescot Cables 0-1
24r Shirebrook Town v Sheffield 0-4
33r Norton United v Rugby Town 1-1q
35r AFC Wulfrunians v Stourport Swifts 4-1e
40r Walsall Wood v Leek Town 2-0
48r Quorn v Basford United 1-1q
49r Rainworth MW v Dunkirk 0-1e
54r Brigg Town v Arnold Town 4-2
68r Whitton United v Waltham Abbey 0-3
73r Newmarket Town v Witham Town 0-2
80r Barking v Maldon & Tiptree 0-1
90r Northampton Spencer v Royston Town 2-3
102r Cirencester Town v Slough Town 1-0
103r Bishop's Cleeve v Ashford Town (Middlesex) 0-1
104r Cheltenham Saracens v Binfield 1-7
116r Alton Town v Raynes Park Vale 1-0
117r Herne Bay v Eastbourne United 1-2
119r Molesey v Folkestone Invicta 2-4
128r Hassocks v Dorking Wanderers 1-0
138r Whitstable Town v Tunbridge Wells 0-2
141r Longwell Green Sports v Moneyfields 1-2
151r Sholing v Totton & Eling 2-1
153r Bridgwater Town v Taunton Town 2-1

Qualifying Round One

1 Marske United v Albion Sports 3-0
2 Blyth Spartans v AFC Fylde 1-3
3 Whitby Town v West Auckland Town 1-1
4 Penrith v Padiham 3-1
5 Spennymoor Town v Lancaster City 0-1
6 Team Northumbria v Scarborough Athletic 0-4
7 Brighouse Town v Crook Town 4-1
8 Guisborough Town v Bishop Auckland 2-2
9 Jarrow Roofing Boldon CA v Morpeth Town 1-0
10 Stocksbridge Park Steels v Ramsbottom United 2-2
11 Marine v Curzon Ashton 2-4
12 Warrington Town v New Mills 0-0
13 Runcorn Linnets v Glossop North End 2-1
14 Prescot Cables v Buxton 0-1
15 FC United of Manchester v Chorley 0-1
16 Ashton United v Witton Albion 2-1
17 Ossett Town v Bamber Bridge 2-2
18 Frickley Athletic v Sheffield 4-1
19 Worksop Parramore v Cammell Laird 1-3
20 Droylsden v Trafford 1-5
21 Worksop Town v Bootle 1-1
22 Burscough v Radcliffe Borough 2-1
23 Northwich Victoria v Skelmersdale United 0-3
24 Tipton Town v Kidsgrove Athletic 2-0

2013/14

25	Atherstone Town v Redditch United	3-3
26	AFC Wulfrunians v Walsall Wood	1-1
27	Evesham United v Stourbridge	0-3
28	Hinckley United v Rushall Olympic	0-3
29	Newcastle Town v Sutton Coldfield Town	2-2
30	Chasetown v Stafford Rangers	0-0
31	Halesowen Town v Brocton	2-1
32	Coventry Sphinx v Tividale	2-1
33	Nantwich Town v Rugby Town	1-2
34	Coalville Town v Long Eaton United	3-2
35	Stamford v Grantham Town	0-0
36	Corby Town v Barwell	3-0
37	Mickleover Sports v Loughborough University	2-0
38	Carlton Town v Brigg Town	1-1
39	Dunkirk v Blaby & Whetstone Athletic	0-0
40	Gresley v Eastwood Town	3-2
41	Ilkeston FC v Belper Town	1-2
42	Basford United v Matlock Town	0-2
43	St Neots Town v Wroxham	3-1
44	Sleaford Town v Huntingdon Town	B
45	King's Lynn Town v Cambridge City	1-5
46	St Ives Town v Dereham Town	4-1
47	Spalding United v Gorleston	1-0
48	Billericay Town v Leiston	2-0
49	Grays Athletic v Romford	2-1
50	Witham Town v Mildenhall Town	1-1
51	Harlow Town v Lowestoft Town	2-1
52	AFC Hornchurch v East Thurrock United	1-1
53	Brentwood Town v FC Clacton	3-3
54	Needham Market v Brantham Athletic	3-2
55	Bury Town v Thurrock	0-2
56	Aveley v Canvey Island	2-5
57	Tilbury v Waltham Abbey	2-1
58	Maldon & Tiptree v Heybridge Swifts	0-2
59	Burnham Ramblers v AFC Sudbury	1-2
60	Hendon v Biggleswade United	7-1
61	Chesham United v Royston Town	1-2
62	Cockfosters v AFC Rushden & Diamonds	2-2
63	Daventry Town v Berkhamsted	6-1
64	Greenhouse London v Bedford Town	2-6
65	Wingate & Finchley v Biggleswade Town	0-0
66	Hitchin Town v Arlesey Town	1-1
67	Uxbridge v Barton Rovers	2-3
68	Harrow Borough v North Greenford United	2-2
69	Wembley v Haringey Borough	0-2
70	St Albans City v Enfield Town	6-1
71	Wealdstone v Kings Langley	6-1
72	Hertford Town v Dunstable Town	0-6
73	St Margaretsbury v Hemel Hempstead Town	0-7
74	Westfield v Aylesbury United	1-1
75	Beaconsfield SYCOB v Burnham	2-4
76	Chertsey Town v Highmoor Ibis	4-0
77	Didcot Town v North Leigh	2-1
78	Hampton & Richmond Boro. v Ashford Town (Middlesex)	4-2
79	Aylesbury v Shortwood United	1-5
80	Hungerford Town v Cove	4-0
81	Chalfont St Peter v Metropolitan Police	0-0
82	Ardley United v Binfield	2-2
83	Hartley Wintney v Camberley Town	0-0
84	Banbury United v Cirencester Town	1-2
85	Leatherhead v Carshalton Athletic	2-1
86	Burgess Hill Town v Alton Town	8-1
87	South Park v Horsham	1-1
88	Merstham v Corinthian Casuals	1-0
89	Peacehaven & Telscombe v Lewes	2-3
90	Three Bridges v Maidstone United (2)	0-1
91	Thamesmead Town v Redhill	2-0
92	Hastings United (2) v Guernsey	2-3
93	Margate v Kingstonian	2-1
94	Folkestone Invicta v Eastbourne United	2-0
95	Sittingbourne v Littlehampton Town	3-2
96	Dulwich Hamlet v Shoreham	6-0
97	Hassocks v Chipstead	1-2
98	Eastbourne Town v Tunbridge Wells	3-2
99	Whyteleafe v Horley Town	3-0
100	Cray Wanderers v Faversham Town	0-3
101	Chatham Town v East Preston	2-1
102	Poole Town v Brockenhurst	2-0
103	Fareham Town v Weymouth	0-1
104	Hallen v Hamworthy United	1-2
105	Sholing v AFC Totton	4-0
106	Frome Town v Bognor Regis Town	1-1
107	Corsham Town v Bristol Manor Farm	4-4
108	Yate Town v Chippenham Town	3-2
109	Winchester City v Mangotsfield United	1-2
110	Horndean v AFC Portchester	0-5
111	Bashley v Moneyfields	2-0
112	Truro City v Street	1-0
113	Bridgwater Town v Merthyr Town (2)	2-1
114	Bideford v Larkhall Athletic	3-0
115	Wells City v Brislington	1-2
116	Clevedon Town v Plymouth Parkway	1-0
3r	West Auckland Town v Whitby Town	4-1
8r	Bishop Auckland v Guisborough Town	0-2
10r	Ramsbottom United v Stocksbridge Park Steels	3-0
12r	New Mills v Warrington Town	0-1
17r	Bamber Bridge v Ossett Town	1-2
21r	Bootle v Worksop Town	0-4
25r	Redditch United v Atherstone Town	1-2
26r	Walsall Wood v AFC Wulfrunians	3-4e
29r	Sutton Coldfield Town v Newcastle Town	2-0
30r	Stafford Rangers v Chasetown	2-0
35r	Grantham Town v Stamford	2-3
38r	Brigg Town v Carlton Town	1-2
39r	Blaby & Whetstone Athletic v Dunkirk	2-1
50r	Mildenhall Town v Witham Town	1-3
52r	East Thurrock United v AFC Hornchurch	1-2
53r	FC Clacton v Brentwood Town	2-1
62r	AFC Rushden & Diamonds v Cockfosters	8-0
65r	Biggleswade Town v Wingate & Finchley	4-3
66r	Arlesey Town v Hitchin Town	2-0
68r	North Greenford United v Harrow Borough	2-1
74r	Aylesbury United v Westfield	2-0
81r	Metropolitan Police v Chalfont St Peter	0-1
82r	Binfield v Ardley United	4-1
83r	Camberley Town v Hartley Wintney	0-2
87r	Horsham v South Park	5-2
106r	Bognor Regis Town v Frome Town	4-0
107r	Bristol Manor Farm v Corsham Town	1-0

Qualifying Round Two

1	Runcorn Linnets v Cammell Laird	1-0
2	Guiseley v Bradford Park Avenue	1-3
3	Frickley Athletic v Marske United	1-3
4	Scarborough Athletic v Penrith	1-1
5	Jarrow Roofing Boldon CA v Guisborough Town	3-3
6	Curzon Ashton v Lancaster City	0-0
7	Workington v Burscough	2-1
8	Stockport County v Brighouse Town	1-0
9	Ossett Town v Warrington Town	1-1
10	AFC Fylde v Ashton United	0-1
11	Colwyn Bay v Harrogate Town	1-0
12	Vauxhall Motors v Chorley	4-0
13	Trafford v Altrincham	2-1
14	Stalybridge Celtic v Worksop Town	3-5
15	Buxton v North Ferriby United	1-4
16	West Auckland Town v Skelmersdale United	5-0
17	Barrow v Ramsbottom United	3-0
18	AFC Telford United v Hednesford Town	1-3
19	Solihull Moors v Leamington	1-1
20	Atherstone Town v Coalville Town	1-0
21	Stamford v AFC Wulfrunians	4-1
22	Stourbridge v Sutton Coldfield Town	3-2
23	Brackley Town v Gresley	1-1
24	Gainsborough Trinity v Rushall Olympic	2-0 D
25	Mickleover Sports v Corby Town	3-3
26	Worcester City v Coventry Sphinx	4-0
27	Belper Town v Daventry Town	1-3
28	Stafford Rangers v Boston United	0-4
29	Blaby & Whetstone Athletic v Rugby Town	0-6
30	Halesowen Town v Tipton Town	5-0
31	Carlton Town v Matlock Town	1-0
32	Grays Athletic v Tilbury	3-0
33	Spalding United v AFC Hornchurch	1-4
34	Concord Rangers v St Ives Town	4-3
35	Royston Town v Histon	0-4
36	FC Clacton v North Greenford United	1-1
37	Needham Market v Dunstable Town	3-1
38	St Albans City v Billericay Town	2-0
39	Hampton & Richmond Boro. v Bedford Town	1-0
40	Arlesey Town v Thurrock	1-0
41	AFC Rushden & Diamonds v Cambridge City	3-2
42	Hemel Hempstead Town v Witham Town	1-1
43	Barton Rovers v Boreham Wood	0-0
44	Biggleswade Town v Chelmsford City	2-0
45	Harlow Town v Heybridge Swifts	2-3
46	Wealdstone v Haringey Borough	4-1
47	Hendon v Bishop's Stortford	0-5
48	AFC Sudbury - Bye	
49	Canvey Island v St Neots Town	2-2
50	Whitehawk v Sutton United	0-1
51	Thamesmead Town v Sittingbourne	1-2
52	Didcot Town v Burnham	2-1
53	Merstham v Maidstone United (2)	1-4
54	Bromley v Burgess Hill Town	1-0
55	Horsham v Faversham Town	2-0
56	Ebbsfleet United v Folkestone Invicta	1-0
57	Guernsey v Dover Athletic	2-3 N
58	Oxford City v Maidenhead United	1-0
59	Eastbourne Town v Hartley Wintney	1-5
60	Whyteleafe v Chatham Town	1-2
61	Chertsey Town v Chipstead	1-2
62	Eastbourne Borough v Farnborough	0-0
63	Margate v Dulwich Hamlet	1-2
64	Binfield v Leatherhead	1-2
65	Aylesbury United v Staines Town	0-3
66	Hayes & Yeading United v Tonbridge Angels	0-0
67	Chalfont St Peter v Lewes	0-1
68	Dorchester Town v Shortwood United	0-1
69	Hamworthy United v Poole Town	2-4
70	Cirencester Town v AFC Portchester	2-0
71	Brislington v Truro City	3-2
72	Bristol Manor Farm v Bridgwater Town	4-4
73	Gloucester City v Havant & Waterlooville	1-1
74	Eastleigh v Mangotsfield United	4-0
75	Basingstoke Town v Weston-Super-Mare	1-3
76	Yate Town v Bideford	2-1
77	Weymouth v Bognor Regis Town	2-2
78	Clevedon Town v Sholing	2-0
79	Bath City v Gosport Borough	2-0
80	Bashley v Hungerford Town	0-3
4r	Penrith v Scarborough Athletic	2-2P
5r	Guisborough Town v Jarrow Roofing Boldon CA	3-1
6r	Lancaster City v Curzon Ashton	1-2
9r	Warrington Town v Ossett Town	1-3e
19r	Leamington v Solihull Moors	1-2
23r	Gresley v Brackley Town	0-1
25r	Corby Town v Mickleover Sports	5-2
36r	North Greenford United v FC Clacton	3-1
42r	Witham Town v Hemel Hempstead Town	3-4
43r	Boreham Wood v Barton Rovers	3-0
49r	St Neots Town v Canvey Island	1-2
62r	Farnborough v Eastbourne Borough	0-2
66r	Tonbridge Angels v Hayes & Yeading United	2-1
72r	Bridgwater Town v Bristol Manor Farm	2-1
73r	Havant & Waterlooville v Gloucester City	2-3
77r	Bognor Regis Town v Weymouth	1-4

Qualifying Round Three

1	Worcester City v Rugby Town	0-0
2	Corby Town v Trafford	4-2
3	Carlton Town v Vauxhall Motors	1-3
4	Marske United v Halesowen Town	3-2
5	Stockport County v Rushall Olympic	0-1
6	Stourbridge v Curzon Ashton	3-0
7	Stamford v Ashton United	4-2
8	Solihull Moors v Worksop Town	4-0
9	Colwyn Bay v Ossett Town	2-1
10	Hednesford Town v West Auckland Town	2-2
11	Atherstone Town v Barrow	0-4
12	Brackley Town v Boston United	2-0
13	North Ferriby United v Runcorn Linnets	2-0
14	Bradford Park Avenue v Penrith	2-1
15	Guisborough Town v Workington	1-4
16	Maidstone United (2) v Boreham Wood	0-2
17	Biggleswade Town v Leatherhead	5-1
18	Dover Athletic v AFC Rushden & Diamonds	3-1
19	Chipstead v Bishop's Stortford	1-6
20	Horsham v Chatham Town	0-1
21	Concord Rangers v Histon	2-1
22	Hampton & Richmond Boro. v Arlesey Town	5-1
23	Needham Market v AFC Sudbury	2-1
24	Staines Town v Sittingbourne	4-1
25	Lewes v Sutton United	0-1
26	St Albans City v Tonbridge Angels	2-1
27	Hemel Hempstead Town v Dulwich Hamlet	3-1
28	AFC Hornchurch v Wealdstone	6-1
29	Canvey Island v North Greenford United	2-1
30	Ebbsfleet United v Eastbourne Borough	2-0
31	Bromley v Heybridge Swifts	1-2
32	Grays Athletic v Daventry Town	0-4
33	Cirencester Town v Weymouth	1-2
34	Weston-Super-Mare v Brislington	2-3
35	Eastleigh v Oxford City	2-3
36	Hartley Wintney v Clevedon Town	1-1
37	Bridgwater Town v Bath City	0-3
38	Poole Town v Hungerford Town	2-0
39	Didcot Town v Shortwood United	0-1
40	Yate Town v Gloucester City	2-2
1r	Rugby Town v Worcester City	0-2
10r	West Auckland Town v Hednesford Town	2-2q
36r	Clevedon Town v Hartley Wintney	3-4
40r	Gloucester City v Yate Town	7-0

Qualifying Round Four

1	Macclesfield Town v Vauxhall Motors	7-0
2	Stamford v Hednesford Town	0-2
3	Grimsby Town v Rushall Olympic	3-0
4	Worcester City v Lincoln City	1-1
5	Bradford Park Avenue v Kidderminster Harriers	1-1
6	Wrexham v Hyde FC	2-0
7	Workington v Stourbridge	1-3
8	Southport v Marske United	6-2
9	Colwyn Bay v Corby Town	1-3
10	Tamworth v Solihull Moors	4-1
11	Nuneaton Town v FC Halifax Town	0-2
12	North Ferriby United v Alfreton Town	1-3
13	Brackley Town v Barrow	0-0
14	Chester FC v Gateshead (2)	0-1
15	Hemel Hempstead Town v Sutton United	3-3
16	AFC Hornchurch v Hereford United	0-1
17	Ebbsfleet United v Dartford	1-1
18	Barnet v Concord Rangers	3-0
19	Chatham Town v St Albans City	0-2
20	Dover Athletic v Oxford City	3-0
21	Boreham Wood v Heybridge Swifts	1-0
22	Bath City v Salisbury City	0-1
23	Gloucester City v Hampton & Richmond Boro.	3-1
24	Weymouth v Braintree Town	1-2
25	Forest Green Rovers v Bishop's Stortford	0-1
26	Needham Market v Cambridge United	0-1
27	Biggleswade Town v Canvey Island	1-0
28	Shortwood United v Aldershot Town	1-1
29	Woking v Luton Town	0-1
30	Brislington v Welling United	0-1
31	Hartley Wintney v Daventry Town	1-6
32	Staines Town v Poole Town	0-0
4r	Lincoln City v Worcester City	3-0
5r	Kidderminster Harriers v Bradford Park Avenue	2-1
13r	Barrow v Brackley Town	0-1e
15r	Sutton United v Hemel Hempstead Town	2-0
17r	Dartford v Ebbsfleet United	1-0
28r	Aldershot Town v Shortwood United	1-2
32r	Poole Town v Staines Town	0-1

Round One

AFC Wimbledon v Coventry City	1-3
Accrington Stanley (2) v Tranmere Rovers	0-1
Bishop's Stortford v Northampton Town	1-2
Boreham Wood v Carlisle United	0-0
Braintree Town v Newport County (2)	1-1

2013/14 to 2014/15

	Brentford v Staines Town	5-0
	Bristol City v Dagenham & Redbridge	3-0
	Bristol Rovers v York City	3-3
	Burton Albion v Hereford United	2-0
	Bury v Cambridge United	0-0
	Chesterfield v Daventry Town	2-0
	Colchester United v Sheffield United	2-3
	Corby Town v Dover Athletic	1-2
	Gillingham v Brackley Town	1-1
	Gloucester City v Fleetwood Town	0-2
	Grimsby Town v Scunthorpe United	0-0
	Hartlepool United v Notts County	3-2
	Hednesford Town v Crawley Town	1-2
	Kidderminster Harriers v Sutton United	4-1
	Leyton Orient v Southport	5-2
	Lincoln City v Plymouth Argyle	0-0
	Macclesfield Town v Swindon Town	4-0
	Milton Keynes Dons v FC Halifax Town	4-1
	Morecambe v Southend United	0-3
	Oldham Athletic v Wolverhampton Wan.	1-1
	Oxford United v Gateshead (2)	2-2
	Peterborough United v Exeter City	2-0
	Preston North End v Barnet	6-0
	Rotherham United v Bradford City	3-0
	Salisbury City v Dartford	4-2
	Shortwood United v Port Vale	0-4
	St Albans City v Mansfield Town	1-8
	Stevenage v Portsmouth	2-1
	Stourbridge v Biggleswade Town	4-1
	Tamworth v Cheltenham Town	1-0
	Torquay United v Rochdale	0-2
	Walsall v Shrewsbury Town	3-0
	Welling United v Luton Town	2-1
	Wrexham v Alfreton Town	3-1
	Wycombe Wanderers v Crewe Alexandra	1-1
r	Brackley Town v Gillingham	1-0
r	Cambridge United v Bury	2-1
r	Carlisle United v Boreham Wood	2-1
r	Crewe Alexandra v Wycombe Wanderers	0-2
r	Gateshead (2) v Oxford United	0-1e
r	Newport County (2) v Braintree Town	1-0
r	Plymouth Argyle v Lincoln City	5-0
r	Scunthorpe United v Grimsby Town	1-2
r	Wolverhampton Wan. v Oldham Athletic	1-2
r	York City v Bristol Rovers	2-3

Round Two

	Bristol Rovers v Crawley Town	0-0
	Cambridge United v Sheffield United	0-2
	Carlisle United v Brentford	3-2
	Chesterfield v Southend United	1-3
	Fleetwood Town v Burton Albion	1-1
	Grimsby Town v Northampton Town	2-0
	Hartlepool United v Coventry City	1-1
	Kidderminster Harriers v Newport County (2)	4-2
	Leyton Orient v Walsall	1-0
	Macclesfield Town v Brackley Town	3-2
	Milton Keynes Dons v Dover Athletic	1-0
	Oldham Athletic v Mansfield Town	1-1
	Peterborough United v Tranmere Rovers	5-0
	Plymouth Argyle v Welling United	3-1
	Port Vale v Salisbury City	4-1
	Rotherham United v Rochdale	1-2
	Stevenage v Stourbridge	4-0
	Tamworth v Bristol City	1-2
	Wrexham v Oxford United	1-2
	Wycombe Wanderers v Preston North End	0-1
r	Burton Albion v Fleetwood Town	1-0
r	Coventry City v Hartlepool United	2-1
r	Crawley Town v Bristol Rovers	1-2
r	Mansfield Town v Oldham Athletic	1-4

Round Three

	Arsenal v Tottenham Hotspur	2-0
	Aston Villa v Sheffield United	1-2
	Barnsley v Coventry City	1-2
	Birmingham City v Bristol Rovers	3-0
	Blackburn Rovers v Manchester City	1-1
	Bolton Wanderers v Blackpool	2-1
	Bournemouth v Burton Albion	4-1
	Brighton & Hove Albion v Reading	1-0
	Bristol City v Watford	1-1
	Charlton Athletic v Oxford United	2-2
	Derby County v Chelsea	0-2
	Doncaster Rovers v Stevenage	2-3
	Everton v Queen's Park Rangers	4-0
	Grimsby Town v Huddersfield Town	2-3
	Ipswich Town v Preston North End	1-1
	Kidderminster Harriers v Peterborough United	0-0
	Liverpool v Oldham Athletic	2-0
	Macclesfield Town v Sheffield Wednesday	1-1
	Manchester United v Swansea City	1-2
	Middlesbrough v Hull City	0-2
	Newcastle United v Cardiff City	1-2
	Norwich City v Fulham	1-1
	Nottingham Forest v West Ham United	5-0
	Port Vale v Plymouth Argyle	2-2
	Rochdale v Leeds United	2-0
	Southampton v Burnley	4-3
	Southend United v Millwall	4-1
	Stoke City v Leicester City	2-1
	Sunderland v Carlisle United	3-1
	West Bromwich Albion v Crystal Palace	0-2
	Wigan Athletic v Milton Keynes Dons	3-3
	Yeovil Town v Leyton Orient	4-0
r	Fulham v Norwich City	3-0
r	Manchester City v Blackburn Rovers	5-0
r	Milton Keynes Dons v Wigan Athletic	1-3e
r	Oxford United v Charlton Athletic	0-3
r	Peterborough United v Kidderminster Harriers	2-3
r	Plymouth Argyle v Port Vale	2-3
r	Preston North End v Ipswich Town	3-2
r	Sheffield Wednesday v Macclesfield Town	4-1
r	Watford v Bristol City	2-0

Round Four

	Arsenal v Coventry City	4-0
	Birmingham City v Swansea City	1-2
	Bolton Wanderers v Cardiff City	0-1
	Bournemouth v Liverpool	0-2
	Chelsea v Stoke City	1-0
	Huddersfield Town v Charlton Athletic	0-1
	Manchester City v Watford	4-2
	Nottingham Forest v Preston North End	0-0
	Port Vale v Brighton & Hove Albion	1-3
	Rochdale v Sheffield Wednesday	1-2
	Sheffield United v Fulham	1-1
	Southampton v Yeovil Town	2-0
	Southend United v Hull City	0-2
	Stevenage v Everton	0-4
	Sunderland v Kidderminster Harriers	1-0
	Wigan Athletic v Crystal Palace	2-1
r	Fulham v Sheffield United	0-1e
r	Preston North End v Nottingham Forest	0-2

Round Five

	Arsenal v Liverpool	2-1
	Brighton & Hove Albion v Hull City	1-1
	Cardiff City v Wigan Athletic	1-2
	Everton v Swansea City	3-1
	Manchester City v Chelsea	2-0
	Sheffield United v Nottingham Forest	3-1
	Sheffield Wednesday v Charlton Athletic	1-2
	Sunderland v Southampton	1-0
r	Hull City v Brighton & Hove Albion	2-1

Round Six

Arsenal v Everton	4-1
Hull City v Sunderland	3-0
Manchester City v Wigan Athletic	1-2
Sheffield United v Charlton Athletic	2-0

Semi Finals

Hull City v Sheffield United	5-3 N
Wigan Athletic v Arsenal	1-1eN

Final

Arsenal v Hull City	3-2eN

2014/15

Extra Preliminary Round

1	Whickham v Bacup & Rossendale Borough	5-0
2	Guisborough Town v Armthorpe Welfare	1-1
3	Seaham Red Star v Liversedge	2-1
4	Jarrow Roofing Boldon CA v Eccleshill United	4-1
5	Bridlington Town (2) v Whitley Bay	1-1
6	North Shields v Pontefract Collieries	1-0
7	Silsden v Consett	0-2
8	Shildon v Crook Town	7-0
9	Billingham Synthonia v Durham City	1-2
10	Thackley v Albion Sports	1-2
11	Holker Old Boys v Ashington	2-2
12	Northallerton Town v Colne	3-1
13	Hebburn Town v West Allotment Celtic	2-2
14	Glasshoughton Welfare v Knaresborough Town	1-2
15	Pickering Town v Washington	0-6
16	Newton Aycliffe v Garforth Town	1-2
17	Bishop Auckland v Sunderland RCA	1-1
18	Nelson v West Auckland Town	1-2
19	Newcastle Benfield v Penrith	2-1
20	Marske United v Billingham Town	7-1
21	Tadcaster Albion v Barnoldswick Town	5-0
22	Morpeth Town v Dunston UTS	0-2
23	West Didsbury & Chorlton v Cammell Laird	wo/s
24	Nostell MW v Stockport Sports	1-2 N
25	Parkgate v Congleton Town	1-3
26	1874 Northwich v Maine Road	2-1
27	Glossop North End v AFC Blackpool	3-0
28	St Helens Town v Atherton Collieries	2-5
29	Runcorn Linnets v Rochdale Town	6-0
30	Bootle v Runcorn Town	0-1
31	AFC Liverpool v Squires Gate	0-3
32	Barton Town Old Boys v Abbey Hey	7-0
33	AFC Emley v Ashton Athletic	2-1
34	Alsager Town v Winterton Rangers	2-3
35	Maltby Main v Wigan Robin Park	2-1
36	Winsford United v Athersley Recreation	0-1
37	Rocester v Stafford Town	1-1
38	Walsall Wood v Heath Hayes	1-0
39	Blaby & Whetstone Athletic v Harborough Town	2-2
40	Heather St Johns v Coventry Sphinx	0-2
41	Kirby Muxloe v Wolverhampton Casuals	3-0
42	Stourport Swifts v Lye Town	2-0
43	Causeway United v Cradley Town	4-1
44	Bolehall Swifts v Dudley Town	1-2
45	St Andrews v Tipton Town	2-2
46	Bromsgrove Sporting v Bewdley Town	2-0
47	Boldmere St Michaels v Desborough Town	4-3
48	Shawbury United v Continental Star	2-1
49	Ellistown & Ibstock United v Studley	2-0
50	Black Country Rangers v Lichfield City	1-3
51	AFC Wulfrunians v Alvechurch	3-2
52	Coleshill Town v Nuneaton Griff	10-0
53	Sporting Khalsa v Pegasus Juniors	0-0
54	Wellington (Hereford) v Ellesmere Rangers	2-1
55	Atherstone Town v Brocton	1-1
56	Gornal Athletic v Westfields	1-2
57	Heanor Town v Long Eaton United	1-0
58	Shirebrook Town v Loughborough University	2-2
59	Quorn v Bottesford Town	3-1
60	Cleethorpes Town v Borrowash Victoria	4-1
61	Shepshed Dynamo v Dunkirk	1-1
62	Clipstone v Harrowby United	2-0
63	Holwell Sports v Graham Street Primitives	3-0
64	Thurnby Nirvana v Lincoln Moorlands Railway	5-1
65	Arnold Town v Basford United	1-4
66	Retford United v Stapenhill	2-2
67	Handsworth Parramore v Oadby Town	5-1
68	Staveley MW v Worksop Town	2-0
69	Peterborough Northern Star v Team Bury	3-0
70	Mildenhall Town v Gorleston	3-0
71	Kirkley & Pakefield v Ely City	3-0
72	Boston Town v Walsham Le Willows	1-1
73	Norwich United v Deeping Rangers	1-0
74	Great Yarmouth Town v Huntingdon Town	1-0
75	Sleaford Town v Wisbech Town	1-3
76	Thetford Town v Swaffham Town	1-0
77	Newmarket Town v Fakenham Town	1-1
78	Yaxley v Godmanchester Rovers	0-3
79	Diss Town v Holbeach United	1-5
80	Clapton v Bowers & Pitsea	1-1
81	Colney Heath v Southend Manor	3-2
82	Halstead Town v St Margaretsbury	0-0
83	Brantham Athletic v Codicote	1-1
84	FC Romania v Haverhill Rovers	0-0
85	Stansted v Ipswich Wanderers	0-2 N
86	Takeley v London Tigers	2-2
87	Whitton United v Eton Manor	2-0
88	London Colney v Woodbridge Town	6-0
89	Wivenhoe Town v Enfield 1893	3-0
90	Sporting Bengal United v FC Clacton	1-2
91	Waltham Forest v Hoddesdon Town	1-2
92	Ilford v Saffron Walden Town	1-2
93	Tower Hamlets v Felixstowe & Walton United	0-1
94	Haverhill Borough v Barking	1-0
95	Basildon United v Stanway Rovers	3-2
96	Hadleigh United v Sawbridgeworth Town	3-2
97	Cockfosters v Hullbridge Sports	5-4
98	Haringey Borough v Hertford Town	0-3
99	Welwyn Garden City v Hadley	1-1
100	Hatfield Town v Baldock Town	0-3
101	Sileby Rangers v Hillingdon Borough	3-0
102	Tring Athletic v Holmer Green	3-4
103	Staines Lammas v Bedfont Sports	3-2
104	Harefield United v Crawley Green	2-1
105	Cogenhoe United v Wembley	1-1
106	Northampton Spencer v AFC Kempston Rovers	0-2
107	Ashford Town (Middlesex) v Berkhamsted	3-1
108	Wellingborough Town (2) v Bedfont & Feltham	2-4
109	Long Buckby v Hanworth Villa	1-1
110	AFC Dunstable v Ampthill Town	2-0
111	Kings Langley v Bedford	3-2
112	AFC Rushden & Diamonds v Oxhey Jets	5-1
113	Stotfold v Biggleswade United	1-3
114	Leverstock Green v Newport Pagnell Town	2-1
115	Hartley Wintney v Frimley Green	2-1
116	Kidlington v Newbury (2)	3-0
117	Cove v Thame United	0-1
118	Fairford Town v Knaphill	1-3
119	Brimscombe & Thrupp v Windsor	1-2
120	Ardley United v Ash United	5-1
121	Holyport v Abingdon United	2-2
122	Slimbridge v Thatcham Town	1-1
123	Reading Town v Shrivenham	0-1
124	Cheltenham Saracens v Camberley Town	1-0
125	Flackwell Heath v Bracknell Town	4-0
126	Chertsey Town v Milton United (Oxon)	1-1
127	Tadley Calleva v Ascot United	1-1
128	Badshot Lea v Binfield	3-0
129	Farnham Town v Highmoor Ibis	1-4
130	Pagham v Woodstock Sports	2-0
131	Erith Town v St Francis Rangers	1-2
132	Horsham YMCA v Alton Town	3-2
133	Sevenoaks Town v East Preston	1-2
134	Ringmer v Corinthian	2-1
135	Guildford City (2) v Ashford United	0-2
136	Chichester City v Mole Valley SCR	2-3
137	Deal Town v Phoenix Sports	2-2
138	Molesey v Haywards Heath Town	11-0
139	Westfield v Horley Town	3-2
140	Dorking Wanderers v Crowborough Athletic	0-0
141	Colliers Wood United v Lordswood	0-1
142	Holmesdale v Tunbridge Wells	4-1
143	Chessington & Hook United v Worthing United	1-0

2014/15

144	Canterbury City v Lingfield	2-1
145	Greenwich Borough v Lancing	2-1
146	Arundel v Croydon	0-1
147	Shoreham v Crawley Down Gatwick	1-1
148	Epsom Athletic v Littlehampton Town	2-5
149	Eastbourne United v Hailsham Town	5-2
150	Erith & Belvedere v AFC Croydon Athletic	2-0
151	Hassocks v Epsom & Ewell	1-3
152	Beckenham Town v Eastbourne Town	1-3
153	Selsey v Fisher	0-3
154	Cray Valley Paper Mills v Raynes Park Vale	1-3
155	Newport (IOW) v Hamworthy United	2-0
156	Whitchurch United v Hallen	1-1
157	Winterbourne United v Hythe & Dibden	3-2
158	Bemerton Heath Harlequins v Totton & Eling	1-0
159	Bridport v Highworth Town	2-3
160	Longwell Green Sports v Melksham Town	1-1
161	Bitton v Blackfield & Langley	1-2
162	Pewsey Vale v Sherborne Town	0-1
163	Folland Sports v Downton	5-1
164	Alresford Town v Christchurch	1-1
165	Bournemouth (Ams) v Verwood Town	4-2
166	AFC Portchester v Fawley	2-1
167	Cadbury Heath v Cribbs	3-4
168	Brockenhurst v Wootton Bassett Town	0-3
169	Bradford Town v Moneyfields	4-3
170	Gillingham Town v Almondsbury UWE	4-1
171	Corsham Town v Horndean	2-3
172	Petersfield Town v Bristol Manor Farm	2-3
173	Romsey Town v Fareham Town	1-3
174	Lymington Town v Winchester City	2-5 N
175	Cowes Sports v Team Solent	1-0
176	Hengrove Athletic v Bodmin Town	0-1
177	Barnstaple Town v Witheridge	0-1
178	Saltash United v Welton Rovers	2-1
179	AFC St Austell v Bishop Sutton	5-0
180	Willand Rovers v Radstock Town	3-1
181	Brislington v Street	2-2
182	Shepton Mallet v Ilfracombe Town	wo/s
183	Torpoint Athletic v Odd Down	2-4
184	Plymouth Parkway v Buckland Athletic	4-1
2r	Armthorpe Welfare v Guisborough Town	2-2P
5r	Whitley Bay v Bridlington Town (2)	0-1
11r	Ashington v Holker Old Boys	3-0
13r	West Allotment Celtic v Hebburn Town	2-0
17r	Sunderland RCA v Bishop Auckland	0-2
37r	Stafford Town v Rocester	2-1
39r	Harborough Town v Blaby & Whetstone Athletic	1-6
45r	Tipton Town v St Andrews	2-1
53r	Pegasus Juniors v Sporting Khalsa	1-2
55r	Brocton v Atherstone Town	2-1
58r	Loughborough University v Shirebrook Town	2-1
61r	Dunkirk v Shepshed Dynamo	2-2q
66r	Stapenhill v Retford United	1-3
72r	Walsham Le Willows v Boston Town	1-3
77r	Fakenham Town v Newmarket Town	0-1
80r	Bowers & Pitsea v Clapton	3-3P
82r	St Margaretsbury v Halstead Town	6-2
83r	Codicote v Brantham Athletic	5-0
84r	Haverhill Rovers v FC Romania	0-3
86r	London Tigers v Takeley	4-0
99r	Hadley v Welwyn Garden City	1-2
105r	Wembley v Cogenhoe United	1-3
109r	Hanworth Villa v Long Buckby	4-0
121r	Abingdon United v Holyport	4-0
122r	Thatcham Town v Slimbridge	1-2
126r	Milton United (Oxon) v Chertsey Town	1-1P
127r	Tadley Calleva v Ascot United	2-4
137r	Phoenix Sports v Deal Town	3-3q
140r	Crowborough Athletic v Dorking Wanderers	0-7
147r	Crawley Down Gatwick v Shoreham	1-3
156r	Hallen v Whitchurch United	2-1
160r	Melksham Town v Longwell Green Sports	0-1
164r	Christchurch v Alresford Town	1-3
181r	Street v Brislington	1-2

Preliminary Round

1	Newcastle Benfield v Kendal Town	0-0
2	Dunston UTS v Durham City	3-0
3	West Auckland Town v Darlington 1883	1-1
4	Garforth Town v Harrogate Railway Athletic	1-2
5	Knaresborough Town v West Allotment Celtic	0-1
6	Tadcaster Albion v Spennymoor Town	0-2
7	Consett v Whickham	2-0
8	Bishop Auckland v Jarrow Roofing Boldon CA	4-4
9	Albion Sports v Ashington	1-2
10	Washington v Lancaster City	0-7
11	Bridlington Town (2) v Northallerton Town	3-0
12	Padiham v Shildon	0-1
13	Armthorpe Welfare v Marske United	1-4
14	Clitheroe v Seaham Red Star	3-2
15	Scarborough Athletic v North Shields	1-1
16	New Mills v Squires Gate	2-3
17	Stockport Sports v Ossett Town	1-5
18	Northwich Victoria v AFC Emley	4-0
19	Winterton Rangers v Ossett Albion	0-3
20	Farsley AFC v Athersley Recreation	4-1
21	Stocksbridge Park Steels v Bamber Bridge	0-2
22	Warrington Town v Barton Town Old Boys	4-1
23	Runcorn Town v Goole AFC	1-1
24	West Didsbury & Chorlton v Brighouse Town	0-3
25	Burscough v Mossley	1-1
26	1874 Northwich v Prescot Cables	3-3
27	Congleton Town v Salford City	0-0
28	Radcliffe Borough v Atherton Collieries	2-2
29	Droylsden v Runcorn Linnets	4-0
30	Maltby Main v Glossop North End	0-7
31	Sporting Khalsa v Tipton Town	0-1
32	Newcastle Town v Chasetown	1-1
33	Walsall Wood v Stafford Rangers	0-3
34	AFC Wulfrunians v Boldmere St Michaels	1-2
35	Shawbury United v Tividale	3-3
36	Leek Town v Lichfield City	5-1
37	Sutton Coldfield Town v Brocton	3-3
38	Coleshill Town v Bromsgrove Sporting	2-2
39	Dudley Town v Market Drayton Town	0-6
40	Stafford Town v Norton United	1-4
41	Westfields v Rugby Town	0-2
42	Coventry Sphinx v Bedworth United	0-0
43	Blaby & Whetstone Athletic v Stratford Town	1-0
44	Evesham United v Kidsgrove Athletic	3-1
45	Wellington (Hereford) v Stourport Swifts	2-3
46	Romulus v Causeway United	3-1
47	Ellistown & Ibstock United v Kirby Muxloe	1-0
48	Lincoln United v Brigg Town	4-0
49	Rainworth MW v Staveley MW	0-3
50	Spalding United v Heanor Town	1-0
51	Basford United v Sheffield	3-3
52	Mickleover Sports v Thurnby Nirvana	3-1
53	Gresley v Cleethorpes Town	0-0
54	Clipstone v Loughborough University	2-1
55	Loughborough Dynamo v Coalville Town	0-2
56	Carlton Town v Handsworth Parramore	2-1
57	Shepshed Dynamo v Quorn	2-0
58	Retford United v Holwell Sports	1-3
59	Dereham Town v St Ives Town	2-2
60	Needham Market v Soham Town Rangers	1-0
61	Peterborough Northern Star v Mildenhall Town	0-2
62	Godmanchester Rovers v Newmarket Town	2-3
63	Thetford Town v Norwich United	0-3
64	Holbeach United v Boston Town	2-4
65	Wisbech Town v Kirkley & Pakefield	2-1
66	Wroxham v Great Yarmouth Town	4-1
67	Royston Town v Brightlingsea Regent	2-3
68	Cheshunt v Thurrock	0-1
69	Baldock Town v Harlow Town	0-3
70	Barkingside v Wivenhoe Town	5-0
71	Brentwood Town v Potters Bar Town	1-0
72	Ware v Felixstowe & Walton United	0-3
73	London Tigers v FC Clacton	2-0
74	Ipswich Wanderers v Hoddesdon Town	2-1
75	Burnham Ramblers v Hadleigh United	1-3
76	Redbridge v AFC Sudbury	1-1
77	FC Romania v Heybridge Swifts	2-1
78	Maldon & Tiptree v London Colney	1-2
79	Aveley v Basildon United	2-0
80	Codicote v Tilbury	1-1
81	Bowers & Pitsea v Colney Heath	1-0
82	Whitton United v Haverhill Borough	0-2
83	Waltham Abbey v Cockfosters	6-3
84	Hertford Town v Great Wakering Rovers	3-2
85	St Margaretsbury v Romford	0-4
86	Saffron Walden Town v Welwyn Garden City	1-1
87	Harefield United v Leverstock Green	1-2
88	AFC Rushden & Diamonds v Bedford Town	1-1
89	Hanworth Villa v North Greenford United	1-1
90	Staines Lammas v Barton Rovers	1-8
91	Northwood v Kings Langley	1-1
92	Aylesbury United v Aylesbury	2-3
93	AFC Kempston Rovers v Sileby Rangers	4-0 D
94	Cogenhoe United v Kettering Town	1-4
95	Bedfont & Feltham v Leighton Town	3-2
96	AFC Hayes v Holmer Green	1-1
97	AFC Dunstable v Uxbridge	2-3
98	Hanwell Town v Biggleswade United	1-2
99	Ashford Town (Middlesex) v Daventry Town	1-1
100	Knaphill v Badshot Lea	2-1
101	Milton United (Oxon) v Marlow	2-1
102	Shrivenham v Shortwood United	1-6
103	Thame United v Highmoor Ibis	3-2
104	North Leigh v Flackwell Heath	1-2
105	Beaconsfield SYCOB v Didcot Town	5-1
106	Ardley United v Hartley Wintney	1-1
107	Windsor v Godalming Town	0-2
108	Slimbridge v Chalfont St Peter	0-1
109	Wantage Town v Kidlington	3-2
110	Cheltenham Saracens v Fleet Town	1-3
111	Bishop's Cleeve v Ascot United	1-0
112	Abingdon United v Egham Town	1-0
113	Chatham Town v Whyteleafe	1-2
114	Greenwich Borough v St Francis Rangers	5-2
115	Lordswood v Hythe Town	2-2
116	Faversham Town v Westfield	2-1
117	Worthing v Guernsey	2-0
118	Cray Wanderers v Molesey	3-1
119	East Preston v Holmesdale	2-1
120	Burgess Hill Town v Eastbourne Town	1-0
121	Ashford United v Chipstead	0-1
122	Redhill v Horsham YMCA	0-0
123	Epsom & Ewell v Croydon	1-1
124	Mole Valley SCR v Carshalton Athletic	1-5
125	Sittingbourne v Dorking Wanderers	0-3
126	Walton & Hersham v Herne Bay	1-2
127	Littlehampton Town v Shoreham	4-2
128	Eastbourne United v Hastings United (2)	2-3
129	Deal Town v Chessington & Hook United	1-1
130	Walton Casuals v Whitstable Town	1-1
131	Tooting & Mitcham United v Three Bridges	0-0
132	Erith & Belvedere v Folkestone Invicta	2-2
133	Fisher v Ramsgate	2-4
134	East Grinstead Town v Raynes Park Vale	2-2
135	South Park v Thamesmead Town	2-1
136	Ringmer v Merstham	0-4
137	Canterbury City v Pagham	0-2
138	Horsham v Corinthian Casuals	1-0
139	Bashley v Winchester City	0-2
140	Alresford Town v Sherborne Town	2-2
141	Cowes Sports v Yate Town	0-1
142	Fareham Town v Longwell Green Sports	0-3
143	Cinderford Town v Horndean	1-2
144	Swindon Supermarine v Hallen	1-0
145	Bradford Town v Wootton Bassett Town	2-1
146	AFC Totton v Gillingham Town	2-0
147	Sholing v Bristol Manor Farm	3-1
148	Newport (IOW) v Winterbourne United	5-2
149	Bemerton Heath Harlequins v Bournemouth (Ams)	0-0
150	Mangotsfield United v Cribbs	4-1
151	Blackfield & Langley v Highworth Town	4-0
152	AFC Portchester v Folland Sports	1-4
153	Taunton Town v Clevedon Town	4-1
154	Merthyr Town (2) v Larkhall Athletic	0-1
155	Bodmin Town v Witheridge	4-1
156	Tiverton Town v Plymouth Parkway	1-0
157	Odd Down v Willand Rovers	0-2
158	Wimborne Town v AFC St Austell	3-2
159	Shepton Mallet v Saltash United	0-0
160	Bridgwater Town v Brislington	1-0
1r	Kendal Town v Newcastle Benfield	0-4
3r	Darlington 1883 v West Auckland Town	3-1
8r	Jarrow Roofing Boldon CA v Bishop Auckland	3-4e
15r	North Shields v Scarborough Athletic	4-4q
23r	Goole AFC v Runcorn Town	0-1
25r	Mossley v Burscough	1-2e
26r	Prescot Cables v 1874 Northwich	2-1
27r	Salford City v Congleton Town	6-4e
28r	Atherton Collieries v Radcliffe Borough	2-2q
32r	Chasetown v Newcastle Town	2-1
35r	Tividale v Shawbury United	5-2
37r	Brocton v Sutton Coldfield Town	0-1e
38r	Bromsgrove Sporting v Coleshill Town	2-3e
42r	Bedworth United v Coventry Sphinx	3-1e
51r	Sheffield v Basford United	2-1e
53r	Cleethorpes Town v Gresley	5-4e
59r	St Ives Town v Dereham Town	3-3q
76r	AFC Sudbury v Redbridge	3-2e
80r	Tilbury v Codicote	2-0
86r	Welwyn Garden City v Saffron Walden Town	1-0e
88r	Bedford Town v AFC Rushden & Diamonds	0-3
89r	North Greenford United v Hanworth Villa	2-1
91r	Kings Langley v Northwood	1-3e
96r	Holmer Green v AFC Hayes	0-4
99r	Daventry Town v Ashford Town (Middlesex)	2-1
106r	Hartley Wintney v Ardley United	0-0q
115r	Hythe Town v Lordswood	2-0
122r	Horsham YMCA v Redhill	0-2
123r	Croydon v Epsom & Ewell	4-1
129r	Chessington & Hook United v Deal Town	2-1
130r	Whitstable Town v Walton Casuals	3-1e
131r	Three Bridges v Tooting & Mitcham United	1-4
132r	Folkestone Invicta v Erith & Belvedere	3-1e
134r	Raynes Park Vale v East Grinstead Town	2-1e
140r	Sherborne Town v Alresford Town	4-0
149r	Bournemouth (Ams) v Bemerton Heath Harlequins	2-3
159r	Saltash United v Shepton Mallet	1-0

Qualifying Round One

1	Marske United v Dunston UTS	2-2
2	West Allotment Celtic v Lancaster City	0-5
3	Darlington 1883 v Blyth Spartans	0-0
4	Newcastle Benfield v Bridlington Town (2)	3-1
5	Ashington v Scarborough Athletic	2-2
6	Shildon v Whitby Town	1-1
7	Workington v Consett	2-0
8	Harrogate Railway Athletic v Clitheroe	3-1
9	Bishop Auckland v Spennymoor Town	2-3
10	Ossett Albion v Droylsden	0-4
11	Salford City v Nantwich Town	2-0
12	Brighouse Town v Ashton United	1-2
13	Northwich Victoria v Glossop North End	0-0
14	FC United of Manchester v Prescot Cables	4-1 N
15	Buxton v Ramsbottom United	3-2
16	Bamber Bridge v Squires Gate	2-2
17	Farsley AFC v Frickley Athletic	2-1
18	Runcorn Town v Witton Albion	5-3
19	Marine v Ossett Town	2-1
20	Burscough v Curzon Ashton	0-1
21	Skelmersdale United v Radcliffe Borough	4-3
22	Warrington Town v Trafford	1-0
23	Rugby Town v Chasetown	1-1
24	Evesham United v Redditch United	0-0
25	Market Drayton Town v Stourbridge	1-3
26	Boldmere St Michaels v Bedworth United	0-3
27	Halesowen Town v Sutton Coldfield Town	3-0
28	Coleshill Town v Barwell	1-2
29	Blaby & Whetstone Athletic v Tipton Town	4-1
30	Rushall Olympic v Romulus	3-2
31	Ellistown & Ibstock United v Hereford United	3-2 N
32	Stafford Rangers v Tividale	0-0
33	Corby Town v Norton United	3-3
34	Leek Town v Stourport Swifts	2-1
35	Lincoln United v Stamford	2-3
36	Mickleover Sports v Staveley MW	3-0
37	Matlock Town v Ilkeston FC	1-2

2014/15

38	Sheffield v Shepshed Dynamo	3-2
39	Spalding United v Holwell Sports	4-0
40	Belper Town v Coalville Town	3-3
41	Cleethorpes Town v Carlton Town	3-2
42	Grantham Town v Clipstone	4-1
43	Mildenhall Town v Wroxham	1-3
44	St Neots Town v Dereham Town	1-1
45	Newmarket Town v Histon	0-3
46	King's Lynn Town v Boston Town	7-0
47	Cambridge City v Needham Market	2-4
48	Norwich United v Wisbech Town	1-0
49	Romford v Bury Town	1-0
50	Billericay Town v Hadleigh United	4-0
51	Hertford Town v Canvey Island	1-4
52	Haverhill Borough v Leiston	0-2
53	Tilbury v Aveley	0-4
54	AFC Hornchurch v East Thurrock United	1-1
55	London Tigers v Brightlingsea Regent	1-0
56	Waltham Abbey v Barkingside	3-1
57	AFC Sudbury v FC Romania	1-3
58	Bowers & Pitsea v Witham Town	0-4
59	Brentwood Town v London Colney	1-0
60	Wingate & Finchley v Ipswich Wanderers	2-2
61	Thurrock v Welwyn Garden City	2-0
62	Grays Athletic v Harlow Town	2-2
63	Enfield Town v Felixstowe & Walton United	5-0
64	Barton Rovers v Northwood	1-1
65	Aylesbury v Kettering Town	1-2
66	Bedfont & Feltham v Uxbridge	0-6
67	Biggleswade United v Leverstock Green	1-2
68	AFC Hayes v Harrow Borough	2-3
69	Hitchin Town v Daventry Town	2-1
70	Sileby Rangers v North Greenford United	1-3
71	Biggleswade Town v Arlesey Town	2-1
72	Dunstable Town v Chesham United	2-2
73	Hendon v AFC Rushden & Diamonds	1-0
74	Abingdon United v Milton United (Oxon)	3-0
75	Flackwell Heath v Wantage Town	3-3
76	Shortwood United v Cirencester Town	1-1
77	Knaphill v Fleet Town	1-2
78	Chalfont St Peter v Hungerford Town	2-1
79	Bishop's Cleeve v Banbury United	0-1
80	Slough Town v Ardley United	1-2
81	Thame United v Burnham	1-2
82	Godalming Town v Beaconsfield SYCOB	0-0
83	Leatherhead v Faversham Town	1-2
84	Hythe Town v Whitstable Town	4-0
85	Ramsgate v Raynes Park Vale	1-2
86	Horsham v Kingstonian	0-4
87	Peacehaven & Telscombe v East Preston	0-0
88	Redhill v Carshalton Athletic	1-0
89	Dorking Wanderers v Pagham	4-2
90	South Park v Metropolitan Police	2-2
91	Dulwich Hamlet v Worthing	0-3
92	Whyteleafe v Hastings United (2)	1-2
93	Folkestone Invicta v Margate	0-0
94	Tonbridge Angels v Herne Bay	6-0
95	Croydon v Burgess Hill Town	2-3
96	Greenwich Borough v Chessington & Hook United	1-0
97	Cray Wanderers v Tooting & Mitcham United	1-2
98	Merstham v Chipstead	2-2
99	Maidstone United (2) v Littlehampton Town	10-0
100	VCD Athletic v Hampton & Richmond Boro.	3-2
101	Bognor Regis Town v Lewes	0-0
102	Blackfield & Langley v Sherborne Town	3-2
103	Horndean v Newport (IOW)	0-1
104	Yate Town v Dorchester Town	1-2
105	Winchester City v Bemerton Heath Harlequins	3-0
106	Sholing v Chippenham Town	0-1
107	Mangotsfield United v Weymouth	0-3
108	Poole Town v Bradford Town	4-0
109	Longwell Green Sports v Folland Sports	0-1
110	AFC Totton v Swindon Supermarine	0-2
111	Bodmin Town v Bridgwater Town	3-3
112	Paulton Rovers v Taunton Town	3-1
113	Tiverton Town v Bideford	0-0
114	Frome Town v Wimborne Town	2-0
115	Truro City v Larkhall Athletic	0-2
116	Willand Rovers v Saltash United	2-1
1r	Dunston UTS v Marske United	2-0
3r	Blyth Spartans v Darlington 1883	3-0
5r	Scarborough Athletic v Ashington	1-0
6r	Whitby Town v Shildon	1-2
13r	Glossop North End v Northwich Victoria	2-2P
16r	Squires Gate v Bamber Bridge	2-3e
23r	Chasetown v Rugby Town	1-3e
24r	Redditch United v Evesham United	0-1
32r	Tividale v Stafford Rangers	4-0
33r	Norton United v Corby Town	2-1
40r	Coalville Town v Belper Town	2-0
44r	Dereham Town v St Neots Town	1-1P
54r	East Thurrock United v AFC Hornchurch	2-2P
60r	Ipswich Wanderers v Wingate & Finchley	3-4
62r	Harlow Town v Grays Athletic	2-4
64r	Northwood v Barton Rovers	2-3
72r	Chesham United v Dunstable Town	1-2
75r	Wantage Town v Flackwell Heath	1-2e
76r	Cirencester Town v Shortwood United	0-1e
82r	Beaconsfield SYCOB v Godalming Town	2-1
87r	East Preston v Peacehaven & Telscombe	2-0
90r	Metropolitan Police v South Park	3-0
93r	Margate v Folkestone Invicta	3-1
98r	Chipstead v Merstham	3-4e
101r	Lewes v Bognor Regis Town	1-0
111r	Bridgwater Town v Bodmin Town	2-1
113r	Bideford v Tiverton Town	1-0

Qualifying Round Two

1	Bradford Park Avenue v AFC Fylde	2-2
2	Curzon Ashton v Scarborough Athletic	1-0
3	Droylsden v Guiseley	0-1
4	Barrow v Runcorn Town	0-1
5	Workington v Bamber Bridge	0-1
6	Harrogate Town v Stockport County	1-2
7	Warrington Town v Sheffield	0-0
8	Shildon v Stalybridge Celtic	1-0
9	Colwyn Bay v Harrogate Railway Athletic	3-2
10	Buxton v Newcastle Benfield	2-0
11	Hyde FC v Marine	4-5
12	Skelmersdale United v Blyth Spartans	1-4
13	Gainsborough Trinity v Farsley AFC	4-1
14	Ashton United v Salford City	1-1
15	Chorley v Glossop North End	1-0
16	FC United of Manchester v Lancaster City	0-1
17	Cleethorpes Town v North Ferriby United	1-2
18	Dunston UTS v Spennymoor Town	1-4
19	Norton United v Spalding United	2-1
20	Bedworth United v Mickleover Sports	1-1
21	Worcester City v Rugby Town	3-1
22	Ellistown & Ibstock United v Halesowen Town	1-7
23	Histon v Evesham United	0-0
24	Boston United v Dereham Town	3-1
25	Barwell v Norwich United	0-0
26	Ilkeston FC v Solihull Moors	1-0
27	Blaby & Whetstone Athletic v Stourbridge	1-1
28	Leamington v Wroxham	4-1
29	Coalville Town v Lowestoft Town	0-0
30	Tamworth v Rushall Olympic	2-1
31	Stamford v Grantham Town	1-2
32	King's Lynn Town v Hednesford Town	1-0
33	Tividale v Leek Town	2-2
34	Redhill v Tonbridge Angels	2-1
35	VCD Athletic v Harrow Borough	0-4
36	Ebbsfleet United v Hythe Town	7-1
37	Needham Market v London Tigers	5-2
38	Hendon v Leiston	4-1
39	Hemel Hempstead Town v Dunstable Town	2-0
40	Hitchin Town v Wingate & Finchley	0-3
41	Chelmsford City v Worthing	6-0
42	Dorking Wanderers v Biggleswade Town	2-2
43	Staines Town v Leverstock Green	5-0
44	Bromley v Uxbridge	5-1
45	Maidstone United (2) v Brentwood Town	2-1
46	Bishop's Stortford v Tooting & Mitcham United	0-0
47	Eastbourne Borough v Enfield Town	1-1
48	Hayes & Yeading United v St Albans City	0-1
49	Boreham Wood v East Preston	3-2
50	Brackley Town v Farnborough	2-2
51	Witham Town v Lewes	4-2
52	Margate v Barton Rovers	1-2
53	Whitehawk v Merstham	2-1
54	FC Romania v Sutton United	2-3
55	Burnham v Canvey Island	0-1
56	Billericay Town v Raynes Park Vale	2-1
57	Grays Athletic v Hastings United (2)	1-0
58	Maidenhead United v Faversham Town	4-0
59	Thurrock v Aveley	0-2
60	Fleet Town v Burgess Hill Town	0-4
61	Wealdstone v Concord Rangers	1-1
62	Waltham Abbey v North Greenford United	1-0
63	Kettering Town v Chalfont St Peter	0-1
64	Beaconsfield SYCOB v Greenwich Borough	1-3
65	Romford v Kingstonian	0-0
66	Metropolitan Police v East Thurrock United	3-4
67	Winchester City v Newport (IOW)	3-3
68	Paulton Rovers v Gloucester City	1-1
69	Folland Sports v Frome Town	1-1
70	Bridgwater Town v Basingstoke Town	0-2
71	Larkhall Athletic v Gosport Borough	3-3
72	Havant & Waterlooville v Swindon Supermarine	3-0
73	Weston-Super-Mare v Banbury United	3-0
74	Blackfield & Langley v Willand Rovers	0-0
75	Abingdon United v Dorchester Town	0-2
76	Shortwood United v Oxford City	2-1
77	Bath City v Poole Town	1-1
78	Weymouth v Bideford	4-1
79	Chippenham Town v Ardley United	1-0
80	Flackwell Heath - Bye	
1r	AFC Fylde v Bradford Park Avenue	2-1e
7r	Sheffield v Warrington Town	1-3
14r	Salford City v Ashton United	0-1
20r	Mickleover Sports v Bedworth United	3-0
23r	Evesham United v Histon	3-1
25r	Norwich United v Barwell	0-2
27r	Stourbridge v Blaby & Whetstone Athletic	4-1
29r	Lowestoft Town v Coalville Town	5-0
33r	Leek Town v Tividale	1-0
42r	Biggleswade Town v Dorking Wanderers	1-0
46r	Tooting & Mitcham United v Bishop's Stortford	3-1
47r	Enfield Town v Eastbourne Borough	4-4q
50r	Farnborough v Brackley Town	0-1
61r	Concord Rangers v Wealdstone	2-0
65r	Kingstonian v Romford	5-3e
67r	Newport (IOW) v Winchester City	0-1
68r	Gloucester City v Paulton Rovers	2-1
69r	Frome Town v Folland Sports	1-0
71r	Gosport Borough v Larkhall Athletic	7-0
74r	Willand Rovers v Blackfield & Langley	1-0
77r	Poole Town v Bath City	0-2

Qualifying Round Three

1	North Ferriby United v Grantham Town	2-1
2	Tamworth v Lowestoft Town	1-0
3	Leamington v Worcester City	1-1
4	Guiseley v Halesowen Town	3-0
5	Runcorn Town v Norton United	2-5
6	Shildon v Stourbridge	0-0
7	AFC Fylde v Buxton	1-0
8	Mickleover Sports v Blyth Spartans	1-2
9	Stockport County v Ilkeston FC	1-0
10	Barwell v Curzon Ashton	2-1
11	Colwyn Bay v Warrington Town	1-1
12	Leek Town v Boston United	2-0
13	Bamber Bridge v Chorley	1-4
14	King's Lynn Town v Lancaster City	3-2
15	Gainsborough Trinity v Marine	4-0
16	Spennymoor Town v Ashton United	1-0
17	Grays Athletic v Bromley	0-0
18	Dorchester Town v Hendon	1-0
19	Barton Rovers v Canvey Island	0-1
20	Frome Town v Boreham Wood	2-2
21	Biggleswade Town v Maidstone United (2)	0-2
22	Evesham United v Chalfont St Peter	4-1
23	Staines Town v Gloucester City	1-1
24	Chippenham Town v Hemel Hempstead Town	0-5
25	Concord Rangers v Winchester City	3-2
26	Willand Rovers v Aveley	3-2
27	East Thurrock United v Tooting & Mitcham United	2-1
28	Billericay Town v Weymouth	0-1
29	Wingate & Finchley v Havant & Waterlooville	0-2
30	Maidenhead United v Gosport Borough	1-1
31	Needham Market v Witham Town	1-2
32	Kingstonian v Eastbourne Borough	2-3
33	Flackwell Heath v Weston-Super-Mare	1-4
34	Greenwich Borough v Redhill	1-0
35	Bath City v Shortwood United	2-2
36	Ebbsfleet United v Basingstoke Town	1-2
37	Harrow Borough v Waltham Abbey	2-1
38	St Albans City v Brackley Town	2-0
39	Sutton United v Burgess Hill Town	1-3
40	Whitehawk v Chelmsford City	4-4
3r	Worcester City v Leamington	2-0
6r	Stourbridge v Shildon	0-2
11r	Warrington Town v Colwyn Bay	1-0
17r	Bromley v Grays Athletic	5-0
20r	Boreham Wood v Frome Town	1-0
23r	Gloucester City v Staines Town	3-2
30r	Gosport Borough v Maidenhead United	3-0
35r	Shortwood United v Bath City	1-3
40r	Chelmsford City v Whitehawk	4-1

Qualifying Round Four

1	Spennymoor Town v AFC Telford United	2-2
2	King's Lynn Town v AFC Fylde	3-4
3	Grimsby Town v Guiseley	3-0
4	Norton United v Shildon	1-1
5	Warrington Town v North Ferriby United	1-0
6	Alfreton Town v Lincoln City	1-1
7	Macclesfield Town v Wrexham	1-1
8	Chorley v FC Halifax Town	0-0
9	Barwell v Altrincham	0-3
10	Leek Town v Blyth Spartans	3-4
11	Stockport County v Chester FC	2-4
12	Gateshead (2) v Gainsborough Trinity	4-0
13	Tamworth v Southport	1-1
14	Dorchester Town v Bristol Rovers	1-7
15	East Thurrock United v Bath City	7-1
16	Gloucester City v Forest Green Rovers	1-4
17	Dartford v Burgess Hill Town	3-1
18	Maidstone United (2) v Welling United	2-1
19	Willand Rovers v Gosport Borough	1-3
20	Witham Town v Weston-Super-Mare	1-2
21	Eastbourne Borough v Dover Athletic	0-0
22	Weymouth v Braintree Town	0-0
23	Worcester City v Greenwich Borough	2-1
24	Canvey Island v Havant & Waterlooville	0-0
25	St Albans City v Concord Rangers	0-1
26	Basingstoke Town v Harrow Borough	1-1
27	Aldershot Town v Torquay United	2-0
28	Kidderminster Harriers v Eastleigh	0-1
29	Evesham United v Bromley	1-2
30	Chelmsford City v Barnet	0-0
31	Nuneaton Town v Hemel Hempstead Town	0-0
32	Woking v Boreham Wood	2-1
1r	AFC Telford United v Spennymoor Town	3-0
4r	Shildon v Norton United	1-2
6r	Lincoln City v Alfreton Town	5-1
7r	Wrexham v Macclesfield Town	5-2
8r	FC Halifax Town v Chorley	5-0
13r	Southport v Tamworth	1-1P
21r	Dover Athletic v Eastbourne Borough	1-0
22r	Braintree Town v Weymouth	5-3e
24r	Havant & Waterlooville v Canvey Island	3-0
26r	Harrow Borough v Basingstoke Town	1-4e
30r	Barnet v Chelmsford City	4-1
31r	Hemel Hempstead Town v Nuneaton Town	2-0e

Round One

Barnet v Wycombe Wanderers	1-3
Barnsley v Burton Albion	5-0
Basingstoke Town v AFC Telford United	1-1
Blyth Spartans v Altrincham	4-1

2014/15 to 2015/16

	Braintree Town v Chesterfield	0-6
	Bromley v Dartford	3-4
	Bury v Hemel Hempstead Town	3-1
	Cambridge United v Fleetwood Town	1-0
	Cheltenham Town v Swindon Town	5-0
	Coventry City v Worcester City	1-2
	Crewe Alexandra v Sheffield United	0-0
	Dagenham & Redbridge v Southport	0-0
	Dover Athletic v Morecambe	1-0
	Eastleigh v Lincoln City	2-1
	FC Halifax Town v Bradford City	1-2
	Forest Green Rovers v Scunthorpe United	0-2
	Gillingham v Bristol City	1-2
	Gosport Borough v Colchester United	3-6
	Grimsby Town v Oxford United	1-3
	Hartlepool United v East Thurrock United	2-0
	Havant & Waterlooville v Preston North End	0-3
	Luton Town v Newport County (2)	4-2
	Mansfield Town v Concord Rangers	1-1
	Northampton Town v Rochdale	0-0
	Norton United v Gateshead (2)	0-4
	Notts County v Accrington Stanley (2)	0-0
	Oldham Athletic v Leyton Orient	1-0
	Peterborough United v Carlisle United	2-1
	Plymouth Argyle v AFC Fylde	2-0
	Port Vale v Milton Keynes Dons	3-4
	Portsmouth v Aldershot Town	2-2
	Southend United v Chester FC	1-2
	Stevenage v Maidstone United (2)	0-0
	Tranmere Rovers v Bristol Rovers	1-0
	Walsall v Shrewsbury Town	2-2
	Warrington Town v Exeter City	1-0
	Weston-Super-Mare v Doncaster Rovers	1-4
	Wrexham v Woking	3-0
	Yeovil Town v Crawley Town	1-0
	York City v AFC Wimbledon	1-1
r	AFC Telford United v Basingstoke Town	2-1
r	AFC Wimbledon v York City	3-1
r	Accrington Stanley (2) v Notts County	2-1
r	Aldershot Town v Portsmouth	1-0
r	Concord Rangers v Mansfield Town	0-1
r	Maidstone United (2) v Stevenage	2-1
r	Rochdale v Northampton Town	2-1
r	Sheffield United v Crewe Alexandra	2-0
r	Shrewsbury Town v Walsall	1-0
r	Southport v Dagenham & Redbridge	2-0

Round Two

	Accrington Stanley (2) v Yeovil Town	1-1
	Aldershot Town v Rochdale	0-0
	Barnsley v Chester FC	0-0
	Bradford City v Dartford	4-1
	Bristol City v AFC Telford United	1-0
	Bury v Luton Town	1-1
	Cambridge United v Mansfield Town	2-2
	Cheltenham Town v Dover Athletic	0-1
	Colchester United v Peterborough United	1-0
	Gateshead (2) v Warrington Town	2-0
	Hartlepool United v Blyth Spartans	1-2
	Milton Keynes Dons v Chesterfield	0-1
	Oldham Athletic v Doncaster Rovers	0-1
	Oxford United v Tranmere Rovers	2-2
	Preston North End v Shrewsbury Town	1-0
	Scunthorpe United v Worcester City	1-1
	Sheffield United v Plymouth Argyle	3-0
	Southport v Eastleigh	2-1
	Wrexham v Maidstone United (2)	3-1
	Wycombe Wanderers v AFC Wimbledon	0-1
r	Chester FC v Barnsley	0-3
r	Luton Town v Bury	1-0
r	Mansfield Town v Cambridge United	0-1
r	Rochdale v Aldershot Town	4-1
r	Tranmere Rovers v Oxford United	2-1
r	Worcester City v Scunthorpe United	1-1q
r	Yeovil Town v Accrington Stanley (2)	2-0

Round Three

	AFC Wimbledon v Liverpool	1-2
	Arsenal v Hull City	2-0
	Aston Villa v Blackpool	1-0
	Barnsley v Middlesbrough	0-2
	Blyth Spartans v Birmingham City	2-3
	Bolton Wanderers v Wigan Athletic	1-0
	Brentford v Brighton & Hove Albion	0-2
	Burnley v Tottenham Hotspur	1-1
	Cambridge United v Luton Town	2-1
	Cardiff City v Colchester United	3-1
	Charlton Athletic v Blackburn Rovers	1-2
	Chelsea v Watford	3-0
	Derby County v Southport	1-0
	Doncaster Rovers v Bristol City	1-1
	Dover Athletic v Crystal Palace	0-4
	Everton v West Ham United	1-1
	Fulham v Wolverhampton Wan.	0-0
	Huddersfield Town v Reading	0-1
	Leicester City v Newcastle United	1-0
	Manchester City v Sheffield Wednesday	2-1
	Millwall v Bradford City	3-3
	Preston North End v Norwich City	2-0
	Queen's Park Rangers v Sheffield United	0-3
	Rochdale v Nottingham Forest	1-0
	Rotherham United v Bournemouth	1-5
	Scunthorpe United v Chesterfield	2-2
	Southampton v Ipswich Town	1-1
	Stoke City v Wrexham	3-1
	Sunderland v Leeds United	1-0
	Tranmere Rovers v Swansea City	2-6
	West Bromwich Albion v Gateshead (2)	7-0
	Yeovil Town v Manchester United	0-2
r	Bradford City v Millwall	4-0
r	Bristol City v Doncaster Rovers	2-0
r	Chesterfield v Scunthorpe United	2-0e
r	Ipswich Town v Southampton	0-1
r	Tottenham Hotspur v Burnley	4-2
r	West Ham United v Everton	2-2P
r	Wolverhampton Wan. v Fulham	3-3q

Round Four

	Aston Villa v Bournemouth	2-1
	Birmingham City v West Bromwich Albion	1-2
	Blackburn Rovers v Swansea City	3-1
	Brighton & Hove Albion v Arsenal	2-3
	Bristol City v West Ham United	0-1
	Cambridge United v Manchester United	0-0
	Cardiff City v Reading	1-2
	Chelsea v Bradford City	2-4
	Derby County v Chesterfield	2-0
	Liverpool v Bolton Wanderers	0-0
	Manchester City v Middlesbrough	0-2
	Preston North End v Sheffield United	1-1
	Rochdale v Stoke City	1-4
	Southampton v Crystal Palace	2-3
	Sunderland v Fulham	0-0
	Tottenham Hotspur v Leicester City	1-2
r	Bolton Wanderers v Liverpool	1-2
r	Fulham v Sunderland	1-3
r	Manchester United v Cambridge United	3-0
r	Sheffield United v Preston North End	1-3

Round Five

	Arsenal v Middlesbrough	2-0
	Aston Villa v Leicester City	2-1
	Blackburn Rovers v Stoke City	4-1
	Bradford City v Sunderland	2-0
	Crystal Palace v Liverpool	1-2
	Derby County v Reading	1-2
	Preston North End v Manchester United	1-3
	West Bromwich Albion v West Ham United	4-0

Round Six

	Aston Villa v West Bromwich Albion	2-0
	Bradford City v Reading	0-0
	Liverpool v Blackburn Rovers	0-0
	Manchester United v Arsenal	1-2
r	Blackburn Rovers v Liverpool	0-1
r	Reading v Bradford City	3-0

Semi Finals

Arsenal v Reading	2-1eN
Aston Villa v Liverpool	2-1 N

Final

Arsenal v Aston Villa	4-0 N

2015/16

Extra Preliminary Round

1	Penrith v Jarrow Roofing Boldon CA	1-2
2	Silsden v West Allotment Celtic	2-1
3	Ashington v Albion Sports	2-2
4	AFC Darwen v Washington	1-2
5	Newcastle Benfield v Yorkshire Amateur	4-2
6	Nelson v Newton Aycliffe	0-4
7	Bedlington Terriers v West Auckland Town	1-1
8	Barnoldswick Town v Colne	0-5
9	Billingham Synthonia v Consett	0-0
10	Hebburn Town v Tadcaster Albion	1-3
11	Bishop Auckland v Shildon	1-1
12	Sunderland RCA v Guisborough Town	4-4
13	Crook Town v Dunston UTS	0-6
14	Holker Old Boys v Liversedge	4-0
15	Pickering Town v Thornaby	4-0
16	Seaham Red Star v Marske United	2-2
17	Garforth Town v Morpeth Town	1-4
18	Heaton Stannington v Norton & Stockton Ancients	3-1
19	Bridlington Town (2) v North Shields	0-2
20	Whitley Bay v Ryhope Colliery Welfare	1-1
21	Whickham v Padiham	1-2
22	Durham City v Thackley	1-3
23	Glasshoughton Welfare v Runcorn Linnets	2-2
24	Chadderton v AFC Liverpool	2-9
25	Congleton Town v Nostell MW	0-0
26	Alsager Town v Athersley Recreation	1-0
27	Winsford United v AFC Blackpool	1-1
28	AFC Emley v Parkgate	7-1
29	Ashton Athletic v Maltby Main	2-2
30	Penistone Church v Pontefract Collieries	0-2
31	Maine Road v St Helens Town	2-1
32	Handsworth Parramore v Staveley MW	6-0
33	1874 Northwich v West Didsbury & Chorlton	3-0
34	Barton Town Old Boys v Squires Gate	2-2
35	Abbey Hey v Worksop Town	3-1
36	Runcorn Town v Bacup Borough	3-0
37	Hemsworth MW v Armthorpe Welfare	1-2
38	Bootle v Atherton Collieries	0-2
39	Hanley Town v Shawbury United	4-2
40	Continental Star v Bolehall Swifts	2-2 N
41	Boldmere St Michaels v Rocester	3-3
42	Hinckley AFC v Walsall Wood	0-0
43	Brocton v Stourport Swifts	1-5
44	Southam United v AFC Wulfrunians	0-2
45	Alvechurch v Heath Hayes	3-0
46	Tipton Town v Cadbury Athletic	0-2
47	AFC Bridgnorth v Wolverhampton Casuals	1-0
48	Malvern Town v Sporting Khalsa	0-5
49	Westfields v Pegasus Juniors	1-0
50	Gornal Athletic v Bromsgrove Sporting	1-2
51	Lye Town v Coventry Sphinx	2-2 N
52	Coleshill Town v Ellesmere Rangers	11-0 N
53	Cleethorpes Town v Brigg Town	5-1
54	Harborough Town v Shirebrook Town	3-2
55	South Normanton Athletic v AFC Mansfield	2-1
56	Shepshed Dynamo v Retford United	1-0
57	Bottesford Town v Rainworth MW	2-2
58	Kirby Muxloe v Heanor Town	3-1
59	Long Eaton United v Harrowby United	2-1
60	Loughborough University v Barrow Town	4-1
61	St Andrews v Clipstone	2-3
62	Radford v Sleaford Town	3-2
63	Quorn v Oadby Town	1-3
64	Bardon Hill v Dunkirk	0-1
65	Ellistown & Ibstock United v Holwell Sports	0-5
66	Blaby & Whetstone Athletic v Leicester Nirvana	0-5
67	Walsham Le Willows v Godmanchester Rovers	0-3
68	Wisbech Town v Diss Town	1-0
69	Yaxley v Gorleston	2-1
70	Peterborough Northern Star v Newmarket Town	1-2
71	Haverhill Rovers v Mildenhall Town	0-1
72	Fakenham Town v Huntingdon Town	0-0
73	Eynesbury Rovers v Peterborough Sports	0-1
74	Swaffham Town v Thetford Town	2-4
75	Great Yarmouth Town v Norwich United	0-3
76	Deeping Rangers v Boston Town	6-1
77	Holbeach United v Ely City	1-1
78	Welwyn Garden City v Haverhill Borough	3-1
79	Hoddesdon Town v Sawbridgeworth Town	4-0
80	FC Romania v Whitton United	0-3 N
81	Southend Manor v Codicote	3-1
82	Wivenhoe Town v Tower Hamlets	1-5
83	Cockfosters v Burnham Ramblers	4-0
84	Hadley v Saffron Walden Town	1-2
85	Hertford Town v Kirkley & Pakefield	2-2
86	Debenham LC v Ipswich Wanderers	0-1
87	Bowers & Pitsea v Ilford	0-1
88	Basildon United v Sporting Bengal United	3-1
89	FC Broxbourne Borough v Brantham Athletic	1-2
90	Long Melford v London Bari	3-0
91	FC Clacton v Eton Manor	3-1
92	Hullbridge Sports v Hadleigh United	2-1
93	Clapton v Stanway Rovers	1-2
94	Stansted v Takeley	2-1 N
95	Enfield 1893 v London Colney	0-4
96	Felixstowe & Walton United v Barking	1-1
97	Waltham Forest v St Margaretsbury	0-3
98	AFC Hayes v Flackwell Heath	3-2
99	Wellingborough Town (2) v Ashford Town (Middlesex)	1-8
100	Berkhamsted v Hanworth Villa	3-2
101	Oxhey Jets v AFC Kempston Rovers	0-0
102	Spelthorne Sports v Stotfold	2-1
103	Windsor v AFC Dunstable	0-1
104	Ampthill Town v Risborough Rangers	0-3
105	Rothwell Corinthians v Thrapston Town	1-2
106	Hillingdon Borough v Wembley	1-1
107	Northampton Sileby Rangers v Sun Sports	2-1
108	Wellingborough Whitworths v Northampton Spencer	0-3
109	Newport Pagnell Town v Holmer Green	6-2
110	Biggleswade United v Desborough Town	2-1
111	Potton United v Bedfont Sports	0-2
112	London Tigers v Bedfont & Feltham	1-1
113	Tring Athletic v Leverstock Green	2-1
114	Bedford v Cogenhoe United	0-6
115	Raunds Town v Crawley Green	1-0
116	Harefield United v Long Buckby	2-2
117	Royal Wootton Bassett Town v Bracknell Town	0-2
118	Ardley United v Tuffley Rovers	1-4
119	Binfield v Westfield	1-1
120	Ascot United v Kidlington	1-2
121	Holyport v Milton United (Oxon)	1-3
122	Hook Norton v Frimley Green	5-0
123	Reading Town v Chertsey Town	0-5
124	Knaphill v Highworth Town	1-3
125	Chinnor v Hartley Wintney	0-2
126	Thame United v Farnham Town	1-1
127	Abingdon United v Brimscombe & Thrupp	0-3
128	Cheltenham Saracens v Winterbourne United	1-0
129	Tadley Calleva v Guildford City (2)	2-3
130	Highmoor Ibis v Thatcham Town	1-2 M
131	Badshot Lea v Camberley Town	2-1
132	Cove v Shrivenham	5-4
133	Banstead Athletic v Rochester United	1-1
134	Hailsham Town v Eastbourne United	2-3
135	Worthing United v Deal Town	0-0
136	Arundel v Raynes Park Vale	3-1
137	Horsham YMCA v AFC Croydon Athletic	2-0
138	Fisher v Corinthian	0-3

2015/16

139 Crawley Down Gatwick v Chichester City 1-3
140 Tunbridge Wells v Glebe wo/s
141 Shoreham v St Francis Rangers 8-0
142 East Preston v Littlehampton Town 1-2
143 Horsham v Lancing 1-0
144 Colliers Wood United v Eastbourne Town 0-2
145 Redhill v Pagham 1-2
146 Holmesdale v Mile Oak 2-0
147 Selsey v Erith Town 1-5
148 Croydon v Sutton Common Rovers 5-1
149 Sevenoaks Town v Seven Acre & Sidcup 1-1
150 Cray Valley Paper Mills v Ashford United 5-1
151 Chessington & Hook United v Crowborough Athletic 1-1
152 Bexhill United v Loxwood 3-1 N
153 Ringmer v Beckenham Town 1-4
154 Lingfield v Canterbury City 0-3 N
155 Greenwich Borough v Lordswood 1-0
156 Epsom & Ewell v Erith & Belvedere 0-4
157 Horley Town v Wick & Barnham United 7-0
158 Christchurch v Cadbury Heath 2-1
159 Melksham Town v Cowes Sports 2-2
160 Longwell Green Sports v Folland Sports 2-1
161 Andover Town v Gillingham Town 2-0
162 Lymington Town v Bitton 0-3 N
163 Alresford Town v Bridport 0-1
164 Hamworthy United v Hallen 1-1
165 Amesbury Town v Bemerton Heath Harlequins 1-2
166 Hythe & Dibden v Moneyfields 1-4
167 Team Solent v Blackfield & Langley 3-4
168 Bradford Town v United Services Portsmouth 2-0
169 Cribbs v Bristol Manor Farm 0-5
170 Verwood Town v Newport (IOW) 2-0
171 Almondsbury UWE v Fawley 3-2
172 Brockenhurst v Fareham Town 2-0
173 Bournemouth (Ams) v AFC Portchester 0-3
174 Sherborne Town v New Milton Town 2-0
175 Whitchurch United v Wincanton Town 1-1
176 Horndean v Sholing 1-3
177 Buckland Athletic v Clevedon Town 3-0
178 Saltash United v AFC St Austell 0-4
179 Bishop Sutton v Street 0-6
180 Witheridge v Welton Rovers 2-0
181 Shepton Mallet v Plymouth Parkway 0-2
182 Bodmin Town v Brislington 3-1
183 Odd Down v Ashton & Backwell United 3-1
184 Barnstaple Town v Willand Rovers 2-0
3r Albion Sports v Ashington 2-3
7r West Auckland Town v Bedlington Terriers 4-0
9r Consett v Billingham Synthonia 8-0
11r Shildon v Bishop Auckland 2-4
12r Guisborough Town v Sunderland RCA 3-2
16r Marske United v Seaham Red Star 3-1
20r Ryhope Colliery Welfare v Whitley Bay 2-3
23r Runcorn Linnets v Glasshoughton Welfare 6-1
25r Nostell MW v Congleton Town 0-4
27r AFC Blackpool v Winsford United 3-2
29r Maltby Main v Ashton Athletic 3-2
34r Squires Gate v Barton Town Old Boys 2-4e
40r Bolehall Swifts v Continental Star 1-3
41r Rocester v Boldmere St Michaels 4-0
42r Walsall Wood v Hinckley AFC 1-3
51r Coventry Sphinx v Lye Town 2-1
57r Rainworth MW v Bottesford Town 1-5
72r Huntingdon Town v Fakenham Town 1-1
77r Ely City v Holbeach United 0-4
85r Kirkley & Pakefield v Hertford Town 2-1
96r Barking v Felixstowe & Walton United 3-1e
101r AFC Kempston Rovers v Oxhey Jets 3-2 N
106r Wembley v Hillingdon Borough 2-1
112r Bedfont & Feltham v London Tigers 2-2p
116r Long Buckby v Harefield United 1-0
119r Westfield v Binfield 0-1
126r Farnham Town v Thame United 1-1p
133r Rochester United v Banstead Athletic 2-1
135r Deal Town v Worthing United 7-1
149r Seven Acre & Sidcup v Sevenoaks Town 1-1p
151r Crowborough Athletic v Chessington & Hook United 1-2e
159r Cowes Sports v Melksham Town 3-1
164r Hallen v Hamworthy United 0-1
175r Wincanton Town v Whitchurch United 3-1

Preliminary Round

1 Whitley Bay v Heaton Stannington 2-1
2 West Auckland Town v Washington 2-3
3 Ashington v Thackley 1-2
4 Pickering Town v Clitheroe 1-5
5 North Shields v Kendal Town 1-1
6 Bishop Auckland v Jarrow Roofing Boldon CA 1-2
7 Silsden v Padiham 0-2
8 Guisborough Town v Newcastle Benfield 4-2
9 Marske United v Lancaster City 1-1
10 Harrogate Railway Athletic v Spennymoor Town 0-0
11 Holker Old Boys v Dunston UTS 0-2
12 Consett v Scarborough Athletic 2-0
13 Tadcaster Albion v Colne 2-5
14 Newton Aycliffe v Morpeth Town 2-0
15 Congleton Town v Handsworth Parramore 4-3
16 Runcorn Linnets v Pontefract Collieries 6-0
17 Armthorpe Welfare v New Mills 1-0
18 Runcorn Town v Northwich Victoria 2-3
19 Alsager Town v Shaw Lane Aquaforce 2-1
20 Ossett Albion v Maine Road 3-0
21 Mossley v Bamber Bridge 1-1
22 Burscough v AFC Emley 3-1
23 Barton Town Old Boys v Droylsden 1-2
24 1874 Northwich v Maltby Main 1-2
25 Abbey Hey v Warrington Town 3-2
26 AFC Blackpool v Ossett Town 1-0
27 Brighouse Town v Atherton Collieries 1-1
28 AFC Liverpool v Radcliffe Borough 3-2
29 Stocksbridge Park Steels v Farsley Celtic FC 1-1
30 Glossop North End v Prescot Cables 2-1
31 Goole AFC v Sheffield 1-1
32 Trafford v Witton Albion 1-2
33 Market Drayton Town v AFC Bridgnorth 2-0
34 Bromsgrove Sporting v Hinckley AFC 2-6
35 Newcastle Town v Continental Star 4-0
36 Leek Town v Rocester 1-1
37 Rugby Town v Coventry Sphinx 1-0
38 Coleshill Town v Stafford Rangers 2-1 N
39 Sporting Khalsa v Cadbury Athletic 4-0
40 Chasetown v Evesham United 2-0
41 Westfields v Kidsgrove Athletic 1-1
42 Stourport Swifts v Alvechurch 1-0
43 AFC Wulfrunians v Romulus 2-0
44 Tividale v Hanley Town 1-0
45 Carlton Town v Shepshed Dynamo 1-2
46 Harborough Town v Oadby Town 0-2
47 Kirby Muxloe v Holwell Sports 0-0
48 Loughborough Dynamo v Basford United 1-3
49 Radford v Spalding United 1-2
50 Dunkirk v Bottesford Town 4-1
51 South Normanton Athletic v Lincoln United 1-1
52 Gresley v Coalville Town 2-2
53 Leicester Nirvana v Belper Town 2-4
54 Loughborough University v Long Eaton United 1-2
55 Clipstone v Cleethorpes Town 1-0
56 Mildenhall Town v Soham Town Rangers 5-2
57 Yaxley v Godmanchester Rovers 4-1
58 Deeping Rangers v Dereham Town 1-0
59 Thetford Town v Bury Town 3-5
60 Wroxham v Fakenham Town 3-2
61 Wisbech Town v Holbeach United 0-1
62 St Ives Town v Norwich United 1-1
63 Newmarket Town v Peterborough Sports 3-5
64 London Colney v Potters Bar Town 1-3
65 St Margaretsbury v AFC Hornchurch 1-5
66 Welwyn Garden City v Waltham Abbey 1-0
67 Ilford v Stanway Rovers 0-2
68 Hullbridge Sports v Maldon & Tiptree 2-0
69 Harlow Town v Southend Manor 5-1
70 Barkingside v Ipswich Wanderers 1-2
71 Barking v Haringey Borough 0-0
72 AFC Sudbury v Ware 4-0
73 Whitton United v Kirkley & Pakefield 0-3
74 Hoddesdon Town v Romford 0-0
75 Stansted v Tilbury 0-0
76 Redbridge v Heybridge Swifts 1-2
77 Cockfosters v Tower Hamlets 3-3
78 Saffron Walden Town v Cheshunt 2-0
79 Great Wakering Rovers v Brantham Athletic 0-2
80 Basildon United v Long Melford 1-0
81 Thurrock v Royston Town 2-2
82 Witham Town v Brightlingsea Regent 1-1
83 FC Clacton v Aveley 2-6
84 Ashford Town (Middlesex) v AFC Kempston Rovers 1-0
85 Long Buckby v Daventry Town 2-1
86 Beaconsfield SYCOB v Raunds Town 3-0
87 Barton Rovers v Berkhamsted 3-1
88 Biggleswade United v Chalfont St Peter 5-3
89 Risborough Rangers v Aylesbury 0-3
90 Wembley v North Greenford United 1-1
91 Northampton Sileby Rangers v Leighton Town 0-3
92 Bedfont & Feltham v AFC Hayes 1-1
93 Newport Pagnell Town v AFC Dunstable 1-1
94 Bedfont Sports v Hanwell Town 1-2
95 Uxbridge v Northampton Spencer 1-0
96 Aylesbury United v Northwood 1-2
97 Bedford Town v Thrapston Town 2-1
98 Cogenhoe United v Spelthorne Sports 3-0
99 Tring Athletic v Arlesey Town 0-2
100 Kings Langley v AFC Rushden & Diamonds 0-1
101 Wantage Town v Didcot Town 3-4
102 Chertsey Town v Kidlington 1-4
103 Binfield v Shortwood United 1-2
104 Badshot Lea v Fleet Town 2-4
105 Marlow v Godalming Town 1-1
106 Brimscombe & Thrupp v Bracknell Town 2-2
107 Tuffley Rovers v Bishop's Cleeve 1-0
108 Cheltenham Saracens v Milton United (Oxon) 1-0
109 Cove v North Leigh 0-7
110 Egham Town v Slimbridge 2-2
111 Thatcham Town v Guildford City (2) 3-2
112 Hartley Wintney v Banbury United 5-2
113 Farnham Town v Highworth Town 4-2
114 Hook Norton v Burnham 1-1
115 Molesey v East Grinstead Town 7-1
116 Chipstead v Rochester United 0-1
117 Deal Town v Horsham 1-1
118 Seven Acre & Sidcup v Sittingbourne 1-2
119 Ramsgate v Tooting & Mitcham United 0-1
120 Folkestone Invicta v Corinthian 3-1
121 Herne Bay v Peacehaven & Telscombe 1-0
122 Hythe Town v Chessington & Hook United 0-2
123 Tunbridge Wells v Croydon 1-1
124 Cray Valley Paper Mills v Hastings United (2) 0-3
125 Holmesdale v South Park 1-10
126 Whitstable Town v Walton Casuals 3-0
127 Three Bridges v Cray Wanderers 0-1
128 Bexhill United v Faversham Town 0-5
129 Eastbourne United v Arundel 1-1
130 Littlehampton Town v Thamesmead Town 0-1
131 Chichester City v Chatham Town 0-4
132 Shoreham v Horley Town 1-1
133 Beckenham Town v Greenwich Borough 0-4
134 Pagham v Corinthian Casuals 3-1
135 Erith Town v Horsham YMCA 2-4
136 Worthing v Walton & Hersham 4-2
137 Eastbourne Town v Whyteleafe 1-1
138 Phoenix Sports v Guernsey 2-2
139 Dorking Wanderers v Canterbury City 6-2
140 Erith & Belvedere v Carshalton Athletic 1-3
141 Winchester City v Wincanton Town 5-1
142 Hamworthy United v Andover Town 4-1 x
Hamworthy United v Andover Town 2-1
143 Longwell Green Sports v Cinderford Town 0-1
144 Brockenhurst v Yate Town 2-1
145 Sholing v Swindon Supermarine 2-4
146 Bradford Town v Christchurch 6-3
147 Cowes Sports v Wimborne Town 0-5
148 Bristol Manor Farm v Bitton 3-2
149 AFC Portchester v AFC Totton 3-1
150 Bashley v Mangotsfield United 0-4
151 Almondsbury UWE v Verwood Town 3-1
152 Moneyfields v Petersfield Town 1-2
153 Blackfield & Langley v Bemerton Heath Harlequins 1-0
154 Bridport v Sherborne Town 3-3
155 Plymouth Parkway v Tiverton Town 4-1
156 Larkhall Athletic v Buckland Athletic 3-2
157 AFC St Austell v Bodmin Town 0-1
158 Barnstaple Town v Bridgwater Town 2-0
159 Street v Witheridge 1-2
160 Taunton Town v Odd Down 5-1
5r Kendal Town v North Shields 2-0
9r Lancaster City v Marske United 1-0
10r Spennymoor Town v Harrogate Railway Athletic 2-0
21r Bamber Bridge v Mossley 3-1
27r Atherton Collieries v Brighouse Town 1-2
29r Farsley Celtic FC v Stocksbridge Park Steels 3-0
31r Sheffield v Goole AFC 0-3
36r Rocester v Leek Town 1-2
41r Kidsgrove Athletic v Westfields 5-6e
47r Holwell Sports v Kirby Muxloe 1-0
51r Lincoln United v South Normanton Athletic 2-1
52r Coalville Town v Gresley 5-0
62r Norwich United v St Ives Town 2-6
71r Haringey Borough v Barking 2-1
74r Romford v Hoddesdon Town 1-1q
75r Tilbury v Stansted 3-0
77r Tower Hamlets v Cockfosters 1-5
81r Royston Town v Thurrock 1-3
82r Brightlingsea Regent v Witham Town 2-3
90r North Greenford United v Wembley 5-1
92r AFC Hayes v Bedfont & Feltham 1-3
93r AFC Dunstable v Newport Pagnell Town 2-1
105r Godalming Town v Marlow 2-1e
106r Bracknell Town v Brimscombe & Thrupp 1-0
110r Slimbridge v Egham Town 3-2e
114r Burnham v Hook Norton 2-4e
117r Horsham v Deal Town 1-2
123r Croydon v Tunbridge Wells 2-1
129r Arundel v Eastbourne United 1-4
132r Horley Town v Shoreham 2-3
137r Whyteleafe v Eastbourne Town 2-3
138r Guernsey v Phoenix Sports 1-2 N
154r Sherborne Town v Bridport 0-1e

Qualifying Round One

1 Jarrow Roofing Boldon CA v Congleton Town 3-4
2 Buxton v Ramsbottom United 2-1
3 Washington v Runcorn Linnets 1-0
4 Padiham v Lancaster City 0-2
5 Spennymoor Town v Blyth Spartans 2-1
6 Droylsden v Ossett Albion 2-1
7 Northwich Victoria v AFC Blackpool 4-0
8 Workington v Colwyn Bay 5-0
9 Consett v Colne 3-1
10 Matlock Town v Whitley Bay 0-0
11 Kendal Town v Dunston UTS 5-2
12 Glossop North End v Skelmersdale United 1-1
13 Maltby Main v Frickley Athletic 0-2
14 Salford City v Whitby Town 1-1
15 Darlington 1883 v Hyde United 1-3
16 AFC Liverpool v Armthorpe Welfare 3-4
17 Ashton United v Guisborough Town 0-0
18 Thackley v Abbey Hey 2-2
19 Alsager Town v Burscough 1-2
20 Witton Albion v Farsley Celtic FC 2-1
21 Brighouse Town v Newton Aycliffe 0-2
22 Marine v Clitheroe 2-0
23 Goole AFC v Bamber Bridge 2-2
24 Spalding United v Nantwich Town 1-0
25 Hinckley AFC v Redditch United 2-1
26 Ilkeston FC v Rugby Town 2-3
27 Tividale v Stourbridge 0-1
28 Leamington v Stamford 1-1
29 Market Drayton Town v Kettering Town 0-5
30 Coleshill Town v Newcastle Town 3-3 N
31 Sutton Coldfield Town v Oadby Town 0-1
32 Sporting Khalsa v AFC Wulfrunians 3-2
33 Clipstone v Lincoln United 1-2
34 Shepshed Dynamo v Rushall Olympic 0-0
35 Holwell Sports v Bedworth United 2-2

2015/16

36	Barwell v Westfields	4-1
37	Halesowen Town v Mickleover Sports	2-1
38	Basford United v Long Eaton United	1-0
39	Chasetown v Grantham Town	3-0
40	Stratford Town v Coalville Town	0-2
41	Holbeach United v Stourport Swifts	2-2
42	Belper Town v Dunkirk	1-3
43	Leek Town v Deeping Rangers	2-2
44	Beaconsfield SYCOB v Kirkley & Pakefield	1-2
45	Long Buckby v Wingate & Finchley	0-4
46	Thurrock v Witham Town	1-2
47	Hanwell Town v Saffron Walden Town	1-0
48	Cogenhoe United v Leighton Town	3-2
49	Billericay Town v Enfield Town	1-1
50	Heybridge Swifts v Uxbridge	1-3
51	Potters Bar Town v Haringey Borough	3-0
52	Northwood v Harrow Borough	0-0
53	Yaxley v East Thurrock United	1-3
54	Leiston v AFC Dunstable	1-0
55	Peterborough Sports v Hitchin Town	1-1
56	Harlow Town v Bedford Town	5-1
57	AFC Sudbury v Hendon	3-1
58	Bury Town v Cockfosters	2-1
59	Bedfont & Feltham v AFC Rushden & Diamonds	1-2
60	Basildon United v Hullbridge Sports	0-1
61	AFC Hornchurch v Cambridge City	2-1
62	Ipswich Wanderers v Canvey Island	1-0
63	Dunstable Town v Barton Rovers	2-1
64	Brantham Athletic v Biggleswade Town	1-2
65	Brentwood Town v Arlesey Town	2-0
66	Hoddesdon Town v Ashford Town (Middlesex)	3-1
67	Histon v Aveley	1-4
68	North Greenford United v Mildenhall Town	0-0
69	Welwyn Garden City v St Ives Town	0-1
70	Tilbury v St Neots Town	2-5
71	King's Lynn Town v Wroxham	4-1
72	Chesham United v Aylesbury	0-0
73	Needham Market v Stanway Rovers	1-1
74	Grays Athletic v Biggleswade United	5-0
75	Tooting & Mitcham United v Farnham Town	2-1
76	Worthing v Thamesmead Town	2-1
77	Metropolitan Police v Sittingbourne	0-0
78	Pagham v Carshalton Athletic	1-2
79	Rochester United v Herne Bay	1-3
80	Greenwich Borough v Slimbridge	2-3
81	Croydon v Molesey	1-0
82	Horsham YMCA v Burgess Hill Town	2-1
83	South Park v Leatherhead	1-1
84	Eastbourne United v Hook Norton	0-1
85	Godalming Town v Kidlington	0-1
86	Shoreham v Eastbourne Town	2-3
87	Tonbridge Angels v Folkestone Invicta	1-1
88	Hampton & Richmond Boro. v Dulwich Hamlet	0-1
89	Phoenix Sports v Lewes	2-0
90	Whitstable Town v Deal Town	1-1
91	Dorking Wanderers v Slough Town	0-1
92	Bognor Regis Town v Merstham	2-1
93	VCD Athletic v Didcot Town	1-1
94	Staines Town v Faversham Town	2-2
95	Chessington & Hook United v North Leigh	2-3
96	Kingstonian v Farnborough	1-1
97	Hartley Wintney v Fleet Town	1-1
98	Hastings United (2) v Thatcham Town	1-0
99	Chatham Town v Cray Wanderers	1-0
100	Swindon Supermarine v Winchester City	0-4
101	Wimborne Town v Witheridge	3-2
102	Shortwood United v Bracknell Town	4-3
103	Cinderford Town v Paulton Rovers	1-2
104	Taunton Town v Tuffley Rovers	3-0
105	Dorchester Town v Cirencester Town	1-1
106	Bridport v Larkhall Athletic	2-5
107	Bristol Manor Farm v AFC Portchester	0-3
108	Hungerford Town v Bradford Town	1-1
109	Poole Town v Barnstaple Town	1-0
110	Frome Town v Chippenham Town	0-0
111	Brockenhurst v Mangotsfield United	3-0
112	Plymouth Parkway v Merthyr Town (2)	0-2
113	Cheltenham Saracens v Blackfield & Langley	1-2
114	Bodmin Town v Almondsbury UWE	2-0
115	Petersfield Town v Weymouth	3-1
116	Bideford v Hamworthy United	3-1
10r	Whitley Bay v Matlock Town	3-3p
12r	Skelmersdale United v Glossop North End	2-1
14r	Whitby Town v Salford City	0-5
17r	Guisborough Town v Ashton United	2-3
18r	Abbey Hey v Thackley	1-0
23r	Bamber Bridge v Goole AFC	4-2
28r	Stamford v Leamington	2-1
30r	Newcastle Town v Coleshill Town	1-3
34r	Rushall Olympic v Shepshed Dynamo	4-1
35r	Bedworth United v Holwell Sports	2-0e
41r	Stourport Swifts v Holbeach United	0-1e
43r	Deeping Rangers v Leek Town	4-2
49r	Enfield Town v Billericay Town	2-0
52r	Harrow Borough v Northwood	0-1
55r	Hitchin Town v Peterborough Sports	4-2e
68r	Mildenhall Town v North Greenford United	1-0
72r	Aylesbury v Chesham United	1-2
73r	Stanway Rovers v Needham Market	3-0
77r	Sittingbourne v Metropolitan Police	1-0
83r	Leatherhead v South Park	1-3
87r	Folkestone Invicta v Tonbridge Angels	1-2
90r	Deal Town v Whitstable Town	2-0
93r	Didcot Town v VCD Athletic	4-3
94r	Faversham Town v Staines Town	1-3
96r	Farnborough v Kingstonian	2-3
97r	Fleet Town v Hartley Wintney	0-4
105r	Cirencester Town v Dorchester Town	3-1
108r	Bradford Town v Hungerford Town	2-0
110r	Chippenham Town v Frome Town	1-0

Qualifying Round Two

1	Chorley v Frickley Athletic	2-0
2	Salford City v Curzon Ashton	2-1
3	Spennymoor Town v Burscough	0-2
4	Abbey Hey v Ashton United	0-5
5	Workington v Harrogate Town	0-1
6	Bamber Bridge v Skelmersdale United	2-0
7	Kendal Town v Stalybridge Celtic	2-3
8	FC United of Manchester v Witton Albion	3-1
9	Hyde United v Northwich Victoria	1-2
10	Whitley Bay v Congleton Town	2-1
11	Droylsden v Lancaster City	2-0
12	Consett v Bradford Park Avenue	1-2
13	Marine v Washington	3-3
14	Armthorpe Welfare v Buxton	1-6
15	AFC Fylde v Stockport County	1-0
16	Newton Aycliffe v North Ferriby United	0-0
17	Holbeach United v Worcester City	1-1
18	Barwell v Cogenhoe United	5-0
19	Basford United v Sporting Khalsa	2-3
20	Rugby Town v Lincoln United	3-2
21	Deeping Rangers v AFC Rushden & Diamonds	0-3
22	Halesowen Town v Nuneaton Town	0-2
23	Kettering Town v AFC Telford United	2-1
24	Gainsborough Trinity v Boston United	2-0
25	Coalville Town v Spalding United	0-3
26	Corby Town v Rushall Olympic	1-1
27	Chasetown v Hinckley AFC	5-2
28	Solihull Moors v Oadby Town	3-1
29	Hednesford Town v Bedworth United	2-0
30	Tamworth v Alfreton Town	2-3
31	Stourbridge v Dunkirk	3-1
32	Coleshill Town v Stamford	2-0 N
33	Grays Athletic v Hullbridge Sports	6-0
34	Maidstone United (2) v South Park	6-2
35	Hanwell Town v Mildenhall Town	1-0
36	Chelmsford City v Ebbsfleet United	0-0
37	Phoenix Sports v AFC Hornchurch	3-5
38	Dunstable Town v Kingstonian	2-0
39	St Albans City v Deal Town	2-1
40	Dartford v Uxbridge	0-1
41	St Ives Town v Harlow Town	0-3
42	St Neots Town v Worthing	1-1
43	Carshalton Athletic v East Thurrock United	0-5
44	Wealdstone v Biggleswade Town	1-1
45	Potters Bar Town v Margate	1-5
46	Wingate & Finchley v Concord Rangers	2-1
47	Eastbourne Borough v AFC Sudbury	2-1
48	Bognor Regis Town v Lowestoft Town	2-1
49	Tooting & Mitcham United v Brackley Town	1-3
50	Whitehawk v Dulwich Hamlet	4-2
51	Bury Town v Hemel Hempstead Town	0-3
52	Horsham YMCA v Aveley	2-2
53	Stanway Rovers v Staines Town	0-1
54	Chatham Town v Eastbourne Town	1-2
55	Brentwood Town v Croydon	3-1
56	Sittingbourne v Hoddesdon Town	1-2
57	Enfield Town v Ipswich Wanderers	1-0
58	Bishop's Stortford v Sutton United	0-2
59	King's Lynn Town v Witham Town	1-0
60	Kirkley & Pakefield v Hitchin Town	0-2
61	Leiston v Tonbridge Angels	3-1
62	Northwood v Didcot Town	1-2
63	Herne Bay v Hastings United (2)	1-1
64	North Leigh v Slimbridge	4-1
65	Hook Norton v Weston-Super-Mare	1-2
66	Larkhall Athletic v Havant & Waterlooville	1-1
67	Merthyr Town (2) v Hartley Wintney	0-1
68	Bradford Town v Chippenham Town	2-3
69	Brockenhurst v AFC Portchester	1-0
70	Paulton Rovers v Chesham United	0-2
71	Bodmin Town v Bath City	1-2
72	Gosport Borough v Bideford	7-0
73	Winchester City v Maidenhead United	1-1
74	Taunton Town v Truro City	2-2
75	Oxford City v Shortwood United	3-1
76	Hayes & Yeading United v Poole Town	2-3
77	Wimborne Town v Blackfield & Langley	1-6
78	Gloucester City v Kidlington	4-2
79	Basingstoke Town v Slough Town	4-2
80	Petersfield Town v Cirencester Town	3-1
13r	Washington v Marine	2-3e
16r	North Ferriby United v Newton Aycliffe	3-0
17r	Worcester City v Holbeach United	2-0
26r	Rushall Olympic v Corby Town	2-1
36r	Ebbsfleet United v Chelmsford City	1-2
42r	Worthing v St Neots Town	2-2p
44r	Biggleswade Town v Wealdstone	0-2
52r	Aveley v Horsham YMCA	4-1
63r	Hastings United (2) v Herne Bay	3-2
66r	Havant & Waterlooville v Larkhall Athletic	4-2
73r	Maidenhead United v Winchester City	4-2
74r	Truro City v Taunton Town	3-1

Qualifying Round Three

1	Harrogate Town v Burscough	3-0
2	Salford City v Bradford Park Avenue	1-1
3	Whitley Bay v Chorley	2-3
4	Stourbridge v Rushall Olympic	1-0
5	Solihull Moors v Worcester City	1-1
6	FC United of Manchester v Buxton	1-1
7	Marine v Northwich Victoria	2-4
8	Chasetown v Stalybridge Celtic	1-1
9	North Ferriby United v Nuneaton Town	2-1
10	AFC Fylde v Coleshill Town	9-0
11	Barwell v King's Lynn Town	1-0
12	Hednesford Town v Alfreton Town	2-4
13	Droylsden v Gainsborough Trinity	3-4
14	Sporting Khalsa v Spalding United	1-1
15	Brackley Town v Rugby Town	1-1
16	Kettering Town v Bamber Bridge	1-1
17	AFC Rushden & Diamonds v Ashton United	2-0
18	Harlow Town v Bath City	2-2
19	East Thurrock United v Staines Town	3-6
20	Bognor Regis Town v Oxford City	4-2
21	Basingstoke Town v Chelmsford City	4-2
22	Maidstone United (2) v Dunstable Town	2-0
23	Eastbourne Borough v Hartley Wintney	3-2
24	Leiston v Gloucester City	1-3
25	Hastings United (2) v Poole Town	0-2
26	Hoddesdon Town v Brentwood Town	0-0
27	Didcot Town v Eastbourne Town	4-1
28	Whitehawk v Gosport Borough	2-2
29	Enfield Town v Hitchin Town	0-0
30	Wingate & Finchley v Weston-Super-Mare	1-3
31	Chesham United v North Leigh	2-0
32	Hanwell Town v Grays Athletic	1-2
33	Margate v Truro City	4-1
34	Brockenhurst v Wealdstone	1-5
35	Uxbridge v Chippenham Town	0-3
36	Hemel Hempstead Town v Sutton United	1-1
37	Petersfield Town v St Albans City	0-1
38	Aveley v Havant & Waterlooville	0-2
39	Worthing v AFC Hornchurch	1-4
40	Blackfield & Langley v Maidenhead United	0-1
2r	Bradford Park Avenue v Salford City	0-1e
5r	Worcester City v Solihull Moors	1-0
6r	Buxton v FC United of Manchester	0-2
8r	Stalybridge Celtic v Chasetown	2-0
14r	Spalding United v Sporting Khalsa	1-2
15r	Rugby Town v Brackley Town	0-2
16r	Bamber Bridge v Kettering Town	3-2
18r	Bath City v Harlow Town	1-2
26r	Brentwood Town v Hoddesdon Town	2-1
28r	Gosport Borough v Whitehawk	1-2
29r	Hitchin Town v Enfield Town	1-2
36r	Sutton United v Hemel Hempstead Town	2-1

Qualifying Round Four

1	Gateshead (2) v Worcester City	1-2
2	AFC Fylde v Barrow	1-0
3	Wrexham v Gainsborough Trinity	0-1
4	Northwich Victoria v Chorley	0-0
5	Harrogate Town v Grimsby Town	1-4
6	Barwell v AFC Rushden & Diamonds	2-2
7	Salford City v Southport	1-0
8	Sporting Khalsa v FC United of Manchester	1-3
9	Stalybridge Celtic v North Ferriby United	1-1
10	FC Halifax Town v Guiseley	2-2
11	Tranmere Rovers v Lincoln City	0-0
12	Stourbridge v Kidderminster Harriers	3-0
13	Macclesfield Town v Alfreton Town	3-2
14	Brackley Town v Bamber Bridge	3-0
15	Altrincham v Chester FC	1-0
16	Whitehawk v Poole Town	2-0
17	Maidenhead United v Woking	3-0
18	Basingstoke Town v Torquay United	3-0
19	Grays Athletic v Welling United	1-1
20	Boreham Wood v AFC Hornchurch	2-1
21	Wealdstone v Bognor Regis Town	2-1
22	Didcot Town v Brentwood Town	4-2
23	Eastbourne Borough v Dover Athletic	1-2
24	Chesham United v Enfield Town	2-1
25	Staines Town v Gloucester City	2-1
26	Aldershot Town v Sutton United	1-0
27	Bromley v Eastleigh	1-2
28	Margate v Forest Green Rovers	1-2
29	Braintree Town v Harlow Town	2-0
30	Havant & Waterlooville v Cheltenham Town	3-3
31	Chippenham Town v Maidstone United (2)	0-2
32	St Albans City v Weston-Super-Mare	2-1
4r	Chorley v Northwich Victoria	1-2
6r	AFC Rushden & Diamonds v Barwell	0-1
9r	North Ferriby United v Stalybridge Celtic	0-0q
10r	Guiseley v FC Halifax Town	1-2
11r	Lincoln City v Tranmere Rovers	2-0
19r	Welling United v Grays Athletic	4-0
30r	Cheltenham Town v Havant & Waterlooville	1-0

Round One

AFC Wimbledon v Forest Green Rovers	1-2
Accrington Stanley (2) v York City	3-2
Aldershot Town v Bradford City	0-0
Altrincham v Barnsley	1-0
Barnet v Blackpool	2-0
Barwell v Welling United	0-2

2015/16 to 2016/17

	Brackley Town v Newport County (2)	2-2
	Braintree Town v Oxford United	1-1
	Bristol Rovers v Chesham United	0-1
	Burton Albion v Peterborough United	0-3
	Bury v Wigan Athletic	4-0
	Cambridge United v Basingstoke Town	1-0
	Coventry City v Northampton Town	1-2
	Crawley Town v Luton Town	1-2
	Crewe Alexandra v Eastleigh	0-1
	Dagenham & Redbridge v Morecambe	0-0
	Didcot Town v Exeter City	0-3
	Doncaster Rovers v Stalybridge Celtic	2-0
	Dover Athletic v Stourbridge	1-2
	FC Halifax Town v Wycombe Wanderers	0-4
	FC United of Manchester v Chesterfield	1-4
	Gainsborough Trinity v Shrewsbury Town	0-1
	Grimsby Town v St Albans City	5-1
	Hartlepool United v Cheltenham Town	1-0
	Leyton Orient v Staines Town	6-1
	Maidstone United (2) v Yeovil Town	0-1
	Mansfield Town v Oldham Athletic	0-0
	Millwall v AFC Fylde	3-1
	Northwich Victoria v Boreham Wood	1-1
	Plymouth Argyle v Carlisle United	0-2
	Port Vale v Maidenhead United	1-1
	Portsmouth v Macclesfield Town	2-1
	Rochdale v Swindon Town	3-1
	Salford City v Notts County	2-0
	Scunthorpe United v Southend United	2-1
	Sheffield United v Worcester City	3-0
	Stevenage v Gillingham	3-0
	Walsall v Fleetwood Town	2-0
	Wealdstone v Colchester United	2-6
	Whitehawk v Lincoln City	5-3
r	Boreham Wood v Northwich Victoria	1-2
r	Bradford City v Aldershot Town	2-0
r	Maidenhead United v Port Vale	1-3
r	Morecambe v Dagenham & Redbridge	2-4
r	Newport County (2) v Brackley Town	4-1
r	Oldham Athletic v Mansfield Town	2-0
r	Oxford United v Braintree Town	3-1

Round Two

	Barnet v Newport County (2)	0-1
	Bradford City v Chesham United	4-0
	Cambridge United v Doncaster Rovers	1-3
	Chesterfield v Walsall	1-1
	Colchester United v Altrincham	3-2
	Dagenham & Redbridge v Whitehawk	1-1
	Exeter City v Port Vale	2-0
	Grimsby Town v Shrewsbury Town	0-0
	Leyton Orient v Scunthorpe United	0-0
	Millwall v Wycombe Wanderers	1-2
	Northampton Town v Northwich Victoria	3-2
	Oxford United v Forest Green Rovers	1-0
	Peterborough United v Luton Town	2-0
	Portsmouth v Accrington Stanley (2)	1-0
	Rochdale v Bury	0-1
	Salford City v Hartlepool United	1-1
	Sheffield United v Oldham Athletic	1-0
	Stourbridge v Eastleigh	0-2
	Welling United v Carlisle United	0-5
	Yeovil Town v Stevenage	1-0
r	Hartlepool United v Salford City	2-0e
r	Scunthorpe United v Leyton Orient	3-0
r	Shrewsbury Town v Grimsby Town	1-0
r	Walsall v Chesterfield	0-0p
r	Whitehawk v Dagenham & Redbridge	2-3e

Round Three

	Arsenal v Sunderland	3-1
	Birmingham City v Bournemouth	1-2
	Brentford v Walsall	0-1
	Bury v Bradford City	0-0
	Cardiff City v Shrewsbury Town	0-1
	Carlisle United v Yeovil Town	2-2
	Chelsea v Scunthorpe United	2-0
	Colchester United v Charlton Athletic	2-1
	Doncaster Rovers v Stoke City	1-2
	Eastleigh v Bolton Wanderers	1-1
	Everton v Dagenham & Redbridge	2-0
	Exeter City v Liverpool	2-2
	Hartlepool United v Derby County	1-2
	Huddersfield Town v Reading	2-2
	Hull City v Brighton & Hove Albion	1-0
	Ipswich Town v Portsmouth	2-2
	Leeds United v Rotherham United	2-0
	Manchester United v Sheffield United	1-0
	Middlesbrough v Burnley	1-2
	Newport County (2) v Blackburn Rovers	1-2
	Northampton Town v Milton Keynes Dons	2-2
	Norwich City v Manchester City	0-3
	Nottingham Forest v Queen's Park Rangers	1-0
	Oxford United v Swansea City	3-2
	Peterborough United v Preston North End	2-0
	Sheffield Wednesday v Fulham	2-1
	Southampton v Crystal Palace	1-2
	Tottenham Hotspur v Leicester City	2-2
	Watford v Newcastle United	1-0
	West Bromwich Albion v Bristol City	2-2
	West Ham United v Wolverhampton Wan.	1-0
	Wycombe Wanderers v Aston Villa	1-1
r	Aston Villa v Wycombe Wanderers	2-0
r	Bolton Wanderers v Eastleigh	3-2
r	Bradford City v Bury	0-0q
r	Bristol City v West Bromwich Albion	0-1
r	Leicester City v Tottenham Hotspur	0-2
r	Liverpool v Exeter City	3-0
r	Milton Keynes Dons v Northampton Town	3-0
r	Portsmouth v Ipswich Town	2-1
r	Reading v Huddersfield Town	5-2
r	Yeovil Town v Carlisle United	1-1q

Round Four

	Arsenal v Burnley	2-1
	Aston Villa v Manchester City	0-4
	Bolton Wanderers v Leeds United	1-2
	Bury v Hull City	1-3
	Carlisle United v Everton	0-3
	Colchester United v Tottenham Hotspur	1-4
	Crystal Palace v Stoke City	1-0
	Derby County v Manchester United	1-3
	Liverpool v West Ham United	0-0
	Milton Keynes Dons v Chelsea	1-5
	Nottingham Forest v Watford	0-1
	Oxford United v Blackburn Rovers	0-3
	Portsmouth v Bournemouth	1-2
	Reading v Walsall	4-0
	Shrewsbury Town v Sheffield Wednesday	3-2
	West Bromwich Albion v Peterborough United	2-2
r	Peterborough United v West Bromwich Albion	1-1q
r	West Ham United v Liverpool	2-1e

Round Five

	Arsenal v Hull City	0-0
	Blackburn Rovers v West Ham United	1-5
	Bournemouth v Everton	0-2
	Chelsea v Manchester City	5-1
	Reading v West Bromwich Albion	3-1
	Shrewsbury Town v Manchester United	0-3
	Tottenham Hotspur v Crystal Palace	0-1
	Watford v Leeds United	1-0
r	Hull City v Arsenal	0-4

Round Six

	Arsenal v Watford	1-2
	Everton v Chelsea	2-0
	Manchester United v West Ham United	1-1
	Reading v Crystal Palace	0-2
r	West Ham United v Manchester United	1-2

Semi Finals

Crystal Palace v Watford	2-1 N
Everton v Manchester United	1-2 N

Final

Manchester United v Crystal Palace	2-1eN

2016/17

Extra Preliminary Round

1	Ashington v Nelson	1-2
2	Heaton Stannington v West Auckland Town	2-3
3	Harrogate Railway Athletic v Albion Sports	1-1
4	Easington Colliery v Northallerton Town	0-1
5	West Allotment Celtic v Consett	0-2 N
6	Shildon v Bedlington Terriers	6-1
7	Seaham Red Star v Morpeth Town	1-3
8	Thornaby v Bishop Auckland	0-4
9	Liversedge v Guisborough Town	2-5
10	North Shields v Jarrow Roofing Boldon CA	0-0
11	Bridlington Town (2) v Silsden	1-1
12	Newcastle Benfield v Thackley	2-0
13	Whitley Bay v Norton & Stockton Ancients	2-2
14	Chester-le-Street Town v Garforth Town	3-0
15	Sunderland Ryhope CW v Pickering Town	2-2
16	Padiham v Team Northumbria	1-0
17	Marske United v South Shields (3)	3-1
18	Penrith v Sunderland RCA	1-0
19	Washington v Newton Aycliffe	2-2
20	Billingham Synthonia v Durham City	4-0
21	Barnoldswick Town v Dunston UTS	2-2
22	Armthorpe Welfare v Handsworth Parramore	0-2
23	Maltby Main v Squires Gate	0-1
24	Penistone Church v Cheadle Town	1-3
25	Alsager Town v Barton Town Old Boys	4-1
26	Pontefract Collieries v Runcorn Town	3-2
27	Parkgate v Irlam	2-1
28	Maine Road v Nostell MW	3-3
29	Congleton Town v New Mills	3-0
30	West Didsbury & Chorlton v AFC Liverpool	0-0
31	Hemsworth MW v Runcorn Linnets	2-1
32	AFC Blackpool v Ashton Athletic	0-1
33	Atherton Collieries v Bacup Borough	3-2
34	AFC Emley v Athersley Recreation	2-1
35	AFC Darwen v Cammell Laird 1907	3-3
36	Abbey Hey v Bootle	1-3
37	1874 Northwich v Barnton	2-1
38	Worksop Town v Hallam	4-2
39	Staveley MW v Winsford United	1-2
40	Lichfield City v Wolverhampton Casuals	0-0
41	Haughmond v Alvechurch	0-2
42	AFC Bridgnorth v Boldmere St Michaels	0-3
43	Heath Hayes v Bromsgrove Sporting	0-3
44	Coleshill Town v Cradley Town	2-2
45	Brocton v Walsall Wood	2-1
46	Lye Town v AFC Wulfrunians	3-2
47	Sporting Khalsa v Hanley Town	1-1
48	Tividale v Wolverhampton Sporting Community	2-1
49	Coventry Sphinx v Highgate United	0-5
50	Stourport Swifts v Westfields	3-4
51	Coventry United v Shawbury United	1-1
52	Dudley Sports v Nuneaton Griff	1-1
53	Malvern Town v Rocester	1-2
54	Brigg Town v Clipstone	2-1
55	Oadby Town v Long Eaton United	1-2
56	Loughborough University v Shirebrook Town	4-4
57	Bottesford Town v Radford	1-0
58	South Normanton Athletic v Aylestone Park	2-0
59	Shepshed Dynamo v AFC Mansfield	0-4
60	Hinckley AFC v Heanor Town	1-1
61	Blaby & Whetstone Athletic v St Andrews	2-0
62	Leicester Nirvana v Dunkirk	1-2
63	Anstey Nomads v Harborough Town	1-3
64	Retford United v Leicester Road	1-1
65	Ashby Ivanhoe v Quorn	4-3
66	Kirby Muxloe v Bardon Hill	wo/s
67	Rainworth MW v Cleethorpes Town	1-3
68	Holbeach United v Swaffham Town	4-1
69	Boston Town v Wisbech Town	1-4
70	Kirkley & Pakefield v Walsham Le Willows	0-0
71	Peterborough Sports v Gorleston	8-0
72	Harrowby United v Thetford Town	2-1
73	Yaxley v Huntingdon Town	12-0
74	Ely City v Deeping Rangers	1-4
75	Fakenham Town v Sleaford Town	0-1
76	Godmanchester Rovers v Great Yarmouth Town	2-0
77	Eynesbury Rovers v Peterborough Northern Star	3-1
78	Haverhill Rovers v Hertford Town	1-2
79	Redbridge v Waltham Forest	1-5
80	Brantham Athletic v Hadley	0-1
81	Enfield 1893 v Tower Hamlets	2-4
82	FC Clacton v Eton Manor	3-5
83	Sporting Bengal United v Ipswich Wanderers	0-0 N
84	Wivenhoe Town v Hullbridge Sports	0-2
85	Barkingside v Hadleigh United	2-1
86	Whitton United v Basildon United	0-0
87	London Bari v Clapton	1-3
88	Barking v Takeley	2-0
89	Sawbridgeworth Town v Southend Manor	0-0
90	Stanway Rovers v FC Romania	1-0
91	Ilford v Burnham Ramblers	9-0
92	FC Broxbourne Borough v Felixstowe & Walton United	1-5
93	Halstead Town v Newmarket Town	2-1
94	St Margaretsbury v Long Melford	2-5
95	Hoddesdon Town v Stansted	1-0
96	Saffron Walden Town v Mildenhall Town	1-0
97	Edgware Town v Holmer Green	5-1
98	Flackwell Heath v Baldock Town	6-3
99	Crawley Green v Rothwell Corinthians	2-1
100	London Tigers v Sun Sports	1-1
101	Leighton Town v Northampton Sileby Rangers	1-2
102	Tring Athletic v Desborough Town	0-1
103	Wellingborough Town (2) v Stotfold	1-3
104	Burnham v Oxhey Jets	0-2
105	Cogenhoe United v Berkhamsted	1-0
106	Bedford v Welwyn Garden City	1-2
107	Cockfosters v Harpenden Town	1-2
108	Newport Pagnell Town v Biggleswade United	0-1
109	Wembley v Daventry Town	4-0
110	Harefield United v Northampton ON Chenecks	1-1
111	Leverstock Green v London Colney	1-2
112	Ascot United v Milton United (Oxon)	2-0
113	Abingdon United v AFC Hayes	0-0
114	Thame United v Abbey Rangers	3-0
115	Binfield v North Greenford United	0-1
116	Thatcham Town v Bracknell Town	2-3
117	Spelthorne Sports v Hartley Wintney	4-3
118	Carterton v Highmoor Ibis	1-2
119	Camberley Town v Cove	6-1
120	Chertsey Town v Hook Norton	2-0
121	Brimscombe & Thrupp v Henley Town	3-1
122	Longlevens v Bedfont & Feltham	4-2
123	Bedfont Sports v Windsor	3-2
124	Ardley United v Tuffley Rovers	3-2
125	Highworth Town v Tadley Calleva	2-1
126	Andover Town v Royal Wootton Bassett Town	5-2
127	Hanworth Villa v Knaphill	2-2
128	Fairford Town v CB Hounslow United	1-5
129	Horsham YMCA v Hollands & Blair	2-3
130	Sevenoaks Town v Sporting Club Thamesmead	2-1
131	Holmesdale v Haywards Heath Town	0-2
132	Chessington & Hook United v Wick	3-1
133	Littlehampton Town v Pagham	1-3
134	Hailsham Town v Crawley Down Gatwick	5-7
135	Beckenham Town v Lancing	1-1
136	Colliers Wood United v AFC Croydon Athletic	5-2
137	Croydon v AFC Uckfield Town	2-1
138	Epsom & Ewell v Gravesham Borough	5-2
139	Erith & Belvedere v Loxwood	0-1
140	Deal Town v Banstead Athletic	0-1
141	Peacehaven & Telscombe v Lordswood	3-3
142	Tunbridge Wells v Eastbourne United	1-1
143	Newhaven v Rochester United	0-0

2016/17

144 Mile Oak v Guildford City (2) 0-3
145 Bridon Ropes v Canterbury City 0-3
146 Raynes Park Vale v Eastbourne Town 0-2
147 Worthing United v Shoreham 0-3
148 East Preston v Horley Town 4-1
149 Whitstable Town v Oakwood 4-0
150 Southwick v Cray Valley Paper Mills 0-4
151 Crowborough Athletic v Farnham Town 1-3
152 St Francis Rangers v Redhill 1-4
153 Sheppey United v Badshot Lea 0-1
154 Ashford United v Corinthian 2-0
155 Erith Town v Sutton Common Rovers 2-2
156 Westfield v Walton & Hersham 0-1
157 Arundel v Chichester City 4-3
158 Moneyfields v Christchurch 4-3
159 Sholing v Bournemouth (Ams) 4-1
160 Bemerton Heath Harlequins v Keynsham Town 1-0
161 Cadbury Heath v Folland Sports 7-0
162 Hengrove Athletic v Verwood Town 2-2
163 Oldland Abbotonians v Newport (IOW) 1-0
164 Lydney Town v Team Solent 0-6
165 Lymington Town v Hamworthy United 0-0 N
166 Bradford Town v Fareham Town 1-3
167 Whitchurch United v Cribbs 0-0
168 Brockenhurst v Laverstock & Ford 2-1
169 United Services Portsmouth v Melksham Town 2-1 N
170 Odd Down v Longwell Green Sports 2-0
171 Sherborne Town v Amesbury Town 0-2
172 Bashley v Horndean 2-1
173 Cowes Sports v Brislington 0-3
174 Fawley v AFC Portchester 0-3
175 Bridport v Alresford Town 1-2
176 Blackfield & Langley v Hallen 2-0
177 Bristol Manor Farm v Gillingham Town 1-1
178 Welton Rovers v Bitton 0-2
179 AFC St Austell v Street 2-2
180 Clevedon Town v Ashton & Backwell United 2-1
181 Wells City v Portishead Town 2-2
182 Shepton Mallet v Willand Rovers 1-1
183 Buckland Athletic v Plymouth Parkway 2-3
184 Bodmin Town v Cheddar 2-2
3r Albion Sports v Harrogate Railway Athletic 0-3
10r Jarrow Roofing Boldon CA v North Shields 0-2
11r Silsden v Bridlington Town (2) 1-3
13r Norton & Stockton Ancients v Whitley Bay 2-1
15r Pickering Town v Sunderland Ryhope CW 3-3P
19r Newton Aycliffe v Washington 0-2
21r Dunston UTS v Barnoldswick Town 4-0
28r Nostell MW v Maine Road 2-3
30r AFC Liverpool v West Didsbury & Chorlton 0-1
35r Cammell Laird 1907 v AFC Darwen 3-2
40r Wolverhampton Casuals v Lichfield City 1-2
44r Cradley Town v Coleshill Town 1-4
47r Hanley Town v Sporting Khalsa 1-3
51r Coventry United v Shawbury United wo/s
52r Nuneaton Griff v Dudley Sports 3-3q
56r Shirebrook Town v Loughborough University 0-3
60r Heanor Town v Hinckley AFC 5-1
64r Leicester Road v Retford United 4-2
70r Walsham Le Willows v Kirkley & Pakefield 1-2
83r Ipswich Wanderers v Sporting Bengal United 0-2
86r Basildon United v Whitton United 5-0
89r Southend Manor v Sawbridgeworth Town 2-2q
100r Sun Sports v London Tigers 2-0
110r Northampton ON Chenecks v Harefield United 1-1qN
113r AFC Hayes v Abingdon United 6-1
127r Knaphill v Hanworth Villa 2-3
135r Lancing v Beckenham Town 3-4
141r Lordswood v Peacehaven & Telscombe 1-3
142r Eastbourne United v Tunbridge Wells 2-1
143r Rochester United v Newhaven 1-4e
155r Sutton Common Rovers v Erith Town 0-2
162r Verwood Town v Hengrove Athletic 3-1
165r Hamworthy United v Lymington Town 1-0 N
167r Cribbs v Whitchurch United 0-1
177r Gillingham Town v Bristol Manor Farm 4-3
179r Street v AFC St Austell 3-0
181r Portishead Town v Wells City 2-1
182r Willand Rovers v Shepton Mallet 0-2
184r Cheddar v Bodmin Town 2-3e

Preliminary Round

1 Harrogate Railway Athletic v Norton & Stockton Anc. 3-1
2 Billingham Synthonia v Northallerton Town 6-0
3 Dunston UTS v Penrith 3-3
4 Shildon v Kendal Town 2-0
5 Padiham v Newcastle Benfield 1-2
6 Nelson v Bishop Auckland 1-4
7 Chester-le-Street Town v Marske United 0-4
8 West Auckland Town v Lancaster City 1-5
9 Clitheroe v Consett 0-1
10 Guisborough Town v Bridlington Town (2) 2-3
11 Washington v Pickering Town 2-2
12 Tadcaster Albion v Scarborough Athletic 3-2
13 North Shields v Morpeth Town 0-1
14 Droylsden v Radcliffe Borough 4-4
15 Prescot Cables v Trafford 0-1
16 Handsworth Parramore v Stocksbridge Park Steels 4-1
17 Congleton Town v Farsley Celtic FC 0-6
18 Alsager Town v Winsford United 1-6
19 Ramsbottom United v Sheffield 1-2
20 Worksop Town v Ashton Athletic 2-2
21 Parkgate v Burscough 1-4
22 Ossett Town v Goole AFC 2-1
23 West Didsbury & Chorlton v Squires Gate 2-3
24 Atherton Collieries v Witton Albion 1-3
25 Mossley v Hemsworth MW 4-0
26 Hyde United v Cammell Laird 1907 4-0
27 Glossop North End v Brighouse Town 2-2
28 Maine Road v AFC Emley 3-2
29 Shaw Lane v Colwyn Bay 0-1
30 Colne v 1874 Northwich 2-2
31 Northwich Victoria v Cheadle Town 2-4
32 Bamber Bridge v Ossett Albion 2-5
33 Pontefract Collieries v Bootle 2-1
34 Coleshill Town v Dudley Sports 4-0
35 Bedworth United v Rocester 3-2
36 Kidsgrove Athletic v Lye Town 2-0
37 Coventry United v Lichfield City 5-1
38 Hereford v Alvechurch 4-2
39 Rugby Town v Bromsgrove Sporting 1-0
40 Leek Town v Newcastle Town 3-2
41 Highgate United v Boldmere St Michaels 1-0
42 Market Drayton Town v Evesham United 0-2
43 Sporting Khalsa v Romulus 1-2
44 Chasetown v Brocton 9-0
45 Westfields v Tividale 5-1
46 Dunkirk v Cleethorpes Town 2-0
47 Heanor Town v Long Eaton United 3-2
48 Lincoln United v Carlton Town 2-1
49 Loughborough Dynamo v Ashby Ivanhoe 1-3
50 Basford United v Belper Town 2-4
51 AFC Mansfield v South Normanton Athletic 2-0
52 Brigg Town v Blaby & Whetstone Athletic 2-1
53 Leicester Road v Harborough Town 3-1
54 Bottesford Town v Kirby Muxloe 1-2
55 Loughborough University v Gresley 1-4
56 Sleaford Town v Stamford 0-3
57 Yaxley v Dereham Town 4-4
58 Soham Town Rangers v Harrowby United 4-1
59 Kirkley & Pakefield v Holbeach United 3-4
60 Deeping Rangers v Wroxham 2-1
61 Wisbech Town v Peterborough Sports 1-4
62 Norwich United v Histon 1-2
63 Eynesbury Rovers v Godmanchester Rovers 1-1
64 Bury Town v Spalding United 0-3
65 Ware v Maldon & Tiptree 0-2
66 Thurrock v Halstead Town 2-3
67 Witham Town v Eton Manor 3-0
68 Waltham Forest v Hoddesdon Town 4-0
69 Haringey Borough v Barkingside 7-2
70 Waltham Abbey v Bowers & Pitsea 2-2
71 Brentwood Town v Tilbury 1-2
72 Sporting Bengal United v Clapton 2-0
73 Long Melford v Saffron Walden Town 0-2
74 Romford v Hullbridge Sports 4-3
75 Barking v Stanway Rovers 0-0
76 Ilford v Felixstowe & Walton United 0-2
77 Brightlingsea Regent v Great Wakering Rovers 2-1
78 Sawbridgeworth Town v Tower Hamlets 4-2
79 Aveley v AFC Hornchurch 0-1
80 Hertford Town v Hadley 0-1
81 Royston Town v Heybridge Swifts 1-4
82 Cheshunt v Basildon United 8-0
83 Kempston Rovers v Oxhey Jets 1-0
84 Stotfold v Welwyn Garden City 3-2
85 Crawley Green v Uxbridge 0-3
86 Bedford Town v AFC Dunstable 1-2
87 Sun Sports v Northwood 2-0
88 Arlesey Town v Potters Bar Town 1-1
89 AFC Rushden&Diamonds v Northampton Sileby Rgs 4-3
90 Desborough Town v London Colney 0-1
91 Chalfont St Peter v Harpenden Town 2-0
92 Edgware Town v Barton Rovers 1-3
93 Aylesbury United v Biggleswade United 0-1
94 Cogenhoe United v Flackwell Heath 1-5
95 Beaconsfield SYCOB v Marlow 2-2
96 Aylesbury v Hanwell Town 1-3
97 Wembley v Harefield United 1-1
98 Bishop's Cleeve v Camberley Town 1-1
99 Highmoor Ibis v Brimscombe & Thrupp 1-2
100 Thame United v North Leigh 1-7
101 Wantage Town v Hanworth Villa 4-2
102 North Greenford United v Kidlington 4-1
103 CB Hounslow United v Petersfield Town 2-1
104 Egham Town v Bracknell Town 2-1
105 Spelthorne Sports v Andover Town 2-3
106 Farnborough v Longlevens 5-1
107 Ascot United v Didcot Town 4-3
108 Slimbridge v Bedfont Sports 3-0
109 Chertsey Town v AFC Hayes 3-0
110 Yate Town v Fleet Town 1-2
111 Shortwood United v Ashford Town (Middlesex) 0-2
112 Ardley United v Highworth Town 0-3
113 Canterbury City v Pagham 1-1
114 Cray Valley Paper Mills v Hastings United (2) 0-2
115 Shoreham v Dorking Wanderers 3-4
116 Greenwich Borough v Walton & Hersham 1-1
117 Hollands & Blair v Whyteleafe 1-1
118 Peacehaven & Telscombe v Haywards Heath Town 2-0
119 Lewes v Redhill 6-1
120 Badshot Lea v Cray Wanderers 0-4
121 Crawley Down Gatwick v Corinthian Casuals 2-3
122 Loxwood v Arundel 0-2
123 Carshalton Athletic v Farnham Town 3-0
124 Whitstable Town v Eastbourne Town 0-0
125 Chipstead v Beckenham Town 2-1
126 South Park v Phoenix Sports 2-0
127 Eastbourne United v Newhaven 2-2
128 Ashford United v Three Bridges 1-0
129 Herne Bay v East Grinstead Town 1-0
130 Molesey v Godalming Town 0-2
131 Faversham Town v Epsom & Ewell 2-1
132 VCD Athletic v Croydon 0-0
133 Sevenoaks Town v Horsham 4-2
134 Tooting & Mitcham United v East Preston 0-1
135 Guernsey v Thamesmead Town 2-2
136 Walton Casuals v Chatham Town 3-3
137 Ramsgate v Erith Town 1-0
138 Banstead Athletic v Colliers Wood United 3-3
139 Sittingbourne v Hythe Town 1-1
140 Guildford City (2) v Chessington & Hook United 1-1
141 Gillingham Town v AFC Totton 2-0
142 Bashley v Sholing 1-2
143 Amesbury Town v Bemerton Heath Harlequins 1-3
144 Blackfield & Langley v Paulton Rovers 1-2
145 Cadbury Heath v Team Solent 4-1
146 AFC Portchester v Mangotsfield United 2-0
147 Whitchurch United v Moneyfields 0-3
148 Wimborne Town v Alresford Town 1-1
149 United Services Portsmouth v Winchester City 0-3
150 Verwood Town v Fareham Town 2-2
151 Swindon Supermarine v Odd Down 5-1
152 Oldland Abbotonians v Brislington 2-3
153 Brockenhurst v Hamworthy United 1-2
154 Salisbury v Bitton 5-0
155 Street v Larkhall Athletic 4-2
156 Bideford v Bodmin Town 1-1
157 Taunton Town v Tiverton Town 4-4
158 Bridgwater Town v Plymouth Parkway 0-6
159 Portishead Town v Shepton Mallet 2-0
160 Clevedon Town v Barnstaple Town 0-1
3r Penrith v Dunston UTS 1-2
11r Pickering Town v Washington 1-2
14r Radcliffe Borough v Droylsden 2-1
20r Ashton Athletic v Worksop Town 2-2P
27r Brighouse Town v Glossop North End 4-2
30r 1874 Northwich v Colne 1-3
57r Dereham Town v Yaxley 1-0
63r Godmanchester Rovers v Eynesbury Rovers 1-3
70r Bowers & Pitsea v Waltham Abbey 2-4
75r Stanway Rovers v Barking 3-2
88r Potters Bar Town v Arlesey Town 4-1
95r Marlow v Beaconsfield SYCOB 3-3q
97r Harefield United v Wembley 2-1
98r Camberley Town v Bishop's Cleeve 2-0
113r Pagham v Canterbury City 2-1e
116r Walton & Hersham v Greenwich Borough 0-3
117r Whyteleafe v Hollands & Blair 4-2
124r Eastbourne Town v Whitstable Town 1-1P
127r Newhaven v Eastbourne United 1-2
132r Croydon v VCD Athletic 1-2
135r Thamesmead Town v Guernsey 1-1P
136r Chatham Town v Walton Casuals 1-2
138r Colliers Wood United v Banstead Athletic 3-0
139r Hythe Town v Sittingbourne 5-0
140r Chessington & Hook United v Guildford City (2) 1-2
148r Alresford Town v Wimborne Town 1-0e
150r Fareham Town v Verwood Town 4-0
156r Bodmin Town v Bideford 1-2
157r Tiverton Town v Taunton Town 0-2

Qualifying Round One

1 Washington v Shildon 2-5
2 Ashton United v Nantwich Town 0-3
3 Brighouse Town v Lancaster City 0-3
4 Blyth Spartans v Frickley Athletic 3-1
5 Hyde United v Colne 1-0
6 Bishop Auckland v Ossett Albion 5-1
7 Whitby Town v Winsford United 3-3
8 Sheffield v Farsley Celtic FC 0-3
9 Marske United v Marine 0-2
10 Newcastle Benfield v Bridlington Town (2) 0-2
11 Morpeth Town v Colwyn Bay 4-1
12 Harrogate Railway Athletic v Consett 0-5
13 Dunston UTS v Skelmersdale United 2-2
14 Ashton Athletic v Mossley 7-2
15 Squires Gate v Handsworth Parramore 2-5
16 Witton Albion v Buxton 3-0
17 Billingham Synthonia v Ossett Town 2-2
18 Pontefract Collieries v Tadcaster Albion 2-3
19 Burscough v Maine Road 4-3
20 Trafford v Cheadle Town 5-2
21 Workington v Warrington Town 3-0
22 Radcliffe Borough v Spennymoor Town 3-5
23 Leek Town v Kettering Town 2-3
24 Hednesford Town v Belper Town 1-2
25 King's Lynn Town v Brigg Town 6-1
26 AFC Mansfield v Stratford Town 2-1
27 Rushall Olympic v Soham Town Rangers 2-2
28 Matlock Town v Heanor Town 4-2
29 Chasetown v Grantham Town 1-1
30 Evesham United v Barwell 2-2
31 Peterborough Sports v Stourbridge 1-3
32 Ashby Ivanhoe v Ilkeston FC 0-6
33 St Neots Town v Stamford 1-1
34 Westfields v St Ives Town 4-0
35 Lincoln United v Dunkirk 6-1
36 Halesowen Town v Coleshill Town 3-0
37 Highgate United v Leamington 3-1
38 Leicester Road v Kirby Muxloe 0-0
39 Coalville Town v Redditch United 2-1
40 Coventry United v Bedworth United 0-2

2016/17

41 Mickleover Sports v Spalding United	3-2
42 Deeping Rangers v Gresley	2-6
43 Romulus v Hereford	1-1
44 Rugby Town v Corby Town	1-0
45 Dereham Town v Holbeach United	2-1
46 Eynesbury Rovers v Sutton Coldfield Town	1-3
47 Stafford Rangers v Kidsgrove Athletic	1-2
48 Brightlingsea Regent v Billericay Town	1-2
49 Hadley v London Colney	1-0
50 Haringey Borough v Witham Town	0-3
51 Kempston Rovers v Harefield United	3-2
52 Hanwell Town v Enfield Town	1-0
53 Sun Sports v Hayes & Yeading United	0-2
54 Hendon v Cheshunt	5-2
55 Maldon & Tiptree v Biggleswade Town	0-1
56 Heybridge Swifts v AFC Dunstable	2-2
57 Chesham United v Saffron Walden Town	5-0
58 Harrow Borough v Sawbridgeworth Town	4-1
59 AFC Sudbury v Halstead Town	6-0
60 Kings Langley v Sporting Bengal United	6-1
61 Felixstowe & Walton United v Tilbury	2-1
62 Chalfont St Peter v Potters Bar Town	0-3
63 Uxbridge v Needham Market	2-0
64 Cambridge City v Flackwell Heath	3-1
65 Harlow Town v Romford	3-1
66 Stanway Rovers v Barton Rovers	0-1
67 Canvey Island v Dunstable Town	2-1
68 Hitchin Town v Biggleswade United	4-2
69 Leiston v Grays Athletic	4-1
70 Waltham Forest v Stotfold	2-1
71 AFC Rushden & Diamonds v AFC Hornchurch	2-0
72 Lowestoft Town v Histon	0-2
73 Waltham Abbey v Wingate & Finchley	0-5
74 Colliers Wood United v Eastbourne Town	2-0
75 Hythe Town v Leatherhead	1-0
76 East Preston v Merstham	1-4
77 Camberley Town v Hastings United (2)	0-2
78 South Park v Dorking Wanderers	2-1
79 Walton Casuals v Greenwich Borough	3-2
80 Burgess Hill Town v Ashford United	2-1
81 Fleet Town v Slimbridge	1-1
82 Andover Town v Farnborough	0-5
83 Brimscombe & Thrupp v Peacehaven & Telscombe	3-0
84 Staines Town v Godalming Town	4-0
85 CB Hounslow United v Metropolitan Police	1-3
86 Herne Bay v Ashford Town (Middlesex)	3-1
87 Eastbourne United v Highworth Town	0-3
88 Faversham Town v Cray Wanderers	1-0
89 Pagham v Dulwich Hamlet	0-3
90 Ascot United v Tonbridge Angels	2-2
91 Arundel v Egham Town	1-5
92 Worthing v Carshalton Athletic	3-3
93 Lewes v Sevenoaks Town	0-0
94 Wantage Town v Beaconsfield SYCOB	1-1
95 VCD Athletic v Kingstonian	4-1
96 Slough Town v Chipstead	6-1
97 Thamesmead Town v Chertsey Town	1-0
98 Corinthian Casuals v North Leigh	2-3
99 Folkestone Invicta v North Greenford United	3-1
100 Bognor Regis Town v Guildford City (2)	5-1
101 Ramsgate v Whyteleafe	1-2
102 Taunton Town v Cinderford Town	2-0
103 Alresford Town v Fareham Town	1-1
104 Barnstaple Town v Merthyr Town (2)	0-4
105 Weymouth v Paulton Rovers	2-1
106 Winchester City v Street	4-2
107 Sholing v Havant & Waterlooville	0-2
108 Salisbury v Frome Town	2-0
109 Portishead Town v Swindon Supermarine	1-4
110 Gillingham Town v Cirencester Town	0-2
111 Cadbury Heath v Plymouth Parkway	3-0
112 Chippenham Town v Moneyfields	9-0
113 Basingstoke Town v Bemerton Heath Harlequins	4-0
114 Dorchester Town v Banbury United	0-3
115 Bideford v AFC Portchester	1-2
116 Brislington v Hamworthy United	5-2
7r Winsford United v Whitby Town	1-2
13r Skelmersdale United v Dunston UTS	1-2
17r Ossett Town v Billingham Synthonia	3-2
27r Soham Town Rangers v Rushall Olympic	0-1
29r Grantham Town v Chasetown	2-2q
30r Barwell v Evesham United	2-0
33r Stamford v St Neots Town	4-1
38r Kirby Muxloe v Leicester Road	3-2e
43r Hereford v Romulus	3-0
56r AFC Dunstable v Heybridge Swifts	2-1
81r Slimbridge v Fleet Town	1-0e
90r Tonbridge Angels v Ascot United	7-0
92r Carshalton Athletic v Worthing	2-6
93r Sevenoaks Town v Lewes	2-1
94r Beaconsfield SYCOB v Wantage Town	6-1
103r Fareham Town v Alresford Town	2-4

Qualifying Round Two

1 Bridlington Town (2) v Harrogate Town	1-1
2 Handsworth Parramore v Burscough	2-0
3 Witton Albion v Stalybridge Celtic	1-1
4 Blyth Spartans v Morpeth Town	2-4
5 Bishop Auckland v Trafford	1-0
6 Nantwich Town v Marine	2-2
7 Ashton Athletic v FC Halifax Town	0-5
8 Curzon Ashton v Consett	1-1
9 Altrincham v Gainsborough Trinity	3-2
10 Kidsgrove Athletic v Matlock Town	1-2
11 Lancaster City v Darlington 1883	2-1
12 Alfreton Town v AFC Fylde	1-0
13 Tadcaster Albion v Farsley Celtic FC	0-2
14 Bradford Park Avenue v Salford City	0-1
15 Workington v Shildon	3-1
16 Dunston UTS v Chorley	0-2
17 Stockport County v Hyde United	2-0
18 Ossett Town v FC United of Manchester	1-7
19 Spennymoor Town v Whitby Town	1-0
20 Rushall Olympic v Kettering Town	1-2
21 Kirby Muxloe v Boston United	1-2
22 Sutton Coldfield Town v Hereford	2-3
23 Brackley Town v Rugby Town	6-0
24 Coalville Town v AFC Mansfield	0-1
25 Mickleover Sports v Stourbridge	1-2
26 Westfields v Highgate United	4-2
27 Kidderminster Harriers v Tamworth	4-0
28 Nuneaton Town v Lincoln United	1-2
29 Halesowen Town v Belper Town	1-0
30 Gresley v Stamford	1-1
31 Barwell v Ilkeston FC	0-1
32 Chasetown v Bedworth United	0-1
33 Worcester City v AFC Telford United	0-0
34 Sevenoaks Town v Chesham United	2-2
35 Concord Rangers v AFC Rushden & Diamonds	1-3
36 Beaconsfield SYCOB v Witham Town	3-1
37 Egham Town v VCD Athletic	2-1
38 Dulwich Hamlet v Hendon	0-2
39 Hythe Town v Walton Casuals	2-4
40 Dereham Town v St Albans City	1-2
41 Wingate & Finchley v Tonbridge Angels	0-3
42 AFC Dunstable v Hampton & Richmond Boro.	1-7
43 Wealdstone v Histon	4-0
44 Chelmsford City v Dartford	2-3
45 Staines Town v Maidenhead United	1-0
46 Hayes & Yeading United v Worthing	0-2
47 Hemel Hempstead Town v Herne Bay	1-1
48 Eastbourne Borough v Metropolitan Police	2-1
49 Kempston Rovers v Burgess Hill Town	1-1
50 South Park v Leiston	1-4
51 Hadley v Kings Langley	2-1
52 Ebbsfleet United v AFC Sudbury	5-0
53 Felixstowe & Walton United v Bishop's Stortford	2-1
54 Cambridge City v Slough Town	1-3
55 Folkestone Invicta v Waltham Forest	3-1
56 Uxbridge v Harrow Borough	1-2
57 East Thurrock United v Whitehawk	2-3
58 Canvey Island v Potters Bar Town	2-2
59 Whyteleafe v Welling United	0-2
60 King's Lynn Town v Harlow Town	1-0
61 Billericay Town v Bognor Regis Town	2-1
62 Faversham Town v Hitchin Town	2-2
63 Hanwell Town v Thamesmead Town	1-1
64 Merstham v Colliers Wood United	0-0
65 Margate v Biggleswade Town	2-0
66 Barton Rovers v Hastings United (2)	0-1
67 Swindon Supermarine v Farnborough	1-0
68 Winchester City v Truro City	4-0
69 Havant & Waterlooville v Highworth Town	5-1
70 Alresford Town v Cadbury Heath	1-3
71 Chippenham Town v Poole Town	4-1
72 Salisbury v Gloucester City	1-2
73 Cirencester Town v Banbury United	1-6
74 Basingstoke Town v Hungerford Town	0-1
75 Weymouth v Gosport Borough	3-2
76 AFC Portchester v Merthyr Town (2)	0-2
77 Taunton Town v Slimbridge	2-0
78 Brislington v Brimscombe & Thrupp	1-2
79 Bath City v Oxford City	1-1
80 North Leigh v Weston-Super-Mare	2-1
1r Harrogate Town v Bridlington Town (2)	3-2
3r Stalybridge Celtic v Witton Albion	2-1 N
6r Marine v Nantwich Town	2-3
8r Consett v Curzon Ashton	0-1
30r Stamford v Gresley	1-0
33r AFC Telford United v Worcester City	1-3
34r Chesham United v Sevenoaks Town	2-1
47r Herne Bay v Hemel Hempstead Town	1-5
49r Burgess Hill Town v Kempston Rovers	3-1
58r Potters Bar Town v Canvey Island	3-2
62r Hitchin Town v Faversham Town	0-1
63r Thamesmead Town v Hanwell Town	4-2e
64r Colliers Wood United v Merstham	1-2e
79r Oxford City v Bath City	1-2e

Qualifying Round Three

1 Halesowen Town v Nantwich Town	1-1
2 Kettering Town v Boston United	2-0
3 Lincoln United v Handsworth Parramore	3-1
4 Farsley Celtic FC v Bishop Auckland	0-1
5 FC Halifax Town v Stalybridge Celtic	2-1
6 Worcester City v Brackley Town	0-3
7 King's Lynn Town v Alfreton Town	0-2
8 Curzon Ashton v Bedworth United	4-0
9 Ilkeston FC v Stourbridge	1-2
10 Lancaster City v Kidderminster Harriers	2-3
11 Matlock Town v Workington	1-1
12 Stockport County v Salford City	2-0
13 Spennymoor Town v Chorley	1-0
14 FC United of Manchester v Harrogate Town	3-3
15 Altrincham v Morpeth Town	3-0
16 AFC Mansfield v Stamford	1-2
17 Faversham Town v Egham Town	1-1
18 North Leigh v Folkestone Invicta	3-1
19 Ebbsfleet United v Havant & Waterlooville	7-0
20 Hungerford Town v Leiston	1-4
21 Potters Bar Town v Bath City	0-0
22 Hendon v AFC Rushden & Diamonds	3-0
23 Margate v Hastings United (2)	2-2
24 Taunton Town v Hampton & Richmond Boro.	2-1
25 Weymouth v Brimscombe & Thrupp	6-0
26 St Albans City v Worthing	6-0
27 Wealdstone v Banbury United	2-1
28 Tonbridge Angels v Hereford	4-2
29 Beaconsfield SYCOB v Felixstowe & Walton United	3-0
30 Whitehawk v Merthyr Town (2)	2-0
31 Chesham United v Staines Town	2-0
32 Burgess Hill Town v Cadbury Heath	6-1
33 Slough Town v Dartford	2-3
34 Billericay Town v Chippenham Town	3-2
35 Welling United v Swindon Supermarine	7-1
36 Gloucester City v Hemel Hempstead Town	2-2
37 Westfields v Walton Casuals	4-0
38 Eastbourne Borough v Hadley	0-0
39 Merstham v Thamesmead Town	5-1
40 Harrow Borough v Winchester City	2-1
1r Nantwich Town v Halesowen Town	2-1
11r Workington v Matlock Town	1-3
14r Harrogate Town v FC United of Manchester	2-0
17r Egham Town v Faversham Town	1-0
21r Bath City v Potters Bar Town	1-1q
23r Hastings United (2) v Margate	1-2e
36r Hemel Hempstead Town v Gloucester City	2-0
38r Hadley v Eastbourne Borough	1-4

Qualifying Round Four

1 Southport v Chester FC	1-0
2 Alfreton Town v Gateshead (2)	2-2
3 North Ferriby United v Macclesfield Town	1-4
4 Harrogate Town v FC Halifax Town	0-2
5 Stockport County v Bishop Auckland	2-0
6 Barrow v Tranmere Rovers	2-1
7 Nantwich Town v Stourbridge	1-3
8 Altrincham v Matlock Town	3-1
9 Lincoln City v Guiseley	0-0
10 Lincoln United v Spennymoor Town	0-3
11 Stamford v Wrexham	1-1
12 York City v Curzon Ashton	1-1
13 Welling United v Whitehawk	0-1
14 Westfields v Leiston	2-1
15 Sutton United v Forest Green Rovers	2-1
16 Chesham United v Potters Bar Town	1-0
17 Dagenham & Redbridge v Wealdstone	3-1
18 Torquay United v Woking	1-1
19 Taunton Town v Hemel Hempstead Town	0-0
20 Braintree Town v Bromley	4-2
21 Beaconsfield SYCOB v Brackley Town	0-5
22 Tonbridge Angels v Dartford	0-3
23 Egham Town v St Albans City	0-1
24 Boreham Wood v Hendon	3-0
25 Aldershot Town v Eastbourne Borough	1-2
26 Harrow Borough v Margate	2-2
27 Maidstone United (2) v Billericay Town	3-1
28 Kidderminster Harriers v Weymouth	6-0
29 Solihull Moors v Kettering Town	3-1
30 Burgess Hill Town v Dover Athletic	0-5
31 Merstham v Ebbsfleet United	2-1
32 Eastleigh v North Leigh	6-0
2r Gateshead (2) v Alfreton Town	2-3e
9r Guiseley v Lincoln City	1-2
11r Wrexham v Stamford	2-3e
12r Curzon Ashton v York City	2-1
18r Woking v Torquay United	2-1
19r Hemel Hempstead Town v Taunton Town	0-1
26r Margate v Harrow Borough	1-3

Round One

Alfreton Town v Newport County (2)	1-1
Blackpool v Kidderminster Harriers	2-0
Bolton Wanderers v Grimsby Town	1-0
Boreham Wood v Notts County	2-2
Bradford City v Accrington Stanley (2)	1-2
Braintree Town v Eastbourne Borough	7-0
Bury v AFC Wimbledon	2-2
Cambridge United v Dover Athletic	1-1
Charlton Athletic v Scunthorpe United	3-1
Cheltenham Town v Crewe Alexandra	1-1
Colchester United v Chesterfield	1-2
Crawley Town v Bristol Rovers	1-1
Dagenham & Redbridge v FC Halifax Town	0-0
Dartford v Sutton United	3-6
Eastleigh v Swindon Town	1-1
Exeter City v Luton Town	1-3
Gillingham v Brackley Town	2-2
Hartlepool United v Stamford	3-0
Lincoln City v Altrincham	2-1
Maidstone United (2) v Rochdale	1-1
Mansfield Town v Plymouth Argyle	1-2
Merstham v Oxford United	0-5
Millwall v Southend United	1-0
Milton Keynes Dons v Spennymoor Town	3-2
Morecambe v Coventry City	1-1
Northampton Town v Harrow Borough	6-0
Oldham Athletic v Doncaster Rovers	2-1
Peterborough United v Chesham United	2-1
Port Vale v Stevenage	1-0
Portsmouth v Wycombe Wanderers	1-2

254

2016/17 to 2017/18

	Sheffield United v Leyton Orient	6-0
	Shrewsbury Town v Barnet	3-0
	Southport v Fleetwood Town	0-0
	St Albans City v Carlisle United	3-5
	Stockport County v Woking	2-4
	Taunton Town v Barrow	2-2
	Walsall v Macclesfield Town	0-1
	Westfields v Curzon Ashton	1-1
	Whitehawk v Stourbridge	1-1
	Yeovil Town v Solihull Moors	2-2
r	AFC Wimbledon v Bury	5-0
r	Barrow v Taunton Town	2-1
r	Brackley Town v Gillingham	4-3e
r	Bristol Rovers v Crawley Town	4-2e
r	Coventry City v Morecambe	2-1
r	Crewe Alexandra v Cheltenham Town	1-4
r	Curzon Ashton v Westfields	3-1
r	Dover Athletic v Cambridge United	2-4e
r	FC Halifax Town v Dagenham & Redbridge	2-1
r	Fleetwood Town v Southport	4-1e
r	Newport County (2) v Alfreton Town	4-1e
r	Notts County v Boreham Wood	2-0
r	Rochdale v Maidstone United (2)	2-0
r	Solihull Moors v Yeovil Town	1-1P
r	Stourbridge v Whitehawk	3-0
r	Swindon Town v Eastleigh	1-3

Round Two

	Blackpool v Brackley Town	1-0
	Bolton Wanderers v Sheffield United	3-2
	Bristol Rovers v Barrow	1-2
	Cambridge United v Coventry City	4-0
	Carlisle United v Rochdale	0-2
	Charlton Athletic v Milton Keynes Dons	0-0
	Chesterfield v Wycombe Wanderers	0-5
	Curzon Ashton v AFC Wimbledon	3-4
	Eastleigh v FC Halifax Town	3-3
	Lincoln City v Oldham Athletic	3-2
	Luton Town v Solihull Moors	6-2
	Macclesfield Town v Oxford United	0-0
	Millwall v Braintree Town	5-2
	Notts County v Peterborough United	2-2
	Plymouth Argyle v Newport County (2)	0-0
	Port Vale v Hartlepool United	4-0
	Shrewsbury Town v Fleetwood Town	0-0
	Stourbridge v Northampton Town	1-0
	Sutton United v Cheltenham Town	2-1
	Woking v Accrington Stanley (2)	0-3
r	FC Halifax Town v Eastleigh	0-2
r	Fleetwood Town v Shrewsbury Town	3-2
r	Milton Keynes Dons v Charlton Athletic	3-1e
r	Newport County (2) v Plymouth Argyle	0-1e
r	Oxford United v Macclesfield Town	3-0
r	Peterborough United v Notts County	2-0

Round Three

	Accrington Stanley (2) v Luton Town	2-1
	Barrow v Rochdale	0-2
	Birmingham City v Newcastle United	1-1
	Blackpool v Barnsley	0-0
	Bolton Wanderers v Crystal Palace	0-0
	Brentford v Eastleigh	5-1
	Brighton & Hove Albion v Milton Keynes Dons	2-0
	Bristol City v Fleetwood Town	0-0
	Cambridge United v Leeds United	1-2
	Cardiff City v Fulham	1-2
	Chelsea v Peterborough United	4-1
	Everton v Leicester City	1-2
	Huddersfield Town v Port Vale	4-0
	Hull City v Swansea City	2-0
	Ipswich Town v Lincoln City	2-2
	Liverpool v Plymouth Argyle	0-0
	Manchester United v Reading	4-0
	Middlesbrough v Sheffield Wednesday	3-0
	Millwall v Bournemouth	3-0
	Norwich City v Southampton	2-2
	Preston North End v Arsenal	1-2
	Queen's Park Rangers v Blackburn Rovers	1-2
	Rotherham United v Oxford United	2-3
	Stoke City v Wolverhampton Wan.	0-2
	Sunderland v Burnley	0-0
	Sutton United v AFC Wimbledon	0-0
	Tottenham Hotspur v Aston Villa	2-0
	Watford v Burton Albion	2-0
	West Bromwich Albion v Derby County	1-2
	West Ham United v Manchester City	0-5
	Wigan Athletic v Nottingham Forest	2-0
	Wycombe Wanderers v Stourbridge	2-1
r	AFC Wimbledon v Sutton United	1-3
r	Barnsley v Blackpool	1-2e
r	Burnley v Sunderland	2-0
r	Crystal Palace v Bolton Wanderers	2-1
r	Fleetwood Town v Bristol City	0-1
r	Lincoln City v Ipswich Town	1-0
r	Newcastle United v Birmingham City	3-1
r	Plymouth Argyle v Liverpool	0-1
r	Southampton v Norwich City	1-0

Round Four

	Blackburn Rovers v Blackpool	2-0
	Burnley v Bristol City	2-0
	Chelsea v Brentford	4-0
	Crystal Palace v Manchester City	0-3
	Derby County v Leicester City	2-2
	Fulham v Hull City	4-1
	Lincoln City v Brighton & Hove Albion	3-1
	Liverpool v Wolverhampton Wan.	1-2
	Manchester United v Wigan Athletic	4-0
	Middlesbrough v Accrington Stanley (2)	1-0
	Millwall v Watford	1-0
	Oxford United v Newcastle United	3-0
	Rochdale v Huddersfield Town	0-4
	Southampton v Arsenal	0-5
	Sutton United v Leeds United	1-0
	Tottenham Hotspur v Wycombe Wanderers	4-3
r	Leicester City v Derby County	3-1e

Round Five

	Blackburn Rovers v Manchester United	1-2
	Burnley v Lincoln City	0-1
	Fulham v Tottenham Hotspur	0-3
	Huddersfield Town v Manchester City	0-0
	Middlesbrough v Oxford United	3-2
	Millwall v Leicester City	1-0
	Sutton United v Arsenal	0-2
	Wolverhampton Wan. v Chelsea	0-3
r	Manchester City v Huddersfield Town	5-1

Round Six

Arsenal v Lincoln City	5-0
Chelsea v Manchester United	1-0
Middlesbrough v Manchester City	0-2
Tottenham Hotspur v Millwall	6-0

Semi Finals

Arsenal v Manchester City	2-1eN
Chelsea v Tottenham Hotspur	4-2 N

Final

Arsenal v Chelsea	2-1 N

2017/18

Extra Preliminary Round

1	Penrith v West Auckland Town	2-1
2	Billingham Town v Pickering Town	0-3
3	Barnoldswick Town v Jarrow Roofing Boldon CA	3-1
4	Sunderland RCA v Garforth Town	3-1
5	Shildon v Morpeth Town	2-0
6	Consett v Bishop Auckland	3-3
7	Washington v Dunston UTS	0-3
8	Bridlington Town (2) v Billingham Synthonia	2-0
9	Newton Aycliffe v Chester-le-Street Town	1-0
10	Seaham Red Star v Whitley Bay	1-1
11	Thackley v Harrogate Railway Athletic	3-4
12	Guisborough Town v Stockton Town	4-2
13	Ashington v Sunderland Ryhope CW	1-0
14	Newcastle Benfield v West Allotment Celtic	1-0
15	Albion Sports v Nelson	2-0
16	Team Northumbria v Heaton Stannington	0-1
17	Marske United v North Shields	4-4
18	Litherland Remyca v AFC Liverpool	2-0
19	AFC Emley v Burscough	0-3
20	Squires Gate v Ashton Athletic	0-4
21	Cammell Laird 1907 v Maltby Main	4-1
22	Padiham v City of Liverpool	1-2
23	Pontefract Collieries v Alsager Town	1-0
24	Hallam v Bootle	3-0
25	Runcorn Town v AFC Darwen	3-2
26	Northwich Victoria v 1874 Northwich	2-2
27	Widnes v Handsworth Parramore	0-5
28	Congleton Town v New Mills	4-2
29	Irlam v Abbey Hey	1-2
30	Armthorpe Welfare v Liversedge	1-1
31	Parkgate v Barnton	4-2
32	Athersley Recreation v West Didsbury & Chorlton	0-5
33	Charnock Richard v Penistone Church	3-4
34	Maine Road v Winsford United	3-2
35	Runcorn Linnets v Hemsworth MW	2-0
36	Hanley Town v Atherstone Town	4-1
37	Coventry United v Rugby Town	1-2
38	Sporting Khalsa v Stourport Swifts	2-2
39	AFC Wulfrunians v Shawbury United	3-0
40	Wolverhampton Sporting Community v Haughmond	2-3
41	Tividale v Highgate United	1-1
42	Walsall Wood v Whitchurch Alport	3-1
43	Coventry Sphinx v Boldmere St Michaels	0-2
44	Daventry Town v Worcester City	0-1
45	Wolverhampton Casuals v Malvern Town	7-0
46	Westfields v Bewdley Town	3-1
47	Coleshill Town v Wellington (Hereford)	6-2
48	Bromsgrove Sporting v Rocester	2-2
49	Brocton v Cadbury Athletic	3-0
50	Kimberley MW v Blaby & Whetstone Athletic	2-4 d
51	Oadby Town v St Andrews	1-1
52	Birstall United v South Normanton Athletic	3-0
53	Bottesford Town v Long Eaton United	6-0
54	Leicester Road v Sleaford Town	2-1
55	Dunkirk v Leicester Nirvana	2-1
56	Kirby Muxloe v Barton Town	4-2
57	AFC Mansfield v Hall Road Rangers	2-1
58	Staveley MW v Loughborough University	2-1
59	Retford United v Quorn	1-1
60	Clipstone v West Bridgford	3-1
61	Heanor Town v Aylestone Park	0-1
62	Worksop Town v Hinckley AFC	1-2
63	Boston Town v Radford	2-2
64	Rainworth MW v Shepshed Dynamo	0-1
65	Harrowby United v Grimsby Borough	0-3
66	Biggleswade v Wisbech Town	1-4
67	Swaffham Town v Rothwell Corinthians	3-1
68	Raunds Town v Yaxley	1-1
69	Peterborough Northern Star v Deeping Rangers	2-3
70	Cogenhoe United v Godmanchester Rovers	3-0
71	Ely City v Holbeach United	0-2
72	Huntingdon Town v Newport Pagnell Town	1-4
73	Eynesbury Rovers v Thetford Town	3-2
74	Northampton Sileby Rangers v Harborough Town	0-5
75	Wellingborough Whitworths v Desborough Town	0-4
76	Fakenham Town v Wellingborough Town (2)	0-2
77	Histon v Northampton ON Chenecks	0-1
78	Potton United v Biggleswade United	0-0
79	Hoddesdon Town v Haverhill Rovers	1-2
80	Sawbridgeworth Town v West Essex	0-3
81	Enfield 1893 v Haverhill Borough	1-2
82	Redbridge v Stansted	3-1
83	Takeley v Wivenhoe Town	3-1
84	Kirkley & Pakefield v Saffron Walden Town	1-2
85	Southend Manor v Wroxham	1-0
86	Framlingham Town v Wadham Lodge	0-0
87	FC Broxbourne Borough v Tower Hamlets	1-1
88	Barkingside v Stowmarket Town	0-4
89	Ilford v Woodbridge Town	1-0
90	FC Clacton v Clapton	0-1
91	Hadleigh United v Sporting Bengal United	3-2
92	FC Romania v Waltham Forest	2-2
93	Hackney Wick v Long Melford	0-1 N
94	Felixstowe & Walton United v Brantham Athletic	2-7
95	Stanway Rovers v Gorleston	2-4
96	Hullbridge Sports v Ipswich Wanderers	5-1
97	St Margaretsbury v Burnham Ramblers	3-2
98	Great Yarmouth Town v Diss Town	5-0
99	Newmarket Town v Great Wakering Rovers	5-1
100	Walsham Le Willows v Basildon United	2-2
101	Welwyn Garden City v North Greenford United	2-4
102	Cockfosters v Risborough Rangers	1-1
103	Holmer Green v AFC Hayes	4-0
104	Lydney Town v Wantage Town	1-3
105	Langford v Hadley	1-9
106	Highworth Town v London Colney	1-1
107	Stotfold v Berkhamsted	1-12
108	Woodley United v Tuffley Rovers	1-2
109	Southall v Harpenden Town	5-1 N
110	Flackwell Heath v Burnham	5-0
111	Highmoor Ibis v Buckingham Town	3-1
112	Fairford Town v Longlevens	1-1
113	Edgware Town v Leverstock Green	1-1
114	Chipping Sodbury Town v Brackley Town Saints	3-1
115	Leighton Town v Oxhey Jets	4-0 N
116	Windsor v Wembley	1-4
117	Brimscombe & Thrupp v Sun Sports	4-0
118	Royal Wootton Bassett Town v Crawley Green	1-2
119	Colney Heath v Tring Athletic	1-0
120	Ardley United v Baldock Town	1-3
121	Corinthian v Deal Town	2-2
122	Hassocks v Hollands & Blair	2-3
123	Sheppey United v AFC Croydon Athletic	3-2
124	Crowborough Athletic v Lingfield	2-0
125	Sutton Common Rovers v Canterbury City	2-0 N
126	Newhaven v Peacehaven & Telscombe	0-0
127	Colliers Wood United v AFC Uckfield Town	2-2
128	Chessington & Hook United v Lancing	2-2
129	East Preston v Saltdean United	2-1
130	Epsom & Ewell v Banstead Athletic	1-2
131	Hailsham Town v Redhill	1-8
132	Loxwood v Holmesdale	3-1
133	Tunbridge Wells v Beckenham Town	1-0
134	Walton & Hersham v Mile Oak	7-0
135	Sevenoaks Town v Broadbridge Heath	3-1
136	Hanworth Villa v Bedfont & Feltham	5-0
137	Glebe v Lordswood	1-0
138	Whitstable Town v Croydon	2-3
139	Worthing United v Steyning Town	2-4
140	Arundel v Pagham	0-4
141	Horley Town v Raynes Park Vale	5-1
142	Abbey Rangers v Cray Valley Paper Mills	1-3
143	Eastbourne Town v Bearsted	2-1
144	Spelthorne Sports v Chertsey Town	1-3
145	Rochester United v Erith Town	1-1
146	Erith & Belvedere v Wick	4-0
147	Crawley Down Gatwick v AC London	2-3
148	Chatham Town v Littlehampton Town	1-1
149	Little Common v Eastbourne United	1-2
150	Rusthall v CB Hounslow United	0-0 N
151	Haywards Heath Town v Bedfont Sports	5-2
152	Horsham YMCA v Three Bridges	0-2
153	Bracknell Town v Cowes Sports	3-0
154	Thatcham Town v Petersfield Town	5-0
155	Christchurch v AFC Portchester	1-5
156	Farnham Town v Fawley	3-2
157	Bashley v Fareham Town	2-4
158	Hamworthy United v Bemerton Heath Harlequins	4-1
159	Team Solent v Brockenhurst	2-5
160	Badshot Lea v Verwood Town	1-1
161	Amesbury Town v Eversley & California	4-0

2017/18

162 Camberley Town v Blackfield & Langley 0-0
163 Whitchurch United v Laverstock & Ford 0-3
164 Ringwood Town v Ascot United 0-6
165 Binfield v Chichester City 4-3
166 Horndean v Melksham Town 2-1
167 Knaphill v Bournemouth (Ams) 0-0
168 Newport (IOW) v Guildford City (2) 2-2
169 Godalming Town v Westfield 2-1
170 Sholing v Alresford Town 1-2
171 Lymington Town v Andover Town 0-2 N
172 Clevedon Town v Bitton 2-2
173 Cadbury Heath v Longwell Green Sports 4-1
174 Plymouth Parkway v Portland United 0-1
175 AFC St Austell v Bridport 1-1
176 Wells City v Cribbs 2-1
177 Shaftesbury v Exmouth Town 0-0
178 Shepton Mallet v Tavistock 1-4
179 Buckland Athletic v Bodmin Town 2-3
180 Cheddar v Willand Rovers 0-2
181 Wellington (Somerset) v Hengrove Athletic 1-3 N
182 Street v Hallen 1-1
183 Brislington v Sherborne Town 6-1
184 Bridgwater Town v Keynsham Town 5-2
185 Bradford Town v Odd Down 3-4
6r Bishop Auckland v Consett 2-5
10r Whitley Bay v Seaham Red Star 4-1
17r North Shields v Marske United 0-1
26r 1874 Northwich v Northwich Victoria 2-0
30r Liversedge v Armthorpe Welfare 5-3
38r Stourport Swifts v Sporting Khalsa 2-3e
41r Highgate United v Tividale 2-3
48r Rocester v Bromsgrove Sporting 0-3
51r Oadby Town v St Andrews 2-2P
59r Quorn v Retford United 3-0
63r Radford v Boston Town 2-2q
68r Yaxley v Raunds Town 4-2e
78r Biggleswade United v Potton United 1-2
86r Wadham Lodge v Framlingham Town 1-3 N
87r Tower Hamlets v FC Broxbourne Borough 1-0
92r Waltham Forest v FC Romania 1-2
100r Basildon United v Walsham Le Willows 3-0
102r Risborough Rangers v Cockfosters 2-2q
106r London Colney v Highworth Town 2-4
112r Longlevens v Fairford Town 5-1
113r Leverstock Green v Edgware Town 5-3
121r Deal Town v Corinthian 4-1
126r Peacehaven & Telscombe v Newhaven 0-2
127r AFC Uckfield Town v Colliers Wood United 0-2
128r Lancing v Chessington & Hook United 1-3
145r Erith Town v Rochester United 5-0
148r Littlehampton Town v Chatham Town 2-1
150r CB Hounslow United v Rusthall 2-1
160r Verwood Town v Badshot Lea 3-3q
162r Blackfield & Langley v Camberley Town 1-2e
167r Bournemouth (Ams) v Knaphill 0-2
168r Guildford City (2) v Newport (IOW) 3-0 N
172r Bitton v Clevedon Town 0-1
175r Bridport v AFC St Austell 1-0
177r Exmouth Town v Shaftesbury 1-2e
182r Hallen v Street 1-4

Preliminary Round

1 Albion Sports v Newton Aycliffe 2-1
2 South Shields (3) v Bridlington Town (2) 3-1
3 Pickering Town v Clitheroe 1-2
4 Sunderland RCA v Ashington 4-0
5 Guisborough Town v Shildon 1-5
6 Goole AFC v Newcastle Benfield 1-2
7 Barnoldswick Town v Dunston UTS 2-1
8 Tadcaster Albion v Colne 0-1
9 Harrogate Railway Athletic v Kendal Town 1-1
10 Scarborough Athletic v Marske United 1-1
11 Consett v Heaton Stannington 4-0
12 Penrith v Whitley Bay 1-1
Whitley Bay v Penrith 3-1
13 Abbey Hey v Maine Road 2-2
14 Sheffield v Ossett Town 0-2
15 Penistone Church v Litherland Remyca 2-0
16 Bamber Bridge v Brighouse Town 3-2
17 Hallam v Atherton Collieries 1-4
18 Frickley Athletic v Runcorn Town 2-1
19 Ramsbottom United v Liversedge 2-3
20 Pontefract Collieries v Skelmersdale United 1-2
21 Ashton Athletic v Runcorn Linnets 4-2
22 Parkgate v Handsworth Parramore 2-4
23 Trafford v Kidsgrove Athletic 2-2
24 Prescot Cables v City of Liverpool 2-2
25 1874 Northwich v West Didsbury & Chorlton 3-3
26 Glossop North End v Mossley 0-2
27 Hyde United v Congleton Town 4-2
28 Ossett Albion v Droylsden 3-4
29 Colwyn Bay v Stocksbridge Park Steels 3-0
30 Radcliffe Borough v Burscough 1-1
31 Leek Town v Cammell Laird 1907 2-0
32 Sporting Khalsa v Market Drayton Town 1-1
33 Alvechurch v Hanley Town 2-0
34 Walsall Wood v Tividale 0-1
35 Bedworth United v Haughmond 0-2
36 Rugby Town v Romulus 2-3
37 Bromsgrove Sporting v Coleshill Town 3-4
38 Wolverhampton Casuals v Boldmere St Michaels 2-2
39 Worcester City v Chasetown 1-1
40 Brocton v Gresley 2-0
41 Newcastle Town v Evesham United 1-1
42 AFC Wulfrunians v Westfields 1-1
43 Birstall United v Cleethorpes Town 0-3
44 Shepshed Dynamo v Kimberley MW 3-0
45 Kirby Muxloe v Dunkirk 0-2
46 Grimsby Borough v Leicester Road 4-1
47 Oadby Town v Loughborough Dynamo 1-3
48 Hinckley AFC v Aylestone Park 4-1
49 Quorn v AFC Mansfield 1-3
50 Staveley MW v Basford United 0-1
51 Boston Town v Carlton Town 3-2
52 Lincoln United v Belper Town 0-0
53 Bottesford Town v Clipstone 4-1
54 Wisbech Town v Spalding United 2-2
55 Dereham Town v Corby Town 3-0
56 Cambridge City v Stamford 1-0
57 Barton Rovers v Deeping Rangers 1-2
58 Yaxley v Harborough Town 5-3
59 Holbeach United v Northampton ON Chenecks 6-1
60 Potton United v AFC Dunstable 2-0
61 Newport Pagnell Town v Kempston Rovers 3-3
62 Arlesey Town v Desborough Town 3-1
63 Soham Town Rangers v Cogenhoe United 3-2
64 Eynesbury Rovers v Peterborough Sports 1-1
65 Wellingborough Town (2) v AFC Rushden & Diamonds 0-4
66 Bedford Town v Swaffham Town 3-1
67 St Margaretsbury v Hullbridge Sports 2-2
68 Bury Town v Tilbury 1-2
69 Southend Manor v Gorleston 2-3
70 Bowers & Pitsea v Haringey Borough 0-2
71 Maldon & Tiptree v Waltham Abbey 5-1
72 AFC Hornchurch v Brentwood Town 2-0
73 Canvey Island v Witham Town 0-2
74 Clapton v Norwich United 2-0
75 Framlingham Town v Mildenhall Town 0-1
76 Haverhill Rovers v Heybridge Swifts 1-1
77 Newmarket Town v Ware 1-2
78 Tower Hamlets v Takeley 0-4
79 Brantham Athletic v Cheshunt 3-6
80 Stowmarket Town v Romford 1-1 N
81 AFC Sudbury v Aveley 4-0
82 Ilford v Haverhill Borough 1-1
83 Hertford Town v Hadleigh United 4-1
84 Great Yarmouth Town v Basildon United 1-0
85 Grays Athletic v Redbridge 2-0
86 Long Melford v FC Romania 1-2
87 Barking v Saffron Walden Town 0-0
88 Potters Bar Town v West Essex 4-1
89 Slimbridge v Cinderford Town 1-2
90 Flackwell Heath v Didcot Town 1-2
91 Baldock Town v North Greenford United 3-1
92 Chalfont St Peter v Beaconsfield Town 2-2
93 Ashford Town (Middlesex) v Wembley 3-0
94 Colney Heath v Shortwood United 2-0
95 Kidlington v Wantage Town 1-0
96 Swindon Supermarine v Northwood 1-0
97 Hayes & Yeading United v Brimscombe & Thrupp 1-0
98 Leighton Town v Tuffley Rovers 2-3
99 Crawley Green v Berkhamsted 2-3
100 Chipping Sodbury Town v Bishop's Cleeve 1-3
101 Leverstock Green v Aylesbury United 1-1
102 Southall v Hadley 2-4 N
103 Aylesbury v Cirencester Town 2-1
104 Uxbridge v Thame United 0-4
105 Highworth Town v Marlow 2-3
106 Hanwell Town v Longlevens 1-0
107 Highmoor Ibis v North Leigh 1-3
108 Cockfosters v Holmer Green 3-0
109 Pagham v Sittingbourne 1-1
110 Hollands & Blair v Crowborough Athletic 1-4
111 Erith & Belvedere v Cray Valley Paper Mills 1-4
112 Whyteleafe v Erith Town 1-1
113 Carshalton Athletic v Walton & Hersham 1-1
114 Haywards Heath Town v South Park 2-0
115 Colliers Wood United v Shoreham 1-1
116 Sutton Common Rovers v Eastbourne Town 1-2
117 Corinthian Casuals v Hythe Town 1-1
118 Greenwich Borough v Three Bridges 4-1
119 Deal Town v Glebe 2-2
120 Walton Casuals v Molesey 3-1 N
121 Redhill v Ashford United 1-3
122 Ramsgate v Hanworth Villa 3-1
123 East Grinstead Town v VCD Athletic 3-2
124 Cray Wanderers v Sevenoaks Town 2-3
125 Banstead Athletic v Loxwood 6-3
126 East Preston v Thamesmead Town 0-8
127 Littlehampton Town v Eastbourne United 3-2
128 Chipstead v Horley Town 2-0
129 Tunbridge Wells v CB Hounslow United 3-1
130 Steyning Town v Phoenix Sports 0-5
131 Chertsey Town v Horsham 1-3
132 Herne Bay v Chessington & Hook United 2-1
133 Lewes v Newhaven 3-3
134 Sheppey United v Hastings United (2) 0-2
135 Croydon v Faversham Town 0-0
136 AC London v Egham Town 1-5
137 Bracknell Town v Winchester City 0-4
138 Fleet Town v AFC Totton 1-1
139 Andover Town v Wimborne Town 3-3
140 Godalming Town v Farnham Town 3-0
141 AFC Portchester v Amesbury Town 3-1
142 Hamworthy United v Ascot United 4-1
143 Binfield v Horndean 1-1
144 Brockenhurst v Hartley Wintney 1-5
145 Guildford City (2) v Camberley Town 4-0 N
146 Salisbury v Fareham Town 3-2
147 Badshot Lea v Moneyfields 0-3
148 Laverstock & Ford v Knaphill 2-4
149 Alresford Town v Thatcham Town 0-2
150 Portland United v Paulton Rovers 0-3
151 Barnstaple Town v Clevedon Town 1-0
152 Tavistock v Shaftesbury 2-1
153 Bideford v Wells City 6-0
154 Cadbury Heath v Yate Town 1-0
155 Bridgwater Town v Brislington 1-0
156 Hengrove Athletic v Bodmin Town 1-4
157 Willand Rovers v Bristol Manor Farm 2-1
158 Odd Down v Mangotsfield United 1-0
159 Taunton Town v Larkhall Athletic 3-0
160 Bridport v Street 3-1
9r Kendal Town v Harrogate Railway Athletic 4-1
10r Marske United v Scarborough Athletic 1-2e
13r Maine Road v Abbey Hey 1-2
23r Kidsgrove Athletic v Trafford 2-0
24r City of Liverpool v Prescot Cables 8-2
25r West Didsbury & Chorlton v 1874 Northwich 1-3
30r Burscough v Radcliffe Borough 0-3
32r Market Drayton Town v Sporting Khalsa 1-1P
38r Boldmere St Michaels v Wolverhampton Casuals 5-0
39r Chasetown v Worcester City 2-0
41r Evesham United v Newcastle Town 2-3e
42r Westfields v AFC Wulfrunians 1-0
52r Belper Town v Lincoln United 1-4
54r Spalding United v Wisbech Town 0-2
61r Kempston Rovers v Newport Pagnell Town 4-1
64r Peterborough Sports v Eynesbury Rovers 2-0
67r Hullbridge Sports v St Margaretsbury 1-1q
76r Heybridge Swifts v Haverhill Rovers 6-1
80r Romford v Stowmarket Town 3-1
82r Haverhill Borough v Ilford 5-2
87r Saffron Walden Town v Barking 3-4
92r Beaconsfield Town v Chalfont St Peter 3-1
101r Aylesbury United v Leverstock Green 4-1
109r Sittingbourne v Pagham 0-1
112r Erith Town v Whyteleafe 3-3P
113r Walton & Hersham v Carshalton Athletic 1-1q
115r Shoreham v Colliers Wood United 3-1e
117r Hythe Town v Corinthian Casuals 1-3
119r Glebe v Deal Town 3-0
133r Newhaven v Lewes 1-4
135r Faversham Town v Croydon 2-1
138r AFC Totton v Fleet Town 5-0
139r Wimborne Town v Andover Town 1-2
143r Horndean v Binfield 3-0

Qualifying Round One

1 Penistone Church v Whitby Town 3-2
2 Albion Sports v Barnoldswick Town 3-2
3 City of Liverpool v Nantwich Town 1-2
4 Warrington Town v Grimsby Borough 1-0
5 Ashton Athletic v Bamber Bridge 2-1
6 Kidsgrove Athletic v Clitheroe 3-2
7 Stalybridge Celtic v Farsley Celtic FC 2-1
8 Marine v Ashton United 1-3
9 Shaw Lane v Radcliffe Borough 3-1
10 Scarborough Athletic v Workington 1-0
11 Bottesford Town v Shildon 0-1
12 Cleethorpes Town v Atherton Collieries 1-2
13 Colne v Lancaster City 0-1
14 Ossett Town v Consett 2-1
15 Hyde United v Kendal Town 1-0
16 Droylsden v Colwyn Bay 4-3
17 Abbey Hey v Altrincham 3-3
18 Skelmersdale United v Handsworth Parramore 1-2
19 Buxton v Frickley Athletic 3-2
20 Whitley Bay v Newcastle Benfield 0-2
21 Sunderland RCA v Liversedge 0-0
22 Mossley v 1874 Northwich 2-2
23 Witton Albion v South Shields (3) 0-2
24 Halesowen Town v Basford United 0-3
25 Boston Town v Hednesford Town 2-0
26 Kempston Rovers v Wisbech Town 2-1
27 Loughborough Dynamo v Stourbridge 1-3
28 Market Drayton Town v Alvechurch 1-5 N
29 AFC Mansfield v Dunkirk 4-0
30 Soham Town Rangers v Westfields 0-0
31 Peterborough Sports v Stafford Rangers 3-4
32 Rushall Olympic v Potton United 1-0
33 Sutton Coldfield Town v Barwell 0-2
34 St Ives Town v Coalville Town 1-0
35 Grantham Town v Holbeach United 2-1
36 Haughmond v Matlock Town 3-2
37 Tividale v AFC Rushden & Diamonds 2-3
38 Lincoln United v Redditch United 0-1
39 Shepshed Dynamo v Leek Town 6-1
40 Romulus v Kettering Town 0-3
41 Stratford Town v Newcastle Town 4-0
42 King's Lynn Town v Coleshill Town 4-1
43 Mickleover Sports v Hinckley AFC 2-1
44 Boldmere St Michaels v Chasetown 0-3
45 Yaxley v Dereham Town 0-1
46 Brocton v Deeping Rangers 2-4
47 Cambridge City v St Neots Town 3-1
48 Maldon & Tiptree v Hayes & Yeading United 3-3
49 Tilbury v Aylesbury United 0-1
50 North Leigh v Biggleswade Town 2-2
51 Romford v AFC Hornchurch 0-1
52 Baldock Town v Thame United 4-3
53 Hendon v Wingate & Finchley 1-1
54 Beaconsfield Town v Marlow 0-2

2017/18

55 Colney Heath v Cockfosters 3-0
56 Berkhamsted v Slough Town 1-3
57 Clapton v Needham Market 0-3
58 Royston Town v Dunstable Town 2-0
59 Billericay Town v Didcot Town 5-0
60 Bedford Town v Lowestoft Town 0-2
61 Ware v Witham Town 2-1
62 Thurrock v Harlow Town 1-1
63 Hadley v FC Romania 2-3
64 Great Yarmouth Town v Chesham United 0-2
65 Hertford Town v Grays Athletic 1-1
66 Haringey Borough v Hitchin Town 1-1
67 Potters Bar Town v Bishop's Stortford 1-0
68 Gorleston v Barking 0-4
69 Arlesey Town v Heybridge Swifts 0-7
70 AFC Sudbury v Mildenhall Town 1-1
71 Aylesbury v Leiston 1-3
72 Hanwell Town v Brightlingsea Regent 4-1
73 St Margaretsbury v Kidlington 1-6
74 Cheshunt v Takeley 2-0
75 Haverhill Borough v Kings Langley 0-8
76 Enfield Town v Harrow Borough 2-1
77 Littlehampton Town v Chipstead 2-2
78 Ashford Town (Middlesex) v Corinthian Casuals 2-0
79 Phoenix Sports v Eastbourne Town 2-0
80 Ramsgate v Egham Town 3-3
81 Margate v East Grinstead Town 3-1
82 Faversham Town v Tonbridge Angels 3-1
83 Crowborough Athletic v Sevenoaks Town 2-0
84 Dulwich Hamlet v Hastings United (2) 3-1
85 Tooting & Mitcham United v Merstham 2-0
86 Thamesmead Town v Lewes 3-0
87 Herne Bay v Walton Casuals 3-1
88 Metropolitan Police v Staines Town 3-2
89 Folkestone Invicta v Greenwich Borough 3-2
90 Dorking Wanderers v Worthing 3-2
91 Horsham v Ashford United 6-0
92 Haywards Heath Town v Tunbridge Wells 2-2
93 Banstead Athletic v Glebe 0-4
94 Carshalton Athletic v Pagham 5-3
95 Kingstonian v Shoreham 3-2
96 Leatherhead v Cray Valley Paper Mills 6-0
97 Erith Town v Burgess Hill Town 0-3
98 Hereford v Godalming Town 8-0
99 Banbury United v Tiverton Town 4-2
100 Bridport v Barnstaple Town 1-0
101 Gosport Borough v Bridgwater Town 1-0
102 Frome Town v AFC Totton 2-1
103 AFC Portchester v Dorchester Town 1-0
104 Farnborough v Salisbury 2-3
105 Odd Down v Weymouth 0-5
106 Tavistock v Taunton Town 2-2
107 Merthyr Town (2) v Willand Rovers 6-1
108 Tuffley Rovers v Swindon Supermarine 0-5
109 Horndean v Bodmin Town 0-2
110 Paulton Rovers v Winchester City 1-0
111 Guildford City (2) v Knaphill 1-3
112 Basingstoke Town v Hartley Wintney 2-2
Hartley Wintney v Basingstoke Town 1-0
113 Bideford v Bishop's Cleeve 5-1
114 Hamworthy United v Thatcham Town 1-5
115 Cinderford Town v Moneyfields 2-1
116 Andover Town v Cadbury Heath 1-2
17r Altrincham v Abbey Hey 2-1
21r Liversedge v Sunderland RCA 0-4
22r 1874 Northwich v Mossley 2-0
30r Westfields v Soham Town Rangers 1-0
48r Hayes & Yeading United v Maldon & Tiptree 4-3e
50r Biggleswade Town v North Leigh 3-2
53r Wingate & Finchley v Hendon 4-2e
62r Harlow Town v Thurrock 2-1
65r Grays Athletic v Hertford Town 2-3e
66r Hitchin Town v Haringey Borough 1-1q
70r Mildenhall Town v AFC Sudbury 2-4
77r Chipstead v Littlehampton Town 4-0
80r Egham Town v Ramsgate 2-4
92r Tunbridge Wells v Haywards Heath Town 3-0e
106r Taunton Town v Tavistock 1-2

Qualifying Round Two

1 Salford City v York City 1-2
2 Darlington v South Shields (3) 0-3
3 Southport v Bradford Park Avenue 0-3
4 Ossett Town v Atherton Collieries 1-0
5 Newcastle Benfield v Ashton United 2-1
6 Warrington Town v Hyde United 1-1
7 Harrogate Town v Penistone Church 3-0
8 Spennymoor Town v Gainsborough Trinity 1-2
9 Handsworth Parramore v FC United of Manchester 1-1
10 Albion Sports v Ashton Athletic 0-4
11 Shildon v Altrincham 1-0
12 Scarborough Athletic v Sunderland RCA 2-0
13 Blyth Spartans v Shaw Lane 1-2
14 1874 Northwich v North Ferriby United 1-0
15 Stockport County v Curzon Ashton 1-0
16 Stalybridge Celtic v Chorley 1-3
17 Lancaster City v Droylsden 4-0
18 Stafford Rangers v Tamworth 1-0
19 Boston United v Haughmond 1-1
20 Shepshed Dynamo v Nantwich Town 0-1
21 Deeping Rangers v Kidderminster Harriers 2-4
22 AFC Mansfield v Rushall Olympic 0-0
23 Kempston Rovers v Hereford 0-4
24 Stratford Town v Redditch United 4-1
25 AFC Telford United v Barwell 2-0
26 Nuneaton Town v King's Lynn Town 3-1
27 Kettering Town v Kidsgrove Athletic 2-0
28 Basford United v Mickleover Sports 1-0
29 Alfreton Town v AFC Rushden & Diamonds 2-2
30 Westfields v Leamington 0-2
31 Grantham Town v Alvechurch 3-4
32 Buxton v Chasetown 4-1
33 Stourbridge v St Ives Town 2-0
34 Dereham Town v Boston Town 1-2
35 Leiston v Crowborough Athletic 4-2
36 Concord Rangers v Tunbridge Wells 4-0
37 Braintree Town v Royston Town 2-2
38 AFC Sudbury v Chipstead 3-0
39 Biggleswade Town v East Thurrock United 0-1
40 St Albans City v Cambridge City 3-3
41 Horsham v Herne Bay 2-5
42 Hemel Hempstead Town v Wingate & Finchley 0-0
43 Lowestoft Town v Harlow Town 0-1
44 Metropolitan Police v Heybridge Swifts 2-2
45 Chelmsford City v Ramsgate 7-0
46 Ware v Leatherhead 2-5
47 Kings Langley v Margate 0-1
48 Thamesmead Town v Billericay Town 1-1
49 Baldock Town v Aylesbury United 1-2
50 Hertford Town v AFC Hornchurch 1-2
51 Glebe v Phoenix Sports 2-2
52 FC Romania v Hayes & Yeading United 2-2
53 Kingstonian v Brackley Town 0-3
54 Eastbourne Borough v Carshalton Athletic 4-3
55 Folkestone Invicta v Tooting & Mitcham United 3-1
56 Cheshunt v Dorking Wanderers 1-3
57 Wealdstone v Faversham Town 4-0
58 Colney Heath v Burgess Hill Town 3-3
59 Welling United v Haringey Borough 1-2
60 Dartford v Barking 3-1
61 Hampton & Richmond Boro. v Potters Bar Town 1-1
62 Whitehawk v Oxford City 1-3
63 Marlow v Ashford Town (Middlesex) 0-2
64 Needham Market v Chesham United 2-0
65 Slough Town v Dulwich Hamlet 3-2
66 Hanwell Town v Enfield Town 0-0
67 Havant & Waterlooville v Merthyr Town (2) 2-1
68 Bodmin Town v Bideford 1-1
69 Bridport v Cadbury Heath 2-2
70 Gosport Borough v Swindon Supermarine 1-2
71 Bognor Regis Town v Weston-Super-Mare 2-1
72 Cinderford Town v Hartley Wintney 1-0
73 Tavistock v Frome Town 1-2
74 Weymouth v Chippenham Town 2-0
75 Banbury United v Thatcham Town 2-0
76 Bath City v Knaphill 6-0
77 Truro City v AFC Portchester 2-0
78 Salisbury v Poole Town 0-2
79 Paulton Rovers v Kidlington 3-2
80 Gloucester City v Hungerford Town 0-3
6r Hyde United v Warrington Town 2-0
9r FC United of Manchester v Handsworth Parramore 6-2
19r Haughmond v Boston United 0-5
22r Rushall Olympic v AFC Mansfield 1-2
29r AFC Rushden & Diamonds v Alfreton Town 1-3
37r Royston Town v Braintree Town 1-2
40r Cambridge City v St Albans City 0-2
42r Wingate & Finchley v Hemel Hempstead Town 1-2e
44r Heybridge Swifts v Metropolitan Police 1-1P
48r Billericay Town v Thamesmead Town 5-0
51r Phoenix Sports v Glebe 1-1P
52r Hayes & Yeading United v FC Romania 2-0e
58r Burgess Hill Town v Colney Heath 3-0
61r Potters Bar Town v Hampton & Richmond Boro. 0-3
66r Enfield Town v Hanwell Town 5-0
68r Bideford v Bodmin Town 1-0
69r Cadbury Heath v Bridport 2-3e

Qualifying Round Three

1 1874 Northwich v Ossett Town 2-2
2 AFC Mansfield v Boston United 0-2
3 Stafford Rangers v AFC Telford United 1-1
4 Newcastle Benfield v Kidderminster Harriers 0-1
5 Nantwich Town v Nuneaton Town 3-1
6 Boston Town v Hyde United 2-3
7 Banbury United v Shildon 2-3
8 Scarborough Athletic v Stratford Town 2-2
9 Basford United v Kettering Town 2-3
10 Shaw Lane v Lancaster City 2-1
11 Buxton v Alvechurch 2-1
12 Stockport County v FC United of Manchester 3-3
13 Ashton Athletic v Chorley 0-1
14 Leamington v Gainsborough Trinity 0-0
15 Stourbridge v Alfreton Town 3-1
16 South Shields (3) v York City 3-2
17 Harrogate Town v Bradford Park Avenue 0-0
18 Swindon Supermarine v Paulton Rovers 2-3
19 Enfield Town v Phoenix Sports 3-0
20 Hayes & Yeading United v Havant & Waterlooville 0-4
21 Hereford v AFC Hornchurch 2-0
22 Slough Town v Poole Town 2-1
23 Brackley Town v Braintree Town 4-1
24 Concord Rangers v Dorking Wanderers 3-0
25 East Thurrock United v Harlow Town 2-2
26 Chelmsford City v Weymouth 2-1
27 Cinderford Town v Hampton & Richmond Boro. 2-3
28 Oxford City v Leiston 4-2
29 Margate v Herne Bay 2-0
30 St Albans City v Bridport 2-1
31 Heybridge Swifts v Frome Town 2-1
32 Truro City v AFC Sudbury 4-1
33 Eastbourne Borough v Bognor Regis Town 0-2
34 Bath City v Hemel Hempstead Town 3-0
35 Needham Market v Dartford 1-6
36 Haringey Borough v Bideford 4-1
37 Folkestone Invicta v Aylesbury United 2-1
38 Hungerford Town v Billericay Town 1-1
39 Burgess Hill Town v Wealdstone 1-0
40 Ashford Town (Middlesex) v Leatherhead 1-2
1r Ossett Town v 1874 Northwich 0-0P
3r AFC Telford United v Stafford Rangers 4-1
8r Stratford Town v Scarborough Athletic 1-4e
12r FC United of Manchester v Stockport County 1-0
14r Gainsborough Trinity v Leamington 2-0
17r Bradford Park Avenue v Harrogate Town 0-2
25r Harlow Town v East Thurrock United 1-2
38r Billericay Town v Hungerford Town 6-1

Qualifying Round Four

1 FC Halifax Town v Tranmere Rovers 1-3
2 Solihull Moors v Ossett Town 1-1
3 South Shields (3) v Hartlepool United 1-2
4 Shaw Lane v Barrow 2-1
5 Chorley v Boston United 0-0
6 AFC Telford United v FC United of Manchester 3-1
7 Harrogate Town v Gainsborough Trinity 1-2
8 Nantwich Town v Kettering Town 1-1
9 Buxton v Gateshead (2) 1-2
10 Guiseley v Shildon 6-0
11 AFC Fylde v Wrexham 1-0
12 Kidderminster Harriers v Chester FC 2-0
13 Scarborough Athletic v Hyde United 0-2
14 Stourbridge v Macclesfield Town 0-5
15 Brackley Town v Billericay Town 3-3
16 Dagenham & Redbridge v Leyton Orient 0-0
17 Eastleigh v Hereford 1-2
18 Aldershot Town v Torquay United 1-0
19 Bath City v Chelmsford City 0-0
20 Oxford City v Bognor Regis Town 1-0
21 Maidenhead United v Havant & Waterlooville 2-1
22 Haringey Borough v Heybridge Swifts 2-4
23 Woking v Concord Rangers 1-1
24 Hampton & Richmond Boro. v Truro City 0-2
25 Dover Athletic v Bromley 0-0
26 Slough Town v Folkestone Invicta 1-0
27 Burgess Hill Town v Dartford 0-1
28 St Albans City v Boreham Wood 1-3
29 Maidstone United (2) v Enfield Town 2-2
30 Margate v Leatherhead 1-2
31 Paulton Rovers v Sutton United 2-3
32 East Thurrock United v Ebbsfleet United 0-0
2r Ossett Town v Solihull Moors 1-2
5r Boston United v Chorley 3-4e
8r Kettering Town v Nantwich Town 0-1
15r Billericay Town v Brackley Town 2-1
16r Leyton Orient v Dagenham & Redbridge 1-0
19r Chelmsford City v Bath City 1-0
23r Concord Rangers v Woking 1-2e
25r Bromley v Dover Athletic 3-0
29r Enfield Town v Maidstone United (2) 1-3e
32r Ebbsfleet United v East Thurrock United 3-0

Round One

AFC Fylde v Kidderminster Harriers 4-2
AFC Wimbledon v Lincoln City 1-0
Blackburn Rovers v Barnet 3-1
Boreham Wood v Blackpool 2-1
Bradford City v Chesterfield 2-0
Cambridge United v Sutton United 1-0
Carlisle United v Oldham Athletic 3-2
Charlton Athletic v Truro City 3-1
Cheltenham Town v Maidstone United (2) 2-4
Chorley v Fleetwood Town 1-2
Colchester United v Oxford City 0-1
Coventry City v Maidenhead United 2-0
Crewe Alexandra v Rotherham United 2-1
Dartford v Swindon Town 1-5
Ebbsfleet United v Doncaster Rovers 2-6
Exeter City v Heybridge Swifts 3-1
Forest Green Rovers v Macclesfield Town 1-0
Gainsborough Trinity v Slough Town 0-6
Gateshead (2) v Chelmsford City 2-0
Gillingham v Leyton Orient 2-1
Guiseley v Accrington Stanley (2) 0-0
Hereford v AFC Telford United 1-0
Hyde United v Milton Keynes Dons 0-4
Leatherhead v Billericay Town 1-1
Luton Town v Portsmouth 1-0
Morecambe v Hartlepool United 3-0
Newport County (2) v Walsall 2-1
Northampton Town v Scunthorpe United 0-0
Notts County v Bristol Rovers 4-2
Peterborough United v Tranmere Rovers 1-1
Plymouth Argyle v Grimsby Town 1-0
Port Vale v Oxford United 2-0
Rochdale v Bromley 4-0
Shaw Lane v Mansfield Town 1-3
Shrewsbury Town v Aldershot Town 5-0
Solihull Moors v Wycombe Wanderers 0-2
Stevenage v Nantwich Town 5-0
Wigan Athletic v Crawley Town 2-1

2017/18 to 2018/19

Woking v Bury 1-1
Yeovil Town v Southend United 1-0
r Accrington Stanley (2) v Guiseley 1-1q
r Billericay Town v Leatherhead 1-3
r Bury v Woking 0-3
r Scunthorpe United v Northampton Town 1-0
r Tranmere Rovers v Peterborough United 0-5

Round Two

AFC Fylde v Wigan Athletic 1-1
AFC Wimbledon v Charlton Athletic 3-1
Blackburn Rovers v Crewe Alexandra 3-3
Bradford City v Plymouth Argyle 3-1
Coventry City v Boreham Wood 3-0
Doncaster Rovers v Scunthorpe United 3-0
Fleetwood Town v Hereford 1-1
Forest Green Rovers v Exeter City 3-3
Gateshead (2) v Luton Town 0-5
Gillingham v Carlisle United 1-1
Mansfield Town v Guiseley 3-0
Milton Keynes Dons v Maidstone United (2) 4-1
Newport County (2) v Cambridge United 2-0
Notts County v Oxford City 3-2
Port Vale v Yeovil Town 1-1
Shrewsbury Town v Morecambe 2-0
Slough Town v Rochdale 0-4
Stevenage v Swindon Town 5-2
Woking v Peterborough United 1-1
Wycombe Wanderers v Leatherhead 3-1
r Carlisle United v Gillingham 3-1
r Crewe Alexandra v Blackburn Rovers 0-1
r Exeter City v Forest Green Rovers 2-1e
r Hereford v Fleetwood Town 0-2
r Peterborough United v Woking 5-2
r Wigan Athletic v AFC Fylde 3-2
r Yeovil Town v Port Vale 3-2e

Round Three

Aston Villa v Peterborough United 1-3
Birmingham City v Burton Albion 1-0
Blackburn Rovers v Hull City 0-1
Bolton Wanderers v Huddersfield Town 1-2
Bournemouth v Wigan Athletic 2-2
Brentford v Notts County 0-1
Brighton & Hove Albion v Crystal Palace 2-1
Cardiff City v Mansfield Town 0-0
Carlisle United v Sheffield Wednesday 0-0
Coventry City v Stoke City 2-1
Doncaster Rovers v Rochdale 0-1
Exeter City v West Bromwich Albion 0-2
Fleetwood Town v Leicester City 0-0
Fulham v Southampton 0-1
Ipswich Town v Sheffield United 0-1
Liverpool v Everton 2-1
Manchester City v Burnley 4-1
Manchester United v Derby County 2-0
Middlesbrough v Sunderland 2-0
Millwall v Barnsley 4-1
Newcastle United v Luton Town 3-1
Newport County (2) v Leeds United 2-1
Norwich City v Chelsea 0-0
Nottingham Forest v Arsenal 4-2
Queen's Park Rangers v Milton Keynes Dons 0-1
Shrewsbury Town v West Ham United 0-0
Stevenage v Reading 0-0
Tottenham Hotspur v AFC Wimbledon 3-0
Watford v Bristol City 3-0
Wolverhampton Wan. v Swansea City 0-0
Wycombe Wanderers v Preston North End 1-5
Yeovil Town v Bradford City 2-0
r Chelsea v Norwich City 1-1P
r Leicester City v Fleetwood Town 2-0
r Mansfield Town v Cardiff City 1-4
r Reading v Stevenage 3-0
r Sheffield Wednesday v Carlisle United 2-0
r Swansea City v Wolverhampton Wan. 2-1
r West Ham United v Shrewsbury Town 1-0e
r Wigan Athletic v Bournemouth 3-0

Round Four

Cardiff City v Manchester City 0-2
Chelsea v Newcastle United 3-0
Huddersfield Town v Birmingham City 1-1
Hull City v Nottingham Forest 2-1
Liverpool v West Bromwich Albion 2-3
Middlesbrough v Brighton & Hove Albion 0-1
Millwall v Rochdale 2-2
Milton Keynes Dons v Coventry City 0-1
Newport County (2) v Tottenham Hotspur 1-1
Notts County v Swansea City 1-1
Peterborough United v Leicester City 1-5
Sheffield United v Preston North End 1-0
Sheffield Wednesday v Reading 3-1
Southampton v Watford 1-0
Wigan Athletic v West Ham United 2-0
Yeovil Town v Manchester United 0-4
r Birmingham City v Huddersfield Town 1-4e
r Rochdale v Millwall 1-0
r Swansea City v Notts County 8-1
r Tottenham Hotspur v Newport County (2) 2-0

Round Five

Brighton & Hove Albion v Coventry City 3-1
Chelsea v Hull City 4-0
Huddersfield Town v Manchester United 0-2
Leicester City v Sheffield United 1-0
Rochdale v Tottenham Hotspur 2-2
Sheffield Wednesday v Swansea City 0-0
West Bromwich Albion v Southampton 1-2
Wigan Athletic v Manchester City 1-0
r Swansea City v Sheffield Wednesday 2-0
r Tottenham Hotspur v Rochdale 6-1

Round Six

Leicester City v Chelsea 1-2e
Manchester United v Brighton & Hove Albion 2-0
Swansea City v Tottenham Hotspur 0-3
Wigan Athletic v Southampton 0-2

Semi Finals

Chelsea v Southampton 2-0 N
Manchester United v Tottenham Hotspur 2-1 N

Final

Chelsea v Manchester United 1-0 N

2018/19

Extra Preliminary Round

1 Consett v North Shields 2-1
2 Thackley v Whitley Bay 2-3
3 Hebburn Town v Dunston UTS 2-3
4 Ashington v Knaresborough Town 0-2
5 Goole AFC v Morpeth Town 1-5
6 Glasshoughton Welfare v Blyth AFC 1-2
7 Newcastle Benfield v Stockton Town 1-1
8 Selby Town v Whickham 3-2
9 Seaham Red Star v Heaton Stannington 1-1
10 Shildon v Team Northumbria wo/s
11 Northallerton Town v Garforth Town 0-4
12 Guisborough Town v Newton Aycliffe 3-3
13 Barnoldswick Town v Billingham Synthonia 1-1
14 Washington v West Auckland Town 0-4
15 Sunderland RCA v Sunderland Ryhope CW 5-2
16 Bridlington Town (2) v Harrogate Railway Athletic 3-0
17 Penrith v Albion Sports 0-3
18 Bishop Auckland v Pickering Town 0-2
19 AFC Darwen v Barnton 3-1
20 Liversedge v Padiham 5-2
21 City of Liverpool v Silsden 2-1
22 AFC Liverpool v Ashton Athletic 2-2
23 Widnes v Northwich Victoria 1-1
24 Burscough v 1874 Northwich 2-2
25 Congleton Town v Eccleshill United 1-0
26 Prestwich Heys v Abbey Hey 2-1
27 West Didsbury & Chorlton v Squires Gate 2-3
28 Winsford United v Irlam 1-2
29 Penistone Church v Bootle 2-1
30 Hemsworth MW v Runcorn Town 1-1
31 Hallam v Runcorn Linnets 0-2
32 Maltby Main v Athersley Recreation 3-0
33 Parkgate v Sandbach United 2-0
34 Litherland Remyca v Charnock Richard 4-2 D
35 Maine Road v Handsworth Parramore 0-1
36 Walsall Wood v Worcester City 1-1
37 Highgate United v AFC Wulfrunians 1-0
38 Boldmere St Michaels v Malvern Town 2-2
39 Atherstone Town v Hanley Town 1-1
40 Stourport Swifts v Shawbury United 2-1
41 Wednesfield v Rocester 2-1
42 Coventry United v Rugby Town 1-2
43 Coventry Sphinx v Whitchurch Alport 0-1
44 Haughmond v Wolverhampton Sporting Community 2-0
45 Racing Club Warwick v Coleshill Town 4-3
46 Romulus v Westfields 6-1
47 Ellesmere Rangers v Leicester Road 0-1
48 Sporting Khalsa v Tividale 2-1
49 Long Eaton United v St Andrews 2-1
50 Sleaford Town v South Normanton Athletic 0-1
51 Heather St Johns v Kimberley MW 3-6
52 Kirby Muxloe v AFC Mansfield 0-6
53 Clipstone v Barton Town 0-0
54 Lutterworth Town v Heanor Town 2-1
55 Hinckley AFC v Anstey Nomads 1-1
56 Worksop Town v Shepshed Dynamo 3-3
57 Rainworth MW v Dunkirk 2-1
58 Staveley MW v Boston Town 4-2
59 Teversal v Loughborough University 1-2
60 Oadby Town v Shirebrook Town 3-1
61 Bottesford Town v Radford 3-1
62 Quorn v Belper United 6-1
63 Leicester Nirvana v Grimsby Borough 0-3
64 Cogenhoe United v Wisbech Town 1-2
65 Wellingborough Whitworths v Harborough Town 0-1
66 Deeping Rangers v Holbeach United 3-2
67 Raunds Town v Eynesbury Rovers 1-2
68 Arlesey Town v Desborough Town 3-4
69 Thetford Town v Fakenham Town 1-0
70 Northampton Sileby Rangers v Ely City 2-0
71 Godmanchester Rovers v Newport Pagnell Town 2-0
72 Biggleswade United v Wellingborough Town (2) 1-1
73 Histon v Peterborough Northern Star 6-1
74 Daventry Town v Potton United 9-2
75 Biggleswade v Northampton ON Chenecks 2-0
76 Swaffham Town v Yaxley 1-3
77 Rothwell Corinthians v Pinchbeck United 3-0
78 Hullbridge Sports v Gorleston 2-1
79 Wroxham v Saffron Walden Town 1-1
80 Hadleigh United v Great Yarmouth Town 3-1
81 Walthamstow v Walsham Le Willows 3-1
82 Kirkley & Pakefield v FC Clacton 2-2
83 Wodson Park v Hoddesdon Town 1-3
84 Tower Hamlets v Stanway Rovers 0-2
85 Norwich United v Takeley 1-2
86 St Margaretsbury v Enfield 1893 2-0
87 Framlingham Town v Whitton United 1-1
88 Southend Manor v FC Romania 1-3
89 Wivenhoe Town v Brantham Athletic 0-5
90 Stowmarket Town v Basildon United 0-2
91 Sporting Bengal United v Ilford 4-3
92 Haverhill Rovers v Haverhill Borough 2-0
93 Ipswich Wanderers v Baldock Town 0-5
94 Barkingside v Leyton Athletic 0-0
95 Cockfosters v Newmarket Town 0-2
96 Woodbridge Town v Clapton 2-2
97 Burnham Ramblers v West Essex 3-5
98 Stansted v Sawbridgeworth Town 2-1 N
99 Redbridge v Long Melford 1-3
100 Oxhey Jets v Wantage Town 3-4
101 Tuffley Rovers v Colney Heath 1-4
102 Winslow United v Easington Sports 2-2
103 Harpenden Town v Edgware Town 1-0
104 Hadley v Fairford Town 2-0
105 Brackley Town Saints v London Colney 1-0 N
106 London Lions v Wembley 2-1
107 Windsor v Highworth Town 3-3
108 Bishop's Cleeve v Stotfold 5-2
109 AFC Hayes v Lydney Town 1-2
110 Flackwell Heath v North Greenford United 0-2
111 Tring Athletic v Berkhamsted 0-2
112 Southall v Leverstock Green 0-1
113 Holmer Green v Longlevens 0-1
114 Ardley United v Shortwood United 7-0
115 Holyport v Brimscombe & Thrupp 1-2
116 Abingdon United v Burnham 2-2
117 Crawley Green v Woodley United 7-1
118 Reading City v Chipping Sodbury Town 1-1
119 Leighton Town v Royal Wootton Bassett Town 0-1
120 Arundel v Chertsey Town 4-1
121 Sutton Common Rovers v CB Hounslow United 0-2
122 Broadbridge Heath v Shoreham 0-2
123 Langney Wanderers v Epsom & Ewell 1-2
124 Bearsted v Chichester City 2-1
125 Redhill v Horley Town 1-3
126 AFC Croydon Athletic v Rochester United 5-0
127 Spelthorne Sports v Peacehaven & Telscombe 3-0
128 Hassocks v Erith Town 1-3
129 Worthing United v Littlehampton Town 1-1
130 Little Common v Bedfont Sports 2-2
131 Crowborough Athletic v Hanworth Villa 1-1
132 Raynes Park Vale v Lingfield 3-0
133 AFC Uckfield Town v Glebe 1-0
134 Abbey Rangers v Newhaven 0-4
135 Cobham v Sheppey United 1-0
136 Fisher v Horsham YMCA 1-2
137 Loxwood v Hollands & Blair 2-1
138 Sevenoaks Town v Lordswood 6-1
139 Crawley Down Gatwick v Three Bridges 0-1
140 Eastbourne United v Hackney Wick 0-2
141 Cray Valley Paper Mills v Eastbourne Town 3-2
142 Croydon v Tunbridge Wells 2-2
143 Erith & Belvedere v Saltdean United 0-0
144 Haywards Heath Town v Lancing 0-2
145 Rusthall v Wick 3-0 N
146 East Preston v Balham FC 0-2
147 K Sports v Pagham 2-2
148 Deal Town v Whitstable Town 2-2
149 Broadfields United v Banstead Athletic 3-0
150 Chatham Town v Walton & Hersham 3-1
151 Corinthian v Canterbury City 3-0
152 Beckenham Town v Colliers Wood United 1-1
153 Hamworthy United v Team Solent 3-2
154 Melksham Town v Badshot Lea 4-0
155 AFC Stoneham v AFC Portchester 0-0
156 Newport (IOW) v Amesbury Town 3-1
157 Knaphill v Sholing 0-3
158 Guildford City (2) v Petersfield Town 0-1
159 Tadley Calleva v Baffins Milton Rovers 1-3
160 Bemerton Heath Harlequins v Cowes Sports 1-0
161 Andover New Street v Romsey Town 4-0
162 United Services Portsmouth v Andover Town 5-2 N
163 Horndean v Godalming Town 5-0
164 Hamble Club v Alresford Town 1-1
165 Farnham Town v Binfield 1-2
166 Brockenhurst v Christchurch 2-2
167 Bashley v Bournemouth (Ams) 0-2
168 Fareham Town v Frimley Green 1-2
169 Ascot United v Camberley Town 2-1
170 Sandhurst Town v Lymington Town 1-1
171 Clevedon Town v Portland United 1-2
172 Westbury United v Cribbs 3-0
173 Hallen v Longwell Green Sports 0-0
174 Wells City v Shaftesbury 2-5
175 Bodmin Town v Keynsham Town 4-4

2018/19

176 Cheddar v Bridgwater Town 3-2
177 Shepton Mallet v Willand Rovers 1-1
178 Bitton v Tavistock 7-0
179 Buckland Athletic v Pewsey Vale 3-0
180 Bridport v Wellington (Somerset) 0-0
181 Hengrove Athletic v Plymouth Parkway 1-5
182 Saltash United v Odd Down 1-0
183 Brislington v Cadbury Heath 1-2
184 Bradford Town v Roman Glass St George 5-2
7r Stockton Town v Newcastle Benfield 0-3
9r Heaton Stannington v Seaham Red Star 4-4q
12r Newton Aycliffe v Guisborough Town 0-2
13r Billingham Synthonia v Barnoldswick Town 0-4
22r Ashton Athletic v AFC Liverpool 4-1
23r Northwich Victoria v Widnes 1-0
24r 1874 Northwich v Burscough 3-3q
30r Runcorn Town v Hemsworth MW 1-0
36r Worcester City v Walsall Wood 1-1q
38r Malvern Town v Boldmere St Michaels 3-2
39r Hanley Town v Atherstone Town 1-4
53r Barton Town v Clipstone 3-4
55r Anstey Nomads v Hinckley AFC 4-3e
56r Shepshed Dynamo v Worksop Town 4-5e
72r Wellingborough Town (2) v Biggleswade United 2-1
79r Saffron Walden Town v Wroxham 3-2e
82r Kirkley & Pakefield v FC Clacton 2-3
87r Whitton United v Framlingham Town 3-1
94r Leyton Athletic v Barkingside 3-0
96r Clapton v Woodbridge Town 1-1q
102r Easington Sports v Winslow United 2-0
107r Highworth Town v Windsor 1-2
116r Burnham v Abingdon United 2-0
118r Chipping Sodbury Town v Reading City 2-1e
129r Littlehampton Town v Worthing United 2-4e
130r Bedfont Sports v Little Common 2-1
131r Hanworth Villa v Crowborough Athletic 2-0
142r Tunbridge Wells v Croydon 2-3e
143r Saltdean United v Erith & Belvedere 2-0
147r Pagham v K Sports 2-0
148r Whitstable Town v Deal Town 4-3
152r Colliers Wood United v Beckenham Town 0-2
155r AFC Portchester v AFC Stoneham 0-3
164r Alresford Town v Hamble Club 0-2
166r Christchurch v Brockenhurst 0-2
170r Lymington Town v Sandhurst Town 5-1 N
173r Longwell Green Sports v Hallen 0-1
175r Keynsham Town v Bodmin Town 1-3
177r Willand Rovers v Shepton Mallet 3-0
180r Wellington (Somerset) v Bridport 0-3 N

Preliminary Round

1 Knaresborough Town v Blyth AFC 5-1
2 Bridlington Town (2) v Garforth Town 1-2
3 Dunston UTS v Pontefract Collieries 4-2
4 Newcastle Benfield v West Auckland Town 1-0
5 Whitley Bay v Barnoldswick Town 6-1
6 Morpeth Town v Marske United 1-0
7 Consett v Seaham Red Star 5-2
8 Tadcaster Albion v Shildon 4-1
9 Clitheroe v Sunderland RCA 6-6
10 Kendal Town v Selby Town 1-1
11 Pickering Town v Colne 0-4
12 Albion Sports v Guisborough Town 2-2
13 Ashton Athletic v Skelmersdale United 2-1
14 Ossett United v Mossley 2-2
15 Burscough v Northwich Victoria 2-0
16 Atherton Collieries v Colwyn Bay 2-1
17 Kidsgrove Athletic v Ramsbottom United 1-1
18 Stocksbridge Park Steels v Bamber Bridge 1-3
19 Prescot Cables v Irlam 1-2
20 Brighouse Town v Parkgate 0-2
21 Prestwich Heys v Radcliffe 0-2
22 Droylsden v Squires Gate 4-4
23 Hyde United v Sheffield 5-1
24 Handsworth Parramore v Congleton Town 0-1
25 Frickley Athletic v Liversedge 10-1
26 Runcorn Linnets v Maltby Main 1-2
27 Penistone Church v Runcorn Town 1-3
28 Charnock Richard v Leek Town 2-2
29 AFC Darwen v Trafford 1-4
30 City of Liverpool v Glossop North End 1-1
31 Stourport Swifts v Sporting Khalsa 2-1
32 Sutton Coldfield Town v Gresley 3-0
33 Alvechurch v Bromsgrove Sporting 4-3
34 Malvern Town v Racing Club Warwick 1-2
35 Bedworth United v Atherstone Town 1-3
36 Romulus v Newcastle Town 4-0
37 Walsall Wood v Whitchurch Alport 2-1
38 Highgate United v Leicester Road 3-0
39 Wednesfield v Chasetown 2-2
40 Rugby Town v Evesham United 1-0
41 Haughmond v Market Drayton Town 1-1
42 Kimberley MW v Oadby Town 0-2
43 Loughborough Dynamo v Bottesford Town 2-4
44 Staveley MW v Lutterworth Town 3-0
45 Belper Town v Lincoln United 2-1
46 Worksop Town v Carlton Town 2-1
47 Loughborough University v Cleethorpes Town 3-3
48 AFC Mansfield v Rainworth MW 1-0
49 Anstey Nomads v Clipstone 4-1
50 Grimsby Borough v Long Eaton United 1-0
51 Quorn v South Normanton Athletic 3-2
52 Stamford v Peterborough Sports 1-1
53 Northampton Sileby Rangers v Wisbech Town 1-1
54 Deeping Rangers v AFC Rushden & Diamonds 1-1
55 Harborough Town v Cambridge City 1-2
56 Corby Town v Dunstable Town 3-3
57 Biggleswade v Soham Town Rangers 3-5
58 Thetford Town v Godmanchester Rovers 0-5
59 Desborough Town v Kempston Rovers 0-3
60 Bedford Town v Dereham Town 4-1
61 Histon v Eynesbury Rovers 1-1
62 Daventry Town v Yaxley 7-5
63 Barton Rovers v Rothwell Corinthians 3-2
64 Spalding United v Wellingborough Town (2) 3-2
65 Waltham Abbey v Bury Town 0-2
66 Felixstowe & Walton United v Walthamstow 0-1
67 AFC Sudbury v Mildenhall Town 2-0
68 Heybridge Swifts v West Essex 3-0
69 Aveley v Potters Bar Town 0-2
70 Hertford Town v Tilbury 5-3
71 Stansted v Takeley 0-1 N
72 Long Melford v St Margaretsbury 3-0
73 Bowers & Pitsea v Barking 1-0 N
74 Coggeshall Town v Witham Town 0-0
75 Haverhill Rovers v Maldon & Tiptree 2-1
76 Brantham Athletic v Welwyn Garden City 1-0
77 Haringey Borough v Stanway Rovers 1-0
78 Cheshunt v Canvey Island 1-0
79 FC Romania v Grays Athletic 2-0 N
80 Woodbridge Town v Hadleigh United 5-1
81 Basildon United v Whitton United 2-1
82 Great Wakering Rovers v Leyton Athletic 4-1
83 FC Clacton v Ware 2-4
84 Newmarket Town v Hullbridge Sports 2-1
85 Saffron Walden Town v Hoddesdon Town 4-1
86 Brentwood Town v Sporting Bengal United 1-1
87 Romford v Baldock Town 3-2
88 Easington Sports v Chipping Sodbury Town 1-2
89 Northwood v Longlevens 3-1
90 Ardley United v Burnham 2-4
91 AFC Dunstable v Swindon Supermarine 0-0
92 Crawley Green v Aylesbury United 2-3
93 Kidlington v Marlow 0-1
94 Thame United v Berkhamsted 0-2
95 Bishop's Cleeve v North Greenford United 5-2
96 Didcot Town v Aylesbury 1-1
97 Brackley Town Saints v Hadley 0-0
98 Slimbridge v Wantage Town 1-1
99 Chalfont St Peter v London Lions 1-0
100 Beaconsfield Town v Uxbridge 2-0
101 Colney Heath v Cinderford Town 1-3
102 Harpenden Town v Leverstock Green 0-6
103 Brimscombe & Thrupp v Hayes & Yeading United 0-7
104 North Leigh v Hanwell Town 2-4
105 Cirencester Town v Windsor 5-0
106 Royal Wootton Bassett Town v Lydney Town 0-0
107 Tooting & Mitcham United v Horley Town 2-1
108 East Grinstead Town v South Park 1-0
109 Walton Casuals v Shoreham 6-0
110 Beckenham Town v Epsom & Ewell 2-2
111 Three Bridges v Phoenix Sports 2-3
112 Arundel v Herne Bay 1-7
113 Sittingbourne v Bearsted 2-0
114 Newhaven v Pagham 0-2
115 Cobham v Egham Town 1-3
116 Cray Valley Paper Mills v Ashford Town (Middlesex) 4-1
117 Molesey v Lewes 0-0
118 AFC Croydon Athletic v Hanworth Villa 1-1
119 Raynes Park Vale v Spelthorne Sports 1-1
120 Carshalton Athletic v Horsham 0-1
121 Ashford United v Horsham YMCA 0-2
122 AFC Uckfield Town v Broadfields United 4-1
123 Greenwich Borough v Lancing 3-7
124 Chipstead v Corinthian 0-1
125 Loxwood v Erith Town 1-1
126 Hythe Town v Worthing United 3-0
127 Whyteleafe v Saltdean United 1-1
128 Corinthian Casuals v Croydon 6-0
129 Ramsgate v Chatham Town 2-1
130 CB Hounslow United v Whitstable Town 0-2
131 Cray Wanderers v Rusthall 1-1
132 Faversham Town v Hackney Wick 4-1
133 Balham FC v Thamesmead Town 0-2
134 Hastings United (2) v VCD Athletic 3-2
135 Sevenoaks Town v Bedfont Sports 1-0
136 Thatcham Town v Bemerton Heath Harlequins 0-0
137 Salisbury v Hamble Club 6-0
138 Binfield v Brockenhurst 2-1
139 Moneyfields v Andover New Street 3-1
140 Hamworthy United v AFC Totton 1-0
141 Lymington Town v Frimley Green 2-0 N
142 Fleet Town v Petersfield Town 3-1
143 United Services Portsmouth v Sholing 1-3
144 AFC Stoneham v Westfield 2-0
145 Baffins Milton Rovers v Hartley Wintney 1-4
146 Wimborne Town v Newport (IOW) 6-0
147 Melksham Town v Blackfield & Langley 1-0
148 Ascot United v Horndean 1-2
149 Winchester City v Bournemouth (Ams) 1-0
150 Bodmin Town v Cadbury Heath 2-2
151 Bideford v Bristol Manor Farm 2-2
152 Bradford Town v Paulton Rovers 0-1
153 Hallen v Bridport 0-5
154 Barnstaple Town v Shaftesbury 0-1
155 Plymouth Parkway v Larkhall Athletic 1-0
156 Portland United v Bitton 0-2
157 Westbury United v Saltash United 3-0
158 Cheddar v Yate Town 0-3
159 Willand Rovers v Street 1-2
160 Buckland Athletic v Mangotsfield United 2-0
9r Sunderland RCA v Clitheroe 2-3
10r Selby Town v Kendal Town 1-1q
12r Guisborough Town v Albion Sports 4-0
14r Mossley v Ossett United 1-1P
17r Ramsbottom United v Kidsgrove Athletic 0-0q
22r Squires Gate v Droylsden 1-0
28r Leek Town v Charnock Richard 3-2
30r Glossop North End v City of Liverpool 2-3e
39r Chasetown v Wednesfield 3-1
41r Market Drayton Town v Haughmond 0-1
47r Cleethorpes Town v Loughborough University 1-0
52r Peterborough Sports v Stamford 4-3
53r Wisbech Town v Northampton Sileby Rangers 0-0P
54r AFC Rushden & Diamonds v Deeping Rangers 3-0
56r Dunstable Town v Corby Town 0-4
61r Eynesbury Rovers v Histon 1-3
74r Witham Town v Coggeshall Town 1-3
86r Sporting Bengal United v Brentwood Town 1-3
91r Swindon Supermarine v AFC Dunstable 3-0
96r Aylesbury v Didcot Town 0-1
97r Hadley v Brackley Town Saints 1-0 N
98r Wantage Town v Slimbridge 1-0
106r Lydney Town v Royal Wootton Bassett Town 5-3
110r Epsom & Ewell v Beckenham Town 0-3e
117r Lewes v Molesey 8-1
118r Hanworth Villa v AFC Croydon Athletic 0-1
119r Spelthorne Sports v Raynes Park Vale 4-3
125r Erith Town v Loxwood 4-1
127r Saltdean United v Whyteleafe 1-2
131r Rusthall v Cray Wanderers 1-1q
136r Bemerton Heath Harlequins v Thatcham Town 3-2
150r Cadbury Heath v Bodmin Town 4-1
151r Bristol Manor Farm v Bideford 4-2e

Qualifying Round One

1 Radcliffe v Stalybridge Celtic 1-0
2 Squires Gate v City of Liverpool 1-5
3 Lancaster City v Trafford 0-2
4 South Shields (3) v Garforth Town 5-1
5 Warrington Town v Burscough 4-0
6 Runcorn Town v Irlam 2-3
7 Whitley Bay v Whitby Town 1-0
8 Marine v Scarborough Athletic 1-1
9 Colne v Hyde United 2-0
10 Newcastle Benfield v Workington 1-1
11 Dunston UTS v North Ferriby United 4-1
12 Knaresborough Town v Kendal Town 7-3
13 Atherton Collieries v Kidsgrove Athletic 1-2
14 Guisborough Town v Farsley Celtic FC 0-4
15 Congleton Town v Consett 0-1
16 Witton Albion v Bottesford Town 5-0
17 Clitheroe v Mossley 2-5
18 Ashton Athletic v Morpeth Town 1-1
19 Maltby Main v Frickley Athletic 1-2
20 Parkgate v Leek Town 2-2
21 Bamber Bridge v Tadcaster Albion 3-1
22 Basford United v Staveley MW 1-3
23 Highgate United v Stourbridge 1-2
24 Cleethorpes Town v Walsall Wood 4-1
25 AFC Mansfield v Stourport Swifts 2-1
26 Romulus v Belper Town 4-0
27 Nantwich Town v Worksop Town 5-2
28 Sutton Coldfield Town v Rushall Olympic 2-2
29 Quorn v Atherstone Town 0-1
30 Coalville Town v Racing Club Warwick 2-1
31 Hednesford Town v Tamworth 2-0
32 Grimsby Borough v Stafford Rangers 1-2
33 Matlock Town v Halesowen Town 1-2
34 Barwell v Buxton 2-5
35 Daventry Town v Grantham Town 0-1
36 Mickleover Sports v Haughmond 6-0
37 Anstey Nomads v Oadby Town 2-1
38 Chasetown v Gainsborough Trinity 1-1
39 Redditch United v Rugby Town 2-4
40 Stratford Town v Alvechurch 0-1
41 Leverstock Green v Hadley 0-0
42 St Neots Town v Bishop's Stortford 2-1
43 Burnham v Bury Town 1-0
44 Cambridge City v Brightlingsea Regent 3-4
45 Aylesbury United v Marlow 0-0
46 Heybridge Swifts v Newmarket Town 2-0
47 Hanwell Town v Potters Bar Town 2-1
48 Brantham Athletic v Spalding United 1-0
49 Corby Town v Hertford Town 2-0
50 AFC Sudbury v Royston Town 3-2
51 Ware v Lowestoft Town 0-1
52 Hendon v Harlow Town 1-1
53 Brentwood Town v Haringey Borough 2-3
54 Haverhill Rovers v Long Melford 0-0
55 AFC Hornchurch v Harrow Borough 1-0
56 Swindon Supermarine v Woodbridge Town 7-1
57 FC Romania v Soham Town Rangers 4-0 N
58 Chesham United v Biggleswade Town 2-1
59 Chalfont St Peter v Kempston Rovers 1-1
60 Great Wakering Rovers v Wisbech Town 3-1
61 Romford v Kettering Town 1-4
62 King's Lynn Town v Histon 2-2
63 Hayes & Yeading United v AFC Rushden & Diamonds 2-1
64 Northwood v Kings Langley 0-0
65 Coggeshall Town v Berkhamsted 1-1
66 Saffron Walden Town v St Ives Town 0-0
67 Walthamstow v Beaconsfield Town 0-2

2018/19

68	Wingate & Finchley v Didcot Town	0-2
69	Cheshunt v Leiston	2-2
70	Hitchin Town v Godmanchester Rovers	3-1
71	Bowers & Pitsea v Takeley	5-1 N
72	Basildon United v Peterborough Sports	0-2
73	Barton Rovers v Needham Market	0-4
74	Enfield Town v Bedford Town	0-3
75	Ramsgate v Sevenoaks Town	1-1
76	Hastings United (2) v Kingstonian	2-1
77	Metropolitan Police v Cray Wanderers	3-2
78	Faversham Town v Worthing	1-3
79	Farnborough v Lewes	2-2
80	AFC Uckfield Town v AFC Croydon Athletic	1-0
81	Fleet Town v East Grinstead Town	1-2
82	Phoenix Sports v Lancing	2-2
83	Merstham v Cray Valley Paper Mills	0-0
84	Spelthorne Sports v Erith Town	1-5
85	Hythe Town v Tonbridge Angels	0-2
86	Egham Town v Staines Town	1-0
87	Corinthian Casuals v Whyteleafe	0-0
88	Margate v Horndean	3-2
89	Moneyfields v Thamesmead Town	1-0
90	Whitstable Town v Bognor Regis Town	0-5
91	Horsham YMCA v Tooting & Mitcham United	1-2
92	Corinthian v Horsham	1-1
93	Pagham v Whitehawk	0-2
94	Leatherhead v Herne Bay	2-0
95	Beckenham Town v Walton Casuals	0-0
96	Burgess Hill Town v Folkestone Invicta	1-0
97	Dorking Wanderers v Hartley Wintney	2-0
98	Sittingbourne v Gosport Borough	0-1
99	Weymouth v Banbury United	1-1
100	Melksham Town v Merthyr Town (2)	1-4
101	Bitton v Westbury United	3-0
102	AFC Stoneham v Cirencester Town	0-7
103	Salisbury v Yate Town	1-1
104	Cadbury Heath v Cinderford Town	0-1
105	Binfield v Buckland Athletic	3-0
106	Frome Town v Winchester City	1-1
107	Wimborne Town v Dorchester Town	1-1
108	Shaftesbury v Poole Town	0-1
109	Sholing v Hamworthy United	0-0
110	Plymouth Parkway v Street	0-0
111	Taunton Town v Bemerton Heath Harlequins	7-1
112	Paulton Rovers v Basingstoke Town	1-1
113	Bridport v Tiverton Town	0-1
114	Bishop's Cleeve v Wantage Town	0-2
115	Chipping Sodbury Town v Bristol Manor Farm	0-2
116	Lymington Town v Lydney Town	2-2
8r	Scarborough Athletic v Marine	2-3
10r	Workington v Newcastle Benfield	5-3
18r	Morpeth Town v Ashton Athletic	1-2
20r	Leek Town v Parkgate	3-0
28r	Rushall Olympic v Sutton Coldfield Town	0-1
38r	Gainsborough Trinity v Chasetown	8-2
41r	Hadley v Leverstock Green	0-1 N
45r	Marlow v Aylesbury United	2-1e
52r	Harlow Town v Hendon	1-2e
54r	Long Melford v Haverhill Rovers	1-2
59r	Kempston Rovers v Chalfont St Peter	2-2P
62r	Histon v King's Lynn Town	0-7
64r	Kings Langley v Northwood	3-1
65r	Berkhamsted v Coggeshall Town	1-2
66r	St Ives Town v Saffron Walden Town	3-1
69r	Leiston v Cheshunt	4-2
75r	Sevenoaks Town v Ramsgate	1-3
79r	Lewes v Farnborough	1-1P
82r	Lancing v Phoenix Sports	0-3 d
83r	Cray Valley Paper Mills v Merstham	3-3P
87r	Corinthian Casuals v Whyteleafe	2-1
92r	Horsham v Corinthian	5-0
95r	Walton Casuals v Beckenham Town	3-0
99r	Banbury United v Weymouth	2-1
103r	Yate Town v Salisbury	1-3
106r	Winchester City v Frome Town	2-1e
107r	Dorchester Town v Wimborne Town	3-0
109r	Hamworthy United v Sholing	0-1
110r	Street v Plymouth Parkway	1-4
112r	Basingstoke Town v Paulton Rovers	2-0
116r	Lydney Town v Lymington Town	1-2

Qualifying Round Two

1	Chester FC v City of Liverpool	4-0
2	Ashton United v Trafford	3-0
3	Radcliffe v Curzon Ashton	1-2
4	Farsley Celtic FC v Southport	0-3
5	Mossley v Kidsgrove Athletic	1-2
6	Staveley MW v Guiseley	0-4
7	South Shields (3) v Stockport County	1-2
8	Knaresborough Town v Workington	1-4
9	Cleethorpes Town v Bamber Bridge	3-3
10	York City v Ashton Athletic	5-0
11	Marine v Frickley Athletic	1-0
12	Dunston UTS v Irlam	2-1
13	FC United of Manchester v Colne	2-0
14	Nantwich Town v Blyth Spartans	3-3
15	Darlington v Bradford Park Avenue	0-1
16	Chorley v Leek Town	3-0
17	Witton Albion v Spennymoor Town	2-1
18	Altrincham v Whitley Bay	5-0
19	Consett v Warrington Town	3-3
20	Sutton Coldfield Town v Alfreton Town	2-2
21	Boston United v Peterborough Sports	0-2
22	St Ives Town v Grantham Town	1-1
23	Kidderminster Harriers v Atherstone Town	5-0
24	Stourbridge v Leamington	3-2
25	Rugby Town v Hednesford Town	1-3
26	St Neots Town v Romulus	4-3
27	Nuneaton Borough v Brackley Town	1-1
28	Alvechurch v Corby Town	1-4
29	Kettering Town v AFC Mansfield	2-1
30	Anstey Nomads v Mickleover Sports	1-7
31	Halesowen Town v Gainsborough Trinity	0-3
32	King's Lynn Town v Stafford Rangers	3-1
33	AFC Telford United v Bedford Town	3-1
34	Buxton v Coalville Town	0-0
35	Hampton & Richmond Boro. v Burgess Hill Town	3-0
36	Kings Langley v Lewes	1-1
37	Wealdstone v Great Wakering Rovers	2-0
38	Welling United v Chesham United	2-1
39	Hendon v Lancing	1-1
40	Woking v Tooting & Mitcham United	4-0
41	Hanwell Town v Lowestoft Town	1-0
42	Egham Town v Brightlingsea Regent	3-3
43	Chelmsford City v Worthing	1-2
44	Concord Rangers v Margate	2-0
45	Leverstock Green v Dorking Wanderers	2-4
46	Haringey Borough v Erith Town	2-0
47	Leiston v Hastings United (2)	3-4
48	Coggeshall Town v Walton Casuals	2-0
49	St Albans City v Corinthian Casuals	1-1
50	Bowers & Pitsea v Hemel Hempstead Town	1-6
51	Billericay Town v Burnham	4-1
52	Kempston Rovers v Marlow	1-0
53	Hitchin Town v Didcot Town	1-1
54	Bognor Regis Town v AFC Sudbury	1-1
55	Haverhill Rovers v Leatherhead	0-6
56	East Thurrock United v Whitehawk	2-3
57	Brantham Athletic v Eastbourne Borough	0-1
58	Oxford City v Cray Valley Paper Mills	5-0
59	Gosport Borough v Ramsgate	2-3
60	AFC Hornchurch v East Grinstead Town	2-1
61	AFC Uckfield Town v Dartford	1-3
62	Hayes & Yeading United v Moneyfields	0-1
63	FC Romania v Beaconsfield Town	0-2
64	Horsham v Heybridge Swifts	4-3
65	Dulwich Hamlet v Tonbridge Angels	3-1
66	Metropolitan Police v Needham Market	2-2
67	Merthyr Town (2) v Winchester City	1-4
68	Lymington Town v Torquay United	0-7
69	Chippenham Town v Swindon Supermarine	2-2
70	Bristol Manor Farm v Basingstoke Town	5-2
71	Gloucester City v Plymouth Parkway	3-1
72	Weston-Super-Mare v Salisbury	2-2
73	Tiverton Town v Dorchester Town	2-0
74	Hereford v Truro City	0-0
75	Poole Town v Cinderford Town	3-0
76	Taunton Town v Bitton	4-0
77	Banbury United v Bath City	0-2
78	Wantage Town v Hungerford Town	2-2q
79	Binfield v Cirencester Town	0-3
80	Slough Town v Sholing	2-2
9r	Bamber Bridge v Cleethorpes Town	0-5
14r	Blyth Spartans v Nantwich Town	1-0
19r	Warrington Town v Consett	2-0
20r	Alfreton Town v Sutton Coldfield Town	3-0
22r	Grantham Town v St Ives Town	0-2
27r	Brackley Town v Nuneaton Borough	2-0
34r	Coalville Town v Buxton	4-1
36r	Lewes v Kings Langley	2-1
39r	Lancing v Hendon	0-4
42r	Brightlingsea Regent v Egham Town	2-1
49r	Corinthian Casuals v St Albans City	0-3 N
53r	Didcot Town v Hitchin Town	0-0q
54r	AFC Sudbury v Bognor Regis Town	3-2e
66r	Needham Market v Metropolitan Police	2-3e
69r	Swindon Supermarine v Chippenham Town	0-1
72r	Salisbury v Weston-Super-Mare	2-3e
74r	Truro City v Hereford	3-4e
80r	Sholing v Slough Town	0-3

Qualifying Round Three

1	Workington v Kidsgrove Athletic	0-0
2	Stockport County v Corby Town	3-0
3	Mickleover Sports v Alfreton Town	1-2
4	Kettering Town v Hednesford Town	4-0
5	Brackley Town v Marine	2-3
6	Peterborough Sports v Chorley	0-3
7	Altrincham v Bradford Park Avenue	4-2
8	Dunston UTS v Chester FC	4-3
9	Stourbridge v Kidderminster Harriers	3-2
10	FC United of Manchester v Witton Albion	1-2
11	Cleethorpes Town v Guiseley	2-2
12	St Neots Town v Coalville Town	2-2
13	King's Lynn Town v Ashton United	0-1
14	Curzon Ashton v Southport	1-2
15	Gainsborough Trinity v Blyth Spartans	1-2
16	York City v St Ives Town	3-0
17	Warrington Town v AFC Telford United	2-1
18	Tiverton Town v Metropolitan Police	3-3
19	Haringey Borough v AFC Sudbury	3-1
20	Gloucester City v Dorking Wanderers	3-3
21	Leatherhead v Hanwell Town	1-1
22	Eastbourne Borough v Dulwich Hamlet	4-3
23	Woking v Kempston Rovers	3-2
24	Taunton Town v St Albans City	5-2
25	Billericay Town v Whitehawk	9-1
26	Hereford v Welling United	0-2
27	Hitchin Town v Hastings United (2)	2-0
28	Concord Rangers v Beaconsfield Town	2-1
29	Hemel Hempstead Town v Ramsgate	5-0
30	Moneyfields v Worthing	2-3
31	Bath City v Lewes	3-0
32	Slough Town v Bristol Manor Farm	2-2
33	Hungerford Town v Wealdstone	1-2
34	Hampton & Richmond Boro. v AFC Hornchurch	1-0
35	Chippenham Town v Hendon	4-1
36	Brightlingsea Regent v Torquay United	0-3
37	Weston-Super-Mare v Coggeshall Town	1-0
38	Horsham v Poole Town	1-1
39	Oxford City v Dartford	4-1
40	Winchester City v Cirencester Town	3-0
1r	Kidsgrove Athletic v Workington	2-1e
11r	Guiseley v Cleethorpes Town	2-1
12r	Coalville Town v St Neots Town	3-3q
18r	Metropolitan Police v Tiverton Town	1-0e
20r	Dorking Wanderers v Gloucester City	0-3
21r	Hanwell Town v Leatherhead	0-0e
32r	Bristol Manor Farm v Slough Town	0-4
38r	Poole Town v Horsham	2-1

Qualifying Round Four

1	Guiseley v Stourbridge	3-1
2	Warrington Town v FC Halifax Town	2-2
3	Chorley v Barrow	3-2
4	Hartlepool United v Kidsgrove Athletic	1-0
5	AFC Fylde v Chesterfield	1-3
6	Southport v Ashton United	2-1
7	Blyth Spartans v York City	0-1
8	Harrogate Town v Wrexham	0-0
9	Dunston UTS v Gateshead (2)	0-4
10	Stockport County v Altrincham	2-0
11	Marine v Salford City	1-2
12	Witton Albion v Solihull Moors	0-2
13	Alfreton Town v St Neots Town	4-0
14	Woking v Welling United	1-0
15	Hitchin Town v Leatherhead	1-1
16	Chippenham Town v Maidenhead United	1-1
17	Eastbourne Borough v Slough Town	1-2
18	Hemel Hempstead Town v Oxford City	1-1
19	Weston-Super-Mare v Bath City	1-0
20	Boreham Wood v Dagenham & Redbridge	2-2
21	Metropolitan Police v Havant & Waterlooville	1-0
22	Gloucester City v Bromley	0-1
23	Aldershot Town v Kettering Town	2-0
24	Torquay United v Winchester City	4-1
25	Billericay Town v Taunton Town	2-2
26	Eastleigh v Hampton & Richmond Boro.	0-1
27	Wealdstone v Sutton United	1-2
28	Ebbsfleet United v Worthing	4-0
29	Maidstone United (2) v Leyton Orient	2-0
30	Haringey Borough v Poole Town	2-1
31	Barnet v Braintree Town	4-2
32	Concord Rangers v Dover Athletic	0-1
2r	FC Halifax Town v Warrington Town	2-0
8r	Wrexham v Harrogate Town	2-0
15r	Leatherhead v Hitchin Town	1-2e
16r	Maidenhead United v Chippenham Town	1-0
18r	Oxford City v Hemel Hempstead Town	5-0
20r	Dagenham & Redbridge v Boreham Wood	0-1
25r	Taunton Town v Billericay Town	0-1

Round One

Accrington Stanley (2) v Colchester United	1-0
Aldershot Town v Bradford City	1-1
Alfreton Town v Fleetwood Town	1-4
Barnet v Bristol Rovers	1-1
Barnsley v Notts County	4-0
Bromley v Peterborough United	1-3
Bury v Dover Athletic	5-0
Chesterfield v Billericay Town	1-1
Chorley v Doncaster Rovers	2-2
Crewe Alexandra v Carlisle United	0-1
Ebbsfleet United v Cheltenham Town	0-0
Exeter City v Blackpool	2-3
Gillingham v Hartlepool United	0-0
Grimsby Town v Milton Keynes Dons	3-1
Guiseley v Cambridge United	4-3
Hampton & Richmond Boro. v Oldham Athletic	1-2
Haringey Borough v AFC Wimbledon	0-1
Hitchin Town v Solihull Moors	0-2
Lincoln City v Northampton Town	3-2
Luton Town v Wycombe Wanderers	2-0
Maidenhead United v Portsmouth	0-4
Maidstone United (2) v Macclesfield Town	2-1
Mansfield Town v Charlton Athletic	1-1
Metropolitan Police v Newport County (2)	0-2
Morecambe v FC Halifax Town	0-0
Oxford United v Forest Green Rovers	0-0
Plymouth Argyle v Stevenage	1-0
Port Vale v Sunderland	1-2
Rochdale v Gateshead (2)	2-1
Scunthorpe United v Burton Albion	2-1
Shrewsbury Town v Salford City	1-1
Southend United v Crawley Town	1-1
Southport v Boreham Wood	2-0
Sutton United v Slough Town	0-0
Swindon Town v York City	2-1
Torquay United v Woking	0-1
Tranmere Rovers v Oxford City	3-3
Walsall v Coventry City	3-2

2018/19 to 2019/20

	Weston-Super-Mare v Wrexham	0-2
	Yeovil Town v Stockport County	1-3
r	Billericay Town v Chesterfield	1-3
r	Bradford City v Aldershot Town	1-1P
r	Bristol Rovers v Barnet	1-2
r	Charlton Athletic v Mansfield Town	5-0
r	Cheltenham Town v Ebbsfleet United	2-0
r	Crawley Town v Southend United	2-6e
r	Doncaster Rovers v Chorley	7-0
r	FC Halifax Town v Morecambe	1-0
r	Forest Green Rovers v Oxford United	0-3
r	Hartlepool United v Gillingham	3-4e
r	Oxford City v Tranmere Rovers	0-2
r	Salford City v Shrewsbury Town	1-3
r	Slough Town v Sutton United	1-1P

Round Two

	Accrington Stanley (2) v Cheltenham Town	3-1
	Barnet v Stockport County	1-0
	Bury v Luton Town	0-1
	Charlton Athletic v Doncaster Rovers	0-2
	Chesterfield v Grimsby Town	0-2
	FC Halifax Town v AFC Wimbledon	1-3
	Guiseley v Fleetwood Town	1-2
	Lincoln City v Carlisle United	2-0
	Maidstone United (2) v Oldham Athletic	0-2
	Peterborough United v Bradford City	2-2
	Plymouth Argyle v Oxford United	1-2
	Rochdale v Portsmouth	0-1
	Shrewsbury Town v Scunthorpe United	1-0
	Slough Town v Gillingham	0-1
	Solihull Moors v Blackpool	0-0
	Southend United v Barnsley	2-4
	Swindon Town v Woking	0-1
	Tranmere Rovers v Southport	1-1
	Walsall v Sunderland	1-1
	Wrexham v Newport County (2)	0-0
r	Blackpool v Solihull Moors	3-2e
r	Bradford City v Peterborough United	4-4q
r	Newport County (2) v Wrexham	4-0
r	Southport v Tranmere Rovers	0-2
r	Sunderland v Walsall	0-1

Round Three

	Accrington Stanley (2) v Ipswich Town	1-0
	Aston Villa v Swansea City	0-3
	Blackpool v Arsenal	0-3
	Bolton Wanderers v Walsall	5-2
	Bournemouth v Brighton & Hove Albion	1-3
	Brentford v Oxford United	1-0
	Bristol City v Huddersfield Town	1-0
	Burnley v Barnsley	1-0
	Chelsea v Nottingham Forest	2-0
	Crystal Palace v Grimsby Town	1-0
	Derby County v Southampton	2-2
	Everton v Lincoln City	2-1
	Fleetwood Town v AFC Wimbledon	2-3
	Fulham v Oldham Athletic	1-2
	Gillingham v Cardiff City	1-0
	Manchester City v Rotherham United	7-0
	Manchester United v Reading	2-0
	Middlesbrough v Peterborough United	5-0
	Millwall v Hull City	2-1
	Newcastle United v Blackburn Rovers	1-1
	Newport County (2) v Leicester City	2-1
	Norwich City v Portsmouth	0-1
	Preston North End v Doncaster Rovers	1-3
	Queen's Park Rangers v Leeds United	2-1
	Sheffield United v Barnet	0-1
	Sheffield Wednesday v Luton Town	0-0
	Shrewsbury Town v Stoke City	1-1
	Tranmere Rovers v Tottenham Hotspur	0-7
	West Bromwich Albion v Wigan Athletic	1-0
	West Ham United v Birmingham City	2-0
	Woking v Watford	0-2
	Wolverhampton Wan. v Liverpool	2-1
r	Blackburn Rovers v Newcastle United	2-4e
r	Luton Town v Sheffield Wednesday	0-1
r	Southampton v Derby County	2-2q
r	Stoke City v Shrewsbury Town	2-3

Round Four

	AFC Wimbledon v West Ham United	4-2
	Accrington Stanley (2) v Derby County	0-1
	Arsenal v Manchester United	1-3
	Barnet v Brentford	3-3
	Brighton & Hove Albion v West Bromwich Albion	0-0
	Bristol City v Bolton Wanderers	2-1
	Chelsea v Sheffield Wednesday	3-0
	Crystal Palace v Tottenham Hotspur	2-0
	Doncaster Rovers v Oldham Athletic	2-1
	Manchester City v Burnley	5-0
	Middlesbrough v Newport County (2)	1-1
	Millwall v Everton	3-2
	Newcastle United v Watford	0-2
	Portsmouth v Queen's Park Rangers	1-1
	Shrewsbury Town v Wolverhampton Wan.	2-2
	Swansea City v Gillingham	4-1
r	Brentford v Barnet	3-1
r	Newport County (2) v Middlesbrough	2-0
r	Queen's Park Rangers v Portsmouth	2-0
r	West Bromwich Albion v Brighton & Hove Albion	1-3e
r	Wolverhampton Wan. v Shrewsbury Town	3-2

Round Five

AFC Wimbledon v Millwall	0-1
Brighton & Hove Albion v Derby County	2-1
Bristol City v Wolverhampton Wan.	0-1
Chelsea v Manchester United	0-2
Doncaster Rovers v Crystal Palace	0-2
Newport County (2) v Manchester City	1-4
Queen's Park Rangers v Watford	0-1
Swansea City v Brentford	4-1

Round Six

Millwall v Brighton & Hove Albion	2-2q
Swansea City v Manchester City	2-3
Watford v Crystal Palace	2-1
Wolverhampton Wan. v Manchester United	2-1

Semi Finals

Manchester City v Brighton & Hove Albion	1-0 N
Watford v Wolverhampton Wan.	3-2eN

Final

Manchester City v Watford	6-0 N

2019/20

Extra Preliminary Round

1	Consett v Dunston UTS	1-1
2	Newton Aycliffe v Northallerton Town	0-2
3	Kendal Town v Hemsworth MW	0-4
4	Shildon v Garforth Town	0-0
5	Whitley Bay v Hebburn Town	1-7
6	Ashington v Albion Sports	2-0
7	Billingham Town v Yorkshire Amateur	3-0
8	West Auckland Town v Bridlington Town (2)	1-3
9	North Shields v Guisborough Town	2-2
10	Bishop Auckland v Thornaby	0-2
11	Sunderland RCA v Sunderland Ryhope CW	0-0
12	Seaham Red Star v Penrith	4-2
13	Harrogate Railway Athletic v Whickham	1-10
14	Nostell MW v Stockton Town	2-2
15	Hall Road Rangers v Goole AFC	0-3
16	Knaresborough Town v Newcastle Benfield	0-3
17	Vauxhall Motors v Winsford United	1-2
18	Charnock Richard v Lower Breck	2-1
19	Thackley v Handsworth Parramore	1-4
20	Longridge Town v Barnoldswick Town	6-1
21	Irlam v Ashton Athletic	4-0
22	Skelmersdale United v Penistone Church	1-1
23	Northwich Victoria v Silsden	2-2
24	AFC Liverpool v Burscough	2-3
25	Avro v Litherland Remyca	3-4
26	Runcorn Town v Rylands	2-0
27	Squires Gate v West Didsbury & Chorlton	1-2
28	Clitheroe v 1874 Northwich	1-2
29	Eccleshill United v Bootle	2-1
30	Athersley Recreation v Padiham	0-4
31	City of Liverpool v Campion	3-1
32	Liversedge v Abbey Hey	5-1
33	Coventry Sphinx v Coventry United	1-1
34	Lye Town v Lutterworth Town	0-3
35	Worcester City v Stone Old Alleynians	4-1
36	Romulus v Wolverhampton Casuals	0-0
37	Lichfield City v Highgate United	3-2
38	Haughmond v Walsall Wood	3-2
39	Atherstone Town v Stourport Swifts	1-3
40	Congleton Town v Westfields	1-1
41	Hanley Town v Leicester Road	2-3
42	Boldmere St Michaels v Daventry Town	3-1
43	Tividale v Wednesfield	2-1
44	Racing Club Warwick v AFC Wulfrunians	0-2
45	Dunkirk v Gresley	1-1 D
46	Sporting Khalsa v Rugby Town	5-4
47	Heather St Johns v Wolverhampton Sporting Community	2-0
48	Malvern Town v Whitchurch Alport	1-2 N
49	Hallam v Staveley MW	0-2
50	Radford v Heanor Town	0-7
51	Winterton Rangers v Grimsby Borough	2-1
52	Quorn v Sherwood Colliery	1-2
53	Shepshed Dynamo v Maltby Main	2-4
54	Leicester Nirvana v Oadby Town	2-1
55	Worksop Town v Melton Town	1-2
56	Sleaford Town v AFC Mansfield	0-7
57	Mulbarton Wanderers v Boston Town	0-0
58	South Normanton Athletic v Selston	5-0
59	Bottesford Town v Long Eaton United	2-8
60	Barton Town v Carlton Town	3-2
61	Anstey Nomads v Kirby Muxloe	0-3
62	Loughborough University v Ilkeston Town	3-1 N
63	Potton United v Ely City	1-2
64	March Town United v Norwich United	2-1
65	Walsham Le Willows v Peterborough Northern Star	1-2
66	Eynesbury Rovers v Wellingborough Town (2)	3-3
67	Desborough Town v Histon	1-3
68	Thetford Town v Rothwell Corinthians	0-1
69	Biggleswade v Mildenhall Town	4-1
70	Holbeach United v Fakenham Town	2-0
71	Bugbrooke St Michaels v Norwich CBS	1-0
72	Biggleswade United v Swaffham Town	1-0
73	Harborough Town v Deeping Rangers	1-2
74	Newmarket Town v Arlesey Town	2-2
75	Gorleston v Pinchbeck United	1-0
76	Northampton ON Chenecks v Godmanchester Rovers	2-3
77	Great Yarmouth Town v Wellingborough Whitworths	4-2
78	Kirkley & Pakefield v Wroxham	2-2
79	Walthamstow v Sporting Bengal United	5-0
80	Framlingham Town v Hackney Wick	3-1
81	Haverhill Rovers v Colney Heath	1-6
82	Crawley Green v Takeley	2-5
83	Hadley v Redbridge	4-2
84	Hoddesdon Town v Brantham Athletic	2-1 N
85	Woodbridge Town v Coggeshall United	1-0
86	Barkingside v Stansted	4-1
87	Clapton v Stowmarket Town	0-6 N
88	Hullbridge Sports v Stanway Rovers	1-2
89	London Colney v Hadleigh United	2-0
90	Sawbridgeworth Town v Halstead Town	1-3
91	FC Clacton v St Margaretsbury	3-0
92	Southend Manor v Long Melford	0-0
93	Cockfosters v Leyton Athletic	1-0
94	Stotfold v Harpenden Town	3-1
95	Ilford v Harwich & Parkeston	1-2
96	Woodford Town v White Ensign	1-1
97	West Essex v Whitton United	1-2 N
98	Saffron Walden Town v Baldock Town	1-0
99	Fairford Town v Enfield 1893	3-2
100	AFC Hayes v Wembley	1-1
101	Clanfield 85 v Shortwood United	1-3
102	Dunstable Town v Chipping Sodbury Town	3-2
103	Slimbridge v Edgware Town	1-0
104	Tuffley Rovers v North Greenford United	1-1
105	Royal Wootton Bassett Town v Aylesbury Vale Dynamos	1-1
106	Abingdon United v Brimscombe & Thrupp	1-2
107	London Tigers v Thame Rangers	0-2
108	Newport Pagnell Town v Cheltenham Saracens	6-2
109	Leverstock Green v Ardley United	1-1
110	Oxhey Jets v Flackwell Heath	0-4
111	Burnham v Tring Athletic	2-1
112	Bishop's Cleeve v Easington Sports	3-0
113	Wantage Town v Brackley Town Saints	1-1
114	Leighton Town v Thornbury Town	4-1
115	Shrivenham v Holmer Green	1-1
116	Harefield United v Lydney Town	3-0
117	Longlevens v Malmesbury Victoria	3-0
118	Winslow United v Roman Glass St George	2-3
119	AFC Croydon Athletic v Virginia Water	1-0
120	Loxwood v Abbey Rangers	1-1
121	Balham FC v Rusthall	1-0
122	Crawley Down Gatwick v Newhaven	0-2
123	Cray Valley Paper Mills v Chatham Town	2-1
124	Erith & Belvedere v Peacehaven & Telscombe	1-1
125	Bridon Ropes v Broadfields United	3-1
126	Tunbridge Wells v Pagham	1-1
127	Corinthian v Little Common	1-2
128	Walton & Hersham v Southall	2-4
129	Horley Town v Bearsted	2-2
130	Egham Town v Lancing	2-2
131	Lordswood v Steyning Town Community	0-1
132	CB Hounslow United v Sheerwater	2-1
133	Horsham YMCA v Croydon	2-1
134	Saltdean United v Eastbourne United	6-1
135	Chertsey Town v Cobham	1-1
136	Tower Hamlets v Selsey	2-1
137	Chichester City v Erith Town	3-1
138	Eastbourne Town v Bexhill United	6-1
139	Hassocks v Langney Wanderers	2-0
140	Arundel v Banstead Athletic	2-0
141	Redhill v K Sports	2-1
142	Glebe v Hollands & Blair	3-1
143	Colliers Wood United v Shoreham	2-3
144	Sheppey United v East Preston	4-1
145	Guildford City (2) v Tooting Bec	3-2
146	Punjab United v Broadbridge Heath	0-1
147	Sutton Athletic v Deal Town	3-2
148	Sutton Common Rovers v Molesey	1-1
149	Spelthorne Sports v Lingfield	1-1
150	Greenwich Borough v Canterbury City	2-3
151	Crowborough Athletic v AFC Varndeanians	1-2
152	Welling Town v AFC Uckfield Town	1-4
153	Hanworth Villa v Fisher	3-2
154	Beckenham Town v Raynes Park Vale	4-3
155	Solent University v Portland United	0-3
156	Shaftesbury v Knaphill	1-4
157	Cowes Sports v Lymington Town	0-4
158	Fleet Town v Farnham Town	2-2
159	Brockenhurst v AFC Stoneham	0-2
160	Bournemouth (Ams) v Frimley Green	2-1
161	Windsor v Reading City	0-3
162	Bemerton Heath Harlequins v Andover New Street	3-3
163	Sholing v Tadley Calleva	1-0
164	Badshot Lea v Ascot United	2-2
165	Binfield v United Services Portsmouth	3-2
166	Romsey Town v Hamble Club	1-5
167	Amesbury Town v Christchurch	2-7
168	Westbury United v Fareham Town	0-1
169	Hamworthy United v Bashley	3-0
170	AFC Portchester v Hythe & Dibden	2-2
171	Horndean v Camberley Town	5-3
172	Alresford Town v Baffins Milton Rovers	0-0
173	Cheddar v Bradford Town	2-3
174	Bitton v Bridport	2-1
175	Cribbs v Wellington (Somerset)	1-1

2019/20

176	Keynsham Town v Brislington	0-1
177	Exmouth Town v Barnstaple Town	2-0
178	Saltash United v Clevedon Town	1-2
179	Plymouth Parkway v Buckland Athletic	1-0
180	Willand Rovers v AFC St Austell	2-1
181	Tavistock v Hengrove Athletic	3-0
182	Street v Odd Down	4-1
183	Shepton Mallet v Cadbury Heath	3-1
184	Bridgwater Town v Hallen	1-0
1r	Dunston UTS v Consett	5-2
4r	Garforth Town v Shildon	3-2
9r	Guisborough Town v North Shields	1-0
11r	Sunderland Ryhope CW v Sunderland RCA	1-2
14r	Stockton Town v Nostell MW	5-1
22r	Penistone Church v Skelmersdale United	2-5
23r	Silsden v Northwich Victoria	3-4
33r	Coventry United v Coventry Sphinx	0-1
36r	Wolverhampton Casuals v Romulus	1-2e
40r	Westfields v Congleton Town	4-1
57r	Boston Town v Mulbarton Wanderers	4-2
66r	Wellingborough Town (2) v Eynesbury Rovers	4-1
74r	Arlesey Town v Newmarket Town	1-0
78r	Wroxham v Kirkley & Pakefield	3-2
92r	Long Melford v Southend Manor	3-3P
96r	White Ensign v Woodford Town	3-1e
100r	Wembley v AFC Hayes	3-2
104r	North Greenford United v Tuffley Rovers	2-1
105r	Aylesbury Vale Dynamos v Royal Wootton Bassett Town	1-0
109r	Ardley United v Leverstock Green	3-1
113r	Brackley Town Saints v Wantage Town	1-2
115r	Holmer Green v Shrivenham	1-1q
120r	Abbey Rangers v Loxwood	2-0
124r	Peacehaven & Telscombe v Erith & Belvedere	1-1q
126r	Pagham v Tunbridge Wells	0-2
129r	Bearsted v Horley Town	0-2
130r	Lancing v Egham Town	4-4q
135r	Cobham v Chertsey Town	2-4
148r	Molesey v Sutton Common Rovers	0-1
149r	Lingfield v Spelthorne Sports	0-4 N
158r	Farnham Town v Fleet Town	1-2
162r	Andover New Street v Bemerton Heath Harlequins	3-2
164r	Badshot Lea v Ascot United	2-1
170r	Hythe & Dibden v AFC Portchester	3-2
172r	Baffins Milton Rovers v Alresford Town	2-1
175r	Cribbs v Wellington (Somerset)	5-1

Preliminary Round

1	Dunston UTS v Goole AFC	2-2
2	Newcastle Benfield v Workington	1-0
3	Seaham Red Star v Guisborough Town	3-1
4	Billingham Town v Ossett United	3-4
5	Whickham v Thornaby	1-2
6	Garforth Town v Colne	0-4
7	Ashington v Marske United	1-3
8	Sunderland RCA v Hemsworth MW	1-0
9	Pickering Town v Bridlington Town (2)	3-1
10	Brighouse Town v Morpeth Town	2-2
11	Pontefract Collieries v Hebburn Town	1-1
12	Frickley Athletic v Tadcaster Albion	0-1
13	Northallerton Town v Stockton Town	0-3
14	Widnes v Mossley	2-2
15	City of Liverpool v Skelmersdale United	2-1
16	Sheffield v Litherland Remyca	2-1
17	Eccleshill United v Glossop North End	1-1
18	Stalybridge Celtic v West Didsbury & Chorlton	0-0
19	Ramsbottom United v Winsford United	3-3
20	Charnock Richard v Longridge Town	1-1
21	Trafford v Burscough	2-0
22	Liversedge v Droylsden	1-0
23	Atherton Collieries v Runcorn Linnets	2-1
24	1874 Northwich v Handsworth Parramore	6-0
25	Northwich Victoria v Prescot Cables	2-1
26	Stocksbridge Park Steels v Irlam	2-3
27	Padiham v Marine	1-1
28	Radcliffe v Runcorn Town	0-0
29	Kidsgrove Athletic v Newcastle Town	1-1
30	Mickleover Sports v Coventry Sphinx	3-0
31	Coleshill Town v Whitchurch Alport	0-3
32	Tividale v Chasetown	0-5
33	AFC Wulfrunians v Leek Town	0-1
34	Stourport Swifts v Boldmere St Michaels	0-0
35	Bromsgrove Sporting v Leicester Road	2-1
36	Bedworth United v Halesowen Town	1-1
37	Belper Town v Sporting Khalsa	1-1
38	Romulus v Market Drayton Town	6-0
39	Heather St Johns v Worcester City	1-0
40	Gresley v Sutton Coldfield Town	1-2
41	Lichfield City v Haughmond	3-0
42	Westfields v Lutterworth Town	2-3
43	Barton Town v Grantham Town	1-3
44	Loughborough Dynamo v Sherwood Colliery	2-2
45	Melton Town v Cleethorpes Town	1-3
46	Boston Town v Leicester Nirvana	0-0
47	Heanor Town v AFC Mansfield	0-0
48	Long Eaton United v South Normanton Athletic	1-1
49	Maltby Main v Loughborough University	4-1
50	Winterton Rangers v Kirby Muxloe	0-1
51	Staveley MW v Lincoln United	2-1
52	Spalding United v Dereham Town	2-4
53	Great Yarmouth Town v Rothwell Corinthians	0-2
54	Peterborough Sports v Bugbrooke St Michaels	7-0
55	Gorleston v Kempston Rovers	0-1
56	Bedford Town v Deeping Rangers	0-1
57	Wisbech Town v Ely City	2-2
58	March Town United v Wellingborough Town (2)	2-1
59	Corby Town v Holbeach United	4-0
60	Wroxham v Stamford	2-4
61	Cambridge City v Barton Rovers	0-2
62	Arlesey Town v Peterborough Northern Star	2-0
63	Biggleswade v Yaxley	4-0
64	Bury Town v Histon	1-2
65	Godmanchester Rovers v St Neots Town	1-1
66	Soham Town Rangers v Biggleswade United	2-0
67	Walthamstow v Great Wakering Rovers	2-0
68	Cockfosters v Coggeshall Town	0-4
69	Harwich & Parkeston v Romford	0-2
70	Long Melford v Colney Heath	0-2
71	Hadley v Hoddesdon Town	2-0
72	London Colney v Halstead Town	5-0
73	Whitton United v Hertford Town	2-1
74	AFC Sudbury v Felixstowe & Walton United	2-1
75	FC Romania v Ware	3-3
76	Grays Athletic v Heybridge Swifts	5-2
77	FC Clacton v Witham Town	1-1
78	Aveley v Barking	1-2
79	Stotfold v Canvey Island	0-2
80	Bowers & Pitsea v Barkingside	4-2
81	Saffron Walden Town v Maldon & Tiptree	1-2
82	Harlow Town v Brentwood Town	1-1
83	Tilbury v Stanway Rovers	3-1
84	Wingate & Finchley v Welwyn Garden City	2-0
85	Cheshunt v Stowmarket Town	1-0
86	Basildon United v Framlingham Town	7-1
87	Waltham Abbey v Woodbridge Town	4-0
88	Takeley v White Ensign	3-3
89	Cirencester Town v North Greenford United	5-0
90	Aylesbury Vale Dynamos v North Leigh	4-5
91	Shrivenham v Chalfont St Peter	0-2
92	Longlevens v Northwood	1-0
93	Wantage Town v Thame Rangers	2-2
94	Bishop's Cleeve v Kidlington	1-4
95	Dunstable Town v Shortwood United	4-1
96	Highworth Town v Ardley United	3-0
97	Marlow v Cinderford Town	2-4
98	Fairford Town v Hanwell Town	2-3
99	Wembley v Berkhamsted	2-3
100	Didcot Town v Roman Glass St George	2-1
101	Thame United v Leighton Town	3-3
102	Evesham United v Harefield United	2-1
103	Slimbridge v Burnham	1-1
104	Brimscombe & Thrupp v Aylesbury United	1-3
105	AFC Dunstable v Hayes & Yeading United	0-0
106	Newport Pagnell Town v Flackwell Heath	1-2
107	Tooting & Mitcham United v Faversham Town	1-0
108	Sittingbourne v Uxbridge	2-0
109	Horsham YMCA v Egham Town	2-1
110	Little Common v Three Bridges	2-1
111	Cray Wanderers v Hythe Town	5-0
112	Sutton Athletic v Ashford Town (Middlesex)	6-0
113	Sutton Common Rovers v Eastbourne Town	3-0
114	Steyning Town Community v Ramsgate	1-4
115	Herne Bay v AFC Croydon Athletic	2-2
116	Chertsey Town v Erith & Belvedere	5-1
117	Sheppey United v Glebe	3-1
118	Whitehawk v Saltdean United	2-0
119	Cray Valley Paper Mills v Whyteleafe	0-2
120	Whitstable Town v Newhaven	3-1
121	Burgess Hill Town v Sevenoaks Town	0-3
122	VCD Athletic v AFC Uckfield Town	3-3
123	Bedfont Sports v Hanworth Villa	3-2
124	Redhill v Balham FC	1-4
125	South Park v Canterbury City	2-1
126	East Grinstead Town v Abbey Rangers	0-1
127	Tower Hamlets v Horsham	1-6
128	Arundel v Shoreham	1-0
129	Beckenham Town v Ashford United	0-1
130	Phoenix Sports v Staines Town	0-6
131	Southall v Spelthorne Sports	1-2
132	Bridon Ropes v Chichester City	2-7
133	Chipstead v Hassocks	0-0
134	Guildford City (2) v AFC Varndeanians	1-2
135	Haywards Heath Town v Tunbridge Wells	2-1
136	CB Hounslow United v Horley Town	0-3
137	Hastings United (2) v Broadbridge Heath	2-1
138	Portland United v Hamworthy United	4-3
139	Hythe & Dibden v Horndean	2-1
140	Hamble Club v Sholing	0-1
141	Moneyfields v Reading City	3-0
142	Christchurch v Badshot Lea	1-2
143	Fleet Town v Baffins Milton Rovers	3-0
144	Bournemouth (Ams) v Bracknell Town	0-5
145	Binfield v Lymington Town	3-2
146	Thatcham Town v Andover New Street	7-1
147	Blackfield & Langley v AFC Totton	2-1
148	Winchester City v AFC Stoneham	1-1
149	Basingstoke Town v Westfield	0-2
150	Knaphill v Fareham Town	0-1
151	Plymouth Parkway v Paulton Rovers	5-2
152	Yate Town v Exmouth Town	2-2
153	Bridgwater Town v Brislington	7-0
154	Cribbs v Bideford	0-1
155	Clevedon Town v Bristol Manor Farm	2-5
156	Tavistock v Frome Town	2-1
157	Shepton Mallet v Melksham Town	1-1
158	Bradford Town v Larkhall Athletic	3-1
159	Street v Willand Rovers	1-5
160	Bitton v Mangotsfield United	2-3
1r	Goole AFC v Dunston UTS	1-4
10r	Morpeth Town v Brighouse Town	3-2
11r	Hebburn Town v Pontefract Collieries	0-4
14r	Mossley v Widnes	2-3
17r	Glossop North End v Eccleshill United	3-1
18r	West Didsbury & Chorlton v Stalybridge Celtic	2-3
19r	Winsford United v Ramsbottom United	1-3
20r	Longridge Town v Charnock Richard	0-2
27r	Marine v Padiham	3-0
28r	Runcorn Town v Radcliffe	2-1
29r	Newcastle Town v Kidsgrove Athletic	1-2
34r	Boldmere St Michaels v Stourport Swifts	4-1
36r	Halesowen Town v Bedworth United	3-1
37r	Sporting Khalsa v Belper Town	1-3e
44r	Sherwood Colliery v Loughborough Dynamo	0-1
46r	Leicester Nirvana v Boston Town	0-1
47r	AFC Mansfield v Heanor Town	2-1
48r	South Normanton Athletic v Long Eaton United	1-0
57r	Ely City v Wisbech Town	0-4
65r	St Neots Town v Godmanchester Rovers	3-1
75r	Ware v FC Romania	2-1
77r	Witham Town v FC Clacton	3-2e
82r	Brentwood Town v Harlow Town	2-1
88r	White Ensign v Takeley	2-3e
93r	Thame Rangers v Wantage Town	2-4e
101r	Leighton Town v Thame United	2-1
103r	Burnham v Slimbridge	1-1P
105r	Hayes & Yeading United v AFC Dunstable	2-1e
115r	AFC Croydon Athletic v Herne Bay	0-1
122r	AFC Uckfield Town v VCD Athletic	1-1q
133r	Hassocks v Chipstead	2-3
148r	AFC Stoneham v Winchester City	1-3
152r	Exmouth Town v Yate Town	2-0
157r	Melksham Town v Shepton Mallet	2-3

Qualifying Round One

1	Thornaby v Ossett United	2-2
2	1874 Northwich v Pickering Town	2-0
3	Scarborough Athletic v Marske United	1-1
4	Lancaster City v Northwich Victoria	0-0
5	FC United of Manchester v Atherton Collieries	2-2
6	Dunston UTS v Sunderland RCA	0-0
7	Liversedge v Stockton Town	0-2
8	Newcastle Benfield v Runcorn Town	2-3
9	Warrington Town v City of Liverpool	2-2
10	Charnock Richard v Irlam	0-4
11	Widnes v Whitby Town	0-4
12	Tadcaster Albion v Ashton United	2-2
13	Stalybridge Celtic v Marine	0-2
14	Trafford v Bamber Bridge	3-0
15	Glossop North End v Pontefract Collieries	1-3
16	South Shields (3) v Colne	0-0
17	Maltby Main v Ramsbottom United	1-5
18	Morpeth Town v Hyde United	3-1
19	Seaham Red Star v Witton Albion	0-1
20	Kirby Muxloe v Boston Town	0-1
21	Lutterworth Town v Hednesford Town	0-3
22	Halesowen Town v Lichfield City	7-1
23	South Normanton Athletic v Coalville Town	0-1
24	Tamworth v Nuneaton Borough	3-1
25	Loughborough Dynamo v Heather St Johns	1-0
26	Barwell v AFC Mansfield	4-1
27	Romulus v Buxton	0-4
28	Banbury United v Gainsborough Trinity	2-2
29	Matlock Town v Basford United	2-1
30	Stratford Town v Boldmere St Michaels	6-1
31	Rushall Olympic v Sheffield	3-1
32	Belper Town v Alvechurch	1-0
33	Nantwich Town v Grantham Town	3-1
34	Kidsgrove Athletic v Cleethorpes Town	2-1
35	Sutton Coldfield Town v Redditch United	1-1
36	Stafford Rangers v Mickleover Sports	3-0
37	Bromsgrove Sporting v Stourbridge	0-1
38	Whitchurch Alport v Leek Town	0-2
39	Chasetown v Staveley MW	1-0
40	Wingate & Finchley v London Colney	4-1
41	Soham Town Rangers v Whitton United	3-0
42	Takeley v Potters Bar Town	0-1
43	Deeping Rangers v AFC Sudbury	2-2
44	Enfield Town v AFC Rushden & Diamonds	1-0
45	Kings Langley v Barking	3-1
46	AFC Hornchurch v Kempston Rovers	6-0
47	Cheshunt v Brightlingsea Regent	1-0
48	Stamford v Witham Town	1-0
49	Biggleswade v Tilbury	2-1
50	Basildon United v Coggeshall Town	2-1
51	Royston Town v Rothwell Corinthians	7-2
52	Histon v Maldon & Tiptree	0-3
53	Waltham Abbey v Canvey Island	2-2
54	Colney Heath v Corby Town	1-3
55	Dunstable Town v Bishop's Stortford	3-5
56	Grays Athletic v March Town United	3-1 D
57	Barton Rovers v Romford	4-0
58	Aylesbury United v Walthamstow	0-3
59	St Ives Town v Berkhamsted	2-1
60	Ware v Leiston	5-1
61	East Thurrock United v Peterborough Sports	1-1
62	Wisbech Town v Hitchin Town	1-2
63	Bowers & Pitsea v Brentwood Town	2-1
64	St Neots Town v Biggleswade Town	2-2
65	Hadley v Arlesey Town	3-2
66	Dereham Town v Needham Market	1-1
67	Lowestoft Town v Leighton Town	2-0
68	Whitstable Town v Folkestone Invicta	0-4
69	Chesham United v Fleet Town	4-2
70	Whyteleafe v Merstham	1-0

2019/20

71	Chertsey Town v Sheppey United	4-1
72	Chichester City v Chalfont St Peter	2-0
73	Hartley Wintney v Spelthorne Sports	3-0
74	Bracknell Town v Carshalton Athletic	0-2
75	Kingstonian v Walton Casuals	2-0
76	Leatherhead v Lewes	2-2
77	Hanwell Town v Staines Town	2-3
78	South Park v Badshot Lea	1-3
79	Tooting & Mitcham United v AFC Varndeanians	3-1
80	Whitehawk v Abbey Rangers	0-1
81	Hastings United (2) v Worthing	3-3
82	Haywards Heath Town v Hayes & Yeading United	0-1
83	Harrow Borough v Binfield	5-0
84	Horley Town v Balham FC	1-3
85	Cray Wanderers v Bedfont Sports	2-1
86	Westfield v Chipstead	0-1
87	Haringey Borough v Herne Bay	3-0
88	Corinthian Casuals v Sevenoaks Town	4-0
89	Sutton Common Rovers v Beaconsfield Town	1-3
90	Ashford United v Farnborough	0-3
91	Ramsgate v Arundel	0-0
92	Sutton Athletic v Flackwell Heath	1-1
93	VCD Athletic v Moneyfields	1-2
94	Bognor Regis Town v Sittingbourne	3-0
95	Little Common v Hendon	0-1
96	Horsham YMCA v Margate	1-2
97	Metropolitan Police v Horsham	1-1
98	Weston-Super-Mare v Fareham Town	3-0
99	Cinderford Town v Bideford	5-3
100	Didcot Town v Poole Town	0-1
101	Truro City v Wimborne Town	2-1
102	Plymouth Parkway v Merthyr Town (2)	0-1
103	Bridgwater Town v Bristol Manor Farm	1-3
104	Winchester City v Taunton Town	0-3
105	Willand Rovers v North Leigh	1-2
106	Burnham v Tiverton Town	2-3
107	Hythe & Dibden v Kidlington	2-4
108	Tavistock v Shepton Mallet	3-3
109	Highworth Town v Exmouth Town	4-2
110	Wantage Town v Swindon Supermarine	0-3
111	Longlevens v Portland United	0-2
112	Thatcham Town v Salisbury	2-3
113	Cirencester Town v Gosport Borough	1-0
114	Evesham United v Dorchester Town	0-2
115	Mangotsfield United v Blackfield & Langley	0-5
116	Sholing v Bradford Town	3-0
1r	Ossett United v Thornaby	6-0
3r	Marske United v Scarborough Athletic	1-2
4r	Northwich Victoria v Lancaster City	1-2
5r	Atherton Collieries v FC United of Manchester	0-1
6r	Sunderland RCA v Dunston UTS	0-5
9r	City of Liverpool v Warrington Town	0-4
12r	Ashton United v Tadcaster Albion	4-2
16r	Colne v South Shields (3)	1-0
28r	Gainsborough Trinity v Banbury United	1-0
35r	Redditch United v Sutton Coldfield Town	1-3
43r	AFC Sudbury v Deeping Rangers	2-3
53r	Canvey Island v Waltham Abbey	2-1
61r	Peterborough Sports v East Thurrock United	3-2
64r	Biggleswade Town v St Neots Town	2-0
66r	Needham Market v Dereham Town	2-1
76r	Lewes v Leatherhead	2-2P
81r	Worthing v Hastings United (2)	3-2
91r	Arundel v Ramsgate	0-4
92r	Flackwell Heath v Sutton Athletic	3-1
97r	Horsham v Metropolitan Police	3-2
108r	Shepton Mallet v Tavistock	1-2

Qualifying Round Two

1	Marine v Dunston UTS	1-2
2	Southport v Scarborough Athletic	5-2
3	Chester FC v Altrincham	1-1
4	Curzon Ashton v Blyth Spartans	4-4
5	Bradford Park Avenue v Morpeth Town	2-4
6	Irlam v York City	0-2
7	Ashton United v Pontefract Collieries	1-0
8	Colne v Ossett United	0-0
9	1874 Northwich v Whitby Town	0-1
10	FC United of Manchester v Warrington Town	1-2
11	Trafford v Darlington	1-3
12	Gateshead (2) v Ramsbottom United	6-0
13	Guiseley v Stockton Town	1-0
14	Lancaster City v Spennymoor Town	0-5
15	Runcorn Town v Farsley Celtic FC	1-3
16	Alfreton Town v King's Lynn Town	1-1
17	Stamford v Boston United	0-4
18	Leamington v Chasetown	2-2
19	Kettering Town v Sutton Coldfield Town	1-1
20	Belper Town v Witton Albion	0-0
21	Loughborough Dynamo v Tamworth	0-3
22	AFC Telford United v Nantwich Town	0-3
23	Rushall Olympic v Gainsborough Trinity	2-0
24	Halesowen Town v Stratford Town	4-1
25	Boston Town v Leek Town	0-4
26	Buxton v Corby Town	5-0
27	Matlock Town v Kidsgrove Athletic	1-2
28	Hednesford Town v Barwell	3-2
29	Kidderminster Harriers v Stafford Rangers	0-0
30	Coalville Town v Stourbridge	1-2
31	Beaconsfield Town v Hemel Hempstead Town	1-0
32	Corinthian Casuals v Chelmsford City	2-0
33	Kingstonian v March Town United	3-0
34	Walthamstow v Abbey Rangers	1-1
35	Balham FC v Royston Town	3-5
36	Tonbridge Angels v Eastbourne Borough	1-2
37	Margate v Concord Rangers	3-1
38	Hendon v Deeping Rangers	3-2
39	St Ives Town v Canvey Island	0-0
40	Maidstone United (2) v Cheshunt	4-1
41	Potters Bar Town v AFC Hornchurch	2-0
42	Bishop's Stortford v Peterborough Sports	1-2
43	Dulwich Hamlet v Bognor Regis Town	6-1
44	Flackwell Heath v Slough Town	0-3
45	Billericay Town v Basildon United	1-0
46	Tooting & Mitcham United v Dorking Wanderers	1-0
47	Hadley v Ramsgate	1-0
48	Lewes v Bowers & Pitsea	1-2
49	Cray Wanderers v Soham Town Rangers	5-2
50	Harrow Borough v Carshalton Athletic	0-1
51	Biggleswade v Chertsey Town	1-3
52	Biggleswade Town v Ware	1-2
53	Badshot Lea v Hayes & Yeading United	0-4
54	Lowestoft Town v Needham Market	4-0
55	Barton Rovers v Hitchin Town	0-1
56	Enfield Town v Braintree Town	2-0
57	Maldon & Tiptree v Wingate & Finchley	4-2
58	Moneyfields v Whyteleafe	0-2
59	Hartley Wintney v Chichester City	0-0
60	Horsham v Dartford	0-2
61	St Albans City v Worthing	2-2
62	Kings Langley v Folkestone Invicta	4-0
63	Haringey Borough v Staines Town	5-0
64	Farnborough v Wealdstone	0-5
65	Welling United v Chipstead	7-0
66	Chesham United v Hampton & Richmond Boro.	1-2
67	Weston-Super-Mare v Merthyr Town (2)	2-1
68	Sholing v Weymouth	0-3
69	Hereford v Truro City	5-2
70	Portland United v Salisbury	0-1
71	Havant & Waterlooville v Taunton Town	2-1
72	Cirencester Town v Chippenham Town	2-2
73	Tavistock v Highworth Town	4-0
74	Tiverton Town v Bristol Manor Farm	2-4
75	Poole Town v Hungerford Town	2-1
76	Swindon Supermarine v Bath City	0-4
77	Oxford City v North Leigh	7-0
78	Kidlington v Gloucester City	0-5
79	Brackley Town v Cinderford Town	4-0
80	Blackfield & Langley v Dorchester Town	1-0
3r	Altrincham v Chester FC	1-0
4r	Blyth Spartans v Curzon Ashton	1-0
8r	Ossett United v Colne	0-4
16r	King's Lynn Town v Alfreton Town	2-1
18r	Chasetown v Leamington	1-2e
19r	Sutton Coldfield Town v Kettering Town	2-1
20r	Witton Albion v Belper Town	0-1e
29r	Stafford Rangers v Kidderminster Harriers	3-0
34r	Abbey Rangers v Walthamstow	2-1
39r	Canvey Island v St Ives Town	3-2e
59r	Chichester City v Hartley Wintney	1-0
61r	Worthing v St Albans City	1-3
72r	Chippenham Town v Cirencester Town	4-3e

Qualifying Round Three

1	Ashton United v Spennymoor Town	2-6
2	Halesowen Town v Altrincham	0-2
3	Hednesford Town v Blyth Spartans	4-2
4	Nantwich Town v Morpeth Town	1-0
5	Peterborough Sports v Guiseley	1-0
6	Leek Town v King's Lynn Town	0-2
7	Whitby Town v Gloucester City	1-1
8	Kidsgrove Athletic v Gateshead (2)	0-1
9	Stourbridge v Stafford Rangers	2-1
10	Belper Town v Rushall Olympic	2-1
11	Buxton v York City	1-2
12	Tamworth v Hereford	0-0
13	Dunston UTS v Colne	2-3
14	Farsley Celtic FC v Southport	0-5
15	Leamington v Darlington	0-2
16	Sutton Coldfield Town v Boston United	0-1
17	Brackley Town v Warrington Town	2-0
18	Oxford City v Hampton & Richmond Boro.	2-0
19	Lowestoft Town v Carshalton Athletic	1-2
20	Dulwich Hamlet v Eastbourne Borough	3-0
21	Canvey Island v Bowers & Pitsea	1-1
22	Bristol Manor Farm v Wealdstone	0-0
23	Kingstonian v Weston-Super-Mare	1-1
24	Haringey Borough v Cray Wanderers	1-0
25	Welling United v Tavistock	4-1
26	Maldon & Tiptree v Chertsey Town	6-1
27	Chippenham Town v Slough Town	3-3
28	Salisbury v Margate	2-4
29	Abbey Rangers v Whyteleafe	0-2
30	Kings Langley v Corinthian Casuals	3-0
31	Ware v Potters Bar Town	1-2
32	Hayes & Yeading United v Hendon	5-4
33	Royston Town v Beaconsfield Town	2-1
34	Tooting & Mitcham United v Poole Town	0-2
35	Havant & Waterlooville v Hadley	3-0
36	Billericay Town v Bath City	4-2
37	Blackfield & Langley v Dartford	1-4
38	Weymouth v St Albans City	4-1
39	Chichester City v Enfield Town	1-0
40	Maidstone United (2) v Hitchin Town	2-1
7r	Gloucester City v Whitby Town	1-3
12r	Hereford v Tamworth	0-0q
21r	Bowers & Pitsea v Canvey Island	1-1P
22r	Wealdstone v Bristol Manor Farm	4-0
23r	Weston-Super-Mare v Kingstonian	1-4
27r	Slough Town v Chippenham Town	2-3

Qualifying Round Four

1	Hednesford Town v Boston United	0-1
2	Gateshead (2) v Colne	5-0
3	Barrow v Solihull Moors	0-1
4	Whitby Town v Stourbridge	1-1
5	Hartlepool United v Brackley Town	1-0
6	Nantwich Town v King's Lynn Town	1-0
7	Chorley v Spennymoor Town	2-0
8	Southport v Altrincham	1-3
9	Tamworth v Darlington	0-3
10	York City v Stockport County	2-0
11	Notts County v Belper Town	2-1
12	Chesterfield v Wrexham	1-1
13	FC Halifax Town v Harrogate Town	1-2
14	AFC Fylde v Peterborough Sports	6-1
15	Whyteleafe v Chippenham Town	0-3
16	Haringey Borough v Yeovil Town	0-3
17	Havant & Waterlooville v Dulwich Hamlet	1-2
18	Ebbsfleet United v Woking	1-1
19	Welling United v Eastleigh	0-0
20	Bromley v Aldershot Town	4-3
21	Maidstone United (2) v Kings Langley	4-1
22	Maidenhead United v Wealdstone	1-1
23	Oxford City v Margate	2-1
24	Bowers & Pitsea v Chichester City	1-2
25	Hayes & Yeading United v Poole Town	1-1
26	Royston Town v Maldon & Tiptree	1-3
27	Potters Bar Town v Barnet	1-1
28	Torquay United v Boreham Wood	3-2
29	Sutton United v Billericay Town	1-1
30	Weymouth v Dover Athletic	1-2
31	Dartford v Kingstonian	2-3
32	Carshalton Athletic v Dagenham & Redbridge	2-1
4r	Stourbridge v Whitby Town	3-2
12r	Wrexham v Chesterfield	1-0
18r	Woking v Ebbsfleet United	0-1
19r	Eastleigh v Welling United	4-2
22r	Wealdstone v Maidenhead United	0-2
25r	Poole Town v Hayes & Yeading United	2-3
27r	Barnet v Potters Bar Town	3-1
29r	Billericay Town v Sutton United	5-2

Round One

	AFC Wimbledon v Doncaster Rovers	1-1
	Accrington Stanley (2) v Crewe Alexandra	0-2
	Barnet v Fleetwood Town	0-2
	Blackpool v Morecambe	4-1
	Bolton Wanderers v Plymouth Argyle	0-1
	Bristol Rovers v Bromley	1-1
	Cambridge United v Exeter City	1-1
	Carshalton Athletic v Boston United	1-4
	Cheltenham Town v Swindon Town	1-1
	Chichester City v Bury	wo/s
	Chippenham Town v Northampton Town	0-3
	Colchester United v Coventry City	0-2
	Crawley Town v Scunthorpe United	4-1
	Dover Athletic v Southend United	1-0
	Dulwich Hamlet v Carlisle United	1-4
	Ebbsfleet United v Notts County	2-3
	Forest Green Rovers v Billericay Town	4-0
	Gateshead (2) v Oldham Athletic	1-2
	Grimsby Town v Newport County (2)	1-1
	Harrogate Town v Portsmouth	1-2
	Hayes & Yeading United v Oxford United	0-2
	Ipswich Town v Lincoln City	1-1
	Leyton Orient v Maldon & Tiptree	1-2
	Macclesfield Town v Kingstonian	0-4
	Maidenhead United v Rotherham United	1-3
	Maidstone United (2) v Torquay United	1-0
	Mansfield Town v Chorley	1-0
	Milton Keynes Dons v Port Vale	0-1
	Nantwich Town v AFC Fylde	0-1
	Oxford City v Solihull Moors	1-5
	Salford City v Burton Albion	1-1
	Shrewsbury Town v Bradford City	1-1
	Stevenage v Peterborough United	1-1
	Stourbridge v Eastleigh	2-2
	Sunderland v Gillingham	1-1
	Tranmere Rovers v Wycombe Wanderers	2-2
	Walsall v Darlington	2-2
	Wrexham v Rochdale	0-0
	Yeovil Town v Hartlepool United	1-4
	York City v Altrincham	0-1
r	Bradford City v Shrewsbury Town	0-1
r	Bromley v Bristol Rovers	0-1
r	Burton Albion v Salford City	4-1
r	Darlington v Walsall	0-1
r	Doncaster Rovers v AFC Wimbledon	2-0
r	Eastleigh v Stourbridge	3-0
r	Exeter City v Cambridge United	1-0
r	Gillingham v Sunderland	1-0e
r	Lincoln City v Ipswich Town	0-1
r	Newport County (2) v Grimsby Town	2-0
r	Peterborough United v Stevenage	2-0
r	Rochdale v Wrexham	1-0
r	Swindon Town v Cheltenham Town	0-1
r	Wycombe Wanderers v Tranmere Rovers	1-2e

2019/20

Round Two

Blackpool v Maidstone United (2)	3-1
Bristol Rovers v Plymouth Argyle	1-1
Cheltenham Town v Port Vale	1-3
Coventry City v Ipswich Town	1-1
Crawley Town v Fleetwood Town	1-2
Eastleigh v Crewe Alexandra	1-1
Exeter City v Hartlepool United	2-2
Forest Green Rovers v Carlisle United	2-2
Gillingham v Doncaster Rovers	3-0
Kingstonian v AFC Fylde	0-2
Maldon & Tiptree v Newport County (2)	0-1
Northampton Town v Notts County	3-1
Oldham Athletic v Burton Albion	0-1
Peterborough United v Dover Athletic	3-0
Portsmouth v Altrincham	2-1
Rochdale v Boston United	0-0
Shrewsbury Town v Mansfield Town	2-0
Solihull Moors v Rotherham United	3-4
Tranmere Rovers v Chichester City	5-1
Walsall v Oxford United	0-1
r Boston United v Rochdale	1-2
r Carlisle United v Forest Green Rovers	1-0
r Crewe Alexandra v Eastleigh	3-1
r Hartlepool United v Exeter City	1-0e
r Ipswich Town v Coventry City	1-2
r Plymouth Argyle v Bristol Rovers	0-1

Round Three

Arsenal v Leeds United	1-0
Birmingham City v Blackburn Rovers	2-1
Bournemouth v Luton Town	4-0
Brentford v Stoke City	1-0
Brighton & Hove Albion v Sheffield Wednesday	0-1
Bristol City v Shrewsbury Town	1-1
Bristol Rovers v Coventry City	2-2
Burnley v Peterborough United	4-2
Burton Albion v Northampton Town	2-4
Cardiff City v Carlisle United	2-2
Charlton Athletic v West Bromwich Albion	0-1
Chelsea v Nottingham Forest	2-0
Crewe Alexandra v Barnsley	1-3
Crystal Palace v Derby County	0-1
Fleetwood Town v Portsmouth	1-2
Fulham v Aston Villa	2-1
Gillingham v West Ham United	0-2
Leicester City v Wigan Athletic	2-0
Liverpool v Everton	1-0
Manchester City v Port Vale	4-1
Middlesbrough v Tottenham Hotspur	1-1
Millwall v Newport County (2)	3-0
Oxford United v Hartlepool United	4-1
Preston North End v Norwich City	2-4
Queen's Park Rangers v Swansea City	5-1
Reading v Blackpool	2-2
Rochdale v Newcastle United	1-1
Rotherham United v Hull City	2-3
Sheffield United v AFC Fylde	2-1
Southampton v Huddersfield Town	2-0
Watford v Tranmere Rovers	3-3
Wolverhampton Wan. v Manchester United	0-0
r Blackpool v Reading	0-2
r Carlisle United v Cardiff City	3-4
r Coventry City v Bristol Rovers	3-0
r Manchester United v Wolverhampton Wan.	1-0
r Newcastle United v Rochdale	4-1
r Shrewsbury Town v Bristol City	1-0
r Tottenham Hotspur v Middlesbrough	2-1
r Tranmere Rovers v Watford	2-1e

Round Four

Bournemouth v Arsenal	1-2
Brentford v Leicester City	0-1
Burnley v Norwich City	1-2
Coventry City v Birmingham City	0-0
Hull City v Chelsea	1-2
Manchester City v Fulham	4-0
Millwall v Sheffield United	0-2
Newcastle United v Oxford United	0-0
Northampton Town v Derby County	0-0
Portsmouth v Barnsley	4-2
Queen's Park Rangers v Sheffield Wednesday	1-2
Reading v Cardiff City	1-1
Shrewsbury Town v Liverpool	2-2
Southampton v Tottenham Hotspur	1-1
Tranmere Rovers v Manchester United	0-6
West Ham United v West Bromwich Albion	0-1
r Birmingham City v Coventry City	2-2P
r Cardiff City v Reading	3-3q
r Derby County v Northampton Town	4-2
r Liverpool v Shrewsbury Town	1-0
r Oxford United v Newcastle United	2-3e
r Tottenham Hotspur v Southampton	3-2

Round Five

Chelsea v Liverpool	2-0
Derby County v Manchester United	0-3
Leicester City v Birmingham City	1-0
Portsmouth v Arsenal	0-2
Reading v Sheffield United	1-2e
Sheffield Wednesday v Manchester City	0-1
Tottenham Hotspur v Norwich City	1-1q
West Bromwich Albion v Newcastle United	2-3

Round Six

Leicester City v Chelsea	0-1
Newcastle United v Manchester City	0-2
Norwich City v Manchester United	1-2e
Sheffield United v Arsenal	1-2

Semi Finals

Arsenal v Manchester City	2-0 N
Chelsea v Manchester United	3-1 N

Final

Arsenal v Chelsea	2-1 N

Ian Rush celebrates his winning goal in the 1989 Final with John Barnes. Rush is the leading FA Cup goal scorer in modern times with 42, including three in Cup Finals. Only England international Harry Cursham of Notts County has more, 48 between seasons 1877/78 and 1888/89.

INDEX TO CLUB APPEARANCES

The following pages provide an index to the 3000 or so clubs that have played in the tournament. The index shows the seasons they entered and the number of times they appear in the listings, including byes and games replayed after protest.

The seasons quoted are the final year of the season; for example, 1956 is season 1955/56. Two seasons on the same line are "from...to"; for example 1914 1935 is "from 1913/14 to 1934/35".

The "war years" 1915/16 to 1918/19, and 1939/40 to 1944/45 are deemed "not to exist", though please note that some clubs did appear in the extra preliminary round of 1939/40.

Take this entry for example:

Abbey United (Cambs)	1928	1931	29
	1933	1946	
	1948	1952	

This shows that Abbey United appear 29 times in the listings. They played between seasons 1927/28 and 1930/31 inclusive, miss season 1931/32, appear between 1932/33 and 1945/46 (ignoring the war years), miss 1946/47, and appear again between 1947/48 and 1951/52. Reference to the list of "other club names" show that they then changed their name to Cambridge United, so it is also necessary to consult that entry for the complete picture of the club.

The club names in use at the time of the matches have been used as far as possible. This means that if a club adds "Town" to its name after playing without it, it may have two entries in the index. The list of "other club names" shows circumstances where the club is known to be the same club after a name change. The list also shows the results of amalgamations of two or more clubs.

Please note that this is an area where historical research is adding to our understanding of club development all the time. Take Chesterfield for example. The club historian Stuart Basson makes a case for four "separate" clubs:
- an original Chesterfield, 1867 to 1881
- Chesterfield Town, 1884 to 1915
- a second "Town", 1915-17
- today's club, from 1919 (though please note that it played as "Chesterfield Municipal" in 1919/20).

I have decided for the sake of simplicity to leave them all as the one club "Chesterfield". After all, what view should we take of clubs such as Middlesbrough, Wolves and Bristol City that were forced to re-form in the 1980s? The return of Accrington Stanley to the Football League has been trumpeted by the media, but strictly the 2006 club is not related to the former club and consequently has a (2) after its name in these pages.

Other "minor" changes have been overlooked in order to avoid undue confusion. Examples are:

Bournemouth played as Bournemouth and Boscombe United until 1972 then became AFC Bournemouth. The other Bournemouth club, formerly an amateur club, is labelled as Bournemouth (Ams) throughout.

Scunthorpe United played as Scunthorpe and Lindsey United.

Sheffield Wednesday played as The Wednesday.

Arsenal were also known as "The Arsenal".

If tracking the progress of League sides, please notice that many of them have played under different names. For example, Birmingham City will be found listed as Small Heath Alliance, Small Heath and (plain) Birmingham. Again, please consult the list of "other club names" in an appendix.

Problems can arise when clubs change their names during the close season, after the draws for the early rounds have been published using their old name. If I have made a mistake in this regard (or anywhere else come to that) correspondence will be most welcome.

Abbreviations of club names have been avoided as far as possible, but some were inevitable. "T" is always "Town" and "C" is always "City". Others are:

Ath.	Athletic
BWI	British Workmen's Institute
Batt.	Battalion
Regm.	Regiment
DS&S	Demobilised Soldiers and Sailors
WM, WMC	Working Men's Club
CW	Colliery Welfare
CI	Colliery Institute
Coms	Comrades
MW	Miners Welfare
Exp.	Expansion
OB	Old Boys

Finally, some clubs were determined to exceed the space allowed for their names! Well done, Steel Peech and Tozer Social Services, Metal and Produce Recovery Depot Number One, Hitchin Blue Cross Temperance Brigade, Portland Prison Officers and Portland United, and Pirelli-General Cable Works Social and Sports!

105th Regiment to Aylesbury

Index of clubs

Club	Start	End	Count
105th Regiment	1876	1879	6
1874 Northwich	2015	2020	23
1st Coldstream Guards	1897 1901	1899	6
1st Grenadier Guards	1906 1909 1915	1912 1920	16
1st Highland Light Infantry	1892	1895	10
1st Kings Royal Rifles	1912	1913	14
1st Scots Guards	1897 1900		7
1st Sherwood Foresters	1893	1894	5
1st South Lancs Regiment	1899	1900	6
1st Surrey Rifles	1873 1876 1886	1874 1878 1887	10
2nd Coldstream Guards	1898 1909 1912	1899 1910	11
2nd Grenadier Guards	1906		2
2nd Lincolnshire Regiment	1907		4
2nd Royal Warwicks	1907		1
2nd Scots Guards	1894		4
2nd West Kent Regiment	1893		4
3rd Coldstream Guards	1899		1
3rd Grenadier Guards	1897 1911	1899 1913	15
4th Divisional Signals Regiment	1932	1934	4
4th Kings Royal Rifles	1908		4
4th Royal Tank Regiment	1938		1
5th Royal Tank Regiment	1928		3
8th Durham Light Infantry	1925		2
93rd Highland Regiment	1891	1892	6
AC London	2018		2
AEC Athletic	1933	1937	5
AFC Blackpool	2009 2012	2017	13
AFC Bridgnorth	2016	2017	3
AFC Croydon Athletic	2014	2020	12
AFC Darwen	2016	2019	6
AFC Dunstable	2012	2020	23
AFC Emley	2008	2018	18
AFC Fylde	2009	2020	40
AFC Hayes	2008	2020	21
AFC Hornchurch	2006	2020	48
AFC Kempston Rovers	2009 2011	2016	16
AFC Liverpool	2011	2020	17
AFC Lymington	1991	1995	19
AFC Mansfield	2016	2020	20
AFC Newbury	1999	2007	20
AFC Portchester	2012	2020	26
AFC Rushden & Diamonds	2014	2020	29
AFC St Austell	2014 2020	2018	10
AFC Stoneham	2019	2020	7
AFC Sudbury	2001	2020	71
AFC Telford United	2005	2020	41
AFC Totton	1983 2000	1996 2020	107
AFC Uckfield	2011	2013	3
AFC Uckfield Town	2017	2020	10
AFC Varndeanians	2020		3
AFC Wallingford	2001 2007	2005 2008	17
AFC Wimbledon	2005	2020	55
AFC Wulfrunians	2009	2020	35
AP Leamington	1974	1988	52
APV Peterborough City	1992		2
Abbey Hey	2001 2013	2011 2020	34
Abbey Rangers	2017	2020	10
Abbey United (Cambs)	1928 1933 1948	1931 1946 1952	29
Aberaman	1903		2
Aberaman & Aberdare	1946	1948	3
Aberaman Athletic	1921	1922	3
Aberaman United	1922		1
Abercarn	1922		1
Aberdare	1913	1914	7
Aberdare (2)	1939		3
Aberdare Amateurs	1920	1921	2
Aberdare Athletic	1921	1929	26
Aberdare Town	1936	1937	4
Abergavenny Thursdays	1964	1972	13
Abertillery	1915	1922	9
Aberystwyth	1897 1910	1901	8
Abingdon Town	1928 1948 1965 1982	1939 1962 1966 2014	102
Abingdon United	1987 2000 2019	1993 2017 2020	59
Accrington	1882	1896	28
Accrington (2)	1965		1
Accrington Stanley	1897 1902	1900 1962	143
Accrington Stanley (2)	1972	2020	130
Achilles (Ipswich)	1949	1950	5
Acomb WMC (York)	1915 1922	1920	4
Acton	1880 1935	1886	14
Acton Town	1947	1950	5
Addlestone	1926 1931 1966 1969	1929 1967 1980	40
Addlestone & Weybridge Town	1981	1985	23
Adlington	1915 1930		8
Albion Sports	2014	2020	18
Alderley Edge United	1912 1926	1915	7
Aldershot	1928	1992	179
Aldershot Albion	1925	1928	7
Aldershot Excelsior	1922	1923	3
Aldershot Institute Albion	1922	1924	7
Aldershot Town	1995	2020	84
Aldershot Traction Company	1925	1933	28
Alford United	1913 1950 1952 1955	1953 1963	25
Alfreton Town	1911 1923 1961	1929 2020	196
Allendale Park	1915		1
Allerton Bywater Colliery	1910 1921	1914 1922	13
Allsops	1903		1
Alma Swanley	1986 1991 1993	1988	9
Almondsbury Greenway	1981	1982	3
Almondsbury Town	2005	2011	16
Almondsbury UWE	2011 2015	2013 2016	11
Alnwick Town	1949 1986 2003	1959 1997 2007	54
Alresford Town	2009	2020	28
Alsager Town	2004	2018	21
Altofts	1899 1908	1902	7
Altofts West Riding Colliery	1922 1928 1936	1930 1938	18
Alton	1907		1
Alton Town	1951 1958 1970 2003	1954 1968 1981 2015	88
Altrincham	1907 1912 1924 1948 1960	1910 1922 1938 1958 2020	307
Alvechurch	1969 2005	1993 2020	115
Amateur Athletic Club	1874		1
Amble	1938	1954	15
Amersham Town	1951 1966 2009 2016	1970 2011 2020	7, 10
Amesbury Town			
Ammanford Town	1977		2
Ampthill Town	1982 1987 2009 2013	1985 2011 2016	16
Andover	1899 1947	2012	134
Andover New Street	2019	2020	5
Andover Town	2016	2019	11
Anglo (Purfleet)	1936	1937	3
Annfield Plain	1907 1977 1987	1974 1984 1993	168
Anstey Nomads	2012 2017 2019	2013 2020	9
Anston Athletic	1922	1928	18
Anston United	1921		1
Apperley Bridge	1920	1922	6
Appleby	1914 1921 1948	1915 1924 1949	10
Appleby Frodingham	1936 1948	1939 1951	12
Appleby Frodingham Athletic	1977	1985	21
Apsley	1902 1907 1910 1913 1923	1905 1908 1911 1914 1947	62
Aquarius	1920	1921	3
Ardley United	2007	2020	30
Ardsley	1894		1
Ardsley Athletic	1921	1933	35
Ardwick	1891	1894	6
Argonauts	1880		2
Arlecdon Red Rose	1921 1928	1923	8
Arlesey Town	1923 1926 1931 1947 1985	1924 1939 1951 2020	108
Arlington	1922		1
Armitage	1976 1981	1977 1987	15
Armitage '90	1994	1996	13
Armthorpe Welfare	1937 1948 1986	1940 1951 2018	82
Arnold	1965	1989	63
Arnold (1)	1904 1906	1908	4
Arnold St Mary's	1914 1962	1923 1964	15
Arnold Town	1990	2015	62
Arnold Town (1)	1926	1927	2
Arsenal	1915	2020	405
Arundel	1951 1955 1959 1970 1979	1961 1976 2020	97
Ascot United	2012	2020	18
Ash United	1995 1997 1999	2015	31
Ashbourne Town	1908	1922	17
Ashby Albion	1896		1
Ashby Institute	1950 1969 1978	1960 1976 1982	34
Ashby Ivanhoe	2017		3
Ashby Town	1921	1927	15
Ashfield United	1997		2
Ashford	1931 1947	1939 1951	48
Ashford Railway Works	1909	1928	32
Ashford Town	1952	2011	173
Ashford Town (1)	1913		1
Ashford Town (Middlesex)	1993 1997	2020	60
Ashford United	1892 1904 1907 2013	1902 1905 1908 2020	39
Ashington	1889 1891 1900 1904 1907 1973 1979 1997	1893 1905 1970 1976 1992 2020	265
Ashton & Backwell United	2016	2017	2
Ashton Athletic	2009	2020	33
Ashton National	1933	1935	5
Ashton North End	1896 1899	1897	7
Ashton Town	2008 2011 2014	2009	5
Ashton Town (1)	1904 1906 1909	1910	6
Ashton United	1948 1969 1971 1982	1966 1980 2020	168
Ashton-under-Lyne	1893		2
Ashtree Highfield	1988	1989	4
Askern Villa	2012		1
Aspatria Athletic	1928	1932	9
Aspatria Spartans	1950	1951	6
Astley Bridge	1881	1889	19
Aston Shakespeare	1888	1889	5
Aston Unity	1883	1888	8
Aston Villa	1880	2020	427
Athersley Recreation	2015	2020	7
Atherstone Town	1909 1912 1931 1947 1950 2007 2018	1927 1936 1948 1980 2015 2020	143
Atherstone United	1986	2004	60
Atherton	1907 1914 1922	1910 1915 1926	31
Atherton Collieries	1949 1995	1951 2020	61
Atherton LR	1990	2013	61
Atlas & Norfolk Works	1910	1924	20
Atlas Hotel	1911		3
Attercliffe	1887	1904	29
Avalon Rovers	1902		1
Aveley	1955	2020	159
Avro	2020		1
Aylesbury	2010	2019	25

266

Aylesbury United to Blaby and Whetstone Athletic

Index of clubs

Club	From	To	No.
Aylesbury United	1898	1903	267
	1906	1911	
	1922		
	1925		
	1927	2020	
Aylesbury Vale	2006	2009	11
Aylesbury Vale Dynamos	2020		3
Aylesford Paper Mills	1934	1939	24
	1948	1951	
Aylestone Park	2017	2018	3
BAT Sports	1996		14
	1999	2006	
BWI Reading	1925	1926	7
	1928		
Babbacombe	1915		3
	1921		
Backwell United	1995	2007	26
Bacup	1895	1897	12
	1903	1904	
	1909	1910	
Bacup & Rossendale Borough	2014	2015	2
Bacup Borough	1924	1928	81
	1948	1969	
	1971	1978	
	1999	2013	
	2016	2017	
Badsey Rangers	1934	1939	9
Badshot Lea	2010	2020	32
Baffins Milton Rovers	2019	2020	5
Baker Perkins	1988	1991	8
Baldock Town	1924	1927	103
	1929	1939	
	1949	1951	
	1968	1971	
	1985	2001	
	2015		
	2017	2020	
Balham FC	2019	2020	6
Bamber Bridge	1993	2020	89
Banbury Spencer	1935	1965	65
Banbury United	1966	2020	135
Bangor City	1897	1899	194
	1925	1986	
	1988	1992	
Banstead Athletic	1951		84
	1969	1972	
	1979	2013	
	2016	2020	
Banstead Mental Hospital	1935	1946	10
Bardon Hill	2010	2013	9
	2016	2017	
Bargoed	1915	1922	7
Barking	1906	1915	258
	1921	1939	
	1947	1957	
	1959	2001	
	2007	2020	
Barking & East Ham United	2002	2006	10
Barking Woodville	1896	1897	4
	1900		
Barkingside	1989	1993	45
	1997	2000	
	2005	2020	
Barnard Castle Athletic	1891		9
	1932		
	1934	1936	
	1938	1939	
Barnes	1872	1883	27
	1885	1886	
Barnet	1920	2020	289
Barnet (1)	1899		1
Barnet (2)	1912		1
Barnet Alston	1906	1915	45
Barnoldswick & District	1949	1951	3
Barnoldswick Park Villa	1925	1928	9
Barnoldswick Town	2012	2020	15
Barnoldswick United	1911	1915	11
Barnsley	1898	2020	311
Barnsley St Peter's	1894	1897	14
Barnstaple Town	1949	1956	174
	1958	2020	
Barnt Green Spartak	2008		2
Barnton	1949	1950	8
	2017	2019	
Barnton Rovers	1893	1897	6
Barnton Victoria	1925	1931	23
	1933	1937	
	1939		
Barri	1993		2
Barrow	1902	2020	309
Barrow (1)	1892	1893	3
Barrow Novocastrians	1909	1911	9
	1913	1915	
Barrow Shipbuilders	1920		1
Barrow St George's	1905	1910	6
Barrow St Luke's	1910	1914	7
Barrow St Mary's	1910		5
	1914	1915	
Barrow Town	2009	2014	14
	2016		
Barrow YMCA	1921		12
	1926	1929	
Barry	1912	1939	79
Barry Town	1946	1968	151
	1970	1992	
Bartley Green	2011	2013	8
Barton Rovers	1977	2020	105
Barton Town	2018	2020	5
Barton Town (1)	1921	1939	53
	1948	1957	
Barton Town (2)	1967	1982	35
Barton Town Old Boys	2009	2017	22
Barwell	1993	2020	70
Barwell Athletic	1950	1953	7
Barwell Swifts	1899	1900	3
Barwell United	1921	1927	16
Basford Rovers	1887	1889	5
Basford United	1909	1955	79
	2014	2020	
Bashley	1989	2020	90
Basildon United	1980	2001	64
	2010	2020	
Basingstoke	1903	1920	48
	1922	1927	
	1929	1933	
	1935		
	1937	1939	
Basingstoke Town	1947	1956	218
	1958	1960	
	1962	2020	
Bath City	1891		345
	1909	1926	
	1928	2020	
Beaconsfield SYCOB	1998	2017	51
Beaconsfield Town	2018	2020	10
Bean (Dudley)	1927		1
Bearsted	2018	2020	5
Beccles	1906		24
	1926	1927	
	1951	1958	
Beckenham	1926	1927	20
	1929	1939	
Beckenham Town	1984	1986	53
	1988	1994	
	2000	2004	
	2011	2020	
Becontree Town	1934		1
Beddington Corner	1930	1937	13
Bedfont	1993	2010	38
Bedfont & Feltham	2015	2018	10
Bedfont Green	2007	2010	7
Bedfont Sports	2012	2020	18
Bedfont Town	2011	2012	2
Bedford	2008		7
	2010	2012	
	2015	2017	
Bedford Avenue	1946	1951	15
Bedford Corinthians	1950	1951	2
Bedford Excelsior	1907		1
Bedford North End	1935		4
Bedford Queens Park Rangers	1934	1935	6
Bedford Queens Works	1902	1903	9
	1948	1949	
	1951		
Bedford St Cuthberts	1950	1951	4
Bedford Town	1996	2020	63
Bedford Town (1)	1911	1983	212
Bedford United	1998	1999	6
	2001	2002	
Bedford United & Valerio	2003	2005	4
Bedlington CW	1968		6
	1970	1972	
Bedlington Mechanics	1960	1963	9
Bedlington Terriers	1987	1993	71
	1996	2013	
	2016	2017	
Bedlington United	1909	1930	50
	1932		
	1935	1936	
Bedminster	1892	1894	19
	1896	1900	
Bedminster Down Sports	1926	1928	4
Bedminster St Pauls	1898		1
Bedouins	1932		4
	1934	1936	
Bedworth Town	1949	1962	53
	1966	1969	
Bedworth United	1970	2020	137
Beeston	1890	1893	6
Beeston Humber	1897	1898	3
Beeston St John's	1889	1890	3
Beighton Miners Welfare	1949	1959	25
Beighton Recreation	1921	1922	2
Beighton WM	1925	1926	2
Belfast North End	1890		2
Belfast YMCA	1889	1890	3
Belper Town	1957	2020	165
Belper Town (1)	1888	1891	49
	1893	1911	
Belper United	2019		1
Belvedere	1922		2
Bemerton Heath Harlequins	1993	2020	54
Bentinck Colliery Welfare	1951	1952	2
Bentley Colliery	1913	1926	48
	1933	1935	
	1937	1940	
	1948	1957	
Benwell Adelaide	1914	1915	5
Berkhamsted	2012	2020	25
Berkhamsted Comrades	1922		1
Berkhamsted Town	1903		124
	1923	1927	
	1929	1931	
	1933	1959	
	1978	2009	
Berwick Rangers	1897	1898	5
	1902		
Bestwood Colliery	1950		7
	1952	1955	
Bethesda Athletic	1970		9
	1975	1977	
Bethnal Green United	2011	2013	9
Betteshanger CW	1935	1939	38
	1948	1954	
	1956	1961	
Beverley Town	1915	1920	4
Bewdley Town	2010	2015	14
	2018		
Bexhill	1929	1939	22
Bexhill Town	1946	1968	57
	1971	1982	
Bexhill United	2016		3
	2020		
Bexley	1933	1940	14
	1948	1950	
Bexley United	1964	1976	45
Bexleyheath & Welling	1932	1937	38
	1953	1963	
Bexleyheath Labour	1921	1922	3
Bexleyheath Town	1923	1931	17
Bicester Town	1931	1940	42
	1947	1956	
	1995	1997	
	2008	2012	
Biddulph Victoria	2003	2011	21
Bideford	1926		242
	1949	2020	
Biggleswade	2018	2020	7
Biggleswade & District	1905	1915	78
	1922	1939	
Biggleswade Town	1947	1949	106
	1951	1976	
	1991	1997	
	2007	2020	
Biggleswade United	2006	2020	34
Biggleswade United (1)	1936	1938	3
Bigrigg United	1915		3
Billericay Town	1978	2020	146
Billingham South	1939		5
Billingham St John	1949		1
Billingham Synthonia	1935	1969	197
	1971	1974	
	1976	2019	
Billingham Town	1985	2015	84
	2018		
	2020		
Bilsthorpe Colliery	1936	1939	7
Bilston	1950	1984	82
Bilston Amateurs	1922		2
Bilston Borough	1935	1939	7
Bilston Town	1985	2002	41
Bilston United	1908	1933	53
Binfield	2010	2020	30
Bingley	1908		1
Birch	1879		1
Birch Coppice Colliery	1955		1
Birdwell	1907	1908	26
	1910	1911	
	1922	1928	
Birdwell Primitive Methodists	1910		1
Birkenhead	1900	1902	11
	1906		
Birkenhead LNWR	1896	1899	5
Birmingham	1906	1921	74
	1923	1939	
Birmingham (1)	1880		2
Birmingham City	1946	2020	216
Birmingham City Transport	1946	1950	6
Birmingham Corp. Tramways	1911	1938	50
Birmingham Excelsior	1884	1888	14
Birmingham St George's	1889	1892	8
Birmingham Transport	1939		7
Birstall United	2018		2
Birtley	1889	1892	75
	1897	1900	
	1913	1934	
	1936	1940	
	1948	1951	
	1955		
Birtley New Town	1925		2
Birtley Town	2010		6
	2012	2013	
Bishop Auckland	1890	2020	363
Bishop Auckland Church Institute	1887	1891	6
Bishop Sutton	2001	2016	32
Bishop's Cleeve	2005	2020	46
Bishop's Stortford	1925	1926	197
	1928	1947	
	1949		
	1951		
	1955	2020	
Bitterne Guild	1908	1912	17
Bitterne Nomads	1948	1949	3
Bitton	2003	2020	42
Blaby & Whetstone Athletic	2013	2018	19

Black Country Rangers to Brotton

Index of clubs

Club	Year 1	Year 2	Num
Black Country Rangers	2014	2015	3
Black Diamonds	1896	1900	11
	1902	1904	
Black Lane Rovers	1925	1928	8
Black Lane Temperance	1902	1906	5
Blackburn Law	1882		1
Blackburn Olympic	1881	1889	25
Blackburn Park Road	1882	1890	26
	1897	1902	
Blackburn Rovers	1880	2020	420
Blackfield & Langley	2002	2004	36
	2010	2020	
Blackhall Colliery Welfare	1932	1959	56
Blackpool	1892	2020	298
Blackpool (Wren) Rovers	1990	1999	14
Blackpool Mechanics	1991		13
	2001	2008	
Blackpool St John's	1883	1884	2
Blackstones	1999	2014	28
Blackwell	1905	1907	9
Blackwell Colliery	1904		27
	1911	1915	
	1921	1924	
	1926		
Blackwood Town	1922		1
Blaenau Ffestiniog	1973	1975	6
Blakebrough & Sons	1922		2
Blakenall	1982	1986	38
	1991	2001	
Blandford	1921	1924	17
	1928	1929	
	1931	1934	
Blandford United	1935	1937	12
	1950	1953	
Blaydon United	1911	1913	6
Bletchley & Wipac Sports	1955	1956	2
Bletchley Town	1964	1974	26
Bletchley Town (1)	1932	1933	2
Blidworth MW	1994	1998	10
Bloxwich Strollers	1915	1932	36
	1955	1956	
Bloxwich Town	1998	1999	2
Bloxwich United	2002		4
	2012	2013	
Blundells	1924		1
Blyth	1893	1898	13
Blyth AFC	2019		2
Blyth Spartans	1910	1929	315
	1931	1939	
	1948	2020	
Bodmin Town	1955	1956	57
	1973		
	2005	2019	
Bognor Regis Town	1909		214
	1927	1931	
	1937	2020	
Boldmere St Michaels	1923		97
	1931		
	1934	1939	
	1947	1959	
	1984	2020	
Boldon CA	1977	1982	11
Boldon CW	1950	1976	44
Boldon Colliery	1915	1920	8
Bolehall Swifts	1995	1997	15
	2008	2011	
	2014	2016	
Boleyn Castle	1903		1
Bollington	1886	1887	2
Bolsover Colliery	1914	1927	45
	1931	1933	
	1935	1939	
	1949	1950	
Bolton & Pauls	1935		1
Bolton Association	1884	1885	4
Bolton Athletic (Rotherham)	1915		2
Bolton Olympic	1883	1884	2
Bolton United	1904		3
	1921		
Bolton Wanderers	1882	1884	411
	1886	2020	
Bookham	2008	2012	7
Boothtown	1913	1922	10
Bootle	1981	2000	70
	2008	2020	
Bootle (1)	1882	1883	21
	1887	1894	
Bootle (2)	1928		2
Bootle Athletic	1950	1954	13
Bootle Celtic	1928		6
	1930		
Boots Athletic	1915	1939	64
	1947	1960	
Boreham Wood	1971	1972	156
	1974	2020	
Borough United	1963	1967	15
Borrowash Victoria	1989	1993	43
	1996	2015	
Boscombe	1910	1911	41
	1913	1923	
Bostall Heath	1921	1939	32
Boston	1966	1986	60
	1989	1994	

Club	Year 1	Year 2	Num
Boston (1)	1888	1892	66
	1901	1906	
	1920	1934	
Boston St James	1921		1
Boston St Nicholas	1922		1
Boston Town	1995	2020	64
Boston Town (1)	1907		8
	1912	1915	
Boston United	1935	2020	264
Botley	1949		1
Bottesford Town	2008	2011	22
	2015	2020	
Botwell Mission	1920	1929	34
Bourne Town	1920		105
	1922		
	1924		
	1948	1960	
	1962	1966	
	1968	1989	
	1991	2010	
Bournemouth	1924	2020	264
Bournemouth (Ams)	1910	1911	113
	1913	1926	
	1928	1929	
	1931	1937	
	1939	1940	
	1947	1951	
	1990	2020	
Bournemouth Gasworks Athletic	1906	1920	54
	1922	1926	
	1940		
	1947	1957	
Bournemouth Rovers	1885	1887	3
Bournemouth Tramways	1915	1936	42
Bournemouth Wanderers	1915		1
Bournville Athletic	1930	1960	34
Bowater Lloyds	1950	1954	9
Bowers & Pitsea	2005	2020	32
Bowers United	1995	1997	13
	1999	2004	
Bowling Albion	1922		2
Bowness Rovers	1910	1911	14
	1915		
	1926	1929	
Bowthorn Recreation	1922	1930	13
Bowthorn United	1948	1951	7
Boxmoor	1926		1
Boxmoor St Johns	1934		4
Brackley Town	1988	1991	91
	1997	2020	
Brackley Town Saints	2018	2020	6
Bracknell Town	1966		98
	1973	2018	
	2020		
Bradford (1)	1898	1899	3
Bradford City	1904	2020	282
Bradford Park Avenue	1909	1974	224
	1993	2020	
Bradford Rovers	1938	1940	3
Bradford Town	2011	2020	20
Bradford United	1947	1949	9
	1952		
Bradford on Avon	1908	1910	5
Brading Town	2009	2012	12
Bradshaw	1884	1886	5
Braintree & Crittall Athletic	1970	1972	11
Braintree Town	1985	2020	102
Brandon CW	1947	1948	7
	1951		
Brandon Rovers	1896		1
Brandon Social	1938	1940	11
Brandon United	1980	2011	67
Brantham Athletic	1939		24
	2011	2020	
Breightmet United	1910		39
	1912	1939	
Brentford	1898	2020	314
Brentwood	2001	2005	6
Brentwood & Warley	1927		53
	1929	1935	
	1947	1965	
Brentwood (1)	1879	1886	21
Brentwood Mental Hospital	1926	1932	11
Brentwood Town	2006	2020	45
Brentwood Town (1)	1966	1970	20
Brereton Social	1974		18
	1976	1977	
	1979	1982	
Bretby Colliery	1921		3
Brett Sports	1970	1971	3
Bridgend Town	1978	1992	34
Bridgend Town (1)	1922		4
Bridgnorth Town	1983	2003	64
	2008	2013	
Bridgwater	1902		2
Bridgwater Town	1997	2020	57
Bridgwater Town (1)	1950	1957	89
	1959	1967	
	1969	1985	
Bridlington Albion	1913		1
Bridlington Central Utd.	1949	1959	21
Bridlington Town	1960	1982	82
	1986	1994	

Club	Year 1	Year 2	Num
Bridlington Town (1)	1921	1924	39
	1929		
	1931	1939	
Bridlington Town (2)	2001	2020	54
Bridlington Trinity	1951	1952	63
	1955		
	1965	1990	
Bridon Ropes	2017		3
	2020		
Bridport	1907		99
	1939		
	1952	1983	
	1994	2001	
	2003	2020	
Brierfield Swifts	1908	1913	8
Brierley Hill & Withymoor	2008	2009	5
Brierley Hill Alliance	1892	1897	169
	1900	1908	
	1910	1928	
	1930	1939	
	1949	1982	
Brierley Hill Town	1995	1996	4
Brigg	1880	1882	4
	1914		
Brigg 2nd Lincs Sugar Company	1933	1936	11
Brigg Brittania	1881	1883	3
Brigg Town	1920		194
	1922	1939	
	1949	1951	
	1953	1960	
	1968	2017	
Briggs Motor Bodies	1936	1937	5
	1939		
Briggs Sports	1949	1959	37
Brigham & Cowan (Hull)	1947		2
Brighouse Town	2011	2020	21
Brightlingsea Regent	2014	2020	14
Brightlingsea United	1934	1939	11
	1949	1950	
	1993	1994	
Brighton & Hove Albion	1902	2020	317
Brighton & Hove Rangers	1901		3
Brighton Amateurs	1904	1905	2
Brighton Athletic	1900	1903	7
Brighton Corp. Tramways	1936	1939	7
Brighton Mental Hospital	1935	1936	7
Brighton Railway Athletic	1924		4
Brighton United	1899	1900	8
Brighton West End	1914		5
	1920		
Brimington Hotspur	1912		1
Brimscombe & Thrupp	2015	2020	15
Brimsdown Rovers	1992	1998	17
	2008	2010	
Brislington	1905	1906	51
	1997	2020	
Bristol Aeroplane Co.	1948	1950	3
Bristol Amateurs	1900		1
Bristol City	1898	2020	313
Bristol East	1900	1907	23
Bristol Manor Farm	1983	1994	80
	1996	1997	
	2001	2020	
Bristol Rovers	1899	2020	321
Bristol South End	1896	1897	3
Bristol St George	1892	1899	68
	1903		
	1922	1934	
	1936	1938	
	1949		
	1951	1954	
British Oil & Cake Mills	1922		15
	1924	1932	
Broadbridge Heath	2005		5
	2018	2020	
Broadfields United	2019	2020	3
Brockenhurst	1983	1987	77
	1992	2020	
Brocton	2009	2018	22
Brodsworth MW	1998	2009	16
Brodsworth Main Colliery	1913	1928	77
	1930	1935	
	1939	1956	
Bromborough	1921		1
Bromley	1899	1900	303
	1902	1906	
	1908	1929	
	1931	2020	
Brompton	1920		2
Bromsgrove Rovers	1911	1920	238
	1922	1938	
	1947	2011	
Bromsgrove Sporting	2015	2020	13
Bromyard Town	2008	2010	4
Brondesbury	1874	1875	2
Bronze Athletic	1912	1914	6
Brook House	1993	1996	30
	1999	2007	
Brookwood Hospital	1936		5
	1938		
	1948	1949	
Brooms	1914	1915	7
Brotherhoods Works	1920	1923	7
Brotton	1908		11
	1915	1924	

Broughton Rangers to Chorley
Index of clubs

Club	From	To	No.
Broughton Rangers	1927 1932	1930 1933	16
Broxbourne Borough V&E	2003	2013	23
Brunswick Institute	1921 1924 1926 1950	1922 1927 1956	15
Brush Sports	1947	1960	51
Brush Works	1920	1922	3
Brynn Central	1905 1909	1907	10
Buckingham Town	1951 1980 2018	2010	82
Buckland Athletic	2010	2020	22
Buckley	1897	1898	4
Buckley United	1921	1922	9
Buckley Victoria	1901		1
Bugbrooke St Michaels	2001 2012 2020	2002 2014	12
Bulford United	1955	1956	8
Bullcroft Main Colliery	1915 1922 1924	1920 1927	16
Bulwell United	1894	1902	17
Bungay Town	1936 1951	1939 1964	32
Burbage	1907	1908	3
Burberry Athletic	1920 1922	1923	4
Burgess Hill Town	1972 1975	1973 2020	110
Burnham	1988	2020	89
Burnham & Hillingdon	1986	1987	2
Burnham (1)	1975	1986	19
Burnham Ramblers	1990	2019	52
Burnhope Institute	1925 1928 1934	1932 1935	14
Burnley	1886	2020	357
Burnley Belvedere	1905	1909	5
Burnley Casuals	1911		2
Burnside (Kendal)	1929 1934		2
Burradon Athletic	1905		1
Burrfield Park	1925	1926	3
Burscough	1948	2020	211
Burscough Rangers	1922	1933	27
Burslem Port Vale	1886	1907	65
Burton Albion	1952	2020	226
Burton All Saints	1921	1924	9
Burton Swifts	1886	1901	44
Burton Town	1912 1925	1939	50
Burton United	1902	1910	35
Burton Wanderers	1886	1901	42
Burton Werneth Rangers	1922		1
Bury	1888 1892	2020	297
Bury St Edmunds	1901 1907 1921	1902 1908 1923	9
Bury Town	1934 1948 1960 1984	1938 1958 1982 2020	201
Bush Hill Park	1925	1926	3
Bushey United	1934 1940	1938	8
Bustleholme	2012		1
Buxton	1892 1921 1931 1935 1937 1947 2001	1915 1926 1932 1940 1999 2020	273
CB Hounslow United	2017	2020	10
CWS Silvertown	1937	1938	3
Cadbury Athletic	2008 2012 2016 2018	2010	8
Cadbury Heath	2012	2020	24
Cadbury Heath YMCA	1932	1935	4
Caerau Rovers	1915	1922	5
Caerleon Athletic	1914	1915	3
Caernarfon Town	1980	1996	41
Caernarvon Athletic	1930	1931	11
Caernarvon Wanderers	1887		1
Caerphilly	1903 1914 1922		4
Caius College	1881	1882	2
Callender Athletic	1929 1933 1947	1931 1939 1950	32
Callington	1951		1
Calne & Harris United	1922 1938 1940 1947 1949	1936 1962	53
Calne Town	1977	2014	60
Calthorpe	1880	1884	5
Calverley	1912	1922	17
Camberley	1949	1951	4
Camberley & Yorktown	1914 1925 1936	1923 1934 1940	40
Camberley Town	1977 1996	1993 2020	88
Cambridge City	1953	2020	198
Cambridge Town	1915 1935	1933 1950	86
Cambridge United	1953	2020	194
Cambridge University	1874	1880	24
Cambridge Utd. (1)	1911	1914	10
Camerton	1909	1915	14
Cammell Laird	2005	2015	29
Cammell Laird (Nottm)	1926		2
Cammell Laird 1907	2017	2018	5
Cammells Sports	1913		2
Campion	2020		1
Cannock Town	1909 1925	1923 1937	50
Cannon	1887		1
Canterbury City	1949 2014	2000 2020	143
Canterbury Waverley	1931 1937	1935 1939	26
Canvey Island	1970 1988	1971 2020	104
Cardiff Albion	1921		2
Cardiff City	1911	2020	267
Cardiff Corinthians	1912 1934	1928 1950	38
Cargo Fleet Works	1936 1948	1951	6
Carlin How	1924 1930 1937	1932	7
Carlisle	1891		1
Carlisle City	1977	1981	8
Carlisle City (1)	1896 1908	1899	5
Carlisle Red Rose	1905	1906	5
Carlisle United	1905	2020	297
Carlton Town	2004	2020	37
Carshalton Athletic	1923 1930 1947	1928 1939 2020	237
Carterton	2006 2014 2017	2010	13
Carterton Town	1997 2000	1998 2005	19
Castle Donnington Town	1911 1915	1913	7
Castle Hill	1930		2
Castle Vale	2008	2012	10
Castle Vale JKS	2011		3
Castleford & Allerton United	1922 1924	1928	17
Castleford Town	1907 1937	1929	69
Castleford United	1913		1
Castleton Gabriels	1995 2001	1998 2002	7
Casuals	1885 1931	1895 1932	26
Catcliffe	1905		2
Catford Southend	1910 1926	1923 1927	27
Causeway United	2003	2015	33
Celtic Nation	2013		2
Central Hull Rangers	1924 1926		4
Chadderton	1984 2016	2013	56
Chalfont St Peter	1978	2020	99
Channing Rovers	1903		1
Chapel-en-le-Frith	1908 1910 1915 1921	1912 1925	16
Chard Town	1978 1989 1998 2002 2012	1986 1992 2010 2013	37
Charlton Athletic	1915	2020	244
Charltons (Grimsby)	1921	1926	12
Charnock Richard	2018	2020	8
Chasetown	1988	2020	100
Chatham	1883 1910 1934 1947	1907 1932 1939 1948	149
Chatham Amateurs	1902		1
Chatham Town	1948 1963 1980	1960 1974 2020	125
Chatteris Engineers	1910 1934	1946	14
Chatteris Town	1931 1947 1993	1939 1990 1995	83
Cheadle	1940		1
Cheadle Town	1996 2017	2014	32
Cheddar	2017	2020	6
Chelmsford	1903 1906 1936	1934 1938	60
Chelmsford City	1939	2020	262
Chelmsford Rollers	1922		1
Chelsea	1906	2020	409
Cheltenham Saracens	2014 2020	2016	10
Cheltenham Town	1915 1926 1928 1932 1934 1975	1922 1929 1973 2020	298
Chepstow	1921	1922	5
Chertsey Town	1951 1965 1970 1976	1967 1972 2020	107
Chesham	1886 1893 1895 1905 1908	1898 1903 1906 1915	21
Chesham Generals	1893		36
Chesham Town	1899	1915	37
Chesham United	1920 1933 1958	1931 1956 2020	271
Cheshunt	1905 1920 1925 1930 1951 1958 1965 1989	1908 1923 1928 1954 1961 1987 2020	166
Chessington & Hook United	2001	2018	39
Chessington United	2002	2005	5
Chester	1887 1902 1906 1908 1922 1931	1899 1920 1929 1983	196
Chester City	1984	2010	69
Chester FC	2013	2020	16
Chester St Oswald's	1888	1892	7
Chester-le-Street	1922 1931 1935	1928 1933	23
Chester-le-Street Town	1982 2017	2013 2018	83
Chesterfield	1893	2020	304
Chesterfield Corinthians	1922 1924	1927	5
Chesterfield Spital	1883	1885	5
Chichester	1928 1932	1930 1939	20
Chichester City	2010	2020	22
Chichester City (1)	1948 1952 1955 1961 1979 1998	1950 1953 1959 1977 1993 2000	82
Chichester City United	2001 2009	2006	15
Chilton & Windlestone	1947		2
Chilton Athletic	1948	1959	17
Chilton Colliery Recreation	1924 1935	1933 1940	45
Chingford Town	1949	1951	8
Chinnor	2014 2016		2
Chippenham Rovers	1921 1927	1925 1938	27
Chippenham Town	1899 1903 1907 1950	1948 2020	258
Chippenham United	1949	1962	34
Chipperfield	1947	1949	5
Chipping Norton Town	1983	1984	2
Chipping Sodbury Town	2018	2020	7
Chipstead	1990	2020	66
Chirk	1885 1891 1898 1901 1905 1910 1922	1889 1899 1903 1908 1925	49
Chiswick	1902		1
Chiswick Town	1921	1922	3
Choppington	1913	1914	3
Chopwell Colliery	1939	1940	2
Chopwell Institute	1920 1927	1925 1934	23
Chorley	1895 1904 1915	1901 1912 2020	347

Christchurch to Darnall Wellington

Index of clubs

Club	From	To	Count
Christchurch	1914	1915	45
	2000	2020	
Church	1883	1888	25
Churchmans Sports (Ipswich)	1950	1951	2
Cinderford Town	1949		138
	1951	1960	
	1965	1985	
	1993	2020	
Cinderhill Colliery	1950		7
	1952	1955	
Cirencester Town	1997	2020	67
City Ramblers	1891		7
	1893		
	1895	1896	
City Wanderers (Norwich)	1924	1928	10
City of Liverpool	2018	2020	13
City of Westminster	1906		9
	1910	1915	
Civil Service	1872	1876	58
	1897		
	1899	1908	
	1927	1929	
	1934	1940	
	1948	1951	
	1972		
Clacton Town	1921	1922	134
	1924	1930	
	1932	1937	
	1939		
	1947		
	1949	1982	
	1989	1992	
	1996	2007	
Clandown	1920	1931	106
	1933	1959	
	1980	1992	
Clanfield 85	2011	2012	3
	2020		
Clapham	1905	1910	14
Clapham Rovers	1872	1887	55
Clapton	1885	1956	248
	1958	1974	
	1976	2020	
Clapton Orient	1905	1946	80
Clarence	1880	1881	2
Clarence Iron & Steel Works	1913	1915	5
Clay Cross & Danesmoor Welfare	1957	1959	5
Clay Cross Town	1894	1896	18
	1910	1911	
	1920	1923	
Clay Cross Works	1909		3
Clay Cross Zingari	1922	1923	2
Clayton West	1908	1910	6
Cleator Moor Celtic	1920	1939	64
	1947	1951	
	1989	1992	
Cleethorpes Town	1887	1889	67
	1912	1931	
	2015	2020	
Clevedon	1910	1911	70
	1913	1959	
Clevedon Town	1977	2020	112
Clevedon United	2002		13
	2004	2010	
Clifton	1891	1898	12
Clifton Colliery	1922	1928	12
Cliftonville	1887	1891	15
Clinton	1890	1891	2
Clipstone	2015	2019	12
Clitheroe	1883	1886	158
	1889	1891	
	1895	1898	
	1926	1927	
	1949	1953	
	1958	1967	
	1969	2020	
Clitheroe Central	1909	1911	6
Clitheroe Low Moor	1884	1886	4
Close Works	1920	1922	14
	1938	1939	
Clove	1909		4
Clowne Colliery	1921		1
Clutton Wanderers	1922	1928	12
Clydesdale	1876		1
Coalville Albion	1898	1899	2
Coalville Swifts	1915	1925	19
Coalville Town	2005	2020	52
Coalville Town (1)	1894	1920	44
Coalville Town (2)	1921	1924	8
	1938	1939	
Coalville Town (3)	1946	1955	17
Coalville United	1905		2
Cobham	1939		40
	1949	1951	
	2000	2013	
	2019	2020	
Cockermouth	1936	1939	14
	1948	1950	
Cockfield	1922	1927	47
	1929	1939	
	1949	1951	
	1955	1959	
Cockfosters	2008	2020	34
Codicote	2014	2016	7
Cogenhoe United	1995	1998	49
	2001	2019	
Coggeshall Town	2019	2020	8
Coggeshall United	2020		1
Colchester Casuals	1949	1950	3
Colchester Town	1900	1901	64
	1910	1938	
Colchester United	1939	2020	195
Coleford Athletic	1923	1933	33
	1935	1936	
	1949	1951	
Coleshill Town	1984	1985	39
	2008	2020	
Collier Row	1987	1996	20
Collier Row and Romford	1997		4
Colliers Wood United	2007	2020	34
Colne	1904	1913	71
	2003	2020	
Colne Carlton	1925	1926	3
Colne Dynamos	1991		1
Colne Town	1927		1
Colney Heath	2007	2015	27
	2018	2020	
Columbia	1932		1
Colwyn Bay	1928	1938	134
	1966	1967	
	1980	2019	
Concord Rangers	1995	2020	55
Congleton Hornets	1899	1900	6
	1906		
Congleton Town	1920	1922	193
	1930	1937	
	1948	1963	
	1965	1971	
	1973	2020	
Conisborough Athletic	1920	1921	2
Conisborough St Peters	1913	1914	4
Connah's Quay	1922		15
	1927	1930	
Connah's Quay & Shotton	1910	1915	15
	1931	1932	
Connah's Quay Nomads	1972	1974	5
Consett	1928	1961	240
	1963	2020	
Consett Celtic	1921	1922	3
Consett Swifts	1923		1
Consett Town Swifts	1905		1
Continental Star	2012	2016	12
Coombs Wood	1911	1913	3
Coppull Central	1913	1914	6
	1925	1927	
Corby Town	1950	2020	212
Corinthian	1989	1998	35
	2012	2020	
Corinthian Casuals	1965	2020	111
Corinthians	1923	1933	27
	1935	1939	
Cornard United	1994	1997	18
	2005	2010	
Cornholme	1922		1
Corsham Town	1951	1953	32
	2003	2015	
Cortonwood	1934		1
Coundon Three Tuns	1985		1
Coundon United	1922	1926	9
Courage & Co.'s Sports	1931	1938	24
Cove	1991	1998	42
	2001	2017	
Coventry Amateurs	1951		2
	1971		
Coventry City	1899	1906	283
	1908	2020	
Coventry Sphinx	2008	2020	35
Coventry Sporting	1975	1990	33
Coventry United	2017	2020	8
Cowes	1924	1926	100
	1929	1930	
	1932	1979	
Cowes (1)	1893	1900	19
Cowes (2)	1905	1922	47
Cowes Sports	1999	2020	38
Cowlairs	1887		3
Cowley	1927	1932	22
	1934	1938	
Cradley Heath	1948	1955	19
	1957	1961	
Cradley Heath St Luke's	1910	1939	73
Cradley Town	2001	2013	29
	2015		
	2017		
Craghead Heros	1920		1
Craghead United	1908	1915	39
	1921	1929	
Cramlington Welfare	1949	1959	20
Cranfield United	2010		2
	2013		
Cranleigh	1913		9
	1934	1939	
Crawcrook Albion	1926	1929	30
	1931	1939	
Crawley Down	2009	2013	9
Crawley Down Gatwick	2014	2020	9
Crawley Green	2010	2020	20
Crawley Town	1959	1962	175
	1964	2020	
Cray Valley Paper Mills	2014	2020	18
Cray Wanderers	1903	1905	145
	1915		
	1921	1922	
	1924		
	1926		
	1928	1932	
	1934	1939	
	1961	1991	
	2000	2020	
Crescent (Hampstead)	1897		2
Creswell Colliery	1922	1926	51
	1949	1965	
Crewe Alexandra	1884	2020	322
Cribbs	2015	2020	10
Crich Town	1914		3
	1924		
Crittall Athletic	1926	1951	59
	1967	1969	
Crockenhill	1985	1989	6
Croft	1907		1
Crofton	1922		1
Cromer	1906	1924	68
	1927	1928	
	1930	1939	
	1948	1956	
Cromptons Recreation	1951		9
	1958	1959	
Crook CW	1947	1950	8
Crook Town	1898	1901	257
	1903	1906	
	1908	1928	
	1931	1939	
	1951	2016	
Crookhall CW	1934	1940	13
Crookhall Rovers	1939		2
Cross Keys	1922		1
Crossens	1933	1939	13
	1947	1951	
Crosswell's Brewery	1887		2
Croston	1925		1
Crouch End	1892	1893	3
Crouch End Vampires	1898	1908	23
Crowborough Athletic	1995	1996	32
	2008	2020	
Crown & Manor	1948	1950	5
Croydon	1973	2020	126
Croydon (1)	1904	1906	25
	1908	1920	
	1922	1923	
Croydon Amateurs	1967	1970	7
Croydon Athletic	1991	2012	47
Croydon Common	1908	1915	29
Croydon Park	1894		1
Croydon Rovers	1952		1
Croydon Wanderers	1903	1907	7
Crusaders	1887	1893	23
Crystal Palace	1906	2020	283
Crystal Palace (1)	1872	1876	12
Crystal Palace Engineers	1891		1
Cudworth St Mary's	1936	1937	3
Cudworth Village	1922	1938	30
Cullompton Rangers	2010		1
Curzon Ashton	1976	2020	107
Custom House	1908	1924	51
	1926	1936	
Cwmbran Town	1989	1992	9
Dagenham	1952	1992	120
Dagenham & Redbridge	1993	2020	87
Dagenham British Legion	1947	1950	6
Dagenham Town	1930	1940	31
Daisy Hill	2007	2009	6
	2011		
	2013		
Dalton Casuals	1921	1922	3
Danesmoor Welfare	1937	1938	4
Darenth Heathside	1987	1992	9
Darenth Park	1938	1939	4
Darenth Training Colony	1936	1937	4
Darfield	1924	1930	15
Darfield St George	1920		3
Darfield United	1907	1908	10
	1910		
	1913	1915	
Darlaston	1908	1927	106
	1930	1932	
	1947	1959	
	1968	1970	
	1972	1983	
	1996		
Darlington	1886	2012	321
	2018	2020	
Darlington 1883	2015	2017	6
Darlington Cleveland Bridge	1986	1993	13
Darlington Cleveland Social	1994	1996	3
Darlington Railway Ath.	1920	1926	9
Darlington Railway Ath. (2)	2007	2009	7
	2013	2014	
Darlington St Augustines	1890	1893	50
	1895	1915	
Darlington St Hilda's	1891		4
	1903	1904	
Darlington West End	1891		2
Darnall Wellington	1922		1

Dartford to Echo

Index of clubs

Club			
Dartford	1896	1898	320
	1900		
	1904	1907	
	1909	1915	
	1921	1939	
	1947	1993	
	1996	2020	
Dartford Amateurs	1915		1
Dartmouth United	1932	1937	35
	1947	1955	
Darwen	1878	1914	283
	1922	1962	
	1966	1970	
	1973	2009	
Darwen Old Wanderers	1885	1888	10
Darwen Ramblers	1883	1885	5
Davenham	1884	1889	15
Daventry Town	1994		33
	2004	2005	
	2010	2020	
Daventry United	2008	2012	9
Daventry United (1)	1910	1912	6
	1914		
Daventry Victoria	1922		1
David Brown Athletic	1949		1
Davis Athletic	1932	1933	2
Dawdon Colliery Recreation	1933	1940	12
Dawdon Colliery Welfare	1947	1957	16
Dawlish Town	1991	1994	20
	2003	2012	
De Havilland (Bolton)	1948	1950	3
De Havilland Vampires	1949		1
Deal Ports	1920		1
Deal Town	1934	1938	137
	1952	1962	
	1964	1978	
	1981	1986	
	1990		
	1993	1994	
	1997	2020	
Dearne	1920		3
Debenham LC	2008	2009	9
	2012	2013	
	2016		
Deeping Rangers	2003	2020	47
Deerfield Athletic	1923		2
Denaby United	1900	1902	260
	1904	1914	
	1920	1964	
	1966	1969	
	1972	2002	
Denbigh Town	1911		1
Denby Dale	1909		2
Denton	1888		19
	1890	1891	
	1907	1915	
Denton United	1935	1936	7
Depot Battalion Royal Engineers	1908	1911	15
Deptford Invicta	1908	1914	8
Deptford Town	1900		4
	1903	1904	
Derby County	1885	2020	352
Derby Hills Ivanhoe	1902	1905	5
Derby Junction	1885	1896	27
Derby Midland	1884	1891	19
Derby St Luke's	1885	1891	12
Derby Town	1882		1
Derbyshire	1881		2
Dereham Town	2003	2020	47
Desborough Town	1900	1904	216
	1907	1939	
	1948	1956	
	1964	1977	
	1979	2020	
Devizes Town	1913	1914	153
	1920	1971	
	1973	1977	
	1980	2010	
	2012		
Dick, Kerrs	1920	1936	41
Dickinsons (Apsley)	1950		1
Didcot Town	1976	1982	80
	1998	2020	
Dilton Rovers	1947	1948	2
Dinnington Athletic	1933	1939	36
	1947	1950	
	1971		
Dinnington Main Colliery	1922	1924	10
	1926	1928	
Dinnington Town	2008	2013	11
Dipton United	1912	1937	40
Diss Town	1951	1960	50
	1995	2016	
	2018		
Distillery	1888		7
	1890		
Distington	1921		3
	1947	1948	
Dobson & Barlow's	1910		3
Dodworth	1922		2
Dominion	1914		1
Doncaster Plant Works	1920		2
Doncaster Rovers	1889	1915	293
	1921	2020	
Doncaster St George	1913		4
Doncaster St James	1908	1911	5
Donnington School	1872		2
Donnington Wood Institute	1922		1
Dorchester Town	1927	1939	217
	1949	2020	
Dorking	1907	1915	79
	1922	1924	
	1926	1935	
	1949	1971	
	1973	1974	
Dorking (2)	1985	2014	69
Dorking Town	1979	1984	13
Dorking Wanderers	2014	2020	21
Dosthill Colts	2011		4
Douglas (Kingswood)	1920	1922	5
	1951		
Dover	1895		120
	1898		
	1900		
	1938	1939	
	1947	1983	
Dover Athletic	1984	2020	124
Downton	1998	2005	27
	2007	2015	
Dreadnought	1881	1884	8
Dresden United	1896	1897	3
Driffield Town	1912		3
	1924		
Dronfield Woodhouse	1920	1922	3
Droylsden	1932	1938	189
	1948		
	1953	1956	
	1959	1960	
	1962	1966	
	1968	2020	
Droylsden United	1950	1951	7
Druids	1877	1878	58
	1883	1888	
	1890	1891	
	1896	1901	
	1905		
	1907	1911	
Drypool Parish Church	1925	1926	3
Dudley	1900		17
	1906	1907	
	1912	1915	
Dudley Phoenix	1913	1914	2
Dudley Sports	2009	2010	9
	2013		
	2017		
Dudley Town	1934	1938	141
	1947	1959	
	1965	1998	
	2008	2011	
	2013	2015	
Dulwich	1885	1890	12
Dulwich Hamlet	1920	1951	229
	1953	2020	
Dunkirk	2009	2020	29
Dunstable	1977	1990	36
	1994	1995	
Dunstable Thursdays	1900		1
Dunstable Town	1951		86
	1953	1961	
	1966	1976	
	2002	2020	
Dunston Federation	2007	2009	7
Dunston Federation Brewery	1992	2006	55
Dunston UTS	2010	2020	48
Durham City	1920	1926	191
	1928	1929	
	1931	1935	
	1937	1938	
	1955	2017	
EFC Cheltenham	1999		1
Eagley	1879	1884	15
	1886		
Earle	1925	1951	38
	1957		
Earles Welfare	1922		1
Earlestown	1901	1912	53
	1948	1950	
	1953	1964	
Earlestown Bohemians	1937		6
	1939		
Earlestown White Star	1939		2
Earlsfield Town	1921	1922	2
Earlswood Town	2013	2014	3
Easington CW	1932	1938	79
	1947	1960	
	1962	1963	
	1976	1981	
Easington Colliery	1984	2005	53
	2017		
Easington Sports	2019	2020	4
East Bierley	1939	1946	4
East Cowes	1926	1929	10
	1936	1940	
East Cowes Victoria	1914		21
	1920	1924	
	1946	1951	
	2000		
East Cowes Victoria Athletic	2013	2014	3
East End Park WMC	1959	1962	8
East Grinstead	1912	1914	58
	1922		
	1924	1935	
	1937	1956	
	1970	1972	
	1978	1982	
	1997		
East Grinstead Town	2004	2011	26
	2014	2020	
East Ham	1906	1915	12
East Ham United	1996		1
East Hull United	1927		1
East Preston	1999	2011	51
	2013	2020	
East Riding Amateurs	1932		1
East Sheen	1888		1
East Tanfield CW	1949		1
East Thurrock United	1990	2020	87
Eastbourne	1895		74
	1899	1902	
	1904		
	1906		
	1915		
	1947		
	1951	1961	
	1963	1970	
Eastbourne Borough	2002	2020	61
Eastbourne Comrades	1935	1939	12
	1948	1951	
Eastbourne Old Comrades	1925	1930	19
	1932	1934	
Eastbourne Old Town	1902	1906	9
Eastbourne St Mary's	1914	1915	7
Eastbourne Swifts	1898	1902	7
Eastbourne Town	1971	1987	90
	1992	1993	
	1995		
	1998	2020	
Eastbourne United	1958	1994	111
	2001	2011	
	2014	2020	
Eastern Coachworks (Lowestoft)	1939		7
	1951		
Eastern Counties United	1937		2
Eastleigh	1982	1985	95
	1987	2020	
Eastleigh Athletic	1899	1900	41
	1902	1920	
	1922	1925	
Eastleigh LSWR	1896	1898	6
Eastville Rovers	1896	1898	11
Eastville Wanderers	1899		1
Eastwood Hanley	1968	1977	51
	1984	1997	
Eastwood Rangers	1908		10
	1910		
	1912		
	1914		
Eastwood Town	1969	2014	138
Eastwood Town (1)	1897	1898	4
Ebbsfleet United	2008	2020	34
Ebbw Vale	1920	1924	59
	1930	1963	
Eccles Borough	1908	1910	21
	1914	1915	
Eccles United	1921	1927	31
	1929		
Ecclesfield	1888	1889	11
	1891		
	1928		
Eccleshall	2006	2013	14
Eccleshill United	1992	2010	43
	2012	2013	
	2015		
	2019	2020	
Eckington Red Rose	1915	1920	5
Eckington Town	1931		1
Eckington Works	1886		20
	1888	1889	
	1891	1896	
	1921	1923	
	1925		
	1927		
Eden CW	1931	1933	21
	1935	1937	
Eden Colliery	1947		1
Edgware Town	1946	1964	117
	1967		
	1974	2005	
	2008		
	2017	2020	
Edmonton	1922	1928	20
Edmonton & Haringey	1974	1977	6
Edmonton (2)	1969	1971	11
	1973		
Edmonton Borough	1948	1949	3
Egham	1923	1940	34
Egham Town	1967		115
	1970		
	1973	2020	
Egremont	1922	1927	21
	1929	1931	
Egremont (1)	1914	1915	2
Ekco (Southend)	1947	1948	5

Eldon Albion to Gitanos

Index of clubs

Club	Year1	Year2	Num
Eldon Albion	1906	1908	4
	1949		
Ellesmere Port Cement	1922	1927	19
	1929	1932	
Ellesmere Port Town	1922	1925	96
	1927		
	1929	1932	
	1935		
	1947	1975	
Ellesmere Rangers	2009	2016	13
	2019		
Ellistown	2010		3
Ellistown & Ibstock United	2015	2016	5
Elmore	1993	2011	37
	2013		
Elsecar Athletic	1907		2
Elsecar Main	1910	1911	6
Elswick Rangers	1888	1891	7
Eltham	1905	1908	7
Ely City	1936		103
	1955	1984	
	1987	1991	
	1998	2001	
	2003	2020	
Emley	1972	2002	98
Emsworth	1926	1930	9
Enderby Town	1973	1983	34
Endsleigh	1997	1998	2
Enfield	1905	2007	308
Enfield (1)	1897		1
Enfield 1893	2010	2020	18
Enfield Town	2004	2020	50
Epping Town	1938		32
	1940		
	1973	1985	
Eppleton CW	1949	1952	27
	1976	1987	
	1995		
Epsom	1936	1950	38
	1952	1961	
Epsom & Ewell	1962	1965	106
	1967	1971	
	1974	2019	
Epsom Athletic	2014	2015	2
Epsom Town	1926	1935	32
Epsom Town (2)	1946	1947	2
Ericssons Athletic	1920	1922	3
Erith	1893		1
Erith & Belvedere	1923	1928	198
	1930	1934	
	1946	2020	
Erith Town	1998	2020	55
Esh Winning	1985	1997	42
	2001	2013	
Esh Winning (1)	1915	1931	24
Esh Winning Rangers	1911	1912	4
Esher Leopold	1882		1
Esso (Purfleet)	1940		1
Eston United	1912	1913	25
	1915	1921	
	1923	1926	
	1929		
Eton Manor	1936		61
	1938	1959	
	1990	1991	
	2005	2017	
Etonian Ramblers	1883		2
Evenwood Town	1930	1939	149
	1947	1963	
	1965	2005	
Eversley & California	2018		1
Everton	1887	2020	434
Everwarm	1974	1977	7
Evesham Town	1924	1925	25
	1929	1939	
Evesham United	1959	1962	116
	1974	1979	
	1981	1982	
	1985		
	1987	2020	
Ewell & Stoneleigh	1938		2
Exeter City	1909	2020	259
Exmouth Town	1935	1939	53
	1951		
	1986	1995	
	2004	2006	
	2018		
	2020		
Exning United	1955	1956	2
Eynesbury Rovers	1936	1939	72
	1947	1959	
	1961	1970	
	1990	2001	
	2014		
	2016	2020	
FC Broxbourne Borough	2016	2018	4
FC Clacton	2008	2020	32
FC Halifax Town	2009	2020	44
FC Romania	2015	2020	19
FC United of Manchester	2008	2020	44
Failsworth	1907	1908	2
Fairfield	1892	1898	24
	1905	1906	
	1908	1909	

Club	Year1	Year2	Num
Fairford Town	2002	2015	32
	2017	2020	
Fakenham Town	1951		37
	1994	2009	
	2013	2020	
Falmouth Town	1963	1984	120
	1989	2012	
Fareham	1925		14
	1930		
	1932	1933	
	1939	1940	
Fareham Town	1956		169
	1959	2020	
Farnborough	2008	2020	30
Farnborough Town	1973	2007	111
Farncombe	1907	1912	9
Farnham	1910	1914	7
Farnham Town	1949	1952	46
	1987		
	1999	2001	
	2003	2020	
Farnham United Breweries	1922	1928	24
Farningham	1874	1875	2
Farsley AFC	2013	2015	7
Farsley Celtic	1929	1930	178
	1932	1933	
	1935	1940	
	1949	1960	
	1962	1992	
	1994	2010	
Farsley Celtic FC	2016	2020	12
Faversham	1896	1897	5
	1899		
	1908		
Faversham Town	1950	1953	80
	1966		
	1972	1988	
	1992	1994	
	2008	2020	
Fawley	2013	2018	6
Felixstowe & Walton United	2001	2002	36
	2005	2020	
Felixstowe Port & Town	1997	2000	4
Felixstowe Town	1929	1939	47
	1978	1996	
Felixstowe United	1950	1951	2
Felling Colliery	1920		21
	1922	1924	
	1927		
	1929	1931	
Felling Red Star	1937	1938	2
Felstead	1905	1906	3
Feltham	1967	1969	41
	1971	1972	
	1974		
	1976	1984	
	1987	1991	
Feltham & Hounslow Borough	1992	1995	6
Feltham (2)	2010		1
Ferndale Athletic	1973		1
Ferrybridge Amateur	1950		1
Ferryhill Athletic	1923	1994	165
	1997		
Filey Town	1921	1923	29
	1926	1939	
	1948	1951	
Filey United	1910		2
Finchley	1879	1882	177
	1905		
	1907	1908	
	1910	1914	
	1922		
	1924	1927	
	1929	1936	
	1938	1991	
Finedon Revellers	1893		10
	1898	1902	
Finedon United	1910		1
Firbeck Main Colliery	1936		8
	1946	1950	
Fisher	2012	2016	11
	2019	2020	
Fisher '93	1994	1996	9
Fisher Athletic	1984	1993	42
Fisher Athletic (London)	1997	2009	37
Fishwick Ramblers	1885	1886	3
Flackwell Heath	1983	2020	90
Fleet Spurs	2012	2013	2
Fleet Town	1967	1974	88
	1983	1986	
	1993	2020	
Fleetwood	1909		117
	1911		
	1920	1928	
	1948	1976	
Fleetwood Freeport	2000	2002	10
Fleetwood Rangers	1887	1889	25
	1892	1899	
Fleetwood Town	1979	1996	118
	2003	2020	
Fletton United	1909		34
	1911	1924	
Flint	1893	1895	8
	1929		
Flint Town United	1951	1962	28

Club	Year1	Year2	Num
Flixton	1992	2011	48
Florence & Ullcoats Utd.	1948	1951	6
Fodens Motor Works (Sandbach)	1939	1949	7
Folkestone	1891	1905	223
	1910	1911	
	1914	1939	
	1947	1974	
	1981	1991	
Folkestone & Shepway	1975	1980	19
Folkestone Invicta	1995	2020	76
Folland Sports	2014	2017	9
Foots Cray	1930		1
Ford Sports (Dagenham)	1935	1950	20
Ford Sports (Daventry)	1999	2007	21
Ford United	1960	1961	65
	1963	1973	
	1990	2004	
Forest Green Rovers	1978	1989	96
	1993	2020	
Forest School	1876	1879	6
Formby	1938	1939	78
	1948	1951	
	1970	1991	
	1993		
	2006	2014	
Framlingham Town	2018	2020	7
Frecheville Community	1977		1
Freemantle	1895	1900	18
	1902	1905	
Freetown	1899	1901	6
Frenchay	1921		1
Friar Lane & Epworth	2008	2012	10
Friar Lane Old Boys	1977	1988	24
	1990	1992	
Fricker Athletic	1921	1925	12
Frickley Athletic	1977	2020	130
Frickley Colliery	1911		189
	1913	1976	
Frimley Green	2005	2011	16
	2014	2016	
	2019	2020	
Frizington Athletic	1914	1930	30
Frizington U (1)	1902	1903	2
Frizington United	1947	1949	8
	1951		
Frizington White Star	1899		12
	1901	1906	
Frodingham & Appleby Ath.	1930	1935	12
Frodingham & Brumby United	1913		2
	1915		
Frodingham Athletic	1920	1921	16
	1924	1929	
Frome Town	1907	1909	240
	1911	1913	
	1915	1939	
	1947	2006	
	2008	2020	
Frosts Athletic	1934	1938	17
Fryston Colliery	1914	1915	16
	1922	1927	
Fulham	1897		322
	1900	2020	
Fulham Amateurs	1911	1913	3
Furness Athletic	1938	1939	2
Furness Vale Rovers	1887		1
GE Hamble	2012	2013	3
GER Loughton	1931		1
GER Romford	1920	1930	26
GKN Sankey	1986	1988	8
GSA Sports	2009		1
Gainsborough Albion	1921		1
Gainsborough Trinity	1886	2020	385
Galgate	1950		1
Garforth Miners	1985		1
Garforth Town	1986	1988	55
	1991	1993	
	1996	2020	
Garrards Athletic	1930	1931	11
	1933	1934	
Garston Copper Works	1898	1899	3
Garston Gasworks	1913		14
	1915	1924	
Garston Woodcutters	1939		4
Gateshead	1931	1974	96
Gateshead (1)	1913	1915	6
Gateshead (2)	1979	2020	127
Gateshead Association	1888		2
	1891		
Gateshead NER	1890		32
	1892	1903	
Gateshead Rodsley	1914	1915	3
Gateshead Town	1906	1909	4
Gateshead Town (2)	1923		2
Gateshead United	1975	1977	10
Gedling Colliery	1926	1927	20
	1948	1955	
Gedling Grove	1892	1897	7
Gedling MW	2009	2012	8
Gedling Town	2001	2011	26
Gilberdyke	1921		4
Gilfach	1922		2
Gillford Park	2012		1
Gillingham	1913	2020	265
Gillingham Town	2009	2017	25
Gitanos	1874		1

272

Glapwell to Harrow Hill

Club	From	To	No.
Glapwell	1998	2011	27
Glasshoughton Colliery	1915	1922	4
Glasshoughton Welfare	1994	2009	33
	2012	2016	
	2019		
Glastonbury	1903	1904	147
	1921	1927	
	1929	1939	
	1947	1954	
	1956	1999	
Glebe	2016		10
	2018	2020	
Glossop	1899	1947	127
	1949	1952	
	1972	1992	
Glossop North End	1895	1898	76
	1993	2020	
Gloucester City	1929		217
	1932		
	1938	1939	
	1947	2020	
Gnome Athletic	1920	1923	16
Godalming	1901	1913	43
	1925		
	1929	1936	
	1938	1939	
Godalming & Guildford	1994	2005	19
Godalming Town	2006	2019	38
Godmanchester Rovers	2005		28
	2010	2020	
Golcar (Huddersfield)	1939		1
Goldenhill	1885	1887	6
Golders Green	1934	1939	18
Goldthorpe Colliery	1921		1
Goldthorpe United	1928		22
	1930	1935	
Goodrich	2009	2010	3
Goole AFC	2000	2020	42
Goole Chevrons	1920		1
Goole Shipyards	1921	1922	3
Goole Town	1907	1920	246
	1926	1931	
	1933	1996	
Gorleston	1910		173
	1912	1913	
	1915	1921	
	1930	1935	
	1937	1939	
	1947	1973	
	1976	2020	
Gornal Athletic	1974	1981	30
	2008	2009	
	2012	2016	
Gorton Villa	1889	1893	8
Gosforth & Coxlodge	1929	1958	36
Gosport	1930		25
	1932	1940	
Gosport Albion	1926	1928	6
Gosport Athletic	1921	1926	29
	1928	1929	
Gosport Borough	1971	1978	125
	1980	2020	
Gosport Borough Athletic	1946	1960	25
Gosport United	1909	1910	13
	1913	1915	
Gothic (Norwich)	1947	1955	28
	1967	1970	
Gradwell Sports	1932	1934	6
Graham Street Primitives	2014	2015	2
Gramophone	1910	1911	9
Grangetown (Sunderland)	1912	1915	4
Grangetown Athletic	1900		24
	1902		
	1904	1906	
	1908		
	1910	1915	
Grangetown St Mary's	1914		24
	1920	1926	
	1935		
	1937	1939	
Grantham	1878	1879	237
	1881	1889	
	1892	1893	
	1913	1931	
	1933	1989	
Grantham Avenue	1901	1909	26
	1913	1915	
Grantham Rovers	1891	1897	13
Grantham Town	1990	2020	78
Grassmoor	1926	1931	17
Grassmoor Comrades	1925		4
Grassmoor Ivanhoe	1922	1924	8
Gravesend	1891	1892	4
Gravesend & Northfleet	1947	2007	192
Gravesend Amateurs	1909		1
Gravesend United	1897	1901	42
	1905		
	1907	1909	
	1911	1915	
	1935	1936	
	1940	1946	
Gravesham Borough	2017		1

Club	From	To	No.
Grays Athletic	1912	1913	251
	1921	1936	
	1938	1972	
	1974	2020	
Grays Sports	1926		1
Grays Thurrock United	1926	1932	15
Grays United	1898	1907	35
Graysons	1921		2
Great Bridge Unity	1888	1891	10
Great Harwood	1900	1901	86
	1909	1924	
	1926	1932	
	1934	1936	
	1938	1939	
	1947	1955	
	1965	1966	
	1968	1978	
Great Harwood Town	1991	1999	35
	2001	2006	
Great Lever	1883	1884	6
	1886	1887	
Great Wakering Rovers	1997	2020	46
Great Yarmouth Town	1901	1906	246
	1908	1910	
	1914	1926	
	1928	1934	
	1936	1939	
	1947	2020	
Green & Silley Weir Ath.	1921	1922	2
Green Waves (Plymouth)	1905	1906	31
	1908		
	1911		
	1924	1930	
	1932	1934	
	1951		
Greenhalgh's	1892	1894	6
Greenhouse London	2014		4
Greenwich Borough	1994		37
	2000	2005	
	2011	2020	
Greenwood Meadows	2010	2012	4
Gresford	1922		1
Gresham	1877		3
	1880		
Gresley	2010	2020	31
Gresley Colliery	1912	1914	22
	1921	1923	
	1926	1930	
Gresley Rovers	1896	1906	242
	1908	1936	
	1939	1960	
	1963	2009	
Gresley Villa	1909	1911	8
Gretna	1984	2003	58
Grey Friars	1879	1881	11
Grimethorpe Athletic	1948	1953	10
Grimethorpe Colliery Institute	1915	1922	22
	1928	1935	
Grimethorpe Rovers	1940	1947	5
Grimethorpe United	1905	1908	21
	1910		
	1912		
Grimsby Albion	1926	1928	5
Grimsby All Saints	1901		1
Grimsby Borough	2012		8
	2018	2020	
Grimsby District	1885	1886	2
Grimsby Haycroft Rovers	1913	1933	36
Grimsby Rangers	1909	1911	5
Grimsby Rovers	1910	1927	31
Grimsby STC	1921		1
Grimsby St John's	1911	1915	7
Grimsby Town	1883	2020	334
Grimsby YMCA	1927		1
Grosvenor Park	2003	2004	4
Guards Depot	1905	1910	14
	1913		
	1920		
Guernsey	2014	2017	8
Guildford	1905	1906	67
	1908	1951	
Guildford & Dorking United	1975	1977	6
Guildford City	1928	1974	119
Guildford City (2)	2007	2020	30
Guildford United	1922	1927	30
Guinness Exports (Ormskirk)	1969	1971	3
Guisborough	1948	1949	3
Guisborough Belmont Ath.	1922		8
	1924	1927	
Guisborough Red Rose	1908		1
Guisborough Town	1979	2020	111
Guiseley	1922	1923	144
	1925	1931	
	1933	1935	
	1937	1946	
	1984	2020	
Guiseley Colliery	1908		5
Gwynnes Athletic	1923	1924	2
HMS Excellent	1937	1939	5
HMS Victory	1935	1940	7
Hackney Wick	2018	2020	4
Hadfield	1924		1
Hadleigh United	1996	1997	28
	2004	2020	
Hadley	2011	2020	31

Club	From	To	No.
Haig United	1947		1
Hailsham Town	1983	2018	63
Halesowen	1899		17
	1901	1903	
	1905	1906	
	1908	1911	
Halesowen Harriers	1988	2003	28
Halesowen Town	1920	1927	204
	1931		
	1934	1935	
	1937	1938	
	1948	1965	
	1967	2009	
	2012	2020	
Halifax (1)	1898		1
Halifax Town	1913	2008	221
Hall Road Rangers	2003	2014	20
	2018		
	2020		
Hallam	1927	1933	63
	1951	1959	
	1995	1997	
	2000	2013	
	2017	2020	
Hallen	2003	2020	49
Halliwell	1883	1893	27
Halliwell Rovers	1896	1899	6
Halliwell Unitarians	1907		2
	1909		
Halstead Town	1989	2001	69
	2004	2015	
	2017		
	2020		
Hamble ASSC	2006	2011	17
Hamble Club	2019	2020	5
Hamilton Central	1920		3
Hammersmith Comrades	1920		1
Hampstead	1898	1906	11
	1908		
Hampstead Heathens	1872		4
Hampstead Town	1913	1933	69
Hampton	1967	1999	81
Hampton & Richmond Borough	2000	2020	56
Hamworthy	1934	1936	12
	1940		
	1949	1951	
Hamworthy United	2005	2020	49
Handley Page	1920		2
Handsworth	1922		2
Handsworth Parramore	2015	2020	18
Hanham Athletic	1913	1939	69
	1947	1955	
Hanley Town	2016	2020	9
Hanover United	1880	1888	14
Hanwell	1904		7
	1907		
	1910		
	1912	1913	
Hanwell Athletic	1923	1924	4
Hanwell Town	1989	1991	54
	1994	1998	
	2000	2020	
Hanwell Town (1)	1925	1927	4
Hanworth Villa	2012	2020	29
Hapton	1899	1900	2
Harborough Town	2014	2020	13
Hardwick Colliery	1913		18
	1915		
	1921	1922	
	1924	1925	
	1949		
Harefield United	1980	1997	71
	2003	2017	
	2020		
Haringey & Waltham Development	2012	2013	5
Haringey Borough	1978	1985	75
	1987	1988	
	1992	1995	
	1997		
	2001	2020	
Harland & Wolffs	1922		10
	1925	1926	
Harlandic	1924		3
	1927		
Harlow Town	1938	1940	167
	1948	1950	
	1963	1993	
	1996	2020	
Harpenden Town	1914		15
	1999	2000	
	2004	2006	
	2017	2020	
Harrisons	1989	1990	2
Harrogate	1920	1922	14
	1929	1930	
Harrogate Hotspurs	1949		1
Harrogate Railway Athletic	1955	1957	82
	1991	2020	
Harrogate Town	1951	1952	121
	1962	1967	
	1983		
Harrow Borough	1967	2020	128
Harrow Chequers	1872		3
	1875	1876	
Harrow Hill	2007	2010	5

Index of clubs

Harrow Town to Horsham YMCA

Index of clubs

Club	From	To	Count
Harrow Town	1940	1966	41
Harrow Weald	1922		7
	1924	1926	
Harrowby	1911	1923	35
	1925	1929	
	1931	1932	
	1934	1939	
	1949		
Harrowby United	2015	2018	5
Hartford & Davenham United	1890		2
Hartford St John's	1884	1887	5
	1889		
Hartlepool	1969	1977	19
Hartlepool United	1978	2020	106
Hartlepools United	1909	1968	133
Hartley Wintney	2004	2005	44
	2009	2020	
Harwich & Parkeston	1899	1902	241
	1904	1905	
	1907		
	1909		
	1911	1915	
	1922	1924	
	1926	1940	
	1947	2010	
	2020		
Harworth Colliery Athletic	1947	1950	11
Harworth Colliery Institute	1989	1994	15
	1996	1997	
Haslingden	1883		36
	1907	1915	
	1998		
Haslington Villa	1936	1940	8
Hassocks	1997	2015	44
	2018	2020	
Hastings & St Leonards	1922		58
	1924	1928	
	1931	1949	
Hastings & St Leonards (1)	1902	1906	18
Hastings & St Leonards United	1907	1910	20
Hastings Town	1982	2002	56
Hastings United	1950	1986	123
Hastings United (2)	2003	2020	56
Haswell	1912		3
Hatfield Main	1930	1933	26
	1969		
	1973	1974	
	1995	1998	
	2001	2004	
Hatfield Town	1950	1951	35
	1965		
	1967	1968	
	1970	1978	
	2009	2015	
Hatfield United	1947		1
Haughmond	2017	2020	12
Havant & Waterlooville	1999	2020	75
Havant Town	1987	1998	28
Haverfordwest County	1982	1985	10
Haverhill Borough	2015	2016	9
	2018	2019	
Haverhill Rovers	1951		108
	1955	1959	
	1965	1968	
	1970	1971	
	1979	1997	
	2004	2020	
Haverton Hill	1921	1925	9
Hawks	1878	1879	3
Haydock	1900	1902	3
Haydock C&B Recreation	1947	1951	11
Hayes	1930	2007	215
Hayes & Yeading United	2008	2020	38
Hayesco Sports	1936	1937	2
Hayling United	2010	2013	5
Haywards Heath	1934	1960	103
	1962	1989	
Haywards Heath Town	1990	1993	14
	2015		
	2017	2020	
Haywards Sports	1928	1931	7
Hazells (Aylesbury)	1970		2
Head Wrightsons	1951	1955	8
Headingley	1929	1939	11
Headington United	1932	1933	62
	1935	1960	
Heanor Athletic	1949	1951	5
Heanor Town	1890	1901	189
	1922	1939	
	1955	1966	
	1968	1998	
	2010	2020	
Heanor United	1910	1912	9
Heart of Midlothian	1886	1887	2
Heath Hayes	2009	2017	13
Heather St Johns	2009	2011	13
	2014	2015	
	2019	2020	
Heaton Stannington	1921		22
	1950	1955	
	1977		
	2016	2019	
Hebburn	1990	2003	26
Hebburn Argyle	1894	1902	48
	1905		
	1907	1915	
Hebburn Colliery	1921		5
Hebburn St Cuthbert's	1933		1
Hebburn Town	2004	2016	36
	2019	2020	
Hebden Bridge	1913	1922	16
	1933		
Heckmondwike	1905		23
	1907	1915	
Hednesford Town	1891	1894	278
	1909	1938	
	1946	1953	
	1955	2020	
Hemel Hempstead Town	1948	1959	163
	1963	2020	
Hemmingfield	1921	1922	4
Hemsworth	1903		2
Hemsworth Colliery	1928		1
Hemsworth MW	2011	2013	15
	2016	2020	
Hemsworth West End	1926	1929	15
Hendon	1947		246
	1949	2020	
Hendon (1)	1878	1889	25
Hendon Town	1927	1934	15
Hengrove Athletic	2012	2015	11
	2017	2020	
Henley	1880	1882	6
	1885		
Henley Comrades	1922	1925	4
Henley Town	1914		48
	1920	1939	
	1947	1950	
	2004	2009	
	2017		
Hereford	2017	2020	18
Hereford (1)	1892	1899	15
	1903		
Hereford City	1910	1911	5
	1913	1915	
Hereford RAOC	1925		1
Hereford St Martins	1922	1924	3
Hereford Thistle	1896	1897	9
	1922	1925	
Hereford United	1925	2015	260
Herne Bay	1966	2020	120
Hersham	1921	1924	26
	1930	1931	
	1934	1939	
Hersham United	1911	1915	7
Hertford Town	1922	1926	187
	1929	1937	
	1939	1947	
	1950	1951	
	1956	2020	
Herts Rangers	1876	1882	11
Hessle	1929		1
Hessle Old Boys (Hull)	1949		1
Hetton United	1923		1
Hexham	1925		7
	1936		
	1938	1939	
Hexham Athletic	1914		1
Hexham Excelsior	1895	1898	4
Hexham Hearts	1949	1956	25
Heybridge	1933	1935	5
Heybridge Swifts	1982	2020	128
Heywood	1892		7
	1900	1901	
	1904		
Heywood Central	1888	1889	13
	1891	1895	
Heywood United	1910	1915	19
Hickleton Main	1909	1915	11
High Duty Alloys (Distington)	1949	1950	5
High Fell	1926	1928	6
High Park	1930		1
High Wycombe	1874	1878	7
Higham Ferrers Town	1922	1936	39
Higham Ferrers YMCI	1909	1911	3
Highbury Union	1877	1878	4
	1882	1883	
Higher Walton	1885	1894	18
Highgate (Rotherham)	1931	1932	8
Highgate United	1970	1993	68
	2008	2013	
	2017	2020	
Highmoor Ibis	2014	2018	10
Highthorn	1905		1
Highworth Town	2002	2020	50
Hillingdon	1984	1985	5
Hillingdon Borough	1965	1983	106
	1995	2016	
Hinckley (1)	1992		1
Hinckley (2)	2011		1
Hinckley AFC	2016	2019	12
Hinckley Athletic	1949	1969	124
	1971		
	1973	1997	
Hinckley Downes	2009	2010	3
Hinckley Town	1988	1997	24
Hinckley Town (1)	1896	1905	25
Hinckley United	1998	2014	61
Hinckley United (1)	1910	1932	62
	1934	1937	
	1939		
Hindley	1899		3
Hindley Green Athletic	1926	1928	4
Hindpool Athletic	1909	1910	4
Histon	1954	1962	118
	1968	1969	
	1971	1982	
	1985	1994	
	1998	2020	
Histon Institute	1933	1936	24
	1938	1939	
	1948	1953	
Hitchin	1872	1873	17
	1875	1876	
	1888	1889	
	1899	1901	
	1904	1905	
Hitchin Athletic	1923		1
Hitchin Blue Cross	1922	1928	10
Hitchin Blue Cross Temperance	1910		1
Hitchin Town	1906	1908	288
	1931	1936	
	1938	2020	
Hitchin Union Jack	1915		2
Hobson Wanderers	1914	1927	19
	1930		
Hoddesdon Town	1885		125
	1932	1951	
	1955	1960	
	1967	1973	
	1975	1997	
	2000	2005	
	2008	2020	
Hoffmann Ath. (Stonehouse)	1947	1951	12
Hoffmann Athletic (Chelmsford)	1913	1921	28
	1926	1927	
	1936	1947	
	1949		
Holbeach United	1939		141
	1948	1992	
	1995	2020	
Holbrook MW	2010		4
Holbrook Sports	2011	2014	9
Holderness Athletic	1921	1928	9
Holiday's Sports	1940		1
Holker Old Boys	2003	2013	28
	2015	2016	
Hollands & Blair	2017	2020	7
Hollington United	1928		4
Holly Bush (Parkgate)	1915		2
Holme	1910		1
Holme Head Works	1932		14
	1934	1938	
	1951		
Holmer Green	2001	2008	24
	2012	2020	
Holmesdale	2010	2018	13
Holt United	1937	1939	8
	1950	1951	
Holwell Sports	2010	2011	14
	2013	2016	
Holwell Works	1911		5
	1913	1915	
Holyhead Town	1965	1966	6
	1968	1969	
	1971		
Holyport	2011	2016	8
	2019		
Hook Norton	2011		7
	2016	2017	
Hook Shipyards	1921	1922	5
Hooley Hill	1910	1911	6
Horden Athletic	1910	1928	48
Horden CW	1930	1939	217
	1947	1994	
	1997	2011	
Horden Colliery	1913		1
Horfield United	1922	1924	7
Horley Town	1983	1986	39
	2007	2020	
Horncastle	1886	1889	9
Horncastle Town	1921	1923	7
	1926		
Horncastle United	1909	1912	5
Hornchurch	1962	2005	104
Hornchurch & Upminster	1958	1961	15
Hornchurch (1)	1883	1884	2
Horndean	1982	1992	38
	2012	2020	
Hornsea Town	1922		2
	1924		
Horsforth	1908		23
	1911	1931	
Horsham	1904	1906	243
	1908	1912	
	1914	1915	
	1923		
	1925		
	1933	2020	
Horsham Trinity	1926	1927	3
Horsham YMCA	1977	2020	97

274

Horwich to Larkhall Athletic

Club	Year	Year	Num
Horwich	1895	1899	9
Horwich Central	1925	1929	6
Horwich RMI	1915	1939	179
	1947	1995	
Hotspur	1880	1883	17
	1885	1888	
Houghton	1920	1924	13
Houghton Main Colliery	1921	1923	9
Houghton Rangers	1950		2
Houghton Rovers	1911		11
	1913	1915	
Hounslow	1899		78
	1907	1910	
	1924	1931	
	1964	1991	
Hounslow Town	1932		60
	1934	1936	
	1938	1963	
Hove	1903		34
	1905		
	1925	1929	
	1931	1939	
	1947		
	1949	1951	
Hove Park	1907		2
Howden Rangers	1894	1895	3
Howden-le-Wear	1896	1897	6
	1899	1901	
Howdon British Legion	1928		12
	1930	1936	
Hoxton Manor	1939		3
Hoylake	1914	1915	20
	1922		
	1924	1925	
	1935	1938	
Hoylake Athletic	1950	1951	3
Hoyland Common Athletic	1949	1950	7
Hoyland Common Wesleyans	1921	1922	2
Hoyland Silkstone	1907	1912	14
Hoyland St Peter's	1921	1922	2
Hoyland Town	1904	1915	30
Hucknall Byron	1920	1923	10
	1926		
	1928	1929	
Hucknall Constitutional	1906		5
Hucknall Portland	1895	1897	11
	1899	1901	
Hucknall St Johns	1894	1899	16
Hucknall Town	1993	2014	60
Hucknall Town (1)	1902		1
Huddersfield (1)	1905		1
Huddersfield Town	1910	2020	285
Hudsons	1901	1902	4
Hugglescote Robin Hood	1899		1
Hull Amateur	1947		1
Hull Brunswick	1966	1970	12
	1972		
Hull City	1905	1939	296
	1947	2020	
Hull Dairycoates	1921		17
	1923	1928	
Hull Day Street Old Boys	1910	1913	6
Hull Old Boys	1914	1929	17
Hull Oriental	1911		1
Hull Papermills	1936		1
Hull St Peter's OB	1921		3
Hull Technical College OB	1925		2
Hull Town	1884	1885	2
Hull Wanderers	1921		1
Hullbridge Sports	2000	2020	33
Humber Graving Dock	1920	1921	4
Humber United	1930	1934	17
	1936	1937	
Hungerford Town	1974	2020	114
Hunslet	1897	1902	19
Huntingdon Town	2012	2018	14
Huntingdon United	1950	1955	11
Huntley & Palmers	1948	1955	34
	1957	1970	
Hunts County	1891	1893	5
Hurst	1884	1886	55
	1888	1889	
	1912	1926	
	1928	1930	
	1946	1947	
Hurst Nook Rovers	1894	1895	2
Hurst Ramblers	1898	1899	4
Hurworth	1891	1894	6
Hyde	1888		22
	1907	1910	
	1912	1915	
Hyde FC	2011	2015	8
Hyde United	1936		218
	1947	2010	
	2016	2020	
Hylton Colliery	1927	1928	4
Hythe & Dibden	2015	2016	6
	2020		
Hythe Town	1986	1993	70
	2002	2020	
Hythe United	1998	2001	9
ICI Alkali	1934	1937	8
Ibstock Colliery	1924	1929	8
Ibstock Penistone Rovers	1938	1939	15
	1947	1953	

Club	Year	Year	Num
Ilford	1891	1897	221
	1899	1979	
	2000	2020	
Ilfracombe Town	1937		50
	1950	1960	
	1990	1995	
	2003		
	2006		
	2008	2015	
Ilkeston	1935	1938	7
Ilkeston FC	2013	2017	14
Ilkeston Town	2020		1
Ilkeston Town (1)	1894	1903	31
Ilkeston Town (2)	1948	1978	160
	1981	2011	
Ilkeston United	1905	1923	73
	1925	1933	
Ilminster Town	1949	1954	27
	1956	1960	
	1977	1982	
Immingham	1913		1
Immingham Town	1993	1996	6
Imperial Paper Mills	1937		1
Industry Inn	1913		4
Ipswich Town	1891	1893	245
	1931	2020	
Ipswich Wanderers	2001	2009	44
	2012	2019	
Ipswich Works	1928	1929	2
Irchester United	1935		5
	1937		
	2012	2014	
Irlam	2011	2013	14
	2017	2020	
Irlam Town	1987	1993	16
Ironbridge	1893	1894	10
	1899	1902	
Ironbridge United	1911		1
Irthlingborough Diamonds	1970	1992	59
Irthlingborough Town	1903	1915	48
	1921	1928	
Irwell Springs	1883	1884	6
	1889		
Islington Town	1920	1921	3
J.S. Fry & Sons	1930		5
	1932	1934	
Jardines (Nottm)	1888	1891	9
Jarrow	1896	1902	105
	1904	1905	
	1909		
	1914	1915	
	1921	1939	
	1949	1950	
Jarrow Blackett	1914	1915	3
Jarrow Caledonians	1911	1913	8
Jarrow Croft	1912	1913	9
Jarrow Roofing Boldon CA	1998	2018	51
Johnson & Barnes	1934		2
Jump Home Guard	1950	1951	3
Jump WMC	1921		2
Jurgens (Purfleet)	1920		15
	1932	1937	
K Sports	2019	2020	3
Kells United	1931	1939	26
Kells Welfare Centre	1946	1951	10
Kells White Star	1920		5
	1922		
Kempston	1911		1
Kempston Rovers	1926	1931	71
	1933	1939	
	1948	1951	
	1978	1983	
	1988	1989	
	1993	1996	
	2000	2003	
	2017	2020	
Kendal Swifts	1910	1912	5
Kendal Town	1923	1924	63
	1926	1930	
	2001	2020	
Kennek Ryhope CA	2000	2001	3
	2005		
Kensal Rise	1905		5
Kensington	1904	1905	2
Kentish Town	2009	2012	7
Keswick	1901	1907	30
	1923	1933	
Kettering	1889	1925	118
Kettering St Mary's	1909	1910	5
Kettering Town	1926	2020	307
Kettering Working Men's	1909	1911	5
Keynsham	1927	1935	23
	1937	1938	
Keynsham Town	1991	1992	16
	1995		
	2003	2005	
	2008	2011	
	2017	2020	
Kibblesworth	1922	1923	2
Kidderminster (1)	1891		6

Index of clubs

Club	Year	Year	Num
Kidderminster Harriers	1896	1925	336
	1927		
	1931		
	1933	1934	
	1936	2020	
Kidlington	1951		30
	2008	2020	
Kidsgrove Athletic	1996	2020	64
Kilburn	1911	1913	8
Kildare	1880	1884	6
Kilnhurst	1891	1898	13
Kilnhurst Colliery	1949	1951	3
Kilnhurst Town	1907	1909	15
	1913	1915	
Kilnhurst United	1920	1922	7
	1926		
Kimberley	1893	1899	14
Kimberley MW	2018	2019	4
Kimberley St John's	1904	1908	7
Kimberley Town	1996	1997	3
Kimberworth Old Boys	1920		6
Kinderton Victoria	1922		2
King's Lynn	1901	1908	328
	1910	2010	
King's Lynn DS&S	1920		1
King's Lynn Town	2012	2020	30
King's Own Rifles	1895		3
Kings Langley	1940	1946	25
	2012	2020	
Kings Norton Town	2000		1
Kingsbury London Tigers	2009	2011	7
Kingsbury Town	1984	2006	41
Kingston Villa	1908	1910	5
Kingston-on-Thames	1907		21
	1910		
	1912	1915	
Kingstonian	1920	2020	288
Kingswood	1925	1935	35
Kingswood Rovers	1909	1910	11
Kippax Parish Church	1908		3
Kirby Muxloe	2010	2020	26
Kirkby Collieries	1921	1922	2
Kirkby Town	1967	1972	16
Kirkby Town (2)	1987	1988	2
Kirkham	1907	1909	6
	1911		
Kirkham & Wesham	1920		1
Kirkley	1900	1909	35
	1911	1914	
	1924	1925	
	1928	1929	
	1933	1936	
Kirkley & Pakefield	2008	2020	32
Kirkley & Waveney	1930	1932	5
Kirkley (2)	2006	2007	3
Kiveton Park Colliery	1921	1923	12
	1947	1950	
Kiveton Park United	1970		1
Knaphill	2015	2020	14
Knaresborough	1911	1913	5
Knaresborough Town	2015		7
	2019	2020	
Knowsley United	1991	1998	27
Knutsford	1950		3
Knypersley Victoria	1996	2002	15
LNWR (Wembley)	1923		3
Laceby	1949	1950	3
Lancaster City	1939	2020	217
Lancaster Town	1907	1909	71
	1914	1915	
	1921	1938	
Lanchester Rangers	1937	1939	4
Lancing	1963	1964	73
	1966	1971	
	1984	1997	
	2000	2020	
Lancing Athletic	1949		22
	1951	1954	
	1956	1962	
Lancing Old Boys	1886		5
	1888	1889	
Langford	1929		38
	1932	1936	
	1938		
	1990	1998	
	2006	2013	
	2018		
Langley Green Victoria	1891		3
Langley Mill Rangers	1893	1899	10
	1908		
Langley Park	1921	1930	33
	1986	1993	
Langley Park (1)	1913	1914	3
Langley Park CW	1947	1951	5
Langley Park Villa	1939		4
Langney Sports	1991	2001	31
Langney Wanderers	2019	2020	2
Langold WMC	1950	1956	16
Langwith Athletic	1923		2
Langwith Colliery	1925	1927	7
Langwith MW	1955	1957	4
Larkhall Athletic	1978	1979	32
	2009	2020	

Laughton Common to Maidenhead United

Club	Year1	Year2	Count
Laughton Common	1922	1923	3
Launceston	2009	2011	5
Laverstock & Ford	2010	2011	6
	2017	2018	
Leadgate Exiles	1894		8
	1896	1899	
Leadgate Park	1893	1897	71
	1899	1911	
	1913	1914	
	1920	1925	
Leagrave & District	1926	1928	5
	1931		
Leagrave United	1910	1911	2
Leamington	2006	2020	37
Leamington Town	1923	1937	30
Leasingthorne	1938		3
Leasingthorne Colliery	1928	1929	13
	1931	1933	
	1935		
	1937	1938	
Leatherhead	1948	1951	181
	1960	2020	
Leatherhead (1)	1910		1
Leavesden	1935	1940	23
	1947	1949	
	1951		
Leavesden Mental Hospital	1915	1924	35
	1926	1927	
	1929	1934	
Ledbury	1929		1
Ledbury Town	2008	2009	3
	2011		
Leeds	1895	1898	5
Leeds Albion	1891	1892	4
Leeds Carnegie	2009	2011	5
Leeds City	1905	1915	22
Leeds Steelworks	1920	1922	5
Leeds United	1921	2020	259
Leeds United (1)	1912		1
Leek	1885	1894	25
Leek CSOB	1999	2009	20
	2011	2012	
Leek Town	1957		146
	1973	2020	
Leicester City	1920	2020	276
Leicester Fosse	1891	1915	72
Leicester Imperial	1908	1915	15
Leicester Nirvana	2016	2020	8
Leicester Nomads	1909	1911	8
	1913		
	1937	1938	
Leicester Road	2017	2020	11
Leicester United	1984	1997	35
Leicester YMCA	1896		1
Leigh Genesis	2009	2011	5
Leigh RMI	1996	2008	31
Leighton Cee Springs	1901	1905	7
Leighton Town	1970	1972	72
	1989	2020	
Leighton Town (1)	1910	1911	3
Leighton United	1924	1931	33
	1933	1951	
Leiston	1946	1959	71
	2005	2020	
Leiston Works Athletic	1920	1926	30
	1928	1935	
Lenton	1921	1927	25
	1929	1934	
Leslies	1923	1924	4
	1932	1933	
Letchworth	2003		2
Letchworth Athletic	1915		4
Letchworth Garden City	1977	1995	39
Letchworth Town	1922	1934	97
	1936	1976	
Leverstock Green	2005	2020	32
Lewes	1913		159
	1920		
	1927		
	1963	1966	
	1972	2020	
Lewisham St Mary's	1897		1
Lewison (Ilkeston)	1927		1
Leyland	1911	1926	25
Leyland DAF	1991	1992	2
Leyland Motors	1923	1924	73
	1934	1959	
	1962	1963	
	1966	1974	
	1976		
	1979	1990	
Leyland Motors (Kingston)	1922		34
	1924	1940	
Leys Recreation (Derby)	1891		1
Leyton	1875	1879	191
	1897	1903	
	1905	1913	
	1920		
	1922	1923	
	1925	1971	
	1973	1975	
	1993	1995	
	2002	2009	
Leyton Athletic	2019	2020	4
Leyton Orient	1947	1966	144
	1988	2020	
Leyton Pennant	1996	2003	17
Leyton-Wingate	1976	1992	55
Leytonstone	1897		196
	1899	1979	
Leytonstone/Ilford	1980	1989	35
Liberty	1913	1915	5
Lichfield City	2015		8
	2017		
	2020		
Limehouse Town	1907	1909	3
Linby Church	1905	1906	3
Linby Colliery	1949	1957	32
Lincoln Albion	1888		1
Lincoln City	1885	2020	311
Lincoln Lindum	1886	1888	4
Lincoln Moorlands	2004	2008	8
Lincoln Moorlands Railway	2009	2015	13
Lincoln Ramblers	1888		1
Lincoln United	1971	1972	86
	1985	1986	
	1992	2020	
Lindley Temperance	1909		1
Linfield Athletic	1889	1891	12
Lingdale Mines	1914	1915	3
Lingfield	2009	2016	22
	2018	2020	
Linotype & Machinery	1930	1931	31
	1933	1939	
	1952		
	1955	1963	
	1967	1970	
Lintz Institute	1915	1925	23
Liskeard Athletic	1979	1983	35
	1991	1992	
	2004	2009	
Litherland Remyca	2018	2020	5
Little Common	2018	2020	6
Littlehampton	1913	1914	20
	1930	1939	
	1947		
Littlehampton Town	1949	2019	144
Liverpool	1893	2020	437
Liverpool Caledonians	1893		4
Liverpool Police	1951	1952	2
Liverpool Ramblers	1883	1885	5
Liverpool South End	1896	1897	3
Liverpool Stanley	1888	1893	10
	1895	1896	
Liversedge	1921	1927	84
	1949		
	1992	2020	
Llandudno	1915		55
	1924	1939	
	1947	1953	
	1955	1965	
	1967		
Llandudno Swifts	1897	1898	4
	1900	1901	
Llanelli	1912	1914	161
	1920	1925	
	1932	1988	
Llangollen	1888	1889	4
Llanhilleth	1922		2
Lloyds (Sittingbourne)	1933	1949	25
Lock Lane Woodville	1913	1915	3
Lockheed Leamington	1949		46
	1951		
	1953	1973	
Lockwood Brothers	1882	1888	18
Loftus	1893		3
Loftus Albion	1914	1930	26
London APSA	2006	2014	15
London Bari	2016	2017	2
London Caledonians	1887	1892	74
	1906	1940	
London Colney	1997	2020	54
London Generals	1921		1
London Labour	1936		2
London Lions	2013	2014	7
	2019		
London Olympic	1883		1
London Paper Mills	1934	1939	26
London Tigers	2014	2017	13
	2020		
London Transport	1947	1949	3
London United	1895		1
London Welsh	1899	1902	5
	1904		
Long Buckby	1992	2016	49
Long Eaton	1915	1928	21
Long Eaton Midland	1890		1
Long Eaton Rangers	1884	1899	35
Long Eaton St Helen's	1904	1905	20
	1907	1911	
	1913	1914	
Long Eaton Town	1951	1953	12
	1955	1957	
Long Eaton United	1958	1991	100
	2004	2020	
Long Melford	1958	1959	28
	2005	2009	
	2012	2013	
	2016	2020	
Longfield	1915		2
Longfleet St Mary's	1904	1920	36
	1948	1951	
Longlevens	2017	2020	10
Longridge Town	2020		3
Longwell Green Sports	2010	2019	22
Lopham Methodists	1938	1939	3
Lordswood	2000	2020	36
Lostock Gralam	1910	1934	65
	1936		
	1938		
	1948	1950	
	1955	1965	
	1967	1971	
Loughborough	1890	1901	37
Loughborough Corinthians	1909	1931	59
	1933	1935	
Loughborough Dynamo	2006	2020	31
Loughborough United	1961	1973	27
Loughborough University	2010	2020	24
Louth Town	1921	1922	33
	1925		
	1928	1930	
	1932	1938	
	2012	2014	
Louth United	1957	1980	64
	1989	1991	
	1993		
	1995	2004	
Lovells Athletic	1922		98
	1927	1969	
Lowca	1913	1915	18
	1921		
	1947	1949	
Lower Breck	2020		1
Lower Darwen	1883	1886	8
Lower Gornal Athletic	1966	1970	17
	1972	1973	
Lowestoft Town	1899	1908	314
	1910	2020	
Loxwood	2016	2020	10
Luddendenfoot	1927	1933	15
	1935	1940	
	1948		
Luddington (Scunthorpe)	1949	1950	2
Ludlow Town	2003	2005	5
Luton Amateur	1903	1906	51
	1913	1915	
	1921	1926	
	1928	1929	
	1931	1932	
	1934	1939	
	1947	1950	
	1952	1954	
Luton Celtic	1909	1911	3
Luton Clarence	1907	1926	36
Luton Crusaders	1912	1914	4
Luton Reliance	1913	1915	6
Luton Town	1886	2020	383
Luton Trinity	1914		2
Luton Wanderers	1885	1887	4
Lutterworth Town	2019	2020	5
Lydney Town	2010	2012	13
	2017	2020	
Lye Town	1949	1955	101
	1958	1959	
	1969	1999	
	2008	2010	
	2012	2017	
	2020		
Lymington	1955	1937	23
	1948	1950	
	1952	1954	
	1996	1998	
Lymington & New Milton	1999	2007	36
Lymington Town	2007	2020	28
Lyndhurst	1887	1890	4
Lynemouth Welfare	1949	1951	6
	1955		
Lynn Swifts	1902		1
Lynton Works (Bedford)	1928		2
	1951		
Lyons Club (Greenford)	1938		10
	1940	1950	
Lysaght's Sports (Scunthorpe)	1934	1955	27
Lysaghts Excelsior	1913	1914	2
Lytham	1923	1939	95
	1947	1967	
	1969	1970	
	1978	1985	
MK Wolverton Town	1989	1990	4
Mablethorpe United	1951		1
Macclesfield (1)	1883	1897	24
Macclesfield Town	1908	1920	277
	1922	1924	
	1929	1937	
	1939		
	1948	2020	
Machynlleth	1922		1
Maesteg Park Athletic	1986	1992	13
Maidenhead	1872	1876	92
	1878	1915	
Maidenhead Norfolkians	1900	1915	34
Maidenhead United	1920	2020	256

276

Maidstone to New Tupton United

Club	From	To	#
Maidstone (1)	1892	1895	4
Maidstone Athletic	1909		2
Maidstone Church Institute	1904	1908	8
Maidstone United	1899	1908	222
	1910	1929	
	1931	1940	
	1947	1948	
	1951	1993	
Maidstone United (2)	2003	2020	66
Maine Road	1990	2019	70
Malden Town	1967	1970	12
Malden Vale	1988	1995	12
Maldon & Heybridge	1936	1939	8
Maldon & Tiptree	2011	2020	31
Maldon Town	1997	1998	35
	2000	2010	
Malmesbury Victoria	2020		1
Maltby MW	1992	1996	11
Maltby Main	1998	1999	38
	2002	2005	
	2008	2020	
Maltby Main Colliery	1921	1928	26
	1930		
	1947	1951	
Malvern Town	1981	1983	52
	1985	1993	
	2006	2013	
	2016	2020	
Manchester	1878		3
	1884		
Manchester Central	1930	1932	13
Manchester City	1896	2020	363
Manchester North End	1924	1930	43
	1932	1938	
Manchester United	1903	1999	433
	2001	2020	
Mangotsfield United	1974	2020	125
Mansfield	1895	1899	8
Mansfield Colliery	1922	1924	5
Mansfield Foresters	1901		2
Mansfield Mechanics	1905	1915	35
Mansfield Town	1911	2020	283
Mansfield Town (1)	1891	1894	9
Mansfield Wesleyans	1910		7
Mansfield Woodhouse Excelsior	1922		2
Mansfield Woodhouse Rangers	1906		2
Manton Colliery	1925	1926	4
Mapperley	1911		4
	1913	1914	
Mapplewell & Staincross Ath.	1926	1930	8
March Great Eastern United	1926	1928	10
	1934		
	1937	1939	
March Town	1948	1950	7
March Town United	1951	1998	143
	2005	2013	
	2020		
Mardy	1911	1915	16
	1922		
Marfleet	1921	1922	28
	1924		
	1926	1939	
Margate	1914	1923	247
	1927	1937	
	1939	1940	
	1947	1981	
	1990	2020	
Margate Holy Trinity	1907	1908	2
Marine	1921	2020	267
Market Drayton Town	2008	2020	31
Market Harborough Town	1903	1904	42
	1908	1915	
	1921	1934	
Markham Main Colliery	1927		2
	1929		
Marlborough Old Boys	1914	1924	9
Marlow	1872	1910	278
	1912	2020	
Marlow United	2008	2010	5
Marsden	1951		2
Marsden Moor	1922		2
Marske United	1999	2020	58
Marston Shelton Rovers	1951		2
Maryport	1914	1915	14
	1924	1925	
	1931	1932	
	1934		
Matlock	1886	1896	19
	1914	1915	
Matlock Town	1921	1935	196
	1947	1955	
	1958	2020	
Mauritius Sports Association UK	2011		1
McLaren Sports	1949	1950	3
Measham Imperial	1950		2
Measham Town	1923	1927	6
Medway	1975	1979	11
Meir KA	2008	2010	9
Melksham	1928	1935	30
	1937	1939	
	1947	1951	
Melksham & Avon United	1921	1927	11

Club	From	To	#
Melksham Town	1910	1911	119
	1914		
	1920		
	1952	1970	
	1972	2020	
Mellors (Nottm)	1886	1889	7
Meltham	1950	1951	2
Meltham Mills	1935		11
	1937	1949	
Melton	1926		2
Melton Town	2020		2
Merstham	1983	1997	67
	2000	2020	
Merthyr Town	1911	1935	59
Merthyr Town (2)	2011	2020	26
Merthyr Tydfil	1947	2010	226
Metal & Produce Recovery Depot	1947	1949	5
Methley Perseverance	1922		17
	1926	1930	
Metrogas	1922	1923	4
Metropolitan Police	1925		220
	1930	1933	
	1935	1963	
	1965	2020	
Metropolitan Railway	1898	1899	6
	1938		
Mexborough	1886		72
	1894	1900	
	1920	1930	
Mexborough Athletic	1931	1936	14
Mexborough Loco. Works	1922		3
Mexborough St John's	1902		2
Mexborough Town	1904	1906	75
	1908	1915	
	1965	1979	
Mexborough Town Athletic	1980	1983	9
Mexborough West End	1904		4
Mickleover RBL	1993		1
Mickleover Sports	2000	2020	52
Mickley	1893		47
	1895	1897	
	1899	1902	
	1904	1923	
Mid Kent	1897	1898	2
Mid Rhondda	1914	1922	29
	1926		
Middlesbrough	1884	2020	373
Middlesbrough Ironopolis	1891	1895	21
Middlesex Wanderers	1905		1
Middleton	1895	1900	16
Middleton Wanderers	1939		1
Middlewich	1911		6
	1923	1925	
Middlewich Athletic	1934	1940	12
Middlewich Rangers	1897	1902	8
	1904		
Mildenhall Town	2001	2020	51
Mile Oak	1997	1998	18
	2005	2012	
	2016	2018	
Mile Oak Rovers & Youth	1983	1991	14
Milford Town	1912		5
	1914	1915	
Millom Town	1951		1
Millwall	1904	2020	298
Millwall Athletic	1890	1903	48
Millwall Rovers	1888	1889	3
Millwall United	1927	1928	4
Milnthorpe Corinthians	1938	1951	38
	1955	1970	
Milton Keynes	1996	1998	4
Milton Keynes Borough	1986	1989	9
	1992	1993	
Milton Keynes City	1975	1985	26
	2000	2004	
Milton Keynes Dons	2005	2020	47
Milton United (Oxon)	2006	2012	16
	2015	2017	
Minehead	1913	1925	151
	1927		
	1929	1935	
	1937	1938	
	1952	2009	
Minerva	1878	1880	5
Mirfield United	1904	1905	23
	1907	1914	
Mirrlees Blackstone	1991	1998	13
Mitcham Wanderers	1924	1932	21
Mitchell's St George's	1882	1888	15
Moira United	1922	1931	28
	1948	1953	
	1955		
Mold	1926	1927	9
Mole Valley Predators	2006		1
Mole Valley SCR	2011	2015	7
Molesey	1969	1970	105
	1973	2020	
Monckton Athletic	1908	1911	39
	1922		
	1924	1946	
	1948	1949	
Mond Nickel Works	1914	1915	2
Moneyfields	2001	2020	51

Club	From	To	#
Monks Hall	1920	1922	10
Monmouth Town	1938	1946	3
Montrose Works	1900	1901	2
Moor Green	1935	1965	136
	1970	2007	
Moor Row Villa Rovers	1922	1924	6
Moore's Athletic	1909		1
Morecambe	1921	1930	243
	1932	1939	
	1947	2020	
Moresby Park	1907	1909	5
	1914		
Moresby Welfare Centre	1949		1
Moreton Town	1980	1985	18
	1994	1995	
Morley	1904	1910	22
	1912	1914	
Morpeth Harriers	1888	1891	31
	1901	1910	
Morpeth Town	1949	1951	69
	1957	1959	
	1996	2011	
	2013	2020	
Morris Motors (Cowley)	1931	1934	17
	1936	1947	
	1951		
Morris Sports (Loughborough)	1949	1951	3
Morton Rangers	1882		1
Mortons Athletic	1915	1921	4
Mosquitos	1880	1884	8
Moss Bay	1947	1949	6
	1951		
Moss Bay (1)	1892		1
Moss Bay Exchange	1896	1898	15
	1900	1904	
Moss Bay United	1924	1931	15
	1933		
Mossley	1949	2020	207
Moulton Verdin	1934	1940	13
Mount Hill Enterprise	1930	1939	24
	1950	1951	
Mount Pleasant	1938		1
Mountsorrel Town	1924	1928	5
Mulbarton Wanderers	2020		2
Murton	1987	1997	24
	2004		
Murton CW	1929	1938	78
	1947	1949	
	1951	1956	
	1960	1962	
	1965	1970	
	1973	1974	
Murton Red Star	1908	1910	7
	1913		
Mytholmroyd	1921	1922	4
N.A.C Athletic (Banbury)	1949	1951	3
Nanpean Rovers	1969	1970	6
Nantwich	1889	1894	108
	1900	1905	
	1907	1925	
	1927	1933	
	1935	1940	
	1947	1952	
	1955	1956	
	1967	1973	
Nantwich Town	1974	1986	103
	1992	2020	
National Radiator Co.	1920		1
Needham Market	2004	2020	50
Nelson	1894	1928	150
	1930	1933	
	1935	1937	
	1947	1969	
	2003	2008	
	2011		
	2015	2018	
Netherfield (1)	1889		1
Netherfield (Kendal)	1926	2000	199
Netherfield Rangers	1910	1922	17
Netherseal Colliery	1922		2
Neville's Athletic	1951		1
New Brighton	1922	1939	135
	1947	1981	
New Brighton Tower	1898	1902	14
New Brighton Tower Amateurs	1910	1914	7
New Brompton	1894	1912	63
New Brompton Athletic	1904		4
	1906		
New Crusaders	1906	1908	13
	1914	1915	
New Gateshead United	1936	1938	8
New Hartley Rovers	1912	1915	6
New Hucknall Colliery	1911	1929	24
New Mills	1924	1927	56
	1933		
	1970	1983	
	2006	2018	
New Milton	1930		3
	1932	1933	
New Milton Town	2008	2013	11
	2016		
New Peterborough Swifts	1932	1933	5
New Tredegar	1922		1
New Tupton United	1922	1923	4
	1925		

277

New Waltham to Post Office Engineers

Index of clubs

Club	From	To	No.
New Waltham	1949		2
New Whittington Exchange	1912		1
Newark	1885	1886	52
	1889		
	1891	1896	
	1898	1908	
Newark Athletic	1920	1924	9
Newark Castle Rovers	1931	1933	6
Newark Town	1925	1939	47
Newbiggin Athletic	1920		5
	1922		
Newbiggin CW	1939		9
	1948	1951	
Newbiggin West End	1935	1938	9
Newburn	1910	1912	61
	1914	1924	
	1935	1956	
	1958	1962	
Newbury	1892	1899	11
Newbury (2)	2012	2015	5
Newbury Town	1915	1922	86
	1924	1946	
	1962	1967	
	1978	1996	
Newcastle Benfield	2008	2020	47
Newcastle Benfield Bay Plastics	2006	2007	7
Newcastle Benfield Saints	2005		1
Newcastle Blue Star	1979	1994	78
	1999	2010	
Newcastle City	1911	1915	19
Newcastle East End	1888	1892	15
Newcastle East End (2)	1896		14
	1907		
	1909	1911	
	1913	1915	
	1933	1934	
Newcastle Town	1992	2020	73
Newcastle United	1893	2020	384
Newcastle West End	1887	1892	17
Newcastle West End (2)	1937		5
	1939	1940	
Newhall Red Rose	1903		2
Newhall St Edward's	1909		1
Newhall Swifts	1907	1912	27
	1915		
	1922	1924	
	1935		
Newhall United	1928		18
	1951	1955	
	1971	1972	
Newhall White Rose	1910	1911	2
Newhaven	1906	1912	74
	1921	1948	
	1950	1951	
	1953	1963	
	1995		
	2017	2020	
Newhaven Cement Works	1903	1905	3
Newland Choir	1921		2
Newmarket Town	1923	1930	155
	1932	1935	
	1938		
	1946	1951	
	1955	1962	
	1966	1972	
	1977	2020	
Newport (IOW)	1930	2019	248
Newport (Monmouth)	1907		2
Newport (Salop)	1898		1
Newport AFC	1993	1999	25
Newport Barbarians	1915	1921	3
Newport County	1914	1931	176
	1933	1989	
Newport County (2)	2000	2020	64
Newport Pagnell Town	1995	1997	35
	2005	2020	
Newportonians	1908	1922	13
Newquay	1927		44
	1951	1960	
	1972	1982	
	2006	2007	
Newquay United	1926		1
Newstead Byron	1895	1898	19
	1900	1902	
Newton Abbot	1952	1954	4
Newton Abbot Spurs	1948	1950	8
	1965		
Newton Aycliffe	2012	2020	19
Newton Common Recreation	1926		2
Newton Corinthians	1939		3
Newton Heath	1887		34
	1890	1902	
Newton Heath Athletic	1907		13
	1912	1915	
Newton YMCA	1947	1950	7
Newton-le-Willows	1906	1911	8
Newtown	1885	1886	21
	1892	1897	
	1899	1900	
Newtown (2)	1991	1992	4
Nomads	1896	1897	2
Normanby Mangnesite	1926	1939	28
Normanby Park Steel Works	1927	1932	17
	1980	1981	
North Derby Ramblers	1936	1938	5
North Engineers (Bootle)	1915		4
	1921		
North Ferriby United	1978	2019	98
North Greenford United	2005	2020	48
North Hants Ironworks	1903	1910	15
North Leigh	2000	2020	48
North Lindsey Midgets	1912		1
North Liverpool	1922		3
	1924		
North Lonsdale Amateurs	1913		4
North Meols	1892	1893	2
North Shields	1931	1993	210
	2005	2009	
	2011	2020	
North Shields Athletic	1906	1915	35
North Skelton	1908		3
North Skelton Athletic	1955	1957	5
North Walsham Athletic	1955		2
North Wingfield	1895		2
Northallerton '94	1996		2
Northallerton Town	1986	1995	60
	1997	2015	
	2017		
	2019	2020	
Northampton Amateurs	1949	1950	2
Northampton Nomads	1926	1927	6
	1931	1932	
	1935		
Northampton ON Chenecks	2017	2020	6
Northampton Sileby Rangers	2016	2019	8
Northampton Spencer	1988	2016	63
Northampton Town	1899	2020	291
Northampton Wanderers	1922	1925	6
Northampton War Team	1921		5
Northern Nomads	1906	1907	45
	1909	1921	
	1926	1938	
Northfleet	1896	1898	8
Northfleet United	1904	1905	83
	1907	1937	
Northmet	1938	1939	3
Northwich Victoria	1883	1898	324
	1913	1925	
	1929	2020	
Northwood	1990	2020	70
Norton & Stockton Ancients	1986	1993	43
	2003	2013	
	2016	2017	
Norton Sports	2011		3
Norton United	2004	2015	36
Norton Woodseats	1927		83
	1929	1933	
	1936	1960	
	1962	1966	
	1968	1974	
Norwich British Legion	1922	1923	3
Norwich CBS	2020		1
Norwich CEYMS	1890	1908	90
	1910		
	1913	1924	
	1927	1938	
	1948	1949	
Norwich City	1903	2020	286
Norwich DS&S	1920		2
Norwich Electricity Works	1940		1
Norwich Priory Athletic	1925	1930	11
Norwich School Old Boys Union	1949	1951	7
Norwich St Barnabas	1934	1939	13
Norwich St James'	1915		3
Norwich Thorpe	1890	1893	6
Norwich United	1993		35
	2004	2020	
Norwich YMCA	1934	1938	11
	1940		
Norwood Association	1908		1
Nostell MW	2009	2017	18
	2020		
Nottingham Forest	1879	2020	397
Notts County	1878	2020	364
Notts Jardines	1909	1913	9
Notts Olympic	1885	1897	30
	1908	1915	
Notts Rangers	1885	1890	20
	1911	1914	
Notts Swifts	1888		2
	1890		
Notts Wanderers	1885	1886	4
	1896		
Nuneaton Borough	1946	2008	243
	2019	2020	
Nuneaton Griff	2008	2015	18
	2017		
Nuneaton Town	1900	1901	105
	1909	1926	
	1928	1937	
	2009	2018	
Nunhead	1906		75
	1908	1939	
Oadby Town	2000	2020	53
Oak Villa	1948	1952	5
Oakdale	1921	1922	2
Oakengates Town	1921	1939	48
Oakham United	1988	1993	13
	1996		
Oakmere (Liverpool)	1937	1939	3
Oakwood	1991	1998	16
	2007		
	2010	2011	
	2017		
Odd Down	1947	1949	55
	1951		
	1994	1996	
	1998	2009	
	2011	2020	
Old Brightonians	1885	1893	22
Old Carthusians	1880	1892	50
Old Castle Swifts	1895		2
Old Cranleighans	1892	1893	2
Old Etonians	1874	1877	80
	1879	1893	
Old Foresters	1878	1889	36
Old Grammarians (Ipswich)	1947	1949	3
Old Harrovians	1877	1882	29
	1886	1891	
	1893		
Old Hill Wanderers	1893	1895	8
Old Hullensians	1938	1939	2
Old Johnians	1929		14
	1931	1940	
Old Kingstonians	1910	1911	14
	1913	1915	
Old Lyonian	1923		26
	1926	1940	
Old Philberdians	1881		1
Old Salopians	1877		1
Old St Mark's	1888	1893	12
Old St Paul's	1890		4
Old St Stephens	1895	1898	8
Old Westminsters	1883	1894	43
Old Whittington Mutuals	1910		1
Old Woodstock Town	2011	2013	6
Old Wykehamists	1877	1878	24
	1884	1893	
Old Xaverians	1921	1928	9
Oldbury Town	1888	1891	5
Oldbury United	1973	2009	74
Oldfields	1909		1
Oldham Athletic	1906	2020	279
Oldham County	1897		3
Oldham Town	1994	2010	29
Oldland Abbotonians	2014		3
	2017		
Oldswinford	1985	1988	8
Ollerton Colliery	1935	1950	20
Olney Town	1979	1980	4
Olympian	1900		1
Olympic	1882		11
	1900	1904	
Oreston Rovers	1933		3
Orient	1967	1987	68
Ormskirk	1972	1975	9
Ormskirk (1)	1915		4
Orpington	1911		1
Orrell	1924		21
	1934	1939	
	1947	1950	
Orwell Works	1923	1925	7
	1937		
	1939		
Osberton Radiator (Oxford)	1935	1951	18
Osborne Athletic	1921	1926	20
	1928	1940	
Ossett Albion	1963	1968	90
	1982	2018	
Ossett Town	1939	1958	100
	1991	2018	
Ossett United	2019	2020	7
Oswaldtwistle Rovers	1885	1889	42
	1893	1907	
	1909	1910	
Oswestry	1883	1889	16
Oswestry Town	1921	1939	146
	1948	1963	
	1965	1987	
Oswestry United	1898	1910	44
	1913	1915	
Ottery St Mary	1981	1983	9
	1986	1988	
Ouston Rovers	1923	1924	4
Ouston United	1938	1939	9
Over Wanderers	1888	1891	6
Overseal Swifts	1912	1914	4
Owlerton	1888	1891	8
Owston Park Rangers	1930		13
	1932	1936	
Oxford City	1896		292
	1898	1989	
	1993	2020	
Oxford Cygnets	1897	1900	5
Oxford United	1961	2020	165
Oxford University	1873	1880	47
Oxhey Jets	2006	2020	31
PO Engineers (Beddington)	1933	1939	20
PO Engineers (Wallington)	1940		2
	1947		

278

Padiham to Raunds Town

Club	Year	Year	Num
Padiham	1884		57
	1886		
	1903	1906	
	1908	1915	
	2005	2020	
Page Green Old Boys	1907		14
	1909		
	1914	1920	
Paget Rangers	1985	2002	31
Pagham	1973	1976	87
	1980	1986	
	1988	1999	
	2002	2020	
Palmers, Jarrow	1920		4
Pandon Temperance	1915	1922	10
	1925	1926	
Panthers	1875	1880	9
Park Grange	1888	1889	5
Park Royal	1931	1936	16
Parkeston Railway	1926	1929	8
	1932	1933	
Parkgate	1998	2019	41
Parkgate & Rawmarsh Utd.	1910	1912	4
Parkgate United	1897	1900	12
	1909		
Parkgate Welfare	1951		2
Parkgate Works Sports	1920		1
Parkhouse Colliery	1950	1951	5
Parliament Street Methodists	1950	1955	6
Parson Drove United	1948	1951	19
	1975	1982	
Partick Thistle	1886	1887	6
Parton Athletic	1921	1922	10
	1925		
	1933		
Parton United	1947	1949	8
Paulton Rovers	1905	1908	190
	1910	1937	
	1939	1954	
	1979	2020	
Paxmans Athletic	1924		2
Peacehaven & Telscombe	1973	1978	81
	1980	1984	
	1987	2005	
	2007	2020	
Pearl Assurance	1920		1
Pease & Partners	1932		10
	1934	1937	
Peasedown MW	1939	1957	25
Peasedown St John's	1913	1920	17
	1922	1926	
Peasley Cross Athletic	1932	1933	7
	1935	1936	
Pegasus Juniors	2006	2016	23
Pegswood United	1935		2
Pelaw	1913		17
	1927	1937	
Pelsall Villa	1993	2004	32
	2008	2009	
	2011		
Pelton Fell	1926		2
Pembroke Dock	1914	1915	4
	1922		
Pendlebury	1907	1909	3
Penistone Church	2016	2020	10
Penrith	1907	1936	207
	1938	1939	
	1947	1951	
	1953	1995	
	1998	2020	
Penryn Athletic	2007		1
Penzance	1953	1962	49
	1968	1971	
	1973	1983	
	2006	2007	
Percy Main Amateurs	1928		2
	1982		
Pershore Town	1994	2000	19
	2009	2010	
Peterborough & Fletton Utd.	1925	1933	43
Peterborough (1)	1895	1897	3
Peterborough City	1993		1
Peterborough City (1)	1908	1915	27
	1924		
Peterborough G.N. Loco	1908	1914	22
	1922	1929	
Peterborough Northern Star	2013	2020	13
Peterborough Sports	2016	2020	21
Peterborough Town	1905		3
	1907		
Peterborough United	1936	2020	289
Peterbro' Westwood Works	1915		32
	1921	1949	
Peterlee Newtown	1980	2006	52
Petersfield Town	2010	2019	16
Petersfield United	1985	1990	11
	1993	1994	
Petter Sports	1963	1965	3
Petters United	1914	1915	3
Pewsey Vale	1948		9
	1951		
	2012	2015	
	2019		
Pewsey YM	1940	1947	4

Club	Year	Year	Num
Phoenix Bessemer	1883		3
Phoenix Sports	2015	2020	16
Phorpres Sports	1934	1935	6
Pica	1948		1
Pickering St George's	1930		1
Pickering Town	1994	2020	61
Pilgrims	1874	1885	24
Pilkington Recreation	1928	1940	32
	1948	1952	
Pilkington XXX	2008	2011	10
	2013		
Pinchbeck United	2019	2020	2
Pinner	1935	1951	14
Pinxton	1907	1912	29
	1922	1925	
Pirelli General Cables	1948	1951	6
Players Athletic	1921		11
	1952	1959	
Pleasley United	1915		1
Plumstead St John's	1907	1911	8
Plymouth & Stonehouse Gas Co.	1936		5
Plymouth Argyle	1904	2020	256
Plymouth Civil Service	1928	1930	10
Plymouth Parkway	2013	2020	24
Plymouth United	1934		5
	1947	1948	
	1951		
Polytechnic	1893	1894	23
	1914	1915	
	1921	1923	
	1925	1930	
	1947		
	1949	1951	
Pontefract Borough	1928	1929	4
Pontefract Collieries	1995	1998	37
	2001	2020	
Pontypridd	1913	1914	22
	1920	1926	
Poole	1892		61
	1903	1911	
	1913	1920	
	1922	1931	
Poole Town	1932		209
	1934	1939	
	1947	1996	
	2007	2020	
Port Clarence	1889	1893	7
Port Sunlight	1896		16
	1904	1905	
	1923	1926	
	1949	1950	
Port Talbot	1913	1915	3
Port Vale	1913	2020	280
Port of London Authority	1939		1
Portfield	1987	2000	29
Porth Athletic	1922	1923	7
Porthleven	2003	2007	6
Porthmadog	1968	1981	22
Portishead Town	2010	2011	8
	2017		
Portland	1912	1913	2
Portland Prison Officers	1908	1910	7
Portland United	1922	1930	94
	1948	1971	
	2003	2006	
	2018	2020	
Portrack Shamrocks	1938	1939	17
	1947	1950	
Portsea Gas Company	1922	1926	17
Portslade	1926		1
Portsmouth	1900	2020	297
Portsmouth Albion	1932		1
Portsmouth Amateurs	1915	1926	16
Portsmouth Electricity	1938	1939	6
	1947		
Portsmouth Gas Company	1927	1930	8
Portsmouth Rovers (Lancs)	1910	1922	18
	1924	1929	
Portsmouth Royal Navy	1997	2001	10
Post Office Telecoms	1949		2
Potters Bar Town	1996	2020	66
Potton United	1949	1956	84
	1969	1982	
	1985		
	1987	1993	
	1996	2001	
	2005	2011	
	2016		
	2018	2020	
Prescot	1892	1893	20
	1921	1928	
Prescot AFC	1991	1995	8
Prescot B.I.C.C	1939		3
	1949	1950	
Prescot Cables	1929	1939	157
	1947	1965	
	1981	1990	
	1996		
	1999	2020	
Prescot Town	1966	1980	22
Prescot Wire Works	1921	1923	6
Pressed Steel	1936	1951	15
Preston Colliery	1921	1928	21
Preston North End	1884		365
	1886	2020	

Index of clubs

Club	Year	Year	Num
Prestwich Heys	1971	1984	29
	2019		
Princes End United	1990	1991	5
Prospect United	1920		16
	1922	1926	
Prudhoe	1900	1901	5
	1904		
Prudhoe Castle	1920	1924	11
Prudhoe East End	1990	1994	10
Prudhoe Town	1995	1997	10
	2004	2007	
Punjab United	2020		1
Purfleet	1989	2003	45
Purton	1932	1933	17
	1935	1951	
Purton West End	1930		1
Pwllheli & District	1954	1964	33
	1968	1972	
	1976		
Pye Radio	1935	1938	6
Pyebank	1900		1
Queen's Park (Glasgow)	1872	1873	39
	1877	1878	
	1880	1887	
Queen's Park Rangers	1896	1926	307
	1928	2020	
Quorn	2003	2020	41
RAE Farnborough	1920		5
	1922	1924	
RAF Cranwell	1921		3
RAF Halton	1935	1937	5
RAF Henlow	1922	1923	12
	1931	1933	
RAF Martlesham	1933		9
	1935	1937	
	1939		
RAF Uxbridge	1929	1931	7
RAMC Aldershot	1923	1927	35
	1929	1939	
RAOC Cosham	1926	1928	6
RAOC Hilsea	1929	1934	28
	1947		
	1949	1951	
RASC	1924	1925	3
RGA Gosport	1922		2
RGA Tynemouth	1913		1
RGA Weymouth	1913	1915	4
RM Chatham	1925	1934	23
RM Deal	1932	1940	15
RM Portsmouth	1926	1930	22
	1934	1935	
RMLI Chatham	1924		1
RN Depot	1921	1922	2
RNVR Mitcham	1932		1
RTM Newcastle	1995	1998	8
Racing Club Warwick	1977	2009	65
	2019	2020	
Radcliffe	2019	2020	5
Radcliffe Borough	1972	1980	105
	1984	2018	
Radcliffe Olympic	2011	2012	8
Radcliffe Welfare United	1948	1949	2
Radford	2010		8
	2016	2020	
Radstock Town	1906	1910	113
	1913		
	1921	1949	
	1951	1956	
	1987	1992	
	2007	2015	
Rainham Town	1948	1951	67
	1955	1964	
	1966	1971	
	1973	1974	
	1977	1994	
Rainworth MW	2008	2019	28
Raleigh Athletic	1931		20
	1938	1939	
	1949	1955	
Ramblers	1876	1879	5
Ramsbottom	1909	1910	3
Ramsbottom United	1999	2020	55
Ramsgate	1974	1981	97
	1983	1984	
	1988	1991	
	1994	1996	
	1999	2020	
Ramsgate (1)	1922	1925	15
	1935	1936	
Ramsgate Athletic	1946	1973	74
Ramsgate Grenville	1938	1939	3
Ramsgate Press Wanderers	1934		3
Ramsgate Town	1912	1915	7
Rangers (Glasgow)	1886	1887	8
Rangers (London)	1881	1882	4
Ranks (Hull)	1937	1939	8
Ransome & Marles	1928	1939	57
	1947	1962	
Raunds St Peter's	1908		1
Raunds Town	1903		82
	1908	1915	
	1921	1922	
	1992	2012	
	2016		
	2018	2019	

279

Ravenscourt Amateurs to Scunthorpe United

Index of clubs

Club	From	To	No.
Ravenscourt Amateurs	1911	1912	5
Ravensthorpe	1937	1940	7
Rawden	1922		1
Rawmarsh Albion	1905	1910	12
Rawmarsh Athletic	1921	1923	4
Rawmarsh Town	1913	1915	4
Rawmarsh Welfare	1931	1955	76
	1969	1974	
Rawtenstall	1885	1889	7
Rayners Lane	1987	1993	14
Raynes Park Vale	1996	1997	41
	1999	2000	
	2004	2020	
Reading	1878	2020	392
Reading Abbey	1881	1882	6
Reading Amateurs	1897	1898	16
	1904	1909	
	1922	1923	
Reading City	2019	2020	4
Reading Hornets	1877	1878	2
Reading Minster	1881	1885	10
Reading Ramblers	1899	1900	5
Reading Town	1998	2016	30
Reading United	1920	1921	4
Reckitt's (Hull)	1912		13
	1924	1929	
	1932		
Redbourne Sports	1936	1938	9
Redbridge	2005	2020	31
Redbridge Forest	1990	1992	6
Redcar	1884	1890	21
	1914	1922	
Redcar Albion	1959	1960	2
Redditch	1911	1936	48
	1955	1957	
	1961	1962	
	1965	1969	
Redditch Town	1894	1897	8
Redditch United	1970	2020	133
Redfearns	1912	1914	5
Redford Sports (Wycombe)	1939	1940	5
	1947	1948	
Redhill	1898		245
	1900	1902	
	1904	1908	
	1910	1924	
	1926	1933	
	1935	2020	
Reigate Priory	1872	1877	13
	1928	1930	
Remnants	1878	1883	12
Rendel	1891	1898	16
Renton	1887		4
Retford Town	1922	1924	73
	1951	1980	
Retford United	2005	2018	33
Reyrolles	1940		1
Rhiwderin	1915	1920	3
	1922		
Rhosllanerchrugog	1891	1893	4
Rhyl	1903		179
	1905	1910	
	1912		
	1932	1934	
	1936	1992	
Rhyl Athletic	1924	1931	39
Rhyl United	1899		4
	1901		
Rhymney Town	1915		5
	1922		
Richmond Association	1899	1907	23
Richmond Town	1903		3
Rickmansworth Town	1949	1950	3
Riddings	1892	1898	8
Riley Brothers	1907		1
Ringmer	1971	2016	80
Ringwood Town	1935	1936	14
	2009	2013	
	2018		
Ripley	1909	1910	7
Ripley Athletic	1904		4
	1909		
Ripley Colliery	1921		2
Ripley Town	1928	1938	28
Ripley Town & Athletic	1911	1915	19
Risborough Rangers	2016		4
	2018		
Risca Stars	1922		2
Rise Carr	1920	1923	7
Road Sea Southampton	1984	1987	14
Rocester	1990	2019	62
Rochdale	1909	2020	254
Rochdale (1)	1898	1903	13
Rochdale Town	2015		1
Rochester	1876	1893	26
Rochester United	2016	2019	9
Rock Ferry	1897	1898	6
Rock-a-Nore	1905	1909	11
	1925	1928	
Rockingham Colliery	1904	1907	10
	1936	1937	
Rogerstone	1920	1922	5
Roman Glass St George	2019	2020	3
Romford	1995	1996	60
	1998	2020	
Romford (1)	1879	1886	50
	1896	1900	
	1904	1915	
Romford (2)	1930		150
	1932	1978	
Romsey Town	1949	1951	35
	1984		
	1989	1993	
	2010	2015	
	2019	2020	
Romulus	2006	2020	37
Rose Green	1935	1937	7
Rosehill	1933	1934	5
Rossendale	1884	1889	25
	1893	1897	
Rossendale United	1899		201
	1901		
	1903	1915	
	1922	1924	
	1934	1939	
	1949	1978	
	1980	1983	
	1985	2011	
Rossington Main	1922	1929	67
	1931	1940	
	1994	1997	
	1999	2013	
Rotherham Amateurs	1920		15
	1922	1929	
Rotherham County	1906	1925	48
Rotherham Main	1906	1909	6
Rotherham Swifts	1889	1891	7
Rotherham Town	1884	1896	123
	1901	1903	
	1905	1925	
Rotherham United	1926	2020	230
Rothwell	1892	1893	4
Rothwell Athletic	1920	1922	7
Rothwell Corinthians	2009	2013	16
	2016	2020	
Rothwell Parish Church	1915	1921	5
Rothwell Town	1908		142
	1923	1934	
	1950		
	1956	1962	
	1964	1966	
	1968	2012	
Rothwell Town Swifts	1898	1902	10
	1904		
Rothwell White Rose	1909	1910	15
	1912	1915	
Roundell	1902		5
	1904		
Roundway Hospital (Devizes)	1950		1
Rowntrees	1920	1922	4
Royal Arsenal	1890	1891	6
Royal Artillery Portsmouth	1897	1899	10
Royal Engineers	1872	1889	65
Royal Engineers United	1900		1
Royal Engs. Aldershot	1910	1914	13
Royal Engs. Comrades (Eastb'rne)	1922	1924	6
Royal Engs. Service Battalion	1904		1
Royal Engs. Training Battalion	1895	1899	10
Royal Ordnance	1895	1897	9
Royal Scots (Chatham)	1896		1
Royal Scots Fusiliers	1895	1896	4
	1900		
Royal Welsh Warehouse	1903		1
Royal Wootton Bassett Town	2016	2020	8
Royston Midland Institute	1912	1913	7
Royston Town	1948	1950	81
	1955		
	1983	2020	
Royston United	1901	1904	10
Royton	1892		1
Rufford Colliery	1920		10
	1922		
	1934	1937	
	1949	1951	
Rugby Town	2006	2020	45
Rugby Town (1)	1913	1924	12
	1934	1935	
Rugby Town (2)	1949	1950	58
	1952	1971	
	1973		
Rugby United	2002	2005	8
Rugeley	1922	1923	2
Ruislip	1989		3
Ruislip Manor	1949	1950	86
	1963		
	1965	1970	
	1976	1983	
	1985	2008	
Ruislip Town	1949	1950	2
Runcorn	1920	1923	219
	1930	1932	
	1937	2002	
Runcorn FC Halton	2003	2006	13
Runcorn Linnets	2009	2020	33
Runcorn Town	2012	2020	28
Runnymede	1879		1
Rushall Olympic	1982	2020	88
Rushall Olympic (1)	1922		2
Rushden	1893	1904	28
Rushden & Diamonds	1993	2011	63
Rushden & Higham United	2012	2014	3
Rushden Fosse	1907	1911	15
	1913	1915	
Rushden Town	1921	1992	146
Rushden Windmill	1909	1915	13
Rusthall	2018	2020	6
Rutherford College	1899		9
	1904		
	1913	1920	
Rycroft Athletic	1922		2
Ryde	1899	1900	12
	1905	1909	
	1911	1912	
Ryde Sports	1922	1953	98
	1959		
	1969	1976	
	1993	1997	
Rye & Iden United	2005	2006	3
Rye United	2007	2009	8
	2013	2014	
Ryhill & Havercroft United	1937	1938	2
Ryhill Liberal	1921		1
Ryhope CW	1962	1973	24
Ryhope Colliery Welfare	2016		2
Ryhope Community Association	1984	1991	28
	1994	1999	
Ryhope Comrades	1920		1
Ryhope Villa	1914	1915	3
Rylands	2020		1
Ryton	2007	2011	10
Ryton & Crawcrook Albion	2012		1
Saffron Walden Town	1877		91
	1879		
	1881		
	1939	1940	
	1947	1950	
	1980	1997	
	2000	2004	
	2006	2012	
	2014	2020	
Sale Holmefield	1907		6
	1909	1910	
Salford City	1991	2020	73
Salford United	1908	1910	7
Salisbury	2017	2020	14
Salisbury (1)	1906	1911	38
	1913		
	1915	1921	
	1923	1928	
Salisbury (2)	1948	1995	165
Salisbury City	1996	2014	69
Salisbury City (1)	1929	1939	41
Salisbury Corinthians	1922	1949	43
Saltash United	1971	1972	76
	1979	1982	
	1984	1997	
	2005		
	2007	2016	
	2019	2020	
Saltburn	1905	1910	18
	1912	1914	
Saltburn Swifts	1895	1897	5
Saltdean United	1998	2008	28
	2018	2020	
Salterbeck	1947		1
Saltney	1910		2
Sandbach Ramblers	1905	1907	55
	1914	1927	
	1929	1934	
	1938	1939	
	1969	1975	
Sandbach United	2019		1
Sandhurst (Liverpool)	1939		2
Sandhurst Town	1999	2014	29
	2019		
Sandiacre Excelsior Foundry	1933	1939	8
Sandiacre Olympic	1906	1908	4
Sandown	1927	1928	13
	1932		
	1939	1950	
Sandwell Borough	1990	2001	28
Sandy Albion	1933	1939	14
Sandygate Excelsior	1905		2
Sankey of Wellington	1962	1965	10
Savoy (Southall)	1927		1
Savoy Hotel	1925		1
Sawbridgeworth	1948	1950	17
	2001	2008	
Sawbridgeworth Town	2012	2020	14
Sawston United	1949		1
Saxons	1877		1
Scalegill	1947	1950	7
Scarborough	1888	1893	272
	1902	1906	
	1908	1926	
	1928	2008	
Scarborough Athletic	2010	2020	31
Scarborough Junior Imperial	1935	1938	4
Scarborough Juniors	1938	1939	4
Scarborough Penguins	1925	1929	7
Scarborough Rangers	1893		1
Schorne College	1889	1891	4
Scotswood	1909	1924	56
	1927	1940	
Scunthorpe United	1910	2020	331

Seaford to Southwick

Club			
Seaford	1910	1912	3
Seaforth Albion	1931		4
	1934	1935	
Seaham Albion	1898	1900	3
Seaham Colliery Welfare	1922		52
	1925	1928	
	1931	1956	
Seaham Harbour	1893		57
	1895		
	1897	1900	
	1910	1929	
Seaham Red Star	1982	2011	75
	2014	2020	
Seaham United	1949	1950	2
Seaham Villa	1911	1912	2
Seaham White Star	1904		10
	1907	1909	
Seaton Delaval	1914	1923	16
	1925	1926	
Selby Mizpah	1909	1910	3
Selby OCO	1927	1935	20
Selby Olympia	1921		6
	1925	1926	
Selby Town	1922	1924	141
	1930	1939	
	1947	1973	
	1976	1980	
	1997	2013	
	2019		
Selsey	1968	1972	64
	1977	1980	
	1991	2016	
	2020		
Selston	2020		1
Seven Acre & Sidcup	2016		3
Sevenoaks Town	2006	2020	36
Severalls Athletic	1929	1931	17
	1933	1939	
	1947		
Shaddongate United	1902	1904	4
Shaftesbury	1910	1911	24
	1933	1935	
	1951	1954	
	2008	2010	
	2018	2020	
Shankhouse	1888	1903	67
	1905	1906	
	1926	1937	
	1939	1947	
	1949	1955	
Shanklin & Lake	1933	1934	2
Sharpness	1986	1991	13
Shaw Lane	2017	2018	6
Shaw Lane Aquaforce	2016		1
Shawbury United	2009	2010	14
	2013	2019	
Sheepbridge Works	1894	1898	10
	1922		
Sheerwater	2020		1
Sheffield	1874	1908	208
	1910	1932	
	1934	1939	
	1947	1960	
	1990	2020	
Sheffield Heeley	1882	1892	22
Sheffield Providence	1880	1882	5
Sheffield Simplex Works	1920		1
Sheffield United	1890	2020	392
Sheffield Walkley	1890	1891	2
Sheffield Wednesday	1881	1886	417
	1888	2020	
Shefford Town	1951		7
	1955	1958	
Shell (Ellesmere Port)	1949	1950	3
Shell Mex	1931	1936	16
Shepherds Bush	1899	1914	55
Sheppey United	1893	1902	220
	1904	1966	
	1968	2001	
	2017	2020	
Shepshed	1898		1
Shepshed Albion	1910	1911	27
	1913	1915	
	1922	1927	
	1950		
	1992	1993	
Shepshed Charterhouse	1982	1991	25
Shepshed Dynamo	1996	2020	61
Shepton Mallet	2002	2010	29
	2014	2020	
Shepton Mallet Town	1951		14
	1979	1986	
Sherborne	1937	1938	4
	1940		
Sherborne Town	2007	2018	27
Sheringham	1928	1939	42
	1948	1962	
Sherwood Colliery	1949	1951	6
	2020		
Shields Albion	1913	1914	3
Shifnal Town	1982	1986	37
	1996	2003	
	2008	2013	
Shilbottle CW	1949	1951	4

Club			
Shildon	1904		296
	1907	2020	
Shildon United	1899		1
Shiphams	1921		1
Shirebrook	1913	1933	67
	1951	1953	
Shirebrook Athletic	1910		1
Shirebrook MW	1954	1962	17
Shirebrook Town	2003	2017	34
	2019		
Shirley Town	1936	1938	7
Shobnall Villa	1912		4
Shoeburyness Garrison	1909	1925	24
Sholing	2011	2020	34
Sholing Athletic	1921	1925	14
Sholing Sports	1984	1993	12
Shoreham	1903	1912	116
	1922	1927	
	1933	1939	
	1947	1956	
	1987	2001	
	2006	2020	
Shorts Sports	1946	1947	2
Shortwood United	1986	1994	73
	2001	2020	
Shotton CW	1933	1939	27
	1948	1951	
	1955		
	1957	1962	
Shotton Comrades	1986		28
	1988	1993	
	1996	2004	
Shredded Wheat	1932		5
	1934		
	1936	1937	
Shrewsbury Town	1888	1891	327
	1899	1904	
	1909	2020	
Shrewton United	2012		2
Shrivenham	2008	2016	18
	2020		
Shropshire Wanderers	1874	1878	12
Sidlesham	2004	2006	3
Sidley United	1974	1979	23
	2006	2014	
Sileby Rangers	2015		3
Silksworth CW	1949	1956	20
	1961	1962	
Silsden	2005	2017	32
	2019	2020	
Silverwood Colliery	1910	1920	35
	1922		
	1930	1936	
Singers (Coventry)	1893	1894	8
	1896	1898	
Sittingbourne	1894	1897	288
	1899	1910	
	1912	1933	
	1935	1939	
	1948	2020	
Sittingbourne Paper Mills	1931		1
Skegness Town	1950	1984	83
	1986		
Skelmersdale United	1906	1907	222
	1915		
	1921	1983	
	1985	1995	
	1998	2020	
Skinningrove Steel Works	1913	1914	3
Skinningrove United	1907	1912	9
Skinningrove Works	1951	1954	4
Skipton Town	1910		1
Slade Green	1991	2010	31
Sleaford Town	2009	2020	21
Slimbridge	2006	2008	29
	2012	2020	
Slipway (Wallsend)	1915		3
Slough	1895	1902	97
	1904	1911	
	1914	1940	
Slough Centre	1949	1951	12
	1953	1956	
Slough Town	1949	2020	258
Slough Trading Estate	1923		1
Slough United	1946	1948	16
Small Heath	1889	1905	46
Small Heath Alliance	1882	1888	17
Smethwick Carriage Works	1895		1
Smith's Dock	1936	1938	10
	1949		
	1951		
Sneinton	1908	1931	29
Snowdown CW	1950	1961	42
	1968	1972	
	1978	1980	
Soham Rangers	1938		1
Soham Town Rangers	1958	1959	100
	1965	1991	
	1995	2020	
Solent University	2020		1
Solihull	1939		2
Solihull Borough	1991	2007	66
Solihull Moors	2008	2020	37
Somerset Rovers	1892	1893	3
Somersett Ambury V&E	2002		3

Club			
Somersham Town	1955		4
	1958	1959	
Somerton Amateurs	1947	1949	3
Soundwell	1947	1951	10
South Ashford Invicta	1909		1
South Bank	1887	1893	228
	1895	1910	
	1912	1939	
	1947	1968	
	1970	1971	
	1975	1993	
South Bank East End	1921	1930	34
	1933	1939	
	1948	1951	
South Bank St Peters	1934	1936	24
	1938	1939	
	1948	1951	
South Farnborough Athletic	1908	1910	11
	1912	1915	
South Hetton CW	1934	1935	12
	1949	1951	
South Kirkby Colliery	1906	1955	99
South Kirkby United	1921		1
South Liverpool	1899	1900	165
	1912	1921	
	1936	1953	
	1955	1991	
South Lynn	1950	1951	3
South Normanton Athletic	2006	2008	19
	2016	2020	
South Normanton Colliery	1912	1931	39
South Normanton MW	1935	1936	36
	1938		
	1949	1963	
South Normanton Rangers	1913		2
South Normanton St Michael's	1909	1911	6
South Norwood	1873	1880	14
South Park	2011	2020	32
South Pontop Villa	1920		6
	1926	1928	
South Reading	1883	1888	15
South Shields	1912	1930	37
South Shields (1)	1899	1901	6
South Shields (2)	1938	1939	96
	1947	1974	
South Shields (3)	1994	2014	54
	2017	2020	
South Shields Adelaide	1908	1911	16
South Shields Albion	1912		1
South Shields Athletic	1902		2
South Shields Corinthians	1932	1933	3
South Shields Ex-schoolboys	1951		2
South Shields Parkside	1910	1915	14
South Shore	1883	1900	57
South Tooting	1913	1914	8
South Weald	1904	1912	20
South West Ham	1897		3
	1933	1934	
Southall	1874	1877	239
	1902	1906	
	1910		
	1912	1975	
	1981	1988	
	1991	2003	
	2006		
	2018	2020	
Southall & Ealing Borough	1976	1980	16
Southall Town	2003	2004	2
Southam United	2008	2014	13
	2016		
Southampton	1898	2020	344
Southampton CS	1926		5
	1928		
Southampton Cambridge	1911	1912	8
	1914	1915	
Southampton St Mary's	1892	1897	23
Southend Amateurs	1913	1914	4
Southend Athletic	1904	1907	5
Southend Corinthians	1921	1922	2
Southend Manor	1997	1998	48
	2000	2020	
Southend United	1908	2020	283
Southern Rail, Croydon	1925		4
Southern United	1905	1907	11
Southfield	1888		1
Southill Park	1878	1879	2
Southport	1920	2020	259
Southport (1)	1883	1886	7
Southport Central	1889		93
	1893	1915	
Southport Leyland Road	1950		1
Southport Park Villa	1911		3
	1914	1915	
Southwick	1910	1912	171
	1915		
	1922	1924	
	1926	1947	
	1949		
	1951	1961	
	1969	1997	
	2000	2005	
	2009	2010	
	2017		
Southwick (1)	1891	1893	23
	1904	1908	

Spalding United to Tate Institute

Club	From	To	Count
Spalding United	1922	1923	183
	1927	1935	
	1938	1939	
	1948	1963	
	1965	2020	
Spelthorne Sports	2016	2020	13
Spen Black & White	1913	1925	30
	1927	1934	
Spencer Melksham	1924	1925	3
Spencer Moulton	1921	1933	49
	1936	1939	
	1947		
	1949	1954	
	1970		
Spennymoor	1892		1
Spennymoor Town	2006	2020	48
Spennymoor United	1906	1929	299
	1931	1964	
	1966	2005	
Spilsby	1881	1885	7
	1921	1922	
Sporting Bengal United	2006	2010	21
	2013	2020	
Sporting Club Thamesmead	2017		1
Sporting Khalsa	2013		26
	2015	2020	
Squires Gate	2001	2020	40
St Albans	1895	1896	9
	1898	1899	
St Albans (Upton)	1881	1882	2
St Albans Abbey	1907	1908	2
St Albans City	1909	2020	289
St Andrews	2010	2011	11
	2013		
	2015	2019	
St Anne's Oldland	1928		2
St Anthony's Institute	1922	1925	11
St Austell	1914	1915	41
	1926	1931	
	1948	1956	
	1958		
	1964	1965	
	1967	1968	
	1991	1992	
St Bart's Hospital	1882		2
St Blazey	1951		126
	1953	1961	
	1963	2012	
	2014		
St Cleopatra's Old Boys	1921		2
St Cuthbert's	1930	1931	3
St Francis Rangers	2010	2017	9
St Frideswides (Oxford)	1949		1
St Helens	1902		3
St Helens Recreation	1903	1913	37
St Helens Town	1903	1915	165
	1927		
	1929		
	1947	1971	
	1975	2016	
St Helens United	1920		1
St Ives Town	1908		41
	1951		
	2006	2020	
St James	1886		1
St Leonards	1999	2004	15
St Leonards (1)	1902	1906	8
St Leonards Amateurs	1912	1914	7
St Leonards Stamcroft	1997	1998	8
St Luke's	1897		1
St Margaretsbury	2001	2020	57
St Mark's	1878		1
St Neots & District	1923		42
	1931	1939	
	1948	1957	
St Neots St Mary	1949	1950	2
St Neots Town	1958	1982	107
	1998	2020	
St Peter's Albion	1898	1901	35
	1921	1924	
	1926	1931	
	1935	1936	
St Peter's Institute	1880	1881	2
St Philips Athletic	1926		14
	1930	1931	
	1933	1938	
St Philips Marsh Adult School	1933	1939	27
	1947	1948	
	1950	1951	
St Stephens	1878		1
Stableford Works	1922	1927	10
Stafford Rangers	1885	1886	287
	1895	1896	
	1902	1933	
	1935	1937	
	1939		
	1948	1966	
	1968	2020	
Stafford Road	1880	1886	21
	1888		
Stafford Town	2001	2004	16
	2014	2015	
Staffordshire Casuals	1949	1950	2
Staines Lagonda	1924	1925	5
Staines Lammas	2012	2015	10
Staines Town	1905	1908	181
	1910		
	1912		
	1926	1935	
	1959	1961	
	1968	2020	
Staithes United	1922		1
Stakeford Albion	1936		4
Stalybridge Celtic	1913	2020	278
Stalybridge Rovers	1895	1908	32
Stamco	1996		1
Stamford	1912	1939	206
	1948	1992	
	1994	2020	
Standard Telephones	1930	1931	2
Stanley	1898		2
Stanley United	1901	1902	126
	1904	1929	
	1931	1934	
	1936		
	1939	1960	
	1962	1975	
Stanlow Social	1938	1939	3
Stansted	1950		38
	1997	2000	
	2003	2020	
Stanton Hill DS&S	1922		3
Stanton Hill Victoria	1907	1910	13
	1912	1913	
Stanton Ironworks	1950		2
Stanway Rovers	2004	2020	42
Stapenhill	1995	2002	20
	2008	2009	
	2015		
Staple Hill	1896	1910	35
Stapleford Brookhill	1935		1
Stapleford Town	1896	1904	18
	1906		
Staveley	1882	1892	35
	1896		
Staveley MW	1998	2020	52
Staveley Town	1914	1930	44
Staveley Welfare	1937	1938	9
	1949	1951	
Steel, Peech & Tozer Social Serv.	1949	1951	6
Sterling Athletic	1922	1924	4
Stevenage	2011	2020	28
Stevenage Athletic	1970	1977	20
Stevenage Borough	1984	2010	93
Stevenage Town	1928	1929	56
	1932	1940	
	1949	1961	
	1963	1968	
Stewartby Works	1938	1939	7
	1948	1951	
Stewarts & Lloyds	1937		8
	1939		
	1947	1949	
Stewarts & Lloyds (2)	1993	1996	35
	1998	2004	
	2008	2014	
Steyning	1905		2
Steyning Town	1981	1985	26
	1987	1997	
	2005	2006	
	2018		
Steyning Town Community	2020		2
Stockport County	1893	2020	287
Stockport Sports	2013	2015	5
Stocksbridge Church	1915		4
Stocksbridge Park Steels	1993	2020	60
Stocksbridge Works	1950	1954	44
	1956	1960	
	1962	1966	
	1973	1976	
Stockton	1889	1893	185
	1895	1956	
	1958	1975	
Stockton (2)	1988	1999	21
Stockton Heath	1957	1960	5
Stockton Malleable Institute	1924	1928	13
Stockton Shamrocks	1929		1
Stockton St John's	1900	1904	6
Stockton Town	2018	2020	8
Stoke	1884	1925	102
Stoke City	1926	2020	244
Stoke United	1949		2
Stokenchurch	1931	1935	5
Stokesley SC	2009	2013	9
Stone Dominoes	2004	2013	19
Stone Old Alleynians	2020		1
Stonehouse	1948	1976	43
Stoneycroft	1939		9
	1948	1951	
Stork	1950		18
	1957	1966	
Stork (Purfleet)	1938	1939	2
Stotfold	1995	2020	64
Stourbridge	1892	1908	317
	1911	1913	
	1915	1939	
	1947	2020	
Stourport Swifts	1993	2020	64
Stourton United	1910		2
Stowmarket	1932	1933	49
	1936	1938	
	1952	1956	
	1958	1963	
	1976	1986	
Stowmarket Corinthians	1949	1951	10
Stowmarket Town	1987	2010	56
	2012		
	2018	2020	
Stratford Town	1967	1971	80
	1977	1979	
	1990	2020	
Streatham Town	1934	1937	12
Street	1900	1904	160
	1911	1939	
	1947	1962	
	1967	1972	
	2000	2020	
Stroud	1990	1992	8
Studley	2003	2015	21
Sudbury Town	1951	2000	146
Sudbury Wanderers	1995	1999	17
Summerstown	1908	1928	48
Sun Sports	2016	2018	6
Sunbeam	1922		1
Sunderland	1885	2020	364
Sunderland Albion	1889	1892	18
Sunderland Black Watch	1904		5
	1906		
Sunderland Nissan	2006	2009	8
Sunderland Olympic	1892		1
Sunderland RCA	2008	2020	28
Sunderland Rovers	1913	1915	21
Sunderland Royal Rovers	1902	1912	31
Sunderland Ryhope CW	2017	2020	6
Sunderland West End	1903	1911	49
	1920	1929	
Sunniside Rangers	1927		1
Surbiton Hill	1893		1
Surbiton Town	1951		1
Surrey Wanderers	1912	1913	5
Sutton (Hull)	1913		5
	1921		
	1925		
Sutton Athletic	2020		4
Sutton Coldfield Town	1957	1960	139
	1972	2020	
Sutton Common Rovers	2016	2020	10
Sutton Court	1915		1
Sutton Junction	1907		60
	1909	1923	
	1925	1934	
Sutton Town	1893	1897	208
	1903	1939	
	1950	1991	
Sutton Town (2)	2004	2007	10
Sutton Town (Birmingham)	1936		23
	1938	1939	
	1949	1956	
Sutton United	1912	1924	305
	1926	2020	
Suttons	1931		1
Swadlincote	1896	1897	10
	1899	1901	
Swaffham Town	2014	2020	9
Swaine Hill United	1908		2
Swallwell Axwell Rovers	1896		1
Swanage Town	1962	1963	2
Swanage Town & Herston	1988	1996	24
Swanley Athletic	1934	1938	6
Swanscombe	1896	1903	20
	1905		
Swansea City	1971	2020	137
Swansea Town	1914	1970	128
Swaythling	1976	1980	9
Swifts	1874	1894	73
Swindon Amateurs	1910		2
Swindon British Rail	1951		2
Swindon Corinthians	1925	1939	32
Swindon GWR Corinthians	1946	1950	10
Swindon Supermarine	2002	2020	52
Swindon Town	1887	2020	347
Swindon Victoria	1912	1951	66
	1955		
Swinton Town	1899	1901	3
Symingtons Recreation	1949	1955	9
Tadcaster Albion	1996	2009	49
	2011	2020	
Tadley Calleva	2014	2017	8
	2019	2020	
Takeley	2011	2020	20
Talbot Stead	1920	1923	10
Tamworth	1935		228
	1937	1946	
	1948	2020	
Tamworth Castle	1915	1920	9
	1922		
Tanfield Lea Rovers	1925	1926	3
	1934		
Tankersley	1912	1922	12
Tankersley United	1928		2
Tate Institute	1933		1

282

Taunton to Walsall Borough

Club	Year1	Year2	Num
Taunton	1949	1957	39
	1959	1960	
	1963	1968	
	1970		
Taunton & Newtons United	1924	1925	8
Taunton Castle	1906		1
Taunton Town	1936		145
	1971	2020	
Taunton Town (1)	1929	1934	21
Taunton United	1926	1927	3
Tavistock	1949	1950	41
	1952	1960	
	2007	2014	
	2018	2020	
Team Bath	2003	2009	27
Team Bury	2011		4
	2013		
	2015		
Team Northumbria	2008	2011	12
	2014		
	2017	2019	
Team Solent	2014	2019	7
Telford United	1970	2004	113
Terrington	1921		1
Teversal	2006	2011	16
	2013	2014	
	2019		
Teversal & Silverhill CW	1930		8
	1938	1939	
	1950	1951	
Thackley	1970		75
	1980	2020	
Thame Rangers	2020		3
Thame United	1932	1936	116
	1939		
	1977	1985	
	1989	2020	
Thames	1930	1932	5
Thames Ironworks	1896	1900	15
Thamesmead Town	1995	2019	58
Thanet United	1982	1989	22
Thatcham	1930	1931	7
	1937	1939	
Thatcham Town	1988	2020	72
Thetford REC	1922		1
Thetford Town	1929	1933	83
	1935	1939	
	1951	1953	
	1955	1960	
	1966		
	1968	1984	
	1989		
	1992		
	2009		
	2011	2020	
Third Lanark	1886	1887	4
Thoresby Colliery	1938		1
Thornaby	1899	1902	35
	1937		
	2002	2009	
	2016	2017	
	2020		
Thornaby St Patrick	1936	1938	3
Thornaby Utopians	1899	1901	6
Thornaby-on-Tees	2000	2001	4
Thornbury Town	2020		1
Thorndale	1936	1939	5
Thorne Colliery	1928	1929	45
	1934	1951	
	1968		
Thornhill Lees Albion	1912	1914	5
Thornhill United	1902	1905	9
Thornley Albion	1923	1927	20
Thornley CW	1933		7
	1935		
Thornton United	1922		2
Thornycroft Athletic	1947	1951	21
	1968	1972	
Thornycrofts (Basingstoke)	1915	1922	37
	1924	1935	
	1937	1946	
Thornycrofts (Woolston)	1920	1925	24
Thorpe Hesley	1905	1911	13
Thrapston Town	2012	2013	8
	2016		
Three Bridges	1977	1998	71
	2000	2020	
Threlkeld	1951		1
Throckley	1946	1948	6
Throckley Welfare	1934	1940	13
Thurnby Nirvana	2012	2015	13
Thurnscoe Park Avenue	1920		3
	1922		
Thurnscoe Victoria	1931	1939	21
	1947	1948	
Thurrock	2004	2018	41
Thynnes Athletic	1936	1937	8
	1939		
	1948	1950	
Tibshelf Colliery	1913	1915	15
	1921		
Tilbury	1928	1930	210
	1933	1939	
	1947	2020	

Club	Year1	Year2	Num
Timperley	1929	1930	14
	1932	1939	
Timsbury Athletic	1914		21
	1920	1924	
	1935	1939	
	1950	1951	
Tinsley Park	1920		5
	1922		
Tipton Town	2007	2016	35
Tiptree United	1981	2010	61
Tiverton Town	1934	1938	146
	1949	1955	
	1976	1984	
	1987	2020	
Tividale	1976	1991	62
	2008	2020	
Tokyngton Manor	2009	2010	2
Ton Pentre	1910		72
	1920	1923	
	1969	1992	
	1949	1996	153
Tonbridge			
Tonbridge Angels	1997	2020	68
Tonge	1895		13
	1909	1911	
Tonge Temperance	1915		1
Tooting	1912	1915	8
Tooting & Mitcham United	1933	2020	253
Tooting Bec	2020		1
Tooting Graveney	1911		3
Tooting Town	1920	1932	26
Torpoint	1907		3
Torpoint Athletic	2011	2012	8
	2015		
Torquay Town	1911	1912	13
	1914	1915	
	1921	1922	
Torquay United	1922	1927	243
	1929	2020	
Torrington	1982	2008	40
Tottenham Hotspur	1895	2020	445
Tottington	1912	1915	4
Totton	1934	1946	26
	1950	1953	
Totton & Eling	2010	2015	16
Tow Law	1892	1905	35
Tow Law Town	1910	1913	207
	1921	1960	
	1962		
	1964	2014	
Tower Hamlets	1995		15
	2014	2020	
Trafalgar	1895		1
Trafalgar Sports (Portsmouth)	1940		2
	1947		
Trafford	1996	2020	64
Tranmere Rovers	1892	1897	298
	1900	1901	
	1904	1908	
	1910	1911	
	1913	2020	
Trawden Forest	1898	1903	10
Treeton	1930		1
Treeton Reading Room	1921	1926	20
	1928	1929	
Treherbert	1922		2
Trent Rovers	1905	1906	4
Trimdon Grange Colliery	1923	1926	29
	1932	1934	
	1936	1938	
	1940		
	1947		
	1955		
Tring Athletic	2006	2020	29
Tring Town	1976	2004	53
Troedryhiw	1949	1954	8
Troedryhiw Stars	1915		3
Trojans	1874		3
	1877		
Trowbridge Town	1896	1899	270
	1902		
	1909	1998	
Truro City	1925		66
	1950	1953	
	1955	1963	
	1971	1974	
	1993		
	2007	2020	
Tuffley Rovers	1996	2006	27
	2016	2020	
Tufnell Park	1909	1951	90
Tufnell Park (2)	1996		3
Tufnell Park Edmonton	1952	1955	9
	1958		
Tufnell Spartan	1912	1920	6
Tunbridge Wells	1970	2020	99
Tunbridge Wells (1)	1903	1906	21
	1908		
	1912	1915	
Tunbridge Wells Rangers	1905	1939	106
Tunbridge Wells Rangers (2)	1965	1967	5
Tunbridge Wells United	1953	1964	38
Turton	1880	1882	13
	1884		
	1901		

Club	Year1	Year2	Num
Tushingham Brick Works	1938	1939	8
Tutbury Town	1915		2
Twerton St Michael's	1937	1939	3
Twickenham	1947	1949	3
Twizell United	1915		10
	1921	1922	
	1925	1928	
Tydesley Albion	1910		3
Tyne Association	1880		2
	1887		
UGB Sports (Charlton)	1933	1936	15
	1939		
UGB St Helens	1949	1951	3
Ulster	1889		2
Ulverston Town	1922		15
	1927	1931	
Union Jack (Bristol)	1926		2
United Hospital	1883		2
United London Swifts	1886		1
United Services Portsmouth	2016	2017	6
	2019	2020	
Unity	1879		1
Upminster	1948	1950	9
Upper Armley	1905	1906	2
Upton Colliery	1937	1960	33
Upton Park	1872	1887	77
	1897	1911	
Upton Rangers	1884		1
Urmston	1937	1938	4
Urmston Old Boys	1934		1
Ushaw Moor	1951	1955	12
Usworth Colliery	1920	1947	47
	1950		
Uxbridge	1874	1875	272
	1884	1886	
	1893	1899	
	1904	1920	
	1922	2020	
V.S. Rugby	1977	2001	86
VCD Athletic	2001	2020	54
VT	2007	2010	13
Vampires	1895	1897	7
Vauxhall G.M.	1990	1992	6
Vauxhall Motors	2002	2014	41
	2020		
Vauxhall Motors (Luton)	1921		95
	1933	1955	
	1957	1971	
	1973	1978	
	1987	1992	
Venner Sports	1938		2
	1940		
Vernon Athletic	1912	1913	34
	1915		
	1921	1935	
	1937	1939	
Verwood Town	2011	2018	14
Vickers (Weybridge)	1955		1
Vickers Armstrong	1940		10
	1947		
	1949	1951	
Vickerstown	1915	1922	4
Viking Greenford	2000	2001	3
Viking Sports	1993	1999	12
Virginia Water	2020		1
Vulcans	1902		1
Wadebridge Town	1951	1965	58
	1968	1981	
	1985		
	2007		
	2009		
Wadebridge United	1931	1933	4
Wadham Lodge	2018		2
Wakefield	1893		17
	2007	2014	
Wakefield & Emley	2003	2006	6
Wakefield City	1908		6
	1922		
Walgrave Amber	1927	1928	2
Walkden Central	1910	1912	13
	1914	1915	
Walker Celtic	1920	1924	61
	1926	1939	
Walker Church Institute	1911	1912	3
	1914		
Walker Parish Church	1907	1910	7
Walker Park	1929	1930	11
	1933	1935	
Wallasey Borough	1915	1920	3
Wallasey Rovers	1914		3
Wallasey Transport	1951		1
Wallasey United	1924	1925	4
Wallingford Town	1948	1949	6
Wallington	1930	1931	2
Wallsend	1914	1925	48
	1927	1933	
	1935		
Wallsend Elm Villa	1912	1915	5
Wallsend Park Villa	1897		52
	1900	1913	
Wallsend Town	1978	1982	6
Walsall	1894	2020	340
Walsall Borough	1983	1986	4

283

Walsall Jolly Club to Whitley and Monkseaton

Index of clubs

Club	From	To	No.
Walsall Jolly Club	1931	1932	6
	1939		
Walsall LMS	1929	1932	9
Walsall Phoenix	1922		14
	1925		
	1927	1933	
	1935	1936	
Walsall Swifts	1883	1886	11
	1888		
Walsall Town	1883	1888	15
Walsall Town Swifts	1889	1893	16
Walsall Wood	1921		37
	1981	1982	
	1987	1993	
	2009	2012	
	2014	2020	
Walsden United	1927	1930	6
Walsham Le Willows	2007	2020	23
Walshaw	1900		2
Waltham	1913		1
Waltham Abbey	1991	1993	45
	1999	2001	
	2006	2020	
Waltham Comrades	1928	1933	10
Waltham Forest	2004	2018	33
Walthamstow	2019	2020	8
Walthamstow Avenue	1922	1988	184
Walthamstow Grange	1909	1924	42
	1926	1931	
Walthamstow Pennant	1990	1995	10
Walthamstow Town	1923	1925	5
Walton & Hersham	1946	1956	203
	1958	2020	
Walton Casuals	2001	2020	42
Walton United	1936		3
	1938	1939	
Walton-on-Thames	1908		37
	1910	1929	
	1932	1940	
Wanderers	1872	1882	44
Wandsworth	1899	1900	5
	1902		
Wandsworth & Norwood	1990		3
Wandsworth United	1938	1939	2
Wanstead	1904		10
	1906	1911	
Wantage Town	2003		38
	2005	2020	
War Office	1903	1904	3
Warboys Town	1955	1959	13
	1998	2001	
Wardle & Barbridge Utd.	1939		1
Wardley Welfare	1933	1936	16
	1950	1951	
Ware	1927	1928	167
	1930		
	1932	1937	
	1939	1940	
	1947	1951	
	1955	2020	
Wareham Town	1914	1915	2
Warley	1972	1973	3
Warley County Borough	1975	1977	4
Warlingham	2012	2013	3
Warminster Town	1921	1929	92
	1947	1970	
	1986		
	1991		
	2000		
	2010	2011	
Warmley	1891	1899	23
Warmley Amateurs	1905		2
Warrington St Elphin's	1895	1900	7
Warrington Town	1984		116
	1986	2020	
Warwick County	1888	1891	8
Washington	1970	1972	52
	1977	1981	
	1990	1993	
	1996	1997	
	2003	2009	
	2013		
	2015	2019	
Washington Chemical Works	1939	1940	2
Washington Colliery	1920		23
	1923	1931	
	1933		
Washington Nissan	2004	2005	4
Washington United	1910	1915	10
Waterlooville	1967	1971	100
	1974	1998	
Waterlows (Dunstable)	1920		65
	1922	1939	
	1947	1949	
	1951		
Watford	1899	2020	338
Watford British Legion	1933	1936	6
	1938	1939	
Watford Old Boys	1922		10
	1926	1930	
Watford Orient	1914		2
Watford Rovers	1887	1892	13
Watford Spartans	1931		1

Club	From	To	No.
Watford St Marys	1897	1898	7
Watford Victoria Works	1908		2
Wath Athletic	1900	1902	87
	1904		
	1908	1935	
Wath Brow United	1920	1928	14
Wath-upon-Dearne	1894	1899	17
Watton United	1988	1989	13
	1992	1998	
	2000		
Wealden	2008	2010	3
Wealdstone	1914	1915	296
	1921	1930	
	1932	1964	
	1966	2020	
Wednesbury Old Athletic	1882	1893	26
Wednesbury Old Athletic (2)	1910	1925	21
Wednesbury Strollers	1879	1882	6
Wednesbury Town	1884	1885	6
Wednesfield	1991	2001	36
	2010	2011	
	2019	2020	
Wednesfield Social	1983	1989	10
Welbeck Colliery	1920	1923	16
Welling Town	2020		1
Welling United	1979	2020	134
Wellingborough Town	1893		180
	1897	1906	
	1920	1934	
	1937	1993	
	1995	2002	
Wellingborough Town (2)	2008	2020	28
Wellingborough Whitworths	2013		5
	2016		
	2018	2020	
Wellingbro Redwell Stars	1907	1915	14
Wellington (Hereford)	2008	2013	17
	2015		
	2018		
Wellington (Somerset)	1982	1985	13
	2010		
	2018	2020	
Wellington St George's	1887	1891	50
	1893	1897	
	1909	1913	
	1921	1929	
	1931		
Wellington Town	1896	1905	177
	1909	1911	
	1913		
	1920	1969	
Wellington Works	1922	1935	26
Wells Amateurs	1949		1
Wells City	1904		84
	1907	1908	
	1924	1939	
	1947	1959	
	2012	2014	
	2017	2019	
Welshpool	1899		11
	1901		
	1903		
	1905	1909	
Welton Rovers	1907	1949	194
	1951	1956	
	1964	2013	
	2015	2017	
Welwyn	1923		2
Welwyn Garden City	1928		66
	1930	1934	
	1939	1950	
	1955	1956	
	1989	1993	
	1995	2001	
	2006	2011	
	2015	2020	
Wembley	1950		159
	1956	2020	
Wesley Rangers	1933	1934	2
West Allotment Celtic	2006	2018	22
West Auckland Town	1906	1912	211
	1915		
	1921		
	1924		
	1926	1928	
	1930	1954	
	1956	1964	
	1966	1971	
	1973	2020	
West Birmingham	1921	1923	3
West Bridgford	2018		1
West Bromwich Albion	1884	2020	408
West Bromwich Town	1993	1994	3
West Croydon	1899	1903	9
West Didsbury & Chorlton	2014	2020	15
West End	1880	1885	13
West End Rovers	1949		1
West Essex	2018	2020	5
West Ham Garfield	1900	1904	8
West Ham United	1901	2020	343
West Hampstead	1900	1906	28
	1908	1911	
West Hartlepool	1902		12
	1904	1910	
	1930		

Club	From	To	No.
West Hartlepool Expansion	1909	1910	7
	1914		
West Hartlepool NER	1895	1898	5
West Hartlepool Rovers	1892	1894	3
West Hartlepool St Josephs	1914	1915	2
West Herts	1893		6
	1895	1898	
West Hull Albion	1921	1922	3
West Kirby	1923	1925	5
West London Old Boys	1913	1915	9
	1921		
West Manchester	1888	1889	13
	1893	1897	
West Midlands Police	1991	2001	23
West Norwood	1897		79
	1899	1922	
	1924	1934	
	1936	1939	
West Sleekburn Welfare	1950	1955	10
West Stanley	1904	1929	91
	1931	1938	
	1948	1951	
West Thurrock Athletic	1948		3
West Vale Ramblers	1912	1914	5
West Wylam CW	1934	1938	9
Westbury United	1922	1928	129
	1931		
	1933	1975	
	1987	2011	
	2019	2020	
Westfield	2003	2009	24
	2012	2020	
Westfield (Sussex)	2010		1
Westfields	1995	1998	58
	2005	2020	
Westham (Weymouth)	1922	1925	5
Westhoughton	1930		6
	1933	1934	
Westland Works	1931		1
Weston-Super-Mare	1912	1915	186
	1926		
	1929	1930	
	1934	1939	
	1950		
	1952		
	1955	1956	
	1958	1967	
	1970	2020	
Weston-Super-Mare St Johns	1947	1951	7
Weybridge	1915		8
	1927	1931	
Weybridge Swallows	1881		2
Weymouth	1894	1906	339
	1908	1939	
	1948	2020	
Weymouth S.A.A.	1947		1
Wheatley Hill Colliery	1925	1928	9
Wheelock Albion	1948	1950	3
Whickham	1990	1997	34
	1999		
	2004	2012	
	2015	2016	
	2019	2020	
Whiston	1922	1924	27
	1926	1935	
Whitburn	1888	1892	11
	1907	1908	
	1910		
Whitburn CW	1935		1
Whitby	1947	1950	9
Whitby (1)	1889	1893	15
	1900		
	1902	1905	
Whitby Albion Rangers	1931	1939	17
	1947	1950	
Whitby Town	1951	1964	185
	1966	1970	
	1972	2020	
Whitby United	1927	1928	38
	1930	1946	
Whitchurch	1906	1912	39
	1922		
	1924		
	1927	1931	
	1933	1939	
Whitchurch Alport	2018	2020	6
Whitchurch United	2001	2004	20
	2012	2018	
White & Co's Sports	1920		1
White Ensign	2020		4
White Star Wanderers	1900	1903	6
White-le-Head Rangers	1922	1931	26
Whitehaven	2011		8
Whitehaven Athletic	1922	1924	35
	1926	1929	
	1931	1936	
Whitehaven Colliery Recreation	1922	1925	13
Whitehaven Wellington Villa	1937	1939	4
Whitehaven White Rose	1937		1
Whitehawk	1983	2020	86
Whiteheads	1902	1910	20
Whitley & Monkseaton	1937	1940	8

Whitley Bay to Youlgrave

Index of clubs

Club	Year	Year	Num
Whitley Bay	1909		168
	1957	1964	
	1966	2020	
Whitstable	1911	1933	74
	1935	1940	
	1947	1952	
	1955	1966	
Whitstable Town	1968	1987	97
	1990	2020	
Whitton United	1948	1960	42
	2009	2017	
	2019	2020	
Whitwell Colliery	1922	1926	8
Whitwick Colliery	1949		19
	1951	1957	
Whitwick Imperial	1913	1929	21
Whitwick White Cross	1902	1904	7
Whyteleafe	1970		104
	1982	2020	
Whyteleafe Athletic	1931		1
Wick	1981	1985	56
	1987	2012	
	2017	2019	
Wick & Barnham United	2016		1
Widnes	2018	2020	6
Widnes County	1912	1915	6
Widnes DS&S	1920		1
Wigan Athletic	1934	2020	260
Wigan Borough	1923	1932	24
Wigan County	1898	1900	12
Wigan Robin Park	2011	2015	6
Wigan Rovers	1968	1970	5
	1973		
Wigan Town	1908		1
Wigan United	1902	1903	4
Wigmore Athletic	1955	1957	8
	1977	1980	
Wigston Fields	1984	1987	9
Wigton Athletic	1912		2
Wigton Harriers	1906	1912	23
	1920		
	1922	1926	
Willand Rovers	2003	2020	41
Willaston White Star	1932	1940	13
Willenhall	1920	1931	33
Willenhall Pickwick	1909	1915	16
Willenhall Swifts	1909	1915	13
Willenhall Town	1978	2013	90
Willesden	1948	1951	20
	1976	1982	
Willesden Town	1901	1903	12
	1905	1906	
William Colliery (Whitehaven)	1947	1948	3
Willington	1912	1986	174
	1988	2005	
Willington Athletic	1892	1915	67
Willington Temperance	1911		2
Wills Sports	1933	1936	8
Wilmslow Albion	1936		5
	1940		
	1948	1950	
Wilts County Mental Hospital	1938	1939	11
	1948	1949	
Wimbledon	1907	1911	254
	1913	1914	
	1920	1923	
	1926	2004	
Wimblington Old Boys	1950	1951	2
Wimborne	1925		1
Wimborne Town	1983	2020	94
Wincanton Town	2016		3
Winchester City	1907	1911	112
	1913		
	1929	1932	
	1934	1940	
	1948	1960	
	1973		
	2004	2020	
Windermere	1908	1915	38
	1922	1930	
	1932	1934	
Windsor	2013	2020	14
Windsor & Eton	1893		230
	1895	1899	
	1902		
	1905	1908	
	1910	1924	
	1926	1929	
	1932	1935	
	1937	2011	
Windsor Home Park	1873		15
	1875		
	1881	1885	
Windsor Phoenix Athletic	1891	1892	3
Windy Nook	1936	1938	5
Wingate	1949	1950	6
	1955		
Wingate & Finchley	1992	2020	73
Wingate (Durham)	1970		28
	1972	1983	
	1986		
Wingate Albion Comrades	1910	1915	33
	1921	1927	
Wingate Constitutional Ath.	1924		1
Wingate Welfare	1951		4
	1957	1958	
Winsford United	1900	1902	243
	1920	1936	
	1938	1939	
	1948	1961	
	1963	2020	
Winslow United	2019	2020	3
Winterbourne United	2013	2016	5
Winterton Rangers	1948	1951	85
	1970	1984	
	1994	1996	
	2003	2015	
	2020		
Wirral Railway	1900		1
Wisbech Town	1924	1946	247
	1948	1963	
	1965	2020	
Witham Town	1987	2020	79
Withdean 2000	2004		1
Witheridge	2015	2016	5
Withernsea	1910		3
	1921		
Witney Town	1924		127
	1930		
	1932	1934	
	1951	1962	
	1971	2002	
	2012	2013	
Witney United	2006	2011	18
Witton	1885	1892	14
Witton Albion	1908	1927	262
	1929	1935	
	1937	2020	
Witton Park Institute	1936		3
	1938		
Wivenhoe Town	1988	2010	65
	2013	2019	
Wodson Park	2012	2013	3
	2019		
Woking	1904	1906	308
	1908	2020	
Wokingham & Emmbrook	2012	2013	4
Wokingham Town	1959	1963	117
	1965	1971	
	1973	2004	
Wolseley Athletic	1923	1925	4
Wolsingham	1897		1
Wolsingham Town	1921		1
Wolsingham Welfare	1955	1959	10
Wolverhampton Amateur	1921	1939	21
Wolverhampton Casuals	2012	2018	16
	2020		
Wolverhampton Sporting Community	2017	2020	4
Wolverhampton Wanderers	1884	2020	387
Wolverton	1991	1992	6
Wolverton (1)	1891	1894	6
Wolverton LNWR	1895	1900	15
Wolverton Town	1903		51
	1915		
	1923	1937	
	1939		
	1947	1949	
	1981	1982	
	1985	1988	
Wolverton Town & BR	1950	1971	50
	1975	1980	
Wombwell	1921	1933	44
Wombwell Athletic	1947	1950	10
Wombwell Main	1907	1910	7
	1921	1922	
Wombwell Main Welfare	1934	1936	5
	1947		
Wombwell Rising Star	1905		1
Wombwell Sporting	1969	1970	5
Wombwell Town	1897	1901	6
Wood Grange	1877	1878	2
Wood Green Town	1910	1914	50
	1921	1935	
	1938	1940	
	1947	1951	
Wood Skinners	1925	1926	6
Woodbridge Town	1996	2015	47
	2018	2020	
Woodford	1901		18
	1903	1909	
Woodford Albion	1915		1
Woodford Bridge	1882	1884	4
Woodford Crusaders	1914	1920	5
Woodford Town	2020		2
Woodford Town (1)	1947	1964	65
	1966	1967	
	1969		
	1971	1972	
	1981	1988	
Woodford United	2005	2014	25
Woodford Wells	1874	1876	7
Woodhouse	1922	1923	12
Woodhouse Brittania	1915		2
Woodley Sports	2000	2012	33
Woodley United	2018	2019	2
Woodstock Sports	2012		2
	2015		
Woolston	1913	1915	5
Woolwich	1915		4
	1922		
Woolwich Arsenal	1892	1914	69
Woolwich Borough Co. Ath.	1932	1937	8
Woolwich Ordnance	1920	1921	7
Woolwich Polytechnic	1906		37
	1910	1912	
	1915	1920	
	1922	1935	
	1937	1950	
Woolwich Royal Artillery	1912		1
Wootton Bassett Town	1939		32
	1947	1951	
	2005		
	2008	2015	
Wootton Blue Cross	1951		50
	1981	1991	
	1995	2010	
Worcester City	1906	1936	312
	1938	1986	
	1988	2020	
Workington	1922	2020	252
Workington (1)	1888	1891	63
	1893	1906	
	1908	1912	
Workington DS&S	1922		4
Worksop Parramore	2014		4
Worksop Town	1894	1906	340
	1908	1940	
	1950	2020	
Worsbrough Bridge MW	1979	1981	7
	2003		
Worthing	1900	1964	299
	1967	2020	
Worthing United	1993		21
	2007	2011	
	2014	2019	
Wren Rovers	1984	1989	11
Wrexham	1889	2020	353
Wrexham Olympic	1884	1888	8
Wrockwardine Wood	1896	1898	12
	1937	1939	
Wroxham	1996	2020	72
Wycliffe	1902		1
Wycombe Wanderers	1896	2020	338
Wymondham Town	1951	1956	9
Yate Town	1987	2020	64
Yaxley	1999	2020	45
Yeading	1987	2007	69
Yeadon Celtic	1921		1
Yeovil	1908	1915	13
Yeovil & Petter's United	1920	1946	86
Yeovil Casuals	1900	1907	13
Yeovil Town	1947	2020	227
Yiewsley	1909	1910	85
	1915	1927	
	1935		
	1937	1964	
York City	1924	2020	286
York City (1)	1910	1915	24
Yorkshire Amateur	1926		137
	1931	1954	
	1956	1962	
	1964	1987	
	1993	2009	
	2012		
	2016		
	2020		
Youlgrave	1922	1927	10
	1948		

APPENDICES

Appendix One is a guide to the date on which most games would have taken place. In the seasons up to 1887/88, the regulations stated that games had to be played "on or before" a certain date. It was left to the clubs concerned to arrange the fixture. They were not always successful in achieving the date required! For these early seasons, the dates shown are generally those of the first game in the round.

The regulations changed in 1888/89 so that rounds were to be played on a designated day. Replays have usually taken place on the Tuesday, Wednesday or Thursday of the following week, often depending on the early closing days of the towns concerned. Policing policies have caused the replays to be delayed a further week in the rounds proper from 1991/92 onwards.

With the advent of greater television coverage, games in any one round can now occur on Friday, Saturday, Sunday and Monday. The Saturday date is the one shown.

The competition of 1896/97 is confusing because, on the same day, some qualifying round groups played games from one round whilst other groups played games from the next!

The actual dates of games played by clubs who were members of the Football League and Premier League in the season concerned will be found at the National Football Archive web site at www.enfa.co.uk.

Season 1925/26 was the first season in which the competition took the form we know today, with (what is now) League One and League Two clubs exempt until Round One, and Premiership and Championship clubs until Round Three.

Appendix Two is a list of the players that have appeared in the FA Cup Final. Goal scorers have the number of goals after their name. The number in brackets after the substitutes name is the player he replaced according to his position on the table, numbered across the page from 1 to 11.

Appendix Three is the list of "other names" by which clubs have been known. Although not intended as the definitive work on this topic, it does at least show you other names used by some of the clubs in the database.

Wembley, April 11 1970, the earliest day in the year for the Final since 1897. 30 minutes gone and Leeds United were in the driving seat. Chelsea, twice behind, scored a late equaliser to force extra time and a replay. The 150-letter display board, by Messrs Hird-Brown of Bolton, was new that year.

APPENDIX ONE: DATES OF FA CUP ROUNDS

PERIOD ONE: 1871/72 to 1887/88

	R1	R2	R3	R4	R5	R6	SF	F	Fr
1871/72	11.11	16.12	20.1	-	-	-	17.2	16.3	-
1872/73	26.10	23.11	9.12	3.2	-	-	-	29.3	-
1873/74	9.10	15.11	6.12	-	-	-	28.1	14.3	-
1874/75	10.10	14.11	23.1	-	-	-	27.2	13.3	16.3
1875/76	23.10	11.12	29.1	-	-	-	19.2	11.3	18.3
1876/77	24.10	29.11	20.1	17.2	-	-	20.3	24.3	-
1877/78	27.10	8.12	12.1	15.2	-	-	16.3	23.3	-
1878/79	19.10	4.12	11.1	13.2	-	-	22.3	29.3	-
1879/80	25.10	29.11	17.1	7.2	21.2	-	27.3	10.4	-
1880/81	16.10	4.12	8.1	5.2	5.3	-	26.3	9.4	-
1881/82	17.10	19.11	20.12	14.1	7.2	-	4.3	25.3	-
1882/83	4.11	18.11	16.12	24.1	20.2	-	17.3	31.3	-
1883/84	6.10	24.11	20.12	19.1	9.2	-	1.3	29.3	-
1884/85	11.10	6.12	20.12	24.1	7.2	21.2	7.3	4.4	-
1885/86	31.10	18.11	19.12	2.1	16.1	13.2	6.3	3.4	10.4
1886/87	23.10	13.11	11.12	15.1	12.2	2.3	5.3	2.4	-
1887/88	15.10	5.11	26.11	17.12	7.1	28.1	18.2	24.3	-

PERIOD TWO: 1888/89 to 1924/25

	EP	PR	Q1	Q2	Q3	Q4	Q5	Q6	IR	R1	R2	R3	R4	SF	F	Fr
1888/89	-	-	6.10	27.10	17.11	8.12	-	-	-	2.2	16.2	2.3	-	16.3	30.3	-
1889/90	-	-	5.10	26.10	16.11	7.12	-	-	-	18.1	1.2	15.2	-	8.3	29.3	-
1890/91	-	27.9	4.10	25.10	15.11	6.12	-	-	-	17.1	31.1	14.2	-	28.2	21.3	-
1891/92	-	-	3.10	24.10	14.11	5.12	-	-	-	16.1	30.1	13.2	-	5.3	19.3	-
1892/93	-	1.10	15.10	29.10	19.11	10.12	-	-	-	21.1	4.2	18.2	-	4.3	25.3	-
1893/94	-	-	14.10	4.11	25.11	16.12	-	-	-	27.1	10.2	24.2	-	10.3	31.3	-
1894/95	-	6.10	13.10	3.11	24.11	15.12	-	-	-	2.2	16.2	2.3	-	16.3	20.4	-
1895/96	-	5.10	12.10	2.11	23.11	14.12	-	-	-	1.2	15.2	29.2	-	21.3	18.4	-
1896/97	-	10.10	31.10	21.11	12.12	2.1	16.1	-	-	30.1	13.2	27.2	-	20.3	10.4	-
1897/98	-	18.9	25.9	16.10	30.10	20.11	11.12	-	-	29.1	12.2	26.2	-	19.3	16.4	-
1898/99	-	17.9	1.10	15.10	29.10	19.11	10.12	-	-	28.1	11.2	25.2	-	18.3	15.4	-
1899/00	-	16.9	30.9	14.10	28.10	18.11	9.12	-	-	27.1	10.2	24.2	-	24.3	21.4	-
1900/01	-	22.9	6.10	20.10	3.11	17.11	8.12	-	5.1	9.2	23.2	23.2	-	6.4	20.4	27.4
1901/02	-	21.9	5.10	19.10	2.11	16.11	30.11	-	14.12	25.1	8.2	22.2	-	15.3	19.4	26.4
1902/03	-	20.9	4.10	18.10	1.11	15.11	29.11	-	13.12	7.2	21.2	7.3	-	21.3	18.4	-
1903/04	12.9	19.9	3.10	17.10	31.10	14.11	28.11	-	12.12	6.2	20.2	5.3	-	19.3	23.4	-
1904/05	10.9	17.9	1.10	15.10	29.10	12.11	26.11	10.12	14.1	4.2	18.2	4.3	-	25.3	15.4	-
1905/06	-	23.9	7.10	28.10	18.11	9.12	-	-	-	13.1	3.2	24.2	10.3	31.3	21.4	-
1906/07	-	22.9	6.10	20.10	3.11	24.11	8.12	-	-	12.1	2.2	23.2	9.3	23.3	20.4	-
1907/08	-	21.9	5.10	19.10	2.11	23.11	7.12	-	-	11.1	1.2	22.2	7.3	28.3	25.4	-
1908/09	12.9	19.9	3.10	17.10	7.11	21.11	5.12	-	-	16.1	6.2	20.2	6.3	27.3	24.4	-
1909/10	11.9	18.9	2.10	16.10	6.11	20.11	4.12	-	-	15.1	5.2	19.2	5.3	26.3	23.4	28.4
1910/11	10.9	17.9	1.10	15.10	5.11	19.11	3.12	-	-	14.1	4.2	25.2	11.3	25.3	22.4	26.4
1911/12	9.9	16.9	30.9	14.10	4.11	18.11	2.12	-	-	13.1	3.2	24.2	9.3	30.3	20.4	24.4
1912/13	14.9	28.9	12.10	2.11	16.11	30.11	14.12	-	-	11.1	1.2	22.2	8.3	29.3	19.4	-
1913/14	13.9	27.9	11.10	1.11	15.11	29.11	13.12	-	-	10.1	31.1	21.2	7.3	28.3	25.4	-
1914/15	12.9	26.9	10.10	24.10	7.11	21.11	5.12	19.12	-	9.1	30.1	20.2	6.3	27.3	24.4	-
1919/20	13.9	27.9	11.10	25.10	8.11	22.11	6.12	20.12	-	10.1	31.1	21.2	6.3	27.3	24.4	-
1920/21	11.9	25.9	9.10	23.10	6.11	20.11	4.12	18.12	-	8.1	29.1	19.2	5.3	19.3	23.4	-
1921/22	10.9	24.9	8.10	22.10	5.11	19.11	3.12	17.12	-	7.1	28.1	18.2	4.3	25.3	29.4	-
1922/23	9.9	23.9	7.10	21.10	4.11	18.11	2.12	16.12	-	13.1	3.2	24.2	10.3	24.3	28.4	-
1923/24	8.9	22.9	6.10	20.10	3.11	17.11	1.12	15.12	-	12.1	2.2	23.2	8.3	29.3	26.4	-
1924/25	6.9	20.9	4.10	18.10	1.11	15.11	29.11	13.12	-	10.1	31.1	21.2	7.3	28.3	25.4	-

PERIOD THREE: 1925/26 to 2019/20

	EP	PR	Q1	Q2	Q3	Q4	R1	R2	R3	R4	R5	R6	SF	F	Fr
1925/26	5.9	19.9	3.10	17.10	31.10	14.11	28.11	12.12	9.1	30.1	20.2	6.3	27.3	24.4	-
1926/27	4.9	18.9	2.10	16.10	30.10	13.11	27.11	11.12	8.1	29.1	19.2	5.3	26.3	23.4	-
1927/28	3.9	17.9	1.10	15.10	29.10	12.11	26.11	10.12	7.1	28.1	18.2	3.3	24.3	21.4	-
1928/29	1.9	15.9	29.9	13.10	27.10	10.11	24.11	8.12	12.1	26.1	16.2	2.3	23.3	27.4	-
1929/30	7.9	21.9	5.10	19.10	2.11	16.11	30.11	14.12	11.1	25.1	15.2	1.3	22.3	26.4	-
1930/31	6.9	20.9	4.10	18.10	1.11	15.11	29.11	13.12	10.1	24.1	14.2	28.2	14.3	25.4	-
1931/32	5.9	19.9	3.10	17.10	31.10	14.11	28.11	12.12	9.1	23.1	13.2	27.2	12.3	23.4	-
1932/33	3.9	17.9	1.10	15.10	29.10	12.11	26.11	10.12	14.1	28.1	18.2	4.3	18.3	29.4	-
1933/34	2.9	16.9	30.9	14.10	28.10	11.11	25.11	9.12	13.1	27.1	17.2	3.3	17.3	28.4	-
1934/35	1.9	15.9	29.9	13.10	27.10	10.11	24.11	8.12	12.1	26.1	16.2	2.3	16.3	27.4	-
1935/36	7.9	21.9	5.10	19.10	2.11	16.11	30.11	14.12	11.1	25.1	15.2	29.2	21.3	25.4	-
1936/37	5.9	19.9	3.10	17.10	31.10	14.11	28.11	12.12	16.1	30.1	20.2	6.3	10.4	1.5	-
1937/38	4.9	18.9	2.10	16.10	30.10	13.11	27.11	11.12	8.1	29.1	12.2	5.3	26.3	30.4	-
1938/39	3.9	17.9	1.10	15.10	29.10	12.11	26.11	10.12	7.1	28.1	11.2	4.3	25.3	29.4	-
1939/40	2.9	*Rest of competition cancelled on declaration of war*													

287

DATES OF ROUNDS (Continued)

	EP	PR	Q1	Q2	Q3	Q4	R1	R2	R3	R4	R5	R6	SF	F	Fr
1945/46	1.9	8.9	22.9	6.10	20.10	3.11	17.11	8.12	5.1	26.1	9.2	2.3	23.3	27.4	-
1946/47	7.9	21.9	5.10	19.10	2.11	16.11	30.11	14.12	11.1	25.1	8.2	1.3	29.3	26.4	-
1947/48	6.9	20.9	4.10	18.10	1.11	15.11	29.11	13.12	10.1	24.1	7.2	28.2	15.3	24.4	-
1948/49	4.9	18.9	2.10	16.10	30.10	13.11	27.11	11.12	8.1	29.1	12.2	26.2	26.3	30.4	-
1949/50	3.9	17.9	1.10	15.10	29.10	12.11	26.11	10.12	7.1	28.1	11.2	4.3	25.3	29.4	-
1950/51	2.9	16.9	30.9	14.10	28.10	11.11	25.11	9.12	6.1	27.1	10.2	24.2	10.3	28.4	-
1951/52	-	15.9	29.9	13.10	27.10	10.11	24.11	15.12	12.1	2.2	23.2	8.3	29.3	3.5	-
1952/53	-	13.9	27.9	11.10	25.10	8.11	22.11	6.12	10.1	31.1	14.2	28.2	21.3	2.5	-
1953/54	-	12.9	26.9	10.10	24.10	7.11	21.11	12.12	9.1	30.1	20.2	13.3	27.3	1.5	-
1954/55	-	11.9	25.9	9.10	23.10	6.11	20.11	11.12	8.1	29.1	19.2	13.3	26.3	7.5	-
1955/56	-	10.9	24.9	8.10	22.10	5.11	19.11	10.12	7.1	28.1	18.2	3.3	17.3	5.5	-
1956/57	-	8.9	22.9	6.10	20.10	3.11	17.11	8.12	5.1	26.1	16.2	2.3	23.3	4.5	-
1957/58	-	7.9	21.9	5.10	19.10	2.11	16.11	7.12	4.1	25.1	15.2	1.3	22.3	3.5	-
1958/59	-	6.9	20.9	4.10	18.10	1.11	15.11	6.12	10.1	24.1	14.2	28.2	14.3	2.5	-
1959/60	-	5.9	19.9	3.10	17.10	31.10	14.11	5.12	9.1	30.1	20.2	12.3	26.3	7.5	-
1960/61	-	27.8	10.9	24.9	8.10	22.10	5.11	26.11	7.1	28.1	18.2	4.3	18.3	6.5	-
1961/62	-	26.8	9.9	23.9	7.10	21.10	4.11	25.11	6.1	27.1	17.2	10.3	31.3	5.5	-
1962/63	-	-	8.9	22.9	6.10	20.10	3.11	24.11	5.1	26.1	16.2	9.3	30.3	25.5	-
1963/64	-	-	7.9	21.9	5.10	19.10	16.11	7.12	4.1	25.1	15.2	29.2	14.3	2.5	-
1964/65	-	-	5.9	19.9	3.10	17.10	14.11	5.12	9.1	30.1	20.2	6.3	27.3	1.5	-
1965/66	-	-	4.9	18.9	2.10	16.10	13.11	4.12	22.1	12.2	5.3	26.3	23.4	14.5	-
1966/67	-	-	3.9	17.9	1.10	15.10	26.11	7.1	28.1	18.2	11.3	8.4	29.4	20.5	-
1967/68	-	2.9	16.9	30.9	14.10	28.10	9.12	6.1	27.1	17.2	9.3	30.3	27.4	18.5	-
1968/69	-	7.9	21.9	5.10	19.10	2.11	16.11	7.12	4.1	25.1	13.2	1.3	22.3	26.4	-
1969/70	-	6.9	20.9	4.10	18.10	1.11	15.11	6.12	3.1	24.1	7.2	21.2	14.3	11.4	29.4
1970/71	-	5.9	19.9	10.10	24.10	7.11	21.11	12.12	2.1	23.1	13.2	6.3	27.3	8.5	-
1971/72	-	4.9	18.9	9.10	23.10	6.11	20.11	11.12	15.1	5.2	26.2	18.3	15.4	6.5	-
1972/73	-	2.9	16.9	7.10	21.10	4.11	18.11	9.12	13.1	3.2	24.2	17.3	7.4	5.5	-
1973/74	-	1.9	15.9	6.10	20.10	3.11	24.11	15.12	5.1	26.1	16.2	9.3	30.3	4.5	-
1974/75	-	31.8	14.9	5.10	19.10	2.11	23.11	14.12	4.1	25.1	15.2	8.3	5.4	3.5	-
1975/76	-	30.8	13.9	4.10	18.10	1.11	22.11	13.12	3.1	24.1	14.2	6.3	3.4	1.5	-
1976/77	-	4.9	18.9	9.10	23.10	6.11	20.11	11.12	8.1	29.1	26.2	19.3	23.4	21.5	-
1977/78	-	3.9	17.9	8.10	22.10	5.11	26.11	17.12	7.1	28.1	18.2	11.3	8.4	6.5	-
1978/79	-	2.9	16.9	29.9	21.10	4.11	25.11	16.12	6.1	27.1	17.2	10.3	31.3	12.5	-
1979/80	-	1.9	15.9	28.9	20.10	3.11	24.11	15.12	5.1	26.1	16.2	8.3	12.4	10.5	-
1980/81	-	30.8	13.9	27.9	18.10	1.11	22.11	13.12	3.1	24.1	14.2	7.3	11.4	9.5	14.5
1981/82	-	5.9	19.9	3.10	17.10	31.10	21.11	12.12	2.1	23.1	13.2	6.3	3.4	22.5	27.5
1982/83	-	4.9	18.9	2.10	16.10	30.10	20.11	11.12	8.1	29.1	19.2	12.3	16.4	21.5	26.5
1983/84	-	3.9	17.9	1.10	15.10	29.10	19.11	10.12	7.1	28.1	18.2	10.3	14.4	19.5	-
1984/85	-	1.9	15.9	29.9	13.10	27.10	17.11	8.12	5.1	26.1	16.2	9.3	13.4	18.5	-
1985/86	-	24.8	7.9	28.9	12.10	26.10	16.11	7.12	4.1	25.1	15.2	8.3	5.4	10.5	-
1986/87	-	30.8	13.9	27.9	11.10	25.10	15.11	6.12	10.1	31.1	21.2	14.3	11.4	16.5	-
1987/88	-	29.8	12.9	26.9	10.10	24.10	14.11	5.12	9.1	30.1	20.2	12.3	9.4	14.5	-
1988/89	-	3.9	17.9	1.10	15.10	29.10	19.11	10.12	7.1	28.1	18.2	18.3	15.4	20.5	-
1989/90	-	2.9	16.9	30.9	14.10	28.10	18.11	9.12	6.1	27.1	17.2	10.3	8.4	12.5	17.5
1990/91	-	1.9	15.9	29.9	13.10	27.10	17.11	8.12	5.1	26.1	16.2	9.3	14.4	18.5	-
1991/92	-	31.8	14.9	28.9	12.10	26.10	16.11	7.12	4.1	25.1	14.2	7.3	5.4	9.5	-
1992/93	-	29.8	12.9	26.9	10.10	24.10	14.11	5.12	2.1	23.1	13.2	6.3	3.4	15.5	20.5
1993/94	-	28.9	11.9	25.9	9.10	23.11	13.11	4.12	8.1	29.1	19.2	12.3	9.4	14.5	-
1994/95	-	27.8	10.9	24.9	8.10	22.11	12.11	3.12	7.1	28.1	18.2	11.3	9.4	20.5	-
1995/96	-	26.8	9.9	23.9	7.10	21.10	11.11	2.12	6.1	27.1	17.2	9.3	31.3	11.5	-
1996/97	-	31.8	14.9	28.9	12.10	26.10	16.11	7.12	4.1	25.1	15.2	8.3	13.4	17.5	-
1997/98	-	30.8	13.9	27.9	11.10	25.10	15.11	6.12	3.1	24.1	14.2	7.3	5.4	16.5	-
1998/99	-	5.9	19.9	3.10	17.10	31.10	14.11	5.12	2.1	23.1	13.2	6.3	11.4	22.5	
1999/00	-	21.8	4.9	18.9	2.10	16.10	30.10	20.11	11.12	8.1	29.1	19.2	9.4	20.5	
2000/01	26.8	2.9	16.9	30.9	14.10	28.10	18.11	9.12	6.1	27.1	17.2	10.3	8.4	12.5	
2001/02	25.8	1.9	15.9	29.9	13.10	27.10	17.11	8.12	5.1	26.1	16.2	9.3	14.4	4.5	
2002/03	24.8	31.8	14.9	28.9	12.10	26.10	16.11	7.12	4.1	25.1	15.2	8.3	13.4	17.5	
2003/04	23.8	30.8	13.9	27.9	11.10	25.10	8.11	6.12	3.1	24.1	14.2	6.3	4.4	22.5	
2004/05	28.8	4.9	18.9	2.10	16.10	30.10	13.11	4.12	8.1	29.1	19.2	12.3	16.4	21.5	
2005/06	20.8	27.8	10.9	24.9	8.10	22.10	5.11	3.12	7.1	28.1	18.2	20.3	22.4	13.5	
2006/07	19.8	2.9	16.9	30.9	14.10	28.10	11.11	2.12	6.1	27.1	17.2	10.3	14.4	19.5	
2007/08	18.8	1.9	15.9	29.9	13.10	27.10	10.11	1.12	5.1	26.1	16.2	19.3	5.4	17.5	
2008/09	16.8	30.8	13.9	27.9	11.10	25.10	8.11	29.11	3.1	24.1	14.2	7.3	18.4	30.5	
2009/10	15.8	29.8	12.9	26.9	10.10	24.10	7.11	28.11	2.1	23.1	13.2	6.3	10.4	15.5	
2010/11	14.8	28.8	11.9	25.9	9.10	23.10	6.11	27.11	8.1	29.1	19.2	12.3	16.4	14.5	
2011/12	20.8	3.9	17.9	1.10	15.10	26.10	12.11	3.12	7.1	28.1	18.2	17.3	14.4	5.5	
2012/13	11.8	25.8	8.9	22.9	6.10	20.10	3.11	1.12	5.1	26.1	16.2	9.3	13.4	11.5	
2013/14	17.8	31.8	14.9	28.9	12.10	26.10	9.11	7.12	4.1	25.1	15.2	8.3	12,4	17,5	
2014/15	16.8	30.8	13.9	27.9	11.10	25.10	8.11	6.12	3.1	24.1	14.2	7.3	18.4	30.5	
2015/16	15.8	29.8	12.9	26.9	10.10	24.10	7.11	5.12	9.1	30.1	20.2	.13.3	23.4	21.5	
2016/17	6.8	20.8	3.9	17.9	1.10	15.10	5.11	3.12	7.1	28.1	18.2	11.3	22.4	27.5	
2017/18	5.8	19.8	2.9	16.9	30.9	14.10	4.11	2.12	.6.1	27.1	17.2	17.3	21.4	19.5	
2018/19	11.8	25.8	8.9	22.9	6.10	20.10	10.11	1.12	5.1	26.1	16.2	16.3	6.4	18.5	
2019/20	10.8	24.8	7.9	21.9	5.10	19.10	9.11	30.11	4.1	25.1	3.3	27.6	18.7	1.8	

APPENDIX TWO: FINAL LINE-UPS 1871/72 to 2019/20

Season	Team	Venue	Att.	1	2	3	4	5	6	7	8	9	10	11
1871/72	Wanderers	Oval	2,000	Welch	E Lubbock	AC Thompson	Alcock	Bowen	Bonsor	Betts	Crake	Hooman	Vidal	Wollaston
	Royal Engineers	1		Merriman	Mandarin	Addison	Goodwyn	Mitchell	Creswell	Renny-Tailyour	Rich	Muirhead	Cotter	Bogle
1872/73	Wanderers	Lillie Bridge		Welch	Howell	Bowen	Wollaston 1	Kingsford	Bonsor	Kenyon-Slaney	Ottaway	Sturgis	Kinnaird	Stewart
	Royal Engineers	0	3,000	Leach	Mackarness	Birley	Longman	AK Smith	Vidal	Maddison		Dixon	Paton	Sumner
1873/74	Oxford University	Oval	2,000	Nepean	Mackarness 1	Birley	Green	Benson	Maddison	Rawson	Ottaway	Johnson	Vidal	Patton 1
	Royal Engineers	0		Merriman	Mandarin	Addison	Onslow	von Donop	Blackburn	Renny-Tailyour	Renny-Tailyour	Olivier	Wood	Digby
1874/75	Royal Engineers	Oval (a.e.t.)	3,000	Merriman	Sim	Onslow	Ruck	Benson	Wood	Rawson	Stafford	Renny-Tailyour 1	Renny-Tailyour 1	Wingfield-Stratford
	Old Etonians	1		Farmer	Wilson	AC Thompson	E Lubbock	von Donop	Kenyon-Slaney	Patton	Bonsor 1	Ottaway	Mein	Stronge
Replay	Royal Engineers	Oval	3,000	Merriman	Sim	Onslow	Ruck	Hammond	Wood	Rawson	Stafford	Renny-Tailyour 2	Mein	Wingfield-Stratford
	Old Etonians	0		Drummond Moray	Farrer	E Lubbock	Wilson	von Donop	A Lubbock	Patton	Bonsor	Farmer	Kinnaird	Stronge
1875/76	Wanderers	Oval	3,500	Greig	Stratford	Lindsay	Maddison	Birley	Wollaston	GHH Heron	CFW Heron	Edwards 1	Hughes	Kenrick
	Old Etonians	1		Hogg	Welldon	AC Thompson	E Lyttleton	Alleyne	Bonsor 1*	Sturgis	A Lyttleton	Kenyon-Slaney	Kinnaird	CM Thompson
Replay	Wanderers	Oval	3,500	Greig	Stratford	Lindsay	Maddison	Birley	Wollaston 1	GHH Heron	CFW Heron	Edwards	Hughes 2	Kenrick
	Old Etonians	0		Wilson	E Lubbock	Farrer	E Lyttleton	Alleyne	Bonsor	Sturgis	A Lyttleton	Kenyon-Slaney	Kinnaird	Stronge
1876/77	Wanderers	Oval (a.e.t.)	3,000	Kinnaird	Stratford	Birley	Waddington	Green	Hughes	Wollaston	GHH Heron	Wace	Denton	Kenrick 1
	Oxford University	1		Allington	Dunell	Rawson	Kinnaird 1*	Savory	Wollaston	Parry	Otter	Todd	Hills	Bain
1877/78	Wanderers	Oval	4,500	Kirkpatrick	Stratford	Lindsay	Kinnaird	Green	Wollaston	GHH Heron	Wylie	Wace	Denton	Kenrick 2
	Royal Engineers	1		Friend	Cowan	Morris	Mayne	Heath	Barnet	Lindsay	Haynes	Hedley	Bond	Ruck
1878/79	Old Etonians	Oval	5,000	Hawtrey	Christian	Bury	Kinnaird	Clarke 1	Rawson	Beaufoy	Goodhart	Chevallier	Pares	Whitfeld
	Clapham Rovers	0		Birkett	Ogilvie	E Field	Bailey	Prinsep	Brougham	Stanley	Stanley	Keith-Falconer	Bevington	Scott
1879/80	Clapham Rovers	Oval	6,000	Birkett	Ogilvie	E Field	Weston	Bailey	Heygate	Hill	Barry	Sparks	Lloyd-Jones	Ram
	Oxford University	0		Parr	Wilson	King	Phillips	Rogers	Hansell	Richards	Crowdy	Eyre	J Lubbock	Childs
1880/81	Old Carthusians	Oval	4,500	Gillett	Colvin	Norris	Vintcent	Prinsep	Fernandez	Parry	Page	Wynyard 1	Parry 1	Tod 1
	Old Etonians	3		Rawlinson	Foley	French	Kinnaird	Farrer	Wollaston	Chevallier	Macaulay	Goodhart	Whitfeld	Novelli
1881/82	Old Etonians	Oval	6,500	Rawlinson	French	de Paravicini	Kinnaird	Foley	Anderson 1	Chevallier	Macaulay	Goodhart	Dunn	Novelli
	Blackburn Rovers	0		Howarth	McIntyre	Suter	F Hargreaves	Sharples	Duckworth	Douglas	Brown	Strachan	Avery	J Hargreaves
1882/83	Blackburn Olympic	Oval (a.e.t.)	8,000	Hacking	Ward	Warburton	Gibson	Astley	Hunter	Dewhurst	Matthews 1	Wilson	Costley 1	Yates
	Old Etonians	1		Rawlinson	French	de Paravicini	Kinnaird	Foley	Anderson	Chevallier	Macaulay	Goodhart 1	Dunn	Bainbridge
1883/84	Blackburn Rovers	Oval	12,000	Arthur	Beverley	Suter	McIntyre	Gow	Forrest 1	Lofthouse	Douglas	Sowerbutts 1	Inglis	Brown
	Queens Park	1		Gillespie	Arnott	McDonald	Campbell	J Hargreaves	Anderson	Watt	Smith	Harrower	Allan	Christie 1
1884/85	Blackburn Rovers	Oval	12,500	Arthur	Turner	Suter	Haworth	McIntyre	Forrest 1	Lofthouse 1	Douglas	Brown 1	Fecitt	Sowerbutts
	Queens Park	0		Gillespie	Arnott	MacLeod	Campbell	McDonald	Hamilton	McWhannel	Anderson	Sellar	Gray	Allan
1885/86	Blackburn Rovers	Oval	15,000	Arthur	Turner	Suter	Heyes	McIntyre	Forrest	Strachan	Douglas	Brown	Fecitt	Sowerbutts
	West Bromwich Alb.	0		Roberts	H Green	H Bell	Horton	Perry	Timmins	Woodhall	T Green	Bayliss	Loach	G Bell
Replay	Blackburn Rovers	Derby	12,000	Arthur	Turner	Suter	Horton	McIntyre	Forrest	Walton	Strachan	Brown 1	Fecitt	Sowerbutts 1
	West Bromwich Alb.	0		Roberts	H Green	H Bell	Horton	Perry	Timmins	Woodhall	T Green	Bayliss	Loach	G Bell
1886/87	Aston Villa	Oval	15,500	Warner	Coulton	Simmonds	Yates	Dawson	Burton	Brown	Hunter 1	Vaughton	Hodgetts 1	Davis
	West Bromwich Alb.	0		Roberts	H Green	Aldridge	Horton	Perry	Timmins	Woodhall 1	T Green	Bayliss 1	Paddock	Pearson
1887/88	West Bromwich Alb.	Oval	19,000	Roberts	Aldridge	H Green	Horton	Perry	Timmins	Bassett	Woodhall 1	Bayliss 1	Pearson	Wilson
	Preston North End	1		Mills-Roberts	Howarth	NJ Ross	Holmes	Russell	Graham	Gordon	JD Ross	Goodall	Dewhurst 1	Drummond
1888/89	Preston North End	Oval	22,000	Mills-Roberts	Howarth	Holmes	Drummond	Russell	Graham	Gordon	JD Ross 1	Goodall	Dewhurst 1	Thomson 1
	Wolverhampton W.	0		Baynton	Baugh	Mason	Fletcher	Allen	Lowder	T Hunter	Wykes	Brodie	Wood	Knight
1889/90	Blackburn Rovers	Oval	20,000	Horne	Jas Southworth	Forbes	Barton	Dewar	Forrest	Lofthouse 1	Campbell	Jo Southworth 1	Walton 1	Townley 3
	Sheffield Wednesday	1		Smith	Morley	Brayshaw	Waller	Betts	Dunqworth	Ingram	Woolhouse	Mumford	Cawley	Bennett 1
1890/91	Blackburn Rovers	Oval	23,000	Pennington	Brandon	Forbes	Barton	Dewar 1	Forrest	Lofthouse	Walton	Jo Southworth 1	Hall	Townley 1
	Notts County	3		Thraves	Ferguson	Hendry	Osborne	Calderhead	A Shelton	McGregor	McInnes	James Oswald	Locker	Daft
1891/92	West Bromwich Alb.	Oval	32,810	Reader	Nicholson	McCulloch	Reynolds 1	Perry	Groves	Bassett	McLeod	Nicholls 1	Pearson	Geddes 1
	Aston Villa	0		Warner	Cox	Evans	H Devey	James Cowan	Baird	Athersmith	Dickson	J Devey	Campbell	Hodgetts
1892/93	Wolverhampton W.	Fallowfield	45,067	Rose	Baugh	Swift	Malpass	Allen 1	Kinsey	Topham	Wykes	Butcher	Griffin	Wood
	Everton	0		Williams	Kelso	Howarth	Boyle	Holt	Stewart	Latta	Gordon	Maxwell	Chadwick	Milward
1893/94	Notts County	Goodison	37,000	Toone	Harper	Hendry	Bramley	Calderhead	A Shelton	Watson 1	Donnelly	Logan 3	Bruce	Daft
	Bolton Wanderers	1		Sutcliffe	Somerville	Jones	Gardiner	Paton	Hughes	Tannahill	Wilson	Cassidy 1	Bentley	Dickenson
1894/95	Aston Villa	Crystal Palace	42,562	Wilkes	Spencer	Welford	Reynolds	James Cowan	Russell	Athersmith	Chatt 1	J Devey	Hodgetts	Smith
	West Bromwich Alb.	0		Reader	Williams	Horton	Perry	Higgins	Taggart	Bassett	McLeod	Richards	Hutchinson	Banks
1895/96	Sheffield Wednesday	Crystal Palace	48,836	Massey	Earp	Langley	Brandon	Crawshaw	Petrie	Brash	Brady	Bell	Davis	Spiksley 2
	Wolverhampton W.	1		Tennant	Baugh	Dunn	Owen	Malpass	Griffiths	Tonks	Henderson	Beats	Wood	Black 1
1896/97	Aston Villa	Crystal Palace	65,891	Whitehouse	Spencer	Evans	Reynolds	James Cowan	Crabtree 1	Athersmith	J Devey	Campbell 1	Wheldon 1	John Cowan
	Everton	2		Menham	Meehan	Storrier	Boyle 1	Holt	Stewart	Taylor	Bell 1	Hartley	Chadwick	Milward
1897/98	Nottingham Forest	Crystal Palace	62,017	Allsop	Ritchie	Scott	Frank Forman	McPherson 1	Wragg	McInnes	Richards	Benbow	Capes 2	Spouncer
	Derby County	1		Fryer	Methven	Leiper	Cox	A Goodall	Turner	J Goodall	Bloomer 1	Boag	Stevenson	McQueen
1898/99	Sheffield United	Crystal Palace	73,833	Foulke	Thickett	Boyle	Johnson	Morren	Needham	Bennett 1	Beers 1	Boag 1	Almond 1	Priest 1
	Derby County	1		Fryer	Methven	Staley	Cox	Paterson	May	Arkesden	Bloomer	Boag 1	MacDonald	Allen
1899/00	Bury	Crystal Palace	68,945	Thompson	Darroch	Pray	Leeming	Ross	Richards	Wood 1	McLuckie 2	Sagar	Plant 1
	Southampton	0		Robinson	Meehan	Durber	Meston	Chadwick	Petrie	Turner	Yates	Farrell	Wood	Milward

289

Year	Opponent		Venue	Att.	1	2	3	4	5	6	7	8	9	10	11
1900/01	Tottenham Hotspur	2	Crystal Palace	114,815	Clawley	Erentz	Tait	Morris	Hughes	Jones	Smith	Cameron	Brown 2	Copeland	Kirwan
Replay	Sheffield United	2			Foulke	Thickett	Boyle	Johnson	Morren	Needham	Bennett 1	Field	Hedley	Priest 1	Lipsham
	Tottenham Hotspur	3	Burnden Park	20,470	Clawley	Erentz	Tait	Morris	Hughes	Jones	Smith 1	Cameron	Brown 1	Copeland 1	Kirwan
1901/02	Sheffield United	1	Crystal Palace	76,914	Foulke	Thickett	Boyle	Johnson	Morren	Needham	Bennett	Field	Hedley	Priest 1	Lipsham
	Southampton	1			Robinson	CB Fry	Molyneux	Meston	Wilkinson	Lee	Common 1	Wood 1	Brown	Chadwick	J Turner
Replay	Sheffield United	2	Crystal Palace	33,068	Foulke	Thickett	Boyle	Johnson	Bowman	Needham	Bennett	Common	Hedley 1	Priest	Lipsham
	Southampton	1			Robinson	CB Fry	Molyneux	Meston	Bowman	Lee	A Turner	Wood 1	Brown 1	Chadwick	J Turner
1902/03	Bury	6	Crystal Palace	63,102	Monteith	Lindsey	Boyle	Johnstone	Thorpe	Ross 1	A Turner	York	Sagar 1	Leeming 2	Plant 1
	Derby County	0			Fryer	Methven	McEwen	Warren	A Goodall	May	Richards	Warrington	Boag	Richards	Davis
1903/04	Manchester City	1	Crystal Palace	61,374	Hillman	McMahon	Morris	Frost	Hynds	Ashworth	Meredith 1	Livingstone	Gillespie	A Turnbull	Booth
	Bolton Wanderers	0			Davies	Brown	Burgess	Clifford	Greenhalgh	Freebairn	Stokes	Marsh	Yenson	White	Taylor
1904/05	Aston Villa	2	Crystal Palace	101,117	George	Spencer	Struthers	Pearson	Leake	Windmill	Brawn	Garraty	Hampton 2	Bache	Hall
	Newcastle United	0			Lawrence	Agnew	Miles	Gardner	Aitken	McWilliam	Rutherford	Howie	Appleyard	Veitch	Gosnell
1905/06	Everton	1	Crystal Palace	75,609	Scott	W Balmer	Carr	Makepeace	Taylor	Abbott	Sharp	Bolton	Young 1	Settle	Hardman
	Newcastle United	0			Lawrence	McCombie	Carr	Gardner	Aitken	McWilliam	Rutherford	Howie	Veitch	Orr	Gosnell
1906/07	Sheffield Wednesday	2	Crystal Palace	84,584	Lyall	Layton	Burton	Brittleton	Crawshaw	Bartlett	Chapman	Bradshaw	Wilson	Stewart 1	Simpson 1
	Everton	1			Scott	W Balmer	Crelley	Makepeace	Taylor	Abbott	Sharp 1	Bolton	Young	Settle	Hardman
1907/08	Wolverhampton W.	3	Crystal Palace	74,697	Lunn	Jones	Collins	Hunt 1	Wooldridge	Bishop	Harrison 1	Shelton	Hedley 1	Radford	Pedley
	Newcastle United	1			Lawrence	McCracken	Pudan	Gardner	Veitch	McWilliam	Rutherford	Howie 1	Appleyard	Speedie	Wilson
1908/09	Manchester United	1	Crystal Palace	71,401	Moger	Stacey	Hayes	Duckworth	Roberts	Bell	Meredith	Halse	J Turnbull	A Turnbull 1	Wall
	Bristol City	0			Clay	Annan	Cottle	Hanlin	Wedlock	Spear	Staniforth	Hardy	Gilligan	Burton	Hilton
1909/10	Newcastle United	1	Crystal Palace	76,980	Lawrence	McCracken	Whitson	Veitch	Low	McWilliam	Rutherford 1	Howie	Shepherd	Higgins	Wilson
	Barnsley	1			Mearns	Downs	Ness	Glendinning	Boyle	Utley	Tufnell 1	Lillycrop	Gadsby	Forman	Bartrop
Replay	Newcastle United	2	Goodison Park	55,364	Lawrence	McCracken	Carr	Veitch	Low	McWilliam	Rutherford	Howie	Shepherd 2(1p)	Higgins	Wilson
	Barnsley	0			Mearns	Downs	Ness	Glendinning	Boyle	Utley	Tufnell	Lillycrop	Gadsby	Forman	Bartrop
1910/11	Bradford City	0	Crystal Palace	69,098	Mellors	Campbell	Taylor	Robinson	Gildea	McDonald	Logan	Stewart	O'Rourke	Devine	Thompson
	Newcastle United	0			Lawrence	McCracken	Whitson	Veitch	Low	Willis	Rutherford	Speirs	Jobey	Higgins	Wilson
Replay	Bradford City	1	Old Trafford	58,000	Mellors	Campbell	Taylor	Robinson	Torrance	McDonald	Logan	Speirs 1	O'Rourke	Devine	Thompson
	Newcastle United	0			Lawrence	McCracken	Whitson	Veitch	Low	Willis	Rutherford	Stewart	Jobey	Higgins	Wilson
1911/12	Barnsley	0	Crystal Palace	54,556	Cooper	Downs	Taylor	Glendinning	Bratley	Utley	Bartrop	Tufnell	Lillycrop	Travers	Moore
	West Bromwich Alb.	0			Pearson	Cook	Pennington	Baddeley	Buck	McNeal	Jephcott	Wright	Pailor	Bowser	Shearman
Replay	Barnsley	1	Bramall Lane	38,555	Cooper	Downs	Taylor	Glendinning	Bratley	Utley	Bartrop	Tufnell 1	Lillycrop	Travers	Moore
	West Bromwich Alb.	0 (a.e.t.)			Pearson	Cook	Pennington	Baddeley	Buck	McNeal	Jephcott	Wright	Pailor	Bowser	Shearman
1912/13	Aston Villa	1	Crystal Palace	121,919	Hardy	Lyons	Weston	Barber 1	Harrop	Leach	Wallace	Halse	Hampton	Stephenson	Bache
	Sunderland	0			Butler	Gladwin	Ness	Cuggy	Thomson	Low	Mordue	Buchan	Richardson	Holley	Martin
1913/14	Burnley	1	Crystal Palace	72,778	Sewell	Bamford	Taylor	Halley	Boyle	Watson	Nesbitt	Lindley	Freeman 1	Hodgson	Mosscrop
	Liverpool	0			Campbell	Longworth	Pursell	Fairfoul	Ferguson	McKinlay	Sheldon	Metcalf	Miller	Nicholl	Lacey
1914/15	Sheffield United	3	Old Trafford	49,557	Gough	Cook	English	Sturgess	Brelsford	Utley	Simmons 1	Fazackerly 1	Kitchen 1	Masterman	Evans
	Chelsea	0			Molyneux	Bettridge	Harrow	Taylor	Logan	Walker	Ford	Halse	Thomson	Croal	McNeil
1919/20	Aston Villa	1	Stamford Bridge	50,018	Hardy	Smart	Weston	Ducat	Barson	Moss	Wallace	Kirton 1	Walker	Stephenson	Dorrell
	Huddersfield Town	0 (a.e.t.)			Mutch	Wood	Bullock	Slade	Wilson	Watson	Richardson	Mann	Taylor	Swann	Islip
1920/21	Tottenham Hotspur	1	Stamford Bridge	72,805	Hunter	Clay	McDonald	Smith	Walters	Grimsdell	Banks	Seed	Cantrell	Bliss	Dimmock 1
	Wolverhampton W.	0			George	Woodward	Marshall	Gregory	Hodnett	Riley	Lea	Burrill	Edmonds	Potts	Brooks
1921/22	Huddersfield Town	1	Stamford Bridge	53,000	Mutch	Wood	Wadsworth	Slade	Wilson	Watson	Richardson	Mann	Islip	Stephenson	WH Smith 1 (p)
	Preston North End	0			JF Mitchell	Hamilton	Doolan	Duxberry	McCall	Williamson	Rawlings	Jefferis	Roberts	Woodhouse	Quinn
1922/23	Bolton Wanderers	2	Wembley	126,047	Pym	Haworth	Finney	Nuttall	Seddon	Jennings	Butler	Jack 1	JR Smith 1	Joe Smith	Vizard
	West Ham United	0			Hufton	Henderson	Young	Bishop	Kay	Tresadern	Richards	Brown	Watson	Moore	Ruffell
1923/24	Newcastle United	2	Wembley	91,645	Bradley	Hampson	Hudspeth	Mooney	Spencer	Gibson	Low	Cowan	Harris 1	McDonald	Seymour 1
	Aston Villa	0			Jackson	Smart	Mort	Moss	Blackburn	Green	York	Kirton	Capewell	Walker	Dorrell
1924/25	Sheffield United	1	Wembley	91,763	Sutcliffe	Cook	Milton	Pantling	King	Green	Mercer	Boyle	Johnson	Gillespie	Tunstall 1
	Cardiff City	0			Farquarson	Nelson	Blair	Wake	Keenor	Hardy	W Davies	Gill	Nicholson	Beadles	D Evans
1925/26	Bolton Wanderers	1	Wembley	91,547	Pym	Haworth	Greenhalgh	Nuttall	Seddon	Jennings	Butler	Jack 1	Johnson	Joe Smith	Vizard
	Manchester City	0			Goodchild	Cookson	McCloy	Pringle	Cowan	McMullan	Austin	Browell	JR Smith	Johnson	Hicks
1926/27	Cardiff City	1	Wembley	91,206	Farquarson	Nelson	Watson	Keenor	Sloan	Hardy	Curtis	Irving	Ferguson 1	L Davies	McLachlan
	Arsenal	0			Lewis	Parker	Kennedy	Baker	Butler	John	Hulme	Buchan	Brain	Blyth	Hoar
1927/28	Blackburn Rovers	3	Wembley	92,041	Crawford	Hutton	Jones	Healless	Rankin	Campbell	Thornewell	Puddefoot	Roscamp 2	McLean 1	Rigby
	Huddersfield Town	1			Mercer	Goodall	Barkas	Redfern	Wilson	Steele	A Jackson 1	Kelly	Brown	Stephenson	WH Smith
1928/29	Bolton Wanderers	2	Wembley	92,576	Pym	Haworth	Finney	Kean	Seddon	Nuttall	Butler	McClelland	Blackmore 1	Gibson	W Cook
	Portsmouth	0			Gilfillan	Mackie	Bell	Nichol	McIlwaine	Thackeray	Forward	Smith	Weddle	Johnson	F Cook
1929/30	Arsenal	2	Wembley	92,486	Preedy	Parker	Hapgood	Baker	Seddon	John	Hulme	Jack	Lambert 1	James 1	Bastin
	Huddersfield Town	0			Turner	Goodall	Spence	Naylor	Wilson	Campbell	Jackson	Kelly	Davies	Raw	Smith
1930/31	West Bromwich Alb.	2	Wembley	92,406	Pearson	Shaw	Trentham	Magee	Seddon	Edwards	Glidden	Carter	WG Richardson 2	Sandford	Wood
	Birmingham	1			Hibbs	Liddell	Barkas	Cringan	Morrall	Leslie	Briggs	Crosbie	Bradford 1	Gregg	Curtis

290

		Venue	Att.	1	2	3	4	5	6	7	8	9	10	11	Subs
1931/32	Newcastle United	2 Wembley	92,298	McInroy	Nelson	Fairhurst	McKenzie	Davidson	Weaver	Boyd	JR Richardson	Allen 2	McMenemy	Lang	
	Arsenal	1		Moss	Parker	Hapgood	Jones	Roberts	Male	Hulme	Jack	Lambert	Bastin	John 1	
1932/33	Everton	3 Wembley	92,900	Sagar	Cook	Cresswell	Britton	White	Thomson	Geldard	Dunn 1	Dean 1	Johnson	Stein 1	
	Manchester City	0		Langford	Cann	Dale	Busby	Cowan	Bray	Toseland	Marshall	Herd	McMullan	Brook	
1933/34	Manchester City	2 Wembley	93,258	Swift	Barnett	Dale	Busby	Cowan	Bray	Toseland	Marshall	Herd	Herd	Brook	
	Portsmouth	1		Gilfillan	Mackie	W Smith	Nichol	Allen	Thackeray	Worrall	J Smith	Tilson 2	Easson	Rutherford 1	
1934/35	Sheffield Wednesday	4 Wembley	93,204	Brown	Nibloe	Catlin	Sharp	Millership	Burrows	Hooper 1	Surtees	Palethorpe 1	Starling	Rimmer 2	
	West Bromwich Alb.	2		Pearson	Shaw	Trentham	Murphy	W Richardson	Edwards	Glidden	Carter	WG Richardson	Sandford 1	Boyes 1	
1935/36	Arsenal	1 Wembley	93,384	Wilson	Male	Hapgood	Crayston	Roberts	Copping	Hulme	Bowden	Drake 1	James	Bastin	
	Sheffield United	0		Smith	Hooper	Wilkinson	Jackson	Johnson	McPherson	Barton	Barclay	Dodds	Pickering	Williams	
1936/37	Sunderland	3 Wembley	93,495	Mapson	Gorman	Hall	Thomson	Johnston	McNab	Duns	Carter 1	Gurney 1	Gallacher	Burbanks 1	
	Preston North End	1		Burns	Gallimore	A Beattie	Shankly	Tremelling	Milne	Dougal	Beresford	F O'Donnell 1	Fagan	H O'Donnell	
1937/38	Preston North End	1 Wembley	93,357	Holdcroft	Gallimore	A Beattie	Shankly	Smith	Batey	Watmough	Mutch 1 (p)	Maxwell	R Beattie	H O'Donnell	
	Huddersfield Town	0 (a.e.t.)		Hesford	Craig	Mountford	Willingham	Young	Boot	Hulme	Isaac	MacFadyen	Barclay	Beasley	
1938/39	Portsmouth	4 Wembley	99,370	Walker	Morgan	Rochford	Guthrie	Rowe	Wharton	Worrall	McAlinden	Anderson 1	Barlow 2	Parker 1	
	Wolverhampton W.	1		Scott	Morris	Taylor	Galley	Cullis	Gardiner	Burton	McIntosh	Westcott	Dorsett 1	Maguire	
1945/46	Derby County	4 Wembley	98,215	Woodley	Nicholas	Howe	Bullions	Leuty	Musson	Harrison	Carter	Stamps 2	Doherty 1	Duncan	
	Charlton Athletic	1 (a.e.t.)		Bartram	Phipps	Shreeve	H Turner	Oakes	Johnson	Fell	Brown	AA Turner	Welsh	Duffy	
1946/47	Charlton Athletic	1 Wembley	98,215	Bartram	Croker	Shreeve	Johnson	Phipps	Whittaker	Hurst	Dawson	Robinson	Welsh	Duffy 1	
	Burnley	0 (a.e.t.)		Strong	Woodruff	Mather	Attwell	Brown	Bray	Chew	Morris	Harrison	Potts	Kippax	
1947/48	Manchester United	4 Wembley	99,000	Crompton	Carey	Aston	Anderson 1	Chilton	Cockburn	Delaney	Morris	Rowley 2	Pearson 1	Mitten	
	Blackpool	2		Robinson	Shimwell 1 (p)	Crosland	Johnston	Hayward	Kelly	Matthews	Munro	Mortensen 1	Dick	Rickett	
1948/49	Wolverhampton W.	3 Wembley	98,920	Williams	Pritchard	Springthorpe	Crook	Shorthouse	Wright	Hancocks	Smyth 1	Pye 2	Dunn	Mullen	
	Leicester City	1		Bradley	Jelly	Scott	W Harrison	Plummer	King	Griffiths 1	Lee	J Harrison	Chisholm	Adam	
1949/50	Arsenal	2 Wembley	100,000	Swindin	Scott	Barnes	Forbes	L Compton	Mercer	Cox	Logie	Goring	Lewis 2	D Compton	
	Liverpool	0		Sidlow	Lambert	Spicer	Taylor	Jones	Hughes	Payne	Baron	Stubbins	Fagan	Liddell	
1950/51	Newcastle United	2 Wembley	100,000	Fairbrother	Cowell	Corbett	Harvey	Brennan	Crowe	Walker	Taylor	Milburn 2	G Robledo	Mitchell	
	Blackpool	0		Farm	Shimwell	Garrett	Johnston	Hayward	Kelly	Matthews	Mudie	Mortensen	Slater	Perry	
1951/52	Newcastle United	1 Wembley	100,000	Simpson	Cowell	McMichael	Harvey	Brennan	E Robledo	Matthews	Foulkes	Milburn	G Robledo 1	Mitchell	
	Arsenal	0		Swindin	Barnes	Smith	Forbes	Daniel	Mercer	Cox	Logie	Holton	Lishman	Roper	
1952/53	Blackpool	4 Wembley	100,000	Farm	Shimwell	Garrett	Fenton	Johnston	Robinson	Matthews	Taylor	Mortensen 3	Mudie	Perry 1	
	Bolton Wanderers	3		Hanson	Ball	Banks	Wheeler	Barrass	Bell 1	Holden	Moir 1	Lofthouse 1	Hassall	Langton	
1953/54	West Bromwich Alb.	3 Wembley	100,000	Sanders	Kennedy	Millard	Dudley	Duddale	Barlow	Griffin 1	Ryan	Allen 2 (1p)	Nicholls	Lee	
	Preston North End	2		Thompson	Cunningham	Walton	Docherty	Marston	Forbes	Finney	Foster	Wayman 1	Baxter	Morrison 1	
1954/55	Newcastle United	3 Wembley	100,000	Simpson	Cowell	Batty	Scoular	Stokoe	Casey	White	Milburn 1	Keeble	Hannah 1	Mitchell 1	
	Manchester City	1		Trautmann	Meadows	Little	Barnes	Ewing	Paul	Spurdle	Hayes	Revie	Johnstone 1	Fagan	
1955/56	Manchester City	3 Wembley	100,000	Trautmann	Leivers	Little	Barnes	Ewing	Paul	Johnstone 1	Hayes 1	Revie	Dyson 1	Clarke	
	Birmingham City	1		Merrick	Hall	Green	Newman	Smith	Boyd	Astall	Kinsey 1	Brown	Murphy	Govan	
1956/57	Aston Villa	2 Wembley	100,000	Sims	Lynn	Aldis	Crowther	Dugdale	Saward	Smith	Sewell	Myerscough	Dixon	McParland 2	
	Manchester United	1		Wood	Foulkes	Byrne	Colman	J Blanchflower	Edwards	Berry	Whelan	T Taylor 1	Charlton	Pegg	
1957/58	Bolton Wanderers	2 Wembley	100,000	Hopkinson	Hartle	Banks	Taylor	Higgins	Edwards	Birch	Stevens	Lofthouse 2	Parry	Holden	
	Manchester United	0		Gregg	Foulkes	Greaves	Hennin	Cope	Crowther	Dawson	E Taylor	Charlton	Viollet	Webster	
1958/59	Nottingham Forest	2 Wembley	100,000	Thomson	Whare	McDonald	Goodwin	McKinlay	Burkitt	Dwight 1	Quigley	Wilson 1	Gray	Imlach	
	Luton Town	1		Baynham	McNally	Hawkes	Groves	Owen	Pacey 1	Bingham	Brown	Morton	Cummins	Gregory	
1959/60	Wolverhampton W.	3 Wembley	100,000	Finlayson	Showell	Harris	Clamp	Slater	Flowers	Deeley 2	Stobart	Murray	Broadbent	Horne	
	Blackburn Rovers	0		Leyland	Bray	Whelan	Clayton	Woods	McGrath	Bimpson	Dobing	Douglas	Allen	MacLeod	
1960/61	Tottenham Hotspur	2 Wembley	100,000	Hanson	Baker	Henry	Blanchflower	Norman	Mackay	Jones	White	Smith 1	White	Dyson 1	
	Leicester City	0		Banks	Chalmers	Norman	McLintock	King	Appleton	Riley	Walsh	McIlmoyle	Keyworth	Cheesebrough	
1961/62	Tottenham Hotspur	3 Wembley	100,000	Brown	Baker	Henry	Blanchflower 1 (p)	Norman	Mackay	Medwin	McIlroy	Smith 1	Greaves 1	Jones	
	Burnley	1		Blacklaw	Angus	Elder	Adamson	Cummings	Miller	Connelly	Pointer	Robson 1	Harris	Charlton	
1962/63	Manchester United	3 Wembley	100,000	Gaskell	Dunne	Cantwell	Crerand	Foulkes	Setters	Giles	Quixall	Herd 2	Law 1	Charlton	
	Leicester City	1		Banks	Sjoberg	Norman	McLintock	King	Appleton	Riley	Cross	Keyworth 1	Gibson	Stringfellow	
1963/64	West Ham United	3 Wembley	100,000	Standen	Bond	Burkett	Bovington	Brown	Moore	Brabrook	Boyce 1	Byrne	Hurst 1	Sissons 1	
	Preston North End	2		Kelly	Ross	Lawton	Smith	Singleton	Kendall	Wilson	Ashworth	Dawson 1	Spavin	Holden 1	
1964/65	Liverpool	2 Wembley	100,000	Lawrence	Lawler	Byrne	Strong	Yeats	Stevenson	Callaghan	Hunt 1	St John 1	Smith	Thompson	
	Leeds United	1 (a.e.t.)		Sprake	Reaney	Bell	Bremner 1	Charlton	Hunter	Giles	Storrie	Peacock	Collins	Johanneson	
1965/66	Everton	3 Wembley	100,000	West	Wright	Wilson	Gabriel	Labone	Harris	Scott	Fantham	Young	Harvey	Temple 1	
	Sheffield Wed	2		Springett	Smith	Megson	Eustace	Ellis	Young	Pugh	Trebilcock 2	McCalliog 1	Ford 1	Quinn	
1966/67	Tottenham Hotspur	2 Wembley	100,000	Jennings	Kinnear	Knowles	Mullery	England	Mackay	Robertson 1	Greaves	Gilzean	Venables	Saul 1	
	Chelsea	1		Bonetti	A Harris	Henry	Hollins	Hinton	R Harris	Cooke	Baldwin	Hateley	Tambling 1	Boyle	
1967/68	West Bromwich	1 Wembley	100,000	Osborne	Fraser	Williams	Brown	Talbot	Kaye	Lovett	Collard	Astle 1	Hope	Clark	Clarke (6)
	Everton	0 (a.e.t)		West	Wright	Wilson	Kendall	Labone	Harvey	Husband	Ball	Royle	Hurst	Morrissey	

291

		Venue		Att.	1	2	3	4	5	6	7	8	9	10	11	Subs
1968/69	Manchester City	1 Wembley		100,000	Dowd	Book	Pardoe	Doyle	Booth	Oakes	Summerbee	Bell	Lee	Young 1	Coleman	Manley (11)
	Leicester City	0			Shilton	Rodrigues	Nish	Roberts	Woollett	Cross	Fern	Gibson	Lochhead	Clarke	Glover	Hinton (6)
1969/70	Chelsea	2 Wembley		100,000	Bonetti	Webb	McCreadie	Hollins	Dempsey	R Harris	Baldwin	Houseman	Osgood	Hutchinson 1	Cooke	
	Leeds United	2	(a.e.t.)		Sprake	Madeley	Cooper	Bremner	Charlton	Hunter	Lorimer	Clarke	Jones 1	Giles	E Gray	Hinton (9)
Replay	Chelsea	2 Old Trafford		62,078	Bonetti	R Harris	Madeley	Hollins	Dempsey	Webb 1	Baldwin	Cooke	Osgood 1	Hutchinson	Houseman	
	Leeds United	1	(a.e.t.)		Harvey	Madeley	Cooper	Bremner	Charlton	Hunter	Lorimer	Clarke	Jones 1	Giles	E Gray	
1970/71	Arsenal	2 Wembley		100,000	Wilson	Rice	McNab	Storey	McLintock	Simpson	Armstrong	Graham	Radford	Kennedy	George 1	Kelly 1 (4)
	Liverpool	1			Clemence	Lawler	Lindsay	Smith	Lloyd	Hughes	Callaghan	Evans	Heighway 1	Toshack	Hall	Thompson (8)
1971/72	Leeds United	1 Wembley		100,000	Harvey	Reaney	Madeley	Bremner	Charlton	Hunter	Lorimer	Clarke 1	Jones	Giles	E Gray	
	Arsenal	0			Barnett	Rice	McNab	Storey	McLintock	Simpson	Armstrong	Ball	Radford	George	Graham	Kennedy (9)
1972/73	Sunderland	1 Wembley		100,000	Montgomery	Malone	Guthrie	Horswill	Watson	Pitt	Kerr	Hughes	Halom	Porterfield 1	Tueart	
	Leeds United	0			Harvey	Reaney	Cherry	Bremner	Madeley	Hunter	Lorimer	Clarke	Jones	Giles	E Gray	Yorath (11)
1973/74	Liverpool	3 Wembley		100,000	Clemence	Smith	Lindsay	Thompson	Cormack	Hughes	Keegan 2	Hall	Heighway 1	Toshack	Callaghan	
	Newcastle United	0			McFaul	Clark	Kennedy	McDermott	Howard	Moncur	Smith	Cassidy	Macdonald	Tudor	Hibbitt	Gibb (7)
1974/75	West Ham United	2 Wembley		100,000	Day	McDowell	Lampard	Bonds	T Taylor	Lock	Jennings	Paddon	A Taylor 2	Brooking	Holland	
	Fulham	0			Mellor	Cutbush	Fraser	Lacy	Moore	Mullery	Conway	Slough	Mitchell	Busby	Barrett	
1975/76	Southampton	1 Wembley		100,000	Turner	Rodrigues	Peach	Holmes	Blyth	Steele	Gilchrist	Channon	Osgood	McCalliog	Stokes 1	
	Manchester United	0			Stepney	Forsyth	Houston	Daly	B Greenhoff	Buchan	Coppell	McIlroy	Pearson	Macari	Hill	McCreery (11)
1976/77	Manchester United	2 Wembley		100,000	Stepney	Nicholl	Albiston	McIlroy	B Greenhoff	Buchan	Coppell	Macari	Pearson 1	Macari	Hill	McCreery (11)
	Liverpool	1			Clemence	Neal	Jones	Smith	Kennedy	Hughes	Keegan	Case 1	Heighway	Johnson	McDermott	Callaghan (10)
1977/78	Ipswich Town	1 Wembley		100,000	Cooper	Burley	Hunter	Beattie	Mills	Osborne 1	Talbot	Walk	Mariner	Geddis	Woods	Lambert (6)
	Arsenal	0			Jennings	Rice	Nelson	Price	O'Leary	Young	Brady	Sunderland	MacDonald	Stapleton	Hudson	Rix (7)
1978/79	Arsenal	3 Wembley		100,000	Jennings	Rice	Nelson	Talbot 1	O'Leary	Young	Brady	Sunderland 1	Stapleton 1	Price	Rix	Walford (10)
	Manchester United	2			Bailey	Nicholl	Albiston	McIlroy 1	McQueen 1	Buchan	Coppell	J Greenhoff	Jordan	Macari	Thomas	
1979/80	West Ham United	1 Wembley		100,000	Parkes	Stewart	Lampard	Bonds	Martin	Devonshire	Brady	Pearson	Cross	Brooking 1	Pike	
	Arsenal	0			Jennings	Rice	Devine	Talbot	O'Leary	Young	Brady	Sunderland	Stapleton	Price	Rix	Nelson (3)
1980/81	Tottenham Hotspur	1 Wembley		100,000	Aleksic	Hughton	Miller	Roberts	Perryman	Villa	Ardiles	Archibald	Galvin	Hoddle	Crooks	Brooke (6)
	Manchester City	1	(a.e.t.)		Corrigan	Ranson	McDonald	Reid	Power	Caton	Bennett	Gow	MacKenzie 1	Hutchinson	Reeves	Henry (7)
Replay	Tottenham Hotspur	3 Wembley		99,500	Aleksic	Hughton	Miller	Roberts	Villa 2	Perryman	Ardiles	Archibald	Galvin	Hoddle	Crooks 1	
	Manchester City	2			Corrigan	Ranson	McDonald	Reid	Power	Caton	Bennett	Gow	MacKenzie	Hutchinson	Reeves 1	Tueart (3)
1981/82	Tottenham Hotspur	1 Wembley		92,000	Clemence	Hughton	Miller	Price	Hazard	Perryman	Roberts	Archibald	Galvin	Hoddle 1	Crooks	Brooke (5)
	QPR	1	(a.e.t.)		Hucker	Fenwick 1	Gillard	Waddock	Hazell	Roeder	Currie	Flanagan	C Allen	Stainrod	Gregory	Mickelwhite (9)
Replay	Tottenham Hotspur	1 Wembley		90,000	Clemence	Hughton	Miller	Price	Hazard	Perryman	Roberts	Archibald	Galvin	Hoddle 1 (p)	Crooks	Brooke (5)
	QPR	0			Hucker	Fenwick	Gillard	Waddock	Hazell	Neill	Currie	Flanagan	Mickelwhite	Stainrod	Gregory	Burke (9)
1982/83	Manchester United	2 Wembley		100,000	Bailey	Duxbury	Albiston	Wilkins 1	Moran	McQueen	Robson	Muhren	Stapleton 1	Whiteside	Davies	
	Brighton & Hove Alb.	2	(a.e.t.)		Moseley	Ramsey	Stevens	Gatting	Pearce	Smillie	Case	Grealish	Howlett	Robinson	Smith	Ryan (2)
Replay	Manchester United	4 Wembley		100,000	Bailey	Duxbury	Albiston	Wilkins	Moran	McQueen	Robson 2	Muhren 1 (p)	Stapleton	Whiteside 1	Davies	
	Brighton & Hove Alb.	0			Moseley	Gatting	Pearce	Grealish	Foster	Stevens	Case	Howlett	Robinson	Smith	Smillie	
1983/84	Everton	2 Wembley		100,000	Southall	Stevens	Bailey	Ratcliffe	Mountfield	Reid	Steven	Heath	Sharp 1	Gray 1	Richardson	
	Watford	0			Sherwood	Bardsley	Price	Taylor	Terry	Sinnott	Callaghan	Johnston	Reilly	Jackett	Barnes	Atkinson (3)
1984/85	Manchester United	1 Wembley		100,000	Bailey	Gidman	Albiston	Whiteside 1	McGrath	Moran	Robson	Strachan	M Hughes	Stapleton	Olsen	Duxbury (3)
	Everton	0	(a.e.t.)		Southall	Stevens	Van Den Hauwe	Ratcliffe	Mountfield	Reid	Steven	Sharp	Gray	Bracewell	Sheedy	
1985/86	Liverpool	3 Wembley		98,000	Grobbelaar	Lawrenson	Beglin	Lawrenson	Whelan	Hansen	Dalglish	Johnston 1	Rush 2	Molby	MacDonald	
	Everton	1			Mimms	Stevens	Van Den Hauwe	Ratcliffe	Mountfield	Reid	Steven	Bennett 1	Sharp	Bracewell	Sheedy	Heath (2)
1986/87	Coventry City	3 Wembley		98,000	Ogrizovic	Phillips	Downs	Peake	Kilcline	McGrath	Bennett	Lineker 1	Gynn	Houchen 1	Pickering	Rodger (5)
	Tottenham Hotspur	2	(a.e.t.)		Clemence	Hughton	Thomas	Hodge	Gough	Mabbutt 1	C Allen 1	P Allen	Waddle	Hoddle	Ardiles	Claesen (2), Stevens (11)
1987/88	Wimbledon	1 Wembley		98,203	Beasant	Goodyear	Phelan	Jones	Young	Thorn	Gibson	Cork	Fashanu	Sanchez 1	Wise	Scales (7), Cunningham (8)
	Liverpool	0			Grobbelaar	Gillespie	Ablett	Nicol	Spackman	Hansen	Beardsley	Aldridge	Houghton	Barnes	McMahon	Molby (5), Johnston (8)
1988/89	Liverpool	3 Wembley		82,800	Grobbelaar	Ablett	Staunton	Nicol	Whelan	Hansen	Beardsley	Aldridge 1	Houghton	Barnes	McMahon	Venison (3), Rush 2 (8)
	Everton	2	(a.e.t.)		Southall	N McDonald	Van Den Hauwe	Ratcliffe	Watson	Bracewell	Nevin	Steven	Sharp	Cottee	Sheedy	McCall 2 (6), Wilson (11)
1989/90	Manchester United	3 Wembley		80,000	Leighton	Ince	Martin	Bruce	Phelan	Pallister	Robson 1	Webb	McClair	M Hughes 2	Wallace	Blackmore (3), Robins (6)
	Crystal Palace	3	(a.e.t.)		Martyn	Pemberton	Shaw	Gray	O'Reilly 1	Thorn	Robson	Barber	Bright	Solako	Pardew	Madden (4), Wright 2 (7)
Replay	Manchester United	1 Wembley		80,000	Sealey	Ince	Martin 1	Bruce	Phelan	Pallister	Robson	Webb	McClair	M Hughes	Wallace	
	Crystal Palace	0			Martyn	Pemberton	Shaw	Gray	O'Reilly	Thorn	Barber	Thomas	Bright	Solako	Pardew	Wright (7), Madden (10)
1990/91	Tottenham Hotspur	2 Wembley		80,000	Thorstvedt	Edinburgh	Van Den Hauwe	Sedgley	Howells	Mabbutt	Stewart 1	Gascoigne	Samways	Lineker	P Allen	Nayim (8), Walsh (9)
	Nottingham Forest	1	(a.e.t.)		Crossley	Charles	Pearce 1	Walker	Chettle	Keane	Crosby	Parker	Clough	Glover	Woan	Laws (10), Hodge (11)
1991/92	Liverpool	2 Wembley		79,544	Grobbelaar	Jones	Burrows	Nicol	Molby	M Wright	Saunders	Houghton	Rush 1	McManaman	Thomas 1	
	Sunderland	0			Norman	Owers	Ball	Bennett	Rogan	D Rush	Bracewell	Davenport	Armstrong	Byrne	Atkinson	
1992/93	Arsenal	1 Wembley		79,347	Seaman	Dixon	Winterburn	Davis	Linighan	Adams	Jensen	Wright 1	Campbell	Merson	Parlour	Hardyman (6), Hawke (11)
	Sheffield Wed	1	(a.e.t.)		Woods	Nilsson	Worthington	Palmer	Anderson	Warhurst	Harkes	Waddle	Hirst 1	Bright	Sheridan	O'Leary (8), AM Smith (11)
Replay	Arsenal	2 Wembley		62,267	Seaman	Dixon	Winterburn	Davis	Linighan 1	Adams	Jensen	Wright 1	AM Smith	Merson	Campbell	Hyde (5), Bart-Williams (8)
	Sheffield Wed	1	(a.e.t.)		Woods	Nilsson	Worthington	Palmer	Harkes	Warhurst	Wilson	Waddle 1	Hirst	Bright	Sheridan	Bart-Williams (2), Hyde (7)

292

Season	Team	Venue	Att.	1	2	3	4	5	6	7	8	9	10	11	Subs
1993/94	Manchester United 4	Wembley	79,634	Schmeichel	Parker	Irwin	Bruce	Kanchelskis	Pallister	Cantona 2 (2p)	Ince	Keane	M Hughes 1	Giggs	Sharpe(3), McClair 1 (5)
	Chelsea 0			Kharine	Clarke	Sinclair	Kjeldbjerg	Johnsen	Burley	Spencer	Newton	Stein	Peacock	Wise	Hoddle (6), Cascarino (9)
1994/95	Everton 1	Wembley	79,592	Southall	Jackson	Ablett	Parkinson	Watson	Unsworth	Limpar	Horne	Stuart	Rideout 1	Hinchcliffe	Amokachi (7), Ferguson (10)
	Manchester United 0			Schmeichel	G Neville	Irwin	Bruce	Sharpe	Pallister	Keane	Ince	McClair	Hughes	Butt	Giggs (4), Scholes (5)
1995/96	Manchester United 1	Wembley	79,007	Schmeichel	Irwin	P Neville	May	Keane	Pallister	Cantona 1	Beckham	Cole	Butt	Giggs	G Neville (8), Scholes (9)
	Liverpool 0			James	McAteer	Jones	Scales	M Wright	Babb	McManaman	Redknapp	Collymore	Barnes	Fowler	Thomas (3), Rush (9)
1996/97	Chelsea 2	Wembley	79,160	Grodas	Petrescu	Minto	Sinclair	Leboeuf	Clarke	Di Matteo 1	Di Matteo	Newton 1	M Hughes	Wise	Vialli (7)
	Middlesbrough 0			Roberts	Blackmore	Fleming	Stamp	Pearson	Festa	Emerson	Mustoe	Ravanelli	Juninho	Hignett	Vickers (8), Beck (9), Kinder (11)
1997/98	Arsenal 2	Wembley	79,183	Seaman	Dixon	Winterburn	Vieira	Keown	Adams	Parlour	Di Matteo	Anelka 1	Wreh	Overmars 1	Platt (10)
	Newcastle United 0			Given	Pistone	Pearce	Batty	Dabizas	Howey	Lee	Barton	Shearer	Ketsbaia	Speed	Andersson (3), Watson (8), Barnes (10)
1998/99	Manchester United 2	Wembley	79,101	Schmeichel	G Neville	Johnsen	P Neville	May	Beckham	Scholes 1	Keane	Giggs	Cole	Solskiaer	Sheringham 1 (8), Stam (7), Yorke (10)
	Newcastle United 0			Harper	Griffin	Charvet	Dabizas	Domi	Lee	Hamann	Speed	Solano	Ketsbaia	Shearer	Ferguson (7), Maric (9), Glass (10)
1999/00	Chelsea 1	Wembley	78,217	De Goey	Melchiot	Babayaro	Deschamps	Leboeuf	Desailly	Poyet	Di Matteo 1	Weah	Zola	Wise	Flo (9), Morris (10)
	Aston Villa 0			James	Delaney	Wright	Southgate	Ehiogu	Barry	Taylor	Boateng	Dublin	Owen 2	Merson	Hendrie (3), Stone (7), Joachim (10)
2000/01	Liverpool 2	Cardiff	74,200	Westerveld	Babbel	Henchoz	Carragher	Hypia	Murphy	Smicer	Grimandi	Gerrard	Wiltord	Heskey	McAllister (7), Berger (6), Fowler (8)
	Arsenal 1			Seaman	Dixon	Adams	Keown	Cole	Ljungberg 1	Vieira	Parlour 1	Pires	Wiltord	Henry	Parlour (10), Kanu (9), Bergkamp (2)
2001/02	Arsenal 2	Cardiff	73,963	Seaman	Lauren	Cole	Vieira	Campbell	Adams	Wiltord	Lampard	Henry	Bergkamp	Ljungberg	Keown (7), Kanu (9), Edu (10)
	Chelsea 0			Cudicini	Melchiot	Babayaro	Petit	Galias	Desailly	Gronkjaer	Parlour	Hasselbaink	Gudjohnsen	Le Saux	Zenden (2), Terry (3), Zola (9)
2002/03	Arsenal 1	Cardiff	73,726	Seaman	Lauren	Cole	Silva	Luzhny	Keown	Ljungberg	Parlour	Henry	Omerod	Pires 1	Wiltord (10)
	Southampton 0			Niemi	Baird	Bridge	Marsden	Lundekvam	M Svensson	Telfer	Oakley	Beattie	Bergkamp	A Svensson	Jones (1), Fernandez (2), Tessem (11)
2003/04	Manchester United 3	Cardiff	72,350	Howard	G Neville	O'Shea	Brown	Keane	Silvestre	Ronaldo 1	Fletcher	van Nistelrooy 2	Scholes	Giggs	Carroll (1), Solskiaer (7), Butt (8)
	Millwall 0			Marshall	Elliott	Ryan	Cahill	Lawrence	Ward	Ifill	Wise	Harris	Livermore	Sweeney	Cogan (3), Weston (8), McCammon (9)
2004/05	Arsenal 0	Cardiff	71,896	Lehmann	Lauren	Cole	Toure	Senderos	Silvestre	Fabregas	Silva	Reyes	Bergkamp	Pires	Van Persie (7), Ljungberg (10), Edu (11)
	Manchester United 0 (a.e.t.)			Carroll	Brown	O'Shea	R Ferdinand	Keane	Silvestre	Fletcher	Scholes	van Nistelrooy	Rooney	Ronaldo	Fortune (3), Giggs (7)

Arsenal won 5-4 on penalties

2005/06	Liverpool 3	Cardiff	71,140	Reina	Finnan	Carragher	Hypia	Rise	Gerrard 2	Alonso	Sissoko	Kewell	Crouch	Cisse 1	Morientes (9), Kronkamp (7), Hamann (10)
	West Ham United 3 (a.e.t.)			Hislop	Scaloni	A Ferdinand	Gabbidon	Konchesky 1	Benayoun	Fletcher	Reo-Coker	Etherington	Ashton 1	Harewood	Zamora (10), Dailly (7), Sheringham (9)

Liverpool won 3-1 on penalties

2006/07	Chelsea 1	Wembley	89,826	Cech	Paulo Ferreira	Bridge	Makelele	Terry	Essien	Wright-Phillips	Lampard	Drogba 1	Mikel	J Cole	Kalou (7), Robben (11), A Cole (13)
	Manchester United 0 (a.e.t.)			Van der Sar	Brown	Heinze	Carrick	Ferdinand	Vidic	Ronaldo 1	Scholes	Rooney	Fletcher	Giggs	O'Shea (4), Smith (10), Solskiaer (11)
2007/08	Portsmouth 1	Wembley	89,874	James	Johnson	Hreidarsson	Diarra	Campbell	Distin	Utaka	Pedro Mendes	Kranjcar	Kanu	Muntari	Nugent (7), Diop (8), Baros (10)
	Cardiff City 0			Enckleman	McNaughton	Capaldi	Rae	Johnson	Loovens	Ledley	McPhail	Hasselbaink	Whittingham	Parry	Sinclair (4), Thompson (9), Ramsey (10)
2008/09	Chelsea 2	Wembley	89,391	Cech	Bosingwa	Cole A	Mikel	Terry	Alex	Essien	Lampard 1	Anelka	Drogba 1	Malouda	Ballack (7)
	Everton 1			Howard	Hibbert	Baines	Yobo	Lescott	Neville P	Osman	Feliani	Saha 1	Cahill	Pienaar	Jacobsen (2), Gosling (7), Vaughan (9)
2009/10	Chelsea 1	Wembley	88,335	Cech	Ivanovic	Cole A	Ballack	Terry	Alex	Kalou	Lampard	Anelka	Drogba 1	Malouda	Belletti (4), Cole J (7), Sturridge (9)
	Portsmouth 0			James	Finnan	Mullins	Boateng	Ricardo Rocha	Mokoena	Brown	Diop	Piquionne	Dindane	O'Hara	Belhadj (3), Utaka (4), Kanu (8)
2010/11	Manchester City 1	Wembley	88,643	Hart	Richards	Kolarov	de Jong	Lescott	Kompany	Barry	Toure Y 1	Balotelli	Tevez	Silva	Johnson A (7), Zabaleta (10), Vieira (11)
	Stoke City 0			Sorensen	Wilkinson	Wilson	Huth	Shawcross	Whelan	Pennant	Delap	Jones	Walters	Etherington	Pugh (6), Carew (8), Whitehead (11)
2011/12	Chelsea 2	Wembley	89,102	Cech	Ivanovic	Cole A	Mikel	Cahill	Ramires 1	Lampard	Mata	Drogba 1	Kalou	Meireles 1	Carroll 1 (9), Kuyt (11)
	Liverpool 1			Reina	Johnson G	Enrique	Aqger	Skrtel	Gerrard	Henderson	Downing	Suarez	Drogba 1	Bellamy	
2012/13	Wigan Athletic 1	Wembley	86,254	Joel	Boyce	Espinoza	Boateng	Alcaraz	Scharner	Gomez	McArthur	McManaman	Kone	Maloney	Watson 1 (8)
	Manchester City 0			Hart	Zabaleta	Clichy	Nastasic	Kompany	Kompany	Nasri	Toure	Aquero	Tevez	Silva	Milner (7), Rodwell (10), Dzeko (4)
2013/14	Arsenal 3	Wembley	89,345	Fabianski	Sagna	Gibbs	Ramsey 1	Mertesacker	Koscielny 1	Cazorla 1	Arteta	Giroud	Ozil	Podolski	Sanogo (11), Wilshere (11), Rosicky (7)
	Hull City 2 (a.e.t.)			McGregor	Elmohamady	Rosenior	Chester 1	Davies 1	Bruce	Livermore	Huddlestone	Fryatt	Meyler	Quinn	McShane (6), Aluko (11), Boyd (3)
2014/15	Arsenal 4	Wembley	89,283	Szczesny	Bellerin	Monreal	Coquelin	Mertesacker	Koscielny	Ramsey	Cazorla	Benteke	Walcott 1	Sanchez 1	Abdonlanor (7), Bacuna (3), Sanchez (6)
	Aston Villa 0			Given	Hutton	Richardson	Vlaar	Okoke	Westwood	N'Zogbia	Delph	Benteke	Cleverley	Grealish	Darmian (3), Young (10), Lingard 1 (7)
2015/16	Manchester United 2	Wembley	88,619	de Gea	Valencia	Rojo	Blind	Smalling	Carrick	Mata 1	Feliani	Martial	Rashford	Rooney	Puncheon 1 (10), Gayle (9), Mariappa (4)
	Crystal Palace 1 (a.e.t.)			Hennessey	Ward	Souare	Dann	Delaney	Jedinak	Zaha	McArthur	Wickham	Cabaye	Bolasie	
2016/17	Arsenal 2	Wembley	89,472	Ospina	Bellerin	Ox-Chamberlain	Holding	Mertesacker	Monreal	Ramsey 1	Diop	Welbeck	Ozil	Sanchez 1	Giroud (9), Coquelin (3), Elneny (11)
	Chelsea 1			Courtois	Azpilicueta	Alonso	Matic	Cahill	David Luiz	Moses	Kante	Costa 1	Hazard	Pedro	Fabregas (4), Willian (11), Batshuayi (9)
2017/18	Chelsea 1	Wembley	87,647	Courtois	Moses	Alonso	Jones	Cahill	Rudiger	Fabregas	Kante	Giroud	Hazard 1 (p)	Bakayoko	Morata (9), Willian (10)
	Manchester United 0			de Gea	Valencia	Young	Smalling	Jones	Matic	Herrera	Pogba	Rashford	Sanchez	Lingard	Lukaku (9), Martial (11), Mata (4)
2018/19	Manchester City 6	Wembley	85,854	Ederson	Walker	Zinchenko	Gundogan	Laporte	Kompany	Mahrez	Silva	Jesus 2	Sterling 2	Silva 1	Success (7), Gray (10), Cleverley (11)
	Watford 0			Gomes	Femenia	Holebas	Capoue	Cathcart	Mariappa	Pereyra	Doucoure	Deeney	Deulofeu	Hughes	Hughes
2019/20	Arsenal 2	Wembley	0	Martinez	Bellerin	Tierney	Xhaka	Holding	Luiz David	Pepe	Ceballos	Lacazette	Maitland-Niles	Aubameyang 2(1p)	Nketiah (9), Sokratis (6), Kolasinac (3)
	Chelsea 1			Caballero	Azpilicueta	James	Jorginho	Zouma	Ridger	Mount	Kovacic	Giroud	Pulisic	Alonso	Christensen (2), Pedro (10), Barkley (7), Abraham (9), Hudson-Odoi (5)

* The Old Etonians goal in 1875/76 is sometimes credited to Bonsor but this cannot be confirmed in contemporary accounts. Similarly, one of the Wanderers goals in 1877/78 is sometimes credited to Kinnaird.

In the 1876/77 final, Kinnaird in goal caught the ball and stepped back over the line. The umpires awarded a goal. Subsequently, an FA Committee accepted Kinnaird's word that he had not stepped over the line. The score was amended to 2-0, although if the score was 1-0 at 90 minutes, extra time would not have been necessary. 2-1 a.e.t. is now the accepted result, with Kinnaird's own goal re-instated.
Own goals are credited to Kinnaird (Wanderers) 1876/77, R Turner (Charlton) 1945/46, McGrath (Blackburn) 1959/60, Hutchison (Manchester City) 1980/81, Mabbutt (Spurs) 1986/87, Walker (Forest) 1990/91 and Carragher (Liverpool) 2005/06.
The Royal Engineers' goal in 1877/78 was scored "in a rush" and is therefore not credited to an individual player.

Line-ups for all cup ties played by Football League and Premier League clubs can be found in the English National Football Archive at www.enfa.co.uk

APPENDIX THREE: OTHER CLUB NAMES

Use this list in conjuction with the main index for a complete record of clubs that have changed their names or amalgamated. Please note this list does not claim to be definitive or complete - an interesting project to document all FA Cup clubs awaits.

Club	See Also	Club	See Also
Abbey United (Cambs)	Cambridge United	Crawley Down	Crawley Down Gatwick
Addlestone	Addlestone & Weybridge Town	Crittall Athletic	Braintree & CA
Aerostructure	Hamble ASSC, GE Hamble	Crook Town	Crook CW
AFC Blackpool	Blackpool Mechanics	Crouch End	Crouch End Vampires
AFC Darwen	Darwen	Croydon	Croydon Amateurs
AFC Kempston Rovers	Kempston Rovers	Croydon Athletic	Wandsworth & Norwood
AFC Lymington	Lymington	Crusaders	Brentwood (1)
AFC Newbury	Newbury	Dagenham	Dagenham & Redbridge
AFC Totton	Totton	Dagenham & Redbridge	Dagenham, Redbridge Forest
AFC Uckfield	Wealden	Darlington 1883	Darlington
AFC Uckfield Town	AGC Uckfield+Uckfield Town	Darlington Cleveland Social	Darlington Cleveland Bridge
Aldershot Albion	Aldershot Institute Albion	Daventry United	Ford Sports (Daventry)
AP Leamington	Lockheed Leamington	Dawdon Colliery Recreation	Dawdon CW
Apsley	Hemel Hempstead	Distington	High Duty Alloys
APV Peterborough City	Baker Perkins, Peterborough City	Dorking	Guildford & Dorking
Ardwick	Man. City	Dorking (2)	Dorking Town
Arnold	Arnold Town	Dudley Town	Dudley
Arnold St Mary's	Arnold	Dunstable Town	Dunstable
Arsenal	Royal Arsenal, Woolwich Arsenal	Dunston UTS	Dunston Federation, Brewery
Ashford	Ashford Town	Easington CW	Easington Colliery
Ashton United	Hurst	Eastbourne	Eastbourne Town
Ashtree Highfield	Sandwell Borough	Eastbourne Borough	Langney Sports
Aylesbury	Aylesbury Vale	Eastbourne Comrades	Eastbourne Utd., Old Comrades
Aylesbury Vale Dynamos	Aylesbury+Bedgrove Dynamos	Eastbourne Old Comrades	Royal Engineers Comrades
Baker Perkins	APV Peterborough City	Eastleigh	Swaythling
Banbury Spencer	Banbury United	Eastleigh LSWR	Eastleigh Ath.
Barking & East Ham United	Barking	Eastville Rovers	Bristol Rovers
Barnet	Barnet Alston	Ebbsfleet United	Gravesend & N'fleet
Barnoldswick Town	United+Park Rovers	Edmonton & Haringey	Haringey Borough
Barnsley	Barnsley St Peter's	Edmonton (2)	Edmonton & Haringey
Barri	Barry Town, Barry	Edmonton Borough	Tufnell Park Edmonton
Barton Town	Barton Town Old Boys	Edmonton Borough	Tufnell Park Edmonton
Barwell	Barwell Athletic, Hinckley	EFC Cheltenham	Endsleigh
Basingstoke	Basingstoke Town	Egham	Egham Town
Bedfont Town	Bedfont Green	Enderby Town	Leicester United
Bedford United & Valerio	Bedford U, Bedford	Endsleigh	EFC Cheltenham
Bedlington Terriers	Bedlington CW, Mechanics	Epsom	Epsom & Ewell
Bedworth United	Bedworth Town	Epsom Town	Epsom
Bexhill	Bexhill Town	Evenwood Town	Spennymoor Town
Bexley United	Bexleyheath & Welling	Everwarm	Bridgend Town
Biddulph Victoria	Knypersley Victoria	Farnborough	Farnborough Town
Billingham Town	Billingham Social	Farsley FC	Farsley Celtic FC
Bilston Town	Bilston	Felixstowe Port & Town	Felixstowe Town
Birmingham	Birmingham City, Small Heath	Felixstowe Town	Felixstowe United
Birmingham City	Small Heath, Small Heath Alliance	Feltham & Hounslow Borough	Feltham, Hounslow
Birmingham Corp. Tramways	Birmingham Transport	Finchley	Wingate & Finchley
Birmingham St George's	Mitchell's St. George's	Fleetwood Freeport	Fleetwood Town
Birmingham Transport	Birmingham City Transport	Folkestone	Folkestone & Shepway
Bitterne Guild	Woolston	Ford Sports (Dagenham)	Ford United
Blackpool (Wren) Rovers	Wren Rovers	Ford United	Briggs Sports + Ford Sports
Blackstone	Mirrlees Blackstone	Forest Green Rovers	Stroud
Blackwell	Blackwell Colliery	Frickley Athletic	Frickley Colliery
Bletchley & Wipac Sports	Bletchley Town	Garforth Town	Garforth Miners
Bletchley Town	Milton Keynes City	Gateshead	South Shields Adelaide, S Shields
Bloxwich Town	Bloxwich United	Gateshead United	South Shields(2)
Boldon Community Association	Boldon CW	Gillingham	New Brompton
Boscombe	Bournemouth	GKN Sankey	Sankey of Wellington
Boston Town	Boston (1)	Glossop	Glossop North End
Botwell Mission	Hayes	Golders Green	Hendon
Bournemouth	Boscombe	Gornal Athletic	Lower Gornal Ath.
Bowater Lloyds	Lloyds	Gosport Borough Athletic	Gosport Borough
Braintree & Crittall Ath.	Braintree Town	Grantham Town	Grantham
Brentwood & Warley	Brentwood Town	Greenhalgh's	Mansfield Town (1)
Brentwood (1)	Crusaders	Grimethorpe Athletic	Grimethorpe Rovers
Brentwood Town	Brentwood & Warley, Brentwood	GSA Sports	Barnt Green Spartak
Bridgend Town	Everwarm	Guildford & Dorking United	Guildford City
Bridlington Central Utd.	Bridlington Town	Guinness Exports (Ormskirk)	Ormskirk
Briggs Sports	Ford United	Hampstead Town	Golders Green
Brightlingsea United	Brightlingsea Regent	Haringey & Waltham Devel.	Mauritius Sports
Brighton & Hove Albion	Brighton & Hove Rangers	Haringey Borough	Edmonton, Edmonton+Haringey
Bristol City	Bristol South End	Harrogate Hotspurs	Harrogate Town
Bristol Rovers	Eastville Rovers	Harrogate Town	Harrogate Hotspurs
Broxbourne Borough V&E	Somersett Ambury V&E	Harrow Town	Harrow Borough
Brunswick Institute	Hull Brunswick	Hartlepool United	Hartlepool, Hartlepools U
Brush Sports	Loughborough United	Harworth Colliery Institute	Harworth Colliery Athletic
Burnham & Hillingdon	Burnham (1), Burnham	Hastings & St Leonards	Hastings Town
Burslem Port Vale	Port Vale	Hatfield Town	Hatfield United
Burton United	Burton Swifts + Burton Wanderers	Havant & Waterlooville	Havant, Waterlooville
Calne & Harris United	Calne Town	Hayes	Botwell Mission
Camberley	Camberley Town	Headington United	Oxford United
Cambridge Town	Cambridge City	Heanor Athletic	Heanor Town
Cambridge United	Abbey United	Hemel Hempstead	Apsley
Cambridge Utd. (1)	Cambridge Town	Hendon	Golders Green
Chatham Town	Medway	Henley Town	Henley
Chesham Town	Chesham	Hereford United	Hereford St Martins
Chesham United	Chesham T, Chesham Generals	High Duty Alloys (Distington)	Distington
Chessington United	Mole Valley Predators	Highmoor Ibis	Reading City
Chester	Chester City	Hillingdon	Burnham
Chichester City	Chichester	Hillingdon Borough	Yiewsley
Chilton Athletic	Chilton & Windlestone	Hinckley	Barwell
City Ramblers	Old St. Paul's	Hinckley Town	Hinckley United
Clapton Orient	Leyton Orient, Orient	Histon Institute	Histon
Clevedon	Clevedon Town	Hitchin	Hitchin Town
Collier Row and Romford	Collier Row, Romford	Hornchurch	Hornchurch & Upminster
Corby Town	Stewarts & Lloyds	Horwich RMI	Leigh RMI
Coventry Amateurs	Coventry Sporting	Hounslow	Feltham & Hounslow
Coventry City	Singers	Hounslow Town	Hounslow
Coventry Sporting	Coventry Amateurs	Howden Rangers	Howden-le-Wear
Cradley Heath St Luke's	Cradley Heath	Hull Brunswick	Brunswick Institute

OTHER CLUB NAMES (CONTINUED)

Club	See Also
Kettering	Kettering Town
Kirkby Town (2)	Knowsley United
Kiveton Park United	Kiveton Park Col.
Knowsley United	Kirkby Town (2)
Lancaster City	Lancaster Town
Lancing Athletic	Lancing
Langley Park CW	Langley Park
Langney Sports	Eastbourne Borough
Leeds Met Carnegie	Leeds Poly
Leicester City	Leicester Fosse
Leicester United	Enderby Town
Leigh RMI	Horwich RMI
Leighton United	Leighton Town
Letchworth Town	Letchworth Garden City
Leyland DAF	Leyland Motors
Leyton	Leyton-Wingate
Leyton Orient	Clapton Orient, Orient
Leyton Pennant	Leyton, Walthamstow Pennant
Leytonstone	Leytonstone/Ilford
Leytonstone/Ilford	Leytonstone, Ilford
Leyton-Wingate	Leyton, Wingate
Littlehampton Town	Littlehampton
Lloyds (Sittingbourne)	Bowater Lloyds
Lockheed Leamington	AP Leamington
Long Eaton United	Long Eaton Town
Loughborough United	Brush Sports
Lower Gornal Athletic	Gornal Ath.
Lymington	AFC Lymington
Lymington & New Milton	Lymington Town
Maltby Main	Malby MW
Manchester City	Ardwick
Manchester United	Newton Heath
Mansfield	Mansfield Town (1) + Greenhalgh's
Mansfield Town	Mansfield Wesley
Mansfield Town (1)	Mansfield, Greenhalgh's
Mansfield Wesley	Mansfield Town
March Town	March Town United
Marconi	Coventry Copsewood
Margate	Thanet U
Matlock Town	Matlock
McLaren Sports	Petter Sports
Medway	Chatham Town
Melksham	Melksham Town
Melksham & Avon United	Melksham
Mellors (Nottm)	Notts Wanderers
Meltham Mills	Meltham
Mexborough Town	Mexborough Town Ath.
Millwall	Millwall Rovers, Millwall Athletic
Millwall Athletic	Millwall
Millwall Rovers	Millwall
Milton Keynes City	Bletchley
Mirrlees Blackstone	Blackstone
Mitchell's St George's	Birmingham St. George's
MK Wolverton Town	Wolverton TBR, Town
Murton	Murton CW
Nantwich Town	Nantwich
New Brompton	Gillingham
Newbury	Newbury Town
Newcastle Blue Star	RTM Newcastle
Newport County	Newport AFC
Newton Heath	Manchester United
North Shields	Preston Col.
Norton Sports	Woodstock Sports
Notts Wanderers	Mellors
Old St Paul's	City Ramblers
Orient	Leyton Orient, Clapton Orient
Ormskirk	Guinness Exports
Ossett United	Ossett Town+Ossett Albion
Over Wanderers	Winsford United
Oxford United	Headington U
Peterborough City	APV P'boro, Baker Perkins
Petter Sports	McLaren Sports
Pewsey Vale	Pewsey YM
PO Engineers (Wallington)	Post Office Telecoms
Port Vale	Burslem Port Vale
Post Office Telecoms	PO Engineers
Prescot Cables	Prescot AFC, Prescot Town
Prescot Town	Prescot Cables
Preston Colliery	North Shields
Prudhoe Town	Prudhoe EE
Purfleet	Thurrock
Radcliffe	Radcliffe Borough
Ramsgate Athletic	Ramsgate
RAOC Cosham	RAOC Hilsea
RAOC Hilsea	RAOC Cosham
Reading City	Highmoor Ibis
Redbridge Forest	Ley/Ilford, Walthamstow Ave
Redditch	Redditch United
Rhyl Athletic	Rhyl
Romford	Collier Row & Romford
Rotherham County	Thornhill Utd.
Rotherham United	Rotherham Town + County
Roundway Hospital (Devizes)	Wilts Co. Mental Hospital
Royal Arsenal	Arsenal, Woolwich Arsenal
Royal Engs. Comrades (Eastb'rne)	Eastbourne Old Comrades
RTM Newcastle	Newcastle Blue Star
Rugby United	Rugby Town
Ruislip	Ruislip Town
Rushden & Diamonds	Rushden T, Irthlingboro' Diamonds
Rushden Town	Rushden & Diamonds

Club	See Also
Salisbury City	Salisbury (2)
Sandwell Borough	Ashtree Highfield
Sankey of Wellington	GKN Sankey
Selby Olympia	Selby OCO
Shaw Lane Aquaforce	Shaw Lane
Shepshed Albion	Shepshed Charterhouse
Shirebrook	Shirebrook MW
Shirley Town	Solihull
Sholing	VT
Singers (Coventry)	Coventry C
Slough United	Slough Town
Small Heath	Birmingham, Birmingham City
Small Heath Alliance	Small Heath, Birmingham
Solihull	Shirley Town
South Shields	Gateshead
South Shields (2)	Gateshead United
South Shields Adelaide	Gateshead
South Shore	Blackpool
Southall	Southall & Ealing Borough
Southampton	Southampton St Mary's
Southport	Southport Central
St Leonards Stamcroft	Stamco, St Leonards
St Neots & District	St Neots Town
Stamco	St Leonards Stamcroft
Stevenage	Stevenage Borough
Stewarts & Lloyds	Corby Town
Steyning Town	Steyning Town Community
Stocksbridge Park Steels	Stocksbridge Works
Stockton	Thornaby
Stockton Heath	Warrington Town
Stoke City	Stoke
Stowmarket	Stowmarket Town
Stowmarket Corinthians	Stowmarket
Stroud	Forest Green Rovers
Sutton Town (Birmingham)	Sutton Coldfield Town
Swanage Town & Herston	Swanage Town
Swansea City	Swansea Town
Swaythling	Eastleigh
Swindon British Rail	Swindon GWR Corinthians
Taunton Town	Taunton
Telford United	Wellington Town
Thames Ironworks	West Ham United
Thanet United	Margate
Thornycroft Athletic	Thornycrofts (Basingstoke)
Tonbridge Angels	Tonbridge
Totton	AFC Totton
Tufnell Park	Tufnell Park Edmonton
Tufnell Park Edmonton	Haringey Borough
Tunbridge Wells Rangers (2)	Tunbridge Wells United
Upminster	Hornchurch & Upminster
V.S. Rugby	Rugby United
Vampires	Crouch End Vampires
Vickers (Weybridge)	Vickers Armstrong
VT	Thornycrofts (Woolston)
Wakefield	Wakefield & Emley, Emley
Walsall	Walsall Town Swifts
Walsall Borough	Walsall Wood
Walsall Wood	Walsall Borough
Waltham Forest	Leyton Pennant
Walthamstow Avenue	Redbridge Forest
Wandsworth & Norwood	Croydon Ath.
Warrington Town	Stockton Heath
Watford Old Boys	Watford Spartans
Wealden	AFC Uckfield
Wealden	AFC Uckfield
Wednesfield Social	Wednesfield
Wellington Town	Telford United
West Ham United	Thames Ironworks
Whitby	Whitby United, Town
Whitstable Town	Whitstable
Wick and Barnham United	Wick
Wigmore Athletic	Worthing United
Wilts County Mental Hospital	Roundway Hospital
Wingate & Finchley	Finchley
Wingate (Durham)	Wingate Welfare
Winsford United	Over Wanderers
Wolverton	Wolverton Town, T&BR
Wolverton Town & BR	Wolverton Town
Woodstock Sports	Norton Sports
Woolston	Bitterne Guild
Woolwich Arsenal	Arsenal
Wootton Bassett Town	Royal Wootton Bassett T
Worthing United	Wigmore Ath.
Wren Rovers	Blackpool Rovers
Yeovil	Yeovil & Petter's United
Yeovil & Petter's United	Yeovil Town
Yeovil Casuals	Yeovil
Yiewsley	Hillingdon Borough

The Everton team return to Liverpool with the Cup following their 3-0 victory over Manchester City in 1933. Dixie Dean holds the trophy. A parade through the streets of the home town is a long established tradition for the winning team, dating back to Olympic's return to Blackburn in 1883. Spurs used a motorised charabanc in 1921, so it is interesting to see Everton preferred four horse power! All photographs in this book © Empics

ACKNOWLEGEMENTS

The first edition of the book was very much a team effort and I am grateful to everyone who participated in the original project. Subsequent editions brought more correspondence and led to changes to the database that continue to this day. Write me at the addresses on the title page.

The British Newspaper Archive is a rich on-line resource for the students of the game, and consequently this 2020 edition contains some changes to the seasons before 1888/89. Research in the 1990s took place at the former Newspaper Library at Colindale, where a "four volumes an hour" rule meant very slow progress when searching for individual games. Such searches can now be done in seconds.

I am indebted to Keith Warsop for changes to line-ups and goal scorer details from the early finals. Keith's account of these finals and biographies of the men that took part will be found in his book "The Early FA Cup Finals".

I do not envy the jobs of the people in the Competitions Department at the Football Association, who keep the Challenge Cup and other competitions running smoothly. I would like to take this opportunity to say "well done" to them.

Tony Brown, August 2020

THE AUTHOR

Tony Brown has worked as a full-time football statistician and publisher since 1995. His interest in personal computers led him to develop the League and Cup databases from which many of his books are written. These include "complete records" of the Football League and cup competitions, and the history of England's oldest professional club, Notts County. His Soccerdata imprint has now published more than 200 titles and his databases are licensed for use by many organisations including the Football Association. A Nottingham man, he splits his affections between Forest and County, after the advice of his grandfather. This gentleman was a Forest fan but only watched County since he couldn't face the trek over Trent Bridge to the City Ground! Tony's only two visits to Wembley for an FA Cup Final were to see the Reds in action. He has also been known to visit the likes of Ilkeston, Long Eaton and Hucknall in search of FA Cup magic. He is a founder-director of the English National Football Archive, the database of which at www.enfa.co.uk contains full line-ups and scorers for all games played by EFL and Premiership club from 1888/89 to date.